Associate Justices (continued)

NAME	YEARS OF SERVICE	STATE APP'T FROM	APPOINTING PRESIDENT	AGE APP'T	POLITICAL AFFILIATION	EDUCATIONAL BACKGROUND
Johnson, William	1804-1834	South Carolina	Jefferson	33	Democratic-Republican	College of New Jersey (Princeton)
Livingston, Henry Brockholst	1807-1823	New York	Jefferson	50	Democratic-Republican	College of New Jersey (Princeton)
Todd, Thomas	1807-1826	Kentucky	Jefferson	42	Democratic-Republican	Liberty Hall (Washington and Lee University)
Duvall, Gabriel	1811-1835	Maryland	Madison	59	Democratic-Republican	Self-taught in law
Story, Joseph	1812-1845	Massachusetts	Madison	33	Democratic-Republican	Harvard
Thompson, Smith	1823-1843	New York	Monroe	55	Democratic-Republican	College of New Jersey (Princeton)
Trimble, Robert	1826-1828	Kentucky	Adams, J. Q.	50	Democratic-Republican	Kentucky Academy (Transylvania University)
McLean, John	1830-1861	Ohio	Jackson	45	Democrat	Read law under Arthur St. Clair, Jr.
Baldwin, Henry	1830-1844	Pennsylvania	Jackson	50	Democrat	Yale College
Wayne, James Moore	1835-1867	Georgia	Jackson	45	Democrat	Princeton
Barbour, Philip Pendleton	1836-1841	Virginia	Jackson	53	Democrat	Read on his own; attended one session at College of William and Mary
Catron, John	1837-1865	Tennessee	Van Buren	51	Democrat	Self-taught in law
McKinley, John	1838-1852	Alabama	Van Buren	58	Democrat	Self-taught in law
Daniel, Peter Vivian	1842-1860	Virginia	Van Buren	58	Democrat	Attended one year at Princeton
Nelson, Samuel	1845-1872	New York	Tyler	53	Democrat	Middlebury College
Woodbury, Levi	1845-1851	New Hampshire	Polk	56	Democrat	Dartmouth College; Tapping Reeve Law School
Grier, Robert Cooper	1846-1870	Pennsylvania	Polk	52	Democrat	Dickinson College
Curtis, Benjamin Robbins	1851-1857	Massachusetts	Fillmore	42	Whig	Harvard; Harvard Law School
Campbell, John Archibald	1853-1861	Alabama	Pierce	42	Democrat	Franklin College; U.S. Military Academy at West Point
Clifford, Nathan	1858-1881	Maine	Buchanan	55	Democrat	Read law in offices of Josiah Quincy
Swayne, Noah Haynes	1862-1881	Ohio	Lincoln	58	Republican	Read law privately
Miller, Samuel Freeman	1862-1890	Iowa	Lincoln	46	Republican	Transylvania University Medical School; read law privately
Davis, David	1862-1877	Illinois	Lincoln	47	Republican	Kenyon College; Yale Law School
Field, Stephen Johnson	1863-1897	California	Lincoln	47	Democrat	Williams College; read law privately
Strong, William	1870-1880	Pennsylvania	Grant	62	Republican	Yale College
Bradley, Joseph P.	1870-1892	New Jersey	Grant	57	Republican	Rutgers
Hunt, Ward	1873-1882	New York	Grant	63	Republican	Union College; read law privately
Harlan, John Marshall	1877-1911	Kentucky	Hayes	61	Republican	Centre College; studied law at Transylvania University
Woods, William Burnham	1881-1887	Georgia	Hayes	57	Republican	Yale
Matthews, Stanley	1881-1889	Ohio	Garfield	57	Republican	Kenyon College
Gray, Horace	1882-1902	Massachusetts	Arthur	54	Republican	Harvard College; Harvard Law School
Blatchford, Samuel	1882-1893	New York	Arthur	62	Republican	Columbia College

BUSINESS LAW
TODAY

Text & Summarized Cases
Legal, Ethical, Regulatory, and
International Environment

Fourth Edition

The Four Versions of
Business Law Today, Fourth Edition

You now have a choice of four different versions of the Fourth Edition of *Business Law Today*, depending on your teaching needs.

Business Law Today: Text & Summarized Cases—Legal, Ethical, Regulatory, and International Environment

- 37 Chapters
- Summarized cases
- Pedagogical features
- A full supplements package
- *Personal Law Handbook*

Business Law Today, Comprehensive Edition: Text & Cases—Legal, Ethical, Regulatory, and International Environment

The ideal text for a complete two-semester course in business law and the legal environment. This version includes additional legal environment chapters and those chapters necessary for students taking the CPA exam.

- 41 Chapters
- Actual case excerpts in the words of the court
- Pedagogical features
- A full supplements package
- *Personal Law Handbook* (as a separate booklet)

Business Law Today, The Essentials: Text & Summarized Cases—Legal, Ethical, Regulatory, and International Environment

This shorter version is aimed at a one-semester introductory course in business law and the legal environment.

- 22 Chapters
- Paraphrased cases
- Pedagogical features
- A full supplements package
- *Personal Law Handbook*

Business Law Today, Alternate Essentials Edition: Text & Hypothetical Examples—Legal, Ethical, Regulatory, and International Environment

This shorter version, with hypotheticals instead of paraphrased cases, is aimed at a one-semester introductory course in business law and the legal environment.

- 22 Chapters
- Hypothetical examples
- Pedagogical features
- A full supplements package
- *Personal Law Handbook*

BUSINESS LAW TODAY

Text & Summarized Cases
Legal, Ethical, Regulatory, and
International Environment

Fourth Edition

ROGER LeROY MILLER
Institute for University Studies
Arlington, Texas

GAYLORD A. JENTZ
Herbert D. Kelleher
Professor in Business Law
MSIS Department
University of Texas at Austin

WEST PUBLISHING COMPANY
St. Paul/Minneapolis   New York   Los Angeles   San Francisco

COPYRIGHT ©1988, 1991, 1994
COPYRIGHT ©1997

By WEST PUBLISHING COMPANY
By WEST PUBLISHING COMPANY
610 Opperman Drive
P.O. Box 64526
St. Paul, MN 55164-0526

Library of Congress Cataloguing-in-Publication Data

Miller, Roger LeRoy.
  Business law today: text, summarized cases, legal, ethical, regulatory, and international environment / Roger LeRoy Miller, Gaylord A. Jentz.—4th ed.
  p.   cm.

  Includes index.
  ISBN 0-314-09488-1 (hb: alk. paper)
  1. Commercial law—United States—Cases. 2. Business law—United States.   I. Jentz, Gaylord A.
  II. Title.
KF888.M553 1997
346.73'07—dc20
[347.3067]
British Library Cataloguing-in-Publication Data. A catalogue record for this book is available from the British Library.

96–15501
∞ CIP

3 UPI/Bettmann; 5 From the painting by Benjamin Ferrers in National Portrait Gallery, photo Corbis-Bettmann; 9 Michael Evans, Sygma; 13 West; 16 Benaytouille Driss, Gamma Liaison, Inc.; 17 UPI/Corbis-Bettmann; 32 David Parker/Science Photo Library, Photo Researchers, Inc.; 34 Cynthia Johnson, The Gamma Liaison Network; 35 Telegraph Colour Library, FPG; 38 Matthew McVay, © Tony Stone Images; 42 Tom Salver, UPI/Bettmann; 49 Chris Brown, Stock Boston, Inc.; 52 Collection, The Supreme Court of the United States, Courtesy The Supreme Court Historical Society; 59 Bettmann; 62 Bill Horsman, Stock Boston, Inc.; 63 Painting by T. Hamilton Crawford, Bettmann; 66 Bob Daemmrich, Bettmann; 70 Photo by Richard Strauss, Smithsonian Institution, Collection of the Supreme Court of the United States; 76 Ron Chapple, FPG; 96 Ted Horowitz, The Stock Market; 101 Joseph Nettiss, Photo Researchers, Inc.; 103 © Mug Shots, The Stock Market; 109 Barbara Alper, Stock Boston, Inc.; 111 Comstock; 129 Frederick D. Bodlin, Stock Boston, Inc.; 134 Comstock; 139 Steve Myerson, International Stock; 143 Thayer Syme, FPG; 159 Mike Mazzaschi, Stock Boston, Inc.; 179 Reuters/Bettmann; 181 Bachmann, Photo Researchers, Inc.; 189 Comstock; 191 Michael Keller, FPG; 212 Stacy Pick, Stock Boston, Inc.; 213 Ron Chapple, FPG; 229 Steve Benbow, Stock Boston, Inc.; 240 Michael Newman, PhotoEdit; 255 Tony Freeman, PhotoEdit; 284 Ewing Galloway, Inc.; 302 David Hanover, Tony Stone Images; 315 Dick Luria, FPG; 321 Stephen Feld Photography; 327 Elizabeth Simpson, FPG; 344 Telegraph Colour Library, FPG; 363 Andy Sacks, Tony Stone Images; 370 Wayne Eastep, Tony Stone Images; 380 Dean Abramson, Stock Boston, Inc.; 385 Joseph Sohm, Tony Stone Images, Inc.; 393 Jeffrey Sylvester, FPG; 397 Phillip Wallick, The Stock Market; 427 West; 430 Collection, The Supreme Court of the United States; 432 Steve Leonard, Black Star; 480 Index Stock Photography, Inc.; 514 West; 570 Tony Freeman, PhotoEdit; 584 Peter Beck, The Stock Market; 594 Comstock; 597 Peter Pearson, Tony Stone Images; 598 Comstock; 621 (top) Jim Erickson, The Stock Market; (bottom) Phil Borden, PhotoEdit; 630 Day Williams, Photo Researchers; 642 Frank Herholdt, Tony Stone Images; 651 Jose L. Pelaez, The Stock Market; 673 McIntyre, Photo Researchers; 678 Paul Barton, The Stock Market; 687 Joe McNally, Sygma; 699 John Terence Turner, FPG; 705 Tom Carroll, International Stock; 709 Myrleen Ferguson, PhotoEdit; 756 Art Montes de Oca, FPG; 770 John Coletti, Stock Boston; 781 Theo Westebberger, Liaison; 798 PhotoEdit; 809 Michael Rosenfeld, Tony Stone Images; 814 Jack Dermid, Photo Researchers, Inc.; 824 Michael Krasowitz, FPG; 829 David R. Frazier Photolibrary, Photo Researchers, Inc.; 831 Malcolm Fielding, Johnson Matthey PLC, Photo Researchers, Inc.; 836 Portrait by Charles Sidney Hopkinson, Collection of the Supreme Court of the United States; 837 Peter M. Fisher, The Stock Market; 861 Dennis Hallinan, FPG; 863 Johnny Stockshooter, International Stock; 883 Ron Sanford, The Stock Market; 895 Peter Vadnai, The Stock Market; 913 Richard Pasley, Stock Boston, Inc.; 915 Tony Freeman, PhotoEdit; 962 Steven Weinberg, Tony Stone Images; 963 D.E. Cox, Tony Stone Images; 973 Bob Daemmrich, Stock Boston, Inc.

Contents in Brief

Contents

Unit Two
Torts and Crimes 119

Chapter 5
Torts 120

Chapter 6
Business Torts and Intellectual Property 150

Chapter 7
Criminal Law 175

Unit Three
Contracts 207

Chapter 8
Nature and Classification 208

Unit Six
Debtor-Creditor Relationships 529

Chapter 21
Secured Transactions 530

Chapter 22
Creditors' Rights and Bankruptcy 558

Unit Seven
Business Organizations 591

Chapter 23
Agency Relationships in Business 592

Chapter 24
The Entrepreneur's Options 620

Chapter 25
Partnerships 641

Preface to the Instructor

We have always felt that business law and the legal environment should be an exciting, contemporary, and interesting course. *Business Law Today*, we believe, imparts this excitement to your students. We have spent a great deal of effort in giving this book a visual appeal that will encourage students to learn the law. We have also worked hard to make sure that *Business Law Today* continues in the established tradition of being the most up-to-date text on the market. The law presented in *Business Law Today* includes new statutes and regulations affecting the legal environment of business, as well as the most recent developments in case law.

We also believe that a thorough understanding of "black letter law" in the traditional business law topics—contracts, sales, torts, agency, business organizations, and other basic topics—is important. You will find that coverage of traditional business law has not been sacrificed in the process of creating this text. Additionally, *Business Law Today* explicitly addresses the American Assembly of Collegiate Schools of Business's (AACSB's) broad array of curriculum requirements. As you will see, many of the features and special pedagogical devices in this text focus on the global, political, ethical, social, environmental, technological, and cultural contexts of business law.

▌A Flexible Teaching/Learning Package

We realize that different people have different teaching philosophies and learning goals. We believe that the Fourth Edition of *Business Law Today* and its extensive supplements offer business law instructors a flexible teaching/learning package. For example, although we have attempted to make the materials flow from chapter to chapter, most of the chapters are self-contained. In other words, generally, you can use the chapters in any order you wish.

Additionally, the extensive number of supplements accompanying *Business Law Today* allows instructors to choose those supplements that will most effectively complement classroom instruction. Suggestions on how you can adapt the *Business Law Today* teaching/learning package to fit your particular teaching and learning goals are given in the *Instructor's Course Planning Guide*. Furthermore, each chapter of the *Instructor's Manual* contains teaching suggestions, possible discussion questions, and additional information on key statutes or other legal sources that you may wish to use in your classroom. These and numerous other supplementary materials (including printed supplements, software, and videos) all contribute to the goal of making *Business law Today* the most flexible teaching/learning package on the market today.

▌ Key Features

Virtually all of the chapters in this text have one or more of the special features described below. These features are designed both to instruct and to pique the interest of the business law and legal environment student. To continue our emphasis on critical thinking, for the Fourth Edition we have added to each feature (except for the *Applications*) a question "For Critical Analysis." These questions, which may serve as a basis for classroom discussion, require the student to reflect on some aspect or implication of the law discussed in the features.

Technology and the Law

A number of chapters in the Fourth Edition of *Business Law Today* contain a special feature focusing on the legal challenges presented by new developments in technology. Some examples of this feature are the following:

- Technology and Free Speech (Chapter 2).
- Technology and Defamation in Cyberspace (Chapter 5).
- Technology and Digital Banking (Chapter 20).

Landmark in the Law

Most of the chapters in this edition have a *Landmark in the Law*. These *Landmarks* discuss important cases, statutes, or other laws affecting business law. Among the *Landmarks* are the following:

- *Palsgraf v. Long Island Railroad Co.* (Chapter 5).
- The Statute of Frauds (Chapter 11).
- The Law of Finders (Chapter 34).

Business Law in Action

A special feature entitled *Business Law in Action* is included in nearly all of the chapters of this text. These features present practical and instructive examples of how the law affects people in the business and/or personal world. Some of the features are as follows:

- Self-Critical Analysis and "Smoking Guns" (Chapter 4).
- Product Liability and the Preemption Issue (Chapter 17).
- The "Slippery Slope" of Privacy Rights (Chapter 32).

Application

Nearly all of the chapters have an *Application* section, which presents the student with some practical advice on how to apply the law discussed in the chapter to real-world business problems. Each *Application* ends with a "Checklist" for the future business-person on how to avoid legal problems. The following are some of the *Applications*:

- Law and the Businessperson—Protecting against Electronic Crimes (Chapter 7).
- Law and the Offeror—Controlling the Terms of the Offer (Chapter 9).
- Law and the Employer—Establishing an E-Mail Policy (Chapter 32).

Ethical Perspectives

In addition to a chapter on ethics, chapter-ending ethical questions, and the *Ethical Considerations* following many of the cases presented in this text, we have included special features called *Ethical Perspectives*. These features are closely integrated with the text so that students can read about some of the ethical implications of topics as they are covered in the text. For example, in Chapter 5, when discussing the potential liability of social hosts, we present an *Ethical Perspective* focusing on the ethical ramifications of holding social hosts liable for harms caused to others by intoxicated guests. Each *Ethical Perspective* concludes with a critical-thinking question about the topic covered.

International Perspectives

As part of the greater emphasis in the Fourth Edition on the global legal environment, nearly every chapter also contains at least one *International Perspective*. These features, like the *Ethical Perspectives*, are closely integrated into the text material and give your students an understanding of the international dimensions of topics that are discussed in the text. For example, in Chapter 33, following a discussion of affirmative action, an *International Perspective* describes how affirmative action programs are also under attack in the European Union. Each *International Perspective* concludes with a critical-thinking question about the topic covered.

Law in the Extreme

Many chapters of this text include a feature entitled *Law in the Extreme*. As the title suggests, this feature discusses some of the more extreme applications of the law. Some examples of this feature are as follows:

- Just Blowing Smoke, or Battery? (Chapter 5).
- Eggshells, Shirts, and Other Negotiable Instruments (Chapter 18).
- Generations and Generations . . . of Tippees (Chapter 29).

Profiles

A number of chapters in this edition include *Profiles* of important jurists and legal scholars, including some from other countries. Some individuals featured in the *Profiles* are as follows:

- Ruth Bader Ginsburg (Chapter 2).
- John Marshall (Chapter 3).
- Mizuho Fukushima (Chapter 37).

▌A Special Case Format

In each chapter, we present cases that have been selected to illustrate the principles of law discussed in the text. The cases are numbered sequentially for easy referencing in class discussions, homework assignments, and examinations. In choosing the cases to be included in this edition, our goal has been to achieve a balance between classic cases and recent cases from the mid-1990s.

Each case is presented in a special format, which begins with the case title and citation. The full citation includes the name of the court deciding the case, the date of the case, and the major parallel reporters in which the case can be found. For federal court cases, the appropriate court seal is also presented. For state court cases, the seal of the state is presented.

For those instructors who like to see the entire set of court opinions for the cases presented in the text in summarized form, we have created a free book, called *Case Printouts for Business Law Today*. This supplement contains the output from WESTLAW (without headnotes) for virtually every case that is included in each chapter. If the instructor wishes, the full set of opinions may be copied and handed out to students.

Company Profiles

Many of the cases in the Fourth Edition of *Business Law Today* are preceded by a *Company Profile*. These profiles give a brief history of the company involved in the particular case and give your students the real-world background to the case.

Historical and Social Settings

A special section entitled *Historical and Social Setting* appears just following the case title and citation. These settings explicitly address the AACSB's curriculum requirements by focusing on the international, political, ethical, social, environmental, technological, or cultural context of each case being presented. Depending on the specific focus, the title of the section varies. For example, for one case the section title might be *Historical and Social Setting*; for another, it may be *Historical and Political Setting* or *Historical and Cultural Setting*.

Basic Case Format

Following the *Historical and Social Setting*, each case is summarized in the following four clearly labeled sections:

- *Facts.*
- *Issue.*
- *Decision.*
- *Reason.*

For Critical Analysis

Each case in this edition of *Business Law Today* concludes with a section entitled *For Critical Analysis*. This section consists of a question that requires the student to think critically about a particular issue raised by the case. The section addresses the AACSB's curriculum requirements by focusing on how particular aspects of the dispute or the court's decision relate to ethical, international, technological, cultural, or other types of issues. Each *For Critical Analysis* section has a subtitle indicating the type of issue to which the question relates. For example, in one case, the subtitle may be *Ethical Consideration*; in another, *Political Consideration*; and so on.

∎ Other Special Pedagogical Devices

We have included in *Business Law Today* a number of additional pedagogical devices, including those discussed below.

Special Pedagogical Devices in the Text

- *Chapter Objectives.*
- *Contents.*
- Margin definitions.
- Quotations.
- Exhibits and forms (almost one hundred).
- Photographs (with critical-thinking questions).
- Cartoons.

Chapter-Ending Pedagogy

- *Key Terms* (with appropriate page references).
- *Chapter Summary* (in graphic format with page references).
- *For Review* (a series of brief review questions).
- *Questions and Case Problems* (including hypotheticals and case problems; many of the case problems are based on cases from the mid-1990s).
- A *Question of Ethics* and *Social Responsibility.*
- *Case Briefing Assignment.*
- *For Critical Analysis.*

Unit-Ending Cumulative Questions

New to the Fourth Edition are unit-ending cumulative hypothetical questions. These questions appear at the end of the *Questions and Case Problems* section in the final chapter of the unit. Each of these questions introduces a hypothetical business firm and then asks a series of questions about how the law applies to various actions taken by the firm. To answer the questions, the student must apply the laws discussed throughout the unit. Suggested answers to the unit-ending cumulative questions are included in the *Answers Manual.*

Accessing the Internet: Business Law and Legal Environment

We have included another special new feature in *Business Law Today,* Fourth Edition, called *Accessing the Internet: Business Law and Legal Environment.* These features, which appear at the ends of more than half of the chapters, indicate how you and your students can access materials relating to chapter topics via the Internet. Specific Internet addresses and "navigational" instructions are included in these features. For more information on how to access legal and other sources on the Internet, you or your students can refer to a new printed supplement accompanying the Fourth Edition of *Business Law Today* entitled *Understanding and Using the Internet,* by Bruce J. McLaren. This book, which is approximately 170 pages in length, includes an *Instructor's Manual.*

∎ Personal Law Handbook

To make sure that your students get a sense of how the law can affect them on a personal level, we have developed a *Personal Law Handbook,* which is placed at the end of the book, just following Chapter 37. We view this handbook as a practical guide to an application of the law to personal, financial, business, and consumer problems.

▌ Appendices

To help students learn how to find and analyze case law, we have added a special appendix at the end of Chapter 1. There your students will find information, including an exhibit, on how to read citations to cases, statutes, and agency regulations. The appendix to Chapter 1 also presents an annotated sample court case to help your students understand how to read and understand the cases presented within this text.

Because the majority of students keep their business law text as a reference source, we have included at the end of the book the following full set of appendices:

A. How to Brief a Case and Selected Cases.
B. The Constitution of the United States.
C. The Uniform Commercial Code (Excerpts—Article 1, Article 2, Article 2A, the Revised Articles 3 and 4, Article 4A, and Article 9).
D. The Uniform Partnership Act.
E. The Revised Model Business Corporation Act.
F. The Restatement (Second) of Torts (Excerpts).
G. The Sherman Antitrust Act of 1890 (Excerpts).
H. The Securities Act of 1933 (Excerpts).
I. The Securities Exchange Act of 1934 (Excerpts).
J. Title VII of the Civil Rights Act of 1964 (Excerpts).
K. The Americans with Disabilities Act of 1990 (Excerpts).
L. The Civil Rights Act of 1991 (Excerpts).
M. The United Nations Convention on Contracts for the International Sale of Goods (Excerpts).
N. Spanish Equivalents for Important Legal Terms in English.

▌ Supplemental Teaching Materials

This edition of *Business Law Today* is accompanied by a vastly expanded number of teaching and learning supplements. Individually and in conjunction with a number of our colleagues, we have developed supplementary teaching materials that we believe are the best available today. The supplements package includes the following components.

Printed Supplements

- *Instructor's Course Planning Guide.*
- *Instructor's Manual.*
- *Study Guide.*
- A comprehensive *Test Bank.*
- *Answers Manual.*
- *Case Printouts* (including printouts of cases referred to in selected features).
- *Handbook on Critical Thinking and Writing.*
- *West's Advanced Topics and Contemporary Issues, Second Edition.*
- *Unrevised Articles 3 and 4 of the Uniform Commercial Code.*
- *Lecture Outline System.*
- *Understanding* and *Using the Internet.*
- *Transparency Acetates.*

- *Citation-At-A-Glance.*
- *Handbook of Selected Statutes.*
- Regional Reporters.

Software and Video Supplements

- Computerized Test Bank *(WESTEST)*.
- Interactive Software—Contracts and Sales.
- "You Be the Judge" software.
- Case-Problem Cases on Diskette.
- WESTLAW.
- West's Business Law and the Legal Environment Audiocassette Library.
- Videocassettes (including new videos on specific legal applications).

▌For Users of the Third Edition

We thought that those of you who have been using *Business Law Today* would like to know some of the major changes that have been made for the Fourth Edition. The book is basically the same, but we think that we have improved it greatly, thanks in part to the many letters, telephone calls, and reviews that we have received.

Organizational Changes

- Constitutional law is now presented as Chapter 2 instead of Chapter 4.
- The ethics chapter now appears as Chapter 4, concluding the first unit of the text.
- More separate units have been created for conceptual clarity. For example, torts and crimes are now covered in Unit Two. Sales and lease contracts now appear in a separate unit (Unit Four) from negotiable instruments (covered in Unit Five) and debtor-creditor relationships (covered in Unit Six).

New or Significantly Revised Chapters

- Chapter 1 (The Legal and International Environment)—The material covered in this chapter has been revised and streamlined to make the text flow more smoothly. The discussion of jurisprudential thought has been greatly condensed, and more coverage is given to classifications of law. Additionally, the entire discussion of how to find and analyze case law has been moved to a special appendix just following Chapter 1.
- Chapter 4 (Ethics and Social Responsibility)—This chapter, which appeared as Chapter 2 in the Third Edition, has been revised extensively. Many sections have been rewritten to reflect today's business environment and current ethical challenges. The discussion of corporate social responsibility is given a more real-world flavor by applying the concepts discussed to a hypothetical business firm. The section on measuring social responsibility has been completely rewritten to reflect today's increased emphasis on corporate process as an important "yardstick" for measuring corporate responsibility.
- Chapter 6 (Business Torts and Intellectual Property)—This chapter includes greater coverage of electronic torts, including the electronic infringement of ownership rights in intellectual property (via the Internet, for example). A *Business Law in Action* entitled "Liability for On-Line Defamation" highlights some of the legal challenges posed by the widespread use of the Internet for communications. A *Landmark*

in the Law on the 1994 Agreement on Trade-Related Aspects of Intellectual Property Rights (TRIPS) emphasizes the growing need for intellectual property protection on a global level. A special feature on *Technology and Software Piracy* explores the ramifications for intellectual property owners of the unauthorized downloading of software from electronic bulletin boards.

● Chapter 7 (Criminal law)—This chapter now includes an exhibit showing the ways in which criminal law differs from civil law and a new section discussing the federal sentencing guidelines.

● Chapter 14 (The Formation of Sales and Lease Contracts)—This chapter now includes lease contracts and references to Article 2A of the Uniform Commercial Code (UCC). Additionally, a special section has been added on the provisions of the United Nations Convention on Contracts for the International Sale of Goods (CISG). The section compares the provisions of the UCC with those of the CISG with respect to specific requirements of sales contracts. The remaining chapters in the sales unit (Chapters 15 through 17) also include coverage of lease contracts and (in *International Perspectives*) comparisons of UCC provisions to those of the CISG.

● Chapter 16 (Performance and Breach of Sales and Lease Contracts)—This chapter has been reorganized to enhance readability. The remedies of the seller or lessor and the buyer or lessee are now grouped according to which party has possession of the goods at the time of the breach.

● Chapter 17 (Warranties and Product Liability)—This chapter includes more detail on actions in strict product liability.

● Chapter 18 (Negotiability and Transferability)—This chapter and the subsequent chapters on negotiable instruments have been revised and rewritten as necessary so that the law discussed is based on the 1990 revision of Articles 3 and 4 of the UCC. Major differences between the revised and unrevised versions of these articles are indicated in footnotes.

● Chapter 20 (Checks and the Banking System)—This chapter now includes a discussion of electronic check presentment and the electronic processing of checks.

● Chapter 22 (Creditors' Rights and Bankruptcy)—The section on bankruptcy has been revised to enhance understandability and to conform with the current Bankruptcy Code, as amended by the 1994 Bankruptcy Reform Act.

● Chapter 25 (Partnerships)—This chapter now includes a section on limited liability partnerships (LLPs). Additionally, we have added footnote references to provisions of the Revised Uniform Partnership Act (RUPA) whenever the RUPA significantly changes or modifies an aspect of partnership law being discussed in the text.

● Chapter 27 (Corporate Directors, Officers, and Shareholders)—This chapter now contains a discussion of shareholder proposals in proxy materials.

● Chapter 29 (Investor Protection)—This chapter has been updated throughout, and the section on exemptions to registration requirements under the 1933 Securities Act has been rewritten to reflect current law. A *Business Law in Action* looks at the current controversy over class-action suits and at the impact of the 1995 Private Securities Litigation Reform Act on such actions.

● Chapter 31 (Consumer and Environmental Law)—This chapter now discusses the most recent consumer protection laws, including the Telephone Consumer Protection Act of 1991, the Telemarketing and Consumer Fraud and Abuse Prevention Act of 1994, the FTC Telemarketing Sales Rule of 1995, the Home Ownership and Equity Protection Act of 1994, and the Truth-in-Lending Act Amendments of 1995.

● Chapter 32 (Employment Relationships) and Chapter 33 (Employment Discrimination)—For the Fourth Edition, we have expanded our coverage of employment laws and now have a separate chapter (Chapter 33) dealing solely with employment discrimination. Chapter 32 contains additional coverage of labor law, a major new section on the Family and Medical Leave Act of 1993, and a more extensive discussion of employee privacy rights. Chapter 33 offers an in-depth examination of the major laws prohibiting employment discrimination. The section on affirmative action has been expanded and updated to include references to the most recent cases on this issue.

What Else Is New?

In addition to the changes noted above, you will find a number of other new items or features in *Business Law Today*, Fourth Edition, as listed below:

NEW FEATURES   The following features are new to the Fourth Edition:

● *Chapter Objectives.*
● *Contents.*
● *Technology and the Law.*
● A greater number of *Ethical Perspectives* and *International Perspectives*, which are also presented in a new format.
● *For Critical Analysis* sections concluding every feature (except for the *Applications*) and every case.
● *Company Profiles* preceding many of the cases.
● *Accessing the Internet: Business Law and Legal Environment.*
● Simplified *For Review* questions placed prior to the standard end-of-chapter *Questions and Case Problems.*
● Unit-ending cumulative questions.

NEW EXHIBITS   We have modified exhibits contained in the Third Edition of *Business Law Today* whenever necessary to achieve greater clarity or accuracy. In addition, the following entirely new exhibits have been added for the Fourth Edition:

● The Legal Systems of Nations (Exhibit 1–1).
● Federal Courts and State Court Systems (Exhibit 3–2).
● Tort Lawsuit and Criminal Prosecution for the Same Act (Exhibit 5–1).
● Civil and Criminal Law Compared (Exhibit 7–1).
● The Check Collection Process (Exhibit 20–6).
● Terminology of Takeover Defenses (Exhibit 28–3).
● Exemptions under the 1993 Securities Act (Exhibit 29–1).
● A Sample Restricted Stock Certificate (Exhibit 29–2).
● A Sample Will (Exhibit 36–3).

NEW CASES AND CASE PROBLEMS   There are 106 new cases and 75 new case problems. Additionally, there are several new hypothetical questions, ethical questions, case briefing assignments, and questions "For Critical Analysis." Of course, all of the unit-ending hypothetical questions are new.

NEW APPENDICES

● Appendix E (The Revised Model Business Corporation Act).
● Appendix M (The United Nations Convention on Contracts for the International Sale of Goods—Excerpts).

Additionally, Appendix C (The Uniform Commercial Code—Excerpts) now includes Article 2A on leases and the revised versions of Articles 3 and 4.

NEW SUPPLEMENTS

● *The Unrevised Articles 3 and 4 of the Uniform Commercial Code.*
● *Handbook of Selected Statutes.*
● *Understanding and Using the Internet.*
● *Citation-At-A-Glance.*

▌ Acknowledgments
. . . .

Numerous careful and conscientious users of *Business Law Today* were kind enough
to help us revise the book. In addition, the staff at West Publishing Company went out
of its way to make sure that this edition came out early and in accurate form. Our production manager and designer, John Orr, along with our production editor, Bette
Darwin, made sure that we came out with an error-free, visually attractive edition. We
will always be in their debt.

We also wish to thank Lavina Leed Miller, who provided expert research, editing,
and proofing services for this project. Additional proofing was done by Suzie Franklin
DeFazio and Roxanna Lee. We must especially thank William Eric Hollowell,
coauthor of the *Instructor's Manual, Study Guide,* and *Test Bank,* for his excellent
research efforts. We were again fortunate to have the copy-editing services of Mary
Berry and the indexing services of Bob Marsh. Our appreciation also goes to Suzanne
Jasin for her many special efforts on the project. In addition, our gratitude goes to
Cecilia Lizama Salvatore for her proofing and for making sure that the work flowed
smoothly through Austin.

Finally, we continue to be in debt to our long-time editor, Clyde Perlee, Jr., who
guided us at all stages of this revision. Our developmental editor, Jan Lamar, deserves
our thanks for her efforts in coordinating reviews and in guaranteeing the timely and
accurate publication of all supplemental materials.

Acknowledgments for the First Edition

John J. Balek
Morton College, Illinois
Brad Botz
Garden City Community College, Kansas
Lee B. Burgunder
*California Polytechnic University — San
  Luis Obispo*
Dale Clark
Corning Community College, New York
Patricia L. DeFrain
Glendale College, California
Joe D. Dillsaver
Northeastern State University, Oklahoma
Larry R. Edwards
*Tarrant County Junior College, South
  Campus, Texas*
George E. Eigsti
Kansas City, Kansas, Community College
Jerry Furniss
University of Montana
Nancy L. Hart
Midland College, Texas
Janine S. Hiller
*Virginia Polytechnic Institute & State
  University*
Sarah Weiner Keidan
Oakland Community College, Michigan
Bradley T. Lutz
Hillsborough Community College, Florida
John D. Mallonee
Manatee Community College, Florida
James K. Miersma
*Milwaukee Area Technical Institute,
  Wisconsin*

Jim Lee Morgan
West Los Angeles College
Jack K. Morton
University of Montana
Solange North
Fox Valley Technical Institute, Wisconsin
Robert H. Orr
Florida Community College of Jacksonville
George Otto
Truman College, Illinois
William M. Rutledge
Macomb Community College, Michigan
Anne W. Schacherl
*Madison Area Technical College,
  Wisconsin*
Edward F. Shafer
Rochester Community College, Minnesota
Lou Ann Simpson
Drake University, Iowa
James E. Walsh, Jr.
Tidewater Community College, Virginia
Edward L. Welsh, Jr.
Phoenix College, Arizona
Clark W. Wheeler
Santa Fe Community College, Florida
James L. Wittenbach
University of Notre Dame, Indiana
Joseph Zavaglia, Jr.
Brookdale Community College, New Jersey

Acknowledgments for the Second Edition

Merlin Bauer
Mid-State Technical College, Wisconsin
Fred Ittner
College of Alameda, California
Susan S. Jarvis
University of Texas, Pan American, Texas
Beverly McCormick
Morehead State University, Kentucky

Robert H. Orr
Florida Community College at Jacksonville
Donald L. Petote
Genessee Community College, New York
Anne W. Schacherl
*Madison Area Technical College,
Wisconsin*

Acknowledgments for the Third Edition

Daryl Barton
Eastern Michigan University
Jere L. Crago
Delgado Community College, Louisiana
Tony Enerva
Lakeland Community College, Ohio
Richard N. Kleeberg
Solano Community College, California
Darlene Mallick
*Anne Arundel Community College,
Maryland*

Susan J. Mitchell
*Des Moines Area Community College,
Iowa*
Thomas L. Palmer
Northern Arizona University
Francis D. Polk
Ocean County College, New Jersey

Acknowledgments for the Fourth Edition

Lorraine K. Bannai
Western Washington University
Claude W. Dotson
Northwest College, Wyoming
Jacolin Eichelberger
Hillsborough Community College, Florida
Phil Harmeson
University of South Dakota
William J. McDevitt
Saint Joseph's University, Pennsylvania
John W. McGee
Southwest Texas State University
Trudi Manuel
Aims Community College, Colorado

Joseph D. Marcus
*Prince George's Community College,
Maryland*
Woodrow J. Maxwell
*Hudson Valley Community College,
New York*
Susan J. Mitchell
*Des Moines Area Community College,
Iowa*
Martha Wright Sartoris
*North Hennepin Community College,
Minnesota*

We know that we are not perfect. If you or your students find something you don't like or want us to change, write to us. That is how we can make *Business Law Today* an even better book in the future.

Roger LeRoy Miller
Gaylord A. Jentz

Unit One

The Legal Environment of Business

UNIT OUTLINE

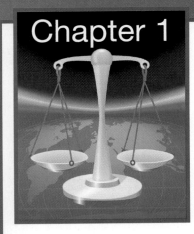

Chapter 1

The Legal and International Environment

"The law is of as much interest to the layman as it is to the lawyer."

Lord Balfour, 1848–1930
(British prime minister, 1902–1905)

CHAPTER OBJECTIVES

After reading this chapter, you should be able to:

1. Explain what is generally meant by the term *law*.
2. Describe the origins and importance of the common *law* tradition.
3. Identify the four major sources of American law.
4. List some important classifications of law.
5. Distinguish between national law and international law.

Lord Balfour's assertion in the quotation above emphasizes the underlying theme of every page in this book—that law is of interest to all persons, not just to lawyers. Those entering the world of business will find themselves subject to numerous laws and government regulations. A basic knowledge of these laws and regulations is beneficial—if not essential—to anyone contemplating a successful career in the business world of today.

In this introductory chapter, we first look at the nature of law and at some concepts that have significantly influenced how jurists and scholars view the nature and function of law. We then examine the common law tradition of the United States, as well as some of the major sources and classifications of American law. The chapter concludes with a discussion of the global legal environment, which frames many of today's business transactions.

▌The Nature of Law

There have been and will continue to be different definitions of *law*. The Greek philosopher Aristotle (384–322 B.C.E.) saw law as a "pledge that citizens of a state will do justice to one another." Aristotle's mentor, Plato (427–347 B.C.E.), believed that law was a form of social control. The Roman orator and politician Cicero (106–43 B.C.E.)

contended that law was the agreement of reason and nature, the distinction between the just and the unjust. The British jurist Sir William Blackstone (1723–1780) described law as "a rule of civil conduct prescribed by the supreme power in a state, commanding what is right, and prohibiting what is wrong." In America, the eminent jurist Oliver Wendell Holmes, Jr. (1841–1935), contended that law was a set of rules that allowed one to predict how a court would resolve a particular dispute—"the prophecies of what the courts will do in fact, and nothing more pretentious, are what I mean by the law."

Although these definitions vary in their particulars, they all are based on the following general observation: **law** consists of enforceable rules governing relationships among individuals and between individuals and their society. In the study of law, often referred to as **jurisprudence,** this very broad statement concerning the nature of law is the point of departure for all legal scholars and philosophers. We look here at three of the most influential schools of legal thought, or philosophies of law: the natural law tradition, legal positivism, and legal realism.

LAW
A body of enforceable rules governing relationships among individuals and between individuals and their society.

JURISPRUDENCE
The science or philosophy of law.

The Natural Law Tradition

The oldest and one of the most significant schools of jurisprudence is the natural law tradition, which dates back to ancient Greece and Rome. **Natural law** denotes a system of moral and ethical principles that are inherent in human nature and that can be discovered by humans through the use of their natural intelligence. The Greek philosopher Aristotle distinguished between natural law (which applies universally to all humankind) and **positive law** (the conventional, or written, law of a particular society at a particular point in time).

In essence, the natural law tradition presupposes that the legitimacy of positive, or conventional, law derives from natural law. Whenever positive law conflicts with natural law, positive law loses its legitimacy and should be changed. A law prohibiting murder, for example, reflects not only the values accepted by a particular society at a particular time (positive law) but also a universally accepted precept that murder is wrong (natural law). To murder someone is thus a violation of natural law. If a law allowed persons to murder each other, that law would be wrong, because it did not accord with natural law. In a sense, the natural law tradition encourages individuals to disobey conventional, or written, laws if those individuals believe that the laws are in conflict with natural law.

NATURAL LAW
The belief that government and the legal system should reflect universal moral and ethical principles that are inherent in human nature. The natural law school is the oldest and one of the most significant schools of legal thought.

POSITIVE LAW
The body of conventional, or written, law of a particular society at a particular point in time.

An international tribunal of judges listens to testimony in the trial of Nazi defendants at Nuremburg, Germany, in 1945. Which school of legal thought influenced these judges to rule that the defendants' crimes against humanity transcended written laws?

Legal Positivism

LEGAL POSITIVISM
A school of legal thought centered on the assumption that there is no law higher than the laws created by the government. Laws must be obeyed, even if they are unjust, to prevent anarchy.

Another school of legal thought is known as **legal positivism.** Legal positivists believe that there can be no higher law than a nation's positive laws—the laws created by a particular society at a particular point in time. Essentially, from the positivist perspective, the law is the law and must be obeyed on pain of punishment. Whether a particular law is bad or good is irrelevant. The merits or demerits of a given law can be discussed, and laws can be changed in an orderly manner through a legitimate lawmaking process. As long as a law exists, however, that law must be obeyed. If people felt justified in disobeying particular laws just because they did not feel the laws were just, anarchy would ensue.

Legal Realism

LEGAL REALISM
A school of legal thought of the 1920s and 1930s that generally advocated a less abstract and more realistic approach to the law, an approach that takes into account customary practices and the circumstances in which transactions take place. The school left a lasting imprint on American jurisprudence.

Legal realism, which became a popular school of legal thought in the 1920s and 1930s, left a strong imprint on American jurisprudence. Contrary to the dominant legal thinking of their time, the legal realists believed that the law could not—and should not—be an abstract body of rules applied uniformly to cases with similar circumstances. According to the legal realists, impartial and uniform application of the law is not possible. After all, judges are human beings with unique personalities, value systems, and intellects. Given this obvious fact, it would be impossible for any two judges to engage in an identical reasoning process when evaluating the same case.

The legal realists argued that each case also involves a unique set of circumstances—no two cases, no matter how similar, are ever exactly the same. Therefore, judges should take into account the specific circumstances of each case, rather than rely on some abstract rule that might not relate to those particular circumstances. When making decisions, judges should also consider extra-legal sources, such as economic and sociological data, to the extent that such sources could illuminate the circumstances and issues involved in specific cases. In other words, the law should take social and economic realities into account.

United States Supreme Court Justice Oliver Wendell Holmes, Jr. (1841–1935), and Karl Llewellyn (1893–1962) were both influential proponents of legal realism. Llewellyn is best known for his dominant role in drafting the Uniform Commercial Code (UCC), a set of rules for commercial transactions that will be discussed later in this chapter. The UCC reflects the influence of legal realism in its emphasis on practicality, flexibility, reasonability, and customary trade practices.

▌ The Common Law Tradition

How jurists view the law is particularly important in a legal system in which judges play a paramount role, as they do in the American legal system. Because of our colonial heritage, much of American law is based on the English legal system. A knowledge of this tradition is necessary to an understanding of the nature of our legal system today.

Early English Courts of Law

COMMON LAW
That body of law developed from custom or judicial decisions in English and U.S. courts, not attributable to a legislature.

In 1066, after the Normans conquered England, William the Conqueror and his successors began the process of unifying the country under their rule. One of the means they used to this end was the establishment of the king's courts, or *curiae regis*. Before the Norman Conquest, disputes had been settled according to the local legal customs and traditions in various regions of the country. The king's courts sought to establish a uniform set of rules for the country as a whole. What evolved in these courts was the beginning of the **common law**—a body of general rules that prescribed social conduct and that was applied throughout the entire English realm.

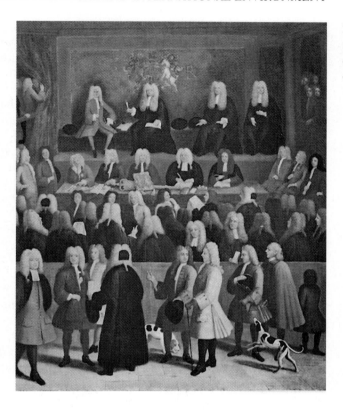

The Court of Chancery in the reign of George I. Early English court decisions formed the basis of what type of law?

Courts developed the common law rules from the principles underlying judges' decisions in actual legal controversies. Judges attempted to be consistent, and whenever possible, they based their decisions on the principles suggested by earlier cases. They sought to decide similar cases in a similar way and considered new cases with care, because they knew that their decisions would make new law. Each interpretation became part of the law on the subject and served as a legal **precedent**—that is, a decision that furnished an example or authority for deciding subsequent cases involving similar legal principles or facts.

In the early years of the common law, there was no single place or publication in which court opinions, or written decisions, could be found. In the late thirteenth and early fourteenth centuries, however, portions of the more important decisions of each year were gathered together and recorded in *Year Books*. The *Year Books* were useful references for lawyers and judges. In the sixteenth century, the *Year Books* were discontinued, and other reports of cases became available. (See the appendix to this chapter for a discussion of how cases are reported, or published, in the United States today.)

Stare Decisis

The practice of deciding new cases with reference to former decisions, or precedents, eventually became a cornerstone of the English and American judicial systems. The practice forms a doctrine called *stare decisis*[1] ("to stand on decided cases"). Under this doctrine, judges are obligated to follow the precedents established within their jurisdictions. For example, if the Supreme Court of California (that state's highest court) has ruled in a certain way on an issue, that decision will control the outcome of future cases on that issue brought before the state courts in California. Similarly, a decision on a given issue by the United States Supreme Court (the nation's highest court) is

"It will not do to decide the same question one way between one set of litigants and the opposite way between another."

Benjamin N. Cardozo, 1870–1938
(Associate justice of the United States Supreme Court, 1932–1938)

PRECEDENT
A court decision that furnishes an example or authority for deciding subsequent cases involving identical or similar facts.

STARE DECISIS
A common law doctrine under which judges are obligated to follow the precedents established in prior decisions.

1. Pronounced *ster*-ay dih-*si*-ses.

BINDING AUTHORITY
Any source of law that a court
must follow when deciding a
case. Binding authorities include
constitutions, statutes, and
regulations that govern the issue
being decided, as well as court
decisions that are controlling
precedents within the
jurisdiction.

binding on all inferior courts. Controlling precedents in a jurisdiction are referred to as **binding authorities,** as are statutes or other laws that must be followed.

The doctrine of *stare decisis* helps the courts to be more efficient, because if other courts have carefully reasoned through a similar case, their legal reasoning and opinions can serve as guides. *Stare decisis* also makes the law more stable and predictable. If the law on a given subject is well settled, someone bringing a case to court can usually rely on the court to make a decision based on what the law has been.

DEPARTURES FROM PRECEDENT Sometimes a court will depart from the rule of precedent if it decides that a given precedent should no longer be followed. If a court decides that a precedent is simply incorrect or that technological or social changes have rendered the precedent inapplicable, the court might rule contrary to the precedent.

Cases that overturn precedent often receive a great deal of publicity. In *Brown v. Board of Education of Topeka,*[2] for example, the United States Supreme Court expressly overturned precedent when it concluded that separate educational facilities for whites and blacks, which had been upheld as constitutional in numerous previous cases,[3] were inherently unequal. The Supreme Court's departure from precedent in *Brown* received a tremendous amount of publicity as people began to realize the ramifications of this change in the law.

WHEN THERE IS NO PRECEDENT Sometimes there is no precedent within a jurisdiction on which to base a decision, or there are conflicting precedents. A court then may look to precedents set in other jurisdictions for guidance. Such precedents, because they are not binding on the court, are referred to as **persuasive authorities.** A court may also consider a number of factors, including legal principles and policies underlying previous court decisions or existing statutes, fairness, social values and customs, public policy, and data and concepts drawn from the social sciences.

Which of these sources is chosen or receives the greatest emphasis will depend on the nature of the case being considered and the particular judge hearing the case. Although judges always strive to be free of subjectivity and personal bias in deciding cases, each judge has his or her own unique personality, set of values or philosophical leanings, and intellectual attributes—all of which necessarily frame the judicial decision-making process.

PERSUASIVE AUTHORITY
Any legal authority or source of
law that a court may look to for
guidance but on which it need
not rely in making its decision.
Persuasive authorities include
cases from other jurisdictions and
secondary sources of law.

Equitable Remedies and Courts of Equity

In law, a **remedy** is the means given to a party to enforce a right or to compensate for the violation of a right. For example, suppose that Shem is injured because of Rowan's wrongdoing. A court may order Rowan to compensate Shem for the harm by paying Shem a certain amount of money.

In the early king's courts of England, the kinds of remedies that could be granted were severely restricted. If one person wronged another, the king's courts could award as compensation either money or property, including land. These courts became known as *courts of law,* and the remedies were called *remedies at law.* Even though this system introduced uniformity in the settling of disputes, when plaintiffs wanted a remedy other than economic compensation, the courts of law could do nothing, so "no remedy, no right."

REMEDIES IN EQUITY Equity is that branch of unwritten law, founded in justice and fair dealing, that seeks to supply a fairer and more adequate remedy than any remedy

REMEDY
The relief given to an innocent
party to enforce a right or
compensate for the violation of a
right.

---

2. 347 U.S. 483, 74 S.Ct. 686, 98 L.Ed. 873 (1954). (See the appendix at the end of this chapter for an explanation of how to read legal citations.)
3. See *Plessy v. Ferguson,* 163 U.S. 537, 16 S.Ct. 1138, 41 L.Ed. 256 (1896).

available at law. In medieval England, when individuals could not obtain an adequate remedy in a court of law, they petitioned the king for relief. Most of these petitions were decided by an adviser to the king called the *chancellor*. The chancellor was said to be the "keeper of the king's conscience." When the chancellor thought that the claim was a fair one, new and unique remedies were granted. In this way, a new body of rules and remedies came into being, and eventually formal *chancery courts*, or *courts of equity*, were established. The remedies granted by these courts were called *remedies in equity*. Thus, two distinct court systems were created, each having a different set of judges and a different set of remedies.

Plaintiffs (those bringing lawsuits) had to specify whether they were bringing an "action at law" or an "action in equity," and they chose their courts accordingly. For example, a plaintiff might ask a court of equity to order a **defendant** (a person against whom a lawsuit is brought) to perform within the terms of a contract. A court of law could not issue such an order, because its remedies were limited to payment of money or property as compensation for damages. A court of equity, however, could issue a decree for *specific performance*—an order to perform what was promised. A court of equity could also issue an *injunction*, directing a party to do or refrain from doing a particular act. In certain cases, a court of equity could allow for the *rescission* (cancellation) of the contract so that the parties would be returned to the positions that they held prior to the contract's formation. Equitable remedies will be discussed in greater detail in Chapter 13.

PLAINTIFF
One who initiates a lawsuit.

DEFENDANT
One against whom a lawsuit is brought; the accused person in a criminal proceeding.

THE MERGING OF LAW AND EQUITY   Today, in most states, the courts of law and equity are merged, and thus the distinction between the two courts has largely disappeared. A plaintiff may now request both legal and equitable remedies in the same action, and the trial court judge may grant either form—or both forms—of relief. The merging of law and equity, however, does not diminish the importance of distinguishing legal remedies from equitable remedies. To request the proper remedy, one must know what remedies are available for the specific kinds of harms suffered. Today, as a rule, courts will grant an equitable remedy only when the remedy at law (money damages) is inadequate.

EQUITABLE PRINCIPLES AND MAXIMS   Over time, a number of **equitable principles and maxims** evolved that have since guided the courts in deciding whether plaintiffs should be granted equitable relief. Because of their importance, both historically and in our judicial system today, these principles and maxims are set forth in the following *Landmark in the Law*.

EQUITABLE PRINCIPLES AND MAXIMS
General propositions or principles of law that have to do with fairness (equity).

Equitable Principles and Maxims

LANDMARK IN THE LAW

In medieval England, courts of equity had the responsibility of using discretion in supplementing the common law. Even today, when the same court can award both legal and equitable remedies, such discretion is exercised. Courts often invoke equitable principles and maxims when making their decisions. Here are some of the more significant equitable principles and maxims:

1. *Whoever seeks equity must do equity.* (Anyone who wishes to be treated fairly must treat others fairly.)
2. *Where there is equal equity, the law must prevail.* (The law will determine the outcome of a controversy in which the merits of both sides are equal.)

(Continued)

Landmark in the Law—Continued

REMEMBER Even though, in most states, courts of law and equity have merged, the principles of equity still apply.

3. *One seeking the aid of an equity court must come to the court with clean hands.* (Plaintiffs must have acted fairly and honestly.)
4. *Equity will not suffer a wrong to be without a remedy.* (Equitable relief will be awarded when there is a right to relief and there is no adequate remedy at law.)
5. *Equity regards substance rather than form.* (Equity is more concerned with fairness and justice than with legal technicalities.)
6. *Equity aids the vigilant, not those who rest on their rights.* (Equity will not help those who neglect their rights for an unreasonable period of time.)

The last maxim has become known as the *equitable doctrine of laches*. The doctrine arose to encourage people to bring lawsuits while the evidence was fresh; if they failed to do so, they would not be allowed to bring a lawsuit. What constitutes a reasonable time, of course, varies according to the circumstances of the case. Time periods for different types of cases are now usually fixed by **statutes of limitations.** After the time allowed under a statute of limitations has expired, no action can be brought, no matter how strong the case was originally.

For Critical Analysis: *Do you think that the government should establish, through statutes of limitations, the time limits within which different types of lawsuits can be brought?*

STATUTE OF LIMITATIONS
A federal or state statute setting the maximum time period during which a certain action can be brought or certain rights enforced.

▌ Sources of American Law

PRIMARY SOURCE OF LAW
A document that establishes the law on a particular issue, such as a constitution, a statute, an administrative rule, or a court decision.

There are numerous sources of American law. **Primary sources of law,** or sources that *establish* the law, include the following:

- The U.S. Constitution and the constitutions of the various states.
- Statutes, or laws, passed by Congress and by state legislatures.
- Regulations created by administrative agencies, such as the federal Food and Drug Administration.
- Case law (court decisions).

We describe each of these important primary sources of law in the following pages.
   Secondary sources of law are books and articles that summarize and clarify the primary sources of law. Examples are legal encyclopedias, treatises, articles in law reviews published by law schools, or other legal journals. Courts often refer to secondary sources of law for guidance in interpreting and applying the primary sources of law discussed here.

SECONDARY SOURCE OF LAW
A publication that summarizes or interprets the law, such as a legal encyclopedia, a legal treatise, or an article in a law review.

Constitutional Law

The federal government and the states have separate written constitutions that set forth the general organization, powers, and limits of their respective governments. **Constitutional law** is the law as expressed in these constitutions.
   The U.S. Constitution is the supreme law of the land. As such, it is the basis of all law in the United States. A law in violation of the Constitution, no matter what its source, will be declared unconstitutional and will not be enforced. Because of its paramount importance in the American legal system, we discuss the Constitution at length in Chapter 2 and present the complete text of the U.S. Constitution in Appendix B.
   The Tenth Amendment to the U.S. Constitution, which defines the powers and limitations of the federal government, reserves all powers not granted to the federal government to the states. Each state in the union has its own constitution. Unless they

CONSTITUTIONAL LAW
Law based on the U.S. Constitution and the constitutions of the various states.

Young students view the U.S. Constitution on display in Washington, D.C. Can a law be in violation of the Constitution and still be enforced? If not, why not?

conflict with the U.S. Constitution or a federal law, state constitutions are supreme within their respective borders.

Statutory Law

Statutes enacted by legislative bodies at any level of government make up another source of law, which is generally referred to as **statutory law.**

FEDERAL STATUTES Federal statutes are laws that are enacted by the U.S. Congress. As mentioned, any law—including a federal statute—that violates the U.S. Constitution will be held unconstitutional.

Examples of federal statutes that affect business operations include laws regulating the purchase and sale of securities, or corporate stocks and bonds (discussed in Chapter 29); consumer protection statutes (discussed in Chapter 31); and statutes prohibiting employment discrimination (discussed in Chapter 33). Whenever a particular statute is mentioned in this text, we usually provide a footnote showing its **citation** (a reference to a publication in which a legal authority—such as a statute or a court decision—or other source can be found). In the appendix following this chapter, we explain how you can use these citations to find statutory law.

STATE AND LOCAL STATUTES AND ORDINANCES State statutes are laws enacted by state legislatures. Any state law that conflicts with the U.S. Constitution, with federal laws enacted by Congress, or with the state's constitution will be deemed unconstitutional. Statutory law also includes the ordinances passed by cities and counties, none of which can violate the U.S. Constitution, the relevant state constitution, or federal or state laws.

STATUTORY LAW
The body of law enacted by legislative bodies (as opposed to constitutional law, administrative law, or case law).

CITATION
A reference to a publication in which a legal authority—such as a statute or a court decision—or other source can be found.

Examples of state statutes include state criminal statutes (discussed in Chapter 7), state corporation statutes (discussed in Chapters 26 through 29), state deceptive trade practices acts (referred to in Chapter 31), state laws governing wills and trusts (discussed in Chapter 36), and state versions of the Uniform Commercial Code (to be discussed shortly). Examples of local ordinances include zoning ordinances and local laws regulating housing construction and such things as the overall appearance of a community.

A federal statute, of course, applies to all states. A state statute, in contrast, applies only within the state's borders. State laws thus vary from state to state.

UNIFORM LAWS   The differences among state laws were particularly notable in the 1800s, when conflicting state statutes frequently made the rapidly developing trade and commerce among the states very difficult. To counter these problems, a group of legal scholars and lawyers formed the National Conference of Commissioners (NCC) on Uniform State Laws in 1892 to draft uniform statutes for adoption by the states. The NCC still exists today and continues to issue uniform statutes.

Adoption of a uniform law is a state matter, and a state may reject all or part of the statute or rewrite it as the state legislature wishes. Hence, even when a uniform law is said to have been adopted in many states, those states' laws may not be entirely "uniform." Once adopted by a state legislature, a uniform act becomes a part of the statutory law of that state.

The earliest uniform law, the Uniform Negotiable Instruments Law, was completed by 1896 and was adopted in every state by the early 1920s (although not all states used exactly the same wording). Over the following decades, other acts were drawn up in a similar manner. In all, over two hundred uniform acts have been issued by the NCC since its inception. The most ambitious uniform act of all, however, was the Uniform Commercial Code.

THE UNIFORM COMMERCIAL CODE (UCC)   The Uniform Commercial Code (UCC), which was created through the joint efforts of the NCC and the American Law Institute,[4] was first issued in 1952. The UCC has been adopted in all fifty states,[5] the District of Columbia, and the Virgin Islands. The UCC facilitates commerce among the states by providing a uniform, yet flexible, set of rules governing commercial transactions. The UCC assures businesspersons that their contracts, if validly entered into, normally will be enforced.

Because of its importance in the area of commercial law, we cite the UCC frequently in this text. We also present excerpts from the latest version of the UCC in Appendix C. (For a discussion of the creation of the UCC, see the *Landmark in the Law* in Chapter 14.)

Administrative Law

An important source of American law consists of **administrative law**—the rules, orders, and decisions of administrative agencies. An **administrative agency** is a federal, state, or local government agency established to perform a specific function. Rules issued by various administrative agencies now affect virtually every aspect of a business's operation, including the firm's capital structure and financing, its hiring and firing procedures, its relations with employees and unions, and the way it manufactures and markets its products.

At the national level, numerous **executive agencies** exist within the cabinet departments of the executive branch. The Food and Drug Administration, for example, is within the Department of Health and Human Services. Executive agencies are subject to the authority of the president, who has the power to appoint and remove

BE CAREFUL Even though uniform laws are intended to be adopted without changes, states often modify them to suit their particular needs.

ADMINISTRATIVE LAW
The body of law created by administrative agencies (in the form of rules, regulations, orders, and decisions) in order to carry out their duties and responsibilities.

ADMINISTRATIVE AGENCY
A federal or state government agency established to perform a specific function. Administrative agencies are authorized by legislative acts to make and enforce rules to administer and enforce the acts.

EXECUTIVE AGENCY
An administrative agency within the executive branch of government. At the federal level, executive agencies are those within the cabinet departments.

---

4.   This institute was formed in the 1920s and consists of practicing attorneys, legal scholars, and judges.
5.   Louisiana has adopted only Articles 1, 3, 4, 5, 7, 8, and 9.

officers of federal agencies. There are also major **independent regulatory agencies** at the federal level, such as the Federal Trade Commission, the Securities and Exchange Commission, and the Federal Communications Commission. The president's power is less pronounced in regard to independent agencies, whose officers serve for fixed terms and cannot be removed without just cause.

There are administrative agencies at the state and local levels as well. Commonly, a state agency (such as a state pollution-control agency) is created as a parallel to a federal agency (such as the Environmental Protection Agency). Just as federal statutes take precedence over conflicting state statutes, so do federal agency regulations take precedence over conflicting state regulations. Because the rules of state and local agencies vary widely, we focus here exclusively on federal administrative law.

AGENCY CREATION Because Congress cannot possibly oversee the actual implementation of all the laws it enacts, it must delegate such tasks to others, particularly when the issues relate to highly technical areas, such as air and water pollution. By delegating some of its constitutional authority to make and implement laws to agencies, Congress is able to monitor indirectly a particular area in which it has passed legislation without becoming bogged down in the many details relating to enforcement—details that are often best left to specialists.

Congress creates an administrative agency by enacting **enabling legislation**, which specifies the name, composition, purpose, and powers of the agency being created. For example, the Federal Trade Commission (FTC) was created in 1914 by the Federal Trade Commission Act.[6] This act prohibits unfair and deceptive trade practices. It also describes the procedures the agency must follow to charge persons or organizations with violations of the act, and it provides for judicial review (review by the courts) of agency orders. Other portions of the act grant the agency powers to "make rules and regulations for the purpose of carrying out the Act," to conduct investigations of business practices, to obtain reports from interstate corporations concerning their business practices, to investigate possible violations of the act, to publish findings of its investigations, and to recommend new legislation. The act also empowers the FTC to hold trial-like hearings and to **adjudicate** (resolve judicially) certain kinds of trade disputes that involve FTC regulations.

Note that the FTC's grant of power incorporates functions associated with the legislative branch of government (rulemaking), the executive branch (investigation and enforcement), and the judicial branch (adjudication). Taken together, these functions constitute what has been termed **administrative process,** which is the administration of law by administrative agencies.

RULEMAKING One of the major functions of an administrative agency is **rulemaking**—creating or modifying rules, or regulations, pursuant to its enabling legislation. The Administrative Procedure Act of 1946[7] imposes strict procedural requirements that agencies must follow in their rulemaking and other functions.

The most common rulemaking procedure involves three steps. First, the agency must give public notice of the proposed rulemaking proceedings, where and when the proceedings will be held, the agency's legal authority for the proceedings, and the terms or subject matter of the proposed rule. The notice must be published in the *Federal Register,* a daily publication of the U.S. government. Second, following this notice, the agency must allow ample time for interested parties to comment in writing on the proposed rule. After the comments have been received and reviewed, the agency takes them into consideration when drafting the final version of the regulation. The third and final step is the drafting of the final version and the publication of the rule in the *Federal Register.* (See the appendix at the end of this chapter for an explanation of how to find agency regulations.)

INDEPENDENT REGULATORY AGENCY
An administrative agency that is not considered part of the government's executive branch and is not subject to the authority of the president. Independent agency officials cannot be removed without cause.

ENABLING LEGISLATION
A statute enacted by Congress that authorizes the creation of an administrative agency and specifies the name, composition, purpose, and powers of the agency being created.

ADJUDICATE
To render a judicial decision. In the administrative process, the proceeding in which an administrative law judge hears and decides on issues that arise when an administrative agency charges a person or a firm with violating a law or regulation enforced by the agency.

ADMINISTRATIVE PROCESS
The procedure used by administrative agencies in the administration of law.

RULEMAKING
The process undertaken by an administrative agency when formally adopting a new regulation or amending an old one. Rulemaking involves notifying the public of a proposed rule or change and receiving and considering the public's comments.

---

6. 15 U.S.C. Sections 45–58.
7. 5 U.S.C. Sections 551–706.

ADMINISTRATIVE LAW JUDGE (ALJ)
One who presides over an administrative agency hearing and who has the power to administer oaths, take testimony, rule on questions of evidence, and make determinations of fact.

INVESTIGATION AND ENFORCEMENT   Agencies have both investigatory and prosecutorial powers. An agency can compel individuals or organizations to hand over specified books, papers, records, or other documents. In addition, agencies may conduct on-site inspections, although a search warrant is normally required for such inspections. Sometimes the search of a home, an office, or a factory is the only means of obtaining evidence needed to prove a regulatory violation. Agencies investigate a wide range of activities, including coal mining, automobile manufacturing, and the industrial discharge of pollutants into the environment.

ADJUDICATION   After conducting its own investigation of a suspected rule violation, an agency may decide to take action against a specific party. The action may involve a trial-like hearing before an **administrative law judge (ALJ)**. The ALJ may compel the charged party to pay fines or may forbid the party to carry on some specified activity. Either side may appeal the ALJ's decision to the commission or board that governs the agency. If the party fails to get relief here, appeal can be made to a federal court.

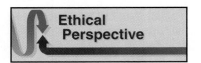
Ethical Perspective

Combining the functions normally divided among the three branches of government into a single governmental entity, such as the FTC, creates institutional flexibility, but it also concentrates a considerable amount of power in a single organization. The broad range of authority exercised by administrative agencies sometimes poses questions of fairness.

For example, when an agency claims that a business firm's practices violate an agency rule, the firm has little recourse against the agency—even if the rule seems somewhat arbitrary. The firm normally must comply with the agency's requests (for documents, for example) during the agency's investigation, and if the dispute is adjudicated, the firm will be subject to the agency's decision. Of course, the firm may be able to appeal the decision to a court, but as long as the agency followed proper procedures when issuing the rule and had some rational basis for the rule, a court will be reluctant to overrule the agency's decision.

The Constitution authorizes only the legislative branch to create laws. Administrative agencies, however, which are not specifically referred to in the Constitution, make rules that are as legally binding as laws passed by Congress. Although the government exercises certain controls over agency powers and functions, in many ways administrative agencies function independently.

For Critical Analysis: *Is there any way to avoid placing so much power in the hands of administrative agencies? Is there any practical alternative?*

Case Law and Common Law Doctrines

The body of law that was first developed in England and that is still used today in the United States consists of the rules of law announced in court decisions. These rules of law include interpretations of constitutional provisions, of statutes enacted by legislatures, and of regulations created by administrative agencies. Today, this body of law is referred to variously as the common law, judge-made law, or **case law.**

CASE LAW
The rules of law announced in court decisions. Case law includes the aggregate of reported cases that interpret judicial precedents, statutes, regulations, and constitutional provisions.

The common law—the doctrines and principles embodied in case law—governs all areas not covered by statutory law (or agency regulations issued to implement various statutes). In disputes concerning contracts for the sale of goods, for example, the Uniform Commercial Code (statutory law) applies instead of the common law of contracts. Similarly, in a dispute concerning a particular employment practice, if a statute regulates that practice, the statute will apply rather than the common law doctrine that applied prior to the enactment of the statute.

THE RELATIONSHIP BETWEEN THE COMMON LAW AND STATUTORY LAW The body of statutory law has expanded greatly since the beginning of this nation, and this expansion has resulted in a proportionate reduction in the scope and applicability of common law doctrines. Nonetheless, there is a significant overlap between statutory law and case law, and thus common law doctrines remain a significant source of legal authority.

For example, many statutes essentially codify existing common law rules, and thus the courts, in interpreting the statutes, often rely on the common law as a guide to what the legislators intended. Additionally, how the courts interpret a particular statute determines how that statute will be applied. If you wanted to learn about the coverage and applicability of a particular statute, for example, you would, of course, need to locate the statute and study it. You would also need to see how the courts in your jurisdiction have interpreted the statute—in other words, what precedents have been established in regard to that statute. Often, the applicability of a newly enacted statute does not become clear until a body of case law develops to clarify how, when, and to whom the statute applies.

RESTATEMENTS OF THE LAW The American Law Institute drafted and published compilations of the common law called Restatements of the Law, which generally summarize the common law rules followed by most states. There are Restatements of the Law in the areas of contracts, torts, agency, trusts, property, restitution, security, judgments, and conflict of laws. The Restatements, like other secondary sources of law, do not in themselves have the force of law but are an important source of legal analysis and opinion on which judges often rely in making their decisions.

Many of the Restatements are now in their second or third editions. We refer to the Restatements frequently in subsequent chapters of this text, indicating in parentheses the edition to which we are referring. For example, we refer to the second edition of the *Restatement of the Law of Contracts* simply as the *Restatement (Second) of Contracts*.

> *"Statutes do not interpret themselves; their meaning is declared by the courts."*
>
> **John Chipman Gray, 1839–1915**
> *(American lawyer and teacher)*

BE AWARE Restatements of the Law are authoritative sources, but they do not have the force of law.

▭ Technology and On-Line Legal Research

Slowly but surely, legal research is changing. In the past, researchers painstakingly had to examine dozens, if not hundreds, of different printed volumes containing court decisions, federal statutes, state statutes, and regulations from administrative agencies. Today, most—if not all—legal research can be done on-line. That is to say, any student who is studying the law and any attorney or other legal practitioner can now search through the millions of pages of available legal sources in minutes.

On-Line Legal Research Services

One of the first and most comprehensive on-line legal research services is WESTLAW, which has been provided for years by West Publishing Company. Powerful computers at West's main headquarters in Eagan, Minnesota, do all of the searching that would otherwise take hours, if not days or weeks. In the last few years, individuals accessing WESTLAW have been able to ask their legal research questions in plain English by using

(Continued)

How has technology changed the methods of legal research?

Technology and On-Line Legal Research—Continued

WIN (WESTLAW Is Natural). A competing system, called LEXIS, is provided by Reed-Elsevier.

The Internet
Finally, anybody with a computer, modem, and a way to access the Internet can obtain certain legal documents, including cases decided by the United States Supreme Court, virtually minutes after they are released for publication. The Internet is a web of educational, corporate, and research computer networks around the world. Today, at least thirty million people are using it, and there are over sixty thousand networks connected to it. Perhaps the most interesting part of the Internet is the World Wide Web, commonly called the Web, which is a vast, interlinked network of computer files all over the world. You can use the Internet to find discussion groups, news groups, and electronic publications. The most common use of the Internet is for electronic mail (E-mail).

Virtually every month a new source of authoritative legal research materials is being put on the Internet. For example, the Securities and Exchange Commission (SEC) recently made available on the Internet, at no cost, its Electronic Data Gathering, Analysis, and Retrieval System (Internet address: http://www.sec.gov/). The chairman of the SEC said that he was committed to maintaining free public access to corporate disclosure documents over the Internet.

CD-ROM Libraries
Increasingly, much of the material that can be accessed on-line is becoming available on CD-ROM. CD stands for *compact disc*. ROM stands for *read-only memory*, meaning that the CDs cannot be erased as a videocassette can be and then reused. Literally hundreds of thousands of pages of legal research materials—cases, statutes, and so on—are recorded on CD-ROM. The equivalent of an entire encyclopedia can be put on one normal CD-ROM. Newer technologies will allow the equivalent of up to ten encyclopedias on one CD-ROM.

For Critical Analysis: *Describe what a law and legal research library might consist of in the future.*

Classifications of Law

SUBSTANTIVE LAW
Law that defines, describes, regulates, and creates legal rights and obligations.

PROCEDURAL LAW
Law that establishes the methods of enforcing the rights established by substantive law.

CIVIL LAW
The branch of law dealing with the definition and enforcement of all private or public rights, as opposed to criminal matters.

CRIMINAL LAW
Law that defines and governs actions that constitute crimes. Generally, criminal law has to do with wrongful actions committed against society for which society demands redress.

The huge body of the law may be broken down according to several classification systems. For example, one classification system divides law into **substantive law** (all laws that define, describe, regulate, and create legal rights and obligations) and **procedural law** (all laws that establish the methods of enforcing the rights established by substantive law).

Another classification system divides law into civil law and criminal law. **Civil law** spells out the rights and duties that exist between persons and between persons and their governments, and the relief available when a person's rights are violated. Contract law, for example, is part of civil law. The whole body of tort law (see Chapters 5 and 6), which deals with the infringement by one person on the legally recognized rights of another, is also an area of civil law. **Criminal law** has to do with a wrong committed against society for which society demands redress (see Chapter 7). Criminal acts are proscribed by local, state, or federal government statutes.

Other classification systems divide law into federal law and state law, private law (dealing with relationships between persons) and public law (addressing the relationship between persons and their government), and so on. One of the broadest classification systems divides law into national law and international law, a topic to which we now turn.

National and International Law

Although the focus of this book is U.S. business law, increasingly businesspersons in this country are engaging in transactions that extend beyond our national borders. In these situations, the laws of other nations or the laws governing relationships among nations may come into play. For this reason, those who pursue a career in business today should have an understanding of the global legal environment.

We examine the laws governing international business transactions in later chapters (including parts of Chapters 14 through 16, which cover contracts for the sale of goods, and all of Chapter 37). It is worthwhile at this point, however, to summarize some important aspects of the international legal environment, because many of the topics covered in this text have international dimensions.

National Law

National law is the law of a particular nation, such as the United States or France. National law, of course, varies from country to country, because each country's law reflects the interests, customs, activities, and values that are unique to that nation's culture. Even though the laws and legal systems of various countries differ substantially, broad similarities do exist.

Basically, there are two legal systems in today's world. One of these systems is the common law system of England and the United States, which we have already discussed. The other system is based on Roman civil law, or "code law." The term *civil law*, as used here, refers not to civil as opposed to criminal law but to *codified* law—an ordered grouping of legal principles enacted into law by a legislature or governing body. In a **civil law system,** the primary source of law is a statutory code, and case precedents are not judicially binding, as they normally are in a common law system. Although judges in a civil law system commonly refer to previous decisions as sources of legal guidance, they are not bound by precedent; in other words, the doctrine of *stare decisis* does not apply.

Exhibit 1–1 lists the countries that today follow either the common law system or the civil law system. Generally, those countries that were once colonies of Great Britain retained their English common law heritage after they achieved their independence. Similarly, the civil law system, which is followed in most of the continental European countries, was retained in the Latin American, African, and Asian countries that were once colonies of the continental European nations. Japan and South Africa also have civil law systems, and ingredients of the civil law system are found in the Islamic courts of predominantly Muslim countries. In the United States, the state of Louisiana, because of its historical ties to France, has in part a civil law system. The legal systems of Puerto Rico, Québec, and Scotland are similarly characterized as having elements of the civil law system.

"*It is perfectly proper to regard and study the law simply as a great anthropological document.*"

Oliver Wendell Holmes, Jr., 1841–1935
(Associate justice of the United States Supreme Court, 1902–1932)

NATIONAL LAW
Law that pertains to a particular nation (as opposed to international law).

CIVIL LAW SYSTEM
A system of law derived from that of the Roman Empire and based on a code rather than case law; the predominant system of law in the nations of continental Europe and the nations that were once their colonies. In the United States, Louisiana is the only state that has a civil law system.

CIVIL LAW		COMMON LAW	
Argentina	Mexico	Australia	United States
Austria	Poland	Bangladesh	Zambia
Brazil	South Korea	Canada	
Chile	Sweden	Ghana	
China	Tunisia	India	
Egypt	Venezuela	Israel	
Finland		Jamaica	
France		Kenya	
Germany		Malaysia	
Greece		New Zealand	
Indonesia		Nigeria	
Iran		Singapore	
Italy		United Kingdom	
Japan			

◆ Exhibit 1–1
The Legal Systems of Nations

International Perspective

The ability to conduct business successfully in a foreign nation requires not only a knowledge of that nation's laws but also some familiarity with its cultural system. One obvious cultural difference among nations is language. Language differences have occasionally confounded efforts to do business abroad. For example, Parker Pen's motto, "Prevent embarrassment, use Parker Ink," was itself an embarrassment in Spanish-speaking countries because the Spanish word *embarazo* means not only "embarrassment" but also "pregnancy."

Perceptions of time, management styles, and conceptions of what kind of behavior is appropriate also vary from one culture to another. In many countries, for example, gift giving is a common practice between contracting companies or between companies and government officials. To Americans, such gift giving may look suspiciously like an unethical (and possibly illegal) bribe.

The role played by women in other countries may also present some difficulties for firms doing business internationally. Equal employment opportunity is a fundamental public policy in the United States. Some other countries, however, largely reject any role for women professionals, which may cause problems for American women who attempt to conduct business transactions in those countries.

For Critical Analysis: *Suppose that John, the president of a U.S. bank, wants to take his top vice president, Carla, with him to a meeting overseas. John is advised that he would lose respect in the eyes of the overseas company if he took Carla, a woman, with him. List some of the pros and cons of taking Carla to the meeting that John should consider in making his decision.*

INTERNATIONAL LAW
The law that governs relations among nations. National laws, customs, treaties, and international conferences and organizations are generally considered to be the most important sources of international law.

Judges at a trial of Islamic extremists on charges of murder. What impact does the use of a civil law system have on rulings in the Islamic courts of predominantly Muslim countries?

International Law

International law can be defined as a body of written and unwritten laws observed by independent nations and governing the acts of individuals as well as governments. The key difference between national law and international law is the fact that national law can be enforced by government authorities. What government, though, can enforce international law? By definition, a *nation* is a sovereign entity, which means that there is no higher authority to which that nation must submit. If a nation violates an international law, the most that other countries or international organizations can do (if

PROFILE

Waleed Sadi (1939–   )

Waleed Sadi has been Jordan's ambassador to Turkey and to the United Nations Human Rights Commission in Geneva, Switzerland. A former editor for the *Jordan Times*, Sadi continues to write a column on human rights for the newspaper.

Sadi's father was a Jordanian army general who served under King Hussein. Despite the animosity generated by conflicts between Israel and its Arab neighbors, including Jordan, Sadi's father insisted that his children respect other people regardless of their religion, nationality, or culture. Sadi attended school in Jerusalem, where his classmates included Muslims, Jews, and Christians. Sadi graduated from a Quaker high school and later obtained a law degree.

At McGill University in Montreal, Québec, Sadi met Irwin Cotler, a professor of international law also involved in human rights work. In 1995, Sadi, a Muslim, and Cotler, a Jew, taught a seminar titled "The Arab-Israeli Conflict: A Case Study in the International Legal Process." They taught about cooperation and the positive effects that can result from respecting different points of view. As part of the course, the students researched legal aspects of the Middle East peace process.

The two professors are committed to the principles they teach. These principles affect their relationship and their individual views. For example, Cotler sees Islam not only as a religion but also as "a comprehensive legal system, an organizing principle, the essential looking glass into an understanding of the Middle East."

Sadi criticizes what he refers to as the culture of hate in which people in the Middle East have been raised for generations. To develop a new culture will take hard work, he says, beginning in the schools. "If," he hopes, "people would only listen." Cotler adds, "If the two of us, coming from different religions, cultures, education, can have so deep a relationship, it augurs well for the culture of peace."[a]

For Critical Analysis: *Are there any acceptable alternatives to respecting and cooperating with those who hold different views?*

a. John Kalbfleisch, "Brothers in Law— Muslim and Jew Teach Course That Aims at Culture of Peace," *Montreal Gazette*, April 9, 1995, p. C3.

---

persuasive tactics fail) is resort to coercive actions against the violating nation. Coercive actions range from severance of diplomatic relations and boycotts to, at the last resort, war.

In essence, international law is the result of centuries-old attempts to reconcile the traditional need of each nation to be the final authority over its own affairs with the desire of nations to benefit economically from trade and harmonious relations with one another. Although no sovereign nation can be compelled to obey a law external to itself, nations can and do voluntarily agree to be governed in certain respects by international law for the purpose of facilitating international trade and commerce, as well as civilized discourse.

International law is an intermingling of rules and constraints derived from a variety of sources. The laws of individual nations are sources of international law, as are the customs that have evolved among nations in their relations with one another. Of increasing importance in regulating international activities, however, are treaties and international organizations.

TREATIES   A **treaty** is an agreement between two or more nations that creates rights and duties binding on the parties to the treaty, just as a private contract creates rights and duties binding on the parties to the contract. To give effect to a treaty, the supreme power of each nation that is a party to the treaty must ratify it. For example, the U.S. Constitution requires approval by two-thirds of the Senate before a treaty executed by the president will be binding on the U.S. government.

Bilateral agreements, as the term implies, occur when only two nations form an agreement that will govern their commercial exchanges or other relations with one

TREATY
An agreement formed between two or more independent nations.

another. Multilateral agreements are those formed by several nations. The European Union (EU), for example, which regulates commercial activities among its fifteen European member nations, is the result of a multilateral trade agreement. The North American Free Trade Agreement (NAFTA), which regulates trade among Canada, the United States, and Mexico, is another example of a multilateral trade agreement.

One treaty of particular significance to the international legal environment of business is the United Nations 1980 Convention on Contracts for the International Sale of Goods (CISG). Essentially, the CISG is to international sales transactions what the Uniform Commercial Code is to domestic sales transactions. The CISG governs the international sale of goods between firms or individuals located in different countries, providing that the countries involved have ratified the CISG. We examine the CISG and its provisions more closely in Chapters 14 through 16, in the context of the law governing the sale of goods.

INTERNATIONAL ORGANIZATIONS   International organizations and conferences also play an important role in the international legal arena. International organizations and conferences adopt resolutions, declarations, and other types of standards that often require a particular behavior of nations. The General Assembly of the United Nations, for example, has adopted numerous resolutions and declarations that embody principles of international law and has sponsored conferences that have led to the formation of international agreements. The United States is a member of more than one hundred multilateral and bilateral organizations, including at least twenty through the United Nations.

Application

Law and the Businessperson—How to Choose and Use a Lawyer

If you are contemplating a career in the business world, sooner or later you will probably face the question, "Do I need a lawyer?" The answer to this question will likely be "Yes," at least at some time during your career. Even individuals who have gone on to law school and later entered into a business often hire an outside lawyer to help them with their legal problems. Today, it is virtually impossible for nonexperts to keep up with the myriad rules and regulations that govern the way in which business can be conducted in the United States. It is also increasingly possible for businesspersons to incur penalties for violating laws or regulations of which they were totally unaware.

Although lawyers may seem expensive—anywhere from $75 to $400 per hour—the cautious businessperson will make sure that he or she is not "penny wise and pound foolish." The consultation fee paid to an attorney may be a drop in the bucket compared with the potential liability facing a businessperson.

Selecting an Attorney
In selecting an attorney, you can ask friends, relatives, or business associates to recommend someone. Alternatively, you can call the local or state bar association to obtain the names of several lawyers. You can also go to your local library (or go on-line) to look at the *Martindale-Hubbell Law Directory*, which includes professional biographies of most of the attorneys engaged in private practice throughout the country. The directory also lists areas of concentration, as well as bank references and representative clients. Some legal aid programs have staff attorneys, and others may refer you to volunteers. You also might investigate legal clinics and prepaid legal service plans.

At your initial meeting with the attorney you have selected, disclose any relevant information about the problem at hand or what kind of legal assistance you need. (Remember that virtually everything you say to your attorney is protected by the attorney-client privilege of confidentiality. In other words, the lawyer is legally prohibited from talking about your case with anyone else except his or her assistants, who may be given information to the extent that they need it to work on your case.) Ask about fees. How are they determined? How much legal work will be required to handle your situation? Can you pay the fee in installments? Will other legal professionals (such as attorneys in the same office, paralegals,

Application—Continued

and other assistants) be working with the lawyer on your case? If so, how are their fees determined? Be specific in questioning your attorney about fees, and ask for a written statement describing them.

Evaluating Your Attorney

Ask yourself the following questions after your first meeting: Did the attorney seem knowledgeable about what is needed to address your concerns? Did he or she seem willing to investigate the law and the facts further to ensure an accurate understanding of your legal situation? Did you communicate well with each other? Did the attorney perceive what issues were of foremost concern to you and address those issues to your satisfaction? Did the attorney "speak your language" when explaining the legal implications of those issues?

Continue to evaluate the relationship as it continues. For many businesspersons, relationships with attorneys last for decades. Make sure that your relationship with your attorney will be a fruitful one.

 Checklist for Choosing and Using a Lawyer

1. If you ever think that you need legal advice, you probably do.
2. When choosing an attorney, try to get recommendations from friends, relatives, or business associates who have had long-standing relationships with their attorneys. If that fails, check with your local or state bar association or with the *Martindale-Hubbell Law Directory.*
3. Do not hesitate to ask about the legal fees that your attorney will charge and for a detailed breakdown of your bill.
4. When you initially consult with an attorney, ask whatever questions are necessary to ensure that you understand what your legal options are. Do not worry about appearing stupid.

▌Key Terms

▌Chapter Summary: The Legal and International Environment

The Nature of Law *(See pages 2–4.)*	Law can be defined as a body of enforceable rules governing relationships among individuals and between individuals and their society. Three important schools of legal thought, or legal philosophies, are the following:
	1. *Natural law tradition*—One of the oldest and most significant schools of legal thought. Those who believe in natural law hold that there is a universal law applicable to all human beings and that this law is of a higher order than positive, or conventional, law.
	2. *Legal positivism*—A school of legal thought centered on the assumption that there is no law higher than the laws created by the government. Laws must be obeyed, even if they are unjust, to prevent anarchy.
	(Continued)

▌Chapter Summary: The Legal and International Environment—Continued

The Nature of Law—Continued	3. *Legal realism*—A popular school of legal thought during the 1920s and 1930s. Legal realists generally advocated a less abstract and more realistic approach to the law, an approach that would take into account customary practices and the circumstances in which transactions take place. The school left a lasting imprint on American jurisprudence.
The Common Law Tradition *(See pages 4-8.)*	1. *Common law*—Law that originated in medieval England with the creation of the king's courts, or *curia regis*, and the development of a body of rules that were common to (or applied throughout) the land. 2. *Stare decisis*—A doctrine under which judges "stand on decided cases"—or follow the rule of precedent—in deciding cases. *Stare decisis* is the cornerstone of the common law tradition. 3. *Remedies*— a. Remedies at law—Money or something else of value. b. Remedies in equity—Remedies that are granted when the remedies at law are unavailable or inadequate. Equitable remedies include specific performance, an injunction, and contract rescission (cancellation).
Sources of American Law *(See pages 8–14.)*	1. *Constitutional law*—The law as expressed in the U.S. Constitution and the various state constitutions. The U.S. Constitution is the supreme law of the land. State constitutions are supreme within state borders to the extent that they do not violate the U.S. Constitution or a federal law. 2. *Statutory law*—Laws or ordinances created by federal, state, and local legislatures and governing bodies. None of these laws can violate the U.S. Constitution or the relevant state constitutions. Uniform laws, when adopted by a state legislature, become statutory law in that state. 3. *Administrative law*—The rules, orders, and decisions of federal or state government administrative agencies. Federal administrative agencies are created by enabling legislation enacted by the U.S. Congress. Agency functions include rulemaking, investigation and enforcement, and adjudication. 4. *Case law and common law doctrines*—Judge-made law, including interpretations of constitutional provisions, of statutes enacted by legislatures, and of regulations created by administrative agencies. The common law—the doctrines and principles embodied in case law—governs all areas not covered by statutory law (or agency regulations issued to implement various statutes).
Classifications of Law *(See page14.)*	The law may be broken down according to several classification systems, such as substantive or procedural law, civil or criminal law, federal or state law, and private or public law.
National and International Law *(See pages 14–18.)*	1. *National law*—Most nations today have either a common law system or a civil law system: a. Common law system—See the summary of the common law tradition above. Generally, those countries that were once colonies of Great Britain retained their English common law heritage after they achieved their independence. Today, nations with common law systems include England, the United States, Ireland, Canada, Australia, New Zealand, and India. b. Civil law system—A legal system stemming from Roman "code law," in which the primary source of law is a statutory code—an ordered grouping of legal principles enacted into law by a legislature or governing body. Precedents are not binding in a civil law system. Most of the continental European countries have a civil law system, as do those African, Latin American, and Asian nations that were once colonies of those European countries. Japan and South Africa also have civil law systems. 2. *International law*—A body of written and unwritten laws observed by independent nations and governing the acts of individuals as well as governments. Sources of international law include national laws, customs, treaties, and international organizations and conferences.

▌For Review

1. What is the common law tradition?
2. What is a precedent? When might a court depart from precedent?
3. What is the difference between remedies at law and remedies in equity?

4. What is the Uniform Commercial Code?
5. What is the difference between civil law and criminal law?

Questions and Case Problems

1–1. Philosophy of Law. After World War II, which ended in 1945, an international tribunal of judges convened at Nuremberg, Germany. The judges convicted several Nazi war criminals of "crimes against humanity." Assuming that the Nazis who were convicted had not disobeyed any law of their country and had merely been following their government's (Hitler's) orders, what law had they violated? Explain.

1–2. Legal Systems. What are the key differences between a common law system and a civil law system? Why do some countries have common law systems and others have civil law systems?

1–3. Reading Citations. Assume that you want to read the entire court opinion in the case of *White v. York International Corp.*, 45 F.3d 357 (10th Cir. 1995). The case deals with the question of whether an employer violated the Americans with Disabilities Act of 1990, a federal statute that prohibits discrimination against persons with disabilities. Read the section entitled "Finding Case Law" in the appendix that follows this chapter, and then explain specifically where you would find the court's opinion.

1–4. Sources of American Law. This chapter discussed a number of sources of American law. Which source of law takes priority in the following situations, and why?

(a) A federal statute conflicts with the U.S. Constitution.

(b) A federal statute conflicts with a state constitution.

(c) A state statute conflicts with the common law of that state.

(d) A state constitutional amendment conflicts with the U.S. Constitution.

(e) A federal administrative regulation conflicts with a state constitution.

1–5. *Stare Decisis.* In the text of this chapter, we stated that the doctrine of *stare decisis* "became a cornerstone of the English and American judicial systems." What does *stare decisis* mean, and why has this doctrine been so fundamental to the development of our legal tradition?

1–6. Court Opinions. Read through the section entitled "Case Titles and Terminology" in the appendix following this chapter. What is the difference between a concurring opinion and a majority opinion? Between a concurring opinion and a dissenting opinion? Why do judges and justices write concurring and dissenting opinions, given the fact that these opinions will not affect the outcome of the case at hand, which has already been decided by majority vote?

1–7. Common Law versus Statutory Law. Courts are able to overturn precedents and thus can change the common law. Should judges have the same authority to overrule statutory law? Explain.

1–8. Philosophy of Law. In the middle of the last century, the United States declared war on Mexico and levied taxes to support the war effort. Henry David Thoreau (author of *Walden*), who felt that the war was unjust, refused to pay taxes to support it and was subsequently imprisoned for violating the law. Thoreau maintained that obeying the law in these circumstances would be unethical. Which of the schools of legal thought discussed in this chapter would be the most sympathetic toward Thoreau's views on law? Explain.

1–9. Statute of Limitations. The equitable principle "Equity aids the vigilant, not those who rest on their rights" means that courts will not aid those who do not pursue a cause of action while the evidence is fresh and while the true facts surrounding the issue can be discovered. State statutes of limitations are based on this principle. Under Article 2 of the Uniform Commercial Code, which has been adopted by virtually all of the states, the statute of limitations governing sales contracts states that parties must bring an action for the breach of a sales contract within four years, although the parties (the seller and the buyer) can reduce this period by agreement to only one year. Which party (the seller or the buyer) would benefit more by a one-year period, and which would benefit more by a four-year period? Discuss.

1–10. Binding versus Persuasive Authority. A county court in Illinois is deciding a case involving an issue that has never been addressed before in that state's courts. The Iowa Supreme Court, however, recently decided a case involving a very similar fact pattern. Is the Illinois court obligated to follow the Iowa Supreme Court's decision on the issue? If the United States Supreme Court had decided a similar case, would that decision be binding on the Illinois court? Explain.

**A QUESTION OF ETHICS
AND SOCIAL RESPONSIBILITY**

1–11. *On July 5, 1884, Dudley, Stephens, and Brooks—"all able-bodied English seamen"—and an English teenage boy were cast adrift in a lifeboat following a storm at sea. They had no water with them in the boat, and all they had for sustenance were two 1-pound tins of turnips. On July 24, Dudley proposed that one of the four in the lifeboat be sacrificed to save the others. Stephens agreed with Dudley, but Brooks refused to consent—and the boy was never asked for his opinion. On July 25, Dudley killed the boy, and the three men then fed upon the boy's body and blood. Four days later, the men were rescued by a passing vessel. They were taken to England and tried for the murder of the boy. If the men had not fed upon the boy's body, they would probably have died of starvation within the four-day period. The boy, who was in a much weaker condition, would likely have died before the rest.* [Regina v. Dudley and Stephens, 14 Q.B.D. (Queen's Bench Division, England) 273 (1884)]

1. The basic question in this case is whether the survivors should be subject to penalties under English criminal law, given the men's unusual circumstances. You be the judge, and decide the issue. Give the reasons for your decisions.

2. Should judges ever have the power to look beyond the written "letter of the law" in making their decisions? Why or why not?

FOR CRITICAL ANALYSIS

1–12. *Courts of equity tend to follow general rules or maxims rather than common law precedents, as courts of law do. Some of these maxims were listed in this chapter's* Landmark in the Law. *Why would equity courts give credence to such general maxims rather than to a hard-and-fast body of law?*

▌Accessing the Internet: Business Law and Legal Environment

A few years ago, only computer fanatics even knew about the Internet. Today, at least 30 million people use it, and by the end of the century it is projected that 100 million people will be using it worldwide. Today, there are over 65,000 networks connected to the Internet with about 4.5 million computers in 91 countries. The Internet is not a centralized system, but rather a collection of networks running the same software standards. You can think of the Internet as a web of educational, corporate, and research computer networks around the world. The Internet has many uses, including transmitting weather reports, doing library searches, and finding addresses of university students and faculty thousands of miles away. On the Internet, you will find discussion groups, news groups, electronic publications, and electronic mail (E-mail), the most common use of the Internet.

Your college or university is probably connected directly to the Internet and pays thousands of dollars a year for this hookup. Faculty, administrators, and students can get an E-mail address and password. The address is just like a mailbox at which you receive electronic information. Addresses differ depending on the gateway that leads from your computer through another computer to the person or address you want to reach. Many chapters of *Business Law Today* end with Internet addresses and activities that you may find useful.

A little advice on hardware: You should use a computer with sufficient RAM (random access memory) to handle the World Wide Web (WWW) protocol, which means at least 4 megabytes, but preferably 8 megabytes. You should also use a modem that runs at least at 14.4 kilobaud, but preferably at 28.8 kilobaud.

Get yourself an address now. Pick up a copy of the handout given to new users, and start playing with E-mail. A good starting point is to roam through the user-friendly **gopher** menus.

Open your connection the way you would to send or receive E-mail. Type **gopher** and hit the return key. You will be presented with a first-level menu of choices. Pick one by moving the arrow up or down to the item you want to open (at the blinking cursor, type in the number of your choice). When you have finished searching or surfing, type **Q**. You may also want to contact the "mother of all gopher" sites, the University of Minnesota, by logging in, typing **gopher**, and then typing **tc.umn.edu.**

Appendix to Chapter 1

Finding and Analyzing the Law

Laws pertaining to business consist of both statutory law and case law. The statutes, agency regulations, and case law referred to in this text establish the rights and duties of businesspersons engaged in various types of activities. The cases presented within the chapters provide you with concise, real-life illustrations of the interpretation and application of the law by the courts. Because of the importance of knowing how to find statutory and case law, this appendix offers a brief introduction to how statutes and cases are published and to the legal "shorthand" employed in referencing these legal sources.

Finding Statutory and Administrative Law

When Congress passes laws, they are collected in a publication titled *United States Statutes at Large*. When state legislatures pass laws, they are collected in similar state publications. Most frequently, however, laws are referred to in their codified form—that is, the form in which they appear in the federal and state codes.

In these codes, laws are compiled by subject. The *United States Code* (U.S.C.) arranges all existing federal laws of a public and permanent nature by subject. Each of the fifty subjects into which the U.S.C. arranges the laws is given a title and a title number. For example, laws relating to commerce and trade are collected in Title 15, which is titled "Commerce and Trade." Titles are subdivided by sections. A citation to the U.S.C. includes title and section numbers. Thus, a reference to "15 U.S.C. Section 1" means that the statute can be found in Section 1 of Title 15. ("Section" may also be designated by the symbol §, and "Sections" by §§.)

Sometimes a citation includes the abbreviation *et seq.*—as in "15 U.S.C. Sections 1 *et seq.*" The term is an abbreviated form of *et sequitur*, which in Latin means "and the following"; when used in a citation, it refers to sections that concern the same subject as the numbered section and follow it in sequence.

State codes follow the U.S.C. pattern of arranging law by subject. The state codes may be called codes, revisions, compilations, consolidations, general statutes, or statutes, depending on the preference of the states. In some codes, subjects are designated by number. In others, they are designated by name. For example, "13 Pennsylvania Consolidated Statutes Section 1101" means the statute can be

found in Title 13, Section 1101, of the Pennsylvania code. "California Commercial Code Section 1101" means the statute can be found under the subject heading "Commercial Code" of the California code in Section 1101. Abbreviations may be used. For example, "13 Pennsylvania Consolidated Statutes Section 1101" may be abbreviated "13 Pa. C.S. § 1101," and "California Commercial Code Section 1101" may be abbreviated "Cal. Com. Code § 1101."

Rules and regulations adopted by federal administrative agencies are compiled in the *Code of Federal Regulations* (C.F.R.). Like the U.S.C., the C.F.R. is divided into fifty titles. Rules within each title are assigned section numbers. A full citation to the C.F.R. includes title and section numbers. For example, a reference to "17 C.F.R. Section 230.504" means that the rule can be found in Section 230.504 of Title 17.

Commercial publications of these laws and regulations are available and are widely used. For example, West Publishing Company publishes the *United States Code Annotated* (U.S.C.A.). The U.S.C.A. contains the complete text of laws included in the U.S.C., as well as notes of court decisions that interpret and apply specific sections of the statutes, plus the text of presidential proclamations and executive orders. The U.S.C.A. also includes research aids, such as cross-references to related statutes, historical notes, and library references. A citation to the U.S.C.A. is similar to a citation to the U.S.C.: "15 U.S.C.A. Section 1."

Finding Case Law

Before discussing the case reporting system, we need to look briefly at the court system. As will be discussed in detail in Chapter 3, there are two types of courts in the United States, federal courts and state courts. Both the federal and state court systems consist of several levels, or tiers, of courts. *Trial courts*, in which evidence is presented and testimony given, are on the bottom tier (which also includes lower courts handling specialized issues). Decisions from a trial court can be appealed to a higher court, which commonly would be an intermediate *court of appeals*, or an *appellate court*. Appellate courts are known as *reviewing courts* because they do not hear evidence or testimony, as trial courts do; rather, an appellate court reviews all of the records relating to a case to determine whether the trial court's decision was correct.

Decisions from these intermediate courts of appeals may be appealed to an even higher court, such as a state supreme court or the United States Supreme Court.

State Court Decisions

Most state trial court decisions are not published. Except in New York and a few other states that publish selected opinions of their trial courts, decisions from the state trial courts are merely filed in the office of the clerk of the court, where the decisions are available for public inspection. Written decisions of the appellate, or reviewing, courts, however, are published and distributed. The reported appellate decisions are published in volumes called *reports* or *reporters*, which are numbered consecutively. State appellate court decisions are found in the state reporters of that particular state.

Additionally, state court opinions appear in regional units of the *National Reporter System*, published by West Publishing Company. Most lawyers and libraries have the West reporters because they report cases more quickly and are distributed more widely than the state-published reports. In fact, many states have eliminated their own reporters in favor of West's National Reporter System. The National Reporter System divides the states into the following geographical areas: *Atlantic* (A. or A.2d), *South Eastern* (S.E. or S.E.2d), *South Western* (S.W. or S.W.2d), *North Western* (N.W. or N.W.2d), *North Eastern* (N.E. or N.E.2d), *Southern* (So. or So.2d), and *Pacific* (P. or P.2d). (The *2d* in the abbreviations refers to *Second Series*.) The states included in each of these regional divisions are indicated in Exhibit 1A–1, which illustrates West's National Reporter System.

After appellate decisions have been published, they are normally referred to (cited) by the name of the case; the volume, name, and page number of the state's official reporter (if different from West's National Reporter System); the volume, unit, and page number of the *National Reporter*; and the volume, name, and page number of any other selected reporter. This information is included in the *citation*. (Citing a reporter by volume number, name, and page number, in that order, is common to all citations.) When more than one reporter is cited for the same case, each reference is called a *parallel citation*. For example, consider the following case: *Williams v. Garraghty*, 249 Va. 224, 455 S.E.2d 209 (1995). We see that the opinion in this case may be found in Volume 249 of the official *Virginia Reports*, on page 224. The parallel citation is to Volume 455 of the *South Eastern Reporter, Second Series*, page 209. In presenting appellate opinions in this text, in addition to the reporter, we give the name of the court hearing the case and the year of the court's decision.

A few of the states—including those with intermediate appellate courts, such as California, Illinois, and New York—have more than one reporter for opinions given by courts within their states. Sample citations from these courts, as well as others, are listed and explained in Exhibit 1A–2.

Federal Court Decisions

Federal district court decisions are published unofficially in West's *Federal Supplement* (F.Supp.), and opinions from the circuit courts of appeals (federal reviewing courts) are reported unofficially in West's *Federal Reporter* (F., F.2d, or F.3d). Cases concerning federal bankruptcy law are published unofficially in West's *Bankruptcy Reporter* (Bankr.). Opinions from the United States Supreme Court are reported in the *United States Reports* (U.S.), West's *Supreme Court Reporter* (S.Ct.), the *Lawyers' Edition of the Supreme Court Reports* (L.Ed. or L.Ed.2d), and other publications.

The *United States Reports* is the official edition of all decisions of the United States Supreme Court for which there are written opinions. Published by the federal government, the series includes reports of Supreme Court cases dating from the August term of 1791, although originally many of the decisions were not reported in the early volumes.

West's *Supreme Court Reporter* is an unofficial edition dating from the Court's term in October 1882. Preceding each case report are a summary of the case and *headnotes* (brief editorial statements of the law involved in the case). The headnotes are given classification numbers that serve to cross-reference each headnote to other headnotes on similar points of law throughout the National Reporter System and other West publications. The numbers facilitate research of all relevant cases on a given point of law. This is important because, as may be evident from the discussion of *stare decisis* in Chapter 1, a lawyer's goal in undertaking legal research is to find an authority that cannot be factually distinguished from his or her case.

The Lawyers Cooperative Publishing Company of Rochester, New York, publishes the *Lawyers' Edition of the Supreme Court Reports*, which is an unofficial edition of the entire series of the Supreme Court reports. The *Lawyers' Edition* contains many of the decisions not reported in the early official volumes. Additionally, among other editorial features, the *Lawyers' Edition*, in its second series, precedes the report of each case with a full summary, includes excerpts from the attorneys' notes on the cases, and discusses in detail selected cases of special interest to the legal profession.

Sample citations for federal court decisions are also listed and explained in Exhibit 1A–2.

Old Case Law

On a few occasions, this text cites opinions from old, classic cases dating to the nineteenth century or earlier; some of these are from the English courts. The citations to these cases appear not to conform to the descriptions given above, because the reporters in which they were published have since been replaced. A sample citation for an English reporter is included in Exhibit 1A–2. Whenever citations to old reporters are made in this text, the citations will be explained as they are presented.

◆ Exhibit 1A–1
National Reporter System—Regional/Federal

Regional Reporters	Coverage Beginning	Coverage
Atlantic Reporter (A. or A.2d)	1885	Connecticut, Delaware, Maine, Maryland, New Hampshire, New Jersey, Pennsylvania, Rhode Island, Vermont, and District of Columbia.
North Eastern Reporter (N.E. or N.E.2d)	1885	Illinois, Indiana, Massachusetts, New York, and Ohio.
North Western Reporter (N.W. or N.W.2d)	1879	Iowa, Michigan, Minnesota, Nebraska, North Dakota, South Dakota, and Wisconsin.
Pacific Reporter (P. or P.2d)	1883	Alaska, Arizona, California, Colorado, Hawaii, Idaho, Kansas, Montana, Nevada, New Mexico, Oklahoma, Oregon, Utah, Washington, and Wyoming.
South Eastern Reporter (S.E. or S.E.2d)	1887	Georgia, North Carolina, South Carolina, Virginia, and West Virginia.
South Western Reporter (S.W. or S.W.2d)	1886	Arkansas, Kentucky, Missouri, Tennessee, and Texas.
Southern Reporter (So. or So.2d)	1887	Alabama, Florida, Louisiana, and Mississippi.

Federal Reporters		
Federal Reporter (F., F.2d, or F.3d)	1880	U.S. Circuit Court from 1880 to 1912; U.S. Commerce Court from 1911 to 1913; U.S. District Courts from 1880 to 1932; U.S. Court of Claims (now called U.S. Court of Federal Claims) from 1929 to 1932 and since 1960; U.S. Court of Appeals since 1891; U.S. Court of Customs and Patent Appeals since 1929; U.S. Emergency Court of Appeals since 1943.
Federal Supplement (F.Supp.)	1932	U.S. Court of Claims from 1932 to 1960; U.S. District Courts since 1932; and U.S. Customs Court since 1956.
Federal Rules Decisions (F.R.D.)	1939	U.S. District Courts involving the Federal Rules of Civil Procedure since 1939 and Federal Rules of Criminal Procedure since 1946.
Supreme Court Reporter (S.Ct.)	1882	U.S. Supreme Court since the October term of 1882.
Bankruptcy Reporter (Bankr.)	1980	Bankruptcy decisions of U.S. Bankruptcy Courts, U.S. District Courts, U.S. Courts of Appeals, and U.S. Supreme Court.
Military Justice Reporter (M.J.)	1978	U.S. Court of Military Appeals and Courts of Military Review for the Army, Navy, Air Force, and Coast Guard.

NATIONAL REPORTER SYSTEM MAP

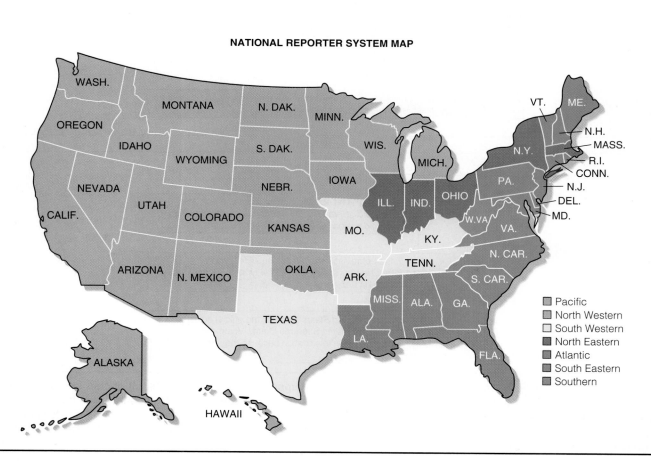

◆ Exhibit 1A–2
How to Read Case Citations

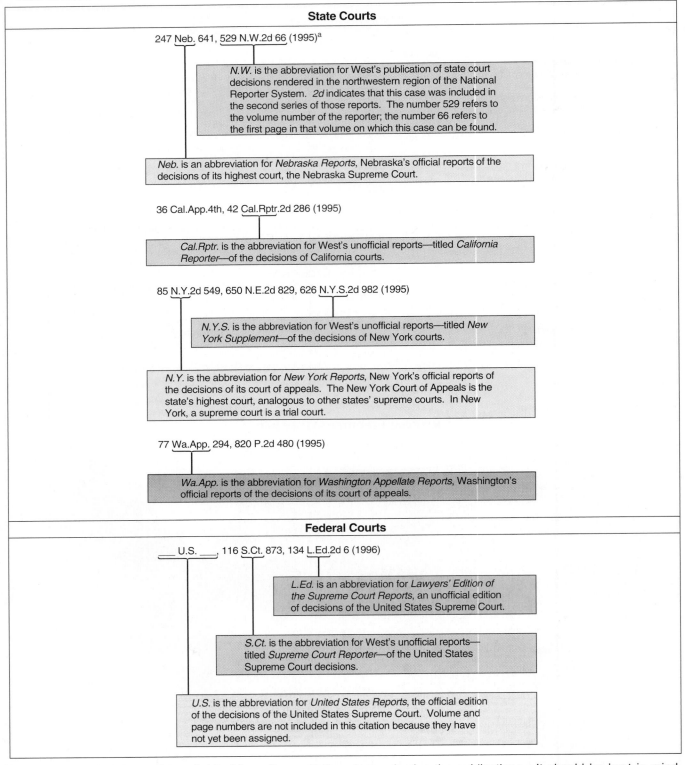

a. The case names have been deleted from these citations to emphasize the publications. It should be kept in mind, however, that the name of a case is as important as the specific page numbers in the volumes in which it is found. If a citation is incorrect, the correct citation may be found in a publication's index of case names. The date of a case is also important because, in addition to providing a check on error in citations, the value of a recent case as an authority is likely to be greater than that of earlier cases.

◆ **Exhibit 1A–2**
How to Read Case Citations—Continued

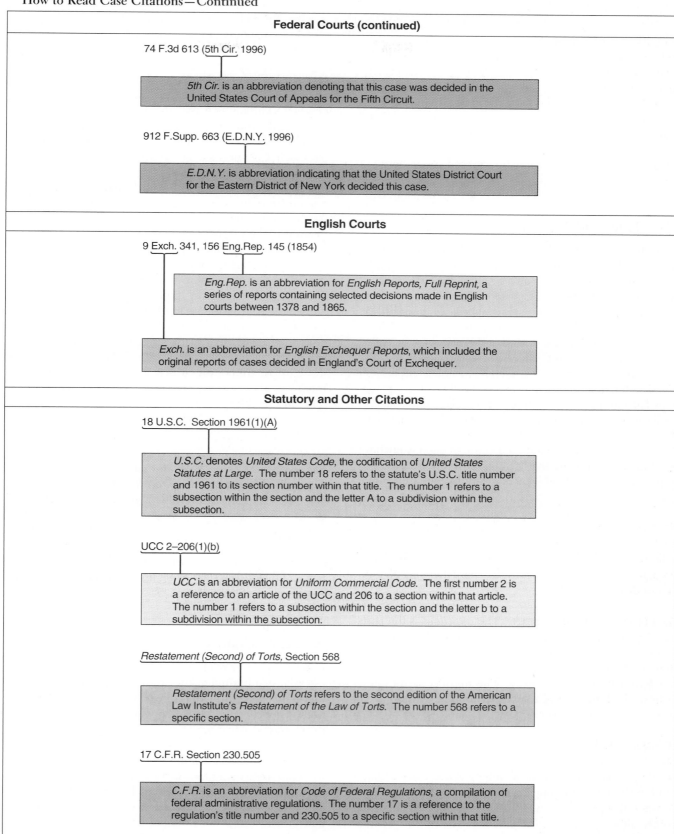

Federal Courts (continued)

74 F.3d 613 (5th Cir. 1996)

5th Cir. is an abbreviation denoting that this case was decided in the United States Court of Appeals for the Fifth Circuit.

912 F.Supp. 663 (E.D.N.Y. 1996)

E.D.N.Y. is abbreviation indicating that the United States District Court for the Eastern District of New York decided this case.

English Courts

9 Exch. 341, 156 Eng.Rep. 145 (1854)

Eng.Rep. is an abbreviation for *English Reports, Full Reprint,* a series of reports containing selected decisions made in English courts between 1378 and 1865.

Exch. is an abbreviation for *English Exchequer Reports,* which included the original reports of cases decided in England's Court of Exchequer.

Statutory and Other Citations

18 U.S.C. Section 1961(1)(A)

U.S.C. denotes *United States Code,* the codification of *United States Statutes at Large.* The number 18 refers to the statute's U.S.C. title number and 1961 to its section number within that title. The number 1 refers to a subsection within the section and the letter A to a subdivision within the subsection.

UCC 2–206(1)(b)

UCC is an abbreviation for *Uniform Commercial Code.* The first number 2 is a reference to an article of the UCC and 206 to a section within that article. The number 1 refers to a subsection within the section and the letter b to a subdivision within the subsection.

Restatement (Second) of Torts, Section 568

Restatement (Second) of Torts refers to the second edition of the American Law Institute's *Restatement of the Law of Torts.* The number 568 refers to a specific section.

17 C.F.R. Section 230.505

C.F.R. is an abbreviation for *Code of Federal Regulations,* a compilation of federal administrative regulations. The number 17 is a reference to the regulation's title number and 230.505 to a specific section within that title.

Reading and Understanding Case Law

Case law is critical to decision making in the business context because businesses must operate within the boundaries established by law. It is thus essential that businesspersons understand case law.

The cases in this text have been rewritten and condensed from the full text of the courts' opinions. For those wishing to review court cases for future research projects or to gain additional legal information, the following sections will provide useful insights into how to read and understand case law.

Case Titles and Terminology

The title of a case, such as *Adams v. Jones*, indicates the names of the parties to the lawsuit. The *v.* in the case title stands for *versus*, which means "against." In the trial court, Adams was the plaintiff—the person who filed the suit. Jones was the defendant. If the case is appealed, however, the appellate court will sometimes place the name of the party appealing the decision first, so that the case may be called *Jones v. Adams*. Because some reviewing courts retain the trial court order of names, it is often impossible to distinguish the plaintiff from the defendant in the title of a reported appellate court decision. You must carefully read the facts of each case to identify each party. Otherwise, the discussion by the appellate court will be difficult to understand.

The following terms and phrases are frequently encountered in court opinions and legal publications. Because it is important to understand what is meant by these terms and phrases, we define and discuss them here.

PLAINTIFFS AND DEFENDANTS   As mentioned in Chapter 1, the *plaintiff* in a lawsuit is the party that initiates the action. The *defendant* is the party against which a lawsuit is brought. Lawsuits frequently involve more than one plaintiff and/or defendant.

APPELLANTS AND APPELLEES   The *appellant* is the party that appeals a case to another court or jurisdiction from the court or jurisdiction in which the case was originally brought. Sometimes, an appellant that appeals a judgment is referred to as the *petitioner*. The *appellee* is the party against which the appeal is taken. Sometimes, the appellee is referred to as the *respondent*.

JUDGES AND JUSTICES   The terms *judge* and *justice* are usually synonymous and represent two designations given to judges in various courts. All members of the United States Supreme Court, for example, are referred to as justices. And justice is the formal title usually given to judges of appellate courts, although this is not always the case. In New York, a justice is a judge of the trial court (which is called the

Supreme Court), and a member of the Court of Appeals (the state's highest court) is called a judge. The term *justice* is commonly abbreviated to J., and *justices* to JJ. A Supreme Court case might refer to Justice Kennedy as Kennedy, J., or to Chief Justice Rehnquist as Rehnquist, C.J.

DECISIONS AND OPINIONS   Most decisions reached by reviewing, or appellate, courts are explained in written *opinions*. The opinion contains the court's reasons for its decision, the rules of law that apply, and the judgment.

There are four possible types of written opinions for any particular case decided by an appellate court. When all judges or justices unanimously agree on an opinion, the opinion is written for the entire court and can be deemed a *unanimous opinion*. When there is not a unanimous opinion, a *majority opinion* is written, outlining the views of the majority of the judges or justices deciding the case. Often, a judge or justice who feels strongly about making or emphasizing a point that was not made or emphasized in the unanimous or majority opinion will write a *concurring opinion*. That means the judge or justice agrees (concurs) with the judgment given in the unanimous or majority opinion but for different reasons. In other than unanimous opinions, a *dissenting opinion* is usually written by a judge or justice who does not agree with the majority. The dissenting opinion is important because it may form the basis of the arguments used years later in overruling the precedential majority opinion.

A NOTE ON ABBREVIATIONS   In court opinions, as well as in other areas of this text, certain terms appearing in the names of firms or organizations will often be abbreviated. The terms *Company*, *Incorporated*, and *Limited*, for example, will frequently appear in their abbreviated forms as *Co.*, *Inc.*, and *Ltd.*, respectively, and *Brothers* is commonly abbreviated to *Bros.* Certain organizations and legislative acts are also frequently referred to by their initials or acronyms. In all such cases, to prevent confusion we will give the complete name of the organization or act upon first mentioning it in a given section of the text.

A Sample Court Case

Knowing how to read and analyze a court opinion is an essential step in undertaking accurate legal research. A further step involves "briefing" the case. Legal researchers routinely brief cases by summarizing and reducing the texts of the opinions to their essential elements. Instructions on how to brief a case and selected cases for briefing are given in Appendix A at the end of this text.

The cases contained within the chapters of this text have already been analyzed and briefed by the authors, and the essential aspects of each case are presented in a convenient format consisting of four basic sections: *Facts*, *Issue*, *Decision*, and *Reason*. This basic format is illustrated in the sample court case shown in Exhibit 1A-3 (see pages 30 and 31), which has also been annotated to illustrate the kind of information that is contained in each section. (Annotated excerpts from the actual court opinion for this case appear as the first case opinion in Appendix A in the back of this book.)

In the remaining chapters of this book, the basic format is expanded to include a special introductory section entitled *Historical and Social Setting*.[1] In some instances, a *Company Profile* is included in place of the *Historical and Social Setting*. These profiles provide a background on one of the parties to the lawsuit. Each case is followed by a brief section entitled *For Critical Analysis*, which presents a question regarding some issue raised by the case.

Diagramming Case Problems

When briefing and analyzing a case problem in *Business Law Today*, you may find it helpful in attempting to understand the facts of the problem to diagram those facts. You might use a square for a plaintiff (the party who files a legal action) and a triangle for a defendant (the party against whom the action is brought), for example, and arrows to indicate who is suing whom. You might also find that it saves time to use symbols in your diagrams. Many symbols are commonly used among law students and lawyers. To indicate a reference to a plaintiff, for example, the pi symbol—π—is often used, and a defendant is noted by delta—Δ—a triangle.

Diagramming the facts helps to emphasize that you should accept the facts as they are given. For example, under some circumstances, the manager of a store may have a duty to warn customers of the hazard presented by a wet floor by putting a sign near the hazard. If there is a statement in a case problem about the existence of a wet floor and the lack of a sign, you should accept that the floor was wet and there was no sign. Arguing with the statement ("Anyone can see when a floor is wet," "Maybe the floor was not too wet," "Maybe an employee was getting a sign to put up," or "Maybe someone stole the sign") only diminishes your ability to learn. When you have learned what the principle is that the case problem involves, then you can ask, "What if the facts were different?"

In analyzing and diagramming case problems, you may find the following method helpful. First, before reading a problem, read the question at the end. Does it ask you to evaluate the facts, the plaintiff's claim, or the defendant's defense? The point is to gain an understanding of the answer toward which the problem is directed. Second, read the

problem, paying special attention to the facts that are directed to the question. As you read, write down the names of the plaintiff and defendant and draw different shapes around them, with an arrow to indicate who is bringing the action against whom. This illustrates the litigation and gives you a framework for answering the question.

For instance, consider the following case problem (Problem 17–5) from Chapter 17.

> George Nesselrode lost his life in an airplane crash. The plane had been manufactured by Beech Aircraft Corp. and sold to Executive Beechcraft, Inc. Shortly before the crash occurred, Executive Beechcraft had conducted a routine inspection of the plane and found that some of the parts needed to be replaced. The new parts were supplied by Beech Aircraft but installed by Executive Beechcraft. These particular parts could be installed backwards, and if they were, the plane would crash. In Nesselrode's case, the crash resulted from just such an incorrect installation of airplane parts. Nesselrode's wife Jane and three daughters sued Beech Aircraft, Executive Beechcraft, and Gerald Hultgren, the pilot who had flown the plane. Beech Aircraft claimed that it was not at fault because it had not installed the parts. Will Beech Aircraft be held liable for Nesselrode's death? [*Nesselrode v. Executive Beechcraft, Inc.*, 707 S.W.2d 371 (Mo. 1986)]

Here is how the facts in this problem might be diagrammed.

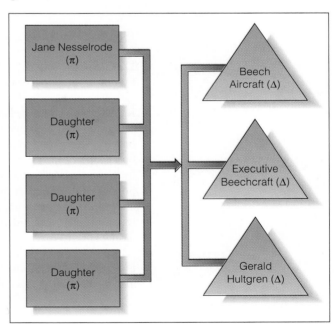

If, after diagramming the facts, you have trouble applying the principle that a problem asks you to discuss, reread the relevant section in the text. The diagramming method may also prove helpful when you are briefing and analyzing cases already analyzed and edited by the authors or cases that you are assigned or that you researched separately.

---

1. The word *Social* in the title of this section may be replaced by *Economic* or *Political* or some other term, depending on the nature of the case and its background.

♦ **Exhibit 1A-3**
A Sample Court Case

1 — [**SUGGS v. SERVICEMASTER EDUCATION FOOD MANAGEMENT**

2 — [United States Court of Appeals,
       Sixth Circuit, 1996.

3 — [72 F.3d 1228.

4 — **HISTORICAL AND CULTURAL SETTING** *For centuries, the division of labor according to gender was a convenient, and sometimes necessary, component of survival. The division was due mainly to the fact that, of the two sexes, women become pregnant and bear children. From this division, some came to believe that women were somehow inferior to men. With the widespread use of family-planning techniques, the ability to prevent most deaths during childbirth, and other social and technological changes, a division of labor according to gender became unnecessary and inconvenient. Despite this change, some still cling to the false notion that women are inferior.*

5 — **FACTS** Sharon Suggs had a B.S. degree in food and nutritional sciences. She operated a food service facility at Tennessee State University (TSU) for ServiceMaster Education Food Management. Ranked fifth among ServiceMaster's twelve area directors, Suggs received satisfactory ratings on performance and client satisfaction, as well as regular merit raises. Six months before ServiceMaster lost the TSU account, Suggs was terminated and replaced by a man. She filed a suit in a federal district court against ServiceMaster, alleging discrimination based on her gender in violation of Title VII of the Civil Rights Act of 1964. ServiceMaster claimed that Suggs was discharged for "client dissatisfaction, operational problems and failure to meet financial and budget commitments." The court awarded Suggs back pay and ordered that she be reinstated. ServiceMaster appealed.

6 — [**ISSUE** Was Suggs's gender a determining factor in ServiceMaster's decision to fire her?

7 — [**DECISION** Yes. The U.S. Court of Appeals for the Sixth Circuit affirmed this part of the lower court's decision.

8 — **REASON** The appellate court concluded "that ServiceMaster's stated reasons for terminating her employment were pretextual and that Suggs was actually terminated because she was a female. Suggs was qualified for the position she held. She was replaced by a man and was not offered another position with the company when she was removed from the TSU account and later terminated, although ServiceMaster had identified positions available at other locations. In contrast to ServiceMaster's treatment of Suggs, other directors in Suggs's area, who had been ranked below Suggs for profitability and client satisfaction, were offered transfers and relocations when their accounts were lost. Those directors were men."

9 — [**FOR CRITICAL ANALYSIS—Cultural Consideration:** *Why do some employers discriminate against employees on the basis of characteristics that have nothing to do with their jobs?*

♦ **Exhibit 1A-3**
    A Sample Court Case—Continued

Review of Sample Court Case

1.   The name of the case is *Suggs v. ServiceMaster Education Food Management.* Suggs is the plaintiff (appellee); ServiceMaster is the defendant (appellant).

2.   The court deciding this case was the U.S. Court of Appeals for the Sixth Circuit, a federal appellate court; the case was decided in 1996.

3.   This citation indicates that the case can be found in Volume 72 of West's *Federal Reporter, Third Series,* on page 1228.

4.   The *Historical and Cultural Setting* section discusses the historical background of gender-based discrimination in the workplace. In other cases presented in this text, this initial section may examine the social, political, international, environmental, technological, or ethical background to the case being presented.

5.   The *Facts* section identifies the parties to the action and describes the events leading up to the lawsuit, the allegations made by the plaintiff, the defendant's response to these allegations, and (because this case is an appellate court decision) the trial court's decision and the party appealing that decision.

6.   The *Issue* section presents the central issue (or issues) to be decided by the court. Cases frequently will involve more than one issue.

7.   The *Decision* section contains the court's decision on the issue or issues before the court. The decision reflects the opinion of the majority of the judges or justices hearing the case. Appellate courts frequently phrase their decisions in reference to the lower courts' decisions. That is, the appellate court may "affirm" the lower court's ruling or "reverse" it. In this particular case, the appellate court affirmed the lower court's judgment.

8.   The *Reason* section indicates what relevant laws and judicial principles were applied in forming the particular conclusion arrived at in the case at bar ("before the court"). In this case, the relevant statute was Title VII of the Civil Rights Act of 1964, which prohibits employment discrimination on the basis of race, color, national origin, religion, and gender. The appellate court concluded that ServiceMaster's treatment of Suggs constituted gender-based discrimination in violation of Title VII.

9.   The *For Critical Analysis—Cultural Consideration* section raises a question to be considered in relation to the case just presented. Here the question involves a "cultural" consideration. In other cases presented in this text, the "consideration" may involve a social, political, international, environmental, technological, or ethical consideration.

▌Accessing the Internet: Business Law and Legal Environment

Realize that you can obtain access to the Internet through many national or regional commercial electronic services, such as Delphi, Prodigy, CompuServe, America Online, GEnie, and The Well. In any event, once you get on the Internet, every site and every document on the Internet has a specific address described by uniform resource locators, known as URLs. You can think of URLs as the phone numbers of information on the Internet. A URL in effect tells computers where a particular site you wish to visit is located. It further tells the computer where the information at that site can be obtained. You have to type the URLs exactly as written: upper and lower case are important. Here are some useful Internet addresses for you to use now:

Legal Information Institute: **http://www.law.cornell.edu**

Legal Dot Net: **http://www.legal.net**

Virtual Law Library: **http://www.law.indiana.edu/law.html**

Yahoo: **http://www.yahoo.com/Government/Law/**

You can also get updated information on legal sites on the Internet by contacting Nolo Press at

http://gnn.com/gnn/bus/nolo/

There are several other collections of law sites that you might want to access. The first is legal information at Rice University. It is one of the most extensive collections of legal data on the Internet. To get to it, type in

gopher://riceinfo.rice.edu:70/11/Subject/Government

Then select

Information by Subject Area

Next select

Government, Political Science and Law

Finally, the 'Lectric Law Library offers a large variety of legal information. Its Internet address on the Web is

http://www.inter-law.com

A scientist updates pages on the World Wide Web (WWW. or Web), a global network of computers connected by the Internet. In what ways does technology contribute to the speed of change in the law?

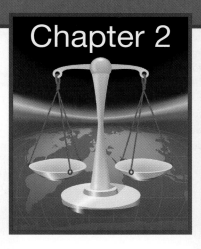

Constitutional Law

"*The United States Constitution has proved itself the most marvelously elastic compilation of rules of government ever written.*"

Franklin D. Roosevelt, 1882–1945
(*Thirty-second president of the United States, 1933–1945*)

CHAPTER OBJECTIVES

After reading this chapter, you should be able to:

1. Describe the form of government created by the U.S. Constitution.
2. Explain the relationship between the national government and state governments as set forth in the Constitution.
3. Identify the constitutional basis for the regulatory power of the federal government.
4. Summarize the fundamental rights protected by the Bill of Rights.
5. Give some examples of how the Bill of Rights affects business.

The U.S. Constitution is brief. It consists of only about seven thousand words, which is less than one-third of the number of words in the average state constitution. Perhaps its brevity explains why it has proved to be so "marvelously elastic," as Franklin Roosevelt pointed out in the above quotation, and why it has survived for over two hundred years—longer than any other written constitution in the world.

Laws that govern business have their origin in the lawmaking authority granted by this document, which is the supreme law in this country.[1] As mentioned in Chapter 1, neither Congress nor any state may pass a law that conflicts with the Constitution.

In this chapter, we first look at some basic constitutional concepts and clauses and their significance for business. Then we examine how certain fundamental freedoms guaranteed by the Constitution affect businesspersons and the workplace.

---

1. See Appendix B for the full text of the U.S. Constitution.

President Bill Clinton, Vice President Al Gore, Senator Bob Dole, and Representative Newt Gingrich meet in the Oval Office of the White House. How does the Constitution prevent any of the branches of government from becoming too powerful?

▌ The Constitutional Powers of Government

FEDERAL FORM OF GOVERNMENT
A system of government in which the states form a union and the sovereign power is divided between a central government and the member states.

The U.S. Constitution established a federal form of government. A **federal form of government** is one in which the states form a union and the sovereign power is divided between a central governing authority and the member states. The Constitution delegates certain powers to the national government, and the states retain all other powers. The relationship between the national government and the state governments is a partnership—neither partner is superior to the other except within the particular area of exclusive authority granted to it under the Constitution.

To prevent the possibility that the national government might use its power arbitrarily, the Constitution provided for three branches of government. The legislative branch makes the laws, the executive branch enforces the laws, and the judicial branch interprets the laws. Each branch performs a separate function, and no branch may exercise the authority of another branch.

CHECKS AND BALANCES
The national government is composed of three separate branches: the executive, the legislative, and the judicial branches. Each branch of the government exercises a check upon the actions of the others.

Each branch, however, has some power to limit the actions of the other two branches. Congress, for example, can enact legislation relating to spending and commerce, but the president can veto that legislation. The executive branch is responsible for foreign affairs, but treaties with foreign governments require the advice and consent of members of the Senate. Although Congress determines the jurisdiction of the federal courts, the United States Supreme Court has the power to hold acts of the other branches of the federal government unconstitutional.[2] Thus, with this system of **checks and balances,** no one branch of government can accumulate too much power.

---

2. See the *Landmark in the Law* in Chapter 3 on *Marbury v. Madison*, 5 U.S. (1 Cranch) 137, 2 L.Ed. 60 (1803), a case in which the doctrine of judicial review was clearly enunciated by Chief Justice John Marshall.

The U.S. Constitution, although brief, delineates the basic structure of the government, the authority of each of the three branches of the government, and the relationship between the national government and the state governments. The first ten amendments to the Constitution spell out the basic rights and liberties of Americans.

International Perspective—Continued

In contrast, Great Britain has no single written document that serves as its constitution. Therefore, it is difficult to obtain a clear outline, in the form of a central body of constitutional rules, that indicates how the British government operates and how the rights of its citizens are protected.

In the place of one document, Britain has a collection of customs and practices, as well as judicial decisions handed down in numerous court cases. In fact, what is regarded as making up the British constitution today is actually a combination of statutes, judicial decisions, conventions, constitutional commentaries, authoritative opinions, letters, and works of scholarship. These include the Magna Carta (1215), the 1689 Bill of Rights, the Reform Act of 1832, and other laws passed by Parliament. Perhaps, then, the distinction between the British "unwritten" constitution and our own is simply that the British constitution exists in written fragments, whereas the U.S. Constitution is contained in one document.

For Critical Analysis: *What are the advantages of having a written constitution, as the United States does? Are there any disadvantages?*

The Commerce Clause

Article I, Section 8, of the U.S. Constitution expressly permits Congress "[t]o regulate Commerce with foreign Nations, and among the several States, and with the Indian Tribes." This clause, referred to as the **commerce clause,** has had a greater impact on business than any other provision in the Constitution. This power was delegated to the federal government to ensure the uniformity of rules governing the movement of goods through the states.

For some time, the commerce power was interpreted as being limited to *interstate* commerce (commerce among the states) and not applicable to *intrastate* commerce (commerce within the states). In 1824, however, in *Gibbons v. Ogden* (see the *Landmark in the Law*), the United States Supreme Court held that commerce within states could also be regulated by the national government as long as the commerce concerned more than one state.

"We are under a Constitution, but the Constitution is what judges say it is."

Charles Evans Hughes, 1862–1948
(American jurist)

COMMERCE CLAUSE
The provision in Article I, Section 8, of the U.S. Constitution that gives Congress the power to regulate interstate commerce.

Ships involved in interstate commerce are loaded with shipping containers. Why do you think Congress was given exclusive power to regulate interstate commerce?

Gibbons v. Ogden (1824)

The commerce clause, which is found in Article I, Section 8, of the U.S. Constitution, gives Congress the power "to regulate Commerce with foreign Nations, and among the several States, and with the Indian Tribes." What exactly does "to regulate commerce" mean? What does "commerce" entail? These questions came before the United States Supreme Court in 1824 in the case of *Gibbons v. Ogden*.[a]

The background of the case was as follows. Robert Fulton, inventor of the steamboat, and Robert Livingston, who was then American minister to France, secured a monopoly on steam navigation on the waters in the state of New York from the New York legislature in 1803. Fulton and Livingston licensed Aaron Ogden, a former governor of New Jersey and a U.S. senator, to operate steam-powered ferryboats between New York and New Jersey. Thomas Gibbons, who had obtained a license from the U.S. government to operate boats in interstate waters, competed with Ogden without New York's permission. Ogden sued Gibbons. The New York state courts granted Ogden an injunction, prohibiting Gibbons from operating in New York waters. Gibbons appealed the decision to the United States Supreme Court.

Sitting as chief justice on the Supreme Court was John Marshall, an advocate of a strong national government. In his decision, Marshall defined the word *commerce* as used in the commerce clause to mean all commercial intercourse—that is, all business dealings that affect more than one state. The Court ruled against Ogden's monopoly, reversing the injunction against Gibbons. Marshall used this opportunity not only to expand the definition of commerce but also to validate and increase the power of the national legislature to regulate commerce. Said Marshall, "What is this power? It is the power . . . to prescribe the rule by which commerce is to be governed." Marshall held that the power to regulate interstate commerce was an exclusive power of the national government and that this power included the power to regulate any intrastate commerce that substantially affects interstate commerce.

For Critical Analysis: *What might have resulted if the Court had held otherwise—that the national government did* not *have the exclusive power to regulate interstate commerce?*

a.   22 U.S. (9 Wheat.) 1, 6 L.Ed. 23 (1824).

THE BREADTH OF THE COMMERCE CLAUSE   As a result of Marshall's decision in *Gibbons v. Ogden*, the commerce clause allowed the national government to exercise increasing authority over all areas of economic affairs throughout the land. In a 1942 case,[3] for example, the Court held that wheat production by an individual farmer intended wholly for consumption on his own farm was subject to federal regulation. The Court reasoned that the home consumption of wheat reduced the demand for wheat and thus could have a substantial effect on interstate commerce. In *McLain v. Real Estate Board of New Orleans, Inc.,* a 1980 case, the Supreme Court acknowledged that the commerce clause had "long been interpreted to extend beyond activities actually in interstate commerce to reach other activities, while wholly local in nature, which nevertheless substantially affect interstate commerce."[4]

In 1995, however, in *United States v. Lopez,*[5] the Supreme Court held—for the first time in sixty years—that there was a limit to the reach of the commerce clause. In

REMEMBER Congress can regulate commerce within states as long as the commerce concerns more than one state.

3.   See *Wickard v. Filburn,* 317 U.S. 111, 63 S.Ct. 82, 87 L.Ed. 122 (1942).
4.   444 U.S. 232, 100 S.Ct. 502, 62 L.Ed.2d 441 (1980).
5.   ___U.S.___, 115 S.Ct. 1624, 131 L.Ed.2d 626 (1995).

the *Lopez* case, the Supreme Court concluded that Congress had exceeded its constitutional authority when it passed the Gun-Free School Zones Act in 1990. The Court stated that the act, which banned the possession of guns within one thousand feet of any school, was unconstitutional because it attempted to regulate an area that had "nothing to do with commerce, or any sort of economic enterprise." The Court held that activities regulated under the commerce clause, to be constitutional, must substantially affect interstate commerce.

The decision in the *Lopez* case was a close one (four of the nine justices dissented), and the extent to which the decision will curb the regulation of purely local business activities under the commerce clause is as yet unclear. It is notable that just a few days after the *Lopez* case was decided, the Supreme Court again declared that what appeared (to many) to be fundamentally local activities sufficiently affected interstate commerce to be subject to a federal statute. In *United States v. Robertson*,[6] the Court held that the activities of an Alaska gold miner involved interstate commerce because the miner purchased some equipment and supplies in Los Angeles for use in his mining enterprise, recruited workers from outside Alaska, and took some gold (about 15 percent of the mine's output) out of state.

Today, at least theoretically, the power over commerce authorizes the national government to regulate every commercial enterprise in the United States. The breadth of the commerce clause permits the national government to legislate in areas in which there is no explicit grant of power to Congress. In the following case, a motel owner challenged the constitutionality of the Civil Rights Act of 1964, alleging that Congress lacked the authority to regulate what the motel owner claimed was "local" business.

RECALL Any law in violation of the U.S. Constitution will not be enforced.

---

6. ___U.S.___, 115 S.Ct. 1732, 131 L.Ed.2d 714 (1995).

CASE 2.1

HEART OF ATLANTA MOTEL v. UNITED STATES

Supreme Court of the United States, 1964.
379 U.S. 241,
85 S.Ct. 348,
13 L.Ed. 2d 258.

HISTORICAL AND SOCIAL SETTING *In the first half of the twentieth century, state governments sanctioned segregation on the basis of race. In 1954, the United States Supreme Court decided that racially segregated school systems violated the Constitution. In the following decade, the Court ordered an end to racial segregation imposed by the states in other public facilities, such as beaches, golf courses, buses, parks, auditoriums, and courtroom seating. Privately owned facilities that excluded or segregated African Americans and others on the basis of race were not subject to the same constitutional restrictions, however. Congress passed the Civil Rights Act of 1964 to prohibit racial discrimination in "establishments affecting interstate commerce." These facilities included "places of public accommodation."*

FACTS The owner of the Heart of Atlanta Motel refused to rent rooms to African Americans in violation of the Civil Rights Act of 1964. The motel owner brought an action in a federal district court to have the act declared unconstitutional, alleging that Congress had exceeded its power to regulate commerce by enacting the act. The owner argued that his motel was not engaged in interstate commerce but was "of a purely local character." The motel, however, was accessible to state and interstate highways. The owner advertised nationally, maintained billboards throughout the state, and accepted convention trade from outside the state (75 percent of the guests were residents of other states). The court sustained the constitutionality of the act and enjoined (prohibited) the owner from discriminating on the basis of race. The owner appealed. The case ultimately went to the United States Supreme Court.

ISSUE Did Congress exceed its constitutional power to regulate interstate commerce by enacting the Civil Rights Act of 1964?

DECISION No. The United States Supreme Court upheld the constitutionality of the act.

(Continued)

Case 2.1—Continued

REASON The Court noted that the act was passed to correct "the deprivation of personal dignity" accompanying the denial of equal access to "public establishments." Testimony before Congress leading to the passage of the act indicated that African Americans in particular experienced substantial discrimination in attempting to secure lodging while traveling. This discrimination impeded interstate travel and thus impeded interstate commerce. As for the owner's argument that his motel was "of a purely local character," the Court said that even if this was true, "if it is interstate commerce that feels the pinch, it does not matter how local the operation that applies the squeeze." Therefore, under the commerce clause, "the power of Congress to promote interstate commerce also includes the power to regulate the local incidents thereof, including local activities."

FOR CRITICAL ANALYSIS—Political Consideration
Suppose that only 5 percent of the motel's guests—or even 2 or 1 percent—were from out of state. In such a situation, would the Court still have been justified in regulating the motel's activities?

THE REGULATORY POWERS OF THE STATES   A problem that frequently arises under the commerce clause concerns a state's ability to regulate matters within its own borders. The U.S. Constitution does not expressly exclude state regulation of commerce, and there is no doubt that states have a strong interest in regulating activities within

Hazardous waste is deposited at a burial site. Can the state in which this site is located regulate this activity? If so, and if those regulations impinge on interstate commerce, will they be held unconstitutional?

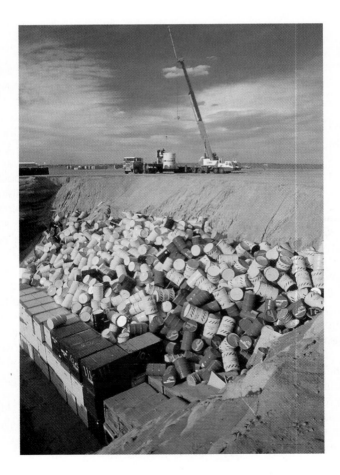

their borders. As part of their inherent sovereignty, states possess **police powers.** The term does not relate solely to criminal law enforcement but also to the right of state governments to regulate private activities to protect or promote the public order, health, safety, morals, and general welfare. Fire and building codes, antidiscrimination laws, parking regulations, zoning restrictions, licensing requirements, and thousands of other state statutes covering virtually every aspect of life have been enacted pursuant to a state's police powers.

When state regulations impinge on interstate commerce, courts must balance the state's interest in the merits and purposes of the regulation against the burden placed on interstate commerce. Generally, state laws enacted pursuant to a state's police powers carry a strong presumption of validity. If state laws substantially interfere with interstate commerce, however, they will be held to violate the commerce clause of the Constitution.

In *Raymond Motor Transportation, Inc. v. Rice,*[7] for example, the United States Supreme Court invalidated Wisconsin administrative regulations limiting the length of trucks traveling on its highways. The Court weighed the burden on interstate commerce against the benefits of the regulations and concluded that the challenged regulations "place a substantial burden on interstate commerce and they cannot be said to make more than the most speculative contribution to highway safety."

Because courts balance the interests involved, it is extremely difficult to predict the outcome in a particular case. The following case concerns an issue that has elicited much controversy in recent years: whether states have the power to discriminate against shipments of out-of-state waste to intrastate disposal facilities.

POLICE POWERS
Powers possessed by states as part of their inherent sovereignty. These powers may be exercised to protect or promote the public order, health, safety, morals, and general welfare.

---

7.   434 U.S. 429, 98 S.Ct. 787, 54 L.Ed.2d 664 (1978).

CASE 2.2

OREGON WASTE SYSTEMS, INC. v. DEPARTMENT OF ENVIRONMENTAL QUALITY OF THE STATE OF OREGON
Supreme Court of the United States, 1994.
511 U.S. 93,
114 S.Ct. 1345,
128 L.Ed.2d 13.

HISTORICAL AND SOCIAL SETTING   *The treatment and disposal of waste is a major industry. The United States leads the world in the production of waste. Almost ten billion tons of waste of all types are generated in the United States every year. This waste includes everybody's garbage and sewage, as well as the by-products of industry, agriculture, mining, demolition, dredging, and energy production. Thus, large quantities of waste move in interstate commerce every day.*

FACTS   Oregon Waste Systems, Inc., operates a waste-disposal facility in Gilliam County, Oregon. The facility receives waste from sources in Oregon and from sources outside the state. In 1989, Oregon imposed a fee ($.85 per ton) on all of the solid waste that such facilities receive from sources in Oregon and imposed a higher fee ($2.25 per ton) on solid waste generated outside the state. Oregon Waste, other operators of waste-disposal facilities in Oregon, and Gilliam County filed a suit against the state in an Oregon court, challenging the higher fee as a violation of, among other things, the commerce clause. The court upheld the higher fee, and the plaintiffs appealed. The Oregon Supreme Court affirmed the ruling. The plaintiffs appealed to the United States Supreme Court.

ISSUE   Does the higher fee imposed by Oregon on solid waste generated outside the state violate the commerce clause?

DECISION   Yes. The Supreme Court held that Oregon's treatment of out-of-state waste was invalid under the commerce clause.

(Continued)

Case 2.2–Continued

REASON The Supreme Court pointed out that the first step in analyzing a law under the commerce clause is to determine whether it "regulates evenhandedly with only 'incidental effects' on interstate commerce." If a restriction is discriminatory—that is, if it favors in-state economic interests over their out-of-state counterparts—it is invalid. The Court concluded that Oregon's out-of-state fee was obviously discriminatory. It "subjects waste from other States to a fee almost three times greater than the *   *   * charge imposed on *   *   * in-state waste." The state argued, among other things, that the higher fee was necessary to make nonresidents pay their "fair share" of the costs imposed on Oregon by the disposal of their waste. The Court noted that the state was unable to specify what waste-disposal costs, in terms of taxes, residents paid that nonresidents did not. Besides, the Court pointed out, in-state shippers of out-of-state waste were charged the higher fee even though they paid all other Oregon taxes.

FOR CRITICAL ANALYSIS—Economic Consideration
In terms of the outcome in this case, would it have mattered if the fee for out-of-state waste was only, say, 10 cents per ton higher than the fee for in-state waste?

The Supremacy Clause

SUPREMACY CLAUSE
The provision in Article VI of the Constitution that provides that the Constitution, laws, and treaties of the United States are "the supreme Law of the Land." Under this clause, state and local laws that directly conflict with federal law will be rendered invalid.

Article VI of the Constitution provides that the Constitution, laws, and treaties of the United States are "the supreme Law of the Land." This article, commonly referred to as the **supremacy clause**, is important in the ordering of state and federal relationships. When there is a direct conflict between a federal law and a state law, the state law is rendered invalid. Because some powers are concurrent (shared by the federal government and the states), however, it is necessary to determine which law governs in a particular circumstance.

When Congress chooses to act exclusively in a concurrent area, it is said to have *preempted* the area. In this circumstance, a valid federal statute or regulation will take precedence over a conflicting state or local law or regulation on the same general subject. Congress, however, rarely makes clear its intent to preempt an entire subject area against state regulation; consequently, the courts must determine whether Congress intended to exercise exclusive dominion over a given area. Consideration of **preemption** often occurs in the commerce clause context.

PREEMPTION
A doctrine under which certain federal laws preempt, or take precedence over, conflicting state or local laws.

No single factor is decisive as to whether a court will find preemption. Generally, congressional intent to preempt will be found if the federal law is so pervasive, comprehensive, or detailed that the states have no room to supplement it. Also, when a federal statute creates an agency—such as the National Labor Relations Board—to enforce the law, matters that may come within the agency's jurisdiction will likely preempt state laws.

The Taxing and Spending Powers

Article I, Section 8, provides that Congress has the "Power to lay and collect Taxes, Duties, Imposts, and Excises." Section 8 further provides that "all Duties, Imposts and Excises shall be uniform throughout the United States." The requirement of uniformity refers to uniformity among the states, and thus Congress may not tax some states while exempting others.

Traditionally, if Congress attempted to regulate indirectly, by taxation, an area over which it had no authority, the tax would be invalidated by the courts. Today, however, if a tax measure bears some reasonable relationship to revenue production, it is generally held to be within the national taxing power. Moreover, the expansive interpretation of the commerce clause almost always provides a basis for sustaining a federal tax.

Under Article I, Section 8, Congress has the power "to pay the Debts and provide for the common Defence and general welfare of the United States." Through the spending power, Congress disposes of the revenues accumulated from the taxing power. Congress can spend revenues not only to carry out its enumerated powers but also to promote any objective it deems worthwhile, so long as it does not violate the Bill of Rights. For example, Congress could not condition welfare payments on the recipients' political views. The spending power necessarily involves policy choices, with which taxpayers may disagree.

▮ Business and the Bill of Rights

The importance of a written declaration of the rights of individuals eventually caused the first Congress of the United States to submit twelve amendments to the Constitution to the states for approval. The first ten of these amendments, commonly known as the **Bill of Rights,** were adopted in 1791 and embody a series of protections for the individual against various types of interference by the federal government.[8] Some constitutional protections apply to business entities as well. For example, corporations exist as separate legal entities, or *legal persons*, and enjoy many of the same rights and privileges as *natural persons* do.

Summarized here are the protections guaranteed by these ten amendments.[9] The due process clause of the Fourteenth Amendment, which we discuss later in this chapter, applies many of the rights guaranteed by these first ten amendments to the states.

1. The First Amendment guarantees the freedoms of religion, speech, and the press and the rights to assemble peaceably and to petition the government.
2. The Second Amendment guarantees the right to keep and bear arms.
3. The Third Amendment prohibits, in peacetime, the lodging of soldiers in any house without the owner's consent.
4. The Fourth Amendment prohibits unreasonable searches and seizures of persons or property.
5. The Fifth Amendment guarantees the rights to indictment by grand jury (see Chapter 7), to due process of law, and to fair payment when private property is taken for public use (see Chapter 35). The Fifth Amendment also prohibits compulsory self-incrimination and double jeopardy (trial for the same crime twice).
6. The Sixth Amendment guarantees the accused in a criminal case the right to a speedy and public trial by an impartial jury and with counsel. The accused has the right to cross-examine witnesses against him or her and to solicit testimony from witnesses in his or her favor.
7. The Seventh Amendment guarantees the right to a trial by jury in a civil case involving at least twenty dollars.[10]
8. The Eighth Amendment prohibits excessive bail and fines, as well as cruel and unusual punishment.
9. The Ninth Amendment establishes that the people have rights in addition to those specified in the Constitution.
10. The Tenth Amendment establishes that those powers neither delegated to the federal government nor denied to the states are reserved for the states.

The rights secured by the Bill of Rights are not absolute. Ultimately, it is the United States Supreme Court, as the interpreter of the Constitution, that both gives meaning to these constitutional rights and determines their boundaries.

"Bills of rights give assurance to the individual of the preservation of his liberty. They do not define the liberty they promise."

Benjamin N. Cardozo, 1870–1938 (*Associate justice of the United States Supreme Court, 1932–1938*)

BILL OF RIGHTS
The first ten amendments to the U.S. Constitution.

BE CAREFUL Although many of these rights apply to actions of the states, some of them apply only to actions of the federal government.

---

8. One of these proposed amendments was ratified 203 years later (in 1992) and became the Twenty-seventh Amendment to the Constitution. See Appendix B.
9. See the Constitution in Appendix B for the complete text of each amendment.
10. Twenty dollars was forty days' pay for the average person when the Bill of Rights was written.

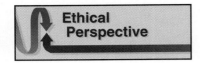

As you can see in the above list, many of the rights guaranteed by the first ten amendments are described in very general terms. For example, the Fourth Amendment prohibits unreasonable searches and seizures, but it does not define what constitutes an "unreasonable" search or seizure. Similarly, the Eighth Amendment prohibits excessive bail or fines, but no definition of *excessive* is contained in that amendment. Clearly, our constitutional rights depend not only on the Constitution but also on how our institutions of government give those rights their specific form and substance. Ultimately, it is the United States Supreme Court, as the interpreter of the Constitution, that defines our rights and determines their boundaries.

Ethical convictions—perceptions of what is right and what is wrong—inevitably enter into the process of interpreting and applying the mandates expressed in the Constitution, including the Bill of Rights. These perceptions naturally change over time—and thus, so do interpretations of the nature of our constitutional rights. For example, although the Supreme Court is obligated to follow precedents it established earlier (see the discussion of *stare decisis* in Chapter 1), it can, and has on occasion, departed from precedent in the interests of serving changed perceptions of fairness and justice.

For Critical Analysis: *Supreme Court justices are not elected by the people but are appointed by the president, with the advice and consent of the Senate. Do you think that the justices exercise too much authority in shaping the rights and liberties of Americans? Can you think of a better alternative?*

Freedom of Speech

The First Amendment freedoms of religion, speech, press, assembly, and petition have all been applied to the states through the due process clause of the Fourteenth Amendment (discussed later in this chapter). As mentioned, however, none of these freedoms confers an absolute right.

UNPROTECTED SPEECH   In interpreting the meaning of the First Amendment's guarantee of free speech, the United States Supreme Court has made it clear that certain types of speech will not be protected. Speech that harms the good reputation of

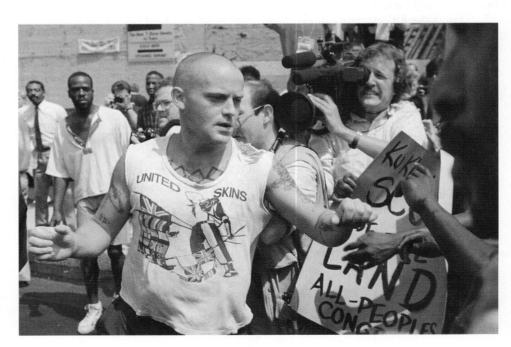

A Ku Klux Klan supporter, in a "United Skins" T-shirt, and an anti-KKK protester exchange blows during a protest. Should all forms of expression be protected under the First Amendment to the Constitution?

another, or defamatory speech (see Chapter 5), will not be protected under the First Amendment. Speech that violates criminal laws (such as threatening speech, pornography, and so on) is not constitutionally protected.

Other unprotected speech includes "fighting words," or words that are likely to incite others to respond violently, and obscene speech. Numerous state and federal statutes make it a crime to disseminate obscene materials. The United States Supreme Court has grappled from time to time with the problem of trying to establish an operationally effective definition of obscene speech, but frequently this determination is left to state and local authorities. Generally, obscenity is still a constitutionally unsettled area, whether it deals with speech, printed materials, or filmed materials. In the interest of protecting against the abuse of children, however, the Supreme Court has upheld state laws prohibiting the sale and possession of child pornography.[11] In the interest of protecting women against sexual harassment in the workplace, at least one court has banned lewd speech and pornographic pinups in the workplace.[12] In recent years, obscenity issues have also arisen in relation to television shows, movies, the lyrics and covers of music albums, and the content of monologues by "shock" comedians. (See this chapter's *Technology and Free Speech* for a discussion of free speech and online communications via the Internet.)

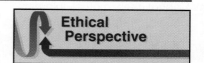

Ethical Perspective

Determining the point at which speech oversteps its constitutionally protected boundaries often poses troublesome ethical questions both for the courts and for society. For example, in recent years several colleges and universities have issued speech or behavioral codes in an attempt to curb the "hate speech" exchanged between members of different ethnic groups on their campuses. The University of Michigan, for instance, established a code that banned "any behavior, verbal or physical, that stigmatizes or victimizes an individual on the basis of race, ethnicity, religion, sex, sexual orientation, creed, national origin, ancestry, age, marital status, handicap or Vietnam-era veterans status." Other universities have issued similar codes. Do such codes go too far in restraining the free speech of students?

Many people contend that forcing students to engage only in "politically correct" speech violates the First Amendment right to freedom of expression. Others argue that hate speech essentially constitutes "fighting words" and thus should not be constitutionally protected. The courts have generally been reluctant to uphold these codes on the ground that they go too far in restricting the free speech of students. The Michigan code, for example, was ruled unconstitutional, as were similar codes issued by the University of Wisconsin and Stanford University.[a]

For Critical Analysis: *Does hate speech equate with fighting words? Should colleges and universities be permitted to regulate speech on their campuses?*

a. See *Doe v. University of Michigan,* 721 F.Supp. 852 (E.D.Mich. 1989); *The UWM Post v. Board of Regents of the University of Wisconsin System,* 774 F.Supp. 1163 (E.D.Wis. 1991); and "California Court Strikes Down Stanford Ban of 'Fighting Words,'" *The New York Times,* March 1, 1995, p. B8.

COMMERCIAL SPEECH—ADVERTISING   Courts often make a distinction between "normal" speech and "commercial" speech, which is speech and communications made by business firms, such as advertising. Although commercial speech is protected by the First Amendment, its protection is not as extensive as that afforded to noncommercial speech. A state may restrict certain kinds of advertising, for example, in the

---

11. See *Osborne v. Ohio,* 495 U.S. 103, 110 S.Ct. 1691, 109 L.Ed.2d 98 (1990).
12. *Robinson v. Jacksonville Shipyards, Inc.,* 760 F.Supp. 1486 (M.D.Fla. 1991).

interest of protecting consumers from being misled by the advertising practices. States also have a legitimate interest in the beautification of roadsides, and this interest allows states to place restraints on billboard advertising.

☐ Technology and Free Speech

When you are talking to someone, you can say just about anything without fear of prosecution. What about a situation in which you are "talking to" someone over the Internet, though? Are there any restrictions on your freedom of speech? The courts are having a hard time dealing with this thorny issue in today's on-line world. In various World Wide Web sites on the Internet, so-called news groups have been set up to allow people to "chat" about their mutual interests. Consequently, there are news groups on virtually every topic under the sun— gardening; political candidates; numerous movie stars, such as Kevin Costner and Winona Ryder; and country-and-western stars, such as the Mavericks and Trisha Yearwood.

What about news groups that deal with pornography, however defined, or even pedophilia? Anyone with a computer and a modem can create a news group in Usenet, which overlaps with the Internet. Indeed, the name of an alternative ("alt.") Usenet news group includes "pedophile," and this news group contains digitized photos that users can download to their own computers. Child pornography violates various federal and state laws. Even if local operators somehow screened out child pornography, users could still exchange digitized photos via electronic mail (E-mail). Moreover, American users can tap into computer systems abroad. There, U.S. obscenity laws do not apply.

Public concern over access to pornographic and obscene materials via the Internet led Congress to enact the Communications Decency Act (CDA) as part of the Telecommunications Act of 1996. The CDA makes it a criminal offense to transmit "indecent" speech or images to minors or to make such speech or images available on-line to minors. The act defines indecent speech as any communication that depicts or describes sexual or execretory activities or organs in such a way that is patently offensive, as measured by current community standards. Violators of the act may be fined up to $250,000 or imprisoned for up to two years.

The American Civil Liberties Union (ACLU) and other organizations immediately challenged the validity of the CDA on the ground that it is unconstitutionally vague—it subjects persons to criminal penalties without specifically identifying the crimes to which these penalties attach. In the first ruling on the issue, a federal district court in Pennsylvania agreed and issued a preliminary injunction against the act's enforcement.[a] The issue will surely come before the United States Supreme Court in the near future.

For Critical Analysis: *The CDA states that indecent speech is to be measured by community standards, but what community standards apply to the Internet, which has no geographic boundaries?*

a. *American Civil Liberties Union v. Reno,* ___ F.Supp.___ (E.D.Pa. 1996)[1996 WL 311865]. This case has not yet been published in West's *Federal Supplement.* Prior to publication, it can be accessed through WESTLAW using the WL citation just given.

Generally, a restriction on commercial speech will be considered valid as long as it meets the following three criteria: (1) it must seek to implement a substantial government interest, (2) it must directly advance that interest, and (3) it must go no further than necessary to accomplish its objective. At issue in the following case is whether a law prohibiting the inclusion of the alcohol content on beer labels unconstitutionally restricts commercial speech.

CASE 2.3

RUBIN v. COORS BREWING CO.

Supreme Court of the United States, 1995.
___ U.S. ___,
115 S.Ct. 1585,
131 L.Ed.2d 532.

HISTORICAL AND SOCIAL SETTING   *In the United States, no federal law regulates the level of alcohol in beer. The most popular beers contain between 3 and 5 percent alcohol. Ice beers are typically between 5 and 6 percent alcohol. Malt liquors may be as much as 7 percent alcohol. Beer is a popular drink among young consumers, who sometimes prefer the more potent brands. In the 1980s, it was widely—and erroneously—believed that beer brewed by the Coors Brewing Company was less potent than other beers.*

FACTS   In 1987, Coors applied to the Bureau of Alcohol, Tobacco and Firearms (BATF), an agency of the Department of the Treasury, for approval of proposed Coors beer labels that disclosed the alcohol content of the beer. The BATF rejected the labels on the ground that the Federal Alcohol Administration Act (FAAA) of 1935**[a]** prohibits the disclosure of the alcohol content of beer on labels. Coors filed a suit in a federal district court against the government to block the enforcement of the FAAA, on the ground that it violated the First Amendment. The government argued that enforcement of the FAAA suppresses the threat of "strength wars" among brewers, who, without the regulation, would compete in the market-

place based on the potency of their products. The district court granted Coors relief, and the government appealed. When the appellate court affirmed, the government appealed to the United States Supreme Court.

ISSUE   Does the FAAA's ban on disclosing the alcohol content of beer on labels violate the First Amendment?

DECISION   Yes. The Supreme Court held that the prohibition violates the First Amendment's protection of commercial speech.

REASON   The Supreme Court held that although the government had a substantial interest in curbing strength wars among brewers, the labeling ban did not directly advance that interest. Other federal laws make the ban effective only in states that also ban the disclosure of alcohol content in advertising. Because most states have no such ban, "brewers remain free to disclose alcohol content in advertisements, but not on labels, in much of the country." Besides, noted the Court, other regulations "allow brewers to signal high alcohol content through use of the term 'malt liquor'" and require the disclosure of alcohol content on the labels of wines and spirits. The Court also noted that there are alternatives to the labeling ban that are less intrusive to the First Amendment's protection of commercial speech. The government can directly limit the alcohol content of beer, prohibit marketing efforts that emphasize high alcohol strength, or limit the ban to malt liquors.

FOR CRITICAL ANALYSIS—Political Consideration
The trend in federal regulation of consumer products appears to favor greater disclosure of information. Whose interests are advanced by the disclosure of more information?

a.   27 U.S.C. Sections 201–220.

POLITICAL SPEECH   Political speech that otherwise would be within the protection of the First Amendment does not lose that protection simply because its source is a corporation. For example, in *First National Bank of Boston v. Bellotti*, national banking associations and business corporations sought United States Supreme Court review of a Massachusetts statute that prohibited corporations from making political contributions or expenditures that individuals were permitted to make. The Court ruled that the Massachusetts law was unconstitutional because it violated the right of corporations to freedom of speech.[13] Similarly, the Court has held that a law forbidding a corporation from using bill inserts to express its views on controversial issues also violates the First Amendment.[14]

Does a state law banning the distribution of anonymous political leaflets unconstitutionally restrain political speech? This question is at issue in the following case.

13.   435 U.S. 765, 98 S.Ct. 1407, 55 L.Ed.2d 707 (1978).
14.   *Consolidated Edison Co. v. Public Service Commission*, 447 U.S. 530, 100 S.Ct. 2326, 65 L.Ed.2d 319 (1980).

CASE 2.4

MCINTYRE v. OHIO ELECTIONS COMMISSION
Supreme Court of the United States, 1995.
___ U.S. ___,
115 S.Ct. 1511,
131 L.Ed.2d 426.

HISTORICAL AND POLITICAL SETTING *Anonymous pamphlets, leaflets, brochures, and books have played an important role in the political life of the United States. Perhaps the most famous embodiment of this tradition is* The Federalist Papers, *a series of essays published in New York City newspapers in 1787 and 1788. Writing under the name "Publius," James Madison, Alexander Hamilton, and John Jay argued in* The Federalist Papers *for the ratification of the Constitution.*

FACTS In April 1988, Margaret McIntyre distributed leaflets to persons attending public meetings at the Blendon Middle School in Westerville, Ohio. The leaflets expressed opposition to a proposed school tax. Some of the leaflets did not identify an author but only purported to express the views of "CONCERNED PARENTS AND TAX PAYERS." A school official filed a complaint with the Ohio Elections Commission under a state statute that prohibits the distribution of campaign literature that does not contain the name and address of the person or official issuing it. The commission imposed a fine of $100. McIntyre appealed to an Ohio state court, arguing that the statute was unconstitutional. The court agreed and dropped the fine. An Ohio appellate court reinstated the fine, and the Ohio Supreme Court affirmed. The state supreme court concluded that the statute was reasonable in light of the state's interests in providing voters with

information and in preventing fraud. McIntyre appealed to the United States Supreme Court.

ISSUE Does a statute prohibiting the anonymous distribution of campaign literature violate the First Amendment?

DECISION Yes. The Supreme Court held that the First Amendment protects the freedom to publish anonymously.

REASON The Supreme Court declared that "handing out leaflets in the advocacy of a politically controversial viewpoint is the essence of First Amendment expression." Thus, Ohio's statute could be upheld "only if it is narrowly tailored to serve an overriding state interest." Ohio's interests in providing information and in preventing fraud were not enough to justify the statute's restraint on speech, the Court concluded. Providing information "does not justify a state requirement that a writer make statements or disclosures that she would otherwise omit. Moreover, in the case of a handbill written by a private citizen unknown to the [reader], the name and address of the author adds little, if anything, to the reader's ability to evaluate the document's message." Regarding the state's interest in preventing fraud, the Court pointed out that the statute covered all documents, regardless of whether they were fraudulent, false, or libelous. Besides, Ohio has other "detailed and specific" regulations covering false statements in political campaigns.

FOR CRITICAL ANALYSIS—Political Consideration *When the source of political speech is a corporation, should the corporation be required to identify itself? Would such a requirement be constitutional?*

Freedom of Religion

ESTABLISHMENT CLAUSE
The provision in the First Amendment to the Constitution that prohibits Congress from creating any law "respecting an establishment of religion."

FREE EXERCISE CLAUSE
The provision in the First Amendment to the Constitution that prohibits Congress from making any law "prohibiting the free exercise" of religion.

The First Amendment states that the government may neither establish any religion nor prohibit the free exercise of religious practices. The first part of this constitutional provision is referred to as the **establishment clause**, and the second part is known as the **free exercise clause.** Government action, both federal and state, must be consistent with this constitutional mandate.

Federal or state regulation that does not promote religion or place a significant burden on religion is constitutional even if it has some impact on religion. "Sunday closing laws," for example, make the performance of some commercial activities on Sunday illegal. These statutes, also known as "blue laws" (from the color of the paper on which an early Sunday law was written), have been upheld on the ground that it is a legitimate function of government to provide a day of rest. The United States Supreme Court has held that the closing laws, although originally of a religious character, have taken on the secular purpose of promoting the health and welfare of

BUSINESS LAW IN ACTION

Religious Symbols Go to Court

Retailers in America know the importance of the Christmas season. Some major retailers obtain 40 percent of their annual sales revenues during the holiday season. Municipalities also spend tax dollars to decorate streets and government offices. Most of these decorations are not religious and apparently offend few individuals. What about blatantly religious scenes, however? Does any government in the United States have the legal right to use public monies for the display of religious scenes or to permit the display of religious symbols on government (public) property? At issue here is the establishment clause of the First Amendment to the U.S. Constitution: "Congress shall make no law respecting an establishment of religion."

A major test of a municipality's ability to spend public funds on religious scenes during the Christmas season occurred in 1984. The city of Pawtucket in Rhode Island included a crèche—a model depicting Mary, Joseph, and others around the crib of Jesus in the stable at Bethlehem—in a larger, nonreligious Christmas display, which included reindeer, candy-striped poles, and a Christmas tree. The entire display, although it was located in a private park, was the city's official display and had been both

erected and maintained by city employees. This case, known as *Lynch v. Donnelly*,[a] was decided in favor of the municipal government. The crèche could be included as long as it was just one part of a holiday display. The presence of the crèche was deemed constitutional; it did not violate the establishment clause.

What about the simultaneous display by local governments of objects that are symbols from various religions? In *County of Allegheny v. American Civil Liberties Union*,[b] the American Civil Liberties Union (ACLU) sued Allegheny County, where Pittsburgh, Pennsylvania, is located, because of what the ACLU claimed were "frankly religious displays." Each year, the county erects a crèche in its county courthouse, and the city of Pittsburgh also displays a menorah (a nine-branched candelabrum used in celebrating Chanukah) near the annual Christmas tree on the steps of its city-county building. Although the county displays nonreligious holiday symbols in the courthouse, they are not displayed alongside the crèche, as they were in the *Lynch* case. Therefore, the Supreme Court held that the presence of the crèche was unconstitutional. Displaying the menorah, however, did not violate the First Amendment, because the menorah was situated in close proximity to the Christmas tree.

a. 465 U.S. 668, 104 S.Ct. 1355, 79 L.Ed.2d 604 (1984).
b. 492 U.S. 573, 109 S.Ct. 3086, 106 L.Ed.2d 472 (1989).

In 1995, the Supreme Court again tangled with religious symbols and the establishment clause. The issue concerned whether the Ku Klux Klan (KKK) should be allowed to place an unattended cross in Capitol Square, the statehouse plaza in Columbus, Ohio, during the Christmas season. The Court ruled in favor of the KKK. Because the square is a forum for the discussion of public questions and for public activities, the presence of the cross would not indicate the government's endorsement of a religious belief. Neither *Allegheny* nor *Lynch*, stated the Court, "even remotely assumes that the government's neutral treatment of private religious expression can be unconstitutional."[c]

Clearly, court judges and justices do not have an easy job. In addition to their other duties, they periodically have to function as, in Justice Kennedy's words, a kind of "theology board."

For Critical Analysis: *During oral arguments before the Supreme Court in the ACLU case discussed above, Justice Scalia asked the attorney representing the city of Pittsburgh the following question: "[M]usn't the city do something for every religion in order to avoid appearing to endorse one religion over another?" How would you answer this question?*

c. *Capitol Square Review and Advisory Board v. Pinette*, ___U.S.___, 115 S.Ct. 2440, 132 L.Ed.2d 650 (1995).

---

workers.[15] Even though closing laws admittedly make it easier for Christians to attend religious services, the Court has viewed this effect as an incidental, not a primary, purpose of Sunday closing laws.

The First Amendment does not require a complete separation of church and state. On the contrary, it affirmatively mandates *accommodation* of all religions and forbids hostility toward any.[16] As indicated in the *Business Law in Action* above, the courts do not have an easy task in determining the extent to which governments can accommodate a religion without appearing to promote that religion and thus violate the

---

15. *McGowan v. Maryland*, 366 U.S. 420, 81 S.Ct. 1101, 6 L.Ed.2d 393 (1961).
16. *Zorach v. Clauson*, 343 U.S. 306, 72 S.Ct. 679, 96 L.Ed. 954 (1952).

establishment clause. For business firms, an important issue involves the accommodation that businesses must make for the religious beliefs of their employees. We examine this issue in Chapter 33, in the context of employment discrimination.

Self-Incrimination

The Fifth Amendment guarantees that no person "shall be compelled in any criminal case to be a witness against himself." Thus, in any federal proceeding, an accused person cannot be compelled to give testimony that might subject him or her to any criminal prosecution. Nor can an accused person be forced to testify against himself or herself in state courts, because the due process clause of the Fourteenth Amendment (discussed later in this chapter) incorporates the Fifth Amendment provision against self-incrimination.

The Fifth Amendment's guarantee against self-incrimination extends only to natural persons. Because a corporation is a legal entity and not a natural person, the privilege against self-incrimination does not apply to it. Similarly, the business records of a partnership do not receive Fifth Amendment protection.[17] When a partnership is required to produce these records, it must give the information even if it incriminates the persons who constitute the business entity. Sole proprietors and sole practitioners (those who fully own their businesses) who have not incorporated cannot be compelled to produce their business records. These individuals have full protection against self-incrimination, because they function in only one capacity; there is no separate business entity.

Searches and Seizures

The Fourth Amendment protects the "right of the people to be secure in their persons, houses, papers, and effects." Before searching or seizing private property, law enforcement officers must obtain a **search warrant**—an order from a judge or other public official authorizing the search or seizure.

SEARCH WARRANTS AND PROBABLE CAUSE   To obtain a search warrant, the officers must convince a judge that they have reasonable grounds, or probable cause, to believe a search will reveal a specific illegality. **Probable cause** requires law enforcement officials to have trustworthy evidence that would convince a reasonable person that the proposed search or seizure is more likely justified than not. Furthermore, the Fourth Amendment prohibits *general* warrants. It requires a particular description of that which is to be searched or seized. General searches through a person's belongings are impermissible. The search cannot extend beyond what is described in the warrant.

There are exceptions to the requirement of a search warrant, as when it is likely that the items sought will be removed before a warrant can be obtained. For example, if a police officer has probable cause to believe an automobile contains evidence of a crime and it is likely that the vehicle will be unavailable by the time a warrant is obtained, the officer can search the vehicle without a warrant.

SEARCHES AND SEIZURES IN THE BUSINESS CONTEXT   Constitutional protection against unreasonable searches and seizures is important to businesses and professionals. As federal and state regulation of commercial activities increased, frequent and unannounced government inspections were conducted to ensure compliance with the regulations. Such inspections were at times extremely disruptive. In *Marshall v. Barlow's, Inc.*,[18] the United States Supreme Court held that government inspectors do not have

---

17.   The privilege has been applied to some small family partnerships. See *United States v. Slutsky*, 352 F.Supp. 1005 (S.D.N.Y. 1972).
18.   436 U.S. 307, 98 S.Ct. 1816, 56 L.Ed.2d 305 (1978).

BE AWARE The Fifth Amendment protection against self-incrimination does not cover partnerships or corporations.

SEARCH WARRANT
An order granted by a public authority, such as a judge, that authorizes law-enforcement personnel to search particular premises or property.

PROBABLE CAUSE
Reasonable grounds to believe the existence of facts warranting certain actions, such as the search or arrest of a person.

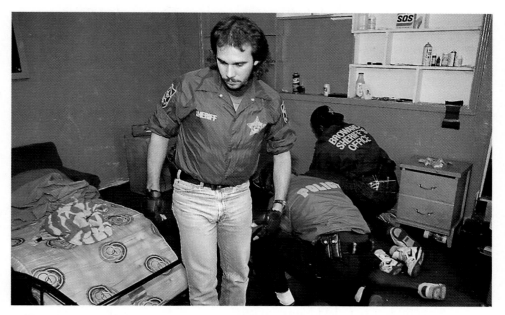

Police search a crack house in Florida. Do the owners and occupants of such houses receive protection from unreasonable searches and seizures under the Constitution? Should they?

the right to enter business premises without a warrant, although the standard of probable cause is not the same as that required in nonbusiness contexts. The existence of a general and neutral enforcement plan will justify issuance of the warrant.

Lawyers and accountants frequently possess the business records of their clients, and inspecting these documents while they are out of the hands of their true owners also requires a warrant. No warrant is required, however, for seizures of spoiled or contaminated food. Nor are warrants required for searches of businesses in such highly regulated industries as liquor, guns, and strip mining. General manufacturing is not considered to be one of these highly regulated industries, however.

Of increasing concern to many government employers is how to maintain a safe and efficient workplace without jeopardizing the Fourth Amendment rights of employees "to be secure in their persons." Requiring government employees to undergo random drug tests, for example, may be held to violate the Fourth Amendment. In Chapter 32, we discuss Fourth Amendment issues in the employment context, as well as the privacy rights of employees in general, in greater detail.

▌Other Constitutional Protections

Two other constitutional guarantees of great significance to Americans are mandated by the *due process clauses* of the Fifth and Fourteenth Amendments and the *equal protection clause* of the Fourteenth Amendment.

Due Process

Both the Fifth and the Fourteenth Amendments provide that no person shall be deprived "of life, liberty, or property, without due process of law." The **due process clause** of these constitutional amendments has two aspects—procedural and substantive.

PROCEDURAL DUE PROCESS *Procedural* due process requires that any government decision to take life, liberty, or property must be made fairly. For example, fair procedures must be used in determining whether a person will be subjected to punishment or have some burden imposed on him or her. Fair procedure has been interpreted as

"What is due process of law depends on circumstances. It varies with the subject matter and necessities of the situation."

Oliver Wendell Holmes, Jr., 1841–1935
(Associate justice of the United States Supreme Court, 1902–1932)

DUE PROCESS CLAUSE
The provisions of the Fifth and Fourteenth Amendments to the Constitution that guarantee that no person shall be deprived of life, liberty, or property without due process of law. Similar clauses are found in most state constitutions.

requiring that the person have at least an opportunity to object to a proposed action before a fair, neutral decision maker (which need not be a judge). Thus, for example, if a driver's license is construed as a property interest, some sort of opportunity to object to its suspension or termination by the state must be provided.

SUBSTANTIVE DUE PROCESS   *Substantive* due process focuses on the content, or substance, of legislation. If a law or other governmental action limits a *fundamental right*, it will be held to violate substantive due process unless it promotes a *compelling or overriding state interest*. Fundamental rights include interstate travel, privacy, voting, and all First Amendment rights. Compelling state interests could include, for example, the public's safety. Thus, laws designating speed limits may be upheld even though they affect interstate travel, if they are shown to reduce highway fatalities, because the state has a compelling interest in protecting the lives of its citizens.

In all other situations, a law or action does not violate substantive due process if it rationally relates to any legitimate governmental end. It is almost impossible for a law or action to fail the "rationality" test. Under this test, virtually any business regulation will be upheld as reasonable—the United States Supreme Court has sustained insurance regulations, price and wage controls, banking controls, and controls of unfair competition and trade practices against substantive due process challenges.

To illustrate, if a state legislature enacted a law imposing a fifteen-year term of imprisonment without a trial on all businesspersons who appeared in their own television commercials, the law would be unconstitutional on both substantive and procedural grounds. Substantive review would invalidate the legislation because it abridges freedom of speech. Procedurally, the law is unfair because it imposes the penalty without giving the accused a chance to defend his or her actions. The lack of procedural due process will cause a court to invalidate any statute or prior court decision. Similarly, a denial of substantive due process requires courts to overrule any state or federal law that violates the Constitution. In the following case, the court considered whether the retroactive application of a statute violated a defendant's due process rights.

CASE 2.5

SHADBURNE-VINTON v. DALKON SHIELD CLAIMANTS TRUST

United States Court of Appeals, Fourth Circuit, 1995.
60 F.3d 1071.

HISTORICAL AND TECHNOLOGICAL SETTING   *An intrauterine device (IUD) is a contraceptive device made of plastic and sometimes containing copper. Today, IUDs are generally reliable, although some women experience painful periods, and there is a risk of pelvic infection. In the 1980s, however, the Dalkon Shield IUD, manufactured by the A. H. Robins Company, was believed to have caused much more serious injuries to many of the women who used it.*

FACTS   Susan Shadburne-Vinton used a Dalkon Shield IUD from 1974 through 1976. Claiming that the IUD had rendered her infertile and caused her to

develop multiple sclerosis, Shadburne-Vinton filed suit against the A. H. Robins Company in a federal district court in 1983. The court dismissed her suit under an Oregon statute that limited the time for filing such suits to "not later than eight years" after the date on which a product was purchased. Shadburne-Vinton appealed, but the appeal was suspended when Robins filed for bankruptcy. During the suspension, the Oregon legislature amended the statute to exclude IUD manufacturers. The amendment expressly stated that it applied retroactively. When Shadburne-Vinton's case went forward, the Dalkon Shield Claimants Trust (which substituted for Robins as a result of the bankruptcy proceeding) argued that retroactive application of the amendment to the statute would violate the trust's due process rights. The court agreed and issued a judgment in favor of the trust. Shadburne-Vinton appealed.

ISSUE   Is the retroactive application of the statute proper under the due process clause of the Fifth Amendment?

DECISION   Yes. The U.S. Court of Appeals for the Fourth Circuit reversed the lower court's ruling and held that the statute could be applied retroactively.

Case 2.5—Continued

REASON The court reasoned that "the Due Process Clause of the Fifth Amendment allows retroactive application of either federal or state statutes as long as the statute serves a legitimate legislative purpose that is furthered by rational means." The court pointed out that after extensive hearings, the Oregon legislature determined that retroactive application of the amendment was "fair and equitable." The court explained that "[b]ecause many of the women suffered injuries from the IUD in the early 1970s, and the link between the IUD and the injuries it caused was not discovered until the early 1980s, the unamended statute * * * barred the claims of many women." The amendment provided these women with "a fair opportunity to litigate their claims."

FOR CRITICAL ANALYSIS—Political Consideration
In whose best interest is it to set a time limit within which a lawsuit must be brought?

Equal Protection

Under the Fourteenth Amendment, a state may not "deny to any person within its jurisdiction the equal protection of the laws." The United States Supreme Court has used the due process clause of the Fifth Amendment to make the **equal protection clause** applicable to the federal government. Equal protection means that the government must treat similarly situated individuals in a similar manner.

Both substantive due process and equal protection require review of the substance of the law or other governmental action rather than review of the procedures used. When a law or action limits the liberty of all persons to do something, it may violate substantive due process; when a law or action limits the liberty of some persons but not others, it may violate the equal protection clause. Thus, for example, if a law prohibits all persons from buying contraceptive devices, it raises a substantive due process question; if it prohibits only unmarried persons from buying the same devices, it raises an equal protection issue.

Basically, in determining whether a law or action violates the equal protection clause, a court will consider questions similar to those previously noted as applicable in a substantive due process review. Under an equal protection inquiry, when a law or action distinguishes between or among individuals, the basis for the distinction—that is, the *classification*—is examined.

STRICT SCRUTINY If the law or action inhibits some persons' exercise of a fundamental right, the law or action will be subject to "strict scrutiny" by the courts. Under this standard, the classification must be necessary to promote a compelling state interest. Also, if the classification is based on a *suspect trait*—such as race, national origin, or citizenship status—the classification must be necessary to promote a compelling state interest. Compelling state interests include remedying past unconstitutional or illegal discrimination but do not include correcting the general effects of "society's" discrimination. Thus, for example, if a city gives preference to minority applicants in awarding construction contracts, the city normally must identify the past unconstitutional or illegal discrimination against minority construction firms that it is attempting to correct.

INTERMEDIATE SCRUTINY Another standard, that of "intermediate scrutiny," is applied in cases involving discrimination based on gender or legitimacy. Laws using these classifications must be *substantially related to important government objectives.* For example, an important government objective is preventing illegitimate teenage pregnancies. Because males and females are not similarly situated in this circumstance—only females can become pregnant—a law that punishes men but not women for statutory rape will be upheld. A state law requiring illegitimate children to bring paternity suits within six years of their births, however, will be struck down if legitimate children are allowed to seek support from their parents at any time.

EQUAL PROTECTION CLAUSE
The provision in the Fourteenth Amendment to the Constitution that guarantees that no state will "deny to any person within its jurisdiction the equal protection of the laws." This clause mandates that the state governments treat similarly situated individuals in a similar manner.

THE "RATIONAL BASIS" TEST In matters of economic or social welfare, the classification will be considered valid if there is any conceivable *rational basis* on which the classification might relate to any legitimate government interest. It is almost impossible for a law or action to fail the rational basis test. Thus, for example, a city ordinance that in effect prohibits all pushcart vendors except a specific few from operating in a particular area of the city will be upheld if the city proffers a rational basis—perhaps regulation and reduction of traffic in the particular area—for the ordinance. In contrast, a law that provides unemployment benefits only to people over six feet tall would violate the guarantee of equal protection. There is no rational basis for determining the distribution of unemployment compensation on the basis of height. Such a distinction could not further any legitimate government objective.

Privacy Rights

Today, virtually all institutions with which an individual has dealings—including schools, doctors and dentists, insurance companies, mail-order houses, banking institutions, credit-card companies, and mortgage firms—obtain information about that individual and store it in their computer files. In addition, numerous government agencies, such as the Census Bureau, the Social Security Administration, and the Internal Revenue Service, collect and store data concerning individuals' incomes, expenses, marital status, and other personal history and habits. Any time an individual applies for a driver's license, a credit card, or even telephone service, information concerning that individual is gathered and stored. Frequently, this personal information finds its way to credit bureaus, marketing departments and firms, or other organizations without the permission or even the knowledge of the individuals concerned.

A personal right to privacy is held to be so fundamental as to be applicable at both the state and the federal levels. Although there is no specific guarantee of a right to privacy in the Constitution, such a right has been derived from guarantees found in the First, Third, Fourth, Fifth, and Ninth Amendments. Invasion of another's privacy is also a civil wrong (see Chapter 5), and over the last several decades legislation has been passed at the federal level to protect the privacy of individuals in several areas of concern (see Exhibit 2–1). In the business context, issues of privacy often arise in the employment context, a topic we will treat in Chapter 32.

♦ **Exhibit 2–1 Federal Legislation Relating to Privacy**

TITLE	PROVISIONS CONCERNING PRIVACY
Freedom of Information Act (1966)	Provides that individuals have a right to obtain access to information about them collected in government files.
Fair Credit Reporting Act (1970)	Provides that consumers have the right to be informed of the nature and scope of a credit investigation, the kind of information that is being compiled, and the names of the firms or individuals who will be receiving the report.
Crime Control Act (1973)	Safeguards the confidentiality of information amassed for certain state criminal systems.
Family and Educational Rights and Privacy Act (1974)	Limits access to computer-stored records of education-related evaluations and grades in private and public colleges and universities.
Privacy Act (1974)	Protects the privacy of individuals about whom the federal government has information. Specifically, the act provides as follows: 1. Agencies originating, using, disclosing, or otherwise manipulating personal information must ensure the reliability of the information and provide safeguards against its misuse. 2. Information compiled for one purpose cannot be used for another without the concerned individual's permission. 3. Individuals must be able to find out what data concerning them are being compiled and how the data will be used. 4. Individuals must be given a means by which to correct inaccurate data.
Tax Reform Act (1976)	Preserves the privacy of personal financial information.
Right to Financial Privacy Act (1978)	Prohibits financial institutions from providing the federal government with access to a customer's records unless the customer authorizes the disclosure.
Electronic Fund Transfer Act (1978)	Requires financial institutions to notify an individual if a third party gains access to the individual's account.
Counterfeit Access Device and Computer Fraud and Abuse Act (1984)	Prohibits the use of a computer without authorization to retrieve data in a financial institution's or consumer reporting agency's files.
Cable Communications Policy Act (1984)	Regulates access to information collected by cable service operators on subscribers to cable services.
Electronic Communications Privacy Act (1986)	Prohibits the interception of information communicated by electronic means.

▌Key Terms

Bill of Rights 41
checks and balances 34
commerce clause 35
due process clause 49
equal protection clause 51

establishment clause 46
federal form of government 34
free exercise clause 46
police powers 39
preemption 40

probable cause 48
search warrant 48
supremacy clause 40

▌Chapter Summary: Constitutional Law

Constitutional Powers of Government *(See pages 34–35.)*	The U.S. Constitution established a federal form of government, in which government powers are shared by the national government and the state governments. At the national level, government powers are divided among the legislative, executive, and judicial branches.
Commerce Clause *(See pages 35–40.)*	1. *The breadth of the commerce clause*—The commerce clause expressly permits Congress to regulate commerce. Over time, courts expansively interpreted this clause, and today the commerce power authorizes the national government, at least theoretically, to regulate virtually every commercial enterprise in the United States. 2. *The regulatory powers of the states*—Under their police powers, state governments may regulate private activities to protect or promote the public order, health, safety, morals, and general welfare. If state regulations substantially interfere with interstate commerce, they will be held to violate the commerce clause of the U.S. Constitution.
Supremacy Clause *(See page 40.)*	The U.S. Constitution provides that the Constitution, laws, and treaties of the United States are "the supreme Law of the Land." Whenever a state law directly conflicts with a federal law, the state law is rendered invalid.
Taxing and Spending Powers *(See pages 40–41.)*	The U.S. Constitution gives Congress the power to impose uniform taxes throughout the United States and to spend revenues accumulated from the taxing power. Congress can spend revenues to promote any objective it deems worthwhile, so long as it does not violate the Bill of Rights.
Business and the Bill of Rights *(See pages 41–49.)*	The Bill of Rights, which consists of the first ten amendments to the U.S. Constitution, was adopted in 1791 and embodies a series of protections for individuals—and in most cases, business entities—against various types of interference by the federal government. Freedoms guaranteed by the Bill of Rights include the following: 1. *Freedom of speech*—Types of speech protected under the First Amendment include commercial speech and political speech. Certain types of speech, such as defamatory speech and lewd or obscene speech, are not protected under the First Amendment. 2. *Freedom of religion*—Under the First Amendment, the government may neither establish any religion (the establishment clause) nor prohibit the free exercise of religion (the free exercise clause). 3. *Self-incrimination*—The Fifth Amendment guarantees that no person "shall be compelled in any criminal case to be a witness against himself." This Fifth Amendment protection against self-incrimination does not apply to corporations or partnerships. 4. *Searches and seizures*—The Fourth Amendment prohibits unreasonable searches and seizures. Normally, law enforcement personnel must obtain a search warrant before they can legitimately conduct a search or seizure.
Other Constitutional Protections *(See pages 49–53.)*	1. *Due process*—Both the Fifth and the Fourteenth Amendments provide that no person shall be deprived of "life, liberty, or property, without due process of law." Procedural due process requires that any government decision to take life, liberty, or property must be made fairly, using fair procedures. Substantive due process focuses on the content of legislation. Generally, a law that is not compatible with the Constitution violates substantive due process unless the law promotes a compelling state interest, such as public safety.

▌ Chapter Summary: Constitutional Law—Continued

Other Constitutional Protections— Continued	2. *Equal protection*—Under the Fourteenth Amendment, a state may not "deny to any person within its jurisdiction the equal protection of the laws." A law or action that limits the liberty of some persons but not others may violate the equal protection clause. Such a law may be deemed valid, however, if there is a rational basis for the discriminatory treatment of a given group or if the law substantially relates to an important government objective.
	3. *Privacy rights*—There is no specific guarantee of a right to privacy in the Constitution, but such a right has been derived from guarantees found in other constitutional amendments.

▌ For Review

1. What is the basic structure of the American government?
2. What constitutional clause gives the federal government the power to regulate commercial activities among the various states?
3. What constitutional clause allows laws enacted by the federal government to take priority over conflicting state laws?

4. What is the Bill of Rights? What rights and liberties does this document establish?
5. Where in the Constitution can the due process clause be found?

▌ Questions and Case Problems

2–1. Government Powers. The framers of the Constitution feared the twin evils of tyranny and anarchy. Discuss how specific provisions of the Constitution and the Bill of Rights reflect these fears and protect against both of these extremes.

2–2. Commercial Speech. A mayoral election is about to be held in a large U.S. city. One of the candidates is Luis Delgado, and his campaign supporters wish to post campaign signs on lampposts and utility posts throughout the city. A city ordinance, however, prohibits the posting of any signs on public property. Delgado's supporters contend that the city ordinance is unconstitutional, because it violates their rights to free speech. What factors might a court consider in determining the constitutionality of this ordinance?

2–3. Commerce Clause. Suppose that Georgia enacts a law requiring the use of contoured rear-fender mudguards on trucks and trailers operating within its state lines. The statute further makes it illegal for trucks and trailers to use straight mudguards. In thirty-five other states, straight mudguards are legal. Moreover, in the neighboring state of Florida, straight mudguards are explicitly required by law. There is some evidence suggesting that contoured mudguards might be a little safer than straight mudguards. Discuss whether this Georgia statute would violate the commerce clause of the U.S. Constitution.

2–4. Freedom of Religion. A business has a backlog of orders, and to meet its deadlines, management decides to run the firm seven days a week, eight hours a day. One of the employees, Marjorie Tollens, refuses to work on Saturday on

religious grounds. Her refusal to work means that the firm may not meet its production deadlines and may therefore suffer a loss of future business. The firm fires Tollens and replaces her with an employee who is willing to work seven days a week. Tollens claims that her employer, in terminating her employment, violated her constitutional right to the free exercise of her religion. Do you agree? Why or why not?

2–5. Equal Protection. In 1988, the Nebraska legislature enacted a statute that required any motorcycle operator or passenger on Nebraska's highways to wear a protective helmet. Eugene Robotham, a licensed motorcycle operator, sued the state of Nebraska to block enforcement of the law. Robotham asserted, among other things, that the statute violated the equal protection clause, because it placed requirements on motorcyclists that were not imposed on other motorists. Will the court agree with Robotham that the law violates the equal protection clause? Why or why not? [*Robotham v. State*, 241 Neb. 379, 488 N.W.2d 533 (1992)]

2–6. Freedom of Religion. A 1988 Minnesota statute required all operators of slow-moving vehicles to display on their vehicles a fluorescent orange-red triangular emblem. Although during the daytime an alternative (a black triangle with a white reflective border and red reflective tape) could be used, at night all slow-moving vehicles had to display the orange-red emblem. Hershberger and the other defendants, who were Amish, claimed that the statute violated their First Amendment freedom of religion because displaying the "loud" colors and "worldly symbols" on their vehicles (black, boxlike buggies) compromised their religious belief that they should remain separate and apart from the modern world. They would not object to displaying a sign similar to the alternative symbol if they could use silver, instead of red, reflective tape and if they did not have to display the "regular" emblem at night. The state argued that although the silver tape was as effective as the red in terms of visibility, the red tape was customarily associated with slow-moving vehicles, and therefore the Amish should comply with the statute as written. What will the court hold? Discuss. [*State v. Hershberger*, 444 N.W.2d 282 (Minn. 1989)]

2–7. Commerce Clause. Taylor owned a bait business in Maine and arranged to have live baitfish imported into the state. The importation of the baitfish violated a Maine statute. Taylor was charged with violating a federal statute that makes it a federal crime to transport fish in interstate commerce in violation of state law. Taylor moved to dismiss the charges on the ground that the Maine statute unconstitutionally burdened interstate commerce. Maine intervened to defend the validity of its statute, arguing that the law legitimately protected the state's fisheries from parasites and nonnative species that might be included in shipments of live baitfish. Were Maine's interests in protecting its fisheries from parasites and nonnative species sufficient to justify the burden placed on interstate commerce by the Maine statute? Discuss. [*Maine v. Taylor*, 477 U.S. 131, 106 S.Ct. 2440, 91 L.Ed.2d 110 (1986)]

2–8. Freedom of Speech. The Allstate Insurance Co. agreed to refer its policyholders to members of the USA-GLAS Network for automobile glass repair and replacement. In response to the concerns of independent glass businesses over the loss of revenue caused by the arrangement, the South Dakota legislature passed a statute prohibiting an insurance company from requiring or recommending that a policyholder "use a particular company or location for the providing of automobile glass replacement or repair services or products." Allstate filed a suit against the state, challenging the validity of the statute as, among other things, an unconstitutional restriction on commercial speech. Will the court agree with Allstate? Why or why not? [*Allstate Insurance Co. v. State of South Dakota*, 871 F.Supp. 355 (D.S.D. 1994)]

2–9. Commerce Clause. South Dakota Disposal Systems, Inc. (SDDS), applied to the South Dakota Department of Water and Natural Resources (DWNR) for a permit to operate a solid-waste-disposal facility (Lonetree). It was estimated that 90 to 95 percent of the waste would come from out of state. The DWNR determined that Lonetree would be environmentally safe and issued a permit. Later, a public referendum was held. The state attorney general issued a pamphlet to accompany the referendum that urged the public to vote against "the out-of-state dump" because "South Dakota is not the nation's dumping grounds." SDDS filed a suit against the state, challenging the referendum as a violation of, among other things, the commerce clause. Was the referendum unconstitutional? Why or why not? [*SDDS, Inc. v. State of South Dakota*, 47 F.3d 263 (8th Cir. 1995)]

2–10. Freedom of Religion. Isaiah Brown was the director of the information services department for Polk County, Iowa. During department meetings in his office, he allowed occasional prayers and, in addressing one meeting, referred to Bible passages related to sloth and "work ethics." There was no apparent disruption of the work routine, but the county admin-

istrator reprimanded Brown. Later, the administrator ordered Brown to remove from his office all items with a religious connotation. Brown sued the county, alleging that the reprimand and the order violated, among other things, the free exercise clause of the First Amendment. Could the county be held liable for violating Brown's constitutional rights? Discuss. [*Brown v. Polk County, Iowa*, 61 F.3d 650 (8th Cir. 1995)]

A QUESTION OF ETHICS AND SOCIAL RESPONSIBILITY

2–11. *Agnes and John Donahue refused to rent an apartment to an unmarried couple, Verna Terry and Robert Wilder. The Donahues were devout Roman Catholics and firmly believed, in accordance with the church's teachings, that engaging in sexual relations outside of marriage was a mortal sin. Renting an apartment to an unmarried couple would, in Agnes Donahue's mind, be aiding the couple in the commission of a sin, and therefore she refused to rent the apartment to Terry and Wilder. Terry and Wilder filed a complaint with the California Fair Employment and Housing Commission, alleging that the Donahues' refusal to rent them an apartment violated a state statute prohibiting discrimination on the basis of marital status. Eventually, the case was heard by a California appellate court. The question before the court was whether the state's interest in prohibiting discrimination based on marital status outweighed the Donahues' state constitutional right to the free exercise of their religion. [Donahue v. Fair Employment and Housing Commission, 7 Cal.App.4th 1498, 2 Cal.Rptr.2d 32 (1991)]*

1. In your opinion, should the court make an exception to the applicability of the state statute prohibiting discrimination on the basis of marital status in the Donahues' case? Why or why not?
2. What if a landlord's religious convictions led him or her to refuse to rent premises to certain prospective tenants for other reasons—because of their race or national origin, for example?

CASE BRIEFING ASSIGNMENT

2–12. *Examine Case A.1 [Austin v. Berryman, 878 F.2d 786 (4th Cir. 1989)] in Appendix A. The case has been excerpted there in great detail. Review and then brief the case, making sure that you include answers to the following questions in your brief.*

1. Who were the plaintiff and defendant in this action?
2. Why did Austin claim that she had been forced to leave her job?
3. Why was Austin refused state unemployment benefits?
4. Did the state's refusal to give Austin unemployment compensation violate her rights under the free exercise clause of the First Amendment?
5. What logic or reasoning did the court employ in arriving at its conclusion?

FOR CRITICAL ANALYSIS

2–13. *In recent years, many people have criticized the film and entertainment industries for promoting violence by exposing the American public, and particularly American youth, to extremely violent films and song lyrics. Do you think that the right to free speech can (or should) be traded off to reduce violence in America?*

▌Accessing the Internet: Business Law and Legal Environment

Although thorough and accurate constitutional research must be conducted through WESTLAW, LEXIS, or a law library, any research that you are doing on a constitutional issue can be initiated by asking experts on-line. You can browse through questions and answers that lawyers have given to specific legal questions in specific Web sites, such as Legal Dot Net, the address of which was given in the *Accessing the Internet* feature following Chapter 1. You can also get E-mail help at

martin@law.mail.cornell.edu

The World Wide Web version of the Constitution provides hypertext links to amendments and other changes. Go to

http://www.law.cornell.edu/constitution/constitution.overview.html/

You can obtain all constitutional decisions of the United States Supreme Court by using a site developed by Cornell Law School at

http://www.law.cornell.edu/syllabi?constituional+unconstitutional

You can always check into the following news group to read what people are saying about the U.S. Constitution:

ALT.POLITICS.USA.CONSTITUTION

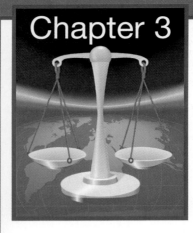

Chapter 3

Courts and Procedures

"The Judicial Department comes home in its effects to every man's fireside: it passes on his property, his reputation, his life, his all."

John Marshall, 1755–1835
(Chief justice of the United States Supreme Court, 1801–1835)

CHAPTER OBJECTIVES

After reading this chapter, you should be able to:

1. Explain the concepts of jurisdiction and venue.
2. State the requirements for federal jurisdiction.
3. Identify the basic components of the federal and state court systems.
4. Compare and contrast the functions of trial courts and appellate courts.
5. Discuss the various ways in which disputes can be resolved outside the court system.

As Chief Justice John Marshall remarked in the above quotation, ultimately, we are all affected by what the courts say and do. This is particularly true in the business world—nearly every businessperson faces either a potential or an actual lawsuit at some time or another in his or her career. For this reason, anyone contemplating a career in business will benefit from an understanding of American court systems, including the mechanics of lawsuits.

In this chapter, after examining the judiciary's overall role in the American governmental scheme, we discuss some basic requirements that must be met before a party may bring a lawsuit before a particular court. We then look at the court systems of the United States in some detail and, to clarify judicial procedures, follow a hypothetical case through a state court system. Even though there are fifty-two court systems—one for each of the fifty states, one for the District of Columbia, plus a federal system—similarities abound. Keep in mind that the federal courts are not superior to the state courts; they are simply an independent system of courts, which derives its authority from Article III, Section 2, of the U.S. Constitution. The chapter concludes with an overview of some alternative methods of settling disputes.

The Judiciary's Role in American Government

As you learned in Chapter 1, the body of American law is vast and complex. It includes the federal and state constitutions, statutes passed by legislative bodies, administrative law, and the case decisions and legal principles that form the common law. These laws would be meaningless, however, without the courts to interpret and apply them. This is the essential role of the judiciary—the courts—in the American governmental system: to interpret and apply the law.

As the branch of government entrusted with interpreting the laws, the judiciary can decide, among other things, whether the laws or actions of the other two branches are constitutional. The process for making such a determination is known as **judicial review.** The power of judicial review enables the judicial branch to act as a check on the other two branches of government, in line with the checks and balances system established by the U.S. Constitution.

The power of judicial review is not mentioned in the Constitution, however. Rather, it was established by the United States Supreme Court's decision in *Marbury v. Madison.*[1] In that case, which was decided in 1803, the Supreme Court stated, "It is emphatically the province and duty of the Judicial Department to say what the law is. . . . If two laws conflict with each other, the courts must decide on the operation of each. . . . So if the law be in opposition to the Constitution . . . [t]he Court must determine which of these conflicting rules governs the case. This is the very essence of judicial duty." Since the *Marbury v. Madison* decision, details of which are offered in the *Landmark in the Law* below, the power of judicial review has remained unchallenged. Today, this power is exercised by both federal and state courts.

---

1.   5 U.S. (1 Cranch) 137, 2 L.Ed. 60 (1803).

"The power vested in the American courts of justice, of pronouncing a statute to be unconstitutional, forms one of the most powerful barriers which has ever been devised against the tyranny of political assemblies."

Alexis de Tocqueville, 1805–1859
(French historian and statesman)

JUDICIAL REVIEW
The process by which a court decides on the constitutionality of legislative enactments and actions of the executive branch.

Marbury v. Madison (1803)

LANDMARK IN THE LAW

In the edifice of American law, the *Marbury v. Madison* decision in 1803 can be viewed as the keystone of the constitutional arch. The facts of the case were as follows. John Adams, who had lost his bid for reelection to Thomas Jefferson in 1800, feared the Jeffersonians' antipathy toward business and toward a strong central government. Adams thus worked feverishly to "pack" the judiciary with loyal Federalists (those who believed in a strong national government) by appointing what came to be called "midnight judges" just before Jefferson took office. All of the fifty-nine judicial appointment letters had to be certified and delivered, but Adams's secretary of state (John Marshall) had only succeeded in delivering forty-two of them by the time Jefferson took over as president. Jefferson, of course, refused to order his secretary of state, James Madison, to deliver the remaining commissions.

William Marbury and three others to whom the commissions had not been delivered sought a writ of *mandamus* (an order directing a government official to fulfill a duty) from the United States Supreme Court, as authorized by Section 13 of the Judiciary Act of 1789. As fate would have it, John Marshall had stepped down as Adams's secretary of state only to become chief justice of the Supreme Court. Marshall faced a dilemma: If he ordered the commissions delivered, the new secretary of state (Madison) could simply refuse to deliver them—and the Court had no way to compel action, because it had no police force. At the same time, if Marshall simply allowed the new administration to do as it wished, the Court's power would be severely eroded.

James Madison. If Madison had delivered the commissions of the Federalist judges, would the U.S. Supreme Court today have the power of judicial review?

(Continued)

Landmark in the Law—Continued

Marshall masterfully fashioned a decision that did not require anyone to do anything but at the same time enlarged the power of the Supreme Court. He stated that the highest court did not have the power to issue a writ of *mandamus* in this particular case. Marshall pointed out that although the Judiciary Act of 1789 specified that the Supreme Court could issue writs of *mandamus* as part of its original jurisdiction, Article III of the Constitution, which spelled out the Court's original jurisdiction, did not mention writs of *mandamus*. Because Congress did not have the right to expand the Supreme Court's jurisdiction, this section of the Judiciary Act of 1789 was unconstitutional—and thus void. The decision still stands today as a judicial and political masterpiece.

For Critical Analysis: *What might result if the courts could not exercise the power of judicial review?*

▌ Basic Judicial Requirements

Before a lawsuit can be brought before a court, certain requirements must first be met. These requirements relate to jurisdiction, venue, and standing to sue. We examine each of these important concepts here.

Jurisdiction

In Latin, *juris* means "law," and *diction* means "to speak." Thus, "the power to speak the law" is the literal meaning of the term **jurisdiction**. Before any court can hear a case, it must have jurisdiction over the person against whom the suit is brought or over the property involved in the suit. The court must also have jurisdiction over the subject matter.

JURISDICTION
The authority of a court to hear and decide a specific action.

JURISDICTION OVER PERSONS   Generally, a court can exercise personal jurisdiction (*in personam* jurisdiction) over residents of a certain geographical area. A state trial court, for example, normally has jurisdictional authority over residents of a particular area of the state, such as a county or district. A state's highest court (often called the state supreme court)[2] has jurisdictional authority over all residents within the state.

In some cases, under the authority of a state **long arm statute,** a court can exercise personal jurisdiction over nonresident defendants as well. Before a court can exercise jurisdiction over a nonresident under a long arm statute, though, it must be demonstrated that the nonresident had sufficient contacts, or *minimum contacts*, with the state to justify the jurisdiction.[3] For example, if an individual has committed a wrong within the state, such as causing an automobile injury or selling defective goods, a court can usually exercise jurisdiction even if the person causing the harm is located in another state. Similarly, a state may exercise personal jurisdiction over a nonresident defendant who is sued for breaching a contract that was formed within the state.

LONG ARM STATUTE
A state statute that permits a state to obtain personal jurisdiction over nonresident defendants. A defendant must have certain "minimum contacts" with that state for the statute to apply.

In regard to corporations,[4] the minimum-contacts requirement is usually met if the corporation does business within the state. Suppose that a corporation incorporated

---

2. As will be discussed shortly, a state's highest court is often referred to as the state supreme court, but there are exceptions. For example, in New York, the supreme court is a trial court.
3. The minimum-contacts standard was established in *International Shoe Co. v. State of Washington,* 326 U.S. 310, 66 S.Ct. 154, 90 L.Ed. 95 (1945).
4. In the eyes of the law, corporations are "legal persons"—entities that can sue and be sued. See Chapter 26.

under the laws of Maine and headquartered in that state has a branch office or manufacturing plant in Georgia. Does this corporation have sufficient minimum contacts with the state of Georgia to allow a Georgia court to exercise jurisdiction over the Maine corporation? Yes, it does. If the Maine corporation advertises and sells its products in Georgia, those activities may also suffice to meet the minimum-contacts requirements. In the following case, the issue is whether an Italian corporation had sufficient minimum contacts with the state of Arizona to permit a suit against the corporation to be brought in an Arizona state court.

CASE 3.1

A. UBERTI AND CO. v. LEONARDO

Supreme Court of Arizona, 1995.
892 P.2d 1354.

HISTORICAL AND SOCIAL SETTING *Colt Industries manufactured the first Peacemaker, a six-shot, single-action revolver, in 1873. The U.S. government adopted it for service that same year, and the gun became known as "the gun that won the West." In 1892, Colt and other gun manufacturers began making safer, more reliable, and more efficient revolvers. The market for the 1873 model declined until the 1950s, when television Westerns created a new market for replica firearms.*

FACTS Aldo Uberti and Company, an Italian corporation, manufactures a replica of the Peacemaker known as the Cattleman. Uberti sells its guns to a U.S. distributor for sale throughout the country. Henry Pacho, a resident of Arizona, bought one of the guns, wrapped it in a towel, and put it under the seat of his car. His two-year-old niece Corrina was helping to clean the car when the gun fell out of the towel, hit the pavement, and discharged. The bullet struck Corrina in the head and killed her. Corrina's parents filed a suit in an Arizona state court against Uberti, alleging that the company was liable for the "design, manufacture, sale, and distribution of a defective and unreasonably dangerous product." Uberti asked the court to dismiss the suit on the ground that the court did not have personal jurisdiction over Uberti. The court refused, and Uberti appealed. The appellate court

reversed. Corrina's parents then appealed to the Supreme Court of Arizona.

ISSUE Does selling a product in the United States in general constitute sufficient "minimum contacts" with Arizona to allow that state's courts to exercise personal jurisdiction over the manufacturer of the product?

DECISION Yes. The Supreme Court of Arizona held that Uberti could be sued in an Arizona state court.

REASON The state supreme court concluded that "the gun, as a replica of an American frontier weapon, was originally and primarily designed and made for the American market." Uberti knew that its products, through its American distributor, "would flow into local markets across America." Corrina's parents did not have to show intent on Uberti's part to sell its guns in Arizona specifically. "An intent to sell across America is enough," concluded the court. If it were otherwise, "no individual state could assert jurisdiction" over Uberti, because Uberti "did not target a particular state or group of states but instead intended to sell its product to all of America. The argument turns common sense on its head. Holding that a defendant intending to sell its products to any and all citizens in the United States could not be held accountable in any jurisdiction where its products caused injury defies any sensible concept of due process."

FOR CRITICAL ANALYSIS—Ethical Consideration
The typical car dealership directs its sales efforts toward the local market in a single state. If a customer buys a car and drives it to another state, where a defect in the car causes an accident, is it fair to allow that state's courts to exercise personal jurisdiction over the dealership located in the other state?

JURISDICTION OVER PROPERTY A court can also exercise jurisdiction over property that is located within its boundaries. This kind of jurisdiction is known as *in rem* jurisdiction, or "jurisdiction over the thing." For example, suppose that a dispute arises over the ownership of a boat in dry dock in Fort Lauderdale, Florida. The boat is owned by

Boat lying in dry dock. Can a state exercise jurisdiction over this boat if its owner is a resident of another state?

an Ohio resident, over whom a Florida court cannot normally exercise personal jurisdiction. The other party to the dispute is a resident of Nebraska. In this situation, a lawsuit concerning the boat could be brought in a Florida state court on the basis of the court's *in rem* jurisdiction.

JURISDICTION OVER SUBJECT MATTER   Jurisdiction over subject matter is a limitation on the types of cases a court can hear. In both the federal and state court systems, there are courts of *general* (unlimited) *jurisdiction* and courts of *limited jurisdiction*. An example of a court of general jurisdiction is a state or federal trial court. An example of a state court of limited jurisdiction is a probate court. **Probate courts** are state courts that handle only matters relating to the transfer of a person's assets and obligations after that person's death, including matters relating to the custody and guardianship of children. An example of a federal court of limited subject-matter jurisdiction is a bankruptcy court. **Bankruptcy courts** handle only bankruptcy proceedings, which are governed by federal bankruptcy law (discussed in Chapter 22). In contrast, a court of general jurisdiction can decide virtually any type of case.

A court's jurisdiction over subject matter is usually defined in the statute or constitution creating the court. In both the federal and state court systems, a court's subject-matter jurisdiction can be limited not only by the subject of the lawsuit but also by the amount of money in controversy, by whether a case is a felony (a more serious type of crime) or a misdemeanor (a less serious type of crime), or by whether the proceeding is a trial or an appeal.

ORIGINAL AND APPELLATE JURISDICTION   The distinction between courts of original jurisdiction and courts of appellate jurisdiction normally lies in whether the case is being heard for the first time. Courts having original jurisdiction are courts of the first instance, or trial courts—that is, courts in which lawsuits begin, trials take place, and evidence is presented. In the federal court system, the *district courts* are trial courts. In the various state court systems, the trial courts are known by various names, as will be discussed shortly.

The key point here is that normally, any court having original jurisdiction is known as a trial court. Courts having appellate jurisdiction act as reviewing courts, or appellate courts. In general, cases can be brought before appellate courts only on appeal from an order or a judgment of a trial court or other lower court.

PROBATE COURT
A state court of limited jurisdiction that conducts proceedings relating to the settlement of a deceased person's estate.

BANKRUPTCY COURT
A federal court of limited jurisdiction that handles only bankruptcy proceedings. Bankruptcy proceedings are governed by federal bankruptcy law.

PROFILE

John Marshall (1755–1835)

It is often said that John Marshall was probably the greatest chief justice ever to head the United States Supreme Court. During his thirty-four-year tenure as chief justice, he penned many decisions of lasting impact on American history and the American judicial system.

Marshall was born in 1755 in a log cabin on the Virginia frontier. He was the first of fifteen children born to parents who were descendants of Welsh and Scottish immigrants. According to John Marshall, his father, Thomas Marshall, had only a "limited education," but in spite of this he educated his son as best he could in English literature and in William Blackstone's *Commentaries on the Laws of England.* (The elder Marshall eventually became a member of the Virginia House of Burgesses and a landowner of some substance.)

Apart from what he learned from his father, John Marshall's education was also limited—to two years of formal schooling. His legal education took even less time and consisted of six weeks of lectures given by George Wythe, America's first law professor, at the College of William and Mary. When he began practicing law six months after attending Wythe's lectures, Marshall's legal library consisted solely of notes he had taken while reading a borrowed copy of a legal text by Francis Bacon. Three years later, he was elected to the Virginia legislature and eventually participated in Virginia's constitutional convention as one of the state's leading Federalists (proponents of a strong central government).

Chief Justice Marshall is most renowned for enunciating the doctrine of judicial review and for establishing the Supreme Court as the final authority in matters concerning constitutional interpretation. Marshall first exercised the power of judicial review in *Marbury v. Madison,* discussed in this chapter's *Landmark in the Law.* This power was also expressed in *Gibbons v. Ogden* (see the *Landmark in the Law* in Chapter 2). In these and other decisions, the Marshall Court, by refusing to hold the national government to the literal limits of its expressed powers, enabled the national government to grow and to meet problems that the framers of the Constitution could not have foreseen.

For Critical Analysis: *Court justices and judges normally maintain that it is not their job to make the law—that is the legislature's province—but to apply it. Is it possible for judges to avoid "making law" when fashioning their decisions?*

JURISDICTION OF THE FEDERAL COURTS Because the federal government is a government of limited powers, the jurisdiction of the federal courts is limited. Article III of the U.S. Constitution establishes the boundaries of federal judicial power. Section 2 of Article III states that "[t]he judicial Power shall extend to all Cases, in Law and Equity, arising under this Constitution, the Laws of the United States, and Treaties made, or which shall be made, under their Authority."

Whenever a plaintiff's cause of action is based, at least in part, on the U.S. Constitution, a treaty, or a federal law, then a **federal question** arises, and the case comes under the judicial power of the federal courts. Any lawsuit involving a federal question can originate in a federal court. People who claim that their constitutional rights have been violated can begin their suits in a federal court.

Federal district courts can also exercise original jurisdiction over cases involving **diversity of citizenship.** Such cases may arise between (1) citizens of different states, (2) a foreign country and citizens of a state or of different states, or (3) citizens of a state and citizens or subjects of a foreign country. The amount in controversy must be more than $50,000 before a federal court can take jurisdiction in such cases. For purposes of diversity jurisdiction, a corporation is a citizen of both the state in which it is incorporated and the state in which its principal place of business is located. A case involving diversity of citizenship can be filed in the appropriate federal district court, or, if the case starts in a state court, it can sometimes be transferred to a federal court. A large percentage of the cases filed in federal courts each year are based on diversity of citizenship.

FEDERAL QUESTION
A question that pertains to the U.S. Constitution, acts of Congress, or treaties. A federal question provides a basis for federal jurisdiction.

DIVERSITY OF CITIZENSHIP
Under Article III, Section 2, of the Constitution, a basis for federal court jurisdiction over a lawsuit between (1) citizens of different states, (2) a foreign country and citizens of a state or of different states, or (3) citizens of a state and citizens or subjects of a foreign country. The amount in controversy must be more than $50,000 before a federal court can take jurisdiction in such cases.

Note that in a case based on a federal question, a federal court will apply federal law. In a case based on diversity of citizenship, however, a federal court will apply the relevant state law (which is often the law of the state in which the court sits).

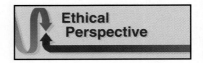
Ethical Perspective

Diversity jurisdiction arose out of what were basically considerations of fairness. Apparently, the authors of the Constitution felt that a state might be biased toward its own citizens, and therefore, when a dispute involved citizens from different states, a federal forum should be available to protect the out-of-state party. Today, the possibility of bringing a case in a federal court when diversity jurisdiction exists is often an attractive option. For example, a California plaintiff who wants to sue a New York business firm for damages that exceed $50,000 can file the suit in a federal court located in California—the plaintiff does not have to initiate the suit in a New York court.

Diversity jurisdiction offers many advantages, but there is also a major disadvantage—the federal courts spend a good deal of their time deciding issues that arise under state law. Like the state courts, the federal courts are increasingly overburdened with cases. Some people see limiting or abolishing diversity jurisdiction as a solution to this problem. In 1994, for example, the Long Range Planning Committee of the Judicial Conference of the United States (the official organization of the federal judiciary) recommended that diversity jurisdiction be eliminated entirely except in cases involving foreigners or in cases in which local prejudice in a state court can be clearly demonstrated. This is not the first such proposal. In fact, since the 1920s bills have been introduced periodically in Congress to curtail or abolish diversity jurisdiction. So far, none of the proposals has been adopted into law.

For Critical Analysis: *Are the benefits of diversity jurisdiction worth its costs to the federal court system?*

CONCURRENT JURISDICTION
Jurisdiction that exists when two different courts have the power to hear a case. For example, some cases can be heard in a federal or a state court.

EXCLUSIVE JURISDICTION
Jurisdiction that exists when a case can be heard only in a particular court or type of court.

VENUE
The geographical district in which an action is tried and from which the jury is selected.

Exclusive versus Concurrent Jurisdiction   When both federal and state courts have the power to hear a case, as is true in suits involving diversity of citizenship, **concurrent jurisdiction** exists. When cases can be tried only in federal courts or only in state courts, **exclusive jurisdiction** exists. Federal courts have exclusive jurisdiction in cases involving federal crimes, bankruptcy, patents, and copyrights; in suits against the United States; and in some areas of admiralty law (law governing transportation on the seas and ocean waters). States also have exclusive jurisdiction in certain subject matters—for example, in divorce and adoption. The concepts of concurrent and exclusive jurisdiction are illustrated in Exhibit 3–1.

Venue

Jurisdiction has to do with whether a court has authority to hear a case involving specific persons, property, or subject matter. **Venue**[5] is concerned with the most appropriate location for a trial. For example, two state courts (or two federal courts) may have the authority to exercise jurisdiction over a case, but it may be more appropriate or convenient to hear the case in one court than in the other.

Basically, the concept of venue reflects the policy that a court trying a suit should be in the geographical neighborhood (usually the county) in which the incident leading to the lawsuit occurred or in which the parties involved in the lawsuit reside. Pretrial publicity or other factors, though, may require a change of venue to another community, especially in criminal cases in which the defendant's right to a fair and impartial jury has been impaired.

---

5. Pronounced *ven*-yoo.

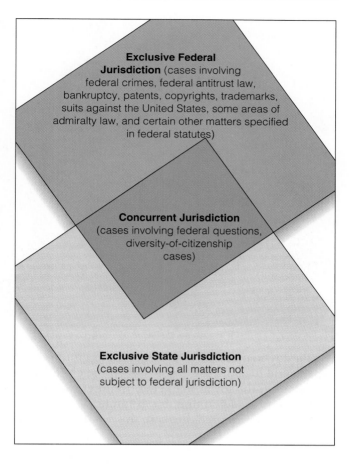

♦ Exhibit 3–1
Exclusive and
Concurrent Jurisdiction

For example, in 1992, when four Los Angeles police officers accused of beating Rodney King were brought to trial, the attorneys defending the police officers requested a change of venue from Los Angeles to Simi Valley, California. The attorneys argued that to try the case in a Los Angeles court would jeopardize the defendants' right to a fair trial. The court agreed and granted the request. For similar reasons, a change of venue from Oklahoma City to Denver, Colorado, was ordered for the trial of Timothy McVeigh and Terry Nichols, who had been indicted in connection with the 1995 bombing of the Federal Building in Oklahoma City.

Standing to Sue

Before a person can bring a lawsuit before a court, the party must have **standing to sue**, or a sufficient "stake" in a matter to justify seeking relief through the court system. In other words, a party must have a legally protected and tangible interest at stake in the litigation in order to have standing. The party bringing the lawsuit must have suffered a harm, or been threatened a harm, by the action about which he or she complained. At times, a person will have standing to sue on behalf of another person. For example, suppose that a child suffered serious injuries as a result of a defectively manufactured toy. Because the child is a minor, a lawsuit could be brought on his or her behalf by another person, such as the child's parent or legal guardian.

Standing to sue also requires that the controversy at issue be a **justiciable**[6] **controversy**—a controversy that is real and substantial, as opposed to hypothetical or academic. For example, in the above example, the child's parent could not

STANDING TO SUE
The requirement that an individual must have a sufficient stake in a controversy before he or she can bring a lawsuit. The plaintiff must demonstrate that he or she either has been injured or threatened with injury.

JUSTICIABLE CONTROVERSY
A controversy that is not hypothetical or academic but real and substantial; a requirement that must be satisfied before a court will hear a case.

---

6. Pronounced jus-*tish*-uh-bul.

Timothy McVeigh, one of the suspects in the bombing of the federal building in Oklahoma City. What is the most important factor requiring a change of venue to another community, especially in a criminal case? What effect does television and the other media have on a court's consideration of a request for a change of venue?

sue the toy manufacturer merely on the ground that the toy was defective. The issue would become justiciable only if the child had actually been injured due to the defect in the toy as marketed. In other words, the parent normally could not ask the court to determine, for example, what damages might be obtained *if* the child had been injured, because this would be merely a hypothetical question.

▌ The State and Federal Court Systems

"The perfect judge fears nothing—he could go front to front before God."

Walt Whitman, 1819–1892
(American poet)

As mentioned earlier in this chapter, each state has its own court system. Additionally, there is a system of federal courts. Although no state court system is the same, Exhibit 3–2 illustrates the basic organizational structure characteristic of the court systems in many states. The exhibit also shows how the federal court system is structured. We turn now to an examination of these court systems, beginning with the state courts.

State Court Systems

Typically a state court system will include several levels, or tiers, of courts. As indicated in Exhibit 3–2, state courts may include (1) trial courts of limited jurisdiction, (2) trial courts of general jurisdiction, (3) appellate courts, and (4) the state's highest court (often called the state supreme court). Judges in the state court system are usually elected by the voters for a specified term.

Generally, any person who is a party to a lawsuit has the opportunity to plead the case before a trial court and then, if he or she loses, before at least one level of appellate court. Finally, if a federal statute or federal constitutional issue is involved in the decision of the state supreme court, that decision may be further appealed to the United States Supreme Court.

TRIAL COURTS   Trial courts are exactly what their name implies—courts in which trials are held and testimony taken. State trial courts have either general or limited jurisdiction. Trial courts that have general jurisdiction as to subject matter may be called county, district, superior, or circuit courts.[7] The jurisdiction of these courts is

---

7.   The name in Ohio is court of common pleas; the name in New York is supreme court.

♦ Exhibit 3–2
Federal Courts and State Court Systems

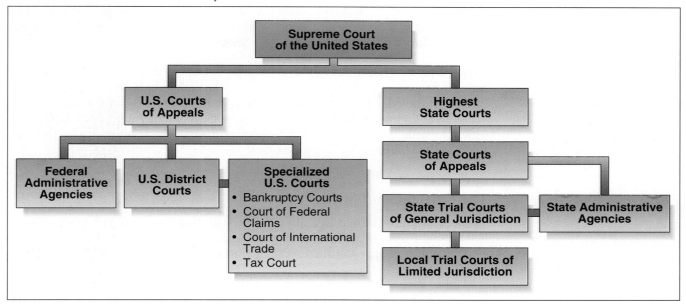

often determined by the size of the county in which the court sits. State trial courts of general jurisdiction have jurisdiction over a wide variety of subjects, including both civil disputes and criminal prosecutions. In some states, trial courts of general jurisdiction may hear appeals from courts of limited jurisdiction.

Some courts of limited jurisdiction are called special inferior trial courts or minor judiciary courts. **Small claims courts** are inferior trial courts that hear only civil cases involving claims of less than a certain amount, such as $2,500—the amount varies from state to state. Suits brought in small claims courts are generally conducted informally, and lawyers are not required. In a minority of states, lawyers are not even allowed to represent people in small claims courts for most purposes. Another example of an inferior trial court is a local municipal court that hears mainly traffic cases. Decisions of small claims courts and municipal courts may be appealed to a state trial court of general jurisdiction.

Other courts of limited jurisdiction as to subject matter include domestic relations courts, which handle only divorce actions and child custody cases, and probate courts, as mentioned earlier.

SMALL CLAIMS COURTS
Special courts in which parties may litigate small claims (usually, claims involving $2,500 or less). Attorneys are not required in small claims courts, and in many states attorneys are not allowed to represent the parties.

COURTS OF APPEALS   Every state has at least one court of appeals (appellate court, or reviewing court), which may be an intermediate appellate court or the state's highest court. About half of the states have intermediate appellate courts. Generally, courts of appeals do not conduct new trials, in which evidence is submitted to the court and witnesses are examined. Rather, an appellate court panel of three or more judges reviews the record of the case on appeal, which includes a transcript of the trial proceedings, and the panel determines whether the trial court committed an error.

Appellate courts look at *questions of law* (on which only a judge, not a jury, can rule) but usually defer to a trial court's findings on *questions of fact* (which may be decided by a judge or a jury based on evidence presented at trial). This is because the trial court judge and jury were in a better position to evaluate testimony—by directly observing witnesses' gestures, demeanor, and nonverbal behavior generally during the trial. At the appellate level, the judges review the written transcript of the trial, which does not include these nonverbal elements.

An appellate court will challenge a trial court's finding of fact only when the finding is clearly erroneous (that is, when it is contrary to the evidence presented at trial) or when there is no evidence to support the finding. For example, if a jury concluded that a manufacturer's product harmed the plaintiff but no evidence was submitted to the court to support that conclusion, the appellate court would hold that the trial court's decision was erroneous. The options exercised by appellate courts will be further discussed later in this chapter.

STATE SUPREME (HIGHEST) COURTS The highest appellate court in a state is usually called the supreme court but may be called by some other name. For example, in both New York and Maryland, the highest state court is called the court of appeals. The decisions of each state's highest court on all questions of state law are final. Only when issues of federal law are involved can a decision made by a state's highest court be overruled by the United States Supreme Court.

BE CAREFUL The decisions of a state's highest court are final on questions of state law.

The Federal Court System

The federal court system is basically a three-tiered model consisting of (1) U.S. district courts (trial courts of general jurisdiction) and various courts of limited jurisdiction, (2) U.S. courts of appeals (intermediate courts of appeals), and (3) the United States Supreme Court.

Unlike state court judges, who are usually elected, federal court judges—including the justices of the Supreme Court—are appointed by the president of the United States, subject to the approval of the U.S. Senate. All federal judges receive lifetime appointments (because under Article III they "hold their offices during Good Behavior").

U.S. DISTRICT COURTS At the federal level, the equivalent of a state trial court of general jurisdiction is the district court. There is at least one federal district court in every state. The number of judicial districts can vary over time, primarily owing to population changes and corresponding caseloads. Currently, there are ninety-six federal judicial districts.

U.S. district courts have original jurisdiction in federal matters. Federal cases typically originate in district courts. There are other trial courts with original, but special (or limited), jurisdiction, such as the federal bankruptcy courts and others shown in Exhibit 3–2.

U.S. COURTS OF APPEALS In the federal court system, there are thirteen U.S. courts of appeals—also referred to as U.S. circuit courts of appeals. The federal courts of appeals for twelve of the circuits hear appeals from the federal district courts located within their respective judicial circuits. The Court of Appeals for the Thirteenth Circuit, called the Federal Circuit, has national appellate jurisdiction over certain types of cases, such as cases involving patent law and cases in which the U.S. government is a defendant.

The decisions of the circuit courts of appeals are final in most cases, but appeal to the United States Supreme Court is possible. Exhibit 3–3 shows the geographical boundaries of U.S. circuit courts of appeals and the boundaries of the U.S. district courts within each circuit.

THE UNITED STATES SUPREME COURT The highest level of the three-tiered model of the federal court system is the United States Supreme Court. According to the language of Article III of the U.S. Constitution, there is only one national Supreme Court. All other courts in the federal system are considered "inferior." Congress is empowered to create other inferior courts as it deems necessary. The inferior courts that Congress has created include the second tier in our model—the U.S. courts of appeals—as well as the district courts and any other courts of limited, or specialized, jurisdiction.

The United States Supreme Court consists of nine justices. Although the United States Supreme Court has original, or trial, jurisdiction in rare instances (set forth in

"We are not final because we are infallible, but we are infallible only because we are final."

Robert H. Jackson, 1892–1954 *(Associate justice of the United States Supreme Court, 1941–1954)*

◆ Exhibit 3–3
U.S. Courts of Appeals and U.S. District Courts

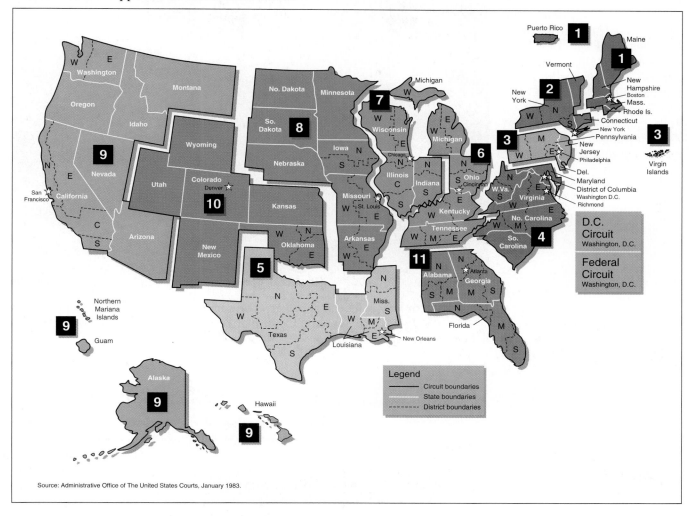

Source: Administrative Office of The United States Courts, January 1983.

Article III, Section 2), most of its work is as an appeals court. The Supreme Court can review any case decided by any of the federal courts of appeals, and it also has appellate authority over some cases decided in the state courts.

To bring a case before the Supreme Court, a party requests the Court to issue a writ of *certiorari*. A **writ of *certiorari***[8] is an order issued by the Supreme Court to a lower court requiring the latter to send it the record of the case for review. The Court will not issue a writ unless at least four of the nine justices approve of it. This is called the **rule of four**. Whether the Court will issue a writ of *certiorari* is entirely within its discretion. The Court is not required to issue one, and most petitions for writs are denied. (Thousands of cases are filed with the Supreme Court each year, yet it hears, on average, less than one hundred of these cases.[9]) A denial is not a decision on the merits of a case, nor does it indicate agreement with the lower court's opinion. Furthermore, denial of the writ has no value as a precedent.

Typically, the petitions granted by the Court involve cases that raise important constitutional questions or cases that conflict with other state or federal court

WRIT OF *CERTIORARI*
A writ from a higher court asking the lower court for the record of a case.

RULE OF FOUR
A rule of the United States Supreme Court under which the Court will not issue a writ of *certiorari* unless at least four justices approve of the decision to issue the writ.

---

8.   Pronounced sur-shee-uh-*rah*-ree.
9.   From the mid-1950s through the early 1990s, the Supreme Court reviewed more cases per year than it has in the last few years. In the Court's 1982–1983 term, for example, the Court issued opinions in 151 cases. In contrast, only 77 cases were scheduled for review during the Court's 1995–1996 term.

The justices of the U.S. Supreme Court are: seated left to right, Antonin Scalia, John Paul Stevens, Chief Justice William H. Rehnquist, Sandra Day O'Connor, and Anthony M. Kennedy; and standing left to right, Ruth Bader Ginsburg, David H. Souter, Clarence Thomas, and Stephen Breyer. Does the fact that these justices are appointed for life have any effect on the decisions they reach in the cases they hear?

decisions. Similarly, if federal appellate courts are rendering inconsistent opinions on an important issue, the Supreme Court may review the case and issue a decision to define the law on the matter.

▌Following a Case through the State Courts

To illustrate the procedures that would be followed in a civil lawsuit brought in a state court, we present a hypothetical case and follow it through the state court system. The case involves an automobile accident in which Kevin Anderson, driving a Mercedes, struck Lisa Marconi, driving a Ford Taurus. The accident occurred at the intersection of Wilshire Boulevard and Rodeo Drive in Beverly Hills, California. Marconi suffered personal injuries, incurring medical and hospital expenses as well as lost wages for four months. Anderson and Marconi are unable to agree on a settlement, and Marconi sues Anderson. Marconi is the plaintiff, and Anderson is the defendant. Both are represented by lawyers.

During each phase of the **litigation** (the process of working a lawsuit through the court system), Marconi and Anderson will be required to observe strict procedural requirements. A large body of law—procedural law—establishes the rules and standards for determining disputes in courts. Procedural rules are very complex, and they vary from court to court. There is a set of federal rules of procedure and various sets of rules for state courts. Additionally, the applicable procedures will depend on whether the case is a civil or criminal case. Generally, the Marconi-Anderson litigation will involve the procedures discussed in the following subsections. Keep in mind that attempts to settle the case may be ongoing throughout the trial. (For an extreme example of how legal fees can spiral during the litigation process, see this chapter's *Law in the Extreme*.)

LITIGATION
The process of resolving a dispute through the court system.

The Pleadings

The complaint and answer (and the counterclaim and reply)—all of which are discussed below—taken together are called the **pleadings**. The pleadings inform each party of the claims of the other and specify the issues (disputed questions) involved in the case.

PLEADINGS
Statements made by the plaintiff and the defendant in a lawsuit that detail the facts, charges, and defenses involved in the litigation; the complaint and answer are part of the pleadings.

IN THE LOS ANGELES MUNICIPAL COURT
FOR THE LOS ANGELES JUDICIAL DISTRICT

CIVIL NO. 8–1026

Lisa Marconi
_____
          Plaintiff

          v.

                                                    COMPLAINT

Kevin Anderson
_____
          Defendant

Comes now the plaintiff and for her cause of action against the defendant alleges and states as follows:

1. The jurisdiction of this court is based on Section 86 of the California Civil Code.
2. This action is between plaintiff, a California resident living at 1434 Palm Drive, Anaheim, California, and defendant, a California resident living at 6950 Garrison Avenue, Los Angeles, California.
3. On September 10, 1996, plaintiff, Lisa Marconi, was exercising good driving habits and reasonable care in driving her car through the intersection of Rodeo Drive and Wilshire Boulevard when defendant, Kevin Anderson, negligently drove his vehicle through a red light at the intersection and collided with plaintiff's vehicle. Defendant was negligent in the operation of the vehicle as to:

    a. Speed,
    b. Lookout,
    c. Management and control.

4. As a result of the collision plaintiff suffered severe physical injury that prevented her from working and property damage to her car. The costs she incurred included $10,000 in medical bills, $9,000 in lost wages, and $5,000 for automobile repairs.

WHEREFORE, plaintiff demands judgment against the defendant for the sum of $24,000 plus interest at the maximum legal rate and the costs of this action.

          By _____
          Roger Harrington
          Attorney for the Plaintiff
          800 Orange Avenue
          Anaheim, CA 91426

♦ **Exhibit 3–4**
Example of a Typical Complaint

COMPLAINT
The pleading made by a plaintiff alleging wrongdoing on the part of the defendant; the document that, when filed with a court, initiates a lawsuit.

SUMMONS
A document informing a defendant that a legal action has been commenced against him or her and that the defendant must appear in court on a certain date to answer the plaintiff's complaint. The document is delivered by a sheriff or any other person so authorized.

THE PLAINTIFF'S COMPLAINT   Marconi's suit against Anderson commences when her lawyer files a **complaint** with the appropriate court. The complaint contains a statement alleging (asserting to the court, in a pleading) the facts necessary for the court to take jurisdiction, a brief summary of the facts necessary to show that the plaintiff is entitled to a remedy, and a statement of the remedy the plaintiff is seeking. Exhibit 3–4 illustrates how the complaint might read in the Marconi-Anderson case. Complaints may be lengthy or brief, depending on the complexity of the case.

After the complaint has been filed, the sheriff, a deputy of the county, or another *process server* (one who delivers a complaint and summons) serves a **summons** and a copy of the complaint on defendant Anderson. The summons notifies Anderson that he must file an answer to the complaint with both the court and the plaintiff's attorney within a specified time period (usually twenty to thirty days). The summons also

LAW IN THE EXTREME

The Price of Principle

Question: How much in legal fees would you pay to settle a $909 dispute? Answer: $73,000—if an important principle is involved. At least, this was the conclusion of the board of a New York housing cooperative (co-op) when litigating a dispute with the owners of one of the co-op's apartments. The dispute began in 1987, when the co-op complied with a New York law that required window guards for all apartments in which children under ten years of age resided. The co-op installed the guards on the windows of a ninth-story apartment owned by Alec and Suzi Diacou, who had children under ten years of age. The co-op's board voted that the Diacous should pay for the window guards. The Diacous refused

to pay, contending that the cost of the guards should be paid jointly by all owners of the co-op's units.

The board asked its law firm to look into the matter. In the ensuing months, the legal fees began to mount as the lawyers devoted time to attempted settlements and other communications with the Diacous. By June 1988, the fees had climbed to over $1,000—more than the cost of installing the window guards. This fact did not deter the board from filing suit against the Diacous the following month, which began a virtual avalanche of legal fees. By January 1989, the attorneys had billed the co-op for over $9,500 for its services. No matter, it was the principle that counted: if the Diacous succeeded in their refusal to pay for the guards, other tenants might follow their example.

The co-op ultimately prevailed— at a cost that exceeded $40,000. The battle to collect legal fees, however, was just beginning. The co-op ownership contract stated that if a dispute arose between the co-op board and an owner of a co-op unit, the loser

was required to reimburse the winner for all legal fees incurred. More legal fees were generated to collect fees, until finally, in March 1994, the case had reached its end: the Diacous were ordered to pay $30,000 of the co-op's legal fees, which by that time totaled $73,000 (this in addition to the Diacous' own legal fees of $70,000).

The court concluded that both parties had "demonstrated a lack of common sense." David Berkey, one of the co-op's lawyers, disagreed: "I think that the expenditures here were appropriate and were kept pretty much to a minimum."[a]

For Critical Analysis: *Should parties who pursue litigation to the point where any result would be economically injurious to their interests be permitted to use the courts (and the public's tax money, which supports the courts) to such ends?*

a. Wade Lambert, "Ever Hear the One about the Lawyers and Window Bars?" *The Wall Street Journal,* March 23, 1994, p. A1.

DEFAULT JUDGMENT
A judgment entered by a court against a defendant who has failed to appear in court to answer or defend against the plaintiff's claim.

ANSWER
Procedurally, a defendant's response to the plaintiff's complaint.

COUNTERCLAIM
A claim made by a defendant in a civil lawsuit that in effect sues the plaintiff.

REPLY
Procedurally, a plaintiff's response to a defendant's answer.

MOTION TO DISMISS
A pleading in which a defendant asserts that the plaintiff's claim fails to state a cause of action (that is, has no basis in law) or that there are other grounds on which a suit should be dismissed.

informs Anderson that failure to answer will result in a **default judgment** for the plaintiff, meaning the plaintiff will be awarded the damages alleged in her complaint.

THE DEFENDANT'S ANSWER   The defendant's **answer** either admits the statements or allegations set forth in the complaint or denies them and outlines any defenses that the defendant may have. If Anderson admits to all of Marconi's allegations in his answer, the court will enter a judgment for Marconi. If Anderson denies any of Marconi's allegations, the litigation will go forward.

Anderson can deny Marconi's allegations and set forth his own claim that Marconi was in fact negligent and therefore owes him money for damages to his Mercedes. This is appropriately called a **counterclaim.** If Anderson files a counterclaim, Marconi will have to answer it with a pleading, normally called a **reply,** which has the same characteristics as an answer.

Anderson can also admit the truth of Marconi's complaint but raise new facts that may result in dismissal of the action. This is called raising an *affirmative defense.* For example, Anderson could assert the running of the relevant statute of limitations (a state or federal statute that sets the maximum time period during which a certain action can be brought or rights enforced) as an affirmative defense.

MOTION TO DISMISS   A **motion to dismiss** requests the court to dismiss the case for stated reasons. The motion to dismiss is often made by a defendant before filing an answer to the plaintiff's complaint. Grounds for dismissal of a case include improper delivery of the complaint and summons, improper venue, and the plaintiff's failure to state a claim for which a court could grant relief (a remedy). For example, if Marconi

Jack had a hunch the case had been thrown out of court.

Toos/Cartoonists & Writers Syndicate.

had suffered no injuries or losses as a result of Anderson's negligence, Anderson could move to have the case dismissed because Marconi had not stated a claim for which relief could be granted.

If the judge grants the motion to dismiss, the plaintiff generally is given time to file an amended complaint. If the judge denies the motion, the suit will go forward, and the defendant must then file an answer.

Note that if Marconi wishes to discontinue the suit because, for example, an out-of-court settlement has been reached, she can likewise move for dismissal. The court can also dismiss the case on its own motion.

Pretrial Motions

Either party may attempt to get the case dismissed before trial through the use of various pretrial motions. We have already mentioned the motion to dismiss. Two other important pretrial motions are the motion for judgment on the pleadings and the motion for summary judgment.

At the close of the pleadings, either party may make a **motion for judgment on the pleadings,** or on the merits of the case. The judge will grant the motion only when there is no dispute over the facts of the case and the only issue to be resolved is a question of law. In deciding on the motion, the judge may only consider the evidence contained in the pleadings.

In contrast, in a **motion for summary judgment,** the court may consider evidence outside the pleadings, such as sworn statements (affidavits) by parties or witnesses or other documents relating to the case. A motion for summary judgment can be made by either party. As with the motion for judgment on the pleadings, a motion for summary judgment will be granted only if there are no genuine questions of fact and the only question is a question of law.

MOTION FOR JUDGMENT ON THE PLEADINGS
A motion by either party to a lawsuit at the close of the pleadings requesting the court to decide the issue solely on the pleadings without proceeding to trial. The motion will be granted only if no facts are in dispute.

MOTION FOR SUMMARY JUDGMENT
A motion requesting the court to enter a judgment without proceeding to trial. The motion can be based on evidence outside the pleadings and will be granted only if no facts are in dispute.

Deciding whether a certain issue presents a question of fact or a question of law is not always easy, and judges sometimes disagree on whether summary judgment is appropriate in a given case. The following case illustrates this point.

CASE 3.2

METZGAR v. PLAYSKOOL, INC.

United States Court of Appeals, Third Circuit, 1994.
30 F.3d 459.

COMPANY PROFILE *Hasbro, Inc., is the world's largest toy maker. Hasbro manufactures and sells many of the most famous, biggest-selling toys—including games, puzzles, and baby items—on the U.S. and world markets. Hasbro products include Cabbage Patch Kids, G.I. Joe, Lincoln Logs, Mr. Potato Head, Monopoly, Scrabble, Trivial Pursuit, Twister, and Yahtzee. Hasbro brand names include Hasbro, Kenner, Milton Bradley, Parker Brothers, Tonka, and Playskool.*

FACTS Ronald Metzgar placed his fifteen-month-old son Matthew, awake and healthy, in his playpen. Ronald left the room for five minutes and on his return found Matthew lifeless. A purple toy block had lodged in the boy's throat, choking him to death. Ronald called 911, but efforts to revive Matthew were to no avail. There was no warning of a choking hazard on the box containing the block. Matthew's parents sued Playskool, Inc., the manufacturer of the block, and others in a federal district court. They alleged, among other things, negligence[a] in failing to warn of the hazard of the block. Playskool filed a motion for summary judgment, arguing that the danger of a young child choking on a small block was obvious.

---

a. *Negligence* is a failure to use the standard of care that a reasonable person would exercise in similar circumstances. See Chapter 5.

The court entered a summary judgment in favor of Playskool. The parents appealed.

ISSUE Is the question of the obviousness of the danger, in the context of a negligence claim, a question of fact for the jury to decide?

DECISION Yes. The U.S. Court of Appeals for the Third Circuit held that the question of the obviousness in this case was not a proper subject for summary judgment and remanded the case for a trial.

REASON The court explained that for purposes of the parents' claim, for a risk to be deemed obvious "there must be general consensus within the relevant community." Reasoned the court, "We cannot see how the purple Playskool block can be deemed as a matter of law an obvious safety hazard in the eyes of the relevant community, when Playskool itself believed the block was safe." The court pointed out that Matthew's parents did not believe the block posed an obvious threat and that Playskool did not offer any evidence to show the danger was obvious. The court concluded that "[u]nder a negligence theory, * * * the question of obviousness is more properly submitted to a jury than disposed on motion for summary judgment. The court's role in deciding a motion for summary judgment is merely to decide whether there is a genuine issue of material fact for trial." The lower court's dismissal of the parents' claim on the basis of a determination that the danger was obvious was "tantamount to holding that no reasonable jury could conclude otherwise. Based on the evidence of record, we cannot agree."

FOR CRITICAL ANALYSIS—Social Consideration
When a case requires a determination of such matters as community standards, summary judgment is not considered appropriate. Such matters are given to juries to determine. Why?

Discovery

DISCOVERY
A phase in the litigation process during which the opposing parties may obtain information from each other and from third parties prior to trial.

Before a trial begins, each party can use a number of procedural devices to obtain information and gather evidence about the case from the other party or from third parties. The process of obtaining such information is known as **discovery**. Discovery includes gaining access to witnesses, documents, records, and other types of evidence.

The Federal Rules of Civil Procedure and similar rules in the states set forth the guidelines for discovery activity. The rules governing discovery are designed to make sure that a witness or a party is not unduly harassed, that privileged material (communications that need not be presented in court) is safeguarded, and that only matters relevant to the case at hand are discoverable.

Discovery prevents surprises at trial by giving parties access to evidence that might otherwise be hidden. This allows both parties to learn as much as they can about what to expect at a trial before they reach the courtroom. It also serves to narrow the issues so that trial time is spent on the main questions in the case. Currently, the trend is toward allowing more discovery and thus fewer surprises.[10]

DEPOSITIONS AND INTERROGATORIES   Discovery can involve the use of depositions or interrogatories, or both. **Depositions** are sworn testimony by a party to the lawsuit or any witness. The person being deposed (the deponent) answers questions asked by the attorneys, and the questions and answers are recorded by an authorized court official and sworn to and signed by the deponent. (Occasionally, written depositions are taken when witnesses are unable to appear in person.) The answers given to depositions will, of course, help the attorneys prepare their cases. They can also be used in court to impeach (challenge the credibility of) a party or a witness who changes testimony at the trial. In addition, the answers given in a deposition can be used as testimony if the witness is not available at trial.

Interrogatories are written questions for which written answers are prepared and then signed under oath. The main difference between interrogatories and written depositions is that interrogatories are directed to a party to the lawsuit (the plaintiff or the defendant), not to a witness, and the party can prepare answers with the aid of an attorney. The scope of interrogatories is broader, because parties are obligated to answer questions, even if it means disclosing information from their records and files.

OTHER INFORMATION   A party can serve a written request to the other party for an admission of the truth of matters relating to the trial. Any matter admitted under such a request is conclusively established for the trial. For example, Marconi can ask Anderson to admit that he was driving at a speed of forty-five miles an hour. A request for admission saves time at trial, because the parties will not have to spend time proving facts on which they already agree.

A party can also gain access to documents and other items not in his or her possession in order to inspect and examine them. Likewise, a party can gain "entry upon land" to inspect the premises. Anderson's attorney, for example, normally can gain permission to inspect and duplicate Marconi's car repair bills.

When the physical or mental condition of one party is in question, the opposing party can ask the court to order a physical or mental examination. If the court is willing to make the order, which it will do only if the need for the information outweighs the right to privacy of the person to be examined, the opposing party can obtain the results of the examination.

Pretrial Conference

Either party or the court can request a pretrial conference, or hearing. Usually, the hearing consists of an informal discussion between the judge and the opposing attorneys after discovery has taken place. The purpose of the hearing is to explore the possibility of a settlement without trial and, if this is not possible, to identify the matters that are in dispute and to plan the course of the trial.

DEPOSITION
The testimony of a party to a lawsuit or a witness taken under oath before a trial.

INTERROGATORIES
A series of written questions for which written answers are prepared and then signed under oath by a party to a lawsuit, usually with the assistance of the party's attorney.

---

10.   This is particularly evident in the 1993 revision of the Federal Rules of Civil Procedure. The revised rules provide that each party must disclose to the other, on an ongoing basis, the types of evidence that will be presented at trial, the names of witnesses that may or will be called, and so on.

Jurors are sworn in. Why might a defendant want the facts in a case to be considered by a jury rather than a judge?

Jury Selection

A trial can be held with or without a jury. If there is no jury, the judge determines the truth of the facts alleged in the case. The Seventh Amendment to the U.S. Constitution guarantees the right to a jury trial for cases in federal courts when the amount in controversy exceeds $20. Most states have similar guarantees in their own constitutions (although the threshold dollar amount is usually higher than $20). The right to a trial by jury does not have to be exercised, and many cases are tried without a jury. In most states and in federal courts, one of the parties must request a jury, or the right is presumed to be waived.

Before a jury trial commences, a jury must be selected. The jury-selection process is known as *voir dire*[11](a French phrase meaning "to speak the truth"). In most jurisdictions, the *voir dire* consists of oral questions that attorneys for the plaintiff and the defendant ask a group of prospective jurors (one at a time) to determine whether a potential jury member is biased or has any connection with a party to the action or with a prospective witness.

During *voir dire*, a party may challenge a certain number of prospective jurors *peremptorily*—that is, ask that an individual not be sworn in as a juror without providing any reason. Alternatively, a party may challenge a prospective juror *for cause*—that is, provide a reason why an individual should not be sworn in as a juror. If the judge grants the challenge, the individual is asked to step down. A prospective juror may not be excluded from the jury by the use of discriminatory challenges, however, such as those based on racial criteria[12] or gender.[13]

VOIR DIRE
A French phrase meaning "to speak the truth." In jury trials, the phrase refers to the process in which the attorneys question prospective jurors to determine whether they are biased or have any connection with a party of the action or with a prospective witness.

---

11.   Pronounced vwahr *deehr.*
12.   *Batson v. Kentucky,* 476 U.S. 79, 106 S.Ct. 1712, 90 L.Ed.2d 69 (1986).
13.   *J.E.B. v. Alabama ex rel. T.B.,* 511 U.S. 127, 114 S.Ct. 1419, 128 L.Ed.2d 89 (1994). (*Ex rel.* is Latin for *ex relatione.* The phrase refers to an action brought on behalf of the state, by the attorney general, at the instigation of an individual who has a private interest in the matter.)

Attorneys naturally want to exclude from the jury people who are unsympathetic to the client's position, and a flourishing new industry—jury consulting—has developed to help attorneys perform this task. Jury consultants decide, based on a demographic analysis of responses to pretrial surveys or other data, what kind of jurors (in terms of age, gender, education, religious background, and so on) would constitute the ideal jury. The consultant then creates questions for the attorney, who uses them during *voir dire* to exclude from the jury (through the use of peremptory challenges) persons who do not fit the "jury profile."

Do jury profiles work? Certainly many attorneys, including those who participated in the O. J. Simpson trial of 1994 to 1995, think they do. The defense retained Jo-Ellan Dimitrius of Los Angeles, who had helped select the jury that acquitted, in 1992, the four white police officers accused of beating Rodney King, an African American. Even before the Simpson trial began, observers were commenting that the mostly African American and female jury boded well for the defense—and Simpson, as it turned out, was acquitted. The prosecution retained Donald Vinson of DecisionQuest, Inc., in Los Angeles.

The growing use of jury consultants raises some disturbing ethical issues. For one thing, jury consultants are expensive, thus giving wealthier litigants a relative advantage in the courtroom. For another, they may be making the truly "impartial" jury a thing of the past.

For Critical Analysis: *In his dissent in the* Batson v. Kentucky *decision (see footnote 12), the late Justice Thurgood Marshall contended that peremptory challenges should be banned entirely. Do you agree?*

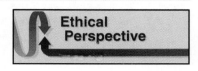

Ethical Perspective

BE CAREFUL A prospective juror cannot be excluded solely on the basis of his or her race or gender.

At the Trial

At the opening of the trial, the attorneys present their opening arguments, setting forth the facts that they expect to provide during the trial. Then the plaintiff's case is presented. In our hypothetical case, Marconi's lawyer would introduce evidence (relevant documents, exhibits, and the testimony of witnesses) to support Marconi's position. The defendant has the opportunity to challenge any evidence introduced and to cross-examine any of the plaintiff's witnesses.

At the end of the plaintiff's case, the defendant's attorney has the opportunity to ask the judge to direct a verdict for the defendant on the ground that the plaintiff has presented no evidence that would justify the granting of the plaintiff's remedy. This is called a **motion for a directed verdict** (known in federal courts as a *motion for judgment as a matter of law*). If the motion is not granted (it seldom is), the defendant's attorney then presents the evidence and witnesses for the defendant's case. The plaintiff's attorney can challenge any evidence introduced and cross-examine the defendant's witnesses.

After the defense concludes its presentation, the attorneys present their closing arguments, each urging a verdict in favor of his or her client. The judge instructs the jury in the law that applies to the case (these instructions are often called *charges*), and the jury retires to the jury room to deliberate a verdict. In the Marconi-Anderson case, the jury will not only decide for the plaintiff or for the defendant but, if it finds for the plaintiff, will also decide on the amount of the **award** (the money to be paid to her).

Posttrial Motions

After the jury has rendered its verdict, either party may make a posttrial motion. If Marconi wins, and Anderson's attorney has previously moved for a directed verdict, Anderson's attorney may make a **motion for judgment** *n.o.v.* (from the Latin

"Proceed. You have my biased attention."

Learned Hand, 1872–1961
(American jurist)

MOTION FOR A DIRECTED VERDICT
In a jury trial, a motion for the judge to take the decision out of the hands of the jury and direct a verdict for the moving party on the ground that the other party has not produced sufficient evidence to support his or her claim.

AWARD
The amount of money awarded to a plaintiff in a civil lawsuit as damages.

MOTION FOR JUDGMENT N.O.V.
A motion requesting the court to grant judgment in favor of the party making the motion on the ground that the jury verdict against him or her was unreasonable and erroneous.

non obstante veredicto, which means "notwithstanding the verdict"—called a *motion for judgment as a matter of law* in the federal courts) in Anderson's favor on the ground that the jury verdict in favor of Marconi was unreasonable and erroneous. If the judge decides that the jury's verdict was reasonable in light of the evidence presented at trial, the motion will be denied. If the judge agrees with Anderson's attorney, then he or she will set the jury's verdict aside and enter a judgment in favor of Anderson.

MOTION FOR A NEW TRIAL
A motion asserting that the trial was so fundamentally flawed (because of error, newly discovered evidence, prejudice, or other reason) that a new trial is necessary to prevent a miscarriage of justice.

Alternatively, Anderson could make a **motion for a new trial,** requesting the judge to set aside the adverse verdict and to hold a new trial. The motion will be granted if the judge is convinced, after looking at all the evidence, that the jury was in error but does not feel it is appropriate to grant judgment for the other side. A new trial may also be granted on the ground of newly discovered evidence, misconduct by the participants or the jury during the trial, or error by the judge. In the following case, the plaintiffs filed a motion for a new trial based on allegations of juror misconduct.

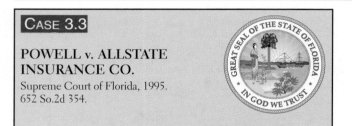

CASE 3.3

POWELL v. ALLSTATE INSURANCE CO.
Supreme Court of Florida, 1995.
652 So.2d 354.

HISTORICAL AND SOCIAL SETTING *One of the principles on which the United States was founded is that all persons are created equal and are entitled to have their individual human dignity respected. This guarantee is in our federal and state constitutions, and there have been long-standing, continual efforts by legislative enactments and judicial decisions to purge our society of racial and other prejudices. Despite these efforts, however, such biases still appear to influence decisions by many people who would deny equal human dignity to those who differ from them in color, religion, or ethnic origin.*

FACTS Derrick and Eugenia Powell, American citizens of Jamaican birth, were in an automobile accident with another motorist, whose insurance liability policy limit was $10,000. Claiming damages in excess of $200,000, the Powells sued their own insurer, Allstate Insurance Company, in a Florida state court to recover the difference. A jury awarded Derrick $29,320 and Eugenia nothing. The next day, one of the jurors—all of whom were white—told the Powells' attorney and the judge that some of the jurors had made racial jokes and statements about the Powells during the trial and the jury deliberations. The Powells filed a motion for a new trial. The court denied the motion, and the appellate court affirmed. The Powells appealed to the Supreme Court of Florida.

ISSUE Do explicit statements of racial bias made by jurors concerning the parties in a case constitute juror misconduct requiring a new trial?

DECISION Yes. The Supreme Court of Florida held that such comments constitute overt juror misconduct and remanded the case for a hearing to determine whether the statements were made and, if so, for a new trial.

REASON The court stated that granting a new trial in this case "may not keep improper bias from being a silent factor with a particular juror, but, hopefully, it will act as a check on such bias and prevent the bias from being expressed so as to overtly influence others." The court also found the racial statements to violate "both the federal and state constitutions which ensure all litigants a fair and impartial jury and equal protection of the law." The court explained that "[t]he obvious difficulty with prejudice in a judicial context is that it prevents the impartial decision-making that both the Sixth Amendment and fundamental fair play require. A racially or religiously biased individual harbors certain negative stereotypes which, despite his protestations to the contrary, may well prevent him or her from making decisions based solely on the facts and law that our jury system requires."

FOR CRITICAL ANALYSIS—Political Consideration
The words "Equal Justice Under Law" are in marble over the entrance to the United States Supreme Court. Should the fact that this principle is not always perfectly implemented allow the courts to consciously ignore it sometimes? Why or why not?

The Appeal

Assume here that any posttrial motion is denied, and Anderson appeals the case. (If Marconi wins but receives a smaller money award than she sought, she can appeal also.) A notice of appeal must be filed with the clerk of the trial court within a prescribed time. Anderson now becomes the appellant, or petitioner, and Marconi becomes the appellee, or respondent.

FILING THE APPEAL   Anderson's attorney files with the appellate court the record on appeal, which includes the pleadings, the trial transcript, the judge's ruling on motions made by the parties, and other trial-related documents. Anderson's attorney will also file with the reviewing court a condensation of the record, known as an abstract, which is filed with the reviewing court along with the brief. The **brief** is a formal legal document outlining the facts and issues of the case, the judge's rulings or jury's findings that should be reversed or modified, the applicable law, and arguments on Anderson's behalf (citing applicable statutes and relevant cases as precedents).

Marconi's attorney will file an answering brief. Anderson's attorney can file a reply to Marconi's brief, although it is not required. The reviewing court then considers the case.

APPELLATE REVIEW   As mentioned earlier, a court of appeals does not hear evidence. Rather, it reviews the record for errors of law. Its decision concerning a case is based on the record on appeal, the abstracts, and the attorneys' briefs. The attorneys can present oral arguments, after which the case is taken under advisement. In general, appellate courts do not reverse findings of fact unless the findings are unsupported or contradicted by the evidence.

If the reviewing court believes that an error was committed during the trial or that the jury was improperly instructed, the judgment will be *reversed*. Sometimes the case will be *remanded* (sent back to the court that originally heard the case) for a new trial. In most cases, the judgment of the lower court is *affirmed*, resulting in the enforcement of the court's judgment or decree.

If the reviewing court is an intermediate appellate court, the losing party normally may appeal to the state supreme court (the highest state court). Such a petition corresponds to a petition for a writ of *certiorari* in the United States Supreme Court. If the petition is granted, new briefs must be filed before the state supreme court, and the attorneys may be allowed or requested to present oral arguments. Like the intermediate appellate courts, the supreme court may reverse or affirm the appellate court's decision or remand the case. At this point, unless a federal question is at issue, the case has reached its end.

BRIEF
A formal legal document submitted by the attorney for the appellant or the appellee (in answer to the appellant's brief) to an appellate court when a case is appealed. The appellant's brief outlines the facts and issues of the case, the judge's rulings or jury's findings that should be reversed or modified, the applicable law, and the arguments on the client's behalf.

KEEP IN MIND An appellate court generally will not overturn a lower court's decision unless there has been an error of law.

Technology and the Courtroom

Many perceive the courtroom as the last bastion of tradition. There you can expect to find gleaming hardwood floors and banisters, judges in somber robes, orderly procedures, and above all, decorum. Even the courts, however, can no longer ignore the benefits of technology. In the past decade, computers, modems, videocassette recorders (VCRs), and yards of electronic cable have slowly been bringing the courts into the modern age—for better or worse.

The Virtual Courtroom
Imagine this "courtroom" scene: A judge in Kansas City sits before several split-level computer screens and orders the trial to begin. The plaintiff and the plaintiff's attorney, sitting in the attorney's Los Angeles teleconferencing room, appear on one of the judge's screens. The defendant and the defendant's attorney, in the attorney's New York offices, appear on another. Both attorneys give their opening arguments. While presenting her

(Continued)

Technology and the Courtroom—Continued

case, the plaintiff's attorney has an expert witness located at a teleconferencing station in Albuquerque, New Mexico, give testimony on the plaintiff's behalf. The defendant's attorney cross-examines the witness, and the plaintiff's attorney then introduces several computerized documents as evidence. The documents appear on the other participants' screens.

The proceedings are being videotaped, and special software converts the spoken words into a written transcript. At any time during the trial, the judge or the attorneys can print out the transcript of the trial to that point. They can also access the pretrial pleadings, which were filed electronically and are instantly retrievable, as well as depositions, interrogatories, and other trial-related documents. The defense, for example, calls up a portion of a witness's deposition for the court to view on one of the screens. At the conclusion of the trial, the trial record is stored electronically and can be accessed immediately by anyone interested in the proceedings.

Into the Future

The scenario just described, of course, depicts the virtual courtroom. Although it may seem futuristic now, it

will not be in the fairly near future. Already, much of the technology exists and is being demonstrated in an experimental courtroom in Williamsburg, Virginia. Set up by the Court Technology Laboratory at the National Center for State Courts in Williamsburg, the court serves as a demonstration center by vendors of what is possible.

Experiments in cyberspace trials are not confined to the United States. Germany, for example, recently held a test trial in which the plaintiff's lawyer was only virtually present—appearing on a television screen. Other tests are being planned, and some anticipate that the "cyber trial" will soon be adopted in German civil trials and labor tribunals—to save lawyers' time and clients' travel costs.

For Critical Analysis: *The virtual courtroom clearly offers many advantages to trial participants in terms of efficiency and lower costs. Are there any disadvantages? Explain.*

Alternative Dispute Resolution

DOCKET
The list of cases entered on a court's calendar and thus scheduled to be heard by the court.

ALTERNATIVE DISPUTE RESOLUTION (ADR)
The resolution of disputes in ways other than those involved in the traditional judicial process. Negotiation, mediation, and arbitration are forms of ADR.

Because the number of court cases filling the **dockets** (court schedules listing the cases to be heard) grows every year and the cost of litigation continues to increase, more and more businesspersons, consumers, and others are turning to **alternative dispute resolution (ADR)** as an alternative to civil lawsuits.

Methods of ADR range from neighbors sitting down over a cup of coffee in an attempt to work out their differences to huge multinational corporations agreeing to resolve a dispute through a formal hearing before a panel of experts. The great advantage of ADR is its flexibility. Normally, the parties themselves can control how the dispute will be settled, what procedures will be used, and whether the decision reached (either by themselves or by a neutral third party) will be legally binding or nonbinding. Today, approximately 95 percent of cases are settled before trial through some form of ADR.

In the following sections, we look at some of the more commonly used methods of ADR. Keep in mind, though, that ADR is an ongoing experiment. In other words, new methods of ADR—or new combinations of existing methods—are continuously being devised and employed.

Negotiation

NEGOTIATION
A process in which parties attempt to settle their dispute informally, with or without attorneys to represent them.

One of the simplest forms of ADR is **negotiation,** a process in which the parties attempt to settle their dispute informally, with or without attorneys to represent them. Attorneys frequently advise their clients to negotiate a settlement voluntarily before they proceed to trial.

Negotiation traditionally involves just the parties themselves and (typically) their attorneys. The attorneys, though, are advocates—they are obligated to put their clients' interests first. Often, parties find it helpful to have the opinion and guidance of a *neutral* (unbiased) third party when deciding whether or how to negotiate a settlement of their dispute. The methods of ADR discussed next all involve neutral third parties.

Mediation

In the **mediation** process, the parties themselves attempt to negotiate an agreement, but with the assistance of a neutral third party, a mediator. The mediator, who need not be a lawyer, usually charges a fee for his or her services (which can be split between the parties).

In mediation, the mediator talks with the parties and allows them to discuss their disagreement openly in a nonadversarial atmosphere. The mediator emphasizes points of agreement, helps the parties evaluate their positions, and proposes solutions. The mediator, however, does not make a decision on the matter being disputed.

Mediation is essentially a form of "assisted negotiation." So are mini-trials, early neutral case evaluations, and summary jury trials—in the sense that the neutral third party in these forms of ADR helps the parties themselves negotiate a settlement.

MEDIATION
A method of settling disputes outside of court by using the services of a neutral third party, who acts as a communicating agent between the parties and assists the parties in negotiating a settlement.

Mini-Trials

A **mini-trial** is a private proceeding in which each party's attorney briefly argues the party's case before the other party. Typically, a neutral third party, who acts as an adviser and an expert in the area being disputed, is also present. If the parties fail to reach an agreement, the adviser renders an opinion as to how a court would likely decide the issue. The proceeding assists the parties in determining whether they should settle their dispute or take it to court.

MINI-TRIAL
A private proceeding in which each party to a dispute argues its position before the other side and vice versa. A neutral third party may be present and act as an adviser if the parties fail to reach an agreement.

Early Neutral Case Evaluation

In **early neutral case evaluation,** the parties select a neutral third party (generally an expert in the subject matter of the dispute) to evaluate their respective positions. The parties explain their positions to the case evaluator however they wish. There is no hearing and no discovery. The case evaluator then evaluates the strengths and weaknesses of the parties' positions, and this evaluation forms the basis for negotiating a settlement.

EARLY NEUTRAL CASE EVALUATION
A form of alternative dispute resolution in which a neutral third party evaluates the strengths and weakness of the disputing parties' positions; the evaluator's opinion forms the basis for negotiating a settlement.

Summary Jury Trials

A form of ADR that has been successfully employed in the federal system is the **summary jury trial (SJT).** In an SJT, the litigants present their arguments and evidence, and the jury then renders a verdict. The jury's verdict is not binding, but it does act as a guide to both sides in reaching an agreement during the mandatory negotiations that immediately follow the trial. Because no witnesses are called, the SJT is much speedier than a regular trial, and frequently the parties are able to settle their dispute without resorting to an actual trial. If no settlement is reached, both sides have the right to a full trial later. Summary jury trials are now held by approximately sixty-five federal judges.

SUMMARY JURY TRIAL (SJT)
A method of settling disputes in which a trial is held, but the jury's verdict is not binding. The verdict acts only as a guide to both sides in reaching an agreement during the mandatory negotiations that immediately follow the summary jury trial.

Arbitration

A more formal method of alternative dispute resolution is **arbitration,** in which an arbitrator (a neutral third party or a panel of experts) hears a dispute and renders a decision.

ARBITRATION
The settling of a dispute by submitting it to a disinterested third party (other than a court), who renders a decision that is (usually) legally binding.

The key difference between arbitration and the forms of ADR just discussed is that in arbitration, the third party's decision normally is legally binding on the parties.[14]

In some respects, formal arbitration resembles a trial, although usually the procedural rules are much less restrictive than those governing litigation. In the typical hearing format, the parties present opening arguments to the arbitrator and state what remedies should or should not be granted. Evidence is then presented, and witnesses may be called and examined by both sides. The arbitrator then renders a decision, which is called an *award*.

An arbitrator's award is usually the final word on the matter. Although the parties may appeal an arbitrator's decision, a court's review of the decision will be much more restricted in scope than an appellate court's review of a trial court's decision. The general view is that because the parties were free to frame the issues and set the powers of the arbitrator at the outset, they cannot complain about the results. The award will only be set aside if the arbitrator's conduct or "bad faith" substantially prejudiced the rights of one of the parties, if the award violates an established public policy, or if the arbitrator exceeded his or her powers (arbitrated issues that the parties did not agree to submit to arbitration).

ARBITRATION CLAUSE

A clause in a contract that provides that, in case of a dispute, the parties will submit the dispute to arbitration rather than litigate the dispute in court.

ARBITRATION CLAUSES AND STATUTES   Virtually any commercial matter can be submitted to arbitration. Frequently, parties include in an **arbitration clause** in a contract (a written agreement—see Chapter 8) that any dispute that arises under the contract will be resolved through arbitration rather than through the court system. Parties can also agree to arbitrate a dispute after a dispute arises.

Most states have statutes (often based in part on the Uniform Arbitration Act of 1955) under which arbitration clauses will be enforced, and some state statutes compel arbitration of certain types of disputes, such as those involving public employees. At the federal level, the Federal Arbitration Act (FAA), enacted in 1925, enforces arbitration clauses in contracts involving maritime activity and interstate commerce. Because of the breadth of the commerce clause (see Chapter 2), arbitration agreements involving transactions only slightly connected to the flow of interstate commerce may fall under the FAA. In the following case, the United States Supreme Court considered whether the FAA applied to an arbitration agreement that, at the time of contracting, the parties did not expect to involve interstate commerce.

---

14.   Depending on the parties' circumstances and preferences, the arbitrator's decision may also be nonbinding on the parties. In some situations, for example, the parties may remain free to reject the arbitrator's decision. Such nonbinding arbitration is more similar to mediation than to binding arbitration. Arbitration that is mandated by the courts (to be discussed shortly) is often not binding on the parties.

CASE 3.4

ALLIED-BRUCE TERMINIX COMPANIES, INC. v. DOBSON

Supreme Court of the United States, 1995.
___ U.S. ___,
115 S.Ct. 834,
130 L.Ed.2d 753.

HISTORICAL AND ENVIRONMENTAL SETTING   *One of the responsibilities of home ownership is to protect the structure from the elements of nature. Those elements*

include termites. Termites feed chiefly on wood, such as the wood used to construct houses. The tiny insects can destroy a home that is unprotected or inadequately protected. In the United States, termites cause over $250 million in losses each year. Common methods to prevent the entry of termites into buildings include using chemically treated wood in the construction of the building or chemically treating the soil on which the building is constructed.

FACTS   Steven Gwin signed a contract with Allied-Bruce Terminix Companies, Inc., a company with operations in many states, to protect his home from termite infestation. The contract specified that any dispute would be resolved by arbitration. After Gwin sold the home to

Case 3.4—Continued

Michael Dobson, the structure became infested with termites. Dobson filed a suit against Gwin and Allied-Bruce in an Alabama state court. Allied-Bruce asked the court to compel arbitration under the Federal Arbitration Act (FAA) section making enforceable a written arbitration provision in "a contract evidencing a transaction involving [interstate] commerce." The court refused to compel arbitration, concluding that at the time of contracting, the parties did not expect their contract to involve interstate commerce. Allied-Bruce appealed. The state supreme court affirmed, and the company appealed again—to the United States Supreme Court.

ISSUE Is an arbitration clause enforceable under the FAA when the contract involves interstate commerce, even if the parties, at the time of contracting, did not expect it to involve interstate commerce?

DECISION Yes. The Supreme Court held that the FAA is written broadly and extends to the limits of Congress's commerce clause power. The Supreme Court reversed

the ruling of the state supreme court and remanded the case for further proceedings.

REASON The Supreme Court acknowledged that the FAA applies only to an arbitration clause in "a contract evidencing a transaction involving commerce." The Court concluded, however, that "involving" means the same thing as "affecting," and "affecting interstate commerce" is the phrase that defines the extent of Congress's power under the commerce clause. The Court also concluded that "evidencing" requires only that a transaction in fact involve commerce. The Court reasoned that permitting parties to argue that they never expected a contract to involve interstate commerce would only lead to more lawsuits, which Congress had sought to avoid in designing the FAA.

FOR CRITICAL ANALYSIS—Ethical Consideration
The Federal Arbitration Act was enacted in 1925, when the commerce clause did not have the reach that it does today. Is it fair to expand the reach of the FAA with the expansion of the reach of the commerce clause?

ARBITRABILITY The role of the courts in the arbitration process is limited. One important role is played at the prearbitration stage. When a dispute arises as to whether or not the parties have agreed in an arbitration clause to submit a particular matter to arbitration, one party may file suit to compel arbitration. The court before which the suit is brought will not decide the basic controversy but must decide the issue of *arbitrability*— that is, whether the matter is one that must be resolved through arbitration.

Even when a claim involves a violation of a statute passed to protect a certain class of people (such as investors), a court may determine that the parties must nonetheless abide by their agreement to arbitrate the dispute. Usually, a court will allow the claim to be arbitrated if the court, in interpreting the statute, can find no legislative intent to the contrary.[15] For example, in *Shearson/American Express, Inc. v. McMahon,*[16] a case decided by the United States Supreme Court in 1987, customers of a brokerage firm alleged that the firm had engaged in fraudulent trading on their accounts in violation of two federal acts—the Racketeer Influenced and Corrupt Organizations Act (see Chapter 6) and the Securities Exchange Act of 1934 (see Chapter 29). When the customers sued the firm, the firm moved to compel arbitration of the claims in accordance with an arbitration clause in the contract. The Court found that when Congress enacted these federal acts, it did not intend to bar enforcement of all predispute arbitration agreements, and thus the claims were arbitrable.

Subsequent to the *Shearson* case, the Court faced a similar question: Should claims involving alleged violations of federal statutes protecting employees from employment discrimination also be arbitrable? The Court answered this question in the following landmark case. (See this chapter's *Business Law in Action* for a discussion of the effects of arbitration on employee rights.)

REMEMBER Litigation—even of a dispute over whether a particular matter should be submitted to arbitration—can be time-consuming and expensive.

---

15.   This general principle for determining the arbitrability of such claims was recently confirmed by the United States Supreme Court in *First Options of Chicago, Inc. v. Kaplan,* ___U.S.___, 115 S.Ct. 1920, 131 L.Ed.2d 985 (1995).
16.   482 U.S. 220, 107 S.Ct. 2332, 96 L.Ed.2d 185 (1987).

CASE 3.5

GILMER v. INTERSTATE/JOHNSON LANE CORP.

Supreme Court of the United States, 1991.
500 U.S. 20,
111 S.Ct. 1647,
114 L.Ed.2d 26.

HISTORICAL AND SOCIAL SETTING *In the nineteenth century, some judges would give little respect to the decisions of private arbitrators. These judges may not have wanted competition for the power to decide cases. In 1925, Congress ordered federal courts to respect the decisions of arbitrators. Today, courts generally enforce arbitration awards without reexamining their correctness. At times, though, it may not be clear whether a certain dispute is arbitrable.*

FACTS Interstate/Johnson Lane Corporation required some of its employees, including Robert Gilmer, to register as securities representatives with the New York Stock Exchange (NYSE). The registration application included an agreement to arbitrate when NYSE rules required it. One of the rules requires the arbitration of any controversy arising out of a registrant's termination of employment. Interstate terminated Gilmer's employment. Gilmer, who was sixty-two years old when he was terminated, filed a suit in a federal district court, alleging that he had been discharged in violation of the Age Discrimination in Employment Act (ADEA) of 1967.[a] (This act prohibits

employers from discriminating against older employees—see Chapter 33.) Interstate asked the court to order the arbitration of Gilmer's claim, according to the agreement in Gilmer's registration application with the NYSE. The court denied the employer's request, but on appeal, the appellate court ordered the arbitration. Gilmer appealed to the United States Supreme Court.

ISSUE Can an age discrimination claim be subject to compulsory arbitration?

DECISION Yes. The United States Supreme Court held that claims of age discrimination are arbitrable.

REASON The Supreme Court pointed out that arbitration is favored under the Federal Arbitration Act (FAA). Thus, to avoid the enforcement of an arbitration clause governed by the FAA on the basis that a dispute concerns a particular statutory right, a party must show that Congress intended "to preclude a waiver of a judicial forum" (regular court). The Supreme Court could find nothing in the text, legislative history, or underlying purposes of the ADEA indicating a congressional intent to preclude enforcement of arbitration agreements. The Court thus affirmed the order of the court of appeals.

FOR CRITICAL ANALYSIS—Ethical Consideration
The decision to compel arbitration may seem to contradict the public policy enunciated in such statutes as the ADEA. For what practical reason might courts favor the arbitration of disputes, even in the employment context?

---

a.   29 U.S.C. Sections 621–634.

Providers of ADR Services

ADR services are provided both by government agencies and by private organizations. A major provider of ADR services is the American Arbitration Association (AAA). Most of the largest law firms in the nation are members of this nonprofit association. Founded in 1926, the AAA now settles nearly sixty thousand disputes a year in its numerous offices around the country. Cases brought before the AAA are heard by an expert or a panel of experts in the area relating to the dispute and are usually settled quickly. Generally, about half of the panel members are lawyers. To cover its costs, the AAA charges a fee, paid by the party filing the claim. In addition, each party to the dispute pays a specified amount for each hearing day, as well as a special additional fee in cases involving personal injuries or property loss.

Hundreds of for-profit firms around the country also provide dispute-resolution services. Typically, these firms hire retired judges to conduct arbitration hearings or otherwise assist parties in settling their disputes. The leading firm in this relatively new private system of justice is JAMS/Endispute, which is based in Santa Ana,

ADR and Employment Discrimination

Over the last three decades, Congress has enacted statutes that give employees significant protection from employers' discriminatory practices. These statutes protect employees from employment discrimination based on race, color, national origin, gender, religion, age, and disability (see Chapter 33).

What happens to these rights, though, if an employee has agreed, in his or her employment contract, to arbitrate any claims arising from the employment relationship? For one thing, the procedural protections available in an arbitral forum can differ significantly from those available in the litigation process. For example, discovery usually is more limited in arbitration than in litigation. If a discrimination claim is arbitrated, an employee may find it difficult to gain access to company documents or other evidence of the discriminatory practice. Remedies also differ. Under Title VII of the Civil Rights Act of

1964, as amended, plaintiffs who can prove that they are victims of intentional discrimination in violation of Title VII may be awarded punitive damages—in addition to actual damages (such as lost wages), reinstatement, and so on. In contrast, arbitration clauses may limit or prohibit entirely an award of punitive damages.

Many people today are concerned about the pitfalls of arbitration for employee rights. For example, JAMS/Endispute, a leading provider of arbitration services, claims that it is unfair of employers to require employees to sign contracts containing arbitration clauses that limit their rights to obtain punitive damages. JAMS has thus adopted a policy of taking only those cases in which an employee retains the same avenues available in court, including the right to obtain punitive damages. In a policy statement issued in 1995, the Equal Employment Opportunity Commission also expressed its disapproval of the mandatory arbitration of employment claims.

The courts, of course, are obligated to follow the precedent set by the United States Supreme Court in the *Gilmer* decision (presented in this chapter as Case 3.5), in which the Court stated that claims of

employment discrimination are arbitrable. Nonetheless, courts are finding grounds not to enforce arbitration clauses. For example, the U.S. Court of Appeals for the Ninth Circuit held that an arbitration clause will not be binding if an employee did not "knowingly" waive his or her rights to statutory remedies when signing the contract containing the clause[a] or if the clause eliminates punitive damages or other remedies provided under federal law.[b] The New Mexico Supreme Court found yet another reason not to enforce an arbitration clause: the clause limited the employee's right to appeal.[c] These and other cases may represent a countertrend against the decisions of the early 1990s, which seemed to expand continuously the scope of arbitrable issues.

For Critical Analysis: *Why do people sign arbitration agreements in the first place?*

a. *Prudential Insurance Co. of America v. Lai,* 42 F.3d 1299 (9th Cir. 1994).
b. *Graham Oil Co. v. ARCO Products Co.,* 43 F.3d 1244 (9th Cir. 1994).
c. *Board of Education of Carlsbad Municipal Schools v. Harrel,* 882 P.2d 511 (N.Mex.1994).

California. Private ADR firms normally allow the parties to decide on the date of the hearing, the presiding judge, whether the judge's decision will be legally binding, and the site of the hearing—which may be a conference room, a law-school office, or a leased courtroom. The judges follow procedures similar to those of the federal courts and use similar rules. Usually, each party to the dispute pays a filing fee and a designated fee for a hearing session or conference.

ADR and the Courts

ADR clearly offers many advantages to disputing parties. It also provides the courts with a means of reducing the number of cases that go to trial. As early as the 1950s, some courts were experimenting with requiring those who filed suits to undergo arbitration before proceeding to trial.

COURT-RELATED ADR Today, at least thirty-five states either require or encourage parties to undergo mediation or arbitration prior to trial. Courts in several federal districts require arbitration prior to trial in cases involving less than $100,000, and

BE AWARE Arbitration can be voluntary, but in some cases, it may be mandatory, and although an arbitrator's decision may be nonbinding, in some cases, the parties are bound.

numerous other federal courts provide for voluntary arbitration. Generally, when a trial court refers cases for arbitration, the arbitrator's decision is not binding on the parties. If they do not agree to the arbitrator's decision, they can go forward with their lawsuit.

The types of court-related ADR programs in use vary widely. In some states, ADR is voluntary. For example, in Missouri, when a party files a lawsuit, he or she is advised of various ADR options and given the names of individuals and organizations that provide ADR services. In other states, such as Minnesota, parties are required to undertake ADR before they can have their case heard in court—as in the federal district courts mentioned above. Some programs refer cases for ADR based on the amount of the claims involved. Hawaii, for example, has a program of mandatory, nonbinding arbitration for disputes involving less than $150,000. Other programs refer cases for ADR according to their subject matter. ADR programs also vary in terms of the types of ADR offered. Some states, such as Minnesota, offer a menu of options. Other states, including Florida (which has a statewide, comprehensive mediation program), offer only one alternative.

ADR programs are not limited to the trial courts. More than forty state appellate courts now also offer some form of ADR to help parties settle civil disputes prior to appellate review.

OTHER COURT-RELATED ALTERNATIVES Today's courts are experimenting with a variety of other alternatives to speed up (and reduce the cost of) justice. These alternatives include summary procedures for commercial litigation, the appointment of special masters to assist judges in deciding complex issues, and permitting an expanded use of paralegals in the handling of routine legal matters.

Some states, including Arizona, California, and Florida, are even experimenting with a type of electronic court. Electronic kiosks (about the size of soda machines) have been installed in shopping malls and other convenient places to allow persons to obtain information, via a computerized system, about certain areas of the law. Arizona's "QuickCourt" system goes a step further. For example, a person who wants to obtain a divorce can go to a QuickCourt, key in the information requested by the computer, and receive a printout of the divorce petition and related forms that can then be filed with the court to initiate divorce proceedings.

International Perspective

The United States is not the only country that encourages mediation, arbitration, and other forms of ADR. Japan, for example, has recently authorized the establishment of neutral panels to act as mediators in product liability suits (suits brought by plaintiffs who have allegedly been injured by a seller's defective product—see Chapter 17). Several industries, including those manufacturing and selling housing materials, automobiles, and appliances, have set up such panels, which follow guidelines published by the Japanese Ministry of International Trade and Industry.

In 1995, China also made it simpler for disputes to be settled through ADR by passing a new arbitration law. The law spells out what types of disputes are arbitrable, the form and content of valid arbitration clauses, and so on. Under the law, although most disputes can be arbitrated, family matters (such as those relating to marriage, adoption, and financial support) cannot be submitted for arbitration. Such disputes will continue to be handled by the relevant administrative agencies of the Chinese government.

For Critical Analysis: *Do you see any reason why certain types of disputes, such as those involving family matters, should* not *be decided by arbitration?*

Application

Law and the Businessperson — To Sue or Not to Sue*

Wrongs are committed every minute of every day in the United States. These wrongs may be committed inadvertently or intentionally. Sometimes businesspersons believe that wrongs have been committed against them by other businesspersons, by consumers, or by the local, state, or federal government. If you are deciding whether or not to sue for a wrong that has been committed against you or your business, you must consider many issues.

The Question of Cost

Competent legal advice is not inexpensive. Good commercial business law attorneys charge $75 to $400 an hour, plus expenses. It is almost always worthwhile to make an initial visit to an attorney who has skills in the area in which you are going to sue to get an estimate of the expected costs of pursuing a redress for your grievance. You may be charged for the initial visit as well.

Note that less than 10 percent of all corporate lawsuits end up in trial—the rest are settled beforehand. You may end up settling for far less than you thought you were "owed" simply because of the length of time it takes your attorney to bring your case to trial and to finish the trial. And then you might not win, anyway!

Basically, then, you must do a cost-benefit analysis to determine whether you should sue. Your attorney can give you the costs, and you can "guesstimate" the benefits. You do this by multiplying the probable size of the award by the probability of obtaining that award.

*This *Application* is not meant to substitute for the services of an attorney who is licensed to practice law in your state.

The Alternatives before You

Another method of settling your grievance is by alternative dispute resolution (ADR). Negotiation, mediation and other forms of "assisted negotiation," and arbitration are all forms of ADR. They are becoming increasingly attractive alternatives to court litigation, because they usually yield quick results at a comparatively low cost. Most disputes relating to business can be mediated or arbitrated through the American Arbitration Association (AAA), and there are numerous other ADR centers as well. You can obtain information on ADR from the AAA, courthouses, chambers of commerce, law firms, state bar associations, or the American Bar Association. The latter is located at 1800 M Street N.W., Washington, DC 20036. The Yellow Pages in large metropolitan areas usually list agencies and firms that could help you settle your dispute out of court; look under "Mediation" or "Social Service Agencies."

✓ Checklist for Deciding Whether to Sue

1. Are you prepared to pay for going to court? Make this decision only after you have consulted an attorney to get an estimate of the costs of preparing the lawsuit.
2. Do you have the patience to follow a court case through the judicial system, even if it takes several years?
3. Is there a way for you to settle your grievance without going to court? Even if the settlement is less than you think you are owed—in net terms corrected for future expenses, lost time, and frustration—you may be better off settling now for the smaller figure.
4. Can you use some form of alternative dispute resolution? Before you say no, investigate these alternatives—they are usually cheaper and quicker to use than the standard judicial process.

▌ Key Terms

(Continued)

▌Key Terms—Continued

long arm statute 60	motion for summary	small claims court 67
mediation 81	judgment 73	standing to sue 65
mini-trial 81	motion to dismiss 72	summary jury trial (SJT) 81
motion for a directed verdict 77	negotiation 80	summons 71
motion for a new trial 78	pleadings 70	venue 64
motion for judgment *n.o.v.* 77	probate court 62	*voir dire* 76
motion for judgment on	reply 72	writ of *certiorari* 69
the pleadings 73	rule of four 69	

▌Chapter Summary: Courts and Procedures

The Judiciary's Role in American Government *(See pages 59–60.)*	The role of the judiciary—the courts—in the American governmental system is to interpret and apply the law. Through the process of judicial review—determining the constitutionality of laws—the judicial branch acts as a check on the executive and legislative branches of government. The power of judicial review was established by Chief Justice John Marshall in *Marbury v. Madison* (1803).

Basic Judicial Requirements *(See pages 60–66.)*	1. *Jurisdiction*—Before a court can hear a case, it must have jurisdiction over the person against whom the suit is brought or the property involved in the suit, as well as jurisdiction over the subject matter.
	   a. Limited versus general jurisdiction—Limited jurisdiction exists when a court is limited to a specific subject matter, such as probate or divorce. General jurisdiction exists when a court can hear any kind of case.
	   b. Original versus appellate jurisdiction—Original jurisdiction exists with courts that have authority to hear a case for the first time (trial courts). Appellate jurisdiction exists with courts of appeals, or reviewing courts; generally, appellate courts do not have original jurisdiction.
	   c. Federal jurisdiction—Arises (1) when a federal question is involved (when the plaintiff's cause of action is based, at least in part, on the U.S. Constitution, a treaty, or a federal law) or (2) when a case involves diversity of citizenship (citizens of different states, for example), and the amount in controversy exceeds $50,000.
	   d. Concurrent versus exclusive jurisdiction—Concurrent jurisdiction exists when two different courts have authority to hear the same case. Exclusive jurisdiction exists when only state courts or only federal courts have authority to hear a case.
	
	 2. *Venue*—Venue has to do with the most appropriate location for a trial, which is usually the geographical area in which the event leading to the dispute took place or where the parties reside.
	
	 3. *Standing to sue*—A requirement that a party must have a legally protected and tangible interest at stake sufficient to justify seeking relief through the court system. The controversy at issue must also be a justiciable controversy—one that is real and substantial, as opposed to hypothetical or academic.

The State and Federal Court Systems *(See pages 66–70.)*	1. *Trial courts*—Courts of original jurisdiction, in which legal actions are initiated.
	   a. State—Courts of general jurisdiction can hear any case; courts of limited jurisdiction include divorce courts, probate courts, traffic courts, small claims courts, etc.
	   b. Federal—The federal district court is the equivalent of the state trial court. Federal courts of limited jurisdiction include the U.S. Tax Court, the U.S. Bankruptcy Court, and the U.S. Court of Federal Claims.
	
	 2. *Intermediate appellate courts*—Courts of appeals, or reviewing courts; generally without original jurisdiction. Many states have an intermediate appellate court; in the federal court system, the U.S. circuit courts of appeals are the intermediate appellate courts.
	
	 3. *Supreme (highest) courts*—Each state has a supreme court, although it may be called by some other name, from which appeal to the United States Supreme Court is only possible if a federal question is involved. The United States Supreme Court is the highest court in the federal court system and the final arbiter of the Constitution and federal law.

▌Chapter Summary: Courts and Procedures—Continued

Procedural Rules *(See pages 70–80.)*	Rules of procedure prescribe the way in which disputes are handled in the courts. Rules differ from court to court, and separate sets of rules exist for federal and state courts, as well as for criminal and civil cases. A sample civil court case in a state court would involve the following procedures:
	
	 1. *The pleadings—*
	   a. Complaint—Filed by the plaintiff with the court to initiate the lawsuit; served with a summons on the defendant.
	   b. Answer—Admits or denies allegations made by the plaintiff; may assert a counterclaim or an affirmative defense.
	   c. Motion to dismiss—A request to the court to dismiss the case for stated reasons, such as the plaintiff's failure to state a claim for which relief can be granted.
	 2. *Pretrial motions (in addition to the motion to dismiss)—*
	   a. Motion for judgment on the pleadings—May be made by either party; will be granted if the parties agree on the facts and the only question is how the law applies to the facts. The judge bases the decision solely on the pleadings.
	   b. Motion for summary judgment—May be made by either party; will be granted if the parties agree on the facts. The judge applies the law in rendering a judgment. The judge can consider evidence outside the pleadings when evaluating the motion.
	 3. *Discovery—*The process of gathering evidence concerning the case. Discovery involves *depositions* (sworn testimony by a party to the lawsuit or any witness), *interrogatories* (written questions and answers to these questions made by parties to the action with the aid of their attorneys), and various requests (for admissions, documents, medical examination, and so on).
	 4. *Pretrial conference—*Either party or the court can request a pretrial conference to identify the matters in dispute after discovery has taken place and to plan the course of the trial.
	 5. *Trial—*Following jury selection (*voir dire*), the trial begins with opening statements from both parties' attorneys. The following events then occur:
	   a. The plaintiff's introduction of evidence (including the testimony of witnesses) supporting the plaintiff's position. The defendant's attorney can challenge evidence and cross-examine witnesses.
	   b. The defendant's introduction of evidence (including the testimony of witnesses) supporting the defendant's position. The plaintiff's attorney can challenge evidence and cross-examine witnesses.
	   c. Closing arguments by attorneys in favor of their respective clients, the judge's instructions to the jury, and the jury's verdict.
	 6. *Posttrial motions—*
	   a. Motion for judgment *n.o.v.* ("notwithstanding the verdict")—Will be granted if the judge is convinced that the jury was in error.
	   b. Motion for a new trial—Will be granted if the judge is convinced that the jury was in error; can also be granted on the grounds of newly discovered evidence, misconduct by the participants during the trial, or error by the judge.
	 7. *Appeal—*Either party can appeal the trial court's judgment to an appropriate court of appeals. After reviewing the record on appeal, the abstracts, and the attorneys' briefs, the appellate court holds a hearing and renders its opinion.

Alternative Dispute Resolution (ADR) *(See pages 80–86.)*	1. *Negotiation—*The parties come together, with or without attorneys to represent them, and try to reach a settlement without the involvement of a third party. 2. *Mediation—*The parties themselves reach an agreement with the help of a neutral third party, called a mediator, who proposes solutions. 3. *Mini-trial—*A private proceeding in which each party's attorney argues the party's case before the other party. Often, a neutral third party renders an opinion on how a court would likely decide the issue. 4. *Early neutral case evaluation—*A private proceeding in which the parties argue their respective cases before a neutral third party, whose decision becomes the basis for negotiating a settlement. 5. *Summary jury trial (SJT)—*A kind of trial employed by some federal courts in which litigants present their arguments and evidence and the jury renders a nonbinding verdict. The verdict guides the parties in reaching an agreement during the mandatory negotiations that immediately follow the trial. *(Continued)*

▮ Chapter Summary: Courts and Procedures—Continued

Alternative Dispute Resolution (ADR) —Continued	6. *Arbitration*—A more formal method of ADR in which the parties submit their dispute to a neutral third party, the arbitrator, who renders a decision. The decision may or may not be legally binding, depending on the circumstances.
	7. *Providers of ADR services*—The leading nonprofit provider of ADR services is the American Arbitration Association. Hundreds of for-profit firms also provide ADR services.
	8. *Court-related ADR*—Many state and federal courts now refer cases for some form of ADR prior to trial. In most cases, pretrial arbitration is nonbinding on the parties.

▮ For Review

1. What is judicial review? How and when was the power of judicial review established?

2. Before a court can hear a case, it must have jurisdiction. Over what must it have jurisdiction? In what circumstances does a federal court have jurisdiction?

3. What is the difference between a trial court and an appellate court?

4. In a lawsuit, what are the pleadings? What is discovery?

5. Name five methods of alternative dispute resolution (ADR). What advantages does ADR offer to the parties?

▮ Questions and Case Problems

3–1. Appellate Process. If a judge enters a judgment on the pleadings, the losing party can usually appeal but cannot present evidence to the appellate court. Does this seem fair? Explain.

3–2. Arbitration. In an arbitration proceeding, the arbitrator need not be a judge or even a lawyer. How, then, can the arbitrator's decision have the force of law and be binding on the parties involved?

3–3. Appellate Process. Sometimes on appeal there are questions concerning whether the facts presented in the trial court support the conclusion reached by the judge or the jury. An appellate court, however, normally defers to the trial court's decision with regard to the facts. Can you see any reason for this?

3–4. Jurisdiction. Marya Callais, a citizen of Florida, was walking near a busy street in Tallahassee one day when a large crate flew off a passing truck and hit her, resulting in numerous injuries to Callais. She incurred a great deal of pain and suffering plus numerous medical expenses, and she could not work for six months. She wishes to sue the trucking firm for $300,000 in damages. The firm's headquarters are in Georgia, although the company does business in Florida. In what court may Marya bring suit—a Florida state court, a Georgia state court, or a federal court? What factors might influence her decision?

3–5. Jurisdiction. Shem and Nadine Maslov, who live in Massachusetts, saw an advertisement in the *Boston Globe* for vacationers that was sponsored by a national hotel chain: "Stay in Maximum Inns' beachfront hotel in Puerto Rico for one week for only $400; continental breakfast included." The Maslovs decided to accept the offer and spent a week at the hotel. On the last day, Nadine fell on a wet floor in the hotel lobby and sustained multiple fractures to her left ankle and hip. Because of her injuries, which were subsequently complicated by infections, she was unable to work at her job as an airline flight attendant for ten months. The hotel chain does not do business in Massachusetts. If Nadine sues Maximum Inns in a Massachusetts state court, can the court exercise jurisdiction over Maximum Inns? What factors should the court consider in deciding this jurisdictional issue?

3–6. Arbitration. Gates worked for Arizona Brewing Co. A contract between Gates's employer and the union to which Gates belonged stated that the employer and the union were to try to settle their differences, but if the parties could not reach a settlement, the matter was to be decided by arbitration. Gates brought a lawsuit against his employer (instead of submitting the dispute to arbitration) to recover wages. The employer argued that Gates could not bring a lawsuit until after arbitration had occurred. Gates claimed that the arbitration clause was void under an Arizona arbitration statute, which stated that "this act shall not apply to collective [bargained] contracts between employers and . . . associations of employ[ees]." Must Gates undergo arbitration before bringing a lawsuit? Explain. [*Gates v. Arizona Brewing Co.*, 54 Ariz. 266, 95 P.2d 49 (1939)]

3–7. Arbitration. Phillip Beaudry, who suffered from mental illness, worked in the Department of Income Maintenance for the state of Connecticut. Beaudry was fired from his job when it was learned that he had misappropriated approximately $1,640 in state funds. Beaudry filed a complaint with his union, Council 4 of the American Federation of State, County, and Municipal Employees (AFSCME), and eventually the dispute was submitted to an arbitrator. The arbitrator concluded that Beaudry had been dismissed without "just cause," because Beaudry's acts were caused by his mental illness and "were not willful or volitional or within his capacity to control." Because Beaudry was disabled, the employer was required, under state law, to transfer him to a position that he was competent to hold. The arbitrator awarded Beaudry reinstatement, back pay, seniority, and other benefits. The state appealed the decision to a court. What public policies (general policies as established by statutes or other laws) must the court weigh in making its decision? How should the court rule? [*State v. Council 4, AFSCME,* 27 Conn.App. 635, 608 A.2d 718 (1992)]

3–8. Arbitration. Randall Fris worked as a seaman on an Exxon Shipping Co. oil tanker for eight years without incident. One night, he boarded the ship for duty while intoxicated, in violation of company policy. This policy also allowed Exxon to discharge employees who were intoxicated and thus unfit for work. Exxon discharged Fris. Under a contract with Fris's union, the discharge was submitted to arbitration. The arbitrators ordered Exxon to reinstate Fris on an oil tanker. Exxon filed a suit against the union, challenging the award as contrary to public policy, which opposes having intoxicated persons operate seagoing vessels. Can a court set aside an arbitration award on the ground that the award violates public policy? Should the court set aside the award in this case? Explain. [*Exxon Shipping Co. v. Exxon Seamen's Union,* 11 F.3d 1189 (3d Cir. 1993)]

3–9. Jurisdiction. Cal-Ban 3000 is a weight loss drug made by Health Care Products, Inc., a Florida corporation, and marketed through CKI Industries, another Florida corporation. Enticed by North Carolina newspaper ads for Cal-Ban, the wife of Douglas Tart bought the drug at Prescott's Pharmacies, Inc., in North Carolina for her husband. Within a week, Tart suffered a ruptured colon. Alleging that the injury was caused by Cal-Ban, Tart sued Prescott's Pharmacies, CKI, the officers and directors of Health Care, and others, in a North Carolina state court. CKI and the Health Care officers and directors argued that North Carolina did not have personal jurisdiction over them because CKI and Health Care were Florida corporations. How will the court hold? Why? [*Tart v. Prescott's Pharmacies, Inc.,* 118 N.C.App. 516, 456 S.E.2d 121 (1995)]

3–10. Procedure. Washoe Medical Center, Inc., admitted Shirley Swisher for the treatment of a fractured pelvis. During her stay, Swisher suffered a fatal fall from her hospital bed. Gerald Parodi, the administrator of her estate, and others, filed an action against Washoe in which they sought damages for the alleged lack of care in treating Swisher. During *voir dire,* when the plaintiffs' attorney returned a few minutes late from a break, the trial judge led the prospective jurors in a standing ovation. The judge joked with one of the prospective jurors, whom he had known in college, about the judge's fitness to serve as a judge and personally endorsed another prospective juror's business. After the trial, the jury returned a verdict in favor of Washoe. The plaintiffs appealed, arguing that the tone set by the judge during *voir dire* prejudiced their right to a fair trial. Should the appellate court agree? Why or why not? [*Parodi v. Washoe Medical Center, Inc.,* 111 Nev. 365, 892 P.2d 588 (1995)]

 A QUESTION OF ETHICS AND SOCIAL RESPONSIBILITY

3–11. *Linda Bender brought an action in a federal court against her supervisor at A. G. Edwards & Sons, Inc., a stock-brokerage firm (the defendants). Bender alleged sexual harassment in violation of Title VII of the Civil Rights Act of 1964, which prohibits, among other things, employment discrimination based on gender. In her application for registration as a stockbroker, Bender had agreed to arbitrate any disputes with her employer. The defendants moved to compel arbitration. The district court judge denied the motion, holding that Bender could not be forced to waive her right to adjudicate Title VII claims in federal court. The appellate court reversed, ruling that Title VII claims are arbitrable. The court held that compelling Bender to submit her claim for arbitration did not deprive her of the right to a judicial forum, because if the arbitration proceedings were somehow legally deficient, she could still take her case to a federal court for review.* [Bender v. A. G. Edwards & Sons, Inc., 971 F.2d 698 (11th Cir. 1992)]

1. Does the right to a postarbitration judicial forum equate to the right to initial access to a judicial forum in employment disputes?
2. Should the fact that reviewing courts rarely set aside arbitrators' awards have any bearing on the arbitrability of certain types of claims, such as those brought under Title VII?

FOR CRITICAL ANALYSIS

3–12. *American courts are forums for adversarial justice, in which attorneys defend the interests of their respective clients before the court. This means that an attorney may end up claiming before a court that his or her client is innocent, even though the attorney knows that the client acted wrongfully. Is it ethical for attorneys to try to "deceive" the court in these situations? Can the adversarial system of justice really lead to "truth"?*

▌Accessing the Internet: Business Law and Legal Environment

You can obtain opinions from all of the U.S. Circuit Courts of Appeals from a site provided by the Villanova Center for Information Law and Policy. Go to

http://www.law.vill.edu/Fed-Ct/fedcourt.html

Decisions from the Supreme Court since 1989 can be accessed at

http://www.law.cornell.edu/supct/supct.table.html

There is also a news group that you can access at

news:courts.usa.federal.supreme

A news group, as explained before, is where you can ask questions or simply read dialogue between individuals interested in the same subject. You can use a very effective bulletin board service (BBS) to access court information from many federal courts. The BBS in question is called the Public Access to Court Electronic Records (PACER). The PACER gives comprehensive summaries of cases. It costs 75¢ a minute, but for many it is well worth it. To access PACER, you have to register by calling 1-800-676-6856, Monday through Friday, between 8 A.M. and 5 P.M. You will receive a form that you can mail or fax in. You can sign up with as many federal courts as you wish, out of a total number of over two hundred.

As yet, there is no centralized service for the fifty state courts. Here are the state court Web addresses that are available now:

- Alaska Supreme Court—**http://www.touchngo.com/sp/sp.html**
- Alaska Court of Appeals—**http://www.touchngo.com/ap/ap.html**
- California Supreme Court and Court of Appeals—**http://www.ljx.com/public/daily/calcourt.html**
- Florida Supreme Court—**http://nersp.nerdc.ufl.edu/~lawinfo/flsupct/**
- Florida Supreme Court and Court of Appeals—**http://www.ljx.com/public/daily/flacourt.html**
- Idaho Supreme Court—**http://www.state.id.us/judicial/scopins.html**
- Idaho Court of Appeals—**http://www.state.id.us/judicial/caopins.html**
- Indiana Supreme Court and Court of Appeals—**http://www.law.indiana.edu/law/incourts/incourts.html**
- Michigan Court of Appeals—**http://www.ljx.com/public/daily/mccourt.html**

- Ohio Supreme Court—**http://winslo.ohio.gov/stgvjud.html**
- Ohio Court of Appeals—**http://winslo.ohio.gov/stgvjud.html**
- Oklahoma Supreme Court and Court of Appeals—**http://www.uoknor.edu/okgov/**
- New York Court of Appeals—**http://www.law.cornell.edu/ny/ctap/overview.html**
- New York Court of Appeals, synopses of decisions by E-mail. To subscribe, send a message to **listserv@lii.law.cornell.edu**. The message should read: "subscribe liibulletin-ny<Your Name>."
- North Carolina Supreme Court—**http://www.nando.net/insider/supreme/supco.html**
- North Carolina Court of Appeals—**http://www.nando.net/insider/appeals/appeals.html**
- Wyoming Supreme Court—**gopher://ferret.state.wy.us:70/11/wqov/jb/decision**

For information on alternative dispute resolution, you should go to ConflictNet at

http://www.igc.apc.org/conflictnet/

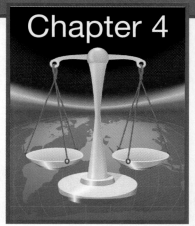

Chapter 4

Ethics and Social Responsibility

"It must be remembered that all trade is and must be in a sense selfish."

John Duke Coleridge, 1821–1892
(English jurist)

CHAPTER OBJECTIVES

After reading this chapter, you should be able to:

1. Define business ethics and its relationship to personal ethics.
2. Explain the relationship between the law and ethics.
3. Compare and contrast duty-based ethics and utilitarian ethics.
4. Identify the various groups to whom corporations are perceived to owe duties.
5. Discuss some of the difficulties involved in measuring corporate social responsibility.

Business and ethics have never been a truly happy couple. This is because, as John Duke Coleridge indicated in the opening quotation, business "must be in a sense selfish." After all, the primary reason for going into business is to make a profit. Throughout history, there has been an underlying tension between the pursuit of profits and the welfare of those groups (employees, consumers, suppliers, creditors, communities, and others) that are affected by this pursuit.

Business owners and managers traditionally have had to ensure that their profit-making activities did not exceed the ethical boundaries established by society. In the past, though, these boundaries were often regarded as being coterminous with the law—that is, if something was legal, it was ethical. Shady business dealings were regarded as "just business" more often than not. In the last few decades, however, the ethical boundaries within which business firms must operate have narrowed significantly. In the rights-conscious world of today, a business firm that decides it has no duties other than those prescribed by law may find it difficult to survive. If a firm's behavior is perceived as unethical—even though it may be legal—that firm may suffer negative publicity, boycotts, and lost profits.

In preparing for a career in business, you will find that a background in business ethics and a commitment to ethical behavior is just as important as a knowledge of the specific laws that you will read about in this text. In this chapter, we first examine the nature of business ethics and some of the sources of ethical standards that have guided others in their business decision making. We then look at some of the obstacles to ethical behavior faced by businesspersons. In the remaining pages of the chapter, which deals with corporate social responsibility, we explore the issue mentioned in the preceding paragraph: How can businesspersons act in an ethically responsible manner and at the same time make profits for their firms or their firms' owners?

▌The Nature of Business Ethics

ETHICS
Moral principles and values applied to social behavior.

To understand the nature of business ethics, we need to define what is meant by ethics generally. **Ethics** can be defined as the study of what constitutes right or wrong behavior. It is the branch of philosophy that focuses on morality and the way in which moral principles are applied to daily life. Ethics has to do with questions relating to the fairness, justness, rightness, or wrongness of an action. What is fair? What is just? What is the right thing to do in this situation?—these are essentially ethical questions.

Often, moral principles serve as the guiding force in an individual's personal ethical system. Although the terms *ethical* and *moral* are often used interchangeably, the terms refer to slightly different concepts. Whereas ethics has to do with the philosophical, rational basis for morality, morals are often defined as universal rules or guidelines (such as those rooted in religious precepts) that determine our actions and character.

Defining Business Ethics

BUSINESS ETHICS
Ethics in a business context; a consensus of what constitutes right or wrong behavior in the world of business and the application of moral principles to situations that arise in a business setting.

Business ethics focuses on what constitutes ethical behavior in the world of business. Personal ethical standards, of course, play an important role in determining what is or is not ethical, or appropriate, business behavior. Business activities are just one part of the human enterprise, and the ethical standards that guide our behavior as, say, mothers, fathers, or students apply equally well to our activities as businesspersons. Businesspersons, though, often must address more complex ethical issues and conflicts in the workplace than they do in their personal lives—as you will learn in this chapter and throughout this book.

Business Ethics and the Law

Because the law reflects and codifies a society's ethical values, many of our ethical decisions are made for us—by our laws. Nevertheless, simply obeying the law does not fulfill all ethical obligations. In the interest of preserving personal freedom, as well as for practical reasons, the law does not—and cannot—codify all ethical requirements. No law says, for example, that it is *illegal* to lie to one's family, but it may be *unethical* to do so. Likewise, in the business world, numerous actions might be unethical but not necessarily illegal. Even though it may be convenient for businesspersons to satisfy themselves by mere compliance with the law, such an approach may not always yield ethical outcomes, as the *International Perspective* below indicates.

In short, the law has its limits—it cannot make all our ethical decisions for us. When it does not, ethical standards must guide the decision-making process.

The production of a new pharmaceutical product is both expensive and time consuming. Because the adverse side effects of a particular drug cannot always be determined in laboratory experiments—especially when symptoms may not manifest themselves for many years—a pharmaceutical company can never be completely certain about the safety of its products when it first brings them to market. Further

CHAPTER 4: ETHICS AND SOCIAL RESPONSIBILITY   95

International Perspective—Continued

complicating the marketing strategies of these companies is the fact that certain drug products may be banned in the United States by the Food and Drug Administration. Because U.S. drug laws are among the toughest in the world, companies with such products will naturally look elsewhere for potential customers—particularly in developing countries that do not have such extensive restrictions on consumer products.

Among the most widely distributed of these banned drugs have been several antidiarrheal products produced by companies such as G. D. Searle, Johnson & Johnson, and Wyeth. Because diarrhea kills several million children in underdeveloped countries each year, the need for effective products is evident. The World Health Organization has said that an inexpensive mixture of sugar, salt, and water can help to rehydrate children much more effectively and safely than any of the drugs available for sale. The lure of an estimated $500 million market, however, has, at least until recently, proved irresistible to many pharmaceutical companies. After a scathing British documentary revealed that a number of infants in Pakistan had died after being given the antidiarrheal drug Immodium, Johnson & Johnson agreed to withdraw its product from all developing countries.

For Critical Analysis: *Is it unethical of U.S. companies to sell banned drugs overseas? Would your answer be different if the drugs significantly benefited the health of consumers in overseas markets?*

▌ Sources of Ethical Standards

Religious and philosophical inquiry into the nature of "the good" is an age-old pursuit. Broadly speaking, though, ethical reasoning relating to business traditionally has been characterized by two fundamental approaches. One approach defines ethical behavior in terms of *duty*. The other approach determines what is ethical in terms of the *consequences*, or *outcome*, of any given action. We examine each of these approaches here.

Duty-Based Ethics

Is it wrong to cheat on an examination, if nobody will ever know that you cheated and if it helps you get into law school so that you can eventually volunteer your legal services to the poor and needy? Is it wrong to lie to your parents if the lie harms nobody but helps to keep family relations congenial? These kinds of ethical questions implicitly weigh the "end" of an action against the "means" used to attain that end. If you believe that you have an ethical *duty* not to lie or cheat, however, then lying and cheating can never be justified by the consequences, no matter how benevolent or desirable those consequences may be. Duty-based ethics may be based on religious precepts or philosophical reasoning.

RELIGION   Duty-based ethical standards are often derived from moral principles rooted in religious sources. In the Judeo-Christian tradition, for example, the Ten Commandments of the Old Testament establish rules for moral action. Other religions have their own sources of revealed truth—such as the Koran in the Muslim world. Within the confines of their influence, moral principles are universal and *absolute*—they are not to be questioned. For example, consider one of the Ten Commandments: "Thou shalt not steal." This is an absolute mandate. Even a benevolent motive for stealing (such as Robin Hood's) cannot justify the act, because the act itself is inherently immoral and thus wrong. When an act is prohibited by religious teachings that serve as the foundation of a person's moral or ethical standards, the act is unethical for that person and should not be undertaken, regardless of its consequences.

Ethical standards based on religious teachings also may involve an element of *compassion*. Therefore, even though it might be profitable for a firm to lay off a less productive employee, if that employee were to find it difficult to find employment elsewhere and his or her family were to suffer as a result, this potential suffering would be given substantial weight by the decision makers. Compassionate treatment of others is also mandated—to a certain extent, at least—by the Golden Rule of the ancients ("Do unto others as you would have them do unto you"), which has been adopted by most religions.

KANTIAN PHILOSOPHY   Ethical standards based on a concept of duty may also be derived solely from philosophical principles. Immanuel Kant (1724–1804), for example, identified some general guiding principles for moral behavior based on what he believed to be the fundamental nature of human beings. Kant held that it is rational to assume that human beings are qualitatively different from other physical objects occupying space. Persons are endowed with moral integrity and the capacity to reason and conduct their affairs rationally. Therefore, their thoughts and actions should be respected. When human beings are treated merely as a means to an end, they are being treated as the equivalent of objects and are being denied their basic humanity.

A central postulate in Kantian ethics is that individuals should evaluate their actions in light of the consequences that would follow if *everyone* in society acted in the same way. This **categorial imperative** can be applied to any action. For example, say that you are deciding whether to cheat on an examination. If you have adopted Kant's categorical imperative, you will decide not to cheat, because if everyone cheated, the examination would be meaningless.

Outcome-Based Ethics

"Thou shalt act so as to generate the greatest good for the greatest number." This is a paraphrase of the major premise of the utilitarian approach to ethics. **Utilitarianism** is a philosophical theory first developed by Jeremy Bentham (1748–1832) and then advanced, with some modifications, by John Stuart Mill (1806–1873)—both British philosophers. In contrast to duty-based ethics, utilitarianism is outcome oriented. It

---

CATEGORICAL IMPERATIVE
A concept developed by the philosopher Immanuel Kant as an ethical guideline for behavior. In deciding whether an action is right or wrong, or desirable or undesirable, a person should evaluate the action in terms of what would happen if everybody else in the same situation, or category, acted the same way.

UTILITARIANISM
An approach to ethical reasoning in which ethically correct behavior is not related to any absolute ethical or moral values but to an evaluation of the consequences of a given action on those who will be affected by it. In utilitarian reasoning, a "good" decision is one that results in the greatest good for the greatest number of people affected by the decision.

A lab worker conducts research for the development of a drug. If the drug proves beneficial to most people but adverse to a few, would it, under a utilitarian model of ethics, be marketed?

focuses on the consequences of an action, not on the nature of the action itself or on any set of preestablished moral values or religious beliefs.

Under a utilitarian model of ethics, an action is morally correct, or "right," when, among the people it affects, it produces the greatest amount of good for the greatest number. When an action affects the majority adversely, it is morally wrong. Applying the utilitarian theory thus requires (1) a determination of which individuals will be affected by the action in question; (2) a **cost-benefit analysis**—an assessment of the negative and positive effects of alternative actions on these individuals; and (3) a choice among alternative actions that will produce maximum societal utility (the greatest positive benefits for the greatest number of individuals).

Utilitarianism is often criticized because it tends to focus on society as a whole rather than on individual human rights. For example, from a utilitarian standpoint, it might be ethically acceptable to test drugs or medicines on human beings because presumably a majority of the population would benefit from the experiments. If, however, one accepts the principle that each individual has basic human rights (to life, freedom, and the pursuit of happiness), then an action that deprives an individual or group of individuals of these rights—even for the greater good of society—is ethically unacceptable. No amount of cost-benefit analysis can justify the action.

COST-BENEFIT ANALYSIS
A decision-making technique that involves weighing the costs of a given action against the benefits of the action.

BE CAREFUL Ethical concepts about what is right and what is wrong can change.

Applying Ethical Standards

Consider the following example: A corporation that markets baby formula in developing countries has learned that mothers in those countries often mix the formula with impure water, to make the formula go further. As a result, babies are suffering from malnutrition, diarrhea, and in some instances, even death. What is the corporation's ethical responsibility in this situation? Should it withdraw the product from those markets (and lose profits), or should it conduct a cost-benefit analysis and let the decision be guided by the results?

If the corporation's decision makers felt that they had an absolute duty not to harm others, then the only ethical response would be to withdraw the product from those markets. If the decision makers approached the problem from a utilitarian perspective, they would engage in a cost-benefit analysis. The cost of the action (the suffering and death of babies) would be weighed against its benefit (the availability of the formula to mothers). Having the formula available frees mothers from the task of breastfeeding and thus allows them to earn money to help raise their incomes and standards of living. The question in a utilitarian analysis would focus on whether the benefit outweighed the cost—not the inherent rightness or wrongness of the action.

In fact, this scenario is not hypothetical. In the 1970s, the Nestlé Company concluded, on the basis of a cost-benefit analysis, that it was ethically justified in continuing to market its baby formula in developing countries. Other companies marketing infant formula in those areas, however, reached a different decision: they pulled out of those markets. Nestlé was severely criticized for its behavior. The company's opponents were outraged, not because the formula had been marketed initially but because of Nestlé's decision to continue marketing the formula based on its cost-benefit analysis.

▌ Obstacles to Ethical Business Behavior

People sometimes behave unethically in the business context, just as they do in their private lives. Some businesspersons knowingly engage in unethical behavior because they think that they can "get away with it"—that no one will ever learn of their unethical actions. Examples of this kind of unethical behavior include padding expense accounts, casting doubts on the integrity of a rival co-worker to gain a job promotion, stealing company supplies or equipment, and so on. Obviously, these acts are unethical, and many of them are illegal as well.

BUSINESS LAW IN ACTION

Self-Critical Analysis and "Smoking Guns"

Under the U.S. Sentencing Guidelines, which were created by the U.S. Department of Justice to provide standardized criminal sentences for federal crimes (see Chapter 7), corporate lawbreakers face sanctions and fines that can be as high as hundreds of millions of dollars. The guidelines allow judges to ease up on penalties, however, if a company can show that it has taken substantial steps to prevent, investigate, and punish wrongdoing by corporate employees. The sentencing guidelines thus provide an incentive for companies to establish ethics programs and procedures for implementing and monitoring corporate behavior. The theory is that companies that attempt to regulate their own behavior through self-critical analysis (SCA)—through internal audits or investigations of corporate conduct—should receive more favorable treatment under the law than those that do not.

Although laws promoting SCA foster ethical behavior, business owners and managers continue to face significant challenges in attempting to prevent wrongdoing within their companies. One of the problems with SCA is that it is virtually impossible to conduct a meaningful internal investigation or undertake an in-depth review process without creating a "paper trail" of some kind. Should the company have to defend itself in a lawsuit, the memos, reports, and other written evidence resulting from an investigation could be subject to discovery (see Chapter 3). If discovered by the plaintiff, these documents could be just the "smoking guns" the plaintiff is seeking—and the company may find it difficult to defend itself.

In an attempt to overcome this disincentive to undertake SCA, several states have passed laws that allow certain types of information resulting from internal audits and reviews to be privileged—that is, not admissible as evidence in a legal proceeding against the company. Some courts have also ruled that the results of a company's internal investigation of corporate conduct are protected by the "privilege of self-critical analysis." These courts hold that the SCA privilege furthers the public policy of encouraging self-evaluation on the part of companies.

In one case, for example, a plaintiff alleging gender discrimination on the part of her employer sought access to the employer's records of an investigation it had conducted on the obstacles faced by women within the company. The court, holding that the records were protected by the SCA privilege, stated that "[f]ew, if any, companies would risk commissioning a candid . . . report if these reports could later be used against the company in litigation.[a] Nonetheless, in most states, there are no real guarantees that the results of internal investigations will be kept confidential.

For Critical Analysis: *List some of the pros and cons of applying the self-critical analysis privilege.*

a. *Flynn v. Goldman, Sachs & Co.* (S.D.N.Y. 1993)[1993 WL 362380]; this case is not reported in West's *Federal Supplement* reporter, but it can be retrieved on WESTLAW using the WL citation given here. See *Sheppard v. Consolidated Edison Co. of New York*, 893 F.Supp. 6 (E.D.N.Y. 1995), for another example of the application of the SCA privilege. For a discussion of the contrary view—that the SCA privilege should not be applied—see *Warren v. Legg Mason Wood Walker, Inc.*, 896 F.Supp. 540 (E.D.N.C. 1995).

REMEMBER There is a constant tension among ethics, social forces, profits, and the law.

In other situations, businesspersons who would choose to act ethically may be deterred from doing so because of situational circumstances or external pressures. We look here at how both the corporate environment and the conduct of management can sometimes act as deterrents to ethical behavior. (See the *Business Law in Action* above for a discussion of another potential deterrent.)

Ethics and the Corporate Environment

Some contend that the nature of the corporate structure itself acts as a deterrent to ethically responsible behavior. We examine the corporate structure in detail in Chapters 26 and 27. Briefly, a corporation is structured as follows: The owners of the corporation are the shareholders—those who purchase shares of stock in the company. The shareholders, however, do not run the corporation. Rather, they elect a board of directors and entrust those directors with the responsibility of directing and overseeing the corporate enterprise. The directors, in turn, hire officers and managers to handle the day-to-day business activities of the firm. A shareholder may also be a director, and a director may also be a corporate officer—the president or chief executive officer, for example.

ETHICS AND COLLECTIVE DECISION MAKING   The corporate setting complicates ethical decision making because (normally) no one person makes a corporate decision. If you are an officer or manager of a large corporation, for example, you may find that the decision as to what is right or wrong for the corporation is not yours to make. Corporate officers and managers, of course, do make decisions that affect the corporation, and your input may weigh in the decision. The ultimate decision makers, however, are the members of the board of directors, who must make decisions as a group.

Collective decision making, because it places emphasis on consensus and unity of opinion, also tends to hinder individual ethical assertiveness. For example, suppose that a director has ethical misgivings about a planned corporate venture that promises to be highly profitable. If the other directors have no such misgivings, the director who does may be swayed by the enthusiasm of the others for the project and downplay his or her own criticisms.

DIMINISHED PERSONAL ACCOUNTABILITY   To some extent, the corporate collectivity may shield corporate personnel from both personal exposure to the consequences of their decisions and personal accountability for those decisions. For example, suppose that a corporate board decides to market a new product that results in several consumers' deaths. Those who made the decision do not witness or deal directly with these consequences. Furthermore, just as normally no one individual is responsible for a corporate decision, so normally no one person is held accountable for the decision. (In recent years, however, the courts have been increasingly willing to look behind the "corporate veil" and hold individual corporate actors liable, or legally responsible, for actions resulting in harm to others—see Chapter 27.)

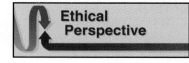
Ethical Perspective

In the corporate setting, complaints by product users about the corporation's products rarely affect corporate decision makers personally. Would the decision makers' view of their ethical responsibilities change significantly if they were personally involved? At least one person, John Swanson, would answer this question in the affirmative.

Swanson was a high-ranking corporate officer at Dow Corning Corporation, which had manufactured and marketed silicone breast implants since 1963. Swanson's wife was among the implant recipients. For years, the company had been receiving complaints about silicone leakage from the implants and consequent adverse health effects. Dow Corning took a defensive stance, maintaining that there was no convincing evidence that linked silicone to the complex of symptoms experienced by the recipients. Swanson supported Dow's position for years—until 1990, when he finally became convinced that his wife's deteriorating health condition was the result of the implants. Swanson urged the company to withdraw the implants from the market, but to no avail. The company continued to manufacture the implants until 1992. In the long run, Dow Corning was forced into bankruptcy due to litigation against the firm by implant recipients.

For Critical Analysis: *Is it likely that Swanson would have criticized Dow Corning's behavior if he had not been personally involved?*

Ethics and Management

Much unethical business behavior occurs simply because it is not always clear what ethical standards and behaviors are appropriate or acceptable in a given context. Although most firms now issue ethical policies or codes of conduct, these policies and codes are not always effective in creating an ethical workplace. At times, this is because a firm's ethical policies are not communicated clearly to employees or do not bear on the real ethical issues confronting decision makers. Additionally, particularly in a large corporation, unethical behavior in one corporate department may simply escape the attention of those in control of the corporation or the corporate officials responsible for implementing and monitoring the company's ethics program.

Another deterrent to ethical behavior exists when corporate management, by its own conduct, indicates that ethical considerations take second place. If management makes no attempt to deter unethical behavior—through reprimands or employment terminations, for example—it will be clear to employees that management is not all that serious about ethics. Likewise, if a company doles out promotions or salary increases to those who obviously engage in unethical tactics to increase the firm's profits, then employees who do not resort to such tactics will be at a disadvantage. An employee in this situation may decide that because "everyone else does it," he or she might as well do so also.

Of course, an even stronger deterrent to ethical behavior occurs when employers engage in blatantly unethical or illegal conduct and expect their employees to do so as well. An employee in this situation faces two options, neither of which is satisfactory: participate in the conduct or "blow the whistle" on (inform authorities of) the employer's actions—and, of course, risk being fired. (See Chapter 32 for a more detailed discussion of "whistleblowing.")

▌Corporate Social Responsibility

CORPORATE SOCIAL
RESPONSIBILITY
The concept that corporations
can and should act ethically
and be accountable to society for their
actions.

REMEMBER Changing ethical
notions about social responsibility
often motivate lawmakers to enact
or repeal laws.

We now return to the question posed in this chapter's introduction: How can businesspersons act in an ethically responsible manner and at the same time make profits for their firms or their firms' owners? This question is at the heart of the debate surrounding the concept of **corporate social responsibility**—the idea that corporations can and should act ethically and be accountable to society for their actions. No one contests the claim that corporations have duties to their shareholders, employers, and product users (consumers). Many of these duties are written into law—that is, they are *legal* duties. The question of corporate social responsibility concerns the extent to which a corporation has ethical duties to various groups in society that go beyond its legally prescribed duties.

To understand the debate over corporate social responsibility, consider a hypothetical firm: the Farthing Company. This firm markets its products, primarily paints and glues, throughout the world. The company is facing a financial crisis and must find a way to increase its profits if it is to survive. In so doing, however, Farthing will need to take into account the ethical ramifications of any decisions it makes. In the following pages, we examine some of the problematic aspects of a corporation's responsibilities in regard to shareholders, employees, consumers, the community, and society. As you will see, corporations like the Farthing Company face difficult conflicts in trying to be ethically responsible.

Duty to Shareholders

Corporate directors and officers have a duty to act in the shareholders' interest. Because of the nature of the relationship between corporate directors and officers and the shareholder-owners, the law holds directors and officers to a high standard of care in business decision making (see Chapter 27).

Traditionally, it was perceived that this duty to shareholders took precedence over all other corporate duties and that the primary goal of corporations should be profit maximization. Milton Friedman, the Nobel Prize–winning economist and a proponent of the profit-maximization view, saw "one and only one" social responsibility of a corporation: "to use its resources and engage in activities designed to increase its profits, so long as it stays within the rules of the game."[1] The "rules of the game" were the "basic rules of society, both those embodied in law and those embodied in ethical custom."[2]

Those who support the profit-maximization view of social responsibility contend that the duty to maximize profits must outweigh any other duty when duties conflict—to the extent, of course, that in maximizing shareholders' profits a firm does not violate the "basic rules of society." The question here is, What are these basic rules?

For example, suppose that our hypothetical firm, the Farthing Company, has suffered a setback because the U.S. government banned the sale of one of its paint thinners. The paint thinner, if allowed to touch the user's skin, can cause severe burns, and many consumers have complained of such injuries. The product is not banned in foreign markets, though, and thus Farthing faces an ethical question: Should it continue marketing the product in other countries? Certainly, it would benefit the shareholders to do so, but would such an action violate society's basic rules and ethical customs? Even if the action violated the ethical rules of even a small minority of Americans, that small minority, through activism and publicity, could harm Farthing's reputation as an ethically responsible corporation.

Duty to Employees

One of the primary concerns of every employer is the ability to control the workplace environment. After all, it is the employer who is responsible for making the business

---

1. *Capitalism and Freedom* (Chicago: University of Chicago Press, 1962), p. 133.
2. Milton Friedman, "Does Business Have Social Responsibility?" *Bank Administration*, April 1971, pp. 13–14.

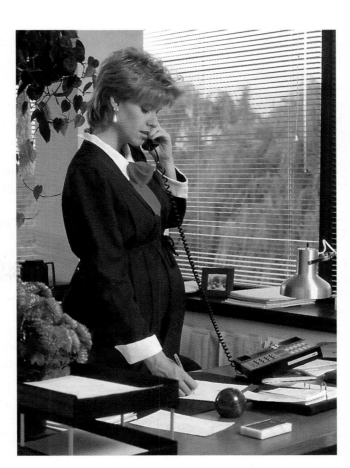

Under the law, pregnant employees must be treated the same as other employees, unless they differ in their ability to perform the duties of their jobs. It is illegal for an employer to discriminate on the basis of pregnancy. Is such discrimination also unethical?

firm a success, and success requires qualified, competent, loyal employees and efficient operations. Employees, however, also have concerns. They want to earn a fair wage; they want to work in an environment free of health-endangering hazards; they want to be treated fairly and equally by their employers; and increasingly in recent years, they want employers to respect their personal integrity and privacy rights.

By law, employers are required to provide a safe workplace, to pay a minimum wage, and to provide equal employment opportunities for all potential and existing employees. Does an employer also have ethical obligations to employees that go beyond these legal duties? Additionally, what if, in fulfillment of one ethical (or legal) obligation, another duty must be violated? We look here at some employment decisions facing employers in which various ethical or legal duties come into conflict. (See Chapters 32 and 33 for other ethical issues that arise in the employment context.)

EMPLOYMENT DISCRIMINATION   As will be discussed in Chapter 33, federal laws require employers to offer equal employment opportunities to all job applicants and employees. These laws prohibit employers from discriminating against existing or potential employees on the basis of race, color, national origin, gender, religion, age, or disability. Many states have similar laws protecting employees. Sometimes, though, employers who are trying to fulfill a perceived ethical obligation to treat employees fairly and equally find themselves in a no-win situation.

The following case illustrates such a situation. (See the *Law in the Extreme* on page 104 for another example.) Even though the employer went substantially beyond minimum legal compliance in attempting to provide a safe workplace for employees, the firm was nonetheless charged by some of its employees with having violated another ethical (and legal) duty—that of providing equal employment opportunities for women.

CASE 4.1

UNITED AUTOMOBILE WORKERS v. JOHNSON CONTROLS, INC.

Supreme Court of the United States, 1991.
499 U.S. 187,
111 S.Ct. 1196,
113 L.Ed.2d 158.

HISTORICAL AND SOCIAL SETTING   *With the Industrial Revolution of the nineteenth century came factories, assembly-line production, and a different way of life for workers. In those days, employees had few rights and often worked long hours in conditions that today would be inconceivable. There was no minimum wage, and the concept of overtime pay was not yet born. Over the course of the twentieth century, the government enacted numerous labor and employee laws to cure these problems. Today, employers who are insensitive to employee needs and working conditions may find themselves subject to lawsuits brought by the affected employees. In the interests of protecting female employees (and protecting their firms against potential liability), some firms have established fetal protection policies.*

FACTS   Johnson Controls, Inc., created its Battery Division in 1978. In 1982, as part of an ongoing attempt to reduce the health hazards that might result from lead exposure, Johnson adopted a "fetal protection policy," under which women of childbearing age were prohibited from working in the Battery Division. Johnson reached this decision after scientific studies indicated that a pregnant woman's exposure to high lead levels could harm the fetus. Employees and their union, United Automobile Workers, brought a suit in a federal court against Johnson, claiming that the fetal protection policy violated Title VII of the Civil Rights Act of 1964, which prohibits discrimination in employment on the basis of gender. The trial court held for Johnson, and the unions and employees appealed. The federal appellate court affirmed the trial court's ruling. The case was then appealed to the United States Supreme Court.

ISSUE   Did the fetal protection policy of Johnson Controls constitute illegal discrimination on the basis of gender?

DECISION   Yes. The Supreme Court reversed the judgment of the appellate court and remanded the case for further proceedings. The fetal protection policy was discriminatory in violation of Title VII of the Civil Rights Act of 1964 and the Pregnancy Discrimination Act of 1978.

Case 4.1—Continued

REASON The Court stated that employers may discriminate on the basis of "religion, sex, or national origin in those certain instances where religion, sex, or national origin is a bona fide occupational qualification [BFOQ]**a** reasonably necessary to the normal operation of that particular business or enterprise." Therefore, the key issue to be decided was whether the BFOQ defense applied in this case. The Court held that it did not. In the eyes of the Court, neither gender nor pregnancy impaired an employee's ability to perform the job. In forming its decision, the Court looked to the Pregnancy Discrimination Act, an amendment to Title VII, which

explicitly states that unless pregnant employees differ from others "in their ability or inability to work," they must be "treated the same" as other employees "for all employment-related purposes." The Court noted that "[f]ertile women, as far as [it] appears in the record, participate in the manufacture of batteries as efficiently as anyone else."

FOR CRITICAL ANALYSIS—Political Consideration
The Court deemed it inappropriate for either the courts or employers "to decide whether a woman's reproductive role is more important to herself and her family than her economic role." Congress, by passing the Pregnancy Discrimination Act, "left this choice to the woman as hers to make." Should Congress have been more concerned about the rights of the unborn?

a. See Chapter 33 for a discussion of this defense to employment discrimination.

SEXUAL HARASSMENT VERSUS WRONGFUL DISCHARGE   Another conflict of duties that sometimes faces employers poises the choice of being sued for sexual harassment against the choice of being sued for wrongful discharge. Lawsuits for *sexual harassment* in the workplace (discussed in Chapter 33) have climbed dramatically in number in the past decade. So have suits for *wrongful discharge*—firing an employee without good cause or for discriminatory reasons (see Chapters 32 and 33). Suppose that an employee of the Farthing Company complains to her supervisor that a co-worker is sexually harassing her—physically touching her in objectionable ways, making lewd comments about her and to her, and so on. The company immediately investigates the claim, and on finding that it is substantiated, promptly fires the harassing employee. The employee then sues the firm for wrongful discharge.

NOTE A business that examines its conduct, and the conduct of its managers and employees, can prevent unethical and illegal acts.

Can a court hold Farthing liable for wrongful discharge when, in firing the employee, the company was complying with a legal requirement? After all, federal law

One employee harasses another. If their employer discharges the harasser, could a court hold the employer liable for wrongful discharge?

LAW IN THE EXTREME

Poor Judgment or Disability?

Laws protecting employees from employment discrimination sometimes lead to bizarre results—at least, in the eyes of those who are untrained in the often arcane workings of legal reasoning. For example, suppose that an employer fired an employee who appeared at work one day toting a loaded gun. Now, a layperson might conclude that the employer's action made perfect sense. After all, loaded guns are dangerous, and the employer has an obligation to provide a safe workplace for his or her employees. A judge, in contrast, is obligated to apply the law, and the law is not always in the business of dispensing common sense.

Replace the word *employer* above with GTE Data Services, Inc., and the word *employee* with Joe Hindman,

and you have the basic factual background for a case brought before a federal district court in 1994.[a] The court had to decide whether GTE, by firing Hindman, had violated the Americans with Disabilities Act (ADA) of 1990, which prohibits discrimination against persons with disabilities. The ADA requires employers to accommodate otherwise qualified persons with disabilities so long as the accommodation does not create an "undue hardship" for the employer. Persons with mental or physical impairments are eligible for protection under the act.

Was Hindman covered by the act? GTE contended that he was not. GTE cited a previous case in which the plaintiff, like Hindman, had exhibited "poor judgment, irresponsible behavior and poor

a. *Hindman v. GTE Data Services, Inc.* (M.D.Fla. 1994) [1994 WL 371396]. This case is not published in West's *Federal Supplement* reporter but may be retrieved on WESTLAW by using the WL citation given here.

impulse control." In that case, the court held that the plaintiff's personality traits were commonplace and "in no way rise to the level of an impairment." The court in the GTE case pointed out, however, that the plaintiff in the previous case, unlike Hindman, did not exhibit such behavior *as a result of* a mental impairment. Hindman claimed that he showed poor judgment and brought a gun to work as a result of his chemical imbalance. The court held that because of Hindman's mental impairment, he fell under the ADA, and GTE should not have fired him; rather, it should have accommodated Hindman's request— to take a leave of absence until he recovered from his problems.

For Critical Analysis: *What if the court had agreed with GTE that the behavior, not the underlying cause of the behavior, should determine whether an employee is covered by the ADA? What would be the implications of such a conclusion?*

and the Equal Employment Opportunity Commission's guidelines require employers to take "immediate and appropriate corrective action" in response to an employee's complaint of sexual abuse. The answer to this question is that under some state laws and employment agreements, employers are prohibited from firing employees without a "just cause," and particular incidents of sexual harassment may or may not constitute just cause for firing the harasser.[3]

CORPORATE RESTRUCTURING AND EMPLOYEE WELFARE   Suppose that our hypothetical firm, the Farthing Company, decided to reduce its costs by downsizing and restructuring its operations. Among other things, this would allow Farthing to cut back on its overhead by consolidating various supervisory and managerial positions. The question for Farthing is, Which employees should be retained and which should be let go? Should the firm retain its highly paid employees who have worked for—and received annual raises from—the firm for years? Alternatively, in the interests of cutting costs, should it retain (or hire) younger, less experienced persons at lower salaries?

The firm would not necessarily be acting illegally if it pursued the second option. Unless a fired employee can prove that the employer has breached an employment contract or violated the Age Discrimination in Employment Act (ADEA) of 1967, he or she will not have a cause of action against the employer. The ADEA prohibits discrimination against workers forty years old and older on the basis

---

3.   See, for example, *Chrysler Motors Corp. v. International Union, Allied Industrial Workers of America,* 959 F.2d 685 (7th Cir. 1992).

of their age, but Farthing can always say that lack of performance or ability, not age, was the deciding factor. The question here is, Would such an action be ethical?

In deciding this issue, remember that Farthing must keep its eye on its profit margin. If it does not, the firm may fail, and the shareholders will lose their investments. Furthermore, why should the firm retain highly paid employees if it can obtain essentially the same work output for a lower price by retaining its less highly paid employees? Does Farthing owe an ethical duty to its employees who have served the firm loyally over a long period of time? Most people would say yes. Should this duty take precedence over Farthing's duty to the firm's owners to maintain or increase the profitability of the firm? Would your answer be the same if the firm faced imminent bankruptcy if it could not lower its operational costs? What if long-time employees were willing to take a slight reduction in pay to help the firm through its financial difficulties? What if they were not?

In the following case, an employer was confronted with a dwindling market and decreasing sales. The employer decided to reduce its costs of doing business by eliminating some of its obligations to its employees.

CASE 4.2

VARITY CORP. v. HOWE
Supreme Court of the United States, 1996.
___ U.S. ___,
116 S.Ct. 1065,
134 L.Ed.2d 130.

HISTORICAL AND ECONOMIC SETTING *Since 1950, the number of U.S. farms has declined as small farms have been driven out of business by huge corporate agribusinesses with assets that small farmers cannot match. Between 1980 and 1996, the number of farms decreased by over 14 percent, to less than 2 million, even as the average acreage per farm increased by 10 percent, to nearly 470 acres. Agribusinesses require fewer workers than do small farms, and thus, the total farm population also decreased by 24 percent in the 1980s. Fewer farmers means a smaller market for those who cater to it.*

FACTS Varity Corporation manufactures and sells farm implements. In 1986, Varity set up a subsidiary, Massey Combines Corporation (MCC), to market its self-propelled combines and four-wheel-drive tractors. The sales of both products were at an all-time low. Varity convinced current and former employees who were, or had been, involved with the products to accept a transfer to MCC of their jobs and retirement benefit plans. Varity did not tell those employees that it expected MCC to fail. Within two years, MCC failed. Among other consequences, some retirees stopped receiving benefits. The retirees and other ex-employees sued Varity in a

federal district court under the Employee Retirement Income Security Act of 1974 (ERISA).[a] They claimed that Varity owed them a fiduciary duty, which it had breached.[b] The court ruled in their favor, and the U.S. Court of Appeals for the Eighth Circuit affirmed the decision. Varity then appealed to the United States Supreme Court.

ISSUE Did Varity owe a fiduciary duty to its employees with respect to their retirement benefits? If so, did it violate that duty?

DECISION Yes, to both questions. The United States Supreme Court affirmed the decision of the lower court.

REASON The Supreme Court pointed out that under ERISA, a fiduciary is required to "discharge his [or her] duties with respect to a [retirement] plan solely in the interest of the participants and beneficiaries." It was on this statute that the Varity retirees based their suit. "To participate knowingly and significantly in deceiving a plan's beneficiaries in order to save the employer money at the beneficiaries' expense, is not to act 'solely in the interest of the participants and beneficiaries.'" The Court stated that "[l]ying is inconsistent with the duty of loyalty owed by all fiduciaries."

FOR CRITICAL ANALYSIS—Ethical Consideration
Should a company continue to market a slow-selling line of products for the sole purpose of employing those who work on the products?

a. 29 U.S.C. Sections 1001–1461. See Chapter 32.
b. A *fiduciary* is a party who, because of something that he or she has undertaken to do, has a duty to act primarily for another's benefit.

Duty to Consumers

Clearly, a corporation has a duty to the users of its products. This is not just an ethical duty but a legal one as well—as you will read in later chapters of this book. The issue, with respect to corporate social responsibility, is the extent to which a corporation has an ethical duty *beyond* those duties mandated by law or when the corporation is uncertain that a legal duty exists. Often, the issue turns on how a firm (or the public or a court) answers the following question: At what point does corporate responsibility for the safety of consumers end and consumer responsibility begin?

PRODUCT MISUSE   Suppose that the Farthing Company learns that one of its products—glue—was being inhaled by thousands of children in several Latin American countries. The health consequences of this misuse can include future kidney disease and brain damage. Consumer activists have launched a media campaign against Farthing, accusing it of being unethical by marketing its glue in those countries when such harms result. What is Farthing's responsibility in this situation? On the one hand, (1) it is not the company's fault that its product is being misused, (2) it has violated no legal duty, and (3) to cease selling the product in those areas would significantly cut into its profits. On the other hand, (1) suspending sales would reduce the suffering of children, and (2) if Farthing ignores the public outcry, the continued adverse publicity could also cause the firm to lose sales—and thus profits. Farthing's solution will rest on the "ethical weight" it attaches to each of these factors.[4]

"A man cannot shift his misfortunes to his neighbor's shoulders."

Oliver Wendell Holmes, Jr., 1841–1935
(**Associate justice of the United States Supreme Court, 1902–1932**)

WHEN IS A RISK "OPEN AND OBVIOUS"?   Whenever a corporation markets a product, the law imposes a duty on the firm to warn consumers, among other things, of the harms that can result from *foreseeable* misuses. When a risk is open and obvious, however, courts tend to hold that no warning is necessary. Sharp knives, for example, can obviously injure their users. Sometimes, a business firm has no way of predicting how a court might rule in deciding whether a particular risk is open and obvious or whether consumers should be warned of the risk. Courts normally decide the issue on a case-by-case basis, and courts often disagree on whether certain types of risks are open and obvious. The following case involves an allegation that an automobile manufacturer failed to warn consumers that seat belts would not necessarily protect them from injuries in head-on collisions.

---

4.   When the H. B. Fuller Company faced this situation a few years ago, its solution was to suspend sales of its glues in some Latin American countries but not others. Fuller's critics contended that it should have suspended sales in all of the Latin American countries in which the product was being misused.

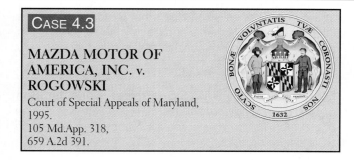

CASE 4.3

MAZDA MOTOR OF AMERICA, INC. v. ROGOWSKI

Court of Special Appeals of Maryland, 1995.
105 Md.App. 318,
659 A.2d 391.

HISTORICAL AND SOCIAL SETTING   *The first motor vehicle death in the United States was reported in New York City on September 14, 1899. Since then, nearly*

3,000,000 people have died in motor vehicle accidents, and many more have been seriously injured. The number of deaths and injuries per 100,000 vehicles has decreased considerably, however—from more than 300 in 1912, for example, to less than 50 today. Much of the decrease can be attributed to such safety measures as seat belts.

FACTS   Francis Rogowski fell asleep at the wheel of his Mazda pickup truck and collided head-on with a large tree. To recover for the cost of his injuries, Rogowski sued Mazda Motor of America, Inc., and others in a Maryland state court. Rogowski claimed, among other things, that Mazda should have warned him the seat belts would not protect him from all injuries if he were in

Case 4.3—Continued

an accident. The court agreed that Mazda was liable for failure to warn and awarded damages of $601,644 to Rogowski. Mazda appealed.

ISSUE   Does an automobile manufacturer have a duty to warn the purchasers of its cars that seat belts cannot protect them from all injuries?

DECISION   No. The Court of Special Appeals of Maryland held that the danger not warned about was clear and obvious, and it reversed and remanded the case to the lower court.

REASON   The court reasoned that "there simply is no necessity to explain that which is obvious—that seat belts do not and cannot protect the occupants of the vehicle from injury no matter how severe the accident." The court also explained that "the giving of unnecessary warnings should be avoided because the presence of superfluous warnings seriously detracts from the efficacy [effectiveness] of warnings that are needed." The court believed that consumers, "[b]ombarded with nearly useless warnings about risks that rarely materialize[,]" might "give up on warnings altogether. And the few persons who might continue to take warnings seriously   *   *   * would probably overreact, investing too heavily in their versions of 'safety.' Given these limits *   *   * , the optimal, rather than the highest, levels of risk information, measured both qualitatively and quantitatively, are what is called for."

FOR CRITICAL ANALYSIS—Social Consideration   *If the notice Rogowski claimed should have been required in his case was required for every automobile manufacturer, presumably every motor vehicle owner's manual would say the same thing. What impact would this have on such a notice?*

Duty to the Community

In some circumstances, the community in which a business enterprise is located has a substantial stake in the firm. Assume, for example, that the Farthing Company employs two thousand workers at one of its plants. If the company decides that it would be profitable to close the plant or move it to another location, the employees—and the community—would suffer as a result. Today, to be considered socially responsible, a corporation must take both employees' needs and community needs into consideration when making such a decision.

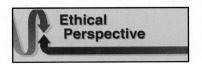

What if a business firm moves into a community? Does it have an obligation to evaluate first the effect its presence there will have on that community? This question has surfaced recently in regard to Wal-Mart's expansion into smaller communities. Generally, most people in such communities welcome the lower prices and wider array of goods that Wal-Mart offers relative to other, smaller stores in the area. A vocal minority of people in some communities, however, claim that smaller stores often find it impossible to compete with Wal-Mart's prices and thus are forced to go out of business. Many of these smaller stores have existed for years and, according to Wal-Mart's critics, enhance the quality of community life. These critics claim that it is unethical of Wal-Mart to disregard a town's interest in the quality and character of its community life.

Recently, beginning in Oklahoma, Wal-Mart has begun to consolidate some of its smaller stores into large "superstores." In the process of this consolidation, Wal-Mart is closing stores in some of the very towns in which it drove its smaller competitors out of business. This development raises yet another ethical question: Does Wal-Mart have an obligation to continue operations in a community once it has driven its competitors out of business?

For Critical Analysis: *Is it fair to blame Wal-Mart for what essentially amounts to its efficiency in supplying consumers with lower-priced products? Does Wal-Mart have an ethical obligation not to drive smaller firms out of business?*

Duty to Society

Perhaps the most disputed area in the controversy surrounding corporate social responsibility is the nature of a corporation's duty to society at large. Generally, the question turns less on whether corporations owe a duty to society than on how that duty can best be fulfilled.

PROFIT MAXIMIZATION   Those who contend that corporations should first and foremost attend to the goal of profit maximization would argue that it is by generating profits that a firm can best contribute to society. Society benefits by profit-making activities, because profits can only be realized when a firm markets products or services that are desired by society. These products and services enhance the standard of living, and the profits accumulated by successful business firms generate national wealth. Our laws and court decisions promoting trade and commerce reflect the public policy that the fruits of commerce (income wealth) are desirable and good. Because our society values income wealth as an ethical goal, corporations, by contributing to income wealth, automatically are acting ethically.

Furthermore, profit maximization results in the efficient allocation of resources. Capital, labor, raw materials, and other resources are directed to the production of those goods and services most desired by society. If capital were directed toward a social goal instead of being reinvested in the corporation, the business operation would become less efficient. For example, if an automobile company contributes $1 million annually to the United Way, that contribution represents $1 million that is not reinvested in making better and safer cars.

Those arguing for profit maximization as a corporate goal also point out that it would be inappropriate to use the power of the corporate business world to fashion society's goals by promoting social causes. Determinations as to what exactly is in society's best interest are essentially political questions, and therefore the public, through the political process, should have a say in making those determinations. The legislature—not the corporate boardroom—is thus the appropriate forum for such decisions.

CRITICS OF PROFIT MAXIMIZATION   Critics of the profit-maximization view believe that corporations should become actively engaged in seeking and furthering solutions to social problems. Because so much of the wealth and power of this country is controlled by business, business in turn has a responsibility to society to use that wealth and power in socially beneficial ways. Corporations should therefore promote human rights, strive for equal treatment of minorities and women in the workplace, take care to preserve the environment, and generally not profit from activities that society has deemed unethical. The critics also point out that it is ethically irresponsible to leave decisions concerning social welfare up to the government, because many social needs are not being met sufficiently through the political process.

▌ The Corporate Balancing Act

Today's corporate decision makers are, in a sense, poised on a fulcrum between profitability and ethical responsibility. If they emphasize profits at the expense of perceived ethical responsibilities, they may become the target of negative media exposure, consumer boycotts, and perhaps lawsuits. If they invest too heavily in good works or social causes, however, their profits may suffer. Striking the right balance on this fulcrum is not always easy, and usually some profits must be sacrificed in the process. Instead of *maximum profits*, many firms today aim for *optimum profits*—profits that can be realized while staying within legal and ethical limits. Notice how PriceCostco's Code of Ethics (see the fold-out exhibit in this chapter) stresses both legal *and* ethical duties.

▌Measuring Corporate Social Responsibility

Measuring corporate social responsibility is difficult because depending on whose yardstick one uses, the answer differs. Traditionally, corporate philanthropy has been used to measure social responsibility. Today, many feel that being ethically responsible involves much more than simply donating funds to charitable causes.

Corporate Philanthropy

Since the nineteenth century and the emergence of giant, wealthy business enterprises in America, corporations have generally contributed some of their shareholders' wealth to meet social needs. Frequently, corporations establish separate nonprofit foundations for this purpose. For example, Honda, Inc., created the American Honda Education Corporation, through which it donated $40 million over a ten-year period to launch and support the Eagle Rock School in Estes Park, Colorado. This school and educator training center gives preference to students who have not been able to succeed in the more rigid, highly structured public school systems. Today, virtually all major corporations routinely donate to hospitals, medical research, the arts, universities, and programs that benefit society.

A related yardstick for measuring corporate social responsibility is the specific causes to which a corporation contributes. One indication of this measure was evident in a worldwide poll conducted a few years ago. Pollsters found that two-thirds of the respondents would switch brands to a manufacturer that supported a social cause that they liked.[5]

"The highest morality almost always is the morality of process."

Alexander M. Bickel, 1924–1974 *(Rumanian-American legal scholar)*

Corporate Process

Increasingly, corporations are being judged less on the basis of their philanthropic activities than on their practices, or corporate process. Corporate process, in this sense,

---

5.   Justin Martin, "Good Citizenship Is Good Business," *Fortune*, March 21, 1992, pp. 15–16.

Ben and Jerry, of Ben and Jerry's Ice Cream, at the One World, One Heart Festival in New York City. According to Ben, "Business has a responsibility to give back to the community." Does giving back to the community conflict with other corporate purposes? If so, can a balance be struck? How?

refers to how a corporation conducts its affairs at all levels of operation. Does it establish and effectively implement ethical policies and take those policies seriously? Does it deal ethically with its shareholders? Does it consider the needs of its employees—for day-care facilities or flexible working hours, for example? Does it promote equal opportunity in the workplace for women, minority groups, and persons with disabilities? Do the corporation's suppliers, particularly those from developing countries, protect the human rights of their employees (provide for safety in the workplace or pay a decent wage, for example)? Does the corporation investigate complaints about its products promptly and, if necessary, take action to improve them?

For many, the answers to these and similar questions are the key factors in determining whether a corporation is socially responsible. From this perspective, no matter how much a corporation may contribute to worthy causes, it will not be socially responsible if it fails to observe ethical standards in its day-to-day activities.

It Pays to Be Ethical

Most corporations today have learned that it pays to be ethically responsible—even if it means less profits in the short run (and it often does). Today's corporations are subject to more intensive scrutiny—both by government agencies and the public—than they ever were in the past. If a corporation fails to conduct its operations ethically or respond quickly to an ethical crisis, its goodwill and reputation (and thus future profits) will likely suffer as a result.

There are other reasons as well for a corporation to behave ethically. As indicated in this chapter's *Business Law in Action*, companies that demonstrate a commitment to ethical behavior—by implementing ethical programs, complying with environmental regulations, and promptly investigating product complaints, for example— often receive more lenient treatment from government agencies or the courts. Furthermore, by keeping their own houses in order, corporations may be able to avoid the necessity for the government to do so—through new laws or regulations.

Additionally, investors may shy away from a corporation's stock if the corporation is perceived to be socially irresponsible. Since the 1970s, certain investment funds have guaranteed to the purchasers of their shares that they will only invest in companies that are ethical. They did not invest in the Dow Chemical Company, for example, because it produced napalm that was used in the Vietnam War (1964–1975). They did not invest in corporations that had any dealings with South Africa because at that time, South Africa practiced *apartheid*, or complete separation of the races. Today, ethical funds base their investments on various ethical criteria. For example, some funds invest money only in corporations that are "environmentally kind."

▍Ethics in the Global Context

Given the varied cultures and religions of the world's nations, one might expect frequent conflicts in ethics between foreign and U.S. businesspersons. In fact, many of the most important ethical precepts are common to virtually all countries. Some important ethical differences do exist, however. In Islamic (Muslim) countries, for example, the consumption of alcohol and certain foods is forbidden by the Koran (the sayings of the prophet Mohammed, which lie at the heart of Islam and Islamic law). It would be thoughtless and imprudent to invite a Saudi Arabian business contact out for a drink.

The role played by women in other countries also may present some difficult ethical problems for firms doing business internationally. Equal employment opportunity is a fundamental public policy in the United States, and Title VII of the Civil Rights Act of 1964 prohibits discrimination against women in the employment context (see Chapter 33). Some other countries, however, largely reject any role for

Engaging in an international business deal can require different cultural courtesies, as shown here. How might cultural differences cause ethical conflicts between U.S. and foreign businesspersons?

women professionals, which may cause difficulties for American women conducting business transactions in those countries.

Another ethical problem in international business dealings has to do with the legitimacy of certain side payments to government officials. In the United States, the majority of contracts are formed within the private sector. In many foreign countries, however, decisions on most major construction and manufacturing contracts are made by government officials because of extensive government regulation and control over trade and industry. Side payments to government officials in exchange for favorable business contracts are not unusual in such countries, nor are they considered to be unethical. In the past, U.S. corporations doing business in developing countries largely followed the dictum, "When in Rome, do as the Romans do."

In the 1970s, however, the U.S. press, and government officials as well, uncovered a number of business scandals involving large side payments by American corporations—such as Lockheed Aircraft—to foreign representatives for the purpose of securing advantageous international trade contracts. In response to this unethical behavior, Congress passed the Foreign Corrupt Practices Act (FCPA) in 1977, which prohibits American businesspersons from bribing foreign officials to secure advantageous contracts. The act, which is the subject of the *Landmark in the Law* that follows, has made it difficult for American companies to compete as effectively as they otherwise might in the global marketplace.

The Foreign Corrupt Practices Act of 1977

LANDMARK IN THE LAW

The Foreign Corrupt Practices Act (FCPA) of 1977 is divided into two major parts. The first part applies to all U.S. companies and their directors, officers, shareholders, employees, and agents. This part of the FCPA prohibits the bribery of most officials of foreign governments if the purpose of the payment is to get the official to act in his or her official capacity to provide business opportunities.

(Continued)

Landmark in the Law—Continued

The FCPA does not prohibit payment of substantial sums to minor officials whose duties are ministerial. These payments are often referred to as "grease," or facilitating payments. They are meant to ensure that administrative services that might otherwise be performed at a slow pace are sped up. Thus, for example, if a firm makes a payment to a minor official to speed up an import licensing process, the firm has not violated the FCPA. Generally, the act, as amended, permits payments to foreign officials if such payments are lawful within the foreign country. The act also does not prohibit payments to private foreign companies or other third parties unless the American firm knows that the payments will be passed on to a foreign government in violation of the FCPA.

The second part of the FCPA is directed toward accountants, because in the past bribes were often concealed in corporate financial records. All companies must keep detailed records that "accurately and fairly" reflect the company's financial activities. In addition, all companies must have an accounting system that provides "reasonable assurance" that all transactions entered into by the company are accounted for and legal. These requirements assist in detecting illegal bribes. The FCPA further prohibits any person from making false statements to accountants or false entries in any record or account.

In 1988, the FCPA was amended to provide that business firms that violated the act may be fined up to $2 million. Individual officers or directors who violate the FCPA may be fined up to $100,000 (the fine cannot be paid by the company) and may be imprisoned for up to five years.

For Critical Analysis: *The FCPA did not change international trade practices in other countries, but it effectively tied the hands of American firms trying to secure foreign contracts. In passing the FCPA, did Congress give too much weight to ethics and too little weight to international economic realities?*

▌ The Ever-Changing Ethical Landscape

"The law is not the same morning and night."

George Herbert, 1593–1633
(English poet and clergyman)

Our sense of what is ethical—what is fair or just or right in a given situation—changes over time. Conduct that might have been considered ethical ten years ago might be considered unethical today. Indeed, most of the ethical and social issues discussed in this chapter and elsewhere in this text either did not exist or were of little public concern at the turn of the twentieth century and, in some cases, even as recently as a decade ago. Technological innovations, the communications revolution, pressing environmental problems, and social movements resulting in greater rights for minorities, women, and consumers have all dramatically changed the society in which we live and, consequently, the business and ethical landscape of America.

This changing ethical landscape is perhaps nowhere more evident than in the evolution of the concept of corporate social responsibility. Today's business manager must not only keep an eye on his or her firm's profit margins but also keep an "ear to the ground" to detect changing social perceptions of what constitutes ethical and socially responsible corporate behavior.

Application

Law and the Manager— How to Create an Ethical Workplace

 The most important factor in creating and maintaining an ethical workplace is the attitude of top management. If you are a manager, rest assured that unless you are totally committed to this goal, you will not succeed in achieving it. In addition to your conduct, two other factors help to create an ethical workplace environment: a written code of ethics, or policy statement, and the effective communication of the firm's ethical policies to employees.

The Role of Management

Surveys of business executives indicate that management's behavior, more than anything else, sets the ethical tone of a firm. If an employee persists in unethical behavior, you should consider discharging the employee as a clear example to other employees that you will not tolerate unethical behavior. Although this may seem harsh, business managers have found that discharging even one employee for ethical reasons has had a tremendous impact as a deterrent to unethical behavior in the workplace. Additionally, you should ensure that your firm's production or marketing goals are realistic. If a sales quota, for example, can only be met through high-pressure, unethical sales tactics, employees trying to act "in the interest of the firm" may think that management is implicitly asking them to behave unethically.

Create a Written Ethical Code

A written ethics code or policy statement helps to make clear to employees how they are expected to relate to their supervisors or managers, to consumers, to suppliers, and to other employees. Above all, it is important to state explicitly what your firm's ethical priorities are. For example, in 1982 Johnson & Johnson (J&J) was confronted with the Tylenol crisis (Tylenol "spiked" with cyanide had caused the deaths of several persons in Chicago). Top management at J&J was able to act swiftly and ethically, because the company had made its goals clear in its ethical code. Its first priority was the welfare of those who used its product; hence the firm decided to withdraw thirty-one million bottles of Tylenol from the market, at a cost of about $100 million.

Communicate Ethical Standards to Employees

For an ethical code to be effective, its provisions must be clearly communicated to employees. A good way to do this is by implementing an ethics training program, in which management discusses with employees—face to face—the firm's policies and the importance of ethical conduct. Some firms hold periodic ethics seminars to allow employees to discuss openly any ethical problems that they may be experiencing and how the firm's ethical policies apply to those specific problems. Generally, the smaller the group, the more effective these discussions are. It is important that employees know that the ethical program is a "two-way street." That is, management must make it clear that feedback from employees and their ethical concerns are a top priority.

Another effective technique is to evaluate periodically the ethical performance of each individual employee. One company, for example, hands out to its employees each week an ethical checklist to fill out and return to their supervisors. This practice serves two purposes: first, employees realize that ethics matters; and second, employees are given an opportunity to reflect on how well they have measured up in terms of ethical performance.

✓ Checklist for Creating an Ethical Workplace

1. Make sure that management is committed to ethical behavior and sets an ethical example.
2. Create, print, and distribute an ethical code clearly stating your firm's ethical goals and priorities, as well as what behavior is expected of employees in their areas of responsibility.
3. Implement an ethics training program to communicate your firm's ethical policies to employees.
4. Hold seminars or small group meetings in which ethical policies and performance can be discussed on an ongoing basis.
5. Devise a method, such as an ethical checklist, for evaluating the ethical performance of each individual employee.

▌ Key Terms

business ethics 94
categorical imperative 96

corporate social responsibility 100
cost-benefit analysis 97

ethics 94
utilitarianism 96

▌ Chapter Summary: Ethics and Social Responsibility

The Nature of Business Ethics *(See pages 94–95.)*	Ethics can be defined as the study of what constitutes right or wrong behavior. Business ethics focuses on how moral and ethical principles are applied in the business context. The law reflects society's convictions on what constitutes right or wrong behavior. The law has its limits, though, and some actions may be legal yet not be ethical.
Sources of Ethical Standards *(See pages 95–97.)*	1. *Duty-based ethics*—Ethics based on religious beliefs and philosophical reasoning, such as that of Immanuel Kant. 2. *Outcome-based ethics (utilitarianism)*—Ethics based on philosophical reasoning, such as that of John Stuart Mill.

Obstacles to Ethical Business Behavior *(See pages 97–100.)*	1. *The corporate structure*—
	  a. Collective decision making tends to deter individual ethical assertiveness.
	  b. The corporate structure tends to shield corporate actors from personal responsibility and accountability.
	2. *Management*—
	  a. Uncertainty on the part of employees as to what kind of behavior is expected of them makes it difficult for them to behave ethically.
	  b. Unethical conduct by management shows employees that ethical behavior is not a priority.

Corporate Social Responsibility *(See pages 100–108.)*	Corporate social responsibility rests on the assumption that corporations should conduct their affairs in a socially responsible manner, but there is disagreement as to what constitutes socially responsible behavior. Corporations are perceived to hold duties to the following groups—duties that often come into conflict: 1. *Duty to shareholders*—Because the shareholders are the owners of the corporation, directors and officers have a duty to act in the shareholders' interest (maximize profits). 2. *Duty to employees*—Employers have numerous legal duties to employees, including providing employees with a safe workplace and refraining from discriminating against employees on the basis of race, color, national origin, gender, religion, age, or disability. These duties sometimes come into conflict. Many believe that employers hold ethical duties to their employees that go beyond those prescribed by law. 3. *Duty to consumers*—Corporate directors and officers have a legal duty to the users of their products. Most people feel that corporations also have an ethical duty that goes beyond what the law requires. Controversy exists over the point at which corporate responsibility for consumer safety ends and consumer responsibility begins. 4. *Duty to the community*—Most people hold that a corporation has a duty to the community in which it operates. The corporation should consider the needs of the community when making decisions that substantially affect the welfare of the community. 5. *Duty to society*—Most people hold that a corporation has a duty to society in general, but they differ in their ideas on how corporations can best fulfill this duty. One view is that corporations serve society's needs most effectively by maximizing profits because profits generally increase national wealth and social welfare. Another view holds that corporations, because they control so much of the country's wealth and power, should use their own wealth and power in socially beneficial ways and not engage in actions that society deems unethical.
The Corporate Balancing Act *(See page 108.)*	Today's corporate decision makers must balance profitability against ethical responsibility when making their decisions. Instead of maximum profits, corporations increasingly aim for optimum profits—the maximum profits that can be realized by the firm while pursuing actions that are not only legal and profitable but also ethical.

∎ Chapter Summary: Ethics and Social Responsibility—Continued

Measuring Corporate Social Responsibility (*See pages 109–110.*)	It is difficult to measure corporate social responsibility because different yardsticks are used. Traditionally, corporate philanthropy has been used as a means of measuring corporate social responsibility. Increasingly, corporate process—how a corporation conducts its business on a day-to-day basis—is a key factor in determining whether a corporation is socially responsible.
Ethics in the Global Context (*See pages 110–112.*)	Despite the cultural and religious differences among nations, the most important ethical precepts are common to virtually all countries. Two notable differences relate to the role of women in society and the practice of giving side payments to foreign officials to secure favorable contracts. The Foreign Corrupt Practices Act (FCPA) of 1977, which prohibits the bribery of foreign officials through such side payments, put U.S. businesspersons at a relative disadvantage to businesspersons from other countries who are not subject to such laws.
The Ever-Changing Ethical Landscape (*See page 112.*)	What is considered ethical in a society may change over time as social customs change and new developments alter our social and business environment.

∎ For Review

1. What is ethics? What is business ethics? What are some sources of ethical standards?
2. What are some of the obstacles to ethical business behavior?
3. To what groups does a corporation owe duties? Why do these duties sometimes come into conflict?

4. What is the difference between maximum profits and optimum profits?
5. What are some of the yardsticks by which corporate social responsibility is measured?

∎ Questions and Case Problems

4–1. Business Ethics. Some business ethicists maintain that whereas personal ethics has to do with right or wrong behavior, business ethics is concerned with appropriate behavior. In other words, ethical behavior in business has less to do with moral principles than with what society deems to be appropriate behavior in the business context. Do you agree with this distinction? Do personal and business ethics ever overlap? Should personal ethics play any role in business ethical decision making?

4–2. Corporate Social Responsibility. Assume that you are a high-level manager for a shoe manufacturer. You know that your firm could increase its profit margin by producing shoes in Indonesia, where you could hire women for $40 a month to assemble them. You also know, however, that a competing shoe manufacturer recently was accused, by human rights advocates, of engaging in exploitative labor practices because the manufacturer sold shoes made by Indonesian women for similarly low wages. You personally do not believe that paying $40 a month to Indonesian women is unethical, because you know that in that impoverished country, $40 a month is a better-than-average wage rate. Assuming that the decision is yours to make, should you have the shoes manufactured in Indonesia and make higher profits for your company? Should you instead avoid the risk of negative publicity and the consequences of that publicity for the firm's reputation and subsequent profits? Are there other alternatives? Discuss fully.

4–3. Corporate Social Responsibility. Do you agree with Milton Friedman's conclusion that there is "one and only one responsibility of business"—to increase its profits? If so, what arguments would you use in defending this statement? If not, what arguments would you raise against it?

4–4. Duty to Consumers. Two eight-year-old boys, Douglas Bratz and Bradley Baughn, were injured while riding a mini–trail bike manufactured by Honda Motor Co. Bratz, who was driving the bike while Baughn rode as a passenger behind him, ran three stop signs and then collided with a truck. Bratz did not see the truck because, at the time of the accident, he was looking behind him at a girl chasing them on another mini–trail bike. Bratz wore a helmet, but it flew off on impact because it was unfastened. Baughn was not wearing a helmet. The owner's manual for the mini–trail bike stated in bold print that the bike was intended for off-the-road use only and urged users to "Always Wear a Helmet." A prominent label on the bike itself also warned that the bike was for off-the-road use only and that it should not be used on public streets or highways. In addition, Bratz's father had repeatedly told the boy not to ride the bike in the street. The parents of the injured boys sued Honda, alleging that the mini–trail bike was unreasonably dangerous. Honda claimed it had sufficiently warned consumers of potential dangers that could result if the bike was not used as directed. Should Honda be held responsible for the boys' injuries? Why or why not? [*Baughn v. Honda Motor Co.*, 107 Wash.2d 127, 727 P.2d 655 (1986)]

4–5. Duty to Employees. In 1984, General Telephone Co. of Illinois, Inc. (GTE), for reasons of efficiency, decided to consolidate its nationwide operations and eliminate unnecessary job positions. One of the positions eliminated was held by John Burnell, a fifty-two-year-old employee who had worked for GTE for thirty-four years and had always received "above average" performance ratings. GTE offered Burnell the choice of either accepting another position within the firm at the same salary or accepting early retirement with a salary continuation for a certain period of time. Burnell did not want to retire, but he was afraid that if he did accept the other position and if the other position was later eliminated, he might not then have the choice of early retirement with the same separation benefit. Because he received no assurances that the other job would be secure in the future, he accepted the early-retirement alternative. Burnell later alleged that he had been "constructively discharged"—that is, that GTE had made his working conditions so intolerable that he was forced to resign. Had GTE constructively discharged Burnell? Can GTE's actions toward Burnell be justified from an ethical standpoint? Discuss. [*Burnell v. General Telephone Co. of Illinois, Inc.*, 181 Ill.App.3d 533, 536 N.E.2d 1387, 130 Ill.Dec. 176 (1989)]

4–6. Duty to Consumers. Beverly Landrine's infant daughter died after the baby swallowed a balloon while playing with a doll known as "Bubble Yum Baby." When a balloon was inserted into the doll's mouth and the doll's arm was pumped, thereby inflating the balloon, the doll simulated the blowing of a bubble gum bubble. The balloon was made by Perfect Product Co. and distributed by Mego Corp. Landrine brought a suit against the manufacturer and distributor, alleging that the balloon was defectively made or inherently unsafe when used by children and that Perfect had failed to warn of the danger associated with the balloon's use. Discuss whether the producer and distributor of the balloon should be held liable for the harm caused by its product. [*Landrine v. Mego Corp.*, 95 A.D.2d 759, 464 N.Y.S.2d 516 (1983)]

4–7. Duty to Consumers. The Seven-Up Co., as part of a marketing scheme, placed two glass bottles of "Like" cola on the front entrance of the Gruenemeier residence. Russell Gruenemeier, a nine-year-old boy, began playing while holding one of the bottles. He tripped and fell, and the bottle broke, severely cutting his right eye and causing him to eventually lose his eyesight in the eye. Russell's mother brought an action against the Seven-Up Co. for damages, claiming that the cause of Russell's injury was Seven-Up's negligence. She claimed that the company was negligent because it placed potentially dangerous instrumentalities—glass bottles—within the reach of small children and that the firm should have used unbreakable bottles for its marketing scheme. Are glass bottles so potentially dangerous that the Seven-Up Co. should be held liable for the boy's harm? If you were the judge, how would you decide the issue? [*Gruenemeier v. Seven-Up Co.*, 229 Neb. 267, 426 N.W.2d 510 (1988)]

4–8. Duty to Consumers. The father of an eleven-year-old child sued the manufacturer of a jungle gym because the manufacturer had failed to warn users of the equipment that they might fall off the gym and get hurt, as the boy did in this case. The father also claimed that the jungle gym was unreasonably dangerous because, as his son began to fall and reached frantically for a bar to grasp, there was no bar within reach. The father based his argument in part on a previous case involving a plaintiff who was injured as a result of somersaulting off a trampoline. In that case [*Pell v. Victor J. Andrew High School*, 123 Ill.App.3d 423, 462 N.E.2d 858, 78 Ill.Dec. 739 (1984)], the court had held that the trampoline's manufacturer was liable for the plaintiff's injuries because it had failed to warn of the trampoline's propensity to cause severe spinal cord injuries if it was used for somersaulting. Should the court be convinced by the father's arguments? Why or why not? [*Cozzi v. North Palos Elementary School District No. 117*, 232 Ill.App.3d 379, 597 N.E.2d 683, 173 Ill.Dec. 709 (1992)]

4–9. Duty to Employees. Matt Theurer, an eighteen-year-old high school senior, worked part-time at a McDonald's restaurant in Oregon. Theurer volunteered to work an extra shift one day, in addition to his regular shifts (one preceding and one following the extra shift). After working about twelve hours during a twenty-four-hour period, Theurer told the manager that he was tired and asked to be excused from his next regularly scheduled shift so that he could rest. The manager agreed. While driving home from work, Theurer fell asleep at the wheel and crashed into a van driven by Frederic Faverty. Theurer died, and Faverty was severely injured. Faverty sued McDonald's, alleging, among other things, that McDonald's was negligent in permitting Theurer to drive a car when it should have known that Theurer was too tired to drive safely. Do employers have a duty to prevent fatigued employees from driving home from work? Should such a duty be imposed on them? How should the court decide this issue? How would you decide the issue if you were the judge? [*Faverty v. McDonald's Restaurants of Oregon, Inc.*, 133 Or.App. 514, 892 P.2d 703 (1994)]

A QUESTION OF ETHICS AND SOCIAL RESPONSIBILITY

4–10. *Hazen Paper Co. manufactured paper and paperboard for use in such products as cosmetic wrap, lottery tickets, and pressure-sensitive items. Walter Biggins, a chemist hired by Hazen in 1977, developed a water-based paper coating that was both environmentally safe and of superior quality. By the mid-1980s, the company's sales had increased dramatically as a result of its extensive use of "Biggins Acrylic." Because of this, Biggins thought he deserved a substantial raise in salary, and from 1984 to 1986, Biggins's persistent requests for a raise became a bone of contention between him and his employers. Biggins ran a business on the side, which involved cleaning up hazardous wastes for various companies. Hazen told Biggins that unless he signed a "confidentiality agreement" promising to restrict his outside activities during the time he was employed by Hazen and for a limited time afterward, he would be fired. Biggins said he would sign the agreement only if Hazen raised his salary to $100,000. Hazen refused to do so, fired Biggins, and hired a younger man to replace him. At the time of his discharge in 1986, Biggins was sixty-two years old, had worked for the company nearly ten years, and was just a few weeks away from being entitled to pension rights worth about $93,000. In view of these circumstances, evaluate and answer the following questions. [Hazen Paper Co. v. Biggins, 507 U.S. 604, 113 S.Ct. 1701, 123 L.Ed.2d 338 (1993)]*

1. Did the company owe an ethical duty to Biggins to increase his salary, given the fact that its sales increased dramatically as a result of Biggins's efforts and ingenuity in developing the coating? If you were one of the company's executives, would you have raised Biggins's salary? Why or why not?

2. Generally, what public policies come into conflict in cases involving employers who, for reasons of cost and efficiency of operations, fire older, higher-paid workers and replace them with younger, lower-paid workers? If you were an employer facing the need to cut back on personnel to save costs, what would you do, and on what ethical premises would you justify your decision?

FOR CRITICAL ANALYSIS

4–11. If a firm engages in "ethically responsible" behavior solely for the purpose of gaining profits from the goodwill it generates, the "ethical" behavior is essentially a means toward a self-serving end (profits and the accumulation of wealth). In this situation, is the firm acting unethically in any way? Should motive or conduct carry greater weight on the ethical scales in this situation?

▌Unit One—Cumulative Hypothetical Problem

4–12. Korman, Inc., a toy manufacturer, has its headquarters in Minneapolis, Minnesota. It markets its toys throughout the United States, as well as in overseas markets. Korman has recently placed on the market a new line of dolls with such irreverent names as "Harass Me," "Spit on Me," "Pull My Hair," "Watch Me Scream," "Cut Me Quick," and "Abuse Me, Please." The dolls are a success commercially and have netted Korman more profits than any of its other toys. Given these "facts," answer the following questions:

1. Jan's Toy Mart, the California distributor of Korman toys, wants to sue Korman for allegedly breaching a contract. If Jan's Toy Mart brought its suit in a California state court, could that court exercise jurisdiction over Korman? Explain.

2. Suppose that in its contract with Korman, Jan's Toy Mart agreed to submit any dispute that arose between the two companies to binding arbitration. Following the arbitration hearing, the arbitrator concludes that Korman did not breach the contract. Jan's Toy Mart is unsatisfied with the arbitrator's award. Can Jan's Toy Mart appeal the arbitrator's decision to a court?

3. Parents and teachers claim that Korman's dolls encourage children to be violent and that it is unethical of Korman to continue marketing the dolls. Parent-teacher groups are organizing boycotts against Korman and the dolls and have launched a media campaign against the company. Recently, they picketed Korman's headquarters in Minneapolis, bearing such signs as "Korman Hates Kids" and "Watch Korman Scream." If you were a Korman executive, would you recommend that the company cease manufacturing the toys? What factors would Korman's directors need to consider in making this decision?

4. Suppose that Korman does business only within the state of Minnesota. A Korman employee claims that the company has violated a federal employment law. Korman argues that it is not liable because the law applies only to employees of companies that are engaged in interstate commerce. What might a court decide? Discuss fully.

Unit Two

Torts and Crimes

UNIT OUTLINE

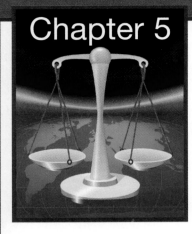

Chapter 5

Torts

TORT
A civil wrong not arising from a
breach of contract. A breach of a
legal duty that proximately causes
harm or injury to another.

*"'Torts' more or less means 'wrongs' . . . . One of
my friends [in law school] said that Torts is the
course which proves that your mother was right."*

Scott Turow, 1949–
(American lawyer and author)

CHAPTER OBJECTIVES

After reading this chapter, you should be able to:

1. Explain how torts and crimes differ.
2. State the purpose of tort law.
3. Identify some intentional torts against persons and property.
4. Name the four elements of negligence.
5. Define strict liability, and list some circumstances in which it will be applied.

As Scott Turow's statement in the above quotation indicates, **torts** are wrongful actions.[1] Through tort law, society compensates those who have suffered injuries as a result of the wrongful conduct of others. Although some torts, such as assault and trespass, originated in the English common law, the field of tort law continues to expand as new ways to commit wrongs are discovered and new conceptions of what is right and wrong in a social or business context emerge.

Tort law covers a wide variety of injuries. Society recognizes an interest in personal physical safety, and tort law provides remedies for acts that cause physical injury or that interfere with physical security and freedom of movement. Society recognizes an interest in protecting personal property, and tort law provides remedies for acts that cause destruction or damage to property. Society also recognizes an interest in protecting certain intangible interests, such as personal privacy, family relations, reputation, and dignity, and tort law provides remedies for invasion of these protected interests.

Certain torts normally occur only in the business context. The important area of business torts will be treated in Chapter 6. In this chapter, we discuss torts that can occur in any context, including the business environment. In fact, as you will see in

---

1. The term *tort* is French for "wrong."

later chapters of this book, many of the lawsuits brought by or against business firms are based on the tort theories discussed in this chapter.

▮ The Basis of Tort Law

Two notions serve as the basis of all torts: wrongs and compensation. Tort law recognizes that some acts are wrong because they cause injuries to others. Of course, a tort is not the only type of wrong that exists in the law; crimes also involve wrongs. A crime, however, is an act so reprehensible that it is considered a wrong against the state or against society as a whole, as well as against the individual victim. Therefore, the *state* prosecutes and punishes (through fines and/or imprisonment—and possibly death) persons who commit criminal acts. A tort action, in contrast, is a civil action in which one person brings a personal suit against another to obtain compensation (money **damages**) or other relief for the harm suffered.

Some torts, such as assault and battery (to be discussed shortly), provide a basis for a criminal prosecution as well as a tort action. For example, Joe is walking down the street, minding his own business, when suddenly a person attacks him. In the ensuing struggle, the attacker stabs Joe several times, seriously injuring Joe. A police officer restrains and arrests the wrongdoer. In this situation, the attacker may be subject both to criminal prosecution by the state and to a tort lawsuit brought by Joe. Exhibit 5–1 illustrates how the same wrongful act can result in both civil (tort) and criminal actions against the wrongdoer.

DAMAGES
Money sought as a remedy for a breach of contract or for a tortious act.

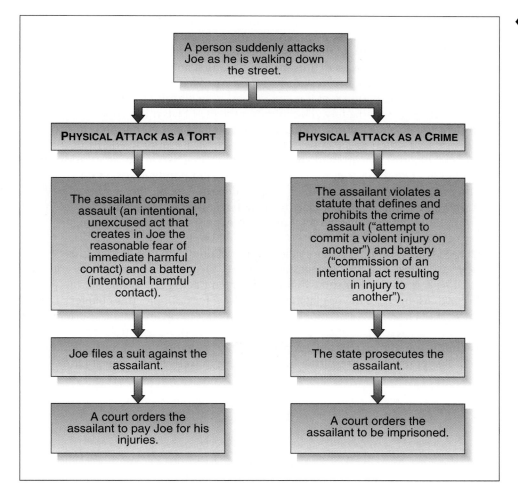

◆ Exhibit 5–1
Tort Lawsuit and Criminal Prosecution for the Same Act

▌ Intentional Torts against Persons

INTENTIONAL TORT
A wrongful act knowingly
committed.

TORTFEASOR
One who commits a tort.

An **intentional tort,** as the term implies, requires *intent.* The **tortfeasor** (the one committing the tort) must intend to commit an act, the consequences of which interfere with the personal or business interests of another in a way not permitted by law. An evil or harmful motive is not required—in fact, the tortfeasor may even have a beneficial motive for committing what turns out to be a tortious act. In tort law, intent only means that the actor intended the consequences of his or her act or knew with substantial certainty that certain consequences would result from the act. The law generally assumes that individuals intend the *normal* consequences of their actions. Thus, forcefully pushing another—even if done in jest and without any evil motive—is an intentional tort (if injury results), because the object of a strong push can ordinarily be expected to go flying.

This section discusses intentional torts against persons, which include assault and battery, false imprisonment, infliction of emotional distress, defamation, invasion of privacy, and misrepresentation.

Assault and Battery

ASSAULT
Any word or action intended to
make another person fearful of
immediate physical harm; a
reasonably believable threat.

Any intentional, unexcused act that creates in another person a reasonable apprehension or fear of immediate harmful or offensive contact is an **assault.** Apprehension is not the same as fear. If a contact is such that a reasonable person would want to avoid it, and if there is a reasonable basis for believing that the contact will occur, then the plaintiff suffers apprehension whether or not he or she is afraid. The interest protected by tort law concerning assault is the freedom from having to expect harmful or offensive contact. The occurrence of apprehension is enough to justify compensation.

BATTERY
The unprivileged, intentional
touching of another.

The *completion* of the act that caused the apprehension, if it results in harm to the plaintiff, is a **battery,** which is defined as an unexcused and harmful or offensive physical contact *intentionally* performed. For example, Ivan threatens Jean with a gun, then shoots her. The pointing of the gun at Jean is an assault; the firing of the gun (if the bullet hits Jean) is a battery. The interest protected by tort law concerning battery is the right to personal security and safety. The contact can be harmful, or it can be merely offensive (such as an unwelcome kiss). Physical injury need not occur. The contact can involve any part of the body or anything attached to it—for example, a hat or other item of clothing, a purse, or a chair or an automobile in which one is sitting. Whether the contact is offensive or not is determined by the *reasonable person standard.*[2] The contact can be made by the defendant or by some force the defendant sets in motion—for example, a rock thrown, food poisoned, or a stick swung.

COMPENSATION   With respect to battery, if the plaintiff shows that there was contact and the jury agrees that the contact was offensive, the plaintiff has a right to compensation. There is no need to show that the defendant acted out of malice; the person could have just been joking or playing around (see, for example, this chapter's *Law in the Extreme*). The underlying motive does not matter, only the intent to bring about the harmful or offensive contact to the plaintiff. In fact, proving a motive is never necessary (but is sometimes relevant). A plaintiff may be compensated for the emotional harm or loss of reputation resulting from a battery, as well as for physical harm.

---

2.   The reasonable person standard is an objective test of how a reasonable person would have acted under the same circumstances. See "The Duty of Care and Its Breach" later in this chapter.

LAW IN THE EXTREME

Just Blowing Smoke, or Battery?

Being the butt of a bad joke is, for most people, not a very pleasant experience. Usually, though, victims of bad jokes either put such experiences behind them or wreak their vengeance on the gag pullers outside the courtroom. Ahron Leichtman decided against both of these alternatives and took his case to court.

Leichtman, who describes himself as a "nationally known" antismoking advocate, was indeed the target of a bad joke. He was invited to appear on a radio talk show, on the date of the

"Great American Smokeout," to discuss the harmful effects of smoking and breathing secondary smoke. During the show, one of the talk show hosts, Furman, lit a cigar and repeatedly blew smoke in Leichtman's face. Leichtman contended that Furman intentionally blew smoke at him "for the purpose of causing physical discomfort, humiliation and distress."

Leichtman claimed that Furman's actions constituted a battery and sued Furman and another talk show host, as well as the owner of the station, WLW Jacor Communications, Inc., for damages. The trial court dismissed the claim for failure to state a cause of action. On appeal, however, the court held that Leichtman had stated a cause of action for battery: tobacco smoke, as "particulate matter," has the "physical properties of making

contact," and "[c]ontact which is offensive to a reasonable sense of personal dignity is offensive contact." The court stated that "[n]o matter how trivial the incident, a battery is actionable [capable of serving as the ground for a lawsuit], even if damages are only one dollar." The court thus remanded the case for trial: "Leichtman's battery claim, previously knocked out by the trial judge in the first round, now survives round two to advance again through the courts into round three."[a]

For Critical Analysis: *Do you think that Leichtman should have used the judicial forum simply to "get back at" Furman? Why or why not?*

a. *Leichtman v. WLW Jacor Communications, Inc.*, 92 Ohio App.3d 232, 634 N.E.2d 697 (1994).

DEFENSES TO ASSAULT AND BATTERY A number of legally recognized **defenses** (reasons why plaintiffs should not obtain what they are seeking) can be raised by a defendant who is sued for assault or battery, or both:

1. *Consent.* When a person consents to the act that damages him or her, there is generally no liability (legal responsibility) for the damage done.
2. *Self-defense.* An individual who is defending his or her life or physical well-being can claim self-defense. In situations of both *real* and *apparent* danger, a person may use whatever force is *reasonably* necessary to prevent harmful contact.
3. *Defense of others.* An individual can act in a reasonable manner to protect others who are in real or apparent danger.
4. *Defense of property.* Reasonable force may be used in attempting to remove intruders from one's home, although force that is likely to cause death or great bodily injury normally cannot be used just to protect property.

DEFENSE
That which a defendant offers and alleges in an action or suit as a reason why the plaintiff should not recover or establish what he or she seeks.

BE AWARE Some of these same defenses can be raised by a defendant who is sued for other torts.

False Imprisonment

False imprisonment is defined as the intentional confinement or restraint of another person's activities without justification. False imprisonment interferes with the freedom to move without restraint. The confinement can be accomplished through the use of physical barriers, physical restraint, or threats of physical force. Moral pressure or future threats do not constitute false imprisonment. It is essential that the person being restrained not comply with the restraint willingly.

Businesspersons are often confronted with suits for false imprisonment after they have attempted to confine a suspected shoplifter for questioning. Under the privilege to detain granted to merchants in some states, a merchant can use the defense of *probable cause* to justify delaying a suspected shoplifter. Probable cause exists when the evidence to support the belief that a person is guilty outweighs the evidence against that belief. The detention, however, must be conducted in a *reasonable* manner and for only a *reasonable* length of time.

Infliction of Emotional Distress

The tort of *infliction of emotional distress* can be defined as an intentional act that amounts to extreme and outrageous conduct resulting in severe emotional distress to another.[3] For example, a prankster telephones an individual and says that the individual's spouse has just been in a horrible accident. As a result, the individual suffers intense mental pain or anxiety. The caller's behavior is deemed to be extreme and outrageous conduct that exceeds the bounds of decency accepted by society and is therefore **actionable** (capable of serving as the ground for a lawsuit). Another example of this tort is "stalking" a person, thus causing that person to experience emotional distress from the fear of possible harm. Stalking is a crime, but courts in many states have concluded that it also constitutes the tort of intentional infliction of emotional distress.

Because infliction of emotional distress is a relatively new tort, it poses some problems. It is difficult to prove the existence of emotional suffering, so a few states require that the emotional disturbance be evidenced by some physical illness. In the following case, the court looks at some of the requirements that plaintiffs must meet in establishing an emotional distress claim.

ACTIONABLE
Capable of serving as the basis of a lawsuit.

---

3.   *Restatement (Second) of Torts*, Section 46, Comment d. The *Restatement (Second) of Torts* is a compilation of the law of torts by the American Law Institute.

CASE 5.1

FUDGE v. PENTHOUSE INTERNATIONAL, LTD.
United States Court of Appeals,
First Circuit, 1988.
840 F.2d 1012.

HISTORICAL AND SOCIAL SETTING *Intentional infliction of emotional distress is a relatively new tort. The law's reluctance to protect freedom from emotional distress as a separate interest may be due to a fear of false claims and a mistrust of the proof that plaintiffs sometimes offer to support their claims for damages for emotional distress. Whatever the reasons may be, the ultimate limits of the tort have not yet been determined.*

FACTS Leslie Fudge was a student at the Oakland Beach Elementary School in Warwick, Rhode Island. In the fall of 1985, because of apparent conflicts between some of the school's male and female students, the school's principal decided to segregate the sexes during recess periods. A Providence, Rhode Island, newspaper ran an item on the story, along with a photograph showing

Leslie Fudge and other girls giving the thumbs-down sign to show their disapproval of the principal's decision. The story and the picture were eventually picked up by *Penthouse* magazine, which printed a one-paragraph story about the girls, along with a slightly cropped version of the photograph that had appeared in the Providence newspaper. The story was headlined "Little Amazons Attack Boys" and appeared in a section of the magazine entitled "Hard Times: A compendium of bizarre, idiotic, lurid, and ofttimes witless driblets of information culled from the nation's press." The brief item told how the Warwick school had segregated the sexes to protect the boys from the girls who "kick them in the shins, pull their hair, and kick them, well, in various painful places." Four of the girls in the picture and their parents brought an action in a federal district court against the owners of *Penthouse* magazine, Penthouse International, Ltd., alleging, among other things, that the publication of the photograph of the girls in a sexually explicit men's magazine constituted the intentional infliction of emotional distress. Penthouse moved for summary judgment, which the district court granted. The plaintiffs—the girls and their parents—appealed.

ISSUE Does the publication of the photograph of the girls in *Penthouse* magazine constitute the tort of intentional infliction of emotional distress?

Case 5.1—Continued

DECISION No. The First Circuit Court of Appeals affirmed the district court's decision to grant Penthouse's motion for summary judgment.

REASON Citing the *Restatement (Second) of Torts,* Section 46, Comment d, the court said that in emotional distress cases, "Liability has been found only where the conduct has been so outrageous in character, and so extreme in degree, as to go beyond all possible bounds of decency, and to be regarded as atrocious, and utterly intolerable in a civilized community." The court could find nothing in the plaintiffs' allegations that was "sufficiently extreme and outrageous to warrant the imposition of liability." There was nothing shocking about the photograph itself; what the plaintiffs objected to was the fact that it had been published in *Penthouse* magazine. The court stated, however, that "[m]agazines such as *Penthouse* are sufficiently a part of the contemporary scene that their reprinting of relatively innocuous news items or photographs that have already appeared in other media simply cannot be characterized as exceeding all possible bounds of decency, atrocious, or utterly intolerable in a civilized society."

FOR CRITICAL ANALYSIS—Social Consideration
What would be the result for society if magazines such as Penthouse were held liable for any and all distress caused by the articles and photographs they publish?

Defamation

Defamation of character involves wrongfully hurting a person's good reputation. The law has imposed a general duty on all persons to refrain from making false, defamatory statements about others. Breaching this duty orally involves the tort of **slander;** breaching it in writing involves the tort of **libel.** The tort of defamation also arises when a false statement is made about a person's product, business, or title to property. We deal with these torts in the following chapter.

The common law defines four types of false utterances that are considered torts *per se* (meaning no proof of injury or harm is required for these false utterances to be actionable):

DEFAMATION
Anything published or publicly spoken that causes injury to another's good name, reputation, or character.

SLANDER
Defamation in oral form.

LIBEL
Defamation in written form.

1. A statement that another has a loathsome communicable disease.
2. A statement that another has committed improprieties while engaging in a profession or trade.
3. A statement that another has committed or has been imprisoned for a serious crime.
4. A statement that an unmarried woman is unchaste.

THE PUBLICATION REQUIREMENT The basis of the tort of defamation is the publication of a statement or statements that hold an individual up to contempt, ridicule, or hatred. *Publication* here means that the defamatory statements are communicated to persons other than the defamed party. If Thompson writes Andrews a private letter accusing him of embezzling funds, the action does not constitute libel. If Peters calls Gordon dishonest, unattractive, and incompetent when no one else is around, the action does not constitute slander. In neither case was the message communicated to a third party.

The courts have generally held that even dictating a letter to a secretary constitutes publication, although the publication may be privileged (privileged communications will be discussed shortly). Moreover, if a third party overhears defamatory statements by chance, the courts usually hold that this also constitutes publication. Defamatory statements made via the Internet are also actionable (see this chapter's *Technology and Defamation in Cyberspace*). Note further that any individual who republishes or repeats defamatory statements is liable even if that person reveals the source of such statements.

"Reputation, reputation, reputation! Oh, I have lost my reputation! I have lost the immortal part of myself, and what remains is bestial."

William Shakespeare,
1564–1616
(English dramatist and poet)

Technology and Defamation in Cyberspace

The widespread use of the Internet for personal and business communications has given rise to a new kind of tort—the "cybertort." Internet users may, without realizing it, commit various wrongs on-line. Here we look at just one wrongful act that may occur in cyberspace—the tort of defamation.

On-Line Defamation

Any defamatory statement that is communicated to a third party is considered "published" under defamation law and thus actionable (capable of providing the basis for a lawsuit). What about defamatory statements made via the Internet? Suppose, for example, that a couple of friends are exchanging thoughts on-line in a chat group. One of them accuses her boss of sexual misconduct. Does this statement constitute defamation? Yes. This is because what may seem like a private on-line "conversation" between just two persons is, in fact, a very public exchange, accessible to millions of people. The fact that those people are unseen at the time a defamatory statement is made makes no difference. The person defamed (the boss, in this example) could suffer serious harm from the statement—loss of reputation and perhaps even the loss of a job. The person who made the defamatory statement could be sued in tort for damages.

Free Speech versus Defamation

As mentioned in Chapter 2, the freedom of speech guaranteed by the First Amendment to the Constitution is not absolute. Speech that harms another person's good name and reputation may be the basis for a defamation suit, and this is true whether the statement is communicated over the radio or television, in a printed publication, or via the Internet.

In one case, for example, an anthropologist, Gilbert Hardwick, posted a message on a worldwide academic network accusing another anthropologist, David Rindos, of engaging in sexual misconduct. According to the judge hearing the case, Hardwick's statements suggested that Rindos engaged in sexual misconduct and that his "professional career and reputation has not been based on appropriate academic research but on 'his ability to berate and bully all and sundry.'" Rindos succeeded in winning a $40,000 judgment against Hardwick for these remarks.[a]

Generally, in determining whether statements are defamatory, the courts distinguish between statements of *fact* and statements of *opinion*. For example, suppose that someone posts a message on an electronic bulletin board accusing a seller of motorcycles of being a "sleazy jerk." In terms of legal liability, the message sender is probably in safe waters. If, however, the message accused the seller of being a "sleazy jerk who sells stolen motorbikes," that statement alleges a fact—that the seller is engaging in criminal behavior. Unless the statement is true, the message sender could be liable in a defamation suit for substantial damages.

For Critical Analysis: *What precautions should Internet users take to avoid liability for defamation?*

a.   As discussed in Deborah Branscum, "Cyberspace Lawsuits," *MacWorld,* May 1995, pp. 149–150.

The following case raises an interesting issue concerning the publication requirement: Can a plaintiff establish the publication of defamatory statements without the testimony of a third person regarding what he or she heard or understood?

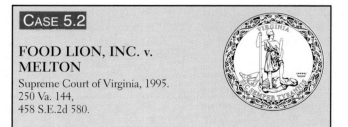

CASE 5.2

FOOD LION, INC. v. MELTON

Supreme Court of Virginia, 1995.
250 Va. 144,
458 S.E.2d 580.

HISTORICAL AND ETHICAL SETTING *In 1992, on ABC's* PrimeTime Live, *reporters claimed that grocery stores owned by Food Lion, Inc., sold contaminated goods and repackaged out-of-date food. The company denied the charges. At the same time, the U.S. government was investigating Food Lion for violations of child labor laws (see Chapter 32), and shareholders in the company had filed a suit alleging that the firm reported misleading information about its financial standing. Meanwhile, Food Lion employees filed their own suits, claiming that the company forced them to work overtime without compensating them for it. In 1994, Food Lion also faced a possible class-action suit alleging racial discrimination.*

Case 5.2—Continued

FACTS In April 1991, after shopping at a Food Lion grocery store, sixty-eight-year-old Christine Melton was walking out of the store when a Food Lion security guard stopped her in the parking lot. The guard accused her of leaving with meat belonging to the store in her purse. According to Melton, the guard questioned her repeatedly, loudly, and in an accusatory manner, and "there were people stopping to listen and see what was going on." Finally, Melton allowed the guard to search her purse. No meat was found. Melton filed a suit against Food Lion in a Virginia state court, in part on the ground of defamation. Food Lion in effect denied that the incident ever happened. Melton was not able to identify any of the people who "stopped to listen" and could not offer proof as to what they heard. On the defamation claim, the court entered a judgment in favor of Food Lion, and Melton appealed to the Virginia Supreme Court.

ISSUE Does a party, to prove publication of defamatory remarks, have to present testimony from any third person?

DECISION No. The Virginia Supreme Court held that a party does not need to present testimony from any third person, or even to identify any such person, to prove publication. The court reversed the judgment of the lower court and remanded the case for a new trial.

REASON The court ruled that "a plaintiff may prove publication of defamatory remarks by * * * evidence that the remarks were heard by a third party who understood these remarks as referring to the plaintiff in a defamatory sense." The court noted that the security guard "made his accusations in a 'very loud tone' of voice" and "during this time, people * * * stopped 'to listen and see what was going on.'" The court concluded that this was enough "to permit a reasonable inference that the accuser's words were heard and understood by a third party as referring to Melton and as imputing the commission of a crime."

FOR CRITICAL ANALYSIS—Social Consideration
Under what circumstances should a court require testimony from third parties in order to prove that a statement was "published" for defamation purposes?

DEFENSES AGAINST DEFAMATION   Truth is normally an absolute defense against a defamation charge. In other words, if the defendant in a defamation suit can prove that his or her allegedly defamatory statements were true, the defendant will not be liable.

Another defense that is sometimes raised is that the statements were **privileged** communications, and thus the defendant is immune from liability. Privileged communications are of two types: absolute and qualified. Only in judicial proceedings and certain legislative proceedings is *absolute* privilege granted. For example, statements made by attorneys and judges during a trial are absolutely privileged. So are statements made by legislators during congressional floor debate, even if the legislators make such statements maliciously—that is, knowing them to be untrue. An absolute privilege is granted in these situations because judicial and legislative personnel deal with matters that are so much in the public interest that the parties involved should be able to speak out fully and freely without restriction.

In other situations, a person will not be liable for defamatory statements because he or she has a *qualified*, or conditional, privilege. For example, statements made in recommendation letters or in written evaluations of employees are qualifiedly privileged. Generally, if the communicated statements are made in good faith and the publication is limited to those who have a legitimate interest in the communication, the statements fall within the area of qualified privilege. The concept of conditional privilege rests on the common law assumption that in some situations, the right to know or speak is of equal importance with the right not to be defamed.

In general, false and defamatory statements that are made about *public figures* (those who exercise substantial governmental power and any persons in the public limelight) and that are published in the press are privileged if they are made without **actual malice.**[4] To be made with actual malice, a statement must be made *with either*

> "Truth is generally the best vindication against slander."
>
> **Abraham Lincoln, 1809–1865**
> **(Sixteenth president of the United States, 1861–1865)**

PRIVILEGE
In tort law, the ability to act contrary to another person's right without that person's having legal redress for such acts. Privilege may be raised as a defense to defamation.

ACTUAL MALICE
Real and demonstrable evil intent. In a defamation suit, a statement made about a public figure normally must be made with actual malice (with either knowledge of its falsity or a reckless disregard of the truth) for liability to be incurred.

---

4. *New York Times Co. v. Sullivan*, 376 U.S. 254, 84 S.Ct. 710, 11 L.Ed.2d 686 (1964).

knowledge of falsity or a reckless disregard of the truth. Statements made about public figures, especially when they are made via a public medium, are usually related to matters of general public interest; they are made about people who substantially affect all of us. Furthermore, public figures generally have some access to a public medium for answering disparaging (belittling, discrediting) falsehoods about themselves; private individuals do not. For these reasons, public figures have a greater burden of proof in defamation cases (they must prove actual malice) than do private individuals.

Invasion of Privacy

A person has a right to solitude and freedom from prying public eyes—in other words, to privacy. Four acts qualify as an invasion of that privacy:

1. The use of a person's name, picture, or other likeness for commercial purposes without permission. This tort, which is usually referred to as the tort of *appropriation,* will be examined in the next chapter.
2. Intrusion in an individual's affairs or seclusion in an area in which the person has a reasonable expectation of privacy.
3. Publication of information that places a person in a false light. This could be a story attributing to the person ideas not held or actions not taken by the person. (Publishing such a story could involve the tort of defamation as well.)
4. Public disclosure of private facts about an individual that an ordinary person would find objectionable.

Misrepresentation—Fraud (Deceit)

A misrepresentation leads another to believe in a condition that is different from the condition that actually exists. This is often accomplished through a false or incorrect statement. Misrepresentations may be innocently made by someone who is unaware of the existing facts, but the tort of **fraudulent misrepresentation,** or **fraud,** involves intentional deceit, usually for personal gain. The tort includes several elements:

FRAUDULENT MISREPRESENTATION (FRAUD)
Any misrepresentation, either by misstatement or omission of a material fact, knowingly made with the intention of deceiving another and on which a reasonable person would and does rely to his or her detriment.

1. Misrepresentation of facts or conditions with knowledge that they are false or with reckless disregard for the truth.
2. Intent to induce another to rely on the misrepresentation.
3. Justifiable reliance by the deceived party.
4. Damages suffered as a result of reliance.
5. Causal connection between the misrepresentation and the injury suffered.

PUFFERY
A salesperson's often exaggerated claims concerning the quality of property offered for sale. Such claims involve opinions rather than facts and are not considered to be legally binding promises or warranties.

For fraud to occur, more than mere **puffery,** or *seller's talk,* must be involved. Fraud exists only when a person represents as a fact something he or she knows is untrue. For example, it is fraud to claim that a roof does not leak when one knows it does. Facts are objectively ascertainable, whereas seller's talk is not. "I am the best accountant in town" is seller's talk. The speaker is not trying to represent something as fact, because the term *best* is a subjective, not an objective, term.[5]

Normally, the tort of misrepresentation or fraud occurs only when there is reliance upon a *statement of fact.* Sometimes, however, reliance on a *statement of opinion* may involve the tort of misrepresentation if the individual making the statement of opinion

---

5. In contracts for the sale of goods, Article 2 of the Uniform Commercial Code distinguishes, for warranty purposes, between statements of opinion ("puffery") and statements of fact. See Chapter 17 for a further discussion of this issue.

has a superior knowledge of the subject matter. For example, when a lawyer makes a statement of opinion about the law, a court would construe reliance on such a statement to be equivalent to reliance on a statement of fact. We examine fraudulent misrepresentation in further detail in Chapter 11, in the context of contract law.

▮ Intentional Torts against Property

Intentional torts against property include trespass to land, trespass to personal property, and conversion. These torts are wrongful actions that interfere with individuals' legally recognized rights with regard to their land or personal property. The law distinguishes real property from personal property (see Chapters 34 and 35). *Real property* is land and things "permanently" attached to the land. *Personal property* consists of all other items, which are basically movable. Thus, a house and lot are real property, whereas the furniture inside a house is personal property. Money and securities are also personal property.

Trespass to Land

A **trespass to land** occurs whenever a person, without permission or legal authorization, enters onto, above, or below the surface of land that is owned by another; causes anything to enter onto the land; remains on the land; or permits anything to remain on it. Actual harm to the land is not an essential element of this tort, because the tort is designed to protect the right of an owner to exclusive possession of his or her property. Common types of trespass to land include walking or driving on the land, shooting a gun over the land, throwing rocks at a building that belongs to someone else, building a dam across a river and thus causing water to back up on someone else's land, and placing part of one's building on an adjoining landowner's property.

TRESPASS CRITERIA, RIGHTS, AND DUTIES   Before a person can be a trespasser, the owner of the real property (or other person in actual and exclusive possession of the property) must establish that person as a trespasser. For example, "posted" trespass signs expressly establish as a trespasser a person who ignores these signs and enters onto the property. A guest in your home is not a trespasser—unless he or she has been asked to leave but refuses. Any person who enters onto your property to commit an illegal act (such as a thief entering a lumberyard at night to steal lumber) is established impliedly as a trespasser, without posted signs.

At common law, a trespasser is liable for damages caused to the property. In addition, a trespasser generally cannot hold the owner liable for injuries sustained on the premises. This common law rule is being abandoned in many jurisdictions in favor of a "reasonable duty of care" rule that varies depending on the status of the parties. For example, a landowner may have a duty to post a notice that the property is patrolled by guard dogs. Furthermore, under the "attractive nuisance" doctrine, children do not assume the risks of the premises if they are attracted to the premises by some object, such as a swimming pool, an abandoned building, or a sand pile. Trespassers normally can be removed from the premises through the use of reasonable force without the owner's being liable for assault and battery.

DEFENSES AGAINST TRESPASS TO LAND   Trespass to land involves wrongful interference with another person's real property rights. If it can be shown that the trespass was warranted, however, as when a trespasser enters to assist someone in danger, a defense exists. Another defense is to show that the purported owner did not actually have the right to possess the land in question.

TRESPASS TO LAND
The entry onto, above, or below the surface of land owned by another without the owner's permission or legal authorization.

Sign warns trespassers. Should a trespasser be allowed to recover from a landowner for injuries sustained on the premises?

Trespass to Personal Property

Whenever any individual unlawfully harms the personal property of another or otherwise interferes with the personal property owner's right to exclusive possession and enjoyment of that property, **trespass to personal property**—also called *trespass to personalty*[6]—occurs. If a student takes another student's business law book as a practical joke and hides it so that the owner is unable to find it for several days prior to a final examination, the student has engaged in a trespass to personal property.

If it can be shown that trespass to personal property was warranted, then a complete defense exists. Most states, for example, allow automobile repair shops to hold a customer's car (under what is called an *artisan's lien*, discussed in Chapter 22) when the customer refuses to pay for repairs already completed.

Conversion

Whenever personal property is wrongfully taken from its rightful owner or possessor and placed in the service of another, the act of **conversion** occurs. Conversion is defined as any act depriving an owner of personal property without that owner's permission and without just cause. When conversion occurs, the lesser offense of trespass to personal property usually occurs as well. If the initial taking of the property was unlawful, there is trespass; retention of that property is conversion. If the initial taking of the property was permitted by the owner or for some other reason is not a trespass, failure to return it may still be conversion. Conversion is the civil side of crimes related to theft. A store clerk who steals merchandise from the store commits a crime and engages in the tort of conversion at the same time.

Even if a person mistakenly believed that he or she was entitled to the goods, a tort of conversion may occur. In other words, good intentions are not a defense against conversion; in fact, conversion can be an entirely innocent act. Someone who buys stolen goods, for example, commits the tort of conversion even if he or she does not know that the goods were stolen. If the true owner brings a tort action against the buyer, the buyer must either return the property to the owner or pay the owner the full value of the property, despite having already paid money to the thief.

A successful defense against the charge of conversion is that the purported owner does not in fact own the property or does not have a right to possess it that is superior to the right of the holder. Necessity is another possible defense against conversion. If Abrams takes Mendoza's cat, Abrams is guilty of conversion. If Mendoza sues Abrams, Abrams must return the cat or pay damages. If, however, the cat has rabies and Abrams took the cat to protect the public, Abrams has a valid defense—necessity (and perhaps even self-defense, if he can prove that he was in danger because of the cat).

▌Unintentional Torts (Negligence)

The tort of **negligence** occurs when someone suffers injury because of another's failure to live up to a required *duty of care*. In contrast to intentional torts, in torts involving negligence, the tortfeasor neither wishes to bring about the consequences of the act nor believes that they will occur. The actor's conduct merely creates a *risk* of such consequences. If no risk is created, there is no negligence.

Many of the actions discussed in the section on intentional torts constitute negligence if the element of intent is missing. For example, if Juarez intentionally shoves Natsuyo, who falls and breaks an arm as a result, Juarez will have committed an intentional tort. If Juarez carelessly bumps into Natsuyo, however, and she falls and breaks an arm as a result, Juarez's action will constitute negligence. In either situation, Juarez has committed a tort.

---

6.   Pronounced *per*-sun-ul-tee.

Drawing by Maslin; © 1990 The New Yorker Magazine, Inc.

"To answer your question. Yes, if you shoot an arrow into the air and it falls to earth you know not where, you could be liable for any damage it may cause."

In examining a question of negligence, one should ask four questions:

1. Did the defendant owe a duty of care to the plaintiff?
2. Did the defendant breach that duty?
3. Did the plaintiff suffer a legally recognizable injury as a result of the defendant's breach of the duty of care?
4. Did the defendant's breach cause the plaintiff's injury?

Each of these elements of neligence is discussed below.

"There is a duty if the court says there is a duty."

William Lloyd Prosser,
1898–1972
(American legal scholar)

The Duty of Care and Its Breach

The concept of a **duty of care** arises from the notion that if we are to live in society with other people, some actions can be tolerated and some cannot; some actions are right and some are wrong; and some actions are reasonable and some are not. The basic principle underlying the duty of care is that people are free to act as they please so long as their actions do not infringe on the interests of others.

When someone fails to comply with the duty of exercising reasonable care, a potentially tortious act may have been committed. Failure to live up to a standard of care may be an act (setting fire to a building) or an omission (neglecting to put out a campfire). It may be an intentional act, a careless act, or a carefully performed but nevertheless dangerous act that results in injury. Courts consider the nature of the act (whether it is outrageous or commonplace), the manner in which the act is performed (cautiously versus heedlessly), and the nature of the injury (whether it is serious or slight) in determining whether the duty of care has been breached.

DUTY OF CARE
The duty of all persons, as established by tort law, to exercise a reasonable amount of care in their dealings with others. Failure to exercise due care, which is normally determined by the "reasonable person standard," constitutes the tort of negligence.

REASONABLE PERSON STANDARD
The standard of behavior expected of a hypothetical "reasonable person." The standard against which negligence is measured and that must be observed to avoid liability for negligence.

THE REASONABLE PERSON STANDARD   Tort law measures duty by the **reasonable person standard.** In determining whether a duty of care has been breached, the courts ask how a reasonable person would have acted in the same circumstances. The reasonable person standard is said to be (though in an absolute sense it cannot be) objective. It is not necessarily how a particular person would act. It is society's judgment on how people *should* act. If the so-called reasonable person existed, he or she would be careful, conscientious, even tempered, and honest. This hypothetical reasonable person is frequently used by the courts in decisions relating to other areas of law as well.

That individuals are required to exercise a reasonable standard of care in their activities is a pervasive concept in business law, and many of the issues dealt with in subsequent chapters of this text have to do with this duty. What constitutes reasonable care varies, of course, with the circumstances.

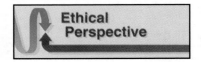

Does a person's duty of care include a duty to come to the aid of a stranger in peril? For example, assume that you are walking down a city street and notice that a pedestrian is about to step directly in front of an oncoming bus. Do you have a legal duty to warn that individual? No. Although most people would probably concede that in this situation, the observer has an *ethical* duty to warn the other, tort law does not impose a general duty to rescue others in peril.

People involved in special relationships, however, have been held to have a duty to rescue other parties within the relationship. A married person, for example, has a duty to rescue his or her child or spouse if either is in danger. Other special relationships, such as those between teachers and students or hiking and hunting partners, may also give rise to a duty to rescue. In addition, if a person who has no duty to rescue undertakes to rescue another, then the rescuer is charged with a duty to follow through with due care on the rescue attempt.

In regard to the duty to rescue, the distinction between legal and ethical duties is clearly evident. Although the law might not require a passerby to save a drowning toddler in a wading pool, society expects that people will aid others who are in danger and cannot help themselves.

For Critical Analysis: *Should the law impose a general duty to rescue others in peril?*

DUTY OF LANDOWNERS   Landowners are expected to exercise reasonable care to protect from harm persons coming onto their property. As mentioned earlier, in some jurisdictions, landowners are held to owe a duty to protect even trespassers against certain risks. Landowners who rent or lease premises to tenants (see Chapter 35) are expected to exercise reasonable care to ensure that the tenants and their guests are not harmed in common areas, such as stairways, entryways, laundry rooms, and the like.

BUSINESS INVITEES
Those people, such as customers or clients, who are invited onto business premises by the owner of those premises for business purposes.

Retailers and other firms that explicitly or implicitly invite persons to come onto their premises are usually charged with a duty to exercise reasonable care to protect those persons, who are considered to be **business invitees.** For example, if you entered a supermarket, slipped on a wet floor, and sustained injuries as a result, the owner of the supermarket would be liable for damages if when you slipped there was no sign warning that the floor was wet. A court would hold that the business owner was negligent because the owner failed to exercise a reasonable degree of care in protecting the store's customers against foreseeable risks about which the owner knew or *should have known.* That a patron might slip on the wet floor and be injured as a result was a foreseeable risk, and the owner should have taken care to avoid this risk or to warn the customer of it. The landowner also has a duty to discover and remove any hidden dangers that might injure a customer or other invitee.

Some risks, of course, are so obvious that the owner need not warn of them. For example, a business owner does not need to warn customers to open a door before attempting to walk through it. Other risks, however, even though they may seem obvious to a business owner, may not be so in the eyes of another, such as a child. For example, a hardware store owner may not think it is necessary to warn customers that a stepladder leaning against the back wall of the store could fall down and harm them. It is possible, though, that a child could tip the ladder over and be hurt as a result and that the store could be held liable. In the following case, the court has to decide whether a supermarket owner should be held liable for a customer's injuries on the premises.

CASE 5.3

DUMONT v. SHAW'S SUPERMARKETS, INC.

Supreme Judicial Court of Maine, 1995.
664 A.2d 846.

HISTORICAL AND POLITICAL SETTING *For more than two decades, the states have been changing their tort laws to reduce what some consider to be excessive advantages given to plaintiffs. In the mid-1970s, for example, some states set limits on the amounts of recovery allowed in medical malpractice cases. In the 1980s, the focus was on reducing liability in cases involving product liability (see Chapter 17). In the 1990s, the debate has concerned other liability issues, lawyers' fees, and the "loser pays" concept. Due in part to these efforts by the states, the number of filings of tort lawsuits has decreased by 6 percent since 1991.*

FACTS At Shaw's Supermarkets, Inc., chocolate-covered peanuts are sold in bulk with other unpackaged, unwrapped candy in bins next to the produce section. Shaw's is aware that self-serve, small, loose, slippery items create a hazard for customers, who may slip and fall if they step on them. Shaw's places mats next to some of the produce and in other locations, but Shaw's does not place mats on the floor next to the candy bins. While shopping at Shaw's, Shirley Dumont slipped on a chocolate-covered peanut, fell, and was injured. Dumont sued Shaw's in a Maine state court, alleging negligence. The court ruled that Dumont could recover only if she proved that Shaw's caused the candy to be on the floor, that Shaw's knew that the candy was on the floor, or that the candy was on the floor for such a length of time that Shaw's should have known it was there. Because Dumont proved none of these things, the court entered a judgment in favor of Shaw's. Dumont appealed to the

state's highest court, the Supreme Judicial Court of Maine.

ISSUE Is a store owner's awareness of the risk of a recurrent hazardous condition on the premises sufficient to hold the owner liable for a customer's injury that is caused by the condition?

DECISION Yes. The Supreme Judicial Court of Maine held that it is not necessary to prove that the owner had actual notice of the specific condition giving rise to the injury. The court vacated (set aside) the lower court's judgment and remanded the case for further proceedings.

REASON Dumont "presented evidence * * * that there existed a foreseeable risk of a recurrent condition and that Shaw's did not exercise reasonable care in failing to place mats next to the bulk candy display." The court emphasized that "Shaw's was aware that items with similar characteristics to the chocolate-covered peanuts created an increased hazard to customers and had placed mats on the floor to mitigate the risk." The court stated that "[i]n those circumstances, a store owner may be chargeable with constructive notice[a] of the existence of the specific condition." The court explained that "a store owner who is aware of the existence of a recurrent condition that poses a potential danger to invitees may not ignore that knowledge and fail reasonably to respond to the foreseeable danger of the likelihood of a recurrence of the condition."

FOR CRITICAL ANALYSIS—Social Consideration
Does the principle applied in this case make a store owner the "absolute insurer" of the store's customers? In other words, is a store owner liable for injuries to customers on the premises even if the owner has taken precautions that are reasonably necessary to protect those customers?

---

a. Notice that is implied or imposed by law, as opposed to actual notice.

Professionals review plans at a construction site. Could they successfully defend against a lawsuit for negligence by claiming that they were not familiar with certain principles of their profession?

DUTY OF PROFESSIONALS   If an individual has knowledge, skill, or intelligence superior to that of an ordinary person, the individual's conduct must be consistent with that status. Professionals—including doctors, dentists, psychiatrists, architects, engineers, accountants, lawyers, and others—are required to have a standard minimum level of special knowledge and ability. Therefore, in determining what constitutes reasonable care in cases involving professionals, their training and expertise is taken into account. In other words, an accountant cannot defend against a lawsuit for negligence by stating, "But I was not familiar with that principle of accounting."

If a professional violates his or her duty of care toward a client, the professional may be sued for **malpractice**. For example, a patient might sue a physician for *medical malpractice*. A client might sue an attorney for *legal malpractice*.

The Injury Requirement and Damages

MALPRACTICE
Professional misconduct or the lack of the requisite degree of skill as a professional. Negligence—the failure to exercise due care—on the part of a professional, such as a physician or an attorney, is commonly referred to as malpractice.

For a tort to have been committed, the plaintiff must have suffered a *legally recognizable* injury. To recover damages (receive compensation), the plaintiff must have suffered some loss, harm, wrong, or invasion of a protected interest. Essentially, the purpose of tort law is to compensate for legally recognized injuries resulting from wrongful acts. If no harm or injury results from a given negligent action, there is nothing to compensate—and no tort exists. For example, if you carelessly bump into a passerby, who stumbles and falls as a result, you may be liable in tort if the passerby is injured in the fall. If the person is unharmed, however, there normally could be no suit for damages, because no injury was suffered. Although the passerby might be angry and suffer emotional distress, few courts recognize negligently inflicted emotional distress as a tort unless it results in some physical disturbance or dysfunction.

COMPENSATORY DAMAGES
A money award equivalent to the actual value of injuries or damages sustained by the aggrieved party.

PUNITIVE DAMAGES
Money damages that may be awarded to a plaintiff to punish the defendant and deter future similar conduct.

As already mentioned, the purpose of tort law is not to punish people for tortious acts but to compensate the injured parties for damages suffered. Occasionally, however, damages awarded in tort lawsuits include both **compensatory damages** (which are intended to reimburse a plaintiff for actual losses—to make the plaintiff whole) and **punitive damages** (which are intended to punish the wrongdoer and deter others from similar wrongdoing). Few negligent acts, however, are so reprehensible that punitive damages are available. (See this chapter's *Business Law in Action* for a further discussion of punitive damages awards in tort litigation.) Unlike in some other nations, in the United States the damages awarded do not depend on whether the tort was intentional or negligent.

The High Cost of Tort Litigation

Americans like to sue, or at least that's what it looks like if you examine the number of lawsuits occurring in this country. We have more than 750,000 lawyers in the United States. Both totally and on a per capita basis, that is more lawyers than most other nations claim. Furthermore, the percentage of total national income devoted to tort costs is higher in the United States than anywhere else. It is five times what it is in Canada, France, Germany, Britain, or Japan. And while tort costs in other nations have remained relatively stable, they have been on the rise in the United States. Currently, the estimated cost of tort litigation in this country exceeds $130 billion annually.

Not surprisingly, if you are in the business world, you should be insured against the possibility of tort litigation. Businesspersons and professionals are potentially subject to a wide array of tort lawsuits brought by clients, customers and consumers, and others. Manufacturers and sellers, for example, are frequently the targets of *product liability* lawsuits—that is, lawsuits brought by consumers who are harmed by a faulty or defective product. To protect against having to pay millions of dollars in damages, manufacturers and sellers purchase liability insurance. The cost of high damages awards and insurance protection against them is borne not just by business but by society in general. This is because those costs are passed on to customers, clients, and consumers in the form of higher prices. Today, about 20 percent of the cost of a $35 stepladder goes to insurance.

High punitive damages awards, which in some cases are hundreds of times higher than the compensatory damages awarded to the plaintiffs, have led some defendants to claim that these awards violate the Eighth Amendment's prohibition against excessive fines or the defendants' constitutional rights to due process. In *BMW of North America v. Gore*,[a] for example, a jury awarded $4,000 in

a. —U.S.—, 115 S.Ct. 1589, 134 L.Ed.2d 809 (1996).

compensatory damages and one thousand times that amount ($4 million) in punitive damages. The Alabama Supreme Court reduced the punitive damages award to $2 million. When the case was appealed to the United States Supreme Court, the Court held that the $2 million award was "grossly excessive" and violated the defendant's due process rights.

Attempts at reducing the number and size of damages awards fall under the rubric of tort reform. Efforts at tort reform in many states are aimed at capping, or putting a ceiling on, high awards. Some states limit the size of punitive awards. New Jersey requires a finding of actual malice or wanton and willful disregard of rights before granting punitive damages. Some states have limited awards for such noneconomic harm as emotional distress. In all, at least thirty states have changed their rules relating to the availability of punitive damages. For some time, members of Congress have been trying to achieve consensus on a tort reform bill, but to date, they have not succeeded.

For Critical Analysis: *Who ultimately pays for extremely large punitive damages awards?*

Among national tort laws, there are many differences—and many different approaches to the calculation of damages. For example, Swiss and Turkish law permit a court to reduce damages if an award of full damages would cause undue hardship to a party who was found negligent. Also, in some nations of northern Africa, different amounts of damages are awarded depending on the type of tortious action committed, whether the tort was intentional or negligent, and so on.

 International Perspective

For Critical Analysis: *Should courts in the United States consider, when awarding damages, whether the awards would cause undue hardship to the defendants?*

Causation

Another element necessary to a tort is *causation.* If a person fails in a duty of care and someone suffers injury, the wrongful activity must have caused the harm for a tort to have been committed.

UNIT TWO: TORTS AND CRIMES

CAUSATION IN FACT
An act or omission without which an event would not have occurred.

PROXIMATE CAUSE
Legal cause; exists when the connection between an act and an injury is strong enough to justify imposing liability.

CAUSATION IN FACT AND PROXIMATE CAUSE   In deciding whether there is causation, the court must address two questions:

1.   *Is there causation in fact?* Did the injury occur because of the defendant's act, or would it have occurred anyway? If an injury would not have occurred without the defendant's act, then there is causation in fact. **Causation in fact** can usually be determined by the use of the *but for* test: "but for" the wrongful act, the injury would not have occurred. Theoretically, causation in fact is limitless. One could claim, for example, that "but for" the creation of the world, a particular injury would not have occurred. Thus, as a practical matter, the law has to establish limits, and it does so through the concept of proximate cause.

2.   *Was the act the proximate cause of the injury?* **Proximate cause,** or legal cause, exists when the connection between an act and an injury is strong enough to justify imposing liability. Consider an example. Ackerman carelessly leaves a campfire burning. The fire not only burns down the forest but also sets off an explosion in a nearby chemical plant that spills chemicals into a river, killing all the fish for a hundred miles downstream and ruining the economy of a tourist resort. Should Ackerman be liable to the resort owners? To the tourists whose vacations were ruined? These are questions of proximate cause that a court must decide.

Probably the most cited case on proximate cause is the *Palsgraf* case discussed in the following *Landmark in the Law.* The question before the court was as follows: Does a defendant's duty of care extend only to those who may be injured as a result of a foreseeable risk, or does it extend also to a person whose injury could not reasonably be foreseen?

LANDMARK IN THE LAW

Palsgraf v. Long Island Railroad Co. (1928)

In 1928, the New York Court of Appeals (that state's highest court) issued its decision in *Palsgraf v. Long Island Railroad Co.*,[a] a case that has become a landmark in negligence law with respect to proximate cause.

The facts of the case were as follows. The plaintiff, Palsgraf, was waiting for a train on a station platform. A man carrying a small package wrapped in newspaper was rushing to catch a train that had begun to move away from the platform. As the man attempted to jump aboard the moving train, he seemed unsteady and about to fall. A railroad guard on the train car reached forward to grab him, and another guard on the platform pushed him from behind to help him board the train. In the process, the man's package fell on the railroad tracks and exploded, because it contained fireworks. The repercussions of the explosion caused scales at the other end of the train platform to fall on Palsgraf, who was injured as a result. She sued the railroad company for damages in a New York state court.

At the trial, the jury found that the railroad guards were negligent in their conduct. On appeal, the question before the New York Court of Appeals was whether the conduct of the railroad guards was the proximate cause of Palsgraf's injuries. In other words, did the guards' duty of care extend to Palsgraf, who was outside the zone of danger and whose injury could not reasonably have been foreseen?

The court stated that the question of whether the guards were negligent *with respect to Palsgraf* depended on whether her injury was *reasonably foreseeable* to the railroad guards. Although the guards may have acted negligently with respect to the man boarding the train, this has no bearing on the question of their negligence

a.   248 N.Y. 339, 162 N.E. 99 (1928).

Landmark in the Law—Continued

with respect to Palsgraf. This is not a situation in which a person commits an act so potentially harmful (for example, firing a gun at a building) that he or she would be held responsible for any harm that resulted. The court stated that here, "by concession, there was nothing in the situation to suggest to the most cautious mind that the parcel wrapped in newspaper would spread wreckage through the station." The court thus concluded that the railroad guards were not negligent with respect to Palsgraf and not liable for her injuries.

For Critical Analysis: *If the guards knew that the package contained fireworks, would the court have ruled otherwise? Would it matter that the guards were motivated by a desire to help the man board the train and not by a desire to harm anyone?*

FORESEEABILITY   Since the *Palsgraf* case, the courts have used *foreseeability* as the test for proximate cause. The railroad guards were negligent, but the railroad's duty of care did not extend to Palsgraf, because her injury was unforeseeable. If the victim of the harm or the consequences of the harm done are unforeseeable, there is no proximate cause. Of course, it is foreseeable that people will stand on railroad platforms and that objects attached to the platforms will fall as the result of explosions nearby; however, this is not a chain of events against which a reasonable person would usually guard. It is difficult to predict when a court will say that something is foreseeable and when it will say that something is not. How far a court stretches foreseeability is determined in part by the extent to which the court is willing to stretch the defendant's duty of care. In the following case, the court considered whether, under the circumstances, the harm caused by arson is a reasonably foreseeable risk.

NOTE Proximate cause can be thought of as a question of social policy: Should the defendant be made to bear the loss instead of the plaintiff?

CASE 5.4

ADDIS v. STEELE

Appeals Court of Massachusetts, 1995.
38 Mass.App.Ct. 433,
648 N.E.2d 773.

HISTORICAL AND ECONOMIC SETTING   *Of major crimes, arson is the easiest to commit, the most difficult to detect, and the hardest to prove. Every year, arson kills as many as a thousand people and injures thousands more. Property worth more than a billion dollars is destroyed, and millions of dollars in jobs and property taxes are lost. One common motive for arson is profit: people in serious financial trouble sometimes burn their own buildings to collect insurance money. Predictably, arson thus causes a significant increase in the price of fire insurance.*

FACTS   On the morning of October 2, 1989, a fire started by an arsonist broke out in the Red Inn in Provincetown, Massachusetts. The inn had a smoke detector, sprinkler, and alarm system, which alerted the guests, but there were no emergency lights or clear exits.

Attempting to escape, Deborah Addis and James Reed, guests at the inn, found the first-floor doors and windows locked. Ultimately, they forced open a second-floor window and jumped out. To recover for their injuries, they filed a suit in a Massachusetts state court against Tamerlane Corporation, which operated the inn under a lease, and others (including Duane Steele, who worked for the owner of the inn). Addis and Reed contended in part that Tamerlane was negligent. Tamerlane responded that harm caused by arson is not a reasonably foreseeable risk. The court entered a judgment against Tamerlane, and Tamerlane appealed. The appellate court affirmed the lower court's judgment. Tamerlane then appealed to a higher state court.

ISSUE   Was the harm caused by the fire set by the arsonist a reasonably foreseeable risk?

DECISION   Yes. The Appeals Court of Massachusetts affirmed the lower courts' judgments against Tamerlane.

REASON   The court pointed out that "the possibility of fire was foreseen and guarded against with * * * smoke detector[s], sprinkler and alarm system[s]." Given the foreseeability of a fire, the court reasoned that Tamerlane should gain "no benefit from the fact that the

(Continued)

Case 5.4—Continued

fire was set." The court held that the duty to protect others against unreasonable risks of harm extends to risks arising from acts of third persons, "whether they be innocent, negligent, intentional, or even criminal." The court concluded that Tamerlane's "failure to provide adequate lighting and egress [exit] created a foreseeable risk that a fire, however started—innocently, negligently, or by a criminal act—would cause harm to its guests."

FOR CRITICAL ANALYSIS—Economic Consideration
Does a business always have a duty to protect its patrons from the harm caused by the criminal activity of third persons? In other words, is the harm caused by all crimes reasonably foreseeable under all circumstances? If not, under what circumstances is harm caused by crime foreseeable?

COMPARE The concept of superseding intervening force is not a question of physics, but is, like proximate cause, a question of responsibility.

SUPERSEDING INTERVENING FORCES   An independent intervening force may break the connection between a wrongful act and an injury to another. If so, it acts as a *superseding cause*—that is, the intervening force or event sets aside, or replaces, the original wrongful act as the cause of the injury. For example, suppose that Derrick keeps a can of gasoline in the trunk of his car. The presence of the gasoline creates a foreseeable risk and is thus a negligent act. If Derrick's car skids and crashes into a tree, causing the gasoline can to explode, Derrick would be liable for injuries sustained by passing pedestrians because of his negligence. If the explosion had been caused by lightning striking the car, however, the lightning would supersede Derrick's original negligence as a cause of the damage, because the lightning was not foreseeable.

In negligence cases, the negligent party will often attempt to show that some act has intervened after his or her action and that this second act was the proximate cause of injury. Typically, in cases in which an individual takes a defensive action, such as swerving to avoid an oncoming car, the original wrongdoer will not be relieved of liability even if the injury actually resulted from the attempt to escape harm. The same is true under the "danger invites rescue" doctrine. Under this doctrine, if Lemming commits an act that endangers Salter and Yokem sustains an injury trying to protect Salter, then Lemming will be liable for Yokem's injury, as well as for any injuries Salter may sustain. Rescuers can injure themselves, or the person rescued, or even a stranger, but the original wrongdoer will still be liable.

Defenses to Negligence

The basic defenses in negligence cases are (1) assumption of risk, (2) contributory negligence, and (3) comparative negligence.

ASSUMPTION OF RISK
A defense against negligence that can be used when the plaintiff is aware of a danger and voluntarily assumes the risk of injury from that danger.

ASSUMPTION OF RISK   A plaintiff who voluntarily enters into a risky situation, knowing the risk involved, will not be allowed to recover. This is the defense of **assumption of risk.** The requirements of this defense are (1) knowledge of the risk and (2) voluntary assumption of the risk. For example, a driver entering a race knows there is a risk of being killed or injured in a crash. The driver has assumed the risk of injury.

The risk can be assumed by express agreement, or the assumption of risk can be implied by the plaintiff's knowledge of the risk and subsequent conduct. Of course, the plaintiff does not assume a risk different from or greater than the risk normally carried by the activity. In our example, the race car driver assumes the risk of being injured in the race but not the risk that the banking in the curves of the racetrack will give way during the race because of a construction defect.

Risks are not deemed to be assumed in situations involving emergencies. Neither are they assumed when a statute protects a class of people from harm and a member of the class is injured by the harm. For example, employees are protected by statute from harmful working conditions and therefore do not assume the risks associated with the workplace. If an employee is injured, he or she will generally be compensated regardless of fault under state workers' compensation statutes (discussed in Chapter 32).

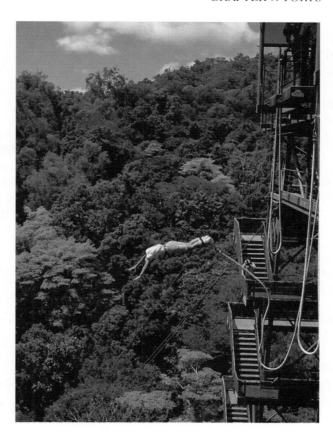

A bungee jumper leaps from a platform. If the jumper is injured and sues the operator of the jump for negligence, what defenses might the operator use to avoid liability?

In the following case, the plaintiff suffered an injury to his pitching arm in a simulated baseball game during a tryout for a major league team. The issue before the court was whether the plaintiff had assumed the risk of the injury, thus precluding him from recovery.

CASE 5.5

WATTENBARGER v. CINCINNATI REDS, INC.

California Court of Appeal, Third District, 1994.
28 Cal.App.4th 746,
33 Cal.Rptr.2d 732.

HISTORICAL AND CULTURAL SETTING *Despite the legend of Abner Doubleday's invention of baseball, most sports historians agree that the game was not the invention of just a single person. Instead, baseball evolved in the nineteenth century from a number of ball-and-stick games (including a game called "base ball") that had been popular earlier in England and colonial America. Segregated until John (Jackie) Robinson integrated the Brooklyn Dodgers in 1947, baseball teams today can include players of all ethnic, cultural, and national backgrounds.*

FACTS In June 1990, in Lodi, California, seventeen-year-old Jeffrey Wattenbarger tried out for the position of pitcher for the Cincinnati Reds. During the tryouts, Wattenbarger's shoulder popped. It occurred on his third pitch to a batter during a simulated game. He stepped off the mound and told the representatives of the Reds. Hearing no response, Wattenbarger stepped back onto the mound and threw another pitch. He immediately experienced severe pain. Later, it was discovered that a portion of the bone and tendons had pulled away sometime during Wattenbarger's pitching, and he underwent an operation on the arm. Seeking damages for the injury, Wattenbarger brought an action in a California state court against the Reds, claiming they had been negligent in allowing him to throw the fourth pitch. The Reds asserted, among other things, the defense of assumption of risk—that is, that Wattenbarger, by participating in the tryout, had assumed the risk of injury—and filed a motion

(Continued)

Case 5.5—Continued

for summary judgment. The court granted the motion, and Wattenbarger appealed to a state appellate court.

ISSUE By taking part in a sport, does an individual assume a risk of injury greater than the risks inherent in the sport?

DECISION No. The California Court of Appeal held, among other things, that a participant does not assume a risk greater than the risks inherent in a sport. The court reversed the lower court's grant of summary judgment and remanded the case.

REASON The court acknowledged that assumption of risk occurs when a person "voluntarily participates in a sporting event or activity involving certain inherent risks." The court stated that if Wattenbarger had stopped after his third pitch, "we would have no difficulty finding *   *   * assumption of risk a bar to recovery." The court explained, however, that the Reds "were not co-participants in the sport or activity but were instead in control of it." Thus, they owed a duty to the tryout participants "not to increase the risks inherent in the game of baseball." When Wattenbarger told them that his arm had popped, "he was seeking guidance as to how to proceed. Hearing nothing to countermand the original instruction *   *   *, [he] threw another pitch, thereby causing further injury."

FOR CRITICAL ANALYSIS—Cultural Consideration
Baseball team managers are aware that young potential players, such as Wattenbarger, sometimes face significant cultural pressure to succeed in the sport. How does this knowledge affect baseball managers' duty of care during tryouts?

CONTRIBUTORY NEGLIGENCE
A theory in tort law under which a complaining party's own negligence contributed to or caused his or her injuries. Contributory negligence is an absolute bar to recovery in a minority of jurisdictions.

CONTRIBUTORY NEGLIGENCE All individuals are expected to exercise a reasonable degree of care in looking out for themselves. In a few jurisdictions, recovery for injury resulting from negligence is prevented if the plaintiff was also negligent (failed to exercise a reasonable degree of care). This is the defense of **contributory negligence.** Under the doctrine of contributory negligence, no matter how insignificant the plaintiff's negligence is relative to the defendant's negligence, the plaintiff will be precluded from recovering any damages.

An exception to the doctrine of contributory negligence may apply if the defendant failed to take advantage of an opportunity to avoid causing the damage. Under the "last clear chance" rule, the plaintiff may recover full damages despite his or her own negligence. For example, if Murphy walks across the street against the light, and Lewis, a motorist, sees her in time to avoid hitting her but hits her anyway, Lewis (the defendant) is not permitted to use Murphy's (the plaintiff's) prior negligence as a defense. The defendant negligently missed the opportunity to avoid injuring the plaintiff. In those states that have adopted the comparative negligence rule, discussed next, the last clear chance doctrine does not apply.

COMPARATIVE NEGLIGENCE
A theory in tort law under which the liability for injuries resulting from negligent acts is shared by all parties who were negligent (including the injured party), on the basis of each person's proportionate negligence.

COMPARATIVE NEGLIGENCE The majority of states now allow recovery based on the doctrine of **comparative negligence.** This doctrine enables both the plaintiff's and the defendant's negligence to be computed and the liability for damages distributed accordingly. Some jurisdictions have adopted a "pure" form of comparative negligence that allows the plaintiff to recover, even if the extent of his or her fault is greater than that of the defendant. For example, if the plaintiff was 80 percent at fault and the defendant 20 percent at fault, the plaintiff may recover 20 percent of his or her damages. Many states' comparative negligence statutes, however, contain a "50 percent" rule by which the plaintiff recovers nothing if he or she was more than 50 percent at fault. In the following case, the court had to determine the meaning of a particular state's comparative negligence statute.

CASE 5.6

RODGERS v. AMERICAN HONDA MOTOR CO.
United States Court of Appeals,
First Circuit, 1995.
46 F.3d 1.

HISTORICAL AND INTERNATIONAL SETTING *Since the nineteenth century, many civil law jurisdictions— including Austria, China, France, Germany, Japan, Portugal, Spain, Switzerland, and Turkey—have apportioned damages in accident cases according to a comparative fault doctrine. In 1945, Great Britain, a common law jurisdiction, began to apply comparative negligence in its accident cases. Britain's law has been followed in Australia, Canada, New Zealand, and North Ireland. In the United States, the first state to adopt a comparative negligence doctrine was Mississippi, in 1910. The doctrine has since been adopted in most of the states.*

FACTS Brian Rodgers, an experienced all-terrain-vehicle (ATV) rider, helped a friend repair a three-wheel ATV. Without putting on a helmet, Rodgers gave the ATV a trial run. It flipped, and Rodgers struck his head, causing injuries to his brain. Rodgers's wife, Debra, and his other guardian filed a suit in a Maine state court against the American Honda Motor Company, the manufacturer of the ATV. During the trial, the plaintiffs asked the court to exclude testimony that Rodgers had not been wearing a helmet. The court ruled that the testimony was admissible, and the plaintiffs appealed to the U.S. Court of Appeals for the First Circuit.

ISSUE Does the doctrine of comparative negligence apply not only to fault for the cause of an accident but also to responsibility for the extent of any damage sustained?

DECISION Yes. The U.S. Court of Appeals for the First Circuit affirmed the ruling of the state court.

REASON Because the accident occurred in Maine, the appellate court reviewed the Maine statute that applied to the case. The statute provides that a reduction in the amount of a recovery is to be "just and equitable, having regard to the claimant's share in the responsibility for the damages * * *. If [a] claimant is found by the jury to be equally at fault, the claimant shall not recover." Noting that the last sentence was added later in the legislative process, the court read "at fault" to mean having "responsibility for the damage sustained." Thus, if a plaintiff was found to be at least equally responsible for the damage sustained, he or she could recover nothing. The court added that in this case, because "the uncontradicted evidence that plaintiff's failure to wear a helmet was responsible for essentially all the damage sustained, this reading of the statute is fatal to his case."

FOR CRITICAL ANALYSIS—International Consideration
When the plaintiff lives in one country and the defendant in another, and the respective countries use different formulas for measuring comparative negligence, which formula should be applied?

Special Negligence Doctrines and Statutes

There are a number of special doctrines and statutes relating to negligence. We examine a few of them here.

RES IPSA LOQUITUR Generally, in lawsuits involving negligence, the plaintiff has the burden of proving that the defendant was negligent. In certain situations, when negligence is very difficult or impossible to prove, the courts may infer that negligence has occurred, in which case the burden of proof rests on the defendant—to prove he or she was *not* negligent. The inference of the defendant's negligence is known as the doctrine of *res ipsa loquitur,* which translates as "the facts speak for themselves." This doctrine is applied only when the event creating the damage or injury is one that ordinarily does not occur in the absence of negligence. *Res ipsa loquitur* has been applied to such events as trains derailing, wheels falling off moving vehicles, and bricks or windowpanes falling from a defendant's premises. For the doctrine to apply, the event must have been within the defendant's power to control, and it must not have been due to any voluntary action or contribution on the part of the plaintiff. Some courts will add still another condition—that the evidence available to explain the event be more accessible to the defendant than to the plaintiff.

RES IPSA LOQUITUR
A doctrine under which negligence may be inferred simply because an event occurred, if it is the type of event that would not occur in the absence of negligence. Literally, the term means "the facts speak for themselves."

NEGLIGENCE *PER SE*
An act (or failure to act) in violation of a statutory requirement.

NEGLIGENCE *PER SE* Certain conduct, whether it consists of an action or a failure to act, may be treated as **negligence *per se*** ("in or of itself"). Negligence *per se* may occur if an individual violates a statute or an ordinance providing for a criminal penalty and that violation causes another to be injured. The injured person must prove (1) that the statute clearly sets out what standard of conduct is expected, when and where it is expected, and of whom it is expected; (2) that he or she is in the class intended to be protected by the statute; and (3) that the statute was designed to prevent the type of injury that he or she suffered. The standard of conduct required by the statute is the duty that the defendant owes to the plaintiff, and a violation of the statute is the breach of that duty.

For example, a statute may require a landowner to keep a building in a safe condition and may also subject the landowner to a criminal penalty, such as a fine, if the building is not kept safe. The statute is meant to protect those who are rightfully in the building. Thus, if the owner, without a sufficient excuse, violates the statute and a tenant is thereby injured, then a majority of courts will hold that the owner's unexcused violation of the statute conclusively establishes negligence—that is, that the owner's violation is negligence *per se*.

GOOD SAMARITAN STATUTE
A state statute that provides that persons who rescue or provide emergency services to others in peril—unless they do so recklessly, thus causing further harm—cannot be sued for negligence.

DRAM SHOP ACT
A state statute that imposes liability on the owners of bars and taverns, as well as those who serve alcoholic drinks to the public, for injuries resulting from accidents caused by intoxicated persons when the sellers or servers of alcoholic drinks contributed to the intoxication.

SPECIAL NEGLIGENCE STATUTES A number of states have enacted statutes prescribing duties and responsibilities in certain circumstances, the violation of which will impose civil liability. For example, most states now have what are called **Good Samaritan statutes.** Under these statutes, persons who are aided voluntarily by others cannot turn around and sue the "Good Samaritans" for negligence. These laws were passed largely to protect physicians and medical personnel who voluntarily render their services in emergency situations to those in need, such as individuals hurt in car accidents.

Many states have also passed **dram shop acts,** under which a tavern owner or bartender may be held liable for injuries caused by a person who became intoxicated while drinking at the bar or who was already intoxicated when served by the bartender. In some states, statutes impose liability on *social hosts* (persons hosting parties) for injuries caused by guests who became intoxicated at the hosts' homes. Under these statutes, it is unnecessary to prove that the tavern owner, bartender, or social host was negligent.

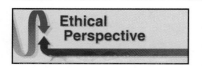 **Ethical Perspective**

Many people question the fairness of state statutes that impose liability on social hosts for injuries caused by guests' intoxication. The trend has been to permit such suits, and currently nearly half of the states allow plaintiffs injured in car accidents to sue social hosts—those who served alcoholic beverages to the defendants. Sometimes, the definition of a "social host" is fashioned broadly. For example, in one case, a person who hosted a "bring your own bottle" party was held liable for injuries caused by a drunken guest.[a] In another case, a passenger in a car who gave the driver an alcoholic beverage was held liable, even though the driver was sober at that time.[b]

The Illinois Supreme Court recently "went against the wind" on this issue when it affirmed the long-established precedent in that state of not permitting social hosts to be liable for their guests' harmful behavior. The court stated that allowing such suits would open a "Pandora's Box of unlimited liability" in which plaintiffs' attorneys could "drag into court any and all adults who may qualify as a social host." According to the Illinois court, the victims of drunk driving "have always had, and will continue to have, a civil remedy. They can sue the drunk driver, who is undoubtedly at

a.   *Dower v. Gamba,* 276 N.J.Super. 319, 647 A.2d 1364 (1994).
b.   *Wheeler v. Murphy,* 452 S.E.2d 416 (W.Va. 1994).

Ethical Perspective—Continued

fault. We have not been presented with any evidence to suggest that this civil remedy is insufficient."[c]

For Critical Analysis: *Explain the differences in the number of lawsuits brought and their outcomes under the "social host" doctrine as opposed to the rule stated by the Illinois court.*

c. *Charles v. Seigfried,* 165 Ill.2d 482, 651 N.E.2d 154, 209 Ill.Dec. 226 (1995).

▌Strict Liability

Another category of torts is called **strict liability,** or *liability without fault.* Intentional torts and torts of negligence involve acts that depart from a reasonable standard of care and cause injuries. Under the doctrine of strict liability, liability for injury is imposed for reasons other than fault. Strict liability for damages proximately caused by an abnormally dangerous or exceptional activity is one application of this doctrine. Courts apply the doctrine of strict liability in such cases because of the extreme risk of the activity. For example, even if blasting with dynamite is performed with all reasonable care, there is still a risk of injury. Balancing that risk against the potential for harm, it is fair to ask the person engaged in the activity to pay for injury caused by that activity. Although there is no fault, there is still responsibility because of the dangerous nature of the undertaking.

STRICT LIABILITY
Liability regardless of fault. In tort law, strict liability may be imposed on defendants in cases involving abnormally dangerous activities, dangerous animals, or defective products.

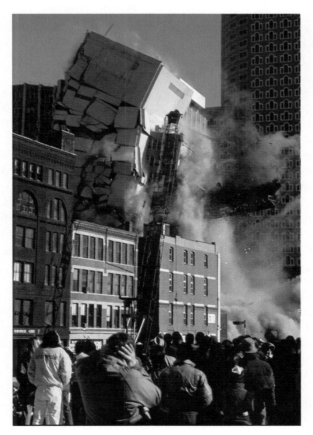

A skyscraper collapses after the detonation of explosive charges placed by a demolition crew. If any of the spectators are injured, would the doctrine of strict liability apply? Why or why not?

There are other applications of the strict liability principle. Persons who keep dangerous animals, for example, are strictly liable for any harm inflicted by the animals. A significant application of strict liability is in the area of *product liability*—liability of manufacturers and sellers for harmful or defective products. Liability here is a matter of social policy and is based on two factors: (1) the manufacturing company can better bear the cost of injury, because it can spread the cost throughout society by increasing prices of goods and services, and (2) the manufacturing company is making a profit from its activities and therefore should bear the cost of injury as an operating expense. We will discuss product liability in greater detail in Chapter 17.

In the following case, the issue before the court is whether a fumigation company should be held strictly liable for injuries caused by the Vikane gas that the company used during the fumigation of a condominium complex.

> **REMEMBER** A business may be considered to have an ethical duty to consumers that goes beyond its legal duty.

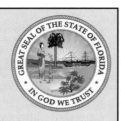

CASE 5.7

OLD ISLAND FUMIGATION, INC. v. BARBEE

District Court of Appeal of Florida,
Third District, 1992.
604 So.2d 1246.

HISTORICAL AND SOCIAL SETTING *The early law of torts was not primarily concerned with whether a wrongdoer was at fault but rather with keeping the peace—providing a remedy in lieu of private vengeance. At that time, a person who hurt another by accident, or even in self-defense, was required to pay for the injury or damage. The rule was "he who breaks must pay." Gradually, the law came to recognize fault as the basis for imposing liability, and it was suggested that there should be no liability without fault. In the late nineteenth century, however, the law began to accept that in some cases, a defendant may be liable not only in the absence of fault but even if he or she has followed a standard of reasonable care. In the context of abnormally dangerous activities, the courts recognized a new doctrine: in the event of harm for which no one is at fault, the party who can best bear the loss will be held liable.*

FACTS Old Island Fumigation, Inc., fumigated Buildings A and B of a condominium complex. Residents in Buildings A and B were evacuated during the procedure, but occupants of Building C were not. Shortly after the fumigation, which involved the use of Vikane gas, several residents of Building C became ill and were treated for sulfuryl fluoride poisoning. Sulfuryl fluoride is the active ingredient of Vikane gas. Several months later, an architect discovered that the fire wall between Buildings B and C was defective and contained an open space measuring four feet by eighteen inches, through which the gas had entered Building C. The defect was visible only

from within the crawl space, and thus it had been missed by various building inspectors, as well as by the fumigating company. Residents of Building C sued Old Island in a Florida state court, alleging that fumigation was an ultrahazardous activity and that Old Island was therefore strictly liable for their injuries. The company asserted that it should not be responsible for injuries caused by the negligence of others—the original architect and contractors for the condominiums, who had failed to note and repair the defect in the fire wall. The trial court granted the plaintiffs' motion for summary judgment against Old Island, and Old Island appealed.

ISSUE The issue in this case is twofold: (1) Is fumigation an ultrahazardous activity? (2) Even if fumigation is an ultrahazardous activity, can Old Island be held liable for damages when the negligence of others (including the building contractors) made the injuries possible?

DECISION Yes, to both questions. The Florida appellate court affirmed the trial court's judgment.

REASON Citing another case, the court stated that the factors to be considered in determining whether an activity is ultrahazardous are "whether [the] activity involves [a] high degree of risk of harm to property of others; whether [the] potential harm is likely to be great; whether [the] risk can be eliminated by [the] exercise of reasonable care; whether [the] activity is [a] matter of common usage; whether [the] activity is appropriate to [the] place where [the activity is] conducted [and] whether [the] activity has substantial value to [the] community." The court held that fumigation is an ultrahazardous activity because it "necessarily involves a risk of serious harm * * * which cannot be eliminated by the exercise of

(Continued)

Case 5.7—Continued

the utmost care, and is not a matter of common usage." Old Island was thus liable regardless of how careful it had been in fumigating the buildings. The court also emphasized that the fact that a third party had also been negligent did not relieve Old Island from liability for a hazard created by the company for its own profit.

FOR CRITICAL ANALYSIS—Social Consideration
Do you agree that business firms should bear the cost of injuries, even though the firms were not at fault, simply because the firms can spread the cost throughout society by increasing the prices of their goods or services?

Application

Law and the Retailer*

Retailers are faced with potential legal problems every day. They face a potential lawsuit not only every time a customer steps onto their property but also whenever a customer purchases a product from them. Here we consider only a few areas in which knowledge of the law can help a retailer prevent a legal problem.

Negligence
Negligence is an important area in tort law. Any retail business firm, whether it is a shoe store or a hamburger stand, must take reasonable care—not be negligent—in providing a safe environment in which the customer can examine products or purchase goods and services. The courts tend to conclude that "the customer is always right." Therefore, if you are a retailer, to assume that your customers will take reasonable care in their behavior or in the management of their small children while on your premises is to invite disaster. In contrast, if you assume that any person on the premises may show a complete lack of common sense, you are going a long way toward preventing a lawsuit for negligence.

For example, even though it might be obvious that an employee is washing a section of the salesroom floor, there should be signs posted that warn the customer what the employee is doing. Also, if your premises include a parking lot used by customers, the parking lot should be periodically inspected to make sure that there are no hazards, such as potholes, that might cause a customer to be injured. Again, even if a risk appears "obvious," the retailer should take steps to remove the risk.

*This *Application* is not meant to substitute for the services of an attorney who is licensed to practice law in your state.

Handling Shoplifters
To what extent can you, the businessperson, detain a suspected shoplifter without being successfully sued for false imprisonment, invasion of privacy, or some other tort, such as defamation or infliction of emotional distress? Suspected shoplifters can be accused and temporarily detained if certain reasonable procedures are used. These procedures differ, depending on the jurisdiction. The word to remember is *reasonable*. Keeping a suspected shoplifter in a locked storeroom for two hours because the manager has not yet got around to contacting the police would usually not be considered reasonable if the individual in question sued the firm for false imprisonment.

When apprehending and questioning a suspected shoplifter, choose your words carefully. Using abusive or accusatory words or otherwise subjecting the person to indignity may result in a lawsuit. In one case, for example, the words "a big fat woman like you" served as the basis for the tort of infliction of emotional distress.[a] If you think someone has shoplifted, act on your suspicion before the suspect leaves the store. Usually, the courts will allow detention only if the suspected shoplifter is still on your premises.

✓ Checklist for the Retailer

1. Obtain adequate liability insurance coverage, if possible.
2. Always assume that the worst can happen; post warnings near all potential hazards no matter how obvious they may seem.

---

a. *Haile v. New Orleans Railway & Light Co.*, 135 La. 229, 65 So. 225 (1914). According to tort scholar William Prosser, this is the mildest insult for which recovery on the grounds of infliction of emotional distress has been allowed. See W. Page Keeton et al., *Prosser and Keeton on Torts*, 5th ed. (St. Paul: West Publishing Co., 1984), p. 58.

(Continued)

Application—Continued

3. Always provide immediate medical care to an individual injured while on your premises.
4. Even for the most minor negligence lawsuit, hire an attorney and be willing to consider an out-of-court settlement (even if you believe that the customer was 100 percent at fault).

5. Employees who handle shoplifters should be appropriately trained in the proper procedure for apprehending and detaining someone suspected of shoplifting. Print out a short list of rules, and have it checked by a local attorney familiar with recent court decisions in your area.

▌Key Terms

actionable 124
actual malice 127
assault 122
assumption of risk 138
battery 122
business invitee 132
causation in fact 136
comparative negligence 140
compensatory damages 134
contributory negligence 140
conversion 130
damages 121

defamation 125
defense 123
dram shop act 142
duty of care 131
fraud 128
fraudulent misrepresentation 128
Good Samaritan statute 142
intentional tort 122
libel 125
malpractice 134
negligence 130
negligence *per se* 142

privilege 127
proximate cause 136
puffery 128
punitive damages 134
reasonable person standard 132
res ipsa loquitur 141
slander 125
strict liability 143
tort 120
tortfeasor 122
trespass to land 129
trespass to personal property 130

▌Chapter Summary: Torts

Intentional Torts against Persons *(See pages 122–129.)*	1. *Assault and battery*—An assault is an unexcused and intentional act that causes another person to be apprehensive of immediate harm. A battery is an assault that results in physical contact.
	2. *False imprisonment*—The intentional confinement or restraint of another person's movement without justification.
	3. *Infliction of emotional distress*—An intentional act that amounts to extreme and outrageous conduct resulting in severe emotional distress to another.
	4. *Defamation (libel or slander)*—A false statement of fact, not made under privilege, that is communicated to a third person and that causes damage to a person's reputation. For public figures, the plaintiff must also prove actual malice.
	5. *Invasion of privacy*—The use of a person's name or likeness for commercial purposes without permission, wrongful intrusion into a person's private activities, publication of information that places a person in a false light, or disclosure of private facts that an ordinary person would find objectionable.
	6. *Misrepresentation—fraud (deceit)*—A false representation made by one party, through misstatement of facts or through conduct, with the intention of deceiving another and on which the other reasonably relies to his or her detriment.
Intentional Torts against Property *(See pages 129–130.)*	1. *Trespass to land*—The invasion of another's real property without consent or privilege. Specific rights and duties apply once a person is expressly or impliedly established as a trespasser.
	2. *Trespass to personal property*—Unlawfully damaging or interfering with the owner's right to use, possess, or enjoy his or her personal property.
	3. *Conversion*—A wrongful act in which personal property is taken from its rightful owner or possessor and placed in the service of another.

❚ Chapter Summary: Torts—Continued

Unintentional Torts—Negligence (See pages 130–143.)	1. *Negligence*—The careless performance of a legally required duty or the failure to perform a legally required act. Elements that must be proved are that a legal duty of care exists, that the defendant breached that duty, and that the breach caused damage or injury to another.
	
	2. *Defenses to negligence*—The basic defenses in negligence cases are (a) assumption of risk, (b) contributory negligence, and (c) comparative negligence.
	
	3. *Special negligence doctrines and statutes*—
	  a. *Res ipsa loquitur*—A doctrine under which a plaintiff need not prove negligence on the part of the defendant because "the facts speak for themselves." *Res ipsa loquitur* has been applied to such events as trains derailing, wheels falling off moving vehicles, and elevators falling.
	  b. Negligence *per se*—A type of negligence that may occur if a person violates a statute or an ordinance providing for a criminal penalty and the violation causes another to be injured.
	  c. Special negligence statutes—State statutes that prescribe duties and responsibilities in certain circumstances, the violation of which will impose civil liability. Dram shop acts and Good Samaritan statutes are examples of special negligence statutes.

Strict Liability (See pages 143–145.)	Under the doctrine of strict liability, a person may be held liable, regardless of the degree of care exercised, for damages or injuries caused by his or her product or activity. Strict liability includes liability for harms caused by abnormally dangerous activities, by wild animals, and by defective products (product liability).

❚ For Review

1. What is the function of tort law?
2. What must a public figure prove to succeed in a defamation suit?
3. What are the four elements of negligence?
4. What defenses are available in an action for negligence?
5. What is strict liability? In what circumstances might this doctrine be applied?

❚ Questions and Case Problems

5–1. Defenses to Negligence. Corinna was riding her bike on a city street. While she was riding, she frequently looked behind her to verify that the books that she had fastened to the rear part of her bike were still attached. On one occasion while she was looking behind her, she failed to notice a car that was entering an intersection just as she was crossing it. The car hit her, causing her to sustain numerous injuries. Three witnesses stated that the driver of the car had failed to stop at the stop sign before entering the intersection. Corinna sued the driver of the car for negligence. What defenses might the defendant driver raise in this lawsuit? Discuss fully.

5–2. Liability to Business Invitees. Kim went to Ling's Market to pick up a few items for dinner. It was a rainy, windy day, and the wind had blown water through the door of Ling's Market each time the door opened. As Kim entered through the door, she slipped and fell in the approximately one-half inch of rainwater that had accumulated on the floor. The manager knew of the weather conditions but had not posted any sign to warn customers of the water hazard. Kim injured her back as a result of the fall and sued Ling's for damages. Can Ling's be held liable for negligence in this situation? Discuss.

5–3. Negligence. In which of the following situations will the acting party be liable for the tort of negligence? Explain fully.

(a) Mary goes to the golf course on Sunday morning, eager to try out a new set of golf clubs she has just purchased. As she tees off on the first hole, the head of her club flies off and injures a nearby golfer.

(b) Mary's doctor gives her some pain medication and tells her not to drive after she takes it, as the medication induces drowsiness. In spite of the doctor's warning, Mary decides to drive to the store while on the medication. Owing to her lack of alertness, she fails to stop at a traffic light and crashes into another vehicle, in which a passenger is injured.

5–4. Causation. Ruth carelessly parks her car on a steep hill, leaving the car in neutral and failing to engage the parking brake. The car rolls down the hill, knocking down an electric line. The sparks from the broken line ignite a grass fire. The fire spreads until it reaches a barn one mile away. The barn houses dynamite, and the burning barn explodes, causing part of the roof to fall on and injure a passing motorist, Jim. Can Jim recover from Ruth? Why or why not?

5–5. Trespass to Land. During a severe snowstorm, Yoshiko parked his car in a privately owned parking lot. The car was later towed from the lot, and Yoshiko had to pay $100 to the towing company to recover his car. Yoshiko sued the owner of the parking lot, Icy Holdings, Inc., to get back the $100 he had paid. Icy Holdings claimed that notwithstanding the severe snowstorm, Yoshiko's parking of his car on its property constituted trespass, and therefore Icy Holdings did not act wrongfully in having the car towed off the lot. Discuss whether Yoshiko can recover his $100.

5–6. Tort Theories. The Yommers operated a gasoline station. In December 1967, the McKenzies, their neighbors, noticed a smell in their well water, which proved to be caused by gasoline in the water. McKenzie complained to the Yommers, who arranged to have one of their underground storage tanks replaced. Nevertheless, the McKenzies were unable to use their water for cooking or bathing until they had a filter and water softener installed. At the time of the trial, in December 1968, they were still bringing in drinking water from an outside source. The McKenzies sued the Yommers for damages. The Yommers claimed that the McKenzies had not proved that there was any intentional wrongdoing or negligence on the part of the Yommers, and therefore they should not be held liable. Under what theory might the McKenzies recover damages even in the absence of any negligence on the Yommers' part? Explain. [*Yommer v. McKenzie*, 255 Md. 220, 257 A.2d 138 (1969)]

5–7. Defenses to Negligence. George Giles was staying at a Detroit hotel owned by the Pick Hotels Corp. While a hotel employee was removing luggage from the back seat of Giles's car, Giles reached into the front seat to remove his briefcase. As he did so, he supported himself by placing his left hand on the center pillar to which the rear door was hinged, with his fingers in a position to be injured if the rear door was closed. The hotel employee closed the rear door, and a part of Giles's left index finger was amputated. Giles sued the hotel for damages. What defense or defenses against negligence discussed in this chapter might relieve the hotel, partially or totally, from liability for Giles's injury? Explain fully. [*Giles v. Pick Hotels Corp.*, 232 F.2d 887 (6th Cir. 1956)]

5–8. Strict Liability. Danny and Marion Klein were injured when an aerial shell at a public fireworks exhibit went astray and exploded near them. They sued the Pyrodyne Corp., the pyrotechnic company that was hired to set up and discharge the fireworks, alleging, among other things, that the company should be strictly liable for damages caused by the fireworks display. Will the court agree with the Kleins? What factors will the court consider in making its decision? Discuss fully. [*Klein v. Pyrodyne Corp.*, 117 Wash.2d 1, 810 P.2d 917 (1991)]

5–9. Duty to Business Invitees. George Ward entered a K-Mart department store in Champaign, Illinois, through a service entrance near the home improvements department. After purchasing a large mirror, Ward left the store through the same door. On his way out the door, carrying the large mirror in front and somewhat to the side of him, he collided with a concrete pole located just outside the door about a foot and a half from the outside wall. The mirror broke, and the broken glass cut Ward's right cheek and eye, resulting in reduced vision in that eye. He later stated that he had not seen the pole, had not realized what was happening, and only knew that he felt "a bad pain, and then saw stars." Ward sued K-Mart Corp. for damages, alleging that the store was negligent. What was the nature of K-Mart's duty of care to Ward? Did it breach that duty by placing the concrete pole just outside the door? What

factors should the court consider when deciding whether K-Mart should be held liable for Ward's injuries? Discuss fully. [*Ward v. K-Mart Corp.*, 136 Ill.2d 132, 554 N.E.2d 223, 143 Ill.Dec. 288 (1990)]

5–10. Duty of Care. As pedestrians exited at the close of an arts and crafts show, Jason Davis, an employee of the show's producer, stood near the exit. Suddenly and without warning, Davis turned around and collided with Yvonne Esposito, an eighty-year-old woman. Esposito was knocked to the ground, fracturing her hip. After hip-replacement surgery, she was left with a permanent physical impairment. Esposito filed a suit in a federal district court against Davis and others, alleging negligence. What are the factors that indicate whether or not Davis owed Esposito a duty of care? What do those factors indicate in these circumstances? [*Esposito v. Davis*, 47 F.3d 164 (5th Cir. 1995)]

5–11. Negligence *Per Se*. A North Carolina Department of Transportation regulation prohibits the placement of telephone booths within public rights of way. Despite this regulation, GTE South, Inc., placed a booth in the right of way near the intersection of Hillsborough and Sparger Roads in Durham County. Laura Baldwin was using the booth when an accident at the intersection caused a dump truck to cross the right of way and smash into the booth. To recover for her injuries, Baldwin filed a suit in a North Carolina state court against GTE and others. Was Baldwin within the class of persons protected by the regulation? If so, did GTE's placement of the booth constitute negligence *per se*? [*Baldwin v. GTE South, Inc.*, 335 N.C. 544, 439 S.E.2d 108 (1995)]

A QUESTION OF ETHICS AND SOCIAL RESPONSIBILITY

5–12. *Ernesto Parra choked to death on a piece of food while eating at a restaurant. The administrator of Parra's estate sued the restaurant, claiming, among other things, that the restaurant breached its duty to rescue Parra while he was choking. The court stressed that under the common law, there is no general duty to aid a person in peril. If Parra had been injured by a dangerous condition in the restaurant, such as a slippery floor, then the restaurant would have had a duty to come to Parra's assistance and ensure that he received any medical treatment necessary. The restaurant, however, had not been responsible for placing Parra in danger; the fact that Parra choked was totally personal to Parra. According to the court, "As a general rule, a restaurateur is not an insurer of his customers' safety against all personal injuries. He has no duty as to 'conditions or risks which are ordinary and are, or should be, known or obvious to the patrons.'"* [Parra v. Tarasco, Inc., 230 Ill.App.3d 819, 595 N.E.2d 1186, 172 Ill.Dec. 516 (1992)]

1. Do you agree with the court's decision that the restaurant had no duty to rescue Parra? Why or why not?
2. Do you think that the law should impose a duty on all persons to rescue others in distress? What would be some of the implications of such a law for society? Discuss fully.

CASE BRIEFING ASSIGNMENT

5–13. *Examine Case A.2 [Burlingham v. Mintz, 891 P.2d 527 (Mont. 1995)] in Appendix A. The case has been excerpted there in great detail. Review and then brief the*

case, making sure that you include answers to the following questions in your brief.

1. Who were the plaintiff and defendant in this action?
2. Describe the events that led up to this lawsuit.
3. What was the central issue on appeal?
4. How did the state supreme court rule on this issue and dispose of the case?

FOR CRITICAL ANALYSIS

5–14. *What general principle underlies the common law doctrine that business owners have a duty of care toward their customers? Does the duty of care unfairly burden business owners? Why or why not?*

▌Accessing the Internet: Business Law and Legal Environment

Within the legal interest group on the commercial service America Online, there is a subcategory on torts and contracts. If you subscribe to America Online, the key word is

LEGAL

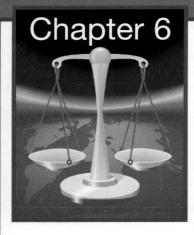

Chapter 6

Business Torts and Intellectual Property

"The language of the law must not be foreign to the ears of those who are to obey it."

Learned Hand, 1872–1961
(American jurist)

BUSINESS TORT
The wrongful interference with another's business rights.

INTELLECTUAL PROPERTY
Property resulting from intellectual, creative processes.

CHAPTER OBJECTIVES

After reading this chapter, you should be able to:

1. Explain the circumstances in which a party will be held liable for the tort of wrongful interference.
2. Indicate how the tort of appropriation occurs.
3. Summarize the laws protecting trademarks, patents, and copyrights.
4. Describe how trade secrets are protected by the law.
5. Point out how the Racketeer Influenced and Corrupt Organizations Act is applied in civil cases.

Our economic system of free enterprise is based on the ability of persons, acting either as individuals or as business firms, to compete freely for customers. Businesses may, generally speaking, engage in whatever is *reasonably* necessary to obtain a fair share of a market or to recapture a share that has been lost. They are not allowed to use the motive of complete elimination of competition to justify certain business activities, however. Those who enter into business should be acquainted with the point at which zealous competition might be construed by a court of law to cross over into tortious interference with the business rights of others. As the opening quotation indicates, businesspersons need to know what the law is if they are to obey it.

Business torts are defined as wrongful interference with another's business rights. Included in business torts are such vaguely worded common law concepts as *unfair competition* and *interfering with the business relations of others.* Some torts that were discussed in the previous chapter, including defamation, also occur in the business context.

Of significant concern to businesspersons is the need to protect their rights in intellectual property. **Intellectual property** is any property resulting from intellectual, creative processes—the products of an individual's mind. Although it is an abstract term for an abstract concept, intellectual property is nonetheless wholly familiar to virtually

150

everyone. The information contained in books and computer files is intellectual property. The software you use, the movies you see, and the music you listen to are all forms of intellectual property. In fact, in today's information age, it should come as no surprise that the value of the world's intellectual property now exceeds the value of physical property, such as machines and houses.

In this chapter, we examine business torts and the protection given to intellectual property rights under trademark, patent, copyright, and other laws. We also look at how the Racketeer Influenced and Corrupt Organizations Act (known more popularly as RICO) has been applied to fraudulent business activities.

▌ Wrongful Interference

Business torts involving wrongful interference are generally divided into two categories: wrongful interference with a contractual relationship and wrongful interference with a business relationship.

Wrongful Interference with a Contractual Relationship

Tort law relating to *intentional interference with a contractual relationship* has expanded greatly in recent years. A landmark case involved an opera singer, Joanna Wagner, who was under contract to sing for a man named Lumley for a specified period of years.[1] A man named Gye, who knew of this contract, nonetheless "enticed" Wagner to refuse to carry out the agreement, and Wagner began to sing for Gye. Gye's action constituted a tort because it interfered with the contractual relationship between Wagner and Lumley. (Of course, Wagner's refusal to carry out the agreement also entitled Lumley to sue Wagner for breach of contract.)

Three elements are necessary for a wrongful interference with a contractual relationship to occur:

1. A valid, enforceable contract must exist between two parties.
2. A third party must *know* that this contract exists.
3. The third party must *intentionally* cause either of the two parties to break the contract.

The contract may be between a firm and its employees or a firm and its customers. Sometimes a competitor of a firm draws away one of the firm's key employees. If the original employer can show that the competitor induced the breach—that is, that the former employee would not otherwise have broken the contract—damages can be recovered from the competitor.

The following, highly publicized case illustrates the requirements for the tort of wrongful interference with a contractual relationship.

REMEMBER It is the intent to do an act that is important in tort law, not the motive behind the intent.

---

1. *Lumley v. Gye*, 118 Eng.Rep. 749 (1853).

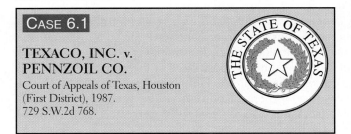

CASE 6.1

TEXACO, INC. v. PENNZOIL CO.
Court of Appeals of Texas, Houston (First District), 1987.
729 S.W.2d 768.

HISTORICAL AND SOCIAL SETTING *The structure of the oil and gas industry changed dramatically in the 1980s, as the price of oil, the number of gasoline stations, and the number of oil industry employees declined. Of the twenty-five largest companies in the industry at the beginning of the decade, by 1990 eleven*

(Continued)

Case 6.1—Continued

were acquired, merged, or dissolved and their assets sold off. Five of these transactions made up five of the ten biggest mergers of the decade. Among the companies that were changed forever were the Pennzoil Company, the Getty Oil Company, and Texaco, Inc.

FACTS The Pennzoil Company agreed to buy control of the Getty Oil Company. Both companies announced the news on January 5, 1984, although details of the agreement remained unsettled. While a formal written document was being negotiated, Texaco, Inc., made a higher bid for Getty, and on January 6, Getty's board of directors accepted it. As part of the deal, Getty insisted that Texaco assume responsibility for any claims brought by Pennzoil against Getty, and Getty's major shareholders insisted on a guaranteed price of at least "the price Pennzoil had agreed to pay." Pennzoil sued Texaco in a Texas state court, alleging wrongful interference with its contract with Getty. The court found that (1) Getty had agreed to Pennzoil's offer; (2) Texaco knowingly interfered with this agreement; (3) as a result, Pennzoil suffered damages of $7.53 billion; (4) Texaco's actions were intentional and in disregard of Pennzoil's rights; and (5) Pennzoil was entitled to additional punitive damages of $3 billion. Texaco appealed.

ISSUE Did Texaco wrongfully interfere with the contractual relationship of Pennzoil and Getty?

DECISION Yes. The Court of Appeals of Texas affirmed the trial court's decision.

REASON As to whether Pennzoil and Getty actually had a contract, the Court of Appeals of Texas pointed out

that if "there is no understanding that a signed writing is necessary before the parties will be bound, and the parties have agreed upon all substantial terms, then an informal agreement can be binding, even though the parties contemplate evidencing their agreement in a formal document later." The court noted that there was sufficient evidence that the parties intended to be bound. Similarly, the court stated that there was sufficient evidence that Texaco knew about the contract—the deal had been announced, and the announcement had been widely reported. As to whether Texaco interfered with the contract, the court again determined that there was sufficient evidence to support the trial court's finding on the issue. As an example of interference, the appellate court pointed to Texaco's "offering [of] better terms or other incentives."[a]

FOR CRITICAL ANALYSIS—Ethical Consideration
Texaco argued that its offer was merely in response to a campaign of active solicitation by the Getty entities, who were dissatisfied with the terms of Pennzoil's offer. Is it fair to hold Texaco liable in these circumstances? Why or why not?

a. On Texaco's subsequent appeal, the Texas Supreme Court found no reversible errors. Other issues in the case were appealed as high as the United States Supreme Court. In 1988, the case was settled for $3 billion. On the day of the payment, Texaco completed its reorganization and emerged from twelve months in bankruptcy proceedings.

Wrongful Interference with a Business Relationship

"Anyone can win unless there happens to be a second entry."

George Ade, 1866–1944
(*American humorist*)

PREDATORY BEHAVIOR
Business behavior, such as the entry into business, that is undertaken with the intention of unlawfully driving competitors out of the market.

Businesspersons devise countless schemes to attract customers, but they are forbidden by the courts to interfere unreasonably with another's business in their attempts to gain a share of the market. There is a difference between competition and **predatory behavior**—actions undertaken with the intention of unlawfully driving competitors completely out of the market.

The distinction usually depends on whether a business is attempting to attract customers in general or to solicit only those customers who have shown an interest in a similar product or service of a specific competitor. If a shopping center contains two shoe stores, an employee of Store A cannot be positioned at the entrance of Store B for the purpose of diverting customers to Store A. This type of activity constitutes the tort of wrongful interference with a business relationship, which is commonly considered to be an unfair trade practice. If this type of activity were permitted, Store A would reap the benefits of Store B's advertising.

Defenses to Wrongful Interference

A person will not be liable for the tort of wrongful interference with a contractual or business relationship if it can be shown that the interference was justified, or permissible. For example, bona fide competitive behavior is a permissible interference even if it results in the breaking of a contract. If Antonio's Meats advertises so effectively that it induces Alex's Restaurant Chain to break its contract with Alvarez Meat Company, Alvarez Meat Company will be unable to recover against Antonio's Meats on a wrongful interference theory. After all, the public policy that favors free competition in advertising outweighs any possible instability that such competitive activity might cause in contractual relations.

REMEMBER What society and the law consider permissible often depends on the circumstances.

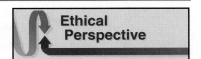

Ethical Perspective

Laws prohibiting unfair competition are based, ultimately, on the ethical conviction that free competition in the marketplace is beneficial to society. The tort of predatory behavior, for example, clearly expresses the public policy against unfair competition in the marketplace. The problem faced by the courts (and business firms), though, is deciding where the line should be drawn between "fair" and "unfair" competition.

That judges may differ in their decisions as to where this line should be drawn is illustrated in a recent case decided by the Arkansas Supreme Court. The case involved allegations by two drugstore owners that a Wal-Mart store located in Faulkner County, Arkansas, was engaging in predatory behavior. Wal-Mart contended that its sales tactics (including frequent sales and using "loss leaders"—selling products below cost—to attract customers) were not predatory and in fact promoted competition. The majority on the court agreed with Wal-Mart. Although Wal-Mart's marketing strategies may have caused the local drugstores to enjoy reduced profits, both of the drugstores nonetheless were still in business and continued to make profits.

Three dissenting judges, however, disagreed. They concluded that the trial court "could have found an intent to injure competitors from the evidence in the record and particularly from the testimony of David Glass, president of Wal-Mart Stores, Inc., who used language such as 'aggressive,' 'do whatever it takes,' 'kill the competition's momentum,' and 'war zones.'"[a]

For Critical Analysis: *Do retail firms such as Wal-Mart have an ethical duty to ensure that their competitors survive in the marketplace?*

a.   *Wal-Mart Stores, Inc. v. American Drugs, Inc.*, 319 Ark. 214, 891 S.W. 2d 30 (1995).

▌ Wrongful Entry into Business

In a freely competitive society it is usually true that any person can enter into any business to compete for the customers of existing businesses. Two situations in which this notion of free competition does not hold, however, are (1) when entering into business is a violation of the law and (2) when competitive behavior is predatory.

Any business or profession not subject to regulatory agencies or occupational licensing standards is open to an individual. No one can open a business for the sole purpose of driving another firm out of business, however; such a motive is considered to be predatory. What the courts consider normal competitive activity is not always easy to ascertain—where does the normal desire to compete and obtain profits end and the tortious action begin? The following landmark case illustrates how a Minnesota court grappled with the question of malicious injury to business.

CASE 6.2

TUTTLE v. BUCK

Supreme Court of Minnesota, 1909.
107 Minn. 145,
119 N.W. 946.

HISTORICAL AND ETHICAL SETTING *We often think of traditional common law as stable, stretching unchanged back in time to old England. This is often contrasted with modern "activist" judicial rulings that allegedly lack respect for precedent. The strength of the common law, however, has always been its flexibility to adapt to new sets of circumstances. Even decades ago, courts would create new torts and expand common law precedents in light of contemporary standards of ethics and justice.*

FACTS The plaintiff, Edward Tuttle, a barber, filed suit in a Minnesota state court against the defendant, Cassius Buck, for malicious interference with his business. The plaintiff had owned and operated a barbershop for the past ten years and had been able to support himself and his family comfortably from the income of the business. The defendant was a banker in the same community. During the previous twelve months, the defendant had "maliciously" established a competitive barbershop, employed a barber to carry on the business, and used his personal influence to attract customers from the plaintiff's barbershop. Apparently, the defendant had circulated false and malicious reports and accusations about the plaintiff and had personally solicited, urged, threatened, and otherwise persuaded many of the plaintiff's patrons to stop using the plaintiff's services and to use the defendant's shop instead. The plaintiff charged that the defendant undertook this entire plan with the sole design of injuring the plaintiff and destroying his business, not to serve any legitimate business interest or to practice fair competition. The defendant filed a general demurrer, which the court did not grant.[a] The defendant appealed to the Supreme Court of Minnesota.

ISSUE Did the defendant's activities constitute malicious interference with the plaintiff's business?

DECISION Yes. The Supreme Court of Minnesota held that the defendant had maliciously interfered with the plaintiff's business.

REASON Based on the facts presented, the court determined that the defendant's sole purpose in establishing the competing barbershop was to deprive the plaintiff of his livelihood. The court was bound by precedent to preserve competition in the marketplace, but at the same time it was supposed to guard against abusive practices. When a person starts a competing business to drive a competitor out of business rather than to earn profits, that person is guilty of a tort and must answer for the harm done. "To call such conduct competition is a perversion of terms. It is simply the application of force without legal justification, which in its moral quality may be no better than highway robbery."

FOR CRITICAL ANALYSIS—International Consideration
The tort of wrongful entry into business may have made sense in nineteenth-century America—an era of mostly small businesses in small towns and rural areas. Does it have any relevance, however, to our time of multinational corporations and international competitors?

a. A *general demurrer* is an objection to a pleading that is the equivalent of a motion to dismiss for failure to state a claim on which relief may be granted.

▌ Appropriation

The use by one person of another person's name, likeness, or other identifying characteristic, without permission and for the benefit of the user, constitutes the tort of **appropriation.** Under the law, an individual's right to privacy includes the right to the exclusive use of his or her identity. For example, in a case involving a Ford Motor Company television commercial in which a Bette Midler "sound-alike" sang a song that Midler had made famous, the court held that Ford "for their own profit in selling their product did appropriate part of her identity."[2]

A court ruled similarly in a case brought by Vanna White, the hostess of the popular television game show *Wheel of Fortune*, against Samsung Electronics America,

APPROPRIATION
In tort law, the use by one person of another person's name, likeness, or other identifying characteristic without permission and for the benefit of the user.

---

2. *Midler v. Ford Motor Co.,* 849 F.2d 460 (9th Cir. 1988).

Inc. Without White's permission, Samsung included in an advertisement for Samsung videocassette recorders (VCRs) a depiction of a robot dressed in a wig, gown, and jewelry, posed in a setting that resembled the *Wheel of Fortune* set, in a stance for which White is famous. The court held in White's favor, holding that the tort of appropriation does not require the use of a celebrity's name or likeness. The court stated that Samsung's robot ad left "little doubt" as to the identity of the celebrity whom the ad was meant to depict.[3]

Often, cases alleging appropriation require the courts to balance a celebrity's right to the exclusive use of his or her identity against the First Amendment right to freedom of speech. For example, in one case, a California newspaper reproduced in poster form various pages from its newspapers that contained a photograph and artist's rendition of Joe Montana, the well-known professional football player. In Montana's suit against the newspaper for the commercial misappropriation of his name, photograph, and likeness, however, the court held that the defendant newspaper's reproduction and sale of the posters was protected speech under the First Amendment.[4]

▌ Defamation in the Business Context

As discussed in Chapter 5, the tort of defamation occurs when an individual makes a false statement that injures another's reputation. Defamation may take the form of libel (defamatory statements in written or printed form) or slander (defamatory statements made orally). Defamation becomes a business tort when the defamatory matter injures someone in a profession, business, or trade or when it adversely affects a business entity in its credit rating and other dealings.

Recently, questions have arisen about the potential liability of on-line computer information services, such as CompuServe and Prodigy, for defamatory statements made in sources included in their databases. This chapter's *Business Law in Action* focuses on this important issue.

> *"Hurl your calumnies boldly; something is sure to stick."*
>
> **Francis Bacon, 1561–1626**
> *(English philosopher and statesman)*

▌ Disparagement of Property

Disparagement of property occurs when economically injurious falsehoods are made not about another's reputation but about another's product or property. Disparagement of property is a general term for torts that can be more specifically referred to as *slander of quality* or *slander of title*.

Slander of Quality

Publication of false information about another's product, alleging that it is not what its seller claims, constitutes the tort of **slander of quality**, or **trade libel**. The plaintiff must prove that actual damages proximately resulted from the slander of quality. In other words, the plaintiff must show not only that a third person refrained from dealing with the plaintiff because of the improper publication but also that there were associated damages. The economic calculation of such damages—they are, after all, conjectural—is often extremely difficult.

An improper publication may be both a slander of quality and a defamation. For example, a statement that disparages the quality of a product may also, by implication, disparage the character of the person who would sell such a product. In one case, for

DISPARAGEMENT OF PROPERTY
An economically injurious falsehood made about another's product or property. A general term for torts that are more specifically referred to as slander of quality or slander of title.

SLANDER OF QUALITY (TRADE LIBEL)
The publication of false information about another's product, alleging that it is not what its seller claims.

---

3. *White v. Samsung Electronics America, Inc.*, 971 F.2d 1395 (9th Cir. 1992).
4. *Montana v. San Jose Mercury News, Inc.*, 34 Cal.App.4th, 40 Cal.Rptr.2d 639 (1995).

BUSINESS LAW IN ACTION

Liability for On-Line Defamation

Not surprisingly, the Information Superhighway—the Internet—has led to legal questions never before posed. One of these questions concerns the liability of on-line information services, such as CompuServe and Prodigy, for defamatory speech generated by the users of those services.

Distributors versus Publishers

Traditionally, the courts have held that libraries, bookstores, newsstands, and other distributors of books and periodicals have no duty to monitor every book or periodical that they distribute. As the United States Supreme Court has held, this would be an unreasonable demand on the seller and a restriction on the public's access to reading matter.[a] If the contents of bookstores and newsstands were restricted to materials that the proprietors had read, they might be nearly empty. Therefore, distributors of defamatory materials are not themselves liable for the defamation— unless they happened to know or had reason to know of the defamatory contents.

A publisher, in contrast, *can* be held liable for defamatory contents in books and periodicals—because one

a. *Smith v. California*, 361 U.S. 147, 80 S.Ct. 215, 4 L.Ed.2d 205 (1959).

who repeats or otherwise republishes a defamatory statement is subject to liability as if he or she had originally published it.

The Status of On-Line Information Services

The question concerning on-line information services thus boils down to this: Should such services, for defamation purposes, be considered *distributors* or *publishers* of information? This question was first addressed in *Cubby, Inc. v. CompuServe, Inc.*,[b] a case decided in 1991. In that case, the plaintiffs alleged that CompuServe, Inc., should be held liable for defamatory statements made against them on one of the information sources provided through CompuServe Information Service (CIS). The court held that CompuServe was a distributor of information and thus could not be held liable for the defamatory statements *unless* there was a showing that it knew or had reason to know of the statements.

Those involved in the electronic distribution of information hoped that *Cubby* was the last word on the matter. In 1995, however, the issue arose again in *Stratton Oakmont, Inc. v. Prodigy Services Co.*,[c] in which the court held that Prodigy was a publisher and thus could be held

b. 776 F.Supp. 135 (S.D.N.Y. 1991).
c. No. 31063/94, Supreme Court of New York, May 24, 1995. This decision is not published in a printed reporter, but may be accessed on WESTLAW by keying in the cite 1995 WL 323710.

liable for defamatory statements posted on Prodigy's "Money Talk" bulletin board by an unidentified Prodigy user. The court reached this conclusion largely because Prodigy, starting in 1990, had held itself out— in its policy statements and in various national newspaper articles—as an on-line service that exercised editorial control over the content of messages posted on its computer bulletin boards. Prodigy expressly differentiated itself from its competition and expressly likened itself to a newspaper. Prodigy also instructed "board leaders" to monitor bulletin board postings and delete notes from its computer bulletin boards if they were offensive or in "bad taste," in accordance with Prodigy's guidelines. The *Stratton* decision indicates that the issue of on-line service providers' liability for defamation is far from resolved.[d]

For Critical Analysis: *What are some of the pros and cons of defining on-line information services as distributors? As publishers?*

d. After the trial court's ruling that Prodigy could be held liable as a publisher, Prodigy prepared to defend itself as any publisher would: by proving that the statements made about Stratton Oakmont were true (and thus not libelous). By October 1995, the parties had decided to end their dispute. Stratton Oakmont agreed to settle for an apology from Prodigy to restore Stratton Oakmont's reputation. Prodigy, in turn, would discontinue its attempts to prove that the statements made about Stratton Oakmont were true.

instance, claiming that a product that was marketed as a sleeping aid contained "habit-forming drugs" was held to constitute defamation.[5]

Trademark law (to be discussed shortly) has, to some extent, made it easier for companies to sue other companies on the basis of purported false advertising. In the past, courts often ruled that companies could be liable for false advertising only when they misrepresented their own products. It mattered little what such companies claimed

5. *Harwood Pharmacal Co. v. National Broadcasting Co.*, 9 N.Y.2d 460, 174 N.E.2d 602, 214 N.Y.S.2d 725 (1961).

about their competitors' brands, particularly in so-called comparative advertisements. Today, false or misleading statements about another firm's products are actionable.

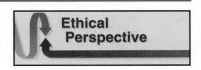

Litigation is expensive. The costs associated with defending against just one lawsuit can cause a small company to go bankrupt. Furthermore, lawsuits also impose costs on society—because it is the public who ultimately pays, through taxes, the salaries of the judges, juries, and court staffs, as well as the overhead for the courtrooms. From an ethical point of view, lawsuits may also be irresponsible—particularly if the suit is brought by a huge, multinational corporation against a small, insignificant company.

Consider, for example, the lawsuit brought by McDonald's Corporation against Dave Morris (an unemployed postal employee) and Helen Steel (a gardener) for libel. Morris and Steel belong to an obscure environmental group in London that published a pamphlet accusing McDonald's of underpaying its employees, torturing animals, corrupting children, and virtually every imaginable sin against consumers and the planet. Chapter headings in the pamphlet range from "McGreedy" to "McRipoff" to "McGarbage."

McDonald's is sparing no expense in pursuing the defendants for their libelous action. In all, McDonald's has arranged for 180 witnesses to testify at the trial, which began in June 1994 and, as of January 1996, had become the longest civil trial in English legal history. McDonald's will have to pay most of the costs of the suit, because the defendants have no money. (As of January 1996, McDonald's had paid $3 million in legal fees.) The taxpayers, though, will have to pay the court costs, which are estimated to be £7,600 (about $11,798) daily!

For Critical Analysis: *Why was McDonald's willing to spend so much money pursuing a lawsuit against such a small, insignificant group?*

Slander of Title

When a publication denies or casts doubt on another's legal ownership of any property, and when this results in financial loss to that property's owner, the tort of **slander of title** may exist. Usually, this is an intentional tort in which someone knowingly publishes an untrue statement about property with the intent of discouraging a third person from dealing with the person slandered. For example, it would be difficult for a car dealer to attract customers after competitors published a notice that the dealer's stock consisted of stolen autos.

SLANDER OF TITLE
The publication of a statement that denies or casts doubt upon another's legal ownership of any property, causing financial loss to that property's owner.

▌Intellectual Property Protection

The need to protect creative works was voiced by the framers of the U.S. Constitution over two hundred years ago: Article I, Section 8, of the Constitution authorized Congress "[t]o promote the Progress of Science and useful Arts, by securing for limited Times to Authors and Inventors the exclusive Right to their respective Writings and Discoveries." Laws protecting patents, trademarks, and copyrights are explicitly designed to protect and reward inventive and artistic creativity.

An understanding of intellectual property law is important because intellectual property has taken on increasing significance, not only in the United States but globally as well. Much of what is sold abroad, including popular American television series, computer programs, and videos, consists of intellectual property.

Trademarks and Related Property

TRADEMARK
A distinctive mark, motto, device, or implement that a manufacturer stamps, prints, or otherwise affixes to the goods it produces so that they may be identified on the market and their origins made known. Once a trademark is established (under the common law or through registration), the owner is entitled to its exclusive use.

A **trademark** is a distinctive mark, motto, device, or implement that a manufacturer stamps, prints, or otherwise affixes to the goods it produces so that they may be identified on the market and their origin vouched for. Statutory protection of trademarks and related property is provided at the federal level by the Lanham Trade-Mark Act of 1946.[6] The Lanham Act was enacted in part to protect manufacturers from losing business to rival companies that used confusingly similar trademarks. The Lanham Act incorporates the common law of trademarks and provides remedies for owners of trademarks who wish to enforce their claims in federal court. Many states also have trademark statutes.

At common law, the person who used a symbol or mark to identify a business or product was protected in the use of that trademark. Clearly, if one used the trademark of another, it would lead consumers to believe that one's goods were made by the other. The law seeks to avoid this kind of confusion. In the following famous case concerning Coca-Cola, the defendants argued that the Coca-Cola trademark was entitled to no protection under the law, because the term did not accurately represent the product.

---

6.   15 U.S.C. Sections 1051–1128.

CASE 6.3

THE COCA-COLA CO. v. KOKE CO. OF AMERICA

Supreme Court of the United States, 1920.
254 U.S. 143,
41 S.Ct. 113,
65 L.Ed. 189.

COMPANY PROFILE *John Pemberton, an Atlanta pharmacist, invented a caramel-colored, carbonated soft drink in 1886. His bookkeeper Frank Robinson named the beverage Coca-Cola after two of the ingredients, coca leaves and kola nuts. Asa Candler bought the Coca-Cola Company in 1891, and within seven years, he made the soft drink available in all of the United States, as well as in parts of Canada and Mexico. Candler continued to sell Coke aggressively and to open up new markets, reaching Europe before 1910. In doing so, however, he attracted numerous competitors, some of whom tried to capitalize directly on the Coke name.*

FACTS The Coca-Cola Company brought an action in a federal district court to enjoin other beverage companies from using the words "Koke" and "Dope" for the defendants' products. The defendants contended that the Coca-Cola trademark was a fraudulent representation and that Coca-Cola was therefore not entitled to any help from the courts. By use of the Coca-Cola name, the defendants alleged, the Coca-Cola Company represented that the beverage contained cocaine (from coca leaves). The district court granted the injunction, but

the federal appellate court reversed. The Coca-Cola Company appealed to the United States Supreme Court.

ISSUE Did the marketing of products called Koke and Dope by the Koke Company of America and other firms constitute an infringement on Coca-Cola's trademark?

DECISION Yes for Koke, but no for Dope. The Supreme Court enjoined the competing beverage companies from calling their products Koke, but the Court did not prevent them from calling their products Dope.

REASON The Court noted that, to be sure, prior to 1900 the Coca-Cola beverage had contained a small amount of cocaine, but this ingredient had been deleted from the formula by 1906 at the latest, and the Coca-Cola Company had advertised to the public that no cocaine was present in its drink. Coca-Cola was a widely popular drink "to be had at almost any soda fountain." Because of the public's widespread familiarity with Coca-Cola, the retention of the name of the beverage (referring to coca leaves and kola nuts) was not misleading: "Coca-Cola probably means to most persons the plaintiff's familiar product to be had everywhere rather than a compound of particular substances." The name Coke was found to be so common a term for the trademarked product Coca-Cola that the defendants' use of the similar-sounding Koke as a name for their beverages was disallowed. The Court could find no reason to restrain the defendants from using the name Dope, however.

FOR CRITICAL ANALYSIS—Social Consideration
How can a court determine when a particular nickname for a branded product has entered into common use?

TRADEMARK REGISTRATION   Trademarks may be registered with the state or with the federal government. To register for protection under federal trademark law, a person must file an application with the U.S. Patent and Trademark Office in Washington, D.C. Under current law, a mark can be registered (1) if it is currently in commerce or (2) if the applicant intends to put the mark into commerce within six months.

Under extenuating circumstances, the six-month period can be extended by thirty months, giving the applicant a total of three years from the date of notice of trademark approval to make use of the mark and file the required use statement. Registration is postponed until actual use of the mark. Nonetheless, during this waiting period, any applicant can legally protect his or her trademark against a third party who previously has neither used the mark nor filed an application for it. Registration is renewable between the fifth and sixth years after the initial registration and every twenty years thereafter (ten years for trademarks registered after 1989).

Registration of a trademark with the U.S. Patent and Trademark Office gives notice on a nationwide basis that the trademark belongs exclusively to the registrant. The registrant is also allowed to use the symbol ® to indicate that the mark has been registered. Whenever that trademark is copied to a substantial degree or used in its entirety by another, intentionally or unintentionally, the trademark has been *infringed* (used without authorization). When a trademark has been infringed, the owner of the mark has a cause of action against the infringer. A person need not have registered a trademark in order to sue for trademark infringement, but registration does furnish proof of the date of inception of the trademark's use.

DISTINCTIVENESS OF MARK   A central objective of the Lanham Act is to reduce the likelihood that registered marks will be so similar to one another that consumers cannot distinguish among them. The Lanham Act states, "No trademark by which the goods of the applicant may be distinguished from the goods of others shall be refused registration."[7] Only those trademarks that are deemed sufficiently distinctive from all competing trademarks will be protected, however. The trademarks must be sufficiently distinct to enable consumers to identify the manufacturer of the goods easily and to differentiate among competing products.

Strong Marks   Fanciful, arbitrary, or suggestive trademarks are generally considered to be the most distinctive (strongest) trademarks, because they are normally taken from outside the context of the particular product and thus provide the best means of distinguishing one product from another.

Fanciful trademarks include invented words, such as "Xerox" for one manufacturer's copiers and "Kodak" for another company's photographic products. Arbitrary trademarks include actual words that have no literal connection to the product such as "English Leather" used as a name for an after-shave lotion (and not for leather processed in England). Suggestive trademarks are those that suggest something about a product without describing the product directly. For example, "Dairy Queen" suggests an association between its products and milk, but it does not directly describe ice cream.

Secondary Meaning   Descriptive terms, geographical terms, and personal names are not inherently distinctive and do not receive protection under the law until they acquire a secondary meaning. A secondary meaning may arise when customers begin to associate a specific term or phrase, such as "London Fog," with specific trademarked items (coats with "London Fog" labels). Whether a secondary meaning becomes attached to a term or name usually depends on how extensively the product is advertised, the market for the product, the number of sales, and other factors. Once a secondary meaning is attached to a term or name, a trademark is considered distinctive and is protected.

---

7.   15 U.S.C. Section 1052.

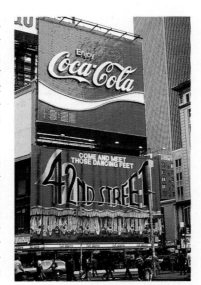

A billboard and theater marquee in New York City. Why are trademarks protected by the law?

An interesting issue in recent years has been whether a color can be trademarked on the basis that it has acquired a secondary meaning. In the following case, the United States Supreme Court addressed this issue.

CASE 6.4

QUALITEX CO. v. JACOBSON PRODUCTS CO.
Supreme Court of the United States, 1995.
___ U.S. ___,
115 S.Ct. 1300,
131 L.Ed.2d 248.

HISTORICAL AND SOCIAL SETTING *For centuries, color has been used to represent affiliations and loyalties and to symbolize various moods and qualities. For example, churches use vestments of different colors for different religious holidays, such as white for Easter. Certain colors are associated with particular political organizations—green with environmental groups, for example. Other colors add distinctive identifying qualities to commercial products, such as the purple and orange of Federal Express.*

FACTS   Since the 1950s, the Qualitex Company has manufactured Sun Glow press pads, which are used in dry cleaning and laundry establishments. The pads are a distinctive green-gold color. In 1989, the Jacobson Products Company began to sell its own press pads, which are a similar green-gold color. Qualitex brought an action against Jacobson in a federal district court, alleging, among other things, trademark infringement. The court entered a judgment in favor of Qualitex, and

Jacobson appealed. The appellate court ruled in favor of Jacobson, and Qualitex appealed to the United States Supreme Court.

ISSUE   Can color alone serve as a trademark?

DECISION   Yes. The United States Supreme Court reversed the ruling of the appellate court and held that color alone can qualify for trademark protection.

REASON   The Supreme Court pointed out that under the Lanham Act, a trademark can consist of "any word, name, symbol, or device, or any combination thereof." The Court noted that the U.S. Patent and Trademark Office has registered, as trademarks, the shape of the Coca-Cola bottle, the sound of NBC's chimes, and the scent of sewing thread. A color may also serve as such a product "symbol," concluded the Court. Furthermore, a color can "identify and distinguish" a product "from those manufactured or sold by others," once customers associate the color with the product. The Court stated that the fact that there is a limited supply of colors does not justify prohibiting their use as trademarks.

FOR CRITICAL ANALYSIS—Technological Consideration
The Court pointed out that there is "no competitive need in the press pad industry for the green-gold color, since other colors are equally usable." If, however, a color were essential to a product's use or purpose, should that color be given trademark protection? Why or why not?

Generic Terms   Generic terms, such as *bicycle* or *computer*, receive no protection, even if they acquire secondary meanings. A particularly thorny problem arises when a trademark acquires generic use. For example, *aspirin* and *thermos* were originally trademarked products, but today the words are used generically. Other examples are *escalator, trampoline, raisin bran, dry ice, lanolin, linoleum, nylon,* and *corn flakes.* Even so, the courts will not allow another firm to use those marks in such a way as to deceive a potential consumer.

SERVICE MARK
A mark used in the sale or the advertising of services, such as to distinguish the services of one person from the services of others. Titles, character names, and other distinctive features of radio and television programs may be registered as service marks.

SERVICE, CERTIFICATION, AND COLLECTIVE MARKS   A **service mark** is similar to a trademark but is used to distinguish the services of one person or company from those of another. For example, each airline has a particular mark or symbol associated with its name. Titles and character names used in radio and television are frequently registered as service marks.

Other marks protected by law include certification marks and collective marks. A *certification mark* is used by one or more persons other than the owner to certify the region, materials, mode of manufacture, quality, or accuracy of the owner's goods or services. When used by members of a cooperative, association, or other organization, it is referred to as a *collective mark*. Examples of certification marks are the "Good Housekeeping Seal of Approval" and "UL Tested." Collective marks appear at the ends of the credits of movies to indicate the various associations and organizations that participated in the making of the movies. The union marks found on the tags of certain products are also collective marks.

TRADE NAMES   Trademarks apply to *products*. The term **trade name** is used to indicate part or all of a business's name, whether the business is a sole proprietorship, a partnership, or a corporation. Generally, a trade name is directly related to a business and its goodwill. Trade names may be protected as trademarks if the trade name is the same as the company's trademarked product—for example, Coca-Cola. Unless also used as a trademark or service mark, a trade name cannot be registered with the federal government. Trade names are protected under the common law, however. As with trademarks, words must be unusual or fancifully used if they are to be protected as trade names. The word *Safeway*, for example, was held by the courts to be sufficiently fanciful to obtain protection as a trade name for a foodstore chain.[8]

Patents

A **patent** is a grant from the government that gives an inventor the exclusive right to make, use, and sell an invention for a period of twenty years from the date of filing the application for a patent. Patents for a fourteen-year period are given for designs, as opposed to inventions. For either a regular patent or a design patent, the applicant must demonstrate to the satisfaction of the U.S. Patent and Trademark Office that the invention, discovery, process, or design is genuine, novel, useful, and not obvious in light of current technology. A patent holder gives notice to all that an article or design is patented by placing on it the word "Patent" or "Pat." plus the patent number.

PATENT INFRINGEMENT   If a firm makes, uses, or sells another's patented design, product, or process without the patent owner's permission, it commits the tort of patent infringement. Patent infringement may exist even though the patent owner has not put the patented product in commerce. Unlike in most other countries, in the United States patent protection is granted to the first person to invent a product, not to the first person to file a patent application. In other words, if two individuals apply for patents, the one who prevails will be the person who first invented the product, not the first person to file for a patent on the product. Patent infringement may also occur even though not all features or parts of an invention are copied. (With respect to a patented process, however, all steps or their equivalent must be copied for infringement to exist.)

Often, litigation for patent infringement is so costly that the patent holder will instead offer to sell to the infringer a license to use the patented design, product, or process. Indeed, in many cases the costs of detection, prosecution, and monitoring are so high that patents are valueless to their owners; the owners cannot afford to protect them.

---

8.   *Safeway Stores v. Suburban Foods*, 130 F.Supp. 249 (E.D.Va. 1955).

TRADE NAME
A term that is used to indicate part or all of a business's name and that is directly related to the business's reputation and goodwill. Trade names are protected under the common law (and under trademark law, if the name is the same as the firm's trademarked property).

PATENT
A government grant that gives an inventor the exclusive right or privilege to make, use, or sell his or her invention for a limited time period. The word *patent* usually refers to some invention and designates either the instrument by which patent rights are evidenced or the patent itself.

• •

"The patent system . . . added the fuel of interest to the fire of genius."

Abraham Lincoln, 1809–1865
(Sixteenth president of the United States, 1861–1865)

• •

In the United States, if someone sells a counterfeit product that infringes on another's patent, the patent owner can bring a suit against the infringer for damages. What happens, though, if counterfeit products are sold in countries that do not offer much protection for those holding patent rights to the products under U.S. law? In such situations, not only do U.S. patent holders lose revenues from the sales of the fake products, but also, at least in some instances, consumers may suffer from the counterfeit products.

(Continued)

International Perspective—Continued

Certainly, the growing trade in counterfeit drugs has not appreciably benefited consumers in developing countries, because such products may consist of inert or even harmful chemicals. The death in 1990 of more than a hundred children in Nigeria after they were given a counterfeit medicine that contained an industrial solvent is just one of the more obvious examples of the dangers posed by these products. Unfortunately, drug counterfeiters are so skilled at duplicating the packaging of the legitimate products that a chemical analysis of the product itself is often necessary to uncover the fraud.

Although U.S. pharmaceutical companies lose billions of dollars in revenues each year to the counterfeiters, the companies have generally been reluctant to acknowledge that such a problem even exists. The fact that developing countries often do not offer any significant legal protection for drugs patented in the United States further complicates efforts to stop the production and sale of phony drugs.

For Critical Analysis: *Why would U.S. pharmaceutical companies be reluctant to acknowledge the fact that counterfeit versions of their drugs are harming consumers?*

PATENTS FOR COMPUTER SOFTWARE   At one time, it was difficult for developers and manufacturers of software to obtain patent protection because many software products simply automate procedures that can be performed manually. In other words, the computer programs do not meet the "novel" and "not obvious" requirements previously mentioned. Also, the basis for software is often a mathematical equation or formula, which is not patentable. In 1981, the United States Supreme Court held that it is possible, however, to obtain a patent for a *process* that incorporates a computer program—providing, of course, that the process itself is patentable.[9] Subsequently, many patents have been issued for software-related inventions. Some critics believe that patents are being issued too readily for software that is not novel or that represents merely an obvious change of another's computer program. According to these critics, a proliferation of software patents will slow down the process of software innovation and application.

Another obstacle to obtaining patent protection for software is the procedure of obtaining patents. The process can be expensive and slow. The time element is a particularly important consideration for someone wishing to obtain a patent on software. In light of the rapid changes and improvements in computer technology, the delay could undercut the product's success in the marketplace.

Despite these difficulties, patent protection is used in the computer industry. If a patent is infringed, the patent holder may sue for an injunction, damages, and the destruction of all infringing copies, as well as attorneys' fees and court costs.

Copyrights

COPYRIGHT
The exclusive right of "authors" to publish, print, or sell an intellectual production for a statutory period of time. A copyright has the same monopolistic nature as a patent or trademark, but it differs in that it applies exclusively to works of art, literature, and other works of authorship (including computer programs).

A **copyright** is an intangible property right granted by federal statute to the author or originator of certain literary or artistic productions. Currently, copyrights are governed by the Copyright Act of 1976,[10] as amended. Works created after January 1, 1978, are automatically given statutory copyright protection for the life of the author plus fifty years. For copyrights owned by publishing houses, the copyright expires seventy-five years from the date of publication or one hundred years from the date of creation, whichever is first. For works by more than one author, the copyright expires fifty years after the death of the last surviving author.

9.   *Diamond v. Diehr,* 450 U.S. 175, 101 S.Ct. 1048, 67 L.Ed.2d 155 (1981).
10.   17 U.S.C. Sections 101 *et seq.*

Copyrights can be registered with the U.S. Copyright Office in Washington, D.C. A copyright owner no longer needs to place a © or "Copr." or "Copyright" on the work, however, to have the work protected against infringement. Chances are that if somebody created it, somebody owns it.

WHAT IS PROTECTED EXPRESSION?   Works that are copyrightable include books, records, films, artworks, architectural plans, menus, music videos, product packaging, and computer software. To obtain protection under the Copyright Act, a work must be original and fall into one of the following categories: (1) literary works; (2) musical works; (3) dramatic works; (4) pantomimes and choreographic works; (5) pictorial, graphic, and sculptural works; (6) films and other audiovisual works; and (7) sound recordings. To be protected, a work must be "fixed in a durable medium" from which it can be perceived, reproduced, or communicated. Protection is automatic. Registration is not required.

BE CAREFUL If a creative work does not fall into a certain category, it may not be copyrighted, but it may be protected by other intellectual property law.

Section 102 of the Copyright Act specifically excludes copyright protection for any "idea, procedure, process, system, method of operation, concept, principle, or discovery, regardless of the form in which it is described, explained, illustrated, or embodied." Note that it is not possible to copyright an *idea*. The underlying ideas embodied in a work may be freely used by others. What is copyrightable is the particular way in which an idea is *expressed*. Whenever an idea and an expression are inseparable, the expression cannot be copyrighted. Generally, anything that is not an original expression will not qualify for copyright protection. Facts widely known to the public are not copyrightable. Page numbers are not copyrightable, because they follow a sequence known to everyone. Mathematical calculations are not copyrightable.

Compilations of facts, however, are copyrightable. Section 103 of the Copyright Act defines a compilation as "a work formed by the collection and assembling of preexisting materials of data that are selected, coordinated, or arranged in such a way that the resulting work as a whole constitutes an original work of authorship." The key requirement in the copyrightability of a compilation is originality. Thus, the White Pages of a telephone directory do not qualify for copyright protection when the information that makes up the directory (names, addresses, and telephone numbers) is not selected, coordinated, or arranged in an original way.[11] In one case, even the Yellow Pages of a telephone directory did not qualify for copyright protection.[12]

COPYRIGHT INFRINGEMENT   Whenever the form or expression of an idea is copied, an infringement of copyright occurs. The reproduction does not have to be exactly the same as the original, nor does it have to reproduce the original in its entirety.

Penalties or remedies can be imposed on those who infringe copyrights. These range from actual damages (damages based on the actual harm caused to the copyright holder by the infringement) or statutory damages (damages provided for under the Copyright Act, not to exceed $100,000) to criminal proceedings for willful violations (which may result in fines and/or imprisonment).

An exception to liability for copyright infringement is made under the "fair use" doctrine. In certain circumstances, a person or organization can reproduce copyrighted material without paying royalties (fees paid to the copyright holder for the privilege of reproducing the copyrighted material). Section 107 of the Copyright Act provides as follows:

> [T]he fair use of a copyrighted work, including such use by reproduction in copies or phonorecords or by any other means specified by [Section 106 of the Copyright Act,] for purposes such as criticism, comment, news reporting, teaching (including multiple copies

---

11.   *Feist Publications, Inc. v. Rural Telephone Service Co.*, 499 U.S. 340, 111 S.Ct. 1282, 113 L.Ed.2d 358 (1991).

12.   *Bellsouth Advertising & Publishing Corp. v. Donnelley Information Publishing, Inc.*, 999 F.2d 1436 (11th Cir. 1993).

for classroom use), scholarship, or research, is not an infringement of copyright. In determining whether the use made of a work in any particular case is a fair use the factors to be considered shall include—

(1) the purpose and character of the use, including whether such use is of a commercial nature or is for nonprofit educational purposes;
(2) the nature of the copyrighted work;
(3) the amount and substantiality of the portion used in relation to the copyrighted work as a whole; and
(4) the effect of the use upon the potential market for or value of the copyrighted work.

Because these guidelines are very broad, the courts determine whether a particular use is fair on a case-by-case basis. Thus, anyone reproducing copyrighted material may be subject to a violation.

A question that sometimes comes before the courts is whether a parody (satire) of a copyrighted work is a "fair use" of that work as a "criticism" or "comment" on the copyrighted version. At issue in the following case is whether a musical group's parody of another's copyrighted song constituted a fair use of the copyrighted music.

CASE 6.5

CAMPBELL v. ACUFF-ROSE MUSIC, INC.

Supreme Court of the United States, 1994.
510 U.S. 569,
114 S.Ct. 1164,
127 L.Ed.2d 500.

HISTORICAL AND SOCIAL SETTING *Rap music started in New York City in the 1970s as part of a subculture called hip-hop. In basement clubs in the South Bronx, DJs played record turntables like musical instruments, picking up bits and pieces from the entire pop music spectrum, cutting from song to song and pushing tracks backward. With this beat as a backdrop, performers spoke, rather than sang, the lyrics in street-jive rhythm, inspired by the experiences and fantasies of mostly young, urban, African American males. One of the most famous rap groups is 2 Live Crew. In Florida in 1991, a federal judge declared one of their albums obscene. The album then sold millions of copies and assured the status of rap as the most controversial music since the early days of rock and roll.*

FACTS The song "Oh, Pretty Woman" was written in 1964 by Roy Orbison and William Dees. Their ownership rights in the song were transferred to Acuff-Rose Music, Inc. In 1989, the rap group 2 Live Crew parodied the song without Acuff-Rose's permission. In 1990, after about 250,000 copies of the parody version had been sold, Acuff-Rose sued 2 Live Crew and its record company in a federal district court, alleging copyright infringement. 2 Live Crew claimed that their parodic use

of the original song fell within the "fair use" exception to the Copyright Act of 1976. 2 Live Crew contended that the parody commented on and satirized the original work, which is considered a fair use under the act in some circumstances. The district court found for 2 Live Crew, holding that the parody version was a fair use. Acuff-Rose appealed. The appellate court reversed, holding that 2 Live Crew's parody carried with it a presumption of unfair use because of its intrinsically commercial nature. 2 Live Crew appealed to the United States Supreme Court.

ISSUE Could the parody version of "Oh, Pretty Woman" be considered a fair use of the original song under the Copyright Act of 1976?

DECISION Yes. The Supreme Court reversed the appellate court's decision and remanded the case.

REASON Section 107 of the Copyright Act sets forth a four-factor test to be used when determining whether the unauthorized use of another's copyrighted work is a "fair use." In regard to the first factor (the "purpose and character of the use, including whether such use is of a commercial nature"), the appellate court had held that the commercial nature of 2 Live Crew's parody rendered the group's use presumptively unfair. The Supreme Court, however, held that the transformative value of parody must also be considered. As to the second factor (the "nature of the copyrighted work"), the Supreme Court affirmed the lower courts' decision that the original version of "Oh, Pretty Woman" warranted copyright protection under the act. As to the third factor (the "amount and substantiality of the portion used in relation to the copyrighted work as a whole"), the appellate court held that 2 Live Crew's parody copied the heart, or essence, of the

Case 6.5—Continued

original work and therefore borrowed too much. The Supreme Court stated that a parody must necessarily "conjure up" enough of the original work for the audience to recognize the "critical wit" intended, and this may require copying the heart of the original version. Whether 2 Live Crew copied musical elements to a greater extent than necessary to accomplish this was an issue to be decided on remand. On the final factor (the "effect of the use upon the potential market for or value of the copyrighted work"), the Supreme Court held that because the original and parodic versions served different market functions, the parodic version would probably not affect the market for the original.

FOR CRITICAL ANALYSIS—Ethical Consideration
Is it fair for one person to realize (sometimes substantial) profits by parodying another's copyrighted material?

COPYRIGHT PROTECTION FOR COMPUTER SOFTWARE   In 1980, Congress passed the Computer Software Copyright Act, which amended the Copyright Act of 1976 to include computer programs in the list of creative works protected by federal copyright law. The 1980 statute, which classifies computer programs as "literary works," defines a computer program as a "set of statements or instructions to be used directly or indirectly in a computer in order to bring about a certain result."

NOTE Technological change is one of the primary factors that lead to changes in the law.

Because of the unique nature of computer programs, the courts have had many problems in applying and interpreting the 1980 act. Traditionally, copyright protection was extended only to literary works that were perceptible to humans—that is, to things written or printed in intelligible notation. Computer programs, however, are expressed in a language "readable" by machines. Determining which elements of a computer program are protectable under copyright law and which are not has been a challenging task for the courts. We look below at the evolution of the case law on this issue. In this chapter's *Technology and Software Piracy*, we look at another problem relating to software: software "piracy," or theft.

Initial Decisions   In a series of cases decided in the 1980s, the courts held that copyright protection extended not only to those parts of a computer program that can be read by humans, such as the "high-level" language of a source code, but also to the binary-language object code of a computer program, which is readable only by the computer.[13] Additionally, such elements as the overall structure, sequence, and organization of a program were deemed copyrightable.[14]

"Look and Feel" Protection   By the early 1990s, the issue had evolved into whether the "look and feel"—the general appearance, command structure, video images, menus, windows, and other screen displays—of computer programs should also be protected by copyright. Although the courts have disagreed on this issue, the tendency has been to not extend copyright protection to "look and feel" aspects of computer programs. For example, in 1992, a federal district court held that the user interface of Apple's Macintosh computer is not protectable under a "look and feel" theory and that Apple's use of windows, icons, and menus, and generally the series of images that Apple calls a "desktop metaphor," are unprotectable "ideas."[15] Similarly, in 1995, the Court of Appeals for the First Circuit held that Lotus Development Corporation's menu command hierarchy for its Lotus 1-2-3 spreadsheet was not protectable under the Copyright Act. The court deemed that the menu command hierarchy was a "method of operation," and Section 102 of the Copyright Act specifically excludes

---

13.   See *Stern Electronics, Inc. v. Kaufman*, 669 F.2d 852 (2d Cir. 1982); and *Apple Computer, Inc. v. Franklin Computer Corp.*, 714 F.2d 1240 (3d Cir. 1983).

14.   *Whelan Associates, Inc. v. Jaslow Dental Laboratory, Inc.*, 797 F.2d 1222 (3d Cir. 1986).

15.   *Apple Computer, Inc. v. Microsoft Corp.*, 799 F.Supp. 1006 (D.N.Cal. 1992). The district court's ruling was not overturned on appeal.

methods of operation from copyright protection.[16] The decision was affirmed by the United States Supreme Court in 1996.[17]

☐ Technology and Software Piracy

Highly skilled programmers must expend thousands of hours of labor to create a commercially successful software program. Each copy of the program may sell for hundreds of dollars. Consequently, there is a tremendous incentive for individuals and companies to purchase a single copy of the program and then make duplicates—to give or sell to others or to distribute to employees within the company. The popularity of such practices in companies throughout Europe and Asia has proved particularly costly for U.S. software manufacturers.

Because U.S. companies lead the world in the production and sale of computer software, they also suffer the greatest losses (billions of dollars annually) from the unauthorized copying of computer programs, referred to as *software piracy*. Over 90 percent of the software in Pakistan, Russia, and China, for example, consists of illegal copies. For Brazil, Malaysia, and Mexico, the figures are slightly lower, but they still exceed 80 percent. In the United States, an estimated 35 percent of the software in use has been pirated.

The development of electronic networks makes it even easier to copy software illegally. Anyone with a computer and a modem can now transmit copies of computer programs to others over the Internet, to which more than 150 countries are now connected. What this means is that a program that retails for, say, $100 can be transmitted via the Internet to someone on the far side of the globe—and that person can sell copies of the program for only a few dollars per copy. Unlike unauthorized copies of videos and musical recordings, pirated software programs are not second-rate versions of the originals. A $2 copy of a computer program often performs as efficiently as the original, which may sell for $100 or more. Of course, the pirated version is not accompanied by a user's manual, which can diminish the usefulness and application of the software.

The ease with which software programs can be duplicated leaves U.S. companies with little choice except to pursue aggressively any available legal remedies in the courts and to pressure the U.S. government to push for protection against software piracy in its trade agreements with other countries. In 1994, for example, a U.S. trade agreement with China provided that the Chinese government would enforce its intellectual property laws more strictly to reduce the high rate of illegal software duplication in that country. For other measures taken against international software piracy, see this chapter's *Landmark in the Law.*

For Critical Analysis: *Is there any practical way to prevent software piracy via the Internet?*

Trade Secrets

TRADE SECRETS
Information or processes that give a business an advantage over competitors who do not know the information or processes.

Some business processes and information that are not or cannot be patented, copyrighted, or trademarked are nevertheless protected against appropriation by a competitor as trade secrets. **Trade secrets** consist of customer lists, plans, research and development, pricing information, marketing techniques, production techniques, and generally anything that makes an individual company unique and that would have value to a competitor.

Virtually all law with respect to trade secrets is common law. Identical types of information reviewed by different courts in similar factual settings have been classified differently. In an effort to reduce the unpredictability of common law with respect to trade secrets, a model act, the Uniform Trade Secrets Act, was presented to the states

---

16. *Lotus Development Corp. v. Borland International Inc.*, 49 F.3d 807 (1st Cir. 1995).
17. *Lotus Development Corp. v. Borland International Inc.*, ___U.S.___, 116 S.Ct. 804, 113 L.Ed.2d 610 (1996). This issue may again come before the Supreme Court for decision, because in this case only eight justices heard the case, and there was a tied vote: four justices voted to affirm the decision, and four justices voted to reverse it. The effect of the tie was to affirm the lower court's decision.

in 1979 for adoption. Parts of it have been adopted in over twenty states. Typically, a state that has adopted parts of the act has adopted only those parts that encompass its own existing common law.

Unlike copyright and trademark protection, protection of trade secrets extends both to ideas and to their expression. (For this reason, and because a trade secret involves no registration or filing requirements, trade secret protection may be well suited for software.) Of course, the secret formula, method, or other information must be disclosed to some persons, particularly to key employees. Businesses generally attempt to protect their trade secrets by having all employees who use the process or information agree in their contracts never to divulge it.

Generally, the law protects an employer against a former employee's disclosure of trade secrets. The court in the following case considered whether an employer is entitled to protection against the *threat* of such a disclosure.

CASE 6.6

PEPSICO, INC. v. REDMOND
United States Court of Appeals,
Seventh Circuit, 1995.
54 F.3d 1262.

HISTORICAL AND ECONOMIC SETTING *Soft drink sales have climbed more than 40 percent since 1980. Although Coca-Cola and Pepsi-Cola (and their different versions) dominate the market as a whole, the sports drink Gatorade and the newer drink Snapple are the dominant brands in their market niches. Gatorade alone accounts for 85 percent of the $1 billion sports drink market. Against these formidable rivals, the Coca-Cola Company and PepsiCo, Inc., are waging a fiercely competitive battle with their own sports and fruit drinks.*

FACTS William Redmond, as the general manager for PepsiCo, Inc., in California, had access to the company's inside information and trade secrets. In 1994, Redmond resigned to become chief operating officer for the Gatorade and Snapple Company, which makes and markets Gatorade and Snapple and is a subsidiary of the Quaker Oats Company. PepsiCo brought an action in a federal district court against Redmond and Quaker Oats, seeking to prevent Redmond from disclosing PepsiCo's

secrets. The court ordered Redmond not to assume new duties that were likely to trigger disclosure of those secrets. Redmond appealed.

ISSUE Can a plaintiff obtain relief for trade secret misappropriation on showing that an ex-employee's new employment will inevitably lead him or her to rely on the plaintiff's trade secrets?

DECISION Yes. The U.S. Court of Appeals for the Seventh Circuit affirmed the order of the district court.

REASON The appellate court acknowledged that this was not a "traditional trade secret case." Under the applicable state statute, however, relief was available for the "actual or threatened" misappropriation of a trade secret. The court determined that Redmond inevitably would disclose PepsiCo's secrets in his new position with Quaker Oats. The court noted that Redmond had "extensive and intimate knowledge" of PepsiCo's goals for its sports and fruit drinks. Redmond and Quaker Oats conceded that the information Redmond obtained at PepsiCo could influence him. The court explained that "PepsiCo finds itself in the position of a coach, one of whose players has left, playbook in hand, to join the opposing team before the big game."

FOR CRITICAL ANALYSIS—Social Consideration
Does the ruling in this case mean that workers cannot pursue their livelihoods if they leave their jobs?

International Protection

For many years, the United States has been a party to various international agreements relating to intellectual property rights. For example, the Paris Convention of 1883, to which about ninety countries are signatory, allows parties in one country to file for patent and trademark protection in any of the other member countries.

International copyright agreements include the Berne Convention and the Universal Copyright Convention. Under the Berne Convention, if an American writes a book, his or her copyright in the book must be recognized by every country that has signed the convention. Also, if a citizen of a country that has not signed the convention first publishes a book in a country that has signed, all other countries that have signed the convention must recognize that author's copyright. Copyright notice is not needed to gain protection under the Berne Convention for works published after March 1, 1989.

These and other international agreements have given some protection to intellectual property on a worldwide level. None of them, however, has been as significant and far reaching in scope as the agreement on Trade-Related Aspects of Intellectual Property Rights, or, more simply, TRIPS—which is the subject of the following *Landmark in the Law*. This agreement was signed by representatives from over one hundred nations in 1994, following the eighth and final round (called the "Uruguay Round") of negotiations among nations that were signatory to the General Agreement on Tariffs and Trade, or GATT.[18] The TRIPS agreement was one of several documents that were annexed to the agreement creating the World Trade Organization, or WTO, which replaced GATT as of 1995—GATT no longer exists.

---

18.   GATT had been originally negotiated in 1947 to minimize trade barriers among nations. Between 1947 and 1994, the GATT nations undertook seven more "rounds" of negotiations relating to tariffs and trade.

| LANDMARK IN THE LAW | **The 1994 Agreement on Trade-Related Aspects of Intellectual Property Rights (TRIPS)** |

The 1994 agreement on Trade-Related Aspects of Intellectual Property Rights (TRIPS) established, for the first time, standards for the international protection of intellectual property rights, including patents, trademarks, and copyrights for movies, computer programs, books, and music.

Prior to the agreement, one of the difficulties faced by U.S. sellers of intellectual property in the international market was either the lack of protection of intellectual property rights under other countries' laws or the lack of enforcement of those laws that do exist. To address this problem, the TRIPS agreement provides that each member country must include in its domestic laws broad intellectual property rights and effective remedies (including civil and criminal penalties) for violations of those rights.

Generally, the TRIPS agreement provides that each member nation must not discriminate (in terms of the administration, regulation, or adjudication of intellectual property rights) against foreign owners of such rights. In other words, a member nation cannot give its own nationals (citizens) favorable treatment without offering the same treatment to nationals of all member countries. For example, if a U.S. software manufacturer brings a suit for the infringement of intellectual property rights under a member nation's national laws, the U.S. manufacturer is entitled to receive the same treatment as a domestic manufacturer. Each member nation must also ensure that legal procedures are available for parties who wish to bring actions for infringement of intellectual property rights. Additionally, in a related document, the Uruguay Round of GATT established a mechanism for settling disputes among member nations.

Particular provisions of the TRIPS agreement refer to patent, trademark, and copyright protection for intellectual property. The agreement specifically provides

Landmark in the Law—Continued

copyright protection for computer programs by stating that compilations of data, databases, or other materials are "intellectual creations" and that they are to be protected as copyrightable works. Other provisions relate to trade secrets and the rental of computer programs and cinematographic works.

For Critical Analysis: *U.S. companies currently hold a 75 percent share of the international market for prepackaged software and a 60 percent share of the international market for other software and related services. How might the TRIPS agreement affect this market share?*

▌RICO

Increasingly in recent years, businesses have been sued for fraudulent or other tortious activities under the Racketeer Influenced and Corrupt Organizations Act.[19] The act, which is commonly known as RICO, was passed by Congress in 1970 as part of the Organized Crime Control Act. The purpose of the act was to curb the apparently increasing entry of organized crime into the legitimate business world.

Activities Prohibited by RICO

Under RICO, it is a federal crime (1) to use income obtained from racketeering activity to purchase any interest in an enterprise, (2) to acquire or maintain an interest in an enterprise through racketeering activity, (3) to conduct or participate in the affairs of an enterprise through racketeering activity, or (4) to conspire to do any of the preceding activities.

Racketeering activity is not a new type of substantive crime created by RICO; rather, RICO incorporates by reference twenty-six separate types of federal crimes and nine types of state felonies[20] and states that if a person commits two of these offenses, he or she is guilty of "racketeering activity." The act provides for both criminal liability (to be discussed in the following chapter) and civil liability.

Civil Liability under RICO

The penalties for violations of the RICO statute are harsh. In the event of a violation, the statute permits the government to seek civil penalties, including the divestiture of a defendant's interest in a business (called forfeiture—discussed in Chapter 7) or the dissolution of the business. Perhaps the most controversial aspect of RICO is that in some cases, private individuals are allowed to recover three times their actual losses (treble damages), plus attorneys' fees, for business injuries caused by a violation of the statute.

The broad language of RICO has allowed it to be applied in cases that have little or nothing to do with organized crime, and an aggressive prosecuting attorney may attempt to show that any business fraud constitutes "racketeering activity." In its 1985 decision in *Sedima, S.P.R.L. v. Imrex Co.*,[21] the United States Supreme Court interpreted RICO broadly and set a significant precedent for subsequent applications of the act. Plaintiffs have used the RICO statute in numerous commercial fraud cases

BE AWARE RICO is often applied in cases that have little to do with what is traditionally thought of as crime.

---

19. 18 U.S.C. Sections 1961–1968.
20. See 18 U.S.C. Section 1961(1)(A).
21. 473 U.S. 479, 105 S.Ct. 3275, 87 L.Ed.2d 346 (1985).

because of the inviting prospect of being awarded treble damages if they win. The most frequent targets of civil RICO lawsuits are insurance companies, employment agencies, commercial banks, and stockbrokerage firms.

One of the requirements of RICO is that there be more than one offense—there must be a "pattern of racketeering activity." What consitutes a "pattern" has been the subject of much litigation. Some courts have interpreted this to mean, in part, that there must be continued criminal activity. This is known as the "continuity" requirement. Part of this requirement is that the activity occur over a "substantial" period of time. The court in the following case considered whether "garden variety" fraud meets this requirement.

CASE 6.7

TABAS v. TABAS

United States Court of Appeals,
Third Circuit, 1995.
47 F.3d 1280.

HISTORICAL AND INTERNATIONAL SETTING *Partnerships as forms of doing business date to the beginning of recorded history. There are references to partnerships in the Code of Hammurabi, which was the law of Babylon in approximately 2300 B.C.E. Three hundred years or so later, the Jews in the Middle East developed a form of partnership known as a* shutolin *to share land and grazing privileges. Later partnerships evolved from the trading caravans that plied Asian and African trade routes. The Romans created a law of partnership that was very similar to current U.S. law, which, as in medieval Europe, evolved from the customs of merchants. One of those customs has always been that agreements between partners should be honored.*

FACTS Charles and Daniel Tabas formed a partnership to conduct real estate and other business ventures. They agreed that if either partner died, the other would distribute the partnership income equally to himself and to the estate of the deceased partner. When Charles died, Daniel agreed to mail monthly partnership income checks to Charles's widow, Harriette. Daniel mailed monthly checks in the same amount to himself. In addition, Daniel drew a salary and paid a variety of personal expenses from partnership income. When Harriette and the executors of Charles's estate learned of Daniel's activities, they confronted him, and he agreed to dissolve the partnership and sell the assets. Continuing dissatisfaction with Daniel's conduct prompted Harriette and the executors (the plaintiffs) to file a suit in a federal district court against Daniel and others (the defendants),

alleging, among other things, that acts of fraud over the previous three and a half years constituted violations of RICO. Daniel filed a motion for summary judgment, which the court granted. The court found no "continuity," reasoning that as soon as the partnership assets were sold, all of the alleged fraud would stop. The plaintiffs appealed to the U.S. Court of Appeals for the Third Circuit.

ISSUE Did the allegations of fraud in the plaintiffs' complaint meet RICO's continuity requirement?

DECISION Yes. The U.S. Court of Appeals for the Third Circuit reversed the district court's ruling and remanded the case for further proceedings.

REASON The appellate court explained that "[e]ach time defendants misrepresented the business nature of an expense, made a questionable charge, or received compensation to which they were not entitled, they lessened the income available" to Charles's estate. The court noted that "these activities, which implemented defendants' purported scheme to defraud the Estate, lasted more than three and a half years." The court concluded that "a scheme lasting over three years extends over a 'substantial' period of time and therefore constitutes the type of 'long-term criminal conduct' that RICO was enacted to address." Thus, the court found that the plaintiffs "made a sufficient showing to survive summary judgment" on the continuity issue.

FOR CRITICAL ANALYSIS—Political Consideration
The United States Supreme Court has consistently struck down the efforts of lower courts to narrow the scope of RICO. Do you think that RICO is applied too broadly? If so, in light of the Supreme Court's decisions, who can narrow RICO's scope?

Application

Law and the Businessperson—Creating and Protecting Your Trademark*

Imagine the following scenario: You have decided to turn your hobby of recording alternative music into a bona fide business. You pick a name for your company— Cruising—and incorporate the company in your state. The secretary of state approves the name because no one else in your state has incorporated under that name or one that could be confused with it. You open for business, and the name Cruising appears in your ads and brochures and in the Yellow Pages. You put out your first CD using the Cruising label. Then you receive a letter in the mail from Tom Cruise's attorneys informing you that Cruising is a federally registered trademark used for all of Tom Cruise's enterprises, and in fact he may someday have a CD label. If you attempt to fight Tom Cruise's attorneys, you will probably lose.

A Trademark Is Not the Same as a Trade Name

When you incorporated in your state, the secretary of state only approved your company's name, Cruising, as a trade name—the formal name for your business that you can use on checks, invoices, and letterhead stationery. You have permission to use Cruising as a trade name only in your state. A trademark (or a service mark) is the word, phrase, slogan, design, or symbol that identifies a specific product brand that you use to market products. If you decide to use your business (trade) name as a trademark, then you need to follow the principles of trademark law. The general rule is that you cannot use a trademark that might lead a customer to think that your product was produced by someone else.

*This *Application* is not meant to substitute for the services of an attorney who is licensed to practice law in your state.

Who Owns a Trademark?

Generally, the first business to use a trademark owns it. The way to qualify as a first user is to be the first company to actually use the trademark in the marketplace or to register the trademark with the U.S. Patent and Trademark Office. First use sometimes takes precedence over federal registration. If Tom Cruise had not registered Cruising as a trademark until two years after you started selling Cruising-labeled CDs throughout the United States, you would probably win your trademark dispute.

Doing a Trademark Search

After you have decided on a trademark, you need to do a search to find out if the trademark is confusingly similar to existing trademarks. You can look at the federal trademark register, as well as the trademark register in your state. You can examine the Yellow Pages in your area of business. You can go to your library to look at *Gale's List of Tradenames*. It is also possible to do a computer search. Finally, you can hire a trademark search firm to do the search for you.

Once you have done an appropriate trademark search and you have not found another trademark that would be confusingly similar to yours, you are probably entitled to register the mark with the U.S. Patent and Trademark Office. Normally, you have to start using the trademark within six months within your state or across state, international, or territorial lines.

Checklist for the Businessperson

1. Remember that a trade name authorized for use by a secretary of state is not the same as a trademark.
2. When deciding on a trademark, be sure that it is not confusingly similar to an existing trademark.
3. There are two ways to own a trademark—being the first to use a trademark or registering the trademark with the U.S. Patent and Trademark Office.
4. Remember that in trademark disputes, first use of a trademark sometimes takes precedence over federal registration.

▌ Key Terms

▍Chapter Summary: Business Torts and Intellectual Property

Wrongful Interference (*See pages 151–153.*)	1. *Wrongful interference with a contractual relationship*—The intentional interference with a valid, enforceable contract by a third party. 2. *Wrongful interference with a business relationship*—The unreasonable interference by one party with another's business relationship.
Wrongful Entry into Business (*See pages 153–154.*)	Entering into business in violation of the law or for the purpose of engaging in predatory behavior.
Appropriation (*See pages 154–155.*)	The use by one person of another's name, likeness, or other identifying characteristic, without permission and for the benefit of the user.
Defamation in the Business Context (*See page 155.*)	A false statement that injures someone in a profession, business, or trade or that adversely affects a business entity in its credit rating and other dealings.
Disparagement of Property (*See pages 155–157.*)	Slanderous or libelous statements made about another's product or property; more specifically referred to as slander of quality (trade libel) or slander of title.
Intellectual Property Protection (*See pages 157–169.*)	1. *Trademark infringement and infringement of related property*—Occurs when one uses the protected trademark, service mark, or trade name of another without permission when marketing goods or services. 2. *Patent infringement*—Occurs when one uses or sells another's patented design, product, or process without the patent owner's permission. Computer software may be patented. 3. *Copyright infringement*—Occurs whenever the form or expression of an idea is copied without the permission of the copyright holder. An exception applies if the copying is deemed a "fair use." The Computer Software Copyright Act of 1980 specifically includes software among the kinds of intellectual property covered by copyright law. 4. *Trade secrets*—Customer lists, plans, research and development, pricing information, and so on are protected under the common law and, in some states, under statutory law against misappropriation by competitors. 5. *International protection*—International protection for intellectual property exists under various international agreements. A landmark agreement is the 1994 agreement on Trade-Related Aspects of Intellectual Property Rights (TRIPS), which provides for the enforcement of intellectual property rights and the establishment of enforcement procedures in all countries signatory to the agreement.
RICO (*See pages 169–170.*)	The Racketeer Influenced and Corrupt Organizations Act (RICO) of 1970 makes it a federal crime (1) to use income obtained from racketeering activity to purchase any interest in an enterprise, (2) to acquire or maintain an interest in an enterprise through racketeering activity, (3) to conduct or participate in the affairs of an enterprise through racketeering activity, or (4) to conspire to do any of the preceding activities. The broad language of RICO has allowed it to be applied in cases that have little or nothing to do with organized crime.

▍For Review

1. What elements are necessary to establish the existence of wrongful interference with a contractual or business relationship?
2. What is the tort of appropriation? How might the tort of defamation occur in the business context?
3. What is intellectual property? How does the law protect intellectual property?
4. What is a trade secret? How are trade secrets protected by law?
5. What is RICO? What activities are prohibited by this act?

▌Questions and Case Problems

6–1. Copyright Infringement. In which of the following situations would a court likely hold Maruta liable for copyright infringement?

(a) At the library, Maruta photocopies ten pages from a scholarly journal relating to a topic on which she is writing a term paper.

(b) Maruta makes leather handbags and sells them in her small leather shop. She advertises her handbags as "Vutton handbags," hoping that customers might mistakenly assume that they were made by Vuitton, the well-known maker of high-quality luggage and handbags.

(c) Maruta owns a video store. She purchases the latest videos from various video manufacturers but buys only one copy of each video. Then, using blank videotapes, she makes copies to rent or sell to her customers.

(d) Maruta teaches Latin American history at a small university. She has a videocassette recorder (VCR) and frequently tapes television programs relating to Latin America. She then takes the videos to her classroom so that her students can watch them.

6–2. Wrongful Interference. Jennings owns a bakery shop. He has been trying to obtain a long-term contract with the owner of Julie's Tea Salon for some time. Jennings starts a local advertising campaign on radio and television and in the newspaper. The campaign is so persuasive that Julie decides to break the contract she has had for some time with Orley's Bakery so that she can patronize Jennings's bakery. Is Jennings liable to Orley's Bakery for the tort of wrongful interference with a contractual relationship? Is Julie liable for this tort? For anything?

6–3. Patent Infringement. John and Andrew Doney invented a hard-bearing device for balancing rotors. Although they registered their invention with the U.S. Patent and Trademark Office, it was never used as an automobile wheel balancer. Some time later, Exetron Corp. produced an automobile wheel balancer that used a hard-bearing device with a support plate similar to that of the Doneys. Given the fact that the Doneys had not used their device for automobile wheel balancing, does Exetron's use of a similar hard-bearing device infringe upon the Doneys' patent?

6–4. Copyright Infringement. Max plots a new Batman adventure and carefully and skillfully imitates the art of DC Comics to create an authentic-looking Batman comic. Max is not affiliated with the owners of the copyright to Batman. Can Max publish the comic without infringing on the owners' copyright?

6–5. Business Tort Theories. After a careful study and analysis, Green Top Airlines decides to expand its operations into Harbor City. Green Top acquires the necessary regulatory authorizations and licenses, negotiates a lease at the airport terminal, and makes substantial capital expenditures renovating airport gates. Immediately thereafter, Red Stripe Airlines, Green Top's major competitor, also undertakes operations in Harbor City, even though (1) Harbor City is nowhere near any of Red Stripe's major existing routes and (2) Red Stripe will lose money by servicing Harbor City. Green Top claims that Red Stripe's entry into Harbor City constitutes a tort. Discuss fully Green Top's claim.

6–6. Copyright Infringement. West Publishing Co. brought a copyright infringement action against Mead Data Central, Inc., then the owner of LEXIS, a computer-assisted legal research system. At issue was a plan for a "star pagination" feature that Mead had developed for use on LEXIS. This feature would incorporate page numbers from West's case reporters into the opinions available on LEXIS and would allow LEXIS users to learn the precise page breaks in a West reporter without ever physically having to refer to a West volume. West claimed that Mead Data's proposed star pagination system would constitute a copyright infringement of its reporting format. Mead Data contended that "mere page numbers" cannot be copyrighted. Can the use of page numbers, which cannot in themselves be copyrighted, fall under copyright protection in this case? If so, under what theory? [*West Publishing Co. v. Mead Data Central, Inc.*, 799 F.2d 1219 (8th Cir. 1986)]

6–7. Copyright Infringement. Jonathan Caven-Atack had been a member of the Church of Scientology for nine years when he decided that the church was a dangerous cult and its leader, L. Ron Hubbard, a vindictive and profoundly disturbed man. Caven-Atack spent the next several years investigating and then writing a book about Hubbard and the church. Caven-Atack's purpose was to expose what he believed was the pernicious nature of the church and the deceit upon which its teachings were based. Approximately 3 percent of Caven-Atack's book consisted of quotations from Hubbard's published works. When New Era Publications International, which held exclusive copyright rights in all of Hubbard's works, learned that the Carol Publishing Group planned to publish Caven-Atack's book, it sued Carol Publishing for copyright infringement. Carol Publishing claimed that Caven-Atack's use of Hubbard's works was a "fair use" of the copyrighted materials. What factors must the court consider in making its decision? How will the court likely decide the issue? [*New Era Publications International, ApS v. Carol Publishing Group*, 904 F.2d 152 (2d Cir. 1990)]

6–8. Trademark Infringement. In 1987, Quality Inns International, Inc., announced a new chain of economy hotels to be marketed under the name "McSleep Inns." McDonald's wrote Quality Inns a letter stating that the use of "McSleep Inns" infringed upon the McDonald's family of trademarks characterized by the prefix "Mc" attached to a generic term. Quality Inns claimed that "Mc" had come into generic use as a prefix, and therefore McDonald's had no trademark rights to the prefix itself. Quality Inns filed an action seeking a declaratory judgment from the court that the mark "McSleep Inns" did not infringe on McDonald's federally registered trademarks or common law rights to its marks and would not constitute an unfair trade practice. What factors must the court consider in deciding this issue? What will be the probable outcome of the case? Explain. [*Quality Inns International, Inc. v. McDonald's Corp.*, 695 F.Supp. 198 (D.Md. 1988)]

6–9. Wrongful Interference. Bombardier Capital, Inc., provides financing to boat and recreational vehicle dealers. Bombardier's credit policy requires dealers to forward immediately to Bombardier the proceeds of boat sales. When Howard Mulcahey, Bombardier's vice president of sales and marketing, learned that a dealer was not complying with this policy, he told

Frank Chandler, Bombardier's credit director, of his concern. Before Chandler could obtain the proceeds, Mulcahey falsely told Jacques Gingras, Bombardier's president, that Chandler was, among other things, trying to hide the problem. On the basis of Mulcahey's statements, Gingras fired Chandler and put Mulcahey in charge of the credit department. Under what business tort theory discussed in this chapter might Chandler recover damages from Mulcahey? Explain. [*Chandler v. Bombardier Capital, Inc.*, 44 F.3d 80 (2d Cir. 1994)]

6–10. RICO. During the 1980s, the Mutual Trading Corp. (MTC) bought and sold tires made by the Uniroyal Goodrich Tire Co. In the 1990s, Uniroyal discovered that MTC had perpetrated at least four separate schemes to swindle money from Uniroyal. As part of one scheme, for example, MTC had submitted fraudulent claims for reimbursement for amounts it had refunded to customers in Saudi Arabia. As part of another scheme, MTC had obtained from Uniroyal twice as much for its advertising costs in Nigeria as the parties had previously agreed. Uniroyal filed a suit against MTC and others in a federal district court, alleging, among other things, that these schemes violated RICO. MTC responded in part that the allegations depicted only a single scheme perpetrated on a single victim and that thus there was no "pattern of racketeering activity." What constitutes a "pattern" of activity to satisfy RICO? Is RICO satisfied in this case? [*Uniroyal Goodrich Tire Co. v. Mutual Trading Corp.*, 63 F.3d 516 (7th Cir. 1995)]

6–11. Trademark Infringement. CBS, Inc., owns and operates Television City, a television production facility in Los Angeles. Home to many television series, the name "Television City" is broadcast each week in connection with each show. CBS sells T-shirts, pins, watches, and so on emblazoned with "CBS Television City." CBS registered "Television City" with the U.S. Patent and Trademark Office as a service mark "for television production services." David and William Liederman wished to open a restaurant in New York City using the name "Television City." Besides food, the restaurant would sell television memorabilia such as T-shirts, sweatshirts, and posters. When CBS learned of the Liedermans' plans, it asked a federal district court to order them not to use "Television City" in connection with their restaurant. Does CBS's registration of "Television City" ensure its exclusive use in all markets and all products? If not, what factors might the court consider to determine whether the Liedermans can use "Television City" in connection with their restaurant? [*CBS, Inc. v. Liederman*, 866 F.Supp. 763 (S.D.N.Y. 1994)]

A QUESTION OF ETHICS AND SOCIAL RESPONSIBILITY

6–12. *Texaco, Inc., conducts research to develop new products and technology in the petroleum industry. As part of the research, Texaco employees routinely photocopy articles from scientific and medical journals without the permission of the copyright holders. The publishers of the journals brought a copyright infringement action against Texaco in a federal district court. The court ruled that the copying was not fair use. The U.S. Court of Appeals for the Second Circuit affirmed this ruling "primarily because the dominant purpose of the use is 'archival'— to assemble a set of papers for future reference, thereby serving the same purpose for which additional subscriptions are normally sold, or . . . for which photocopying licenses may be obtained."* [American Geophysical Union v. Texaco, Inc., 37 F.3d 881(2d Cir. 1994)]

1. Do you agree with the court's decision that the copying was not a fair use? Why or why not?
2. Do you think that the law should impose a duty on every person to obtain permission to photocopy or reproduce any article under any circumstance? What would be some of the implications of such a duty for society? Discuss fully.

FOR CRITICAL ANALYSIS

6–13. *Patent protection in the United States is granted to the first person to invent a given product or process, even though another person might be the first to file for a patent on the same product or process. What are the advantages of this patenting procedure? Can you think of any disadvantages? Explain.*

▌Accessing the Internet: Business Law and Legal Environment

For basic U.S. patent, trademark, and copyright information, you can access a Web site developed by Franklin Pierce Law Center at

http://www.fplc.edu/tfield/orde.html

For a thorough presentation of the Copyright Act, you can access

http://www.law.cornell.edu//usc/17/overview.html

To obtain intellectual property rights decisions of the U.S. Supreme Court, go to

http://www.law.cornell.edu/syllabi?copyright+patent+trademark

To study the text of the Paris Treaty, called the Paris Convention for the Protection of Industrial Property, go to

http://www.law.cornell.edu:70/00/foreign/fletcherUNTS11851.txt

There is also a specific copyright Web site at

http://www.benedict.com/

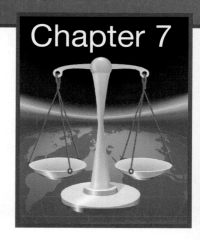

Chapter 7

Criminal Law

"No state shall make or enforce any law which shall abridge the privileges or immunities of citizens of the United States; nor shall any State deprive any person of life, liberty, or property without due process of law, nor deny to any person within its jurisdiction the equal protection of the laws."

Fourteenth Amendment to the U.S. Constitution, July 28, 1868

CHAPTER OBJECTIVES

After reading this chapter, you should be able to:

1. Explain the difference between criminal offenses and other types of wrongful conduct.
2. Indicate the essential elements of criminal liability.
3. Describe the constitutional safeguards that protect the rights of persons accused of crimes.
4. Identify and define the crimes that affect business.
5. Summarize the defenses to criminal liability.

Various sanctions are used to bring about a society in which individuals engaging in business can compete and flourish. These sanctions include damages for various types of tortious conduct (as discussed in the preceding chapters), damages for breach of contract (to be discussed in Chapter 13), and the equitable remedies discussed in Chapter 1. Additional sanctions are imposed under criminal law. Many statutes regulating business provide for criminal as well as civil sanctions. Therefore, criminal law joins civil law as an important element in the legal environment of business.

In this chapter, following a brief summary of the major differences between criminal and civil law, we look at how crimes are classified and what elements must be present for criminal liability to exist. We then examine criminal procedural law, which attempts to ensure that a criminal defendant's right to "due process of law" (see the above quotation) is enforced. In the remainder of the chapter, we focus on crimes affecting business and the defenses that can be raised to avoid liability for criminal actions.

▌ Civil Law and Criminal Law

Civil law spells out the duties that exist between persons or between citizens and their governments, excluding the duty not to commit crimes. Contract law, for example, is part of civil law. The whole body of tort law, which deals with the infringement by one person on the legally recognized rights of another, is also an area of civil law. The right of people engaged in business to compete and flourish is sustained by the civil law, which imposes damages for various types of tortious conduct (as discussed in the preceding chapters) and damages for breach of contract (to be discussed in Chapter 13).

Criminal law, in contrast, has to do with crime. A **crime** can be defined as a wrong against society proclaimed in a statute and, if committed, punishable by society through fines and/or imprisonment—and, in some cases, death. Because crimes are *offenses against society as a whole*, they are prosecuted by a public official, not by victims. Exhibit 7–1 presents additional ways in which criminal and civil law differ.

▌ Classification of Crimes

Depending on their degree of seriousness, crimes are classified as felonies or misdemeanors. **Felonies** are serious crimes punishable by death or by imprisonment in a federal or state penitentiary for more than a year. The Model Penal Code[1] provides for four degrees of felony: (1) capital offenses, for which the maximum penalty is death; (2) first degree felonies, punishable by a maximum penalty of life imprisonment; (3) second degree felonies, punishable by a maximum of ten years' imprisonment; and (4) third degree felonies, punishable by a maximum of five years' imprisonment.

Under federal law and in most states, any crime that is not a felony is considered a **misdemeanor.** Misdemeanors are crimes punishable by a fine or by confinement for up to a year. If incarcerated (imprisoned), the guilty party goes to a local jail instead of a penitentiary. Disorderly conduct and trespass are common misdemeanors. Some states have different classes of misdemeanors. For example, in Illinois misdemeanors are either Class A (confinement for up to a year), Class B (not more than six months), or Class C (not more than thirty days). Whether a crime is a felony or a misdemeanor

---

1.   The American Law Institute issued the Official Draft of the Model Penal Code in 1962. The Model Penal Code is not a uniform code. Uniformity of criminal law among the states is not as important as uniformity in other areas of the law. Types of crimes vary with local circumstances, and it is appropriate that punishments vary accordingly. The Model Penal Code contains four parts: (1) general provisions, (2) definitions of special crimes, (3) provisions concerning treatment and corrections, and (4) provisions on the organization of correction.

CRIME
A wrong against society proclaimed in a statute and, if committed, punishable by society through fines and/or imprisonment—and, in some cases, death.

FELONY
A crime—such as arson, murder, rape, or robbery—that carries the most severe sanctions, usually ranging from one year in a state or federal prison to the forfeiture of one's life.

MISDEMEANOR
A lesser crime than a felony, punishable by a fine or imprisonment for up to one year in other than a state or federal penitentiary.

♦ Exhibit 7–1
Civil and Criminal Law
Compared

ISSUE	CIVIL LAW	CRIMINAL LAW
Area of concern	Rights and duties between individuals	Offenses against society as a whole
Wrongful act	Harm to a person	Violation of a statute that prohibits some type of activity
Party who brings suit	Person who suffered harm	The state
Standard of proof	Preponderance of the evidence	Beyond a reasonable doubt
Remedy	Damages to compensate for the harm	Punishment (fine or imprisonment)

can also determine whether the case is tried in a magistrate's court (for example, by a justice of the peace) or a general trial court.

In most jurisdictions, **petty offenses** are considered to be a subset of misdemeanors. Petty offenses are minor violations, such as violations of building codes. Even for petty offenses, however, a guilty party can be put in jail for a few days, fined, or both, depending on state law.

PETTY OFFENSE
In criminal law, the least serious kind of criminal offense, such as a traffic or building-code violation.

❚ Criminal Liability

Two elements must exist simultaneously for a person to be convicted of a crime: (1) the performance of a prohibited act and (2) a specified state of mind or intent on the part of the actor. Every criminal statute prohibits certain behavior. Most crimes require an act of *commission*; that is, a person must *do* something in order to be accused of a crime.[2] In some cases, an act of *omission* can be a crime, but only when a person has a legal duty to perform the omitted act. Failure to file a tax return is an example of an omission that is a crime.

The *guilty act* requirement is based on one of the premises of criminal law—that a person is punished for harm done to society. Thinking about killing someone or about stealing a car may be wrong, but the thoughts do no harm until they are translated into action. Of course, a person can be punished for attempting murder or robbery, but normally only if he or she took substantial steps toward the criminal objective.

A wrongful mental state[3] is as necessary as a wrongful act in establishing criminal liability. What constitutes such a mental state varies according to the wrongful action. For murder, the act is the taking of a life, and the mental state is the intent to take life. For theft, the guilty act is the taking of another person's property, and the mental state involves both the knowledge that the property belongs to another and the intent to deprive the owner of it. Without the mental state required by law for a particular crime, there is no crime, as the following case illustrates.

"A man may have as bad a heart as he chooses, if his conduct is within the rules."

Oliver Wendell Holmes, Jr., 1841–1935
(*Associate justice of the United States Supreme Court, 1902–1932*)

---

2. Called the *actus reus* (pronounced *ak*-tuhs *ray*-uhs), or "guilty act."
3. Called the *mens rea* (pronounced mehns *ray*-uh), or "evil intent."

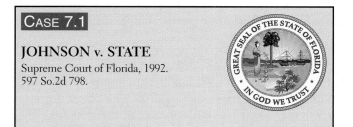

CASE 7.1

JOHNSON v. STATE
Supreme Court of Florida, 1992.
597 So.2d 798.

HISTORICAL AND SOCIAL SETTING *During the early days of the development of crimes at common law, judges often held an act to be criminal even if the perpetrator had no criminal intent. Starting in the early seventeenth century, judges began to require, in addition to the commission of a criminal act, some sort of criminal intent. Today, criminal liability still generally requires criminal intent.*

FACTS Raymond Johnson allegedly snatched a purse left in an unattended car at a gas station. Because the purse contained both money and a firearm, among other items, the state trial court convicted and sentenced Johnson for burglary of a conveyance (vehicle), grand theft of property (cash and payroll checks), and grand theft of a firearm. On appeal, Johnson claimed that he could not be guilty of grand theft of a firearm because he did not know that the purse contained a firearm. In other words, intent to commit the latter crime was lacking, and therefore that crime had not been committed.

ISSUE Can Johnson be convicted and sentenced for the crime of grand theft of a firearm even though he did not know that the firearm was in the purse?

DECISION No. There can be only one conviction for grand theft in this case.

(Continued)

Case 7.1—Continued

REASON The Supreme Court of Florida held that Johnson had committed the crime of theft and that it was grand theft because of the value of the property contained in the purse, including the value of the firearm. Only one crime of theft had occurred, however. The court stated that "a separate crime occurs only when there are separate distinct acts of seizing the property of another."

In this case, the crime occurred "in one swift motion." Johnson saw the purse and snatched it without knowing what it contained: "there was one intent and one act[.]"

FOR CRITICAL ANALYSIS—Social Consideration
Why didn't the court conclude that because Johnson intended to steal the purse, he therefore intended to steal everything contained in the purse?

▮ Procedure in Criminal Law

"A search is not to be made legal by what it turns up."

Robert H. Jackson, 1892–1954
(Associate justice of the United States Supreme Court, 1941–1954)

Criminal law brings the force of the state, with all its resources, to bear against the individual. Criminal procedures are designed to protect the constitutional rights of individuals and to prevent the arbitrary use of power on the part of the government.

Constitutional Safeguards

The U.S. Constitution provides specific safeguards for those accused of crimes. The United States Supreme Court has ruled that most of these safeguards apply not only in federal but also in state courts by virtue of the due process clause of the Fourteenth Amendment. These safeguards include the following:

1. The Fourth Amendment protection from unreasonable searches and seizures.
2. The Fourth Amendment requirement that no warrants for a search or an arrest can be issued without probable cause.
3. The Fifth Amendment requirement that no one can be deprived of "life, liberty, or property without due process of law."

DOUBLE JEOPARDY
A situation occurring when a person is tried twice for the same criminal offense; prohibited by the Fifth Amendment to the Constitution.

4. The Fifth Amendment prohibition against **double jeopardy** (trying someone twice for the same criminal offense).[4]
5. The Fifth Amendment requirement that no person can be required to be a witness against (incriminate) himself or herself.
6. The Sixth Amendment guarantees of a speedy trial, a trial by jury, a public trial, the right to confront witnesses, and the right to a lawyer at various stages of criminal proceedings.
7. The Eighth Amendment prohibitions against excessive bail and fines and cruel and unusual punishment.

EXCLUSIONARY RULE
In criminal procedure, a rule under which any evidence that is obtained in violation of the accused's constitutional rights guaranteed by the Fourth, Fifth, and Sixth Amendments, as well as any evidence derived from illegally obtained evidence, will not be admissible in court.

THE EXCLUSIONARY RULE Under what is known as the **exclusionary rule**, all evidence obtained in violation of the constitutional rights spelled out in the Fourth, Fifth, and Sixth Amendments normally must be excluded, as well as all evidence derived from the illegally obtained evidence. Evidence derived from the illegally obtained evidence is known as the "fruit of the poisonous tree." For example, if a confession is obtained after an illegal arrest, the arrest would be "the poisonous tree," and the confession, if "tainted" by the arrest, would be the "fruit."

---

4. The prohibition against double jeopardy means that once a criminal defendant is acquitted (found "not guilty") of a particular crime, the government may not reindict the person and retry him or her for the same crime. The prohibition against double jeopardy does not preclude the crime victim from bringing a *civil* suit against the same person to recover damages. For example, a person found "not guilty" of assault and battery in a criminal case may be sued by the victim in a civil tort case for damages. Additionally, a state's prosecution of a crime will not prevent a separate federal prosecution of the same crime, and vice versa. For example, a defendant found "not guilty" of violating a federal law can be tried in a state court for the same act, if the act is defined as a crime under state law.

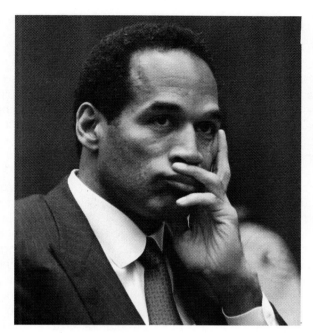

O. J. Simpson in court. After being acquitted of charges that he murdered Nicole Brown Simpson and Ron Goldman, Simpson was the defendant in a civil suit stemming from the same double murder. Do such suits violate the Fifth Amendment's prohibition against double jeopardy?

The purpose of the exclusionary rule is to deter police from conducting warrantless searches and other misconduct. The rule is sometimes criticized because it can lead to injustice. Many a defendant has "gotten off on a technicality" because law enforcement personnel failed to observe procedural requirements based on the above-mentioned constitutional amendments. Even though a defendant may be obviously guilty, if the evidence of that guilt is obtained improperly (without a valid search warrant, for example), it normally cannot be used against the defendant in court.

The courts, however, can exercise a certain amount of discretion in determining whether evidence is obtained improperly, thus balancing the scales somewhat. For example, in a 1995 case heard by the U.S. Court of Appeals for the Ninth Circuit, the judges had to decide whether evidence obtained from a legally conducted wiretap surveillance operation overseas violated the defendant's Fourth Amendment rights. If it did, the evidence would be inadmissible under the exclusionary rule. The court held that even though the wiretapping would have been illegal in the United States, the evidence legally obtained overseas was admissible. The court stated that the extent to which an American was protected from surveillance in another country is determined by the law of that country.[5]

The following case presents another interesting issue: Does the exclusionary rule require the suppression of evidence obtained during an arrest that was made on the basis of an erroneous computer record?

NOTE A person may be convicted despite police misconduct, because knowledge of facts obtained independently of the misconduct are admissible.

---

5. *United States v. Barona,* 56 F.3d 1087 (9th Cir. 1995).

CASE 7.2

ARIZONA v. EVANS
Supreme Court of the United States, 1995.
___ U.S. ___,
115 S.Ct. 1185,
131 L.Ed.2d 34.

HISTORICAL AND ETHICAL SETTING *For centuries, U.S. courts allowed the introduction of relevant evidence in criminal trials even if the evidence had been acquired unlawfully. Beginning at the end of the nineteenth century, however, some federal courts thought that to protect the integrity of the judicial process, unlawfully acquired*

(Continued)

Case 7.2—Continued

evidence should not be used in criminal trials. In 1914, the United States Supreme Court agreed that a federal court should not be a party to a wrong by allowing prosecutors to use the "fruits" of a police violation of the Fourth Amendment.[a] Over the last thirty years, there has been a steady attack on this rule, in part on the ground that evidence should not be excluded, even if it was seized illegally, when it clearly shows the guilt of the person charged.

FACTS During a routine traffic stop in Phoenix, Arizona, a police officer arrested Isaac Evans when the police computer indicated that there was an outstanding warrant for his arrest. In fact, the warrant had been quashed (voided) more than two weeks earlier, but court employees had wrongly failed to remove the warrant from the computer. The police searched Evans's car and discovered marijuana. Evans was charged, in an Arizona state court, with possession of marijuana. He moved to suppress the evidence (marijuana), on the ground that the arrest was unlawful because the warrant had already been quashed. The court granted Evans's motion, but on appeal, the state appellate court reversed. The state supreme court vacated (set aside) the appellate court's ruling, and the case was appealed to the United States Supreme Court.

ISSUE Is evidence admissible in a criminal trial if it was obtained during an arrest made on the basis of a computer

a. *Weeks v. United States,* 232 U.S. 383, 34 S.Ct. 341, 58 L.Ed. 652 (1914).

record that was incorrect as a result of mistakes by court employees?

DECISION Yes. The United States Supreme Court held that evidence seized in violation of the Fourth Amendment as a result of errors of court employees, causing an incorrect computer record, is admissible in a criminal trial. The Court reversed and remanded the case.

REASON The Court explained that "the exclusionary rule was * * * designed as a means of deterring police misconduct, not mistakes by court employees." Evans offered no evidence that "court employees are inclined to ignore or subvert the Fourth Amendment or that lawlessness among these actors requires application of the extreme sanction of exclusion." In fact, the Court noted, this kind of mistake happens only once every three or four years. Additionally, the Court believed that application of the exclusionary rule in this case would not have "a significant effect on court employees responsible for informing police that a warrant has been quashed," because court employees "have no stake in the outcome of particular criminal prosecutions." Finally, application of the rule could not be expected to alter police officers' behavior. "There is no indication that the arresting officer was not acting * * * reasonably when he relied upon the police computer record."

FOR CRITICAL ANALYSIS—Social Consideration
What if police department personnel (instead of court employees) had been responsible for the computer error? How would this circumstance affect the Court's reasoning?

THE MIRANDA RULE In *Miranda v. Arizona,* the United States Supreme Court established the rule that individuals who are arrested must be informed of certain constitutional rights, including their right to remain silent and their right to counsel. If the arresting officers fail to inform a criminal suspect of these constitutional rights, any statements the suspect makes will not be admissible in court. Because of its importance in criminal procedure, the *Miranda* case is presented as this chapter's *Landmark in the Law.*

LANDMARK IN THE LAW	*Miranda v. Arizona* (1966)

The United States Supreme Court's decision in *Miranda v. Arizona*[a] has been cited in more court decisions than any other case in the history of American law. Through television shows and other media, the case has also become familiar to most of America's

a.   384 U.S. 436, 86 S.Ct. 1602, 16 L.Ed.2d 694 (1966).

Landmark in the Law—Continued

adult population. The case arose after Ernesto Miranda was arrested in his home, on March 13, 1963, for the kidnapping and rape of an eighteen-year-old woman. Miranda was taken to a Phoenix, Arizona, police station and questioned by two police officers. Two hours later, the officers emerged from the interrogation room with a written confession signed by Miranda. The confession was admitted into evidence at the trial, and Miranda was convicted and sentenced to prison for twenty to thirty years.

Miranda appealed the decision, claiming that he had not been informed of his constitutional rights. He did not claim that he was innocent of the crime or that his confession was false or made under duress. He only claimed that he would not have confessed to the crime if he had been advised of his right to remain silent and to have an attorney. Nonetheless, the Supreme Court of Arizona held that Miranda's constitutional rights had not been violated and affirmed his conviction. In forming its decision, the court emphasized the fact that Miranda had not specifically requested an attorney. The *Miranda* case was subsequently consolidated with three other cases involving similar issues and reviewed by the United States Supreme Court.

In its decision, the Supreme Court stated that whenever an individual is taken into custody, "the following measures are required: He must be warned prior to any questioning that he has the right to remain silent, that anything he says can be used against him in a court of law, that he has the right to the presence of an attorney, and that if he cannot afford an attorney one will be appointed for him prior to any questioning if he so desires." If the accused waives his or her rights to remain silent and to have counsel present, the government must be able to demonstrate that the waiver was made knowingly, intelligently, and voluntarily.

Today, both on television and in the real world, police officers routinely advise suspects of their "*Miranda* rights" upon arrest. When Ernesto Miranda himself was later murdered, the suspected murderer was "read his *Miranda* rights."

For Critical Analysis: *Should illegally seized evidence be excluded from a criminal trial even if the evidence clearly shows the guilt of the person charged? Why should defendants who have admitted that they are guilty be allowed to avoid criminal liability because of procedural violations?*

Police officers take a suspect into custody. Why must a criminal suspect be informed of his or her legal rights?

THE EROSION OF THE *MIRANDA* RULE   The Supreme Court and lower courts have enforced the *Miranda* rule hundreds of times since the *Miranda* decision. Over time, however, several exceptions to the rule have been created. Congress in 1968 passed the Omnibus Crime Control and Safe Streets Act, which provided—among other things—that in federal cases a voluntary confession could be used in evidence even if the accused was not informed of his or her rights. The United States Supreme Court has carved out other exceptions. In 1984, for example, the Court recognized a "public safety" exception to the *Miranda* rule. The need to protect the public warranted the admissibility of statements made by the defendant (in this case, indicating where he placed the gun) as evidence in a trial, even when the defendant had not been informed of his *Miranda* rights.[6] Today, juries can even accept confessions without being convinced of their voluntariness.

> **REMEMBER** Once a suspect has been informed of his or her rights, anything he or she says can be used as evidence in a trial.

---

6.   *New York v. Quarles*, 467 U.S. 649, 104 S.Ct. 2626, 81 L.Ed.2d 550 (1984).

International Perspective

The right to remain silent is rooted in the Fifth Amendment prohibition against self-incrimination (no person "shall be compelled in any criminal case to be a witness against himself"). This protection against self-incrimination is a fundamental element in U.S. criminal procedure. For example, as will be discussed shortly, in a criminal trial a defendant need not say anything in his or her defense; rather, the burden is on the state to prove that the defendant committed the crime with which he or she is charged. Juries are not permitted to infer that a defendant is guilty simply because he or she remains silent.

The right to remain silent has long been a legal hallmark in Great Britain also. Until recently, a British police officer, upon arresting a suspect, was required to tell the suspect, "You do not have to say anything unless you wish to do so, but what you say may be given in evidence." In 1994, however, the British Parliament passed an act that provides that a criminal defendant's silence may be interpreted as evidence of the defendant's guilt. British police officers are now required, when making arrests, to inform the suspects, "You do not have to say anything. But if you do not mention now something which you later use in your defense, the court may decide that your failure to mention it now strengthens the case against you. A record will be made of everything you say, and it may be given in evidence if you are brought to trial."

For Critical Analysis: *Should U.S. judges and juries be allowed to make inferences from a defendant's silence?*

Criminal Process

As mentioned, a criminal prosecution differs significantly from a civil case in several respects. These differences reflect the desire to safeguard the rights of the individual against the state. Exhibit 7–2 summarizes the major steps in processing a criminal case. We discuss below in more detail three phases of the criminal process—arrest, indictment or information, and trial.

ARREST   Before a warrant for arrest can be issued, there must be probable cause for believing that the individual in question has committed a crime. As discussed in Chapter 2, *probable cause* can be defined as a substantial likelihood that the person has committed or is about to commit a crime. Note that probable cause involves a likelihood, not just a possibility. Arrests may sometimes be made without a warrant if there is no time to get one, but the action of the arresting officer is still judged by the standard of probable cause.

♦ Exhibit 7–2
Major Steps in Processing a Criminal Case

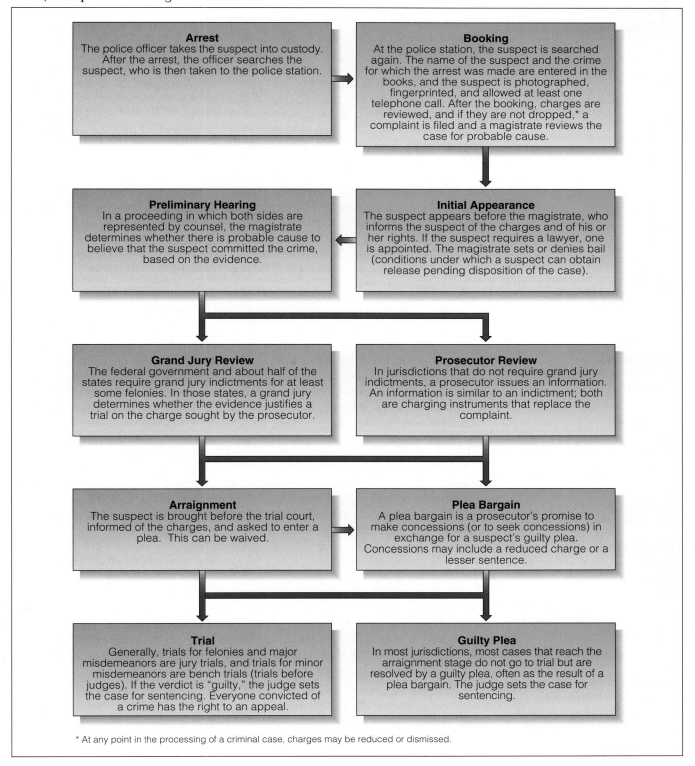

Arrest
The police officer takes the suspect into custody. After the arrest, the officer searches the suspect, who is then taken to the police station.

Booking
At the police station, the suspect is searched again. The name of the suspect and the crime for which the arrest was made are entered in the books, and the suspect is photographed, fingerprinted, and allowed at least one telephone call. After the booking, charges are reviewed, and if they are not dropped,* a complaint is filed and a magistrate reviews the case for probable cause.

Preliminary Hearing
In a proceeding in which both sides are represented by counsel, the magistrate determines whether there is probable cause to believe that the suspect committed the crime, based on the evidence.

Initial Appearance
The suspect appears before the magistrate, who informs the suspect of the charges and of his or her rights. If the suspect requires a lawyer, one is appointed. The magistrate sets or denies bail (conditions under which a suspect can obtain release pending disposition of the case).

Grand Jury Review
The federal government and about half of the states require grand jury indictments for at least some felonies. In those states, a grand jury determines whether the evidence justifies a trial on the charge sought by the prosecutor.

Prosecutor Review
In jurisdictions that do not require grand jury indictments, a prosecutor issues an information. An information is similar to an indictment; both are charging instruments that replace the complaint.

Arraignment
The suspect is brought before the trial court, informed of the charges, and asked to enter a plea. This can be waived.

Plea Bargain
A plea bargain is a prosecutor's promise to make concessions (or to seek concessions) in exchange for a suspect's guilty plea. Concessions may include a reduced charge or a lesser sentence.

Trial
Generally, trials for felonies and major misdemeanors are jury trials, and trials for minor misdemeanors are bench trials (trials before judges). If the verdict is "guilty," the judge sets the case for sentencing. Everyone convicted of a crime has the right to an appeal.

Guilty Plea
In most jurisdictions, most cases that reach the arraignment stage do not go to trial but are resolved by a guilty plea, often as the result of a plea bargain. The judge sets the case for sentencing.

* At any point in the processing of a criminal case, charges may be reduced or dismissed.

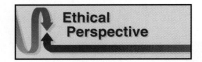

Ethical Perspective

Criminal suspects may waive their *Miranda* rights (see this chapter's *Landmark in the Law*), but the waiver must be made voluntarily. Evidence that the accused was tricked into waiving his or her rights will show that the rights were not voluntarily waived. What happens, though, if a suspect is tricked into confessing to a crime *after* the suspect has waived his or her rights?

Lying to criminal suspects to induce them to confess to crimes has occurred. In one case, for example, a police officer told a suspect accused of stabbing a person that the suspect's fingerprints had been found on the knife (which was not true). The suspect then confessed to the crime.[a] In another case, a suspect was told that a co-defendant had said something that, in fact, the co-defendant had not said.[b] In both of these cases, the courts held that the confessions induced by the lies were admissible. Coercion was not involved, no threats of harm were made, no bribes were tendered, and generally, in each case, the defendant's will was not "overcome" by the police. The central question remains, however: Where does society draw the line between trickery and coercion? Other kinds of police actions, such as "reverse sting" operations carried out by undercover agents, raise similar ethical questions.

For Critical Analysis: *Trickery may lead to more guilty criminal defendants being convicted. What cost is nonetheless imposed on society by such actions?*

a. *State v. Barner,* 486 N.W.2d 1 (Minn.App. 1992).
b. *Frazier v. Cupp,* 394 U.S. 731, 89 S.Ct. 1420, 22 L.Ed.2d 684 (1969).

INDICTMENT
A charge by a grand jury that a named person has committed a crime.

GRAND JURY
A group of citizens called to decide, after hearing the state's evidence, whether a reasonable basis (probable cause) exists for believing that a crime has been committed and whether a trial ought to be held.

INFORMATION
A formal accusation or complaint (without an indictment) issued in certain types of actions (usually criminal actions involving lesser crimes) by a law officer, such as a magistrate.

BEYOND A REASONABLE DOUBT
The standard of proof used in criminal cases. If there is any reasonable doubt that a criminal defendant did not commit the crime with which he or she has been charged, then the verdict must be "not guilty."

INDICTMENT OR INFORMATION   Individuals must be formally charged with having committed specific crimes before they can be brought to trial. If issued by a grand jury, this charge is called an **indictment**.[7] A **grand jury** usually consists of a greater number of jurors than the ordinary trial jury. A grand jury does not determine the guilt or innocence of an accused party; rather, its function is to determine, after hearing the state's evidence, whether a reasonable basis (probable cause) exists for believing that a crime has been committed and whether a trial ought to be held.

Usually, grand juries are called in cases involving serious crimes, such as murder. For lesser crimes, an individual may be formally charged with a crime by what is called an **information,** or criminal complaint. An information will be issued by a magistrate (a public official vested with judicial authority) if the magistrate determines that there is sufficient evidence to justify bringing the individual to trial.

TRIAL   At a criminal trial, the accused person does not have to prove anything; the entire burden of proof is on the prosecutor (the state). The prosecution must show that, based on all the evidence presented, the defendant's guilt is established **beyond a reasonable doubt.** If there is any reasonable doubt that a criminal defendant did not commit the crime with which he or she has been charged, then the verdict must be "not guilty." Note that giving a verdict of "not guilty" is not the same as stating that the defendant is innocent; it merely means that not enough evidence was properly presented to the court to prove guilt beyond all reasonable doubt.

The requirement that a defendant's guilt be proved beyond a reasonable doubt is a stricter standard of proof than the standard normally used in civil proceedings, in which a defendant's liability is usually decided based on a preponderance of the evidence. A *preponderance of the evidence* means that the evidence offered in support of

---

7.   Pronounced in-*dyte*-ment.

a certain claim outweighs the evidence offered to negate the claim. The higher standard of proof in criminal cases reflects a fundamental social value—a belief that it is worse to convict an innocent individual than to let a guilty person go free.

Courts have complex rules about what types of evidence may be presented and how the evidence may be brought out in criminal cases, especially in jury trials. These rules are designed to ensure that evidence in trials is relevant, reliable, and not prejudicial against the defendant.

"Our procedure has been always haunted by the ghost of the innocent man convicted."

Learned Hand, 1872–1961 *(American jurist)*

Ethical Perspective

Jurors in a criminal case must find the defendant guilty "beyond a reasonable doubt." What, though, does "reasonable doubt" mean? Traditionally in the United States, judges have told jurors that guilt beyond a reasonable doubt equates to a "moral certainty" that a defendant is guilty. Some defendants have claimed, however, that the "moral certainty" test of guilt is too subjective and invites the jurors to ignore objective evidence presented at trial—thus violating the defendants' constitutional rights to due process of law.

In a 1994 case, the United States Supreme Court held otherwise, stating that "so long as the court instructs the jury on the necessity that the defendant's guilt be proven beyond a reasonable doubt, the Constitution does not require that any particular form of words be used in advising the jury of the government's burden of proof." After delving into modern dictionaries, Justice Sandra Day O'Connor concluded that although the phrase "moral certainty," standing alone, "might not be recognized by modern jurors as a synonym for 'proof beyond a reasonable doubt,' its use in conjunction with the abiding conviction language" did not invite "conviction on less than the constitutionally required proof."[a]

Justice Ruth Bader Ginsburg, in a separate opinion, suggested that courts adopt a model jury instruction devised by the Federal Judicial Center, which defines reasonable doubt as "proof that leaves you firmly convinced of the defendant's guilt." Clearly, the debate over reasonable doubt indicates that law is not yet an exact science.

For Critical Analysis: *Judges are often reluctant to explain to juries what the phrase "reasonable doubt" means, fearing that the more they explain it, the less clear it will be. Do you think that judges should explain to juries what "reasonable doubt" means? Or should the definition of this phrase be left to the jurors?*

NOTE Reasonable doubt is, as its name implies, doubt based on reason. It is not doubt based on wishes, or imagination, or a desire to avoid doing something unpleasant.

a. *Victor v. Nebraska*, 511 U.S. 1, 114 S.Ct. 1239, 127 L.Ed.2d 583 (1994).

Federal Sentencing Guidelines

In 1984, Congress enacted the Sentencing Reform Act. This act created the U.S. Sentencing Commission, which was charged with the task of standardizing sentences for federal crimes. The commission fulfilled its task, and in 1987 its sentencing guidelines for all federal crimes became effective. The guidelines establish a range of possible penalties for each federal crime. Depending on the defendant's criminal record, the seriousness of the offense, and other factors specified in the guidelines, federal judges must select a sentence from within this range when sentencing criminal defendants.

The commission also created specific guidelines for the punishment of crimes committed by corporate employees (white-collar crimes). These guidelines, which went into effect in 1991, established stiffer penalties for criminal violations of securities laws (see Chapter 29), antitrust laws (see Chapter 30), employment laws (see

Chapters 32 and 33), mail and wire fraud, commercial bribery, and kickbacks and money laundering (all discussed later in this chapter). The guidelines allow federal judges to take into consideration a number of factors when selecting from the range of possible penalties for a specified crime. These factors include the defendant company's history of past violations, the extent of management's cooperation with federal investigators, and the extent to which the firm has undertaken specific programs and procedures to prevent criminal activities by its employees.

Criminal cases are sometimes appealed on the ground that the sentence imposed was too severe. In the following case, for example, the defendant, because of a check-kiting scheme, had been charged with bank fraud. Obtaining the property—including money—of a financial institution such as a bank is a federal crime. The issue before the appellate court is whether the defendant's sentence should be reduced in light of the fact that he immediately repaid the amount that he obtained through the fraudulent scheme.

CASE 7.3

UNITED STATES v. ASHER
United States Court of Appeals,
Seventh Circuit, 1995.
59 F.3d 622.

HISTORICAL AND POLITICAL SETTING   *At one time, the Interstate Commerce Commission regulated the routes and rates of trucking companies. Congress deregulated the industry in 1980, allowing truckers to ship freight anywhere and charge whatever they wanted. The immediate effect was a huge number of small, start-up companies—more than twelve thousand in the first few years. The most successful of the truckers, however, were the large national companies that could carry freight anywhere. Most of the new, small outfits failed.*

FACTS   Asher Truck & Trailer, Inc., had facilities in Evansville, Indiana, and Mount Vernon, Illinois. Guy Asher, the company's owner and operator, kept separate bank accounts for the two facilities. When the business began to have cash flow problems, Asher began to write checks on the Evansville account and deposit them in the Mount Vernon account, and vice versa, knowing that the accounts on which the checks were drawn did not have sufficient funds to cover the checks. When the scheme was discovered, the Mount Vernon account was overdrawn by $160,000, which Asher promptly repaid. Asher was charged in a federal district court with bank fraud, and he pleaded guilty to the charge. Asher argued, however, that his sentence should be reduced because he had immediately repaid the bank. The court refused to reduce his sentence, and Asher appealed.

ISSUE   For purposes of sentencing in bank fraud cases, should the amount of the loss be measured at the time the scheme is discovered or after a defendant has repaid the funds?

DECISION   The U.S. Court of Appeals for the Seventh Circuit affirmed the district court's judgment that the amount of the loss should be measured at the time the scheme is discovered.

REASON   The appellate court acknowledged that Asher's decision to repay the amount of the bank's loss when his scheme was uncovered "may indicate that he accepted responsibility for his fraudulent practices." The court pointed out, however, that "it does not indicate that his fraudulent practices created no loss to the bank." According to the court, the loss is the value of whatever is unlawfully taken. The argument that there was no loss to the bank because Asher promptly repaid the full amount "does not carry the day. *   *   * The mere fortuity that he had the financial resources available to him to repay the victim bank in full after his *   *   * scheme was discovered does not negate the fact that he engaged in fraudulent conduct which resulted in the loss of $160,000."

FOR CRITICAL ANALYSIS—Economic Consideration
Do you think that the court's decision in this case will discourage criminals from repaying their victims?

Twenty-Five Years in Prison—All for a Slice of Pizza

Many states have enacted "three strikes and you're out" legislation. Typically, this legislation states that any "career" criminal who already has two violent felony convictions on his or her record will go to jail (in some states, for life and without parole) if convicted of a third similar felony. A federal crime bill enacted in 1994 adopted this provision as well. A California law, enacted in 1994, requires longer prison sentences for felons who have had at least one prior conviction for a serious or violent felony.

Although the purpose of these laws may be laudatory (note, however, that they have been criticized by many), they can lead to extreme situations. In January 1995, Williams was convicted of felony petty theft for stealing a slice of pizza from a group of children on a pier in Redondo Beach, California. Because Williams had prior convictions for robbery and other felonies, he was sentenced to twenty-five years in prison for the theft of the slice of pizza![a]

Some criminal defendants have argued that "three strikes" laws are unconstitutional because they deprive judges of too much power, thus violating the constitutional separation of powers between the legislative and judicial branches. This issue recently reached the California Supreme Court, when it reviewed a case in which a judge had disregarded two previous "strikes" against a repeat offender and sentenced him to six years instead of the twenty-five-years-to-life sentence prescribed by the "three strikes" law. The California high court held that the law did not preclude the court from striking allegations of prior convictions.[b]

For Critical Analysis: *What are some of the costs and benefits to society of three-strikes-and-you're-out laws?*

a. "Theft of Pizza Slice Nets a 25-Year Term," *The New York Times*, March 5, 1995, p. 11.

b. *People v. Superior Court*, 53 Cal.4th 497, 917 P.2d 628, 53 Cal.Rptr.2d 789 (1996).

▌Crimes Affecting Business

Many of the crimes that occur in the business context and that are discussed in the following pages are popularly referred to as **white-collar crimes.** Although there is no official definition of white-collar crime, the term is popularly used to mean an illegal act or series of acts committed by an individual or business entity using some nonviolent means to obtain a personal or business advantage. Usually, this kind of crime is committed in the course of a legitimate occupation. Corporate crimes, which are not treated here, also fall under the category of white-collar crimes. The liability of corporations and corporate personnel for criminal actions will be discussed in detail in Chapters 26 and 27.

WHITE-COLLAR CRIME
Nonviolent crime committed by individuals or corporations to obtain a personal or business advantage.

Forgery

The fraudulent making or altering of any writing in a way that changes the legal rights and liabilities of another is **forgery.** If, without authorization, Severson signs Bennett's name to the back of a check made out to Bennett, Severson is committing forgery. Forgery also includes changing trademarks, falsifying public records, counterfeiting, and altering a legal document.

FORGERY
The fraudulent making or altering of any writing in a way that changes the legal rights and liabilities of another.

Robbery

At common law, **robbery** was defined as forcefully and unlawfully taking personal property of any value from another. The use of force or intimidation is usually necessary for an act of theft to be considered a robbery. Thus, picking pockets is not robbery, because the action is unknown to the victim. Typically, states have more severe penalties for *aggravated* robbery—robbery with the use of a deadly weapon.

ROBBERY
The act of forcefully and unlawfully taking personal property of any value from another; force or intimidation is usually necessary for an act of theft to be considered a robbery.

Burglary

At common law, **burglary** was defined as breaking and entering the dwelling of another at night with the intent to commit a felony. Originally, the definition was aimed at protecting an individual's home and its occupants. Most state statutes have eliminated some of the requirements found in the common law definition. The time at which the breaking and entering occurs, for example, is usually immaterial. State statutes frequently omit the element of breaking, and some states do not require that the building be a dwelling. Aggravated burglary, which is defined as burglary with the use of a deadly weapon, burglary of a dwelling, or both, incurs a greater penalty.

Larceny

Any person who wrongfully or fraudulently takes and carries away another person's personal property is guilty of **larceny.** Larceny includes the fraudulent intent to deprive an owner permanently of property. Many business-related larcenies entail fraudulent conduct. Whereas robbery involves force or fear, larceny does not. Therefore, picking pockets is larceny, not robbery.

As society becomes more complex, the question often arises as to what is property. In most states, the definition of property that is subject to larceny statutes has expanded. Stealing computer programs may constitute larceny even though the "property" consists of magnetic impulses. Stealing computer time can also constitute larceny. So, too, can the theft of natural gas. Trade secrets can be subject to larceny statutes. Intercepting cellular phone calls to obtain another's phone card number—and then using that number to place long-distance calls, often overseas—is a form of property theft. These types of larceny are covered by "theft of services" statutes in many jurisdictions.

The common law distinction between grand and petit larceny depends on the value of the property taken. Many states have abolished this distinction, but in those that have not, grand larceny is a felony and petit larceny, a misdemeanor.

Obtaining Goods by False Pretenses

It is a criminal act to obtain goods by means of false pretenses—for example, buying groceries with a check, knowing that one has insufficient funds to cover it. Statutes dealing with such illegal activities vary widely from state to state.

Receiving Stolen Goods

It is a crime to receive stolen goods. The recipient of such goods need not know the true identity of the owner or the thief. All that is necessary is that the recipient knows or should have known that the goods are stolen, which implies an intent to deprive the owner of those goods.

Embezzlement

When a person entrusted with another person's property or money fraudulently appropriates it, **embezzlement** occurs. Typically, embezzlement involves an employee who steals money. Banks face this problem, and so do a number of businesses in which corporate officers or accountants "jimmy" the books to cover up the fraudulent conversion of money for their own benefit. Embezzlement is not larceny, because the wrongdoer does not physically take the property from the possession of another, and it is not robbery, because force or fear is not used.

A businessperson places a call with a cellular phone. If this call is intercepted to obtain the phone number and that number is used without permission to place long-distance calls, what crime is committed?

It does not matter whether the accused takes the money from the victim or from a third person. If, as the financial officer of a large corporation, Saunders pockets a certain number of checks from third parties that were given to her to deposit into the corporate account, she is embezzling.

Ordinarily, an embezzler who returns what has been taken will not be prosecuted, because the owner usually will not take the time to make a complaint, give depositions, and appear in court. That the accused intended eventually to return the embezzled property, however, does not constitute a sufficient defense to the crime of embezzlement. The role of intention in establishing whether embezzlement has occurred is emphasized in the following case.

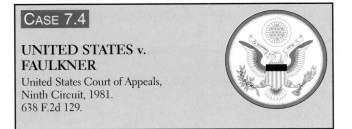

CASE 7.4

UNITED STATES v. FAULKNER

United States Court of Appeals, Ninth Circuit, 1981.
638 F.2d 129.

HISTORICAL AND SOCIAL SETTING *At one time, the law generally divided theft into three separate crimes— larceny, false pretenses, and embezzlement. Statutes prohibiting embezzlement often listed the kinds of persons who might have lawful possession of another's property (store clerks, bank employees, merchants, and so on) and provided that any such person who fraudulently converted the property to his or her own use was guilty of embezzlement. Today, in those jurisdictions that*

have enacted new criminal codes, the three separate crimes have been replaced with a single crime. With regard to the once-separate crime of embezzlement, these statutes may simply provide that one who is in lawful possession of another's property and intends to convert it to his or her own use is guilty.

FACTS Faulkner, a truck driver, was hauling a load of refrigerators from San Diego to New York for the trucking company that employed him. He departed from his assigned route and stopped in Las Vegas, where he attempted to display and sell some of the refrigerators to a firm. Although the refrigerators never left the truck, to display them he had to break the truck's seals, enter the cargo department, and open two refrigerator cartons. The store owner refused to purchase the appliances, and when Faulkner left the store, he was arrested. He was later convicted under federal law for the embezzlement

(Continued)

Case 7.4—Continued

of an interstate shipment. Faulkner appealed, claiming that there were no grounds for the charge, because he had never removed any equipment from the truck.

ISSUE   Does the charge of embezzlement apply when the property has not been physically removed from the owner's possession?

DECISION   Yes. The U.S. Court of Appeals for the Ninth Circuit affirmed the judgment of the lower court.

REASON   The federal appellate court held that if a person has possession and control over the property of another and has the *intent* of converting the goods to his or her own use, then embezzlement occurs. By leaving his assigned route in order to sell the refrigerators and keep the proceeds, Faulkner exercised control over the property, with the intent to convert it to his own use.

FOR CRITICAL ANALYSIS—Social Consideration
By definition, a crime involves both intent and a criminal act. What criminal act did Faulkner commit?

••••••••••••••••••••••••••••••
"A large number of houses deserve to be burnt."

H. G. Wells, 1866–1946
(English author)
••••••••••••••••••••••••••••••

ARSON
The malicious burning of another's dwelling. Some statutes have expanded this to include any real property regardless of ownership and the destruction of property by other means—for example, by explosion.

Arson

The willful and malicious burning of a building (and in some states, personal property) owned by another is the crime of **arson**. At common law, arson applied only to burning down another person's house. The law was designed to protect human life. Today, arson statutes have been extended to cover the destruction of any building, regardless of ownership, by fire or explosion.

Every state has a special statute that covers a person's burning a building for the purpose of collecting insurance. If Smith owns an insured apartment building that is falling apart and sets fire to it himself or pays someone else to do so, he is guilty not only of arson but also of defrauding insurers, which is an attempted larceny. Of course, the insurer need not pay the claim when insurance fraud is proved.

Mail and Wire Fraud

One of the most potent weapons against white-collar criminals is the Mail Fraud Act of 1990.[8] Under this act, it is a federal crime to use the mails to defraud the public. Illegal use of the mails must involve (1) mailing or causing someone else to mail a writing—something written, printed, or photocopied—for the purpose of executing a scheme to defraud and (2) a contemplated or an organized scheme to defraud by false pretenses. If, for example, Johnson advertises by mail the sale of a cure for cancer that he knows to be fraudulent because it has no medical validity, he can be prosecuted for fraudulent use of the mails.

Federal law also makes it a crime to use wire, radio, or television transmissions to defraud.[9] Violators may be fined up to $1,000, imprisoned for up to five years, or both. If the violation affects a financial institution, the violator may be fined up to $1 million, imprisoned for up to thirty years, or both.

COMPUTER CRIME
Any act that is directed against computers and computer parts, that uses computers as instruments of crime, or that involves computers and constitutes abuse.

Computer Crime

The American Bar Association defines **computer crime** as any act that is directed against computers and computer parts, that uses computers as instruments of crime, or that involves computers and constitutes abuse. Frequently our laws are inadequate to deal with the various types of computer crimes that are committed. As mentioned earlier, larceny statutes were originally passed to prohibit the taking and carrying away of physical property belonging to another.

---

8.   18 U.S.C. Sections 1341–1342.
9.   18 U.S.C. Section 1343.

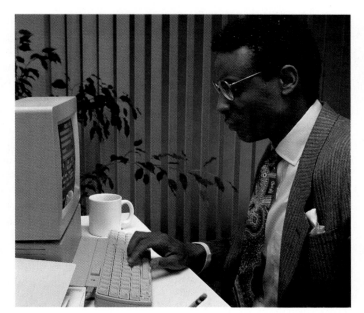

A businessperson works with a computer. If the work being done is copied by another employee without permission and given to a business competitor, what crime has been committed?

Computer crimes, however, such as those involving the theft of computer data or services, frequently do not require a physical "taking and carrying away" of another's property. Some states have expanded their definitions of property to allow computer crimes to fall within their larceny statutes, but in other states prosecutors have to rely on other criminal statutes. People committing computer crimes often receive lenient punishments, which has led lawmakers to put forth various proposals to deal with this type of crime.

A variety of different types of crime can be committed with or against computers. We look here at some of the ways in which computers have been involved in criminal activity, as well as at some of the difficulties involved in prosecuting computer crime.

FINANCIAL CRIMES Many computer crimes fall into the broad category of financial crimes. In addition to using computers for information storage and retrieval, businesses commonly use computers to conduct financial transactions. This is equally true of the government, which handles virtually all of its transactions via computer. These circumstances provide opportunities for employees and others to commit crimes that can involve serious economic losses. For example, employees of accounting and computer departments can transfer monies among accounts with little effort and without the risk involved in transactions evidenced by paperwork. Thus, not only is the potential for crime in the area of financial transactions great, but also most monetary losses from computer crime are suffered in this area.

BE AWARE Technological change is one of the primary factors that lead to new types of crime.

SOFTWARE PIRACY As discussed in the *Technology and Software Piracy* feature in Chapter 6, given the expense of software, many individuals and businesses have been tempted to steal software by decoding and making unauthorized copies of software programs. Under most state laws, software piracy is classified as a crime. At the federal level, the traditional laws protecting intellectual property (such as patent and copyright laws) have been amended in the last decade or so to extend coverage to computer programs (see Chapter 6). In 1990, in an attempt to control further the unauthorized copying of computer programs, the federal government passed a law that prohibits, with some exceptions, the renting, leasing, or lending of computer software without the express permission of the copyright holder.

PROPERTY THEFT Computer crimes can also involve property theft. One type is the theft of computer equipment (hardware), which has become easier in recent years as computer components have become smaller and more readily transportable. Another type of property theft is the theft of computer-related property, which may involve taking goods that are controlled and accounted for by means of a computer application program. For example, an employee in a company's accounting department could manipulate inventory records to conceal unauthorized shipments of goods. The theft of computer equipment and the theft of goods with the aid of computers are subject to the same criminal and tort laws covering thefts of other physical property.

VANDALISM AND DESTRUCTIVE PROGRAMMING   Another form of computer crime is the intentional destruction of computer hardware or software. In one instance, an individual erased a company's records merely by walking past computer storage banks with an electromagnet. Other destructive acts have required greater technical awareness and facility. A knowledgeable individual, such as an angry employee whose job has just been terminated, can do a considerable amount of damage to computer data and files. One ongoing problem for businesspersons and other computer users today is guarding against computer "viruses"—computer programs that are designed to rearrange, replace, or destroy data. This form of vandalism is difficult to combat because of the difficulty of locating and prosecuting those responsible for "unleashing" such programs.

THEFT OF DATA OR SERVICES   Many people would agree that when an individual uses another's computer or computer information system without authorization, the individual is stealing. For example, an employee who used a computer system or data stored in a computer system for private gain and without the employer's authorization would likely be considered a thief, as would a politician who used a government computer to send out campaign brochures. Under an increasing number of revised criminal codes and broad judicial interpretations of existing statutes, the unauthorized use of computer data or services is considered larceny. The following case illustrates how one court interpreted a statute to cover the theft of computer time and storage.

CASE 7.5

UNITED STATES v. COLLINS
United States Court of Appeals,
District of Columbia Circuit, 1995.
56 F.3d 1416.

HISTORICAL AND TECHNOLOGICAL SETTING
Early computers used vacuum tubes. The Electronic Numerical Integrator and Calculator (ENIAC) required 18,000 vacuum tubes to operate in 1946. The ENIAC took up 2,000 square feet and weighed 50 tons. It could perform approximately 10,000 calculations per second but had an internal memory capacity of only 20 words. By comparison, in the early 1990s a single silicon chip less than ¼ inch across was more than a million times as fast and could store 800,000 words. If cars had become as efficient, a Rolls Royce would cost $1 and get 1,000,000 miles per gallon.

FACTS   Peter Collins worked for the U.S. Defense Intelligence Agency (DIA) and had access to the DIA's classified computer system. Collins was also involved in amateur ballroom dancing through the U.S. Amateur Ballroom Dance Association. Over a five-year period, Collins used the DIA's computer system to create hundreds of documents, including newsletters, mailing lists, and calendars, relating to his ballroom dance activities. Collins was subsequently prosecuted and convicted in a federal district court of, among other things, converting to his own use government computer time and storage. Collins appealed to the U.S. Court of Appeals for the District of Columbia Circuit. He argued in part that his conviction should be reversed on the ground that the statute under which he was convicted for the conversion of computer time and storage does not cover intangible property (property that, like computer data and services, does not have a physical existence).

ISSUE   Does the statute cover the theft of such intangible property as computer time and storage?

DECISION   Yes. The U.S. Court of Appeals for the District of Columbia Circuit affirmed the district court's judgment.

Case 7.5—Continued

REASON   The U.S. Court of Appeals for the District of Columbia Circuit pointed out that the statute under which Collins was convicted provides for liability on the part of any person who "knowingly converts to his use or the use of another * * * any * * * thing of value of the United States or of any * * * agency thereof." The court emphasized that "Congress did not limit those things which could be converted to 'tangible property,' but rather any 'thing of value.'" The court explained that

"Congress intended to enact a broad prohibition against the misappropriation of anything belonging to the national government, unrestrained by * * * fine and technical distinctions." This intent "clearly confirms" that the statute "covers the misappropriation of intangible property."

FOR CRITICAL ANALYSIS—Technological Considera-tion   *When computer time is stolen, it may never affect others' use of the computer. Why, then, is such an action prosecuted?*

PROSECUTING COMPUTER CRIME   In attempting to control computer crime, governments at both the federal and state levels have undertaken protective measures. The Counterfeit Access Device and Computer Fraud and Abuse Act of 1984, as amended, prohibits unauthorized access to certain types of information, such as restricted government information, information contained in a financial institution's financial records, and information contained in a consumer reporting agency's files on consumers. Penalties for violations include up to five years' imprisonment and a fine of up to $250,000 or twice the amount that was gained by the thief or lost by the victim as a result of the crime. Several states have also passed legislation specifically addressing the problem of computer crime.

One of the major problems in attempting to control computer crime is that it cannot be prosecuted if it is not reported. It seems clear to many people that the reason many computer crimes go unreported is because business firms are reluctant to disclose the vulnerability of their systems. Companies adversely affected by such crime do not want to publicize the fact, because they are afraid customers will doubt the accuracy and security of computer-generated material. Cases involving computer crimes are thus often settled out of court to avoid publicity. (See this chapter's *Technology and Prosecuting Computer Crime* for a discussion of the problems faced by prosecutors in trying to control the alleged crimes committed via the Internet.)

☐ Technology and Prosecuting Computer Crime

Technology has always been just a few steps ahead of the law. This is particularly true in respect to the Internet, the use of which has given rise to perplexing legal issues. Consider, for example, a case brought by the government against David LaMacchia. LaMacchia, a student at the Massachusetts Institute of Technology (MIT), used MIT's computer network to gain entry to the Internet. Using pseudonyms and an encrypted address, LaMacchia set up an electronic bulletin board, which he called Cynosure, and encouraged his correspondents to upload popular software applications and computer games onto it. He then transferred the software to a second encrypted address (Cynosure II), where it could be downloaded by other users with access to the Cynosure password.

Eventually, the worldwide traffic generated by LaMacchia's offer of free software came to the attention of federal authorities, who arrested LaMacchia for conspiring with "persons unknown" to violate the federal law prohibiting wire fraud. The government alleged that LaMacchia's scheme facilitated, on an international scale, the "illegal copying and distribution of copyrighted software" and that the scheme caused losses of more than a million dollars to software copyright holders.

The problem in LaMacchia's case, however, was that the court could not find that he had committed any crime. The court held that for wire fraud to exist, LaMacchia would have had to defraud people of

(Continued)

money. If LaMacchia had sold the software, he would have committed a criminal act. LaMacchia also had not violated the Copyright Act, which imposes criminal penalties only when copyrighted products are copied without authorization "willfully and for purposes of commercial advantage or private financial gain." LaMacchia's actions, however, had not resulted in any "commercial advantage or private gain" for LaMacchia.

The court concluded that in arriving at its decision, it did not mean "to suggest that there is anything edifying about what LaMacchia is alleged to have done . . . . [O]ne might at best describe [LaMacchia's] actions as heedlessly irresponsible, and at worst as nihilistic, self-indulgent, and lacking in any fundamental sense of values. Criminal as well as civil penalties should probably attach to willful, multiple infringements of copy-

righted software even absent a commercial motive on the part of the infringer. One can envision ways that the copyright law could be modified to permit such prosecution. But, '[i]t is the legislature, not the Court which is to define a crime, and ordain its punishment.'"[a]

This is but one example of how ill-equipped existing criminal laws are to handle new kinds of issues emerging in an on-line era. The problem will become even greater as the use of the Internet becomes more widespread.

For Critical Analysis: *Do you think that the easy pirating of software via the Internet will eventually stifle innovation on the part of software manufacturers?*

a. *United States v. LaMacchia,* 871 F.Supp. 535 (D.Mass. 1994).

> *"[It is] very much better to bribe a person than kill him."*
>
> **Sir Winston Churchill, 1874–1965**
> *(British prime minister, 1940–1945, 1951–1955)*

Bribery

Basically, three types of bribery are considered crimes: bribery of public officials, commercial bribery, and bribery of foreign officials.

BRIBERY OF PUBLIC OFFICIALS The attempt to influence a public official to act in a way that serves a private interest is a crime. As an element of this crime, intent must be present and proved. The bribe can be anything the recipient considers to be valuable. It is important to realize that *the commission of the crime of bribery occurs when the bribe is offered.* The recipient does not have to agree to perform whatever action is desired by the person offering the bribe, nor does the recipient have to accept the bribe, for the crime of bribery to occur.

COMMERCIAL BRIBERY Typically, people make commercial bribes to obtain proprietary information, cover up an inferior product, or secure new business. Industrial espionage sometimes involves commercial bribes. For example, a person in one firm may offer an employee in a competing firm some type of payoff in exchange for trade secrets and pricing schedules. So-called kickbacks or payoffs for special favors or services are a form of commercial bribery in some situations.

BRIBERY OF FOREIGN OFFICIALS Bribing foreign officials to obtain favorable business contracts is a crime. This crime and the Foreign Corrupt Practices Act of 1977, which was passed to curb the practice of bribery by American businesspersons in securing foreign contracts, are discussed in detail in the *Landmark in the Law* in Chapter 4.

Bankruptcy Fraud

Today, federal bankruptcy law (see Chapter 22) allows individuals and businesses to be relieved of oppressive debt through bankruptcy proceedings. Numerous white-collar crimes may be committed during the many phases of a bankruptcy proceeding. A creditor, for example, may file a false claim against the debtor, which is a crime. Also, a debtor may fraudulently transfer assets to favored parties before or after the petition for bankruptcy is filed. For example, a company-owned automobile may be "sold" at a bargain price to a trusted friend or relative. Closely related to the crime of fraudulent transfer of property is the crime of fraudulent concealment of property, such as hiding gold coins.

Money Laundering

The profits from illegal activities amount to billions of dollars a year, particularly the profits from illegal drug transactions and, to a lesser extent, from racketeering, prostitution, and gambling. Under federal law, banks, savings and loan associations, and other financial institutions are required to report currency transactions of over $10,000. Consequently, those who engage in illegal activities face difficulties in placing their cash profits from illegal transactions.

As an alternative to simply placing cash from illegal transactions in bank deposits, wrongdoers and racketeers have invented ways to launder "dirty" money to make it "clean." This **money laundering** is done through legitimate businesses. For example, a successful drug dealer might become a partner with a restaurateur. Little by little, the restaurant shows an increasing profit. As a shareholder or partner in the restaurant, the wrongdoer is able to report the "profits" of the restaurant as legitimate income on which federal and state taxes are paid. The wrongdoer can then spend those monies without worrying about whether his or her lifestyle exceeds the level possible with his or her reported income. The Federal Bureau of Investigation estimates that organized crime alone has invested tens of billions of dollars in as many as a hundred thousand business establishments in the United States for the purpose of money laundering.

MONEY LAUNDERING
Falsely reporting income that has been obtained through criminal activity as income obtained through a legitimate business enterprise—in effect, "laundering" the "dirty money."

Insider Trading

An individual who obtains "inside information" about the plans of large corporations can often make stock-trading profits by using such information to guide decisions relating to the purchase or sale of corporate securities. **Insider trading** is a violation of securities law and will be considered more fully in Chapter 29. At this point, it may be said that one who possesses inside information and who has a duty not to disclose it to outsiders may not profit from the purchase or sale of securities based on that information until the information is available to the public.

INSIDER TRADING
The purchase or sale of securities on the basis of "inside information" (information that has not been made available to the public) in violation of a duty owed to the company whose stock is being traded.

Criminal RICO Violations

The Racketeer Influenced and Corrupt Organizations Act (RICO) was passed in an attempt to prevent the use of legitimate business enterprises as shields for racketeering activity and to prohibit the purchase of any legitimate business interest with illegally obtained funds (see the discussion of RICO in Chapter 6).

Most of the criminal RICO offenses have little, if anything, to do with normal business activities, for they involve gambling, arson, and extortion. Securities fraud (involving the sale of stocks and bonds), as well as mail fraud, wire fraud, welfare fraud, embezzlement, and numerous other crimes defined by state or federal statutes, however, are also criminal RICO violations, and RICO has become an effective tool in attacking these white-collar crimes in recent years. Under criminal provisions of RICO, any individual found guilty of a violation is subject to a fine of up to $25,000 per violation, imprisonment for up to twenty years, or both.

▌ Defenses to Crimes

There are numerous defenses that the law deems sufficient to excuse a defendant's criminal behavior. Among the most important defenses to criminal liability are infancy, intoxication, insanity, mistake, consent, duress, justifiable use of force, entrapment, and the statute of limitations. Also, in some cases, defendants are given *immunity* and thus relieved, at least in part, of criminal liability for crimes they committed. We look at each of these defenses here.

Note that procedural violations (such as obtaining evidence without a valid search warrant) may operate as defenses also—because evidence obtained in violation of a defendant's constitutional rights may not be admitted in court. If the evidence is suppressed, then there may be no basis for prosecuting the defendant.

Infancy

The term *infant*, as used in the law, refers to any person who has not yet reached the age of majority (see Chapter 10). Exhibit 7–3 indicates the relationship between age and responsibility for criminal acts under the common law.

In all states, certain courts handle cases involving children who are alleged to have violated the law. In some states, juvenile courts handle children's cases exclusively. In most states, however, courts that handle children's cases also have jurisdiction over other matters, such as traffic offenses. Originally, juvenile court hearings were informal, and lawyers were rarely present. Since 1967, however, when the United States Supreme Court ordered that a child charged with delinquency must be allowed to consult with an attorney before being committed to a state institution,[10] juvenile court hearings have become more formal. In some states, a child will be treated as an adult and tried in a regular court if he or she is above a certain age (usually fourteen) and is guilty of a felony, such as rape or murder.

Intoxication

The law recognizes two types of intoxication, whether from drugs or from alcohol: *involuntary* and *voluntary*. Involuntary intoxication occurs when a person either is physically forced to ingest or inject an intoxicating substance or is unaware that a substance contains drugs or alcohol. Involuntary intoxication is a defense to a crime if its effect was to make a person incapable of understanding that the act committed was wrong or incapable of obeying the law.

Using voluntary drug or alcohol intoxication as a defense is based on the theory that extreme levels of intoxication may negate the state of mind that a crime requires. Many courts are reluctant to allow voluntary intoxication as a defense to a crime, however. After all, the defendant, by definition, voluntarily chose to put himself or herself into an intoxicated state. Voluntary intoxication as a defense may be effective in cases in which the defendant was *extremely* intoxicated when committing the wrong.

Insanity

"Insanity is often the logic of an accurate mind overtaxed."

Oliver Wendell Holmes, Jr., 1841–1935
(Associate justice of the United States Supreme Court, 1902–1932)

Just as a child is often judged incapable of the state of mind required to commit a crime, so also may be someone suffering from a mental illness. Thus, insanity may be a defense to a criminal charge. The courts have had difficulty deciding what the test for legal insanity should be, and psychiatrists as well as lawyers are critical of the tests used. Almost all federal courts and some states use the relatively liberal standard set forth in the Model Penal Code:

> A person is not responsible for criminal conduct if at the time of such conduct as a result of mental disease or defect he lacks substantial capacity either to appreciate the wrongfulness of his conduct or to conform his conduct to the requirements of the law.

---

10.   *In re Gault*, 387 U.S.1, 87 S.Ct. 1428, 18 L.Ed.2d 527 (1967).

Age 0–7	Absolute presumption of incompetence.
Age 7–14	Presumption of incompetence, but government may oppose.
Age 14+	Presumption of competence, but infant may oppose.

◆ **Exhibit 7–3
Responsibility of Infants for
Criminal Acts under the
Common Law**

Some states use the *M'Naghten* test,[11] under which a criminal defendant is not responsible if, at the time of the offense, he or she did not know the nature and quality of the act or did not know that the act was wrong. Other states use the irresistible-impulse test. A person operating under an irresistible impulse may know an act is wrong but cannot refrain from doing it.

Mistake

Everyone has heard the saying, "Ignorance of the law is no excuse." Ordinarily, ignorance of the law or a mistaken idea about what the law requires is not a valid defense. In some states, however, that rule has been modified. People who claim that they honestly did not know that they were breaking a law may have a valid defense if (1) the law was not published or reasonably made known to the public or (2) the people relied on an official statement of the law that was erroneous.

A *mistake of fact*, as opposed to a *mistake of law*, operates as a defense if it negates the mental state necessary to commit a crime. If, for example, Oliver Wheaton mistakenly walks off with Julie Tyson's briefcase because he thinks it is his, there is no theft. Theft requires knowledge that the property belongs to another.

COMPARE "Ignorance" is a lack of information. "Mistake" is a confusion of information.

Consent

What if a victim consents to a crime or even encourages the person intending a criminal act to commit it? The law allows **consent** as a defense if the consent cancels the harm that the law is designed to prevent. In each case, the question is whether the law forbids an act that was committed against the victim's will or forbids the act without regard to the victim's wish. The law forbids murder, prostitution, and drug use whether the victim consents to it or not. Also, if the act causes harm to a third person who has not consented, there is no escape from criminal liability. Consent or forgiveness given after a crime has been committed is not really a defense, though it can affect the likelihood of prosecution. Consent operates as a defense most successfully in crimes against property.

CONSENT
Voluntary agreement to a proposition or an act of another. A concurrence of wills.

Duress

Duress exists when the *wrongful threat* of one person induces another person to perform an act that he or she would not otherwise perform. In such a situation, duress is said to negate the mental state necessary to commit a crime. For duress to qualify as a defense, the following requirements must be met:

1. The threat must be of serious bodily harm or death.
2. The harm threatened must be greater than the harm caused by the crime.
3. The threat must be immediate and inescapable.
4. The defendant must have been involved in the situation through no fault of his or her own.

DURESS
Unlawful pressure brought to bear on a person, causing the person to perform an act that he or she would not otherwise perform.

---

11. A rule derived from *M'Naghten's Case*, 8 Eng.Rep. 718 (1843).

One crime that cannot be excused by duress is murder. It is difficult to justify taking a life even if one's own life is threatened.

Justifiable Use of Force

SELF-DEFENSE
The legally recognized privilege to protect one's self or property against injury by another. The privilege of self-defense protects only acts that are reasonably necessary to protect one's self or property.

Probably the most well-known defense to criminal liability is **self-defense.** Other situations, however, also justify the use of force: the defense of one's dwelling, the defense of other property, and the prevention of a crime. In all of these situations, it is important to distinguish between the use of deadly and nondeadly force. Deadly force is likely to result in death or serious bodily harm. Nondeadly force is force that reasonably appears necessary to prevent the imminent use of criminal force.

Generally speaking, people can use the amount of nondeadly force that seems necessary to protect themselves, their dwellings, or other property or to prevent the commission of a crime. Deadly force can be used in self-defense if there is a *reasonable belief* that imminent death or grievous bodily harm will otherwise result, if the attacker is using unlawful force (an example of lawful force is that exerted by a police officer), and if the defender has not initiated or provoked the attack. Deadly force normally can be used to defend a dwelling only if the unlawful entry is violent and the person believes deadly force is necessary to prevent imminent death or great bodily harm or—in some jurisdictions—if the person believes deadly force is necessary to prevent the commission of a felony (such as arson) in the dwelling.

Entrapment

ENTRAPMENT
In criminal law, a defense in which the defendant claims that he or she was induced by a public official—usually an undercover agent or police officer—to commit a crime that he or she would otherwise not have committed.

Entrapment is a defense designed to prevent police officers or other government agents from encouraging crimes in order to apprehend persons wanted for criminal acts. In the typical entrapment case, an undercover agent *suggests* that a crime be committed and somehow pressures or induces an individual to commit it. The agent then arrests the individual for the crime.

For entrapment to be considered a defense, both the suggestion and the inducement must take place. The defense is intended not to prevent law enforcement agents from setting a trap for an unwary criminal but rather to prevent them from pushing the individual into it. The crucial issue is whether a person who committed a crime was predisposed to commit the crime or did so because the agent induced it.

An interesting variation of the entrapment defense is "sentencing entrapment." This occurs when undercover police officers induce a criminal suspect to commit a more serious crime than the crime contemplated by the suspect, thus causing the person, if convicted, to receive a harsher penalty under the federal sentencing guidelines discussed earlier. In the following case, the defendants claimed that they had been the victims of this form of entrapment.

CASE 7.6

UNITED STATES v. CANNON
United States District Court,
District of North Dakota, 1995.
886 F.Supp. 705.

HISTORICAL AND POLITICAL SETTING *The Bureau of Alcohol, Tobacco, and Firearms (BATF) was established in 1972. Among its criminal enforcement objectives is the suppression of illegal trafficking, possession, and use of firearms. During the 1990s, the BATF came under fire for overzealousness in the pursuit of some of its criminal enforcement activities. Although this criticism was sometimes interpreted as rhetoric on the part of*

Case 7.6—Continued

antigovernment radicals, Congress initiated hearings into BATF conduct, and it was proposed that perhaps the agency should be dissolved and its duties transferred to other government agencies.

FACTS   Keith and Stephanie Cannon sold crack cocaine to a deputy sheriff, who was operating undercover as a drug buyer. The Cannons asked the undercover officer to help them procure some handguns. He arranged for an agent of the BATF to pose as an illegal gun seller. The BATF agent, on his own initiative, brought a machine gun to the meeting with the Cannons. At that meeting, the Cannons again sold crack to the sheriff and bought three handguns from the agent. After the undercover officers exercised some persuasive sales tactics, the Cannons also bought the machine gun. They were promptly arrested and charged with using firearms during and in relation to drug trafficking. The Cannons were tried in a federal district court and convicted. Because one of the weapons was a machine gun, their convictions required minimum prison sentences of thirty years. At their sentencing hearing, the Cannons argued in part that they should receive a different minimum term (five years—the

minimum mandatory sentence for the use of a firearm generally), on the ground of sentencing entrapment.

ISSUE   Does the sale of an illegal machine gun by a government agent to drug traffickers constitute entrapment when the traffickers sought to buy only illegal handguns?

DECISION   Yes. The federal district court ordered that the Cannons be sentenced as though no machine gun had been present during their offense.

REASON   The court looked at all of the evidence, including video and audio recordings of the Cannons' transactions with the undercover officers, and read the trial transcripts, including the testimony of the BATF agent. The court reasoned, "based on all the evidence cognizable in imposing sentence," that "the defendants have met their burden of proving * * * that [they] were not predisposed to purchase a machine gun and that they were induced to do so by the government."

FOR CRITICAL ANALYSIS—Ethical Consideration
Should there be any legal limits on the degree of temptation to which law enforcement officers can subject persons who are under investigation? Why or why not?

Statute of Limitations

With some exceptions, such as for the crime of murder, statutes of limitations apply to crimes just as they do to civil wrongs. In other words, criminal cases must be prosecuted within a certain number of years. If a criminal action is brought after the statutory time period has expired, the accused person can raise the statute of limitations as a defense.

Immunity

At times, the state may wish to obtain information from a person accused of a crime. Accused persons are understandably reluctant to give information if it will be used to prosecute them, and they cannot be forced to do so. The privilege against self-incrimination is granted by the Fifth Amendment to the Constitution, which reads, in part, "nor shall [any person] be compelled in any criminal case to be a witness against himself." In cases in which the state wishes to obtain information from a person accused of a crime, the state can grant *immunity* from prosecution or agree to prosecute for a less serious offense in exchange for the information. Once immunity is given, the person can no longer refuse to testify on Fifth Amendment grounds, because he or she now has an absolute privilege against self-incrimination.

Often a grant of immunity from prosecution for a serious crime is part of the **plea bargaining** between the defendant and the prosecuting attorney. The defendant may be convicted of a lesser offense, while the state uses the defendant's testimony to prosecute accomplices for serious crimes carrying heavy penalties.

PLEA BARGAINING
The process by which a criminal defendant and the prosecutor in a criminal case work out a mutually satisfactory disposition of the case, subject to court approval; usually involves the defendant's pleading guilty to a lesser offense in return for a lighter sentence.

Application

Law and the Businessperson— Protecting against Electronic Crimes*

 In addition to protecting their physical property, businesspersons today also are concerned about protecting their intangible property—such as computer data or files—from outside access. Another concern is the need to protect confidential communications, such as messages left on voice mail, from being "stolen" by competitors.

Protecting against Computer Crimes

One way to prevent unauthorized access to computer data is to restrict access to information in a computer system through the use of various security measures. For example, the data might be made available only to those with special security clearances. Establishing a system of security clearances may involve organizing data in specific categories. The category to which an individual is given access is related to the information the individual needs to perform his or her job. For example, the names of account holders can be kept separate from the accounts' balances. In this way, a party who needs to work with the balances can be prevented from learning the holders' identities. Passwords may be attached to a system or to a portion of the data within a system to preclude unauthorized access. Considering the relative ease with which unauthorized individuals have discovered passwords in the past, however, it is advisable to change the passwords frequently.

Another means of limiting access to computer information is to encrypt (translate into a secret code) the data contained within the system. Data can be encoded before they are stored or communicated to another party. The data can be decoded when they are taken from storage or when the other party receives them. As a further protective measure, a copy of the data can be stored in outside facilities to ensure against the destruction or loss of data.

Protecting against Voice Mail Theft

Voice mail theft is of relatively recent vintage, but there have been several cases in which former employees or others have accessed a company's voice mail boxes to learn of confidential trade secrets and other sensitive

information. In one case, for example, a person was hired by a competitor of his former employer to search through the former employer's voice mail boxes for confidential sales information. It took months before the activity was uncovered by the former employer. In another case, a small oil service company in Dallas was bidding on a drilling contract. While negotiations were under way, one of the oil company's officers called a colleague and left a voice mail message indicating the terms of the company's bids. The next day, a competitor won the contract. On investigation, it turned out that the voice mail message had been intercepted by the competitor.[a]

You can do several things to protect against voice mail theft. First, consider using long passwords that contain both numbers and letters—to make them more difficult to discover by unauthorized persons. Change the passwords often. Second, if possible, subscribe to a caller identification service, to make it easier to trace telephone activity. Third, instruct those with whom you do business, as well as your family and friends, not to refer to sensitive information when leaving a message. Fourth, get rid of old voice mail messages. Fifth, consider hiring a security consultant to evaluate your voice mail system. Finally, the surest solution to the problem is not to use voice mail if you do not really need to do so.

✓ Checklist for the Businessperson

1. To protect against computer crimes, (a) limit employees' access to computer data and files through the establishment of a system of security clearances, (b) make sure that the passwords are changed frequently, (c) consider encrypting (encoding) computer data before storage or communication of the data to another party, and (d) store a copy of computer files in outside facilities to ensure against the destruction or loss of data.

2. To protect against voice mail theft, (a) use long passwords, and change them frequently; (b) subscribe to a caller identification service, if possible; (c) tell your business associates, as well as your family and friends, not to refer to sensitive information when leaving voice mail; (d) destroy old voice mail messages; (e) consider hiring a security consultant to evaluate your voice mail system; and (f) do not even use voice mail if you do not need to do so.

---

*This *Application* is not meant to substitute for the services of an attorney who is licensed to practice law in your state.

a. William G. Flanagan and Toddi Gutner, "The Perils of Voice Mail," *Forbes*, January 17, 1994, pp. 106–107.

▌Key Terms

▌Chapter Summary: Criminal Law

Civil Law and Criminal Law *(See page 176.)*	1. *Civil law*—Spells out the duties that exist between persons or between citizens and their governments, excluding the duty not to commit crimes. In a civil case, damages are awarded to compensate those harmed by others' wrongful acts, or equitable remedies may be granted. 2. *Criminal law*—Has to do with crimes, which are defined as wrongs against society proclaimed in statutes and, if committed, punishable by society through fines and/or imprisonment—and, in some cases, death. Because crimes are *offenses against society as a whole*, they are prosecuted by a public official, not by victims. (See Exhibit 7–1 for a summary of how criminal and civil laws differ.)
Classification of Crimes *(See pages 176–177.)*	1. *Felonies*—Serious crimes punishable by death or by imprisonment in a penitentiary for more than a year. 2. *Misdemeanors*—Under federal law and in most states, any crime that is not a felony.
Criminal Liability *(See pages 177–178.)*	1. *Guilty act*—In general, some form of harmful act must be committed for a crime to exist. 2. *Intent*—An intent to commit a crime, or a wrongful mental state, is required for a crime to exist.
Procedure in Criminal Law *(See pages 178–185.)*	1. *Constitutional safeguards*—The rights of accused persons are protected under the Constitution, particularly by the Fourth, Fifth, Sixth, and Eighth Amendments. Under the exclusionary rule, evidence obtained in violation of the constitutional rights of the accused will not be admissible in court. In *Miranda v. Arizona*, the United States Supreme Court ruled that individuals must be informed of their constitutional rights (such as their rights to counsel and to remain silent) on being taken into custody. 2. *Criminal process*—Procedures governing arrest, indictment, and trial for a crime are designed to safeguard the rights of the individual against the state. See Exhibit 7–2 for the steps involved in prosecuting a criminal case.
Federal Sentencing Guidelines *(See pages 185–187.)*	Guidelines established by the U.S. Sentencing Commission indicating a range of penalties for each federal crime; federal judges must abide by these guidelines when imposing sentences on those convicted of federal crimes.
Crimes Affecting Business *(See pages 187–195.)*	1. *Forgery*—The fraudulent making or altering of any writing in a way that changes the legal rights and liabilities of another. 2. *Robbery*—The forceful and unlawful taking of personal property of any value from another. 3. *Burglary*—At common law, defined as breaking and entering the dwelling of another at night with the intent to commit a felony. State statutes now vary in their definitions of burglary. 4. *Larceny*—The wrongful or fraudulent taking and carrying away of another's personal property with the intent to deprive the owner permanently of the property. 5. *Obtaining goods by false pretenses*—Such as cashing a check knowing that there are insufficient funds in the bank to cover it.

(Continued)

▌Chapter Summary: Criminal Law—Continued

Crimes Affecting Business—Continued	6. *Receiving stolen goods*—A crime if the recipient knew or should have known that the goods were stolen. 7. *Embezzlement*—The fraudulent appropriation of another person's property or money by a person to whom the property or money was entrusted. 8. *Arson*—The willful and malicious burning of a building or (in some states) personal property owned by another. 9. *Mail and wire fraud*—Using the mails, wires, radio, or television to defraud the public. 10. *Computer crime*—Any act that is directed against computers and computer parts, that uses computers as instruments of crime, or that involves computers and constitutes abuse. Computer crime includes financial crimes that involve computers; theft of computer software, equipment, data, or services; and vandalism and destructive programming of computers. 11. *Bribery*—Includes bribery of public officials, commercial bribery, and bribery of foreign officials. The crime of bribery is committed when the bribe is tendered. 12. *Bankruptcy fraud*—Encompasses crimes committed in connection with bankruptcy proceedings, including false claims of creditors and fraudulent transfers of assets by debtors. 13. *Money laundering*—Establishing legitimate enterprises through which "dirty" money (obtained through criminal activities) can be "laundered." 14. *Insider trading*—The buying or selling of corporate securities by a person in possession of material nonpublic information in violation of securities laws. 15. *Criminal RICO violations*—Include the use of legitimate business enterprises to shield racketeering activity, securities fraud, and mail fraud.
Defenses to Criminal Liability (*See pages 195–199.*)	1. *Infancy.* 5. *Consent.* 9. *Statute of limitations.* 2. *Intoxication.* 6. *Duress.* 10. *Immunity.* 3. *Insanity.* 7. *Justifiable use of force.* 4. *Mistake.* 8. *Entrapment.*

▌For Review

1. How are crimes distinguished from other wrongful acts?
2. What two elements must exist before a person can be held liable for a crime?
3. What constitutional safeguards exist to protect persons accused of crimes?

4. List and describe five crimes affecting business.
5. What defenses might be raised by criminal defendants to avoid liability for criminal acts?

▌Questions and Case Problems

7–1. Criminal versus Civil Trials. In criminal trials, the defendant must be proved guilty beyond a reasonable doubt, whereas in civil trials, the defendant need only be proved guilty by a preponderance of the evidence. Discuss why a higher standard of proof is required in criminal trials.

7–2. Types of Crimes. Determine from the facts below what type of crime has been committed in each situation.

   (a) Carlos is walking through an amusement park when his wallet, with $2,000 in it, is "picked" from his pocket.

   (b) Carlos walks into a camera shop. Without force and without the owner's noticing, Carlos walks out of the store with a camera.

7–3. Types of Crimes. The following situations are similar (all involve the theft of Makoto's television set), yet they represent three different crimes. Identify the three crimes, noting the differences among them.

   (a) While passing Makoto's house one night, Sarah sees a portable television set left unattended on Makoto's lawn. Sarah takes the television set, carries it home, and tells everyone she owns it.

(b) While passing Makoto's house one night, Sarah sees Makoto outside with a portable television set. Holding Makoto at gunpoint, Sarah forces him to give up the set. Then Sarah runs away with it.

(c) While passing Makoto's house one night, Sarah sees a portable television set in a window. Sarah breaks the front-door lock, enters, and leaves with the set.

7–4. Types of Crimes. Which, if any, of the following crimes necessarily involve illegal activity on the part of more than one person?

(a) Bribery.
(b) Forgery.
(c) Embezzlement.
(d) Larceny.
(e) Receiving stolen property.

7–5. Double Jeopardy. Armington, while robbing a drugstore, shot and seriously injured a drugstore clerk, Jennings. Armington was subsequently convicted in a criminal trial of armed robbery and assault and battery. Jennings later brought a civil tort suit against Armington for damages. Armington contended that he could not be tried again for the same crime, as that would constitute double jeopardy, which is prohibited by the Fifth Amendment to the Constitution. Is Armington correct? Explain.

7–6. Receiving Stolen Property. Rafael stops Laura on a busy street and offers to sell her an expensive wristwatch for a fraction of its value. After some questioning by Laura, Rafael admits that the watch is stolen property, although he says he was not the thief. Laura pays for and receives the wristwatch. Has Laura committed any crime? Has Rafael? Explain.

7–7. Embezzlement. Slemmer, who had been a successful options trader, gave lectures to small groups about stock options. Several persons who attended his lectures decided to invest in stock options and have Slemmer advise them. They formed an investment club called Profit Design Group (PDG). Slemmer set up an account for PDG with a brokerage firm. Slemmer had control of the PDG account and could make decisions on which stock options to buy or sell. He was not authorized to withdraw money from the account for his own benefit. Nonetheless, he withdrew money from the PDG account to make payments on real estate that he owned. Slemmer made false representations to the members of PDG, and he eventually lost all the money in their account. A jury found him guilty of first degree theft by embezzlement. Slemmer objected to the trial court's failure to instruct the jury that an intent to permanently deprive was an element of the crime charged. Is intent to permanently deprive another of property a required element for the crime of embezzlement? Explain. [*State v. Slemmer*, 48 Wash.App. 48, 738 P.2d 281 (1987)]

7–8. Self-Defense. Bernardy came to the defense of his friend Harrison in a fight with Wilson. Wilson started the fight, and after Harrison knocked Wilson down, Bernardy (who was wearing tennis shoes) kicked Wilson several times in the head. Bernardy stated that he did so because he believed an onlooker, Gowens, would join forces with Wilson against Harrison. Bernardy maintained that his use of force was justifiable because he was protecting another (Harrison) from injury. Discuss whether Bernardy's use of force to protect Harrison from

harm was justified. [*State v. Bernardy*, 25 Wash.App. 146, 605 P.2d 791(1980)]

7–9. Criminal Liability. In January 1988, David Ludvigson was hired as chief executive officer of Leopard Enterprises, a group of companies that owned funeral homes and cemeteries in Iowa and sold "pre-need" funeral contracts. Under Iowa law, 80 percent of monies obtained under such a contract must be set aside in trust until the death of the person for whose benefit the funds were paid. Shortly after Ludvigson was hired, the firm began having financial difficulties. Ludvigson used money from these contracts to pay operating expenses until the company went bankrupt and was placed in receivership. Ludvigson was charged and found guilty on five counts of second degree theft stemming from the misappropriation of these funds. He appealed, alleging, among other things, that because none of the victims whose trust funds were used to cover operating expenses was denied services, no injury was done and thus no crime was committed. Will the court agree with Ludvigson? Explain. [*State v. Ludvigson*, 482 N.W.2d 419 (Iowa 1992)]

7–10. Defenses to Criminal Liability. The Child Protection Act of 1984 makes it a crime to receive knowingly through the mails sexually explicit depictions of children. After this act was passed, government agents found Keith Jacobson's name on a bookstore's mailing list. (Jacobson previously had ordered and received from a bookstore two *Bare Boys* magazines containing photographs of nude preteen and teenage boys.) To test Jacobson's willingness to break the law, government agencies sent mail to him, through five fictitious organizations and a bogus pen pal, over a period of two and a half years. Many of these "organizations" claimed that they had been founded to protect sexual freedom, freedom of choice, and so on. Jacobson eventually ordered a magazine. He testified at trial that he ordered the magazine because he was curious about "all the trouble and the hysteria over pornography and I wanted to see what the material was." When the magazine was delivered, he was arrested for violating the 1984 act. What defense discussed in this chapter might Jacobson raise to avoid criminal liability under the act? Explain fully. [*Jacobson v. United States*, 503 U.S. 540, 112 S.Ct. 1535, 118 L.Ed.2d 174 (1992)]

7–11. Entrapment. When Sharon Shepherd attempted to sell cocaine powder to an undercover law enforcement officer, the officer insisted that she first convert the powder to crack cocaine—which she did by "cooking" the powder in a microwave for a few minutes. The agent then purchased the cocaine in its converted state. The agent's purpose in requesting Shepherd to convert the powder to crack was to cause Shepherd to receive a more severe sentence. Under the federal sentencing guidelines, the mandatory sentence for the sale of crack cocaine is from 120 to 135 months in prison, whereas the sentence for the sale of cocaine powder is only 60 months. Was Shepherd a victim of "sentencing entrapment"? What factors should the court consider in deciding this issue? Discuss fully. [*United States v. Shepherd*, 857 F.Supp. 105 (D.C. 1994)]

A QUESTION OF ETHICS AND SOCIAL RESPONSIBILITY

7–12. A *troublesome issue concerning the constitutional privilege against self-incrimination has to do with "jail plants"—that is, placing undercover police officers in cells* *with criminal suspects to gain information from the suspects. For example, in one case the police placed an undercover agent, Parisi, in a jail cellblock with Lloyd Perkins, who had been imprisoned on charges unrelated to the murder that Parisi was investigating. When Parisi asked Perkins if he had ever killed anyone, Perkins made statements implicating himself in the murder. Perkins was then charged with the murder. [Illinois v. Perkins, 496 U.S. 914, 110 S.Ct. 2394, 110 L.Ed.2d 243 (1990)]*

1. Review the discussion of *Miranda v. Arizona* in this chapter's *Landmark in the Law.* Should Perkins's statements be suppressed—that is, not be treated as admissible evidence at trial—because he was not "read his rights," as required by the *Miranda* decision, prior to making his self-incriminating statements? Does *Miranda* apply to Perkins's situation?

2. Do you think that it is fair for the police to resort to trickery and deception to bring those who have committed crimes to justice? Why or why not? What rights or public policies must be balanced in deciding this issue?

FOR CRITICAL ANALYSIS

7–13. *Do you think that criminal procedure in this country is weighted too heavily in favor of accused persons? Can you think of a fairer way to balance the constitutional rights of accused persons against the right of society to be protected against criminal behavior? Explain.*

▌Unit Two—Cumulative Hypothetical Problem

7–14. *CompTac, Inc., is one of the leading software manufacturers in the United States. The company invests millions of dollars in researching and developing new software applications and games that are sold worldwide. It also has a large service department and has taken great pains to offer its customers excellent support services. Recently, CompTac has been losing sales to a new competitor in the field, the Geminex Co. In view of these "facts," answer the following questions:*

1. Geminex has launched a new advertising campaign in which it compares its prices and support services to those offered by CompTac. The advertising campaign is so effective that many of CompTac's customers have switched to Geminex software and services. One of Comp-Tac's most important customers, Allotran Corp., breached its contract with CompTac and started purchasing its software and services from Geminex instead. As a result of Allotran's breach of contract, CompTac stood to lose nearly $2 million in revenues. CompTac sues Geminex for wrongful interference with a contractual relationship. Will CompTac succeed in its suit? Why or why not?

2. In its advertising campaign against CompTac, Geminex claims that CompTac, instead of fully testing and debugging the computer programs before they are marketed, has its customers test the software. CompTac knows this is not true and that it is unfair of Geminex to make such a claim. Could CompTac sue Geminex for the harm Geminex is causing to CompTac's reputation? If so, on what grounds? Explain.

3. CompTac has just developed a new software application that the company hopes will reap lucrative profits. It has taken the company two years and a substantial investment of money to create the program. CompTac learns that its competitor, Geminex, has already filed for a patent on a nearly identical program and has sold the software to many of its customers. CompTac learns from a reliable source that Geminex paid one of CompTac's employees a substantial sum of money to obtain a copy of the program. What legal recourse does CompTac have against Geminex? Discuss fully.

4. The head of CompTac's accounting department, Roy Olson, has to pay his daughter's college tuition within a week, or his daughter will not be able to continue taking classes. The payment due is over $20,000. Roy would be able to make the payment in two months, but cannot do so until then. The college refuses to wait that long. In desperation, Roy—through a fictitious bank account and some clever accounting—"borrows" funds from Comp-Tac. Before Roy can pay back the borrowed funds, an auditor discovers what Roy did. CompTac's president alleges that Roy has "stolen" company funds and informs the police of the theft. Has Roy committed a crime? If so, what crime did he commit? Explain.

▌Accessing the Internet: Business Law and Legal Environment

The National Institute of Justice (NIJ) is the research and development agency of the U.S. Department of Justice. It has a Web site relating to the National Criminal Justice Reference Service. To locate it, use

gopher://ncjrs.aspensys.com:71/1

Once you get to that site, the gopher address is

ncjrs.aspensys.com

Within the gopher you should select

National Criminal Justice Reference Service

You can get updated information on California criminal law as well as a glossary of criminal law terms and jargon at

http://starbase.ingress.com/tsw/alawyer/criminal.html

If you are still interested in the O. J. Simpson trial, go to

http://www.timeinc.com:80pathfinder/features/oj/central1.html

Unit Three

Contracts

UNIT OUTLINE

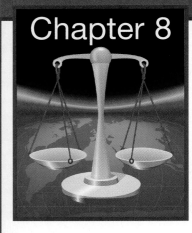

Chapter 8

Nature and Classification

PROMISE
A declaration that something either will or will not happen in the future.

> "The social order rests upon the stability and predictability of conduct, of which keeping promises is a large item."
>
> **Roscoe Pound, 1870–1964**
> *(American jurist)*

CHAPTER OBJECTIVES

After reading this chapter, you should be able to:

1. Explain the function of contract law.
2. Define the term *contract,* and list the basic elements that are required for contract formation.
3. Discuss the objective theory of contracts.
4. Identify the various types of contracts.
5. Outline the rules that govern the courts' interpretation of contracts.

As Roscoe Pound—an eminent jurist—observed in the above quotation, "keeping promises" is important to a stable social order. Contract law deals with, among other things, the formation and keeping of promises. A **promise** is a declaration that something either will or will not happen in the future.

Like other types of law, contract law reflects our social values, interests, and expectations at a given point in time. It shows, for example, what kinds of promises our society thinks should be legally binding. It shows what excuses our society accepts for breaking such promises. Additionally, it shows what promises are considered to be contrary to public policy and therefore legally void. If a promise goes against the interests of society as a whole, it will be invalid. Also, if it was made by a child or a mentally incompetent person, or on the basis of false information, a question will arise as to whether the promise should be enforced. Resolving such questions is the essence of contract law.

In business law and the legal environment of business, questions and disputes concerning contracts arise daily. Although aspects of contract law vary from state to state, much of it is based on the common law. In 1932, the American Law Institute compiled the *Restatement of the Law of Contracts.* This work is a nonstatutory, authoritative exposition of the present law on the subject of contracts and is presently in its second edition (although a third edition is in the process of being drafted). Throughout the following chapters on contracts, we will refer to the second edition of the *Restatement of the Law of Contracts* as simply the *Restatement (Second) of Contracts.*

The Uniform Commercial Code (UCC), which governs contracts and other transactions relating to the sale of goods, occasionally departs from common law contract rules. Generally, the different treatment of contracts falling under the UCC stems from the general policy of encouraging commerce. The ways in which the UCC changes common law contract rules will be discussed extensively in later chapters. In this unit covering the common law of contracts (Chapters 8 through 13), we only indicate briefly or in footnotes which common law rules have been altered by the UCC for sales contracts.

▌The Function of Contracts

No aspect of modern life is entirely free of contractual relationships. Indeed, even the ordinary consumer in his or her daily activities acquires rights and obligations based on contract law. You acquire rights and obligations, for example, when you borrow money to make a purchase or when you buy a house. Contract law is designed to provide stability and predictability for both buyers and sellers in the marketplace.

Contract law assures the parties to private agreements that the promises they make will be enforceable. Clearly, many promises are kept because of a moral obligation to do so or because keeping a promise is in the mutual self-interest of the parties involved, not because the **promisor** (the person making the promise) or the **promisee** (the person to whom the promise is made) is conscious of the rules of contract law. Nevertheless, the rules of contract law are often followed in business agreements to avoid potential problems.

By supplying procedures for enforcing private agreements, contract law provides an essential condition for the existence of a market economy. Without a legal framework of reasonably assured expectations within which to plan and venture, businesspersons would be able to rely only on the good faith of others. Duty and good faith are usually sufficient, but when dramatic price changes or adverse economic factors make it costly to comply with a promise, these elements may not be enough. Contract law is necessary to ensure compliance with a promise or to entitle the innocent party to some form of relief.

PROMISOR
A person who makes a promise.

PROMISEE
A person to whom a promise is made.

▌Definition of a Contract

A **contract** is an agreement that can be enforced in court. It is formed by two or more parties who agree to perform or to refrain from performing some act now or in the future. Generally, contract disputes arise when there is a promise of future performance. If the contractual promise is not fulfilled, the party who made it is subject to the sanctions of a court (see Chapter 13). That party may be required to pay money damages for failing to perform; in limited instances, the party may be required to perform the promised act.

In determining whether a contract has been formed, the element of intent is of prime importance. In contract law, intent is determined by what is referred to as the **objective theory of contracts,** not by the personal or subjective intent, or belief, of a party. The theory is that a party's intention to enter into a contract is judged by outward, objective facts as interpreted by a *reasonable* person, rather than by the party's own secret, subjective intentions. Objective facts include (1) what the party said when entering into the contract, (2) how the party acted or appeared, and (3) the circumstances surrounding the transaction. As will be discussed later in this chapter, in the section on express versus implied contracts, intent to form a contract may be manifested not only in words, oral or written, but also by conduct.

CONTRACT
An agreement that can be enforced in court; formed by two or more parties who agree to perform or to refrain from performing some act now or in the future.

OBJECTIVE THEORY OF CONTRACTS
A theory under which the intent to form a contract will be judged by outward, objective facts (what the party said when entering into the contract, how the party acted or appeared, and the circumstances surrounding the transaction) as interpreted by a reasonable person, rather than by the party's own secret, subjective intentions.

International Perspective

U.S. courts routinely adhere to the objective theory of contracts. Courts in some nations, however, give more weight to subjective intentions. Under French law, for example, when there is a conflict between an objective interpretation and a subjective interpretation of a contract, the French civil law code prefers the subjective construction. Other nations that have civil law codes take this same approach. French courts, nonetheless, will look to writings and other objective evidence to determine a party's subjective intent. In operation, the difference between the French and U.S. approaches is therefore perhaps not as significant as it may seem at first blush.

For Critical Analysis: *What problems may arise when a court attempts to look at the subjective basis of a contract?*

▌Requirements of a Contract

The following list describes the requirements of a contract. Each item will be explained more fully in the chapter indicated. Although we pair these requirements in subsequent chapters (for example, agreement and consideration are treated in Chapter 9), it is important to stress that each requirement is separate and independent. They are paired merely for reasons of space.

1. *Agreement.* An agreement includes an *offer* and an *acceptance.* One party must offer to enter into a legal agreement, and another party must accept the terms of the offer (Chapter 9).
2. *Consideration.* Any promises made by parties must be supported by legally sufficient and bargained-for *consideration* (something of value received or promised, to convince a person to make a deal) (Chapter 9).
3. *Contractual capacity.* Both parties entering into the contract must have the contractual *capacity* to do so; the law must recognize them as possessing characteristics that qualify them as competent parties (Chapter 10).
4. *Legality.* The contract's purpose must be to accomplish some goal that is *legal* and not against public policy (Chapter 10).
5. *Genuineness of assent.* The apparent consent of both parties must be *genuine* (Chapter 11).
6. *Form.* The contract must be in whatever *form* the law requires; for example, some contracts must be in writing to be enforceable (Chapter 11).

The first four items in this list are formally known as the *elements of a contract.* The last two are possible *defenses to the formation or the enforcement of a contract.*

▌Freedom of Contract ▌and Freedom from Contract

As a general rule, the law recognizes everyone's ability to enter freely into contractual arrangements. This recognition is called *freedom of contract,* a freedom protected by the U.S. Constitution in Article I, Section 10 (see this chapter's *Business Law in Action* for a discussion of the contracts clause of the Constitution). Because freedom of contract is a fundamental public policy of the United States, courts rarely interfere with contracts that have been voluntarily made.

Of course, as in other areas of the law, there are many exceptions to the general rule that contracts voluntarily negotiated will be enforced. For example, illegal bargains, agreements unreasonably in restraint of trade, and certain unfair contracts made between one party with a great amount of bargaining power and another with little

The Contracts Clause Is Alive and Well

The public policy supporting freedom of contract is expressed in the contracts clause of Article I, Section 10, of the U.S. Constitution. This clause mandates that no state shall make any "Law impairing the Obligation of Contracts." In the past, particularly in the 1920s and 1930s, the contracts clause was often used by the courts to invalidate legislation regulating business activities if (1) the legislation substantially impaired an existing contractual relationship and (2) the state could not demonstrate a significant and legitimate public purpose behind the regulation. Today, in contrast, the contracts clause is rarely used to render regulatory legislation invalid.

Many of the regulatory laws passed by the states impair existing contractual relationships, but generally the courts give the states broad discretion to determine whether the public purposes of the laws are legitimate. For example, suppose that Wickman contracts with the Shell Oil

Company to operate a Shell service station. The contract stipulates that if either party wants to terminate the contractual relationship, the other party must be given sixty days' notice. Now suppose that the state passes a law stating that all oil companies must give ninety days' notice to their dealers, and vice versa, before a dealership is terminated. Even though this law impairs (alters) the contract between Wickman and Shell, it normally will be upheld as valid if it serves a legitimate public purpose.

Although today's courts rarely invoke the contracts clause, it remains viable—as illustrated by a 1995 federal court decision in which the court held that a Minnesota state statute violated the contracts clause. The statute, which was passed in 1993, changed the way in which surplus funds in the state workers' compensation system were to be distributed. (As will be discussed in Chapter 32, under state workers' compensation laws, funds are established to pay workers who are injured on the job.) A 1979 Minnesota law required insurance companies and self-insured employers to contribute money to a pool designed to provide extra coverage for unusually large claims. The original terms of the fund—which, according to the court, constituted a contract—

provided that any surplus funds in the pool would be distributed to the insurance companies and the employers that had contributed to the pool. The 1993 statute, however, called for the excess funds to be distributed only to the employers that had contributed, and not to the insurance companies.

When the insurance companies challenged the constitutionality of the statute, a federal appellate court agreed with the insurance companies that the 1993 statute was unconstitutional. The statute both interfered with the contractual relationship between the insurance companies and the state and served no legitimate public purpose. Although the state legislature claimed that the new law would benefit employers—by reducing the amount they had to pay for workers' compensation coverage—the court pointed out that the statute did not benefit *all* employers.[a]

For Critical Analysis: *How might critics of today's new regulatory legislation utilize the above case?*

a. *In re Workers' Compensation Refund,* 46 F.3d 813 (8th Cir. 1995).

power are generally not enforced. In addition, certain contracts with consumers, as well as certain clauses within those contracts, may not be enforceable if they are contrary to public policy, fairness, and justice (see Chapter 10 for a discussion of contracts contrary to public policy). These exceptions provide *freedom from contract* for persons who may have been forced into making contracts unfavorable to themselves.

❚ Types of Contracts

There are numerous types of contracts. The categories into which contracts are placed involve legal distinctions as to formation, enforceability, or performance. The best method of explaining each type of contract is to compare one type with another.

Bilateral versus Unilateral Contracts

Every contract involves at least two parties. The **offeror** is the party making the offer. The **offeree** is the party to whom the offer is made. The offeror always promises to do

OFFEROR
A person who makes an offer.

OFFEREE
A person to whom an offer is made.

What would make the contract illustrated here a bilateral contract rather than a unilateral contract?

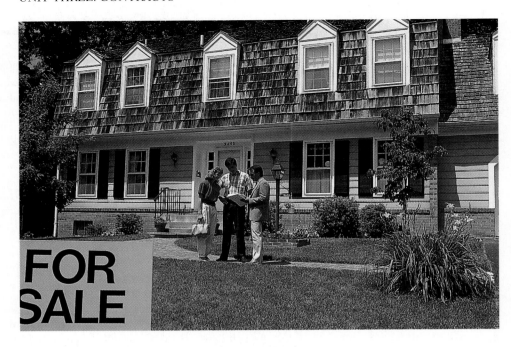

or not to do something and thus is also a promisor. Whether the contract is classified as *unilateral* or *bilateral* depends on what the offeree must do to accept the offer and to bind the offeror to a contract.

BILATERAL CONTRACT
A type of contract that arises when a promise is given in exchange for a return promise.

BILATERAL CONTRACTS   If to accept the offer the offeree must only *promise* to perform, the contract is a **bilateral contract.** Hence, a bilateral contract is a "promise for a promise." An example of a bilateral contract is a contract in which one person agrees to buy another person's automobile for a specified price. No performance, such as the payment of money or delivery of goods, need take place for a bilateral contract to be formed. The contract comes into existence at the moment the promises are exchanged.

UNILATERAL CONTRACT
A contract that results when an offer can only be accepted by the offeree's performance.

UNILATERAL CONTRACTS   If the offer is phrased so that the offeree can accept only by completing the contract performance, the contract is a **unilateral contract.** Hence, a unilateral contract is a "promise for an act."

A classic example of a unilateral contract is as follows: Joe says to Celia, "If you walk across the Brooklyn Bridge, I'll give you $10." Joe promises to pay only if Celia walks the entire span of the bridge. Only upon Celia's complete crossing does she fully accept Joe's offer to pay $10. If she chooses not to undertake the walk, there are no legal consequences. Contests, lotteries, and other prize-winning competitions are also examples of offers for unilateral contracts. If a person complies with the rules of the contest—such as by submitting the right lottery number at the right place and time—a unilateral contract is formed, binding the organization offering the prize to a contract to perform as promised in the offer.

REVOCATION OF OFFERS FOR UNILATERAL CONTRACTS   A problem arises in unilateral contracts when the promisor attempts to *revoke* (cancel) the offer after the promisee has begun performance but before the act has been completed. For example, suppose that Roberta offers to buy Ed's sailboat, moored in San Francisco, upon delivery of the boat to Roberta's dock in Newport Beach, three hundred miles south of San Francisco. Ed rigs the boat and sets sail. Shortly before his arrival at Newport Beach, Ed receives a radio message from Roberta withdrawing her offer. Roberta's offer is an offer for a unilateral contract, and only Ed's delivery of the sailboat at her dock is an acceptance.

In contract law, offers are normally *revocable* (capable of being taken back, or canceled) until accepted. Under the traditional view of unilateral contracts, Roberta's revocation would terminate the offer. Because of the harsh effect on the offeree of the revocation of an offer to form a unilateral contract, the modern-day view is that once performance has been substantially undertaken, the offeror cannot revoke the offer. Thus, in our example, even though Ed has not yet accepted the offer by complete performance, Roberta is prohibited from revoking it. Ed can deliver the boat and bind Roberta to the contract.

Express versus Implied Contracts

An **express contract** is one in which the terms of the agreement are fully and explicitly stated in words, oral or written. A signed lease for an apartment or a house is an express written contract. If a classmate calls you on the phone and agrees to buy your textbooks from last semester for $50, an express oral contract has been made.

A contract that is implied from the conduct of the parties is called an **implied-in-fact contract,** or an implied contract. This type of contract differs from an express contract in that the *conduct* of the parties, rather than their words, creates and defines the terms of the contract. For example, suppose that you need an accountant to fill out your tax return this year. You look through the Yellow Pages and find an accounting firm located in your neighborhood. You drop by the firm's office, explain your problem to an accountant, and learn what fees will be charged. The next day you return, giving the receptionist all of the necessary information and documents, such as canceled checks, W-2 forms, and so on. You say nothing expressly to the receptionist; rather, you walk out the door. In this situation, you have entered into an implied-in-fact contract to pay the accountant the usual and reasonable fees for the accounting services. The contract is implied by your conduct. The accountant expects to be paid for completing your tax return. By bringing in the records the accountant will need to do the work, you have implied an intent to pay for the services.

EXPRESS CONTRACT
A contract in which the terms of the agreement are fully and explicitly stated in words, oral or written.

IMPLIED-IN-FACT CONTRACT
A contract formed in whole or in part from the conduct of the parties (as opposed to an express contract).

"Outward actions are a clue to hidden secrets."

(Legal maxim)

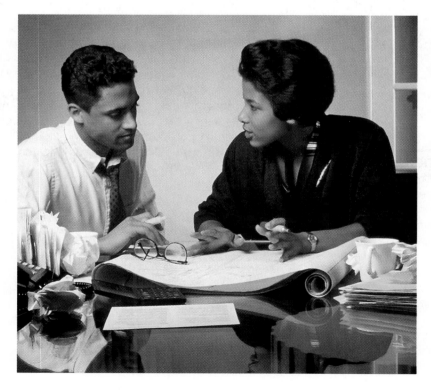

What determines whether a contract for accounting, tax preparation, or any other service is an express contract or an implied-in-fact contract?

The following three steps establish an implied-in-fact contract:

1.   The plaintiff furnished some service or property.
2.   The plaintiff expected to be paid for that service or property, and the defendant knew or should have known that payment was expected (by using the objective-theory-of-contracts test, discussed previously).
3.   The defendant had a chance to reject the services or property and did not.

QUASI CONTRACT
A fictional contract imposed on parties by a court in the interests of fairness and justice; usually, quasi contracts are imposed to avoid the unjust enrichment of one party at the expense of another.

Quasi Contracts—Contracts Implied in Law

Quasi contracts, or contracts *implied in law*, are wholly different from actual contracts. Express contracts and implied-in-fact contracts are actual, or true, contracts. Quasi contracts, as the term suggests, are not true contracts. They do not arise from any agreement, express or implied, between the parties themselves. Rather, quasi contracts are fictional contracts imposed on parties by courts in the interests of fairness and justice. Quasi contracts are therefore equitable, rather than contractual, in nature. Usually, quasi contracts are imposed to avoid the *unjust enrichment* of one party at the expense of another.

For example, suppose that a vacationing doctor is driving down the highway and comes upon Emerson, who is lying unconscious on the side of the road. The doctor renders medical aid that saves Emerson's life. Although the injured, unconscious Emerson did not solicit the medical aid and was not aware that the aid had been rendered, Emerson received a valuable benefit, and the requirements for a quasi contract were fulfilled. In such a situation, the law will impose a quasi contract, and Emerson will have to pay the doctor for the reasonable value of the medical services rendered. The following case represents an example of circumstances in which unjust enrichment can occur.

CASE 8.1

SERVICEMASTER OF ST. CLOUD v. GAB BUSINESS SERVICES, INC.
Court of Appeals of Minnesota, 1995.
530 N.W.2d 558.

HISTORICAL AND INTERNATIONAL SETTING   *The United States leads the world in insurance coverage. For example, more than 3,500 American companies offer property insurance (coverage for property, such as cars and homes, against fire, theft, and other catastrophes). During the early 1990s, after a string of costly hurricanes, earthquakes, and fires, insurance companies worldwide began to stop insuring against certain risks and even began to stop insuring altogether in geographical areas where, they complained, they could not charge rates high enough to make a profit.*

FACTS   Nancy Mollinedo's house was damaged in a fire. Her insurance company, Sentry Insurance, hired

GAB Business Services, Inc., an independent insurance claims adjuster, to investigate the claim. GAB hired ServiceMaster of St. Cloud to repair the damage. While ServiceMaster worked on the house, Sentry decided to deny Mollinedo's claim on the ground that she deliberately set the fire. Sentry allowed the repairs to be continued, however, without informing either ServiceMaster or GAB that it would deny the claim. When the work was done, Sentry sent a check for the amount ServiceMaster charged for the work (a little more than $30,000) to the Federal Housing Administration (FHA), Mollinedo's mortgagee,[a] as required under the insurance policy's mortgagee clause. Sentry received in return a partial mortgage on the house. ServiceMaster received nothing. Subsequently, ServiceMaster filed a suit in a Minnesota state court against Sentry and GAB for, among other things, unjust enrichment. The court awarded damages to ServiceMaster. Sentry appealed.

ISSUE   Was Sentry unjustly enriched by the work performed by ServiceMaster?

a.   A *mortgagee* is a creditor who takes an interest in a debtor's real property as security for the payment of a debt.

Case 8.1—Continued

DECISION Yes. The Court of Appeals of Minnesota affirmed the award of the trial court.

REASON The appellate court stated that "[t]o establish its unjust enrichment claim, ServiceMaster had to show that Sentry knowingly received something of value, while not being entitled to the benefit, and under circumstances that would make it unjust to permit its retention." Sentry argued in part that it did not receive a benefit but "suffered a loss because it had to pay out on the claim." ServiceMaster responded by pointing out that in return for Sentry's payment to the FHA, Sentry received a partial mortgage, which increased in value on completion of the repairs. ServiceMaster also argued that "Sentry allowed ServiceMaster to continue the repairs long after Sentry suspected that Mollinedo's claim would be denied." The trial court found these circumstances to be unjust. The appellate court concluded that "the trial court's findings * * * are not clearly erroneous."

FOR CRITICAL ANALYSIS—Ethical Consideration
Is the mere fact that a person confers a benefit on another enough to require the other to pay? For example, a property owner who improves her property benefits her neighbors to some extent, but should she be entitled to payment from them?

LIMITATIONS ON QUASI-CONTRACTUAL RECOVERY Although quasi contracts exist to prevent unjust enrichment, situations exist in which the party who obtains a benefit will not be deemed to have been unjustly enriched by that benefit. Basically, the quasi-contractual principle cannot be invoked by the party who has conferred a benefit on someone else unnecessarily or as a result of misconduct or negligence.

REMEMBER Quasi contract is an equitable concept, but most courts can apply the doctrine, because in most states, courts of law and equity have merged.

Consider the following example. You take your car to the local car wash and ask to have it run through the washer and to have the gas tank filled. While your car is being washed, you go to a nearby shopping center for two hours. In the meantime, one of the workers at the car wash has mistakenly believed that your car is the one that he is supposed to hand wax. When you come back, you are presented with a bill for a full tank of gas, a wash job, and a hand wax. Clearly, a benefit has been conferred on you, but this benefit has been conferred because of a mistake by the car wash employee. You have not been *unjustly* enriched under these circumstances. People cannot normally be forced to pay for benefits "thrust" upon them.

Quasi contracts, or contracts implied in law, arise to establish justice and fairness. The term *quasi contract* is misleading, because a quasi contract is not really a contract at all. It does not arise from any agreement between two individuals. Rather, a court imposes a quasi contract on the parties when justice so requires to prevent unjust enrichment. The doctrine of unjust enrichment is based on the theory that individuals should not be allowed to profit or enrich themselves inequitably at the expense of others. This belief is fundamental in our society and is clearly inspired by ethical considerations.

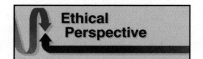

Ethical Perspective

For Critical Analysis: *Why is the term* contract *used in situations involving quasi-contractual recovery, in view of the fact that no agreement between the parties exists?*

WHEN A CONTRACT ALREADY EXISTS The doctrine of quasi contract generally cannot be used when an actual contract covers the area in controversy. For example, Martinez contracts with Stevenson to deliver a furnace to a building project owned by Richards. Martinez delivers the furnace, but Stevenson never pays Martinez. Stevenson has been unjustly enriched in this situation, to be sure. Martinez, however, cannot collect from Richards in quasi contract, because Martinez had an existing contract with Stevenson. Martinez already has a remedy—he can sue for breach of contract to recover the price of the furnace from Stevenson. No quasi contract need be imposed by the court in this instance to achieve justice. In the following case, the issue concerned whether a party could recover in quasi contract even though an express contract covering the area in controversy already existed.

CASE 8.2

INDUSTRIAL LIFT TRUCK SERVICE CORP. v. MITSUBISHI INTERNATIONAL CORP.

Appellate Court of Illinois,
First District, Fourth Division, 1982.
104 Ill.App.3d 357,
432 N.E.2d 999,
60 Ill.Dec. 100.

HISTORICAL AND SOCIAL SETTING *Quasi contracts have sometimes been applied in contractual contexts. These contexts, however, usually involve contracts that are unenforceable. A contract may be unenforceable because its terms are too indefinite, because each party has a different reasonable understanding of the agreement, or because the agreement is illegal. A contract may also be unenforceable because it is not in the correct form; because it involves fraud, duress, mistake, or incapacity; or because of other circumstances that allow a contract to be avoided. In none of the situations in which the doctrine of quasi contract is applied, however, is there an enforceable contract covering the area in controversy.*

FACTS   In 1973 and again in 1976, an agreement was executed between Industrial Lift Truck Service Corporation (IL) and Mitsubishi International Corporation calling for IL to purchase forklift trucks from Mitsubishi and to use its best efforts to sell and service the trucks. The agreement also allowed Mitsubishi to terminate the agreement without just cause by giving ninety days' notice. From 1973 to 1977, IL allegedly became the nation's largest dealer of Mitsubishi forklift trucks. During this period, IL made design changes in the trucks to better suit the American market. Mitsubishi did not request these changes but later incorporated them into the

trucks it sold to other dealers. In 1978, Mitsubishi terminated the agreement. IL sued Mitsubishi in an Illinois state court under quasi-contractual principles to recover the benefits conferred upon Mitsubishi by the design changes. The suit was dismissed, and IL appealed.

ISSUE   Could IL's quasi-contractual claim overcome the written contract attesting to the companies' relationship?

DECISION   No. The Illinois appellate court affirmed the lower court's dismissal, holding that the written contract between the parties defined their entire relationship.

REASON   The court reasoned that, in the absence of a valid amendment to the agreement, Mitsubishi had a right to assume that it did not have to compensate IL for any acts performed in relation to the subject matter of the contract except in accordance with the express provisions of the contract. The court characterized a contract implied in law (a quasi contract) as "fictitious and arising by implication of law wholly apart from the usual rules" of contract formation. At times, the court said, when one party confers a benefit on another party and the other party accepts the benefit, the law will impose a duty on the benefited party to pay for the services—provided that the benefit was not intended as a gift. When there is already a written contract concerning the same subject matter, however, the usual rule is that no quasi-contractual claim can arise. In this case, IL understood the terms of the existing contract, and it knew the risks involved in initiating the design changes it made. The court found that IL, by suing, attempted to unilaterally circumvent the contract into which it had freely entered. The contract controlled the relationship between the parties, and the suit had to be dismissed.

FOR CRITICAL ANALYSIS—Ethical Consideration   *Is it fair, in a case such as the one presented above, for the court to hold that quasi-contractual recovery is unavailable if an existing contract covers the disputed area?*

Formal versus Informal Contracts

FORMAL CONTRACT
A contract that by law requires for its validity a specific form, such as executed under seal.

Formal contracts require a special form or method of creation (formation) to be enforceable. They include (1) contracts under seal, (2) recognizances, (3) negotiable instruments, and (4) letters of credit.[1] *Contracts under seal* are formalized writings with

1. *Restatement (Second) of Contracts*, Section 6.

a special seal attached.[2] The significance of the seal has lessened, although about ten states require no consideration when a contract is under seal. A *recognizance* is an acknowledgment in court by a person that he or she will perform some specified obligation or pay a certain sum if he or she fails to perform. One form of recognizance is the surety bond.[3] Another is the personal recognizance bond used as bail in a criminal matter. As will be discussed at length in subsequent chapters, *negotiable instruments* include checks, notes, drafts, and certificates of deposit; *letters of credit* are agreements to pay contingent on the purchaser's receipt of invoices and bills of lading (documents evidencing receipt of, and title to, goods shipped).

Informal contracts (also called *simple contracts*) include all other contracts. No special form is required (except for certain types of contracts that must be in writing), as the contracts are usually based on their substance rather than on their form.

INFORMAL CONTRACT
A contract that does not require a specified form or formality in order to be valid.

Executed versus Executory Contracts

Contracts are also classified according to their state of performance. A contract that has been fully performed on both sides is called an **executed contract.** A contract that has not been fully performed on either side is called an **executory contract.** If one party has fully performed but the other has not, the contract is said to be executed on the one side and executory on the other, but the contract is still classified as executory.

For example, assume that you agree to buy ten tons of coal from the Western Coal Company. Further assume that Western has delivered the coal to your steel mill, where it is now being burned. At this point, the contract is an executory contract—it is executed on the part of Western and executory on your part. After you pay Western for the coal, the contract will be executed on both sides.

EXECUTED CONTRACT
A contract that has been completely performed by both parties.

EXECUTORY CONTRACT
A contract that has not as yet been fully performed.

Valid, Void, Voidable, and Unenforceable Contracts

A **valid contract** has the elements necessary for contract formation. Those elements consist of (1) an agreement (offer and an acceptance) (2) supported by legally sufficient consideration (3) for a legal purpose and (4) made by parties who have the legal capacity to enter into the contract. As mentioned, we will discuss each of these elements in the following chapters.

A **void contract** is no contract at all. The terms *void* and *contract* are contradictory. A void contract produces no legal obligations on the part of any of the parties. For example, a contract can be void because one of the parties was adjudged by a court to be legally insane (and thus lacked the legal capacity to enter into a contract) or because the purpose of the contract was illegal.

A **voidable contract** is a *valid* contract but one that can be avoided at the option of one or both of the parties. The party having the option can elect either to avoid any duty to perform or to *ratify* (make valid) the contract. If the contract is avoided, both parties are released from it. If it is ratified, both parties must fully perform their respective legal obligations.

As a general rule, contracts made by minors are voidable at the option of the minor (see Chapter 10). Contracts entered into under fraudulent conditions are voidable at the option of the defrauded party. In addition, contracts entered into under legally defined duress or undue influence are voidable (see Chapter 11).

An **unenforceable contract** is one that cannot be enforced because of certain legal defenses against it. It is not unenforceable because a party failed to satisfy a legal requirement of the contract; rather, it is a valid contract rendered unenforceable by

VALID CONTRACT
A contract that results when elements necessary for contract formation (agreement, consideration, legal purpose, and contractual capacity) are present.

VOID CONTRACT
A contract having no legal force or binding effect.

VOIDABLE CONTRACT
A contract that may be legally avoided (canceled, or annulled) at the option of one of the parties.

UNENFORCEABLE CONTRACT
A valid contract rendered unenforceable by some statute or law.

---

2.   A seal may be actual (made of wax or some other durable substance), impressed on the paper, or indicated simply by the word *seal* or the letters *L.S.* at the end of the document. *L.S.* stands for *locus sigilli* and means "the place for the seal."

3.   An obligation of a party guaranteeing that a second party will be paid if a third party does not perform.

© Glick. Reprinted with permission from *Lawyer's Weekly USA*, *The National Newspaper for Small-Firm Lawyers* (June 19, 1995).

"No, Mr. Foster, I'm afraid that keeping your fingers crossed during the signing of the contract did not render it unenforceable."

some statute or law. For example, certain contracts must be in writing (see Chapter 11), and if they are not, they will not be enforceable except in certain exceptional circumstances.

Interpretation of Contracts

Common law rules of contract interpretation have evolved over time to provide the courts with guidelines for determining the meaning of contracts.

The Plain Meaning Rule

NOTE No one can avoid a contract by claiming that he or she did not read it. A contract is interpreted as if each party read every word carefully.

When the writing is clear and unequivocal, a court will enforce it according to its plain terms (what is clearly stated in the contract), and there is no need for the court to interpret the language of the contract. The meaning of the terms must be determined from *the face of the instrument*—from the written document alone. This is sometimes referred to as the *plain meaning rule*. Under this rule, if a contract's words appear to be clear and unambiguous, a court cannot consider *extrinsic evidence*, which is any evidence not contained in the document itself. Admissibility of extrinsic evidence can significantly affect how a court may interpret ambiguous contractual provisions and thus the outcome of litigation.

Other Rules of Interpretation

When the writing contains ambiguous or unclear terms, a court will interpret the language to give effect to the parties' intent *as expressed in their contract*. This is the primary purpose of the rules of interpretation—to determine the parties' intent from the language used in their agreement and to give effect to that intent. A court normally will not make or remake a contract, nor will it normally interpret the language according to what the parties *claim* their intent was when they made it. The following rules are used by the courts in interpreting ambiguous contractual terms:

1.   Insofar as possible, a reasonable, lawful, and effective meaning will be given to all of a contract's terms.
2.   A contract will be interpreted as a whole; individual, specific clauses will be considered subordinate to the contract's general intent. All writings that are a part of the same transaction will be interpreted together.
3.   Terms that were the subject of separate negotiation will be given greater consideration than standardized terms and terms that were not negotiated separately.
4.   A word will be given its ordinary, commonly accepted meaning, and a technical word or term will be given its technical meaning, unless the parties clearly intended something else.
5.   Specific and exact wording will be given greater consideration than general language.
6.   Written or typewritten terms prevail over preprinted terms.
7.   Because a contract should be drafted in clear and unambiguous language, a party who uses ambiguous expressions is held to be responsible for the ambiguities. Thus, when the language has more than one meaning, it will be interpreted against the party who drafted the contract.
8.   Evidence of trade usage, prior dealing, and course of performance may be admitted to clarify the meaning of an ambiguously worded contract. (We define and discuss these terms in Chapter 14.) What each of the parties does pursuant to the contract will be interpreted as consistent with what the other does and with any relevant usage of trade and course of dealing or performance. Express terms (terms expressly stated in the contract) are given the greatest weight, followed by course of performance, course of dealing, and usage of trade—in that order. When considering custom and usage, a court will look at the trade customs and usage common to the particular business or industry and to the locale in which the contract was made or is to be performed.

KEEP IN MIND Not every contract is a document with the word "Contract" printed in block letters at the top. A contract can be expressed in a letter, a memo, or another document.

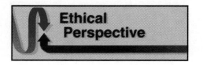
Ethical Perspective

Point number 7 in the above list—that a party who uses ambiguous expressions will be held responsible for the ambiguities—expresses the ethical conviction that those who draft contracts should not be allowed to reap benefits from vague language. Often, the party responsible for drafting a contract has superior bargaining power relative to the other party. For example, if a person wants to obtain life or health insurance, that person must either accept the terms of the insurance company's policy, as drafted, or not obtain insurance coverage from the company that is offering it.

Insurance contracts are essentially *adhesion* contracts. An adhesion contract is a contract drafted by the dominant party and then presented to the other (adhering) party on a "take it or leave it" basis (see Chapter 10). If an insurance policy contains an ambiguous clause, the insurance company could, by interpreting the clause in its favor, deny coverage to the policyholder in the event of a claim. To prevent such unfairness, the courts interpret vague or ambiguous statements *against* the party that drafted the contract.

For Critical Analysis: *Is it fair to apply the rule just discussed even if the party who drafted a contractual agreement had the same—or even less—bargaining power than the other party to the contract? Why or why not?*

Plain Language Laws

To avoid disputes over contract interpretation, business managers should make sure that their intentions are clearly expressed in their contracts. A Harvard Law School study indicated that approximately one-fourth of all contract disputes resulted from poorly worded contracts.[4] Careful drafting of contracts not only helps prevent potential disputes over the meaning of certain terms but also may be crucial if the firm brings or needs to defend against a lawsuit for breach of contract.

In the interests of helping consumers, as well as easing the work of the courts, the government has been active in the push for more clearly written legal contracts by enacting "plain language laws." These laws, which are the subject of the following *Landmark in the Law*, deal with private contracts in their entirety. Plain language laws attempt to reach a broad variety of consumer agreements relating to personal, family, and household matters, including residential leases.

---

4. Rick Schmitt, "Law Schools, Firms Sending a Message: Polish Your Prose," *The Wall Street Journal*, August 28, 1995, p. B6.

LANDMARK IN THE LAW

Plain Language Laws

Plain language is increasingly being required in contracts, and for a good reason: parties to contracts cannot genuinely assent to contractual terms that they do not understand. Compare, for example, the following words from a Citibank loan agreement:

> In the event of default in the payment of this or any other Obligation or the performance or observance of any term or covenant contained herein or in any note or other contract or agreement evidencing or relating to any Obligation or any Collateral on the Borrower's part to be performed or observed . . .

with this phrase: "If I don't pay an installment on time . . . "[a]

The difference is obvious: one statement is in "legalese," and the other is in "plain English." Citibank's use of the plain language version in loan agreements has led to fewer *defaults* (failures to pay) by borrowers.

---

a. As quoted in Scott J. Burnham, "The Hazards of Using Plain English: A New Look at Contracts," *The Compleat Lawyer,* Summer 1991, pp. 46–47.

Landmark in the Law—Continued

Today, the federal government and a majority of the states regulate legal writing through "plain language laws." The New York law, which has strongly influenced the plain language laws adopted by other states, illustrates how such statutes address the language problem. In New York, an agreement must be (1) "written in a clear and coherent manner using words with common and everyday meanings" and (2) "appropriately divided and captioned by its various sections."**b**

If a party to a contract, such as an insurance company, violates a plain language statute, the contract may be void—unless it can be shown that the party made a good faith effort to comply with the statute. Some state statutes even allow proposed contracts to be submitted to the state attorney general, whose approval then eliminates any liability for damages because of supposed violation of the plain language statute.

In response to plain language laws, the legal profession has attempted to abandon the traditional preference for often turgid and verbose language in favor of clear and easily understandable legal writing. Judges and clients also are pressuring lawyers to make legal concepts and documents more comprehensible. At one point during the O. J. Simpson murder trial in 1994–1995, for example, the judge ordered the defense attorneys to redraft what the judge called an "incoherent" motion relating to certain evidence in the case.

DON'T FORGET Most law, like most contracts, can be expressed in ordinary English.

For Critical Analysis: *What are the potential hazards in "translating" legalese into plain English?*

b.   N.Y. Gen. Oblig. Law, Section 5–702.

Application

Law and the Employer— Avoiding Unintended Employment Contracts*

Employers have learned many lessons from court decisions. In recent years, for example, the message has been becoming clear that promises made in an employment manual may create an implied-in-fact employment contract. If an employment handbook contains a statement that employees will be fired only for specific causes, the employer may be held to that "promise." Even if, by state law, employment is "at will"—that is, the employer is allowed to hire and fire employees at will, with or without cause—the at-will doctrine will not apply if the terms of employment are subject to a contract between the employer and employee. If a court holds that an implied employment contract exists—on the basis of promises made in an employment manual in effect—the employment is no

longer at will. The employer will be bound by the contract and liable for damages for breaching the contract.

Employers who wish to avoid potential liability for breaching unintended employment contracts should therefore make it clear to employees that the policies expressed in an employment manual are not to be interpreted as contractual promises. An effective way to do this is to inform employees, when initially giving them the handbook or discussing its contents with them, that the handbook is not intended as a contract and to include a disclaimer to that effect in the employment application. The disclaimer might read as follows: "I understand and agree that, if hired, my employment is for no definite period and may be terminated at any time without any prior notice." The employer should make the disclaimer clear and prominent so that the applicant cannot later claim that it was the employer's fault that the employee did not see the disclaimer. A disclaimer will be clear and prominent if it is set off from the surrounding text by the use of larger type, a different color, all capital letters, or some other device that calls the reader's attention to it.

*This *Application* is not meant to substitute for the services of an attorney who is licensed to practice law in your state.

(Continued)

Application—Continued

In the handbook, the employer should avoid making definite promises that employees will be fired only for cause, that they will not be fired after they have worked for a certain length of time except for certain reasons, or the like. The handbook itself should include a clear and prominent disclaimer of contractual liability for its contents.

 Checklist for the Employer

1. Inform new employees that statements in an employment handbook are not intended as contractual terms.

2. Include a clear and prominent disclaimer to this effect in employment applications.
3. Avoid including in the handbook any definite promises relating to job security.
4. Include in the handbook a clear and prominent disclaimer of contractual liability for any statements made within it.
5. Last but not least: check with your attorney concerning your state's employment laws.

▮ Key Terms

▮ Chapter Summary: Nature and Classification

The Function of Contracts *(See page 209.)*	Contract law establishes what kinds of promises will be legally binding and supplies procedures for enforcing legally binding promises, or agreements.
Requirements of a Contract *(See page 210.)*	1. *Elements of a valid contract*—Agreement, consideration, contractual capacity, and legality. 2. *Possible defenses to the enforcement of a contract*—Genuineness of assent and form.
Types of Contracts *(See pages 211–218.)*	1. *Bilateral*—A promise for a promise. 2. *Unilateral*—A promise for an act (acceptance is the completed—or substantial—performance of the act). 3. *Express*—Formed by words (oral, written, or a combination). 4. *Implied in fact*—Formed by the conduct of the parties. 5. *Quasi contract (contract implied in law)*—Imposed by law to prevent unjust enrichment. 6. *Formal*—Requires a special form for creation. 7. *Informal*—Requires no special form for creation. 8. *Executed*—A fully performed contract. 9. *Executory*—A contract not yet fully performed.

Chapter Summary: Nature and Classification—Continued

Types of Contracts—Continued	10. *Valid*—The contract has the necessary contractual elements of offer and acceptance, consideration, parties with legal capacity, and having been made for a legal purpose.
	11. *Void*—No contract exists, or there is a contract without legal obligations.
	12. *Voidable*—One party has the option of avoiding or enforcing the contractual obligation.
	13. *Unenforceable*—A contract exists, but it cannot be enforced because of a legal defense.
Interpretation of Contracts *(See pages 218–221.)*	When the terms of a contract are unambiguous, a court will enforce the contract according to its plain terms, the meaning of which must be determined from the written document alone. (Plain language laws enacted by the federal government and the majority of the states require contracts to be clearly written and easily understandable.) When the terms of a contract are ambiguous, the following rules are used by the courts in interpreting the terms:
	1. A reasonable, lawful, and effective meaning will be given to all contract terms.
	2. A contract will be interpreted as a whole, specific clauses will be considered subordinate to the contract's general intent, and all writings that are a part of the same transaction will be interpreted together.
	3. Terms that were negotiated separately will be given greater consideration than standardized terms and terms not negotiated separately.
	4. Words will be given their commonly accepted meanings and technical words their technical meanings, unless the parties clearly intended otherwise.
	5. Specific wording will be given greater consideration than general language.
	6. Written or typewritten terms prevail over preprinted terms.
	7. A party who uses ambiguous expressions is held to be responsible for the ambiguities.
	8. Evidence of prior dealing, course of performance, or usage of trade is admissible to clarify an ambiguously worded contract. In these circumstances, express terms are given the greatest weight, followed by course of performance, course of dealing, and usage of trade—in that order.

For Review

1. What is a contract? What is the objective theory of contracts?
2. What are the four basic elements necessary to the formation of a valid contract?
3. What is the difference between an implied-in-fact contract and an implied-in-law contract (quasi contract)?
4. What is a void contract? How does it differ from a voidable contract? What is an unenforceable contract?
5. What rules guide the courts in interpreting contracts?

Questions and Case Problems

8–1. Express versus Implied Contracts. Suppose that McDougal, a local businessperson, is a good friend of Krunch, the owner of a local candy store. Every day at his lunch hour McDougal goes into Krunch's candy store and spends about five minutes looking at the candy. After examining Krunch's candy and talking with Krunch, McDougal usually buys one or two candy bars. One afternoon, McDougal goes into Krunch's candy shop, looks at the candy, and picks up a $1 candy bar. Seeing that Krunch is very busy, he waves the candy bar at Krunch without saying a word and walks out. Is there a contract? If so, classify it within the categories presented in this chapter.

8–2. Contractual Promises. Rosalie, a wealthy widow, invited an acquaintance, Jonathan, to her home for dinner. Jonathan accepted the offer and, eager to please her, spent lavishly in preparing for the evening. His purchases included a new blazer, new shoes, an expensive floral arrangement, and champagne. On the appointed evening, Jonathan arrived at Rosalie's house only to find that she had left for the evening. Jonathan wants to sue Rosalie to recover some of his expenses. Can he? Why or why not?

8–3. Contract Classification. Jennifer says to her neighbor, Gordon, "If you mow my lawn, I'll pay you $25." Gordon orally accepts her offer. Is there a contract? If so, is it a bilateral or a unilateral contract? What is the legal significance of the distinction?

8–4. Contract Classification. High-Flying Advertising, Inc., contracted with Big Burger Restaurants to fly an advertisement above the Connecticut beaches. The advertisement offered $5,000 to any person who could swim from the Connecticut beaches to Long Island across the Long Island Sound in less than a day. McElfresh saw the streamer and accepted the challenge. He started his marathon swim that same day at 10 A.M. After he had been swimming for four hours and was about halfway across the sound, McElfresh saw another plane pulling a streamer that read, "Big Burger revokes." Is there a contract between McElfresh and Big Burger? If there is a contract, what type(s) of contract is (are) formed?

8–5. Equitable Doctrines. Ashton Co., which was engaged in a construction project, leased a crane from Artukovich & Sons, Inc., and hired the Reliance Truck Co. to deliver the crane to the construction site. Reliance, while the crane was in its possession and without permission from either Ashton or Artukovich, used the crane to install a transformer for a utility company, which paid Reliance for the job. Reliance then delivered the crane to the Ashton construction site at the appointed time of delivery. When Artukovich learned of the unauthorized use of the crane by Reliance, it sued Reliance for damages. What equitable doctrine could be used as a basis for awarding damages to Artukovich? [*Artukovich & Sons, Inc. v. Reliance Truck Co.*, 126 Ariz. 246, 614 P.2d 327 (1980)]

8–6. Bilateral versus Unilateral Contracts. William Greene began working for Grant Building, Inc., in 1959. Greene allegedly agreed to work at a pay rate below union scale in exchange for a promise that Grant would employ him "for life." In 1975, Oliver Realty, Inc., took over the management of Grant Building. Oliver Realty's president assured former Grant employees that existing employment contracts would be honored. During that same year, Greene explained the terms of his agreement to an Oliver Realty supervisor. The supervisor stated that he would look into the matter but never got back to Greene. After twenty-four years of service, Greene was fired by the new owners of the business. Greene sued Oliver Realty for breach of a unilateral contract. Discuss fully whether Greene and Oliver Realty had a unilateral contract. [*Greene v. Oliver Realty, Inc.*, 363 Pa.Super. 534, 526 A.2d 1192 (1987)]

8–7. Recovery for Services Rendered. Sosa Crisan, an eighty-seven-year-old widow, collapsed while shopping at a local grocery store. The Detroit police took her to the Detroit city hospital by ambulance. She was admitted to the hospital and remained there for fourteen days. Then she was transferred to another hospital, where she died some eleven months later. Crisan had never regained consciousness after her collapse at the grocery store. After she died, the city of Detroit sued her estate to recover the expenses of both the ambulance that took her to the Detroit city hospital and her Detroit city hospital stay. Is there a contract between Sosa Crisan and the Detroit city hospital? If so, how much can the hospital recover? [*In re Estate of Crisan*, 362 Mich. 569, 107 N.W.2d 907 (1961)]

8–8. Bilateral versus Unilateral Contracts. Nichols is the principal owner of Samuel Nichols, Inc., a real estate firm. Nichols signed an exclusive brokerage agreement with Molway to find a purchaser for Molway's property within ninety days. This type of agreement entitles the broker to a commission if the property is sold to any purchaser to whom the property is shown during the ninety-day period. Molway tried to cancel the brokerage agreement before the ninety-day term had expired. Nichols had already advertised the property, put up a "for sale" sign, and shown the property to prospective buyers. Molway claimed that the brokerage contract was unilateral and that she could cancel the contract at any time before Nichols found a buyer. Nichols claimed the contract was bilateral and that Molway's cancellation breached the contract. Discuss who should prevail at trial. [*Samuel Nichols, Inc. v. Molway*, 25 Mass.App. 913, 515 N.E.2d 598 (1987)]

8–9. Recovery for Services Rendered. Garris Briggs died on October 11, 1990, leaving $782 in unpaid medical bills. Following his death, insurance checks in the amount of $676.72, payable to Briggs, were sent to his widow, Beatrice Briggs. The Briggses had been living apart for the previous five years and during that time had not had any financial connections. Under state law, a surviving spouse, upon the execution of an affidavit (a statement signed under oath) before the appropriate county official, was entitled to all of the estate's assets without administration, and the assets of the estate up to $5,000 were free from all debts of the decedent (the person who died). Garris Briggs's estate was worth less than $5,000, so Beatrice Briggs signed the necessary affidavit, cashed the checks, and deposited the funds. The physicians who had provided medical services for Garris Briggs sued the widow in a New Jersey state court to recover the insurance proceeds. Should the physicians be able to recover the proceeds? If so, under what legal theory? Explain. [*Drs. Laves, Sarewitz and Walko v. Briggs*, 259 N.J.Super. 368, 613 A.2d 506 (1992)]

8–10. Recovery for Services Rendered. After Walter Washut had suffered a heart attack and could no longer take care of himself, he asked Eleanor Adkins, a friend who had previously refused Washut's proposal to marry him, to move to his ranch. For the next twelve years, Adkins lived with Washut, although she retained ownership of her own house and continued to work full-time at her job. Adkins took care of Washut's personal needs, cooked his meals, cleaned and maintained his house, cared for the livestock, and handled other matters for Washut. According to Adkins, Washut told her on numerous occasions that "everything would be taken care of" and that she would never have to leave the ranch. After Washut's death, Adkins sought to recover in quasi contract for the value of the services she had rendered to Washut. Adkins stated in her deposition that she performed the services because she loved Washut, not because she expected to be paid for them. What will the court decide, and why? [*Adkins v. Lawson*, 892 P.2d 128 (Wyo. 1995)]

**A QUESTION OF ETHICS
AND SOCIAL RESPONSIBILITY**

8–11. *In 1982, in the closing days of Minnesota's gubernatorial campaign, Dan Cohen offered a reporter from the* Minneapolis Star and Tribune *some documents—copies of two public court records of a rival party's candidate for lieutenant governor—if the reporter promised not to reveal the source of the information. The reporter promised to keep the source confidential. The editor of the* Tribune, *however, in spite of the reporter's objections, decided to name Cohen as the source of the information so as not to mislead the public into thinking that the information came from an unbiased source. On the day the* *newspaper article was published, Cohen was fired by his employer. Cohen sued the newspaper's owner, Cowles Media Co., for breach of contract. Given these facts, discuss the following questions.* [Cohen v. Cowles Media Co., 501 U.S. 663, 111 S.Ct. 2513, 115 L.Ed.2d 586 (1991)]

1. Should the editor's ethical duty to provide the reading public with unbiased news coverage have overridden the editor's ethical duty to honor the reporter's promise to Cohen?
2. Did the reporter's promise to keep Cohen's identity confidential create solely an ethical obligation, or did it create an enforceable contract?
3. If the court decides that an enforceable contract was formed between Cohen and the reporter, would the deci-sion be counter to society's valuation—as expressed in the First Amendment to the Constitution—that freedom of the press should not be constrained?

 FOR CRITICAL ANALYSIS
8–12. *Review the list of basic requirements for contract formation given at the beginning of this chapter. In view of those requirements, analyze the relationship entered into when a student enrolls in a college or university. Has a contract been formed? If so, is it a bilateral contract or a unilateral contract? Discuss.*

▌Accessing the Internet: Business Law and Legal Environment

Within the legal interest group on the commercial service America Online, there is a subcategory on torts and contracts. If you subscribe to America Online, the key word is:

LEGAL

If you wish to partake in discussions of contract law and the teaching of contract law, you can peruse a news group about contracts, provided you subscribe to it. To subscribe by E-mail, contact

listserv@austin.onu.edu

Subject: **<anything>**
Message: **Subscribe Contracts <Your Name>**

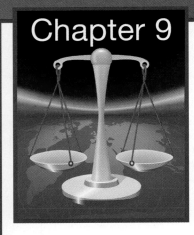

Chapter 9

Agreement and Consideration

"It is necessity that makes laws."

Voltaire, 1749–1832
(French philosopher and writer)

CHAPTER OBJECTIVES

After reading this chapter, you should be able to:

1. Identify the elements of contractual agreement.
2. State the requirements of an offer.
3. Describe how an offer can be accepted.
4. List and define the elements of consideration.
5. Explain the circumstances in which a promise will be enforced despite a lack of consideration.

Voltaire's statement that it is "necessity that makes laws" is certainly true in regard to contracts. In Chapter 8, we pointed out that promises and agreements, and the knowledge that certain of those promises and agreements will be legally enforced, are essential to civilized society. The homes we live in, the food we eat, the clothes we wear, the cars we drive, the books we read, the recordings we listen to—all of these have been purchased through contractual agreements that we have made with sellers. Contract law developed over time, through the common law tradition, to meet society's need to know with certainty the kinds of promises, or contracts, that will be enforced and the point at which a valid and binding contract is formed.

For a contract to be considered valid and enforceable, the requirements listed in Chapter 8 must be met. In this chapter, we look closely at two of these requirements, *agreement* and *consideration*.

AGREEMENT
A meeting of two or more minds in regard to the terms of a contract; usually broken down into two events—an offer by one party to form a contract, and an acceptance of the offer by the person to whom the offer is made.

▌ Agreement

An essential element for contract formation is **agreement**—the parties must agree on the terms of the contract. Ordinarily, agreement is evidenced by two events: an *offer* and an *acceptance*. One party offers a certain bargain to another party, who then accepts that bargain.

Because words often fail to convey the precise meaning intended, the law of contracts generally adheres to the *objective theory of contracts,* as discussed in Chapter 8. Under this theory, a party's words and conduct are held to mean whatever a reasonable person in the offeree's position would think they meant. The court will give words their usual meanings even if "it were proved by twenty bishops that [the] party . . . intended something else."[1]

Requirements of the Offer

An **offer** is a promise or commitment to perform or refrain from performing some specified act in the future. As discussed in Chapter 8, the party making an offer is called the *offeror,* and the party to whom the offer is made is called the *offeree.*

Three elements are necessary for an offer to be effective:

1. There must be a *serious, objective intention* by the offeror.
2. The terms of the offer must be reasonably *certain,* or *definite,* so that the parties and the court can ascertain the terms of the contract.
3. The offer must be communicated to the offeree.

Once an effective offer has been made, the offeree has the power to accept the offer. If the offeree accepts, the offer is translated into an agreement (and into a contract, if other essential elements are present).

INTENTION   The first requirement for an effective offer to exist is a serious, objective intention on the part of the offeror. Intent is not determined by the *subjective* intentions, beliefs, or assumptions of the offeror. Rather, it is determined by what a reasonable person in the offeree's position would conclude the offeror's words and actions meant. Offers made in obvious anger, jest, or undue excitement do not meet the serious-and-objective-intent test. Because these offers are not effective, an offeree's acceptance does not create an agreement.

For example, you and three classmates ride to school each day in Julio's new automobile, which has a market value of $18,000. One cold morning the four of you get into the car, but Julio cannot get it started. He yells in anger, "I'll sell this car to anyone for $500!" You drop $500 in his lap. A reasonable person, taking into consideration Julio's frustration and the obvious difference in value between the car's market price and the purchase price, would declare that Julio's offer was not made with serious and objective intent and that you do not have an agreement. The concept of intention can be further explained by distinctions between offers and nonoffers.

Expressions of Opinion   An expression of opinion is not an offer. It does not evidence an intention to enter into a binding agreement. In *Hawkins v. McGee,*[2] for example, Hawkins took his son to McGee, a doctor, and asked McGee to operate on the son's hand. McGee said that the boy would be in the hospital three or four days and that the hand would *probably* heal few days later. The son's hand did not heal for a month, but nonetheless the father did not win a suit for breach of contract. The court held that McGee did not make an offer to heal the son's hand in three or four days. He merely expressed an opinion as to when the hand would heal.

OFFER
A promise or commitment to perform or refrain from performing some specified act in the future.

• • • • • • • • • • • • • • • • • • • •

"[Contracts] must not be the sports of an idle hour, mere matters of pleasantry and badinage, never intended by the parties to have any serious effect whatever."

William Stowell, 1745–1836 (English jurist)

• • • • • • • • • • • • • • • • • • • •

BE CAREFUL   An opinion is not an offer and not a contract term. Goods or services can be "perfect" in one party's opinion and "poor" in another's.

---

1.   Judge Learned Hand in *Hotchkiss v. National City Bank of New York,* 200 F. 287 (2d Cir. 1911), aff'd 231 U.S. 50, 34 S.Ct. 20, 58 L.Ed. 115 (1913). (The term *aff'd* is an abbreviation for *affirmed;* an appellate court can affirm a lower court's judgment, decree, or order, thereby declaring that it is valid and must stand as rendered.)
2.   *Hawkins v. McGee,* 84 N.H. 114, 146 A. 641 (1929).

Statements of Intention   If Ari says "I *plan* to sell my stock in Novation, Inc., for $150 per share," a contract is not created if John "accepts" and tenders the $150 per share for the stock. Ari has merely expressed his intention to enter into a future contract for the sale of the stock. If John accepts and tenders the $150 per share, no contract is formed, because a reasonable person would conclude that Ari was only *thinking about* selling his stock, not promising to sell it.

Preliminary Negotiations   A request or invitation to negotiate is not an offer; it only expresses a willingness to discuss the possibility of entering into a contract. Examples are statements such as "Will you sell Forest Acres?" and "I wouldn't sell my car for less than $1,000." A reasonable person in the offeree's position would not conclude that such a statement evidenced an intention to enter into a binding obligation. Likewise, when the government and private firms need to have construction work done, contractors are invited to submit bids. The *invitation* to submit bids is not an offer, and a contractor does not bind the government or private firm by submitting a bid. (The bids that the contractors submit are offers, however, and the government or private firm can bind the contractor by accepting the bid.)

   In the following case, the court addressed the question of whether a letter informing several people that a cottage was for sale was an offer or merely a preliminary negotiation.

CASE 9.1

MELLEN v. JOHNSON
Supreme Judicial Court of Massachusetts,
1948.
322 Mass. 236,
76 N.E.2d 658.

HISTORICAL AND ENVIRONMENTAL SETTING
Nahant, Massachusetts, is one of the small communities on the North Shore of Greater Boston Harbor. An area of rugged coast and ocean beaches, the North Shore has been a desirable place to live since the Puritans landed in Salem in 1628. The area's many rivers and marshes supply the region with drinking water. Plum Island includes an important wildlife refuge. The fish population has been decimated, but lobsters and clams abound. Residents say no place is as perfect or as pristine.[a] As for Nahant, even in years in which other North Shore communities saw declines in the prices of housing, Nahant saw increases.

FACTS   Johnson, who owned a three-bedroom cottage in Nahant, Massachusetts, sent a letter to Mellen saying that he was putting the cottage on the market. Earlier, Mellen had expressed an interest in purchasing the cot-

a.   Beth Daley, "South vs. North," *The Boston Globe*, September 3, 1995, p. 1.

tage. The letter indicated that several other people, who had also expressed an interest in purchasing the property, were being informed by letter of its availability at the same time. Mellen, interpreting the letter as an offer, promptly accepted. Johnson sold the property to a higher bidder, and Mellen sued Johnson in a Massachusetts state court. The court found that the letter was an offer and ordered Johnson to convey the property to Mellen upon Mellen's payment of the purchase price. Johnson appealed.

ISSUE   Was Johnson's letter to Mellen an offer?

DECISION   No. The Supreme Judicial Court of Massachusetts (that state's highest court) reversed the lower court's decision. The letter did not constitute an offer.

REASON   The court held that the letter merely expressed Johnson's desire to sell the property and thus was not an offer but instead an attempt to negotiate. Because the letter announced that Johnson was sending the same letter to other people, Mellen "could not reasonably understand this to be more than an attempt at negotiation. It was a mere request or suggestion that an offer be made to the defendant [Johnson]."

FOR CRITICAL ANALYSIS—Social Consideration
How can the kind of confusion that arose in this case be prevented? Is it enough to say to prospective purchasers that other parties have also been informed that certain property is for sale?

Advertisements, Catalogues, and Circulars   In general, mail-order catalogues, price lists, and circular letters (meant for the general public) are treated not as offers to contract but as invitations to negotiate.[3] Suppose that Tartop & Company advertises a used paving machine. The ad is mailed to hundreds of firms and reads, "Used Case Construction Co. paving machine. Builds curbs and finishes cement work all in one process. Price $11,250." If General Paving, Inc., calls Tartop and says, "We accept your offer," no contract is formed. A reasonable person must conclude that Tartop was not promising to sell the paving machine but rather was soliciting offers to purchase it, because the seller never has an unlimited supply of goods. If advertisements were offers, then everyone who "accepted" after the retailer's supply was exhausted could sue for breach of contract.

KEEP IN MIND Advertisements are not binding, but they cannot be deceptive.

Consider another example. You put an ad in the classified section of your local newspaper offering to sell your guitar for $75. Seven people call and "accept" your "offer" before you can remove the ad from the newspaper. If the ad were truly an offer, you would be bound by seven contracts to sell your guitar. Because *initial* advertisements are treated as *invitations* to make offers rather than offers, however, you would have seven offers to choose from, and you could accept the best one without incurring any liability for the six you rejected. On rare occasions, though, courts have construed advertisements to be offers because the ads contained such definite terms. (One such occasion is discussed in this chapter's *Business Law in Action*.)

Price lists are another form of invitation to negotiate or trade. A seller's price list is not an offer to sell at that price; it merely invites the buyer to offer to buy at that price. In fact, the seller usually puts "prices subject to change" on the price list. Only in rare circumstances will a price quotation be construed as an offer.[4]

Auctions   In an auction, a seller "offers" goods for sale through an auctioneer. This is not, however, an offer for purposes of contract. The seller is really only expressing a willingness to sell. Unless the terms of the auction are explicitly stated to be *without reserve*, the seller (through the auctioneer) may withdraw the goods at any time before the auctioneer closes the sale by announcement or by fall of the hammer. The seller's right to withdraw the goods characterizes an auction *with reserve*; all auctions are

---

3. *Restatement (Second) of Contracts*, Section 26, Comment b.
4. See, for example, *Fairmount Glass Works v. Grunden-Martin Woodenware Co.*, 106 Ky. 659, 51 S.W. 196 (1899).

An auction in progress at Christie's in London. A seller's putting goods up for bid, in an auction with reserve, is not an offer for purposes of contract law. Why not?

BUSINESS LAW IN ACTION

When Is an Ad an Offer?

Although most advertisements are treated as invitations to negotiate, this does not mean that an advertisement can never be an offer. If the ad makes a promise so definite in character that it is apparent that the offeror is binding himself or herself to the terms stated, then the ad is treated as an offer. That was the situation in a case brought before the Supreme Court of Minnesota in 1957.[a] The case arose when a merchant refused to sell to a customer a fur stole for $1, as promised in a newspaper advertisement. The customer, Lefkowitz, had read the following ad on April 13, 1956, in a Minneapolis newspaper:

a. *Lefkowitz v. Great Minneapolis Surplus Store, Inc.*, 251 Minn. 188, 86 N.W.2d 689 (1957).

"Saturday 9 a.m.
2 Brand New Pastel
Mink 3-Skin Scarfs
Selling for $89.50
Out they go
Saturday. Each . . . $1.00
1 Black Lapin Stole
Beautiful,
worth $139.50 . . . $1.00
First Come
First Served"

Lefkowitz was the first to appear at the appropriate counter on the Saturday morning of the sale. He was told, however, that according to a "house rule," the offer was intended for women only and that men could not make the purchase.

Lefkowitz then sued the store for breach of contract, and the trial court awarded him damages. The store appealed the decision, contending that no contract existed because no offer had been made. The advertisement was solely an invitation to customers to make offers to buy the goods on the terms given in the ad—offers that, when forthcoming, could be accepted or rejected by the store.

In evaluating the claim, the Supreme Court of Minnesota held for Lefkowitz. The court stated, "We are

of the view on the facts before us that the offer by the defendant of the sale of the Lapin fur was clear, definite, and explicit, and left nothing open for negotiation." Lefkowitz's acceptance of the offer (by being the first one to appear at the store and by offering the stated purchase price) created a binding contract between the parties. As to the "house rule," the court stated that the defendant did "not have the right, after acceptance, to impose new or arbitrary conditions not contained in the published offer."[b]

In short, the advertisement in this case was sufficiently definite to create an offer. The quantity was specified (one fur stole), as were the price ($1), the value ($139.50), and the person who could accept (first come, first served).

For Critical Analysis: *What words might the store have omitted from its advertisement to avoid having it being construed as an offer?*

b. Note that today, the surplus store could have been charged with violating Federal Trade Commission rules that prohibit deceptive advertising (see Chapter 31).

---

assumed to be of this type unless a clear statement to the contrary is made.[5] At auctions without reserve, the goods cannot be withdrawn and must be sold to the highest bidder.

In an auction with reserve, there is no obligation to sell, and the seller may refuse the highest bid. The bidder is actually the offeror. Before the auctioneer strikes the hammer, which constitutes acceptance of the bid, a bidder may revoke his or her bid, or the auctioneer may reject that bid or all bids. Typically, an auctioneer will reject a bid that is below the price the seller is willing to accept. When the auctioneer accepts a higher bid, he or she rejects all previous bids. Because rejection terminates an offer (as will be pointed out later), those bids represent offers that have been terminated. Thus, if the highest bidder withdraws his or her bid before the hammer falls, none of the previous bids is reinstated. If the bid is not withdrawn or rejected, the contract is formed when the auctioneer announces, "Going once, going twice, sold!" (or something similar) and lets the hammer fall.

In auctions with reserve, the seller may reserve the right to confirm or reject the sale even after the "hammer has fallen." In this situation, the seller is obligated to notify those attending the auction that sales of goods made during the auction are not final until confirmed by the seller. The following case illustrates this point.

---

5. See UCC 2–328.

CASE 9.2

LAWRENCE PAPER CO. v. ROSEN & CO.

United States Court of Appeals,
Sixth Circuit, 1991.
939 F.2d 376.

HISTORICAL AND SOCIAL SETTING *More than two hundred years ago, it was established at common law that when an auctioneer says, "What am I bid?" the auctioneer is not making an offer to sell but is inviting offers to buy, which the auctioneer is free to accept or reject. More than one hundred years ago, it was established that in some cases, even if an auctioneer announces, "I will sell to the highest bidder," the statement still does not constitute an offer. These common law rules relating to auctions plus auctions "without reserve" were adopted by the Uniform Commercial Code, which has governed most sales of goods since the 1950s. It is also generally held that when a seller reserves the right to refuse to accept a bid, a binding sale is not made until the seller accepts the bid.*

FACTS This dispute arose when some equipment, which had been used as security for a loan obtained by North Coast Corrugator Company from Ameritrust Company, was sold at auction to satisfy North Coast's debt to Ameritrust. Ameritrust Company employed Rosen & Company to conduct the sale. Included in Rosen's extensive advertisements of the sale was the announcement that the sale was subject to confirmation by Ameritrust. The auctioneer made a similar announcement at the time of the sale. Sixty bidders attended the

auction. The auctioneer first offered the equipment in bulk, but only one bid—from Alpine Company for $50,000—was received. Then the equipment was offered piecemeal, and total bids of $139,000 were received. Two bids from Lawrence Paper Company and American Corrugated Machine Corporation (ACMC) were accepted, and both companies submitted checks for 25 percent of their bid totals, as requested. After the auction, Alpine offered $175,000 for the equipment, and Ameritrust sold the entire lot to Alpine. Lawrence and ACMC sued in a federal district court for breach of contract. The trial judge dismissed the suit, and the plaintiffs appealed.

ISSUE Did contracts exist between Rosen and Lawrence and between Rosen and ACMC as a result of the auctioneer's acceptance of the two companies' bids?

DECISION No. The district court's decision was affirmed.

REASON The district court judge had found that the auction was clearly "with reserve" and therefore there was "no acceptance of the bid, because the sale was not confirmed by the secured party." The appellate court agreed, concluding that "there was no binding contract and the sellers were free to accept the subsequent offer." The court stated that "where a sale is with reserve and subject to 'confirmation' by the seller, the bids are subject to rejection after the sale, even though accepted by the auctioneer."

FOR CRITICAL ANALYSIS—Ethical Consideration
Are auctions with reserve unfair to the bidders, whose bids and partial payments toward the purchase prices of the items being sold may be freely ignored later by the seller?

Agreements to Agree Traditionally, agreements to agree—that is, agreements to agree to a material term of a contract at some future date—were not considered to be binding contracts. More recent cases illustrate the view that agreements to agree serve valid commercial purposes and often can be enforced if the parties clearly intended to be bound by the agreements. For example, suppose that Zahn Consulting leases office space from Leon Properties, Inc. Their lease agreement includes a clause permitting Zahn to extend the lease at an amount of rent to be agreed on when the lease is extended. Under the traditional rule, because the amount of rent was not specified in the lease clause itself, the clause would be too indefinite in its terms to be enforced. Under the modern view, a court could hold that the parties intended the future rent to be a reasonable amount and could enforce the clause.[6]

In other words, under the modern view, the emphasis is on the parties' intent rather than on form. For example, when the Pennzoil Company discussed with the

---

6. *Restatement (Second) of Contracts*, Section 33. See also UCC 2–204, 2–305.

Getty Oil Company the possible purchase of Getty's stock, a memorandum of agreement was drafted to reflect the terms of the conversations. After more negotiations over the price, both companies issued press releases announcing an agreement in principle on the terms of the memorandum. The next day, Texaco, Inc., offered to buy all Getty's stock at a higher price. The day after that, Getty's board of directors voted to accept Texaco's offer, and Texaco and Getty signed a merger agreement. When Pennzoil sued Texaco for tortious interference with its "contractual" relationship with Getty, a jury concluded that Getty and Pennzoil had intended to form a binding contract before Texaco made its offer, with only the details left to be worked out. Texaco was held liable for wrongfully interfering with this contract.[7]

DEFINITENESS   The second requirement for an effective offer involves the definiteness of its terms. An offer must have reasonably definite terms so that a court can determine if a breach has occurred and give an appropriate remedy.[8]

An offer may invite an acceptance to be worded in such specific terms that the contract is made definite. For example, suppose that Marcus Business Machines contacts your corporation and offers to sell "from one to ten MacCool copying machines for $1,600 each; state number desired in acceptance." Your corporation agrees to buy two copiers. Because the quantity is specified in the acceptance, the terms are definite, and the contract is enforceable.

Definiteness is also required when a contract is modified. The terms of a contract as modified must be reasonably definite so that a court can determine if there has been a breach. The following case illustrates this point.

---

7. *Texaco, Inc. v. Pennzoil Co.*, 729 S.W.2d 768 (Tex.App—Houston [1st Dist.] 1987, writ ref'd n.r.e.). (Generally, a complete Texas court of appeals citation includes the writ-of-error history showing the Texas Supreme Court's disposition of the case. In this case, *writ ref'd n.r.e.* is an abbreviation for "writ refused, no reversible error," which means that Texas's highest court refused to grant the appellant's request to review the case, because the court did not consider there to be any reversible error.) This case is presented in Chapter 6 as Case 6.1.
8. *Restatement (Second) of Contracts*, Section 33. The UCC has relaxed the requirements regarding the definitiveness of terms in contracts for the sale of goods. See UCC 2–204(3).

CASE 9.3

RUUD v. GREAT PLAINS SUPPLY, INC.
Supreme Court of Minnesota, 1995.
526 N.W.2d 369.

COMPANY PROFILE *Michael Wigley bought Great Plains Supply, Inc. (GPS), a building materials supplier, in 1989. GPS had suffered losses in nine of the previous ten years. To turn GPS around, Wigley closed unprofitable stores and concentrated business on contractors. By 1994, sales exceeded $100 million—up more than 40 percent over 1993—and sales from GPS's truss manufacturing facilities doubled for the fifth straight year. GPS plants, lumberyards, and distribution centers are located primarily in the Midwest. Successful salespersons are*

promoted to management, and managers are compensated according to their performance.

FACTS The corporate manual of Great Plains Supply, Inc., states that employees can be discharged at any time for any reason. This manual constitutes an employment contract between GPS and its employees. Kevin Ruud was a store manager for GPS. Before accepting an offer to transfer to an unprofitable store, he expressed worries about job security to Michael Wigley, GPS's owner, and Ronald Nelson, a GPS vice president. Wigley and Nelson each responded, "Good employees are taken care of." Ruud accepted the transfer, but when the store closed as he had feared, he was offered only lesser jobs at lower pay. Ruud quit his job and filed a suit in a Minnesota state court against GPS, Wigley, and Nelson for, among other things, breach of contract. Ruud alleged that their statements modified the terms of his contract with GPS to include permanent employment. The court dismissed the claims against Wigley and Nelson and granted GPS's motion for summary judg-

Case 9.3—Continued

ment. Ruud appealed, and the appellate court reversed the trial court's summary judgment on the issue. The case was then appealed to the state supreme court.

ISSUE Were the statements of Wigley and Nelson sufficiently definite to modify the terms of Ruud's employment contract?

DECISION No. The Supreme Court of Minnesota reinstated the order for summary judgment in favor of GPS.

REASON The state supreme court interpreted the statements of Wigley and Nelson as "policy statements as to the general goodwill of the company toward Kevin Ruud and its other employees." Even if there was an intent to modify the terms of Ruud's contract, the court concluded that the statements were "so vague as to leave undeterminable the nature of that modification."

FOR CRITICAL ANALYSIS—Ethical Consideration
Are there any circumstances under which an employer would intend to make a promise of permanent employment to any prospective or actual employee?

COMMUNICATION A third requirement for an effective offer is communication, resulting in the offeree's knowledge of the offer. Suppose that Tolson advertises a reward for the return of her lost cat. Dirlik, not knowing of the reward, finds the cat and returns it to Tolson. Ordinarily, Dirlik cannot recover the reward, because an essential element of a reward contract is that the one who claims the reward must have known it was offered. A few states would allow recovery of the reward, but not on contract principles—Dirlik would be allowed to recover on the basis that it would be unfair to deny him the reward just because he did not know about it. The following case is one of the classic reward suits in common law.

CASE 9.4

GLOVER v. JEWISH WAR VETERANS OF THE UNITED STATES, POST NO. 58
Municipal Court of Appeals
for the District of Columbia, 1949.
68 A.2d 233.

HISTORICAL AND SOCIAL SETTING *Rewards have been offered for the capture of criminals since the days of the Old West. Such rewards gave rise to the bounty hunters who tried to make a living by finding alleged criminals. After World War II, which ended in 1945, the professional bounty-hunting business had died, but some rewards continued to be given. The purpose of these rewards remained the same as in the Old West— to provide incentives for persons to make an extra effort to find those accused of committing crimes.*

FACTS The Jewish War Veterans of the United States placed in the newspaper an offer of a reward of $500 "to the person or persons furnishing information resulting in the apprehension and conviction of the persons guilty of the murder of Maurice L. Bernstein." Mary Glover gave police information that led to the arrest and conviction of the murderers, not knowing that a reward had been

offered and not learning of it until the next day. In an action brought before a District of Columbia trial court, the court held that no contract existed because Mary Glover did not know about the reward at the time she gave the police the information. Glover appealed.

ISSUE Does a contract between Glover and the Jewish War Veterans exist, given the fact that Glover did not know of the reward when she delivered the requested information?

DECISION No. The appellate court affirmed the trial court's judgment. Glover's act did not constitute an acceptance, because she did not act in response to the offer.

REASON Glover was not entitled to the $500 reward because she was not aware of the nongovernmental offer when she gave the police the information. The *Restatement of the Law of Contracts* says: "It is impossible that there should be an acceptance unless the offeree knows of the existence of the offer."

FOR CRITICAL ANALYSIS—Political Consideration
With respect to awards offered by the government, should it be assumed by the government that members of the public have knowledge of government actions and that members of the public should receive government rewards without further proof of knowledge?

Termination of the Offer

The communication of an effective offer to an offeree gives the offeree the power to transform the offer into a binding, legal obligation (a contract) by an acceptance. This power of acceptance, however, does not continue forever. It can be terminated by *action of the parties* or by *operation of law*.

TERMINATION BY ACTION OF THE PARTIES   An offer can be terminated by the action of the parties in any of three ways: by revocation, by rejection, or by counteroffer.

Revocation of the Offer   The offeror's act of withdrawing an offer is referred to as **revocation.** Unless an offer is irrevocable, the offeror usually can revoke the offer (even if he or she has promised to keep the offer open), as long as the revocation is communicated to the offeree before the offeree accepts. Revocation may be accomplished by express repudiation of the offer (for example, with a statement such as "I withdraw my previous offer of October 17") or by performance of acts inconsistent with the existence of the offer, which are made known to the offeree.

REVOCATION
In contract law, the withdrawal of an offer by an offeror; unless the offer is irrevocable, it can be revoked at any time prior to acceptance without liability.

For example, Geraldine offers to sell some land to Gary. A week passes, and Gary, who has not yet accepted the offer, learns from his friend Konstantine that Geraldine has in the meantime sold the property to Nunan. Gary's knowledge of Geraldine's sale of the land to Nunan, even though Gary learned of it through a third party, effectively revokes Geraldine's offer to sell the land to Gary. Geraldine's sale of the land to Nunan is inconsistent with the continued existence of the offer to Gary, and thus the offer to Gary is revoked.

The general rule followed by most states is that a revocation becomes effective when the offeree or offeree's agent (a person who acts on behalf of another) actually receives it. Therefore, a letter of revocation mailed on April 1 and delivered at the offeree's residence or place of business on April 3 becomes effective on April 3.

An offer made to the general public can be revoked in the same manner the offer was originally communicated. Suppose that a department store offers a $10,000 reward to anyone giving information leading to the apprehension of the persons who burglarized its downtown store. The offer is published in three local papers and four papers in neighboring communities. To revoke the offer, the store must publish the revocation in all seven papers for the same number of days it published the offer. The revocation is then accessible to the general public, and the offer is revoked even if some particular offeree does not know about it.

Irrevocable Offers   Although most offers are revocable, some can be made irrevocable. Increasingly, courts refuse to allow an offeror to revoke an offer when the offeree has changed position because of justifiable reliance on the offer (under the doctrine of detrimental reliance, or promissory estoppel, discussed later in the chapter). In some circumstances, "firm offers" made by merchants may also be considered irrevocable. We discuss these offers in Chapter 14.

OPTION CONTRACT
A contract under which the offeror cannot revoke his or her offer for a stipulated time period, and the offeree can accept or reject the offer during this period without fear that the offer will be made to another person. The offeree must give consideration for the option (the irrevocable offer) to be enforceable.

Another form of irrevocable offer is an option contract. An **option contract** is created when an offeror promises to hold an offer open for a specified period of time in return for a payment (consideration) given by the offeree. An option contract takes away the offeror's power to revoke an offer for the period of time specified in the option. If no time is specified, then a reasonable period of time is implied. For example, suppose that you are in the business of writing movie scripts. Your agent contacts the head of development at New Line Cinema and offers to sell New Line your new movie script. New Line likes your script and agrees to pay you $5,000 for a six-month option. In this situation, you (through your agent) are the offeror, and New Line is the offeree. You cannot revoke your offer to sell New Line your script for the next six months. If after six months no contract has been formed, however, New Line loses the $5,000, and you are free to sell the script to another firm.

Option contracts are also frequently used in conjunction with the sale of real estate. For example, you might agree with a landowner to lease a home and include in the lease contract a clause stating that you will pay $2,000 for an option to purchase the home within a specified period of time. If you decide not to purchase the home after the specified period has lapsed, you forfeit the $2,000, and the landlord is free to sell the property to another buyer.

Rejection of the Offer by the Offeree The offer may be rejected by the offeree, in which case the offer is terminated. Any subsequent attempt by the offeree to accept will be construed as a new offer, giving the original offeror (now the offeree) the power of acceptance. A rejection is ordinarily accomplished by words or by conduct evidencing an intent not to accept the offer.

As with revocation, rejection of an offer is effective only when it is actually received by the offeror or the offeror's agent. Suppose that Growgood Farms mails a letter to Campbell Soup Company offering to sell carrots at ten cents a pound. Campbell Soup Company could reject the offer by sending or faxing a letter to Growgood Farms expressly rejecting the offer, or by mailing the offer back to Growgood, evidencing an intent to reject it. Alternatively, Campbell could offer to buy the carrots at eight cents per pound (a counteroffer), necessarily rejecting the original offer.

Merely inquiring about the offer does not constitute rejection. For example, a friend offers to buy your CD-ROM library for $300. You respond, "Is this your best offer?" or "Will you pay me $375 for it?" A reasonable person would conclude that you did not reject the offer but merely made an inquiry for further consideration of the offer. You can still accept and bind your friend to the $300 purchase price. When the offeree merely inquires as to the firmness of the offer, there is no reason to presume that he or she intends to reject it.

Counteroffer by the Offeree A **counteroffer** is a rejection of the original offer and the simultaneous making of a new offer. Suppose that Burke offers to sell his home to Lang for $170,000. Lang responds, "Your price is too high. I'll offer to purchase your house for $165,000." Lang's response is termed a counteroffer because it rejects Burke's offer to sell at $170,000 and creates a new offer by Lang to purchase the home at a price of $165,000.

At common law, the **mirror image rule** requires that the offeree's acceptance match the offeror's offer exactly. In other words, the terms of the acceptance must "mirror" those of the offer. If the acceptance materially changes or adds to the terms of the original offer, it will be considered not an acceptance but a counteroffer—which, of course, need not be accepted. The original offeror can, however, accept the terms of the counteroffer and create a valid contract.[9]

TERMINATION BY OPERATION OF LAW The offeree's power to transform an offer into a binding, legal obligation can be terminated by operation of the law if any of four conditions occur: lapse of time, destruction of the subject matter, death or incompetence of the offeror or offeree, or supervening illegality of the proposed contract.

Lapse of Time An offer terminates automatically by law when the period of time specified in the offer has passed. For example, Jane offers to sell her boat to Jonah if he accepts within twenty days. Jonah must accept within the twenty-day period, or the offer will lapse (terminate). The time period specified in an offer normally begins to run when the offer is actually received by the offeree, not when it is drawn up or sent.

BE CAREFUL The way in which a response to an offer is phrased can determine whether the offer is accepted or rejected.

COUNTEROFFER
An offeree's response to an offer in which the offeree rejects the original offer and at the same time makes a new offer.

MIRROR IMAGE RULE
A common law rule that requires, for a valid contractual agreement, that the terms of the offeree's acceptance adhere exactly to the terms of the offeror's offer.

9. The mirror image rule has been greatly modified in regard to contracts for the sale of goods. Section 2–207 of the UCC provides that a contract is formed if the offeree makes a definite expression of acceptance (such as signing the form in the appropriate location), even though the terms of the acceptance modify or add to the terms of the original offer (see Chapter 14).

When the offer is delayed (through the misdelivery of mail, for example), the period begins to run from the date the offeree would have received the offer, but only if the offeree knows or should know that the offer is delayed.[10] For example, if Jane used improper postage when mailing the offer to Jonah, and Jonah knew about the improper mailing, the offer would lapse twenty days after the day Jonah would ordinarily have received the offer had Jane used proper postage.

If no time for acceptance is specified in the offer, the offer terminates at the end of a *reasonable* period of time. A reasonable period of time is determined by the subject matter of the contract, business and market conditions, and other relevant circumstances. An offer to sell farm produce, for example, will terminate sooner than an offer to sell farm equipment, because farm produce is perishable and subject to greater fluctuations in market value.

Destruction of the Subject Matter   An offer is automatically terminated if the specific subject matter of the offer is destroyed before the offer is accepted. For example, if Bekins offers to sell his cow to Yatsen, but the cow dies before Yatsen can accept, the offer is automatically terminated.

Death or Incompetence of the Offeror or Offeree   An offeree's power of acceptance is terminated when the offeror or offeree dies or is deprived of legal capacity to enter into the proposed contract, unless the offer is irrevocable.[11] An offer is personal to both parties and normally cannot pass to the decedent's heirs, guardian, or estate. This rule applies whether or not the one party had notice of the death or incompetence of the other party.

Supervening Illegality of the Proposed Contract   A statute or court decision that makes an offer illegal will automatically terminate the offer. If Acme Finance Corporation offers to lend Jack $20,000 at 15 percent annually, and a state statute is enacted prohibiting loans at interest rates greater than 12 percent before Jack can accept, the offer is automatically terminated. (If the statute is enacted after Jack accepts the offer, a valid contract is formed, but the contract may still be unenforceable—see Chapter 10.)

Acceptance

ACCEPTANCE
A voluntary act by the offeree that shows assent, or agreement, to the terms of an offer; may consist of words or conduct.

An **acceptance** is a voluntary act by the offeree that shows assent, or agreement, to the terms of an offer. The offeree's act may consist of words or conduct. The acceptance must be unequivocal and must be communicated to the offeror.

WHO CAN ACCEPT?   Generally, a third person cannot substitute for the offeree and effectively accept the offer. After all, the identity of the offeree is as much a condition of a bargaining offer as any other term contained therein. Thus, except in special circumstances, only the person to whom the offer is made or that person's agent can accept the offer and create a binding contract. For example, Lottie makes an offer to Paul. Paul is not interested, but Paul's friend José accepts the offer. No contract is formed.

UNEQUIVOCAL ACCEPTANCE   To exercise the power of acceptance effectively, the offeree must accept unequivocally. This is the *mirror image rule* previously discussed. If the acceptance is subject to new conditions or if the terms of the acceptance mate-

---

10.   *Restatement (Second) of Contracts*, Section 49.
11.   *Restatement (Second) of Contracts*, Section 48. If the offer is irrevocable, it is not terminated when the offeror dies. Also, if the offer is such that it can be accepted by the performance of a series of acts, and those acts began before the offeror died, the offeree's power of acceptance is not terminated.

"It's a deal, but just to be on the safe side let's have our lawyers look at this handshake."

Dollars and Nonsense reprinted by permission of United Feature Syndicate, Inc. © 1996 Robert Mankoff from the Cartoon Bank™, Inc.

rially change the original offer, the acceptance may be deemed a counteroffer that implicitly rejects the original offer.

Certain terms, when added to an acceptance, will not qualify the acceptance sufficiently to constitute rejection of the offer. Suppose that in response to a person offering to sell a painting by a well-known artist, the offeree replies, "I accept; please send a written contract." The offeree is requesting a written contract but is not making it a condition for acceptance. Therefore, the acceptance is effective without the written contract. If the offeree replies, "I accept if you send a written contract," however, the acceptance is expressly conditioned on the request for a writing, and the statement is not an acceptance but a counteroffer. (Notice how important each word is!)[12]

DON'T FORGET When an offer is rejected, it is terminated.

The following case illustrates that the language in an offer or acceptance should be considered together. That is, a few unequivocal words or phrases should not be taken out of context and be given a meaning that they do not have.

---

12.   As noted in footnote 9, in regard to sales contracts, the UCC provides that an acceptance may still be valid even if some terms are added. The new terms are simply treated as proposals for additions to the contract, or become part of the contract. See UCC 2–207(2).

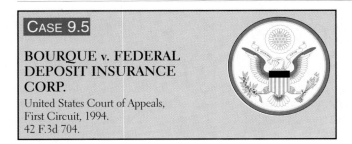

CASE 9.5

BOURQUE v. FEDERAL DEPOSIT INSURANCE CORP.

United States Court of Appeals, First Circuit, 1994.
42 F.3d 704.

HISTORICAL AND ECONOMIC SETTING *Banks sometimes go out of business when many of their loans cannot be repaid. From 1945 to 1980, U.S. banks failed at the rate of about six per year. The number increased dramatically in the 1980s and 1990s: there were more than two hundred failures in 1989 and nearly five hundred in 1992. Many of the more recent bank failures were*

(Continued)

Case 9.5—Continued

due to loans that could not be repaid because they had been used to finance commercial real estate developments that did not provide a sufficient return. Among those banks that failed in the early 1990s was the Eastland Savings Bank of Woonsocket, Rhode Island. Newmark Investments, Inc., was a subsidiary of Eastland.

FACTS   The Federal Deposit Insurance Corporation (FDIC) was selling all of the real estate owned by Newmark Investments, Inc. Raymond Bourque offered to buy a certain parcel of the property for $105,500. Curtis Cain, an FDIC account officer, responded in a letter to Bourque's attorney that "the FDIC is unable to accept Mr. Bourque's offer. FDIC's counteroffer is $130,000.00. All offers are subject to approval by the appropriate FDIC delegated authority." Bourque filled in an FDIC purchase-and-sale form to indicate a $130,000 selling price, signed it, and sent it to the FDIC. Elizabeth Carroll, another FDIC account officer, responded that the FDIC would not accept $130,000 for the property, but that Bourque could submit another offer. Bourque made no other offer, and the FDIC refused to sell the property to him. Bourque filed a suit in a federal district court against the FDIC and Newmark (the defendants) for breach of contract. The court issued a summary judgment in favor of the defendants. Bourque appealed to the U.S. Court of Appeals for the First Circuit.

ISSUE   Can unequivocal language, such as the term *counteroffer* in Cain's letter to Bourque, be considered in

isolation from other, qualifying language in the offer or acceptance?

DECISION   No. The U.S. Court of Appeals for the First Circuit held that in the context of offers and acceptances, the qualifying language is likely to control. The court affirmed the district court's judgment.

REASON   The appellate court stated that "[w]hen read as a whole, as it must be read," Cain's letter "sets forth with sufficient clarity that the recipient may 'accept' Cain's 'counteroffer' of $130,000, but only subject to final approval by the appropriate FDIC authority." In other words, Cain's response to Bourque's first offer was not itself an offer—even though Cain used the word "counteroffer." Instead, Cain was only inviting Bourque to make another offer. The court pointed out that Bourque made another offer, but the FDIC never accepted it, "so as a matter of law, no contract was ever formed between the parties."

FOR CRITICAL ANALYSIS—International Consideration
If Cain had not used the word counteroffer *in his letter, would Bourque have had any support for his argument that they had a contract? What are the implications of the importance of such terms in international deals, when more than one language is involved?*

SILENCE AS ACCEPTANCE   Ordinarily, silence cannot constitute acceptance, even if the offeror states, "By your silence and inaction, you will be deemed to have accepted this offer." This general rule applies because an offeree should not be put under a burden of liability to act affirmatively in order to reject an offer. No consideration—that is, nothing of value—has passed to the offeree to impose such a liability.

In some instances, however, the offeree does have a duty to speak, in which case his or her silence or inaction will operate as an acceptance. For example, silence may be an acceptance when an offeree takes the benefit of offered services even though he or she had an opportunity to reject them and knew that they were offered with the expectation of compensation. Suppose Jameson watches while a stranger mows her lawn, even though the stranger has not been asked to mow the lawn. Jameson knows the stranger expects to be paid and does nothing to stop him. Here, her silence constitutes an acceptance, and an implied-in-fact contract is created. She is bound to pay a reasonable value for the stranger's work. This rule normally applies only when the offeree has received a benefit from the goods or services.

Silence can also operate as acceptance when the offeree has had prior dealings with the offeror. If a merchant, for example, routinely receives shipments from a supplier and in the past has always notified the supplier of rejection of defective goods, then silence constitutes acceptance. Also, if a person solicits an offer specifying that certain terms and conditions are acceptable, and the offeror makes the offer in response to the solicitation, the offeree has a duty to reject—that is, a duty to tell the offeror that the offer is not acceptable. Failure to reject (silence) would operate as an acceptance.

COMMUNICATION OF ACCEPTANCE Whether the offeror must be notified of the acceptance depends on the nature of the contract. In a bilateral contract, communication of acceptance is necessary, because acceptance is in the form of a promise (not performance), and the contract is formed when the promise is made (rather than when the act is performed). The offeree must communicate the acceptance to the offeror. Communication of acceptance is not necessary, however, if the offer dispenses with the requirement. Also, if the offer can be accepted by silence, no communication is necessary.[13]

Because in a unilateral contract the full performance of some act is called for, acceptance is usually evident, and notification is therefore unnecessary. Exceptions do exist, however. When the offeror requests notice of acceptance or has no adequate means of determining whether the requested act has been performed, or when the law requires such notice of acceptance, then notice is necessary.[14]

MODE AND TIMELINESS OF ACCEPTANCE The general rule is that acceptance in a bilateral contract is timely if it is effected within the duration of the offer. Problems arise, however, when the parties involved are not dealing face to face. In such cases, the offeree may use an authorized mode of communication. Acceptance takes effect, thus completing formation of the contract, at the time the offeree sends the communication via the mode expressly or impliedly authorized by the offeror. This is the so-called **mailbox rule,** also called the "deposited acceptance rule," which the majority of courts uphold. Under this rule, if the authorized mode of communication is the mail, then an acceptance becomes valid when it is dispatched—not when it is received by the offeror. The mailbox rule was formed to prevent the confusion that arises when an offeror sends a letter of revocation but, before this letter is received by the offeree, the offeree sends a letter of acceptance. Thus, whereas a revocation becomes effective only when it is *received* by the offeree, an acceptance becomes effective upon *dispatch* (even if it is never received), providing that an *authorized* means of communication is used.

Authorized means can be either expressly authorized—that is, expressly stipulated in the offer—or impliedly authorized by facts or law.[15] When an offeror specifies how acceptance should be made (for example, by first-class mail or express delivery), *express authorization* is said to exist. Moreover, both the offeror and the offeree are bound in contract the moment that such means of acceptance are employed.

Most offerors do not specify expressly the means by which the offeree is to accept. Thus, the common law recognizes the following implied authorized means of acceptance:[16]

1.   The choice of a particular means by the offeror in making the offer implies that the offeree is authorized to use the *same* or a *faster* means for acceptance.
2.   When two parties are at a distance, *mailing* is impliedly authorized.

REMEMBER A bilateral contract is a promise for a promise, and a unilateral contract is performance for a promise.

MAILBOX RULE
A rule providing that an acceptance of an offer becomes effective upon dispatch (upon being placed in a mailbox), if mail is, expressly or impliedly, an authorized means of communication of acceptance to the offeror.

---

13.   Under the UCC, an order or other offer to buy goods that are to be promptly shipped may be treated as either a bilateral or a unilateral offer and can be accepted by a promise to ship or by actual shipment. See UCC 2–206 (1)(b).
14.   UCC 2–206(2).
15.   *Restatement (Second) of Contracts*, Section 30, provides that an offer invites acceptance "by any medium reasonable in the circumstances," unless the offer is specific about the means of acceptance. Under Section 65, a medium is reasonable if it is one used by the offeror or one customary in similar transactions, unless the offeree knows of circumstances that would argue against the reasonableness of a particular medium (the need for speed because of rapid price changes, for example).
16.   Note that under the UCC, acceptance of an offer for the sale of goods can be made by any medium that is *reasonable* under the circumstances. See UCC 2–206 (1)(a).

If an offeror expressly authorizes acceptance of his or her offer by first-class mail or express delivery, can the offeree accept by a faster means, such as a fax?

There are three basic exceptions to the rule that a contract is formed when acceptance is sent by authorized means:

1.   If the acceptance is not properly dispatched (if a letter is incorrectly addressed, for example, or is without the proper postage), in most states it will not be effective until it is received by the offeror.
2.   The offeror can specifically condition his or her offer upon the receipt of an acceptance by a certain time, in which case, to be effective, the acceptance must be received prior to the end of the time period.
3.   Sometimes an offeree sends a rejection first, then later changes his or her mind and sends an acceptance. Obviously, this chain of events could cause confusion and even detriment to the offeror, depending on whether the rejection or the acceptance arrived first. In such cases, the law cancels the rule of acceptance upon dispatch, and the first communication received by the offeror determines whether a contract is formed. If the rejection comes first, there is no contract.[17]

An acceptance given by means not expressly or impliedly authorized is not effective until it is received by the offeror.

_____

17.   *Restatement (Second) of Contracts*, Section 40.

▭ Technology and the Mailbox Rule

The world of offer and acceptance has changed in recent years. To a certain extent, this change has been brought about by the emergence of express delivery services. When an offer is sent via Federal Express (or some other express delivery service), for example, express delivery is the impliedly authorized means of acceptance. The "mailbox rule," which states that an acceptance is effective on dispatch, does not come into play, because mail (other than express mail) is not an impliedly authorized means of acceptance in this situation. Electronic communications systems have even more significantly altered the ways in which offers and acceptances are exchanged by businesspersons today.

Technology and the Mailbox Rule—Continued

Faxed Offers and Acceptances

What happens when an offer or acceptance is faxed, rather than mailed? In effect, because of the nearly instantaneous sending and receiving of faxes, the mailbox rule becomes irrelevant. Another legal issue raised by the use of faxes is whether faxed documents are valid in light of the fact that faxed signatures are not "original." To date, courts that have addressed this issue generally have held that signatures on faxed documents are legally binding unless an "original" signature is specifically required. Usually, in cases involving faxed documents, the courts simply assume that they are valid.[a]

What happens when an acceptance is faxed to the offeror's office but for some reason is not received by the offeror in a timely fashion? This is similar to a situation in which a letter goes astray because of an incorrect address. In such a situation, the mailbox rule that an acceptance is "effective on dispatch" does not apply, and the acceptance will not be effective until received by the offeror. Very likely, if a fax transmitted to the offeror failed to reach the offeror for some reason, a court would look closely at the circumstances. For

a.   See, for example, *Bazak v. Mast Industries,* 73 N.Y.2d 113, 535 N.E.2d 633, 538 N.Y.S. 503 (1989); and *Hessenthaler v. Farzin,* 388 Pa.Super., 564 A.2d 990 (1989).

example, if the offeror did not receive the fax because her fax machine was out of paper, and the offeree had reason to suspect or know that the offeror did not receive the fax, then the court might hold that the faxed acceptance was not effective.

Digital Signatures

A current issue presented by technology in regard to contracts (as well as other areas of the law) is how to create and verify "digital signatures" for use in electronic communications via computer networks, including those on the Internet. The Science and Technology section of the American Bar Association is currently preparing digital signature guidelines, as well as a Model Digital Signature Act. These efforts are in response to the growing need for certainty in regard to how traditional legal principles apply to electronically communicated documents. Among other things, such transmissions will require some kind of "CyberNotary" to provide legal authentication and certification of electronic documents. Efforts are already under way to create this new "legal specialization."

For Critical Analysis: *What other types of issues, other than signature problems, might arise when transmitting offers and acceptances via the Internet?*

▌ Consideration and Its Requirements

In every legal system, some promises will be enforced, and some promises will not be enforced. The simple fact that a party has made a promise, then, does not mean the promise is enforceable. Under the common law, a primary basis for the enforcement of promises is consideration. **Consideration** is usually defined as the value given in return for a promise. We look here at the basic elements of consideration and then at some other contract doctrines relating to consideration.

Elements of Consideration

Often, consideration is broken down into two parts: (1) something of *legally sufficient value* must be given in exchange for the promise, and (2) there must be a *bargained-for* exchange.

LEGAL VALUE   The "something of legally sufficient value" may consist of (1) a promise to do something that one has no prior legal duty to do (to pay money on receipt of certain goods, for example), (2) the performance of an action that one is otherwise not obligated to undertake (such as providing accounting services), or (3) the refraining from an action that one has a legal right to undertake. Generally, to be legally sufficient, consideration must be either *detrimental to the promisee* or *beneficial to the promisor*. Note that legal detriment (creating, modifying, or giving up a legal right) is not the same as economic, or actual, detriment (paying money or suffering economic losses).

CONSIDERATION
Generally, the value given in return for a promise. The consideration, which must be present to make the contract legally binding, must result in a detriment to the promisee (something of legally sufficient value and bargained for) or a benefit to the promisor.

Consider the following example. Jerry says to his son, "When you finish painting the garage, I will pay you $100." Jerry's son paints the garage. The act of painting the garage is the consideration that creates Jerry's contractual obligation to pay his son $100. In this situation, the consideration is both detrimental to the promisee (the son) and beneficial to the promisor (Jerry). Jerry's garage was painted, and his son undertook an action that the son was not otherwise legally obligated to undertake.

What if, in return for a promise to pay, a person forbears to pursue harmful habits, such as the use of tobacco and alcohol? Does such forbearance represent a legal detriment to the promisee and thus create consideration for the contract, or does it in fact benefit the promisee and thus *not* create consideration for the contract? This was the issue before the court in *Hamer v. Sidway*, a classic case concerning consideration, which we present here as this chapter's *Landmark in the Law*.

<table>
<tr><td>LANDMARK IN
THE LAW</td><td>*Hamer v. Sidway* (1891)</td></tr>
</table>

In *Hamer v. Sidway*,[a] the issue before the court arose from a contract created in 1869 between William Story, Sr., and his nephew, William Story II. The uncle promised his nephew that if the nephew refrained from drinking alcohol, using tobacco, and playing billiards and cards for money until he reached the age of twenty-one, the uncle would pay him $5,000. The nephew, who indulged occasionally in all of these "vices," agreed to refrain from them and did so for the next six years. Following his twenty-first birthday in 1875, the nephew wrote to his uncle that he had performed his part of the bargain and was thus entitled to the promised $5,000. A few days later, the uncle wrote the nephew a letter stating, "[Y]ou shall have the five thousand dollars, as I promised you." The uncle said that the money was in the bank, and that the nephew could "consider this money on interest."

The nephew left the money in the care of his uncle, who held it for the next twelve years. When the uncle died in 1887, however, the executor of the uncle's estate refused to pay the $5,000 claim brought by Hamer, a third party to whom the promise had been *assigned*. (The law allows parties to assign, or transfer, rights in contracts to third parties; see Chapter 12.) The executor, Sidway, contended that the contract was invalid because there was insufficient consideration to support it. He argued that neither a benefit to the promisor (the uncle) nor a detriment to the promisee (the nephew) existed in this case. The uncle had received nothing, and the nephew had actually benefited by fulfilling the uncle's wishes. Therefore, no contract existed.

Although a lower court upheld Sidway's position, the New York Court of Appeals reversed and ruled in favor of the plaintiff, Hamer. "The promisee used tobacco, occasionally drank liquor, and he had a legal right to do so," the court stated. "That right he abandoned for a period of years upon the strength of the promise of the testator [one who makes a will] that for such forbearance he would give him $5,000. We need not speculate on the effort which may have been required to give up the use of those stimulants. It is sufficient that he restricted his lawful freedom of action within certain prescribed limits upon the faith of his uncle's agreement."

For Critical Analysis: *How might one argue that this contract also benefited the promisor (Story, Sr.)?*

a.   124 N.Y. 538, 27 N.E. 256 (1891).

BARGAINED-FOR EXCHANGE   The second element of consideration is that it must provide the basis for the bargain struck between the contracting parties. The consideration given by the promisor must induce the promisee to incur a legal detriment either now or in the future, and the detriment incurred must induce the promisor to make the promise. This element of bargained-for exchange distinguishes contracts from gifts.

For example, suppose that Jerry says to his son, "In consideration of the fact that you are not as wealthy as your brothers, I will pay you $500." This promise is not enforceable, because Jerry's son has not given any return consideration for the $500 promised.[18] The son (the promisee) incurs no legal detriment; he does not have to promise anything or undertake (or refrain from undertaking) any action to receive the $500. Here, Jerry has simply stated his motive for giving his son a gift. The fact that the word *consideration* is used does not, alone, mean that consideration has been given.

---

18. See *Fink v. Cox*, 18 Johns. 145, 9 Am.Dec. 191 (N.Y. 1820).

> "It is the essence of a consideration, that, by the terms of the agreement, it is given and accepted as the motive or inducement of the promise."
>
> **Oliver Wendell Holmes, Jr., 1841–1935**
> *(Associate justice of the United States Supreme Court, 1902–1932)*

Many of the principles of contract law are common around the globe. There are some differences, however, including differences in what constitutes consideration for contractual purposes. In the United States, as just discussed, consideration is a required element for a valid contract. Promises to make gifts are normally not enforceable, because the donee does not give consideration for the gift. In Germany, in contrast, the exchange of consideration is not required for a contract to be legally binding.

International Perspective

For Critical Analysis: *Do you think that promises to make gifts should be enforceable in the United States? Why or why not?*

Adequacy of Consideration

Legal sufficiency of consideration involves the requirement that consideration be something of value in the eyes of the law. Adequacy of consideration involves "how much" consideration is given. Essentially, adequacy of consideration concerns the fairness of the bargain. On the surface, fairness would appear to be an issue when the values of items exchanged are unequal. In general, however, courts do not question the adequacy of consideration if the consideration is legally sufficient. Under the doctrine of freedom of contract, parties are usually free to bargain as they wish. If people could sue merely because they had entered into an unwise contract, the courts would be overloaded with frivolous suits.

In extreme cases, however, a court of law may look to the amount or value (the adequacy) of the consideration, because apparently inadequate consideration can indicate that fraud, duress, or undue influence was involved or that a gift was made (if a father "sells" a $100,000 house to his daughter for only $1, for example). Additionally, in cases in which the consideration is grossly inadequate, the courts may declare the contract unenforceable on the ground that it is *unconscionable*[19]—that is, generally speaking, it is so one sided under the circumstances as to be overly unfair. (Unconscionability is discussed further in Chapter 10.)

BE AWARE A consumer's signature on a contract does not always guarantee that the contract will be enforced. Ultimately, the terms must be fair.

---

19. Pronounced un-*kon*-shun-uh-bul.

In the United States, as just mentioned, the courts rarely inquire into the adequacy of the consideration given for contracts. Generally, only contracts that are so extremely one sided as to "shock the conscience" of the court have been found to be unconscionable—and thus unenforceable. In some countries, however, such as India, the courts look to the adequacy of consideration when evaluating whether the parties'

International Perspective

(Continued)

International Perspective—Continued

assent to a contract was truly genuine and therefore whether the contract should be enforced.

For Critical Analysis: *Should U.S. courts, in determining whether a contract should be enforced, routinely evaluate how much consideration was given for the contract by each party? If they did, how would such actions affect the doctrine of free-*

Contracts That Lack Consideration

Sometimes, one of the parties (or both parties) to a contract may think that they have exchanged consideration when in fact they have not. Here we look at some situations in which the parties' promises or actions do not qualify as contractual consideration.

PREEXISTING DUTY   Under most circumstances, a promise to do what one already has a legal duty to do does not constitute legally sufficient consideration, because no legal detriment is incurred.[20] The preexisting legal duty may be imposed by law or may arise out of a previous contract. A sheriff, for example, cannot collect a reward for information leading to the capture of a criminal if the sheriff already has a legal duty to capture the criminal. Likewise, if a party is already bound by contract to perform a certain duty, that duty cannot serve as consideration for a second contract.

For example, suppose that Bauman-Bache, Inc., begins construction on a seven-story office building and after three months demands an extra $75,000 on its contract. If the extra $75,000 is not paid, it will stop working. The owner of the land, having no one else to complete construction, agrees to pay the extra $75,000. The agreement is not enforceable, because it is not supported by legally sufficient consideration; Bauman-Bache had a preexisting contractual duty to complete the building.

Unforeseen Difficulties   The rule regarding preexisting duty is meant to prevent extortion and the so-called holdup game. What happens, though, when an honest contractor, who has contracted with a landowner to build a house, runs into extraordinary difficulties that were totally unforeseen at the time the contract was formed? In the interests of fairness and equity, the courts sometimes allow exceptions to the preexisting duty rule. In the example just mentioned, if the landowner agrees to pay extra compensation to the contractor for overcoming the unforeseen difficulties, the court may refrain from applying the preexisting duty rule and enforce the agreement. When the "unforeseen difficulties" that give rise to a contract modification are the types of risks ordinarily assumed in business, however, the courts will usually assert the preexisting duty rule.[21]

Rescission and New Contract   The law recognizes that two parties can mutually agree to rescind their contract, at least to the extent that it is executory (still to be carried out). **Rescission**[22] is defined as the unmaking of a contract so as to return the parties to the positions they occupied before the contract was made. When rescission and the making of a new contract take place at the same time, the courts frequently are given a choice of applying the preexisting duty rule or allowing rescission and letting the new contract stand.

RESCISSION
A remedy whereby a contract is canceled and the parties are returned to the positions they occupied before the contract was made; may be effected through the mutual consent of the parties, by their conduct, or by court decree.

---

20.   See *Foakes v. Beer*, 9 App.Cas. 605 (1884).
21.   Note that under the UCC, any agreement modifying a contract within Article 2 on Sales needs no consideration to be binding. See UCC 2–209(1).
22.   Pronounced reh-*sih*-zhen.

PAST CONSIDERATION Promises made in return for actions or events that have already taken place are unenforceable. These promises lack consideration in that the element of bargained-for exchange is missing. In short, you can bargain for something to take place now or in the future but not for something that has already taken place. Therefore, **past consideration** is no consideration.

Suppose, for example, that Elsie, a real estate agent, does her friend Judy a favor by selling Judy's house and not charging any commission. Later, Judy says to Elsie, "In return for your generous act, I will pay you $3,000." This promise is made in return for past consideration and is thus unenforceable; in effect, Judy is stating her intention to give Elsie a gift.

ILLUSORY PROMISES If the terms of the contract express such uncertainty of performance that the promisor has not definitely promised to do anything, the promise is said to be *illusory*—without consideration and unenforceable. For example, suppose that the president of Tuscan Corporation says to his employees, "All of you have worked hard, and if profits continue to remain high, a 10 percent bonus at the end of the year will be given—if management thinks it is warranted." This is an *illusory promise*, or no promise at all, because performance depends solely on the discretion of the president (the management). There is no bargained-for consideration. The statement declares merely that management may or may not do something in the future.

Option-to-cancel clauses in contracts for specified time periods sometimes present problems in regard to consideration. For example, suppose that Abe contracts to hire Chris for one year at $5,000 per month, reserving the right to cancel the contract at any time. On close examination of these words, you can see that Abe has not actually agreed to hire Chris, as Abe could cancel without liability before Chris started performance. Abe has not given up the opportunity of hiring someone else. This contract is therefore illusory. Now suppose that Abe contracts to hire Chris for a one-year period at $5,000 per month, reserving the right to cancel the contract at any time after Chris has begun performance by giving Chris thirty days' notice. Abe, by saying that he will give Chris thirty days' notice, is relinquishing the opportunity (legal right) to hire someone else instead of Chris for a thirty-day period. If Chris works for one month, at the end of which Abe gives him thirty days' notice, Chris has a valid and enforceable contractual claim for $10,000 in salary.

Settlement of Claims

Businesspersons or others can settle legal claims in several ways. It is important to understand the nature of consideration given in these kinds of settlement agreements, or contracts. A common means of settling a claim is through an *accord and satisfaction*, in which a debtor offers to pay a lesser amount than the creditor purports to be owed. Two other methods that are commonly used to settle claims are the release and the covenant not to sue.

ACCORD AND SATISFACTION The concept of **accord and satisfaction** deals with a debtor's offer of payment and a creditor's acceptance of a lesser amount than the creditor originally purported to be owed. The *accord* is defined as the agreement under which one of the parties undertakes to give or perform, and the other to accept, in satisfaction of a claim, something other than that which was originally agreed on. *Satisfaction* takes place when the accord is executed. Accord and satisfaction deal with an attempt by the obligor to extinguish an obligation. A basic rule is that there can be no satisfaction unless there is first an accord.

For accord and satisfaction to occur, the amount of the debt *must be in dispute*. If a debt is *liquidated*, accord and satisfaction cannot take place. A liquidated debt is one whose amount has been ascertained, fixed, agreed on, settled, or exactly determined. For example, if Baker signs an installment loan contract with her banker in which she

PAST CONSIDERATION
An act done before the contract is made, which ordinarily, by itself, cannot be consideration for a later promise to pay for the act.

ACCORD AND SATISFACTION
An agreement for payment (or other performance) between two parties, one of whom has a right of action against the other. After the payment has been accepted or other performance has been made, the "accord and satisfaction" is complete and the obligation is discharged.

agrees to pay a specified rate of interest on a specified sum of borrowed money at monthly intervals for two years, that is a liquidated debt. The amount owing is precisely known to both of the parties, and reasonable persons will not differ over the amount owed. Suppose that Baker misses her last two payments on the loan and the creditor demands that she pay the overdue debt. Baker makes a partial payment and states that she believes that is all that she should have to pay and that, if the creditor accepts the payment, the debt will be satisfied, or discharged. In the majority of states, acceptance of a lesser sum than the entire amount of a liquidated debt is not satisfaction, and the balance of the debt is still legally owed. The rationale for this rule is that no consideration is given by the debtor to satisfy the obligation of paying the balance to the creditor—because the debtor has a preexisting legal obligation to pay the entire debt.

An *unliquidated debt* is the opposite of a liquidated debt. Here, reasonable persons may differ over the amount owed. It is not settled, fixed, agreed on, ascertained, or determined. In these circumstances, acceptance of payment of the lesser sum can operate as a satisfaction, or discharge, or the debt. For example, suppose that Devereaux goes to the dentist's office. The dentist tells him that he needs three special types of gold inlays. The price is not discussed, and there is no standard fee for this type of work. Devereaux leaves the office. At the end of the month, the dentist sends him a bill for $3,000. Devereaux, believing that this amount is grossly out of proportion with what a reasonable person would believe to be the debt owed, sends a check for $2,000. On the back of the check he writes "payment in full for three gold inlays." The dentist cashes the check. Because we are dealing with an unliquidated debt—the amount has not been agreed on—payment accepted by the dentist normally will eradicate the debt. One argument to support this rule is that the parties give up a legal right to contest the amount in dispute, and thus consideration is given.

RELEASE
A contract in which one party forfeits the right to pursue a legal claim against the other party.

RELEASE A **release** is a contract in which one party forfeits the right to pursue a legal claim against the other party. For example, suppose that you are involved in an automobile accident caused by Raoul's negligence. Raoul offers to give you $1,000 if you will release him from further liability resulting from the accident. You believe that this amount will cover your damages, so you agree to the release. Later you discover that it will cost $1,200 to repair your car.

Can you collect the balance from Raoul? The answer is normally no; you are limited to the $1,000 in the release. Why? Because a valid contract existed. You and Raoul both assented to the bargain (hence, agreement existed), and sufficient consideration was present. Your consideration for the contract was the legal detriment you suffered (by releasing Raoul from liability, you forfeited your right to sue to recover damages, should they be more than $1,000). This legal detriment was induced by Raoul's promise to give you the $1,000. Raoul's promise was, in turn, induced by your promise not to pursue your legal right to sue him for damages.

Releases will generally be binding if they are (1) given in good faith, (2) stated in a signed writing (required by many states), and (3) accompanied by consideration.[23] Clearly, persons are better off if they know the extent of their injuries or damages before signing releases.

COVENANT NOT TO SUE
An agreement to substitute a contractual obligation for some other type of legal action based on a valid claim.

COVENANT NOT TO SUE A **covenant not to sue,** unlike a release, does not always bar further recovery. The parties simply substitute a contractual obligation for some other type of legal action based on a valid claim. Suppose (following the earlier example) that you agree with Raoul not to sue for damages in a tort action if he will pay for the damage to your car. If Raoul fails to pay, you can bring an action for breach of contract.

---

23.   Under the UCC, a written, signed waiver or renunciation by an aggrieved party discharges any further liability for a breach, even without consideration. See UCC 1–107.

"You should have signed a contract. A high-five just isn't binding."

Promises Enforceable without Consideration—Promissory Estoppel

Sometimes individuals rely on promises, and such reliance may form a basis for contract rights and duties. Under the doctrine of **promissory estoppel** (also called *detrimental reliance*), a person who has reasonably relied on the promise of another can often hope to obtain some measure of recovery. For the doctrine of promissory estoppel to be applied, the following elements are required:

1. There must be a clear and definite promise.
2. The promisee must justifiably rely on the promise.
3. The reliance normally must be of a substantial and definite character.
4. Justice will be better served by the enforcement of the promise.

Consider some examples. Your uncle tells you, "I'll pay you $150 a week so you won't have to work anymore." You quit your job, but your uncle refuses to pay you. Under the doctrine of promissory estoppel, you may be able to enforce such a promise.[24] Now your uncle makes a promise to give you $10,000 with which to buy a car. If you buy the car and he does not pay you, you may once again be able to enforce the promise under this doctrine. When the doctrine of promissory estoppel is applied, the promisor (the offeror) is **estopped** (barred, or impeded) from revoking the promise.

"To break an oral agreement which is not legally binding is morally wrong."

The Talmud,
Bava Metzi'a

PROMISSORY ESTOPPEL
A doctrine that applies when a promisor makes a clear and definite promise on which the promisee justifiably relies; such a promise is binding if justice will be better served by the enforcement of the promise.

ESTOPPED
Barred, impeded, or precluded.

---

24. *Ricketts v. Scothorn*, 57 Neb. 51, 77 N.W. 365 (1898).

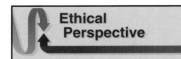

Ethical Perspective

Ethical standards certainly underlie the doctrine of promissory estoppel, under which a person who has reasonably relied on the promise of another can often obtain some measure of recovery. Essentially, promissory estoppel allows a variety of promises to be enforced despite the fact that they lack what is formally regarded as consideration.

In the business world, a person who relies to his or her detriment on the promise of another can often recover damages, particularly when justice is better served by estopping the other party from denying that a contractual promise was made. An oral promise made by an insurance agent to a business owner, for example, may be binding if the owner relies on that promise to his or her detriment. Employees who rely to their detriment on an employer's promise may be able to recover under the doctrine of promissory estoppel. A contractor who, when bidding for a job, relies on a subcontractor's promise to perform certain construction work at a certain price may be able to recover any damages sustained by the subcontractor's failure to perform on the basis of promissory estoppel. These are but a few examples of the many ways in which the courts, in the interests of fairness and justice, have estopped a promisor from denying that a contract existed.

For Critical Analysis: *Can you think of any other contract doctrine under which, to ensure justice, courts will allow a party to recover based on detrimental reliance?*

Application

Law and the Offeror— Controlling the Terms of the Offer*

 The courts normally attempt to "save" contracts whenever possible, but sometimes it is simply impossible to do so. Two common reasons why contracts fail is because (1) the terms of the offer were too unclear or indefinite to constitute a binding contract on the offer's acceptance and (2) the acceptance was not timely. If you are an offeror, you can control both of these factors: you can determine what the terms of the future contract will be, as well as the time and mode of acceptance.

Include Clear and Definite Terms
If a contract's terms are too unclear or indefinite, the contract will fail. Unless a court can ascertain what exactly the rights and duties of the parties are under a particular contract, the court cannot enforce those rights and duties. Therefore, as an offeror, make sure that the terms of your offer are sufficiently definite to constitute a binding contract if the offer is accepted. A term such as

*This *Application* is not meant to substitute for the services of an attorney who is licensed to practice law in your state.

"Price to be determined later" may allow the offeree, after acceptance, to claim that a contract was never formed, because the price term was too indefinite.

Another reason why an offeror, in drafting the offer, should make sure that the offer's terms are clear and definite is that if a contract results, any ambiguous provision may be interpreted against the party that drafted the contract (see Chapter 8).

Specify the Time and Mode of Acceptance
Problems concerning contract formation also arise when it is unclear whether an acceptance is effective. To avoid such problems, you should take some precautions when phrasing the offer. Whether your offer is made via fax, express delivery, or mail, you can specify that the offer must be accepted (or even that the acceptance must be received by you) by a certain time, and if it is not, the offer will terminate. Similarly, you can specify the mode of acceptance. If you make an offer and want the acceptance to be faxed to you, for example, make sure that you clearly indicate that the acceptance must be faxed to you at a given fax number by a specific time or it will not be effective.

 Checklist for the Offeror

1. Make sure that the terms of the offer are sufficiently clear and definite to allow both the parties and a

Application—Continued

court to determine the specific rights and obligations of the parties. Otherwise, the contract may
fail for indefiniteness.

2. Specify in the offer the date on which the offer will
terminate and the authorized mode of accep-
tance. For example, you can indicate that an
acceptance, to be effective, must be faxed to you
at a specific fax number by a specific time or date.

▌Key Terms

▌Chapter Summary: Agreement and Consideration

AGREEMENT	
Requirements of the Offer *(See pages 227–233.)*	1. *Intent*—There must be a serious, objective intention by the offeror to become bound by the offer. Nonoffer situations include (a) expressions of opinion; (b) statements of intention; (c) preliminary negotiations; (d) generally, advertisements, catalogues, and circulars; (e) solicitations for bids made by an auctioneer; and (f) agreements to agree in the future. 2. *Definiteness*—The terms of the offer must be sufficiently definite to be ascertainable by the parties or by a court. 3. *Communication*—The offer must be communicated to the offeree.

Termination of the Offer *(See pages 234–236.)*	1. *By action of the parties—*
	   a. Revocation—Unless the offer is irrevocable, it can be revoked at any time before acceptance without liability. Revocation is not effective until received by the offeree or the offeree's agent. Some offers, such as the merchant's firm offer and option contracts, are irrevocable.
	   b. Rejection—Accomplished by words or actions that demonstrate a clear intent not to accept the offer; not effective until received by the offeror or the offeror's agent.
	   c. Counteroffer—A rejection of the original offer and the making of a new offer.
	
	 2. *By operation of law—*
	   a. Lapse of time—The offer terminates (a) at the end of the time period specified in the offer or (b) if no time period is stated in the offer, at the end of a reasonable time period.
	   b. Destruction of the specific subject matter of the offer—Automatically terminates the offer.
	   c. Death or incompetence—Terminates the offer unless the offer is irrevocable.
	   d. Illegality—Supervening illegality terminates the offer.

Acceptance *(See pages 236–241.)*	1. Can be made only by the offeree or the offeree's agent.
	
	 2. Must be unequivocal. Under the common law (mirror image rule), if new terms or conditions are added to the acceptance, it will be considered a counteroffer.
	
	 3. Acceptance of a unilateral offer is effective upon full performance of the requested act. Generally, no communication is necessary.
	
	 4. Acceptance of a bilateral offer can be communicated by the offeree by any authorized mode of communication and is effective upon dispatch. Unless the mode of communication is expressly specified by the offeror, the following methods are impliedly authorized:
	   a. The same mode used by the offeror (or a faster mode) or, in the sale of goods, any reasonable medium.
	   b. Mail, when the two parties are at a distance.
	
	 (Continued)

▌ Chapter Summary: Agreement and Consideration—Continued

CONSIDERATION	
Elements of Consideration (*See pages 241–243.*)	Consideration is broken down into two parts: (1) something of *legally sufficient value* must be given in exchange for the promise, and (2) there must be a *bargained-for* exchange. To be legally sufficient, consideration must involve a legal detriment to the promisee, a legal benefit to the promisor, or both. One incurs a legal detriment by doing (or refraining from doing) something that one had no prior legal duty to do (or to refrain from doing).
Adequacy of Consideration (*See pages 243–244.*)	Adequacy of consideration relates to "how much" consideration is given and whether a fair bargain was reached. Courts will inquire into the adequacy of consideration (if the consideration is legally sufficient) only when fraud, undue influence, duress, a gift, or unconscionability may be involved.
Contracts That Lack Consideration (*See pages 244–245.*)	Consideration is lacking in the following situations: 1. *Preexisting duty*—Consideration is not legally sufficient if one is either by law or by contract under a *preexisting duty* to perform the action being offered as consideration for a new contract. 2. *Past consideration*—Actions or events that have already taken place do not constitute legally sufficient consideration. 3. *Illusory promises*—When the nature or extent of performance is too uncertain, the promise is rendered illusory (without consideration and unenforceable).
Settlement of Claims (*See pages 245–246.*)	1. *Accord and satisfaction*—An *accord* is an agreement in which a debtor offers to pay a lesser amount than the creditor purports to be owed. *Satisfaction* takes place when the accord is executed. 2. *Release*—An agreement by which, for consideration, a party is barred from further recovery beyond the terms specified in the release. 3. *Covenant not to sue*—An agreement not to sue on a present, valid claim.
Promises Enforceable without Consideration— Promissory Estoppel	The equitable doctrine of promissory estoppel applies when a promisor reasonably expects a promise to induce definite and substantial action or forbearance by the promisee, and the promisee does act in reliance on the promise. Such a promise is binding if injustice can be avoided only by enforcement of the promise. Also known as the doctrine of detrimental reliance.

▌ For Review

1. What elements are necessary for an effective offer? What are some examples of nonoffers?
2. In what circumstances will an offer be irrevocable?
3. What elements are necessary for an effective acceptance?

4. What is consideration? What is required for consideration to be legally sufficient?
5. In what circumstances might a promise be enforced despite a lack of what is normally thought of as consideration?

▌ Questions and Case Problems

9–1. Offer. Chernek, operating a sole proprietorship, has a large piece of used farm equipment for sale. He offers to sell the equipment to Bollow for $10,000. Discuss the legal effects of the following events on the offer.

(a) Chernek dies prior to Bollow's acceptance, and at the time she accepts, Bollow is unaware of Chernek's death.

(b) The night before Bollow accepts, fire destroys the equipment.

(c) Bollow pays $100 for a thirty-day option to purchase the equipment. During this period Chernek dies, and

later Bollow accepts the offer, knowing of Chernek's death.

(d) Bollow pays $100 for a thirty-day option to purchase the equipment. During this period Bollow dies, and Bollow's estate accepts Chernek's offer within the stipulated time period.

9–2. Offers versus Nonoffers. On June 1, Jason placed an ad in a local newspaper, to be run on the following Sunday, June 5, offering a reward of $100 to anyone who found his wallet. When his wallet had not been returned by June 12, he purchased another wallet and took steps to obtain duplicates of his driver's license, credit cards, and other items that he had lost. On June 15, Sharith, who had seen Jason's ad in the paper, found Jason's wallet, returned it to Jason, and asked for the $100. Is Jason obligated to pay Sharith the $100? Why or why not?

9–3. Offer and Acceptance. Carrie offered to sell a set of legal encyclopedias to Antonio for $300. Antonio said that he would think about her offer and let her know his decision the next day. Norvel, who had overheard the conversation between Carrie and Antonio, said to Carrie, "I accept your offer" and gave her $300. Carrie gave Norvel the books. The next day, Antonio, who had no idea that Carrie had already sold the books to Norvel, told Carrie that he accepted her offer. Has Carrie breached a valid contract with Antonio? Explain.

9–4. Consideration. Ben hired Lewis to drive his racing car in a race. Tuan, a friend of Lewis, promised to pay Lewis $3,000 if he won the race. Lewis won the race, but Tuan refused to pay the $3,000. Tuan contended that no legally binding contract had been formed, because he had received no consideration from Lewis for his promise to pay the $3,000. Lewis sued Tuan for breach of contract, arguing that winning the race was the consideration given in exchange for Tuan's promise to pay the $3,000. What rule of law discussed in this chapter supports Tuan's claim? Explain.

9–5. Acceptance. On Saturday, Arthur mailed Tanya an offer to sell his car to her for $2,000. On Monday, having changed his mind and not having heard from Tanya, Arthur sent her a letter revoking his offer. On Wednesday, before she had received Arthur's letter of revocation, Tanya mailed a letter of acceptance to Arthur. When Tanya demanded that Arthur sell his car to her as promised, Arthur claimed that no contract existed because he had revoked his offer prior to Tanya's acceptance. Is Arthur correct? Explain.

9–6. Promissory Estoppel. Red Owl Stores, Inc., induced the Hoffmans to give up their current business and run a Red Owl franchise. Although no contract was ever signed, the Hoffmans incurred numerous expenses in reliance upon Red Owl's representations. When the deal ultimately fell through because of Red Owl's failure to keep its promise concerning the operation of the franchise agency store, the Hoffmans brought suit to recover their losses under the doctrine of promissory estoppel. What is this doctrine, and what elements must exist before it will be applied by the court? Will the Hoffmans likely succeed in their suit? Discuss fully. [*Hoffman v. Red Owl Stores, Inc.*, 26 Wis.2d 683, 133 N.W.2d 267 (1965)]

9–7. Offers versus Nonoffers. The Olivers were planning to sell some of their ranch land and mentioned this fact to Southworth, a neighbor. Southworth expressed interest in purchasing the property and later notified the Olivers that he had the money available to buy it. The Olivers told Southworth they would let him know shortly about the details concerning the sale. The Olivers later sent a letter to Southworth—and (unknown to Southworth) to several other neighbors—giving information about the sale, including the price, the location of the property, and the amount of acreage involved. When Southworth received the letter, he sent a letter to the Olivers "accepting" their offer. The Olivers stated that the information letter had not been intended as an "offer" but merely as a start-

ing point for negotiations. Southworth brought suit against the Olivers to enforce the "contract." Did a contract exist? Why or why not? Explain fully. [*Southworth v. Oliver*, 284 Or. 361, 587 P.2d 994 (1978)]

9–8. Consideration. Martino was a police officer in Atlantic City. Gray, who lost a significant amount of her jewelry during a burglary of her home, offered a reward for the recovery of the property. Incident to his job, Martino possessed certain knowledge concerning the theft of Gray's jewelry. When Martino informed Gray of his knowledge of the theft, Gray offered Martino $500 to help her recover her jewelry. As a result of Martino's police work, the jewelry was recovered and returned to Gray. Gray, however, did not pay Martino the $500. Martino sued Gray for the reward he claimed she promised him. Was there a valid contract between Gray and Martino? [*Gray v. Martino*, 91 N.J.L. 462, 103 A. 24 (1918)]

9–9. Offer and Acceptance. James sent invitations to a number of potential buyers to submit bids for some timber he wanted to sell. Two bids were received as a result, the highest one submitted by Eames. James changed his mind about selling the timber and did not accept Eames's bid. Eames claimed that a contract for sale existed and sued James for breach. Did a contract exist? Explain. [*Eames v. James*, 452 So.2d 384 (La.App.3d 1984)]

9–10. Acceptance. On September 5, 1987, Ralph Defeo and others offered to purchase a farm that Amfarms Associates had listed for sale in 1986. At one point during the subsequent negotiations, Amfarms made a counteroffer to Defeo and the others, stating that the offer would be valid only until 5 P.M. on October 17. Amfarms's attorney sent the offer to Defeo's attorney via Federal Express. On October 16, Defeo and the others sent their acceptance by certified mail to Amfarms's real estate broker, and Amfarms received it on October 19. On October 16, however, Amfarms had accepted an offer from another party. Defeo and the others sued Amfarms, claiming that their acceptance on October 16 was effective on the day that it was sent. How should the court decide? Discuss fully. [*Defeo v. Amfarms Associates*, 161 A.D.2d 904, 557 N.Y.S.2d 469 (1990)]

9–11. Consideration. In 1972, Thomas L. Weinsaft signed a written agreement with his son, Nicholas L. Weinsaft. Thomas agreed that during his lifetime he would not transfer any interest in his 765 shares of stock of Crane Manufacturing Co. unless he first gave Nicholas an opportunity to purchase it, and upon Thomas's death, Nicholas would have the "option and right to purchase all of the stock" from the estate. The agreement stated that it was entered into "In consideration of $10.00 and other good and valuable consideration, including the inducement of Second Party [Nicholas] to remain the chief executive officer of said company." Thomas died in 1980. Nicholas gave notice that he intended to buy the stock, but one of the beneficiaries under Thomas's will objected, contending that there was no consideration for Thomas's promises. Nicholas sued to force the estate to transfer the shares. Discuss whether this contract is supported by consideration. [*In re Estate of Weinsaft*, 647 S.W.2d 179 (Mo.App. 1983)]

9–12. Offer and Acceptance. Cora Payne was involved in an automobile accident with Don Chappell, an employee of E & B Carpet Cleaning, Inc. E & B's insurance company offered Payne $18,500 to settle her claim against E & B. Payne did not accept the offer at that time but instead filed suit against E & B and its insurance company (the defendants). Later Payne offered to settle the case for $50,000, but the defendants refused her offer. Ultimately, Payne told the defendants that she would accept the insurance company's original settlement offer of $18,500, but the insurance company stated that the offer was no longer open for acceptance. When Payne sought to compel the defendants to perform the original settlement offer, the defendants contended that Payne's filing of her lawsuit terminated the insurance company's earlier settlement offer. Will the court agree with the defendants? Discuss. [*Payne v. E & B Carpet Cleaning, Inc.*, 896 S.W.2d 650 (Mo.App. 1995)]

 A QUESTION OF ETHICS
AND SOCIAL RESPONSIBILITY

9–13. *Roy Suess worked as a salesperson for Curtis 1000, Inc., which sells customized stationery, business forms, and printing services to business firms. In 1993, after having worked for Curtis for twenty-four years, Suess resigned and went to work for a competitor of Curtis's. When Suess proceeded to solicit current and recent customers of Curtis's, Curtis sued Suess, claiming that Suess's activities violated a covenant not to compete that Suess had signed while a Curtis employee. Suess had signed several covenants over the years, the last one dating to eight years prior to his termination. The final covenant provided that Suess, for a two-year period following the termination of his* employment with Curtis, would not solicit customers whom he had solicited on Curtis's behalf during the two years prior to his termination and to whom Curtis had made at least one sale during that period. In view of these facts, consider the following questions. [Curtis 1000, Inc. v. Suess, 24 F.3d 941 (7th Cir. 1994)]

1. Suess argued that the covenant not to compete was not valid because Curtis had given no consideration (such as extra pay or a guarantee of permanent employment) for Suess's promise not to compete. Suess, though, had to sign the covenant if he wanted to remain employed by Curtis. Did Curtis's retention of Suess as an employee for eight years following the signing of the final covenant constitute consideration? If you were the judge, how would you decide this issue?

2. Suppose that a company has an employee sign a covenant not to compete and then fires the employee the next day. Would that one day's continued employment constitute consideration? Should it? (Remember, courts rarely inquire into the adequacy of consideration.)

FOR CRITICAL ANALYSIS

9–14. *Discuss the implications of new communications technology for the communication requirements relating to offers and acceptances.*

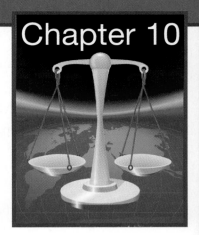

Capacity and Legality

"Liberty of contract is not an absolute concept. It is relative to many conditions of time and place and circumstance."

Benjamin Cardozo, 1870–1938
(Associate justice of the United States Supreme Court, 1932–1938)

CHAPTER OBJECTIVES

After reading this chapter, you should be able to:

1. Explain the contractual rights and obligations of minors.
2. Indicate how intoxication affects contractual liability.
3. Outline the effects of mental incompetency on contractual liability.
4. Give examples of some contracts that are contrary to state or federal statutes.
5. Discuss why certain types of contracts and clauses are contrary to public policy.

Courts generally want contracts to be enforceable, and much of the law is made to aid in the enforceability of contracts. Nonetheless, as indicated in the opening quotation, "liberty of contract" is not absolute. In other words, not all people can make legally binding contracts at all times. Contracts entered into by persons lacking the capacity to do so may be unenforceable. Similarly, contracts calling for the performance of an illegal act are illegal and thus void—they are not contracts at all. In this chapter, we examine contractual capacity and some aspects of illegal bargains.

▮ Contractual Capacity

Although the parties to a contract must assume certain risks, the law indicates that neither party should be allowed to benefit from the other party's lack of **contractual capacity**—the legal ability to enter into a contractual relationship. Courts generally presume the existence of contractual capacity, but there are some situations in which capacity is lacking or may be questionable. A person *adjudged by a court* to be mentally incompetent, for example, cannot form a legally binding contract with another party. In other situations, a party may have the capacity to enter into a valid contract

CONTRACTUAL CAPACITY
The threshold mental capacity required by the law for a party who enters into a contract to be bound by that contract.

253

but also have the right to avoid liability under it. For example, minors usually are not legally bound by contracts. In this section, we look at the effect of youth, intoxication, and mental incompetence on contractual capacity.

Minors

Today, in virtually all states, the *age of majority* (when a person is no longer a minor) for contractual purposes is eighteen years for both sexes.[1] In addition, some states provide for the termination of minority upon marriage. Subject to certain exceptions, the contracts entered into by a minor are voidable at the option of that minor.

The general rule is that a minor can enter into any contract an adult can, provided that the contract is not one prohibited by law for minors (for example, the sale of alcoholic beverages). Although minors have the right to avoid their contracts, there are exceptions (to be discussed later).

DISAFFIRMANCE
The legal avoidance, or setting aside, of a contractual obligation.

DISAFFIRMANCE   For a minor to exercise the option to avoid a contract, he or she need only manifest an intention not to be bound by it. The minor "avoids" the contract by disaffirming it. The technical definition of **disaffirmance** is the legal avoidance, or setting aside, of a contractual obligation. Words or conduct may serve to express this intent. The contract can ordinarily be disaffirmed at any time during minority or for a reasonable time after the minor comes of age. In some states, however, when there is a contract for the sale of land by a minor, the minor cannot disaffirm the contract until he or she reaches the age of majority. When a minor disaffirms a contract, all property that he or she has transferred to the adult as consideration can be recovered, even if it is then in the possession of a third party.[2]

Disaffirmance must be timely. If, for example, an individual wishes to disaffirm an executed contract made as a minor but fails to do so until two years after he or she has reached the age of majority, a court will likely hold that the contract has been ratified (see the discussion of ratification below). Additionally, if a minor disaffirms a contract, he or she must disaffirm the *entire* contract. The minor cannot decide to keep part of the goods contracted for and return the remainder.

Note that an adult who enters into a contract with a minor cannot avoid his or her contractual duties on the ground that the minor can do so. Unless the minor exercises the option to disaffirm the contract (to be discussed shortly), the adult party normally is bound by it.

---

1.   The age of majority may still be twenty-one for other purposes, such as the purchase and consumption of alcohol. The word *infant* is usually used synonymously with the word *minor*.
2.   The Uniform Commercial Code, in Section 2–403(1), allows an exception if the third party is a "good faith purchaser for value." See Chapter 15.

International Perspective

Like courts in the United States, courts in Great Britain may permit minors' contracts to be avoided on the ground that minors lack contractual capacity. Great Britain, however, has no single, fixed age limit for lack of capacity. British courts deal with contracts on a case-by-case basis. In deciding whether a minor can avoid a particular contract, a British court will consider a number of factors, including the specific circumstances of the case, the nature of the item contracted for, and the psychological maturity of the minor.

For Critical Analysis: *What benefit is there to the U.S. system, which lacks flexibility with respect to the contractual capacity of minors?*

When a minor disaffirms a contract, such as a contract to buy a computer, most states require the minor to return whatever consideration he or she received, if it is within his or her control. Why do some states require more?

Minor's Obligations on Disaffirmance   All state laws permit minors to disaffirm contracts (with certain exceptions—to be discussed shortly), including executed contracts. States differ, however, on the extent of a minor's obligations on disaffirmance. Courts in a majority of states hold that the minor need only return the goods (or other consideration) subject to the contract, provided the goods are in the minor's possession or control. For example, suppose that Jim Garrison, a seventeen-year-old, purchases a computer from Radio Shack. While transporting the computer to his home, Garrison, through no fault of his own, is involved in a car accident. As a result of the accident, the plastic casing of the computer is broken. The next day, he returns the computer to Radio Shack and disaffirms the contract. Under the majority view, this return fulfills Garrison's duty even though the computer is now damaged. Garrison is entitled to get a refund of the purchase price (if paid in cash) or to be relieved of any further obligations under an agreement to purchase the computer on credit.

A growing number of states, either by statute or by court decision, place an additional duty on the minor—the duty to restore the adult party to the position he or she held before the contract was made. In the example just given, Garrison would be required not only to return the computer but also to pay Radio Shack for damages to the computer.

In the following case, a minor's father brought an action on behalf of his son to disaffirm the minor's purchase of an automobile and to recover the money paid for the car from a seller who knew that the purchaser was a minor when the contract was made.

CASE 10.1

QUALITY MOTORS, INC. v. HAYS

Supreme Court of Arkansas, 1949.
216 Ark. 264,
225 S.W.2d 326.

HISTORICAL AND ECONOMIC SETTING   *In 1949, a business recession produced a decline in the cost of living. United Automobile Workers at General Motors plants accepted a slight wage cut, after they had obtained a wage increase the year before. Unemployment jumped more than two percentage points, while prices of shares*

(Continued)

Case 10.1—Continued

on the stock market fell more than 10 percent. The cost of housing and health care rose, while other consumer prices fell. A gallon of gasoline cost 21 cents. A new Cadillac cost $5,000. The average steelworker, after taxes, made $3,000 a year, and the average high school teacher made $4,700 a year. The typical car salesperson made, after taxes, $8,000 annually.

FACTS Sixteen-year-old Johnny Hays went to Quality Motors, Inc., to purchase a car. The salesperson refused to sell the car unless the purchase was made by an adult, so Johnny left and later returned with a young man of twenty-three. Hays paid for the car, and a bill of sale was made out to the twenty-three-year-old. The salesperson then drove the two boys into town to a notary public, the young man transferred the title to the car to Johnny, and the salesperson delivered the car to Johnny. Johnny's father attempted to return the car to Quality Motors for a full refund, but Quality Motors refused it. Subsequently, Johnny wrecked the car in an accident. Johnny, through his father, brought suit in an Arkansas state court to disaffirm the contract and recover the purchase price. The trial court ordered the purchase price to be refunded to Hays on his return of the car to Quality Motors. Quality Motors appealed.

ISSUE Can Johnny disaffirm this contract even though it was nominally (in name only) made by an adult?

DECISION Yes. The Supreme Court of Arkansas held that Johnny could disaffirm the contract and return the car. He was not held liable for any damages.

REASON The court reasoned that because the salesperson knew that Johnny was a minor, aided Johnny in obtaining the car by selling it to an adult, and assisted in the transfer of title to Johnny, the sale was essentially made to Johnny. When goods—*other than necessaries* (food, clothing, and so on, as will be discussed shortly)—are sold to a minor, the minor can disaffirm the contract of sale. The court quoted the law as follows: "The law is well settled * * * that an infant may disaffirm his contracts, except those made for necessaries, without being required to return the consideration received, except such part as may remain * * * in his hands."

FOR CRITICAL ANALYSIS—Cultural Consideration
What societal values have led to laws governing disaffirmance that weigh so heavily in favor of minors?

NOTE In most circumstances, misrepresentation justifies the cancellation of a contract by the innocent party and can also result in tort liability.

Disaffirmance and Misrepresentation of Age Suppose that a minor tells a seller she is twenty-one years old when she is really seventeen. Ordinarily, the minor can disaffirm the contract even though she has misrepresented her age. Moreover, the minor is not liable in certain jurisdictions for the tort of deceit for such misrepresentation, the rationale being that such a tort judgment might indirectly force the minor to perform the contract.

Many jurisdictions, however, do find circumstances under which a minor can be bound by a contract when the minor has misrepresented his or her age. First, several states have enacted statutes for precisely this purpose. In these states, misrepresentation of age is enough to prohibit disaffirmance. Other statutes prohibit disaffirmance by a minor who has engaged in business as an adult.

Second, some courts refuse to allow minors to disaffirm executed (fully performed) contracts unless they can return the consideration received. The combination of the minors' misrepresentations and their unjust enrichment has persuaded these courts to *estop* (prevent) minors from asserting contractual incapacity.

Third, some courts allow a misrepresenting minor to disaffirm the contract, but they hold the minor liable for damages in tort. Here, the defrauded party may sue the minor for misrepresentation or fraud. A split in authority exists on this point, because some courts, as previously noted, have recognized that allowing a suit in tort is equivalent to the indirect enforcement of the minor's contract.

Liability for Necessaries, Insurance, and Loans A minor who enters into a contract for necessaries may disaffirm the contract but remains liable for the reasonable value of the goods. **Necessaries** are basic needs, such as food, clothing, shelter, and medical services. In some cases, however, courts have not limited necessaries to items required for physical existence but have interpreted the term to include whatever is believed to

NECESSARIES
Necessities required for life, such as food, shelter, clothing, and medical attention; may include whatever is believed to be necessary to maintain a person's standard of living or financial and social status.

be necessary to maintain a person's standard of living or financial and social status. Thus, what will be considered a necessary for one person may be a luxury for another.

Traditionally, insurance has not been viewed as a necessary, so minors can ordinarily disaffirm their insurance contracts and recover all premiums paid. Some jurisdictions, however, prohibit the right to disaffirm insurance contracts—for example, when minors contract for life insurance on their own lives. Financial loans are seldom considered to be necessaries, even if the minor spends the money borrowed on necessaries. If, however, a lender makes a loan to a minor for the express purpose of enabling the minor to purchase necessaries, and the lender personally makes sure the money is so spent, the minor normally is obligated to repay the loan.

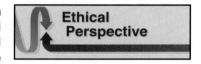

Ethical Perspective

A minor's legal duty to pay for the reasonable value of necessaries does not arise from the contract itself. Rather, it is imposed by law under the equitable theory of quasi contract. One approach is that the minor should not be unjustly enriched and should therefore be liable for purchases that fulfill basic needs. This theory expresses the basic principle that laws protecting minors should act as a shield to protect minors against the sometimes harsh consequences of contractual obligations—and not as a sword by which minors can be unjustly enriched at the expense of adult parties to contracts.

Another approach focuses on the economic ramifications of a contrary rule: if minors could not be held liable for necessaries, merchants would be reluctant to enter into contracts for such items. The result would be that minors would find it more difficult to meet their basic needs.

For Critical Analysis: *What arguments might a court use in order to include as necessaries whatever is believed to be necessary to maintain a person's financial and social status, and not just items necessary for physical existence?*

RATIFICATION   In contract law, **ratification** is the act of accepting and giving legal force to an obligation that previously was not enforceable. A minor who has reached the age of majority can ratify a contract expressly or impliedly.

Express ratification occurs when the minor expressly states, orally or in writing, that he or she intends to be bound by the contract. Implied ratification exists when the conduct of the minor is inconsistent with disaffirmance (as when the minor enjoys the benefits of the contract) or when the minor fails to disaffirm an executed (fully performed) contract within a reasonable time after reaching the age of majority. If the contract is still executory (not yet performed or only partially performed), however, failure to disaffirm the contract will not necessarily imply ratification.

Generally, the courts base their determination on whether the minor, after reaching the age of majority, has had ample opportunity to consider the nature of the contractual obligations he or she entered into as a minor and the extent to which the adult party to the contract has performed.

PARENTS' LIABILITY   As a general rule, parents are not liable for the contracts made by minor children acting on their own. This is why businesses ordinarily require parents to cosign any contract made with a minor. The parents then become personally obligated under the contract to perform the conditions of the contract, even if their child avoids liability.

Generally, a minor is held personally liable for the torts he or she commits. Therefore, minors cannot disaffirm their liability for their tortious conduct. The parents of the minor can *also* be held liable under certain circumstances. For example, if the minor commits a tort under the direction of a parent or while performing an act requested by a parent, the injured party can hold the parent liable. In addition, parents

RATIFICATION
The act of accepting and giving legal force to an obligation that previously was not enforceable.

are liable in many states up to a statutory amount for malicious torts committed by a minor child living in their home.

EMANCIPATION   The release of a minor by his or her parents is known as emancipation. **Emancipation** occurs when a child's parent or legal guardian relinquishes the legal right to exercise control over the child. Normally, a minor who leaves home to support himself or herself is considered emancipated. Several jurisdictions permit minors to petition a court for emancipation themselves. For business purposes, a minor may petition a court to be treated as an adult. If the court grants the minor's request, it removes the minor's lack of contractual capacity and right of disaffirmance for those contracts entered into in conducting the business.

Intoxicated Persons

Another situation in which contractual capacity becomes an issue is when a contract is formed by a person who claims to have been intoxicated at the time the contract was made. The general rule is that if a person who is sufficiently intoxicated to lack mental capacity enters into a contract, the contract is voidable at the option of the intoxicated person. This is true even if the intoxication was purely voluntary. For the contract to be voidable, it must be proved that the intoxicated person's reason and judgment were impaired to the extent that he or she did not comprehend the legal consequences of entering into the contract. If the person was intoxicated but understood these legal consequences, the contract is enforceable.

Simply because the terms of the contract are foolish or are obviously favorable to the other party does not mean the contract is voidable (unless the other party fraudulently induced the person to become intoxicated). Problems often arise in determining whether a party was sufficiently intoxicated to avoid legal duties. Generally, contract avoidance on the ground of intoxication is rarely permitted.

The following case involves an unusual business transaction in which boasts and dares "after a few drinks" resulted in a contract to sell certain property. The issue before the court is whether the seller was sufficiently intoxicated to render the contract voidable at the seller's option.

EMANCIPATION
In regard to minors, the act of being freed from parental control; occurs when a child's parent or legal guardian relinquishes the legal right to exercise control over the child. Normally, a minor who leaves home to support himself or herself is considered emancipated.

CASE 10.2

LUCY v. ZEHMER
Supreme Court of Appeals of Virginia, 1954.
196 Va. 493,
84 S.E.2d 516.

HISTORICAL AND SOCIAL SETTING   *In part because intoxication is usually self-induced, the emphasis in cases that concern lack of capacity on the ground of intoxication is sometimes different from the emphasis in cases that concern lack of capacity on other grounds. Particularly in older cases, there is often a discussion of the parties' morals. Rather than focusing on whether the person was sober enough to understand what he or she was doing, the issue was whether the law should allow someone who becomes intoxicated voluntarily to avoid*

the consequences of his or her behavior. At least one court at the turn of the century held that intoxication is never a defense.[a]

FACTS   Lucy and Zehmer had known each other for fifteen or twenty years. For some time, Lucy had been wanting to buy Zehmer's farm. Zehmer had always told Lucy that he was not interested in selling. One night, Lucy stopped in to visit with the Zehmers at a restaurant they operated. Lucy said to Zehmer, "I bet you wouldn't take $50,000 for that place." Zehmer replied, "Yes, I would, too; you wouldn't give fifty." Throughout the evening, the conversation returned to the sale of the farm. At the same time, the parties were drinking whiskey. Eventually, Zehmer wrote up an agreement, on the back of a restaurant check, for the sale of the farm, and he asked his wife to sign it—which she did. When Lucy brought an action in a Virginia state court to enforce the agreement, Zehmer argued that he had been "high

a.   *Cook v. Bagnell Timber Co.,* 78 Ark. 47, 94 S.W. 695 (1906).

Case 10.2—Continued

as a Georgia pine" at the time and that the offer had been made in jest: "two doggoned drunks bluffing to see who could talk the biggest and say the most." Lucy claimed that he had not been intoxicated and did not think Zehmer had been, either, given the way Zehmer handled the transaction. The trial court ruled in favor of the Zehmers, and Lucy appealed.

ISSUE　Can the agreement be avoided on the basis of intoxication?

DECISION　No. The agreement to sell the farm was binding.

REASON　The opinion of the court was that the evidence given about the nature of the conversation, the

appearance and completeness of the agreement, and the signing all tended to show that a serious business transaction, not a casual jest, was intended. The court had to look into the objective meaning of the words and acts of the Zehmers: "An agreement or mutual assent is of course essential to a valid contract, but the law imputes to a person an intention corresponding to the reasonable meaning of his words and acts. If his words and acts, judged by a reasonable standard, manifest an intention to agree, it is immaterial what may be the real but unexpressed state of mind."

FOR CRITICAL ANALYSIS—Cultural Consideration
How does the court's decision in this case relate to the objective theory of contracts discussed in Chapter 8?

Mentally Incompetent Persons

If a person has been adjudged mentally incompetent by a court of law and a guardian has been appointed, any contract made by the mentally incompetent person is *void*—no contract exists. Only the guardian can enter into a binding contract on behalf of the mentally incompetent person.

If a mentally incompetent person not previously so adjudged by a court enters into a contract, the contract may be *voidable* if the person does not know he or she is entering into the contract or lacks the mental capacity to comprehend its nature, purpose, and consequences. In such situations, the contract is voidable at the option of the mentally incompetent person but not the other party. The contract may then be disaffirmed or ratified. Ratification must occur after the person has regained mental competence or after a guardian is appointed and ratifies the contract. Like minors and intoxicated persons, mentally incompetent persons are liable for the reasonable value of any necessaries they receive.

A contract entered into by a mentally incompetent person (but not previously so adjudged by a court) may also be deemed valid and enforceable if the contract was formed during a lucid interval. For such a contract to be valid, it must be shown that the person was able to comprehend the nature, purpose, and consequences of the contract *at the time the contract was formed.*

BE CAREFUL A contract will almost always be enforced if both parties knew what they were signing.

▌Legality

To this point, we have discussed three of the requirements for a valid contract to exist—agreement, consideration, and contractual capacity. Now we examine a fourth—legality. For a contract to be valid and enforceable, it must be formed for a legal purpose. A contract to do something that is prohibited by federal or state statutory law is illegal and, as such, void from the outset and thus unenforceable. Additionally, a contract to commit a tortious act or to commit an action that is contrary to public policy is illegal and unenforceable.

Contracts Contrary to Statute

Statutes sometimes prescribe the terms of contracts. In some instances, the laws are specific, even providing for the inclusion of certain clauses and their wording. Other statutes prohibit certain contracts on the basis of their subject matter, the time at which they are entered into, or the status of the contracting parties. We examine here several ways in which contracts may be contrary to a statute and thus illegal.

USURY
Charging an illegal rate of interest.

USURY   Virtually every state has a statute that sets the maximum rate of interest that can be charged for different types of transactions, including ordinary loans. A lender who makes a loan at an interest rate above the lawful maximum commits **usury**. The maximum rate of interest varies from state to state.

Although usury statutes place a ceiling on allowable rates of interest, exceptions have been made to facilitate business transactions. For example, many states exempt corporate loans from the usury laws. In addition, almost all states have adopted special statutes allowing much higher interest rates on small loans to help those borrowers who are in need of money but simply cannot get loans at interest rates below the normal lawful maximum.

The effects of a usurious loan differ from state to state. A number of states allow the lender to recover only the principal of a loan along with interest up to the legal maximum. In effect, the lender is denied recovery of the excess interest. In other states, the lender can recover the principal amount of the loan but not the interest. In a few states, a usurious loan is a void transaction, and the lender cannot recover either the principal or the interest.

GAMBLING   In general, gambling contracts are illegal and thus void. All states have statutes that regulate gambling—defined as any scheme that involves the distribution of property by chance among persons who have paid valuable consideration for the opportunity (chance) to receive the property.[3] Gambling is the creation of risk for the purpose of assuming it. In some states, such as Nevada and New Jersey, casino gambling is legal. In other states, certain other forms of gambling are legal. California, for example, has not defined draw poker as a crime, although criminal statutes prohibit numerous other types of gambling games. Several states allow horse racing, and about half of the states have recognized the substantial revenues that can be obtained from gambling and have legalized state-operated lotteries, as well as lotteries (such as bingo) arranged for charitable purposes. Many states also allow gambling on Indian reservations.

BE AWARE The risk inherent in a contract—that the value of goods may change, for instance—is almost never a defense to its enforcement.

Sometimes it is difficult to distinguish a gambling contract from the risk sharing inherent in almost all contracts. Suppose that Isaacson takes out a life insurance policy on Donohue, naming himself as beneficiary under the policy. At first glance, this may seem entirely legal; but further examination shows that Isaacson is simply gambling on how long Donohue will live. To prevent that type of practice, insurance contracts can be entered into only by someone with an *insurable interest* (see Chapter 36).

SABBATH (SUNDAY) LAWS   Statutes called Sabbath (Sunday) laws prohibit the formation or performance of certain contracts on a Sunday. Under the common law, such contracts are legal in the absence of this statutory prohibition. Under some state and local laws, all contracts entered into on a Sunday are illegal. Laws in other states or municipalities prohibit only the sale of certain types of merchandise, such as alcoholic beverages, on a Sunday.

BLUE LAWS
State or local laws that prohibit the performance of certain types of commercial activities on Sunday.

These laws, which date back to colonial times, are often called **blue laws.** Blue laws get their name from the blue paper on which New Haven, Connecticut, printed its new town ordinance in 1781. The ordinance prohibited all work on Sunday and required all shops to close on the "Lord's Day." A number of states and municipalities enacted laws forbidding the carrying on of "all secular labor and business on the Lord's Day." Exceptions to Sunday laws permit contracts for necessities (such as food) and

3.   See *Wishing Well Club v. Akron,* 66 Ohio Law Abs. 406, 112 N.E.2d 41 (1951).

works of charity. A fully performed (executed) contract that was entered into on a Sunday normally cannot be rescinded (canceled).

Sunday laws are often not enforced, and some of these laws have been held to be unconstitutional on the ground that they are contrary to the freedom of religion. Nonetheless, as a precaution, business owners contemplating doing business in a particular locality should check to see if any Sunday statutes or ordinances will affect their business activities.

RECALL Under the First Amendment, the government cannot promote or place a significant burden on religion.

LICENSING STATUTES   All states require that members of certain professions obtain licenses allowing them to practice. Physicians, lawyers, real estate brokers, architects, electricians, and stockbrokers are but a few of the people who must be licensed. Some licenses are obtained only after extensive schooling and examinations, which indicate to the public that a special skill has been acquired. Others require only that the particular person be of good moral character.

Generally, business licenses provide a means of regulating and taxing certain businesses and protecting the public against actions that could threaten the general welfare. For example, in nearly all states, a stockbroker must be licensed and must file a bond with the state to protect the public from fraudulent transactions in stock. Similarly, a plumber must be licensed and bonded to protect the public against incompetent plumbers and to protect the public health. Only persons or businesses possessing the qualifications and complying with the conditions required by statute are entitled to licenses. Typically, for example, an owner of a saloon or tavern is required to sell food as a condition of obtaining a license to sell liquor for consumption on the premises.

When a person enters into a contract with an unlicensed individual, the contract may still be enforceable depending on the nature of the licensing statute. Some states expressly provide that the lack of a license in certain occupations bars the enforcement of work-related contracts. If the statute does not expressly state this, one must look to the underlying purpose of the licensing requirements for a particular occupation. If the purpose is to protect the public from unauthorized practitioners, a contract involving an unlicensed individual is illegal and unenforceable. If, however, the underlying purpose of the statute is to raise government revenues, a contract with an unlicensed practitioner is enforceable—although the unlicensed person is usually fined. In the following case, the court looked at the purpose of an attorney registration statute to decide whether an unregistered attorney could collect fees for legal services.

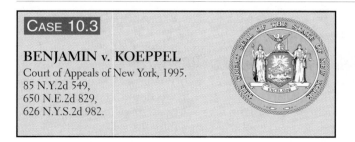

CASE 10.3

BENJAMIN v. KOEPPEL
Court of Appeals of New York, 1995.
85 N.Y.2d 549,
650 N.E.2d 829,
626 N.Y.S.2d 982.

HISTORICAL AND ECONOMIC SETTING   *State taxes generally follow patterns that are typical of normal business cycles. During a recession, for example, there is usually a drop in state revenue at the same time that there is a rise in the demand for state services (welfare, unemployment compensation, and so on). As a result, during recessions many states raise taxes. At the end of*

the 1970s, during a period of double-digit inflation and high unemployment, legislators in New York State looked for ways to increase revenues. Finding that New York was the only state that did not impose a special registration fee on attorneys, the legislature enacted a law in 1981 to overcome this oversight.

FACTS   Donald Benjamin, an attorney, agreed to a fee-sharing arrangement with Koeppel, Del Casino & Martone, P.C. (professional corporation), a law firm. Under the agreement, Benjamin was to receive one-third of any fees the firm obtained from a client whom Benjamin referred to it. When the firm refused to pay, Benjamin filed a suit against it and Adolph Koeppel, one of the partners, in a New York state court. The firm discovered

(Continued)

Case 10.3—Continued

that Benjamin was not registered with the state according to the state's attorney registration rules and claimed that payment to Benjamin would therefore violate public policy. The court ruled in Benjamin's favor, and the firm appealed. The appellate court affirmed the lower court's ruling, and the law firm appealed to New York's highest state court, the New York Court of Appeals.

ISSUE   May an attorney who has not complied with a state's statutory registration requirements recover fees for legal services provided in that state?

DECISION   Yes. The New York Court of Appeals affirmed the lower court's ruling. The appellate court held, among other things, that the registration requirements were revenue-raising measures.

REASON   The court determined that the state's attorney registration system "more closely resembles a revenue-raising measure than a program for 'the protection of public health or morals or the prevention of fraud.'" The court pointed out that when the registration statute was enacted, its express purpose was to "generate $1,750,000 in estimated [annual] fee revenues." The court also found that amendments to the statute "only serve to underscore [its] essential purpose as a revenue-raising mechanism." For example, "[t]he 1990 amendments tripled the $100 biannual fee and provided for the allocation of the resulting revenues."

FOR CRITICAL ANALYSIS—Political Consideration
When a licensing statute provides for a fine for noncompliance, is it still appropriate to deny an individual his or her fee, even after the fine has been paid?

"Public policy is in its nature so uncertain and fluctuating, varying with the habits of the day, . . . that it is difficult to determine its limits with any degree of exactness."

Joseph Story, 1779–1845
(Associate justice of the United States Supreme Court, 1811–1845)

Contracts Contrary to Public Policy

Although contracts involve private parties, some are not enforceable because of the negative impact they would have on society. These contracts are said to be *contrary to public policy*. Examples include a contract to commit an immoral act (such as a surrogate-parenting contract, which several courts and state statutes equate with "baby selling") and a contract that prohibits marriage. As an example of the latter, suppose that Everett offers a young man $500 if he refrains from marrying Everett's daughter. If the young man accepts, no contract is formed (the contract is void) because it is contrary to public policy. Thus, if the man marries Everett's daughter, Everett cannot sue him for breach of contract. Business contracts that may be contrary to public policy include contracts in restraint of trade and unconscionable contracts or clauses.

CONTRACTS IN RESTRAINT OF TRADE   Contracts in restraint of trade (anticompetitive agreements) usually adversely affect the public, which favors competition in the economy. Typically, such contracts also violate one or more federal or state statutes.[4] An exception is recognized when the restraint is reasonable and it is *ancillary to* (is a subsidiary part of) a contract, such as a contract for the sale of a business or an employment contract. Many such exceptions involve a type of restraint called a *covenant not to compete*, or a restrictive covenant.

Covenants Not to Compete   Covenants not to compete are often contained in contracts concerning the sale of an ongoing business. A covenant not to compete is created when a seller agrees not to open a new store in a certain geographical area surrounding the old store. Such an agreement, when it is ancillary to a sales contract and reasonable in terms of time and geographic area, enables the seller to sell, and the purchaser to buy, the "goodwill" and "reputation" of an ongoing business. If, for example, a well-known merchant sells his or her store and opens a competing business a block away, many of the merchant's customers will likely do business at the new store. This renders valueless the good name and reputation sold to the other merchant for a price. If a covenant not to compete was not ancillary to a sales agreement, however, it would be void, because it unreasonably restrains trade and is contrary to public policy.

---

4.   Such as the Sherman Antitrust Act, the Clayton Act, and the Federal Trade Commission Act (see Chapter 30).

Agreements not to compete can also be contained in employment contracts. It is common for many people in middle-level and upper-level management positions to agree not to work for competitors or not to start a competing business for a specified period of time after terminating employment. Such agreements are legal so long as the specified period of time is not excessive in duration and the geographical restriction is reasonable. Basically, the restriction on competition must be reasonable—that is, not any greater than necessary to protect a legitimate business interest. The following case illustrates this point.

CASE 10.4

SUPERIOR CONSULTING CORP. v. WALLING

United States District Court,
Eastern District of Michigan, 1994.
851 F.Supp. 839.

COMPANY PROFILE *The Superior Consulting Corporation (SCC) provides information systems and management consulting services to large, multifacility health-care institutions. SCC's business is national and international in scope, involving employees in approximately thirty states and clients in forty-three states and Canada, France, Saudi Arabia, Singapore, and other nations. SCC competes with national and international consulting companies for clients, consultants, and managers.*

FACTS Michael Walling began work for SCC as an executive director in 1990. Two years later, when he was promoted to vice president, he signed a new employment contract that contained a covenant not to compete. The covenant prohibited Walling from accepting a job with "any health-care information systems consulting business for a period of six months following his termination" of employment with SCC. The express purpose of the agreement was to protect SCC's trade secrets. Walling resigned from SCC in 1994. In less than a week, he agreed to work for Ernst & Young to provide health-

care information systems consulting services. SCC filed a suit in a federal district court against Walling to enforce the covenant not to compete.

ISSUE Were the terms of this covenant not to compete reasonable?

DECISION Yes. The court ordered Walling to comply with the covenant not to compete.

REASON Six months was reasonable, the court concluded, pointing out that "[l]onger periods have been approved, particularly * * * to protect proprietary information learned by the employee." The agreement had no geographical limitations, but the court explained that this was reasonable "if the employer actually has legitimate business interests throughout the world," as SCC did. Finally, the agreement was reasonable as to "line of work," because, as limited by the court, it applied only to "actual consulting and management work for competitors of SCC, and only in the competitors' health-care information systems consulting businesses."

FOR CRITICAL ANALYSIS—Social Consideration
Why wouldn't every company want all of its employees to sign covenants not to compete?

Reformation of an Illegal Covenant Not to Compete On occasion, when a covenant not to compete is unreasonable in its essential terms, the court may *reform* the covenant, converting its terms into reasonable ones. Instead of declaring the covenant illegal and unenforceable, the court applies the rule of reasonableness and changes the contract so that its basic, original intent can be enforced. This presents a problem, however, in that the judge becomes a party to the contract. Consequently, contract **reformation** is usually carried out by a court only when necessary to prevent undue burdens or hardships. (See this chapter's *Business Law in Action* for a further discussion of this topic.)

REFORMATION
A court-ordered correction of a written contract so that it reflects the true intentions of the parties.

Should Courts Reform Covenants Not to Compete?

Essentially, when a contract is illegal, any purported contractual obligations under that contract can be avoided because there is no contract. What happens, though, when a court reforms an illegal contract or contract clause, such as an illegal covenant not to compete? In such a situation, the court in effect is rewriting the contract and *creating* an obligation where there was none initially (due to the illegality of the contract)—regardless of whether the parties have agreed to such a modification. Is it within the power of the courts to construct what essentially amount to private agreements?

Many courts have faced this question in recent years. In the majority of cases, the courts have concluded that they do have such powers. These courts have modified such covenants by either "blue penciling" (striking out) unreasonable restrictions from a covenant and then enforcing the modified covenant or applying a "rule of reasonableness." The rule of reasonableness allows a

court to fashion an agreement that reasonably protects the interests of a party seeking to enforce the covenant while preventing the other party from suffering undue hardship. A minority of courts, however, take the opposite position. These courts maintain that reformation of a covenant not to compete is tantamount to the creation of a private agreement, and the courts do not have the power to do this.

An interesting twist on this issue arose in a case heard by the Nebraska Supreme Court: What if the parties themselves, in their covenant not to compete, agree to allow a court to reform any unreasonable provision of the covenant? The case involved a covenant not to compete signed by an employee in conjunction with the purchase of stock in his employer's company. Among other things, the covenant prohibited the employee from divulging the company's trade secrets and from competing with the company for five years "anywhere in the United States, the continent of North America, or anywhere else on earth." The covenant also provided as follows: "In the event that any portion of this Covenant may be held to be invalid or unenforceable for any reason, it is agreed that said invalidity or unenforceability shall not affect the other portions of this Covenant, and that the remaining covenants, terms and conditions or portions thereof

shall remain in full force and effect and any court of competent jurisdiction may so modify the objectionable provision as to make it valid, reasonable and enforceable."

When the employer sought to enforce the agreement, the Nebraska trial court reformed the covenant by striking certain clauses and phrases, including the phrase "anywhere else on earth," from the covenant. It then deemed the covenant enforceable as modified. The state's highest court, though, concluded that "[t]he provision of the agreement which states that a court may reform the covenant is of no effect. Private parties may not confer upon the court powers which it does not possess. This court has stated repeatedly that courts may not rewrite a contract for parties. Because we find that the covenant is not subject to modification, we must either enforce it as written or not enforce it at all. The trial court found as a matter of law that the covenant not to compete was unenforceable as written. That finding was not challenged, and we let it stand."[a]

For Critical Analysis: *What argument could be made in support of reforming (and then enforcing) illegal covenants not to compete?*

a.   *CAE Vanguard, Inc. v. Newman*, 246 Neb. 334, 518 N.W.2d 652 (1994).

UNCONSCIONABLE CONTRACT (OR UNCONSCIONABLE CLAUSE)
A contract or clause that is void on the basis of public policy because one party, as a result of his or her disproportionate bargaining power, is forced to accept terms that are unfairly burdensome and that unfairly benefit the dominating party.

UNCONSCIONABLE CONTRACTS OR CLAUSES   Ordinarily, a court does not look at the fairness or equity of a contract; in other words, it does not inquire into the adequacy of consideration. Persons are assumed to be reasonably intelligent, and the court does not come to their aid just because they have made unwise or foolish bargains. In certain circumstances, however, bargains are so oppressive that the courts relieve innocent parties of part or all of their duties. Such a bargain is called an **unconscionable contract** (or **unconscionable clause**). Both the Uniform Commercial Code (UCC) and the Uniform Consumer Credit Code (UCCC) embody the unconscionability concept—the former with regard to the sale of goods and the latter with regard to consumer loans and the waiver of rights.[5]

Procedural Unconscionability   Procedural unconscionability has to do with how a term becomes part of a contract and relates to factors bearing on a party's lack of

---

5.   See, for example, UCC Sections 2–302 and 2–719 (see Chapters 14 and 16, respectively) and UCCC Sections 5.108 and 1.107 (see Chapter 31).

knowledge or understanding of the contract terms because of inconspicuous print, unintelligible language ("legalese"), lack of opportunity to read the contract, lack of opportunity to ask questions about its meaning, and other factors. Procedural unconscionability sometimes relates to purported lack of voluntariness because of a disparity in bargaining power between the two parties. Contracts entered into because of one party's vastly superior bargaining power may be deemed unconscionable. These situations usually involve an **adhesion contract,** which is a contract drafted by the dominant party and then presented to the other—the adhering party—on a "take it or leave it" basis.[6] The following case involved an adhesion contract.

ADHESION CONTRACT
A "standard form" contract, such as that between a large retailer and a consumer, in which the stronger party dictates the terms.

CASE 10.5

PHOENIX BAPTIST HOSPITAL & MEDICAL CENTER, INC. v. AIKEN
Court of Appeals of Arizona,
Division 1, Department B, 1994.
179 Ariz. 289,
877 P.2d 1345.

HISTORICAL AND SOCIAL SETTING *The health-care industry is the largest industry in the United States. Expenditures on health care absorb an increasing percentage of total national income every year. The health-care industry consists mostly of small firms, private doctors, and hospitals. Of these, the largest component is hospital care. Nearly 40 percent of the money that pays for health care is spent in hospitals.*

FACTS Patricia Aiken suffered a heart attack and was hospitalized at Phoenix Baptist Hospital and Medical Center, Inc. At the time of her admission, the Aikens told the hospital that they did not have the money to pay for medical care. At the same time, her husband, Thomas, signed an agreement to pay her medical expenses. He did not read what he signed, no one explained the agreement to him, and he later claimed to have been so upset that he could not remember having signed anything. When the bills were not paid, the hospital filed a suit in an Arizona state court against the Aikens. The court ruled in favor of the hospital, and the Aikens

appealed. They argued that the agreement was an adhesion contract obtained under circumstances that made it unenforceable.

ISSUE Were the circumstances such that the agreement may have been unenforceable?

DECISION Yes. The state court of appeals reversed the ruling of the lower court and remanded the case. The lower court was instructed to look at the circumstances surrounding Thomas's signing of the agreement.

REASON The appellate court held that the agreement was "undeniably a contract of adhesion." Whether it was enforceable depended on "the reasonable expectations of the adhering party and whether the contract is unconscionable." The court concluded that there was "a material issue of fact as to Thomas' reasonable expectation," considering the stressful circumstances under which he signed the agreement. As to the form's unconscionability, the court stated that, given the circumstances—Thomas's haste, the failure of the hospital to explain the agreement, and the small print of the form—Thomas either may not have understood "the implications of the agreement" or may have "felt he had no choice but to immediately sign the preprinted form."

FOR CRITICAL ANALYSIS—Ethical Consideration
Under what circumstances would an adhesion contract to pay for medical services be enforceable when an emergency admission to a hospital is at issue?

Substantive Unconscionability Substantive unconscionability characterizes those contracts, or portions of contracts, that are oppressive or overly harsh. Courts generally focus on provisions that deprive one party of the benefits of the agreement or leave that party without remedy for nonperformance by the other. For example, suppose that a welfare recipient with a fourth-grade education agrees to purchase a refrigerator for $2,000 and signs a two-year installment contract. The same type of refrigerator usually

---

6.   See, for example, *Henningsen v. Bloomfield Motors, Inc.*, 32 N.J. 358, 161 A.2d 69 (1960).

sells for $400 on the market. Some courts have held this type of contract to be unconscionable, despite the general rule that the courts will not inquire into the adequacy of the consideration, because the contract terms are so oppressive as to "shock the conscience" of the court.[7]

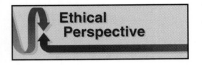

Ethical Perspective

The doctrine of unconscionability represents a good example of how the law attempts to enforce ethical behavior. Under this doctrine, a contract may be deemed to be so unfair to one party as to be unenforceable—even though that party voluntarily agreed to the contract's terms. Unconscionable action, like unethical action, is incapable of precise definition. Information about the particular facts and specific circumstances surrounding the contract is essential. For example, a contract with a marginally literate consumer might be seen as unfair and unenforceable, whereas the same contract with a major business firm would be upheld by the courts.

Section 2–302 of the Uniform Commercial Code (UCC), which incorporates the common law concept of unconscionability, similarly does not define the concept with any precision. Rather, it leaves it up to the courts to determine when a contract is so one sided and unfair to one party as to be unconscionable and thus unenforceable.

Usually, courts will do all they can to save contracts rather than render them unenforceable. Thus, only in extreme situations, as when a contract or clause is so one sided as to "shock the conscience" of the court, will a court hold a contract or contractual clause unconscionable.

For Critical Analysis: *The requirement that contracts be performed as promised is one of the cornerstones of contract law. How can the doctrine of unconscionability be reconciled with this requirement?*

EXCULPATORY CLAUSE
A clause that releases a contractual party from liability in the event of monetary or physical injury, no matter who is at fault.

EXCULPATORY CLAUSES   Often closely related to the concept of unconscionability are **exculpatory clauses,** defined as clauses that release a party from liability in the event of monetary or physical injury, *no matter who is at fault.* Indeed, some courts refer to such clauses in terms of unconscionability. Suppose, for example, that Madison Manufacturing Company hires a laborer and has him sign a contract containing the following clause:

> Said employee hereby agrees with employer, in consideration of such employment, that he will take upon himself all risks incident to his position and will in no case hold the company liable for any injury or damage he may sustain, in his person or otherwise, by accidents or injuries in the factory, or which may result from defective machinery or carelessness or misconduct of himself or any other employee in service of the employer.

This contract provision attempts to remove Madison's potential liability for injuries occurring to the employee, and it would usually be held contrary to public policy.[8] Exculpatory clauses found in agreements to lease commercial property are also, in the majority of cases, held to be contrary to public policy. Additionally, such clauses are almost universally held to be illegal and unenforceable when they are included in residential property leases.

---

7.   See, for example, *Jones v. Star Credit Corp.*, 59 Misc.2d 189, 298 N.Y.S.2d 264 (1969). This case is presented in Chapter 14 as Case 14.4.

8.   For a case with similar facts, see *Little Rock & Fort Smith Railway Co. v. Eubanks*, 48 Ark. 460, 3 S.W. 808 (1887). In such a case, the exculpatory clause may also be illegal on the basis of a violation of a state workers' compensation law.

Generally, an exculpatory clause will not be enforced if the party seeking its enforcement is involved in a business that is important to the public interest. These businesses include public utilities, common carriers, and banks. Because of the essential nature of these services, the companies offering them have an advantage in bargaining strength and could insist that anyone contracting for their services agree not to hold them liable. This would tend to relax their carefulness and increase the number of injuries. Imagine the results, for example, if all exculpatory clauses in contracts between airlines and their passengers were enforced.

Exculpatory clauses may be enforced, however, when the parties seeking their enforcement are not involved in businesses considered important to the public interest. These businesses have included health clubs, amusement parks, horse-rental concessions, golf-cart concessions, and skydiving organizations. Because these services are not essential, the firms offering them are sometimes considered to have no relative advantage in bargaining strength, and anyone contracting for their services is considered to do so voluntarily. The following case involved an exculpatory clause that purported to absolve an alarm company from liability for its own negligence.

REMEMBER Virtually everyone is liable for his or her own torts, and this responsibility cannot be contracted away.

CASE 10.6

NEW LIGHT CO. v. WELLS FARGO ALARM SERVICES
Supreme Court of Nebraska, 1994.
247 Neb. 57,
525 N.W.2d 25.

HISTORICAL AND SOCIAL SETTING *"We Feed the World" is the motto of the city of Omaha, Nebraska. Omaha is a major transportation hub of the midwestern United States, with seven important railroads and, operating out of the Port of Omaha, fourteen barge lines. Omaha's major food products include pasta, potato chips, coffee, pancake mixes, frozen dinners, and Omaha steaks.*

FACTS The New Light Company, which owned and operated the Great Wall Restaurant in Omaha, Nebraska, contracted with Wells Fargo Alarm Services to install and maintain a fire alarm system in the restaurant. The agreement included an exculpatory clause that relieved Wells Fargo of liability for its "negligent acts or omissions." A fire in the restaurant rendered the alarm system inoperative. New Light sued Wells Fargo in a Nebraska state court, claiming in part that the alarm company's failure to install an alarm system that would detect a fire before the system was rendered inoperative amounted to willful, wanton, and intentional misconduct and thus constituted gross negligence. Based on the exculpatory clause, the court issued a summary judgment in favor of Wells Fargo, and New Light appealed. The state appellate court affirmed, and New Light appealed to the Supreme Court of Nebraska.

ISSUE Is an exculpatory clause that relieves a party of liability for its gross negligence or willful and wanton misconduct against public policy?

DECISION Yes. The state supreme court reversed the decision of the lower court and remanded the case for a determination as to whether Wells Fargo had in fact been grossly negligent or was guilty of any willful and wanton misconduct.

REASON There was, the court found, "a sufficiently compelling reason to prevent Wells Fargo from insulating itself by contractual agreement from damages caused by its own gross negligence or willful and wanton misconduct. Such an agreement would have a tendency to be injurious to the public." The court explained that "[t]he right of contract may be restricted for the public good. The greater the threat to the general safety of the community, the greater the restriction on the party's freedom to contractually limit the party's liability." The court stated that "[t]his limitation on the freedom to contract is imposed by law because of the potential risks to human life and property and is, therefore, independent of the agreement of the parties."

FOR CRITICAL ANALYSIS—Ethical Consideration
Under what circumstances should a court uphold an exculpatory clause that partially eliminates a party's duty of care?

The Effect of Illegality

In general, an illegal contract is void: the contract is deemed never to have existed, and the courts will not aid either party. In most illegal contracts, both parties are considered to be equally at fault—*in pari delicto*. If the contract is executory (not yet fulfilled), neither party can enforce it. If it is executed, there can be neither contractual nor quasi-contractual recovery.

That one wrongdoer in an illegal contract is unjustly enriched at the expense of the other is of no concern to the law—except under certain circumstances (to be discussed shortly). The major justification for this hands-off attitude is that it is improper to place the machinery of justice at the disposal of a plaintiff who has broken the law by entering into an illegal bargain. Another justification is the hoped-for deterrent effect of this general rule. A plaintiff who suffers a loss because of an illegal bargain should presumably be deterred from entering into similar illegal bargains in the future.

There are exceptions to the general rule that neither party to an illegal bargain can sue for breach and neither can recover for performance rendered. We look at these exceptions here.

JUSTIFIABLE IGNORANCE OF THE FACTS   When one of the parties to a contract is relatively innocent (has no knowledge or any reason to know that the contract is illegal), that party can often obtain restitution or recovery of benefits conferred in a partially executed contract. The courts do not enforce the contract but do allow the parties to return to their original positions.

It is also possible for an innocent party who has fully performed under the contract to enforce the contract against the guilty party. For example, Debbie contracts with Tucker to purchase ten crates of goods that cannot legally be bought or sold. Tucker hires a trucking firm to deliver the shipment to Debbie and agrees to pay the firm the normal fee of $500. Although the law specifies that the shipment, use, and sale of the goods were illegal, the carrier, being an innocent party, can legally collect the $500 from Tucker.

MEMBERS OF PROTECTED CLASSES   When a statute protects a certain class of people, a member of that class can enforce an illegal contract even though the other party cannot. For example, there are statutes that prohibit certain employees (such as flight attendants) from working more than a specified number of hours per month. These employees thus constitute a class protected by statute. An employee who is required to work more than the maximum can recover for those extra hours of service.

Another example of statutes designed to protect a particular class of people are **blue sky laws**, which are state laws that regulate and supervise investment companies for the protection of the public. (The phrase *blue sky laws* dates to a 1917 decision by the United States Supreme Court in which the Court declared that the purpose of such laws was to prevent "speculative schemes which have no more basis than so many feet of 'blue sky.'")[9] These laws are intended to stop the sale of stock in fly-by-night concerns, such as visionary oil wells and distant and perhaps nonexistent gold mines. Investors are protected as a class and can sue to recover the purchase price of stock issued in violation of such laws.

Most states also have statutes regulating the sale of insurance. If an insurance company violates a statute when selling insurance, the purchaser can nevertheless enforce the policy and recover from the insurer.

WITHDRAWAL FROM AN ILLEGAL AGREEMENT   If the illegal part of a bargain has not yet been performed, the party tendering performance can withdraw from the bargain and recover the performance or its value. For example, suppose that Martha and Andy

BLUE SKY LAWS
State laws that regulate the offer and sale of securities.

---

9. *Hall v. Geiger-Jones Co.*, 242 U.S. 539, 37 S.Ct. 217, 61 L.Ed. 480 (1917).

decide to wager (illegally) on the outcome of a boxing match. Each deposits money with a stakeholder, who agrees to pay the winner of the bet. At this point, each party has performed part of the agreement, but the illegal part of the agreement will not occur until the money is paid to the winner. Before such payment occurs, either party is entitled to withdraw from the agreement by giving notice to the stakeholder of his or her withdrawal.

FRAUD, DURESS, OR UNDUE INFLUENCE   Whenever a plaintiff has been induced to enter into an illegal bargain as a result of fraud, duress, or undue influence, he or she can either enforce the contract or recover for its value.

Application

Law and the Retailer— Sales Personnel and Contracts with Minors*

Sales personnel, particularly those who are paid on a commission basis, are often eager to make contracts. Sometimes, however, these salespersons must deal with minors and intoxicated persons, both of whom have limited contractual capacity. Therefore, if you are a retailer, you should make sure that your employees are acquainted with the law governing minors and intoxicated persons.

If in your business you sell consumer durables, such as entertainment centers or automobiles, your sales personnel must be careful in forming contracts with minors and should heed the adage, "When in doubt, check." Remember that a contract signed by a minor (unless it is for necessaries) normally is voidable, and the minor may exercise the option to disaffirm the contract. Employees should demand legal proof of age of a customer when they have any doubt concerning the customer's age.

In addition, because the law governing minors' rights varies substantially from state to state, you should check with your attorney concerning the laws governing disaf-

firmance in your state. You and those you hire to sell your products should know, for example, what the consequences will be if a minor has misrepresented his or her age when forming a sales contract. Similarly, you need to find out whether and in what circumstances a minor, on disaffirming a contract, can be required to pay for damage to goods sold under the contract.

Little need be said about a salesperson's dealings with obviously intoxicated persons. If the customer, despite intoxication, understands the legal consequences of the contract being signed, the contract is enforceable. Nonetheless, it may be extremely difficult to establish that the intoxicated customer understood the consequences of entering into the contract if the customer claims that he or she did not understand those consequences. Therefore, the best advice is, "When in doubt, don't." In other words, if you suspect a customer may be intoxicated, do not sign a contract with him or her.

 Checklist for the Salesperson

1. When in doubt about the age of a customer to whom you are about to sell major consumer durable goods or anything other than necessaries, require legal proof of age.
2. If such proof is not forthcoming, require that a parent or guardian also sign the contract.
3. Check with an attorney about the laws governing minors' contracts in your state.
4. Do not sign contracts with intoxicated customers.

*This *Application* is not meant to substitute for the services of an attorney who is licensed to practice law in your state.

▌Key Terms

adhesion contract 265
blue law 260
blue sky law 268
contractual capacity 253
disaffirmance 254

emancipation 258
exculpatory clause 266
necessaries 256
ratification 257
reformation 263

unconscionable contract (or unconscionable clause) 264
usury 260

▌Chapter Summary: Capacity and Legality

CONTRACTUAL CAPACITY	

Minors
(See pages 254–258.)
	A minor is a person who has not yet reached the age of majority. In most states, the age of majority is eighteen for contract purposes. Contracts with minors are voidable at the option of the minor.
	
	1. *Disaffirmance*—Defined as the legal avoidance of a contractual obligation.
	  a. Can take place (in most states) at any time during minority and within a reasonable time after the minor has reached the age of majority.
	  b. If a minor disaffirms a contract, the entire contract must be disaffirmed.
	  c. When disaffirming executed contracts, the minor has a duty to return received goods if they are still in the minor's control or (in some states) to pay their reasonable value.
	  d. A minor who has committed an act of fraud (such as misrepresentation of age) will be denied the right to disaffirm by some courts.
	  e. A minor may disaffirm a contract for necessaries but remains liable for the reasonable value of the goods.
	
	2. *Ratification*—Defined as the affirmation of a voidable legal obligation; may be express or implied.
	  a. Express ratification—Exists when the minor, through a writing or an oral agreement, explicitly assumes the obligations imposed by the contract.
	  b. Implied ratification—Exists when the conduct of the minor is inconsistent with disaffirmance or when the minor fails to disaffirm an executed contract within a reasonable time after reaching the age of majority.
	
	3. *Parents' liability*—Generally, parents are not liable for the contracts made by minor children acting on their own, nor are parents liable for minors' torts except in certain circumstances.
	
	4. *Emancipation*—Occurs when a child's parent or legal guardian relinquishes the legal right to exercise control over the child. Normally, a minor who leaves home to support himself or herself is considered emancipated. In some jurisdictions, minors themselves are permitted to petition for emancipation for limited purposes.

Intoxicated Persons *(See pages 258–259.)*	1. A contract entered into by an intoxicated person is voidable at the option of the intoxicated person if the person was sufficiently intoxicated to lack mental capacity, even if the intoxication was voluntary. 2. A contract with an intoxicated person is enforceable if, despite being intoxicated, the person understood the legal consequences of entering into the contract.
Mentally Incompetent Persons *(See page 259.)*	1. A contract made by a person adjudged by a court to be mentally incompetent is void. 2. A contract made by a mentally incompetent person not adjudged by a court to be mentally incompetent is voidable at the option of the mentally incompetent person.
LEGALITY	
Contracts Contrary to Statute *(See pages 259–262.)*	1. *Usury*—Occurs when a lender makes a loan at an interest rate above the lawful maximum. The maximum rate of interest varies from state to state. 2. *Gambling*—Gambling contracts that contravene (go against) state statutes are deemed illegal and thus void. 3. *Sabbath (Sunday) laws*—Laws prohibiting the formation or the performance of certain contracts on Sunday. Such laws vary widely from state to state, and many states do not enforce them. 4. *Licensing statutes*—Contracts entered into by persons who do not have a license, when one is required by statute, will not be enforceable *unless* the underlying purpose of the statute is to raise government revenues (and not to protect the public from unauthorized practitioners).
Contracts Contrary to Public Policy *(See pages 262–267.)*	1. *Contracts in restraint of trade*—Contracts to reduce or restrain free competition are illegal. Most such contracts are now prohibited by statutes. An exception is a *covenant not to compete*. It is usually enforced by the courts if the terms are ancillary to a contract (such as a contract for the sale of a business or an employment contract) and are reasonable as to time and area of restraint. Courts tend to scrutinize covenants not to compete closely. If a covenant is overbroad, a court may either reform the covenant to fall within reasonable constraints and then enforce the reformed contract or declare the covenant void and thus unenforceable.

▌Chapter Summary: Capacity and Legality—Continued

Contracts Contrary to Public Policy —Continued	2. *Unconscionable contracts and clauses*—When a contract or contract clause is so unfair that it is oppressive to one party, it can be deemed unconscionable; as such, it is illegal and cannot be enforced.
	3. *Exculpatory clauses*—An exculpatory clause is a clause that releases a party from liability in the event of monetary or physical injury, no matter who is at fault. In certain situations, exculpatory clauses may be contrary to public policy and thus unenforceable.
Effect of Illegality (*See pages 268–269.*)	In general, an illegal contract is void, and the courts will not aid either party when both parties are considered to be equally at fault (*in pari delicto*). If the contract is executory, neither party can enforce it. If the contract is executed, there can be neither contractual nor quasi-contractual recovery. Exceptions (situations in which recovery is allowed):
	1. When one party to the contract is relatively innocent.
	2. When one party to the contract is a member of a group of persons protected by statute.
	3. When either party seeks to recover consideration given for an illegal contract before the illegal act is performed.
	4. When one party was induced to enter into an illegal bargain through fraud, duress, or undue influence.

▌For Review

1. Generally, a minor can disaffirm any contract. What are some exceptions to this rule?
2. Under what circumstances does intoxication make a contract voidable?
3. Does mental incompetence necessarily render a contract void?

4. Under what circumstances will a covenant not to compete be enforceable? When will such covenants not be enforced?
5. What is an exculpatory clause? In what circumstances might exculpatory clauses be enforced? When will they not be enforced?

▌Questions and Case Problems

10–1. Contracts by Minors. Kalen is a seventeen-year-old minor who has just graduated from high school. He is attending a university two hundred miles from home and has contracted to rent an apartment near the university for one year at $500 per month. He is working at a convenience store to earn enough money to be self-supporting. After living in the apartment and paying monthly rent for four months, a dispute arises between him and the landlord. Kalen, still a minor, moves out and returns the key to the landlord. The landlord wants to hold Kalen liable for the balance of the payments due under the lease. Discuss fully Kalen's liability in this situation.

10–2. Covenants Not to Compete. Joseph, who owns the only pizza parlor in Middletown, learns that Giovanni is about to open a competing pizza parlor in the same small town, just a few blocks from Joseph's restaurant. Joseph offers Giovanni $10,000 in return for Giovanni's promise not to open a pizza parlor in the Middletown area. Giovanni accepts the $10,000 but goes ahead with his plans, in spite of the agreement. When Giovanni opens his restaurant for business, Joseph sues to enjoin (prevent) Giovanni's continued operation of his restaurant or to recover the $10,000. The court denies recovery. On what basis?

10–3. Intoxication. After Katie has several drinks one night, she sells Emily a valuable fur stole for $10. The next day, Katie offers the $10 to Emily and requests the return of her stole. Emily refuses, claiming that they had a valid contract of sale. Katie explains that she was intoxicated at the time the bargain was made, and thus the contract is voidable at her option. Who is right? Explain.

10–4. Mental Incompetence. Jermal has been the owner of a car dealership for a number of years. One day, Jermal sold one of his most expensive cars to Kessler. At the time of the sale, Jermal thought Kessler acted in a peculiar manner, but he gave the matter no further thought until four months later, when Kessler's court-appointed guardian appeared at Jermal's office, tendered back the car, and demanded Kessler's money back. The guardian informed Jermal that Kessler had been adjudicated mentally incompetent two months earlier by a proper court.

(a) Discuss the rights of the parties in this situation.
(b) If Kessler had been adjudicated mentally incompetent before the contract was formed, what would be the legal effect of the contract?

10–5. Licensing Statutes. State X requires that persons who prepare and serve liquor in the form of drinks at commercial establishments be licensed by the state to do so. The only requirement for obtaining a yearly license is that the person be at least eighteen years old. Mickey, aged thirty-five, is hired as a bartender for the Southtown Restaurant. Gerald, a staunch alumnus of a nearby university, brings twenty of his friends to the restaurant to celebrate a football victory one afternoon. Gerald orders four rounds of drinks, and the bill is nearly $200. Gerald learns that Mickey has failed to renew his bartender's license, and Gerald refuses to pay, claiming that the contract is unenforceable. Discuss whether Gerald is correct.

10–6. Contracts by Minors. In 1982, Webster Street Partnership, Ltd. (Webster), entered into a lease agreement with Matthew Sheridan and Pat Wilwerding. Webster was aware that both Sheridan and Wilwerding were minors. Both tenants were living away from home, apparently with the understanding that they could return home at any time. Sheridan and Wilwerding paid the first month's rent but then failed to pay the rent for the next month and vacated the apartment. Webster sued them for breach of contract. They claimed that the lease agreement was voidable because they were minors. Who will win, and why? [*Webster Street Partnership, Ltd. v. Sheridan*, 220 Neb. 9, 368 N.W.2d 439 (1985)]

10–7. Contracts by Minors. Smith purchased a car on credit from Bobby Floars Toyota, Inc., a month before his eighteenth birthday. Smith made regular monthly payments for eleven months but then returned the car to the dealer and made no further payments on it. The dealer sold the car and sued Smith to recover the difference between the amount obtained by the sale of the car and the money Smith still owed to the dealer. Smith refused to pay on the ground that he had been a minor at the time of purchase and had disaffirmed the contract after he had reached the age of majority. Will the car dealer succeed in its claim that the ten monthly payments made after Smith turned eighteen constituted a ratification of the purchase contract? Discuss. [*Bobby Floars Toyota, Inc. v. Smith*, 48 N.C.App. 580, 269 S.E.2d 320 (1980)]

10–8. Unconscionability. Carolyn Murphy was a welfare recipient with four minor children. After seeing Brian McNamara's advertisement for "rent to own" televisions, Murphy signed a lease agreement with McNamara for a twenty-five-inch Philco color TV at $16 per week. The lease payments were to run for seventy-eight weeks, after which Murphy would become the owner. At no time did McNamara tell Murphy that the total lease payments amounted to $1,268, including the delivery charge. The retail sale price of the set was $499. Murphy had paid about $436 when she read a newspaper article criticizing the lease plan. When she learned that she was required to pay $1,268, Murphy stopped making payments. McNamara's employees attempted to take possession of the TV and made threats through telephone and written communications. Murphy filed suit, alleging, among other things, that the contract terms were unconscionable. Discuss her allegation and whether a court might find the contract unconscionable. [*Murphy v. McNamara*, 36 Conn.Supp. 183, 416 A.2d 170 (1979)]

10–9. Usury. Tony's Tortilla Factory, Inc., had two checking accounts with First Bank. Due to financial difficulties, Tony's wrote a total of 2,165 checks (totaling $88,000) for which there were insufficient funds in the accounts. First Bank paid the overdrawn checks but imposed an "NSF" (nonsufficient funds) fee of $20 for each check paid. The owners of Tony's sued First Bank and one of its officers, alleging, among other things, that the $20-per-check fee was essentially "interest" charged by the bank for Tony's use of the bank's money (the money the bank advanced to cover the bad checks); because the rate of "interest" charged by the bank ($20 per check) exceeded the rate allowed by law, it was usurious. First Bank claimed that its NSF fees were not interest but fees charged to cover its costs in processing checks drawn on accounts with insufficient funds. How should the court decide this issue? Discuss fully. [*First Bank v. Tony's Tortilla Factory, Inc.*, 877 S.W.2d 285 (Tex. 1994)]

10–10. Gambling Contracts. No law prohibits citizens in a state that does not sponsor a state-operated lottery from purchasing lottery tickets in a state that does have such a lottery. Because Georgia did not have a state-operated lottery, Talley and several other Georgia residents allegedly agreed to purchase a ticket in a lottery sponsored by Kentucky and to share the proceeds if they won. They did win, but apparently Talley had difficulty collecting his share of the proceeds. In Talley's suit to obtain his share of the funds, a Georgia trial court held that the "gambling contract" was unenforceable because it was contrary to Georgia's public policy. On appeal, how should the court rule on this issue? Discuss. [*Talley v. Mathis*, 265 Ga. 179, 453 S.E.2d 704 (1995)]

A QUESTION OF ETHICS AND SOCIAL RESPONSIBILITY

10–11. *Michael Niemiec and Judith Polek (the plaintiffs) joined a buyer's club after they had been invited via telephone to visit the club's premises. A salesperson told them that in exchange for a $1,160 membership fee, members could order items from various catalogues at supposedly low prices, but they had to sign the contract then and there or forgo the "once in a lifetime opportunity" to join the club. They signed the contract. When they sought to cancel the contract three days later, they learned that they could not do so. The contract stated that no dues were refundable, even on a member's death; that a membership could not be transferred for any reason; that orders for merchandise could not be canceled even prior to shipment; and that merchandise could not be returned once accepted. Further, although members were to rely on warranties of the supplier for all merchandise, they were forbidden to make any "contact with the suppliers of merchandise." The plaintiffs then sought relief in court. The court held that the contract was unconscionable. [Niemiec v. Kellmark Corp., 153 Misc.2d 347, 581 N.Y.S.2d 569 (1992)]*

1. Courts will sometimes hold contracts unconscionable because of gross inadequacy of consideration. Is that a possibility here? What, for example, did the club offer as consideration for the contract?

2. What might be some other possible reasons for the court's conclusion that this contract was unconscionable?

FOR CRITICAL ANALYSIS

10–12. *Do you think that the advent of legalized forms of gambling, such as state-operated lotteries, is consistent with a continued public policy against the enforcement of gambling contracts? Why or why not?*

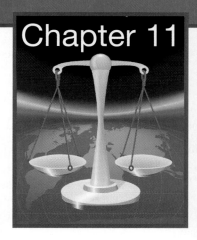

Chapter 11

Assent and Form

"Law is a pledge that the citizens of a state will do justice to one another."

Aristotle, 384–322 B.C.E.
(Greek philosopher)

CHAPTER OBJECTIVES

After reading this chapter, you should be able to:

1. Distinguish between a mistake of value or quality and a mistake of fact.
2. Describe fraudulent misrepresentation and its elements.
3. Discuss the effects of undue influence and duress on contract enforceability.
4. Identify the types of contracts that must be in writing to be enforceable.
5. State the parol evidence rule, and indicate when parol evidence will be admissible.

A contract has been entered into by two parties, each with full legal capacity and for a legal purpose. The contract is also supported by consideration. Nonetheless, the contract may be unenforceable if the parties have not genuinely assented to the terms. Lack of genuine assent is a *defense* to the enforcement of a contract. As Aristotle stated in the above quotation, the law seeks to ensure that "the citizens of a state will do justice to one another." If the law were to enforce contracts not genuinely assented to by the contracting parties, injustice would result. The first part of this chapter focuses on what kinds of factors indicate that genuineness of assent to a contract may be lacking.

A contract that is otherwise valid may also be unenforceable if it is not in the proper form. For example, if a contract is required by law to be in writing, and there is no written evidence of the contract, it may not be enforceable. In the second part of this chapter, we examine the kinds of contracts that require a writing under what is called the *Statute of Frauds*. The chapter concludes with a discussion of the *parol evidence rule*, under which courts determine the admissibility at trial of evidence extraneous (external) to written contracts.

▌ Genuineness of Assent

Genuineness of assent may be lacking because of mistake, fraudulent misrepresentation, undue influence, or duress. Generally, a party who demonstrates that he or she did not genuinely assent to the terms of a contract can choose either to carry out the contract or to rescind (cancel) it, and thus avoid the entire transaction.

Mistakes

We all make mistakes, and it is not surprising that mistakes are made when contracts are created. In certain circumstances, contract law allows a contract to be avoided on the basis of mistake. Realize, though, that the concept of mistake in contract law has to do with mistaken assumptions relating to contract formation. For example, if you send your monthly bank loan payment to your plumber "by mistake," that is a kind of mistake totally different from the kind of mistake that we are discussing here. In contract law, a mistake may be a defense to the enforcement of a contract if it can be proved that the parties entered into the contract under different assumptions relating to the subject matter of the contract.

Courts have considerable difficulty in specifying the circumstances that justify allowing a mistake to invalidate a contract. Thus, the results in cases with similar facts can be different, and finding clearly defined rules governing the effects of mistakes can be difficult. Generally, though, courts distinguish between *mistakes as to judgment of market value or conditions* and *mistakes as to fact.* Only the latter normally have legal significance.

Suppose, for example, that Jud Wheeler contracts to buy ten acres of land because he believes that he can resell the land at a profit to Bart. Can Jud escape his contractual obligations if it later turns out that he was mistaken? Not likely. Jud's overestimation of the value of the land or of Bart's interest in it is an ordinary risk of business for which a court will not normally provide relief. Now suppose that Jud purchases a painting of a landscape from Roth's Gallery. Both Jud and Roth believe that the painting is by the artist Van Gogh. Jud later discovers that the painting is a very clever fake. Because neither Jud nor Roth was aware of this fact when they made their deal, Jud can rescind the contract and recover the purchase price of the painting.

Mistakes occur in two forms—*unilateral* and *bilateral (mutual)*. A unilateral mistake is made by only one of the contracting parties; a mutual mistake is made by both.

UNILATERAL MISTAKES　A unilateral mistake involves some *material fact*—that is, a fact important to the subject matter of the contract. In general, a unilateral mistake does not afford the mistaken party any right to relief from the contract. In other words, the contract normally is enforceable. For example, Ellen intends to sell her motor home for $17,500. When she learns that Chin is interested in buying a used motor home, she faxes him an offer to sell her vehicle to him, but when typing the fax, she mistakenly keys in the price of $15,700. Chin writes back, accepting Ellen's offer. Even though Ellen intended to sell her motor home for $17,500, she has made a unilateral mistake and is bound by contract to sell the vehicle to Chin for $15,700.

There are at least two exceptions.[1] First, if the *other* party to the contract knows or should have known that a mistake of fact was made, the contract may not be enforceable. In the above example, if Chin knew that Ellen intended to sell her motor home for $17,500, then Ellen's unilateral mistake (stating $15,700 in her offer) may render the resulting contract unenforceable. The second exception arises when a unilateral mistake of fact was due to a mathematical mistake in addition, subtraction, division, or multiplication and was made inadvertently and without gross (extreme) negligence. If a contractor's bid was low because he or she made a mistake in addition when totaling the estimated costs, any contract resulting from the bid may be rescinded. Of course, in both situations, the mistake must still involve some *material* fact. In the following

---

1.　*The Restatement (Second) of Contracts,* Section 153, liberalizes the general rule to take into account the modern trend of allowing avoidance in some circumstances even though only one party has been mistaken.

case, a unilateral mistake was made when a typist erroneously transformed $500 to $500,000 in a settlement offer.

CASE 11.1

WHITAKER v. ASSOCIATED CREDIT SERVICES, INC.

United States Court of Appeals,
Sixth Circuit, 1991.
946 F.2d 1222.

HISTORICAL AND ETHICAL SETTING *At one time, courts of law generally enforced all contracts without regard to the equity of the circumstances in a particular case. It was at this time that the law regarding mistakes developed in the courts of equity. Today, although the law regarding mistakes is part of the law of contracts, it is still applied and interpreted as a matter of equity. Thus, when deciding an issue concerning a mistake, a court may make use of the concepts of fault, good faith, unconscionability, unjust enrichment, and fairness. In other words, the basic rules of the law concerning mistakes are subject, in a particular case, to considerations of what is fair under the circumstances.*

FACTS Kenneth and Linda Whitaker had filed an action against Trans Union Corporation and others, alleging violations of the Fair Credit Reporting Act. The lawyer for Trans Union drafted an offer of settlement and presented it to the Whitakers' attorney. The amount of the settlement was supposed to be $500, but the first draft contained a typographical error showing the amount as $500,000. The error went undetected, and the $500,000 figure was typed into the second draft, which was forwarded to Linda Gosnell, Trans Union's attorney, who also did not detect the mistake. Gosnell filed the offer with the clerk of the court and mailed a copy to the Whitakers' lawyer. The Whitakers filed an acceptance of the settlement and forwarded it to Gosnell, who at that time noticed the typing error. The Whitakers refused a substitute offer, and Trans Union filed a motion in a federal district court to set aside the settlement. The district court found for Trans Union, and the Whitakers appealed.

ISSUE Could the settlement be set aside on the basis of mistake, notwithstanding the fact that the mistake was unilateral?

DECISION Yes. The U.S. Court of Appeals for the Sixth Circuit affirmed the district court's decision.

REASON In this case, a clerical error was indisputably the cause of the mistake. The court stated that "any reasonable person would have been shocked by the offer in light of the circumstances of this case[:] * * * that before they filed their action, plaintiffs had made no demands for monetary damages; * * * that plaintiffs in their complaint had specified only $3,600 in actual damages caused by Trans Union's conduct; and that the purported $500,000 offer was the first offer of any kind that plaintiffs had received from defendants." If the offer was allowed to stand, it would result in unjust enrichment. The court found that there was, in fact, no "meeting of the minds," because the Whitakers were aware of the outrageousness of the $500,000 offer.

FOR CRITICAL ANALYSIS—Social Consideration
What would be the social ramifications if everybody who received benefits as a result of a mistake retained those benefits?

MUTUAL MISTAKES When both parties are mistaken about the same material fact, the contract can be rescinded by either party.[2] Note that, as with unilateral mistakes, the mistake must be about a *material fact* (one that is important and central to the contract). If, instead, a mutual mistake concerns the later market value or quality of the object of the contract, the contract normally can be enforced by either party. This rule is based on the theory that both parties assume certain risks when they enter into a contract. Without this rule, almost any party who did not receive what he or she considered a fair bargain could argue bilateral mistake. In essence, this would make adequacy of consideration a factor in determining whether a contract existed, and as

---

2. *Restatement (Second) of Contracts*, Section 152.

discussed previously, the courts normally do not inquire into the adequacy of the consideration.

A word or term in a contract may be subject to more than one reasonable interpretation. In that situation, if the parties to the contract attach materially different meanings to the term, their mutual misunderstanding may allow the contract to be rescinded. The following classic case on mutual misunderstanding involved a ship named *Peerless* that was to sail from Bombay with certain cotton goods on board. More than one ship named *Peerless* sailed from Bombay that winter, however.

CASE 11.2

RAFFLES v. WICHELHAUS
Court of Exchequer, England, 1864.
159 Eng.Rep. 375.

HISTORICAL AND POLITICAL SETTING *Before the Civil War, the states in the southern United States were largely agricultural. By the mid-nineteenth century, the staple of this agricultural area had become cotton. Cotton was important to the economy of the South and to the economy of the European textile industry, which by 1860 was booming. In the 1860s, when the southern states seceded from the United States to form the Confederate States, the United States announced a blockade of southern ports. The states of the Confederacy knew that cotton was important to the European economy, and they were confident that Europe would exert pressure on the United States to lift the blockade. Instead, to obtain cotton, European merchants turned to other sources, including India.*

FACTS Wichelhaus purchased a shipment of cotton from Raffles to arrive on a ship called the *Peerless* from Bombay, India. Wichelhaus meant a ship called the *Peerless* sailing from Bombay in October; Raffles meant another ship called the *Peerless* sailing from Bombay in December. When the goods arrived on the December *Peerless,* Raffles delivered them to Wichelhaus. By that time, however, Wichelhaus was no longer willing to accept them.

ISSUE Was there a bilateral mistake of fact, which would release Wichelhaus from the contract?

DECISION Yes. The court adjudged that a bilateral mistake of fact had occurred, and hence there was no contract.

REASON When both parties contract under the mistaken, but reasonable, belief that a certain fact is true from an objective viewpoint, neither one is bound by the contract. The British court hearing the case stated, "There is nothing on the face of the contract to show that any particular ship called the 'Peerless' was meant; but the moment it appears that two ships called the 'Peerless' were about to sail from Bombay there is a latent ambiguity. * * * That being so, there was no consensus * * * and therefore no binding contract."

FOR CRITICAL ANALYSIS—Social Consideration
What policy considerations underlie the general rule that contracts involving mutual mistakes of fact may be rescinded, whereas contracts involving unilateral mistakes of fact (with the exceptions discussed earlier) may not be?

"It was beautiful and simple as all truly great swindles are."

O. Henry, 1862–1910
(American author)

Fraudulent Misrepresentation

Although fraud is a tort, the presence of fraud also affects the genuineness of the innocent party's consent to a contract. When an innocent party consents to a contract with fraudulent terms, the contract usually can be avoided, because he or she has not *voluntarily* consented to the terms.[3] Normally, the innocent party can either rescind (cancel) the contract and be restored to his or her original position or enforce the contract and seek damages for injuries resulting from the fraud.

---

3. *Restatement (Second) of Contracts,* Sections 163 and 164.

Typically, there are three elements of fraud:

1. A misrepresentation of a material fact must occur.
2. There must be an intent to deceive.
3. The innocent party must justifiably rely on the misrepresentation.

Additionally, to collect damages, a party must have been injured as a result of the misrepresentation.

> **REMEMBER** To collect damages in almost any lawsuit, there must be some sort of injury.

MISREPRESENTATION MUST OCCUR   The first element of proving fraud is to show that misrepresentation of a material fact has occurred. This misrepresentation can take the form of words or actions. For example, an art gallery owner's statement "This painting is a Picasso" is a misrepresentation of fact if the painting was done by another artist.

A statement of opinion is generally not subject to a claim of fraud. For example, claims such as "This computer will never break down" and "This car will last for years and years" are statements of opinion, not fact, and contracting parties should recognize them as such and not rely on them. A fact is objective and verifiable; an opinion is usually subject to debate. Therefore, a seller is allowed to "huff and puff his wares" without being liable for fraud. In certain cases, however, particularly when a naïve purchaser relies on a so-called expert's opinion, the innocent party may be entitled to rescission or reformation (an equitable remedy granted by a court in which the terms of a contract are altered to reflect the true intentions of the parties). The issue in the following case is whether the statements made by instructors at a dancing school to one of the school's dance students qualified as statements of opinion or statements of fact.

CASE 11.3

VOKES v. ARTHUR MURRAY, INC.

District Court of Appeal of Florida,
Second District, 1968.
212 So.2d 906.

HISTORICAL AND SOCIAL SETTING   *In the seventeenth century, in some of the new American colonies, the law prohibited professional performances of music. By the time of the Revolutionary War, however, the bans had generally been lifted, and the nineteenth century saw the founding of opera companies, city orchestras, and music schools. In the South, gospel music gave birth to the blues, which in turn gave birth to ragtime and jazz. With the development of radio and the recording industries in the first decades of the twentieth century, music became available to an ever-growing American audience, and social dancing became increasingly popular. Dancing skills often led to popularity on the dance floor and—because dancing was popular—to social popularity, especially for the generations that came of age in the 1920s, 1930s, and 1940s. With the popularity of social dancing came dancing schools.*

FACTS   Audrey Vokes was a fifty-one-year-old widow. While she was attending a dance party at Davenport's School of Dancing, an Arthur Murray dancing school, an instructor sold her eight half-hour dance lessons for the sum of $14.50. Thereafter, over a period of less than sixteen months, she was sold a total of fourteen dance courses, which amounted to 2,302 hours of dancing lessons for a total cash outlay of $31,090.45. All of these lessons were sold to her by salespersons who continually assured her that she was very talented, that she was progressing in her lessons, that she had great dance potential, and that they were "developing her into a beautiful dancer." Vokes contended that, in fact, she was not progressing in her dancing ability, had no "dance aptitude," and had difficulty even "hearing the musical beat." She filed suit against the school in a Florida state court, seeking rescission of her contract on the ground of fraudulent misrepresentation. When the trial court dismissed her complaint, she appealed.

ISSUE   Could Vokes's contract be rescinded because the salespersons misrepresented her dancing ability?

DECISION   Yes. The Florida appellate court reinstated Vokes's complaint and remanded the case to the trial

(Continued)

Case 11.3—Continued

court for further proceedings consistent with the appellate court's opinion.

REASON   The court held that Vokes could avoid the contract because it was procured by false representations that she had a promising career in dancing. The court acknowledged that ordinarily, to be grounds for rescission, a misrepresentation must be one of fact rather than of opinion. The court concluded that "[a] statement of a party having *   *   * superior knowledge may be regarded as a statement of fact although it would

be considered as opinion if the parties were dealing on equal terms. It could be reasonably supposed here that defendants [the dance studio] had 'superior knowledge' as to whether plaintiff had 'dance potential.'"

FOR CRITICAL ANALYSIS—Social Consideration   *If the law imposed liability for fraudulent misrepresentation on all persons who make false statements of opinion (such as "This car is the best on the road"), as well as on those persons who make false statements of fact (such as "This car has only been driven twelve thousand miles"), would society benefit? Explain.*

Misrepresentation by Conduct   Misrepresentation can occur by conduct, as well as through express oral or written statements. For example, if a seller, by his or her actions, prevents a buyer from learning of some fact that is material to the contract, such an action constitutes misrepresentation by conduct. Suppose that Cummings contracts to purchase a racehorse from Garner. The horse is blind in one eye, but when Garner shows the horse, he skillfully conceals this fact by keeping the horse's head turned so that Cummings does not see the defect. The concealment constitutes fraud.[4] Another example of misrepresentation by conduct is the false denial of knowledge or information concerning facts that are material to the contract when such knowledge or information is requested.

> "Ignorance of the law is no excuse in any country. If it were, the laws would lose their effect, because ignorance can always be pretended."
>
> **Thomas Jefferson, 1743–1826 (***Third president of the United States, 1801–1809***)**

Misrepresentation of Law   Misrepresentation of law does not *ordinarily* entitle a party to be relieved of a contract. For example, Debbie has a parcel of property that she is trying to sell to Barry. Debbie knows that a local ordinance prohibits building anything higher than three stories on the property. Nonetheless, she tells Barry, "You can build a condominium fifty stories high if you want to." Barry buys the land and later discovers that Debbie's statement is false. Normally, Barry cannot avoid the contract, because under the common law, people are assumed to know state and local laws. Exceptions to this rule occur, however, when the misrepresenting party is in a profession known to require greater knowledge of the law than the average citizen possesses.

Misrepresentation by Silence   Ordinarily, neither party to a contract has a duty to come forward and disclose facts, and a contract normally will not be set aside because certain pertinent information has not been volunteered. For example, suppose that you are selling a car that has been in an accident and has been repaired. You do not need to volunteer this information to a potential buyer. If, however, the purchaser asks you if the car has had extensive body work and you lie, you have committed a fraudulent misrepresentation.

Generally, if a *serious* defect or a *serious* potential problem is known to the seller but cannot reasonably be suspected to be known by the buyer, the seller may have a duty to speak. For example, suppose a city fails to disclose to bidders for sewer-construction contracts the fact that subsoil conditions will cause great expense in constructing the sewer. In this situation, the city has committed fraud.[5] Also, when the

---

4.   *Restatement (Second) of Contracts*, Section 160.
5.   *City of Salinas v. Souza & McCue Construction Co.*, 66 Cal. 2d 217, 424 P.2d 921, 57 Cal.Rptr. 337 (1967). Normally, the seller must disclose only "latent" defects—that is, defects that would not readily be discovered. Thus, termites in a house would not be a latent defect, because a buyer could normally discover their presence.

parties are in a fiduciary relationship (one of trust, such as partners, doctor and patient, or attorney and client), there is a duty to disclose material facts; failure to do so may constitute fraud. (See this chapter's *Business Law in Action* for a discussion of whether an employer has a duty to disclose pertinent information concerning a company's financial situation to a potential employee.)

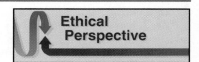
Ethical Perspective

In recent years, some courts have faced an issue with some interesting ethical implications: Does a seller of property have a duty to disclose "psychological damage" to real estate? Ordinarily, as mentioned, under the common law, sellers do not have a duty to volunteer information about property being sold unless the information concerns a serious defect or potential problem. What if a purchaser buys a house that has a reputation for being haunted, and the seller failed to disclose this history? Would the purchaser be able to rescind the contract on the basis of misrepresentation by silence? What if a gruesome murder had taken place on the property? Would this be a ground for rescission?

The essential question here is whether the law should come to the aid of people who suffer emotional distress on learning about such events—after they have purchased property. Does "psychological damage" to property qualify as a serious defect or potential problem that must be disclosed? Some people, at least, believe that it does. Recently, for example, a New Hampshire couple filed suit against a seller for failing to disclose that a terminally ill man shot himself in the living room of the home they purchased.[a] At least one court has allowed a purchaser to rescind a contract to purchase a home that had a reputation for being "haunted" because this history was not disclosed to the purchaser by the seller.[b]

For Critical Analysis: *When does so-called psychological damage rise to a level where it can serve as a ground for contract rescission due to the seller's failure to disclose the damage?*

a. As reported in *Lawyers Weekly USA*, February 27, 1995, p. 20.
b. See *Stambovsky v. Ackley*, 169 A.D.2d 254, 572 N.Y.S.2d 672 (1991).

INTENT TO DECEIVE The second element of fraud is knowledge on the part of the misrepresenting party that facts have been falsely represented. This element, normally called *scienter*,[6] or "guilty knowledge," generally signifies that there was an *intent to deceive*. *Scienter* clearly exists if a party knows that a fact is not as stated. *Scienter* also exists if a party makes a statement that he or she believes not to be true or makes a statement recklessly, without regard to whether it is true or false. Finally, this element is met if a party says or implies that a statement is made on some basis, such as personal knowledge or personal investigation, when it is not.

For example, suppose that Rolando, when selling a house to Cariton, tells Cariton that the plumbing pipe is of a certain quality. Rolando knows nothing about the quality of the pipe but does not believe it to be what she is representing it to be (and in fact it is not what she says it is). Rolando's statement induces Cariton to buy the house. Rolando's statement is a misrepresentation, because Rolando does not believe that what she says is true and because she knows that she does not have any basis for making the statement. Cariton can avoid the contract.

SCIENTER
Knowledge by the misrepresenting party that material facts have been falsely represented or omitted with an intent to deceive.

6. Pronounced sy-*en*-ter.

BUSINESS LAW IN ACTION

"Silent Fraud" in the Employment Context

The "silent fraud" doctrine dates back to at least 1886. In that year, the Michigan Supreme Court held that "[a] fraud arising from the suppression of the truth is as prejudicial as that which springs from the assertion of a falsehood, and courts have not hesitated to sustain recoveries where the truth has been suppressed with the intent to defraud."[a]

One of the problems with claims of silent fraud, as indicated in the *Ethical Perspective* on this topic, is that it is not always clear what information a party to a contract is required to disclose to the other party. For example, does a company have a duty to disclose to prospective employees information concerning the financial health of the company? That question arose in a recent case brought by Karen Clement-Rowe against the Michigan Health Care

Corporation.[b] The corporation hired Clement-Rowe as a health nurse in 1990. Upon accepting the job, Clement-Rowe sold her home in Saginaw, Michigan, and moved to Detroit. About a month after she was hired, the company fired 150 of its employees, including Clement-Rowe, in response to a severe financial crisis.

In her lawsuit, Clement-Rowe alleged, among other things, silent fraud. She claimed that the corporation had a duty to disclose its adverse financial condition when it hired her and that she would not have taken a job with the company if such information had been disclosed. According to Clement-Rowe, the nondisclosure was intentional—the corporation intended to induce her to rely on the nondisclosure in accepting employment. In evaluating the case, the Court of Appeals of Michigan held that Clement-Rowe had met the requirements for a claim of silent fraud; therefore the trial court's decision to grant the defendant corporation's request for summary judgment on this issue was in error.

The final words of the appellate court's opinion contain an important

message for any company that seeks to hire new personnel while facing serious financial difficulties: "Today's employment market is both tenuous and difficult. Nearly all employment is at-will.[c] The economic well-being and financial stability of a potential employer is an important factor in accepting a job offer. Consequently, an employer who succeeds in asserting its economic health to attract qualified employees knowing the assertions are untrue may not later hide behind an at-will employment contract. Neither may it be permitted to avoid liability after omitting to disclose, when asked, known economic instability which later leads to economically-based layoffs."

For Critical Analysis: *If employers were required to disclose adverse financial conditions to prospective employees, how would employers be able to induce qualified personnel (who may be able to help the companies recover financially) to come to work for their companies?*

a.   *Tompkins v. Hollister*, 60 Mich. 470, 27 N.W. 651 (1886).

b.   *Clement-Rowe v. Michigan Health Care Corp.*, 212 Mich.App. 503, 538 N.W.2d 20 (1995).

c.   Under the common law doctrine of employment at will, an employer can fire employees "at will"—that is, with or without cause (see Chapter 32).

REMEMBER An opinion is not a contract offer, not a contract term, and not fraud.

RELIANCE ON THE MISREPRESENTATION   The third element of fraud is *justifiable reliance* on the misrepresentation of fact. The deceived party must have a justifiable reason for relying on the misrepresentation, and the misrepresentation must be an important factor (but not necessarily the sole factor) in inducing the party to enter into the contract.

Reliance is not justified if the innocent party knows the true facts or relies on obviously extravagant statements. Suppose that a used-car dealer tells you, "This old Cadillac will get over sixty miles to the gallon." You normally would not be justified in relying on this statement. Suppose, however, that Merkel, a bank director, induces O'Connell, a co-director, to sign a statement that the bank's assets will satisfy its liabilities by telling O'Connell, "We have plenty of assets to satisfy our creditors." If O'Connell knows the true facts, he is not justified in relying on Merkel's statement. If O'Connell does not know the true facts, however, *and has no way of finding them out*, he may be justified in relying on the statement. The same rule applies to defects in property sold. If the defects are obvious, the buyer cannot justifiably rely on the seller's representations. If the defects are hidden or latent (that is, not apparent on examination), the buyer is justified in relying on the seller's statements.

Can a lawyer justifiably rely on the representations of another lawyer, when the two are on opposite sides in a lawsuit? That was one of the questions in the following case.

CASE 11.4

FIRE INSURANCE EXCHANGE v. BELL

Supreme Court of Indiana, 1994.
643 N.E.2d 310.

HISTORICAL AND ETHICAL SETTING *Lawyers' statements on behalf of clients are sometimes perceived to go beyond the truth. This perception is not new, but it seems to have become more widespread as the number of lawyers has increased. At the same time, however, legislatures, courts, and bar associations have nearly eliminated any rules allowing an attorney to keep a fact hidden from opposing counsel. Surprise witnesses, testimony, and evidence are not common tools of an attorney's trade. To the extent that they ever were, they have generally become artifacts of the past.*

FACTS A fire at the Indianapolis home of Joseph Moore severely burned Moore's sixteen-month-old grandson, Jason Bell. Jason's mother, Ruby, hired attorney Robert Collins to negotiate a payment for Jason's injuries with Moore's insurer, the Fire Insurance Exchange. Phillip Scaletta, the attorney for the insurer, told Collins that the limit on Moore's policy was $100,000. After the parties settled, Ruby learned that the limit was

actually $300,000. Through Ruby, Jason filed a suit in an Indiana state court against Scaletta and others, alleging, among other things, fraudulent misrepresentation of the policy limits. The defendants filed a motion for summary judgment, which the court denied. The defendants appealed, the state court of appeals affirmed, and the defendants appealed to the Supreme Court of Indiana.

ISSUE Did Jason's attorney have a right to rely on the allegedly fraudulent misrepresentations of the insurer's attorney?

DECISION Yes. The Supreme Court of Indiana affirmed this part of the lower court's decision and remanded the case for further proceedings.

REASON The state supreme court reasoned that it would "burden unnecessarily the courts and litigation process with discovery to verify the truthfulness of material representations made by opposing counsel." Relying on such statements "is an integral component of the fair and efficient administration of justice." The court believed that "[t]he law should promote lawyers' care in making statements that are accurate and trustworthy and should foster the reliance upon such statements by others."

FOR CRITICAL ANALYSIS—Economic Consideration *If attorneys were not held to the standard the court upholds in this case, what would be the effect on negotiations and trial tactics in the course of litigation?*

INJURY TO THE INNOCENT PARTY Most courts do not require a showing of injury when the action is to *rescind* the contract—these courts hold that because rescission returns the parties to the positions they held before the contract was made, a showing of injury to the innocent party is unnecessary.[7]

For a person to recover damages caused by fraud, however, proof of an injury is universally required. The measure of damages is ordinarily equal to the property's value had it been delivered as represented, less the actual price paid for the property. In actions based on fraud, courts often award *punitive,* or *exemplary, damages*—which are granted to a plaintiff over and above the proved, actual compensation for the loss. Punitive damages are based on the public-policy consideration of punishing the defendant or setting an example to deter similar wrongdoing by others.

Undue Influence

Undue influence arises from relationships in which one party can greatly influence another party, thus overcoming that party's free will. Minors and elderly people, for example, are often under the influence of guardians. If a guardian induces a young or elderly *ward* (a person placed by a court under the care of a guardian) to enter into a contract that benefits the guardian, the guardian may have exerted undue influence.

CONTRAST Even when there is no undue influence, a minor can avoid a contract.

7. See, for example, *Kaufman v. Jaffe,* 244 App.Div. 344, 279 N.Y.S. 392 (1935).

LAW IN THE EXTREME

Promises, Promises

Sometimes, divorcing spouses resort to rather extreme legal tactics to gain title to property that is jointly held by the couple. Certainly, Ronald Askew did, when he and his wife, Bonnette, were divorcing. Ronald wanted to obtain sole title to certain properties owned jointly by the couple. When Bonnette refused to grant his request for them, Ronald faced a problem: How could he succeed in gaining title to the properties?

His solution to the problem was played out before a trial court judge in California. In a suit against Bonnette, Ronald claimed that she had misrepresented to him, prior to their marriage, that she loved him and was sexually attracted to him. (Bonnette, after they were married, admitted as

much—that she had only pretended to love Ronald.) Ronald argued that it was only in reliance on Bonnette's fraudulent misrepresentations that he married her and gave her joint-ownership rights in property formerly owned solely by Ronald. Therefore, because Bonnette's statements fraudulently induced him to marry her, she had no right to keep the property—it should go to him.

Ronald's tactic worked at trial. Among other things, the jury found that Bonnette had made a false representation as to a "past or existing material fact" for the purpose of inducing Ronald to rely on that representation. In all, Ronald was awarded over $240,000 in damages. On appeal, however, his tactic failed miserably. The California appellate court held that the trial court should have dismissed Ronald's complaint.

The court laced its opinion with references to Gilbert and Sullivan's operetta *Trial by Jury*, which lampooned "breach of promise" suits.

Such suits, which at one time allowed plaintiffs to recover for breach of promises of love and affection, had long ago been banned by state "anti-heart-balm" statutes. These statutes expressed a public policy against "litigation of the affairs of the heart." Quoting a line from one of Gilbert's later scripts, the court concluded, "'Gild the farthing if you will, But it is a farthing still.' So it is with lawsuits. This one is still a breach of promise action even if it is titled fraud."[a]

For Critical Analysis: *What would be the results for society if "breach of promise" suits were still allowed?*

a. *Askew v. Askew*, 22 Cal.App.4th 942, 28 Cal.Rptr.2d 284 (1994). (A farthing is an old British coin worth one-fourth of a penny. Here, the court is merely pointing out that regardless of whether the farthing is gilded, or plated, with gold or other precious metal, it still remains a farthing.)

Undue influence can arise from a number of confidential relationships or relationships founded on trust, including attorney-client, doctor-patient, guardian-ward, parent-child, husband-wife, and trustee-beneficiary relationships. The essential feature of undue influence is that the party being taken advantage of does not, in reality, exercise free will in entering into a contract. A contract entered into under excessive or undue influence lacks genuine assent and is therefore voidable.[8]

Duress

Assent to the terms of a contract is not genuine if one of the parties is *forced* into the agreement. Forcing a party to enter into a contract because of the fear created by threats is legally defined as *duress*.[9] In addition, blackmail or extortion to induce consent to a contract constitutes duress. Duress is both a defense to the enforcement of a contract and a ground for rescission, or cancellation, of a contract. Therefore, a party who signs a contract under duress can choose to carry out the contract or to avoid the entire transaction. (The wronged party usually has this choice in cases in which assent is not real or genuine.)

Economic need is generally not sufficient to constitute duress, even when one party exacts a very high price for an item the other party needs. If the party exacting the price also creates the need, however, economic duress may be found. For example, the Internal Revenue Service (IRS) assessed a large tax and penalty against Weller. Weller retained Eyman to resist the assessment. Two days before the deadline for

---

8. *Restatement (Second) of Contracts*, Section 177.
9. *Restatement (Second) of Contracts*, Sections 174 and 175.

filing a reply with the IRS, Eyman declined to represent Weller unless Weller agreed to pay a very high fee for Eyman's services. The agreement was unenforceable.[10] Although Eyman had threatened only to withdraw his services, something that he was legally entitled to do, he was responsible for delaying his withdrawal until the last days. Because it would have been impossible at that late date to obtain adequate representation elsewhere, Weller was forced into either signing the contract or losing his right to challenge the IRS assessment.

The Statute of Frauds— Requirement of a Writing

Today, almost every state has a statute that stipulates what types of contracts must be in writing. In this text, we refer to such statutes as the **Statute of Frauds.** The primary purpose of the statute is to ensure that there is reliable evidence of the existence and terms of certain classes of contracts deemed historically to be important or complex. Although the statutes vary slightly from state to state, all require the following types of contracts to be in writing or evidenced by a written memorandum:

STATUTE OF FRAUDS
A state statute under which certain types of contracts must be in writing to be enforceable.

1.   Contracts involving interests in land.
2.   Contracts that cannot *by their terms* be performed within one year from the date of formation.
3.   Collateral contracts, such as promises to answer for the debt or duty of another.
4.   Promises made in consideration of marriage.
5.   Contracts for the sale of goods priced at $500 or more.

Certain exceptions are made to the applicability of the Statute of Frauds in some circumstances. These exceptions are discussed later in this section.

The actual name of the Statute of Frauds is misleading, because it does not apply to fraud. Rather, the statute denies enforceability to certain contracts that do not comply with its requirements. The name derives from an English act passed in 1677 and presented here as this chapter's *Landmark in the Law.*

---

10.   *Thompson Crane & Trucking Co. v. Eyman*, 123 Cal.App.2d 904, 267 P.2d 1043 (1954).

The Statute of Frauds

LANDMARK IN THE LAW

On April 12, 1677, the English Parliament passed "An Act for the Prevention of Frauds and Perjuries." Four days later, the act was signed by King Charles II and became the law of the land. The act contained twenty-five sections and required that certain types of contracts, if they were to be enforceable by the courts, would henceforth have to be in writing or evidenced by a written memorandum.[a]

The British act was created specifically to prevent the further perpetration of the many frauds that had been brought about through the perjured testimony of witnesses in cases involving breached oral agreements, for which no written evidence existed. Although in the early history of common law in England, oral contracts were generally not enforced by the courts, they began to be enforced in the fourteenth century in

a.   These contracts are discussed in the text of this chapter.

(Continued)

Landmark in the Law—Continued

King Charles II, under whose reign Parliament enacted the Statute of Frauds. What reasons support the application of the statute today?

certain *assumpsit* actions.**b** These actions, to which the origins of modern contract law are traced, allowed a party to sue and obtain relief in cases in which a promise or contract had been breached. Enforcement of oral promises in actions in *assumpsit* became a common practice in the king's courts during the next two centuries.

Because courts enforced oral contracts on the strength of oral testimony by witnesses, it was not too difficult to evade justice by alleging that a contract had been breached and then procuring "convincing" witnesses to support the claim. The possibility of fraud in such actions was enhanced by the fact that in seventeenth-century England, courts did not allow oral testimony to be given by the parties to a lawsuit— or by any parties with an interest in the litigation, such as husbands or wives. Defense against actions for breach of contract was thus limited to written evidence and the testimony given by third parties.

Essentially, the Statute of Frauds offers a defense against oral contracts that fall under the statute. If a contract is oral when it is required to be in writing, it will not, as a rule, be enforced by the courts.

For Critical Analysis: *How does the Statute of Frauds benefit society economically—that is, in terms of the costs associated with litigation?*

b.   *Assumpsit* is Latin for "he undertook" or "he promised." The emergence of remedies given on the basis of breached promises dates to these actions. One of the earliest occurred in 1370, when the court allowed an individual to sue a person who, in trying to cure the plaintiff's horse, had acted so negligently that the horse died. Another such action was permitted in 1375, when a plaintiff obtained relief for having been maimed by a surgeon hired to cure him.

Contracts Involving Interests in Land

Land is real property, which includes not only land but all physical objects that are permanently attached to the soil, such as buildings, plants, trees, and the soil itself. Under the Statute of Frauds, a contract involving an interest in land, to be enforceable, must be evidenced by a writing.[11] If Carol, for example, contracts orally to sell Seaside Shelter to Axel but later decides not to sell, Axel cannot enforce the contract. Similarly, if Axel refuses to close the deal, Carol cannot force Axel to pay for the land by bringing a lawsuit. The Statute of Frauds is a *defense* to the enforcement of this type of oral contract.

A contract for the sale of land ordinarily involves the entire interest in the real property, including buildings, growing crops, vegetation, minerals, timber, and anything else affixed to the land. Therefore, a *fixture* (personal property so affixed or so used as to become a part of the realty—see Chapter 35) is treated as real property.

The Statute of Frauds requires written contracts not just for the sale of land but also for the transfer of other interests in land, such as mortgages and leases. We describe these other interests in Chapter 35.

The One-Year Rule

Contracts that cannot, *by their own terms*, be performed within one year from the day after the contract is formed must be in writing to be enforceable. Because disputes over such contracts are unlikely to occur until some time after the contracts are made, resolution of these disputes is difficult unless the contract terms have been put in writing.

---

11.   In some states, the contract will be enforced, however, if each party admits to the existence of the oral contract in court or admits to its existence during discovery before trial (see Chapter 3).

♦ **Exhibit 11–1**
The One-Year Rule

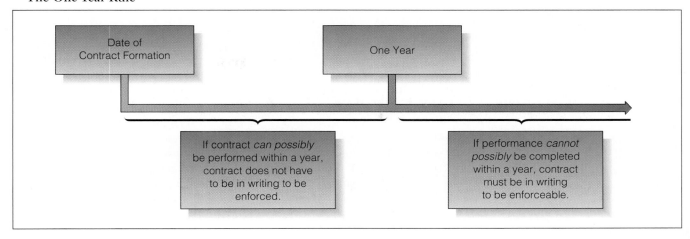

The one-year period begins to run *the day after the contract is made*.[12] Exhibit 11–1 illustrates the one-year rule.

The test for determining whether an oral contract is enforceable under the one-year rule of the statute is not whether the agreement is *likely* to be performed within one year from the date of contract formation but whether performance within a year is *possible*. When performance of a contract is objectively impossible during the one-year period, the oral contract will be unenforceable.

Collateral Promises

A **collateral promise,** or secondary promise, is one that is ancillary (subsidiary) to a principal transaction or primary contractual relationship. In other words, a collateral promise is one made by a third party to assume the debts or obligations of a primary party to a contract if that party does not perform. Any collateral promise of this nature falls under the Statute of Frauds and therefore must be in writing to be enforceable. To understand this concept, it is important to distinguish between primary and secondary promises and obligations.

PRIMARY VERSUS SECONDARY OBLIGATIONS Suppose that Kenneth orally contracts with Joanne's Floral Boutique to send his mother a dozen roses for Mother's Day. Kenneth promises to pay the boutique when he receives the bill for the flowers. Kenneth is a direct party to this contract and has incurred a *primary* obligation under the contract. Because he is a party to the contract and has a primary obligation to Joanne's Floral Boutique, this contract does *not* fall under the Statute of Frauds and does not have to be in writing to be enforceable. If Kenneth fails to pay the florist and the florist sues him for payment, Kenneth cannot raise the Statute of Frauds as a defense. He cannot claim that the contract is unenforceable because it was not in writing.

Now suppose that Kenneth's mother borrows $1,000 from the Medford Trust Company on a promissory note payable six months later. Kenneth promises the bank officer handling the loan that he will pay the $1,000 *if his mother does not pay the loan on time*. Kenneth, in this situation, becomes what is known as a *guarantor* on the loan. That is, he is guaranteeing to the bank (the *creditor*) that he will pay the loan if his mother fails to do so. This kind of collateral promise, in which the guarantor states that he or she will become responsible *only* if the primary party does not perform, must be

COLLATERAL PROMISE
A secondary promise that is ancillary (subsidiary) to a principal transaction or primary contractual relationship, such as a promise made by one person to pay the debts of another if the latter fails to perform. A collateral promise normally must be in writing to be enforceable.

---

12.   Arthur Corbin, *Corbin on Contracts* (St. Paul: West Publishing Co., 1952), Section 444.

in writing to be enforceable. We return to the concept of guaranty and the distinction between primary and secondary obligations in Chapter 22, in the context of creditors' rights.

AN EXCEPTION—THE "MAIN PURPOSE" RULE   An oral promise to answer for the debt of another is covered by the Statute of Frauds *unless* the guarantor's main purpose in accepting secondary liability is to secure a personal benefit. Under the "main purpose" rule, this type of contract need not be in writing.[13] The assumption is that a court can infer from the circumstances of a case whether the "leading objective" of the promisor was to secure a personal benefit and thus, in effect, to answer for his or her own debt.

Consider an example. Oswald contracts with Machine Manufacturing Company to have some machines custom-made for Oswald's factory. She promises Allrite Materials Supply Company, Machine Manufacturing's supplier, that if Allrite continues to deliver materials to Machine Manufacturing, she will guarantee payment. This promise need not be in writing, even though the effect may be to pay the debt of another, because Oswald's main purpose is to secure a benefit for herself.[14]

Another typical application of the so-called main purpose doctrine is the situation in which one creditor guarantees the debtor's debt to another creditor to forestall litigation. This allows the debtor to remain in business long enough to generate profits sufficient to pay *both* creditors.

Promises Made in Consideration of Marriage

A unilateral promise to pay a sum of money or to give property in consideration of a promise to marry must be in writing. If Mr. Baumann promises to pay Joe Villard $10,000 if Villard promises to marry Baumann's daughter, the promise must be in writing. The same rule applies to **prenuptial agreements**—agreements made before marriage (also called *antenuptial agreements*) that define each partner's ownership rights in the other partner's property. For example, a prospective wife may wish to limit the amount her prospective husband could obtain if the marriage ended in divorce. Prenuptial agreements made in consideration of marriage must be in writing to be enforceable.

Generally, courts tend to give more credence to prenuptial agreements that are accompanied by consideration. For example, assume that Maureen, who has little money, marries Kaiser, who has a net worth of $300 million. Kaiser has several children, and he wants them to receive most of his wealth upon his death. Prior to their marriage, Maureen and Kaiser draft and sign a prenuptial agreement in which Kaiser promises to give Maureen $100,000 per year for the rest of her life should they divorce. As consideration for her consenting to this amount, Kaiser offers Maureen $500,000. If Maureen consents to the agreement and accepts the $500,000, very likely a court would hold this to be a valid prenuptial agreement should the agreement ever be contested.

Contracts for the Sale of Goods

The Uniform Commercial Code (UCC) contains several Statute of Frauds provisions that require written evidence of a contract. Section 2–201 contains the major provision, which generally requires a writing or memorandum for the sale of goods priced at $500 or more. A writing that will satisfy the UCC requirement need only state the quantity term; other terms agreed upon need not be stated "accurately" in the writing, as long as they adequately reflect both parties' intentions. The contract will not be

PRENUPTIAL AGREEMENT
An agreement made before marriage that defines each partner's ownership rights in the other partner's property. Prenuptial agreements must be in writing to be enforceable.

---

13.   *Restatement (Second) of Contracts*, Section 116.
14.   See *Kampman v. Pittsburgh Contracting and Engineering Co.*, 316 Pa. 502, 175 A. 396 (1934).

Schwadron/Cartoonists & Writers Syndicate.

"And do you, Bob, agree to the wording of Alice's pre-nuptial agreements, and do you, Alice, agree to wording of Bob's?"

enforceable, however, for any quantity greater than that set forth in the writing. In addition, the writing must be signed by the person against whom enforcement is sought. Beyond these two requirements, the writing need not designate the buyer or the seller, the terms of payment, or the price.

International Perspective

Recall from Chapter 1 that the Convention on Contracts for the International Sale of Goods (CISG) provides rules that govern international sales contracts between countries that have ratified the convention, or agreement. Article 11 of the CISG does not incorporate any Statute of Frauds provisions. Rather, it states that a "contract for sale need not be concluded in or evidenced by writing and is not subject to any other requirements as to form."[a]

Article 11 accords with the legal customs of most nations, in which contracts no longer need to meet certain formal or writing requirements to be enforceable. Ironically, even England, the nation that created the original Statute of Frauds in 1677, has repealed all of it except the provisions relating to collateral promises and to transfers of interests in land. Many other countries that once had such statutes have also repealed all or parts of them. Civil law countries, such as France, never have required certain types of contracts to be in writing.

For Critical Analysis: *If there were no Statute of Frauds and if a dispute arose concerning an oral agreement, how would the parties substantiate their respective positions?*

a.   We examine the provisions of the CISG in more detail in Chapters 14 through 16, in the context of sales law.

Exceptions to the Statute of Frauds

Exceptions to the applicability of the Statute of Frauds are made in certain situations. We describe those situations here.

PARTIAL PERFORMANCE   In cases involving contracts relating to the transfer of interests in land, if the purchaser has paid part of the price, taken possession, and made permanent improvements to the property, and if the parties cannot be returned to their status quo prior to the contract, a court may grant *specific performance* (performance of the contract according to its precise terms). Whether the courts will enforce an oral contract for an interest in land when partial performance has taken place is usually determined by the degree of injury that would be suffered if the court chose *not* to enforce the oral contract. In some states, mere reliance on certain types of oral contracts is enough to remove them from the Statute of Frauds.

Under the UCC, an oral contract is enforceable to the extent that a seller accepts payment or a buyer accepts delivery of the goods.[15] For example, if Ajax Corporation ordered by telephone twenty crates of bleach from Cloney, Inc., and repudiated the contract after ten crates had been delivered and accepted, Cloney could enforce the contract to the extent of the ten crates accepted by Ajax.

ADMISSIONS　In some states, if a party against whom enforcement of an oral contract is sought "admits" in pleadings, testimony, or otherwise in court proceedings that a contract for sale was made, the contract will be enforceable.[16] A contract subject to the UCC will be enforceable, but only to the extent of the quantity admitted.[17] Thus, if the president of Ajax Corporation admits under oath that an oral agreement was made with Cloney, Inc., for twenty crates of bleach, the agreement will be enforceable to that extent.

PROMISSORY ESTOPPEL　In some states, an oral contract that would otherwise be unenforceable under the Statute of Frauds may be enforced under the doctrine of promissory estoppel, or detrimental reliance. Recall from Chapter 9 that if a promisor makes a promise on which the promisee justifiably relies to his or her detriment, a court may *estop* (prevent) the promisor from denying that a contract exists. Section 139 of the *Restatement (Second) of Contracts* provides that in these circumstances, an oral promise can be enforceable notwithstanding the Statute of Frauds if the reliance was foreseeable to the person making the promise and if injustice can be avoided only by enforcing the promise.

15.　UCC 2–201(3)(c). See Chapter 14.
16.　*Restatement (Second) of Contracts*, Section 133.
17.　UCC 2–201(3)(b). See Chapter 14.

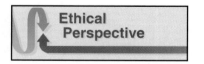
Ethical Perspective

Enforcing an oral contract on the basis of a party's reliance arguably undercuts the essence of the Statute of Frauds. The reason that such an exception is made is to prevent the statute—which was created to prevent injustice—from being used to promote injustice. Nevertheless, this use of the doctrine is controversial, as is the Statute of Frauds itself.

Since its inception three hundred years ago, the statute has been criticized by some because, although it was created to protect the innocent, it can also be used as a technical defense by a party breaching a genuine, mutually agreed-on oral contract—if the contract falls within the Statute of Frauds. For this reason, some legal scholars believe the act has caused more fraud than it has prevented. Thus, exceptions are sometimes made, such as under the doctrine of promissory estoppel, to prevent unfairness and injustice. Generally, the courts are slow to apply the statute if its application will result in obvious injustice. In some instances, this has required a good deal of inventiveness on the part of the courts.[a]

a.　See, for example, *Bader v. Hiscox,* 188 Iowa 986, 174 N.W. 565 (1919). According to the eminent contracts scholar Arthur Corbin, the court "worked indefatigably [tirelessly] to prevent the defendant from using the statute to defeat the enforcement of his promise." See *Corbin on Contracts* (St. Paul: West Publishing Co., 1952), Section 275, footnote 2.

Ethical Perspective—Continued

For Critical Analysis: *What are some of the costs and benefits to society of the Statute of Frauds?*

SPECIAL EXCEPTIONS UNDER THE UCC   Special exceptions to the applicability of the Statute of Frauds apply to sales contracts. Oral contracts for customized goods may be enforced in certain circumstances. Another exception has to do with oral contracts *between merchants* that have been confirmed in writing. We will examine these exceptions in Chapter 14.

▌The Statute of Frauds—
▌Sufficiency of the Writing

A written contract will satisfy the writing requirement of the Statute of Frauds. A *written memorandum* signed by the party against whom enforcement is sought will also satisfy the writing requirement.[18] A writing can consist of any confirmation, invoice, sales slip, check, or fax—or such items in combination. The writing need not consist of a single document to constitute an enforceable contract. One document may incorporate another document by expressly referring to it. Several documents may form a single contract if they are physically attached, by staple, paper clip, or glue. Several documents may form a single contract even if they are only placed in the same envelope.

The signature need not be placed at the end of the document but can be anywhere in the writing; it can even be initials rather than the full name. For example, Sam orally agrees to sell to Terry some land next to a shopping mall. Sam gives to Terry an unsigned memo that contains a legal description of the property, and Terry gives to Sam an unsigned first draft of their contract. Sam writes a signed letter to Terry that refers to the memo and to the first and final drafts of the contract. Terry sends to Sam an unsigned copy of the final draft of the contract with a signed check stapled to it. Together, the documents can constitute a writing sufficient to satisfy the Statute of Frauds and bind both parties to the terms of the contract.

A memorandum evidencing the oral contract need only contain the essential terms of the contract. Under most provisions of the Statute of Frauds, the writing must name the parties, subject matter, consideration, and quantity. With respect to contracts for the sale of land, some states require that the memorandum also state the essential terms of the contract, such as location and price, with sufficient clarity to allow the terms to be determined from the memo itself, without reference to any outside sources.[19] Under the UCC, in regard to the sale of goods, the writing need only name the quantity term and be signed by the party against whom enforcement is sought.

Because only the party against whom enforcement is sought need have signed the writing, a contract may be enforceable by one of its parties but not by the other. Suppose that Rock agrees to buy Devlin's lake house and lot for $150,000. Devlin writes Rock a letter confirming the sale by identifying the parties and the essential terms of the sales contract—price, method of payment, and legal address—and signs the letter. Devlin has made a written memorandum of the oral land contract. Because she signed the letter, she normally can be held to the oral contract by Rock. Rock, however, because he has not signed or entered into a written contract or memorandum, can plead the Statute of Frauds as a defense, and Devlin cannot enforce the contract against him. The following classic case illustrates what may be considered a "signed writing" by the court.

---

18.   Under the UCC Statute of Frauds, a writing is only required for contracts for the sale of goods priced at $500 or more. See Chapter 14.
19.   *Rhodes v. Wilkins*, 83 N.M. 782, 498 P.2d 311 (1972).

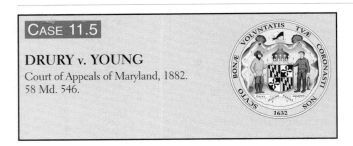

CASE 11.5

DRURY v. YOUNG

Court of Appeals of Maryland, 1882.
58 Md. 546.

HISTORICAL AND ECONOMIC SETTING   *Changes in the weather have sometimes affected U.S. harvests dramatically. In 1880, U.S. wheat production was up more than 200 percent over production a dozen years before. Due in part to this greater quantity of wheat on the market, the price was down nearly 30 percent. Corn production was so high, and prices so low, that many corn farmers burned corn for fuel because it was cheaper than shipping the crop to market. The next year, drought struck the United States, and harvests were poor. This caused prices to rise in 1882. At the time, one popular dish was sliced tomatoes with sugar and vinegar.*

FACTS   The plaintiff, Young, formed an oral agreement with the defendant, Drury, to buy several carloads of tomatoes. Afterward, Drury wrote a memorandum concerning the agreement and all its terms for his own records and put it in his safe. The memo, which Drury did not sign, was created on Drury's letterhead (which is a sufficient signing in the eyes of the court) and con-

tained Young's name in the text. Subsequently, Drury wrote a letter to Young stating he was not going to sell Young the tomatoes as agreed. When Young sued Drury in a Maryland state court for breach of contract, Drury used the Statute of Frauds as a defense. The trial court held in Young's favor, claiming that Drury's memo (even if it was never delivered to Young), combined with the subsequent letter, satisfied the writing requirement of the Statute of Frauds. Drury appealed. Ultimately, the Court of Appeals of Maryland (that state's highest court) reviewed the case.

ISSUE   Does the memo written by Drury satisfy the writing requirement under the Statute of Frauds?

DECISION   Yes. The Court of Appeals of Maryland affirmed the trial court's judgment.

REASON   The court stated that the Statute of Frauds is not concerned with whether or not a writing has been delivered, or with the custody of a writing, but just with the *existence* of a writing evidencing the agreement. Drury's memo with the terms of the agreement, kept in his own safe, in conjunction with the subsequent letter to Young denying delivery, provided sufficient evidence to the court that the Statute of Frauds had been satisfied.

FOR CRITICAL ANALYSIS—Technological Consideration
How does the existence of electronic mail (E-mail) affect the writing requirements under the Statute of Frauds?

▌The Parol Evidence Rule

PAROL EVIDENCE RULE
A substantive rule of contracts under which a court will not receive into evidence the parties' prior negotiations, prior agreements, or contemporaneous oral agreements if that evidence contradicts or varies the terms of the parties' written contract.

The **parol evidence rule** prohibits the introduction at trial of evidence of the parties' prior negotiations, prior agreements, or contemporaneous oral agreements if that evidence contradicts or varies the terms of written contracts. The written contract is ordinarily assumed to be the complete embodiment of the parties' agreement. Because of the rigidity of the parol evidence rule, however, courts make several exceptions:

1.   Evidence of a *subsequent modification* of a written contract can be introduced in court. Keep in mind that the oral modifications may not be enforceable if they come under the Statute of Frauds—for example, if they increase the price of the goods for sale to $500 or more or increase the term for performance to more than one year. Also, oral modifications will not be enforceable if the original contract provides that any modification must be in writing.[20]
2.   Oral evidence can be introduced in all cases to show that the contract was voidable or void (for example, induced by mistake, fraud, or misrepresentation). In this situation, if deception led one of the parties to agree to the terms of a written contract, oral evidence indicating fraud should not be excluded. Courts frown upon bad faith and are quick to allow such evidence when it establishes fraud.

---

20.   UCC 2–209(2), (3). See Chapter 14.

3. When the terms of a written contract are ambiguous, evidence is admissible to show the meaning of the terms.

4. Evidence is admissible when the written contract is incomplete in that it lacks one or more of the essential terms. The courts allow evidence to "fill in the gaps."

5. Under the UCC, evidence can be introduced to explain or supplement a written contract by showing a prior dealing, course of performance, or usage of trade.[21] We discuss these terms in further detail in Chapter 14, in the context of sales contracts. Here, it is sufficient to say that when buyers and sellers deal with each other over extended periods of time, certain customary practices develop. These practices are often overlooked in the writing of the contract, so courts allow the introduction of evidence to show how the parties have acted in the past.

6. The parol evidence rule does not apply if the existence of the entire written contract is subject to an orally agreed-on condition. Proof of the condition does not alter or modify the written terms but affects the *enforceability* of the written contract. Suppose, for example, that Jelek agrees to purchase Armand's car for $4,000, but only if Jelek's mechanic, Frank, inspects the car and approves of the purchase. Armand agrees to this condition, but because he is leaving town for the weekend and Jelek wants to use the car (if he buys it) before Armand returns, Jelek writes up a contract of sale, and they both sign it. Frank does not approve of the purchase, and when Jelek does not buy the car, Armand sues him, alleging that he breached the contract. In this case, Jelek's oral agreement did not alter or modify the terms of the written agreement but concerned whether or not the contract would exist at all.

7. When an *obvious* or *gross* clerical (or typographic) error exists that clearly would not represent the agreement of the parties, parol evidence is admissible to correct the error. For example, Sharon agrees to lease 1,000 square feet of office space at the current monthly rate of $3 per square foot from Stone Enterprises. The signed written lease provides for a monthly lease payment of $300 rather than the $3,000 agreed to by the parties. Because the error is obvious, Stone Enterprises would be allowed to admit parol evidence to correct the mistake.

The determination of whether evidence will be allowed basically depends on whether the written contract is intended to be a complete and final embodiment of the terms of the agreement. If it is so intended, it is referred to as an **integrated contract**, and extraneous evidence is excluded. If it is only partially integrated, evidence of consistent additional terms is admissible to supplement the written agreement.[22]

---

21. UCC 1–205, 2–202.
22. *Restatement (Second) of Contracts*, Section 216.

NOTE The parol evidence rule and its exceptions relate to the rules concerning the interpretation of contracts.

INTEGRATED CONTRACT
A written contract that constitutes the final expression of the parties' agreement. If a contract is integrated, evidence extraneous to the contract that contradicts or alters the meaning of the contract in any way is inadmissible.

Application

Law and the Businessperson— The Problem with Oral Contracts*

As a general rule, most business contracts should be in writing even when they fall outside the Statute of Frauds requirement. Businesspersons frequently make oral contracts over the telephone, however, partic-

ularly when the parties have done business with each other in the past.

Any time an oral contract is made, it is advisable for one of the parties to send either a written memorandum or a confirmation of the oral agreement by fax to the other party. This accomplishes two purposes: (1) it demonstrates a party's clear intention to form a contract, and (2) it provides the terms that at least one of the parties believes were agreed on. If the party receiving the memorandum or confirmation then disagrees with the

*This *Application* is not meant to substitute for the services of an attorney who is licensed to practice law in your state.

(Continued)

Application—Continued

terms as described, the issue can be addressed before performance begins.

What about the sale of goods between merchants? Under the UCC, written confirmation received by one merchant removes the Statute of Frauds requirement of a writing unless the merchant receiving the confirmation objects in writing within ten days of its receipt. This law (discussed in Chapter 14) points out clearly the need for the merchant receiving the confirmation to review it carefully to ascertain that the confirmation conforms to the oral contract. If the writing does not so conform, the merchant can object in writing (the Statute of Frauds still applies), and the parties can resolve misunderstandings without legal liability. If the merchant fails to object, the written confirmation can be used as evidence to prove the terms of the oral contract. Note, however, that this ten-day rule does not apply to contracts for interests in realty or for services.

 Checklist for Oral Contracts

1. When feasible, use written contracts.
2. If you enter into an oral contract over the telephone, fax a written confirmation outlining your understanding of the oral contract.
3. If you receive the other party's written or faxed confirmation, read it carefully to make sure that its terms agree with what you believed was already agreed on in the oral contract.
4. If you have any objections, notify the other party of these objections, in writing, within ten days.

Key Terms

collateral promise 285
integrated contract 291
parol evidence rule 290
prenuptial agreement 286
scienter 279
Statute of Frauds 283

Chapter Summary: Assent and Form

GENUINENESS OF ASSENT	
Mistakes (*See pages 274–276.*)	1. *Unilateral*—Generally, the mistaken party is bound by the contract *unless* (a) the other party knows or should have known of the mistake or (b) the mistake is an inadvertent mathematical error—such as an error in addition or subtraction—committed without gross negligence. 2. *Mutual (bilateral)*—When both parties are mistaken about the same material fact, such as identity, either party can avoid the contract. If the mistake concerns value or quality, either party can enforce the contract.
Fraudulent Misrepresentation (*See pages 276–281.*)	When fraud occurs, usually the innocent party can enforce or avoid the contract. The elements necessary to establish fraud are as follows: 1. A misrepresentation of a material fact must occur. 2. There must be an intent to deceive. 3. The innocent party must justifiably rely on the misrepresentation.
Undue Influence (*See pages 281–282.*)	Undue influence arises from special relationships, such as fiduciary or confidential relationships, in which one party's free will has been overcome by the undue influence exerted by the other party. Usually, the contract is voidable.
Duress (*See pages 282–283.*)	Duress is defined as the tactic of forcing a party to enter a contract under the fear of a threat—for example, the threat of violence or serious economic loss. The party forced to enter the contract can rescind the contract.

❚ Chapter Summary: Assent and Form—Continued

FORM	
Contracts Subject to the Statute of Frauds *(See pages 283–289.)*	*Applicability*—The following types of contracts fall under the Statute of Frauds and must be in writing to be enforceable: 1. *Contracts involving interests in land*—The statute applies to any contract for an interest in realty, such as a sale, a lease, or a mortgage. 2. *Contracts whose terms cannot be performed within one year*—The statute applies only to contracts objectively impossible to perform fully within one year from (the day after) the contract's formation. 3. *Collateral promises*—The statute applies only to express contracts made between the guarantor and the creditor whose terms make the guarantor secondarily liable. Exception: "main purpose" rule. 4. *Promises made in consideration of marriage*—The statute applies to promises to pay money or give property in consideration of a promise to marry and to prenuptial agreements made in consideration of marriage. 5. *Contracts for the sale of goods priced at $500 or more*—Under the UCC Statute of Frauds provision in UCC 2–201. *Exceptions*—Partial performance, admissions, and promissory estoppel.
Sufficiency of the Writing *(See pages 289–290.)*	To constitute an enforceable contract under the Statute of Frauds, a writing must be signed by the party against whom enforcement is sought, must name the parties, must identify the subject matter, and must state with reasonable certainty the essential terms of the contract. In a sale of land, the price and a description of the property may need to be stated with sufficient clarity to be determined without reference to outside sources. Under the UCC, a contract for a sale of goods is not enforceable beyond the quantity of goods shown.
Parol Evidence Rule *(See pages 290–291.)*	The parol evidence rule prohibits the introduction at trial of evidence of the parties' prior negotiations, prior agreements, or contemporaneous oral agreements that contradicts or varies the terms of written contracts. The written contract is assumed to be the complete embodiment of the parties' agreement. Exceptions are made in the following circumstances: 1. To show that the contract was subsequently modified. 2. To show that the contract was voidable or void. 3. To clarify the meaning of ambiguous terms. 4. To clarify the terms of the contract when the written contract lacks one or more of its essential terms. 5. Under the UCC, to explain the meaning of contract terms in light of a prior dealing, course of performance, or usage of trade. 6. To show that the entire contract is subject to an orally agreed-on condition. 7. When an obvious clerical or typographic error was made.

❚ For Review

1. In what types of situations might genuineness of assent to a contract's terms be lacking?

2. What is the difference between a mistake of value or quality and a mistake of fact?

3. What elements must exist for fraudulent misrepresentation to occur?

4. What contracts must be in writing to be enforceable?

5. What is parol evidence? When is it admissible to clarify the terms of a written contract?

∎ Questions and Case Problems

11–1. Genuineness of Assent. Jerome is an elderly man who lives with his nephew, Philip. Jerome is totally dependent on Philip's support. Philip tells Jerome that unless Jerome transfers a tract of land he owns to Philip for a price 15 percent below market value, Philip will no longer support and take care of him. Jerome enters into the contract. Discuss fully whether Jerome can set aside this contract.

11–2. Collateral Promises. Gemma promises a local hardware store that she will pay for a lawn mower that her brother is purchasing on credit if the brother fails to pay the debt. Must this promise be in writing to be enforceable? Why or why not?

11–3. One-Year Rule. On January 1, Dominic, for consideration, orally promised to pay Francis $300 a month for as long as Francis lived, with the payments to be made on the first day of every month. Dominic made the payments regularly for nine months and then made no further payments. Francis claimed that Dominic had breached the oral contract and sued Dominic for damages. Dominic contended that the contract was unenforceable because, under the Statute of Frauds, contracts that cannot be performed within one year must be in writing. Discuss whether Dominic will succeed in this defense.

11–4. Fraudulent Misrepresentation. Larry offered to sell Stanley his car and told Stanley that the car had been driven only 25,000 miles and had never been in an accident. Stanley hired Cohen, a mechanic, to appraise the condition of the car, and Cohen said that the car probably had at least 50,000 miles on it and probably had been in an accident. In spite of this information, Stanley still thought the car would be a good buy for the price, so he purchased it. Later, when the car developed numerous mechanical problems, Stanley sought to rescind the contract on the basis of Larry's fraudulent misrepresentation of the auto's condition. Will Stanley be able to rescind his contract? Discuss.

11–5. Collateral Promises. Jeffrey took his mother on a special holiday to Mountain Air Resort. Jeffrey was a frequent patron of the resort and was well known by its manager. The resort required of each of its patrons a large deposit to ensure payment of the room rental. Jeffrey asked the manager to waive the requirement for his mother and told the manager that if his mother for any reason failed to pay the resort for her stay there, he would cover the bill. Relying on Jeffrey's promise, the manager waived the deposit requirement for Jeffrey's mother. After she returned home from her holiday, Jeffrey's mother refused to pay the resort bill. The resort manager tried to collect the sum from Jeffrey, but Jeffrey also refused to pay, stating that his promise was not enforceable under the Statute of Frauds. Is Jeffrey correct? Explain.

11–6. Genuineness of Assent. Steven Lanci was involved in an automobile accident with an uninsured motorist. Lanci was insured with Metropolitan Insurance Co., although he did not have a copy of the insurance policy. Lanci and Metropolitan entered settlement negotiations, during which Lanci told Metropolitan that he did not have a copy of his policy. Ultimately, Lanci agreed to settle all claims for $15,000, noting in a letter to Metropolitan that $15,000 was the "sum you have represented to be the . . . policy limits applicable to this claim." After signing a release, Lanci learned that the policy limits were actually $250,000, and he refused to accept the settlement proceeds. What defense could Lanci assert to avoid his obligations under the release (contract)? Explain. [*Lanci v. Metropolitan Insurance Co.*, 388 Pa.Super. 1, 564 A.2d 972 (1989)]

11–7. Statute of Frauds. The plaintiffs—the Nicols, Hoerrs, Turners, and Andersons—purchased subdivision lots from Ken Nelson. The lots bordered an undeveloped tract and offered scenic views of an adjacent lake. When Nelson and his partners began taking steps to develop the previously undeveloped tract, the plaintiffs sued to enjoin (prevent) the development of the tract. The plaintiffs argued (and the trial court found) that the plaintiffs had purchased their lots only after receiving oral assurances from Nelson that (1) the tract would remain undeveloped open space, (2) the property was owned by a company that had no plans to build on the land, (3) he held an option to purchase the property if it became available, and (4) he would not develop the land if it came under his ownership. Nelson argued that the Statute of Frauds barred the enforcement of his oral promises. Did it? Explain. [*Nicol v. Nelson*, 776 P.2d 1144 (Colo.App. 1989)]

11–8. Fraudulent Misrepresentation. Nosrat, a citizen of Iran, owned a hardware store with his brother-in-law, Edwin. Edwin induced Nosrat to sign a promissory note written in English, for $11,400, payable to a third party, telling Nosrat that the document was a credit application for the hardware store. Although Nosrat could read and write English, he failed to read the note or to notice that the document was clearly entitled "PROMISSORY NOTE (SECURED) and Security Agreement." Edwin and others spent the money received from the third party in exchange for the note. When the third party sued for payment, Nosrat sought to void the note on the basis of Edwin's fraudulent inducement. Will Nosrat succeed in his attempt? Discuss. [*Waldrep v. Nosrat*, 426 So.2d 822 (Ala. 1983)]

11–9. One-Year Rule. Fernandez orally promised Pando that if Pando helped her win the New York state lottery, she would share the proceeds equally with him. Pando agreed to purchase the tickets in Fernandez's name, select the lottery numbers, and pray for the divine intervention of a saint to help them win. Fernandez won $2.8 million in the lottery, which was to be paid over a ten-year period. When Fernandez failed to share the winnings equally, Pando sued for breach of her contractual obligation. Fernandez countered that their contract was unenforceable under the Statute of Frauds, because the contract could not be performed within one year. Could the contract be performed within one year? Explain. [*Pando by Pando v. Fernandez*, 127 Misc.2d 224, 485 N.Y.S.2d 162 (1984)]

11–10. Genuineness of Assent. Linda Lorenzo purchased Lurlene Noel's home in 1988 without having it inspected. The basement started leaking in 1989. In 1991, Lorenzo had the paneling removed from the basement walls and discovered that the walls were bowed inward and cracked. Lorenzo then had a civil engineer inspect the basement walls, and he found that the cracks had been caulked and painted over before the paneling was installed. He concluded that the "wall failure" had existed "for at least thirty years" and that the basement walls were "structurally unsound." Does Lorenzo have a cause of action against Noel? If so, on what ground? Discuss. [*Lorenzo v. Noel*, 206 Mich.App. 682, 522 N.W.2d 724 (1994)]

11–11. One-Year Rule. Adam Curry worked as a videodisc jockey for MTV Networks (MTVN). In discussions during 1993, Curry and MTVN executives orally agreed that Curry could develop, at his own expense, an Internet site address ("mtv.com") and that MTVN would not interfere with Curry's development of the site. By early 1994, Curry's mtv.com address had been accessed by millions of Internet users, in part because of a computer bulletin board (developed by Curry) that facilitated communication between performers and other music professionals. In the meantime, MTVN decided to offer on-line services through America On-Line. These services were to include a bulletin board similar to that developed by Curry. In mid-January 1994, MTVN requested that Curry cease using the mtv.com address. A dispute ensued, and eventually MTVN sued Curry on several grounds. Curry counterclaimed that MTVN had breached its oral contract with him. MTVN argued that because the contract could not be performed within one year, the Statute of Frauds barred its enforcement. How should the court decide this issue? Explain. [*MTV Networks, A Division of Viacom International, Inc. v. Curry*, 867 F.Supp. 202 (S.D.N.Y. 1994)]

**A QUESTION OF ETHICS
AND SOCIAL RESPONSIBILITY**

11–12. *Mark Van Wagoner, an attorney experienced in real estate transactions, and his wife, Kathryn, were interested in buying certain property being sold by Carol Klas for her former*

husband, John Klas. When the Van Wagoners asked Carol Klas if there had been any appraisals of the property, she replied that there had been several appraisals, ranging from $175,000 to $192,000. (At trial, Carol claimed that she understood the term appraisal to mean any opinion as to the market value of the house.) The Van Wagoners did not request a written appraisal of the property until after signing an agreement to purchase the property for $175,000. Carol Klas then provided them with a written appraisal that listed the house's value as $165,000. When the Van Wagoners refused to go through with the deal, John Klas brought suit to recover the difference between the agreement price and the price for which the house was later sold. In view of these facts, answer the following questions. [Klas v. Van Wagoner, 829 P.2d 135 (Utah App.1992)]

1. The Van Wagoners claimed that the contract should be rescinded on the basis of their mistaken assumption as to the value of the house. What kind of mistake was made in this situation (mutual or unilateral, mistake of value or mistake of fact)? How should the court rule on this issue?

2. Mark Van Wagoner was an attorney experienced in real estate transactions. Should the court take this fact into consideration when making its decision?

3. Generally, what ethical principles, as expressed in public policies, are in conflict here and in similar situations in which parties enter into a contract with mistaken assumptions?

 FOR CRITICAL ANALYSIS

11–13. *Describe the types of individuals who might be capable of exerting undue influence on others.*

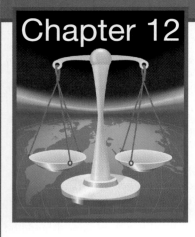

Chapter 12

Third Party Rights and Discharge

PRIVITY OF CONTRACT
The relationship that exists
between the promisor and the
promisee of a contract.

*"The laws of a state change with the changing
times."*

               Aeschylus, 525–456 B.C.E.
               (Greek dramatist)

CHAPTER OBJECTIVES

After reading this chapter, you should be able to:

1. Identify noncontracting parties who have rights under a contract.
2. Discuss assignments of contract rights, and describe what rights can or cannot be assigned.
3. Explain what a contract condition is and the different kinds of conditions that may exist.
4. Indicate how contract obligations are commonly discharged.
5. Differentiate between complete and substantial performance of a contract, and indicate when a breach of contract occurs.

Because a contract is a private agreement between the parties who have entered into it, it is fitting that these parties alone should have rights and liabilities under the contract. This concept is referred to as **privity of contract,** and it establishes the basic principle that third parties have no rights in contracts to which they are not parties.

You are probably convinced by now that for every rule of contract law there is an exception. As times change, so must the laws, as indicated in the opening quotation. When justice cannot be served by adherence to a rule of law, exceptions to the rule must be made. There are two important exceptions to the rule of privity of contract. One exception allows a party to a contract to transfer the rights arising from the contract to another or to free himself or herself from the duties of a contract by having another person perform them. Legally, the first of these actions is referred to as an *assignment of rights* and the second, as a *delegation of duties*. A second exception to the rule of privity of contract involves a *third party beneficiary* contract. Here, the rights of a third party against the promisor arise from the original contract, as the parties to the original contract normally make it with the intent to benefit the third party. We discuss the law relating to assignments, delegations, and third party beneficiary contracts in the first half of this chapter.

At some point, parties to a contract must know when their duties are at an end and when their contract is terminated. The second part of this chapter deals with the *discharge* of a contract, which is normally accomplished when both parties have performed the acts promised in the contract. We look at the degree of performance required, as well as at some other ways in which contract discharge can occur.

Assignments and Delegations

When third parties acquire rights or assume duties arising from contracts to which they were not parties, the rights are transferred to them by *assignment,* and the duties are transferred by *delegation*. Assignment and delegation occur *after* the original contract is made, when one of the parties transfers to another party a right or obligation arising from the contract.

Assignments

In a bilateral (mutual) contract, the two parties have corresponding rights and duties. One party has a right to require the other to perform some task, and the other has a duty to perform it. The transfer of *rights* to a third person is known as an **assignment.** When rights under a contract are assigned unconditionally, the rights of the *assignor* (the party making the assignment) are extinguished.[1] The third party (the *assignee,* or party receiving the assignment) has a right to demand performance from the other original party to the contract (the *obligor*).

   Consider Exhibit 12–1, which illustrates assignment relationships. Suppose that Brent owes Alex $1,000, and Alex assigns to Carmen the right to receive the $1,000. Here, a valid assignment of a debt exists. Once Alex has assigned to Carmen his rights under the original contract with Brent, Carmen can enforce the contract against Brent if Brent fails to perform.

   The assignee takes only those rights that the assignor originally had. Furthermore, the assignee's rights are subject to the defenses that the obligor has against the assignor. For example, assume that in the above example, Brent owes Alex the $1,000 under a contract in which Brent agreed to buy Alex's personal computer. Brent, in deciding to

ASSIGNMENT
The act of transferring to another all or part of one's rights arising under a contract.

---

1. *Restatement (Second) of Contracts,* Section 317.

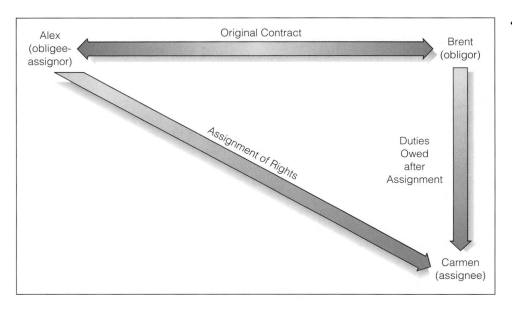

◆ **Exhibit 12–1**
Assignment Relationships
In the assignment relationship illustrated here, Alex assigns his *rights* under a contract that he made with Brent to a third party, Carmen. Alex thus becomes the *assignor* and Carmen the *assignee* of the contractual rights. Brent, the *obligor* (the party owing performance under the contract), now owes performance to Carmen instead of Alex. Alex's original contract rights are extinguished after assignment.

purchase the computer, relied on Alex's fraudulent misrepresentation that the computer's hard drive had a storage capacity of 1 gigabyte. When Brent discovered that the computer could store only 500 megabytes, he told Alex that he was going to return the computer to him and cancel the contract. Even though Alex had assigned his "right" to receive the $1,000 to Carmen, Brent need not pay Carmen the $1,000—Brent can raise the defense of Alex's fraudulent misrepresentation to avoid payment.

Assignments are important because they are involved in much business financing. Banks, for example, frequently assign the rights to receive payments under their loan contracts to other firms, which pay for those rights. For example, if you obtain a loan from your local bank to purchase a car, you might later receive in the mail a notice stating that your bank has transferred (assigned) its rights to receive payments on the loan to another firm and that, when the time comes to repay your loan, you must make the payments to that other firm.

Banks that make *mortgage loans* (loans to allow prospective home buyers to purchase land or a home) often assign their rights to collect the mortgage payments to a third party, such as GMAC Mortgage Corporation. Following the assignment, the home buyers are notified that they must make future payments not to the bank that loaned them the funds but to the third party. Millions of dollars change hands daily in the business world in the form of assignments of rights in contracts. If it were not possible to transfer (assign) contractual rights, many businesses could not continue to operate.

RIGHTS THAT CANNOT BE ASSIGNED   As a general rule, all rights can be assigned. Exceptions are made, however, in the following special circumstances:

1. If a statute expressly prohibits assignment, the particular right in question cannot be assigned. Suppose that Marn is a new employee of CompuFuture, Inc. CompuFuture is an employer under workers' compensation statutes (see Chapter 32) in this state, and thus Marn is a covered employee. Marn has a relatively high-risk job. In need of a loan, Marn borrows some money from Stark, assigning to Stark all workers' compensation benefits due her should she be injured on the job. The assignment of *future* workers' compensation benefits is prohibited by state statute, and thus such rights cannot be assigned.

2. When a contract is *personal* in nature, the rights under the contract cannot be assigned unless all that remains is a money payment.[2] Suppose that Brent signs a contract to be a tutor for Alex's children. Alex then attempts to assign to Carmen his right to Brent's services. Carmen cannot enforce the contract against Brent. Brent may not like Carmen's children or may for some other reason not want to tutor them. Because personal services are unique to the person rendering them, rights to receive personal services cannot be assigned.

3. A right cannot be assigned if assignment will materially increase or alter the risk or duties of the obligor.[3] Assume that Alex has a hotel, and to insure it he takes out a policy with Northwest Insurance Company. The policy insures against fire, theft, floods, and vandalism. Alex attempts to assign the insurance policy to Carmen, who also owns a hotel. The assignment is ineffective because it may substantially alter the insurance company's duty of performance and the risk that the company undertakes. An insurance company evaluates the particular risk of a certain party and tailors its policy to fit that risk. If the policy is assigned to a third party, the insurance risk is materially altered.

4. If a contract stipulates that the right cannot be assigned, then *ordinarily* it cannot be assigned. For example, suppose that Brent agrees to build a house for Alex. The contract between Brent and Alex states, "This contract cannot be assigned by Alex without Brent's consent. Any assignment without such consent renders this contract

---

2. *Restatement (Second) of Contracts*, Sections 317 and 318.
3. See UCC 2–210(2).

void, and all rights hereunder will thereupon terminate." Alex then assigns his rights to Carmen, without first obtaining Brent's consent. Carmen cannot enforce the contract against Brent.

There are several exceptions to the fourth rule. These exceptions are as follows:

1. A contract cannot prevent an assignment of the right to receive money. This exception exists to encourage the free flow of money and credit in modern business settings.
2. The assignment of rights in real estate often cannot be prohibited, because such a prohibition is contrary to public policy. Prohibitions of this kind are called restraints against **alienation** (transfer of land ownership).
3. The assignment of *negotiable instruments* (see Chapter 18) cannot be prohibited.
4. In a contract for the sale of goods, the right to receive damages for breach of contract or for payment of an account owed may be assigned even though the sales contract prohibits such assignment.[4]

ALIENATION
A term used to define the process of transferring land out of one's possession (thus "alienating" the land from oneself).

In the following case, the central issue was whether a covenant not to compete contained in an employment contract could be assigned.

---

4. UCC 2–210(2).

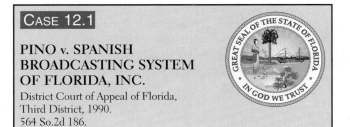

CASE 12.1

PINO v. SPANISH BROADCASTING SYSTEM OF FLORIDA, INC.
District Court of Appeal of Florida, Third District, 1990.
564 So.2d 186.

HISTORICAL AND CULTURAL SETTING *Owing to waves of immigration from Latin American countries in the 1960s and 1980s, more than half of the population of Dade County, Florida, is of Hispanic ancestry. In more than half of the households of this group, the language spoken at home is Spanish. Spanish-language radio and television stations are integral parts of the local entertainment spectrum, and therefore Spanish-speaking radio announcers and disc jockeys are in demand. Employment contracts between these stations and Spanish-speaking announcers or disc jockeys may contain covenants not to compete.*

FACTS In October 1985, Beatriz Pino signed a five-year employment contract as a radio announcer and disc jockey with two radio stations. The contract provided that Pino would not "engage directly or indirectly in the broadcasting business * * * in Dade or Broward Counties, Florida, for a period of twelve (12) months after the termination of her employment by the stations." The

contract also provided that it was assignable. In December 1986, the stations sold their assets to Spanish Broadcasting System of Florida, Inc. (SBS), and as part of the sale, Pino's contract was assigned to SBS. In October 1989, Pino contracted with Viva, a broadcasting competitor of SBS, to begin working for Viva when her SBS contract terminated in March 1990. SBS asked a Florida state court to grant a temporary injunction to enforce the agreement not to compete. Pino contended that the assignment of the clause containing the covenant not to compete was invalid. Although a Florida statute provided that covenants not to compete could be enforced, it said nothing about such covenants being assignable. The trial court held for SBS, and Pino appealed.

ISSUE Was the covenant not to compete assignable?

DECISION Yes. The appellate court affirmed the trial court's decision.

REASON The appellate court held that because the contract contained a provision permitting its assignment, the covenant not to compete was assignable. The court explained that its holding "conform[ed] with the policy of preserving the sanctity of contract and providing uniformity and certainty in commercial transactions."

FOR CRITICAL ANALYSIS—Social Consideration
What interests must a court balance when deciding whether a covenant not to compete is assignable?

NOTICE OF ASSIGNMENT   Once a valid assignment of rights has been made to a third party, the third party should notify the obligor of the assignment (for example, in Exhibit 12–1, Carmen should notify Brent). Giving notice is not legally necessary to establish the validity of the assignment, because an assignment is effective immediately, whether or not notice is given. Two major problems arise, however, when notice of the assignment is not given to the obligor:

1.   If the assignor assigns the same right to two different persons, the question arises as to which one has priority—that is, which one has the right to the performance by the obligor. Although the rule most often observed in the United States is that the first assignment in time is the first in right, some states follow the English rule, which basically gives priority to the first assignee who gives notice. For example, suppose that Brent owes Alex $1,000 on a contractual obligation. On May 1, Alex assigns this monetary claim to Carmen. Carmen gives no notice of the assignment to Brent. On June 1, for services Dorman has rendered to Alex, Alex assigns the same monetary claim (to collect $1,000 from Brent) to Dorman. Dorman immediately notifies Brent of the assignment. In the majority of states, Carmen would have priority, because the assignment to Carmen was first in time. In some states, however, Dorman would have priority, because Dorman gave first notice.

2.   Until the obligor has notice of assignment, the obligor can discharge his or her obligation by performance to the assignor, and performance by the obligor to the assignor constitutes a discharge to the assignee. Once the obligor receives proper notice, only performance to the assignee can discharge the obligor's obligations. To illustrate: Suppose that in the above example Alex assigns to Carmen his right to collect $1,000 from Brent. Carmen does not give notice to Brent. Brent subsequently pays Alex the $1,000. Although the assignment was valid, Brent's payment to Alex was a discharge of the debt, and Carmen's failure to give notice to Brent of the assignment caused her to lose the right to collect the money from Brent. If Carmen had given Brent notice of the assignment, however, Brent's payment to Alex would not have discharged the debt.

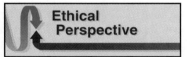

Ethical Perspective

Clearly, the rule governing notification of assignments rests on notions of fairness. The obligor must know to whom his or her obligations flow under a contract, and an assignee must be able to enforce the rights that have been assigned to him or her by the assignor (obligee).

The rules relating to notification of assignments reflect the attempt of the courts to balance the rights of parties. Nonetheless, seeming unfairness sometimes results when contract rights are assigned. For example, the English rule—that the first assignee to give notice, not the first assignee in time, can enforce the assigned rights—means that the first person to receive assigned rights may lose out.

Another problem arises when a party (the obligor) pays the other original party to the contract (the assignor), notwithstanding the assignee's notice to the obligor that the party must pay the assignee instead. For example, suppose that Brent owes Alex $1,000, and Alex assigns his right to that $1,000 to Carmen. Carmen notifies Brent that he is to pay her the $1,000 instead of Alex. If Brent pays Alex instead of Carmen, he will still owe Carmen the $1,000. Thus, in effect, Brent will have to pay the debt twice. Of course, Brent could try to recover the payment made to Alex, but this would involve spending time and money to litigate the matter, as well as the risk that Alex may not have funds available to recover.

For Critical Analysis: *What argument could you make in support of the English rule (that the first assignment to give notice is the first in right)?*

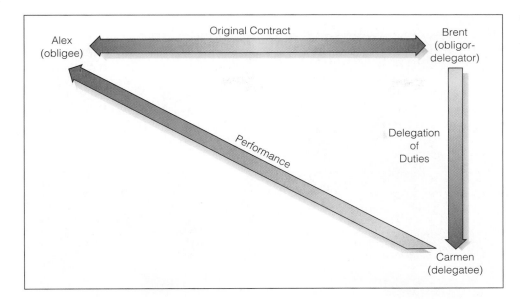

◆ **Exhibit 12–2**
Delegation Relationships
In the delegation relationship illustrated here, Brent delegates his *duties* under a contract that he made with Alex to a third party, Carmen. Brent thus becomes the *delegator* and Carmen the *delegatee* of the contractual duties. Carmen now owes performance of the contractual duties to Alex. Note that a delegation of duties does not normally relieve the delegator (Brent) of liability if the delegatee (Carmen) fails to perform the contractual duties.

Delegations

Just as a party can transfer rights to a third party through an assignment, a party can also transfer duties. Duties are not assigned, however; they are *delegated*. Normally, a **delegation of duties** does not relieve the party making the delegation (the *delegator*) of the obligation to perform in the event that the party to whom the duty has been delegated (the *delegatee*) fails to perform. No special form is required to create a valid delegation of duties. As long as the delegator expresses an intention to make the delegation, it is effective; the delegator need not even use the word *delegate*. Exhibit 12–2 graphically illustrates delegation relationships.

DELEGATION OF DUTIES
The act of transferring to another all or part of one's duties arising under a contract.

DUTIES THAT CANNOT BE DELEGATED   As a general rule, any duty can be delegated. There are, however, some exceptions to this rule. Delegation is prohibited in the following circumstances:

1.   When performance depends on the *personal* skill or talents of the obligor.
2.   When special trust has been placed in the obligor.
3.   When performance by a third party will vary materially from that expected by the obligee (the one to whom performance is owed) under the contract.
4.   When the contract expressly prohibits delegation.

The following examples will help to clarify the kinds of duties that can and cannot be delegated:

1.   Brent contracts with Alex to tutor Alex in the various aspects of financial underwriting and investment banking. Brent, an experienced businessperson known for his expertise in finance, delegates his duties to a third party, Carmen. This delegation is ineffective, because Brent contracted to render a service that is founded on Brent's *expertise,* and the delegation changes Alex's expectancy under the contract.
2.   Brent contracts with Alex *personally* to mow Alex's lawn during June, July, and August. Then Brent decides that he would rather spend the summer at the beach. Brent delegates his lawn-mowing duties to Carmen, who is in the business of mowing lawns and doing other landscaping work to earn money to pay for college. The delegation is not effective, no matter how competent Carmen is, without Alex's consent. The contract was for *personal* performance.

A contract to perform personal services, such as an interior designer's contract to decorate offices with a unique personal touch, cannot be delegated. Why not?

3. Brent contracts with Alex to pick up and deliver heavy construction machinery to Alex's property. Brent delegates this duty to Carmen, who is in the business of delivering heavy machinery. This delegation is effective. The performance required is of a *routine* and *nonpersonal* nature, and the delegation does not change Alex's expectancy under the contract.

EFFECT OF A DELEGATION   If a delegation of duties is enforceable, the *obligee* (the one to whom performance is owed) must accept performance from the delegatee (the one to whom the duties are delegated). Consider the third example in the above list, in which Brent delegates his duty (to pick up and deliver heavy construction machinery to Alex's property) to Carmen. In that situation, Alex (the obligee) must accept performance from Carmen (the delegatee), because the delegation was effective. The obligee can legally refuse performance from the delegatee only if the duty is one that cannot be delegated.

     A valid delegation of duties does not relieve the delegator of obligations under the contract.[5] For example, in the above example, if Carmen (the delegatee) fails to perform, Brent (the delegator) is still liable to Alex (the obligee). The obligee can also hold the delegatee liable if the delegatee made a promise of performance that will directly benefit the obligee. In this situation, there is an "assumption of duty" on the part of the delegatee, and breach of this duty makes the delegatee liable to the obligee. For example, if Carmen (the delegatee) promises Brent (the delegator), in a contract, to pick up and deliver the construction equipment to Alex's property but fails to do so, Alex (the obligee) can sue Brent, Carmen, or both. Although there are many exceptions, the general rule today is that the obligee can sue both the delegatee and the delegator.

"Assignment of All Rights"

Sometimes, a contract provides for an "assignment of all rights." The traditional view was that under this type of assignment, the assignee did not assume any duties. This view was based on the theory that the assignee's agreement to accept the benefits of the contract was not sufficient to imply a promise to assume the duties of the contract.

COMPARE In an assignment, the assignor's original contract rights are extinguished after assignment. In a delegation, the delegator remains liable for performance under the contract if the delegatee fails to perform.

---

5.   *Crane Ice Cream Co. v. Terminal Freezing & Heating Co.*, 147 Md. 588, 128 A. 280 (1925).

Modern authorities, however, take the view that the probable intent in using such general words is to create both an assignment of rights and an assumption of duties.[6] Therefore, when general words are used (for example, "I assign the contract" or "all my rights under the contract"), the contract is construed as implying both an assignment of rights and an assumption of duties.

▌ Third Party Beneficiaries

To have contractual rights, a person normally must be a party to the contract. In other words, privity of contract must exist. As mentioned earlier in this chapter, an exception to the doctrine of privity exists when the original parties to the contract intend at the time of contracting that the contract performance directly benefit a third person. In this situation, the third person becomes a **third party beneficiary** of the contract. As an **intended beneficiary** of the contract, the third party has legal rights and can sue the promisor directly for breach of the contract.

Who, though, is the promisor? In bilateral contracts, both parties to the contract are promisors, because they both make promises that can be enforced. In third party beneficiary contracts, courts will determine the identity of the promisor by asking which party made the promise that benefits the third party—that person is the promisor. Allowing a third party to sue the promisor directly in effect circumvents the "middle person" (the promisee) and thus reduces the burden on the courts. Otherwise, a third party would sue the promisee, who would then sue the promisor.

A classic case in the area of third party beneficiary contracts is *Lawrence v. Fox*—a case decided in 1859. In *Lawrence*, which is presented below as this chapter's *Landmark in the Law*, the court set aside the traditional requirement of privity and allowed a third party to bring a suit directly against the promisor. At the time, this was a novel idea and represented a radical departure from contract law. Prior to that time, contractual liability had always been limited to the parties to the contract.

THIRD PARTY BENEFICIARY
One for whose benefit a promise is made in a contract but who is not a party to the contract.

INTENDED BENEFICIARY
A third party for whose benefit a contract is formed; an intended beneficiary can sue the promisor if such a contract is breached.

---

6. See UCC 2–210(1), (4); *Restatement (Second) of Contracts*, Section 328.

Lawrence v. Fox (1859)

LANDMARK IN THE LAW

In 1859, the New York Court of Appeals (that state's highest court) decided a case, *Lawrence v. Fox*,[a] involving the following facts: Holly had borrowed $300 from Lawrence. Shortly thereafter, Holly loaned $300 to Fox, who in return promised Holly that he would pay Holly's debt to Lawrence on the following day. When Lawrence failed in his attempts to obtain the $300 from Fox, he sued Fox to recover the money. The issue before the court was whether Lawrence, who was not a party to the Holly-Fox contract, could sue Fox directly to recover the $300. The court held that Lawrence could do so. It was manifestly "just," declared the court, to allow Lawrence to recover the money from Fox. The principle of law enunciated was that "[in the case of] a promise made for the benefit of another, he for whose benefit it is made may bring an action for its breach."

Why didn't Lawrence sue Holly directly, rather than pursue the unusual route of suing Fox, which meant that his chances at recovery were much slimmer? According

a.   20 N.Y. 268 (1859).

(Continued)

to one scholar, the answer to this question is that the "Holly" in this case was probably Merwin Spencer Hawley. Both Hawley and the defendant, Arthur Wellesley Fox, were prominent members of the Buffalo, New York, business community. Evidence at trial suggested that the debt Hawley owed Lawrence was a gambling debt. Because gambling was illegal under New York law, Lawrence could not recover from Hawley directly in court, as the contract would have been deemed illegal.[b]

Although privity of contract remained the guiding principle until after the turn of the century, in two leading cases decided in 1916[c] and 1918,[d] the New York Court of Appeals cited *Lawrence v. Fox* in justifying its departure from the privity of contract principle. Since then, the third party beneficiary rule has been continuously expanded in scope.

For Critical Analysis: *What argument could be made in favor of not abandoning the concept of privity of contract in any circumstances?*

b.   See Antony Jon Waters, "The Property in the Promise: A Study of the Third Party Beneficiary Rule," 98 *Harvard Law Review* 1109, 1168 (1985).
c.   *MacPherson v. Buick Motor Co.*, 217 N.Y. 382, 111 N.E. 1050 (1916). This case is presented as the *Landmark in the Law* in Chapter 17.
d.   *Seaver v. Ransom*, 224 N.Y. 233, 120 N.E. 639 (1918).

Types of Intended Beneficiaries

The law distinguishes between *intended* beneficiaries and *incidental* beneficiaries. Only intended beneficiaries acquire legal rights in a contract. One type of intended beneficiary is a *creditor beneficiary*. A creditor beneficiary is one who, like Lawrence in the case discussed in this chapter's *Landmark in the Law*, benefits from a contract in which one party (the promisor) promises another party (the promisee) to pay a debt that the promisee owes to a third party (the creditor beneficiary). As an intended beneficiary, the creditor beneficiary can sue the promisor directly to enforce the contract.

Another type of intended beneficiary is a *donee beneficiary*. When a contract is made for the express purpose of giving a *gift* to a third party, the third party (the donee beneficiary) can sue the promisor directly to enforce the promise.[7] The most common donee beneficiary contract is a life insurance contract. Consider the following example of a typical life insurance contract: Akins (the promisee) pays premiums to Standard Life, a life insurance company, and Standard Life (the promisor) promises to pay a certain amount of money on Akins's death to anyone Akins designates as a beneficiary. The designated beneficiary is a donee beneficiary under the life insurance policy and can enforce the promise made by the insurance company to pay him or her on Akins's death.

As the law concerning third party beneficiaries evolved, numerous cases arose in which the third party beneficiary did not fit readily into either category—creditor beneficiary or donee beneficiary. Thus, the modern view, and the one adopted by the *Restatement (Second) of Contracts*, does not draw such clear lines and distinguishes only between intended beneficiaries (who can sue to enforce contracts made for their benefit) and incidental beneficiaries (who cannot sue, as will be discussed shortly).

Can an intended beneficiary recover on the basis of a contract between an attorney and client for legal services, if a transfer of property from the client to the beneficiary fails due to the attorney's negligence? That is the issue in the following case.

7.   *Seaver v. Ransom*, 224 N.Y. 233, 120 N.E. 639 (1918).

CASE 12.2

HOLSAPPLE v. McGRATH

Supreme Court of Iowa, 1994.
521 N.W.2d 711.

HISTORICAL AND ENVIRONMENTAL SETTING
The two great rivers of the central United States, the Mississippi and the Missouri, border the state of Iowa. The state contains a quarter of the finest, richest soil in the country. With 90 percent of this land farmed, Iowa farmers lead the nation in the production of corn, as well as providing much of our cattle, hogs, and other livestock. Three-quarters of the state's residents work in agriculture-related industries.

FACTS Don and Beulah DeVoss hired attorney James McGrath to handle the transfer of title to a farm they wished to give to Bobby and Barbara Holsapple. The transfer failed because McGrath did not have the new deed notarized. The DeVosses died before a corrected deed could be signed. The Holsapples filed a suit in an Iowa state court against McGrath, alleging negligence. McGrath filed a motion to dismiss for failure to state a claim, which the court granted on the ground that the Holsapples were not parties to the lawyer-client relationship between McGrath and the DeVosses and thus McGrath owed them no duty. The Holsapples appealed to the Supreme Court of Iowa.

ISSUE Can the Holsapples recover by establishing that they were intended beneficiaries of the DeVosses' transfer of their property and that the transfer failed only because of McGrath's negligence?

DECISION Yes. The Supreme Court of Iowa reversed the decision of the lower court and remanded the case.

REASON The state supreme court held that plaintiffs such as the Holsapples must plead two elements for their cases to proceed. First, a cause of action for professional negligence arises only when a plaintiff is a "specifically identifiable" beneficiary, as expressed by the grantor (the DeVosses). The court explained that "more than an unrealized expectation of benefits must be shown; a plaintiff must show that the * * * grantor attempted to put the donative wishes into effect and failed to do so only because of the intervening negligence of a lawyer." Second, "a cause of action ordinarily will arise only when as a direct result of the lawyer's professional negligence * * * the [benefit] is * * * lost." Because the Holsapples' petition alleged both elements, "it was error for the district court to dismiss it."

FOR CRITICAL ANALYSIS—Social Consideration
What are the policy reasons for allowing intended beneficiaries to enforce contracts made between other parties for their benefit (or, as in the Holsapple *case, to sue for negligence in the execution of such a contract)?*

When the Rights of an Intended Beneficiary Vest

An intended third party beneficiary cannot enforce a contract against the original parties until the rights of the third party have *vested*, which means the rights have taken effect and cannot be taken away. Until these rights have vested, the original parties to the contract—the promisor and the promisee—can modify or rescind the contract without the consent of the third party. When do the rights of third parties vest? Generally, the rights vest when either of the following occurs:

1. When the third party demonstrates *manifest assent* to the contract, such as sending a letter or note acknowledging awareness of and consent to a contract formed for his or her benefit.
2. When the third party materially alters his or her position in *detrimental reliance* on the contract.

If the contract expressly reserves to the contracting parties the right to cancel, rescind, or modify the contract, the rights of the third party beneficiary are subject to any changes that result. In such a situation, the vesting of the third party's rights does

BUSINESS LAW IN ACTION

Expanding the Rights of Third Parties

As discussed in this chapter's *Landmark in the Law*, since the early twentieth century, courts have continuously expanded the third party beneficiary rule. One way of protecting third parties is to apply the third party beneficiary rule, thus allowing an intended beneficiary to sue the promisor to enforce a contract. For example, in *Holsapple v. McGrath* (presented as Case 12.2), even though the plaintiffs (the Holsapples) were not in privity of contract with the attorney (McGrath), the court allowed them to sue McGrath directly on the ground that they were intended beneficiaries of the contract between McGrath and his clients (the DeVosses). Another example is a case decided by the Virginia Supreme Court in 1995, *Levine v. Selective Insurance Co. of America.*[a]

In the *Levine* case, Barry and Patricia Levine had contracted with Henry Elmore to construct a house on

some property they owned. The contract provided that Elmore would obtain construction hazard insurance, which would provide coverage for loss of materials and personal injuries on the job site, with the Levines named as beneficiaries on the policy. Elmore obtained the insurance from Selective Insurance Company of America, but the Levines were not shown as beneficiaries on the policy. During construction, a windstorm caused damage to the partially completed house. Selective's delay in reviewing and paying the insurance claim caused even further damage. Even though the Levines were not named as beneficiaries on the policy, the Virginia Supreme Court held that they could sue the company directly because the contract insured their property, and "all parties expressly understood that the beneficiaries of such [insurance contract] were the Levines." According to the court, the Levines had "pled sufficient facts . . . to support their claim that they are third-party beneficiaries to the contract between Elmore and Selective."

In another case, *Stinson v. Physicians Immediate Care, Ltd.,*[b] an

Illinois appellate court held that an employee who lost his job due to erroneous drug-testing results could sue the drug-testing laboratory. Rather than allowing the employee to recover as an intended third party beneficiary, however, the court held that the employee could sue the laboratory for negligence. In response to the defendant laboratory's claim that it had no duty to the employee (Bradford Stinson), the court stated that "the defendant confuses concepts of contract and tort law. There need not be a contract between the plaintiff [Stinson] and the defendant for the defendant to owe a tort duty." The court went on to state, "We find that drug testing laboratories . . . owe a duty of care to the testee/employee, regardless of the contractual arrangement between the lab and the employer. Privity of contract should never excuse a duty imposed by law on the conduct of individuals towards another in a reasonable society."

For Critical Analysis: *If courts allowed employees to be intended third party beneficiaries of contracts between their employers and drug-testing labs, how would you measure the duty that the drug-testing labs owed to the employees?*

a.   462 S.E.2d 81 (Va. 1995).

b.   269 Ill.App.3d 659, 646 N.E.2d 930, 207 Ill.Dec. 96 (1995).

not terminate the power of the original contracting parties to alter their legal relationships.[8] This is particularly true in most life insurance contracts, in which the right to change the beneficiary is reserved to the policyholder.

8. Defenses that can be raised against third party beneficiaries are given in *Restatement (Second) of Contracts*, Section 309.

 International Perspective

Among the common law countries, the third party beneficiary rule is unique to the United States. In all other common law countries, privity of contract is required before a party can sue to have a contract enforced—unless a statutory exception exists to counter common law.

For Critical Analysis: *Can you think of any reason why U.S. courts allow exceptions to the privity requirement with respect to third party beneficiaries, while other common law countries do not?*

Incidental Beneficiaries

The benefit that an **incidental beneficiary** receives from a contract between two parties is unintentional. Therefore, an incidental beneficiary cannot enforce a contract to which he or she is not a party. The following are examples of *incidental* beneficiaries:

1.   Jules contracts with Vivian to build a cottage on Vivian's land. Jules's plans specify that Super Insulation Company's insulation materials must be used in constructing the house. Super Insulation Company is an incidental beneficiary and cannot enforce the contract against Jules.

2.   Ed contracts with Ona to build a recreational facility on Ona's land. Once the facility is constructed, it will greatly enhance the property values in the neighborhood. If Ed subsequently refuses to build the facility, Tandy, Ona's neighbor, cannot enforce the contract against Ed.

Intended versus Incidental Beneficiaries

In determining whether a third party beneficiary is an intended or an incidental beneficiary, the courts generally use the *reasonable person* test. That is, a beneficiary will be considered an intended beneficiary if a reasonable person in the position of the beneficiary would believe that the promisee *intended* to confer upon the beneficiary the right to bring suit to enforce the contract. In determining whether a party is an intended or an incidental beneficiary, the courts also look at a number of other factors. The presence of one or more of the following factors strongly indicates that the third party is an *intended* (rather than an incidental) beneficiary to the contract:

1.   Performance is rendered directly to the third party.
2.   The third party has the right to control the details of performance.
3.   The third party is expressly designated as a beneficiary in the contract.

▌ Contract Discharge

The most common way to **discharge**, or terminate, one's contractual duties is by the **performance** of those duties. The duty to perform under a contract may be *conditioned* on the occurrence or nonoccurrence of a certain event, or the duty may be *absolute*. In addition to performance, there are numerous other ways in which a contract can be discharged, including discharge by agreement of the parties and discharge based on impossibility of performance.

Conditions of Performance

In most contracts, promises of performance are not expressly conditioned or qualified. Instead, they are *absolute promises*. They must be performed, or the party promising the act will be in breach of contract. For example, JoAnne contracts to sell Alfonso a painting for $1,000. The parties' promises are unconditional: JoAnne's transfer of the painting to Alfonso and Alfonso's payment of $1,000 to JoAnne. The payment does not have to be made if the painting is not transferred.

In some situations, however, contractual promises are conditioned. A **condition** is a possible future event, the occurrence or nonoccurrence of which will trigger the performance of a legal obligation or terminate an existing obligation under a contract. If the condition is not satisfied, the obligations of the parties are discharged. Suppose that Alfonso, in the above example, offers to purchase JoAnne's painting only if an independent appraisal indicates that it is worth at least $1,000. JoAnne accepts Alfonso's offer. Their obligations (promises) are conditioned upon the outcome of the appraisal.

INCIDENTAL BENEFICIARY
A third party who incidentally benefits from a contract but whose benefit was not the reason the contract was formed; an incidental beneficiary has no rights in a contract and cannot sue to have the contract enforced.

DISCHARGE
The termination of an obligation. In contract law, discharge occurs when the parties have fully performed their contractual obligations or when events, conduct of the parties, or operation of the law releases the parties from performance.

PERFORMANCE
In contract law, the fulfillment of one's duties arising under a contract with another; the normal way of discharging one's contractual obligations.

CONDITION
A qualification, provision, or clause in a contractual agreement, the occurrence of which creates, suspends, or terminates the obligations of the contracting parties.

Should this condition not be satisfied (for example, if the appraiser deems the value of the painting to be only $500), their obligations to each other are discharged and cannot be enforced.

We look here at three types of conditions that can be present in any given contract: conditions precedent, conditions subsequent, and concurrent conditions.

CONDITION PRECEDENT
In a contractual agreement, a condition that must be met before a party's promise becomes absolute.

CONDITIONS PRECEDENT   A condition that must be fulfilled before a party's promise becomes absolute is called a **condition precedent.** The condition precedes the absolute duty to perform. For example, in the JoAnne-Alfonso example just given, Alfonso's promise is subject to the condition precedent that the appraised value of the painting be at least $1,000. Until the condition is fulfilled, Alfonso's promise is not absolute. Insurance contracts frequently specify that certain conditions, such as passing a physical examination, must be met before the insurance company will be obligated to perform under the contract. The issue in the following case involves a condition precedent.

CASE 12.3

CAL WADSWORTH CONSTRUCTION v. CITY OF ST. GEORGE
Supreme Court of Utah, 1995.
898 P.2d 1372.

HISTORICAL AND ECONOMIC SETTING *Partly because economic growth in the 1990s has been uneven, some state and local governments, including counties, cities, and towns, have struggled to balance their books. The economy has shifted from a manufacturing base to a service base, and growth in personal income has been slow, which affects the amount of state revenues. The federal government has also reduced the amount of money that it provides to states and municipalities. Consequently, state and local governments have raised taxes and fees, even while they have cut spending. The goal is to become more responsible with the funds that are available.*

FACTS   The city of St. George asked for bids to expand its municipal airport terminal. Cal Wadsworth Construction submitted the lowest bid. Because even the lowest (Wadsworth's) bid was more than the city had budgeted, the city council accepted the bid only on the condition that Wadsworth reduce it to conform to the city's budget. When Wadsworth did not meet the condition, the city reopened the bidding process. Wadsworth sued the city in a Utah state court for breach of contract. The court ruled in favor of the city on the ground that there was no contract, and Wadsworth appealed. The state appellate court affirmed. Wadsworth appealed to the Supreme Court of Utah.

ISSUE   Did Wadsworth's failure to fulfill the condition regarding reduction of the bid mean that there was no contract between Wadsworth and the city?

DECISION   Yes. The Supreme Court of Utah affirmed the lower court's decision.

REASON   The Supreme Court of Utah pointed out that "the City Council clearly and unambiguously imposed a condition of price reduction on its acceptance of Wadsworth's bid." The court stated that Wadsworth's bid constituted an offer, and the city's modification of the offer (the condition that the price be reduced) constituted a counteroffer, which Wadsworth had not accepted unconditionally. According to the court, "Merely expressing confidence that the requested reduction could be made later [as Wadsworth had done] was insufficient as an acceptance. We therefore hold *   *   * that the court of appeals did not err in concluding that a contract did not come into existence between Wadsworth and the City."

FOR CRITICAL ANALYSIS—Political Consideration
Why would a government agency impose a price reduction as a condition rather than reject the bidder's offer outright and request the bidder to submit a lower bid?

CONDITIONS SUBSEQUENT When a condition operates to terminate a party's absolute promise to perform, it is called a **condition subsequent.** The condition follows, or is subsequent to, the absolute duty to perform. If the condition occurs, the party need not perform any further. For example, assume that a law firm hires Julia Darby, a recent law-school graduate and a newly licensed attorney. Their contract provides that the firm's obligation to continue employing Darby is discharged if Darby fails to maintain her license to practice law. This is a condition subsequent, because a failure to maintain the license would discharge a duty that has already arisen.[9]

Generally, conditions precedent are common; conditions subsequent are rare. The *Restatement (Second) of Contracts* deletes the terms *condition subsequent* and *condition precedent* and refers to both simply as "conditions."[10]

CONCURRENT CONDITIONS When each party's absolute duty to perform is conditioned on the other party's absolute duty to perform, there are **concurrent conditions.** These conditions exist only when the parties expressly or impliedly are to perform their respective duties *simultaneously.* For example, if a buyer promises to pay for goods when they are delivered by the seller, each party's absolute duty to perform is conditioned upon the other party's absolute duty to perform. The buyer's duty to pay for the goods does not become absolute until the seller either delivers or attempts to deliver the goods. Likewise, the seller's duty to deliver the goods does not become absolute until the buyer pays or attempts to pay for the goods. Therefore, neither can recover from the other for breach without first tendering performance.

Discharge by Performance

The contract comes to an end when both parties fulfill their respective duties by performance of the acts they have promised. Performance can also be accomplished by tender. **Tender** is an unconditional offer to perform by a person who is ready, willing, and able to do so. Therefore, a seller who places goods at the disposal of a buyer has tendered delivery and can demand payment according to the terms of the agreement. A buyer who offers to pay for goods has tendered payment and can demand delivery of the goods. Once performance has been tendered, the party making the tender has done everything possible to carry out the terms of the contract. If the other party then refuses to perform, the party making the tender can consider the duty discharged and sue for **breach of contract**.

COMPLETE VERSUS SUBSTANTIAL PERFORMANCE Normally, conditions expressly stated in the contract must fully occur in all aspects for *complete performance* (strict performance) of the contract to occur. Any deviation breaches the contract and discharges the other party's obligations to perform. Although in most contracts the parties fully discharge their obligations by complete performance, sometimes a party fails to fulfill all of the duties or completes the duties in a manner contrary to the terms of the contract. The issue then arises as to whether the performance was nonetheless sufficiently substantial to discharge the contractual obligations.

To qualify as *substantial performance*, the performance must not vary greatly from the performance promised in the contract, and it must create substantially the same benefits as those promised in the contract. If performance is substantial, the other party's duty to perform remains absolute (less damages, if any, for the minor deviations).

CONDITION SUBSEQUENT
A condition in a contract that operates to terminate a party's absolute promise to perform.

CONCURRENT CONDITIONS
Conditions that must occur or be performed at the same time; they are mutually dependent. No obligations arise until these conditions are simultaneously performed.

• • • • • • • • • • • • • • • • • • • •
"The law is not exact upon the subject, but leaves it open to a good man's judgment."

Hugo Grotius, 1583–1645
(Dutch jurist, political leader, and theologian)
• • • • • • • • • • • • • • • • • • • •

TENDER
An unconditional offer to perform an obligation by a person who is ready, willing, and able to do so.

BREACH OF CONTRACT
The failure, without legal excuse, of a promisor to perform the obligations of a contract.

---

9. The difference between conditions precedent and conditions subsequent is relatively unimportant from a substantive point of view but very important procedurally. Normally, the plaintiff must prove conditions precedent, because usually it is he or she who claims there is a duty to be performed. Similarly, the defendant must usually prove conditions subsequent, because usually it is he or she who claims that a duty no longer exists.
10. *Restatement (Second) of Contracts*, Section 224.

For example, a couple contracts with a construction company to build a house. The contract specifies that Brand X plasterboard be used for the walls. The builder cannot obtain Brand X plasterboard, and the buyers are on holiday in France and virtually unreachable. The builder decides to install Brand Y instead, which he knows is identical in quality and durability to Brand X plasterboard. All other aspects of construction conform to the contract. Does this deviation constitute a breach of contract? Can the buyers avoid their contractual obligation to pay the builder because Brand Y plasterboard was used instead of Brand X? Very likely, a court would hold that the builder had substantially performed his end of the bargain, and therefore the couple is obligated to pay the builder.[11]

What if the plasterboard substituted for Brand X had been inferior in quality to Brand X, reducing the value of the house by $1,000? Again, a court would likely hold that the contract was substantially performed and that the contractor should be paid the price agreed on in the contract, less that $1,000.

PERFORMANCE TO THE SATISFACTION OF ANOTHER   Contracts often state that completed work must personally satisfy one of the parties or a third person. The question is whether this satisfaction becomes a condition precedent, requiring actual personal satisfaction or approval for discharge, or whether the test of satisfaction is performance that would satisfy a *reasonable person* (substantial performance).

When the subject matter of the contract is personal, a contract to be performed to the satisfaction of one of the parties is conditioned, and performance must actually satisfy that party. For example, contracts for portraits, works of art, and tailoring are considered personal. Therefore, only the personal satisfaction of the party fulfills the condition—unless a jury finds the party is expressing dissatisfaction only to avoid payment or otherwise is not acting in good faith.

Contracts that involve mechanical fitness, utility, or marketability need only be performed to the satisfaction of a reasonable person unless they *expressly state otherwise*. When such contracts require performance to the satisfaction of a third party (for example, "to the satisfaction of Robert Ames, the supervising engineer"), the courts are divided. A majority of courts require the work to be satisfactory to a reasonable person, but some courts hold that the personal satisfaction of the third party (Robert Ames) must be met. Again, the personal judgment must be made honestly, or the condition will be excused.

MATERIAL BREACH OF CONTRACT   When a breach of contract is *material*[12]—that is, when performance is not deemed substantial—the nonbreaching party is excused from the performance of contractual duties and has a cause of action to sue for damages caused by the breach. If the breach is *minor* (not material), the nonbreaching party's duty to perform can sometimes be suspended until the breach is remedied, but the duty is not entirely excused. Once the minor breach is cured, the nonbreaching party must resume performance of the contractual obligations undertaken.

A breach entitles the nonbreaching party to sue for damages, but only a material breach discharges the nonbreaching party from the contract. The policy underlying these rules is that contracts should go forward when only minor problems occur, but contracts should be terminated if major problems arise.[13] The issue in the following case is whether performance was substantial or so inferior as to constitute a material breach of contract.

---

11.   For a classic case on substantial performance, see *Jacobs & Young, Inc. v. Kent*, 230 N.Y. 239, 129 N.E. 889 (1921).
12.   *Restatement (Second) of Contracts*, Section 241.
13.   See UCC 2–612, which provides that an installment contract for the sale of goods is breached only when one or more nonconforming installments *substantially impairs* the value of the *whole* contract.

CASE 12.4

WARREN v. DENISON
Court of Appeals of Texas, Amarillo, 1978.
563 S.W.2d 299.

HISTORICAL AND ECONOMIC SETTING *In the late 1960s, the condition of the U.S. economy was excellent. In 1968, the average price of an existing single-family home was $20,000. In 1970, however, average corporate share prices fell and unemployment rose. The next year, because of increasing inflation, President Richard Nixon imposed a ninety-day freeze on wages and prices. As the 1970s progressed, prices increased at a rapid pace. By 1973, the median price of an existing single-family house was $28,900, and by 1976, the price was $38,100. By 1978, the annual inflation rate was double digit.*

FACTS Denison was a building contractor hired by the Warrens to construct a house on their property. The parties formed a written contract in which the Warrens agreed to pay Denison $73,400 for the work. Further writings gave Denison the right to foreclose on the house if the Warrens refused to make payments. After the Warrens took possession of the house, they noted several flaws in the construction of the home and refused to

pay the $48,400 that they still owed to Denison. Denison initiated foreclosure proceedings, and the Warrens sued Denison in a Texas state court, alleging that Denison had breached their contract by his poor workmanship. The trial court ruled for Denison, and the Warrens appealed.

ISSUE Had Denison, despite his poor workmanship, discharged his duty under the contract?

DECISION Yes. The Texas appellate court affirmed the trial court's judgment.

REASON The court noted that "literal performance of each and every particular of such [construction] contracts is virtually impossible. * * * [S]ubstantial performance is regarded as full performance in allowing the builder to recover on the contract. * * * [A] job can be substantially performed with some breaches of workmanlike construction preventing * * * perfect performance." The Warrens were thus ordered to pay the $48,400 still owed to Denison, minus $2,161.50, which the Warrens felt was necessary to undertake repairs on the house necessitated by Denison's "construction flaws."

FOR CRITICAL ANALYSIS—Economic Consideration
If courts routinely held that only strict (complete) performance could discharge contractual obligations, how would this affect the construction industry? How would it affect homeowners?

ANTICIPATORY REPUDIATION OF A CONTRACT Before either party to a contract has a duty to perform, one of the parties may refuse to perform his or her contractual obligations. This is called **anticipatory repudiation**.[14] When anticipatory repudiation occurs, it is treated as a material breach of contract, and the nonbreaching party is permitted to bring an action for damages immediately, even though the scheduled time for performance under the contract may still be in the future.[15] Until the nonbreaching party treats this early repudiation as a breach, however, the breaching party can retract his or her anticipatory repudiation by proper notice and restore the parties to their original obligations.[16]

There are two reasons for treating an anticipatory repudiation as a present, material breach. First, the nonbreaching party should not be required to remain ready and willing to perform when the other party has already repudiated the contract. Second, the nonbreaching party should have the opportunity to seek a similar contract elsewhere and should have the duty to do so to minimize his or her loss.

ANTICIPATORY REPUDIATION
An assertion or action by a party indicating that he or she will not perform an obligation that the party is contractually obligated to perform at a future time.

14. *Restatement (Second) of Contracts*, Section 253, and UCC 2–610.
15. The doctrine of anticipatory repudiation first arose in the landmark case of *Hochster v. De La Tour*, 2 Ellis and Blackburn Reports 678 (1853), when the English court recognized the delay and expense inherent in a rule requiring a nonbreaching party to wait until the time of performance before suing on an anticipatory repudiation. See the *Ethical Perspective* in Chapter 16, on page 400, for a discussion of this case.
16. See UCC 2–611.

Quite often, an anticipatory repudiation occurs when a sharp fluctuation in market prices creates a situation in which performance of the contract would be extremely unfavorable to one of the parties. For example, Shasta Manufacturing Company contracts to manufacture and sell 100,000 personal computers to New Age, Inc., a computer retailer with 500 outlet stores. Delivery is to be made eight months from the date of the contract. One month later, three suppliers of computer parts raise their prices to Shasta. Because of these higher prices, Shasta stands to lose $500,000 if it sells the computers to New Age at the contract price. Shasta writes to New Age, informing New Age that it cannot deliver the 100,000 computers at the agreed-on contract price. Even though you might sympathize with Shasta, its letter is an anticipatory repudiation of the contract, allowing New Age the option of treating the repudiation as a material breach and proceeding immediately to pursue remedies, even though the actual contract delivery date is still seven months away.[17]

REMEMBER The risks that prices will fluctuate and values will change are ordinary business risks for which the law does not provide relief.

"Agreement makes law."

(Legal maxim)

Discharge by Agreement

Any contract can be discharged by the agreement of the parties. The agreement can be contained in the original contract, or the parties can form a new contract for the express purpose of discharging the original contract.

DISCHARGE BY RESCISSION As discussed in an earlier chapter, *rescission* is the process in which the parties cancel the contract and are returned to the positions they occupied prior to the contract's formation. For *mutual rescission* to take place, the parties must make another agreement that also satisfies the legal requirements for a contract—there must be an *offer*, an *acceptance*, and *consideration*. Ordinarily, if the parties agree to rescind the original contract, their promises *not* to perform those acts promised in the original contract will be legal consideration for the second contract.

Mutual rescission can occur in this manner when the original contract is executory on both sides (that is, neither party has completed performance). The agreement to rescind an executory contract is generally enforceable, even if it is made orally and even if the original agreement was in writing.[18] When one party has fully performed, however, an agreement to rescind the original contract is not usually enforceable. Because the performing party has received no consideration for the promise to call off the original bargain, additional consideration is necessary.[19]

NOVATION
The substitution, by agreement, of a new contract for an old one, with the rights under the old one being terminated. Typically, there is a substitution of a new person who is responsible for the contract and the removal of the original party's rights and duties under the contract.

DISCHARGE BY NOVATION The process of **novation** substitutes a third party for one of the original parties. Essentially, the parties to the original contract and one or more new parties all get together and agree to the substitution. The requirements of a novation are as follows:

1. The existence of a previous, valid obligation.
2. Agreement by all of the parties to a new contract.
3. The extinguishing of the old obligation (discharge of the prior party).
4. A new, valid contract.

An important distinction between an assignment or delegation and a novation is that a novation involves a new contract, and an assignment or delegation involves the old contract.

---

17. Another illustration can be found in *Reliance Cooperage Corp. v. Treat*, 195 F.2d 977 (8th Cir. 1952).
18. Agreements to rescind contracts involving transfers of realty, however, must be evidenced by a writing. Another exception has to do with the sale of goods under the UCC, when the sales contract requires written rescission.
19. Under UCC 2–209(1), however, no consideration is needed to modify a contract for a sale of goods. See Chapter 14. Also see UCC 1–107.

Suppose that you contract with A. Logan Enterprises to sell it your office-equipment business. Logan later learns that it should not expand at this time but knows of another party, MBI Corporation, that is interested in purchasing your business. All three of you get together and agree to a novation. As long as the new contract is supported by consideration, the novation discharges the original contract between you and Logan and replaces it with the new contract between you and MBI Corporation. Logan prefers the novation to an assignment because it discharges all the contract liabilities stemming from its contract with you. For example, if an installment sales contract had been involved, requiring twelve monthly payments, and Logan had merely assigned the contract (assigned its rights *and* delegated its duties under the contract) to MBI Corporation, Logan would have remained liable to you for the payments if MBI Corporation defaulted.

DISCHARGE BY ACCORD AND SATISFACTION As discussed in Chapter 9, in an *accord and satisfaction,* the parties agree to accept performance different from the performance originally promised. An *accord* is defined as an executory contract (one that has not yet been performed) to perform some act in order to satisfy an existing contractual duty that is not yet discharged.[20] A *satisfaction* is the performance of the accord agreement. An *accord* and its *satisfaction* discharge the original contractual obligation.

Once the accord has been made, the original obligation is merely suspended until the accord agreement is fully performed. If it is not performed, the party to whom performance is owed can bring an action on the original obligation. Suppose that Shea obtains a judgment against Marla for $4,000. Later, both parties agree that the judgment can be satisfied by Marla's transfer of her automobile to Shea. This agreement to accept the auto in lieu of $4,000 in cash is the accord. If Marla transfers her automobile to Shea, the accord agreement is fully performed, and the $4,000 debt is discharged. If Marla refuses to transfer her car, the accord is breached. Because the original obligation is merely suspended, Shea can bring an action to enforce the judgment for $4,000 in cash.

When Performance Is Impossible

After a contract has been made, performance may become impossible in an objective sense. This is known as **impossibility of performance** and may discharge a contract.[21]

OBJECTIVE IMPOSSIBILITY *Objective impossibility* ("It can't be done") must be distinguished from *subjective impossibility* ("I'm sorry, I simply can't do it"). Examples of subjective impossibility include contracts in which goods cannot be delivered on time because of a freight car shortage[22] and contracts in which money cannot be paid on time because the bank is closed.[23] In effect, the nonperforming party is saying, "It is impossible for *me* to perform," not "It is impossible for *anyone* to perform." Accordingly, such excuses do not discharge a contract, and the nonperforming party is normally held in breach of contract. Four basic types of situations will generally qualify as grounds for the discharge of contractual obligations based on impossibility of performance:[24]

1. *When one of the parties to a personal contract dies or becomes incapacitated prior to performance.* For example, Fred, a famous dancer, contracts with Ethereal Dancing Guild to play a leading role in its new ballet. Before the ballet can be performed, Fred

"Law is a practical matter."

Roscoe Pound, 1870–1964
(American jurist)

IMPOSSIBILITY OF PERFORMANCE
A doctrine under which a party to a contract is relieved of his or her duty to perform when performance becomes impossible or totally impracticable (through no fault of either party).

---

20. *Restatement (Second) of Contracts,* Section 281.
21. *Restatement (Second) of Contracts,* Section 261.
22. *Minneapolis v. Republic Creosoting Co.,* 161 Minn. 178, 201 N.W. 414 (1924).
23. *Ingham Lumber Co. v. Ingersoll & Co.,* 93 Ark. 447, 125 S.W. 139 (1910).
24. *Restatement (Second) of Contracts,* Sections 262–266, and UCC 2–615.

becomes ill and dies. His personal performance was essential to the completion of the contract. Thus, his death discharges the contract and his estate's liability for his non-performance.

2. *When the specific subject matter of the contract is destroyed.* For example, A-1 Farm Equipment agrees to sell Gudgel the green tractor on its lot and promises to have it ready for Gudgel to pick up on Saturday. On Friday night, however, a truck veers off the nearby highway and smashes into the tractor, destroying it beyond repair. Because the contract was for this specific tractor, A-1's performance is rendered impossible owing to the accident.

3. *When a change in the law renders performance illegal.* An example is a contract to build an apartment building, when the zoning laws are changed to prohibit the construction of residential rental property at this location. This change renders the contract impossible to perform.

4. *When performance becomes commercially impracticable.* The inclusion of this type of "impossibility" as a basis for contract discharge results from a growing trend to allow parties to discharge contracts in which the originally contemplated performance turns out to be much more difficult or expensive than anticipated. In such situations, courts may excuse parties from their performance obligations under the doctrine of *commercial impracticability*. For example, in one case, a court held that a contract could be discharged because a party would have to pay ten times more than the original estimate to excavate a certain amount of gravel.[25] We will discuss this doctrine in more detail in Chapter 16, in the context of sales contracts.

NOTE The doctrine of commercial impracticability does not provide relief from such events as ordinary price increases or predictable changes in the weather.

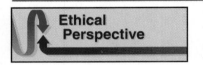
Ethical Perspective

Until the latter part of the nineteenth century, courts were reluctant to discharge a contract even when it appeared that performance was literally impossible. Just as society's ethics change with the passage of time, however, so law also makes a transition to reflect new perceptions of ethical behavior. Today, courts are much more willing to discharge a contract when its performance has become literally impossible. Holding a party in breach of contract in such circumstances no longer coincides with society's notions of fairness.

The doctrine of impossibility is applied only when the parties could not have reasonably predicted, at the time the contract was formed, the event or events that rendered performance impossible. The doctrine also rests on the assumption that the party claiming the defense of impossibility has acted ethically. In other words, a party cannot arrange events intentionally to make performance impossible.

For Critical Analysis: *What factors might a court examine to determine whether the events claimed to render performance impossible were not reasonably foreseeable?*

TEMPORARY IMPOSSIBILITY An occurrence or event that makes performance temporarily impossible operates to *suspend* performance until the impossibility ceases. Then, ordinarily, the parties must perform the contract as originally planned. If, however, the lapse of time and the change in circumstances surrounding the contract make it substantially more burdensome for the parties to perform the promised acts, the contract is discharged.

The leading case on the subject, *Autry v. Republic Productions*,[26] involved an actor who was drafted into the army in 1942. Being drafted rendered the actor's contract temporarily impossible to perform, and it was suspended until the end of the war. When the actor got out of the army, the value of the dollar had so changed that performance of the contract would have been substantially burdensome to him. Therefore, the contract was discharged.

25. *Mineral Park Land Co. v. Howard*, 172 Cal. 289, 156 P. 458 (1916).
26. 30 Cal.2d 144, 180 P.2d 888 (1947).

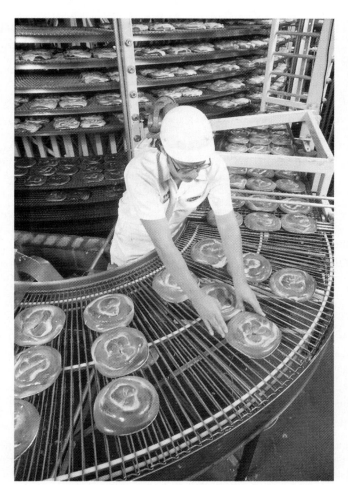

A production line in a commercial bakery. If a fire incapacitated the bakery's oven, would the bakery be excused from performing its contracts until the oven was fixed? If a contract involved a holiday order and the oven could not be fixed until after the holiday, would the contract be discharged?

▌ Key Terms

. . . .

▌ Chapter Summary: Third Party Rights and Discharge

. . . .

THIRD PARTY RIGHTS	
Assignment *(See pages 297–300.)*	1. An assignment is the transfer of rights under a contract to a third party. The person assigning the rights is the *assignor*, and the party to whom the rights are assigned is the *assignee*. The assignee has a right to demand performance from the other original party to the contract. 2. Generally, all rights can be assigned, except in the following circumstances: a. When assignment is expressly prohibited by statute (for example, workers' compensation benefits). *(Continued)*

▌Chapter Summary: Third Party Rights and Discharge—Continued

Assignment—Continued	b. When a contract calls for the performance of personal services. c. When the assignment will materially increase or alter the risks or duties of the *obligor* (the party that is obligated to perform). d. When the contract itself stipulates that the rights cannot be assigned (except a money claim). 3. Notice of the assignment should be given by the assignee to the obligor. a. If the assignor assigns the same right to two different persons, generally the first assignment in time is the first in right, although in some states the first assignee to give notice takes priority. b. Until the obligor is notified of the assignment, the obligor can tender performance to the assignor; and if performance is accepted by the assignor, the obligor's duties under the contract are discharged without benefit to the assignee.
Delegation *(See pages 301–303.)*	1. A delegation is the transfer of duties under a contract to a third party (the delegatee), who then assumes the obligation of performing the contractual duties previously held by the one making the delegation (the delegator). 2. As a general rule, any duty can be delegated, except in the following circumstances: a. When performance depends on the personal skill or talents of the obligor. b. When special trust has been placed in the obligor. c. When performance by a third party will vary materially from that expected by the obligee (the one to whom the duty is owed) under the contract. d. When the contract expressly prohibits delegation. 3. A valid delegation of duties does not relieve the delegator of obligations under the contract. If the delegatee fails to perform, the delegator is still liable to the obligee. 4. An "assignment of all rights" or an "assignment of contract" is often construed to mean that both the rights and duties arising under the contract are transferred to a third party.
Third Party Beneficiary Contract *(See pages 303–307.)*	A third party beneficiary contract is one made for the purpose of benefiting a third party. 1. *Intended beneficiary*—One for whose benefit a contract is created. When the promisor (the one making the contractual promise that benefits a third party) fails to perform as promised, the third party can sue the promisor directly. Examples of third party beneficiaries are creditor beneficiaries and donee beneficiaries. 2. *Incidental beneficiary*—A third party who indirectly (incidentally) benefits from a contract but for whose benefit the contract was not specifically intended. Incidental beneficiaries have no rights to the benefits received and cannot sue to have the contract enforced.
WAYS TO DISCHARGE A CONTRACT	
Conditions of Performance *(See pages 307–309.)*	Contract obligations may be subject to the following types of conditions: 1. *Condition precedent*—A condition that must be fulfilled before a party's promise becomes absolute. 2. *Condition subsequent*—A condition that operates to terminate a party's absolute promise to perform. 3. *Concurrent conditions*—Each party's absolute duty to perform is conditioned on the other party's absolute duty to perform.
Discharge by Performance *(See pages 309–312.)*	A contract may be discharged by complete (strict) or by substantial performance. In some cases, performance must be to the satisfaction of another. Totally inadequate performance constitutes a material breach of contract. An anticipatory repudiation of a contract allows the other party to sue immediately for breach of contract.
Discharge by Agreement *(See pages 312–313.)*	Parties may agree to discharge their contractual obligations in several ways: 1. *By rescission*—The parties mutually agree to rescind (cancel) the contract. 2. *By novation*—A new party is substituted for one of the primary parties to a contract. 3. *By accord and satisfaction*—The parties agree to render performance different from that originally agreed on. *(Continued)*

▌ Chapter Summary: Third Party Rights and Discharge—Continued

Discharge by Objective Impossibility of Performance *(See pages 313–314.)*	Parties' obligations under contracts may be discharged by objective impossibility of performance owing to one of the following events: 1. The death or incapacity of a person whose performance is essential to the completion of the contract. 2. The destruction of the specific subject matter of the contract prior to transfer. 3. A change in the law that renders the performance called for by the contract illegal. 4. Commercial impracticability of performance.

▌ For Review

1. What is the difference between an assignment and a delegation?

2. State what rights can be assigned despite a contract clause expressly prohibiting assignment.

3. What factors indicate that a third party beneficiary is an intended beneficiary?

4. How are most contracts discharged?

5. What is a contractual condition, and how might a condition affect contractual obligations?

▌ Questions and Case Problems

12–1. Substantial Performance. Complete performance is strict performance according to the terms of a contract. What is substantial performance?

12–2. Third Party Beneficiaries. Wilken owes Rivera $2,000. Howie promises Wilken to pay Rivera the $2,000 in return for Wilken's promise to give Howie's children guitar lessons. Is Rivera an intended beneficiary of the Howie-Wilken contract? Explain.

12–3. Assignments. Aron is a student attending college. He signs a one-year lease agreement that runs from September 1 to August 31. The lease agreement specifies that the lease cannot be assigned without the landlord's consent. In late May, Aron decides not to go to summer school and assigns the balance of the lease (three months) to a close friend, Erica. The landlord objects to the assignment and denies Erica access to the apartment. Aron claims that Erica is financially sound and should be allowed the full rights and privileges of an assignee. Discuss fully whether the landlord or Aron is correct.

12–4. Novation versus Accord and Satisfaction. Doug owes creditor Cartwright $1,000, which is due and payable on June 1. Doug has a car accident, misses several months of work, and consequently does not have the money to pay Cartwright on June 1. Doug's father, Bert, offers to pay Cartwright $1,100 in four equal installments if Cartwright will discharge Doug from any further liability on the debt. Cartwright accepts. In view of these events, answer the following questions.

    (a) Is the transaction a novation, or is it an accord and satisfaction? Explain.

    (b) Does the contract between Bert and Cartwright have to be in writing to be enforceable? (Review the Statute of Frauds.) Explain.

12–5. Impossibility of Performance. Millie contracted to sell Frank 1,000 bushels of corn to be grown on Millie's farm. Owing to drought conditions during the growing season, Millie's yield was much less than anticipated, and she could deliver only 250 bushels to Frank. Frank accepted the lesser amount but sued Millie for breach of contract. Can Millie defend successfully on the basis of objective impossibility of performance? Explain.

12–6. Third Party Beneficiaries. Rensselaer Water Co. was under contract to the city of Rensselaer, New York, to provide water to the city, including water at fire hydrants. A warehouse owned by H. R. Moch Co. was totally destroyed by a fire that could not be extinguished because of inadequate water pressure at the fire hydrants. Moch brought suit against Rensselaer Water Co. for damages, claiming that Moch was a third party beneficiary to the city's contract with the water company. Will Moch be able to recover damages from the water company on the basis that the water company breached its contract with the city? Explain. [*H. R. Moch Co. v. Rensselaer Water Co.*, 247 N.Y. 160, 159 N.E. 896 (1928)]

12–7. Third Party Beneficiaries. Owens, a federal prisoner, was transferred from federal prison to the Nassau County Jail pursuant to a contract between the U.S. Bureau of Prisons and the county. The contract included a policy statement that required the receiving prison to provide for the safekeeping and protection of transferred federal prisoners. While in the Nassau County Jail, Owens was beaten severely by prison officials and suffered lacerations, bruises, and a lasting impairment that caused blackouts. Can Owens, as a third party beneficiary, sue the county for breach of its agreement with the U.S. Bureau of Prisons? [*Owens v. Haas*, 601 F.2d 1242 (2d Cir. 1979)]

12–8. Performance and Discharge. John Agosta and his brother Salvatore had formed a corporation, but disagreements between the two brothers caused John to petition for voluntary dissolution of the corporation. According to the dissolution agreement, the total assets of the corporation, which included a warehouse and inventory, would be split between the brothers by Salvatore's selling his stock to John for $500,000. This agreement was approved, but shortly before the payment was made, a fire totally destroyed the warehouse and inventory, which were the major assets of the corporation. John refused to pay Salvatore the $500,000, and Salvatore brought suit for breach of contract. Discuss whether the destruction of the major assets of the corporation affects John's required performance under the contract. [*In the Matter of Fontana v. D'Oro Foods, Inc.*, 122 Misc.2d 1091, 472 N.Y.S.2d 528 (1983)]

12–9. Assignments. Abby's Cakes on Dixie, Inc., agreed in a lease contract to lease space in a shopping center from Colonial Palms Plaza, Ltd. The contract provided that Colonial would pay Abby's a construction allowance of up to $11,250 after Abby's had satisfactorily completed certain improvements to the rented premises. The contract also prohibited any "assignment, encumbrance or subletting" of the premises by Abby's without Colonial's prior consent. Before the improvements were completed, Abby's assigned its right to receive the first $8,000 of the construction allowance to Robert Aldana (without first obtaining Colonial's consent). In return, Aldana loaned Abby's $8,000 to finance the construction. Aldana notified Colonial of the assignment by certified mail. After Abby's had completed the improvements, Colonial ignored the assignment and paid Abby's the construction allowance. Will Aldana succeed in his suit against Colonial for the $8,000 due him pursuant to the assignment? Explain. [*Aldana v. Colonial Palms Plaza, Ltd.*, 591 So.2d 953 (Fla.App. 1992)]

12–10. Conditions Precedent. Larry McLanahan's 1985 Lamborghini was stolen, and by the time McLanahan recovered the car, it had been extensively damaged. The car was insured by Farmers Insurance Co. of Washington under a policy providing comprehensive coverage, including theft. A provision in the policy stated that the coverage for theft damages was subject to certain terms and conditions, including the condition that any person claiming coverage under the policy must allow Farmers "to inspect and appraise the damaged vehicle before its repair or disposal." McLanahan, without notifying Farmers and without giving Farmers an opportunity to inspect the vehicle, sold the car to a wholesale car dealer. Farmers then denied coverage, and McLanahan brought suit to recover for the damages caused to his car by the theft. Did McLanahan have a valid claim against the insurance company? Explain. [*McLanahan v. Farmers Insurance Co. of Washington*, 66 Wash.App. 36, 831 P.2d 160 (1992)]

12–11. Third Party Beneficiaries. When Charles and Judy Orr were divorced in 1970, their divorce agreement included a provision that Charles would pay for the college or professional school education of the couple's two children, then minors. In 1990, when Charles's daughter Jennifer was attending college,

Charles refused to pay her college tuition. Can Jennifer, who was not a party to her parents' divorce agreement, bring a court action to compel her father to pay her college expenses? Discuss fully. [*Orr v. Orr*, 228 Ill.App.3d 234, 592 N.E.2d 553, 170 Ill.Dec. 117 (1992)]

12–12. Assignments. Joseph LeMieux, of Maine, won $373,000 in a lottery operated by the Tri-State Lotto Commission. The lottery is sponsored by the three northern New England states and is administered in Vermont. Per its usual payment plan, Tri-State was to pay the $373,000 to LeMieux in annual installments over a twenty-year period. LeMieux assigned his rights to the lottery installment payments for the years 1996 through 2006 to Singer Freidlander Corp. for the sum of $80,000. LeMieux and Singer Freidlander (the plaintiffs) sought a declaratory judgment from a court authorizing the assignment agreement between them despite Tri-State's regulation barring the assignment of lottery proceeds. The trial court granted Tri-State's motion for summary judgment. On appeal, the plaintiffs argued that Tri-State's regulation was invalid. Is it? Discuss. [*LeMieux v. Tri-State Lotto Commission*, 666 A.2d 1170 (Vt. 1995)]

**A QUESTION OF ETHICS
AND SOCIAL RESPONSIBILITY**

12–13. *Bath Iron Works (BIW) offered a job to Thomas Devine, contingent on Devine's passing a drug test. The testing was conducted by NorDx, a subcontractor of Roche Biomedical Laboratories. When NorDx found that Devine's urinalysis showed the presence of opiates, a result confirmed by Roche, BIW refused to offer Devine permanent employment. Devine claimed that the ingestion of poppy seeds can lead to a positive result and that he tested positive for opiates only because of his daily consumption of poppy seed muffins. In Devine's suit against Roche, Devine argued, among other things, that he was a third party beneficiary of the contract between his employer (BIW) and NorDx (Roche). Given this factual background, consider the following questions.* [Devine v. Roche Biomedical Laboratories, 659 A.2d 868 (Me. 1995)]

1. Is Devine an intended third party beneficiary of the BIW-NorDx contract? In deciding this issue, should the court focus on the nature of the promises made in the contract itself or on the consequences of the contract for Devine, a third party?

2. Should employees whose job security and reputation have suffered as a result of false test results be allowed to sue the drug-testing labs for the tort of negligence (review this chapter's *Business Law in Action*)? In such situations, do drug-testing labs have a duty to the employees to exercise reasonable care in conducting the tests?

FOR CRITICAL ANALYSIS

12–14. *The concept of substantial performance permits parties to be discharged from their contracts even though they have breached those contracts (albeit in minor ways). Is this fair? What policy interests are at issue here?*

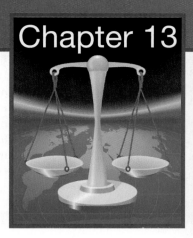
Chapter 13

Breach and Remedies

*"Men keep their engagements when it is to the
advantage of both not to break them."*

Solon, sixth century B.C.E.
(Athenian legal reformer)

CHAPTER OBJECTIVES

After reading this chapter, you should be able to:

1. Define the different types of damages that may be obtainable on the breach of a contract.
2. Describe the usual measure of damages for breach of various types of contracts.
3. Distinguish between liquidated damages and penalties.
4. List the equitable remedies that may be granted by courts, and indicate when they will be granted.
5. Explain the common law doctrine of election of remedies.

CONTENTS

DAMAGES
Types of Damages
Mitigation of Damages
Liquidated Damages versus
Penalties
RESCISSION AND RESTITUTION
SPECIFIC PERFORMANCE
REFORMATION
RECOVERY BASED ON QUASI
CONTRACT
ELECTION OF REMEDIES
PROVISIONS LIMITING
REMEDIES

As the Athenian political leader Solon instructed centuries ago, a contract will not be broken so long as "it is to the advantage of both" parties not to break it. Normally, the reason a person enters into a contract with another is to secure an advantage. When it is no longer advantageous for a party to fulfill his or her contractual obligations, breach of contract may result. As discussed in Chapter 12, a *breach of contract* occurs when a party fails to perform part or all of the required duties under a contract.[1] Once a party fails to perform or performs inadequately, the other party—the nonbreaching party—can choose one or more of several remedies.

The most common remedies available to a nonbreaching party include damages, rescission and restitution, specific performance, and reformation. As discussed in Chapter 1, courts distinguish between *remedies at law* and *remedies in equity*. Today, the remedy at law is normally money damages. We discuss this remedy in the first part of this chapter. Equitable remedies include rescission and restitution, specific performance, and reformation, all of which we examine later in the chapter. Usually a court will not award an equitable remedy unless the remedy at law is inadequate. In the final pages of this chapter, we look at some special legal doctrines and concepts relating to remedies.

---

1. *Restatement (Second) of Contracts*, Section 235(2).

319

▌Damages

A breach of contract entitles the nonbreaching party to sue for money damages. As you read in Chapter 5, damages are designed to compensate a party for harm suffered as a result of another's wrongful act. In the context of contract law, damages are designed to compensate the nonbreaching party for the loss of the bargain. Often, courts say that innocent parties are to be placed in the position they would have occupied had the contract been fully performed.[2]

Types of Damages

There are basically four kinds of damages: compensatory, consequential, punitive, and nominal damages.

COMPENSATORY DAMAGES As discussed in Chapter 5, *compensatory damages* compensate an injured party for injuries or damages actually sustained by that party. The nonbreaching party must prove that the actual damages arose directly from the loss of the bargain caused by the breach of contract. The amount of compensatory damages is the difference between the value of the breaching party's promised performance under the contract and the value of his or her actual performance. This amount is reduced by any loss that the injured party has avoided, however.

Suppose that you contract with Marinot Industries to perform certain personal services exclusively for Marinot during August for a payment of $3,500. Marinot cancels the contract and is in breach. You are able to find another job during August but can only earn $1,000. You normally can sue Marinot for breach and recover $2,500 as compensatory damages. You may also recover from Marinot the amount you spent to find the other job. Expenses or costs that are caused directly by a breach of contract—such as those incurred to obtain performance from another source—are *incidental damages*.

The measurement of compensatory damages varies by type of contract. Certain types of contracts deserve special mention—contracts for the sale of goods, contracts for the sale of land, and construction contracts.

Sale of Goods In a contract for the sale of goods, the usual measure of compensatory damages is an amount equal to the difference between the contract price and the market price.[3] Suppose that MediQuick Laboratories contracts with Cal Computer Industries to purchase ten Model X-15 computer workstations for $8,000 each. If Cal Computer fails to deliver the ten workstations, and the current market price of the workstations is $8,150, MediQuick's measure of damages is $1,500 (10 × $150). In cases in which the buyer breaches and the seller has not yet produced the goods, compensatory damages normally equal the lost profits on the sale, not the difference between the contract price and the market price.

Sale of Land The measure of damages in a contract for the sale of land is ordinarily the same as it is for contracts involving the sale of goods—that is, the difference between the contract price and the market price of the land. The majority of states follow this rule regardless of whether it is the buyer or the seller who breaches the contract.

A minority of states, however, follow a different rule when the seller breaches the contract and the breach is not deliberate. An example of a nondeliberate breach of a contract to sell land occurs when a previously unknown easement (a right of use over

---

2.   *Restatement (Second) of Contracts*, Section 347, and UCC 1–106(1).
3.   That is, the difference between the contract price and the market price at the time and place at which the goods were to be delivered or tendered. See UCC 2–708 and 2–713 (discussed in Chapter 16).

PARTY IN BREACH	TIME OF BREACH	MEASUREMENT OF DAMAGES
Owner	Before construction begins	Profits (contract price less cost of materials and labor)
Owner	After construction begins	Profits plus costs incurred up to time of breach
Owner	After construction is completed	Contract price
Contractor	Before construction is completed	Generally, all costs incurred by owner to complete construction

◆ **Exhibit 13–1**
Measurement of Damages—Breach of Construction Contracts

the property of another) is discovered and renders title to the land unmarketable. (In real property law, *title* means the right to own property or the evidence of that right.) In such a situation, these states allow the prospective purchaser to recover any down payment plus any expenses incurred (such as fees for title searches or attorneys). This minority rule effectively places a purchaser in the position that he or she occupied prior to the contract of sale.

What factors influence the measure of damages on the breach of a construction contract?

Construction Contracts   With construction contracts, the measure of damages often varies depending on which party breaches and at what stage the breach occurs. See Exhibit 13–1 for illustrations. In the following case, the issue centers on the proper measure of damages in a breached construction contract.

CASE 13.1

**SHADOW LAKES, INC. v.
CUDLIPP CONSTRUCTION
AND DEVELOPMENT CO.**

District Court of Appeal of Florida,
Second District, 1995.
658 So.2d 116.

HISTORICAL AND ECONOMIC SETTING *In the last
half of the twentieth century, the housing industry has
experienced extraordinary growth. Since 1960, nearly
sixty million units (including single-family houses, apartments, and mobile homes) have been built—twenty million more than in the previous forty years. Since 1920,
however, the population has increased by only about 150
million. In other words, between 1920 and 1995, a new
unit was built for every one and a half persons. Much of
this growth has occurred in Florida, which is now the
fourth most populous state.*

FACTS Cudlipp Construction and Development
Company agreed to build up to 375 houses for Shadow
Lakes, Inc., near Tampa, Florida. Under the contract, the
parties were bound to complete fourteen of the houses,
but either party had the right to terminate the agreement
with regard to future houses if prices could not be mutually agreed on by the parties. For each house, Shadow
Lakes agreed to pay a fixed price, which included the
costs of construction and a fee for Cudlipp's services.
The contract indicated that the fee covered "off-site and
on-site supervision, office overhead and general support," as well as Cudlipp's profit—which, according to
Cudlipp's testimony at trial—was to be $10,000 per
house. Problems developed between the parties after
Cudlipp had begun to construct eight houses. Cudlipp
filed a suit in a Florida state court against Shadow Lakes,

alleging, among other things, breach of contract. The
damages Cudlipp sought included lost profits of
$3,670,000 ($10,000 for 367 houses—375 houses less
the 8 houses already under construction). The jury
awarded Cudlipp $3,670,000 in lost profits, and Shadow
Lakes appealed.

ISSUE   Was $10,000 an accurate figure for the amount
of Cudlipp's lost profits for each house?

DECISION   No. The District Court of Appeal of Florida
reversed the award and remanded for a new trial on the
amount.

REASON   The state appellate court concluded in part
that the amount of profit to be realized on each home was
"speculative." Additionally, stated the court, "Whether or
not the parties would have come to a meeting of the
minds regarding other houses beyond the original fourteen is pure speculation and conjecture. Not only did the
parties have to agree on price, but the acreage needed
for the project had to be purchased by Shadow Lakes."
The court pointed out that the contract indicated, and
Cudlipp later acknowledged, that "certain overhead and
other expenses should be subtracted from" the $10,000
per house. Moreover, Cudlipp's owner testified that "the
$10,000 figure also included possible upgrades to the
houses by the ultimate purchasers."

FOR CRITICAL ANALYSIS—Economic Consideration
*What might be an appropriate measure of damages if in
fact a contractor was realizing no profit, or was even
actually losing money, on a contract?*

CONSEQUENTIAL DAMAGES
Special damages that compensate
for a loss that is not direct or
immediate (for example, lost
profits). The special damages
must have been reasonably
foreseeable at the time the
breach or injury occurred in
order for the plaintiff to collect
them.

CONSEQUENTIAL DAMAGES   Foreseeable damages that result from a party's breach of
contract are referred to as **consequential damages,** or *special damages.* Consequential
damages differ from compensatory damages in that they are caused by special circumstances beyond the contract itself. When a seller does not deliver goods, *knowing*
that a buyer is planning to resell those goods immediately, consequential damages are
awarded for the loss of profits from the planned resale. For example, Gilmore contracts
to have a specific item shipped to her—one that she desperately needs to repair her
printing press. In contracting with the shipper, Gilmore tells him that she must receive
the item by Monday or she will not be able to print her paper and will lose $750. If
the shipper is late, Gilmore normally can recover the consequential damages caused
by the delay (that is, the $750 in losses).

   For a nonbreaching party to recover consequential damages, the breaching party
must know (or have reason to know) that special circumstances will cause the non-

breaching party to suffer an additional loss.[4] This rule was enunciated in *Hadley v. Baxendale*, a case decided in England in 1854 and presented below as this chapter's *Landmark in the Law*. Today, the rule still applies. When damages are awarded, compensation is given only for those injuries that the defendant *could reasonably have foreseen* as a probable result of the usual course of events following a breach. If the injury complained of is outside the usual and foreseeable course of events, the plaintiff must show specifically that the defendant had reason to know the facts and foresee the injury.

NOTE A seller who does not wish to take on the risk of consequential damages can limit the buyer's remedies.

---

4. UCC 2–715(2). See Chapter 16.

Hadley v. Baxendale (1854)

LANDMARK IN
THE LAW

A landmark case in establishing the rule that notice of special ("consequential") circumstances must be given if consequential damages are to be recovered is *Hadley v. Baxendale*,[a] decided in 1854. This case involved a broken crankshaft used in a flour mill run by the Hadley family in Gloucester, England. The crankshaft attached to the steam engine in the mill broke, and the shaft had to be sent to a foundry located in Greenwich so that a new shaft could be made to fit the other parts of the engine. The Hadleys hired Baxendale, a common carrier, to transport the shaft from Gloucester to Greenwich. Baxendale received payment in advance and promised to deliver the shaft the following day. It was not delivered for several days, however. As a consequence, the mill was closed during those days because the Hadleys had no extra crankshaft on hand to use. The Hadleys sued Baxendale to recover the profits they lost during that time. Baxendale contended that the loss of profits was "too remote."

In the mid-1800s, it was normal for large mills, such as that run by the Hadleys, to have more than one crankshaft in case the main one broke and had to be repaired, as it did in this case. Also, in those days it was common knowledge that flour mills did indeed have spares. It is against this background that the parties argued their respective positions on whether the damages resulting from loss of profits while the crankshaft was out for repair were "too remote" to be recoverable.

The crucial issue before the court was whether the Hadleys had informed the carrier, Baxendale, of the special circumstances surrounding the crankshaft's repair, particularly of the fact that the mill would have to shut down while the crankshaft was being repaired. If Baxendale had been notified of this circumstance at the time the contract was formed, then the remedy for breaching the contract would have been the amount of damages that would reasonably follow from the breach—including the Hadleys' lost profits. In the court's opinion, however, the only circumstances communicated by the Hadleys to Baxendale at the time the contract was made were that the item to be transported was a broken crankshaft of a mill and that the Hadleys were the owners and operators of that mill. The court concluded that these circumstances did not reasonably indicate that the mill would have to stop operations if the delivery of the crankshaft was delayed.

For Critical Analysis: *If it had not been the custom in the mid-1800s for mills to have extra crankshafts on hand, how would this circumstance have affected the court's ruling?*

a. 9 Exch. 341, 156 Eng.Rep. 145 (1854).

324   UNIT THREE: CONTRACTS

> *"The duty to keep a contract at common law means a prediction that you must pay damages if you do not keep it—and nothing else."*
>
> **Oliver Wendell Holmes, Jr., 1841–1935**
> (*Associate justice of the United States Supreme Court, 1902–1932*)

PUNITIVE DAMAGES Recall from Chapter 5 that *punitive damages* are designed to punish a wrongdoer and set an example to deter similar conduct in the future. Punitive damages, which are also referred to as *exemplary damages*, are generally not recoverable in an action for breach of contract. Such damages have no legitimate place in contract law because they are, in essence, penalties, and a breach of contract is not unlawful in a criminal sense. A contract is simply a civil relationship between the parties. The law may compensate one party for the loss of the bargain—no more and no less.

In a few situations, a person's actions can cause both a breach of contract and a tort. For example, the parties can establish by contract a certain reasonable standard or duty of care. Failure to live up to that standard is a breach of contract, and the act itself may constitute negligence. An intentional tort (such as fraud) may also be tied to a breach of contract. In such a situation, it is possible for the nonbreaching party to recover punitive damages for the tort in addition to compensatory and consequential damages for the breach of contract.

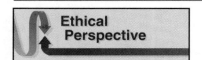

Ethical Perspective

The reason punitive damages are awarded in tort actions while they normally are not in contract actions has to do with the different purposes of tort and contract law. The social policies reflected in each body of law are particularly evident in the different remedies available under tort and contract law. Tort damages are awarded to compensate a victim for harms proximately caused by a tortious act, regardless of whether the full extent of those harms could have been anticipated. Because intentional torts are generally viewed as morally wrongful actions, punitive damages are sometimes awarded to deter particularly egregious conduct.

Contract damages, in contrast, are generally limited to those damages that could be reasonably foreseen when the parties entered into the contract. This limitation on contract damages allows parties to estimate in advance the risks they assume in entering into contracts and thus furthers the public policy of encouraging commerce. Unlike an intentional tort, an intentional breach of contract is often viewed as morally neutral (unless the breach also involves a tort). This is because a breach of contract can sometimes create a net gain for society. For example, a businessperson may be economically more productive by breaching a contract (and paying damages for the breach) for the purpose of performing another contract that will yield higher benefits to the breaching party.

For Critical Analysis: *Can a breach of contract ever be viewed as "morally neutral" by the nonbreaching party to that contract?*

> *"Nominal damages are, in effect, only a peg to hang costs on."*
>
> **Sir William Henry Maule, 1788–1858**
> (*British jurist*)

NOMINAL DAMAGES
A small monetary award (often one dollar) granted to a plaintiff when no actual damage was suffered.

NOMINAL DAMAGES Damages that are awarded to an innocent party when only a technical injury is involved and no actual damage (no financial loss) has been suffered are called **nominal damages.** Nominal damage awards are often small, such as one dollar, but they do establish that the defendant acted wrongfully.

For example, suppose that Parrott contracts to buy potatoes at fifty cents a pound from Lentz. Lentz breaches the contract and does not deliver the potatoes. Meanwhile, the price of potatoes falls. Parrott is able to buy them in the open market at half the price he agreed to pay Lentz. Parrott is clearly better off because of Lentz's breach. Thus, in a suit for breach of contract, Parrott may be awarded only nominal damages for the technical injury he sustained, as no monetary loss was involved. Most lawsuits for nominal damages are brought as a matter of principle under the theory that a breach has occurred and some damages must be imposed regardless of actual loss.

Mitigation of Damages

In most situations, when a breach of contract occurs, the injured party is held to a duty to mitigate, or reduce, the damages that he or she suffers. Under this doctrine of **mitigation of damages,** the required action depends on the nature of the situation. For example, in the majority of states, wrongfully terminated employees have a duty to mitigate damages suffered by their employers' breach. The damages they will be awarded are their salaries less the incomes they would have received in similar jobs obtained by reasonable means. It is the employer's burden to prove the existence of such jobs and to prove that the employee could have been hired. An employee is, of course, under no duty to take a job that is not of the same type and rank. This is illustrated in the following case.

MITIGATION OF DAMAGES
A rule requiring a plaintiff to have done whatever was reasonable to minimize the damages caused by the defendant.

CASE 13.2

PARKER v. TWENTIETH CENTURY-FOX FILM CORP.
Supreme Court of California, 1970.
3 Cal.3d 176,
474 P.2d 689,
89 Cal.Rptr. 737.

COMPANY PROFILE *Daryl Zanuck and Joseph Schenk formed the Twentieth Century Company in 1933 to make movies. Two years later, they merged with the Fox Film Company, which had been founded by William Fox, and became Twentieth Century-Fox Film Corporation. Today, Twentieth Century-Fox produces movies and television shows as part of the News Corporation Limited, which is headquartered in Australia. The News Corporation also has interests in the production and distribution of newspapers, magazines, books, television programs, and films in Great Britain, Hong Kong, New Zealand, and other countries.*

FACTS Twentieth Century-Fox Film Corporation planned to produce a musical, *Bloomer Girl,* and contracted with Shirley MacLaine Parker to play the leading female role. According to the contract, Fox was to pay Parker $53,571.42 per week for fourteen weeks, for a total of $750,000. Fox later decided not to produce *Bloomer Girl* and tried to substitute another contract for the existing contract. Under the terms of this second contract, Parker would play the leading role in a Western movie for the same amount of money guaranteed by the first contract. Fox gave Parker one week in which to accept the new contract. Parker filed suit in a California state court against Fox to recover the amount of compensation guaranteed in the first contract because, she maintained, the two roles were not at all equivalent. The

Bloomer Girl production was a musical, to be filmed in California, and it could not be compared with a "western-type" production that Fox tentatively planned to produce in Australia. When the trial court held for Parker, Fox appealed. Ultimately, the California Supreme Court reviewed the case.

ISSUE May Fox's substitute offer of the Western movie contract be used in mitigating the damages ensuing from the breach of the first contract?

DECISION No. The California Supreme Court affirmed the judgment for Parker.

REASON The court noted that the "measure of recovery by a wrongfully discharged employee is the amount of salary agreed upon for the period of service, less the amount which the employer affirmatively proves the employee has earned or with reasonable effort might have earned from other employment. Before projected earnings from other employment opportunities not sought or accepted by the discharged employee can be applied in mitigation, however, the employer must show that the other employment was comparable, or substantially similar, to that of which the employee has been deprived." The court held that the two roles were substantially dissimilar—that is, one called for Parker's dancing and acting abilities, and the other was simply an acting role in a Western movie. The court asserted that "by no stretch of the imagination" could the latter "be considered the equivalent of or substantially similar to the lead in a song-and-dance production."

FOR CRITICAL ANALYSIS—International Consideration
Many legal systems, including that of France, have no clear requirement that damages must be mitigated. Can justice be better served by requiring that damages be mitigated? If so, how?

Liquidated Damages versus Penalties

LIQUIDATED DAMAGES
An amount, stipulated in the contract, that the parties to a contract believe to be a reasonable estimation of the damages that will occur in the event of a breach.

PENALTY
A sum inserted into a contract, not as a measure of compensation for its breach but rather as punishment for a default. The agreement as to the amount will not be enforced, and recovery will be limited to actual damages.

A **liquidated damages** provision in a contract specifies that a certain amount of money is to be paid in the event of a future default or breach of contract. (*Liquidated* means determined, settled, or fixed.) Liquidated damages differ from penalties. A **penalty** specifies a certain amount to be paid in the event of a default or breach of contract and is designed to penalize the breaching party. Liquidated damages provisions normally are enforceable; penalty provisions are not.[5]

To determine whether a particular provision is for liquidated damages or for a penalty, the court must answer two questions: First, at the time the contract was formed, was it difficult to estimate the potential damages that would be incurred if the contract was not performed on time? Second, was the amount set as damages a reasonable estimate of those potential damages and not excessive?[6] If the answers to both questions are yes, the provision will be enforced. If either answer is no, the provision will normally not be enforced. In a construction contract, it is difficult to estimate the amount of damages that might be caused by a delay in completing construction, so liquidated damages clauses are often used.

The following case involved a contract clause that required a client to pay an attorney substantial damages if the client terminated its relationship with the attorney. The issue before the court was whether the clause was a liquidated damages clause or a penalty clause.

---

5. This is also the rule under the Uniform Commercial Code. See UCC 2–718(1).
6. *Restatement (Second) of Contracts*, Section 356(1).

CASE 13.3

AFLAC, INC. v. WILLIAMS
Supreme Court of Georgia, 1994.
264 Ga. 351,
444 S.E.2d 314.

HISTORICAL AND SOCIAL SETTING *Historically, lawyers and law firms concentrated their efforts on the practice of law, but they also traditionally held a position as general counselor to their clients. In the 1980s and 1990s, according to some observers, lawyers began to focus too narrowly on legal issues. Consequently, attorneys lost ground, in their traditional role as general counselors, to financial advisers, accounting firms, banks, actuaries, and other consultants who were looking for new areas in which to do business when they found their own traditional markets shrinking.*

FACTS AFLAC, Inc., hired Peter Williams, an attorney, under a seven-year contract to give the company legal advice as needed. The contract provided that if AFLAC terminated the relationship, it would pay Williams 50 percent of whatever amount was due for the remaining term. After four years, AFLAC terminated the contract with

Williams and asked a Georgia state court to determine the enforceability of the termination payment provision. The court declared the provision unenforceable, and Williams appealed. The state appellate court reversed this decision, and AFLAC appealed.

ISSUE Does a contract clause that requires a client to pay his or her attorney unreasonably high damages for discharging the attorney constitute an improper penalty?

DECISION Yes. The Supreme Court of Georgia, holding that the provision was an unenforceable penalty clause, reversed the decision of the intermediate appellate court.

REASON The state supreme court explained that the contract "requires AFLAC to pay an unreasonably high sum as damages, requires payment without considering Williams' duty to mitigate his damages, and obligates AFLAC to pay even if Williams is discharged for cause." Thus, the provision "is not a reasonable estimate of Williams' damages and instead is a penalty imposed to punish AFLAC."

FOR CRITICAL ANALYSIS—Ethical Consideration
Why shouldn't parties to a contract be allowed to agree to the imposition of whatever penalty they wish in the event of a breach?

When is specific performance the appropriate remedy for a breach of contract?

▌ Rescission and Restitution

As discussed in Chapter 12, *rescission* is essentially an action to undo, or cancel, a contract—to return nonbreaching parties to the positions that they occupied prior to the transaction. When fraud, mistake, duress, or failure of consideration is present, rescission is available. The failure of one party to perform under a contract entitles the other party to rescind the contract.[7] The rescinding party must give prompt notice to the breaching party. Furthermore, both parties must make **restitution** to each other by returning goods, property, or money previously conveyed.[8] If the goods or property can be restored *in specie*—that is, if they can be returned—they must be. If the goods or property have been consumed, restitution must be made in an equivalent amount of money.

Essentially, restitution refers to the recapture of a benefit conferred on the defendant through which the defendant has been unjustly enriched. For example, Andrea pays $10,000 to Miles in return for Miles's promise to design a house for her. The next day Miles calls Andrea and tells her that he has taken a position with a large architectural firm in another state and cannot design the house. Andrea decides to hire another architect that afternoon. Andrea can get restitution of $10,000, because she conferred an unjust benefit of $10,000 on Miles. (See this chapter's *Business Law in Action* for a further discussion of restitution and the distinction between restitution and damages.)

RESTITUTION
An equitable remedy under which a person is restored to his or her original position prior to loss or injury, or placed in the position he or she would have been in had the breach not occurred.

CONTRAST The advantages of obtaining restitution instead of damages include the possibility of recovering specific property, the possibility of making a recovery when damages cannot be proved, and the possibility of obtaining a greater award.

---

7. The rescission discussed here refers to *unilateral* rescission, in which only one party wants to undo the contract. In *mutual* rescission, both parties agree to undo the contract. Mutual rescission discharges the contract; unilateral rescission is generally available as a remedy for breach of contract.
8. *Restatement (Second) of Contracts*, Section 370.

Restitution versus Damages

The remedy of rescission and restitution, which attempts to restore the parties to their precontractual status, rests on the equitable principle that a person should not be unjustly enriched. Whereas damages are measured by the amount of the plaintiff's loss, restitution is measured by the amount of the defendant's gain. In some cases, this distinction has little practical effect, because the plaintiff's loss is equal to the defendant's gain. In other cases, however, the defendant's gain is greater than the plaintiff's loss.

Suppose, for example, that Andrea gives Miles $10,000 in return for Miles's promise to design a house for her. The next day, Miles uses the $10,000 to purchase an old Ferrari, which he immediately sells to another person for $12,000. He then notifies Andrea that he cannot perform the contract. If Andrea sued for damages, she could obtain $10,000. If she sues to rescind the contract and obtain restitution, however, the question arises as to whether the $2,000 profit

Miles made on the purchase and sale of the Ferrari should be included as restitution (and be given to Andrea) or be retained by Miles.

This thorny issue came before the Colorado Supreme Court in a case brought by Hydrosphere Resource Consultants, Inc., against EarthInfo, Inc., for breach of contract. Under the contract, EarthInfo was obligated to package and market CD-ROM players and software that had been developed by Hydrosphere and to pay Hydrosphere a percentage of its net sales as royalties. A dispute arose, and EarthInfo refused to pay Hydrosphere any royalties after June 30, 1990. Hydrosphere sued EarthInfo for rescission and restitution, and the court had to decide whether the amount of restitution should include just Hydrosphere's unpaid royalties on sales made after the breach or all of EarthInfo's profits made on those sales.

The court noted that in similar cases, some courts have refused to award the breaching party's profits to the nonbreaching party under the theory that a breach of contract is not a "wrong." Other courts, however, have concluded that the breaching party should be stripped of the profits—they should go to the nonbreaching party. The Colorado

court adopted neither approach, concluding that the question should be decided on a case-by-case basis. The outcome should depend on "the nature of the defendant's wrong, the relative extent of his or her contribution, and the feasibility of separating this from the contribution traceable to the plaintiff's interest."

The court stated that if "the defendant's wrongdoing is intentional or substantial, or there are no other means of measuring the wrongdoer's enrichment, recovery of profits must be granted." Because EarthInfo intentionally breached the contract, the breach was substantial, and damages were difficult to assess, the court held that the amount of restitution should include EarthInfo's profits from the sale of Hydrosphere's products—less the costs incurred by EarthInfo in packaging and marketing the products.[a]

For Critical Analysis: *Is there any reason why a nonbreaching party would seek rescission and restitution as a remedy, instead of damages, if the amount of restitution would be equal to the damages sought?*

a. *EarthInfo, Inc. v. Hydrosphere Resource Consultants, Inc.*, 900 P.2d 113 (Colo. 1995).

▎Specific Performance

SPECIFIC PERFORMANCE
An equitable remedy requiring *exactly* the performance that was specified in a contract; usually granted only when money damages would be an inadequate remedy and the subject matter of the contract is unique (for example, real property).

The equitable remedy of **specific performance** calls for the performance of the act promised in the contract. This remedy is often attractive to a nonbreaching party, because it provides the exact bargain promised in the contract. It also avoids some of the problems inherent in a suit for money damages. First, the nonbreaching party need not worry about collecting the judgment.[9] Second, the nonbreaching party need not look around for another contract. Third, the actual performance may be more valuable than the money damages. Although the equitable remedy of specific performance is often preferable to other remedies, normally it is not granted unless the party's legal remedy (money damages) is inadequate.[10]

---

9. Courts dispose of cases, after trials, by entering judgments. A judgment may order the losing party to pay money damages to the winning party. Collection of judgments, however, poses problems—such as when the judgment debtor is insolvent (cannot pay his or her bills when they become due) or has only a small net worth, or when the debtor's assets cannot be seized, under exemption laws, by a creditor to satisfy a debt (see Chapter 22).
10. *Restatement (Second) of Contracts*, Section 359.

For example, contracts for the sale of goods that are readily available on the market rarely qualify for specific performance. Money damages ordinarily are adequate in such situations, because substantially identical goods can be bought or sold in the market. If the goods are unique, however, a court of equity will decree specific performance. For example, paintings, sculptures, and rare books and coins are often unique, and money damages will not enable a buyer to obtain substantially identical substitutes in the market. The same principle applies to contracts relating to sales of land or interests in land, because each parcel of land is unique by legal description.

Courts normally refuse to grant specific performance of contracts for personal services. Sometimes the remedy at law may be adequate if substantially identical services are available from other persons (as with lawn-mowing services). Even for individually tailored personal-service contracts, courts are very hesitant to order specific performance by a party, because public policy strongly discourages involuntary servitude.[11] Moreover, the courts do not want to monitor a personal-service contract. For example, if you contract with a brain surgeon to perform brain surgery on you and the surgeon refuses to perform, the court would not compel (and you certainly would not want) the surgeon to perform under these circumstances. There is no way the court can assure meaningful performance in such a situation.[12]

Specific performance is a remedy of grace and not a matter of right, and the test of whether or not it should be granted depends on the particular circumstances of each case."

George Bushnell, 1887–1965 *(American jurist)*

In the United States, the general rule is that the equitable remedy of specific performance will be granted only if the remedy at law (money damages) is inadequate. In Germany, however, the typical remedy for a breach of contract is specific performance. In other words, a German court normally would order the breaching party to go forward and perform the contract. German courts will award damages for breach of contract in some circumstances, but damages are available only after notice and other procedures have been employed to seek performance.

For Critical Analysis: *If U.S. courts commonly granted the remedy of specific performance, as German courts do, would parties be less likely to breach their contracts?*

▌Reformation

When the parties have imperfectly expressed their agreement in writing, the equitable remedy of *reformation* allows the contract to be rewritten to reflect the parties' true intentions. This remedy applies most often when fraud or mutual mistake (for example, a clerical error) has occurred. If Keshan contracts to buy a certain piece of equipment from Shelley but the written contract refers to a different piece of equipment, a mutual mistake has occurred. Accordingly, a court could reform the contract so that the writing conforms to the parties' original intention as to which piece of equipment is being sold.

Two other examples deserve mention. The first involves two parties who have made a binding oral contract. They further agree to reduce the oral contract to writing, but in doing so, they make an error in stating the terms. Universally, the courts

---

11.   The Thirteenth Amendment to the U.S. Constitution prohibits involuntary servitude, but negative injunctions (that is, prohibiting rather than ordering certain conduct) are possible. Thus, you may not be able to compel a person to perform under a personal-service contract, but you may be able to restrain that person from engaging in similar contracts with others for a period of time.

12.   Similarly, courts often refuse to order specific performance of construction contracts, because courts are not set up to operate as construction supervisors or engineers.

"What burns me up is that the answer is right here somewhere, staring us in the face."

allow into evidence the correct terms of the oral contract, thereby reforming the written contract.

The second example has to do with written covenants not to compete. As discussed in Chapter 10, if a covenant not to compete is for a valid and legitimate purpose (such as the sale of a business), but the area or time restraints of the covenant are unreasonable, some courts reform the restraints by making them reasonable and enforce the entire contract as reformed. Other courts throw the entire restrictive covenant out as illegal.

▌ Recovery Based on Quasi Contract

DON'T FORGET The function of a quasi contract is to impose a legal obligation on parties who made no actual promises.

Recall from Chapter 8 that a quasi contract is not a true contract but a fictional contract that is imposed on the parties to obtain justice and prevent unjust enrichment. Hence, a quasi contract becomes an equitable basis for relief. Generally, when one party confers a benefit on another, justice requires that the party receiving the benefit pay a reasonable value for it so as not to be unjustly enriched at the other party's expense.

Quasi-contractual recovery is useful when one party has *partially* performed under a contract that is unenforceable. It can be an alternative to suing for damages, and it allows the party to recover the reasonable value of the partial performance. For quasi-contractual recovery to occur, the party seeking recovery must show the following:

1. A benefit was conferred on the other party.
2. The party conferring the benefit did so with the expectation of being paid.
3. The party seeking recovery did not act as a volunteer in conferring the benefit.
4. Retaining the benefit without paying for it would result in an unjust enrichment of the party receiving the benefit.

For example, suppose that Ericson contracts to build two oil derricks for Petro Industries. The derricks are to be built over a period of three years, but the parties do not create a written contract. Enforcement of the contract will therefore be barred by the Statute of Frauds.[13] Ericson completes one derrick, and then Petro Industries informs him that it will not pay for the derrick. Ericson can sue in quasi contract because (1) a benefit (one oil derrick) has been conferred on Petro Industries; (2) Ericson conferred the benefit (built the derrick) expecting to be paid; (3) Ericson did not volunteer to build the derrick but built it under an unenforceable oral contract; and (4) allowing Petro Industries to retain the derrick without paying would enrich the company unjustly. Therefore, Ericson should be able to recover the reasonable value of the oil derrick (under the theory of *quantum meruit*[14]—"as much as he deserves"). The reasonable value is ordinarily equal to the fair market value.

∎ Election of Remedies

In many cases, a nonbreaching party has several remedies available. Because the remedies may be inconsistent with one another, the common law of contract requires the party to choose which remedy to pursue. This is called *election of remedies*.

The purpose of the doctrine of election of remedies is to prevent double recovery. Suppose that Jefferson agrees to sell his land to Adams. Then Jefferson changes his mind and repudiates the contract. Adams can sue for compensatory damages or for specific performance. If she receives damages as a result of the breach, she should not also be granted specific performance of the sales contract, because that would mean she would end up with both the land *and* damages, which would be unfair. In effect, she would recover twice for the same breach of contract. The doctrine of election of remedies requires Adams to choose the remedy she wants, and it eliminates any possibility of double recovery.

Unfortunately, the doctrine has been applied in a rigid and technical manner, leading to some harsh results. For example, in a Wisconsin case, a man named Carpenter was fraudulently induced to buy a piece of land for $100. He spent $140 moving onto the land and then discovered the fraud. Instead of suing for damages, Carpenter sued to rescind the contract. The court denied recovery of the $140 because the seller, Mason, had not received the $140 and was therefore not required to reimburse Carpenter for his moving expenses. So Carpenter suffered a net loss of $140 on the transaction. If Carpenter had sued for damages, he could have recovered the $100 purchase price and the $140.[15]

In the following case, the frustrated sellers of a house were apparently attempting to avoid the doctrine of election of remedies in order to, as the old saying goes, "have their cake and eat it, too."

BE AWARE Which remedy a plaintiff elects depends on the subject of the contract, the defenses of the breaching party, the advantages that might be gained in terms of tactics against the defendant, and what the plaintiff can prove with respect to the remedy sought.

---

13. Contracts that by their terms cannot be performed within one year must be in writing to be enforceable. See Chapter 11.
14. Pronounced *kwahn*-tuhm *mehr*-oo-wuht.
15. See *Carpenter v. Mason*, 181 Wis. 114, 193 N.W. 973 (1923). Because of the harsh results of the doctrine of election of remedies, the Uniform Commercial Code expressly rejects it. Remedies under the UCC, discussed in Chapter 16, are essentially *cumulative* in nature (see UCC 2–703 and 2–711).

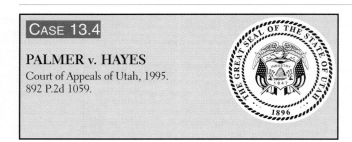

CASE 13.4

PALMER v. HAYES
Court of Appeals of Utah, 1995.
892 P.2d 1059.

HISTORICAL AND ECONOMIC SETTING   *Real estate transactions have long involved the same steps as those that shape a deal today. A transaction starts with a seller who wants to sell and a buyer who wants to buy. The buyer makes a bid on the property. This bid usually takes the form of a proposed contract of sale and includes a deposit of 1 or 2 percent of the price offered for the property. In transactions involving single-family homes, unsophisticated buyers often do not realize how binding their bids can be. If a seller accepts a buyer's proposal, the buyer is bound to it.*

FACTS   Kenneth and Rebecca Palmer wanted to sell their house. Edward and Stephanie Hayes signed a proposed contract of sale, under which they agreed to give the Palmers' real estate agent, Maple Hills Realty, $2,000 as a deposit on the house. The agreement provided that in the event of default, the Palmers could either keep the deposit or sue to enforce their rights. The Palmers accepted the Hayeses' offer and signed the contract. Before the property changed hands, however, the

Hayeses changed their minds and asked for the return of their deposit. The Palmers refused and filed a suit against the Hayeses in a Utah state court, seeking damages. The Hayeses filed a motion for summary judgment on the ground that, by not releasing the deposit, the Palmers had elected their remedy. The court ruled in favor of the Hayeses on this point, and the Palmers appealed.

ISSUE   Did the Palmers' failure to release the deposit money before filing their suit for damages constitute an election of remedies?

DECISION   Yes. The Court of Appeals of Utah, concluding that the Palmers had elected the remedy of retaining the deposit, affirmed the lower court's ruling.

REASON   The state appellate court held that "a seller's failure to offer to return * * * deposits precludes the seller from pursuing other remedies." The court explained that the Palmers "needed only to indicate to Maple Hills Realty, in writing, that they released the deposit money to the Hayeses. Then they could have proceeded with their suit for damages." The court concluded that "by failing to release the deposit money, the Palmers elected to retain it as liquidated damages."

FOR CRITICAL ANALYSIS—Economic Consideration
What are the reasons for applying the doctrine of election of remedies to preclude sellers who keep deposits from suing for damages?

▌Provisions Limiting Remedies

A contract may include provisions stating that no damages can be recovered for certain types of breaches or that damages must be limited to a maximum amount. The contract may also provide that the only remedy for breach is replacement, repair, or refund of the purchase price. Provisions stating that no damages can be recovered are called *exculpatory clauses* (see Chapter 11). Provisions that affect the availability of certain remedies are called *limitation-of-liability clauses*.

RECALL Exculpatory clauses are often held unconscionable, depending on the relative bargaining positions of the parties and the importance to the public interest of the business seeking to enforce the clause.

Whether these contract provisions and clauses will be enforced depends on the type of breach that is excused by the provision. For example, a provision excluding liability for fraudulent or intentional injury will not be enforced. Likewise, a clause excluding liability for illegal acts or violations of law will not be enforced. A clause excluding liability for negligence may be enforced in some cases. When an exculpatory clause for negligence is contained in a contract made between parties who have roughly equal bargaining positions, the clause usually will be enforced.

The UCC provides that in a contract for the sale of goods, remedies can be limited. We will examine the UCC's provisions on limited remedies in Chapter 16, in the context of the remedies available on the breach of a sales contract.

Application

Law and the Contractor—When You Cannot Perform*

Not every contract can be performed. If you are a contractor, you may take on a job that, for one reason or another, you cannot or do not wish to perform. Simply walking away from the job and hoping for the best is not normally the most effective way to avoid litigation—which can be costly, time consuming, and emotionally draining. Instead, you should consider avoidance of litigation through *compromise.*

For example, suppose that you are a building contractor and you sign a contract to build a home for the Andersons. Performance is to begin on June 15. On June 1, Central Enterprises offers you a position that will yield you two and a half times the amount of net income you could earn as an independent builder. To take the job, you have to start on June 15. You cannot be in two places at the same time, so to accept the new position you must breach the contract with the Andersons.

What to do? One option is to subcontract the work to another builder and oversee the work yourself to make

sure it conforms to the contract. Another option is to negotiate with the Andersons for a *release.* You can offer to find another qualified builder who will build a house of the same quality at the same price. Alternatively, you can offer to pay any additional costs if another builder takes the job and is more expensive. In any event, this additional cost would be the measure of damages that a court would impose on you if the Andersons sued you for breach of contract and the Andersons prevailed. Thus, by making the offer, you might be able to avoid the expense of litigation—if the Andersons accept your offer.

Often, parties are reluctant to propose compromise settlements because they fear that what they say will be used against them in court if litigation ensues. The general rule, however, is that offers for settlement cannot be used in court to prove that you are liable for a breach of contract.

 Checklist for the Contractor Who Cannot Perform

1. Consider a compromise.
2. Subcontract out the work and oversee it.
3. Offer to find an alternative contractor to fulfill your obligation.
4. Make a cash offer to "buy" a release from your contract. If anything other than an insignificant amount of money is involved, however, work with an attorney in making the offer.

*This *Application* is not meant to substitute for the services of an attorney who is licensed to practice law in your state.

▌Key Terms

consequential damages 322
liquidated damages 326
mitigation of damages 325

nominal damages 324
penalty 326

restitution 327
specific performance 328

▌Chapter Summary: Breach and Remedies

COMMON REMEDIES AVAILABLE TO THE NONBREACHING PARTY	
Damages *(See pages 320–326.)*	The legal remedy of damages is designed to compensate the nonbreaching party for the loss of the bargain. By awarding money damages, the court tries to place the parties in the positions that they would have occupied had the contract been fully performed. The nonbreaching party frequently has a duty to *mitigate* (lessen or reduce) the damages incurred as a result of the contract's breach. There are five broad categories of damages: 1. *Compensatory damages*—Damages that compensate the nonbreaching party for injuries actually sustained and proved to have arisen directly from the loss of the bargain resulting from the breach of contract. *(Continued)*

▌Chapter Summary: Breach and Remedies—Continued

Damages— Continued	a. In breached contracts for the sale of goods, the usual measure of compensatory damages is an amount equal to the difference between the contract price and the market price. b. In breached contracts for the sale of land, the measure of damages is ordinarily the same as in contracts for the sale of goods. c. In breached construction contracts, the measure of damages depends on which party breaches and at what stage of construction the breach occurs. 2. *Consequential damages*—Damages resulting from special circumstances beyond the contract itself; the damages flow only from the consequences of a breach. For a party to recover consequential damages, the damages must be the foreseeable result of a breach of contract, and the breaching party must have known at the time the contract was formed that special circumstances existed and that the nonbreaching party would incur additional loss upon breach of the contract. Also called *special damages*. 3. *Punitive damages*—Damages awarded to punish the breaching party. Usually not awarded in an action for breach of contract unless a tort is involved. 4. *Nominal damages*—Damages small in amount (such as one dollar) that are awarded when a breach has occurred but no actual damages have been suffered. Awarded only to establish that the defendant acted wrongfully. 5. *Liquidated damages*—Damages that may be specified in a contract as the amount to be paid to the nonbreaching party in the event the contract is later breached. Clauses providing for liquidated damages are enforced if the damages were difficult to estimate at the time the contract was formed and if the amount stipulated is reasonable. If construed to be a penalty, the clause will not be enforced.
Rescission and Restitution *(See pages 327–328.)*	1. *Rescission*—A remedy whereby a contract is canceled and the parties are restored to the original positions that they occupied prior to the transaction. Available when fraud, a mistake, duress, or failure of consideration is present. The rescinding party must give prompt notice of the rescission to the breaching party. 2. *Restitution*—When a contract is rescinded, both parties must make restitution to each other by returning the goods, property, or money previously conveyed. Restitution prevents the unjust enrichment of the defendant.
Specific Performance *(See pages 328–329.)*	An equitable remedy calling for the performance of the act promised in the contract. Specific performance is only available in special situations—such as those involving contracts for the sale of unique goods or land—and when monetary damages would be an inadequate remedy. Specific performance is not available as a remedy in breached contracts for personal services.
Reformation *(See pages 329–330.)*	An equitable remedy allowing a contract to be "reformed," or rewritten, to reflect the parties' true intentions. Available when an agreement is imperfectly expressed in writing.
Recovery Based on Quasi Contract *(See pages 330–331.)*	An equitable theory imposed by the courts to obtain justice and prevent unjust enrichment in a situation in which no enforceable contract exists. The party seeking recovery must show the following: 1. A benefit was conferred on the other party. 2. The party conferring the benefit did so with the expectation of being paid. 3. The benefit was not volunteered. 4. Retaining the benefit without paying for it would result in the unjust enrichment of the party receiving the benefit.
CONTRACT DOCTRINES RELATING TO REMEDIES	
Election of Remedies *(See pages 331–332.)*	A common law doctrine under which a nonbreaching party must choose one remedy from those available. This doctrine prevents double recovery.
Provisions Limiting Remedies *(See page 332.)*	A contract may provide that no damages (or only a limited amount of damages) can be recovered in the event the contract is breached. Clauses excluding liability for fraudulent or intentional injury or for illegal acts cannot be enforced. Clauses excluding liability for negligence may be enforced if both parties hold roughly equal bargaining power. Under the UCC, in contracts for the sale of goods, remedies may be limited.

▌ For Review

1. What is the difference between compensatory damages and consequential damages? What are nominal damages, and when might they be awarded by a court?
2. What is the usual measure of damages on a breach of contract for a sale of goods?
3. Under what circumstances will the remedy of rescission and restitution be available?

4. When might specific performance be granted as a remedy?
5. What is the rationale underlying the doctrine of election of remedies? Does the UCC accept or reject the doctrine?

▌ Questions and Case Problems

13–1. Liquidated Damages. Carnack contracts to sell his house and lot to Willard for $100,000. The terms of the contract call for Willard to pay 10 percent of the purchase price as a deposit toward the purchase price, or as a down payment. The terms further stipulate that should the buyer breach the contract, the deposit will be retained by Carnack as liquidated damages. Willard pays the deposit, but because her expected financing of the $90,000 balance falls through, she breaches the contract. Two weeks later Carnack sells the house and lot to Balkova for $105,000. Willard demands her $10,000 back, but Carnack refuses, claiming that Willard's breach and the contract terms entitle him to keep the deposit. Discuss who is correct.

13–2. Election of Remedies. Perez contracts to buy a new Oldsmobile from Central City Motors, paying $2,000 down and agreeing to make twenty-four monthly payments of $350 each. He takes the car home and, after making one payment, learns that his Oldsmobile has a Chevrolet engine in it rather than the famous Olds Super V-8 engine. Central City never informed Perez of this fact. Perez immediately notifies Central City of his dissatisfaction and returns the car to Central City. Central City accepts the car and returns to Perez the $2,000 down payment plus the one $350 payment. Two weeks later Perez, without a car and feeling angry, files a suit against Central City, seeking damages for breach of warranty and fraud. Discuss the effect of Perez's actions.

13–3. Specific Performance. In which of the following situations might a court grant specific performance as a remedy for the breach of contract?

  (a) Tarrington contracts to sell her house and lot to Rainier. Then, on finding another buyer willing to pay a higher purchase price, she refuses to deed the property to Rainier.

  (b) Marita contracts to sing and dance in Horace's nightclub for one month, beginning June 1. She then refuses to perform.

  (c) Juan contracts to purchase a rare coin from Edmund, who is breaking up his coin collection. At the last minute, Edmund decides to keep his coin collection intact and refuses to deliver the coin to Juan.

  (d) There are three shareholders of Astro Computer Corp.: Coase, who owns 48 percent of the stock; De Valle, who owns 48 percent; and Cary, who owns 4 percent. Cary contracts to sell his 4 percent to De Valle but later refuses to transfer the shares to him.

13–4. Measure of Damages. Johnson contracted to lease a house to Fox for $700 a month, beginning October 1. Fox stipulated in the contract that before he moved in, the interior of the house had to be completely repainted. On September 9, Johnson hired Keever to do the required painting for $1,000. He told Keever that the painting had to be finished by October 1 but did not explain why. On September 28, Keever quit for no reason, having completed approximately 80 percent of the work. Johnson then paid Sam $300 to finish the painting, but Sam did not finish until October 4. Fox, when the painting had not been completed as stipulated in his contract with Johnson, leased another home. Johnson found another tenant who would lease the property at $700 a month, beginning October 15. Johnson then sued Keever for breach of contract, claiming damages of $650. This amount included the $300 Johnson paid Sam to finish the painting and $350 for rent for the first half of October, which Johnson had lost as a result of Keever's breach. Johnson had not yet paid Keever anything for Keever's work. Can Johnson collect the $650 from Keever? Explain.

13–5. Measure of Damages. Ben owns and operates a famous candy store. He makes most of the candy sold in the store, and business is particularly heavy during the Christmas season. Ben contracts with Sweet, Inc., to purchase ten thousand pounds of sugar, to be delivered on or before November 15. Ben informs Sweet that this particular order is to be used for the Christmas season business. Because of production problems, the sugar is not tendered to Ben until December 10, at which time Ben refuses the order because it is so late. Ben has been unable to purchase the quantity of sugar needed to meet the Christmas orders and has had to turn down numerous regular customers, some of whom have indicated that they will purchase candy elsewhere in the future. The sugar that Ben has been able to purchase has cost him ten cents per pound above Sweet's price. Ben sues Sweet for breach of contract, claiming as damages the higher price paid for the sugar from others, lost profits from this year's lost Christmas sales, future lost profits from customers who have indicated that they will discontinue doing business with him, and punitive damages for failure to meet the contracted-for delivery date. Sweet claims Ben is limited to compensatory damages only. Discuss who is correct and why.

13–6. Consequential Damages. Kerr Steamship Co. delivered to Radio Corp. of America (RCA) a twenty-nine-word, coded message to be sent to Kerr's agent in Manila. The message included instructions on loading cargo onto one of Kerr's vessels. Kerr's profits on the carriage of the cargo were to be about $6,600. RCA mislaid the coded message, and it was never sent. Kerr sued RCA for the $6,600 in profits that it lost because RCA failed to send the message. Can Kerr recover? Explain. [*Kerr Steamship Co. v. Radio Corp. of America*, 245 N.Y. 284, 157 N.E. 140 (1927)]

13–7. Liquidated Damages versus Penalties. Dewerff was a teacher and basketball coach for Unified School District No. 315. The employment contract included a clause that read, in part: "Penalty for breaking contracts: . . . In all cases where a teacher under contract fails to honor the full term of his or her contract, a lump sum of $400 is to be collected if the contract is broken before August 1." Dewerff resigned on June 28, 1978, and he was told that the school would accept his resignation on his payment of the $400 stipulated in the contract. When Dewerff refused to make the $400 payment, the school district sued for $400 as "liquidated damages" on the basis of the contract clause. Dewerff argued that the contract provision was a "penalty" clause and unenforceable in this situation. Is Dewerff correct? Discuss. [*Unified School District No. 315, Thomas County v. Dewerff*, 6 Kan.App.2d 77, 626 P.2d 1206 (1981)]

13–8. Limitation of Liability. Westinghouse Electric Corp. entered into a contract with New Jersey Electric to manufacture and install a turbine generator for producing electricity. The contract price was over $10 million. The parties engaged in three years of negotiations and bargaining before they agreed on a suitable contract. The ultimate contract provided, among other things, that Westinghouse would not be liable for any injuries to the property belonging to the utility or to its customers or employees. Westinghouse warranted only that it would repair any defects in workmanship and materials appearing within one year of installation. After installation, part of New Jersey Electric's plant was damaged, and several of its employees were injured because of a defect in the turbine. New Jersey Electric sued Westinghouse, claiming that Westinghouse was liable for the damages because the exculpatory provisions in the contract were unconscionable. What was the result? [*Royal Indemnity Co. v. Westinghouse Electric Corp.*, 385 F.Supp. 520 (S.D.N.Y. 1974)]

13–9. Liquidated Damages versus Penalties. The Ivanovs, who were of Russian origin, agreed to purchase the Sobels' home for $300,000. A $30,000 earnest money deposit was placed in the trust account of Kotler Realty, Inc., the broker facilitating the transaction. Tiasia Buliak, one of Kotler's salespersons, negotiated the sale because she spoke fluent Russian. To facilitate the closing without the Ivanovs' having to be present, Buliak suggested they form a Florida corporation, place the cash necessary to close the sale in a corporate account, and give her authority to draw checks against it. The Ivanovs did as Buliak had suggested. Before the closing date of the sale, Buliak absconded with all of the closing money, which caused the transaction to collapse. Subsequently, because the Ivanovs had defaulted, Kotler Realty delivered the $30,000 earnest money deposit in its trust account to the Sobels. The Ivanovs then sued the Sobels, seeking to recover the $30,000. Was the clause providing that the seller could retain the earnest money if the buyer defaulted an enforceable liquidated damages clause or an unenforceable penalty clause? Discuss. [*Ivanov v. Sobel*, 654 So.2d 991 (Fla.App.3d 1995)]

13–10. Mitigation of Damages. Charles Kloss had worked for Honeywell, Inc., for over fifteen years when Honeywell decided to transfer the employees at its Ballard facility to its Harbour Pointe facility. Honeywell planned to hire a medical person at the Harbour Pointe facility and promised Kloss that if he completed a nursing program and became a registered nurse (RN), the company would hire him for the medical position. When Kloss graduated from his RN program, however, Honeywell did not assign him to a nursing or medical position. Instead, the company gave Kloss a job in its maintenance department. Shortly thereafter, Kloss left the company and eventually sued Honeywell for damages (lost wages) resulting from Honeywell's breach of the employment contract. One of the issues facing the court was whether Kloss, by voluntarily leaving the maintenance job at Honeywell, had failed to mitigate his damages. How should the court rule on this issue? Discuss. [*Kloss v. Honeywell, Inc.*, 77 Wash.App. 294, 890 P.2d 480 (1995)]

A QUESTION OF ETHICS AND SOCIAL RESPONSIBILITY

13–11. *In 1984, Robert Ryan, a widower with a ninth-grade education, fell behind in his mortgage payments and faced foreclosure. Norman Weiner told Ryan that he could loan him money to help him keep his house if Ryan signed over the deed to the house as "security" for the loan. When Weiner left, he took Ryan's deed to the property with him for "safekeeping." The next day, Ryan signed several papers without reading them, believing that he was signing loan documents, because he trusted Weiner. In fact, he had signed documents that conveyed ownership of his house to Weiner. Weiner brought the mortgage payments up to date, continued to make the payments on the house, and paid for utilities and services necessary to maintain the house. Ryan continued to live in the house and made monthly payments to Weiner. The payments steadily increased from $100 to $310 a month. During that time, the mortgage payments increased also, from $93 in 1984 to $120 in 1991. In May 1991, Ryan concluded that he had paid off his mortgage and also his "loan" from Weiner and refused to make further payments. When Weiner initiated legal proceedings to evict Ryan, Ryan sought to rescind his transfer of the property to Weiner. Based on these facts, answer the following questions.* [Ryan v. Weiner, 610 A.2d 1377 (Del. 1992)]

1. In view of the fact that Ryan voluntarily signed a document (contract) conveying his property to Weiner, should he be allowed to rescind that contract? What public policies are in conflict here?
2. When the equitable remedy of rescission and restitution is granted, the parties are restored to their status quo prior to the contract's formation. Is it possible in this case to restore the parties to their status quo prior to the 1984 transaction? Discuss.

U.S. v. CASE BRIEFING ASSIGNMENT

13–12. *Examine Case A.3* [Potter v. Oster, 426 N.W.2d 148 (Iowa 1988)] *in Appendix A. The case has been excerpted there in great detail. Review and then brief the case, making sure that you include answers to the following questions in your brief.*

1. Why was Oster appealing the trial court's decision?

2. Why did Oster assert that allowing the remedy of rescission and restitution in this case would lead to an inequitable result?
3. According to the court, what three requirements must be met before rescission will be granted?
4. Did the Potters meet these three requirements, and if so, why?
5. What reasons did the court give for its conclusion that remedies at law were inadequate in this case?

6. Why are remedies at law presumed to be inadequate for breach of real estate contracts?

 FOR CRITICAL ANALYSIS
13–13. *Review the discussion of the doctrine of election of remedies in this chapter. What are some of the advantages and disadvantages of this doctrine?*

▌Unit Three—Cumulative Hypothetical Problem

 13–14. *Corelli offers to purchase Bach's coin collection for $5,000, and Bach accepts Corelli's offer. Assuming that the contract has met all of the requirements for a valid contract, answer the questions raised in each of the following situations.*

1. The contract is in writing. Bach is a minor, and Corelli is an adult. Bach gives the coin collection to Corelli and receives the $5,000. Bach then has a change of heart and wants to recover his coin collection from Corelli. Can he do so? Explain. What if Bach was a minor at the time of the sale but did not decide that he wanted the coin collection back until a year after he had turned eighteen?
2. The contract is oral, and both parties are adults. Bach creates a memorandum of the transaction, indicating the names of the parties, the date, and the exact terms of the contract; Bach places the memorandum in his file. Corelli refuses to go through with the agreement. Is the contract enforceable against Corelli? Against Bach?
3. The contract is in writing, and both parties are adults. Although Bach represented to Corelli that the coin collection was worth at least $5,000, in fact, Bach had just

had it appraised and knew that it was worth only $2,000. Corelli later learns that the collection is worth only $2,000 and wants to sue Bach. What remedies are available to Corelli?
4. The contract is in writing, and both parties are adults. Corelli pays Bach $5,000, but Bach, having had a change of heart, decides to keep the collection and offers to return the $5,000 to Corelli. Corelli wants the coin collection, not the money. In Corelli's suit against Bach, will the court grant the equitable remedy of specific performance? Explain.
5. The contract is in writing, and both parties are adults. Corelli takes possession of the coin collection and promises to pay Bach the $5,000 in three weeks. Bach, in urgent need of money, borrows $5,000 from his friend Viva and assigns to Viva his rights to collect $5,000 from Corelli in return for the loan. Viva notifies Corelli of the assignment. Corelli pays Bach the $5,000 on the date stipulated in their contract. Bach refuses to give the money to Viva, and Viva sues Corelli. Is Corelli obligated to pay Viva $5,000 also? Discuss.

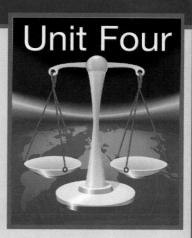

Unit Four

Sales and Lease Contracts

UNIT OUTLINE

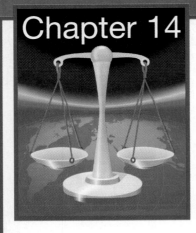

Chapter 14

The Formation of Sales and Lease Contracts

"The great object of the law is to encourage commerce."

J. Chambre, 1739–1823
(British jurist)

CHAPTER OBJECTIVES

After reading this chapter, you should be able to:

1. Discuss the scope of the UCC's Article 2 (on sales of goods) and Article 2A (on leases of goods).
2. Indicate the ways in which the UCC changes the common law of contracts in respect to contract formation.
3. Describe how the UCC attempts to avoid the "battle of the forms."
4. Identify some rules that apply only to contracts between merchants.
5. Compare and contrast the law governing domestic contracts with the law governing contracts for the international sale of goods.

When we turn to sales and lease contracts, we move away from common law principles and into the area of statutory law. State statutory law governing sales and lease transactions is based on the Uniform Commercial Code (UCC). The opening quotation states that the object of the law is to encourage commerce. This is particularly true with respect to the UCC. The UCC facilitates commercial transactions by making the laws governing sales and lease contracts clearer, simpler, and more readily applicable to the numerous difficulties that can arise during such transactions.

We open this chapter with a discussion of the general coverage of the UCC and its significance as a legal landmark. We then look at the scope of the UCC's Article 2 (on sales) and Article 2A (on leases) as a background to the focus of this chapter, which is the formation of contracts for the sale and lease of goods. Because international sales transactions are increasingly commonplace in the business world, the chapter concludes with an examination of the United Nations Convention on Contracts for the International Sale of Goods (CISG), which governs international sales contracts.

▌The Scope of the UCC

The UCC attempts to provide a consistent and integrated framework of rules to deal with all phases *ordinarily arising* in a commercial sales transaction from start to finish. For example, consider the following events, all of which may be involved in a single sales transaction:

1. *A contract for the sale or lease of goods is formed and performed.* Article 2 and Article 2A of the UCC provide rules governing all the facets of this transaction.
2. *The transaction may involve a payment—by check, electronic fund transfer, or other means.* Article 3 (on negotiable instruments), Article 4 (on bank deposits and collections), and Article 4A (on fund transfers) cover this part of the transaction.
3. *If the goods purchased are shipped or stored, they may be covered by a bill of lading or a warehouse receipt.* Article 7 (on documents of title) deals with this subject.
4. *The transaction may involve the acceptance of some form of security for a remaining balance owed.* Article 9, on secured transactions, covers this part of the transaction.

Two articles of the UCC seemingly do not address the "ordinary" commercial sales transaction. Article 6, on bulk transfers, has to do with merchants who sell off the major part of their inventory. Such bulk sales are not part of the ordinary course of business. Article 8, which covers investment securities, deals with transactions involving negotiable securities (stocks and bonds), transactions that do not involve the sale of *goods*. The subject matter of Articles 6 and 8, however, was considered by the UCC's drafters to be related *sufficiently* to commercial transactions to warrant its inclusion in the UCC. Excerpts from the most recent version of the UCC are included in Appendix C in this text.

The UCC has been adopted by all of the states, and it is impossible for a person to be in the business world without coming into contact with some aspect of the UCC. Because of its importance in the area of commercial transactions, we present the UCC as this chapter's *Landmark in the Law*.

"When there's no law, there's no bread."

Benjamin Franklin, 1706–1790
(American diplomat, author, and scientist)

BE CAREFUL Although the UCC has been widely adopted without many changes, states have modified some of the details to suit their particular needs.

The Uniform Commercial Code

LANDMARK IN THE LAW

Of all the attempts in the United States to produce a uniform body of laws relating to commercial transactions, none has been as comprehensive or successful as the Uniform Commercial Code (UCC). The UCC was the brainchild of William A. Schnader, president of the National Conference of Commissioners on Uniform State Laws (NCC). The drafting of the UCC began in 1945. The most significant individual involved in the project was its chief editor, Karl N. Llewellyn, of the Columbia University Law School. Llewellyn's intellect, continuous efforts, and ability to compromise made the first version of the UCC (1949) a legal landmark. Over the next several years, the UCC was substantially accepted by virtually every state in the Union.

Various articles and sections of the UCC are periodically changed or supplemented to clarify certain rules or to establish new rules when changes in business customs render the existing UCC provisions inapplicable. For example, because of the increasing importance of leases of goods in the commercial context, Article 2A, governing leases, was added to the UCC. To clarify the rights of parties to commercial fund transfers, particularly electronic fund transfers, Article 4A was issued. Articles 3 and 4, on negotiable instruments and banking relationships, recently underwent a significant revision. Because of other changes in business and in the law, the

(Continued)

Landmark in the Law—Continued

NCC has recommended the repeal of Article 6 (on bulk transfers), offering a revised Article 6 to those states that prefer not to repeal it. Currently, Article 8 (on investment securities) and Article 9 (covering secured transactions) are in the process of being revised.

Recently, the NCC drafted a revision of Article 2, on sales transactions. Since its issuance as part of the UCC over three decades ago, Article 2 has remained virtually unchanged. Business practices, however, have changed—electronic communications systems have significantly altered commercial practices in regard to sales transactions. Among other things, the revised Article 2 attempts to clarify the law in regard to these new business practices. (See this chapter's *Business Law in Action* for a further discussion of proposed changes to Article 2.)

For Critical Analysis:	*What are the benefits of having uniform laws among the states in regard to commercial transactions?*

▌The Scope of Article 2—Sales

SALES CONTRACT
A contract for the sale of goods under which the ownership of goods is transferred from a seller to a buyer for a price.

Article 2 of the UCC governs **sales contracts,** or contracts for the sale of goods. To facilitate commercial transactions, Article 2 modifies some of the common law contract requirements that were discussed in the previous chapters. To the extent that it has not been modified by the UCC, however, the common law of contracts also applies to sales contracts. For example, the common law requirements for a valid contract—agreement (offer and acceptance), consideration, capacity, and legality—are applicable to sales contracts as well. Thus, you should reexamine these common law principles when studying sales. In general, the rule is that whenever there is a conflict between a common law contract rule and the UCC, the UCC controls. In other words, when a UCC provision addresses a certain issue, the UCC governs; when the UCC is silent, the common law governs.

In regard to Article 2, you should keep in mind two things. First, Article 2 deals with the sale of *goods*; it does not deal with real property (real estate), services, or intangible property such as stocks and bonds. Thus, if the subject matter of a dispute is goods, the UCC governs. If it is real estate or services, the common law applies. The relationship between general contract law and the law governing sales of goods is illustrated in Exhibit 14–1. Second, in some cases, the rules may vary quite a bit, depending on whether the buyer or the seller is a *merchant*. We look now at how the UCC defines a *sale, goods,* and *merchant status.*

What Is a Sale?

SALE
The passing of title to property from the seller to the buyer for a price.

The UCC defines a **sale** as "the passing of title from the seller to the buyer for a price," where *title* refers to the formal right of ownership of property [UCC 2–106(1)]. The price may be payable in money or in other goods, services, or realty (real estate).

What Are Goods?

TANGIBLE PROPERTY
Property that has physical existence and can be distinguished by the senses of touch, sight, and so on. A car is tangible property; a patent right intangible property.

To be characterized as a *good,* the item of property must be *tangible,* and it must be *movable.* **Tangible property** has physical existence—it can be touched or seen. Intangible property—such as corporate stocks and bonds, patents and copyrights, and ordinary contract rights—have only conceptual existence and thus do not come under Article 2. A *movable* item can be carried from place to place. Hence, real estate is excluded from Article 2.

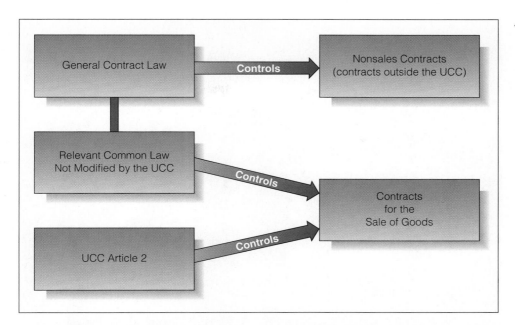

♦ **Exhibit 14–1**
Law Governing Contracts
This exhibit graphically illustrates the relationship between general contract law and the law governing contracts for the sale of goods. Sales contracts are not governed exclusively by Article 2 of the Uniform Commercial Code but also by general contract law whenever it is relevant and has not been modified by the UCC.

Two areas of dispute arise in determining whether the object of the contract is goods and thus whether Article 2 is applicable. One problem has to do with *goods associated with real estate,* such as crops or timber, and the other concerns contracts involving a combination of *goods and services.*

GOODS ASSOCIATED WITH REAL ESTATE   Goods associated with real estate often fall within the scope of Article 2. Section 2–107 provides the following rules:

1.   A contract for the sale of minerals or the like (including oil and gas) or a structure (such as a building) is a contract for the sale of goods *if severance, or separation, is to be made by the seller.* If the *buyer* is to sever (separate) the minerals or structure from the land, the contract is considered to be a sale of real estate governed by the principles of real property law, not the UCC.
2.   A sale of growing crops or timber to be cut is considered to be a contract for the sale of goods *regardless of who severs them.*
3.   Other "things attached" to realty but capable of severance without material harm to the land are considered goods *regardless of who severs them.*[1] Examples of "things attached" that are severable without harm to realty are a heater, a window air conditioner in a house, and counters and stools in a restaurant. Thus, removal of one of these things would be considered a sale of goods. The test is whether removal will cause substantial harm to the real property to which the item is attached.

GOODS AND SERVICES COMBINED   In cases in which goods and services are combined, courts disagree. For example, is the blood furnished to a patient during an operation a "sale of goods" or the "performance of a medical service"? Some courts say it is a good; others say it is a service. Similarly, contracts to sell and install software have posed the question of whether such contracts are primarily contracts for the sale of goods or contracts for the sale of services.[2] Because the UCC does not provide the answers to such questions, the courts try to determine which factor is predominant—the good or the service.

KEEP IN MIND Technological change is one of the primary sources of legal disputes.

---

1.   The UCC avoids the term *fixtures* here because of the numerous definitions of the word. A fixture is anything so firmly or permanently attached to land or to a building as to become a part of it. Once personal property becomes a fixture, it is governed by real estate law. See Chapter 35.
2.   See, for example, *Richard Haney Ford v. Ford Dealer Computer Services,* 218 Ga.App. 315, 461 S.E.2d 282 (1995).

Sunflowers in bloom. Does Article 2 apply to the sale of sunflower seeds to a snack foods company?

The UCC does stipulate, however, that serving food or drink to be consumed either on or off restaurant premises is a "sale of goods," at least for the purpose of an implied warranty of merchantability (to be explained in Chapter 17) [UCC 2–314(1)]. Other special transactions are also explicitly characterized as sales of goods by the UCC, including sales of unborn animals and rare coins. Whether the transaction in question involves the sale of goods or services is important, because the majority of courts treat services as being excluded by the UCC. If the transaction is not covered by the UCC, then UCC provisions, including those relating to implied warranties, would not apply. The court in the following case considered whether electricity is a "product" and thus subject to laws that apply to goods.

CASE 14.1

BRYANT v. TRI-COUNTY ELECTRIC MEMBERSHIP CORP.

United States District Court,
Western District of Kentucky, 1994.
844 F.Supp. 347.

HISTORICAL AND TECHNOLOGICAL SETTING
Electricity generated on a commercial scale has been available since the 1880s. Electricity is generated at power stations at about 25,000 volts. A transformer steps this up to 400,000 volts or more for transmission to a network of power stations and distribution centers covering a large area. Local substations receive the electricity and reduce the voltage in step-down transformers to distrib-

ute it to consumers. Some of the dangers of electricity, including voltage surges, have been recognized since it was first widely available.

FACTS   A fire in April 1988 destroyed the sawmill at the Bryant Lumber Company. The fire started when an electrical switch on one of the machines exploded. The mill owners claimed that the switch failed because of voltage surges that had plagued the mill for years. Seeking to recover for the damage, the owners filed a suit in a federal district court against the Tri-County Electric Membership Corporation (the utility that supplied the electricity causing the surges) and others. The owners argued in part that electricity is a "product" and thus subject to warranty laws and other laws that apply to goods. The defendants filed motions for summary judgment, contending in effect that electricity is not a "product."

ISSUE   Is ordinary electricity a product?

Case 14.1—Continued

DECISION   Yes. The court refused to grant Tri-County's motion for summary judgment.

REASON   The court pointed out that "the majority rule * * * considers ordinary electricity to be a 'product.'" The court explained that this view "sensibly accounts for the fact that electricity is created, harnessed, measured, transported, bought and sold, like products generally." The court recognized, however, that "in some respects electricity is different from traditional products. These real differences will be considered by the Court and by the jury" in determining, during the trial, whether Tri-County is liable.

FOR CRITICAL ANALYSIS—Social Consideration   *If electricity was not considered a "product," under what legal theory might a supplier be held liable for injuries attributable to its actions in connection with providing the electricity?*

Who Is a Merchant?

Article 2 governs the sale of goods in general. It applies to sales transactions between all buyers and sellers. In a limited number of instances, however, the UCC presumes that in certain phases of sales transactions involving merchants, special business standards ought to be imposed because of the merchants' relatively high degree of commercial expertise.[3] Such standards do not apply to the casual or inexperienced seller or buyer ("consumer"). Section 2–104 defines three ways in which merchant status can arise:

1.   A merchant is a person who *deals in goods of the kind* involved in the sales contract. Thus, a retailer, a wholesaler, or a manufacturer is a merchant of those goods sold in the business. A merchant for one type of goods is not necessarily a merchant for another type. For example, a sporting-equipment retailer is a merchant when selling tennis equipment but not when selling a used computer.
2.   A merchant is a person who, by occupation, holds himself or herself out as having knowledge and skill unique to the practices or goods involved in the transaction. This broad definition may include banks or universities as merchants.
3.   A person who *employs a merchant as a broker, agent, or other intermediary* has the status of merchant in that transaction. Hence, if a "gentleman farmer" who ordinarily does not run the farm hires a broker to purchase or sell livestock, the farmer is considered a merchant in the transaction.

In summary, a person is a **merchant** when he or she, acting in a mercantile capacity, possesses or uses an expertise specifically related to the goods being sold. This basic distinction is not always clear-cut. For example, courts in some states have determined that farmers may be merchants, while courts in other states have determined that it was not within the contemplation of the drafters of the UCC to include farmers as merchants.

MERCHANT
A person who is engaged in the purchase and sale of goods. Under the UCC, a person who deals in goods of the kind involved in the sales contract; for further definitions, see UCC 2–104.

▌ The Scope of Article 2A—Leases

In the past few decades, leases of personal property (goods) have become increasingly common. Consumers and business firms lease automobiles, industrial equipment, items for use in the home (such as floor sanders), and many other types of goods. Until

---

3.   The provisions that apply only to merchants deal principally with the Statute of Frauds, firm offers, confirmatory memoranda, warranties, and contract modification. These special rules reflect expedient business practices commonly known to merchants in the commercial setting. They will be discussed later in this chapter.

Article 2A was added to the UCC, no specific body of law addressed the legal problems that arose when goods were leased, rather than sold. In cases involving leased goods, the courts generally applied a combination of common law rules, real estate law, and principles expressed in Article 2 of the UCC.

Article 2A of the UCC was created to fill the need for uniform guidelines in this area. Article 2A covers any transaction that creates a lease of goods, as well as subleases of goods [UCC 2A–102, 2A–103(k)]. Article 2A is essentially a repetition of Article 2, except that it applies to leases of goods, rather than sales of goods, and thus varies to reflect differences between sale and lease transactions.

Definition of a Lease

LEASE AGREEMENT
In regard to the lease of goods, an agreement in which one person (the lessor) agrees to transfer the right to the possession and use of property to another person (the lessee) in exchange for rental payments.

LESSOR
A person who sells the right to the possession and use of goods to another in exchange for rental payments.

LESSEE
A person who acquires the right to the possession and use of another's goods in exchange for rental payments.

Article 2A defines a **lease agreement** as the lessor and lessee's bargain, as found in their language and as implied by other circumstances, including course of dealing and usage of trade or course of performance [UCC 2A–103(k)]. A **lessor** is one who sells the right to the possession and use of goods under a lease [UCC 2A–103(p)]. A **lessee** is one who acquires the right to the possession and use of goods under a lease [UCC 2A–103(o)]. Article 2A applies to all types of leases of goods, including commercial leases and consumer leases. Special rules apply to certain types of leases, however, including consumer leases and finance leases.

Consumer Leases

A *consumer lease* involves three elements: (1) a lessor who regularly engages in the business of leasing or selling, (2) a lessee (except an organization) who leases the goods "primarily for a personal, family, or household purpose," and (3) total lease payments that are less than $25,000 [UCC 2A–103(1)(e)]. In the interest of providing special protection for consumers, certain provisions of Article 2A apply only to consumer leases. For example, one provision states that a consumer may recover attorneys' fees if a court finds that a term in a consumer lease contract is unconscionable [UCC 2A–108(a)].

Finance Leases

A *finance lease* involves a lessor, a lessee, and a supplier. The lessor buys or leases goods from a supplier and leases or subleases them to the lessee [UCC 2A–103(g)]. Typically, in a finance lease, the lessor is simply financing the transaction. For example, suppose that Marlin Corporation wants to lease a crane for use in its construction business. Marlin's bank agrees to purchase the equipment from Jennco, Inc., and lease the equipment to Marlin. In this situation, the bank is the lessor-financer, Marlin is the lessee, and Jennco is the supplier.

Article 2A, unlike ordinary contract law, makes the lessee's obligations under a commercial finance lease irrevocable and independent from the financer's obligations [UCC 2A–407]. That is, the lessee must perform whether or not the financer performs. The lessee also must look almost entirely to the supplier for warranties.

▌The Formation of Sales and Lease Contracts

In regard to the formation of sales and lease contracts, the UCC modifies the common law in several ways. We look here at how Article 2 and Article 2A of the UCC modify common law contract rules. Remember that parties to sales contracts are free to establish whatever terms they wish. The UCC comes into play when the parties have not, in their contract, provided for a contingency that later gives rise to a dispute. The UCC makes this very clear time and again by its use of such phrases as "unless the parties otherwise agree" or "absent a contrary agreement by the parties."

Offer

In general contract law, the moment a definite offer is met by an unqualified acceptance, a binding contract is formed. In commercial sales transactions, the verbal exchanges, the correspondence, and the actions of the parties may not reveal exactly when a binding contractual obligation arises. The UCC states that an agreement sufficient to constitute a contract can exist even if the moment of its making is undetermined [UCC 2–204(2), 2A–204(2)].

NOTE Under the UCC, it is the actions of the parties that determine whether they intended to form a contract.

OPEN TERMS   According to contract law, an offer must be definite enough for the parties (and the courts) to ascertain its essential terms when it is accepted. The UCC states that a sales or lease contract will not fail for indefiniteness even if one or more terms are left open as long as (1) the parties intended to make a contract and (2) there is a reasonably certain basis for the court to grant an appropriate remedy [UCC 2–204(3), 2A–204(3)].

For example, Mike agrees to lease from CompuQuik a highly specialized computer workstation. Mike and one of CompuQuick's sales representatives sign a lease agreement that leaves some of the details blank, to be "worked out" the following week, when the leasing manager will be back from her vacation. In the meantime, CompuQuick obtains the necessary equipment from one of its suppliers and spends several days modifying the equipment to suit Mike's needs. When the leasing manager returns, she calls Mike and tells him that his workstation is ready. Mike says he is no longer interested in the workstation, as he has arranged to lease the same type of equipment for a lower price from another firm. CompuQuik sues Mike to recover its costs in obtaining and modifying the equipment, and one of the issues before the court is whether the parties had an enforceable contract. The court will likely hold that they did, based on their intent and conduct, despite the blanks in their written agreement.

Although the UCC has radically lessened the requirement of definiteness of terms, keep in mind that the more terms left open, the less likely a court will find that the parties intended to form a contract.

Open Price Term   If the parties have not agreed on a price, the court will determine a "reasonable price at the time for delivery" [UCC 2–305(1)]. If either the buyer or the seller is to determine the price, the price is to be fixed in good faith [UCC 2–305(2)].

Sometimes the price fails to be fixed through the fault of one of the parties. In that case, the other party can treat the contract as canceled or fix a reasonable price. For example, Johnson and Merrick enter into a contract for the sale of goods and agree that Johnson will fix the price. Johnson refuses to fix the price. Merrick can either treat the contract as canceled or set a reasonable price [UCC 2–305(3)].

As mentioned, if the buyer or the seller is to determine the price, the UCC requires that the price be fixed in good faith. This is but one of many UCC provisions requiring good faith in the formation and performance of sales contracts. In fact, the concepts of *good faith* and *commercial reasonableness* permeate the UCC. Section 1–203 states, "Every contract or duty within this act imposes an obligation of good faith in its performance or enforcement." Good faith in the case of a merchant is defined to mean honesty in fact and the observance of reasonable commercial standards of fair dealing in the trade [UCC 2–103(1)(b)]. Good faith means that honesty in fact is a condition *precedent* to a contract, and good faith exists if a party can meet the subjective test of innocence—sometimes called the "pure heart and empty head" test—when entering into the contract.

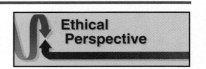
Ethical Perspective

(Continued)

The concept of commercial reasonableness means not only that sellers and buyers are expected to perform contracts in a reasonable manner but also that performance may be excused when circumstances render performance unreasonable or impracticable. The fact that the word *reasonable* appears about ninety times in Article 2 of the UCC demonstrates the UCC's opposition to imposing undue hardship on merchants and on those with whom they deal. A merchant is expected to act in a reasonable manner according to reasonable commercial customs.

For Critical Analysis: *How would a court objectively measure "good faith" and "commercial reasonableness"?*

CONTRAST The common law requires that the parties make their terms definite before they have a contract. The UCC applies general commercial standards to make the terms of a contract definite.

Open Payment Term　When parties do not specify payment terms, payment is due at the time and place at which the buyer is to receive the goods [UCC 2–310(a)]. The buyer can tender payment using any commercially normal or acceptable means, such as a check or credit card. If the seller demands payment in cash, however, the buyer must be given a reasonable time to obtain it [UCC 2–511(2)]. This is especially important when the contract states a definite and final time for performance.

Open Delivery Term　When no delivery terms are specified, the buyer normally takes delivery at the seller's place of business [UCC 2–308(a)]. If the seller has no place of business, the seller's residence is used. When goods are located in some other place and both parties know it, delivery is made there. If the time for shipment or delivery is not clearly specified in the sales contract, the court infers a "reasonable" time for performance [UCC 2–309(1)].

Duration of an Ongoing Contract　A single contract might specify successive performances but not indicate how long the parties are required to deal with each other. Although either party may terminate the ongoing contractual relationship, principles of good faith and sound commercial practice call for reasonable notification before termination so as to give the other party reasonable time to seek a substitute arrangement [UCC 2–309(2), (3)].

Options and Cooperation Regarding Performance　When specific shipping arrangements have not been made but the contract contemplates shipment of the goods, the *seller* has the right to make these arrangements in good faith, using commercial reasonableness in the situation [UCC 2–311].

When terms relating to the assortment of goods are omitted from a sales contract, the *buyer* can specify the assortment. For example, Marconi's Dental Supply and Petry Drugs, Inc., contract for the sale of one thousand toothbrushes. The toothbrushes come in a variety of colors, but the contract does not specify color. Petry, the buyer, has the right to take six hundred blue toothbrushes and four hundred green ones if it wishes. Petry, however, must exercise good faith and commercial reasonableness in making the selection [UCC 2–311].

Open Quantity Term　Normally, if the parties do not specify a quantity, a court will have no basis for determining a remedy. The UCC recognizes two exceptions in requirements and output contracts [UCC 2–306(1)]. In a **requirements contract,** the buyer agrees to purchase and the seller agrees to sell all or up to a stated amount of what the buyer *needs* or *requires*. There is implicit consideration in a requirements contract, for the buyer gives up the right to buy from any other seller, and this forfeited right creates a legal detriment. Requirements contracts are common in the business world and are normally enforceable. If, however, the buyer promises to purchase only if the buyer *wishes* to do so, or if the buyer reserves the right to buy the goods from

REQUIREMENTS CONTRACT
An agreement in which a buyer agrees to purchase and the seller agrees to sell all or up to a stated amount of what the buyer needs or requires.

someone other than the seller, the promise is illusory (without consideration) and unenforceable by either party.

In an **output contract**, the seller agrees to sell and the buyer agrees to buy all or up to a stated amount of what the seller *produces.* Again, because the seller essentially forfeits the right to sell goods to another buyer, there is implicit consideration in an output contract.

The UCC imposes a *good faith limitation* on requirements and output contracts. The quantity under such contracts is the amount of requirements or the amount of output that occurs during a *normal* production year. The actual quantity purchased or sold cannot be unreasonably disproportionate to normal or comparable prior requirements or output [UCC 2–306].

OUTPUT CONTRACT
An agreement in which a seller agrees to sell and a buyer agrees to buy all or up to a stated amount of what the seller produces.

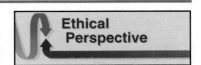

Ethical Perspective

The obligation of good faith is particularly important in requirements and output contracts. Without the obligation of good faith, the potential for abuse would be tremendous. For example, suppose that Tarpec Corporation contracts with Elfax, Inc., to purchase all of the electrical cable Tarpec needs for a three-year period. The contract sale price of the cable is pegged only to the annual rate of inflation for the whole economy, so it will increase by that amount each year. A year after the contract is formed, the market price of electrical cable doubles. Tarpec claims that its needs are now equivalent to the entire output of Elfax. It buys all of Elfax's output at a price that turns out to be substantially below the market price and then turns around and resells the cable that it does not need in its business at the new, higher market price.

Under the UCC, this type of unethical behavior is prohibited. Even though contracts that call for the buyer to purchase all of his or her needs from the seller are explicitly authorized under the UCC, such contracts are construed to involve *actual* requirements that may occur in good faith. Under UCC 2–306(1), no quantity "unreasonably disproportionate to any stated estimate or in the absence of a stated estimate to any normal or otherwise comparable prior output or requirements may be tendered or demanded." Thus, the UCC reflects ethical considerations in prohibiting the abuse of such contracts.

For Critical Analysis: *What type of clause could a seller include in a requirements contract to protect against the possibility that the buyer will do as Tarpec Corporation did in the hypothetical situation discussed above?*

MERCHANT'S FIRM OFFER Under regular contract principles, an offer can be revoked at any time before acceptance. The major common law exception is an *option contract* (discussed in Chapter 9), in which the offeree pays consideration for the offeror's irrevocable promise to keep the offer open for a stated period. The UCC creates a second exception, which applies only to firm offers for the sale or lease of goods made by a merchant (regardless of whether or not the offeree is a merchant). A **firm offer** arises when a merchant-offeror gives *assurances* in a *signed writing* that the offer will remain open. The merchant's firm offer is irrevocable without the necessity of consideration[4] for the stated period or, if no definite period is stated, a reasonable period (neither to exceed three months) [UCC 2–205, 2A–205].

It is necessary that the offer be both *written* and *signed* by the offeror.[5] When a firm offer is contained in a form contract prepared by the offeree, the offeror must also sign

FIRM OFFER
An offer (by a merchant) that is irrevocable without consideration for a period of time (not longer than three months). A firm offer by a merchant must be in writing and must be signed by the offeror.

---

4.   If the offeree pays consideration, then an option contract (not a merchant's firm offer) is formed.
5.   "Signed" includes any symbol executed or adopted by a party with a present intention to authenticate a writing [UCC 1–201(39)]. A complete signature is not required. Therefore, initials, a thumbprint, a trade name, or any mark used in lieu of a written signature will suffice, regardless of its location on the document.

a separate firm offer assurance also. This requirement ensures that the offeror will be made aware of the offer. If the firm offer is buried amid copious language in one of the pages of the offeree's form contract, the offeror may inadvertently sign the contract without realizing that there is a firm offer, thus defeating the purpose of the rule—which is to give effect to a merchant's deliberate intent to be bound to a firm offer.

International Perspective

As just mentioned, under the UCC a merchant's firm offer is irrevocable, even without consideration, if the offer gives assurances in a signed writing that the offer will remain open. The United Nations Convention on Contracts for the International Sale of Goods (CISG), which will be discussed later in this chapter, takes a different approach in regard to international sales contracts. Article 16(2) of the CISG provides that an offer will be irrevocable if the merchant-offeror simply states orally that the offer is irrevocable or if the offeree reasonably relies on the offer as being irrevocable. In either of these situations, the offer will be irrevocable even without a writing and without consideration.

For Critical Analysis: *What are the advantages and disadvantages of the CISG's provisions on firm offers relative to the UCC's provisions?*

Acceptance

BE AWARE The UCC's rules on means of acceptance illustrate the UCC's flexibility. The rules have been adapted to new forms of communication, such as faxes and E-mail.

The following sections examine the UCC's provisions governing acceptance. As you will see, acceptance of an offer to buy, sell, or lease goods generally may be made in any reasonable manner and by any reasonable means.

METHODS OF ACCEPTANCE   The general common law rule is that an offeror can specify, or authorize, a particular means of acceptance, making that means the only one effective for contract formation. Even an unauthorized means of communication is effective, however, as long as the acceptance is received by the specified deadline. For example, suppose that the offer states, "Answer by fax within five days." If the offeree sends a letter, and the offeror receives it within five days, a valid contract is formed. (For a review of the requirements relating to mode and timeliness of acceptance, see Chapter 9.)

Any Reasonable Means   When the offeror does not specify a means of acceptance, the UCC provides that acceptance can be made by any means of communication reasonable under the circumstances [UCC 2–206(1), 2A–206(1)]. This broadens the common law rules concerning authorized means of acceptance.

For example, Anodyne Corporation writes Bethlehem Industries a letter offering to lease $1,000 worth of goods. The offer states that Anodyne will keep the offer open for only ten days from the date of the letter. Before the ten days have lapsed, Bethlehem sends Anodyne an acceptance by fax. The fax is misdirected by someone at Anodyne's offices and does not reach the right person at Anodyne until after the ten-day deadline has passed. Is a valid contract formed? The answer is yes, because acceptance by fax is a commercially reasonable medium of acceptance under the circumstances. Acceptance would be effective upon Bethlehem's transmission of the fax, which occurred before the offer lapsed.

Promise to Ship or Prompt Shipment   The UCC permits acceptance of an offer to buy goods for current or prompt shipment by either a prompt *promise* to ship the goods to the buyer or the *prompt shipment* of conforming goods (that is, goods that accord with the contract's terms) to the buyer [UCC 2–206(1)(b)]. The prompt shipment of *nonconforming goods* constitutes both an acceptance (a contract) and a *breach* of that contract. This rule does not apply if the seller **seasonably** (within a reasonable amount of time) notifies the buyer that the nonconforming shipment is offered only as an *accommodation,* or as a favor. The notice of accommodation must clearly indicate to the buyer that the shipment does not constitute an acceptance and that, therefore, no contract has been formed.

For example, suppose that McIntosh orders five thousand *blue* widgets from Halderson. If Halderson ships five thousand *black* widgets instead, the shipment acts as both an acceptance of McIntosh's offer and a *breach* of the resulting contract. McIntosh may sue Halderson for any appropriate damages. If, however, Halderson notifies McIntosh that the black widgets are being shipped *as an accommodation*—because Halderson has only black widgets in stock—the shipment will not constitute an acceptance but a counteroffer. A contract will be formed only if McIntosh (the buyer) accepts the black widgets.

NOTICE OF ACCEPTANCE   Under the common law, because a unilateral offer invites acceptance by a performance, the offeree need not notify the offeror of performance unless the offeror would not otherwise know about it. The UCC is more stringent than the common law, stating that when "the beginning of requested performance is a reasonable mode of acceptance[,] an offeror who is not notified of acceptance within a reasonable time may treat the offer as having lapsed before acceptance" [UCC 2–206(2), 2A–206(2)].

ADDITIONAL TERMS   Under the common law, if Alderman makes an offer to Beale, and Beale in turn accepts but adds some slight modification, there is no contract. The so-called *mirror image rule,* which requires that the terms of the acceptance exactly match those of the offer (see Chapter 9), makes Beale's action a rejection of—and a counteroffer to—Alderman's offer. This rule often results in the so-called *battle of the forms.*

Say, for example, that a buyer negotiates with a seller over the phone to purchase a certain piece of equipment. The parties agree to all of the specific terms of the sale—price, quantity, delivery date, and so on. The buyer then offers to buy the equipment, using its standard purchase order form, and sends the form to the seller. At the same time, the seller accepts the offer, using its standard sales form. Because the parties presume that they have reached an agreement, discrepancies in the terms and conditions contained in their respective forms may go unnoticed. (See Exhibit 14–2 for an illustration of the kinds of terms and conditions that may be included in a standard purchase order form.) If a dispute arises, however, the discrepancies become significant, and a "battle of the forms" begins, in which each party claims that its form represents the true terms of the agreement.

Under the common law, the courts tended to resolve this difficulty by holding that no contract was formed, because the last form to be sent was not an acceptance but a counteroffer. To avoid the battle of the forms, the UCC dispenses with the mirror image rule. The UCC generally takes the position that if the offeree's response indicates a *definite* acceptance of the offer, a contract is formed, even if the acceptance includes additional or different terms from those contained in the offer [UCC 2–207(1)]. What happens to these additional terms? The answer to this question depends, in part, on whether the parties are nonmerchants or merchants.

One Party or Both Parties Are Nonmerchants   If one (or both) of the parties is a *nonmerchant,* the contract is formed according to the terms of the original offer submitted by the original offeror and not according to the additional terms of the acceptance [UCC 2–207(2)]. For example, Tolsen offers in writing to sell his personal computer to Valdez for $1,500. Valdez faxes a reply to Tolsen in which Valdez states, "I accept your offer to purchase your computer for $1,500. I *would like* a box of computer paper and ten diskettes to be included in the purchase price." Valdez has given Tolsen a definite expression of acceptance (creating a contract), even though Valdez's acceptance also suggests an added term for the offer. Because Tolsen is not a

SEASONABLY
Within a specified time period, or, if no period is specified, within a reasonable time.

DON'T FORGET The UCC recognizes that a proposed deal is a contract if, in commercial understanding, the deal has been closed.

♦ Exhibit 14–2
An Example of a Purchase Order (Front)

IBM®   **Purchase Order**

IBM DATA

SUPPLIER	MACH	U/M	O C	SUC	P P	R E C	E X P	COMMODITY	M M	DEPT. ORDER	A L T	JOB NO.	DEPT. CHG.	APPROP.	C C	PR ORIG.	CHG. RN

NUMBER   DATE

REC. NO.	B.J. S.O. OR REF. NO.	ACCOUNT NO.	COMMITMENT

REMIT TO →

NOTIFY BUYER IMMEDIATELY IF REMIT TO
ADDRESS IS DIFFERENT ON INVOICE

CODE	**TAXES**	**SPECIFICATION CODE**
	DO NOT CHARGE TEXAS SALES USE TAX SINCE WE PAY DIRECT OUR DIRECT PAY AUTHORIZATION NUMBER IS: **3-000001-7281-4**	1. Print Attached. 2. Specifications Attached. 3. Sample Attached. 4. Print in Your Possession. 5. Specification in Your Possession. 6. Sample in your Possession.

SHIP TO

IBM®   11400 BURNET ROAD   AUSTIN, TEXAS 78758 | BLDG.

OTHER THAN ABOVE

SEE CODE BELOW	SHIP VIA	IBM DATA	F.O.B. SHIP POINT	DESTINATION	IBM DATA	YOUR TERMS OF PAYMENT

TRANSPORTATION ROUTING GUIDELINES
(DO NOT INSURE OR DECLARE VALUE)

0-99 (45kg.) United Parcel Service, if available. If not,
0-40 (18kg.) Parcel Post (Zones 1-8) up to $1000 value.
All other Ship as indicated in "ship via" block.

IMPORTANT
1. SHOW OUR COMPLETE ORDER NUMBER, ITEM NUMBER AND IBM PART NUMBER (IF ANY) ON ALL INVOICES, SHIPPING CONTAINERS, PACKING LISTS AND CORRESPONDENCE.
2. SECURELY ATTACH PACKING SLIP TO OUTSIDE OF CARTON.
3. PACKAGES WEIGHING OVER 75 LBS. MUST BE PACKAGED FOR HANDLING WITH A MECHANICAL DEVICE.

ITEM	PART NUMBER	E/C LEVEL	SHIP TO ARRIVE	QUANTITY	U/M	UNIT PRICE	U/M

*TOTAL QUANTITY OF ITEM ORDERED

"SUBJECT TO THE TERMS AND CONDITIONS ON THE BACK HEREOF WHICH ARE IN-CORPORATED AND MADE A PART HEREOF"

ADDRESS ALL INVOICES TO:
INTERNATIONAL BUSINESS MACHINES CORP.
Attn: Accounts Payable
P.O. Box 9928
Austin, Texas 78766

AUTHORIZED SIGNATURE   512-838-3300

EXT.

942-0262-4

♦ **Exhibit 14–2—Continued**
An Example of a Purchase Order (Back)

STANDARD TERMS AND CONDITIONS
IBM EXPRESSLY LIMITS ACCEPTANCE TO THE TERMS SET FORTH ON THE FACE AND REVERSE SIDE OF THIS PURCHASE ORDER AND ANY ATTACHMENTS HERETO:

PURCHASE ORDER CONSTITUTES COMPLETE AGREEMENT	This Purchase order, including the terms and conditions on the face and reverse side hereof and any attachments hereto, contains the complete and final agreement between International Business Machines Corporation (IBM) and Seller. Reference to Seller's bids or proposals, if noted on this order, shall not affect terms and conditions hereof, unless specifically provided to the contrary herein, and no other agreement or quotation in any way modifying any of said terms and conditions will be binding upon IBM unless made in writing and signed by IBM's authorized representative.
ADVERTISING	Seller shall not, without first obtaining the written consent of IBM, in any manner advertise, publish or otherwise disclose the fact that Seller has furnished, or contracted to furnish to IBM, the material and/or services ordered hereunder.
APPLICABLE LAW	The agreement arising pursuant to this order shall be governed by the laws of the State of New York. No rights, remedies and warranties available to IBM under this contact or by operation of law are waived or modified unless expressly waived or modified by IBM in writing.
CASH DISCOUNT OR NET PAYMENT PERIOD	Calculations will be from the date an acceptable invoice is received by IBM. Any other arrangements agreed upon must appear on this order and on the invoice.
CONFIDENTIAL INFORMATION	Seller shall not disclose to any person outside of its employ, or use for any purpose other than to fulfill its obligations under this order, any information received from IBM pursuant to this order, which has been disclosed to Seller by IBM in confidence, except such information which is otherwise publicly available or is publicly disclosed by IBM subsequent to Seller's receipt of such information or is rightfully received by Seller from a third party. Upon termination of this order, Seller shall return to IBM upon request all drawings, blueprints, descriptions or other material received from IBM and all materials containing said confidential information. Also, Seller shall not disclose to IBM any information which Seller deems to be confidential, and it is understood that any information received by IBM, including all manuals, drawings and documents will not be of a confidential nature or restrict, in any manner, the use of such information by IBM. Seller agrees that any legend or other notice on any information supplied by Seller, which is inconsistent with the provisions of this article, does not create any obligation on the part of IBM.
GIFTS	Seller shall not make or offer gifts or gratuities of any type to IBM employees or members of their families. Such gifts or offerings may be construed as Seller's attempt to improperly influence our relationship.
IBM PARTS	All parts and components bailed by IBM to Seller for incorporation in work being performed for IBM shall be used solely for such purposes.
OFF-SPECIFICATION	Seller shall obtain from IBM written approval of all off-specification work.
PACKAGES	Packages must bear IBM's order number and show gross, tare and net weights and/or quantity.
PATENTS	Seller will settle or defend, at Seller's expense (and pay any damages, costs or fines resulting from), all proceedings or claims against IBM, its subsidiaries and affiliates and their respective customers, for infringement, or alleged infringement, by the goods furnished under this order, or any part or use thereof of patents (including utility models and registered designs) now or hereafter granted in the United States or in any country where Seller, its subsidiaries or affiliates, heretofore has furnished similar goods. Seller will, at IBM's request, identify the countries in which Seller, its subsidiaries or affiliates, heretofore has furnished similar goods.
PRICE	If price is not stated on this order, Seller shall invoice at lowest prevailing market price.
QUALITY	Material is subject to IBM's inspection and approval within a reasonable time after delivery. If specifications are not met, material may be returned at Seller's expense and risk for all damages incidental to the rejection. Payment shall not constitute an acceptance of the material nor impair IBM's right to inspect or any of its remedies.
SHIPMENT	Shipment must be made within the time stated on this order, failing which IBM reserves the right to purchase elsewhere and charges Seller with any loss incurred, unless delay in making shipment is due to unforeseeable causes beyond the control and without the fault or negligence of Seller.
SUBCONTRACTS	Seller shall not subcontract or delegate its obligations under this order without the written consent of IBM. Purchase of parts and materials normally purchased by Seller or required by this order shall be construed as subcontracts or delegations.
(NON-U.S. LOCATIONS ONLY)	Seller further agrees that during the process of bidding or production of goods and services hereunder, it will not re-export or divert to others any IBM specifications, drawing or other data, or any product of such data.
TAXES	Unless otherwise directed, Seller shall pay all sales and use taxes imposed by law upon or on account of this order. Where appropriate, IBM will reimburse Seller for this expense.
TOOLS	IBM owned tools held by Seller are to be used only for making parts for IBM. Tools of any kind held by Seller for making IBM's parts must be repaired and renewed by Seller at Seller's expense.
TRANSPORTATION	<u>Routing</u>—As indicated in transportation routing guidelines on face of this order. <u>F.O.B.</u>—Unless otherwise specified, ship collect, F.O.B. origin. <u>Prepaid Transportation (when specified)</u>—Charges must be supported by a paid freight bill or equivalent. <u>Cartage</u>) No charge allowed <u>Premium Transportation</u>) unless authorized <u>Insurance</u>) by IBM <u>Consolidation</u>—Unless otherwise instructed, consolidate all daily shipments to one destination on one bill of lading.
COMPLIANCE WITH LAWS AND REGULATIONS	Seller shall at all times comply with all applicable Federal, State and local laws, rules and regulations.
EQUAL EMPLOYMENT OPPORTUNITY	There are incorporated in this order the provisions of Executive Order 11246 (as amended) of the President of the United States on Equal Employment Opportunity and the rules and regulations issued pursuant thereto with which the Seller represents that he will comply, unless exempt.
EMPLOYMENT AND PROCUREMENT PROGRAMS	There are incorporated in this order the following provisions as they apply to performing work under Government procurement contracts: Utilization of Small Business Concerns (if in excess of $10,000) (Federal Procurement Regulation (FPR) 1-1.710-3(a)); Small Business Subcontracting Program (if in excess of $500,000) (FPR 1-1.710-3 (b)); Utilization of Labor Surplus Area Concerns (if in excess of $10,000) (FPR 1-1.805-3(a)); Labor Surplus Area Subcontracting Program (if in excess of $500,000) (FPR 1-1.805-3 (b)); Utilization of Minority Enterprises (if in excess of $10,000) (FPR 1-1.1310-2 (a)); Minority Business Enterprises Subcontracting Program (if in excess of $50,000) (FPR 1-1.1310-2(b)); Affirmative Action for Handicapped Workers (if $2,500 or more) (41 CFR 60-741.4); Affirmative Action for Disabled Veterans and Veterans of the Vietnam Era (if $10,000 or more) (41 CFR 60-250.4); Utilization of Small Business Concerns and Small Business Concerns Owned and Controlled by Socially and Economically Disadvantaged Individuals (if in excess of $10,000) (44 Fed. Reg. 23610 (April 20, 1979)); Small Business and Small Disadvantaged Business Subcontracting Plan (if in excess of $500,000) (44 Fed. Reg. 23610 (April 20, 1979)).
WAGES AND HOURS	Seller warrants that in the performance of this order Seller has complied with all of the provisions of the Fair Labor Standards Act of 1938 of the United States as amended.
WORKERS' COMPENSATION, EMPLOYERS' LIABILITY INSURANCE	If Seller does not have Workers' Compensation or Employer's Liability Insurance, Seller shall indemnify IBM against all damages sustained by IBM resulting from Seller's failure to have such insurance.

merchant, the additional term is merely a proposal (suggestion), and Tolsen is not legally obligated to comply with that term.

Both Parties Are Merchants   In contracts *between merchants* (that is, when both parties to the contract are merchants), the additional terms automatically become part of the contract unless (1) the original offer expressly limits acceptance to the terms of the offer, (2) the new or changed terms materially alter the contract, or (3) the offeror objects to the new or changed terms within a reasonable period of time [UCC 2–207(2)].

What constitutes a material alteration is frequently a question of fact that only a court can decide. Generally, if the modification involves no unreasonable element of surprise or hardship for the offeror, the court will hold that the modification did not materially alter the contract. The issue in the following case concerns whether an additional term in the acceptance (subjecting any disputes to arbitration) constituted a material alteration of the contract terms.

CASE 14.2

WILSON FERTILIZER & GRAIN, INC. v. ADM MILLING CO.
Court of Appeals of Indiana, 1995.
654 N.E.2d 848.

COMPANY PROFILE   *The Archer-Daniels-Midland Company had its beginnings in 1878 in Minneapolis, Minnesota, when John Daniels started crushing flaxseed to produce linseed oil. Today, Archer-Daniels-Midland, with more processing capacity than any other agricultural enterprise, calls itself the "supermarket to the world." Its customers include virtually every U.S. food company. Archer-Daniels-Midland is the leading global processor and producer of oilseed, ethanol, and soy protein, and it handles nearly 10 percent of the world grain trade. The division of Archer-Daniels-Midland that handles barley, corn, oats, rice, and wheat is the ADM Milling Company.*

FACTS   In October 1992, Wilson Fertilizer & Grain, Inc., agreed to sell grain to the ADM Milling Company. ADM sent Wilson a confirmation stating that "[t]his contract is also subject to the Trade Rules of the National Grain and Feed Association [NGFA]." The NGFA rules require the arbitration of disputes and limit the time for filing a complaint to one year. Wilson did not respond to the confirmation. A dispute arose under the contract, and Wilson filed suit against ADM in an Indiana state court. ADM moved to dismiss the action, claiming that the Trade Rules of the NGFA require the parties to arbitrate the dispute. Wilson argued that the arbitration provisions were not included within the terms of its agreement with ADM.

The trial court granted ADM's motion and ordered the parties to arbitration. By that time, however, the one-year limit had expired. Wilson appealed, arguing in part that ADM's confirmation materially altered the contract and thus did not become a part of the contract, because the one-year limit imposed a hardship on Wilson.

ISSUE   Was the confirmation clause that required the arbitration of disputes a material alteration of the contract terms?

DECISION   No. The Court of Appeals of Indiana affirmed the order of the lower court.

REASON   The state appellate court pointed out that "the test for whether additional terms materially alter an agreement is whether their 'incorporation into the contract without express awareness by the other party would result in surprise or hardship.'" The court concluded that the arbitration provision and the requirement that claims must be filed within one year did not impose an undue hardship on Wilson. First, the court stated that the UCC "specifically permits parties to a contract for sale to reduce the time for filing claims to one year." Second, "and even more significantly," the court noted "Wilson's apparent ability to have submitted its claim for arbitration within the one-year limit." The court explained that the contract was formed in October 1992, and Wilson filed the complaint in September 1993. "If Wilson was able to file its complaint in court within one year" after ADM allegedly breached the contract, "we fail to see how a contract provision requiring Wilson to submit its claim for arbitration in the same time period imposes a hardship."

FOR CRITICAL ANALYSIS—Social Consideration
For what reasons might a company prefer to litigate a dispute rather than submit it to arbitration?

Conditioned on Offeror's Assent   Regardless of merchant status, the UCC provides that the offeree's expression cannot be construed as an acceptance if additional or different terms in the acceptance are expressly conditioned on the offeror's assent to the additional or different terms [UCC 2–207(1)]. For example, Philips offers to sell Hundert 650 pounds of turkey thighs at a specified price and with specified delivery terms. Hundert responds, "I accept your offer for 650 pounds of turkey thighs *on the condition that you agree that the weight will be evidenced by a city scale weight certificate.*" Hundert's response will be construed not as an acceptance but as a counteroffer, which Philips may or may not accept.

Additional Terms May Be Stricken   The UCC provides yet another option for dealing with conflicting terms in the parties' writings. Section 2–207(3) states that conduct by both parties that recognizes the existence of a contract is sufficient to establish a contract for sale even though the writings of the parties do not otherwise establish a contract. In this situation, "the terms of the particular contract will consist of those terms on which the writings of the parties agree, together with any supplementary terms incorporated under any other provisions of this Act." In a dispute over contract terms, this provision allows a court simply to strike from the contract those terms on which the parties do not agree. (See this chapter's *Business Law in Action* for an application of this UCC provision.)

Consideration

The common law rule that a contract requires consideration also applies to sales and lease contracts. Unlike the common law, however, the UCC does not require a contract modification to be supported by new consideration. An agreement modifying a contract for the sale or lease of goods "needs no consideration to be binding" [UCC 2–209(1), 2A–208(1)].

MODIFICATIONS MUST BE MADE IN GOOD FAITH   Of course, contract modification must be sought in good faith [UCC 1–203]. For example, Jim agrees to lease certain goods to Louise for a stated price. Subsequently, a sudden shift in the market makes it difficult for Jim to lease the items to Louise at the given price without suffering a loss. Jim tells Louise of the situation, and Louise agrees to pay an additional sum for the goods. Later Louise reconsiders and refuses to pay more than the original price. Under the UCC, Louise's promise to modify the contract needs no consideration to be binding. Hence, Louise is bound by the modified contract.

In this example, a shift in the market is a *good faith* reason for contract modification. What if there really was no shift in the market, however, and Jim knew that Louise needed the goods immediately but refused to deliver them unless Louise agreed to pay an additional sum of money? This sort of extortion of a modification without a legitimate commercial reason would be ineffective, because it would violate the duty of good faith. Jim would not be permitted to enforce the higher price.

WHEN MODIFICATION WITHOUT CONSIDERATION REQUIRES A WRITING   In some situations, modification of a sales or lease contract without consideration must be in writing to be enforceable. For example, if the contract itself prohibits any changes to the contract unless they are in a signed writing, only those changes agreed to in a signed writing are enforceable. If a consumer (nonmerchant buyer) is dealing with a merchant *and* the merchant supplies the form that contains a prohibition against oral modification, the consumer must sign a separate acknowledgment of such a clause [UCC 2–209(2), 2A–208(2)].

Also, any modification that brings a sales contract under the Statute of Frauds must usually be in writing to be enforceable. Thus, if an oral contract for the sale of goods priced at $400 is modified so that the contract goods are now priced at $600, the modification must be in writing to be enforceable [UCC 2–209(3)]. If, however, the buyer

The Ongoing Battle of the Forms

The drafters of UCC Section 2–207 attempted to avoid the "battle of the forms" by providing that a contract can be formed even though the acceptance includes additional terms. Nonetheless, the battle continues in earnest. Indeed, one of the results of Section 2–207 is that buyers and sellers go to great lengths to draft their acceptances as "offers" or "counteroffers" (instead of acceptances) so that their terms will control the resulting contracts.

Consider, for example, the events that unfolded in *Ionics, Inc. v. Elmwood Sensors, Inc.*[a] Ionics, Inc., purchased approximately sixteen thousand thermostats from Elmwood Sensors, Inc., during 1990 and 1991. Ionics installed the thermostats as component parts in water dispensers that were then leased to third parties. Soon after they were placed in use, several Ionics water dispensers caused fires, which, according to Ionics, resulted from defects in Elmwood's sensors. When Ionics filed suit against

a.   896 F.Supp. 66 (D.Mass. 1995).

Elmwood to recover damages, a classic "battle of the forms" ensued.

Ionics pointed to the purchase order form that it had used for each of its orders for the thermostats. The form included a condition that Ionics would be entitled to all remedies if Elmwood breached the contract and stated that the purchase order could only be accepted "upon the exact terms herein set forth." Elmwood then pointed to its acknowledgment form, which it had enclosed in each of its shipments to Ionics. The form stated that Elmwood would ship the goods but only on the terms and conditions set forth in its form, which was labeled a "counteroffer." Ionics would be deemed to have accepted the counteroffer unless it objected to the terms within ten days. The conditions in Elmwood's form included one that disclaimed warranties and another that limited the buyer's remedies to the repair or replacement of defective goods.

The issue in this case—as in many other "battle of the forms" cases—was not whether the parties had a contract. Clearly, their conduct established that they did. Rather, the issue turned on which party's terms became part of the contract. In deciding the case, the court virtually ignored the problem of offer-acceptance by applying UCC 2–207(3). The court held that the parties' contract consisted of only

those terms on which the parties agreed, and all conflicting terms were stricken from the contract. The end result was that Ionics was able to recover from Elmwood for breach of an implied warranty. (See Chapter 17 for a discussion of the UCC's provisions regarding implied warranties.)

One of the goals in the proposed revision of Article 2 of the UCC is to redesign UCC 2–207 so that the "battle of the forms" can be avoided. Some have suggested that this section should be revised so that it focuses less on contract formation (offer-acceptance) and more on the approach currently provided under UCC 2–207(3)—that the terms of a contract are only those on which the parties have agreed.[b]

For Critical Analysis: *What argument could be made in favor of the requirement that a definite expression of acceptance by the offeree results in a contract* on the offeror's terms *unless the offeree specifically conditions the acceptance on the offeror's assent to additional or different terms?*

b.   Mark E. Roszkowski and John D. Wladis, "Revised U.C.C. Section 2–207: Analysis and Recommendations," *The Business Lawyer* (Chicago: Section of Business Law, American Bar Association, May 1994), pp. 1065–1080.

accepts delivery of the goods after the modification, he or she is bound to the $600 price [UCC 2–201(3)(c)]. Unlike Article 2, Article 2A does not say whether a lease as modified needs to satisfy the Statute of Frauds.

⬜ Technology and Electronic Sales Contracts

An increasing number of sellers today engage in so-called trading partner or partnering agreements with purchasers. In a partnering agreement, a seller and buyer who frequently do business with each other can agree ahead of time on the general terms and conditions that will apply to all transactions subsequently

conducted via computer modem or fax. The agreement can also establish special access and identification codes to be used by the buyer and seller when transacting business electronically. The buyer can then submit an order for specific goods (indicating the quantity, price, and so on) via fax or modem without having to

Technology and Electronic Sales Contracts—Continued

include all of the terms and conditions of the purchase. Similarly, the seller can respond to the purchase order with a brief message, indicating that the requested goods will be shipped.

Trading partner agreements thus set the stage for simpler and more efficient sales transactions. The parties would only have to focus on the specific components of a particular order or sale, without having to worry about future disputes over conflicting contractual terms and conditions. The time saved through the electronic purchase and sale of goods is, of course, beneficial to both buyers and sellers. The traditional delays caused by sending orders and acknowledgments through the mails are avoided. Moreover, the partnering agreement reduces the likelihood of a "battle of the forms," because the buyer and seller have agreed to the terms and conditions that will accompany each sale. The parties can also agree to the computerized forms that will be used before specific sales and purchases are made.

The idea of contracting in advance as to what terms and conditions will govern future sales is not really new. "Master purchase agreements" and similar contracts have been used in the past to establish general terms and conditions of future sales. What is new, however, is the use of trading partner agreements to agree in advance to use electronic data interchange (EDI) to form valid and enforceable contracts.

With electronic purchasing systems, just as with other, similar computerized systems, unauthorized transactions are easier to make than when paper forms are used. After all, when the seller receives a purchase order on a computer system, the seller cannot see the buyer, nor is there any written signature to authenticate the transaction. Therefore, if an unauthorized person uses a purchaser's designated access number and identification code, it may be some time before the problem is discovered. In the meantime, who is liable for the loss, the seller or the buyer? Legal problems of this kind can be avoided if, in the partnering agreement, a special "signature code" for the buyer is established in addition to the other buyer codes and identification numbers. The seller and buyer can agree that only purchase orders including this special signature code will be filled.

For Critical Analysis: *Who do you think should be responsible for the damages that occur when a computer system fails and orders do not get processed under an EDI system?*

Statute of Frauds

The UCC contains Statute of Frauds provisions covering sales and lease contracts. Under these provisions, sales contracts for goods priced at $500 or more and lease contracts requiring payments that are $1,000 or more must be in writing to be enforceable [UCC 2–201(1), 2A–201(1)].

SUFFICIENCY OF THE WRITING   The UCC has greatly relaxed the requirements for the sufficiency of a writing to satisfy the Statute of Frauds. A writing or a memorandum will be sufficient as long as it indicates that the parties intended to form a contract and as long as it is signed by the party (or agent of the party) against whom enforcement is sought. The contract normally will not be enforceable beyond the quantity of goods shown in the writing, however. All other terms can be proved in court by oral testimony. For leases, the writing must reasonably identify and describe the goods leased and the lease term.

WRITTEN CONFIRMATION BETWEEN MERCHANTS   Once again, the UCC provides a special rule for merchants. Merchants can satisfy the requirements of a writing for the Statute of Frauds if, after the parties have agreed orally, one of the merchants sends a signed written confirmation to the other merchant. The communication must indicate the terms of the agreement, and the merchant receiving the confirmation must have reason to know of its contents. Unless the merchant who receives the confirmation gives written notice of objection to its contents within ten days after receipt, the writing is sufficient against the receiving merchant, even though he or she has not signed anything [UCC 2–201(2)].[6]

For example, Alfonso is a merchant buyer in Cleveland. He contracts over the telephone to purchase $4,000 worth of goods from Goldstein, a New York City merchant seller. Two days later, Goldstein sends written confirmation detailing the terms of the oral contract, and Alfonso subsequently receives it. If Alfonso does not give Goldstein written notice of objection to the contents of the written confirmation within ten days of receipt, Alfonso cannot raise the Statute of Frauds as a defense against the enforcement of the oral contract.

EXCEPTIONS   The UCC defines three exceptions to the writing requirements of the Statute of Frauds. An oral contract for the sale of goods priced at $500 or more or the lease of goods involving total payments of $1,000 or more will be enforceable despite the absence of a writing in the following circumstances [UCC 2–201(3), 2A–201(4)]. These exceptions and other ways in which sales law differs from general contract law are summarized in Exhibit 14–3.

Specially Manufactured Goods   An oral contract is enforceable if it is for (1) goods that are specially manufactured for a particular buyer or specially manufactured or obtained for a particular lessee, (2) these goods are not suitable for resale or lease to others in the ordinary course of the seller's or lessor's business, and (3) the seller or lessor has substantially started to manufacture the goods or has made commitments for the manufacture or procurement of the goods. In this situation, once the seller or lessor has taken action, the buyer or lessee cannot repudiate the agreement claiming the Statute of Frauds as a defense.

For example, suppose Womach orders custom-made draperies for her new boutique. The price is $1,000, and the contract is oral. When the merchant seller manufactures the draperies and tenders delivery to Womach, Womach refuses to accept them even though the quality of the work is satisfactory and the job has been completed on time. Womach claims that she is not liable because the contract was oral. Clearly, if the unique style and color of the draperies makes it improbable that the seller can find another buyer. Womach is liable to the seller. Note that the seller must have made a substantial beginning in manufacturing the specialized item prior to the buyer's repudiation. (Here, the manufacture was completed.) Of course, the court must still be convinced by evidence of the terms of the oral contract.

REMEMBER An admission can be made in documents revealed during discovery, including internal memos and employee reports.

Admissions   An oral contract for the sale or lease of goods is enforceable if the party against whom enforcement of a contract is sought admits in pleadings, testimony, or other court proceedings that a contract for sale was made. In this situation, the contract will be enforceable even though it was oral, but enforceability will be limited to the quantity of goods admitted.

For example, Lane and Sugg negotiate an agreement over the telephone. During the negotiations, Lane requests a delivery price for five hundred gallons of gasoline and a separate price for seven hundred gallons of gasoline. Sugg replies that the price would be the same, $1.10 per gallon. Lane orally orders five hundred gallons. Sugg honestly believes that Lane ordered seven hundred gallons and tenders that amount. Lane refuses the shipment of seven hundred gallons, and Sugg sues for breach. In his pleadings and testimony, Lane admits that an oral contract was made, but only for five hundred gallons. Because Lane admits the existence of the oral contract, Lane cannot

---

6. According to the Comments accompanying UCC 2A–201 (Article 2A's Statute of Frauds), the "between merchants" provision was not included because the number of such transactions involving leases, as opposed to sales, was thought to be modest.

	CONTRACT LAW	**SALES LAW**
Contract Terms	Contract must contain all material terms.	Open terms are acceptable if parties intended to form a contract, but contract not enforceable beyond quantity term.
Acceptance	Mirror image rule applies. If additional terms are added in acceptance, counteroffer is created.	Additional terms will not negate acceptance unless acceptance is made expressly conditional on assent to the additional terms.
Contract Modification	Requires consideration.	Does not require consideration.
Irrevocable Offers	Option contracts (with consideration).	Merchants' firm offers (without consideration).
Statute of Frauds Requirements	All material terms must be included in the writing.	Writing required only in sale of goods of $500 or more but not enforceable beyond quantity specified. *Between merchants:* Contract is enforceable if merchant fails to object in writing to confirming memorandum within ten days. *Exceptions:* 1. Contracts for specially manufactured goods. 2. Contracts admitted to by party against whom enforcement is sought. 3. Contracts will be enforced to extent goods delivered or paid for.

◆ Exhibit 14–3
Major Differences between Contract Law and Sales Law

plead the Statute of Frauds as a defense. The contract is enforceable, however, only to the extent of the quantity admitted (five hundred gallons).

Partial Performance   An oral contract for the sale or lease of goods is enforceable if payment has been made and accepted or goods have been received and accepted. This is the "partial performance" exception. The oral contract will be enforced at least to the extent that performance *actually* took place.

Suppose that Allan orally contracts to lease Opus a thousand chairs at $1 each to be used during a one-day rock concert. Before delivery, Opus sends Allan a check for $500, which Allan cashes. Later, when Allan attempts to deliver the chairs, Opus refuses delivery, claiming the Statute of Frauds as a defense, and demands the return of his $500. Under the UCC's partial performance rule, Allan can enforce the oral contract by tender of delivery of five hundred chairs for the $500 accepted. Similarly, if Opus had made no payment but had accepted the delivery of five hundred chairs from Allan, the oral contract would have been enforceable against Opus for $500, the price of the five hundred chairs delivered.

Parol Evidence

If the parties to a contract set forth its terms in a confirmatory memorandum (a writing expressing offer and acceptance of the deal) or in a writing intended as their final expression, the terms of the contract cannot be contradicted by evidence of any prior agreements or contemporaneous oral agreements. The terms of the contract may, however, be explained or supplemented by *consistent additional terms* or by *course of dealing, usage of trade,* or *course of performance* [UCC 2–202, 2A–202].

CONSISTENT ADDITIONAL TERMS   If the court finds an ambiguity in a writing that is supposed to be a complete and exclusive statement of the agreement between the parties, it may accept evidence of consistent additional terms to clarify or remove the ambiguity. The court will not, however, accept evidence of contradictory terms. This is the rule under both the UCC and the common law of contracts.

COURSE OF DEALING AND USAGE OF TRADE   Under the UCC, the meaning of any agreement, evidenced by the language of the parties and by their actions, must be interpreted in light of commercial practices and other surrounding circumstances. In interpreting a commercial agreement, the court will assume that the *course of prior dealing* between the parties and the *usage of trade* were taken into account when the agreement was phrased.

COURSE OF DEALING
Prior conduct between parties to a contract that establishes a common basis for their understanding.

A **course of dealing** is a sequence of previous actions and communications between the parties to a particular transaction that establishes a common basis for their understanding [UCC 1–205(1)]. A course of dealing is restricted to the sequence of actions and communications between the parties that has occurred prior to the agreement in question. The UCC states, "A course of dealing between the parties and any usage of trade in the vocation or trade in which they are engaged or of which they are or should be aware give particular meaning to [the terms of the agreement] and supplement or qualify the terms of [the] agreement" [UCC 1–205(3)].

USAGE OF TRADE
Any practice or method of dealing having such regularity of observance in a place, vocation, or trade as to justify an expectation that it will be observed with respect to the transaction in question.

Usage of trade is defined as any practice or method of dealing having such regularity of observance in a place, vocation, or trade as to justify an expectation that it will be observed with respect to the transaction in question [UCC 1–205(2)]. Further, the express terms of an agreement and an applicable course of dealing or usage of trade will be construed to be consistent with each other whenever reasonable. When such a construction is *unreasonable,* however, the express terms in the agreement will prevail [UCC 1–205(4)]. In the following case, the issue concerned whether evidence of usage and custom in the trade could be used to explain the meaning of the quantity figures specified by the parties when the contract was formed.

CASE 14.3

HEGGBLADE-MARGULEAS-TENNECO, INC. v. SUNSHINE BISCUIT, INC.

Court of Appeal of California,
Fifth District, 1976.
59 Cal.App.3d 948,
131 Cal.Rptr. 183.

unknown outside the northeastern United States for nearly seventy years, potato chips began to become popular in other areas of the country in the 1920s. After 1945, their popularity soared, particularly with the creation of California dip, which was perfect for the casual entertaining that was part of the growing middle-class, suburban lifestyle. In the late 1960s and early 1970s, however, it became fashionable among some groups to reject all things perceived to be middle class or suburban. This may have contributed to a decline in the demand for potato chips during those years.

HISTORICAL AND SOCIAL SETTING *George Crumb cooked the first known potato chips at the Moon Lake Lodge in Saratoga, New York, in 1853. Generally*

FACTS In 1970, Heggblade-Marguleas-Tenneco, Inc. (HMT), contracted with Sunshine Biscuit, Inc., to supply potatoes to be used in the 1971 production of snack

Case 14.3—Continued

foods. HMT had never marketed processing potatoes before. The quantity mentioned in its contract negotiations was 100,000 sacks of potatoes. The parties agreed that the amount of potatoes to be supplied would vary somewhat with Sunshine Biscuit's needs. Subsequently, a decline in demand for Sunshine Biscuit's products severely reduced its need for potatoes. Sunshine Biscuit was able to take only 60,105 sacks out of the 100,000 previously estimated. HMT filed suit against Sunshine Biscuit in a California state court. Sunshine Biscuit attempted to introduce evidence that it is customary in the potato-processing industry for the number of potatoes specified in sales contracts to be reasonable estimates rather than exact numbers that a buyer intends to purchase. The trial court held for Sunshine Biscuit, and HMT appealed.

ISSUE   Could evidence of custom in the potato-processing trade be admissible?

DECISION   Yes. The California appellate court affirmed the trial court's decision.

REASON   UCC Section 2–202 states that even though evidence of prior agreements or contemporaneous oral agreements that contradict a written contract is inadmissible, evidence of a course of dealing or of trade usage is admissible to explain or supplement a written contract. The fact that specific numbers were used to designate what quantities of potatoes Sunshine Biscuit thought it would need does not dispose of the issue. In its statement that evidence of trade usage was admissible, the court quoted an official comment to the UCC: "[I]n order that the true understanding of the parties as to the agreement may be [reached, such] writings are to be read on the assumption that * * * the usages of trade were taken for granted when the document was phrased. Unless carefully negated they have become an element of the meaning of the words used." HMT was held to have sufficient knowledge of the "trade custom."

FOR CRITICAL ANALYSIS—Ethical Consideration   *If HMT had not been aware of the prevailing customs in the potato-processing trade, would evidence of those customs still be admissible? Should it be?*

COURSE OF PERFORMANCE   A **course of performance** is the conduct that occurs under the terms of a particular agreement. Presumably, the parties themselves know best what they meant by their words, and the course of performance actually undertaken under their agreement is the best indication of what they meant [UCC 2–208(1), 2A–207(1)].

For example, suppose that Janson's Lumber Company contracts with Barrymore to sell Barrymore a specified number of "2 by 4s." The lumber in fact does not measure 2 inches by 4 inches but rather 1⅞ inches by 3¾ inches. Janson's agrees to deliver the lumber in five deliveries, and Barrymore, without objection, accepts the lumber in the first three deliveries. On the fourth delivery, however, Barrymore objects that the two-by-fours do not measure 2 inches by 4 inches.

The course of performance in this transaction—that is, the fact that Barrymore accepted three deliveries without objection under the agreement—is relevant in determining that here the words "2 by 4" actually mean "1⅞ by 3¾." Janson's can also prove that two-by-fours need not be exactly 2 inches by 4 inches by applying usage of trade, course of prior dealing, or both. Janson's can, for example, show that in previous transactions, Barrymore took 1⅞-inch-by-3¾-inch lumber without objection. In addition, Janson's can show that in the trade, two-by-fours are commonly 1⅞ inches by 3¾ inches.

RULES OF CONSTRUCTION   The UCC provides *rules of construction* for interpreting contracts. Express terms, course of performance, course of dealing, and usage of trade are to be construed together when they do not contradict one another. When such a construction is unreasonable, however, the following order of priority controls: (1) express terms, (2) course of performance, (3) course of dealing, and (4) usage of trade [UCC 1–205(4), 2–208(2), 2A–207(2)].

> "Merchants know perfectly well what they mean when they express themselves, not in the language of lawyers, but in the language of courteous mercantile communication."
>
> **Lord Cairn, 1819–1885 (British jurist)**

COURSE OF PERFORMANCE
The conduct that occurs under the terms of a particular agreement; such conduct indicates what the parties to an agreement intended it to mean.

Unconscionability

As discussed in Chapter 10, an unconscionable contract is one that is so unfair and one sided that it would be unreasonable to enforce it. The UCC allows the court to evaluate a contract or any clause in a contract, and if the court deems it to have been unconscionable *at the time it was made*, the court can (1) refuse to enforce the contract, (2) enforce the remainder of the contract without the unconscionable clause, or (3) limit the application of any unconscionable clauses to avoid an unconscionable result [UCC 2–302, 2A–108].

The inclusion of Sections 2–302 and 2A–108 in the UCC reflects an increased sensitivity to certain realities of modern commercial activities. Classical contract theory holds that a contract is a bargain in which the terms have been worked out *freely* between parties that are equals. In many modern commercial transactions, this premise is invalid. Standard-form contracts and leases are often signed by consumer-buyers who understand few of the terms used and who often do not even read them. Virtually all of the terms are advantageous to the party supplying the standard-form contract. The UCC's unconscionability provisions give the courts a powerful weapon for policing such transactions, as the next case illustrates.

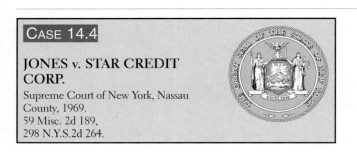

CASE 14.4

JONES v. STAR CREDIT CORP.

Supreme Court of New York, Nassau County, 1969.
59 Misc. 2d 189,
298 N.Y.S.2d 264.

HISTORICAL AND ECONOMIC SETTING   *In the sixth century, under Roman civil law, the rescission of a contract was allowed when the court determined that the market value of the goods that were the subject of the contract equaled less than half the contract price. This same ratio has appeared over the last thirty years in many cases in which courts have found contract clauses to be unconscionable under UCC 2–302 on the ground that the price was excessive. In a Connecticut case, for example, the court held that a contract requiring a welfare recipient to make payments totaling $1,248 for a television set that retailed for $499 was unconscionable.[a] The seller had not told the buyer the full purchase price. Most of the litigants who have used UCC 2–302 successfully have been consumers who are poor or otherwise at a disadvantage. In one New York case, for example, the court held that a contract requiring a Spanish-speaking consumer to make payments totaling nearly $1,150 for a freezer that wholesaled for less than*

$350 was unconscionable.[b] The contract was in English, and the salesperson did not translate or explain it.

FACTS   The Joneses, the plaintiffs, were welfare recipients who agreed to purchase a freezer for $900 as the result of a salesperson's visit to their home. Tax and financing charges raised the total price to $1,234.80. At trial, the freezer was found to have a maximum retail value of approximately $300. The plaintiffs, who had made payments totaling $619.88, brought a suit in a New York state court to have the purchase contract declared unconscionable under the UCC.

ISSUE   Can this contract be denied enforcement on the ground of unconscionability?

DECISION   Yes. The court held that the contract was not enforceable as it stood, and the contract was reformed so that no further payments were required.

REASON   The court relied on UCC 2–302(1), which states that if "the court as a matter of law finds the contract or any clause of the contract to have been unconscionable at the time it was made the court may *   *   * so limit the application of any unconscionable clause as to avoid any unconscionable result." The court then examined the disparity between the $900 purchase price and the $300 retail value, as well as the fact that the credit charges alone exceeded the retail value. These

---

a.   *Murphy v. McNamara*, 36 Conn.Supp. 183, 416 A.2d 170 (1979).

b.   *Frostifresh Corp. v. Reynoso*, 52 Misc.2d 26, 274 N.Y.S.2d 757 (Dist. 1966); rev'd on issue of relief, 54 Misc.2d 119, 281 N.Y.S.2d 946 (Sup. 1967).

Case 14.4—Continued

excessive charges were exacted despite the seller's knowledge of the plaintiffs' limited resources. The court reformed the contract so that the plaintiffs' payments, amounting to more than $600, were regarded as payment in full.

FOR CRITICAL ANALYSIS—Ethical Consideration
What if the plaintiffs had made payments totaling $300—the retail value of the freezer? Would the court regard that $300 as "payment in full"? Should the court consider the seller's interests in a case such as this one, in which the seller was deemed to have acted unconscionably?

Contracts for the International Sale of Goods

International sales contracts between firms or individuals located in different countries are governed by the 1980 United Nations Convention on Contracts for the International Sale of Goods (CISG)—if the countries of the parties to the contract have ratified the CISG (and if the parties have not agreed that some other law will govern their contract). As of 1996, thirty-eight countries had ratified or acceded to the CISG, including the United States, Canada, Mexico, some Central and South American countries, and most of the European nations. Four other nations have signed the CISG and indicated their intent to ratify it.

Applicability of the CISG

Essentially, the CISG is to international sales contracts what Article 2 of the UCC is to domestic sales contracts. As discussed in this chapter, in domestic transactions the UCC applies when the parties to a contract for a sale of goods have failed to specify in writing some important term concerning price, delivery, or the like. Similarly, whenever the parties to international transactions have failed to specify in writing the precise terms of a contract, the CISG will be applied. Although the UCC applies to consumer sales, the CISG does not, and neither applies to contracts for services.

Businesspersons must take special care when drafting international sales contracts to avoid problems caused by distance, including language differences and different national laws. The fold-out exhibit contained within this chapter, which shows an

A production line in a globe factory. If, in the United States, a contract for a sale of globes is not in writing, is it enforceable? Is a contract for an international sale of the globes enforceable if it is not in writing?

actual international sales contract used by Starbucks Coffee Company, illustrates many of the special terms and clauses that are typically contained in international contracts for the sale of goods. Annotations in the exhibit explain the meaning and significance of specific clauses in the contract. (See Chapter 37 for a discussion of other laws that frame global business transactions.)

A Comparison of CISG and UCC Provisions

The provisions of the CISG, although similar for the most part to those of the UCC, differ from them in some respects. We have already mentioned some of these differences. In the *International Perspective* in Chapter 11, for example, we pointed out that the CISG does not include the requirements imposed by the UCC's Statute of Frauds. Rather, Article 11 of the CISG states that an international sales contract "need not be concluded in or evidenced by writing and is not subject to any other requirements as to form." Other differences between the UCC and the CISG were indicated in this chapter's *International Perspective* discussing merchants' firm offers.

In respect to contract formation, some other differences between the CISG and the UCC merit attention. First, under the UCC, if the price term is left open, the court will determine "a reasonable price at the time for delivery" [UCC 2–305(1)]. Under the CISG, however, the price term must be specified, or at least provisions for its specification must be included in the agreement; otherwise, normally no contract will exist.

Second, like UCC 2–207, the CISG provides that a contract can be formed even though the acceptance contains additional terms, unless the additional terms materially alter the contract. The definition of a "material alteration" under the CISG, however, involves virtually any differences in terms. In its effect, then, the CISG requires that the terms of the acceptance mirror those of the offer.

Third, under the UCC, an acceptance is effective on dispatch. Under the CISG, however, a contract is created not at the time the acceptance is transmitted but only on its receipt by the offeror. (The offer becomes *irrevocable*, however, when the acceptance is sent.) Additionally, in contrast to the UCC, the CISG provides that acceptance by performance does not require that the offeror be notified of the performance.

In the following chapters, we continue to point out differences between the CISG and the UCC as they relate to the topics covered. These topics include risk of loss, performance, remedies, and warranties.

BE AWARE It has been proposed that the UCC be revised to eliminate the Statute of Frauds.

Key Terms

Chapter Summary: The Formation of Sales and Lease Contracts

The Scope of the UCC *(See pages 341–342.)*	The UCC attempts to provide a consistent and integrated framework of rules to deal with all phases *ordinarily arising* in a commercial sales or lease transaction, including contract formation, passage of title and risk of loss, performance, remedies, payment for goods, warehoused goods, and secured transactions. If there is a conflict between a common law rule and the UCC, the UCC controls.
The Scope of Article 2—Sales *(See pages 342–345.)*	Article 2 governs contracts for the sale of goods (tangible, movable personal property). The common law of contracts also applies to sales contracts to the extent that the common law has not been modified by the UCC.

▌ Chapter Summary: The Formation of Sales and Lease Contracts—Continued

The Scope of Article 2A—Leases *(See pages 345–346.)*	Article 2A governs contracts for the lease of goods. Article 2A is essentially a repetition of Article 2, except that it applies to leases, instead of sales, of goods and thus varies to reflect differences between sale and lease transactions.

Offer and Acceptance *(See pages 346–355.)*	1. *Offer*—
	  a. Not all terms have to be included for a contract to be formed (only the subject matter and quantity term must be specified).
	  b. The price does not have to be included for a contract to be formed.
	  c. Particulars of performance can be left open.
	  d. A written and signed firm offer by a *merchant*, covering a period of three months or less, is irrevocable without payment of consideration.
	
	2. *Acceptance*—
	  a. Acceptance may be made by any reasonable means of communication; it is effective when dispatched.
	  b. The acceptance of a unilateral offer can be made by a promise to ship or by prompt shipment of conforming goods.
	  c. Acceptance by performance requires notice within a reasonable time; otherwise, the offer can be treated as lapsed.
	  d. A definite expression of acceptance creates a contract even if the terms of the acceptance vary from those of the offer.

Consideration *(See pages 355–357.)*	A modification of a contract for the sale of goods does not require consideration.

Requirements under the Statute of Frauds *(See pages 357–359.)*	1. All contracts for the sale of goods priced at $500 or more must be in writing. A writing is sufficient as long as it indicates a contract between the parties and is signed by the party against whom enforcement is sought. A contract is not enforceable beyond the quantity shown in the writing.
	
	2. When written confirmation of an oral contract *between merchants* is not objected to in writing by the receiver within ten days, the contract is enforceable.
	
	3. Exceptions to the requirement of a writing exist in the following situations:
	  a. When the oral contract is for specially manufactured goods not suitable for resale to others, and the seller has substantially started to manufacture the goods.
	  b. When the defendant admits in pleadings, testimony, or other court proceedings that an oral contract for the sale of goods was made. In this case, the contract will be enforceable to the extent of the quantity of goods admitted.
	  c. The oral agreement will be enforceable to the extent that payment has been received and accepted or to the extent that the goods have been received and accepted.

Parol Evidence Rule *(See pages 360–361.)*	1. The terms of a clearly and completely worded written contract cannot be contradicted by evidence of prior agreements or contemporaneous oral agreements.
	
	2. Evidence is admissible to clarify the terms of a writing in the following situations:
	  a. If the contract terms are ambiguous.
	  b. If evidence of course of dealing, usage of trade, or course of performance is necessary to learn or to clarify the intentions of the parties to the contract.

Unconscionability *(See pages 362–363.)*	An unconscionable contract or clause is one that is so unfair and one sided that it would be unreasonable to enforce it. If the court deems a contract to have been unconscionable at the time it was made, the court can (1) refuse to enforce the contract, (2) refuse to enforce the unconscionable clause of the contract, or (3) limit the application of any unconscionable clauses to avoid an unconscionable result.
Contracts for the International Sale of Goods *(See pages 363–364.)*	International sales contracts are governed by the United Nations Convention on Contracts for the International Sale of Goods (CISG)—if the countries of the parties to the contract have ratified the CISG (and if the parties have not agreed that some other law will govern their contract). Essentially, the CISG is to international sales contracts what Article 2 of the UCC is to domestic sales contracts. Whenever the parties to international transactions have failed to specify in writing the precise terms of a contract, the CISG will be applied.

▌For Review

1. Describe the scope and coverage of Article 2 and Article 2A of the UCC.
2. What is a merchant's firm offer?
3. If an offeree includes additional or different terms in an acceptance, will a contract result? If so, what happens to these terms?

4. Article 2 and Article 2A of the UCC both define three exceptions to the writing requirements of the Statute of Frauds. What are these three exceptions?
5. What law governs contracts for the international sale of goods?

▌Questions and Case Problems

14–1. Terms of the Offer. The UCC changes the effect of the common law of contracts in several ways. For instance, at common law, an offer must be definite enough for the parties to ascertain its essential terms when it is accepted. What happens under the UCC if some of an offer's terms—the price term, for example—are left open? What if the quantity term is left open?

14–2. Statute of Frauds. Fresher Foods, Inc., orally agreed to purchase from Dale Vernon, a farmer, one thousand bushels of corn for $1.25 per bushel. Fresher Foods paid $125 down and agreed to pay the remainder of the purchase price upon delivery, which was scheduled for one week later. When Fresher Foods tendered the balance of $1,125 on the scheduled day of delivery and requested the corn, Vernon refused to deliver it. Fresher Foods sued Vernon for damages, claiming that Vernon had breached their oral contract. Can Fresher Foods recover? If so, to what extent?

14–3. Merchant's Firm Offer. On September 1, Jennings, a used-car dealer, wrote a letter to Wheeler in which he stated, "I have a 1955 Thunderbird convertible in mint condition that I will sell you for $13,500 at any time before October 9. [signed] Peter Jennings." By September 15, having heard nothing from Wheeler, Jennings sold the Thunderbird to another party. On September 29, Wheeler accepted Jennings's offer and tendered the $13,500. When Jennings told Wheeler he had sold the car to another party, Wheeler claimed Jennings had breached their contract. Is Jennings in breach? Explain.

14–4. Accommodation Shipments. M. M. Salinger, Inc., a retailer of television sets, orders one hundred Model Color-X sets from manufacturer Fulsom. The order specifies the price and that the television sets are to be shipped via Interamerican Freightways on or before October 30. Fulsom receives the order on October 5. On October 8, Fulsom writes Salinger a letter indicating that it has received the order and that it will ship the sets as directed, at the specified price. Salinger receives this letter on October 10. On October 28, Fulsom, in preparing the shipment, discovers it has only ninety Color-X sets in stock. Fulsom ships the ninety Color-X sets and ten television sets of a different model, stating clearly on the invoice that the ten sets are being shipped only as an accommodation. Salinger claims that Fulsom is in breach of contract. Fulsom claims that the shipment was not an acceptance, and therefore no contract was formed. Explain who is correct, and why.

14–5. Statute of Frauds. Loeb & Co. entered into an oral agreement with Schreiner, a farmer, in which Schreiner agreed to sell Loeb 150 bales of cotton, each weighing 480

pounds. Shortly thereafter, Loeb sent Schreiner a letter confirming the terms of the oral contract. Schreiner neither acknowledged receipt of the letter nor objected to its terms. When delivery came due, Schreiner ignored the oral agreement and sold his cotton on the open market, because the price of cotton had more than doubled (from 37 cents to 80 cents per pound) since the oral agreement had been made. In the lawsuit by Loeb & Co. against Schreiner, did Loeb recover? Explain. [*Loeb & Co. v. Schreiner*, 294 Ala. 722, 321 So.2d 199 (1975)]

14–6. Additional Terms in Acceptance. The Carpet Mart, a carpet dealer, telephoned an order (offer) for carpet to Collins & Aikman Corp., a carpet manufacturer. Collins & Aikman then sent Carpet Mart an acknowledgment form (acceptance), which specified the quantity and price agreed to in the telephone conversation. The reverse side of the printed acknowledgment form stated that Collins & Aikman's acceptance was subject to the buyer's agreement to submit all disputes to arbitration. Collins & Aikman shipped the carpet to Carpet Mart, which received the acknowledgment form and shipment without objection. Later, a dispute arose, and Carpet Mart brought a civil suit against Collins & Aikman, claiming misrepresentation as to the quality of the carpet. Collins & Aikman filed a motion to compel arbitration. Will the court enforce the arbitration clause? Discuss. [*Dorton v. Collins & Aikman Corp.*, 453 F.2d 1161 (6th Cir. 1972)]

14–7. Statute of Frauds. Peggy Holloway was a real estate broker who guaranteed payment for shipment of over $11,000 worth of mozzarella cheese sold by Cudahy Foods Co. to Pizza Pride in Jamestown, North Carolina. The entire arrangement was made orally. Cudahy mailed to Holloway an invoice for the order, and Holloway did not object in writing to the invoice within ten days of receipt. Later, when Cudahy demanded payment from Holloway, Holloway denied ever having guaranteed payment for the cheese and raised the Statute of Frauds [UCC 2–201] as a defense. Cudahy claimed that the Statute of Frauds could not be used as a defense, as both Cudahy and Holloway were merchants and Holloway failed to object within ten days to Cudahy's invoice. Discuss Cudahy's argument. [*Cudahy Foods Co. v. Holloway*, 286 S.E.2d 606 (N.C.App. 1982)]

14–8. Statute of Frauds. Harry Starr orally contracted to purchase a new automobile from Freeport Dodge, Inc. Starr signed an order form describing the car and made a down payment of $25. The dealer did not sign the form, and the form stated that "this order is not valid unless signed and accepted by the dealer." The dealer deposited the $25, and that was noted on the order form. On the day scheduled for delivery, a sales representative for the dealer told Starr that an error had been made in determining the price and that Starr would be required to pay an additional $175 above the price on the order form. Starr refused to pay the additional amount and sued for breach of contract. Freeport Dodge claimed that the contract fell under the Statute of Frauds and that because Freeport Dodge had not signed the contract, the oral contract was not enforceable. Discuss Freeport Dodge's contention. [*Starr v. Freeport Dodge, Inc.*, 54 Misc.2d 271, 282 N.Y.S.2d 58 (Dist. 1967)]

14–9. Statute of Frauds. R-P Packaging, Inc., is a manufacturer of cellophane wrapping material. The plant manager for Flowers Baking Co. decided to improve its packaging of cookies. The plant manager contacted R-P Packaging for the possible purchase of cellophane wrap imprinted with designed "artwork." R-P took measurements to determine the appropriate size of the wrap and submitted to Flowers a sample size with the artwork to be imprinted. After agreeing that the artwork was satisfactory, Flowers gave a verbal order to R-P for the designed cellophane wrap at a price of $13,000. When the wrap was tendered, although it conformed to the measurements and design, Flowers complained that the wrap was too short and the design off center. Flowers rejected the shipment. R-P sued. Flowers contended that the oral contract was unenforceable under the Statute of Frauds. Discuss this contention. [*Flowers Baking Co. v. R-P Packaging, Inc.*, 229 Va. 370, 329 S.E.2d 462 (1985)]

14–10. Merchant Status. Albert Reifschneider was raised on a farm and had been in the business of selling corn and in the business of selling other crops under futures contracts (contracts for goods to be harvested in the future) for twenty years. In April 1988, Reifschneider orally agreed to sell Colorado-Kansas Grain Co. 12,500 bushels of corn after the harvest in the fall. The company sent Reifschneider a written confirmation of the agreement with instructions to sign it and return it. In June, Reifschneider told the company that he would not sign the confirmation and that no contract existed between the parties. The company demanded that Reifschneider deliver the corn, but the demand was to no avail. The company sued Reifschneider for breach of contract, and the issue turned on whether Reifschneider was a "merchant" within the meaning of the UCC. How should the court rule? Discuss. [*Colorado-Kansas Grain Co. v. Reifschneider*, 817 P.2d 637 (Colo.App. 1991)]

14–11. Goods and Services Combined. Jane Pittsley contracted with Donald Houser, who was doing business as the Hilton Contract Carpet Co., for the installation of carpet in her home. Following installation, Pittsley complained to Hilton that some seams were visible, gaps appeared, the carpet did not lie flat in all areas, and the carpet failed to reach the wall in certain locations. Although Hilton made various attempts to fix the installation by attempting to stretch the carpet and other methods, Pittsley was not satisfied with the work and eventually sued Hilton to recover the $3,500 she had paid

toward the $4,319.50 contract price for the carpet and its installation. Hilton paid the installers $700 for the work done in laying Pittsley's carpet. One of the issues before the court was whether the contract was a contract for the sale of goods or a contract for the sale of services. How should the court decide this issue? Discuss fully. [*Pittsley v. Houser*, 125 Idaho 820, 875 P.2d 232 (1994)]

**A QUESTION OF ETHICS
AND SOCIAL RESPONSIBILITY**

14–12. *John Schwanbeck entered into negotiations with Federal-Mogul Corp. to purchase Federal-Mogul's Vellumoid Division. The two parties drew up a letter of intent stating that "[n]o further obligation will arise until a definitive agreement is reduced to writing" and that it was the parties' intention "to proceed in good faith in the negotiation of such binding definitive agreement." At another place in the letter of intent were the following words: "Of course, this letter is not intended to create, nor do you or we presently have any binding legal obligation whatever in any way relating to such sale and purchase." Federal-Mogul eventually sold the Vellumoid Division to another party. Schwanbeck sued Federal-Mogul, alleging, among other things, that Federal-Mogul had breached an agreement to negotiate in good faith the proposed contract with Schwanbeck. Given these facts, consider the following questions.* [*Schwanbeck v. Federal-Mogul Corp.*, 412 Mass. 703, 592 N.E.2d 1289 (1992)]

1. Did the letter of intent create a legally binding obligation, or was the letter merely an "agreement to agree" in the future? (You may wish to review the section on "Agreements to Agree" in Chapter 9 before you answer this question.)
2. Regardless of its legal duties, did Federal-Mogul have an ethical duty to proceed in negotiating a contract with Schwanbeck? Discuss.

CASE BRIEFING ASSIGNMENT

14–13. *Examine Case A.4 [Goldkist, Inc. v. Brownlee, 182 Ga.App. 287, 355 S.E.2d 733 (1987)] in Appendix A. The case has been excerpted there in great detail. Review and then brief the case, making sure that you include answers to the following questions in your brief.*

1. What defense did the Brownlees raise against Goldkist's claim that the Brownlees had formed a contract with Goldkist for the sale of goods?
2. Why is the question as to whether the Brownlees were merchants significant?
3. Summarize the court's reasons for reversing the trial court's summary judgment for the Brownlees.

FOR CRITICAL ANALYSIS

14–14. *Why is the designation "merchant" or "nonmerchant" important?*

▌Accessing the Internet: Business Law and Legal Environment

If you are interested in getting advice and averting legal problems with a lease contract for your property, and if you are a subscriber to the commercial service America Online, you can go to "Legal advice from the Microsoft Small Business Center." The key word is

microsoft

Then click on the **Small Business Center** icon and select **Legal Issues.**

    For the most updated information on the Uniform Commercial Code, including drafts of revised articles, go to

http://www.law.cornell.edu/ucc/ucc.table.html

Or go to

http://www.kentlaw.edu/ulc/ulc.html

    You can obtain information on current commercial law topics from the law firm of Hale and Dorr at

http://www.haledorr.com/

    The Web browser Yahoo has a subcategory on commercial law. Go to

http://www.yahoo.com/Government/Law/

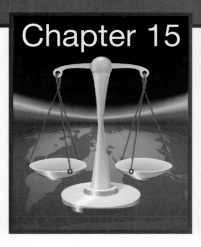

Chapter 15

Title and Risk of Loss

"Now, it is of great moment that well-drawn laws should themselves define all the points they possibly can and leave as few as may be to the decision of the judges."

Aristotle, 384–322 B.C.E.
(Greek philosopher)

CHAPTER OBJECTIVES

After reading this chapter, you should be able to:

1. Indicate when title to goods passes from seller to buyer.
2. Explain the problems that can arise when persons who acquire goods with imperfect title attempt to resell the goods.
3. Define various contract terms that help to determine when the risk of loss passes from a seller or lessor to a buyer or lessee.
4. Identify who bears the risk of loss when a contract is breached.
5. Indicate when each party to a sales or lease contract has an insurable interest in the goods.

The sale of goods transfers ownership (title) from the seller to the buyer. Often, a sales contract is signed before the actual goods are available. For example, a sales contract for oranges might be signed in May, but the oranges may not be ready for picking and shipment until October. Any number of things can happen between the time the sales contract is signed and the time the goods are actually transferred to the buyer's possession. For example, fire, flood, or frost may destroy the orange groves, or the oranges may be lost or damaged in transit. The same problems may occur under a lease contract. Because of these possibilities, it is important to know the rights and liabilities of the parties between the time the contract is formed and the time the goods are actually received by the buyer or lessee.

Before the creation of the Uniform Commercial Code (UCC), *title*—the right of ownership—was the central concept in sales law, controlling all issues of rights and remedies of the parties to a sales contract. There were numerous problems attending

A freeze can destroy an orange grove. If a contract for a sale of the oranges had already been signed, who would suffer the loss?

KEEP IN MIND Most issues that arise between a seller and a buyer are dealt with by the UCC in terms of performance or nonperformance under their contract rather than in terms of whether or not "title" has passed.

this concept. For example, frequently it was difficult to determine when title actually passed from a seller to a buyer, and therefore it was also difficult to predict which party a court would decide had title at the time of a loss. Because of such problems, the UCC divorced the question of title as completely as possible from the question of the rights and obligations of buyers, sellers, and third parties (such as subsequent purchasers, creditors, or the tax collector).

In some situations, title is still relevant under the UCC, and the UCC has special rules for locating title. These rules will be discussed in the sections that follow. In most situations, however, the UCC has replaced the concept of title with three other concepts: (1) identification, (2) risk of loss, and (3) insurable interest. By breaking down the transfer of ownership into these three components, the drafters of the UCC have essentially followed Aristotle's advice in the chapter-opening quotation and created greater precision in the law governing sales—leaving as few points of law as possible "to the decision of the judges."

In lease contracts, of course, title to the goods is retained by the lessor-owner of the goods. Hence, the UCC's provisions relating to passage of title do not apply to leased goods. Other concepts discussed in this chapter, though, including identification, risk of loss, and insurable interest, relate to lease contracts as well as to sales contracts.

▌Identification

IDENTIFICATION
In a sale of goods, the express designation of the goods provided for in the contract.

Before any interest in specific goods can pass from the seller or lessor to the buyer or lessee, two conditions must prevail: (1) the goods must be in existence, and (2) they must be identified as the specific goods designated in the contract. **Identification** is a designation of goods as the subject matter of a sales or lease contract. Title cannot pass from buyer to seller unless the goods are identified to the contract. (As mentioned, title to leased goods remains with the lessor—or, if the owner is a third party, with that party. The lessee does not acquire title to leased goods.) Identification is significant because it gives the buyer or lessee the right to insure (or an insurable interest in) the goods and the right to recover from third parties who damage the goods.

In their contract, the parties can agree on when identification will take place. If they do not so specify, however, the UCC provisions discussed here determine when identification takes place [UCC 2–501(1), 2A–217].

Existing Goods

If the contract calls for the sale or lease of specific and ascertained goods that are already in existence, identification takes place at the time the contract is made. For example, you contract to purchase or lease a fleet of five cars by the serial numbers listed for the cars.

Future Goods

If a sale involves unborn animals to be born within twelve months after contracting, identification takes place when the animals are conceived. If a lease involves any unborn animals, identification occurs when the animals are conceived. If a sale involves crops that are to be harvested within twelve months (or the next harvest season occurring after contracting, whichever is longer), identification takes place when the crops are planted or begin to grow. In a sale or lease of any other future goods, identification occurs when the goods are shipped, marked, or otherwise designated by the seller or lessor as the goods to which the contract refers.

Goods That Are Part of a Larger Mass

Goods that are part of a larger mass are identified when the goods are marked, shipped, or somehow designated by the seller or lessor as the particular goods to pass under the contract. Suppose that a buyer orders 1,000 cases of beans from a 10,000-case lot. Until the seller separates the 1,000 cases of beans from the 10,000-case lot, title and risk of loss remain with the seller.

A common exception to this rule deals with fungible goods. **Fungible goods** are goods that are alike by physical nature, by agreement, or by trade usage. Typical examples are specific grades or types of wheat, oil, and wine, usually stored in large containers. If these goods are held or intended to be held by owners as tenants in common (owners having shares undivided from the entire mass), a seller-owner can pass title and risk of loss to the buyer without an actual separation. The buyer replaces the seller as an owner in common [UCC 2–105(4)].

For example, Anselm, Braudel, and Carpenter are farmers. They deposit, respectively, 5,000 bushels, 3,000 bushels, and 2,000 bushels of grain of the same grade and quality in a bin. The three become owners in common, with Anselm owning 50 percent of the 10,000 bushels, Braudel 30 percent, and Carpenter 20 percent. Anselm could contract to sell 5,000 bushels of grain to Tareyton and, because the goods are fungible, pass title and risk of loss to Tareyton without physically separating 5,000 bushels. Tareyton now becomes an owner in common with Braudel and Carpenter.

FUNGIBLE GOODS
Goods that are alike by physical nature, by agreement, or by trade usage. Examples of fungible goods are wheat, oil, and wine that are identical in type and quality.

▌Passage of Title

Once goods exist and are identified, the provisions of UCC 2–401 apply to the passage of title. In virtually all subsections of UCC 2–401, the words "unless otherwise explicitly agreed" appear, meaning that any explicit understanding between the buyer and the seller determines when title passes. Unless an agreement is explicitly made, title passes to the buyer at the time and the place the seller performs the *physical* delivery of the goods [UCC 2–401(2)]. This rule is applied in the following case.

CASE 15.1

SYNERGISTIC TECHNOLOGIES, INC. v. IDB MOBILE COMMUNICATIONS, INC.

United States District Court,
District of Columbia, 1994.
871 F.Supp. 24.

HISTORICAL AND TECHNOLOGICAL SETTING *The former Soviet Union (now fifteen independent countries, of which the most important is Russia) launched the first artificial satellite, Sputnik I, into orbit around the earth in 1957. Today, several thousand artificial satellites circle our planet. They are used for weather forecasting, for communications, and for military, scientific, and other purposes. For example, the maritime and aviation industries use the International Maritime Satellite (INMARSAT) system for navigation and communication purposes. In the United States, one of the few providers of INMARSAT service is IDB Mobile Communications, Inc.*

FACTS   Synergistic Technologies, Inc. (SynTech), developed three computer software systems for IDB Mobile Communications, Inc., to provide IDB's customers with satellite voice and data communications services. SynTech installed the systems in IDB's computers under a "Statement of Work" negotiated between the two firms. During the installation, IDB discovered that the systems would not allow it to make back-up copies of the

software. If IDB's computers crashed, a return to full operation would thus be delayed. When IDB hired another company to make back-up copies, SynTech filed a suit in a federal district court against IDB, seeking damages and other relief for, among other things, alleged infringement of SynTech's copyrights. IDB responded in part by filing a motion for summary judgment. One of the issues was whether IDB was the "owner" of the software.

ISSUE   Had title to the software passed to IDB?

DECISION   Yes. The federal district court granted IDB's motion for summary judgment on this issue.

REASON   The court found that the parties' "Statement of Work is not clear on the issue of transfer of ownership of the software," adding that "[i]f this matter turned solely on the Statement of Work, the Court would be unable to resolve the issue." The court pointed out, however, that the question was "also governed by [Section] 2–401 of the Uniform Commercial Code, which provides that '[u]nless otherwise explicitly agreed title passes to the buyer at the time and place at which the seller completes his performance with reference to the physical delivery of the goods.'" Thus, because the parties had not explicitly agreed otherwise, title to "the software passed to IDB at the time of delivery of the goods."

FOR CRITICAL ANALYSIS—Technological Consideration
Why would Synergistic Technologies be concerned about the fact that its client was making back-up copies of the software?

SHIPMENT CONTRACT
A contract for the sale of goods in which the seller is required or authorized to ship the goods by carrier. The seller assumes liability for any losses or damage to the goods until they are delivered to the carrier.

DESTINATION CONTRACT
A contract for the sale of goods in which the seller is required or authorized to ship the goods by carrier and deliver them at a particular destination. The seller assumes liability for any losses or damage to the goods until they are tendered at the destination specified in the contract.

Shipment and Destination Contracts

Delivery arrangements can determine when title passes from the seller to the buyer. In a **shipment contract,** the seller is required or authorized to ship goods by carrier, such as a trucking company. Under a shipment contract, the seller is required only to deliver conforming goods into the hands of a carrier, and title passes to the buyer at the time and place of shipment [UCC 2–401(2)(a)]. Generally, *all contracts are assumed to be shipment contracts if nothing to the contrary is stated in the contract.*

In a **destination contract,** the seller is required to deliver the goods to a particular destination, usually directly to the buyer, but sometimes the buyer designates that the goods should be delivered to another party. Title passes to the buyer when the goods are *tendered* at that destination [UCC 2–401(2)(b)]. A tender of delivery is the seller's placing or holding of conforming goods at the buyer's disposition (with any necessary notice), enabling the buyer to take delivery [UCC 2–503(1)].

Delivery without Movement of the Goods

When the contract of sale does not call for the seller's shipment or delivery of the goods (when the buyer is to pick up the goods), the passage of title depends on whether the seller must deliver a **document of title,** such as a bill of lading or a warehouse receipt, to the buyer. A *bill of lading* is a receipt for goods that is signed by a carrier and that serves as a contract for the transportation of the goods. A *warehouse receipt* is a receipt issued by a warehouser for goods stored in a warehouse. (See Exhibits 15–1 and 15–2.)

When a document of title is required, title passes to the buyer *when and where the document is delivered.* Thus, if the goods are stored in a warehouse, title passes to the buyer when the appropriate documents are delivered to the buyer. The goods never move. In fact, the buyer can choose to leave the goods at the same warehouse for a period of time, and the buyer's title to those goods will be unaffected.

When no documents of title are required, and delivery is made without moving the goods, title passes at the time and place the sales contract is made, if the goods have already been identified. If the goods have not been identified, title does not pass until identification occurs. Consider an example. Rogers sells lumber to Bodan. It is agreed that Bodan will pick up the lumber at the yard. If the lumber has been identified (segregated, marked, or in any other way distinguished from all other lumber), title passes to Bodan when the contract is signed. If the lumber is still in storage bins at the mill, title does not pass to Bodan until the particular pieces of lumber to be sold under this contract are identified [UCC 2–401(3)].

Sales or Leases by Nonowners

Problems occur when persons who acquire goods with imperfect titles attempt to sell or lease them. Sections 2–402 and 2–403 of the UCC deal with the rights of two parties who lay claim to the same goods, sold with imperfect titles. Generally, a buyer acquires at least whatever title the seller has to the goods sold.

The UCC also protects a person who leases such goods from the person who bought them. Of course, a lessee does not acquire whatever title the lessor has to the goods. A lessee acquires a right to possess and use the goods—that is, a *leasehold interest.* A lessee acquires whatever leasehold interest the lessor has or has the power to transfer, subject to the lease contract [UCC 2A–303, 2A–304, 2A–305].

VOID TITLE   A buyer may unknowingly purchase goods from a seller who is not the owner of the goods. If the seller is a thief, the seller's title is *void*—legally, no title exists. Thus, the buyer acquires no title, and the real owner can reclaim the goods from the buyer. The same result would occur if the goods were only leased, because the lessor has no leasehold interest to transfer.

For example, if Jim steals goods owned by Maren, Jim has a *void title* to those goods. If Jim sells the goods to Shidra, Maren can reclaim them from Shidra even though Shidra acted in good faith and honestly was not aware that the goods were stolen. Article 2A contains similar provisions for leases.

VOIDABLE TITLE   A seller has a *voidable title* if the goods that he or she is selling were obtained by fraud, paid for with a check that is later dishonored, purchased from a minor, or purchased on credit when the seller was insolvent. (Under the UCC, a person is **insolvent** when that person ceases to pay "his debts in the ordinary course of business or cannot pay his debts as they become due or is insolvent within the meaning of federal bankruptcy law" [UCC 1–201(23)].)

In contrast to a seller with *void title,* a seller with *voidable title* has the power to transfer a good title to a good faith purchaser for value. A **good faith purchaser** is one who buys without knowledge of circumstances that would make a person of ordinary prudence inquire about the validity of the seller's title to the goods. One who purchases *for value* gives legally sufficient consideration (value) for the goods purchased. The real, or original, owner cannot recover goods from a good faith purchaser for value

DOCUMENT OF TITLE
Paper exchanged in the regular course of business that evidences the right to possession of goods (for example, a bill of lading or warehouse receipt).

REMEMBER Theft is a crime (larceny, embezzlement, and so on) and a tort (conversion). Receiving goods that the recipient knows were stolen is also a crime and a tort.

INSOLVENT
Under the UCC, a term describing a person who ceases to pay "his debts in the ordinary course of business or cannot pay his debts as they become due or is insolvent within the meaning of federal bankruptcy law" [UCC 1–201(23)].

GOOD FAITH PURCHASER
A purchaser who buys without notice of any circumstance that would put a person of ordinary prudence on inquiry as to whether the seller has valid title to the goods being sold.

Exhibit 15–1
A Sample Negotiable Bill of Lading

UNIFORM MOTOR CARRIER ORDER BILL OF LADING

Original—Domestic

1st Sheet

Shipper's No. _____

Agent's No. _____

CENTRAL FREIGHT LINES INC.

RECEIVED, subject to the classifications and tariffs in effect on the date of the issue of this Bill of Lading,

From _____   Date _____ 19__

At _____ Street _____ City _____ County _____ State

the property described below, in apparent good order, except as noted (contents and condition of contents of packages unknown) marked, consigned and destined as shown below, which said company (the word company being understood throughout this contract as meaning any person or corporation in possession of the property under the contract) agrees to carry to its usual place of delivery at said destination, if within the scope of its lawful operations, otherwise to deliver to another carrier on the route to said destination. It is mutually agreed, as to each carrier of all or any of said property over all or any portion of said route to destination, and as to each party at any time interested in all or any of said property, that every service to be performed hereunder shall be subject to all the conditions not prohibited by law, whether printed or written, herein contained, including the conditions on back hereof, which are hereby agreed to by the shipper and accepted for himself and his assigns.

The surrender of this Original ORDER Bill of Lading properly indorsed shall be required before the delivery of the property. Inspection of property covered by this bill of lading will not be permitted unless provided by law or unless permission is indorsed on this original Bill of lading or given in writing by the shipper.

Consigned to Order of _____

Destination _____ Street, _____ City, _____ County, _____ State

Notify _____

At _____ Street, _____ City, _____ County, _____ State

I.C.C. No. _____ Vehicle No. _____

Routing _____

No. Pack-ages	Description of Articles, Special Marks, and Exceptions	*Weight (Subject to Correction)	Class or Rate	Check Column	Subject to Section 7 of Conditions, if this shipment is to be delivered to the consignee without recourse on the consignor, the consignor shall sign the following statement:
					The carrier shall not make delivery of this shipment without payment of freight and all other lawful charges.
					_____
					(signature of consignor.)
					If charges are to be prepaid write or stamp here, "To be Prepaid."
					_____
					Received $_____
					to apply in prepayment of the charges of the property described hereon.
					Agent or Cashier.
					Per _____ (the signature here acknowledges only the amount prepaid.)

SAMPLE

*If the shipment moves between two ports by a carrier by water, the law requires that the bill of lading shall state whether it is "carrier's or shipper's weight."

Note--Where the rate is dependent on value, shippers are required to state specifically in writing the agreed or declared value of the property.

The agreed or declared value of the property is hereby specifically stated by the shipper to be not exceeding _____ per _____

Charges Advanced:

$ _____

Shipper _____   Agent. _____

Per _____   Per _____

Permanent address of Shipper _____ Street _____ City, _____ State

MOORE BUSINESS FORMS, INC. WACO, TEX. M

Source: Reprinted with permission of Central Freight Lines, Inc. © 1985 Central Freight Lines, Inc.
Note: This form is printed in yellow to warn holders that it is a bill lading. The back of the form permits negotiation by indorsement.

♦ **Exhibit 15–2**
A Sample Nonnegotiable Warehouse Receipt

HART

Warehouse Receipt – Not Negotiable

Agreement No. _____   Vault No. _____

Service Order _____   _____

Receipt and
Lot Number _____   Date of Issue _____ 19 ____

Received for the account of and deliverable to • _____

whose latest known address is _____ **SAMPLE** _____

_____ the goods enumerated on the inside or attached schedule to be

stored in Company warehouse, located at _____
which goods are accepted only upon the following conditions set forth below:

READ CAREFULLY ➤ That the value of all goods stored, including the contents of any container, and all goods hereafter stored for Depositor's account to be not over $ _____ per pound† per article unless a higher value is noted in the schedule, for which an additional monthly storage charge of _____ ¢ on each $_____ valuation in excess of $ _____ per pound † per article or fraction thereof will be made.

If there are any items enumerated in this receipt valued in excess of the above limitations per pound per article and not so noted in the schedule, return this receipt within 10 days with proper values so indicated in writing in order that the receipt may be re-issued and proper higher storage rates assessed.

OWNERSHIP. The Customer, Shipper, Depositor, or Agent represents and warrants that he is lawfully possessed of goods to be stored and/or has the authority to store or ship said goods. (If the goods are mortgaged, notify the Company the name and address of the mortgagee.)

PAYMENT OF CHARGES. Storage bills are payable monthly in advance for each month's storage or fraction thereof. Labor charges, cartage and other services rendered are payable upon completion of work. All charges shall be paid at the warehouse location shown hereon, and if delinquent, shall incur interest monthly at the rate of _____ per cent ( ) per year.
The Depositor will pay reasonable attorney's fee incurred by The Company in collecting delinquent accounts.

LIABILITY OF COMPANY. The company shall be liable for any loss or injury to the goods caused by its failure to exercise such care as a reasonably careful man would exercise under like circumstances. The company will not be liable for loss or damage to fragile articles not packed, or articles packed or unpacked by other than employees of this company. Depositor specifically agrees that the warehouse will not be liable for contamination of or for insect damage to articles placed in drawer of furniture by the depositor. Periodic spraying of the warehouse premises shall constitute ordinary and proper care, unless the depositor requests in writing and pays for anti-infestation treatment of articles in drawers and compartments of stored furniture.

CHANGE OF ADDRESS. Notice of change of address must be given the Company in writing, and acknowledged in writing by the Company.

TRANSFER OR WITHDRAWAL OF GOODS. The warehouse receipt is not negotiable and shall be produced and all charges must be paid before delivery to the Depositor, or transfer of goods to another person; however, a written direction to the Company to transfer the goods to another person or deliver the goods may be accepted by the Company at its option without requiring tender of the warehouse receipt

ACCESS TO STORAGE PARTIAL WITHDRAWAL. A signed order from the person in whose name the receipt is issued is required to enable others to remove or have access to goods. A charge is made for stacking and unstacking, and for access to stored goods.
BUILDING-FIRE-WATCHMAN. The Company does not represent or warrant that its building cannot be destroyed by fire or that the contents of said buildings including the said property cannot be destroyed by fire. The Company shall not be required to maintain a watchman or sprinkler system and its failure to do so shall not constitute negligence.
CLAIMS OR ERRORS. All claims for non-delivery of any article or articles and for damage, breakage, etc., must be made in writing within ninety (90) days from delivery of goods stored or they are waived. Failure to return the warehouse receipt for correction within ( ) days after receipt thereof by the depositor will be conclusive that it is correct and delivery will be made only in accordance therewith.
FUTURE SERVICE. This Contract shall extend and apply to future services rendered to the Depositor by the Company and to any additional goods deposited with the Company by the Depositor.
WAREHOUSEMAN'S LIEN. The Company reserves the right to sell the goods stored, in accordance with the provisions of the Uniform Commercial Code (Business and Commerce Code if stored in Texas), for all lawful charges in arrears.
TERMINATION OF STORAGE. The Company reserves the right to terminate the storage of the goods at any time by giving to the Depositor thirty (30) days' written notice of its intention so to do, and, unless the Depositor removes such goods within that period, the Company is hereby empowered to have the same removed at the cost and expense of the Depositor, or the Company may sell them at auction in accordance with state law.

DEPOSITOR WILL PAY REASONABLE LEGAL FEES INCURRED BY WAREHOUSE IN COLLECTING DELINQUENT CHARGES.

THIS DOCUMENT CONTAINS THE WHOLE CONTRACT BETWEEN THE PARTIES AND THERE ARE NO OTHER TERMS, WARRANTIES, REPRESENTATIONS, OR AGREEMENTS OF EITHER DEPOSITOR OR COMPANY NOT HEREIN CONTAINED.

Storage per month
or fraction thereof. . . . $_____
Warehouse labor . . . . . $_____
Cartage. . . . . $_____
Packing at residence . . . $_____
Wrapping and preparing
for storage. . . . . . $_____
Charges advanced . . . . $_____
_____ $_____
_____ $_____

By _____

• Insert "Mr. and/or Mrs." or, if military personnel, appropriate rank or grade.
†Delete the words "per pound" if the declared value is per article.
For goods stored for military personnel under PL 245, the contractor's liability for care of goods is as provided in Basic Agreement with U.S. Goverment

THIS PROPERTY HAS NOT BEEN INSURED BY THIS COMPANY FOR FIRE OR ANY OTHER CASUALTY
SCHEDULE OF GOODS ON FOLLOWING PAGE OR ATTACHED

W-1 (9-81) Approved by SW WT4©   Re-order from Hart Graphics, Austin, Texas

---

Source: Reprinted with permission of Hart Graphics, Inc. of Austin, Texas. © 1985 Hart Graphics, Inc.

◆ **Exhibit 15–3**
Void and Voidable Title
If goods are transferred from their owner to another by theft, the thief acquires no ownership rights. Because the thief's title is *void*, a later buyer can acquire no title, and the owner can recover the goods. If the transfer occurs by fraud, the transferee acquires a *voidable* title. A later good faith purchaser for value can acquire good title, and the original owner cannot recover the goods.

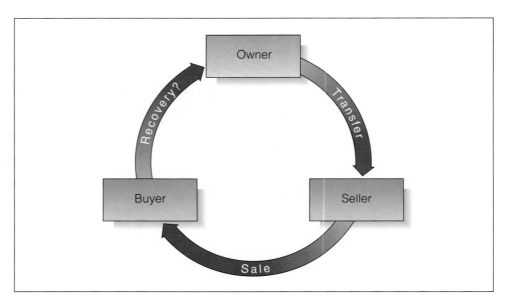

[UCC 2–403(1)].[1] If the buyer of the goods is not a good faith purchaser for value, then the actual owner of the goods can reclaim them from the buyer (or from the seller, if the goods are still in the seller's possession). Exhibit 15–3 illustrates these concepts.

The same rules apply in circumstances involving leases. A lessor with voidable title has the power to transfer a valid leasehold interest to a good faith lessee for value. The real owner cannot recover the goods, except as permitted by the terms of the lease. The real owner can, however, receive all proceeds arising from the lease, as well as a transfer of all rights, title, and interest as lessor under the lease, including the lessor's interest in the return of the goods when the lease expires.

---

1. The real, or original, owner could, of course, sue the purchaser who initially obtained voidable title to the goods.

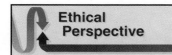
Ethical Perspective

The concept of the good faith purchaser reflects the UCC's emphasis on protecting innocent parties. If you innocently and in good faith purchase a boat, for example, from someone who appears to have good title and who demands and receives from you a fair market price, then the UCC believes that you should be protected from the possibility that the real owner—from whom the seller may have fraudulently obtained the boat—may later appear and demand his or her boat back. (Nothing, however, prevents the true owner from bringing suit against the party who defrauded him or her.)

Ethical questions arise in situations in which the purchaser has reason to suspect that the seller may not have good title to the goods being sold but nonetheless lets the transaction go forward because it is a "good deal." At what point does the buyer, in such a situation, cross over the boundary that separates the good faith purchaser from one who purchases in bad faith? This boundary is a significant one in the law of sales, because the UCC will not be a refuge for those who purchase in bad faith. The term *good faith purchaser* means just that—one who enters into a contract for the purchase of goods without knowing, or having any reason to know, that there is anything shady or illegal about the deal.

For Critical Analysis: *Why does the UCC protect innocent persons (good faith purchasers) who buy goods from sellers with* voidable *title but not innocent persons who buy goods from sellers with* void *title?*

THE ENTRUSTMENT RULE According to Section 2–403(2), entrusting goods to a merchant *who deals in goods of that kind* gives the merchant the power to transfer all rights to a *buyer in the ordinary course of business.* Entrusting includes both delivering the goods to the merchant and leaving the purchased goods with the merchant for later delivery or pickup [UCC 2–403(3)]. A buyer in the ordinary course of business is a person who, in good faith and without knowledge that the sale violates the ownership rights or security interest of a third party, buys in ordinary course from a person (other than a pawnbroker) in the business of selling goods of that kind [UCC 1–201(9)]. (A *security interest* is any interest in personal property that secures payment or the performance of an obligation—see Chapter 21.)

For example, Jan leaves her watch with a jeweler to be repaired. The jeweler sells both new and used watches. The jeweler sells Jan's watch to Kim, a customer, who does not know that the jeweler has no right to sell it. Kim, as a good faith buyer, gets good title against Jan's claim of ownership.[2] Kim, however, obtains only those rights held by the person entrusting the goods (here, Jan). Suppose that in the example just given, Jan had stolen the watch from Greg and then left it with the jeweler to be repaired. The jeweler then sells it to Kim. Kim gets good title against Jan, who entrusted the watch to the jeweler, but not against Greg (the real owner), who neither entrusted the watch to Jan nor authorized Jan to entrust it.

Article 2A provides a similar rule for leased goods. If a lessor entrusts goods to a lessee-merchant who deals in goods of that kind, the lessee-merchant has the power to transfer all of the rights the lessor had in the goods to a buyer or sublessee in the ordinary course of business [UCC 2A–305(2)].

The following case involved the application of the entrustment doctrine to protect a good faith buyer.

> **BE AWARE** The purpose of most goods held in inventory is to turn those goods into cash by selling them. That is the reason for the entrustment rule.

---

2. Jan, of course, can sue the jeweler for the equivalent money value of the watch.

CASE 15.2

HEINRICH v. TITUS-WILL SALES, INC.

Court of Appeals of Washington, Division 2, 1994.
73 Wash.App. 147,
868 P.2d 169.

HISTORICAL AND INTERNATIONAL SETTING *U.S. manufacturers once held a virtual lockhold on the world auto and truck market. Even at the beginning of the 1980s, the Big Three—Chrysler Corporation, Ford Motor Company, and General Motors Corporation—held more than three-quarters of the U.S. market. By the end of the decade, however, their share of the U.S. market was barely more than two-thirds. Japanese manufacturers had absorbed the rest. In California, for example, the Japanese share was 40 percent. Despite these losses in market share, Ford still sold more trucks in the United States than did any other manufacturer.*

FACTS James Wilson held himself out as a dealer/broker, licensed to buy and sell motor vehicles. Michael

Heinrich hired Wilson to buy a new Ford pickup. Wilson made a deal with Titus-Will Ford Sales, Inc., for the truck. Heinrich gave Wilson checks totaling more than $22,000. Titus-Will gave Wilson a variety of documents, including the owner's manual, an odometer disclosure statement, and a warranty card, as well as the keys to the truck. Wilson gave Titus-Will a check for half of the purchase price. Because the check was dated for three days later, Titus-Will did not release the truck's certificate of origin, which a buyer needs to obtain title. When Wilson's check bounced, Titus-Will refused to give up title to the truck. Heinrich sued Titus-Will and Wilson in a Washington state court to obtain the title and damages. The court applied the entrustment doctrine to award Heinrich what he asked for, and Titus-Will appealed. Titus-Will argued that the entrustment doctrine did not apply.

ISSUE Did Titus-Will "entrust" the truck to Wilson for purposes of applying the entrustment doctrine?

DECISION Yes. The Court of Appeals of Washington affirmed the award of the lower court.

(Continued)

Case 15.2—Continued

REASON The state appellate court pointed out that "[t]he UCC definition of 'entrusting' is broad." Under UCC 2–403, "any delivery and any acquiescence in retention of possession" can constitute entrustment. The court explained that "[a] person can entrust goods to a merchant by a variety of methods, such as consigning them, creating a bailment, taking a security interest in inventory, leaving them with the merchant after purchase, and delivering them for purposes of repair." The court also noted that "[a] sale can * * * constitute an entrustment when some aspect of the transaction remains incomplete."

FOR CRITICAL ANALYSIS—Social Consideration
What policies support protecting innocent buyers, such as Heinrich, under the entrustment doctrine?

▌Risk of Loss

"This doing of something about disputes, this doing of it reasonably, is the business of law."

Karl N. Llewellyn, 1893–1962
(American legal scholar)

Under the UCC, risk of loss does not necessarily pass with title. When risk of loss passes from a seller or lessor to a buyer or lessee is generally determined by the contract between the parties. Sometimes, the contract states expressly when the risk of loss passes. At other times, it does not, and a court must interpret the performance and delivery terms of the contract to determine whether the risk has passed. In the following case, the court had to decide whether, under the terms of the parties' agreement, the risk of loss had passed from the seller to the buyer.

CASE 15.3

IN RE THOMAS[a]
United States Bankruptcy Court,
Southern District of Florida, 1995.
182 Bankr. 347,
26 UCC Rep.Serv.2d 774.

HISTORICAL AND CULTURAL SETTING *By the beginning of the 1990s, almost 15 million crimes were being reported each year. The largest increase in the numbers and rates of crimes has occurred in the suburbs, with nearly 5,500 offenses per 100,000 inhabitants. The emotional cost to victims and their families, and the total cost to society, cannot be estimated. With property crimes, however, the most measurable cost is the value of the property stolen. In a typical year, property worth approximately $20 billion is stolen. Only about a third of this stolen property is recovered.*

FACTS Marilyn Thomas contracted with Sunkissed Pools for an "installed pool heater" for her home. One afternoon, Thomas noticed that a heating unit had been placed in her driveway. When Sunkissed returned to install the heater, it had been stolen. Thomas subsequently filed for personal bankruptcy. Sunkissed filed a claim for the price of the heater. Thomas objected. She argued that when she had noticed the heater in her driveway, she had called Sunkissed and told them they needed to move the unit because the neighborhood was not safe. She said that the unit sat in her driveway for four days before it disappeared, after which she again called Sunkissed and was told "not to worry." Sunkissed's president testified that the firm did not receive any calls from Thomas and that he had gone to her home the day after the unit was left in her driveway and found that it was gone.

ISSUE Had the risk of loss of the pool heater passed from the seller to the buyer?

DECISION No. The court dismissed Sunkissed's claim.

REASON The court stated that the parties' "conflicting views of the events" were "worrisome" but pointed out that "they are not controlling or truly relevant." Instead, the court found it more significant that both parties "testified that [Thomas] had purchased an 'installed' pool heater, and that the pool heater had not been installed as agreed and contracted for." Thus, the court concluded that "there simply was no delivery by the seller." For this reason, "the risk of loss always remained with the seller, and never shifted."

---

a. *In re* means "in the matter of, concerning, or regarding." The use of *in re* is the usual method of entitling a judicial proceeding in which judicial action is to be taken on some matter, such as a debtor's estate in bankruptcy, in which there are no adversary parties. *In re, Matter of,* and *Estate of,* or some combination of these phrases (such as *In re Estate of*) , are all commonly used in the titles of cases involving actions of the kind just mentioned.

Case 15.3—Continued

FOR CRITICAL ANALYSIS—Social Consideration
What if Thomas had purchased a different product, such

as a set of poolside chairs, and Sunkissed Pools simply delivered them to her driveway? Would the risk have passed to Thomas in such a situation?

Delivery with Movement of the Goods—Carrier Cases

When there is no specification in the agreement, the following rules apply to cases involving movement of the goods (carrier cases).

SHIPMENT CONTRACTS   In a shipment contract, if the seller or lessor is required or authorized to ship goods by carrier (but not required to deliver them to a particular destination), risk of loss passes to the buyer or lessee when the goods are duly delivered to the carrier [UCC 2–509(1)(a), 2A–219(2)(a)].

   For example, a seller in Texas sells five hundred cases of grapefruit to a buyer in New York, F.O.B. Houston (free on board in Houston—that is, the buyer pays the transportation charges from Houston). The contract authorizes a shipment by carrier; it does not require that the seller tender the grapefruit in New York. Risk passes to the buyer when conforming goods are properly placed in the possession of the carrier. If the goods are damaged in transit, the loss is the buyer's. (Actually, buyers have recourse against carriers, subject to certain limitations, and they usually insure the goods from the time the goods leave the seller.)

The possibility that goods will be lost or damaged in transit or at some time before the buyer takes possession of the goods is enhanced when goods are shipped great distances, as is normally the situation with international sales contracts. Therefore, those who form international sales contracts should safeguard their interests by indicating in the contract the point at which risk of loss passes from the seller to the buyer. Note that the international sales contract between Starbucks Coffee Company and one of its coffee suppliers, shown in the fold-out exhibit included in Chapter 14, includes a specific (insurance) clause indicating when risk of loss will pass to the buyer.

   The United Nations Convention on Contracts for the International Sale of Goods (CISG), which governs international sales contracts (see Chapter 14), contains provisions relating to risk of loss. Article 67 of the CISG provides that unless the contract requires the seller to hand the goods over at a particular place, the risk passes to the buyer when the goods identified to the contract "are handed over to the first carrier for transmission to the buyer in accordance with the contract of sale." In regard to goods sold in transit, Article 68 provides that risk of loss "passes to the buyer from the time of the conclusion of the contract." If the seller knew or should have known that the contract goods were lost or damaged, however, and failed to disclose this to the buyer, then the seller bears the risk.

For Critical Analysis: *Why would buyers of goods that are to be shipped internationally ever agree to shipment contracts—which subject them to liability for any loss or damage to the goods while they are in transit?*

DESTINATION CONTRACTS   In a destination contract, the risk of loss passes to the buyer or lessee when the goods are tendered to the buyer or lessee at the specified destination [UCC 2–509(1)(b), 2A–219(2)(b)]. In the preceding example, if the contract had been F.O.B. New York, risk of loss during transit to New York would have been the seller's.

If the goods on board this train were damaged, what determines who bears the loss?

CONTRACT TERMS   Specific terms in the contract help determine when risk of loss passes to the buyer. These terms, which are listed and defined in Exhibit 15–4, relate generally to the determination of which party will bear the costs of delivery.

Delivery without Movement of the Goods

The UCC also addresses situations in which the seller or lessor is required neither to ship nor to deliver the goods. Frequently, the buyer or lessee is to pick up the goods from the seller or lessor, or the goods are held by a bailee. Under the UCC, a **bailee** is a party who, by a bill of lading, warehouse receipt, or other document of title, acknowledges possession of goods and contracts to deliver them. A warehousing company, for example, or a trucking company that normally issues documents of title for the goods it receives is a bailee. (Bailments are discussed in detail in Chapter 34.)

GOODS HELD BY THE SELLER   If the goods are held by the seller, a document of title is usually not used. If the seller is a merchant, risk of loss to goods held by the seller passes to the buyer when the buyer *actually takes physical possession of the goods* [UCC 2–509(3)]. If the seller is not a merchant, the risk of loss to goods held by the seller passes to the buyer upon *tender of delivery* [UCC 2–509(3)].

In respect to leases, the risk of loss passes to the lessee on the lessee's receipt of the goods if the lessor—or supplier, in a finance lease (see Chapter 14)—is a merchant. Otherwise, the risk passes to the lessee on tender of delivery [UCC 2A–219(c)].

GOODS HELD BY A BAILEE   When a bailee is holding goods for a person who has contracted to sell them and the goods are to be delivered without being moved, the goods are usually represented by a negotiable or nonnegotiable document of title (a bill of lading or a warehouse receipt—see Exhibits 15–1 and 15–2). Risk of loss passes to the buyer when (1) the buyer receives a negotiable document of title for the goods, (2) the bailee acknowledges the buyer's right to possess the goods, or (3) the buyer receives a nonnegotiable document of title *and* has had a *reasonable time* to present the document to the bailee and demand the goods. Obviously, if the bailee refuses to honor the document, the risk of loss remains with the seller [UCC 2–503(4)(b), 2–509(2)].

BAILEE
Under the UCC, a party who, by a bill of lading, warehouse receipt, or other document of title, acknowledges possession of goods and contracts to deliver them.

COMPARE A merchant who is to make delivery at his or her own place has control of the goods and can be expected to insure his or her interest in them. The buyer has no control of the goods and will likely not carry insurance on goods that he or she does not possess.

◆ **Exhibit 15–4**
Contract Terms—
Definitions

F.O.B. (free on board)—Indicates that the selling price of goods includes transportation costs (and that the seller carries risk of loss) to the specific F.O.B. place named in the contract. The place can be either the place of initial shipment (for example, the seller's city or place of business) or the place of destination (for example, the buyer's city or place of business) [UCC 2–319(1)].
F.A.S. (free alongside)—Requires that the seller, at his or her own expense and risk, deliver the goods alongside the ship before risk passes to the buyer [UCC 2–319(2)].
C.I.F. or **C.&F.** (cost, insurance, and freight, or just cost and freight)—Requires, among other things, that the seller "put the goods in possession of a carrier" before risk passes to the buyer [UCC 2–320(2)]. (These are basically pricing terms, and the contracts remain shipment contracts, not destination contracts.)
Delivery ex-ship (delivery from the carrying ship)—Means that risk of loss does not pass to the buyer until the goods leave the ship or are otherwise properly unloaded [UCC 2–322].

In respect to leases, if goods held by a bailee are to be delivered without being moved, the risk of loss passes to the lessee on acknowledgment by the bailee of the lessee's right to possession of the goods [UCC 2A–219(2)(b)].

Conditional Sales

Buyers and sellers sometimes form sales contracts that are conditioned either on the buyer's approval of the goods or on the buyer's resale of the goods. Under such contracts, the buyer is in possession of the goods. Sometimes, however, problems arise as to whether the buyer or seller should bear the loss if, for example, the goods are damaged or stolen while in the possession of the buyer.

SALE OR RETURN   A **sale or return** (sometimes called a *sale and return*) is a type of contract by which the seller delivers a quantity of goods to the buyer on the understanding that if the buyer wishes to retain any portion of those goods (for use or resale), the buyer will consider the portion retained as having been sold to him or her and will pay accordingly. The balance will be returned to the seller. When the buyer receives possession of the goods under a sale-or-return contract, the title and risk of loss pass to the buyer. Title and risk of loss remain with the buyer until the buyer returns the goods to the seller within the time period specified. If the buyer fails to return the goods within this time period, the sale is finalized. The return of the goods is made at the buyer's risk and expense. Goods held under a sale-or-return contract are subject to the claims of the buyer's creditors while they are in the buyer's possession (even if the buyer has not paid for the goods).

The UCC treats a **consignment** as a sale or return. Under a consignment, the owner of goods (the *consignor*) delivers them to another (the *consignee*) for the consignee to sell. If the consignee sells the goods, the consignee must pay the consignor for them. If the consignee does not sell the goods, they may simply be returned to the consignor. While the goods are in the possession of the consignee, the consignee holds title to them, and creditors of the consignee will prevail over the consignor in any action to repossess the goods [UCC 2–326(3)].

SALE ON APPROVAL   When a seller offers to sell goods to a buyer and permits the buyer to take the goods on a trial basis, a **sale on approval** is usually made. The term *sale* here is a misnomer, as only an *offer* to sell has been made, along with a *bailment* created by the buyer's possession. (A bailment is a temporary delivery of personal property into the care of another—see Chapter 34.)

SALE OR RETURN
A type of conditional sale in which title and possession pass from the seller to the buyer; however, the buyer retains the option to return the goods during a specified period even though the goods conform to the contract.

CONSIGNMENT
A transaction in which an owner of goods (the consignor) delivers the goods to another (the consignee) for the consignee to sell. The consignee pays the consignor for the goods when they are sold by the consignee.

SALE ON APPROVAL
A type of conditional sale in which the buyer may take the goods on a trial basis. The sale becomes absolute only when the buyer approves of (or is satisfied with) the goods being sold.

Therefore, title and risk of loss (from causes beyond the buyer's control) remain with the seller until the buyer accepts (approves) the offer. Acceptance can be made expressly, by any act inconsistent with the *trial* purpose or the seller's ownership, or by the buyer's election not to return the goods within the trial period. If the buyer does not wish to accept, the buyer may notify the seller of that fact within the trial period, and the return is made at the seller's expense and risk [UCC 2–327(1)]. Goods held on approval are not subject to the claims of the buyer's creditors until acceptance.

It is often difficult to determine from a particular transaction which exists—a contract for a sale on approval, a contract for a sale or return, or a contract for sale. The UCC states that (unless otherwise agreed) "if the goods are delivered primarily for use," the transaction is a sale on approval; "if the goods are delivered primarily for resale," the transaction is a sale or return [UCC 2–326(1)]. The court in the following case had to determine whether a particular transaction was a contract for a sale on approval or a contract for sale.

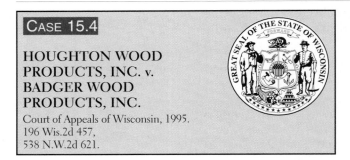

CASE 15.4

HOUGHTON WOOD PRODUCTS, INC. v. BADGER WOOD PRODUCTS, INC.

Court of Appeals of Wisconsin, 1995.
196 Wis.2d 457,
538 N.W.2d 621.

HISTORICAL AND SOCIAL SETTING *Small businesses make up over 90 percent of all nonagricultural businesses in the United States. They employ more than half of the work force in the private sector, make nearly half of the sales, and produce almost 40 percent of the annual national income. Over the last twenty years, the number of small businesses has increased by about 60 percent. Despite these inspiring statistics, however, small businesses also fail at a high rate.*

FACTS Badger Wood Products, Inc., a manufacturer of cabinets and other wood products, owed Associated Bank Green Bay over $3.7 million dollars. As collateral for the debt, Badger had promised all of its raw materials and work in process. When Badger failed to repay the money, it gave its assets to the bank, including three shipments of wood that had been delivered to Badger from Houghton Wood Products, Inc., but that had not been paid for. Houghton filed a suit in a Wisconsin state court against Badger and the bank, seeking the wood or the full purchase price of the wood. Houghton contended that it owned the wood because it was delivered pursuant to a sale on approval. The court agreed and issued a judgment in Houghton's favor. The bank appealed.

ISSUE Was the transaction between Badger and Houghton a sale on approval?

DECISION No. The Court of Appeals of Wisconsin reversed the lower court's ruling and remanded the case with an order to enter a judgment in the bank's favor.

REASON The court explained that "the wood delivered to Badger was to be made into cabinets that Badger would then sell to customers. Once the wood is made into cabinets, it undergoes substantial transformation and cannot be returned." If the sale was on approval, "title in the transformed wood would remain with Houghton until payment is made." The court reasoned that it "violates common sense and the rules of commerce to permit transformed goods to remain titled to the seller." Thus, the court held that "when a good is used in the manufacturing process where it undergoes transformation and is subsequently resold, it is not delivered for 'use,'" as that term is used in the UCC. Because the transaction was not a delivery for use, the court concluded that it was a contract for sale, not a sale on approval.

FOR CRITICAL ANALYSIS—Economic Consideration
For what reasons would a seller ever agree to a sale on approval, given the fact that in a sale on approval the seller retains the risk of loss and is also responsible for the expenses involved in the buyer's returning of the goods?

Risk of Loss When a Sales or Lease Contract Is Breached

There are many ways to breach a sales or lease contract, and the transfer of risk operates differently depending on which party breaches. Generally, the party in breach bears the risk of loss.

WHEN THE SELLER OR LESSOR BREACHES   If the goods are so nonconforming that the buyer has the right to reject them, the risk of loss does not pass to the buyer until the defects are **cured** (that is, until the goods are repaired, replaced, or discounted in price by the seller) or until the buyer accepts the goods in spite of their defects (thus waiving the right to reject). For example, a buyer orders blue widgets from a seller, F.O.B. seller's plant. The seller ships black widgets instead. The black widgets (nonconforming goods) are damaged in transit. The risk of loss falls on the seller. Had the seller shipped blue widgets (conforming goods) instead, the risk would have fallen on the buyer [UCC 2–510(2)].

CURE
The right of a party who tenders nonconforming performance to correct his or her performance within the contract period [UCC 3–508].

If a buyer accepts a shipment of goods and later discovers a defect, acceptance can be revoked. Revocation allows the buyer to pass the risk of loss back to the seller, at least to the extent that the buyer's insurance does not cover the loss [UCC 2–510(2)].

In regard to leases, Article 2A states a similar rule. If the lessor or supplier tenders goods that are so nonconforming that the lessee has the right to reject them, the risk of loss remains with the lessor or the supplier until cure or acceptance [UCC 2A–220(1)(a)]. If the lessee, after acceptance, revokes his or her acceptance of nonconforming goods, the revocation passes the risk of loss back to the seller or supplier, to the extent that the lessee's insurance does not cover the loss [UCC 2A–220(1)(b)].

In the following case, the buyer claimed that the seller should bear the risk of loss for nonconforming goods that were stolen before the buyer was able to return them to the seller.

CASE 15.5

GRAYBAR ELECTRIC CO. v. SHOOK

Supreme Court of North Carolina, 1973.
283 N.C. 213,
195 S.E.2d 514.

HISTORICAL AND SOCIAL SETTING   *The UCC clearly provides that a party who breaches a contract bears the risk of loss. There have been relatively few cases arising under this provision of the UCC. This is in part because it seems reasonable that, for example, a seller should bear the risk when he or she has delivered goods that are nonconforming or clearly defective.*

FACTS   Harold Shook agreed with Graybar Electric Company to purchase three reels of burial cable for use in Shook's construction work. When the reels were delivered, each carton was marked "burial cable," but two of the reels were in fact aerial cable. Shook accepted the conforming reel of cable and notified Graybar that he was rejecting the two reels of aerial cable. Because of a truckers' strike, Shook was unable to return the reels to Graybar. He stored the reels in a well-lighted space near a grocery store owner's dwelling, which was close to Shook's work site. About four months later, Shook noticed that one of the reels had been stolen. On the following day, he notified Graybar of the loss and, worried about the safety of the second reel, arranged to have it transported to a garage for storage. Before the second reel was transferred, however, it was also stolen, and Shook notified Graybar of the second theft. Graybar sued Shook in a North Carolina state court for the purchase price, claiming that Shook had agreed to return to Graybar the nonconforming reels and had failed to do so. Shook contended that he had agreed only to contact a trucking company to return the reels, and because he had contacted three trucking firms to no avail (owing to the strike), his obligation had been fulfilled. The trial court ruled for Shook, and Graybar appealed.

ISSUE   Who should bear the risk of loss for the reels?

DECISION   Graybar. The Supreme Court of North Carolina affirmed the lower court's judgment in Shook's favor.

(Continued)

Case 15.5—Continued

REASON   The court relied on UCC 2–510(1), which states, "Where tender or delivery of goods so fails to conform to the contract as to give a right of rejection the risk of their loss remains on the seller until cure or acceptance." The court held that Shook had formed no contract with Graybar to return the nonconforming goods, although Shook had attempted to facilitate the aerial cable's return at the owner's request. Graybar, however, "with full notice of the place of storage which was at the place of delivery did nothing but sleep on its rights for more than three months." Thus, Graybar had evidenced neither promptness of action nor good faith.

FOR CRITICAL ANALYSIS—Ethical Consideration
Did the fact that Graybar "did nothing but sleep on its rights for more than three months" have anything to do with the outcome of this case? Should it have?

WHEN THE BUYER OR LESSEE BREACHES   The general rule is that when a buyer or lessee breaches a contract, the risk of loss *immediately* shifts to the buyer or lessee. There are three important limitations to this rule:

1.   The seller or lessor must already have identified the contract goods.
2.   The buyer or lessee bears the risk for only a *commercially reasonable time* after the seller has learned of the breach.
3.   The buyer or lessee is liable only to the extent of any deficiency in the seller's insurance coverage [UCC 2–510(3), 2A–220(2)].

▌Insurable Interest

"When the praying does no good, insurance does help."

Bertolt Brecht, 1898–1956
(*German playwright and poet*)

Parties to sales and lease contracts often obtain insurance coverage to protect against damage, loss, or destruction of goods. Any party purchasing insurance, however, must have a sufficient interest in the insured item to obtain a valid policy. Insurance laws—not the UCC—determine sufficiency. The UCC is helpful, however, because it contains certain rules regarding insurable interests in goods.

Insurable Interest of the Buyer or Lessee

INSURABLE INTEREST
In regard to the sale or lease of goods, a property interest in the goods that is sufficiently substantial to permit a party to insure against damage to the goods.

A buyer or lessee has an **insurable interest** in *identified* goods. The moment the contract goods are identified by the seller or lessor, the buyer or lessee has a special property interest that allows the buyer or lessee to obtain necessary insurance coverage for those goods even before the risk of loss has passed [UCC 2–501(1), 2A–218(1)].

Consider an example: In March, a farmer sells a cotton crop he hopes to harvest in October. The buyer acquires an insurable interest in the crop when it is planted, because those goods (the cotton crop) are identified to the sales contract between the seller and the buyer. The rule stated in UCC 2–501(1)(c) is that such buyers obtain an insurable interest in crops by identification, which occurs when the crops are planted or otherwise become growing crops, providing that the contract is for "the sale of crops to be harvested within twelve months or the next normal harvest season after contracting, whichever is longer."

Insurable Interest of the Seller or Lessor

A seller has an insurable interest in goods as long as he or she retains title to the goods. Even after title passes to a buyer, however, a seller who has a security interest in the goods (a right to secure payment—see Chapter 21) still has an insurable interest and can insure the goods [UCC 2–501(2)]. Hence, both a buyer and a seller can have an

Goods, such as these B52s at an Air Force base in Arizona, must be delivered from seller to buyer. What determines which party has an insurable interest in the goods before and during delivery?

insurable interest in identical goods at the same time. Of course, the buyer or seller must sustain an actual loss to have the right to recover from an insurance company. In regard to leases, the lessor retains an insurable interest in leased goods until an option to buy has been exercised by the lessee and the risk of loss has passed to the lessee [UCC 2A–218(3)].

▌Bulk Transfers

Bulk transfers are the subject of UCC Article 6. A *bulk transfer* is defined as any transfer of a major part of the transferor's material, supplies, merchandise, or other inventory *not made in the ordinary course of the transferor's business* [UCC 6–102(1)]. Difficulties sometimes occur with bulk transfers. For example, when a business that owes debts to numerous creditors sells a substantial part of its equipment and inventories to a buyer, the business should use the proceeds to pay off the debts. What happens, though, if the merchant instead spends the money on a trip, leaving the creditors without payment? Can the creditors lay any claim to the goods that were transferred in bulk to the buyer?

The purpose of Article 6 is to protect creditors in such situations. UCC 6–104 and 6–105 provide that the following requirements must be met when a bulk transfer is undertaken:

1.   The seller must furnish to the buyer a sworn list of his or her existing creditors. The list must include those whose claims are disputed and must state names, business addresses, and amounts due.
2.   The buyer and the seller must prepare a schedule of the property to be transferred.
3.   The buyer must preserve the list of creditors and the schedule of property for six months and permit inspection of the list by any creditor of the seller or must file the list and the schedule of property in a designated public office.
4.   The buyer must give notice of the proposed bulk transfer to each of the seller's creditors at least ten days before the buyer takes possession of the goods or makes payments for them, whichever happens first.

WATCH OUT The notice provisions of Article 6 can sometimes interfere with and delay normal business transactions.

If these requirements are met, the buyer acquires title to the goods free of all claims by the seller's creditors. If the requirements are not met, goods in the possession of the buyer continue to be subject to the claims of the unpaid creditors of the seller for six months [UCC 6–111].

In 1988, the National Conference of Commissioners on Uniform State Laws recommended that those states that have adopted Article 6 repeal it, because changes in the business and legal contexts in which bulk sales are conducted have made their regulation unnecessary. For states disinclined to do so, Article 6 has been revised to provide creditors with better protection while reducing the burden imposed on good faith purchasers. To date, over half of the states have repealed Article 6, and an increasing number of states have opted for the revised version.

The revised Article 6 limits its application to bulk sales by sellers whose principal business is the sale of inventory from bulk stock. It does not apply to transactions involving property valued at less than $10,000 or more than $25 million. If a seller has more than two hundred creditors, a buyer, rather than having to send individual notice to each creditor, can give notice by public filing (for example, in the office of a state's secretary of state). The notice period is increased from ten to forty-five days, and the statute of limitations is extended from six months to one year.

Application

Law and the Shipper or Buyer— Who Bears the Risk of Loss?*

 A major aspect of commercial transactions involves the shipment of goods. Many issues arise when the unforeseen occurs, such as fire, theft, or other forms of damage to goods in transit. The UCC uses a three-part checklist to determine risk of loss:

1. If the contract includes terms allocating risk of loss, those terms are binding and must be applied.
2. If the contract is silent as to risk, and either party breaches the contract, the breaching party is liable for risk of loss.
3. When a contract makes no reference to risk, and neither party breaches, risk of loss is borne by the party having control over the goods.

If you are a seller of goods to be shipped, realize that as long as you have control over the goods, you are liable for any loss unless the buyer is in breach or the contract contains an explicit agreement to the contrary. When there is no explicit agreement, the UCC uses the delivery terms in your contract as a basis for determining control. Thus, "F.O.B. buyer's business" is a destination-delivery term, and risk of loss for goods shipped under these terms does not pass to the buyer until there is a tender of delivery at the point of destination. Any loss or damage in transit falls on the seller, because the seller has control until proper tender has been made.

From the buyer's point of view, it is important to remember that most sellers prefer "F.O.B. seller's business" as a delivery term. Under these terms, once the goods are delivered to the carrier, the buyer bears the risk of loss. Thus, if conforming goods are completely destroyed or lost in transit, the buyer not only suffers the loss but is obligated to pay the seller the contract price.

At the time of contract negotiation, both the seller and the buyer should determine the importance of risk of loss. In some circumstances, risk is relatively unimportant (such as when ten boxes of copier paper are being sold), and the delivery terms should simply reflect costs and price. In other circumstances, risk is extremely important (such as when a fragile piece of equipment is being sold), and the parties will need an express agreement as to the moment risk is to pass so that they can insure the goods accordingly. The point is that risk should be considered before the loss occurs, not after.

A major consideration relating to risk is when to insure goods against possible losses. Buyers and sellers should determine the point at which they have an insurable interest in the goods and obtain insurance coverage to protect them against loss from that point.

*This *Application* is not meant to substitute for the services of an attorney who is licensed to practice law in your state.

Application—Continued

 Checklist for the Shipment of Goods

1. Prior to entering a contract, determine the importance of risk of loss for a given sale.
2. If risk is extremely important, the contract should expressly state the moment risk of loss will pass from the seller to the buyer. This clause could even provide that risk will not pass until the goods are "delivered, installed, inspected, and tested (or in running order for a period of time)."
3. If an express clause is not agreed on, delivery terms determine passage of risk of loss.
4. When appropriate, either party or both parties should consider the need to obtain insurance.

▌Key Terms

bailee 380	fungible goods 371	insurable interest 384
consignment 381	good faith purchaser 373	sale on approval 381
cure 383	identification 370	sale or return 381
destination contract 372	insolvent 373	shipment contract 372
document of title 373		

▌Chapter Summary: Title and Risk of Loss

Shipment Contracts *(See pages 372 and 379.)*	In the absence of an agreement, title and risk pass upon the seller's or lessor's delivery of conforming goods to the carrier [UCC 2–401(2)(a), 2–509(1)(a), 2A–219(2)(a)].
Destination Contracts *(See pages 372 and 379.)*	In the absence of an agreement, title and risk pass upon the seller's or lessor's *tender* of delivery of conforming goods to the buyer or lessee at the point of destination [UCC 2–401(2)(b), 2–509(1)(b), 2A–219(2)(b)].

Delivery without Movement of the Goods *(See pages 372–373 and pages 380–381.)*	1. In the absence of an agreement, if the goods are not represented by a document of title:
	   a. Title passes upon the formation of the contract [UCC 2–401(3)(b)].
	   b. Risk passes to the buyer or lessee, if the seller or lessor (or supplier, in a finance lease) is a merchant, upon the buyer's or lessee's receipt of the goods or, if the seller or lessor is a nonmerchant, upon the seller's or lessor's *tender* of delivery of the goods [UCC 2–509(3), 2A–219(c)].
	
	 2. In the absence of an agreement, if the goods are represented by a document of title:
	   a. If the document is negotiable and the goods are held by a bailee, title and risk pass upon the buyer's *receipt* of the document [UCC 2–401(3)(a), 2–509(2)(a)].
	   b. If the document is nonnegotiable and the goods are held by a bailee, title passes upon the buyer's receipt of the document, but risk does *not* pass until the buyer, after receipt of the document, has had a reasonable time to present the document to demand the goods [UCC 2–401(3)(a), 2–509(2)(c), 2–503(4)(b)].
	
	 3. In the absence of an agreement, if the goods are held by a bailee and no document of title is transferred, risk passes to the buyer when the bailee acknowledges the buyer's right to the possession of the goods [UCC 2–509(2)(b)].
	
	 4. In respect to leases, if goods held by a bailee are to be delivered without being moved, the risk of loss passes to the lessee upon acknowledgment by the bailee of the lessee's right to possession of the goods [UCC 2A–219(2)(b)].

Sales by Nonowners *(See pages 373–378.)*	Between the owner and a good faith purchaser or sublessee: 1. *Void title*—Owner prevails [UCC 2–403(1)]. 2. *Voidable title*—Buyer prevails [UCC 2–403(1)]. 3. *Entrusting to a merchant*—Buyer or sublessee prevails [UCC 2–403(2), (3); 2A–305(2)]. *(Continued)*

▌Chapter Summary: Title and Risk of Loss—Continued

Sale-or-Return Contracts *(See page 381.)*	When the buyer receives possession of the goods, title and risk of loss pass to the buyer, with the buyer's option to return to the seller the goods, title, and risk [UCC 2–327(2)].
Sale-on-Approval Contracts *(See pages 381–382.)*	Title and risk of loss (from causes beyond the buyer's control) remain with the seller until the buyer approves (accepts) the offer [UCC 2–327(1)].
Risk of Loss When a Sales or Lease Contract Is Breached *(See pages 383–384.)*	1. If the seller or lessor breaches by tendering nonconforming goods that are rejected by the buyer or lessee, the risk of loss does not pass to the buyer or lessee until the defects are cured (unless the buyer or lessee accepts the goods in spite of their defects, thus waiving the right to reject) [UCC 2–510(1), 2A–220(1)]. 2. If the buyer or lessee breaches the contract, the risk of loss to identified goods immediately shifts to the buyer or lessee. Limitations to this rule are as follows [UCC 2–510(3), 2A–220(2)]: a. The seller or lessor must already have identified the contract goods. b. The buyer or lessee bears the risk for only a commercially reasonable time after the seller or lessor has learned of the breach. c. The buyer or lessee is liable only to the extent of any deficiency in the seller's or lessor's insurance coverage.
Insurable Interest *(See pages 384–385.)*	1. Buyers and lessees have an insurable interest in goods the moment the goods are identified to the contract by the seller or the lessor [UCC 2–510(3), 2A–218(1)]. 2. Sellers have an insurable interest in goods as long as they have (1) title to the goods or (2) a security interest in the goods [UCC 2–501(2)]. Lessors have an insurable interest in leased goods until an option to buy has been exercised by the lessee and the risk of loss has passed to the lessee [UCC 2A–218(3)].
Bulk Transfers *(See pages 385–386.)*	1. In a bulk transfer of assets, in those states that have not repealed Article 6 of the UCC or replaced it with the revised Article 6, the buyer acquires title to the goods free of all claims of the seller's creditors if the following requirements are met: a. The transferor (seller) furnishes to the transferee (buyer) a sworn list of existing creditors, listing their names, business addresses, amounts due, and any disputed claims [UCC 6–104(1)(a)]. b. The buyer and seller prepare a schedule of the property to be transferred [UCC 6–104(1)(b)]. c. The buyer preserves the list of creditors and the schedule of property for six months, allowing any creditors of the seller to inspect it, or files the list and schedule of property in a designated public office [UCC 6–104(1)(c)]. d. Notice of the proposed bulk transfer is given by the buyer to each creditor of the seller at least ten days before the buyer takes possession of the goods or pays for them, whichever happens first [UCC 6–105]. 2. The revised Article 6 limits its application to bulk sales by sellers whose principal business is the sale of inventory from bulk stock and to transactions involving property valued between $10,000 and $25 million. If a seller has more than two hundred creditors, the buyer can give notice of the sale to the creditors by public filing.

▌For Review

1. What is the significance of identifying goods to a contract?

2. If the parties to a contract do not expressly agree on when title to goods passes, what determines when title passes?

3. Risk of loss does not necessarily pass with title. If the parties to a contract did not expressly agree when risk passes and the goods are to be delivered without movement by the seller, when does risk pass?

4. Under what circumstances will the seller's title to goods being sold be void? Under what circumstances will a seller have voidable title? What is the legal effect on a good faith purchaser of the goods of the seller's having a void title versus a voidable title?

5. At what point does the buyer acquire an insurable interest in goods subject to a sales contract? Can the buyer and seller both have an insurable interest in the goods simultaneously?

▌Questions and Case Problems

15–1. Sales by Nonowners. In the following situations, two parties lay claim to the same goods sold. Discuss which of the parties would prevail in each situation.

(a) Terry steals Dom's television set and sells the set to Blake, an innocent purchaser, for value. Dom learns that Blake has the set and demands its return.

(b) Karlin takes her television set for repair to Orken, a merchant who sells new and used television sets. By accident, one of Orken's employees sells the set to Grady, an innocent purchaser-customer, who takes possession. Karlin wants her set back from Grady.

15–2. Risk of Loss. When will risk of loss pass from the seller to the buyer under each of the following contracts, assuming the parties have not expressly agreed on when risk of loss would pass?

(a) A New York seller contracts with a San Francisco buyer to ship goods to the buyer F.O.B. San Francisco.

(b) A New York seller contracts with a San Francisco buyer to ship goods to the buyer in San Francisco. There is no indication as to whether the shipment will be F.O.B. New York or F.O.B. San Francisco.

(c) A seller contracts with a buyer to sell goods located on the seller's premises. The buyer pays for the goods and makes arrangements to pick them up the next week at the seller's place of business.

(d) A seller contracts with a buyer to sell goods located in a warehouse.

15–3. Sales by Nonowners. Julian Makepeace, who had been declared mentally incompetent by a court, sold his diamond ring to Golding for value. Golding later sold the ring to Carmichael for value. Neither Golding nor Carmichael knew that Makepeace had been adjudged mentally incompetent by a court. Farrel, who had been appointed as Makepeace's guardian, subsequently learned that the diamond ring was in Carmichael's possession and demanded its return from Carmichael. Who has legal ownership of the ring? Why?

15–4. Risk of Loss. Alberto's Food Stores contracts to purchase from Giant Food Distributors, Inc., one hundred cases of Golden Rod corn to be shipped F.O.B. seller's warehouse by Janson Truck Lines. Giant Food Distributors, by mistake, delivers one hundred cases of Gold Giant corn to Janson Truck Lines. While in transit, the Gold Giant corn is stolen. Between Alberto's and Giant Food Distributors, who suffers the loss? Explain.

15–5. Sale on Approval. Chi Moy, a student, contracted to buy a television set from Ted's Electronics. Under the terms of the contract, Moy was to try out the set for thirty days, and if he liked it, he was to pay for the set at the end of the thirty-day period. If he did not want to purchase the set after thirty days, he could return the TV to Ted's Electronics with no obligation. Ten days after Moy took the set home, it was stolen from Moy's apartment, although Moy had not been negligent in his care of the set in any way. Ted's Electronics claimed that Moy had to pay for the stolen set. Moy argued that the risk of loss fell on Ted's Electronics. Which party will prevail?

15–6. Risk of Loss. Isis Foods, Inc., located in St. Louis, wanted to purchase a shipment of food from Pocasset Food Sales, Inc. The sale of food was initiated by a purchase order

from Isis stating that the shipment was to be made "F.O.B. St. Louis." Pocasset made the shipment by delivery of the goods to the carrier. Pocasset's invoices contained a provision stating, "Our liability ceases upon delivery of merchandise to carrier." The shipment of food was destroyed before it reached St. Louis. Discuss which party bears the risk of loss, and why. [*In re Isis Foods, Inc.*, 38 Bankr. 48 (Bankr.W.D.Mo. 1983)]

15–7. Sales by Nonowners. A new car owned by a New Jersey car-rental agency was stolen in 1967. The agency collected the full price of the car from its insurance company, Home Indemnity Co., and assigned all its interest in the automobile to the insurer. Subsequently, the thief sold the car to an automobile wholesaler, who in turn sold it to a retail car dealer. Schrier purchased the car from the dealer without knowledge of the theft. Home Indemnity sued Schrier to recover the car. Can Home Indemnity recover? [*Schrier v. Home Indemnity Co.*, 273 A.2d 248 (D.C. 1971)]

15–8. Sales by Nonowners. Fred Lane was the owner of Lane's Outboard and was engaged in the business of selling boats, motors, and trailers. He sold a new boat, motor, and trailer to a person who called himself John Willis. Willis took possession of the goods and paid for them with a check for $6,285. The check was later dishonored. About six months later, Jimmy Honeycutt bought the boat, motor, and trailer from a man identified as "Garrett," who was renting a summer beach house to the Honeycutts that year and whom Honeycutt had known for several years. Honeycutt paid $2,500 for the boating equipment and did not receive an official certificate of title. Lane sought to recover the boat, motor, and trailer from Honeycutt. Honeycutt's sole defense was that he was a good faith purchaser and therefore Lane should not be able to recover from him. Discuss whether Honeycutt will succeed in his defense. [*Lane v. Honeycutt*, 14 N.C.App. 436, 188 S.E.2d 604 (1972)]

15–9. Sale or Return. Hargo Woolen Mills had purchased bales of surplus wool fibers, which Hargo used in its manufacture of woolen cloth, from Shabry Trading Co. for many years. On one occasion, however, Shabry shipped twenty-four bales to Hargo without an order. Rather than pay for reshipment, both parties decided that Hargo would retain possession of the bales and pay for what it used. Hargo kept the bales separate inside its warehouse and eventually used, and was billed for, eight bales. Hargo still kept the remaining sixteen bales separate. Hargo went bankrupt, and the receiver, Meinhard-Commercial Corp., took everything in Hargo's warehouse. Shabry claimed that it was the owner and title holder of the bales and requested their return, but Meinhard-Commercial refused to return them. Should Shabry be able to retake possession of the bales? [*Meinhard-Commercial Corp. v. Hargo Woolen Mills*, 112 N.H.500, 300 A.2d 321 (1972)]

15–10. Risk of Loss. Donald Hayward agreed to buy a thirty-foot Revel Craft Playmate Yacht from Herbert F. Postma, a yacht dealer, on February 7, 1967. The boat was to be delivered to a slip on Lake Macatawa during April 1967. Hayward signed a security agreement on March 1, 1967, and gave a promissory note for $13,095.60 to Postma's dealership. The note was subsequently assigned to a bank. The security agreement contained clauses requiring the buyer to keep the boat in first-class order or repair and to keep the boat fully insured at all times. After Hayward had made some payments, but before the boat was delivered to Hayward, it was destroyed by fire. Neither Postma nor Hayward had insured the boat, and Hayward requested that Postma pay off the note or reimburse him for payments made. Postma refused, and Hayward sued. Discuss whether Hayward or Postma bears the risk of loss as to the boat destroyed in the fire. [*Hayward v. Postma*, 31 Mich.App. 720, 188 N.W.2d 31 (1971)]

15–11. Entrustment Rule. Bobby Locke, the principal stockholder and chief executive officer (CEO) of Worthco Farm Center, Inc., hired Mr. Hobby as the company's manager. Subsequently, it was discovered that during the approximately thirteen months of Locke's tenure as CEO, Hobby had sold corn stored with Worthco to Arabi Grain & Elevator Co. and pocketed the proceeds. When Locke brought an action against Arabi to recover the corn, Arabi alleged, among other things, that Locke had entrusted the corn to Hobby and that because Arabi was a purchaser in the ordinary course of business, Hobby had transferred ownership rights in the corn to Arabi. Assuming that Arabi was a buyer in the ordinary course of business, how should the court rule? Discuss. [*Locke v. Arabi Grain & Elevator Co.*, 197 Ga.App. 854, 399 S.E.2d 705 (1991)]

15–12. Sales by Nonowners. Doyle Alexander sold his 1986 Mercury to another person (called the "initial buyer," because the identity of this person was not disclosed in the court record). Alexander signed the back of the certificate of title to the car but did not indicate the name of the person to whom he was selling the car. The initial buyer, posing as Doyle Alexander, then sold the car to Express Drive Away. Express Drive Away resold the car to Hodges Wholesale Cars through an auction conducted by Auto Dealer's Exchange of Birmingham. The car was later resold several other times. In the meantime, Alexander, upon learning that the initial buyer's check had bounced, informed the authorities that his car had been "stolen." Ultimately, Hodges Wholesale Cars sued Auto Dealer's Exchange and Express to recover payments that Hodges Wholesale Cars had made to a later purchaser (who had demanded a refund of the purchase price it had paid for the "stolen" car). A central issue before the court was whether the initial buyer had acquired voidable title or void title to the car. How should the court rule on this issue, and why? Discuss fully. [*Hodges Wholesale Cars v. Auto Dealer's Exchange of Birmingham*, 628 So.2d 608 (Ala. 1993)]

A QUESTION OF ETHICS AND SOCIAL RESPONSIBILITY

15–13. *Toby and Rita Kahr accidentally included a small bag containing their sterling silver in a bag of used clothing that they had donated to Goodwill Industries, Inc. The*

silverware, which was valued at over $3,500, had been given to them twenty-seven years earlier by Rita's father as a wedding present and had great sentimental value for them. The Kahrs realized what had happened shortly after Toby returned from Goodwill, but when Toby called Goodwill, he was told that the silver had immediately been sold to a customer, Karon Markland, for $15. Although Goodwill called Markland and asked her to return the silver, Markland refused to return it. The Kahrs then brought an action against Markland to regain the silver, claiming that Markland did not have good title to it. In view of these circumstances, discuss the following issues. [Kahr v. Markland, 187 Ill.App.3d 603, 543 N.E.2d 579, 135 Ill.Dec. 196 (1989)]

1. The basic issue in this case is whether the silver was "lost property" (defined as property unintentionally separated from its owner) or property entrusted to a merchant, Goodwill Industries. If the court decides that the silver was lost, the party in possession of the property will have good title against all parties except the true owner—in which case, the Kahrs will be able to recover the silver from Markland. If the court decides that the Kahrs entrusted the silver to Goodwill, then the entrustment rule will be applied—in which case, the Kahrs will be unable to recover the silver from Markland, a good faith purchaser. If you were the judge, how would you decide the issue? Why?

2. Did Karon Markland act wrongfully in any way by not returning the silver to Goodwill when requested to do so? What would you have done in her position?

3. Goodwill argued that the entrustment rule should apply. Is this ethical behavior on the part of Goodwill? Why or why not? How might Goodwill justify its argument from an ethical point of view?

 FOR CRITICAL ANALYSIS

15–14. *Under the UCC, passage of title does not always occur simultaneously with passage of risk of loss. Why is this? Give some examples of what might result if risk of loss and title always passed from the buyer to the seller at the same time.*

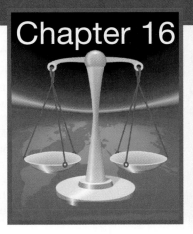

Chapter 16

Performance and Breach of Sales and Lease Contracts

"It has been uniformly laid down . . . , as far back as we can remember, that good faith is the basis of all mercantile transactions."

J. Buller, 1746–1800
(British jurist)

CHAPTER OBJECTIVES

After reading this chapter, you should be able to:

1. Outline the performance obligations of sellers and lessors under the UCC.
2. State the perfect tender rule, and identify and discuss its exceptions.
3. Describe the performance obligations of buyers and lessees under the UCC.
4. Point out the options available in the event that one of the parties to a sales or lease contract repudiates the contract prior to the time for performance.
5. List and discuss the remedies available to the nonbreaching party when a sales or lease contract is breached.

Billions of sales and lease contracts are carried out every year in the United States. Most of these contracts involve virtually no problems. This is because most people try to fulfill their contractual obligations.

The performance that is required of the parties under a sales or lease contract consists of the duties and obligations each party has assumed under the terms of the contract. Keep in mind that "duties and obligations" under the terms of the contract include those specified by the agreement, by custom, and by the Uniform Commercial Code (UCC). In this chapter, we examine the basic performance obligations of the parties under a sales or lease contract.

Sometimes circumstances make it difficult for a person to carry out the promised performance, in which case the contract may be breached. When breach occurs, the aggrieved party looks for remedies—which we deal with in the second half of the chapter.

▌ Performance Obligations

As discussed in the *Ethical Perspective* in Chapter 14 and stressed in the opening quotation to this chapter, the standards of good faith and commercial reasonableness are read into every contract. These standards provide a framework in which the parties can specify particulars of performance. Thus, when one party delays specifying particulars of performance for an unreasonable period of time or fails to cooperate with the other party, the innocent party is excused from any resulting delay in performance. In addition, the innocent party can proceed to perform in any reasonable manner. If the innocent party has performed as far as is reasonably possible under the circumstances, the other party's failure to specify particulars or to cooperate can be treated as a breach of contract. Good faith is a question of fact for the jury.

In the performance of a sales or lease contract, the basic obligation of the seller or lessor is to *transfer and deliver conforming goods*. The basic obligation of the buyer or lessee is to *accept and pay for conforming goods* in accordance with the contract [UCC 2–301, 2A-516(1)]. Overall performance of a sales or lease contract is controlled by the agreement between the parties. When the contract is unclear and disputes arise, the courts look to the UCC.

▌ Obligations of the Seller or Lessor

"It is only when merchants dispute about their own rules that they invoke the law."

J. Brett, 1815–1899
(British jurist)

The major obligation of the seller or lessor under a sales or lease contract is to *tender* conforming goods to the buyer or lessee.

Tender of Delivery

Tender of delivery requires that the seller or lessor have and hold *conforming* goods at the disposal of the buyer or lessee and give the buyer or lessee whatever notification is reasonably necessary to enable the buyer or lessee to take delivery [UCC 2–503(1), 2A–508(1)].

Tender must occur at a *reasonable hour* and in a *reasonable manner*. In other words, a seller cannot call the buyer at 2:00 A.M. and say, "The goods are ready. I'll give you twenty minutes to get them." Unless the parties have agreed otherwise, the goods must be tendered for delivery at a reasonable time and kept available for a reasonable period of time to enable the buyer to take possession of them [UCC 2–503(1)(a)].

All goods called for by a contract must be tendered in a single delivery unless the parties agree otherwise, or the circumstances are such that either party can rightfully request delivery in lots [UCC 2–307, 2–612, 2A–510]. Hence, an order for 1,000 shirts cannot be delivered 2 shirts at a time. If, however, the seller and the buyer contemplate that the shirts will be delivered in four orders of 250 each, as they are produced (for summer, fall, winter, and spring stock), and the price can be apportioned accordingly, it may be commercially reasonable to deliver the shirts in this way.

Place of Delivery

The UCC provides for the place of delivery pursuant to a contract if the contract does not. Of course, the parties may agree on a particular destination, or their contract's terms or the circumstances may indicate the place.

NONCARRIER CASES   If the contract does not designate the place of delivery for the goods, and the buyer is expected to pick them up, the place of delivery is the *seller's place of business* or, if the seller has none, the *seller's residence* [UCC 2–308]. If the contract involves the sale of *identified goods*, and the parties know when they enter into

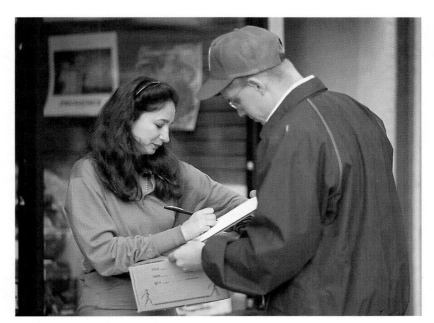

Under what circumstances can a buyer reject goods without breaching the sales contract?

the contract that these goods are located somewhere other than at the seller's place of business (such as at a warehouse), then the *location of the goods* is the place for their delivery [UCC 2–308].

For example, Rogers and Aguirre live in San Francisco. In San Francisco, Rogers contracts to sell Aguirre five used trucks, which both parties know are located in a Chicago warehouse. If nothing more is specified in the contract, the place of delivery for the trucks is Chicago. The seller may tender delivery by either giving the buyer a *negotiable or nonnegotiable document of title* or obtaining the *bailee's (warehouser's) acknowledgment* that the buyer is entitled to possession.[1]

CARRIER CASES   In many instances, attendant circumstances or delivery terms in the contract make it apparent that the parties intend that a carrier be used to move the goods. There are two ways a seller can complete performance of the obligation to deliver the goods in carrier cases—through a shipment contract and through a destination contract.

KEEP IN MIND If goods never arrive, the buyer usually has at least some recourse against the carrier. Also, a buyer normally insures the goods from the time they leave the seller's possession.

Shipment Contracts   Recall from Chapter 15 that a *shipment contract* requires or authorizes the seller to ship goods by a carrier. The contract does not require that the seller deliver the goods at a particular destination [UCC 2–319, 2–509]. Unless otherwise agreed, the seller must do the following:

1. Put the goods into the hands of the carrier.
2. Make a contract for their transportation that is reasonable according to the nature of the goods and their value. (For example, certain types of goods need refrigeration in transit.)
3. Obtain and promptly deliver or tender to the buyer any documents necessary to enable the buyer to obtain possession of the goods from the carrier.
4. Promptly notify the buyer that shipment has been made [UCC 2–504].

---

1. If the seller delivers a nonnegotiable document of title or merely writes instructions to the bailee to release the goods to the buyer without the bailee's *acknowledgment* of the buyer's rights, this is also a sufficient tender, unless the buyer objects [UCC 2–503(4)]. Risk of loss, however, does not pass until the buyer has a reasonable amount of time in which to present the document or the instructions.

If the seller fails to notify the buyer that shipment has been made or fails to make a proper contract for transportation, and a *material loss* of the goods or a significant *delay* results, the contract has been breached and the buyer can reject the shipment. Of course, the parties can agree that a lesser amount of loss or any delay will be grounds for rejection.

Destination Contracts   Under a *destination contract*, the seller agrees to see that conforming goods will be duly tendered to the buyer at a particular destination. The goods must be tendered at a reasonable hour and held at the buyer's disposal for a reasonable length of time. The seller must also give the buyer appropriate notice. In addition, the seller must provide the buyer with any documents of title necessary to enable the buyer to obtain delivery from the carrier. This is often done by tendering the documents through ordinary banking channels [UCC 2–503].

The Perfect Tender Rule

As previously noted, the seller or lessor has an obligation to ship or tender *conforming goods*, and this entitles the buyer or lessee to accept and pay for the goods according to the terms of the contract. Under the common law, the seller was obligated to deliver goods in conformity with the terms of the contract in every detail. This was called the *perfect tender* doctrine. The UCC preserves the perfect tender doctrine by stating that if goods or tender of delivery fail *in any respect* to conform to the contract, the buyer or lessee has the right to accept the goods, reject the entire shipment, or accept part and reject part [UCC 2–601, 2A–509].

For example, a lessor contracts to lease fifty Vericlear computers to be delivered at the lessee's place of business on or before October 1. On September 28, the lessor discovers that there are only thirty Vericlear computers in inventory, but there will be another forty Vericlear computers within the next two weeks. The lessor tenders delivery of the thirty Vericlear computers on October 1, with the promise that the other computers will be delivered within three weeks. Because the lessor failed to make a perfect tender of fifty Vericlear computers, the lessee has the right to reject the entire shipment and hold the lessor in breach.

Exceptions to Perfect Tender

Because of the rigidity of the perfect tender rule, several exceptions to the rule have been created, some of which are discussed here.

"It is the duty of a judge to inquire not only into the matter but into the circumstances of the matter."

Ovid, 43 B.C.E.–17 C.E.
(Roman poet)

AGREEMENT OF THE PARTIES   Exceptions to the perfect tender rule may be established by agreement. If the parties have agreed, for example, that defective goods or parts will not be rejected if the seller or lessor is able to repair or replace them within a reasonable period of time, the perfect tender rule does not apply.

CURE   The UCC does not specifically define the term *cure*, but it refers to the right of the seller or lessor to repair, adjust, or replace defective or nonconforming goods [UCC 2–508, 2A–513]. When any tender of delivery is rejected because of nonconforming goods and the time for performance has not yet expired, the seller or lessor can notify the buyer or lessee promptly of the intention to cure and can then do so *within the contract time for performance* [UCC 2–508(1), 2A–513(1)]. Once the time for performance under the contract has expired, the seller or lessor can still exercise the right to cure in respect to the rejected goods if he or she had *reasonable grounds to believe that the nonconforming tender would be acceptable to the buyer or lessee* [UCC 2–508(2), 2A–513(2)].

Sometimes, a seller or lessor will tender nonconforming goods with some type of price allowance. The allowance serves as the "reasonable grounds" for the seller or lessor to believe that the nonconforming tender will be acceptable to the buyer or lessee. Other reasons might also serve as the basis for the assumption that a buyer or lessee will accept a nonconforming tender. For example, if in the past a buyer frequently accepted a particular substitute for a good when the good ordered was not available, the seller has reasonable grounds to believe the buyer will again accept such a substitute. If the buyer rejects the substitute good on a particular occasion, the seller nonetheless had reasonable grounds to believe that the substitute would be acceptable. Therefore, the seller can cure within a reasonable time, even though conforming delivery will occur after the time limit for performance allowed under the contract.

The right to cure substantially restricts the right of the buyer or lessee to reject goods. For example, if a lessee refuses a tender of goods as nonconforming but does not disclose the nature of the defect to the lessor, the lessee cannot later assert the defect as a defense if the defect is one that the lessor could have cured. Generally, buyers and lessees must act in good faith and state specific reasons for refusing to accept goods [UCC 2–605, 2A–514].

SUBSTITUTION OF CARRIERS   When an agreed-on manner of delivery (such as which carrier will be used to transport the goods) becomes impracticable or unavailable through no fault of either party, but a commercially reasonable substitute is available, the seller must use this substitute performance, which is sufficient tender to the buyer [UCC 2–614(1)]. For example, a sales contract calls for the delivery of a large piece of machinery to be shipped by Roadway Trucking Corporation on or before June 1. The contract terms clearly state the importance of the delivery date. The employees of Roadway Trucking go on strike. The seller will be entitled to make a reasonable substitute tender, perhaps by rail. Note that the seller here is responsible for any additional shipping costs, unless contrary arrangements have been made in the sales contract.

INSTALLMENT CONTRACTS   An **installment contract** is a single contract that requires or authorizes delivery in two or more separate lots to be accepted and paid for separately. In an installment contract, a buyer or lessee can reject an installment *only if the nonconformity substantially impairs the value* of the installment and cannot be cured [UCC 2–612(2), 2–307, 2A–510(1)].

Unless the contract provides otherwise, the entire installment contract is breached only when one or more nonconforming installments *substantially* impair the value of the *whole contract*. If the buyer or lessee subsequently accepts a nonconforming installment and fails to notify the seller or lessor of cancellation, however, the contract is reinstated [UCC 2–612(3), 2A–510(2)].

A major issue to be determined is what constitutes substantial impairment of the "value of the whole contract." For example, consider an installment contract for the sale of twenty carloads of plywood. The first carload does not conform to the contract because 9 percent of the plywood deviates from the thickness specifications. The buyer cancels the contract, and immediately thereafter the second and third carloads of plywood arrive at the buyer's place of business. If a lawsuit ensued, the court would have to grapple with the question of whether the 9 percent of nonconforming plywood substantially impaired the value of the whole.[2]

The point to remember is that the UCC substantially alters the right of the buyer or lessee to reject the entire contract if the contract requires delivery to be made in several installments. The UCC strictly limits rejection to cases of *substantial* nonconformity.

COMMERCIAL IMPRACTICABILITY   As mentioned in Chapter 12, occurrences unforeseen by either party when a contract was made may make performance commercially

INSTALLMENT CONTRACT
Under the UCC, a contract that requires or authorizes delivery in two or more separate lots to be accepted and paid for separately.

"Inability suspends the law."

(Legal maxim)

---

2.   *Continental Forest Products, Inc. v. White Lumber Sales, Inc.,* 256 Or. 466, 474 P.2d 1 (1970). The court held that the deviation did not substantially impair the value of the whole contract. Additionally, the court stated that the nonconformity could be cured by an adjustment in the price.

impracticable. When this occurs, the rule of perfect tender no longer holds. According to UCC 2–615(a) and 2A–405(a), delay in delivery or nondelivery in whole or in part is not a breach when performance has been made impracticable "by the occurrence of a contingency the nonoccurrence of which was a basic assumption on which the contract was made." The seller or lessor must, however, notify the buyer or lessee as soon as practicable that there will be a delay or nondelivery.

Foreseeable versus Unforeseeable Contingencies   An increase in cost resulting from inflation does not in and of itself excuse performance, as this kind of risk is ordinarily assumed by a seller or lessor conducting business. The unforeseen contingency must be one that would have been impossible to contemplate in a given business situation. For example, a major oil company that receives its supplies from the Middle East has a contract to supply a buyer with 100,000 gallons of oil. Because of an oil embargo by the Organization of Petroleum Exporting Countries (OPEC), the seller is prevented from securing oil supplies to meet the terms of the contract. Because of the same embargo, the seller cannot secure oil from any other source. This situation comes fully under the commercial-impracticability exception to the perfect tender doctrine.

Can unanticipated increases in a seller's costs, which make performance "impracticable," constitute a valid defense to performance on the basis of commercial impracticability? The court deals with this question in the following case.

CASE 16.1

MAPLE FARMS, INC. v. CITY SCHOOL DISTRICT OF ELMIRA

Supreme Court of New York, 1974.
76 Misc.2d 1080,
352 N.Y.S.2d 784.

HISTORICAL AND ECONOMIC SETTING   *In 1972, the former Soviet Union suffered its worst drought in ten years, forcing it to buy American grain, including 25 percent of the U.S. wheat crop. This led to higher U.S. grain prices, which consequently forced up the prices of other food, including dairy products. In response, U.S. farmers planted more grain. Nevertheless, food prices continued to rise. Consumers organized boycotts in protest. On June 13, 1973, President Richard Nixon ordered a temporary freeze on all retail prices, including those for food. On June 27, Nixon ordered a temporary embargo on soybean exports. The embargo shocked foreign buyers. Although the embargo was lifted after five days, amounts due under previous contracts were cut 40 to 50 percent. Fearing that further controls would be applied, foreign buyers doubled their purchases of U.S. grain. In response, U.S. farmers held back their crops as prices were bid up.*

FACTS   On June 15, 1973, Maple Farms, Inc., formed an agreement with the city school district of Elmira, New York, to supply the school district with milk for the 1973–1974 school year. The agreement was in the form of a requirements contract, under which Maple Farms would sell to the school district all the milk the district required at a fixed price—which was the June market price of milk. By December 1973, the price of raw milk had increased by 23 percent over the price specified in the contract. This meant that if the terms of the contract were fulfilled, Maple Farms would lose $7,350. Because it had similar contracts with other school districts, Maple Farms stood to lose a great deal if it was held to the price stated in the contracts. When the school district would not agree to release Maple Farms from its contract, Maple Farms brought an action in a New York state court for a declaratory judgment (a determination of the parties' rights under a contract). Maple Farms contended that the substantial increase in the price of raw milk was an event not contemplated by the parties when the contract was formed and that, given the increased price, performance of the contract was commercially impracticable.

ISSUE   Can Maple Farms be released from the contract on the ground of commercial impracticability?

DECISION   No. The court ruled that performance in this case was not impracticable.

REASON   The court reasoned that commercial impracticability arises when an event occurs that is totally unexpected and unforeseeable by the parties. The increased price of raw milk was not totally unexpected, given the facts that in the previous year the price of milk had risen 10 percent and that the price of milk had traditionally varied. Additionally, the general inflation of prices in the

Case 16.1—Continued

United States should have been anticipated. Maple Farms had reason to know these facts and could have placed a clause in its contract with the school district to protect itself from its present situation. The court also noted that the primary purpose of the contract, on the part of the school district, was to protect itself (for budgeting purposes) against price fluctuations.

FOR CRITICAL ANALYSIS—Economic Consideration
What would be the result for society if courts routinely allowed parties to avoid their contractual obligations because of steep price increases?

Partial Performance Sometimes the unforeseen event only *partially* affects the capacity of the seller or lessor to perform, and the seller or lessor is thus able to fulfill the contract *partially* but cannot tender total performance. In this event, the seller or lessor is required to allocate in a fair and reasonable manner any remaining production and deliveries among those to whom it is contractually obligated to deliver the goods [UCC 2–615(b), 2A–405(b)]. The buyer or lessee must receive notice of the allocation and has the right to accept or reject the allocation [UCC 2–615(c), 2A–405(c)].

For example, a Florida orange grower, Best Citrus, Inc., contracts to sell this season's production to a number of customers, including Martin's grocery chain. Martin's contracts to purchase two thousand crates of oranges. Best Citrus has sprayed *some* of its orange groves with a chemical called Karmoxin. The Department of Agriculture discovers that persons who eat products sprayed with Karmoxin may develop cancer. The department issues an order prohibiting the sale of these products. Best Citrus picks all of the oranges not sprayed with Karmoxin, but the quantity does not fully meet all the contracted-for deliveries. In this situation, Best Citrus is required to allocate its production, and it notifies Martin's that it cannot deliver the full quantity agreed on in the contract and specifies the amount it will be able to deliver under the circumstances. Martin's can either accept or reject the allocation, but Best Citrus has no further contractual liability.

DESTRUCTION OF IDENTIFIED GOODS The UCC provides that when an unexpected event, such as a fire, totally destroys *goods identified at the time the contract is formed* through no fault of either party and *before risk passes to the buyer or lessee*, the parties

A flood can destroy a farmer's crop. If a contract for a sale of the crop had already been signed, would the farmer be in breach of the contract?

are excused from performance [UCC 2–613, 2A–221]. If the goods are only partially destroyed, however, the buyer or lessee can inspect them and either treat the contract as void or accept the damaged goods with a reduction of the contract price.

Consider an example. Atlas Sporting Equipment agrees to lease to River Bicycles sixty of a particular model of bicycle that has been discontinued. No other bicycles of that model are available. River specifies that it needs the bicycles to rent to tourists. Before Atlas can deliver the bikes, they are destroyed by a fire. In this situation, Atlas is not liable to River for failing to deliver the bikes. The goods were destroyed through no fault of either party, before the risk of loss passed to the lessee. The loss was total, so the contract is avoided. Clearly, Atlas has no obligation to tender the bicycles, and River has no obligation to pay for them.

▌ Obligations of the Buyer or Lessee

Once the seller or lessor has adequately tendered delivery, the buyer or lessee is obligated to accept the goods and pay for them according to the terms of the contract. In the absence of any specific agreements, the buyer or lessee must make payment at the time and place the buyer or lessee *receives* the goods [UCC 2–310(a), 2A–516(1)].

Payment

When a sale is made on credit, the buyer is obliged to pay according to the specified credit terms (for example, 60, 90, or 120 days), *not* when the goods are received. The credit period usually begins on the *date of shipment* [UCC 2–310(d)]. Under a lease contract, a lessee must pay the lease payment specified in the contract [2A–516(1)].

Payment can be made by any means agreed on between the parties—cash or any other method generally acceptable in the commercial world. If the seller demands cash when the buyer offers a check, credit card, or the like, the seller must permit the buyer reasonable time to obtain legal tender [UCC 2–511].

Right of Inspection

Unless otherwise agreed, or for C.O.D. (collect on delivery) transactions, the buyer or lessee has an absolute right to inspect the goods. This right allows the buyer or lessee to verify, before making payment, that the goods tendered or delivered are what were contracted for or ordered. If the goods are not what the buyer or lessee ordered, the buyer or lessee has no duty to pay. An *opportunity for inspection is therefore a condition precedent to the right of the seller or lessor to enforce payment* [UCC 2–513(1), 2A–515(1)].

Unless otherwise agreed, inspection can take place at any reasonable place and time and in any reasonable manner. Generally, what is reasonable is determined by custom of the trade, past practices of the parties, and the like. Costs of inspecting conforming goods are borne by the buyer unless otherwise agreed [UCC 2–513(2)].

C.O.D. SHIPMENTS   If a seller ships goods to a buyer C.O.D. (or under similar terms) and the buyer has not agreed to a C.O.D. shipment in the contract, the buyer can rightfully *reject* the goods. This is because a C.O.D. shipment does not permit inspection before payment, which is a denial of the buyer's right of inspection. When the buyer has agreed to a C.O.D. shipment in the contract, however, or has agreed to pay for the goods upon the presentation of a bill of lading, no right of inspection exists, because it was negated by the agreement [UCC 2–513(3)].

PAYMENT DUE—DOCUMENTS OF TITLE   Under certain contracts, payment is due upon the receipt of the required documents of title even though the goods themselves may not have arrived at their destination. With C.I.F. and C.&F. contracts (see Exhibit 15–4 in Chapter 15), payment is required upon receipt of the documents unless the parties have agreed otherwise. Thus, payment may be required prior to inspection, and payment must be made unless the buyer knows that the goods are nonconforming [UCC 2–310(b), 2–513(3)].

Acceptance

A buyer or lessee can manifest assent to the delivered goods in the following ways, each of which constitutes acceptance:

1. The buyer or lessee can expressly accept the shipment by words or conduct. For example, there is an acceptance if the buyer or lessee, after having had a reasonable opportunity to inspect the goods, signifies agreement to the seller or lessor that the goods are either conforming or are acceptable despite their nonconformity [UCC 2–606(1)(a), 2A–515(1)(a)].
2. Acceptance is presumed if the buyer or lessee has had a reasonable opportunity to inspect the goods and has failed to reject them within a reasonable period of time [UCC 2–606(1)(b), 2–602(1), 2A–515(1)(b)].

Additionally, in sales contracts, the buyer will be deemed to have accepted the goods if he or she performs any act inconsistent with the seller's ownership. For example, any use or resale of the goods generally constitutes an acceptance. Limited use for the sole purpose of testing or inspecting the goods is not an acceptance, however [UCC 2–606(1)(c)].

If some of the goods delivered do not conform to the contract and the seller or lessor has failed to cure, the buyer or lessee can make a *partial* acceptance [UCC 2–601(c), 2A–509(1)]. The same is true if the nonconformity was not reasonably discoverable before acceptance. (In the latter situation, the buyer or lessee may be able to revoke the acceptance, as will be discussed later in this chapter.) A buyer or lessee cannot accept less than a single commercial unit, however. A *commercial unit* is defined by the UCC as a unit of goods that, by commercial usage, is viewed as a "single whole" for purposes of sale, division of which would materially impair the character of the unit, its market value, or its use [UCC 2–105(6), 2A–103(c)]. A commercial unit can be a single article (such as a machine), a set of articles (such as a suite of furniture or an assortment of sizes), a quantity (such as a bale, a gross, or a carload), or any other unit treated in the trade as a single whole.

In the following case, the court considered whether a buyer's actions, in regard to goods shipped to it by the seller, were "inconsistent with the seller's ownership" so as to constitute acceptance under UCC 2–606(1)(c).

CASE 16.2

INDUSTRIA de CALCADOS MARTINI LTDA.[a] v. MAXWELL SHOE CO.
Appeals Court of Massachusetts, 1994.
36 Mass.App.Ct. 268,
630 N.E.2d 299.

HISTORICAL AND SOCIAL SETTING *In the middle of the nineteenth century, New England was the shoe capital of the United States. Except for expensive, custom-made footwear, men's and women's shoes were essentially all the same: black and functional. Near the end of the century, shoemakers in the Midwest began to mass-produce more fashionable dress shoes. The new lines met with instant success. Then, during the 1980s, more casual shoes (tennis shoes, sneakers, and the like), often made out of canvas and other material, became popular. Indeed, sales of all athletic-type footwear soared. Traditional leather-shoe manufacturing*

a. *Ltda.* is an abbreviation for *Limitada*, a business organization form involving limited liability for the owners (see Chapter 24).

(Continued)

Case 16.2—Continued

in the United States saw a concomitant decline. Today, most shoes sold in the United States are manufactured elsewhere.

FACTS　The Maxwell Shoe Company agreed to buy 12,042 pairs of shoes from Industria de Calcados Martini Ltda. (Martini), a Brazilian shoe manufacturer. Maxwell paid part of the price with a check. When the shoes arrived, they were cracked and peeling. Maxwell stopped payment on the check and told Martini that it was rejecting the shoes. Martini did not respond. Two months later, Maxwell shipped the shoes to Maine to have them refinished, sold the refinished shoes, and kept the money. Martini filed a suit in a Massachusetts state court against Maxwell for, among other things, breach of contract. The court held in part that Maxwell had accepted the shoes when it shipped them to Maine to be refinished, "on the grounds that an alteration or repair of a defect in goods is an act inconsistent with the seller's

ownership" under UCC 2–606(1)(c). The court awarded damages to Martini, reduced by the amount that Maxwell had paid for the refinishing. Both parties appealed.

ISSUE　Did Maxwell accept the shoes?

DECISION　Yes. The Appeals Court of Massachusetts affirmed the lower court's decision.

REASON　The court pointed out that "Maxwell received no * * * instructions from Martini" and instead "acted on its own in sending the shoes for refinishing and then selling them and retaining the proceeds for its own benefit." The court concluded, "Accordingly, we do not think the judge's ruling * * * was clearly erroneous."

FOR CRITICAL ANALYSIS—Economic Consideration
What might have been Maxwell's recovery if, instead of refinishing and reselling the shoes, Maxwell had simply sent them back?

∎ Anticipatory Repudiation

What if, before the time for contract performance, one party clearly communicates to the other the intention not to perform? Such an action is a breach of the contract by *anticipatory repudiation*. When anticipatory repudiation occurs, the nonbreaching party has a choice of two responses. He or she can treat the repudiation as a final breach by pursuing a remedy; or he or she can wait, hoping that the repudiating party will decide to honor the obligations required by the contract despite the avowed intention to renege [UCC 2–610, 2A–402]. In either situation, the nonbreaching party may suspend performance.

Should the latter course be pursued, the UCC permits the breaching party (subject to some limitations) to "retract" his or her repudiation. This can be done by any method that clearly indicates an intent to perform. Once retraction is made, the rights of the repudiating party under the contract are reinstated [UCC 2–611, 2A–403].

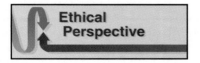
Ethical Perspective

The doctrine of anticipatory repudiation, which arose for both ethical and practical reasons, was first enunciated in an 1853 English case, *Hochster v. De La Tour.*[a] In that case, De La Tour, in April 1852, had agreed to employ Hochster as a courier for three months, beginning June 1. On May 11, De La Tour told Hochster that he would not need a courier after all. On May 22, Hochster sued De La Tour for damages for the breach of contract. De La Tour maintained that Hochster could not sue for damages, as no "breach" could possibly occur before the scheduled time for performance, which was June 1. Hochster would have to stand "ready and willing" to work for De La Tour until June 1 and then sue for breach.

Hochster, however, had been offered a job elsewhere, to begin on May 22, which he could not accept if he had to stand "ready and willing" to work for De La Tour until June 1. In view of these circumstances, the English court allowed Hochster to sue for damages, holding that a nonbreaching party should not have to wait until the time for

a.　2 Ellis and Blackburn Reports 678 (1853).

Ethical Perspective—Continued

performance to sue for breach of the contract. The doctrine of anticipatory repudiation, which has since been incorporated into the UCC, is not only fair to the nonbreaching party but is also efficient—in the sense that the nonbreaching party may not only sue for damages on the breached contract but also look for another contract prior to the time for performance.

For Critical Analysis: *In what way might allowing a nonbreaching party to sue for damages prior to the time for performance be beneficial to the breaching party?*

▌Remedies of the Seller or Lessor

There are numerous remedies available under the UCC to a seller or lessor when the buyer or lessee is in breach. Generally, the remedies available to the seller or lessor depend on the circumstances existing at the time of the breach, such as which party has possession of the goods, whether the goods are in transit, whether the buyer or lessee has rejected or accepted the goods, and so on.

"Life is so terrifyingly dependent on the law."

Karl N. Llewellyn, 1893–1962
(American legal scholar)

When the Goods Are in the Possession of the Seller or Lessor

Under the UCC, if the buyer or lessee breaches the contract before the goods have been delivered to the buyer or lessee, the seller or lessor has the right to pursue the remedies discussed here.

NOTE A buyer or lessee breaches a contract by wrongfully rejecting the goods, revoking acceptance, refusing to pay, or repudiating the contract.

THE RIGHT TO CANCEL THE CONTRACT   One of the options available to a seller or lessor when the buyer or lessee breaches the contract is simply to cancel the contract [UCC 2–703(f), 2A–523(1)(a)]. The seller must notify the buyer or lessee of the cancellation, and at that point all remaining obligations of the seller or lessor are discharged. The buyer or lessee is not discharged from all remaining obligations, however; he or she is in breach, and the seller or lessor can pursue remedies available under the UCC for breach.

THE RIGHT TO WITHHOLD DELIVERY   In general, sellers and lessors can withhold or discontinue performance of their obligations under sales or lease contracts when the buyers or lessees are in breach. If a buyer or lessee has wrongfully rejected or revoked acceptance of contract goods (rejection and revocation of acceptance will be discussed later), failed to make proper and timely payment, or repudiated a part of the contract, the seller or lessor can withhold delivery of the goods in question [UCC 2–703(a), 2A–523(1)(c)]. If the breach results from the buyer's or the lessee's insolvency (inability to pay debts as they become due), the seller or lessor can refuse to deliver the goods unless the buyer or lessee pays in cash [UCC 2–702(1), 2A–525(1)].

THE RIGHT TO RESELL OR DISPOSE OF THE GOODS   When a buyer or lessee breaches or repudiates a sales contract while the seller or lessor is still in possession of the goods, the seller or lessor can resell or dispose of the goods, retaining any profits made as a result of the breach or holding the buyer or lessee liable for any loss [UCC 2–703(d), 2–706(1), 2A–523(1)(e), 2A–527(1)].

When the goods contracted for are unfinished at the time of breach, the seller or lessor can do one of two things: (1) cease manufacturing the goods and resell them for scrap or salvage value or (2) complete the manufacture and resell or dispose of them, holding the buyer or lessee liable for any deficiency. In choosing between these two alternatives, the seller or lessor must exercise reasonable commercial judgment in order to mitigate the loss and obtain maximum value from the unfinished goods

INCIDENTAL DAMAGES
Damages resulting from a breach of contract, including all reasonable expenses incurred because of the breach.

[UCC 2–704(2), 2A–524(2)]. Any resale of the goods must be made in good faith and in a commercially reasonable manner.

In sales transactions, the seller can recover any deficiency between the resale price and the contract price, along with **incidental damages,** defined as those costs to the seller resulting from the breach [UCC 2–706(1), 2–710]. The resale can be private or public, and the goods can be sold as a unit or in parcels. The seller must give the original buyer reasonable notice of the resale, unless the goods are perishable or will rapidly decline in value [UCC 2–706(2), (3)]. A good faith purchaser in a resale takes the goods free of any of the rights of the original buyer, even if the seller fails to comply with these requirements of the UCC [UCC 2–706(5)].

In lease transactions, the lessor may lease the goods to another party and recover from the original lessee, as damages, any unpaid lease payments up to the beginning date of the lease term under the new lease. The lessor can also recover any deficiency between the lease payments due under the original lease contract and under the new lease contract, along with incidental damages [UCC 2A–527(2)].

THE RIGHT TO RECOVER THE PURCHASE PRICE OR LEASE PAYMENTS DUE   Under the UCC, an unpaid seller or lessor can bring an action to recover the purchase price or payments due under the lease contract, plus incidental damages, if the seller or lessor is unable to resell or dispose of the goods [UCC 2–709(1), 2A–529(1)].

For example, suppose that Southern Realty contracts with Gem Point, Inc., to purchase one thousand pens with Southern Realty's name inscribed on them. Gem Point tenders delivery of the one thousand pens, but Southern Realty wrongfully refuses to accept them. In this situation, Gem Point has, as a proper remedy, an action for the purchase price. Gem Point tendered delivery of conforming goods, and Southern Realty, because it failed to accept the goods, is in breach. Gem Point obviously cannot sell to anyone else the pens inscribed with the buyer's business name, so this situation falls under UCC 2–709.

If a seller or lessor sues for the contract price of, or lease payments for, goods that he or she has been unable to resell or dispose of, the goods must be held for the buyer or lessee. The seller or lessor can resell or dispose of the goods at any time prior to collection (of the judgment) from the buyer or lessee, but the net proceeds from the sale must be credited to the buyer or lessee. This is an example of the duty to mitigate damages. In the following case, the court had to determine whether a seller was entitled to recover the purchase price of specially manufactured goods after the buyer had breached the sales contract.

CASE 16.3

ROYAL JONES & ASSOCIATES, INC. v. FIRST THERMAL SYSTEMS, INC.
District Court of Appeal of Florida, 1990.
566 So.2d 853.

HISTORICAL AND TECHNOLOGICAL SETTING
Manufacturing plants in the chemical process industries (CPI) use heat-transfer equipment that in many instances was designed thirty or more years ago. CPI plants need to update their designs and equipment partly because they need to improve energy efficiency. They are reluctant to do so, however, because, for one thing, they are expected *to comply with environmental emission standards that increase energy costs. Also, economic pressures are forcing CPI manufacturers to develop smaller markets. This means that their equipment must be highly specialized. Consequently, the equipment is relatively expensive.*

FACTS   Royal Jones & Associates, Inc., ordered three steel rendering tanks from First Thermal Systems, Inc., for use in its business of constructing rendering plants (factories that process livestock carcasses into hides, fertilizer, and so on). The contract provided that First Thermal would manufacture the tanks according to Royal Jones's specifications for a price of $64,350. When the manufacture of the tanks was completed, Royal Jones refused to accept or pay for the tanks. First Thermal brought an action in a Florida state court for the contract price of the tanks. The trial court, finding that Royal

Case 16.3—Continued

Jones had breached the contract and that the specially manufactured goods were not suitable for sale in the ordinary course of First Thermal's business, awarded First Thermal the full contract price as damages. Royal Jones appealed.

ISSUE Is First Thermal entitled to the full contract price as damages?

DECISION Yes. The Florida appellate court affirmed the trial court's judgment.

REASON The appellate court held that First Thermal was entitled to the full contract price of the specially manufactured tanks as damages because the evidence showed that efforts to resell the tanks would be useless.

The court pointed to evidence that the rendering tanks "were the only ones First Thermal ever made, the tanks were manufactured according to Royal Jones's specifications, [and] First Thermal had no other customers to which it could resell the tanks[.]" Furthermore, First Thermal did not know how to market the tanks for resale, and the "tanks were built without needed internal components and to a special size" and "could not be used as rendering tanks without special engineering to which First Thermal had no access." The court also noted that the scrap value of the tanks to First Thermal was only about $700.

FOR CRITICAL ANALYSIS—Social Consideration
What factors must a court consider when determining whether to allow a seller to recover the purchase price for specially manufactured goods?

THE RIGHT TO RECOVER DAMAGES If a buyer or lessee repudiates a contract or wrongfully refuses to accept the goods, a seller or lessor can maintain an action to recover the damages that were sustained. Ordinarily, the amount of damages equals the difference between the contract price or lease payments and the market price or lease payments (at the time and place of tender of the goods), plus incidental damages [UCC 2–708(1), 2A–528(1)]. The time and place of tender are frequently given by such terms as F.O.B., F.A.S., C.I.F., and the like, which determine whether there is a shipment or destination contract.

If the difference between the contract price or payments due under the lease contract and the market price or payments due under a new lease contract is too small to place the seller or lessor in the position that he or she would have been in if the buyer or lessee had fully performed, the proper measure of damages is the lost profits of the seller or lessor, including a reasonable allowance for overhead and other expenses [UCC 2–708(2), 2A–528(2)].

When the Goods Are in Transit

If the seller or lessor has delivered the goods to a carrier or a bailee but the buyer or lessee has not as yet received them, the goods are said to be *in transit*. If, while the goods are in transit, the seller or lessor learns that the buyer or lessee is insolvent, the seller or lessor can stop the carrier or bailee from delivering the goods, regardless of the quantity of goods shipped. If the buyer or lessee is in breach but is not insolvent, the seller or lessor can stop the goods in transit only if the quantity shipped is at least a carload, a truckload, a planeload, or a larger shipment [UCC 2–705(1), 2A–526(1)].

To stop delivery, the seller or lessor must *timely notify* the carrier or other bailee that the goods are to be returned or held for the seller or lessor. If the carrier has sufficient time to stop delivery, the goods must be held and delivered according to the instructions of the seller or lessor, who is liable to the carrier for any additional costs incurred [UCC 2–705(3), 2A–526(3)].

UCC 2–705(2) and 2A–526(2) provide that the right of the seller or lessor to stop delivery of goods in transit is lost when any of the following events occur:

1. The buyer or lessee obtains possession of the goods.

2. The carrier acknowledges the rights of the buyer or lessee by reshipping or storing the goods for the buyer or lessee.

3. A bailee of the goods other than a carrier acknowledges that he or she is holding the goods for the buyer or lessee.

Additionally, in sales transactions, the seller loses the right to stop delivery of goods in transit when a negotiable document of title covering the goods has been negotiated (properly transferred, giving the buyer ownership rights in the goods) to the buyer [UCC 2–705(2)].

Once the seller or lessor reclaims the goods in transit, he or she can pursue the remedies allowed to sellers and lessors when the goods are in their possession. In other words, the seller or lessor who has reclaimed goods may do the following:

1. Cancel the contract.

2. Resell the goods and recover any deficiency.

3. Sue for any deficiency between the contract price (or lease payments due) and the market price (or market lease payments).

4. Sue to recover the purchase price or lease payments due if the goods cannot be resold.

When the Goods Are in the Possession of the Buyer or Lessee

When the buyer or lessee breaches a sales or lease contract and the goods are in the buyer's or lessee's possession, the UCC gives the seller or lessor the right to choose among various remedies.

THE RIGHT TO RECOVER THE PURCHASE PRICE OR PAYMENTS DUE UNDER THE LEASE CONTRACT If the buyer or lessee has accepted the goods but refuses to pay for them, the seller or lessor can sue for the purchase price of the goods or for the lease payments due, plus incidental damages [UCC 2–709(1), 2A–529(1)].

RECALL Incidental damages include all reasonable expenses incurred because of a breach of contract.

THE RIGHT TO RECLAIM THE GOODS In regard to sales contracts, if a seller discovers that the buyer has received goods on credit and is insolvent, the seller can demand return of the goods, if the demand is made within ten days of the buyer's receipt of the goods. The seller can demand and reclaim the goods at any time if the buyer misrepresented his or her solvency in writing within three months prior to the delivery of the goods [UCC 2–702(2)]. The seller's right to reclaim the goods, however, is subject to the rights of a good faith purchaser or other buyer in the ordinary course of business who purchases the goods from the buyer before the seller reclaims.

Under the UCC, a seller seeking to exercise the right to reclaim goods receives preferential treatment over the buyer's other creditors—the seller need only demand the return of the goods within ten days after the buyer has received them.[3] Because of this preferential treatment, the UCC provides that reclamation *bars* the seller from pursuing any other remedy as to these goods [UCC 2–702(3)].

In regard to lease contracts, if the lessee is in default (fails to make payments that are due, for example), the lessor may reclaim the leased goods that are in the possession of the lessee [UCC 2A–525(2)].

---

3. A seller who has delivered goods to an insolvent buyer also receives preferential treatment if the buyer enters into bankruptcy proceedings (discussed in Chapter 22).

❚ Remedies of the Buyer or Lessee

Under the UCC, there are numerous remedies available to the buyer or lessee when the seller or lessor breaches the contract. As with the remedies available to sellers and lessors, the remedies of buyers and lessees depend on the circumstances existing at the time of the breach.

NOTE A seller or lessor breaches a contract by wrongfully failing to deliver the goods, delivering nonconforming goods, making an improper tender of the goods, or repudiating the contract.

When the Seller or Lessor Refuses to Deliver the Goods

If the seller or lessor refuses to deliver the goods to the buyer or lessee, the remedies available to the buyer or lessee include those discussed here.

THE RIGHT TO CANCEL THE CONTRACT   When a seller or lessor fails to make proper delivery or repudiates the contract, the buyer or lessee can cancel, or rescind, the contract. Upon notice of cancellation, the buyer or lessee is relieved of any further obligations under the contract but retains all rights to other remedies against the seller [UCC 2–711(1), 2A–508(1)(a)].

THE RIGHT TO RECOVER THE GOODS   If a buyer or lessee has made a partial or full payment for goods that remain in the possession of the seller or lessor, the buyer or lessee can recover the goods if the seller or lessor becomes insolvent within ten days after receiving the first payment and if the goods are identified to the contract. To exercise this right, the buyer or lessee must tender to the seller any unpaid balance of the purchase price [UCC 2–502, 2A–522].

THE RIGHT TO OBTAIN SPECIFIC PERFORMANCE   A buyer or lessee can obtain specific performance when the goods are unique and when the remedy at law is inadequate [UCC 2–716(1), 2A–521(1)]. Ordinarily, a suit for money damages is sufficient to place a buyer or lessee in the position he or she would have occupied if the seller or lessor had fully performed. When the contract is for the purchase of a particular work of art or a similarly unique item, however, money damages may not be sufficient. Under these circumstances, equity will require that the seller or lessor perform exactly by delivering the particular goods identified to the contract (a remedy of specific performance).

THE RIGHT OF COVER   In certain situations, buyers and lessees can protect themselves by obtaining **cover**—that is, by substituting goods for those that were due under the sales contract. This option is available when the seller or lessor repudiates the contract or fails to deliver the goods. (The right to obtain cover is also available to a buyer or lessee who has rightfully rejected goods or revoked acceptance.)

In obtaining cover, the buyer or lessee must act in good faith and without unreasonable delay [UCC 2–712, 2A–518]. After purchasing or leasing substitute goods, the buyer or lessee can recover from the seller or lessor the difference between the cost of cover and the contract price (or lease payments), plus incidental and consequential damages, less the expenses (such as delivery costs) that were saved as a result of the breach [UCC 2–712, 2–715, 2A–518]. Consequential damages are any losses suffered by the buyer or lessee that the seller or lessor could have foreseen (had reason to know about) at the time of contract and any injury to the buyer's or lessee's person or property proximately resulting from the contract's breach [UCC 2–715(2), 2A–520(2)].

Buyers and lessees are not required to cover, and failure to do so will not bar them from using any other remedies available under the UCC. A buyer or lessee who fails to cover, however, may *not* be able to collect consequential damages that could have been avoided had he or she purchased or leased substitute goods.

If, by obtaining cover and reselling the substitute goods, a buyer is able to recoup all or most of his or her loss from a source other than the breaching party, should the

COVER
Under the UCC, a remedy of the buyer that allows the buyer or lessee, on the seller's or lessor's breach, to purchase the goods from another seller or lessor and substitute them for the goods due under the contract. If the cost of cover exceeds the cost of the contract goods, the breaching seller or lessor will be liable to the buyer or lessee for the difference. In obtaining cover, the buyer or lessee must act in good faith and without unreasonable delay.

buyer's recovery under UCC 2–712 be reduced? That was the issue confronting the court in the following case.

CASE 16.4

KGM HARVESTING CO. v. FRESH NETWORK

California Court of Appeal,
Sixth District, 1995.
36 Cal.App.4th 376,
42 Cal.Rptr.2d 286.

HISTORICAL AND ECONOMIC SETTING   *After 1950, the United States experienced an unprecedented economic boom in car sales, an increase in highway building, and a movement to the suburbs. With the growth of suburbs came a new type of restaurant—the fast-food restaurant, such as McDonald's. Attracted by the efficiency of the early McDonald's restaurants, Ray Kroc bought the small chain in 1954. Over the next thirty years, Kroc built McDonald's into an international, corporate giant. Business associates who worked with Kroc from the beginning became rich.*

FACTS   McDonald's buys its lettuce from the KGM Harvesting Company, which also sells lettuce to other companies. For example, in 1988, KGM also agreed to deliver fourteen loads of lettuce each week to Fresh Network. Fresh Network then sold the lettuce to the Castellini Company, which in turn sold it to Club Chef. Club Chef then chopped and shredded it for Burger King, Taco Bell, and Pizza Hut. In the spring of 1991, the market price of lettuce rose dramatically. KGM chose to sell only to McDonald's and some of its other customers rather than to deliver to Fresh Network the usual fourteen loads at the contract price. Consequently, to fulfill its obligation to Castellini, Fresh Network bought lettuce on the open market at a higher price. Castellini agreed to pay the difference, which it charged to its customer, Club Chef, which in turn passed the higher price on to its cus-

tomers. In an attempt to recover the extra amount it had to pay for lettuce, Fresh Network refused to pay KGM for previous shipments. KGM filed a suit in a California state court for the balance due. Fresh Network responded with a demand for damages. The court awarded Fresh Network an amount equal to the difference between the contract price and the price it had paid for the substitute lettuce, minus the amount that it owed KGM. KGM appealed, arguing that the court should have taken into consideration the fact that Fresh Network had passed on most of its loss to Castellini.

ISSUE   In assessing a buyer's recovery under the UCC's cover provision, should all of the events affecting the buyer's ultimate profit or loss be taken into consideration?

DECISION   No. The California Court of Appeal affirmed the lower court's award.

REASON   The court pointed out that "the object of contract damages is to give the aggrieved party as nearly as possible the equivalent of the benefits of performance." The court explained that buying replacement lettuce did not put Fresh Network in "as good a position as if the other party had fully performed," because Fresh Network paid more than the contract price for the replacement lettuce. Only when Fresh Network was reimbursed for the additional cost could it "truly receive the benefit of the bargain." This, the court held, is the measure of damages set forth in UCC 2–712. "What the buyer chooses to do with that bargain is not relevant."

FOR CRITICAL ANALYSIS—Economic Consideration
Is it fair for Fresh Network to, in essence, recover twice—once from KGM and once from Castellini?

REPLEVIN
An action to recover specific goods in the hands of a party who is wrongfully withholding them from the other party.

THE RIGHT TO REPLEVY GOODS   Buyers and lessees also have the right to replevy goods. **Replevin**[4] is an action to recover specific goods in the hands of a party who is wrongfully withholding them from the other party. Outside the UCC, the term *replevin* refers to a prejudgment process (a proceeding that takes place prior to a court's judgment) that permits the seizure of specific personal property in which a party

---

4.   Pronounced ruh-*pleh*-vun.

claims a right or an interest. Under the UCC, the buyer or lessee can replevy goods subject to the contract if the seller or lessor has repudiated or breached the contract. To maintain an action to replevy goods, buyers and lessees must usually show that they are unable to cover for the goods after a reasonable effort [UCC 2–716(3), 2A–521(3)].

THE RIGHT TO RECOVER DAMAGES   If a seller or lessor repudiates the sales contract or fails to deliver the goods, the buyer or lessee can sue for damages. The measure of recovery is the difference between the contract price (or lease payments) and the market price of (or lease payments that could be obtained for) the goods at the time the buyer (or lessee) *learned* of the breach. The market price or market lease payments are determined at the place where the seller or lessor was supposed to deliver the goods. The buyer or lessee can also recover incidental and consequential damages less the expenses that were saved as a result of the breach [UCC 2–713, 2A–519].

> RECALL Consequential damages compensate for a loss (such as lost profits) that is not direct but that is reasonably foreseeable at the time of the breach.

Consider an example. Schilling orders ten thousand bushels of wheat from Valdone for $5 a bushel, with delivery due on June 14 and payment due on June 20. Valdone does not deliver on June 14. On June 14, the market price of wheat is $5.50 per bushel. Schilling chooses to do without the wheat. He sues Valdone for damages for nondelivery. Schilling can recover $0.50 × 10,000, or $5,000, plus any expenses the breach may have caused him. The measure of damages is the market price less the contract price on the day Schilling was to have received delivery. (Any expenses Schilling saved by the breach would be deducted from the damages.)

When the Seller or Lessor Delivers Nonconforming Goods

When the seller or lessor delivers nonconforming goods, the buyer or lessee has several remedies available under the UCC.

THE RIGHT TO REJECT THE GOODS   If either the goods or the tender of the goods by the seller or lessor fails to conform to the contract *in any respect*, the buyer or lessee can reject the goods. If some of the goods conform to the contract, the buyer or lessee can keep the conforming goods and reject the rest [UCC 2–601, 2A–509]. If the buyer or lessee rejects the goods, he or she may then obtain cover, cancel the contract, or sue for damages for breach of contract, just as if the seller or lessor had refused to deliver the goods (see the earlier discussion of these remedies).

Timeliness and Reason for Rejection Required   The buyer or lessee must reject the goods within a reasonable amount of time, and the seller or lessor must be notified seasonably—that is, in a timely fashion or at the proper time [UCC 2–602(1), 2A–509(2)]. Furthermore, the buyer or lessee must designate defects that would have been apparent to the seller or lessor on reasonable inspection. Failure to do so precludes the buyer or lessee from using such defects to justify rejection or to establish breach when the seller could have cured the defects if they had been stated seasonally [UCC 2–605, 2A–514].

Duties of Merchant Buyers and Lessees When Goods Are Rejected   If a *merchant buyer or lessee* rightfully rejects goods, and the seller or lessor has no agent or business at the place of rejection, the buyer or lessee is required to follow any reasonable instructions received from the seller or lessor with respect to the goods controlled by the buyer or lessee. The buyer or lessee is entitled to reimbursement for the care and cost entailed in following the instructions [UCC 2–603, 2A–511]. The same requirements hold if the buyer or lessee rightfully revokes his or her acceptance of the goods at some later time [UCC 2–608(3), 2A–517(5)]. (Revocation of acceptance will be discussed shortly.)

If no instructions are forthcoming and the goods are perishable or threaten to decline in value quickly, the buyer or lessee can resell the goods in good faith, taking the appropriate reimbursement from the proceeds [UCC 2–603(1), 2A–511(1)]. If the goods are not perishable, the buyer or lessee may store them for the seller or lessor or reship them to the seller or lessor [UCC 2–604, 2A–512].

Buyers who rightfully reject goods that remain in their possession or control have a *security interest* in the goods (basically, a legal claim to the goods to the extent necessary to recover expenses, costs, and the like—see Chapter 21). The security interest encompasses any payments the buyer has made for the goods, as well as any expenses incurred with regard to inspection, receipt, transportation, care, and custody of the goods [UCC 2–711(3)]. A buyer with a security interest in the goods is a "person in the position of a seller." This gives the buyer the same rights as an unpaid seller. Thus, the buyer can resell, withhold delivery of, or stop delivery of the goods. A buyer who chooses to resell must account to the seller for any amounts received in excess of the security interest [UCC 2–711, 2–706(6)].

REVOCATION OF ACCEPTANCE Acceptance of the goods precludes the buyer or lessee from exercising the right of rejection, but it does not necessarily preclude the buyer or lessee from pursuing other remedies. In certain circumstances, a buyer or lessee is permitted to *revoke* his or her acceptance of the goods. Acceptance of a lot or a commercial unit can be revoked if the nonconformity *substantially* impairs the value of the lot or unit and if one of the following factors is present:

1. If acceptance was predicated on the reasonable assumption that the nonconformity would be cured, and it has not been cured within a reasonable period of time [UCC 2–608(1)(a), 2A–517(1)(a)].
2. If the buyer or lessee did not discover the nonconformity before acceptance, either because it was difficult to discover before acceptance or because assurances made by the seller or lessor that the goods were conforming kept the buyer or lessee from inspecting the goods [UCC 2–608(1)(b), 2A–517(1)(b)].

Revocation of acceptance is not effective until notice is given to the seller or lessor, which must occur within a reasonable time after the buyer or lessee either discovers *or should have discovered* the grounds for revocation. Additionally, revocation must occur before the goods have undergone any substantial change (such as spoilage) not caused by their own defects [UCC 2–608(2), 2A–517(4)]. (See this chapter's *Business Law in Action* for a further discussion of revocation of acceptance.)

International Perspective

Under the UCC, a buyer or lessee who has accepted goods may be able to revoke acceptance in the circumstances just mentioned. Provisions of the United Nations Convention on Contracts for the International Sale of Goods (CISG) similarly allow buyers to rescind their contracts after they have accepted the goods. The CISG, however, takes a somewhat different—and more direct—approach to the problem than the UCC does. Circumstances that would permit a buyer to revoke acceptance under the UCC would, under the CISG, allow the buyer simply to declare that the seller has *fundamentally* breached the contract. Article 25 of the CISG states that a "breach of contract committed by one of the parties is fundamental if it results in such detriment to the other party as substantially to deprive him of what he is entitled to expect under the contract."

For Critical Analysis: *What is the essential difference between revocation of acceptance and bringing a suit for breach of contract?*

BUSINESS LAW IN ACTION

Can a Buyer Revoke Acceptance and Continue to Use the Goods?

In certain situations, courts permit buyers to revoke their acceptance. This exceptional remedy will only be allowed, however, if the requirements specified by UCC 2–608 are met. These requirements are fashioned broadly, thus leaving many questions for the courts to decide on a case-by-case basis.

One question largely unanswered by the UCC—and a question that the courts must decide—is the following: Can a buyer, after notifying the seller of his or her revocation of acceptance, continue to use the goods? This question came before the Supreme Judicial Court of Massachusetts (that state's highest court) in *Liarikos v. Mello.*[a] The court's analysis of the

issue sheds some light on how courts generally approach this question.

The facts of the case were as follows: In 1988, Kathleen Liarikos purchased a 1984 Jaguar XJS from Pine Grove Auto Sales, in part because of the low mileage on the vehicle. Over the next year or so, she experienced various mechanical problems. In 1990, after discovering that Pine Grove had turned back the odometer on the car prior to selling it to her, she notified Pine Grove that she was revoking her acceptance. Pine Grove never responded to her notice, and eventually she brought a court action against Pine Grove. In the meantime, she continued to use the vehicle, which she needed for her business.

One of the issues before the court was whether Liarikos's continued use of the car following her revocation invalidated the revocation. The trial court held that Liarikos's use of the car after revocation was reasonable and that the revocation was valid. On appeal, the state supreme court noted that the courts are divided on this issue. Some courts hold that the continued use of an automobile after a revocation of acceptance operates as a second, or continuing, acceptance,

"thereby invalidating the revocation." Other courts, however, hold that a general rule prohibiting a buyer from continuing to use the goods after revocation is inconsistent with the UCC's rule of reasonableness. These courts emphasize that, as a practical matter, a person who buys an automobile "may very well be unable, without extraordinary financial difficulty," to return the car on revocation and do without it until the dispute is settled.

The Massachusetts court agreed with the latter view, holding that "[t]he continued reasonable use of an automobile should not as a matter of law prevent the buyer from revoking acceptance." What constituted "reasonable use" was a question of fact for the jury. In this case, the trial court jury had found that Liarikos's use of the car was reasonable, and the state's highest court saw no reason not to affirm that decision.

For Critical Analysis: *Can you think of other types of personal property that a court might reasonably allow a person to continue to use after revocation of acceptance?*

a.   418 Mass. 669, 639 N.E.2d 716 (1994).

THE RIGHT TO RECOVER DAMAGES FOR ACCEPTED GOODS   A buyer or lessee who has accepted nonconforming goods may also keep the goods and recover damages caused by the breach. The buyer or lessee, however, must *notify* the seller or lessor of the breach within a reasonable time after the defect was or should have been discovered. Failure of the buyer or lessee to give notice of the defects (breach) to the seller or lessor bars the buyer or lessee from pursuing any remedy to recover damages. [UCC 2–607(3), 2A–516(3)]. In addition, the parties to a sales or lease contract can insert a provision requiring that the buyer or lessee give notice of any defects in the goods within a prescribed period.

When the goods delivered are not as promised, the measure of damages equals the difference between the value of the goods as accepted and their value if they had been delivered as promised [UCC 2–714(2), 2A–519(4)]. For this and other types of breaches in which the buyer or lessee has accepted the goods, the buyer or lessee is entitled to recover for any loss "resulting in the ordinary course of events . . . as determined in any manner which is reasonable" [UCC 2–714(1), 2A–519(3)]. The UCC also permits the buyer or lessee, with proper notice to the seller or lessor, to deduct all or any part of the damages from the price or lease payments still due and payable to the seller or lessor [UCC 2–717, 2A–516(1)].

International Perspective

The United Nations Convention on Contracts for the International Sale of Goods (CISG), like the UCC, establishes notice requirements for international sales transactions. In other words, before a buyer can recover damages for defective goods, the buyer must notify the seller that the goods are defective within a reasonable time. The CISG's notice requirements are not as strict as those imposed by the UCC, however. The CISG requires notice by the buyer only when the seller is reasonably unaware that the goods that were shipped did not conform to the contract. Thus, the lack of prompt notice of nonconformity need not necessarily defeat a buyer's claim.

For Critical Analysis: *What purpose is served by the UCC's requirement that, to be entitled to recover damages or pursue other remedies, the buyer must notify the seller of the breach within a reasonable time—even if the seller knew that the goods were nonconforming?*

▌Statute of Limitations

An action for breach of contract under the UCC must be commenced *within four years after the cause of action accrues*—that is, within four years after the breach occurs. In addition to filing suit within the four-year period, an aggrieved party who has accepted nonconforming goods usually must notify the breaching party of the breach within a reasonable time, or the buyer or lessee is barred from pursuing any remedy [UCC 2–607(3)(a), 2A–516(3)]. By agreement in the contract, the parties can reduce this period to not less than one year but *cannot* extend it beyond four years [UCC 2–725(1), 2A–506(1)]. A cause of action accrues for breach of warranty when the seller or lessor *tenders* delivery. This is the rule even if the aggrieved party is unaware that the cause of action has accrued [UCC 2–725(2), 2A–506(2)].

▌Limitation of Remedies

The parties to a sales or lease contract can vary their respective rights and obligations by contractual agreement. For example, a seller and buyer can expressly provide for remedies in addition to those provided in the UCC. They can also provide remedies in lieu of those provided in the UCC, or they can change the measure of damages. The seller can provide that the buyer's only remedy upon breach of warranty will be repair or replacement of the item, or the seller can limit the buyer's remedy to return of the goods and refund of the purchase price. In sales and lease contracts, an agreed-on remedy is in addition to those provided in the UCC unless the parties expressly agree that the remedy is exclusive of all others [UCC 2–719(1), 2A–503(1)].

If the parties state that a remedy is exclusive, then it is the sole remedy. When circumstances cause an exclusive remedy to fail in its essential purpose, however, it is no longer exclusive [UCC 2–719(2), 2A–503(2)]. For example, a sales contract that limits the buyer's remedy to repair or replacement fails in its essential purpose if the item cannot be repaired and no replacements are available.

A contract can limit or exclude consequential damages, provided the limitation is not unconscionable. When the buyer or lessee is a consumer, the limitation of consequential damages for personal injuries resulting from nonconforming goods is *prima facie* (on its face) unconscionable. The limitation of consequential damages is not necessarily unconscionable when the loss is commercial in nature—for example, lost profits and property damage [UCC 2–719(3), 2A–503(3)]. In the following case, the court had to decide whether a contract clause that excluded liability for consequential damages was unconscionable.

CASE 16.5

TRANSPORT CORP. OF AMERICA, INC. v. INTERNATIONAL BUSINESS MACHINES CORP.

United States Court of Appeals,
Eighth Circuit, 1994.
30 F.3d 953.

COMPANY PROFILE *Transport Corporation of America, Inc. (TCA), provides a wide range of services to its customers, which include Ford Motor Company, General Mills, 3M Company, and Sears, Roebuck & Company. From ten regional centers, with a fleet of more than 1,100 tractors and 2,600 trailers, TCA provides temperature-controlled trailers, multistop loading and unloading, and time-definite pickup and delivery. In 1994, at a cost of more than $1.5 million, TCA began to develop a more sophisticated computer information system. The system was to combine operational data, through satellite communications, with information such as maintenance, billing, and accounting.*

FACTS Innovative Computing Corporation (ICC) sold an International Business Machines Corporation (IBM) computer to TCA. As part of the deal, TCA expressly agreed to a disclaimer that stated, in part, "IN NO EVENT SHALL ICC BE LIABLE FOR ANY * * * CONSEQUENTIAL DAMAGES * * * IN CONNECTION WITH * * * THIS AGREEMENT." One year later, the computer failed. The downtime was nearly thirty-four hours. TCA spent more than $4,500 to replace lost data and purportedly lost nearly $470,000 in income while the computer was down. TCA filed a suit in a Minnesota state court against IBM and ICC, alleging, among other things, breach of warranty. The case was moved to a federal district court, and IBM and ICC filed a motion for summary judgment. The court granted the motion, based in part on the disclaimer. TCA appealed, arguing in part that the disclaimer was unconscionable.

ISSUE Was the disclaimer of consequential damages unconscionable?

DECISION No. The U.S. Court of Appeals for the Eighth Circuit affirmed the lower court's decision.

REASON The court explained that "[t]he U.C.C. encourages negotiated agreements in commercial transactions * * *. It is at the time of contract formation that experienced parties define the product, identify the risks, and negotiate a price of the goods that reflects the relative benefits and risks to each. An exclusion of consequential damages set forth in advance in a commercial agreement between experienced business parties represents a bargained-for allocation of risk that is conscionable." The court concluded that "the damages claimed by TCA, for business interruption losses and replacement media, were consequential damages," but that "TCA and ICC were sophisticated business entities of relatively equal bargaining power." Thus "ICC's disclaimer was not unconscionable and TCA is * * * precluded from recovering consequential damages."

FOR CRITICAL ANALYSIS—Social Consideration
Why is a limitation on consequential damages considered unconscionable when one of the parties is a consumer but not when both parties are business entities?

Application

Law and the Seller or Buyer—Breach of Contract*

A contract for the sale of goods has been breached. Can such a breach be settled without a trip to court? The answer depends on the willingness of the parties to agree on an appropriate remedy. First, the parties by contract may already have agreed on the remedy applicable in the event of a

*This *Application* is not meant to substitute for the services of an attorney who is licensed to practice law in your state.

breach. This may take the form of a contract provision restricting or expanding remedies provided for under the Uniform Commercial Code [UCC 2–719].

Consider an example. When defective goods are delivered and accepted, usually it is preferable for the buyer and seller to reach an agreement on a reduced purchase price. Practically speaking, the buyer may be unable to obtain a partial refund from the seller. UCC 2–717 allows the buyer in such circumstances to give notice of the intention to deduct the damages from any part of the purchase price not yet paid. If you are a buyer who has accepted defective goods and has not yet paid in full, it may be appropriate for you to exercise your rights

(Continued)

Application—Continued

under UCC 2–717 and not pay in full when you make your final payment.

If there is nothing in your agreement to cover a breach of contract and you are the nonbreaching party, the UCC gives you a variety of alternatives. What you need to do is analyze the remedies that would be available if you were to go to court, put these remedies in order of priority, and then predict how successful you might be in pursuing each remedy. Next, look at the position of the breaching party to determine the basis for negotiating a settlement, including whether it is actually worth your trouble to go to court. Remember that most breaches of contract do not end up in court—they are settled beforehand.

✓ **Checklist for the Nonbreaching Party to a Contract**

1. Ascertain what remedy is explicitly written into your contract. Use that remedy, if possible, to avoid litigation.
2. If no specific remedy is available, look to the UCC.
3. Assess how successful you might be in pursuing a remedy if you went to court.
4. Analyze the position of the breaching party.
5. Determine whether a negotiated settlement is preferable to a lawsuit, which is best done by consulting your attorney.

▌ Key Terms

cover 405   incidental damages 402   installment contract 395   replevin 406

▌ Chapter Summary: Performance and Breach of Sales and Lease Contracts

PERFORMANCE OBLIGATIONS	
Obligations of the Seller or Lessor *(See pages 392–398.)*	1. The seller or lessor must tender *conforming* goods to the buyer. Tender must take place at a *reasonable hour* and in a *reasonable manner*. Under the perfect tender doctrine, the seller or lessor must tender goods that exactly conform to the terms of the contract [UCC 2–503(1), 2A–508(1)].
	2. If the seller or lessor tenders nonconforming goods and the buyer or lessee rejects them, the seller or lessor may *cure* (repair or replace the goods) within the contract time for performance [UCC 2–508(1), 2A–513(1)]. If the seller or lessor has reasonable grounds to believe the buyer or lessee would accept the goods, on the buyer's or lessee's rejection, the seller or lessor has a reasonable time to substitute conforming goods without liability [UCC 2–508(2), 2A–513(2)].
	3. If the agreed-on means of delivery becomes impracticable or unavailable, the seller must substitute a reasonable alternative means (such as a different carrier) if one is available [UCC 2–614(1)].
	4. If a seller or lessor tenders nonconforming goods in any one installment under an installment contract, the buyer or lessee may reject the installment only if its value is substantially impaired and cannot be cured. The entire installment contract is breached when one or more installments *substantially* impair the value of the *whole* contract [UCC 2–612, 2A–510].
	5. When performance becomes commercially impracticable owing to circumstances unforeseen when the contract was formed, the perfect tender rule no longer holds [UCC 2–615, 2A–405].
Obligations of the Buyer or Lessee *(See pages 398–400.)*	1. Upon tender of delivery by the seller, the buyer or lessee must pay for the goods at the time and place the buyer or lessee *receives* the goods, even if the place of shipment is the place of delivery, unless the sale is made on credit. Payment may be made by any method generally acceptable in the commercial world [UCC 2–310, 2–511]. In lease contracts, the lessee must pay lease payments in accordance with the contract [UCC 2A–516(1)].
	2. Unless otherwise agreed, the buyer or lessee has an absolute right to inspect the goods before acceptance [UCC 2–513(1), 2A–515(1)].
	3. The buyer or lessee can manifest acceptance of delivered goods expressly in words or by conduct, or by failing to reject the goods after a reasonable period of time following inspection or after

▌Chapter Summary: Performance and Breach—Continued

Obligations of the Buyer or Lessee—Continued	having had a reasonable opportunity to inspect them [UCC 2–606(1), 2A–515(1)]. A buyer will be deemed to have accepted goods if he or she performs any act inconsistent with the seller's ownership [UCC 2–606(1)(c)].
	
	4. Following the acceptance of delivered goods, the buyer or lessee may revoke acceptance only if the nonconformity *substantially* impairs the value of the unit or lot and if one of the following factors is present:
	  a. Acceptance was predicated on the reasonable assumption that the nonconformity would be cured and it was not cured within a reasonable time [UCC 2–608(1)(a), 2A–517(1)(a)].
	  b. The buyer or lessee did not discover the nonconformity before acceptance, either because it was difficult to discover before acceptance or because the seller's or lessor's assurance that the goods were conforming kept the buyer or lessee from inspecting the goods [UCC 2–608(1)(b), 2A–517(1)(b)].

Anticipatory Repudiation *(See pages 400–401.)*	If, before the time for performance, either party clearly indicates to the other an intention not to perform, under UCC 2–610 and 2A–402 the aggrieved party may do the following: 1. Await performance by the repudiating party for a commercially reasonable time. 2. Resort to any remedy for breach. 3. In either situation, suspend performance.
REMEDIES FOR BREACH OF CONTRACT	

Remedies of the Seller or Lessor *(See pages 401–404.)*	1. *When the goods are in the possession of the seller or lessor*—The seller or lessor may do the following:
	  a. Cancel the contract [UCC 2–703(f), 2A–523(1)(a)].
	  b. Withhold delivery [UCC 2–703(a), 2A–523(1)(c)].
	  c. Resell or dispose of the goods [UCC 2–703(d), 2–706(1), 2A–523(1)(e), 2A–527(1)].
	  d. Sue to recover the purchase price or lease payments due [UCC 2–709(1), 2A–529(1)].
	  e. Sue to recover damages [UCC 2–708, 2A–528].
	
	2. *When the goods are in transit*—The seller may stop the carrier or bailee from delivering the goods [UCC 2–705, 2A–526].
	
	3. *When the goods are in the possession of the buyer or lessee*—The seller or lessor may do the following:
	  a. Sue to recover the purchase price or lease payments due [UCC 2–709(1), 2A–529(1)].
	  b. Reclaim the goods. A seller may reclaim goods received by an insolvent buyer if the demand is made within ten days of receipt (excludes all other remedies on reclamation) [UCC 2–702]; a lessor may repossess goods if the lessee is in default [UCC 2A–525(2)].

Remedies of the Buyer or Lessee *(See pages 405–410.)*	1. *When the seller or lessor refuses to deliver the goods*—The buyer or lessee may do the following:
	  a. Cancel the contract [UCC 2–711(1), 2A–508(1)(a)].
	  b. Recover the goods if the seller or lessor becomes insolvent within ten days after receiving the first payment and the goods are identified to the contract [UCC 2–502, 2A–522].
	  c. Obtain specific performance (when the goods are unique or when the remedy at law is inadequate) [UCC 2–716(1), 2A–521(1)].
	  d. Obtain cover [UCC 2–712, 2A–518].
	  e. Replevy the goods (if cover is unavailable) [UCC 2–716(3), 2A–521(3)].
	  f. Sue to recover damages [UCC 2–713, 2A–519].
	
	2. *When the seller or lessor delivers nonconforming goods*—The buyer or lessee may do the following:
	  a. Reject the goods [UCC 2–601, 2A–509].
	  b. Revoke acceptance (in certain circumstances) [UCC 2–608, 2A–517].
	  c. Sue to recover damages [UCC 2–607, 2–714, 2A–519].

Statute of Limitations *(See page 410.)*	The UCC has a four-year statute of limitations for actions involving breach of contract. By agreement, the parties to a sales or lease contract can reduce this period to not less than one year, but they cannot extend it beyond four years [UCC 2–725(1), 2A–506(1)].
Limitation of Remedies *(See pages 410–411.)*	Remedies may be limited in sales or lease contracts by agreement of the parties. If the contract states that a remedy is exclusive, then that is the sole remedy—unless the remedy fails in its essential purpose. Sellers and lessors can also limit the rights of buyers and lessees to receive consequential damages—unless the limitation is unconscionable [UCC 2–719, 2A–503].

▌For Review

1. What are the respective obligations of the parties under a contract for the sale or lease of goods?

2. What is the perfect tender rule? What are some important exceptions to this rule that apply to sales and lease contracts?

3. What options are available to the nonbreaching party when the other party to a sales or lease contract repudiates the contract prior to the time for performance?

4. What remedies are available to a seller or lessor when the buyer or lessee breaches the contract? What remedies are available to a buyer or lessee if the seller or lessor breaches the contract?

5. In contracts subject to the UCC, are parties free to limit the remedies available to the nonbreaching party on a breach of contract?

▌Questions and Case Problems

16–1. Revocation of Acceptance. What events or circumstances must occur before a buyer can rightfully revoke his or her acceptance of a sales contract?

16–2. Remedies. Genix, Inc., has contracted to sell Larson five hundred washing machines of a certain model at list price. Genix is to ship the goods on or before December 1. Genix produces one thousand washing machines of this model but has not yet prepared Larson's shipment. On November 1, Larson repudiates the contract. Discuss the remedies available to Genix in this situation.

16–3. Right of Inspection. Cummings ordered two Model-X Super Fidelity speakers from Jamestown Wholesale Electronics, Inc. Jamestown shipped the speakers via United Parcel Service, C.O.D. (collect on delivery), although Cummings had not requested or agreed to a C.O.D. shipment of the goods. When the speakers were delivered, Cummings refused to accept them because he would not be able to inspect them before payment. Jamestown claimed that Cummings had breached their contract, because Jamestown had shipped conforming goods. Had Cummings breached the contract? Explain.

16–4. Anticipatory Repudiation. Moore contracted in writing to sell her 1994 Ford Taurus to Hammer for $8,500. Moore agreed to deliver the car on Wednesday, and Hammer promised to pay the $8,500 on the following Friday. On Tuesday, Hammer informed Moore that he would not be buying the car after all. By Friday, Hammer had changed his mind again and tendered $8,500 to Moore. Moore, although she had not sold the car to another party, refused the tender and refused to deliver. Hammer claimed that Moore had breached their contract. Moore contended that Hammer's repudiation released her from her duty to perform under the contract. Who is correct, and why?

16–5. Remedies. Rodriguez is an antique car collector. He contracts to purchase spare parts for a 1938 engine from Gerrard. These parts are not made anymore and are scarce. To get the contract with Gerrard, Rodriguez has to pay 50 percent of the purchase price in advance. On May 1, Rodriguez sends the payment, which is received on May 2. On May 3, Gerrard, having found another buyer willing to pay substantially more for the parts, informs Rodriguez that he will not deliver as contracted. That same day, Rodriguez learns that Gerrard is insolvent. Gerrard has the parts, and Rodriguez wants them.

Discuss fully any available remedies that would allow Rodriguez to obtain these car parts.

16–6. Commercial Impracticability. In November 1975, Sun Maid Raisin Growers of California contracted to purchase 1,900 tons of raisins from Victor Packing Co. The first 100 tons were priced at 39 cents per pound and the remainder at 40 cents per pound. No delivery date was specified in the contract. On August 10, 1976, Victor informed Sun Maid that it would not complete performance, as it was unable to deliver the last 610 tons. Sun Maid was able to purchase 200 tons of raisins at 43 cents per pound from another supplier. In September 1976, heavy rains damaged the new crop of raisins, causing the price of raisins to increase dramatically. Sun Maid sued Victor for damages, including lost profits (consequential damages). Victor claimed that it should not be liable for lost profits because the disastrous rain was not foreseeable. Discuss Victor's claim. [*Sun Maid Raisin Growers of California v. Victor Packing Co.*, 146 Cal.App.3d 787, 194 Cal.Rptr. 612 (1983)]

16–7. Right to Cure. Wilson purchased a new television set from Scampoli in 1965. When the set was delivered, Wilson found that it did not work properly; the color was defective. Scampoli's repairperson could not correct the problem, and Wilson refused to allow the repairperson to dismantle the set and take it back to the shop to determine the cause of the difficulty. Instead, Wilson demanded that Scampoli deliver a new television set or return the purchase price. Scampoli refused to refund Wilson's money and insisted that he receive the opportunity to correct the malfunctioning of Wilson's set before replacing it or issuing a refund. Discuss whether Scampoli has the right to attempt to cure the product, according to UCC 2–508. [*Wilson v. Scampoli*, 228 A.2d 848 (D.C.App. 1967)]

16–8. Measure of Damages. Bigelow-Sanford, Inc., entered into a contract to buy 100,000 yards of jute (a strong, coarse fiber used for sacking and cordage) at $0.64 per yard from Gunny Corp. Gunny delivered 22,228 yards to Bigelow but informed the company that it would deliver no more. Several other suppliers to Bigelow defaulted, and Bigelow was forced to go into the market one month later to purchase a total of 164,503 yards of jute for $1.21 per yard. Bigelow sued Gunny for the difference between the market price and the contract price of the amount of jute that Gunny had not delivered.

Discuss whether Bigelow could recover this amount from Gunny. [*Bigelow-Sanford, Inc. v. Gunny Corp.*, 649 F.2d 1060 (5th Cir. 1981)]

16–9. Limited Remedies. In 1983, Canal Electric Co. purchased some new rotating blades from Westinghouse Electric Corp. to use in a generator that Canal had purchased several years earlier from Westinghouse. The contract for the sale of the blades warranted that Westinghouse would repair or replace any defective parts for a one-year period and limited Westinghouse's total liability under the contract to the purchase price of the blades, which was $40,750. Liability for incidental and consequential damages was specifically disclaimed. A few months later, the blades developed cracks, and Canal had to shut down operations for 124 days while the blades were being replaced. As a result, Canal incurred costs (which were significantly higher than the purchase price of the blades) to obtain replacement power during this period. Ultimately, Canal sued Westinghouse for breach of warranty and negligence. Westinghouse claimed that its liability to Canal was limited to the purchase price of the blades, $40,750. Will the court enforce the limitation-of-liability clause? What factors will the court consider in deciding the issue? Discuss fully. [*Canal Electric Co. v. Westinghouse Electric Corp.*, 756 F.Supp. 620 (D.Mass. 1991)]

16–10. Remedies of the Buyer or Lessee. Marine Indemnity Insurance Co. of America purchased a "toploader" (a piece of ship-loading equipment) from Hapag-Lloyd, A.G. (A.G. is an abbreviation of the German *Aktiengesellschaft*—the German equivalent of the English term *company*.) Marine Indemnity was aware of the fact that the wiring in the toploader's engine was defective but nevertheless used the equipment in its defective state without notifying the seller. After Marine Indemnity had used the toploader for about four weeks, the wiring caused an explosion in the engine, which severely damaged the equipment. Marine Indemnity then sued Hapag-Lloyd for breach of express warranty. The trial court held for Marine Indemnity. Hapag-Lloyd appealed, contending that Marine Indemnity's failure to give timely notice of the breach barred it from pursuing any remedy. Will the appellate court agree with Hapag-Lloyd? Discuss fully. [*Hapag-Lloyd, A.G. v. Marine Indemnity Insurance Co. of America*, 576 So.2d 1330 (Fla.App.3d 1991)]

16–11. Notice of Defect. Rachel Hebron bought an Isuzu Trooper four-wheel-drive sports vehicle from American Isuzu Motors, Inc. Their contract required her to give notice of any defects in the car within two years of their discovery. In June 1991, Hebron was driving the Trooper when another vehicle pulled in front of her. She swerved to avoid hitting it, and the Trooper rolled over, causing her permanent injuries. Hebron waited, for no apparent reason, until July 1993 to file a suit in a federal district court against American, seeking damages for alleged defects in the car. She had already disposed of the Trooper, without notifying American. American filed a motion for summary judgment based on the contract requirement of

notice within two years. How should the court rule? Discuss fully. [*Hebron v. American Isuzu Motors, Inc.*, 60 F.3d 1095 (4th Cir. 1995)]

16–12. Limitation of Remedies. Wilk Paving, Inc., bought a street-paving asphalt roller from Southworth-Milton, Inc. In large capital letters, on the front of the contract, was printed, "ADDITIONAL TERMS AND CONDITIONS ON REVERSE SIDE." A clause on the back stated that "under no circumstances shall seller . . . be held liable for any . . . consequential damages." In a hurry to close the deal, Wilk's representative did not notice this clause, and Southworth's representative did not call attention to it. Within sixty days, the roller needed the first of what became continuous repairs for mechanical problems. Wilk asked Southworth for its money back. When Southworth refused, Wilk sued Southworth, seeking the purchase price and consequential damages. Was the clause limiting damages enforceable in these circumstances? Explain. [*Wilk Paving, Inc. v. Southworth-Milton, Inc.*, 649 A.2d 778 (Vt. 1995)]

A QUESTION OF ETHICS AND SOCIAL RESPONSIBILITY

16–13. *In March 1985, Bruce Young purchased from Hessel Tractor & Equipment Co., a John Deere equipment dealer, a machine to shear trees in his logging business. The only warranty in the contract was a one-year warranty against defects in the equipment with an exclusive remedy of repair and replacement for any defect in materials or workmanship. All other warranties were expressly and conspicuously disclaimed. Young began to have serious problems with the equipment after less than a month of use. After over a year of continuing unsuccessful attempts at repair and after the one-year warranty had expired, Hessel stopped repairing the machine. Given these facts, consider the following questions.* [Young v. Hessel Tractor & Equipment Co., 782 P.2d 164 (Or.App. 1989)]

1. Do you think that it is fair for a seller to limit available remedies under a sales contract to just one exclusive remedy, such as repair and replacement of parts? Is there anything unethical about this practice?
2. When an exclusive remedy leads to unfair results, as in this case, what, if anything, can be done about it?
3. What UCC provisions might Young cite to persuade the court that he is entitled to revoke his acceptance of the machine and recover the purchase price? How do these provisions reflect the UCC's attempt to balance freedom of contract against the need for fairness and justice in commercial transactions?

FOR CRITICAL ANALYSIS

16–14. *What are the circumstances under which courts should not allow fully informed contracting parties to agree to limit remedies?*

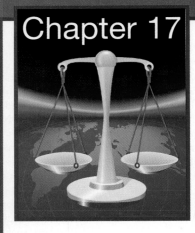

Chapter 17

Warranties and Product Liability

"I'll warrant him heart-whole."

William Shakespeare, 1564–1616
(English dramatist and poet)

CHAPTER OBJECTIVES

After reading this chapter, you should be able to:

1. Describe the types of warranties that may arise in a sales or lease transaction.
2. Indicate how warranties may be disclaimed and the legal effect of warranty disclaimers.
3. Discuss how negligence and misrepresentation can provide a basis for a product liability action.
4. List the requirements for an action in strict liability.
5. Summarize the defenses that can be raised against product liability claims.

Warranty is an age-old concept. In sales and lease law, a warranty is an assurance by one party of the existence of a fact upon which the other party can rely. Just as William Shakespeare's character warranted his friend "heart-whole" in the play *As You Like It*, so sellers and lessors warrant to those who purchase or lease their goods that the goods are as represented or will be as promised.

The Uniform Commercial Code (UCC) has numerous rules governing the concept of product warranty as it occurs in sales and lease contracts. That will be the subject matter of the first part of this chapter. A natural addition to the discussion is *product liability:* Who is liable to consumers, users, and bystanders for physical harm and property damage caused by a particular good or the use thereof? Product liability encompasses the contract theory of warranty, as well as the tort theories of negligence and strict liability (discussed in Chapter 5).

▌Warranties

Article 2 (on sales) and Article 2A (on leases) of the UCC designate several types of warranties that can arise in a sales or lease contract, including warranties of title, express warranties, and implied warranties.

Warranties of Title

Title warranty arises automatically in most sales contracts. The UCC imposes three types of warranties of title.

GOOD TITLE   In most cases, sellers warrant that they have good and valid title to the goods sold and that transfer of the title is rightful [UCC 2–312(1)(a)]. For example, Sharon steals goods from Miguel and sells them to Carrie, who does not know that the goods are stolen. If Miguel reclaims the goods from Carrie, which he has a right to do, Carrie can then sue Sharon for breach of warranty. When Sharon sold Carrie the goods, Sharon *automatically* warranted to her that the title conveyed was valid and that its transfer was rightful. Because this was not in fact the case, Sharon breached the warranty of title imposed by UCC 2–312(1)(a) and became liable to the buyer for the appropriate damages.

NO LIENS   A second warranty of title provided by the UCC protects buyers who are *unaware* of any encumbrances (claims, charges, or liabilities—usually called **liens**[1]) against goods at the time the contract was made [UCC 2–312(1)(b)]. This warranty protects buyers who, for example, unknowingly purchase goods that are subject to a creditor's security interest (see Chapter 21). If a creditor legally repossesses the goods from a buyer *who had no actual knowledge of the security interest*, the buyer can recover from the seller for breach of warranty.

Article 2A affords similar protection for lessees. Section 2A–211(1) provides that during the term of the lease, no claim of any third party will interfere with the lessee's enjoyment of the leasehold interest.

NO INFRINGEMENTS   A merchant is also deemed to warrant that the goods delivered are free from any copyright, trademark, or patent claims of a third person[2] [UCC 2–312(3), 2A–211(2)]. If this warranty is breached and the buyer is sued by the party holding copyright, trademark, or patent rights in the goods, the buyer *must notify the seller* of litigation within a reasonable time to enable the seller to decide whether to defend the lawsuit. If the seller states in writing that he or she has decided to defend and agrees to bear all expenses, including that of an adverse judgment, then the buyer must let the seller undertake litigation; otherwise, the buyer loses all rights against the seller if any infringement liability is established [UCC 2–607(3)(b), 2–607(5)(b)].

Article 2A provides for the same notice of litigation in situations that involve leases rather than sales [UCC 2A–516(3)(b), 2A–516(4)(b)]. There is an exception for leases to individual consumers for personal, family, or household purposes. A consumer who fails to notify the lessor within a reasonable time does not lose his or her remedy against the lessor for any liability established in the litigation [UCC 2A–516(3)(b)].

DISCLAIMER OF TITLE WARRANTY   In an ordinary sales transaction, the title warranty can be disclaimed or modified only by *specific language* in the contract [UCC 2–312(2)]. For example, sellers can assert that they are transferring only such rights, title, and interest as they have in the goods. In a lease transaction, the disclaimer must "be specific, be by a writing, and be conspicuous" [UCC 2A–214(4)].

Express Warranties

A seller or lessor can create an **express warranty** by making representations concerning the quality, condition, description, or performance potential of the goods. Under

LIEN
An encumbrance upon a property to satisfy a debt or protect a claim for payment of a debt.

EXPRESS WARRANTY
A seller's or lessor's oral or written promise, ancillary to an underlying sales or lease agreement, as to the quality, description, or performance of the goods being sold or leased.

---

1. Pronounced *leens*. The term *lien* is derived from the Latin word *liqare*, which means "to bind."
2. Recall from Chapter 14 that a *merchant* is defined in UCC 2–104(1) as a person who deals in goods of the kind involved in the sales contract or who, by occupation, presents himself or herself as having knowledge or skill peculiar to the goods involved in the transaction.

UCC 2–313 and 2A–210, express warranties arise when a seller or lessor indicates any of the following:

1.   That the goods conform to any *affirmation or promise* of fact that the seller or lessor makes to the buyer or lessee about the goods. Such affirmations or promises are usually made during the bargaining process. Statements such as "these drill bits will penetrate stainless steel—and without dulling" are express warranties.
2.   That the goods conform to any *description* of them. For example, a label that reads "Crate contains one 150-horsepower diesel engine" or a contract that calls for the delivery of a "camel's-hair coat" creates an express warranty.
3.   That the goods conform to any *sample or model* of the goods shown to the buyer or lessee.

To create an express warranty, a seller or lessor does not have to use formal words such as *warrant* or *guarantee*. It is only necessary that a reasonable buyer or lessee would regard the representation as part of the basis of the bargain [UCC 2–313(2), 2A–210(2)].

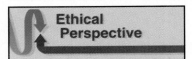
Ethical Perspective

The UCC, by recognizing descriptions as express warranties, injects greater fairness into contractual transactions. If goods that are sold fail to conform to the seller's description of those goods, the seller may be held to have breached an express warranty. The UCC thus acknowledges the fact that a buyer may often reasonably believe that a seller is warranting his or her product, even though the seller or lessor may not use formal words such as *warrant* or *guarantee*. In effect, the law, by statute, imposes an obligation on sellers to act ethically.

For Critical Analysis: *If an express warranty arises because an employee-salesperson exaggerates the qualities of a product sold, who should be held responsible if the buyer sues for breach of warranty?*

BASIS OF THE BARGAIN   The UCC requires that for an express warranty to be created, the affirmation, promise, description, or sample must become part of the "basis of the bargain" [UCC 2–313(1), 2A–210(1)]. Just what constitutes the basis of the bargain is hard to say. The UCC does not define the concept, and it is a question of fact in each case whether a representation was made at such a time and in such a way that it induced the buyer or lessee to enter into the contract. In the following case, the issue was whether warranties contained in a booklet in the glove compartment of a new truck were part of the basis of the bargain for the purchase of the truck.

CASE 17.1

HARRIS v. FORD MOTOR CO.
United States District Court, Middle District of Alabama, 1994.
845 F.Supp. 1511.

a platform in place of a back seat. They were used almost exclusively by farmers for hauling. Pickups remained solely practical, functional workhorses for farmers, cowboys, and oil-rig workers until the mid-1970s, when they became fashionable for some suburbanites. By the late 1980s, pickups were as likely to be used to commute to white-collar jobs as they were to do chores on a farm or a ranch. Today, 20 percent of all new vehicles bought in the United States are pickups. Many of these are strictly show vehicles, unsuited to any useful task besides transportation. They may be coated with expensive paint, outfitted with fancy wheels, or upholstered in velour.

HISTORICAL AND SOCIAL SETTING   *The first pickup trucks, in the 1910s and 1920s, were Ford Model Ts with*

Case 17.1—Continued

FACTS   William Harris purchased a new 1989 Ford F350 pickup truck from Quality Motors, Inc. The truck came with a "New Car Warranty" booklet, which had been placed in the glove compartment of the truck. A few months later, after the right rear fender on the truck began to discolor, Harris discovered that the truck's fender had been scratched in transit from the manufacturer (Ford Motor Company) to the dealership (Quality Motors) and that Quality Motors had repaired the scratched fender and repainted the truck before it sold the truck to Harris. Harris sued Quality Motors and Ford in a federal district court for, among other things, breach of express warranty, claiming in part that the truck was represented as being "new" when in fact it was not—it was damaged. In defending against Harris's claim, the defendants pointed to a clause in the "New Car Warranty" booklet. The clause provided as follows: "A defect or damage may occur in an appearance item while a vehicle is being assembled at the factory or shipped to the dealer. Usually such a defect or damage is found and repaired during the inspection processes at the factory and the dealership." Harris, in response, contended that the warranty booklet was not a part of the "basis of the bargain," because the booklet was delivered long after Harris obligated himself to purchase the vehicle. All of the parties filed motions for summary judgment.

ISSUE   Was the warranty expressed in the booklet part of the basis of the bargain?

DECISION   Yes. The court granted summary judgment in favor of the defendants.

REASON   According to the court, "[t]he evidence demonstrates that, at the time William Harris purchased the vehicle, the 'New Car Warranty' was in the glove compartment of the truck and that the plaintiff was aware of its presence." The court thus held that "the warranty was delivered to the plaintiff at the time of the sale and was part of the 'basis of the bargain.'"

FOR CRITICAL ANALYSIS—Social Consideration
What are some of the factors that a court must consider in deciding whether a seller's oral or written statement about a product, such as the new car in this case, was part of the "basis of the bargain"?

STATEMENTS OF OPINION   Statements of fact create express warranties. If the seller or lessor merely makes a statement that relates to the value or worth of the goods, or makes a statement of opinion or recommendation about the goods, however, the seller or lessor is not creating an express warranty [UCC 2–313(2), 2A–210(2)].

For example, a seller claims that "this is the best used car to come along in years; it has four new tires and a 350-horsepower engine just rebuilt this year." The seller has made several *affirmations of fact* that can create a warranty: the automobile has an engine; it has a 350-horsepower engine; it was rebuilt this year; there are four tires on the automobile; and the tires are new. The seller's *opinion* that the vehicle is "the best used car to come along in years," however, is known as "puffing" and creates no warranty. (Puffing is the expression of opinion by a seller or lessor that is not made as a representation of fact.) A statement relating to the value of the goods, such as "it's worth a fortune" or "anywhere else you'd pay $10,000 for it," does not usually create a warranty. If the seller or lessor is an expert and gives an opinion as an expert to a layperson, however, then a warranty can be created.

It is not always easy to determine what constitutes an express warranty and what constitutes puffing. The reasonableness of the buyer's or lessee's reliance appears to be the controlling criterion in many cases. For example, a salesperson's statements that a ladder "will never break" and will "last a lifetime" are so clearly improbable that no reasonable buyer should rely on them. Additionally, the context within which a statement is made might be relevant in determining the reasonableness of the buyer's or lessee's reliance. For example, a reasonable person is more likely to rely on a written statement made in an advertisement than on a statement made orally by a salesperson.

Implied Warranties

An **implied warranty** is one that *the law derives* by implication or inference from the nature of the transaction or the relative situation or circumstances of the parties. In an

IMPLIED WARRANTY
A warranty that the law derives by implication or inference from the nature of the transaction or the relative situation or circumstances of the parties.

action based on breach of implied warranty, it is necessary to show that an implied warranty existed and that the breach of the warranty proximately caused the damage sustained. We look here at some of the implied warranties that arise under the UCC.

IMPLIED WARRANTY OF MERCHANTABILITY Every sale or lease of goods made *by a merchant* who deals in goods of the kind sold or leased automatically gives rise to an **implied warranty of merchantability** [UCC 2–314, 2A–212]. Thus, a merchant who is in the business of selling ski equipment makes an implied warranty of merchantability every time the merchant sells a pair of skis, but a neighbor selling his or her skis at a garage sale does not.

IMPLIED WARRANTY OF MERCHANTABILITY

A warranty that goods being sold or leased are reasonably fit for the general pupose for which they are sold, are properly packaged and labeled, and are of proper quality. The warranty automatically arises in every sale or lease of goods made by a merchant who deals in goods of the kind sold or leased.

Merchantable Goods Goods that are *merchantable* are "reasonably fit for the ordinary purposes for which such goods are used." They must be of at least average, fair, or medium-grade quality. The quality must be comparable to quality that will pass without objection in the trade or market for goods of the same description. To be merchantable, the goods must also be adequately packaged and labeled as provided by the agreement, and they must conform to the promises or affirmations of fact made on the container or label, if any.

An implied warranty of merchantability also imposes on the merchant liability for the safe performance of the product. It makes no difference whether the merchant knew of or could have discovered a defect that makes the product unsafe—he or she is liable in either situation. Of course, merchants are not absolute insurers against *all* accidents arising in connection with the goods. For example, a bar of soap is not unmerchantable merely because a user could slip and fall by stepping on it.

Merchantable Food The UCC recognizes the serving of food or drink to be consumed on or off the premises as a sale of goods subject to the implied warranty of merchantability [UCC 2–314(1)]. "Merchantable" food means food that is fit to eat. Courts generally determine whether food is fit to eat on the basis of consumer expectations. For example, the courts assume that consumers should reasonably expect to find on occasion bones in fish fillets, cherry pits in cherry pie, a nutshell in a package of shelled nuts, and so on—because such substances are natural incidents of the food. In contrast, consumers would not reasonably expect to find an inchworm in a can of peas or a piece of glass in a soft drink—because these substances are not natural to the food product.[3] In the following classic case, the court had to determine whether a fish bone was a substance that one should reasonably expect to find in fish chowder.

---

3. See, for example, *Mexicali Rose v. Superior Court*, 1 Cal.4th 617, 4 Cal.Rptr.2d 145, 822 P.2d 1292 (1992).

CASE 17.2

WEBSTER v. BLUE SHIP TEA ROOM, INC.

Supreme Judicial Court of Massachusetts, 1964.
347 Mass. 421,
198 N.E.2d 309.

HISTORICAL AND CULTURAL SETTING *Chowder, a soup or stew made with fresh fish, possibly originated in the fishing villages of Brittany (a French province located*

*west of Paris) and was probably carried to Canada and New England by Breton fishermen. In the nineteenth century and earlier, recipes for chowder did not call for the removal of the fish bones. Chowder recipes in the first half of the twentieth century remained as they had in previous centuries, sometimes specifying that the fish head, tail, and backbone were to be broken in pieces and boiled, with the "liquor thus produced * * * added to the balance of the chowder."* [a] *By the mid–twentieth century, there was a considerable body of case law involving*

---

a. Fannie Farmer, *The Boston Cooking School Cook Book* (Boston: Little Brown Co., 1937), p. 166.

Case 17.2—Continued

implied warranties and foreign and natural substances in food. It was perhaps inevitable that sooner or later, a consumer injured by a fish bone in chowder would challenge the merchantability of chowder containing fish bones.

FACTS Blue Ship Tea Room, Inc., was located in Boston in an old building overlooking the ocean. Webster, who had been born and raised in New England, went to the restaurant and ordered fish chowder. The chowder was milky in color. After three or four spoonfuls, she felt something lodged in her throat. As a result, she underwent two esophagoscopies; in the second esophagoscopy, a fish bone was found and removed. Webster filed suit against the restaurant in a Massachusetts state court for breach of the implied warranty of merchantability. The jury rendered a verdict for Webster, and the restaurant appealed to the state's highest court.

ISSUE Does serving fish chowder that contains a bone constitute the breach of an implied warranty of merchantability on the part of the restaurant?

DECISION No. The Supreme Judicial Court of Massachusetts held that Webster could not recover against Blue Ship Tea Room, because no breach of warranty had occurred.

REASON The court, citing UCC Section 2–314, stated that "a warranty that goods shall be merchantable is implied in a contract for their sale if the seller is a merchant with respect to goods of that kind. Under this section the serving for value of food or drink to be consumed either on the premises or elsewhere is a sale. * * * Goods to be merchantable must at least be * * * fit for the ordinary purposes for which such goods are used." The question here is whether a fish bone made the chowder unfit for eating. In the judge's opinion, "the joys of life in New England include the ready availability of fresh fish chowder. We should be prepared to cope with the hazards of fish bones, the occasional presence of which in chowders is, it seems to us, to be anticipated, and which, in the light of a hallowed tradition, do not impair their fitness or merchantability."

FOR CRITICAL ANALYSIS—Cultural Consideration
If the fish chowder had been served in a restaurant located in, say, Nebraska, instead of a restaurant in New England, would the outcome of this case have been different? Should it have?

IMPLIED WARRANTY OF FITNESS FOR A PARTICULAR PURPOSE The **implied warranty of fitness for a particular purpose** arises when *any seller or lessor* (merchant or nonmerchant) knows the particular purpose for which a buyer or lessee will use the goods *and* knows that the buyer or lessee is relying on the skill and judgment of the seller or lessor to select suitable goods [UCC 2–315, 2A–213].

A "particular purpose" of the buyer or lessee differs from the "ordinary purpose for which goods are used" (merchantability). Goods can be merchantable but unfit for a particular purpose. For example, suppose that you need a gallon of paint to match the color of your living room walls—a light shade somewhere between coral and peach. You take a sample to your local hardware store and request a gallon of paint of that color. Instead, you are given a gallon of bright blue paint. Here, the salesperson has not breached any warranty of implied merchantability—the bright blue paint is of high quality and suitable for interior walls—but he or she has breached an implied warranty of fitness for a particular purpose.

A seller or lessor does not need to have actual knowledge of the buyer's or lessee's particular purpose. It is sufficient if a seller or lessor "has reason to know" the purpose. The buyer or lessee, however, must have *relied* on the skill or judgment of the seller or lessor in selecting or furnishing suitable goods for an implied warranty to be created.

For example, Bloomberg leases a computer from Future Tech, a lessor of technical business equipment. Bloomberg tells the clerk that she wants a computer with enough memory to operate certain brands of software and to produce and store complicated engineering graphics and plans. Future Tech leases Bloomberg an Architex One computer. The computer works, but its memory is too limited. Bloomberg wants her money back. Here, because Future Tech has breached the implied warranty of fitness for a particular purpose, Bloomberg normally will be able to recover. The clerk knew specifically that Bloomberg wanted a computer with enough memory to run

IMPLIED WARRANTY OF FITNESS FOR A PARTICULAR PURPOSE
A warranty that goods sold or leased are fit for a particular purpose. The warranty arises when any seller or lessor knows the particular purpose for which a buyer or lessee will use the goods and knows that the buyer or lessee is relying on the skill and judgment of the seller or lessor to select suitable goods.

certain software and store certain information. Furthermore, Bloomberg relied on the clerk to furnish a computer that would fulfill this purpose. Because Future Tech did not do so, the warranty was breached.

OTHER IMPLIED WARRANTIES Implied warranties can also arise (or be excluded or modified) as a result of course of dealing, course of performance, or usage of trade [UCC 2–314(3), 2A–212(3)]. In the absence of evidence to the contrary, when both parties to a sales or lease contract have knowledge of a well-recognized trade custom, the courts will infer that both parties intended for that custom to apply to their contract. For example, if an industry-wide custom is to lubricate a new car before it is delivered and a dealer fails to do so, the dealer can be held liable to a buyer for damages resulting from the breach of an implied warranty. This, of course, would also be negligence on the part of the dealer.

Overlapping Warranties

Sometimes two or more warranties are made in a single transaction. An implied warranty of merchantability, an implied warranty of fitness for a particular purpose, or both, can exist in addition to an express warranty. For example, when a sales contract for a new car states that "this car engine is warranted to be free from defects for 36,000 miles or thirty-six months, whichever occurs first," there is an express warranty against all defects and an implied warranty that the car will be fit for normal use.

The rule under the UCC is that express and implied warranties are construed as *cumulative* if they are consistent with one another [UCC 2–317, 2A–215]. If the warranties are *inconsistent*, the courts usually hold as follows:

1. *Express* warranties displace inconsistent *implied* warranties, except implied warranties of fitness for a particular purpose.
2. Samples take precedence over inconsistent general descriptions.
3. Technical specifications displace inconsistent samples or general descriptions.

In the example described earlier, suppose that when Bloomberg leases the computer from Future Tech, the contract contains an express warranty concerning the amount of memory in the computer and the application programs that the computer is capable of running. Bloomberg does not realize that the memory expressly warranted in the contract is insufficient for her needs. When she tries to load the software and some engineering plans, the computer memory is quickly filled. Bloomberg claims that Future Tech has breached the implied warranty of fitness for a particular purpose. Here, although the express warranty would take precedence over any implied warranty of merchantability, it normally would not take precedence over an implied warranty of fitness for a particular purpose. Bloomberg therefore has a good claim for the breach of implied warranty of fitness for a particular purpose, because she made it clear that she was leasing the computer to perform certain tasks.

Third Party Beneficiaries of Warranties

One of the general principles of contract law is that unless you are one of the parties to a contract, you have no rights under the contract. In other words, *privity of contract* must exist between a plaintiff and a defendant before any action based on a contract can be maintained. Two notable exceptions to the rule of privity are assignments and third party beneficiary contracts (discussed in Chapter 12). Another exception is made under warranty laws so that third parties can recover for harms suffered as a result of breached warranties.

There is sharp disagreement among the states as to how far warranty liability should extend, however. In view of this disagreement, the UCC offers three alternatives for liability to third parties [UCC 2–318, 2A–216]. All three alternatives are intended to eliminate the privity requirement with respect to certain enumerated types of injuries (personal versus property) for certain beneficiaries (for example, household members or bystanders). The following case involves a third party who suffered injuries as a result of a faulty lock on the door of a walk-in freezer, which was located in a church. The issue is whether the seller's express and implied warranties extended to the injured third party under the UCC alternative adopted by the state of North Carolina.

CASE 17.3

CREWS v. W. A. BROWN & SON, INC.

Court of Appeals of North Carolina, 1992.
106 N.C.App. 324,
416 S.E.2d 924.

HISTORICAL AND SOCIAL SETTING *In most states, personal injury claims that do not meet the privity requirement can be brought on the ground of strict liability (discussed in Chapter 5 and also later in this chapter). Lack of privity is no defense to a suit brought on this ground by a product's user or consumer. If a state does not recognize strict liability or the case is brought under a warranty claim, however, an injured party may look to UCC 2–318. This section, as it was drafted in 1962 ("Alternative A" of the current version), extends warranty liability to "any natural person who is in the family or household of [the] buyer or who is a guest in his home" and who could reasonably be expected to use, consume, or be affected by the goods.*

FACTS Thirteen-year-old Vickie Crews was working as a volunteer at her church on the evening of July 2, 1985. At about 8:45 P.M., Vickie went to the church's kitchen and thought she heard a noise in the walk-in freezer. Crews, barefoot and wearing shorts, stepped inside the freezer, and the door closed behind her. She pushed the red emergency release button on the inside of the door, but the door did not open. At approximately 10:00 P.M., someone discovered Crews, and she was taken to a hospital and treated for severe frostbite. During the next two months, she endured five separate operations and the amputation of most of her toes. Crews and her mother (the plaintiffs) brought suit in a North Carolina state court against W. A. Brown & Son, Inc. (the manufacturer of the

freezer), Foodcraft Equipment Company (the firm that had assembled and installed the freezer and sold it to the church), and the church. The plaintiffs alleged, among other things, breach of express and implied warranties. The court granted Foodcraft's motion for summary judgment, holding that the plaintiffs' claims were barred by a lack of privity with Foodcraft. The plaintiffs appealed.

ISSUE Were the plaintiffs' breach of warranty claims barred by a lack of privity with Foodcraft?

DECISION Yes. The appellate court affirmed the trial court's decision.

REASON The court stated that under North Carolina law, the ultimate purchaser of a product may sue a seller for breach of express or implied warranties. Additionally, "any natural person who is in the family or household of [the] buyer or who is a guest in his home if it is reasonable to expect that such person may use, consume or be affected by the goods and who is injured in person by breach of the warranty" has standing to sue a seller for breach of warranty. The court stressed that the statute did not extend warranty coverage to persons beyond those specifically enumerated, and Vickie Crews was not among them. "Because a church does not have a 'family' or a 'household' in the ordinary meanings of those terms, Crews cannot be classified as a member of [the church's] 'family' or 'household.'" Furthermore, because "a church is not a 'home,' * * * she was not a guest in the buyer's 'home.'"

FOR CRITICAL ANALYSIS—Social Consideration *For what reasons might a state, such as North Carolina in this case, restrict recovery for breach of implied warranties to only those persons who are in the family or household of the buyer or who are guests in the buyer's home?*

Warranty Disclaimers

Because each type of warranty is created in a special way, the manner in which warranties can be disclaimed or qualified by a seller or lessor varies depending on the type of warranty.

EXPRESS WARRANTIES   As already stated, any affirmation of fact or promise, description of the goods, or use of samples or models by a seller or lessor creates an express warranty. Obviously, then, express warranties can be excluded if the seller or lessor carefully refrains from making any promise or affirmation of fact relating to the goods, describing the goods, or using a sample or model.

The UCC does permit express warranties to be negated or limited by specific and unambiguous language, provided that this is done in a manner that protects the buyer or lessee from surprise. Therefore, a written disclaimer in language that is clear and conspicuous, and called to a buyer's or lessee's attention, could negate all oral express warranties not included in the written sales contract [UCC 2–316(1), 2A–214(1)]. This allows the seller or lessor to avoid false allegations that oral warranties were made, and it ensures that only representations made by properly authorized individuals are included in the bargain.

Note, however, that a buyer or lessee must be made aware of any warranty disclaimers or modifications *at the time the contract is formed*. In other words, any oral or written warranties—or disclaimers—made during the bargaining process cannot be modified at a later time by the seller or lessor.

WATCH OUT Courts generally view warranty disclaimers unfavorably, especially when consumers are involved.

IMPLIED WARRANTIES   Generally speaking, unless circumstances indicate otherwise, the implied warranties of merchantability and fitness are disclaimed by the expressions "as is," "with all faults," and other similar expressions that in common understanding for *both* parties call the buyer's or lessee's attention to the fact that there are no implied warranties [UCC 2–316(3)(a), 2A–214(3)(a)].

The UCC also permits a seller or lessor to specifically disclaim an implied warranty either of fitness or of merchantability [UCC 2–316(2), 2A–214(2)]. To disclaim an implied warranty of fitness for a particular purpose, the disclaimer *must* be in writing and be conspicuous. The word *fitness* does not have to be mentioned in the writing; it is sufficient if, for example, the disclaimer states, **"THERE ARE NO WARRANTIES THAT EXTEND BEYOND THE DESCRIPTION ON THE FACE HEREOF."**

A merchantability disclaimer must be more specific; it must mention *merchantability*. It need not be written; but if it is, the writing must be conspicuous [UCC 2–316(2), 2A–214(4)]. According to UCC 1–201(10),

> A term or clause is conspicuous when it is so written that a reasonable person against whom it is to operate ought to have noticed it. A printed heading in capitals . . . is conspicuous. Language in the body of a form is conspicuous if it is in larger or other contrasting type or color.

For example, Forbes, a merchant, sells Maves a particular lawn mower selected by Forbes with the characteristics clearly requested by Maves. At the time of the sale, Forbes orally tells Maves that he does not warrant the merchantability of the mower, as it is last year's model. If the mower proves to be defective and does not work, Maves can hold Forbes liable for breach of the warranty of fitness for a particular purpose but not for breach of the warranty of merchantability. Forbes's oral disclaimer mentioning the word *merchantability* is a proper disclaimer. For Forbes to have disclaimed the implied warranty of fitness for a particular purpose, however, a conspicuous writing would have been required. Because he made no written disclaimer, Forbes can still be held liable.

BUYER'S OR LESSEE'S REFUSAL TO INSPECT If a buyer or lessee actually examines the goods (or a sample or model) as fully as desired before entering into a contract, or if the buyer or lessee refuses to examine the goods on the seller's or lessor's demand that he or she do so, *there is no implied warranty with respect to defects that a reasonable examination would reveal or defects that are accidentally found* [UCC 2–316(3)(b), 2A–214(2)(b)].

For example, suppose that Joplin buys an ax at Gershwin's Hardware Store. No express warranties are made. Joplin, even after Gershwin asks, refuses to inspect the ax before buying it. Had she done so, she would have noticed that the handle of the ax was obviously cracked. If she is later injured by the defective ax, she normally will not be able to hold Gershwin liable for breach of the warranty of merchantability, because she could have spotted the defect during an inspection.

WARRANTY DISCLAIMERS AND UNCONSCIONABILITY The UCC sections dealing with warranty disclaimers do not refer specifically to unconscionability as a factor. Ultimately, however, the courts will test warranty disclaimers with reference to the UCC's unconscionability standards [UCC 2–302, 2A–108]. Such things as lack of bargaining position, "take-it-or-leave-it" choices, and a buyer's or lessee's failure to understand or know of a warranty disclaimer will become relevant to the issue of unconscionability. In the following landmark decision, which was decided before the UCC was effective in New Jersey, the court gave significant weight to a consumer's lack of bargaining power with respect to a large auto manufacturer in determining whether a warranty disclaimer was unconscionable.

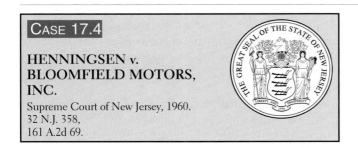

CASE 17.4

HENNINGSEN v. BLOOMFIELD MOTORS, INC.

Supreme Court of New Jersey, 1960.
32 N.J. 358,
161 A.2d 69.

HISTORICAL AND SOCIAL SETTING *The Uniform Sales Act of 1906 imposed obligations on sellers by operation of law, rather than depending on the express agreement of the parties. Of particular significance was the act's recognition of the right to sue on the basis of personal injury arising from a breach of warranty. The Uniform Sales Act also provided, however, that a warranty could be varied by express agreement. Through trade associations, manufacturers and sellers drafted standardized contracts with broad disclaimer clauses. For example, a uniform warranty disclaimer was standard with the members of the Automobile Manufacturers Association, which represented almost 94 percent of automobile production in the United States in 1958.*

FACTS Henningsen purchased a new Chrysler from Bloomfield Motors, Inc., for his wife. Subsequently, his wife suffered severe injuries as a result of an apparent defect in the steering wheel mechanism. The standard-form purchase order used in the transaction contained an express ninety-day/four-thousand-mile warranty. In addition, the purchase order contained a disclaimer, in fine print, of any and all other express or implied warranties. Thus, Bloomfield Motors and Chrysler Corporation refused to pay for Mrs. Henningsen's injuries, asserting that the sales contract, which warranted that Bloomfield would repair defects at no charge, disclaimed warranty liabilities for injuries suffered. A lawsuit in a New Jersey state court followed, based in part on breach of the implied warranty of merchantability. The trial court held for the Henningsens, and Bloomfield appealed.

ISSUE Can the Henningsens recover from Bloomfield Motors and Chrysler despite the disclaimer contained in the sales contract?

DECISION Yes. The Supreme Court of New Jersey affirmed the trial court's judgment.

REASON The liability of Bloomfield Motors and Chrysler Corporation was based on an implied warranty of merchantability contained in the Uniform Sales Act (the warranty is now included in the UCC). The court stated that the legislature's purpose in implying a warranty of merchantability in the sale of goods was to protect buyers and "not to limit the liability of the seller or

(Continued)

Case 17.4—Continued

manufacturer." In the opinion of the court, "[t]he disclaimer of the implied warranty and exclusion of all obligations except those specifically assumed by the express warranty signify a studied effort to frustrate the protection." Although the Uniform Sales Act allowed parties to modify warranty obligations, "[t]he lawmakers did not authorize the automobile manufacturer to use its grossly disproportionate bargaining power [and the unfair surprise of fine print] to relieve itself from liability and to impose on the ordinary buyer, who in effect has no real freedom of choice, the grave danger of injury to himself and others that attends the sale of such a dangerous instrumentality as a defectively made automobile."

FOR CRITICAL ANALYSIS—Economic Consideration
Why would a buyer ever accept a deal in which the seller disclaims all warranties?

Magnuson-Moss Warranty Act

The Magnuson-Moss Warranty Act of 1975[4] was designed to prevent deception in warranties by making them easier to understand. The act is mainly enforced by the Federal Trade Commission (FTC). Additionally, the attorney general or a consumer who has been injured can enforce the act if informal procedures for settling disputes prove to be ineffective. The act modifies UCC warranty rules to some extent when *consumer* transactions are involved. The UCC, however, remains the primary codification of warranty rules for industrial and commercial transactions.

No seller or lessor is *required* to give a written warranty for consumer goods sold under the Magnuson-Moss Act. If a seller or lessor chooses to make an express written warranty, however, and the cost of the consumer goods is more than $10, the warranty must be labeled as "full" or "limited." In addition, if the cost of the goods is more than $15, by FTC regulation, the warrantor must make certain disclosures fully and conspicuously in a single document in "readily understood language." This disclosure states the names and addresses of the warrantor(s), what specifically is warranted, procedures for enforcement of the warranty, any limitations on warranty relief, and that the buyer has legal rights.

FULL WARRANTY   Although a *full warranty* may not cover every aspect of the consumer product sold, what it covers ensures some type of consumer satisfaction in case the product is defective. A full warranty requires free repair or replacement of any defective part; if the product cannot be repaired within a reasonable time, the consumer has the choice of either a refund or a replacement without charge. The full warranty frequently does not have a time limit on it. Any limitation on consequential damages must be *conspicuously* stated. Additionally, the warrantor need not perform warranty services if the problem with the product was caused by damage to the product or unreasonable use by the consumer.

REMEMBER When a buyer or lessee is a consumer, a limitation on consequential damages for personal injuries resulting from nonconforming goods is *prima facie* unconscionable.

LIMITED WARRANTY   A *limited warranty* arises when the written warranty fails to meet one of the minimum requirements of a full warranty. The fact that only a limited warranty is being given must be conspicuously designated. If it is only a time limitation that distinguishes a limited warranty from a full warranty, the Magnuson-Moss Warranty Act allows the warrantor to identify the warranty as a full warranty by such language as "full twelve-month warranty."

IMPLIED WARRANTIES   Implied warranties are not covered under the Magnuson-Moss Warranty Act; they continue to be created according to UCC provisions. When an express warranty is made, the Magnuson-Moss Warranty Act prevents disclaimers or modifications of the implied warranties of merchantability and fitness for a particular

---

4.   15 U.S.C. Sections 2301–2312.

Lemon laws were enacted in response to the frustrations of the buyers of defective automobiles. What does a lemon law provide for a frustrated buyer?

purpose. A warrantor can impose a time limit on the duration of an implied warranty, but it has to correspond to the duration of the express warranty.[5]

▌Lemon Laws

Some purchasers of defective automobiles—called "lemons"—found that the remedies provided by the UCC, after limitations had been imposed by the seller, were inadequate. In response to the frustrations of these buyers, the majority of states have enacted *lemon laws.* Basically, lemon laws provide that if an automobile under warranty possesses a defect that significantly affects the vehicle's value or use, and the defect has not been remedied by the seller within a specified number of opportunities (usually four), the buyer is entitled to a new car, replacement of defective parts, or return of all consideration paid.

In most states, lemon laws require an aggrieved new-car owner to notify the dealer or manufacturer of the problem and to provide the dealer or manufacturer with an opportunity to solve it. If the problem remains, the owner must then submit complaints to the arbitration program specified in the manufacturer's warranty before taking the case to court. Decisions by arbitration panels are binding on the manufacturer (that is, cannot be appealed by the manufacturer to the courts) but are not usually binding on the purchaser.

Most major automobile companies use their own arbitration panels. Some companies, however, subscribe to independent arbitration services, such as those provided by the Better Business Bureau. Although arbitration boards must meet state and/or federal standards of impartiality, industry-sponsored arbitration boards have been criticized for not being truly impartial in their decisions. In response to this criticism, some states have established mandatory, government-sponsored arbitration programs for lemon-law disputes.

"The biggest corporation, like the humblest private citizen, must be held to strict compliance with the will of the people."

Theodore Roosevelt, 1858–1919
(Twenty-sixth president of the United States, 1901–1909)

---

5. The time limit on an implied warranty occurring by virtue of the warrantor's express warranty must, of course, be reasonable, conscionable, and set forth in clear and conspicuous language on the face of the warranty.

PRODUCT LIABILITY
The legal liability of manufacturers, sellers, and lessors of goods to consumers, users, and bystanders for injuries or damages that are caused by the goods.

▌Product Liability

Manufacturers, sellers, and lessors of goods can be held liable to consumers, users, and bystanders for physical harm or property damage that is caused by the goods. This is called **product liability.** Product liability may be based on the warranty theories just discussed, as well as on the theories of negligence, misrepresentation, and strict liability.

American manufacturers have discovered that just about anything they produce can result in a product liability lawsuit, even if the consumer has used the product incorrectly or in violation of the manufacturer's printed instructions. The fear of huge liability lawsuits may discourage companies from engaging in the kind of research and development necessary to be internationally competitive in certain markets thought to have unusually high product liability claims. Some manufacturers feel that they cannot afford to produce any product that is not completely risk free, because they may face excessive liability.

Americans are among the most litigious people in the world. Although other industrialized countries are developing more stringent consumer product laws, thus affording injured parties greater opportunities to sue manufacturers for injuries caused by defective products, most of these countries do not hold their manufacturers to standards of strict liability (discussed later in this chapter). Consequently, foreign companies are able to undertake research programs and produce products that American companies, fearful of potential liability, may not consider economically justifiable. Of course, foreign producers that sell their products in the United States must abide by U.S. liability rules.

For Critical Analysis: *How do expansive product liability laws and court decisions affect the growth of small businesses?*

Negligence

RECALL The elements of negligence include a duty of care, a breach of the duty, and an injury to the plaintiff proximately caused by the breach.

Chapter 5 defined *negligence* as the failure to exercise the degree of care that a reasonable, prudent person would have exercised under the circumstances. If a manufacturer fails to exercise "due care" to make a product safe, a person who is injured by the product may sue the manufacturer for negligence.

Due care must be exercised in designing the product, in selecting the materials, in using the appropriate production process, in assembling and testing the product, and in placing adequate warnings on the label informing the user of dangers of which an ordinary person might not be aware. The duty of care also extends to the inspection and testing of any purchased products that are used in the final product sold by the manufacturer.

A product liability action based on negligence does not require privity of contract between the injured plaintiff and the negligent defendant-manufacturer. Section 395 of the *Restatement (Second) of Torts* states as follows:

> A manufacturer who fails to exercise reasonable care in the manufacture of a chattel [movable good] which, unless carefully made, he should recognize as involving an unreasonable risk of causing physical harm to those who lawfully use it for a purpose for which the manufacturer should expect it to be used and to those whom he should expect to be endangered by its probable use, is subject to liability for physical harm caused to them by its lawful use in a manner and for a purpose for which it is supplied.

In other words, a manufacturer is liable for its failure to exercise due care to any person who sustained an injury proximately caused by a negligently made (defective) product, regardless of whether the injured person is in privity of contract with the negligent defendant-manufacturer or lessor. Relative to the long history of the common law, this exception to the privity requirement is a fairly recent development, dating to the early part of the twentieth century. A leading case in this respect is *MacPherson v. Buick Motor Co.*, which is presented here as this chapter's *Landmark in the Law*.

MacPherson v. Buick Motor Co. (1916)

In the landmark case of *MacPherson v. Buick Motor Co.*,[a] the New York Court of Appeals—New York's highest court—dealt with the liability of a manufacturer that failed to exercise reasonable care in manufacturing a finished product. The case was brought by Donald MacPherson, who suffered injuries while riding in a Buick automobile that suddenly collapsed because one of the wheels was made of defective wood. The spokes crumbled into fragments, throwing MacPherson out of the vehicle and injuring him.

MacPherson had purchased the car from a Buick dealer, but he brought suit against the manufacturer, Buick Motor Company. The wheel itself had not been made by Buick; it had been bought from another manufacturer. There was evidence, though, that the defects could have been discovered by reasonable inspection by Buick and that no such inspection had taken place. MacPherson charged Buick with negligence for putting a human life in imminent danger. The major issue before the court was whether Buick owed a duty of care to anyone except the immediate purchaser of the car (that is, the Buick dealer).

In deciding the issue, Justice Benjamin Cardozo (see the *Profile* of Cardozo in this chapter) stated that "[i]f the nature of a thing is such that it is reasonably certain to place life and limb in peril when negligently made, it is then a thing of danger. . . . If to the element of danger there is added knowledge that the thing will be used by persons other than the purchaser, and used without new tests, then, irrespective of contract, the manufacturer of this thing of danger is under a duty to make it carefully." The court concluded that "[b]eyond all question, the nature of an automobile gives warning of probable danger if its construction is defective. This automobile was designed to go 50 miles an hour. Unless its wheels were sound and strong, injury was almost certain."

Although Buick had not manufactured the wheel itself, the court held that Buick had a duty to inspect the wheels and that Buick "was responsible for the finished product." Therefore, Buick was liable to MacPherson for the injuries he sustained when he was thrown from the car.

For Critical Analysis: *To what extent, if any, have technological developments contributed to the courts' placing less emphasis on the doctrine of* caveat emptor *("let the buyer beware") and more emphasis on the doctrine of* caveat venditor *("let the seller beware")?*

a.   217 N.Y. 382, 111 N.E. 1050 (1916).

Misrepresentation

When a fraudulent misrepresentation has been made to a user or consumer, and that misrepresentation ultimately results in an injury, the basis of liability may be the tort of fraud. Examples are the intentional mislabeling of packaged cosmetics and the intentional concealment of a product's defects.

"One may smile, and smile, and be a villain."

William Shakespeare, 1564–1616
(English dramatist and poet)

PROFILE

Benjamin Cardozo (1870–1938)

Benjamin Nathan Cardozo, one of the most notable liberal jurists of the twentieth century and an eminent legal scholar, was born in New York City on May 24, 1870. He studied law at Columbia University Law School, after which he entered private practice in New York. Over the next twenty

years, Cardozo's skill as an attorney and his legal knowledge became well known to the legal community— eventually leading Charles Evans Hughes, a United States Supreme Court chief justice, to refer to Cardozo as "a walking encyclopedia of the law."

During Cardozo's nearly twenty years on the bench of the New York Court of Appeals (New York's highest court) and later as a United States Supreme Court justice, his opinions had a profound effect on American jurisprudence. One of his most significant and far-reaching decisions was *MacPherson v. Buick Motor Co.* This case, which is presented as this chapter's *Landmark in the Law*, laid the foundation for the product liability law accepted by the courts today.

Generally, Cardozo sided with the liberal voices of the Court (such as Louis Brandeis and Harlan Stone) in his decisions. He believed that the Constitution was flexible enough to allow the government considerable latitude in matters relating to the public welfare. The conviction that

legal principles must be flexible and must change over time permeates all of Cardozo's writing.

In *The Nature of the Judicial Process* (1921), one of his most influential and widely read works, he wrote of the "uncertainty" that such flexibility must ultimately lend to the law and of the creative nature of the judicial process that naturally follows this uncertainty. Cardozo advised judges and lawmakers to look beyond the specific principles, precedents, and policies of American jurisprudence to the delicate, integrating web of justice that holds them all together. Those who do so, Cardozo suggests, will find, as he did, that ultimately the judicial process involves more creation than discovery.

For Critical Analysis: *Given that the role of judges is to apply the law, how can the judicial process involve "more creation than discovery," as Cardozo suggests?*

"The assault upon the citadel of privity [of contract] is proceeding in these days apace."

Benjamin Cardozo,
1870–1938
(Associate justice of the United States Supreme Court, 1932–1938)

Strict Liability

Under the doctrine of strict liability (discussed in Chapter 5), people may be liable for the results of their acts regardless of their intentions or their exercise of reasonable care. Under this doctrine, liability does not depend on privity of contract. The injured party does not have to be the buyer or a third party beneficiary, as required under contract warranty theory. Indeed, this type of liability in law is not governed by the provisions of the UCC because it is a tort doctrine, not a principle of contract law.

The *Restatement (Second) of Torts* designates how the doctrine of strict liability should be applied. It is a precise and widely accepted statement of the liabilities of sellers of goods (including manufacturers, processors, assemblers, packagers, bottlers, wholesalers, distributors, retailers, and lessors) and deserves close attention. Section 402A of the *Restatement (Second) of Torts* states as follows:

(1) One who sells any product in a defective condition unreasonably dangerous to the user or consumer or to his property is subject to liability for physical harm thereby caused to the ultimate user or consumer or to his property, if
  (a) the seller is engaged in the business of selling such a product, and
  (b) it is expected to and does reach the user or consumer without substantial change in the condition in which it is sold.
(2) The rule stated in Subsection (1) applies although
  (a) the seller has exercised all possible care in the preparation and sale of his product, and
  (b) the user or consumer has not bought the product from or entered into any contractual relation with the seller.

Strict liability is imposed by law as a matter of public policy. This policy rests on the threefold assumption that (1) consumers should be protected against unsafe products; (2) manufacturers and distributors should not escape liability for faulty products simply because they are not in privity of contract with the ultimate user of those products; and (3) manufacturers, sellers, and lessors of products are in a better position to bear the costs associated with injuries caused by their products—costs that they can ultimately pass on to all consumers in the form of higher prices.

California was the first state to impose strict liability in tort on manufacturers. In the landmark decision that follows, the California Supreme Court sets out the reason for applying tort law rather than contract law to cases in which consumers are injured by defective products.

CASE 17.5

GREENMAN v. YUBA POWER PRODUCTS, INC.
Supreme Court of California, 1962.
59 Cal.2d 57,
377 P.2d 897,
27 Cal.Rptr. 697.

HISTORICAL AND SOCIAL SETTING *From the earliest days of the common law, English courts applied a doctrine of strict liability. Often, persons whose conduct resulted in the injury of another were held liable for damages, even if they had not intended to injure anyone and had exercised reasonable care. This approach was abandoned around 1800 in favor of the* fault *approach, in which an action was considered tortious only if it was wrongful or blameworthy in some respect. Strict liability began to be reapplied to manufactured goods in several landmark cases in the 1960s, a decade during which many traditional assumptions were being challenged.*

FACTS The plaintiff, Greenman, wanted a Shopsmith—a combination power tool that could be used as a saw, drill, and wood lathe—after seeing a Shopsmith demonstrated by a retailer and studying a brochure prepared by the manufacturer. The plaintiff's wife bought and gave him one for Christmas. More than a year later, a piece of wood flew out of the lathe attachment of the Shopsmith while the plaintiff was using it, inflicting serious injuries on him. About ten and a half months later, the plaintiff filed suit in a California state court against both the retailer and the manufacturer for breach of warranties and negligence. The trial court jury found for the plaintiff. The case was ultimately appealed to the Supreme Court of California.

ISSUE Can the manufacturer and retailer be held liable for the plaintiff's injuries?

DECISION Yes. The Supreme Court of California upheld the verdict for the plaintiff.

REASON The plaintiff had successfully proved that the design and construction of the Shopsmith were defective, that statements in the manufacturer's brochure constituted express warranties and were untrue, and that the plaintiff's injuries were caused by the breach of these express warranties. The manufacturer argued that the plaintiff had waited too long to give notice of the breach of warranty, but the court, in imposing strict liability upon the manufacturer, held that it was not necessary for the plaintiff to establish an express warranty or a breach of warranty. The court stated that "a manufacturer is strictly liable in tort when an article he places on the market, knowing that it is to be used without inspection for defects, proves to have a defect that causes injury to a human being." The court stated that the "purpose of such liability is to [e]nsure that the costs of injuries resulting from defective products are borne by the manufacturers * * * rather than by the injured persons who are powerless to protect themselves."

FOR CRITICAL ANALYSIS—Ethical Consideration
What UCC rule did the manufacturer refer to when it argued that the plaintiff had "waited too long" to give notice of the breach of warranty? What ethical doctrine underlies this rule?

REQUIREMENTS OF STRICT PRODUCT LIABILITY—SUMMARIZED The bases for an action in strict liability as set forth in Section 402A of the *Restatement (Second) of Torts* and as the doctrine is commonly applied can be summarized as a series of six

If a child is injured by a toy, does he or she have a cause of action against the manufacturer?

requirements, which are listed here. If these requirements are met, the manufacturer's liability to an injured party may be virtually unlimited.[6]

1.   The product must be in a defective condition when the defendant sells it.
2.   The defendant must normally be engaged in the business of selling (or otherwise distributing) that product.
3.   The product must be unreasonably dangerous to the user or consumer because of its defective condition (in most states).
4.   The plaintiff must incur physical harm to self or property by use or consumption of the product.
5.   The defective condition must be the proximate cause of the injury or damage.
6.   The goods must not have been substantially changed from the time the product was sold to the time the injury was sustained.

Thus, in any action against a manufacturer, seller, or lessor, the plaintiff does not have to show why or in what manner the product became defective. To recover damages, however, the plaintiff must show that the product was so defective as to be unreasonably dangerous; that the product caused the plaintiff's injury; and that at the time the injury was sustained, the condition of the product was essentially the same as when it left the hands of the defendant manufacturer, seller, or lessor.

UNREASONABLY DANGEROUS PRODUCT
In product liability, a product that is defective to the point of threatening a consumer's health and safety. A product will be considered unreasonably dangerous if it is dangerous beyond the expectation of the ordinary consumer or if a less dangerous alternative was economically feasible for the manufacturer, but the manufacturer failed to produce it.

PRODUCT DEFECT AND STRICT LIABILITY CLAIMS   A court may consider a product so defective as to be an **unreasonably dangerous product** if either (1) the product was dangerous beyond the expectation of the ordinary consumer or (2) a less dangerous alternative was economically feasible for the manufacturer, but the manufacturer failed to produce it. Generally, claims that a product is so defective as to be unreasonably dangerous fall into the three categories discussed here.

---

6.   Some states have enacted what are called *statutes of repose*. Basically, these statutes provide that after a specific statutory period of time from the date of manufacture or sale, a plaintiff is precluded from pursuing a cause of action for injuries or damages sustained from a product, even though the product is defective. The states of Illinois, Indiana, Alabama, Tennessee, Florida, Texas, and Nebraska are illustrative.

Flaw in the Manufacturing Process A plaintiff may allege that a product was unreasonably dangerous because of a flaw in the manufacturing process. As discussed earlier, manufacturers are required to use due care in the manufacture, assembly, and testing of the goods they produce. A manufacturer that fails to exercise proper care in manufacturing a product may be liable in strict liability for harms suffered by users of the product.

NOTE Although a failure to exercise due care can result in strict liability, proof of such a failure is not required, as it is in an action based on negligence.

Design Defect A product, although perfectly manufactured, may nonetheless be unreasonably dangerous because of a defect in design. Generally, a plaintiff claiming a design defect must show that a safer alternative was available and economically feasible for the manufacturer, but the manufacturer failed to produce it. When determining whether a less dangerous alternative was economically feasible for the manufacturer, courts will consider a number of factors, including the product's social utility and desirability, the availability of—and economic feasibility of producing—a safer alternative, the obviousness of the danger posed by the product, the probability of injury and its likely seriousness, and the possibility of eliminating the danger without appreciably impairing the product's function.

People often cut themselves on knives, but because there is no way to avoid injuries without making the product useless and because the danger is obvious to users, a court normally would not find a knife to be unreasonably dangerous and would not hold a supplier of knives liable. In contrast, a court may consider a snowblower without a safety guard over the opening through which the snow is blown to be in a condition that is unreasonably dangerous, even if the snowblower carries warnings to stay clear of the opening. The danger may be within the users' expectations, but the court will also consider the likelihood of injury and its probable seriousness, as well as the cost of putting a guard over the opening and the guard's effect on the blower's operation.

Some products are safe when used as their manufacturers and distributors intend but not safe when used in other ways. Suppliers are generally required to expect reasonably foreseeable misuses and to design products that are either safe when misused or marketed with some protective device—for example, a childproof cap. The following case required the court to determine whether a misuse of a product was reasonably foreseeable.

CASE 17.6

LUTZ v. NATIONAL CRANE CORP.
Supreme Court of Montana, 1994.
884 P.2d 455.

HISTORICAL AND TECHNOLOGICAL SETTING
Industrial cranes are often used in close proximity to power lines. Operators must take extreme care to avoid contact with the lines. Sideloading (dragging) with a crane causes the crane cable to extend its slack in unpredictable ways, increasing the risk of contact with one of the lines. If this happens, electricity can be conducted through the crane and electrocute anyone who is touching it. There are 2,300 crane/power line contacts in the United States each year, and crane/power line elec-

trocutions are the fifth leading cause of work-related deaths in the United States. For this reason, insulated links, which stop the conduction of electricity, are available to crane manufacturers.

FACTS Gerald Lutz and another employee of Montana Ready-Mix were using a crane to retrieve drilling pipe from beneath power lines when the crane cable touched one of the lines. The cable did not have an insulated link and thus conducted electricity from the line to the pipe, electrocuting Lutz. Lutz's widow, Lori Lutz, filed a suit in a Montana state court against the National Crane Corporation, which manufactured the crane, and others, alleging, among other things, that the crane—without an insulated link—was defectively designed and unreasonably dangerous. National Crane argued, among other things, that the employees had been using the crane to sideload and that sideloading was an unreasonable misuse. The court awarded Lori Lutz $815,400, less

(Continued)

Case 17.6—Continued

20 percent, which it attributed, in part, to Gerald Lutz's unreasonable misuse. Both parties appealed. Lori Lutz sought the full $815,400. She admitted that sideloading was a misuse but claimed that it was reasonably foreseeable.

ISSUE Was sideloading a reasonably foreseeable misuse of the crane?

DECISION Yes. The Supreme Court of Montana remanded the case to the lower court with the instruction to reinstate the full award.

REASON The Supreme Court of Montana explained that "cranes are often operated in close proximity to live electrical lines and that * * * sideloading is not an uncommon, albeit improper, practice." The court pointed out that National Crane admitted that its cranes could be misused through sideloading and knew that if sideloading occurred near power lines, the crane cables might contact the lines. The court reasoned that the alleged misuse was thus reasonably foreseeable, making the defense of "unreasonable misuse" unavailable to National Crane.

FOR CRITICAL ANALYSIS—Social Consideration
Who would bear the consequences if the law did not allow for reasonably foreseeable misuses?

Inadequate Warning A plaintiff in a strict liability action may claim that a product is unreasonably dangerous because it lacks adequate warnings or instructions. Manufacturers and other suppliers of products have a duty to warn product users of product-associated risks and dangers, unless the risks and dangers are commonly known. (As will be discussed later in this chapter, an assertion that a danger is commonly known can be used as a defense to product liability.) A pharmaceutical company, for example, must warn of possible side effects of its drugs or of the risks associated with using a certain drug in conjunction with other medications.

Generally, a manufacturer must warn those who purchase its product of the harms that can result from the misuse of the product as well. If a particular misuse of a product is foreseeable, a court normally will hold that the manufacturer had a duty to warn of the dangers associated with such misuse. (See this chapter's *Law in the Extreme* for a discussion of some of the problems facing manufacturers in regard to warning requirements.)

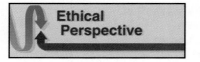 **Ethical Perspective**

Cases alleging inadequate warnings often present thorny issues for the courts to decide. For example, should a manufacturer of an opaque windshield sunscreen have to warn a consumer not to drive his or her car without first removing the sunscreen? Should a manufacturer of swimming pools have to warn swimmers not to dive into the shallow end of the pool? These and similar questions raise the issue addressed in Chapter 4: At what point does the manufacturer's responsibility for consumer safety end and the consumer's responsibility for his or her own safety begin?

In deciding cases involving this issue, the courts generally try to balance the policy of protecting consumers against harmful products with the policy that manufacturers cannot be absolute insurers of the safety of all products on the market. Sometimes, though, common sense seems to give way to the principle that consumers should be warned of *all* foreseeable harms associated with products, even if those harms are obvious. When this happens, other plaintiffs are encouraged to bring suits for injuries for which, at least in the minds of many (including many courts), the sellers should not be held responsible.

For Critical Analysis: *Why weren't issues of product liability and strict liability important a hundred years ago?*

LAW IN THE EXTREME

Can an "Unread" Warning Be Inadequate?

Product liability laws attempt to shield consumers from the harmful effects of defective and unreasonably dangerous products. It sometimes appears, though, as if product liability laws also try to shield consumers from the harmful effects of their own negligence or poor judgment.

Consider, for example, the facts in *Rowson v. Kawasaki Heavy Industries, Ltd.*[a] The plaintiff in the case, Bryan Rowson, was injured while riding a borrowed all-terrain vehicle (ATV) manufactured by Kawasaki Heavy Industries, Ltd. The injury occurred

a. 886 F.Supp. 1221 (N.D.Iowa 1994).

when the ATV rolled over backward while Rowson was riding it up an embankment by a creek. The ATV bore six safety labels containing operating information and warnings. All labels were in good condition and legible. Additionally, an operator's manual for the ATV was available for Rowson to read. Although Rowson had never ridden an ATV, he did not ask the friend from whom he borrowed the vehicle how to operate it, nor did he look at the operator's manual. Furthermore, in a pretrial proceeding, Rowson admitted that he had not read any of the warning labels on the ATV. (Rowson later changed his mind. In an affidavit filed with the court after he had been shown pictures of the ATV and one of the warning labels, Rowson said that he thought he had read at least part of the label.)

Rowson sued Kawasaki, claiming that the warnings provided were inadequate. Kawasaki moved for

summary judgment, contending that a complaint as to the adequacy of a warning "necessarily presupposes that the operator has read the warning"—and in this case, it was not clear that Rowson had indeed read the warnings. No matter, said the court. Failure to read the warnings would not bar Rowson's inadequate-warning claims as a matter of law, because Rowson had also alleged that the warnings were inadequate in presentation and location, regardless of their content. In other words, no matter how many warnings are posted on a product, a plaintiff injured while misusing the product may still be able to sue the manufacturer on the ground that the warnings were "inadequate"—even if the plaintiff never read the existing warnings!

For Critical Analysis: *How can a court determine whether warnings are inadequate if the warnings were never read by the product user?*

MARKET-SHARE LIABILITY   Generally, in all cases involving product liability, a plaintiff must prove that the defective product that caused his or her injury was the product of a specific defendant. In the last decade or so, in cases in which plaintiffs could not prove which of many distributors of a harmful product supplied the particular product that caused the plaintiffs' injuries, courts have dropped this requirement.

This has occurred, for example, in several cases involving DES (diethylstilbestrol), a drug administered in the past to prevent miscarriages. DES's harmful character was not realized until, a generation later, daughters of the women who had taken DES developed health problems, including vaginal carcinoma, that were linked to the drug. Partly because of the passage of time, a plaintiff-daughter often could not prove which pharmaceutical company—out of as many as three hundred—had marketed the DES her mother had ingested. In these cases, some courts applied *market-share liability*, holding that all firms that manufactured and distributed DES during the period in question were liable for the plaintiffs' injuries in proportion to the firms' respective shares of the market.[7]

Market-share liability has also been applied in other situations. In one case, for example, a plaintiff who was a hemophiliac received injections of a blood protein known as antihemophiliac factor (AHF) concentrate. The plaintiff later tested positive for the AIDS (acquired immune deficiency syndrome) virus. Because it was not known which manufacturer was responsible for the particular AHF received by the plaintiff, the court held that all of the manufacturers of AHF could be held liable under a market-share theory of liability.[8] In another case, the New York Court of Appeals (that

---

7.   See, for example, *Martin v. Abbott Laboratories*, 102 Wash.2d 581, 689 P.2d 368 (1984).
8.   *Smith v. Cutter Biological, Inc.*, 72 Haw. 416, 823 P.2d 717 (1991).

state's highest court) held that even if a firm can prove that it did not manufacture the particular product that caused injuries to the plaintiff, the firm can be held liable based on the firm's share of the national market.[9]

OTHER APPLICATIONS OF STRICT LIABILITY   Although the drafters of the *Restatement (Second) of Torts*, Section 402A, did not take a position on bystanders, all courts extend the strict liability of manufacturers and other sellers to injured bystanders. For example, in one case, an automobile manufacturer was held liable for injuries caused by the explosion of a car's motor. A cloud of steam that resulted from the explosion caused multiple collisions because other drivers could not see well.[10]

The rule of strict liability also applies to suppliers of component parts. Thus, if General Motors buys brake pads from a subcontractor and puts them in Chevrolets without changing their composition, and those pads are defective, both the supplier of the brake pads and General Motors will be held strictly liable for the damages caused by the defects.

Defenses to Product Liability

There are several defenses that manufacturers, sellers, or lessors can raise to avoid liability for harms caused by their products. We look at some of these defenses here.

ASSUMPTION OF RISK   Assumption of risk can sometimes be used as a defense in a product liability action. To establish such a defense, the defendant must show that (1) the plaintiff knew and appreciated the risk created by the product defect and (2) the plaintiff voluntarily assumed the risk, even though it was unreasonable to do so. (See Chapter 5 for a more detailed discussion of assumption of risk.)

BE CAREFUL A defendant cannot successfully claim that the plaintiff assumed a risk different from or greater than the risk normally associated with a product.

PRODUCT MISUSE   Similar to the defense of voluntary assumption of risk is that of misuse of the product. Here, the injured party *does not know that the product is dangerous for a particular use* (contrast this with assumption of risk), but the use is not the one for which the product was designed. The courts have severely limited this defense, however. Even if the injured party does not know about the inherent danger of using the product in a wrong way, if the misuse is foreseeable, the seller must take measures to guard against it.

COMPARATIVE NEGLIGENCE   Developments in the area of comparative negligence (discussed in Chapter 5) have even affected the doctrine of strict liability—the most extreme theory of product liability. Whereas previously the plaintiff's conduct was not a defense to strict liability, today many jurisdictions consider the negligent or intentional actions of both the plaintiff and the defendant in the apportionment of liability and damages. This means that even if a product was misused by the plaintiff, the plaintiff may nonetheless be able to recover at least some damages for injuries caused by the defendant's defective product.

COMMONLY KNOWN DANGERS   The dangers associated with certain products (such as sharp knives and guns) are so commonly known that manufacturers need not warn users of those dangers. If a defendant succeeds in convincing the court that a plaintiff's injury resulted from a *commonly known danger*, the defendant will not be liable.

A classic case on this issue involved a plaintiff who was injured when an elastic exercise rope that she had purchased slipped off her foot and struck her in the eye, causing a detachment of the retina. The plaintiff claimed that the manufacturer

9.   *Hymowitz v. Eli Lilly and Co.*, 73 N.Y.2d 487, 539 N.E.2d 1069, 541 N.Y.S.2d 941 (1989).
10.   *Giberson v. Ford Motor Co.*, 504 S.W.2d 8 (Mo. 1974).

should be liable because it had failed to warn users that the exerciser might slip off a foot in such a manner. The court stated that to hold the manufacturer liable in these circumstances "would go beyond the reasonable dictates of justice in fixing the liabilities of manufacturers." After all, stated the court, "[a]lmost every physical object can be inherently dangerous or potentially dangerous in a sense. . . . A manufacturer cannot manufacture a knife that will not cut or a hammer that will not mash a thumb or a stove that will not burn a finger. The law does not require [manufacturers] to warn of such common dangers."[11]

A related defense is the *knowledgeable user* defense. If a particular danger (such as electrical shock) is or should be commonly known by particular users of the product (such as electricians), the manufacturer of electrical equipment need not warn these users of the danger. The following case illustrates this concept.

---

11.   *Jamieson v. Woodward & Lothrop*, 247 F.2d 23, 101 D.C.App. 32 (1957).

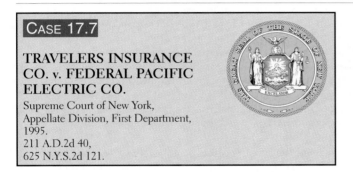

CASE 17.7

TRAVELERS INSURANCE CO. v. FEDERAL PACIFIC ELECTRIC CO.

Supreme Court of New York,
Appellate Division, First Department,
1995.
211 A.D.2d 40,
625 N.Y.S.2d 121.

COMPANY PROFILE   *The Federal Pacific Electric Company makes electrical equipment, including Stab-Lok circuit breakers. The Reliance Electric Company bought Federal from UV Industries Liquidating Trust, Inc., in 1979. In 1980, Federal revealed that it had obtained Underwriters Laboratories (UL) certification for its Stab-Lok circuit breakers by cheating on UL tests. Reliance sued UV Industries. A cash settlement ended the lawsuit in 1984. Two years later, Reliance sold Federal to the Challenger Electric Equipment Corporation. The federal Consumer Product Safety Commission later concluded that the Stab-Lok circuit breakers "did not present a serious risk of injury."*

FACTS   A water pipe burst, flooding a switchboard at the offices of RCA Global Communications, Inc. This tripped the switchboard circuit breakers. RCA employees assigned to reactivate the switchboard included an electrical technician with twelve years of on-the-job training, a licensed electrician, and an electrical engineer with twenty years of experience who had studied power engineering in college. The employees attempted to switch one of the circuit breakers back on without testing for short circuits, which they later admitted they knew

how to do and should have done. The circuit breaker failed to engage but ignited an explosive fire. RCA filed a claim with its insurer, the Travelers Insurance Company. Travelers paid the claim and filed a suit in a New York state court against, among others, the Federal Pacific Electric Company, the supplier of the circuit breakers. Travelers alleged that Federal had been negligent in failing to give RCA adequate warnings and instructions regarding the circuit breakers. The court apportioned 15 percent of the responsibility for the fire to Federal. Federal appealed.

ISSUE   Did Federal fail to give RCA adequate warnings and instructions regarding the circuit breakers?

DECISION   No. The Supreme Court of New York, Appellate Division, reversed the judgment of the lower court and dismissed the complaint against Federal.

REASON   The appellate court explained that "[t]here is 'no necessity to warn a customer already aware—through common knowledge or learning—of a specific hazard.'" The court concluded that, "[g]iven the * * * common knowledge of the minimal accepted practices in the field and the level of expertise, training and experience of the RCA electricians which encompassed the specific situation they faced, the * * * court should have found that there was no necessity on the part of Federal to warn RCA."

FOR CRITICAL ANALYSIS—Technological Consideration   *What might have been the result in this case if the training, experience, and expertise of the employees dispatched to check the circuit breakers had been with a different, out-of-date technology?*

BUSINESS LAW IN ACTION

Product Liability and the Preemption Issue

If a manufacturer, such as an automobile manufacturer, complies with federal safety standards in manufacturing its products, can it nonetheless be held liable under state product liability laws? The answer to this question, which has significant implications for businesses and consumers alike, depends on whether the federal standards are held to preempt relevant state laws. Recall from Chapter 2 that when Congress chooses to act exclusively in an area in which the federal government and the states have concurrent (shared) powers, Congress is said to have *preempted* the area, thus precluding claims brought under a conflicting state or local law on the same subject.

A leading case on this issue, *Cipollone v. Liggett Group, Inc.,*[a] was decided by the United States Supreme Court in 1992. In that case, the Court held that the Federal Cigarette Labeling and Advertising Act of 1965, which requires specific warnings to be included on cigarette packages, preempted state laws requiring cigarette manufacturers to sufficiently

warn consumers of the potential dangers associated with cigarette smoking. The Court stated, however, that there was no indication that Congress intended to preempt state laws that fall *outside* the scope of the federal law, such as laws governing fraudulent misrepresentation.

In *Cipollone* and other cases involving preemption issues, the courts must decide whether Congress, when enacting a particular statute, *intended* to preempt state law claims. In determining congressional intent, courts look at the wording of the statute itself, as well as at the legislative history of the statute (such as congressional committee reports on the topic). For example, in *Tebbetts v. Ford Motor Co.,*[b] a plaintiff alleged that a 1988 Ford Escort was defectively designed because it did not contain an air bag on the driver's side. The defendant-manufacturer contended that it had complied with federal safety regulations authorized by the National Traffic and Motor Vehicle Safety Act of 1966 and that those regulations preempted recovery under state product-safety laws. The court interpreted House and Senate reports on the issue, as well as a clause included in the act itself, to mean that all state law claims were not preempted by the federal regulations. (The relevant clause stated that "[c]ompliance with any Federal motor vehicle safety standard issued under

this [act] does not exempt any person from any liability under common law.")

Generally, manufacturers should be wary in assuming that just because they comply with federally mandated product-safety standards they will not be subject to liability under state laws. Courts differ in their interpretations of congressional intent, and the outcomes in cases involving similar facts can thus also differ. For example, numerous cases have been brought by plaintiffs who have suffered injuries from the use of certain pesticides or herbicides. Some courts have held that the Federal Insecticide, Fungicide, and Rodenticide Act (FIFRA) of 1947, which imposes labeling requirements on manufacturers of these products, preempts actions under state laws.[c] Other courts, however, have held that FIFRA does not preempt all state law claims—for example, those based on negligence or misrepresentation.[d]

For Critical Analysis: *Does the trend toward giving states more authority to regulate their own affairs and away from federal regulation further argue against federal preemption of state law claims?*

a. 505 U.S. 504, 112 S.Ct. 2608, 120 L.Ed.2d 407 (1992).
b. 665 A.2d 345 (N.H. 1995).
c. See, for example, *TaylorAg Industries v. Pure-Gro*, 54 F.3d 555 (9th Cir. 1995).
d. See, for example, *Gorton v. American Cyanamid Co.*, 533 N.W.2d 746 (Wisc. 1995).

OTHER DEFENSES A defendant can also defend against product liability by showing that there is no basis for the plaintiff's claim. For example, suppose that a plaintiff alleges that a seller breached an implied warranty. If the seller can prove that he or she effectively disclaimed all implied warranties, the plaintiff cannot recover. Similarly, in a product liability case based on negligence, a defendant who can show that the plaintiff has not met the requirements (such as causation) for an action in negligence will not be liable. In regard to strict liability, a defendant could claim that the plaintiff failed to meet one of the requirements for an action in strict liability. For example, if the defendant establishes that the goods have been subsequently altered, the defendant will not be held liable. (See the *Business Law in Action* above for a discussion of how federal preemption of state law claims can, in effect, serve as a defense to liability in some situations.)

Application

Law and the Salesperson— The Creation of Warranties*

Warranties are important in both commercial and consumer purchase transactions. There are three types of product warranties: express warranties, implied warranties of merchantability, and implied warranties of fitness for a particular purpose. If you are a seller of products, you can make or create any one of these warranties, which are available to both consumers and commercial purchasers.

First and foremost, sellers and buyers need to know whether warranties have been created. Express warranties do not have to be labeled as such, but statements of simple opinion generally do not constitute express warranties. Express warranties can be made by descriptions of the goods. Express warranties can be found in a seller's advertisement, brochure, or promotional materials or can be made orally or in an express writing. A sales representative should use care in describing the merits of a product; otherwise, the seller could be held to an express warranty. If an express warranty is not intended, the sales pitch should not promise too much.

In most sales, because the seller is a merchant, the purchased goods carry the implied warranty of merchantability. If you are a seller, you must also be aware of the importance of the implied warranty of fitness for a particular purpose. Assume that a customer comes to

your sales representative, describes the job to be done in detail, and says, "I really need something that can do the job." Your sales representative replies, "This product will do the job." An implied warranty that the product is fit for that particular purpose has been created.

Many sellers, particularly in commercial sales, try to limit or disclaim warranties. The Uniform Commercial Code permits all warranties, including express warranties, to be excluded or negated. Conspicuous statements—such as "THERE ARE NO WARRANTIES WHICH EXTEND BEYOND THE DESCRIPTION ON THE FACE HEREOF" or "THERE ARE NO IMPLIED WARRANTIES OF FITNESS FOR A PARTICULAR PURPOSE OR MERCHANTABILITY WHICH ACCOMPANY THIS SALE"—can be used to disclaim the implied warranties of fitness and merchantability. Used goods are sometimes sold "as is" or "with all faults" so that implied warranties of fitness and merchantability are disclaimed. Whenever these warranties are disclaimed, a purchaser should be aware that the product may not be of even average quality.

✓ Checklist for the Salesperson

1. If you wish to limit warranties, do so by means of a carefully worded and prominently placed written or printed provision that a reasonable person would understand and accept.

2. As a seller, you might wish to have the buyer sign a statement certifying that he or she has read all of your warranty disclaimer provisions.

3. If you do not intend to make an express warranty, do not make a promise or an affirmation of fact concerning the performance or quality of a product you are selling.

*This *Application* is not meant to serve as a substitute for the services of an attorney who is licensed to practice law in your state.

▌ Key Terms

▌Chapter Summary: Warranties and Product Liability

WARRANTIES	
Warranties of Title *(See page 417.)*	The UCC provides for the following warranties of title [UCC 2–312, 2A–211]: 1. *Good title*—A seller warrants that he or she has the right to pass good and rightful title to the goods. 2. *No liens*—A seller warrants that the goods sold are free of any encumbrances (claims, charges, or liabilities—usually called *liens*). A lessor warrants that the lessee will not be disturbed in his or her possession of the goods by the claims of a third party. 3. *No infringements*—A merchant seller warrants that the goods are free from infringement claims (claims that a patent, trademark, or copyright has been infringed) by third parties. Lessors make similar warranties.
Express Warranties *(See pages 417–419* *and pages 426–427.)*	1. *Under the UCC*—An express warranty arises under the UCC when a seller or lessor indicates any of the following [UCC 2–313, 2A–210]: a. An affirmation or promise of fact. b. A description of the goods. c. A sample shown as conforming to the contract goods. 2. *Under the Magnuson-Moss Warranty Act*—Express written warranties covering consumer goods priced at more than $10, *if made,* must be labeled as one of the following: a. Full warranty—Free repair or replacement of defective parts; refund or replacement for goods if they cannot be repaired in a reasonable time. b. Limited warranty—When less than a full warranty is being offered.
Implied Warranty **of Merchantability** *(See pages 420–421.)*	When a seller or lessor is a merchant who deals in goods of the kind sold or leased, the seller or lessor warrants that the goods sold or leased are properly packaged and labeled, are of proper quality, and are reasonably fit for the ordinary purposes for which such goods are used [UCC 2–314, 2A–212].
Implied Warranty **of Fitness for a** **Particular Purpose** *(See pages 421–422.)*	Arises when the buyer's or lessee's purpose or use is expressly or impliedly known by the seller or lessor, and the buyer or lessee purchases or leases the goods in reliance on the seller's or lessor's selection [UCC 2–315, 2A–213].
Other Implied **Warranties** *(See page 422.)*	Other implied warranties can arise as a result of course of dealing, course of performance, or usage of trade [UCC 2–314(3), 2A–212(3)].
PRODUCT LIABILITY	
Liability Based **on Negligence** *(See pages 428–429.)*	1. Due care must be used by the manufacturer in designing the product, selecting materials, using the appropriate production process, assembling and testing the product, and placing adequate warnings on the label or product. 2. Privity of contract is not required. A manufacturer is liable for failure to exercise due care to any person who sustains an injury proximately caused by a negligently made (defective) product.
Liability Based on **Misrepresentation** *(See page 429.)*	Fraudulent misrepresentation of a product may result in product liability based on the tort of fraud.
Strict Liability— **Requirements** *(See pages 430–432.)*	1. The defendant must sell the product in a defective condition. 2. The defendant must normally be engaged in the business of selling that product. 3. The product must be unreasonably dangerous to the user or consumer because of its defective condition (in most states). A court may consider a product so defective as to be unreasonably dangerous if either (a) the product was dangerous beyond the expectation of the ordinary consumer or (b) a less dangerous alternative was economically feasible for the manufacturer, but the manufacturer failed to produce it. 4. The plaintiff must incur physical harm to self or property by use or consumption of the product. (Courts will also extend strict liability to include injured bystanders.) 5. The defective condition must be the proximate cause of the injury or damage.

▊ Chapter Summary: Warranties and Product Liability—Continued

Strict Liability—Requirements—Continued	6. The goods must not have been substantially changed from the time the product was sold to the time the injury was sustained.
Strict Liability—Product Defect *(See pages 432–435.)*	Claims that a product is so defective as to be unreasonably dangerous generally allege that the product is unreasonably dangerous for one of the following reasons: 1. Because of a flaw in the manufacturing process. 2. Because of a design defect. 3. Because the manufacturer failed to warn adequately of harms associated with the product's use.
Market-Share Liability *(See pages 435–436.)*	In cases in which plaintiffs cannot prove which of many distributors of a harmful product supplied the particular product that caused the plaintiffs' injuries, some courts have applied market-share liability. All firms that manufactured and distributed the harmful product during the period in question are then held liable for the plaintiffs' injuries in proportion to the firms' respective shares of the market, as directed by the court.
Other Applications of Strict Liability *(See page 436.)*	1. Manufacturers and other sellers are liable for harms suffered by injured bystanders due to defective products. 2. Suppliers of component parts are strictly liable for defective parts that, when incorporated into a product, cause injuries to users.
Defenses to Product Liability *(See pages 436–438.)*	1. *Assumption of risk*—The user or consumer knew of the risk of harm and voluntarily assumed it. 2. *Product misuse*—The user or consumer misused the product in a way unforeseeable by the manufacturer. 3. *Comparative negligence*—Liability may be distributed between plaintiff and defendant under the doctrine of comparative negligence. 4. *Commonly known dangers*— If a defendant succeeds in convincing the court that a plaintiff's injury resulted from a commonly known danger, such as the danger associated with using a sharp knife, the defendant will not be liable. 5. *Other defenses*—A defendant can also defend against a strict liability claim by showing that there is no basis for the plaintiff's claim (that the plaintiff has not met the requirements for an action in negligence or strict liability, for example).

▊ For Review

1. What factors determine whether a seller's or lessor's statement constitutes an express warranty or merely "puffing"?

2. What implied warranties arise under the UCC?

3. Can a manufacturer be held liable to *any* person who suffers an injury proximately caused by the manufacturer's negligently made product?

4. What are the elements of a cause of action in strict product liability?

5. What defenses to liability can be raised in a product liability lawsuit?

▊ Questions and Case Problems

17–1. Product Liability. Under what contract theory can a seller be held liable to a consumer for physical harm or property damage that is caused by the goods sold? Under what tort theories can the seller be held liable?

17–2. Product Liability. Carmen buys a television set manufactured by AKI Electronics. She is going on vacation, so she takes the set to her mother's house for her mother to use. Because the set is defective, it explodes, causing considerable

damage to her mother's house. Carmen's mother sues AKI for the damages to her house. Discuss the theories under which Carmen's mother can recover from AKI.

17–3. Warranty Disclaimers. Tandy purchased a washing machine from Marshall Appliances. The sales contract included a provision explicitly disclaiming all express or implied warranties, including the implied warranty of merchantability. The disclaimer was printed in the same size and color as the rest of the contract. The machine turned out to be a "lemon" and never functioned properly. Tandy sought a refund of the purchase price, claiming that Marshall had breached the implied warranty of merchantability. Can Tandy recover her money, notwithstanding the warranty disclaimer in the contract? Explain.

17–4. Implied Warranties. Sam, a farmer, needs to place a two-thousand-pound piece of equipment in his barn. The equipment must be lifted thirty feet into a hayloft. Sam goes to Durham Hardware and tells Durham that he needs some heavy-duty rope to be used on his farm. Durham recommends a one-inch-thick nylon rope, and Sam purchases two hundred feet of it. Sam ties the rope around the piece of equipment, puts it through a pulley, and with the aid of a tractor lifts the equipment off the ground. Suddenly the rope breaks. In the crash to the ground, the equipment is extensively damaged. Sam files suit against Durham for breach of the implied warranty of fitness for a particular purpose. Discuss how successful Sam will be with his suit.

17–5. Product Liability. George Nesselrode lost his life in an airplane crash. The plane had been manufactured by Beech Aircraft Corp. and sold to Executive Beechcraft, Inc. Shortly before the crash occurred, Executive Beechcraft had conducted a routine inspection of the plane and found that some of the parts needed to be replaced. The new parts were supplied by Beech Aircraft but installed by Executive Beechcraft. These particular airplane parts could be installed backward, and if they were, the plane would crash. Nesselrode's crash resulted from just such an incorrect installation of the airplane parts. Nesselrode's wife, Jane, and three daughters sued Executive Beechcraft, Beech Aircraft, and Gerald Hultgren, the pilot who had flown the plane, for damages. Beech Aircraft claimed that it was not at fault because it had not installed the parts. Will Beech Aircraft be held liable for Nesselrode's death? Discuss. [*Nesselrode v. Executive Beechcraft, Inc.*, 707 S.W.2d 371 (Mo. 1986)]

17–6. Strict Liability. Embs was buying some groceries at Stamper's Cash Market. Unnoticed by her, a carton of 7-Up was sitting on the floor at the edge of the produce counter about one foot from where she was standing. Several of the 7-Up bottles exploded. Embs's leg was injured severely enough that she had to be taken to the hospital by a managing agent of the store. Embs sued the manufacturer of 7-Up, Pepsi-Cola Bottling Co. of Lexington, Kentucky, Inc., claiming that the manufacturer should be held strictly liable for the harm caused by its products. The trial court dismissed her claim. On appeal, what will the court decide? Discuss fully. [*Embs v. Pepsi-Cola Bottling Co. of Lexington, Kentucky, Inc.*, 528 S.W.2d 703 (Ky.App. 1975)]

17–7. Duty to Warn. William Mackowick, who had worked as an electrician for thirty years, was installing high-voltage capacitors in a switchgear room in a hospital when he noticed that a fellow electrician had removed the cover from an existing capacitor manufactured by Westinghouse Electric Corp. A warning label that Westinghouse had placed inside the cover of the metal box containing the capacitor instructed users to ground the electricity before handling. Nothing was said on the label about the propensity of electricity to arc. (Arcing occurs when electricity grounds itself by "jumping" to a nearby object or instrument.) Mackowick, while warning the other

electrician of the danger, pointed his screwdriver toward the capacitor box. The electricity flowing through the fuses arced to the screwdriver and sent a high-voltage electric current through Mackowick's body. As a result, he sustained severe burns and was unable to return to work for three months. Should Westinghouse be held liable because it failed to warn users of arcing—a principle of electricity? Discuss. [*Mackowick v. Westinghouse Electric Corp.*, 575 A.2d 100 (Pa. 1990)]

17–8. Strict Liability. David Jordon, a ten-year-old boy, lost control of his sled, hit a tree, and was injured. The sled was a plastic toboggan-like sled that had been purchased from K-Mart. David's parents brought suit against K-Mart, alleging that the sled was defective and unreasonably dangerous because (1) the sled contained design defects (the molded runners on the sled rendered the sled unsteerable, and the sled lacked any independent steering or braking mechanisms), and (2) there were no warnings of the dangers inherent in the use of the sled. K-Mart moved for summary judgment. Should the court grant K-Mart's motion? Discuss fully. [*Jordon v. K-Mart Corp.*, 416 Pa.Super. 186, 611 A.2d 1328 (1992)]

17–9. Defenses to Product Liability. The Campbell Soup Co. manufactured, sold, and shipped packages of chicken-flavored Campbell's Ramen Noodle Soup to a distributor. The distributor sold and shipped the packages to Associated Grocers. Associated Grocers shipped the packages to Warehouse Foods, a retail grocer. Six weeks after Campbell first shipped the soup to the distributor, Warehouse Foods sold it to Kathy Jo Gates. Gates prepared the soup. Halfway through eating her second bowl, she discovered beetle larvae in the noodles. She filed a product liability suit against Campbell and others. Gates argued, in effect, that the mere presence of the bugs in the soup was sufficient to hold Campbell strictly liable. How might Campbell defend itself? [*Campbell Soup Co. v. Gates*, 319 Ark. 54, 889 S.W.2d 750 (1994)]

17–10. Product Liability. John Whitted bought a Chevrolet Nova from General Motors Corp. (GMC). Six years later, Whitted crashed the Nova into two trees. During the impact, the seat belt broke, and Whitted was thrust against the steering wheel, which broke, and the windshield, which shattered. He suffered fractures in his left arm and cuts to his forehead. Whitted sued GMC and the manufacturer, asserting, among other things, that because the seat belt broke, the defendants were strictly liable for his injuries. What does Whitted have to show in order to prove his case? [*Whitted v. General Motors Corp.*, 58 F.3d 1200 (7th Cir. 1995)]

A QUESTION OF ETHICS AND SOCIAL RESPONSIBILITY

17–11. *Three-year-old Randy Welch, the son of Steve and Teresa Griffith, climbed up to a shelf and obtained a disposable butane cigarette lighter. Randy then used the lighter to ignite a flame, which set fire to his pajama top. Welch and his parents sued the lighter's manufacturer, Scripto-Tokai Corp., for damages, alleging that the lighter was defective and unreasonably dangerous because it was not child resistant. In view of this factual background, consider the following questions. [Welch v. Scripto-Tokai Corp., 651 N.E.2d 810 (Ind.App. 1995)]*

1. One of the questions raised in this case was whether the risks attending the lighter were sufficiently "open and obvious" that the manufacturer did not need to warn of

those risks. If you were the judge, how would you decide this issue? Explain your reasoning.

2. If a product is not dangerous to an extent beyond that contemplated by the ordinary consumer, should the manufacturer nonetheless be held liable if it could have made the product safer? Explain.

3. How can a court decide what kinds of risks should be open and obvious for the ordinary consumer?

FOR CRITICAL ANALYSIS

17–12. *The United States has the strictest product liability laws in the world today. Why do you think many other countries, particularly developing countries, are more lax with respect to holding manufacturers liable for product defects?*

❚ Unit Four—Cumulative Hypothetical Problem

17–13. *Lesa, who owns a small restaurant on the Oregon coast, orders three new tables and twelve new chairs from Larson's Furniture Plaza, a local furniture store. She gives the store a check for $2,000, the purchase price of the tables and chairs, and Larson, the store's owner, agrees to have the furniture delivered to her restaurant the following week.*

1. Larson only has only one table-and-chair set in stock. When he calls the manufacturer and orders two more sets, however, he learns that the manufacturer has increased the price of the furniture. Larson telephones Lesa and informs her of the price increase. Lesa agrees to pay the additional price for the remaining two sets when they are delivered. After the furniture is delivered, however, Lesa refuses to pay the extra amount. She claims that her oral agreement to pay the extra cost is not enforceable because the modification of her contract with Larson was not supported by any new consideration. Is Lesa correct? Why or why not?

2. The manufacturer shipped the furniture to Larson via truck, F.O.B. Portland, from its warehouse located in Portland, Oregon. If the manufacturer and Larson do not specify when risk of loss will pass from the seller to the buyer, when will risk pass? Explain.

3. Suppose that when Lesa receives the furniture, she notices a large crack in the top of one of the tables. She tells Larson about the problem and asks him to replace the cracked table with a new, undamaged one. Larson refuses to do so. What remedies might Lesa pursue in this situation?

4. One day, Jane, an elderly diner, was sitting at one of the new tables in Lesa's restaurant. The table leg suddenly buckled under, causing the table to fall on Jane and injure her hip. In spite of several hip operations, Jane was never able to walk normally again. Under what theories discussed in Chapter 17 might Jane be able to recover damages from the manufacturer of the table?

Unit Five

Negotiable Instruments

UNIT OUTLINE

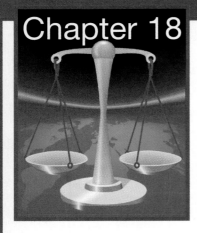

Chapter 18

Negotiability and Transferability

NEGOTIABLE INSTRUMENT
A signed writing that contains an unconditional promise or order to pay an exact sum of money on demand or at an exact future time to a specific person or order, or to bearer.

"Convenience is the basis of mercantile law."

Lord Mansfield, 1705–1793
(British jurist)

CHAPTER OBJECTIVES

After reading this chapter, you should be able to:

1. Identify the four types of negotiable instruments.
2. Summarize the requirements that must be met for an instrument to be negotiable.
3. Indicate the factors that do not affect an instrument's negotiability.
4. Explain the process of negotiation.
5. List the types of indorsements, and describe the legal effect of each type of indorsement.

The vast number of commercial transactions that take place daily in the modern business world would be inconceivable without negotiable instruments. A **negotiable instrument** can be defined as a signed writing that contains an unconditional promise or order to pay an exact sum of money on demand or at an exact future time to a specific person or order, or to bearer. The checks you write to pay for groceries and other items are negotiable instruments.

A negotiable instrument can function in two ways—as a substitute for money or as an extension of credit. For example, when a buyer writes a check to pay for goods, the check serves as a substitute for money. When a buyer gives a seller a promissory note in which the buyer promises to pay the seller the purchase price within sixty days, the seller has essentially extended credit to the buyer for a sixty-day period. For a negotiable instrument to operate *practically* as either a substitute for money or a credit device, or both, it is essential that the instrument be easily transferable without danger of being uncollectible. This is an essential function of negotiable instruments. Each rule described in the following pages can be examined in light of this function.

In the opening quotation, Lord Mansfield stresses the element of convenience in the evolution of mercantile law, and the law governing negotiable instruments did indeed grow out of commercial necessity. In the medieval world, merchants dealing in foreign trade used negotiable instruments to finance and conduct their affairs. Problems in transportation and in the safekeeping of gold or coins had prompted this practice. Because the English king's courts of those times did not recognize the validity of negotiable instruments, the merchants had to develop their own rules governing its use, and these rules were enforced by "fair" or "borough" courts. Eventually, these decisions became a distinct set of laws known as the *Lex Mercatoria* (Law Merchant).

The Law Merchant was codified in England in the Bills of Exchange Act of 1882. In 1896, in the United States, the National Conference of Commissioners on Uniform State Laws drafted the Uniform Negotiable Instruments Law, which is presented here as this chapter's *Landmark in the Law*.

The Uniform Negotiable Instruments Law

LANDMARK IN THE LAW

The early history of American commercial law was strongly influenced by several conditions—the instability of the monetary system, the large number of separate jurisdictions, and the diversity of nationalities among settlers in America. Although English common law was influential, each state generally adopted statutory rules governing the use of negotiable instruments. Thus, in contrast to the practice in England prior to 1882, the use of negotiable instruments in the early years of the United States was regulated by written law.

Although statutes governing the use of negotiable instruments had been created in the various states for the purpose of facilitating commerce, in fact they produced as many problems as they solved. The variance of statutes from one state to the next often impeded commerce, particularly the interstate commerce that was rapidly developing in the nineteenth century. Consequently, when the American Bar Association was formed in 1878, one of its major goals was the establishment of some degree of uniformity of law among the states to avoid the problems created by conflicting state statutes. This concern eventually led to the creation of the National Conference of Commissioners on Uniform State Laws, and it was a committee of this conference that drafted the Uniform Negotiable Instruments Law.

Modeled on the English Bills of Exchange Act of 1882, the law was drafted primarily by John J. Crawford of New York, who submitted it to the National Conference in 1896. Having approved the draft, the conference urged its enactment by the states. Twenty-eight years later, all of the states had adopted the new law.

Although uniformity and certainty in negotiable instruments were to some extent achieved by the Uniform Negotiable Instruments Law, the long-term result was even greater uncertainty, because the courts rarely applied the act uniformly. Some did not use it at all but relied on the common law instead; others relied solely on the uniform law. In general, the law's application in a particular case depended on the state and the particular judge's views. By 1940, it was apparent that the original goal of the conference to create a uniform law governing negotiable instruments was far from realized. The conference, in studying solutions to this problem—and to similar problems stemming from uniform acts enacted in other areas of commercial law—eventually drafted the Uniform Commercial Code (UCC), Article 3 of which replaced the Uniform Negotiable Instruments Law.

For Critical Analysis: *Can "uniform" laws ever be truly uniform? Explain.*

▌Article 3 of the UCC

Negotiable instruments must meet special requirements relating to form and content. These requirements, which are imposed by Article 3 of the Uniform Commercial

Code (UCC), will be discussed at length in this chapter. When an instrument is negotiable, its transfer from one person to another is also governed by Article 3. Indeed, UCC 3–104(b) defines *instrument* as a "negotiable instrument." For that reason, whenever the term *instrument* is used in this book, it refers to a negotiable instrument.

In 1990, a revised version of Article 3 was promulgated for adoption by the states. Many of the changes to Article 3 simply clarified old sections; some significantly altered the former UCC Article 3 provisions. As of this writing, most of the states have adopted the revised article. Therefore, references to Article 3 in this chapter and in the following two chapters are to the *revised* Article 3. When the revised Article 3 has made important changes in the law, however, we discuss the previous law in footnotes.

Article 4 of the UCC, which governs bank deposits and collections (discussed in Chapter 20), was also revised in 1990. In part, these changes were necessary to reflect changes in Article 3 that affect Article 4 provisions. The revised Articles 3 and 4 are included in their entirety in Appendix C.

■ Types of Instruments

The UCC specifies four types of negotiable instruments: *drafts, checks, promissory notes,* and *certificates of deposit (CDs)*. These instruments are frequently divided into the two classifications that we will discuss in the following subsections: *orders to pay* (drafts and checks) and *promises to pay* (promissory notes and CDs).

Negotiable instruments may also be classified as either demand instruments or time instruments. A *demand instrument* is payable on demand; that is, it is payable immediately after it is issued and thereafter for a reasonable period of time. All checks are demand instruments, because by definition, they must be payable on demand. A *time instrument* is payable at a future date.

Drafts and Checks (Orders to Pay)

A **draft** (bill of exchange) is an unconditional written order that involves *three parties*. The party creating the draft (the **drawer**) orders another party (the **drawee**) to pay money, usually to a third party (the **payee**). A *time draft* is payable at a definite future time. A *sight draft* (or demand draft) is payable on sight—that is, when it is presented for payment. A draft can be both a time and a sight draft; such a draft is one payable at a stated time after sight.

Exhibit 18–1 shows a typical time draft. The drawee must be obligated to the drawer either by agreement or through a debtor-creditor relationship for the drawee to be obligated to the drawer to honor the order. For example, on November 16, the Bank of Ourtown orders $1,000 worth of office supplies from Stephen Eastman, with payment due January 16. On December 16, Eastman borrows $1,000 from the First National Bank of Whiteacre, with payment also due January 16. The First National Bank of Whiteacre might agree to accept a draft drawn by Eastman on the Bank of Ourtown as payment for the loan.

A **trade acceptance** is a type of draft that is frequently used in the sale of goods. The seller is both the drawer and the payee on this draft. Essentially, the draft orders the buyer to pay a specified sum of money to the seller, usually at a stated time in the future. For example, Jackson River Fabrics sells fabric priced at $50,000 to Comfort Creations, Inc., each fall on terms requiring payment to be made in ninety days. One year Jackson River needs cash, so it draws a *trade acceptance* (see Exhibit 18–2) that orders Comfort Creations to pay $50,000 to the order of Jackson River Fabrics ninety days hence. Jackson River presents the paper to Comfort Creations. Comfort Creations *accepts* the draft, by signing the face of the draft, and returns it to Jackson River Fabrics. The acceptance by Comfort Creations creates an enforceable obliga-

---

DRAFT

Any instrument drawn on a drawee (such as a bank) that orders the drawee to pay a certain sum of money, usually to a third party (the payee), on demand or at a definite future time.

DRAWER

The party that initiates a draft (such as a check), thereby ordering the drawee to pay.

DRAWEE

The party that is ordered to pay a draft or check. With a check, a financial institution is always the drawee.

PAYEE

A person to whom an instrument is made payable

TRADE ACCEPTANCE

A draft that is drawn by a seller of goods ordering the buyer to pay a specified sum of money to the seller, usually at a stated time in the future. The buyer accepts the draft by signing the face of the draft, thus creating an enforceable obligation to pay the draft when it comes due. On a trade acceptance, the seller is both the drawer and the payee.

♦ **Exhibit 18–1**
A Typical Time Draft

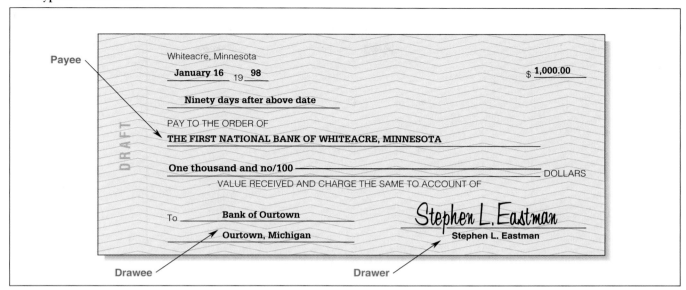

tion to pay the draft when it comes due in ninety days. Jackson River can then sell the trade acceptance in the commercial money market.

The most commonly used type of draft is a **check.** The writer of the check is the drawer, the bank upon which the check is drawn is the drawee, and the person to whom the check is payable is the payee. As mentioned earlier, checks, because they are payable on demand, are demand instruments.

Checks will be discussed more fully in Chapter 20, but it should be noted here that with certain types of checks, such as *cashier's checks,* the bank is both the drawer and the drawee. The bank customer purchases a cashier's check from the bank—that is, pays the bank the amount of the check—and indicates to whom the check should be made payable. The bank, not the customer, is the drawer of the check (as well as the drawee).

CHECK
A draft drawn by a drawer ordering the drawee bank or financial institution to pay a certain amount of money to the holder on demand.

♦ **Exhibit 18–2**
A Typical Trade Acceptance

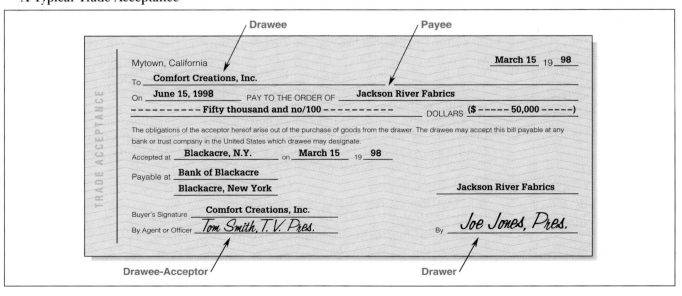

♦ Exhibit 18–3
A Typical Promissory Note

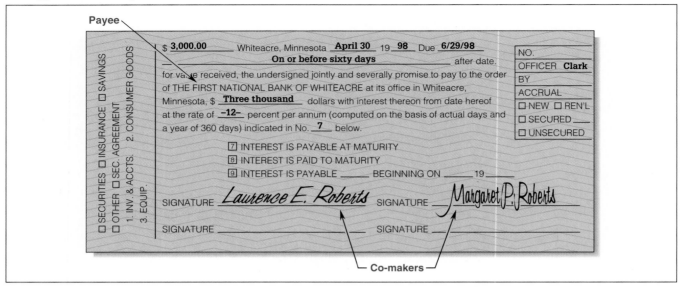

Promissory Notes and Certificates of Deposit (Promises to Pay)

PROMISSORY NOTE
A written promise made by one person (the maker) to pay a fixed sum of money to another person (the payee or a subsequent holder) on demand or on a specified date.

MAKER
One who promises to pay a certain sum to the holder of a promissory note or certificate of deposit (CD).

CERTIFICATE OF DEPOSIT (CD)
A note of a bank in which a bank acknowledges a receipt of money from a party and promises to repay the money, with interest, to the party on a certain date.

A **promissory note** is a written promise made by one person (the **maker** of the promise to pay) to another (the payee, or the one to whom the promise is made). A promissory note, which is often referred to simply as a *note*, can be made payable at a definite time or on demand. It can name a specific payee or merely be payable to bearer (bearer instruments are discussed later in this chapter). For example, on April 30, Laurence and Margaret Roberts sign a writing unconditionally promising to pay "to the order of" the First National Bank of Whiteacre $3,000 (with 12 percent interest) on or before June 29. This writing is a promissory note. A typical promissory note is shown in Exhibit 18–3.

Notes are used in a variety of credit transactions and often carry the name of the transaction involved. For example, a note that is secured by personal property, such as an automobile, is called a *collateral note*, because the property pledged as security for the satisfaction of the debt is called *collateral* (see Chapter 21). A note payable in installments, such as for payment for an entertainment center over a twelve-month period, is called an *installment note*.

A **certificate of deposit (CD)** is a type of note. A CD is issued when a party deposits money with a bank, and the bank promises to repay the money, with interest, on a certain date [UCC 3–104(j)]. The bank is the maker of the note, and the depositor is the payee. For example, on February 15, Sara Levin deposits $5,000 with the First National Bank of Whiteacre. The bank promises to repay the $5,000, plus 7½ percent interest, on August 15.

Certificates of deposit in small denominations (for amounts up to $100,000) are often sold by savings and loan associations, savings banks, and commercial banks. Certificates of deposit for amounts over $100,000 are called large (or jumbo) CDs. Exhibit 18–4 shows a typical small CD.

"A negotiable bill or note is a courier without luggage."

John B. Gibson, 1780–1853 (American jurist)

▌Requirements for Negotiability

For an instrument to be negotiable, it must meet the following requirements:

1. Be in writing.
2. Be signed by the maker or the drawer.

♦ **Exhibit 18–4**
A Typical Small CD

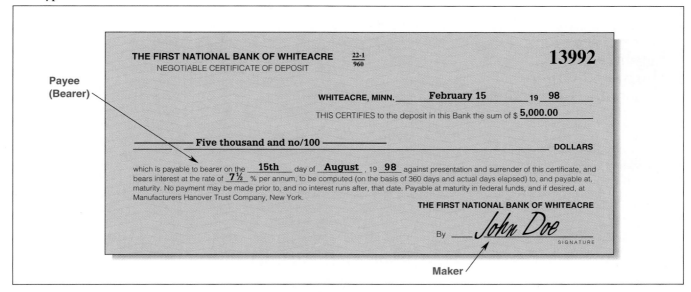

3. Be an unconditional promise or order to pay.
4. State a fixed amount of money.
5. Be payable on demand or at a definite time.
6. Be payable to order or to bearer, unless it is a check.

Written Form

Negotiable instruments must be in written form [UCC 3–103(a)(6)]. This is because negotiable instruments must possess the quality of certainty that only formal, written expression can give. The writing must have the following qualities:

1. The writing must be on material that lends itself to *permanence*. Instruments carved in blocks of ice or recorded on other impermanent surfaces would not qualify as negotiable instruments. Suppose that Suzanne writes in the sand, "I promise to pay $500 to the order of Jack." This cannot be a negotiable instrument because, although it is in writing, it lacks permanence.
2. The writing must also have *portability*. Although this is not a spelled-out legal requirement, if an instrument is not movable, it obviously cannot meet the requirement that it be freely transferable. For example, Charles writes on the side of a cow, "I promise to pay $500 to the order of Jason." Technically, this meets the requirements of a negotiable instrument, but as a cow cannot easily be transferred in the ordinary course of business, the "instrument" is nonnegotiable. (See this chapter's *Law in the Extreme* for some examples of unusual forms of negotiable instruments.)

Signatures

For an instrument to be negotiable, it must be signed by (1) the maker, if it is a note or a certificate of deposit, or (2) the drawer, if it is a draft or a check [UCC 3–103(a)(3)]. If a person signs an instrument as an authorized *agent* of the maker or drawer, the maker or drawer has effectively signed the instrument. (Agents' signatures will be discussed in Chapter 19.)

The UCC grants extreme latitude in regard to what constitutes a signature. UCC 1–201(39) provides that a **signature** may include "any symbol executed or adopted by a party with present intention to authenticate a writing." UCC 3–401(b) expands on

SIGNATURE
Under the UCC, "any symbol executed or adopted by a party with a present intention to authenticate a writing."

LAW IN THE EXTREME

Eggshells, Shirts, and Other Negotiable Instruments

The UCC leaves a lot of room for imagination when it comes to negotiable instruments. Bearer instruments, for example, need not always be written to "cash" or to "bearer." They can be written to "Merry Christmas" or "Happy New Year" or just about any nonexistent or inanimate object. Even more extraordinary is the UCC's lack of specificity as to the form of a negotiable instrument. When we think of a check, for example, we normally envision a preprinted form with the "normal" terms and phrases on it, including the bank's name and address, "Pay to," and so on. The UCC, however, says nothing to indicate that negotiable instruments must be typed or printed or placed on any specific kind of material. The UCC only stipulates that a negotiable instrument must be in writing, the writing must lend itself to permanence, and the writing must be portable.

As might be imagined, this lack of specificity has led to some extraordinary negotiable instruments. Checks and notes have been written on napkins, menus, tablecloths, and a variety of other materials. According to one legal scholar, Marianne Jennings, in one case a check was written on an eggshell.[a] Another legal scholar, Douglas Whaley, contends that the Internal Revenue Service frequently receives checks written on shirts.[b]

Probably the most famous (or infamous) negotiable instrument, though, is a fictitious one created by Sir Alan Herbert in his memorable story entitled *"Board of Inland Revenue v. Haddock:* The Negotiable Cow."[c] In the story, Albert Haddock, disgusted over the high amount of taxes he has

to pay for government services from which he does not benefit, wrote in large red lettering on the side of his white cow the following words: "Pay the Collector of Taxes, who is no gentleman, or Order, the sum of fifty-seven pounds (and may he rot!). 'Albert Haddock.'" The tax collector refused to accept the check, mostly because the cow would not let the tax collector indorse it. Summoned into court for failing to pay his income taxes, Haddock told his story to the judge. The judge, who clearly sided with Haddock in regard to government spending policies, also agreed with Haddock on the issue of the cow's negotiability: "an order to pay is an order to pay, whether it is made on the back of an envelope or on the back of a cow."

For Critical Analysis: *What if a check were filled out and signed using invisible ink that is visible only when heated? Would the check meet the requirements for a negotiable instrument?*

a. Marianne M. Jennings, "I Want to Know What Bearer Paper Is and I Want to Meet a Holder in Due Course: Reflections on Instruction in UCC Articles Three and Four," 1992 *Brigham Young University Law Review* 385 (1992). Jennings also tells of negotiable instruments written on a tractor fender, a tamale, and a watermelon.
b. Douglas J. Whaley, *Problems and Materials on Negotiable Instruments*, 2d ed. (New York: Little, Brown, 1988).
c. In M. Kossler, ed., *Masterpieces of Legal Fiction* (Rochester, N.Y.: Lawyer's Cooperative Publishing Co., 1964).

this by stating that a "signature may be made (i) manually or by means of a device or machine, and (ii) by the use of any name, including a trade or assumed name, or by a word, mark, or symbol executed or adopted by a person with present intention to authenticate a writing." Thus, initials, an X, or a thumbprint will suffice as a signature. A trade name or an assumed name is also sufficient. Signatures that are placed onto instruments by means of rubber stamps are permitted and frequently used in the business world. If necessary, parol evidence (discussed in Chapter 11) is admissible to identify the signer. When the signer is identified, the signature becomes effective.

The location of the signature on the document is unimportant, although the usual place is the lower right-hand corner. A *handwritten* statement on the body of the instrument, such as "I, Jerome Cavallo, promise to pay Elaine Grant," is sufficient to act as a signature.

There are virtually no limitations on the manner in which a signature can be made, but one should be careful about receiving an instrument that has been signed in an unusual way. Furthermore, an unusual signature clearly decreases the *marketability* of an instrument, because it creates uncertainty.

Unconditional Promise or Order to Pay

The terms of the promise or order must be included in the writing on the face of a negotiable instrument. The terms must also be *unconditional*—that is, they cannot be conditioned on the occurrence or nonoccurrence of some other event or agreement [UCC 3–104(a)].

PROMISE OR ORDER   For an instrument to be negotiable, it must contain an express order or promise to pay. A mere acknowledgment of the debt, which might logically *imply* a promise, is not sufficient under the UCC, because the promise must be an *affirmative* (express) undertaking [UCC 3–103(a)(9)]. For example, the traditional I.O.U. is only an acknowledgment of indebtedness. Although the I.O.U. might logically *imply* a promise, it is not a negotiable instrument, because it does not contain an express promise to repay the debt. If such words as "to be paid on demand" or "due on demand" are added to the I.O.U., however, the need for an express promise is satisfied. Thus, if a buyer executes a promissory note using the words "I promise to pay $1,000 to the order of the seller for the purchase of X goods," then this requirement for a negotiable instrument is satisfied.

> **REMEMBER** Negotiable instruments are classified as promises to pay and orders to pay.

A certificate of deposit is exceptional in this respect. No express promise is required in a CD, because the bank's acknowledgment of the deposit and the other terms of the instrument clearly indicate a promise by the bank to repay the sum of money [UCC 3–104(j)].

An *order* is associated with three-party instruments, such as trade acceptances, checks, and drafts. An order directs a third party to pay the instrument as drawn. In the typical check, for example, the word *pay* (to the order of a payee) is a command to the drawee bank to pay the check when presented, and thus it is an order. The order is mandatory even if it is written in a courteous form with words like "Please pay" or "Kindly pay." Generally, precise language must be used. An order stating "I wish you would pay" does not fulfill the requirement of precision. The order to the drawee may be addressed to one person or to more than one person, either jointly ("to A *and* B") or alternatively ("to A *or* B") [UCC 3–103(a)(6)].

UNCONDITIONALITY OF PROMISE OR ORDER   A negotiable instrument's utility as a substitute for money or as a credit device would be dramatically reduced if it had conditional promises attached to it. Suppose, for example, that Andrew promises in a note to pay Frances $10,000 only on the condition that a certain ship reaches port. No one could safely purchase the promissory note without first investigating whether the ship had arrived. Even then, the facts disclosed by the investigation might be incorrect. To avoid such problems, the UCC provides that only unconditional promises or orders can be negotiable [UCC 3–104(a)].

A promise or order is conditional (and *not* negotiable) if it states (1) an express condition to payment, (2) that the promise or order is subject to or governed by another writing, or (3) that the rights or obligations with respect to the promise or order are stated in another writing. A reference to another writing, however, does not of itself make the promise or order conditional [UCC 3–106(a)]. For example, the words "As per contract" or "This debt arises from the sale of goods X and Y" do not render an instrument nonnegotiable.

Similarly, a statement in the instrument that payment can be made only out of a particular fund or source will not render the instrument nonnegotiable [UCC 3–106(b)(ii)].[1] Thus, for example, terms in a note that include the condition that payment will be made out of the proceeds of next year's cotton crop will not make the note

---

1. Section 3–105(2)(b) of the unrevised Article 3 provided just the opposite: an instrument with a term providing that payment could be made only out of a particular fund or source rendered the instrument nonnegotiable.

nonnegotiable. (The payee of such a note, however, may find the note commercially unacceptable and refuse to take it.)

Finally, a simple statement in an otherwise negotiable note indicating that the note is secured by a mortgage does not destroy its negotiability. Realize, though, that the statement that a note is secured by a mortgage must not stipulate that the maker's promise to pay is *subject* to the terms and conditions of the mortgage.

In the following case, the court had to decide whether a loan guaranty contained an unconditional promise to pay and therefore constituted a negotiable instrument.

CASE 18.1

FEDERAL DEPOSIT INSURANCE CORP. v. F.S.S.S.

United States District Court,
District of Alaska, 1993.
829 F.Supp. 317.

HISTORICAL AND ECONOMIC SETTING   *Banks often fail because of too many bad loans. When a federally insured bank fails, the Federal Deposit Insurance Corporation (FDIC) normally pays off each depositor, up to a certain amount, and then sells the bank's assets to obtain some repayment. Sometimes, the FDIC is repaid a percentage of what it pays out by negotiating another bank's acquisition of the failed bank. To arrange a deal, the FDIC may subsidize the acquisition. To obtain other funds, the FDIC may also attempt to collect on some of the failed bank's outstanding loans.*

FACTS   Thomas Fink, Donald Schroer, David Swanson, and Marie Swanson—doing business as F.S.S.S., a partnership—signed two promissory notes to borrow money from the Alaska Mutual Bank (AMB), providing the same real estate as collateral for both loans. Patricia Fink and LaVonne Schroer signed guaranties of repayment for the second note. AMB failed. The first note ended up in the hands of the First Interstate Bank of Oregon. The second fell into the possession of the Federal Deposit Insurance Corporation (FDIC). When Fink, Schroer, and the Swansons

were unable to repay the first note, the Oregon bank agreed to accept a lesser amount if the FDIC would approve. The FDIC refused and filed a suit in a federal district court against the Finks, the Schroers, and the Swansons to collect the money due on the note that the FDIC now owned. On the FDIC's motion for summary judgment, one of the issues was whether Patricia and LaVonne's guaranties were negotiable instruments. If so, Patricia and LaVonne could have asserted a certain defense under which they might have been able to avoid liability.

ISSUE   Did the guaranties satisfy the requirements for negotiable instruments?

DECISION   No. The court granted the FDIC's motion for summary judgment.

REASON   The court pointed out that "[t]o constitute a negotiable instrument, a document must * * * contain an unconditional promise to pay." The court acknowledged that "Patricia Fink and LaVonne Schroer executed separate documents apart from the promissory notes that they guaranteed." The court concluded, however, that neither guaranty contained an "unconditional promise" to pay a fixed amount. Thus, according to the court, "[n]either guaranty is a negotiable instrument."

FOR CRITICAL ANALYSIS—Economic Consideration
If the defendants in this case had avoided the repayment of their note to the FDIC, who would have ultimately had to pay for their default?

A Fixed Amount of Money

Negotiable instruments must state with certainty a fixed amount of money to be paid at any time the instrument is payable [UCC 3–104(a)]. This requirement promises clarity and certainty in determining the value of the instrument.

FIXED AMOUNT   The term *fixed amount* means an amount that is ascertainable from the face of the instrument. A demand note payable with 12 percent interest meets the requirement of a fixed amount because its amount can be determined at the time it is payable [UCC 3–104(a)].[2] The rate of interest also may be determined with reference to information that is not contained in the instrument but that is readily ascertainable by reference to a formula or a source described in the instrument [UCC 3–112(b)].[3] For example, when an instrument is payable at the *legal rate of interest* (a rate of interest fixed by statute), the instrument is negotiable. Mortgage notes tied to a variable rate of interest (a rate that fluctuates as a result of market conditions) can also be negotiable. The requirement that to be negotiable a writing must contain a promise or order to pay a fixed amount applies only to the principal [UCC 3–104].

BE AWARE Interest payable on an instrument normally cannot exceed the maximum limit on interest under a state's usury statute.

During the 1980s, variable-rate mortgages became increasingly popular. This led to problems, because Article 3, prior to the 1990 revision, stated that an amount or rate of interest could be determined only from the instrument without reference to any outside source. The 1990 revision of Article 3 brought the UCC into line with current business practices by providing that notes tied to a variable interest rate can be negotiable.

As part of an ongoing effort to make international law consistent for negotiable instruments, the United Nations Convention on International Bills of Exchange and International Promissory Notes (CIBN) has established rules to govern international transactions. The CIBN, like revised Article 3 of the UCC, considers an instrument with a variable interest rate to be negotiable.

For Critical Analysis: *Can you think of any reasons why an instrument with a variable interest rate should* not *be negotiable?*

Payable in Money   UCC 3–104(a) provides that a fixed amount is to be *payable in money*. The UCC defines money as "a medium of exchange authorized or adopted by a domestic or foreign government as a part of its currency" [UCC 1–201(24)].

Suppose that the maker of a note promises "to pay on demand $1,000 in U.S. gold." Because gold is not a medium of exchange adopted by the U.S. government, the note is not payable in money. The same result would occur if the maker promises "to pay $1,000 and fifty liters of 1964 Château Lafite-Rothschild wine," because the instrument is not payable *entirely* in money. An instrument payable in government bonds or in shares of IBM stock is not negotiable, because neither is a medium of exchange recognized by the U.S. government. The statement "Payable in $1,000 U.S. currency or an equivalent value in gold" would render the instrument nonnegotiable if the maker reserved the option of paying in money *or* gold. If the option were left to the payee, some legal scholars argue that the instrument would be negotiable. Any instrument payable in the United States with a face amount stated in a foreign currency is negotiable and can be paid in the foreign money or in the equivalent in U.S. dollars [UCC 3–107].

Payable on Demand or at a Definite Time

A negotiable instrument must "be payable on demand or at a definite time" [UCC 3–104(a)(2)]. Clearly, to ascertain the value of a negotiable instrument, it is necessary to know when the maker, drawee, or acceptor (an **acceptor** is a drawee that promises to pay an instrument when it is presented later for payment) is required to pay. It is also

ACCEPTOR
A drawee that promises to pay an instrument when the instrument is presented later for payment.

---

2.   Under Section 3–104(1)(b) of the unrevised Article 3, the amount to be paid was called a *sum certain.*
3.   This was not possible under the unrevised Article 3, which required that an amount or rate of interest could be determined only from the instrument without reference to any outside source [UCC 3–106].

necessary to know when the obligations of secondary parties, such as indorsers[4] (to be discussed later in this chapter), will arise. Furthermore, it is necessary to know when an instrument is due in order to calculate when the statute of limitations may apply [UCC 3–118(a)]. Finally, with an interest-bearing instrument, it is necessary to know the exact interval during which the interest will accrue to determine the present value of the instrument.

PAYABLE ON DEMAND   Instruments that are payable on demand include those that contain the words "Payable at sight" or "Payable upon presentment." **Presentment** occurs when a person presents an instrument to the party liable on the instrument to collect payment; presentment also occurs when a person presents an instrument to a drawee for acceptance—see the discussion of trade acceptances earlier in this chapter.

The very nature of the instrument may indicate that it is payable on demand. For example, a check, by definition, is payable on demand [UCC 3–104(f)]. If no time for payment is specified and the person responsible for payment must pay on the instrument's presentment, the instrument is payable on demand [UCC 3–108(a)].

PAYABLE AT A DEFINITE TIME   If an instrument is not payable on demand, to be negotiable it must be payable at a definite time. An instrument is payable at a definite time if it states that it is payable (1) on a specified date, (2) within a definite period of time (such as thirty days) after sight or acceptance, or (3) on a date or time readily ascertainable at the time the promise or order is issued [UCC 3–108(b)]. The maker or drawee is under no obligation to pay until the specified time.

Suppose that an instrument dated June 1, 1998, states, "One year after the death of my grandfather, Henry Adams, I promise to pay to the order of James Harmon $500. [Signed] Jacqueline Wells." This instrument is nonnegotiable. Because the date of the grandfather's death is uncertain, the instrument is not payable at a definite time, even though the event is bound to occur or has already occurred.

When an instrument is payable on or before a stated date, it is clearly payable at a definite time, although the maker has the option of paying before the stated maturity date. This uncertainty does not violate the definite-time requirement. Suppose that Levine gives Hirsch an instrument dated May 1, 1998, that indicates on its face that it is payable on or before May 1, 1999. This instrument satisfies the requirement. In contrast, an instrument that is undated and made payable "one month after date" is clearly nonnegotiable. There is no way to determine the maturity date from the face of the instrument.

ACCELERATION CLAUSE   An **acceleration clause** allows a payee or other holder of a time instrument to demand payment of the entire amount due, with interest, if a certain event occurs, such as a default in the payment of an installment when due. (A **holder** is any person in the possession of an instrument drawn, issued, or indorsed to him or her, to his or her order, to bearer, or in blank [see UCC 1–201(20)]. (The terms *indorse*, *bearer*, and *in blank* will be explained later in the chapter.) There must be, of course, a good faith belief that payment will not be made for an acceleration clause to be invoked.

Assume that Martin lends $1,000 to Ruth. Ruth makes a negotiable note promising to pay $100 per month for eleven months. The note contains an acceleration provision that permits Martin or any holder to demand at once all the payments plus the interest owed to date if Ruth fails to pay an installment in any given month. If, for example, Ruth fails to make the third payment, the note will be due and payable in full. If Martin accelerates the unpaid balance, Ruth will owe Martin the remaining principal plus any unpaid interest.

PRESENTMENT
The act of presenting an instrument to the party liable on the instrument to collect payment; presentment also occurs when a person presents an instrument to a drawee for acceptance.

ACCELERATION CLAUSE
A clause that allows a payee or other holder of a time instrument to demand payment of the entire amount due, with interest, if a certain event occurs, such as a default in the payment of an installment when due.

HOLDER
Any person in the possession of an instrument drawn, issued, or indorsed to him or her, to his or her order, to bearer, or in blank.

---

4.   We should note here that because the UCC uses the spelling *indorse* (*indorsement*, etc.), rather than *endorse* (endorsement, etc.), we adopt that spelling here and in other chapters in the text.

Under the UCC, instruments that include acceleration clauses are negotiable, because (1) the exact value of the instrument can be ascertained and (2) the instrument will be payable on a specified date if the event allowing acceleration does not occur [UCC 3–108(b)(ii)]. Thus, the specified date is the outside limit used to determine the value and negotiability of the instrument.

EXTENSION CLAUSE   The reverse of an acceleration clause is an **extension clause,** which allows the date of maturity to be extended into the future [UCC 3–108(b)(iii), (iv)]. To keep the instrument negotiable, the interval of the extension must be specified if the right to extend is given to the maker of the instrument. If, however, the holder of the instrument can extend it, the extended maturity date does not have to be specified.

Suppose that a note reads, "The maker has the right to postpone the time of payment of this note beyond its definite maturity date of January 1, 1999. This extension, however, shall be for no more than a reasonable time." A note with this language is not negotiable, because it does not satisfy the definite-time requirement. The right to extend is the maker's, and the maker has not indicated when the note will become due after the extension.

In contrast, a note that reads, "The holder of this note at the date of maturity, January 1, 1999, can extend the time of payment until the following June 1 or later, if the holder so wishes," is a negotiable instrument. The length of the extension does not have to be specified, because the option to extend is solely that of the holder. After January 1, 1999, the note is, in effect, a demand instrument.

Payable to Order or to Bearer

Because one of the functions of a negotiable instrument is to serve as a substitute for money, freedom to transfer is an essential requirement. To assure a proper transfer, the instrument must be "payable to order or to bearer" at the time it is issued or first comes into the possession of the holder [UCC 3–104(a)(1)]. An instrument will not be negotiable unless it meets this requirement.

ORDER INSTRUMENTS   An **order instrument** is an instrument that is payable (1) "to the order of an identified person" or (2) "to an identified person or order" [UCC 3–109(b)]. An identified person is the person "to whom the instrument is initially payable" as determined by the intent of the maker or drawer [UCC 3–110(a)]. The identified person, in turn, may transfer the instrument to whomever he or she wishes. Thus, the maker or drawer is agreeing to pay either the person specified on the instrument or whomever that person might designate. In this way, the instrument retains its transferability. Suppose an instrument states, "Payable to the order of Rocky Reed" or "Pay to Rocky Reed or order." Clearly, the maker or drawer has indicated that a payment will be made to Reed or to whomever Reed designates. The instrument is negotiable.

Except for bearer instruments (explained in the following paragraph), the person specified must be named with *certainty*, because the transfer of an order instrument requires an indorsement. (An **indorsement** is a signature placed on an instrument, such as on the back of a check, for the purpose of transferring one's ownership rights in the instrument.) If an instrument states, "Payable to the order of my kissing cousin," the instrument is nonnegotiable, because a holder could not be sure that the person who indorsed the instrument was actually the "kissing cousin" who was supposed to have indorsed it.

BEARER INSTRUMENTS   A **bearer instrument** is an instrument that does not designate a specific payee [UCC 3–109(a)]. The term **bearer** refers to a person in the possession of an instrument that is payable to bearer or indorsed in blank (with a signature only,

---

EXTENSION CLAUSE
A clause in a time instrument that allows the instrument's date of maturity to be extended into the future.

ORDER INSTRUMENT
A negotiable instrument that is payable "to the order of an identified person" or "to an identified person or order."

INDORSEMENT
A signature placed on an instrument for the purpose of transferring one's ownership rights in the instrument.

BEARER INSTRUMENT
Any instrument that is not payable to a specific person, including instruments payable to the bearer or to "cash."

BEARER
A person in the possession of an instrument payable to bearer or indorsed in blank.

as will be discussed shortly) [UCC 1–201(5), 3–109(a), 3–109(c)]. This means that the maker or drawer agrees to pay anyone who presents the instrument for payment. Any instrument containing the following terms is a bearer instrument:

NOTE An instrument that purports to be payable both to order and bearer is a contradiction in terms. Such an instrument is a bearer instrument.

- "Payable to the order of bearer."
- "Payable to Rocky Reed or bearer."
- "Payable to bearer."
- "Pay cash."
- "Pay to the order of cash."

In addition, an instrument that "indicates that it is not payable to an identified person" is bearer paper [UCC 3–109(a)(3)]. Thus, an instrument "payable to X" can be negotiated as bearer paper, as though it were payable to cash. The UCC does not accept an instrument issued to a nonexistent organization as payable to bearer, however [UCC 3–109, Comment 2]. An instrument "payable to the order of the Camrod Company," if no such company exists, therefore would not be bearer paper.

▌Factors That Do *Not* Affect Negotiability

Certain ambiguities or omissions will not affect the negotiability of an instrument. The UCC's rules for clearing up ambiguous terms include the following:

1. Unless the date of an instrument is necessary to determine a definite time for payment, the fact that an instrument is undated does not affect its negotiability. A typical example is an undated check [UCC 3–113(b)].
2. Postdating or antedating an instrument does not affect the instrument's negotiability [UCC 3–113(a)].
3. Handwritten terms outweigh typewritten and printed terms (preprinted terms on forms, for example), and typewritten terms outweigh printed terms [UCC 3–114]. For example, if your check is printed, "Pay to the order of," and in handwriting you insert in the blank, "Anita Delgado or bearer," the check is a bearer instrument.
4. Words outweigh figures unless the words are ambiguous [UCC 3–114]. This is important when the numerical amount and written amount on a check differ.
5. When a particular interest rate is not specified but the instrument simply states "with interest," the interest rate is the *judgment rate of interest* (a rate of interest fixed by statute that is applied to a monetary judgment awarded by a court until the judgment is paid or terminated) [UCC 3–112(b)].

▌Transfer of Instruments

Once issued, a negotiable instrument can be transferred by *assignment* or by *negotiation*.

Transfer by Assignment

Recall from Chapter 12 that an assignment is a transfer of rights under a contract. Under general contract principles, a transfer by assignment to an assignee gives the assignee only those rights that the assignor possessed. Any defenses that can be raised against an assignor can normally be raised against the assignee. This same principle applies when an instrument, such as a promissory note, is transferred by assignment. The transferee is then an *assignee* rather than a *holder*. Sometimes, a transfer fails to qualify as a negotiation because it fails to meet one or more of the requirements of a negotiable instrument, discussed above. When this occurs, the transfer becomes an assignment.

Transfer by Negotiation

Negotiation is the transfer of an instrument in such form that the transferee (the person to whom the instrument is transferred) becomes a holder [UCC 3–201(a)]. Under UCC principles, a transfer by negotiation creates a holder who, at the very least, receives the rights of the previous possessor [UCC 3–203(b)]. Unlike an assignment, a transfer by negotiation can make it possible for a holder to receive *more* rights in the instrument than the prior possessor had [UCC 3–202(b), 3–305, 3–306]. A holder who receives greater rights is known as a *holder in due course*, a concept we discuss in Chapter 19.

There are two methods of negotiating an instrument so that the receiver becomes a holder. The method used depends on whether the instrument is order paper or bearer paper.

NEGOTIATING ORDER INSTRUMENTS   An order instrument contains the name of a payee capable of indorsing, as in "Pay to the order of Lloyd Sorenson." An order instrument is also an instrument that has as its last or only indorsement a *special* indorsement, as in "Pay to Sorenson. [Signed] Adams." (Special indorsements are discussed in more detail later in this chapter.) If the instrument is an order instrument, it is negotiated by delivery with any necessary indorsements. For example, National Express Corporation issues a payroll check "to the order of Lloyd Sorenson." Sorenson takes the check to the supermarket, signs his name on the back (an indorsement), gives it to the cashier (a delivery), and receives cash. Sorenson has *negotiated* the check to the supermarket [UCC 3–201(b)]. In the following case, the court had to decide whether a promissory note had been assigned or negotiated.

> *"Money has little value to its possessor unless it also has value to others."*
>
> **Leland Stanford, 1824–1893**
> (*U.S. senator and founder of Stanford University*)

NEGOTIATION
The transfer of an instrument in such form that the transferee (the person to whom the instrument is transferred) becomes a holder.

CASE 18.2

ALVES v. BALDAIA
Court of Appeals of Ohio,
Third District, 1984.
14 Ohio App.3d 187,
470 N.E.2d 459.

HISTORICAL AND SOCIAL SETTING   *Checks and promissory notes have been in use for centuries. Nearly everyone can identify a check, and most people can explain its general legal effect. Most people can also explain the general obligation of a promissory note, particularly when it is pointed out that a note is usually an instrument that is signed when money is borrowed. Despite this familiarity with checks and notes, many people are not aware of some of the most important consequences of dealing with negotiable instruments, including the consequences of indorsements.*

FACTS   In January 1973, Keith and Joyce Alves loaned Joyce Alves's parents, Beatrice and William Baldaia, $15,000. In return, the Baldaias executed a promissory note payable to Joyce Alves. In February 1978, Keith and Joyce Alves divorced. The separation agreement contained the following provision: "Wife agrees to assign to Husband any and all right, title, and interest she may have in a certain note, executed by her parents, dated January 3, 1973 on or before date of final hearing." Joyce Alves later wrote on the promissory note, "Pay to the order of Keith R. Alves. [Signed] Joyce Ann Alves." Some time later, Keith Alves tried to collect payment on the note from the Baldaias, who refused to pay it. Alves then brought an action in an Ohio state court, seeking payment from his former wife, who had since remarried and taken the name of Schaller. Schaller claimed that her transfer of the promissory note to Alves, pursuant to the separation agreement, constituted an "assignment" of her rights and interests in the note and not a formal "negotiation" of the note. The trial court held that Schaller's signature on the note operated as an indorsement. Schaller and her parents, the Baldaias, appealed the decision, claiming that the trial court had been in error by dismissing their motion for summary judgment.

ISSUE   Was the transfer of the promissory note an assignment or a negotiation?

DECISION   The Ohio appellate court affirmed the trial court's judgment that the transfer had been a negotiation and, hence, Schaller was secondarily liable (liable in the event that her parents failed to pay the note—see Chapter 19).

(Continued)

Case 18.2—Continued

REASON The court reasoned that if Schaller had wished only to "assign" the note, she should not have indorsed it. As it stood, the indorsement of the note technically gave Keith Alves the rights of a holder. Although the divorce agreement made it clear that Joyce Alves had intended an assignment of the note, as a matter of law such extraneous evidence could not be used to determine the intent of the parties. The decision had to rest on what the instrument itself stated or reflected, and parol evidence was inadmissible in this case. The court stated that an "indorser may disclaim his liability on the contract of indorsement, *but only if the indorsement itself*

so specifies. * * * *The customary manner of disclaiming the indorser's liability is* * * * *to indorse 'without recourse.'*" (Emphasis added.) Because no disclaimer was written on the instrument, Schaller's signature on the note meant that "she contracted to pay the instrument, according to its tenor [its exact words], to the holder thereof if the maker dishonored the note at maturity."

FOR CRITICAL ANALYSIS—Ethical Consideration
Sometimes, the application of negotiable instruments law has seemingly unfair results, as in this case. What problems would courts face if subjective intentions were considered in determining whether a note is negotiable or nonnegotiable?

NEGOTIATING BEARER INSTRUMENTS If an instrument is payable to bearer, it is negotiated by delivery—that is, by transfer into another person's possession. Indorsement is not necessary [UCC 3–201(b)]. The use of bearer instruments thus involves more risk through loss or theft than the use of order instruments.

Assume that Richard Kraychek writes a check "payable to cash" and hands it to Jessie Arnold (a delivery). Kraychek has issued the check (a bearer instrument) to Arnold. Arnold places the check in her wallet, which is subsequently stolen. The thief has possession of the check. At this point, negotiation has not occurred, because delivery must be *voluntary* on the part of the transferor. If the thief "delivers" the check to an innocent third person, however, negotiation will be complete. All rights to the check will be passed *absolutely* to that third person, and Arnold will lose all right to recover the proceeds of the check from him or her [UCC 3–306]. Of course, Arnold can recover the money from the thief if the thief can be found.

> RECALL A person convicted of theft may be sued for conversion. Conversion is the civil side of crimes of theft.

CONVERTING ORDER INSTRUMENTS TO BEARER INSTRUMENTS AND VICE VERSA
The method used for negotiation depends on the character of the instrument at the time the negotiation takes place. For example, a check originally payable to "cash" but subsequently indorsed with the words "Pay to Arnold" must be negotiated as an order instrument (by indorsement and delivery), even though it was previously a bearer instrument [UCC 3–205(a)].

An instrument payable to the order of a named payee and indorsed in blank (by the holder's signature only, as will be discussed shortly) becomes a bearer instrument [UCC 3–205(b)]. For example, a check made payable to the order of Jessie Arnold is issued to Arnold, and Arnold indorses it by signing her name on the back. The instrument, which is now a bearer instrument, can be negotiated by delivery without indorsement. Arnold can negotiate the check to whomever she wishes merely by delivery, and that person can negotiate by delivery without indorsement. If Arnold loses the check after she indorses it, then a finder can negotiate it further. Exhibit 18–5 illustrates how indorsements can convert an order instrument into a bearer instrument and vice versa.

▌Indorsements

Indorsements are required whenever the instrument being negotiated is classified as an order instrument. An *indorsement* is a signature with or without additional words or statements. It is most often written on the back of the instrument itself. If there is no room on the instrument, indorsements can be written on a separate piece of paper,

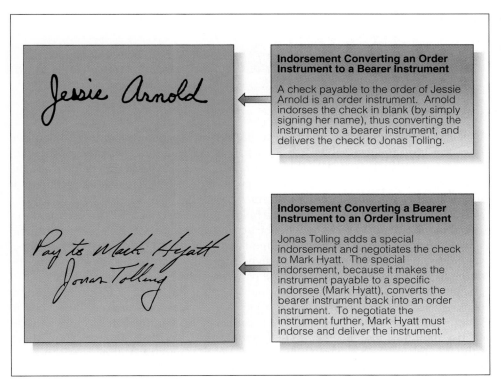

◆ Exhibit 18–5
Converting an Order
Instrument to a Bearer
Instrument and Vice Versa

Indorsement Converting an Order Instrument to a Bearer Instrument

A check payable to the order of Jessie Arnold is an order instrument. Arnold indorses the check in blank (by simply signing her name), thus converting the instrument to a bearer instrument, and delivers the check to Jonas Tolling.

Indorsement Converting a Bearer Instrument to an Order Instrument

Jonas Tolling adds a special indorsement and negotiates the check to Mark Hyatt. The special indorsement, because it makes the instrument payable to a specific indorsee (Mark Hyatt), converts the bearer instrument back into an order instrument. To negotiate the instrument further, Mark Hyatt must indorse and deliver the instrument.

called an **allonge.**[5] The allonge must be "so firmly affixed [to the instrument] as to become a part thereof" [UCC 3–204(a)]. Pins or paper clips will not suffice. Most courts hold that staples are sufficient.

A person who transfers an instrument by signing (indorsing) it and delivering it to another person is an **indorser.** For example, Martha receives a graduation check for $100. She can transfer the check to her mother (or to anyone) by signing it on the back and delivering it. Martha is an indorser. If Martha indorses the check by writing "Pay to Mary Grimes," Mary Grimes is the **indorsee.**

One purpose of an indorsement is to effect the negotiation of order paper. Sometimes the transferee of a bearer instrument will request the holder-transferor to indorse the instrument to impose liability on the indorser (the liability of indorsers will be discussed in Chapter 19), although the UCC does not require bearer instruments to be indorsed.

We examine here four categories of indorsements: blank indorsements, special indorsements, qualified indorsements, and restrictive indorsements.

Blank Indorsements

A **blank indorsement** specifies no particular indorsee and can consist of a mere signature [UCC 3–205(b)]. Hence, a check payable "to the order of Alan Luberda" can be indorsed in blank simply by having Luberda's signature written on the back of the check. An instrument payable to order and indorsed in blank becomes a bearer instrument and can be negotiated by delivery alone, as already discussed. Exhibit 18–6 shows a blank indorsement.

ALLONGE
A piece of paper firmly attached to a negotiable instrument, upon which transferees can make indorsements if there is no room left on the instrument itself.

INDORSER
A person who transfers an instrument by signing (indorsing) it and delivering it to another person.

INDORSEE
The person to whom a negotiable instrument is transferred by indorsement.

BLANK INDORSEMENT
An indorsement that specifies no particular indorsee and that can consist of a mere signature. An order instrument that is indorsed in blank becomes a bearer instrument.

---

5. Pronounced uh-*lohnj.*

◆ **Exhibit 18–6**
  A Blank Indorsement

Alan Luberda

SPECIAL INDORSEMENT
An indorsement on an instrument that indicates the specific person to whom the indorser intends to make the instrument payable; that is, it names the indorsee.

Special Indorsements

A **special indorsement** indicates the specific person to whom the indorser intends to make the instrument payable; that is, it names the indorsee [UCC 3–205(a)]. For example, words such as "Pay to the order of Storr" or "Pay to Storr," followed by the signature of the indorser, create a special indorsement. When an instrument is indorsed in this way, it is an order instrument.

To avoid the risk of loss from theft, a holder may convert a blank indorsement to a special indorsement. This changes the bearer instrument back to an order instrument. A holder may "convert a blank indorsement that consists only of a signature into a special indorsement by writing, above the signature of the indorser, words identifying the person to whom the instrument is made payable" [UCC 3–205(c)].

For example, a check is made payable to Arthur Rabe. He indorses his name in blank (signs his name only) on the back of the check and delivers the check to Anthony Alfono. Anthony, not wishing to cash the check immediately, wants to avoid any risk should he lose the check. He therefore writes "Pay to Anthony Alfono" above Arthur's blank indorsement (see Exhibit 18–7). In this manner, Anthony has converted Arthur's blank indorsement into a special indorsement. Further negotiation now requires Anthony Alfono's indorsement plus delivery.

◆ **Exhibit 18–7**
  A Special Indorsement

Pay to Anthony Alfono

Arthur Rabe

QUALIFIED INDORSEMENT
An indorsement on a negotiable instrument in which the indorser disclaims any contract liability on the instrument; the notation "without recourse" is commonly used to create a qualified indorsement.

Qualified Indorsements

Generally, an indorser, *merely by indorsing,* impliedly promises to pay the holder, or any subsequent indorser, the amount of the instrument in the event that the drawer or maker defaults on the payment [UCC 3–415(b)]. An indorser uses a **qualified indorsement** to disclaim this contract liability on the instrument. The notation "without recourse" is commonly used to create a qualified indorsement, such as the one shown in Exhibit 18–8.

◆ **Exhibit 18–8**
  A Qualified Indorsement

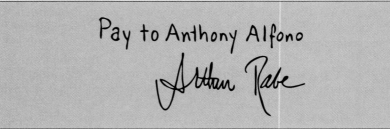

Pay to Elvie Ling, without recourse.

Bridgett Cage

Qualified indorsements are often used by persons acting in a representative capacity. For example, insurance agents sometimes receive checks payable to them that are really intended as payment to the insurance company. The agent is merely indorsing the payment through to the insurance company and should not be required to make good on the check if it is later dishonored. The "without recourse" indorsement relieves the agent from any contract liability on a check. If the instrument is dishonored, the holder cannot obtain recovery from the agent who indorsed "without recourse" unless the indorser has breached one of the transfer warranties discussed in Chapter 19, which relate to good title, authorized signature, no material alteration, and so forth.

Usually, then, blank and special indorsements are *unqualified indorsements.* That is, the blank or special indorser is guaranteeing payment of the instrument in addition to transferring title to it. The qualified indorser is not guaranteeing payment. Nonetheless, an instrument bearing a qualified indorsement can be negotiated.

A qualified indorsement is accompanied by either a special or a blank indorsement that determines further negotiation. Accordingly, a special qualified indorsement makes the instrument an order instrument, and it requires an indorsement plus delivery for negotiation. A blank qualified indorsement makes the instrument a bearer instrument, and only delivery is required for negotiation.

Assume that a check is made payable to the order of Bridgett Cage and that Bridgett wants to negotiate the check specifically to Elvie Ling with a qualified indorsement. Bridgett would indorse the check as follows: "Pay to Elvie Ling, without recourse. [Signed] Bridgett Cage." For Elvie to negotiate the check further to Joe Nantz, Elvie would have to indorse the check and deliver it to Joe. The qualified indorsement shown earlier in Exhibit 18–8 is an example of a special qualified indorsement.

Restrictive Indorsements

The **restrictive indorsement** requires indorsees to comply with certain instructions regarding the funds involved. A restrictive indorsement does not prohibit the further negotiation of an instrument [UCC 3–206(a)]. Restrictive indorsements come in many forms, some of which we discuss here.

CONDITIONAL INDORSEMENTS   When payment depends on the occurrence of some event specified in the indorsement, the instrument has a conditional indorsement [UCC 3–205(a)]. For example, suppose that Ken Barton indorses a check as follows: "Pay to Lars Johansen if he completes the renovation of my kitchen by June 1, 1998. [Signed] Ken Barton." Article 3 states that an indorsement conditioning the right to receive payment "does not affect the right of the indorsee to enforce the instrument" [UCC 3–206(b)].[6] A person paying or taking for value an instrument can disregard the condition without liability.

A conditional indorsement does not prevent further negotiation of the instrument. If conditional language appears on the *face* of an instrument, however, the instrument is not negotiable, because it does not meet the requirement that it contain an unconditional promise to pay.

INDORSEMENTS PROHIBITING FURTHER INDORSEMENT   An indorsement such as "Pay to Makoto Chi only. [Signed] Jerome Edelman" does not destroy transfer by negotiation. Chi can negotiate the instrument to a holder just as if it had read "Pay to Makoto Chi. [Signed] Jerome Edelman" [UCC 3–206(a)]. If the holder gives value

RESTRICTIVE INDORSEMENT
Any indorsement on a negotiable instrument that requires the indorsee to comply with certain instructions regarding the funds involved. A restrictive indorsement does not prohibit the further negotiation of the instrument.

---

6.   Under the unrevised Article 3, neither the indorsee nor any subsequent holder had the right to enforce payment against an indorser who indorsed a check conditionally until the specified condition was met [UCC 3–206(3)].

to Chi, this type of restrictive indorsement has the same legal effect as a special indorsement.

INDORSEMENTS FOR DEPOSIT OR COLLECTION   A common type of restrictive indorsement is one that makes the indorsee (almost always a bank) a collecting agent of the indorser [UCC 3–206(c)]. For example, if Stephanie Mallak wants to deposit a check she has received into her checking account at the bank, she could indorse the check "For deposit only. [Signed] Stephanie Mallak." (See Exhibit 18–9.) A "Pay any bank or banker" or "For deposit" indorsement has the effect of locking the instrument into the bank collection process, because only a bank can acquire the rights of a holder following this indorsement.

♦ **Exhibit 18–9**
For Deposit/For
Collection Indorsements

For deposit
Stephanie Mallak

or

For Collection only
Stephanie Mallak

TRUST INDORSEMENT
An indorsement for the benefit of the indorser or a third person; also known as an agency indorsement. The indorsement result in legal title vesting in the original indorsee.

TRUST INDORSEMENTS   An indorsement indicating that the indorsee is to hold or use the funds for the benefit of the indorser or a third party is called a **trust indorsement** (also known as an *agency indorsement*) [UCC 3–206(d)]. For example, assume that Ramon Martinez asks his accountant, Ada Alvarez, to pay some bills for him while he is out of the country. He indorses a check as follows: "Pay to Ada Alvarez as Agent for Ramon Martinez." This agency indorsement obligates Alvarez to use the funds only for the benefit of Martinez. Exhibit 18–10 shows sample trust and agency indorsements.

♦ **Exhibit 18–10**
Trust Indorsements

Pay to Ada Alvarez in
trust for José Martinez
Ramon Martinez

or

Pay to Ada Alvarez as Agent
for Ramon Martinez
Ramon Martinez

The result of a trust indorsement is that legal rights in the instrument are transferred to the original indorsee (Ada Alvarez, in the example just given). To the extent that the original indorsee pays or applies the proceeds consistently with the indorsement (for example, "in trust for José Martinez"), the indorsee is a holder and can become a holder in due course (described in Chapter 19).

The fiduciary restrictions (restrictions mandated by a relationship involving trust and loyalty) on the instrument do not reach beyond the original indorsee [UCC 3–206(d), (e)]. Any subsequent purchaser can qualify as a holder in due course unless he or she has actual notice that the instrument was negotiated in breach of the fiduciary duty.[7]

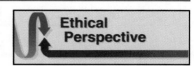

One of the basic goals of the UCC, including Article 3, is to encourage the free flow of commerce by making the laws practical and reasonable. Article 3's provisions relating to trust indorsements provide just one example of the many ways in which the UCC balances this goal against other ethical principles.

For example, by holding only the original indorsee to the fiduciary restrictions on an instrument with a trust indorsement, the UCC furthers the goal of encouraging commerce. If all subsequent holders were obligated to verify that the terms of the trust indorsement were fulfilled, it would impair the ease with which instruments could be transferred—and thus impair their function as substitutes for money. At the same time, Article 3 gives the force of law to the ethical duties of the indorsees on trust instruments to use the funds in accordance with the wishes of the indorsers.

For Critical Analysis: *Why doesn't Article 3 impose the same obligation (to fulfill the terms of an indorsement) on the indorsee of an instrument containing a conditional indorsement?*

▊ Miscellaneous Indorsement Problems

Of course, a significant problem in relation to indorsements occurs when an indorsement is forged or unauthorized. The UCC rules concerning unauthorized or forged signatures and indorsements will be discussed in Chapter 19, in the context of signature liability, and again in Chapter 20, in the context of the bank's liability for payment of an instrument over an unauthorized signature. Two other problems that may arise with indorsements concern misspelled names and multiple payees.

An indorsement should be identical to the name that appears on the instrument. The payee or indorsee whose name is misspelled can indorse with the misspelled name, the correct name, or both [UCC 3–204(d)]. For example, if Sheryl Kruger receives a check payable to the order of Sherrill Krooger, she can indorse the check either "Sheryl Kruger" or "Sherrill Krooger." The usual practice is to indorse the name as it appears on the instrument and follow it by the correct name.

An instrument payable to two or more persons *in the alternative* (for example, "Pay to the order of Tuan or Johnson") requires the indorsement of only one of the payees. If, however, an instrument is made payable to two or more persons *jointly* (for example, "Pay to the order of Sharrie and Bob Covington"), all of the payees' indorsements are necessary for negotiation. If an instrument payable to two or more persons does not clearly indicate whether it is payable in the alternative or jointly (for example, "Pay to the order of John and/or Sara Fitzgerald"), then the instrument is payable to the persons alternatively [UCC 3–110(d)]. The same principles apply to special indorsements that indicate more than one identified person to whom the indorser intends to make the instrument payable [UCC 3–205(a)]. The following case raises some interesting questions concerning checks payable to two parties jointly.

BE AWARE An indorsement in a name different from the name that appears on an instrument raises questions about validity. Anyone paying or taking the instrument can require indorsement in both names.

---

7. See *In re Quantum Development Corp.*, 397 F.Supp. 329 (D.V.I. 1975).

CASE 18.3

GENERAL MOTORS ACCEPTANCE CORP. v. ABINGTON CASUALTY INSURANCE CO.

Supreme Judicial Court of Massachusetts, 1992.
413 Mass. 583,
602 N.E.2d 1085.

COMPANY PROFILE *One of the major divisions of the General Motors Corporation (GM) is the General Motors Acceptance Corporation (GMAC). Created by William Durant, the founder of General Motors and president of GM before he resigned in 1920, GMAC originally loaned money only to buyers of GM vehicles. Over time, however, GMAC became the second largest mortgage banker in the United States. In the 1980s, GMAC was sometimes more profitable than the GM automotive divisions. In 1996, GMAC held outstanding loans worth more than $97 billion. This was more than was held by any commercial bank in the United States except Citicorp.*

FACTS Abington Casualty Insurance Company issued an insurance policy to Robert Azevedo. The policy covered Azevedo's 1984 Jeep. GMAC held a security interest in the vehicle, and the insurance policy named GMAC as the beneficiary. In other words, if the Jeep was damaged and a claim submitted, Abington was to pay GMAC for the amount of appraised damages. The Jeep was later damaged, and Abington appraised the loss and issued a check payable jointly "to the order of Robert A. Azevedo and G.M.A.C." The check was delivered to Azevedo, who then indorsed the check and presented it to the bank. The bank accepted the check, which had not been indorsed by GMAC, and Azevedo received full payment. GMAC never received the funds. GMAC filed suit in a Massachusetts state court against the drawer of the check, Abington, to recover the insurance payment it should have received. The trial court dismissed the action, and GMAC appealed.

ISSUE The two issues in this case were as follows: (1) Does the delivery of a negotiable instrument to one joint payee operate as a delivery to all joint payees? (2) Is the drawer's underlying obligation to joint payees discharged when one joint payee cashes a check without the indorsement of the other?

DECISION Yes, to the first question; no, to the second.

REASON The Supreme Judicial Court of Massachusetts, that state's highest court, concluded that delivery to one joint payee constituted delivery to all joint payees. The court reasoned that because state law required that every payee had to indorse an instrument before it could be negotiated, transferred, or discharged, "delivery of the instrument to one payee does not jeopardize the rights of the other payees." Abington's delivery of the check to Azevedo therefore was held to constitute delivery to both payees. As to the second issue—whether Abington's obligations to GMAC were discharged when Azevedo cashed the check—the court held that "a negotiable instrument cannot be discharged by the actions of only one payee." The UCC "expressly prohibits the discharge of an instrument except by all the payees." The court stated that if it were not for this rule, "there would be no assurance that all the joint payees would receive payment." Because GMAC, as a joint payee, had not received payment, Abington had not discharged its obligation to GMAC.

FOR CRITICAL ANALYSIS—Ethical Consideration
The general principle in negotiable instruments law is that the loss should fall on the party in the best position to prevent it. In the case just presented, which party was in the best position to prevent the loss?

Application

Law and the Consumer—Writing and Indorsing Checks*

As a consumer or as a businessperson, you will certainly be writing and receiving checks. There are pitfalls involved in both activities.

The danger in signing a blank check is clear. Anyone can write in an unauthorized amount and cash the check. Although you may be able to assert lack of authorization against the person who filled in the unauthorized amount, subsequent holders of the properly indorsed check may be able to enforce the check as completed. While you are haggling with the person who inserted the unauthorized figure and who may not be able to repay the amount, you may also have to honor the check for the unauthorized amount to a subsequent holder.

It is equally dangerous to write out and sign a check payable to "cash" until you are actually at the bank.

* This *Application* is not meant to substitute for the services of an attorney who is licensed to practice law in your state.

Remember that checks payable to "cash" are bearer instruments. This means that if you lose or misplace the check, anybody who finds it can present it to the bank for payment.

Just as a check signed in blank or payable to cash may be dangerous, a negotiable instrument with a blank indorsement also has dangers, because as a bearer instrument, it is as easily transferred as cash. When you make a bank deposit, therefore, you should sign (indorse) the back of the check in blank only in the presence of a teller. If you choose to sign it ahead of time, make sure you insert the words "For deposit only" before you sign your name.

✓ Checklist for the Use of Negotiable Instruments

1. A good rule of thumb is never to sign a blank check.
2. Another good rule of thumb is never to write and sign a check payable to "cash" until you are actually at the bank.
3. Be wary of indorsing a check in blank unless a bank teller is simultaneously giving you a receipt for your deposit.

▌ Key Terms

▌ Chapter Summary: Negotiability and Transferability

Article 3 of the UCC (See pages 447–448.)	Article 3 of the Uniform Commercial Code governs the negotiability and transferability of negotiable instruments. Article 3 was significantly revised in 1990. Most states have adopted the revised article.
Types of Instruments (See pages 448–450.)	The UCC specifies four types of negotiable instruments: drafts, checks, promissory notes, and certificates of deposit (CDs). These instruments fall into two basic classifications: 1. *Demand instruments versus time instruments*—A demand instrument is payable on demand (when the holder presents it to the maker or drawer). A time instrument is payable at a future date. *(Continued)*

▌Chapter Summary: Negotiability and Transferability—Continued

Types of Instruments —Continued	2. *Orders to pay versus promises to pay*—Checks and drafts are *orders* to pay. Promissory notes and certificates of deposit (CDs) are *promises* to pay.
Requirements for Negotiability *(See pages 450–458.)*	1. Must be in writing. 2. Must be signed by the maker or drawer. 3. Must be an unconditional promise or order to pay. 4. Must state a fixed amount of money. 5. Must be payable on demand or at a definite time. 6. Must be payable to order or bearer.
Factors Not Affecting Negotiability *(See page 458.)*	1. The fact that an instrument is undated does not affect its negotiability unless the date is necessary to determine a definite time for payment. 2. Postdating or antedating an instrument does not affect negotiability. 3. Handwritten terms outweigh typewritten and printed terms. 4. Words outweigh figures unless the words are ambiguous. 5. An instrument that states "with interest" but that does not state the interest rate is payable at the judgment rate of interest.
Transfer of Instruments *(See pages 458–460.)*	1. *Transfer by assignment*— A transfer by assignment to an assignee gives the assignee only those rights that the assignor possessed. Any defenses that can be raised against an assignor can normally be raised against the assignee. 2. *Transfer by negotiation*—An order instrument is negotiated by indorsement and delivery; a bearer instrument is negotiated by delivery only.
Indorsements *(See pages 460–465.)*	1. *Blank* (for example, "Alan Luberda"). 2. *Special* (for example, "Pay to Anthony Alfono. [Signed] Arthur Rabe"). 3. *Qualified* (for example, "Without recourse. [Signed] Bridgett Cage"). 4. *Restrictive* (for example, "For deposit only. [Signed] Stephanie Mallak" or "Pay to Ada Alvarez in trust for José Martinez. [Signed] Ramon Martinez").
Miscellaneous Indorsement Problems *(See pages 465–466.)*	A payee or indorsee whose name is misspelled can indorse with the misspelled name, the correct name, or both. An instrument payable to two or more persons in the alternative requires the indorsement of only one of the payees. An instrument payable to two or more persons jointly requires all of the payees' indorsements for negotiation. If an instrument payable to two or more persons does not clearly indicate whether it is payable in the alternative or jointly, it is payable to the persons alternatively. The same principle applies to special indorsements that contain multiple indorsees.

▌For Review

1. What are the four types of negotiable instruments with which Article 3 of the UCC is concerned? Which of these instruments are *orders* to pay, and which are *promises* to pay?

2. What requirements must an instrument meet to be negotiable?

3. To whom is a bearer instrument payable?

4. What is the difference between an indorsement in blank and a special indorsement?

5. What is a restrictive indorsement? Does a restrictive indorsement prohibit further negotiation of the instrument?

▌Questions and Case Problems

18–1. Parties to Negotiable Instruments. A note has two original parties. What are these parties called? A check has three original parties. What are these parties called?

18–2. Indorsements. Bertram writes a check for $200, payable to "cash." He puts the check in his pocket and drives to the bank to cash the check. As he gets out of his car in the bank's parking lot, the check slips out of his pocket and falls to the pavement. Jerrod walks by moments later, picks up the check, and later that day delivers it to Amber, to whom he owes $200. Amber indorses the check "For deposit only. [Signed] Amber Dowel" and deposits it into her checking account. In light of these circumstances, answer the following questions:

(a) Is the check a bearer instrument or an order instrument?

(b) Did Jerrod's delivery of the check to Amber constitute a valid negotiation? Why or why not?

(c) What type of indorsement did Amber make?

(d) Does Bertram have a right to recover the $200 from Amber? Explain.

18–3. Requirements for Negotiability. The following note is written by Muriel Evans on the back of an envelope: "I, Muriel Evans, promise to pay Karen Marvin or bearer $100 on demand." Is this a negotiable instrument? Discuss fully.

18–4. Requirements for Negotiability. The following instrument was written on a sheet of paper by Jeff Nolan: "I, the undersigned, do hereby acknowledge that I owe Stephanie Craig one thousand dollars, with interest, payable out of the proceeds of the sale of my horse, Swiftfoot, next month. Payment is to be made on or before six months from date." Discuss specifically why this instrument is not negotiable.

18–5. Indorsements. A check drawn by David for $500 is made payable to the order of Matthew and issued to Matthew. Matthew owes his landlord $500 in rent and transfers the check to his landlord with the following indorsement: "For rent paid. [Signed] Matthew." Matthew's landlord has contracted to have Juarez do some landscaping on the property. When Juarez insists on immediate payment, the landlord transfers the check to Juarez without indorsement. Later, to pay for some palm trees purchased from Green's Nursery, Juarez transfers the check with the following indorsement: "Pay to Green's Nursery, without recourse. [Signed] Juarez." Green's Nursery sends the check to its bank indorsed "For deposit only. [Signed] Green's Nursery."

(a) Classify each of these indorsements.

(b) Was the transfer from Matthew's landlord to Juarez, without indorsement, an assignment or a negotiation? Explain.

18–6. Requirements for Negotiation. Dynamics Corp. and Marine Midland Bank–New York had a long-standing agreement under which Marine Midland received checks payable to Dynamics and indorsed and deposited them into Dynamics's account. Dynamics never saw the checks. They were made out to the order of Dynamics and delivered directly to Marine Midland. Marine Midland stamped the backs of the checks with Dynamics's name and insignia and transferred them. Within the meaning of the UCC, is the act of sending checks to Marine Midland Bank a negotiation? If Marine Midland transfers the checks to other parties, is this a negotiation? [*Marine Midland Bank–New York v. Graybar Electric Co.*, 41 N.Y.2d 703, 363 N.E.2d 1139, 395 N.Y.S.2d 403 (1977)]

18–7. Undated Instruments. During a three-year period, Appliances, Inc., performed electrical heating and plumbing work for Yost Construction worth approximately $7,000. Yost never paid Appliances for any of these jobs. Yost, in both his capacity as president of the construction company and his individual capacity, signed an undated ninety-day promissory note in favor of Appliances to reduce Yost Construction's debt and to have Appliances perform services for Yost as an individual. Neither Yost in his individual capacity nor Yost Construction paid the note, and Appliances filed suit. The trial court held that the undated note was totally unenforceable. Should Appliances prevail on appeal by arguing that the note was negotiable? [*Appliances, Inc. v. Yost*, 181 Conn. 207, 435 A.2d 1 (1980)]

18–8. Indorsements. James Liddell, who was doing business under the corporate name of JHL & Associates, Inc., agreed to invest Jan Mumma's funds in Fidelity, a nationally traded mutual fund management company. Mumma indorsed a cashier's check for $13,904.48 to "Fidelity/JHL & Associates." Liddell indorsed the check with JHL's indorsement stamp and deposited the check, without Fidelity's indorsement, into JHL's bank account at Rainier National Bank. Liddell never invested the funds in Fidelity. Mumma was unable to recover her money from JHL, which had become insolvent, or from Liddell, who was serving a jail sentence for fraud stemming from this incident and others like it. Mumma then attempted to recover from Rainier National Bank, claiming that the bank was negligent by not requiring *both* Fidelity and JHL & Associates to indorse the check. Was Mumma correct? Explain. [*Mumma v. Rainier National Bank*, 60 Wash.App. 937, 808 P.2d 767 (1991)]

18–9. Words versus Figures. Eugene Kindy, a seller of diesel engine parts, agreed to buy four diesel engines from Tony Hicks. Kindy transferred $6,500 by wire and issued a check for the remainder of the purchase price. Kindy placed two different amounts on the check, because he did not want the check honored until Hicks had delivered the engine parts. Using a check-imprinting machine, Kindy imprinted $5,550 on the check in the space where the dollar amount is normally written in words, but he wrote $6,550 in figures in the box usually reserved for numbers. An employee of Galatia Community State Bank, noticing the discrepancy, altered the figures to read "$5,550," initialed the change, and accepted the check. The check was returned to Galatia by Kindy's bank at his request, because Hicks had not delivered the engine parts. In the litigation that followed, a key issue was whether the machine-imprinted figure took precedence over the handwritten figure. What should the court decide on this issue? Discuss. [*Galatia Community State Bank v. Kindy*, 807 Ark. 467, 821 S.W.2d 765 (1991)]

18–10. Requirements for Negotiability. Emil Amberboy and others invested in oil and gas partnerships formed by Vanguard Group International, Inc. Each investor made a down payment in cash and signed a promissory note payable to the partnership for the balance of the investment. Each note stated that its interest rate was to be determined by reference to a certain bank's published prime rate. Several months later, Vanguard sold the notes to Société de Banque Privée. Suspecting that the investments were being handled fraudulently, Amberboy and the other investors stopped making payments on the notes and filed a lawsuit against Société de Banque Privée and others. One of the issues before the court was whether the notes were negotiable. The plaintiffs contended that because the interest rate on the notes could be calculated only by reference to a source outside the notes, the notes could not be negotiable instruments. How should the court rule?

[*Amberboy v. Société de Banque Privée,* 831 S.W.2d 793 (Tex. 1992)]

18–11. Fixed Amount of Money. William Bailey and William Vaught, as officers for Bailey, Vaught, Robertson, and Co. (BVR), signed a promissory note to borrow $34,000 from the Forestwood National Bank. The interest rate was variable: "the lender's published prime rate" plus 1 percent. Forestwood went out of business, and ultimately, the note was acquired by Remington Investments, Inc. When BVR failed to make payments, Remington filed a suit in a Texas state court against BVR. BVR contended in part that the note was not negotiable because after Forestwood closed, there was no "published lender's prime rate" to use to calculate the interest. Did the note provide for payment of a "fixed amount of money"? [*Bailey, Vaught, Robertson, and Co. v. Remington Investments, Inc.,* 888 S.W.2d 860 (Tex.App.—Dallas, 1994)]

A QUESTION OF ETHICS AND SOCIAL RESPONSIBILITY

18–12. *Richard Caliendo, an accountant, prepared tax returns for various clients. To satisfy their tax liabilities, the clients issued checks payable to various state taxing entities and gave them to Caliendo. Between 1977 and 1979, Caliendo forged indorsements on these checks, deposited them in his own bank account, and subsequently withdrew the proceeds. In 1983, after learning of these events and after Caliendo's death, the state brought an action against Barclays Bank of New York, N.A., the successor to Caliendo's bank, to recover the amount of the checks. Barclays moved for dismissal on the ground that because the checks had never been delivered to the state, the state never acquired the status of holder and therefore never acquired any rights in the instruments. The trial court held for the state, but the appellate court reversed. The state then appealed the case to the state's highest court. That court ruled that the state could not recover the amount of the checks from the bank because, although the state was the named payee on the checks, the checks* had never been delivered to the payee. [State v. Barclays Bank of New York, N.A., 561 N.Y.2d 533, 563 N.E.2d 11, 561 N.Y.S.2d 697 (1990)]

1. If you were deciding this case, would you make an exception to the rule and let the state collect the funds from Barclays Bank? Why or why not? What ethical policies must be balanced in this situation?

2. Under agency law, which will be discussed in Chapter 23, delivery to the agent of a given individual or entity constitutes delivery to that person or entity. The court deemed that Caliendo was not an agent of the state but an agent of the taxpayers. Does it matter that the taxpayers may not have known this principle of agency law and might have thought that, by delivering their checks to Caliendo, they were delivering them to the state?

CASE BRIEFING ASSIGNMENT

18–13. *Examine Case A.5 [Federal Deposit Insurance Corp. v. Trans Pacific Industries, Inc., 14 F.3d 10 (5th Cir. 1994] in Appendix A. The case has been excerpted there in great detail. Review and then brief the case, making sure that you include answers to the following questions in your brief.*

1. What was the procedural background to this case?
2. What issue was being appealed and by which party?
3. Which UCC provision applied to this issue?
4. How did the appellate court rule on the issue, and why?

FOR CRITICAL ANALYSIS

18–14. *The UCC requirements for negotiable instruments are generally strict. In regard to what constitutes a signature on an instrument, however, the UCC grants extreme latitude—X marks, initials, and rubber-stamped signatures are all permitted. Given the potential for forgery of these kinds of signatures, why does the UCC permit them?*

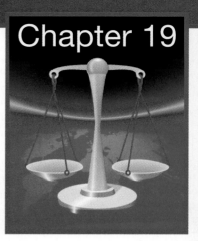

Chapter 19

Rights and Liabilities of Parties

"Wealth, in a commercial age, is made up largely of promises."

Roscoe Pound, 1870–1964
(American jurist)

CHAPTER OBJECTIVES

After reading this chapter, you should be able to:

1. Summarize the requirements for HDC status.
2. Explain the liability of parties who sign negotiable instruments.
3. Describe the effect of forged or unauthorized signatures on the liability of those persons whose names are signed.
4. Identify the defenses that can be raised to avoid liability for payment on negotiable instruments.
5. Indicate how liability on a negotiable instrument is discharged.

As discussed in Chapter 18, negotiable instruments function as substitutes for money; they also function as an extension of credit. Any note in which a person promises to pay another a sum of money creates a debtor (the one promising) and a creditor (the one to be paid). As the eminent jurist Roscoe Pound indicated in this chapter's opening quotation, wealth "is made up largely of promises." The extensive exchange of negotiable instruments that takes place daily in the United States is predicated, ultimately, on the existence of law and a government capable of enforcing the promises made by parties to negotiable instruments.

The outcome of litigation concerning negotiable instruments usually turns on whether a holder is entitled to obtain payment on an instrument when it is due. Often, whether a holder is entitled to obtain payment will depend on whether the holder is a *holder in due course (HDC)*, a concept we examine in the opening pages of this chapter. We then discuss the liability of the parties to negotiable instruments. In the remainder of the chapter, we consider the defenses available for avoiding liability and, briefly, the ways in which a person can be discharged from an obligation on a negotiable instrument.

▌Holder versus Holder in Due Course (HDC)

As pointed out in Chapter 18, the Uniform Commercial Code (UCC) defines a *holder* as a person in the possession of an instrument drawn, issued, or indorsed to him or her, to his or her order, or to bearer or in blank [UCC 1–201(20)]. An ordinary holder obtains only those rights that the transferor had in the instrument. In this respect, a holder has the same status as an assignee (see Chapter 12). Like an assignee, a holder normally is subject to the same defenses that could be asserted against the transferor.

In contrast, a **holder in due course (HDC)** is a holder who, by meeting certain acquisition requirements (to be discussed shortly), takes the instrument *free* of most of the defenses and claims that could be asserted against the transferor. Stated another way, an HDC can normally acquire a higher level of immunity than can an ordinary holder in regard to defenses against payment on the instrument or ownership claims to the instrument by other parties.

An example will help to clarify the distinction between the rights of an ordinary holder and the rights of an HDC. Marcia Morrison signs a $500 note payable to Alex Jerrod in payment for goods. Jerrod negotiates the note to Lesley Larson, who promises to pay Jerrod for it in thirty days. During the next month, Larson learns that Jerrod has breached his contract with Morrison by delivering defective goods and that, for this reason, Morrison will not honor the $500 note. Whether Larson can hold Morrison liable on the note depends on whether Larson has met the requirements for HDC status. If Larson has met these requirements and thus has HDC status, Larson is entitled to payment on the note. If Larson has not met these requirements, she has the status of an ordinary holder, and Morrison's defense against payment to Jerrod will also be effective against Larson.

HOLDER IN DUE COURSE (HDC)
A holder who acquires a negotiable instrument for value; in good faith; and without notice that the instrument is overdue, that it has been dishonored, that any person has a defense against it or a claim to it, or that the instrument contains unauthorized signatures, alterations, or is so irregular or incomplete as to call into question its authenticity.

▌Requirements for HDC Status

The basic requirements for attaining HDC status are set forth in UCC 3–302. A holder of a negotiable instrument is an HDC if he or she takes the instrument (1) for value; (2) in good faith; and (3) without notice that it is overdue, that it has been dishonored, that any person has a defense against it or a claim to it, or that the instrument contains unauthorized signatures, alterations, or is so irregular or incomplete as to call into question its authenticity. We now examine each of these requirements.

Taking for Value

An HDC must have given *value* for the instrument [UCC 3–302(a)(2)(i)]. A person who receives an instrument as a gift or who inherits it has not met the requirement of value. In these situations, the person normally becomes an ordinary holder and does not possess the rights of an HDC.

The concept of *value* in the law of negotiable instruments is not the same as the concept of *consideration* in the law of contracts. A promise to give value in the future is clearly sufficient consideration to support a contract [UCC 1–201(44)]. A promise to give value in the future, however, normally does not constitute value sufficient to make one an HDC. A holder takes an instrument for value only to the extent that the promise has been performed [UCC 3–303(a)(1)]. Therefore, if the holder plans to pay for the instrument later or plans to perform the required services at some future date, the holder has not yet given value. In that situation, the holder is not yet an HDC.

In the Larson-Morrison example presented earlier, Larson is not an HDC, because she did not take the instrument (Morrison's note) for value—she had not yet paid

◆ **Exhibit 19–1**
Taking for Value
By exchanging defective goods for the note, Jerrod breached his contract with
Morrison. Morrison could assert this defense if Jerrod presented the note to her
for payment. Jerrod exchanged the note for Larson's promise to pay in thirty days,
however. Because Larson did not take the note for value, she is not a holder in
due course. Thus, Morrison can assert against Larson the defense of Jerrod's
breach when Larson submits the note to Morrison for payment. If Larson had
taken the note for value, Morrison could not assert that defense and would be
liable to pay the note.

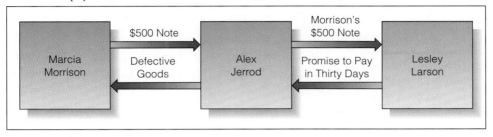

Jerrod for the note. Thus, Morrison's defense of breach of contract is valid not only
against Jerrod but also against Larson. If Larson had paid Jerrod for the note at the time
of transfer (which would mean she had given value for the instrument), she would be
an HDC. As an HDC, she could hold Morrison liable on the note even though
Morrison has a valid defense against Jerrod on the basis of breach of contract. Exhibit
19–1 illustrates these concepts.

Under UCC 3–303(a), a holder can take an instrument for value in one of five ways:

1. By performing the promise for which the instrument was issued or transferred.
2. By acquiring a security interest or other lien in the instrument, excluding a lien
obtained by a judicial proceeding. (Security interests and liens are discussed in
Chapters 21 and 22.)
3. By taking an instrument in payment of (or as security for) an antecedent debt.
4. By giving a negotiable instrument as payment.
5. By giving an irrevocable commitment as payment.

Taking in Good Faith

The second requirement for HDC status is that the holder take the instrument in *good
faith* [UCC 3–302(a)(2)(ii)]. This means that the holder must have acted honestly in
the process of acquiring the instrument. Article 3 defines *good faith* as "honesty in fact
and the observance of reasonable commercial standards of fair dealing." The good
faith requirement applies only to the *holder*. It is immaterial whether the transferor
acted in good faith. Thus, even a person who in good faith takes a negotiable instrument from a thief may become an HDC.

Because of the good faith requirement, one must ask whether the purchaser, when
acquiring the instrument, honestly believed that the instrument was not defective. If a
person purchases a $10,000 note for $300 from a stranger on a street corner, the issue
of good faith can be raised on the grounds of both the suspicious circumstances and
the grossly inadequate consideration (value). The UCC does not provide clear guidelines to determine good faith, so each situation must be examined separately. In the
following case, the court considered whether a casino fulfilled the good faith requirement to qualify as an HDC.

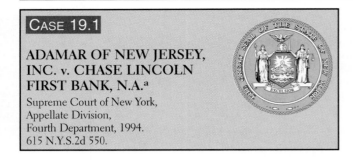

CASE 19.1

ADAMAR OF NEW JERSEY, INC. v. CHASE LINCOLN FIRST BANK, N.A.[a]

Supreme Court of New York,
Appellate Division,
Fourth Department, 1994.
615 N.Y.S.2d 550.

HISTORICAL AND ECONOMIC SETTING *Gambling is a multibillion-dollar industry that has enjoyed tremendous growth in the 1990s. In the mid-1990s, people wagered about $500 billion each year. Most of this amount was wagered in twenty-seven states in casinos built in the previous five years. Cities and towns with casinos have generally experienced increases in crime, even while the crime rate for the United States as a whole has been dropping. Gambling's new frontier is the Internet, with nearly three hundred gambling-related sites on the World Wide Web. Because such services probably violate U.S. law, however, on-line casinos are based elsewhere—on islands in the Caribbean, for example.*

FACTS Joseph Thomas stole two signed cashier's checks from a loan officer's desk at Chase Lincoln First Bank, N.A. Thomas wrote $200,000 as the amount of one check and $300,000 as the amount of the other, and made them payable to the order of his brother-in-law. Posing as his brother-in-law, Thomas presented the checks to the Tropicana Casino. A casino employee who contacted Chase was told that the $200,000 check was "good," that there were adequate funds to cover it, and

a. The initials *N.A.* stand for National Association.

that there was no stop-payment order on the $300,000 check. Thomas gambled away most of the money before Chase stopped payment on the checks. The owner of the Tropicana, Adamar of New Jersey, Inc., filed a suit in a New York state court against the bank to recover the $500,000. When the court denied Adamar's motion for summary judgment, Adamar appealed.

ISSUE Had Adamar taken the checks in good faith, as required for HDC status?

DECISION Yes. The Supreme Court of New York, Appellate Division, held that the casino was entitled to payment.

REASON The court framed the issue as follows: Did the casino have "knowledge of some fact which would prevent a commercially honest individual from taking up the instruments"? The court pointed out that the casino did not violate either state gaming regulations or its own internal procedures in verifying Thomas's identity and the validity of the checks. The court concluded that the Chase employee's statement, in response to the casino's inquiries, that the $200,000 check was "good," with adequate funds to cover it, satisfied a relevant state regulation. The regulation required that "[p]rior to acceptance of any cash equivalent from a patron, the general cashier shall determine the validity of such cash equivalent by performing the necessary verification for each type of cash equivalent." Besides, the court added, "the Casino was expressly informed that there was no stop payment on the $300,000 check."

FOR CRITICAL ANALYSIS—Ethical Consideration *Why should good faith be a requirement to attain HDC status?*

International Perspective

Good faith is an issue not only in domestic transactions involving negotiable instruments but also internationally. Under the United Nations Convention on International Bills of Exchange and International Promissory Notes (CIBN), the equivalent of a holder in due course is known as a "protected holder." As under the UCC, the protected holder is afforded greater protection than an ordinary holder. The CIBN, however, unlike the UCC, does not provide any objective test by which to measure good faith. Article 3 of the UCC, as revised in 1990, added to the subjective definition of *good faith* (which was defined under the unrevised Article 3 as simply "honesty in fact") the phrase, "and the observance of reasonable commercial standards of fair dealing." Thus, courts applying the UCC can have some objective guidelines as to what constitutes good faith. The CIBN, in contrast, simply qualifies someone as a protected holder if he or she was "without knowledge" of a fraud or other defense against the instrument.

For Critical Analysis: *What might be a reason why the CIBN contains only a very broad and subjective definition of good faith?*

Taking without Notice

The final requirement for HDC status involves *notice* [UCC 3–302]. A person will not be afforded HDC protection if he or she acquires an instrument and is *on notice* (knows or has reason to know) that it is defective in any one of the following ways [UCC 3–302(a)]:

1. It is overdue.
2. It has been dishonored.
3. There is an uncured (uncorrected) default with respect to another instrument issued as part of the same series.
4. The instrument contains an unauthorized signature or has been altered.
5. There is a defense against the instrument or a claim to the instrument.
6. The instrument is so irregular or incomplete as to call into question the instrument's authenticity.

WHAT CONSTITUTES NOTICE?   Notice of a defective instrument is given whenever the holder (1) has actual knowledge of the defect; (2) has received a notice of the defect (such as a bank's receipt of a letter listing the serial numbers of stolen bearer instruments); or (3) has reason to know that a defect exists, given all the facts and circumstances known at the time in question [UCC 1–201(25)]. The holder must also have received the notice "at a time and in a manner that gives a reasonable opportunity to act on it" [UCC 3–302(f)]. A purchaser's knowledge of certain facts, such as insolvency proceedings against the maker or drawer of the instrument, does not constitute notice that the instrument is defective [UCC 3–302(b)].

OVERDUE INSTRUMENTS   What constitutes notice that an instrument is overdue depends on whether it is a demand instrument (payable on demand) or a time instrument (payable at a definite time).

> REMEMBER Demand instruments are payable immediately. Time instruments are payable at a future date.

     A purchaser has notice that a *demand instrument* is overdue if he or she either takes the instrument knowing that demand has been made or takes the instrument an unreasonable length of time after its issue. A "reasonable time" for the taking of a check is ninety days, but for other demand instruments, what will be considered a reasonable time depends on the circumstances [UCC 3–304(a)].[1]

     A holder of a *time instrument* who takes the instrument at any time after its expressed due date is on notice that it is overdue [UCC 3–304(b)(2)]. Nonpayment by the due date should indicate to any purchaser that the instrument may be defective. Thus, a promissory note due on May 15 must be acquired before midnight on May 15. If it is purchased on May 16, the purchaser will be an ordinary holder, not an HDC.

     Sometimes, an instrument reads, "Payable in thirty days." A promissory note dated December 1 that is payable in thirty days is due by midnight on December 31. If the payment date falls on a Sunday or holiday, the instrument is payable on the next business day. If a debt is to be paid in installments or through a series of notes, the maker's default on any installment of prinicpal (not interest) or on any one note of the series will constitute notice to the purchaser that the instrument is overdue [UCC 3–304(b)(1)].

DISHONORED INSTRUMENTS   An instrument is *dishonored* when the party to which the instrument is presented refuses to pay it. If a holder has actual knowledge that an instrument has been dishonored or has knowledge of facts that would lead him or her

---

1.   Under the unrevised Article 3, a reasonable time for the taking of a domestic check is *presumed* to be thirty days [UCC 3–304(3)(c)].

to suspect that an instrument has been dishonored, the holder is on notice [UCC 3–302(a)(2)].

For example, Condor holds a demand note dated September 1 made by JWB Enterprises, Inc., a local business firm. On September 17, Condor demands payment, and JWB refuses to pay (that is, JWB dishonors the instrument). On September 22, Condor negotiates the note to Bream, a purchaser who lives in another state. Bream does not know, and has no reason to know, that the note has been dishonored, so Bream is *not* put on notice and therefore can become an HDC.

NOTICE OF CLAIMS OR DEFENSES   A holder cannot become an HDC if he or she has notice of any claim to the instrument or any defense against it [UCC 3–302(a)]. Knowledge of claims or defenses can be imputed to the purchaser if these claims or defenses are apparent on the face of the instrument or if the purchaser otherwise had reason to know of them from facts surrounding the transaction.

A purchaser cannot expect to become an HDC of an instrument so incomplete on its face that an element of negotiability is lacking (for example, the amount is not filled in). Minor omissions (such as the omission of the date—see Chapter 18) are permissible, because these do not call into question the validity of the instrument. Similarly, when a person accepts an instrument that has been completed without knowing that it was incomplete when issued, the person can take it as an HDC.

Suppose, for example, that Carrie asks Barron to buy a textbook for her at the campus bookstore. Carrie writes a check payable to the bookstore, leaves the amount blank, and tells Barron to fill in the price of the textbook. The cost of the textbook is $45. If Barron fills in the check for $75 before he gets to the bookstore, the bookstore cashier sees only a properly completed instrument. Therefore, because the bookstore had no notice that the check was incomplete when it was issued, the bookstore can take the check for $75 and become an HDC.

Any irregularity on the face of an instrument (such as an obvious forgery) that calls into question its validity or terms of ownership, or that creates an ambiguity as to the party to pay, will bar HDC status. A careful forgery of a signature, however, or the careful alteration of an instrument can go undetected by reasonable examination; therefore, the purchaser can qualify as an HDC.

NOTE A difference between the handwriting in the body of a check and the handwriting in the signature does not affect the validity of the check.

▌ Holder through an HDC

A person who does not qualify as an HDC but who derives his or her title through an HDC can acquire the rights and privileges of an HDC. According to UCC 3–203(b),

> Transfer of an instrument, whether or not the transfer is a negotiation, vests in the transferee any right of the transferor to enforce the instrument, including any right as a holder in due course, but the transferee cannot acquire rights of a holder in due course by a transfer, directly or indirectly, from a holder in due course if the transferee engaged in fraud or illegality affecting the instrument.

SHELTER PRINCIPLE
The principle that the holder of a negotiable instrument who cannot qualify as a holder in due course (HDC), but who derives his or her title through an HDC, acquires the rights of an HDC.

Under this rule, which is sometimes called the **shelter principle,** anyone—no matter how far removed from an HDC—who can trace his or her title ultimately back to an HDC has the rights of an HDC.

There are some limitations on the shelter principle, however. Certain persons who formerly held instruments cannot improve their positions by later reacquiring the instruments from HDCs [UCC 3–203(b)]. Thus, if a holder was a party to fraud or illegality affecting the instrument or if, as a prior holder, he or she had notice of a claim or defense against an instrument, that holder is not allowed to improve his or her status by repurchasing from a later HDC.

The shelter principle seems counter to the reasoning underlying the HDC doctrine—that only those who fulfill the requirements for HDC status should be allowed immunity from most claims and defenses against payment on instruments. The shelter principle is, however, in line with the concept of encouraging the marketability and free transferability of commercial paper, because it aids HDCs in readily disposing of instruments. The shelter principle is also consistent with contract law, which provides that assignees acquire the rights of assignors.

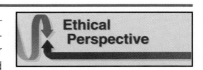

Ethical Perspective

Furthermore, the limitations on the shelter principle are designed to curb potential abuses of it. As an example of how the shelter principle can be abused, consider the following events. Barry and Sheila collaborate to defraud Helen. Sheila induces Helen to give her a negotiable note payable to Sheila's order. Sheila specially indorses the note for value to Joseph, who then becomes an HDC. Barry and Sheila split the proceeds. Joseph negotiates the note to Paul, another HDC. Paul then negotiates the note for value to Barry. Barry, even though he got the note through an HDC, does not acquire the rights of an HDC, because he participated in the original fraud and can never acquire HDC rights in this note. Essentially, the limitations on the shelter principle imposed by UCC 3–203(b) are designed to prevent a person from "laundering" an instrument by passing it into the hands of an HDC and then buying it back again.

For Critical Analysis: *In the Barry-Sheila example just given, what would result if Paul had fraudulently acquired the note from Joseph? Would Paul nonetheless have the rights of an HDC?*

▌Signature Liability

The key to liability on a negotiable instrument is a *signature*.[2] The general rule is as follows: Every party, except a qualified indorser,[3] who signs a negotiable instrument is either primarily or secondarily liable for payment of that instrument when it comes due. The following subsections discuss these two types of liability, as well as the conditions that must be met before liability can arise.

"Most men are admirers of justice—when justice happens to be on their side."

Richard Whately, 1787–1863 (English theologian and logician)

Primary Liability

A person who is primarily liable on a negotiable instrument is absolutely required to pay the instrument—unless, of course, he or she has a valid defense to payment [UCC 3–305]. Only *makers* and *acceptors* of instruments are primarily liable.

The maker of a promissory note promises to pay the note. It is the maker's promise to pay that makes the note a negotiable instrument. The words "I promise to pay" embody the maker's obligation to pay the instrument according to the terms as written at the time of the signing. If the instrument is incomplete when the maker signs it, then the maker's obligation is to pay it to an HDC according to the terms written when it is completed [UCC 3–115, 3–407(a), 3–412].

A drawee that promises to pay an instrument when it is presented later for payment is called an *acceptor*, as discussed in Chapter 18. A drawee's acceptance of a draft, which it makes by signing the draft, guarantees that the drawee will pay the draft when it is presented in the future for payment [UCC 3–409(a)]. A drawee that refuses to accept a draft that requires the drawee's acceptance (such as a trade acceptance, discussed in Chapter 18) has dishonored the instrument. Acceptance of a check is called

---

2. See Chapter 18 for a discussion of how the UCC defines a *signature*.
3. A qualified indorser—one who indorses "without recourse"—undertakes no contractual obligation to pay. A qualified indorser merely assumes warranty liability, which is discussed later in this chapter.

certification (discussed in Chapter 20). Certification is not necessary on checks, and a bank is under no obligation to certify checks. Upon certification, however, the drawee bank occupies the position of an acceptor and is primarily liable on the check to any holder [UCC 3–409(d)].

Secondary Liability

Drawers and indorsers are secondarily liable. Secondary liability on a negotiable instrument is similar to the liability of a guarantor in a simple contract (described in Chapter 12) in the sense that it is *contingent liability*. In other words, a drawer or an indorser will be liable only if the party that is primarily liable on the instrument dishonors it or, in regard to drafts and checks, the drawee fails to pay or to accept the instrument, whichever is required [UCC 3–412, 3–415].

Dishonor of an instrument thus triggers the liability of parties who are secondarily liable on the instrument—that is, the drawer and *unqualified* indorsers. For example, Nina Lee writes a check on her account at Universal Bank payable to the order of Stephen Miller. Universal Bank refuses to pay the check when Miller presents it for payment, thus dishonoring the check. In this situation, Lee will be liable to Miller on the basis of her secondary liability. Drawers are secondarily liable on drafts unless they disclaim their liability by drawing the instruments "without recourse" (unless the draft is a check, in which circumstance a drawer cannot disclaim liability) [UCC 3–414(e)].

Parties that are secondarily liable on a negotiable instrument promise to pay on that instrument only if the following events occur:[4]

1. The instrument is properly and timely presented.
2. The instrument is dishonored.
3. Timely notice of dishonor is given to the secondarily liable party.

PROPER AND TIMELY PRESENTMENT   The UCC requires that presentment by a holder must be made to the proper person, must be made in a proper manner, and must be timely [UCC 3–414(f), 3–415(e), 3–501]. The party to whom the instrument must be presented depends on what type of instrument is involved. A note or certificate of deposit (CD) must be presented to the maker for payment. A draft is presented by the holder to the drawee for acceptance, payment, or both, whichever is required. A check is presented to the drawee for payment [UCC 3–501(a), 3–502(b)].

Presentment can be properly made in any of the following ways, depending on the type of instrument involved [UCC 3–501(b)]:

1.   By any commercially reasonable means, including oral, written, or electronic communication (but presentment is not effective until the demand for payment or acceptance is received).
2.   Through a clearinghouse procedure used by banks, such as for deposited checks (see Chapter 20).
3.   At the place specified in the instrument for acceptance or payment.

One of the most crucial criteria for proper presentment is timeliness [UCC 3–414(f), 3–415(e), 3–501(b)(4)]. Failure to present on time is the most common reason for improper presentment and consequent discharge of unqualified indorsers from secondary liability. The time for proper presentment for different types of instruments is shown in Exhibit 19–2.

---

4.   These requirements are necessary for a secondarily liable party to have signature liability on a negotiable instrument, but they are not necessary for a secondarily liable party to have warranty liability (to be discussed later in the chapter).

◆ Exhibit 19–2
Time for Proper Presentment

TYPE OF INSTRUMENT	FOR ACCEPTANCE	FOR PAYMENT
Time	On or before due date.	On due date.
Demand	Within a reasonable time (after date or issue or after secondary party becomes liable on the instrument).	
Check	Not applicable.	Within thirty days of its date, to hold drawer secondarily liable Within thirty days of indorsement to hold indorser secondarily lliable.[a]
a. Under the unrevised Article 3, these periods were *presumed* to be thirty days to hold drawer secondarily liable, and seven days to hold indorser secondarily liable.		

DISHONOR An instrument is dishonored when the required acceptance or payment is refused or cannot be obtained within the prescribed time, or when required presentment is excused (as it would be, for example, if the maker had died) and the instrument is not properly accepted or paid [UCC 3–502(e), 3–504].

PROPER NOTICE Once an instrument has been dishonored, proper notice must be given to secondary parties for them to be held liable. Notice may be given in any reasonable manner. This includes oral notice, written notice (including notice by fax, E-mail, and the like), and notice written or stamped on the instrument itself. Any necessary notice must be given by a bank before its midnight deadline (midnight of the next banking day after receipt). Notice by any party other than a bank must be given within thirty days following the day on which the person receives notice of dishonor [UCC 3–503].[5]

Accommodation Parties

An **accommodation party** is one who signs an instrument for the purpose of lending his or her name as credit to another party on the instrument [UCC 3–419(a)]. Accommodation parties are one form of security against nonpayment on a negotiable instrument. For example, a bank about to lend money wants some reasonable assurance that the debt will be paid. If the prospective borrower's financial condition is uncertain, the bank may be reluctant to rely solely on the borrower's ability to pay. To reduce the risk of nonpayment, the bank can require the joining of a third person as an accommodation party on the borrower's promissory note. When one person (such as a parent) cosigns a promissory note with the maker (such as the parent's son or daughter), the cosigner is an accommodation party.

If the accommodation party signs on behalf of the *maker*, he or she becomes an *accommodation maker* and is primarily liable on the instrument. If the accommodation party indorses an instrument on behalf of a *payee or other holder* (usually to make the instrument more marketable), he or she is an *accommodation indorser* and is secondarily liable. An accommodation party is never liable to the party accommodated, however. If the accommodation party pays the instrument, he or she has a right to recover the amount paid from the party that was accommodated.

ACCOMMODATION PARTY
A person who signs an instrument for the purpose of lending his or her name as credit to another party on the instrument.

---

5. Under the unrevised Article 3, notice by a person other than a bank has to be given "before midnight of the third business day after dishonor or receipt of notice of dishonor" [UCC 3–508(2)].

A family looks at a van on a dealer's lot. If, as prospective borrowers, the family's financial condition were uncertain, how could an accommodation party help them to obtain the money to pay for the van?

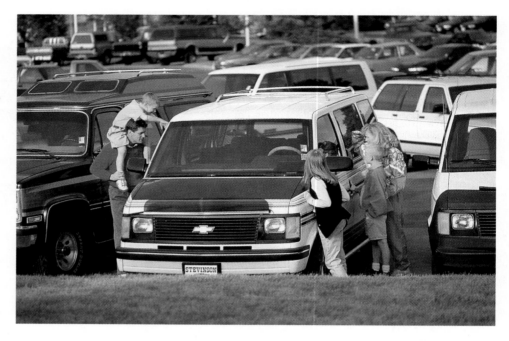

Agents' Signatures

The general law of agency, covered in Chapter 23, applies to negotiable instruments. An **agent** is a person who agrees to represent or act for another, called the **principal.** Agents can sign negotiable instruments and thereby bind their principals [UCC 3–401(a)(ii), 3–402(a)]. Without such a rule, all corporate commercial business would stop—as every corporation can and must act through its agents.

AUTHORIZED AGENT   Generally, an *authorized* agent does not bind a principal on an instrument unless the agent *clearly names* the principal in his or her signature. The agent may or may not add his or her own name, but if the signature shows clearly that it is made on behalf of the principal, the agent is not liable on the instrument. For example, either of the following two signatures by Joan Collingsworth as agent for Brian Peterson would bind Peterson (but not Collingsworth) on the instrument, and Collingsworth would not be personally liable for payment on it:

1.   Peterson, by Collingsworth, agent.
2.   Peterson.

    If Collingsworth (the agent) signed just her own name, however, she would be personally liable to an HDC who has no notice that the agent was not intended to be liable. In respect to other holders, the agent can escape liability if the agent proves that the original parties did not intend the agent to be liable on the instrument [UCC 3–402(a), 3–402(b)(2)]. In either situation, the principal is bound if the party entitled to enforce the instrument can prove the agency relationship.[6]
    There are two other situations in which an authorized agent can be held personally liable on a negotiable instrument. When the instrument is signed in both the agent's name and the principal's name (for example, "Collingsworth, Peterson"), but nothing on the instrument indicates the agency relationship (so the agent cannot be distinguished from the principal), the agent may be held personally liable. An agent

AGENT
A person who agrees to represent or act for another, called the principal.

PRINCIPAL
In agency law, a person who agrees to have another, called the agent, act on his or her behalf.

---

6.   Under the unrevised Article 3, a principal is not liable on an instrument unless his or her signature appears on it, even if the parties are aware of the agency relationship [UCC 3–401(1)].

LAW IN THE EXTREME

A Word of Warning to Agents: Read the UCC

Troublesome issues sometimes arise in respect to the signature liability of agents. This is because it is not always too clear to an agent just how specifically he or she must spell out—on the instrument itself—the fact that he or she is signing in a representative capacity. Even though an agent takes seemingly sufficient precautions against the risk of personal liability on an instrument, the agent may still face liability under the UCC.

An extreme example of this situation arose when Donald Galt, the president of Woodside Construction, Inc., signed a promissory note to a bank for $912,000. In an attempt to

clarify his relationship to the company, Galt signed the note in two places. Beneath the first signature appeared the typed words, "Woodside Construction, Inc." Beneath the second signature appeared the typed words, "Donald A. Galt, President." Woodside defaulted on its payments on the note, which had in the meantime been acquired by the Federal Deposit Insurance Corporation (FDIC), along with other assets of the bank that loaned Galt the funds.

The FDIC sued Galt personally to collect on the note. Galt contended that he could not be held personally liable on the note because the two signatures, taken together, clearly indicated that he had signed in a representative capacity. The court, however, held that "the first signature above the principal designation fails to indicate the representative capacity, and the second signature above the representative capacity designation fails to indicate the principal."

Because neither signature indicated both elements—Galt's representative capacity and the name of the principal—Galt was held personally liable on the note.[a]

The court's decision in this case, albeit a harsh one,[b] contains an important message for agents who sign negotiable instruments: a little knowledge of the law can go a long way toward avoiding significant liability!

For Critical Analysis: *How could Donald Galt have avoided this problem?*

a. *Federal Deposit Insurance Corp. v. Woodside Construction, Inc.,* 979 F.2d 172 (9th Cir. 1992).
b. Another court might have reached a different conclusion. See, for example, *Federal Deposit Insurance Corp. v. Trans Pacific Industries, Inc.,* 14 F.3d 10 (5th Cir. 1994) for a similar situation in which the court reached the opposite conclusion.

may also be held personally liable when the agent indicates agency status in signing a negotiable instrument but fails to name the principal (for example, "Joan Collingsworth, agent") [UCC 3–402(b)(2)]. (See this chapter's *Law in the Extreme* for a strict application of this rule.)

An important exception to the above rules is made for checks that are signed by agents. If an agent signs his or her own name on a check that is *payable from the account of the principal*, and the principal is identified on the check, the agent will not be personally liable on the check [UCC 3–402(c)]. For example, suppose that Collingsworth, who is authorized to draw checks on Peterson Company's account, signs a check that is preprinted with Peterson Company's name. The signature reads simply "Joan Collingsworth." In this situation, Collingsworth would not be personally liable on the check. (Contrast this rule with the rule under the unrevised Article 3, which is discussed in this chapter's *Business Law in Action.*)

UNAUTHORIZED AGENT If an agent is *not authorized* to sign the principal's name, the principal is not bound—the agent is personally liable [UCC 3–403(a)]. Assume that Maria Ortega is the principal and Justin Cohen is her agent. Cohen, without authority, signs a promissory note as follows: "Maria Ortega, by Justin Cohen, agent." Because Maria Ortega's "signature" is unauthorized, she cannot be held liable on the note, but Cohen is liable. This would be true even if Cohen had merely signed the note "Maria Ortega," without indicating any agency. In either situation, the unauthorized signer, Cohen, is liable on the instrument.

Unauthorized Signatures

People normally are not liable to pay on negotiable instruments unless their signatures appear on the instruments. As already stated, the general rule is that an unauthorized

Relief for Agents Who Sign Checks

Before Article 3 of the UCC was revised in 1990, a corporate agent who signed a corporate check without indicating his or her representative status risked being held personally liable on the check. This was true even if the check was clearly imprinted with the name of the corporation. In the language of the unrevised Section 3–403, "[a]n authorized representative who signs his own name to an instrument . . . is personally obligated if the instrument names the person represented but does not show that the representative signed in a representative capacity, or if the instrument does not name the person represented but does show that the representative signed in a representative capacity."

A classic case in which this provision of the unrevised Article 3 was applied is *Griffin v. Ellinger.*[a]

a.   538 S.W.2d 97 (Tex. 1976).

Griffin, the president of Greenway Building Company, issued three checks to Ellinger, drawn on Greenway's account. Griffin signed his name on the checks without revealing his representative capacity. The name of the company was on the face of each check, and Griffin was authorized to sign checks as president of the company. At the time the checks were issued, neither Ellinger (the payee) nor Griffin discussed who was responsible for paying the checks. The drawee bank refused to honor the checks because of insufficient funds in the Greenway account, and Ellinger sought recovery from Griffin personally.

The Texas Supreme Court held that Griffin was personally liable on the three checks because "the burden is on the signer to relieve himself of personal liability by disclosing his agency," and Griffin had failed to meet that burden. One may surmise that many an agent fell into this trap of personal liability by signing imprinted company checks without indicating the agent's representative capacity.

Fortunately for those who sign corporate checks, the 1990 revision of Article 3 changed this rule. Under the revised article, if a corporate agent signs his or her name on a check that clearly indicates the name of the principal (the corporation), the agent will not be held liable even if the agent does not indicate his or her representative capacity [UCC 3–402(c)].

Why did the drafters of the revised Article 3 change this rule? Clearly, it is no less important today than it has been in the past to know who will be liable on an instrument signed by an agent. The reason for the change is given in Official Comment 3 to UCC 3–402(c): "Virtually all checks used today are in personalized form which identify the person on whose account the check is drawn. In this case, nobody is deceived into thinking that the person signing the check is meant to be liable. The subsection is meant to overrule cases decided under former Article 3 such as *Griffin v. Ellinger.*"

For Critical Analysis: *Does the above analysis apply to promissory notes?*

signature is wholly inoperative and will not bind the person whose name is forged. Assume, for example, that Parra finds Dolby's checkbook lying on the street, writes out a check to himself, and forges Dolby's signature. If a bank fails to ascertain that Dolby's signature is not genuine (which banks normally have a duty to do) and cashes the check for Parra, the bank will generally be liable to Dolby for the amount. (The liability of banks for paying over forged signatures is discussed further in Chapter 20.) There are two exceptions to this rule:

1.   Any unauthorized signature will bind the person whose name is forged if the person whose name is signed ratifies (affirms) it [UCC 3–403(a)]. For example, a signature made by an agent who exceeded the scope of his or her authority can be ratified by the principal, either expressly, by affirming the validity of the signature, or impliedly, by other conduct, such as keeping any benefits received in the transaction or failing to repudiate the signature. The parties involved need not be principal and agent. For example, a mother may ratify her daughter's forgery of the mother's name so that her daughter will not be prosecuted for forgery. A person may be precluded from denying the effectiveness of an unauthorized signature, however, if the person's negligence led to the forgery. For example, Jonathan signs a check, leaving blank the amount and the name of the payee, and then leaves the check in a public place. Jonathan can be estopped (prevented), on the basis of negligence, from denying liability for payment of the check [UCC 3–115, 3–406, 4–401(d)(2)].

2. An unauthorized signature operates as the signature of the unauthorized signer in favor of an HDC. A person who forges a check, for example, can be held personally liable for payment by an HDC [UCC 3–403(a)].

Special Rules for Unauthorized Indorsements

Generally, when there is a forged or unauthorized indorsement, the burden of loss falls on the first party to take the instrument with the forged or unauthorized indorsement. If the indorsement was made by an imposter or by a fictitious payee, however, the loss falls on the maker or drawer. We look at these two situations here.

IMPOSTERS An **imposter** is one who, by use of the mails, telephone, or personal appearance, induces a maker or drawer to issue an instrument in the name of an impersonated payee. If the maker or drawer believes the imposter to be the named payee at the time of issue, the indorsement by the imposter is not treated as unauthorized when the instrument is transferred to an innocent party. This is because the maker or drawer *intended* the imposter to receive the instrument. In this situation, under the UCC's *imposter rule*, the imposter's indorsement will be effective—that is, not considered a forgery—insofar as the drawer or maker is concerned [UCC 3–404(a)].

In the following case, a financial adviser pretended to be one of his clients so that he could obtain checks in the client's name and then cash the checks. The court had to decide whether the financial adviser was an imposter or a mere forger.

IMPOSTER
One who, by use of the mails, telephone, or personal appearance, induces a maker or drawer to issue an instrument in the name of an impersonated payee. Indorsements by imposters are not treated as unauthorized under Article 3 of the UCC.

CASE 19.2

DOMINION BANK, N.A. v. HOUSEHOLD BANK, F.S.B.[a]
United States District Court,
Southern District of Ohio, 1993.
827 F.Supp. 463.

HISTORICAL AND ECONOMIC SETTING *Annuities affect most of us at some time, even though many of us do not know what an annuity is. An* annuity *is a certain number of payments of a specific amount over a definite period of time. Modern annuities are better known as pensions or retirement benefits and can be purchased from numerous insurance companies. They form an essential part of the retirement plans of many workers, as a supplement to public-benefit programs, such as Social Security. Many people fear that in the near future, Social Security, which has existed since 1935, may not provide sufficient retirement benefits. In that event, an annuity will be all the more valuable.*

FACTS Lawrence Pompili was in charge of his firm's employee-benefits plans. Robert Grossman was a financial

adviser. Pompili gave Grossman over $80,000 to buy an annuity from the Fidelity Bankers' Life Insurance Company. After buying the annuity, Grossman wrote to Fidelity by mail, using Pompili's name and personal stationery, and asked for a check for $35,000. Later, Grossman followed the same procedure to request a check for $29,037.17. Both times, Fidelity issued checks payable to Pompili and mailed them to Grossman. Grossman forged Pompili's signature on the checks, added his own indorsement, and deposited them into his own account in Household Bank. Household obtained payment for the checks from the Dominion Bank, Fidelity's bank. When the scam was uncovered, Dominion filed a suit in a federal district court against Household. Household filed a motion for summary judgment, arguing that Grossman was an imposter and that under the imposter rule Household was not liable for the amount of the checks.

ISSUE Was Grossman an imposter?

DECISION Yes. The court held that Grossman was an imposter. Household was thus not liable for the amount of the checks.

---

a. *F.S.B.* is an abbreviation of Federal Savings Bank.

(Continued)

(Case 19.2—Continued

REASON The court explained that a "distinction exists between impersonation and mere forgery." If a person, through simple forgery, causes a drawer "to issue a check to him in the name of another, his actions do not trigger the application of the [imposter] rule." Instead, said the court, "the forger must have actively impersonated the payee by holding himself out to be that person." The court pointed out that Grossman corresponded with Fidelity in the name of Pompili, using Pompili's stationery. In fact, emphasized the court, throughout the letters were references by Grossman to himself as Pompili. "The record is so replete with such references" that the only conclusion to be drawn is that Grossman assumed the identity of * * * Pompili in all of his communications with Fidelity and did not merely forge * * * Pompili's signature."

FOR CRITICAL ANALYSIS—Social Consideration
Why should the drawer of a check suffer the loss under the imposter rule?

FICTITIOUS PAYEE
A payee on a negotiable instrument whom the maker or drawer does not intend to have an interest in the instrument. Indorsements by fictitious payees are not treated as unauthorized under Article 3 of the UCC.

FICTITIOUS PAYEES Another situation in which an unauthorized indorsement will be effective is when a person causes an instrument to be issued to a payee who will have *no interest* in the instrument [UCC 3–404(b), 3–405]. In this situation, the payee is referred to as a **fictitious payee**. Situations involving fictitious payees most often arise when (1) a dishonest employee deceives the employer into signing an instrument payable to a party with no right to receive payment on the instrument or (2) a dishonest employee or agent has the authority to issue an instrument on behalf of the employer. Under the UCC's *fictitious payee rule*, the payee's indorsement is not treated as a forgery, and the employer can be held liable on the instrument by an innocent holder.

Assume that Flair Industries, Inc., gives its bookkeeper, Axel Ford, general authority to issue checks in the company name drawn on First State Bank so that Ford can pay employees' wages and other corporate bills. Ford decides to cheat Flair Industries out of $10,000 by issuing a check payable to Erica Nied, an old acquaintance. Neither Flair nor Ford intends Nied to receive any of the money, and Nied is not an employee or creditor of the company. Ford indorses the check in Nied's name, naming himself as indorsee. He then cashes the check at a local bank, which collects payment from the drawee bank, First State Bank. First State Bank charges the Flair Industries account $10,000. Flair Industries discovers the fraud and demands that the account be recredited.

Who bears the loss? UCC 3–404(b)(2) provides the answer. Neither the local bank that first accepted the check nor First State Bank is liable. Because Ford's indorsement in the name of a payee with no interest in the instrument is "effective," there is no "forgery." Hence, the collecting bank is protected in paying on the check, and the drawee bank is protected in charging Flair's account. It is the employer-drawer, Flair Industries, that bears the loss. Of course, Flair Industries has recourse against Axel Ford, if Ford has not absconded with the money.

Regardless of whether a dishonest employee actually signs the check or merely supplies his or her employer with names of fictitious creditors (or with true names of creditors having fictitious debts), the UCC makes no distinction in result. Assume that Nathan Holtz draws up the payroll list from which employees' salary checks are written. He fraudulently adds the name Sally Slight (a fictitious person) to the payroll, thus causing checks to be issued to her. Again, it is the employer-drawer who bears the loss. In the following case, the court must determine whether a bank should bear the loss for forged indorsements on checks payable to fictitious payees.

CASE 19.3

GOLDEN YEARS NURSING HOME (NO. 2), INC. v. GABBARD

Court of Appeals of Ohio,
Butler County, 1994.
640 N.E.2d 1186.

HISTORICAL AND SOCIAL SETTING *People who reach age sixty-five have a 44 percent chance of spending at least some time in a nursing home before they die. Nursing homes have nearly two million residents, more than 90 percent of whom are over age sixty-five and nearly half of whom are over age eighty-five. Women constitute about three-quarters of these residents. The cost of nursing home care is high and increasing. In the mid-1990s, the average annual cost was $30,000 per resident, for a total of nearly $60 billion. Almost half this amount is covered by government funds.*

FACTS Nancy Gabbard was the office manager at Golden Years Nursing Home (No. 2), Inc. She was given a signature stamp to issue checks to the nursing home's employees for up to $100 as advances on their pay. The checks were drawn on Golden Years's account at the First National Bank. Over a seven-year period, Gabbard wrote a number of checks to employees exclusively for the purpose of embezzling the money. She forged the employees' indorsements on the checks, signed her name as a second indorser, and deposited the checks in her personal account at Star Bank. The employees whose names were on the checks never actually requested them. When the scheme was uncovered, Golden Years filed a suit in an Ohio state court against Gabbard, Star Bank, and others to recover the money. Star Bank filed a motion for summary judgment, which the court granted. Golden Years appealed.

ISSUE Did the fictitious payee rule bar Golden Years from recovering the amount of the checks from the bank?

DECISION Yes. The Court of Appeals of Ohio affirmed this part of the lower court's decision.

REASON The appellate court pointed out that "[t]he padded-payroll or fictitious-payee defense * * * validates a forged payee's indorsement whenever the drawer or his employee has designated as payee someone who is not really intended to have an interest in the instrument." In that situation, "the instrument will be properly payable out of the drawer/employer's bank account." The court explained that because Gabbard provided her employer with the names of employees "who had not really requested loans for the specific purpose of embezzling money without ever intending that the employees have an interest in the checks, * * * the padded-payroll defense * * * precluded Golden Years, the drawer of the checks, from asserting the forged payee indorsements against Star Bank."

FOR CRITICAL ANALYSIS—Social Consideration
Why should an employer, rather than a bank, have to suffer the loss in a fictitious payee case?

Warranty Liability

In addition to the signature liability discussed in the preceding pages, transferors make certain implied warranties regarding the instruments that they are negotiating. Liability under these warranties is not subject to the conditions of proper presentment, dishonor, or notice of dishonor. These warranties arise even when a transferor does not indorse the instrument (as in the delivery of a bearer instrument) [UCC 3–416, 3–417]. Warranties fall into two categories: those that arise on the *transfer* of a negotiable instrument and those that arise on *presentment*. Both transfer and presentment warranties attempt to shift liability back to a wrongdoer or to the person who dealt face to face with the wrongdoer and thus was in the best position to prevent the wrongdoing.

Transfer Warranties

The UCC describes five **transfer warranties** [UCC 3–416]. These warranties provide that any person who transfers an instrument *for consideration* makes the following

TRANSFER WARRANTIES
Implied warranties, made by any person who transfers an instrument for consideration to subsequent transferees and holders who take the instrument in good faith, that (1) the transferor is entitled to enforce the instrument, (2) all signatures are authentic and authorized, (3) the instrument has not been altered, (4) the instrument is not subject to a defense or claim of any party that can be asserted against the transferor, and (5) the transferor has no knowledge of any insolvency proceedings against the maker, the acceptor, or the drawer of the instrument.

warranties to all subsequent transferees and holders who take the instrument in good faith (with some exceptions, as will be noted shortly):

1.   The transferor is entitled to enforce the instrument.
2.   All signatures are authentic and authorized.
3.   The instrument has not been altered.
4.   The instrument is not subject to a defense or claim of any party that can be asserted against the transferor.[7]
5.   The transferor has no knowledge of any insolvency proceedings against the maker, the acceptor, or the drawer of the instrument.

The manner of transfer and the negotiation that is used determine how far and to whom a transfer warranty will run. Transfer by indorsement and delivery of order paper extends warranty liability to any subsequent holder who takes the instrument in good faith. The warranties of a person who transfers without indorsement (by the delivery of a bearer instrument), however, will extend the transferor's warranties only to the immediate transferee [UCC 3–416(a)].

Suppose that Abraham forges Peter's name as a maker of a promissory note. The note is made payable to Abraham. Abraham indorses the note in blank, negotiates it to Carla, and then leaves the country. Carla, without indorsement, delivers the note to Frank. Frank, in turn without indorsement, delivers the note to Ricardo. On Ricardo's presentment of the note to Peter, the forgery is discovered. Ricardo can hold Frank (the immediate transferor) liable for breach of the transfer warranty that all signatures are genuine. Ricardo cannot hold Carla liable, because the transfer warranties made by Carla, who negotiated the bearer instrument by delivery only, extend only to Frank, the immediate transferee.

Note that if Abraham had added a special indorsement ("Payable to Carla") instead of a blank indorsement, the instrument would have remained an order instrument. In that situation, to negotiate the instrument to Frank, Carla would have had to indorse the instrument, and her transfer warranties would extend to all subsequent holders, including Ricardo. This example shows the importance of the distinction between a transfer by indorsement and delivery (of an order instrument) and a transfer by delivery only, without indorsement (of a bearer instrument).

Presentment Warranties

Any person who presents an instrument for payment or acceptance makes the following **presentment warranties** to any other person who in good faith pays or accepts the instrument [UCC 3–417(a), 3–417(d)]:

1.   The person obtaining payment or acceptance is entitled to enforce the instrument or is authorized to obtain payment or acceptance on behalf of a person who is entitled to enforce the instrument. (This is, in effect, a warranty that there are no missing or unauthorized indorsements.)
2.   The instrument has not been altered.
3.   The person obtaining payment or acceptance has no knowledge that the signature of the issuer of the instrument is unauthorized.

These warranties are referred to as presentment warranties because they protect the person to whom the instrument is presented. The second and third warranties do not apply in certain situations (to certain persons). It is assumed, for example, that a

PRESENTMENT WARRANTIES
Implied warranties, made by any person who presents an instrument for payment or acceptance, that (1) the person obtaining payment or acceptance is entitled to enforce the instrument or is authorized to obtain payment or acceptance on behalf of a person who is entitled to enforce the instrument, (2) the instrument has not been altered, and (3) the person obtaining payment or acceptance has no knowledge that the signature of the drawer of the instrument is unauthorized.

---

7.   Under the unrevised Article 3, a qualified indorser who indorses an instrument "without recourse" limits this warranty to a warranty that he or she has "no knowledge" of such a defense (rather than that there is no defense). This limitation does not apply under the revised Article 3.

drawer or a maker will recognize his or her own signature and that a maker or an acceptor will recognize whether an instrument has been materially altered.

▌Defenses to Liability

Persons who would otherwise be liable on negotiable instruments may be able to avoid liability by raising certain defenses. There are two general categories of defenses—*universal defenses* and *personal defenses*.

Universal Defenses

Universal defenses (also called *real defenses*) are valid against *all* holders, including HDCs and holders who take through an HDC. Universal defenses include those described here.

FORGERY   Forgery of a maker's or drawer's signature cannot bind the person whose name is used unless that person ratifies (approves or validates) the signature or is precluded from denying it (because the forgery was made possible by the maker's or drawer's negligence, for example) [UCC 3–403(a)]. Thus, when a person forges an instrument, the person whose name is used normally has no liability to pay any holder or any HDC the value of the forged instrument.

FRAUD IN THE EXECUTION   If a person is deceived into signing a negotiable instrument, believing that he or she is signing something other than a negotiable instrument (such as a receipt), *fraud in the execution*, or fraud in the inception, is committed against the signer. For example, a salesperson asks a consumer to sign a paper, which the salesperson says is a request for an estimate. In fact, the paper is a promissory note, but the consumer, who is unfamiliar with the English language, does not realize this. In this situation, even if the note is negotiated to an HDC, the consumer has a valid defense against payment [UCC 3–305(a)(1)].

The defense of fraud in the execution cannot be raised, however, if a reasonable inquiry would have revealed the nature and terms of the instrument.[8] Thus, the signer's age, experience, and intelligence are relevant, because they frequently determine whether the signer should have known the nature of the transaction before signing. The following case concerns a farmer who signed a negotiable instrument under the mistaken assumption that he was signing a receipt for funds received.

> **UNIVERSAL DEFENSES**
> Defenses that are valid against all holders of a negotiable instrument, including holders in due course (HDCs) and holders with the rights of HDCs.

---

8. *Burchett v. Allied Concord Financial Corp.*, 74 N.M. 575, 396 P.2d 186 (1964).

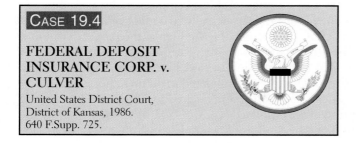

CASE 19.4

FEDERAL DEPOSIT INSURANCE CORP. v. CULVER

United States District Court, District of Kansas, 1986. 640 F.Supp. 725.

strong. *In early 1984, Nasib Ed Kalliel approached the bank with what he said was a plan to rescue farmers who were seeking to avoid possible bankruptcy. If the bank would loan the funds to keep the farmers in operation, Kalliel would guarantee repayment. Over the next year, the bank loaned $2 million to forty farmers in nine states. Not all of the money went to the borrowers, however. Kalliel diverted about $536,000 to himself and his companies. In less than two years, the bank failed.*

COMPANY PROFILE   *At the end of 1983, the Rexford State Bank had very few bad loans and was financially*

(Continued)

Case 19.4—Continued

FACTS Nasib Ed Kalliel agreed with Gary Culver, the owner of a Missouri farm, to manage the business end of the enterprise while Culver did the actual farming. When Culver told Kalliel that he needed money, Kalliel arranged with the Rexford State Bank to deposit $50,000 in Kalliel's account and send $30,000 of the money to Culver. Culver did not know about the $50,000 deposit and assumed that Kalliel was responsible for repayment of the $30,000. The bank asked Culver to sign a promissory note, assuring him that it was merely a receipt. The amount on the note read "$50,000," but the other terms— maturity date, interest rate, and so on—were blank. When the bank went broke, the Federal Deposit Insurance Corporation (FDIC) bought Culver's note and filed a suit in a federal district court against Culver to recover the amount. Culver argued that the bank had misrepresented the nature of the note and thus had committed fraud in the execution.

ISSUE Did the circumstances constitute fraud in the execution?

DECISION No. The court ruled in favor of the FDIC.

REASON The court noted that "[i]t is obvious from reading defendant's deposition that he is able to read and understand the English language." The court concluded that Culver was negligent in relying on the bank's assurance that the note was only a receipt. The court pointed out that Culver had a "reasonable opportunity to obtain knowledge of [the note's] character" before he signed it. Furthermore, "one who signs an instrument before all essential terms have been completed creates a 'blank check' that may be enforced by a subsequent holder in due course according to any terms that are completed by an intervening holder."

FOR CRITICAL ANALYSIS—Social Consideration
What factors should be taken into account in determining whether a party had a reasonable opportunity to know what he or she was signing?

MATERIAL ALTERATION An alteration is material if it changes the contract terms between any two parties in any way. Examples of material alterations include completing an incomplete instrument, adding words or numbers to an instrument, or making any other change to an instrument in an unauthorized manner that affects the obligation of a party to the instrument [UCC 3–407(a)].

Thus, cutting off part of the paper of a negotiable instrument; adding clauses; or making any change in the amount, the date, or the rate of interest—even if the change is only one penny, one day, or 1 percent—is material. It is not a material alteration, however, to correct the maker's address, for example, or to change the figures on a check so that they agree with the written amount (recall from Chapter 18 that words outweigh figures if there is a conflict between the written amount and the amount given in figures). If the alteration is not material, any holder is entitled to enforce the instrument according to its terms.

Material alteration is a *complete defense* against an ordinary holder. An ordinary holder can recover nothing on an instrument if it has been materially altered [UCC 3–407(b)]. Material alteration, however, may be only a *partial defense* against an HDC. When the holder is an HDC, if an original term, such as the monetary amount payable, has been *altered*, the HDC can enforce the instrument against the maker or drawer according to the original terms but not for the altered amount. If the instrument was originally incomplete and was later completed in an unauthorized manner, however, alteration no longer can be claimed as a defense against an HDC, and the HDC can enforce the instrument as completed [UCC 3–407(b)]. This is because the drawer or maker of the instrument, by issuing an incomplete instrument, will normally be held responsible for the alteration, which could have been avoided by the exercise of greater care. If the alteration is readily apparent, then obviously the holder has notice of some defect or defense and therefore cannot be an HDC [UCC 3–302(a)(1)].

DISCHARGE IN BANKRUPTCY   Discharge in bankruptcy is an absolute defense on any instrument regardless of the status of the holder, because the purpose of bankruptcy is to settle finally all of the insolvent party's debts [UCC 3–305(a)(1)].

MINORITY   Minority, or infancy, is a universal defense only to the extent that state law recognizes it as a defense to a simple contract (see Chapter 10). Because state laws on minority vary, so do determinations of whether minority is a universal defense against an HDC [UCC 3–305(a)(1)(i)].

ILLEGALITY   Certain types of illegality constitute universal defenses. Other types constitute personal defenses—that is, defenses that are effective against ordinary holders but not against HDCs. The difference lies in the state statutes or ordinances that make the transactions illegal. If a statute provides that an illegal transaction is *void*, then the defense is universal—that is, absolute against both an ordinary holder and an HDC. If the law merely makes the instrument *voidable*, then the illegality is still a defense against an ordinary holder but not against an HDC. The courts are sometimes prone to treat the word *void* in a statute as meaning *voidable* to protect an HDC [UCC 3–305(a)(1)(ii)].

MENTAL INCAPACITY   If a person is adjudged mentally incompetent by state proceedings, then any instrument issued by that person thereafter is void. The instrument is *void ab initio* (void from the beginning) and unenforceable by any holder or HDC [UCC 3–305(a)(1)(ii)]. Mental incapacity in these circumstances is thus a universal defense. If a person has not been adjudged mentally incompetent by state proceedings, mental incapacity operates as a defense against an ordinary holder but not against an HDC.

EXTREME DURESS   When a person signs and issues a negotiable instrument under such extreme duress as an immediate threat of force or violence (for example, at gunpoint), the instrument is void and unenforceable by any holder or HDC [UCC 3–305(a)(1)(ii)]. (Ordinary duress is a defense against ordinary holders but not against HDCs.)

> **CONTRAST** Minority, illegality, mental incapacity, and duress can be universal defenses or personal defenses, depending in some cases on state law other than the UCC.

Personal Defenses

Personal defenses (sometimes called *limited defenses*), such as those described here, can be used to avoid payment to an ordinary holder of a negotiable instrument, but not an HDC or a holder with the rights of an HDC.

BREACH OF CONTRACT OR BREACH OF WARRANTY   When there is a breach of the underlying contract for which the negotiable instrument was issued, the maker of a note can refuse to pay it, or the drawer of a check can order his or her bank to stop payment on the check. Breach of warranty can also be claimed as a defense to liability on the instrument.

For example, Rhodes purchases several sets of imported china from Livingston. The china is to be delivered in four weeks. Rhodes gives Livingston a promissory note for $2,000, which is the price of the china. The china arrives, but many of the pieces are broken, and several others are chipped or cracked. Rhodes refuses to pay the note on the basis of breach of contract and breach of warranty. (Under sales law, a seller impliedly promises that the goods are at least merchantable—see Chapter 17.) The payee-seller cannot enforce payment on the note because of the breach of contract and breach of warranty. If the payee-seller has negotiated the note to a third party, however, and the third party is an HDC, the maker-buyer will not be able to use breach of contract or warranty as a defense against liability on the note.

> **PERSONAL DEFENSES** Defenses that can be used to avoid payment to an ordinary holder of a negotiable instrument but not a holder in due course (HDC) or a holder with the rights of an HDC.

LACK OR FAILURE OF CONSIDERATION   The absence of consideration (value) may be a successful defense in some instances [UCC 3–303(b), 3–305(a)(2)]. For example, Tara gives Clem, as a gift, a note that states "I promise to pay you $100,000," and Clem accepts the note. There is no consideration for Tara's promise, and a court will not enforce the promise.

FRAUD IN THE INDUCEMENT (ORDINARY FRAUD)   A person who issues a negotiable instrument based on false statements by the other party will be able to avoid payment on that instrument, unless the holder is an HDC. Suppose that Jerry agrees to purchase Howard's used tractor for $24,500. Howard, knowing his statements to be false, tells Jerry that the tractor is in good working order and that it has been used for only one harvest. In addition, he tells Jerry that he owns the tractor free and clear of all claims. Jerry pays Howard $4,500 in cash and issues a negotiable promissory note for the balance. As it turns out, Howard still owes the original seller $10,000 on the purchase of the tractor. In addition, the tractor is three years old and has been used in three harvests. Jerry can refuse to pay the note if it is held by an ordinary holder. If Howard has negotiated the note to an HDC, however, Jerry must pay the HDC. Of course, Jerry can then sue Howard to recover the money.

ILLEGALITY   As mentioned, if a statute provides that an illegal transaction is void, a universal defense exists. If, however, the statute provides that an illegal transaction is voidable, the defense is personal. For example, a state may make gambling contracts illegal and void but be silent on payments of gambling debts. Thus, the payment of a gambling debt becomes voidable and is a personal defense. The effect that a void contract might have on a check issued in payment under that contract is at issue in the following case.

CASE 19.5

KEDZIE AND 103RD STREET CURRENCY EXCHANGE, INC. v. HODGE
Supreme Court of Illinois, 1993.
156 Ill.2d 112,
619 N.E.2d 732,
189 Ill.Dec. 31.

HISTORICAL AND ETHICAL SETTING   *There are always those who view federal, state, and local administrative regulations with disdain. This is particularly true with local and state regulations concerning home repairs and construction. Some people believe that they are qualified to construct or repair a house, for example, without first passing a test or obtaining a license that a local ordinance, state law, or federal law requires. Some of those with whom they do business agree. These customers are fully aware that their contractors are not licensed, but they expect to get the work done cheaply or quickly. Other customers have no idea whether their*

contractors are unlicensed and simply trust that whoever they deal with will perform the work more or less satisfactorily.

FACTS   Beulah Hodge made out a check to Fred Fentress for $500 as a partial payment in advance for plumbing services at her home. When Fentress failed to appear on the date work was to begin, Hodge ordered her bank to stop payment on the check. Fentress, however, had already cashed the check at Kedzie and 103rd Street Currency Exchange, Inc. When the check was returned to Kedzie marked "payment stopped," Kedzie filed a suit in an Illinois state court against Hodge to recover the amount of the check. In the meantime, Hodge discovered that Fentress was not a licensed plumber and that under state law, engaging in the plumbing trade without a license was a crime. Hodge filed a motion to dismiss Kedzie's claim on the ground that the plumbing contract was illegal and void. The court granted Hodge's motion, the appellate court affirmed, and Kedzie appealed to the Supreme Court of Illinois.

ISSUE   Is the check void?

Case 19.5—Continued

DECISION   No. The Supreme Court of Illinois reversed the lower court's ruling.

REASON   The state supreme court pointed out that "[a] holder in due course is an innocent third party * * * without knowledge of the circumstances of the contract upon which the instrument was initially exchanged." Thus, "unless the instrument arising from a contract or transaction is, itself, made void by statute, the 'illegality'

defense" does not bar the claim of an HDC. Here, the state plumbing license law "is relevant only to determine whether [it] provides that any obligation arising from a contract for plumbing services made in violation of its requirements is void. It does not."

FOR CRITICAL ANALYSIS—Economic Consideration
How could Hodge have avoided this situation?

MENTAL INCAPACITY   As mentioned, if a maker or drawer has been declared by a court to be mentally incompetent, any instrument issued by the maker or drawer is void. Hence, mental incapacity can serve as a universal defense [UCC 3–305(a)(1)(ii)]. If a maker or drawer issues a negotiable instrument while mentally incompetent but before a formal court hearing has declared him or her to be so, however, the instrument is voidable. In this situation, mental incapacity can serve only as a personal defense.

OTHER PERSONAL DEFENSES   Other personal defenses can be used to avoid payment to an ordinary holder of a negotiable instrument, including the following:

1.   Discharge by payment or cancellation [UCC 3–601(b), 3–602(a), 3–603, 3–604].
2.   Unauthorized completion of an incomplete instrument [UCC 3–115, 3–302, 3–407, 4–401(d)(2)].
3.   Nondelivery of the instrument [UCC 1–201(14), 3–105(b), 3–305(a)(2)].
4.   Ordinary duress or undue influence rendering the contract voidable [UCC 3–305(a)(1)(ii)].

∎ Federal Limitations on the Rights of HDCs

Because of the sometimes harsh effects of the HDC doctrine on consumers, the federal government limits HDC rights in certain circumstances. To understand the harsh effects of the HDC doctrine, consider an example. A consumer purchases a used car under express warranty from an automobile dealer. The consumer pays $1,000 down and signs a promissory note to the dealer for the remaining $5,000 due on the car. The dealer sells the bank this promissory note, which is a negotiable instrument, and the bank then becomes the creditor, to whom the consumer makes payments.

The car does not perform as warranted. The consumer returns the car and requests return of the down payment and cancellation of the contract. Even if the dealer refunded the $1,000, however, under the traditional HDC rule, the consumer would normally still owe the remaining $5,000, because the consumer's claim of breach of warranty is a personal defense, and the bank is a holder in due course. Thus, the traditional HDC rule leaves consumers who have purchased defective products liable to HDCs.

To protect consumers, the Federal Trade Commission issued a rule in 1976 that effectively abolished the HDC doctrine in consumer transactions. This rule, because of its significance in curbing the rights of HDCs, is presented here as this chapter's *Landmark in the Law.*

FTC Rule 433

In 1976, the Federal Trade Commission (FTC) issued Rule 433,[a] which severely limited the rights of HDCs who purchase instruments arising out of *consumer* credit transactions. The rule, entitled "Preservation of Consumers' Claims and Defenses," applies to any seller of goods or services who takes or receives a consumer credit contract. The rule also applies to a seller who accepts as full or partial payment for a sale the proceeds of any purchase-money loan[b] made in connection with any consumer credit contract. Under the rule, these parties must include in the consumer credit contract the following provision:

NOTICE
ANY HOLDER OF THIS CONSUMER CREDIT CONTRACT IS SUBJECT TO ALL CLAIMS AND DEFENSES WHICH THE DEBTOR COULD ASSERT AGAINST THE SELLER OF GOODS OR SERVICES OBTAINED PURSUANT HERETO OR WITH THE PROCEEDS HEREOF. RECOVERY HEREUNDER BY THE DEBTOR SHALL NOT EXCEED AMOUNTS PAID BY THE DEBTOR HEREUNDER.

Thus, a consumer who is party to a consumer credit transaction can now bring any defense he or she has against the seller of a product against a subsequent holder as well. In essence, the FTC rule places a holder in due course of the negotiable instrument in the position of a contract assignee. The rule makes the buyer's duty to pay conditional on the seller's full performance of the contract. The rule also makes both the seller and the creditor responsible for the seller's misconduct. Finally, the rule clearly reduces the degree of transferability of negotiable instruments resulting from consumer credit contracts.

What if the seller does not include the notice in a promissory note and then sells the note to a third party, such as a bank? While the seller has violated the rule, the bank has not. Because the FTC rule does not prohibit third parties from purchasing notes or credit contracts that do *not* contain the required rule, the third party does not become subject to the buyer's defenses against the seller. Thus, some consumers remain unprotected by the FTC rule.

For Critical Analysis: *How has FTC Rule 433 affected the ease with which consumer credit instruments can be negotiated?*

a.   16 C.F.R. Section 433.2. The rule was enacted pursuant to the FTC's authority under the Federal Trade Commission Act, 15 U.S.C. Sections 41–58.
b.   A purchase-money loan is one in which a seller or lessor advances money to a buyer or lessee, through a credit contract, to purchase or lease goods. See Chapter 21.

WATCH OUT Under the UCC, there can be no holder in due course of an instrument that complies with the FTC rule.

▌Discharge from Liability

Discharge from liability on an instrument can occur in several ways. The liability of all parties to an instrument is discharged when the party primarily liable on it pays to a holder the amount due in full [UCC 3–602, 3–603]. Payment by any other party discharges only the liability of that party and subsequent parties.

Intentional cancellation of an instrument discharges the liability of all parties [UCC 3–604]. Intentionally writing "Paid" across the face of an instrument cancels it. Intentionally tearing up an instrument cancels it. If a holder intentionally crosses out a party's signature, that party's liability and the liability of subsequent indorsers who have already indorsed the instrument are discharged. Materially altering an instrument may discharge the liability of any party affected by the alteration, as previously discussed [UCC 3–407(b)]. (An HDC may be able to enforce a materially altered instrument against its maker or drawer according to the instrument's original terms, however.)

Discharge of liability can also occur when a party's right of recourse is impaired [UCC 3–605]. A right of recourse is a right to seek reimbursement. Ordinarily, when a holder collects the amount of an instrument from an indorser, the indorser has a right of recourse against prior indorsers, the maker or drawer, and accommodation parties. If the holder has adversely affected the indorser's right to seek reimbursement from these other parties, however, the indorser is not liable on the instrument. This occurs when, for example, the holder releases or agrees not to sue a party against whom the indorser has a right of recourse.

Application

Law and the Purchaser of a Negotiable Instrument*

 Negotiable instruments are transferred every business day of the year. Most purchasers of negotiable instruments do not encounter any problems in further negotiating and transferring the instruments or in collecting payment on them if they are time instruments. Potential problems exist, however, and purchasers should take precautions against them.

For example, suppose that you wish to purchase a demand instrument. By definition, such an instrument has no stated time for payment and therefore may be overdue—that is, payment may have been demanded but not made, or a reasonable amount of time may have passed. (With checks, a reasonable amount of time is ninety days from the date on the check.) If you have any doubt about whether a demand instrument is overdue, you should investigate.

With any negotiable instrument, as a prospective holder, you cannot afford to ignore a defect in the instrument. A four-month-old date on a check, for example, constitutes notice that the instrument is overdue. Whenever a defect in an instrument exists, you will not qualify as a holder in due course (HDC), and you may be unable to obtain payment. In other words, it is prudent to determine whether the instrument is complete and whether the transfer is such as to qualify you for HDC status.

 Checklist for the Purchaser of Negotiable Instruments

1. Make sure that a demand instrument is not overdue before purchasing it.
2. Make sure that the negotiable instrument has no defects—undertake a good faith attempt to determine whether the maker or drawer of the instrument might have a valid reason for refusing to pay.

*This *Application* is not meant to substitute for the services of an attorney who is licensed to practice law in your state.

▌ Key Terms

▌Chapter Summary: Rights and Liabilities of Parties

Holder versus Holder in Due Course (HDC) *(See page 472.)*	1. *Holder*—A person in the possession of an instrument drawn, issued, or indorsed to him or her, to his or her order, or to bearer or in blank. A holder obtains only those rights that the transferor had in the instrument [UCC 1–201(20)]. 2. *Holder in due course (HDC)*—A holder who, by meeting certain acquisition requirements (summarized next), takes the instrument free of most defenses and claims to which the transferor was subject.

Requirements for HDC Status *(See pages 472–476.)*	To be an HDC, a holder must take the instrument:
	
	 1. *For value*—A holder can take an instrument for value in one of five ways [UCC 3–303]:
	    a. By performing the promise for which the instrument was issued or transferred.
	    b. By acquiring a security interest or other lien in the instrument, excluding a lien obtained by a judicial proceeding.
	    c. By taking an instrument in payment of (or as security for) an antecedent debt.
	    d. By giving a negotiable instrument as payment.
	    e. By giving an irrevocable commitment as payment.
	
	 2. *In good faith*—Good faith is defined as "honesty in fact and the observance of reasonable commercial standards of fair dealing" [UCC 3–103(a)(4)].
	
	 3. *Without notice*—To be an HDC, a holder must not be on notice that the instrument is defective in any of the following ways [UCC 3–302, 3–304]:
	    a. It is overdue.
	    b. It has been dishonored.
	    c. There is an uncured (uncorrected) default with respect to another instrument issued as part of the same series.
	    d. The instrument contains an unauthorized signature or has been altered.
	    e. There is a defense against the instrument or a claim to the instrument.
	    f. The instrument is so irregular or incomplete as to call into question its authenticity.

The Shelter Principle *(See pages 476–477.)*	A holder who cannot qualify as an HDC has the *rights* of an HDC if he or she derives title through an HDC unless the holder engaged in fraud or illegality affecting the instrument [UCC 3–203(b)].

Signature Liability *(See pages 477–485.)*	Every party (except a qualified indorser) who signs a negotiable instrument is either primarily or secondarily liable for payment of the instrument when it comes due.
	
	 1. *Primary liability*—Makers and acceptors are primarily liable (an acceptor is a drawee that promises to pay an instrument when it is presented for payment at a later time) [UCC 3–115, 3–407, 3–409, 3–412].
	
	 2. *Secondary liability*—Drawers and indorsers are secondarily liable [UCC 3–412, 3–414, 3–415, 3–501, 3–502, 3–503]. Parties who are secondarily liable on an instrument promise to pay on that instrument only if the following events occur:
	    a. The instrument is properly and timely presented.
	    b. The instrument is dishonored.
	    c. Timely notice of dishonor is given to the secondarily liable party.
	
	 3. *Accommodation parties*—An accommodation party is one who signs his or her name as credit to another party on an instrument [UCC 3–419]. Accommodation *makers* are primarily liable; accommodation *indorsers* are secondarily liable.
	
	 4. *Agents' signatures*—An *agent* is a person who agrees to represent or act for another, called the *principal*. Agents can sign negotiable instruments and therefore bind their principals. Liability on the instrument depends on whether the agent is authorized and on whether the agent's representative capacity and the principal's identity are both indicated on the instrument [UCC 3–401, 3–402, 3–403]. Agents need not indicate their representative capacity on *checks*—provided the checks clearly identify the principal and are drawn on the principal's account.
	
	 5. *Unauthorized signatures*—An unauthorized signature is wholly inoperative *unless*:
	    a. The person whose name is signed ratifies (affirms) it or is precluded from denying it [UCC 3–115, 3–401, 3–403, 3–406].
	    b. The instrument has been negotiated to an HDC [UCC 3–403].

▌Chapter Summary: Rights and Liabilities of Parties—Continued

Signature Liability—Continued	6. *Special rules for unauthorized indorsements*—An unauthorized signature will not bind the person whose name is forged except in the following circumstances: a. When an imposter induces the maker or drawer of an instrument to issue it to the imposter (imposter rule) [UCC 3–404(a)]. b. When a person signs as or on behalf of a maker or drawer, intending that the payee will have no interest in the instrument, or when an agent or employee of the maker or drawer has supplied him or her with the name of the payee, also intending the payee to have no such interest (fictitious payee rule) [UCC 3–404(b), 3–405].
Warranty Liability *(See pages 485–487.)*	1. *Transfer warranties*—Any person who transfers an instrument for consideration makes the following warranties to all subsequent transferees and holders who take the instrument in good faith (but when a bearer instrument is transferred by delivery only, the transferor's warranties extend only to the immediate transferee) [UCC 3–416]: a. The transferor is entitled to enforce the instrument. b. All signatures are authentic and authorized. c. The instrument has not been altered. d. The instrument is not subject to a defense or claim of any party that can be asserted against the transferor. e. The transferor has no knowledge of any insolvency proceedings against the maker, the acceptor, or the drawer of the instrument. 2. *Presentment warranties*—Any person who presents an instrument for payment or acceptance makes the following warranties to any other person who in good faith pays or accepts the instrument [UCC 3–417(a), 3–417(d)]: a. The person obtaining payment or acceptance is entitled to enforce the instrument or is authorized to obtain payment or acceptance on behalf of a person who is entitled to enforce the instrument. (This is, in effect, a warranty that there are no missing or unauthorized indorsements.) b. The instrument has not been altered. c. The person obtaining payment or acceptance has no knowledge that the signature of the drawer of the instrument is unauthorized.
Defenses to Liability *(See pages 487–491.)*	1. *Universal (real) defenses*—The following defenses are valid against all holders, including HDCs and holders with the rights of HDCs [UCC 3–305, 3–401, 3–403, 3–407]: a. Forgery. b. Fraud in the execution. c. Material alteration. d. Discharge in bankruptcy. e. Minority—if the contract is voidable under state law. f. Illegality, mental incapacity, or extreme duress—if the contract is void under state law. 2. *Personal (limited) defenses*—The following defenses are valid against ordinary holders but not against HDCs or holders with the rights of HDCs [UCC 3–105, 3–115, 3–302, 3–305, 3–306, 3–407, 3–601, 3–602, 3–603, 3–604, 4–401]: a. Breach of contract or breach of warranty. b. Lack or failure of consideration. c. Fraud in the inducement. d. Illegality and mental incapacity—if the contract is voidable. e. Previous payment of the instrument. f. Unauthorized completion of the instrument. g. Nondelivery of the instrument. h. Ordinary duress or undue influence that renders the contract voidable.
Federal Limitations on the Rights of HDCs *(See pages 491–492.)*	Rule 433 of the Federal Trade Commission, issued in 1976, limits the rights of HDCs who purchase instruments arising out of consumer credit transactions. Under the rule, a consumer who is a party to a consumer credit transaction is permitted to bring any defense he or she has against the seller against a subsequent holder as well, even if the subsequent holder is an HDC.
Discharge from Liability *(See pages 492–493.)*	All parties to a negotiable instrument will be discharged when the party primarily liable on it pays to a holder the amount due in full. Discharge can also occur in other circumstances (if the instrument has been canceled, materially altered, and so on) [UCC 3–601 through 3–606].

▌ For Review

1. What are the requirements for attaining HDC status?

2. How can a person who does not qualify as an HDC acquire the rights and privileges of an HDC?

3. What is the key to liability on a negotiable instrument? What is the difference between signature liability and warranty liability?

4. Certain defenses are valid against all holders, including HDCs. What are these defenses called? Name four defenses that fall within this category.

5. Certain defenses can be used to avoid payment to an ordinary holder of a negotiable instrument but are not effective against an HDC. What are these defenses called? Name four defenses that fall within this category.

▌ Questions and Case Problems

19–1. Unauthorized Indorsements. What are the exceptions to the rule that a bank will be liable for paying a check over an unauthorized indorsement?

19–2. Agents' Signatures. Karen Thorpe is a purchasing agent for GymNast, Inc., a manufacturer of sports equipment. Karen has authority to sign checks in payment of purchases made by GymNast. Karen makes out three checks to suppliers and signs each one differently, as follows:

   (a) GymNast, Inc., by Karen Thorpe, purchasing agent.

   (b) Karen Thorpe, purchasing agent.

   (c) Karen Thorpe.

Discuss briefly whether Karen is personally liable on each signature and whether parol evidence is admissible to hold GymNast, Inc., liable.

19–3. Defenses. Jules sold Alfred a small motorboat for $1,500; Jules maintained to Alfred that the boat was in excellent condition. Alfred gave Jules a check for $1,500, which Jules indorsed and gave to Sherry for value. When Alfred took the boat for a trial run, he discovered that the boat leaked, needed to be painted, and needed a new motor. Alfred stopped payment on his check, which had not yet been cashed. Jules has disappeared. Can Sherry recover from Alfred as a holder in due course? Discuss.

19–4. Defenses. Fox purchased a used car from Emerson for $1,000. Fox paid for the car with a check, written in pencil, payable to Emerson for $1,000. Emerson, through careful erasures and alterations, changed the amount on the check to read $10,000 and negotiated the check to Sanderson. Sanderson took the check for value, in good faith, and without notice of the alteration and thus met the UCC requirements for holder-in-due-course status. Can Fox successfully raise the universal defense of material alteration to avoid payment on the check? Explain.

19–5. Signature Liability. Marion makes a promissory note payable to the order of Perry. Perry indorses the note by writing "without recourse, Perry" and transfers the note for value to Steven. Steven, in need of cash, negotiates the note to Harriet by indorsing it with the words "Pay to Harriet, Steven." On the due date, Harriet presents the note to Marion for payment, only to learn that Marion has filed for bankruptcy and will have all debts (including the note) discharged in bankruptcy. Discuss fully whether Harriet can hold Marion, Perry, or Steven liable on the note.

19–6. HDC Status. An employee of Epicycle Corp. cashed a payroll check at Money Mart Check Cashing Center, Inc. Money Mart deposited the check, with others, into its bank account. When the check was returned marked "Payment stopped," Money Mart sought to recover from Epicycle for the value of the check. Money Mart claimed that it was a holder in due course on the instrument because it had accepted the check for value, in good faith, and without notice that a stop-payment order had been made. Epicycle argued that Money Mart was not a holder in due course, because it had failed to verify that the check was good before it cashed the check. Did Money Mart's failure to inquire into the validity of the check preclude it from being a holder in due course? Explain. [*Money Mart Check Cashing Center, Inc. v. Epicycle Corp.*, 667 P.2d 1372 (Colo. 1983)]

19–7. Unauthorized Indorsements. Mowatt worked as a bookkeeper for the law firm of McCarthy, Kenney & Reidy, P.C., which had several branch offices in the Boston area. Part of Mowatt's job involved preparing checks payable to the partners in other offices for the authorized signature of a partner of the firm. On numerous occasions, Mowatt wrote such checks with no intention of transmitting them to the payee-partners. Instead, after an authorized partner had signed the checks, Mowatt forged indorsements on them and then either cashed them or deposited them in one of three bank accounts that he had opened for this purpose. The fraudulent scheme went on for a year and a half. When the forgeries were finally discovered, the law firm demanded that the bank credit its account with the full amount of loss that it had sustained as a result of the forgeries. The bank refused to do so, and the law firm brought an action against the bank. Which party had to bear the loss arising from the forgeries, the law firm or the drawee bank? Discuss. [*McCarthy, Kenney & Reidy, P.C. v. First National Bank of Boston*, 402 Mass. 630, 524 N.E.2d 390 (1988)]

19–8. Unauthorized Indorsements. While Wanda Snow was married to Cary Byron, Byron established an account with Shearson Lehman Hutton, Inc.—a securities brokerage firm—for Wanda's son by a previous marriage. Wanda was designated as the account custodian. After Wanda and Byron had separated but before their divorce became final, Byron wrote a letter to Shearson instructing Shearson to close the account and send the proceeds (about $44,000) to a Florida bank account. Byron forged Wanda's signature on the letter. Later, Byron called Shearson, identified himself, and asked that the proceeds be sent instead to Wanda Snow in care of Byron's cousin in Connecticut. Byron obtained the check, forged Wanda's indorsement on it, and deposited the check into his bank account, later personally using the proceeds. Wanda sued Byron, Shearson, and the bank to recover the funds. In her claim against the bank, Wanda alleged that the bank was liable for paying the check over a forged indorsement. The bank raised the "imposter rule" as a defense. Is the imposter rule applicable in these circumstances? Why or why not? [*Snow v. Byron*, 580 So.2d 238 (Fla.App.1st 1991)]

19–9. Unauthorized Indorsements. Edward Bauerband contacted Minster State Bank by phone and requested a $25,000 loan, purportedly on behalf of himself and his wife, Michelle. The Bauerbands had a long-standing relationship with the bank, and the request was not so unusual as to put the bank on notice. The bank mailed a promissory note to Edward to be signed by both him and his wife. Edward forged his wife's signature on the note, signed it himself, and returned the note and other loan documents to the bank. On its receipt of the documents, the bank issued a cashier's check in the amount of $25,000, payable to Edward and Michelle jointly, and mailed the check to the Bauerbands' home. Edward indorsed the check in his name, forged his wife's indorsement, and deposited the check in his business account at another bank, Baybank Middlesex. Michelle knew nothing about the loan transaction or the check. Ultimately, the forgery was discovered, and Minster State Bank sued Baybank Middlesex to recover the funds. Baybank contended that it was precluded from liability under the UCC's "imposter rule." Was it? Explain. [*Minster State Bank v. Bauerband*, 1992 Mass.App.Div. 61 (1992)]

19–10. Discharge. Richard and Coralea Triplett signed two promissory notes—one for $14,000 and one for $3,500—in favor of FirsTier Bank, N.A. The Tripletts sent the bank a check for $7,200 as payment on the notes. A clerk divided the $7,200 payment to pay the second note in full and to reduce the amount owed on the first note. The clerk then incorrectly stamped the first note "PAID," signed it, and mailed it to the Tripletts. Later, a different clerk stamped the second note "PAID," signed it, and returned it to the Tripletts. When FirsTier sued the Tripletts in a Nebraska state court for the rest of the money due on the first note, the Tripletts asserted that the bank had stamped "PAID" on the note and returned it.

The bank contended that it had not intended to release both notes. In deciding whether the first note was discharged, what factors should the court take into consideration? [*FirsTier Bank, N.A. v. Triplett*, 242 Neb. 614, 497 N.W.2d 339 (1993)]

A QUESTION OF ETHICS AND SOCIAL RESPONSIBILITY

19–11. *One day, while Ort, a farmer, was working alone in his field, a stranger approached him. The stranger said he was the state agent for a manufacturer of iron posts and wire fence. Eventually the stranger persuaded Ort to accept a township-wide agency for the same manufacturer. The stranger then asked Ort to sign a document that purportedly was an agency agreement. Because Ort did not have his glasses with him and could read only with great difficulty, he asked the stranger to read what the document said. The stranger then pretended to read the document to Ort, not mentioning that it was a promissory note. Both men signed the note, and Ort assumed that he was signing a document of agency. The stranger later negotiated the note to a good faith purchaser for value. When that person sued Ort, Ort attempted to defend on the basis of fraud in the execution. In view of these facts, consider the following questions. [Ort v. Fowler, 31 Kan. 478, 2 P. 580 (1884)]*

1. Although this classic case was decided long before the UCC was drafted, the court applied essentially the same rule that would apply under Article 3. What is this rule, and how would it be applied to Ort's attempted defense on the ground of fraud in the execution?

2. This case provides a clear example of a situation in which one of two innocent parties (Ort and the purchaser of the note) must bear the loss caused by a third party (the stranger, who was the perpetrator of the fraud). Under Article 3, which party should bear the loss, and why?

FOR CRITICAL ANALYSIS

19–12. *How does the concept of holder in due course further Article 3's general goal of encouraging the negotiability of commercial paper? How does it further Article 3's goal of balancing the rights of parties to negotiable instruments?*

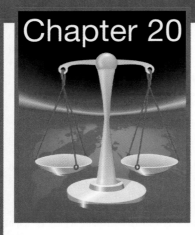

Chapter 20

Checks and the Banking System

"[E]very man will take money."

Jonathan Swift, 1667–1745
(Irish-born English satirist)

CHAPTER OBJECTIVES

After reading this chapter, you should be able to:

1. Identify the different types of checks.
2. Indicate when a bank may dishonor a customer's check without liability to the customer.
3. Outline a bank's responsibilities regarding stale checks, stop-payment orders, and forged or altered checks.
4. Describe how banks collect payment on checks deposited by their customers.
5. Explain the laws governing consumer electronic fund transfers and commercial fund transfers.

Checks are the most common kind of negotiable instruments regulated by the Uniform Commercial Code (UCC). It is estimated that over sixty billion personal and commercial checks are written each year in the United States. Checks are more than a daily convenience; they are an integral part of the American economic system. Just as "every man will take money," according to Jonathan Swift in the chapter-opening quotation, so most people accept checks—because they serve as substitutes for money.

Issues relating to checks are governed by Article 3 and Article 4 of the UCC. Recall from Chapters 18 and 19 that Article 3 establishes the requirements that all negotiable instruments, including checks, must meet. Article 3 also sets forth the rights and liabilities of parties to negotiable instruments. Article 4 of the UCC governs the relationships of banks with one another as they process checks for payment, and it establishes a framework for deposit and checking agreements between a bank and its customers. A check therefore may fall within the scope of Article 3 and yet be subject to the provisions of Article 4 while the check is in the course of collection. If a conflict between Article 3 and Article 4 arises, Article 4 controls [UCC 4–102(a)].

In this chapter, we first identify the legal characteristics of checks and the legal duties and liabilities that arise when a check is issued. Then we examine the check deposit and collection process—that is, the actual procedure by which the checks deposited into bank accounts move through banking channels, causing the underlying cash dollars to be shifted from one bank account to another. Increasingly, credit cards, debit cards, and other devices and methods to transfer funds electronically are being used to pay for goods and services. In the latter part of this chapter, we look at the law governing electronic fund transfers.

▌Checks

A **check** is a special type of draft that is drawn on a bank, ordering the bank to pay a fixed amount of money on demand [UCC 3–104(f)]. Article 4 defines a *bank* as "a person engaged in the business of banking, including a savings bank, savings and loan association, credit union or trust company" [UCC 4–105(1)]. If any other institution handles a check for payment or for collection, the check is not covered by Article 4.

    Recall from the discussion of negotiable instruments in Chapters 18 and 19 that a person who writes a check is called the *drawer*. The drawer is a depositor in the bank on which the check is drawn. The person to whom the check is payable is the *payee*. The bank or financial institution on which the check is drawn is the *drawee*. If Anita Cruzak writes a check from her checking account to pay her college tuition, she is the drawer, her bank is the drawee, and her college is the payee. We now look at some special types of checks.

CHECK
A draft drawn by a drawer ordering the drawee bank or financial institution to pay a fixed amount of money to the holder on demand.

Cashier's Checks

Checks are usually three-party instruments, but on certain types of checks, the bank can serve as both the drawer and the drawee. For example, when a bank draws a check upon itself, the check is called a **cashier's check** and is a negotiable instrument upon issue (see Exhibit 20–1) [UCC 3–104(g)]. Normally, a cashier's check indicates a specific payee. In effect, with a cashier's check, the bank assumes responsibility for paying the check, thus making the check more readily negotiable.

    For example, Kramer needs to pay a moving company $6,000 for moving his household goods to a new home in another state. The moving company requests

CASHIER'S CHECK
A check drawn by a bank on itself.

♦ **Exhibit 20–1**
   A Cashier's Check

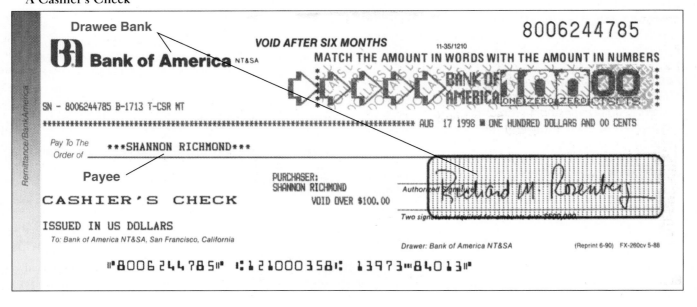

payment in the form of a cashier's check. Kramer goes to a bank (he need not have an account at the bank) and purchases a cashier's check, payable to the moving company, in the amount of $6,000. Kramer has to pay the bank the $6,000 for the check, plus a small service fee. He then gives the check to the moving company.

Cashier's checks are sometimes used in the business community as nearly the equivalent of cash. Except in very limited circumstances, the issuing bank must honor its cashier's checks when they are presented for payment. If a bank wrongfully dishonors a cashier's check, a holder can recover from the bank all expenses incurred, interest, and consequential damages [UCC 3–411]. This same rule applies if a bank wrongfully dishonors a certified check (to be discussed shortly) or a teller's check. (A *teller's check* is a check drawn by a bank on another bank or, when drawn on a nonbank, payable at or through a bank [UCC 3–104(h)]). In the following case, the court considered whether a bank could legitimately refuse to honor its own cashier's checks.

CASE 20.1

FIRST RAILROAD COMMUNITY FEDERAL CREDIT UNION v. COLUMBIA COUNTY BANK

United States District Court,
Middle District of Florida,
Jacksonville Division, 1994.
849 F.Supp. 780.

HISTORICAL AND ECONOMIC SETTING *In the 1980s, the share of the U.S. auto market held by U.S. auto makers declined by 10 percent relative to imports. With sales dropping, U.S. manufacturers closed plants, replaced blue-collar workers with robots, substituted computers for white-collar workers, and sometimes used creative bookkeeping to satisfy their shareholders. Domestic auto dealers began to sell foreign models. Instead of selling only Chevrolets, for example, dealers also began to sell Mazdas, Hondas, or BMWs. Some dealers, however, were unable to meet the challenges resulting from declining profits and engaged in criminal schemes to bolster their finances.*

FACTS Clark Crapps operated two automobile dealerships with bank accounts in the First Railroad Community Federal Credit Union and the Columbia County Bank. On one occasion, checks drawn on the account with First Railroad were deposited into the Columbia account. Unaware that the First Railroad account did not have enough funds to pay the checks, Columbia credited the account in its bank and issued two cashier's checks,

each for $300,000, based on the credit. Both checks were immediately deposited into the First Railroad account. When Columbia learned of the financial misdealings, it refused to honor the cashier's checks. Seeking payment, First Railroad filed a suit in a federal district court against Columbia. Both parties filed motions for summary judgment.

ISSUE Did Columbia have to pay its cashier's checks?

DECISION Yes. The court held that First Railroad was entitled to payment and granted summary judgment in its favor.

REASON The court explained that unlike an ordinary check, a cashier's check "stands on its own foundation as an independent, unconditional, and primary obligation of the bank. People accept a cashier's check as a substitute for cash because the bank stands behind the check, rather than an individual." The court reasoned that "the parties' expectation is that the cashier's check will remove doubt as to whether the instrument will be returned to the holder unpaid due to insufficient funds in the account, a stop payment order, or insolvency." Therefore, "the only inquiry a bank may make upon presentment of a cashier's check is whether or not the payee or [i]ndorsee is in fact a legitimate holder, i.e., whether the cashier's check is being presented by a thief or one who simply found a lost check, or whether the check has been materially altered."

FOR CRITICAL ANALYSIS—Economic Consideration
Why are the grounds on which a bank can refuse to pay a cashier's check so limited?

Traveler's Checks

A **traveler's check** has the characteristics of a teller's check. It is an instrument that is payable on demand, drawn on or payable at a bank, and designated as a traveler's

◆ **Exhibit 20–2**
  A Traveler's Check

check. The institution is directly obligated to accept and pay its traveler's check according to the check's terms. The purchaser is required to sign the check at the time it is bought and again at the time it is used [UCC 3–104(i)]. Exhibit 20–2 shows an example of a traveler's check.

Certified Checks

A **certified check** is a check that has been *accepted* by the bank on which it is drawn [UCC 3–409(d)]. When a drawee bank certifies (accepts) a check, it immediately charges the drawer's account with the amount of the check and transfers those funds to its own certified check account. In effect, the bank is agreeing in advance to accept that check when it is presented for payment and to make payment from those funds reserved in the certified check account. Essentially, certification prevents the bank from denying liability. It is a promise that sufficient funds are on deposit and *have been set aside* to cover the check. Exhibit 20–3 shows a sample certified check.

A drawee bank is not obligated to certify a check, and failure to do so is not a dishonor of the check [UCC 3–409(d)]. If a bank does certify a check, however, the bank should write on the check the amount that it will pay. If the certification does not state an amount, and the amount is later increased and the instrument negotiated to a holder in due course (HDC), the obligation of the certifying bank is the amount of the instrument when it was taken by the HDC [UCC 3–413(b)].

Certification may be requested by a holder (to ensure that the check will not be dishonored for insufficient funds) or by the drawer. In either circumstance, on certification the drawer and any prior indorsers are completely discharged from liability on the instrument [UCC 3–414(c), 3–415(d)].[1]

TRAVELER'S CHECK
A check that is payable on demand, drawn on or payable through a bank, and designated as a traveler's check.

CERTIFIED CHECK
A check that has been accepted by the bank on which it is drawn. Essentially, the bank, by certifying (accepting) the check, promises to pay the check at the time the check is presented.

---

1. Under Section 3–411 of the unrevised Article 3, the legal liability of a drawer varies according to whether certification is requested by the drawee or a holder. The drawer who obtains certification remains *secondarily liable* on the instrument if the certifying bank does not honor the check when it is presented for payment. If the check is certified at the request of a holder, the drawer and anyone who indorses the check before certification are completely discharged.

♦ Exhibit 20–3
A Certified Check

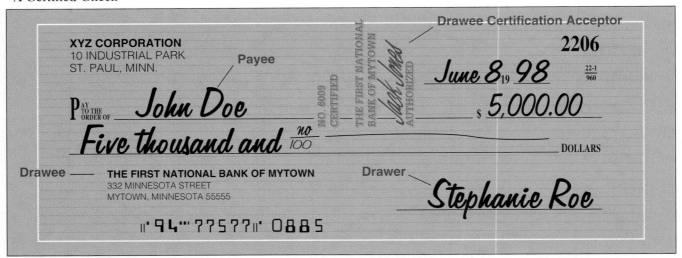

The Bank-Customer Relationship

The bank-customer relationship begins when the customer opens a checking account and deposits money that the bank will use to pay for checks written by the customer. The rights and duties of the bank and the customer are contractual and depend on the nature of the transaction.

A creditor-debtor relationship is created between a customer and a bank when, for example, the customer makes cash deposits into a checking account. When a customer makes a deposit, the customer becomes a creditor, and the bank a debtor, for the amount deposited.

An agency relationship also arises between the customer and the bank when the customer writes a check on his or her account. In effect, the customer is ordering the bank to pay the amount specified on the check to the holder when the holder presents the check to the bank for payment. In this situation, the bank becomes the customer's agent and is obligated to honor the customer's request. Similarly, if the customer deposits a check into his or her account, the bank, as the customer's agent, is obligated to collect payment on the check from the bank on which the check was drawn. To transfer checkbook dollars among different banks, each bank acts as the agent of collection for its customer [UCC 4–201(a)].

Whenever a bank-customer relationship is established, certain contractual rights and duties arise. The respective rights and duties of banks and their customers are discussed in detail in the following pages.

Bank's Duty to Honor Checks

When a commercial bank provides checking services, it agrees to honor the checks written by its customers with the usual stipulation that there be sufficient funds available in the account to pay each check [UCC 4–401(a)]. The customer is generally obligated to keep sufficient money on deposit to cover all checks written. The customer is liable to the payee or to the holder of a check in a civil suit if a check is dishonored for insufficient funds. If intent to defraud can be proved, the customer can also be subject to criminal prosecution for writing a bad check.

When the bank properly dishonors a check for insufficient funds, it has no liability to the customer. When a drawee bank *wrongfully* fails to honor a customer's check, however, it is liable to its customer for damages resulting from its refusal to pay [UCC 4–402].

Clearly, the bank's duty to honor its customers' checks is not absolute. As noted, the bank, is under no duty to honor a check when there are insufficient funds in the customer's account. There are other circumstances as well in which the bank may rightfully refuse payment on a customer's check. We look here at the rights and duties of both the bank and its customers in relation to specific situations.

Overdrafts

When the bank receives an item properly payable from its customer's checking account but there are insufficient funds in the account to cover the amount of the check, the bank has two options. It can either (1) dishonor the item or (2) pay the item and charge the customer's account, thus creating an **overdraft**, providing that the customer has authorized the payment and the payment does not violate any bank-customer agreement [UCC 4–401(a)].[2] The bank can subtract the difference from the customer's next deposit, because the check carries with it an enforceable implied promise to reimburse the bank. A bank can expressly agree with a customer to accept overdrafts through what is sometimes called an "overdraft protection agreement." If such an agreement is formed, any failure of the bank to honor a check because it would create an overdraft breaches this agreement and is treated as wrongful dishonor [UCC 4–402(a)].

When a check "bounces," a holder can resubmit the check, hoping that at a later date sufficient funds will be available to pay it. The holder must notify any indorsers on the check of the first dishonor, however; otherwise, they will be discharged from their signature liability.

OVERDRAFT
A check written on a checking account in which there are insufficient funds to cover the check.

Postdated Checks

A bank may also charge a postdated check against a customer's account, unless the customer notifies the bank not to pay the check until the stated date in a timely manner—that is, in time to allow the bank to act on the notice before the bank commits itself to pay on the check. If the bank receives timely notice from the customer and nonetheless charges the customer's account before the date on the postdated check, the bank may be liable for any damages incurred by the customer as a result [UCC 4–401(c)].[3]

Stale Checks

Commercial banking practice regards a check that is presented for payment more than six months from its date as a **stale check**. A bank is not obligated to pay an uncertified check presented more than six months from its date [UCC 4–404]. When receiving a stale check for payment, the bank has the option of paying or not paying the check. The bank may consult the customer before paying the check. If a bank pays a stale

STALE CHECK
A check, other than a certified check, that is presented for payment more than six months after its date.

---

2.   If there is a joint account, the bank cannot hold any joint-account customer liable for payment of an overdraft unless the customer has signed the check or has benefited from the proceeds of the check [UCC 4–401(b)].

3.   Under the UCC, postdating does not affect the negotiability of a check. Instead of treating postdated checks as checks payable on demand, however, many courts treat them as time drafts. Thus, regardless of whether the customer notified the bank of the postdating, a bank could not charge a customer's account for a postdated check without facing potential liability for the payment of later checks. Under the automated check-collection system in use today, however, a check is usually paid without respect to its date.

check in good faith without consulting the customer, however, the bank has the right to charge the customer's account for the amount of the check.

Stop-Payment Orders

STOP-PAYMENT ORDER
An order by a bank customer to his or her bank not to pay or certify a certain check.

A **stop-payment order** is an order by a customer to his or her bank not to pay or certify a certain check. Only a customer or a person authorized to draw on the account can order the bank not to pay the check when it is presented for payment [UCC 4–403(a)]. For a deceased customer, any person claiming a legitimate interest in the account may issue a stop-payment order [UCC 4–405]. A customer has no right to stop payment on a check that has been certified or accepted by a bank, however. Also, a stop-payment order must be received within a reasonable time and in a reasonable manner to permit the bank to act on it [UCC 4–403(a)]. Although a stop-payment order can be given orally, usually by phone, it is binding on the bank for only fourteen calendar days unless confirmed in writing.[4] A written stop-payment order (see Exhibit 20–4) or an oral order confirmed in writing is effective for six months, at which time it must be renewed in writing [UCC 4–403(b)].

If the bank pays the check over the customer's properly instituted stop-payment order, the bank will be obligated to recredit the customer's account—but only for the amount of the actual loss suffered by the drawer because of the wrongful payment [UCC 4–403(c)]. For example, Arlene Drury orders six bamboo palms from a local nursery at $50 each and gives the nursery a check for $300. Later that day, the nursery tells Drury that it will not deliver the palms as arranged. Drury immediately calls her bank and stops payment on the check. If the bank nonetheless honors the check, the bank will be liable to Drury for the full $300. The result would be different, however, if the nursery had delivered five palms. In that situation, Drury would owe the nursery $250 for the delivered palms, and her actual losses would be only $50. Consequently, the bank would be liable to Drury for only $50.

A stop-payment order has its risks for a customer. The customer-drawer must have a *valid legal ground* for issuing such an order; otherwise, the holder can sue the drawer for payment. Moreover, defenses sufficient to refuse payment against a payee may not

---

4. Some states do not recognize oral stop-payment orders; they must be in writing.

♦ Exhibit 20–4
  A Stop-Payment Order

| **B** Bank of America | | **Checking Account**
Stop Payment Order |

be valid grounds to prevent payment against a subsequent holder in due course [UCC 3–305, 3–306]. A person who wrongfully stops payment on a check not only will be liable to the payee for the amount of the check but also may be liable for consequential damages incurred by the payee as a result of the wrongful stop-payment order.

At issue in the following case was whether a bank wrongfully honored a check by making payment on the check after its customer had given the bank a stop-payment order.

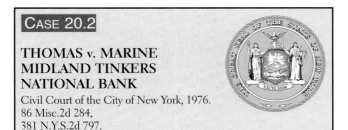

CASE 20.2

THOMAS v. MARINE MIDLAND TINKERS NATIONAL BANK

Civil Court of the City of New York, 1976.
86 Misc.2d 284,
381 N.Y.S.2d 797.

HISTORICAL AND TECHNOLOGICAL SETTING
Changing conditions constantly call for new procedures. Between 1950 and 1990, the volume of checks written grew from less than seven billion annually to more than sixty billion annually. Banks could not have handled this increase if they had not developed in the 1950s and 1960s an automated system for check processing based on encoding checks according to the Magnetic Ink Character Recognition (MICR) system. During the same decades, banks began to computerize their operations. Of course, computerized transactions are not always flawless. In the mid-1970s, banks had not yet designed and implemented software to identify and stop payment on checks from a specific account simply by account number and dollar amount.

FACTS On December 8, 1973, the plaintiff (Thomas) gave Ralph Gallo a check for $2,500 as a down payment on two rugs that Thomas was purchasing from Gallo. The check was postdated December 10 and drawn on the Marine Midland Tinkers National Bank. Having changed his mind about the purchase, Thomas went to the Marine Midland bank on the morning of December 10 and arranged with a bank officer whom he knew to have a stop-payment order placed on the check. Thomas gave the bank officer all the required information but described the check as #22 instead of #221, the correct number. On the afternoon of the following day, the check

was presented for payment at the same bank, and the bank cashed it and debited the plaintiff's account in the amount of the $2,500. When Thomas called Gallo, demanding the return of the $2,500, Gallo refused to pay and threatened to enforce the purchase agreement. Thomas then brought an action in a New York court against the bank for wrongful payment. The bank moved for dismissal of the charge on the basis of the incorrect information (the erroneous check number) given by Thomas on the stop-payment order.

ISSUE Can Thomas recover the $2,500 from the bank?

DECISION Yes. The bank was held responsible for its act of improperly making payment on the check.

REASON The court held that "[a] day and a half is more than reasonable notice to enforce a stop order on a check presented at the very same branch, and payment of the item by the bank thereafter constitutes a breach of its obligations to honor the stop order. The normal problem of reasonable computer lag when dealing with a great number of other branches of a large bank has no relevancy to the facts at bar [the facts in this case], where all transactions occurred in a single branch." As to the error regarding the check number, the court stated, "The single digital mistake in describing the check in the stop order is deemed trivial, and insignificant. Enough information was supplied to the bank to reasonably provide it with sufficient information to comply with the stop payment order. The bank is therefore held responsible for its act of improperly making payment upon the check."

FOR CRITICAL ANALYSIS—Economic Consideration
If Thomas did not have a legally sufficient reason to stop payment on the check, would that circumstance affect the court's decision that the bank had improperly paid the check? Should it?

Death or Incompetence of a Customer

A customer's death or incompetence does not affect the bank's authority to honor a check until the bank knows of the situation and has had a reasonable period of time to act on the information. Article 4 provides that if, at the time a check is issued or its collection has been undertaken, a bank does not know of an adjudication of incompetence or of the death of its customer, an item can be paid, and the bank will not incur liability.

Even when a bank knows of the death of its customer, for ten days after the *date of death*, it can pay or certify checks drawn on or before the date of death—unless a person claiming an interest in that account, such as an heir, orders the bank to stop payment [UCC 4–405]. Without this provision, banks would constantly be required to verify the continued life and competence of their drawers.

Forged Drawers' Signatures

When a bank pays a check on which the drawer's signature is forged, generally the bank is liable. A bank, however, may be able to recover at least some of the loss—from the customer (if the customer's negligence contributed to the forgery), from the forger of the check (if he or she can be found), or from the holder who presented the check for payment (if the holder knew that the signature was forged).

International Perspective

Attempts by the United Nations to form an international law for negotiable instruments have proved to be complicated, because different legal traditions handle liability for forged instruments differently. In the United States, for example, forgery is a universal defense. In other words, the person whose signature is forged normally will not be liable for paying on the instrument even if the holder is a holder in due course. In civil law systems, however, such as that of France, a good faith taker of a forged instrument is protected by the rule that the person whose signature is forged is liable on the instrument.

For Critical Analysis: *Who benefits the most under the French rule?*

THE GENERAL RULE   A forged signature on a check has no legal effect as the signature of a drawer [UCC 3–403(a)]. For this reason, banks require signature cards from each customer who opens a checking account. Signature cards allow the bank to verify whether the signatures on their customers' checks are genuine. The general rule, illustrated in the following case, is that the bank must recredit the customer's account when it pays a check with a forged signature.

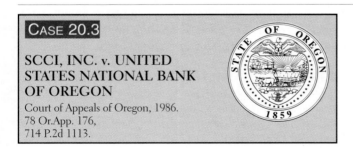

CASE 20.3

SCCI, INC. v. UNITED STATES NATIONAL BANK OF OREGON

Court of Appeals of Oregon, 1986.
78 Or.App. 176,
714 P.2d 1113.

HISTORICAL AND SOCIAL SETTING *The earliest cases in the common law were concerned with compensation for the victims of property crimes, such as trespass. In the 1990s, it continued to be widely acceptable for the victims of crimes, and sometimes relatives of the victims, to seek restitution from those convicted of the crimes. Sometimes, a criminal suspect is willing to "pay"* a victim to avoid the consequences of a conviction, such as imprisonment. The victim may be more willing to accept such a "payment" when the crime is a property offense, such as theft, and the victim knows the suspect—or the suspect's parents.

FACTS Susan Wolf, who was employed as a secretary and bookkeeper for SCCI, Inc., a construction contractor, forged her employer's name on more than ninety checks drawn on SCCI's account at the United States National Bank of Oregon. The bank cashed the checks and debited SCCI's account, and Susan Wolf wrongfully received a total of approximately $22,600. SCCI brought a criminal action against Wolf when the forgeries were discovered but later dropped the charges because SCCI's president "was acquainted with the parents of Susan Wolf, had no desire that [she] go to jail and was content

Case 20.3—Continued

to let the attorneys work the matter out." Wolf and her father gave SCCI a signed promissory note for $10,000. Meanwhile, SCCI demanded that the bank credit its account for the $22,600 worth of forged checks. The bank refused, claiming that the out-of-court settlement between SCCI and Wolf would undermine its ability to collect from Wolf (which it would attempt to do if it credited SCCI's account). SCCI filed a suit in an Oregon state court against the bank, arguing that it was the bank's duty, under its contractual responsibilities to SCCI, to cash checks only when they were authorized by SCCI. The court granted the bank's request for summary judgment. SCCI appealed.

ISSUE Can the bank be held liable for cashing the forged checks?

DECISION Yes. The Oregon appellate court reversed the trial court's judgment and remanded the case.

REASON The court reasoned that because there was no evidence that "plaintiff's [SCCI's] negligence substantially contributed to the forgery, plaintiff was not obligated for the forged checks that the bank had honored * * * and the bank lacked authority to debit plaintiff's account for the checks. Plaintiff was entitled to have the bank credit its account."

FOR CRITICAL ANALYSIS—Ethical Consideration
One of the general principles underlying the UCC's provisions governing negotiable instruments is that between two innocent parties, the one in the better position to prevent the loss should bear the burden of the loss. How might one argue that in the above case, SCCI, and not the bank, was in the better position to prevent the loss?

CUSTOMER NEGLIGENCE When the customer's negligence substantially contributes to the forgery, the bank will not normally be obligated to recredit the customer's account for the amount of the check [UCC 3–406]. Suppose, for example, that Gemco Corporation uses special check-writing equipment to write its payroll and business checks. Gemco discovers that one of its employees used the equipment to write himself a check for $10,000 and that the bank subsequently honored it. Gemco requests the bank to recredit $10,000 to its account for improperly paying the forged check.

If the bank can show that Gemco failed to take reasonable care in controlling access to the check-writing equipment, Gemco cannot require the bank to recredit its account for the amount of the forged check. Gemco's liability may be reduced, however, by the amount of loss caused by negligence on the part of the bank (or other "person") paying the instrument or taking it for value if the negligence substantially contributes to the loss [UCC 3–406(b)].[5]

Timely Examination of Bank Statements Required Banks typically send their customers monthly statements detailing activity on their checking accounts. Banks are not obligated to include the canceled checks themselves with the statement sent to the customer. If the bank does not send the canceled checks (or photocopies of the canceled checks), however, it must provide the customer with information (check number, amount, and date of payment) on the statement that will allow the customer to reasonably identify the checks that the bank has paid [UCC 4–406(a), 4–406(b)]. If the bank retains the canceled checks, it must keep the checks—or legible copies of the checks—for a period of seven years [UCC 4–406(b)]. The customer may obtain a check (or a copy of the check) during this period of time.

The customer has a duty to examine bank statements (and canceled checks or photocopies, if they are included with the statements) promptly and with reasonable care, and to report any alterations or forged signatures promptly [UCC 4–406(c)]. This

---

5. The unrevised Article 4 does not include a similar provision.

includes forged signatures of indorsers, to be discussed later. If the customer fails to fulfill this duty and the bank suffers a loss as a result, the customer will be liable for the loss [4–406(d)]. Even if the customer can prove that he or she took reasonable care against forgeries, the UCC provides that discovery of such forgeries and notice to the bank must take place within specific time frames in order for the customer to require the bank to recredit his or her account.

Consequences of Failing to Detect Forgeries When a series of forgeries by the same wrongdoer has taken place, the UCC provides that the customer, to recover for all the forged items, must have discovered and reported the first forged check to the bank within thirty calendar days of the receipt of the bank statement (and canceled checks or copies, if they are included) [UCC 4–406(d)(2)].[6] Failure to notify the bank within this period of time discharges the bank's liability for all forged checks that it pays prior to notification.

When the Bank Is Also Negligent There is one situation in which a bank customer can escape liability, at least in part, for failing to notify the bank of forged or altered checks within the required thirty-day period. If the customer can prove that the bank was also negligent—that is, that the bank failed to exercise ordinary care—then the bank will also be liable, and an allocation of the loss between the bank and the customer will be made on the basis of comparative negligence [UCC 4–406(e)].[7] In other words, even though a customer may have been negligent, the bank may still have to recredit the customer's account for a portion of the loss if the bank failed to exercise ordinary care.

Does a bank fail to exercise ordinary care if it fails to examine *every* signature on every check? Not according to UCC 3–103(a)(7). That section defines *ordinary care* to mean the "observance of reasonable commercial standards, prevailing in the area in which [a] person is located, with respect to the business in which that person is engaged." It is customary in the banking industry to manually examine signatures only on checks over a certain amount (such as $1,000, $2,500, or some higher amount). Thus, if a bank, in accordance with prevailing banking standards, fails to examine a signature on a particular check, the bank has not breached its duty to exercise ordinary care.

Prior to the 1990 revision of Article 3, bank customers whose own negligence contributed to forgeries sometimes sought to avoid liability by claiming that their banks were also negligent—that is, customers claimed that the banks' failure to examine *every* signature on the checks they paid constituted a breach of the banks' duty to exercise ordinary care. Some courts agreed; others did not. The revised Article 3 put an end to the problem by clarifying the meaning of ordinary care in the context of today's banking system.

Regardless of the degree of care exercised by the customer or the bank, the UCC places an absolute time limit on the liability of a bank for paying a check with a forged customer signature. A customer who fails to report a forged signature within one year from the date that the statement was made available for inspection loses the legal right to have the bank recredit his or her account [UCC 4–406(f)].

Forged Indorsements

A bank that pays a customer's check bearing a forged indorsement must recredit the customer's account or be liable to the customer-drawer for breach of contract. Suppose that Brian issues a $50 check "to the order of Antonio." Jimmy steals the check, forges

KEEP IN MIND If a bank is forced to recredit a customer's account, the bank may recover from the forger or from the party that cashed the check (usually a different customer or a collecting bank).

---

6. The unrevised Article 4 limits the period for examining and reporting to *fourteen* days [UCC 4–406(2)(b)].

7. Under the unrevised Article 4, if both parties are negligent, the bank is wholly liable [UCC 4–406(3)].

Antonio's indorsement, and cashes the check. When the check reaches Brian's bank, the bank pays it and debits Brian's account. The bank must recredit the $50 to Brian's account because it failed to carry out Brian's order to pay "to the order of Antonio" [UCC 4–401(a)]. Of course, Brian's bank can in turn recover—under breach of warranty principles (see Chapter 19)—from the bank that paid the check when Jimmy presented it [UCC 4–207(a)(2)].

Eventually, the loss usually falls on the first party to take the instrument bearing the forged indorsement, because, as discussed in Chapter 19, a forged indorsement does not transfer title. Thus, whoever takes an instrument with a forged indorsement cannot become a holder.

In any event, the customer has a duty to examine the returned checks (or copies of the checks) and statements received from the bank and to report forged indorsements promptly. A customer's failure to report forged indorsements within a three-year period after the forged items have been made available to the customer relieves the bank of liability [UCC 4–111].

COMPARE Three years is also the limit for bringing actions for breach of warranty and to enforce other obligations, duties, and rights under Article 3.

Altered Checks

The customer's instruction to the bank is to pay the exact amount on the face of the check to the holder. The bank has a duty to examine each check before making final payment. If it fails to detect an alteration, it is liable to its customer for the loss, because it did not pay as the customer ordered. The loss is the difference between the original amount of the check and the amount actually paid. Suppose that a check written for $11 is raised to $111. The customer's account will be charged $11 (the amount the customer ordered the bank to pay). The bank will normally be responsible for the $100 [UCC 4–401(d)(1)].

The bank is entitled to recover the amount of loss from the transferor, who, by presenting the check for payment, warrants that the check has not been materially altered. If the bank is the drawer (as it is on a cashier's check and a teller's check), however, it cannot recover on this ground from the presenting party if the party is an HDC acting in good faith [UCC 3–417(a)(2), 4–208(a)(2)]. The reason is that an instrument's drawer is in a better position than an HDC to know whether the instrument has been altered. Similarly, an HDC, acting in good faith in presenting a certified check for payment, does not warrant that the check was not altered before the HDC acquired it [UCC 3–417(a)(2), 4–207(a)(2)].

For example, Selling draws a check for $500 payable to Deffen. Deffen alters the amount to $5,000. The First National Bank of Whiteacre, the drawee bank, certifies the check for $5,000. Deffen negotiates the check to Evans, an HDC. The drawee bank pays Evans $5,000. On discovering the mistake, the bank cannot recover from Evans the $4,500 paid by mistake, even though the bank was not in a superior position to detect the alteration. This is in accord with the purpose of certification, which is to obtain the definite obligation of a bank to honor a definite instrument.

As in a situation involving a forged drawer's signature, when payment is made on an altered check, a customer's negligence can shift the loss (unless the bank was also negligent). A common example occurs when a person carelessly writes a check and leaves large gaps around the numbers and words so that additional numbers and words can be inserted (see Exhibit 20–5). Similarly, a person who signs a check and leaves the dollar amount for someone else to fill in is barred from protesting when the bank unknowingly and in good faith pays whatever amount is shown [UCC 4–401(d)(2)]. Finally, if the bank can trace its loss on successive altered checks to the customer's failure to discover the initial alteration, then the bank can reduce its liability for reimbursing the customer's account [UCC 4–406]. The law governing the customer's duty to examine monthly statements and canceled checks (or copies), and to discover and report unauthorized signatures to the drawee bank, applies to altered instruments as well as forgeries.

"Opportunity makes the thief."

Thomas Fuller, 1608–1661
(English clergyman and writer)

♦ **Exhibit 20–5**
A Poorly Filled-Out Check

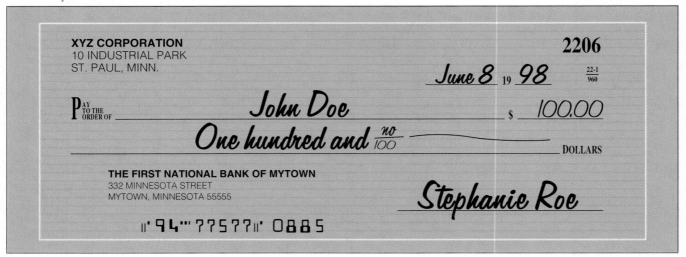

▌Bank's Duty to Accept Deposits

A bank has a duty to its customer to accept the customer's deposits of cash and checks. When checks are deposited, the bank must make the funds represented by those checks available within certain time frames. A bank also has a duty to collect payment on any checks payable or indorsed to its customer and deposited by the customer into his or her account. Cash deposits made in U.S. currency are received into the customer's account without being subject to further collection procedures.

Availability Schedule for Deposited Checks

BE AWARE With respect to checks, the Expedited Funds Availability Act of 1987 supersedes UCC Article 4.

The Expedited Funds Availability Act of 1987[8] and Regulation CC,[9] which was issued by the Federal Reserve Board of Governors (the Federal Reserve System will be discussed shortly) to implement the act, require that any local check deposited must be available for withdrawal by check or as cash within one business day from the date of deposit. A check is classified as a local check if the first bank to receive the check for payment and the bank on which the check is drawn are located in the same check processing region (check processing regions are designated by the Federal Reserve Board of Governors). For nonlocal checks, the funds must be available for withdrawal within not more than five business days.

In addition, the act requires the following:

1.   That funds be available on the *next business day* for cash deposits and wire transfers, government checks, the first $100 of a day's check deposits, cashier's checks, certified checks, and checks for which the depositary and payor banks are branches of the same institution.

2.   That the first $100 of any deposit be available for cash withdrawal on the opening of the next business day after deposit. If a local check is deposited, the next $400 is to be available for withdrawal by no later than 5:00 P.M. the next business day. If, for example, you deposit a local check for $500 on Monday, you can withdraw $100 in cash at the opening of the business day on Tuesday, and an additional $400 must be available for withdrawal by no later than 5:00 P.M. on Wednesday.

---

8.   12 U.S.C. Sections 4001–4010.
9.   12 C.F.R. Sections 229.1–229.42.

A different availability schedule applies to deposits made at *nonproprietary* auto-mated teller machines (ATMs). These are ATMs that are not owned or operated by the depositary institution. Basically, a five-day hold is permitted on all deposits, including cash deposits, made at nonproprietary ATMs.

Other exceptions also exist. A depository institution has eight days to make funds available in new accounts (those open less than thirty days). It has an extra four days on deposits over $5,000 (except deposits of government and cashier's checks), on accounts with repeated overdrafts, and on checks of questionable collectibility (if the institution tells the depositor it suspects fraud or insolvency).

Truth-in-Savings Act

Under the Truth-in-Savings Act (TISA) of 1991[10] and Regulation DD,[11] the act's implementing regulation, banks must pay interest on the full balance of a customer's account each day. For example, Furman has an interest-bearing checking account with the First National Bank. Furman keeps a $500 balance in the account for most of the month but withdraws all but $50 the day before the bank posts the interest. The bank cannot pay interest on only the $50. The interest must be adjusted to account for all of the days that Furman's balance was higher.

Before opening a deposit account, new customers must be given certain information in a brochure, pamphlet, or other handout. The information, which must also appear in all advertisements, includes the following:

1. The minimum balance required to open an account and to be paid interest.
2. The interest, stated in terms of the annual percentage yield on the account.
3. Whether interest is calculated daily.
4. Any fees, charges, and penalties, and how they are calculated.

Also, under the TISA and Regulation DD, a customer's monthly statement must declare the interest earned on the account, any fees that were charged, how the fees were calculated, and the number of days that the statement covers.

The Collection Process

Usually, deposited checks involve parties who do business at different banks, but sometimes checks are written between customers of the same bank. Either situation brings into play the bank collection process as it operates within the statutory framework of Article 4 of the UCC.

DESIGNATIONS OF BANKS INVOLVED IN THE COLLECTION PROCESS The first bank to receive a check for payment is the **depositary bank.**[12] For example, when a person deposits an IRS tax-refund check into a personal checking account at the local bank, that bank is the depositary bank. The bank on which a check is drawn (the drawee bank) is called the **payor bank.** Any bank except the payor bank that handles a check during some phase of the collection process is a **collecting bank.** Any bank except the payor bank or the depositary bank to which an item is transferred in the course of this collection process is called an **intermediary bank.**

DEPOSITARY BANK
The first bank to receive a check for payment.

PAYOR BANK
The bank on which a check is drawn (the drawee bank).

COLLECTING BANK
Any bank handling an item for collection, except the payor bank.

INTERMEDIARY BANK
Any bank to which an item is transferred in the course of collection, except the depositary or payor bank.

10. 12 U.S.C. Sections 4301–4313.
11. 12 C.F.R. Sections 230.1–230.9.
12. All definitions in this section are found in UCC 4–105. The terms *depositary* and *depository* have different meanings in the banking context. A depository bank refers to a *physical* place (a bank or other institution) in which deposits or funds are held or stored.

♦ **Exhibit 20–6**
The Check Collection Process

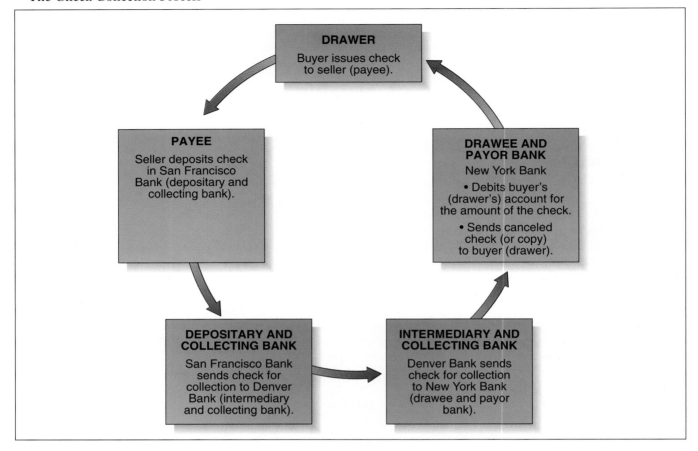

During the collection process, any bank can take on one or more of the various roles of depositary, payor, collecting, and intermediary bank. To illustrate: A buyer in New York writes a check on her New York bank and sends it to a seller in San Francisco. The seller deposits the check in her San Francisco bank account. The seller's bank is both a *depositary bank* and a *collecting bank*. The buyer's bank in New York is the *payor bank*. As the check travels from San Francisco to New York, any collecting bank handling the item in the collection process (other than the ones acting as a depositary bank and a payor bank) is also called an *intermediary bank*. Exhibit 20–6 illustrates how various banks function in the collection process.

CHECK COLLECTION BETWEEN CUSTOMERS OF THE SAME BANK An item that is payable by the depositary bank (also the payor bank) that receives it is called an "on-us item." If the bank does not dishonor the check by the opening of the second banking day following its receipt, the check is considered paid [UCC 4–215(e)(2)]. For example, Williams and Merkowitz both have checking accounts at State Bank. On Monday morning, Merkowitz deposits into his own checking account a $300 check drawn by Williams. That same day, State Bank issues Merkowitz a "provisional credit" for $300. When the bank opens on Wednesday, Williams's check is considered honored, and Merkowitz's provisional credit becomes a final payment.

CHECK COLLECTION BETWEEN CUSTOMERS OF DIFFERENT BANKS Once a depositary bank receives a check, it must arrange to present it either directly or through intermediary banks to the appropriate payor bank. Each bank in the collection chain must pass the check on before midnight of the next banking day following its receipt [UCC

4–202(b)].[13] A "banking day" is any part of a day that the bank is open to carry on substantially all of its banking functions. Thus, if a bank has only its drive-through facilities open, a check deposited on Saturday would not trigger a bank's midnight deadline until the following Monday. When the check reaches the payor bank, unless the payor bank dishonors the check or returns it by midnight on the next banking day following receipt, the payor bank is accountable for the face amount of the check [UCC 4–302].[14]

Because of this deadline and because banks need to maintain an even work flow in the many items they handle daily, the UCC permits what is called *deferred posting*. According to UCC 4–108, "a bank may fix an afternoon hour of 2:00 P.M. or later as a cutoff hour for the handling of money and items and the making of entries on its books." Any checks received after that hour "may be treated as being received at the opening of the next banking day." Thus, if a bank's "cutoff hour" is 3:00 P.M., a check received by a payor bank at 4:00 P.M. on Monday would be deferred for posting until Tuesday. In this situation, the payor bank's deadline would be midnight Wednesday.

HOW THE FEDERAL RESERVE SYSTEM CLEARS CHECKS The **Federal Reserve System** is a network of twelve central banks, located around the country and headed by the Federal Reserve Board of Governors. Most banks in the United States have Federal Reserve accounts. The Federal Reserve System has greatly simplified the check collection process by acting as a **clearinghouse**—a system or a place where banks exchange checks and drafts drawn on each other and settle daily balances.

For example, suppose that Pamela Moy of Philadelphia writes a check to Jeanne Sutton in San Francisco. When Sutton receives the check in the mail, she deposits it in her bank. Her bank then deposits the check in the Federal Reserve Bank of San Francisco, which transfers it to the Federal Reserve Bank of Philadelphia. That Federal Reserve bank then sends the check to Moy's bank, which deducts the amount of the check from Moy's account. Exhibit 20–7 on page 515 illustrates this process.

ELECTRONIC CHECK PRESENTMENT In the past, most checks were processed manually—the employees of each bank in the collection chain would physically handle each check that passed through the bank for collection or payment. Today, however, most checks are being processed electronically. In contrast to manual check processing, which can take days, *electronic check presentment* can be done on the day of the deposit. With electronic check presentment, items may be encoded with information (such as the amount of the check) that is read and processed by other banks' computers. In some situations, a check may be retained at its place of deposit, and only its image or information describing it is presented for payment under a Federal Reserve agreement, clearinghouse rule, or truncation agreement [UCC 4–110]. The term *truncation* refers to presentment by notice rather than by delivery.

FEDERAL RESERVE SYSTEM
A network of twelve central banks, located around the country and headed by the Federal Reserve Board of Governors. Most banks in the United States have Federal Reserve accounts.

CLEARINGHOUSE
A system or place where banks exchange checks and drafts drawn on each other and settle daily balances.

---

13. A bank may take a "reasonably longer time," such as when the bank's computer system is down due to a power failure, but the bank must show that it is still timely [UCC 4–202(b)].
14. Most checks are cleared by a computerized process, and communication and computer facilities may fail because of weather, equipment malfunction, or other conditions. If such conditions arise and a bank fails to meet its midnight deadline, the bank is "excused" from liability if the bank has exercised "such diligence as the circumstances require" [UCC 4–109(d)].

Electronic check presentment means that customers cannot take advantage of *float time*—the time between the check's issuance and final payment on the check by the bank. In the past, check drawers would often have a float time of several days (depending on where the payee was located). During this time, they could deposit funds to their accounts if they did not have sufficient funds to cover the checks when they wrote them. With electronic banking, this float time is lost.

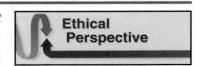
Ethical Perspective

(Continued)

Ethical Perspective—Continued

The lack of float time, though, also has helped to prevent check fraud, particularly in the form of check kiting. *Check kiting* occurs when a person takes advantage of float time to obtain unauthorized credit from a bank during the time it takes checks to clear. For example, assume that Ron has two checking accounts, one with Bank A and one with Bank B. Ron writes a check drawn on Bank A for $2,000, knowing there are insufficient funds in that account to cover the check. He then writes a check drawn on an account with Bank B for $2,000, even though he has insufficient money in that account to cover the check, and deposits this check in his account with Bank A—thus covering the first check. Then he writes another check on Bank A to cover the check drawn on Bank B, and so on. In other words, Ron is enjoying the *use* of $2,000 that, in essence, belongs to the bank. In some check-kiting schemes, several bank accounts—and substantial sums of money—have been involved.

For Critical Analysis: *What are some of the implications of the lack of float time for buyers and sellers in the marketplace?*

"Money is a poor man's credit card."

(Herbert) Marshall McLuhan, 1911–1980
(Canadian educator and author)

ELECTRONIC FUND TRANSFER (EFT)
A transfer of funds with the use of an electronic terminal, a telephone, a computer, or magnetic tape.

The advantages of using an automated teller machine are obvious. What are some of the disadvantages?

▌Electronic Fund Transfers

The application of computer technology to banking, in the form of *electronic fund transfer systems*, has been helping to relieve banking institutions of the burden of having to move mountains of paperwork to process fund transfers. An **electronic fund transfer (EFT)** is a transfer of money made by the use of an electronic terminal, a telephone, a computer, or magnetic tape.

The benefits of electronic banking are obvious. Automatic payments, direct deposits, and other fund transfers are now made electronically; no physical transfers of cash, checks, or other negotiable instruments are involved. Through the use of EFT systems, transactions that would otherwise take days can now be completed in seconds. For example, Harlan in New York can pay a debt to Lesley in Los Angeles by entering into a computer a bank order to pay it. Chase Manhattan, the drawee bank, can

♦ **Exhibit 20–7**
How a Check Is Cleared

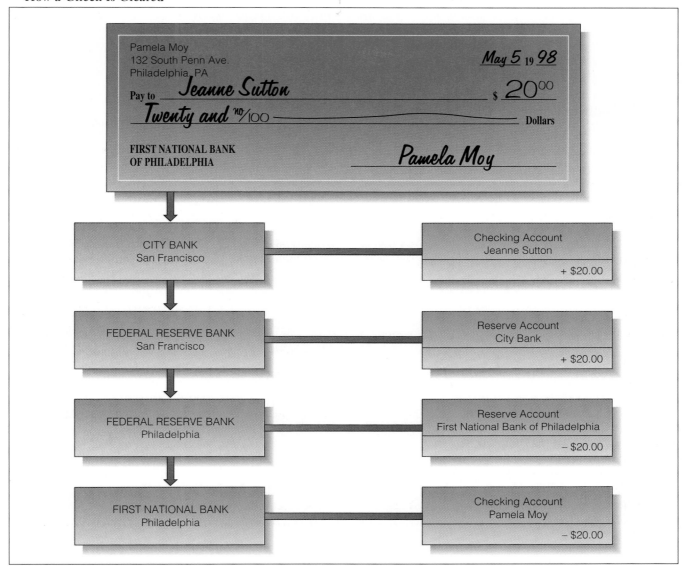

instantly debit Harlan's account and transfer the credit to the Bank of America, Lesley's bank, which can immediately credit her account. Not surprisingly, though, electronic banking also poses difficulties on occasion, including the following:

1. It is difficult to issue stop-payment orders.
2. Fewer records are available to prove or disprove that a transaction took place.
3. The possibilities for tampering (with a resulting decrease in privacy) are increased.
4. The time between the writing of a check and its deduction from an account (float time) is lost.

Types of EFT Systems

Most banks today offer EFT services to their customers. The four most common types of EFT systems used by bank customers are (1) automated teller machines, (2) point-of-sale systems, (3) systems handling direct deposits and withdrawals, and (4) pay-by-telephone systems. We look here at each of these types of EFT systems. Vast amounts of money are also transferred daily through electronic transfers between financial institutions. We look at these *commercial transfers* of funds later in the chapter. (See this chapter's *Technology and Digital Banking* for a discussion of still other, newer forms of fund transfers.)

▭ Technology and Digital Banking

For decades, Americans have been talking about the "cashless society." Now it seems as if it is truly becoming a reality. Americans spend millions of dollars without ever seeing those dollars. For example, an employer deposits an employee's paycheck directly into the employee's bank account. The employee uses debit or credit cards to pay for merchandise, groceries, fast food, newspapers, and even—in some areas—taxi and subway fares.

Recently, even newer types of cashless transactions have emerged. For example, customers of two British banks, National Westminster and Midland, can obtain a plastic and silicone cash substitute called Mondex. A Mondex card is like an ATM card, but it carries a computer chip inside and contains *data money.* The banks' customers can load data money into their cards over the phone if they have a "smart phone" (a phone with a special device attached) in their house. These cards can then be used, along with a PIN, to purchase goods and services—until the data money in the card is depleted.

Another development is the use of *electronic money,* called E-money or E-cash. Companies other than banks have already started their own forms of E-cash.

Some of the companies in the E-cash game are well known, such as Microsoft and Xerox; others are less well known, such as CyberCash and DigiCash. Perhaps E-cash's biggest success will be on the Internet, where electronic commerce is growing daily. People will be able to download money to their hard drives in their personal computers or to palm-sized electronic wallets and then transfer that money to Internet merchants.

With the growth of E-cash, the traditional definition of money will certainly no longer hold. E-cash moves along completely outside the network of banks, checks, and paper currency. Thus, E-cash—at least as yet—is not subject to government regulation. Furthermore, E-cash may provide problems if it is stored in computer systems. What if the systems crash? Additionally, electronic counterfeiting may be a serious problem. Computer hackers who break into an E-cash system might be able to steal money from thousands or even hundreds of thousands of individuals all at once. Finally, E-cash may allow for more tax evasion and money laundering.

For Critical Analysis: *What is the disadvantage of having, say, a Mondex money card instead of cash?*

AUTOMATED TELLER MACHINES   Automated teller machines (ATMs) are located either on the bank's premises or at convenient locations such as supermarkets, drugstores and other stores, airports, and shopping centers. Automated teller machines receive deposits, dispense funds from checking or savings accounts, make credit-card advances, and receive payments. The devices are connected on-line to the banks' computers. To access an account through an ATM, the bank customer uses a plastic card (debit card, access card), issued to him or her by the bank, plus a secret *personal identification number (PIN)*. The PIN protects the customer from someone else's use of a lost or stolen access card.

POINT-OF-SALE SYSTEMS   Point-of-sale systems allow consumers to transfer funds to merchants to pay for purchases. On-line terminals are located in, for example, grocery stores. When a purchase is made, the customer's *debit card* (issued by the bank to the customer) is inserted into the terminal, which reads the data encoded on it. The computer at the customer's bank verifies that the card and identification code are valid and that there is enough money in the customer's account to cover the purchase. After the purchase is made, the customer's account is debited for the amount of the purchase.

DIRECT DEPOSITS AND WITHDRAWALS   A direct deposit may be made to a customer's account through an electronic terminal when the customer has authorized the deposit in advance. The federal government often uses this type of EFT to deposit Social Security payments directly into beneficiaries' accounts. Similarly, an employer may agree to make payroll and pension payments directly into an employee's account at specified intervals.

A customer may also authorize the bank (or other financial institution at which the customer's funds are on deposit) to make automatic payments at regular, recurrent intervals to a third party. For example, insurance premiums, utility bills, and automobile installment loan payments may often be made automatically.

PAY-BY-TELEPHONE SYSTEMS   When it is undesirable to arrange in advance for an automatic payment—as, for example, when the amount of a regular payment varies—some financial institutions permit customers to pay bills through a pay-by-telephone system. This allows the customer to access the institution's computer system by telephone and direct a transfer of funds. Customers frequently pay utility bills directly using pay-by-telephone systems. Customers may also be permitted to transfer funds between accounts—for example, to withdraw funds from a savings account and make a deposit in a checking account—in this way.

Consumer Fund Transfers

Consumer fund transfers are governed by the Electronic Fund Transfer Act (EFTA)[15] of 1978. This act provides a basic framework for the rights, liabilities, and responsibilities of users of EFT systems. Additionally, the act gave the Federal Reserve Board authority to issue rules and regulations to help implement the act's provisions. The Federal Reserve Board's implemental regulation is called Regulation E.

The EFTA governs financial institutions that offer electronic fund transfers involving consumer accounts. The types of accounts covered include checking accounts, savings accounts, and any other asset accounts established for personal, family, or household purposes. Note that telephone transfers are covered by the EFTA only if they are made in accordance with a prearranged plan under which periodic or recurring transfers are contemplated.[16]

Because of its importance in establishing the rights of consumers who engage in EFT transactions, the EFTA is presented as this chapter's *Landmark in the Law*. In the subsections that follow the *Landmark*, we look more closely at the act's provisions concerning two important issues: unauthorized transfers and error resolution.

---

15. 15 U.S.C. Sections 1693 *et seq.* The EFTA is Title IX of the Consumer Credit Protection Act.
16. *Kashanchi v. Texas Commerce Medical Bank, N.A.*, 703 F.2d 936 (5th Cir. 1983).

The Electronic Fund Transfer Act (1978)

LANDMARK IN THE LAW

Congress stated in 1978 that the use of electronic systems to transfer funds promised to provide substantial benefits for consumers. At the same time, Congress acknowledged that existing laws provided inadequate protection for consumers with respect to electronic fund transfers. Thus, Congress passed the Electronic Fund Transfer Act

(Continued)

Landmark in the Law—Continued

(EFTA) "to provide a basic framework establishing the rights, liabilities, and responsibilities of participants in electronic fund transfers." The EFTA is designed to protect consumers. It is not concerned with commercial electronic fund transfers—transfers between businesses or between businesses and financial institutions. (Commercial fund transfers are governed by Article 4A of the UCC.)

The EFTA is essentially a disclosure law benefiting consumers. The act requires financial institutions to inform consumers of their rights and responsibilities, including those listed here, with respect to EFT systems.

1. If a customer's debit card is lost or stolen and used without his or her permission, the customer may be required to pay no more than $50. The customer, however, must notify the bank of the loss or theft within two days of learning about it. Otherwise, the liability increases to $500. The customer may be liable for more than $500 if he or she does not report the unauthorized use within sixty days after it appears on the customer's statement. (Even the $50 limit does not apply if the customer gives his or her card to someone who uses it improperly or if fraud is committed.)

2. The customer must discover any error on the monthly statement within sixty days, and he or she must notify the bank. The bank then has ten days to investigate and must report its conclusions to the customer in writing. If the bank takes longer than ten days, it must return the disputed amount of money to the customer's account until it finds the error. If there is no error, the customer has to return the money to the bank.

3. The bank must furnish receipts for transactions made through computer terminals, but it is not obligated to do so for telephone transfers.

4. The bank must make a monthly statement for every month in which there is an electronic transfer of funds. Otherwise, the bank must make statements every quarter. The statement must show the amount and date of the transfer, the names of the retailers or other third parties involved, the location or identification of the terminal, and the fees. Additionally, the statement must give an address and a phone number for inquiries and error notices.

5. Any authorized prepayment for utility bills and insurance premiums can be stopped three days before the scheduled transfer.

BE CAREFUL The EFTA does not provide for the reversal of an electronic transfer of funds once it has occurred.

For Critical Analysis: *Few individuals are required to use electronic transfer systems, but many do. Why?*

UNAUTHORIZED ELECTRONIC FUND TRANSFERS Unauthorized electronic fund transfers are one of the hazards of electronic banking. A paper check leaves visible evidence of a transaction, and a customer can easily detect a forgery or an alteration on a check with ordinary vigilance. Evidence of an electronic transfer, however, is in many cases only an entry in a computer printout of the various debits and credits made to a particular account during a specified time period.

Because of the vulnerability of EFT systems to fraudulent activities, the EFTA of 1978 clearly defined what constitutes an unauthorized transfer. Under the act, a transfer is unauthorized if (1) it is initiated by a person other than the consumer who has no actual authority to initiate the transfer; (2) the consumer receives no benefit from it; and (3) the consumer did not furnish the person "with the card, code, or other means of access" to his or her account.

In the following case, the court had to determine whether an account holder had authorized an imposter to withdraw funds from the customer's account. The first two parts of the definition of an unauthorized transfer just cited were obviously not relevant—the customer had not initiated or authorized the transfer, nor had he benefited from it. He had, however, unwittingly furnished the imposter with his EFT card and bank code. The case contains a lesson for all ATM users.

CASE 20.4

OGNIBENE v. CITIBANK, N.A.

Civil Court of New York City, 1981.
112 Misc.2d 219,
446 N.Y.S.2d 845.

HISTORICAL AND ECONOMIC SETTING *Many bank customers avoid automated teller machines (ATMs) located outside banks because they feel that the machines are unsafe. At some outside ATMs, muggings and thefts have been frequent occurrences. Sophisticated security devices can reduce the number of these incidents. Such innovations cost money that banks are reluctant to spend, however, considering that, as a system, ATMs have not resulted in significant cost savings. Also, some customers have practiced fraud in connection with ATMs, claiming that their bank statements reflect withdrawals they never made. The banking industry estimates that 10 percent of its losses from ATMs are from customer fraud.*

FACTS Frederick Ognibene stopped at an ATM outside a Citibank branch to make a $20 withdrawal from his account. Two ATMs were close together. In between them was a customer service telephone that a man appeared to be using. After Ognibene made his withdrawal, the man asked if he could try Ognibene's card in the other ATM to see if it would activate the machine. Ognibene, who thought the man was a bank employee, gave the man his card. The man inserted it in the other machine and punched in Ognibene's personal identification number (which the man had seen when Ognibene made his withdrawal). The man said into the phone that the machine was functioning and then hung up, returned Ognibene's card, thanked him, and left. Later, Ognibene

realized that $400 had been withdrawn from his account at that time. He brought an action against Citibank in a New York court to recover the money.

ISSUE Was the stranger's withdrawal from Ognibene's account "authorized" by Ognibene, in view of the fact that Ognibene had voluntarily allowed the stranger to use his card?

DECISION No. The court ordered the bank to credit the $400 to Ognibene's account.

REASON The court emphasized that Ognibene did not intend to authorize the stranger's withdrawal of funds from his account. The court also concluded that Ognibene was not negligent—he believed he was assisting a bank employee. Instead, the court pointed out that the bank had received reports of fraudulent withdrawals conducted by imposters posing as bank employees and gaining access to accounts in the same manner as in Ognibene's case. Because "the bank had knowledge of the scam and its operational details," it was in a better position than Ognibene to prevent the fraud. Thus, the court concluded that the bank "was negligent in failing to provide plaintiff-customer with information sufficient to alert him to the danger," so that, for example, he could have kept his personal identification number private.

FOR CRITICAL ANALYSIS—Ethical Consideration *Was the bank really in a better position than the customer to protect against fraud in this case? What kind of message does this case send to bank customers?*

ERROR RESOLUTION AND DAMAGES Banks must strictly follow the error-resolution procedures prescribed by the EFTA and described briefly in the *Landmark in the Law*. If a bank fails to investigate an error and report its conclusion promptly to the customer, in the specific manner designated by the EFTA, it will be in violation of the act and subject to civil liability. Its liability extends to any actual damages sustained by a customer and to all the costs of a successful action brought against the bank by a customer, including attorneys' fees. In addition, the bank may be liable for punitive damages ranging from $100 to $1,000 in an individual action. Failure to investigate an error in good faith makes the bank liable for treble damages. Even when a customer has sustained no actual damage, the bank may be liable for legal costs and punitive damages if it fails to follow the proper procedures outlined by the EFTA in regard to error resolution.

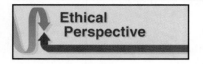

Ethical Perspective

The courts normally show little sympathy for a bank that breaches one of the procedural duties required by the EFTA, even if the bank has acted in good faith. For example, if a customer asks his or her bank to investigate a problem, the bank must look into the matter and report its findings to the customer *in writing* within ten days. Suppose, though, that a bank simply telephones the customer and explains that no error has been made. In this situation, the customer may sue the bank for violating the requirements of the EFTA—because the bank failed to inform the customer in writing of its conclusions. Even though the bank acted in good faith and had not committed any error in regard to the customer's account, a court would probably hold the bank liable because of its failure to comply with procedures required under the EFTA.[a]

Although it may seem unfair to hold the bank liable in these circumstances, the reasoning behind holding banks to strict compliance with EFTA requirements is clear: overall, strict compliance will ensure more fairness to more consumers. As with any consumer protection statute, there will be times when consumers take unfair advantage of the letter of the law for personal gain.

For Critical Analysis: *Do you agree with the reasoning in the above paragraph? Why or why not?*

a. See, for example, *Bisbey v. D.C. National Bank,* 253 D.C.App. 244, 793 F.2d 315 (1986).

Commercial Transfers

The transfer of funds "by wire" between commercial parties is another way in which funds are transferred electronically. In fact, the dollar volume of payments by wire transfer is more than $1 trillion a day—an amount that far exceeds the dollar volume of payments made by other means. The two major wire payment systems are the Federal Reserve wire transfer network (Fedwire) and the New York Clearing House Interbank Payments Systems (CHIPS).

Unauthorized wire transfers are obviously possible and, indeed, have become a problem. If an imposter, for example, succeeds in having funds wired from another's account, the other party will bear the loss (unless he or she can recover from the imposter). In the past, any disputes arising as a result of unauthorized or incorrectly made transfers were settled by the courts under the common law principles of tort law or contract law. To clarify the rights and liabilities of parties involved in fund transfers not subject to the EFTA or other federal or state statutes, Article 4A of the UCC was promulgated in 1989. Most states have adopted this article.

NOTE If any part of an electronic fund transfer is covered by the EFTA, the entire transfer is excluded from UCC Article 4A.

The type of fund transfer covered by Article 4A is illustrated in the following example. Jellux, Inc., owes $5 million to Perot Corporation. Instead of sending Perot a check or some other instrument that would enable Perot to obtain payment, Jellux tells its bank, East Bank, to credit $5 million to Perot's account in West Bank. East Bank instructs West Bank to credit $5 million to Perot's account. In more complex transactions, additional banks would be involved.

In these and similar circumstances, ordinarily a financial institution's instruction is transmitted electronically. Any means may be used, however, including first-class mail. To reflect this fact, Article 4A uses the term *funds transfer* rather than *wire transfer* to describe the overall payment transaction. The full text of Article 4A is included in Appendix C, following Article 4 of the Uniform Commercial Code.

BUSINESS LAW IN
ACTION

Time Zones and EFT Transactions

Today, because most checks are cleared electronically, bank customers often have little time in which they can stop payment on a check. This problem is even more pronounced with respect to electronic fund transfers. When a bank customer requests that funds be transferred electronically from the customer's account to a party's account in another bank, there may be very little time indeed within which the customer can cancel the request—particularly if the parties are in different time zones.

In one case, for example, a vice president of Aleo International, Ltd., in New York, instructed its bank, Citibank, N.A., to transfer $284,563 to a party's account in a Berlin bank. The request was made late in the day. Aleo decided to cancel the transfer and instructed Citibank to do so at

9 A.M. the next morning, when the bank opened. Unfortunately for Aleo, it was too late to cancel the payment. Citibank had sent the payment order electronically to the Berlin bank at around 5:30 P.M. the preceding day, shortly after Aleo had requested the transfer. The Berlin bank had also already notified Citibank that the funds had been paid to the beneficiary (credited to the recipient's account) at 9:59 A.M. Because Berlin time is six hours ahead of New York time, that meant that the Berlin bank already had paid the beneficiary at 3:59 A.M. New York time.

Aleo sued Citibank for negligence, but to no avail. For one thing, stated the court, Article 4A of the UCC governed the dispute, and Article 4 "does not include any provision for a cause of action in negligence"; rather, Article 4A was intended to be "the exclusive means of determining the rights, duties and liabilities of the affected parties in any situation covered by particular provisions of the Article." Furthermore, under UCC 4A–211, a sender's cancellation order is effective only "if notice of the communication is received at a time

and in a manner affording the receiving bank a reasonable opportunity to act on the communication before the bank accepts the payment order." Acceptance, in turn, occurs when the bank pays the beneficiary or notifies the beneficiary that the beneficiary's account has been credited [UCC 4A–209]. The court concluded that when the Berlin bank credited the beneficiary's account, it had "paid the beneficiary." In short, there was no way that Citibank could be held liable for failing to honor Aleo's request to cancel the payment.[a]

Businesspersons who arrange for the international transfer of funds electronically clearly may have little time within which to cancel the transactions if they have a change of heart.

For Critical Analysis: *What type of similar situations might arise in transferring money to Asia from the United States?*

a. *Aleo International, Ltd. v. Citibank, N.A.*, 160 Misc.2d 950, 612 N.Y.S.2d 540 (1994).

Application

Law and the Bank Customer— Stop-Payment Orders*

For a variety of reasons, a drawer should not misuse stop-payment orders. One reason is monetary: the bank's charges for stop-payment orders (which usually range between $15 and $20) are not small in relation to checks written for small amounts. Another reason is the risk attached to the issuance of a stop-payment order for any drawer-

customer. The bank is entitled to take a reasonable amount of time to enforce your stop order before it has liability for improper payment. Hence, the payee or another holder may be able to cash the check despite your stop order if he or she acts quickly. Indeed, you could be writing out a stop order in the bank lobby while the payee or holder cashes the check in the drive-in facility next door. In addition, even if a bank pays over your proper stop-payment order, the bank is only liable to the drawer-customer for the amount of loss the drawer suffers from the improper payment.

Remember that a drawer must have a legal reason for issuing a stop-payment order. You cannot legally stop payment on a check simply because you have had a change of heart about the wisdom of your purchase.

*This *Application* is not meant to substitute for the services of an attorney who is licensed to practice law in your state.

(Continued)

Application—Continued

Generally, you can safely stop payment if you clearly did not get what you paid for or were fraudulently induced to make a purchase. You can also stop payment if a "cooling-off" law governs the transaction—that is, if you legally have a few days in which to change your mind about a purchase. Any wrongful stop order subjects the *drawer* to liability to the payee or a holder, and this liability may include special damages that resulted from the order. When all is considered, it may be unwise to order a stop payment hastily on a check because of a minor dispute with the payee.

✓ **Checklist for Stop-Payment Orders**

1. Compare the stop-payment fee with the disputed sum to make sure it is worthwhile to issue a stop-payment order.
2. Make sure that your stop-payment order will be honored by your bank prior to the time the payee cashes the check.
3. Make sure that you have a legal reason for issuing the stop-payment order.

▌Key Terms

cashier's check 499
certified check 501
check 499
clearinghouse 513
collecting bank 511

depositary bank 511
electronic fund transfer (EFT) 514
Federal Reserve System 513
intermediary bank 511
overdraft 503

payor bank 511
stale check 503
stop-payment order 504
traveler's check 501

▌Chapter Summary: Checks and the Banking System

Checks *(See pages 499–502.)*	1. *Cashier's check*—A check drawn by a bank on itself (the bank is both the drawer and the drawee) and purchased by a customer. In effect, the bank lends its credit to the purchaser of the check, thus making the funds available for immediate use in banking circles. 2. *Teller's check*—A check drawn by a bank on another bank or, when drawn on a nonbank, payable at or through a bank. 3. *Traveler's check*—An instrument payable on demand, drawn on or through a bank, and designated as a traveler's check. The purchaser must provide his or her signature for a traveler's check to become a negotiable instrument. 4. *Certified check*—A check for which the drawee bank certifies that it will set aside funds in the drawer's account to ensure payment of the check upon presentation. On certification, the drawer and all prior indorsers are completely discharged from liability on the check.
The Bank-Customer Relationship *(See page 502.)*	1. *Contractual relationship*—The bank's relationship with its customer is contractual; both the bank and the customer assume certain contractual duties when a customer opens a bank account. 2. *Creditor-debtor relationship*—The relationship is also a creditor-debtor relationship (the bank is the debtor, because it holds the customer's funds on deposit). 3. *Agency relationship*—Because a bank must act in accordance with the customer's orders in regard to the customer's deposited money, an agency relationship also arises—the bank is the agent for the customer, who is the principal.
Bank's Duty to Honor Checks *(See pages 502–510.)*	Generally, a bank has a duty to honor its customers' checks, provided that the customers have sufficient funds on deposit to cover the checks [UCC 4–401(a)]. The bank is liable to its customers for actual damages caused by the bank's wrongful dishonor. The following list summarizes the rights and liabilities of the bank and the customer in various situations.

▌Chapter Summary: Checks and the Banking System—Continued

Bank's Duty to Honor Checks— Continued	1. *Overdrafts*—The bank has the right to charge a customer's account for any item properly payable, even if the charge results in an overdraft [UCC 4–401(a)].
	2. *Postdated checks*—A bank may charge a postdated check against a customer's account, unless the customer notifies the bank of the postdating in time to allow the bank to act on the notice before the bank commits itself to pay on the check [UCC 4–401(c)].
	3. *Stale checks*—The bank is not obligated to pay an uncertified check presented more than six months after its date, but it may do so in good faith without liability [UCC 4–404].
	4. *Stop-payment orders*—The customer must make a stop-payment order in time for the bank to have a reasonable opportunity to act. Oral orders are binding for only fourteen days unless they are confirmed in writing. Written orders are effective for only six months unless renewed in writing. The bank is liable for wrongful payment over a timely stop-payment order, but only to the extent of the loss suffered by the drawer-customer [UCC 4–403].
	5. *Death or incompetence of a customer*—So long as the bank does not know of the death or incompetence of a customer, the bank can pay an item without liability to the customer's estate. Even with knowledge of a customer's death, a bank can honor or certify checks (in the absence of a stop-payment order) for ten days after the date of the customer's death [UCC 4–405].
	6. *Forged drawers' signatures, forged indorsements, and altered checks*—The customer has a duty to examine account statements with reasonable care upon receipt and to notify the bank promptly of any forged or unauthorized signatures or indorsements, or alterations. On a series of unauthorized signatures or alterations by the same wrongdoer, examination and report must occur within thirty calendar days of receipt of the statement. Failure to comply releases the bank from any liability unless the bank failed to exercise ordinary care. Regardless of care or lack of care, the customer is estopped from holding the bank liable after one year for unauthorized customer signatures or alterations and after three years for unauthorized indorsements [UCC 3–403, 4–111, 4–401(a), 4–406].
Bank's Duty to Accept Deposits *(See pages 510–511.)*	A bank has a duty to accept deposits made by its customers into their accounts. Funds represented by checks deposited must be made available to the customer according to a schedule mandated by the Expedited Funds Availability Act of 1987 and Regulation CC. A bank also has a duty to collect payment on any checks deposited by its customers. When checks deposited by a customer are drawn on other banks, as they often are, the check collection process comes into play (discussed next). Under the Truth-in-Savings Act of 1991 and its implementing regulation, banks must pay interest on the full balance of a customer's account each day on any interest-bearing account.

The Collection Process *(See pages 511–514.)*	1. *Definitions of banks*—UCC 4–105 provides the following definitions of banks involved in the collection process:
	  a. Depositary bank—The first bank to accept a check for payment.
	  b. Payor bank—The bank on which a check is drawn.
	  c. Collecting bank—Any bank except the payor bank that handles a check during the collecting process.
	  d. Intermediary bank—Any bank except the payor bank or the depositary bank to which an item is transferred in the course of the collection process.

	2. *Check collection between customers of the same bank*—A check payable by the depositary bank that receives it is an "on-us item"; if the bank does not dishonor the check by the opening of the second banking day following its receipt, the check is considered paid [UCC 4–215(e)(2)].
	3. *Check collection between customers of different banks*—Each bank in the collection process must pass the check on to the next appropriate bank before midnight of the next banking day following its receipt [UCC 4–108, 4–202(b), 4–302].
	4. *How the Federal Reserve System clears checks*—The Federal Reserve System facilitates the check clearing process by serving as a clearinghouse for checks.
	5. *Electronic check presentment*—When checks are presented electronically, items may be encoded with information (such as the amount of the check) that is read and processed by other banks' computers. In some situations, a check may be retained at its place of deposit, and only its image or information describing it is presented for payment under a Federal Reserve agreement, clearinghouse rule, or other agreement [UCC 4–110].

(Continued)

▌Chapter Summary: Checks and the Banking System—Continued

Electronic Fund Transfers (See pages 514–521.)	1. *Types of EFT systems—*
	   a. Automated teller machines (ATMs).
	   b. Point-of-sale systems.
	   c. Direct deposits and withdrawals.
	   d. Pay-by-telephone systems.
	
	 2. *Consumer fund transfers—*Consumer fund transfers are governed by the Electronic Fund Transfer Act (EFTA) of 1978. The EFTA is basically a disclosure law that sets forth the rights and duties of the bank and the customer in respect to electronic fund transfer systems. Banks must comply strictly with EFTA requirements.
	
	 3. *Commercial transfers—*Disputes arising as a result of unauthorized or incorrectly made fund transfers between financial institutions are not covered under the EFTA. Article 4A of the UCC, which has been adopted by the majority of the states, governs fund transfers not subject to the EFTA or other federal or state statutes.

▌For Review

1. Checks are usually three-party instruments. On what type of check, however, does a bank serve as both the drawer and the drawee? What type of check does a bank agree in advance to accept when the check is presented for payment?

2. When may a bank properly dishonor a customer's check without liability to the customer?

3. In what circumstances might a bank not be liable for payment of a check containing a forged signature of the drawer?

4. Under the Electronic Fund Transfer Act, under what conditions will a bank be liable for an unauthorized fund transfer? When will the consumer be liable?

5. Are commercial electronic fund transfers between businesses governed by the Electronic Fund Transfer Act? If not, what law governs commercial fund transfers?

▌Questions and Case Problems

20–1. Error Resolution. Sheridan has a checking account at Gulf Bank. She frequently uses her access card to obtain money from the automatic teller machines. She always withdraws $50 when she makes a withdrawal, but she never withdraws more than $50 in any one day. When she received the April statement on her account, she noticed that on April 13 two withdrawals for $50 each had been made from the account. Believing this to be a mistake, she went to her bank on May 10 to inform the bank of the error. A bank officer told her that the bank would investigate and inform her of the result. On May 26, the bank officer called her and said that bank personnel were having trouble locating the error but would continue to try to find it. On June 20, the bank sent her a full written report advising her that no error had been made. Sheridan, unhappy with the bank's explanation, filed suit against the bank, alleging that it had violated the Electronic Fund Transfer Act. What was the outcome of the suit? Would it matter if the bank could show that on the day in question it had deducted $50 from Sheridan's account to cover a check that Sheridan had written to a local department store and that had cleared the bank on that day?

20–2. Forged Signatures. Gary goes grocery shopping and carelessly leaves his checkbook in his shopping cart. Dolores

steals his checkbook, which has two blank checks remaining. On May 5, Dolores forges Gary's name on a check for $10 and cashes the check at Gary's bank, Citizens Bank of Middletown. Gary has not reported the theft of his blank checks to his bank. On June 1, Gary receives his monthly bank statement and canceled checks from Citizens Bank, including the forged check, but he does not examine the canceled checks. On June 20, Dolores forges Gary's last check. This check is for $1,000 and is cashed at Eastern City Bank, a bank with which Dolores has previously done business. Eastern City Bank puts the check through the collection process, and Citizens Bank honors it. On July 1, Gary receives his bank statement and canceled checks. On July 4, Gary discovers both forgeries and immediately notifies Citizens Bank. Dolores cannot be found. Gary claims that Citizens Bank must recredit his account for both checks, as his signature was forged. Discuss fully Gary's claim.

20–3. Death of Bank Customer/Stale Checks. Brian, on January 5, drafts a check for $3,000 drawn on the Southern Marine Bank and payable to his assistant, Shanta. Brian puts last year's date on the check by mistake. On January 7, before Shanta has had a chance to go to the bank, Brian is killed in an automobile accident. Southern Marine is aware of Brian's death. On January 10, Shanta presents the check to the bank, and the bank honors the check by payment to Shanta. Brian's widow, Joyce, claims that the bank wrongfully paid Shanta, because it knew of Brian's death and also paid a check that was by date over one year old. Joyce, as executor of Brian's estate and sole heir by his will, demands that Southern Marine recredit Brian's estate for the check paid to Shanta. Discuss fully Southern Marine's liability in light of Joyce's demand.

20–4. Overdrafts. In September 1976, Edward and Christine McSweeney opened a joint checking account with the United States Trust Co. of New York. Between April 1978 and July 1978, 195 checks totaling $99,063 were written. In July 1978, activity in the account ceased. Christine wrote 95 of the 195 checks, totaling $16,811, and Edward wrote the rest of the checks. After deposits were credited for that period, the checks created a cumulative overdraft of $75,983. Can a bank knowingly honor a check when payment creates an overdraft, or must the bank dishonor the check? If the bank pays a check and thereby creates an overdraft, can the bank collect the amount of the overdraft from its customer? [*United States Trust Co. of New York v. McSweeney*, 91 A.D.2d 7, 457 N.Y.S.2d 276 (1982)]

20–5. Unauthorized Transfers. Parviz Haghighi Abyaneh and Iran Haghighi were co-owners of a savings account at First State Bank. On May 23, 1984, a person identifying himself as Abyaneh entered the Raleigh, North Carolina, office of Citizens Savings and Loan Association of Rocky Mount and opened a savings account. He then called First State Bank and asked a bank employee to transfer funds from Abyaneh's First State account into the newly created account. As a result, $53,825.66 was transferred to the new account, and subsequently the funds were withdrawn. When the true owners of the First State Bank account learned of the transfer, they filed suit against Merchants Bank, North, successor by merger to First State Bank, for violating the Electronic Fund Transfer Act. Discuss whether Abyaneh will be able to recover the $53,825.66. [*Abyaneh v. Merchants Bank, North*, 670 F.Supp. 1298 (M.D.Pa. 1987)]

20–6. Commercial Transfers. Dr. As'ad M. Masri and his wife borrowed $150,000 from First Virginia Bank–Colonial (FVBC). Masri then signed a wire-transfer request directing FVBC to transfer the funds to the Amro Bank in Amsterdam. The request also stated that the funds were to be deposited to the Lenex Corporation's account in that bank. FVBC transferred the funds to the Bank of Nova Scotia, an intermediary bank, and sent disbursal instructions directly to Amro. The following day, the funds were credited to the Lenex account at the Amro Bank. They were withdrawn, however, by someone other than the person intended by Masri to do so. When the Masris later defaulted on the loan, FVBC sought full repayment. The Masris claimed that FVBC breached the wire-transfer agreement. Has FVBC breached the transfer agreement? Where does FVBC's responsibility end? Discuss fully. [*First Virginia Bank–Colonial v. Masri, M.D.*, 245 Va. 461, 428 S.E.2d 903 (1993)]

20–7. Stale Checks. RPM Pizza, Inc., issued a $96,000 check to Systems Marketing but immediately placed a written stop-payment order on the check. Three weeks after the order expired, Systems cashed the check. Bank One Cambridge, RPM's bank, paid the check with funds from RPM's account. Because the check was more than six months old, it was stale

and thus, according to standard banking procedures as well as Bank One's own procedures, the signature on the check should have been specially verified. RPM filed a suit in a federal district court against Bank One to recover the amount of the check. What should the court consider in deciding whether the bank's payment of the check violated the UCC? [*RPM Pizza, Inc. v. Bank One Cambridge*, 69 F.Supp. 517 (E.D.Mich. 1994)]

20–8. Article 3 versus Article 4. Gary Morgan Chevrolet and Oldsmobile, Inc., issued four checks payable to General Motors Acceptance Corp. (GMAC) on Morgan's account with the Bank of Richmondville. There were insufficient funds in Morgan's account, and the bank gave GMAC oral notice of dishonor. The bank returned the checks two days later. GMAC filed a suit against the bank in a New York state court, claiming that the bank failed to dishonor the checks before its midnight deadline, because notice of dishonor must be in writing under Article 4. The bank countered that notice of dishonor may be made orally under Article 3. Which article controls when there is such a conflict? [*General Motors Acceptance Corp. v. Bank of Richmondville*, 203 A.D.2d 851, 611 N.Y.S.2d 338 (1994)]

A QUESTION OF ETHICS AND SOCIAL RESPONSIBILITY

20–9. *Lorine Daniels worked as a bookkeeper for Wilder Binding Co., which had a checking account with Oak Park Trust and Savings Bank. Among Daniels's responsibilities was the reconciliation of the bank statements with the firm's checkbook each month. Daniels forged signatures on forty-two checks, each for an amount under $1,000, which she made payable to herself. Over a six-month period, she embezzled a total of $25,254.78 in this way. When the forgeries were discovered, Wilder demanded that the bank recredit Wilder's account with the $25,254.78. In the lawsuit that followed, a key issue was whether the bank's custom of manually verifying signatures only on checks drawn for more than $1,000 constituted a breach of its duty of ordinary care. The bank testified that such policies and procedures were customary and routine and that its adherence to the policies and procedures therefore did not violate its duty of care. Given these facts, consider the following questions.* [Wilder Binding Co. v. Oak Park Trust and Savings Bank, 135 Ill.2d 121, 552 N.E.2d 783, 142 Ill.Dec. 1192 (1990)]

1. This case was decided under Article 3 before it was revised in 1990. The court held that whether the bank had breached its duty of care was a question of fact for the jury. How would a court decide this issue under the revised Article 3?
2. Does the fact that a practice is "customary and routine" in a certain industry, such as the banking industry, mean that it is necessarily ethical?

FOR CRITICAL ANALYSIS

20–10. *Under the 1990 revision of Article 4, banks are not required to send, with their monthly statements to customers, the customers' canceled checks. Banks may simply itemize the checks (by number, date, and amount) or, in addition* *to this itemization, also provide photocopies of the checks. Often, even when photocopies are included, the photocopies are reduced in size, so they are harder to read than the original canceled*

checks would be. What implications do the revised rules have for bank customers in terms of liability for unauthorized signatures and indorsements?

▌Unit Five—Cumulative Hypothetical Problem

 20–11. *Marva Cummings works as a bookkeeper for Albatross Printing Corp., a small printing firm. Marva has worked for the firm for years. She is authorized to sign company checks, on which Albatross's name and address are printed, and generally handles the firm's accounts. One of her tasks is to reconcile the monthly bank statement from the firm's bank.*

1. Albatross owes White Paper Co. $350 for paper supplies that Albatross ordered and received. Marva, who is distracted by personal problems, writes a check to White Paper but inadvertently fails to add the date. She also enters $300 in the box on the check indicating the amount in figures, but writes out "Three hundred and fifty and no/100" before the word "Dollars"—which is preprinted on the check. Is this check negotiable? If so, for what amount? If White Paper Co. crosses out the numerical amount $300 and writes "$350" above it, will this constitute a material alteration of the check?

2. Marva writes a check for $250 to Tony Malmo for some repairs Tony performed on the printing press. Tony indorses the check in blank and delivers it to Amber, who qualifies as a holder in due course. Amber loses the check. Felix finds it, indorses the check in blank, and deposits it into his bank account. In the meantime, Marva's employer discovers that Tony had not performed the repairs as promised on the printing press and asks Marva to stop payment on the check, which she does. Describe the rights and liabilities of each of the parties in this situation.

3. Marva writes and signs a corporate check for $3,500 payable to Latham Manufacturing Co. to pay for new printing equipment ordered and received by Albatross. When the check reaches Albatross's bank for collection, the bank refuses payment because Albatross has insufficient funds in its account to cover the check. Latham learns that Albatross is having financial difficulties and decides to sue Marva, claiming that she is personally liable on the check because she signed her name without indicating in her signature that she was acting as an agent for Albatross. Will the court hold Marva liable? Why or why not?

4. Business at Albatross is booming, and its profits have been increasing each month for over a year. Marva's employer refuses to give her a raise, which she feels she deserves. She decides to pay herself some extra money by engaging in some deception. Each month, she writes a check payable to Ann Barkley for $500, indorses Ann's name on the check, and then deposits the check in her bank account, indorsing the check "For deposit only." Marva assumes that Albatross will never learn of her deception, because normally she is the only one who sees the bank statements and copies of the canceled checks. Unfortunately for Marva, after she has written six monthly checks in this way, for a total of $3,000, her employer discovers the scheme. The employer insists that the bank recredit its account for the $3,000 it paid to Marva over the forged indorsements. Must the bank recredit Albatross's account? Why or why not?

▐ Accessing the Internet: Business Law and Legal Environment

To discover the major legal issues in banking and finance today, you can use the Legal Research Center of the commercial service CompuServe. When on CompuServe type in

Go legal

Select

Legal Research Center

The law firm of Reinhart et al. offers current information on banking law at

http://www.rbvdnr.com/

You can obtain a tremendous amount of information on banking regulation from the Federal Deposit Insurance Corporation (FDIC) at

http://www.fdic.gov/

Additional information about banking can be obtained from the Federal Reserve System at

gopher://marvel.loc.gov:70/11/federal/fedinfo/byagency/
executive/fedreserve

The gopher address is

marvel.loc.gov

The gopher directions are

1. Select **Government Information**
2. Select **Federal Information Resources**
3. Select **Information by Branch of Federal Government**
4. Select **Executive Branch**
5. Select **Federal Reserve System**

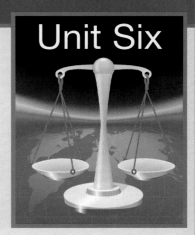

Unit Six

Debtor-Creditor Relationships

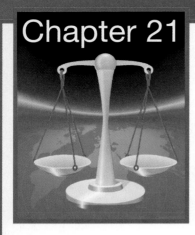

Chapter 21

Secured Transactions

"Article 9 is clearly the most novel and probably the most important article of the Code . . . and covers the entire range of transactions in which the debts are secured by personal property."

Walter D. Malcolm, 1904–1979
*(**President of the National Conference of Commissioners on Uniform State Laws,** 1963–1966)*

CHAPTER OBJECTIVES

After reading this chapter, you should be able to:

1. List and define the various terms used in secured transactions.
2. State what is necessary to create an enforceable security interest.
3. Explain how and why security interests are perfected.
4. Indicate how priority disputes among creditors are decided.
5. Discuss the remedies available to a secured creditor when the debtor defaults.

SECURED TRANSACTION
Any transaction in which the payment of a debt is guaranteed, or secured, by personal property owned by the debtor or in which the debtor has a legal interest.

Whenever the payment of a debt is guaranteed, or *secured*, by personal property owned by the debtor or in which the debtor has a legal interest, the transaction becomes known as a **secured transaction**. The concept of the secured transaction is as basic to modern business practice as the concept of credit. Logically, sellers and lenders do not want to risk nonpayment, so they usually will not sell goods or lend money unless the promise of payment is somehow guaranteed. Indeed, business as we know it could not exist without laws permitting and governing secured transactions.

The significance of Article 9 of the Uniform Commercial Code (UCC), which governs secured transactions, is related in the following *Landmark in the Law.* As will become evident, the law of secured transactions tends to favor the rights of creditors; but to a lesser extent, it offers debtors some protection, too.

Article 9 Security Interest

Prior to the drafting and adoption by the states of Article 9 of the Uniform Commercial Code, secured transactions were governed by a patchwork of security devices. These devices were replete with variations that, according to many, made no logical sense. Additionally, each device had its own jargon. Depending on the device used, for example, a debtor could be called variously a pledgor, a mortgagor, a conditional vendee, an assignor, or a borrower.

One of the earliest security devices, historically, is the pledge. A *pledge* is called a possessory security interest because the secured party acquires or holds possession of the property involved, called the *collateral,* to secure the payment or performance of the secured obligation. The pledge has existed since at least the fourth or fifth century. One security device that developed from the pledge concept involved obtaining a security interest in goods that could not be conveniently moved from the debtor's property. In such a situation, the creditor would have an independent warehouser establish a warehouse on the debtor's premises to obtain possession of the goods. This was called a field warehouse and dates from about 1900.

There were many other types of security devices. Nonetheless, creditors still faced several legal problems. For example, in many states, a security interest could not be taken in inventory or a stock in trade, such as cars for a car dealer or chocolate for a candy manufacturer. Sometimes, highly technical limitations were placed on the use of a particular device. If a court determined that a particular device was not appropriate for a given transaction, it might void the security interest.

The drafters of Article 9 concluded that the two elements common to all security devices were (1) the objective of conferring on a creditor or secured party priority in certain property (the collateral) against the risk of the debtor's nonpayment of the debt or the debtor's insolvency or bankruptcy and (2) a means of notifying other creditors of this prior security interest. With these two elements in mind, the drafters created a new, simplified security device with a single set of terms to cover all situations. What is this device called? It is called, simply, an Article 9 security interest.

Although the law of secured transactions still remains far from simple, it is now—thanks to the drafters of Article 9—far more rational and uniform than it was in the days prior to the UCC.

For Critical Analysis: *Clearly, creditors benefit from secured transactions. How do debtors also benefit from the existence of secured transactions?*

▌ The Terminology of Secured Transactions

The UCC's terminology is now uniformly adopted in all documents used in situations involving secured transactions. A brief summary of the UCC's definitions of terms relating to secured transactions follows.

1. A **security interest** is any interest "in personal property or fixtures which secures payment or performance of an obligation" [UCC 1–201(37)].
2. A **secured party** is a lender, a seller, or any person in whose favor there is a security interest, including a person to whom accounts or *chattel paper* (any writing evidencing a debt secured by personal property) has been sold [UCC 9–105(1)(m)]. The terms *secured party* and *secured creditor* are used interchangeably.

SECURITY INTEREST
Any interest "in personal property or fixtures which secures payment or performance of an obligation" [UCC 1–201(37)].

SECURED PARTY
A lender, seller, or any other person in whose favor there is a security interest, including a person to whom accounts or chattel paper has been sold.

◆ **Exhibit 21–1**
 Secured Transactions—Concept and Terminology
In a security agreement, a debtor and creditor agree that the creditor will have a
security interest in collateral in which the debtor has rights. In essence, the collateral
secures the loan and ensures the creditor of payment should the debtor default.

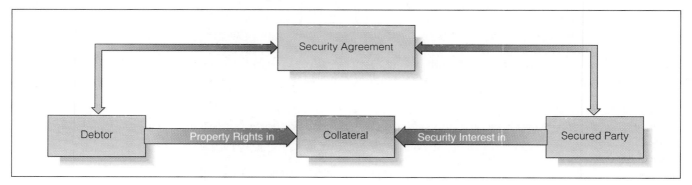

DEBTOR
Under Article 9 of the UCC, a
debtor is any party who owes
payment or performance of a
secured obligation, whether or
not the party actually owns or has
rights in the collateral.

SECURITY AGREEMENT
An agreement that creates or
provides for a security interest
between the debtor and a
secured party.

COLLATERAL
Under Article 9 of the UCC, the
property subject to a security
interest, including accounts and
chattel paper that have been sold.

DEFAULT
The failure to observe a promise
or discharge an obligation. The
term is commonly used to mean
the failure to pay a debt when it
is due.

3. A **debtor** is the party who owes payment or performance of the secured obligation,
whether or not that party actually owns or has rights in the collateral [UCC
9–105(1)(d)].
4. A **security agreement** is the agreement that creates or provides for a security interest between the debtor and a secured party [UCC 9–105(1)(*l*)].
5. **Collateral** is the property subject to a security interest, including accounts and
chattel paper that have been sold [UCC 9–105(1)(c)].

These basic definitions form the concept under which a debtor-creditor relationship becomes a secured transaction relationship (see Exhibit 21–1).

▌Creating and Perfecting a Security Interest

A creditor has two main concerns if the debtor **defaults** (fails to pay the debt as
promised): (1) satisfaction of the debt through the possession and (usually) sale of the
collateral and (2) priority over any other creditors or buyers who may have rights in the
same collateral. We look here at how these two concerns are met through the creation
and perfection of a security interest.

Creating a Security Interest

To become a secured party, the creditor must obtain a security interest in the collateral of the debtor. Three requirements must be met for a creditor to have an
enforceable security interest:

1. Either (a) the collateral must be in the possession of the secured party in
accordance with an agreement, or (b) there must be a written security agreement
describing the collateral and signed by the debtor.
2. The secured party must give value.
3. The debtor must have rights in the collateral.

ATTACHMENT
In a secured transaction, the
process by which a security
interest in the property of another
becomes enforceable.

Once these requirements have been met, the creditor's rights are said to *attach* to
the collateral. **Attachment** gives the creditor an enforceable security interest in the
collateral [UCC 9–203].

_____

Date

Name	No. and Street	City	County	State

(hereinafter called "Debtor") hereby grants to _____

Name

_____

No. and Street	City	County	State

(hereinafter called "Secured Party") a security interest in the following property (hereinafter called the "Collateral"): _____

_____

_____

_____

to secure payment and performance of obligations identified or set out as follows (hereinafter called the "Obligations"): _____

_____

_____

_____

   Default in payment or performance of any of the Obligations or default under any agreement evidencing any of the Obligations is a default under this agreement. Upon such default Secured Party may declare all Obligations immediately due and payable and shall have the remedies of a secured party under the _____ Uniform Commercial Code.
   Signed in (duplicate) triplicate.

_____

Debtor

By_____

Secured Party

By_____

WRITTEN SECURITY AGREEMENT When the collateral is not in the possession of the secured party, a security agreement must be in writing to be enforceable. To be effective, (1) the security agreement must be signed by the debtor, (2) it must contain a description of the collateral, and (3) the description must reasonably identify the collateral [UCC 9–203(1), 9–110]. See Exhibit 21–2 above for a sample security agreement.

   At issue in the following case was whether a security agreement had reasonably identified the collateral and had, in fact, been signed by the debtor.

CASE 21.1

IN RE ZILUCK
United States District Court,
Southern District of Florida, 1992.
139 Bankr. 44.

HISTORICAL AND SOCIAL SETTING *UCC 9–110 provides that a description of collateral is sufficient "whether or not it is specific if it reasonably identifies what is described." In cases decided before Article 9 of the UCC was adopted, courts often held that descriptions were insufficient unless they were "of the most*

(Continued)

Case 21.1—Continued

exact and detailed nature, the so-called 'serial number' test." In the Comment to UCC 9–110, the drafters of the UCC recognized that a description is sufficient if it does "the job assigned to it—that it make possible the identification of the thing described." Of course, in some situations, only a specific description will reasonably identify the collateral. In holding that a description is too general, a court may believe that it is protecting a debtor against a clause that would otherwise subject much of his or her property to the claim of a single creditor.

FACTS David Ziluck applied for a Radio Shack credit card. The front of the application contained blanks for various personal and employment information and a space for the applicant to sign. Above the signature line was the following statement: "I have read the Radio Shack Credit Account and Security Agreement, including the notice provisions in the last paragraph, and it contains no blanks or blank spaces. I agree to the terms of the Agreement and acknowledge a copy of the agreement." The back of the application contained a "Radio Shack Credit Account and Security Agreement," which stated in part, "We retain a security interest under the Uniform Commercial Code in all merchandise charged to your Account. If you do not make payments on your Account as agreed, the security interest allows us to repossess only the merchandise that has not been paid in full." When Ziluck later filed for bankruptcy protection, the bankruptcy court had to decide whether the application form constituted a valid security agreement. The court concluded that it did not, for two reasons. First,

Ziluck's signature was not effective, because it was not on the back side of the form, which stated the terms of the security agreement. Second, the security agreement's description of the collateral ("all merchandise charged to your Account") was not sufficiently descriptive. The bankruptcy court's decision was appealed.

ISSUE The issue in this case is twofold: (1) Had Ziluck effectively signed the security agreement? (2) Was the security agreement's description of the collateral sufficient?

DECISION Yes, to both questions.

REASON As to whether Ziluck had signed the security agreement, the court found that the language on the front of the credit-card application, above the signature line, made it clear that Ziluck was signing a security agreement. As to whether the collateral had been adequately described, the court stated that under UCC 9–110, "any description of personal property * * * is sufficient whether or not it is specific if it reasonably identifies what is described." In the court's view, the words "all merchandise charged to your Account" reasonably identified "the property subject to the security interest—namely any property purchased with the subject credit card."

FOR CRITICAL ANALYSIS—Ethical Consideration
Should the court have considered whether Ziluck had actually read the full agreement?

SECURED PARTY MUST GIVE VALUE The secured party must give value. Value, according to UCC 1–201(44), is any consideration that supports a simple contract, security given for a preexisting (antecedent) obligation, or any binding commitment to extend credit. Normally, the value given by a secured party is in the form of a direct loan, or it involves a commitment to sell goods on credit.

DEBTOR MUST HAVE RIGHTS IN THE COLLATERAL The debtor must have rights in the collateral; that is, the debtor must have some ownership interest or right to obtain possession of that collateral. The debtor's rights can represent either a current or a future legal interest in the collateral. For example, a retail seller-debtor can give a secured party a security interest not only in existing inventory owned by the retailer but also in *future* inventory to be acquired by the retailer.

In the following case, a creditor held a security interest in a pharmacist's accounts receivable (payments yet to be made to the pharmacist by his customers). Among these receivables were Medicaid payments—payments to be made to the pharmacist by the state government for services rendered to customers who received government assistance through the Medicaid program. Federal and state laws prohibit the assignment of Medicaid payments. Did this mean that the pharmacist had insufficient rights in these accounts to use them as collateral for a loan?

CASE 21.2

ESTATE OF ANGIULLI

Surrogate's Court, Oneida County, 1990.
148 Misc.2d 796,
561 N.Y.S.2d 626.

HISTORICAL AND SOCIAL SETTING *In the early 1980s, much of the northeastern United States was experiencing an economic recession. At the same time, in many small communities, hometown businesses found themselves in competition with regional or national retail companies, which could open stores in or near small communities at comparatively low cost and undersell hometown competitors. Meanwhile, health-care costs were soaring. In 1986, Congress passed a law making it illegal for hospitals to turn away patients who could not afford to pay. Nearly one-third of U.S. citizens, particularly those who were unemployed or living in depressed areas, had inadequate health insurance or none at all. To pay for providing medical care to those whose incomes fell below a certain level, the Medicaid program used government funds. Many physicians avoided taking Medicaid patients, however, because the payments were considered too low.*

FACTS When Frank Angiulli died in 1988, the pharmacy he owned in Utica, New York, was insolvent. At the time of his death, Angiulli owed H. K. Hineline Company, a supplier of pharmaceutical supplies, $34,469.63. The debt was secured by the pharmacy's accounts receivable, in which Hineline had earlier acquired a security interest. The administrator of Angiulli's estate collected funds from several accounts due to the pharmacy, including Medicaid payments, and used the monies to pay funeral and administrative costs. Hineline objected to this use of the funds, contending that Hineline's security interest in the accounts receivable entitled it to receive the payments. When the issue came before a New York state court, the administrator moved to dismiss Hineline's objections. The administrator argued that because Medicaid payments are not assignable under either federal or state law, Angiulli never acquired sufficient rights in those accounts to use them as collateral. Therefore, Hineline's security interest in the Medicaid accounts was not valid, because the security interest had never attached to the collateral.

ISSUE Did Hineline have a valid security interest in the Medicaid accounts receivable?

DECISION Yes. The court denied the administrator's motion to dismiss Hineline's objection.

REASON The court acknowledged that under both federal and state law, Medicaid payments were not assignable. In other words, the New York State Department of Social Services, the agency that issued Medicaid payments, could not issue them to anyone other than the provider of the services that were being paid for by the Medicaid payments. The administrator had argued that in view of this law, it necessarily followed that the Medicaid receivables could not have served as collateral for a security interest. The court disagreed. The court found that the reason behind the law prohibiting assignments of Medicaid payments was "to enable the social services district to pay the supplier regardless of any assignment and to relieve the district from the potential liability and increased administrative burdens involved in such assignments." The law did not prohibit the recipient of the payments from assigning them to another party once the funds had been disbursed by the relevant government agency, however. The court therefore concluded that "Hineline's security interest in the Medicaid Receivable attached once the Department approved decedent's claim and authorized payment." Hineline's security interest was therefore effective, and Hineline was entitled to the payments. The payments "could not properly be used to pay funeral and administrative expenses."

FOR CRITICAL ANALYSIS—Economic Consideration
What was the significance of the fact that Angiulli's pharmacy was insolvent?

Perfecting a Security Interest

Perfection represents the legal process by which secured parties protect themselves against the claims of third parties who may wish to have their debts satisfied out of the same collateral. Usually, perfection is accomplished by the filing of a financing statement with the appropriate government official. In some circumstances, however, a security interest becomes perfected without the filing of a financing statement. The

PERFECTION
The legal process by which secured parties protect themselves against the claims of third parties who may wish to have their debts satisfied out of the same collateral; usually accomplished by the filing of a financing statement with the appropriate government official.

♦ Exhibit 21–3
Types of Collateral and Methods of Perfection

TYPE OF COLLATERAL	DEFINITION	PERFECTION METHOD	UCC SECTIONS
Tangible	All things that are *movable* at the time the security interest attaches or that are *fixtures* [UCC 9–105(1)(h)]. This includes timber to be cut, growing crops, and unborn animals.		
1. Consumer Goods	Goods used or bought primarily for personal, family, or household purposes—for example, household furniture [UCC 9–109(1)].	For purchase-money security interest, attachment is sufficient; for boats, motor vehicles, and trailers, there is a requirement of filing or compliance with a certificate of title statute; for other consumer goods, general rules of filing or possession apply.	9–302(1)(d), (3), (4); 9–305
2. Equipment	Goods bought for or used primarily in business—for example, a delivery truck [UCC 9–109(2)].	Filing or possession by secured party.	9–302(1); 9–305
3. Farm Products	Crops, livestock, and supplies used or produced in a farming operation in the possession of a farmer-debtor. This includes products of crops or livestock—for example, milk, eggs, maple syrup, and ginned cotton [UCC 9–109(3)].	Filing or possession by secured party.	9–302(1); 9–305
4. Inventory	Goods held for sale or lease and materials used or consumed in the course of business—for example, raw materials or floor stock of a retailer [UCC 9–109(4)].	Filing or possession by secured party.	9–302(1); 9–305
5. Fixtures	Goods that become so affixed to realty that an interest in them arises under real estate law—for example, a central air-conditioning unit [UCC 9–313(1)(a)].	Filing only.	9–313(1)

classification of collateral is important in determining the proper method of perfection. Exhibit 21–3 summarizes the various classifications of collateral and the methods of perfecting a security interest in them.

FINANCING STATEMENT
A document prepared by a secured creditor, and filed with the appropriate state or local official, to give notice to the public that the creditor claims an interest in collateral belonging to the debtor named in the statement. The financing statement must be signed by the debtor, contain the addresses of both the debtor and the creditor, and describe the collateral by type or item.

PERFECTION BY FILING   A secured party can perfect a security interest by filing a financing statement (or the security agreement) with the appropriate state or local official. The UCC requires a **financing statement** to contain (1) the signature of the debtor, (2) the addresses of both the debtor and the secured party, and (3) a description of the collateral by type or item [UCC 9–402(1)]. Filing is the most common means of perfection to use. A sample financing statement is shown in Exhibit 21–4 on page 539.

An improper filing reduces a secured party's claim in bankruptcy to that of an unsecured creditor. If the debtor's name on the financing statement is inaccurate, for example, or the collateral is not sufficiently described on the statement, the filing may not be effective.

◆ Exhibit 21–3
Types of Collateral and Methods of Perfection—Continued

TYPE OF COLLATERAL	DEFINITION	PERFECTION METHOD	UCC SECTIONS
Intangible	Nonphysical property that exists only in connection with something else.		
1. Chattel Paper	Any writing that evidences both a *monetary obligation and a security interest*—for example, a thirty-six-month-payment retail security agreement signed by a buyer to purchase a car [UCC 9–105(1)(b)].	Filing or possession by secured party.	9–304(1); 9–305
2. Documents of Title	Papers that entitle the person in possession to hold, receive, or dispose of the paper or goods the documents cover—for example, bills of lading, warehouse receipts, and dock warrants [UCC 9–105(1)(f), 1–201(15), 7–201].	Filing or posession by secured party.	9–304(1), (3); 9–305
3. Instruments	Any writing that evidences a right to payment of money that is not a security agreement or lease, and any negotiable instrument or certificated security that in the ordinary course of business is transferred by delivery with any necessary indorsement or assignment—for example, stock certificates, promissory notes, and certificates of deposit [UCC 9–105)1)(i), 3–104, 8–102(1)(a)].	Except for temporary perfected status, possession only.	9–304(1), (4), (5); 9–305
4. Accounts	Any right to payment for goods sold or leased or for services *rendered* that is not evidenced by an instrument or chattel paper—for example, accounts receivable and contract right payments [UCC 9–106].	Filing required (with exceptions).	9–302(1)(e), (g)
5. General Intangibles	Any personal property other than that defined above—for example, a patent, a copyright, goodwill, or a trademark [UCC 9–106].	Filing only.	9–302(1)

The Debtor's Name   The UCC requires that a financing statement be filed under the name of the debtor [UCC 9–402(1)]. If the debtor is an individual, the financing statement must be filed under the name of the individual, but if the debtor is a partnership or a corporation, the financing statement must be filed under the partnership or corporate name [UCC 9–402(7)]. If a financing statement identifies the debtor by an incorrect name, the statement may be ineffective to perfect a security interest.

Creditors are expected to exercise good faith when naming the debtor on a financing statement. The good faith requirement of UCC 1–203 applies to all transactions subject to the UCC, including secured transactions under Article 9. In one case, for example, a creditor filed a financing statement that identified the debtors by their individual names even though the creditor knew that the collateral would be transferred immediately to the debtors' newly formed corporation. Later, a second creditor perfected

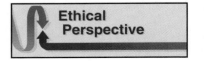
Ethical Perspective

(Continued)

Ethical Perspective—Continued

a security interest in the same collateral, and a dispute arose over which creditor's security interest took priority.

In the lawsuit that followed, the court held that the first creditor had violated the duty of good faith by including only the debtors' individual names—and not the name of the corporation—on the financing statement. According to the court, the first creditor "had to realize that the financing statement he was filing—while technically correct—contained an imminently misleading debtor designation." As a result of the creditor's "misleading debtor designation," the financing statement was ineffective to perfect the security interest, and the second creditor's perfected security interest prevailed.[a]

For Critical Analysis: *How can a creditor who is inexperienced in secured transactions know when he or she is acting in good faith? Should compliance with the "technical" requirements of Article 9 be sufficient to indicate good faith?*

a.   *Wollenberg v. Phoenix Leasing, Inc.,* 182 Ariz. 4, 893 P.2d 4 (1994).

Description of the Collateral   The UCC requires that both the security agreement and the financing statement contain a description of the collateral in which the secured party has a security interest. The security agreement must include a description of the collateral because no security interest in goods can exist unless the parties agree on which goods are subject to the security interest. The financing statement must include a description of the collateral because the purpose of filing the statement is to give public notice of the fact that certain goods in the debtor's possession are subject to a security interest. Other parties who might later wish to lend money to the debtor or buy the collateral can thus learn of the security interest by checking with the state or local office in which a financing statement for that type of collateral would be filed (where financing statements are filed will be discussed shortly).

Sometimes, the descriptions in the two documents vary, with the description in the security agreement being more precise and the description in the financing statement more general. For example, a security agreement for a commercial loan to a manufacturer may list all of the manufacturer's equipment subject to the loan by serial number, whereas the financing statement may simply state "all equipment owned or hereafter acquired." To avoid problems arising from such variations in descriptions, a secured party may repeat exactly the security agreement's description in the financing statement or file the security agreement itself as a financing statement—assuming the security agreement meets the previously discussed criteria. (Whether the reverse is true—that is, a financing statement can serve as a security agreement—is the topic of the *Business Law in Action* on page 540.) Alternatively, where permitted, the secured party might file a combination security agreement–financing statement form. If the financing statement is too general or vague, a court may find it insufficient to perfect a security interest.

> **NOTE** To create a security interest in a fixture, the description of real estate to which the fixture is attached does not need to be the same as the description in a deed or mortgage. Such a description provides a familiar form of notice, however, to those searching the records.

Where to File   Depending on how collateral is classified, filing is done either centrally with the secretary of state, locally with the county clerk or other official, or both, according to state law. According to UCC 9–401, a state may choose one of three alternatives.[1] In general, financing statements for consumer goods should be filed with the county clerk. Other kinds of collateral require filing with the secretary of state [UCC 9–401].

---

1.   See UCC 9–401 in Appendix C for these three alternatives. Approximately half the states have adopted the second alternative. Filing fees range from as low as $3 to as high as $25.

♦ **Exhibit 21–4**
A Sample Financing Statement

This FINANCING STATEMENT is presented for filing pursuant to the California Uniform Commercial Code.

1. DEBTOR (LAST NAME FIRST—IF AN INDIVIDUAL)	**1A.** SOCIAL SECURITY OR FEDERAL TAX NO.

1B. MAILING ADDRESS	**1C.** CITY, STATE	**1D.** ZIP CODE

2. ADDITIONAL DEBTOR (IF ANY) (LAST NAME FIRST—IF AN INDIVIDUAL)	**2A.** SOCIAL SECURITY OR FEDERAL TAX NO.

2B. MAILING ADDRESS	**2C.** CITY, STATE	**2D.** ZIP CODE

3. DEBTOR'S TRADE NAMES OR STYLES (IF ANY)	**3A.** FEDERAL TAX NUMBER

4. SECURED PARTY NAME MAILING ADDRESS CITY STATE ZIP CODE	**4A.** SOCIAL SECURITY NO., FEDERAL TAX NO. OR BANK TRANSIT AND A.B.A. NO.

5. ASSIGNEE OF SECURED PARTY (IF ANY) NAME MAILING ADDRESS CITY STATE ZIP CODE	**5A.** SOCIAL SECURITY NO., FEDERAL TAX NO. OR BANK TRANSIT AND A.B.A. NO.

6. This FINANCING STATEMENT covers the following types or items of property **(include description of real property on which located and owner of record when required by instruction 4)**.

As security for and in consideration of all present and any future advances or other obligations debtor hereby grants United California Bank a security interest in all of the following types or items of property ("Collateral" herein) in which the debtor now has or hereafter acquires any right, title, or interest, or rights present and future, wheresoever located and whether in the possession of the debtor, a warehouseman, bailee, trustee or any other person, and all increases, therein and replacements, products, and proceeds thereof. Proceeds include but are not limited to inventory, returned merchandise, accounts, chattel paper, general intangibles, insurance proceeds, documents, money, goods, equipment, instruments, and any other tangible or intangible property arising under the sale, lease or other disposition of collateral:

7. CHECK ☒ IF APPLICABLE	**7A.** ☐ PRODUCTS OF COLLATERAL ARE ALSO COVERED	**7B.** DEBTOR(S) SIGNATURE NOT REQUIRED IN ACCORDANCE WITH INSTRUCTION 5(c) ITEM: ☐ (1) ☐ (2) ☐ (3) ☐ (4)
8. CHECK ☒ IF APPLICABLE	☐ DEBTOR IS A "TRANSMITTING UTILITY" IN ACCORDANCE WITH UCC § 9105 (1) (n)	

9. ► DATE:	C O D E	**10.** THIS SPACE FOR USE OF FILING OFFICER (DATE, TIME, FILE NUMBER AND FILING OFFICER)
SIGNATURE(S) of DEBTOR(S)		
TYPE OR PRINT NAME(S) OF DEBTOR(S)	1	
►	2	
SIGNATURE(S) OF SECURED PARTY(IES)	3	
	4	
TYPE OR PRINT NAME(S) OF SECURED PARTY(IES)	5	
11. *Return copy to:*	6	
NAME	7	
ADDRESS		
CITY	8	
STATE	9	
ZIP CODE		
	0	
(1) FILING OFFICER COPY FORM UCC-1—FILING FEE $3.00 *Approved by the Secretary of State*		

MS-336 10-78

BUSINESS LAW IN ACTION

Can a Financing Statement Serve as a Security Agreement?

Typically, a financing statement is filed to perfect an existing security interest. In fact, often the security agreement doubles as a financing statement. What about the reverse situation? Can a financing statement also serve as a security agreement?

For example, suppose that a creditor loans money to a farmer, and the parties orally agree that the loan is to be secured by certain crops to be raised by the farmer. Further suppose that the creditor files a completed standard-form UCC-1 financing statement (see Exhibit 21–4) to perfect the security interest in the collateral. The financing statement identifies the creditor, is signed by the debtor, and contains a description of the collateral securing the loan. The financing statement does not, however, create or provide for a security interest in the collateral—which is the basic requirement for a written security agreement under UCC 9–201(1). Can the financing statement nonetheless serve as a written security agreement in this situation? In other words, can the fact that the financing statement was filed imply an agreement to create a security interest?

Because the UCC is silent on this issue, the courts have been left to decide the matter. As might be expected, the courts' conclusions on the matter vary widely. At one end of the spectrum is the view, first expressed by the Rhode Island Supreme Court, that it is "not possible for a financing statement which does not contain the debtor's Grant of a security interest to serve as a security agreement."[a] At the other end of the spectrum is the view that "as a matter of law," a financing statement is sufficient to satisfy the requirements for a security agreement.[b] Somewhere in the middle of the spectrum is the view, adopted by most courts, that a "composite document rule" should be applied. Under this rule, although a financing statement cannot by itself be considered a security agreement, "an adequate agreement can be found when a financing statement is considered together with other documents."[c]

When the question came before the Indiana Supreme Court in 1994, the court devised a solution that fell somewhere in the middle of the spectrum: "Although we are not willing to go so far as to hold that a

a. *American Card Co. v. H.M.H. Co.*, 97 R.I. 59, 196 A.2d 150 (1963).
b. See, for example, *Evans v. Everett*, 279 N.C. 352, 183 S.E.2d 109 (1971); and *In re Numeric Corp.*, 485 F.2d 1328 (1st Cir. 1973).
c. See *In re Amex-Protein Development Corp.*, 504 F.2d 1056 (9th Cir. 1974).

standard-form UCC-1 financing statement alone is, as a matter of law, sufficient evidence that the parties intended to create a security interest, we do hold that once the Writing Requirement of [UCC] 9–203(1) is satisfied, whether the parties intended the writing to create a security interest is a question of fact for the trier of fact [the trial court] to determine." In this case, the trial court had found that the parties (who had no written security agreement but who had filed a UCC-1 financing statement) had intended to form a security agreement. Although the Indiana Supreme Court affirmed the trial court's decision, it added a footnote to clarify its ruling: "This is not to say that we condone or in any way approve the use of bare-bones UCC-1 financing statements as security agreements. We do not. . . . Had the trial court found that no security interest had been created, we would have been compelled to affirm that finding as well."[d]

For Critical Analysis: *Which of the views described above best furthers the UCC's twin goals of encouraging commercial transactions on the one hand and protecting the rights of the parties on the other? Why?*

d. *Gibson County Farm Bureau Cooperative Association, Inc. v. Greer*, 643 N.E.2d 313 (Ind. 1994).

PERFECTION WITHOUT FILING   In two types of situations, security interests can be perfected without the secured party's having to file a financing statement. First, when the collateral is transferred into the possession of the secured party, the secured party's security interest in the collateral is perfected. Second, a purchase-money security interest in consumer goods and an assignment of a beneficial interest in a trust or a decedent's estate are perfected automatically.

PLEDGE
A common law security device (retained in Article 9 of the UCC) in which personal property is turned over to the creditor as security for the payment of a debt and retained by the creditor until the debt is paid.

Perfection by Possession   Under the common law, as discussed in this chapter's *Landmark in the Law*, one of the most common means of obtaining financing was to **pledge** certain collateral as security for the debt and transfer the collateral into the creditor's possession. When the debt was paid, the collateral would be returned to the debtor. Usually, the transfer of collateral was accompanied by a written security agreement, but the agreement did not have to be in writing. In other words, an oral security agreement was effective as long as the secured party possessed the collateral. Article 9 of the UCC retained the common law pledge and the principle that the security agreement need not be in writing to be enforceable if the collateral is transferred to the secured party [UCC 9–203(1)(a)].

For most collateral, possession by the secured party is impractical because it denies the debtor the right to use or derive income from the property to pay off the debt. For example, if a farmer took out a loan to finance the purchase of a piece of heavy farm equipment, using the equipment as collateral, the purpose of the purchase would be defeated if the farmer transferred the collateral into the creditor's possession. Certain items, however, such as stocks, bonds, and jewelry, are commonly transferred into the creditor's possession when they are used as collateral for loans. With respect to negotiable instruments and certain securities (such as stocks and bonds), with a few exceptions, the *only* way to properly perfect a security interest is through possession by the secured party.

If a secured party is in possession of the collateral, he or she must use reasonable care in preserving it. Otherwise, the secured party is liable to the debtor [UCC 9–207(1), 9–207(3)].

Purchase-Money Security Interest   Often, sellers of consumer goods (defined as goods bought or used by the debtor primarily for personal, family, or household purposes) agree to extend credit for part or all of the purchase price of those goods. Additionally, lenders, such as financial institutions, that are not necessarily in the business of selling such goods often agree to lend much of the purchase price for them. There is a special name for the security interest that the seller or the lender obtains when such a transaction occurs. It is called a **purchase-money security interest (PMSI)**, because the lender or seller has essentially provided a buyer with the "purchase money" to buy goods [UCC 9–107].

Suppose that Jamie wants to purchase a new entertainment center from ABC Electronics. The purchase price is $1,500. Not being able to pay cash, Jamie signs a purchase agreement to pay $300 down and $100 per month until the balance plus interest is fully paid. ABC Electronics is to retain a security interest in the purchased goods until full payment has been made. Because the security interest was created as part of the purchase agreement, it is a PMSI.

A PMSI in consumer goods is perfected automatically at the time of a credit sale—that is, at the time that the PMSI is created. The seller in this situation need do nothing more to protect his or her interest. There are exceptions to this rule, however, that cover security interests in fixtures and in motor vehicles [UCC 9–302(1)(d)]. In a few states, a PMSI in farm equipment under a certain statutory value may also be perfected automatically by attachment.

PERFECTION OF SECURITY INTERESTS IN MOTOR VEHICLES   Most states require a certificate of title for any motor vehicle, boat, or motor home. The normal methods described above for the perfection of a security interest typically do not apply to such vehicles. Rather, the perfection of a security interest only occurs when a notation of such an interest appears on the certificate of title that covers the vehicle.

As an example, suppose that your commercial bank lends you 80 percent of the money necessary to purchase a new BMW. You live in a state that requires certificates of title for all automobiles. If your bank fails to have its security interest noted on the certificate of title, its interest is not perfected. That means that a good faith purchaser of your BMW would take it free of the bank's interest. In most states, purchasers of motor vehicles can buy vehicles with the confidence that no security interest exists that is not disclosed on the certificate of title.[2]

"I will pay you some, and, as most debtors do, promise you infinitely."

William Shakespeare, 1564–1616 *(English dramatist)*

PURCHASE-MONEY SECURITY INTEREST (PMSI) A security interest that arises when a seller or lender extends credit for part or all of the purchase price of goods purchased by a buyer.

---

2. In the few states that do not require title registration of motor vehicles, one must examine the appropriate statutes to determine the priority of conflicting security interests.

COLLATERAL MOVED TO ANOTHER JURISDICTION Obviously, collateral may be moved by the debtor from one jurisdiction (state) to another. In general, a properly perfected security interest in collateral moved into a new jurisdiction continues to be perfected in the new jurisdiction for priority purposes (priority disputes will be examined later in the chapter) for a period of up to four months from the date the collateral was moved into the new jurisdiction or for the period of time remaining under the perfection in the original jurisdiction, whichever expires first [UCC 9–103(1)(d), 9–103(3)(e)]. Collateral moved from county to county within a state (if local filing is required), rather than from one state to another, however, may not have a four-month limitation [UCC 9–403(3)].

To illustrate: Suppose that on January 1, Wheeler secures a loan from a Nebraska bank by putting up all his wheat-threshing equipment as security. The Nebraska bank files the security interest centrally with the secretary of state. In June, Wheeler has an opportunity to harvest wheat crops in South Dakota and moves his equipment into that state on June 15. The law just mentioned means that the Nebraska bank's perfection remains effective in South Dakota for a period of four months from June 15. If the Nebraska bank wishes to retain its perfection priority, the bank must perfect properly in South Dakota during this four-month period. Should the bank fail to do so, its perfection would be lost after four months, and subsequent perfected security interests in the same collateral in South Dakota would prevail.

Among mobile goods, automobiles pose one of the biggest problems. If the original jurisdiction does not require a certificate of title as part of its perfection process for an automobile, perfection automatically ends four months after the automobile is moved into another jurisdiction. When a security interest exists on an automobile in a state in which title registration is required and when the security interest is noted on the certificate of title, the perfection of the security interest continues after the automobile is moved to another state requiring a certificate of title until the automobile is registered in the new state [UCC 9–103(2)]. This rule protects the secured party against anyone purchasing the car in the new state prior to the new registration. Moreover, because each certificate-of-title state requires that the old certificate of title be surrendered to obtain a new one, and because the secured party typically holds the certificate, the secured party usually is able to ensure that the security interest is noted on the new certificate of title.

CONTINUATION STATEMENT

A statement that, if filed within six months prior to the expiration date of the original financing statement, continues the perfection of the original security interest for another five years. The perfection of a security interest can be continued in the same manner indefinitely.

EFFECTIVE TIME OF PERFECTION A financing statement is effective for five years from the date of filing [UCC 9–403(2)]. If a **continuation statement** is filed *within six months* prior to the expiration date, the effectiveness of the original statement is continued for another five years, starting with the expiration date of the first five-year period [UCC 9–403(3)]. The effectiveness of the statement can be continued in the same manner indefinitely.

In the following case, a perfected secured party filed a continuation statement two days early—that is, six months and two days before the expiration date of the original filing. At issue was whether the filing had occurred "within six months," as required under UCC 9–403(3).

CASE 21.3

BANQUE WORMS v. DAVIS CONSTRUCTION CO.
Court of Appeals of Kentucky, 1992.
831 S.W.2d 921.

HISTORICAL AND ECONOMIC SETTING *Seventy-five years ago, ten mining companies were among the one hundred largest U.S. manufacturers. Today, no mining company is among those one hundred. There are three basic reasons for the change. First, in the 1970s, oil companies flush with profits from the high price of oil used some of the money to buy mining companies. Second, during the 1980s, the prices of the products of*

Case 21.3—Continued

many mines dropped significantly. For example, the price of copper fell below the cost of mining it. Third, environmental regulations greatly affect mining companies, whose foreign competitors may not be restricted in the same way.

FACTS   A New York bank, Banque Worms, provided the Big Oak Coal Company and the Dollar Branch Coal Corporation with a loan. As collateral for the loan, the mining companies granted Banque Worms a security interest in a "Euclid R-25 rock truck," as well as in other mining equipment. Banque Worms properly perfected its security interest in the equipment by filing a financing statement, effective for five years, on October 12, 1982. Banque Worms later filed a continuation statement on April 10, 1987, to maintain its priority status as a perfected secured party. Later that year, on November 23, the mining companies sold the rock truck to the Davis Construction Company to satisfy a $36,192 debt. Davis filed suit in a Kentucky state court to clear title to the rock truck once it became aware of Banque Worms's security interest. The trial court, holding in favor of Davis, found that Banque Worms had failed to comply with UCC 9–403. Banque Worms appealed.

ISSUE   Is the continuation statement effective?

DECISION   No. The Court of Appeals of Kentucky held that Banque Worms became an unperfected secured creditor on the lapse of the five-year perfection period.

REASON   The court stated that "[b]ecause the continuation statement was not filed within six months prior to the lapse of the financing statement's effective period, [Banque Worms's] security interest in the rock truck became unperfected on October 12, 1987, which was five years after the date on which the financing statement was filed." In response to Banque Worms's argument for liberal construction of the UCC's time-limiting provision, the court stated that "the statute cannot be employed to overlook and defeat the clear and unambiguous statutory requirement as to timely filing which is imposed by [UCC 9–403(3)]."

FOR CRITICAL ANALYSIS—Ethical Consideration
Is it ever appropriate for a court to "overlook" a "clear and unambiguous statutory requirement"? Did the court in the above case have any alternative option?

▌The Scope of a Security Interest

In addition to covering collateral already in the debtor's possession, a security agreement can cover various other types of property, including the proceeds of the sale of collateral, after-acquired property, and future advances.

Proceeds

Proceeds include whatever is received when collateral is sold or otherwise disposed of, such as by exchange. A secured party's security interest in the collateral includes a security interest in the proceeds of the sale of that collateral. For example, suppose that a bank has a perfected security interest in the inventory of a retail seller of heavy farm machinery. The retailer sells a tractor out of this inventory to a farmer, a buyer in the ordinary course of business. The farmer agrees, in a retail security agreement, to pay monthly payments for a period of twenty-four months. If the retailer should go into default on the loan from the bank, the bank is entitled to the remaining payments the farmer owes to the retailer as proceeds.

A security interest in proceeds perfects automatically upon perfection of the secured party's security interest in the collateral and remains perfected for ten days after receipt of the proceeds by the debtor. One way to extend the ten-day automatic period is to provide for such extended coverage in the original security agreement. This is typically done when the collateral is the type that is likely to be sold, such as a retailer's inventory. The UCC provides that in the following circumstances the

PROCEEDS
Under Article 9 of the UCC, whatever is received when the collateral is sold or otherwise disposed of, such as by exchange.

LAW IN THE EXTREME

The Disappearing Proceeds

One of the ways in which the legal system protects secured parties is by making it possible for a secured party to have not only a security interest in collateral but also an interest in the proceeds from the sale of the collateral. Sometimes, though, proceeds have a way of disappearing. For example, when flour is the collateral and it is turned into bread, the flour does not exist anymore, but the bread does, so the security interest persists in the bread. What about cattle or hog feed? If there is a security interest in the feed and it is fed to animals, does the security interest continue in the animals? If we based

our logic on the flour example just given, the answer would have to be yes. At least one court, however, has come up with the opposite conclusion. Basically, the court reasoned that because the hogs were the same before and after feeding, there were "no traceable proceeds."[a]

As another example, what happens if the collateral is a car, and the car is damaged in an accident? The "proceeds" in this situation consist of the insurance payment made to the debtor. If the debtor fails to pay off the outstanding loan on the car, though, what can the creditor do? If the car has been totaled and turned over to the insurance company in return for the insurance payment, the creditor no longer has any collateral to repossess. In one case, a creditor in this situation sued the debtor's

a. *Farmers Cooperative Elevator Co. v. Union State Bank*, 409 N.W.2d 178 (Iowa 1987).

insurance company to recover the insurance payment—the proceeds that were wrongfully (according to the creditor) given to the debtor. The court found, however, that the insurance company's only obligation was to the owner of the insurance policy (the debtor). To make a long story short, the proceeds had again simply vanished, and the creditor was left with nothing securing the outstanding debt.[b] Creditors facing similar problems of "disappearing" proceeds are probably also wondering about why they are left empty-handed even though they had perfected security interests in the proceeds.

For Critical Analysis: *What distinction is there between flour made into bread and cattle feed made into cattle beef?*

b. *Fidelity Financial Services v. Blaser*, 889 P.2d 268 (Okla. 1994).

security interest in proceeds remains perfected for longer than ten days after the receipt of the proceeds by the debtor:

1. When a filed financing statement covers the original collateral and the proceeds are collateral in which a security interest may be perfected by a filing in the office or offices with which the financing statement has been filed. Furthermore, a secured party's interest automatically perfects in property that the debtor acquires with cash proceeds, if the original filing would have been effective as to that property and the financing statement indicates that type of property [UCC 9–306(3)(a)]. Thus, in the farm equipment example above, if the retailer used the farmer's monthly payments to acquire additional inventory, the bank would be entitled to that inventory, providing that the bank's original filing was effective as to that property and the financing statement indicated that type of property.
2. Whenever there is a filed financing statement that covers the original collateral and the proceeds are identifiable cash proceeds [UCC 9–306(3)(b)].
3. Whenever the security interest in the proceeds is perfected before the expiration of the ten-day period [UCC 9–306(3)(c)].

After-Acquired Property

AFTER-ACQUIRED PROPERTY
Property of the debtor that is acquired after the execution of a security agreement.

After-acquired property of the debtor is property acquired after the execution of the security agreement. The security agreement may provide for coverage of after-acquired property [UCC 9–204(1)]. This is particularly useful for inventory financing arrangements, because a secured party whose security interest is in existing inventory knows that the debtor will sell that inventory, thereby reducing the collateral subject to the security interest. Generally, the debtor will purchase new inventory to replace the inventory sold. The secured party wants this newly acquired inventory to be subject to the original security interest. Thus, the after-acquired property clause continues the secured party's claim to any inventory acquired thereafter. This is not to say that the original security interest will be superior to the rights of all other creditors with regard to this after-acquired inventory, as will be discussed later.

Consider a typical example. Amato buys factory equipment from Bronson on credit, giving as security an interest in all of her equipment—both what she is buying and what she already owns. The security interest with Bronson contains an after-acquired property clause. Six months later, Amato pays cash to another seller of factory equipment for more equipment. Six months after that, Amato goes out of business before she has paid off her debt to Bronson. Bronson has a security interest in all of Amato's equipment, even the equipment bought from the other seller.

Future Advances

Often, a debtor will arrange with a bank to have a continuing *line of credit* under which the debtor can borrow funds intermittently. Advances against lines of credit can be subject to a properly perfected security interest in certain collateral. The security agreement may provide that any future advances made against that line of credit are also subject to the security interest in the same collateral. For example, Stroh is the owner of a small manufacturing plant with equipment valued at $1 million. He has an immediate need for $50,000 of working capital, so he obtains a loan from Midwestern Bank and signs a security agreement, putting up all of his equipment as security. The security agreement provides that Stroh can borrow up to $500,000 in the future, using the same equipment as collateral for any future advances. In this situation, Stroh does not have to execute a new security agreement and perfect a security interest in the collateral each time an advance is made [UCC 9–204(3)].

The Floating-Lien Concept

A security agreement that provides for a security interest in proceeds, in after-acquired property, or in property purchased under a line of credit (or in all three) is often characterized as a **floating lien.** When a creditor places a lien on a debtor's property, the creditor's rights are bound (attached) to the property, and the creditor acquires the right to sell or hold the property of a debtor as security or payment for a debt (see Chapter 22 for a further discussion of liens). Floating liens commonly arise in the financing of inventories. A creditor is not interested in specific pieces of inventory, because they are constantly changing, so the lien "floats" from one item to another, as the inventory changes.

For example, suppose that Cascade Sports, Inc., a cross-country ski dealer, has a line of credit with Portland First Bank to finance an inventory of cross-country skis. Cascade and Portland First enter into a security agreement that provides for coverage of proceeds, after-acquired inventory, present inventory, and future advances. This security interest in inventory is perfected by filing centrally (with the secretary of state). One day, Cascade sells a new pair of the latest cross-country skate skis, for which it receives a used pair in trade. That same day, it purchases two new pairs of skate skis from a local manufacturer with an additional amount of money obtained from Portland First. Portland First gets a perfected security interest in the used pair of skis under the proceeds clause, has a perfected security interest in the two new pairs of skis purchased from the local manufacturer under the after-acquired property clause, and has the new amount of money advanced to Cascade secured by the future-advances clause. All of this is accomplished under the original perfected security agreement. The various items in the inventory have changed, but Portland First still has a perfected security interest in Cascade's inventory, and hence it has a floating lien on the inventory.

FLOATING LIEN
A security interest in proceeds, after-acquired property, or property purchased under a line of credit (or all three); a security interest in collateral that is retained even when the collateral changes in character, classification, or location.

The concept of the floating lien can also apply to a shifting stock of goods. Under Section 9–205, the lien can start with raw materials; follow them as they become finished goods and inventories; and continue as the goods are sold and are turned into accounts receivable, chattel paper, or cash.

▌Priorities among Security Interests

Whether a secured party's security interest is perfected or unperfected may have serious consequences for the secured party if the debtor defaults on the debt or files for bankruptcy. For example, what if the debtor has borrowed money from two different creditors, using the same property as collateral for both loans? If the debtor defaults on both loans, which of the two creditors has first rights to the collateral? In this situation, the creditor with a perfected security interest will prevail. Generally, the following UCC rules apply when more than one creditor claims rights in the same collateral:

KEEP IN MIND Secured creditors—perfected or not—have priority over unsecured creditors.

1. *Conflicting perfected security interests.* When two or more secured parties have perfected security interests in the same collateral, generally the first to perfect (file or take possession of the collateral) has priority [UCC 9–312(5)(a)].
2. *Conflicting unperfected security interests.* When two conflicting security interests are unperfected, the first to attach has priority [UCC 9–312(5)(b)].
3. *Conflicting perfected security interests in commingled or processed goods.* When goods to which two or more perfected security interests attach are so manufactured or commingled that they lose their identities into a product or mass, the perfected parties' security interests attach to the new product or mass "according to the ratio that the cost of goods to which each interest originally attached bears to the cost of the total product or mass" [UCC 9–315(2)].

Under certain circumstances, on the debtor's default, the perfection of a security interest will not protect a secured party against certain other third parties having claims to the collateral. For example, the UCC provides that under certain conditions a PMSI, properly perfected, will prevail over another security interest in after-acquired collateral, even though the other was perfected first [UCC 9–312].

Because buyers should not be required to find out if there is an outstanding security interest in, for example, a merchant's inventory, the UCC also provides that a person who buys "in the ordinary course of business" will take the goods free from any security interest created by the seller in the purchased collateral.[3] This is so even if the security interest is perfected and *even if the buyer knows of its existence* [UCC 9–307(1)]. The UCC defines a *buyer in the ordinary course of business* as any person who in good faith, and without knowledge that the sale is in violation of the ownership rights or security interest of a third party in the goods, buys in ordinary course from a person in the business of selling goods of that kind [UCC 1–201(9)]. The priority of claims to a debtor's collateral is detailed in Exhibit 21–5.

▌Rights and Duties of Debtors and Creditors

"Let us live in a small circle as we will, we are either debtors or creditors before we have had time to look round."

Johann Wolfgang von Goethe, 1749–1832
(German poet and dramatist)

The security agreement itself determines most of the rights and duties of the debtor and the secured party. The UCC, however, imposes some rights and duties that are applicable in the absence of a security agreement to the contrary.

---

3.   Under the Food Security Act of 1985, buyers in the ordinary course of business include buyers of farm products from a farmer. Under this act, these buyers are protected from prior perfected security interests unless the secured parties perfected centrally by a special form called an effective financing statement (EFS) or the buyers received proper notice.

♦ Exhibit 21–5
Priority of Claims to a Debtor's Collateral

PARTIES	PRIORITY
Unperfected Secured Party	Prevails over unsecured creditors and creditors who have obtained judgments against the debtor but who have not begun the legal process to collect on those judgments [UCC 9–301].

Purchaser of Debtor's Collateral	1. Goods purchased in the ordinary course of the seller's business—Purchaser prevails over a secured party's security interest, even if perfected and even if the purchaser knows of the security interest [UCC 9–307(1)].
	
	2. Consumer goods purchased out of the ordinary course of business—Purchaser prevails over a secured party's interest, even if perfected, providing purchaser purchased as follows:
	  a. For value.
	  b. Without actual knowledge of the security interest.
	  c. For use as a consumer good.
	  d. Prior to secured party's perfection by *filing* [UCC 9–307(2)].

Perfected Secured Parties to Same Collateral	Between two perfected secured parties in the same collateral, the general rule is that first in time of perfection is first in right to the collateral [UCC 9–312(5)]. Exceptions follow:
	
	1. Crops—New value to produce crops given within three months of planting has priority over prior six-month perfected interest [UCC 9–312(2)].
	2. Purchase-money security interest—Even if second in time of perfection, it has priority, providing the following:
	  a. Inventory—PMSI is perfected and proper written notice is given to the other security-interest holder *on* or *before* the time that debtor takes possession [UCC 9–312(3)].
	  b. Other collateral—PMSI has priority, providing it is perfected within ten days after debtor receives possession [UCC 9–312(4)].

Information Requests

Under UCC 9–407(1), a secured party has the option, when making the filing, of asking the filing officer to make a note of the file number, the date, and the hour of the original filing on a copy of the financing statement. The filing officer must send this copy to the person making the request. Under UCC 9–407(2), a filing officer must also give information to a person who is contemplating obtaining a security interest from a prospective debtor. The filing officer must give a certificate that provides information on possible perfected financing statements with respect to the named debtor. The filing officer will charge a fee for the certification and for any information copies provided.

Assignment, Amendment, and Release

Whenever desired, a secured party of record can release part or all of the collateral described in a filed financing statement. This ends his or her security interest in the collateral [UCC 9–406]. A secured party can assign part or all of the security interest to another, called the assignee. That assignee becomes the secured party of record if, for example, he or she either makes a notation of the assignment somewhere on the financing statement or files a written statement of assignment [UCC 9–405(2)].

It is also possible to amend a financing statement that has already been filed. The amendment must be signed by both parties. The debtor signs the security agreement, the original financing statement, and the amendments [UCC 9–402]. All other secured transaction documents, such as releases, assignments, continuations of perfection, perfections of collateral moved into another jurisdiction, and termination statements, need only be signed by the secured party.

The Status of the Debt

At any time that the secured debt is outstanding, the debtor may wish to know the status of the debt. If so, the debtor need only sign a statement that indicates the aggregate amount of the unpaid debt at a specific date (and perhaps a list of the collateral covered by the security agreement). The secured party (creditor) must then approve or correct this statement in writing. The creditor must comply with the request within two weeks of receipt; otherwise, the creditor is liable for any loss caused to the debtor by the failure to comply [UCC 9–208(2)]. One such request is allowed without charge every six months. For each additional request, the secured party (creditor) can require a fee not exceeding $10 per request [UCC 9–208(3)].

Termination Statement

When a secured debt is paid, the secured party generally must send a termination statement to the debtor or file such a statement with the filing officer to whom the original financing statement was given. If the financing statement covers consumer goods, the termination statement must be filed by the secured party within one month after the debt is paid, or—if the debtor requests the termination statement in writing—it must be filed within ten days of receipt of such request after the debt is paid, whichever is earlier [UCC 9–404(1)].

In all other circumstances, the termination statement must be filed or furnished to the debtor within ten days after a written request is made by the debtor. If the affected secured party fails to file such a termination statement, as required by UCC 9–404(1), or fails to send the termination statement within ten days after proper demand, the secured party will be liable to the debtor for $100. Additionally, the secured party will be liable for any loss caused to the debtor.

▌ Default

"Nothing so cements and holds together all the parts of society as faith or credit, which can never be kept up unless men are under some force or necessity of honestly paying what they owe."

Cicero, 106–43 B.C.E.
(Roman politician, orator, and philosopher)

Article 9 defines the rights, duties, and remedies of the secured party and of the debtor upon the debtor's default. Should the secured party fail to comply with his or her duties, the debtor is afforded particular rights and remedies.

The topic of default is one of great concern to secured lenders and to the lawyers who draft security agreements. What constitutes default is not always clear. In fact, Article 9 does not define the term. Consequently, parties are encouraged in practice and by the UCC to include in their security agreements certain standards to be applied should default occur. In so doing, parties can stipulate the conditions that will constitute a default [UCC 9–501(1)]. Typically, because of the disparity in bargaining position between a debtor and a creditor, these critical terms are shaped by the creditor in an attempt to provide the maximum protection possible. The ultimate terms, however, are not allowed to go beyond the limitations imposed by the good faith requirement of UCC 1–203 and the unconscionability doctrine.

Although any breach of the terms of the security agreement can constitute default, default occurs most commonly when the debtor fails to meet the scheduled payments that the parties have agreed on or when the debtor becomes bankrupt. Another breach that could constitute default is a debtor's breach of the warranty of title (see Chapter 17) to property offered as collateral.

Basic Remedies

EXECUTION
An action to carry into effect the directions in a court decree or judgment.

A secured party's remedies can be divided into two basic categories:

1. A secured party can relinquish a security interest and proceed to judgment on the underlying debt, followed by execution and levy. (**Execution** is an action to carry into

effect the directions in a court decree or judgment. **Levy** is the obtaining of money by legal process through the seizure and sale of property, usually done after a writ of execution has been issued.) Execution and levy are rarely undertaken unless the value of the secured collateral has been reduced greatly below the amount of the debt and the debtor has other assets available that may be legally seized to satisfy the debt [UCC 9–501(1)].[4]

2. A secured party can take possession of the collateral covered by the security agreement [UCC 9–503]. Upon taking possession, the secured party can either retain the collateral for satisfaction of the debt [UCC 9–505(2)] or resell the goods and apply the proceeds toward the debt [UCC 9–504].

The rights and remedies under UCC 9–501(1) are *cumulative*. Therefore, if a creditor is unsuccessful in enforcing rights by one method, he or she can pursue another method.[5]

When a security agreement covers both real and personal property, the secured party can proceed against the personal property in accordance with the remedies of Article 9. Alternatively, the secured party can proceed against the entire collateral under procedures set down by local real estate law, in which case the UCC does not apply [UCC 9–501(4)]. Determining whether particular collateral is personal or real property can prove difficult, especially in dealing with fixtures—things affixed to real property. Under certain circumstances, the UCC allows the removal of fixtures upon default; such removal, however, is subject to the provisions of Article 9 [UCC 9–313].

Repossession of Collateral

UCC 9–503 states that "[u]nless otherwise agreed, a secured party has on default the right to take possession of the collateral. In taking possession, a secured party may proceed without judicial process if this can be done without a breach of the peace." The underlying rationale for this "self-help" provision of Article 9 is that it simplifies the process of repossession for creditors and reduces the burden on the courts. Because the UCC does not define *breach of the peace*, however, it is not always easy to predict what will or will not constitute a breach of the peace.

Generally, the secured party or the secured party's agent cannot enter a debtor's house, garage, or place of business without permission. Consider a situation in which an automobile is collateral. If the repossessing party walks onto the debtor's premises, proceeds up the driveway, enters the vehicle without entering the garage, and drives off, it probably will not amount to a breach of the peace. In some states, however, an action for wrongful trespass could start a cause of action for breach of the peace or other tortious action.

LEVY
The obtaining of money by legal process through the seizure and sale of property, usually done after a writ of execution has been issued.

RECALL A trespass to land occurs when a person, without permission, enters onto another's land.

---

4.   Some assets are exempt from creditors' claims—see Chapter 22.
5.   See James J. White and Robert S. Summers, *Uniform Commercial Code*, 4th ed. (St. Paul: West Publishing Co., 1995), pp. 908–909.

The underlying rationale for the "self-help" provision of Article 9 is that it simplifies the process of repossession for secured parties and reduces the burden on the courts. Nonetheless, the provision has generated substantial controversy because of its potential adverse consequences, for both secured parties and debtors. If a repossession attempt results in a "breach of the peace," the secured party may be barred from recovering the remainder of the debt from the debtor.

A breach of the peace can, in turn, be emotionally distressful for the debtor. For example, suppose that someone hired by the secured party appears on the debtor's property in the middle of the night to repossess collateral. A debtor in this situation

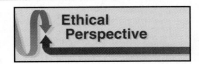

Ethical Perspective

(Continued)

Ethical Perspective—Continued

may logically assume that someone is trying to steal his or her property; thus, violence and a "breach of the peace" may ensue. Additionally, in some cases, secured parties (or persons hired by them) have engaged in outrageous conduct when repossessing collateral, which again may result in a breach of the peace (see, for example, the *Question of Ethics and Social Responsibility* at the end of this chapter). Additionally, the "self-help" provision may implicitly give debtors a motive for resorting to violence and forcing a confrontation when collateral is being repossessed—because if the secured party breaches the peace, the debtor will ultimately benefit.

For Critical Analysis: *Do debtors benefit in any way from the "self-help" provision of Article 9?*

Disposition of Collateral

Once default has occurred and the secured party has obtained possession of the collateral, the secured party may sell, lease, or otherwise dispose of the collateral in any commercially reasonable manner [UCC 9–504(1)]. Any sale is always subject to procedures established by state law.

RETENTION OF COLLATERAL BY THE SECURED PARTY   The UCC acknowledges that parties are sometimes better off if they do not sell the collateral. Therefore, a secured party can retain collateral, but this general right is subject to several conditions. The secured party must send written notice of the proposal to the debtor if the debtor has not signed a statement renouncing or modifying his or her rights after default. If the collateral is consumer goods, the secured party does not need to give any other notice. In all other situations, the secured party must also send notice to any other secured party from whom the secured party has received written notice of a claim of interest in the collateral in question.

    If within twenty-one days after the notice is sent, the secured party receives an objection in writing from a person entitled to receive notification, then the secured party must sell or otherwise dispose of the collateral in accordance with the provisions of UCC 9–504 (disposition procedures under UCC 9–504 will be discussed shortly). If no such written objection is forthcoming, the secured party can retain the collateral in full satisfaction of the debtor's obligation [UCC 9–505(2)].

CONSUMER GOODS   When the collateral is consumer goods with a PMSI and the debtor has paid 60 percent or more of the purchase price, then the secured party must sell or otherwise dispose of the repossessed collateral in accordance with the provisions of UCC 9–504 within ninety days. Failure to comply opens the secured party to an action for conversion or other liability under UCC 9–507(1) unless the consumer-debtor signed a written statement *after default* renouncing or modifying the right to demand the sale of the goods [UCC 9–505(1)].

REMEMBER Conversion is a tort that consists of an act depriving an owner of personal property without the owner's permission.

DISPOSITION PROCEDURES   A secured party who does not choose to retain the collateral must resort to the disposition procedures prescribed under UCC 9–504. The UCC allows a great deal of flexibility with regard to disposition. The only real limitations are that (1) the sale must be accomplished in a commercially reasonable manner and (2) the debtor must be notified of the sale.

What Qualifies as a Commercially Reasonable Sale?   A secured party is not compelled to resort to public sale to dispose of the collateral. The party is given latitude under the UCC to seek out the best terms possible in a private sale. Generally, no specific time requirements must be met; however, the time must ultimately meet the standard of commercial reasonableness. Additionally, UCC 9–507(2) states as follows:

> The fact that a better price could have been obtained by a sale at a different time or in a different method from that selected by the secured party is not of itself sufficient to establish that the sale was not made in a commercially reasonable manner. If the secured party either sells the collateral in the usual manner in any recognized market therefor or if he sells at the price current in such a market at the time of sale or if he has otherwise sold in conformity with reasonable commercial practices among dealers in the type of property sold, he has sold in a commercially reasonable manner.

In the following case, the court had to decide whether a sale was conducted in a commercially reasonable manner.

CASE 21.4

FIRST WESTSIDE BANK v. FOR-MED, INC.

Supreme Court of Nebraska, 1995.
247 Neb. 641,
529 N.W.2d 66.

HISTORICAL AND SOCIAL SETTING *In the 1950s, the United States began building its interstate highway system. Wally Byam, known as "Mr. Trailer," organized caravans of cars and trailers to tour the new roads and to journey into Canada, Mexico, Central America, Europe, Africa, and the Middle East. Twenty years later, trailers had evolved into motor homes. Blue Bird motor homes have been described as the top of the line. There is a limited supply of Blue Birds, because the manufacturer does not want to saturate the market. Nationwide, there are less than a dozen Blue Bird dealers. A new Blue Bird can cost up to $200,000, depending on equipment, but depreciates at about 8 percent a year for the first decade.*

FACTS David Anderson and For-Med, Inc., signed a security agreement with the First Westside Bank for $79,924.89, plus interest. The collateral for the loan was Anderson's Blue Bird motor home. Anderson and For-Med defaulted, and the bank took possession of the Blue Bird. The bank solicited bids for the motor home by word of mouth from other financial institutions, Blue Bird dealers, and some of its customers. Ultimately, the bank sold the motor home to a bank customer for $60,000. The buyer repaired the motor home at a cost of $22,000 and sold it two and a half years later for $58,000. Meanwhile, the bank sued For-Med and Anderson in a Nebraska state court for the difference between the amount due on

the loan and the proceeds from the Blue Bird's sale. The court entered a judgment in favor of the bank. For-Med and Anderson appealed, acknowledging that although the price in the bank's sale had not been "wholly unreasonable," the sale had not been commercially reasonable, because it had not been advertised sufficiently.

ISSUE Was the sale of the collateral commercially reasonable, despite the bank's failure to advertise?

DECISION Yes. The Supreme Court of Nebraska affirmed the lower court's decision.

REASON The state supreme court agreed that a secured party must "use all fair and reasonable means to obtain the best price under the circumstances," but the court added that "the creditor need not use extraordinary means." Depending on the circumstances, the court stated, "a sale may be commercially reasonable notwithstanding the lack of advertising." Factors to be considered in determining whether a sale was commercially reasonable include "the adequacy or insufficiency of the price at which [the collateral] was sold. Here, the collateral was resold 2½ years after the purchaser acquired it, for an amount far less than he had invested in its purchase and repair. In light of that circumstance and the admission of For-Med and Anderson that the price * * * was not 'wholly unreasonable,' it cannot be said that the [lower] court's finding that the sale was commercially reasonable is clearly wrong."

FOR CRITICAL ANALYSIS—Economic Consideration
Why should a court consider what the buyer of collateral does with it, or sells it for, after the secured party has disposed of it?

Notice to the Debtor The secured party must send to the debtor notice of any sale if the debtor has not signed a statement renouncing or modifying the right to notification of the sale after default. For consumer goods, no other notification need be sent. In all other cases, notification must be sent to any other secured party from whom the secured party has received written notice of a claim of interest in the collateral [UCC 9–504(3)]. Such notice is not necessary, however, when the collateral is perishable or threatens to decline speedily in value, or when it is of a type customarily sold on a recognized market. Generally, notice of the place, time, and manner of the sale is required if the sale is to be classified as a sale conducted in a commercially reasonable manner.

International Perspective

To prevent challenges to the reasonability of sales of collateral, banks have sought to include clauses in loan contracts that essentially constitute waivers of the important right of debtors to be notified of sales of collateral. In other words, a clause might state that if the debtor defaults and the bank chooses to repossess and sell the collateral, the debtor waives any right to be notified of the sale. In some countries, such as England, such waivers are enforceable. In the United States, however, they are generally not enforceable, because they are inconsistent with the UCC's requirement that foreclosure sales be conducted in a commercially reasonable manner.

For Critical Analysis: *How does Article 9's requirement that the debtor be notified of any sale of the collateral benefit the debtor?*

PROCEEDS FROM DISPOSITION Proceeds from the disposition of collateral after default on the underlying debt must be applied in the following order:

1. Reasonable expenses stemming from the retaking, holding, or preparing for sale are paid first. When authorized by law and if provided for in the agreement, these can include reasonable attorneys' fees and other legal expenses.
2. Satisfaction of the balance of the debt owed to the secured party is then made.
3. Creditors with subordinate security interests whose written demands have been received prior to the completion of distribution of the proceeds are then entitled to receive the remaining proceeds from the sale [UCC 9–504(1)].
4. Any surplus generally goes to the debtor.

DEFICIENCY JUDGMENT Often, after proper disposition of the collateral, the secured party has not collected all that the debtor still owes. Unless otherwise agreed, the debtor is liable for any deficiency, and the creditor can obtain a **deficiency judgment** from a court to collect the deficiency. Note, however, that if the underlying transaction was a sale of accounts or of chattel paper, the debtor is entitled to any surplus or is liable for any deficiency only if the security agreement so provides [UCC 9–504(2)].

DEFICIENCY JUDGMENT
A judgment against a debtor for the amount of a debt remaining unpaid after collateral has been repossessed and sold.

REDEMPTION RIGHTS At any time before the secured party disposes of the collateral or enters into a contract for its disposition, or before the debtor's obligation has been discharged through the secured party's retention of the collateral, the debtor or any other secured party can exercise the right of *redemption* of the collateral. The debtor or other secured party can do this by tendering performance of all obligations secured by the collateral and by paying the expenses reasonably incurred by the secured party in retaking and maintaining the collateral [UCC 9–506].

Application

Law and the Creditor— Perfecting Your Security Interest*

The importance of perfecting your security interest cannot be overemphasized, particularly when the debt is large and you wish to maximize the priority of your security interest in the debtor's collateral. Failure to perfect or to perfect properly may result in your becoming the equivalent of an unsecured creditor.

The filing of a financing statement, either locally or centrally with the secretary of state, is the most common method of perfection. Generally, the moment the filing takes place, your priority over the other creditors is established, as well as your priority over some purchasers of the collateral and a subsequent trustee in bankruptcy.

We have noted that as a secured party, you do not have to file to perfect a purchase-money security interest in consumer goods. Nonetheless, you are advised to do so. A public filing can reduce the chances that another creditor will secure a loan with the same collateral.

When you create a financing statement, describe the collateral—not necessarily in detailed terms but, then again, not in too general a way. If your description is too general, your security interest will not be perfected. For example, instead of stating, "All equipment located at (address)," state specifically the equipment that will serve as the collateral.

*This *Application* is not meant to substitute for the services of an attorney who is licensed to practice law in your state.

Sometimes, credit transactions occur outside normal business relationships. You may be asked, for example, to aid an associate, a relative, or a friend. At that moment, you should reflect on your need for security for any debt that will be owed to you. If there is a need for security, then you should perfect your security interest, even if you believe this is an unnecessary action because the debtor is a friend or a relative. That particular friendship or blood relationship is irrelevant should he or she ever be forced into bankruptcy. Bankruptcy law does not allow friends or relatives to be paid ahead of nonfriends or nonrelatives. You will end up standing in line with the other unsecured creditors if you have not perfected your security interest in the collateral. The best way to protect your security interest by perfection is to have your friend, relative, or associate transfer to your possession the collateral—stocks, bonds, jewelry, or whatever. By possessing such collateral, you can keep the transaction private but still have security for the loan.

✓ Checklist for Perfecting Your Security Interest

1. File a financing statement promptly.
2. Describe the collateral well—it is better to err by giving too much detail than by giving too little detail.
3. Even with friends, relatives, or associates, be sure to perfect your security interest, perhaps by having the debtor transfer the collateral to your possession.

▮ Key Terms

after-acquired property 544
attachment 532
collateral 532
continuation statement 542
debtor 532
default 532
deficiency judgment 552

execution 548
financing statement 536
floating lien 545
levy 549
perfection 535
pledge 540
proceeds 543

purchase-money security interest (PMSI) 541
secured party 531
secured transaction 530
security agreement 532
security interest 531

▌Chapter Summary: Secured Transactions

Creating a Security Interest *(See pages 532–535.)*	1. Unless the creditor has possession of the collateral, there must be an agreement in writing, signed by the debtor, describing and reasonably identifying the collateral. 2. The secured party must give value to the debtor. 3. The debtor must have rights in the collateral—some ownership interest or right to obtain possession of the specified collateral.

Perfecting a Security Interest *(See pages 535–543.)*	1. *Perfection by filing*—The most common method of perfection is by filing a financing statement containing the names and addresses of the secured party and the debtor and describing the collateral by type or item. The financing statement must be signed by the debtor.
	    a. State laws determine where the financing statement is to be filed—with the secretary of state, county clerk (or other local official), or both.
	    b. Classification of collateral determines whether filing is necessary and the place of filing (see Exhibit 21–3).
	
	2. *Perfection without filing*—
	    a. By transfer of collateral—The debtor can transfer possession of the collateral itself to the secured party. This type of transfer is called a *pledge.*
	    b. By attachment of a *purchase-money security interest* in consumer goods—If the secured party has a purchase-money security interest in consumer goods (goods bought or used by the debtor for personal, family, or household purposes), the secured party's security interest is perfected automatically. Exceptions: security interests in fixtures or motor vehicles.

The Scope of a Security Interest *(See pages 543–546.)*	A security agreement can cover the following types of property: 1. *Collateral in the present possession of the debtor.* 2. *Proceeds from a sale, exchange, or disposition of secured collateral.* 3. *After-acquired property*—A security agreement may provide that property acquired after the execution of the security agreement will also be secured by the agreement. This provision often accompanies security agreements covering a debtor's inventory. 4. *Future advances*—A security agreement may provide that any future advances made against a line of credit will be subject to the security interest in the same collateral.
Priorities among Security Interests *(See page 546.)*	See Exhibit 21–5.

Rights and Duties of Debtors and Creditors *(See pages 546–548.)*	1. *Information requests*—Upon request by any person, the filing officer must send a statement listing the file number, the date, and the hour of original filing of financing statements covering collateral of a particular debtor; a fee is charged.
	
	2. *Assignment, amendment, and release*—A secured party may (a) release part or all of the collateral described in a filed financing statement, thus ending the creditor's security interest; (b) assign part or all of the security interest to another party; and (c) amend a filed financing statement.
	
	3. *The status of the debt*—If a debtor wishes to know the status of a secured debt, he or she may sign a descriptive statement of the amount of the unpaid debt (and may include a list of the covered collateral) as of a specific date. The creditor must then approve or correct this statement in writing within two weeks of receipt or be liable for any loss caused to the debtor by failure to do so. Only one request without charge is permitted per six-month period.
	
	4. *Termination statement*—When a debt is paid, the secured party generally must send to the debtor or file with the filing officer to whom the original financing statement was given a *termination statement.* Failure to comply results in the secured party's liability to the debtor for $100 plus any loss caused to the debtor.
	    a. If the financing statement covers consumer goods, the termination statement must be filed by the secured party within one month after the debt is paid, or if the debtor requests the termination statement in writing, it must be filed within ten days of the request after the debt is paid—whichever is earlier.
	    b. In all other cases, the termination statement must be filed or furnished to the debtor within ten days after a written request is made by the debtor.

▌Chapter Summary: Secured Transactions—Continued

Default *(See pages 548–552.)*	On the debtor's default, the secured party may do either of the following:
	1. Relinquish the security interest and proceed to judgment on the underlying debt, followed by execution and levy on the nonexempt assets of the debtor. This remedy is rarely pursued.
	2. Take possession (peacefully or by court order) of the collateral covered by the security agreement and then pursue one of two alternatives:
	a. Retain the collateral (unless the secured party has a purchase-money security interest in consumer goods and the debtor has paid 60 percent or more of the selling price or loan), in which case the secured party—
	(1) Must give written notice to the debtor if the debtor has not signed a statement renouncing or modifying his or her rights after default. With consumer goods, no other notice is necessary.
	(2) Must send notice to any other secured party with an interest in the same collateral. If an objection is received from the debtor or any other secured party within twenty-one days, in writing, the creditor must dispose of the collateral according to the requirements of UCC 9–504. Otherwise, the secured party may retain the collateral in full satisfaction of the debt.
	b. Sell the collateral, in which case the secured party—
	(1) Must sell the goods in a commercially reasonable manner at a public or private sale.
	(2) Must notify the debtor and (except in sales of consumer goods) other secured parties who have notified the secured party of claims to the collateral of the sale (unless the collateral is perishable or will decline rapidly in value).
	(3) Must generally apply the proceeds in the following order:
	(a) Expenses incurred by the sale (which may include reasonable attorneys' fees and other legal expenses).
	(b) Balance of the debt owed to the secured party.
	(c) Subordinate security interests of creditors whose written demands have been received prior to the completion of the distribution of the proceeds.
	(d) Surplus to the debtor.

▌For Review

1. What is a security interest? Who is a secured party? What is a security agreement? What is a financing statement?
2. What three requirements must be met to create an enforceable security interest?
3. What is the most common method of perfecting a security interest under Article 9?
4. If two secured parties have perfected security interests in the collateral of the debtor, which party has priority to the collateral on the debtor's default?
5. What rights does a secured creditor have on the debtor's default?

▌Questions and Case Problems

21–1. Priority Disputes. Redford is a seller of electric generators. He purchases a large quantity of generators from a manufacturer, Mallon Corp., by making a down payment and signing an agreement to make the balance of payments over a period of time. The agreement gives Mallon Corp. a security interest in the generators and the proceeds. Mallon Corp. files a financing statement on its security interest centrally. Redford receives the generators and immediately sells one of them to Garfield on an installment contract, with payment to be made in twelve equal installments. At the time of sale, Garfield knows of Mallon's security interest. Two months later Redford goes into default on his payments to Mallon. Discuss Mallon's rights against purchaser Garfield in this situation.

21–2. Oral Security Agreements. Marsh has a prize horse named Arabian Knight. Marsh is in need of working capital. She borrows $5,000 from Mendez, with Mendez's taking possession of Arabian Knight as security for the loan. No written agreement is signed. Discuss whether, in the absence of a written agreement, Mendez has a security interest in Arabian Knight. If Mendez does have a security interest, is it a perfected security interest?

21–3. Default. Delgado is a retail seller of television sets. He sells a color television set to Cummings for $600. Cummings cannot pay cash, so she signs a security agreement, paying $100 down and agreeing to pay the balance in twelve equal installments of $50 each. The security agreement gives Delgado a security interest in the television set sold. Cummings makes six payments on time; then she goes into default because of unexpected financial problems. Delgado repossesses the set and wants to keep it in full satisfaction of the debt. Discuss Delgado's rights and duties in this matter.

21–4. The Scope of a Security Interest. Edward owned a retail sporting goods shop. A new ski resort was being created in his area, and to take advantage of the potential business, Edward decided to expand his operations. He borrowed a large sum of money from his bank, which took a security interest in his present inventory and any after-acquired inventory as collateral for the loan. The bank properly perfected the security interest by filing a financing statement. A year later, just a few months after the ski resort had opened, an avalanche destroyed the ski slope and lodge. Edward's business consequently took a turn for the worse, and he defaulted on his debt to the bank. The bank sought possession of his entire inventory, even though the inventory was now twice as large as it had been when the loan was made. Edward claimed that the bank only had rights to half his inventory. Is Edward correct? Explain.

21–5. Sale of Collateral. In 1969, Jones and Percell executed a promissory note and a security agreement covering a converted military aircraft built in the 1950s. Upon their default, the Bank of Nevada repossessed the aircraft. After providing the required notice to Jones and Percell, the bank placed advertisements to sell the aircraft in several trade journals, as well as in major newspapers in several large cities. In addition, the bank sent 2,000 brochures to 240 sales organizations. It hired a sales representative to market the aircraft. The plane was later sold for $71,000 to an aircraft broker, who in turn resold it for $123,000 after spending $33,000 on modifications. Because the price obtained on the sale of the plane was about $75,000 less than the amount Jones and Percell owed the bank, the bank initiated a lawsuit to obtain the amount of the deficiency. Jones and Percell claim that the sale was not conducted in a commercially reasonable manner. Will they succeed in their claim? Why or why not? [*Jones v. Bank of Nevada*, 91 Nev. 368, 535 P.2d 1279 (1975)]

21–6. Priority Disputes. In 1977, the Marcuses sold their drugstore business to Mistura, Inc. Mistura made a down payment on the purchase price, and the Marcuses took a security interest in the fixtures and personal property of the business for the unpaid portion of the debt. Arizona law requires that financing statements relating to security interests in personal property be filed with the secretary of state. Because the Marcuses had filed their statement with the Maricopa County recorder, only their security interest in the fixtures was properly perfected. Mistura later obtained a loan from McKesson, using the same property secured by its transaction with the Marcuses as collateral. McKesson properly perfected a security interest in this collateral by filing with the secretary of state. McKesson had actual knowledge at the time of the loan that the Marcuses had not properly perfected their security interest in the personal property of Mistura's business. A few days after McKesson's filing, the Marcuses filed a financing statement with the secretary of state. Which party had a superior security interest in the collateral, McKesson or the Marcuses? Explain. [*In re Mistura, Inc.*, 705 F.2d 1496 (9th Cir. 1983)]

21–7. Oral Security Agreements. John and Melody Fish bought various pieces of expensive jewelry, including a diamond ring, a diamond necklace, and a wedding band, from Odom's Jewelers. The Fishes agreed to make monthly installment payments to Odom's until the purchase price was paid in full. In 1988, the Fishes fell behind in their monthly payments on the account. The Fishes and Odom's orally agreed that the Fishes would return the jewelry to Odom's and that Odom's would hold the items for the Fishes until the account was paid. In 1991, the Fishes filed for bankruptcy protection. The jewelry was still in the possession of Odom's. One of the issues before the bankruptcy court was whether Odom's had a security interest in the jewelry. Did it? Explain. [*In re Fish*, 128 Bankr. 468 (N.D.Okla. 1991)]

21–8. Purchase-Money Security Interest. Barbara Wiegert and her daughter, Darcie Wiegert, went shopping at Sears, and Darcie bought a mattress and box spring for $396.11. Barbara later purchased from Sears a television set for $239.96. Both purchases of consumer goods were charged to the credit card of Barbara (and her husband, Harold). On both credit slips was printed the following statement: "I grant Sears a security interest or lien in this merchandise, unless prohibited by law, until paid in full." When the Wiegerts filed their bankruptcy petition, the balance due to Sears was $587.26, plus interest. The Wiegerts claimed that Sears was an unsecured creditor. Sears claimed that it had a purchase-money security interest in the goods and that the security interest was perfected. Was Sears correct in making these claims? Discuss fully. [*In the Matter of Wiegert*, 145 Bankr. 621 (D.Neb. 1991)]

21–9. Perfection. Richard E. Walker, Kelly E. Walker, and Kenneth W. Walker were partners in the Walker Brothers Dairy, a general partnership located in Florida. The Walkers purchased a "Model 2955 utility tractor, a round bale saw, and a feed mixer box" from the John Deere Co. John Deere took a security interest in the equipment. The security agreement stated that the debtor was a partnership known as "Walker Brothers Dairy." John Deere filed a financing statement, however, that listed the debtors as "Richard Walker, Kelly Walker, and Kenneth Wendell Walker." Each of the three partners signed the statement. Their signatures were followed by a typewritten statement indicating that the partners were doing business as "Walker Brothers Dairy." When Walker Brothers Dairy voluntarily filed for bankruptcy, John Deere sought to repossess the equipment. The issue before the court was whether the financing statement, which listed as debtors the partners rather than the partnership, was sufficient to perfect John Deere's security interest in the partnership equipment. What should the court decide? Discuss. [*In re Walker*, 142 Bankr. 482 (M.D.Fla. 1992)]

21–10. Sale of Collateral. To pay for the purchases of several aircraft, Robert Wall borrowed money from the Cessna Finance Corp., using the aircraft as collateral. Wall defaulted on the loans. Cessna took possession of the collateral (the aircraft) and sold it. Cessna filed a suit in a federal district court against Wall for the difference between the amount due on the loans and the amount received from the sale of the aircraft. Wall claimed that he could have obtained a higher price for the aircraft if he had sold it himself. What effect does the issue concerning whether a better price could have been obtained have on whether the sale was commercially reasonable? Discuss. [*Cessna Finance Corp. v. Wall*, 876 F.Supp. 273 (M.D.Ga. 1994)]

**A QUESTION OF ETHICS
AND SOCIAL RESPONSIBILITY**

21–11. *Raymond and Joan Massengill borrowed money from Indiana National Bank (INB) to purchase a van. Toward the end of the loan period, the Massengills were notified by mail that they were delinquent on their last two loan payments. Joan called INB and said that she and her husband would go to the bank the following Monday morning and take care of the matter. In the meantime, INB had made arrangements for the van to be repossessed. At 1:30 A.M. Sunday morning, two men appeared at the Massengills' driveway and began to hook up the van to a tow truck. Raymond, assuming that the van was being stolen, went outside to intervene and did so vociferously. During the course of events, Massengill became entangled in machinery at the rear of the tow truck and was dragged down the street and* then run over by his towed van. The "repo men"—those hired by INB to repossess the van—knew of Raymond's plight but sped away. The trial court granted summary judgment for the bank, ruling that the bank was not liable for the injuries caused by the repossession company. On appeal, however, the court ruled that the bank could be liable for the acts of the repossession company and remanded the case for the determination of damages. [Massengill v. Indiana National Bank, 550 N.E.2d 97 (Ind.App.1st Dist. 1990)]

1. Frequently, courts must decide, as in this case, whether the secured party should be held liable for the wrongful acts of persons hired by the secured party to undertake an actual repossession effort. Is it fair to hold the secured party liable for acts that the creditor did not commit? Why or why not?

2. Given the potential for violence during repossession efforts, why do you think Article 9 permits secured parties to resort to "self-help" repossessions?

3. Should repossession companies be prohibited from taking collateral from debtors' property during the middle of the night, when debtors are more likely to conclude that the activity is wrongful?

 FOR CRITICAL ANALYSIS

21–12. *Review the three requirements for an enforceable security interest. Why is each of these requirements necessary?*

Chapter 22

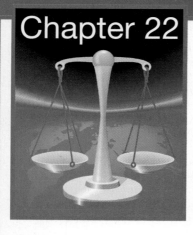

Creditors' Rights and Bankruptcy

"Creditors are . . . great observers of set days and times."

Benjamin Franklin, 1706–1790
(American diplomat, author, and scientist)

CHAPTER OBJECTIVES

After reading this chapter, you should be able to:

1. Summarize the various remedies available to creditors, and indicate how and when creditors use these remedies to collect debts.
2. Differentiate between suretyship and guaranty arrangements.
3. Outline the typical steps in a bankruptcy proceeding.
4. Describe what property constitutes a debtor's estate in a bankruptcy proceeding and what property is exempt.
5. Compare and contrast the types of relief available under Chapter 7, Chapter 11, Chapter 12, and Chapter 13 of the Bankruptcy Code.

America's font of practical wisdom, Benjamin Franklin, observed a truth known to all debtors—that creditors do observe "set days and times" and will expect to recover their money at the agreed-on times. Historically, debtors and their families have been subjected to punishment, including involuntary servitude and imprisonment, for their inability to pay debts. The modern legal system, however, has moved away from a punishment philosophy in dealing with debtors. In fact, many observers say that it has moved too far in the other direction, to the detriment of creditors.

Normally, creditors have no problem collecting the debts owed to them. When disputes arise over the amount owed, however, or when the debtor simply cannot or will not pay, what happens? What remedies are available to creditors when debtors default? We have already discussed, in Chapter 21, the remedies available to secured creditors under Article 9 of the Uniform Commercial Code (UCC). In the first part of this chapter, we focus on other laws that assist the debtor and creditor in resolving their disputes without the debtor's having to resort to bankruptcy. The second part of this chapter discusses bankruptcy as a last resort in resolving debtor-creditor problems.

▌Laws Assisting Creditors

Both the common law and statutory laws other than Article 9 of the UCC create various rights and remedies for creditors. We discuss here some of these rights and remedies.

Liens

As discussed earlier in this text, a *lien* is an encumbrance on property to satisfy a debt or protect a claim for the payment of a debt. Creditors' liens include the mechanic's lien, the artisan's lien, the innkeeper's lien, and judicial liens.

MECHANIC'S LIEN   When a person contracts for labor, services, or materials to be furnished for the purpose of making improvements on real property (land and things attached to the land, such as buildings and trees—see Chapter 35) but does not immediately pay for the improvements, the creditor can file a **mechanic's lien** on the property. This creates a special type of debtor-creditor relationship in which the real estate itself becomes security for the debt.

For example, a painter agrees to paint a house for a homeowner for an agreed-on price to cover labor and materials. If the homeowner refuses to pay for the work or pays only a portion of the charges, a mechanic's lien against the property can be created. The painter is the lienholder, and the real property is encumbered with a mechanic's lien for the amount owed. If the homeowner does not pay the lien, the property can be sold to satisfy the debt. Notice of the *foreclosure* (the process by which the creditor deprives the debtor of his or her property) and sale must be given to the debtor in advance, however. Note that state law governs mechanic's liens. The time period within which a mechanic's lien must be filed is usually 60 to 120 days from the last date labor or materials were provided.

ARTISAN'S LIEN   An **artisan's lien** is a security device created at common law through which a creditor can recover payment from a debtor for labor and materials furnished in the repair or improvement of personal property. For example, Cindy leaves her diamond ring at the jeweler's to be repaired and to have her initials engraved on the band. In the absence of an agreement, the jeweler can keep the ring until Cindy pays for the services that the jeweler provides. Should Cindy fail to pay, the jeweler has a lien on Cindy's ring for the amount of the bill and normally can sell the ring in satisfaction of the lien.

In contrast to a mechanic's lien, an artisan's lien is *possessory*. The lienholder ordinarily must have retained possession of the property and have expressly or impliedly agreed to provide the services on a cash, not a credit, basis. Usually, the lienholder retains possession of the property. When this occurs, the lien remains in existence as long as the lienholder maintains possession, and the lien is terminated once possession is voluntarily surrendered—unless the surrender is only temporary. If it is a temporary surrender, there must be an agreement that the property will be returned to the lienholder. Even with such an agreement, if a third party obtains rights in that property while it is out of the possession of the lienholder, the lien is lost. The only way that a lienholder can protect a lien and surrender possession at the same time is to record notice of the lien (if state law so permits) in accordance with state lien and recording statutes.

Modern statutes permit the holder of an artisan's lien to foreclose and sell the property subject to the lien to satisfy payment of the debt. As with the mechanic's lien, the holder of an artisan's lien is required to give notice to the owner of the property prior to foreclosure and sale. The sale proceeds are used to pay the debt and the costs of the legal proceedings, and the surplus, if any, is paid to the former owner.

In the following case, a creditor with a purchase-money security interest (PMSI) in an automobile tried to repossess the property but failed to do so because an artisan's lien had also been placed on the car.

"Creditor: One of a tribe of savages dwelling beyond the Financial Straits and dreaded for their desolating incursions."

Ambrose Bierce, 1842–1914 (American writer)

MECHANIC'S LIEN
A statutory lien upon the real property of another, created to ensure payment for work performed and materials furnished in the repair or improvement of real property, such as a building.

ARTISAN'S LIEN
A possessory lien given to a person who has made improvements and added value to another person's personal property as security for payment for services performed.

CASE 22.1

NATIONAL BANK OF JOLIET v. BERGERON CADILLAC, INC.

Appellate Court of Illinois, 1977.
66 Ill.2d 140,
361 N.E.2d 116,
5 Ill.Dec. 588.

HISTORICAL AND SOCIAL SETTING *Before the UCC, there was generally no specific statutory rule concerning the priority of artisan's or mechanic's liens over other security interests (except for Section 11 of the Uniform Trust Receipts Act of 1933). Under the case law existing at that time, some courts ruled that the priority of the liens turned on whether the secured party had "title." The drafters of the UCC clarified the law in respect to the priority of liens. Article 9 provides that liens securing claims that arise from work intended to enhance or preserve the value of collateral take priority over earlier security interests, even if the earlier interests have been perfected [UCC 9–310]. The work must have been performed in the ordinary course of the lienholder's business, and the lienholder must possess the collateral. Of course, another state statute may make the lien subordinate to an earlier, perfected security interest. If there is a state statute creating artisan's or mechanic's liens but the statute is silent regarding priorities, UCC 9–310 provides that an artisan's or mechanic's lien takes priority.*

FACTS In February 1973, Gladys Schmidt borrowed $4,120 from the National Bank of Joliet to finance the purchase of a Cadillac. The bank held a security interest in the automobile and had perfected this interest by filing in the office of the secretary of state. In August 1973, Schmidt took the car to Bergeron Cadillac, Inc., for repairs, which cost approximately $2,000. When Schmidt failed to pay for the repairs, Bergeron Cadillac retained possession of the car and placed an artisan's lien on it. In September, Schmidt defaulted on her payments to the bank, and the bank later filed an action in an Illinois state court to gain possession of the Cadillac from Bergeron. The trial court held for Bergeron Cadillac, and the bank appealed.

ISSUE Which party has a right to possession of the vehicle—Bergeron Cadillac or the National Bank?

DECISION Bergeron Cadillac. The Illinois appellate court affirmed the trial court's judgment.

REASON The court looked to both the common law and the UCC in its determination: "The plain language of Section 9–310 gives the lien of persons furnishing services or materials upon goods in their possession priority over a perfected security interest unless the lien is created by statute and the statute expressly provides otherwise." In response to the bank's contention that the common law possessory lien had been superseded in Illinois by two statutes providing for artisan's liens, the court ruled that in both cases "the statutes expressly provide that the liens created shall be in addition to, and shall not exclude, any lien existing by virtue of the common law."

FOR CRITICAL ANALYSIS—Ethical Consideration
Is the fact that artisan's liens "arise from work intended to enhance or preserve the value of collateral" a sufficient reason to give artisan's liens priority over perfected security interests?

INNKEEPER'S LIEN
A possessory lien placed on the luggage of hotel guests for hotel charges that remain unpaid.

INNKEEPER'S LIEN An **innkeeper's lien** is another security device created at common law. An innkeeper's lien is placed on the baggage of guests for the agreed-on hotel charges that remain unpaid. If no express agreement has been made on the amount of those charges, then the lien will be for the reasonable value of the accommodations furnished. The innkeeper's lien is terminated either by the guest's payment of the hotel charges or by the innkeeper's surrender of the baggage to the guest, unless the surrender is temporary. Additionally, the lien is terminated by the innkeeper's foreclosure and sale of the property.

JUDICIAL LIENS When a debt is past due, a creditor can bring a legal action against the debtor to collect the debt. If a creditor is successful in the action, the court awards the creditor a judgment against the debtor (usually for the amount of the debt plus any interest and legal costs incurred in obtaining the judgment). Frequently, however, the creditor is unable to collect the awarded amount.

To ensure that a judgment in the creditor's favor will be collectible, creditors are permitted to request that certain nonexempt property of the debtor be seized to satisfy the debt. (As will be discussed later in this chapter, under state or federal statutes, certain property is exempt from attachment by creditors.) If the court orders the debtor's property to be seized prior to a judgment in the creditor's favor, the court's order is referred to as a *writ of attachment*. If the court orders the debtor's property to be seized following a judgment in the creditor's favor, the court's order is referred to as a *writ of execution*.

Attachment Recall from Chapter 21 that *attachment*, in the context of secured transactions, refers to the process through which a security interest in a debtor's collateral becomes enforceable. In the context of judicial liens, **attachment** is a court-ordered seizure and taking into custody of property prior to the securing of a judgment for a past-due debt. Attachment rights are created by state statutes. Attachment is a *prejudgment* remedy, because it occurs either at the time of or immediately after the commencement of a lawsuit and before the entry of a final judgment. By statute, the restrictions and requirements for a creditor to attach before judgment are specific and limited. The due process clause of the Fourteenth Amendment to the Constitution limits the courts' power to authorize seizure of a debtor's property without notice to the debtor or a hearing on the facts.

To use attachment as a remedy, the creditor must have an enforceable right to payment of the debt under law, and the creditor must follow certain procedures. Otherwise, the creditor can be liable for damages for wrongful attachment. He or she must file with the court an *affidavit* (a written or printed statement, made under oath or sworn to) stating that the debtor is in default and stating the statutory grounds under which attachment is sought. The creditor must also post a bond to cover at least court costs, the value of the loss of use of the good suffered by the debtor, and the value of the property attached. When the court is satisfied that all the requirements have been met, it issues a **writ of attachment,** which directs the sheriff or other officer to seize nonexempt property. If the creditor prevails at trial, the seized property can be sold to satisfy the judgment.

ATTACHMENT
In the context of judicial liens, a court-ordered seizure and taking into custody of property prior to the securing of a judgment for a past-due debt.

WRIT OF ATTACHMENT
A court's order, prior to a trial to collect a debt, directing the sheriff or other officer to seize nonexempt property of the debtor; if the creditor prevails at trial, the seized property can be sold to satisfy the judgment.

Under the principle of comity (discussed in Chapter 37), a court in one country may enforce a judgment rendered by a court in another country. For example, suppose that a German court enters a judgment ordering the attachment of a debtor's assets that are located in the United States. A U.S. court will give full effect to that judgment unless the procedures underlying the German court's judgment seem too unfair. For example, in one case, a U.S. court refused to enforce a pretrial writ of attachment issued by a Spanish court. The U.S. court refused to "tie up all the assets of an enterprise in Illinois," because the defendant had no opportunity to appear before the Spanish court to contest the order.[a]

For Critical Analysis: *What criteria should a U.S. court use to determine the fairness of a foreign court's writ of attachment?*

a. *Carezo v. Babson Brothers Co.,* No. 91 C 7622 (N.D.Ill. 1992).

Writ of Execution If the debtor will not or cannot pay the judgment, the creditor is entitled to go back to the court and obtain a court order, directing the sheriff to seize (levy) and sell any of the debtor's nonexempt real or personal property that is within

WRIT OF EXECUTION
A court's order, after a judgment has been entered against the debtor, directing the sheriff to seize (levy) and sell any of the debtor's nonexempt real or personal property. The proceeds of the sale are used to pay off the judgment, accrued interest, and costs of the sale; any surplus is paid to the debtor.

GARNISHMENT
A legal process used by a creditor to collect a debt by seizing property of the debtor (such as wages) that is being held by a third party (such as the debtor's employer).

the court's geographical jurisdiction (usually the county in which the courthouse is located). This order is called a **writ of execution.** The proceeds of the sale are used to pay off the judgment, accrued interest, and the costs of the sale. Any excess is paid to the debtor. The debtor can pay the judgment and redeem the nonexempt property any time before the sale takes place. Because of exemption laws and bankruptcy laws, however, many judgments are virtually uncollectible.

Garnishment

Garnishment occurs when a creditor is permitted to collect a debt by seizing property of the debtor that is being held by a third party. Typically, a garnishment judgment is served on a debtor's employer so that part of the debtor's usual paycheck will be paid to the creditor. As a result of a garnishment proceeding, the court orders the debtor's employer to turn over a portion of the debtor's wages to pay the debt.

The legal proceeding for a garnishment action is governed by state law, and garnishment operates differently from state to state. According to the laws in some states, the creditor needs to obtain only one order of garnishment, which will then continuously apply to the debtor's weekly wages until the entire debt is paid. In other states, the creditor must go back to court for a separate order of garnishment for each pay period.

Both federal laws and state laws limit the amount of money that can be garnished from a debtor's weekly take-home pay.[1] Federal law provides a minimal framework to protect debtors from losing all their income in order to pay judgment debts.[2] State laws also provide dollar exemptions, and these amounts are often larger than those provided by federal law. Under federal law, garnishment of an employee's wages for any one indebtedness cannot be a ground for dismissal of an employee.

One of the questions courts have faced in recent years has to do with whether a debtor's pension fund can be attached by creditors, through garnishment or other proceedings, to satisfy a debt. Under federal law, certain types of pension funds may not be attached. The law is less clear, however, on whether pension funds, *after* they have been received by a retiree, can be subject to attachment by creditors. This issue is before the court in the following case.

---

1.   Some states (for example, Texas) do not permit garnishment of wages by private parties except under a child-support order.
2.   For example, the federal Consumer Credit Protection Act of 1968, 15 U.S.C. Sections 1601–1693r, provides that a debtor can retain either 75 percent of the disposable earnings per week or the sum equivalent to thirty hours of work paid at federal minimum wage rates, whichever is greater.

CASE 22.2

UNITED STATES v. SMITH
United States Court of Appeals,
Fourth Circuit, 1995.
47 F.3d 681.

HISTORICAL AND ETHICAL SETTING   *Pension plans have a significant financial impact on the lives of millions of Americans. At one time, some employees with long years of service were deprived of their pension benefits*

through a variety of purportedly unethical methods. For these and other reasons, Congress enacted the Employee Retirement Income Security Act of 1974 (ERISA).[a] *ERISA provides that certain pension benefits "may not be alienated [transferred]." Some courts have interpreted this to mean that even after a retiree has received his or her benefit, the amount received cannot be subject to any court-ordered transfer.*

FACTS   For nine years, Charles Smith asked his friends and acquaintances to invest their money in his business schemes. Smith used most of the money—estimated to

---

a.   29 U.S.C. Sections 1001–1461.

Case 22.2—Continued

be more than $350,000—for personal expenses. Smith was indicted for criminal fraud and pleaded guilty to that crime in a federal district court. The court imposed a prison sentence and ordered Smith to repay his victims as much as possible by turning over, each month, the entire amount of his pension benefits. Smith appealed the order, claiming that it violated the "anti-alienation" provision of ERISA.

ISSUE   Was the order to Smith to turn over his pension benefits in violation of federal law?

DECISION   Yes. The U.S. Court of Appeals for the Fourth Circuit vacated (removed) the lower court's order and remanded the case. The appellate court ordered the lower court to redetermine the amount that Smith should pay to his victims, based on "a balance of the victims'

interest in compensation and Smith's other financial resources."

REASON   The appellate court "recognized a 'strong public policy against the alienability [transferability] of * * * ERISA [pension] benefits.'" The court pointed out that the "Supreme Court, as well, has found that it is not 'appropriate to approve any * * * exception.'" The appellate court acknowledged that "[u]nderstandably, there may be a natural distaste for the result we reach here" but reasoned that "[t]he statute * * * is clear. Congress has made a policy decision to protect the ERISA income of retirees, even if that decision prevents others from securing relief for the wrongs done them."

FOR CRITICAL ANALYSIS—Political Consideration
Why does the law protect certain pension benefits from court-ordered transfers?

Creditors' Composition Agreements

Creditors may contract with the debtor for discharge of the debtor's liquidated debts (debts that are definite, or fixed, in amount) on payment of a sum less than that owed. These agreements are called **creditors' composition agreements** or *composition agreements* and are usually held to be enforceable.

CREDITORS' COMPOSITION AGREEMENT
An agreement formed between a debtor and his or her creditors in which the creditors agree to accept a lesser sum than that owed by the debtor in full satisfaction of the debt.

Mortgage Foreclosure

Mortgage holders have the right to foreclose on mortgaged property in the event of a debtor's default. The usual method of foreclosure is by judicial sale of the property, although the statutory methods of foreclosure vary from state to state. If the proceeds of the foreclosure sale are sufficient to cover both the costs of the foreclosure and the mortgaged debt, the debtor receives any surplus. If the sale proceeds are insufficient to cover the foreclosure costs and the mortgaged debt, however, the **mortgagee** (the creditor-lender) can seek to recover the difference from the **mortgagor** (the debtor) by obtaining a *deficiency judgment* representing the difference between the mortgaged debt and the amount actually received from the proceeds of the foreclosure sale. The mortgagee obtains a deficiency judgment in a separate legal action that he or she pursues subsequent to the foreclosure action. The deficiency judgment entitles the mortgagee to recover the amount of the deficiency from other property owned by the debtor.

MORTGAGEE
Under a mortgage agreement, the creditor who takes a security interest in the debtor's property.

MORTGAGOR
Under a mortgage agreement, the debtor who gives the creditor a security interest in the debtor's property in return for a mortgage loan.

Suretyship and Guaranty

When a third person promises to pay a debt owed by another in the event the debtor does not pay, either a *suretyship* or a *guaranty* relationship is created. Suretyship and guaranty have a long history under the common law and provide creditors with the right to seek payment from the third party if the primary debtor defaults on his or her obligations. Exhibit 22–1 illustrates the relationship between a suretyship or guaranty party and the creditor.

♦ **Exhibit 22–1**
Suretyship and Guaranty Parties
In a suretyship or guaranty arrangement, a third party promises to be responsible for a debtor's obligations. A third party who agrees to be responsible for the debt even if the primary debtor does not default is known as a surety; a third party who agrees to be *secondarily* responsible for the debt only if the primary debtor defaults is known as a guarantor. As noted in Chapter 11, normally a promise of guaranty (a collateral, or secondary, promise) must be in writing to be enforceable.

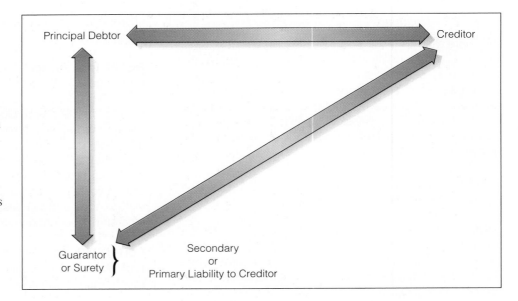

SURETYSHIP
An express contract in which a third party to a debtor-creditor relationship (the surety) promises to be primarily responsible for the debtor's obligation.

SURETY
A person, such as a cosigner on a note, who agrees to be primarily responsible for the debt of another.

GUARANTOR
A person who agrees to satisfy the debt of another (the debtor) *only* after the principal debtor defaults; a guarantor's liability is thus secondary.

SURETY   A contract of strict **suretyship** is a promise made by a third person to be responsible for the debtor's obligation. It is an express contract between the **surety** (the third party) and the creditor. The surety in the strictest sense is *primarily* liable for the debt of the principal. The creditor need not exhaust all legal remedies against the principal debtor before holding the surety responsible for payment. The creditor can demand payment from the surety from the moment the debt is due.

For example, Robert Delmar wants to borrow money from the bank to buy a used car. Because Robert is still in college, the bank will not lend him the money unless his father, Joseph Delmar, who has dealt with the bank before, will cosign the note (add his signature to the note, thereby becoming a surety and thus jointly liable for payment of the debt). When Joseph Delmar cosigns the note, he becomes primarily liable to the bank. On the note's due date, the bank has the option of seeking payment from either Robert or Joseph Delmar, or both jointly.

GUARANTY   A guaranty contract is similar to a suretyship contract in that it includes a promise to answer for the debt or default of another. With a guaranty arrangement, the **guarantor**—the third person making the guaranty—is *secondarily* liable. The guarantor can be required to pay the obligation *only after the principal debtor defaults*, and default usually takes place only after the creditor has made an attempt to collect from the debtor.

For example, a small corporation, BX Enterprises, needs to borrow money to meet its payroll. The bank is skeptical about the creditworthiness of BX and requires Dawson, its president, who is a wealthy businessperson and the owner of 70 percent of BX Enterprises, to sign an agreement making himself personally liable for payment if BX does not pay off the loan. As a guarantor of the loan, Dawson cannot be held liable until BX Enterprises is in default.

The Statute of Frauds requires that a guaranty contract between the guarantor and the creditor must be in writing to be enforceable unless the *main purpose* exception applies. As discussed in Chapter 11, this exception provides that if the main purpose of the guaranty agreement is to benefit the guarantor, then the contract need not be in writing to be enforceable.

DEFENSES OF THE SURETY AND THE GUARANTOR   The defenses of the surety and the guarantor are basically the same. Therefore, the following discussion applies to both, although it refers only to the surety.

Certain actions will release the surety from the obligation. For example, any binding material modification in the terms of the original contract made between the principal debtor and the creditor—including the awarding of a binding extension of time for making payment—without first obtaining the consent of the surety will discharge a gratuitous surety completely and a compensated surety to the extent that the surety suffers a loss. (An example of a gratuitous surety is a father who agrees to assume responsibility for his daughter's obligation; an example of a compensated surety is a venture capitalist who will profit from a loan made to the principal debtor.)

Naturally, if the principal obligation is paid by the debtor or by another person on behalf of the debtor, the surety is discharged from the obligation. Similarly, if valid tender of payment is made, and the creditor rejects it with knowledge of the surety's existence, then the surety is released from any obligation on the debt.

Generally, the surety can use any defenses available to a principal debtor to avoid liability on the obligation to the creditor. Defenses available to the principal debtor that the surety *cannot* use include the principal debtor's incapacity or bankruptcy and the statute of limitations. The ability of the surety to assert any defenses the debtor may have against the creditor is the most important concept in suretyship, because most of the defenses available to the surety are also those of the debtor.

Obviously, a surety may also have his or her own defenses—for example, incapacity or bankruptcy. If the creditor fraudulently induced the surety to guarantee the debt of the debtor, the surety can assert fraud as a defense. In most states, the creditor has a legal duty to inform the surety, prior to the formation of the suretyship contract, of material facts known by the creditor that would substantially increase the surety's risk. Failure to do so is fraud and makes the suretyship obligation voidable. In addition, if a creditor surrenders the collateral to the debtor or impairs the collateral while knowing of the surety and without the surety's consent, the surety is released to the extent of any loss suffered from the creditor's actions. The primary reason for this requirement is to protect the surety who agreed to become obligated only because the debtor's collateral was in the possession of the creditor.

RIGHTS OF THE SURETY AND THE GUARANTOR   The rights of the surety and the guarantor are basically the same. Therefore, again, the following discussion applies to both.

When the surety pays the debt owed to the creditor, the surety is entitled to certain rights. First, the surety has the legal **right of subrogation.** Simply stated, this means that any right the creditor had against the debtor now becomes the right of the surety. Included are creditor rights in bankruptcy, rights to collateral possessed by the creditor, and rights to judgments secured by the creditor. In short, the surety now stands in the shoes of the creditor and may pursue any remedies that were available to the creditor against the debtor.

Second, the surety has the **right of reimbursement** from the debtor. Basically, the surety is entitled to receive from the debtor all outlays made on behalf of the suretyship arrangement. Such outlays can include expenses incurred as well as the actual amount of the debt paid to the creditor.

Third, in the case of **co-sureties** (two or more sureties on the same obligation owed by the debtor), a surety who pays more than his or her proportionate share on a debtor's default is entitled to recover from the co-sureties the amount paid above the surety's obligation. This is the **right of contribution.** Generally, a co-surety's liability either is determined by agreement or, in the absence of agreement between the co-sureties, can be specified in the suretyship contract itself.

For example, assume that two co-sureties are obligated under a suretyship contract to guarantee the debt of a debtor. Together, the sureties' maximum liability is $25,000. As specified in the suretyship contract, surety A's maximum liability is $15,000, and surety B's is $10,000. The debtor owes $10,000 and is in default. Surety A pays the creditor the entire $10,000. In the absence of any agreement between the two co-sureties, surety A can recover $4,000 from surety B ($10,000/$25,000 $\times$ $10,000 = $4,000).

RIGHT OF SUBROGATION
The right of a person to stand in the place of (be substituted for) another, giving the substituted party the same legal rights that the original party had.

RIGHT OF REIMBURSEMENT
The legal right of a person to be restored, repaid, or indemnified for costs, expenses, or losses incurred or expended on behalf of another.

CO-SURETY
A joint surety; a person who assumes liability jointly with another surety for the payment of an obligation.

RIGHT OF CONTRIBUTION
The right of a co-surety who pays more than his or her proportionate share upon a debtor's default to recover the excess paid from other co-sureties.

▌Laws Assisting Debtors

HOMESTEAD EXEMPTION
A law permitting a debtor to retain the family home, either in its entirety or up to a specified dollar amount, free from the claims of unsecured creditors or trustees in bankruptcy.

The law protects debtors as well as creditors. Certain property of the debtor, for example, is exempt from creditors' actions. Probably the most familiar of these exemptions is the **homestead exemption.** Each state permits the debtor to retain the family home, either in its entirety or up to a specified dollar amount, free from the claims of unsecured creditors or trustees in bankruptcy. The purpose of the homestead exemption is to ensure that the debtor will retain some form of shelter.

Suppose that Van Cleave owes Acosta $40,000. The debt is the subject of a lawsuit, and the court awards Acosta a judgment of $40,000 against Van Cleave. The homestead of Van Cleave is valued at $50,000, and the state exemption on homesteads is $25,000. There are no outstanding mortgages or other liens on his homestead. To satisfy the judgment debt, Van Cleave's family home is sold at public auction for $45,000. The proceeds of the sale are distributed as follows:

1. Van Cleave is given $25,000 as his homestead exemption.
2. Acosta is paid $20,000 toward the judgment debt, leaving a $20,000 deficiency judgment that can be satisfied from any other nonexempt property (personal or real) that Van Cleave may have, if allowed by state law.

State exemption statutes usually include both real and personal property. Personal property that is most often exempt from satisfaction of judgment debts includes the following:

1. Household furniture up to a specified dollar amount.
2. Clothing and certain personal possessions, such as family pictures or a Bible.
3. A vehicle (or vehicles) for transportation (at least up to a specified dollar amount).
4. Certain classified animals, usually livestock but including pets.
5. Equipment that the debtor uses in a business or trade, such as tools or professional instruments, up to a specified dollar amount.

Consumer protection statutes (see Chapter 31) also protect debtors' rights. Of course, bankruptcy laws, which are discussed in the next section, are designed specifically to assist debtors in need of relief from their debts.

▌Bankruptcy and Reorganization

"How often have I been able to trace bankruptcies and insolvencies to some lawsuit, . . . the costs of which have mounted up to large sums."

Henry Peter Brougham,
1778–1868
(English politician)

At one time, debtors who could not pay their debts as they came due faced harsh consequences, including imprisonment and involuntary servitude. Today, in contrast, debtors have numerous rights. Some of these rights have already been mentioned. We now look at another significant right of debtors: the right to petition for bankruptcy relief under federal law.

Bankruptcy law in the United States has two goals—to protect a debtor by giving him or her a fresh start, free from creditors' claims; and to ensure equitable treatment to creditors who are competing for a debtor's assets. Bankruptcy law is federal law, but state laws on secured transactions, liens, judgments, and exemptions also play a role in federal bankruptcy proceedings.

Current bankruptcy law is based on the Bankruptcy Reform Act of 1978, as amended. In this chapter, we refer to this act, as amended, as the Bankruptcy Code (or, more simply, the Code). The following *Landmark in the Law* traces the historical evolution of bankruptcy law and the importance of the 1978 Bankruptcy Reform Act.

| The Bankruptcy Reform Act of 1978 | LANDMARK IN THE LAW |

Article I, Section 8, of the U.S. Constitution gives Congress the power to establish "uniform Laws on the subject of Bankruptcies throughout the United States." Congress initially exercised this power in 1800, when the first bankruptcy law was enacted as a result of the business crisis created by restraints imposed on American trade by the British and French. In 1803, the law was repealed, and during the rest of the century—always in response to some crisis—Congress periodically enacted (and later repealed) other bankruptcy legislation. The National Bankruptcy Act of 1898, however, was not repealed, and since that time the United States has had ongoing federal statutory laws concerning bankruptcy. The 1898 act allowed only for *liquidation* in bankruptcy proceedings (which occurs when the debtor's assets are sold and the proceeds distributed to creditors). Some relief through reorganization was first allowed by amendments to the 1898 act in the 1930s.

Modern bankruptcy law is based on the Bankruptcy Reform Act of 1978, which repealed the 1898 act and represented a major overhaul of federal bankruptcy law. The 1978 act attempted to remedy previous abuses of bankruptcy law, introduced more clarity into bankruptcy procedures, and generally made it easier for debtors to obtain bankruptcy relief. A major organizational change in the 1978 act was the establishment of a new system of bankruptcy courts, in which each federal judicial district would have an adjunct bankruptcy court with exclusive jurisdiction over bankruptcy cases. The act also specified that, in contrast to the lifetime terms of judges in other federal courts, bankruptcy court judges would have a fourteen-year term.

The 1978 act, referred to now simply as the Bankruptcy Code, has been amended several times since its passage. Amendments to the Code have created additional bankruptcy judgeships, placed bankruptcy court judges under the authority of the U.S. district courts, extended the bankruptcy trustee system nationally, granted more power to bankruptcy trustees in the handling of bankruptcy matters, and added a new chapter to the Bankruptcy Code (Chapter 12) to aid financially troubled farmers. The most significant amendments to the Bankruptcy Code were made by the Bankruptcy Reform Act of 1994. Among the many important changes of the 1994 act was the creation of a "fast-track" procedure for small-business debtors (those not involved in owning or managing real estate and with debts of less than $2 million) under Chapter 11 of the Code.

RECALL Congress regulates the jursidiction of the federal courts, within the limits set by the Constitution. Congress can expand or reduce the number of federal courts at any time.

For Critical Analysis: *The Code no longer refers to persons who file for bankruptcy as "bankrupts" but simply as "debtors." What does this change in terminology signify, if anything?*

Bankruptcy Courts

Bankruptcy proceedings are held in federal bankruptcy courts. A bankruptcy court's primary function is to hold *core proceedings*[3] dealing with the procedures required to administer the estate of the debtor in bankruptcy. Bankruptcy courts are under the authority of U.S. district courts (see Exhibit 3–2 on the federal court system in Chapter 3), and rulings from bankruptcy courts can be appealed to the district courts. Fundamentally, a bankruptcy court fulfills the role of an administrative

---

3. Core proceedings are procedural functions, such as allowance of claims, decisions on preferences, automatic-stay proceedings, confirmation of bankruptcy plans, discharge of debts, and so on. These terms and procedures are defined and discussed in the following sections of this chapter.

court for the district court concerning matters in bankruptcy. A bankruptcy court can conduct a jury trial if the appropriate district court has authorized it and if the parties to the bankruptcy consent to a jury trial.

Types of Bankruptcy Relief

LIQUIDATION
The sale of all of the nonexempt assets of a debtor and the distribution of the proceeds to the debtor's creditors. Chapter 7 of the Bankruptcy Code provides for liquidation bankruptcy proceedings.

The Bankruptcy Code is contained in Title 11 of the U.S. Code (U.S.C.). Chapters 1, 3, and 5 of the Code include general definitional provisions and provisions governing case administration and procedures, creditors, the debtor, and the estate. These three chapters of the Code apply generally to all types of bankruptcies. The next five chapters set forth the different types of relief that debtors may seek. Chapter 7 provides for **liquidation** proceedings (the selling of all nonexempt assets and the distribution of the proceeds to the debtor's creditors). Chapter 9 governs the adjustment of the debts of municipalities. Chapter 11 governs reorganizations. Chapter 12 (for family farmers) and Chapter 13 (for individuals) provide for adjustment of the debts of parties with regular income.[4]

In the following pages, we deal first with liquidation proceedings under Chapter 7 of the Code. We then examine the procedures required for Chapter 11 reorganizations and for Chapter 12 and Chapter 13 plans.

▌ Chapter 7—Liquidation

Liquidation is the most familiar type of bankruptcy proceeding and is often referred to as an *ordinary*, or *straight*, *bankruptcy*. Put simply, debtors in straight bankruptcies state their debts and turn their assets over to trustees. The trustees sell the assets and distribute the proceeds to creditors. With certain exceptions, the remaining debts are then **discharged** (extinguished), and the debtors are relieved of the obligation to pay the debts.

DISCHARGE
In bankruptcy proceedings, the extinction of the debtor's dischargeable debts.

Any "person"—defined as including individuals, partnerships, and corporations— may be a debtor under Chapter 7. Railroads, insurance companies, banks, savings and loan associations, investment companies licensed by the Small Business Administration, and credit unions *cannot* be Chapter 7 debtors, however. Other chapters of the Code or other federal or state statutes apply to them. A husband and wife may file jointly for bankruptcy under a single petition.

Filing the Petition

A straight bankruptcy may be commenced by the filing of either a voluntary or an involuntary **petition in bankruptcy**—the document that is filed with a bankruptcy court to initiate bankruptcy proceedings.

PETITION IN BANKRUPTCY
The document that is filed with a bankruptcy court to initiate bankruptcy proceedings. The official forms required for a petition in bankruptcy must be completed accurately, sworn to under oath, and signed by the debtor.

VOLUNTARY BANKRUPTCY A voluntary petition is brought by the debtor, who files official forms designated for that purpose in the bankruptcy court. A consumer-debtor (defined as an individual whose debts are primarily consumer debts) who has selected Chapter 7 must state in the petition, at the time of filing, that he or she understands the relief available under other chapters and has chosen to proceed under Chapter 7. If the consumer-debtor is represented by an attorney, the attorney must file an affidavit stating that he or she has informed the debtor of the relief available under each chapter. Any debtor who is liable on a claim held by a creditor can file a voluntary petition.

CONSUMER-DEBTOR
An individual whose debts are primarily consumer debts (debts for purchases made primarily for personal or household use).

---

4. There are no Chapters 2, 4, 6, 8, or 10 in Title 11. Such "gaps" are not uncommon in the U.S.C. This is because chapter numbers (or other subdivisional unit numbers) are sometimes reserved for future use when a statute is enacted. (A gap may also appear if a law has been repealed.)

The debtor does not even have to be insolvent to do so.[5] The voluntary petition contains the following schedules:

1.   A list of both secured and unsecured creditors, their addresses, and the amount of debt owed to each.
2.   A statement of the financial affairs of the debtor.
3.   A list of all property owned by the debtor, including property claimed by the debtor to be exempt.
4.   A listing of current income and expenses.

The official forms must be completed accurately, sworn to under oath, and signed by the debtor. To conceal assets or knowingly supply false information on these schedules is a crime under the bankruptcy laws. If the voluntary petition for bankruptcy is found to be proper, the filing of the petition will itself constitute an order for relief. An **order for relief** relieves the debtor of the immediate obligation to pay the debts listed in the petition. Once a consumer-debtor's voluntary petition has been filed, the clerk of the court (or person directed) must give the trustee and creditors mailed notice of the order for relief not more than twenty days after the entry of the order.

As mentioned previously, debtors do not have to be insolvent to file for voluntary bankruptcy. Debtors do not have unfettered access to Chapter 7 bankruptcy proceedings, however. Section 707(b) of the Bankruptcy Code allows a bankruptcy court to dismiss a petition for relief under Chapter 7 if the granting of relief would constitute "substantial abuse" of Chapter 7.

For example, the court might determine, after evaluating the debtor's schedule listing current income and expenses, that the debtor would be able to pay creditors a reasonable amount from future income. In this situation, the court might conclude that it would be a substantial abuse of Chapter 7 to allow the debtor to have his or her debts completely discharged. The court might dismiss the consumer-debtor's Chapter 7 petition after a hearing and encourage the debtor to file a repayment plan under Chapter 13 of the Code, when that would result in a substantial improvement in a creditor's receipt of payment. In the following case, the court had to decide whether granting a Chapter 7 discharge to the debtor would constitute substantial abuse.

ORDER FOR RELIEF
A court's grant of assistance to a complainant. In bankruptcy proceedings, the order relieves the debtor of the immediate obligation to pay the debts listed in the bankruptcy petition.

5.   The inability to pay debts as they become due is known as *equitable* insolvency. A *balance-sheet* insolvency, which exists when a debtor's liabilities exceed assets, is not the test. Thus, it is possible for debtors to petition voluntarily for bankruptcy even though their assets far exceed their liabilities. This situation may occur when a debtor's cash flow problems become severe.

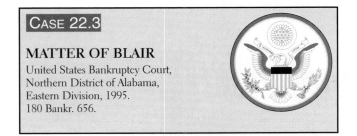

CASE 22.3

MATTER OF BLAIR
United States Bankruptcy Court, Northern District of Alabama, Eastern Division, 1995. 180 Bankr. 656.

HISTORICAL AND POLITICAL SETTING   *In the early 1980s, retailers and consumer lenders complained to Congress of an increasing number of Chapter 7 discharges being granted to debtors who creditors felt could actually afford to pay their debts. In response, Congress enacted the substantial abuse provision. The*

provision illustrates the tension between two principles underlying bankruptcy law: to give debtors the opportunity for a fresh start and to help creditors thwart the abuse of consumer credit. An indication of this tension is the fact that Congress did not define "substantial abuse" but left the task to the courts.

FACTS   James Blair, Jr., owed primarily consumer debts of less than $7,000, and his income exceeded his living expenses by more than $200 a month. When he filed a petition for relief under Chapter 7, the court concluded that if he were to file a repayment plan under Chapter 13, his debts would be paid off in forty months. The bankruptcy administrator filed a motion to dismiss Blair's petition.

(Continued)

Case 22.3—Continued

ISSUE Should Blair's petition be dismissed on the ground of substantial abuse?

DECISION Yes. The court dismissed the petition.

REASON The court held that substantial abuse must be determined on a case-by-case basis, according to the following factors: "(1) Whether the bankruptcy petition was filed because of sudden illness, calamity, disability, or unemployment; (2) Whether the debtor incurred cash advances and made consumer purchases far in excess of his ability to pay; (3) Whether the debtor's proposed family budget is excessive or unreasonable; (4) Whether the debtor's schedules and statement of current income and expenses reasonably and accurately reflect the true financial condition; and (5) Whether the petition was filed in good faith." The court indicated that the "single most important indicator of substantial abuse is the presence of enough disposable income to realistically enable the debtor to repay a significant portion of his debts through a Chapter 13 plan." The court concluded that to grant Blair relief under Chapter 7 would constitute substantial abuse, because he could pay off most, if not all, of his debt under a Chapter 13 repayment plan.

FOR CRITICAL ANALYSIS—Economic Consideration
The court also stated that granting Blair relief under Chapter 7 would be "perverting the purpose of the Bankruptcy Code." What did the court mean by this statement?

INVOLUNTARY BANKRUPTCY An involuntary bankruptcy occurs when the debtor's creditors force the debtor into bankruptcy proceedings. An involuntary case cannot be commenced against a farmer[6] or a charitable institution (or those entities not eligible for Chapter 7 relief—mentioned earlier), however. For an involuntary action to be filed against other debtors, the following requirements must be met: If the debtor has twelve or more creditors, three or more of those creditors having unsecured claims totaling at least $10,000 must join in the petition. If a debtor has fewer than twelve creditors, one or more creditors having a claim of $10,000 may file.

---

6. *Farmers* are defined as persons who receive more than 80 percent of their gross income from farming operations, such as tilling the soil; dairy farming; ranching; or the production or raising of crops, poultry, or livestock. Corporations and partnerships, as well as individuals, can be farmers.

A store advertises a court-ordered bankruptcy sale. On what basis might a court enter an order for relief in an involuntary bankruptcy proceeding initiated by the store's creditors?

If the debtor challenges the involuntary petition, a hearing will be held, and the bankruptcy court will enter an order for relief if it finds either of the following:

1. That the debtor is generally not paying debts as they become due.
2. That a general receiver, custodian, or assignee took possession of, or was appointed to take charge of, substantially all of the debtor's property within 120 days before the filing of the petition.

If the court grants an order for relief, the debtor will be required to supply the same information in the bankruptcy schedules as in a voluntary bankruptcy.

An involuntary petition should not be used as an everyday debt-collection device, and the Code provides penalties for the filing of frivolous (unjustified) petitions against debtors. Judgment may be granted against the petitioning creditors for the costs and attorneys' fees incurred by the debtor in defending against an involuntary petition that is dismissed by the court. If the petition is filed in bad faith, damages can be awarded for injury to the debtor's reputation. Punitive damages may also be awarded.

Automatic Stay

The filing of a petition, either voluntary or involuntary, operates as an **automatic stay** on (suspension of) virtually all litigation and other action by creditors against the debtor or the debtor's property. In other words, once a petition is filed, creditors cannot commence or continue most legal actions against the debtor to recover claims or to repossess property in the hands of the debtor. A secured creditor, however, may petition the bankruptcy court for relief from the automatic stay in certain circumstances. Additionally, the automatic stay does not apply to paternity, alimony, or family maintenance and support debts.

A creditor's failure to abide by an automatic stay imposed by the filing of a petition can be costly. If a creditor *knowingly* violates the automatic-stay provision (a willful violation), any party injured is entitled to recover actual damages, costs, and attorneys' fees and may also be entitled to recover punitive damages.

AUTOMATIC STAY
In bankruptcy proceedings, the suspension of virtually all litigation and other action by creditors against the debtor or the debtor's property; the stay is effective the moment the debtor files a petition in bankruptcy.

Creditors' Meeting and Claims

Within a reasonable time after the order of relief is granted (not less than ten days or more than thirty days), the bankruptcy court must call a meeting of the creditors listed in the schedules filed by the debtor. The bankruptcy judge does not attend this meeting. The debtor must attend this meeting (unless excused by the court) and submit to an examination under oath. Failure to appear or making false statements under oath may result in the debtor's being denied a discharge of bankruptcy. At the meeting, the trustee ensures that the debtor is advised of the potential consequences of bankruptcy and of his or her ability to file under a different chapter.

In a bankruptcy case in which the debtor has no assets (called a "no-asset" case), creditors are notified of the debtor's petition for bankruptcy but are instructed not to file a claim. In such a situation, the creditors will receive no payment, and most, if not all, of the debtor's debts will be discharged. If there are sufficient assets to be distributed to creditors, however, each creditor must normally file a *proof of claim* with the bankruptcy court clerk within ninety days of the creditors' meeting to be entitled to receive a portion of the debtor's estate. The proof of claim lists the creditor's name and address, as well as the amount that the creditor asserts is owed to the creditor by the debtor. If a creditor fails to file a proof of claim, the bankruptcy court or trustee may file the proof of claim on the creditor's behalf but is not obligated to do so. If a claim is for a disputed amount, the bankruptcy court will set the value of the claim.

Creditors' claims are automatically allowed unless contested by the trustee, the debtor, or another creditor. The Code, however, does not allow claims for breach of

BE AWARE In most cases, creditors' meetings take only five or ten minutes. But a debtor who lies, commits bribery, conceals assets, uses a false name, or makes false claims is subject to a $5,000 fine and up to five years in prison.

employment contracts or real estate leases for terms longer than one year. These claims are limited to one year's wages or rent, despite the remaining length of either contract in breach.

Property of the Estate

ESTATE IN PROPERTY
In bankruptcy proceedings, all of the debtor's legal and equitable interests in property presently held, wherever located, together with certain jointly owned property, property transferred in transactions voidable by the trustee, proceeds and profits from the property of the estate, and certain property interests to which the debtor becomes entitled within 180 days after filing for bankruptcy.

Upon the commencement of a liquidation proceeding under Chapter 7, an **estate in property** is created. The estate consists of all the debtor's legal and equitable interests in property presently held, wherever located, together with certain jointly owned property, property transferred in transactions voidable by the trustee, proceeds and profits from the property of the estate, and certain after-acquired property. Interests in certain property—such as gifts, inheritances, property settlements (resulting from divorce), or life insurance death proceeds—to which the debtor becomes entitled *within 180 days after filing* may also become part of the estate. Thus, the filing of a bankruptcy petition generally fixes a dividing line: property acquired prior to the filing becomes property of the estate, and property acquired after the filing, except as just noted, remains the debtor's.

Exempted Property

Any individual debtor is entitled to exempt certain property from the property of the estate. The Bankruptcy Code establishes a federal exemption scheme under which the following property is exempt:[7]

1. Up to $15,000 in equity in the debtor's residence and burial plot (the homestead exemption).
2. Interest in a motor vehicle up to $2,400.
3. Interest in household goods and furnishings, wearing apparel, appliances, books, animals, crops, and musical instruments up to $400 in a particular item but limited to $8,000 in total.
4. Interest in jewelry up to $1,000.
5. Any other property worth up to $800, plus any unused part of the $15,000 homestead exemption up to an amount of $7,500.
6. Interest in any tools of the debtor's trade, up to $1,500.
7. Certain life insurance contracts owned by the debtor.
8. Certain interests in accrued dividends or interests under life insurance contracts owned by the debtor.
9. Professionally prescribed health aids.
10. The right to receive Social Security and certain welfare benefits, alimony and support payments, and certain pension benefits.
11. The right to receive certain personal injury and other awards, up to $15,000.

Individual states have the power to pass legislation precluding debtors in their states from using the federal exemptions. At least thirty-five states have done this. In those states, debtors may use only state (not federal) exemptions. In the rest of the states, an individual debtor (or husband and wife who file jointly) may choose between the exemptions provided under state law and the federal exemptions. State laws may provide significantly greater protection for debtors than federal law. For example, Florida and Texas traditionally have provided for generous exemptions for homeowners. State laws may also define the property coming within an exemption differently than the federal law.

---

7. The dollar amounts stated in the Bankruptcy Code will be adjusted automatically on April 1, 1998, and every three years thereafter based on changes in the Consumer Price Index.

The Trustee's Role

Promptly after the order for relief has been entered, an interim, or provisional, trustee is appointed by the **U.S. trustee** (a government official who performs certain administrative tasks that a bankruptcy judge would otherwise have to perform). The interim trustee administers the debtor's estate until the first meeting of creditors, at which time either a permanent trustee is elected or the interim trustee becomes the permanent trustee. Trustees are entitled to compensation for services rendered, plus reimbursement for expenses.

The basic duty of the trustee is to collect the debtor's available estate and reduce it to money for distribution, preserving the interests of *both* the debtor and unsecured creditors. In other words, the trustee is accountable for administering the debtor's estate. To enable the trustee to accomplish this duty, the Code gives him or her certain powers, stated in both general and specific terms.

TRUSTEE'S POWERS The trustee has the power to require persons holding the debtor's property at the time the petition is filed to deliver the property to the trustee. To enable the trustee to implement this power, the Code provides that the trustee occupies a position equivalent in rights to that of certain other parties. For example, in some situations, the trustee has the same rights as creditors and can obtain a judicial lien or levy execution on the debtor's property. This means that a trustee has priority over an unperfected secured party to the debtor's property. The trustee also has rights equivalent to those of the debtor.

In addition, the trustee has the power to avoid (cancel) certain types of transactions, including those transactions that the debtor could rightfully avoid, *preferences*, certain statutory *liens*, and *fraudulent transfers* by the debtor. Avoidance powers must be exercised within two years of the order for relief (the period runs even if a trustee has not been appointed). These powers of the trustee are discussed in more detail in the following subsections.

VOIDABLE RIGHTS A trustee steps into the shoes of the debtor. Thus, any reason that a debtor can use to obtain the return of his or her property can be used by the trustee as well. These grounds (for recovery) include fraud, duress, incapacity, and mutual mistake.

For example, Rob sells his boat to Inga. Inga gives Rob a check, knowing that there are insufficient funds in her bank account to cover the check. Inga has committed fraud. Rob has the right to avoid that transfer and recover the boat from Inga. Once an order for relief has been entered for Rob, the trustee can exercise the same right to recover the boat from Inga. If the trustee does not take action to enforce one of his or her rights, the debtor in a Chapter 7 bankruptcy will nevertheless be able to enforce that right.[8]

PREFERENCES A debtor is not permitted to transfer property or to make a payment that favors—or gives a **preference** to—one creditor over others. The trustee is allowed to recover payments made both voluntarily and involuntarily to one creditor in preference over another.

To have made a preferential payment that can be recovered, an *insolvent* debtor generally must have transferred property, for a *preexisting* debt, within *ninety days* of the filing of the petition in bankruptcy. The transfer must give the creditor more than the creditor would have received as a result of the bankruptcy proceedings. The trustee does not have to prove insolvency, as the Code provides that the debtor is presumed to be insolvent during this ninety-day period.

U.S. TRUSTEE
A government official who performs certain administrative tasks that a bankruptcy judge would otherwise have to perform.

PREFERENCE
In bankruptcy proceedings, property transfers or payments made by the debtor that favor (give preference to) one creditor over others. The bankruptcy trustee is allowed to recover payments made both voluntarily and involuntarily to one creditor in preference over another.

---

8. In a Chapter 11 reorganization (to be discussed later), for which generally no trustee is appointed, the debtor has the same avoiding powers as a trustee in a Chapter 7 liquidation. In repayment plans under Chapters 12 and 13 (also to be discussed later), a trustee must be appointed.

Sometimes the creditor receiving the preference is an insider—an individual, a partner, a partnership, or an officer or a director of a corporation (or a relative of one of these) who has a close relationship with the debtor. If this is the case, the avoidance power of the trustee is extended to transfers made within *one year* before filing; however, the *presumption* of insolvency is confined to the ninety-day period. Therefore, the trustee must prove that the debtor was insolvent at the time of an earlier transfer.

Not all transfers are preferences. To be a preference, the transfer must be made for something other than current consideration. Therefore, it is generally assumed by most courts that payment for services rendered within ten to fifteen days prior to the payment of the current consideration is not a preference. If a creditor receives payment in the ordinary course of business, such as payment of last month's telephone bill, the payment cannot be recovered by the trustee in bankruptcy. To be recoverable, a preference must be a transfer for an antecedent (preexisting) debt, such as a year-old printing bill. In addition, the Code permits a consumer-debtor to transfer any property to a creditor up to a total value of $600, without the transfer's constituting a preference. Also, payment of paternity, alimony, maintenance, and support debts is not a preference.

If a preferred creditor has sold the property to an innocent third party, the trustee cannot recover the property from the innocent party. The creditor, however, generally can be held accountable for the value of the property.

NOTE What the trustee does with property recovered as a preference, in most cases, is to sell it and distribute the proceeds to the debtor's creditors.

LIENS ON DEBTOR'S PROPERTY   The trustee is permitted to avoid the fixing of certain statutory liens, such as a mechanic's lien, on property of the debtor. Liens that first become effective at the time of the bankruptcy or insolvency of the debtor are voidable by the trustee. Liens that are not perfected or enforceable against a good faith purchaser on the date of the petition are also voidable.

FRAUDULENT TRANSFERS   The trustee may avoid fraudulent transfers or obligations if they were made within one year of the filing of the petition or if they were made with actual intent to hinder, delay, or defraud a creditor. Transfers made for less than a reasonably equivalent consideration are also vulnerable if the debtor thereby became insolvent, was left engaged in business with an unreasonably small amount of capital, or intended to incur debts that would be beyond his or her ability to pay. When a fraudulent transfer is made outside the Code's one-year limit, creditors may seek alternative relief under state laws. State laws often allow creditors to recover for transfers made up to three years prior to the filing of a petition.

The court in the following case had to determine whether the debtors' contributions to their church, in the year preceding their filing of a Chapter 7 petition, could be recovered as "fraudulent transfers."

CASE 22.4

IN RE NEWMAN
United States Bankruptcy Court,
District of Kansas, 1995.
183 Bankr. 239.

HISTORICAL AND POLITICAL SETTING   *Commercial and religious laws have coexisted for at least as long as humans have attempted to write down either. English bankruptcy law can trace its origin to early Jewish cus-* *toms and medieval Jewish commercial and bankruptcy law. Bankruptcy courts descend from English religious courts. U.S. bankruptcy law derives from English practices. Over the centuries, the recovery of fraudulent transfers has become a central tenet of bankruptcy law.*

FACTS   Paul and Myrtle Newman filed a Chapter 7 petition. They listed their monthly income as $1,556 and monthly expenses as $2,458. Their debts totaled more than $25,000, consisting mostly of credit-card and medical bills. Despite the Newmans' circumstances, within the year preceding their petition, they had donated more than $2,400 to the Midway Southern Baptist Church. The donations were pursuant to their "sincere and firmly held

Case 22.4—Continued

belief in tithing."[a] In return for most of the donations, the Newmans received "spiritual benefits" but nothing tangible. Michael Morris, the Newmans' bankruptcy trustee, filed a suit in a federal bankruptcy court against the church to recover the money that the Newmans had donated in the preceding year.

ISSUE Did the Newmans' donations to their church constitute a fraudulent transfer?

DECISION Yes. The court granted the trustee's request.

REASON The court acknowledged that the Newmans and the church had no fraudulent intent but pointed out

---

a. *Tithing* means contributing part of one's income (the term *tithe* means "one-tenth") to a church to support the clergy and church administration costs.

that fraudulent intent was not required. The Code allows for recovery of those transfers of a debtor's property that occur within one year of the bankruptcy filing, while the debtor is insolvent, and that are not given in exchange for "reasonably equivalent value." The court concluded that "[t]he transfers in question involved interests of the debtors in property, occurred within one year of the debtors' bankruptcy filing, and * * * the debtors were insolvent" when they made their donations. As to whether the Newmans received "reasonably equivalent value," the court noted that in bankruptcy statutes and cases, the term "has long meant tangible benefit or economic value." The court concluded that "[s]uch economic benefit is clearly lacking in this case."

FOR CRITICAL ANALYSIS—Economic Consideration
What is the policy behind allowing for the recovery of certain transfers made prior to bankruptcy? Who benefits from this recovery?

Property Distribution

Creditors are either secured or unsecured. As discussed in Chapter 21, a *secured* creditor has a security interest in collateral that secures the debt. An *unsecured* creditor does not have any security interest.

SECURED CREDITORS The Code provides that a consumer-debtor, within thirty days of the filing of a Chapter 7 petition or before the date of the first meeting of the creditors (whichever is first), must file with the clerk a statement of intention with respect to the secured collateral. The statement must indicate whether the debtor will retain the collateral or surrender it to the secured party. Additionally, if applicable, the debtor must specify whether the collateral will be claimed as exempt property and whether the debtor intends to redeem the property or reaffirm the debt secured by the collateral. The trustee is obligated to enforce the debtor's statement within forty-five days after the statement is filed.

If the collateral is surrendered to the perfected secured party, the secured creditor can enforce the security interest either by accepting the property in full satisfaction of the debt or by foreclosing on the collateral and using the proceeds to pay off the debt. Thus, the secured party has priority over unsecured parties to the proceeds from the disposition of the secured collateral. Indeed, the Code provides that if the value of the secured collateral exceeds the secured party's claim, the secured party also has priority to the proceeds in an amount that will cover reasonable fees (including attorneys' fees, if provided for in the security agreement) and costs incurred because of the debtor's default. Any excess over this amount is used by the trustee to satisfy the claims of unsecured creditors. Should the secured collateral be insufficient to cover the secured debt owed, the secured creditor becomes an unsecured creditor for the difference.

UNSECURED CREDITORS Bankruptcy law establishes an order or priority for classes of debts owed to *unsecured* creditors, and they are paid in the order of their priority. Each class of debt must be fully paid before the next class is entitled to any of the proceeds—if there are sufficient funds to pay the entire class. If not, the proceeds are distributed *proportionately* to each creditor in the class, and all classes lower in priority on the list receive nothing. The order of priority among classes of unsecured creditors is as follows:

1.   Administrative expenses—including court costs, trustee fees, and bankruptcy attorneys' fees.
2.   In an involuntary bankruptcy, expenses incurred by the debtor in the ordinary course of business from the date of the filing of the petition up to the appointment of the trustee or the issuance by the court of an order for relief.
3.   Unpaid wages, salaries, and commissions earned within ninety days of the filing of the petition, limited to $4,000 per claimant. Any claim in excess of $4,000 is treated as a claim of a general creditor (listed as number 9 below).
4.   Unsecured claims for contributions to be made to employee benefit plans, limited to services performed during 180 days prior to the filing of the bankruptcy petition and $4,000 per employee.
5.   Claims by farmers and fishers, up to $4,000, against debtor operators of grain storage or fish storage or processing facilities.
6.   Consumer deposits of up to $1,800 given to the debtor before the petition was filed in connection with the purchase, lease, or rental of property or the purchase of services that were not received or provided. Any claim in excess of $1,800 is treated as a claim of a general creditor (listed as number 9 below).
7.   Paternity, alimony, maintenance, and support debts.
8.   Certain taxes and penalties due to government units, such as income and property taxes.
9.   Claims of general creditors.

If any amount remains after the priority classes of creditors have been satisfied, it is turned over to the debtor.

Discharge

BE AWARE Ordinarily, a discharge in bankruptcy—even under Chapter 7—does not free a debtor of *all* of his or her debts.

From the debtor's point of view, the purpose of a liquidation proceeding is to obtain a fresh start through the discharge of debts.[9] Certain debts, however, are not dischargeable in a liquidation proceeding. Also, certain debtors may not qualify—because of their conduct—to have all debts discharged in bankruptcy.

EXCEPTIONS TO DISCHARGE   Claims that are not dischargeable under Chapter 7 include the following:

1.   Claims for back taxes accruing within three years prior to bankruptcy.
2.   Claims for amounts borrowed by the debtor to pay federal taxes.
3.   Claims against property or money obtained by the debtor under false pretenses or by false representations.
4.   Claims by creditors who were not notified of the bankruptcy; these claims did not appear on the schedules the debtor was required to file.
5.   Claims based on fraud or misuse of funds by the debtor while he or she was acting in a fiduciary capacity or claims involving the debtor's embezzlement or larceny.
6.   Alimony, child support, and (with certain exceptions) property settlements.
7.   Claims based on willful or malicious conduct by the debtor toward another or the property of another.
8.   Certain government fines and penalties.
9.   Certain student loans, unless payment of the loans imposes an undue hardship on the debtor and the debtor's dependents.

---

9.   Discharges are granted under Chapter 7 only to *individuals*, not to corporations or partnerships. The latter may use Chapter 11, or they may terminate their existence under state law.

10. Consumer debts of more than $1,000 for luxury goods or services owed to a single creditor incurred within sixty days of the order for relief. This denial of discharge is a rebuttable presumption (that is, the denial may be challenged by the debtor), however, and any debts reasonably incurred to support the debtor or dependents are not classified as luxuries.

11. Cash advances totaling more than $1,000 that are extensions of open-end consumer credit obtained by the debtor within sixty days of the order for relief. A denial of discharge of these debts is also a rebuttable presumption.

12. Judgments or consent decrees against a debtor as a result of the debtor's operation of a motor vehicle while intoxicated.

In the following case, the debtor sought to have her student loans discharged in bankruptcy. The question before the court was whether payment of the loan would constitute an "undue hardship" for the debtor. (See this chapter's *Business Law in Action* for more detail on the Code's provisions on the nondischargeability of certain student loans.)

CASE 22.5

IN RE BAKER
United States Bankruptcy Court,
Eastern District of Tennessee, 1981.
10 Bankr. 870.

HISTORICAL AND SOCIAL SETTING *In 1980, about 53 percent of married women in the United States were working, compared with about 41 percent ten years earlier. More than 60 percent of wives who were separated from their husbands worked outside the home in 1980, compared with about 52 percent in 1970; for divorced women, the figures were about 74 percent and 72 percent, respectively. On average, however, in 1980, women earned only 62 cents for every dollar that men earned. In American families, husbands averaged nearly $21,000 in earnings and wives, $8,600. At the same time, of mothers who were entitled to child support, less than 75 percent actually received any payments. Of mothers living below the poverty line, more than 60 percent received nothing at all.*

FACTS Mary Lou Baker attended three different institutions of higher learning. At these three schools, she received educational loans totaling $6,635. After graduation, she was employed, but her monthly take-home pay was less than $650. Monthly expenses for herself and her three children were approximately $925. Her husband had left town and provided no child or other financial support. She received no public aid and had no other income. In January 1981, just prior to this action, Baker's church paid her gas bill so that she and her

children could have heat in their home. One child had reading difficulty, and another required expensive shoes. Baker had not been well and had been unable to pay her medical bills. She filed for bankruptcy. In her petition, she sought a discharge of her educational loans based on the hardship provision.

ISSUE Would paying the debt pose an undue hardship for Baker?

DECISION Yes. The student loans were discharged.

REASON The purpose of the prohibition against discharge was "to remedy an abuse by students who, immediately upon graduation, would file bankruptcy to secure a discharge of educational loans." In this case, Baker did not file bankruptcy to secure a discharge only from her educational loans. The bankruptcy court found that Baker could reduce her expenses somewhat but that her reasonable expenses each month far exceeded her income. Given Baker's circumstances, the court found that forcing payment of Baker's debts would create an undue hardship and that the Bankruptcy Code was drafted to provide a fresh start for those such as Baker "who have truly fallen on hard times."

FOR CRITICAL ANALYSIS— Economic Consideration
Why does the Bankruptcy Code generally prohibit the discharge of student loans, such as those obtained through government-guaranteed educational loan programs?

BUSINESS LAW IN ACTION

The Loan That Got Away

Section 523(a)(8) of the Bankruptcy Code provides that certain educational debts are not dischargeable in bankruptcy—unless paying the debt causes "undue hardship" for the debtor (see, for example, Case 22.5). This section of the Code is designed to deter students from financing their education with funds borrowed through government-guaranteed loan programs or nonprofit scholarship programs and then, once they have graduated, filing for bankruptcy to discharge the educational debt.

Student loans come in many forms, and thus Section 523(a)(8) of the Code attempts to define fairly specifically the types of student loans that are not dischargeable. The Code states that a nondischargeable student debt is any debt "for an educational benefit overpayment or loan made, insured or guaranteed by a governmental unit, or made under any program funded in whole or in part by a governmental unit or nonprofit institution, or for an

obligation to repay funds received as an educational benefit, scholarship or stipend." Given this lengthy definition, is it possible for a dispute to arise over whether a particular loan qualifies as a nondischargeable student loan?

Yes, it is, as evidenced by a case decided by the U.S. Court of Appeals for the Third Circuit in 1995. The case involved a $200,000 loan made by Santa Fe Medical Services, Inc., to a physician, Dr. Elizabeth Crowe, to entice Crowe to accept a job offer. Crowe needed the money to pay off an educational loan she had received through the U.S. National Health Service Corps (NHSC) Scholarship Program while she was in medical school. Crowe used the $200,000 to pay her debt to the NHSC, but then, a few years later—after she had repaid Santa Fe only about $5,000—she declared bankruptcy. During the bankruptcy proceedings, Santa Fe claimed that the debt was not dischargeable because it was an educational loan. When the bankruptcy court discharged the debt, Santa Fe appealed.

On appeal, Santa Fe urged the court to consider the purpose of the loan—which was to pay off an educational debt. The court, however, concluded that the real reason

Santa Fe loaned the money to Crowe was not to facilitate her education, "which had long since been completed," but rather to induce Crowe to accept employment with Santa Fe "by providing her with a means to repay her obligation to the NHSC." Furthermore, stated the court, the purpose of this section of the Code was "principally to protect government entities and nonprofit institutions of higher education—places which lend money or guarantee loans to individuals for educational purposes—from bankruptcy discharge." If Crowe did not repay Santa Fe, neither the federal Treasury nor the solvency of the NHSC would be affected.

In sum, the court held that this section of the Code simply "does not reach the particular type of loan at issue in this case." Loans made "pursuant to the terms of an employment contract" that are used to repay educational debts are not dischargeable in bankruptcy.[a]

For Critical Analysis: *If a student, after graduating from college, took out a loan from a bank to pay off an educational debt, should that loan be dischargeable in bankruptcy? Why does this issue rarely come before the courts?*

a.   *In re Segal,* 57 F.3d 342 (3d Cir. 1995).

OBJECTIONS TO DISCHARGE   In addition to the exceptions to discharge previously listed, the following circumstances (relating to the debtor's *conduct* and not the debt) will cause a discharge to be denied:

1.   The debtor's concealment or destruction of property with the intent to hinder, delay, or defraud a creditor.
2.   The debtor's fraudulent concealment or destruction of financial records.
3.   The granting of a discharge to the debtor within six years of the filing of the petition.[10]

When a discharge is denied under these circumstances, the assets of the debtor are still distributed to the creditors, but the debtor remains liable for the unpaid portions of all claims.

---

10.   A discharge under Chapter 13 of the Code within six years of the filing of the petition does not bar a subsequent Chapter 7 discharge when a good faith Chapter 13 plan paid at least 70 percent of all allowed unsecured claims and was the debtor's "best effort."

EFFECT OF DISCHARGE   The primary effect of a discharge is to void, or set aside, any judgment on a discharged debt and prohibit any action to collect a discharged debt. A discharge does not affect the liability of a co-debtor.

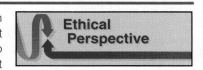

Ethical Perspective

The obvious effect of a discharge in bankruptcy is that the individual debtor is given a "fresh start" financially and can go forward without worrying about old debts that cannot be paid. The other consequences of a discharge in bankruptcy may not be so immediately apparent, however. The most notable of these consequences is the fact that the debtor's credit rating may be affected for years to come. A poor credit rating, in turn, may foreclose future opportunities for the debtor, including job opportunities.

There is no law prohibiting private employers from discriminating against job applicants on the basis of the applicants' prior bankruptcy status. The Bankruptcy Code does provide that the *government* may not "deny employment to, terminate the employment of, or discriminate with respect to employment against" a person who has been a bankruptcy debtor. In the parallel provision concerning private employers, however, the Code omits the phrase "deny employment to." Therefore, although a private employer may not fire an employee who has filed for bankruptcy protection, the employer may refuse to hire a job applicant who has done so. The courts provide little relief for job applicants who encounter such experiences, generally holding that the wording of the Code's provisions in these respects reflects the specific intentions of legislators who drafted those provisions.[a]

For Critical Analysis: *Can an employer's discrimination against job applicants on the basis of their history of bankruptcy ever be justified?*

a.   See, for example, *Pastore v. Medford Savings Bank,* 186 Bankr. 553 (D.Mass. 1995).

REVOCATION OF DISCHARGE   The Code provides that a debtor's discharge may be revoked. Upon petition by the trustee or a creditor, the bankruptcy court may, within one year, revoke the discharge decree if it is discovered that the debtor was fraudulent or dishonest during the bankruptcy proceedings. The revocation renders the discharge void, allowing creditors not satisfied by the distribution of the debtor's estate to proceed with their claims against the debtor.

REAFFIRMATION OF DEBT   A debtor may voluntarily agree to pay off a debt—for example, a debt owed to a family member, close friend, or some other party—notwithstanding the fact that the debt could be discharged in bankruptcy. An agreement to pay a debt dischargeable in bankruptcy is referred to as a *reaffirmation agreement.* To be enforceable, reaffirmation agreements must be made before a debtor is granted a discharge, and they must be filed with the court. If the debtor is represented by an attorney, court approval is not required if the attorney files a declaration or affidavit stating that (1) the debtor has been fully informed of the consequences of the agreement (and a default under the agreement), (2) the agreement is made voluntarily, and (3) the agreement does not impose undue hardship on the debtor or the debtor's family. If the debtor is not represented by an attorney, court approval is required, and the agreement will be approved only if the court finds that the agreement will result in no undue hardship to the debtor and is in the best interest of the debtor.

The agreement must contain a clear and conspicuous statement advising the debtor that reaffirmation is not required. The debtor can rescind, or cancel, the agreement at any time prior to discharge or within sixty days of filing the agreement, whichever is later. This rescission period must be stated *clearly* and *conspicuously* in the reaffirmation agreement.

▌Chapter 11—Reorganization

WORKOUT
An out-of-court agreement between a debtor and his or her creditors in which the parties work out a payment plan or schedule under which the debtor's debts can be discharged.

The type of bankruptcy proceeding used most commonly by a corporate debtor is the Chapter 11 *reorganization*. In a reorganization, the creditors and the debtor formulate a plan under which the debtor pays a portion of his or her debts and is discharged of the remainder. The debtor is allowed to continue in business. Although this type of bankruptcy is commonly a corporate reorganization, any debtor (except a stockbroker or a commodities broker) who is eligible for Chapter 7 relief is eligible for relief under Chapter 11.[11] Railroads are also eligible.

The same principles that govern the filing of a liquidation petition apply to reorganization proceedings. The case may be brought either voluntarily or involuntarily. The same principles govern the entry of the order for relief. The automatic-stay provision is also applicable in reorganizations.

In some instances, creditors may prefer private, negotiated debt-adjustment agreements, also known as **workouts,** to bankruptcy proceedings. Often these out-of-court workouts are much more flexible and thus more conducive to a speedy settlement. Speed is critical, because delay is one of the most costly elements in any bankruptcy proceeding. Another advantage of workouts is that they avoid the various administrative costs of bankruptcy proceedings.

A bankruptcy court, after notice and a hearing, may dismiss or suspend all proceedings in a case at any time if dismissal or suspension would better serve the interests of the creditors. The Code also allows a court, after notice and a hearing, to dismiss a case under reorganization "for cause." *Cause* includes the absence of a reasonable likelihood of rehabilitation, the inability to effect a plan, and an unreasonable delay by the debtor that is prejudicial to (may harm the interests of) creditors.[12] In the following widely publicized case, creditors of Johns-Manville Corporation sought to dismiss a voluntary Chapter 11 petition filed by Manville.

---

11.   *Toibb v. Radloff,* 501 U.S. 157, 111 S.Ct. 2197, 115 L.Ed.2d 145 (1991).
12.   See 11 U.S.C. Section 1112(b).

CASE 22.6

IN RE JOHNS-MANVILLE CORP.
United States Bankruptcy Court, Southern District of New York, 1984.
36 Bankr. 727.

HISTORICAL AND ENVIRONMENTAL SETTING   *In the late 1970s and early 1980s, the number of claims for injuries caused by asbestos in the products manufactured and sold by Johns-Manville Corporation was mounting. Studies projected runaway asbestos-related health costs for the company within the foreseeable future. The accounting firm of Price Waterhouse advised the company that at least $1.9 billion would be needed as a reserve fund to meet those costs. This figure took into account only the moderate to severe asbestos disease cases, assumed that Manville's insurance companies would pay many of*

the costs, and did not include punitive damages. As the number of claims accelerated, Manville's insurance companies disavowed their liability. Asbestos-related property damage claims began to present another source of liability. Schools sought damages for their unknowing use of asbestos products in ceilings, walls, piping, ductwork, and boilers in school buildings. Manville estimated that it could need another $500 million to $1.4 billion to cover this liability. In addition, Manville had debts in the amount of approximately $700 million not related to the asbestos problem.

FACTS   On August 26, 1982, Johns-Manville Corporation a highly successful industrial enterprise, filed for protection under Chapter 11 of the Bankruptcy Code. This filing came as a surprise to some of Manville's creditors, as well as to some of the other corporations that were also being sued, along with Manville, for injuries caused by asbestos exposure. Manville asserted that the approximately sixteen thousand lawsuits pending as of the filing date and the potential lawsuits of people who had been exposed but who would not manifest the asbestos-related diseases until

Case 22.6—Continued

sometime in the future necessitated its filing. Manville's creditors, on motion to the bankruptcy court, contended that Manville did not file in good faith, that Manville was not insolvent, and that therefore the voluntary Chapter 11 petition should be dismissed.

ISSUE Was Manville eligible to file a voluntary petition for Chapter 11 reorganization under the Bankruptcy Code?

DECISION Yes. The court held that bankruptcy proceedings were appropriate in this situation and denied the motions to dismiss Manville's petition.

REASON With respect to voluntary petitions, the court noted that "it is no longer necessary for a petitioner for reorganization to allege or show insolvency or inability to pay debts as they mature." Manville clearly met all of the threshold eligibility requirements for filing a voluntary petition. Furthermore, in determining whether to dismiss a Chapter 11 case, a court is not necessarily required to

consider the debtor's good faith in filing, because "good faith" is not specifically necessary for filing under the Code. Rather, good faith emerges as a requirement for confirmation of the plan; that is, good faith is required to come out of Chapter 11, but not to get into it. A "principal goal" of the Code is to provide open and easy access to the bankruptcy process. Here, liquidation would be inefficient and wasteful; it would destroy the utility of Manville's assets, as well as jobs. More important, liquidation would preclude compensation of future asbestos claimants. Ultimately, the court concluded that Manville needed the protection of the Bankruptcy Code and should not be required to wait until its economic picture deteriorated beyond salvation to file for reorganization.

FOR CRITICAL ANALYSIS—Ethical Consideration
In view of the fact that Manville was a solvent corporation, did it deserve the "fresh start" it achieved through Chapter 11 proceedings?

Debtor in Possession

Upon entry of the order for relief, the debtor generally continues to operate his or her business as a **debtor in possession (DIP)**. The court, however, may appoint a trustee (often referred to as a *receiver*) to operate the debtor's business if gross mismanagement of the business is shown or if appointing a trustee is in the best interests of the estate.

The DIP's role is similar to that of a trustee in a liquidation. The DIP is entitled to avoid preferential payments made to creditors and fraudulent transfers of assets that occurred prior to the filing of the Chapter 11 petition. The DIP has the power to decide whether to cancel or assume obligations under executory contracts (contracts that have not yet been performed) that were made prior to the petition.

DEBTOR IN POSSESSION (DIP)
In Chapter 11 bankruptcy proceedings, a debtor who is allowed to continue in possession of the estate in property (the business) and to continue business operations.

Chapter 11 reorganizations have become the target of substantial criticism. One of the arguments against Chapter 11 is that it allows the very managers who "bankrupted" a firm to continue to manage the firm as debtors in possession while the firm is in Chapter 11 proceedings. According to some critics, the main beneficiaries of Chapter 11 corporate reorganizations are not the shareholder-owners of the corporations but attorneys and current management. Basically, these critics argue that reorganizations do not preserve companies' assets, because large firms must pay millions of dollars for attorneys and accountants during the reorganization process, which can take years to complete.

Because of the expenses associated with reorganization proceedings, the chance that any one company will survive Chapter 11 proceedings is less than 7 percent. Only the very largest corporations seem to have a real chance of emerging from Chapter 11 proceedings as viable business entities.

For Critical Analysis: *Should Chapter 11 be scrapped, as some critics recommend? Should it be amended to set time limits on reorganization proceedings?*

Creditors' Committees

As soon as practicable after the entry of the order for relief, a creditors' committee of unsecured creditors is appointed. The committee may consult with the trustee or the DIP concerning the administration of the case or the formulation of the reorganization plan. Additional creditors' committees may be appointed to represent special interest creditors. Orders affecting the estate generally will not be entered without either the consent of the committee or a hearing in which the judge hears the position of the committee.

Businesses with debts of less than $2 million that do not own or manage real estate can avoid creditors' committees. In these cases, orders can be entered without a committee's consent.

The Reorganization Plan

A reorganization plan to rehabilitate the debtor is a plan to conserve and administer the debtor's assets in the hope of an eventual return to successful operation and solvency. The plan must be fair and equitable and must do the following:

1. Designate classes of claims and interests.
2. Specify the treatment to be afforded the classes. (The plan must provide the same treatment for each claim in a particular class.)
3. Provide an adequate means for execution.

FILING THE PLAN   Only the debtor may file a plan within the first 120 days after the date of the order for relief. If the debtor does not meet the 120-day deadline, however, or if the debtor fails to obtain the required creditor consent (see below) within 180 days, any party may propose a plan. The plan need not provide for full repayment to unsecured creditors. Instead, unsecured creditors receive a percentage of each dollar owed to them by the debtor. If a small-business debtor chooses to avoid creditors' committees, the time for the debtor's filing is shortened to 100 days, and any other party's plan must be filed within 160 days.

ACCEPTANCE AND CONFIRMATION OF THE PLAN   Once the plan has been developed, it is submitted to each class of creditors for acceptance. Each class must accept the plan unless the class is not adversely affected by the plan. A class has accepted the plan when a majority of the creditors, representing two-thirds of the amount of the total claim, vote to approve it. Even when all classes of claims accept the plan, the court may refuse to confirm it if it is not "in the best interests of the creditors." A spouse or child of the debtor can block the plan if it does not provide for payment of his or her claims in cash.

Even if only one class of claims has accepted the plan, the court may still confirm the plan under the Code's so-called **cram-down provision**. In other words, the court may confirm the plan over the objections of a class of creditors. Before the court can exercise this right of cram-down confirmation, it must be demonstrated that the plan "does not discriminate unfairly" against any creditors and that the plan is "fair and equitable."

The plan is binding on confirmation. The debtor is given a reorganization discharge from all claims not protected under the plan. This discharge does not apply to any claims that would be denied discharge under liquidation.

CRAM-DOWN PROVISION
A provision of the Bankruptcy Code that allows a court to confirm a debtor's Chapter 11 reorganization plan even though only one class of creditors has accepted it. To exercise the court's right under this provision, the court must demonstrate that the plan does not discriminate unfairly against any creditors and is fair and equitable.

▌ Chapter 13—Repayment Plan

Chapter 13 of the Bankruptcy Code provides for the "Adjustment of Debts of an Individual with Regular Income." Individuals (not partnerships or corporations) with regular income who owe fixed unsecured debts of less than $250,000 or fixed secured debts of less than $750,000 may take advantage of bankruptcy repayment plans. This includes salaried employees; individual proprietors; and individuals who live on welfare, Social Security, fixed pensions, or investment income. Many small-business debtors have a choice of filing under either Chapter 11 or Chapter 13. There are several advantages to repayment plans. One advantage is that they are less expensive and less complicated than reorganization proceedings or liquidation proceedings.

A Chapter 13 case can be initiated only by the filing of a voluntary petition by the debtor. Certain liquidation and reorganization cases may be converted to Chapter 13 cases with the consent of the debtor. A Chapter 13 case may be converted to a Chapter 7 case at the request of either the debtor or, under certain circumstances, a creditor. A Chapter 13 case also may be converted to a Chapter 11 case after a hearing. Upon the filing of a petition under Chapter 13, a trustee must be appointed. The automatic stay previously discussed also takes effect. Although the stay applies to all or part of a consumer debt, it does not apply to any business debt incurred by the debtor.

> **REMEMBER** A secured debt is a debt in which a security interest in personal property or fixtures assures payment of the obligation.

The Repayment Plan

Shortly after the petition is filed, the debtor must file a repayment plan. This plan may provide either for payment of all obligations in full or for payment of a lesser amount. A plan of rehabilitation by repayment provides for the turnover to the trustee of such future earnings or income of the debtor as is necessary for execution of the plan. The time for payment under the plan may not exceed three years unless the court approves an extension. The term, with extension, may not exceed five years.

The Code requires the debtor to make "timely" payments, and the trustee is required to ensure that the debtor commences these payments. The debtor must begin making payments under the proposed plan within thirty days after the plan has been filed with the court. If the plan has not been confirmed, the trustee is instructed to retain the payments until the plan is confirmed and then distribute them accordingly. If the plan is denied, the trustee will return the payments to the debtor less any costs. Failure of the debtor to make timely payments or to begin payments within the thirty-day period will allow the court to convert the case to a liquidation bankruptcy or to dismiss the petition.

CONFIRMATION OF THE PLAN   After the plan is filed, the court holds a confirmation hearing, at which interested parties may object to the plan. The court will confirm a plan with respect to each claim of a secured creditor under any of the following circumstances:

1.   If the secured creditors have accepted the plan.
2.   If the plan provides that creditors retain their claims against the debtor's property and if the value of the property to be distributed to the creditors under the plan is not less than the secured portion of their claims.
3.   If the debtor surrenders the property securing the claim to the creditors.

OBJECTION TO THE PLAN   Unsecured creditors do not have a vote to confirm a repayment plan, but they can object to it. The court can approve a plan over the objection of the trustee or any unsecured creditor only in either of the following situations:

1.   When the value of the property to be distributed under the plan is at least equal to the amount of the claims.
2.   When all the debtor's projected disposable income to be received during the three-year plan period will be applied to making payments. Disposable income is all

income received *less* amounts needed to support the debtor and dependents and/or amounts needed to meet ordinary expenses to continue the operation of a business.

MODIFICATION OF THE PLAN   Prior to the completion of payments, the plan may be modified at the request of the debtor, the trustee, or an unsecured creditor. If any interested party has an objection to the modification, the court must hold a hearing to determine approval or disapproval of the modified plan.

Discharge

BE CAREFUL Courts, trustees, and creditors carefully monitor Chapter 13 debtors. If payments are not made, a court can require a debtor to explain why and may allow a creditor to take back his or her property.

After the completion of all payments, the court grants a discharge of all debts provided for by the repayment plan. Except for allowed claims not provided for by the plan, certain long-term debts provided for by the plan, and claims for alimony and child support, all other debts are dischargeable. A discharge of debts under a Chapter 13 repayment plan is sometimes referred to as a "superdischarge." One of the reasons for this is that the law allows a Chapter 13 discharge to include fraudulently incurred debt and claims resulting from malicious or willful injury. Therefore, a discharge under Chapter 13 may be much more beneficial to some debtors than a liquidation discharge under Chapter 7 might be.

Even if the debtor does not complete the plan, a hardship discharge may be granted if failure to complete the plan was due to circumstances beyond the debtor's control and if the value of the property distributed under the plan was greater than creditors would have received in a liquidation proceeding. A discharge can be revoked within one year if it was obtained by fraud.

▌Chapter 12—Family-Farmer Plan

The Bankruptcy Code defines a *family farmer* as one whose gross income is at least 50 percent farm dependent and whose debts are at least 80 percent farm related. The total debt must not exceed $1.5 million. A partnership or closely held corporation that is at least 50 percent owned by the farm family can also take advantage of Chapter 12.

A farmer examines his crop in a soybean field. If the farmer is forced to petition for bankruptcy relief under Chapter 12, what happens to the crop?

The procedure for filing a family-farmer bankruptcy plan is very similar to the procedure for filing a repayment plan under Chapter 13. The farmer-debtor must file a plan not later than ninety days after the order for relief. The filing of the petition acts as an automatic stay against creditors' actions against the estate.

The content of a family-farmer plan is basically the same as that of a Chapter 13 repayment plan. The plan can be modified by the farmer-debtor but, except for cause, must be confirmed or denied within forty-five days of the filing of the plan.

Court confirmation of the plan is the same as for a repayment plan. In summary, the plan must provide for payment of secured debts at the value of the collateral. If the secured debt exceeds the value of the collateral, the remaining debt is unsecured. For unsecured debtors, the plan must be confirmed if either the value of the property to be distributed under the plan equals the amount of the claim or the plan provides that all of the farmer-debtor's disposable income to be received in a three-year period (or longer, by court approval) will be applied to making payments. Completion of payments under the plan discharges all debts provided for by the plan.

A farmer who has already filed a reorganization or repayment plan may convert the plan to a family-farmer plan. The farmer-debtor may also convert a family-farmer plan to a liquidation plan.

Application

Law and the Small-Business Owner—Preparing for Bankruptcy*

Chapter 11 of the Bankruptcy Code expresses the broad public policy of encouraging commerce. To this end, Chapter 11 allows financially troubled business firms to petition for reorganization in bankruptcy even while they are still solvent, so that the firms' business can continue. Small businesses, however, do not fare very well under Chapter 11. Although many megacorporations entering Chapter 11 emerge as functioning entities, very few smaller companies survive the process. The reason is that Chapter 11 proceedings are prolonged and extremely costly, and whether a firm survives is largely a matter of size. The greater the firm's assets, the greater the likelihood it will emerge from Chapter 11 intact.

If you ever are a small-business owner contemplating Chapter 11 reorganization, you can improve your chances of being among the survivors by planning ahead. You should take action before, not after, entering bankruptcy proceedings to ensure the greatest possibility of success. Your first step, of course, should be to do everything possible to avoid having to resort to Chapter 11. Discuss your financial troubles openly and cooperatively with creditors to see if you can agree on a workout or some other arrangement.

If it appears that you have no choice but to file for Chapter 11 protection, try to interest a lender in loaning you funds to see you through the bankruptcy. If your business is a small corporation, you might try to negotiate a favorable deal with a major investor. For example, you could offer to transfer stock ownership to the investor in return for a loan to pay the costs of the bankruptcy proceedings and an option to repurchase the stock when the firm becomes profitable again.

Most important, you should form a Chapter 11 plan prior to entering bankruptcy proceedings. Consult with creditors in advance to see what kind of a plan would be acceptable to them, and prepare your plan accordingly. Having an acceptable plan prepared before you file will help expedite the proceedings and thus save substantially on costs.

 Checklist for the Small-Business Owner

1. Try to negotiate workouts with creditors to avoid costly Chapter 11 proceedings.
2. If your business is a small corporation, see if a major investor will loan you funds to help you pay bankruptcy costs in return for stock ownership.
3. Consult with creditors in advance, and have an acceptable Chapter 11 plan prepared before filing in order to expedite bankruptcy proceedings and save on costs.

*This *Application* is not meant to substitute for the services of an attorney who is licensed to practice law in your state.

▌Key Terms

▌Chapter Summary: Creditors' Rights and Bankruptcy

LAWS ASSISTING CREDITORS	
Liens *(See pages 559–562.)*	1. *Mechanic's lien*—A nonpossessory, filed lien on an owner's real estate for labor, services, or materials furnished to or made on the realty. 2. *Artisan's lien*—A possessory lien on an owner's personal property for labor performed or value added. 3. *Innkeeper's lien*—A possessory lien on a hotel guest's baggage for hotel charges that remain unpaid. 4. *Judicial Liens*— a. *Attachment*—A court-ordered seizure of property prior to a court's final determination of the creditor's rights to the property. Attachment is available only on the creditor's posting of a bond and in strict compliance with the applicable state statutes. b. *Writ of execution*—A court order directing the sheriff to seize (levy) and sell a debtor's nonexempt real or personal property to satisfy a court's judgment in the creditor's favor.
Garnishment *(See pages 562–563.)*	A collection remedy that allows the creditor to attach a debtor's money (such as wages owed) and property that are held by a third person.
Creditors' Composition Agreement *(See page 563.)*	A contract between a debtor and his or her creditors by which the debtor's debts are discharged by payment of a sum less than the sum that is actually owed.
Mortgage Foreclosure *(See page 563.)*	On the debtor's default, the entire mortgage debt is due and payable, allowing the creditor to foreclose on the realty by selling it to satisfy the debt.
Suretyship or Guaranty *(See pages 563–565.)*	Under contract, a third person agrees to be primarily or secondarily liable for the debt owed by the principal debtor. A creditor can turn to this third person for satisfaction of the debt.
LAWS ASSISTING DEBTORS	
Exemptions *(See page 566.)*	Numerous laws, including consumer protection statutes, assist debtors. Additionally, state laws exempt certain types of real and personal property from levy of execution or attachment. 1. *Real property*—Each state permits a debtor to retain the family home, either in its entirety or up to a specified dollar amount, free from the claims of unsecured creditors or trustees in bankruptcy (homestead exemption). 2. *Personal property*—Personal property that is most often exempt from satisfaction of judgment debts includes the following: a. Household furniture up to a specified dollar amount. b. Clothing and certain personal possessions.

▌Chapter Summary: Creditors' Rights and Bankruptcy—Continued

Exemptions—Continued	c. Transportation vehicles up to a specified dollar amount. d. Certain classified animals, such as livestock and pets. e. Equipment used in a business or trade up to a specified dollar amount.		
BANKRUPTCY—A COMPARISON OF CHAPTERS 7, 11, 12, AND 13 *(See pages 566–585.)*			
ISSUE	**CHAPTER 7**	**CHAPTER 11**	**CHAPTERS 12 AND 13**
Purpose	Liquidation.	Reorganization.	Adjustment.
Who Can Petition	Debtor (voluntary) or creditors (involuntary).	Debtor (voluntary) or creditors (involuntary).	Debtor (voluntary) only.
Who Can Be a Debtor	Any "person" (including partnerships and corporations) except railroads, insurance companies, banks, savings and loan institutions, investment companies licensed by the Small Business Administration, and credit unions. Farmers and charitable institutions cannot be involuntarily petitioned.	Any debtor eligible for Chapter 7 relief; railroads are also eligible.	*Chapter 12*—Any family farmer (one whose gross income is at least 50 percent farm dependent and whose debts are at least 80 percent farm related) or any partnership or closely held corporation at least 50 percent owned by a farm family, when total debt does not exceed $1.5 million. *Chapter 13*—Any individual (not partnerships or corporations) with regular income who owes fixed unsecured debts of less than $250,000 or fixed secured debts of less than $750,000.
Procedure Leading to Discharge	Nonexempt property is sold with proceeds to be distributed (in order) to priority groups. Dischargeable debts are terminated.	Plan is submitted; if it is approved and followed, debts are discharged.	Plan is submitted and must be approved if the debtor turns over disposable income for a three-year period; if the plan is followed, debts are discharged.
Advantages	Upon liquidation and distribution, most debts are discharged, and the debtor has an opportunity for a fresh	Debtor continues in business. Creditors can either accept the plan, or it can be "crammed down" on them. The plan allows for the reorganization and liquidation of debts over the plan period.	Debtor continues in business or possession of assets. If the plan is approved, most debts are discharged after a three-year period.

▌For Review

1. What is a prejudgment attachment? What is a writ of execution? How does a creditor use these remedies?
2. What is garnishment? When might a creditor undertake a garnishment proceeding?
3. In a bankruptcy proceeding, what constitutes the debtor's estate in property? What property is exempt from the estate under federal bankruptcy law?

4. What is the difference between an exception to discharge and an objection to discharge?
5. In a Chapter 11 reorganization, what is the role of the debtor in possession?

■ Questions and Case Problems

22–1. Creditors' Remedies. In what circumstances would a creditor resort to each of the following remedies when trying to collect on a debt?

    (a) Mechanic's lien.

    (b) Artisan's lien.

    (c) Innkeeper's lien.

    (d) Writ of attachment.

    (e) Writ of execution.

    (f) Garnishment.

22–2. Rights of the Surety. Meredith, a farmer, borrowed $5,000 from Farmer's Bank and gave the bank $4,000 in bearer bonds to hold as collateral for the loan. Meredith's neighbor, Peterson, who had known Meredith for years, signed as a surety on the note. Because of a drought, Meredith's harvest that year was only a fraction of what it normally was, and he was forced to default on his payments to Farmer's Bank. The bank did not immediately sell the bonds but instead requested $5,000 from Peterson. Peterson paid the $5,000 and then demanded that the bank give him the $4,000 in securities. Can Peterson enforce this demand? Explain.

22–3. Rights of the Guarantor. Sabrina is a student at Sunnyside University. In need of funds to pay for tuition and books, she attempts to secure a short-term loan from University Bank. The bank agrees to make a loan if Sabrina will have someone financially responsible guarantee the loan payments. Abigail, a well-known businessperson and a friend of Sabrina's family, calls the bank and agrees to pay the loan if Sabrina cannot. Because of Abigail's reputation, the bank makes the loan. Sabrina makes several payments on the loan, but because of illness she is not able to work for one month. She requests that University Bank extend the loan for three months. The bank agrees and raises the interest rate for the extended period. Abigail has not been notified of the extension (and therefore has not consented to it). One month later, Sabrina drops out of school. All attempts to collect from Sabrina have failed. University Bank wants to hold Abigail liable. Will the bank succeed? Explain.

22–4. Distribution of Property. Runyan voluntarily petitions for bankruptcy. He has three major claims against his estate. One is by Calvin, a friend who holds Runyan's negotiable promissory note for $2,500; one is by Kohak, an employee who is owed three months' back wages of $4,500; and one is by the First Bank of Sunny Acres on an unsecured loan of $5,000. In addition, Martinez, an accountant retained by the trustee, is owed $500, and property taxes of $1,000 are owed to Micanopa County. Runyan's nonexempt property has been liquidated, with the proceeds totaling $5,000. Discuss fully what amount each party will receive, and why.

22–5. Creditors' Remedies. Orkin owns a relatively old home valued at $45,000. He notices that the bathtubs and fixtures in both bathrooms are leaking and need to be replaced. He contracts with Pike to replace the bathtubs and fixtures. Pike replaces them and submits her bill of $4,000 to Orkin. Because of financial difficulties, Orkin does not pay the bill. Orkin's only asset is his home, which under state law is exempt up to $40,000 as a homestead. Discuss fully Pike's remedies in this situation.

22–6. Writ of Attachment. Topjian Plumbing and Heating, Inc., the plaintiff, sought prejudgment writs of attachment to satisfy an anticipated judgment in a contract action against Bruce Topjian, Inc., the defendant. The plaintiff did not petition the court for permission to effect the attachments but merely completed the forms, served them on the defendant and on the Fencers (the owners of a parcel of land that had previously belonged to the defendant), and recorded them at the registry of deeds. On what grounds might the court invalidate the attachments? [*Topjian Plumbing and Heating, Inc. v. Bruce Topjian, Inc.*, 129 N.H. 481, 529 A.2d 391 (1987)]

22–7. Rights of the Guarantor. Hallmark Cards, Inc., sued Edward Peevy, who had guaranteed an obligation owed to Hallmark by Garry Peevy. At the time of Edward Peevy's guaranty, Hallmark had in its possession property pledged as security by Garry Peevy. Before the suit was filed, Hallmark sold the pledged property without giving notice to Edward Peevy. Because the property sold did not cover the loan balance, Hallmark sued for the balance, seeking a deficiency judgment. Edward Peevy contended that because Hallmark had sold the property pledged by Garry Peevy as security for the obligation without notifying him (Edward Peevy), Hallmark was not entitled to a deficiency judgment against him. Hallmark contended that Edward Peevy was not entitled to notice of the sale of the collateral and was not required to give consent. Which party will prevail in court? Discuss. [*Hallmark Cards, Inc. v. Peevy*, 293 Ark. 594, 739 S.W.2d 691 (1987)]

22–8. Preferences. Fred Currey purchased cattle from Itano Farms, Inc. As payment for the cattle, Currey gave Itano Farms worthless checks in the amount of $50,250. Currey was later convicted of passing bad checks, and the state criminal court ordered him to pay Itano Farms restitution in the amount of $50,250. About four months after this court order, Currey and his wife filed for Chapter 7 bankruptcy protection. During the ninety days prior to the filing of the petition, Currey had made three restitution payments to Itano, totaling $14,821. The Curreys sought to recover these payments as preferences. What should the court decide? Explain. [*In re Currey*, 144 Bankr. 490 (D.Ida. 1992)]

22–9. Dismissal of Chapter 7 Case. Ellis and Bonnie Jarrell filed a Chapter 7 petition. The petition was not filed due to a calamity, sudden illness, disability, or unemployment—both Jarrells were employed. Their petition was full of inaccuracies that understated their income and overstated their obligations. For example, they declared as an expense a monthly contribution to an investment plan. The truth was that they had monthly income of $3,197.45 and expenses of $2,159.44. They were attempting to discharge a total of $15,391.64 in unsecured debts. Most of these were credit-card debts, at least half of which had been taken as cash advances. Should the court dismiss the petition? If so, why? Discuss. [*In re Jarrell*, 189 Bankr. 374 (M.D.N.C. 1995)]

A QUESTION OF ETHICS
AND SOCIAL RESPONSIBILITY

22–10. *In September 1986, Edward and Debora Davenport pleaded guilty in a Pennsylvania court to welfare* fraud and were sentenced to probation for one year. As a condition of their probation, the Davenports were ordered to make monthly restitution payments to the county probation department, which would forward the payments to the Pennsylvania Department of Public Welfare, the victim of the Davenports' fraud. In May 1987, the Davenports filed a petition for Chapter 13 relief and listed the restitution payments among their debts. The bankruptcy court held that the restitution obligation was a dischargeable debt. Ultimately, the United States Supreme Court reviewed the case. The Court noted that under the Bankruptcy Code, a debt is defined as a liability on a claim, and a claim is defined as a right to payment. Because the restitution obligations clearly constituted a right to payment, the Court held that the obligations were dischargeable in bankruptcy. [Pennsylvania Department of Public Welfare v. Davenport, 495 U.S. 552, 110 S.Ct. 2126, 109 L.Ed.2d 588 (1990)]

1. Critics of this decision contend that the Court adhered to the letter, but not the spirit, of bankruptcy law in arriving at its conclusion. In what way, if any, did the Court not abide by the "spirit" of bankruptcy law?

2. Do you think that Chapter 13 plans, which allow nearly all types of debts to be discharged, tip the scales of justice too far in favor of debtors?

CASE BRIEFING ASSIGNMENT

22–11. *Examine Case A.6 [Hawley v. Cement Industries, Inc., 51 F.3d 246 (11th Cir. 1995)] in Appendix A. The case has been excerpted there in great detail.*

Review and then brief the case, making sure that you include answers to the following questions in your brief.

1. How did the case originate, and who are the parties?
2. What was the central issue to be decided?
3. What law governs the issue?
4. How did the lower court decide the case?
5. What was the appellate court's decision on the matter?

FOR CRITICAL ANALYSIS

22–12. *Since the reform of bankruptcy law in 1978, the number of annual bankruptcy filings has increased significantly. Just in the last decade, for example, the number of filings has more than tripled. By the mid-1990s, more than 900,000 bankruptcy petitions were being filed each year. Has the Bankruptcy Code made it too easy for debtors to avoid their obligations by filing for bankruptcy? What are the implications of the increased number of bankruptcy filings for future potential debtors who seek to obtain credit?*

▌ Unit Six—Cumulative Hypothetical Problem

22–13. *Dmitri Peter ("Pete") Darin is president of Southside Equipment Corp., a small electronics store. Darin owns 80 percent of the corporation's shares, and Oliver Castle owns the remaining 20 percent. Business is booming, and Darin and Castle decide to expand their business. To do so, they borrow $50,000 from First Bank and Trust. As collateral for the loan, Southside agrees to give the bank a security interest in all of the firm's current and after-acquired inventory. The bank properly perfects its interest in Southside's collateral by filing a financing statement with the appropriate government office.*

1. Southside later obtains a loan from Central Bank, using the same inventory as collateral. Central Bank properly perfects its security interest by filing a financing statement. In a priority contest, which bank will have superior rights to the inventory? If First Bank, on its financial statement, had identified the debtor only as "Pete Darin," which creditor would have superior rights to the collateral?

2. Southside is experiencing financial setbacks and defaults on its payments to First Bank. Assuming that First Bank's security interest was properly perfected and that no other creditor has rights in the collateral, what basic remedies are available to First Bank?

3. Suppose that Darin has done business with First Bank for years, and First Bank knows that Darin is a good credit risk. The bank also knows that Darin has substan-

tial personal assets. Instead of taking a security interest in Southside's inventory to secure the $50,000 loan, First Bank asks Darin to promise that if Southside defaults, Darin will personally pay the loan. Is Darin a surety or a guarantor in this situation? Is Darin's liability on the loan primary or secondary? Must Darin's promise be in writing to be enforceable? Explain.

4. Darin is experiencing personal financial problems. The amount of income he receives from the corporation is barely sufficient to cover his living expenses, the payments due on his mortgage, various credit-card debts, and some loans that he took out to pay for his son's college tuition. He would like to file for Chapter 7 liquidation to just be rid of the debts entirely, but he knows that he could probably pay them off over a four-year period if he really scrimped and used every cent available to pay his creditors. Darin decides to file for bankruptcy relief under Chapter 7. Are all of Darin's debts dischargeable under Chapter 7, including the debts incurred for his son's education? Given the fact that Darin could foreseeably pay off his debts over a four-year period, will the court allow Darin to obtain relief under Chapter 7? Why or why not?

▌Accessing the Internet: Business Law and Legal Environment

You can get answers to the most frequently asked questions about personal bankruptcy at

http://www.bhs.com/art/bkfq.html

If you want to read discussions about bankruptcy law and related subjects, you can go directly to

http://www.law.indiana.edu/ftp/archives/bankrlaw/bankrlaw.html

If you subscribe to the commercial service CompuServe, you can get legal and legislative information on money, banking, and credit by typing in

Go government

Then select

Information U.S.A.

There is an Internet bankruptcy library that offers documentation on worldwide troubled company resources. Go to

http://bankrupt.com/

Virtually all of the federal bankruptcy courts are accessible on a bulletin board service (BBS) or through PACER (see an explanation of PACER at the end of Chapter 3).

Unit Seven

Business Organizations

UNIT OUTLINE

Chapter 23

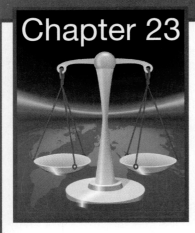

Agency Relationships in Business

AGENCY
A relationship between two parties in which one party (the agent) agrees to represent or act for the other (the principal).

"[It] is a universal principle in the law of agency, that the powers of the agent are to be exercised for the benefit of the principal only, and not of the agent or of third parties."

Joseph Story, 1779–1845
***(Associate justice of the United States
Supreme Court, 1811–1844)***

CHAPTER OBJECTIVES

After reading this chapter, you should be able to:

1. Distinguish between employees and independent contractors.
2. Outline the ways in which an agency relationship can arise.
3. Specify the duties that agents and principals owe to each other.
4. Describe the liability of the principal and the agent with respect to third parties.
5. List the ways in which an agency relationship can be terminated.

One of the most common, important, and pervasive legal relationships is that of **agency.** As discussed in Chapter 19, in an agency relationship between two parties, one of the parties, called the *agent,* agrees to represent or act for the other, called the *principal.* The principal has the right to control the agent's conduct in matters entrusted to the agent, and the agent must exercise his or her powers "for the benefit of the principal only," as Justice Joseph Story indicated in the above quotation. By using agents, a principal can conduct multiple business operations simultaneously in various locations. Thus, for example, contracts that bind the principal can be made at different places with different persons at the same time.

A familiar example of an agent is a corporate officer who serves in a representative capacity for the owners of the corporation. In this capacity, the officer has the authority to bind the principal (the corporation) to a contract. Indeed, agency law is essential to the existence and operation of a corporate entity, because only through its agents can a corporation function and enter into contracts. Because agency relationships permeate the business world, an understanding of the law of agency is crucial to understanding business law.

∎ Agency Relationships

Section 1(1) of the *Restatement (Second) of Agency*[1] defines *agency* as "the fiduciary relation which results from the manifestation of consent by one person to another that the other shall act in his behalf and subject to his control, and consent by the other so to act." The term **fiduciary** is at the heart of agency law. The term can be used both as a noun and as an adjective. When used as a noun, it refers to a person having a duty created by his or her undertaking to act primarily for another's benefit in matters connected with the undertaking. When used as an adjective, as in "fiduciary relationship," it means that the relationship involves trust and confidence.

In a principal-agent relationship, the parties have agreed that the agent will act *on behalf and instead of* the principal in negotiating and transacting business with third persons. Agency relationships commonly exist between employers and employees. A salesperson in a department store, for example, is an agent of the store's owner (the principal) and acts on the owner's behalf. Any sale of goods made by the salesperson to a customer is binding on the principal. Similarly, most representations of fact made by the salesperson with respect to the goods sold are binding on the principal. Agency relationships may sometimes also exist between employers and independent contractors who are hired to perform special tasks or services.

FIDUCIARY
As a noun, a person having a duty created by his or her undertaking to act primarily for another's benefit in matters connected with the undertaking. As an adjective, a relationship founded upon trust and confidence.

Employer-Employee Relationships

Normally, all employees who deal with third parties are deemed to be agents. All employment laws (state and federal) apply only to the employer-employee relationship. Statutes governing Social Security, withholding taxes, workers' compensation, unemployment compensation, workplace safety laws, employment discrimination, and the like (see Chapters 32 and 33) are applicable only if there is an employer-employee status. *These laws do not apply to the independent contractor.*

Because employees who deal with third parties are normally deemed agents of their employers, agency law and employment law overlap considerably. Agency relationships, though, as will become apparent, can exist outside an employee-employer relationship and thus have a broader reach than employment laws do. Additionally, bear in mind that agency law is based on the common law. In the employment realm, many common law doctrines have been displaced by statutory law and government regulations governing employment relationships.

Employer–Independent Contractor Relationships

Independent contractors are not employees, because by definition, those who hire them have no control over the details of their physical performance. Section 2 of the *Restatement (Second) of Agency* defines an **independent contractor** as follows:

> [An independent contractor is] a person who contracts with another to do something for him but who is not controlled by the other nor subject to the other's right to control with respect to his physical conduct in the performance of the undertaking. He may or may not be an agent.

INDEPENDENT CONTRACTOR
One who works for, and receives payment from, an employer but whose working conditions and methods are not controlled by the employer. An independent contractor is not an employee but may be an agent.

Building contractors and subcontractors are independent contractors, and a property owner does not control the acts of either of these professionals. Truck drivers who own their equipment and hire out on a per-job basis are independent contractors, but truck drivers who drive company trucks on a regular basis are usually employees.

---

1. The *Restatement (Second) of Agency* is an authoritative summary of the law of agency and is often referred to by jurists in their decisions and opinions.

A truck driver shakes hands with his employer. What are the factors for determining whether the driver is an employee or an independent contractor?

The relationship between a person or firm and an independent contractor may or may not involve an agency relationship. To illustrate: An owner of real estate who hires a real estate broker to negotiate a sale of his or her property not only has contracted with an independent contractor (the real estate broker) but also has established an agency relationship for the specific purpose of assisting in the sale of the property. Another example is an insurance agent, who is both an independent contractor and an agent of the insurance company for which he or she sells policies. (Note that an insurance *broker*, in contrast to an insurance agent, normally is not an agent of the insurance company but of the person obtaining insurance.)

Criteria for Determining Employee Status

A question the courts frequently face in determining liability under agency law is whether a person hired by another to do a job is an employee or an independent contractor (see, for example, this chapter's *Business Law in Action* on page 597). Because employers are normally held liable as principals for the actions made by their employee-agents within the scope of employment (as will be discussed later in this chapter), the court's decision as to employee versus independent-contractor status can be significant for the parties. In making this determination, courts often consider the following questions:

1.   How much control can the employer exercise over the details of the work? (If an employer can exercise considerable control over the details of the work, this would indicate employee status.)
2.   Is the worker engaged in an occupation or business distinct from that of the employer? (If so, this would point to independent-contractor status, not employee status.)
3.   Is the work usually done under the employer's direction or by a specialist without supervision? (If the work is usually done under the employer's direction, this would indicate employee status.)
4.   Does the employer supply the tools at the place of work? (If so, this would indicate employee status.)
5.   For how long is the person employed? (If the person is employed for a long period of time, this would indicate employee status.)
6.   What is the method of payment—by time period or at the completion of the job? (Payment by time period, such as once every two weeks or once a month, would indicate employee status.)

7. What degree of skill is required of the worker? (If a great degree of skill is required, this may indicate that the person was an independent contractor who was hired for a specialized job and not an employee.)

Often, the criteria for determining employee status are established by a statute or administrative agency regulation. The Internal Revenue Service (IRS), for example, establishes its own criteria for determining whether a worker is an independent contractor or an employee. In the past, these criteria consisted of a list of twenty factors. In 1996, however, these twenty factors were abolished in favor of rules that essentially encourage IRS examiners to look more closely at just one of the factors—the degree of control the business exercises over the worker.

The IRS tends to scrutinize closely a firm's classification of a worker as an independent contractor rather than an employee, because independent contractors can avoid certain tax liabilities by taking advantage of business organizational forms available to small businesses (see Chapter 24). Regardless of the firm's classification of a worker's status as an independent contractor, if the IRS decides that the worker should be classified as an employee, then the employer will be responsible for paying any applicable Social Security, withholding, and unemployment taxes.

Sometimes, it is advantageous to have independent-contractor status—for tax purposes, for example. At other times, employee status may confer desirable benefits on the worker. In the following case, for example, an insurance broker who lost her job wanted to take advantage of the protection against discrimination offered to employees under a state statute. Because that statute governed only employer-employee relationships, the plaintiff tried to convince the court that she was an employee rather than an independent contractor.

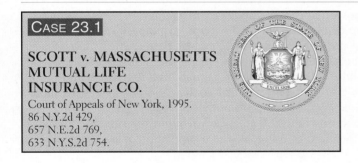

CASE 23.1

SCOTT v. MASSACHUSETTS MUTUAL LIFE INSURANCE CO.

Court of Appeals of New York, 1995.
86 N.Y.2d 429,
657 N.E.2d 769,
633 N.Y.S.2d 754.

HISTORICAL AND SOCIAL SETTING *As recently as thirty-five years ago, some types of discrimination in employment were almost routine. Positions were filled, promotions were granted, and workers were terminated on the basis of gender, age, ethnicity, marital status, or some other irrelevant characteristic. Today, U.S. workers enjoy substantial employment rights, among the most significant of which is the right of equality in employment opportunity (see Chapter 33). The right of employees to be free from discriminatory employment practices has affected employees in virtually all workplaces.*

FACTS James Blatt hired Marilyn Scott to sell insurance for the Massachusetts Mutual Life Insurance Company. Their contract stated, "Nothing in this contract shall be construed as creating the relationship of employer and employee," and that the contract was terminable at will by either party. Scott hired and trained other agents according to Massachusetts Mutual's guidelines, but she financed her own office and staff, was paid according to performance, had no taxes withheld from her checks, and could sell products of Massachusetts Mutual's competitors. When Blatt terminated their contract, Scott filed a suit in a New York state court against him and Massachusetts Mutual. Scott claimed that she had been discriminated against on the basis of her gender, age, and marital status in violation of a state law prohibiting employment discrimination. The defendants filed a motion for summary judgment on the ground that the law applied only to employees and Scott was an independent contractor. The court granted the motion, which an appellate court upheld. Scott appealed to New York's highest state court.

ISSUE Was Scott an independent contractor?

DECISION Yes. The Court of Appeals of New York dismissed Scott's claim.

REASON The court emphasized that Scott "was responsible for financing her own operating expenses and support staff, was paid by performance rather than a salary,

(Continued)

Case 23.1—Continued

did not have Federal, State or local taxes withheld from her pay, could sell competitors' products and had agreed by contract to operate as an independent contractor." The court acknowledged that one of Scott's duties was "to recruit and train agents according to defendant Massachusetts Mutual's guidelines" but pointed out that "that was true only for agents whose hiring was financed by defendant * * * . [A]t most, * * * defendants

exercised minimal control over plaintiff's own daily work product." The court concluded that Scott "operated her office with a high degree of independence not found in a traditional employer/employee relationship."

FOR CRITICAL ANALYSIS—Social Consideration
Which factor seems to have most influenced the court to rule that Scott was an independent contractor?

▌Agency Formation

Agency relationships are *consensual*; that is, they come about by voluntary consent and agreement between the parties. Generally, the agreement need not be in writing,[2] and consideration is not required.

A principal must have contractual capacity. A person who cannot legally enter into contracts directly should not be allowed to do so indirectly through an agent. Because an agent derives the authority to enter into contracts from the principal and because a contract made by an agent is legally viewed as a contract of the principal, it is immaterial whether the agent personally has the legal capacity to make that contract. Thus, a minor can be an agent but in some states cannot be a principal appointing an agent.[3] (When a minor is permitted to be a principal, however, any resulting contracts will be voidable by the minor principal but not by the adult third party.) In sum, any person can be an agent, regardless of whether he or she has the capacity to contract. Even a person who is legally incompetent can be appointed an agent.

An agency relationship can be created for any legal purpose. An agency relationship created for an illegal purpose or contrary to public policy is unenforceable. If Sharp (as principal) contracts with Blesh (as agent) to sell illegal narcotics, the agency relationship is unenforceable, because selling illegal narcotics is a felony and is contrary to public policy. It is also illegal for medical doctors and other licensed professionals to employ unlicensed agents to perform professional actions.

Generally, there are four ways in which an agency relationship can arise: by agreement of the parties, by ratification, by estoppel, and by operation of law. We look here at each of these possibilities.

Agency by Agreement

Because an agency relationship is, by definition, consensual, normally it must be based on an express or implied agreement that the agent will act for the principal and the principal agrees to have the agent so act. An agency agreement can take the form of an express written contract. For example, Renato enters into a written agreement with Troy, a real estate agent, to sell Renato's house. An agency relationship exists between

---

2.   There are two main exceptions to the statement that agency agreements need not be in writing: (1) Whenever agency authority empowers the agent to enter into a contract that the Statute of Frauds requires to be in writing, then the agent's authority from the principal must likewise be in writing (this is called the *equal dignity rule*, to be discussed later in this chapter). (2) A power of attorney, which confers authority to an agent, must be in writing.
3.   Some courts have granted exceptions to allow a minor to appoint an agent for the limited purpose of contracting for the minor's necessities of life. See *Casey v. Kastel*, 237 N.Y. 305, 142 N.E. 671 (1924).

BUSINESS LAW IN ACTION

Who Owns "Works for Hire"?

Under the Copyright Act of 1976, any copyrighted work created by an *employee* during the scope of his or her employment at the request of the employer is called a "work for hire." The employer owns and holds the copyright to such a work. What happens, though, when a firm hires independent contractors—freelance artists, writers, or computer programmers, for example—to create a work? In this situation, the freelancer/independent contractor will be the owner of the work created *unless* the parties agree in writing that the work is "for hire" *and if* the work falls into one of nine categories stipulated by the act, such as audiovisual works, translations, supplementary works, and others.

As might be expected, when disputes arise between firms and freelancers over copyright ownership, the firms often argue that the freelancers are not really independent contractors but employees. It is not always easy, though, for a court to make this determination. When the United States Supreme Court decided a case involving this issue in 1989, the Court set out thirteen factors that should be considered in determining the worker's status.[a] (The factors are similar to those for determining employee status listed on pages 594–595.) The Court did not indicate, however, the relative weight that should be attached to each factor. Therefore, it is still difficult to predict with accuracy when a freelancer will or will not be deemed an employee for copyright purposes.

Consider a case that came before the U.S. Court of Appeals for the Sixth Circuit in 1995. The case involved a

©1996 Estate of Pablo Picasso/Artists Rights Society (ARS), New York.

Picasso sculpture displayed in front of the Daley Civic Arts Center in Chicago. Who owns the copyright on commissioned art?

claim of copyright infringement brought by Hi-Tech Video Productions, Inc., against Capital Cities/ABC, Inc. (ABC). Hi-Tech, which had produced a travel video entitled *Mackinac Island: The Mackinac Video*, claimed that ABC had infringed Hi-Tech's copyright in the video when ABC featured parts of the video on ABC's television program *Good Morning America* without Hi-Tech's permission. ABC claimed that Hi-Tech had no valid copyright in the video, because the video had been created by independent contractors hired by Hi-Tech and with whom Hi-Tech had no written agreement stating that the video was a "work for hire."

The issue thus turned on whether Hi-Tech's hired workers (two videographers and a scriptwriter/narrator) were employees or independent contractors. The federal district court, applying the Supreme Court precedent mentioned above to the circumstances of this case, determined that the workers were employees; thus, Hi-Tech had a valid copyright in the video. In arriving at its conclusion, the district court gave substantial weight to the

control factor—the fact that Hi-Tech exercised substantial control over the workers' activities. On appeal, however, the federal appellate court stressed other factors, including the parties' perception of their relationship. The appellate court concluded that the workers were not employees; thus, the video was not a "work for hire," and Hi-Tech had no copyright in the work.[b]

Clearly courts can disagree on whether a worker should be classified as an employee or an independent contractor. Therefore, a firm that wishes to own the copyright in a work created by a freelancer should make sure that it has a written agreement with the freelancer specifying that the work is a "work for hire."

For Critical Analysis: *What policy is served by the law that employers do not have copyright ownership in works created by independent contractors (unless there is a written "work for hire" agreement)?*

a. *Community for Creative Non-Violence v. Reid*, 490 U.S. 730, 109 S.Ct. 2166, 104 L.Ed.2d 811 (1989).

b. *Hi-Tech Video Productions, Inc. v. Capital Cities/ABC, Inc.*, 58 F.3d 1093 (6th Cir. 1995).

Renato and Troy for the sale of the house and is detailed in a document that both parties sign.

Many express agency agreements are oral. If Renato asks Cary, a gardener, to contract with others for the care of his lawn on a regular basis, and Cary agrees, an agency relationship exists between Renato and Cary for the lawn care.

An agency agreement can also be implied by conduct. For example, a hotel expressly allows only Boris Koontz to park cars, but Boris has no employment contract there. The hotel's manager tells Boris when to work, as well as where and how to park the cars. The hotel's conduct amounts to a manifestation of its willingness to have Boris park its customers' cars, and Boris can infer from the hotel's conduct that he has authority to act as a parking valet. It can be inferred that Boris is an agent for the hotel, his purpose being to provide valet parking services for hotel guests.

Agency by Ratification

On occasion, a person who is in fact not an agent (or who is an agent acting outside the scope of his or her authority) may make a contract on behalf of another (a principal). If the principal approves or affirms that contract by word or by action, an agency relationship is created by **ratification.** Ratification is a question of intent, and intent can be expressed by either words or conduct. The basic requirements for ratification are discussed later in this chapter.

RATIFICATION
In agency law, the confirmation by one person of an act or contract performed or entered into on his or her behalf by another, who assumed, without authority, to act as his or her agent.

Agency by Estoppel

When a principal causes a third person to believe that another person is his or her agent, and the third person deals with the supposed agent, the principal is "estopped to deny" the agency relationship. In such a situation, the principal's actions create the *appearance* of an agency that does not in fact exist.

Suppose that Andrew accompanies Charles, a seed sales representative, to call on a customer, Steve, the proprietor of the General Seed Store. Andrew has done independent sales work but has never signed an employment agreement with Charles at this time. Charles boasts to Steve that he wishes he had three more assistants "just like Andrew." Steve has reason to believe from Charles's statements that Andrew is an

A proprietor reviews the inventory in her clothing store. Under what circumstances might a clothing importer be considered to act as an agent for the store?

agent for Charles. Steve then places seed orders with Andrew. If Charles does not correct the impression that Andrew is an agent, Charles will be bound to fill the orders just as if Andrew were really Charles's agent. Charles's representation to Steve created the impression that Andrew was Charles's agent and had authority to solicit orders.

The acts or declarations of a purported *agent* in and of themselves do not create an agency by estoppel. Rather, it is the deeds or statements of the *principal* that create an agency by estoppel. Suppose that Olivia walks into Dru's Dress Boutique and claims to be a sales agent for an exclusive Paris dress designer, Pierre Dumont. Dru has never had business relations with Pierre Dumont. Based on Olivia's claim, however, Dru gives Olivia an order and prepays 15 percent of the sales price. Olivia is not an agent, and the dresses are never delivered. Dru cannot hold Pierre Dumont liable. Olivia's acts and declarations alone do not create an agency by estoppel.

In addition, to assert the creation of an agency by estoppel, the third person must prove that he or she *reasonably* believed that an agency relationship existed and that the agent had authority. Facts and circumstances must show that an ordinary, prudent person familiar with business practice and custom would have been justified in concluding that the agent had authority.

The court in the following case considered whether an agency existed by estoppel between the owner of a jewelry cart in a mall and the seller of "The Only Completely Safe, Sterile Ear Piercing Method."

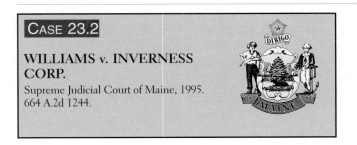

CASE 23.2

WILLIAMS v. INVERNESS CORP.
Supreme Judicial Court of Maine, 1995.
664 A.2d 1244.

COMPANY PROFILE *Inverness Corporation is the world's largest maker of body-piercing equipment. Sam Mann founded Inverness in 1975 with a design for piercing equipment that was more sterile and less threatening than the products then in use. The first year's sales totaled more than $750,000. Today, the company makes disposable ear-piercing kits, skin-care products, hair-removal waxes, electrolysis kits, and jewelry dips. Based in Fair Lawn, New Jersey, Inverness sells its products in fifty-two countries.*

FACTS The Inverness Corporation markets the Inverness Ear Piercing System, which includes a training course, an "eye-catching assortment of selling aids" such as counter displays, and release forms that tout the system as "The Only Completely Safe, Sterile Ear Piercing Method." Margaret Barrera, the owner of a jewelry cart in a mall, bought the system, took the course, and set up the displays. Seventeen-year-old Angela Williams paid Barrera to pierce Williams's ear. The ear became infected, which led to complications. Williams's mother filed a suit on Angela's behalf in a Maine state court against Inverness and Barrera, claiming in part that Inverness was liable on a theory of agency by estoppel. When the court issued a judgment in Williams's favor, Inverness appealed to Maine's highest court.

ISSUE Was there an agency by estoppel between Inverness and Barrera?

DECISION Yes. The Supreme Judicial Court of Maine affirmed the lower court's judgment.

REASON The Supreme Judicial Court of Maine pointed to evidence that Inverness held Barrera out as its agent. "Most important," said the court, "a jury reasonably could infer that Inverness knew, or should have known, that Barrera distributed Inverness's release forms * * * , that Barrera was using the Inverness Ear Piercing System, that she displayed Inverness's 'eye-catching assortment of selling aids,' and that she used Inverness's training program." The court also referred to "evidence that Angela believed that Barrera was Inverness's agent, that Angela relied on Inverness's manifestations of agency, and that Angela's reliance on Barrera's care and skill was justifiable." For example, "[t]he release form and display promote the Inverness Ear Piercing System as 'The Only Completely Safe, Sterile Ear Piercing Method.' "

FOR CRITICAL ANALYSIS—Social Consideration
What are the policy reasons for holding a firm liable on a theory of agency by estoppel?

Agency by Operation of Law

There are other situations also in which the courts will find an agency relationship in the absence of a formal agreement. This may occur in family relationships. For example, suppose one spouse purchases certain basic necessaries and charges them to the other spouse's charge account. The courts will often rule that the latter is liable for payment of the necessaries, either because of a social policy of promoting the general welfare of the spouse or because of a legal duty to supply necessaries to family members.

Agency by operation of law may also occur in emergency situations, when the agent's failure to act outside the scope of his or her authority would cause the principal substantial loss. If the agent is unable to contact the principal, the courts will often grant this emergency power. For example, a railroad engineer may contract on behalf of his or her employer for medical care for an injured motorist hit by the train.

▌Duties of Agents and Principals

"I am 'in a fiduciary position'—which is always a _____ uncomfortable position."

Frederic W. Maitland, 1850–1906
(English jurist and historian)

Once the principal-agent relationship has been created, both parties have duties that govern their conduct. As discussed previously, the principal-agent relationship is *fiduciary*—one of trust. In a fiduciary relationship, each party owes the other the duty to act with the utmost good faith.

We now examine the various duties of agents and principals. In general, for every duty of the principal, the agent has a corresponding right, and vice versa. When one party to the agency relationship violates his or her duty to the other party, the remedies available to the party not in breach arise out of contract and tort law. These remedies include monetary damages, termination of the agency relationship, injunction, and required accountings.

Agent's Duties to the Principal

Generally, the agent owes the principal five duties—performance, notification, loyalty, obedience, and accounting.

PERFORMANCE   An implied condition in every agency contract is the agent's agreement to use reasonable diligence and skill in performing the work. When an agent fails to perform his or her duties entirely, liability for breach of contract normally will result. The degree of skill or care required of an agent is usually that expected of a reasonable person under similar circumstances. Generally, this is interpreted to mean ordinary care. An agent may, however, have represented himself or herself as possessing special skills (such as those that an accountant or attorney possesses). In these situations, the agent is expected to exercise the skill or skills claimed. Failure to do so constitutes a breach of the agent's duty.

Not all agency relationships are based on contract. In some situations, an agent acts gratuitously—that is, not for money. A gratuitous agent cannot be liable for breach of contract, as there is no contract; he or she is subject only to tort liability. Once a gratuitous agent has begun to act in an agency capacity, he or she has the duty to continue to perform in that capacity in an acceptable manner and is subject to the same standards of care and duty to perform as other agents. For example, Peterson's friend, Stendhof, is a real estate broker. Stendhof gratuitously offers to sell Peterson's farm. If Stendhof never attempts to sell the farm, Peterson has no legal cause of action to force Stendhof to do so. If Stendhof does find a buyer, however, but fails to provide a sales contract within a reasonable period of time, thus causing the buyer to seek other property, then Peterson has a cause of action in tort for negligence.

NOTIFICATION There is a maxim in agency law that notice to the agent is notice to the principal. An agent is thus required to notify the principal of all matters that come to his or her attention concerning the subject matter of the agency. This is the duty of notification. The law assumes that the principal knows of any information acquired by the agent that is relevant to the agency—regardless of whether the agent actually passes on this information to the principal.

LOYALTY Loyalty is one of the most fundamental duties in a fiduciary relationship. Basically stated, the agent has the duty to act solely for the benefit of his or her principal and not in the interest of the agent or a third party. For example, an agent cannot represent two principals in the same transaction unless both know of the dual capacity and consent to it. The duty of loyalty also means that any information or knowledge acquired through the agency relationship is considered confidential. It would be a breach of loyalty to disclose such information either during the agency relationship or after its termination. Typical examples of confidential information are trade secrets and customer lists compiled by the principal.

> **BE AWARE** An agent's disclosure of confidential information could constitute the business tort of misappropriation of trade secrets.

In short, the agent's loyalty must be undivided. The agent's actions must be strictly for the benefit of the principal and must not result in any secret profit for the agent. For example, suppose that Ryder contracts with Alton, a real estate agent, to sell Ryder's property. Alton knows that he can find a buyer who will pay substantially more for the property than Ryder is asking. If Alton secretly purchased Ryder's property, however, and then sold it at a profit to another buyer, Alton would breach his duty of loyalty as Ryder's agent. Alton has a duty to act in Ryder's best interests and can only become the purchaser in this situation with Ryder's knowledge and approval.

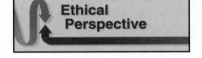

The duty of loyalty to one's employer-principal is fundamentally an ethical duty that has been written into law. The duty is rooted in the principle that a person cannot serve two masters at the same time. In an agency relationship, the agent's loyalty must be undivided. There are times, however, when the ethical duty of loyalty may come into conflict with another duty, such as one's duty to society. For example, consider the situation faced by employees of Firestone in regard to faulty tires produced by that company in the early 1980s. The employees who knew of the defective tires presumably could have divulged that information to the public (at the risk of losing their jobs, of course). Some scholars have argued that many of the greatest "evils" in the past twenty-five years have been accomplished in the name of "duty" to the principal. Duty in this context means placing the well-being of the principal above that of the public.

For Critical Analysis: *Agency law does not impose on the principal a duty of loyalty to the agent. Why is this? What would result if the law did not impose a duty of loyalty on agents?*

OBEDIENCE When an agent is acting on behalf of the principal, a duty is imposed on that agent to follow all lawful and clearly stated instructions of the principal. Any deviation from such instructions is a violation of this duty. During emergency situations, however, when the principal cannot be consulted, the agent may deviate from such instructions without violating this duty. Whenever instructions are not clearly stated, the agent can fulfill the duty of obedience by acting in good faith and in a manner reasonable under the circumstances.

ACCOUNTING Unless an agent and a principal agree otherwise, the agent has the duty to keep and make available to the principal an account of all property and money received and paid out on behalf of the principal. This includes gifts from third persons in connection with the agency. For example, a gift from a customer to a salesperson for prompt deliveries made by the salesperson's firm belongs to the firm. The agent has a duty to maintain separate accounts for the principal's funds and for the agent's personal funds, and no intermingling of these accounts is allowed. Whenever a licensed professional (such as an attorney) violates this duty to account, he or she may be subject to disciplinary proceedings carried out by the appropriate regulatory institution (such as the state bar association) in addition to being liable to the principal (the professional's client) for failure to account.

Principal's Duties to the Agent

The principal also has certain duties to the agent. These duties relate to compensation, reimbursement and indemnification, cooperation, and safe working conditions.

COMPENSATION In general, when a principal requests certain services from an agent, the agent reasonably expects payment. The principal therefore has a duty to pay the agent for services rendered. For example, when an accountant or an attorney is asked to act as an agent, an agreement to compensate the agent for such service is implied. The principal also has a duty to pay that compensation in a timely manner. Except in a gratuitous agency relationship, in which an agent does not act for money, the principal must pay the agreed-on value for an agent's services. If no amount has been expressly agreed on, then the principal owes the agent the customary compensation for such services.

REIMBURSEMENT AND INDEMNIFICATION Whenever an agent disburses sums of money to fulfill the request of the principal or to pay for necessary expenses in the course of a reasonable performance of his or her agency duties, the principal has the duty to reimburse the agent for these payments. Agents cannot recover for expenses incurred by their own misconduct or negligence, however.

Subject to the terms of the agency agreement, the principal has the duty to compensate, or *indemnify*, an agent for liabilities incurred because of authorized and lawful acts and transactions. For example, if the agent, on the principal's behalf, forms a contract with a third party, and the principal fails to perform the contract, the third party may sue the agent for damages. In this situation, the principal is obligated to compensate the agent for any costs incurred by the agent as a result of the principal's failure to perform the contract. Additionally, the principal must indemnify (pay) the agent for the value of benefits that the agent confers upon the principal. The amount of indemnification is usually specified in the agency contract. If it is not, the courts will look to the nature of the business and the type of loss to determine the amount.

COOPERATION A principal has a duty to cooperate with the agent and to assist the agent in performing his or her duties. The principal must do nothing to prevent such performance. For example, when a principal grants an agent an exclusive territory, creating an *exclusive agency*, the principal cannot compete with the agent or appoint or allow another agent to so compete in violation of the exclusive agency. If the principal did so, he or she would be exposed to liability for the agent's lost sales or profits.

SAFE WORKING CONDITIONS The common law requires the principal to provide safe working premises, equipment, and conditions for all agents and employees. The principal has a duty to inspect working conditions and to warn agents and employees about any unsafe areas. When the agency is one of employment, the employer's

REMEMBER An agent who signs a negotiable instrument on behalf of a principal may be personally liable on the instrument. Liability depends in part on whether the identity of the principal is disclosed and whether the parties intend the agent to be bound.

liability and the safety standards with which the employer must comply normally are covered by federal and state statutes and regulations (see Chapter 32).

▋ Agent's Authority

An agent's authority to act can be either *actual* (express or implied) or *apparent.* If an agent contracts outside the scope of his or her authority, the principal may still become liable by ratifying the contract.

Actual Authority

As indicated, an agent's actual authority can be express or implied. *Express authority* is authority declared in clear, direct, and definite terms. Express authority can be given orally or in writing. The **equal dignity rule** in most states requires that if the contract being executed is or must be in writing, then the agent's authority must also be in writing.[4] Failure to comply with the equal dignity rule can make a contract voidable *at the option of the principal.* The law regards the contract at that point as a mere offer. If the principal decides to accept the offer, acceptance must be in writing. Assume that Klee (the principal) orally asks Parkinson (the agent) to sell a ranch that Klee owns. Parkinson finds a buyer and signs a sales contract (a contract for an interest in realty must be in writing) on behalf of Klee to sell the ranch. The buyer cannot enforce the contract unless Klee subsequently ratifies Parkinson's agency status *in writing.* Once Parkinson's agency status is ratified, either party can enforce rights under the contract.

The equal dignity rule does not apply when an agent acts in the presence of a principal or when the agent's act of signing is merely perfunctory. Thus, if Dickens (the principal) negotiates a contract but is called out of town the day it is to be signed and orally authorizes Santini to sign the contract, the oral authorization is sufficient.

Giving an agent a **power of attorney** confers express authority.[5] The power of attorney normally is a written document and is usually notarized. (A document is notarized when a **notary public**—a public official authorized to attest to the authenticity of signatures—signs and dates the document and imprints it with his or her seal of authority.) A power of attorney can be special (permitting the agent to do specified acts only), or it can be general (permitting the agent to transact all business for the principal). An agent holding a power of attorney for a client is authorized to act *only* on the principal's behalf when exercising that power. An ordinary power of attorney terminates on the incapacity of the person giving the power.[6] Exhibit 23–1 shows a sample power of attorney.

Implied authority can be (1) conferred by custom, (2) inferred from the position the agent occupies, or (3) inferred as being reasonably necessary to carry out express authority. For example, Mueller is employed by Al's Supermarket to manage one of its

EQUAL DIGNITY RULE
In most states, a rule stating that express authority given to an agent must be in writing if the contract to be made on behalf of the principal is required to be in writing.

POWER OF ATTORNEY
A written document, which is usually notarized, authorizing another to act as one's agent; can be special (permitting the agent to do specified acts only) or general (permitting the agent to transact all business for the principal).

NOTARY PUBLIC
A public official authorized to attest to the authenticity of signatures.

---

4. An exception to the equal dignity rule exists in modern business practice. An executive officer of a corporation, when acting for the corporation in an ordinary business situation, is not required to obtain written authority from the corporation.

5. An agent who holds the power of attorney is called an *attorney-in-fact* for the principal. The holder does not have to be an attorney-at-law (and often is not).

6. A *durable* power of attorney, however, provides an agent with very broad powers to act and make decisions for the principal and specifies that it is not affected by the principal's incapacity. An elderly person, for example, might grant a durable power of attorney to provide for the handling of property and investments should he or she become incompetent.

♦ Exhibit 23–1   A Sample Power of Attorney

POWER OF ATTORNEY
GENERAL

Know All Men by These Presents: That I, _____

_____

the undersigned (jointly and severally, if more than one) hereby make, constitute and appoint _____

_____

as a true and lawful Attorney for me and in my name, place and stead and for my use and benefit:

(a)   To ask, demand, sue for, recover, collect and receive each and every sum of money, debt, account, legacy, bequest, interest, dividend, annuity and demand (which now is or hereafter shall become due, owing or payable) belonging to or claimed by me, and to use and take any lawful means for the recovery thereof by legal process or otherwise, and to execute and deliver a satisfaction or release therefore, together with the right and power to compromise or compound any claim or demand;

(b) To exercise any or all of the following powers as to real property, any interest therein and/or any building thereon: To contract for, purchase, receive and take possession thereof and or evidence of title thereto; to lease the same for any term or purpose, including leases for business, residence, and oil and/or mineral development; to sell, exchange, grant or convey the same with or without warranty; and to mortgage, transfer in trust, or otherwise encumber or hypothecate the same to secure payment of a negotiable or non-negotiable note or performance of any obligation or agreement;

(c)   To exercise any or all of the following powers as to all kinds of personal property and goods, wares and merchandise, choses in action and other property in possession or in action: To contract for, buy, sell, exchange, transfer and in any legal manner deal in and with the same; and to mortgage, transfer in trust, or otherwise encumber or hypothecate the same to secure payment of a negotiable or non-negotiable note or performance of any obligation or agreement;

(d) To borrow money and to execute and deliver negotiable or non-negotiable notes therefore with or without security; and to loan money and receive negotiable or non-negotiable notes therefore with such security as he shall deem proper;

(e) To create, amend, supplement and terminate any trust and to instruct and advise the trustee of any trust wherein I am or may be trustor or beneficiary; to represent and vote stock, exercise stock rights, accept and deal with any dividend, distribution or bonus, join in any corporate financing, reorganization, merger, liquidation, consolidation or other action and the extension, compromise, conversion, adjustment, enforcement or foreclosure, singly or in conjunction with others, of any corporate stock, bond, note, debenture or other security; to compound, compromise, adjust, settle and satisfy any obligation, secured or unsecured, owing by or to me and to give or accept any property and/or money whether or not equal to or less in value than the amount owing in payment, settlement or satisfaction thereof;

(f) To transact business of any kind or class and as my act and deed to sign, execute, acknowledge and deliver any deed, lease, assignment of lease, covenant, indenture, indemnity, agreement, mortgage, deed of trust, assignment of mortgage or of the beneficial interest under deed of trust, extension or renewal of any obligation, subordination or waiver of priority, hypothecation, bottomry, charter-party, bill of lading, bill of sale, bill, bond, note, whether negotiable or non-negotiable, receipt, evidence of debt, full or partial release or satisfaction of mortgage, judgment and other debt, request for partial or full reconveyance of deed of trust and such other instruments in writing of any kind or class as may be necessary or proper in the premises.

Giving and Granting unto my said Attorney full power and authority to do so and perform all and every act and thing whatsoever requisite, necessary or appropriate to be done in and about the premises as fully to all intents and purposes as I might or could do if personally present, hereby ratifying all that my said Attorney shall lawfully do or cause to be done by virtue of these presents. The powers and authority hereby conferred upon my said Attorney shall be applicable to all real and personal property or interests therein now owned or hereafter acquired by me and wherever situated.

My said Attorney is empowered hereby to determine in his sole discretion the time when, purpose for and manner in which any power herein conferred upon him shall be exercised, and the conditions, provisions and covenants of any instrument or document which may be executed by him pursuant hereto; and in the acquisition or disposition of real or personal property, my said Attorney shall have exclusive power to fix the terms thereof for cash, credit and/or property, and if on credit with or without security.

The undersigned, if a married woman, hereby further authorizes and empowers my said Attorney, as my duly authorized agent, to join in my behalf, in the execution of any instrument by which any community real property or any interest therein, now owned or hereafter acquired by my spouse and myself, or either of us, is sold, leased, encumbered, or conveyed.

When the context so requires, the masculine gender includes the feminine and/or neuter, and the singular number includes the plural.

WITNESS my hand this _____ day of _____ , 19 _____

_____   _____

_____   _____

State of California
    County of _____   } SS.
On _____ , before me, the undersigned, a Notary Public in and for said
State, personally appeared _____

_____
known to me to be the person _____ whose name _____ subscribed
to the within instrument and acknowledged that _____ executed the same.
                                                    (Seal) _____
Witness my hand and official seal.   Notary Public in and for said State.

stores. Al has not expressly stated that Mueller has authority to contract with third persons. In this situation, however, authority to manage a business implies authority to do what is reasonably required (as is customary or can be inferred from a manager's position) to operate the business. Reasonably required actions include creating contracts to hire employees, to buy merchandise and equipment, and to arrange for advertising the products sold in the store.

Apparent Authority

Actual authority arises from what the principal manifests *to the agent*. Apparent authority exists when the principal, by either words or actions, causes a *third party* reasonably to believe that an agent has authority to act, even though the agent has no express or implied authority. If the third party changes his or her position in reliance on the principal's representations, the principal may be *estopped* from denying that the agent had authority. Note that here, in contrast to agency formation by estoppel, the issue has to do with the apparent authority of an *agent*, not the apparent authority of a person who is in fact not an agent.

To illustrate: Suppose that a traveling salesperson, Anderson (the agent), is authorized to take customers' orders. Anderson, however, does not deliver the ordered goods and is not authorized to collect payments for the goods. A customer, Byron, pays Anderson for a solicited order. Anderson then takes the payment to the principal's accounting department, and an accountant accepts the payment and sends Byron a receipt. This procedure is thereafter followed for other orders solicited and paid for by Byron. Later, Anderson solicits an order, and Byron pays her as before. This time, however, Anderson absconds with the money. Can Byron claim that the payment to the agent was authorized and was thus, in effect, a payment to the principal?

The answer is normally yes, because the principal's *repeated* acts of accepting Byron's payment led Byron reasonably to expect that Anderson had authority to receive payments for goods solicited. Although Anderson did not have express or implied authority, the principal's conduct gave Anderson *apparent* authority to collect. In this situation, the principal would be estopped from denying that Anderson had authority to collect payments.

"The law is not a series of calculating machines where definitions and answers come tumbling out when the right levers are pushed."

**William O. Douglas,
1898–1980**
(*Associate justice of the United States Supreme Court, 1939–1975*)

Ratification

As already mentioned, ratification is the affirmation of a previously unauthorized contract. Ratification can be either express or implied. If the principal does not ratify, there is no contract binding on the principal, and the third party's agreement with the agent is viewed merely as an unaccepted offer. The third party can revoke the offer at any time prior to the principal's ratification without liability. Death or incapacity of the third party before ratification will void an unauthorized contract.

The requirements for ratification can be summarized as follows:

BE AWARE An agent who exceeds his or her authority to enter into a contract that the principal does not ratify may be liable to the third party on the ground of misrepresentation.

1.   The purported agent must have acted on behalf of a principal who subsequently ratified the action.
2.   The principal must know of all material facts involved in the transaction.
3.   The agent's act must be affirmed in its entirety by the principal.
4.   The principal must have the legal capacity to authorize the transaction at the time the agent engages in the act and at the time the principal ratifies.
5.   The principal's affirmance must occur prior to the withdrawal of the third party from the transaction.
6.   The principal must observe the same formalities when he or she approves the act purportedly done by the agent on his or her behalf as would have been required to authorize it initially.

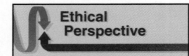

A principal may impliedly ratify an agent's unauthorized contract simply by remaining silent and not renouncing the contract. This form of implied ratification is ultimately based on the ethical concept that people should pursue their rights in a timely fashion, a concept expressed in the equitable maxim "Equity aids the vigilant, not those who rest on their rights." This is commonly called the doctrine of *laches* (discussed in Chapter 1). If a principal learns that his or her agent formed an unauthorized contract with a third party, the principal has a duty to act within a reasonable period of time—or the principal will forfeit his or her right to be free of any obligations under the contract. The principal's silence and inaction may be construed to mean that the principal intended to ratify the contract and thus be bound by it.

For Critical Analysis: *In what other situations might a party's intent be construed from the party's silence or inaction?*

▮ Liability in Agency Relationships

Frequently, the issue arises as to which party, the principal or the agent, should be held liable for the contracts formed by the agent or for the torts or crimes committed by the agent. We look here at these aspects of agency law.

Liability for Contracts

An important consideration in determining liability for a contract formed by an agent is whether the third party knew the identity of the principal at the time the contract was made. The *Restatement (Second) of Agency*, Section 4, classifies principals as disclosed, partially disclosed, or undisclosed.

DISCLOSED PRINCIPAL
A principal whose identity is known to a third party at the time the agent makes a contract with the third party.

PARTIALLY DISCLOSED PRINCIPAL
A principal whose identity is unknown by a third person, but the third person knows that the agent is or may be acting for a principal at the time the agent and the third person form a contract.

DISCLOSED OR PARTIALLY DISCLOSED PRINCIPAL   A principal whose identity is known to the third party at the time the agent makes the contract is a **disclosed principal.** For example, Joan, a purchasing agent for Maxwell Graphics, signs a contract for the purchase of office supplies. Joan signs her name on the contract as purchasing agent for Maxwell Graphics. In this situation, Maxwell Graphics is a disclosed principal.

The identity of a **partially disclosed principal** is not known by the third party, but the third party knows that the agent is or may be acting for a principal at the time the contract is made. For example, a seller of real estate may wish to keep his or her identity a secret, yet the agent with whom the seller has contracted can make it perfectly clear to the purchaser of the real estate that the agent is acting in an agency capacity for a principal.

A disclosed or partially disclosed principal is liable to a third party for a contract made by an agent who is acting within the scope of his or her authority. Ordinarily, if the principal is disclosed, the agent has no contractual liability if the principal or the third party does not perform the contract. If the agent *exceeds* the scope of his or her authority and the principal fails to ratify the contract, however, the third party cannot hold the principal liable for nonperformance. In such situations, the agent is generally liable unless the third party knew of the agent's lack of authority.

In the following case, the issue was whether an agent, through a written agreement, had incurred liability for a contract with a third party when the identity of the principal was fully disclosed to the third party.

CASE 23.3

FAIRCHILD PUBLICATIONS DIVISION OF CAPITAL CITIES MEDIA, INC. v. ROSSTON, KREMER & SLAWTER, INC.

Supreme Court, New York County, 1992.
584 N.Y.S.2d 389.

HISTORICAL AND SOCIAL SETTING *The American Association of Advertising Agencies, Inc. (AAAA), represents approximately 750 advertising agencies. These agencies place ads that account for 80 percent of all national advertising revenues. For the use of its members in placing ads with the media, the AAAA has adopted form contracts. Clauses in the contracts impose sole liability on the advertising agencies for the cost of the ads. These clauses reflect what has been the custom and practice of the print media advertising industry for more than forty years. One reason for the practice is that in accepting ads, publications customarily rely on the credit ratings of the agencies, not the advertisers, in assessing whether to extend credit. Sometimes, in a particular instance, changes are made to a contract to ensure that an advertiser is solely liable.*

FACTS Fabrican, Inc., a home furnishings manufacturer, hired an advertising agency, Rosston, Kremer & Slawter, Inc. (RKS), to advertise Fabrican's products in national magazines. In early 1989, RKS arranged for Fabrican's ads to be placed in two magazines published by Fairchild Publications Division of Capital Cities Media, Inc. Daniel Kremer of RKS signed two contracts covering the advertising arrangement, both of which clearly designated Fabrican as the "advertiser." Both contracts, which consisted of preprinted forms containing filled-in blanks and typed and handwritten additions, provided that Fairchild agreed to publish the ads subject to the terms of advertising contracts adopted by the AAAA, "which terms are hereby incorporated herein and made part of this contract." The attached AAAA form stated that the advertising agency and the publisher agreed that the publisher would hold the advertising agency solely liable for payment. Fairchild published Fabrican's ads and sent invoices to RKS totaling $85,157. Neither Fabrican (which had since filed for bankruptcy) nor RKS paid the invoices, and Fairchild Publications sued RKS in a New York state court to recover the price of the ads. RKS argued that it could not be liable, because (1) RKS was unaware of the AAAA term holding the advertising agency solely liable for payment and (2) RKS was acting as an agent for a disclosed principal.

ISSUE Can RKS be held liable for payment of the price of the ads?

DECISION Yes.

REASON The court stated that "in order to prevail, Fairchild must prove either that RKS agreed to be liable for Fabrican's debts or that custom and usage rendered RKS liable." The court concluded that based on the evidence, Fairchild "met its burden of proof on both grounds." Even though Kremer was unaware that the AAAA terms regarding agency liability were incorporated by reference into the contracts, Kremer's lack of awareness "does not affect their validity. Under these terms, RKS is liable for payment." Furthermore, the court found that when the contracts were formed, RKS had been placing ads in Fairchild publications for more than forty years and, as a regular customer of Fairchild's, knew or should have known of Fairchild's policy of holding advertising agencies solely liable for payment of the ads. "RKS acknowledged familiarity with the concept of sole agency liability, and did not dispute its liability, despite receiving regular bills, invoices, and dunning letters, until a number of months after executing the Contracts. All these factors combine to estop RKS from denying liability."

FOR CRITICAL ANALYSIS—Ethical Consideration *If RKS had never contracted with Fairchild before for the placement of ads for a third party, would the court have viewed the matter differently?*

UNDISCLOSED PRINCIPAL The identity of an **undisclosed principal** is totally unknown to the third party. Furthermore, the third party has no knowledge that the agent is acting in an agency capacity at the time the contract is made. For example, Albright agrees to sell two truckloads of apples to Zimmer. Zimmer believes that he is buying the apples from Albright; but actually Albright is the agent for Henderson, who legally owns the apples. In this situation, Henderson is an undisclosed principal.

When neither the fact of agency nor the identity of the principal is disclosed, a third party is deemed to be dealing with the agent personally, and the agent is liable as a party to the contract. If an agent has acted within the scope of his or her authority, the

UNDISCLOSED PRINCIPAL
A principal whose identity is unknown by a third person, and the third person has no knowledge that the agent is acting for a principal at the time the agent and the third person form a contract.

undisclosed principal is also liable as a party to the contract, just as if the principal had been fully disclosed at the time the contract was made. Conversely, the undisclosed principal can hold the third party to the contract, unless (1) the undisclosed principal was expressly excluded as a party in the contract, (2) the contract is a negotiable instrument signed by the agent with no indication of signing in a representative capacity, or (3) the performance of the agent is personal to the contract, allowing the third party to refuse the principal's performance.

Liability for Torts and Crimes

Obviously, an agent is liable for his or her own torts and crimes. Whether the principal can also be held liable depends on several factors, which we examine here. In some situations, a principal may be held liable not only for the torts of an agent but also for the torts committed by an independent contractor.

LIABILITY FOR AGENT'S TORTS   As mentioned, an agent is liable for his or her own torts. A principal may also be liable for an agent's torts under the doctrine of ***respondeat superior***,[7] a Latin term meaning "let the master respond." This doctrine, which is discussed in the following *Landmark in the Law*, is similar to the theory of strict liability discussed in Chapter 5. The doctrine imposes vicarious (indirect) liability on the employer without regard to the personal fault of the employer for torts committed by an employee in the course or scope of employment.

RESPONDEAT SUPERIOR
In Latin, "Let the master respond." A doctrine under which a principal or an employer is held liable for the wrongful acts committed by agents or employees while acting within the scope of their agency or employment.

---

7.   Pronounced ree-*spahn*-dee-uht soo-*peer*-ee-your.

LANDMARK IN
THE LAW

The Doctrine of *Respondeat Superior*

The idea that a master (employer) must respond to third persons for losses negligently caused by the master's servant (employee) first appeared in Lord Holt's opinion in *Jones v. Hart* (1698).[a] By the early nineteenth century, this maxim had been adopted by most courts and was referred to as the doctrine of *respondeat superior*.

The vicarious (indirect) liability of the master for the acts of the servant has been supported primarily by two theories. The first theory rests on the issue of *control,* or *fault:* the master has control over the acts of the servant and is thus responsible for injuries arising out of such service. The second theory is economic in nature: because the master takes the benefits or profits of the servant's service, he or she should also suffer the losses; moreover, the master is better able than the servant to absorb such losses.

The *control* theory is clearly recognized in the *Restatement (Second) of Agency,* in which the master is defined as "a principal who employs an agent to perform service in his affairs and who controls, or has the right to control, the physical conduct of the other in the performance of the service." Accordingly, a servant is defined as "an agent employed by a master to perform service in his affairs whose physical conduct in his performance of the service is controlled, or is subject to control, by the master."

There are limitations on the master's liability for the acts of the servant, however. An employer (master) is only responsible for the wrongful conduct of an employee (servant) that occurs in "the scope of the employment." The criteria used by the

---

a.   K.B. [King's Bench] 642, 90 Eng. Reprint 1255 (1698).

Landmark in the Law—Continued

courts in determining whether an employee is acting within the scope of employment are stated in the *Restatement (Second) of Agency* and will be discussed shortly. Generally, the act must be of a kind the servant was employed to do; must have occurred within "authorized time and space limits"; and must have been "activated, at least in part, by a purpose to serve the master."

The courts have accepted the doctrine of *respondeat superior* for nearly two centuries. This theory of vicarious liability is laden with practical implications in all situations in which a principal-agent (master-servant, employer-employee) relationship exists. The small-town grocer with one clerk and the multinational corporation with thousands of employees are equally subject to the doctrinal demand of "let the master respond."

For Critical Analysis: *How does the doctrine of* respondeat superior *relate to the doctrine of strict product liability?*

Scope of Employment   The key to determining whether a principal may be liable for the torts of the agent under the doctrine of *respondeat superior* is whether the torts are committed within the scope of the agency or employment. The *Restatement (Second) of Agency*, Section 229, indicates the factors that courts will consider in determining whether or not a particular act occurred within the course and scope of employment. These factors are as follows:

> NOTE An employee going to or from work or meals is not usually considered to be within the scope of employment. An employee whose job requires travel, however, is considered to be within the scope of employment for the entire trip, including the return.

1.   Whether the act was authorized by the employer.
2.   The time, place, and purpose of the act.
3.   Whether the act was one commonly performed by employees on behalf of their employers.
4.   The extent to which the employer's interest was advanced by the act.
5.   The extent to which the private interests of the employee were involved.
6.   Whether the employer furnished the means or instrumentality (for example, a truck or a machine) by which the injury was inflicted.
7.   Whether the employer had reason to know that the employee would do the act in question and whether the employee had ever done it before.
8.   Whether the act involved the commission of a serious crime.

A useful insight into the "scope of employment" concept may be gained from Baron Parke's classic distinction between a "detour" and a "frolic" in the case of *Joel v. Morison* (1834):[8]

> If the servants, being on their master's business took a *detour* . . . the master will be responsible. . . . The master is only liable where the servant is acting in the course of his employment. If he was going out of his way, against his master's implied commands, when driving on his master's business, he will make his master liable; but if he was going on a *frolic of his own*, without being at all on his master's business, the master will not be liable.

Courts often refer to the "detour-frolic" distinction when deciding whether a given action was within the scope of employment. At issue in the following case is whether a truck driver's actions fell within the scope of employment or constituted a "frolic of his own."

---

8.   6 Car. & P. 501, 172 Eng. Reprint 1338 (1834).

CASE 23.4

McNAIR v. LEND LEASE TRUCKS, INC.

United States Court of Appeals,
Fourth Circuit, 1995.
62 F.3d 651.

HISTORICAL AND SOCIAL SETTING   *The illegal use of controlled substances and the misuse of alcohol in particular have long had terrible consequences on U.S. highways. Sometimes, the abusers are professional drivers of large trucks and other commercial vehicles. To curb this abuse, Congress enacted the Omnibus Transportation Employee Testing Act of 1991. This act requires that, beginning in 1996, all employers test for drugs and alcohol whomever they hire to operate a commercial motor vehicle. Of course, the tests are too late for the millions who have already died on our nation's highways.*

FACTS   Lend Lease Trucks, Inc., employed Thomas Jones as an interstate truck driver. While on an assignment, Jones parked on the shoulder of U.S. Highway 301 near Kenly, North Carolina, and crossed the highway to the Dry Dock Lounge. In the lounge, Jones drank enough liquor for his blood-alcohol level to rise to eighteen points above the level at which he could legally drive his truck. After a few hours, Jones left the lounge. As he started across the highway to his truck, he darted into the path

of a motorcycle driven by Edward McNair. In the collision, Jones and McNair were killed. McNair's wife, Catherine, filed a suit in a North Carolina state court against Lend Lease Trucks, Inc., and others, claiming in part that Jones was acting within the scope of employment at the time of the accident. The case was removed to a federal district court. Lend Lease filed a motion to dismiss, the court granted the motion, and Catherine appealed.

ISSUE   Was Jones acting within the scope of employment at the time of the accident?

DECISION   No. The U.S. Court of Appeals for the Fourth Circuit affirmed the order of the lower court.

REASON   The court held that "an employee can go 'on a frolic of his own' *   *   * by engaging in conduct which *   *   * is in no way 'about,' or 'in furtherance of,' 'his master's business.' " The court explained that Jones departed from the scope of his employment when he took a break of three to fours hours, "during which he consume[d] sufficient alcohol to make it illegal for him to drive his truck." The court concluded that this departure "could only have ceased *   *   * when his blood-alcohol content dropped at least to the legal limit for performing his duty. That obviously had not occurred by the time of the collision."

FOR CRITICAL ANALYSIS—Social Consideration
What effect might it have had on the outcome of this case if, during his break, Jones had not "consume[d] sufficient alcohol to make it illegal for him to drive his truck"?

Misrepresentation   A principal is exposed to tort liability whenever a third person sustains a loss due to the agent's misrepresentation. The principal's liability depends on whether or not the agent was actually or apparently authorized to make representations and whether such representations were made within the scope of the agency. The principal is always directly responsible for an agent's misrepresentation made within the scope of the agent's authority, whether the misrepresentation was made fraudulently or simply by the agent's mistake or oversight.

The doctrine of *respondeat superior* is well established in the legal systems of the United States and most Western countries. Middle Eastern countries, however, do not employ the principle. Islamic law, codified in the *Shari'a,* holds to a strict principle that responsibility for human actions lies with the individual and cannot be vicariously extended to others. This principle and other concepts of Islamic law are based on the sayings of Mohammed, the seventh-century prophet and founder of Islam.

For Critical Analysis: *How would American society be affected if employers could not be held vicariously liable for their employees' torts?*

LIABILITY FOR INDEPENDENT CONTRACTOR'S TORTS   Generally, the principal is not liable for physical harm caused to a third person by the negligent act of an independent contractor in the performance of the contract. This is because the employer does not have the *right to control* the details of an independent contractor's performance. An exception to this doctrine is made when exceptionally hazardous activities are involved, such as blasting operations, the transportation of highly volatile chemicals, or the use of poisonous gases. In these situations, a principal cannot be shielded from liability merely by using an independent contractor. Strict liability is imposed on the principal as a matter of law and, in some states, by statute. In the following case, one of the issues before the court was whether the "self-help" repossession of collateral is an inherently dangerous activity, in which case the secured creditor could be held liable for damages caused by the independent contractor's tortious actions.

CASE 23.5

SANCHEZ v. MBANK OF EL PASO

Court of Appeals of Texas—El Paso, 1990.
792 S.W.2d 530.

HISTORICAL AND SOCIAL SETTING   *Under uniform laws that predated the Uniform Commercial Code (UCC), a secured party could take possession of collateral on a debtor's default without judicial process. The drafters of the UCC followed these provisions in UCC 9–503. Taking possession of collateral on default must be done without a breach of the peace, however. Among the acts that have been considered to be peaceable, in connection with repossession, is the removal of an automobile from the debtor's driveway without the debtor's knowledge. Acts that have been considered to constitute a breach of the peace, in connection with repossession, include the removal of an automobile over the debtor's objection and the removal of an automobile after a threat of violence.*

FACTS   MBank of El Paso contracted with El Paso Recovery Service (El Paso) to have El Paso repossess Yvonne Sanchez's 1978 Pontiac Trans Am, which had been purchased through MBank financing. Two men hired by El Paso went to Sanchez's home with a tow truck and proceeded to hook the tow truck to the car, which was in the driveway. Sanchez, who was in the yard cutting the grass at the time, asked them their purpose and demanded that they cease their attempt to take the automobile and leave the premises. When they ignored her, she entered and locked herself in the car in an effort to stall them until the police or her husband could arrive. It was only after they got the automobile in the street that they identified their purpose and told her to get out of the car, which she refused to do. They then took the vehicle,

with Sanchez locked in it, on a high-speed ride from her home to the repossession lot and parked the car in a fenced and locked yard with a loose guard dog. She was rescued some time later by her husband and the police. Sanchez filed suit in a Texas state court against MBank for damages, alleging that El Paso and its employees were MBank's agents and that they had willfully breached the peace in violation of UCC 9–503. The trial court granted the bank's motion for summary judgment, holding that the bank could not be liable, because El Paso was an independent contractor and not an employee or agent of MBank. Sanchez appealed.

ISSUE   Can MBank be held liable for the tortious actions of El Paso, notwithstanding the fact that El Paso was an independent contractor?

DECISION   Yes. The Texas appellate court reversed the trial court's decision and remanded the case for trial.

REASON   The appellate court pointed out that two situations represent exceptions to the general rule that an employer is not liable for the tortious acts of an independent contractor: "(1) where the employer is by the statute * * * under a duty to provide specific safeguards for the safety of others" and "(2) where the employer employs an independent contractor to do work involving a special or inherent danger to others." The court concluded that MBank had a nondelegable duty under UCC 9–503 to avoid breaching the peace when repossessing collateral and thus could be liable to Sanchez for a breach of the peace by El Paso. The court also concluded that self-help repossession—"[a]lways bordering on the edge of illegality if not carried out carefully"—is an inherently dangerous activity.

FOR CRITICAL ANALYSIS—Economic Consideration
In determining liability for a breach of the peace under UCC 9–503, should the court take into consideration the behavior of the person from whom the collateral was possessed (in this case, Sanchez)?

LIABILITY FOR AGENT'S CRIMES   An agent is liable for his or her own crimes. A principal or employer is not liable for an agent's crime even if the crime was committed within the scope of authority or employment—unless the principal participated by conspiracy or other action. In some jurisdictions, under specific statutes, a principal may be liable for an agent's violation, in the course and scope of employment, of regulations, such as those governing sanitation, prices, weights, and the sale of liquor.

▌Agency Termination

Agency law is similar to contract law in that both an agency and a contract can be terminated by an act of the parties or by operation of law. Once the relationship between the principal and the agent has ended, the agent no longer has the right to bind the principal. For an agent's apparent authority to be terminated, third persons may also need to be notified when the agency has been terminated.

Termination by Act of the Parties

An agency may be terminated by act of the parties in several ways, including those discussed here.

LAPSE OF TIME   An agency agreement may specify the time period during which the agency relationship will exist. If so, the agency ends when that time period expires. Thus, if Allen signs an agreement of agency with Proust "beginning January 1, 1998, and ending December 31, 1999," the agency is automatically terminated on December 31, 1999. Of course, the parties can agree to continue the relationship, in which case the same terms will apply. If no definite time is stated, then the agency continues for a reasonable time and can be terminated at will by either party. What constitutes a "reasonable time" depends, of course, on the circumstances and the nature of the agency relationship.

PURPOSE ACHIEVED   An agent can be employed to accomplish a particular objective, such as the purchase of stock for a cattle rancher. In that situation, the agency automatically ends after the cattle have been purchased. If more than one agent is employed to accomplish the same purpose, such as the sale of real estate, the first agent to complete the sale automatically terminates the agency relationship for all the others.

OCCURRENCE OF A SPECIFIC EVENT   An agency can be created to terminate upon the happening of a certain event. If Posner appoints Rubik to handle his business affairs while he is away, the agency automatically terminates when Posner returns.

Sometimes, one aspect of the agent's authority terminates on the occurrence of a particular event, but the agency relationship itself does not terminate. Suppose that William, a banker, permits Calvin, the bank's credit manager, to grant a credit line of $2,000 to certain depositors who maintain $2,000 in a savings account. If any customer's savings account falls below $2,000, Calvin can no longer continue making the credit line available to that customer. Calvin's right to extend credit to the other customers maintaining the minimum balance will continue, however.

MUTUAL AGREEMENT   Recall from the chapters on contract law that parties can cancel (rescind) a contract by mutually agreeing to terminate the contractual relationship. The same holds true under agency law regardless of whether the agency contract is in writing or whether it is for a specific duration.

TERMINATION BY ONE PARTY   As a general rule, either party can terminate the agency relationship. The agent's act is called a *renunciation of authority*. The principal's act is referred to as a *revocation of authority*. Although both parties have the *power* to terminate the agency, however, they may not possess the *right*. Wrongful termination can subject the canceling party to a suit for damages. For example, Rawlins has a one-year employment contract with Munro to act as an agent in return for $35,000. Munro can discharge Rawlins before the contract period expires (Munro has the *power* to breach the contract); however, Munro will be liable to Rawlins for money damages, because Munro has no *right* to breach the contract.

A special rule applies in an agency *coupled with an interest*. This type of agency is not an agency in the usual sense, because it is created for the agent's benefit instead of for the principal's benefit. For example, suppose that Julie borrows $5,000 from Rob, giving Rob some of her jewelry and signing a letter giving Rob the power to sell the jewelry as her agent if she fails to repay the loan. Julie, after she has received the $5,000 from Rob, then attempts to revoke Rob's authority to sell the jewelry as her agent. Julie would not succeed in this attempt, because a principal cannot revoke an agency created for the agent's benefit.

NOTICE OF TERMINATION   If the parties themselves have terminated the agency, it is the principal's duty to inform any third parties who know of the existence of the agency that it has been terminated (although notice of the termination may be given by others).

An agent's authority continues until the agent receives some notice of termination. Notice to third parties follows the general rule that an agent's *apparent* authority continues until the third person receives notice (from any source of information) that such authority has been terminated. The principal is expected to notify directly any third person who the principal knows has dealt with the agent. For third persons who have heard about the agency but have not yet dealt with the agent, *constructive notice* is sufficient.[9]

No particular form is required for notice of agency termination to be effective. The principal can actually notify the agent, or the agent can learn of the termination through some other means. For example, Manning bids on a shipment of steel, and Stone is hired as an agent to arrange transportation of the shipment. When Stone learns that Manning has lost the bid, Stone's authority to make the transportation arrangement terminates.

If the agent's authority is written, it must be revoked in writing, and the writing must be shown to all people who saw the original writing that established the agency relationship. Sometimes, a written authorization (such as a power of attorney) contains an expiration date. The passage of the expiration date is sufficient notice of termination for third parties.

Termination by Operation of Law

Termination of an agency by operation of law occurs in the circumstances discussed here. Note that when an agency terminates by operation of law, there is no duty to notify third persons—unless the agent's authority is coupled with an interest.

DEATH OR INSANITY   The general rule is that the death or mental incompetence of either the principal or the agent automatically and immediately terminates the ordinary agency relationship. Knowledge of the death is not required. Suppose that Geer

---

9. Constructive notice is information or knowledge of a fact imputed by law to a person if he or she could have discovered the fact by proper diligence. Constructive notice is often accomplished by newspaper publication.

sends Pyron to the Far East to purchase a rare painting. Before Pyron makes the purchase, Geer dies. Pyron's agent status is terminated at the moment of Geer's death, even though Pyron does not know that Geer has died. Some states, however, have changed this common law rule by statute, and death does not terminate an agency coupled with an interest.

An agent's transactions that occur after the death of the principal are not binding on the principal's estate.[10] Assume that Carson is hired by Perry to collect a debt from Thomas (a third party). Perry dies, but Carson, not knowing of Perry's death, still collects the money from Thomas. Thomas's payment to Carson is no longer legally sufficient to discharge Thomas's debt to Perry, because Carson's authority to collect the money ended on Perry's death. If Carson absconds with the money, Thomas is still liable for the debt to Perry's estate.

IMPOSSIBILITY   When the specific subject matter of an agency is destroyed or lost, the agency terminates. If Bullard employs Gonzalez to sell Bullard's house, but prior to the sale the premises are destroyed by fire, then Gonzalez's agency and authority to sell Bullard's house terminate. When it is impossible for the agent to perform the agency lawfully, the agency terminates.

CHANGED CIRCUMSTANCES   When an event occurs that has such an unusual effect on the subject matter of the agency that the agent can reasonably infer that the principal will not want the agency to continue, the agency terminates. For example, Roberts hires Mullen to sell a tract of land for $20,000. Subsequently, Mullen learns that there is oil under the land and that the land is worth $1 million. The agency and Mullen's authority to sell the land for $20,000 are terminated.

BANKRUPTCY AND WAR   Bankruptcy of the principal or the agent usually terminates the agency relationship. When the principal's country and the agent's country are at war with each other, the agency is terminated or at least suspended.

---

10.   There is an exception to this rule in banking under which the bank, as the agent of the customer, can continue to exercise specific types of authority even after the customer has died or become mentally incompetent unless it has knowledge of the death or incompetence [UCC 4–405]. Even with knowledge of the customer's death, the bank has authority for ten days following the customer's death to honor checks in the absence of a stop-payment order.

Application

Law and the Employer—Using Independent Contractors*

As an employer, you may at some time consider hiring an independent contractor. One reason for using an independent contractor is that it may reduce your susceptibility to tort liability. If, however, an

This *Application* is not meant to substitute for the services of an attorney who is licensed to practice law in your state.

independent contractor's words or conduct leads another party to believe that the independent contractor is your employee, you may not escape liability for the worker's torts.

To minimize the possibility of your being legally liable for negligence on the part of an independent contractor, you should, prior to hiring that contractor, inquire about his or her qualifications. The degree to which you should investigate depends, of course, on the nature of the work. A more thorough investigation is necessary when there is a potential danger to the public from the contractor's activities (as in delivering explosives).

Generally, it is a good idea to have the independent contractor assume, in a written contract, liability for harms caused to third parties by the independent con-

Application—Continued

tractor's negligence. You should also require the independent contractor to purchase liability insurance to cover the costs of potential lawsuits for harms caused to third persons by the independent contractor's hazardous activities or negligence.

Another reason for hiring an independent contractor is that you need not pay or deduct Social Security and unemployment taxes on behalf of such individuals. The independent contractor is the party responsible for paying these taxes. Additionally, the independent contractor is not eligible for any retirement or medical plans or other fringe benefits that you have for yourself and your employees, and this is a cost saving to you.

A word of caution, though: simply designating a person as an independent contractor does not make him or her one. Under Internal Revenue Service (IRS) rules, an individual will be treated as an employee if he or she is "in fact" an employee, regardless of any classification that you might have made. For example, a secretary will not be treated by the IRS as an independent contractor simply because you designate him or her as such. If, however, you contract with a secretarial service, the secretary is an employee of the service and not your employee directly. In this situation, even though you are utilizing an independent contractor (the secretarial service), you still retain the right to supervise and inspect work to make sure that it meets your contract specifications.

If you improperly designate an employee as an independent contractor, the penalty may be high. Usually, you will be liable for back Social Security and unemployment taxes, plus interest and penalties. When in doubt, seek professional assistance in such matters.

Checklist for Using Independent Contractors

1. Check the qualifications of any independent contractor you plan to use to reduce the potential for negligent actions.
2. It is best to require in any contract with an independent contractor that the contractor assume liability for harm to a third person caused by the contractor's negligence.
3. Require any independent contractor working for you to carry liability insurance. Examine the policy to make sure that it is current, particularly when the contractor will be undertaking actions that are more than normally hazardous to the public.
4. Make sure that independent contractors do not represent themselves as your employees to the rest of the world.
5. Regularly inspect the work of the independent contractor to make sure that it is being performed in accordance with contract specifications. Such supervision on your part will not change the worker's status as an independent contractor.

▌ Key Terms

agency 592
disclosed principal 606
equal dignity rule 603
fiduciary 593

independent contractor 593
notary public 603
partially disclosed principal 606
power of attorney 603

ratification 598
respondeat superior 608
undisclosed principal 607

▌ Chapter Summary: Agency Relationships in Business

Agency Relationships (*See pages 593–596.*)	In a *principal-agent* relationship, an agent acts on behalf of and instead of the principal, using a certain degree of his or her own discretion. An employee who deals with third parties is normally an agent. An independent contractor is not an employee, and the employer has no control over the details of physical performance. The independent contractor is not usually an agent.
Agency Formation (*See pages 596–600.*)	1. *By agreement*—Through express consent (oral or written) or implied by conduct. 2. *By ratification*—The principal, either by act or agreement, ratifies the conduct of an agent who acted outside the scope of authority or the conduct of a person who is in fact not an agent. *(Continued)*

▌Chapter Summary: Agency Relationships in Business—Continued

Agency Formation —Continued	3. *By estoppel*—When the principal causes a third person to believe that another person is his or her agent, and the third person deals with the supposed agent, the principal is "estopped to deny" the agency relationship. 4. *By operation of law*—Based on a social duty (such as the need to support family members) or created in emergency situations when the agent is unable to contact the principal.

Duties of Agents and Principals *(See pages 600–603.)*	1. *Duties of the agent*—
	  a. Performance—The agent must use reasonable diligence and skill in performing his or her duties.
	  b. Notification—The agent is required to notify the principal of all matters that come to his or her attention concerning the subject matter of the agency.
	  c. Loyalty—The agent has a duty to act solely for the benefit of his or her principal and not in the interest of the agent or a third party.
	  d. Obedience—The agent must follow all lawful and clearly stated instructions of the principal.
	  e. Accounting—The agent has a duty to make available to the principal records of all property and money received and paid out on behalf of the principal.
	
	2. *Duties of the principal*—
	  a. Compensation—Except in a gratuitous agency relationship, the principal must pay the agreed-on value (or reasonable value) for an agent's services.
	  b. Reimbursement and indemnification—The principal must reimburse the agent for all sums of money disbursed at the request of the principal and for all sums of money the agent disburses for necessary expenses in the course of reasonable performance of his or her agency duties.
	  c. Cooperation—A principal must cooperate with and assist an agent in performing his or her duties.
	  d. Safe working conditions—A principal must provide safe working conditions for the agent-employee.

Agent's Authority *(See pages 603–606.)*	1. *Actual authority*—
	  a. Express authority—Can be oral or in writing. Authorization must be in writing if the agent is to execute a contract that must be in writing.
	  b. Implied authority—Authority customarily associated with the position of the agent or authority that is deemed necessary for the agent to carry out expressly authorized tasks.
	
	2. *Apparent authority*—Exists when the principal, by word or action, causes a third party reasonably to believe that an agent has authority to act, even though the agent has no express or implied authority.
	
	3. *Ratification*—The affirmation by the principal of an agent's unauthorized action or promise. For the ratification to be effective, the principal must be aware of all material facts.

Liability in Agency Relationships *(See pages 606–612.)*	1. *Liability for contracts*—If the principal's identity is disclosed or partially disclosed at the time the agent forms a contract with a third party, the principal is liable to the third party under the contract (if the agent acted within the scope of his or her authority). If the principal's identity is undisclosed at the time of contract formation, the agent is liable to the third party. If the agent acted within the scope of authority, the principal is bound by the contract.
	
	2. *Liability for torts and crimes*—
	  a. Liability for agent's torts—Under the doctrine of *respondeat superior*, the principal is liable for any harm caused to another through the agent's torts if the agent was acting within the scope of his or her employment at the time the harmful act occurred. The principal is also liable for an agent's misrepresentation, whether made knowingly or by mistake.
	  b. Liability for independent contractor's torts—A principal is not liable for harm caused by an independent contractor's negligence, unless hazardous activities are involved (in which situation the principal is strictly liable for any resulting harm).
	  c. Liability for agent's crimes—An agent is responsible for his or her own crimes, even if the crimes were committed while the agent was acting within the scope of authority or employment. A principal will be liable for an agent's crime only if the principal participated by conspiracy or other action or (in some jurisdictions) if the agent violated certain government regulations in the course of employment.

▮ Chapter Summary: Agency Relationships in Business—Continued

Agency Termination *(See pages 612–614.)*	1. *By act of the parties—*
	  a. Lapse of time (when a definite time for the duration of the agency was agreed on when the agency was established).
	  b. Purpose achieved.
	  c. Occurrence of a specific event.
	  d. Mutual rescission (requires mutual consent of principal and agent).
	  e. Termination by act of either the principal (revocation) or the agent (renunciation). (A principal cannot revoke an agency coupled with an interest.)
	  f. When an agency is terminated by act of the parties, all third persons who have previously dealt with the agency must be directly notified; constructive notice will suffice for all other third parties.
	
	2. *By operation of law—*
	  a. Death or mental incompetence of either the principal or the agent (except in an agency coupled with an interest).
	  b. Impossibility (when the purpose of the agency cannot be achieved because of an event beyond the parties' control).
	  c. Changed circumstances (in which it would be inequitable to require that the agency be continued).
	  d. Bankruptcy of the principal or the agent, or war between the principal's and agent's countries.
	  e. When an agency is terminated by operation of law, no notice to third parties is required (unless the agent's authority is coupled with an interest).

▮ For Review

1. What formalities are required to create an agency relationship?

2. What duties does the agent owe to the principal? What duties does the principal owe to the agent?

3. How does an agent's apparent authority differ from an agent's actual authority? If an agent acts outside the scope of his or her authority, how might a principal still be held liable for the act?

4. If an agent, acting within the scope of authority, forms a contract with a third party on behalf of an undisclosed principal, will the principal be held liable on the contract?

5. Under what doctrine can a principal-employer be held liable for the torts committed by an agent-employee?

▮ Questions and Case Problems

23–1. Agency Formation. Pete Gaffrey is a well-known, wealthy financier living in the city of Takima. Alan Winter, Gaffrey's friend, tells Til Borge that he (Winter) is Gaffrey's agent for the purchase of rare coins. Winter even shows Borge a local newspaper clipping mentioning Gaffrey's interest in coin collecting. Borge, knowing of Winter's friendship with Gaffrey, contracts with Winter to sell to Gaffrey a rare coin valued at $25,000. Winter takes the coin and disappears with it. On the date of contract payment, Borge seeks to collect from Gaffrey, claiming that Winter's agency made Gaffrey liable. Gaffrey does not deny that Winter was a friend, but he claims that Winter was never his agent. Discuss fully whether an agency was in existence at the time the contract for the rare coin was made.

23–2. Ratification by Principal. Springer was a political candidate running for congressional office. He was operating on a tight budget and instructed his campaign staff not to purchase any campaign materials without his explicit authorization. In

spite of these instructions, one of his campaign workers ordered Dubychek Printing Co. to print some promotional materials for Springer's campaign. When the printed materials were received, Springer did not return them but instead used them during his campaign. When Dubychek failed to obtain payment from Springer for the materials, he sued for recovery of the price. Springer contended that he was not liable on the sales contract, because he had not authorized his agent to purchase the printing services. Dubychek argued that Springer's use of the materials constituted ratification of his agent's unauthorized purchase. Is Dubychek correct? Explain.

23–3. Agent's Duties to Principal. Iliana is a traveling sales agent. Iliana not only solicits orders but also delivers the goods and collects payments from her customers. Iliana places all payments in her private checking account and at the end of each month draws sufficient cash from her bank to cover the payments made. Giberson Corp., Iliana's employer, is totally unaware of this procedure. Because of a slowdown in the economy, Giberson tells all its sales personnel to offer 20 percent discounts on orders. Iliana solicits orders, but she offers only 15 percent discounts, pocketing the extra 5 percent paid by customers. Iliana has not lost any orders by this practice, and she is rated as one of Giberson's top salespersons. Giberson now learns of Iliana's actions. Discuss fully Giberson's rights in this matter.

23–4. Liability for Agent's Contracts. Michael Mosely works as a purchasing agent for Suharto Coal Supply, a partnership. Mosely has authority to purchase the coal needed by Suharto to satisfy the needs of its customers. While Mosely is leaving a coal mine from which he has just purchased a large quantity of coal, his car breaks down. He walks into a small roadside grocery store for help. While there, he runs into Wiley, who owns 360 acres back in the mountains with all mineral rights. Wiley, in need of money, offers to sell Mosely the property at $1,500 per acre. Upon inspection, Mosely concludes that the subsurface may contain valuable coal deposits. Mosely contracts to purchase the property for Suharto, signing the contract, "Suharto Coal Supply, Michael Mosely, agent." The closing date is set for August 1. Mosely takes the contract to the partnership. The managing partner is furious, as Suharto is not in the property business. Later, just before August 1, both Wiley and the partnership learn that the value of the land is at least $15,000 per acre. Discuss the rights of Suharto and Wiley concerning the land contract.

23–5. Agent's Duties to Principal. Sam Kademenos was about to sell a $1 million life insurance policy to a prospective customer when he resigned from his position with Equitable Life Assurance Society. Before resigning from the company, he had expended substantial amounts of company money and had utilized Equitable's medical examiners to procure the $1 million sale. After resigning, Kademenos joined a competing insurance firm, Jefferson Life Insurance Co., and made the sale through it. Has he breached any duty to Equitable? Explain. [*Kademenos v. Equitable Life Assurance Society*, 513 F.2d 1073 (3d Cir. 1975)]

23–6. Respondeat Superior. Richard Lanno worked for Thermal Equipment Corp. as a project engineer. Lanno was allowed to keep a company van and tools at his home because he routinely drove to work sites directly from his home and because he was often needed for unanticipated business trips during his off hours. The arrangement had been made for the convenience of Thermal Equipment, even though Lanno's managers permitted him to make personal use of the van. Lanno was involved in a collision with Lazar while driving the van home from work one day. At the time of the accident, Lanno had taken a detour in order to stop at a store—he had intended to purchase a few items and then go home. Lazar sued Thermal Equipment, claiming that Lanno had acted within the scope of his employment. Discuss whether Lazar was able to recover from Thermal Equipment. Can employees act on behalf of their employers and themselves at the same time? Discuss. [*Lazar v. Thermal Equipment Corp.*, 148 Cal.App.3d 458, 195 Cal.Rptr. 890 (1983)]

23–7. Authority of Agent. The Federal Land Bank (FLB) filed an action to foreclose a mortgage on Tom and Judith Sullivan's real estate. Before the trial, FLB's attorney wrote to the Sullivans' attorney to invite settlement offers. A copy of the letter was sent to Wayne Williamson, an FLB vice president.

Nine days later, on September 3, the Sullivans' attorney wrote to FLB's attorney expressing interest in settling the case. A copy of this letter was sent to Williamson. On September 11, FLB's attorney replied with an offer that "[m]y client has authorized me to extend . . . to you." The Sullivans accepted the offer. Three weeks later, FLB's attorney wrote the following to the Sullivans' attorney: "Any compromises regarding Federal Land Bank loans must be cleared through [FLB's] Omaha [office]. The proposed compromise was not approved and therefore we have been requested to proceed through the foreclosure process." The case went to trial, and FLB obtained a judgment of foreclosure. The trial court found that FLB was not bound by the offer made by its attorney. The Sullivans appealed, arguing that the attorney had or appeared to have had authority to settle the case. What should the appellate court decide? [*Federal Land Bank v. Sullivan*, 430 N.W.2d 700 (S.Dak. 1988)]

23–8. Ratification by Principal. Fred Hash worked for Van Stavern Construction Co. as a field supervisor in charge of constructing a new plant facility. Hash entered into a contract with Sutton's Steel & Supply, Inc., to supply steel to the construction site in several installments. Hash gave the name of B. D. Van Stavern, the president and owner of the construction firm, instead of the firm's name as the party for whom he was acting. The contract and the subsequent invoices all had B. D. Van Stavern's name on them. Sutton delivered several loads. All of the invoices were signed by Van Stavern employees, and corporate checks were made out to Sutton. When Sutton Steel later sued Van Stavern personally for unpaid debts totaling $40,437, it claimed that Van Stavern had ratified the acts of his employee, Hash, by allowing payment on previous invoices. Although Van Stavern had had no knowledge of the unauthorized arrangement, had he legally ratified the agreement by his silence? Explain. [*Sutton's Steel & Supply, Inc. v. Van Stavern*, 496 So.2d 1360 (La.App. 3d Cir. 1986)]

23–9. Respondeat Superior. Justin Jones suffered from genital herpes and sought treatment from Dr. Steven Baisch of Region West Pediatric Services. A nurse's assistant, Jeni Hallgren, who was a Region West employee, told her friends and some of Jones's friends about Jones's condition. This was a violation of the Region West employee handbook, which required employees to maintain the confidentiality of patients' records. Jones filed a suit in a federal district court against Region West, among others, alleging that Region West should be held liable for its employee's actions on the basis of *respondeat superior*. On what basis might the court hold that Region West is not liable for Hallgren's acts? Discuss fully. [*Jones v. Baisch, M.D.*, 40 F.3d 252 (8th Cir. 1994)]

23–10. Employee versus Independent Contractor. Stephen Hemmerling was a driver for the Happy Cab Co. Hemmerling paid certain fixed expenses and abided by a variety of rules relating to the use of the cab, the hours that could be worked, the solicitation of fares, and so on. Rates were set by the state. Happy Cab did not withhold taxes from Hemmerling's pay. While driving a cab, Hemmerling was injured in an accident and filed a claim against Happy Cab in a Nebraska state court for workers' compensation benefits. Such benefits are not available to independent contractors. On what basis might the court hold that Hemmerling is an employee? Explain. [*Hemmerling v. Happy Cab Co.*, 247 Neb. 919, 530 N.W.2d 916 (1995)]

A QUESTION OF ETHICS AND SOCIAL RESPONSIBILITY

23–11. *Kimberly Sierra, suffering from a severe asthma attack, went to Southview Hospital & Family Health Center. She was treated in the emergency room by Dr. Thomas Mucci. At the time, as a result of statements by Southview administrators, brochures, and ads, Sierra believed that the physicians at Southview were "hospital doctors." In fact, however, Mucci's contract with Southview stated, "The relationship between [Southview and Mucci] shall be that of independent contractor." Within a few hours, Sierra was pronounced dead. Sierra's mother, Edna Clark, filed a suit in an Ohio state court against Southview and others, alleging, in part, negligent medical care. Southview argued that it was not responsible for the acts of its independent contractors. Ultimately, the Supreme Court of Ohio heard the case and held that Southview was liable, under the doctrine of agency by estoppel, based primarily on its "hold[ing] itself out to the public as a provider of medical services." [Clark v. Southview Hospital & Family Health Center, 68 Ohio St.3d 435, 628 N.E.2d 46 (1994)]*

1. Could Southview have avoided liability if Sierra had known that Mucci was an independent contractor? If so, would a sign in the emergency room have been enough? If not, how might Southview have avoided liability? Is it ethical for a hospital to attempt to avoid such responsibility?

2. Some department stores rent space in their stores to vendors of individual lines of products, such as cosmetics. In doing so, does a department store hold itself out to the public as a "provider" of cosmetics, subjecting itself to liability for the negligent acts of the independent contractors on its premises? Should the holding in the *Southview* case be applied in such contexts?

FOR CRITICAL ANALYSIS

23–12. *When a worker is injured on the job, normally the sole remedy is provided through state workers' compensation statutes, regardless of fault or the employer's negligence. On average, recoveries under these statutes are less than half what recoveries in tort lawsuits would be. In view of the law's increasing concern with compensating injured parties, why are these statutes retained? What policy considerations underlie their retention?*

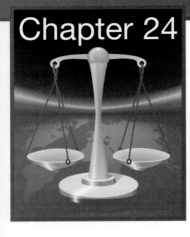

Chapter 24

The Entrepreneur's Options

ENTREPRENEUR
One who initiates and assumes the financial risks of a new enterprise and undertakes to provide or control its management.

"[E]veryone thirsteth after gaine."

Sir Edward Coke, 1552–1634
(English jurist and politician)

CHAPTER OBJECTIVES

After reading this chapter, you should be able to:

1. Identify and describe the three major traditional forms of business organization.
2. Summarize the advantages and disadvantages of doing business as a partnership and as a corporation, respectively.
3. Specify how the limited liability company addresses needs that are not met by traditional forms of business.
4. Describe the basic characteristics of joint ventures and other business forms.
5. Define the term *franchise*, and indicate how a franchising relationship arises.

Many Americans would agree with Sir Edward Coke that most people, at least, "thirsteth after gaine." Certainly, an entrepreneur's primary motive for undertaking a business enterprise is to make profits. An **entrepreneur** is by definition one who initiates and *assumes the financial risks* of a new enterprise and undertakes to provide or control its management.

One of the questions faced by any entrepreneur who wishes to start up a business is what form of business organization he or she should choose for the business endeavor. In this chapter, we first examine the basic features of the three major traditional business forms—sole proprietorships, partnerships, and corporations. We then look at a relatively new, but significant, business form: the limited liability company, or LLC. The LLC is rapidly becoming an attractive alternative to the traditional corporate form. (The limited liability partnership, or LLP, which is a variation of the LLC, will be discussed in Chapter 25.) Other forms touched on in this chapter include joint ventures, syndicates, joint stock companies, business trusts, and cooperatives. A discussion of private franchises concludes the chapter.

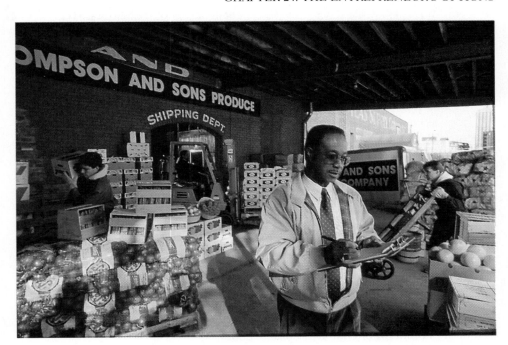

A manager checks a shipment of the products that his firm sells. What form of organization would this firm likely find to be best for doing business and why?

▌Major Traditional Business Forms

Traditionally, entrepreneurs have used three major forms to structure their business enterprises: the sole proprietorship, the partnership, and the corporation.

Sole Proprietorships

The simplest form of business is a **sole proprietorship.** In this form, the owner is the business; thus, anyone who does business without creating a separate business organization has a sole proprietorship. Sole proprietorships constitute over two-thirds of all American businesses. They are also usually small enterprises—about 1 percent of the sole proprietorships existing in the United States have revenues that exceed $1 million per year. Sole proprietors can own and manage any type of business from an informal, home-office undertaking to a large restaurant or construction firm.

A major advantage of the sole proprietorship is that the proprietor receives all of the profits (because he or she assumes all of the risk). In addition, it is often easier and less costly to start a sole proprietorship than to start any other kind of business, as few legal forms are involved. This type of business organization also entails more flexibility than does a partnership or a corporation. The sole proprietor is free to make any decision he or she wishes to concerning the business—whom to hire, when to take a vacation, what kind of business to pursue, and so on. A sole proprietor pays only personal income taxes on profits, which are reported as personal income on the proprietor's personal income tax form. Sole proprietors are also allowed to establish tax-exempt retirement accounts in the form of Keogh plans.[1]

The major disadvantage of the sole proprietorship is that, as sole owner, the proprietor alone bears the burden of any losses or liabilities incurred by the business enterprise. In other words, the sole proprietor has unlimited liability, or legal responsibility, for all obligations incurred in doing business. This unlimited liability is a major factor

SOLE PROPRIETORSHIP
The simplest form of business, in which the owner is the business; the owner reports business income on his or her personal income tax return and is legally responsible for all debts and obligations incurred by the business.

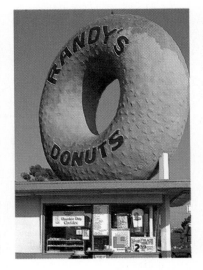

What are the advantages of doing business as a sole proprietorship?

---

1. A *Keogh plan* is a retirement program designed for self-employed persons through which a certain percentage of their income can be contributed to the plan, and interest earnings will not be taxed until funds are withdrawn from the plan.

to be considered in choosing a business form. Another disadvantage is that the proprietor's opportunity to raise capital is limited to personal funds and the funds of those who are willing to make loans. The sole proprietorship also has the disadvantage of lacking continuity upon the death of the proprietor. When the owner dies, so does the business—it is automatically dissolved. If the business is transferred to family members or other heirs, a new proprietorship is created.

Partnerships

Traditionally, partnerships have been classified as either general partnerships or limited partnerships. The two forms of partnership differ considerably in regard to legal requirements and the rights and liabilities of partners. We look here at the basic characteristics of each of these forms (both forms are examined in greater detail in Chapter 25).

GENERAL PARTNERSHIPS A **partnership** arises from an agreement, express or implied, between two or more persons to carry on a business for profit. Partners are co-owners of a business and have joint control over its operation and the right to share in its profits. No particular form of partnership agreement is necessary for the creation of a partnership, but for practical reasons, the agreement should be in writing. Basically, the partners may agree to almost any terms when establishing the partnership so long as they are not illegal or contrary to public policy.

A partnership is a legal entity only for limited purposes, such as the partnership name and title of ownership and property. A key advantage of the partnership is that the firm itself does not pay federal income taxes, although the firm must file an information return with the Internal Revenue Service (IRS). A partner's profit from the partnership (whether distributed or not) is taxed as individual income to the individual partner. The main disadvantage of the partnership is that the partners are subject to personal liability for partnership obligations. In other words, if the partnership cannot pay its debts, the personal assets of the partners are subject to creditors' claims.

LIMITED PARTNERSHIPS A special and quite popular form of partnership is the **limited partnership,** which consists of at least one general partner and one or more limited partners. A limited partnership is a creature of statute, because it does not come into existence until a *certificate of partnership* is filed with the appropriate state office. A **general partner** assumes responsibility for the management of the partnership and liability for all partnership debts. A **limited partner** has no right to participate in the general management or operation of the partnership and assumes no liability for partnership debts beyond the amount of capital he or she has contributed. Thus, one of the major benefits of becoming a limited partner is this limitation on liability, both with respect to lawsuits brought against the partnership and the amount of money placed at risk.

PARTNERSHIP
An agreement by two or more persons to carry on, as co-owners, a business for profit.

LIMITED PARTNERSHIP
A partnership consisting of one or more general partners (who manage the business and are liable to the full extent of their personal assets for debts of the partnership) and of one or more limited partners (who contribute only assets and are liable only up to the amount contributed by them).

GENERAL PARTNER
In a limited partnership, a partner who assumes responsibility for the management of the partnership and liability for all partnership debts.

LIMITED PARTNER
In a limited partnership, a partner who contributes capital to the partnership but has no right to participate in the management and operation of the business. The limited partner assumes no liability for partnership debts beyond the capital contributed.

International Perspective

Many nations permit businesspersons to establish limited partnerships. Often, as in the United States, limited partnerships must comply with statutory requirements. In Argentina, for example, the limited partnership (called a *sociedad en comandita*) is closely regulated by the government. Additionally, as in the United States, other nations commonly provide that in a limited partnership, the limited partners cannot participate in management. In Argentina, for example, limited partners are known as "sleeping partners" and have limited liability so long as they do not participate in management.

For Critical Analysis: *The right to participate in management is an important right of partners in an ordinary partnership. Why are limited partners in a limited partnership prohibited from exercising this right?*

Corporations

A third and widely used type of business organizational form is the **corporation**. Corporations are owned by *shareholders*—those who have purchased ownership shares in the business. A *board of directors*, elected by the shareholders, manages the business. The board of directors normally employs *officers* to oversee day-to-day operations.

The corporation, like the limited partnership, is a creature of statute. The corporation's existence as a legal entity, which can be perpetual, depends generally on state law. The law governing the formation, management and operation, liability, and termination of corporations will be discussed in detail in Chapters 26 through 29.

One of the key advantages of the corporate form of business is that the liability of its owners (shareholders) is limited to their investments. The shareholders usually are not personally liable for the obligations of the corporation. Another advantage is that a corporation can raise capital by selling shares of corporate stock to investors. A key disadvantage of the corporate form is that any distributed corporate income is taxed twice. The corporate entity pays taxes on the firm's income, and when income is distributed to shareholders, the shareholders again pay taxes on that income.

Some small corporations are able to avoid this double-taxation feature of the corporation by electing to be treated, for tax purposes, as an **S corporation**. Subchapter S of the Internal Revenue Code allows qualifying corporations to be taxed in a way similar to the way a partnership is taxed. In other words, an S corporation is not taxed at the corporate level. As in a partnership, the income is taxed only once—when it is distributed to the shareholder-owners, who pay personal income taxes on their respective shares of the profits. (See Chapter 26 for a further discussion of S corporations.)

▌ Major Traditional Business Forms Compared

Exhibit 24–1 lists the essential advantages and disadvantages of each of the three major traditional forms of business organization. We select for discussion here four important concerns for anyone starting a business—the ease of creation, the liability of the owners, tax features, and the need for capital.

Ease of Creation

No formalities are required in starting a business as a sole proprietorship. A general partnership can be organized easily and inexpensively. A corporation must be organized according to specific statutory procedures, must have sufficient capitalization, and must pay other costs of formal incorporation. In fact, throughout its life, a corporation is subject to more governmental supervision and reporting requirements than a partnership or a sole proprietorship normally is.

Liability of Owners

Generally, sole proprietors and general partners have personal liability, whereas the liability of limited partners and shareholders of corporations is limited to their investments. The issue of liability is an important one for the firm's owners, who may not want to place their personal assets at risk in the event the business cannot meet its obligations. The form of the organization does not always in and of itself determine the liability of the owners, however. For example, a court may "pierce the corporate veil" in certain circumstances (as will be discussed in Chapter 26) and hold corporate shareholders personally liable for corporate obligations.

Furthermore, creditors may not be willing to extend credit to a newly formed or small corporation precisely because of the limited liability of corporate owners. Typically, if a corporation has relatively few shareholders, a bank or other lender will

CORPORATION
A legal entity formed in compliance with statutory requirements. The entity is distinct from its shareholders-owners.

S CORPORATION
A close business corporation that has met certain requirements as set out by the Internal Revenue Code and thus qualifies for special income-tax treatment. Essentially, an S corporation is taxed the same as a partnership, but its owners enjoy the privilege of limited liability.

♦ Exhibit 24–1
Major Business Forms Compared

CHARACTERISTIC	SOLE PROPRIETORSHIP	PARTNERSHIP	CORPORATION
Method of Creation	Created at will by the owner.	Created by agreement of the parties.	Charter issued by the state—created by statutory authorization.
Legal Position	Not a separate entity; the owner is the business.	Not a separate legal entity in some states.	Always a legal entity separate and distinct from its owners—a legal fiction for the purposes of owning property and being a party to litigation
Liability	Unlimited liability.	Unlimited liability.	Limited liability of shareholders—shareholders are not liable for the debts of the corporation.
Duration	Determined by the owner; automatically dissolved on the owner's death.	Terminated by agreement of the partners, by the death of one or more of the partners, by withdrawal of a partner, by bankruptcy, and so on.	Can have perpetual existence.
Transferability of Interest	Interest can be transferred, but the individual's proprietorship then ends.	Although a partnership interest can be assigned, the assignee normally does not have the full rights of a partner.	Shares of stock can be transferred.
Management	Completely at the owner's discretion.	Each general partner has a direct and equal voice in management unless expressly agreed otherwise in the partnership agreement.	Shareholders elect directors, who set policy and appoint officers.
Taxation	The owner pays personal taxes on business income.	Each partner pays income taxes based on a pro rata share of net profits, whether or not they are distributed.	Double taxation—the corporation pays income tax on net profits, with no deduction for dividends, and shareholders pay income tax on disbursed dividends they receive.
Organizational Fees, Annual License Fees, and Annual Reports	None.	None.	All required.
Transaction of Business in Other States	Generally no limitation.	Generally no limitation.[a]	Normally must qualify to do business and obtain a certificate of authority.

a. A few states have enacted statutes requiring that foreign (out-of-state) partnerships qualify to do business there—for example, 3 N.H.Rev.Stat.Ann. Chapter 305-A in New Hampshire.

require the shareholders to cosign or guarantee personally any loans made to the corporation. That is, the shareholders agree to become personally liable for the loan if the corporation cannot meet its debts or goes bankrupt. In essence, the shareholders become guarantors for the corporation's debt. Hence, the corporate form of business does not prevent the shareholders from having personal liability in such a situation, because they have assumed the liability voluntarily.

Tax Considerations

Various tax considerations must be taken into account when one decides how best to organize a business. As discussed earlier, income earned by a sole proprietor is simply taxed as personal income. Tax aspects of partnerships and corporations are summarized in Exhibit 24–2.

The Need for Capital

One of the most common reasons for changing from a sole proprietorship to a partnership or a corporation is the need for additional capital to finance expansion. A sole proprietor can seek partners who will bring capital with them. The partnership might be able to secure more funds from potential lenders than could the sole proprietor.

"What is the difference between a taxidermist and a tax collector? The taxidermist takes only your skin."

Samuel Clemens (Mark Twain), 1835–1910 *(American author and humorist)*

♦ **Exhibit 24–2**
Tax Aspects of Partnerships and Corporations[a]

TAX ASPECT	PARTNERSHIP	CORPORATION
Federal Income Tax	Partners are taxed on proportionate shares of partnership income, even if not distributed; the partnership files information returns only.	The income of the corporation is taxed; stockholders are also taxed on distributed dividends. The corporation files corporate income tax forms.
Accumulation	Partners are taxed on accumulated as well as distributed earnings.	Corporate stockholders are not taxed on accumulated earnings. There is, however, a penalty tax, in some instances, that the corporation must pay for "unreasonable" accumulations of income.
Capital Gains	Partners are taxed on their proportionate shares of capital gains, which are taxed at the ordinary income rate.	The corporation is taxed on capital gains and losses.
Exempt Income	Partners are not taxed on exempt income received from the firm.	Any exempt income distributed by a corporation is fully taxable income to the stockholders.
Pension Plan	Partners can adopt a Keogh plan, an Individual Retirement Account (IRA), or a 401-K plan.	Employees and officers who are also stockholders can be beneficiaries of a pension trust. The corporation can deduct its payments to the trust.
Social Security	Partners must pay a self-employment tax (in 1996, 12.4 percent on income up to $62,700, plus 2.9 percent Medicare tax on all income).	All compensation to officers and employee-stockholders is subject to Social Security taxation up to the maximum.
Death Benefits (excluding those provided by insurance)	There is no exemption for payments to partners' beneficiaries.	Benefits up to $5,000 can be received tax-free by employees' beneficiaries.
State Taxes	The partnership is not subject to taxes. State income taxes are paid by each partner.	The corporation is subject to state income taxes (although these taxes can be deducted on federal returns).

a. As of 1996.

When a firm wants to expand greatly, however, simply increasing the number of partners can result in too many partners and make it difficult for the firm to operate effectively. Therefore, incorporation might be the best choice for an expanding business organization because a corporation can obtain more capital by issuing shares of stock. The original owners will find that, although their proportionate ownership of the company is reduced, they are able to expand much more rapidly by selling shares in the company.

☐ Technology and the Entrepreneur

Technology via the Internet has allowed those with relatively small capital needs to access, easily and inexpensively, a large number of potential investors. Today, there are several on-line "matching services." These services specialize in matching potential investors with companies seeking investors. A small company seeking capital investment could pay a fee to a service provider, which would then include a description of the company in a list that it makes available to investors—also for a fee.

For example, one on-line service provider, American Venture, charges each company $150 for a six-month listing that includes a one-page summary of the company's business. Investors, for a fee of $95, can have access to American Venture's list of companies for a year. If an investor is interested in a particular company, he or she can contact the company directly. Other on-line providers offer even more services for entrepreneurs, including franchising opportunities.

Matching services are not new. For decades, several companies have provided such services by using computerized databases to match business firms' investment needs with potential investors. What is new is that many of these service providers are now going on-line and expanding the geographical scope of their operations.

For Critical Analysis: *How can an investor who uses on-line matching services protect himself or herself against fraud?*

▌Limited Liability Companies

The two most common forms of business organization selected by two or more persons entering into business together are the partnership and the corporation. As already explained—and summarized in Exhibits 24–1 and 24–2—each form has distinct advantages and disadvantages. For partnerships, the advantage is that partnership income is taxed only once (all income is "passed through" the partnership entity to the partners themselves, who are taxed only as individuals); the disadvantage is the personal liability of the partners. For corporations, the advantage is the limited liability of shareholders; the disadvantage is the double taxation of corporate income. For many entrepreneurs and investors, the ideal business form would combine the tax advantages of the partnership form of business with the limited liability of the corporate enterprise.

The limited partnership and the S corporation partially address these needs. The limited liability of limited partners, however, is conditional: limited liability exists only so long as the limited partner does *not* participate in management. The problem with S corporations is that only small corporations (those with thirty-five or fewer shareholders) may acquire S corporation status. Furthermore, with few exceptions, only *individuals* may be shareholders in an S corporation; partnerships and corporations cannot be shareholders. Finally, no nonresident alien can be a shareholder in an S corporation. This means that if, say, a European investor wanted to purchase shares in an S corporation, it would not be permissible.

LIMITED LIABILITY COMPANY (LLC)
A hybrid form of business enterprise that offers the limited liability of the coporation but the tax advantages of a partnership.

Since 1977, an increasing number of states have authorized a new form of business organization called the **limited liability company (LLC)**. The LLC is a hybrid form of business enterprise that offers the limited liability of the corporation but the tax advantages of a partnership. The origins and characteristics of this increasingly significant form of business organization are discussed in the following *Landmark in the Law*. State statutes also now provide for limited liability partnerships (LLPs), which are similar in structure to limited liability companies. LLPs will be discussed in Chapter 25.

Limited Liability Company (LLC) Statutes

In 1977, the state of Wyoming passed legislation authorizing the creation of a limited liability company (LLC). Interest in LLCs mushroomed after a 1988 ruling by the Internal Revenue Service that Wyoming LLCs would be taxed as partnerships instead of as corporations. Before that ruling, the only other state to enact a statute authorizing LLCs was Florida, in 1982. By 1996, all but a few states had enacted LLC statutes. The various state LLC statutes are far from uniform, but generally they are based on the Wyoming act's provisions, with variations based on the corporate and partnership laws of whatever state is enacting the LLC statute.

A major advantage of the LLC is that, like the partnership and the S corporation, the LLC does not pay taxes as an entity; rather, profits are "passed through" the LLC and paid personally by the members of the company. Another advantage is that the liability of members is limited to the amount of their investments. In an LLC, members are allowed to participate fully in management activities, and under at least one state's statute, the firm's managers need not even be members of the LLC. Yet another advantage is that corporations and partnerships, as well as foreign investors, can be LLC members, whereas these entities cannot be shareholders in S corporations. Also in contrast to S corporations, there is no limit on the number of shareholder-members of the LLC.

The disadvantages of the LLC are relatively few. Perhaps the greatest disadvantage is that LLC statutes differ from state to state, and thus any firm engaged in multi-state operations may face difficulties. In an attempt to promote some uniformity among the states in respect to LLC statutes, the National Conference of Commissioners on Uniform State Laws drafted a uniform limited liability company statute for submission to the states to consider for adoption. Until all of the states have adopted the uniform law, however, an LLC in one state will have to check the rules in the other states in which the firm does business to ensure that it retains its limited liability.

Although LLCs emerged in the United States only in 1977, they have been in existence for over a century in other areas, including several European and South American nations. Part of the impetus behind creating LLCs in this country is that foreign investors are allowed to become LLC members. Generally, in an era increasingly characterized by global business efforts and investments, the LLC offers U.S. firms and potential investors from other countries flexibility and opportunities greater than those available through partnerships or corporations.

For Critical Analysis: *Given the fact that the tax and liability characteristics of partnerships and corporations have long been in existence, why is it that LLC statutes have emerged only recently?*

CONTRAST A partnership must have at least two partners. In many states, an LLC can be created with only one shareholder-member.

▮ Other Organizational Forms

Besides the business forms already discussed, there are several other forms that can be used to organize a business. For the most part, these other business forms are hybrid organizations—that is, they have characteristics similar to those of partnerships or corporations or combine features of both. We look at several of these forms here.

Joint Venture

When two or more persons or entities combine their interests in a particular business enterprise and agree to share in losses or profits equally or in proportion to their contributions, they are engaged in a *joint venture*. The joint venture is treated much like a partnership, but it differs in that it is created in contemplation of a limited activity or a single transaction.

     Members of a joint venture usually have limited powers to bind their co-venturers. A joint venture is normally not a legal entity and therefore cannot be sued as such, but its members can be sued individually. Usually, joint ventures are taxed like partnerships. They range in size from very small activities to huge, multimillion-dollar joint actions engaged in by some of the world's largest corporations.

CONTRAST A partnership involves a continuing relationship of the partners. A joint venture is essentially a one-time association.

Syndicate

A group of individuals getting together to finance a particular project, such as the building of a shopping center or the purchase of a professional basketball franchise, is called a *syndicate* or an *investment group.* The form of such groups varies considerably. A syndicate may exist as a corporation or as a general or limited partnership. In some cases, the members merely own property jointly and have no legally recognized business arrangement.

Joint Stock Company

A *joint stock company* or *association* is a true hybrid of a partnership and a corporation. It has many characteristics of a corporation in that (1) its ownership is represented by transferable shares of stock, (2) it is usually managed by directors and officers of the company or association, and (3) it can have a perpetual existence. Most of its other features, however, are more characteristic of a partnership, and it is usually treated like a partnership. As with a partnership, it is formed by agreement (not statute), property is usually held in the names of the members, shareholders have personal liability, and generally the company is not treated as a legal entity for purposes of a lawsuit. In a joint stock company, however, shareholders are not considered to be agents of each other, as would be the case if the company were a true partnership (see Chapter 25).

Business Trust

A *business trust* is created by a written trust agreement that sets forth the interests of the beneficiaries and the obligations and powers of the trustees. With a business trust, legal ownership and management of the property of the business stay with one or more of the trustees, and the profits are distributed to the beneficiaries.

     The business trust was started in Massachusetts in an attempt to obtain the limited liability advantage of corporate status while avoiding certain restrictions on a corporation's ownership and development of real property. The business trust resembles a corporation in many respects. Beneficiaries of the trust, for example, are not personally responsible for the debts or obligations of the business trust. In fact, in a number of states, business trusts must pay corporate taxes.

Cooperative

A *cooperative* is an association, either incorporated or not, that is organized to provide an economic service, without profit, to its members (or shareholders). An incorporated cooperative is subject to state laws governing nonprofit corporations. It will make distributions of dividends, or profits, to its owners on the basis of their transactions with the cooperative rather than on the basis of the amount of capital they contributed. Cooperatives that are unincorporated are often treated like partnerships. The members have joint liability for the cooperative's acts.

This form of business is generally adopted by groups of individuals who wish to pool their resources to gain some advantage in the marketplace. Consumer purchasing co-ops are formed to obtain lower prices through quantity discounts. Seller marketing co-ops are formed to control the market and thereby obtain higher sales prices from consumers. Often cooperatives are exempt from certain federal laws, such as *antitrust* laws (laws prohibiting anticompetitive practices—see Chapter 30), because of their special status.

▌ Private Franchises

Times have changed dramatically since Ray Kroc, the late founder of McDonald's, launched the franchising boom more than thirty-five years ago. Today, over a third of all retail sales and an increasing part of the total annual national output of the United States are generated by private franchises.

A **franchise** is defined as any arrangement in which the owner of a trademark, a trade name, or a copyright licenses others to use the trademark, trade name, or copyright in the selling of goods or services. A **franchisee** (a purchaser of a franchise) is generally legally independent of the **franchisor** (the seller of the franchise). At the same time, the franchise is economically dependent on the franchisor's integrated business system. In other words, a franchisee can operate as an independent businessperson but still obtain the advantages of a regional or national organization. Well-known franchises include McDonald's, KFC, and Burger King.

Types of Franchises

Because the franchising industry is so extensive (at least sixty-five types of distinct businesses sell franchises), it is difficult to summarize the many types of franchises that now exist. Generally, though, the majority of franchises fall into one of the following three classifications: distributorships, chain-style business operations, or manufacturing or processing-plant arrangements. We briefly describe these types of franchises here.

DISTRIBUTORSHIP A *distributorship* arises when a manufacturing concern (franchisor) licenses a dealer (franchisee) to sell its product. Often, a distributorship covers an exclusive territory. An example of this type of franchise is an automobile dealership.

CHAIN-STYLE BUSINESS OPERATION A *chain-style business operation* exists when a franchise operates under a franchisor's trade name and is identified as a member of a select group of dealers that engages in the franchisor's business. Often, the franchisor requires that the franchisee maintain certain standards of operation. In addition, sometimes the franchisee is obligated to deal exclusively with the franchisor to obtain materials and supplies. Examples of this type of franchise are McDonald's and most other fast-food chains.

MANUFACTURING OR PROCESSING-PLANT ARRANGEMENT A *manufacturing or processing-plant arrangement* exists when the franchisor transmits to the franchisee the essential ingredients or formula to make a particular product. The franchisee then

FRANCHISE
Any arrangement in which the owner of a trademark, trade name, or copyright licenses another to use that trademark, trade name, or copyright, under specified conditions or limitations, in the selling of goods and services.

FRANCHISEE
One receiving a license to use another's (the franchisor's) trademark, trade name, or copyright in the sale of goods and services.

FRANCHISOR
One licensing another (the franchisee) to use his or her trademark, trade name, or copyright in the sale of goods or services.

Familiar franchises compete for business. What laws govern the relationship between franchisors and franchisees?

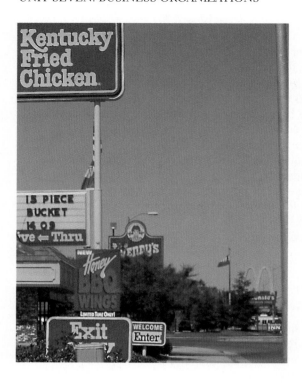

markets the product either at wholesale or at retail in accordance with the franchisor's standards. Examples of this type of franchise are Coca-Cola and other soft-drink bottling companies.

Laws Governing Franchising

KEEP IN MIND Because a franchise involves the licensing of a trademark, a trade name, or a copyright, the law governing intellectual property may apply in some cases.

Because a franchise relationship is primarily a contractual relationship, it is governed by contract law. If the franchise exists primarily for the sale of products manufactured by the franchisor, the law governing sales contracts as expressed in Article 2 of the Uniform Commercial Code applies (see Chapters 14 through 17). Additionally, the federal government and most states have enacted laws governing certain aspects of franchising. Generally, these laws are designed to protect prospective franchisees from dishonest franchisors and to prohibit franchisors from terminating franchises without good cause.

FEDERAL REGULATION OF FRANCHISING   Automobile dealership franchisees are protected from automobile manufacturers' bad faith termination of their franchises by the Automobile Dealers' Franchise Act[2]—also known as the Automobile Dealers' Day in Court Act—of 1965. If a manufacturer-franchisor terminates a franchise because of a dealer-franchisee's failure to comply with unreasonable demands (for example, failure to attain an unrealistically high sales quota), the manufacturer may be liable for damages.

Another federal statute is the Petroleum Marketing Practices Act (PMPA)[3] of 1979, which prescribes the grounds and conditions under which a franchisor may terminate or decline to renew a gasoline station franchise. Federal antitrust laws (discussed in Chapter 30), which prohibit certain types of anticompetitive agreements, may also apply in certain circumstances.

---

2.   15 U.S.C. Sections 1221 *et seq.*
3.   15 U.S.C. Sections 2801 *et seq.*

In 1979, the Federal Trade Commission (FTC) issued regulations that require franchisors to disclose material facts necessary to a prospective franchisee's making an informed decision concerning the purchase of a franchise.

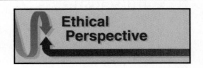

Ethical Perspective

A franchising relationship is based on a contract, and contract law thus applies. Why, then, has the government deemed it necessary to enact laws to protect franchisees from the consequences of contracts into which they have voluntarily entered? One reason is that a franchisee often relies heavily on information about the business provided by the franchisor when deciding to purchase a franchise. Disclosure laws, such as the FTC rule and disclosure requirements under state statutes, help to ensure that prospective franchisees have accurate information when deciding whether to enter into a franchise contract.

Another reason is that many franchise contracts are essentially adhesion contracts—in the sense that the purchaser of a franchise often has little bargaining power relative to the franchisor and little say in the contract provisions. Additionally, franchise contracts are typically lengthy documents, consisting of perhaps fifty pages (McDonald's eleven-page contract is an exception). A franchisee who is relatively inexperienced in business may not realize the economic and legal consequences of particular clauses in the contract or of the absence of certain clauses—such as a clause granting the franchisee exclusive rights to sell the franchisor's products in a particular territory.

For Critical Analysis: *Are lengthy franchise contracts necessarily disadvantageous to franchisees? Explain.*

REMEMBER Unfair contracts between a party with a great amount of bargaining power and another with little power are generally not enforced. This is part of the freedom *from* contract.

STATE REGULATION OF FRANCHISING   State legislation tends to be similar to federal statutes and the FTC regulations. For example, to protect franchisees, a state law might require the disclosure of information that is material to making an informed decision regarding the purchase of a franchise. This could include such information as the actual costs of operation, recurring expenses, and profits earned, along with facts substantiating these figures. State deceptive trade practices acts may also prohibit certain types of actions on the part of franchisors.

In response to the need for a uniform franchise law, the National Conference of Commissioners on Uniform State Laws drafted a model law that standardizes the various state franchise regulations. Because the uniform law represents a compromise of so many diverse interests, it has met with little success in being adopted as law by the various states.

The Franchise Contract

The franchise relationship is defined by a contract between the franchisor and the franchisee. The franchise contract specifies the terms and conditions of the franchise and spells out the rights and duties of the franchisor and the franchisee. If either party fails to perform the contractual duties, that party may be subject to a lawsuit for breach of contract. (If a franchisee is induced to enter into a franchise contract by the franchisor's fraudulent misrepresentation, the franchisor may also be liable for damages. See, for example, the case discussed in this chapter's *Business Law in Action.*)

Because each type of franchise relationship has its own characteristics, it is difficult to describe the broad range of details a franchising contract may include. In the remaining pages of this chapter, we look at some of the major issues that typically are addressed in a franchise contract.

A Case of Nondisclosure

Franchisors usually have numerous statistics and market studies available for prospective franchisees to examine. These data enable prospective franchisees to evaluate the likely return on their investments and to make an informed decision. What if a franchisor does not disclose certain data to a prospective franchisee—data that might dissuade the prospective franchisee from purchasing the franchise? Ford Motor Company learned the answer to this question when it was ordered to pay over $7.5 million in damages (including $6 million in punitive damages) to its franchisees who sued it for fraudulent misrepresentation.

In 1988, the plaintiffs, Samuel Foster II and Dee-Witt Sperau, had acquired a Ford dealership in Selma, Alabama. Foster was an African American, and he and Sperau had purchased the dealership pursuant to Ford's minority dealership program. Since the 1960s, Ford had actively recruited minority dealers and provided them with a number of

special benefits, including training and financial assistance. In 1987, Cornelius Willingham, an employee in Ford's district sales office in Charlotte, North Carolina, discussed the minority program with Foster. Foster later testified that Willingham had told him that the vast majority of African American dealers participating in the program were making profits and receiving a good return on their investments. Other Ford representatives with whom Foster dealt confirmed Willingham's representations.

In fact, the Ford representatives knew from studies of the minority program that the failure rate of minority dealers during the first two years was extremely high. None of the Ford representatives disclosed this information to either Foster or Sperau, however. If they had disclosed the information, Foster and Sperau probably would not have invested $1 million in the business—which went bankrupt after three years of operation.

When Foster and Sperau sued Ford for fraud, the trial court awarded damages to the plaintiffs. On appeal, the Alabama Supreme Court affirmed the trial court's judgment. The state's highest court held that "[t]here was evidence from which the jury could find, by a clear and convincing

standard, that Ford defrauded the Plaintiffs by using sales and profit forecasts and capitalization requirements which were deceptive based upon facts known to Ford." The court emphasized that "at the same time that it was aggressively recruiting African American dealer candidates, including Samuel Foster, with high sales and profits forecasts, Ford management was telling its board of directors that it expected these same new minority dealer candidates to be 'loss dealers.'"[a]

For Critical Analysis: *Ford argued that providing negative information to African American dealer candidates would discourage their participation in Ford's minority program. If you were the judge, how would you respond to this argument?*

a. *Sperau v. Ford Motor Co.,* 674 S.2d. 24 (Ala. 1995) The damages awarded in this case will likely be reduced substantially. In 1996, the United States Supreme Court remanded the case to the Alabama Supreme Court for further consideration in light of the Court's ruling on the issue of excessive damages in *BMW of North America, Inc. v. Gore,* ___ U.S. ___, 116 S.Ct. 1589, 134 L.Ed.2d 809 (1996)—see the *Business Law in Action* in Chapter 5.

PAYMENT FOR THE FRANCHISE   The franchisee ordinarily pays an initial fee or lump-sum price for the franchise license (the privilege of being granted a franchise). This fee is separate from the various products that the franchisee purchases from or through the franchisor. In some industries, the franchisor relies heavily on the initial sale of the franchise for realizing a profit. In other industries, the continued dealing between the parties brings profit to both. In most situations, the franchisor will receive a stated percentage of the annual sales or annual volume of business done by the franchisee. The franchise agreement may also require the franchisee to pay a percentage of advertising costs and certain administrative expenses.

LOCATION AND BUSINESS ORGANIZATION OF THE FRANCHISE   Typically, the franchisor will determine the territory to be served. The franchise agreement may specify whether the premises for the business must be leased or purchased outright. In some cases, construction of a building is necessary to meet the terms of the agreement. Often, the franchise contract will indicate whether the franchisee has exclusive rights, or "territorial rights," to a certain geographical area.

LAW IN THE EXTREME

The Letter of the Law

In the past decade or so, businesspersons have increasingly resorted to private express delivery services, such as Federal Express, to transport and deliver documents. Express delivery services offer not only speedier delivery but also security. Computerized tracking devices help to prevent important documents from being lost; also, normally the recipient must sign for the package, thus providing evidence of receipt.

The law, though, will not be rushed into new definitions and adaptations. If the law requires that a certain type of document be sent by mail, then sending the document by, for example, Federal Express may not suffice. Just this situation occurred in a North Carolina case. A Nissan dealer, who wished to relocate his business site, notified Nissan of the proposed relocation. Under North Carolina law, Nissan, if it objected to the relocation, had to notify the dealer of its objection in writing, by "registered or certified mail, return receipt requested," within thirty days. If Nissan failed to do so, it would waive its rights to object to the dealer's relocation. Nissan, however, sent its notice of objection via Federal Express, and thus the issue arose as to whether delivery by Federal Express satisfied the statute's requirements.

Eventually, the issue reached the North Carolina Supreme Court. Nissan argued that the legislature, when enacting the statute, "easily could have inserted language that would have provided for exclusive use of the U.S. Mail if it had intended for franchisors to send notice exclusively in this manner." The court held otherwise, concluding that the legislature "intended for the phrase 'registered or certified mail, return receipt requested' to refer exclusively to the delivery service offered by the U.S. Mail and not to notice delivered by any private delivery service." The court went on to say that "[o]ne reasonable purpose for requiring notice by registered or certified mail is to distinguish the [franchisor's] notice of objection from the correspondence that dealers receive daily from their franchisors by Federal Express and regular U.S. Mail. The dealership will be made aware of the notice if it is sent in an exclusive manner."[a] No doubt, Nissan is still pondering the mysterious ways of the law!

For Critical Analysis: *As long as a notice, such as Nissan's, is received within the time period specified by the statute, should the mode of delivery matter? Why would a statute ever specify a particular mode of delivery?*

a. *Nissan Division of Nissan Motor Corp. in U.S.A. v. Fred Anderson Nissan,* 337 N.C. 424, 445 S.E.2d 600 (1994).

Certainly the agreement will specify whether the franchisor supplies equipment and furnishings for the premises or whether this is the responsibility of the franchisee. When the franchise is a service operation, such as a motel, the contract often provides that the franchisor will establish certain standards for the facility and will make inspections to ensure that the standards are being maintained in order to protect the franchise's name and reputation.

The business organization of the franchisee is of great concern to the franchisor. Depending on the terms of the franchise agreement, the franchisor may specify particular requirements for the form and capital structure of the business. The franchise agreement can provide that standards of operation—relating to such aspects of the business as sales quotas, quality, and record keeping—be met by the franchisee. Furthermore, a franchisor may wish to retain stringent control over the training of personnel involved in the operation and over administrative aspects of the business. Although the day-to-day operation of the franchise business is normally left up to the franchisee, the franchise agreement may provide for the amount of supervision and control agreed on by the parties.

One area of franchising that often raises questions of fairness is the territorial exclusivity of the franchise. Some franchise contracts, while they define the territory allotted to a particular franchise, either specifically state that the franchise is nonexclusive or are silent on the issue of territorial rights. In either situation, the franchisee may suffer lost profits if the franchisor allows a competing franchise to be established nearby.

(Continued)

Ethical Perspective—Continued

Even when a contract is silent on the issue of territorial rights, though, courts may prohibit a franchisor from establishing new franchises in a particular geographical area at the expense of an existing franchise. In one case, for example, the court held that a franchisor's denial of exclusive rights did not mean that the franchisor could establish another franchise in the area. To construe a franchise agreement in such a fashion, said the court, "would run afoul of the principle that a contract contains such implied conditions as are necessary to make sense of the contract. Taken to its logical extreme," such a construction of a franchise agreement "would entitle [the franchisor] to set up a competing franchise next door to an existing franchise the day after the existing franchise had opened for business."[a]

For Critical Analysis: *Why would a prospective franchisee ever sign a franchise contract that did* not *provide for exclusive territorial rights?*

a.   *Burger King Corp. v. Weaver,* 798 F.Supp. 684 (S.D.Fla. 1992).

PRICE AND QUALITY CONTROLS OF THE FRANCHISE   Franchises provide the franchisor with an outlet for the firm's goods and services. Depending on the nature of the business, the franchisor may require the franchisee to purchase certain supplies from the franchisor at an established price.[4] A franchisor cannot, however, set the prices at which the franchisee will resell the goods, because this is a violation of state or federal antitrust laws, or both. A franchisor can suggest retail prices but cannot mandate them.

As a general rule, the validity of a provision permitting the franchisor to enforce certain quality standards is unquestioned. Because the franchisor has a legitimate interest in maintaining the quality of the product or service to protect its name and reputation, it can exercise greater control in this area than would otherwise be tolerated. Increasingly, however, franchisors are finding that if they exercise too much control over the operations of their franchisees, they may incur liability, as principals, for the torts of their franchisees' employees.

RECALL Under the doctrine of *respondeat superior,* an employer may be liable for the torts of his or her employees if they occur within the scope of employment, without regard to the personal fault of the employer.

TERMINATION OF THE FRANCHISE   The duration of the franchise is a matter to be determined between the parties. Generally, a franchise will start out for a short period, such as a year, so that the franchisee and the franchisor can determine whether they want to stay in business with one another. Usually, the franchise agreement will specify that termination must be "for cause," such as death or disability of the franchisee, insolvency of the franchisee, breach of the franchise agreement, or failure to meet specified sales quotas. Most franchise contracts provide that notice of termination must be given. If no set time for termination is specified, then a reasonable time, with notice, will be implied. A franchisee must be given reasonable time to wind up the business—that is, to do the accounting and return the copyright or trademark or any other property of the franchisor.

Because a franchisor's termination of a franchise often has adverse consequences for the franchisee, much franchise litigation involves claims of wrongful termination. Generally, the termination provisions of contracts are more favorable to the franchisor. This means that the franchisee, who normally invests a substantial amount of time and money in the franchise operation to make it successful, may receive little or nothing for the business on termination. The franchisor owns the trademark and hence the business.

---

4.   Although a franchisor can require franchisees to purchase supplies from it, requiring a franchisee to purchase exclusively from the franchisor may violate federal antitrust laws (see Chapter 30). For two landmark cases in these areas, see *United States v. Arnold, Schwinn & Co.,* 388 U.S. 365, 87 S.Ct. 1956, 18 L.Ed.2d (1967); and *Fortner Enterprises, Inc. v. U.S. Steel Corp.,* 394 U.S. 495, 89 S.Ct. 1252, 22 L.Ed.2d 495 (1969).

It is in this area that statutory and case law become important. The federal and state laws discussed earlier attempt, among other things, to protect franchisees from the arbitrary or unfair termination of their franchises by the franchisors. Generally, both statutory and case law emphasize the importance of good faith and fair dealing in terminating a franchise relationship.

In determining whether a franchisor has acted in good faith when terminating a franchise agreement, the courts generally try to balance the rights of both parties. If a court perceives that a franchisor has arbitrarily or unfairly terminated a franchise, the franchisee will be provided with a remedy for wrongful termination. If a franchisor's decision to terminate a franchise was made in the normal course of the franchisor's business operations, however, and reasonable notice of termination was given to the franchisee, normally a court would not consider such a termination wrongful. At issue in the following case is whether Domino's Pizza, Inc., had acted wrongfully when it terminated one of its franchises.

CASE 24.1

BENNETT ENTERPRISES, INC. v. DOMINO'S PIZZA, INC.
United States Court of Appeals, District of Columbia Circuit, 1995. 45 F.3d 493.

HISTORICAL AND SOCIAL SETTING *Pizza was originally an Italian dish, but its popularity exploded in the United States as part of the fast-food revolution that began in the 1950s. Today, the American appetite for pizza is more than eight pounds per person per year. U.S. pizza franchisors have spread their operations overseas to open pizza stores and restaurants in more than fifty countries. Pizza Hut, Inc., is the leader in sales in pizza restaurants. Domino's Pizza, Inc., is number one in pizza delivery sales.*

FACTS Bennett Enterprises, Inc., entered into a franchise agreement with Domino's Pizza, Inc., to operate a Domino's pizza store. The agreement stated that Domino's had the right to terminate the franchise if Bennett failed to comply with any provision, including a promise to comply with "all applicable laws." For most of its first year in business, Bennett did not turn a profit and did not pay any taxes. Domino's told Bennett that if it did not resolve its tax problems, Domino's would terminate the franchise. Bennett did not pay the taxes or work out a payment plan with the government, but instead sold the franchise and filed a suit against Domino's in a federal district court. Bennett charged Domino's with, among other things, breach of contract, on the ground that the franchise agreement did not entitle Domino's to

declare Bennett in default on the basis of unpaid taxes. The court ruled in Bennett's favor. Domino's appealed.

ISSUE Did Domino's have the right, under the franchise agreement, to consider Bennett in default for failing to pay taxes?

DECISION Yes. The U.S. Court of Appeals for the District of Columbia Circuit reversed the lower court's judgment.

REASON The court reasoned that the franchise agreement "is not ambiguous * * * because it is not reasonably or fairly susceptible to an interpretation that does not encompass compliance with state and federal tax laws." The court stated that "any reasonable construction" of the phrase "all applicable laws" in the franchise agreement includes tax laws "at the very minimum." The court concluded that "[t]o that extent the contract is unambiguous, and that is the only extent with which we are concerned."

FOR CRITICAL ANALYSIS—Economic Consideration *Would violations of other laws, such as parking ordinances or speed limits, have been sufficient grounds for Domino's to terminate Bennett's franchise?*

Application

Law and the Franchisee*

A franchise arrangement appeals to many prospective businesspersons for several reasons. Entrepreneurs who purchase franchises can operate independently and without the risks associated with products that have never been marketed before. Additionally, the franchisee can usually rely on the assistance and guidance of a management network that is regional or national in scope and that has been in place for some time.

Franchisees do face potential problems, however. Consider the franchise fee. Virtually all franchise contracts require a franchise fee payable up front or in installments. This fee often ranges between $5,000 and $35,000. For nationally known franchises, such as McDonald's, the fee may be $500,000 or more. The true cost of the franchise, however, must also include fees that are paid once the franchisee opens for business. For example, as a franchisee, you would probably pay royalties to the franchisor (for the use of the franchisor's trademark, for example) of anywhere from 2 to 8 percent of your gross sales. Another 1 to 2 percent of gross sales might go to the franchisor to cover advertising costs. Although your business would benefit from the advertising, the cost of that advertising might exceed the benefits you would realize.

Another problem that many franchisees do not anticipate is the adverse effects on their businesses of so-called electronic encroachment. For example, suppose that a franchise contract gives the franchisee exclusive rights to operate a franchise in a certain territory. Nothing in the contract, though, indicates what will happen if the franchisor sells its products to customers located within the franchisee's territory via telemarketing methods, mail-order catalogues, or on-line services over the Internet. Additionally, many franchisees today are feeling the effects of competition from kiosks, carts, or slimmed-down "express franchises" located in such places as airports, hospitals, and shopping malls. As a prospective franchisee, you should make sure that your franchise contract covers such contingencies and protects you against any losses you might incur if you face these types of competition in your area.

*This *Application* is not meant to substitute for the services of an attorney who is licensed to practice law in your state.

A major economic consequence, usually of a negative nature, will occur if the franchisor terminates your franchise agreement. Before you sign a franchise contract, make sure that the contract provisions regarding termination are reasonable and clearly specified.

Generally, to avoid potentially significant economic and legal problems, it is imperative that you obtain all relevant details about the business and that you have an attorney evaluate the franchise contract for possible pitfalls.

✓ Checklist for the Franchisee

1. Find out all you can about the franchisor: How long has the franchisor been in business? How profitable is the business? Is there a healthy market for the product?

2. Obtain the most recent financial statement from the franchisor and a complete description of the business.

3. Obtain a clear and complete statement of all fees that you will be required to pay.

4. Will the franchisor help you in training management and employees? With promotion and advertising? By supplying capital or credit? In finding a good location for your business?

5. Visit other franchisees in the same business. Ask them about their experiences with the product, the market, and the franchisor.

6. Evaluate your training and experience in the business upon which you are about to embark. Are they sufficient to ensure success as a franchisee?

7. Carefully examine the franchise contract provisions relating to termination of the franchise agreement. Are they specific enough to allow you to sue for breach of contract in the event the franchisor wrongfully terminates the contract? Find out how many franchises have been terminated in the past several years.

8. Will you have an exclusive geographical territory and, if so, for how many years? What plans does the franchisor have in regard to telemarketing, electronic marketing, and mail-order sales to customers within the territory?

9. Finally, the most important way to protect yourself is to have an attorney familiar with franchise law examine the contract before you sign it.

▌Key Terms

▌Chapter Summary: The Entrepreneur's Options

Major Traditional Business Forms *(See pages 621–626.)*	1. *Sole proprietorships*—The simplest form of business; used by anyone who does business without creating an organization. The owner is the business. The owner pays personal income taxes on all profits and is personally liable for all business debts. 2. *Partnerships*— a. General partnerships—Created by agreement of the parties; not treated as an entity except for limited purposes. Partners have unlimited liability for partnership debts, and each partner normally has an equal voice in management. Income is "passed through" the partnership to the individual partners, who pay personal taxes on the income. b. Limited partnerships—Must be formed in compliance with statutory requirements. A limited partnership consists of one or more general partners, who have unlimited liability for partnership losses, and one or more limited partners, who are liable only to the extent of their contributions. Only general partners can participate in management. 3. *Corporations*—A corporation is formed in compliance with statutory requirements, is a legal entity separate and distinct from its owners, and can have perpetual existence. The shareholder-owners elect directors, who set policy and hire officers to run the day-to-day business of the corporation. Shareholders normally are not personally liable for the debts of the corporation. The corporation pays income tax on net profits; shareholders pay income tax on disbursed dividends.
Limited Liability Companies *(See pages 626–627.)*	The limited liability company (LLC) is a hybrid form of business organization that offers the limited liability feature of corporations but the tax benefits of partnerships. Unlike limited partners, LLC members participate in management. Unlike shareholders in S corporations, members of LLCs may be corporations or partnerships, are not restricted in number, and may be residents of other countries.
Other Organizational Forms *(See pages 627–629.)*	1. *Joint venture*—An organization created by two or more persons in contemplation of a limited activity or a single transaction; otherwise, similar to a partnership. 2. *Syndicate*—An investment group that undertakes to finance a particular project; may exist as a corporation or as a general or limited partnership. 3. *Joint stock company*—A business form similar to a corporation in some respects (transferable shares of stock, management by directors and officers, perpetual existence), but otherwise resembling a partnership. 4. *Business trust*—Created by a written trust agreement that sets forth the interests of the beneficiaries and obligations and powers of the trustee(s). Similar to a corporation in many respects. Beneficiaries are not personally liable for the debts or obligations of the business trust. 5. *Cooperative*—An association organized to provide an economic service, without profit, to its members. May take the form of a corporation or a partnership.
Private Franchises *(See pages 629–635.)*	1. *Types of franchises*— a. Distributorship (for example, automobile dealerships). b. Chain-style operation (for example, fast-food chains). c. Manufacturing/processing-plant arrangement (for example, soft-drink bottling companies, such as Coca-Cola). 2. *Laws governing franchising*—Franchises are governed by contract law, occasionally by agency law, and by federal and state statutory and regulatory laws. *(Continued)*

▌Chapter Summary: The Entrepreneur's Options—Continued

Private Franchises—Continued	3. *The franchise contract—* a. Ordinarily requires the franchisee (purchaser) to pay a price for the franchise license. b. Specifies the territory to be served by the franchisee's firm. c. May require the franchisee to purchase certain supplies from the franchisor at an established price. d. May require the franchisee to abide by certain standards of quality relating to the product or service offered but cannot set retail resale prices. e. Usually provides for the date and/or conditions of termination of the franchise arrangement. Both federal and state statutes attempt to protect certain franchisees from franchisors who unfairly or arbitrarily terminate franchises.

▌For Review

1. Which form of business organization is the simplest? Which form arises from an agreement between two or more persons to carry on a business for profit? Which form consists of shareholders and is managed by officers appointed by a board of directors? What is a limited liability company?

2. Generally, the liability of a limited partner or a corporate shareholder is limited to the amount of his or her investment. Under what circumstances might a limited partner or a shareholder be held liable for the obligations of his or her partnership or corporation?

3. How are business profits taxed in each of the three major forms of business organization discussed in this chapter? How are business profits taxed in a limited liability company?

4. Besides sole proprietorships, partnerships, corporations, and limited liability companies, what other forms of business organization exist?

5. What is a franchise? What are the most common types of franchises? What terms and conditions are typically included in a franchise contract?

▌Questions and Case Problems

24–1. Forms of Business Organization. In each of the following situations, determine whether Georgio's Fashions is a sole proprietorship, a partnership, a limited partnership, or a corporation.

(a) Georgio's defaults on a payment to supplier Dee Creations. Dee sues Georgio's and each of the owners of Georgio's personally for payment of the debt.

(b) Georgio's raises $200,000 through the sale of shares of its stock.

(c) At tax time, Georgio's files a tax return with the IRS and pays taxes on the firm's net profits.

(d) Georgio's is owned by three persons, two of whom are not allowed to participate in the firm's management.

24–2. Choice of Business Form. Jorge, Marta, and Jocelyn are college graduates, and Jorge has come up with an idea for a new product that he believes could make the three of them very rich. His idea is to manufacture soft-drink dispensers for home use and market them to consumers throughout the Midwest. Jorge's personal experience qualifies him to be both first-line supervisor and general manager of the new firm. Marta is a born salesperson. Jocelyn has little interest in sales or management but would like to invest a large sum of money that she has inherited from her aunt. What factors should

Jorge, Marta, and Jocelyn consider in deciding which form of business organization to adopt?

24–3. Business Forms and Liability. The limited liability of corporate shareholders is one of the most important reasons that firms choose to organize as corporations rather than as partnerships or sole proprietorships. Limited liability means that if a corporation is not able to meet its obligations with corporate assets, creditors will not be allowed to look to the owners (stockholders) of the corporation to satisfy their claims. Assume that Jorge and Marta (in Question 24–2) do not have a wealthy friend like Jocelyn who wishes to go into business with them, and they therefore must borrow money to start their business. Jorge and Marta decide to incorporate. What do you think a lender will ask them when they seek a loan? What effect does this request have on the "advantage" of limited liability under state corporation statutes?

24–4. Business Forms and Liability. Assume that Faraway Corp. is considering entering into two contracts, one with a joint stock company that distributes home products east of the Mississippi River and the other with a business trust formed by a number of sole proprietors who are sellers of home products on the West Coast. Both contracts involve large capital outlays for Faraway, which will supply each business with soft-drink dispensers. In both business organizations, at least two share-holders or beneficiaries are personally wealthy, but each business organization has limited financial resources. The owner-managers of Faraway are not familiar with either form of business organization. Because each form resembles a corporation, they are concerned about whether they will be able to collect payments from the wealthy members of the business organizations in the event that either business organization breaches the contract by failing to make the payments. Discuss fully Faraway's concern.

24–5. Franchise Termination. H. C. Blackwell Co., Inc., was a truck dealership owned by the Blackwell family. In 1961, they had purchased a franchise from Kenworth Truck Co. to sell Kenworth trucks, and the franchise contract had been renewed several times. On February 4, 1976, Kenworth wrote a letter to the Blackwells informing them that the franchise would be terminated in ninety days unless they met twelve specific demands made by Kenworth. In trying to meet these demands—which included increased sales and capital improvements at the dealership—Blackwell spent approximately $90,000. By the end of the ninety-day period, however, the Blackwells had not met the demands, so Kenworth terminated the franchise. Blackwell sued Kenworth for damages on the ground that Kenworth had wrongfully terminated the franchise agreement and, in so doing, had violated the Automobile Dealers' Franchise Act. During the trial, Kenworth's regional sales manager stated that the demands imposed by Kenworth on Blackwell would have taken at least a year to meet. Did Kenworth wrongfully terminate the franchise under the Automobile Dealers' Franchise Act? [*H. C. Blackwell Co., Inc. v. Kenworth Truck Co.*, 620 F.2d 104 (5th Cir. 1980)]

24–6. Franchise Termination. In 1953, Atlantic Richfield Co. (ARCO) and Razumic signed a printed form titled "Dealer Lease." The agreement, which referred to the parties as lessor and lessee, authorized Razumic to operate an ARCO service station and provided, among other things, for ARCO's signs and trade name to be prominently displayed at the service station and for ARCO gasoline and other related products to be sold. The agreement detailed other aspects of the parties' business relationship, including Razumic's obligation to operate the service station in such a manner as to reflect favorably on ARCO's goodwill. These basic terms were in all renewal agreements made by the parties over the years. In 1973, ARCO notified Razumic that the agreement was being terminated and gave him thirty days to vacate the premises. Razumic refused, and ARCO filed suit to force termination of the agreement. Did the "Dealer Lease" constitute a franchise contract? If so—as the Petroleum Marketing Practices Act had not yet been passed when this case was decided—on what grounds might the court hold that ARCO could not terminate the franchise at will? [*Atlantic Richfield Co. v. Razumic*, 480 Pa. 366, 390 A.2d 736 (1978)]

24–7. Joint Ventures. Gustave Peterson contacted his family doctor, Leland Reichelt, complaining of abdominal pain. The doctor recommended gallbladder surgery. Another doctor, George Fortier, performed the surgery, and Reichelt assisted. It was Reichelt's normal practice to refer patients to Fortier for surgery, and each doctor charged the patient separately for his services. During the operation, a metal clip was inadvertently left inside Peterson's abdominal cavity. It eventually formed a

stone, which later caused Peterson to have chest and gastric pain. Peterson repeatedly complained to Reichelt, who diagnosed the problem as being related to either a hernia or stress. Peterson finally sought the advice of another physician, who, on performing surgery, discovered the metal clip. Peterson filed suit against both Reichelt and Fortier for malpractice under the theory that Fortier and Reichelt were engaged in a joint enterprise (joint venture). Discuss whether the two doctors were joint venturers. [*Peterson v. Fortier*, 406 N.W.2d 563 (Minn.App. 1987)]

24–8. Good Faith in Franchising Relationships. Ernst and Barbara Larese entered into a ten-year franchise agreement with Creamland Dairies, Inc. The agreement provided that the franchisee "shall not assign, transfer or sublet this franchise, or any of [the] rights under this agreement, without the prior written consent of Area Franchisor [Creamland] and Baskin Robbins, any such authorized assignment, transfer or subletting being null and without effect." The Lareses attempted to sell their franchise rights in February and August of 1979, but Creamland refused to consent to the sales. The Lareses brought suit, alleging that Creamland had interfered with their contractual relations with the prospective buyers by unreasonably withholding its consent; they claimed that Creamland had a duty to act in good faith and in a commercially reasonable manner when a franchisee sought to transfer its rights under the franchise agreement. Creamland contended that the contract gave it an unqualified right to refuse to consent to proposed sales of the franchise rights. Which party prevailed? Explain. [*Larese v. Creamland Dairies, Inc.*, 767 F.2d 716 (10th Cir. 1985)]

24–9. Franchise Termination. Texaco Refining & Marketing, Inc. (TRMI), a wholly owned subsidiary of Texaco, Inc., refines and markets motor fuels and other petroleum products for wholesale and retail distribution. After acquiring the Getty Oil Co., Texaco formed TRMI as part of Texaco's reorganization under Chapter 11 of the Bankruptcy Code. The Beck Oil Co. and four other firms each held distribution franchises with TRMI, the franchisor. TRMI withdrew from the geographical areas in which the franchisees had been distributing TRMI petroleum products; closed its outdated Lawrenceville, Illinois, refinery; and terminated the franchise agreements with Beck and the others. The franchisees sued TRMI in a federal district court for terminating the franchise agreements. The question before the court was whether TRMI had acted in good faith and in the normal course of business when it withdrew from the plaintiffs' marketing area. What federal statute will the court apply to this case? How should the court decide this issue? [*Beck Oil Co. v. Texaco Refining & Marketing, Inc.*, 822 F.Supp. 1326 (C.D.Ill. 1993)]

24–10. Franchise Termination. Ormsby Motors, Inc. (OMI), was a General Motors Corp. (GM) dealership. Their agreement provided for termination if OMI submitted "false . . . claims for any payment." Larry Kain was in charge of OMI's warranty claims. After several years of excessive claims, GM complained to OMI. When nothing changed, GM conducted a dealer audit. The audit uncovered, among other things, over eighty claims in one ten-day period for paint repair work that was never done. OMI denied knowledge of Kain's activities. GM terminated its dealership agreement with OMI. OMI asked a federal district court to stop the termination, arguing in part that GM did not have good cause. Did GM have good cause? Explain. [*Ormsby Motors, Inc. v. General Motors Corp.*, 842 F.Supp. 344 (N.D.Ill. 1994)]

24–11. Good Faith in Franchise Relations. Barn-Chestnut, Inc. (BCI), entered into a franchise agreement with Grocers Development Corp. (GDC) for a Convenient Food Mart "for as long as [BCI] . . . shall have a good and valid lease" to the property. GDC sold its interest in the franchise and the property to CFM Development Corp. When the lease was about to expire, CFM offered to enter into a new lease and franchise agreement with BCI at a significantly higher price. BCI refused. When CFM refused to make another deal, BCI filed a suit against CFM in a West Virginia state court on the ground that CFM had to offer BCI a lease because the franchise was contingent on a lease. The court did not agree. BCI then argued that the implied obligation of good faith required CFM to offer to renew the lease. Essentially, the question on appeal was whether a franchisor had an obligation to renew a franchise even though there was no clause in the contract requiring that the lease/franchise be renewed. Is BCI correct in contending that the franchisor does have such an obligation? Explain. [*Barn-Chestnut, Inc. v. CFM Development Corp.*, 193 W.Va. 565, 457 S.E.2d 502 (1995)]

**A QUESTION OF ETHICS
AND SOCIAL RESPONSIBILITY**

24–12. *Graham Oil Co. (Graham) had been a distributor of ARCO gasoline in Coos Bay, Oregon, for nearly forty years under successive distributorship agreements. ARCO notified Graham that it intended to terminate the franchise because Graham had not been purchasing the minimum amount of gasoline required under their most recent agreement. Graham sought a preliminary injunction against ARCO, arguing that ARCO*

had violated the Petroleum Marketing Practices Act (PMPA) by deliberately raising its prices so that Graham would be unable to meet the minimum gasoline requirements; thus, ARCO should not be allowed to terminate the agreement. The court ordered Graham to submit the claim to arbitration, in accordance with an arbitration clause in the distributorship agreement. Graham refused to do so, and the court granted summary judgment for ARCO. On appeal, Graham claimed that the arbitration clause was invalid because it forced him to forfeit rights given to franchisees under the PMPA, including the right to punitive damages and attorneys' fees. The appellate court agreed with Graham and remanded the case for trial. In view of these facts, answer the following questions. [Graham Oil Co. v. ARCO Products Co., A Division of Atlantic Richfield Co., 43 F.3d 1244 (9th Cir. 1994)]

1. Do you agree with Graham and the appellate court that statutory rights cannot be forfeited contractually, through an arbitration clause?
2. Review the discussion of arbitration in Chapter 3. Does the decision in the above case conflict with any established public policy concerning arbitration? Is the decision in the case consistent with other court decisions on arbitration discussed in Chapter 3, including decisions of the United States Supreme Court?

FOR CRITICAL ANALYSIS

24–13. *As indicated in this chapter, the law permits individuals to exercise the option of organizing their business enterprises in many different forms. What policy interests are served by granting entrepreneurs these options? Would it be better if the law required that everyone organize his or her business in the same form? Discuss.*

▌ Accessing the Internet: Business Law and Legal Environment

There is an Entrepreneurs' Forum on the commercial service CompuServe. There you can find answers to questions about incorporating and the like. When on CompuServe, type in the following:

Go usen

From the library menu, choose

Browse

Then select

Legalities

You can also obtain legal advice from the Microsoft Small Business Center if you subscribe to America Online. On that commercial service, the key word is

microsoft

Then click

The Small Business Center

And select

Legal Issues

You can get useful information from the Small Business Administration about financial assistance and the like from

http://www.sbaonline.sba.gov/

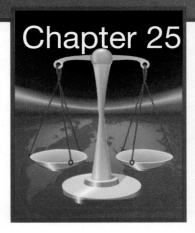

Chapter 25

Partnerships

"Many forms of conduct permissible in a
workaday world for those acting at arm's length,
are forbidden to those bound by fiduciary ties."

Benjamin Cardozo, 1870–1938
*(Associate justice of the United States
Supreme Court, 1932–1938)*

CHAPTER OBJECTIVES

After reading this chapter, you should be able to:

1. Identify the essential elements of a partnership.
2. Outline the rights, duties, and powers of partners.
3. Point out how general principles of agency apply to partnerships.
4. Explain how a partnership can be terminated.
5. Indicate the similarities and differences between limited partnerships and general partnerships.

When two or more persons agree to do business as partners, they enter into a special relationship with one another. To an extent, their relationship is similar to an agency relationship, because each partner is deemed to be the agent of the other partners and of the partnership. The agency concepts outlined in Chapter 23 thus apply—specifically, the imputation of knowledge of, and responsibility for, acts done within the scope of the partnership relationship. In their relations with one another, partners, like agents, are bound by the "fiduciary ties" referred to by Benjamin Cardozo in the opening quotation.

In one important way, however, partnership law is distinct from agency law. A partnership is based on a voluntary contract between two or more competent persons who agree to place money, labor, and skill in a business with the understanding that profits and losses will be shared. In a nonpartnership agency relationship, the agent usually does not have an ownership interest in the business, nor is he or she obliged to bear a portion of the ordinary business losses.

The Uniform Partnership Act (UPA) governs the operation of partnerships *in the absence of express agreement* and has done much to reduce controversies in the law relating to partnerships. Except for Louisiana, all of the states, as well as the District of Columbia, have adopted the UPA. The entire text of the UPA is presented in Appendix D of this book. A revised version of the UPA, known as the Revised Uniform Partnership Act (RUPA), was formally adopted by the National Conference of Commissioners on Uniform State Laws in 1992 and has already been adopted in some states. The RUPA significantly changes some of the rules governing partnerships. We indicate the most important changes in footnotes throughout this chapter.

In this chapter, we first examine the law governing the formation, operation, and termination of general partnerships. We then look at two special types of partnerships—the limited partnership and the limited liability partnership.

▌ Definition of Partnership

KEEP IN MIND Two or more persons are required to form a partnership. Most other forms of business can be organized by a single individual.

Conflicts commonly arise over whether a business enterprise is legally a partnership, especially in the absence of a formal, written partnership agreement. The UPA defines a *partnership* as "an association of two or more persons to carry on as co-owners a business for profit" [UPA 6(1)]. The *intent* to associate is a key element of a partnership, and one cannot join a partnership unless all other partners consent [UPA 18(g)].

Partnership Status

In resolving disputes over whether partnership status exists, courts will usually look for the following three essential elements of partnership implicit in the UPA's definition of the term:

1. A sharing of profits and losses.
2. A joint ownership of the business.
3. An equal right in the management of the business.

Businesspersons review documents. What elements would establish their association as a partnership rather than some other form of business organization?

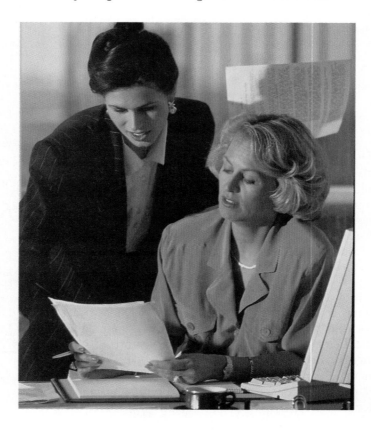

If the evidence in a particular case is insufficient to establish all three factors, the UPA provides a set of guidelines to be used. For example, the sharing of profits and losses from a business is considered *prima facie* ("on the face of it") evidence that a partnership has been created. No such inference is made, however, if the profits were received as payment of any of the following [UPA 7(4)]:

1. A debt by installments or interest on a loan.
2. Wages of an employee.
3. Rent to a landlord.
4. An annuity to a widow or representative of a deceased partner.
5. A sale of goodwill of a business or property.

Joint ownership of property, obviously, does not in and of itself create a partnership. Therefore, if Ablat and Burke own real property as joint tenants or as tenants in common (forms of joint ownership, to be discussed in Chapter 34), this does not mean that they are partners in a partnership. In fact, the sharing of gross returns and even profits from such ownership is usually not enough to create a partnership [UPA 7(2), (3)]. Thus, if Ablat and Burke jointly own a piece of rural property and lease the land to a farmer, the sharing of the profits from the farming operation conducted by the farmer in lieu of set rental payments would ordinarily not make Ablat, Burke, and the farmer partners. Note, though, that although the sharing of profits in itself does not prove the existence of a partnership, sharing *both profits and losses* usually does.

In the following case, three brothers and their sister bought a ranch from their parents. They owned the property as tenants in common. The issue was whether their ownership was a partnership.

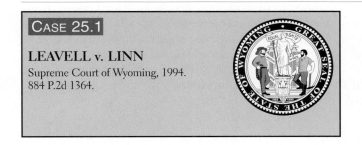

CASE 25.1

LEAVELL v. LINN
Supreme Court of Wyoming, 1994.
884 P.2d 1364.

HISTORICAL AND ENVIRONMENTAL SETTING *Anyone who is at least forty years old has seen the population of the world double in his or her lifetime. Over the same period, the population of the United States has also nearly doubled. This has meant an unprecedented expansion of cities into rural areas, turning farmland and ranch land that was once cheap into very valuable suburban property. Of course, such land is more valuable if, rather than being maintained as a farm or ranch, it is subdivided for the development of sites for homes and businesses.*

FACTS Connie, Bennie, Peter, and Eugene Linn agreed, in writing, to buy a ranch from their parents. The intent was to keep the property in the family, not to run the ranch as a business for profit. The siblings decided specifically not to form a partnership, but they routinely referred to themselves as "partners," and each year they filed a partnership tax return. Many years later, Connie and her husband, Harold Leavell, wanted to obtain sole ownership of a large part of the ranch. When the brothers refused to accommodate their sister, the Leavells filed a suit against the brothers and their spouses in a Wyoming state court. Among other things, the Leavells sought to have the siblings' ownership of the ranch declared to be a partnership (so that the property could then be divided according to partnership law, which the Leavells believed would be to their advantage). The court concluded that there was no partnership. The Leavells appealed to the Supreme Court of Wyoming.

ISSUE Did a partnership exist among the siblings?

DECISION No. The Supreme Court of Wyoming affirmed the lower court's decision.

REASON The state supreme court pointed out that one of the basic indications of partnership status was lacking: the agreement to carry on a business as co-owners for a profit. The court held that "the most obvious inference which might be drawn from the evidence" in this case is that "the agreement entered into by this family was not one intended to be a business for profit." The

(Continued)

Case 25.1—Continued

court also emphasized that the siblings did not intend to form a partnership when they bought the ranch. "While it cannot be denied that the agreement in question has many of the characteristics which might also be found in a partnership agreement," reasoned the court, "on its face it is not a partnership agreement." The court pointed out that the agreement did not use the words "partner" or "partnership" and that "the parties specifically decided not to form a partnership." The court concluded that

"unless the intent is clearly proved, this court will not construe a family arrangement as a partnership. * * * It is in just such circumstances of disagreement and disarray as those in which this family finds itself that it is especially important to read and strictly construe formal agreements."

FOR CRITICAL ANALYSIS—Economic Consideration
Which, if any, of the requirements for the creation of a partnership did the agreement among the Linn siblings satisfy?

Entity versus Aggregate

A partnership is sometimes called a *firm* or a *company*, terms that connote an entity separate and apart from its aggregate members. Sometimes the law of partnership recognizes a partnership as an *independent entity*, but for most other purposes, the law treats it as an *aggregate of the individual partners.*

At common law, a partnership was never treated as a separate legal entity. Thus, at common law a suit could never be brought by or against the firm in its own name; each individual partner had to sue or be sued. Today, most states provide specifically that the partnership can be treated as an entity for certain purposes. For example, a partnership usually can sue or be sued, collect judgments, and have all accounting procedures in the name of the partnership entity. In addition, the UPA recognizes that partnership property may be held in the name of the partnership rather than in the names of the individual partners. Finally, federal procedural laws frequently permit the partnership to be treated as an entity in such matters as suits in federal courts, bankruptcy proceedings, and informational federal tax returns.

When the partnership is not regarded as a separate legal entity, it is treated as an aggregate of the individual partners. For example, as discussed in Chapter 24, for federal income tax purposes, a partnership is not a tax-paying entity. The income and losses it incurs are passed through the partnership framework and attributed to the partners on their individual tax returns.

"Mr. Morgan buys his partners; I grow my own."

Andrew Carnegie, 1835–1918
(American industrialist and philanthropist)

▌Partnership Formation

A partnership is ordinarily formed by an explicit agreement among the parties, although the law recognizes another form of partnership—*partnership by estoppel*—which arises when persons who are not partners represent themselves as partners when dealing with third parties. This section will describe the requirements for the creation of a partnership, including references to the liability of alleged partners.

International Perspective

American businesspersons who wish to operate a partnership in another country need to check to see what that country requires in terms of local participation. If a country requires local participation, this means that a specific share of the business must be owned by nationals of the host country. In other words, the American businesspersons would need to admit to the partnership a partner or partners who live in the host country.

Sometimes, Americans seeking to establish partnerships (or to undertake joint ventures) in a country that requires local participation are reluctant to do so. This is

International Perspective—Continued

because the technology and expertise developed by the partnership business may end up in the hands of a future competitor if the partnership breaks up—and the American parties may have little recourse against their former partner's use of their intellectual property under the host country's law.

For Critical Analysis: *Do local participation rules benefit countries in the long run?*

The Partnership Agreement

As a general rule, agreements to form a partnership can be oral, written, or implied by conduct. Some partnership agreements, however, must be in writing to be legally enforceable within the Statute of Frauds (discussed in Chapter 11). For example, a partnership agreement that, by its terms, is to continue for more than one year must be evidenced by a sufficient writing.

A partnership agreement, called **articles of partnership,** usually specifies the name and location of the business, the duration of the partnership, the purpose of the business, each partner's share of the profits, how the partnership will be managed, how assets will be distributed on dissolution, and other provisions. As mentioned, the UPA applies only in the absence of the parties' agreement on a particular issue. The partnership agreement is thus binding on the parties, even if certain provisions, such as the distribution of profits, seem to be unfair. A sample partnership agreement is shown in Exhibit 25–1.[1]

ARTICLES OF PARTNERSHIP
A written agreement that sets forth each partner's rights and obligations with respect to the partnership.

---

1. The RUPA provides for the voluntary filing of a partnership statement, containing such information as the agency authority of the partners, with the secretary of state. The statement must be executed by at least two partners, a copy must be sent to all of the partners, and a certified copy must be filed in the office for recording transfers of real property (in most states, in the county in which the property is located).

Practically speaking, the provisions of any partnership agreement should always be in writing. For one thing, the amicable relations characteristic of a partnership at the outset may deteriorate over time. If a dispute arises and there is no written evidence of the partners' initial agreement on the matter being disputed, it will be one partner's word against the other's should the dispute come before a court. Additionally, the act of drafting a written agreement forces the partners to contemplate potential problems that may arise and to deal with those problems in advance.

For example, Turino and Crowder decide to create a partnership to sell tires. They orally agree that Turino will provide two-thirds of the capital to start up the business and will receive two-thirds of the profits in return. After the business is under way, Crowder claims that he is working harder at the business than Turino is, and thus at least one-half of the profits should be his. If the dispute ends up in court, Turino, because he has no evidence of the oral agreement, may indeed end up with only one half of the profits. This is because the law assumes that members of a partnership share profits and losses equally unless a partnership agreement provides otherwise, as will be discussed later in this chapter [UPA 18(a)]. Turino and Crowder could have avoided this problem by creating a written partnership agreement that specified how the profits would be shared.

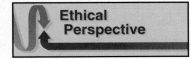

Ethical Perspective

For Critical Analysis: *How can members in a small partnership consisting of, say, three partners decide in advance what an equitable distribution of the firm's profits would be?*

◆ Exhibit 25–1
A Sample Partnership Agreement

PARTNERSHIP AGREEMENT

This agreement, made and entered into as of the _____ , by and among _____ _____ (hereinafter collectively sometimes referred to as "Partners").

WITNESSETH:

Whereas, the Parties hereto desire to form a General Partnership (hereinafter referred to as the "Partnership"), for the term and upon the conditions hereinafter set forth;

Now, therefore, in consideration of the mutual covenants hereinafter contained, it is agreed by and among the Parties hereto as follows:

Article I
BASIC STRUCTURE

Form. The Parties hereby form a General Partnership pursuant to the Laws of _____ _____ .

Name. The business of the Partnership shall be conducted under the name of _____ _____ .

Place of Business. The principal office and place of business of the Partnership shall be located at _____ , or such other place as the Partners may from time to time designate.

Term. The Partnership shall commence on _____ , and shall continue for _____ years, unless earlier terminated in the following manner: (a) By the completion of the purpose intended, or (b) Pursuant to this Agreement, or (c) By applicable _____ law, or (d) By death, insanity, bankruptcy, retirement, withdrawal, resignation, expulsion, or disability of all of the then Partners.

Purpose—General. The purpose for which the Partnership is organized is _____ _____ .

Article II
FINANCIAL ARRANGEMENTS

Each Partner has contributed to the initial capital of the Partnership property in the amount and form indicated on Schedule A attached hereto and made a part hereof. Capital contributions to the Partnership shall not earn interest. An individual capital account shall be maintained for each Partner. If at any time during the existence of the Partnership it shall become necessary to increase the capital with which the said Partnership is doing business, then (upon the vote of the Managing Partner(s)): each party to this Agreement shall contribute to the capital of this Partnership within _____ days notice of such need in an amount according to his then Percentage Share of Capital as called for by the Managing Partner(s).

The Percentage Share of Profits and Capital of each Partner shall be (unless otherwise modified by the terms of this Agreement) as follows:

Names	Initial Percentage Share of Profits and Capital

No interest shall be paid on any contribution to the capital of the Partnership. No Partner shall have the right to demand the return of his capital contributions except as herein provided. Except as herein provided, the individual Partners shall have no right to any priority over each other as to the return of capital contributions except as herein provided.

Distributions to the Partners of net operating profits of the Partnership, as hereinafter defined, shall be made at _____ . Such contributions shall be made to the Partners simultaneously.

For the purpose of this Agreement, net operating profit for any accounting period shall mean the gross receipts of the Partnership for such period, less the sum of all cash expenses of operation of the Partnership, and such sums as may be necessary to establish a reserve for operating expenses. In determining net operating profit, deductions for depreciation, amortization, or other similar charges not requiring actual current expenditures of cash shall *not* be taken into account in accordance with generally accepted accounting principles.

♦ Exhibit 25–1
A Sample Partnership Agreement—Continued

No partner shall be entitled to receive any compensation from the Partnership, nor shall any Partner receive any drawing account from the Partnership.

Article III
MANAGEMENT

The Managing Partner(s) shall be _____.

The Managing Partner(s) shall have the right to vote as to the management and conduct of the business of the Partnership as follows:

Names   **Vote**

Article IV
DISSOLUTION

In the event that the Partnership shall hereafter be dissolved for any reason whatsoever, a full and general account of its assets, liabilities and transactions shall at once be taken. Such assets may be sold and turned into cash as soon as possible and all debts and other amounts due the Partnership collected. The proceeds thereof shall thereupon be applied as follows:

(a) To discharge the debts and liabilities of the Partnership and the expenses of liquidation.

(b) To pay each Partner or his legal representative any unpaid salary, drawing account, interest or profits to which he shall then be entitled and in addition, to repay to any Partner his capital contributions in excess of his original capital contribution.

(c) To divide the surplus, if any, among the Partners or their representatives as follows: (1) First (to the extent of each Partner's then capital account) in proportion to their then capital accounts. (2) Then according to each Partner's then Percentage Share of [*Capital/Income*].

No Partner shall have the right to demand and receive property in kind for his distribution.

Article V
MISCELLANEOUS

The Partnership's fiscal year shall commence on January 1st of each year and shall end on December 31st of each year. Full and accurate books of account shall be kept at such place as the Managing Partner(s) may from time to time designate, showing the condition of the business and finances of the Partnership; and each Partner shall have access to such books of account and shall be entitled to examine them at any time during ordinary business hours. At the end of each year, the Managing Partner(s) shall cause the Partnership's accountant to prepare a balance sheet setting forth the financial position of the Partnership as of the end of that year and a statement of operations (income and expenses) for that year. A copy of the balance sheet and statement of operations shall be delivered to each Partner as soon as it is available.

Each Partner shall be deemed to have waived all objections to any transaction or other facts about the operation of the Partnership disclosed in such balance sheet and/or statement of operations unless he shall have notified the Managing Partner(s) in writing of his objections within thirty (30) days of the date on which statement is mailed.

The Partnership shall maintain a bank account or bank accounts in the Partnership's name in a national or state bank in the State of _____. Checks and drafts shall be drawn on the Partnership's bank account for Partnership purposes only and shall be signed by the Managing Partner(s) or their designated agent.

Any controversy or claim arising out of or relating to this Agreement shall only be settled by arbitration in accordance with the rules of the American Arbitration Association, one Arbitrator, and shall be enforceable in any court having competent jurisdiction.

Witnesses   **Partners**

_____   _____

_____   _____

Date: _____

Partnership Duration

The partnership agreement can specify the duration of the partnership in terms of a date or the completion of a particular project. A partnership that is specifically limited in duration is called a *partnership for a term*. A dissolution without the consent of all the partners prior to the expiration of the partnership term constitutes a breach of the agreement, and the responsible partner can be liable for any losses resulting from it. If no fixed duration is specified, the partnership is a *partnership at will*. This type of partnership can be dissolved at any time by any partner without violating the agreement and without incurring liability for losses to other partners resulting from the termination.

The Corporation as Partner

REMEMBER A limited liability company provides many of the advantages of partnerships and corporations without all of the same restrictions.

General partners are personally liable for the debts incurred by the partnership. If one of the general partners is a corporation, however, what does personal liability mean? Basically, the capacity of corporations to contract is a question of corporation law. Many states have restrictions on corporations becoming partners, although such restrictions have become less common over the years. The Revised Model Business Corporation Act (discussed in Chapter 26), however, generally allows corporations to make contracts and incur liabilities, and the UPA specifically permits a corporation to be a partner. By definition, "a partnership is an association of two or more persons," and the UPA defines *person* as including corporations [UPA 2].

Partnership by Estoppel

Parties who are not partners sometimes represent themselves as such and cause third persons to rely on their representations. The law of partnership does not confer any partnership rights on these persons, but it may impose liability on them. This is also true when a partner represents, expressly or impliedly, that a nonpartner is a member of the firm. Whenever a third person has reasonably and detrimentally relied on the representation that a nonpartner was part of the partnership, *partnership by estoppel* is deemed to exist. When this occurs, the nonpartner is regarded as an agent whose acts are binding on the partnership. In the following case, an attorney's corporate client claimed to have relied on a representation that the attorney was a partner in a law firm.

CASE 25.2

ATLAS TACK CORP. v. DIMASI

Appeals Court of Massachusetts, Suffolk, 1994.
37 Mass.App.Ct. 66,
637 N.E.2d 230.

"professional associations." A professional association is a group of professionals organized to practice their profession together. This "association" need not be organized as a corporation or a partnership.

HISTORICAL AND SOCIAL SETTING *Professionals (accountants, attorneys, physicians, and others) commonly share office space with members of the same profession. They usually do not wish to share responsibility, however, for the wrongful acts of those with whom they share offices. To obtain the advantages of working near others in the same profession, professionals often form*

FACTS Attorneys Salvatore DiMasi, Ralph Donabed, and Stephen Karll shared office space, which they designated the "Law Offices of DiMasi, Donabed, & Karll, A Professional Association." They also shared stationery that bore the same heading and that listed their names, along with the names of other attorneys, in the margin. Atlas Tack Corporation hired Donabed to handle a certain legal matter. All correspondence and invoices from Donabed to Atlas were on the "Law Offices" stationery, and Atlas's payment for the services was in the form of checks payable to "DiMasi, Donabed & Karll." Believing that Donabed had done something wrong in his handling of its matter, Atlas filed a suit in a Massachusetts state

Case 25.2—Continued

court against Donabed, DiMasi, and Karll. Donabed settled out of court, but Atlas maintained the suit against DiMasi and Karll, alleging that they were Donabed's partners and were thus liable for Donabed's acts. The court granted the defendants' motion for summary judgment, and Atlas appealed.

ISSUE   Can the members of a professional association be considered partners by estoppel?

DECISION   Yes. The Appeals Court of Massachusetts reversed the lower court's judgment and remanded the case for trial.

REASON   The appeals court pointed out that DiMasi and Karll consented to Donabed's use of stationery with the heading "DiMasi, Donabed & Karll," as well as the legend "a professional association" and a list in the margin of attorneys "including themselves [and] Donabed." The court pointed out that the bills to Atlas came on stationery with this letterhead, with no indication that payment should be made to Donabed specifically "or that the bill was submitted by Donabed instead of the law office of DiMasi, Donabed & Karll." The court also reasoned that "the use of the term 'professional association' may well suggest a partnership to the public * * *. At the very least, the use of the term in the circumstances of this case presents a question * * * as to whether a partnership by estoppel exists."

FOR CRITICAL ANALYSIS—Social Consideration
What could the members of a professional association do to avoid liability for the wrongful acts of other members?

▌ Rights among Partners

The rights and duties of partners are governed largely by the specific terms of their partnership agreement. In the absence of provisions to the contrary in the partnership agreement, the law imposes the rights and duties discussed here. The character and nature of the partnership business generally influence the application of these rights and duties.

Interest in the Partnership

A partner's interest in the partnership is a personal asset consisting of a proportionate share of the profits earned [UPA 26] and a return of capital after the partnership is terminated. Each partner is entitled to the proportion of business profits and losses designated in the partnership agreement.

PROFITS AND LOSSES   If the agreement does not apportion profits or losses, the UPA provides that *profits shall be shared equally* and *losses shall be shared in the same ratio as profits* [UPA 18(a)]. To illustrate: The partnership agreement for Ponce and Brent provides for capital contributions of $6,000 from Ponce and $4,000 from Brent, but it is silent as to how Ponce and Brent will share profits or losses. In this situation, Ponce and Brent will share both profits and losses equally. If the partnership agreement provided for profits to be shared in the same ratio as capital contributions, however, 60 percent of the profits would go to Ponce, and 40 percent of the profits would go to Brent. If their partnership agreement was silent as to losses, losses would be shared in the same ratio as profits (60 percent to 40 percent).

ASSIGNMENT OF PARTNERSHIP INTEREST   A partner may assign (transfer) his or her interest in the partnership to another party. When a partner's interest is assigned, the assignee (the person to whom the interest was transferred) has the right to receive the partner's share of the profits and, on the partnership's termination, the partner's capital contribution. The assignee, however, does not become a partner in the partnership and thus has no say in the management or administration of the partnership affairs and

....

....

no right to inspect the partnership books. Rather, the partner who assigned his or her interest remains a partner with the full rights of a partner with respect to those rights that cannot be assigned.

CREDITOR'S LIEN ON PARTNERSHIP INTEREST   A partner's interest is also subject to a judgment creditor's lien (described in Chapter 22). A judgment creditor can attach a partner's interest by petitioning the court that entered the judgment to grant the creditor a **charging order.** This order entitles the creditor to the profits of the partner and to any assets available to the partner on the firm's dissolution [UPA 28].

Management Rights

Under the UPA, all partners have equal rights in managing the partnership [UPA 18(e)]. Each partner has one vote in management matters *regardless of the proportional size of his or her interest in the firm.* Often, in a large partnership, partners will agree to delegate daily management responsibilities to a management committee made up of one or more of the partners.

   The majority rule controls decisions in ordinary matters connected with partnership business, unless otherwise specified in the agreement. Decisions to undertake any of the actions listed below, however, if they are to be binding on the partnership, require the *unanimous* consent of the partners. This is because these decisions significantly affect the nature of the partnership.

1.   To alter the essential nature of the firm's business as expressed in the partnership agreement or to alter the capital structure of the partnership.
2.   To admit new partners or to enter a wholly new business [UPA 18(g), (h)].
3.   To assign partnership property into a trust for the benefit of creditors.
4.   To dispose of the partnership's goodwill.
5.   To confess judgment against the partnership or to submit partnership claims to arbitration. (A **confession of judgment** is the act of a debtor in permitting a judgment to be entered against him or her by a creditor, for an agreed sum, without the institution of legal proceedings.)
6.   To undertake any act that would make further conduct of partnership business impossible [UPA 9(3)].
7.   To amend the articles of the partnership agreement.

Compensation

A partner has a duty to expend time, skill, and energy on behalf of the partnership business, and such services are generally not compensable in the form of a salary. Rather, as mentioned, a partner's income from the partnership takes the form of a distribution of profits according to the partner's share in the business. Partners can, however, agree otherwise. For example, the managing partner of a law firm often receives a salary in addition to his or her share of profits for performing special administrative duties in office and personnel management. When a partnership must be terminated because a partner dies, a surviving partner is entitled to reasonable compensation for services relating to the final settlement of partnership affairs (and reimbursement for expenses incurred in the process) above and apart from his or her share in the partnership profits [UPA 18(f)].

   Each partner impliedly promises to subordinate his or her interests to those of the partnership. Assume that Hall, Banks, and Porter enter into a partnership. Porter undertakes independent consulting, in the same area in which the partnership specializes, for an outside firm without the consent of Hall and Banks. Porter's compensation from the outside firm is considered partnership income [UPA 21]. A partner cannot engage in any independent business that involves the partnership's time unless expressly agreed on by the partnership.

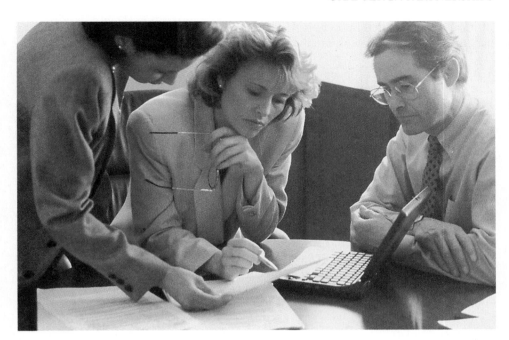

Businesspersons examine accounting records. Are there any restrictions on the right of a partner to inspect his or her firm's books and records? Why or why not?

Inspection of Books

Partnership books and records must be kept accessible to all partners. Each partner has the right to receive (and each partner has the corresponding duty to produce) full and complete information concerning the conduct of all aspects of partnership business [UPA 20]. Each firm keeps books in which to record and preserve such information. Partners contribute the information, and a bookkeeper or an accountant typically has the duty to preserve it. The books must be kept at the firm's principal business office and cannot be removed without the consent of all of the partners [UPA 19]. Every partner, whether active or inactive, is entitled to inspect all books and records on demand and can make copies of the materials. The personal representative of a deceased partner's estate has the same right of access to partnership books and records that the decedent would have had.

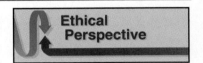

Ethical Perspective

The right to inspect partnership books and records helps to ensure that partners abide by their fiduciary duties to one another. If one partner suspects that another partner is using the partnership assets for personal gain, for example, an inspection of the partnership records will help to either confirm or dispel the suspicion. If partners did not have the right of inspection, there would be no way for them to monitor the nature and types of business transactions undertaken by the partnership. Furthermore, the partner's interest in the partnership is essentially a property right—a right to own a share of partnership assets and profits. This right would be meaningless if the partner did not have access to information indicating how his or her property was being used.

For Critical Analysis: *How can a partnership avoid having to give partners access to the books at all times for any reason, even a frivolous reason?*

Accounting of Assets

An accounting of partnership assets or profits is required to determine the value of each partner's share in the partnership. An accounting can be performed voluntarily, or it can be compelled by a court. Under UPA 22, a partner has the right to a formal accounting in the following situations:

1.   When the partnership agreement provides for a formal accounting.
2.   When a partner is wrongfully excluded from the business, from access to the books, or both.
3.   When any partner is withholding profits or benefits belonging to the partnership in breach of the fiduciary duty.
4.   When circumstances "render it just and reasonable."

Formal accounting also occurs by right in connection with *dissolution* proceedings (discussed later in this chapter). Generally, the principal remedy of a partner against co-partners is a suit for dissolution, an accounting, or both. With minor exceptions, a partner cannot maintain an action against other firm members for damages until partnership affairs are settled and an accounting is done. This rule is necessary because legal disputes between partners invariably involve conflicting claims to shares in the partnership. Logically, the value of each partner's share must first be determined by an accounting.

Property Rights

One of the property rights of partners—the right to a share of the profits made by the partnership—has already been discussed. A partner also has ownership rights in any real or personal property owned by the partnership. Property owned by the partnership, or *partnership property*, is defined by the UPA as "all property originally brought into the partnership's stock or subsequently acquired, by purchase or otherwise, on account of the partnership" [UPA 8(1)].

For example, in the formation of a partnership, a partner may bring into the partnership any property that he or she owns as a part of his or her capital contribution. This property becomes partnership property even though title to it may still be in the name of the contributing partner. The intention that certain assets are to be partnership assets is the heart of the phrase "on account of the partnership." Thus, the more closely an asset is associated with the business operations of the partnership, the more likely it is to be a partnership asset.[2]

UPA 25(1) states that partners are *tenants in partnership*. This means that every partner is a co-owner with all other partners of specific partnership property, such as office equipment, paper supplies, and vehicles. Each partner has equal rights to possess partnership property for business purposes or in satisfaction of firm debts, but not for any other purpose without the consent of all the other partners. Tenancy in partnership has several important effects. If a partner dies, the surviving partners, not the heirs of the deceased partner, have the right of survivorship to the specific property. Although surviving partners are entitled to possession, they have a duty to account to the decedent's estate for the *value* of the deceased partner's interest in the property [UPA 25(2)(d), (e)].

A partner has no right to sell, assign, or in any way deal with a particular item of partnership property as an exclusive owner [UPA 25(2)(a), (b)]. Therefore, creditors cannot use partnership property to satisfy the personal debts of a partner. Partnership

CONTRAST The death of a sole proprietor or the death of a partner can result in the dissolution of a business. The death of a corporate shareholder, however, rarely causes the dissolution of a corporation.

---

2.   Under the RUPA, property that is not acquired in the name of the partnership is nonetheless partnership property if the instrument transferring title either refers to (1) a person who is taking title as a partner or (2) indicates the existence of the partnership [RUPA 204(a)(2)]. Also, the property is presumed to be partnership property if it is acquired with partnership funds [RUPA 204(c)]. If none of the above occurs, the property is presumed to be the property of individual partners, even if it is used in the partnership business [RUPA 204(d)].

property is available only to satisfy partnership debts, to enhance the firm's credit, or to achieve other business purposes of the partnership.

▌ Duties and Liabilities of Partners

The duties and liabilities of partners are basically derived from agency law. Each partner is an agent of every other partner and acts as both a principal and an agent in any business transaction within the scope of the partnership agreement. Each partner is also a general agent of the partnership in carrying out the usual business of the firm.[3] Thus, every act of a partner concerning partnership business and every contract signed in the partnership name bind the firm [UPA 9(1)]. The UPA affirms general principles of agency law that pertain to the authority of a partner to bind a partnership in contract or tort.

We examine here the fiduciary duties of partners, the authority of partners, the joint and several liability that characterizes partnerships, and the limitations imposed on the liability of incoming partners for preexisting partnership debts.

"Of legal knowledge I acquired such a grip, that they took me into the partnership."

William S. Gilbert, 1836–1911 *(English playwright; Arthur Sullivan's collaborator in comic opera)*

Fiduciary Duties

Partners stand in a fiduciary relationship to one another just as principals and agents do (see Chapter 23). A fiduciary relationship is one of extraordinary trust and loyalty. Each partner has a fiduciary duty to act in good faith and for the benefit of the partnership. Each partner must also subordinate his or her personal interests to those of the partnership if a conflict of interests arises.[4]

This fiduciary duty underlies the entire body of law pertaining to partnership and agency. From it, certain other duties are commonly implied. Thus, a partner must account to the partnership for personal profits or benefits derived from any partnership transaction that is undertaken without the consent of all of the partners.[5] The following case illustrates this underlying principle of partnership law.

---

3. The RUPA adds "or business of the kind carried on by the partnership" [RUPA 301(1)]. Basically, this addition gives added protection to third persons who deal with an unfamiliar partnership.
4. The RUPA states that partners may pursue their own interests without automatically violating their fiduciary duties [RUPA 404(e)].
5. In this sense, to account to the partnership means not only to divulge the information but also to determine the value of any benefits or profits derived and to hold that money or property in trust on behalf of the partnership.

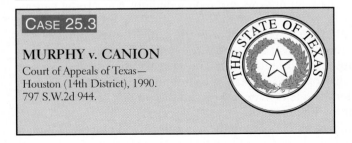

CASE 25.3

MURPHY v. CANION

Court of Appeals of Texas—
Houston (14th District), 1990.
797 S.W.2d 944.

HISTORICAL AND ETHICAL SETTING   *In an opinion written nearly seventy years ago, Justice Benjamin Cardozo stated, in words that are often quoted in cases,*

textbooks, treatises, and legal publications of all kinds, that partners "owe to one another, while the enterprise continues, the duty of the finest loyalty. Many forms of conduct permissible in a workaday world for those acting at arm's length, are forbidden to those bound by fiduciary ties. A trustee is held to something stricter than the morals of the market place. Not honesty alone, but the punctilio [meticulous observation] of an honor the most sensitive, is then the standard of behavior. As to this there has developed a tradition that is unbending and inveterate [of long standing]. Uncompromising rigidity

(Continued)

Case 25.3—Continued

has been the attitude of courts of equity when petitioned to undermine the rule of undivided loyalty by the 'disintegrating erosion' of particular exceptions. Only thus has the level of conduct for fiduciaries been kept at a level higher than that trodden by the crowd." **a**

FACTS   David Murphy and James Canion formed a partnership to conduct real estate business. A provision in their partnership agreement provided that all personal earnings from personal services would be included as partnership income and that any real estate or other partnership business conducted by either partner during the term of the partnership agreement should be for the joint account of the partnership. Through his business associates and contacts, Canion learned of several profitable real estate opportunities. Canion never informed Murphy of these opportunities but instead secretly took advantage of them for his own gain. When Murphy found out about Canion's activities, he told Canion that he was canceling the partnership under a clause in the partnership agreement that allowed termination by a partner with ninety days' notice. In the lawsuit that followed, Murphy alleged that Canion had breached the partnership agreement and his fiduciary duty to the partnership. The trial court agreed with Murphy and awarded him, as damages, half of the profits made by Canion from certain

real estate sales made by Canion without Murphy's knowledge. On appeal, Canion contended, among other things, that because he received income from those sales only after the partnership had been terminated, Murphy had no claim to that income.

ISSUE   Is Murphy entitled to his share of the income received by Canion after the partnership's termination?

DECISION   Yes. The appellate court affirmed the trial court's ruling that Murphy had a right to his share of the income, even though it was received by Canion after the partnership had ended.

REASON   The appellate court concluded, as had the trial court, that the income Canion received after the partnership's dissolution resulted from efforts undertaken during the life of the partnership. By these efforts, Canion had taken advantage of partnership opportunities secretly, for his self-gain, in breach of his fiduciary duty to Murphy. Therefore, Murphy had a right to his share of the profits from Canion's usurpation of partnership opportunities.

FOR CRITICAL ANALYSIS—Historical Consideration
How does the imposition of fiduciary duties on partners affect the value of the partnership as a business form?

a.   *Meinhard v. Salmon,* 249 N.Y. 458, 164 N.E. 545 (1928).

Authority of Partners

Agency concepts relating to actual authority (express and implied), apparent authority, and ratification are also applicable to partnerships. In an ordinary partnership, firm members can exercise all implied powers reasonably necessary and customary to carry on that particular business. Some customarily implied powers include the authority to make warranties on goods in the sales business, the power to convey real property in the firm's name when such conveyances are part of the ordinary course of partnership business, the power to enter into contracts consistent with the firm's regular course of business, and the power to make admissions and representations concerning partnership affairs [UPA 11].

When a partner acts within the scope of authority, the partnership is bound to third parties by these acts. For example, a partner's authority to sell partnership products carries with it the implied authority to transfer title and to make the usual warranties. Hence, in a partnership that operates a retail tire store, any partner negotiating a contract with a customer for the sale of a set of tires can warrant that "each tire will be warranted for normal wear for 40,000 miles."

This same partner, however, does not have the authority to sell office equipment, fixtures, or the partnership office building without the consent of all of the other partners. In addition, because partnerships are formed to create profits, a partner does not generally have the authority to make charitable contributions without the consent of the other partners. Such actions are not binding on the partnership unless they are ratified by all of the other partners.

As in the law of agency, the law of partnership imputes one partner's knowledge to all other partners, because members of a partnership stand in a fiduciary relationship to one another. This relationship implies that each partner will fully disclose to every other partner all information pertaining to the business of the partnership.

Joint Liability

In most states, partners are subject to joint liability on partnership debts and contracts [UPA 15(b)]. **Joint liability** means that if a third party sues a partner on, for example, a partnership debt, the partner has the right to insist that the other partners be sued with him or her. If the third party does not sue all of the partners, the partners sued cannot be required to pay a judgment, and the assets of the partnership cannot be used to satisfy the judgment. (Similarly, a release of one partner releases all partners.) In other words, to bring a successful claim against the partnership on a debt or contract, a plaintiff must name all the partners as defendants.

To simplify this rule, some states, such as California, have enacted statutes providing that a partnership may be sued in its own name and that a judgment will bind the partnership's and the individual partners' property even though not all the partners are named in the complaint. If the third party is successful, he or she may collect on the judgment against the assets of one or more of the partners. Otherwise stated, each partner is liable and may be required to pay the entire amount of the judgment. When one partner pays the entire amount, the partnership is required to indemnify that partner [UPA 18(b)]. If the partnership cannot do so, the obligation falls on the other partners.

Joint and Several Liability

In some states, partners are both jointly liable and *severally*, or individually, liable for partnership debts and contracts. In all states, partners are jointly and severally liable for torts and breaches of trust [UPA 15(a)].[6] **Joint and several liability** means that a third party may sue any one or more of the partners without suing all of them or the partnership itself. In other words, a third party may sue one or more of the partners separately (severally) or all of the partners together (jointly), at his or her option. This is true even if the partner did not participate in, ratify, or know about whatever it was that gave rise to the cause of action.[7]

A judgment against one partner on his or her several liability does not extinguish the others' liability. (Similarly, a release of one partner discharges the partners' joint but not several liability.) Thus, those not sued in the first action may be sued subsequently. The first action, however, may have been conclusive on the question of liability. If, for example, in an action against one partner, the court held that the partnership was in no way liable, the third party cannot bring an action against another partner and succeed on the issue of the partnership's liability.

If the third party is successful, he or she may collect on the judgment only against the assets of those partners named as defendants. The partner who committed the tort is required to indemnify the partnership for any damages it pays.

Liability of Incoming Partner

A newly admitted partner to an existing partnership normally has limited liability for whatever debts and obligations the partnership incurred prior to the new partner's

JOINT LIABILITY
Shared liability. In partnership law, partners incur joint liability for partnership obligations and debts. For example, if a third party sues a partner on a partnership debt, the partner has the right to insist that the other partners be sued with him or her.

JOINT AND SEVERAL LIABILITY
In partnership law, a doctrine under which a plaintiff may sue, and collect a judgment from, one or more of the partners separately (severally, or individually) or all of the partners together (jointly). This is true even if one of the partners sued did not participate in, ratify, or know about whatever it was that gave rise to the cause of action.

---

6. Under the RUPA, partners' liability is joint and several for all debts [RUPA 306].
7. The RUPA prevents creditors from bringing an action to collect debts from the partners of a non-bankrupt partnership without first attempting unsuccessfully to collect from the partnership (or convincing a court that the attempt would be unsuccessful) [RUPA 307(d)].

admission. The new partner's liability can be satisfied only from partnership assets [UPA 17]. This means that the new partner usually has no personal liability for these debts and obligations, but any capital contribution made by him or her to the partnership is subject to these debts.

In cases involving old debts and new partners, there are two dates of great significance: the date on which the debt arose and the date on which the partner joined the firm. The court in the following case had to determine the date on which a partnership debt arose.

CASE 25.4

CITIZENS BANK OF MASSACHUSETTS v. PARHAM-WOODMAN MEDICAL ASSOCIATES

United States District Court, Eastern District of Virginia, Richmond Division, 1995.
874 F.Supp. 705.

HISTORICAL AND ECONOMIC SETTING   *Some of the most talented professionals do not have any special competence outside their fields. For example, the history of business is full of stories concerning brilliant artists, architects, dentists, and other professionals who made poor choices when investing their money. In the 1980s, many of these unwise investments were in real estate and construction projects. At the time, some of the most expert businesspersons and financial institutions also made wrong choices in deciding where and in what to invest and nearly put themselves out of business.*

FACTS   The Citizens Bank of Massachusetts agreed to lend Parham-Woodman Medical Associates, a partnership, $2 million to construct a new office building. Their agreement, which was signed on April 30, 1985, provided for the money to be disbursed in installments. Most of the funds had been disbursed before Richard Hunley, Nada Tas, and Joseph Tas joined the firm. When the partnership failed to repay the loan, the bank sold the building and obtained a deficiency judgment for more than

$1.2 million. The bank filed a suit in a federal district court against the firm and the partners to recover this amount.

ISSUE   Were the partners who joined the firm after the date of the loan, but before disbursement of all of the funds, liable for the debt beyond the amount of their interest in partnership assets?

DECISION   No. The court held that Hunley and the Tases were liable only to the extent of the partnership property.

REASON   The court noted that UPA 17 makes an incoming partner liable for "all the obligations of the partnership arising before his admission" but provides that "this liability shall be satisfied only out of partnership property." The court concluded that "a partnership obligation arises *   *   * when the creditor extends the credit to the partnership." In this case, "that occurred on April 30, 1985 and not on the occasion when the bank disbursed each advance." In other words, "long before Dr. Hunley and the Tases joined Parham-Woodman," the loan documents "were binding obligations on both Citizens Bank and the partnership. That is not changed," said the court, "merely because the passage of part of the consideration was delayed pursuant to a schedule which also was set before Dr. Hunley and the Tases became partners."

FOR CRITICAL ANALYSIS—Economic Consideration
Does the rule of UPA 17 favor debtors or creditors? Why?

▌Partnership Termination

Any change in the relations of the partners that demonstrates unwillingness or inability to carry on partnership business dissolves the partnership, resulting in termination [UPA 29]. If one of the partners wishes to continue the business, he or she is free to reorganize into a new partnership with the remaining members.

The termination of a partnership has two stages, both of which must take place before termination is complete. The first stage, **dissolution,** occurs when any partner (or partners) indicates an intention to disassociate from the partnership. The second stage, **winding up,**[8] is the actual process of collecting and distributing the partnership assets.

Dissolution

Dissolution of a partnership can be brought about by the acts of the partners, by the operation of law, and by judicial decree. Each of these events will be discussed here.

DISSOLUTION BY ACTS OF PARTNERS   Dissolution of a partnership may come about through the acts of the partners in several ways. First, the partnership can be dissolved by the partners' agreement. For example, when a partnership agreement expresses a fixed term or a particular business objective to be accomplished, the passing of the date or the accomplishment of the objective dissolves the partnership.

Second, because a partnership is a voluntary association, a partner has the power to disassociate himself or herself from the partnership at any time and thus dissolve the partnership. (See this chapter's *Business Law in Action* for a discussion of a problem facing many law firms today—partners who leave the firm and take their clients with them.) Any change in the partnership, whether by the withdrawal of a partner or by the admission of a new partner, results in dissolution.[9] In practice, this is modified by the provision that the remaining or new partners may continue in the firm's business. Nonetheless, a new partnership arises. Creditors of the prior partnership become creditors of the new partnership [UPA 41].

Finally, the UPA provides that neither a voluntary assignment of a partner's interest nor an involuntary sale of a partner's interest for the benefit of creditors [UPA 28] by itself dissolves the partnership. Either occurrence, however, can ultimately lead to judicial dissolution of the partnership (judicial dissolution will be discussed shortly).

DISSOLUTION BY OPERATION OF LAW   If one of the partners dies, the partnership is dissolved by operation of law, even if the partnership agreement provides for carrying on the business with the executor of the decedent's estate.[10] The bankruptcy of a partner will also dissolve a partnership, and naturally, the bankruptcy of the firm itself will result in dissolution.

Additionally, any event that makes it unlawful for the partnership to continue its business or for any partner to carry on in the partnership will result in dissolution. Note, however, that even if the illegality of the partnership business is a cause for dissolution, the partners can decide to change the nature of their business and continue in the partnership. When the illegality applies to an individual partner, then dissolution is mandatory. For example, suppose the state legislature passes a law making it illegal for judges to engage in the practice of law. If an attorney in a law firm is appointed a judge, the attorney must leave the law firm, and the partnership must be dissolved.

DISSOLUTION BY JUDICIAL DECREE   For dissolution of a partnership by judicial decree to occur, an application or petition must be made in an appropriate court.

DISSOLUTION
The formal disbanding of a partnership or a corporation. It can take place by (1) acts of the partners or, in a corporation, of the shareholders and board of directors; (2) the death of a partner; (3) the expiration of a time period stated in a partnership agreement or a certificate of incorporation; or (4) judicial decree.

WINDING UP
The second of two stages involved in the termination of a partnership or corporation. Once the firm is dissolved, it continues to exist legally until the process of winding up all business affairs (collecting and distributing the firm's assets) is complete.

---

8. Although "winding down" would seem to describe more accurately the process of settling accounts and liquidating the assets of a partnership, "winding up" has been traditionally used in English and U.S. statutory and case law to denote this final stage of a partnership's existence.
9. The RUPA distinguishes the withdrawal of a partner that causes a breakup of a partnership from a withdrawal that causes only the end of a partner's participation in the business (and results in a buyout of that partner's interest) [RUPA 601, 701, 801]. Dissolution results only if the partnership must be liquidated [RUPA 801].
10. Under the RUPA, the death of a partner represents that partner's "dissociation" from the partnership, but it is not an automatic ground for the partnership's dissolution [RUPA 601(7)].

BUSINESS LAW IN ACTION

Departing Partners—and Profits

An ongoing problem faced by partnerships is that of the departing partner who joins a competing firm or sets up a competing practice. This is particularly true in law firms, because attorneys are prohibited by state codes of ethics (which are adopted as law in each state) from signing agreements not to compete. For example, the Model Rules of Professional Conduct, a model ethical code drafted by the American Bar Association and adopted by many states, reads as follows: "A lawyer shall not participate in the offering or making" of "a partnership or employment agreement that restricts the right of a lawyer to practice after termination of the relationship, except an agreement concerning benefits upon retirement." Virtually all state codes of ethics contain this rule, although the specific wording may vary.

Thus, if a law firm's partnership agreement contains any clause prohibiting withdrawing partners from competing with the firm, the clause normally will be deemed an unenforceable restraint on the practice of law. For the same reason, a clause in a partnership agreement that essentially "punishes" departing partners (by withholding the partner's share of earned but uncollected revenues, for example) would likely be deemed unenforceable.[a] Additionally, an individual's right to choose an attorney is a widely held public policy in this country. Therefore, if a withdrawing law partner's clients follow the partner to his or her new firm, there is little the old firm can do about it—except suffer a loss in profits.

A New York law firm, faced with the challenge of deterring partners from leaving the firm while remaining within the boundaries of law, came up with an unusual solution. The firm included a clause in its partnership agreement providing that on withdrawal, a partner would receive, among other payments (such as the partner's capital contribution), supplemental payments, spread out over five years, amounting to "150% of the withdrawing partner's final percentage of the firm's profits, calculated by averaging the firm's net profit for the three years preceding the withdrawal." The payments, however, were to be "reduced dollar-for-dollar to the extent that the withdrawing partner's annual earned income, from any source, exceeds $100,000."

Is such a provision enforceable? A partner who withdrew from the firm to join another law firm (and who subsequently earned an annual income that was substantially higher than $100,000 a year) contended that it was not, because it constituted an impermissible restraint on the practice of law. The arbitrator who initially decided the matter held otherwise. The arbitrator noted that "[t]he Partnership makes no bones about the fact that a primary motive for adopting [the clause] was to avoid payments to withdrawing partners who competed." Nonetheless, the clause did not effectively restrain the withdrawing partner's ability to practice law. Furthermore, the clause provided a "safety net" for those partners who left the firm "for lower-income pursuits."

When the issue ultimately came before the New York Court of Appeals (that state's highest court), the court, like the arbitrator, could find nothing contrary to law or public policy in the arbitrator's decision. Thus, the decision was allowed to stand.[b]

For Critical Analysis: *Is there any way a law firm can avoid the problems created by withdrawing partners who take their clients with them?*

---

a. See, for example, *Cohen v. Lord, Day & Lord*, 75 N.Y.2d 95, 550 N.E.2d 410, 551 N.Y.S.2d 157 (1989).

b. *Hackett v. Milbank, Tweed, Hadley & McCloy*, 86 N.W.2d 146, 654 N.E.2d 95, 630 N.Y.S.2d 274 (1995).

The court then either denies the petition or grants a decree of dissolution. UPA 32 cites situations in which a court can dissolve a partnership. One situation occurs when a partner is adjudicated mentally incompetent or is shown to be of unsound mind. Another situation arises when a partner appears incapable of performing his or her duties under the partnership agreement. If the incapacity is likely to be permanent and to affect substantially the partner's ability to discharge his or her duties to the firm, a court will dissolve the partnership by decree.

Dissolution may also be ordered by a court when it becomes obviously impractical for the firm to continue—for example, if the business can only be operated at a loss. Additionally, a partner's impropriety involving partnership business (for example, fraud perpetrated on the other partners) or improper behavior reflecting unfavorably on the firm may provide grounds for a judicial decree of dissolution. Finally, if dissension between partners becomes so persistent and harmful as to undermine the confidence and cooperation necessary to carry on the firm's business, dissolution may also be granted.

NOTICE OF DISSOLUTION   The intent to dissolve or to withdraw from a firm must be communicated clearly to each partner. A partner can express this notice of intent by either actions or words. All partners will share liability for the acts of any partner who continues conducting business for the firm without knowing that the partnership has been dissolved.

Dissolution of a partnership by the act of a partner requires notice to all affected third persons as well. Any third person who has extended credit to the firm must receive *actual notice* (notice given to the party directly and personally). For all others, *constructive notice* (a newspaper announcement or similar public notice) is sufficient. Dissolution resulting from the operation of law generally requires no notice to third parties.[11]

Winding Up

Once dissolution occurs and the partners have been notified, the partners cannot create new obligations on behalf of the partnership. Their only authority is to complete transactions begun but not finished at the time of dissolution and to wind up the business of the partnership. *Winding up* includes collecting and preserving partnership assets, discharging liabilities (paying debts), and accounting to each partner for the value of his or her interest in the partnership.

> **DON'T FORGET** Secured creditors have priority over unsecured creditors to any assets that serve as collateral for a partnership's debts.

Both creditors of the partnership and creditors of the individual partners can make claims on the partnership's assets. In general, creditors of the partnership have priority over creditors of individual partners in the distribution of partnership assets; the converse priority is usually followed in the distribution of individual partner assets, except under bankruptcy law. The priorities in the distribution of a partnership's assets are as follows:[12]

1. Payment of third party debts.
2. Refund of advances (loans) made to or for the firm by a partner.
3. Return of capital contribution to a partner.
4. Distribution of the balance, if any, to partners in accordance with their respective shares in the profits.

If the partnership's liabilities are greater than its assets, the partners bear the losses—in the absence of a contrary agreement—in the same proportion in which they shared the profits (rather than, for example, in proportion to their contributions to the partnership's capital). Partners continue in their fiduciary relationship until the winding-up process is completed.

▌Limited Partnerships

In many ways, *limited partnerships* are like general partnerships, but they also differ from general partnerships in several ways. Because of this, they are sometimes referred to as *special partnerships*. As discussed in Chapter 24, limited partnerships consist of at least one *general partner* and one or more *limited partners*. The general partner (or partners) assumes management responsibility for the partnership and so has full responsibility for the partnership and for all debts of the partnership. The limited partner (or partners) contributes cash (or other property) and owns an interest in the firm but does not undertake any management responsibilities and is not personally liable for partnership debts beyond the amount of his or her investment. A limited partner

---

11.   *Childers v. United States,* 442 F.2d 1299 (5th Cir. 1971).
12.   Under the RUPA, partner creditors are included among creditors who take first priority [RUPA 808(a)]. Capital contributions and profits or losses are then calculated together to determine the amounts that the partners receive or the amounts that they must pay.

can forfeit limited liability by taking part in the management of the business. A comparison of the basic characteristics of partnerships appears in Exhibit 25–2.[13]

Until 1976, the law governing limited partnerships in all states except Louisiana was the Uniform Limited Partnership Act (ULPA) of 1916. In 1976, the ULPA was revised, and most states and the District of Columbia have adopted its revision, which is known as the Revised Uniform Limited Partnership Act (RULPA). Because the RULPA is the dominant law governing limited partnerships in the United States, we will refer to the RULPA in our discussion of limited partnerships.

---

13.   Under the RUPA, a general partnership can be converted into a limited partnership and vice versa [RUPA 901, 902]. The RUPA also provides for the merger of a general partnership with one or more general or limited partnerships under rules that are similar to those governing corporate mergers [RUPA 905].

♦ Exhibit 25–2
A Comparison of General Partnerships and Limited Partnerships

CHARACTERISTIC	GENERAL PARTNERSHIP (UPA)	LIMITED PARTNERSHIP (RULPA)
Creation	By agreement of two or more persons to carry on a business as co-owners for profit.	By agreement of two or more persons to carry on a business as co-owners for profit. Must include one or more general partners and one or more limited partners. Filing of a certificate with the secretary of state is required.
Sharing of Profits and Losses	By agreement; or, in the absence of agreement, profits are shared equally by the partners, and losses are shared in the same ratio as profits.	Profits are shared as required in the certificate agreement, and losses are shared likewise, up to the amount of the limited partners' capital contributions. In the absence of a provision in the certificate agreement, profits and losses are shared on the basis of percentages of capital contributions.
Liability	Unlimited personal liability of all partners.	Unlimited personal liability of all general partners; limited partners liable only to the extent of their capital contributions.
Capital Contribution	No minimum or mandatory amount; set by agreement.	Set by agreement.
Management	By agreement, or in the absence of agreement, all partners have an equal voice.	General partners by agreement, or else each has an equal voice. Limited partners have no voice or else are subject to liability as general partners (but *only* if a third party has reason to believe that the limited partner is a general partner). A limited partner may act as an agent or employee of the partnership and vote on amending the certificate or on the sale or dissolution of the partnership.
Duration	By agreement, or can be dissolved by action of the partners (withdrawal), operation of law (death or bankruptcy), or court decree.	By agreement in the certificate or by withdrawal, death, or mental incompetence of a general partner in the absence of the right of the other general partners to continue the partnership. Death of a limited partner, unless he or she is the only remaining limited partner, does not terminate the partnership.
Distribution of Assets on Liquidation—Order of Priorities	1. Outside creditors. 2. Partner creditors. 3. Partners, according to capital contributions. 4. Partners, according to profits.	1. Outside creditors and partner creditors. 2. Partners and former partners entitled to distributions before withdrawal under the agreement or the RULPA. 3. Partners, according to capital contributions. 4. Partners, according to profits.

Formation

Compared with the informal, private, and voluntary agreement that usually suffices for a general partnership, the formation of a limited partnership is a public and formal proceeding that must follow statutory requirements. A limited partnership must have at least one general partner and one limited partner, as mentioned previously. Additionally, the partners must sign a **certificate of limited partnership,** which requires information similar to that found in a corporate charter (see Chapter 26). The certificate must be filed with the designated state official—under the RULPA, the secretary of state. The certificate is usually open to public inspection.

CERTIFICATE OF LIMITED PARTNERSHIP The basic document filed with a designated state official by which a limited partnership is formed.

Rights and Liabilities of Partners

General partners, unlike limited partners, are personally liable to the partnership's creditors; thus, at least one general partner is necessary in a limited partnership so that someone has personal liability. This policy can be circumvented in states that allow a corporation to be the general partner in a partnership. Because the corporation has limited liability by virtue of corporate laws, if a corporation is the general partner, no one in the limited partnership has personal liability.

RIGHTS OF LIMITED PARTNERS   Subject to the limitations that will be discussed here, limited partners have essentially the same rights as general partners, including the right of access to partnership books and the right to other information regarding partnership business. Upon dissolution, limited partners are entitled to a return of their contributions in accordance with the partnership certificate [RULPA 201(a)(10)]. They can also assign their interests subject to the certificate [RULPA 702, 704].

The RULPA provides a limited partner with the right to sue an outside party on behalf of the firm if the general partners with authority to do so have refused to file suit [RULPA 1001]. In addition, investor protection legislation, such as securities laws (discussed in Chapter 29), may give some protection to limited partners.

LIABILITIES OF LIMITED PARTNERS   In contrast to the virtually unlimited liability of a general partner for partnership indebtedness, the liability of a limited partner is limited to the capital that he or she contributes or agrees to contribute to the partnership [RULPA 502].

A limited partnership is formed by good faith compliance with the requirements for signing and filing the certificate, even if it is incomplete or defective. When a limited partner discovers a defect in the formation of the limited partnership, he or she can avoid future liability by causing an appropriate amendment or certificate to be filed or by renouncing an interest in the profits of the partnership [RULPA 304]. If the limited partner takes neither of these actions on the discovery of the defect, however, the partner can be held personally liable by the firm's creditors. Liability for false statements in a partnership certificate runs in favor of persons relying on the false statements and against members who know of the falsity but still sign the certificate [RULPA 207].

NOTE A limited partner is also liable to the extent of any contribution that he or she made to the partnership but later took back from the firm.

LIMITED PARTNERS AND MANAGEMENT   Limited partners enjoy limited liability so long as they do not participate in management [RULPA 303]. A limited partner who participates in management will be just as liable as a general partner to any creditor who transacts business with the limited partnership and believes, based on a limited partner's conduct, that the limited partner is a general partner [RULPA 303]. How much actual review and advisement a limited partner can engage in before being exposed to liability is an unsettled question.[14] A limited partner who knowingly permits

---

14.   It is an unsettled question partly because there are differences among the laws in different states. Factors to be considered under the RULPA are listed in RULPA 303(b), (c).

his or her name to be used in the name of the limited partnership is liable to creditors who extend credit to the limited partnership without knowledge that the limited partner is not a general partner [RULPA 102, 303(d)].

Dissolution

A limited partnership is dissolved in much the same way as an ordinary partnership. The retirement, death, or mental incompetence of a general partner can dissolve the partnership, but not if the business can be continued by one or more of the other general partners in accordance with their certificate or by the consent of all of the members [RULPA 801]. The death or assignment of interest of a limited partner does not dissolve the limited partnership [RULPA 702, 704, 705]. A limited partnership can be dissolved by court decree [RULPA 802].

RECALL The test for bankruptcy is not that a debtor's liabilities exceed his or her assets, but that the debtor is not able to pay his or her debts as they come due.

Bankruptcy or the withdrawal of a general partner dissolves a limited partnership. Bankruptcy of a limited partner, however, does not dissolve the partnership unless it causes the bankruptcy of the firm. The retirement of a general partner causes a dissolution unless the members consent to a continuation by the remaining general partners or unless this contingency is provided for in the certificate.

Upon dissolution, creditors' rights, including those of partners who are creditors, take first priority. Then partners and former partners receive unpaid distributions of partnership assets and, except as otherwise agreed, amounts representing returns on their contributions and amounts proportionate to their shares of the distributions [RULPA 804].

∎ Limited Liability Partnerships

Many professionals, such as attorneys and accountants, work together using the business form of the partnership. As discussed in Chapter 24, one of the major advantages of a partnership is that the partnership's income is "passed through" to the partners as personal income. Consequently, partners avoid the double-taxation feature of the corporate form of business. There is a price to pay for this tax advantage, however: partners face unlimited personal liability.

Consider a group of lawyers operating as a partnership. A client sues one of the attorneys for malpractice and wins a large judgment. When the firm's malpractice insurance is insufficient to cover the obligation and that attorney's personal assets are exhausted, the personal assets of the other, innocent partners can be used to satisfy the judgment.

The limited partnership offers the advantage of limited liability for limited partners, but to retain that limited liability, the limited partners must refrain from participating in management. Thus, this form of business organization is unsuitable for professionals who wish to have a voice in management. The professional corporation (discussed in Chapter 26) is another option for professionals who wish to limit their liability. By incorporating as a professional corporation, attorneys or accountants, for example, can obtain the limited liability of corporate shareholders. The trade-off here, however, is that they then have to pay corporate income taxes.

LIMITED LIABILITY PARTNERSHIP
A form of partnership that allows professionals to enjoy the tax benefits of a partnership while avoiding personal liability for the malpractice of other partners.

The **limited liability partnership (LLP)** is a relatively new form of partnership that allows professionals to enjoy the tax benefits of a partnership while avoiding personal liability for the malpractice of other partners. If a professional group organizes as an LLP, innocent partners are not personally liable for the wrongdoing of the other partners. The LLP is similar to the limited liability company (LLC) discussed in Chapter 24. The difference is that LLPs are designed more for professionals who normally do business as partners in a partnership. As with limited liability companies, LLPs must be formed and operated in compliance with state statutes. LLP statutes, because of their importance to professionals, are discussed in the following *Landmark in the Law*.

Limited Liability Partnership (LLP) Statutes

The first state to enact a limited liability partnership (LLP) statute was Texas, in August 1991. Delaware, Louisiana, North Carolina, and Washington, D.C., quickly followed suit. By 1996, the majority of states had enacted LLP statutes.

Limitations on Liability

LLP statutes, like the limited liability company statutes discussed in Chapter 24, vary from state to state. Generally, though, each state statute limits in some way the normal joint and several liability of partners. For example, Delaware law protects each innocent partner from the "debts and obligations of the partnership arising from negligence, wrongful acts, or misconduct." In North Carolina, Texas, and Washington, D.C., the statutes protect innocent partners from obligations arising from "errors, omissions, negligence, incompetence, or malfeasance." Louisiana also includes "willful or intentional misconduct." Although the language of these statutes seems to apply specifically to attorneys, virtually any group of professionals can use the LLP.

Setting Up an LLP

One of the reasons why LLPs are becoming so popular among professionals is that most LLP statutes make it relatively easy to establish an LLP. This is particularly true for a partnership. For example, to become an LLP in Texas, all a partnership must do is fulfill the following requirements:

1. File the appropriate form with the secretary of state.
2. Pay an annual fee of $200 per partner.
3. Maintain at least $100,000 in professional liability insurance.
4. Add either "L.L.P." or "Registered Limited Liability Partnership" to its name.

Converting from a partnership to an LLP is also easy because the firm's basic organizational structure remains the same. Additionally, all of the statutory and common law rules governing partnerships still apply (apart from those modified by the LLP statute). Normally, LLP statutes are simply amendments to a state's already existing partnership law.

For Critical Analysis: *Is there anything unethical about allowing professionals to limit their liability for the negligence of their partners?*

▌ Key Terms

▌ Chapter Summary: Partnerships

General Partnership *(See pages 642–659.)*	1. Created by agreement of the parties. 2. Not treated as an entity except for limited purposes.

(Continued)

▌Chapter Summary: Partnerships—Continued

General Partnership— Continued	3. Partners have unlimited liability for partnership debts.
	4. Each partner has an equal voice in management unless otherwise provided for in the partnership agreement.
	5. The capital contribution of each partner is determined by agreement.
	6. Each partner pays a proportionate share of income taxes on the net profits of the partnership, whether or not they are distributed; the partnership files only an information return with the Internal Revenue Service.
	7. Terminated by agreement or can be dissolved by action of the partners (withdrawal), operation of law (death or bankruptcy), or court decree.
Limited Partnership (*See pages 659–662.*)	1. Must be formed in compliance with statutory requirements.
	2. Consists of one or more general partners and one or more limited partners.
	3. Only general partners can participate in management. Limited partners have no voice in management; if they do participate in management activities, they risk having general-partner liability.
	4. General partners have unlimited liability for partnership losses; limited partners are liable only to the extent of their contributions.
Limited Liability Partnership (LLP) (*See pages 662–663.*)	1. Must be formed in compliance with statutory requirements.
	2. Most state statutes make it relatively easy to establish an LLP, particularly if a firm is already doing business as a partnership.
	3. Statutes vary from state to state, but generally, each state statute limits in some way the personal liability of innocent partners for the wrongful acts of other partners.

▌For Review

1. What are the three essential elements of a partnership?

2. What is meant by joint and several liability? Why is this often considered to be a disadvantage of the partnership form of business?

3. Can a partner continue the business of a terminated partnership if he or she wishes to do so? How?

4. What are the key differences between the rights and liabilities of general partners and limited partners?

5. What is the limited liability partnership (LLP)? How does this relatively new form of business organization meet the needs of today's professionals, such as accountants and lawyers?

▌Questions and Case Problems

25–1. Distribution of Partnership Assets. Shawna and David formed a partnership. At the time of the partnership's formation, Shawna's capital contribution was $10,000, and David's was $15,000. Later, Shawna made a $10,000 loan to the partnership when it needed working capital. The partnership agreement provided that profits were to be shared, 40 percent for Shawna and 60 percent for David. The partnership was dissolved by David's death. At the end of the dissolution and the winding up of the partnership, the partnership's assets were $50,000, and the partnership's debts were $8,000. Discuss fully how the assets should be distributed.

25–2. Partnership Property. Schwartz and Zenov were partners in an accounting firm. Because business was booming and profits were better than ever, they decided to invest some

of the firm's profits in Munificent Corp. stock. The investment turned out to be a good one, as the stock continued to increase in value. On Schwartz's death several years later, Zenov assumed full ownership of the business, including the Munificent Corp. stock, a partnership asset. Schwartz's daughter Rosalie, however, claimed a 50 percent ownership interest in the Munificent Corp. stock as Schwartz's sole heir. Can Rosalie enforce her claim? Explain.

25–3. Liability of Limited Partners. Asher and Breem form a limited partnership with Asher as the general partner and Breem as the limited partner. Breem puts up $15,000, and Asher contributes some office equipment that he owns. A certificate of limited partnership is properly filed, and business is begun. One month later, Asher becomes ill. Instead of hiring someone to manage the business, Breem takes over complete management himself. While Breem is in control, he makes a contract with Thaler involving a large sum of money. Asher returns to work. Because of other commitments, Asher and Breem breach the Thaler contract. Thaler contends that Asher and Breem will be personally liable for damages caused by the breach if the damages cannot be satisfied out of the assets of the limited partnership. Discuss this contention.

25–4. Partner's Property Rights. Maruta, Samms, and Ortega were partners in a business firm. The firm's business equipment included several expensive computers. One day, Maruta borrowed one of the computers for use in his home, but he never bothered to return it. When the other partners asked him about it, Maruta claimed that because the computer represented less than one-third of the computers owned by the partnership, and because he owned one-third of the business, he had a right to keep the equipment. Was he right? Explain.

25–5. Partnership by Estoppel. Alvin and Carol Volkman negotiated with David McNamee, a construction contractor, to have a house built. McNamee informed the Volkmans that he was going into business with Phillip Carroll. Carroll was present on several occasions when the Volkmans went to McNamee's offices, and by all indications he was a partner in the decisions concerning the construction of the Volkmans' house. On one occasion, for example, Carroll said to the Volkmans, "I hope we'll be working together." Correspondence to the Volkmans from McNamee was written on stationery carrying the letterhead "DP Associates," and the Volkmans assumed the "DP" represented David and Phillip. When the construction contract was not performed as agreed, the Volkmans brought suit against DP Associates, McNamee, and Carroll. Carroll petitioned the trial court to dismiss the suit against him, as he was not a partner in DP Associates. Will the court find Carroll to be a partner by estoppel? Explain. [*Volkman v. DP Associates*, 48 N.C.App. 155, 268 S.E.2d 265 (1980)]

25–6. Rights among Partners. Jebeles and Costellos were partners in "Dino's Hot Dogs," doing business on the Montgomery Highway in Alabama. From the outset, Costellos worked at the business full-time, while Jebeles involved himself only to a small extent in the actual running of the business. Jebeles was married to Costellos's sister, and when marital difficulties developed between Jebeles and his wife, Costellos barred Jebeles from the premises. Jebeles sued for an accounting of the partnership's profits and for dissolution of the partnership, claiming a partnership at will and that the relationship between the partners made it impossible to conduct partnership business. Will the court grant the petition? Explain. [*Jebeles v. Costellos*, 391 So.2d 1024 (Ala. 1980)]

25–7. Partnership Dissolution. Carola and Grogan were partners in a law firm. The partnership began business in 1974 and was created by an oral agreement. On September 6, 1976, Carola withdrew from the partnership some of its files, furniture, and books, along with various other items of office equipment. The next day, Carola informed Grogan he had withdrawn from the partnership. Discuss whether Carola's actions on September 6, 1976, constituted effective notice of dissolution to Grogan. [*Carola v. Grogan*, 102 A.D.2d 934, 477 N.Y.S.2d 525 (1984)]

25–8. Liability of General Partners. Pat McGowan, Val Somers, and Brent Roberson were general partners in Vermont Place, a limited partnership formed to construct duplexes on a tract of land in Fort Smith, Arkansas. In 1984, the partnership mortgaged the property so that it could build there. McGowan owned a separate company, Advance Development Corp., which was hired by the partnership to develop the project. On September 3, 1984, Somers and Roberson discovered that McGowan had not been paying the suppliers to the project, including National Lumber Co., and had not been making the mortgage payments. The suppliers and the bank sued the partnership and the general partners individually. Discuss whether Somers and Roberson could be held individually liable for the debts incurred by McGowan. [*National Lumber Co. v. Advance Development Corp.*, 293 Ark. 1, 732 S.W.2d 840 (1987)]

25–9. Distribution of Assets. Robert Lowther, Fred Riggleman, and Granville Zopp were equal partners in the Four Square Partnership. The partnership was created to acquire and develop real estate for commercial retail use. In the course of the partnership, Riggleman loaned $30,000 to the partnership, and Zopp loaned the partnership $50,000. Donald H. Lowther, Robert's brother and not a partner in the firm, loaned Four Square $80,000 and took a promissory note signed by the three partners. Four Square encountered financial difficulties shortly after the commercial venture began and eventually defaulted on payments due on a construction loan it had received from a bank. The bank foreclosed on the property securing the debt. The proceeds of the subsequent foreclosure sale satisfied the bank's interest and left a surplus of $87,783 to be returned to the partnership. In the meantime, the partnership had been dissolved and was in the process of winding up its affairs. Donald H. Lowther maintained that, as a nonpartner creditor, his claim against the firm's assets took priority over those of Riggleman and Zopp. Is Lowther correct? Explain. [*Lowther v. Riggleman*, 189 W.Va. 68, 428 S.E.2d 49 (1993)]

25–10. Rights among Partners. B&R Communications was a general partner in Amarillo CellTelco. Under the partnership agreement, each partner had the right to inspect partnership records "at reasonable times during business hours," so long as the inspection did not "unreasonably interfere with the operation of the partnership." B&R believed that the managers of the firm were using partnership money to engage in lawsuits that were too costly. B&R and other general partners filed a suit in a Texas state court against the managers. B&R wanted to inspect the firm's records to discover information about the lawsuits, but the court denied B&R's request. B&R asked a state appellate court to order the trial judge to grant the request. On what ground did the appellate court issue the order? [*B&R Communications v. Lopez*, 890 S.W.2d 224 (Tex.App.—Amarillo 1994)]

25–11. Liability of Incoming Partner. Conklin Farm sold land to LongView Estates, a general partnership, to build condominiums. LongView gave a promissory note to Conklin for $9 million as payment. A few years later, Doris Leibowitz joined LongView as a general partner. Leibowitz left the firm before the note came due, but while she was a partner, interest accrued on the balance. The condominium project failed, and LongView went out of business. Conklin filed a suit in a New Jersey state court against Leibowitz to recover some of the interest on the note. Conklin acknowledged that Leibowitz was not liable for debt incurred before she joined the firm but argued that the interest that accrued while she was a partner was "new" debt for which she was personally liable. To what extent, if any, is Leibowitz liable to Conklin? [*Conklin Farm v. Leibowitz*, 140 N.J. 417, 658 A.2d 1257 (1995)]

A QUESTION OF ETHICS AND SOCIAL RESPONSIBILITY

25–12. *Mt. Hood Meadows Oregon, Ltd., was a limited partnership established to carry on the business of constructing and operating a winter sports development in the Hood River area of Oregon. Elizabeth Brooke and two of the other limited partners were dissatisfied because, for all the years in which profits were earned after 1974, the general partner distributed only 50 percent of the limited partners' taxable profits. The remaining profits were retained and reinvested in the business. Each of the limited partners was taxed on his or her distributable share of the profits, however, regardless of whether the cash was actually distributed. Brooke and the others brought an action to compel the general partner to distribute all of the limited partnership's profits. The court held that, in the absence of a limited partnership agreement concerning the distribution of profits, the decision to reinvest profits was strictly a managerial one. Unless the limited partners could prove that the general partner's conduct was inappropriate or violated a fiduciary duty, the decision of the general partner was binding on the limited partners. [Brooke v. Mt. Hood Meadows Oregon, Ltd., 81 Ore.App. 387, 725 P.2d 925 (1986)]*

1. The major attraction of limited partnerships is that the investors, as limited partners, are not liable for partnership obligations beyond the amount that they have invested. The "price" paid for this limited liability, however, is that limited partners have no say in management—as is well illustrated by the case described here. What ethical considerations are expressed in the rule that limited partners cannot participate in management? Do you think such a rule is fair?

2. This case also illustrates how relatively helpless the limited partners are when faced with a general partner whose actions do not correspond to the limited partners' wishes. Apart from selling their partnership shares to others (and at times, buyers are hard to find) or participating in management (and losing their limited liability as a result), limited partners have little recourse against the decisions of general partners so long as the general partners have not violated their fiduciary duties or the partnership agreement. Do you think that, because limited partners cannot participate in management, general partners have ethical duties to limited partners that go beyond those prescribed by law? If not, why not? If so, how would you describe or define such duties?

FOR CRITICAL ANALYSIS

25–13. *Given the option in most states of converting a partnership to a limited liability partnership, will the traditional partnership eventually disappear?*

Chapter 26

Corporate Formation and Financing

"A corporation is an artificial being, invisible, intangible, and existing only in contemplation of law."

John Marshall, 1755–1835
(*Chief justice of the United States Supreme Court, 1801–1835*)

CHAPTER OBJECTIVES

After reading this chapter, you should be able to:

1. Describe the basic characteristics of the corporate entity.
2. Identify the express and implied powers of a corporation.
3. Summarize the ways in which corporations are classified.
4. Outline the steps involved in forming a corporation, and point out the effects of improper incorporation.
5. Indicate how corporations are financed, and discuss the difference between stocks and bonds.

A corporation can be owned by a single person, or it can have hundreds, thousands, or even millions of shareholders. The shareholder form of business organization was developed in Europe at the end of the seventeenth century. Called *joint stock companies,* these organizations frequently collapsed because their organizers absconded with the funds or proved to be incompetent. Because of this history of fraud and collapse, organizations resembling corporations were regarded with suspicion in the United States during its early years. Although several business corporations were formed after the Revolutionary War, it was not until the nineteenth century that the corporation came into common use for private business. Today, the corporation is one of the most important forms of business organization in the United States.

As John Marshall indicated in the opening quotation, a corporation is an artificial being, existing in law only and neither tangible nor visible. The corporation is a creature of statute. Its existence depends generally on state law, although some corporations, especially public organizations, can be created under federal law.

Each state has its own body of corporate law, and these laws are not entirely uniform. The Model Business Corporation Act (MBCA) is a codification of modern corporation law that has been influential in the drafting and revision of state corporation statutes. Today, the majority of state statutes are guided by the revised version of the MBCA, known as the Revised Model Business Corporation Act (RMBCA). You should keep in mind, however, that there is considerable variation among the statutes of the states that have used the MBCA or the RMBCA as a basis for their statutes, and several states do not follow either act. Because of this, individual state corporation laws should be relied on rather than the MBCA or RMBCA.

▮ The Nature of the Corporation

A *corporation* can consist of one or more *natural* persons (as opposed to the artificial "person" of the corporation) identified under a common name. The corporation substitutes itself for its shareholders in conducting corporate business and in incurring liability, yet its authority to act and the liability for its actions are separate and apart from the individuals who own it. (In certain limited situations, the "corporate veil" can be pierced; that is, liability for the corporation's obligations can be extended to shareholders, a topic to be discussed later in this chapter.)

Corporate Personnel

Responsibility for the overall management of the corporation is entrusted to a *board of directors*, which is elected by the shareholders. The board of directors hires *corporate officers* and other employees to run the daily business operations of the corporation.

When an individual purchases a share of stock in a corporation, that person becomes a *shareholder* and an owner of the corporation. Unlike the members in a partnership, the body of shareholders can change constantly without affecting the continued existence of the corporation. A shareholder can sue the corporation, and the corporation can sue a shareholder. Additionally, under certain circumstances, a shareholder can sue on behalf of a corporation. The rights and duties of all corporate personnel will be examined in Chapter 27.

Corporate Taxation

Corporate profits are taxed by state and federal governments. Corporations can do one of two things with corporate profits—retain them or pass them on to shareholders in the form of **dividends.** The corporation receives no tax deduction for dividends distributed to shareholders. Dividends are again taxable (except when they represent distributions of capital) as ordinary income to the shareholder receiving them. This double-taxation feature of the corporation is one of its major disadvantages, as mentioned in Chapter 24.

Profits not distributed are retained by the corporation. These **retained earnings,** if invested properly, will yield higher corporate profits in the future and thus normally cause the price of the company's stock to rise. Individual shareholders can then reap the benefits of these retained earnings in the capital gains they receive when they sell their shares.

The consequences of a failure to pay corporate taxes can be severe. As will be discussed in Chapter 28, the state may dissolve a corporation for this reason. Alternatively, corporate status may be suspended until the taxes are paid. In the following case, the state had suspended a corporation's **corporate charter** (the document issued by a state agency or authority—usually the secretary of state—that grants a corporation legal existence and the right to function) because of the corporation's failure to pay certain taxes. The issue before the court is whether a shareholder who was unaware of the suspension could be held personally liable on a corporate contract.

DIVIDEND
A distribution to corporate shareholders of corporate profits or income, disbursed in proportion to the number of shares held.

RETAINED EARNINGS
The portion of a corporation's profits that has not been paid out as dividends to shareholders.

CORPORATE CHARTER
The document issued by a state agency or authority (usually the secretary of state) that grants a corporation legal existence and the right to function.

CASE 26.1

CHARLES A. TORRENCE CO. v. CLARY

Court of Appeals of North Carolina, 1995.
464 S.E.2d 502.

HISTORICAL AND POLITICAL SETTING   *At one time, opening a small business was relatively simple in terms of the obligations to the government. Today, however, many businesspersons feel that there is an ocean of federal, state, and local laws that threatens to swamp even the least regulated of small businesses. For example, all states require proof of financial responsibility and compliance with other requirements before they issue a license to engage in certain businesses or occupations. Even a business that is exempt from state regulations may be required to obtain a county or city permit or license. Every level of government also imposes taxes and penalties for not paying them.*

FACTS   In 1989, the architectural firm of Clary, Martin, McMullen & Associates, Inc. (CMMA, Inc.), failed to pay its North Carolina franchise taxes,[a] and the state suspended its corporate charter. Between April 1991 and March 1992, the Charles A. Torrence Company provided graphics services for the firm. In September 1992, Moodye Clary—a shareholder, the president, and the director of marketing of CMMA, Inc.—learned that his firm's corporate charter had been suspended. When

CMMA, Inc., failed to pay Torrence's bill, Torrence filed a suit in a North Carolina state court against CMMA, Inc., as well as against Moodye Clary personally, for the money. The court dismissed the claim against Moodye Clary, and Torrence appealed.

ISSUE   Is a corporate officer who does not know that the firm's corporate charter has been suspended personally liable for debts incurred by the firm during the suspension?

DECISION   No. The Court of Appeals of North Carolina affirmed the lower court's decision.

REASON   The state appellate court explained that "the suspension was only designed to put 'additional bite' into the collection of franchise taxes, but not to deprive the shareholders of the normal protection of limited liability." The court acknowledged that "directors and officers are personally liable for corporate obligations incurred by them on behalf of the corporation, or by others with their acquiescence, if at that time they were aware that the corporate charter was suspended." Moodye Clary, however, "had no knowledge, at the time the debt was incurred on behalf of the Corporation, that the corporate charter was suspended."

FOR CRITICAL ANALYSIS—Social Consideration
Why wouldn't a court permit a shareholder who knows that the charter of his or her firm has been suspended to retain limited liability for corporate debts?

a.   A *franchise tax* is an annual tax imposed for the privilege of doing business in a state.

Constitutional Rights of Corporations

A corporation is recognized under state and federal law as a "person," and it enjoys many of the same rights and privileges that U.S. citizens enjoy. The Bill of Rights guarantees a person, as a citizen, certain protections, and corporations are considered persons in most instances. Accordingly, a corporation has the same right as a natural person to equal protection of the laws under the Fourteenth Amendment. It has the right of access to the courts as an entity that can sue or be sued. It also has the right of due process before denial of life, liberty, or property, as well as freedom from unreasonable searches and seizures and from double jeopardy.

Under the First Amendment, corporations are entitled to freedom of speech. As we pointed out in Chapter 2, however, commercial speech (such as advertising) and political speech (such as contributions to political causes or candidates) receive significantly less protection than noncommercial speech.

Only the corporation's individual officers and employees possess the Fifth Amendment right against self-incrimination.[1] Additionally, the privileges and immunities clause of the Constitution (Article IV, Section 2) does not protect corporations.[2] This clause requires each state to treat citizens of other states equally with respect to access to courts, travel rights, and so forth.

Torts and Criminal Acts

A corporation is liable for the torts committed by its agents or officers within the course and scope of their employment. This principle applies to a corporation exactly as it applies to the ordinary agency relationships discussed in Chapter 23. It follows the doctrine of *respondeat superior.*

Under modern criminal law, a corporation can sometimes be held liable for the criminal acts of its agents and employees, provided the punishment is one that can be applied to the corporation. Corporate criminal prosecutions were at one time relatively rare, but in the past decade they have increased significantly in number. Obviously, corporations cannot be imprisoned, but they can be fined. (Of course, corporate directors and officers can be imprisoned, and in recent years, many have faced criminal penalties for their own actions or for the actions of employees under their supervision. The liability of corporate directors and officers is examined in Chapter 27.)

Recall from Chapter 7 that the U.S. Sentencing Commission, which was established by the Sentencing Reform Act of 1984, created standardized sentencing guidelines for federal crimes. These guidelines went into effect in 1987. The commission subsequently created specific sentencing guidelines for crimes committed by corporate employees (white-collar crimes). The net effect of the guidelines has been a fivefold to tenfold increase in criminal penalties for crimes committed by corporate personnel. Because of their importance in the corporate world, we examine these corporate sentencing guidelines in the following *Landmark in the Law.*

---

1. *In re Grand Jury No. 86–3 (Will Roberts Corp.),* 816 F.2d 569 (11th Cir. 1987).
2. *W. C. M. Window Co. v. Bernardi,* 730 F.2d 486 (7th Cir. 1984).

LANDMARK IN THE LAW

Corporate Sentencing Guidelines

The Federal Organizational Corporate Sentencing Guidelines became effective in 1991. The guidelines cover thirty-two levels of offenses. The punishment for each offense depends on such things as the seriousness of the charge, the amount of money involved, and the extent to which top company executives are involved. Under the sentencing guidelines, corporate lawbreakers face sanctions and fines that can be as high as hundreds of millions of dollars. The guidelines allow judges to ease up on penalties, however, when companies have taken substantial steps to prevent, investigate, and punish wrongdoing. Additionally, if companies cooperate with government investigators, the penalties may be less severe.

The guidelines present judges with a complicated formula for determining penalties for businesses based on the seriousness of the offense and the degree of the company's guilt. The so-called *culpability score* of a company depends on what role senior management had in the alleged wrongdoing as well as the company's history of past violations and the extent of management's cooperation with federal investigators. Additionally, the effectiveness of the company's compliance program is impor-

Landmark in the Law—Continued

tant. Firms can establish "credits" against potential penalties if they have undertaken the measures listed below.

• The firm must establish and put in writing crime-prevention standards and procedures for all employees and agents, and these standards must be communicated to all employees and agents in writing, training programs, or both.
• The standards must be enforced by high-level employees.
• When an employee has demonstrated an apparent propensity to engage in criminal activities, the company must prevent that employee from exercising discretionary authority.
• All anticrime standards of the company must include methods of detecting as well as preventing crimes.
• Whistleblowers must be protected from reprisals.

For Critical Analysis: *What if cooperating with federal investigators means disclosing incriminating materials? In this situation, should the company cooperate with the investigators?*

▌Corporate Powers

When a corporation is created, the express and implied powers necessary to achieve its purpose also come into existence. The express powers of a corporation are found in its **articles of incorporation** (a document containing information about the corporation, including its organization and functions), in the law of the state of incorporation, and in the state and federal constitutions. Corporate **bylaws** (rules of management adopted by the corporation at its first organizational meeting) and the resolutions of the corporation's board of directors also grant or restrict certain powers. The following order of priority is used when conflicts arise among documents involving corporations:

1. The U.S. Constitution.
2. State constitutions.
3. State statutes.
4. The articles of incorporation.
5. Bylaws.
6. Resolutions of the board of directors.

Certain implied powers attach when a corporation is created. Barring express constitutional, statutory, or other prohibitions, the corporation has the implied power to perform all acts reasonably appropriate and necessary to accomplish its corporate purposes. For this reason, a corporation has the implied power to borrow money within certain limits, to lend money or to extend credit to those with whom it has a legal or contractual relationship, and to make charitable contributions.[3] To borrow money, the corporation acts through its board of directors to authorize the loan. Most often, the president or chief executive officer of the corporation will execute the necessary papers on behalf of the corporation. In so doing, corporate officers have the implied power to

ARTICLES OF INCORPORATION
The document filed with the appropriate governmental agency, usually the secretary of state, when a business is incorporated; state statutes usually prescribe what kind of information must be contained in the articles of incorporation.

BYLAWS
A set of governing rules adopted by a corporation or other association.

---

3. A corporation is prohibited from making political contributions in federal elections by the Federal Elections Campaign Act of 1974 (18 U.S.C. Section 321). Early law held that a corporation had no implied authority to make charitable contributions, because charitable activities were contrary to the primary purpose of the corporation to make a profit. Modern law, by statutes and court decisions, holds that a corporation has such implied authority.

bind the corporation in matters directly connected with the *ordinary* business affairs of the enterprise.

ULTRA VIRES
A Latin term meaning "beyond the powers"; in corporate law, acts of a corporation that are beyond its express and implied powers to undertake.

The term ***ultra vires*** means "beyond the powers." In corporate law, acts of a corporation that are beyond its express and implied powers are *ultra vires* acts. Under Section 3.04 of the RMBCA, the following remedies are available for *ultra vires* acts:

1. The shareholders may sue on behalf of the corporation to obtain an injunction (to prohibit the corporation from engaging in the *ultra vires* transactions) or to obtain damages for the harm caused by the transactions.
2. The corporation itself can sue the officers and directors who were responsible for the *ultra vires* transactions to recover damages.
3. The attorney general of the state may institute a proceeding to obtain an injunction against the *ultra vires* transactions or to institute dissolution proceedings against the corporation for *ultra vires* acts.

In the following case, the court had to decide whether the board of directors of a cooperative housing corporation had exceeded its authority when it set minimum prices for the cooperative's housing units.

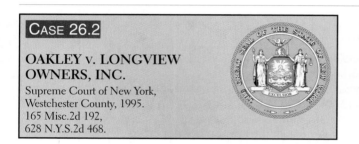

CASE 26.2

OAKLEY v. LONGVIEW OWNERS, INC.

Supreme Court of New York, Westchester County, 1995.
165 Misc.2d 192,
628 N.Y.S.2d 468.

HISTORICAL AND ECONOMIC SETTING *Cooperative housing corporations are a special form of ownership of real property. A cooperative takes out a mortgage on, for example, an entire apartment building. Residents buy shares in the corporation representing their apartments (or units) and make payments to the cooperative to cover their proportionate shares of the cooperative's mortgage payment. The board of directors of a cooperative housing corporation often has the power to disapprove sales of units to protect other residents' stake in the building. In the early 1990s, the prices for units in some New York cooperatives were dropping.*

FACTS Dorothy Oakley owned shares in Longview Owners, Inc., a cooperative housing corporation in New York. When she tried to sell her shares—that is, her apartment—the Longview board of directors refused to approve the sale, in part because the price was less than a minimum price for the apartments set by the board two months earlier. The board set the minimum in a resolution without notifying the shareholder-owners or giving them the opportunity to vote on it. Neither the Longview bylaws nor the certificate of incorporation gave the board the

authority to set prices. Oakley filed a suit in a New York state court against the board, alleging that it had exceeded its authority in refusing to approve the sale. The board filed a motion to dismiss.

ISSUE Did the Longview board have the authority to set minimum prices for apartments in the cooperative?

DECISION No. The court denied the board's motion to dismiss the suit and scheduled the case for trial.

REASON The court explained that "[a] cooperative board of directors may only act upon the authority which they are given. That authority may be found by looking to the by-laws of the corporation * * * and the certificate of incorporation." In this case, the board was not granted "by language expressed, or implied," authority to impose price restraints. The court also pointed out that the shareholder-owners had not been given prior notice of the restraints or an opportunity to vote on "this significant restriction affecting the stock of the corporation."

FOR CRITICAL ANALYSIS—Economic Consideration
Is it possible that the setting of a minimum sale price by the cooperative's board could somehow benefit the owners of the cooperative?

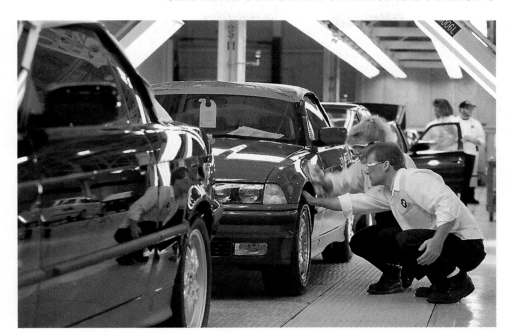

BMW automobiles are inspected at a plant in the United States. BMW is classified as an alien corporation. What is the difference between an alien corporation and a foreign corporation?

▌ Classification of Corporations

The classification of a corporation depends on its purpose, ownership characteristics, and location.

Domestic, Foreign, and Alien Corporations

A corporation is referred to as a **domestic corporation** by its home state (the state in which it incorporates). A corporation formed in one state but doing business in another is referred to in that other state as a **foreign corporation**. A corporation formed in another country—say, Mexico—but doing business in the United States is referred to in the United States as an **alien corporation.**

A corporation does not have an automatic right to do business in a state other than its state of incorporation. It normally must obtain a *certificate of authority* in any state in which it plans to do business. Once the certificate has been issued, the powers conferred upon a corporation by its home state generally can be exercised in the other state.

DOMESTIC CORPORATION
In a given state, a corporation that does business in, and is organized under the law of, that state.

FOREIGN CORPORATION
In a given state, a corporation that does business in the state without being incorporated therein.

ALIEN CORPORATION
A designation in the United States for a corporation formed in another country but doing business in the United States.

International Perspective

If a U.S. consumer is injured by a product manufactured by a corporation located in another country, can the consumer sue the corporation in a U.S. state court? In other words, may a U.S. state court exercise personal jurisdiction over an alien corporation? The answer depends on whether the defendant corporation has sufficient "contacts" with the state in which the lawsuit is filed. As discussed in Chapter 3, if the defendant corporation meets the "minimum-contacts" requirement, then the state court can exercise jurisdiction over the corporation. Generally, the minimum-contacts requirement is satisfied if a corporation does business within the state, advertises or sells its

(Continued)

products within the state, or places its goods into the "stream of commerce" with the intent that the goods be sold in the state.

Alien corporations that are sued in U.S. courts sometimes claim that it is essentially unfair to force them to travel to the United States to defend against the suits—because the transportation of witnesses, documents, and other evidence can be very costly. In response to such arguments, U.S. courts generally hold that alien corporations, by marketing their goods in the United States, should expect to be "haled into court" in this country. As one court stated, any such inconvenience "must be weighed against a public policy which favors providing a forum for an injured resident to bring an action against a non-resident manufacturer."[a]

For Critical Analysis: *Is there any way a foreign manufacturer that sells its products in the United States can avoid being "haled into court" in this country to defend against a product liability action?*

a.   *Loral Fairchild Corp. v. Victor Co. of Japan, Ltd.,* 803 F.Supp. 626 (E.D.N.Y. 1992).

Public and Private Corporations

A public corporation is one formed by the government to meet some political or governmental purpose. Cities and towns that incorporate are common examples. In addition, many federal government organizations, such as the U.S. Postal Service, the Tennessee Valley Authority, and AMTRAK, are public corporations. Note that a public corporation is not the same as a *publicly held* corporation. A publicly held corporation is any corporation whose shares are publicly traded in securities markets, such as the New York Stock Exchange or the over-the-counter market.

In contrast to public corporations, private corporations are created either wholly or in part for private benefit. Most corporations are private. Although they may serve a public purpose, as a public utility does, they are owned by private persons rather than by the government.[4]

NOTE A private corporation is a voluntary association, but a public corporation is not.

Nonprofit Corporations

Corporations formed without a profit-making purpose are called *nonprofit* or *not-for-profit* corporations. Private hospitals, educational institutions, charities, and religious organizations, for example, are frequently organized as nonprofit corporations. The nonprofit corporation is a convenient form of organization that allows various groups to own property and to form contracts without the individual members' being personally exposed to liability.

Close Corporations

CLOSE CORPORATION
A corporation whose shareholders are limited to a small group of persons, often including only family members. The rights of shareholders of a close corporation usually are restricted regarding the transfer of shares to others.

Most corporate enterprises in the United States fall into the category of close corporations. A **close corporation** is one whose shares are held by members of a family or by relatively few persons. Close corporations are also referred to as *closely held, family,* or *privately held* corporations. Usually, the members of the small group constituting a

4.   For a landmark case on the distinction between private and public corporations, and the rights of private corporations, see *The Trustees of Dartmouth College v. Woodward,* 17 U.S. (4 Wheaton) 518, 4 L.Ed. 629 (1819).

close corporation are personally known to each other. Because the number of shareholders is so small, there is no trading market for the shares.

Some states have enacted special statutory provisions that apply to close corporations. These provisions expressly permit close corporations to depart significantly from certain formalities required by traditional corporation law.[5] Additionally, Section 7.32 of the RMBCA, a provision added to the RMBCA in 1991 and adopted in several states, gives close corporations a substantial amount of flexibility in determining the rules by which they will operate. Under Section 7.32, if all of the shareholders of a corporation agree in writing, the corporation can operate without directors, bylaws, annual or special shareholders' or directors' meetings, stock certificates, or formal records of shareholders' or directors' decisions.[6]

MANAGEMENT OF CLOSE CORPORATIONS   The close corporation has a single shareholder or a closely knit group of shareholders, who usually hold the positions of directors and officers. Management of a close corporation resembles that of a sole proprietorship or a partnership. As a corporation, however, the firm must meet specific legal requirements, as mentioned previously.

To prevent a majority shareholder from dominating a close corporation, the corporation may require that action can be taken by the board only on approval of more than a simple majority of the directors. Typically, this would not be required for ordinary business decisions but only for extraordinary actions, such as changing the amount of dividends or dismissing an employee-shareholder.

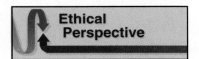

Ethical Perspective

Close corporations that are owned by family members may face severe problems when relations among the family deteriorate. For example, suppose that three sisters are equal shareholders in a close corporation. Each sister is both a director and an officer of the corporation. Disagreements over how the corporation should be operated arise, and two of the sisters, as the majority on the board of directors, vote to fire the other sister from her position as corporate president.

Although the sister who is fired remains a shareholder and a member of the board, she is deprived of her job (and her salary), which may have important economic consequences. Furthermore, she may be prevented by the corporate articles or by a shareholder agreement (to be discussed shortly) from selling her shares and investing her money elsewhere.

What can the fired sister do? Often, the only option in this kind of situation is to petition a court to dissolve the corporation or force the majority shareholders to buy the minority shareholder's shares. Although courts generally are reluctant to interfere with corporate decisions, they have held, in some cases, that majority shareholders owe a fiduciary duty to minority shareholders (see Chapter 27). A breach of this duty may cause a court to order the majority shareholders to buy out the minority shareholder's interest in the firm or, as a last resort, to dissolve the corporation.

For Critical Analysis: *Is there any way that shareholders in a small, family-owned (close) corporation can prevent, in advance, oppressive actions by a majority of the shareholders against minority shareholders?*

---

5.   For example, in some states (such as Maryland), the close corporation need not have a board of directors.

6.   Shareholders cannot agree, however, to eliminate certain rights of shareholders, such as the right to inspect corporate books and records or the right to bring derivative actions (lawsuits on behalf of the corporation—see Chapter 27).

TRANSFER OF SHARES IN CLOSE CORPORATIONS   Because, by definition, a close corporation has a small number of shareholders, the transfer of one shareholder's shares to someone else can cause serious management problems. The other shareholders may find themselves required to share control with someone they do not know or like.

Consider an example. Three brothers, Terry, Damon, and Henry Johnson, are the only shareholders of Johnson's Car Wash, Inc. Terry and Damon do not want Henry to sell his shares to an unknown third person. To avoid this situation, the articles of incorporation could restrict the transferability of shares to outside persons by stipulating that shareholders must offer their shares to the corporation or other shareholders before selling them to an outside purchaser. In fact, a few states have statutes under which close corporation shares cannot be transferred unless certain persons—including shareholders, family members, and the corporation—are first given the opportunity to purchase the shares for the same price.

Another way that control of a close corporation can be stabilized is through the use of a shareholder agreement. A shareholder agreement can provide that when one of the original shareholders dies, his or her shares of stock in the corporation will be divided in such a way that the proportionate holdings of the survivors, and thus their proportionate control, will be maintained. Courts are generally reluctant to interfere with private agreements, including shareholder agreements. Whether a shareholder agreement should be enforced is at issue in the following case.

CASE 26.3

ROSINY v. SCHMIDT
New York Supreme Court,
Appellate Division, 1992.
185 A.D.2d 727,
587 N.Y.S.2d 929.

COMPANY PROFILE   *During the 1940s and 1950s, C. L. McGuire & Company operated an automobile repair business in a building in Manhattan. Auto mechanics Charles (C. L.) McGuire and Theodore Schmidt were shareholders in the company. In 1957, an opportunity arose to buy the building, and Ched Realty was formed for the purpose. Ched's initial shareholders were McGuire and Schmidt, who each owned 25 percent, and Edward Rosiny, who owned 50 percent. In 1964, Rosiny transferred his Ched shares to his wife, Annabelle, with whom McGuire and Schmidt executed a new shareholder agreement. In 1971, after Schmidt died, McGuire and Annabelle signed a new shareholder agreement with Schmidt's widow, Jeanette. In 1981, Annabelle transferred her shares to Allen and Frank, her sons.*

FACTS   In 1981, the four shareholders of Ched Realty, each of whom held 25 percent of the shares, formed a shareholder agreement. The agreement provided that in the event of a shareholder's death, the surviving shareholders could buy the decedent's shares at "book value"

or $200 per share, whichever was greater. Two of the shareholders, Allen and Frank Rosiny, were young, well-educated attorneys. The other two shareholders, Charles McGuire and Jeanette Priddy, were elderly, and neither of them had completed high school. Both, however, had signed several shareholder agreements prior to 1981, and a 1971 agreement included basically the same "book value" buy-out agreement. The other agreements provided for a book value formula to determine the value of a decedent's shares. At the time of the 1981 agreement, the book value was negative, but the market value was $4,225 per share and gaining. When Priddy and McGuire died in 1988, their stock had a market value of $41,500 per share. The Rosinys sued in a New York state court to enforce the buy-out provision of the shareholder agreement. The heirs of McGuire and Priddy argued that there was no mutual assent when the 1981 agreement was formed. They also claimed that the agreement was unconscionable, because the younger shareholders, knowing that neither McGuire nor Priddy was aware of what was being signed, took advantage of this fact. The court agreed with the heirs, and the Rosinys appealed.

ISSUE   Is the shareholder agreement enforceable?

DECISION   Yes. The appellate court ruled in favor of the Rosinys.

REASON   The court pointed out that this was the fourth Ched shareholders' agreement, three of which provided for a book value formula to determine the value of a

Case 26.3—Continued

decedent's shares. There was no evidence that "because of the disparity in age and educational background, the decedents were deceived by the young attorneys." Additionally, "[d]espite representation by counsel, neither Priddy nor McGuire opted to sell the property or dissolve the corporation during the seven years following their execution of the 1981 agreement," which included those options. The court also noted that a 1971 shareholder agreement, which was signed by Priddy and McGuire before the Rosinys became shareholders, contained the identical buy-out provision in rejection of a fair market value approach contained in an earlier agreement. "The return to the use of 'book value,' an unambiguous term, from fair market value, as well as the use of this term in previous agreements, evinces a meeting of the minds as to this term of the agreement."

FOR CRITICAL ANALYSIS—Social Consideration
Even assuming (as the court did) that Priddy's and McGuire's consent to the agreement was genuine, were there any other grounds on which the court might have decided that the agreement was unenforceable?

S Corporations

The Subchapter S Revision Act of 1982 was passed "to permit the incorporation and operation of certain small businesses without the incidence of income taxation at both the corporate and shareholder level."[7] Additionally, Congress divided corporations into two groups: **S corporations,** which have elected Subchapter S treatment, and *C corporations*, which are all other corporations. Certain close corporations can choose to qualify under Subchapter S of the Internal Revenue Code to avoid the imposition of income taxes at the corporate level while retaining many of the advantages of a corporation, particularly limited liability.

S CORPORATION
A close business corporation that has met certain requirements as set out by the Internal Revenue Code and thus qualifies for special income-tax treatment. Essentially, an S corporation is taxed the same as a partnership, but its owners enjoy the privilege of limited liability.

QUALIFICATION REQUIREMENTS FOR S CORPORATIONS   Among the numerous requirements for S corporation status, the following are the most important:

1.   The corporation must be a domestic corporation.
2.   The corporation must not be a member of an affiliated group of corporations.
3.   The shareholders of the corporation must be individuals, estates, or certain trusts. Corporations, partnerships, and nonqualifying trusts cannot be shareholders. (See this chapter's *Business Law in Action* on page 680 for a discussion of how a shareholder of an S corporation attempted to use this requirement to his advantage.)
4.   The corporation must have seventy-five or fewer shareholders.
5.   The corporation must have only one class of stock, although not all shareholders need have the same voting rights.
6.   No shareholder of the corporation may be a nonresident alien.

BENEFITS OF S CORPORATIONS   At times, it is beneficial for a regular corporation to elect S corporation status. Benefits include the following:

1.   When the corporation has losses, the S election allows the shareholders to use the losses to offset other income.
2.   When the shareholder's tax bracket is lower than the corporation's tax bracket, the S election causes the corporation's pass-through net income to be taxed in the

---

7.   Senate Report No. 640, 97th Congress, 1st Session (1981).

Doctors discuss a patient's case. What are the advantages to these doctors of incorporating as a professional corporation?

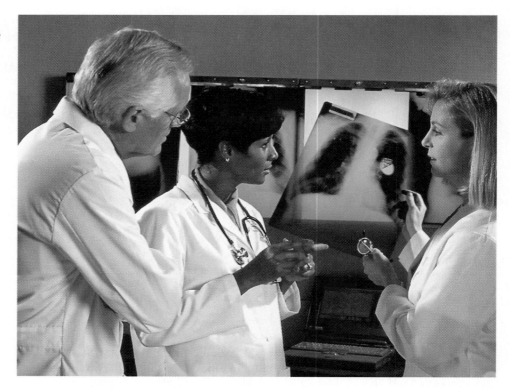

shareholder's bracket. This is particularly attractive when the corporation wants to accumulate earnings for some future business purpose.

3.　As mentioned, a single tax on corporate income is imposed at individual income tax rates at the shareholder level. (The income is taxable to shareholders whether or not it is actually distributed.)

Professional Corporations

CONTRAST Unlike the shareholders of most other corporations, the shareholders of professional corporations must generally be licensed professionals.

Professional persons such as physicians, lawyers, dentists, and accountants can incorporate. Professional corporations are typically identified by the letters S.C. (service corporation), P.C. (professional corporation), or P.A. (professional association). In general, the laws governing professional corporations are similar to those governing ordinary business corporations, but three basic areas of liability deserve special attention.

First, a court might, for liability purposes, regard the professional corporation as a partnership in which each partner can be held liable for whatever malpractice liability is incurred by the others within the scope of the partnership. Second, a shareholder in a professional corporation is protected from the liability imposed because of any torts (unrelated to malpractice) committed by other members. Third, many professional corporation statutes retain personal liability of professional persons for their acts and the professional acts performed under their supervision.

In the following case, a law partnership incorporated as a professional corporation in 1977 primarily for the purpose of obtaining certain tax benefits. In fact, however, the firm continued to operate as a partnership. A central question before the court in this case was whether the firm should be governed by partnership law or corporation law.

CASE 26.4

BOYD, PAYNE, GATES & FARTHING, P.C. v. PAYNE, GATES, FARTHING & RADD, P.C.
Supreme Court of Virginia, 1992.
422 S.E.2d 784.

HISTORICAL AND SOCIAL SETTING *Professional corporations or associations are authorized by the statutes of all states and the District of Columbia. To be treated as a corporation, however, a professional corporation must act as a corporation, just as any individuals coming together to conduct business as a corporation must act as a corporation. This is not a new proposition. The principle applied to ordinary corporations before professional corporations were common. For example, in the late 1920s, two businesspersons entered into a partnership to manufacture and sell radio cabinets. They formed a corporation to carry out the purpose, but no stock was issued, and no capital was invested. In a suit to determine what amounts creditors should receive from the funds of the company, the court held that although the company "became technically a corporate entity," the two businesspersons dealt with it as if it were a partnership. Consequently, the court decided that in settling the company's accounts, the company should be treated as a partnership.*[a]

FACTS Robert Boyd, Charles Payne, Ronald Gates, and Philip Farthing practiced law together as a partnership. In 1977, for tax advantages, the partners formed a professional corporation—Boyd, Payne, Gates & Farthing, P.C. (Boyd P.C.). Corporate stock was issued to each partner in proportion to the amount of profit his work generated for the firm. No partnership assets were transferred to the corporation. The members of the firm continued to refer to one another as "partners" and to Boyd as the "managing partner." "Partner" meetings

were held to discuss business matters. In 1983, Anthony Radd joined the practice, but four years later, Radd, Payne, Gates, and Farthing formed their own professional corporation—Payne, Gates, Farthing & Radd, P.C. In a dispute over Boyd P.C.'s assets, a Virginia state court found that Boyd P.C. was a partnership and applied partnership law to distribute the assets. Boyd P.C. appealed.

ISSUE Was the trial court justified in applying partnership law to Boyd P.C.?

DECISION Yes. The Supreme Court of Virginia affirmed the trial court's judgment.

REASON The Supreme Court of Virginia found, as the trial court had, that Boyd P.C. was merely a corporate "shell" formed to gain tax advantages. The evidence sufficiently indicated that the firm continued to operate as a partnership. The court also found it significant that after the corporation had been formed, the partners "executed an agreement dealing with the possibility of a tax audit" in which it was provided that if the firm was audited, each partner's tax liability would be based on the percentage of profits that the partner received in that particular year. This agreement effectively indicated that "tax liability was apportioned on the basis of partnership percentages, not stock ownership." The court cited a previous case in which partnership law was applied to a corporation because members of the corporation "utterly disregarded [the] corporate entity, and dealt with its rights, property and business as if they belonged to a partnership." The court concluded that "[b]ecause Boyd P.C. was a close corporation and its shareholders validly conducted the internal affairs of their law practice as a partnership, we hold that the trial court properly settled their rights and liabilities according to partnership law."

FOR CRITICAL ANALYSIS—Economic Consideration
What benefits can be gained by switching from a partnership form of business to a corporation?

a.   *Deeds v. Gilmer,* 162 Va. 157, 174 S.E. 37 (1934).

▌Corporate Formation

Up to this point, we have discussed some of the general characteristics of corporations. We now examine the process in which corporations come into existence. Generally, this process involves two steps: (1) preliminary organizational and promotional undertakings—particularly obtaining capital for the future corporation—and (2) the legal process of incorporation.

BUSINESS LAW IN ACTION

A Case of Shareholder Blackmail

What happens if a family member cannot sell his or her shares in a close corporation? Arthur Chesterton faced this situation when he wanted to leave his family-owned company. The A. W. Chesterton Company had been owned by Chesterton family members since it was founded in 1885. The corporate articles provided that if any shareholder attempted to transfer his or her shares to anyone other than a family member, the shareholder first had to notify the company of his or her intention to do so. Then, after receiving the shareholder's notice, the company would have thirty days to either purchase the shares itself or designate a purchaser of the shares.

For years, the family member–shareholders of the Chesterton Company had disagreed over the control and direction of the company. Arthur Chesterton tried unsuccessfully to convince the other shareholders to sell all of the assets of the company. He also tried to sell his

shares in the corporation but could not find a buyer.

Arthur's solution was to force the company's hand. Taking advantage of the above-mentioned provision in the corporate articles, Arthur notified the company that he intended to transfer some of his shares to two different corporations, one located in Florida and the other in the Cayman Islands. This meant that the Chesterton Company had to either purchase the shares itself or designate another purchaser within thirty days. In effect, Arthur was "blackmailing" the company into purchasing his shares— because the company was an S corporation, and its S corporation status would be lost if a corporation became a shareholder. In other words, if Arthur went through with his intended transfer of shares to the two corporations, Chesterton Company would forfeit the tax advantages it enjoyed as an S corporation. At the same time, the company was in no position to pay the $40 million that it would cost to purchase Arthur's shares itself, nor could it find another buyer for the shares within the allotted time period of thirty days.

The company and the majority shareholders, seeing no other solution to the problem, filed a lawsuit against

Arthur, seeking a preliminary injunction against his intended transfer of the shares to the two corporations. The court concluded, as did the company and the majority shareholders, that Arthur's proposed transfer was simply a sham. The court stated that the plaintiffs (the company and the majority shareholders) "are likely to show that Chesterton has engaged in a scheme to coerce the Company to repurchase his shares, that his purpose is to pursue his own financial interests, and that his plan jeopardizes the Company's ability to operate as an S-corporation." The court held that these findings were "sufficient to merit granting Plaintiffs' request for preliminary injunctive relief."[a]

For Critical Analysis: *What tax advantages did the company and the majority shareholders enjoy as a result of S corporation status?*

---

a. *A. W. Chesterton Co. v. Chesterton,* 907 F.Supp. 19 (D.Mass. 1995).

Promotional Activities

Before a corporation becomes a reality, **promoters**—those who, for themselves or others, take the preliminary steps in organizing a corporation—frequently make contracts with investors and others on behalf of the future corporation. One of the tasks of the promoter is to issue a prospectus. A **prospectus** is a document required by federal or state securities laws (discussed in Chapter 29) that describes the financial operations of the corporation, thus allowing investors to make informed decisions. The promoter also secures the corporate charter.

PROMOTER'S LIABILITY   A promoter may purchase or lease property with a view to selling it to the corporation when the corporation is formed. A promoter may also enter into contracts with attorneys, accountants, architects, or other professionals whose services will be needed in planning for the proposed corporation. Finally, a promoter induces people to purchase stock in the corporation.

As a general rule, a promoter is held personally liable on preincorporation contracts. Courts simply hold that promoters are not agents when a corporation has yet to come into existence. If, however, the promoter secures the contracting party's agreement to hold only the corporation (and not the promoter) liable on the contract, the promoter will not be liable in the event of any breach of contract. Basically, the personal liability of the promoter continues even after incorporation unless the third party *releases* the promoter. In most states, this rule is applied whether or not the promoter made the agreement in the name of, or with reference to, the proposed corporation.

Once the corporation is formed (the charter issued), the promoter remains personally liable until the corporation assumes the preincorporation contract by *novation* (discussed in Chapter 12). Novation releases the promoter and makes the corporation liable for performing the contractual obligations. In some situations, the corporation *adopts* the promoter's contract by undertaking to perform it. Most courts hold that adoption in and of itself does not discharge the promoter from contractual liability. A corporation cannot normally *ratify* a preincorporation contract, as no principal was in existence at the time the contract was made.

SUBSCRIBERS AND SUBSCRIPTIONS   Prior to the actual formation of the corporation, the promoter can contact potential individual investors, and they can agree to purchase capital stock in the future corporation. This agreement is usually called a *subscription agreement*, and the potential investor is called a *subscriber*. Depending on state law, subscribers become shareholders as soon as the corporation is formed or as soon as the corporation accepts the agreement.

Most courts view preincorporation subscriptions as continuing offers to purchase corporate stock. On or after its formation, the corporation can choose to accept the offer to purchase stock. Many courts also treat a subscription as irrevocable except with the consent of all of the subscribers. A subscription is irrevocable for a period of six months unless the subscription agreement provides otherwise or unless all the subscribers agree to the revocation of the subscription [RMBCA 6.20]. In some courts and jurisdictions, the preincorporation subscriber can revoke the offer to purchase before acceptance without liability, however.

Incorporation Procedures

Exact procedures for incorporation differ among states, but the basic requirements are similar.

STATE CHARTERING   The first step in the incorporation procedure is to select a state in which to incorporate. Because state incorporation laws differ, individuals often incorporate in a state that offers the most advantageous tax or incorporation provisions. Delaware has historically had the least restrictive laws. Consequently, many corporations, including a number of the largest, have incorporated there. Delaware's statutes permit firms to incorporate in Delaware and carry out business and locate operating headquarters elsewhere. (Most other states now permit this.) Closely held corporations, however, particularly those of a professional nature, generally incorporate in the state in which their principal shareholders live and work.

ARTICLES OF INCORPORATION   The primary document needed to begin the incorporation process is called the *articles of incorporation* (see Exhibit 26–1). The articles include basic information about the corporation and serve as a primary source of authority for its future organization and business functions. The person or persons who execute the articles are called *incorporators*. Generally, the articles of incorporation should include the elements discussed in the following subsections.

Corporate Name   The choice of a corporate name is subject to state approval to ensure against duplication or deception. State statutes usually require that the secretary of state run a check on the proposed name in the state of incorporation. Some

"A man to carry on a successful business must have imagination. He must see things as in a vision, a dream of the whole thing."

Charles M. Schwab, 1862–1939
(American industrialist)

RECALL Most offers to form a contract can be revoked, without liability, before they are accepted. Exceptions include option contracts, merchants' firm offers, and offers on which the offerees changed postion in justifiable reliance.

♦ Exhibit 26–1   Articles of Incorporation

ARTICLE ONE

The name of the corporation is _____ .

ARTICLE TWO

The period of its duration is perpetual (may be a number of years or until a certain date).

ARTICLE THREE

The purpose (or purposes) for which the corporation is organized is (are) _____
_____ .

ARTICLE FOUR

The aggregate number of shares that the corporation shall have authority to issue is _____ of the par value of
_____ dollar(s) each (or without par value).

ARTICLE FIVE

The corporation will not commence business until it has received for the issuance of its shares consideration of the
value of $1,000 (can be any sum not less that $1,000).

ARTICLE SIX

The address of the corporation's registered office is _____ ,
New Pacum, and the name of its registered agent at such address is _____
_____ .

(Use the street or building or rural address of the registered office, not a post office box number.)

ARTICLE SEVEN

The number of initial directors is _____ , and the names and addresses of the directors are
_____
_____ .

ARTICLE EIGHT

The name and address of the incorporator is _____
_____ .

(signed) _____

                                                          Incorporator

Sworn to on _____ by the above-named incorporator.
              (date)

                                      _____
                                      Notary Public _____ County, New Pacum

(Notary Seal)

---

states require that the incorporators, at their own expense, run a check on the proposed name for the newly formed corporation. Once cleared, a name can be reserved for a short time, for a fee, pending the completion of the articles of incorporation. All corporate statutes require the corporation name to include the word *Corporation, Incorporated, Company,* or *Limited,* or abbreviations of these terms.

A corporate name is prohibited from being the same as (or deceptively similar to) the name of an existing corporation doing business within the state. For example, if an existing corporation is named General Dynamics, Inc., the state will not allow another corporation to be called General Dynamic, Inc.—because that name is deceptively similar to the first, and it impliedly transfers a part of the goodwill established by the first corporate user to the second corporation.

Duration   A corporation can have perpetual existence under most state corporate statutes. A few states, however, prescribe a maximum duration, after which the corporation must formally renew its existence.

Nature and Purpose   The articles must specify the intended business activities of the corporation, and naturally, these activities must be lawful. A general statement of corporate purpose is usually sufficient to give rise to all of the powers necessary or convenient to the purpose of the organization. The articles of incorporation can state, for example, that the corporation is organized "to engage in the production and sale of agricultural products." There is a trend toward allowing corporate articles to state that the corporation is organized for "any legal business," with no mention of specifics, to avoid unnecessary future amendments to the corporate articles.

Capital Structure   The articles generally set forth the capital structure of the corporation. A few state statutes require a very small capital investment for ordinary business corporations but a greater capital investment for those engaged in insurance or banking. The articles often must outline the number of shares of stock authorized for issuance; their valuation; the various types or classes of stock authorized for issuance; and other relevant information concerning equity, capital, and credit.

Internal Organization   The articles should describe the internal management structure of the corporation, although this can be included in bylaws adopted after the corporation is formed. The articles of incorporation commence the corporation; the bylaws are formed after commencement by the board of directors. Bylaws cannot conflict with the incorporation statute or the corporation's charter [RMBCA 2.06].

KEEP IN MIND Unlike the articles of incorporation, bylaws do not need to be filed with a state official.

Under the RMBCA, shareholders may amend or repeal bylaws. The board of directors may also amend or repeal bylaws unless the articles of incorporation or provisions of the incorporation statute reserve this power to shareholders exclusively [RMBCA 10.20]. Typical bylaw provisions describe such things as voting requirements for shareholders, the election of the board of directors, the methods of replacing directors, and the manner and time of scheduling shareholder and board meetings (these corporate activities will be discussed in Chapter 27).

Registered Office and Agent   The corporation must indicate the location and address of its registered office within the state. Usually, the registered office is also the principal office of the corporation. The corporation must give the name and address of a specific person who has been designated as an *agent* and who can receive legal documents (such as orders to appear in court) on behalf of the corporation.

Incorporators   Each incorporator must be listed by name and must indicate an address. An incorporator is a person—often, the corporate promoter—who applies to the state on behalf of the corporation to obtain its corporate charter. The incorporator need not be a subscriber and need not have any interest at all in the corporation. Many states do not impose residency or age requirements for incorporators. States vary on the required number of incorporators; it can be as few as one or as many as three. Incorporators are required to sign the articles of incorporation when they are submitted to the state; often this is their only duty. In some states, they participate at the first organizational meeting of the corporation.

CERTIFICATE OF INCORPORATION
The primary document that evidences corporate existence (referred to as articles of incorporation in some states).

CERTIFICATE OF INCORPORATION   Once the articles of incorporation have been prepared, signed, and authenticated by the incorporators, they are sent to the appropriate state official, usually the secretary of state, along with the appropriate filing fee. In many states, the secretary of state then issues a **certificate of incorporation** representing the state's authorization for the corporation to conduct business. (This may be referred to as the *corporate charter*.) The certificate and a copy of the articles are returned to the incorporators.

FIRST ORGANIZATIONAL MEETING   The first organizational meeting is provided for in the articles of incorporation but is held after the charter has actually been granted. At this meeting, the incorporators elect the first board of directors and complete the routine business of incorporation (pass bylaws and issue stock, for example). Some-times, the meeting is held after the election of the board, and the business transacted depends on the requirements of the state's incorporation statute, the nature of the busi-ness, the provisions made in the articles, and the desires of the promoters. Adoption of bylaws—the internal rules of management for the corporation—is probably the most important function of the meeting. The shareholders, directors, and officers must abide by the bylaws in conducting corporate business.

▌ Corporate Status

The procedures for incorporation are very specific. If they are not followed precisely, others may be able to challenge the existence of the corporation.

Errors in the incorporation procedures can become important when, for example, a third person who is attempting to enforce a contract or bring suit for a tort injury learns of them. On the basis of improper incorporation, the plaintiff could seek to make the would-be shareholders personally liable. Additionally, when the corporation seeks to enforce a contract against a defaulting party, if the defaulting party learns of a defect in the incorporation procedure, he or she may be able to avoid liability on that ground.

To prevent injustice, courts will sometimes attribute corporate status to an improp-erly formed corporation by holding it to be a *de jure* corporation or a *de facto* corpora-tion. Occasionally, a corporation may be held to exist by estoppel. Additionally, in certain circumstances involving abuse of the corporate form, a court may disregard the corporate entity and hold the shareholders personally liable.

De Jure and *De Facto* Corporations

In the event of substantial compliance with all conditions precedent to incorporation, the corporation is said to have *de jure* (rightful and lawful) existence. In most states and under the RMBCA, the certificate of incorporation is viewed as evidence that all mandatory statutory provisions have been met. This means that the corporation is properly formed, and neither the state nor a third party can attack its existence. If, for example, an incorporator's address was incorrectly listed, this would technically mean that the corporation was improperly formed; but the law does not regard such incon-sequential procedural defects as detracting from substantial compliance, and courts will uphold the *de jure* status of the corporate entity.

Sometimes, there is a defect in complying with statutory mandates—for example, the corporation charter may have expired. Under these circumstances, the corporation may have *de facto* (actual) status, meaning that the corporation in fact exists, even if not rightfully or lawfully. A corporation with *de facto* status cannot be challenged by third persons (except for the state). The following elements are required for *de facto* status:

1.   There must be a state statute under which the corporation can be validly incorporated.

2.   The parties must have made a good faith attempt to comply with the statute.

3.   The enterprise must already have undertaken to do business as a corporation.

Corporation by Estoppel

If an association that is neither an actual corporation nor a *de facto* or *de jure* corporation holds itself out as being a corporation, it normally will be estopped from denying
corporate status in a lawsuit by a third party. This usually occurs when a third party
contracts with an association that claims to be a corporation but does not hold a certificate of incorporation. When the third party brings suit naming the so-called corporation as the defendant, the association may not escape from liability on the ground
that no corporation exists. When justice requires, the courts treat an alleged corporation as if it were an actual corporation for the purpose of determining the rights and
liabilities involved in a particular situation. Corporation by estoppel is thus determined by the situation. It does not extend recognition of corporate status beyond the
resolution of the problem at hand.

COMPARE Corporation by estoppel, agency by estoppel, and promissory estoppel all involve situations in which a party's own conduct prevents him or her from claiming a right to the detriment of one who relied on that conduct.

Disregarding the Corporate Entity

Occasionally, the owners use a corporate entity to perpetuate a fraud, circumvent the
law, or in some other way accomplish an illegitimate objective. In these situations, the
court will ignore the corporate structure by "piercing the corporate veil" and exposing
the shareholders to personal liability. The following are some of the factors that frequently cause the courts to pierce the corporate veil:

1.   A party is tricked or misled into dealing with the corporation rather than the
individual.

2.   The corporation is set up never to make a profit or always to be insolvent, or it is
too "thinly" capitalized—that is, it has insufficient capital at the time of formation to
meet its prospective debts or potential liabilities.

3.   Statutory corporate formalities, such as holding required corporation meetings,
are not followed.

4.   Personal and corporate interests are **commingled** (mixed together) to the extent
that the corporation has no separate identity.

COMMINGLE
To mix together. In corporate law, if personal and corporate interests are commingled to the extent that the corporation has no separate identity, a court may "pierce the corporate veil" and expose the shareholders to personal liability.

To elaborate on the fourth factor in the preceding list, consider a close corporation
that is formed according to law by a single person or by a few family members. In such
a situation, the separate status of the corporate entity and the sole stockholder (or family-
member stockholders) must be carefully preserved. Certain practices invite trouble for
the one-person or family-owned corporation: the commingling of corporate and personal funds, the failure to hold and record minutes of board of directors' meetings, or
the shareholders' continuous personal use of corporate property (for example, vehicles).

Corporation laws usually do not specifically prohibit a stockholder from lawfully
lending money to his or her corporation. When an officer or director lends the corporation money and takes back security in the form of corporate assets, however, the
courts will scrutinize the transaction closely. Any such transaction must be made in
good faith and for fair value.

Generally, when the corporate privilege is abused for personal benefit or when the
corporate business is treated in such a careless manner that the corporation and the
shareholder in control are no longer separate entities, the court usually will require an
owner to assume personal liability to creditors for the corporation's debts. In short,
when the facts show that great injustice would result from the use of a corporation to
avoid individual responsibility, a court of equity will look behind the corporate structure to the individual stockholder. The following case is illustrative.

CASE 26.5

J-MART JEWELRY OUTLETS, INC. v. STANDARD DESIGN
Court of Appeals of Georgia, 1995.
218 Ga.App. 459,
462 S.E.2d 406.

HISTORICAL AND CULTURAL SETTING *A gem is a mineral that is valuable because of its durability, rarity, and beauty. Gems are usually cut and polished for use in jewelry. At least 120 minerals have been classified as gems over the centuries, but only two dozen are used in jewelry today. Precious gems include diamonds, emeralds, sapphires, and rubies. These can be mined from the earth or produced synthetically. All other gems are classified as semiprecious.*

FACTS Jim Halter, the sole shareholder of J-Mart Jewelry Outlets, Inc., knew that as a result of financial difficulties, J-Mart would soon go out of business. Eight days before the firm stopped doing business, it paid the balance due on Halter's personal credit card. At the same time, Halter paid J-Mart $1 for a Cadillac that the firm had bought new for his personal use and on which it had made three payments. Four of J-Mart's creditors, including Standard Design, filed a suit in a Georgia state court against Halter and others to recover for J-Mart's unpaid debts. The jury "pierced the corporate veil" to hold Halter personally responsible. Halter appealed.

ISSUE Is it proper to pierce the corporate veil when, shortly before a corporation goes out of business, the corporation pays the balance on its sole shareholder's personal credit card and makes unauthorized payments on a car for the shareholder's personal benefit?

DECISION Yes. The Court of Appeals of Georgia affirmed the judgment of the lower court.

REASON The state appellate court explained that "[t]he concept of piercing the corporate veil is applied in Georgia to remedy injustices which arise where a party has overextended his privilege in the use of a corporate entity in order to defeat justice, perpetrate fraud or to evade contractual or tort responsibility." The court noted that shortly before J-Mart went out of business, it paid off the balance on Halter's personal credit card and made unauthorized payments on a car for his personal benefit.

FOR CRITICAL ANALYSIS—Ethical Consideration
Why shouldn't the sole owner of a corporation be held liable for all corporate acts?

▌Corporate Financing

Part of the process of corporate formation involves corporate financing. Corporations are financed by the issuance and sale of corporate securities. **Securities** (stocks and bonds) evidence the obligation to pay money or the right to participate in earnings and the distribution of corporate property. **Stocks,** or *equity securities*, represent the purchase of ownership in the business firm. **Bonds** (debentures), or *debt securities*, represent the borrowing of money by firms (and governments). Of course, not all debt is in the form of debt securities. For example, some debt is in the form of accounts payable and notes payable. Accounts and notes payable are typically short-term debts. Bonds are simply a way for the corporation to split up its long-term debt so that it can market it more easily.

Bonds

Bonds are issued by business firms and by governments at all levels as evidence of the funds they are borrowing from investors. Bonds normally have a designated

SECURITIES
Corporate stocks and bonds; evidence of an ownership interest in the corporation or a promise of repayment by the corporation.

STOCK
An equity (ownership) interest in a corporation, measured in units of shares.

BOND
A certificate that evidences a corporate (or government) debt. It is a security that involves no ownership interest in the issuing entity.

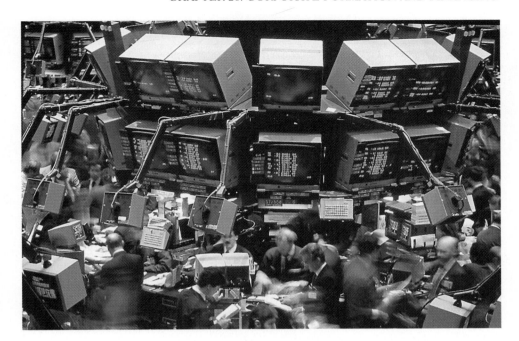

Corporations are financed by the issuance and sale of securities, which are bought and sold in such places as the New York Stock Exchange. What are securities, and what do they represent?

maturity date—the date when the principal, or face, amount of the bond is returned to the investor. They are sometimes referred to as *fixed-income securities* because their owners (that is, the creditors) receive fixed-dollar interest payments during the period of time prior to maturity, usually semiannually.

Because debt financing represents a legal obligation on the part of the corporation, various features and terms of a particular bond issue are specified in a lending agreement called a **bond indenture.** A corporate trustee, often a commercial bank trust department, represents the collective well-being of all bondholders in ensuring that the corporation meets the terms of the bond issue. The bond indenture specifies the maturity date of the bond and the pattern of interest payments until maturity. The different types of corporate bonds are described in Exhibit 26–2.

BOND INDENTURE
A contract between the issuer of a bond and the bondholder.

Stocks

Issuing stocks is another way that corporations can obtain financing. The ways in which stocks differ from bonds are summarized in Exhibit 26–3. Basically, as

Debenture Bonds	Bonds for which no specific assets of the corporation are pledged as backing. Rather, they are backed by the general credit rating of the corporation, plus any assets that can be seized if the corporation allows the debentures to go into default.
Mortgage Bonds	Bonds that pledge specific property. If the corporation defaults on the bonds, the bondholders can take the property.
Convertible Bonds	Bonds that can be exchanged for a specified number of shares of common stock under certain conditions.
Callable Bonds	Bonds that may be called in and the principal repaid at specified times or under conditions specified in the bond when it is issued.

♦ **Exhibit 26–2**
Types of Corporate Bonds

♦ Exhibit 26–3
How Do Stocks and Bonds Differ?

STOCKS	BONDS
1. Stocks represent ownership.	1. Bonds represent debt.
2. Stocks (common) do not have a fixed dividend rate.	2. Interest on bonds must always be paid, whether or not any profit is earned.
3. Stockholders can elect a board of directors, which controls the corporation.	3. Bondholders usually have no voice in, or control over, management of the corporation.
4. Stocks do not have a maturity date; the corporation does not usually repay the stockholder.	4. Bonds have a maturity date, when the corporation is to repay the bondholder the face value of the bond.
5. All corporations issue or offer to sell stocks. This is the usual definition of a corporation.	5. Corporations do not necessarily issue bonds.
6. Stockholders have a claim against the property and income of a corporation after all creditors' claims have been met.	6. Bondholders have a claim against the property and income of a corporation that must be met before the claims of stockholders.

"There are two times in a man's life when he should not speculate: when he can't afford it and when he can."

Samuel Clemens (Mark Twain), 1835–1910
(*American author and humorist*)

COMMON STOCK
Shares of ownership in a corporation that give the owner of the stock a proportionate interest in the corporation with regard to control, earnings, and net assets; shares of common stock are lowest in priority with respect to payment of dividends and distribution of the corporation's assets upon dissolution.

mentioned, stocks represent ownership in a business firm, whereas bonds represent borrowing by the firm.

The most important characteristics of stocks are as follows:

1. Stockholders need not be paid back.
2. Stockholders receive dividends only when so voted by the directors.
3. Stockholders are the last investors to be paid off on dissolution.
4. Stockholders vote for management and on major issues.

Exhibit 26–4 summarizes the types of stocks issued by corporations. We look now at the two major types of stock—*common stock* and *preferred stock*.

COMMON STOCK The true ownership of a corporation is represented by **common stock.** Common stock provides a proportionate interest in the corporation with regard to (1) control, (2) earnings, and (3) net assets. A shareholder's interest is generally in proportion to the number of shares he or she owns out of the total number of shares issued.

Voting rights in a corporation apply to the election of the firm's board of directors and to any proposed changes in the ownership structure of the firm. For example, a holder of common stock generally has the right to vote in a decision on a proposed merger, as mergers can change the proportion of ownership. State corporation law specifies the types of actions for which shareholder approval must be obtained.

Firms are not obligated to return a principal amount per share to each holder of common stock, because no firm can ensure that the market price per share of its common stock will not decline over time. The issuing firm also does not have to guarantee a dividend; indeed, some corporations never pay dividends.

Holders of common stock are a group of investors who assume a *residual* position in the overall financial structure of a business. In terms of receiving payment for their

Common Stock	Voting shares that represent ownership interest in a corporation. Common stock has the lowest priority with respect to payment of dividends and distribution of assets on the corporation's dissolution.
Preferred Stock	Shares of stock that have priority over common-stock shares as to payment of dividends and distribution of assets on dissolution. Dividend payments are usually a fixed percentage of the face value of the share.
Cumulative Preferred Stock	Required dividends not paid in a given year must be paid in a subsequent year before any common-stock dividends are paid.
Participating Preferred Stock	Stock entitling the owner to receive the preferred-stock dividend and additional dividends after the corporation has paid dividends on common stock.
Convertible Preferred Stock	Stock entitling the owners to convert their shares into a specified number of common shares either in the issuing corporation or, sometimes, in another corporation.
Redeemable, or Callable, Preferred Stock	Preferred shares issued with the express condition that the issuing corporation has the right to repurchase the shares as specified.

◆ Exhibit 26–4
Types of Stocks

investments, they are last in line. The earnings to which they are entitled are those left after preferred stockholders, bondholders, suppliers, employees, and other groups have been paid. Once those groups are paid, however, the owners of common stock may be entitled to *all* the remaining earnings as dividends. (The board of directors is not normally under any duty to declare the remaining earnings as dividends, however.)

PREFERRED STOCK   **Preferred stock** is stock with *preferences*. Usually, this means that holders of preferred stock have priority over holders of common stock as to dividends and as to payment on dissolution of the corporation. Holders of preferred stock may or may not have the right to vote.

Preferred stock is not included among the liabilities of a business, because it is equity. Like other equity securities, preferred shares have no fixed maturity date on which the firm must pay them off. Although occasionally firms buy back preferred stock, they are not legally obligated to do so. A sample cumulative convertible preferred-stock certificate is shown in Exhibit 26–5.

Holders of preferred stock are investors who have assumed a rather cautious position in their relationship to the corporation. They have a stronger position than common shareholders with respect to dividends and claims on assets, but as a result, they will not share in the full prosperity of the firm if it grows successfully over time. This is because the value of preferred shares will not rise as rapidly as that of common shares during a period of financial success. Preferred stockholders do receive fixed dividends periodically, however, and they may benefit to some extent from changes in the market price of the shares.

The return and the risk for preferred stock lie somewhere between those for bonds and those for common stock. Preferred stock is more similar to bonds than to common stock, even though preferred stock appears in the ownership section of the firm's balance sheet. As a result, preferred stock is often categorized with corporate bonds as a fixed-income security, even though the legal status is not the same.

PREFERRED STOCK
Classes of stock that have priority over common stock both as to payment of dividends and distribution of assets upon the corporation's dissolution.

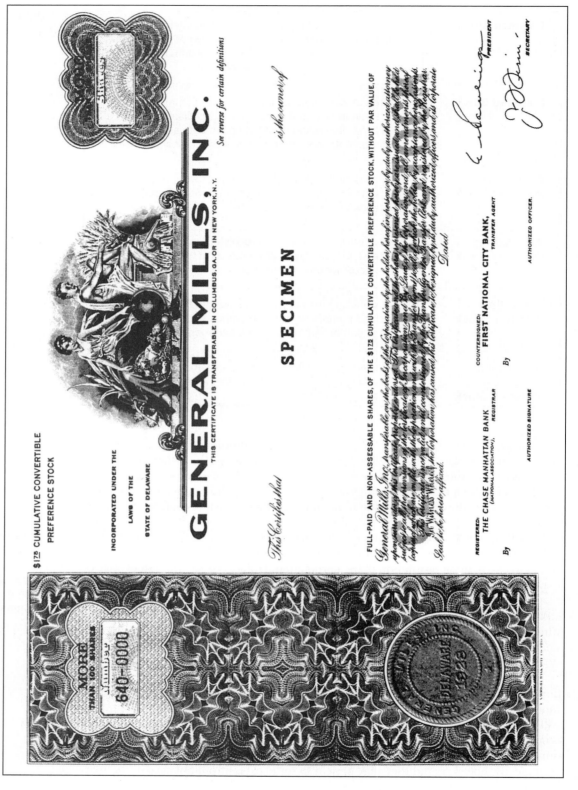

◆ Exhibit 26–5
Cumulative Convertible Preferred-Stock Certificate

Application

Law and the Entrepreneur—How to Incorporate*

Incorporation generally involves a very modest investment in legal fees and filing fees. Indeed, just about anybody can form a corporation for any lawful purpose in any state. The requirements differ from state to state. You do not have to form your corporation in the state in which you live or the state in which you are doing business, however. In fact, many individuals obtain their corporate charters from the state of Delaware, because it has the fewest legal restrictions on corporate formation and operation. Delaware also limits the liability of directors, so a number of large companies have obtained their charters from that state.

Delaware is also the state most often chosen for "mail-order incorporation." Perhaps you have even seen the ads—"You, too, can incorporate"—in various national and regional magazines. Those ads are usually generated by organizations in Delaware that have preprinted incorporation forms for you to fill out and

send back with a small fee. The employees of these organizations send or take your forms to the appropriate state office in Delaware to obtain your certificate of incorporation.

Such "do-it-yourself" incorporating may be sufficient for those who are interested in starting small businesses but who have no serious aspirations that their companies will grow much larger. If you believe that the business in which you are going to engage has growth potential and may require significant financing in the future, though, you are best advised to contact a local attorney to take you through the necessary steps in incorporating your business.

Checklist of Factors to Discuss with an Attorney Concerning Incorporation

1. Tax considerations.
2. The initial cost of incorporation and any continuing costs.
3. The formalities that are necessary.
4. The amount of record keeping that will be required.
5. What should be included in the bylaws.

*This *Application* is not meant to substitute for the services of an attorney who is licensed to practice law in your state.

▌Key Terms

▌Chapter Summary: Corporate Formation and Financing

The Nature of the Corporation (See pages 668–671.)	The corporation is a legal entity distinct from its owners. Formal statutory requirements, which vary somewhat from state to state, must be followed in forming a corporation. The corporation can have perpetual existence or be chartered for a specific period of time.
	1. *Corporate personnel*—The shareholders own the corporation. They elect a board of directors to govern the corporation. The board of directors hires corporate officers and other employees to run the daily business of the firm.

(Continued)

▌Chapter Summary: Corporate Formation and Financing—Continued

The Nature of the Corporation— Continued	2. *Corporate taxation*—The corporation pays income tax on net profits; shareholders pay income tax on the disbursed dividends that they receive from the corporation (double-taxation feature).
	3. *Torts and criminal acts*—The corporation is liable for the torts committed by its agents or officers within the course and scope of their employment (under the doctrine of *respondeat superior*). In some circumstances, a corporation can be held liable (and be fined) for the criminal acts of its agents and employees. In certain situations, corporate officers may be held personally liable for corporate crimes.
Corporate Powers *(See pages 671–672.)*	1. *Express powers*—The express powers of a corporation are granted by the following laws and documents (listed according to their priority): federal constitution, state constitutions, state statutes, articles of incorporation, bylaws, and resolutions of the board of directors.
	2. *Implied powers*—Barring express constitutional, statutory, or other prohibitions, the corporation has the implied power to do all acts reasonably appropriate and necessary to accomplish its corporate purposes.
	3. *Ultra vires doctrine*—Any act of a corporation that is beyond its express or implied powers to undertake is an *ultra vires* act. a. *Ultra vires* contracts may or may not be enforced by the courts, depending on the circumstances. b. The corporation (or shareholders on behalf of the corporation) may sue to enjoin or recover damages for *ultra vires* acts of corporate officers or directors. In addition, the state attorney general may bring an action either to institute an injunction against the transaction or to institute dissolution proceedings against the corporation for *ultra vires* acts.
Classification of Corporations *(See pages 673–679.)*	1. *Domestic, foreign, and alien corporations*—A corporation is referred to as a *domestic corporation* within its home state (the state in which it incorporates). A corporation is referred to as a *foreign corporation* by any state that is not its home state. A corporation is referred to as an *alien corporation* if it originates in another country but does business in the United States.
	2. *Public and private corporations*—A public corporation is one formed by government (e.g., cities, towns, and public projects). A private corporation is one formed wholly or in part for private benefit. Most corporations are private corporations.
	3. *Nonprofit corporations*—Corporations formed without a profit-making purpose (e.g., charitable, educational, and religious organizations and hospitals).
	4. *Close corporations*—Corporations owned by a family or a relatively small number of individuals; transfer of shares is usually restricted, and the corporation cannot make a public offering of its securities.
	5. *S corporations*—Small domestic corporations (must have thirty-five or fewer shareholders as members) that, under Subchapter S of the Internal Revenue Code, are given special tax treatment. These corporations allow shareholders to enjoy the limited legal liability of the corporate form but avoid its double-taxation feature (taxes are paid by shareholders as personal income, and the S corporation is not taxed separately).
	6. *Professional corporations*—Corporations formed by professionals (e.g., doctors, lawyers) to obtain the benefits of incorporation (such as tax benefits and limited liability). In most situations, the professional corporation is treated like other corporations, but sometimes the courts will disregard the corporate form and treat the shareholders like partners.
Corporate Formation *(See pages 679–684.)*	1. *Promotional activities*—A corporate promoter is one who takes the preliminary steps in organizing a corporation (issues a prospectus, secures the charter, interests investors in the purchase of corporate stock, forms subscription agreements, and so on).
	2. *Incorporation procedures*— a. A state in which to incorporate is selected. b. The articles of incorporation are prepared and filed. The articles generally should include the corporate name, duration, nature and purpose, capital structure, internal organization, registered office and agent, and incorporators. c. The certificate of incorporation (or charter), which authorizes the corporation to conduct business, is received from the appropriate state office (usually the secretary of state) after the articles of incorporation have been filed.

▌Chapter Summary: Corporate Formation and Financing—Continued

Corporate Formation —Continued	d. The first organizational meeting is held after the charter is granted. The board of directors is elected and other business completed (bylaws passed, stock issued, and so on).
Corporate Status (*See pages 684–686.*)	1. *De jure or de facto corporation*—If a corporation has been improperly incorporated, courts will sometimes impute corporate status to the firm by holding that the firm is a *de jure* corporation (cannot be challenged by the state or third persons) or a *de facto* corporation (can be challenged by the state but not by third persons). 2. *Corporation by estoppel*—If a firm is neither a *de jure* nor a *de facto* corporation but represents itself to be a corporation and is sued as such by a third party, it may be held to be a corporation by estoppel. 3. *Disregarding the corporate entity*—To avoid injustice, courts may "pierce the corporate veil" and hold a shareholder or shareholders personally liable for a judgment against the corporation. This usually occurs only when the corporation was established to circumvent the law, when the corporate form is used for an illegitimate or fraudulent purpose, or when the controlling shareholder commingles his or her own interests with those of the corporation to such an extent that the corporation no longer has a separate identity.
Corporate Financing—Bonds (*See pages 686–687.*)	Corporate bonds are securities representing *corporate debt*—money borrowed by a corporation. Types of corporate bonds include the following: 1. *Debenture bonds*—Bonds backed by the general credit rating of the corporation; no corporate assets are pledged as security. 2. *Mortgage bonds*—Bonds pledging as security specific corporate property. 3. *Convertible bonds*—Bonds that can be exchanged for a specified number of shares of common stock at the option of the bondholder. 4. *Callable bonds*—Bonds that may be called in and the principal repaid at specified times or under specified conditions.

Corporate Financing—Stocks (*See pages 687–690.*)	Stocks are equity securities issued by a corporation that represent the purchase of ownership in the business firm.
	
	1. *Important characteristics of stocks*—
	  a. Stockholders need not be paid back.
	  b. Stockholders receive dividends only when so voted by the directors.
	  c. Stockholders are the last investors to be paid on dissolution.
	  d. Stockholders vote for management and on major issues.
	
	2. *Types of stock (see Exhibit 26–4 for details)*—
	  a. Common stock—Represents the true ownership of the firm. Holders of common stock share in the control, earning capacity, and net assets of the corporation. Common stockholders carry more risk than preferred stockholders but, if the corporation is successful, are compensated for this risk by greater returns on their investments.
	  b. Preferred stock—Stock whose holders have a preferred status. Preferred stockholders have a stronger position than common stockholders with respect to dividends and claims on assets, but as a result, they will not share in the full prosperity of the firm if it grows successfully over time. The return and risk for preferred stock lie somewhere between those for bonds and common stock.

▌For Review

1. What are the express and implied powers of corporations? On what sources are these powers based?

2. What are the steps for bringing a corporation into existence? Who is liable for preincorporation contracts?

3. What is the difference between a *de jure* corporation and a *de facto* corporation?

4. In what circumstances might a court disregard the corporate entity ("pierce the corporate veil") and hold the shareholders personally liable?

5. How are corporations financed? What is the difference between stocks and bonds?

▌Questions and Case Problems

26–1. Corporate Status. Three brothers inherited a small paper-supply business from their father, who had operated the business as a sole proprietorship. The brothers decided to incorporate under the name of Gomez Corp. and retained an attorney to draw up the necessary documents. The attorney drew up the papers and had the brothers sign them but neglected to send the application for a corporate charter to the secretary of state's office. The brothers assumed that all necessary legal work had been taken care of, and they proceeded to do business as Gomez Corp. One day, a Gomez Corp. employee, while making a delivery to one of Gomez's customers, negligently ran a red light and caused a car accident. Baxter, the driver of the other vehicle, was injured as a result and sued Gomez Corp. for damages. Baxter then learned that no state charter had ever been issued to Gomez Corp., so he sued each of the brothers personally for damages. Can the brothers avoid personal liability for the tort of their employee? Explain.

26–2. Liability for Preincorporation Contracts. Christy, Briggs, and Dobbs are recent college graduates who want to form a corporation to manufacture and sell personal computers. Perez tells them that he will set in motion the formation of their corporation. Perez first makes a contract with Oliver for the purchase of a parcel of land for $25,000. Oliver does not know of the prospective corporate formation at the time the contract is signed. Perez then makes a contract with Kovac to build a small plant on the property being purchased. Kovac's contract is conditional on the corporation's formation. Perez secures all necessary subscription agreements and capitalization, and he files the articles of incorporation. A charter is issued.

    (a) Discuss whether the newly formed corporation or Perez (or both) is liable on the contracts with Oliver and Kovac.

    (b) Discuss whether the corporation, on coming into legal existence, is automatically liable to Kovac.

26–3. Corporate Powers. Kora Nayenga and two business associates formed a corporation called Nayenga Corp. for the purpose of selling computer services. Kora, who owned 50 percent of the corporate shares, served as the corporation's president. Kora wished to obtain a personal loan from his bank for $250,000, but the bank required the note to be cosigned by a third party. Kora cosigned the note in the name of the corporation. Later, Kora defaulted on the note, and the bank sued the corporation for payment. The corporation asserted, as a defense, that Kora had exceeded his authority when he cosigned the note. Had he? Explain.

26–4. Liability of Shareholders. Charles Wolfe was the sole shareholder and president of Wolfe & Co., a firm that leased tractor-trailers. The corporation had no separate bank account. Banking transactions were conducted through Wolfe's personal accounts, and employees were paid from them. Wolfe never consulted with any other corporate directors. During the tax years 1974–1976, the corporation incurred $114,472.91 in federal tax liabilities. The government held Wolfe personally liable for the taxes. Wolfe paid the tax bill and then brought an action against the government for disregarding his corporate

entity. Discuss whether the government can "pierce the corporate veil" in Wolfe's case and hold Wolfe personally liable for corporate taxes. [*Wolfe v. United States*, 798 F.2d 124 (9th Cir. 1961)]

26–5. Liability for Preincorporation Contracts. Skandinavia, Inc., manufactured and sold polypropylene underwear. Following two years of poor sales, Skandinavia entered into negotiations to sell the business to Odilon Cormier, an individual who was an experienced textile manufacturer. Skandinavia and Cormier agreed that Cormier would take Skandinavia's underwear inventory and use it in a new corporation, which would be called Polypro, Inc. In return, Skandinavia would receive a commission on future sales from Polypro. Polypro was subsequently established and began selling the underwear. Skandinavia, however, having never received any commissions from the sales, sued Polypro and Cormier to recover its promised commissions. Is Cormier personally liable for the contract he signed in the course of setting up a new corporation? Discuss. [*Skandinavia, Inc. v. Cormier*, 128 N.H. 215, 214 A.2d 1250 (1986)]

26–6. Professional Corporations. Cohen, Stracher & Bloom, P.C., a law firm organized as a professional corporation under New York law, entered into an agreement with We're Associates Co. for the lease of office space located in Lake Success, New York. The lease was signed for We're Associates by one of the partners of that company and for the professional corporation by Paul J. Bloom, as vice president. Bloom, Cohen, and Stracher were the sole officers, directors, and shareholders of the professional corporation. The corporation became delinquent in paying its rent, and We're Associates brought an action to recover rents and other charges of approximately $9,000 alleged to be due under the lease. The complaint was filed against the professional corporation and each individual shareholder of the corporation. The individual shareholders moved to dismiss the action against them individually. Will the court grant their motion? Discuss. [*We're Associates Co. v. Cohen, Stracher & Bloom, P.C.*, 103 A.D.2d 130, 478 N.Y.S.2d 670 (1984)]

26–7. *Ultra Vires* Acts. The Midtown Club, Inc., was a nonprofit corporation whose certificate of incorporation stated that the sole purpose of the club was "to provide facilities for the serving of luncheon or other meals to members." Samuel Cross, a member of the club, brought a female guest to lunch at the club, but he and his friend were both refused seating. On several occasions, Cross made applications on behalf of females for their admission to the club, but the club ignored or rejected them. Cross brought an action against the club, alleging that its actions were *ultra vires*. Did he succeed? Explain. [*Cross v. Midtown Club, Inc.*, 33 Conn.Supp. 150, 365 A.2d 127 (1976)]

26–8. Liability of Shareholders. In the early 1950s, Mary Emmons opened an account at M&M Wholesale Florist, Inc., to purchase flowers and florist supplies for her flower shop, called Bay Minette Flower Shop, which she operated as a sole proprietorship. In 1973, the flower shop was incorporated as Bay Minette Flower Shop, Inc. Emmons continued to order supplies from M&M, as did her son when he began to manage the day-to-day operations of the shop during the 1980s. M&M,

which had no knowledge that Bay Minette was now a corporation, sued Emmons and her son personally to recover a balance due on the Bay Minette account (for purchases made after Bay Minette had incorporated). Is the fact that M&M was never informed of the incorporation of Bay Minette Flower Shop a sufficient ground for piercing the corporate veil and holding Emmons and her son personally liable for the debt? Explain. [*M & M Wholesale Florist, Inc. v. Emmons*, 600 So.2d 998 (Ala. 1992)]

26–9. Liability of Shareholders. Moseley Group Management Co. (MGM) provided management services to apartment complexes. MGM's only assets were equipment worth $500 and a bank account with an average balance of $1,500. Richard Moseley ran the company and owned half of the stock. MGM contracted with Property Tax Research Co. (PTR) to obtain a lower property tax assessment on one of its complexes. PTR performed, but MGM refused to pay and transferred its assets and employees to Terrace Management, Inc., a corporation controlled by Moseley. PTR filed a suit in a Missouri state court against Moseley and others to recover the unpaid fees. Should the court pierce the corporate veil and hold Moseley personally liable for the debt? If so, on what basis? [*Sansone v. Moseley*, 912 S.W.2d 666 (Mo.App., W.D. 1995)]

26–10. Corporate Powers. Soda Dispensing Systems, Inc., was owned by two shareholders, each of whom owned half of the stock. One shareholder was the president of the corporation, and the other was vice president. Their shareholder agreement stated that neither shareholder could "encumber any corporate property . . . without the written consent of the other." When Soda Dispensing went out of business, the two shareholders agreed to sell the assets, split the proceeds, and pay $9,900 to their accountants, Cooper, Selvin & Strassberg. Later, the president committed Soda Dispensing to pay Cooper, Selvin more than $24,000, claiming that he had the authority, as president, to make that commitment. When the accountants tried to collect, the vice president objected, asserting that the president had exceeded his authority. Will the court order Soda Dispensing to pay? Explain. [*Cooper, Selvin & Strassberg v. Soda Dispensing Systems, Inc.*, 212 A.D.2d 498, 622 N.Y.S.2d 312 (1995)]

A QUESTION OF ETHICS AND SOCIAL RESPONSIBILITY

26–11. *On November 3, 1981, Garry Fox met with a representative of Coopers & Lybrand (Coopers), a national accounting firm, to obtain tax advice and other accounting services on behalf of a corporation Fox was in the process of forming. Coopers agreed to perform the services. The new corporation, G. Fox and Partners, Inc., was incorporated on December 4, 1981. Coopers had completed its work by mid-December and billed G. Fox and Partners for $10,827 for its accounting services. When neither the new corporation nor Fox paid the bill, Coopers sued Garry Fox personally for the amount. Coopers claimed that Fox had breached express and implied contracts and that, as a corporate promoter, Fox was liable for the unpaid debt. Fox argued that Coopers had agreed to look solely to the corporation for payment. The trial court found that there was no agreement, either express or implied, that would obligate Fox individually to pay Coopers's fee, because Coopers failed to prove the existence of any such agreement. On appeal, however, the trial court's judgment was reversed. Fox was held liable as a corporate promoter for the unpaid debt. [Coopers & Lybrand v. Fox, 758 P.2d 683 (Colo. 1988)]*

1. In view of the fact that Coopers & Lybrand knew that Fox was acting on behalf of a future corporation, do you think that it is fair that Fox should be held personally liable for the contract?
2. Undertaking preliminary organization and promotion is an essential step in the process of corporate formation. Do you think that imposing risks on promoters by holding them personally liable for preincorporation contracts counters the public policy of promoting business enterprises?
3. What might result if corporate promoters could never be held personally liable for preincorporation contracts? Would such a law also pose a barrier to commerce by increasing the difficulty in obtaining necessary preincorporation contracts, such as for office space, equipment, credit, and so on?

 FOR CRITICAL ANALYSIS

26–12. *What are some of the ways in which the limited liability of corporate shareholders serves the public interest? Can you think of any ways in which this limited liability is harmful to the public interest? Explain.*

▌Accessing the Internet: Business Law and Legal Environment

If you want to find out about the benefits of incorporation, you can access the Company Corporation at

http://amber.ora./gnn/bus/compcorp/index.html

More information about business organizations can be found by accessing the law firm of Reinhart et al. at

http://www.rbvdnr.com/

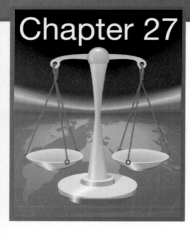

Chapter 27

Corporate Directors, Officers, and Shareholders

*"They [corporations] cannot commit treason, nor
be outlawed nor excommunicated, because they
have no soul."*

Sir Edward Coke, 1552–1634
(English jurist and legal scholar)

CHAPTER OBJECTIVES

After reading this chapter, you should be able to:

1. Describe the role of corporate directors and officers.
2. Summarize the duties owed to the corporation by directors and officers.
3. Explain the effect of the business judgment rule on directors' liability for their decisions.
4. Identify the rights of shareholders, including the right to bring a derivative suit.
5. Discuss the liability of shareholders and the duties owed by majority shareholders.

Sir Edward Coke's observation that a corporation has no "soul" is based on the fact that a corporation is not a "natural" person but a legal fiction. No one individual shareholder or director bears sole responsibility for the corporation and its actions. Rather, a corporation joins the efforts and resources of a large number of individuals for the purpose of producing returns greater than the returns those persons could have obtained individually.

Sometimes, actions that benefit the corporation as a whole do not coincide with the separate interests of the individuals making up the corporation. In such situations, it is important to know the rights and duties of all participants in the corporate enterprise. This chapter focuses on the rights and duties of directors, managers, and shareholders and the ways in which conflicts among them are resolved.

▌ Role of Directors

A corporation typically is governed by a board of directors. A director occupies a position of responsibility unlike that of other corporate personnel. Directors are sometimes inappropriately characterized as *agents* because they act on behalf of the corporation.

No *individual* director, however, can act as an agent to bind the corporation; and as a group, directors collectively control the corporation in a way that no agent is able to control a principal. Directors are often incorrectly characterized as *trustees* because they occupy positions of trust and control over the corporation. Unlike trustees, however, they do not own or hold title to property for the use and benefit of others.

Election of Directors

Subject to statutory limitations, the number of directors is set forth in the corporation's articles or bylaws. Historically, the minimum number of directors has been three, but today many states permit fewer. Indeed, the Revised Model Business Corporation Act (RMBCA), in Section 8.01, permits corporations with fewer than fifty shareholders to eliminate the board of directors.

The first board of directors is normally appointed by the incorporators on the creation of the corporation, or directors are named by the corporation itself in the articles. The first board serves until the first annual shareholders' meeting. Subsequent directors are elected by a majority vote of the shareholders.

The term of office for a director is usually one year—from annual meeting to annual meeting. Longer and staggered terms are permissible under most state statutes. A common practice is to elect one-third of the board members each year for a three-year term. In this way, there is greater management continuity.

A director can be removed *for cause* (that is, for failing to perform a required duty), either as specified in the articles or bylaws or by shareholder action. Even the board of directors itself may be given power to remove a director for cause, subject to shareholder review. In most states, unless the shareholders have reserved the right at the time of election, a director cannot be removed without cause.

> **BE AWARE** The articles of incorporation may provide that a director can be removed only for cause.

Vacancies can occur on the board of directors because of death or resignation, or when a new position is created through amendment of the articles or bylaws. In these situations, either the shareholders or the board itself can fill the position, depending on state law or on the provisions of the bylaws.

Directors' Qualifications and Compensation

Few legal requirements exist concerning directors' qualifications. Only a handful of states impose minimum age and residency requirements. A director is sometimes a shareholder, but this is not a necessary qualification—unless, of course, statutory provisions or corporate articles or bylaws require ownership.

Compensation for directors is ordinarily specified in the corporate articles or bylaws. Because directors have a fiduciary relationship to the shareholders and to the corporation, an express agreement or provision for compensation often is necessary for them to receive money from the funds that they control and for which they have responsibilities.

Board of Directors' Meetings

The board of directors conducts business by holding formal meetings with recorded minutes. The date on which regular meetings are held is usually established in the articles or bylaws or by board resolution, and no further notice is customarily required. Special meetings can be called, with notice sent to all directors.

Quorum requirements can vary among jurisdictions. (A **quorum** is the minimum number of members of a body of officials or other group that must be present in order for business to be validly transacted.) Many states leave the decision as to quorum requirements to the corporate articles or bylaws. In the absence of specific state statutes, most states provide that a quorum is a majority of the number of directors

> **QUORUM**
> The number of members of a decision-making body that must be present before business may be transacted.

authorized in the articles or bylaws. Voting is done in person (unlike voting at share-holders' meetings, which can be done by proxy, as discussed later in this chapter).[1] The rule is one vote per director. Ordinary matters generally require a simple major-ity vote; certain extraordinary issues may require a greater-than-majority vote.

Rights of Directors

A director of a corporation has a number of rights, including the rights of participation, inspection, compensation, and indemnification.

PARTICIPATION AND INSPECTION   A corporate director must have certain rights to function properly in that position. The main right is one of participation—meaning that the director must be notified of board of directors' meetings so as to participate in them. As pointed out earlier in this chapter, regular board meetings are usually estab-lished by the bylaws or by board resolution, and no notice of these meetings is required. If special meetings are called, however, notice is required unless waived by the director.

A director must have access to all of the corporate books and records to make deci-sions and to exercise the necessary supervision over corporate officers and employees. This right of inspection is virtually absolute and cannot be restricted.

COMPENSATION AND INDEMNIFICATION   Historically, directors have had no inherent right to compensation for their services as directors. Nominal sums are often paid as honorariums to directors, however. In many corporations, directors are also chief cor-porate officers (president or chief executive officer, for example) and receive compen-sation in their managerial positions. Most directors, however, gain through indirect benefits, such as business contacts, prestige, and other rewards, such as stock options. There is a trend toward providing more than nominal compensation for directors, especially in large corporations in which directorships can be enormous burdens in terms of time, work, effort, and risk. Many states permit the corporate articles or bylaws to authorize compensation for directors, and in some cases the board can set its own compensation unless the articles or bylaws provide otherwise.

Corporate directors may become involved in lawsuits by virtue of their positions and their actions as directors. Most states (and RMBCA 8.51) permit a corporation to indemnify (guarantee reimbursement to) a director for legal costs, fees, and judgments involved in defending corporation-related suits. Many states specifically permit a cor-poration to purchase liability insurance for the directors and officers to cover indem-nification. When the statutes are silent on this matter, the power to purchase such insurance is usually considered to be part of the corporation's implied power.

Management Responsibilities

Directors have responsibility for all policymaking decisions necessary to the manage-ment of corporate affairs. Just as shareholders cannot act individually to bind the cor-poration, the directors must act as a body in carrying out routine corporate business. One director has one vote, and generally the majority rules. The general areas of responsibility of the board of directors include the following:

1. Declaration and payment of corporate dividends to shareholders.
2. Authorization for major corporate policy decisions—for example, the initiation of proceedings for the sale or lease of corporate assets outside the regular course of

---

1. Except in Louisiana, which allows a director to vote by proxy under certain circumstances. Some states, such as Michigan and Texas, and Section 8.20 of the RMBCA permit telephone conferences for board of directors' meetings.

business, the determination of new product lines, and the overseeing of major contract negotiations and major management-labor negotiations.

3. Appointment, supervision, and removal of corporate officers and other managerial employees and the determination of their compensation.

4. Financial decisions, such as the issuance of authorized shares and bonds.

The board of directors can delegate some of its functions to an executive committee or to corporate officers. In doing so, the board is not relieved of its overall responsibility for directing the affairs of the corporation, but corporate officers and managerial personnel are empowered to make decisions relating to ordinary, daily corporate affairs within well-defined guidelines.

▍Role of Corporate Officers and Executives

The officers and other executive employees are hired by the board of directors or, in rare instances, by the shareholders. In addition to carrying out the duties articulated in the bylaws, corporate and managerial officers act as agents of the corporation, and the ordinary rules of agency (discussed in Chapter 23) normally apply to their employment. The qualifications required of officers and executive employees are determined at the discretion of the corporation and are included in the articles or bylaws. In most states, a person can hold more than one office and can be both an officer and a director of the corporation.

The rights of corporate officers and other high-level managers are defined by employment contracts, because these persons are employees of the company. Corporate officers normally can be removed by the board of directors at any time with or without cause and regardless of the terms of the employment contracts—although in so doing, the corporation may be liable for breach of contract. The duties of corporate officers are the same as those of directors, because both groups are involved in decision making and are in similar positions of control. Hence, officers are viewed as having the same fiduciary duties of care and loyalty in their conduct of corporate affairs as directors have, a subject to which we now turn.

CONTRAST Shareholders own a corporation and directors make policy decisions, but officers who run the daily business of the corporation often have significant decision-making power.

Corporate executives discuss the business of their firm. How do the rights and duties of corporate officers differ from those of corporate directors?

∎ Duties of Directors and Officers

Directors and officers are deemed *fiduciaries* of the corporation, because their relationship with the corporation and its shareholders is one of trust and confidence. The fiduciary duties of the directors and officers include the duty of care and the duty of loyalty.

"It is not the crook in modern business that we fear but the honest man who does not know what he is doing."

Owen D. Young, 1874–1962
(*American corporate executive and public official*)

Duty of Care

Directors and officers must exercise due care in performing their duties. The standard of *due care* has been variously described in judicial decisions and codified in many corporation codes. Generally, a director or officer is expected to act in good faith, to exercise the care that an ordinarily prudent person would exercise in similar circumstances, and to act in what he or she considers to be the best interests of the corporation.[2] Directors and officers who have not exercised the required duty of care can be held liable for the harms suffered by the corporation as a result of their negligence.

DUTY TO MAKE INFORMED AND REASONABLE DECISIONS   Directors and officers are expected to be informed on corporate matters. To be informed, the director or officer must do what is necessary to become informed: attend presentations, ask for information from those who have it, read reports, review other written materials such as contracts—in other words, carefully study a situation and its alternatives. Depending on the nature of the business, directors and officers are often expected to act in accordance with their own knowledge and training. Most states (and Section 8.30 of the RMBCA), however, allow a director to make decisions in reliance on information furnished by competent officers or employees, professionals such as attorneys and accountants, or even an executive committee of the board without being accused of acting in bad faith or failing to exercise due care if such information turns out to be faulty.

Directors are also expected to make reasonable decisions. For example, a director should not accept a **tender offer** (an offer to purchase shares in the company that is made by another company directly to the shareholders, sometimes referred to as a "takeover" bid) with only a moment's consideration based solely on the market price of the corporation's shares.

TENDER OFFER
An offer to purchase made by one company directly to the shareholders of another (target) company; often referred to as a "takeover bid."

2.   RMBCA 8.30.

If a director fails to exercise due care in making a decision, the director may face significant liability. For example, in *Smith v. Van Gorkom*,[a] directors were held liable for accepting an offer for the purchase of a corporation because they allegedly failed to investigate the value of the business and whether a higher price could be obtained; they also made the decision after considering the matter for only two hours. The Supreme Court of Delaware remanded the case for a hearing on the fair value of the shares. If the value was determined to be higher than the price for which the shares were sold, the shareholders were to be paid the difference as damages.

The court in *Smith* (and in many subsequent cases involving similar claims) focused more on the sale *process* than on the sale price. In 1995, however, the Delaware Supreme Court seemed to take just the opposite approach. The case was brought by a shareholder of Technicolor, Inc., in 1982, after Technicolor's directors decided to sell the company to billionaire Ronald O. Perelman. The shareholder alleged that the directors had breached their fiduciary duties because, among other things, they sold the company at $23 a share without investigating whether a higher

a.   488 A.2d 858 (Del. 1985).

Ethical Perspective—Continued

price could be obtained. After over a decade of litigation, the Supreme Court of Delaware held that the directors were not liable. The court stated that although the directors had shown an "undisputed lack of care" (some of the directors had even hidden a list of potential bidders from the others!), Technicolor had obtained the "highest price reasonably available."**b**

For Critical Analysis: *Should directors be liable for breaching their duty of care even though the breach does not harm the shareholders' interests?*

b. *Cinerama, Inc. v. Technicolor, Inc.,* 663 A.2d 1156 (Del. 1995).

DUTY TO EXERCISE REASONABLE SUPERVISION Directors are also expected to exercise a reasonable amount of supervision when they delegate work to corporate officers and employees. For example, suppose that a corporate bank director fails to attend any board of directors' meetings for five years, never inspects any of the corporate books or records, and generally fails to supervise the efforts of the bank president and the loan committee. Meanwhile, a corporate officer, the bank president, makes various improper loans and permits large overdrafts. In this situation, the corporate director may be held liable to the corporation for losses resulting from the unsupervised actions of the bank president and the loan committee.

DISSENTING DIRECTORS Directors are expected to attend board of directors' meetings, and their votes should be entered into the minutes of corporate meetings. Unless a dissent is entered, the director is presumed to have assented. Directors who dissent are rarely held individually liable for mismanagement of the corporation. For this reason, a director who is absent from a given meeting sometimes registers with the secretary of the board a dissent to actions taken at the meeting.

Duty of Loyalty

Loyalty can be defined as faithfulness to one's obligations and duties. In the corporate context, the duty of loyalty requires directors and officers to subordinate their personal interests to the welfare of the corporation.

For example, directors may not use corporate funds or confidential corporate information for personal advantage. Similarly, they must refrain from self-dealing. For instance, a director should not oppose a tender offer that is in the corporation's best interest simply because its acceptance may cost the director his or her position. Cases dealing with fiduciary duty typically involve one or more of the following:

1. Competing with the corporation.
2. Usurping (taking advantage of) a corporate opportunity.
3. Having an interest that conflicts with the interest of the corporation.
4. Engaging in insider trading (using information that is not public to make a profit trading securities, as discussed in Chapter 29).
5. Authorizing a corporate transaction that is detrimental to minority shareholders.
6. Selling control over the corporation.

The usurping of a corporate opportunity occurs when an officer or director, for his or her personal gain, takes advantage of a business opportunity that is financially within the corporation's reach, is in line with the firm's business, is to the firm's practical advantage, and is one in which the corporation has an interest. Whether buying certain stock constitutes the usurping of a corporate opportunity is at issue in the following case.

> *"It is not within the lawful powers of a board of directors to shape and conduct the affairs of a corporation for the merely incidental benefit of the shareholders."*
>
> **Russell C. Ostrander, 1851–1919**
> *(Michigan jurist)*

CASE 27.1

YIANNATSIS v. STEPHANIS

Supreme Court of Delaware, 1995.
653 A.2d 275.

HISTORICAL AND SOCIAL SETTING *More than 90 percent of all U.S. corporations have ten or fewer shareholders. Many of these corporations are family-owned firms organized to own and operate relatively small businesses. A close corporation can ignore some of the formalities that a more widely owned corporation must observe. In regard to board meetings and shareholder votes, however, a close corporation cannot avoid some requirements, particularly those mandated by an agreement among the shareholders.*

FACTS Demos and Stella Yiannatsis and Demos's cousins John and Costas Stephanis were the directors of the Sunview Corporation. Demos, John, and Costas were also Sunview's shareholders. In 1975, the three shareholders agreed that if any shareholder—or after the shareholder's death, the executor of his or her estate—wished to sell Sunview stock, the stock must be offered to the corporation first. If the shareholders could not agree on a price, they would hire appraisers to determine the value. The purpose of this agreement was to prevent the stock from being sold to a fourth party. In 1984, Costas died. At the next Sunview board meeting, Costas's executor offered to sell Costas's stock for $150,000 cash plus $55,000 payable over time. The directors (Demos, Stella, and John) voted to refuse the

offer. The next day, Stella offered to buy the stock, on slightly different terms. The executor agreed. John filed a suit in a Delaware state court against Stella and Demos, alleging that they had usurped a corporate opportunity. The court ruled in John's favor, and the defendants appealed.

ISSUE Did buying the stock without complying with the shareholder agreement constitute the usurping of a corporate opportunity?

DECISION Yes. The Supreme Court of Delaware affirmed the judgment of the lower court.

REASON The state supreme court found that "Sunview's opportunity to purchase the Costas Stock was never properly presented to Sunview, and that Demos and Stella acted without regard for the 1975 Agreement or the fiduciary duties they owed to Sunview and John." The court pointed out that "the Costas Stock price was determined at the meeting where Stella agreed to purchase the Costas Stock. Given this fact," noted the court, "it would be impossible for Sunview to explore adequately the possibility of purchasing the relevant stock before Stella decided to buy it." The court concluded that "Demos' and Stella's actions are classic examples of the acts of faithless fiduciaries, and they should not benefit from their wrongful actions."

FOR CRITICAL ANALYSIS—Ethical Consideration
How could Stella and Demos have met their fiduciary obligations to the corporation?

Conflicts of Interest

The duty of loyalty also requires officers and directors to disclose fully to the board of directors any possible conflict of interest that might occur in conducting corporate transactions. The various state statutes contain different standards, but a contract will generally *not* be voidable if it was fair and reasonable to the corporation at the time it was made, if there was a full disclosure of the interest of the officers or directors involved in the transaction, and if the contract was approved by a majority of the disinterested directors or shareholders.

For example, Southwood Corporation needs office space. Lambert Alden, one of its five directors, owns the building adjoining the corporation's main office building. He negotiates a lease with Southwood for the space, making a full disclosure to Southwood and the other four board directors. The lease arrangement is fair and reasonable, and it is unanimously approved by the corporation's board of directors. In this situation, Alden has not breached his duty of loyalty to the corporation, and the contract is thus valid. The rule is one of reason. If it were otherwise, directors would be prevented from ever giving financial assistance to the corporations they serve.

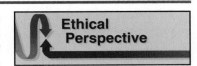

Corporate directors often have many business affiliations, and they may even sit on the board of more than one corporation. (Of course, directors generally are precluded from sitting on the boards of directors of competing companies.) The duty of loyalty can become cloudy when corporate directors sit on the board of more than one corporation. Because of the potential for abuse in transactions negotiated between corporations whose boards have some members in common, courts tend to scrutinize such actions closely.

For example, suppose that four individuals own a total of 70 percent of the shares of Company A and 100 percent of the shares of Company B. All four of these shareholders sit on the boards of directors of both corporations. Company A decides to purchase all of Company B's stock for $6 million, when in fact it is worth only $3 million. The shareholder-directors of both firms have not breached their duty to Company B, because the $6 million price is beneficial to that company. A court would likely hold that the directors breached their duty to the other shareholders of Company A (who owned the remaining 30 percent of Company A's shares), however, because these other shareholders had nothing to gain by the transaction and much to lose by Company A's purchase of Company B at an inflated price.[a]

For Critical Analysis: *Given the potential for conflicts of interest, why are individuals allowed to sit on two or more boards of directors simultaneously?*

a. See, for example, *Gries Sports Enterprises, Inc. v. Cleveland Browns Football Co.*, 26 Ohio St.3d 15, 496 N.E.2d 959 (1986).

▌ Liability of Directors and Officers

Directors and officers are exposed to liability on many fronts. Shareholders may perceive that the corporate directors are not acting in the best interests of the corporation and may sue the directors, in what is called a *shareholder's derivative suit,* on behalf of the corporation. (This type of action is discussed later in this chapter, in the context of shareholders' rights.) In addition, corporate directors and officers may be held liable for the torts and crimes committed by themselves or by corporate employees under their supervision.

In this section, we first examine the so-called *business judgment rule,* under which a corporate director or officer may be able to avoid liability to the corporation or to its shareholders for poor business judgments. We then look at the liability of corporate directors and officers for torts and crimes.

The Business Judgment Rule

Directors and officers are expected to exercise due care and to use their best judgment in guiding corporate management, but they are not insurers of business success. Honest mistakes of judgment and poor business decisions on their part do not make them liable to the corporation for resulting damages. This is the **business judgment rule.** The rule generally immunizes directors and officers from liability for the consequences of a decision that is within managerial authority, as long as the decision complies with management's fiduciary duties and as long as acting on the decision is within the powers of the corporation. Consequently, if there is a reasonable basis for a business decision, it is unlikely that the court will interfere with that decision, even if the corporation suffers as a result.

To benefit from the rule, directors and officers must act in good faith, in what they consider to be the best interests of the corporation, and with the care that an ordinarily prudent person in a similar position would exercise in similar circumstances. This

"All business proceeds on beliefs, or judgments of probabilities, and not on certainties."

Charles Eliot, 1834–1936
(American educator and editor)

BUSINESS JUDGMENT RULE
A rule that immunizes corporate management from liability for actions that result in corporate losses or damages if the actions are undertaken in good faith, and are within both the power of the corporation and the authority of management to make.

requires an informed decision, with a rational basis, and with no conflict between the decision maker's personal interest and the interest of the corporation.

Liability for Torts and Crimes

As mentioned in previous chapters, the corporation as an entity is liable for the torts and crimes that corporate agents and employees commit when they are acting within the scope of their employment. Liability for the actions of its corporate agents and employees is imputed to the corporation (the principal) under agency law. Directors, officers, and corporate employees also are personally liable for the torts and crimes that they commit within the scope of their employment. In other words, even though the corporation as an entity may assume liability for, say, a corporate agent's tort, that does not mean that the agent can avoid personal liability for the tort. Additionally, directors and officers can be held criminally liable under federal or state statutes (antitrust, environmental, or employment laws, for example—see Chapters 30 through 33).

Corporate directors and officers may also be held personally liable for the torts and crimes committed by corporate personnel under their direct supervision. Normally, the court must show that the wrongful actions were committed at the officer's direction or with his or her permission. Increasingly, however, liability is imposed on corporate officers because of their failure to supervise adequately their employees or because of their ability to exercise such pervasive control over corporate affairs that they should be treated as employers. We look now at these two bases of liability.

REMEMBER If a director is sued and wins, the corporation may be required to indemnify the director for his or her expenses in connection with the suit.

"RESPONSIBLE CORPORATE OFFICER" DOCTRINE   Under what has become known as the "responsible corporate officer" doctrine, a court may impose criminal liability on a corporate officer regardless of whether he or she participated in, directed, or even knew about a given criminal violation. In *United States v. Park,*[3] for example, the chief executive officer of a national supermarket chain was held personally liable for sanitation violations in corporate warehouses in which food was exposed to contamination by rodents. The court imposed personal liability on the corporate officer not because he intended the crime[4] or even knew about it. Rather, liability was imposed because the officer was in a "responsible relationship" to the corporation and had the power to prevent the violation. Since the *Park* decision, courts have applied this "responsible corporate officer" doctrine numerous times to hold corporate officers liable for their employees' statutory violations.

PERVASIVENESS OF CONTROL   In *United States v. Cusack,*[5] the court enunciated yet another basis for imposing personal liability on a corporate officer. In that case, the court held that a corporate officer's control over corporate operations was so pervasive that, in effect, the officer was not only a corporate agent-employee but also an employer. Therefore, as an employer, the officer could be subject to liability for the statutory violations of corporate employees.

▌ Role of Shareholders

The acquisition of a share of stock makes a person an owner and shareholder in a corporation. Shareholders thus own the corporation. Although they have no legal title

---

3.   421 U.S. 658, 95 S.Ct. 1903, 44 L.Ed.2d 489 (1975).
4.   Recall from Chapter 7 that two elements must be present for a crime to exist: a criminal act and criminal intent. In *Park*, the court dispensed with the latter requirement.
5.   806 F.Supp. 47 (D.N.J. 1992).

to corporate property, such as buildings and equipment, they do have an *equitable* (ownership) interest in the firm.

As a general rule, shareholders have no responsibility for the daily management of the corporation, although they are ultimately responsible for choosing the board of directors, which does have such control. Ordinarily, corporate officers and other employees owe no direct duty to individual shareholders. Their duty is to the corporation as a whole. A director, however, is in a fiduciary relationship to the corporation and therefore serves the interests of the shareholders. Generally, there is no legal relationship between shareholders and creditors of the corporation. Shareholders can, in fact, be creditors of the corporation and thus have the same rights of recovery against the corporation as any other creditor.

In this section, we look at the powers and voting rights of shareholders, which are generally established in the articles of incorporation and under the state's general incorporation law.

BE AWARE Shareholders are not normally agents of their corporation.

Shareholders' Powers

Shareholders must approve fundamental corporate changes before the changes can be effected. Hence, shareholders are empowered to amend the articles of incorporation (charter) and bylaws, approve a merger or the dissolution of the corporation, and approve the sale of all or substantially all of the corporation's assets. Some of these powers are subject to prior board approval.

Directors are elected to (and removed from) the board of directors by a vote of the shareholders. The first board of directors is either named in the articles of incorporation or chosen by the incorporators to serve until the first shareholders' meeting. From that time on, the selection and retention of directors are exclusively shareholder functions.

Directors usually serve their full terms; if they are unsatisfactory, they are simply not reelected. Shareholders have the inherent power, however, to remove a director from office *for cause* (breach of duty or misconduct) by a majority vote.[6] Some state statutes (and some corporate charters) even permit removal of directors *without cause* by the vote of a majority of the holders of outstanding shares entitled to vote.

---

6. A director can often demand court review of removal for cause.

Shareholders meet to vote on corporate issues. What issues must be put before shareholders for their vote?

Shareholders' Meetings

Shareholders' meetings must occur at least annually, and additional, special meetings can be called as needed to take care of urgent matters.

NOTICE OF MEETINGS   Each shareholder must receive written notice of the date, time, and place of a shareholders' meeting.[7] The notice must be received within a reasonable length of time prior to the date of the meeting. Notice of a special meeting must include a statement of the purpose of the meeting, and business transacted at the meeting is limited to that purpose.

PROXY

In corporation law, a written agreement between a stockholder and another under which the stockholder authorizes the other to vote the stockholder's shares in a certain manner.

PROXIES AND PROXY MATERIALS   Because it is usually not practical for owners of only a few shares of stock of publicly traded corporations to attend shareholders' meetings, such stockholders normally give third parties written authorization to vote their shares at the meeting. This authorization is called a **proxy** (from the Latin *procurare*, "to manage, take care of"). Proxies are often solicited by management, but any person can solicit proxies to concentrate voting power. Proxies have been used by a group of shareholders as a device for taking over a corporation (corporate takeovers are discussed in Chapter 28). Proxies are normally revocable (that is, they can be withdrawn), unless they are specifically designated as irrevocable. Under RMBCA 7.22(c), proxies last for eleven months, unless the proxy agreement provides for a longer period.

When shareholders want to change a company policy, they can put their idea up for a shareholder vote. They can do this by submitting a shareholder proposal to the board of directors and asking the board to include the proposal in the proxy materials that are sent to all shareholders before meetings. The Securities and Exchange Commission (SEC), which regulates the purchase and sale of securities (see Chapter 29), has special provisions relating to proxies and shareholder proposals. SEC Rule 14a-8 requires that when a company sends proxy materials to its shareholders, the company must also include whatever proposals will be considered at the meeting and provide shareholders with the opportunity to vote on the proposals by marking and returning their proxy cards. SEC Rule 14a-8 provides that all shareholders who own stock worth at least $1,000 are eligible to submit proposals for inclusion in corporate proxy material. Only those proposals that relate to significant policy considerations must be included, however (see this chapter's *Business Law in Action* for further details).

Shareholder Voting

Shareholders exercise ownership control through the power of their votes. Each shareholder is entitled to one vote per share, although the voting techniques that will be discussed shortly all enhance the power of the shareholder's vote. The articles of incorporation can exclude or limit voting rights, particularly for certain classes of shares. For example, owners of preferred shares are usually denied the right to vote.

BE CAREFUL Once a quorum is present, a vote can be taken even if some shareholders leave without casting their votes.

QUORUM REQUIREMENTS   For shareholders to act during a meeting, a quorum must be present. Generally, a quorum exists when shareholders holding more than 50 percent of the outstanding shares are present. Corporate business matters are presented in the form of *resolutions*, which shareholders vote to approve or disapprove. Some state statutes have set forth specific voting requirements, and corporations' articles or bylaws must abide by these statutory requirements. Some states provide that the unanimous

---

7.   The shareholder can waive the requirement of written notice by signing a waiver form. In some states, a shareholder who does not receive written notice, but who learns of the meeting and attends without protesting the lack of notice, is said to have waived notice by such conduct. State statutes and corporate bylaws typically set forth the time within which notice must be sent, what methods can be used, and what the notice must contain.

BUSINESS LAW IN ACTION

Proxies and Shareholder Proposals

As mentioned, SEC Rule 14a-8 requires companies to include shareholder proposals in their proxy materials, provided that the proposals relate to significant policy issues and not merely to ordinary business activities. It is often difficult, however, to determine whether a proposal relates to ordinary business activities or significant policy issues—as can be seen by the SEC's inconsistent rulings on shareholder proposals.

For example, in 1994, shareholders of Amoco Corporation submitted a proposal requesting that the company cease operations in Burma (Myanmar) until political prisoners were released and power was transferred to a democratically elected government. The SEC, concluding in part that the policy issue raised by the proposal was not significant, ruled that Amoco could omit the proposal from its proxy materials. In the same year, however, the SEC ruled that W. R. Grace & Company could not exclude from its proxy materials a shareholder proposal asking the company to assess environmental and human rights

issues with respect to its business in Mexico. The SEC viewed this issue as significant.

A major concern for many shareholders is their companies' policies and actions relating to equal employment opportunity and affirmative action. Are these issues significant policy issues? In a 1976 ruling, the SEC stated that shareholder proposals concerning equal opportunity and affirmative action relate to significant policy issues on which shareholders should be allowed to vote. In 1992, however, the SEC reversed its position when it ruled that the Cracker Barrel Old Country Store, Inc., could omit from its proxy materials a shareholder proposal asking that the company adopt a policy favoring nondiscrimination on the basis of sexual orientation.[a]

The following year, Wal-Mart Stores, Inc., relying on the 1992 ruling, refused to include a shareholder proposal requesting

a.   The shareholders sued the SEC, claiming that the SEC violated federally mandated rulemaking procedures in issuing the rule. In 1995, a federal appellate court held that the rule was a valid and properly issued interpretive rule. See *New York City Employees' Retirement System v. Securities and Exchange Commission*, 45 F.3d 7 (2d Cir. 1995).

Wal-Mart's directors to report on the company's equal opportunity and affirmative action policies, among other things. When the shareholders sued Wal-Mart, a federal district court sided with the shareholders. The court stated that the SEC could not "eliminate this avenue of shareholder communication with management and other shareholders on a topic of broad social import simply because it finds the line between proper and improper issues for communication hard to draw."[b] Following this court decision and in the wake of substantial criticism of its 1992 rule, the SEC has since changed its stance.

Clearly, SEC officials do not have an easy job in deciding what is or is not a significant policy issue. Some critics claim that because of the SEC's inconsistent rulings, the "significant policy issues" requirement should be abandoned entirely.

For Critical Analysis: *Should the SEC staff be the group that decides whether equal opportunity, human rights, and environmental issues (and other issues that are essentially social or political in nature) are sufficiently significant to include in proxy materials?*

b.   *Amalgamated Clothing and Textile Workers Union v. Wal-Mart Stores, Inc.*, 821 F.Supp. 877 (S.D.N.Y. 1993).

written consent of shareholders is a permissible alternative to holding a shareholders' meeting. Once a quorum is present, a majority vote of the shares represented at the meeting is usually required to pass resolutions.

For example, assume that Novo Pictures, Inc., has 10,000 outstanding shares of voting stock. Its articles of incorporation set the quorum at 50 percent of outstanding shares and provide that a majority vote of the shares present is necessary to pass resolutions concerning ordinary matters. Therefore, for this firm, a quorum of shareholders representing 5,000 outstanding shares must be present at a shareholders' meeting to conduct business. If exactly 5,000 shares are represented at the meeting, a vote of at least 2,501 of those shares is needed to pass a resolution. If 6,000 shares are represented, a vote of 3,001 will be required, and so on.

At times, a larger-than-majority vote will be required either by a statute or by the corporate charter. Extraordinary corporate matters, such as a merger, consolidation, or dissolution of the corporation (see Chapter 28), require a higher percentage of the representatives of all corporate shares entitled to vote, not just a majority of those present at that particular meeting.

VOTING LISTS   Voting lists are prepared by the corporation prior to each shareholders' meeting. Persons whose names appear on the corporation's shareholder records as owners are the ones ordinarily entitled to vote.[8] The voting list contains the name and address of each shareholder as shown on the corporate records on a given cutoff date, or record date. (Under RMBCA 7.07, the record date may be as much as seventy days before the meeting.) The voting list also includes the number of voting shares held by each owner. The list is usually kept at the corporate headquarters and is available for shareholder inspection.

CUMULATIVE VOTING   Most states permit or even require shareholders to elect directors by *cumulative voting*, a method of voting designed to allow minority shareholders representation on the board of directors.[9] When cumulative voting is allowed or required, the number of members of the board to be elected is multiplied by the total number of voting shares. The result equals the number of votes a shareholder has, and this total can be cast for one or more nominees for director. All nominees stand for election at the same time. When cumulative voting is not required either by statute or under the articles, the entire board can be elected by a simple majority of shares at a shareholders' meeting.

Cumulative voting can best be understood by an example. Suppose that a corporation has 10,000 shares issued and outstanding. One group of shareholders (the minority shareholders) holds only 3,000 shares, and the other group of shareholders (the majority shareholders) holds the other 7,000 shares. Three members of the board are to be elected. The majority shareholders' nominees are Acevedo, Barkley, and Craycik. The minority shareholders' nominee is Drake. Can Drake be elected by the minority shareholders?

If cumulative voting is allowed, the answer is yes. The minority shareholders have 9,000 votes among them (the number of directors to be elected times the number of shares held by the minority shareholders equals 3 times 3,000, which equals 9,000 votes). All of these votes can be cast to elect Drake. The majority shareholders have 21,000 votes (3 times 7,000 equals 21,000 votes), but these votes have to be distributed among their three nominees. The principle of cumulative voting is that no matter how the majority shareholders cast their 21,000 votes, they will not be able to elect all three directors if the minority shareholders cast all of their 9,000 votes for Drake, as illustrated in Exhibit 27–1.

OTHER VOTING TECHNIQUES   A group of shareholders can agree in writing prior to a shareholders' meeting, in a *shareholder voting agreement*, to vote their shares together in a specified manner. Such agreements usually are held to be valid and enforceable.

---

8.   When the legal owner is deceased, bankrupt, incompetent, or in some other way under a legal disability, his or her vote can be cast by a person designated by law to control and manage the owner's property.

9.   See, for example, California Corporate Code Section 708. Under RMBCA 7.28, however, no cumulative voting rights exist unless the articles of incorporation so provide.

♦ **Exhibit 27–1   Results of Cumulative Voting**
This exhibit illustrates how cumulative voting gives minority shareholders a greater chance of electing a director of their choice. By casting all of their 9,000 votes for one candidate (Drake), the minority shareholders will succeed in electing Drake to the board of directors.

BALLOT	MAJORITY SHAREHOLDERS' VOTES			MINORITY SHAREHOLDERS' VOTES	DIRECTORS ELECTED
	Acevedo	Barkley	Craycik	Drake	
1	10,000	10,000	1,000	9,000	Acevedo/Barkley/Drake
2	9,001	9,000	2,999	9,000	Acevedo/Barkley/Drake
3	6,000	7,000	8,000	9,000	Barkley/Craycik/Drake

A shareholder can also appoint a voting agent and vote by proxy. As mentioned, a proxy is a written authorization to cast the shareholder's vote, and a person can solicit proxies from a number of shareholders in an attempt to concentrate voting power.

Another technique is for shareholders to enter into a **voting trust,** which is an agreement (a trust contract) under which legal title (record ownership on the corporate books) is transferred to a trustee who is responsible for voting the shares. The agreement can specify how the trustee is to vote, or it can allow the trustee to use his or her discretion. The trustee takes physical possession of the stock certificate and in return gives the shareholder a *voting trust certificate.* The shareholder retains all of the rights of ownership (for example, the right to receive dividend payments) except for the power to vote the shares.

VOTING TRUST
An agreement (trust contract) under which legal title to shares of corporate stock is transferred to a trustee who is authorized by the shareholders to vote the shares on their behalf.

▮ Rights of Shareholders

Shareholders possess numerous rights. A significant right—the right to vote their shares—has already been discussed. We now look at some additional rights of shareholders.

Stock Certificates

A **stock certificate** is a certificate issued by a corporation that evidences ownership of a specified number of shares in the corporation. In jurisdictions that require the issuance of stock certificates, shareholders have the right to demand that the corporation issue certificates. In most states (and under RMBCA 6.26), boards of directors may provide that shares of stock be uncertificated (that is, that physical stock certificates need not be issued). In that circumstance, the corporation may be required to send the holders of uncertificated shares letters or some other form of notice containing the same information as that included on stock certificates.

Stock is intangible personal property, and the ownership right exists independently of the certificate itself. A stock certificate may be lost or destroyed, but ownership is not destroyed with it. A new certificate can be issued to replace one that has been lost or

STOCK CERTIFICATE
A certificate issued by a corporation evidencing the ownership of a specified number of shares in the corporation.

Why does a corporation issue stock certificates?

destroyed.[10] Notice of shareholders' meetings, dividends, and operational and financial reports are all distributed according to the recorded ownership listed in the corporation's books, not on the basis of possession of the certificate.

Preemptive Rights

PREEMPTIVE RIGHTS
Rights held by shareholders that entitle them to purchase newly issued shares of a corporation's stock, equal in percentage to shares presently held, before the stock is offered to any outside buyers. Preemptive rights enable shareholders to maintain their proportionate ownership and voice in the corporation.

A **preemptive right** is a common law concept under which a preference is given to shareholders over all other purchasers to subscribe to or purchase shares of a *new issue* of stock in proportion to the percentage of total shares they already hold. This allows each shareholder to maintain his or her portion of control, voting power, or financial interest in the corporation. Most statutes either (1) grant preemptive rights but allow them to be negated in the corporation's articles or (2) deny preemptive rights except to the extent that they are granted in the articles. The result is that the articles of incorporation determine the existence and scope of preemptive rights. Generally, preemptive rights apply only to additional, newly issued stock sold for cash, and the preemptive rights must be exercised within a specified time period (usually thirty days).

For example, Detering Corporation authorizes and issues 1,000 shares of stock. Lebow purchases 100 shares, making her the owner of 10 percent of the company's stock. Subsequently, Detering, by vote of the shareholders, authorizes the issuance of another 1,000 shares (by amending the articles of incorporation). This increases its capital stock to a total of 2,000 shares. If preemptive rights have been provided, Lebow can purchase one additional share of the new stock being issued for each share she currently owns—or 100 additional shares. Thus, she can own 200 of the 2,000 shares outstanding, and she will maintain her relative position as a shareholder. If preemptive rights are not allowed, her proportionate control and voting power may be diluted from that of a 10 percent shareholder to that of a 5 percent shareholder because of the issuance of the additional 1,000 shares.

Preemptive rights can be very important for shareholders in close corporations. This is because of the relatively small number of shares and the substantial interest that each shareholder controls in a close corporation. Without preemptive rights, it would be possible for a shareholder to lose his or her proportionate control over the firm.

Stock Warrants

STOCK WARRANT
A certificate that grants the owner the option to buy a given number of shares of stock, usually within a set time period.

Usually, when preemptive rights exist and a corporation is issuing additional shares, each shareholder is given **stock warrants,** which are transferable options to acquire a given number of shares from the corporation at a stated price. Warrants are often publicly traded on securities exchanges. When the option to purchase is in effect for a short period of time, the stock warrants are usually referred to as *rights*.

Dividends

As mentioned in Chapter 26, a *dividend* is a distribution of corporate profits or income *ordered by the directors* and paid to the shareholders in proportion to their respective shares in the corporation. Dividends can be paid in cash, property, stock of the corporation that is paying the dividends, or stock of other corporations.[11]

---

10. For a lost or destroyed certificate to be reissued, a shareholder normally must furnish an indemnity bond to protect the corporation against potential loss should the original certificate reappear at some future time in the hands of a bona fide purchaser [UCC 8–302, 8–405(2)].

11. Technically, dividends paid in stock are not dividends. They maintain each shareholder's proportional interest in the corporation. On one occasion, a distillery declared and paid a "dividend" in bonded whiskey.

State laws vary, but each state determines the general circumstances and legal requirements under which dividends are paid. State laws also control the sources of revenue to be used; only certain funds are legally available for paying dividends. Depending on state law, dividends may be paid from the following sources:

1.　*Retained earnings.* All state statutes allow dividends to be paid from the undistributed net profits earned by the corporation, including capital gains from the sale of fixed assets. The undistributed net profits are called *retained earnings.*
2.　*Net profits.* A few state statutes allow dividends to be issued from current net profits without regard to deficits in prior years.
3.　*Surplus.* A number of statutes allow dividends to be paid out of any surplus.

ILLEGAL DIVIDENDS　A dividend paid while the corporation is insolvent is automatically an illegal dividend, and shareholders may be liable for returning the payment to the corporation or its creditors. Furthermore, as just discussed, dividends are generally required by statute to be distributed only from certain authorized corporate accounts. Sometimes dividends are improperly paid from an unauthorized account, or their payment causes the corporation to become insolvent. Generally, in such cases, shareholders must return illegal dividends only if they knew that the dividends were illegal when they received them. Whenever dividends are illegal or improper, the board of directors can be held personally liable for the amount of the payment. When directors can show that a shareholder knew that a dividend was illegal when it was received, however, the directors are entitled to reimbursement from the shareholder.

DIRECTORS' FAILURE TO DECLARE A DIVIDEND　When directors fail to declare a dividend, shareholders can ask a court to compel the directors to meet and to declare a dividend. For the shareholders to succeed, they must show that the directors have acted so unreasonably in withholding the dividend that the directors' conduct is an abuse of their discretion.

Often, large money reserves are accumulated for a bona fide purpose, such as expansion, research, or other legitimate corporate goals. The mere fact that sufficient corporate earnings or surplus is available to pay a dividend is not enough to compel directors to distribute funds that, in the board's opinion, should not be paid. The courts are circumspect about interfering with corporate operations and will not compel directors to declare dividends unless abuse of discretion is clearly shown. In the following classic case, the shareholders brought a court action to compel Ford Motor Company to declare a dividend.

CASE 27.2

DODGE v. FORD MOTOR CO.
Supreme Court of Michigan, 1919.
204 Mich. 459,
170 N.W. 668.

HISTORICAL AND SOCIAL SETTING　*Corporations are owned by shareholders but run by directors and officers. Practical and ethical problems are inevitable. Directors are supposed to act in the best interests of the corporation, which is presumed to be the same as the* *best interests of the shareholders. Directors and shareholders may have different views about the corporation's best interests, however. Directors who look toward long-term growth and future profitability may want to reinvest profits in the firm. Shareholders may be more interested in receiving those profits as current dividends.*

FACTS　Henry Ford was the president and major shareholder of Ford Motor Company. In the company's early years, business expanded rapidly, and in addition to regular quarterly dividends, special dividends were often paid. By 1916, surplus above capital was still $111,960,907. That year, however, Henry Ford declared

(Continued)

Case 27.2—Continued

that the company would no longer pay special dividends but would put back into the business all the earnings of the company above the regular dividend of 5 percent. According to the court, Ford stated as follows: "My ambition is to employ still more men, to spread the benefits of this industrial system to the greatest possible number, to help them build up their lives and their homes. To do this, we are putting the greatest share of our profits back into the business." The minority shareholders (who owned 10 percent of the stock) filed a lawsuit in a Michigan state court against Ford and others to force the declaration of a dividend. The court ordered the Ford directors to declare a dividend, and the plaintiffs appealed.

ISSUE   Was Ford's refusal to pay a dividend an abuse of managerial discretion?

DECISION   Yes. Because of the special circumstances of this case, the court compelled Ford to pay a dividend.

REASON   The undisputed facts were that Ford had a surplus of $112 million—approximately $54 million in cash on hand. It had made profits of $59 million in the

past year and expected to make $60 million in the coming year. The board of directors gave no reason to justify withholding a dividend. Thus, in doing so, it violated the stated purpose of the corporation's existence. According to the court, "Courts of equity will not interfere in the management of the directors unless it is clearly made to appear that they are guilty of fraud or misappropriation of the corporate funds, or refuse to declare a dividend when the corporation has a surplus of net profits which it can, without detriment to its business, divide among its stockholders, and when a refusal to do so would amount to such an abuse of discretion as would constitute a fraud, or breach of that good faith which they are bound to exercise towards the stockholders."

FOR CRITICAL ANALYSIS—Social Consideration
Generally, how can a court determine when directors should pay dividends?

Inspection Rights

Shareholders in a corporation enjoy both common law and statutory inspection rights.[12] The shareholder's right of inspection is limited, however, to the inspection and copying of corporate books and records for a *proper purpose*, provided the request is made in advance. The shareholder can inspect in person, or an attorney, agent, accountant, or other type of assistant can do so. The RMBCA requires the corporation to maintain an alphabetical voting list of shareholders with addresses and number of shares owned; this list must be kept open at the annual meeting for inspection by any shareholder of record [RMBCA 7.20].

     The power of inspection is fraught with potential abuses, and the corporation is allowed to protect itself from them. For example, a shareholder can properly be denied access to corporate records to prevent harassment or to protect trade secrets or other confidential corporate information. Some states require that a shareholder must have held his or her shares for a minimum period of time immediately preceding the demand to inspect or must hold a minimum number of outstanding shares. The RMBCA provides, however, that every shareholder is entitled to examine specified corporate records [RMBCA 16.02].

     In the following case, a shareholder sought to inspect and copy corporate records in order to locate other shareholders who might want to join in an action against the corporation for alleged wrongdoing. The question before the court was whether the shareholder's reason for inspecting the corporate records, given these circumstances, qualified as a "proper purpose."

---

12.   See, for example, *Schwartzman v. Schwartzman Packing Co.*, 99 N.M. 436, 659 P.2d 888 (1983).

CASE 27.3

COMPAQ COMPUTER CORP. v. HORTON

Supreme Court of Delaware, 1993.
631 A.2d 1.

HISTORICAL AND TECHNOLOGICAL SETTING *In the 1990s, the technology revolution has been transforming life in the home, workplace, and institutions of higher education in ways that were unimaginable only a few years ago. Among the leaders in this revolution are IBM, Apple Corporation, Microsoft Corporation, and Compaq Computer Corporation. For the leaders, success has come in part from an emphasis on cutting-edge technology. For example, three former Texas Instruments engineers formed Compaq in 1982, and the company shipped its first computer the same year. The next year, the firm introduced a portable computer—eighteen months before IBM did so—and experienced unprecedented growth, with sales of $111 million.*

FACTS In July 1991, Charles Horton and seventy-eight other shareholders of Compaq Computer Corporation sued Compaq and some of its advisors and managers in a Delaware state court, alleging fraud and other misconduct. The plaintiffs contended that Compaq misled the public as to the true value of its stock at a time when members of management were selling their shares. In September 1992, Horton sought to inspect Compaq's stock ledger and related records. Horton's demand letter stated that the purpose of the request was to inform other Compaq shareholders of the lawsuit and to learn whether any of them wanted to join in the action against the defendants. Compaq refused Horton's demand, stating that the purpose described in the letter was not a "proper purpose" under Delaware law. The court entered a judgment in the plaintiffs' favor, and Compaq appealed.

ISSUE Was Horton's purpose for inspecting Compaq's records a "proper purpose" under Delaware law?

DECISION Yes. The Supreme Court of Delaware affirmed the lower court's decision.

REASON Compaq argued that because Horton's objective to solicit additional parties to the litigation could impose substantial expenses on the company, it was *per se* ("in itself") improper. The court reasoned, however, that Horton, as a current stockholder, had nothing to gain "by harming the legitimate interests of the company," that the litigation posed "no legitimate threat to Compaq's interests," and that "the litigation [was] already pending with seventy-nine plaintiffs." The court stated that the "real risk to Compaq is that any additional plaintiffs [may] potentially increase the damage award against the company. Yet, * * * for breaches of their duties to shareholders Compaq has no legitimate interest in avoiding the payment of compensatory damages which it, its management or advisors may owe to those who own the enterprise. Thus, common sense and public policy dictate that a proper purpose may be stated in these circumstances, notwithstanding the lack of a direct benefit flowing to the corporation." The court also pointed out that if damages were assessed, Compaq could seek indemnification from its "co-defendant managers and advisors" or pursue its own claims against them, thus diminishing any possible harm suffered by Compaq.

FOR CRITICAL ANALYSIS—Ethical Consideration
What did the court mean when it stated that Horton had nothing to gain "by harming the legitimate interests of the company"?

Transfer of Shares

Stock certificates generally are negotiable and freely transferable by indorsement and delivery. Transfer of stock in closely held corporations, however, usually is restricted by the bylaws, by a restriction stamped on the stock certificate, or by a shareholder agreement (see Chapter 26). The existence of any restrictions on transferability must always be noted on the face of the stock certificate, and these restrictions must be reasonable.

Sometimes, corporations or their shareholders restrict transferability by reserving the option to purchase any shares offered for resale by a shareholder. This **right of first refusal** remains with the corporation or the shareholders for only a specified time or a reasonable time. Variations on the purchase option are possible. For example, a

RIGHT OF FIRST REFUSAL
The right to purchase personal or real property—such as corporate shares or real estate—before the property is offered for sale to others.

shareholder might be required to offer the shares to other shareholders first or to the corporation first.

When shares are transferred, a new entry is made in the corporate stock book to indicate the new owner. Until the corporation is notified and the entry is complete, the current record owner has the right to be notified of (and attend) shareholders' meetings, the right to vote the shares, the right to receive dividends, and all other shareholder rights.

Corporate Dissolution

When a corporation is dissolved and its outstanding debts and the claims of its creditors have been satisfied, the remaining assets are distributed to the shareholders in proportion to the percentage of shares owned by each shareholder. Certain classes of preferred stock can be given priority. If no preferences to distribution of assets on liquidation are given to any class of stock, then the shareholders are entitled to the remaining assets.

In some circumstances, shareholders may petition a court to have the corporation dissolved. Suppose, for example, that a minority shareholder knows that the board of directors is mishandling corporate assets. The minority shareholder is not powerless to intervene. He or she can petition a court to appoint a **receiver**—who will wind up corporate affairs and liquidate the business assets of the corporation.

The RMBCA permits any shareholder to initiate such an action in any of the following circumstances [RMBCA 14.30]:

1.   The directors are deadlocked in the management of corporate affairs. Shareholders are unable to break that deadlock, and irreparable injury to the corporation is being suffered or threatened.
2.   The acts of the directors or those in control of the corporation are illegal, oppressive, or fraudulent.
3.   Corporate assets are being misapplied or wasted.
4.   The shareholders are deadlocked in voting power and have failed, for a specified period (usually two annual meetings), to elect successors to directors whose terms have expired or would have expired with the election of successors.

When the shareholders themselves are deadlocked, a court may order the dissolution of a corporation. This was the circumstance in the following case.

RECEIVER
In a corporate dissolution, a court-appointed person who winds up corporate affairs and liquidates corporate assets.

CASE 27.4

BLACK v. GRAHAM
Supreme Court of Georgia, 1996.
464 S.E.2d 814.

HISTORICAL AND ECONOMIC SETTING   *Despite the continued expansion of the economy in the early 1990s, there was negative growth in the market for construction materials. At the time, there were nearly 72,000 building materials and garden supplies establishments. In*

contrast, there were more than 500,000 construction contractors. Most contractors and building supplies firms are small businesses. In the construction industry, a business is classified as small if it has gross annual receipts between $7 million and $15 million.

FACTS   Black and Graham each owned 50 percent of the stock of a building supplies corporation; they also served as the corporation's directors. When the two shareholder-directors deadlocked over differences of opinion on how to run their business, Graham filed a petition in a Georgia state court to dissolve the corporation. The parties agreed to the appointment of a custodian to run their firm while the court considered Graham's petition. Ultimately, the court ordered each shareholder to offer to buy the other out. This attempt to resolve the

Case 27.4—Continued

matter failed. The court then converted the custodian into a receiver, directed him to wind up the affairs of the business, and told him to liquidate the corporation. Both parties appealed to the Supreme Court of Georgia.

ISSUE   Were the shareholders and directors so dead-locked that dissolution was warranted?

DECISION   Yes. The Supreme Court of Georgia affirmed the orders of the lower court.

REASON   The state supreme court explained that a deadlock occurs "[w]here stock of [a] corporation is owned in equal shares by two contending parties, which condition threatens to result in destruction of business, and it appears that [the] parties cannot agree upon management of [the] business, and under existing circumstances neither one is authorized to impose its views upon the other." This case, the court said, "portrays a classic situation of deadlock. Black and Graham as sole and equal shareholders functioned as *de facto* directors who were wholly unable to agree on the management of the business. Neither had the authority to prevail in his view and the hostile and static situation threatened irreparable injury to the corporation."

FOR CRITICAL ANALYSIS—Political Consideration
What steps might a corporation with an even number of shareholders and directors take to avoid a deadlock?

Shareholder's Derivative Suit

When those in control of a corporation—the corporate directors—fail to sue in the corporate name to redress a wrong suffered by the corporation, shareholders are permitted to do so "derivatively" in what is known as a **shareholder's derivative suit.** Some wrong must have been done to the corporation, and before a derivative suit can be brought, the shareholders must first state their complaint to the board of directors. Only if the directors fail to solve the problem or take appropriate action can the derivative suit go forward.

The right of shareholders to bring a derivative action is especially important when the wrong suffered by the corporation results from the actions of corporate directors or officers. This is because the directors and officers would probably want to prevent any action against themselves.

The shareholder's derivative suit is singular in that those suing are not pursuing rights or benefits for themselves personally but are acting as guardians of the corporate entity. Therefore, any damages recovered by the suit normally go into the corporation's treasury, not to the shareholders personally.

SHAREHOLDER'S DERIVATIVE SUIT
A suit brought by a shareholder to enforce a corporate cause of action against a third person.

In the United States, the 1980s and early 1990s saw a dramatic increase in the number of shareholder suits brought against directors and officers for alleged breaches of duties. Today, most of the claims brought against directors and officers are those alleged in shareholders' derivative suits. Other nations, however, are more restrictive in regard to the use of such suits. In Germany, for example, there is no provision for derivative litigation, and a corporation's duty to its employees is just as significant as its duty to the shareholder-owners of the company. The United Kingdom has no statute authorizing derivative actions, which are permitted only to challenge directors' actions that the shareholders could not legally ratify. Japan authorizes derivative

(Continued)

International Perspective—Continued

actions but also permits a company to sue the shareholder-plaintiff for damages if the action is unsuccessful.

For Critical Analysis: *Do corporations benefit from shareholders' derivative suits? If so, how?*

▌Liability of Shareholders

One of the hallmarks of the corporate organization is that shareholders are not personally liable for the debts of the corporation. If the corporation fails, shareholders can lose their investments, but that is generally the limit of their liability. As discussed in Chapter 26, in certain instances of fraud, undercapitalization, or careless observance of corporate formalities, a court will pierce the corporate veil (disregard the corporate entity) and hold the shareholders individually liable. These situations are the exception, however, not the rule. Although they are rare, certain other instances arise where a shareholder can be personally liable. One relates to illegal dividends, which were discussed previously. Two others relate to *stock subscriptions* and *watered stock*, which we discuss here.

Sometimes stock-subscription agreements—written contracts by which one agrees to buy capital stock of a corporation—exist prior to incorporation. Normally, these agreements are treated as continuing offers and are irrevocable (for up to six months under RMBCA 6.20). Once the corporation has been formed, it can sell shares to shareholder investors. In either situation, once the subscription agreement or stock offer is accepted, a binding contract is formed. Any refusal to pay constitutes a breach resulting in the personal liability of the shareholder.

Shares of stock can be paid for by property or by services rendered instead of cash. They cannot be purchased with promissory notes, however. The general rule is that for **par-value shares** (shares that have a specific face value, or formal cash-in value, written on them, such as one penny or one dollar), the corporation must receive a value at least equal to the par-value amount. For **no-par shares** (shares that have no face value—no specific amount printed on their face), the corporation must receive the value of the shares as determined by the board or the shareholders when the stock was issued. When the corporation issues shares for less than these stated values, the shares are referred to as **watered stock**.[13] Usually, the shareholder who receives watered stock must pay the difference to the corporation (the shareholder is personally liable). In some states, the shareholder who receives watered stock may be liable to creditors of the corporation for unpaid corporate debts.

To illustrate the concept of watered stock, suppose that during the formation of a corporation, Gomez, one of the incorporators, transfers his property, Sunset Beach, to the corporation for ten thousand shares of stock. The stock has a par value of $100 per share, and thus the total price of the ten thousand shares is $1 million. After the property is transferred and the shares are issued, Sunset Beach is carried on the corporate books at a value of $1 million. Upon appraisal, it is discovered that the market value of the property at the time of transfer was only $500,000. The shares issued to Gomez are therefore watered stock, and he is liable to the corporation for the difference.

PAR-VALUE SHARES
Corporate shares that have a specific face value, or formal cash-in value, written on them, such as one dollar.

NO-PAR SHARES
Corporate shares that have no face value—that is, no specific dollar amount is printed on their face.

WATERED STOCK
Shares of stock issued by a corporation for which the corporation receives, as payment, less than the stated value of the shares.

---

13. The phrase *watered stock* was originally used to describe cattle that—kept thirsty during a long drive—were allowed to drink large quantities of water just prior to their sale. The increased weight of the "watered stock" allowed the seller to reap a higher profit.

▮ Duties of Majority Shareholders

In some cases, a majority shareholder is regarded as having a fiduciary duty to the corporation and to the minority shareholders. This occurs when a single shareholder (or a few shareholders acting in concert) owns a sufficient number of shares to exercise *de facto* control over the corporation. In these situations, majority shareholders owe a fiduciary duty to the minority shareholders when they sell their shares, because such a sale would be, in fact, a transfer of control of the corporation. Whether the controlling majority of shareholders owed a fiduciary duty to a minority shareholder was at issue in the following case.

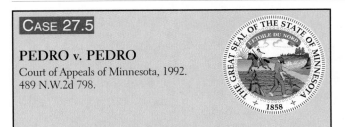

CASE 27.5

PEDRO v. PEDRO
Court of Appeals of Minnesota, 1992.
489 N.W.2d 798.

HISTORICAL AND SOCIAL SETTING   *The purchase of a minority shareholder's shares in a corporation by the majority shareholders is termed a buy-out. In litigation, when fashioning relief involving the buy-out of shareholders in a close corporation, trial courts have broad equitable powers. For example, Minnesota Statutes Section 302A.751(3a) allows courts to look to a shareholder's reasonable expectations when awarding damages. Besides the shareholder's ownership interest in the corporation, "[t]he reasonable expectations of such a shareholder are a job, salary, a significant place in management, and economic security for his family."*[a]

FACTS   Alfred, Carl, and Eugene Pedro each owned a one-third interest in The Pedro Companies (TPC), a close corporation that manufactured and sold luggage and leather products. All of the brothers had worked for the corporation for most of their adult lives. The relationship between Alfred and the other two brothers began to deteriorate in 1987 after Alfred discovered a discrepancy between the internal accounting records and the TPC checking account. At Alfred's insistence, two different accountants examined the records, but neither could identify the source of a $140,000 discrepancy, and one accountant said that he was denied access to numerous documents during the investigation. Alfred stated that his brothers told him that if he did not forget about the discrepancy, they would fire him—which they did in

December 1987. Alfred filed suit in a Minnesota state court against his brothers, alleging that they had breached their fiduciary duties and that he had been wrongfully discharged. The trial court held for Alfred and awarded him over $1.8 million in damages, plus interest, for the value of his shares, lost wages, and attorneys' fees. The brothers appealed.

ISSUE   Had the brothers breached their fiduciary duties to Alfred by terminating his employment with TPC?

DECISION   Yes. The Minnesota Court of Appeals affirmed the trial court's judgment.

REASON   The appellate court emphasized that the relationship among shareholders in closely held corporations is "analogous to that of partners" and that they owe one another a fiduciary duty. "Owing a fiduciary duty," stated the court, "includes dealing 'openly, honestly and fairly with other shareholders.'" The court found that the brothers had not acted openly, honestly, and fairly with Alfred. Furthermore, the court found that Alfred justifiably assumed that he had an implied contract with the corporation for lifetime employment, a contract that the brothers breached when they fired him. Given the fact that Alfred's father had worked for the company until his death and that Eugene, who had worked for TPC for over fifty years, testified that he intended to always work for the company, Alfred's expectation of a lifetime job was reasonable. The court concluded that "[b]ased upon this evidence[,] it was reasonable for the trial court to determine that the parties did in fact have a contract that was not terminable at will."

FOR CRITICAL ANALYSIS—Economic Consideration
Is there anything Alfred could have done to ensure that he would be employed "for life" by the corporation?

a.   Joseph Olson, "A Statutory Elixir for the Oppression Malady," 36 *Mercer Law Review* 627 (1985).

Application

Law and the Corporation— Developing a Document- Retention Policy*

If a corporation becomes the target of a civil lawsuit or criminal investigation, the company may be required to turn over any documents in its files relating to the matter during the discovery stage of litigation. These documents may consist of legal documents, contracts, faxes, letters, interoffice memorandums, notebooks, diaries, and other materials, even if they are kept in personal files in the homes of directors or officers.

At one time, document-retention policies referred only to paper documents. Today, a document-retention policy must also take into consideration electronic documents and data. Under the current Federal Rules of Civil Procedure, which govern civil litigation procedures (see Chapter 3), a defendant in a lawsuit must disclose all relevant electronic data compilations and documents, as well as all relevant paper documents. Although certain documents or data might free a company of any liability arising from a claim, others might serve to substantiate a civil claim or criminal charge. It is also possible that information in a document—an interoffice E-mail memo, for example (or even a memo referring to that memo)—could be used to convince a jury that the company or its directors or officers condoned a certain action when they deny it.

To be fully prepared in the event of a lawsuit or criminal investigation, many companies today have created document-retention policies to determine what paper and electronic documents to keep. How does a company decide which documents should be retained and which should be destroyed? By law, corporations are required to

keep certain types of documents, such as those specified in the Code of Federal Regulations and in regulations issued by government agencies, such as the Occupational Safety and Health Administration. Generally, any records that the company is not legally required to keep or that the company is sure it will have no legal need for should be removed from the files and destroyed. A joint-venture agreement, for example, should be kept. A memo about last year's company picnic, however, should be removed from the files and destroyed; obviously, it is just taking up storage space.

If the company becomes the target of an investigation, it usually must modify its document-retention policy until the investigation has been completed. Company officers, after receiving a subpoena to produce specific types of documents, should instruct the appropriate employees not to destroy relevant papers that would otherwise be disposed of as part of the company's normal document-retention program.

Generally, company officials must always exercise good faith in deciding what documents should or should not be destroyed when attempting to comply with a subpoena to avoid being charged with the obstruction of justice. The specter of criminal prosecution would appear to encourage the retention of even those documents that are only remotely related to the dispute—at least until it has been resolved.

 Checklist for a Document- Retention Policy

1. Find out which documents must be retained under the Code of Federal Regulations and under other government agency regulations to which your corporation is subject.

2. Retain other paper and electronic documents only if the retention is in the corporation's interest.

3. If certain corporate documents are subpoenaed, modify your document-retention policy to retain any document that is even remotely related to the dispute until the legal action has been resolved.

*This *Application* is not meant to substitute for the services of an attorney who is licensed to practice law in your state.

▌Key Terms

business judgment rule 703
no-par share 716
par-value share 716
preemptive right 710
proxy 706

quorum 697
receiver 714
right of first refusal 713
shareholder's derivative suit 715
stock certificate 709

stock warrant 710
tender offer 700
voting trust 709
watered stock 716

▌Chapter Summary: Corporate Directors, Officers, and Shareholders

Role of Directors *(See pages 696–699.)*	1. *Election of directors*—The first board of directors is usually appointed by the incorporators; thereafter, directors are elected by the shareholders. Directors usually serve a one-year term, although longer and staggered terms are permitted under most state statutes. 2. *Directors' qualifications and compensation*—Few qualifications are required; a director can be a shareholder but is not required to be. Compensation is usually specified in the corporate articles or bylaws. 3. *Board of directors' meetings*—The board of directors conducts business by holding formal meetings with recorded minutes. The date of regular meetings is usually established in the corporate articles or bylaws; special meetings can be called, with notice sent to all directors. Quorum requirements vary from state to state; usually, a quorum is the majority of the corporate directors. Voting must usually be done in person, and in ordinary matters only a majority vote is required. 4. *Rights of directors*—Directors' rights include the rights of participation, inspection, compensation, and indemnification. 5. *Directors' management responsibilities*—Directors are responsible for declaring and paying corporate dividends to shareholders; authorizing major corporate decisions; appointing, supervising, and removing corporate officers and other managerial employees; determining employees' compensation; making financial decisions necessary to the management of corporate affairs; and issuing authorized shares and bonds. Directors may delegate some of their responsibilities to executive committees and corporate officers and executives.
Role of Corporate Officers and Executives *(See page 699.)*	Corporate officers and other executive employees are normally hired by the board of directors. In most states, a person can hold more than one office and can be both an officer and a director of a corporation. The rights of corporate officers and executives are defined by employment contracts. The duties of corporate officers are the same as those of directors.
Duties of Directors and Officers *(See pages 700–703.)*	1. *Duty of care*—Directors are obligated to act in good faith, to use prudent business judgment in the conduct of corporate affairs, and to act in the corporation's best interests. If a director fails to exercise this duty of care, he or she can be answerable to the corporation and to the shareholders for breaching the duty. 2. *Duty of loyalty*—Directors have a fiduciary duty to subordinate their own interests to those of the corporation in matters relating to the corporation. 3. *Conflicts of interest*—To fulfill their duty of loyalty, directors and officers must make a full disclosure of any potential conflicts of interest between their personal interests and those of the corporation.
Liability of Directors and Officers *(See pages 703–704.)*	1. *Business judgment rule*—This rule immunizes a director from liability for a corporate decision as long as the decision was within the powers of the corporation and the authority of the director to make and was an informed, reasonable, and loyal decision. 2. *Liability for torts and crimes*—Corporate directors and officers are personally liable for their own torts and crimes; additionally, they may be held personally liable for the torts and crimes committed by corporate personnel under their direct supervision.
Role of Shareholders *(See pages 704–709.)*	1. *Shareholders' powers*—Shareholders' powers include the approval of all fundamental changes affecting the corporation and the election of the board of directors. 2. *Shareholders' meetings*—Shareholders' meetings must occur at least annually; special meetings can be called when necessary. Notice of the date, time, and place of the meeting (and its purpose, if it is specially called) must be sent to shareholders. Shareholders may vote by proxy (authorizing someone else to vote their shares) and may submit proposals to be included in the company's proxy materials sent to shareholders before meetings. 3. *Shareholder voting*—Shareholder voting requirements and procedures are as follows: a. A minimum number of shareholders (a quorum—generally, more than 50 percent of shares held) must be present at a meeting for business to be conducted; resolutions are passed (usually) by simple majority vote. *(Continued)*

▌Chapter Summary: Corporate Directors, Officers, and Shareholders—Continued

Role of Shareholders— Continued	b. The corporation must prepare voting lists of shareholders on record prior to each shareholders' meeting.
	c. Cumulative voting may or may not be required or permitted. Cumulative voting gives minority shareholders a better chance to be represented on the board of directors.
	d. A shareholder voting agreement (an agreement of shareholders to vote their shares together) is usually held to be valid and enforceable.
	e. A shareholder may appoint a proxy (substitute) to vote his or her shares.
	f. A shareholder may enter into a voting trust agreement by which title (record ownership) of his or her shares is given to a trustee, and the trustee votes the shares in accordance with the trust agreement.
Rights of Shareholders (See pages 709–716.)	Shareholders have numerous rights, which may include the following:
	1. The right to a stock certificate, preemptive rights, and the right to stock warrants (depending on the corporate charter).
	2. The right to obtain a dividend (at the discretion of the directors).
	3. Voting rights.
	4. The right to inspect the corporate records.
	5. The right to transfer shares (this right may be restricted in close corporations).
	6. The right to a share of corporate assets when the corporation is dissolved.
	7. The right to sue on behalf of the corporation (bring a shareholder's derivative suit) when the directors fail to do so.
Liability of Shareholders (See page 716.)	Shareholders may be liable for the retention of illegal dividends, for breach of a stock-subscription agreement, and for the value of watered stock.
Duties of Majority Shareholders (See page 717.)	In certain situations, majority shareholders may be regarded as having a fiduciary duty to minority shareholders and will be liable if that duty is breached.

▌For Review

1. What are the duties of the directors and officers of a corporation?
2. Directors are expected to use their best judgment in managing the corporation. What must directors do to avoid liability for honest mistakes of judgment and poor business decisions?
3. What is a voting proxy? What is cumulative voting?

4. If a group of shareholders perceives that the corporation has suffered a wrong and the directors refuse to take action, can the shareholders compel the directors to act? If so, how?
5. From what sources may dividends be paid legally? In what circumstances is a dividend illegal? What happens if a dividend is illegally paid?

▌Questions and Case Problems

27–1. Rights of Shareholders. Dmitri has acquired one share of common stock of a multimillion-dollar corporation with over 500,000 shareholders. Dmitri's ownership is so small that he is questioning what his rights are as a shareholder. For example, he wants to know whether this one share entitles him to attend and vote at shareholders' meetings, inspect the corporate books, and receive periodic dividends. Discuss Dmitri's rights in these matters.

27–2. Voting Techniques. Algonquin Corp. has issued and has outstanding 100,000 shares of common stock. Four stockholders own 60,000 of these shares, and for the past six years they have nominated a slate of people for membership on the board, all of whom have been elected. Sergio and twenty other shareholders, owning 20,000 shares, are dissatisfied with corporate management and want a representative on the board who shares their views. Explain under what circumstances

Sergio and the minority shareholders can elect their representative to the board.

27–3. Duties of Directors. Starboard, Inc., has a board of directors consisting of three members (Ellsworth, Green, and Morino) and approximately five hundred shareholders. At a regular meeting of the board, the board selects Tyson as president of the corporation by a two-to-one vote, with Ellsworth dissenting. The minutes of the meeting do not register Ellsworth's dissenting vote. Later, during an audit, it is discovered that Tyson is a former convict and has openly embezzled $500,000 from Starboard. This loss is not covered by insurance. The corporation wants to hold directors Ellsworth, Green, and Morino liable. Ellsworth claims no liability. Discuss the personal liability of the directors to the corporation.

27–4. Liability of Shareholders. Mallard has made a preincorporation subscription agreement to purchase 500 shares of a newly formed corporation. The shares have a par value of $100 per share. The corporation is formed, and it accepts Mallard's subscription. Mallard transfers a piece of land he owns to the corporation as payment for 250 of the shares, and the corporation issues 250 shares for it. Mallard pays for the other 250 shares with cash. One year later, with the corporation in serious financial difficulty, the board declares and pays a $5-per-share dividend. It is now learned that the land transferred by Mallard had a market value of $18,000. Discuss any liability that shareholder Mallard has to the corporation or to the creditors of the corporation.

27–5. Duties of Directors. Overland Corp. is negotiating with Wharton Construction Co. for the renovation of Overland's corporate headquarters. Wharton, the owner of Wharton Construction, is also one of the five members of the board of directors of Overland. The contract terms are standard for this type of contract. Wharton has previously informed two of the other Overland directors of his interest in the construction company. Overland's board approves the contract on a three-to-two vote, with Wharton voting with the majority. Discuss whether this contract is binding on the corporation.

27–6. Duties of Directors. Midwest Management Corp. was looking for investment opportunities. Morris Stephens, one of Midwest's directors and the chairman of the investment committee, proposed that Midwest provide financing for Stephens's son and his business colleagues, who were in need of financing to open a broker-dealer business. Midwest agreed to propose to the shareholders for their approval an investment of $250,000 in the new business on the condition that Stephens would manage the business and would purchase 100,000 shares of stock in the new firm. At each of two shareholders' meetings, the directors informed the shareholders that Stephens had agreed to the condition. Stephens was present at both meetings and did not deny that he had agreed to purchase the 100,000 shares of stock and manage the new corporation. On the shareholders' approval, the $250,000 investment was made, and later another $150,000 was invested when the new business suffered losses. About a year after it had opened, the business closed, and Midwest ended up losing over $325,000. Midwest then learned that Stephens had not kept his agreement to purchase stock in and manage the corporation. Midwest sued Stephens for breaching his fiduciary duties and asked for compensatory and punitive damages. Did Midwest

succeed? Explain. [*Midwest Management Corp. v. Stephens*, 353 N.W.2d 76 (Iowa 1984)]

27–7. Duties of Directors and Officers. Klinicki and Lundgren formed Berlinair, a closely held Oregon corporation, to provide air transportation out of West Germany. Klinicki, who owned 33 percent of the company stock, was the vice president and a director. Lundgren, who also owned 33 percent of the stock, was the president and a director. Lelco, Inc., a corporation owned by Lundgren and his family, owned 33 percent of Berlinair, and Berlinair's attorney owned the last 1 percent of stock. One of the goals of Berlinair was to obtain a contract with BFR, a West German consortium of travel agents, to provide BFR with air charter service. Later, Lundgren learned that the BFR contract might become available. Lundgren then incorporated Air Berlin Charter Co., of which he was the sole owner, and bid for the BFR contract. Lundgren won the BFR contract for Air Berlin while using Berlinair working time, staff, money, and facilities without the knowledge of Klinicki. Has Lundgren breached any fiduciary duty to Berlinair or to Klinicki? If so, what duty, and how was it breached? Explain. [*Klinicki v. Lundgren*, 67 Or.App. 160, 678 P.2d 1250 (1984)]

27–8. Rights of Shareholders. Jacob Schachter and Herbert Kulik, the founders of Ketek Electric Corp., each owned 50 percent of the corporation's shares and served as the corporation's only officers. Arnold Glenn, as trustee, and Kulik brought a shareholder's derivative suit in a New York state court against Schachter, alleging that Schachter had diverted Ketek assets and opportunities to Hoteltron Systems, Inc., a corporation wholly owned by Schachter. The trial court held for Glenn and Kulik, and it awarded damages to Kulik, not to Ketek. On appeal, the appellate court ruled that the damages should be awarded to the injured corporation, Ketek, rather than to the innocent shareholder, Kulik. Kulik appealed to the state supreme court, arguing that awarding damages to the corporation was inequitable because Schachter, as a shareholder of Ketek, would ultimately share in the proceeds of the award. How should the state supreme court rule, and why? [*Glenn v. Hoteltron Systems, Inc.*, 74 N.Y.2d 386, 547 N.E.2d 71, 547 N.Y.S.2 816 (1989)]

27–9. Duties of Directors and Officers. While working for Veco Corp., an Illinois financial services company, officers Robert Babcock and Margaret Michails, after discussions with other employees, prepared a business plan for their own financial services company, CorMac, Inc. The plan listed other Veco employees who would join CorMac and detailed the "taking over" of an important Veco client. Veco's founder and sole shareholder, David Vear, discovered what Babcock had done and fired him. Michails and other Veco employees quit to work for CorMac. As a result, Veco was left with no personnel who were experienced in handling one of its major accounts. Veco sued Babcock and Michails, alleging that they had breached their fiduciary duties to Veco. Had they breached any fiduciary duty? If so, what duty had they breached? How should the court rule on this issue? [*Veco Corp. v. Babcock*, 243 Ill.App.3d 153, 611 N.E.2d 1054, 183 Ill.Dec. 406 (1993)]

27–10. Rights of Shareholders. Melissa and Gary Callicoat each owned 50 percent of Callicoat, Inc. They were also Callicoat's only directors. They could not agree on the day-today management of the firm. They also could not agree on whether a debt owed to Arthur Baz was a personal or corporate debt. Melissa suggested that they dissolve the corporation. Gary refused and shut her out from the operations of the firm. Melissa filed a petition in an Ohio state court against Gary and Callicoat, asking the court to dissolve the corporation. On what basis might the court order the dissolution? [*Callicoat v. Callicoat*, 73 Ohio Misc.2d 38, 657 N.E.2d 874 (1994)]

27–11. Business Judgment Rule. William Bear was the president of the William R. Bear Agency, Inc. (Bear Agency). Timothy Schirmer was a shareholder. In 1990, the YMCA was an important client of Bear Agency, and Bear spent company funds for family memberships in the YMCA. The same year, Bear put his wife on the payroll because, at the time, she was the only one in the office with computer experience. He decided not to declare a bonus for the employees in 1990, in part to invest the money in computers for the firm. The next April, Bear bought a BMW with company funds to use as a company car. Disapproving these actions, Schirmer filed a suit against Bear, Bear Agency, and others in an Illinois state court, asking the court to dissolve the corporation, among other things. Discuss how the decision not to dissolve Bear Agency might be supported by the business judgment rule. [*Schirmer v. Bear*, 271 Ill.App.3d 778, 648 N.E.2d 1131, 208 Ill.Dec. 209 (1994)]

A QUESTION OF ETHICS AND SOCIAL RESPONSIBILITY

27–12. *McQuade was the manager of the New York Giants baseball team. McQuade and John McGraw purchased shares in the National Exhibition Co., the corporation that owned the Giants, from Charles Stoneham, who owned a majority of National Exhibition's stock. As part of the transaction, each of the three agreed to use his best efforts to ensure that the others continued as directors and officers of the organization. Stoneham and McGraw, however, subsequently failed to use their best efforts to ensure that McQuade continued as the treasurer and a director of the corporation, and McQuade sued to compel specific performance of the agreement. A court reviewing the matter noted that McQuade had been "shabbily" treated by the others but refused to grant specific performance on the ground that the agreement was void because it interfered with the duty of the others as directors to do what was best for all the shareholders. Although shareholders may join to elect corporate directors, they may not join to limit the directors' discretion in managing the business affairs of an organization; the directors must retain their independent judgment. Consider the implications of the case, and address the following questions. [McQuade v. Stoneham, 263 N.Y. 323, 189 N.E. 234 (1934)]*

1. Given that even the court sympathized with McQuade, was it ethical to put the business judgment of the directors ahead of an otherwise valid promise they had made?
2. Are there practical considerations that support the court's decision? How can directors perform the tasks dictated to them if their judgment is constrained by earlier agreements with some of the shareholders?
3. Can you think of any circumstances in which it would be fair to the shareholders, as a group, to interfere with the directors' business judgment by holding some of the directors to a similar prior agreement with some or all of the other directors?

CASE BRIEFING ASSIGNMENT

27–13. *Examine Case A.7 [Maschmeier v. Southside Press, Ltd., 435 N.W.2d 377 (Iowa App. 1989)] in Appendix A. The case has been excerpted there in great detail. Review and then brief the case, making sure that you include answers to the following questions in your brief.*

1. What was the primary reason for this lawsuit?
2. What restriction did the corporate bylaws place on the transfer of corporate shares? Upon transfer, how was the price of shares to be determined?
3. How did the majority shareholders (the parents) effectively "freeze out" or "squeeze out" the minority shareholders (the sons)?
4. Why was it necessary for the court to determine the fair value of shares, as the shareholders had agreed in the bylaws on a method for accomplishing this?
5. Why was it necessary to establish that the majority shareholders had acted oppressively toward the minority shareholders or wasted corporate assets before the court could fashion its particular remedy in this case?

FOR CRITICAL ANALYSIS

27–14. *In recent years, some courts have held corporate officers personally liable for corporate employees' violations of environmental and safety regulations in the workplace solely on the ground that the officers were in a position to prevent the violations. From a policy point of view, evaluate the public interests that are traded off in holding corporate officers liable on this basis.*

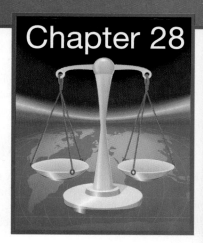

Chapter 28

Corporate Merger, Consolidation, and Termination

"Business is a combination of war and sport."

André Maurois, 1885-1967
(French author and historian)

CHAPTER OBJECTIVES

After reading this chapter, you should be able to:

1. Summarize the procedures involved in a merger or a consolidation.
2. Indicate what appraisal rights are and how they function.
3. Analyze the effects of a corporation's purchase of all or substantially all of another corporation's assets.
4. Discuss the effects of a corporation's purchase of a substantial number of voting shares of another corporation's stock.
5. Explain the phases of corporate termination.

Corporations increase the size of their operations for a number of reasons. They may wish to enlarge their physical plants, for example, or to increase their property or investment holdings. They may wish to acquire the assets, know-how, or goodwill of another corporation. Sometimes, the acquisition of another company is motivated by a desire to eliminate a competitor, to accomplish diversification, or to ensure adequate resources and markets for the acquiring corporation's product. Whatever the reason, during the 1980s, the acquisition of corporations by other corporations became a common phenomenon, and corporate takeovers continue in the 1990s. Observers of the numerous corporate takeovers occurring in the business world today might well conclude, as André Maurois did, that business is indeed a "combination of war and sport."

A corporation typically extends its operations by combining with another corporation through a merger, a consolidation, a purchase of assets, or a purchase of a controlling interest in the other corporation. This chapter will examine these four types of corporate expansion. Dissolution and liquidation are the combined processes by which a corporation terminates its existence. The last part of this chapter will discuss the typical reasons for—and methods used in—terminating a corporation's existence.

▌ Merger and Consolidation

The terms *merger* and *consolidation* often are used interchangeably, but they refer to two legally distinct proceedings. The rights and liabilities of the corporation, its shareholders, and its creditors are the same for both, however.

Merger

MERGER
A contractual and statutory process in which one corporation (the surviving corporation) acquires all of the assets and liabilities of another corporation (the merged corporation). The shareholders of the merged corporation receive either payment for their shares or shares in the surviving corporation.

A **merger** involves the legal combination of two or more corporations in such a way that only one of the corporations continues to exist. For example, Corporation A and Corporation B decide to merge. It is agreed that A will absorb B, so upon merger, B ceases to exist as a separate entity, and A continues as the *surviving corporation*. Exhibit 28–1 graphically illustrates this process.

After the merger, A is recognized as a single corporation, possessing all the rights, privileges, and powers of itself and B. It automatically acquires all of B's property and assets without the necessity of formal transfer. Additionally, A becomes liable for all of B's debts and obligations. Finally, A's articles of incorporation are deemed *amended* to include any changes that are stated in the *articles of merger* (a document setting forth the terms and conditions of the merger that is filed with the secretary of state).

CHOSE IN ACTION
A right that can be enforced in court to recover a debt or to obtain damages.

In a merger, the surviving corporation inherits the disappearing corporation's preexisting legal rights and obligations. For example, if the disappearing corporation had a right of action against a third party, the surviving corporation can bring suit after the merger to recover the disappearing corporation's damages. The corporation statutes of many states provide that a successor (surviving) corporation inherits a **chose**[1] **in action** (a right to sue for a debt or sum of money) from a merging corporation as a matter of law. The common law similarly recognizes that, following a merger, a chose in action to enforce a property right will vest with the successor (surviving) corporation, and no right of action will remain with the disappearing corporation.

Consolidation

CONSOLIDATION
A contractual and statutory process in which two or more corporations join to become a completely new corporation. The original corporations cease to exist, and the new corporation acquires all their assets and liabilities.

In a **consolidation,** two or more corporations combine in such a way that each corporation ceases to exist and a new one emerges. For example, Corporation A and Corporation B consolidate to form an entirely new organization, Corporation C. In the process, A and B both terminate, and C comes into existence as an entirely new entity. Exhibit 28–2 graphically illustrates this process.

---

1.   The word *chose* is French for "thing."

♦ **Exhibit 28–1**
  Merger
  In this illustration, Corporation A and Corporation B decide to merge. They agree that A will absorb B, so after the merger, B no longer exists as a separate entity, and A continues as the surviving corporation.

FRANK AND ERNEST ®by Bob Thaves

Reprinted with permission of Bob Thaves.

As a result of the consolidation, C is recognized as a new corporation and a single entity; A and B cease to exist. C inherits all of the rights, privileges, and powers that A and B previously held. Title to any property and assets owned by A and B passes to C without formal transfer. C assumes liability for all of the debts and obligations owed by A and B. The terms and conditions of the consolidation are set forth in the *articles of consolidation*, which are filed with the secretary of state. These articles *take the place of* A's and B's original corporate articles and are thereafter regarded as C's corporate articles.

Procedure for Merger or Consolidation

All states have statutes authorizing mergers and consolidations for domestic (in-state) corporations, and most states allow the combination of domestic and foreign (out-of-state) corporations. Although the procedures vary somewhat among jurisdictions, the basic requirements for a merger or a consolidation are as follows:

1. The board of directors of each corporation involved must approve a merger or consolidation plan.
2. The shareholders of each corporation must approve the plan, by vote, at a shareholders' meeting. Most state statutes require the approval of two-thirds of the outstanding shares of voting stock, although some states require only a simple majority, and others require a four-fifths vote. Frequently, statutes require that each class of stock approve the merger; thus, the holders of nonvoting stock must also approve. A corporation's bylaws can provide for a stricter requirement.
3. Once approved by all of the directors and shareholders, the plan (articles of merger or consolidation) is filed, usually with the secretary of state.

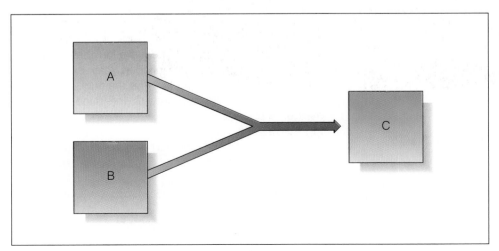

♦ **Exhibit 28–2**
Consolidation
In this illustration, Corporation A and Corporation B consolidate to form an entirely new organization, Corporation C. In the process, A and B terminate, and C comes into existence as an entirely new entity.

4.   When state formalities are satisfied, the state issues a certificate of merger to the surviving corporation or a certificate of consolidation to the newly consolidated corporation.

SHORT-FORM MERGER
A merger between a subsidiary corporation and a parent corporation that owns at least 90 percent of the outstanding shares of each class of stock issued by the subsidiary corporation. Short-form mergers can be accomplished without the approval of the shareholders of either corporation.

RMBCA 11.04 provides for a simplified procedure for the merger of a substantially owned subsidiary corporation into its parent corporation. Under these provisions, a **short-form merger** can be accomplished *without the approval of the shareholders* of either corporation. The short-form merger can be used only when the parent corporation owns at least 90 percent of the outstanding shares of each class of stock of the subsidiary corporation. The simplified procedure requires that a plan for the merger be approved by the board of directors of the parent corporation before it is filed with the state. A copy of the merger plan must be sent to each shareholder of record of the subsidiary corporation. In the following case, a minority group of shareholders objected to a short-form merger undertaken to "cash out" public shareholders (including the plaintiffs in this case).

CASE 28.1

ROLAND INTERNATIONAL CORP. v. NAJJAR
Supreme Court of Delaware, 1979.
407 A.2d 1032.

HISTORICAL AND SOCIAL SETTING *Corporate property belongs to all shareholders, and those in control of a corporation are accountable to all owners of the corporate property. These concepts underlie the rule that majority shareholders—who have the power to control corporate property—owe a fiduciary duty to minority shareholders. This duty is violated when those who control a corporation's voting machinery use that power to exclude minority shareholders from continued participation in the corporate life for no reason other than to eliminate them. In a case decided in 1977, the Supreme Court of Delaware held that "when a freeze-out of minority stockholders on a cash-out basis is alleged to be [a merger's] sole purpose," and it is alleged that "the purpose is improper," a court must consider the allegation "because of the fiduciary obligation owed to the minority."*[a] *The case involved a regular merger. Undecided at that time was whether the same rule applied to a short-form merger.*

FACTS   Roland International Corporation was 97.6 percent owned by Hyatt Corporation and others. This controlling group of shareholders created Landro Corporation for the purpose of merging it with Roland. All

of the statutory requirements for a short-form merger were met, and the minority (public) shareholders were offered $5.25 per share for each share of Roland stock that they owned. If this price was not acceptable, the minority group could have their shares evaluated under the Delaware appraisal statute. Najjar brought a class-action suit in a Delaware state court on behalf of the minority shareholders, seeking damages. Najjar claimed that the merger was simply an effort to eliminate the public shareholders and that it had been grossly unfair to those shareholders. The defendants (the majority group) moved for dismissal, contending that a proper purpose is conclusively presumed when the conditions of the short-form merger statutes are met; thus the plaintiffs had no cause of action. The trial court denied the motion, and the defendants appealed.

ISSUE   May a court examine a short-form merger to see if it was undertaken for a proper purpose?

DECISION   Yes. The Supreme Court of Delaware affirmed the trial court's denial of the defendants' motion to dismiss.

REASON   The court held that the short-form merger statute does not create a presumption that the merger serves a valid purpose. The court may examine such mergers to determine whether the majority shareholders have met their fiduciary duty to the minority. When a merger is undertaken with the sole purpose of eliminating the minority shareholders, it constitutes a breach of that duty. The plaintiff thus had a cause of action, and the defendants' motion to dismiss was properly denied.

FOR CRITICAL ANALYSIS—Social Consideration
Why do state laws allow short-form mergers to be undertaken without shareholder approval?

a.   *Singer v. Magnavox Co.*, 380 A.2d 969 (Del.Sup. 1977).

Shareholder Approval

Shareholders invest in a corporate enterprise with the expectation that the board of directors will manage the enterprise and will approve ordinary business matters. Actions taken on extraordinary matters must be authorized by the board of directors and the shareholders. Often, modern statutes require that the shareholders approve certain types of extraordinary matters—such as the sale, lease, or exchange of all or substantially all corporate assets outside of the corporation's regular course of business. Other examples of matters requiring shareholder approval include amendments to the articles of incorporation, transactions concerning merger or consolidation, and dissolution.

Hence, when any extraordinary matter arises, the corporation must proceed as authorized by law to obtain the approval of the shareholders and the board of directors. Sometimes, a transaction can be characterized in such a way as not to require shareholder approval, but in that event, a court will use its equity powers to require such approval. To determine the nature of the transaction, the courts will look not only to the details of the transaction but also to its consequences.

REMEMBER State statutes, articles of incorporation, and corporate bylaws can require the approval of more than a majority of shares for some extraordinary matters.

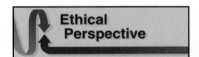
Ethical Perspective

The rule requiring shareholder approval for certain types of corporate actions protects the shareholders' interests in the corporate enterprise. Clearly, the shareholder-owners have a stake in the corporation's survival and profitability. Sometimes, corporate directors and officers may take certain actions—such as selling various corporate assets—over a period of time so that the shareholders do not realize how significantly the total number of assets is dwindling. In such a situation, however, a court normally will use its equity powers to require the approval of the shareholders.

For example, in one case, a corporation was formed for the purpose of engaging in the restaurant business. One of the three shareholders, who was the corporate president, sold off the assets of the company until only one restaurant remained. When the president entered into a contract to sell this remaining asset, the other two shareholders sought to have a court issue an injunction prohibiting the sale. The court did so, in accordance with state law, which prohibited the sale of all or substantially all of a corporation's assets without shareholder approval. The court stated that the purpose of the law was "to protect the shareholders from . . . the destruction of the means to accomplish the purpose or objects for which the corporation was incorporated and actually performs."[a]

For Critical Analysis: *Recall from Chapter 1 that the equitable remedy of an injunction normally will be granted only if the remedy at law (money damages) is inadequate. Why would damages be inadequate in the case just described?*

a. *Schwadel v. Uchitel*, 455 So.2d 401 (Fla.App. 1984).

Appraisal Rights

What if a shareholder disapproves of a merger or a consolidation but is outvoted by the other shareholders? The law recognizes that a dissenting shareholder should not be forced to become an unwilling shareholder in a corporation that is new or different from the one in which the shareholder originally invested. The shareholder has the right to dissent and may be entitled to be paid the *fair value* for the number of shares held on the date of the merger or consolidation. This right is referred to as the shareholder's **appraisal right.**

Appraisal rights are available only when a state statute specifically provides for them. Appraisal rights normally extend to regular mergers, consolidations, short-form

APPRAISAL RIGHT
The right of a dissenting shareholder, if he or she objects to an extraordinary transaction of the corporation (such as a merger or consolidation), to have his or her shares appraised and to be paid the fair value of his or her shares by the corporation.

> *"The greatest of all gifts is the power to estimate things at their true worth."*
>
> **François La Rochefoucauld, 1613–1680**
> *(French writer and moralist)*

mergers, and sales of substantially all of the corporate assets not in the ordinary course of business.

Shareholders may lose their appraisal rights if they do not follow precisely the elaborate statutory procedures. Whenever they lose the right to an appraisal, dissenting shareholders must go along with the transaction despite their objections. One of the usual basic requirements is a written notice of dissent filed by dissenting shareholders prior to the vote of the shareholders on the proposed transaction. This notice of dissent is also basically a notice to all shareholders of the costs that dissenting shareholders may impose should the merger or consolidation be approved. In addition, after approval, the dissenting shareholders must make a written demand for payment and for the fair value of their shares.

Valuation of shares is often a point of contention between the dissenting shareholder and the corporation. RMBCA 13.01 provides that the "fair value of shares" normally is the value on the day prior to the date on which the vote was taken. The corporation must make a *written* offer to purchase a dissenting shareholder's stock, accompanying the offer with a current balance sheet and income statement for the corporation. If the shareholder and the corporation do not agree on the fair value, a court will determine it.

Once a dissenting shareholder elects appraisal rights under a statute, in some jurisdictions, the shareholder loses his or her shareholder status. Without that status, a shareholder cannot vote, receive dividends, or sue to enjoin whatever action prompted his or her dissent. In some of those jurisdictions, statutes provide, or courts have held, that shareholder status may be reinstated during the appraisal process (for example, if the shareholder decides to withdraw from the process and the corporation approves). In other jurisdictions, shareholder status may not be reinstated until the appraisal is concluded. Even if an individual loses his or her shareholder status, courts may allow the individual to sue on the ground of fraud or other illegal conduct associated with the merger.

A shareholder cannot sue on the ground of fraud or other illegal conduct, however, if the shareholder's complaint is really about the price that he or she received for the stock. For complaints about price, appraisal rights are the exclusive remedy, as illustrated in the following case.

GRACE BROTHERS, LTD. v. FARLEY INDUSTRIES, INC.

Supreme Court of Georgia, 1994.
264 Ga. 817,
450 S.E.2d 814.

COMPANY PROFILE *West Point–Pepperell (WPP) started business in the nineteenth century as separate textile companies, West Point in Georgia and Pepperell in Maine. After the merger of the two companies in the 1960s, WPP became a large, successful conglomerate. Its success attracted William Farley, who had founded Farley Industries, Inc., in 1976. Owner of Fruit of the Loom, Inc., and other textile companies, Farley attempted a takeover of WPP. The firm fought back, and the Georgia legislature passed an antitakeover statute to block Farley's bid.*

FACTS William Farley, through Farley Industries, Inc., and other companies, made a tender offer (an offer to purchase shares in the company made by another company directly to the target company's shareholders) of $58 per share for the stock of WPP. This was far more than the price of WPP stock on the New York Stock Exchange. WPP's board of directors approved the offer and sold 95 percent of the stock to Farley. WPP also agreed to merge with West Point Tender Corporation (WPTC), a Farley entity, after which the last 5 percent of WPP shareholders would be paid $58 per share. Before the WPP-WPTC merger could take place, Farley encountered financial troubles and announced that he could pay no more than $46 per share to Grace Brothers, Ltd., and other minority shareholders. Grace and the others filed a suit in a Georgia state court against Farley, alleging, among other things, that Farley breached a fiduciary duty by not paying $58 per share, as promised in the merger agreement. The court dismissed the claim, and the plaintiffs appealed.

Case 28.2—Continued

ISSUE   Are appraisal rights the exclusive remedy for dissenting shareholders' complaints about stock prices?

DECISION   Yes. The Supreme Court of Georgia affirmed the dismissal.

REASON   The state supreme court concluded that the shareholders' claim "boils down to nothing more than a complaint about stock price." For such complaints, "our statutory appraisal remedy is exclusive. It permits a dissenting shareholder to be paid the fair value of his shares and preempts any other remedy." As for the alleged wrongdoing, "any facts which shed light on the value of the dissenting shareholders' interests are to be considered in arriving at 'fair value.'"

FOR CRITICAL ANALYSIS—Economic Consideration
Besides Farley's "alleged wrongdoing," what other facts might "shed light on the value of the dissenting shareholders' interests" in determining the fair value of shares?

▌ Purchase of Assets

When a corporation acquires all or substantially all of the assets of another corporation by direct purchase, the purchasing, or *acquiring*, corporation simply extends its ownership and control over more physical assets. Because no change in the legal entity occurs, the acquiring corporation is not required to obtain shareholder approval for the purchase.[2]

Although the acquiring corporation may not be required to obtain shareholder approval for such an acquisition, the U.S. Department of Justice and the Federal Trade Commission have issued guidelines that significantly constrain and often prohibit mergers that could result from a purchase of assets, including takeover bids. These guidelines are discussed in Chapter 30, in the context of federal antitrust laws.

Note that the corporation that is selling all its assets is substantially changing its business position and perhaps its ability to carry out its corporate purposes. For that reason, the corporation whose assets are acquired must obtain the approval of both the board of directors and the shareholders. In most states and under RMBCA 13.02, a dissenting shareholder of the selling corporation can demand appraisal rights.

Generally, a corporation that purchases the assets of another corporation is not responsible for the liabilities of the selling corporation. Exceptions to this rule are made in the following circumstances:

1.   When the purchasing corporation impliedly or expressly assumes the seller's liabilities.
2.   When the sale amounts to what in fact is a merger or consolidation.
3.   When the purchaser continues the seller's business and retains the same personnel (same shareholders, directors, and officers).
4.   When the sale is fraudulently executed to escape liability.

In any of these situations, the acquiring corporation will be held to have assumed both the assets and the liabilities of the selling corporation.

There are several factors for determining whether a purchase of assets is in fact a merger. The court considers these factors in the following case.

RECALL In a merger or consolidation, the surviving corporation inherits the disappearing corporation's rights and obligations.

---

2.   If the acquiring corporation plans to pay for the assets with its own corporate stock and not enough authorized unissued shares are available, the shareholders must vote to approve issuance of additional shares by amendment of the corporate articles. Additionally, acquiring corporations whose stock is traded in a national stock exchange can be required to obtain their own shareholders' approval if they plan to issue a significant number of shares, such as a number equal to 20 percent or more of the outstanding shares.

CASE 28.3

SEDBROOK v. ZIMMERMAN DESIGN GROUP, LTD.
Court of Appeals of Wisconsin, 1994.
190 Wis.2d 14,
526 N.W.2d 758.

HISTORICAL AND ECONOMIC SETTING *Since 1970, the public has generally opposed what is sometimes perceived as attempts by plaintiffs in product liability suits against big companies to collect fat awards and "retire." In fact, however, the average award of damages in product liability suits between 1989 and 1992 was about $400,000, and in 1993 and 1994, about $500,000. Over the same period, the number of suits actually declined. The percentage of plaintiffs who recovered also declined, from 55 percent in 1989 to 42 percent in 1994.*

FACTS When EG&G, Inc., took over the E. Van Noorden Company, the manufacturer of Vanco-brand skylights, Van Noorden shareholders traded their stock for EG&G stock. Van Noorden ceased to exist. EG&G assumed Van Noorden's customer and supplier relationships and acquired all of Van Noorden's assets. EG&G continued to make Vanco skylights, using the same factory and employees, as well as at least two key Van Noorden officers. EG&G also assumed all of the obligations of Van Noorden necessary for uninterrupted operations. Clarence Sedbrook fell through a Vanco skylight on a hospital roof and suffered permanent injuries. Sedbrook and his family filed a suit in a Wisconsin state court against Zimmerman Design Group, Ltd. (the firm

that designed the roof), EG&G, and others. EG&G asked to be dismissed from the suit on the ground that Van Noorden had manufactured the skylight before EG&G had purchased Van Noorden's assets. The court granted the request. Sedbrook appealed.

ISSUE Did EG&G, when it acquired Van Noorden's assets, assume Van Noorden's liability for manufacturing a defective product?

DECISION Yes. The Court of Appeals of Wisconsin reversed the lower court's decision and remanded the case for trial.

REASON The state appellate court held, among other things, that EG&G's acquisition of Van Noorden qualified as a merger. The court listed four factors for determining whether a purchase of assets is in fact a merger: "(1) the assets of the seller corporation are acquired with shares of the stock in the buyer corporation * * * ; (2) the seller ceases operations and dissolves soon after the sale; (3) the buyer continues the enterprise of the seller corporation so that there is a continuity of management, employees, business location, assets and general business operations; and (4) the buyer assumes those liabilities of the seller necessary for the uninterrupted continuation of normal business operations." The court found all of those factors present in this case. "[A]s a result, there is no legal bar to Sedbrook's asserting a * * * claim against EG&G for its predecessor's potential liability."

FOR CRITICAL ANALYSIS—Social Consideration *In determining whether a merger occurred, which of the four factors listed by the court do you think was the most important, and why?*

▊ Purchase of Stock

An alternative to the purchase of another corporation's assets is the purchase of a substantial number of the voting shares of its stock. This enables the acquiring corporation to control the acquired corporation. The acquiring corporation deals directly with the target company's shareholders in seeking to purchase the shares they hold. It does this by making a *tender offer* to all of the shareholders of the corporation to be acquired, or the **target corporation.** The tender offer is publicly advertised and addressed to all shareholders of the target company. The price of the stock in the tender offer is generally higher than the market price of the target stock prior to the announcement of the tender offer. The higher price induces shareholders to tender their shares to the acquiring firm.

The tender offer can be conditioned on the receipt of a specified number of outstanding shares by a specified date. The offering corporation can make an *exchange tender offer* in which it offers target stockholders its own securities in exchange for their

TARGET CORPORATION
The corporation to be acquired in a corporate takeover; a corporation to whose shareholders a tender offer is submitted.

♦ Exhibit 28–3
The Terminology of Takeover Defenses

TERM	DEFINITION
Crown Jewel	When threatened with a takeover, management makes the company less attractive to the raider by selling to a third party the company's most valuable asset (hence the term *crown jewel*).
Golden Parachute	When a takeover is successful, top management is usually changed. With this in mind, a company may establish special termination or retirement benefits that must be paid to top management if they are "retired." In other words, a departing high-level manager's parachute will be "golden" when he or she is forced to "bail out" of the company.
Greenmail	To regain control, a target company may pay a higher-than-market price to repurchase the stock that the acquiring corporation bought. When a takeover is attempted through a gradual accumulation of target stock rather than a tender offer, the intent may be to get the target company to buy back the accumulated shares at a premium price—a concept similar to blackmail.
Lobster Trap	Lobster traps are designed to catch large lobsters but to allow small lobsters to escape. In the "lobster trap" defense, holders of convertible securities (corporate bonds or stock that is convertible into common shares) are prohibited from converting the securities into common shares if the holders already own, or would own after conversion, 10 percent or more of the voting shares of stock.
Pac-Man	Named after the Atari video game, this is an aggressive defense by which the target corporation attempts its own takeover of the acquiring corporation.
Poison Pill	The target corporation issues to its stockholders shares that can be turned in for cash if a takeover is successful. This makes the takeover undesirably or even prohibitively expensive for the acquiring corporation.
Scorched Earth	The target corporation sells off assets or divisions or takes out loans that it agrees to repay in the event of a takeover, thus making itself less financially attractive to the acquiring corporation.
Shark Repellent	To make a takeover more difficult, a target company may change its articles of incorporation or bylaws. For example, the bylaws may be amended to require that a large number of shareholders approve the firm's combination. This tactic casts the acquiring corporation in the role of a shark that must be repelled.
White Knight	The target corporation solicits a merger with a third party, which then makes a better (often simply a higher) tender offer to the target's shareholders. The third party that "rescues" the target is the "white knight."

target stock. In a *cash tender offer,* the offering corporation offers the target stockholders cash in exchange for their target stock.

Federal securities laws strictly control the terms, duration, and circumstances under which most tender offers are made. In addition, a majority of states have passed takeover statutes that impose additional regulations on tender offers.

A firm may respond to a tender offer in numerous ways. Sometimes, a target firm's board of directors will see a tender offer as favorable and will recommend to the shareholders that they accept it. To resist a takeover, a target company may make a *self-tender,* which is an offer to acquire stock from its own shareholders and thereby retain corporate control. Alternatively, a target corporation might resort to one of several other tactics to resist a takeover (see Exhibit 28–3).

▌ Termination

The termination of a corporation's existence has two phases. **Dissolution** is the legal death of the artificial "person" of the corporation. **Liquidation** is the process by which

DISSOLUTION
The formal disbanding of a partnership or a corporation. Dissolution of a corporation can take place by (1) an act of the state legislature, (2) agreement of the shareholders and the board of directors, (3) the expiration of a time period stated in the certificate of incorporation, or (4) court order.

LIQUIDATION
In regard to corporations, the process by which corporate assets are converted into cash and distributed among creditors and shareholders according to specific rules of preference.

BUSINESS LAW IN ACTION

Hostile Takeovers— Who Wins, and Who Loses?

During the 1980s and 1990s, the tactics of corporate raiders, arbitrageurs, boards of directors, and investment banking firms have caught the attention of the press, politicians, and laypersons alike. A number of corporate raiders have become famous—some because they have gone to jail for resorting to illegal activities. Why do hostile takeovers occur? Who benefits from hostile takeovers?

To answer these thorny questions, consider an example. A corporate raider learns, through diligent research and personal contacts, that a certain publicly traded company seems to be undervalued in the marketplace. In other words, the public, or market, value of the company appears to be less than its true value. The corporate raider starts to acquire shares of stock of the company. Eventually, word gets out that he or she is doing this, and typically, the market value of the stock rises. At some point, the corporate raider may make a tender offer to purchase a certain percentage of the

outstanding shares of stock at a price that exceeds the current market price. If the corporate raider succeeds, he or she will acquire voting control of the corporation, oust the board of directors, put in his or her own men and women, and take over the corporation. Often, after this is done, the new board of directors will sell off certain parts of the company and restructure other parts. In the process, the lives of the previous managers and employees are altered—many of them are fired.

Clearly, in this situation, the corporate raider—providing that the new management can increase the company's profits—will gain. It could also be argued that the shareholders, who received a higher-than-market price for their shares, benefited from the takeover. The losers here are the corporate directors, officers, and managers who are fired.

Often, the ethics of corporate raiders have been called into question. Realize, though, that typically a corporate raider will target only a corporation that is poorly managed—for if a corporation is well managed, its profits and its profit potential will be high and will be reflected in a high market value, thus making it an unlikely candidate for a takeover. When a corporate raider chooses a poorly managed company as his or her target, a certain group of individuals will gain—current

shareholders. Another group will lose—current management and some employees.

Sometimes, corporate raiders may go past any well-reasoned ethical boundary. This occurs in the case of *greenmail*. In a greenmail situation, the purported corporate raider has no intention of actually making a raid on the corporation, but he or she gives the impression that a takeover attempt is going to occur. The raider purchases a large block of stock and dangles a threat of purchasing more of the stock in front of current management. Often, the board of directors, in an attempt to make sure that no corporate raid occurs, will agree to buy back this large block of stock at an inflated price. In this situation, the winners include both the corporate raider (who obtains a handsome profit) and current management (who have made sure that their jobs are protected). The actual losers are the shareholders.

For Critical Analysis: *Is it ever ethical for corporate directors and managers to resist a takeover attempt if the shareholders would benefit from the takeover?*

corporate assets are converted into cash and distributed among creditors and shareholders according to specific rules of preference (see Chapter 26).

"Lots of folks confuse bad management with destiny."

Kin (F. McKinney) Hubbard, 1868–1930
(American humorist and journalist)

Dissolution

Dissolution of a corporation can be brought about in any of the following ways:

1. An act of a legislature in the state of incorporation.
2. Expiration of the time provided in the certificate of incorporation.
3. Voluntary approval of the shareholders and the board of directors.
4. Unanimous action by all shareholders.
5. A court decree brought about by the attorney general of the state of incorporation for any of the following reasons: (a) the failure to comply with administrative requirements (for example, failure to pay annual franchise taxes, to submit an annual report,

or to have a designated registered agent), (b) the procurement of a corporation charter through fraud or misrepresentation on the state, (c) the abuse of corporate powers (*ultra vires* acts), (d) the violation of the state criminal code after the demand to discontinue has been made by the secretary of state, (e) the failure to commence business operations, or (f) the abandonment of operations before starting up [RMBCA 14.20].

As discussed in Chapter 27, sometimes a shareholder or a group of shareholders petitions a court for corporate dissolution. For example, the board of directors may be deadlocked. Courts hesitate to order involuntary dissolution in such circumstances unless there is specific statutory authorization to do so. If the deadlock cannot be resolved by the shareholders and if it will irreparably injure the corporation, however, the court will proceed with an involuntary dissolution. Courts can also dissolve a corporation in other circumstances, such as when the controlling shareholders or directors are committing fraudulent or oppressive acts or when management is misapplying or wasting corporate assets [RMBCA 14.30].

In Canada, ownership of corporations is frequently concentrated in the hands of a few controlling shareholders. Unlike the United States, Canada does not recognize a fiduciary duty of controlling shareholders toward minority shareholders. Canada does have a doctrine of "fraud on the minority," however. This doctrine applies only to extreme situations. Canada also has "oppression statutes" that place some restrictions on the actions of majority shareholders.

For Critical Analysis: *Courts in both the United States and Canada will grant minority shareholders' petitions to dissolve a corporation only in extreme circumstances. How else (other than petitioning for dissolution) can minority shareholders protect themselves against majority shareholders' actions that are adverse to their interests?*

Liquidation

When dissolution takes place by voluntary action, the members of the board of directors act as trustees of the corporate assets. As trustees, they are responsible for winding up the affairs of the corporation for the benefit of corporate creditors and shareholders. This makes the board members personally liable for any breach of their fiduciary trustee duties.

Liquidation can be accomplished without court supervision unless the members of the board do not wish to act as trustees of the corporate assets, or unless shareholders or creditors can show cause to the court why the board should not be permitted to assume the trustee function. In either case, the court will appoint a receiver to wind up the corporate affairs and liquidate corporate assets. A receiver is always appointed by the court if the dissolution is involuntary.

CONTRAST Except during liquidation, directors do not act as trustees of the corporate assets. Although they are in positions of control over the corporation, they do not hold title to its property.

▌Key Terms

appraisal right 727	dissolution 731	short-form merger 726
chose in action 724	liquidation 731	target corporation 730
consolidation 725	merger 724	

▌Chapter Summary: Corporate Merger, Consolidation, and Termination

Merger and Consolidation
(See pages 724–729.)
	1. *Merger*—The legal combination of two or more corporations, the result of which is that the surviving corporation acquires all the assets and obligations of the other corporation, which then ceases to exist.
	2. *Consolidation*—The legal combination of two or more corporations, the result of which is that each corporation ceases to exist and a new one emerges. The new corporation assumes all the assets and obligations of the former corporations.
	3. *Procedure*—Determined by state statutes. Basic requirements are the following:
	  a. The board of directors of each corporation involved must approve the merger or consolidation plan.
	  b. The shareholders of each corporation must approve the merger or consolidation plan at a shareholders' meeting.
	  c. Articles of merger or consolidation (the plan) must be filed, usually with the secretary of state.
	  d. The state issues a certificate of merger (or consolidation) to the surviving (or newly consolidated) corporation.
	4. *Short-form merger (parent-subsidiary merger)*—Possible when the parent corporation owns at least 90 percent of the outstanding shares of each class of stock of the subsidiary corporation.
	  a. Shareholder approval is not required.
	  b. The merger must be approved only by the board of directors of the parent corporation.
	  c. A copy of the merger plan must be sent to each shareholder of record.
	  d. The merger plan must be filed with the state.
	5. *Appraisal rights*—Rights of shareholders (given by state statute) to receive the *fair value* for their shares when a merger or consolidation takes place. If the shareholder and the corporation do not agree on the fair value, a court will determine it.

Purchase of Assets (See pages 729–730.)	A purchase of assets occurs when one corporation acquires all or substantially all of the assets of another corporation. 1. *Acquiring corporation*—The acquiring (purchasing) corporation is not required to obtain shareholder approval; the corporation is merely increasing its assets, and no fundamental business change occurs. 2. *Acquired corporation*—The acquired (purchased) corporation is required to obtain the approval of both its directors and its shareholders for the sale of its assets, because this creates a substantial change in the corporation's business position.
Purchase of Stock (See pages 730–731.)	A purchase of stock occurs when one corporation acquires a substantial number of the voting shares of the stock of another (target) corporation. 1. *Tender offer*—A public offer to all shareholders of the target corporation to purchase its stock at a price generally higher than the market price of the target stock prior to the announcement of the tender offer. Federal and state securities laws strictly control the terms, duration, and circumstances under which most tender offers are made. 2. *Target responses*—Ways in which target corporations respond to takeover bids. These include self-tender (the target firm's offer to acquire its own shareholders' stock), the Pac-Man defense (the target firm's takeover of the acquiring corporation), and numerous other strategies (see Exhibit 28–3).

Termination
(See pages 731–733.)
	The termination of a corporation involves the following two phases:
	1. *Dissolution*—The legal death of the artificial "person" of the corporation. Dissolution can be brought about in any of the following ways:
	  a. An act of a legislature in the state of incorporation.
	  b. Expiration of the time provided in the corporate charter.
	  c. Voluntary approval of the shareholders and the board of directors.
	  d. Unanimous action by all shareholders.
	  e. Court decree.
	2. *Liquidation*—The process by which corporate assets are converted into cash and distributed to creditors and shareholders according to specified rules of preference. May be supervised by members of the board of directors (when dissolution is voluntary) or by a receiver appointed by the court to wind up corporate affairs.

■ For Review

1. What is the difference between a merger and a consolidation?
2. What are the four steps of the merger or consolidation procedure?
3. Under what circumstances is a corporation that purchases the assets of another corporation responsible for the liabilities of the selling corporation?

4. A target corporation can use a number of defenses to resist a takeover. Name five such defenses.
5. What are the two ways in which a corporation can be voluntarily dissolved? Under what circumstances might a corporation be involuntarily dissolved by state action?

■ Questions and Case Problems

28–1. Consolidations. Determine which of the following situations describes a consolidation:
   (a) Arkon Corp. purchases all of the assets of Botrek Co.
   (b) Arkon Corp. and Botrek Co. combine their firms, with Arkon Corp. as the surviving corporation.
   (c) Arkon Corp. and Botrek Co. agree to combine their assets, dissolve their old corporations, and form a new corporation under a new name.
   (d) Arkon Corp. agrees to sell all its accounts receivable to Botrek Co.

28–2. Corporate Combinations. Jolson is chairman of the board of directors of Artel, Inc., and Douglas is chairman of the board of directors of Fox Express, Inc. Artel is a manufacturing corporation, and Fox Express is a transportation corporation. Jolson and Douglas meet to consider the possibility of combining their corporations and activities into a single corporate entity. They consider two alternative courses of action: Artel could acquire all of the stock and assets of Fox Express, or the corporations could combine to form a new corporation, called A&F Enterprises, Inc. Both chairmen are concerned about the necessity of a formal transfer of property, liability for existing debts, and the problem of amending the articles of incorporation. Discuss what the two proposed combinations are called and the legal effect each has on the transfer of property, the liabilities of the combined corporations, and the need to amend the articles of incorporation.

28–3. Mergers. Tally Ho Co. was merged into Perfecto Corp., with Perfecto being the surviving corporation in the merger. Hanjo, a creditor of Tally Ho, brought suit against Perfecto Corp. for payment of the debt. The directors of Perfecto refused to pay, stating that Tally Ho no longer existed and that Perfecto had never agreed to assume any of Tally Ho's liabilities. Discuss fully whether Hanjo will be able to recover from Perfecto.

28–4. Purchase of Assets. Fuju Enterprises, Inc., purchased all the assets of Grosmont Corp. The directors of both corporations approved the sale, and 80 percent of Grosmont's shareholders approved. The shareholders of Fuju Enterprises, however, were never consulted. Some of these shareholders claimed that the purchase was invalid. Are they correct?

28–5. Corporate Dissolution. Two brothers, Albert and Raymond Martin, each owned 50 percent of the stock in Martin's News Service, Inc. Albert and Raymond had difficulty working together and communicated only through their accountant. For ten years, there were no corporate meetings, elections to the board of directors, or other corporate formalities. During that time, Raymond operated the business much as a sole proprietorship, failing to consult Albert on any matter and making all of the decisions himself. The corporation, however, was a viable concern that had grown successfully through the years. Albert sued to have the corporation dissolved. Should he succeed? Discuss. [*Martin v. Martin's News Service, Inc.*, 9 Conn.App. 304, 518 A.2d 951 (1986)]

28–6. Corporate Dissolution. I. Burack, Inc., was a family-operated close corporation that sold plumbing supplies in New York. The founder, Israel Burack, transferred his shares in the corporation to other family members, and when Israel died in 1974, the position of president passed to his son, Robert Burack. Robert held a one-third interest in the company, and the remainder was divided among Israel's other children and grandchildren. All of the shareholders participated in the corporation as employees or officers and thus relied on salaries and bonuses, rather than dividends, for distribution of the corporation's earnings. In 1976, several of the family-member employees requested a salary increase from Robert, who claimed that company earnings were not sufficient to warrant any employee salary increases. Shortly thereafter, a shareholders' meeting was held (the first in the company's fifty-year history), and Robert was removed from his position as president and denied the right to participate in any way in the corporation. Robert sued to have the company dissolved because he had been "frozen out" of the business by the allegedly oppressive tactics of the other shareholders. Discuss whether Robert should succeed in his suit or whether the court would choose another alternative. [*Burack v. I. Burack, Inc.*, 137 A.D.2d 523, 524 N.Y.S.2d 457 (1988)]

28–7. Mergers and Consolidations. Edward Antar and William Markowitz were the sole stockholders and directors of E.B.M., Inc., a corporation formed for the purpose of buying and managing real estate. Antar and Markowitz were also the controlling shareholders and directors of Acousti-Phase, Inc., a corporation that manufactured and sold stereo speakers. In 1982, Acousti-Phase was effectively shut down when a fire destroyed the manufacturing and storage facility that it was renting from E.B.M. Shortly after the fire, E.B.M. contracted with a New York firm to assemble the speakers, affix the Acousti-Phase name, and sell the final product, primarily to former customers of Acousti-Phase. At the time of the fire, Acousti-Phase owed $26,470 to Cab-Tek, Inc., a corporation that supplied it with cabinet housings for its stereo speakers. In

1985, Cab-Tek sued E.B.M. to recover the debt owed by Acousti-Phase. Discuss fully whether E.B.M. can be held liable for Acousti-Phase's debt. [*Cab-Tek, Inc. v. E.B.M., Inc.*, 153 Vt. 432, 571 A.2d 671 (1990)]

28–8. Purchase of Assets. In 1987, William Myers sustained injuries to his hand while operating a concrete cement pump that had been designed and manufactured by Thomsen Equipment Co. and purchased from Thomsen in 1981. Myers alleged that the pump was unreasonably dangerous because it had an "unguarded nip point in a flapper valve." Putzmeister, Inc., had purchased Thomsen's assets in 1982. Assuming that Myers has a valid product liability claim, what factors will the court consider in determining whether Putzmeister, as a successor corporation, can be held liable for injuries caused by Thomsen's product? [*Myers v. Putzmeister, Inc.*, 232 Ill.App.3d 419, 596 N.E.2d 754, 173 Ill.Dec. 130 (1992)]

28–9. Purchase of Assets. Lori Nilsson, while working as a machine operator, was injured by a pipe and tube cutoff machine that had been manufactured and sold by Continental Machine Co. (CM) prior to 1978. In 1986, Fredor Corp. purchased all of the production assets of CM, including the pipe and tube machine product line, and formed Continental Machine Manufacturing Co. (CMM). CMM continued to manufacture the same product lines as CM had. The shareholders of CM did not become shareholders, officers, or employees of Fredor or CMM. Most of the employees of CM became employees of CMM, however. There was no evidence that the transaction was undertaken for a fraudulent purpose, nor did Fredor or CMM agree to assume CM's liabilities. After the sale of assets, CM continued to exist, but it had no productive assets. CM continued to own the building in which the assets had been located, however, and leased the building to CMM. Nilsson brought a product liability suit against CMM. Should CMM be held liable for injuries caused by a machine manufactured by CM? How will the court decide this issue? Discuss fully. [*Nilsson v. Continental Machine Manufacturing Co.*, 251 Ill.App.3d 415, 621 N.E.2d 1032, 190 Ill.Dec. 579 (1993)]

28–10. Purchase of Assets. MRS Manufacturing, Inc., manufactured tractors, which it sold to Glades Equipment, Inc. Glades Equipment sold one of the tractors to the U.S. Sugar Corp. Later, Glade and Grove Supply, Inc., bought the Glades Equipment dealership under a contract that stated the sale covered only such property "as [Glades Equipment] has on hand at the time of the . . . sale." Daniel Brown, an employee of the U.S. Sugar Corp., was operating an MRS tractor when it rolled over and killed him. His wife, Patricia, filed a product liability suit against, among others, Glade and Grove. What factors will the court consider in determining whether Glade and Grove is liable? [*Brown v. Glade and Grove Supply, Inc.*, 647 So.2d 1033 (Fla.App. 1994)]

28–11. Appraisal Rights. Travelers Corp. announced that it would merge with Primerica Corp. At a special shareholders

meeting, a vote of the Travelers shareholders revealed that 95 percent approved of the merger. Robert Brandt and other shareholders who did not approve of the merger sued Travelers and others, complaining that the defendants had not obtained "the highest possible price for shareholders." Travelers asked the court to dismiss the suit, contending that Brandt and the others had, as a remedy for their complaint, their statutory appraisal rights. On what basis might the court dismiss the suit? Discuss. [*Brandt v. Travelers Corp.*, 44 Conn.Supp. 12, 665 A.2d 616 (1995)]

A QUESTION OF ETHICS AND SOCIAL RESPONSIBILITY

28–12. *In a corporate merger, Diamond Shamrock retained its corporate identity, and Natomas Corp. was absorbed into Diamond's corporate hierarchy. Five inside directors (directors who are also officers of the corporation) of Natomas had golden parachutes, which were incorporated into the merger agreement. The terms of the parachute agreements provided that each of the five individuals would receive a payment equal to three years' compensation in the event that they left their positions at Natomas at any time for any reason other than termination for just cause. Three of the five voluntarily left their positions after three years. Under the terms of their parachute agreements, they collected over $10 million. A suit challenging the golden parachutes was brought by Gaillard, a Natomas shareholder. A trial court granted the defendants' motion for summary judgment; the court sustained the golden parachutes on the ground that the directors were protected by the business judgment rule in effecting the agreement. The appellate court held that the business judgment rule does not apply in a review of the conduct of inside directors and remanded the case for trial. [Gaillard v. Natomas, 208 Cal.App.3d 1250, 256 Cal.Rptr. 702 (1989)]*

1. Regardless of the legal issues, are golden parachutes ethical in a general sense? Discuss.

2. What practical considerations would lead a corporation to *want* to grant its top management such seemingly one-sided agreements?

3. In the *Gaillard* case, how would your views be affected by evidence showing that the golden parachutes had been developed and presented to the board by the very individuals who were the beneficiaries of the agreements—that is, by the five inside directors?

FOR CRITICAL ANALYSIS

28–13. *A corporation that purchases the assets of another corporation generally is not liable for the obligations and duties of the predecessor corporation. Exceptions to this rule are made when the purchasing corporation assumes the liabilities, fraud is involved, or the transaction is actually a merger or merely a change of name. Why are these exceptions made?*

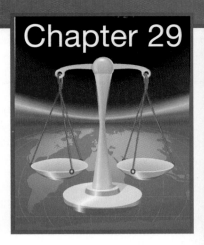

Investor Protection

*"It shall be unlawful for any person in the offer or sale
of any security . . . to engage in any transaction,
practice, or course of business which operates or
would operate as a fraud or deceit upon the purchaser."*

Securities Act of 1933, Section 17

CHAPTER OBJECTIVES

After reading this chapter, you should be able to:

1. Define what is meant by the term *securities*.
2. Describe the purpose and provisions of the Securities Act of 1933.
3. Explain the purpose and provisions of the Securities Exchange Act of 1934.
4. Identify federal laws that specifically regulate investment companies.
5. Point out some of the features of state securities laws.

After the great stock market crash of 1929, various studies showed a need for regulating securities markets. Basically, legislation for such regulation was enacted to provide investors with more information to help them make buying and selling decisions about **securities**—generally defined as any documents evidencing corporate ownership (stock) or debts (bonds)—and to prohibit deceptive, unfair, and manipulative practices. Today, the sale and transfer of securities are heavily regulated by federal and state statutes and by government agencies.

This chapter will discuss the nature of federal securities regulations and their effects on the business world. First, though, it is necessary to understand the paramount role played by the Securities and Exchange Commission (SEC) in the regulation of federal securities laws. Because of its importance in this area, we examine the origin and functions of the SEC in the following *Landmark in the Law*.

SECURITY
Generally, a stock certificate, bond, note, debenture, warrant, or other document given as evidence of an ownership interest in a corporation or as a promise of repayment by a corporation.

737

The Securities and Exchange Commission

The creation of the Securities and Exchange Commission (SEC) was a direct result of the stock market crash of October 29, 1929. The crash and the ensuing economic depression caused the public to focus on the importance of securities markets in the economic well-being of the nation. The feverish trading in securities during the preceding decade became the subject of widespread attention, and numerous reports circulated concerning the purportedly speculative and manipulative trading that occurred in the stock market.

NOTE Congress intended the federal securities laws to protect the public from unethical business practices.

As a result, in 1931, the Senate passed a resolution calling for an extensive investigation of securities trading. The investigation led, ultimately, to the passage by Congress of the Securities Act of 1933, which is also known as the *truth-in-securities* bill. In the following year, Congress passed the Securities Exchange Act. This 1934 act created the Securities and Exchange Commission as an independent regulatory agency whose function was to administer the 1933 and 1934 acts. Its major responsibilities in this respect are as follows:

1. Requiring disclosure of facts concerning offerings of securities listed on national securities exchanges and of certain securities traded over the counter (OTC).
2. Regulating the trade in securities on the thirteen national and regional securities exchanges and in the over-the-counter markets.
3. Investigating securities fraud.
4. Regulating the activities of securities brokers, dealers, and investment advisers and requiring their registration.
5. Supervising the activities of mutual funds.
6. Recommending administrative sanctions, injunctive remedies, and criminal prosecution against those who violate securities laws. (The SEC can bring enforcement actions for civil violations of federal securities laws. The Fraud Section of the Criminal Division of the Department of Justice prosecutes criminal violations.)

Since its creation, the SEC's regulatory functions have gradually been increased by legislation granting it authority in different areas. We look at the expanding powers of the SEC later in the chapter.

For Critical Analysis: *What is the source of the national government's authority to regulate the securities industry?*

■ Securities Act of 1933

The Securities Act of 1933[1] was designed to prohibit various forms of fraud and to stabilize the securities industry by requiring that all essential information concerning the issuance of securities be made available to the investing public. Essentially, the purpose of this act is to require disclosure.

---

1.   15 U.S.C. Sections 77–77aa.

What Is a Security?

Section 2(1) of the Securities Act states that securities include the following:

[A]ny note, stock, treasury stock, bond, debenture, evidence of indebtedness, certificate of interest or participation in any profit-sharing agreement, collateral-trust certificate, preorganization certificate or subscription, transferable share, investment contract, voting-trust certificate, certificate of deposit for a security, fractional undivided interest in oil, gas, or other mineral rights, or, in general, any interest or instrument commonly known as a "security," or any certificate of interest or participation in, temporary or interim certificate for, receipt for, guarantee of, or warrant or right to subscribe to or purchase, any of the foregoing.[2]

Generally, the courts have interpreted Section 2(1) of the Securities Act to mean that a security exists in any transaction in which a person (1) invests (2) in a common enterprise (3) reasonably expecting profits (4) derived *primarily* or *substantially* from others' managerial or entrepreneurial efforts.[3]

For our purposes, it is probably most convenient to think of securities in their most common forms—stocks and bonds issued by corporations. Bear in mind, however, that securities can take many forms and have been held to include whiskey, cosmetics, worms, beavers, boats, vacuum cleaners, muskrats, and cemetery lots, as well as investment contracts in condominiums, franchises, limited partnerships, oil or gas or other mineral rights, and farm animals accompanied by care agreements.

Registration Statement

Section 5 of the Securities Act of 1933 broadly provides that if a security does not qualify for an exemption, that security must be *registered* before it is offered to the public either through the mails or through any facility of interstate commerce, including securities exchanges. Issuing corporations must file a *registration statement* with the SEC. Investors must be provided with a *prospectus* that describes the security being sold, the issuing corporation, and the investment or risk attaching to the security. In principle, the registration statement and the prospectus supply sufficient information to enable unsophisticated investors to evaluate the financial risk involved.

CONTENTS OF THE REGISTRATION STATEMENT The registration statement must include the following:

1. A description of the significant provisions of the security offered for sale, including the relationship between that security and the other capital securities of the registrant. Also, the corporation must disclose how it intends to use the proceeds of the sale.
2. A description of the registrant's properties and business.
3. A description of the management of the registrant and its security holdings; remuneration; and other benefits, including pensions and stock options. Any interests of directors or officers in any material transactions with the corporation must be disclosed.
4. A financial statement certified by an independent public accounting firm.
5. A description of pending lawsuits.

In 1996, the SEC undertook steps to simplify corporate securities-offering procedures that will make it easier for small businesses to raise capital. Generally, the SEC intends to eliminate many of its regulations and required forms, and streamline the disclosure process, so that requirements will be easier to understand. The SEC may also create broader exemptions from registration requirements for small businesses (exemptions under the 1933 act will be discussed shortly).

"Spending and investing differ only in degree, depending on the length of time elapsing between the expenditure and the enjoyment."

Irving Fisher, 1867–1947 *(American economist)*

DON'T FORGET The purpose of the Securities Act of 1933 is disclosure—the SEC does not consider whether a security is worth the investment.

---

2. 15 U.S.C. Section 77b(1). Amendments in 1982 added stock options.
3. *SEC v. W. J. Howey Co.*, 328 U.S. 293, 66 S.Ct. 1100, 90 L.Ed. 1244 (1946).

OTHER REQUIREMENTS   Before filing the registration statement and the prospectus with the SEC, the corporation is allowed to obtain an underwriter—a company that agrees to purchase the new issue of securities for resale to the public. There is a twenty-day waiting period (which can be accelerated by the SEC) after registration before the sale can take place. During this period, oral offers between interested investors and the issuing corporation concerning the purchase and sale of the proposed securities may take place; very limited written advertising is allowed. At this time, the so-called **red herring** prospectus may be distributed. It gets its name from the red legend printed across it stating that the registration has been filed but has not become effective.

After the waiting period, the registered securities can be legally bought and sold. Written advertising is allowed in the form of a **tombstone ad,** so named because historically the format resembles a tombstone. Such ads simply tell the investor where and how to obtain a prospectus. Normally, any other type of advertising is prohibited.

VIOLATIONS   As mentioned, the SEC has the power to investigate and bring civil enforcement actions against companies that violate federal securities laws, including the Securities Act of 1933. Criminal violations are prosecuted by the Department of Justice. When the SEC was formed, Congress intended that the SEC also would rely on private lawsuits as a supplement to its efforts to enforce securities laws. Thus, private parties, such as shareholders, can bring suits against those who violate federal securities laws. (See the *Business Law in Action* later in this chapter for a discussion of shareholder class-action suits.)

Registration violations of the 1933 act are not treated lightly. In the following classic case, purchasers of the corporation's debentures (debentures were discussed in Chapter 26) sued BarChris Construction Corporation under Section 11 of the Securities Act of 1933. Section 11 imposes liability when a registration statement contains material false statements or material omissions.

RED HERRING

A preliminary prospectus that can be distributed to potential investors after the registration statement (for a securities offering) has been filed with the Securities and Exchange Commission. The name derives from the red legend printed across the prospectus stating that the registration has been filed but has not become effective.

TOMBSTONE AD

An advertisement, historically in a format resembling a tombstone, of a securities offering. The ad informs potential investors of where and how they may obtain a prospectus.

CASE 29.1

ESCOTT v. BARCHRIS CONSTRUCTION CORP.

United States District Court,
Southern District of New York, 1968.
283 F.Supp. 643.

HISTORICAL AND TECHNOLOGICAL SETTING
Automatic pin-setting equipment became widely available to bowling alleys in the early 1950s. Partly because of this development, bowling became the leading U.S. indoor sport. Not all lanes in older bowling alleys could accommodate the new equipment. Business was good for those who built new facilities. Because the buyers of the new alleys could not always pay cash, the builders would sometimes accept a promissory note for most of the price. Ordinarily, the builders' suppliers would not accept promises to pay in the future, however, but insisted on cash. For these reasons, the builders were often in need of capital.

FACTS   BarChris Construction Corporation was an expanding company that built bowling alleys and was in constant need of cash to finance its operations. In 1961,

BarChris issued securities, in the form of debenture bonds, after filing the appropriate registration statement with the Securities and Exchange Commission. By early 1962, the company's financial difficulties had become insurmountable, and BarChris defaulted on the interest due on the debentures one month after petitioning for bankruptcy. Purchasers of the BarChris bonds sued BarChris in a federal district court, alleging that BarChris had violated Section 11 of the Securities Act of 1933. The plaintiffs challenged the accuracy of the registration statement filed with the Securities and Exchange Commission and charged that the text of the prospectus was false and that material information had been omitted. There were three categories of defendants: BarChris and all of the signers of the registration statement, the underwriters, and BarChris's auditors.

ISSUE   Had BarChris violated the 1933 Securities Act requirements concerning the registration statement and prospectus accompanying its bond issue?

DECISION   Yes. The court held that BarChris and all of the signers of the registration statement, the underwriters, and the corporation's auditors were all liable.

REASON   The court found that the registration statement contained false statements of fact and omitted

Case 29.1—Continued

other facts that should have been included to prevent the statement from being misleading. The misstatements included overstatement of sales and gross profits; understatement of contingent liabilities; overstatement of orders on hand; and failure to disclose true facts with respect to officers' loans, customers' delinquencies, application of proceeds, and the prospective operation of several bowling alleys. The facts that were falsely stated or omitted were "material" within the meaning of the Securities Act of 1933. The court found that "[t]he average prudent investor is not concerned with minor inaccuracies or with errors as to matters which are of no interest to him. The facts which tend to deter him from purchasing a security are facts which have an important bearing upon the nature or condition of the issuing corporation or its business. Judged by this test, there is no doubt that many of the misstatements and omissions in this prospectus were material."

FOR CRITICAL ANALYSIS—Social Consideration
Under what common law theory might a buyer sue a seller for the seller's failure to disclose material facts about the goods being sold?

Exempt Securities

A number of specific securities are exempt from the registration requirements of the Securities Act of 1933. These securities—which can also generally be resold without being registered—include the following:[4]

1. All bank securities sold prior to July 27, 1933.
2. Commercial paper, if the maturity date does not exceed nine months.
3. Securities of charitable organizations.
4. Securities resulting from a corporate reorganization issued for exchange with the issuer's existing security holders and certificates issued by trustees, receivers, or debtors in possession under the bankruptcy laws (bankruptcy is discussed in Chapter 22).
5. Securities issued exclusively for exchange with the issuer's existing security holders, provided no commission is paid (for example, stock dividends and stock splits).
6. Securities issued to finance the acquisition of railroad equipment.
7. Any insurance, endowment, or annuity contract issued by a state-regulated insurance company.
8. Government-issued securities.
9. Securities issued by banks, savings and loan associations, farmers' cooperatives, and similar institutions subject to supervision by governmental authorities.
10. In consideration of the "small amount involved,"[5] an issuer's offer of up to $5 million in securities in any twelve-month period (including up to $1.5 million in nonissuer resales).

For the last exemption, under Regulation A,[6] the issuer must file with the SEC a notice of the issue and an offering circular, which must also be provided to investors before the sale. This is a much simpler and less expensive process than the procedures associated with full registration. Companies are allowed to "test the waters" for potential interest before preparing the offering circular. To *test the waters* means to determine potential interest without actually selling any securities or requiring any commitment on the part of those who are interested. Small-business issuers (companies with less than $25 million in annual revenues and less than $25 million in outstanding voting stock) can also use an integrated registration and reporting system that uses simpler forms than the full registration system.

BE AWARE The issuer of an exempt security does not have to disclose the same information that other issuers do.

Exhibit 29–1 summarizes the securities and transactions (discussed next) that are exempt from the registration requirements under the Securities Act of 1933 and SEC regulations.

---

4. 15 U.S.C. Section 77c.
5. 15 U.S.C. Section 77c(b).
6. 17 C.F.R. Sections 230.251–230.263.

◆ **Exhibit 29–1**
Exemptions under the 1933 Securities Act

Exempt Transactions

An issuer of securities that are not exempt under one of the categories listed above can avoid the high cost and complicated procedures associated with registration by taking advantage of certain transaction exemptions. An offering may qualify for more than one exemption. These exemptions are very broad, and thus most sales occur without registration. The exemptions are available only in the transaction in which the securities are issued, however (except for securities issued under Rule 504, which will be discussed shortly). A resale may be made only after registration (unless the resale qualifies as an exempt transaction).

REGULATION D   The SEC's Regulation D contains four separate exemptions from registration requirements for limited offers (offers that involve either a small amount of money or are made in a limited manner). Regulation D provides that any of these offerings made during any twelve-month period are exempt from the registration requirements.

Rule 504   Noninvestment company offerings up to $1 million in any one year are exempt.[7] In contrast to investment companies (discussed later in this chapter),

---

7.   17 C.F.R. Section 230.504. Rule 504 is the exemption currently used by most small businesses, but that could change if the SEC adopts proposed Rule 135(d). The proposed rule would permit "testing the waters" for offerings of up to $5 million *per transaction.*

noninvestment companies are firms that are not engaged primarily in the business of investing or trading in securities.

Rule 504a   Offerings up to $500,000 in any one year by so-called blank check companies—companies with no specific business plans except to locate and acquire presently unknown businesses or opportunities—are exempt if no general solicitation or advertising is used; the SEC is notified of the sales; and precaution is taken against nonexempt, unregistered resales.[8] The limits on advertising and unregistered resales do not apply if the offering is made solely in states that provide for registration and disclosure and the securities are sold in compliance with those provisions.[9]

Rule 505   Private, noninvestment company offerings up to $5 million in any twelve-month period are exempt, regardless of the number of **accredited investors** (banks, insurance companies, investment companies, the issuer's executive officers and directors, and persons whose income or net worth exceeds certain limits), so long as there are no more than thirty-five unaccredited investors; no general solicitation or advertising is used; the SEC is notified of the sales; and precaution is taken against nonexempt, unregistered resales. If the sale involves *any* unaccredited investors, *all* investors must be given material information about the offering company, its business, and the securities before the sale. The issuer is not required to believe that each unaccredited investor "has such knowledge and experience in financial and business matters that he is capable of evaluating the merits and the risks of the prospective investment."[10]

ACCREDITED INVESTORS
In the context of securities offerings, "sophisticated" investors, such as banks, insurance companies, investment companies, the issuer's executive officers and directors, and persons whose income or net worth exceeds certain limits.

Rule 506   Private offerings in unlimited amounts that are not generally solicited or advertised are exempt if the SEC is notified of the sales; precaution is taken against nonexempt, unregistered resales; and the issuer believes that each unaccredited investor has sufficient knowledge or experience in financial matters to be capable of evaluating the investment's merits and risks. There may be no more than thirty-five unaccredited investors, although there may be an unlimited number of accredited investors. If there are *any* unaccredited investors, the issuer must provide to *all* purchasers material information about itself, its business, and the securities before the sale.[11]

This exemption is perhaps most important to those firms that want to raise funds through the sale of securities without registering them. It is often referred to as the *private placement* exemption, because it exempts "transactions not involving any public offering."[12] This provision applies to private offerings to a limited number of persons who are sufficiently sophisticated and in a sufficiently strong bargaining position to be able to assume the risk of the investment (and who thus have no need for federal registration protection), as well as to private offerings to similarly situated institutional investors.

KEEP IN MIND An investor can be "sophisticated" by virtue of his or her education and experience or by investing through a knowledgeable, experienced representative.

RULE 147—INTRASTATE ISSUES   Also exempt are intrastate transactions involving purely local offerings.[13] This exemption applies to most offerings that are restricted to residents of the state in which the issuing company is organized and doing business. For nine months after the last sale, virtually no resales may be made to nonresidents, and precautions must be taken against this possibility. These offerings remain subject to applicable laws in the state of issue.

---

8. Precautions to be taken against nonexempt, unregistered resales include asking the investor whether he or she is buying the securities for others; before the sale, disclosing to each purchaser in writing that the securities are unregistered and thus cannot be resold, except in an exempt transaction, without first being registered; and indicating on the certificates that the securities are unregistered and restricted.
9. 17 C.F.R. Section 230.504a.
10. 17 C.F.R. Section 230.505.
11. 17 C.F.R. Section 230.506.
12. 15 U.S.C. Section 77d(2).
13. 15 U.S.C. Section 77c(a)(11); 17 C.F.R. Section 230.147.

SECTION 4(6) Under Section 4(6) of the Securities Act of 1933, an offer made *solely* to accredited investors is exempt if its amount is not more than $5 million. Any number of accredited investors may participate, but no unaccredited investors may do so. No general solicitation or advertising may be used; the SEC must be notified of all sales; and precaution must be taken against nonexempt, unregistered resales (because these are restricted securities and may be resold only by registration or in an exempt transaction).[14]

RESALES Most securities can be resold without registration (although some resales may be subject to certain restrictions, which were discussed previously in connection with specific exemptions). The Securities Act of 1933 provides exemptions for resales by most persons other than issuers or underwriters. Resales of restricted securities acquired under Rule 504a, Rule 505, Rule 506, or Section 4(6), however, trigger the registration requirements unless the party selling them complies with Rule 144 or Rule 144A. These rules are sometimes referred to as "safe harbors."

Rule 144 Rule 144 exempts restricted securities from registration on resale if there is adequate current public information about the issuer, the person selling the securities has owned them for at least two years, they are sold in certain limited amounts in unsolicited brokers' transactions, and the SEC is given notice of the resale.[15] "Adequate current public information" consists of the reports that certain companies are required to file under the Securities Exchange Act of 1934.

Rule 144A Securities that at the time of issue are not of the same class as securities listed on a national securities exchange or quoted in a U.S. automated interdealer quotation system may be resold under Rule 144A.[16] They may be sold only to a qualified institutional buyer (an institution, such as an insurance company, an investment company, or a bank, that owns and invests at least $100 million in securities). The seller must take reasonable steps to ensure that the buyer knows that the seller is relying on the exemption under Rule 144A. A sample restricted stock certificate is shown in Exhibit 29–2.

CONTRAST Securities do not have to be held for two years to be exempt from registration on a resale under Rule 144A, as they do under Rule 144.

▌Securities Exchange Act of 1934

The Securities Exchange Act of 1934 provides for the regulation and registration of securities exchanges; brokers; dealers; and national securities associations, such as the National Association of Securities Dealers (NASD). The SEC regulates the markets in which securities are traded by maintaining a continuous disclosure system for all corporations with securities on the securities exchanges and for those companies that have assets in excess of $10 million and five hundred or more shareholders. These corporations are referred to as Section 12 companies, because they are required to register their securities under Section 12 of the 1934 act.

The act regulates proxy solicitation for voting (discussed in Chapter 27) and allows the SEC to engage in market surveillance to regulate undesirable market practices such as fraud, market manipulation, misrepresentation, and stabilization. (*Stabilization* is a market-manipulating technique by which securities underwriters bid for securities to stabilize the prices of securities during their issuance.)

14. 15 U.S.C. Section 77d(6).
15. 17 C.F.R. Section 230.144.
16. 17 C.F.R. Section 230.144A.

◆ Exhibit 29–2
A Sample Restricted Stock Certificate

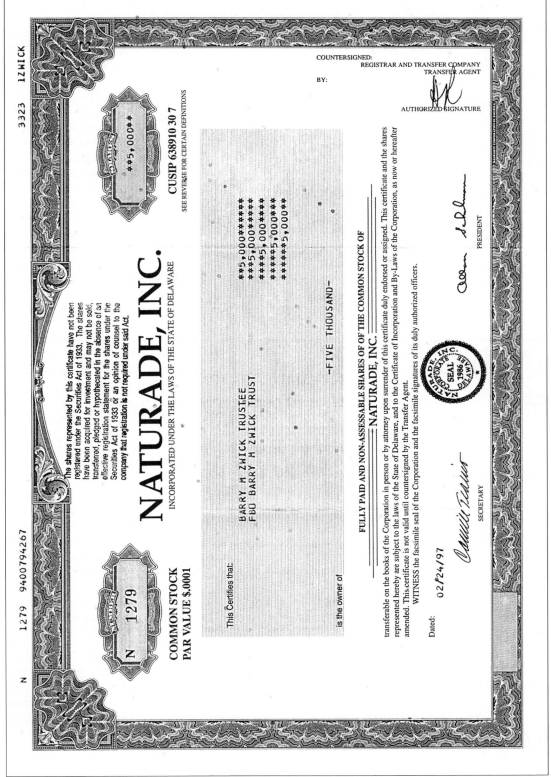

N   1279   9400794267   3323   1ZWICK

COMMON STOCK
PAR VALUE $.0001

N   1279

CUSIP 638910 30 7
SEE REVERSE FOR CERTAIN DEFINITIONS

5,000

NATURADE, INC.

INCORPORATED UNDER THE LAWS OF THE STATE OF DELAWARE

The shares represented by this certificate have not been registered under the Securities Act of 1933. The shares have been acquired for investment and may not be sold, transferred, pledged or hypothecated in the absence of an effective registration statement for the shares under the Securities Act of 1933 or an opinion of counsel to the company that registration is not required under said Act.

This Certifies that:

BARRY M ZWICK TRUSTEE
FBO BARRY M ZWICK TRUST

5,000******
5,000******
****5,000*******
******5,000****
*******5,000***

is the owner of

—FIVE THOUSAND—

FULLY PAID AND NON-ASSESSABLE SHARES OF OF THE COMMON STOCK OF

NATURADE, INC.

transferable on the books of the Corporation in person or by attorney upon surrender of this certificate duly endorsed or assigned. This certificate and the shares represented hereby are subject to the laws of the State of Delaware, and to the Certificate of Incorporation and By-Laws of the Corporation, as now or hereafter amended. This certificate is not valid until countersigned by the Transfer Agent.

WITNESS the facsimile seal of the Corporation and the facsimile signatures of its duly authorized officers.

Dated: 02/24/97

SECRETARY

PRESIDENT

COUNTERSIGNED:
REGISTRAR AND TRANSFER COMPANY
TRANSFER AGENT

BY:

AUTHORIZED SIGNATURE

Section 10(b), SEC Rule 10b-5, and Insider Trading

Section 10(b) is one of the most important sections of the Securities Exchange Act of 1934. This section proscribes the use of "any manipulative or deceptive device or contrivance in contravention of such rules and regulations as the [SEC] may prescribe." Among the rules that the SEC has promulgated pursuant to the 1934 act is **SEC Rule 10b-5,** which prohibits the commission of fraud in connection with the purchase or sale of any security.

One of the most important purposes of Section 10(b) and SEC Rule 10b-5 relates to so-called **insider trading.** Because of their positions, corporate directors and officers often obtain advance inside information that can affect the future market value of the corporate stock. Obviously, their positions can give them a trading advantage over the general public and shareholders. The 1934 Securities Exchange Act defines inside information and extends liability to officers and directors for taking advantage of such information in their personal transactions when they know that it is unavailable to the persons with whom they are dealing.

Section 10(b) of the 1934 act and SEC Rule 10b-5 cover not only corporate officers, directors, and majority shareholders but also any persons having access to or receiving information of a nonpublic nature on which trading is based.[17] Those found liable under SEC Rule 10b-5 have a right to seek reimbursement from persons or entities that may have shared responsibility for the violations, including accountants, attorneys, and corporations.[18]

SEC RULE 10b-5
A rule of the Securities and Exchange Commission that makes it unlawful, in connection with the purchase or sale of any security, to make any untrue statement of a material fact or to omit a material fact if such omission causes the statement to be misleading.

INSIDER TRADING
The purchase or sale of securities on the basis of information that has not been made available to the public.

International Perspective

Traditionally, Germany has resisted any legal prohibition against insider trading. Instead, insider trading was regulated by voluntary guidelines that were included in employment contracts with banks and stock corporations. The guidelines prohibited trading by corporate insiders but were not consistently enforced. Generally, German banks and stock companies contended that moral codes were more effective than legal prohibitions in controlling insider trading.

German attitudes toward insider trading began to change in the early 1990s, however, in the wake of insider-trading scandals. In 1994, Germany made insider trading a criminal offense, thus bringing that country in line with other European nations. Germany now has a government agency, similar to the SEC, that regulates insider trading, and German business firms are changing the ways in which they traditionally have disseminated information. For example, in the past, companies frequently disclosed their sales and earnings information to various securities analysts. They also often sent copies of their annual reports to members of the press days before the announcement of the information in the reports at news conferences.

For Critical Analysis: *How can you explain the fact that, relative to the United States, Germany waited so long to create a securities regulation agency?*

"There are three kinds of lies: lies, damned lies, and statistics."

Benjamin Disraeli, 1804–1881
(British prime minister, 1868, 1874–1880)

DISCLOSURE UNDER SEC RULE 10b-5   Any material omission or misrepresentation of material facts in connection with the purchase or sale of a security may violate not only Section 11 of the Securities Act of 1933 but also the antifraud provisions of Section 10(b) and SEC Rule 10b-5 of the 1934 act. The key to liability (which can be

---

17. Note that a private cause of action under Section 10(b) and SEC Rule 10b-5 cannot be brought against accountants, attorneys, and others who "aid and abet" violations of the act. Only the SEC can bring actions against so-called aiders and abettors. See *Central Bank of Denver, N.A. v. First Interstate Bank of Denver, N.A.,* 511 U.S. 164, 114 S.Ct. 1439, 128 L.Ed.2d 119 (1994).

18. *Musick, Peeler & Garrett v. Employers Insurance of Wausau,* 508 U.S. 286, 113 S.Ct. 2085, 124 L.Ed.2d 194 (1993).

civil or criminal) under Section 10(b) and SEC Rule 10b-5 is whether the insider's information is *material*. The following are some examples of material facts calling for a disclosure under the rule:

1. A new ore discovery.
2. Fraudulent trading in the company stock by a broker-dealer.
3. A dividend change (whether up or down).
4. A contract for the sale of corporate assets.
5. A new discovery (process or product).
6. A significant change in the firm's financial condition.

Courts have struggled with the problem of when information becomes public knowledge. Clearly, when inside information becomes public knowledge, all insiders should be allowed to trade without disclosure. The courts have suggested that insiders should refrain from trading for a "reasonable waiting period" when the news is not readily translatable into investment action. Presumably, this gives the news time to filter down to, and to be evaluated by, the investing public.

The following is one of the landmark cases interpreting SEC Rule 10b-5. The SEC sued Texas Gulf Sulphur Company for issuing a misleading press release. The release underestimated the magnitude and the value of a mineral discovery. The SEC also sued several of Texas Gulf Sulphur's directors, officers, and employees under SEC Rule 10b-5 for purchasing large amounts of the corporate stock prior to the announcement of the corporation's rich ore discovery.

CASE 29.2

SEC v. TEXAS GULF SULPHUR CO.
United States Court of Appeals,
Second Circuit, 1968.
401 F.2d 833.

HISTORICAL AND ENVIRONMENTAL SETTING *No court has ever held that every buyer or seller is entitled to all of the information relating to all of the circumstances in every stock transaction. By the mid-1950s, however, significant understatement of the value of the assets of a company had been held to be materially misleading.[a] In 1957, the Texas Gulf Sulphur Company (TGS) began exploring for minerals in eastern Canada. In March 1959, aerial geophysical surveys were conducted over more than fifteen thousand square miles of the area. The operations revealed numerous and extraordinary variations in the conductivity of the rock, which indicated a remarkable concentration of commercially exploitable minerals. One site of such variations was near Timmins, Ontario. On October 29 and 30, 1963, a ground survey of the site near Timmins indicated a need to drill for further evaluation.*

FACTS The Texas Gulf Sulphur Company drilled a hole on November 12, 1963, that appeared to yield a core with an exceedingly high mineral content. TGS kept secret the results of the core sample. Officers and employees of the company made substantial purchases of TGS's stock or accepted stock options after learning of the ore discovery, even though further drilling was necessary to establish whether there was enough ore to be mined commercially. On April 11, 1964, an unauthorized report of the mineral find appeared in the newspapers. On the following day, April 12, TGS issued a press release that played down the discovery and stated that it was too early to tell whether the ore finding would be a significant one. Later on, TGS announced a strike of at least twenty-five million tons of ore, substantially driving up the price of TGS stock. The SEC brought suit in a federal district court against the officers and employees of TGS for violating the insider-trading prohibition of SEC Rule 10b-5. The officers and employees argued that the prohibition did not apply. They reasoned that the information on which they had traded was not material, as the mine had not been commercially proved. The court held that most of the defendants had not violated SEC Rule 10b-5, and the SEC appealed.

ISSUE Had the officers and employees of TGS violated SEC Rule 10b-5 by purchasing the stock, even though they did not know the full extent and profit potential of the mine at the time they purchased the stock?

a. *Speed v. Transamerica Corp.,* 99 F.Supp. 808 (D.Del. 1951).

(Continued)

Case 29.2—Continued

DECISION   Yes. The federal appellate court reversed the lower court's decision and remanded the case to the trial court, holding that the employees and officers violated SEC Rule 10b-5's prohibition against insider trading.

REASON   For SEC Rule 10b-5 purposes, the test of materiality is whether the information would affect the judgment of reasonable investors. Reasonable investors include speculative as well as conservative investors. "[A] major factor in determining whether the * * * discovery [of the ore] was a material fact is the importance attached to the drilling results by those who knew about it. * * * [T]he timing by those who knew of it of their stock purchases and their purchases of short-term calls [rights to buy shares at a specified price within a specified time period]—purchases in some cases by individuals who had never before purchased calls or even TGS stock—virtually compels the inference that the insiders were influenced by the drilling results. * * * We hold, therefore, that all transactions in TGS stock or calls by individuals apprised of the drilling results * * * were made in violation of Rule 10b-5."

FOR CRITICAL ANALYSIS—Economic Consideration
Who is hurt by insider trading?

APPLICABILITY OF SEC RULE 10b-5   SEC Rule 10b-5 applies in virtually all cases concerning the trading of securities, whether on organized exchanges, in over-the-counter markets, or in private transactions. The rule covers notes, bonds, certificates of interest and participation in any profit-sharing agreement, agreements to form a corporation, and joint-venture agreements; in short, it covers just about any form of security. It is immaterial whether a firm has securities registered under the 1933 act for the 1934 act to apply.

Although SEC Rule 10b-5 is applicable only when the requisites of federal jurisdiction—such as the use of the mails, of stock exchange facilities, or of any instrumentality of interstate commerce—are present, virtually no commercial transaction can be completed without such contact. In addition, the states have corporate securities laws, many of which include provisions similar to SEC Rule 10b-5.

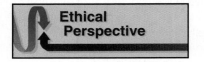
Ethical Perspective

Clearly, SEC Rule 10b-5 has broad applicability. As will be discussed shortly, the rule covers not only corporate insiders but even "outsiders"—those who receive and trade on tips received from insiders. Investigating and prosecuting violations of SEC Rule 10b-5 is costly, both for the government and for those convicted of insider trading.

Some people doubt that such extensive regulation is necessary and even contend that insider trading should be legal. Would there be any benefit from the legalization of insider trading? To evaluate this question, review the facts in *SEC v. Texas Gulf Sulphur Co.* (Case 29.2 in this chapter). If insider trading were legal, the discovery of the ore sample would probably have caused many more company insiders to purchase stock. Consequently, the price of Texas Gulf's stock would have increased fairly quickly. These increases presumably would have attracted the attention of outside investors, who would have learned sooner that something positive had happened to the company and would thus have had the opportunity to purchase the stock. The higher demand for the stock would have more quickly translated into higher prices for the stock and hence, perhaps, a more efficient capital market.

For Critical Analysis: *How would you argue against the legalization of insider trading?*

OUTSIDERS AND SEC RULE 10b-5   The traditional insider-trading case involves true insiders—corporate officers, directors, and majority shareholders who have access to (and trade on) inside information. Increasingly, liability under Section 10(b) of the 1934 act and SEC Rule 10b-5 has been extended to include certain "outsiders"—those

LAW IN THE EXTREME

Generations and Generations . . . of Tippees

How far down the chain of tippees does liability under SEC Rule 10b-5 extend? For example, consider an insider-trading case that the SEC investigated in 1995. The insider (tipper) in the case was a paralegal who learned of a pending takeover bid. The paralegal told a friend about the bid. The friend then told his father (an IBM executive), who told a colleague at IBM, who told a friend (an executive of R. H. Macy), who told a friend (a co-owner of Frost & Sullivan, a broker-dealer), who told another co-owner of Frost & Sullivan, who told a sales representative of Frost & Sullivan, who told a classmate (the president of Greenwald Securities, a broker-dealer), who told a Greenwald sales representative. In all, there were nine "generations" of tippees. (The SEC refers to the first person to receive a tip as the "first generation," the person to whom the first person passes on the information as the "second generation," and so on.)[a]

The information passed quickly from one tippee to another, and all

a. Floyd Norris, "The Labyrinth of Two Insider Cases," *The Wall Street Journal*, March 8, 1995, p. C1.

tippees apparently traded on the basis of the information. The question is, are all nine generations liable under SEC Rule 10b-5 for insider trading? The answer is a resounding yes—provided that they all knew that the insider-tipper had breached a fiduciary duty by passing on the information. The problem for the SEC, of course, is proving that the tippees—particularly those in the third and fourth (and subsequent) generations—knew that the original tipper breached a fiduciary duty.

For Critical Analysis: *Why wouldn't a tippee, particularly one who is several generations removed from the tipper, simply not ask about the origins of the inside information?*

---

who trade on inside information acquired *indirectly*. Two theories have been developed under which outsiders may be held liable for insider trading: the *tipper/tippee theory* and the *misappropriation theory*.

Tipper/Tippee Theory   Anyone who acquires inside information as a result of a corporate insider's breach of his or her fiduciary duty can be liable under SEC Rule 10b-5. This liability extends to **tippees** (those who receive "tips" from insiders) and even remote tippees (tippees of tippees).

The key to liability under this theory is that the inside information be obtained as a result of someone's breach of a fiduciary duty to the corporation whose shares are involved in the trading. Unless there is a breach of a duty not to disclose inside information, the disclosure was in exchange for personal benefit, and the tippee knows of this breach (or should know of it) and benefits from it, there is no liability under this theory.[19]

TIPPEE
A person who receives inside information.

Misappropriation Theory   Liability for insider trading may also be established under the misappropriation theory. This theory holds that if an individual wrongfully obtains (misappropriates) inside information and trades on it for his or her personal gain, then the individual should be held liable because, in essence, the individual stole information rightfully belonging to another.

The misappropriation theory significantly extends the reach of SEC Rule 10b-5 to outsiders who would not ordinarily be deemed fiduciaries of the corporations in whose stock they trade. Courts will normally hold, however, that some fiduciary duty to some lawful possessor of material nonpublic information must have been violated and some harm to the defrauded party must have occurred for liability to exist. For example, suppose that an employee of a printing shop that handles takeover bids learns of a takeover and trades on the information. Clearly, the employee has no fiduciary duty to the shareholders of either corporation involved in the takeover. The employee does, however,

---

19.   See, for example, *Chiarella v. United States*, 445 U.S. 222, 100 S.Ct. 1108, 63 L.Ed.2d 348 (1980); and *Dirks v. SEC*, 463 U.S. 646, 103 S.Ct. 3255, 77 L.Ed.2d 911 (1983).

have a duty of loyalty to his or her employer—who lawfully possesses material nonpublic information.[20]

The following case raises the question of whether, for the tippee to be held liable under SEC Rule 10b-5, the tipper must have known that his or her breach of a fiduciary obligation would lead to the tippee's trading on the misappropriated information.

---

20.   Note that in contrast to several other federal circuit courts of appeals, the U.S. Court of Appeals for the Fourth Circuit has refused to impose liability under the misappropriation theory for SEC Rule 10b-5 violations. See *United States v. Bryan,* 58 F.3d 933 (4th Cir. 1994).

CASE 29.3

UNITED STATES v. LIBERA

United States Court of Appeals,
Seventh Circuit, 1993.
989 F.2d 596.

COMPANY PROFILE   *Two weeks before the stock market crash in October 1929, the McGraw-Hill Book Company started* Business Week *magazine. In the first issue, the editors expressed concern about the health of the U.S. economy. This view was contrary to current opinion but certainly proved correct—the stock market crash occurred two weeks later and heralded the start of the Great Depression. Today,* Business Week *is one of the top U.S. business magazines. It is available, as are most of McGraw-Hill's magazines and other products, in multimedia versions.*

FACTS   R. R. Donnelley & Sons Company operates a printing plant that prints *Business Week* (owned by McGraw-Hill, Inc.). McGraw-Hill and Donnelley had a policy of keeping the contents of each issue confidential until 5:00 P.M. on Thursday, because the contents could affect the price of particular stocks and, before release, were regarded as inside information by the Securities and Exchange Commission. William Dillon observed that trading in stocks mentioned favorably in the magazine often began increasing on the Wednesday before publication and continued through the next Monday. Dillon, recognizing the value of receiving advance copies of *Business Week*, sought out Donnelley employees who would give him copies on Thursday mornings. Dillon, Benjamin Libera, and Francis Sablone used the information to trade regularly on Thursday mornings in the securities reported in *Business Week*. When their scheme was discovered, Dillon pleaded guilty to certain criminal charges and testified against Libera and Sablone, who were convicted of violations of Section 10(b) under the

misappropriation theory. Libera and Sablone appealed, arguing that they could not be liable for insider trading unless the tipper (in this case, the Donnelly employees who gave them advance copies) knew that the breach of a fiduciary obligation would lead to the tippee's trading on the misappropriated information.

ISSUE   Must the tipper know that a tippee will trade on misappropriated information for the tippee to be held liable under Section 10(b)?

DECISION   No. The U.S. Court of Appeals for the Seventh Circuit affirmed the convictions of Libera and Sablone.

REASON   The federal appellate court stated that "[t]he misappropriation theory requires the establishment of two elements: (i) a breach by the tipper of a duty owed to the owner of the nonpublic information; and (ii) the tippee's knowledge that the tipper had breached the duty." The court held that "these two elements, without more, are sufficient for tippee liability. The tipper's knowledge that he or she was breaching a duty to the owner of confidential information suffices to establish the tipper's expectation that the breach will lead to some kind of a misuse of the information," because "it may be presumed that the tippee's interest in the information is, in contemporary jargon, not for nothing. To allow a tippee to escape liability solely because the government cannot prove *   *   * that the tipper knew exactly what misuse would result from the tipper's wrongdoing would not fulfill the purpose of the misappropriation theory, which is to protect property rights in information."

FOR CRITICAL ANALYSIS—Social Consideration
From whom was the information misappropriated?

▭ Technology and Securities Laws

We have stressed elsewhere how technological advances have affected business practices as well as the law governing those practices. Not surprisingly, technology is also affecting practices in the securities industry—and securities law. More than ever before, today's investors have access to information that can help them make informed decisions. Information on the Internet, for example, ranges from the data concerning the financial performance of various companies to securities laws and regulations. (See *Accessing the Internet: Business Law and Legal Environment* at the end of this chapter.)

As might be expected, the on-line era has opened the door to new forms of fraud. Officials in several states are undertaking investigations into numerous on-line schemes perpetrated via electronic "investor bulletin boards." For example, a purported investment adviser or stockbroker might offer his or her investment services to Internet users. Then, once the investor sends funds to invest, the scam artist walks off with the money. Securities officials in some states are planning to establish their own bulletin boards to warn users of these problems and answer questions concerning investments.

An interesting question raised by the extensive amount of on-line information available to investors is whether a court can reasonably assume that investors should know about that information. In other words, do investors have a duty to "surf the Net"? At least one court—the U.S. Court of Appeals for the Seventh Circuit—has suggested that they do. The case involved allegations by Whirlpool Financial Corporation that GN Holdings, Inc., had violated securities laws by issuing a misleading financial forecast in connection with a securities offering. GN contended that the suit was barred by the statute of limitations. (Under federal securities laws, a plaintiff must file a claim within one year from the time that the cause of action accrues. Normally, an action under securities laws accrues when the plaintiff is put on notice of the fraud.) The question before the court was whether Whirlpool had been put on notice that GN's representations were misleading more than a year before Whirlpool filed its claim.

The court held that Whirlpool had constructive notice of the fraud the moment that the information needed to discover the fraud (discrepancies between GN's financial projections and the actual results) was in the public domain. Information in the public domain included information available on the Internet. The court stated that "with the advent of the 'information superhighway,' federal and state legislation and regulations, as well as information regarding industry trends, are easily accessed. A reasonable investor is presumed to have information available in the public domain, and therefore Whirlpool is imputed with constructive knowledge of this information." The court concluded, based on the date of Whirlpool's constructive notice, that Whirlpool's action against GN was barred by the statute of limitations.[a]

For Critical Analysis: *How might the "Information Superhighway" affect securities trading and regulation in the future?*

a. *Whirlpool Financial Corp. v. GN Holdings, Inc.,* 67 F.3d 605 (7th Cir. 1995).

Insider Reporting and Trading—Section 16(b)

Officers, directors, and certain large stockholders[21] of Section 12 corporations (corporations that are required to register their securities under Section 12 of the 1934 act) must file reports with the SEC concerning their ownership and trading of the corporations' securities.[22] To discourage such insiders from using nonpublic information about their companies for their personal benefit in the stock market, Section 16(b) of the 1934 act provides for the recapture by the corporation of all profits realized by an insider on any purchase and sale or sale and purchase of the corporation's stock within any six-month period.[23] It is irrelevant whether the insider actually uses inside information; all such *short-swing* profits must be returned to the corporation.

---

21.   Those stockholders owning 10 percent of the class of equity securities registered under Section 12 of the 1934 act.

22.   15 U.S.C. Section 78*l*.

23.   When a decline is predicted in the market for a particular stock, one can realize profits by "selling short"—selling at a high price and repurchasing later at a lower price to cover the "short sale." The short seller typically has to borrow the stock in the meantime (and pay interest on the borrowed stock).

Section 16(b) applies not only to stock but to warrants, options, and securities convertible into stock. In addition, the courts have fashioned complex rules for determining profits. Corporate insiders are wise to seek competent counsel prior to trading in the corporation's stock. Exhibit 29–3 compares the effects of SEC Rule 10b-5 and Section 16(b).

People resort to various tactics to avoid liability under Section 16(b). These tactics include creative forms for the exchange of money for stock, as illustrated by the following case.

CASE 29.4

TRISTAR CORP. v. FREITAS

United States District Court,
Eastern District of New York, 1994.
867 F.Supp. 149.

HISTORICAL AND ETHICAL SETTING *Between 1932 and 1934, the Senate Banking Committee held hearings on the securities markets. It discovered widespread fraud and abuse in securities financing and market practices. This discovery helped to propel the securities acts through Congress. The most important aspect of these acts is their requirement of full disclosure. All important information about a company, its securities, and the transaction must be disclosed. The parties can then make a free choice to deal (or not to deal) based on that information. Because of this unregulated freedom to deal, it is vital that the disclosed information be truthful and complete.*

FACTS Ross Freitas and Carolyn Kenner were officers and directors of the Tristar Corporation. They were also Tristar shareholders, as they had bought Tristar stock between February 2 and June 15, 1989. Meanwhile, on May 31, they agreed to transfer their Tristar shares to Starion International Ltd. Under a contract titled "Periodic Loan Agreement," Freitas and Kenner gave their shares

to Starion's attorney. Starion paid Freitas and Kenner in periodic installments. With each payment, the attorney gave a block of the stock to Starion. When Tristar learned of the deal, the firm filed a suit in a federal district court against Freitas and Kenner, under Section 16(b), to obtain their profits. Tristar filed a motion for summary judgment.

ISSUE For the purposes of Section 16(b), was the so-called Periodic Loan Agreement actually a contract to sell shares?

DECISION Yes. The federal district court ruled in favor of Tristar on this point. The court set for trial the issue of how much money Freitas and Kenner should pay to Tristar.

REASON The court pointed out that under Section 16(b), a sale occurs when "the insider has incurred an 'irrevocable liability' to dispose of the stock so that his 'rights and obligations' have become fixed." The court was "persuaded that the Loan Agreement has the ordinary indicia [signs or indications] of an installment sales contract." The court found that Freitas and Kenner did "contract to sell or otherwise dispose of" their stock on May 31.

FOR CRITICAL ANALYSIS—Economic Consideration
Had the shares of stock simply been used as collateral, would this case have been decided differently?

Insider-Trading Sanctions

The Insider Trading Sanctions Act of 1984 permits the SEC to bring suit in a federal district court against anyone violating or aiding in a violation of the 1934 act or SEC rules by purchasing or selling a security while in the possession of material nonpublic information.[24] The violation must occur on or through the facilities of a national securities exchange or through a broker or dealer. Transactions connected with a public offering by an issuer of securities are excepted.

---

24. 15 U.S.C. Section 78u–1(a)(1).

	SEC RULE 10b-5	SECTION 16(b)
What is the subject matter of the transaction?	Any security (does not have to be registered).	Any security (does not have to be registered).
What transactions are covered?	Purchase or sale.	Short-swing purchase and sale or short-swing sale and purchase.
Who is subject to liability?	Virtually anyone with inside information under a duty to disclose—including officers, directors, controlling stockholders, and tippees.	Officers, directors, and certain 10 percent stockholders.
Is omission or misrepresentation necessary for liability?	Yes.	No.
Are there any exempt transactions?	No.	Yes, there are a variety of exemptions.
Is direct dealing with the party necessary?	No.	No.
Who may bring an action?	A person transacting with an insider, the SEC, or a purchaser or seller damaged by a wrongful act.	A corporation or a shareholder by derivative action.

♦ **Exhibit 29–3**
Comparison of Coverage, Application, and Liabilities under SEC Rule 10b-5 and Section 16(b)

The Insider Trading and Securities Fraud Enforcement Act of 1988 extended the class of persons who may be subject to civil liability for insider-trading violations and gave the SEC authority to award **bounty payments** (rewards given by government officials for acts beneficial to the state) to persons providing information leading to the prosecution of insider-trading violations. The act also gave the SEC rulemaking authority to require specific policies and procedures in order to prevent insider trading, in addition to increasing the criminal penalties for violations. Maximum jail terms were increased from five to ten years, and fines were increased to $1 million for individuals and $2.5 million for partnerships and corporations.[25] Neither act has any effect on other actions the SEC or private investors may take.

In imposing sanctions for insider trading, the court may assess as a penalty as much as triple the profits gained or the loss avoided by the guilty party. For purposes of the act, profit or loss is defined as "the difference between the purchase or sale price of the security and the value of that security as measured by the trading price of the security at a reasonable period of time after public dissemination of the nonpublic information."[26] The following case provides an example, in a securities fraud case, of the computation of "avoided losses"—that is, the amount of the loss a violator avoids by selling his or her stock before a disclosure of negative information about a company.

BOUNTY PAYMENT
A reward (payment) given to a person or persons who perform a certain service—such as informing legal authorities of illegal actions.

---

25. 15 U.S.C. Section 78ff(a).
26. 15 U.S.C. Section 78u–1(d)(5)(f).

CASE 29.5

SEC v. PATEL
United States Court of Appeals,
Second Circuit, 1995.
61 F.3d 137.

HISTORICAL AND SOCIAL SETTING *A drug cannot be copyrighted or trademarked, but it can be patented. (Patents are discussed in Chapter 6.) When a drug's patent expires, the patented product falls into the public domain, and the patent owner is no longer protected against infringement. Other pharmaceutical manufacturers can make and market the drug as a "generic" drug. A generic drug is one that is produced without a brand name but that is identical to a product with a brand name. Generic drugs are cheaper than their brand-name counterparts.*

FACTS In November 1987, Par Pharmaceutical, Inc., submitted to the Food and Drug Administration (FDA) an application for a new generic drug. The application falsely stated that the drug had been tested as required. Ratilal Patel, an officer and director of Par Pharmaceutical, knew that the application contained false information and subsequently (in early 1988) sold 75,000 shares of his stock in Par Pharmaceutical at a price of approximately $21 per share. In 1988 and 1989, Par Pharmaceutical became the target of investigations and indictments for various improprieties, including bribery. By Friday, July 21, 1989, the price of Par stock was $10 per share. On Monday, July 24, Par Pharmaceutical publicly disclosed the facts about the falsified drug application. On

Tuesday, the price of Par Pharmaceutical stock dropped to $7.125 per share. The SEC filed a suit in a federal district court against Patel, alleging that he had violated securities laws. The court ordered Patel to, among other things, pay the amount of the loss he avoided by selling his stock before the announcement of the false FDA application. The court computed the amount based on the difference between the price of Par Pharmaceutical stock on July 21 and the price on July 25. Patel appealed, contending in part that the earlier investigations and indictments had affected the price of the stock.

ISSUE Did the computation of Patel's "avoided losses" reasonably approximate the amount that was causally connected to his securities fraud violations?

DECISION Yes. The U.S. Court of Appeals for the Second Circuit affirmed this part of the lower court's decision.

REASON The federal appellate court acknowledged that "calculations of this nature are not capable of exactitude" but added that any "risk of uncertainty [in calculating losses] should fall on the wrongdoer whose illegal conduct created that uncertainty." At any rate, the court stated that "[t]here certainly was a rational basis" to conclude that the investigations and indictments "had been fully taken into account by the market and that the July 24, 1989 disclosure alone accounted for the 28.75% decline identified as of July 25."

FOR CRITICAL ANALYSIS—Social Consideration
What penalty, among those that a court can impose, might a corporate officer and director consider worse than paying out "avoided losses"?

Proxy Statements

Section 14(a) of the Securities Exchange Act of 1934 regulates the solicitation of proxies from shareholders of Section 12 companies. The SEC regulates the content of proxy statements, which (as discussed in Chapter 27) are statements sent to shareholders by corporate officials who are requesting authority to vote on behalf of the shareholders in a particular election on specified issues. Whoever solicits a proxy must fully and accurately disclose in the proxy statement all of the facts that are pertinent to the matter on which the shareholders are to vote. SEC Rule 14a-9 is similar to the antifraud provisions of SEC Rule 10b-5. Remedies for violation are extensive; they range from injunctions that prevent a vote from being taken to monetary damages.

▌The Expanding Powers of the SEC

In recent years, Congress has expanded significantly the SEC's powers. For example, to further curb securities fraud, the Securities Enforcement Remedies and Penny

BUSINESS LAW IN ACTION

Curbing Class-Action Securities-Fraud Suits

Traditionally, the SEC has encouraged companies to disclose quantitative, forward-looking information—such as financial forecasts—to investors in prospectuses and other documents in connection with securities offerings. Ironically, one of the effects of SEC Rule 10b-5 is to deter such disclosure. To understand why, consider an example. A company announces that its projected earnings in a certain time period will be X amount. It turns out that the forecast was wrong. The earnings are in fact much lower, and the price of the company's stock is affected—negatively. The shareholders then bring a class-action suit against the company's managers, alleging that the directors violated SEC Rule 10b-5 by disclosing misleading financial information.

In many class-action suits, the accused managers are innocent of any intentional fraud; they simply made mistaken forecasts. The cost of such mistakes can be high, however, if the managers are sued for securities fraud. Rather than risk being sued—and risk potential liability under SEC Rule 10b-5—for publicizing misleading or deceptive financial information, many companies understandably prefer to say less, rather than more, about their future prospects.

In part because of the controversy over class-action suits, in 1995 Congress passed the Private Securities Litigation Reform Act. The act provides, among other things, a "safe harbor" for publicly held companies that make forward-looking statements, such as financial forecasts. Those who make such statements are protected against liability for securities fraud as long as the statements are accompanied by "meaningful cautionary statements identifying important factors that could cause actual results to differ materially from those in the forward-looking statement." The act also deters class-action suits in other ways, such as by limiting attorneys' fees in class actions.

Critics of the legislation—including trial lawyers, consumer groups, and a number of others—contend that the safe harbor in essence gives corporate managers a "license to lie" about the companies' future prospects. Opponents of the law also believe that other provisions of the act, such as those that in effect make it more difficult for plaintiffs to bring a claim of securities fraud, will make it harder for investors to recover for losses caused by fraud. The full effect of the legislation on investors and corporate decision makers depends, of course, on how the courts interpret and apply the act.

A United States Supreme Court decision in 1996 may also curb the extent of class-action suits alleging securities fraud, or at least alter the legal options available to shareholders. In *Matsushita Electric Industrial Co. v. Lawrence Epstein*,[a] the Court held that state-court settlements of class-action securities suits will be respected by federal courts. In other words, plaintiffs who are unsatisfied with a state-court settlement are barred from bringing the same suit in a federal forum in order to obtain better results.

For Critical Analysis: *How do class-action securities-fraud suits benefit society? Does the 1995 legislation go too far in curbing shareholders' rights?*

a. ___U.S.___, 116 S.Ct. 873, 134 L.Ed.2d 6 (1996).

Stock Reform Act of 1990 amended existing securities laws to expand greatly the types of securities violation cases that SEC administrative law judges can hear and the SEC's enforcement options. The act also provides that courts may bar persons who have engaged in securities fraud from serving as officers and directors of publicly held corporations.

The 1990 Securities Acts Amendments authorized the SEC to seek sanctions against those who violate foreign securities laws. These amendments increase the ability of the SEC to cooperate in international securities law enforcement. Under the Market Reform Act of 1990, the SEC can suspend trading in securities in the event that the prices rise and fall excessively in a short period of time.

▌ Regulation of Investment Companies

Investment companies, and mutual funds in particular, grew rapidly after World War II. **Investment companies** act on behalf of many smaller shareholders by buying a large portfolio of securities and professionally managing that portfolio. A **mutual fund** is a specific type of investment company that continually buys or sells to investors

INVESTMENT COMPANY
A company that acts on behalf of many smaller shareholders/owners by buying a large portfolio of securities and professionally managing that portfolio.

MUTUAL FUND
A specific type of investment company that continually buys or sells to investors shares of ownership in a portfolio.

A stockbroker checks investments with a computer. What restrictions does the SEC place on a broker's investment activities?

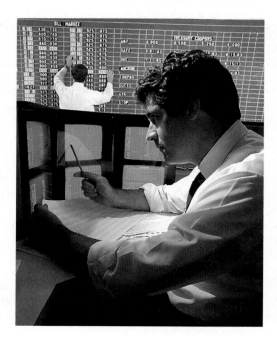

shares of ownership in a portfolio. Such companies are regulated by the Investment Company Act of 1940,[27] which provides for SEC regulation of their activities. The act was expanded by the 1970 amendments to the Investment Company Act. Further minor changes were made in the Securities Act Amendments of 1975 and in later years.

The 1940 act requires that every investment company register with the SEC and imposes restrictions on the activities of these companies and persons connected with them. For the purposes of the act, an investment company is defined as any entity that (1) is engaged primarily "in the business of investing, reinvesting, or trading in securities" or (2) is engaged in such business and has more than 40 percent of its assets in investment securities. Excluded from coverage by the act are banks, insurance companies, savings and loan associations, finance companies, oil and gas drilling firms, charitable foundations, tax-exempt pension funds, and other special types of institutions, such as closely held corporations.

All investment companies must register with the SEC by filing a notification of registration. Each year, registered investment companies must file reports with the SEC. To safeguard company assets, all securities must be held in the custody of a bank or stock exchange member, and that bank or stock exchange member must follow strict procedures established by the SEC.

No dividends may be paid from any source other than accumulated, undistributed net income. Furthermore, there are some restrictions on investment activities. For example, investment companies are not allowed to purchase securities on the margin (pay only part of the total price, borrowing the rest), sell short (sell shares not yet owned), or participate in joint trading accounts.

∎ State Securities Laws

BE AWARE Federal securities laws do not supersede state securities laws.

Today, all states have their own corporate securities laws, or "blue sky laws," that regulate the offer and sale of securities within individual state borders.[28] (As mentioned in

---

27. 15 U.S.C. Sections 80a–1 to 80a–64.
28. These laws are catalogued and annotated in the Commerce Clearing House's *Blue Sky Law Reporter*, a loose-leaf service.

Chapter 10, the phrase *blue sky laws* dates to a 1917 decision by the United States Supreme Court in which the Court declared that the purpose of such laws was to prevent "speculative schemes which have no more basis than so many feet of 'blue sky.' ")[29] Article 8 of the Uniform Commercial Code, which has been adopted by all of the states, also imposes various requirements relating to the purchase and sale of securities. State securities laws apply only to intrastate transactions. Since the adoption of the 1933 and 1934 federal securities acts, the state and federal governments have regulated securities concurrently. Issuers must comply with both federal and state securities laws, and exemptions from federal law are not exemptions from state laws.

There are differences in philosophy among state statutes, but certain features are common to all state blue sky laws. Typically, state laws have disclosure requirements and antifraud provisions, many of which are patterned after Section 10(b) of the Securities Exchange Act of 1934 and SEC Rule 10b-5. State laws also provide for the registration or qualification of securities offered or issued for sale within the state and impose disclosure requirements. Unless an applicable exemption from registration is found, issuers must register or qualify their stock with the appropriate state official, often called a *corporations commissioner*. Additionally, most state securities laws regulate securities brokers and dealers. The Uniform Securities Act, which has been adopted in part by several states, was drafted to be acceptable to states with differing regulatory philosophies.

---

29. *Hall v. Geiger-Jones Co.*, 242 U.S. 539, 37 S.Ct. 217, 61 L.Ed. 480 (1917).

▌Key Terms

accredited investor 743	mutual fund 755	tippee 749
bounty payment 753	red herring 740	tombstone ad 740
insider trading 746	SEC Rule 10b-5 746	
investment company 755	security 737	

▌Chapter Summary: Investor Protection

The Securities Act of 1933 *(See pages 738–744.)*	Prohibits fraud and stabilizes the securities industry by requiring disclosure of all essential information relating to the issuance of stocks to the investing public. 1. *Registration requirements*—Securities, unless exempt, must be registered with the SEC before being offered to the public through the mails or any facility of interstate commerce (including securities exchanges). The *registration statement* must include detailed financial information about the issuing corporation; the intended use of the proceeds of the securities being issued; and certain disclosures, such as interests of directors or officers and pending lawsuits. 2. *Prospectus*—A *prospectus* must be provided to investors, describing the security being sold, the issuing corporation, and the risk attaching to the security. 3. *Exemptions*—The SEC has exempted certain offerings from the requirements of the Securities Act of 1933. Exemptions may be determined on the basis of the size of the issue, whether the offering is private or public, and whether advertising is involved. Exemptions are summarized in Exhibit 29–1.
The Securities Exchange Act of 1934 *(See pages 744–754.)*	Provides for the regulation and registration of securities exchanges, brokers, dealers, and national securities associations (such as the NASD). Maintains a continuous disclosure system for all corporations with securities on the securities exchanges and for those companies that have assets in excess of $10 million and five hundred or more shareholders (Section 12 companies). *(Continued)*

▌Chapter Summary: Investor Protection—Continued

The Securities Exchange Act of 1934—Continued	1. *SEC Rule 10b-5 [under Section 10(b) of the 1934 act]* —
	  a. Applies to insider trading by corporate officers, directors, majority shareholders, and any persons receiving information not available to the public who base their trading on this information.
	  b. Liability for violation can be civil or criminal.
	  c. May be violated by failing to disclose "material facts" that must be disclosed under this rule.
	  d. Applies in virtually all cases concerning the trading of securities—a firm does not have to have its securities registered under the 1933 act for the 1934 act to apply.
	  e. Applies only when the requisites of federal jurisdiction (such as use of the mails, stock exchange facilities, or any facility of interstate commerce) are present.
	
	2. *Insider trading [under Section 16(b) of the 1934 act]* —To prevent corporate officers and directors from taking advantage of inside information (information not available to the investing public), the 1934 act requires officers, directors, and shareholders owning 10 percent or more of the issued stock of a corporation to turn over to the corporation all short-term profits (called short-swing profits) realized from the purchase and sale or sale and purchase of corporate stock within any six-month period.
	
	3. *Proxies [under Section 14(a) of the 1934 act]* —The SEC regulates the content of proxy statements sent to shareholders by corporate managers of Section 12 companies who are requesting authority to vote on behalf of the shareholders in a particular election on specified issues. Section 14(a) is essentially a disclosure law, with provisions similar to the antifraud provisions of SEC Rule 10b-5.

Regulation of Investment Companies *(See pages 755–756.)*	The Investment Company Act of 1940 provides for SEC regulation of investment company activities. It was altered and expanded by the amendments of 1970 and 1975.
State Securities Laws *(See pages 756–757.)*	All states have corporate securities laws (*blue sky laws*) that regulate the offer and sale of securities within state borders; designed to prevent "speculative schemes which have no more basis than so many feet of 'blue sky.'" States regulate securities concurrently with the federal government.

▌For Review

1. What is the essential purpose of the Securities Act of 1933? What is the essential purpose of the Securities Exchange Act of 1934?

2. What is a registration statement? What must it include? What is a prospectus?

3. Basically, what constitutes a *security* under the Securities Act of 1933?

4. What is SEC Rule 10b-5? What is the key to liability under this rule? To what kinds of transactions does SEC Rule 10b-5 apply?

5. Name two theories under which "outsiders" can be held liable for violating SEC Rule 10b-5.

▌Questions and Case Problems

29–1. Registration Requirements. Langley Brothers, Inc., a corporation incorporated and doing business in Kansas, decides to sell no-par common stock worth $1 million to the public. The stock will be sold only within the state of Kansas. Joseph Langley, the chairman of the board, says the offering need not be registered with the SEC. His brother, Harry, disagrees. Who is right? Explain.

29–2. Registration Requirements. Huron Corp. had 300,000 common shares outstanding. The owners of these outstanding shares lived in several different states. Huron decided to split the 300,000 shares two for one. Will Huron Corp. have

to file a registration statement and prospectus on the 300,000 new shares to be issued as a result of the split? Explain.

29–3. Definition of a Security. The W. J. Howey Co. (Howey) owned large tracts of citrus acreage in Lake County, Florida. For several years, it planted about five hundred acres annually, keeping half of the groves itself and offering the other half to the public to help finance additional development. Howey-in-the-Hills Service, Inc., was a service company engaged in cultivating and developing these groves, including the harvesting and marketing of the crops. Each prospective customer was offered both a land sales contract and a service contract, after being told that it was not feasible to invest in a grove unless service arrangements were made. Of the acreage sold by Howey, 85 percent was sold with a service contract with Howey-in-the-Hills Service. Howey did not register with the SEC or meet the other administrative requirements that issuers of securities must fulfill. The SEC sued to enjoin Howey from continuing to offer the land sales and service contracts. Howey responded that no SEC violation existed, because no securities had been issued. Evaluate the definition of a security given in this chapter, and then determine which party should prevail in court, Howey or the SEC. [*SEC v. W. J. Howey Co.*, 328 U.S. 293, 66 S.Ct. 1100, 90 L.Ed. 1244 (1946)]

29–4. Definition of a Security. U.S. News & World Report, Inc., set up a profit-sharing plan in 1962 that allotted to certain employees specially issued stock known as bonus or anniversary stock. The stock was given to the employees for past services and could not be traded or sold to anyone other than the corporate issuer, U.S. News. This special stock was issued only to employees and for no other purpose than as bonuses. Because there was no market for the stock, U.S. News hired an independent appraiser to estimate the fair value of the stock so that the employees could redeem the shares. Charles Foltz and several other employees held stock through this plan and sought to redeem the shares with U.S. News, but Foltz disputed the value set by the appraisers. Foltz sued U.S. News for violation of securities regulations. What defense would allow U.S. News to resist successfully Foltz's claim? [*Foltz v. U.S. News & World Report, Inc.*, 627 F.Supp. 1143 (D.D.C. 1986)]

29–5. Short-Swing Profits. Emerson Electric Co. purchased 13.2 percent of Dodge Manufacturing Co.'s stock in an unsuccessful takeover attempt in June 1967. Less than six months later, when Dodge merged with Reliance Electric Co., Emerson decided to sell its shares. To avoid being subject to the short-swing profit restrictions of Section 16(b) of the Securities Exchange Act of 1934, Emerson decided on a two-step selling plan. First, it sold off sufficient shares to reduce its holdings to 9.96 percent [owners with less than 10 percent are exempt from Section 16(b)], and then it sold the remaining stock—all within a six-month period. Emerson in this way succeeded in avoiding Section 16(b) requirements. Reliance demanded that Emerson return the profits made on both sales. Emerson sought a declaratory judgment from the court that it was not liable, arguing that because at the time of the second sale it had not owned 10 percent of Dodge stock, Section 16(b) did not apply. Does Section 16(b) of the Securities Exchange Act of 1934 apply to Emerson's transactions, and is Emerson liable to Reliance for its profits? Discuss fully. [*Reliance Electric Co. v. Emerson Electric Co.*, 404 U.S. 418, 92 S.Ct. 596, 30 L.E.2d 575 (1972)]

29–6. SEC Rule 10b-5. Energy Resource Group, Inc. (ERG), entered into a written agreement with Ivan West by which West was to find an investor willing to purchase ERG stock. West later formed a partnership, called Investment Management Group (IMG), with Don Peters and another person. According to the terms of the partnership agreement, West's consulting work for ERG was excluded from the work of the IMG partnership. West learned through his consulting position with ERG that ERG was to be acquired by another corporation for $6.00 per share. At the time West learned of the acquisition, ERG stock was trading at $3.50 per share.

Apparently, Peters learned of the acquisition from papers on West's desk in the IMG office and then shared the information with Ken Mick, his stockbroker. Mick then encouraged several clients to buy ERG stock prior to the public announcement of the acquisition. Mick, in return for leaking this inside information to clients, received a special premium from the enriched investors. Mick then paid a portion of the premium to Peters. The SEC brought an action against Peters for violating SEC Rule 10b-5. Under what theory might Peters be held liable for insider trading in violation of SEC Rule 10b-5? Discuss fully. [*SEC v. Peters*, 735 F.Supp. 1505 (D.Kans. 1990)]

29–7. Securities Fraud. William Gotchey owned 50 percent of the shares of First American Financial Consultants, Inc. (FAFC), an investment company registered with the SEC. In the fall of 1987, Paul Hatfield, a client of FAFC, spoke with Gotchey about investing. As a result of their conversations, Hatfield invested $5,000 with FAFC. In December, Hatfield told Gotchey that he wished to invest $20,000, $15,000 of which he wished to place in a secure investment. Gotchey told Hatfield that he would place this $15,000 in mortgage-backed securities to be invested through a mortgage company. For a time, Hatfield received interest payments from FAFC, purportedly from the mortgage-backed investment. He also received statements confirming that the investment had been made. In fact, Gotchey had deposited the entire $20,000 in an FAFC bank account. When Hatfield did not receive the interest payment due at the beginning of July 1988, he confronted Gotchey. Gotchey responded by asking Hatfield to sign an agreement whereby FAFC would repay the $15,000 in monthly installments over ten years. Hatfield refused. Gotchey did not account for the $15,000, and Hatfield received no interest payments after June 1988. Has Gotchey violated Section 10(b) of the Securities Exchange Act? Why or why not? [*SEC v. Gotchey*, 981 F.2d 1251 (4th Cir. 1992)]

29–8. SEC Rule 10b-5. Danny Cherif worked for a Chicago bank from 1979 until 1987, when his position was eliminated because of an internal reorganization. Cherif, through a forged memo to the bank's security department, caused his magnetic identification (ID) card—which he had received as an employee to allow him to enter the bank building—to remain activated after his employment was terminated. Cherif used his ID card to enter the building at night to obtain confidential financial information regarding extraordinary business transactions, such as tender offers. During 1988 and 1989, Cherif made substantial profits by using this information in securities trading. Eventually, Cherif's activities were investigated by the SEC, and he was charged with violating Section 10(b) and SEC Rule 10b-5 by misappropriating and trading on inside information in violation of his fiduciary duties to his former employer. Cherif argued that the SEC had wrongfully applied the misappropriation theory to his activities, because as a former employee, he no longer had a fiduciary duty to the bank. Will the court agree with Cherif? Discuss fully. [*SEC v. Cherif*, 933 F.2d 403 (7th Cir. 1991)]

29–9. SEC Rule 10b-5. In early 1985, FMC Corp. made plans to buy some of its own stock as part of a restructuring of its balance statement. Unknown to FMC management, the brokerage firm FMC employed—Goldman, Sachs & Co.—disclosed information on the stock purchase that found its way to Ivan Boesky. FMC was one of the seven major corporations in whose stock Boesky allegedly traded using inside information. Boesky made purchases of FMC's stock between February 18 and February 21, 1986, and between March 12 and April 4, 1986. Boesky's purchases amounted to a substantial portion of the total volume of FMC stock traded during these periods. The price of FMC stock increased from $71.25 on February 20, 1986, to $97.00 on April 25, 1986. As a result, FMC paid substantially more for the repurchase of its own stock than anticipated. When FMC discovered Boesky's knowledge of its recapitalization plan, FMC sued Boesky for the excess price it had paid—approximately $220 million. Discuss whether FMC should recover under Section 10(b) of the Securities Exchange Act and SEC Rule 10b-5. [*In re Ivan F. Boesky Securities Litigation*, 36 F.3d 255 (2d Cir. 1994)]

29–10. SEC Rule 10b-5. Louis Ferraro was the chairman and president of Anacomp, Inc. In June 1988, Ferraro told his good friend Michael Maio that Anacomp was negotiating a tender offer for stock in Xidex Corp. Maio passed on the information to Patricia Ladavac, a friend of both Ferraro and Maio. Maio and Ladavac immediately purchased shares in Xidex stock. On the day that the tender offer was announced—an announcement that caused the price of Xidex shares to increase—Maio and Ladavac sold their Xidex stock and made substantial profits (Maio made $211,000 from the transactions, and Ladavac gained $78,750). The SEC brought an action against the three individuals, alleging that they had violated, among other laws, SEC Rule 10b-5. Maio and Ladavac claimed that they had done nothing illegal. They argued that they had no fiduciary duty either to Anacomp or to Xidex, and therefore they had no duty to disclose or abstain from trading in the stock of those corporations. Had Maio and Ladavac violated SEC Rule 10b-5? Discuss fully. [*SEC v. Maio*, 51 F.3d 623 (7th Cir. 1995)]

29–11. Definition of a Security. Life Partners, Inc. (LPI), facilitates the sale of life insurance policies that are owned by persons suffering from AIDS (acquired immune deficiency syndrome) to investors at a discount. The investors pay LPI, and LPI pays the policyholder. Typically, the policyholder, in turn, assigns the policy to LPI, which also obtains the right to make LPI's president the beneficiary of the policy. On the policyholder's death, LPI receives the proceeds of the policy and pays the investor. In this way, the terminally ill sellers secure much-needed income in the final years of life, when employment is unlikely and medical bills are often staggering. The SEC sought to enjoin (prevent) LPI from engaging in further transactions on the ground that the investment contracts were securities, which LPI had failed to register with the SEC in violation of securities laws. Do the investment contracts meet the definition of a security discussed in this chapter? Discuss fully. [*SEC v. Life Partners, Inc.*, 87 F.3d 536 (D.C.Cir. 1996)]

A QUESTION OF ETHICS AND SOCIAL RESPONSIBILITY

29–12. *Susan Waldbaum was a niece of the president and controlling shareholder of Waldbaum, Inc. Susan's mother (the president's sister) told Susan that the company was going to be sold at a favorable price and that a tender offer was soon to be made. She told Susan not to tell anyone except her husband, Keith Loeb, about the sale. (Loeb did not work for the company and was never brought into the family's inner circle, in which family members discussed confidential business information.) The next day, Susan told her husband of the sale and cautioned him not to tell anyone, because "it could possibly ruin the sale." The day after he learned of the sale, Loeb told Robert Chestman, his broker, about the sale, and Chestman purchased shares of the company for both Loeb and himself. Chestman was later convicted by a jury of, among other things, trading on misappropriated inside information in violation of SEC Rule 10b-5. [United States v. Chestman, 947 F.2d 551 (2d Cir. 1991)]*

1. On appeal, the central question was whether Chestman had acquired the inside information about the tender offer as a result of an insider's breach of a fiduciary duty. Could Loeb—the "tipper" in this case—be considered an insider?

2. If Loeb was not an insider, did he owe any fiduciary (legal) duty to his wife or his wife's family to keep the information confidential? Would it be fair of the court to impose such a legal duty on Loeb?

FOR CRITICAL ANALYSIS

29–13. *Do you think that the tipper/tippee and misappropriation theories extend liability under SEC Rule 10b-5 too far? Why or why not?*

▌Unit Seven—Cumulative Hypothetical Problem

29–14. *Samuel Polson established a publishing business, and over the years it became quite profitable. On his death, three of his children—Joan, Harley, and Kevin Polson—took over the business.*

1. When Samuel Polson ran the business, one of Polson's employees routinely used the firm's van to make deliveries. One day, while delivering some pamphlets to a customer, the employee negligently drove through a red light and crashed into another car. A passenger in the other car was seriously injured and sued both the employee and Samuel Polson for damages. Is the employee liable? Can Polson be held liable for his employee's negligence? Explain.

2. While he lived, Samuel Polson was the sole owner of the business and paid no business income taxes. What was the form of Samuel's business organization? After Samuel died, his children wanted to continue the business. What options, in terms of business organizational forms, do they have? What are the advantages and disadvantages of each option?

3. Joan, Harley, and Kevin decide to incorporate the business under the name Polson Publishing, Inc. They also want to expand the business by setting up branch offices in two other cities. What steps will they need to take to incorporate the business and obtain the capital needed for expansion?

4. Polson Publishing, now a thriving corporate enterprise, decides to merge with another publishing firm, with Polson as the surviving corporation. What procedures must Polson follow in carrying out the merger? After the merger, would Polson be liable for the debts and obligations of the other company? What if a minority of the shareholders disagree with the merger? What rights and remedies are available to these shareholders?

5. One of Polson Publishing's employees learned that Polson was contemplating a takeover of a rival publishing house. The employee told her husband about the possibility. The husband called their broker, who purchased shares in the target corporation for the employee and her husband, as well as for himself. Has the employee violated any securities law? Has her husband? Has the broker? Explain.

▌Accessing the Internet: Business Law and Legal Environment

If you want to look up the Securities Act of 1933, go to

http://www.law.uc.edu/CCL/33Act/index.html

Likewise, you can examine the Securities Exchange Act of 1934 at

http://www.law.uc.edu/CCL/34Act/index.html

The Center for Corporate Law examines all of the acts outlined in this chapter. Go to

http://www.law.uc.edu/CCL/

The Securities and Exchange Commission has developed its own database called EDGAR. To find out more about EDGAR, log on the Web at

http://www.town.hall.org/edgar/edgar.html

If you subscribe to the commercial service GEnie, you can access the Corporate, Securities, & Business Law section. Once on GEnie, select

Career/Professional Services

Then select

Law RT

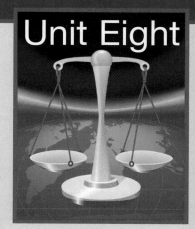

Unit Eight

Government Regulation

UNIT OUTLINE

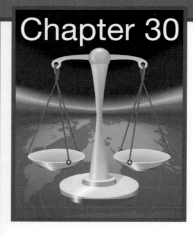

Chapter 30

Antitrust Law

ANTITRUST LAWS
Laws protecting commerce from
unlawful restraints.

*"Free competition is worth more to society than
it costs."*

Oliver Wendell Holmes, Jr., 1841–1935
*(Associate justice of the United States
Supreme Court, 1902–1932)*

CHAPTER OBJECTIVES

After reading this chapter, you should be able to:

1. Explain the purpose of antitrust laws, and identify the major federal antitrust statutes.
2. Summarize the types of activities prohibited by Sections 1 and 2 of the Sherman Act, respectively.
3. Indicate why the Clayton Act was passed, and describe the types of activities prohibited by this act.
4. Describe how the antitrust laws are enforced.
5. Name several exemptions to the antitrust laws.

Today's antitrust laws are the direct descendants of common law actions intended to limit *restraints on trade* (agreements between firms that have the effect of reducing competition in the marketplace). Such actions date to the fifteenth century in England. In America, concern over monopolistic practices arose following the Civil War with the growth of large corporate enterprises and their attempts to reduce or eliminate competition. To thwart competition they legally tied themselves together in *trusts*, legal entities in which trustees hold title to property for the benefit of others. The most powerful of these trusts, the Standard Oil trust, is discussed in this chapter's *Landmark in the Law*.

Many states attempted to control such monopolistic behavior by enacting statutes outlawing the use of trusts. That is why all of the laws that regulate economic competition today are referred to as **antitrust laws**. At the national level, the government recognized the problem in 1887 and passed the Interstate Commerce Act. Congress passed the Sherman Antitrust Act in 1890. In 1914, Congress passed the Clayton Act and the Federal Trade Commission Act to further curb anticompetitive or unfair business practices. Since their passage, the 1914 acts have been amended by Congress to broaden and strengthen their coverage.

This chapter examines these major antitrust statutes, focusing particularly on the Sherman Act and the Clayton Act, as amended, and the types of activities prohibited by those acts. Remember in reading this chapter that the basis of antitrust legislation is the desire to foster competition. Antitrust legislation was initially created—and continues to be enforced—because of our belief that competition leads to lower prices, generates more product information, and results in a better distribution of wealth between consumers and producers. As Oliver Wendell Holmes, Jr., indicated in the opening quotation, free competition is worth more to our society than the cost we pay for it. The cost is, of course, government regulation of business behavior.

▌The Sherman Antitrust Act

In 1890, Congress passed "An Act to Protect Trade and Commerce against Unlawful Restraints and Monopolies"—commonly known as the Sherman Antitrust Act or, more simply, as the Sherman Act. The Sherman Act was and remains one of the government's most powerful weapons in the struggle to maintain a competitive economy. Because of the act's significance, we examine its passage more closely in the following *Landmark in the Law.*

The Sherman Antitrust Act of 1890

LANDMARK IN THE LAW

The author of the Sherman Antitrust Act of 1890, Senator John Sherman, was the brother of the famed Civil War general and a recognized financial authority. Sherman had been concerned for years with the diminishing competition within American industry. This concern led him to introduce into Congress in 1888, in 1889, and again in 1890 bills designed to destroy the large combinations of capital that were, he felt, creating a lack of balance within the nation's economy. He told Congress that the Sherman Act "does not announce a new principle of law, but applies old and well-recognized principles of the common law."[a]

The common law regarding trade regulation was not always consistent. Certainly it was not very familiar to the legislators of the Fifty-first Congress of the United States. The public concern over large business integrations and trusts was familiar, however. By 1890, the Standard Oil trust had become the foremost petroleum manufacturing and marketing combination in the United States. Streamlined, integrated, and centrally and efficiently controlled, its monopoly over the industry could not be disputed. Standard Oil controlled 90 percent of the U.S. market for refined petroleum products, and small manufacturers were incapable of competing with such an industrial leviathan.

The increasing consolidation occurring in American industry, and particularly the Standard Oil trust, did not escape the attention of the American public. In March 1881, Henry Demarest Lloyd, a young journalist from Chicago, published an article in the *Atlantic Monthly* entitled "The Story of a Great Monopoly," which discussed the success of the Standard Oil Company. The article brought to the public's attention for the first time the fact that the petroleum industry in America was dominated by one firm—Standard Oil. Lloyd's article, which was so popular that the issue was reprinted six times, marked the beginning of the American public's growing awareness of, and

a. 21 Congressional Record 2456 (1890).

(Continued)

Landmark in the Law—Continued

concern over, the growth of monopolies, a concern that eventually prompted Congress to pass the Sherman Act in 1890.

In the pages that follow, we look closely at the major provisions of this act. Generally, the act prohibits business combinations and conspiracies that restrain trade and commerce, as well as certain monopolistic practices.

For Critical Analysis: *Is monopoly power (the ability to control a particular market) necessarily harmful to society's interests?*

- - - - - - - - - - - - - - - - - - -

"As a charter of freedom, the [Sherman] Act has a generality and adaptability comparable to that found to be desirable in constitutional provisions."

Charles Evans Hughes, 1862–1948 (Associate justice of the United States Supreme Court, 1930–1941)

- - - - - - - - - - - - - - - - - - -

MONOPOLY
A term generally used to describe a market in which there is a single seller or a limited number of sellers.

MONOPOLY POWER
The ability of a monopoly to dictate what takes place in a given market.

MARKET POWER
The power of a firm to control the market price of its product. A monopoly has the greatest degree of market power.

Major Provisions of the Sherman Act

Sections 1 and 2 contain the main provisions of the Sherman Act:

> 1: Every contract, combination in the form of trust or otherwise, or conspiracy, in restraint of trade or commerce among the several States, or with foreign nations, is hereby declared to be illegal [and is a felony punishable by fine and/or imprisonment].
>
> 2: Every person who shall monopolize, or attempt to monopolize, or combine or conspire with any other person or persons, to monopolize any part of the trade or commerce among the several States, or with foreign nations, shall be deemed guilty of a felony [and is similarly punishable].

These two sections of Sherman Act are quite different. Violation of Section 1 requires two or more persons, as a person cannot contract or combine or conspire alone. Thus, the essence of the illegal activity is *the act of joining together.* Section 2 applies both to several people who have joined together and to individual persons, because it specifies "[e]very person who . . . ." Thus, unilateral conduct can result in a violation of Section 2.

The cases brought to court under Section 1 of the Sherman Act differ from those brought under Section 2. Section 1 cases are often concerned with finding an agreement (written or oral) that leads to a restraint of trade. Section 2 cases deal with the structure of a monopoly that already exists in the marketplace. The term **monopoly** is generally used to describe a market in which there is a single or a limited number of sellers. Whereas Section 1 focuses on agreements that are restrictive—that is, agreements that have a wrongful purpose—Section 2 looks at the so-called misuse of **monopoly power** in the marketplace. Monopoly power exists when a firm has an extremely great amount of **market power**—the power to affect the market price of its product. We return to a discussion of these two sections of the Sherman Act after we look at the act's jurisdictional requirements.

Jurisdictional Requirements

Because Congress can regulate only interstate commerce, the Sherman Act applies only to restraints that affect interstate commerce. As discussed in Chapter 2, courts have construed the meaning of *interstate commerce* broadly, bringing even local activities within the regulatory power of the national government. In regard to the Sherman Act, courts have generally held that any activity that substantially affects interstate commerce is covered by the act. The Sherman Act also extends to nationals abroad who are engaged in activities that have an effect on U.S. foreign commerce. (The extraterritorial application of U.S. antitrust laws is discussed in Chapter 37.)

▌Section 1 of the Sherman Act

The underlying assumption of Section 1 of the Sherman Act is that society's welfare is harmed if rival firms are permitted to join in an agreement that consolidates their market power or otherwise restrains competition. The types of trade restraints that Section 1 of the Sherman Act prohibits generally fall into two broad categories: *horizontal restraints* and *vertical restraints*. Some restraints are so blatantly and substantially anticompetitive that they are deemed ***per se* violations**—illegal *per se* (on their face, or inherently)—under Section 1. Other agreements, however, even though they result in enhanced market power, do not *unreasonably* restrain trade. Under what is called the **rule of reason,** anticompetitive agreements that allegedly violate Section 1 of the Sherman Act are analyzed with the view that they may, in fact, constitute reasonable restraints on trade.

PER SE VIOLATION
A type of anticompetitive agreement—such as a horizontal price-fixing agreement—that is considered to be so injurious to the public that there is no need to determine whether it actually injures market competition; rather, it is in itself (*per se*) a violation of the Sherman Act.

Per Se Violations versus the Rule of Reason

The need for a rule-of-reason analysis of some agreements in restraint of trade is obvious—if the rule of reason had not been developed, virtually any business agreement could conceivably be held to violate the Sherman Act. Justice Louis Brandeis effectively phrased this sentiment in *Chicago Board of Trade v. United States*, a case decided in 1918:

> Every agreement concerning trade, every regulation of trade, restrains. To bind, to restrain, is of their very essence. The true test of legality is whether the restraint imposed is such as merely regulates and perhaps thereby promotes competition or whether it is such as may suppress or even destroy competition.[1]

RULE OF REASON
A test by which a court balances the positive effects (such as economic efficiency) of an agreement against its potentially anticompetitive effects. In antitrust litigation, many practices are analyzed under the rule of reason.

When analyzing an alleged Section 1 violation under the rule of reason, a court will consider several factors. These factors include the purpose of the agreement, the parties' power to implement the agreement to achieve that purpose, and the effect or potential effect of the agreement on competition. Yet another factor that a court might consider is whether the parties could have relied on less restrictive means to achieve their purpose.

The dividing line between agreements that constitute *per se* violations and agreements that should be judged under a rule of reason is seldom clear. Moreover, in some cases, the United States Supreme Court has stated that it is applying a *per se* rule, and yet a careful reading of the Court's analysis suggests that the Court is weighing benefits against harms under a rule of reason. Some have termed this a "soft," or "limited," *per se* rule. Others have called it a "narrow" rule of reason. Perhaps the most that can be said with certainty is that although the distinction between the two rules seems clear in theory, in the actual application of antitrust laws, the distinction has not always been so clear.

Section 1—Horizontal Restraints

The term **horizontal restraint** is encountered frequently in antitrust law. A horizontal restraint is any agreement that in some way restrains competition between rival firms competing in the same market. In the following subsections, we look at several types of horizontal restraints.

HORIZONTAL RESTRAINT
Any agreement that in some way restrains competition between rival firms competing in the same market.

---

1. 246 U.S. 231, 38 S.Ct. 242, 62 L.Ed. 683 (1918).

PRICE-FIXING AGREEMENT
An agreement between competitors in which the competitors agree to fix the prices of products or services at a certain level; prohibited by the Sherman Act.

PRICE FIXING   Any agreement among competitors to fix prices constitutes a *per se* violation of Section 1. Perhaps the definitive case regarding **price-fixing agreements** remains the 1940 case of *United States v. Socony-Vacuum Oil Co.*[2] In that case, a group of independent oil producers in Texas and Louisiana were caught between falling demand due to the Great Depression of the 1930s and increasing supply from newly discovered oil fields in the region. In response to these conditions, a group of the major refining companies agreed to buy "distress" gasoline (excess supplies) from the independents so as to dispose of it in an "orderly manner." Although there was no explicit agreement as to price, it was clear that the purpose of the agreement was to limit the supply of gasoline on the market and thereby raise prices.

The United States Supreme Court recognized the dangerous effects that such an agreement could have on open and free competition. The Court held that the asserted reasonableness of a price-fixing agreement is never a defense; any agreement that restricts output or artificially fixes price is a *per se* violation of Section 1. The rationale of the *per se* rule was best stated in what is now the most famous portion of the Court's opinion—footnote 59. In that footnote, Justice William O. Douglas compared a freely functioning price system to a body's central nervous system, condemning price-fixing agreements as threats to "the central nervous system of the economy."

GROUP BOYCOTT
The refusal to deal with a particular person or firm by a group of competitors; prohibited by the Sherman Act.

GROUP BOYCOTTS   A **group boycott** is an agreement by two or more sellers to boycott, or refuse to deal with, a particular person or firm. Such group boycotts have been held to constitute *per se* violations of Section 1 of the Sherman Act. Section 1 has been violated if it can be demonstrated that the boycott or joint refusal to deal was undertaken with the intention of eliminating competition or preventing entry into a given market. Some boycotts, such as group boycotts against a supplier for political reasons, may be protected under the First Amendment right to freedom of expression, however.

HORIZONTAL MARKET DIVISION   It is a *per se* violation of Section 1 of the Sherman Act for competitors to divide up territories or customers. For example, manufacturers A, B, and C compete against each other in the states of Kansas, Nebraska, and Iowa. By agreement, A sells products only in Kansas; B sells only in Nebraska; and C sells only in Iowa. This concerted action reduces marketing costs and allows all three (assuming there is no other competition) to raise the price of the goods sold in their respective states. The same violation would take place if A, B, and C simply agreed that A would sell only to institutional purchasers (such as school districts, universities, state agencies and departments, and municipalities) in all three states, B only to wholesalers, and C only to retailers.

In the following case, after a partnership's dissolution, the former partners agreed to restrict future advertising to certain geographical regions. At issue is whether the agreement constituted a *per se* violation of Section 1 of the Sherman Act.

---

2.   310 U.S. 150, 60 S.Ct. 811, 84 L.Ed.2d 1129 (1940).

CASE 30.1

BLACKBURN v. SWEENEY
United States Court of Appeals,
Seventh Circuit, 1995.
53 F.3d 825.

HISTORICAL AND SOCIAL SETTING   *Disagreements over money often lead to the breakup of partnerships and other business associations—because money is the most common reason for going into business. Perhaps the most common mistake of partners—including lawyers who practice law together—is failing to adopt the common-sense approach of putting their partnership agreement in writing when business begins. It is the*

Case 30.1—Continued

wrong time to attempt to come to an agreement after relations have become hostile, especially if the partnership has already dissolved.

FACTS Thomas Blackburn, Raymond Green, Charles Sweeney, and Daniel Pfeiffer practiced law together as partners, relying on advertising to attract clients. When they came to a disagreement over the use of partnership funds, they split into separate partnerships—Blackburn and Green, and Sweeney and Pfeiffer. After the split, they negotiated and signed an agreement that restricted, for an indefinite time, the geographical area within which each partnership could advertise. Less than a year later, the Blackburn firm filed a suit in a federal district court against the Sweeney firm, alleging in part that the restriction on advertising was a *per se* violation of the Sherman Act. The court ruled in favor of Sweeney, and Blackburn appealed.

ISSUE Was the agreement to restrict advertising a horizontal agreement to divide markets among competitors?

DECISION Yes. The U.S. Court of Appeals for the Seventh Circuit reversed the ruling of the lower court.

REASON The federal appellate court pointed out that the purpose of the agreement was, as Sweeney testified, to "really trade markets *   *   * . We, in effect, said that'll be your market." The court emphasized that the partnerships "rely heavily on advertising as their primary source of clients." The court concluded that the agreement "to limit advertising to different geographical regions was intended to be, and sufficiently approximates[,] an agreement to allocate markets so that the *per se* rule of illegality applies."

FOR CRITICAL ANALYSIS—Ethical Consideration
Why didn't the court see the agreement to limit advertising as a reasonable covenant not to compete?

TRADE ASSOCIATIONS Businesses in the same general industry or profession frequently organize trade associations to pursue common interests. A trade association's activities may include facilitating exchanges of information, representing members' business interests before governmental bodies, conducting advertising campaigns, and setting regulatory standards to govern the industry or profession. Generally, the rule of reason is applied to many of these horizontal actions.

For example, if a court finds that a trade association practice or agreement that restrains trade is sufficiently beneficial both to the association and to the public, it may deem the restraint reasonable. Other trade association agreements may have such substantially anticompetitive effects that the court will consider them to be in violation of Section 1 of the Sherman Act. In *National Society of Professional Engineers v. United States*,[3] for example, it was held that the society's code of ethics—which prohibited members from discussing prices with a potential customer until after the customer had chosen an engineer—was a Section 1 violation. The United States Supreme Court found that this ban on competitive bidding was "nothing less than a frontal assault on the basic policy of the Sherman Act."

JOINT VENTURES Joint ventures undertaken by competitors are also subject to antitrust laws. As discussed in Chapter 24, a *joint venture* is an undertaking by two or more individuals or firms for a specific purpose. If a joint venture does not involve price fixing or market divisions, the agreement will be analyzed under the rule of reason. Whether the venture will then be upheld under Section 1 depends on an overall assessment of the purposes of the venture, a strict analysis of the potential benefits relative to the likely harms, and—in some cases—an assessment of whether there are less restrictive alternatives for achieving the same goals.[4]

3.   453 U.S. 679, 98 S.Ct. 1355, 55 L.Ed.2d 637 (1978).
4.   See, for example, *United States v. Morgan*, 118 F.Supp. 621 (S.D.N.Y. 1953). This case is often cited as a classic example of how to judge joint ventures under the rule of reason.

A retail store displays a well-known designer's clothing. Why is an agreement between the manufacturer and an independent retailer to sell the clothing at a certain price considered a violation of the Sherman Act?

Section 1—Vertical Restraints

A **vertical restraint** of trade is one that results from an agreement between firms at different levels in the manufacturing and distribution process. In contrast to horizontal relationships, which occur at the same level of operation, vertical relationships encompass the entire chain of production: the purchase of inventory, basic manufacturing, distribution to wholesalers, and eventual sale of a product at the retail level. For some products, these distinct phases may be carried out by different firms. If a single firm may carry out two or more of the different functional phases involved in bringing a product to the final consumer, the firm is considered to be a **vertically integrated firm.**

Even though firms operating at different functional levels are not in direct competition with one another, they are in competition with other firms. Thus, agreements between firms standing in a vertical relationship do significantly affect competition. Some vertical restraints are *per se* violations of Section 1; others are judged under the rule of reason.

RESALE PRICE MAINTENANCE AGREEMENTS   An agreement between a manufacturer and a distributor or retailer in which the manufacturer specifies what the retail prices of its products must be is referred to as a **resale price maintenance agreement.** Resale price maintenance agreements, which are also known as *fair trade agreements*, were authorized for many years under *fair trade laws*. Today, these vertical price-fixing agreements are normally considered to be *per se* violations of Section 1 of the Sherman Act. Although manufacturers can determine the retail prices of their products when they are sold through their own stores or outlets, they may only *suggest* retail prices for their products when the products are sold by independent retailers.

TERRITORIAL OR CUSTOMER RESTRICTIONS   In arranging for the distribution of its product, a manufacturing firm often wishes to insulate dealers from direct competition with other dealers selling the product. To this end, it may institute territorial restrictions, or it may attempt to prohibit wholesalers or retailers from reselling the product to certain classes of buyers, such as competing retailers. There may be legitimate, procompetitive reasons for imposing such territorial or customer restrictions. For example, a computer manufacturer may wish to prevent a dealer from cutting costs and

VERTICAL RESTRAINT
Any restraint on trade created by agreements between firms at different levels in the manufacturing and distribution process.

VERTICALLY INTEGRATED FIRM
A firm that carries out two or more functional phases (manufacture, distribution, retailing, and so on) of a product.

RESALE PRICE MAINTENANCE AGREEMENT
An agreement between a manufacturer and a retailer in which the manufacturer specifies the minimum retail price of its products. Resale price maintenance agreements are illegal *per se* under the Sherman Act.

undercutting rivals by providing computers without promotion or customer service, while relying on nearby dealers to provide these services. This is an example of the "free rider" problem.

Vertical territorial and customer restrictions are judged under a rule of reason. The following case, *Continental T.V., Inc. v. GTE Sylvania, Inc.*, overturned the United States Supreme Court's earlier stance, which had been set out in *United States v. Arnold, Schwinn & Co.*[5] In *Schwinn*, the Court had held vertical territorial and customer restrictions to be *per se* violations of Section 1 of the Sherman Act. The *Continental* case has been heralded as one of the most important antitrust cases since the 1940s. It marked a definite shift from rigid characterization of these kinds of vertical restraints to a more flexible, economic analysis of the restraints under the rule of reason.

5.　388 U.S. 365, 87 S.Ct. 1856, 18 L.Ed.2d 1249 (1967).

CASE 30.2

CONTINENTAL T.V., INC. v. GTE SYLVANIA, INC.

Supreme Court of the United States, 1977.
433 U.S. 36,
97 S.Ct. 2549,
53 L.Ed.2d 568.

HISTORICAL AND ECONOMIC SETTING *Since the passage of the antitrust laws around the turn of the century, the courts have been skeptical of any business action that appeared to restrain commerce, having long agreed that the "heart of our national economic policy [is] faith in the value of competition."* **a** *In determining what is or is not permitted under the antitrust laws, the courts have sometimes applied a rigid standard to business conduct. The trend, however, has been to establish a flexible standard, rather than a rigid one, particularly in regard to conduct that is considered to have procompetitive benefits. Under a flexible standard, a business practice that is considered a criminal offense in one decade may be judged a corporate virtue in the next. In the mid-1970s, for example, the United States Supreme Court began to qualify or overrule many of its previous decisions that prohibited certain business practices as* per se *violations of the antitrust laws. The Court appeared to be focusing on economic considerations, such as consumer welfare,* **b** *economic efficiency,* **c** *and interbrand versus intrabrand competition.*

a.　*Standard Oil Co. v. Federal Trade Commission*, 340 U.S. 231, 71 S.Ct. 240, 95 L.Ed. 239 (1951).
b.　*Reiter v. Sonotone Corp.*, 442 U.S. 330, 99 S.Ct. 2326, 60 L.Ed.2d 931 (1979).
c.　*Broadcast Music, Inc. v. Columbia Broadcasting System, Inc.*, 441 U.S. 1, 99 S.Ct. 1551, 60 L.Ed.2d 1 (1979).

FACTS GTE Sylvania, Inc., a manufacturer of television sets, adopted a franchise plan that limited the number of franchises granted in any given geographical area and that required each franchise to sell only Sylvania products from the location or locations at which they were franchised. A franchise did not constitute an exclusive territory, and Sylvania retained sole discretion to increase the number of retailers in an area, depending on the success or failure of existing retailers in developing their market. Continental T.V., Inc., was a retailer under Sylvania's franchise plan. Shortly after Sylvania proposed a new franchise that would compete with Continental, Sylvania terminated Continental's franchise, and a suit was brought in a federal district court for money owed. Continental claimed that Sylvania's vertically restrictive franchise system violated Section 1 of the Sherman Act. The district court held for Continental, and Sylvania appealed. The appellate court reversed the trial court's decision. Continental appealed to the United States Supreme Court.

ISSUE Was Sylvania's action a *per se* violation of Section 1 of the Sherman Act?

DECISION No. The United States Supreme Court upheld the appellate court's reversal of the district court's decision. Sylvania's vertical system, which was not price restrictive, did not constitute a *per se* violation of Section 1 of the Sherman Act.

REASON The fact that Sylvania restricted franchise retailers in their locations, even though title in the televisions had passed to the retailers, was a violation of the Sherman Act only if the facts and circumstances indicated that the restrictions were unreasonable. Two facts militated against a *per se* rule here. The restrictions were between a manufacturer and a retailer instead of

(Continued)

Case 30.2—Continued

between two entities on the same level (for example, two retailers or two manufacturers), and no price restrictions were involved. The Court noted that although vertical restrictions may reduce competition, they can also stimulate interbrand competition, because the restrictions may allow the manufacturer "to achieve certain efficiencies in the distribution of his products." The court concluded that "[w]hen anticompetitive effects are shown to result from particular vertical restrictions[,] they can be adequately policed under the rule of reason."

FOR CRITICAL ANALYSIS—Economic Consideration
Could the same argument made by the Court in this case (as to the effect of restrictions on market efficiency) be made in regard to resale price maintenance agreements (fair trade laws)?

REFUSALS TO DEAL   As discussed previously, joint refusals to deal (group boycotts) are subject to close scrutiny under Section 1 of the Sherman Act. A single manufacturer acting unilaterally, however, is generally free to deal, or not to deal, with whomever it wishes. In vertical arrangements, even though a manufacturer cannot set retail prices for its products, it can refuse to deal with retailers or dealers that cut prices to levels substantially below the manufacturer's suggested retail prices. In *United States v. Colgate & Co.*,[6] for example, the United States Supreme Court held that a manufacturer's advance announcement that it would not sell to price cutters was not a violation of the Sherman Act.

There are instances, however, in which a unilateral refusal to deal violates antitrust laws. These instances involve offenses proscribed under Section 2 of the Sherman Act and occur only if (1) the firm refusing to deal has—or is likely to acquire—monopoly power and (2) the refusal is likely to have an anticompetitive effect on a particular market.

▌ Section 2 of the Sherman Act

Section 1 of the Sherman Act proscribes certain concerted, or joint, activities that restrain trade. In contrast, Section 2 condemns "every person who shall monopolize, or attempt to monopolize." There are two distinct types of behavior that are subject to sanction under Section 2: *monopolization* and *attempts to monopolize*. A tactic that may be involved in either offense is **predatory pricing**. Predatory pricing involves an attempt by one firm to drive its competitors from the market by selling its product at prices substantially *below* the normal costs of production; once the competitors are eliminated, the firm will attempt to recapture its losses and go on to earn very high profits by driving prices up far above their competitive levels.

PREDATORY PRICING
The pricing of a product below cost with the intent to drive competitors out of the market.

Monopolization

In *United States v. Grinnell Corp.*,[7] the United States Supreme Court defined the offense of **monopolization** as involving the following two elements: "(1) the possession of monopoly power in the relevant market and (2) the willful acquisition or maintenance of the power as distinguished from growth or development as a consequence

MONOPOLIZATION
The possession of monopoly power in the relevant market and the willful acquisition or maintenance of the power, as distinguished from growth or development as a consequence of a superior product, business acumen, or historic accident. A violation of Section 2 of the Sherman Act requires that both of these elements be established.

---

6.   250 U.S. 300, 39 S.Ct. 465, 63 L.Ed. 992 (1919).
7.   384 U.S. 563, 86 S.Ct. 1698, 16 L.Ed.2d 778 (1966).

of a superior product, business acumen, or historic accident." A violation of Section 2 requires that both these elements—monopoly power and an intent to monopolize—be established.

MONOPOLY POWER The Sherman Act does not define *monopoly*. In economic parlance, monopoly refers to control by a single entity. It is well established in antitrust law, however, that a firm may be a monopolist even though it is not the sole seller in a market. Additionally, size alone does not determine whether a firm is a monopoly. For example, a "mom and pop" grocery located in an isolated desert town is a monopolist if it is the only grocery serving that particular market. Size in relation to the market is what matters, because monopoly involves the power to affect prices and output. *Monopoly power*, as mentioned earlier in this chapter, exists when a firm has an extremely great amount of market power. If a firm has sufficient market power to control prices and exclude competition, that firm has monopoly power.

As difficult as it is to define market power precisely, it is even more difficult to measure it. Courts often use the so-called **market-share test**[8]—a firm's percentage share of the "relevant market"—in determining the extent of the firm's market power. A firm may be considered to have monopoly power if its share of the relevant market is 70 percent or more. This is merely a rule of thumb, however; it is not a binding principle of law. In some cases, a smaller share may be held to constitute monopoly power.[9]

The relevant market consists of two elements: (1) a relevant product market and (2) a relevant geographical market. What should the relevant product market include? No doubt, it must include all products that, although produced by different firms, have identical attributes, such as sugar. Products that are not identical, however, may sometimes be substituted for one another. Coffee may be substituted for tea, for example. In defining the relevant product market, the key issue is the degree of interchangeability between products. If one product is a sufficient substitute for another, the two products are considered to be part of the same product market.

The second component of the relevant market is the geographical boundaries of the market. For products that are sold nationwide, the geographical boundaries of the market encompass the entire United States. If a producer and its competitors sell in only a limited area (one in which customers have no access to other sources of the product), then the geographical market is limited to that area. A national firm may thus compete in several distinct areas and have monopoly power in one area but not in another. (See this chapter's *Business Law in Action* for a further discussion of the concept of relevant market.)

THE INTENT REQUIREMENT Monopoly power, in and of itself, does not constitute the offense of monopolization under Section 2 of the Sherman Act. The offense also requires an intent to monopolize. A dominant market share may be the result of business acumen or the development of a superior product. It may simply be the result of historical accident. In these situations, the acquisition of monopoly power is not an antitrust violation. Indeed, it would be counter to society's interest to condemn every firm that acquired a position of power because it was well managed, efficient, and marketed a product desired by consumers. If, however, a firm possesses market power as a result of carrying out some purposeful act to acquire or maintain that power through anticompetitive means, then it is in violation of Section 2. In most monopolization

> "A *rule of such a nature as to bring all trade or traffic into the hands of one company, or one person, and to exclude all others, is illegal.*"
>
> **Sir Edward Coke, 1552–1634** (*British jurist and legal scholar*)

MARKET-SHARE TEST
The primary measure of monopoly power. A firm's market share is the percentage of a market that the firm controls.

KEEP IN MIND Section 2 of the Sherman Act essentially condemns the act of monopolizing, not the possession of monopoly power.

---

8. Other measures of market power have been devised, but the market-share test is the most widely used.
9. This standard was first articulated by Justice Learned Hand in *United States v. Aluminum Co. of America*, 148 F.2d 416 (2d Cir. 1945). A 90 percent share was held to be clear evidence of monopoly power. Anything less than 64 percent, said Justice Hand, made monopoly power doubtful, and anything less than 30 percent was clearly not monopoly power.

Relevant Market versus Trade Area

One of the difficulties in analyzing alleged violations of Section 2 of the Sherman Act is determining the relevant market. For example, consider a case that was brought by Gilbert Bathke and other gasoline retailers (the plaintiffs) located in small Iowa communities against Casey's General Stores, Inc. During the 1980s, Casey's, a multistate retailer of gasoline and other goods, had begun to lose profits to its competitors. In an attempt to increase its sales, Casey's directed its stores that were losing sales to reduce gas prices. The plaintiffs claimed that Casey's price reductions amounted to predatory pricing in violation of, among other laws, Section 2 of the Sherman Act.

One of the central issues in the case concerned Casey's share of the relevant geographical market. The plaintiffs contended that the relevant geographical market consisted of the small towns in which Casey's operated its stores. After all, contended the plaintiffs, consumers preferred to buy their gasoline in the towns in which they lived, and gasoline retailers' trade came mostly from in-town customers. The court held, however, that the plaintiffs had failed to produce "evidence on a critical question: where those gasoline consumers could practically turn for alternatives."

The court pointed out that a geographical market "is determined by inquiring into the 'commercial realities' faced by consumers." Essentially, the question is not where consumers go for their gasoline but where they *could* go. Evidence of consumers' actual habits is not enough, said the court, to establish the relevant geographical market. To demonstrate the "logic and necessity of applying such a requirement in this case," the court illustrated the difference between a "trade area" and a "relevant market."

"Consider the following illustration," stated the court. "Fifteen miles outside of City A is a small town, Town B, which contains a single shoe store, Smith's Clothing. The only people who ever shop in Smith's Clothing are residents of Town B. When Smith's is accused of monopolization, the plaintiffs argue that Town B defines the relevant geographic market, since all of the store's customers come from there. In that case, Smith's market share is 100%. But further inquiry shows the following. Last year 800 residents of Town B purchased shoes. 400 of them purchased from Smith's Clothing, and the other 400 purchased from the numerous shoe stores in City A. Note that this conclusion is absolutely consistent with the proposition that Smith's 'trade area' is Town B. . . . In sum, 'trade area' considers the extent to which customers will travel in order to do business at Smith's. 'Relevant market' considers the extent to which customers will travel in order to avoid doing business at Smith's."

The court concluded that the plaintiffs' evidence, at best, demonstrated only the "trade area" of Casey's stores. The plaintiffs looked at the issue "only from the perspective of Casey's rivals, not from the perspective of the consumer. This is not the correct approach to use in antitrust cases."[a]

For Critical Analysis: *How can plaintiffs in antitrust cases similar to this one obtain evidence concerning where consumers can "practically turn for alternatives"?*

a. *Bathke v. Casey's General Stores, Inc.,* 64 F.3d 340 (8th Cir. 1995).

cases, intent may be inferred from evidence that the firm had monopoly power and engaged in anticompetitive behavior.

Attempts to Monopolize

**ATTEMPTED
MONOPOLIZATION**
Any actions by a firm to eliminate competition and gain monopoly power.

Section 2 also prohibits **attempted monopolization** of a market. Any action challenged as an attempt to monopolize must have been specifically intended to exclude competitors and garner monopoly power. In addition, the attempt must have had a "dangerous" probability of success—only *serious* threats of monopolization are condemned as violations. The probability cannot be dangerous unless the alleged offender possesses some degree of market power. In the following case, the United States Supreme Court summarizes the requirements that a plaintiff must meet to demonstrate that the defendant has attempted to monopolize a market.

CASE 30.3

SPECTRUM SPORTS, INC. v. McQUILLAN

Supreme Court of the United States, 1993.
506 U.S. 447,
113 S.Ct. 884,
122 L.Ed.2d 247.

HISTORICAL AND TECHNOLOGICAL SETTING
Plastics are synthetic materials derived principally from petroleum. Because they are light, easy to clean, durable, and can be made strong, plastics are used in place of many natural substances. Most plastics are what are called polymers, made up of long chains of identical molecules. Bakelite was the world's first polymer. Bakelite was developed in 1909 and used originally in electrical insulation. Sorbothane is an elastic polymer with characteristics that make it useful in a variety of products.

FACTS BTR, Inc., owns the patent rights to sorbothane. In 1980, BTR granted Shirley and Larry McQuillan the distribution rights to sorbothane. In 1981, BTR split the rights between the McQuillans and Spectrum Sports, Inc. Over the next two years, BTR further undercut the McQuillans' once-exclusive rights. Finally, BTR refused to accept their orders, and the McQuillans' business failed. They filed a suit in a federal district court against BTR and Spectrum for, among other things, attempted monopolization in violation of the Sherman Act. The jury found in favor of the McQuillans, and the court ruled accordingly. BTR and Spectrum appealed, and the appellate court affirmed. The defendants appealed to the United States Supreme Court.

ISSUE Had the defendants violated Section 2 of the Sherman Act, which prohibits attempted monopolization?

DECISION No. The United States Supreme Court reversed the decision of the appellate court and remanded the case.

REASON The Supreme Court stated that "[t]o demonstrate attempted monopolization[,] a plaintiff must prove (1) that the defendant has engaged in predatory or anticompetitive conduct with (2) a specific intent to monopolize and (3) a dangerous probability of achieving monopoly power. In order to determine whether there is a dangerous probability of monopolization[,] * * * it [is] necessary to consider the relevant market and the defendant's ability to lessen or destroy competition in that market." The Court pointed out that in this case, the jury inferred "specific intent and dangerous probability of success from the defendants' predatory conduct, without any proof of the relevant market or of a realistic probability that the defendants could achieve monopoly power in that market." The Court explained that the purpose of the Sherman Act "is not to protect businesses from the working of the market; it is to protect the public from the failure of the market. The law directs itself not against conduct which is competitive, even severely so, but against conduct which unfairly tends to destroy competition itself." It is not enough, the Court said, to ask "only whether the defendant has engaged in 'unfair' or 'predatory' tactics."

FOR CRITICAL ANALYSIS—Economic Consideration
Is predatory conduct always anticompetitive?

▌ The Clayton Act

In 1914, Congress attempted to strengthen federal antitrust laws by enacting the Clayton Act. The Clayton Act was aimed at specific anticompetitive or monopolistic practices that the Sherman Act did not cover. The substantive provisions of the act deal with four distinct forms of business behavior, which are declared illegal but not criminal. With regard to each of the four provisions, the act's prohibitions are qualified by the general condition that the behavior is illegal only if it substantially tends to lessen competition or tends to create monopoly power. The major offenses under the Clayton Act are set out in Sections 2, 3, 7, and 8 of the act.

"The commerce of the world is conducted by the strong, and usually it operates against the weak."

Henry Ward Beecher,
1813–1887
(American abolitionist leader)

Section 2—Price Discrimination

PRICE DISCRIMINATION
Setting prices in such a way that two competing buyers pay two different prices for an identical product or service.

Section 2 of the Clayton Act prohibits **price discrimination,** which occurs when a seller charges different prices to competitive buyers for identical goods. Because businesses frequently circumvented Section 2 of the act, Congress strengthened this section by amending it with the passage of the Robinson-Patman Act in 1936.

As amended, Section 2 prohibits price discrimination that cannot be justified by differences in production costs, transportation costs, or cost differences due to other reasons. To violate Section 2, the seller must be engaged in interstate commerce, and the effect of the price discrimination must be to substantially lessen competition or create a competitive injury. Under the Robinson-Patman Act, a seller is prohibited from reducing a price to one buyer below the price charged to that buyer's competitor.

An exception is made if the seller can justify the price reduction by demonstrating that he or she charged the lower price temporarily and in good faith to meet another seller's equally low price to the buyer's competitor. To be predatory, a seller's pricing policies must also include a reasonable prospect of the seller's recouping its losses.[10]

Section 3—Exclusionary Practices

Under Section 3 of the Clayton Act, sellers or lessors cannot sell or lease goods "on the condition, agreement or understanding that the . . . purchaser or lessee thereof shall not use or deal in the goods . . . of a competitor or competitors of the seller." In effect, this section prohibits two types of vertical agreements involving exclusionary practices—exclusive-dealing contracts and tying arrangements.

**EXCLUSIVE-DEALING
CONTRACT**
An agreement under which a seller forbids a buyer to purchase products from the seller's competitors.

EXCLUSIVE-DEALING CONTRACTS   A contract under which a seller forbids a buyer to purchase products from the seller's competitors is called an **exclusive-dealing contract.** A seller is prohibited from making an exclusive-dealing contract under Section 3 if the effect of the contract is "to substantially lessen competition or tend to create a monopoly."

The leading exclusive-dealing decision was made by the Supreme Court in the case of *Standard Oil Co. of California v. United States.*[11] In this case, the then-largest gasoline seller in the nation made exclusive-dealing contracts with independent stations in seven western states. The contracts involved 16 percent of all retail outlets, whose sales were approximately 7 percent of all retail sales in that market. The Court noted that the market was substantially concentrated because the seven largest gasoline suppliers all used exclusive-dealing contracts with their independent retailers and together controlled 65 percent of the market. Looking at market conditions after the arrangements were instituted, the Court found that market shares were extremely stable, and entry into the market was apparently restricted. Thus, the Court held that Section 3 of the Clayton Act had been violated, because competition was "foreclosed in a substantial share" of the relevant market.

TYING ARRANGEMENT
An agreement between a buyer and a seller in which the buyer of a specific product or service becomes obligated to purchase additional products or services from the seller.

TYING ARRANGEMENTS   When a seller conditions the sale of a product (the tying product) on the buyer's agreement to purchase another product (the tied product) produced or distributed by the same seller, a **tying arrangement,** or *tie-in sales agreement,* results. The legality of a tie-in agreement depends on many factors, particularly the purpose of the agreement and the agreement's likely effect on competition in the relevant markets (the market for the tying product and the market for the tied product).

---

10.   See, for example, *Brooke Group, Ltd. v. Brown & Williamson Tobacco Corp.,* 509 U.S. 209, 113 S.Ct. 2578, 125 L.Ed.2d 168 (1993), in which the Supreme Court held that a seller's price-cutting policies could not be predatory "[g]iven the market's realities"—the size of the seller's market share, the expanding output by other sellers, plus other factors.
11.   37 U.S. 293, 69 S.Ct. 1051, 93 L.Ed. 1371 (1949).

In 1936, for example, the United States Supreme Court held that International Business Machines and Remington Rand had violated Section 3 of the Clayton Act by requiring the purchase of their own machine cards (the tied product) as a condition to the leasing of their tabulation machines (the tying product). Because only these two firms sold completely automated tabulation machines, the Court concluded that each possessed market power sufficient to "substantially lessen competition" through the tying arrangements.[12]

Section 3 of the Clayton Act has been held to apply only to commodities, not to services. Tying arrangements, however, also can be considered agreements that restrain trade in violation of Section 1 of the Sherman Act. Thus, those cases involving tying arrangements of services have been brought under Section 1 of the Sherman Act. Traditionally, the courts have held tying arrangements brought under the Sherman Act to be illegal *per se*. In recent years, however, courts have shown a willingness to look at factors that are important in a rule-of-reason analysis. This is another example of the "soft" *per se* rule referred to earlier in this chapter.

What if a tying arrangement affects only one customer? Can the arrangement nonetheless violate Section 1 of the Sherman Act? The following case addresses this issue.

---

12. *International Business Machines Corp. v. United States*, 298 U.S. 131, 56 S.Ct. 701, 80 L.Ed. 1085 (1936).

CASE 30.4

DATAGATE, INC. v. HEWLETT-PACKARD CO.

United States Court of Appeals,
Ninth Circuit, 1995.
60 F.3d 1421.

HISTORICAL AND TECHNOLOGICAL SETTING *Military investment in the 1940s fueled the growth of the electronics industry. Computers made at this time weighed several tons and required the space of a warehouse to store operating components. With the advent of smaller components in the 1960s, computers and other technological equipment became more compact. The Hewlett-Packard Company (HP) produced the first handheld scientific calculator in 1972. In the decades since then, the growth of the electronics and computer industries has seemed unstoppable. Today, HP makes a variety of electronic products, including computer hardware and software.*

FACTS Datagate, Inc., provided repair service for computer hardware made by the Hewlett-Packard Company (HP). HP offered the same service. HP also offered support for those who used its software, but the company refused to provide software support to those

who did not buy its hardware service. Datagate filed a suit in a federal district court against HP, claiming in part that HP's practice constituted an illegal tying arrangement. The arrangement had been imposed on only one HP customer, Rockwell International, but the Rockwell hardware service contract was worth $100,000 per year. The court held that one customer was not enough and entered a judgment in favor of HP. Datagate appealed.

ISSUE Can a tying arrangement affecting only one customer be illegal *per se* under the Sherman Act?

DECISION Yes. The U.S. Court of Appeals for the Ninth Circuit reversed the decision of the lower court and remanded the case for trial.

REASON The federal appellate court pointed out that one of the elements establishing an illegal tying arrangement is that the arrangement "affects a not insubstantial volume of commerce." This element can be met "by the foreclosure of a single purchaser, so long as the purchaser represents a 'not insubstantial' dollar-volume of sales." The court concluded that $100,000 per year is sufficient.

FOR CRITICAL ANALYSIS—Economic Consideration
Did Rockwell International have an alternative to the tying arrangement required by HP?

MARKET CONCENTRATION The percentage of a particular firm's market sales in a relevant market area.

Section 7—Mergers

Under Section 7 of the Clayton Act, a person or business organization cannot hold stock and/or assets in another business "where the effect . . . may be to substantially lessen competition." Section 7 is the statutory authority for preventing mergers that could result in monopoly power or a substantial lessening of competition in the marketplace. Section 7 applies to three types of mergers: horizontal mergers, vertical mergers, and conglomerate mergers. We discuss each type of merger in the following subsections.

A crucial consideration in most merger cases is **market concentration.** Determining market concentration involves allocating percentage market shares among the various companies in the relevant market. When a small number of companies share a larger part of the market, the market is concentrated. For example, if the four largest grocery stores in Chicago accounted for 80 percent of all retail food sales, the market clearly would be concentrated in those four firms. Competition, however, is not necessarily diminished solely as a result of market concentration, and other factors will be considered in determining whether a merger will violate Section 7. One factor of particular importance in evaluating the effects of a merger is whether the merger will make it more difficult for potential competitors to enter the relevant market.

International Perspective

U.S. firms involved in mergers in other countries may find themselves subject to the antitrust laws of those countries. In India, for example, the government regulates any company that has a market share in excess of 25 percent and may bar mergers and other practices that are deemed contrary to the public interest. Taiwan prohibits mergers when the total resulting market share of the firms would exceed 33 percent.

In Germany, a company with more than 20 percent of a major market segment must inform the relevant government agency of this fact, and acquisitions or mergers that would cause undesirable market concentration can be prohibited. Mergers of particularly large companies in European nations are also subject to regulations issued by the European Union. A 1989 regulation gave the European Commission the authority to approve or reject mergers between firms with annual sales exceeding a specified threshold amount.

Other countries may have little or no regulation in respect to mergers. In Egypt, for example, private firms are generally not subject to antitrust restrictions on mergers and acquisitions.

For Critical Analysis: *If firms from different countries are contemplating a merger, what other differences in the law of the two countries—that is, other than different antitrust laws—should be considered?*

HORIZONTAL MERGER A merger between two firms that are competing in the same marketplace.

HORIZONTAL MERGERS   Mergers between firms that compete with each other in the same market are called **horizontal mergers**. If a horizontal merger creates an entity with anything other than a small percentage market share, the merger will be presumed illegal. This is because of the United States Supreme Court's interpretation that Congress, in amending Section 7 of the Clayton Act in 1950, intended to prevent mergers that increase market concentration.[13] Three other factors that the courts also consider in analyzing the legality of a horizontal merger are overall concentration of the relevant market, the relevant market's history of tending toward concentration, and

---

13.   *Brown Shoe v. United States*, 370 U.S. 294, 82 S.Ct. 1502, 8 L.Ed.2d 510 (1962).

whether the apparent design of the merger is to establish market power or to restrict competition.

The Federal Trade Commission (FTC) and the Department of Justice (DOJ) have established guidelines indicating which mergers will be challenged. Under the guidelines, the first factor to be considered in determining whether a merger will be challenged is the degree of concentration in the relevant market. In determining market concentration, the FTC and DOJ employ what is known as the **Herfindahl-Hirschman Index (HHI).** The HHI is the sum of the squares of the percentage market shares of the firms in the relevant market. For example, if there are four firms with shares of 30 percent, 30 percent, 20 percent, and and 20 percent, respectively, then the HHI equals 2,600 ($30^2 + 30^2 + 20^2 + 20^2 = 2,600$). If the premerger HHI is less than 1,000, then the market is unconcentrated, and the merger will not likely be challenged. If the premerger HHI is between 1,000 and 1,800, the industry is moderately concentrated, and the merger will be challenged only if it increases the HHI by 100 points or more. If the premerger HHI is greater than 1,800, the market is highly concentrated. In a highly concentrated market, a merger that produces an increase in the HHI between 50 and 100 points raises significant competitive concerns. Mergers that produce an increase in the HHI of more than 100 points in a highly concentrated market are deemed likely to enhance the market power of the surviving corporation. Thus, any attempted merger by the above four firms would be challenged by the FTC or the DOJ.

The FTC and the DOJ will also look at a number of other factors, including the ease of entry into the relevant market, economic efficiency, the financial condition of the merging firms, the nature and price of the product or products involved, and so on. If a firm is a leading one—having at least a 35 percent share and twice that of the next leading firm—any merger with a firm having as little as a 1 percent share will be challenged.

VERTICAL MERGERS A **vertical merger** occurs when a company at one stage of production acquires a company at a higher or lower stage of production. An example of a vertical merger is a company merging with one of its suppliers or retailers. Courts in the past have almost exclusively focused on "foreclosure" in assessing vertical mergers. Foreclosure occurs because competitors of the merging firms lose opportunities to either sell or buy products from the merging firms.

For example, in *United States v. E. I. du Pont de Nemours & Co.,*[14] du Pont was challenged for acquiring a considerable amount of General Motors (GM) stock. In holding that the transaction was illegal, the United States Supreme Court noted that stock acquisition would enable du Pont to prevent other sellers of fabrics and finishes from selling to GM, which then accounted for 50 percent of all auto fabric and finishes purchases.

Today, whether a vertical merger will be deemed illegal generally depends on several factors, including market concentration, barriers to entry into the market, and the apparent intent of the merging parties. Mergers that do not prevent competitors of either of the merging firms from competing in a segment of the market will not be condemned as "foreclosing" competition and are legal.

CONGLOMERATE MERGERS There are three general types of **conglomerate mergers:** market-extension, product-extension, and diversification mergers. A market-extension merger occurs when a firm seeks to sell its product in a new market by merging with a firm already established in that market. A product-extension merger occurs when a firm seeks to add a closely related product to its existing line by merging with a firm already producing that product. For example, a manufacturer might seek to extend its

HERFINDAHL-HIRSCHMAN INDEX (HHI)
An index of market power used to calculate whether a merger of two corporations will result in sufficient monopoly power to violate antitrust laws.

VERTICAL MERGER
The acquisition by a company at one stage of production of a company at a higher or lower stage of production (such as a company merging with one of its suppliers or retailers).

CONGLOMERATE MERGER
A merger between firms that do not compete with each other because they are in different markets (as opposed to horizontal and vertical mergers).

---

14. 353 U.S. 586, 77 S.Ct. 872, 1 L.Ed.2d 1057 (1957).

line of household products to include floor wax by acquiring a leading manufacturer of floor wax. Diversification occurs when a firm merges with another firm that offers a product or service wholly unrelated to the first firm's existing activities. An example of a diversification merger is an automobile manufacturer's acquisition of a motel chain. The following classic case involves a product-extension conglomerate merger.

CASE 30.5

FEDERAL TRADE COMMISSION v. PROCTER & GAMBLE CO.

Supreme Court of the United States, 1967.
386 U.S. 568,
87 S.Ct. 1224,
18 L.Ed.2d 303.

COMPANY PROFILE *The Procter & Gamble Company (P&G) started in 1837 in Cincinnati, Ohio, when William Procter and James Gamble merged their candle-making and soap-making businesses. In 1878, P&G, which had by then become one of the largest companies in the city of Cincinnati, introduced The White Soap. The White Soap's appeal was that it floated. Renamed Ivory in 1882, the soap was advertised as "99 and 44/100ths percent pure." The advertising campaign for Ivory was one of the first to advertise directly to the consumer. Between 1930 and 1959, P&G became the largest seller of packaged consumer goods in the United States. The company has introduced or acquired more than 160 products under such familiar brand names as Bounce, Charmin, Cheer, Crest, Crisco, Duncan Hines, Folgers Coffee, Hawaiian Punch, Head & Shoulders, Icy Hot, Old Spice, Safeguard, Spic and Span, Tide, and Vicks.*

FACTS P&G, a large and diversified producer of high-turnover household products, acquired Clorox Chemical Company. At the time, Clorox was the leading manufacturer of household bleach in a highly concentrated market. Purex, the major competitor, did not sell its product in some markets, primarily in the northeastern and mid-Atlantic states. P&G's large advertising budget, along with other factors, allowed it to enjoy economic advantages in advertising its products. The Federal Trade Commission (FTC) brought an action against P&G,

claiming that P&G's acquisition of Clorox substantially lessened competition in the market for liquid bleach and thus violated Section 7 of the Clayton Act. Arguing that the merger prevented other bleach products from entering the market, thereby eliminating potential competitors, the FTC ordered P&G to divest itself of (give up) the Clorox Chemical Company. P&G appealed. The appellate court reversed the FTC order and directed that the FTC's complaint be dismissed. The FTC appealed to the United States Supreme Court.

ISSUE Did the merger between P&G and Clorox violate Section 7 of the Clayton Act?

DECISION Yes. The United States Supreme Court upheld the FTC order that P&G divest itself of the Clorox Chemical Company.

REASON P&G had sought to expand its product line by adding household bleach to it. The Court noted that the markets for the products of P&G and Clorox were highly concentrated; that is, they were already dominated by a few companies. Thus, barriers to entry by potential competitors were already high, and competition was at a minimum. The Court concluded that "[i]n the marketing of soaps, detergents and cleansers, as in the marketing of household liquid bleach, advertising and sales promotion are vital. * * * [T]he substitution of Procter, with its huge assets and advertising advantages, for the already dominant Clorox would dissuade new entrants and discourage active competition from the firms already in the industry due to fear of retaliation by Procter."

FOR CRITICAL ANALYSIS—Economic Consideration
How should a court determine when potential competition is sufficiently injured to require that a corporate acquisition be prevented?

Section 8—Interlocking Directorates

Section 8 of the Clayton Act deals with *interlocking directorates*—that is, the practice of having individuals serve as directors on the boards of two or more competing companies simultaneously. Specifically, no person may be a director in two or more competing corporations at the same time if either of the corporations has capital, surplus, or undivided profits aggregating more than $13,239,000 or competitive sales of

$1,323,900 or more. The threshold amounts are adjusted each year by the Federal Trade Commission (FTC). (The amounts given here are those announced by the FTC in 1996.)

▌ The Federal Trade Commission Act

The Federal Trade Commission Act was enacted in 1914, the same year the Clayton Act was written into law. Section 5 is the sole substantive provision of the act. It provides, in part, as follows: "Unfair methods of competition in or affecting commerce, and unfair or deceptive acts or practices in or affecting commerce are hereby declared illegal." Section 5 condemns all forms of anticompetitive behavior that are not covered under other federal antitrust laws. The act also created the Federal Trade Commission to implement the act's provisions.

CONTRAST Section 5 of the Federal Trade Commission Act is broader than the other antitrust laws. It covers virtually all anticompetitve behavior, including conduct that does not violate either the Sherman Act or the Clayton Act.

▌ Enforcement of Antitrust Laws

The federal agencies that enforce the federal antitrust laws are the U.S. Department of Justice (DOJ) and the Federal Trade Commission (FTC). The DOJ can prosecute violations of the Sherman Act as either criminal or civil violations. Violations of the Clayton Act are not crimes, and the DOJ can enforce that statute only through civil proceedings. The various remedies that the DOJ has asked the courts to impose include **divestiture** (making a company give up one or more of its operating functions) and dissolution. The DOJ might force a group of meat packers, for example, to divest itself of control or ownership of butcher shops.

The FTC also enforces the Clayton Act (but not the Sherman Act) and has sole authority to enforce violations of Section 5 of the Federal Trade Commission Act. FTC actions are effected through administrative orders, but if a firm violates an FTC order, the FTC can seek court sanctions for the violation.

A private party can sue for treble damages and attorneys' fees under Section 4 of the Clayton Act if the party is injured as a result of a violation of any of the federal antitrust laws, except Section 5 of the Federal Trade Commission Act. In some

DIVESTITURE
The act of selling one or more of a company's parts, such as a subsidiary or plant; often mandated by the courts in merger or monopolization cases.

Janet Reno, the Attorney General of the United States, is the head of the U.S. Department of Justice (DOJ). Who, besides the DOJ, can enforce the antitrust laws?

NOTE In a suit under the Federal Trade Commission Act, a private party can obtain damages, but not treble damages.

instances, private parties may also seek injunctive relief to prevent antitrust violations. The courts have determined that the ability to sue depends on the directness of the injury suffered by the would-be plaintiff. Thus, a person wishing to sue under the Sherman Act must prove (1) that the antitrust violation either caused or was a substantial factor in causing the injury that was suffered and (2) that the unlawful actions of the accused party affected business activities of the plaintiff that were protected by the antitrust laws.

In recent years, more than 90 percent of all antitrust actions have been brought by private plaintiffs. One reason for this is, of course, that successful plaintiffs may recover three times the damages that they have suffered as a result of the violation. Such recoveries by private plaintiffs for antitrust violations have been rationalized as encouraging people to act as "private attorneys general" who will vigorously pursue antitrust violators on their own initiative.

International Perspective

As mentioned earlier in this chapter, the reach of U.S. antitrust laws extends beyond the territorial borders of the United States. The U.S. government (the DOJ or the FTC) and private parties may bring an action against a foreign party that has violated Section 1 of the Sherman Act, and the FTC act may also be applied to foreign trade. Foreign mergers, if Section 7 of the Clayton Act applies, may also be brought within the jurisdiction of U.S. courts.

The 1994 revision of the Antitrust Enforcement Guidelines for International Operations (the guidelines are jointly created by the DOJ and the FTC) provides as follows: "Anti-competitive conduct that affects U.S. domestic or foreign commerce may violate the U.S. antitrust laws regardless of where such conduct occurs or the nationality of the parties involved." Before U.S. courts will exercise jurisdiction and apply antitrust laws to actions occurring in other countries, however, normally it must be shown that the alleged violation had a *substantial effect* on U.S. commerce. (See Chapter 37 for a further discussion of the extraterritorial application of U.S. antitrust laws.)

For Critical Analysis: *Should U.S. business firms operating within the United States similarly be subject to the antitrust laws of other countries?*

∎ Exemptions from Antitrust Laws

There are many legislative and constitutional limitations on antitrust enforcement. Most statutory and judicially created exemptions to the antitrust laws apply to the following areas or activities:

1. *Labor.* Section 6 of the Clayton Act generally permits labor unions to organize and bargain without violating antitrust laws. Section 20 of the Clayton Act specifies that strikes and other labor activities are not violations of any law of the United States. A union can lose its exemption, however, if it combines with a nonlabor group rather than acting simply in its own self-interest.

2. *Agricultural associations and fisheries.* Section 6 of the Clayton Act (along with the Capper-Volstead Act of 1922) exempts agricultural cooperatives from the antitrust laws. The Fisheries Cooperative Marketing Act of 1976 exempts from antitrust legislation individuals in the fishing industry who collectively catch, produce, and prepare for market their products. Both exemptions allow members of such co-ops to combine and set prices for a particular product, but they do not allow them to engage in exclusionary practices or restraints of trade directed at competitors.

3. *Insurance.* The McCarran-Ferguson Act of 1945 exempts the insurance business from the antitrust laws whenever state regulation exists. This exemption does not cover boycotts, coercion, or intimidation on the part of insurance companies.

4. *Foreign trade.* Under the provisions of the 1918 Webb-Pomerene Act, American exporters may engage in cooperative activity to compete with similar foreign associations. This type of cooperative activity may not, however, restrain trade within the United States or injure other American exporters. The Export Trading Company Act of 1982 broadened the Webb-Pomerene Act by permitting the Department of Justice to certify properly qualified export trading companies. Any activity within the scope described by the certificate is exempt from public prosecution under the antitrust laws.

5. *Professional baseball.* In 1922, the United States Supreme Court held that professional baseball was not within the reach of federal antitrust laws because it did not involve "interstate commerce."[15] (See the *Ethical Perspective* below on this topic.)

6. *Oil marketing.* The 1935 Interstate Oil Compact allows states to determine quotas on oil that will be marketed in interstate commerce.

7. *Cooperative research and production.* Cooperative research among small business firms is exempt under the Small Business Administration Act of 1958, as amended. Research or production of a product, process, or service by joint ventures consisting of competitors is exempt under special federal legislation, including the National Cooperative Research Act of 1984 and the National Cooperative Production Amendments of 1993.

8. *Joint efforts by businesspersons to obtain legislative or executive action.* This is often referred to as the *Noerr-Pennington doctrine.*[16] For example, video producers might jointly lobby Congress to change the copyright laws, or a video-rental company might sue another video-rental firm, without being held liable for attempting to restrain trade. Though selfish rather than purely public-minded conduct is permitted, there is an exception: an action will not be protected if it is clear that the action is "objectively baseless in the sense that no reasonable [person] could reasonably expect success on the merits" and it is an attempt to make anticompetitive use of government processes.[17]

9. *Other exemptions.* Other activities exempt from antitrust laws include activities approved by the president in furtherance of the defense of our nation (under the Defense Production Act of 1950, as amended); state actions, when the state policy is clearly articulated and the policy is actively supervised by the state;[18] and activities of regulated industries (such as the communication and banking industries) when federal commissions, boards, or agencies (such as the Federal Communications Commission and the Federal Maritime Commission) have primary regulatory authority.

NOTE State actions include the regulation of public utilities, whose rates may be set by the states in which they do business.

---

15. *Federal Baseball Club of Baltimore, Inc. v. National League of Professional Baseball Clubs,* 259 U.S. 200, 42 S.Ct. 465, 66 L.Ed. 898 (1922).

16. See *United Mine Workers of America v. Pennington,* 381 U.S. 657, 89 S.Ct. 1585, 14 L.Ed.2d 626 (1965), and *Eastern Railroad Presidents Conference v. Noerr Motor Freight, Inc.,* 365 U.S. 127, 81 S.Ct. 523, 5 L.Ed.2d 464 (1961).

17. *Professional Real Estate Investors, Inc. v. Columbia Pictures Industries, Inc.,* 508 U.S. 49, 113 S.Ct. 1920, 123 L.Ed.2d 611 (1993).

18. See *Parker v. Brown,* 347 U.S. 341, 63 S.Ct. 307, 87 L.Ed. 315 (1943).

The fact that baseball remains exempt from antitrust laws not only seems unfair to many but also defies logic: Why is an exemption made for baseball but not for other professional sports? This perfectly reasonable question has been asked innumerable times, and the answer is always the same: baseball is exempt because the United

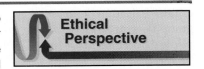

Ethical Perspective

(Continued)

Ethical Perspective—Continued

States Supreme Court, in 1922, said that it was. The Court held that baseball is not subject to antitrust laws because baseball leagues' activities did not involve interstate commerce—and thus did not meet the requirement for federal jurisdiction.

Under modern interpretations of what constitutes interstate commerce, the Court's decision in the 1922 case would clearly be erroneous. Nonetheless, based on that decision, professional baseball continues to retain its extraordinary status as the only professional sport exempt from antitrust laws.

For Critical Analysis: *How can you explain professional baseball's continued exempt status under the antitrust laws?*

Application

Law and the Businessperson— Avoiding Antitrust Problems

Business managers need to be aware of how antitrust legislation may affect their activities. In addition to federal antitrust laws covered in this chapter, numerous state antitrust laws also exist. States also now have the power to bring civil suits to enforce federal antitrust laws. Additionally, antitrust law is subject to various interpretations by the court. Unless businesspersons exercise caution, a court may decide that their actions are in violation of a federal or state statute.

If you are a business manager or owner, you should thus be careful when communicating with a direct competitor that offers products or services that are similar to those of your own company. If you know that such communications might cause problems in your line of business, you should probably arrange for the appropriate employees to attend a seminar given by professionals who will let your employees know what is legal and what is not in dealing with competitors. Generally, any businessperson who is worried about potential antitrust violations should seek counsel from a competent attorney specializing in antitrust law.

 Checklist for Avoiding Antitrust Problems

1. Exercise caution when communicating and dealing with competitors.
2. Seek the advice of an attorney specializing in antitrust law to assure that your business practices and agreements do not violate antitrust laws.

▌Key Terms

▌ Chapter Summary: Antitrust Law

Sherman Antitrust Act (1890) *(See pages 765–775.)*	1. *Major provisions—*
	  a. Section 1—Prohibits contracts, combinations, and conspiracies in restraint of trade.
	    (1) Horizontal restraints subject to Section 1 include price-fixing agreements, group boycotts (joint refusals to deal), horizontal market division, trade association agreements, and joint ventures.
	    (2) Vertical restraints subject to Section 1 include resale price maintenance agreements, territorial or customer restrictions, and refusals to deal.
	  b. Section 2—Prohibits monopolies and attempts to monopolize.
	
	2. *Jurisdictional requirements*—The Sherman Act applies only to activities that have a significant impact on interstate commerce.
	
	3. *Interpretative rules—*
	  a. *Per se* rule—Applied to restraints on trade that are so inherently anticompetitive that they cannot be justified and are deemed illegal as a matter of law.
	  b. Rule of reason—Applied when an anticompetitive agreement may be justified by legitimate benefits. Under the rule of reason, the lawfulness of a trade restraint will be determined by the purpose and effects of the restraint.

Clayton Act (1914) *(See pages 775–781.)*	The major provisions are as follows:
	
	1. *Section 2*—As amended in 1936 by the Robinson-Patman Act, prohibits price discrimination that substantially lessens competition and prohibits a seller engaged in interstate commerce from selling to two or more buyers goods of similar grade and quality at different prices when the result is a substantial lessening of competition or the creation of a competitive injury.
	
	2. *Section 3*—Prohibits exclusionary practices, such as exclusive-dealing contracts and tying arrangements, when the effect may be to substantially lessen competition.
	
	3. *Section 7*—Prohibits mergers when the effect may be to substantially lessen competition or to tend to create a monopoly.
	  a. Horizontal mergers—The acquisition by merger or consolidation of a competing firm engaged in the same relevant market. Will be unlawful only if a merger results in the merging firms' holding a disproportionate share of the market, resulting in a substantial lessening of competition, and if the merger does not enhance consumer welfare by increasing efficiency of production or marketing.
	  b. Vertical mergers—The acquisition by a seller of one of its buyers or vice versa. Will be unlawful if the merger prevents competitors of either merging firm from competing in a segment of the market that otherwise would be open to them, resulting in a substantial lessening of competition.
	  c. Conglomerate mergers—The acquisition of a noncompeting business.
	
	4. *Section 8*—Prohibits interlocking directorates.

Federal Trade Commission Act (1914) *(See page 781.)*	Prohibits unfair methods of competition; established and defined the powers of the Federal Trade Commission.
Enforcement of Antitrust Laws *(See pages 781–782.)*	Antitrust laws are enforced by the Department of Justice, by the Federal Trade Commission, and in some cases by private parties, who may be awarded treble damages and attorneys' fees.
Exemptions from Antitrust Laws *(See pages 782–784.)*	1. Labor unions (under Section 6 of the Clayton Act of 1914). 2. Agricultural associations and fisheries (under Section 6 of the Clayton Act of 1914, the Capper-Volstead Act of 1922, and the Fisheries Cooperative Marketing Act of 1976). 3. Insurance—when state regulation exists (under the McCarran-Ferguson Act of 1945). 4. Export trading companies (under the Webb-Pomerene Act of 1918 and the Export Trading Company Act of 1982). 5. Professional baseball (by a 1922 judicial decision). 6. Oil marketing (under the Interstate Oil Compact of 1935).

(Continued)

▮ Chapter Summary: Antitrust Law—Continued

Exemptions from Antitrust Laws— Continued	7. Cooperative research and production (under various acts, including the Small Business Administration Act of 1958, as amended, the National Cooperative Research Act of 1984, and the National Cooperative Production Amendments of 1993).
	8. Joint efforts by businesspersons to obtain legislative or executive action (under the *Noerr-Pennington* doctrine).
	9. Other activities, including certain national defense actions, state actions, and actions of certain regulated industries.

▮ For Review

1. What is a monopoly? What is market power? How do these concepts relate to each other?

2. What type of activity is prohibited by Section 1 of the Sherman Act? What type of activity is prohibited by Section 2 of the Sherman Act?

3. What are the four major provisions of the Clayton Act, and what types of activities do these provisions prohibit?

4. What federal agencies enforce the federal antitrust laws?

5. Name four activities that are exempt from the antitrust laws.

▮ Questions and Case Problems

30–1. Sherman Act. An agreement that is blatantly and substantially anticompetitive is deemed a *per se* violation of Section 1 of the Sherman Act. Under what rule is an agreement analyzed if it appears to be anticompetitive but is not a *per se* violation? In making this analysis, what factors will a court consider?

30–2. Antitrust Laws. Allitron, Inc., and Donovan, Ltd., are interstate competitors selling similar appliances, principally in the states of Indiana, Kentucky, Illinois, and Ohio. Allitron and Donovan agree that Allitron will no longer sell in Ohio and Indiana and that Donovan will no longer sell in Kentucky and Illinois. Have Allitron and Donovan violated any antitrust laws? If so, which law? Explain.

30–3. Antitrust Laws. The partnership of Alvaredo and Parish is engaged in the oil-wellhead service industry in the states of New Mexico and Colorado. The firm presently has about 40 percent of the market for this service. Webb Corp. competes with the Alvaredo-Parish partnership in the same state area. Webb has approximately 35 percent of the market. Alvaredo and Parish acquire the stock and assets of the Webb Corp. Do the antitrust laws prohibit the type of action undertaken by Alvaredo and Parish? Discuss fully.

30–4. Horizontal Restraints. Jorge's Appliance Corp. was a new retail seller of appliances in Sunrise City. Because of its innovative sales techniques and financing, Jorge's caused a substantial loss of sales from the appliance department of No-Glow Department Store, a large chain store with a great deal of buying power. No-Glow told a number of appliance manufacturers that if they continued to sell to Jorge's, No-Glow

would discontinue its large volume of purchases from them. The manufacturers immediately stopped selling appliances to Jorge's. Jorge's filed suit against No-Glow and the manufacturers, claiming that their actions constituted an antitrust violation. No-Glow and the manufacturers were able to prove that Jorge's was a small retailer with a small portion of the market. They claimed that because the relevant market was not substantially affected, they were not guilty of restraint of trade. Discuss fully whether there was an antitrust violation.

30–5. Exclusionary Practices. Instant Foto Corp. is a manufacturer of photography film. At the present time, Instant Foto has approximately 50 percent of the market. Instant Foto advertises that the purchase price for Instant Foto film includes photo processing by Instant Foto Corp. Instant Foto claims that its film processing is specially designed to improve the quality of photos taken with Instant Foto film. Is Instant Foto's combination of film purchase and film processing an antitrust violation? Explain.

30–6. Sherman Act, Section 2. For some time, the four major and independently owned downhill skiing facilities in Aspen, Colorado—Ajax, Aspen Highlands, Buttermilk, and Snowmass—offered an "all-Aspen" skiing ticket that could be used at any of the four facilities. The proceeds of the all-Aspen ticket sales were distributed to the four facilities in proportion to the number of skiers using each one. By 1977, Aspen Skiing Co. had acquired ownership of Ajax, Buttermilk, and Snowmass. The company discontinued the all-Aspen ticket, offering instead a ticket that could be used by skiers only at its three facilities. As a result of Aspen Skiing Co.'s activities, Aspen

Highlands's share of the skiing market declined from 20 percent in 1977 to only 11 percent by 1981. Aspen Highlands brought an action against Aspen Skiing Co., alleging that the latter had monopolized the Aspen skiing market and that its discontinuation of the all-Aspen ticket sales constituted an intentional attempt to misuse that power in violation of Section 2 of the Sherman Act. Aspen Skiing Co. claimed that its actions represented nothing more than a refusal to participate in a cooperative venture with a competitor and therefore could not possibly be illegal under antitrust laws. Which party will prevail in court, and why? [*Aspen Skiing Co. v. Aspen Highlands Skiing Corp.*, 472 U.S. 585, 105 S.Ct. 2847, 86 L.Ed.2d 467 (1985)]

30–7. Sherman Act, Section 1. Hartwell and Business Electronics Corp. were both authorized by Sharp Electronics Corp. to sell Sharp electronic products in the Houston, Texas, area. Business Electronics continuously sold Sharp products at below suggested retail prices. Hartwell complained to Sharp Electronics about its rival's price-cutting tactics, and Sharp Electronics eventually terminated Business Electronics's dealership. Business Electronics brought an action, claiming that Sharp and Hartwell had conspired together to create a vertical restraint of trade that was illegal *per se* under Section 1 of the Sherman Act. Does Sharp's termination of Business Electronics's dealership constitute a *per se* violation of Section 1, or should the rule of reason apply? Discuss fully. [*Business Electronics Corp. v. Sharp Electronics Corp.*, 485 U.S. 717, 108 S.Ct. 1515, 99 L.Ed.2d 806 (1988)]

30–8. Sherman Act, Section 1. Harcourt Brace Jovanovich Legal and Professional Publications (HBJ), the nation's largest provider of bar review materials and lecture services, began offering a Georgia bar review course in 1976. It was in direct, and often intense, competition with BRG of Georgia, Inc., the other main provider of bar review courses in Georgia, from 1977 to 1979. In early 1980, HBJ and BRG entered into an agreement that gave BRG the exclusive right to market HBJ's materials in Georgia and to use its trade name, Bar/Bri. The parties agreed that HBJ would not compete with BRG in Georgia and that BRG would not compete with HBJ outside of Georgia. Immediately after the 1980 agreement, the price of BRG's course was increased from $150 to over $400. Jay Palmer, a former law student, brought an action against the two firms, alleging that the 1980 agreement violated Section 1 of the Sherman Act. What will the court decide? Discuss fully. [*Palmer v. BRG of Georgia, Inc.*, 498 U.S. 46, 111 S.Ct. 401, 112 L.Ed.2d 349 (1990)]

30–9. Clayton Act. Ford Motor Co. purchased Autolite Co., a manufacturer of spark plugs. Ford, Chrysler, and General Motors together produced 90 percent of American automobiles. The spark plug market was dominated by Champion (50 percent), General Motors (30 percent), and Autolite (15 percent). Ford had planned to begin manufacturing its own spark plugs but decided to buy Autolite instead. Following Ford's purchase of Autolite, Champion was the only independent spark plug manufacturer, and five years after Ford's acquisition of Autolite, Champion's share of the spark plug market had been reduced from 50 percent to about 33 percent. The United States brought an action against Ford, claiming that its acquisition of Autolite violated Section 7 of the Clayton Act because it substantially lessened competition in the spark plug market. Did Ford's acquisition of Autolite violate Section 7 of the Clayton Act by foreclosing a sufficiently large segment of the spark plug market to competition? Discuss fully. [*Ford Motor Co. v. United States*, 405 U.S. 562, 92 S.Ct. 1142, 31 L.Ed.2d 492 (1972)]

30–10. Tying Arrangements. Eastman Kodak Co. has about a 20 percent share of the highly competitive market for high-volume photocopiers and microfilm equipment and controls nearly the entire market for replacement parts for its equipment (which are not interchangeable with parts for other manufacturers' equipment). Prior to 1985, Kodak sold replacement parts for its equipment without significant restrictions. As a result, a number of independent service organizations (ISOs) purchased Kodak parts to use when repairing and servicing Kodak copiers. In 1985, Kodak changed its policy to prevent the ISOs from competing with Kodak's own service organizations. It ceased selling parts to ISOs and refused to sell replacement parts to its customers unless they agreed *not* to have their equipment serviced by ISOs. In 1987, Image Technical Services, Inc., and seventeen other ISOs sued Kodak, alleging that Kodak's policy was a tying arrangement in violation of Section 1 of the Sherman Act. Assuming that Kodak does not have market power in the market for photocopying and microfilm equipment, does Kodak's restrictive policy constitute an illegal tying arrangement? Does it violate antitrust laws in any way? Discuss fully. [*Eastman Kodak Co. v. Image Technical Services, Inc.*, 504 U.S. 451, 112 S.Ct. 2072, 119 L.Ed.2d 265 (1992)]

30–11. Robinson-Patman Act. Stelwagon Manufacturing Co. agreed with Tarmac Roofing Systems, Inc., to promote and develop a market for Tarmac's products in the Philadelphia area. In return, Tarmac promised not to sell its products to other area distributors. In 1991, Stelwagon learned that Tarmac had been selling its products to Stelwagon's competitors—the Standard Roofing Co. and the Celotex Corp.—at substantially lower prices. Stelwagon filed a suit against Tarmac in a federal district court. What is the principal factor in determining whether Tarmac violated the Robinson-Patman Act? Did Tarmac violate the act? [*Stelwagon Manufacturing Co. v. Tarmac Roofing Systems, Inc.*, 63 F.3d 1267 (3d Cir. 1995)]

30–12. Antitrust Laws. Great Western Directories, Inc. (GW), is an independent publisher of telephone directory Yellow Pages. GW buys information for its listings from Southwestern Bell Telephone Co. (SBT). Southwestern Bell Corp. owns SBT and Southwestern Bell Yellow Pages (SBYP), which publishes a directory in competition with GW. In June 1988, in some markets, SBT raised the price for its listing information, and SBYP lowered the price for advertising in its Yellow Pages. GW feared that these companies would do the same thing in other local markets, and it would then be too expensive to compete in those markets. Because of this fear, GW left one market and declined to compete in another. Consequently, SBYP had a monopoly in those markets. GW and another independent publisher filed a suit in a federal district court against Southwestern Bell Corp. What antitrust law, if any, did Southwestern Bell Corp. violate? Should the independent companies be entitled to damages? [*Great Western Directories, Inc. v. Southwestern Bell Telephone Co.*, 74 F.3d 613 (5th Cir. 1996)]

A QUESTION OF ETHICS
AND SOCIAL RESPONSIBILITY

30–13. A group of lawyers in the District of Columbia regularly acted as court-appointed attorneys for indigent defendants in District of Columbia criminal cases. At a meeting of the Superior Court Trial Lawyers Association (SCTLA), the attorneys agreed to stop providing this representation until the district increased their compensation. Their subsequent boycott had a severe impact on the district's criminal justice system, and the District of Columbia gave in to the lawyers' demands for higher pay. After the lawyers had returned to work, the Federal Trade Commission filed a complaint against the SCTLA and four of its officers and, after an investigation, ruled that the SCTLA's activities constituted an illegal group boycott in violation of antitrust laws. [Federal Trade Commission v. Superior Court Trial Lawyers Association, 493 U.S. 411, 110 S.Ct. 768, 107 L.Ed.2d 851 (1990)]

1. The SCTLA obviously was aware of the negative impact its decision would have on the district's criminal justice system. Given this fact, do you think the lawyers behaved ethically?

2. On appeal, the SCTLA claimed that its boycott was undertaken to publicize the fact that the attorneys were underpaid and that the boycott thus constituted an expression protected by the First Amendment. Do you agree with this argument?

3. Labor unions have the right to strike when negotiations between labor and management fail to result in agreement. Is it fair to prohibit members of the SCTLA from "striking" against their employer, the District of Columbia, simply because the SCTLA is a professional organization and not a labor union?

 FOR CRITICAL ANALYSIS

30–14. Critics of antitrust law claim that in the long run, competitive market forces will eliminate private monopolies unless they are fostered by government regulation. Do you agree with these critics? Why or why not?

▌Accessing the Internet: Business Law and Legal Environment

You can find out what the Antitrust Division of the U.S. Department of Justice is doing by addressing the following:

http://www.usdoj.gov/

If you use the Yahoo browser, you can access valuable information about antitrust law. Go to

http://www.yahoo.com/Government/Law/

If you have any problems with Yahoo, you can get E-mail help at

admin@yahoo.com

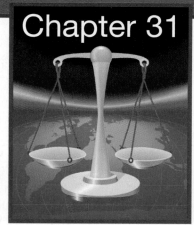

Chapter 31

Consumer and Environmental Law

"*Subject to specific constitutional limitations, when the legislature has spoken, the public interest has been declared in terms well nigh conclusive.*"

William O. Douglas, 1898–1980
(Associate justice of the United States Supreme Court, 1939–1975)

CHAPTER OBJECTIVES

After reading this chapter, you should be able to:

1. Summarize the major consumer protection laws.
2. Indicate some specific ways in which consumers are protected against deceptive advertising and sales practices.
3. Explain how the government protects consumers who are involved in credit transactions.
4. List and describe the major statutes that regulate environmental pollution.
5. Identify the purpose and functions of Superfund.

The "public interest" referred to by Justice William O. Douglas in the opening quotation was evident during the 1960s and 1970s in what has come to be known as the consumer movement. Some have labeled the 1960s and 1970s "the age of the consumer," because so much legislation was passed to protect consumers against purportedly unfair practices and unsafe products of sellers. Since the 1980s, the impetus driving the consumer movement has lessened, to a great extent because so many of its goals have been achieved.

Consumer protection law consists of all statutes, agency rules, and common law judicial rulings that serve to protect the interest of consumers. State and federal laws regulate how businesses may advertise, engage in mail-order and telemarketing transactions, package and label their products, and so on. In addition, numerous local, state, and federal agencies now exist to aid the consumer in settling his or her grievances with sellers and producers. In the first part of this chapter, we examine some of the sources and some of the major issues of consumer protection.

The urban industrial society of our century has apparently strained the environment's capacity to handle the pollution being discharged into the air and water. In the last two decades, a growing body of *environmental law* has been created, most of which is statutory or administrative in nature. In the latter part of this chapter, we will examine some of the major federal statutes that have been enacted in an attempt to protect our environment.

▮ Consumer Protection Laws

Sources of consumer protection exist at all levels of government. At the federal level, a number of laws have been passed to define the duties of sellers and the rights of consumers. Exhibit 31–1 lists the major federal consumer protection statutes. Federal administrative agencies, such as the Federal Trade Commission (FTC), also provide an important source of consumer protection. Nearly every agency and department of the government has an office of consumer affairs, and most states have one or more such offices to assist consumers.

Because of the wide variation among state consumer protection laws, our primary focus here will be on federal legislation—specifically, on legislation governing deceptive advertising, telemarketing and fax advertising, labeling and packaging, sales, health protection, product safety, and credit protection. Realize, though, that state laws often provide more sweeping and significant protections for the consumer than do federal laws. State consumer protection laws will be discussed later in this section.

Deceptive Advertising

One of the earliest—and still one of the most important—federal consumer protection laws was the Federal Trade Commission Act of 1914 (discussed in Chapter 30). The act created the FTC to carry out the broadly stated goal of preventing unfair and deceptive trade practices, including deceptive advertising, within the meaning of Section 5 of the act.

DECEPTIVE ADVERTISING
Advertising that misleads consumers, either by unjustified claims concerning a product's performance or by the omission of a material fact concerning the product's composition or performance.

DEFINING DECEPTIVE ADVERTISING   Generally, **deceptive advertising** occurs if a reasonable consumer would be misled by the advertising claim. Vague generalities and obvious exaggerations are permissible. These claims are known as *puffing*. When a claim takes on the appearance of literal authenticity, however, it may create problems. Advertising that would *appear* to be based on factual evidence but that in fact is scientifically untrue will be deemed deceptive. A classic example is provided by a 1944 case in which the claim that a skin cream would restore youthful qualities to aged skin was deemed deceptive.[1]

Some advertisements contain "half-truths," meaning that the presented information is true but incomplete, and it leads consumers to a false conclusion. For example, the makers of Campbell's soups advertised that "most" Campbell's soups were low in fat and cholesterol and thus were helpful in fighting heart disease. What the ad did not say was that Campbell's soups are high in sodium, and high-sodium diets may increase the risk of heart disease. The FTC ruled that Campbell's claims were thus deceptive. Advertising that contains an endorsement by a celebrity may be deemed deceptive if the celebrity actually makes no use of the product.

BAIT-AND-SWITCH ADVERTISING   The FTC has promulgated rules to govern specific forms of advertising. One of the more important rules is contained in the FTC's

---

1. *Charles of the Ritz Distributing Corp. v. Federal Trade Commission*, 143 F.2d 676 (2d Cir. 1944).

♦ Exhibit 31–1
Federal Consumer Protection Statutes

Statute or Regulation	Purpose
ADVERTISING	
Federal Trade Commission Act (1914)	Prohibits deceptive and unfair trade practices.
Public Health Cigarette Smoking Act (1970)	Prohibits radio and TV cigarette advertising.
FTC Rules of Negative Options (1973)	Federal Trade Commission rules regulating advertising of book and record clubs.
Smokeless Tobacco Health Education Act (1986)	Prohibits radio and TV advertising of smokeless tobacco products; requires special labeling to warn consumers of potential health hazards associated with smokeless tobacco.
Telephone Consumer Protection Act (1991)	Prohibits telephone solicitation using an automatic telephone dialing system or a prerecorded voice; prohibits the transmission of advertisements by fax machine without the permission of the recipient.
Telemarketing and Consumer Fraud and Abuse Prevention Act (1994)	Directed the Federal Trade Commission to establish rules governing telemarketing.
FTC Telemarketing Sales Rule (1995)	Federal Trade Commission rule requiring telemarketers to make specific types of disclosures to recipients to prevent fraudulent telemarketing practices.
CREDIT	
Consumer Credit Protection Act (Truth-in-Lending Act) (1968)	Offers comprehensive protection covering all phases of credit transactions.
Fair Credit Reporting Act (1970)	Protects consumers' credit reputations.
Equal Credit Opportunity Act (1974)	Prohibits discrimination in the extending of credit.
Fair Credit Billing Act (1974)	Protects consumers from credit-card billing errors and in other disputes.
Fair Debt Collection Practices Act (1977)	Prohibits debt collectors' abuses.
Counterfeit Access Device and Computer Fraud and Abuse Act (1984)	Prohibits the production, use, and sale of counterfeit credit cards or other access devices used to obtain money, goods, services, or other things of value.
Fair Credit and Charge Card Disclosure Act (1988)	Requires full disclosure of terms and conditions in credit-card and charge-card applications and solicitations.
Home Equity Loan Consumer Protection Act (1988)	Prohibits lenders from changing the terms of a loan after the contract has been signed; requires full disclosure in home equity loans of interest-rate formulas and repayment terms.
Consumer Leasing Act (1988)	Amended the Truth-in-Lending Act to provide protection for consumers who lease automobiles and other goods.
Home Ownership and Equity Protection Act (1994)	Requires home equity lenders to make written disclosures to borrowers of payment amounts, of the consequences of default, and of the borrowers' right to cancel loans within a certain time period.
Truth-in-Lending Act Amendments (1995)	Prevents borrowers from rescinding loans for minor clerical errors in loan documents.
HEALTH AND SAFETY	
Pure Food and Drugs Act (1906)	Prohibits the adulteration and mislabeling of food and drugs sold in interstate commerce.
Meat Inspection Act (1906)	Provides for the inspection of meat.

(Continued)

♦ Exhibit 31–1
Federal Consumer Protection Statutes—Continued

Statute or Regulation	Purpose
HEALTH AND SAFETY—CONTINUED	
Federal Food, Drug and Cosmetic Act (1938)	Protects consumers from unsafe food products and from unsafe and/or ineffective drugs (superseded the Pure Food and Drugs Act of 1906).
Flammable Fabrics Act (1953)	Prohibits the sale of highly flammable clothing.
Poultry Products Inspection Act (1957)	Provides for the inspection of poultry.
National Traffic and Motor Vehicle Safety Act (1966)	Requires manufacturers to inform new-car dealers of any safety defects found after the manufacture and sale of automobiles.
Wholesome Meat Act (1967)	Updated the Meat Inspection Act of 1906 to provide for stricter standards for processing plants where red-meat animals are slaughtered.
Child Protection and Toy Safety Act (1969)	Requires childproof devices and special labeling.
Consumer Product Safety Act (1972)	Established the Consumer Product Safety Commission to regulate all potentially hazardous consumer products.
Department of Transportation Rule on Passive Restraints in Automobiles (1984)	Requires automatic restraint systems in all new cars sold after September 1, 1990.
Toy Safety Act (1984)	Allows the Consumer Product Safety Commission to recall quickly toys and other articles intended for use by children that present a substantial risk of injury.
Drug-Price Competition and Patent-Term Restoration Act (Generic Drug Act) (1984)	Speeds up and simplifies the Food and Drug Administration's approval of generic versions of drugs on which patents have expired.
LABELING AND PACKAGING	
Wool Products Labeling Act (1939)	Requires accurate labeling of wool products.
Fur Products Labeling Act (1951)	Prohibits misbranding of fur products.
Textile Fiber Products Identification Act (1958)	Prohibits false labeling and advertising of all textile products not covered under the Wool Products Labeling Act and the Fur Products Labeling Act.
The Federal Hazardous Substances Act (1960)	Requires warning labels on all items containing dangerous chemicals.
Cigarette Labeling and Advertising Act (1965)	Requires labels warning of the possible health hazards associated with smoking cigarettes.
Fair Packaging and Labeling Act (1966)	Requires that accurate names, quantities, and weights be given on product labels.
Child Protection and Toy Safety Act (1969)	Requires childproof devices and special labeling.
Smokeless Tobacco Health Education Act (1986)	Requires labels disclosing possible health hazards of smokeless tobacco; prohibits radio and TV advertising of smokeless tobacco products.
Nutrition Labeling and Education Act (1990)	Requires standard nutrition facts (for example, fat content) on food labels; regulates the use of such terms as *fresh* and *low-fat*; and subject to the Food and Drug Administration's approval, authorizes certain health claims.
SALES AND WARRANTIES	
Interstate Land Sales Full Disclosure Act (1968)	Requires disclosure in interstate land sales.
Odometer Act (1972)	Protects consumers against odometer fraud in used-car sales.

♦ Exhibit 31–1
Federal Consumer Protection Statutes—Continued

Statute or Regulation	Purpose
SALES AND WARRANTIES—CONTINUED	
FTC Door-to-Door Sales Rule (1973)	Federal Trade Commission rule regulating door-to-door sales contracts.
Real Estate Settlement Procedures Act (1974)	Requires disclosure of home-buying costs.
FTC Mail Order Rule (1975)	Federal Trade Commission rule providing protection for consumers who purchase goods through the mails.
Magnuson-Moss Warranty Act (1975)	Provides rules governing the content of warranties.
FTC Vocational and Correspondence School Rule (1980)	Federal Trade Commission rule regulating contracts with these types of schools.
FTC Used-Car Rule (1984)	Federal Trade Commission rule requiring dealers in used-car sales to disclose specified types of information in a "Buyer's Guide" affixed to the automobile.
FTC Funeral Home Rule (1984)	Federal Trade Commission rule requiring disclosure by funeral homes regarding prices and services.
FTC Mail or Telephone Order Merchandise Rule (1993)	Federal Trade Commission rule amending the FTC Mail Order Rule of 1975 to provide specific protections for consumers who purchase goods via phone lines, as well as through the mails.

"Guides on Bait Advertising." [2] The rule is designed to prohibit what is referred to as **bait-and-switch advertising**—that is, advertising a very low price for a particular item that will likely be unavailable to the consumer, who will then be encouraged to purchase a more expensive item. The low price is the "bait" to lure the consumer into the store. The salesperson is instructed to "switch" the consumer to a different item. According to the FTC guidelines, bait-and-switch advertising occurs if the seller refuses to show the advertised item, fails to have adequate quantities of it available, fails to promise to deliver the advertised item within a reasonable time, or discourages employees from selling the item.

FTC ACTIONS AGAINST DECEPTIVE ADVERTISING The FTC receives complaints from many sources, including competitors of alleged violators, consumers, consumer organizations, trade associations, Better Business Bureaus, government organizations, and state and local officials. If enough consumers complain and the complaints are widespread, the FTC will investigate the problem and perhaps take action. If, after its investigations, the FTC believes that a given advertisement is unfair or deceptive, it drafts a formal complaint, which it sends to the alleged offender. The company may agree to settle the complaint without further proceedings.

If the company does not agree to settle a complaint, the FTC can conduct a hearing—which is similar to a trial—in which the company can present its defense. The hearing is held before an administrative law judge (ALJ) instead of a federal district court judge (see the discussion of administrative law in Chapter 1). If the FTC succeeds in proving that an advertisement is unfair or deceptive, it usually issues a **cease-and-desist order** requiring that the challenged advertising be stopped. It might also impose a sanction known as **counteradvertising** by requiring the company to advertise anew—in print, on radio, and on television—to inform the public about the earlier misinformation.

BAIT-AND-SWITCH ADVERTISING
Advertising a product at a very attractive price (the "bait") and then informing the consumer, once he or she is in the store, that the advertised product is either not available or is of poor quality; the customer is then urged to purchase ("switched" to) a more expensive item.

CEASE-AND-DESIST ORDER
An administrative or judicial order prohibiting a person or business firm from conducting activities that an agency or court has deemed illegal.

COUNTERADVERTISING
New advertising that is undertaken pursuant to a Federal Trade Commission order for the purpose of correcting earlier false claims that were made about a product.

_____
2. 16 C.F.R. Section 288.

When an ALJ rules against a company, the company can appeal to the full commission. The FTC commissioners listen to the parties' arguments and may uphold, modify, or reverse the ALJ's decision. If the commission rules against a company, the company can appeal the FTC's order through judicial channels, but a reviewing court generally accords great weight to the FTC's judgment. This is because the court recognizes that the FTC, as the administrative agency that deals continually with such claims, is often in a better position than the courts to determine when a practice is deceptive within the meaning of the Federal Trade Commission Act.

Is it false or misleading to advertise a product as effective when its only effectiveness results from its users' belief that it works? The court addresses this issue in the following case.

CASE 31.1

FEDERAL TRADE COMMISSION v. PANTRON I CORP.

United States Court of Appeals,
Ninth Circuit, 1994.
33 F.3d 1088.

HISTORICAL AND SOCIAL SETTING   *Hair has been part of our self-image since primitive men and women first adorned it with clay, trophies, and badges. Sometimes, an abundance of hair is interpreted as characteristic of virility. At other times, a bald pate is seen as a trait of masculinity. Regardless of how it is viewed, male pattern baldness (the loss of hair from the upper scalp) results from an individual's genetic background and hormone levels. There is no "cure," and even hair transplants may have no lasting effect.*

FACTS   Pantron I Corporation sold the Helsinki Formula as a "cure" for baldness. Pantron claimed that the product reduced hair loss and promoted hair growth. The Federal Trade Commission filed a suit in a federal district court against Pantron and its owner, Hal Lederman, alleging that these claims were an unfair or deceptive trade practice. The court concluded in part that the product had a "placebo effect"—that is, that it worked when

its users believed it would. The court issued an order that, among other things, allowed Pantron to continue claiming its product "works some of the time for a lot of people." The FTC appealed this order.

ISSUE   Were the claims regarding the product's effectiveness likely to deceive or mislead consumers?

DECISION   Yes. The U.S. Court of Appeals for the Ninth Circuit reversed this part of the lower court's order and remanded the case.

REASON   The appellate court held that it is false to advertise a product as effective when its effectiveness results solely from a placebo effect. The court concluded that the "claim is 'misleading' because the [product] is not inherently effective, its results being attributable to the psychosomatic effect produced by * * * advertising." The court reasoned that "were we to hold otherwise, advertisers would be encouraged to foist unsubstantiated claims on an unsuspecting public in the hope that consumers would believe the ads and the claims would be self-fulfilling."

FOR CRITICAL ANALYSIS—Political Consideration
What other government agencies might have taken action against Pantron and the Helsinki Formula, which is classified as a drug and sold through the mail?

Telemarketing and Fax Advertising

The pervasive use of the telephone to market goods and services to the home and other businesses led to the passage in 1991 of the Telephone Consumer Protection Act (TCPA).[3] The act prohibits telephone solicitation using an automatic telephone

---

3.   47 U.S.C. Sections 227 *et seq.*

dialing system or a prerecorded voice. Most states also have laws regulating telephone solicitation.[4]

REMEMBER Changes in technology are often the motivation for changes in the law.

Not surprisingly, the widespread use of facsimile (fax) machines has led to the use of faxes as a tool for direct marketing. Advertising by fax is less expensive than mailing a letter, and faxes normally receive greater attention than "junk mail." At the same time, unsolicited fax messages tie up the recipient's fax machine and impose a cost on the recipient, who must pay for fax paper, toner, and other supplies. The TCPA also makes it illegal to transmit ads via fax without first obtaining the recipient's permission.

The act is enforced by the Federal Communications Commission and also provides for a private right of action. Consumers can recover any actual monetary loss resulting from a violation of the act or receive $500 in damages for each violation, whichever is greater. If a court finds that a defendant willfully or knowingly violated the act, the court has the discretion to treble the damages awarded.

The Telemarketing and Consumer Fraud and Abuse Prevention Act[5] of 1994 directed the FTC to establish rules governing telemarketing and to bring actions against fraudulent telemarketers. The FTC's Telemarketing Sales Rule[6] of 1995 requires telemarketers, before making a sales pitch, to inform recipients that the call is a sales call and to identify the seller's name and the product being sold. The rule makes it illegal for telemarketers to misrepresent information (including facts about their goods or services, earnings potential, profitability, the risk attending an investment, or the nature of a prize). Additionally, telemarketers must inform the people they call of the total cost of the goods being sold, any restrictions on obtaining or using them, and whether a sale will be considered to be final and nonrefundable.

Labeling and Packaging

In addition to broadly restricting advertising, a number of federal and state laws deal specifically with the information given on labels and packages. The restrictions are designed to provide accurate information about the product and to warn about possible dangers from its use or misuse. In general, labels must be accurate. That is, they must use words that are understood by the ordinary consumer. For example, a box of cereal cannot be labeled "giant" if it would exaggerate the amount of cereal contained in the box. In some instances, labels must specify the raw materials used in the product, such as the percentage of cotton, nylon, or other fibers used in a garment. In other instances, the products must carry a warning. Cigarette packages and advertising, for example, must include one of several warnings about the health hazards associated with smoking.[7]

Federal laws regulating the labeling and packaging of products include the Wool Products Labeling Act of 1939,[8] the Fur Products Labeling Act of 1951,[9] the Flammable Fabrics Act of 1953,[10] the Fair Packaging and Labeling Act of 1966,[11] and the Smokeless Tobacco Health Education Act of 1986.[12] The Smokeless Tobacco Health Education Act, for example, requires that producers, packagers, and importers of smokeless tobacco label their product with one of several warnings about the health

4. For a discussion of the constitutionality of the TCPA, which some plaintiffs have alleged goes too far in restricting free speech, see *Moser v. FCC*, 46 F.3d 970 (9th Cir. 1995); *cert.* denied ___ U.S. ___, 115 S.Ct. 2615, 132 L.Ed.2d 857 (1995).
5. 15 U.S.C. Sections 6101–6108.
6. 16 C.F.R. Sections 310.1–310.8.
7. 15 U.S.C. Sections 1331 *et seq.*
8. 15 U.S.C. Section 68.
9. 15 U.S.C. Section 69.
10. 15 U.S.C. Section 1191.
11. 15 U.S.C. Sections 1451 *et seq.*
12. 15 U.S.C. Sections 4401–4408.

hazards associated with the use of smokeless tobacco; the warnings are similar to those contained on cigarette packages.

The Fair Packaging and Labeling Act requires that products possess labels that identify the product; the net quantity of the contents, as well as the quantity of servings, if the number of servings is stated; the manufacturer; and the packager or distributor. The act also provides authority to add requirements concerning words used to describe packages, terms that are associated with savings claims, information disclosures for ingredients in nonfood products, and standards for the partial filling of packages. Food products must bear labels detailing nutrition, including how much fat a product contains and what kind of fat it is. These restrictions are enforced by the Department of Health and Human Services, as well as the Federal Trade Commission.

Sales

A number of statutes that protect the consumer in sales transactions concern the disclosure of certain terms in sales and provide rules governing home or door-to-door sales, mail-order transactions, referral sales, and unsolicited merchandise. The Federal Reserve Board of Governors, for example, has issued **Regulation Z,** which governs credit provisions associated with sales contracts, and numerous states have passed laws governing the remedies available to consumers in home sales. Furthermore, states have provided a number of consumer protection provisions, such as implied warranties, through the adoption of the Uniform Commercial Code. In some states, the Uniform Consumer Credit Code's requirements, including disclosure requirements, also protect consumers in credit transactions.

REGULATION Z
A set of rules promulgated by the Federal Reserve Board to implement the provisions of the Truth-in-Lending Act.

DOOR-TO-DOOR SALES Door-to-door sales are singled out for special treatment in the laws of most states. This special treatment stems in part from the nature of the sales transaction. Because repeat purchases are not as likely as they are in stores, the seller has less incentive to cultivate the goodwill of the purchaser. Furthermore, the seller is unlikely to present alternative products and their prices. Thus, a number of states have passed **"cooling off"** laws that permit the buyers of goods sold door-to-door to cancel their contracts within a specified period of time, usually two to three days after the sale.

An FTC regulation also requires sellers to give consumers three days to cancel any door-to-door sale. Because this rule applies in addition to the relevant state statutes, consumers are given the most favorable benefits of the FTC rule and their own state statutes. In addition, the FTC rule requires that consumers be notified in Spanish of this right if the oral negotiations for the sale were in that language.

"COOLING OFF" LAWS
Laws that allow buyers a period of time, such as two to three days, in which to cancel door-to-door sales contracts.

TELEPHONE AND MAIL-ORDER SALES Sales made by telephone or mail order are the greatest source of complaints to the nation's Better Business Bureaus. Many mail-order houses are far removed from the buyers to whom the houses sell, thus making it more difficult for a consumer to bring a complaint against a seller. To a certain extent, consumers are protected under federal laws prohibiting mail fraud, which were discussed in Chapter 7, and under state consumer protection laws that parallel and supplement the federal laws.

The FTC "Mail or Telephone Order Merchandise Rule" of 1993, which amended the FTC "Mail Order Rule" of 1975,[13] provides specific protections for consumers who purchase goods via phone lines or through the mails. The 1993 rule, which became effective in March 1994, extended the 1975 rule to include sales in which orders are transmitted using computers, fax machines, or some similar means involving telephone lines. Among other things, the rule requires mail-order merchants to

13. 16 C.F.R. Sections 435.1–435.2.

ship orders within the time promised in their catalogues or advertisements, to notify consumers when orders cannot be shipped on time, and to issue a refund within a specified period of time when a consumer cancels an order.

In addition, the Postal Reorganization Act of 1970[14] provides that *unsolicited* merchandise sent by U.S. mail may be retained, used, discarded, or disposed of in any manner the recipient deems appropriate, without the recipient's incurring any obligation to the sender.

FTC REGULATION OF SPECIFIC INDUSTRIES Over the last decade, the FTC has begun to target certain sales practices on an industry-wide basis. Two examples are the used-car business and the funeral-home trade. In 1984, the FTC enacted the "Used Motor Vehicle Regulation Rule,"[15] which is more commonly known as the "Used-Car Rule." This rule requires used-car dealers to affix a "Buyers Guide" label to all cars sold on their lots. The label must disclose the following information: (1) the car's warranty or a statement that the car is being sold "as is," (2) information regarding any service contract or promises being made by the dealer, and (3) a suggestion that the purchaser obtain both an inspection of the car and a written statement of any promises made by the dealer.

In 1984, the FTC also enacted rules requiring that funeral homes provide customers with itemized prices of all charges incurred for a funeral.[16] In addition, the regulations prohibit funeral homes from requiring specific embalming procedures or specific types of caskets for bodies that are to be cremated.

DON'T FORGET A seller's puffery—his or her opinion about the goods—is not a legally binding warranty or promise.

REAL ESTATE SALES Various federal and state laws apply to consumer transactions involving real estate. The goal of these laws is to prevent fraud and to provide buyers with certain types of information. Some of these protections mirror those provided for other types of sales. The disclosure requirements of the Truth-in-Lending Act, which will be discussed shortly, apply to a number of real estate transactions. There are differences, however, between the disclosure requirements for real estate transactions and those for other types of transactions. For example, in certain real estate transactions, consumers are given a right to rescind their purchase contracts if certain disclosures are not made to them. Moreover, under certain circumstances—such as the lender's failure to give the borrower the required number of copies of certain loan documents—the Truth-in-Lending Act provides the consumer with a right to cancel the contract even though a creditor has made all of the required disclosures.[17]

Health and Safety Protection

Laws discussed earlier regarding the labeling and packaging of products go a long way toward promoting consumer health and safety. There is a significant distinction, however, between regulating the information dispensed about a product and regulating the content of the actual product. The classic example is tobacco products. Tobacco products have not been altered by regulation or banned outright despite their obvious hazards. What has been regulated are the warnings that producers are required to give consumers about the hazards of tobacco.[18] This section focuses on laws that regulate the actual products made available to consumers.

---

14. 39 U.S.C. Section 3009.
15. 16 C.F.R. Part 455.
16. 16 C.F.R. Section 453.2.
17. 15 U.S.C. Section 1635.
18. We are ignoring recent civil litigation concerning the liability of tobacco product manufacturers for injuries that arise from the use of tobacco.

A warning appears on a package of cigarettes, as required by federal law. Why is Congress concerned with protecting consumers against purportedly unsafe products?

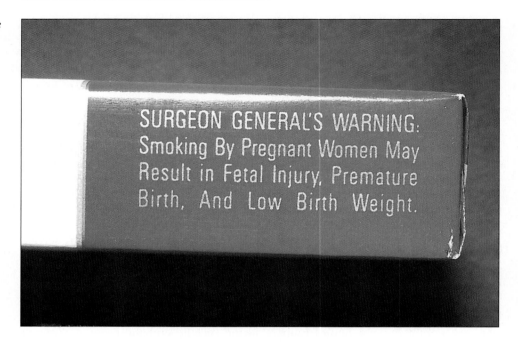

FOODS AND DRUGS   The first federal legislation regulating food and drugs was enacted in 1906 as the Pure Food and Drugs Act.[19] That law, as amended in 1938, exists presently as the Federal Food, Drug and Cosmetic Act (FFDCA).[20] The act protects consumers against adulterated and misbranded foods and drugs. More recent amendments have added additional substantive and procedural requirements to the act. In its present form, the act establishes food standards, specifies safe levels of potentially hazardous food additives, and sets classifications of food and food advertising.

Most of these statutory requirements are monitored and enforced by the Food and Drug Administration (FDA). Under an extensive set of procedures established by the FDA, drugs must be shown to be effective as well as safe before they may be marketed to the public, and the use of some food additives suspected of being carcinogenic is prohibited. A 1975 amendment to the FFDCA[21] authorizes the FDA to regulate medical devices, such as pacemakers and other health devices or equipment, and to withdraw from the market any such device that is mislabeled.

BE AWARE The Food and Drug Administration is authorized to obtain, among other things, orders for the recall and seizure of certain products.

CONSUMER PRODUCT SAFETY   Consumer product-safety legislation began in 1953 with the enactment of the Flammable Fabrics Act, which prohibits the sale of highly flammable clothing or materials. Over the next two decades, Congress enacted legislation regarding the design or composition of specific classes of products. Then in 1972, Congress, by enacting the Consumer Product Safety Act,[22] created a comprehensive scheme of regulation over matters concerning consumer safety. The act also established far-reaching authority over consumer safety under the Consumer Product Safety Commission (CPSC).

The CPSC conducts research on the safety of individual products, and it maintains a clearinghouse on the risks associated with different consumer products. The Consumer Product Safety Act authorizes the CPSC to set standards for consumer products and to ban the manufacture and sale of any product that the commission

---

19.   21 U.S.C. Sections 1–5, 7–15.
20.   21 U.S.C. Section 301.
21.   21 U.S.C. Sections 360(c) *et seq.*
22.   15 U.S.C. Section 2051.

deems to be potentially hazardous to consumers. The CPSC also has authority to remove from the market any products it believes to be imminently hazardous and to require manufacturers to report on any products already sold or intended for sale if the products have proved to be hazardous. Additionally, the CPSC administers other product-safety legislation, such as the Child Protection and Toy Safety Act of 1969,[23] the Federal Hazardous Substances Act of 1960,[24] and the Flammable Fabrics Act.

The CPSC's authority is sufficiently broad to allow it to ban any product that the CPSC believes poses merely an "unreasonable risk" to the consumer. Some of the products that the CPSC has banned include various types of fireworks, cribs, and toys, as well as many products containing asbestos or vinyl chloride.

Credit Protection

Because of the extensive use of credit by American consumers, credit protection has become one of the more important areas regulated by consumer protection legislation. One of the most significant statutes regulating the credit and credit-card industry is the Truth-in-Lending Act (TILA), the name commonly given to Title 1 of the Consumer Credit Protection Act (CCPA),[25] which was passed by Congress in 1968.

TRUTH IN LENDING The TILA is basically a *disclosure law*. The TILA is administered by the Federal Reserve Board and requires sellers and lenders to disclose credit terms or loan terms so that individuals can shop around for the best financing arrangements. TILA requirements apply only to persons who, in the ordinary course of business, lend money, sell on credit, or arrange for the extension of credit. Thus, sales or loans made between two consumers do not come under the protection of the act. Additionally, only debtors who are *natural* persons (as opposed to the artificial "person" of the corporation) are protected by this law; other legal entities are not.

The disclosure requirements are found in Regulation Z, which, as mentioned earlier in this chapter, was promulgated by the Federal Reserve Board. If the contracting parties are subject to the TILA, the requirements of Regulation Z apply to any transaction involving an installment sales contract in which payment is to be made in more than four installments. Transactions subject to Regulation Z typically include installment loans, retail and installment sales, car loans, home improvement loans, and certain real estate loans if the amount of financing is less than $25,000.

Under the provisions of the TILA, all of the terms of a credit instrument must be clearly and conspicuously disclosed. The TILA provides for contract rescission (cancellation) if a creditor fails to follow *exactly* the procedures required by the act.[26] TILA requirements are strictly enforced.

NOTE The Federal Reserve Board is part of the Federal Reserve System, which influences the lending and investing activities of commercial banks and the cost and availability of credit.

---

23. 15 U.S.C. Section 1262(e).
24. 15 U.S.C. Sections 1261–1273.
25. 15 U.S.C. Sections 1601–1693r. The act was amended in 1980 by the Truth-in-Lending Simplification and Reform Act.
26. Note, however, that amendments to the TILA enacted in 1995 prevent borrowers from rescinding loans for minor clerical errors in closing documents [15 U.S.C. Sections 1605, 1631, 1635, 1640, and 1641].

In some cases, consumers have taken unfair advantage of the TILA's requirements to avoid genuine obligations that they voluntarily assumed. For example, under the TILA, borrowers are allowed three business days to rescind, without penalty, a consumer loan that uses their principal dwelling as security. The lender must state specifically the last day on which the borrower can rescind the agreement. If the lender fails to do so, the borrower can rescind the loan within three years after it was made. This is true

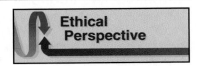

Ethical Perspective

(Continued)

Ethical Perspective—Continued

even if the lender inadvertently (unintentionally) failed to comply with the TILA's requirements.

Is it fair to hold creditors liable for TILA violations regardless of whether the violations were intentional or unintentional? According to the courts, the answer to this question is yes. The courts reason that, overall, consumers will benefit from strict compliance requirements, even though some consumers may abuse the act. In essence, the TILA is a "strict liability" statute (this is generally true of most consumer protection statutes). In other words, intention normally is irrelevant in determining whether a consumer protection statute has been violated.

For Critical Analysis: *In your opinion, should the courts give more weight to the circumstances surrounding a transaction and the intent factor in deciding cases involving alleged TILA violations? Why or why not?*

Equal Credit Opportunity In 1974, Congress enacted the Equal Credit Opportunity Act (ECOA)[27] as an amendment to the TILA. The ECOA prohibits the denial of credit solely on the basis of race, religion, national origin, color, sex, marital status, or age. The act also prohibits credit discrimination on the basis of whether an individual receives certain forms of income, such as public-assistance benefits. Under the ECOA, a creditor may not require the signature of an applicant's spouse, other than a joint applicant, on a credit instrument if the applicant qualifies under the creditor's standards of creditworthiness for the amount and terms of the credit request. Creditors are permitted to request any information from a credit applicant except that which would be used for the type of discrimination covered in the act or its amendments. In the following case, the issue concerned whether a creditor had violated the ECOA by requesting a spouse to cosign a loan guaranty.

---

27.   15 U.S.C. Section 1643.

CASE 31.2

FEDERAL DEPOSIT INSURANCE CORP. v. MEDMARK, INC.
United States District Court,
District of Kansas, 1995.
897 F.Supp. 511.

HISTORICAL AND ECONOMIC SETTING *The health-care industry is the largest single industry in the United States. Some major corporations, such as Abbott Laboratories, Inc., and Johnson & Johnson, have sold medical equipment and other health-care products to doctors and hospitals for more than one hundred years. The industry is made up primarily of new, small firms, however, as well as private doctors and hospitals. Probably the* *most difficult problem that such small organizations face is a lack of capital.*

FACTS Bruce Shalberg was a director of Medmark, Inc., a small medical equipment supply company. As a condition of a loan to Medmark, the Merchants Bank asked Shalberg—whom the bank found to be independently creditworthy—to sign a guaranty of repayment. Later, for another loan, the bank required Shalberg's wife, Mary—who had nothing to do with Medmark—to sign the guaranty. When the bank failed, the Federal Deposit Insurance Corporation (FDIC) took over its assets. The FDIC filed a suit in a federal district court against Medmark and the Shalbergs to recover the amount of the loans. Mrs. Shalberg filed a motion for summary judgment, contending that the bank, in requiring her to sign the guaranty, had violated the Equal Credit Opportunity Act (ECOA).

Case 31.2—Continued

ISSUE   Did the bank violate the ECOA when it required Mrs. Shalberg to cosign a loan guaranty with her husband, in spite of her husband's independent creditworthiness?

DECISION   Yes. The court issued a summary judgment in favor of Mrs. Shalberg, which relieved her from any obligation on the loans.

REASON   The court pointed out that a regulation issued under the ECOA "specifically provides that a creditor may not require the signature of an applicant's spouse if the applicant qualifies under the creditor's standards of creditworthiness for the amount and terms of the credit requested." The court noted that "[t]he record contains no evidence that Mr. Shalberg was not creditworthy, in his own right, in the Bank's eyes."

FOR CRITICAL ANALYSIS—Political Consideration
Why does the ECOA prohibit lenders from requiring a spouse's signature on a credit application if the applicant independently qualifies for the credit?

Credit-Card Rules   The TILA also contains provisions regarding credit cards. One provision limits the liability of a cardholder to $50 per card for unauthorized charges made before the creditor is notified that the card has been lost. Another provision prohibits a credit-card company from billing a consumer for any unauthorized charges if the credit card was improperly issued by the company. For example, if a consumer receives an unsolicited credit card in the mail and the card is later stolen and used by the thief to make purchases, the consumer to whom the card was sent will not be liable for the unauthorized charges.

COMPARE   The Electronic Fund Transfer Act also limits, under certain circumstances, the liability of a consumer to $50 for unauthorized transfers made before the issuer of an access card is notified that the card is lost.

Further provisions of the act concern billing disputes related to credit-card purchases. If a debtor thinks that an error has occurred in billing or wishes to withhold payment for a faulty product purchased by credit card, the act outlines specific procedures for both the consumer and the credit-card company in settling the dispute.

Consumer Leases   The Consumer Leasing Act (CLA) of 1988[28] amended the TILA to provide protection for consumers who lease automobiles and other goods. The CLA applies to those who lease or arrange to lease consumer goods in the ordinary course of their business. The act only applies if the goods are priced at $25,000 or less and if the lease term exceeds four months. The CLA and its implementing regulation, Regulation M,[29] requires lessors to disclose in writing all of the material terms of the lease.

FAIR CREDIT REPORTING ACT   In 1970, to protect consumers against inaccurate credit reporting, Congress enacted the Fair Credit Reporting Act (FCRA).[30] The act provides that consumer credit reporting agencies may issue credit reports to users only for specified purposes, including the extension of credit, the issuance of insurance policies, compliance with a court order, and compliance with a consumer's request for a copy of his or her own credit report. The act further provides that any time a consumer is denied credit or insurance on the basis of the consumer's credit report, or is charged more than others ordinarily would be for credit or insurance, the consumer must be notified of that fact and of the name and address of the credit reporting agency that issued the credit report.

Under the act, consumers may request the source of any information being given out by a credit agency, as well as the identity of anyone who has received an agency's report. Consumers are also permitted to have access to the information contained

---

28.   15 U.S.C. Sections 1667–1667e .
29.   12 C.F.R. Part 213.
30.   15 U.S.C. Sections 1681 *et seq.*

about them in a credit reporting agency's files. If a consumer discovers that a credit reporting agency's files contain inaccurate information about the consumer's credit standing, the agency, on the consumer's written request, must investigate the matter and delete any unverifiable or erroneous information within a reasonable period of time. The following case illustrates the potential liability exposure of companies that maintain credit reports and ratings.

CASE 31.3

GUIMOND v. TRANS UNION CREDIT INFORMATION CO.

United States Court of Appeals,
Ninth Circuit, 1995.
45 F.3d 1329.

HISTORICAL AND ECONOMIC SETTING *A credit report reflects a consumer's bill-paying history. It lists the consumer's creditors and whether he or she has made payments on time. Inaccurate information can keep an individual from obtaining credit, through a creditor's denial of it or the consumer's decision not to apply for it out of fear it will be denied. The major credit reporting agencies are Equifax, Inc.; TRW, Inc.; and the Trans Union Credit Information Company.*

FACTS Renie Guimond learned that the Trans Union Credit Information Company had inaccurate information in its file on her. She notified Trans Union, which told her the file would be corrected; however, it was not corrected for a year. Guimond filed a suit in a federal district court against Trans Union, in part to recover damages under the Fair Credit Reporting Act (FCRA) for the company's failure to correct the information more quickly. Trans Union

countered that Guimond had no claim, because she had not been denied credit before the information was corrected. The court ruled in favor of Trans Union, and Guimond appealed.

ISSUE Is denial of credit a prerequisite to recovery under the FCRA?

DECISION No. The U.S. Court of Appeals for the Ninth Circuit reversed this part of the lower's court ruling and remanded the case for trial.

REASON The federal appellate court pointed out that the FCRA states, "Whenever a consumer reporting agency prepares a consumer report it shall follow reasonable procedures to assure maximum possible accuracy of the information." Liability is based on "the reasonableness of the credit reporting agency's procedures." For this reason, "the focus should not have been on Guimond's damage claims." Guimond made out a *prima facie* case under the FCRA. "The district court was then required to consider whether Trans Union was liable * * * before it determined that Guimond had suffered no recoverable damages."

FOR CRITICAL ANALYSIS—Social Consideration
How do the policies underlying the FCRA support the court's interpretation of the statute in Guimond's case?

FAIR DEBT COLLECTION PRACTICES ACT In 1977, Congress enacted the Fair Debt Collection Practices Act (FDCPA)[31] in an attempt to curb what were perceived to be abuses by collection agencies. The act applies only to specialized debt-collection agencies that, usually for a percentage of the amount owed, regularly attempt to collect debts on behalf of someone else. Creditors who attempt to collect a debt are not covered by the act unless, by misrepresenting themselves to the debtor, they cause the debtor to believe they are a collection agency. The act explicitly prohibits a collection agency from using any of the following tactics:

1. Contacting the debtor at the debtor's place of employment if the debtor's employer objects.

---

31. 15 U.S.C. Section 1692.

2. Contacting the debtor during inconvenient or unusual times (for example, calling the debtor at three o'clock in the morning) or at any time if the debtor is being represented by an attorney.

3. Contacting third parties other than the debtor's parents, spouse, or financial adviser about payment of a debt unless a court authorizes such action.

4. Using harassment or intimidation (for example, using abusive language or threatening violence), or employing false and misleading information (for example, posing as a police officer).

5. Communicating with the debtor at any time after receiving notice that the debtor is refusing to pay the debt, except to advise the debtor of further action to be taken by the collection agency.

The FDCPA also requires collection agencies to include a "validation notice" whenever they initially contact a debtor for payment of a debt or within five days of that initial contact. The notice must state that the debtor has thirty days within which to dispute the debt and to request a written verification of the debt from the collection agency. The debtor's request for debt validation must be in writing.

The enforcement of the FDCPA is primarily the responsibility of the Federal Trade Commission. The act provides that a debt collector who fails to comply with the act is liable for actual damages, plus additional damages not to exceed $1,000[32] and attorneys' fees.

In the following case, the United States Supreme Court considered whether lawyers engaged in consumer debt-collection litigation were exempt from the FDCPA.

---

32. According to the U.S. Court of Appeals for the Sixth Circuit, the $1,000 limit on damages applies to each lawsuit, not to each violation. See *Wright v. Finance Service of Norwalk, Inc.*, 22 F.3d 647 (6th Cir. 1994).

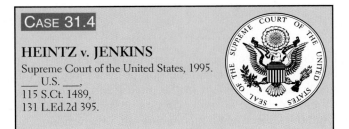

CASE 31.4

HEINTZ v. JENKINS

Supreme Court of the United States, 1995.
___ U.S. ___,
115 S.Ct. 1489,
131 L.Ed.2d 395.

HISTORICAL AND ECONOMIC SETTING *For seven decades, the financing of automobile purchases has been a very profitable business. Sometimes, when a car dealer needs funds to increase its inventory, a lender will agree to loan the dealer money at low, competitive rates in return for the dealer's promise to arrange its customers' financing of their vehicle purchases through the lender. Such loans are attractive to lenders because of the relatively high rate of interest and the relatively low rate of default.*

FACTS Darlene Jenkins borrowed money from the Gainer Bank to buy a car. The terms of the loan required her to keep the car insured. When she let her insurance

expire, the bank bought a policy. Jenkins defaulted on the loan, and the bank asked George Heintz, a lawyer, to recover its money. Heintz began legal proceedings against Jenkins to recover the amount due on the loan, plus the cost of the insurance. Jenkins filed a suit in a federal district court against Heintz under the Fair Debt Collection Practices Act (FDCPA), claiming that Heintz was trying to collect an amount that was not part of the loan agreement. The court dismissed the suit, holding that the FDCPA does not apply to lawyers engaging in litigation. Jenkins appealed, and the U.S. Court of Appeals for the Seventh Circuit reversed. Heintz appealed to the United States Supreme Court.

ISSUE Does the FDCPA apply to a lawyer engaged in consumer debt-collection litigation?

DECISION Yes. The Supreme Court upheld the decision of the appellate court.

REASON The Supreme Court gave two reasons for applying the FDCPA to lawyers engaged in litigation.

(Continued)

Case 31.4—Continued

First, the Court reasoned that a lawyer who regularly tries to obtain payment of consumer debts through legal proceedings meets the FDCPA's definition of "debt collector"—that is, one who "regularly collects or attempts to collect, directly or indirectly, [consumer] debts owed *   *   * another." Second, the Court pointed out that although an earlier version of the FDCPA's defin-

ition of "debt collector" expressly excluded "any attorney-at-law collecting a debt as an attorney on behalf of and in the name of a client," Congress had repealed this exemption ten years ago.

FOR CRITICAL ANALYSIS—Political Consideration
Why do you think Congress repealed the FDCPA exemption for lawyers collecting debts?

State Consumer Protection Laws

Thus far, our primary focus has been on federal legislation. State laws, however, often provide more sweeping and significant protections for the consumer than do federal laws. The warranty and unconscionability provisions of the Uniform Commercial Code (discussed in Chapters 14 through 17) offer important protections for consumers against unfair practices on the part of sellers. Far less widely adopted than the UCC is the Uniform Consumer Credit Code (UCCC), which has provisions concerning truth in lending, maximum credit ceilings, door-to-door sales, fine-print clauses, and other practices affecting consumer transactions.

Virtually all states have specific consumer protection acts, often titled "deceptive trade practices acts." Although state consumer protection statutes vary widely in their provisions, a common thread runs through most of them. Typically, state consumer protection laws are directed at sellers' deceptive practices, such as providing false or misleading information to consumers. As just mentioned, some of the legislation provides broad protection for consumers. A prime example is the Texas Deceptive Trade Practices Act of 1973, which forbids a seller from selling to a buyer anything that the buyer does not need or cannot afford.

▌Environmental Law

"Man, however much he may like to pretend the contrary, is part of nature."

Rachel Carson, 1907–1964
(American writer and conservationist)

To this point, this chapter has dealt with government regulation of business in the interest of protecting consumers. We now turn to a discussion of the various ways in which businesses are regulated by the government in the interest of protecting the environment. Concern over the degradation of the environment has increased over time in response to the environmental effects of population growth, urbanization, and industrialization. Environmental protection is not without a price, however. For many businesses, the costs of complying with environmental regulations are high, and for some they are too high. There is a constant tension between the desirability of increasing profits and productivity and the need to attain a higher quality in the environment.

To a great extent, environmental law consists of statutes passed by federal, state, or local governments and regulations issued by administrative agencies. Before examining statutory and regulatory environmental laws, however, we look at the remedies available under the common law against environmental pollution.

Common Law Actions

Common law remedies against environmental pollution originated centuries ago in England. Those responsible for operations that created dirt, smoke, noxious odors, noise, or toxic substances were sometimes held liable under common law theories of nuisance or negligence. Today, injured individuals continue to rely on the common law to obtain damages and injunctions against business polluters.

NUISANCE   Under the common law doctrine of **nuisance,** persons may be held liable if they use their property in a manner that unreasonably interferes with others' rights to use or enjoy their own property. In these situations, the courts commonly balance the equities between the harm caused by the pollution and the costs of stopping it.

Courts have often denied injunctive relief on the ground that the hardships to be imposed on the polluter and on the community are relatively greater than the hardships to be suffered by the plaintiff. For example, a factory that causes neighboring landowners to suffer from smoke, dirt, and vibrations may be left in operation if it is the core of a local economy. The injured parties may be awarded only their money damages. These damages may include compensation for the decreased value of the neighbors' property that results from the factory's operation.

A property owner may be given relief from pollution in situations in which he or she can identify a distinct harm separate from that affecting the general public. This is referred to as a "private" nuisance. Under the common law, citizens were denied standing (access to the courts—see Chapter 3) unless they suffered a harm distinct from the harm suffered by the public at large. Some states still require this. Therefore, a group of citizens who wished to stop a new development that would cause significant water pollution was denied access to the courts on the ground that the harm to them did not differ from the harm to the general public.[33] A public authority (such as a state's attorney general) can sue to abate a "public" nuisance.

NEGLIGENCE AND STRICT LIABILITY   An injured party may sue a business polluter in tort under the negligence and strict liability theories discussed in Chapter 5. The basis for a negligence action is the business's alleged failure to use reasonable care toward the party whose injury was foreseeable and, of course, caused by the lack of reasonable care. For example, employees might sue an employer whose failure to use proper pollution controls contaminated the air and caused the employees to suffer respiratory illnesses.

Businesses that engage in ultrahazardous activities—such as the transportation of radioactive materials—are strictly liable for whatever injuries the activities cause. In a strict liability action, the injured party does not need to prove that the business failed to exercise reasonable care.

State and Local Regulation

Many states regulate the degree to which the environment may be polluted. Thus, for example, even when state zoning laws permit a business's proposed development, the proposal may have to be altered to change the development's impact on the environment. State laws may restrict a business's discharge of chemicals into the air or water or regulate its disposal of toxic wastes. States may also regulate the disposal or recycling of other wastes, including glass, metal, and plastic containers and paper. Additionally, states may restrict the emissions from motor vehicles.

City, county, and other local governments control some aspects of the environment. For instance, local zoning laws control some land use. These laws may be designed to inhibit or direct the growth of cities and suburbs or to protect the natural environment. Other aspects of the environment may be subject to local regulation for other reasons. Methods of waste and garbage removal and disposal, for example, can have a substantial impact on a community. The appearance of buildings and other structures, including advertising signs and billboards, may affect traffic safety, property values, or local aesthetics. Noise generated by a business or its customers may be annoying, disruptive, or damaging to neighbors. The location and condition of parks, streets, and other publicly used land subject to local control affect the environment and can also affect business.

NUISANCE
A common law doctrine under which persons may be held liable for using their property in a manner that unreasonably interferes with others' rights to use or enjoy their own property.

• •

"A nuisance may be merely a right thing in the wrong place, like a pig in the parlor instead of the barnyard."

George Sutherland, 1862–1942
(American jurist)
• •

---

33.   *Save the Bay Committee, Inc. v. Mayor of City of Savannah,* 227 Ga. 436, 181 S.E.2d 351 (1971).

Federal Regulation

Congress has passed a number of statutes to control the impact of human activities on the environment. Some of these have been passed to improve the quality of air and water. Some of them specifically regulate toxic chemicals—including pesticides, herbicides, and hazardous wastes.

ENVIRONMENTAL IMPACT STATEMENT (EIS)

A statement required by the National Environmental Policy Act for any major federal action that will significantly affect the quality of the environment. The statement must analyze the action's impact on the environment and explore alternative actions that might be taken.

NATIONAL ENVIRONMENTAL POLICY ACT (NEPA) The National Environmental Policy Act (NEPA)[34] of 1969 imposes environmental responsibilities on all agencies of the federal government. NEPA requires that all agencies consider environmental factors when making significant decisions. For every major federal action that significantly affects the quality of the environment, an **environmental impact statement (EIS)** must be prepared. An action qualifies as "major" if it involves a substantial commitment of resources, monetary or otherwise. An action is "federal" if a federal agency has the power to control it. For example, building a new nuclear reactor involves federal action, because a federal license is required.

An EIS must analyze (1) the impact on the environment that the action will have, (2) any adverse effects to the environment and alternative actions that might be taken, and (3) irreversible effects the action might generate. If an agency decides that an EIS is unnecessary, it must issue a statement supporting this conclusion. EISs have become instruments by which private citizens, consumer and environmental interest groups, businesses, and others challenge federal agency actions on the basis that the actions improperly threaten the environment. For example, an environmental interest group can use an EIS as evidence in court when challenging a federal agency action on the basis that the action violates the Clean Air Act. Today, almost all environmental litigation involves disputes with government agencies rather than disputes between private parties.

THE ENVIRONMENTAL PROTECTION AGENCY (EPA) In 1970, the Environmental Protection Agency (EPA) was created to coordinate federal environmental responsibilities. The EPA administers most federal environmental policies and statutes. Other federal agencies that have authority to regulate specific environmental matters include the Department of the Interior, the Department of Defense, the Department of Labor, the Food and Drug Administration, and the Nuclear Regulatory Commission.

---

34.   42 U.S.C. Sections 4321–4370d.

International Perspective

Today's business managers can no longer afford to ignore the effect of their decisions on the environment. This is true not only in the United States but in other countries around the globe as well. As discussed in Chapter 4, those companies that engage in activities harmful to the environment may be subject to negative sanctions (criticism in the press, boycotts, and so on) for their "ethically irresponsible" behavior.

To guide companies in their attempts to be environmentally responsible, the Geneva-based International Organization for Standardization has created fourteen thousand universally applicable standards for the development of environmental management systems. The standards are the outgrowth of the nine thousand quality management and quality assurance standards published by the organization in 1987. The nine thousand standards achieved wide acceptance in the United States, Europe, and Asia.

The standards are not regulatory in nature and do not impose any restrictions on polluting activities. Rather, they offer a variety of management tools and devices to help companies perform their environmental obligations. Essentially, the standards set forth a series of recommendations on how a company can establish an effective

International Perspective—Continued

and totally integrated environmental management system. The standards reflect the commercial reality that firms doing business internationally, because they are subject to different national environmental laws, need a consistent set of environmental standards to guide them.

For Critical Analysis: *Why don't the standards impose restrictions on polluting activities?*

Air Pollution

Federal involvement with air pollution goes back to the 1950s, when Congress authorized funds for air-pollution research. In 1963, the federal government passed the Clean Air Act,[35] which focused on multistate air pollution and provided assistance to states. Various amendments, particularly in 1970, 1977, and 1990, strengthened the government's authority to regulate the quality of air. These laws provide the basis for issuing regulations to control pollution coming primarily from mobile sources (such as automobiles) and stationary sources (such as electric utilities and industrial plants).

MOBILE SOURCES   Regulations governing air pollution from automobiles and other mobile sources specify pollution standards and time schedules. Under the 1990 amendments to the Clean Air Act, for example, automobile manufacturers must cut new automobiles' exhaust emission of nitrogen oxide by 60 percent and emission of other pollutants by 35 percent. Beginning in 1994, increasing numbers of new automobiles had to meet these standards. By 1999, all new automobiles will have had to do so. Another set of emission controls may be ordered after 2000.

   To ensure compliance, the EPA may inspect production models. If a vehicle does not meet the standards in actual driving, the EPA can order a recall and the repair or replacement of pollution-control equipment at the manufacturer's expense. The 1990 amendments also required service stations in specified areas to sell gasoline with a higher oxygen content. In the following case, the court reviewed an EPA order regulating the lead content of gasoline, the validity of which had been challenged.

---

35.   42 U.S.C. Sections 7401 *et seq.*

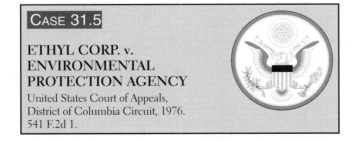

CASE 31.5

ETHYL CORP. v.
ENVIRONMENTAL
PROTECTION AGENCY

United States Court of Appeals,
District of Columbia Circuit, 1976.
541 F.2d 1.

HISTORICAL AND ENVIRONMENTAL SETTING
Among the obstacles to effective control of air pollution is the lack of scientific knowledge about the extent of the threat posed by specific pollutants. Sometimes, for example, it is unclear how much of a particular sub-

stance can be released into the air before it becomes a hazard to human health. Even when it is known how much of a substance is a health hazard, it can be difficult to regulate the sources of the substance if no single source releases enough of the substance to be hazardous. For instance, it is well known that lead is toxic. Because people are exposed to lead from many sources, however, it can be difficult to determine the negative health effects of an increase in the amount of lead in the environment from any one source. Notwithstanding these problems, the EPA has a mandate to protect the public health.

(Continued)

Case 31.5—Continued

FACTS   Ethyl Corporation, a leading producer of gasoline additives, sought court review of the Environmental Protection Agency's order that required annual reductions in the lead content of gasoline. The Clean Air Act authorized the agency to regulate gasoline additives that are a danger to public health or welfare. Ethyl Corporation claimed that the EPA had exceeded its authority by requiring annual reductions in the lead content of gasoline.

ISSUE   Had the EPA exceeded its authority by requiring a reduction in the lead content of gasoline?

DECISION   No. The court found that the EPA had not abused its discretion by requiring a reduction in the lead content of gasoline.

REASON   The record in this case was massive—over ten thousand pages. The EPA had relied on this evidence in making its decision, and although the evidence was not wholly unassailable, it did provide a reasonable basis on which to make a decision. The court defined its scope of review as follows: "Our scope * * * requires us to strike 'agency action, findings, and conclusions' [only if] we find [them] to be 'arbitrary, capricious, an abuse of discretion, or otherwise not in accordance with law.' This standard of review is a highly deferential one. It presumes agency action to be valid. Moreover, it forbids the court's substituting its judgment for that of the agency."

FOR CRITICAL ANALYSIS—Political Consideration
Why do the courts generally defer to administrative agency actions, as the court did in this case?

STATIONARY SOURCES   The Clean Air Act authorizes the EPA to establish air quality standards for stationary sources (such as manufacturing plants) also but recognizes that the primary responsibility for preventing and controlling air pollution rests with state and local governments. The EPA sets two levels (primary and secondary) of ambient standards—that is, the maximum level of certain pollutants—and the states formulate plans to achieve those standards. The plans are to provide for the attainment of primary standards within three years and secondary standards within a reasonable time. For economic, political, or technological reasons, however, the deadlines are often subject to change.

Different standards apply to existing sources of pollution and major new sources. Different standards also apply to sources in clean areas and sources in polluted areas. Major new sources include existing sources modified by a change in a method of operation that increases emissions. Performance standards for these sources require the use of the maximum achievable control technology, or MACT, to reduce emissions from the combustion of fossil fuels (coal and oil).

Hazardous air pollutants are those likely to cause an increase in mortality or in serious irreversible or incapacitating illness, such as cancer or neurological damage. These pollutants include asbestos, benzene, beryllium, cadmium, mercury, and vinyl chloride. The pollutants may be emitted by a variety of business activities, such as smelting, dry cleaning, house painting, and commercial baking. Instead of establishing specific emissions standards for each hazardous air pollutant, the law requires industry to use the best available technology to limit those emissions. The EPA may strengthen this requirement if necessary to protect the public health.

PENALTIES   For violations of emission limits under the Clean Air Act, the EPA can assess civil penalties of up to $25,000 per day. To penalize those for whom this amount makes a violation more cost effective than compliance, the EPA can obtain a penalty equal to the violator's economic benefits from noncompliance. Private citizens can also sue violators. Those who knowingly violate the act may be subject to criminal penalties.

....

"Among the treasures of our land is water—fast becoming our most valuable, most prized, most critical resource."

Dwight D. Eisenhower,
1890–1969
(*Thirty-fourth president of the United States, 1953–1961*)
....

Water Pollution

The major sources of water pollution are industrial, municipal, and agricultural. Pollutants entering streams, lakes, and oceans include organic wastes, heated water,

A scientist tests water from an industrial source that has been cleaned of pollutants. How "clean" should such water be before it is released into the environment?

sediments from soil runoff, nutrients (including detergents, fertilizers, and human and animal wastes), and toxic chemicals and other hazardous substances. We look here at laws and regulations governing water pollution.

NAVIGABLE WATERS   Federal regulations governing the pollution of water can be traced back to the Rivers and Harbors Appropriations Act of 1899.[36] These regulations required a permit for discharging or depositing refuse in navigable waterways. In 1948, Congress passed the Federal Water Pollution Control Act (FWPCA),[37] but its regulatory system and enforcement powers proved to be inadequate.

In 1972, amendments to the FWPCA—known as the Clean Water Act—established the following goals: (1) make waters safe for swimming, (2) protect fish and wildlife, and (3) eliminate the discharge of pollutants into the water. The amendments set forth specific time schedules, which were extended by amendment in 1977 and by the Water Quality Act of 1987.[38] Under these schedules, the EPA establishes limitations for discharges of types of pollutants based on the technology available for controlling them. The 1972 amendments also required municipal and industrial polluters to apply for permits before discharging wastes into navigable waters.

Under the act, violators are subject to a variety of civil and criminal penalties. Civil penalties for each violation range from $10,000 per day to as much as $25,000 per day or per violation. Criminal penalties range from a fine of $2,500 per day and imprisonment of up to one year to a fine of $1 million and fifteen years' imprisonment. Injunctive relief and damages can also be imposed. The polluting party can be required to clean up the pollution or pay for the cost of doing so.

The Clean Water Act prohibits the filling or dredging of **wetlands** unless a permit is obtained from the Army Corps of Engineers. The EPA defines wetlands as "those areas that are inundated or saturated by surface or ground water at a frequency and duration sufficient to support, and that under normal circumstances do support, a prevalence of vegetation typically adapted for life in saturated soil conditions." In recent years, federal regulatory policy in regard to wetlands has elicited substantial

WETLANDS
Areas of land designated by government agencies (such as the Army Corps of Engineers or the Environmental Protection Agency) as protected areas that support wildlife and that therefore cannot be filled in or dredged by private contractors or parties.

---

36.   33 U.S.C. Sections 401–418.
37.   33 U.S.C. Sections 1251–1387.
38.   This act amended 33 U.S.C. Section 1251.

controversy because of the broad interpretation of what constitutes a wetland subject to the regulatory authority of the federal government. The following case is illustrative (see also this chapter's *Law in the Extreme*).[39]

---

39.   Note that Congress is now considering bills that would alter the current regulatory scheme.

CASE 31.6

HOFFMAN HOMES, INC. v. ADMINISTRATOR, UNITED STATES ENVIRONMENTAL PROTECTION AGENCY

United States Court of Appeals,
Seventh Circuit, 1993.
999 F.2d 256.

COMPANY PROFILE   *Sam and Jack Hoffman started F&S Construction in Phoenix in 1947. Over the next few years, the company—renamed the Hoffman Group—built thousands of low-priced houses throughout the United States, becoming the nation's third largest builder by 1955. Norman Hassinger, a residential marketing expert, became president of the Hoffman Group in 1982 and gradually took over the firm. In 1987, the Hoffman Group became the Hassinger Companies. Hassinger created Hoffman Homes, Inc., as a home-building subsidiary.*

FACTS   Hoffman Homes, Inc., in preparation for the construction of a housing subdivision, filled and graded a bowl-shaped depression covering an area of 0.8 acre ("Area A"), located on property owned by Hoffman in Hoffman Estates, Illinois. Before Hoffman filled Area A, rainwater periodically collected there. The EPA issued an order stating that Hoffman had filled wetlands without a permit in violation of the Clean Water Act and ordered Hoffman, among other things, to cease its filling activities and pay a fine of $50,000 for violating the act. In response to Hoffman's protests that the EPA had no regulatory authority over Area A because the area in no way affected *inter*state commerce, the EPA stated that it had authority to regulate discharges of fill materials into *intra*state wetlands that have a "minimal, potential effect"

on interstate commerce. The EPA found that Area A had such a minimal, potential effect on interstate commerce because migratory birds could *potentially* use the area. Hoffman appealed the EPA's decision.

ISSUE   Was Area A subject to regulation under the Clean Water Act?

DECISION   No. The U.S. Court of Appeals for the Seventh Circuit vacated the EPA's order requiring Hoffman Homes to pay a $50,000 administrative penalty for the filling of Area A.

REASON   The appellate court concluded that there was no evidence to support the contention that filling Area A affects interstate commerce. The court stated, "It is true, of course, that migratory birds can alight most anywhere. As [a witness] testified, he has seen mallards in parking lot puddles." The court stressed, however, that the evidence in this case simply does not support the conclusion that Area A had characteristics whose use by, and value to, migratory birds is well established. "The migratory birds are better judges of what is suitable for their welfare than are we [or the EPA]. Having avoided Area A[,] the migratory birds have thus spoken and submitted their own evidence. We see no need to argue with them. No justification whatsoever is seen from the evidence to interfere with private ownership based on what appears to be no more than a well intentioned effort in these particular factual circumstances to expand government control beyond reasonable or practical limits. After April showers not every temporary wet spot necessarily becomes subject to government control."

FOR CRITICAL ANALYSIS—Political Consideration
In evaluating cases concerning wetlands, does it matter that the EPA, and not Congress, defines specifically what constitutes a "wetland"?

DRINKING WATER   Another statute governing water pollution is the Safe Drinking Water Act.[40] Passed in 1974, this act requires the EPA to set maximum levels for

---

40.   42 U.S.C. Sections 300f to 300j–25.

LAW IN THE EXTREME

Facing a No-Win Situation

Sometimes, a company that attempts to comply with environmental laws faces a no-win situation. Consider, for example, the experience of the Leslie Salt Company, which owned a large tract of land southeast of San Francisco, across the highway from the San Francisco Bay National Wildlife Refuge. Leslie Salt's predecessor had dug various shallow basins to facilitate the manufacture of salt. After Leslie Salt discontinued salt production in 1959, the area remained dry most of the year. During the winter and spring months, however, rainwater occasionally created temporary ponds, which were visited by migratory birds. The usually dry basins created a dust problem, and as a result, Leslie Salt eventually was cited for violating federal air-pollution standards.

To prevent further citations, Leslie Salt began to plow the basins, dig ditches, and discharge fill material into the basins to create conditions more hospitable to plant growth. Ironically, these actions subjected it to penalties under the Clean Water Act. When the Army Corps of Engineers (the Corps) learned of Leslie Salt's filling activities, it issued a cease-and-desist order. The Corps claimed that the filling of the basins violated the Clean Water Act, which prohibits the discharge of any pollutant—including dredged or fill materials—into "navigable waters" without a permit from the Corps. Under a regulation promulgated by the Corps, "navigable waters" include, among other things, "mudflats, sandflats, wetlands, sloughs, prairie potholes, wet meadows, . . . or natural ponds, the use, degradation or destruction of which could affect interstate or foreign commerce."

Leslie Salt, claiming that the ponds had nothing to do with interstate commerce, filed a suit challenging the Corps's jurisdiction over its property. A federal district court concluded that the presence of migratory birds created a sufficient

connection to interstate commerce to sustain the Corps's (federal) jurisdiction. On appeal, a federal appellate court affirmed the decision.[a] A further appeal to the United States Supreme Court fared no better: the high court refused to grant *certiorari*. Justice Thomas, who strongly dissented to the denial of *certiorari*, stated that "[o]ther than the occasional presence of migratory birds, there was no showing that petitioner's land use would have any effect on interstate commerce, much less a substantial effect."[b]

For Critical Analysis: *In the Clean Water Act, Congress defined "navigable waters" as simply "waters of the United States." Why didn't Congress create a more specific definition, rather than leaving it up to administrative agencies to provide a specific definition?*

a. *Leslie Salt Co. v. United States*, 55 F.3d 1388 (9th Cir. 1995).
b. *Cargill, Inc. v. United States*, ___U.S.___, 116 S.Ct. 407, 133 L.Ed.2d 325 (1995). (Cargill, Inc., is the corporate successor of Leslie Salt Co.)

pollutants in public water systems. Public water system operators must come as close as possible to meeting the EPA's standards by using the best available technology that is economically and technologically feasible. The EPA is particularly concerned with contamination from underground sources.

OCEAN DUMPING The Marine Protection, Research, and Sanctuaries Act[41] of 1972 (popularly known as the Ocean Dumping Act), as amended in 1983, regulates the transportation and dumping of material into ocean waters. It prohibits entirely the ocean dumping of radiological, chemical, and biological-warfare agents and high-level radioactive waste. A violation of any provision may result in a civil penalty of $50,000, and a knowing violation is a criminal offense that may result in a $50,000 fine, imprisonment for not more than a year, or both.

OIL SPILLS In 1989, the supertanker *Exxon Valdez* caused the worst oil spill in North American history in the waters of Alaska's Prince William Sound. A quarter of a million barrels of crude oil—more than ten million gallons—leaked out of the ship's broken hull. In response to the *Exxon Valdez* oil spill disaster, Congress passed the Oil Pollution Act of 1990.[42] Any onshore or offshore oil facility, oil shipper, vessel owner,

---

41. 16 U.S.C. Sections 1401–1445.
42. 33 U.S.C. Sections 2701–2761.

or vessel operator that discharges oil into navigable waters or onto an adjoining shore may be liable for clean-up costs, as well as damages.

The act provides for civil penalties of $1,000 per barrel spilled or $25,000 for each day of the violation. The party held responsible for the clean-up costs can bring a civil suit, however, for contribution from other potentially liable parties. The act also created a $1 billion oil clean-up and economic compensation fund and decreed that by the year 2011, oil tankers using U.S. ports must be double hulled to limit the severity of accidental spills.

Noise Pollution

Regulations concerning noise pollution include the Noise Control Act of 1972.[43] This act directed the EPA to establish noise-emission standards (maximum noise levels below which no harmful effects occur due to interference with speech or other activity). The standards must be achievable by the best available technology, and they must be economically within reason. The act prohibits, among other things, the distribution of products manufactured in violation of the noise-emission standards and tampering with noise-control devices. Either of these activities can result in an injunction or whatever other remedy "is necessary to protect the public health and welfare." Violations of provisions of the Noise Control Act can result in penalties of not more than $50,000 per day and imprisonment for not more than two years.

Toxic Chemicals

> "All property in this country is held under the implied obligation that the owner's use of it shall not be injurious to the community."
>
> **John Harlan, 1899–1971**
> (*Associate justice of the United States Supreme Court, 1955–1971*)

Originally, most environmental clean-up efforts were directed toward reducing smog and making water safe for fishing and swimming. Over time, however, it became clear that chemicals released into the environment in relatively small amounts could pose a threat to human life and health. Control of these toxic chemicals has become an important part of environmental law.

PESTICIDES AND HERBICIDES   The first toxic chemical problem to receive widespread public attention was that posed by pesticides and herbicides. Using these chemicals to kill insects and weeds has increased agricultural productivity, but their residue remains in the environment. In some instances, accumulations of this residue have killed animals, and scientists have identified potential long-term effects that are detrimental to people.

The federal statute regulating pesticides and herbicides is the Federal Insecticide, Fungicide, and Rodenticide Act (FIFRA) of 1947.[44] Under FIFRA, pesticides and herbicides must be (1) registered before they can be sold, (2) certified and used only for approved applications, and (3) used in limited quantities when applied to food crops. It is a violation of FIFRA to sell a pesticide or herbicide that is unregistered or that is marketed with a false or misleading label. The act's labeling requirements include directions for the use of the pesticide or herbicide, warnings to protect human health and the environment, a statement of treatment in the case of poisoning, and a list of the ingredients.

A private party can petition the EPA to suspend or cancel the registration of a pesticide or herbicide. If the EPA fails to act, the private party can petition a federal court to review the EPA's failure. Penalties for registrants and producers for violating FIFRA include imprisonment for up to one year and a fine of no more than $50,000. Penalties for commercial dealers include imprisonment for up to one year and a fine of no

---

43.   42 U.S.C. Sections 4901–4918.
44.   7 U.S.C. Sections 135–136y.

more than $25,000. Farmers and other private users of pesticides or herbicides who violate the act are subject to a $1,000 fine and imprisonment for up to thirty days.

TOXIC SUBSTANCES   The first comprehensive law covering toxic substances was the Toxic Substances Control Act of 1976.[45] The act was passed to regulate chemicals and chemical compounds that are known to be toxic—such as asbestos and polychlorinated biphenyls, popularly known as PCBs—and to institute investigation of any possible harmful effects from new chemical compounds. The regulations authorize the EPA to require that manufacturers, processors, and other organizations planning to use chemicals first determine their effects on human health and the environment. The EPA can regulate substances that potentially pose an imminent hazard or an unreasonable risk of injury to health or the environment. The EPA may require special labeling, limit the use of a substance, set production quotas, or prohibit the use of a substance altogether.

Hazardous Waste Disposal

Some industrial, agricultural, and household wastes pose more serious threats than others. If not properly disposed of, these toxic chemicals may present a substantial danger to human health and the environment. If released into the environment, they may contaminate public drinking water resources.

RESOURCE CONSERVATION AND RECOVERY ACT   In 1976, Congress passed the Resource Conservation and Recovery Act (RCRA)[46] in reaction to an ever-increasing concern over the effects of hazardous waste materials on the environment. The RCRA required the EPA to establish regulations to monitor and control hazardous waste disposal and to determine which forms of solid waste should be considered hazardous and thus subject to regulation. The EPA has promulgated various technical requirements for limited types of facilities for storage and treatment of hazardous waste. The act also requires all producers of hazardous waste materials to label and package properly any hazardous waste to be transported.

> BE CAREFUL Under the Resource Conservation and Recovery Act, anyone who generates, treats, stores, or transports hazardous waste must obtain a permit.

The RCRA was amended in 1984 and 1986 to add several new regulatory requirements to those already monitored and enforced by the EPA.[47] The basic aims of the amendments were to decrease the use of land containment in the disposal of hazardous waste and to require compliance with the act by some generators of hazardous waste—such as those generating less than 1,000 kilograms (2,200 pounds) a month— that had previously been excluded from regulation under the RCRA.

Under the RCRA, a company may be assessed a civil penalty based on the seriousness of the violation, the probability of harm, and the extent to which the violation deviates from RCRA requirements. The assessment may be up to $25,000 for each violation.[48] Criminal penalties include fines up to $50,000 for each day of violation, imprisonment for up to two years (in most instances), or both.[49] Criminal fines and the time of imprisonment can be doubled for certain repeat offenders.

SUPERFUND   In 1980, Congress passed the Comprehensive Environmental Response, Compensation, and Liability Act (CERCLA),[50] commonly known as Superfund. The basic purpose of Superfund is to regulate the clean-up of leaking hazardous waste disposal sites. A special federal fund was created for that purpose. Because

---

45.   15 U.S.C. Sections 2601–2692.
46.   42 U.S.C. Sections 6901 *et seq.*
47.   42 U.S.C. Sections 6901 *et seq.*
48.   42 U.S.C. Section 6929(g).
49.   42 U.S.C. Section 6929(d).
50.   42 U.S.C. Sections 9601–9675.

of its impact on the business community, the act is presented here as this chapter's *Landmark in the Law.*

Superfund

The origins of the Comprehensive Environmental Response, Compensation, and Liability Act (CERCLA) of 1980, which is commonly referred to as Superfund, can be traced to drafts that the Environmental Protection Agency (EPA) started to circulate in 1978. EPA officials emphasized the political necessity of new legislation by pointing to what they thought were "ticking time bombs"—dump sites around the country that were ready to explode and injure the public with toxic fumes.

The popular press also gave prominence to hazardous waste dump sites at the time. The New York Love Canal disaster began to make the headlines in 1978 after residents in the area complained about health problems, contaminated sludge oozing into their basements, and chemical "volcanoes" erupting in their yards as a result of Hooker Chemical's dumping of approximately 21,000 tons of chemicals into the canal from 1942 to 1953. The Love Canal situation made the national news virtually every day from the middle of May to the middle of June in 1980.

The basic purpose of CERCLA, which was amended in 1986 by the Superfund Amendments and Reauthorization Act, is to regulate the clean-up of leaking hazardous waste disposal sites. The act has four primary elements:

• It established an information-gathering and analysis system that allows federal and state governments to characterize chemical dump sites and to develop priorities for appropriate action.
• It authorized the EPA to respond to hazardous substance emergencies and to clean up leaking sites directly through contractors or through cooperative agreements with the states if the persons responsible for the problem fail to clean up the site.
• It created a Hazardous Substance Response Trust Fund (Superfund) to pay for the clean-up of hazardous sites. Monies for the fund are obtained through taxes on

A warning to trespassers is posted at a hazardous waste site. Who should pay the cost of cleaning up the site?

Landmark in the Law—Continued

certain businesses, including those processing or producing petroleum and chemical feed stock.

• It allowed the government to recover the cost of clean-up from the persons who were (even remotely) responsible for hazardous-substance releases.

For Critical Analysis: *Must all of the contamination be removed from a hazardous waste site to ensure that it no longer poses any threat of harm to life? Would some lesser amount satisfy a reasonable degree of environmental quality?*

POTENTIALLY RESPONSIBLE PARTY (PRP)
A liable party under the Comprehensive Environmental Response, Compensation, and Liability Act (CERCLA). Any person who generated the hazardous waste, transported the hazardous waste, owned or operated a waste site at the time of disposal, or currently owns or operates a site may be responsible for some or all of the clean-up costs involved in removing the hazardous chemicals.

Potentially Responsible Parties under Superfund   Superfund provides that when a release or a threatened release of hazardous chemicals from a site occurs, the EPA can clean up the site and recover the cost of the clean-up from the following persons: (1) the person who generated the wastes disposed of at the site, (2) the person who transported the wastes to the site, (3) the person who owned or operated the site at the time of the disposal, or (4) the current owner or operator. A person falling within one of these categories is referred to as a **potentially responsible party (PRP).**

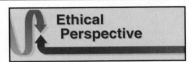

Deciding who qualifies as a PRP under Superfund is not always easy; nor are the results of such decisions always necessarily fair. For example, one controversial issue has centered on whether a bank that holds a mortgage on a company's real property should be liable for clean-up costs as an "owner or operator" of the property. Some courts have followed the lead of the Eleventh Circuit Court of Appeals, which held that a bank can be held liable as a PRP if the bank has the "capacity to influence" a borrower's decisions about toxic waste.[a] Other courts have held to the contrary. For example, one court pointed out that "[s]ecured lenders frequently have some routine involvement in the financial affairs of their debtors in order to insure that their interests are being adequately protected." The court held that to impose liability on a bank for involving itself in the debtor's affairs would be to "punish the Bank for engaging in its normal course of business."[b]

Other parties who have been deemed liable as PRPs by the courts include parent companies, successor corporations, and trustees who manage property held in trust.[c] In some cases, courts have even "pierced the corporate veil" to hold corporate shareholder-officers personally liable because of the degree of control they exercised over their corporations.[d]

Decisions as to who qualifies as a PRP have important ramifications, because liability under Superfund can be extensive. Proposed Superfund legislation, if passed, would significantly limit the liability of PRPs, but in the meantime it remains difficult to predict when and to what extent parties may be liable under Superfund.

For Critical Analysis: *Should the cost of clean-up operations to PRPs ever be a factor in determining how "clean" the site must be?*

a.   See *United States v. Fleet Factors Corp.,* 901 F.2d 1550 (11th Cir. 1990).
b.   *Z & Z Leasing, Inc. v. Graying Reel, Inc.,* 873 F.Supp. 51 (E.D.Mich. 1995).
c.   See *United States v. Kayser-Roth Corp.,* 910 F.2d 24 (1st Cir. 1990); *Anspec Co. v. Johnson Controls, Inc.,* 922 F.2d 1240 (6th Cir. 1991); and *Phoenix v. Garbage Services Co.,* 816 F.Supp. 564 (D.Ariz. 1993), respectively. (Trusts are discussed in Chapter 36.)
d.   See, for example, *United States v. TIC Investment Corp.,* 68 F.3d 1082 (8th Cir. 1995).

Joint and Several Liability   Liability under Superfund is usually joint and several—that is, a person who generated only a fraction of the hazardous waste disposed of at the site may nevertheless be liable for *all* of the clean-up costs. CERCLA authorizes a party who has incurred clean-up costs to bring a "contribution action" against any other person who is liable or potentially liable for a percentage of the costs.[51]

51.   Note that the Superfund reauthorization bill currently before Congress would abolish joint and several liability for clean-up costs.

Application

Law and the Businessperson—Keeping Abreast of Environmental Laws*

Businesspersons today increasingly face the threat of severe civil or criminal penalties if they violate environmental laws and regulations. It therefore is necessary that every person in the business world be aware of what those laws and regulations are and how to monitor changes in them. At a minimum, knowledge of the changing and complex nature of environmental law will help a businessperson to know when to contact an attorney during the normal course of business.

Consider some areas of concern that affect businesses. Businesspersons often purchase business property. When engaging in such purchases, you must keep in mind the environmental problems that may arise. Realize that it is up to you as a purchaser of the property to raise environmental issues. This is because sellers, title insurance companies, and real estate brokers will rarely pursue such matters. (A bank financing the property may worry about the potential environmental hazards of the property, however.)

As a purchaser of business property, you should learn whether there are any restrictions regarding the use of the land, such as whether the land can be cleared of trees for construction purposes. The most prominent environmental concern, however, is whether the property has been contaminated by hazardous wastes created by the previous owners. There seems to be an unending number of ways in which purchasers of property can be held liable under the Comprehensive Environmental Response, Compensation, and Liability Act (CERCLA)

of 1980 for the clean-up of hazardous wastes dumped by previous property owners. Although it is true that current property owners who are sued under CERCLA for clean-up costs can sue the previous owners, such litigation is uncertain and usually costly. Clearly, a more prudent course when purchasing property is to investigate the history of the use of the land. If you purchase business property, you would be well advised to hire a private environmental site inspector to determine, at a minimum, whether the land has any obvious signs of former contamination.

There is also an incentive for today's companies to discover their own environmental wrongdoings. As mentioned in Chapters 7 and 26, the federal sentencing guidelines encourage companies to promptly detect, disclose, and correct wrongdoing, including environmental crimes. Companies that do so are subject to lighter penalties for violations of environmental laws. Under the guidelines, a company that regularly conducts comprehensive audits of its compliance with environmental requirements, immediately reports a violation to the government, disciplines the responsible people within the corporation, and provides their names to the government should qualify for leniency.

Small businesses will find it particularly advantageous to investigate and correct environmental violations. Under the EPA's "Common Sense Compliance Policy," which became effective in 1995, the EPA will waive all fines if a company corrects environmental violations within 180 days (or 360 days if pollution-prevention techniques are involved). The policy applies to companies with one hundred or fewer employees. The policy does not apply to criminal violations of environmental laws or to actions that pose a significant threat to public health, safety, or the environment.

*This *Application* is not meant to substitute for the services of an attorney who is licensed to practice law in your state.

Application—Continued

Checklist for the Businessperson

1. If you are in business or plan to open a business that is going to purchase real estate, use land, or engage in activities that might cause environmental damage, check with your attorney immediately.
2. If you want to avoid liability for violating environmental regulations or statutes, conduct environ-

mental compliance audits on a regular basis. To learn whether you are doing so appropriately, check with your attorney.

3. If you are ever charged with violating an environmental regulation or law, you must check with your attorney.
4. In short, environmental law is sufficiently complex that you should never attempt to deal with it without the help of an attorney.

▌Key Terms

bait-and-switch advertising 793
cease-and-desist order 793
"cooling off" law 796
counteradvertising 793

deceptive advertising 790
environmental impact statement
  (EIS) 806
nuisance 805

potentially responsible
  party (PRP) 815
Regulation Z 796
wetlands 809

▌Chapter Summary: Consumer and Environmental Law

CONSUMER PROTECTION LAWS	

Deceptive Advertising
(See pages 790–794.)
	1. *Definition of deceptive advertising*—Generally, an advertising claim will be deemed deceptive if it would mislead a reasonable consumer.
	2. *Bait-and-switch advertising*—Advertising a lower-priced product (the "bait") when the intention is not to sell the advertised product but to lure consumers into the store and convince them to buy a higher-priced product (the "switch") is prohibited by the FTC.
	3. *FTC actions against deceptive advertising*—
	  a. Cease-and-desist orders—Requiring the advertiser to stop the challenged advertising.
	  b. Counteradvertising—Requiring the advertiser to advertise to correct the earlier misinformation.

Telemarketing and Fax Advertising *(See pages 794–795.)*	The Telephone Consumer Protection Act of 1991 prohibits telephone solicitation using an automatic telephone dialing system or a prerecorded voice, as well as the transmission of advertising materials via fax without first obtaining the recipient's permission to do so.
Labeling and Packaging *(See pages 795–796.)*	Manufacturers must comply with labeling or packaging requirements for their specific products. In general, all labels must be accurate and not misleading.
Sales *(See pages 796–797.)*	1. *Door-to-door sales*—The FTC requires all door-to-door sellers to give consumers three days (a "cooling-off" period) to cancel any sale. States also provide for similar protection. 2. *Telephone and mail-order sales*—Federal and state statutes and regulations govern certain practices of sellers who solicit over the telephone or through the mails and prohibit the use of the mails to defraud individuals. 3. *Regulations affecting specific industries*—The FTC has regulations that apply to specific industries, such as the used-car business and funeral homes. 4. *Real estate sales*—Various federal and state laws apply to consumer transactions involving real estate. *(Continued)*

▌Chapter Summary: Consumer and Environmental Law—Continued

Health and Safety Protection *(See pages 797–799.)*	1. *Food and drugs*—The Federal Food, Drug and Cosmetic Act of 1938, as amended, protects consumers against adulterated and misbranded foods and drugs. The act establishes food standards, specifies safe levels of potentially hazardous food additives, and sets classifications of food and food advertising. 2. *Consumer product safety*—The Consumer Product Safety Act of 1972 seeks to protect consumers from risk of injury from hazardous products. The Consumer Product Safety Commission has the power to remove products that are deemed imminently hazardous from the market and to ban the manufacture and sale of hazardous products.

Credit Protection *(See pages 799–804.)*	1. *Consumer Credit Protection Act, Title I (Truth-in-Lending Act, or TILA)*—A disclosure law that requires sellers and lenders to disclose credit terms or loan terms in certain transactions, including retail and installment sales and loans, car loans, home improvement loans, and certain real estate loans. Additionally, the TILA provides for the following:
	  a. Equal credit opportunity—Creditors are prohibited from discriminating on the basis of race, religion, marital status, gender, and so on.
	  b. Credit-card protection—Credit-card users may withhold payment for a faulty product sold, or for an error in billing, until the dispute is resolved; liability of cardholders for unauthorized charges is limited to $50, providing notice requirements are met; consumers are not liable for unauthorized charges made on unsolicited credit cards.
	  c. Consumer leases—The Consumer Leasing Act (CLA) of 1988 protects consumers who lease automobiles and other goods priced at $25,000 or less if the lease term exceeds four months.
	2. *Fair Credit Reporting Act*—Entitles consumers to request verification of the accuracy of a credit report and to have unverified information removed from their files.
	3. *Fair Debt Collection Practices Act*—Prohibits debt collectors from using unfair debt-collection practices, such as contacting the debtor at his or her place of employment if the employer objects or at unreasonable times, contacting third parties about the debt, harassing the debtor, and so on.

State Consumer Protection Laws *(See page 804.)*	State laws often provide for greater consumer protection against deceptive trade practices than do federal laws. In addition, the warranty and unconscionability provisions of the Uniform Commercial Code protect consumers against sellers' deceptive practices. The Uniform Consumer Credit Code, which has not been widely adopted by the states, provides credit protection for consumers.
ENVIRONMENTAL LAW	
Common Law Actions *(See pages 804–805.)*	1. *Nuisance*—A common law doctrine under which actions against pollution-causing activities may be brought. An action is permissible only if an individual suffers a harm separate and distinct from that of the general public. 2. *Negligence and strict liability*—Parties may recover damages for injuries sustained as a result of pollution-causing activities of a firm if it can be demonstrated that the harm was a foreseeable result of the firm's failure to exercise reasonable care (negligence); businesses engaging in ultrahazardous activities are liable for whatever injuries the activities cause, regardless of whether the firms exercise reasonable care.
State and Local Regulation *(See page 805.)*	Activities affecting the environment are controlled at the local and state levels through regulations relating to land use, the disposal and recycling of garbage and waste, and pollution-causing activities in general.
Federal Regulation *(See pages 806–816.)*	The National Environmental Policy Act of 1969 imposes environmental responsibilities on all federal agencies and requires for every major federal action the preparation of an environmental impact statement (EIS). An EIS must analyze the action's impact on the environment, its adverse effects and possible alternatives, and its irreversible effects on environmental quality. The Environmental Protection Agency was created in 1970 to coordinate federal environmental programs; it administers most federal environmental policies and statutes. Important areas regulated by the federal government include the following: 1. *Air pollution*—Regulated under the authority of the Clean Air Act of 1963 and its amendments, particularly those of 1970, 1977, and 1990. 2. *Water pollution*—Regulated under the authority of the Rivers and Harbors Appropriations Act of 1899, as amended, and the Federal Water Pollution Control Act of 1948, as amended by the Clean Water Act of 1972.

▌ Chapter Summary: Consumer and Environmental Law—Continued

Federal Regulation—Continued	3. *Noise pollution*—Regulated by the Noise Control Act of 1972.
	4. *Toxic chemicals*—Pesticides and herbicides, toxic substances, and hazardous waste are regulated under the authority of the Federal Insecticide, Fungicide, and Rodenticide Act of 1947, the Toxic Substances Control Act of 1976, and the Resource Conservation and Recovery Act of 1976, respectively. The Comprehensive Environmental Response, Compensation, and Liability Act (CERCLA) of 1980, as amended, regulates the clean-up of hazardous waste disposal sites.

▌ For Review

1. When will advertising be deemed deceptive?
2. How does the Federal Food, Drug and Cosmetic Act protect consumers? What are the major federal statutes providing for consumer protection in credit transactions?
3. Under what common law theories may polluters be held liable?

4. What is an environmental impact statement, and who must file one? What does the Environmental Protection Agency do?
5. What major federal statutes regulate air and water pollution? What is Superfund? To what categories of persons does liability under Superfund extend?

▌ Questions and Case Problems

31–1. Clean Air Act. Current scientific knowledge indicates that there is no safe level of exposure to a cancer-causing agent. In theory, even one molecule of such a substance has the potential for causing cancer. Section 112 of the Clean Air Act requires that all cancer-causing substances be regulated to ensure a margin of safety. Some environmental groups have argued that all emissions of such substances must be eliminated in order for such a margin of safety to be reached. Such a total elimination would likely shut down many major U.S. industries. Should the Environmental Protection Agency totally eliminate all emissions of cancer-causing chemicals? Discuss.

31–2. Environmental Laws. Fruitade, Inc., is a processor of a soft drink called Freshen Up. Fruitade uses returnable bottles and uses a special acid to clean its bottles for further beverage processing. The acid is diluted with water and then allowed to pass into a navigable stream. Fruitade crushes its broken bottles and also throws the crushed glass into the stream. Discuss *fully* any environmental laws that Fruitade has violated.

31–3. Sales. On June 28, a sales representative for Renowned Books called on the Guevaras at their home. After listening to a very persuasive sales pitch, the Guevaras agreed in writing to purchase a twenty-volume set of historical encyclopedias from Renowned Books for a total of $299. An initial down payment of $35 was required, with the remainder of the price to be paid in monthly payments over a one-year period. Two days later, the Guevaras, having second thoughts about the purchase, contacted the book company and stated that they had decided to rescind the contract. Renowned Books said this would be impossible. Has Renowned Books violated any consumer law by not allowing the Guevaras to rescind their contract? Explain.

31–4. Credit Protection. Maria Ochoa receives two new credit cards on May 1. She had solicited one of them from Midtown Department Store, and the other had arrived unsolicited from High-Flying Airlines. During the month of May, Ochoa makes numerous credit-card purchases from Midtown Store, but she does not use the High-Flying Airlines card. On May 31, a burglar breaks into Ochoa's home and steals both credit cards, along with other items. Ochoa notifies the Midtown Department Store of the theft on June 2, but she fails to notify High-Flying Airlines. Using the Midtown credit card, the burglar makes a $500 purchase on June 1 and a $200 purchase on June 3. The burglar then charges a vacation flight on the High-Flying Airlines card for $1,000 on June 5. Ochoa receives the bills for these charges and refuses to pay them. Discuss Ochoa's liability in these situations.

31–5. Deceptive Advertising. Dennis and Janice Geiger saw an advertisement in a newspaper for a Kimball Whitney spinet piano on sale for $699 at McCormick Piano & Organ Co. Because the style of the piano drawn in the advertisement matched their furniture, the Geigers were particularly interested in the Kimball. When they went to McCormick Piano & Organ, however, they learned that the drawing closely resembled another, more expensive Crest piano and that the Kimball spinet looked quite different from the piano sketched in the drawing. The salesperson told the Geigers that she was unable to order the spinet piano in the style requested by the Geigers. When the Geigers asked for the names of other customers who had purchased the advertised pianos, the salesperson became hysterical and said she would not, under any circumstances, sell the Geigers a piano. The Geigers then brought suit against the piano store, alleging that the store had engaged in deceptive advertising in violation of Indiana law. Had McCormick

Piano & Organ Co. engaged in deceptive advertising? Explain. [*McCormick Piano & Organ Co. v. Geiger,* 412 N.E.2d 842 (Ind.App. 1980)]

31–6. Deceptive Advertising. Thompson Medical Co. marketed a new cream, called Aspercreme, which was supposed to help people with arthritis and others suffering from minor aches. Aspercreme contained no aspirin. Thompson's television advertisements stated that the product provided "the strong relief of aspirin right where you hurt" and showed the announcer holding up aspirin tablets, as well as a tube of Aspercreme. The Federal Trade Commission held that the advertisements were misleading, because they led consumers to believe that Aspercreme contained aspirin. Thompson Medical Co. appealed this decision and argued that the advertisements never actually stated that its product contained aspirin. How should the court rule? Discuss. [*Thompson Medical Co. v. Federal Trade Commission,* 791 F.2d 189 (D.C. Cir. 1986)]

31–7. Debt Collection. Swanson owed $262.20 to a hospital in southern Oregon for medical services he had received. When Swanson failed to pay the debt, the hospital turned the account over to a local collection agency, which sent Swanson a letter requesting payment of the bill. Swanson alleged that the letter violated Section 809(a) of the Fair Debt Collection Practices Act (FDCPA), which mandates that any debt collector or agency subject to the act must notify the consumer early in the collection process that the consumer has thirty days within which to request validation of the debt. In the meantime, the consumer may withhold payment on the debt until assured that he or she actually owes the money. The letter did contain notice that the consumer had thirty days in which to demand verification of the debt, but the notice was, according to Swanson, overshadowed and effectively negated by the following statement—which was printed in boldface type, underlined, and set in a larger-than-standard typeface: IF THIS ACCOUNT IS PAID WITHIN THE NEXT 10 DAYS IT WILL NOT BE RECORDED IN OUR MASTER FILE AS AN UNPAID COLLECTION ITEM. A GOOD CREDIT RATING IS YOUR MOST VALUABLE ASSET. Had the collection agency violated Section 809(a) of the FDCPA? Explain. [*Swanson v. Southern Oregon Credit Service, Inc.,* 869 F.2d 1222 (9th Cir. 1989)]

31–8. Superfund. During the 1970s, a number of chemical companies disposed of their wastes at a facility maintained by South Carolina Recycling and Disposal, Inc. Hazardous chemical wastes were stored rather haphazardly; some leaked into the ground, and fires occurred on several occasions. Eventually, the Environmental Protection Agency (EPA) conducted clean-up operations under Superfund and sued companies that had used the site for the costs of the clean-up. Five of the defendant companies claimed that they should not be liable for the clean-up costs because there was no evidence that their waste materials had contributed in any way to the leakage problem or to any other hazard posed by the site. The EPA asserted that causation was not required for the companies' liability, only evidence that the companies had sent waste to the site. Will the EPA succeed in its claim? Discuss. [*United States v. South Carolina Recycling and Disposal, Inc.,* 653 F.Supp. 984 (D.S.C. 1986)]

31–9. Truth in Lending. On December 5, 1988, John and Carol Rowland met with a sales representative from Nu View Window of Illinois, Inc., and agreed to buy six windows for $4,364. On the same day, the Rowlands and the sales representative also partially completed a "Retail Installment Contract" and a "Notice of Right of Rescission," a copy of which was given to the Rowlands. The copy, however, was nearly illegible, and it was impossible to read the finance charges, the total price, the total number of payments, and other information. A few days later, the Rowlands gave Magna Millikin Bank of Decatur, N.A., a mortgage on their home in return for a loan of $4,364. On January 18, 1989, Magna Millikin dated its copy of the retail installment contract. On February 5, 1991, the Rowlands, having had second thoughts about the purchase, by letter to Magna Millikin, rescinded the transaction and demanded release from their mortgage on their residence. Magna Millikin refused to terminate the transaction or release the mortgage. Should the Rowlands be allowed to rescind the transaction? Why or why not? Discuss fully. [*Rowland v. Magna Millikin Bank of Decatur, N.A.,* 812 F.Supp. 875 (C.D.Ill. 1992)]

31–10. Equal Credit Opportunity. The Riggs National Bank of Washington, D.C., loaned more than $11 million to Samuel Linch and Albert Randolph. To obtain the loan, Linch and Randolph provided personal financial statements. Linch's statement included substantial assets that he owned jointly with his wife, Marcia. As a condition of the loan, Riggs required that Marcia, as well as Samuel and Albert, sign a personal guaranty for repayment. When the borrowers defaulted, Riggs filed a suit in a federal district court to recover its money, based on the personal guaranties. The court ruled against the borrowers, who appealed. On what basis might the borrowers argue that Riggs violated the Equal Credit Opportunity Act (ECOA)? [*Riggs National Bank of Washington, D.C. v. Linch,* 36 F.3d 370 (4th Cir. 1994)]

31–11. Debt Collection. Equifax A.R.S., a debt-collection agency, sent Donna Russell a notice about one of her debts. The front of the notice stated that "[i]f you do not dispute this claim (see reverse side) and wish to pay it within the next 10 days we will not post this collection to your file." The reverse side set out Russell's rights under the Fair Debt Collection Practices Act (FDCPA), including that she had thirty days to decide whether to contest the claim. Russell filed a suit in a federal district court against Equifax. The court ruled against Russell, who appealed. On what basis might Russell argue that Equifax violated the FDCPA? [*Russell v. Equifax A.R.S.,* 74 F.3d 30 (2d Cir. 1996)]

A QUESTION OF ETHICS AND SOCIAL RESPONSIBILITY

31–12. *The Endangered Species Act of 1973 makes it unlawful for any person to "take" endangered or threatened species. The act defines* take *to mean to "harass, harm, pursue," "wound," or "kill." The secretary of the Interior (Bruce Babbitt) issued a regulation that further defined* harm *to include "significant habitat modification or degradation where it actually kills or injures wildlife." A group of businesses and individuals involved in the timber industry brought an action against the secretary of the Interior and others. The group complained that the* *application of the "harm" regulation to the red-cockaded wood-pecker and the northern spotted owl had injured the group economically, because it prevented logging operations (habitat modification) in Pacific Northwest forests containing these species. The group challenged the regulation's validity, contending that Congress did not intend the word* take *to include habitat modification. The case ultimately reached the United States Supreme Court, which held that the secretary reasonably construed Congress's intent when he defined* harm *to include habitat modification.* [Babbitt v. Sweet Home Chapter of Communities for a Great Oregon, ___U.S.___, 115 S.Ct. 2407, 132 L.Ed.2d 597 (1995)]

1. Traditionally, the term *take* has been used to refer to the capture or killing of wildlife, usually for private gain. Is the secretary's regulation prohibiting habitat modification consistent with this definition?
2. One of the issues in this case was whether Congress intended to protect existing generations of species or future generations. How do the terms *take* and *habitat modification* relate to this issue?
3. Three dissenting Supreme Court justices contended that construing the act as prohibiting habitat modification "imposes unfairness to the point of financial ruin—not just upon the rich, but upon the simplest farmer who finds his land conscripted to national zoological use." Should private parties be required to bear the burden of preserving habitats for wildlife?
4. Generally, should the economic welfare of private parties be taken into consideration when creating and applying environmental statutes and regulations?

 CASE BRIEFING ASSIGNMENT

31–13. *Examine Case A.8 [Roberts v. Walmart Stores, Inc., 736 F.Supp. 1527 (E.D.Mo. 1990)] in Appendix A. The case has been excerpted there in great detail. Review and then brief the case, making sure that you include answers to the following questions in your brief.*

1. What was the basis of the plaintiffs' claim?
2. What defense did Walmart raise?
3. What was the court's decision?

FOR CRITICAL ANALYSIS

31–14. *It has been estimated that for every dollar spent cleaning up hazardous waste sites, administrative agencies spend seven dollars in overhead. Can you think of any way to trim the administrative costs associated with the clean-up of contaminated sites?*

▌Accessing the Internet: Business Law and Legal Environment

If you subscribe to the commercial service CompuServe, there is a Consumer Forum that you might find useful. Once on CompuServe, type in the following:

Go legal

Then select

Consumer Forum

From the Library Menu, choose

Browse

The Alexander law firm offers consumer law articles at

http://tsw.ingress.com/tsw/talf/talf.html

The Nolo Press, which is also available on the commercial services America Online and CompuServe, has a section called Money and Consumer Matters. You can access it at

http://gnn.com/gnn/bus/nolo/

If you want to get a full listing of legal and historical resources available on-line concerning consumer issues, you need to go to Citizen Rights at

gopher://una.hh.lib.umich.edu:70/00/inetdirsstacks/citizens: bachpfaff

The gopher address is

una.hh.lib.umich.edu

Once you are in that gopher address, you should select

inetdirsstacks

Then select

Citizens' Rights; M. Plaff, D. Bachman

To access the central environmental law and resources part of the World Wide Web virtual library, you need to go directly to

http://www.law.indiana.edu/

If you are interested in environmental treaties and agreements on an international level, you should go to

gopher:infoserver.ciesin.org:70/11/catalog/Politics/go_policy/intl/ treaties

If you use the on-line Net browser Yahoo, you can access

Environmental

Simply type in

http://www.yahoo.com/Government/Law/

You might want to see what is happening at the National Resources Defense Council by typing in

http://www.nrdc.org/nrdc

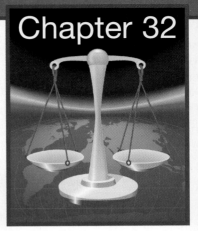

Chapter 32

Employment Relationships

"Show me the country in which there are no strikes, and I'll show you the country in which there is no liberty."

Samuel Gompers, 1850–1924
(American labor leader)

CHAPTER OBJECTIVES

After reading this chapter, you should be able to:

1. Discuss the employment-at-will doctrine.
2. Identify the leading federal statute governing wages and working hours.
3. List the major laws governing labor unions.
4. Describe the major laws relating to health and safety in the workplace.
5. Summarize the laws governing the rights of employees in regard to pension plans, family and medical leave, and privacy.

Before the industrial revolution, workers and employers in the United States enjoyed relatively equal bargaining power, and most employer-employee relationships were "at will." Under the common law doctrine of **employment at will**, either party may terminate the employment relationship at any time and for any reason—provided, of course, that the employment termination does not violate the provisions of an employment contract. Other common law concepts governing employment relationships were those of contract, agency, and tort law.

In the 1930s, during the Great Depression, however, both state and federal governments began to regulate employment relationships. Legislation during the 1930s and subsequent decades established the right of employees to form labor unions. At the heart of labor rights is the right to unionize and bargain with management for improved working conditions, salaries, and benefits. The ultimate weapon of labor is, of course, the strike. As noted in the opening quotation, the labor leader Samuel Gompers concluded that without the right to strike, there could be no liberty. A succession of other laws during and since the 1930s provided further protection for employees. Today's employers must comply with a myriad of laws and regulations to ensure that employee rights are protected.

CONTENTS

EMPLOYMENT AT WILL
A common law doctrine under which either party may terminate an employment relationship at any time for any reason, unless a contract specifies otherwise.

823

A restaurant worker rings up a sale. Persons under eighteen years of age often work in restaurants. What restrictions do employers face in employing teenagers?

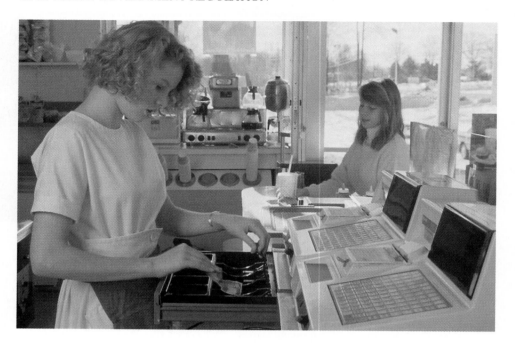

In this chapter, we look at the most significant laws regulating employment relationships. We deal with other significant laws regulating the workplace—those that prohibit employment discrimination—in the next chapter.

▌Wage-Hour Laws

In the 1930s, Congress enacted several laws regulating the wages and working hours of employees. In 1931, Congress passed the Davis-Bacon Act,[1] which requires the payment of "prevailing wages" to employees of contractors and subcontractors working on government construction projects. In 1936, the Walsh-Healey Act[2] was passed. This act requires that a minimum wage, as well as overtime pay of time and a half, be paid to employees of manufacturers or suppliers entering into contracts with agencies of the federal government.

In 1938, Congress passed the Fair Labor Standards Act[3] (FLSA). This act extended wage-hour requirements to cover all employers engaged in interstate commerce or engaged in the production of goods for interstate commerce, plus selected types of businesses. We examine here the FLSA's provisions in regard to child labor, maximum hours, and minimum wages.

Child Labor

The FLSA prohibits oppressive child labor. Children under fourteen years of age are allowed to do certain types of work, such as deliver newspapers, work for their parents, and work in the entertainment and (with some exceptions) agricultural areas. Children who are fourteen or fifteen years of age are allowed to work, but not in hazardous occupations. There are also numerous restrictions on how many hours per day

---

1.   40 U.S.C. Sections 276a–276a-5.
2.   41 U.S.C. Sections 35–45.
3.   29 U.S.C. Sections 201–260.

and per week they can work. For example, they cannot work during school hours, for more than three hours on a school day (or eight hours on a nonschool day), for more than eighteen hours during a school week (or forty hours during a nonschool week), or before 7 A.M. or after 7 P.M. (9 P.M. during the summer). Most states require persons under sixteen years of age to obtain work permits.

Persons between the ages of sixteen and eighteen do not face such restrictions on working times and hours, but they cannot be employed in hazardous jobs or in jobs detrimental to their health and well-being. Persons over the age of eighteen are not affected by any of the above-mentioned restrictions.

RECALL Special provisions also cover minors in the areas of tort law, contract law, agency law, and the law governing negotiable instruments.

Hours and Wages

Under the FLSA, any employee who agrees to work more than forty hours per week must be paid no less than one and a half times his or her regular pay for all hours over forty. Certain employees are exempt from the overtime provisions of the act. Exempt employees fall into four categories: executives, administrative employees, professional employees, and outside salespersons. Generally, to fall into one of these categories, an employee must earn more than a specified amount of income per week and devote a certain percentage of work time to the performance of specific types of duties, as determined by the FLSA. To qualify as an outside salesperson, the employee must regularly engage in sales work away from the office and spend no more than 20 percent of work time per week performing duties other than sales.

The FLSA provides that a **minimum wage** of a specified amount must be paid to employees in covered industries. Congress periodically revises such minimum wages. For example, in 1996, Congress raised the minimum wage from $4.25 an hour to $5.15 an hour. The increase will be implemented incrementally, with the $5.15 wage becoming effective on September 1, 1997. Under the FLSA, the term *wages* includes the reasonable cost of the employer in furnishing employees with board, lodging, and other facilities if they are customarily furnished by that employer.

MINIMUM WAGE
The lowest wage, either by government regulation or union contract, that an employer may pay an hourly worker.

▌ Labor Unions
. . . .

In the 1930s, in addition to wage-hour laws, the government also enacted the first of several labor laws. These laws protect employees' rights to join labor unions, to bargain with management over the terms and conditions of employment, and to conduct strikes.

Federal Labor Laws

Federal labor laws governing union-employer relations have developed considerably since the first law was enacted in 1932. Initially, the laws were concerned with protecting the rights and interests of workers. Subsequent legislation placed some restraints on unions and granted rights to employers. We look here at four major federal statutes regulating union-employer relations.

NORRIS-LAGUARDIA ACT   Congress protected peaceful strikes, picketing, and boycotts in 1932 in the Norris-LaGuardia Act.[4] The statute restricted federal courts in their power to issue injunctions against unions engaged in peaceful strikes. In effect, this act declared a national policy permitting employees to organize.

---

4. 29 U.S.C. Sections 101–110, 113–115.

NATIONAL LABOR RELATIONS ACT One of the foremost statutes regulating labor is the National Labor Relations Act (NLRA) of 1935.[5] This act established the rights of employees to engage in collective bargaining and to strike. The act also specifically defined a number of employer practices as unfair to labor:

1. Interference with the efforts of employees to form, join, or assist labor organizations or to engage in concerted activities for their mutual aid or protection.
2. An employer's domination of a labor organization or contribution of financial or other support to it.
3. Discrimination based on union affiliation in the hiring or awarding of tenure to employees.
4. Discrimination against employees for filing charges under the act or giving testimony under the act.
5. Refusal to bargain collectively with the duly designated representative of the employees.

The act also created the National Labor Relations Board (NLRB) to oversee union elections and to prevent employers from engaging in unfair and illegal union activities and unfair labor practices. The purpose of the NLRA was to secure for employees the rights to organize; to bargain collectively through representatives of their own choosing; and to engage in concerted activities for organizing, collective bargaining, and other purposes.

The NLRB has the authority to investigate employees' charges of unfair labor practices and to serve complaints against employers in response to these charges. The NLRB may also issue cease-and-desist orders—orders compelling employers to cease engaging in the unfair practices—when violations are found. Cease-and-desist orders can be enforced by a circuit court of appeals if necessary. Arguments over alleged unfair labor practices are first decided by the NLRB and may then be appealed to a federal court.

To be protected under the NLRA, an individual must be an "employee," as that term is defined in the statute. Courts have long held that job applicants fall within the definition (otherwise, the NLRA's ban on discrimination in regard to hiring would mean nothing). In the following case, the United States Supreme Court considered whether an individual may be a company's "employee" if, at the same time, a union pays the individual to organize the company.

---

5. 29 U.S.C. Section 151–169.

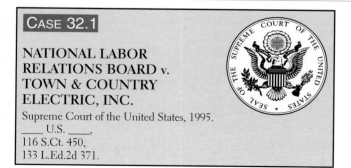

HISTORICAL AND SOCIAL SETTING *Over the last two decades, the percentage of private-sector workers* *who are union members has declined. Perhaps this is due, at least in part, to a popular belief that unions represent only a level of interference between a company's making money and the workers' getting paid. In the public sector, however, unions are becoming more popular and are growing in force. Unions themselves are consolidating and still attempting to organize workers.*

FACTS Town & Country Electric, Inc., advertised for job applicants but refused to interview ten of eleven applicants who were members of a union, the International Brotherhood of Electrical Workers. The applicants were union "salts"—persons paid by the union to apply for a job with a company and then, when hired, to unionize the

Case 32.1—Continued

company (in this case, Town & Country's work force). The applicants filed a complaint with the National Labor Relations Board (NLRB), alleging that the company had committed an unfair labor practice by discriminating against the applicants on the basis of union membership. The issue turned on whether job applicants paid by a union to organize a company could be considered "employees" under the National Labor Relations Act (NLRA). The NLRB determined that the applicants were employees and ruled in their favor. Town & Country appealed, and the U.S. Court of Appeals for the Eighth Circuit reversed. The applicants appealed to the United States Supreme Court.

ISSUE Can a worker be a company's "employee," under the NLRA, if, at the same time, a union pays that worker to organize the company?

DECISION Yes. The United States Supreme Court reversed the decision of the appellate court and remanded the case.

REASON The Supreme Court reasoned that the NLRB's "decision is consistent with the broad language" of the NLRA. The Court pointed out that the "ordinary dictionary definition of 'employee' includes any 'person who works for another in return for financial or other compensation.'" The NLRA states that "[t]he term 'employee' shall include any employee." This, the Court said, "seems to reiterate the breadth of the ordinary dictionary definition." The Court also reasoned that this interpretation is consistent with the NLRA's purposes, such as protecting "the right of employees to organize for mutual aid without employer interference."

FOR CRITICAL ANALYSIS—Social Consideration
How would the relationship between labor and management be affected if job applicants did not have rights under the NLRA?

LABOR-MANAGEMENT RELATIONS ACT The Labor-Management Relations Act (LMRA) of 1947[6] was passed to proscribe certain unfair union practices, such as the *closed shop*. A **closed shop** is a firm that requires union membership by its workers as a condition of employment. Although the act made the closed shop illegal, it preserved the legality of the union shop. A **union shop** does not require membership as a prerequisite for employment but can, and usually does, require that workers join the union after a specified amount of time on the job.

The LMRA also prohibited unions from refusing to bargain with employers, engaging in certain types of picketing, and featherbedding (causing employers to hire more employees than necessary). The act also allowed individual states to pass their own **right-to-work laws**—laws making it illegal for union membership to be required for *continued* employment in any establishment. Thus, union shops are technically illegal in states with right-to-work laws.

LABOR-MANAGEMENT REPORTING AND DISCLOSURE ACT The Labor-Management Reporting and Disclosure Act (LMRDA) of 1959[7] established an employee bill of rights and reporting requirements for union activities. The act strictly regulates internal union business procedures. Union elections, for example, are regulated by the LMRDA, which requires that regularly scheduled elections of officers occur and that secret ballots be used. Ex-convicts and Communists are prohibited from holding union office. Moreover, union officials are accountable for union property and funds. Members have the right to attend and to participate in union meetings, to nominate officers, and to vote in most union proceedings.

CLOSED SHOP
A firm that requires union membership by its workers as a condition of employment. The closed shop was made illegal by the Labor-Management Relations Act of 1947.

UNION SHOP
A place of employment in which all workers, once employed, must become union members within a specified period of time as a condition of their continued employment.

RIGHT-TO-WORK LAW
A state law providing that employees are not to be required to join a union as a condition of obtaining or retaining employment.

---

6. 29 U.S.C. Sections 141 *et seq.*
7. 29 U.S.C. Sections 401 *et seq.*

HOT-CARGO AGREEMENT
An agreement in which employers voluntarily agree with unions not to handle, use, or deal in nonunion-produced goods of other employers; a type of secondary boycott explicitly prohibited by the Labor-Management Reporting and Disclosure Act of 1959.

SECONDARY BOYCOTT
A union's refusal to work for, purchase from, or handle the products of a secondary employer, with whom the union has no dispute, for the purpose of forcing that employer to stop doing business with the primary employer, with whom the union has a labor dispute.

COLLECTIVE BARGAINING
The process by which labor and management negotiate the terms and conditions of employment, including working hours and workplace conditions.

The act also outlawed **hot-cargo agreements**—agreements in which employers voluntarily agree with unions not to handle, use, or deal in nonunion-produced goods of other employers. The act made all such **secondary boycotts** illegal.

Union Organization

Suppose that the workers of a particular firm want to join a union. How is a union formed? Typically, the first step in the process is to have the workers sign authorization cards. An authorization card usually states that the worker desires to have a certain union, such as the American Federation of Labor and Congress of Industrial Organizations (AFL-CIO), represent the work force. If those in favor of the union can obtain authorization cards from a majority of the workers, they may present the cards to the employer and ask the employer to recognize the union formally. If the employer refuses to do so, the union organizers (unionizers) can petition the NLRB for an election.

UNION ELECTIONS For an election to be held, the unionizers must demonstrate that at least 30 percent of the workers to be represented support a union or an election on unionization. The NLRB supervises the election and ensures secret voting and voter eligibility. If the election is a fair one and if the proposed union receives majority support, the NLRB certifies the union as the bargaining representative for the employees.

UNION ELECTION CAMPAIGNS Many labor-management disputes arise during union election campaigns. Generally, the employer has control over unionizing activities that take place on company property and during working hours. Employers may thus limit the campaign activities of union supporters. For example, an employer may prohibit all solicitations and pamphlets on company property as long as the employer has a legitimate business reason for doing so. Suppose that a union sought to organize clerks at a department store. Courts have found that an employer can prohibit all solicitation in areas of the store open to the public. Union campaign activities in these circumstances could seriously interfere with the store's business. The employer may not, however, discriminate in its prohibition against solicitation in the workplace. For example, the employer could not prohibit union solicitation but allow solicitation for charitable causes.

An employer may also campaign among its workers against the union, but the NLRB carefully monitors and regulates campaign tactics by management. Otherwise, management might use its economic power to coerce the workers into voting against unionization. For example, an employer might tell its workers, "If the union wins, you'll all be fired." The NLRB prohibits employers from making such threats. If the employer issues threats or engages in other unfair labor practices, the NLRB may certify the union even though it lost the election. Alternatively, the NLRB may ask a court to order a new election.

Collective Bargaining

If a fair election is held and the union wins, the NLRB will certify the union as the *exclusive bargaining representative* of the workers. The central legal right of a union is to engage in collective bargaining on the members' behalf. **Collective bargaining** can be defined as the process by which labor and management negotiate the terms and conditions of employment, including wages, benefits, working conditions, and other matters. Collective bargaining allows union representatives to be elected by union members and to speak on behalf of the members at the bargaining table.

When a union is officially recognized, it may make a demand to bargain with the employer and negotiate new terms or conditions of employment. In collective bargaining, as in most other business negotiations, each side uses its economic power to pressure or persuade the other side to grant concessions.

Bargaining is a somewhat vague term. Bargaining does not mean that one side must give in to the other or that compromises must be made. It does mean that a demand to bargain with the employer must be taken seriously and that both sides must bargain in "good faith." Good faith bargaining means that management, for example, must be willing to meet with union representatives and consider the union's wishes when negotiating a contract. Examples of bad faith bargaining on the part of management include engaging in a campaign among workers to undermine the union, constantly shifting positions on disputed contract terms, and sending bargainers who lack authority to commit the company to a contract. If an employer (or a union) refuses to bargain in good faith without justification, it has committed an unfair labor practice, and the other party may petition the NLRB for an order requiring good faith bargaining.

Strikes

Even when labor and management have bargained in good faith, they may be unable to reach a final agreement. When extensive collective bargaining has been conducted and an impasse results, the union may call a strike against the employer to pressure it into making concessions. A **strike** occurs when the unionized workers leave their jobs and refuse to work. The workers also typically picket the plant, standing outside the facility with signs that complain of management's unfairness.

A strike is an extreme action. Striking workers lose their rights to be paid, and management loses production and may lose customers, whose orders cannot be filled. Labor law regulates the circumstances and conduct of strikes. Most strikes take the form of "economic strikes," which are initiated because the union wants a better contract. A union may also strike when the employer has engaged in unfair labor practices.

The right to strike is guaranteed by the NLRA, within limits, and strike activities, such as picketing, are protected by the free speech guarantee of the First Amendment to the Constitution. Nonworkers have a right to participate in picketing an employer. The NLRA also gives workers the right to refuse to cross a picket line of fellow workers who are engaged in a lawful strike. Employers are permitted to hire replacement workers to substitute for the workers who are on strike.

An important issue concerns the rights of strikers after a strike ends. In a typical economic strike over working conditions, the strikers have no right to return to their jobs. If satisfactory replacement workers are found, the strikers may find themselves out of work. The law does prohibit the employer from discriminating against former strikers, however. Employers must give former strikers preferential rights to any new vacan-

STRIKE
An extreme action undertaken by unionized workers when collective bargaining fails; the workers leave their jobs, refuse to work, and (typically) picket the employer's workplace.

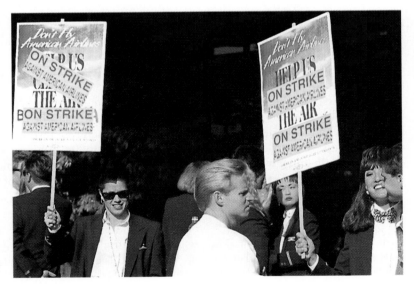

Striking workers picket to publicize their labor dispute. Why is the right to strike important to unions?

cies that arise and also retain their seniority rights. Different rules apply when a union strikes because the employer has engaged in unfair labor practices. In this situation, the employer may still hire replacements but must give the strikers back their jobs once the strike is over.

▮ Worker Health and Safety

Under the common law, employees injured on the job had to rely on tort law or contract law theories in suits they brought against their employers. Additionally, workers had some recourse under the common law governing agency relationships (discussed in Chapter 23), which imposes a duty on a principal-employer to provide a safe workplace for his or her agent-employee. Today, numerous state and federal statutes protect employees and their families from the risk of accidental injury, death, or disease resulting from their employment. This section discusses the primary federal statute governing health and safety in the workplace, along with state workers' compensation acts.

The Occupational Safety and Health Act

At the federal level, the primary legislation for employee health and safety protection is the Occupational Safety and Health Act of 1970.[8] Congress passed this act in an attempt to ensure safe and healthful working conditions for practically every employee in the country. The act provides for specific standards that employers must meet, plus a general duty to keep workplaces safe.

ENFORCEMENT AGENCIES   Three federal agencies develop and enforce the standards set by the Occupational Safety and Health Act. The Occupational Safety and Health Administration (OSHA) is part of the Department of Labor and has the authority to promulgate standards, make inspections, and enforce the act. OSHA has safety standards governing many workplace details, such as the structural stability of ladders and the requirements for railings. OSHA also establishes standards that protect employees against exposure to substances that may be harmful to their health.

The National Institute for Occupational Safety and Health is part of the Department of Health and Human Services. Its main duty is to conduct research on safety and health problems and to recommend standards for OSHA to adopt. Finally, the Occupational Safety and Health Review Commission is an independent agency set up to handle appeals from actions taken by OSHA administrators.

BE CAREFUL To check for compliance with safety standards without being cited for violations, an employer can often obtain advice from an insurer, a trade association, or a state agency.

PROCEDURES AND VIOLATIONS   OSHA compliance officers may enter and inspect facilities of any establishment covered by the Occupational Safety and Health Act.[9] Employees may also file complaints of violations. Under the act, an employer cannot discharge an employee who files a complaint or who, in good faith, refuses to work in a high-risk area if bodily harm or death might result.

Employers with eleven or more employees are required to keep occupational injury and illness records for each employee. Each record must be made available for inspection when requested by an OSHA inspector. Whenever a work-related injury or disease occurs, employers must make reports directly to OSHA. Whenever an employee is killed in a work-related accident or when five or more employees are hospitalized in one accident, the employer must notify the Department of Labor within

---

8.   29 U.S.C. Sections 553, 651–678.
9.   In the past, warrantless inspections were conducted. In 1978, however, the United States Supreme Court held that warrantless inspections violated the warrant clause of the Fourth Amendment to the Constitution. See *Marshall v. Barlow's, Inc.*, 436 U.S. 307, 98 S.Ct. 1816, 56 L.Ed.2d 305 (1978).

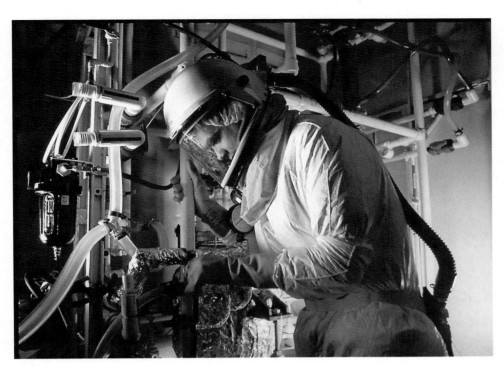

A scientist complies with safety standards in manufacturing drugs for the treatment of cancer. Should the government regulate such standards for all businesses?

forty-eight hours. If the company fails to do so, it will be fined. Following the accident, a complete inspection of the premises is mandatory.

Criminal penalties for willful violation of the Occupational Safety and Health Act are limited. Employers may be prosecuted under state laws, however. In other words, the act does not preempt state and local criminal laws.[10] In the following case, an employer argued that it should not be penalized by OSHA for violating a regulation of which the employer was ignorant.

10. *Pedraza v. Shell Oil Co.*, 942 F.2d 48 (1st Cir. 1991); *cert.* denied, *Shell Oil Co. v. Pedraza*, 502 U.S. 1082, 112 S.Ct. 993, 117 L.Ed.2d 154 (1992).

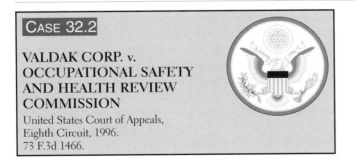

CASE 32.2

VALDAK CORP. v. OCCUPATIONAL SAFETY AND HEALTH REVIEW COMMISSION

United States Court of Appeals, Eighth Circuit, 1996.
73 F.3d 1466.

HISTORICAL AND SOCIAL SETTING *Since the Occupational Safety and Health Act was enacted in 1970, the rates of deaths and injuries in the workplace have been cut in half. In 1970, for example, eighteen of every one hundred thousand workers were killed on the job. In 1996, the rate was eight per one hundred thousand. To prevent accidental injuries and deaths, employers often impose safety measures. Such measures are particularly important when an employer's work force is young and inexperienced, as in many restaurants, retail establishments, and car washes.*

FACTS The Valdak Corporation operates a car wash that uses an industrial dryer to spin-dry towels. The dryer was equipped with a device that was supposed to keep it locked while it spun, but the device often did not work. An employee reached into the dryer while it was spinning, and his arm was cut off above the elbow. OSHA cited Valdak for, among other things, a willful violation of a

(Continued)

Case 32.2—Continued

machine-guarding regulation and assessed a $28,000 penalty. Valdak appealed to the Occupational Safety and Health Review Commission, which upheld the penalty. Valdak appealed to the U.S. Court of Appeals for the Eighth Circuit, arguing in part that it did not know about the specific regulation.

ISSUE Can an employer who is not aware of a specific Occupational Safety and Health Act regulation be cited for a "willful" violation of it?

DECISION Yes. The U.S. Court of Appeals for the Eighth Circuit upheld the agency's finding.

REASON The federal appellate court reasoned that "[w]illfulness can be proved by 'plain indifference' to the [Occupational Safety and Health Act's] requirements. Plain indifference to the machine guarding requirement is amply demonstrated by the facts that the dryer was equipped with an interlocking device, the interlocking device did not work, and Valdak continued to use the dryer with the broken interlock device."

FOR CRITICAL ANALYSIS—Ethical Consideration *For what policy reasons might an employer set up a formal safety program or issue a written safety manual?*

Workers' Compensation

WORKERS' COMPENSATION LAWS
State statutes establishing an administrative procedure for compensating workers' injuries that arise out of—or in the course of—their employment, regardless of fault.

State **workers' compensation laws** establish an administrative procedure for compensating workers injured on the job. Instead of suing, an injured worker files a claim with the administrative agency or board that administers the local workers' compensation claims.

Most workers' compensation statutes are similar. No state covers all employees. Typically excluded are domestic workers, agricultural workers, temporary employees, and employees of common carriers (companies that provide transportation services to the public). Typically, the statutes cover minors. Usually, the statutes allow employers to purchase insurance from a private insurer or a state fund to pay workers' compensation benefits in the event of a claim. Most states also allow employers to be *self-insured*—that is, employers who show an ability to pay claims do not need to buy insurance.

In general, the right to recover benefits is predicated wholly on the existence of an employment relationship and the fact that the injury was *accidental* and *occurred on the job* or *in the course of employment*, regardless of fault. Intentionally inflicted self-injury, for example, would not be considered accidental and hence would not be covered. If an injury occurred while an employee was commuting to or from work, it would not usually be considered to have occurred on the job or in the course of employment and hence would not be covered. (See the *Law in the Extreme* on page 834 for an example of an unusual situation concerning this issue.)

An employee must notify his or her employer promptly (usually within thirty days) of an injury. Generally, an employee also must file a workers' compensation claim with the appropriate state agency or board within a certain period (sixty days to two years) from the time the injury is first noticed, rather than from the time of the accident.

An employee's acceptance of workers' compensation benefits bars the employee from suing for injuries caused by the employer's negligence. By barring lawsuits for negligence, workers' compensation laws also bar employers from raising common law defenses to negligence, such as contributory negligence or assumption of risk. A worker may sue an employer who *intentionally* injures the worker, however.

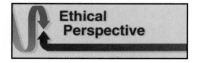

Ethical Perspective

We have stated elsewhere that today's employers sometimes face situations in which responsible corporate behavior is made difficult because of conflicting statutory or regulatory requirements. One example of conflicting requirements involves workers' compensation laws. In the interests of promoting safety in the workplace, more than a dozen states have amended their workers' compensation laws in the last several

Ethical Perspective—Continued

years to require employers to establish safety and health committees. The goal of these laws is to reduce workplace injuries by having management and employees work together in promoting safety and health in the workplace. Ironically, companies that comply with these laws and establish such committees may end up violating the National Labor Relations Act (NLRA).

For example, suppose that a company's employees are unionized. In this situation, the union is the sole representative of the employees in respect to working conditions, such as wage rates, hours of employment, grievances, labor disputes, and so on. If a company establishes a management-sponsored safety committee, union representatives may complain to the National Labor Relations Board (NLRB) that the committees are, in fact, "labor organizations"[a] that are dominated by the employer. If the NLRB agrees, the company will be held to have violated the NLRA, because that act, which prohibits employers from dominating labor organizations, preempts state laws.

For Critical Analysis: *What is the constitutional basis for federal preemption of conflicting state laws?*

a.   The NLRB has defined a labor organization as having three essential elements: (1) employees participate in the committee; (2) the committee exists for the purpose of dealing with the employer, and (3) these dealings concern working conditions or topics subject to collective bargaining agreements. See *Electromation, Inc. v. National Labor Relations Board*, 35 F.3d 1148 (7th Cir. 1994).

▌ Income Security

Federal and state governments participate in insurance programs designed to protect employees and their families by covering the financial impact of retirement, disability, death, hospitalization, and unemployment. The key federal law on this subject is the Social Security Act of 1935.[11]

Social Security and Medicare

The Social Security Act provides for old age (retirement), survivors, and disability insurance. The act is therefore often referred to as OASDI. Both employers and employees must "contribute" under the Federal Insurance Contributions Act (FICA)[12] to help pay for the employees' loss of income on retirement. The basis for the employee's and the employer's contribution is the employee's annual wage base— the maximum amount of the employee's wages that are subject to the tax. The employer withholds the employee's FICA contribution from the employee's wages and then matches this contribution. (In 1996, employers were required to withhold 6.2 percent of each employee's wages, up to a maximum wage base of $62,700, and to match this contribution.)

Retired workers are then eligible to receive monthly payments from the Social Security Administration, which administers the Social Security Act. Social Security benefits are fixed by statute but increase automatically with increases in the cost of living.

Medicare, a health-insurance program, is administered by the Social Security Administration for people sixty-five years of age and older and for some under the age

BE AWARE Social Security currently covers almost all jobs in the United States. Nine out of ten workers contribute to this protection for themselves and their families.

11.   42 U.S.C. Sections 301–1397e.
12.   26 U.S.C. Sections 3101–3125.

LAW IN THE EXTREME

It's All in the Course of Employment

One of the challenges faced by state workers' compensation boards is determining whether particular injuries occur on the job or in the course of employment. Because the circumstances surrounding each injury are unique, it is difficult to predict how a state workers' compensation board will rule on a given claim. For example, one might reasonably conclude that injuries incurred during a fistfight in the workplace would not be classified as injuries arising "out of or in the course of" employment. It is always possible, however, that a court might hold otherwise—as the Montana Supreme Court did when evaluating just such a claim.

The case involved Jerry Pinyerd, who was assaulted by a co-worker, Robert Jacobson. Both employees worked as sales representatives for Prestige Toyota in Billings, Montana. Prestige divided its salespeople into two teams, which competed against each other, and imposed quota requirements on each member. In addition, team members competed against their own "teammates" for commissions and quotas. Pinyerd and Jacobson were sales representatives on the same team. At one point, Jacobson, who was losing sales and becoming increasingly annoyed at Pinyerd's successful sales tactics, approached Pinyerd on the auto lot and hit him several times. While he was punching Pinyerd, Jacobson yelled, "Get off the lot. Get out of this town. You'll never work in this town again. You have no business working here to begin with."

When Pinyerd submitted a claim for workers' compensation for his injuries, the workers' compensation board denied the claim, on the ground that the assault did not arise out of and in the course of employment. On appeal, however, the Montana Supreme Court held that Pinyerd's injuries did indeed arise out of and in the course of his employment. The court concluded that there was a "reasonable connection between Pinyerd's injury and the conditions under which he pursued his employment." That connection was the employer's competitive policies, which "created daily friction among its sales staff and were substantial cause for animosity."[a]

For Critical Analysis: *Would Pinyerd be eligible for workers' compensation if Jacobson, for the same reasons, had assaulted him somewhere else than in the workplace?*

a. *Pinyerd v. State Compensation Insurance Fund,* 271 Mont. 115, 894 P.2d 932 (1995).

of sixty-five who are disabled. It has two parts, one pertaining to hospital costs and the other to nonhospital medical costs, such as visits to doctors' offices. People who have Medicare hospital insurance can also obtain additional federal medical insurance if they pay small monthly premiums, which increase as the cost of medical care increases. As with Social Security contributions, both the employer and the employee contribute to Medicare. Currently, 2.9 percent of the amount of all wages and salaries paid to employees goes toward financing Medicare. Unlike Social Security contributions, there is no cap on the amount of wages subject to the Medicare tax.

Private Pension Plans

There has been significant legislation to regulate employee retirement plans set up by employers to supplement Social Security benefits. The major federal act covering these retirement plans is the Employee Retirement Income Security Act (ERISA) of 1974.[13] This act empowers the Labor Management Services Administration of the Department of Labor to enforce its provisions governing employers who have private pension funds for their employees. ERISA does not require an employer to establish a pension plan. When a plan exists, however, ERISA establishes standards for its management.

A key provision of ERISA concerns **vesting**. Vesting gives an employee a legal right to receive pension benefits at some future date when he or she stops working. Before ERISA was enacted, some employees who had worked for companies for as long as

VESTING
The creation of an absolute or unconditional right or power.

_____

13.   29 U.S.C. Sections 1001 *et seq.*

thirty years received no pension benefits when their employment terminated, because those benefits had not vested. ERISA establishes complex vesting rules. Generally, however, all employee contributions to pension plans vest immediately, and employee rights to employer pension-plan contributions vest after five years of employment.

In an attempt to prevent mismanagement of pension funds, ERISA has established rules on how they must be invested. Pension managers must be cautious in their investments and refrain from investing more than 10 percent of the fund in securities of the employer. ERISA also contains detailed record-keeping and reporting requirements.

Unemployment Insurance

The United States has a system of unemployment insurance in which employers pay into a fund, the proceeds of which are paid out to qualified unemployed workers. The Federal Unemployment Tax Act of 1935[14] created a state system that provides unemployment compensation to eligible individuals. Employers that fall under the provisions of the act are taxed at regular intervals. Taxes are typically paid by the employers to the states, which then deposit them with the federal government. The federal government maintains an unemployment insurance fund, in which each state has an account.

WATCH OUT A state government can place a lien on the property of an employer who does not pay unemployment taxes.

▌COBRA

Federal legislation also addresses the issue of health insurance for workers whose jobs have been terminated—and who are thus no longer eligible for group health-insurance plans. The Consolidated Omnibus Budget Reconciliation Act (COBRA) of 1985[15] prohibits the elimination of a worker's medical, optical, or dental insurance coverage on the voluntary or involuntary termination of the worker's employment. Employers, with some exceptions, must comply with COBRA if they employ twenty or more workers and provide a benefit plan to those workers. They must inform an employee of COBRA's provisions when a group health plan is established and if that worker faces termination or a reduction of hours that would affect his or her eligibility for coverage under the plan.

The worker has sixty days (beginning with the date that the group coverage would stop) to decide whether to continue with the employer's group insurance plan. If the worker chooses to discontinue the coverage, then the employer has no further obligation. If the worker chooses to continue coverage, however, the employer is obligated to keep the policy active for up to eighteen months. If the worker is disabled, the employer must extend coverage up to twenty-nine months. The coverage provided must be the same as that enjoyed by the worker prior to the termination or reduction of work. If family members were originally included, for example, COBRA would prohibit their exclusion. This is not a free ride for the worker, however. To receive continued benefits, he or she may be required to pay all of the premium, as well as a 2 percent administrative charge.

The employer is relieved of the responsibility to provide benefit coverage if it completely eliminates its group benefit plan. An employer is also relieved of responsibility when the worker becomes eligible for Medicare, falls under a spouse's health plan, becomes insured under a different plan (with a new employer, for example), or fails to pay the premium. An employer that fails to comply with COBRA risks substantial penalties, such as a tax of up to 10 percent of the annual cost of the group plan or $500,000, whichever is less.[16]

---

14.   26 U.S.C. Sections 3301–3310.
15.   29 U.S.C. Sections 1161–1169.
16.   Health-care legislation proposed in 1996 by the Clinton administration may supersede COBRA.

Oliver Wendell Holmes, Jr. (1841–1935)

The task of a judge or justice can be awesome—especially a justice on the United States Supreme Court. How do you decide what cases are significant enough to warrant the attention of the Court? How do you decide which precedent to apply when more than one possibility exists? How do you decide at what point justice requires that a well-established precedent be overturned? These kinds of questions escape few jurists, and certainly they were among those that preoccupied Oliver Wendell Holmes, Jr., during his long tenure as a jurist on the Supreme Judicial Court of Massachusetts (twenty years) and then as a United States Supreme Court justice (thirty years).

Holmes was a man of ideas. He was an intellectual, a scholar, and a prolific writer. He read avidly and even kept a notebook in which he recorded the books he read each year. According to the notebook entries for 1910–1911, Holmes, while serving on the United States Supreme Court, also somehow found the time to read forty-nine books, including works by Plato (in Greek), Dante, and Alfred North Whitehead. During his tenure on the bench, Holmes—who was frequently referred to as the "court scholar"—became celebrated for his pithy philosophical statements concerning law and the human condition in general. He remains probably the most widely quoted of American jurists.

In Holmes's view, just as society is in a constant state of evolution, so, too, must the law remain fluid and open to the moral, political, and economic evolution of the times. In *The Common Law*, written in 1881 and one of Holmes's best-known works, he wrote of the practical, experiential nature of the law: "The life of the law has not been logic, it has been experience"; it is affected by the "prejudices which judges share with their fellow men" and corresponds, "as far as it goes, with what is . . . understood to be convenient." Probably one of Holmes's greatest insights into the common law was that the same legal rules can be manipulated by judges to serve different policies at different times. The task of judges, in Holmes's opinion, must be to keep their own prejudices and biases out of their decisions, insofar as possible, and to be ever vigilant in distinguishing between conclusions based on objective legal reasoning and those stemming from purely subjective biases and attitudes.

For Critical Analysis: *Can judges ever keep their own prejudices and biases out of their decisions? Should they?*

"It is the job of the legislature to follow the spirit of the nation, provided it is not contrary to the principles of government."

Charles-Louis de Secondat, Baron de Montesquieu, 1689–1755
(French philosopher and jurist)

▌Family and Medical Leave

In 1993, Congress passed the Family and Medical Leave Act (FMLA)[17] to assist employees who need time off work for family or medical reasons. A majority of the states also have legislation allowing for a leave from employment for family or medical reasons, and many employers maintain private family-leave plans for their workers.

The FMLA requires employers who have fifty or more employees to provide employees with up to twelve weeks of family or medical leave during any twelve-month period. During the employee's leave, the employer must continue the worker's health-care coverage and guarantee employment in the same position or a comparable position when the employee returns to work. An important exception to the FMLA, however, allows the employer to avoid reinstatement of a *key employee*—defined as an employee whose pay falls within the top 10 percent of the firm's work force. Additionally, the act does not apply to employees who have worked less than one year or less than twenty-five hours a week during the previous twelve months.

---

17. 29 U.S.C. Sections 2601, 2611–2619, 2651–2654.

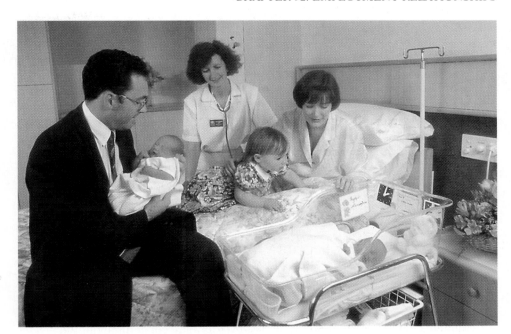

A family welcomes their newborn babies. Under federal law, how much leave can the father take from his job to care for the family?

Generally, an employee may take family leave when he or she wishes to care for a newborn baby, an adopted child, or a foster child.[18] An employee may take medical leave when the employee or the employee's spouse, child, or parent has a "serious health condition" requiring care. For most absences, the employee must demonstrate that the health condition requires continued treatment by a health-care provider and includes a period of incapacity of more than three days. Under regulations issued by the Department of Labor (DOL) in 1995, employees suffering from certain chronic health conditions may take FMLA leave for their own incapacities that require absences of less than three days. For example, an employee who has asthma or diabetes may have periodic episodes of illness, rather than episodes continuing over an extended period of time. Similarly, pregnancy may involve periodic visits to a health-care provider and episodes of morning sickness. According to the DOL's regulations, employees with such conditions are covered by the FMLA.

Remedies for violations of the FMLA include damages for unpaid wages (or salary), lost benefits, denied compensation, actual monetary losses (such as the cost of providing for care) up to an amount equivalent to the employee's wages for twelve weeks, job reinstatement, and promotion. The successful plaintiff is entitled to court costs; attorneys' fees; and in cases involving bad faith on the part of the employer, double damages.

18. The foster care must be state sanctioned to fall within the coverage of the FMLA.

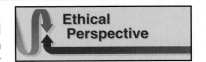
Ethical Perspective

In a dynamic society such as the United States, the law cannot stand still for too long. The FMLA provides a clear example of a law that was necessitated by social changes. The law reflects the realities of today's world. Nearly two-thirds of women with children now work outside the home, by choice or necessity. Additionally, about a fourth of all adults now provide care for elderly relatives or anticipate the need to provide this care within the next five years. With so many women now working, there is often no caretaker available to attend to medical emergencies or other family needs

(Continued)

Ethical Perspective—Continued

in the home. By allowing employees to take a leave from work for family or medical reasons, the FMLA recognizes the changing face of America.

From an ethical perspective, the act may be viewed as a choice on the part of society to shift to the employer family burdens caused by changing economic and social needs. In effect, Congress, by passing the act, addressed the pressing needs of the so-called baby boomer (or "sandwich") generation—caught between the pressures of providing child care on the one hand and care for aging parents on the other.

For Critical Analysis: *Who ultimately pays for increased rights for employees?*

"We are rapidly entering the age of no privacy, where everyone is open to surveillance at all times; where there are no secrets."

William O. Douglas, 1898–1980
(Associate justice of the United States Supreme Court, 1939–1975)

▌Employee Privacy Rights

Recall from Chapter 2 that there is no provision in the U.S. Constitution that guarantees a right to privacy. A personal right to privacy, however, has been inferred from other constitutional guarantees provided by the First, Third, Fourth, Fifth, and Ninth Amendments to the Constitution. In the last two decades, concerns about the privacy rights of employees have arisen in response to the sometimes invasive tactics used by employers in their efforts to monitor and screen workers. Lie-detector tests, drug tests, and other practices have increasingly been subject to challenge as violations of employee privacy rights.

Lie-Detector Tests

At one time, many employers required employees or job applicants to take polygraph examinations (lie-detector tests) in connection with their employment. To protect the privacy interests of employees and job applicants, in 1988 Congress passed the Employee Polygraph Protection Act.[19] The act prohibits employers from (1) requiring or causing employees or job applicants to take lie-detector tests or suggesting or requesting that they do so; (2) using, accepting, referring to, or asking about the results of lie-detector tests taken by employees or applicants; and (3) taking or threatening negative employment-related action against employees or applicants based on results of lie-detector tests or on their refusal to take the tests.

Employers excepted from these prohibitions include federal, state, and local government employers; certain security service firms; and companies manufacturing and distributing controlled substances. Other employers may use polygraph tests when investigating losses attributable to theft—including embezzlement and the theft of trade secrets.

Drug Testing

In the interests of public safety and to reduce unnecessary costs, many of today's employers, including the government, require their employees to submit to drug testing. State laws relating to the privacy rights of private-sector employees vary from state to state. Some state constitutions may prohibit private employers from testing for drugs, and state statutes may restrict drug testing by private employers in any number of ways. A collective bargaining agreement may also provide protection against drug testing. In some instances, employees have brought an action against the employer for the tort of invasion of privacy (discussed in Chapter 5).

---

19.   29 U.S.C. Sections 2001 *et seq.*

Constitutional limitations apply to the testing of government employees. The Fourth Amendment provides that individuals have the right to be "secure in their persons" against "unreasonable searches and seizures" conducted by government agents. Drug tests have been held constitutional, however, when there was a reasonable basis for suspecting government employees of using drugs. Additionally, when drug use in a particular government job could threaten public safety, testing has been upheld. For example, a Department of Transportation rule that requires employees engaged in oil and gas pipeline operations to submit to random drug testing was upheld, even though the rule did not require that before being tested the individual must have been suspected of drug use.[20] The court held that the government's interest in promoting public safety in the pipeline industry outweighed the employees' privacy interests.

In the following case, employees of the Department of Labor claimed that drug testing based on the reasonable suspicion of off-duty drug use violated their constitutional rights under the Fourth Amendment.

20.   *Electrical Workers Local 1245 v. Skinner*, 913 F.2d 1454 (9th Cir. 1990).

CASE 32.3

AMERICAN FEDERATION OF GOVERNMENT EMPLOYEES, AFL-CIO, LOCAL 2391 v. MARTIN
United States Court of Appeals, Ninth Circuit, 1992.
969 F.2d 788.

HISTORICAL AND POLITICAL SETTING   *In the 1980s, the greatest threat to domestic tranquillity appeared to be an increasing use of illegal drugs. As part of a war on drugs, President Ronald Reagan issued Executive Order 12564, which prohibited illegal drug use by federal employees both on and off duty.*

FACTS   In 1988, the Department of Labor (DOL) designated certain DOL employment positions as "sensitive" in regard to public health and safety or national security. Employees holding these positions, called "testing-designated positions" (TDPs), could be subjected to drug testing based on a reasonable suspicion of *on-duty or off-duty* drug use. The American Federation of Government Employees (AFGE) and others asked a federal district court to, among other things, order the DOL to stop testing based on a reasonable suspicion of *off-duty* drug use. The court issued the order, and the DOL appealed.

ISSUE   Does drug testing based on a reasonable suspicion of off-duty drug use by DOL employees in TDPs violate the Fourth Amendment?

DECISION   No. The U.S. Court of Appeals for the Ninth Circuit reversed the district court's ruling in respect to this issue.

REASON   The court stated at the outset that "urinalysis drug tests necessarily invade reasonable expectations of privacy rendering [the tests] searches within the meaning of the Fourth Amendment." Whether the government can require its employees to submit to drug testing, and thus intrude on employees' privacy rights, depends on whether these rights are outweighed by "legitimate governmental interests." The court found in the circumstances of this case that the employees' interests in privacy were "outweighed by the DOL's interest in preventing on-duty or off-duty drug use from impairing TDP employees in the performance of their duties." In the court's opinion, the safety-sensitive and security-sensitive nature of TDPs justified the DOL's drug testing of TDP employees based on a reasonable suspicion arising from observed off-duty illegal drug use or impairment. "We are convinced," concluded the court, "that under these limited circumstances the reasonable suspicion requirement of the DOL's Plan adequately protects its TDP employees from arbitrary and unreasonable drug testing."

FOR CRITICAL ANALYSIS—Political Consideration
If the DOL's plan had required drug testing regardless of whether there was a "reasonable suspicion" of on-duty or off-duty drug use, would the plan have violated the Fourth Amendment?

The "Slippery Slope" of Privacy Rights

Employers have an interest not only in maintaining a safe workplace but also in cutting health-insurance costs. Does this mean that employers can refuse to hire individuals who are more likely than others to become ill because of off-duty habits, such as smoking? This thorny question was addressed by the Supreme Court of Florida in *Kurtz v. City of North Miami.*[a] The case involved Arlene Kurtz, who had applied for a job as a clerk-typist with the city of North Miami. When she was interviewed for the job, she was informed of a new city regulation that required all job applicants to sign an affidavit stating that they had not used tobacco products for at least one year preceding their application for employment. Kurtz, a smoker, refused to sign the affidavit—and did not get the job for this reason. Kurtz then sued the city of North Miami, alleging that the employer's request violated her constitutional right to privacy.

The case was ultimately appealed to the Supreme Court of Florida,

a.   653 So.2d 1025 (Fla. 1995).

which held that the employer's request did not violate Kurtz's privacy rights. In the court's eyes, the city had a compelling interest in reducing the costs of employee health care, which was paid for by the public, through taxes. Evidence submitted by the city indicated that each smoking employee costs the city as much as $4,611 per year over what it incurs for nonsmoking employees. The court also concluded that Kurtz had no fundamental "right to smoke" or even a "legitimate expectation of privacy" in regard to questions relating to smoking. The court pointed out that "[i]n today's society, smokers are constantly required to reveal whether they smoke"—when they enter restaurants, hotels, and car-rental agencies, for example.

Perhaps even more interesting than the majority's opinion in this case is the dissenting opinion. The dissent was troubled by the "slippery-slope" problem, referring to the concept that one step taken in a certain direction makes it easier to "slide" further in that direction. According to the dissent, "There is a 'slippery-slope' problem here because, if governmental employers can inquire too extensively into off-job-site behavior, a point eventually will be reached at which the right of privacy under [the state constitution] clearly will be breached. An obvious example would be an inquiry into the lawful

sexual behavior of job applicants in an effort to identify those with the 'most desirable' lifestyles." The dissent also noted that the city's health-based concerns present a "definite slippery slope to the courts. The time is fast approaching, for example, when human beings can be genetically tested so thoroughly that susceptibility to particular diseases can be identified years in advance. To my mind, any governmental effort to identify those who might eventually suffer from cancer or heart disease, for instance, itself is a violation of bodily integrity guaranteed by [the state constitution]."[b]

For Critical Analysis: *Should judges consider the "slippery-slope" problem when deciding cases involving employees' privacy rights? Why or why not?*

b.   Note that about two-thirds of the states now have laws prohibiting discrimination against employees based on off-duty conduct. At least six of these states allow off-duty employees to use any legal product. Florida, however, has no such law.

AIDS Testing

An increasing number of employers are testing their workers for acquired immune deficiency syndrome (AIDS). Few public issues are more controversial than this practice. Some state laws restrict AIDS testing, and federal statutes offer some protection to employees or job applicants who have AIDS or have tested positive for the AIDS virus. The federal Americans with Disabilities Act of 1990[21] (discussed in Chapter 33), for example, prohibits discrimination against persons with disabilities and the term *disability* has been broadly defined to include those individuals with diseases such as

21.   42 U.S.C. Sections 12102–12118.

AIDS. The law also requires employers to reasonably accommodate the needs of persons with disabilities. As a rule, although the law may not prohibit AIDS testing, it may prohibit the discharge of employees based on the results of those tests.

Performance Monitoring

A particularly troublesome privacy issue concerns employers' monitoring of their employees' computer files, voice mail, E-mail, or other electronic communications. Electronic monitoring by employers may violate the Electronic Communications Privacy Act (ECPA) of 1986.[22] This act amended existing federal wiretapping law to cover electronic forms of communications, such as communications via cellular telephones or E-mail. The ECPA prohibits the intentional interception of any wire or electronic communication or the intentional disclosure or use of the information obtained by the interception.

The act excludes from coverage, however, any electronic communications through devices that are "furnished to the subscriber or user by a provider of wire or electronic communication service" and that are being used by the subscriber or user, or by the provider of the service, "in the ordinary course of its business." This "business-extension exception" to the ECPA permits employers to monitor employee telephone conversations in the ordinary course of their businesses. It does not, however, permit employers to monitor employees' personal communications. Under another exception to the ECPA, employers may also avoid liability under the act if the employees consent to having their electronic communications intercepted by the employer.

Generally, there is little specific government regulation of monitoring activities, and an employer may be able to avoid what laws do exist by simply informing employees that they are subject to monitoring. Then, if employees later challenge the monitoring practice, the employer can raise the defense of consent by claiming that the employees consented to the monitoring.[23] Employers should be cautious, however, when monitoring employees, because if an employee brings an action for invasion of privacy, a court may decide that the employee's reasonable expectation of privacy outweighs the employer's need for surveillance. Similarly, an employer should consider alternatives before searching an employee's desk, filing cabinet, or office. If a search is conducted and the employee sues, a court may balance the purposes of the search against its intrusiveness. The court may also consider the availability of less intrusive alternatives that would have accomplished the same purposes.

Screening Procedures

An area of concern to potential employees has to do with preemployment screening procedures. What kinds of questions on an employment application or a preemployment test are permissible? What kinds of questions go too far in terms of invading the potential employee's privacy? Is it an invasion of the potential employee's privacy, for example, to ask questions about his or her sexual orientation or religious convictions? Although an employer may believe that such information is relevant to the job for which the individual has applied, the applicant may feel differently about the matter.

KEEP IN MIND An employer may act on the basis of any professionally developed test, provided the test relates to the employment and does not violate the law.

A key factor in determining whether preemployment screening tests violate the privacy rights of potential employees is whether there exists a nexus, or connection, between the questions and the job for which an applicant is applying. The following case illustrates this distinction.

---

22. 18 U.S.C. Sections 2510–2521.
23. See, for example, *Griffin v. Milwaukee*, 74 F.3d 824 (7th Cir. 1996).

CASE 32.4

SOROKA v. DAYTON HUDSON CORP.

California Court of Appeal,
First District, Division 4, 1991.
7 Cal.App.4th 203,
1 Cal.Rptr.2d 77.

COMPANY PROFILE   *In 1881, Joseph Hudson opened a clothing store in Detroit. Using marketing techniques that were new at the time, Hudson marked his goods with prices (instead of bargaining with the customers) and accepted merchandise returns. By 1891, Hudson's was the largest retailer of men's clothing in the United States. In 1902, in Minneapolis, George Dayton established Dayton's, a department store that, like Hudson's, accepted customers' returns of merchandise. In 1969, Dayton's bought Hudson's and formed the Dayton Hudson Corporation. Dayton Hudson operates Target Stores, which account for nearly 60 percent of the corporation's sales.*

FACTS   Target Stores hire store security officers (SSOs) to observe, apprehend, and arrest suspected shoplifters. Target views good judgment and emotional stability as important SSO job skills. All SSO job applicants must take a test, called the Psychscreen. Some of the test questions relate to religious beliefs; other questions concern sexual orientation. Sibi Soroka and two other applicants (the plaintiffs) found the test objectionable and brought a class-action suit in a California state court against Dayton Hudson; the suit challenged the test as violating their privacy rights. The court found that Target's use of the test was reasonable, and the plaintiffs appealed.

ISSUE   Did Target's use of the Psychscreen violate the job applicants' right to privacy?

DECISION   Yes. The appellate court reversed the trial court's decision and remanded the case.

REASON   Target conceded that the Psychscreen intruded upon the privacy rights of job applicants. The question before the court was therefore whether this intrusion could be justified. The court concluded that it could not: "While Target unquestionably has an interest in employing emotionally stable persons to be SSO's, testing applicants about their religious beliefs and sexual orientation does not further this interest. To justify the invasion of privacy resulting from the use of the Psychscreen, Target must demonstrate a compelling interest and must establish that the test serves a job-related purpose. * * * Target made no showing that a person's religious beliefs or sexual orientation have any bearing on emotional stability or on the ability to perform an SSO's job responsibilities. It did no more than to make generalized claims about the Psychscreen's relationship to emotional fitness and to assert that it has seen an overall improvement in SSO quality and performance since it implemented the Psychscreen. This is not suffi-cient to constitute a compelling interest, nor does it sat-isfy the nexus [job-relatedness] requirement. Therefore Target's inquiry into the religious beliefs and sexual ori-entation of SSO applicants unjustifiably violates the state constitutional right to privacy."

FOR CRITICAL ANALYSIS—Ethical Consideration
Should the privacy rights of job applicants be given the same consideration as the privacy rights of employees? Why or why not?

∎ Employment-Related Immigration Laws

The most important immigration laws governing employer-employee relationships are the Immigration Reform and Control Act (IRCA) of 1986[24] and the Immigration

---

24.   29 U.S.C. Section 1802.

Act of 1990.[25] The IRCA, which is administered by the U.S. Immigration and Naturalization Service (INS), prohibits employers from hiring illegal immigrants. Employers must complete a special form—called INS Form I-9—for each employee and indicate on it that the employer has verified that the employee is either a U.S. citizen or is otherwise entitled to work in this country.

The Immigration Act of 1990 limits the number of legal immigrants entering the United States by capping the number of visas (entry permits) that are issued each year. Under the act, employers recruiting workers from other countries must complete a certification process and satisfy the Department of Labor that there is a shortage of qualified U.S. workers capable of performing the work. The employer must also establish that bringing immigrants into this country will not adversely affect the existing labor market in that particular area. In this way, the act attempts to serve two purposes: encouraging skilled workers to enter this country and at the same time restricting competition for American jobs.

▌Wrongful Discharge

Whenever an employer discharges an employee in violation of an employment contract or laws protecting employees, the employee may bring an action for **wrongful discharge.** An employee who is protected by a statute, such as one prohibiting employment discrimination (see Chapter 33), may bring a cause of action under that statute. If an employer's actions do not violate any statute, then the question is whether the employer has violated an employment contract or a common law doctrine.

As mentioned, under the employment-at-will doctrine, an employer may hire and fire employees at will (regardless of the employees' performance) without liability, unless the decision violates the terms of an employment contract or statutory law. Because of the harsh effects of the employment-at-will doctrine for employees, courts have carved out various exceptions to the doctrine. These exceptions are based on contract theory, tort theory, and public policy.

WRONGFUL DISCHARGE
An employer's termination of an employee's employment in violation of an employment contract or laws that protect employees.

Exceptions Based on Contract Theory

Some courts have held that an *implied* employment contract exists between the employer and the employee. If the employee is fired outside the terms of the implied contract, he or she may succeed in an action for breach of contract even though no written employment contract exists.

For example, an employer's manual or personnel bulletin may state that, as a matter of policy, workers will be dismissed only for good cause. If the employee is aware of this policy and continues to work for the employer, a court may find that there is an implied contract based on the terms stated in the manual or bulletin. Promises that an employer makes to employees regarding discharge policy may also be considered part of an implied contract. If the employer fires a worker in a manner contrary to the manner promised, a court may hold that the employer has violated the implied contract and is liable for damages. Most state courts will consider this claim and judge it by traditional contract standards.

A few states have gone further and held that all employment contracts contain an implied covenant of good faith. This means that both sides promise to abide by the contract in good faith. If an employer fires an employee for an arbitrary or unjustified reason, the employee can claim that the covenant of good faith was breached and the contract violated.

REMEMBER An implied contract may exist if a party furnishes a service expecting to be paid, and the other party, who knows (or should know) of this expectation, has a chance to reject the service and does not.

---

25. This act amended various provisions of the Immigration and Nationality Act of 1952, 8 U.S.C. Sections 1101 *et seq.*

In the following case, one of the issues was whether there existed between an employer and its employees an implied-in-fact contract not to demote the employees without good cause.

CASE 32.5

SCOTT v. PACIFIC GAS AND ELECTRIC CO.

Supreme Court of California, 1995.
11 Cal.4th 454,
904 P.2d 834,
46 Cal.Rptr.2d 427.

HISTORICAL AND SOCIAL SETTING *Faced with more regulations than they believe they can afford to enforce and supported by the popular belief that fewer regulations help businesses prosper, many states are attempting to deregulate some industries. California is leading the way in the deregulation of the power industry. For this reason, utilities in California are facing increased competition. In response, utility firms are cutting costs to increase efficiency. Some of these cuts involve the elimination of jobs. Others involve the investigation of possible employee misconduct, such as time card fraud and conflict of interest.*

FACTS The Pacific Gas and Electric Company (PG&E) had a system called "Positive Discipline" that, according to its personnel manual, was to apply to all employees. The basic principle was to discipline employees only for good cause. Byron Scott and Al Johnson were engineers working for PG&E as senior managers when they were demoted, allegedly for a conflict of interest from their outside consulting practice. They filed a suit in a California state court against PG&E, claiming that there was no good cause for the demotions. The court issued a judg-

ment in their favor, and PG&E appealed. The state appellate court reversed, and the engineers appealed to the Supreme Court of California.

ISSUE Was there an implied-in-fact contract between PG&E and its employees not to demote the employees without good cause? If so, did PG&E breach it?

DECISION Yes, to both questions. The Supreme Court of California reversed the decision of the intermediate appellate court and remanded the case.

REASON The state supreme court explained that "PG&E employees had a reasonable expectation that the company would follow its own human resources policy, which had as its basic premise the disciplining of its employees only for good cause." The court pointed out that the trial court had found that "Scott and Johnson committed no significant conflict of interest violations." PG&E failed to give them the chance to correct any relatively minor offenses through the positive discipline process. Therefore, the trial court "reasonably concluded that PG&E had breached its implied contractual agreement by wrongfully demoting Scott and Johnson."

FOR CRITICAL ANALYSIS—Political Consideration
What incentives do employers have to use basic principles of due process in disciplining employees?

Exceptions Based on Tort Theory

In a few cases, the discharge of an employee may give rise to an action for wrongful discharge under tort theories. Abusive discharge procedures may result in intentional infliction of emotional distress or defamation. In one case, a restaurant had suffered some thefts of supplies, and the manager announced that he would start firing waitresses alphabetically until the thief was identified. The first waitress fired said that she suffered great emotional distress as a result. The state's highest court upheld her claim as stating a valid cause of action.[26]

---

26. *Agis v. Howard Johnson Co.*, 371 Mass. 140, 355 N.E.2d 315 (1976).

Exceptions Based on Public Policy

The most widespread common law exception to the employment-at-will doctrine is an exception made on the basis of public policy. Courts may apply this exception when an employer fires a worker for reasons that violate a fundamental public policy of the jurisdiction. For example, a court may prevent an employer from firing a worker who serves on a jury and therefore cannot work during his or her normally scheduled working hours.

Sometimes, an employer will direct an employee to do something that violates the law. If the employee refuses to perform the illegal act, the employer might decide to fire the worker. Similarly, employees who "blow the whistle" on the wrongdoing of their employers often find themselves disciplined or even out of a job. **Whistleblowing** occurs when an employee tells a government official, upper-management authorities, or the press that his or her employer is engaged in some unsafe or illegal activity. Whistleblowers on occasion have been protected from wrongful discharge for reasons of public policy. For example, a bank was held to have wrongfully discharged an employee who pressured the employer to comply with state and federal consumer credit laws.[27] In the following case, the plaintiff alleged that his discharge for refusing to participate in illegal eavesdropping was wrongful because it violated public policy.

WHISTLEBLOWING
An employee's disclosure to government, the press, or upper-management authorities that the employer is ingaged in unsafe or illegal activities.

---

27. *Harless v. First National Bank in Fairmont*, 162 W.Va. 116, 246 S.E.2d 270 (1978).

CASE 32.6

NAGY v. WHITTLESEY AUTOMOTIVE GROUP
California Court of Appeal,
Fourth District, Division 3, 1995.
40 Cal.App.4th 1238,
47 Cal.Rptr.2d 395.

HISTORICAL AND TECHNOLOGICAL SETTING
Technology has made significant advances in the last century—particularly in the last thirty years—and the United States generally leads the way. These advances include easier and less obtrusive electronic monitoring of activities. For example, satellites can take photos that clearly depict relatively small objects. There is a device that can pick up the number of a cellular phone, while the phone is in use, in a car driving by. Eavesdropping on a cellular phone conversation is easy and inexpensive.

FACTS Gabor Nagy was a car salesperson for Whittlesey Automotive Group. Whittlesey asked Nagy to allow some of his phone conversations with "customers" to be recorded. The "customers" were actually employees of a company Whittlesey hired to conduct a sales training program. Nagy refused to consent. He was eventually fired for his "negative attitude." Nagy filed a suit in a California state court against Whittlesey. He cited a state statute that makes eavesdropping a crime and alleged in part that he was wrongfully terminated in violation of public policy. The court dismissed the suit, and Nagy appealed.

ISSUE Is it a violation of public policy to terminate an employee for refusing to be a "victim" of the employer's crime of eavesdropping?

DECISION Yes. The California Court of Appeal reversed the judgment of the lower court and remanded the case.

REASON The state appellate court pointed out that "[a]n employer may be held liable in tort for terminating an otherwise 'at will' employee if the termination violates public policy." The court explained that "otherwise the threat of discharge could be used to coerce employees into committing crimes, concealing wrongdoing, or taking other action harmful to the public." The court reasoned that "[w]here, as here, employment is conditioned on the employee's agreement to be a crime victim, public policy is equally violated."

FOR CRITICAL ANALYSIS—Ethical Consideration
Consent is a defense to some crimes. Could it also be a defense to charges of violations of public policy in the employment context?

▌Whistleblower Statutes

To encourage workers to report employer wrongdoing, such as fraud, a number of states have enacted so-called whistleblower statutes.[28] These statutes protect whistleblowers from subsequent retaliation on the part of employers. On the federal level, the Whistleblower Protection Act of 1989[29] protects federal employees who blow the whistle on their employers from their employers' retaliatory actions. Whistleblower statutes may also provide an incentive to disclose information by providing the whistleblower with a monetary reward. For example, the federal False Claims Reform Act of 1986[30] requires that a whistleblower who has disclosed information relating to a fraud perpetrated against the U.S. government receive between 15 and 25 percent of the proceeds if the government brings suit against the wrongdoer.

---

28.   At least thirty-seven states now have whistleblower statutes.
29.   5 U.S.C. Section 1201.
30.   31 U.S.C. Sections 3729–3733. This act amended the False Claims Act of 1863.

International Perspective

England also provides legal protection for whistleblowers to some extent. The English Parliament has passed legislation protecting workers who report health and safety violations by their employers. In one case, a company dismissed a worker who reported unsafe levels of a chemical, lindane, and called in a health and safety inspector. After the company fired the worker, the worker sued the employer for violating the law protecting whistleblowers and recovered approximately $12,000 in damages.

For Critical Analysis: *Why might a government be reluctant to come to the aid of all whistleblowers at all times?*

Application

Law and the Employer— Establishing an E-Mail Policy*

Employers that make electronic communications systems (such as access to the Internet and E-mail) available to their employees face some obvious risks. One risk is that E-mail could be used to harass employees. In one case, for example, Chevron Corporation had to pay $2.2 million to four female employees who claimed that they had been sexually harassed by E-mail messages.[a] Another risk is that employees could subject the employer to liability by reproducing, without authorization, copyright-protected materials on the Internet. Still another risk is that confidential information contained in E-mail messages transmitted via the Internet could be intercepted by an outside party. Finally, those employers who monitor employees' E-mail in an attempt to avoid these risks face yet another risk: the risk of being held liable for violating the employees' privacy rights.

If you are an employer and find it prudent to monitor employees' E-mail messages, you should take certain

---

*This *Application* is not meant to substitute for the services of an attorney who is licensed to practice law in your state.

a.   Tamar Lewin, "Chevron Settles Sexual Harassment Charges," *The New York Times*, February 21, 1995, p. A14.

Application—Continued

precautions. First, you might consider establishing a comprehensive E-mail policy statement. The statement should indicate to employees why you will be monitoring their E-mail and what methods you will use in doing so. The statement should also include specific instructions concerning the form and content of E-mail messages. You might advise your employees, for example, that E-mail may only be used for business communications and that they should use the same degree of care in drafting E-mail messages as they do when drafting communications printed on company letterhead. To underscore the importance of this rule, you can point out that E-mail messages may be subject to discovery in litigation. To avoid liability for copyright infringement, you might inform your employees that they should regard all information available on the Internet as protected by copyright.

Second, you should make sure that those in charge of monitoring E-mail messages restrict their monitoring to business communications only. As stated elsewhere, the Electronic Communications Privacy Act (ECPA) of 1986 prohibits the intentional and unauthorized interception of electronic communications, including E-mail, and imposes both civil and criminal liability on violators. An exception to the act is made, however, when the interception, or monitoring, is conducted in the ordinary course of business for business-related purposes.

Third, to protect yourself as fully as possible against liability under the ECPA, you should obtain each employee's direct consent to have his or her E-mail messages monitored. This is because another exception to liability under the ECPA is made when electronic monitoring is conducted with the employees' consent.

Finally, you should realize that state laws relating to privacy issues vary widely. Furthermore, new federal or state statutes may give more specific guidance to employers on the extent to which they can monitor their employees' communications. Additionally, case law interpreting existing state and federal statutes may change over time. For these reasons, to protect your interests fully and make sure your actions are legal, you should discuss your proposed monitoring policy with an attorney before implementing it.

 Checklist for the Employer

1. Develop a comprehensive policy statement stating how E-mail should and should not be used, why employees' E-mail messages are being monitored, and the methods used for monitoring.
2. Make sure that only business-related communications are monitored.
3. Obtain employees' consent to having their E-mail messages monitored.
4. Discuss your proposed monitoring policy with an attorney to make sure you fully protect your interests and stay within the limits allowed by law.

▮ Key Terms

closed shop 827
collective bargaining 828
employment at will 823
hot-cargo agreement 828
minimum wage 825

right-to-work law 827
secondary boycott 828
strike 829
union shop 827

vesting 834
whistleblowing 845
workers' compensation laws 832
wrongful discharge 843

▮ Chapter Summary: Employment Relationships

Wage-Hour Laws (See pages 824–825.)	1. *Davis-Bacon Act (1931)*—Requires the payment of "prevailing wages" to employees of contractors and subcontractors working on government construction projects.
	2. *Walsh-Healey Act (1936)*—Requires that a minimum wage and overtime pay be paid to employees of firms that contract with federal agencies.
	3. *Fair Labor Standards Act (1938)*—Extended wage-hour requirements to cover all employers whose activities affected interstate commerce. The act has specific requirements in regard to child labor, maximum hours, and minimum wages.

(Continued)

▌Chapter Summary: Employment Relationships—Continued

Labor Unions
(See pages 825–830.)
	1. *Federal labor laws*—
	   a. Norris-LaGuardia Act (1932)—Protects peaceful strikes, picketing, and boycotts.
	   b. National Labor Relations Act (1935)—Established the rights of employees to engage in collective bargaining and to strike; also defined specific employer practices as unfair to labor. The National Labor Relations Board (NLRB) was created to administer and enforce the act.
	   c. Labor-Management Relations Act (1947)—Proscribes certain unfair union practices, such as the closed shop.
	   d. Labor-Management Reporting and Disclosure Act (1959)—Established an employee bill of rights and reporting requirements for internal control of union activities.
	
	2. *Union organization*—Union campaign activities and elections must comply with the requirements established by federal labor laws and the NLRB.
	
	3. *Collective bargaining*—The process by which labor and management negotiate the terms and conditions of employment (wages, benefits, working conditions, and so on). The central legal right of a labor union is to engage in collective bargaining on the members' behalf.
	
	4. *Strikes*—When collective bargaining reaches an impasse, union members may use their ultimate weapon in labor-management struggles—the strike. A strike occurs when unionized workers leave their jobs and refuse to work.

Worker Health and Safety *(See pages 830–833.)*	1. The Occupational Safety and Health Act of 1970 requires employers to meet specific safety and health standards that are established and enforced by the Occupational Safety and Health Administration (OSHA). 2. State workers' compensation laws establish an administrative procedure for compensating workers who are injured in accidents that occur on the job, regardless of fault.
Income Security *(See pages 833–835.)*	1. *Social Security and Medicare*—The Social Security Act of 1935 provides for old-age (retirement), survivors, and disability insurance. Both employers and employees must make contributions under the Federal Insurance Contributions Act (FICA) to help pay for the employees' loss of income on retirement. The Social Security Administration administers Medicare, a health-insurance program for older or disabled persons. 2. *Private pension plans*—The federal Employee Retirement Income Security Act (ERISA) of 1974 establishes standards for the management of employer-provided pension plans. 3. *Unemployment insurance*—The Federal Unemployment Tax Act of 1935 created a system that provides unemployment compensation to eligible individuals. Covered employers are taxed to help cover the costs of unemployment compensation.
COBRA *(See page 835.)*	The Consolidated Omnibus Budget Reconciliation Act (COBRA) of 1985 requires employers to give employees, on termination of employment, the option of continuing their medical, optical, or dental insurance coverage for a certain period.
Family and Medical Leave *(See pages 836–838.)*	The Family and Medical Leave Act (FMLA) of 1993 requires employers with fifty or more employees to provide their employees (except for key employees) with up to twelve weeks of unpaid family or medical leave during any twelve-month period for the following reasons: 1. *Family leave*—May be taken to care for a newborn baby, an adopted child, or a foster child. 2. *Medical leave*—May be taken when the employee or the employee's spouse, child, or parent has a serious health condition requiring care.
Employee Privacy Rights *(See pages 838–842.)*	A right to privacy has been inferred from guarantees provided by the First, Third, Fourth, Fifth, and Ninth Amendments to the U.S. Constitution. State laws may also provide for privacy rights. Employer practices that are often challenged by employees as invasive of their privacy rights include lie-detector tests, drug testing, AIDS testing, performance monitoring, and screening procedures.
Employment-Related Immigration Laws *(See pages 842–843.)*	1. *Immigration Reform and Control Act (1986)*—Prohibits employers from hiring illegal immigrants; administered by the U.S. Immigration and Naturalization Service. 2. *Immigration Act (1990)*—Limits the number of legal immigrants entering the United States by capping the number of visas (entry permits) that are issued each year.

▌Chapter Summary: Employment Relationships—Continued

Wrongful Discharge (See pages 843–845.)	Wrongful discharge occurs whenever an employer discharges an employee in violation of the law or of an employment contract. To protect employees from some of the harsh results of the common law employment-at-will doctrine (under which employers may hire or fire employees "at will" unless a contract indicates to the contrary), courts have made exceptions to the doctrine on the basis of contract theory, tort theory, and public policy.
Whistleblower Statutes (See page 846.)	Most states have passed whistleblower statutes specifically to protect employees who "blow the whistle" on their employers from subsequent retaliation by those employers. The federal Whistleblower Protection Act of 1989 protects federal employees who report their employers' wrongdoing. The federal False Claims Reform Act of 1986 provides monetary rewards for whistleblowers who disclose information relating to fraud perpetrated against the U.S. government.

▌For Review

1. What is the employment-at-will doctrine? When and why are exceptions to this doctrine made?
2. What federal statute governs working hours and wages? What federal statutes govern labor unions and collective bargaining?
3. What federal act was enacted to protect the health and safety of employees? What are workers' compensation laws?

4. Under the Family and Medical Leave Act of 1993, under what circumstances may an employee take family or medical leave?
5. Does drug testing violate employees' privacy rights? Name three other types of activities undertaken by employers that might violate the privacy rights of employees.

▌Questions and Case Problems

32–1. Labor Laws. Calzoni Boating Co. is an interstate business engaged in manufacturing and selling boats. The company has five hundred nonunion employees. Representatives of these employees are requesting a four-day, ten-hours-per-day workweek, and Calzoni is concerned that this would require paying time and a half after eight hours per day. Which federal act is Calzoni thinking of that might require this? Will the act in fact require paying time and a half for all hours worked over eight hours per day if the employees' proposal is accepted? Explain.

32–2. Health and Safety Regulations. Denton and Carlo were employed at an appliance plant. Their job required them to do occasional maintenance work while standing on a wire mesh twenty feet above the plant floor. Other employees had fallen through the mesh, one of whom had been killed by the fall. When Denton and Carlo were asked by their supervisor to do work that would likely require them to walk on the mesh, they refused due to their fear of bodily harm or death. Because of their refusal to do the requested work, the two employees were fired from their jobs. Was their discharge wrongful? If so, under what federal employment law? To what federal agency or department should they turn for assistance?

32–3. Unfair Labor Practices. Suppose that Consolidated Stores is undergoing a unionization campaign. Prior to the union election, management says that the union is unnecessary to protect workers. Management also provides bonuses and wage increases to the workers during this period. The

employees reject the union. Union organizers protest that the wage increases during the election campaign unfairly prejudiced the vote. Should these wage increases be regarded as an unfair labor practice? Discuss.

32–4. Workers' Compensation. Galvin Strang worked for a tractor company in one of its factories. Near his work station there was a conveyor belt that ran through a large industrial oven. Sometimes, the workers would use the oven to heat their meals. Thirty-inch-high flasks containing molds were fixed at regular intervals on the conveyor and were transported into the oven. Strang had to walk between the flasks to get to his work station. One day, the conveyor was not moving, and Strang used the oven to cook a frozen pot pie. As he was removing the pot pie from the oven, the conveyor came on. One of the flasks struck Strang and seriously injured him. Strang sought recovery under the state workers' compensation law. Should he recover? Why or why not?

32–5. Health and Safety Regulations. At an REA Express, Inc., shipping terminal, a conveyor belt was inoperative because an electrical circuit had shorted out. The manager called a licensed electrical contractor. When the contractor arrived, REA's maintenance supervisor was in the circuit breaker room. The floor was wet, and the maintenance supervisor was using sawdust to try to soak up the water. While the licensed electrical contractor was standing on the wet floor and attempting to fix the short circuit, he was electrocuted. Simultaneously, REA's maintenance supervisor, who was standing on a wooden platform, was burned and knocked unconscious. The Occupational Safety and Health Administration (OSHA) sought to fine REA Express $1,000 for failure to furnish a place of employment free from recognized hazards. Will the court uphold OSHA's decision? Discuss fully. [*REA Express, Inc. v. Brennan*, 495 F.2d 822 (2d Cir. 1974)]

32–6. Whistleblowing. Richard Winters was an at-will employee for the Houston *Chronicle* from April 1977 to June 1986. Beginning in 1980, he became aware of alleged illegal activities carried out by other employees. He claimed that the *Chronicle* was falsely reporting an inflated number of paid subscribers, that several employees were engaged in inventory theft, and that his supervisor had offered him an opportunity to participate in a kickback scheme with the manufacturers of plastic bags. Winters reported all these activities to upper-level management in January 1986 but made no report to law enforcement agencies. He was fired six months later. He sued the *Chronicle* for wrongful termination. How should the court decide? Discuss fully. [*Winters v. Houston Chronicle Publishing*, 795 S.W.2d 723 (Tex. 1990)]

32–7. Employment at Will. Robert Adams worked as a delivery truck driver for George W. Cochran & Co. Adams persistently refused to drive a truck that lacked a required inspection sticker and was subsequently fired as a result of his refusal. Adams was an at-will employee, and Cochran contended that because there was no written employment contract stating otherwise, Cochran was entitled to discharge Adams at will—that is, for cause or no cause. Adams sought to recover $7,094 in lost wages and $200,000 in damages for the "humiliation, mental anguish and emotional distress" that he had suffered as a result of being fired from his job. Under what legal doctrines discussed in this chapter—or exceptions to those doctrines—might Adams be able to recover damages from Cochran? Discuss fully. [*Adams v. George W. Cochran & Co.*, 597 A.2d 28 (D.C.App. 1991)]

32–8. Workers' Compensation. Linda Burnett Kidwell, employed as a state traffic officer by the California Highway Patrol (CHP), suffered an injury at home, off duty, while practicing the standing long jump. The jump is part of a required test during the CHP's annual physical performance program fitness test. Kidwell filed a claim for workers' compensation benefits. The CHP and the California workers' compensation appeals board denied her claim. Kidwell appealed to a state appellate court. What is the requirement for granting a workers' compensation claim? Should Kidwell's claim be granted? [*Kidwell v. Workers' Compensation Appeals Board*, 33 Cal.App.4th 1130, 39 Cal.Rptr.2d 540 (1995)]

32–9. Privacy Rights. The city of Los Angeles requires a polygraph examination for police officers who ask to be promoted or transferred into a few specialized divisions where the work is unusually sensitive and requires a high level of integrity. Generally, those who fail the test are not promoted or transferred, but neither are they demoted or otherwise penalized. The Los Angeles Protective League filed a suit against the city in a California state court, asking the court, among other things, to order the city to stop the testing. On what basis might

the court grant the league's request? On what basis might it refuse to do so? [*Los Angeles Protective League v. City of Los Angeles*, 35 Cal.App.4th 1535, 42 Cal.Rptr.2d 23 (1995)]

32–10. Whistleblowing. Barbara Kraus was vice president of nursing at the New Rochelle Hospital Medical Center. She learned that a certain doctor had written on the charts of some patients that he had performed procedures for them that he had not performed, and in fact, he had not obtained consent forms from the patients to perform those procedures. She reported this to the doctor's superiors, who took little action against the doctor. Some time later, Kraus was terminated. She filed a suit in a New York state court against the hospital in order to recover damages for wrongful termination. What is required for the court to rule in Kraus's favor? [*Kraus v. New Rochelle Hospital Medical Center*, 628 N.Y.S.2d 360 (1995)]

A QUESTION OF ETHICS AND SOCIAL RESPONSIBILITY

32–11. *Salvatore Monte was president of Kenrich Petrochemicals, Inc. Helen Chizmar had been Kenrich's office manager since 1963. Among the staff that Chizmar supervised were her sister, daughter, and daughter-in-law. In 1987, Chizmar's relatives and four other staff members designated the Oil, Chemical, and Atomic Workers International Union as their bargaining representative. Chizmar was not involved, but when Monte was notified that his office was unionizing, he told Chizmar that someone else could do her job for "$20,000 less" and fired her. He told another employee that one of his reasons for firing Chizmar was that he "was not going to put up with any union bullsh——." During negotiations with the union, Monte said that he planned to "get rid of the whole family." Chizmar's family complained to the National Labor Relations Board (NLRB) that the firing was an unfair labor practice. The NLRB agreed and ordered that Chizmar be reinstated with back pay. Kenrich appealed. In view of these facts, consider the following questions. [Kenrich Petrochemicals, Inc. v. National Labor Relations Board, 907 F.2d 400 (3d Cir. 1990)]*

1. The National Labor Relations Act does not protect supervisors who engage in union activities. Should the appellate court affirm the NLRB's order nonetheless?
2. If the appellate court does not affirm the NLRB's order, what message would be sent to the supervisors and employees of Kenrich?
3. Is there anything Kenrich could (legally) do to avoid the unionization of its employees? Would it be ethical to counter the wishes of the employees to unionize?
4. What are the advantages of unionization for employees? Are there any disadvantages?

 FOR CRITICAL ANALYSIS

32–12. *Employees have a right to privacy, but employers also have a right to create and maintain an efficient and safe workplace. Do you think that existing laws strike an appropriate balance between employers' rights and employees' rights?*

▌Accessing the Internet: Business Law and Legal Environment

You can find an extensive index of labor-law resources that have been compiled by the Institute of Labor Relations at Cornell University. Go to

http://www.ilr.cornell.edu/othersites/

The U.S. Department of Labor is on the Internet at

gopher://marvel.loc.gov:70/11/federal/fedinfo/byagency/executive/labor

You can also access the National Institute for Occupational Safety and Health at

http://www.cdc.gov/niosh/homepage.html

The Legal Information Institute at Cornell Law School provides introductions to various labor and employment topics at

http://fatty.law.cornell.edu/topics/topics2.html#employment_law

You can visit the 'Lectric Law Library Web site concerning law and employment at

http://www.inter=law.com/temp.html

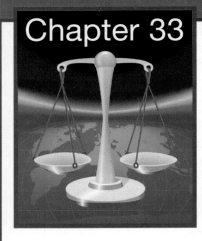

Chapter 33

Employment Discrimination

"Nor shall any State . . . deny to any person within its jurisdiction the equal protection of the laws."

The Fourteenth Amendment to the U.S. Constitution

CHAPTER OBJECTIVES

After reading this chapter, you should be able to:

1. Indicate what types of discrimination are prohibited by federal laws.
2. List and describe the three major federal statutes that prohibit employment discrimination.
3. Distinguish between disparate-treatment discrimination and disparate-impact discrimination.
4. Summarize the remedies available to victims of employment discrimination.
5. Discuss how employers can defend against claims of employment discrimination.

During the early 1960s we, as a nation, focused our attention on the civil rights of all Americans, including our rights under the Fourteenth Amendment to the equal protection of the laws. Out of this movement to end racial and other forms of discrimination grew a body of law protecting workers against discrimination in the workplace. This protective legislation further eroded the employment-at-will doctrine, which was discussed in the previous chapter. In the past several decades, judicial decisions, administrative agency actions, and legislation have restricted the ability of employers, as well as unions, to discriminate against workers on the basis of race, color, religion, national origin, gender, age, or disability. A class of persons defined by one or more of these criteria is known as a *protected class*.

Several federal statutes prohibit discrimination in the employment context against members of protected classes. The most important statute is Title VII of the Civil Rights Act of 1964.[1] Title VII prohibits discrimination on the basis of race, color, religion, national origin, and gender. Discrimination on the basis of age and disability are

---
1. 42 U.S.C. Sections 2000e–2000e-17.

prohibited by the Age Discrimination in Employment Act of 1967[2] and the Americans with Disabilities Act of 1990,[3] respectively.

The focus of this chapter is on the kinds of discrimination prohibited by these federal statutes. Note, however, that discrimination against employees on the basis of any of the above-mentioned criteria may also violate state human rights statutes or other state laws prohibiting discrimination.

▮ Title VII of the Civil Rights Act of 1964

Title VII of the Civil Rights Act of 1964 and its amendments prohibit **employment discrimination** against employees, applicants, and union members on the basis of race, color, national origin, religion, and gender at any stage of employment. Title VII applies to employers with fifteen or more employees, labor unions with fifteen or more members, labor unions that operate hiring halls (to which members go regularly to be rationed jobs as they become available), employment agencies, and state and local governing units or agencies. A special section of the act prohibits discrimination in most federal government employment.

Compliance with Title VII is monitored by the Equal Employment Opportunity Commission (EEOC). A victim of alleged discrimination, before bringing a suit against the employer, must first file a claim with the EEOC. The EEOC may investigate the dispute and attempt to obtain the parties' voluntary consent to an out-of-court settlement. If voluntary agreement cannot be reached, the EEOC may then file a suit against the employer on the employee's behalf. If the EEOC decides not to investigate the claim, the victim may bring his or her own lawsuit against the employer.

Until recently, the EEOC investigated every claim of employment discrimination, regardless of the merits of the claim. In 1996, however, in its "National Enforcement Plan," the EEOC stated that it will investigate only "priority cases." The plan contains a list of the types of cases that the EEOC wants to investigate and take to litigation and those that it does not. Generally, priority cases are cases that affect many workers, cases involving retaliatory discharge (firing an employee in retaliation for submitting a claim to the EEOC), and cases involving types of discrimination that are of particular concern to the EEOC.

Types of Discrimination

Title VII prohibits both intentional and unintentional discrimination. Intentional discrimination by an employer against an employee is known as **disparate-treatment discrimination**. Because intent may sometimes be difficult to prove, courts have established certain procedures for resolving disparate-treatment cases. Suppose that a woman applies for employment with a construction firm and is rejected. If she sues on the basis of disparate-treatment discrimination in hiring, she must show that (1) she is a member of a protected class, (2) she applied and was qualified for the job in question, (3) she was rejected by the employer, and (4) the employer continued to seek applicants for the position or filled the position with a person not in a protected class.

If the woman can meet these relatively easy requirements, she makes out a *prima facie* **case** of illegal discrimination. Making out a *prima facie* case of discrimination means that the plaintiff has met her initial burden of proof and will win in the absence

EMPLOYMENT DISCRIMINATION
Treating employees or job applicants unequally on the basis of race, color, national origin, religion, gender, age, or disability; prohibited by federal statutes.

DISPARATE-TREATMENT DISCRIMINATION
A form of employment discrimination that results when an employer intentionally discriminates against employees who are members of protected classes.

***PRIMA FACIE* CASE**
A case in which the plaintiff has produced sufficient evidence of his or her conclusion that the case can go to to a jury; a case in which the evidence compels the plaintiff's conclusion if the defendant produces no evidence to disprove it.

2. 29 U.S.C. Sections 621–634.
3. 42 U.S.C. Sections 12102–12118.

of a legally acceptable employer defense (defenses to claims of employment discrimination will be discussed later in this chapter). The burden then shifts to the employer-defendant, who must articulate a legal reason for not hiring the plaintiff. For example, the employer might say that the plaintiff was not hired because she lacked sufficient experience or training. To prevail, the plaintiff must then show that the employer's reason is a *pretext* (not the true reason) and that discriminatory intent actually motivated the employer's decision.

DISPARATE-IMPACT DISCRIMINATION

A form of employment discrimination that results from certain employer practices or procedures that, although not discriminatory on their face, have a discriminatory effect.

Employers often find it necessary to use interviews and testing procedures to choose from among a large number of applicants for job openings. Minimum educational requirements are also common. Employer practices, such as those involving educational requirements, may have an unintended discriminatory impact on a protected class. **Disparate-impact discrimination** occurs when, as a result of educational or other job requirements or hiring procedures, an employer's work force does not reflect the percentage of nonwhites, women, or members of other protected classes that characterizes qualified individuals in the local labor market. If a person challenging an employment practice having a discriminatory effect can show a connection between the practice and the disparity, he or she makes out a *prima facie* case, and no evidence of discriminatory intent needs to be shown. Disparate-impact discrimination can also occur when an educational or other job requirement or hiring procedure excludes members of a protected class from an employer's work force at a substantially higher rate than nonmembers, regardless of the racial balance in the employer's work force.

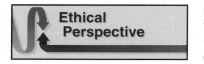

Ethical Perspective

Clearly, employers have an interest in the appearance of their employees, because the appearance of the employees affects the company's image in the eyes of the public. For this reason, many employers have dress or grooming policies for their employees. What if these policies result in disparate-impact discrimination? For example, suppose that a dress code requires that men may not wear ponytails, whereas women are allowed to do so. Is this an illegal form of disparate-impact gender discrimination?

Generally, the courts have held that employers have a right to establish and enforce dress and grooming requirements. In other words, even though the requirements may result in disparate-impact discrimination, the discrimination is not illegal—so long as there is no discrimination in the enforcement of the policy. If an employer enforces dress codes for men more strictly than it enforces dress codes for women, for example, then a male employee may succeed in a suit for unlawful disparate-impact discrimination based on gender.

For Critical Analysis: *How do dress codes affect employees' free speech (expression) rights under the First Amendment to the Constitution?*

Discrimination Based on Race, Color, and National Origin

If a company's standards or policies for selecting or promoting employees have the effect of discriminating against employees or job applicants on the basis of race, color, or national origin, they are illegal—unless (except for race) they have a substantial, demonstrable relationship to realistic qualifications for the job in question. Discrimination against these protected classes in regard to employment conditions and benefits is also illegal.

In such cases, there are two basic questions—whether a standard or policy has a discriminatory impact and, if it does, whether the standard or policy nevertheless has a substantial, demonstrable relationship to the job. These were the questions in the following case.

CASE 33.1

FICKLING v. NEW YORK STATE DEPARTMENT OF CIVIL SERVICE

United States District Court,
Southern District of New York, 1995.
909 F.Supp. 185.

HISTORICAL AND POLITICAL SETTING *Two principles form the core of Americans' beliefs about the workplace: all of us deserve equal opportunities, and hard work—not privilege, race, or gender—should determine who succeeds. In the early 1990s, the public debate about the role of race in the workplace became angrier and more divisive than at any time since the 1960s. Perhaps the real root of the discontent was the slow-growing economy, stagnant middle-class incomes, and corporate downsizing, all of which inflamed the debate over who should be hired and fired.*

FACTS Job applicants for the position of Social Welfare Eligibility Examiner for Westchester County, New York, must pass a New York State Department of Civil Service examination. In 1989 and 1990, the exam tested mainly reading comprehension and arithmetic, skills that were of relatively little importance to the job. When it was revealed that fewer than two African Americans and about one Hispanic passed the exam for every three whites who passed, Juliette Fickling and seven other minority members who failed the test (the plaintiffs) filed a suit in a federal district court against the state and the county. The plaintiffs alleged violations of, among other things, Title VII.

ISSUE Did the exam have a racially disparate impact? Did the exam lack a substantial, demonstrable relationship to the job?

DECISION Yes, to both questions. The court ruled in favor of the plaintiffs.

REASON The court pointed out that "[a] selection rate for any race, sex, or ethnic group which is less than four-fifths *   *   * (or 80%) of the rate for the group with the highest rate" is evidence of disparate impact. "Here," noted the court, "the disparate racial impact *   *   * was far below the 80% standard." The court also found that, despite the exam's emphasis on reading and arithmetic, neither ability was important to success on the job, while written and oral expression were generally not tested, "despite the fact that these abilities were found to be very important to successful job performance."

FOR CRITICAL ANALYSIS—Social Consideration
What are reasons, other than equal opportunity under Title VII, for insisting that a job test have a "substantial, demonstrable relationship" to the job?

Discrimination Based on Religion

Title VII of the Civil Rights Act of 1964 also prohibits government employers, private employers, and unions from discriminating against persons because of their religion. An employer must "reasonably accommodate" the religious practices of its employees, unless to do so would cause undue hardship to the employer's business. For example, if an employee's religion prohibits him or her from working on a certain day of the week or at a certain type of job, the employer must make a reasonable attempt to accommodate these religious requirements. Employers must reasonably accommodate an employee's religious belief even if the belief is not based on the tenets or dogma of a particular church, sect, or denomination. The only requirement is that the belief be sincerely held by the employee.[4]

---

4. *Frazee v. Illinois Department of Employment Security,* 489 U.S. 829, 109 S.Ct. 1514, 103 L.Ed.2d 914 (1989).

Discrimination Based on Gender

Under Title VII, as well as other federal acts, employers are forbidden to discriminate against employees on the basis of gender. Employers are prohibited from classifying jobs as male or female and from advertising in help-wanted columns that are designated male or female unless the employer can prove that the gender of the applicant is essential to the job. Furthermore, employers cannot have separate male and female seniority lists. Generally, to succeed in a suit for gender discrimination, a plaintiff must demonstrate that gender was a determining factor in the employer's decision to hire, fire, or promote him or her. Typically, this involves looking at all of the surrounding circumstances.

The Pregnancy Discrimination Act of 1978,[5] which amended Title VII, expanded the definition of gender discrimination to include discrimination based on pregnancy. Women affected by pregnancy, childbirth, or related medical conditions must be treated—for all employment-related purposes, including the receipt of benefits under employee-benefit programs—the same as other persons not so affected but similar in ability to work. An employer is required to treat an employee temporarily unable to perform her job owing to a pregnancy-related condition in the same manner as the employer would treat other temporarily disabled employees. The employer must change work assignments, grant paid disability leaves, or grant leaves without pay if that is how it would treat other temporarily disabled employees. Policies concerning an employee's return to work, accrual of seniority, pay increases, and so on must also result in equal treatment.[6]

Sexual Harassment

SEXUAL HARASSMENT
In the employment context, the granting of job promotions or other benefits in return for sexual favors, or language or conduct that is so sexually offensive that it creates a hostile working environment.

Title VII also protects employees against **sexual harassment** in the workplace. Sexual harassment can take two forms: *quid-pro-quo* harassment and hostile-environment harassment. *Quid pro quo* is a Latin phrase that is often translated to mean "something in exchange for something else." *Quid-pro-quo* harassment occurs when job opportunities, promotions, salary increases, and so on are given in return for sexual favors.

Hostile-environment harassment occurs when an employee is subjected to sexual conduct or comments that he or she perceives as offensive. The EEOC's guidelines on harassment state that the following types of verbal or physical conduct constitute hostile-environment harassment:

1. Conduct that has the purpose or effect of creating an intimidating, hostile, or offensive working environment.
2. Conduct that has the purpose or effect of unreasonably interfering with an individual's work performance.
3. Conduct that otherwise adversely affects an individual's employment opportunities.

HARASSMENT BY SUPERVISORS AND CO-WORKERS   What if an employee is harassed by a manager or supervisor of a large firm, and the firm itself (the "employer") is not

---

5.   42 U.S.C. Section 2000e(k).
6.   A cause of action under the Pregnancy Discrimination Act is not limited to women—a man may also have standing to sue for discrimination under the act. In *Nicol v. Imagematrix, Inc.,* 773 F.Supp. 802 (E.D.Va. 1991), the court held that the husband of a pregnant woman had standing to sue his former employer. The husband alleged that he had been fired because his wife (who worked for the same employer and was also fired) was pregnant.

aware of the harassment? Does the employee nonetheless have a cause of action against the employer? The answer to this question is often yes. Employers are generally liable for Title VII violations by the firm's managerial or supervisory personnel. Usually, in *quid-pro-quo* harassment cases, the courts hold employers strictly liable for the harassment. In other words, the employer will be held liable regardless of whether the employer knew about the harassment. In hostile-environment cases, however, the majority of courts tend to hold employers liable only if the employer knew or should have known of the harassment and failed to take prompt remedial action. (Note that if the employer takes reasonable steps to discover and remedy acts of sexual harassment, these actions may shield the employer from liability—see the *Business Law in Action* on this topic on page 859.)

In some cases, high-level supervisors and managers have been held personally liable for harassment under the theory that the supervisors exercised sufficient control to be deemed "employers." There is a growing consensus among the courts, however, that supervisors cannot be held liable, as employers, under Title VII.[7]

Often, employees alleging harassment complain that the actions of co-workers, not supervisors, are responsible for creating a hostile working environment. In such cases, the employee still has a cause of action against the employer. Normally, though, the employer will be held liable only if it knew, or should have known, about the harassment and failed to take immediate remedial action.

The following case raises the issue of whether an employer can be held responsible for doing nothing in a situation involving harassment even though the harassing employee had voluntarily ceased the harassment.

---

7. See, for example, *Williams v. Banning*, 72 F.3d 552 (7th Cir. 1995); and *Sheridan v. E. I. du Pont de Nemours and Co.*, 74 F.3d 1439 (3d Cir. 1996).

CASE 33.2

FULLER v. CITY OF OAKLAND, CALIFORNIA
United States Court of Appeals,
Ninth Circuit, 1995.
47 F.3d 1522.

HISTORICAL AND SOCIAL SETTING   *At one time, a fear of false reporting limited the testimony of women in the prosecution of rape cases. In the 1970s, this same fear of false reporting was one of the reasons some observers initially opposed the recognition of sexual harassment as discrimination on the basis of gender. Others believed that harassment reflects a conflict between personalities, or that it is based on sexual attractiveness, not gender. Some felt that even if some conduct was harassment, once it stopped, the employer should not be held responsible for it.*

FACTS   Patricia Fuller and Antonio Romero were police officers with the city of Oakland, California, when they had a brief romantic relationship. When Fuller broke it off, Romero—who was promoted to a supervisory position—began to harass her on and off duty. Fuller complained to their superiors. Romero stopped harassing her, and the superiors took no action, except to officially call Fuller's complaint "[u]nfounded." Fuller resigned and filed a suit against the city in a federal district court under Title VII. The city argued that when the harassment stopped, its own responsibility ceased. The court agreed. Fuller appealed to the U.S. Court of Appeals for the Ninth Circuit.

ISSUE   Does an employer have a responsibility to take action in a case of harassment even if the harassment has stopped?

DECISION   Yes. The U.S. Court of Appeals for the Ninth Circuit reversed the judgment of the lower court and remanded the case.

(Continued)

Case 33.2—Continued

REASON   The appellate court concluded that "Title VII does not permit employers to stand idly by once they learn that sexual harassment has occurred. To do so amounts to a ratification of the prior harassment." The court explained that "[o]nce an employer knows or should know of harassment, a remedial obligation kicks in. That obligation will not be discharged until action— prompt, effective action—has been taken." The court reasoned that the effectiveness of the action is "measured by the twin purposes of ending the current harass-ment and deterring future harassment—by the same offender or others."

FOR CRITICAL ANALYSIS—Social Consideration
What steps should an employer take, once harassment has ceased, to deter future misconduct?

HARASSMENT BY NONEMPLOYEES   Employers may also be liable for harassment by *nonemployees* in certain circumstances. For example, if a restaurant owner or manager knows that a certain customer repeatedly harasses a waitress and permits the harass-ment to continue, the restaurant owner may be liable under Title VII even though the customer is not an employee of the restaurant. The issue turns on the control that the employer exerts over a nonemployee. In the situation just described, a court would likely conclude that the restaurant manager or owner could have taken action to pre-vent the customer from harassing the waitress.

PROVING SEXUAL HARASSMENT   One of the major problems faced by employees who are sexually harassed is that such harassment can be very difficult to prove. Often, there are no third parties who have witnessed the harassment and no written evidence of it. The question thus comes down to who is more believable, the alleged victim or the alleged offender.

Even if an employee can prove that sexually offensive conduct occurred, at what point does such conduct result in an "intimidating, hostile, or offensive working environment" or otherwise qualify as hostile-environment harassment under the EEOC's guidelines? Courts have had to struggle with such questions and usually render their decisions on a case-by-case basis. At least one court has concluded that even one incident of sexually offensive conduct can result in a hostile, offensive working environment.[8]

In *Harris v. Forklift Systems, Inc.*,[9] the United States Supreme Court addressed another controversial issue relating to hostile-environment claims. Prior to this deci-sion, many jurisdictions had held that a worker claiming to be a victim of hostile-environment harassment must establish that he or she suffered serious psychological effects as a result of the offensive conduct. In the *Harris* case, the Supreme Court held that "Title VII bars conduct that would seriously affect a reasonable person's psycho-logical well-being, but the statute is not limited to such conduct. So long as the envi-ronment would reasonably be perceived, and is perceived, as hostile or abusive, there is no need for it also to be psychologically injurious."

In *Harris*, the Court also attempted to settle disagreements among the courts on the standard to be applied in harassment cases. Should a neutral and objective "reasonable person" standard apply, or should a more subjective "reasonable female" or "reasonable male" standard be used? The Court adopted a broad standard by

---

8.   See *Radtke v. Everett*, 442 Mich. 368, 501 N.W.2d 155 (1993).
9.   510 U.S. 17, 114 S.Ct. 367, 126 L.Ed.2d 295 (1993).

BUSINESS LAW IN ACTION

Harassment Policies May Shield Employers from Liability

The courts do not look kindly on employers that fail to take prompt remedial action when learning of sexual-harassment complaints (see, for example, Case 33.2). Employers that *do* take prompt action to remedy the problem, however, often can avoid liability for the harassment. Even more significantly, employers that provide specific guidelines for their employees on sexual harassment—guidelines that indicate how to report incidents of harassment—may not be held liable if employees fail to complain of the harassment through the "proper channels."

The case of *Baskerville v. Culligan International Co.*[a] is illustrative in this respect. In that case, an employee, Valerie Baskerville, complained that she was being sexually harassed by her supervisor, Michael Hall. Baskerville alleged that Hall had harassed her over a period of seven months through such incidents as the following: he had called her "pretty girl" on several

a. 50 F.3d 428 (7th Cir. 1995).

occasions; once, when she was wearing a leather skirt, he made a grunting sound that sounded like "um um um" as she turned to leave his office; another time, when she commented on how hot his office was, he raised his eyebrows and said, "Not until you stepped your foot in here."

The federal district court held that these actions constituted sexual harassment in violation of Title VII and awarded damages to Baskerville. On appeal, the U.S. Court of Appeals for the Seventh Circuit reversed the district court's judgment. The appellate court pointed out that Hall had never touched the plaintiff and had never invited her—explicitly or implicitly—to have sex with him or even to go on a date together. The court held that "Mr. Hall, whatever his qualities as a sales manager, is not a man of refinement; but neither is he a sexual harasser."

It is interesting that the appellate court also stated that even if Hall's actions had created a hostile environment—that is, if they did give rise to a cause of action for harassment—the company could still avoid liability for Hall's actions. The reason is that Baskerville did not follow the company's established guidelines, well known to her, for reporting incidents of sexual harassment. Instead of immediately going through proper channels and reporting the problem to the human

resources department, as required by the company, Baskerville first complained to Hall's supervisor. The supervisor reprimanded Hall, but the purported harassing actions continued. Eventually, Baskerville reported the problem to the company's human resources department, and the company took prompt action. The matter was promptly investigated, Hall was told to cease his offensive behavior immediately, and he was placed on probation for several months. Hall got the point, and there was no recurrence of the offensive behavior.

Clearly, employers who wish to avoid liability for harassment would be wise to establish and implement effective harassment policies and grievance procedures. Employers are charged with a duty to discover and rectify acts of sexual harassment in the workplace, and the employer's negligence is often the key factor in hostile-environment cases. Effective harassment guidelines and procedures can be used as evidence that the employer was not negligent in this duty.

For Critical Analysis: *In what circumstances might a court not allow an employer to avoid liability for harassment simply because the employee failed to complain through the "proper channels"?*

holding that in cases of alleged sexual harassment, the conduct at issue must be abusive both objectively (as perceived by a reasonable person) and subjectively (as perceived by the victim).

SAME-GENDER HARASSMENT   Recently, the courts have had to address the issue of whether men who are harassed by other men, or women who are harassed by other women, are also protected by laws that prohibit gender-based discrimination in the workplace. For example, what if the male president of a firm demands sexual favors from a male employee? Does this action qualify as sexual harassment? The courts are widely split on this issue. In some jurisdictions, courts have held that plaintiffs may bring actions under Title VII for same-gender harassment;[10] in other jurisdictions, courts have held to the contrary.[11]

10.   See, for example, *McCoy v. Johnson Controls World Services, Inc.,* 878 F.Supp. 229 (S.D.Ga. 1995).
11.   See, for example, *McWilliams v. Fairfax County Board of Supervisors,* 72 F.3d 1191 (4th Cir. 1996).

Remedies under Title VII

Employer liability under Title VII may be extensive. If the plaintiff successfully proves that unlawful discrimination occurred, he or she may be awarded reinstatement, back pay, retroactive promotions, and damages. Prior to the Civil Rights Act of 1991, damages were not available under Title VII. Plaintiffs alleging racial discrimination therefore often brought actions under 42 U.S.C. Section 1981. Section 1981, which was enacted as part of the Civil Rights Act of 1866, prohibits discrimination on the basis of race or ethnicity in the formation or enforcement of contracts. Until the 1991 Civil Rights Act, however, damages were not available for victims of intentional employment discrimination based on sex, religion, age, or disability. The 1991 act, however, allowed compensatory damages to be awarded in cases brought under other employment laws, such as Title VII, thus significantly broadening the rights of victims of employment discrimination.

Under the 1991 act, compensatory damages are available only in cases of intentional discrimination. The statute also stipulates that compensatory damages shall not include back pay, interest on back pay, or other relief already available under Title VII. Punitive damages may be recovered against a private employer only if the employer acted with malice or reckless indifference to an individual's rights. The sum of the amount of compensatory and punitive damages is limited by the statute to specific amounts against specific employers—ranging from $50,000 against employers with one hundred or fewer employees to $300,000 against employers with more than five hundred employees.

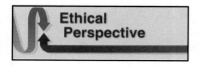
Ethical Perspective

Title VII was not intended to be the sole remedy for employment discrimination based on race, color, national origin, religion, or gender. Plaintiffs who suffer from employment discrimination on these bases may also bring actions under other laws. In fact, it is often advantageous for some plaintiffs to do so. For example, a plaintiff alleging racial discrimination may choose to sue under Section 1981, because there are no caps on damages available under that law. Plaintiffs may also bring suits under state laws prohibiting discrimination, if the state laws allow for greater recovery than Title VII. For example, a plaintiff may recover damages for emotional distress (which are not available under Title VII) under a state statute.[a] (See also Case 33.5 later in this chapter for other advantages of bringing a discrimination suit under state law.)

Some employees may opt to sue under the equal protection clause of the Fifth and Fourteenth Amendments (discussed in Chapter 2). For example, in *Beardsley v. Webb,*[b] a former deputy sheriff sued her supervisor and the sheriff, alleging sexual harassment and employment discrimination. The court held that the equal protection clause confers a right to be free from gender discrimination that is not substantially related to important governmental objectives. Furthermore, the court held that standards developed in Title VII litigation could be applied to similar litigation under the equal protection clause.

For Critical Analysis: *Can you think of any other reasons why plaintiffs might want to bring discrimination suits under laws other than Title VII?*

a.   *Luciano v. Olsten Corp.,* 912 F.Supp. 663 (E.D.N.Y. 1996).
b.   30 F.3d 524 (4th Cir. 1994).

▎Equal Pay Act of 1963

The Equal Pay Act of 1963 was enacted as an amendment to the Fair Labor Standards Act of 1938. Basically, the act prohibits gender-based discrimination in the wages paid for equal work on jobs when their performance requires equal skill, effort, and responsibility under similar conditions. It is job content rather than job description that controls in all cases. To determine whether the Equal Pay Act has been violated, a court will thus look to the primary duties of the two jobs. The jobs of a barber and a beautician, for example, are considered essentially "equal." So, too, are those of a tailor and a seamstress. For the equal pay requirements to apply, the act requires that male and female employees must work at the same establishment.

A wage differential for equal work is justified if it is shown to be because of (1) seniority, (2) merit, (3) a system that pays according to quality or quantity of production, or (4) any factor other than gender. Small differences in job content, however, do not justify higher pay for one gender.

RECALL The Fair Labor Standards Act of 1938 extends wage-hour requirements to nearly all employers.

▎Discrimination Based on Age

Age discrimination is potentially the most widespread form of discrimination, because anyone—regardless of race, color, national origin, or gender—could be a victim at some point in life. The Age Discrimination in Employment Act (ADEA) of 1967, as amended, prohibits employment discrimination on the basis of age against individuals forty years of age or older. An amendment to the act prohibits mandatory retirement for nonmanagerial workers. For the act to apply, an employer must have twenty or more employees, and the employer's business activities must affect interstate commerce.

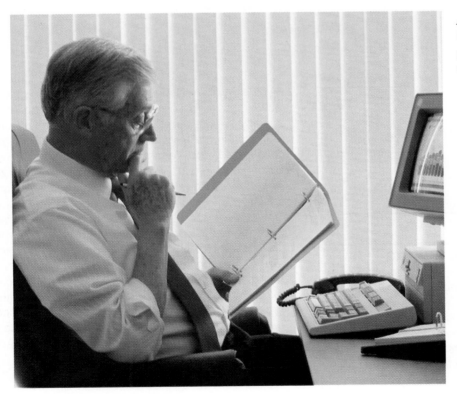

A worker reviews documents at his desk. Why did Congress prohibit employment discrimination based on age?

862

UNIT EIGHT: GOVERNMENT REGULATION

The burden-shifting procedure under the ADEA is similar to that under Title VII. If a plaintiff can establish that he or she (1) was a member of the protected age group, (2) was qualified for the position from which he or she was discharged, and (3) was discharged under circumstances that give rise to an inference of discrimination, the plaintiff has established a *prima facie* case of unlawful age discrimination. The burden then shifts to the employer, who must articulate a legitimate reason for the discrimination. If the plaintiff can prove that the employer's reason is only a pretext and that the plaintiff's age was a determining factor in the employer's decision, the employer will be held liable under the ADEA.

Numerous cases of alleged age discrimination have been brought against employers who, to cut costs, replaced older, higher-salaried employees with younger, lower-salaried workers. Whether a firing is discriminatory or simply part of a rational business decision to prune the company's ranks is not always clear. Companies generally defend a decision to discharge a worker by asserting that the worker could no longer perform his or her duties or that the worker's skills were no longer needed. The employee must prove that the discharge was motivated, at least in part, by age bias. Proof that qualified older employees are generally discharged before younger employees or that co-workers continually made unflattering age-related comments about the discharged worker may be enough.

In the past, courts had sometimes held that to establish a *prima facie* case of age discrimination, the plaintiff must also prove that he or she was replaced by a person outside the protected class—that is, by a person under the age of forty years. In 1996, however, in *O'Connor v. Consolidated Coin Caterers Corp.*,[12] the United States Supreme Court held that a cause of action for age discrimination under the ADEA does not require the replacement worker to be outside the protected class. Rather, the issue in all ADEA cases turns on whether age discrimination has, in fact, occurred, regardless of the age of the replacement worker. In the following case, the court had to decide whether there was sufficient evidence to support a jury's finding of discrimination on the basis of age.

---

12. ___U.S.___, 116 S.Ct. 1307, 134 L.Ed.2d 433 (1996).

CASE 33.3

RHODES v. GUIBERSON OIL TOOLS

United States Court of Appeals, Fifth Circuit, 1996.
75 F.3d 989.

HISTORICAL AND ECONOMIC SETTING *Exploring and drilling for oil is an expensive operation; drills, pipes, pumps, testing and measuring equipment, trucks, tankers, helicopters, and a variety of services are utilized. Suppliers of these products and services depend entirely on the activities of oil companies in the field. If no one is drilling for oil, the suppliers are out of business. In 1986, the oil industry was in the throes of a severe economic downturn.*

FACTS Calvin Rhodes sold oil field equipment for Guiberson Oil Tools. When he was discharged in 1986 at age fifty-six, he was told that the discharge was part of a reduction in the work force (RIF), and that he would be considered for reemployment. Within six weeks, Guiberson hired a forty-two-year-old person to do the same job. Rhodes filed a suit in a federal district court against Guiberson under the Age Discrimination in Employment Act. At the trial, Guiberson officials testified that they had not told Rhodes the truth about why they discharged him and that they had intended to replace him. Guiberson offered as a defense Rhodes's "poor work performance" but did not present any company sales records or goals. Rhodes countered with customers' testimony about his expertise and diligence. The jury found that Rhodes was discharged because of his age. Guiberson appealed to the U.S. Court of Appeals for the Fifth Circuit.

Case 33.3—Continued

ISSUE Was the evidence in this case sufficient to support the verdict?

DECISION Yes. The U.S. Court of Appeals for the Fifth Circuit affirmed the jury's finding.

REASON The appellate court concluded that "the jury was entitled to find that the reasons given for Rhodes' discharge were pretexts for age discrimination. The jury was entitled to find that Guiberson's stated reason for discharging Rhodes—RIF—was false. Additionally, the reason for discharge that Guiberson Oil proffered in court * * * was countered with evidence from which the jury could have found that Rhodes was an excellent salesman who met Guiberson Oil's legitimate productivity expectations. * * * [A] reasonable jury could have found that Guiberson Oil discriminated against Rhodes on the basis of his age."

FOR CRITICAL ANALYSIS—Social Consideration *If age is not the sole reason for an adverse employment decision, how significant a factor do you think it should be to support a finding of discrimination?*

▌Discrimination Based on Disability

The Americans with Disabilities Act (ADA) of 1990 is designed to eliminate discriminatory employment practices that prevent otherwise qualified workers with disabilities from fully participating in the national labor force. Prior to 1990, the major federal law providing protection to those with disabilities was the Rehabilitation Act of 1973. That act covered only federal government employees and those employed under federally funded programs. The ADA extends federal protection against disability-based discrimination to all workplaces with fifteen or more workers. Basically, the ADA requires

"[I]n order to treat some persons equally, we must treat them differently."

Harry A. Blackmun, 1908–
(Associate justice of the United States Supreme Court, 1970–1994)

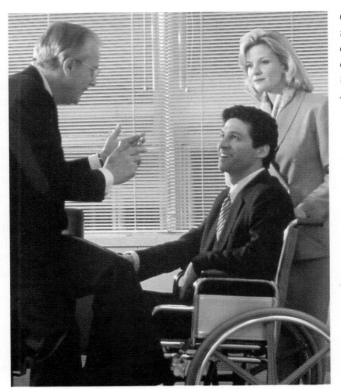

Co-workers discuss business matters. Which workers with disabilities are protected from employment discrimination by the Americans with Disabilities Act?

that employers "reasonably accommodate" the needs of persons with disabilities unless to do so would cause the employer to suffer an "undue hardship."

To prevail on a claim under the ADA, a plaintiff must show that he or she (1) has a disability, (2) is otherwise qualified for the employment in question, and (3) was excluded from the employment solely because of the disability. As in Title VII cases, a claim alleging violation of the ADA may be commenced only after the plaintiff has pursued the claim through the EEOC. Plaintiffs may sue for many of the same remedies available under Title VII. They may seek reinstatement, back pay, a limited amount of compensatory and punitive damages (for intentional discrimination), and certain other forms of relief. Repeat violators may be ordered to pay fines of up to $100,000.

What Is a Disability?

The ADA is broadly drafted to define persons with disabilities as persons with a physical or mental impairment that "substantially limits" their everyday activities. More specifically, the ADA defines *disability* as "(1) a physical or mental impairment that substantially limits one or more of the major life activities of such individuals; (2) a record of such impairment; or (3) being regarded as having such an impairment."

Generally, the determination of whether an individual has a disability as defined by the ADA is made on a case-by-case basis. Unlike plaintiffs in cases brought under Title VII or the ADEA, who clearly either are or are not members of the classes protected by those acts, a plaintiff suing under the ADA must *prove* that he or she has a disability—and thus falls under the protection of the ADA. Meeting this first requirement for a case of disability-based discrimination is often difficult.

Health conditions that have been considered disabilities under federal law include blindness, alcoholism, heart disease, cancer, muscular dystrophy, cerebral palsy, paraplegia, diabetes, acquired immune deficiency syndrome (AIDS), and morbid obesity (defined as existing when an individual's weight is two times that of the normal person)[13] The ADA excludes from coverage certain conditions, including homosexuality and kleptomania.

Reasonable Accommodation

The ADA does not require that *unqualified* applicants with disabilities be hired or retained. Therefore, employers are not obligated to accommodate the needs of job applicants or employees with disabilities who are not otherwise qualified for the work. If a job applicant or an employee with a disability, with reasonable accommodation, can perform essential job functions, however, then the employer must make the accommodation. Required modifications may include installing ramps for a wheelchair, establishing more flexible working hours, creating or modifying job assignments, and creating or improving training materials and procedures.

Generally, employers should give primary consideration to employees' preferences in deciding what accommodations should be made. What happens if a job applicant or employee does not indicate to the employer how his or her disability can be accommodated so that the employee can perform essential job functions? In this situation, the employer may avoid liability for failing to hire or retain the individual on the ground that the applicant or employee has failed to meet the "otherwise qualified" requirement.[14]

---

13. *Cook v. Rhode Island Department of Mental Health*, 10 F.3d 17 (1st Cir. 1993).
14. See, for example, *Beck v. University of Wisconsin Board of Regents*, 75 F.3d 1130 (7th Cir. 1996); and *White v. York International Corp.*, 45 F.3d 357 (10th Cir. 1995).

Employers who do not accommodate the needs of persons with disabilities must demonstrate that the accommodations will cause "undue hardship." Generally, the law offers no uniform standards for identifying what is an undue hardship other than the imposition of a "significant difficulty or expense" on the employer. Usually, the courts decide whether an accommodation constitutes an undue hardship on a case-by-case basis. In one case, the court decided that paying for a parking space near the office for an employee with a disability was not an undue hardship.[15] In another case, the court held that accommodating the request of an employee with diabetes for indefinite leave until his disease was under control would create an undue hardship for the employer, because the employer would not know when the employee was returning to work. The court stated that reasonable accommodation under the ADA means accommodation so that the employee can perform the job now or "in the immediate future" rather than at some unspecified distant time.[16]

We now look at some specific requirements of the ADA in regard to the extent to which employers must reasonably accommodate the needs of employees with disabilities.

JOB APPLICATIONS AND PREEMPLOYMENT PHYSICAL EXAMS   Employers must modify their job-application process so that those with disabilities can compete for jobs with those who do not have disabilities. A job announcement that only has a phone number, for example, would discriminate against potential job applicants with hearing impairments. Thus, the job announcement must also provide an address.

Employers are restricted in the kinds of questions they may ask on job-application forms and during preemployment interviews (see the *Application* at the end of this chapter on this subject). Furthermore, they cannot require persons with disabilities to submit to preemployment physicals unless such exams are required of all other applicants. Employers can condition an offer of employment on the employee's successfully passing a medical examination, but disqualifications must result from the discovery of problems that render the applicant unable to perform the job for which he or she is to be hired.

DANGEROUS WORKERS   Employers are not required to hire or retain workers who, because of their disabilities, pose a "direct threat to the health or safety" of their co-workers. This danger must be substantial and immediate; it cannot be speculative. In the wake of the AIDS epidemic, many employers are concerned about hiring or continuing to employ a worker who has AIDS under the assumption that the worker might pose a direct threat to the health or safety of others in the workplace. Courts have generally held, however, that AIDS is not so contagious as to disqualify employees in most jobs. Therefore, employers must reasonably accommodate job applicants or employees who have AIDS or who test positive for the human immunodeficiency virus (HIV), the virus that causes AIDS.[17]

As mentioned, the ADA does not require that *unqualified* disabled applicants be hired or retained. Employers sometimes argue that persons with AIDS are not "otherwise qualified" for particular positions because they pose a direct threat to the health or safety of others that cannot be eliminated or reduced by reasonable accommodation. This was the employer's argument in the following case.

DON'T FORGET Preemployment screening procedures must be applied carefully in regard to all job applicants.

---

15.   See *Lyons v. Legal Aid Society,* 68 F.3d 1512 (2d Cir. 1995).
16.   *Myers v. Hase,* 50 F.3d 278 (4th Cir. 1995).
17.   Courts have disagreed on whether HIV-positive persons who do not have any symptoms of AIDS have a disability under the ADA. See *Doe v. Kohn Nast & Graf, P.C.,* 866 F.Supp. 190 (E.D.Pa. 1994); and *Ennis v. National Association of Business and Educational Radio, Inc.,* 53 F.3d 55 (4th Cir. 1995) for two views on this issue.

CASE 33.4

MAURO v. BORGESS MEDICAL CENTER

United States District Court,
Western District of Michigan,
Southern Division, 1995.
886 F.Supp. 1349.

HISTORICAL AND SOCIAL SETTING *Acquired immune deficiency syndrome (AIDS) was unknown until the first cases were reported in the United States in 1981. AIDS, which is fatal and for which there is no known cure, is caused by the human immunodeficiency virus (HIV). HIV can be transmitted from one person to another by contact of the infected blood of one person with an open wound of another. A person infected with HIV remains infected for the rest of his or her life. Although an infected person may not show any symptoms for years, he or she can still infect others.*

FACTS   William Mauro was an operating room surgical technician for the Borgess Medical Center. Surgical technicians must occasionally place their hands into a patient's surgical incision. Borgess officials had reason to believe that Mauro was infected with HIV. When Borgess asked Mauro to be tested for HIV, however, Mauro refused. He also refused to accept a job outside the operating room and, as a consequence, was laid off. Mauro filed a suit in a federal district court against Borgess, alleging, among other things, discrimination in

violation of the Americans with Disabilities Act (ADA). Borgess filed a motion for summary judgment. Mauro argued that the probability of transmission of HIV is small and that a reasonable accommodation would be to add a person to the surgical team to work in or near a patient's incision.

ISSUE   Does a person who poses a small but permanent risk of lethal consequences pose a sufficiently direct threat to the health and safety of others to make the person not "otherwise qualified" under the ADA?

DECISION   Yes. The court granted Borgess's motion for summary judgment.

REASON   The court recognized that the risk of an HIV-positive surgical technician infecting others is small, but it reasoned that "[b]ecause there is a real possibility of transmission, * * * and because the consequence of transmission is invariably death, the threat to patient safety posed by plaintiff's presence in the operating room performing the functions of a surgical technician is direct and significant." As for the proposed accommodation, the court concluded that it "is not reasonable." It "would entail a job restructuring in the operating room, a burden the law does not impose."

FOR CRITICAL ANALYSIS—Ethical Consideration
Some people believe that AIDS is as contagious as an influenza virus. Are employers justified in taking such fears into account in making employment-related decisions?

HEALTH-INSURANCE PLANS   Workers with disabilities must be given equal access to any health insurance provided to other employees. Employers can exclude from coverage preexisting health conditions and certain types of diagnostic or surgical procedures, however. An employer can also put a limit, or cap, on health-care payments in its particular group-health policy—as long as such caps are "applied equally to all insured employees" and do not "discriminate on the basis of disability." Whenever a group health-care plan makes a disability-based distinction in its benefits, the plan violates the ADA. The employer must then be able to justify the distinction by proving one of the following:

1.   That limiting coverage of certain ailments is required to keep the plan financially sound.
2.   That coverage of certain ailments would cause a significant increase in premium payments or their equivalent such that the plan would be unappealing to a significant number of workers.
3.   That the disparate treatment is justified by the risks and costs associated with a particular disability.

THE ADA AND SUBSTANCE ABUSERS   Drug addiction is a disability under the ADA, because drug addiction is a substantially limiting impairment. Those who are

Kweisi Mfume
(1948–   )

"Life is a short commodity," says Kweisi Mfume, one of the co-authors of the Americans with Disabilities Act (ADA) of 1990. "You have to do all you can when you can."[a] Mfume appears to have lived by his own words.

Mfume, a Democratic representative from Maryland, served five terms in Congress. He chaired the Congressional Black Caucus for two years and sat on the Banking and Finance Committee. Besides the ADA, Mfume championed the Civil Rights Act of 1991, the federal ban on assault weapons, important amendments to the Equal Credit Opportunity Act, and other legislation.

a.   Hollis Towns, "New Leader Pledges New Life for NAACP: Kweisi Mfume Has a Vision for the NAACP—Relevance," *The Atlanta Journal-Constitution*, December 10, 1995.

Born Frizzell Gerard Gray in Baltimore, Mfume found himself living on the streets after his mother died of cancer when he was sixteen years old. He dropped out of school and hung around with gangs until he decided, after several years, to return to school and do something more with his life. As a symbol of his change in attitude, he changed his name to Kweisi Mfume, which means "conqueror of kings" in one of the languages spoken in Ghana. Mfume graduated from Morgan State University in 1976 and earned a master's degree in international studies at Johns Hopkins University.

Mfume taught briefly at Morgan State and also worked as a radio station program director and talk show host. In 1979, he was elected to the Baltimore City Council, where he served two terms before being elected to his first term in the U.S. House of Representatives.

Recently, Mfume resigned his seat in the House to become president and chief executive officer of the National Association for the Advancement of Colored People (NAACP). When he assumed control of the NAACP, he

said, "The task before us will be significant, but I hasten to point out that all challenge is significant. The greater challenge, my friends, will not be measured, however, by its size, but by our willingness to accept it."[b]

For Critical Analysis: *How does legislation such as the Americans with Disabilities Act of 1990 challenge those it is designed to help?*

b.   Kweisi Mfume, "Press Conference with Rep. Kweisi Mfume (D-Md) Following the Announcement of His Appointment as Head of the NAACP," Transcript by Federal News Service Group, Inc., December 10, 1995.

currently using illegal drugs are not protected by the act. The ADA only protects persons with *former* drug addictions—those who have completed a supervised drug-rehabilitation program or who are currently in a supervised rehabilitation program. Individuals who have used drugs casually in the past are not protected under the act. They are not considered addicts and therefore do not have a disability (addiction).

People recovering from alcoholism are protected by the ADA. Employers cannot legally discriminate against employees simply because they are suffering from alcoholism and must treat them in the same way as they treat other employees. In other words, an employee suffering from alcoholism cannot be disciplined any differently than anyone else simply because he or she was drinking the night before and came to work late. Of course, employers have the right to prohibit the use of alcohol in the workplace and can require that employees not be under the influence of alcohol while working. Employers can also fire or refuse to hire a person suffering from alcoholism if he or she poses a substantial risk of harm to either himself or herself or to others and the risk cannot be reduced by reasonable accommodation.

▌ Defenses to Employment Discrimination

The first line of defense for an employer charged with employment discrimination is, of course, to assert that the plaintiff has failed to meet his or her initial burden of proof—proving that discrimination in fact occurred. As noted, plaintiffs bringing cases under the ADA often find it difficult to meet this initial burden, because they must prove that their alleged disabilities are disabilities covered by the ADA. Furthermore, plaintiffs in ADA cases must prove that they were otherwise qualified for the job and that the reason they were not hired or were fired was solely because of their disabilities.

Once a plaintiff succeeds in proving that discrimination occurred, then the burden shifts to the employer to justify the discriminatory practice. Often, employers attempt to justify the discrimination by claiming that it was a result of a business necessity, a bona fide occupational qualification, or a seniority system. As mentioned in this chapter's *Business Law in Action*, an effective anti-harassment policy and prompt remedial action when harassment occurs also may shield employers from liability under Title VII for sexual harassment in some cases.

Business Necessity

BUSINESS NECESSITY
A defense to allegations of employment discrimination in which the employer demonstrates that an employment practice that discriminates against members of a protected class is related to job performance.

An employer may defend against a claim of discrimination by asserting that a practice that has a discriminatory effect is a business necessity. If requiring a high school diploma, for example, is shown to have a discriminatory effect, an employer might argue that a high school education is required for workers to perform the job at a required level of competence. If the employer can demonstrate to the court's satisfaction that there exists a definite connection between a high school education and job performance, then the employer will succeed in this **business necessity** defense.

Bona Fide Occupational Qualification

BONA FIDE OCCUPATIONAL QUALIFICATION (BFOQ)
Identifiable characteristics reasonably necessary to the normal operation of a particular business. These characteristics can include gender, national origin, and religion, but not race.

Another defense applies when discrimination against a protected class is essential to a job—that is, when a particular trait is a **bona fide occupational qualification (BFOQ)**. For example, a men's fashion magazine might legitimately hire only male models. Similarly, the Federal Aviation Administration can legitimately impose age limits for airline pilots. Race, however, can never be a BFOQ. Generally, courts have restricted the BFOQ defense to instances in which the employee's gender is essential to the job. In 1991, the United States Supreme Court held that even a fetal-protection policy that was adopted to protect the unborn children of female employees from the harmful effects of exposure to lead was an unacceptable BFOQ.[18]

Seniority Systems

SENIORITY SYSTEM
In regard to employment relationships, a system in which those who have worked longest for the company are first in line for promotions, salary increases, and other benefits; they are also the last to be laid off if the work force must be reduced.

An employer with a history of discrimination may have no members of protected classes in upper-level positions. Even if the employer now seeks to be unbiased, it may face a lawsuit seeking an order that minorities be promoted ahead of schedule to compensate for past discrimination. If no present intent to discriminate is shown, and promotions or other job benefits are distributed according to a fair **seniority system** (in which workers with more years of service are promoted first, or laid off last), however, the employer has a good defense against the suit.

After-Acquired Evidence Is No Defense

In some situations, employers have attempted to avoid liability for employment discrimination on the basis of "after-acquired evidence" of an employee's misconduct. For example, suppose that an employer fires a worker, and the employee sues the

---

18. *United Auto Workers v. Johnson Controls, Inc.,* 113 U.S. 158, 111 S.Ct. 1196, 113 L.Ed.2d 158 (1991). (This case is presented in Chapter 4 as Case 4.1.)

employer for employment discrimination. During pretrial investigation, the employer learns that the employee made material misrepresentations on his or her employment application — misrepresentations that, had the employer known about them, would have served as a ground to fire the individual. Can this after-acquired evidence be used as a defense?

The United States Supreme Court addressed this question in *McKennon v. Nashville Banner Publishing Co.*,[19] a case decided in 1995. The Court stated that both Title VII and the ADEA share a common purpose: "the elimination of discrimination in the workplace." The Court held that allowing employers to avoid liability for discrimination on the basis of after-acquired evidence did "not accord" with this purpose. After-acquired evidence of wrongdoing should not operate, "in every instance, to bar all relief for an earlier violation of the Act." Since this decision, the courts have generally held that after-acquired evidence cannot be used to shield employers from liability for employment discrimination, although it may be a factor in determining the amount of damages awarded to plaintiffs.

▌Affirmative Action

Federal statutes and regulations providing for equal opportunity in the workplace were designed to reduce or eliminate discriminatory practices with respect to hiring, retaining, and promoting employees. **Affirmative action** programs go a step further and attempt to "make up" for past patterns of discrimination by giving members of protected classes preferential treatment in hiring or promotion.

Affirmative action programs have caused much controversy, particularly when they result in what is frequently called "reverse discrimination" — discrimination against "majority" workers, such as white males (or discrimination against other minority groups that may not be given preferential treatment under a particular affirmative action program). At issue is whether affirmative action programs, because of their inherently discriminatory nature, violate the equal protection clause of the Fourteenth Amendment to the Constitution.

AFFIRMATIVE ACTION
Job-hiring policies that give special consideration to members of protected classes in an effort to overcome present effects of past discrimination.

The *Bakke* Case

An early case addressing this issue, *Regents of the University of California v. Bakke*,[20] involved an affirmative action program implemented by the University of California at Davis. Allan Bakke, who had been turned down for medical school at the Davis campus, sued the university for reverse discrimination after he discovered that his academic record was better than those of some of the minority applicants who had been admitted to the program.

The United States Supreme Court held that affirmative action programs were subject to "intermediate scrutiny." Recall from the discussion of the equal protection clause in Chapter 2 that any law or action evaluated under a standard of intermediate scrutiny, to be constitutionally valid, must be substantially related to important government objectives. Applying this standard, the Court held that the university could give favorable weight to minority applicants as part of a plan to increase minority enrollment so as to achieve a more culturally diverse student body. The Court stated, however, that the use of a quota system, in which a certain number of places is explicitly reserved for minority applicants, violated the equal protection clause of the Fourteenth Amendment.

---

19. ___ U.S.___, 115 S.Ct. 879, 130 L.Ed.2d 852 (1995).
20. 438 U.S. 265, 98 S.Ct. 2733, 57 L.Ed.2d 750 (1978).

The *Adarand* Case and Subsequent Developments

Although the *Bakke* case and later court decisions alleviated the harshness of the quota system, today's courts are going even further in questioning the constitutional validity of affirmative action programs. For example, in *Adarand Constructors, Inc. v. Peña*,[21] the plaintiff (Adarand Constructors, Inc.) was not awarded a federal highway construction project even though it had submitted the lowest bid. Instead, the project went to an Hispanic-owned firm pursuant to a federal program designed to give at least 5 percent of highway construction projects to disadvantaged business enterprises. Adarand sued Federico Peña, the secretary of the Transportation Department, alleging that the federal program violated the equal protection clause.

The Supreme Court held that any federal, state, or local affirmative action program that uses racial or ethnic classifications as the basis for making decisions is subject to "strict scrutiny" by the courts. As discussed in Chapter 2, under a strict-scrutiny analysis, to be constitutional, a discriminatory law or action must be narrowly tailored to meet a *compelling* government interest. In effect, the Court's opinion in *Adarand* means that an affirmative action program cannot make use of quotas or preferences for unqualified persons, and once the program has succeeded, it must be changed or dropped.

Since the *Adarand* decision, the lower courts have followed the Supreme Court's lead in subjecting affirmative action programs to strict scrutiny. In several cases, the lower courts have held that the affirmative action programs being challenged do violate the equal protection clause. The first federal appellate ruling on the issue, in *Hopwood v. State of Texas*,[22] involved two white law-school applicants who sued the University of Texas School of Law in Austin, alleging that they were denied admission because of the school's affirmative action program. The program allowed admitting officials to take racial and other factors into consideration when determining which students would be admitted. The Court of Appeals for the Fifth Circuit held that the program violated the equal protection clause because it discriminated in favor of minority applicants. Significantly, the court directly challenged the *Bakke* decision by stating that the use of race even as a means of achieving diversity on college campuses "undercuts the Fourteenth Amendment." Although these decisions do not directly relate to affirmative action programs in the employment context, clearly they indicate a trend that will affect employers' affirmative action programs as well.

---

21.   ___U.S.___, 115 S.Ct. 2097, 132 L.Ed.2d 158 (1995).
22.   84 F.3d. 720 (5th Cir. 1996).

> REMEMBER The Fourteenth Amendment prohibits any state from denying any person "the equal protection of the laws." This prohibition applies to the *federal* government through the due process clause of the Fifth Amendment.

International Perspective

Affirmative action programs are under attack not only in the United States but also in Europe. In 1995, the European Court of Justice delivered a landmark ruling on government-imposed affirmative action programs that give women preference in jobs and promotions. The rulings of the court, which is located in Luxembourg, are not necessarily binding on the fifteen member nations of the European Union (EU), but the court's ruling in this case is likely to have significant implications for affirmative action programs throughout the EU.

The case was brought by Eckhard Kalanke, a landscaper who works for the Parks Department in the city of Bremen, Germany. Kalanke alleged that a promotion he sought was given to a woman because of an affirmative action law requiring public agencies to give preference to qualified women for positions in which women were underrepresented. When the case reached the European Court of Justice, the court held that the Bremen affirmative action policy violated a 1976 directive of the European Economic Community (EEC), which has since become the EU. The directive barred "discrimination on the grounds of sex either directly or indirectly." The

International Perspective—Continued

court concluded that although the 1976 directive allows countries to remove barriers to employment opportunities for women, the Bremen program went too far. The court stated that "[n]ational rules which guarantee women absolute and unconditional priority for appointment or promotion go beyond promoting equal opportunities and overstep the limits of EU law."**a**

For Critical Analysis: *How can the goal of equal employment opportunities for women be achieved without affirmative action programs?*

a. *The New York Times International,* October 18, 1995, p. A11.

▌ State Statutes

Although the focus of this chapter is on federal legislation, most states also have statutes that prohibit employment discrimination. Generally, the kinds of discrimination prohibited under federal legislation are also prohibited by state laws. In addition, state statutes often provide protection for certain individuals, such as homosexuals, who are not protected under Title VII. Furthermore, state laws prohibiting discrimination may provide additional damages, such as damages for emotional distress, that are not provided for under Title VII.

One of the problems faced by employees of very small business firms is that they may have no cause of action for discrimination under federal statutes (because the statutes apply only to firms with a specified number of employees). Some state statutes have similar requirements. In California, for example, the state employment antidiscrimination statute—the Fair Employment and Housing Act—applies only to employers with five or more employees. Many small businesses, like the medical office in the following case, employ less than five people.

CASE 33.5

BADIH v. MYERS

California Court of Appeal,
First District, Division 1, 1995.
36 Cal.App.4th 1289,
43 Cal.Rptr.2d 229.

HISTORICAL AND SOCIAL SETTING *The number of divorces—and single-parent families—increased dramatically between 1970 and 1980. Since 1990, however, these numbers have decreased, and the number of two-parent families with children has risen by almost 800,000. The U.S. marriage rate is the highest in the industrialized world. Despite these numbers, factors that undercut the stability of a traditional family still exist.*

FACTS Fatmeh Badih was a medical assistant for Dr. Leonard Myers. When Badih married her boyfriend and became pregnant, Myers fired her. Badih filed a suit in a

California state court against Myers, alleging in part discrimination on the basis of pregnancy in violation of public policy. The court awarded Badih damages. Myers appealed, asserting that he was not subject to any state law prohibiting discrimination in employment on the basis of pregnancy. Badih argued that pregnancy discrimination in employment is a form of sex discrimination prohibited by the California Constitution, which states that "[a] person may not be disqualified from * * * employment because of sex."

ISSUE Is pregnancy discrimination a form of sex discrimination under the California Constitution?

DECISION Yes. The state appellate court affirmed the lower court's decision.

REASON The court agreed with Badih that the state constitution "expresses a fundamental public policy against sex discrimination in employment." The court

(Continued)

Case 33.5—Continued

reasoned that, although there were no cases interpreting this provision of the state constitution, federal and state laws "strongly support the notion that pregnancy discrimination in employment should be treated as a form of sex discrimination." In the context of the state constitu-tion, "there is no reason why a different definition of sex discrimination should be applied."

FOR CRITICAL ANALYSIS—Political Consideration
Why are state antidiscrimination laws necessary?

Application

Law and the Employer— Interviewing Workers with Disabilities*

 Many employers have been held liable under the Americans with Disabilities Act (ADA) of 1990 simply because they asked the wrong questions when interviewing job applicants with disabilities. If you are an employer, you can do several things to avoid violating the ADA.

As a preliminary matter, you should familiarize your-self with the EEOC's "final rules" on how the ADA's pro-visions should be applied. These rules, which were issued in 1995, replace the EEOC's interim rules that were issued shortly after the ADA was enacted. The final rules indicate the kinds of questions that employers cur-rently may—and may not—ask job applicants with dis-abilities. Often, the line between permissible and impermissible questions is a fine one. Consider these examples:

• *Ability to perform the job*: As an employer, you may ask a job applicant, "Can you do the job?" You may also ask whether the applicant can perform specific tasks related to the job. You may not ask the candidate, "How would you do the job?"—*unless* the disability is obvious, the applicant brings up the subject during the interview, or you ask the question of all applicants.
• *Absenteeism*: You may ask, "Can you meet our atten-dance requirements?" or "How many days were you absent last year?" You may not ask, "How many days were you sick last year?"
• *Drug use*: Generally, employers may ask about the current or past use of illegal drugs but not about drug addiction. Therefore, as an employer, you may ask,

"Have you ever used illegal drugs?" or "Have you done so in the last six months?" You may not ask, "How often did you use illegal drugs?" or "Have you been treated for drug abuse?"
• *Alcohol use*: Generally, employers may ask about a candidate's drinking habits but not about alcoholism. Therefore, you may ask, "Do you drink alcohol?" or "Have you been arrested for driving while intoxicated?" but you may not ask, "How often do you drink?"
• *History of job-related injuries*: Employers may not ask a job candidate with a disability any questions about the applicant's previous job-related injuries or about work-ers' compensation claims submitted in the past.

Once you have made a job offer, however, you may ask the applicant questions concerning his or her dis-ability, including questions about previous workers' com-pensation claims or about the extent of a drinking problem. You may also ask for medical documents veri-fying the nature of the applicant's disability. Generally, though, you should ask such questions only if you ask them of all applicants or if they are follow-up questions concerning the applicant's disability that he or she already disclosed during a job interview.

To avoid liability under the ADA, the wisest thing you can do is consult with an attorney. You should inform the attorney of the kinds of questions you typi-cally ask job applicants during interviews or following employment offers. Then, you should work with the attorney in modifying these questions so that they are consistent with the EEOC's final rules on permissible and impermissible questions. Finally, you should make sure that anyone on your staff who interviews job appli-cants receives thorough instructions on what questions may and may not be asked of candidates with disabilities. You might also remind your staff that under the ADA, the words and phraseology the interviewer uses may result in a violation of the ADA regardless of the inter-viewer's intentions.

*This *Application* is not meant to substitute for the services of an attorney who is licensed to practice law in your state.

Application—Continued

 Checklist for the Employer

1. Familiarize yourself with the EEOC's final rules indicating what questions are and are not permissible while interviewing job applicants with disabilities.
2. Work with an attorney to create a list of particular types of questions that are or are not permissible

under the EEOC's rules in respect to job candidates with disabilities.

3. Make sure that everyone in your firm who interviews job applicants is thoroughly instructed as to the types of questions that they may and may not ask when interviewing job applicants with disabilities.

▮ Key Terms

affirmative action 869
bona fide occupational
    qualification (BFOQ) 868
business necessity 868

disparate-impact
    discrimination 854
disparate-treatment
    discrimination 853

employment discrimination 853
prima facie case 853
seniority system 868
sexual harassment 856

▮ Chapter Summary: Employment Discrimination

Title VII of the Civil Rights Act of 1964 (*See pages 853–860.*)	Title VII prohibits employment discrimination based on race, color, national origin, religion, or gender. 1. *Procedures*—Employees must file a claim with the Equal Employment Opportunity Commission (EEOC). The EEOC may sue the employer on the employee's behalf; if not, the employee may sue the employer directly. 2. *Intentional versus unintentional discrimination*—Title VII prohibits both intentional (disparate-treatment) and unintentional (disparate-impact) discrimination. Disparate-impact discrimination occurs when an employer's practice, such as hiring only persons with a certain level of education, has the effect of discriminating against a class of persons protected by Title VII. 3. *Remedies for discrimination under Title VII*—If a plaintiff proves that unlawful discrimination occurred, he or she may be awarded reinstatement, back pay, and retroactive promotions. Damages (both compensatory and punitive) may be awarded for intentional discrimination.
Discrimination Based on Age (*See pages 861–863.*)	The Age Discrimination in Employment Act (ADEA) of 1967 prohibits employment discrimination on the basis of age against individuals forty years of age or older. Procedures for bringing a case under the ADEA are similar to those for bringing a case under Title VII.
Discrimination Based on Disability (*See pages 863–867.*)	The Americans with Disabilities Act (ADA) of 1990 prohibits employment discrimination against persons with disabilities who are otherwise qualified to perform the essential functions of the jobs for which they apply. 1. *Procedures and remedies*—To prevail on a claim under the ADA, the plaintiff must show that he or she has a disability, is otherwise qualified for the employment in question, and was excluded from the employment solely because of the disability. Procedures under the ADA are similar to those required in Title VII cases; remedies are also similar to those under Title VII. 2. *Definition of disability*—The ADA defines the term *disability* as a physical or mental impairment that substantially limits one or more major life activities; a record of such impairment; or being regarded as having such an impairment. 3. *Reasonable accommodation*—Employers are required to reasonably accommodate the needs of persons with disabilities. Reasonable accommodations may include altering job-application *(Continued)*

▌Chapter Summary: Employment Discrimination—Continued

Discrimination Based on Disability— Continued	procedures, modifying the physical work environment, and permitting more flexible work schedules. Employers are not required to accommodate the needs of all workers with disabilities. For example, employers need not accommodate workers who pose a definite threat to health and safety in the workplace or those who are not otherwise qualified for their jobs.
Defenses to Employment Discrimination *(See pages 867–869.)*	If a plaintiff proves that employment discrimination occurred, employers may avoid liability by successfully asserting certain defenses. Employers may assert that the discrimination was required for reasons of business necessity, to meet a bona fide occupational qualification, or to maintain a legitimate seniority system. Evidence of prior employee misconduct acquired after the employee has been fired is not a defense to discrimination.
Affirmative Action *(See pages 869–871.)*	Affirmative action programs attempt to "make up" for past patterns of discrimination by giving members of protected classes preferential treatment in hiring or promotion. Increasingly, such programs are being strictly scrutinized by the courts.
State Statutes *(See pages 871–872.)*	Generally, the kinds of discrimination prohibited by federal statutes are also prohibited by state laws. State laws may provide for more extensive protection and remedies than federal laws.

▌For Review

1.   Generally, what kind of conduct is prohibited by Title VII of the Civil Rights Act of 1964, as amended?

2.   What is the difference between disparate-treatment discrimination and disparate-impact discrimination?

3.   What remedies are available under Title VII of the 1964 Civil Rights Act, as amended?

4.   What federal acts prohibit discrimination based on age and discrimination based on disability?

5.   Name three defenses to claims of employment discrimination.

▌Questions and Case Problems

33–1. Title VII Violations. Discuss fully whether any of the following actions would constitute a violation of Title VII of the 1964 Civil Rights Act, as amended:

   (a)   Tennington, Inc., is a consulting firm and has ten employees. These employees travel on consulting jobs in seven states. Tennington has an employment record of hiring only white males.

   (b)   Novo Films, Inc., is making a film about Africa and needs to employ approximately one hundred extras for this picture. Novo advertises in all major newspapers in southern California for the hiring of these extras. The ad states that only African Americans need apply.

33–2. Discrimination Based on Age. Tavo Jones had worked since 1974 for Westshore Resort, where he maintained golf carts. During the first decade, he received positive job evaluations and numerous merit pay raises. He was promoted to the position of supervisor of golf-cart maintenance at three courses. Then a new employee, Ben Olery, was placed in charge of the golf courses. He demoted Jones, who was over the age of forty, to running only one of the three cart facilities, and he froze Jones's salary indefinitely. Olery also demoted five other men over the age of forty. Another cart facility was placed under the supervision of Blake Blair. Later, the cart facilities for the three

courses were again consolidated, but Blair—not Jones—was put in charge. At the time, Jones was still in his forties, and Blair was in his twenties. Jones overheard Blair say that "we are going to have to do away with these . . . old and senile" men. Jones quit and sued Westshore for employment discrimination. Should he prevail? Explain.

33–3. Disparate-Impact Discrimination. Several African American employees of the Connecticut Department of Income Maintenance who sought promotion to supervisory positions took the required written examination but failed to pass it. Of all who took the examination, 54 percent of the African American employees passed it, whereas nearly 80 percent of the white employees passed. Following the examination, the state of Connecticut promoted eleven African Americans (representing 23 percent of all African American employees) and thirty-five white employees (representing 14 percent of all white employees). Teal and three other African American employees who failed the test sued the state of Connecticut and the Department of Income Maintenance. The employees asserted that the written test excluded a disproportionate number of African American employees from promotion to supervisory positions and therefore violated Title VII of the Civil Rights Act. The state argued that because a greater percentage of African American employees had been promoted, relative to white employees, the test was not discriminatory. Which party was correct?

33–4. Disparate-Impact Discrimination. Chinawa, a major processor of cheese sold throughout the United States, employs one hundred workers at its principal processing plant. The plant is located in Heartland Corners, which has a population that is 50 percent white and 25 percent African American, with the balance Hispanic American, Asian American, and others. Chinawa requires a high school diploma as a condition of employment for its cleaning crew. Three-fourths of the white population complete high school, compared with only one-fourth of those in the minority groups. Chinawa has an all-white cleaning crew. Has Chinawa violated Title VII of the Civil Rights Act of 1964? Explain.

33–5. Discrimination Based on Gender. Beginning in June 1966, Corning Glass Works started to open up jobs on the night shift to women. The previously separate male and female seniority lists were consolidated, and the women became eligible to exercise their seniority on the same basis as men and to bid for higher-paid night inspection jobs as vacancies occurred. On January 20, 1969, however, a new collective bargaining agreement went into effect; it established a new job evaluation system for setting wage rates. This agreement abolished (for the future) separate base wages for night-shift and day-shift inspectors and imposed a uniform base wage for inspectors that exceeded the wage rate previously in effect for the night shift. The agreement, though, did allow for a higher "red circle" rate for employees hired prior to January 20, 1969, when they were working as inspectors on the night shift. This "red circle" wage served essentially to perpetuate the differential in base wages between day and night inspectors. Had Corning violated Title VII of the Civil Rights Act of 1964? Discuss. [*Corning Glass Works v. Brennan*, 417 U.S. 188, 94 S.Ct. 2223, 41 L.Ed.2d 1 (1974)]

33–6. Burden of Proof. Melvin Hicks, an African American, was a shift supervisor at St. Mary's Honor Center, a halfway house operated by the Missouri Department of Corrections and Human Resources. After being demoted and eventually terminated from his job, Hicks brought an action under Title VII, alleging racial discrimination. Hicks successfully presented a *prima facie* case: he was a member of a protected class, he was qualified for the job of shift commander, he was demoted and then discharged, and the position he vacated was filled by a white man. St. Mary's Honor Center asserted that it had demoted and fired Hicks for legitimate, nondiscriminatory reasons—Hicks had violated procedures and threatened his supervisor. The district court found the claims to be a mere pretext (a fabricated reason for dismissing Hicks). The court nonetheless held for the center, because Hicks had failed to prove that the center's actions were motivated by any racial bias—in other words, Hicks had not been discriminated against on the basis of race, as he had contended. The appellate court reversed, holding that once the district court had found that the center's reasons were pretextual, Hicks was entitled to judgment as a matter of law. The case was appealed to the United States Supreme Court. Discuss how the Supreme Court should decide this case, and why. [*St. Mary's Honor Center v. Hicks*, 509 U.S. 502, 113 S.Ct. 2742, 125 L.Ed.2d 407 (1993)]

33–7. Defenses to Employment Discrimination. Dorothea O'Driscoll had worked as a quality control inspector for Hercules, Inc., for six years when her employment was terminated in 1986. O'Driscoll, who was over forty years of age, sued Hercules for age discrimination in violation of the Age Discrimination in Employment Act of 1967. While preparing for trial, Hercules discovered evidence of misconduct on the part of O'Driscoll that it had been unaware of when it terminated her employment. Among other things, Hercules learned that O'Driscoll had misrepresented her age on both her employment application and her application for a government security clearance (necessary to handle confidential information). She also did not disclose a previous employer, falsely represented that she had never applied for work with Hercules before, and falsely stated that she had completed two quarters of study at a technical college. Additionally, on her application for group insurance coverage, she misrepresented the age of her son, who would otherwise have been ineligible for coverage as her dependent. Hercules defended against O'Driscoll's claim of age discrimination by stating that had it known of this misconduct, it would have terminated her employment anyway. What should the court decide? Discuss fully. [*O'Driscoll v. Hercules, Inc.*, 12 F.3d 176 (10th Cir. 1994)]

33–8. Discrimination Based on National Origin. Phanna Xieng was sent by the Cambodian government to the United States in 1974 for "advanced military training." When the Cambodian government fell in 1975, Xieng remained in the United States and eventually was employed by Peoples National Bank of Washington in 1979. In performance appraisals from 1980 through 1985, Xieng was rated by his supervisors as "capable of dealing effectively with customers" and qualified for promotion, although in each appraisal it was noted that Xieng might improve his communication skills to maximize his possibilities for future advancement. Xieng sought job promotions on numerous occasions but was never promoted. In 1986, he filed a complaint against the bank, alleging employment discrimination based on national origin. The employer argued that its refusal to promote Xieng because of his accent or communication skills did not amount to discrimination based on national origin. Is it possible to separate discrimination based on an employee's accent and communication skills from discrimination based on national origin? How should the court rule on this issue? [*Xieng v. Peoples National Bank of Washington*, 120 Wash.2d 512, 844 P.2d 389 (1993)]

33–9. Disparate-Impact Discrimination. Local 1066 of the Steamship Clerks Union accepted only new members who were sponsored by existing members. All of the existing members were white. During a six-year period, the local admitted thirty new members, all of whom were relatives of present members and also white. The Equal Employment Opportunity Commission filed a suit in a federal district court against the union, alleging that this practice constituted disparate-impact discrimination under Title VII. The union argued that it was only continuing a family tradition. What does each party have to prove to win its case? Should the union be required to change its practice? [*EEOC v. Steamship Clerks Union, Local 1066*, 48 F.3d 594 (1st Cir. 1995)]

33–10. Discrimination Based on Disability. When the University of Maryland Medical System Corp. learned that one of its surgeons was HIV positive, the university offered him transfers to positions that did not involve surgery. The surgeon refused, and the university terminated him. The surgeon filed a suit in a federal district court against the university, alleging in part a violation of the Americans with Disabilities Act. The surgeon claimed that he was "otherwise qualified" for his former position. What does he have to prove to win his case? Should he be reinstated? [*Doe v. University of Maryland Medical System Corp.*, 50 F.3d 1261 (4th Cir. 1995)]

A QUESTION OF ETHICS AND SOCIAL RESPONSIBILITY

33–11. *Luz Long and three other Hispanic employees (the plaintiffs) worked as bank tellers for the Culmore branch of the First Union Corp. of Virginia. The plaintiffs often conversed with one another in Spanish, their native language. In 1992, the Culmore branch manager adopted an "English-only" policy, which required all employees to speak English during working hours unless they had to speak another language to assist customers. The plaintiffs refused to cooperate with the new policy and were eventually fired. In a suit against the bank, the plaintiffs alleged that the English-only policy discriminated against them on the basis of their national origin. The court granted the bank's motion for summary judgment, concluding that "[t]here is nothing in Title VII which . . . provides that an employee has a right to speak his or her native tongue while on the job." [Long v. First Union Corp. of Virginia, 894 F.Supp. 933 (E.D.Va. 1995)]*

1. The bank argued that the policy was implemented in response to complaints made by fellow employees that the Spanish-speaking employees were creating a hostile environment by speaking Spanish among themselves in the presence of other employees. From an ethical perspective, is this a sufficient reason to institute an English-only policy?
2. Is it ever ethically justifiable for employers to deny bilingual employees the opportunity to speak their native language while on the job?
3. Might there be situations in which English-only policies are necessary to promote worker health and safety?
4. Generally, what are the pros and cons of English-only policies in the workplace?

FOR CRITICAL ANALYSIS

33–12. *The Equal Employment Opportunity Commission (EEOC) decided, pursuant to its "National Employment Policy" of 1996, not to investigate every complaint of discrimination, as it once did. In the same policy statement, the EEOC stated that it will place more emphasis on the mediation and arbitration of employee-employer disputes. Who will benefit more from this policy, employers or employees?*

▌Unit Eight—Cumulative Hypothetical Problem

33–13. *Falwell Motors, Inc., is a large corporation that manufactures automobile batteries.*

1. Falwell faces stiff competition from Alchem, Inc., another battery manufacturer. To acquire control over Alchem, Falwell makes a tender offer to Alchem's shareholders. If Falwell succeeds in its attempt and Alchem is merged into Falwell, will the merger violate any antitrust laws? Suppose that the merger falls through. The vice president of Falwell's battery division and the president of Alchem agree to divide up the market between them, so they will not have to compete for customers. Is this agreement legal? Explain.
2. The Federal Trade Commission (FTC) has learned that one of the retail stores that sells Falwell's batteries has engaged in deceptive advertising practices. What actions can the FTC take against the retailer?
3. For years, Falwell has shipped the toxic waste created by its manufacturing process to a waste-disposal site in the next county. The waste site became contaminated by leakage from toxic waste containers delivered to the site by other manufacturers. Can Falwell be held liable for clean-up costs, even though its containers were not the ones that leaked? If so, what is the extent of its liability?
4. One day Gina, a Falwell employee, suffered a serious burn when she accidentally spilled some acid on her hand. The accident occurred because another employee, who was suspected of using illegal drugs, carelessly

bumped into her. The hand required a series of skin-grafting operations before it healed sufficiently to allow Gina to return to work. Can Gina obtain compensation for her lost wages and medical expenses? If so, how? After the accident, Falwell decides to conduct random drug tests on all of its employees. Several employees claim that the testing violates their privacy rights. If the dispute is litigated, what factors will the court consider in deciding whether the random drug testing is legally permissible?
5. Aretha, a Falwell employee, is disgusted by the sexually offensive behavior of several male employees. She has complained to her supervisor on several occasions about the offensive behavior, but the supervisor merely laughs at her concerns. Aretha decides to bring a legal action against the company for sexual harassment. Does Aretha's complaint concern *quid-pro-quo* harassment or hostile-environment harassment? What federal statute protects employees from sexual harassment? What remedies are available under that statute? What procedures must Aretha follow in pursuing her legal action?

▌Accessing the Internet: Business Law and Legal Environment
....

The U.S. Department of Labor is on the Internet at

**gopher://marvel.loc.gov:70/11/federal/
fedinfo/byagency/executive/labor**

The Legal Information Institute at Cornell Law School provides introductions to various labor and employment topics at

http://fatty.law.cornell.edu/topics/topics2.html#employment_law

You can visit the 'Lectric Law Library Web site concerning law and employment at

http://www.inter=law.com/temp.html

The most information available about discrimination with respect to disabilities is included in the Americans with Disabilities Act document center at

http://janweb.icdi.wvu.edu./kinder

Additional information on the Americans with Disabilities Act is available via the U.S. Department of Justice, Civil Rights Division, at

gopher://justice2.usdoj.gov/11/crt

For perspectives on sexual harassment court opinions, go to the following Web site:

http://www.vix.com/pub/men/harass/harass.html

Unit NINE

Property and Its Protection

UNIT OUTLINE

Chapter 34

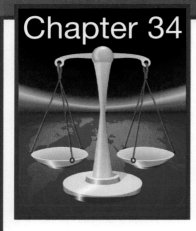

Personal Property and Bailments

PROPERTY
Legally protected rights and interests in anything with an ascertainable value that is subject to ownership.

REAL PROPERTY
Land and everything attached to it, such as foliage and buildings.

PERSONAL PROPERTY
Property that is movable; any property that is not real property.

CHATTEL
All forms of personal property.

"The great and chief end . . . of men united into commonwealths, and putting themselves under government, is the preservation of their property."

John Locke, 1632–1704
(English political philosopher)

CHAPTER OBJECTIVES

After reading this chapter, you should be able to:

1. Distinguish between personal property and real property.
2. Discuss different types of property ownership and the ways in which property can be acquired.
3. Identify who has rights to mislaid, lost, or abandoned property.
4. List the elements of a bailment.
5. Outline the rights and duties of a bailee and a bailor.

Property consists of the legally protected rights and interests a person has in anything with an ascertainable value that is subject to ownership. Property would have little value (and the word would have little meaning) if the law did not define the right to use it, to sell or dispose of it, and to prevent trespass on it. In the United States, the ownership of property receives unique protection under the law. The Bill of Rights states that "no person shall . . . be deprived of life, liberty, or property, without due process of law; nor shall private property be taken for public use, without just compensation." The Fourteenth Amendment provides that "no State shall . . . deprive any person of life, liberty, or property, without due process of law." Indeed, John Locke, as indicated in the opening quotation, considered the preservation of property to be the primary reason for the establishment of government.

Property is divided into real property and personal property. **Real property** (sometimes called *realty* or *real estate*) means the land and everything permanently attached to it. Everything else is **personal property,** or *personalty*. Attorneys sometimes refer to personal property as **chattel,** a term used under the common law to denote all forms of personal property. Personal property can be tangible or intangible. *Tangible* personal property, such as a TV set or a car, has physical substance. *Intangible* personal property represents some set of rights and interests but has no real physical existence. Stocks and bonds, patents, and copyrights are examples of intangible personal property.

In the first part of this chapter, we look at the ways in which title to property is held; the methods of acquiring ownership of personal property; and issues relating to mislaid, lost, and abandoned personal property. In the second part of the chapter, we examine bailment relationships. A **bailment** is created when personal property is temporarily delivered into the care of another without a transfer of title. This is the distinguishing characteristic of a bailment compared with a sale or a gift—there is no passage of title and no intent to transfer title.

▌Property Ownership

Property ownership[1] can be viewed as a bundle of rights, including the right to possess property and to dispose of it—by sale, gift, lease, or other means.

Fee Simple

A person who holds the entire bundle of rights to property is said to be the owner in **fee simple.** The owner in fee simple is entitled to use, possess, or dispose of the property as he or she chooses during his or her lifetime, and on this owner's death, the interests in the property descend to his or her heirs. We will return to this form of property ownership in Chapter 35, in the context of ownership rights in real property.

Concurrent Ownership

Persons who share ownership rights simultaneously in a particular piece of property are said to be *concurrent* owners. There are two principal types of concurrent ownership: tenancy in common and joint tenancy. Other types of concurrent ownership include tenancy by the entirety and community property.

TENANCY IN COMMON   The term **tenancy in common** refers to a form of co-ownership in which each of two or more persons owns an undivided interest in the property. The interest is *undivided* because each tenant has rights in the *whole* property. For example, Rosa and Chad own a rare-stamp collection as tenants in common. This does not mean that Rosa owns some particular stamps and Chad others. Rather, it means that Rosa and Chad each have rights in the entire collection. (If Rosa owned some stamps and Chad owned others, then the interest would be *divided.*)

On the death of a tenant in common, that tenant's interest in the property passes to his or her heirs. For example, should Rosa die before Chad, a one-half interest in the stamp collection would become the property of Rosa's heirs. If Rosa sold her interest to Fred before she died, Fred and Chad would be co-owners as tenants in common. If Fred died, his interest in the personal property would pass to his heirs, and they in turn would own the property with Chad as tenants in common.

JOINT TENANCY   In a **joint tenancy,** each of two or more persons owns an undivided interest in the property, and a deceased joint tenant's interest passes to the surviving joint tenant or tenants. The rights of a surviving joint tenant to inherit a deceased joint tenant's ownership interest, which are referred to as *survivorship rights,* distinguish the joint tenancy from the tenancy in common. A joint tenancy can be terminated before a joint tenant's death by gift or by sale, in which situation the person who received the

---

1. The principles discussed in this section apply equally to real property ownership, which is discussed in Chapter 35.

BAILMENT
A situation in which the personal property of one person (a bailor) is entrusted to another (a bailee), who is obligated to return the bailed property to the bailor or dispose of it as directed.

FEE SIMPLE
An absolute form of property ownership entitling the property owner to use, possess, or dispose of the property as he or she chooses during his or her lifetime. Upon death, the interest in the property descends to the owner's heirs.

TENANCY IN COMMON
Co-ownership of property in which each party owns an undivided interest that passes to his or her heirs at death.

JOINT TENANCY
The joint ownership of property by two or more co-owners of property in which each co-owner owns an undivided portion of the property. Upon the death of one of the joint tenants, his or her interest automatically passes to the surviving joint tenants.

property as a gift or who purchased the property would become a tenant in common, not a joint tenant.

To illustrate: In the preceding example, if Rosa and Chad held their stamp collection in a joint tenancy and if Rosa died before Chad, the entire collection would become the property of Chad; Rosa's heirs would receive absolutely no interest in the collection. If Rosa, while living, sold her interest to Fred, however, the sale would terminate the joint tenancy, and Fred and Chad would become owners as tenants in common.

International Perspective

Islamic law, which is followed in Muslim countries, makes no provision for joint tenancy with rights of survivorship. Instead, concurrent owners of property are normally regarded as tenants in common. In regard to survivorship rights, Islamic law provides that an owner can transfer no more than one-third of an estate by will. The rest of the estate must be inherited by those who are designated as legal heirs under Islamic law.

For Critical Analysis: *What policy considerations might motivate a government to restrict the transfer of property to legally designated heirs (such as spouses, children, and so on)?*

TENANCY BY THE ENTIRETY
The joint ownership of property by a husband and wife. Neither party can transfer his or her interest in the property without the consent of the other.

TENANCY BY THE ENTIRETY   Concurrent ownership of property can also take the form of a **tenancy by the entirety**—a form of co-ownership between a husband and wife that is similar to a joint tenancy, except that a spouse cannot transfer his or her interest during his or her lifetime without the consent of the other spouse.

COMMUNITY PROPERTY
A form of concurrent ownership of property in which each spouse technically owns an undivided one-half interest in property acquired during the marriage. This form of joint ownership occurs in only nine states and Puerto Rico.

COMMUNITY PROPERTY   When property is held as **community property**, each spouse technically owns an undivided one-half interest in property acquired during the marriage. The community property form of ownership occurs in only nine states and Puerto Rico.

▌Acquiring Ownership of Personal Property

The most common way of acquiring personal property is by purchasing it. We have already discussed the purchase and sale of personal property (goods) in Chapters 14 through 17. Often, property is acquired by will or inheritance, a topic we cover in Chapter 36. Here we look at additional ways in which ownership of personal property can be acquired, including acquisition by possession, production, gift, accession, and confusion.

"In no country in the world is the love of property more active and more anxious than in the United States."

Alexis de Tocqueville, 1805–1859
(French historian and statesman)

Possession

One example of acquiring ownership by possession is the capture of wild animals. Wild animals belong to no one in their natural state, and the first person to take possession of a wild animal normally owns it. The killing of a wild animal amounts to assuming ownership of it. Merely being in hot pursuit does not give title, however. There are two exceptions to this basic rule. First, any wild animals captured by a trespasser are the property of the landowner, not the trespasser. Second, if wild animals are captured or killed in violation of wild-game statutes, the capturer does not obtain title to the animals; rather, the state does.

Those who find lost or abandoned property also can acquire ownership rights through mere possession of the property, as will be discussed later in the chapter.

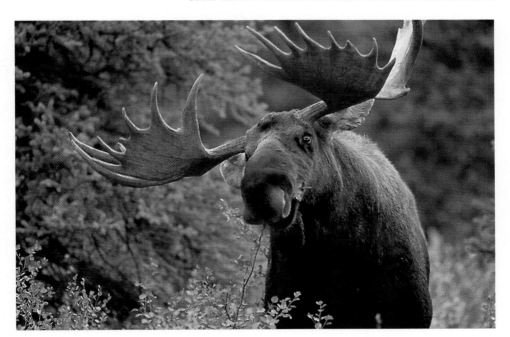

A moose stands in the woods. In its natural state, to whom does a wild animal belong?

(Ownership rights in real property can also be acquired through possession, such as adverse possession—see Chapter 35.)

Production

Production—the fruits of labor—is another means of acquiring ownership of personal property. For example, writers, inventors, and manufacturers all produce personal property and thereby acquire title to it. (In some situations—for example, when a researcher is hired to invent a new product or technique—the producer may not own what is produced, however.)

Gifts

A **gift** is another fairly common means of acquiring and transferring ownership of real and personal property. A gift is essentially a voluntary transfer of property ownership for which no consideration is given. As discussed in Chapter 9, the presence of consideration is what distinguishes a contract from a gift. Certain conditions must exist, however, before a gift will be deemed effective in the eyes of the law. The donor (the one making the gift) must intend to make the gift, the gift must be delivered to the donee (the recipient of the gift), and the donee must accept the gift. We examine each of these requirements here, as well as the requirements of a gift made in contemplation of imminent death.

GIFT
Any voluntary transfer of property made without consideration, past or present.

DONATIVE INTENT When a gift is challenged in court, the court will determine whether donative intent exists by looking at the surrounding circumstances. For example, the court may look at the relationship between the parties and the size of the gift in relation to the donor's other assets. A gift to a mortal enemy is viewed with suspicion. Similarly, when a gift represents a large portion of a person's assets, the courts scrutinize the transaction closely to determine the mental capacity of the donor and whether there is any element of fraud or duress present.

DELIVERY The gift must be delivered to the donee. An effective delivery requires giving up complete control and **dominion** (ownership rights) over the subject matter of

DOMINION
Ownership rights in property, including the right to possess and control the property.

the gift. Delivery is obvious in most cases. Suppose, though, that you want to make a gift of various old rare coins that you have stored in a safe-deposit box. You certainly cannot deliver the box itself to the donee, and you do not want to take the coins out of the bank. In such a situation, when the physical object cannot be delivered, a symbolic, or *constructive*, delivery will be sufficient. **Constructive delivery** is a general term for all those acts that the law holds to be equivalent to acts of real delivery. In the preceding example, the delivery of the key to the safe-deposit box constitutes a constructive delivery of the contents of the box. The delivery of intangible property—such as stocks, bonds, insurance policies, contracts, and so on—is always accomplished by symbolic, or constructive, delivery. This is because the documents represent rights and are not, by themselves, the true property.

CONSTRUCTIVE DELIVERY
An act equivalent to the actual, physical delivery of property that cannot be physically delivered because of difficulty or impossibility; for example, the transfer of a key to a safe constructively delivers the contents of the safe.

Delivery may be accomplished by means of a third party. If the third party is the agent of the donor, the delivery is effective when the agent delivers the gift to the donee. If the third party is the agent of the donee, then the gift is effectively delivered when the donor delivers the property to the donee's agent.[2] Naturally, no delivery is necessary if the gift is already in the hands of the donee.

In the following case, the court focused on the requirement that a donor must give up complete control and dominion over property given to the donee before a gift can be effectively delivered.

_____

2. *Bickford v. Mattocks*, 95 Me. 547, 50 A. 894 (1901).

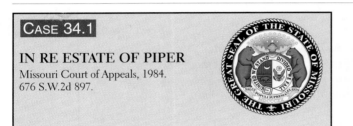

CASE 34.1

IN RE ESTATE OF PIPER
Missouri Court of Appeals, 1984.
676 S.W.2d 897.

HISTORICAL AND CULTURAL SETTING   *The rule that there must be a delivery for a gift to be valid originated at a time when handing over possession of an item was the only method of transferring it. The policy behind the rule is to protect alleged donors and their heirs from fraudulent claims based only on parol evidence. It is too easy for an alleged donee to claim that a gift was made when, in fact, it was not. For this reason, courts are wary of purported gifts that have not been delivered, except when the alleged donee is a member of the family.*

FACTS   Gladys Piper died intestate (without a will) in 1982. At her death, she owned miscellaneous personal property worth $5,000 and had in her purse $200 in cash and two diamond rings, known as the Andy Piper rings. The contents of her purse were taken by her niece Wanda Brown, allegedly to preserve them for the estate. Clara Kaufmann, a friend of Piper's, filed a claim against the estate for $4,800. From October 1974 until Piper's death, Kaufmann had taken Piper to the doctor, beauty shop, and grocery store; had written her checks

to pay her bills; and had helped her care for her home. Kaufmann maintained that Piper had promised to pay her for these services and had given her the diamond rings as a gift. A Missouri state trial court denied her request for payment; the court found that her services had been voluntary. Kaufmann then filed a petition for delivery of personal property, the rings, which was granted by the trial court. Brown, other heirs, and the administrator of Piper's estate appealed.

ISSUE   Had Gladys Piper made an effective gift of the rings to Clara Kaufmann?

DECISION   No. The state appellate court reversed the judgment of the trial court on the ground that Piper had never delivered the rings to Kaufmann.

REASON   Kaufmann claimed that the rings belonged to her by reason of a "consummated gift long prior to the death of Gladys Piper." Two witnesses testified for Kaufmann at the trial that Piper had told them the rings belonged to Kaufmann but that she was going to wear them until she died. The appellate court found "no evidence of any actual delivery." The court held that the essentials of a gift are (1) a present intention to make a gift on the part of the donor, (2) a delivery of the property by the donor to the donee, and (3) an acceptance by the donee. The evidence in the case showed only an intent to make a gift. Because there was no delivery—either actual or constructive—a valid gift was not made. For Piper to have made a gift, her intention would have

Case 34.1—Continued

to have been executed by the complete and unconditional delivery of the property or the delivery of a proper
written instrument evidencing the gift. As this did not
occur, the court found that there had been no gift.

FOR CRITICAL ANALYSIS—Social Consideration
*What could Piper have done to ensure that Kaufmann
received the rings on Piper's death?*

ACCEPTANCE   The final requirement of a valid gift is acceptance by the donee. This
rarely presents any problem, as most donees readily accept their gifts. The courts generally assume acceptance unless shown otherwise.

GIFTS *INTER VIVOS* AND GIFTS *CAUSA MORTIS*   Gifts *inter vivos* are gifts made during one's lifetime, whereas **gifts *causa mortis*** (so-called *deathbed gifts*) are made in
contemplation of imminent death. A gift *causa mortis* does not become absolute until
the donor dies from the contemplated illness, and it is automatically revoked if the
donor recovers from the illness. Moreover, the donee must survive to take the gift. To
be effective, a gift *causa mortis* must also meet the three requirements discussed earlier—donative intent, delivery, and acceptance by the donee. The question of whether
a gift *causa mortis* had been effectively delivered is at issue in the following case.

GIFT *INTER VIVOS*
A gift made during one's lifetime
and not in contemplation of
imminent death, in contrast to a
gift *causa mortis*.

GIFT *CAUSA MORTIS*
A gift made in contemplation of
death. If the donor does not die
of that ailment, the gift is
revoked.

CASE 34.2

KESTERSON v. CRONAN
Court of Appeals of Oregon, 1991.
105 Or.App. 551,
806 P.2d 134.

HISTORICAL AND ETHICAL SETTING   *Gifts* causa
mortis *were accepted by courts of equity before they
were accepted by courts of law. The basis for giving
effect to these gifts is a religious premise that a person
expresses his or her true feelings when facing death and
settles debts and disburses property to ease his or her
soul. Today, some of the religious basis may be evapo-
rating, and partly for this reason, gifts* causa mortis *are
not entirely favored by courts of law. Another reason for
the courts' disfavor of gifts* causa mortis *is that these gifts
defeat the purpose of the statutes that require specific
forms for the transfer of property at death. Additionally,
because the donor is no longer available to testify, the
donee may be tempted to commit fraud. For these and
other reasons, the delivery requirement is a particularly
important element of a gift* causa mortis.

FACTS   James Wilson, after learning that he had terminal
cancer, arranged for a friend, Harold Buell, to have joint
access to his safe-deposit box. Wilson gave Buell a key to
the box, which contained, among other things, a copy of a

promissory note for $65,000 from Michael Cronan. Wilson
told Buell that the debt represented by the note was to be
forgiven when he died and that on his (Wilson's) death,
Buell was to deliver the copy of the note to Cronan. After
Cronan had learned of Wilson's illness, Wilson told Cronan
on at least two occasions that Cronan's debt was to be forgiven on Wilson's death. In the meantime, Cronan continued to make payments on the note. On the day after Wilson
died, Buell delivered the copy of the note to Cronan, as
directed. Wilson's personal representative (a person
appointed to look after the deceased's affairs), Carol
Kesterson, brought an action in an Oregon state court to
recover from Cronan the balance owing on the $65,000
note, the original of which was found among Wilson's
personal effects after his death. Cronan claimed that the
debt had been forgiven, as a gift to Cronan. The trial
court held that the gift had not been adequately delivered prior to Wilson's death, and therefore Cronan was
liable on the debt. Cronan appealed.

ISSUE   Had Wilson effectively delivered the gift?

DECISION   No. The appellate court affirmed the trial
court's decision. Wilson's gift to Cronan—the forgiveness
of Cronan's debt—was never adequately delivered to
Cronan during Wilson's lifetime.

REASON   The court stated that "[f]or a gift of personal
property *   *   * to be valid, there must be a donative

(Continued)

Case 34.2—Continued

intent, coupled with the delivery of the subject of the gift to the donee with the intent that the donee have a present interest in it and an acceptance by the donee. * * * The one claiming a gift has the burden to prove the elements by clear and convincing evidence." Cronan argued that Wilson had delivered the copy of the note to Buell and that Buell was acting as Cronan's agent, but the court noted that the evidence did not support the finding that an agency relationship between Buell and Cronan existed. The court found "no evidence that [Cronan] knew that Buell had the key to the safe deposit box or that he had possession of the envelope" that contained the copy of the note, or even that Cronan had given instructions to Buell. Because Buell acted on Wilson's instructions and essentially served as Wilson's agent, the court found that there was no delivery of the note to Cronan before Wilson died.

FOR CRITICAL ANALYSIS—Ethical Consideration
Why does the law impose such strict legal requirements for a gift to be effective?

Accession

ACCESSION
Occurs when an individual adds value to personal property by either labor or materials. In some situations, a person may acquire ownership rights in another's property through accession.

Accession, which means "adding on" to something, occurs when someone adds value to an item of personal property by either labor or materials. Generally, there is no dispute about who owns the property after accession has occurred, especially when the accession is accomplished with the owner's consent. When accession occurs without the permission of the owner, the courts will tend to favor the owner over the improver—the one who improves the property—provided that the accession was wrongful and undertaken in bad faith. In addition, many courts will deny the improver any compensation for the value added; for example, a car thief who puts new tires on the stolen car will obviously not be compensated for the value of the new tires.

If the accession is performed in good faith, however, even without the owner's consent, ownership of the improved item most often depends on whether the accession has increased the value of the property or changed its identity. The greater the increase in value, the more likely it is that ownership will pass to the improver. If ownership so passes, the improver obviously must compensate the original owner for the value of the property prior to the accession. If the increase in value is not sufficient for ownership to pass to the improver, most courts will require the owner to compensate the improver for the value added.

Confusion

CONFUSION
The mixing together of goods belonging to two or more owners so that the separately owned goods cannot be identified.

Confusion is defined as the commingling (mixing together) of goods so that one person's personal property cannot be distinguished from another's. Confusion frequently occurs when the goods are *fungible*, meaning that each particle is identical with every other particle, as with grain and oil. For example, if two farmers put their Number 2–grade winter wheat into the same storage bin, confusion would occur.

If confusion of goods is caused by a person who wrongfully and willfully mixes the goods for the purpose of rendering them indistinguishable, the innocent party acquires title to the whole. If confusion occurs as a result of agreement, an honest mistake, or the act of some third party, the owners share ownership as tenants in common and will share any loss in proportion to their shares of ownership of the property.

▌ Mislaid, Lost, and Abandoned Property

As already mentioned, one of the methods of acquiring ownership of property is to possess it. Simply finding something and holding onto it, however, does not necessarily give the finder any legal rights in the property. Different rules apply, depending on whether the property was mislaid, lost, or abandoned.

Mislaid Property

Property that has been placed somewhere by the owner voluntarily and then inadvertently forgotten is **mislaid property.** Suppose that you go to the theater and leave your gloves on the concession stand. The gloves are mislaid property, and the theater owner is entrusted with the duty of reasonable care for them. When mislaid property is found, the finder does not obtain title to the goods. Instead, the owner of the place where the property was mislaid becomes the caretaker of the property, because it is highly likely that the true owner will return.[3]

Lost Property

Property that is involuntarily left and forgotten is **lost property.** A finder of the property can claim title to the property against the whole world, *except the true owner.*[4] If the true owner demands that the lost property be returned, the finder must return it. If a third party attempts to take possession of lost property from a finder, however, the third party cannot assert a better title than the finder. When a finder knows who the true owner of the property is and fails to return it to that person, the finder is guilty of the tort of *conversion* (the wrongful taking of another's property—see Chapter 5). Finally, many states require the finder to make a reasonably diligent search to locate the true owner of lost property.

For example, suppose that Kormian works in a large library at night. In the courtyard on her way home, she finds a piece of gold jewelry set with stones that look like precious stones to her. She takes it to a jeweler to have it appraised. While pretending to weigh the jewelry, an employee of the jeweler removes several of the stones. If Kormian brings an action to recover the stones from the jeweler, she normally will win, because she found lost property and holds valid title against everyone *except the true owner.* Because the property was lost, rather than mislaid, the finder is not the caretaker of the jewelry. Instead, the finder acquires title good against the whole world (except the true owner).

Many states have laws that encourage and facilitate the return of property to its true owner and then reward a finder for honesty if the property remains unclaimed. These laws, called **estray statutes,** provide an incentive for finders to report their discoveries by making it possible for them, after the passage of a specified period of time, to acquire legal title to the property they have found. The statute usually requires the county clerk to advertise the property in an attempt to enhance the opportunity of the owner to recover what has been lost. Some preliminary questions must always be resolved before the estray statute can be employed. The item must be lost property, not merely mislaid property. When the situation indicates that the property was probably lost and not mislaid or abandoned, loss is presumed as a matter of public policy, and the estray statute applies.

The law that finders of lost property may obtain good title to the property has a long history. The cases discussed in the following *Landmark in the Law* on the origin of the law of finders illustrate the doctrine of *relativity of title.* Under this doctrine, if two contestants are before the court, neither of whom can claim absolute title to the property, the one who can claim prior possession will likely have established sufficient rights to the property to win the case.

MISLAID PROPERTY
Property with which the owner has voluntarily parted and then cannot find or recover.

LOST PROPERTY
Property with which the owner has involuntarily parted and then cannot find or recover.

ESTRAY STATUTE
A statute defining finders' rights in property when the true owners are unknown.

---

3. The finder of mislaid property is an involuntary bailee (to be discussed later in this chapter).
4. See *Armory v. Delamirie,* 93 Eng.Rep. 664 (K.B. [King's Bench] 1722), discussed in this chapter's *Landmark in the Law.*

The Law of Finders

The well-known children's adage, "Finders keepers, losers weepers," is actually written into law—provided that the loser (the rightful owner) cannot be found, that is. A finder of lost property may acquire good title to found personal property *against everyone except the true owner*. A number of landmark cases have made this principle clear. An early English case, *Armory v. Delamirie,*[a] is considered a landmark in Anglo-American jurisprudence concerning finders' rights in property.

The plaintiff in the case was Armory, a chimney sweep who found a jewel in its setting during the course of his work. He took the jewel to a goldsmith to have it appraised. The goldsmith refused to return the jewel to Armory, claiming that Armory was not the rightful owner of the property. The court held that the finder, as prior possessor of the item, had rights to the jewel superior to those of all others except the rightful owner. The court stated, "The finder of a jewel, though he does not by such finding acquire an absolute property or ownership, yet . . . has such a property as will enable him to keep it against all but the rightful owner."

A curious situation arises when goods wrongfully obtained by one person are in turn wrongfully obtained by another, and the two parties contest their rights to possession. In such a situation, does the *Armory* rule still apply—that is, does the first (illegal) possessor have more rights in the property than the second (illegal) possessor? In a case that came before the Minnesota Supreme Court in 1892, *Anderson v. Gouldberg,*[b] the court said yes.

In the *Anderson* case, the plaintiffs had trespassed on another's land and wrongfully cut timber. The defendants later took the logs from the mill site, allegedly in the name of the owner of the property on which the timber had been cut. The evidence at trial indicated that both parties had illegally acquired the property. The court instructed the jury that even if the plaintiffs were trespassers when they cut the logs, they were entitled to recover them from later possessors—except the true owner or an agent of the true owner. The jury found for the plaintiffs, a decision affirmed later by the Minnesota Supreme Court. The latter court held that the plaintiffs' possession, "though wrongfully obtained," justified an action to repossess the property from another who took it from them.

BE AWARE A finder who appropriates the personal property of another, knowing who the true owner is, can be guilty of conversion.

For Critical Analysis: *As will be discussed in Chapter 36, if a person dies without a valid will and has no legal heirs, that person's property is transferred to the state. Why doesn't the state similarly claim ownership of found property when the property's true owner cannot be located?*

---

a.   93 Eng.Rep. 664 (K.B. [King's Bench] 1722).
b.   51 Minn. 294, 53 N.W. 636 (1892).

Abandoned Property

ABANDONED PROPERTY
Property with which the owner has voluntarily parted, with no intention of recovering it.

Property that has been discarded by the true owner, who has no intention of reclaiming title to it, is **abandoned property.** Someone who finds abandoned property acquires title to it, and such title is good against the whole world, *including the original owner.* The owner of lost property who eventually gives up any further attempt to find the lost property is frequently held to have abandoned the property. In situations in which the finder is trespassing on the property of another and finds abandoned property, title vests not in the finder but in the owner of the land.

▌ Bailments

A bailment is formed by the delivery of personal property, without transfer of title, by one person, called a **bailor,** to another, called a **bailee,** usually under an agreement for a particular purpose (for example, for storage, repair, or transportation). Upon completion of the purpose, the bailee is obligated to return the bailed property to the bailor or to a third person or to dispose of it as directed.

Bailments usually are created by agreement but not necessarily by contract, because in many bailments not all of the elements of a contract (such as mutual assent and consideration) are present. For example, if you loan your bicycle to a friend, a bailment is created, but not by contract, because there is no consideration. Many commercial bailments, such as the delivery of your suit to the cleaners for dry cleaning, are based on contract, however.

Virtually every individual or business is affected by the law of bailments at one time or another (and sometimes even on a daily basis). When individuals deal with bailments, whether they realize it or not, they are subject to the obligations and duties that arise from the bailment relationship. The number, scope, and importance of bailments created daily in the business community and in everyday life make it desirable for every person to understand the elements necessary for the creation of a bailment and to know what rights, duties, and liabilities flow from bailments.

BAILOR
One who entrusts goods to a bailee.

BAILEE
One to whom goods are entrusted by a bailor.

Elements of a Bailment

Not all transactions involving the delivery of property from one person to another create a bailment. For such a transfer to become a bailment, three conditions must be met. We look here at each of these conditions.

RECALL Transactions that involve the delivery of property from one person to another but that do not create a bailment include sales of goods and leases of real property.

PERSONAL PROPERTY   Bailment involves only personal property; there can be no bailment of persons. Although a bailment of your luggage is created when it is transported by an airline, as a passenger you are not the subject of a bailment. Additionally, you cannot bail realty; thus, leasing your house to a tenant does not create a bailment.

DELIVERY OF POSSESSION   In a voluntary bailment, possession of the property must be transferred to the bailee in such a way that (1) the bailee is given exclusive possession and control over the property and (2) the bailee *knowingly* accepts the personal property. If either of these conditions for effective delivery of possession is lacking, there is no bailment relationship. For example, suppose that you take a friend out to dinner at an expensive restaurant. When you enter the restaurant, your friend checks her coat. In the pocket of the coat is a $20,000 diamond necklace. The bailee, by accepting the coat, does not *knowingly* also accept the necklace; thus, a bailment of the coat exists—because the restaurant has exclusive possession and control over the coat and knowingly accepted it—but a bailment of the necklace does not exist.

Two types of delivery—*physical* and *constructive*—will result in the bailee's exclusive possession of and control over the property. As discussed earlier, in the context of gifts, constructive delivery is a substitute, or symbolic, delivery. What is delivered to the bailee is not the actual property bailed (such as a car) but something so related to the property (such as the car keys) that the requirement of delivery is satisfied.

In certain unique situations, a bailment is found despite the apparent lack of the requisite elements of control and knowledge. In particular, the rental of a safe-deposit box is usually held to create a bailor-bailee relationship between the bank and its customer, despite the bank's lack of knowledge of the contents and its inability to have exclusive control of the property.[5] Another example of such a situation occurs when

---

5. By statute or by express contract, the rental of a safe-deposit box may be regarded as a lease of space or a license instead of a bailment.

the bailee acquires the property accidentally or by mistake—as in finding someone else's lost or mislaid property. A bailment is created even though the bailor did not voluntarily deliver the property to the bailee. Such bailments are called *constructive* or *involuntary* bailments.

To what extent is a parking lot attendant responsible for undisclosed articles left in the trunk of a car placed in his or her care? This is the question in the following case.

CASE 34.3

JACK BOLES SERVICES, INC. v. STAVELY

Court of Appeals of Texas,
Austin, 1995.
906 S.W.2d 185.

HISTORICAL AND CULTURAL SETTING *The value of artwork fluctuates as much as the value of other investments. Vincent van Gogh, for example, sold less than a handful of his paintings in his lifetime in the 1800s, and those were sold for very low prices. Today, van Gogh's paintings are some of the most expensive works in the market; they cost as much as tens of millions of dollars each. Van Gogh is regarded as a master, but the price of other artists' work may have nothing to do with their importance to the art world.*

FACTS   Gerald Stavely entrusted a valuable painting to the care of Patricia Bolger. Bolger put the painting in the trunk of her husband's Cadillac. Her husband left the car at his country club in the care of a parking attendant who worked for Jack Boles Services, Inc. The car and painting were stolen. Bolger's car was eventually returned to

him, but the painting was missing. Stavely filed a suit in a Texas state court against Jack Boles Services, Inc., arguing that the bailee was responsible for the theft. The court agreed. Boles appealed.

ISSUE   Is a bailee responsible for the unknown contents of bailed property if the presence of those contents is not reasonably foreseeable?

DECISION   No. The Court of Appeals of Texas (Austin) reversed the lower court's judgment.

REASON   The state appellate court concluded that "[i]t cannot be said * * * that a country club parking attendant should reasonably foresee the presence of valuable artwork in each member's car trunk." Thus, Boles could not be said to have had actual or implied notice of the painting. Without notice, it could "not expressly or implicitly accept Stavely's painting as a bailed piece of property. Without acceptance, no bailor-bailee relationship existed in regard to the painting, and accordingly, Jack Boles had no duty of care in regard to the painting."

FOR CRITICAL ANALYSIS—Social Consideration
Why did Stavely file suit against Boles instead of against the parking attendant?

BAILMENT AGREEMENT   A bailment agreement can be express or implied. Although a written agreement is not required for bailments of less than one year (that is, the Statute of Frauds does not apply—see Chapter 11), it is a good idea to have one, especially when valuable property is involved.

The bailment agreement expressly or impliedly provides for the return of the bailed property to the bailor or to a third person, or it provides for disposal by the bailee. The agreement presupposes that the bailee will return the identical goods originally given by the bailor. In certain types of bailments, however, such as bailments of fungible goods, the property returned need only be equivalent property.

For example, if Holman stores his grain (fungible goods) in Joe's Warehouse, a bailment is created. At the end of the storage period, however, the warehouse is not obligated to return to Holman exactly the same grain that he stored. As long as the warehouse returns goods of the same *type*, *grade*, and *quantity*, the warehouse—the bailee—has performed its obligation.

Ordinary Bailments

Bailments are either *ordinary* or *special (extraordinary)*. There are three types of ordinary bailments. The distinguishing feature among them is *which party receives a benefit from the bailment*. Ultimately, the courts may use this factor to determine the standard of care required of the bailee in possession of the personal property, and this factor will dictate the rights and liabilities of the parties. The three types of ordinary bailments are as follows:

1. *Bailment for the sole benefit of the bailor.* This is a gratuitous bailment (a bailment without consideration) for the convenience and benefit of the bailor. For example, if Allen asks his friend, Sumi, to store Allen's car in Sumi's garage, and Sumi agrees to do so, the bailment of the car would be for the sole benefit of the bailor (Allen).

2. *Bailment for the sole benefit of the bailee.* This type of bailment typically occurs when one person loans an item to another person (the bailee) solely for the bailee's convenience and benefit. For example, Allen asks his friend Sumi to borrow Sumi's boat so that Allen can go sailing over the weekend. The bailment of the boat is for Allen's (the bailee's) sole benefit.

3. *Bailment for the mutual benefit of the bailee and the bailor.* This is the most common kind of bailment and involves some form of compensation for storing items or holding property while it is being serviced. It is a contractual bailment and is often referred to as a bailment for hire. For example, leaving your car at a service station for an oil change is a mutual-benefit bailment.

RIGHTS OF THE BAILEE   Certain rights are implicit in the bailment agreement. A hallmark of the bailment agreement is that the bailee acquires the *right to control and possess the property temporarily*. The bailee's right of possession permits the bailee to recover damages from any third person for damage or loss of the property. If the property is stolen, the bailee has a legal right to regain possession of it or to obtain damages from any third person who has wrongfully interfered with the bailee's possessory rights. The bailee's right to regain possession of the property or to obtain damages is important because, as you will read shortly, a bailee is liable to the bailor for any loss or damage to bailed property resulting from the bailee's negligence.

Depending on the type of bailment and the terms of the bailment agreement, a bailee also may have a *right to use the bailed property*. For example, if you borrow a friend's car to drive to the airport, you, as the bailee, would obviously be expected to use the car. In a bailment involving the long-term storage of a car, however, the bailee is not expected to use the car, because the ordinary purpose of a storage bailment does not include use of the property.

Except in a gratuitous bailment, a bailee has a *right to be compensated* as provided for in the bailment agreement, a right to be reimbursed for costs and services rendered in the keeping of the bailed property, or both. Even in a gratuitous bailment, a bailee has a right to be reimbursed or compensated for costs incurred in the keeping of the bailed property. For example, Margo loses her pet dog, which Judith finds. Judith takes Margo's dog to her home and feeds it. Even though she takes good care of the dog, it becomes ill, and she calls a veterinarian. Judith pays the bill for the veterinarian's services and the medicine. Judith normally will be entitled to be reimbursed by Margo for all reasonable costs incurred in the keeping of Margo's dog. To enforce the right of compensation, the bailee has a right to place a *possessory lien* (which entitles a creditor to retain possession of the debtor's goods until a debt is paid) on the specific bailed property until he or she has been fully compensated. This type of lien, sometimes referred to as an *artisan's lien* or a *bailee's lien*, was discussed in Chapter 22.

Ordinary bailees have the *right to limit their liability* as long as the limitations are called to the attention of the bailor and are not against public policy. It is essential that the bailor in some way know of the limitation. Even if the bailor has notice, certain types of disclaimers of liability have been considered to be against public policy and therefore illegal. For example, certain exculpatory clauses limiting a person's liability for his or her own wrongful acts are often scrutinized by the courts and, in the case of bailments, are routinely held to be illegal. This is particularly true in bailments for the mutual benefit of the bailor and the bailee. Whether a bailee could disclaim liability for the loss of bailed property is at issue in the following case.

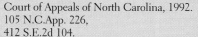

CASE 34.4

BROCKWELL v. LAKE GASTON SALES AND SERVICE

Court of Appeals of North Carolina, 1992.
105 N.C.App. 226,
412 S.E.2d 104.

HISTORICAL AND TECHNOLOGICAL SETTING *Navigation is the science and technology of finding the position, course, and distance traveled by a boat, ship, plane, or other craft. Traditionally, sailors used a magnetic compass and a sextant to plot their courses. Today, sailors and others use highly sophisticated electronic methods employing radio signals transmitted by satellites. Modern navigation satellites enable users to calculate their positions to within a few feet. When navigating in deep waters, such as freshwater lakes, or when fishing, sailors use charts that represent underwater depths.*

FACTS R. W. Brockwell took his boat and its motor to Lake Gaston Sales and Service (Gaston) to be repaired. At the time Brockwell delivered the boat to Gaston, the boat contained many items of personal property, including fishing gear, navigation equipment, and electronic equipment. Before the boat could be repaired, Brockwell had to sign a repair order that contained the following disclaimer: "It is understood and agreed that [Gaston] assumes no responsibility whatsoever for loss or damage by theft, fire, vandalism, water or weather related damages, nor for any items of personal property left with the unit placed with [Gaston] for repair, storage or sale." About ten days later, after the boat had been repaired, Brockwell learned that equipment and other personal

property worth over $2,000 were missing from the boat. Gaston contended that the disclaimer in the repair order absolved it from any liability for the missing property. Brockwell sued Gaston in a North Carolina state court for negligence. The trial court held for Brockwell and awarded him damages. Gaston appealed.

ISSUE Did the disclaimer in the repair order absolve Gaston from liability for the missing property?

DECISION No. The appellate court affirmed the trial court's decision. Gaston could not, by contract, disclaim liability for its own negligence.

REASON The court stated that as a general rule, in mutual-benefit bailment contracts, bailees can relieve themselves from the liability imposed on them under the common law so long as contract provisions are not contrary to public policy. The court noted that many courts have held that "where the bailee makes it his business to act as bailee for hire, on a uniform and not an individual basis, it is against the public interest to permit him to exculpate himself from his own negligence. And the decided trend of modern decisions is against the validity of such exculpatory clauses or provisions * * * ." Gaston, the bailee, was in the business of acting as a bailee for hire on a uniform basis and took Brockwell's boat and its contents and attachments "into its sole possession in order to perform repairs on the boat in the regular course of its business, and we hold it was against public policy for [Gaston] to attempt to exculpate itself from the duty of ordinary care it owed to [Brockwell]. We therefore hold the liability disclaimer in the present case is void and unenforceable as a matter of law."

FOR CRITICAL ANALYSIS—Ethical Consideration *Would it matter, in terms of the outcome of this case, whether Brockwell had or had not read the disclaimer?*

DUTIES OF THE BAILEE The bailee has two basic responsibilities: (1) to take proper care of the property and (2) to surrender to the bailor or dispose of the property in accordance with the bailor's instructions at the end of the bailment. The bailee must exercise reasonable care in preserving the bailed property. What constitutes reasonable care in a bailment situation normally depends on the nature and specific circumstances of the bailment. Traditionally, courts have determined the appropriate standard of care on the basis of the type of bailments involved. In a bailment for the sole

◆ **Exhibit 34–1**
Degree of Care Required of a Bailee

A bailee's failure to exercise appropriate care in handling the bailor's property results in tort liability. The duty to relinquish the property at the end of the bailment is grounded in both contract and tort law principles. Failure to return the property constitutes a breach of contract or the tort of conversion, and with one exception, the bailee is liable for damages. The exception is when the obligation is excused because the goods or chattels have been destroyed, lost, or stolen through no fault of the bailee (or claimed by a third party with a superior claim).

Under the law of bailments, a bailor's proof that damage or loss to the property has occurred will, in and of itself, raise a *presumption* that the bailee is guilty of negligence or conversion. In other words, whenever a bailee fails to return bailed property, the bailee's negligence will be *presumed* by the court.

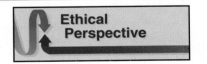

The standard of care expected of a bailee clearly illustrates how the law reflects ethical principles. For example, suppose that a friend asks to borrow your business law text for the weekend. You agree to loan your friend the book. In this situation, which is a bailment for the sole benefit of the bailee (your friend), most people would agree that your friend has an ethical obligation to take great care of your book. After all, if your friend lost your book, you would incur damages. You would have to purchase another one, and if you could not, you might find it difficult to do well in your homework assignments, examinations, and so on. Traditionally, the law has reflected this ethical principle by holding that in a bailment for the sole benefit of the bailee, the bailee must exercise great care to preserve the bailed property.

It would be different if you had loaned your book to your friend totally for your own benefit. For example, suppose that you are leaving town during the summer, and a friend offers to store several boxes of books for you until you return in the fall. In this situation, a benefit for the sole benefit of the bailor (you) exists. If your books are destroyed through the bailee's (your friend's) negligence and you sue the bailee for damages, a court will likely take into consideration the fact that the bailee was essentially doing you a favor by storing the books. Although bailees generally have a duty to exercise reasonable care over bailed property, what constitutes reasonable care in a specific situation normally depends on the surrounding circumstances—including the reason for the bailment and who stood to benefit from the arrangement.

For Critical Analysis: *What would result if bailees were held to a standard of great care for all types of bailments and in all circumstances?*

DUTIES OF THE BAILOR   It goes without saying that the rights of a bailor are essentially the same as the duties of a bailee. The major duty of the bailor is to provide the bailee with goods or chattels that are free from known defects that could cause injury to the bailee. In the case of a mutual-benefit bailment, the bailor must also notify the bailee of any hidden defects that the bailor could have discovered with reasonable diligence and proper inspection.

The bailor's duty to reveal defects is based on a negligence theory of tort law. A bailor who fails to give the appropriate notice is liable to the bailee and to any other person who might reasonably be expected to come into contact with the defective article. For example, if an equipment rental firm leases equipment with a *discoverable* defect, and the lessee (bailee) is not notified of such a defect and is harmed because of it, the rental firm is liable for negligence under tort law.

An exception to this rule exists if the bailment was created for the sole benefit of the bailee. Thus, if you loaned your car to a friend as a favor to your friend and not for any direct return benefit to yourself, you would be required to notify your friend of any *known* defect of the automobile that could cause injury but not of a defect of which you were unaware (even if it was a *discoverable* defect). If your friend was injured in an accident as a result of a defect unknown to you, you would normally not be liable.

A bailor can also incur *warranty liability* based on contract law (see Chapter 17) for injuries resulting from the bailment of defective articles. Property leased by a bailor must be *fit for the intended purpose of the bailment*. Warranties of fitness arise by law in sales contracts and leases and by judicial interpretation in the case of bailments for hire. Article 2A of the Uniform Commercial Code extends implied warranties of merchantability and fitness for a particular purpose to bailments whenever the bailments include rights to use the bailed goods.[6]

The resolution of the following case depended on the degree of care owed by a bailor—the Atlanta Coca-Cola Bottling Company—to an injured third party. In determining the required degree of care, the court evaluates whether the bailment was a bailment for hire or a gratuitous bailment (a bailment without consideration).

6.   UCC 2A–212, 2A–213.

CASE 34.5

PRINCE v. ATLANTA COCA-COLA BOTTLING CO.
Court of Appeals of Georgia, 1993.
210 Ga.App. 108,
435 S.E.2d 482.

COMPANY PROFILE   *In 1886, John Pemberton, a druggist in Atlanta, invented Coca-Cola. Within a few years, Asa Candler, another Atlanta druggist, bought the Coca-Cola Company for $2,300. In less than a decade, Candler made Coca-Cola available throughout the United States, and in Canada and Mexico. In 1899, Candler sold most of the U.S. bottling rights to Benjamin Thomas and John Whitehead, who, with John Lupton, developed the* regional franchise bottling system that is still in use. In 1919, Candler sold the Coca-Cola Company for $25 million to the Woodruff family. Robert Woodruff introduced the advertising slogans "The Pause that Refreshes" and "It's the Real Thing." Coca-Cola introduced Sprite in 1961, TAB in 1963, Diet Coke in 1982, and New Coke in 1985. Today, Coca-Cola dominates the global soft drink market. Coca-Cola products are available in nearly two hundred countries, and the company produces four of the world's five most popular carbonated beverages. In the U.S. market, however, Coca-Cola Classic barely has the lead over PepsiCo's Pepsi.*

FACTS   Phar-Mor arranged with the Atlanta Coca-Cola Bottling Company (ACCBC) to use one of its "special events wagons" during a promotion in the store's parking lot. An ACCBC employee delivered the wagon and parked it in accordance with a Phar-Mor employee's

Case 34.5—Continued

instructions. ACCBC did not charge Phar-Mor for the use of the wagon, but only for the beverages and food items (provided by ACCBC) that Phar-Mor employees sold during the event. Water leaked from the wagon, causing a puddle to form. Lisa Prince stepped in the puddle, slipped, fell, and sustained injuries. ACCBC was not aware of the accident for several months. Prince sued ACCBC for negligence in a Georgia state court, claiming, among other things, that ACCBC had failed in its duty, as a bailor, to maintain the premises around the wagon. The trial court granted summary judgment in ACCBC's favor, and Prince appealed.

ISSUE Did ACCBC have a legal duty to maintain the premises around the wagon?

DECISION No. The appellate court affirmed the lower court's decision.

REASON The court reasoned that a gratuitous bailment existed between Phar-Mor and ACCBC, because there was no evidence of Prince's claim that "appellee contracted with Phar-Mor to provide refreshments in the Coca-Cola special events wagon under a bailment for hire." As a gratuitous bailor, ACCBC had no legal duty to maintain the area around the wagon, no legal duty to prevent drain water from accumulating, and no legal duty to warn "of any slippery, dangerous, or unsafe conditions existing in the vicinity," particularly as to water that drained and accumulated after the wagon was delivered and placed under Phar-Mor's sole control.

FOR CRITICAL ANALYSIS—Social Consideration
What might result if bailors were held to the same standard of care in gratuitous bailments as in bailments for hire?

Special Types of Bailments

Up to this point, our discussion of bailments has been concerned with ordinary bailments—bailments in which bailees are expected to exercise ordinary care in the handling of bailed property. Some bailment transactions warrant special consideration. These include bailments in which the bailee's duty of care is *extraordinary*—that is, his or her liability for loss or damage to the property is absolute—as is generally true in cases involving common carriers and innkeepers. Warehouse companies have the same duty of care as ordinary bailees; but, like carriers, they are subject to extensive regulation under federal and state laws, including Article 7 of the Uniform Commercial Code (UCC).

A truck travels a highway. Why are common carriers, such as most trucking companies, held to a higher standard of care than ordinary bailees?

COMMON CARRIER
An owner of a truck, railroad, airline, ship, or other vehicle who is licensed to offer transportation services to the public, generally in return for compensation or a payment.

COMMON CARRIERS Transportation providers that are publicly licensed to provide transportation services to the general public are known as **common carriers.** Common carriers are distinguished from private carriers, which operate transportation facilities for a select clientele. Whereas a private carrier is not bound to provide service to every person or company making a request, a common carrier must arrange carriage for all who apply, within certain limitations.[7]

The delivery of goods to a common carrier creates a bailment relationship between the shipper (bailor) and the common carrier (bailee). Unlike ordinary bailees, the common carrier is held to a standard of care based on *strict liability*, rather than reasonable care, in protecting the bailed personal property. This means that the common carrier is absolutely liable, regardless of negligence, for all loss or damage to goods except damage caused by one of the following common law exceptions: (1) an act of God, (2) an act of a public enemy, (3) an order of a public authority, (4) an act of the shipper, or (5) the inherent nature of the goods.

Common carriers cannot contract away their liability for damaged goods. Subject to government regulations, however, they are permitted to limit their dollar liability to an amount stated on the shipment contract or rate filing.[8]

WAREHOUSE COMPANIES Warehousing is the business of providing storage of property for compensation.[9] A warehouse company is a professional bailee whose responsibility differs from an ordinary bailee's in two important aspects. First, a warehouse company is empowered to issue documents of title—in particular, warehouse receipts.[10] Second, warehouse companies are subject to an extraordinary network of state and federal statutes, including Article 7 of the UCC.

A warehouse company accepts goods for storage and issues a warehouse receipt describing the property and the terms of the bailment contract. The warehouse receipt can be negotiable or nonnegotiable, depending on how it is written. It is negotiable if its terms provide that the warehouse company will deliver the goods "to the bearer" of the receipt or "to the order of" a person named on the receipt.[11]

The warehouse receipt serves multiple functions. It is a receipt for the goods stored; it is a contract of bailment; it also represents the goods (that is, it indicates title) and hence has value and utility in financing commercial transactions. For example, Ossip, a processor and canner of corn, delivers 6,500 cases of corn to Shaneyfelt, the owner of a warehouse. Shaneyfelt issues a negotiable warehouse receipt payable "to bearer" and gives it to Ossip. Ossip sells and delivers the warehouse receipt to a large supermarket chain, Better Foods, Inc. Better Foods is now the owner of the corn and has the right to obtain the cases from Shaneyfelt. It will present the warehouse receipt to Shaneyfelt, who in return will release the cases of corn to the grocery chain.

Like ordinary bailees, a warehouse company is liable for loss or damage to property resulting from *negligence* (and therefore does not have the same liability as a common carrier). As a professional bailee, however, it is expected to exercise a high degree of care to protect and preserve the goods. A warehouse company can limit the dollar

---

7. A common carrier is not required to take any and all property anywhere in all instances. Public regulatory agencies govern common carriers, and carriers can be restricted to geographical areas. They can also be limited to carrying certain kinds of goods or to providing only special types of transportation equipment.

8. Federal laws require common carriers to offer shippers the opportunity to obtain higher dollar limits for loss by paying a higher fee for the transport.

9. UCC 7–102(h) defines the person engaged in the storing of goods for hire as a "warehouseman."

10. A document of title is defined in UCC 1–201(15) as any "document which in the regular course of business or financing is treated as adequately evidencing that the person in possession of it is entitled to receive, hold, and dispose of the document and the goods it covers. To be a document of title, a document must purport to be issued by or addressed to a bailee and purport to cover goods in the bailee's possession."

11. UCC 7–104.

amount of its liability, but the bailor must be given the option of paying an increased storage rate for an increase in the liability limit.

INNKEEPERS   At common law, innkeepers, hotel owners, and similar operators were held to the same strict liability as common carriers with respect to property brought into the rooms by guests. Today, only those who provide lodging to the public for compensation as a *regular* business are covered under this rule of strict liability. Moreover, the rule applies only to those who are guests, as opposed to lodgers. A lodger is a permanent resident of the hotel or inn, whereas a guest is a traveler.

In many states, innkeepers can avoid strict liability for loss of guests' valuables and money by providing a safe in which to keep them. Each guest must be clearly notified of the availability of such a safe. Statutes often limit the liability of innkeepers with regard to articles that are not kept in the safe or that are of such a nature that they are not normally kept in a safe. These statutes may limit the amount of monetary damages or even provide for no liability in the absence of innkeeper negligence.

Suppose that Joyce stays for a night at the Harbor Hotel. When she returns from eating breakfast in the hotel restaurant, she discovers that the people in the room next door have forced the lock on the door between the two rooms and stolen her suitcase. Joyce claims that the hotel is liable for her loss. The hotel maintains that because it was not negligent, it is not liable. At common law, the hotel would have been liable, because innkeepers were actually insurers of the property of their guests. Today, however, state statutes limit strict liability by limiting the amount of monetary damages for which the innkeeper is liable or providing that the innkeeper has no liability in the absence of negligence. Most statutes require these limitations to be posted or the guest to be notified. Such postings, or notices, are frequently found on the doors of the rooms in the motel or hotel.

Normally, the innkeeper (a motel keeper, for example) assumes no responsibility for the safety of a guest's automobile, because the guest usually retains possession and control over it. If, however, the innkeeper provides parking facilities and the guest's car is entrusted to the innkeeper or to an employee, the innkeeper will be liable under the rules that pertain to parking-lot bailments (which are ordinary bailments).

> *"All saints can do miracles, but few of them can keep a hotel."*
>
> **Samuel Clemens (Mark Twain), 1835–1910** *(American author and humorist)*

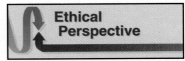

Ethical Perspective

Problems sometimes arise when persons who are not hotel guests attend conferences held in hotels. For example, suppose that you attend a meeting held in a local hotel's conference room. You enter the hotel, hang your coat on a rack near the door of the conference room, and attend the meeting. At the lunch break, you decide to retrieve something from your coat, which is no longer hanging where you left it. Hotel employees search everywhere, but your coat is not to be found. Is the hotel responsible for the loss or theft of the coat? Probably not. A court would likely hold that no bailor-bailee relationship had come into existence, because you had not entrusted, or delivered, your coat to any employee of the hotel.[a]

Should the hotel be held responsible? Most people would probably conclude that in these circumstances, it would be unfair to the hotel to hold it responsible for your loss. In effect, such a rule would mean that hotels would have to hire extra employees to watch over all personal property left temporarily anywhere on the hotel's premises. Therefore, a hotel's liability normally arises only if a patron checks his or her coat at the hotel's coat-checking area.

For Critical Analysis: *If the hotel was an extremely expensive one that catered only to elite groups, should that fact affect the hotel's liability for the lost coat in the hypothetical situation described above?*

a.   See, for example, *Augustine v. Marriott Hotel*, 132 Misc.2d 180, 503 N.Y.S.2d 498 (1986).

898 UNIT NINE: PROPERTY AND ITS PROTECTION

Application

What to Do with Lost Property*

If you are walking down a street in New York City and chance upon a valuable diamond ring that is lying next to a gutter, what should you do with the ring? The tempting thing would be to keep it or sell it and enjoy the proceeds. That would be unethical, however; it would also be illegal under New York laws governing the finding of lost property. New York law defines *lost property* to include lost property, mislaid property, abandoned property, "waifs [goods to which all ownership rights have been waived, such as goods that are found but unclaimed] and treasure trove, and other property which is found." Property includes "money, goods, chattels and tangible personal property," with some exceptions. Generally, the finder of property worth $20 or more must deposit it with police authorities (or with the owner of the premises on which the property was found) within ten days. Failure to do so is a misdemeanor, subject to a fine of up to $100 and imprisonment for not more than six months.

Many states have enacted lost-property statutes. The statutes differ significantly from state to state, but typically, they eliminate the distinction between lost property, mislaid property, abandoned property, and treasure trove, as the New York statute does. Many statutes also require the finder to deposit found property with local authorities, although the penalty imposed for failure to do so may not be as severe as under New York's statute

(in Illinois, for example, a finder who fails to comply with the requirements of that state's lost-property statute may be fined $10). Lost-property statutes also typically require the police to attempt to find the true owner—by calling the owner or person in charge of the premises on which the property was found, for example. Sometimes, the finder must advertise, at the county court, the property and its discovery.

Generally, if the true owner cannot be located within a certain period of time, which varies depending on the value of the property and whether the property is perishable, the finder gets the property. If the finder does not appear after the period of time has lapsed, the property may be sold and the proceeds disposed of as specified by the statute. In California, for instance, the proceeds from such a sale go into a state abandoned-property fund (if the state police had custody of the lost property) or become the property of the city, county, town, or village (if other police had custody).

Every statute has exceptions, of course. In some situations, an employer may have rights to property found by an employee. Property found in a safe-deposit area in a bank may also be subject to different rules.

✓ Checklist for the Finder of Lost Property

1. To maximize your chances of legally keeping lost property, take the found property to the nearest police station.

*This *Application* is not meant to substitute for the services of an attorney who is licensed to practice law in your state.

▮ Key Terms

abandoned property 888
accession 886
bailee 889
bailment 881
bailor 889
chattel 880
common carrier 896
community property 882

confusion 886
constructive delivery 884
dominion 883
estray statute 887
fee simple 881
gift 883
gift *causa mortis* 885
gift *inter vivos* 885

joint tenancy 881
lost property 887
mislaid property 887
personal property 880
property 880
real property 880
tenancy by the entirety 882
tenancy in common 881

▌Chapter Summary: Personal Property and Bailments

PERSONAL PROPERTY	
Definition of Personal Property *(See pages 880–881.)*	Personal property (personalty) is considered to include all property not classified as real property (realty). Personal property can be tangible (such as a TV set or a car) or intangible (such as stocks or bonds). Personal property may be referred to legally as *chattel*—a term used under the common law to denote all forms of personal property.

Property Ownership *(See pages 881–882.)*	1. *Fee simple*—Exists when individuals have the right to use, possess, or dispose of the property as they choose during their lifetimes and to pass on the property to their heirs at death.
	
	2. *Concurrent ownership*—
	  a. Tenancy in common—Co-ownership in which two or more persons own an undivided interest in the property; on one tenant's death, the property interest passes to his or her heirs.
	  b. Joint tenancy—Exists when two or more persons own an undivided interest in property; on the death of a joint tenant, the property interest transfers to the remaining tenant(s), not to the heirs of the deceased.
	  c. Tenancy by the entirety—A form of co-ownership between a husband and wife that is similar to a joint tenancy, except that a spouse cannot transfer separately his or her interest during his or her lifetime without the consent of the other spouse.
	  d. Community property—A form of co-ownership in which each spouse technically owns an undivided one-half interest in property acquired during the marriage. This type of ownership occurs in only a few states.

Acquiring Ownership of Personal Property *(See pages 882–886.)*	The most common means of acquiring ownership in personal property is by purchasing it (see Chapters 14 through 17). Another way in which personal property is often acquired is by will or inheritance (see Chapter 36). The following are additional methods of acquiring personal property:
	
	1. *Possession*—Ownership may be acquired by possession if no other person has ownership title (for example, capturing wild animals or finding abandoned property).
	
	2. *Production*—Any product or item produced by an individual (with some exceptions) becomes the property of that individual.
	
	3. *Gift*—An effective gift exists when the following conditions exist:
	  a. There is evidence of *intent* to make a gift of the property in question.
	  b. The gift is *delivered* (physically or constructively) to the donee or the donee's agent.
	  c. The gift is *accepted* by the donee or the donee's agent.
	
	4. *Accession*—When someone adds value to a piece of personal property by labor or materials, the added value generally becomes the property of the owner of the original property (includes accessions made in bad faith or wrongfully). Good faith accessions that substantially increase the property's value or change the identity of the property may cause title to pass to the improver.
	
	5. *Confusion*—In the case of fungible goods, if a person wrongfully and willfully commingles goods with those of another in order to render them indistinguishable, the innocent party acquires title to the whole. Otherwise, the owners become tenants in common of the commingled goods.

Mislaid, Lost, and Abandoned Property *(See pages 886–888.)*	1. *Mislaid property*—Property that is placed somewhere voluntarily by the owner and then inadvertently forgotten. A finder of mislaid property will not acquire title to the goods, and the owner of the place where the property was mislaid becomes a caretaker of the mislaid property. 2. *Lost property*—Property that is involuntarily left and forgotten. A finder of lost property can claim title to the property against the whole world *except the true owner.* 3. *Abandoned property*—Property that has been discarded by the true owner, who has no intention of claiming title to the property in the future. A finder of abandoned property can claim title to it against the whole world, *including the original owner.*
BAILMENTS	
Elements of a Bailment *(See pages 889–890.)*	1. *Personal property*—Bailments involve only personal property. 2. *Delivery of possession*—For an effective bailment to exist, the bailee (the one receiving the property) must be given exclusive possession and control over the property, and in a voluntary bailment, the bailee must knowingly accept the personal property. *(Continued)*

▌Chapter Summary: Personal Property and Bailments—Continued

Elements of a Bailment–Continued	3. *The bailment agreement*—Expressly or impliedly provides for the return of the bailed property to the bailor or a third party, or for the disposal of the bailed property by the bailee.

Ordinary Bailments *(See pages 891–895.)*	1. *Types of bailments*—
	   a. Bailment for the sole benefit of the bailor—A gratuitous bailment undertaken for the sole benefit of the bailor (for example, as a favor to the bailor).
	   b. Bailment for the sole benefit of the bailee—A gratuitous bailment of an article to a person (the bailee) solely for the bailee's benefit.
	   c. Mutual-benefit (contractual) bailment—The most common kind of bailment; involves compensation between the bailee and bailor for the service provided.
	
	 2. *Rights of a bailee (duties of a bailor)*—
	   a. The right of possession—Allows actions against third persons who damage or convert the bailed property and allows actions against the bailor for wrongful breach of the bailment.
	   b. The right to be compensated and reimbursed for expenses—In the event of nonpayment, the bailee has the right to place a possessory (bailee's) lien on the bailed property.
	   c. The right to limit liability—An ordinary bailee can limit his or her liability for loss or damage, provided proper notice is given and the limitation is not against public policy. In special bailments, limitations on types of liability are usually not allowed, but limitations on the monetary amount of liability are permitted.
	
	 3. *Duties of a bailee (rights of a bailor)*—
	   a. A bailee must exercise appropriate care over property entrusted to him or her. What constitutes appropriate care normally depends on the nature and circumstances of the bailment.
	   b. Bailed goods in a bailee's possession must be either returned to the bailor or disposed of according to the bailor's directions. A bailee's failure to return the bailed property constitutes a breach of contract or the tort of conversion.

Special Types of Bailments *(See pages 895–897.)*	1. *Common carriers*—Carriers that are publicly licensed to provide transportation services to the general public. The common carrier is held to a standard of care based on *strict liability* unless the bailed property is lost or destroyed due to (a) an act of God, (b) an act of a public enemy, (c) an order of a public authority, (d) an act of a shipper, or (e) the inherent nature of the goods. 2. *Warehouse companies*—Professional bailees that differ from ordinary bailees because they (a) can issue documents of title (warehouse receipts) and (b) are subject to state and federal statutes, including Article 7 of the UCC (as are common carriers). They must exercise a high degree of care over the bailed property and are liable for loss or damage of property due to negligence. 3. *Innkeepers (hotel operators)*—Those who provide lodging to the public for compensation as a *regular* business. The common law standard of strict liability to which innkeepers were once held is limited today by state statutes, which vary from state to state.

▌For Review

1. What is real property? What is personal property?
2. What does it mean to own property in fee simple? What is the difference between a joint tenancy and a tenancy in common?
3. What are the three elements necessary for an effective gift? How else can property be acquired?
4. What are the three elements of a bailment?
5. What are the basic rights and duties of the bailee? What are the rights and duties of the bailor?

▌Questions and Case Problems

34–1. Duties of the Bailee. Discuss the standard of care traditionally required of the bailee for the bailed property in each of the following situations, and determine whether the bailee breached that duty.

(a) Ricardo borrows Steve's lawn mower because his own lawn mower needs repair. Ricardo mows his front yard. To mow the back yard, he needs to move some hoses and lawn furniture. He leaves the mower in front of his house while doing so. When he returns to the front yard, he discovers that the mower has been stolen.

(b) Alicia owns a valuable speedboat. She is going on vacation and asks her neighbor, Maureen, to store the boat in one stall of Maureen's double garage. Maureen consents, and the boat is moved into the garage. Maureen needs some grocery items for dinner and drives to the store. She leaves the garage door open while she is gone, as is her custom, and the speedboat is stolen during that time.

34–2. Gifts. Reineken, very old and ill, wanted to make a gift to his nephew, Gerald. He had a friend obtain $2,500 in cash for him from his bank account, placed this cash in an envelope, and wrote on the envelope, "This is for my nephew, Gerald." Reineken then placed the envelope in his dresser drawer. When Reineken died a month later, his family found the envelope, and Gerald got word of the intended gift. Gerald then demanded that Reineken's daughter, the executor of Reineken's estate (the person appointed by Reineken to handle his affairs after his death), turn over the gift to him. The daughter refused to do so. Discuss fully whether Gerald can successfully claim ownership rights to the $2,500.

34–3. Gifts. In 1968, Armando was about to be shipped to Vietnam for active duty with the U.S. Marines. Shortly before he left, he gave an expensive stereo set and other personal belongings to his girlfriend, Sara, saying, "I'll probably not return from this war, so I'm giving these to you." Armando returned eighteen months later and requested that Sara return the property. Sara said that because Armando had given her these items to keep, she was not required to return them. Was a gift made in this instance, and can Armando recover his property? Discuss fully.

34–4. Requirements of a Bailment. Calvin is an executive on a business trip to the West Coast. He has driven his car on this trip and checks into the Hotel Ritz. The hotel has a guarded underground parking lot. Calvin gives his car keys to the parking-lot attendant but fails to notify the attendant that his wife's $10,000 diamond necklace is in a box in the trunk. The next day, upon checking out, he discovers that his car has been stolen. Calvin wants to hold the hotel liable for both the car and the necklace. Discuss the probable success of his claim.

34–5. Gifts. Welton, an experienced businessperson, transferred to Gallagher some bearer bonds. He stated that the bonds were hers with "no strings attached" and that she should place the bonds in her safe-deposit box for safekeeping. Later, Welton wanted Gallagher to return the bonds to him, claiming that he was still the owner. Gallagher refused, claiming that Welton's transfer was a gift. Was it? Discuss fully. [*Welton v. Gallagher*, 2 Haw.App. 242, 630 P.2d 1077 (1981)]

34–6. Abandoned Property. Danny Smith and his brother discovered a sixteen-foot boat lying beside a roadway in Alabama. Smith informed the police, who immediately impounded the boat and stored it in a city warehouse. Although Smith acquiesced to the police action, he told the police that if the true owner did not claim the boat, he wanted it. When the true owner did not come forward, the police refused to relinquish the boat to Smith and instead told Smith that they planned to auction it to the highest bidder on behalf of the city. Smith sued for custody of the boat. Because Smith

never physically held the boat but rather allowed the police to take possession, should Smith succeed in his claim to title as finder? Could Smith defeat a claim if the true owner sought to retake the boat? Discuss fully. [*Smith v. Purvis*, 474 So.2d 1131 (Ala.Civ.App. 1985)]

34–7. Duties of the Bailee. Wanda Perry, who had an account with Farmers Bank of Greenwood, wanted to rent a safe-deposit box from the bank. The boxes were available only to bank customers, and no fee was charged. When renting the box, Wanda was asked to sign a signature card that stated as follows: "The undersigned customer holds the Farmers Bank harmless for loss of currency or coin left in the box." A little over four years later, the bank was burglarized, and most of the safe-deposit boxes were broken into. Wanda's box was among those burglarized, and she lost all the currency and coins it contained. At trial, evidence showed that the bank had been negligent in failing to restore a burglar alarm system that had been inoperative for more than a week when the bank was burglarized. Wanda sued the bank to recover the value of the currency and coins, alleging negligence on the part of the bank. Discuss fully whether the bank should be held liable for the loss. [*Farmers Bank of Greenwood v. Perry*, 301 Ark. 547, 787 S.W.2d 645 (1990)]

34–8. Gifts. William Yee and S. Hing Woo had been lovers for nearly twenty years. They held themselves out as husband and wife, and Woo wore a wedding band. Two days before his death, Yee told Woo that he felt "terribly bad" and believed he would die. He gave Woo three checks, for $42,700, $80,000, and $1,900, and told her that if he died, he wanted her "to be taken care of." After Yee's death, Woo cashed the $42,700 check and the $1,900 check. She never cashed the $80,000 check. The administrator of Yee's estate petitioned a Virginia state court to declare that Woo was not entitled to the money represented by the checks. What will the court decide, and why? [*Woo v. Smart*, 247 Va. 365, 442 S.E.2d 690 (1994)]

34–9. Bailments. Jole Liddle, a high school student in Salem School District No. 600, played varsity basketball. A letter from Monmouth College of West Long Branch, New Jersey, addressed to Liddle in care of the coach, was delivered to Liddle's school a few days after it was mailed on July 18, 1990. The letter notified Liddle that he was being recruited for a basketball scholarship. The school, which had a policy of delivering promptly any mail sent to students in care of the school, did not deliver the letter to Liddle until seven months later. Because Monmouth College had not heard from Liddle, the college discontinued its efforts to recruit him. Liddle sued the school district, alleging that the coach was negligent in his duties as a bailee of the letter. The school district filed a motion to dismiss the case, arguing that the letter was not bailable property. Was the letter bailable property? Discuss fully. [*Liddle v. Salem School District No. 600*, 249 Ill.App.3d 768, 619 N.E.2d 530, 188 Ill.Dec. 905 (1993)]

34–10. Gifts. Mabel Meredith gave Jeanette Taylor and Ann Dumler each a $25,000 check. Although Meredith owned property worth more than $2 million, she did not have enough in her checking account to cover the checks. Meredith died six years later, and Taylor and Dumler filed claims in a Maryland state court against her estate, represented by William Dulany, to recover the amounts of the checks. Does the receipt of a check represent a completed gift? Should Taylor and Dumler be awarded $25,000 each? [*Dulany v. Taylor*, 105 Md.App. 619, 660 A.2d 1046 (1995)]

A QUESTION OF ETHICS AND SOCIAL RESPONSIBILITY

34–11. *George Cook stayed at a Day's Inn Motel in Nashville, Tennessee, while attending a trade show. At the trade show, Cook received orders for 225 cases of his firm's product, representing $17,336.25 in profits to the company. On the third day of his stay, Cook's room was burglarized while he was gone from the room. The burglar took Cook's order lists, as well as $174 in cash and medicine worth about $10. Cook sued the owner of the motel, Columbia Sussex Corp., alleging negligence. The motel defended by stating that it had posted a notice on the door of Cook's room informing guests of the fact that the motel would not be liable for any valuable property not placed in the motel safe for safekeeping. Given these circumstances, evaluate and answer the following questions. [Cook v. Columbia Sussex Corp., 807 S.W.2d 567 (Tenn.App. 1990)]*

1. The relevant state statute governing the liability of innkeepers allowed motels to disclaim their liability by posting a notice such as the one posted by Day's Inn, but the statute also required that the notice be posted "in a conspicuous manner." The notice posted by Day's Inn on the inside of the door to Cook's room was six-by-three inches in size. In your opinion, is the notice sufficiently conspicuous? If you were the guest, would you notice the disclaimer? Is it fair to guests to assume that they will notice such disclaimers? Discuss fully.

2. Should hotels or motels ever be allowed to disclaim liability by posting such notices? From a policy point of view, evaluate the implications of your answer.

CASE BRIEFING ASSIGNMENT

34–12. *Examine Case A.9 [Strang v. Hollowell, 387 S.E.2d 664 (N.C.App. 1990)] in Appendix A. The case has been excerpted there in great detail. Review and then brief the case, making sure that you include answers to the following questions in your brief.*

1. Are there any facts in dispute in this case?
2. What was the only issue presented on appeal?
3. How was the bailment contract breached?
4. Why did the defendant, Hollowell, contend that he should not be held personally liable for the damages to the plaintiff's automobile?

FOR CRITICAL ANALYSIS

34–13. *Suppose that a certificate of deposit (CD) owned by two joint tenants (with the right of survivorship) is given by one of the joint tenants as security for a loan (without the other joint tenant's knowledge). Further suppose that the joint tenant died after defaulting on the loan. Who has superior rights in the CD, the creditor or the other surviving joint tenant?*

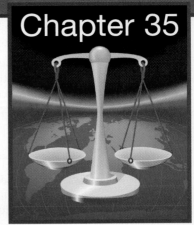

Chapter 35

Real Property

"The right of property is the most sacred of all the rights of citizenship."

Jean-Jacques Rousseau, 1712–1778
(French writer and philosopher)

CHAPTER OBJECTIVES

After reading this chapter, you should be able to:

1. Distinguish among different types of possessory ownership interests in real property.
2. Identify three types of nonpossessory interests in real property.
3. Discuss how ownership interests in real property can be transferred.
4. Indicate what a leasehold estate is and how a landlord-tenant relationship comes into existence.
5. Outline the respective rights of landlords and tenants concerning the possession, use, and maintenance of leased property.

From earliest times, property has provided a means for survival. Primitive peoples lived off the fruits of the land, eating the vegetation and wildlife. Later, as the wildlife was domesticated and the vegetation cultivated, property provided pasturage and farmland. In the twelfth and thirteenth centuries, the power of feudal lords was determined by the amount of land that they held; the more land they held, the more powerful they were. After the age of feudalism passed, property continued to be an indicator of family wealth and social position. In the Western world, the protection of an individual's right to his or her property has become, in the words of Jean-Jacques Rousseau, one of the "most sacred of all the rights of citizenship."

In this chapter, we first examine closely the nature of real property. We then look at the various ways in which real property can be owned and at how ownership rights in real property are transferred from one person to another. We conclude the chapter with a discussion of leased property and landlord-tenant relationships.

▌The Nature of Real Property

Real property consists of land and the buildings, plants, and trees that it contains. Real property also includes subsurface and air rights, as well as personal property that has become permanently attached to real property. Whereas personal property is movable, real property—also called *real estate* or *realty*—is immovable.

Land

Land includes the soil on the surface of the earth and the natural or artificial structures that are attached to it. It further includes all the waters contained on or under the surface and much, but not necessarily all, of the airspace above it. The exterior boundaries of land extend down to the center of the earth and up to the farthest reaches of the atmosphere (subject to certain qualifications).

Air and Subsurface Rights

The owner of real property has relatively exclusive rights to the airspace above the land, as well as to the soil and minerals underneath it.

AIR RIGHTS   Early cases involving air rights dealt with matters such as the right to run a telephone wire across a person's property when the wire did not touch any of the property[1] and whether a bullet shot over a person's land constituted trespass.[2] Today, disputes concerning air rights may involve the right of commercial and private planes to fly over property and the right of individuals and governments to seed clouds and produce artificial rain. Flights over private land do not normally violate the property owners' rights unless the flights are low and frequent enough to cause a direct interference with the enjoyment and use of the land.[3] Leaning walls or buildings and projecting eave spouts or roofs may also violate the air rights of an adjoining property owner.

SUBSURFACE RIGHTS   In many states, the owner of the surface of a piece of land is not the owner of the subsurface, and hence the land ownership may be separated. Subsurface rights can be extremely valuable, as these rights include the ownership of minerals and, in most states, oil and natural gas. Water rights are also extremely valuable, especially in the West. When the ownership is separated into surface and subsurface rights, each owner can pass title to what he or she owns without the consent of the other owner. Each owner has the right to use the land owned, and in some cases a conflict arises between a surface owner's use and the subsurface owner's need to extract minerals, oil, and natural gas. When this occurs, one party's interest may become subservient to the other party's interest, either by statute or case decision.

> **BE AWARE** If, during an excavation, a subsurface owner causes the land to subside, he or she may be liable to the owner of the surface.

Significant limitations on either air rights or subsurface rights normally have to be indicated on the deed transferring title at the time of purchase. (Deeds and the types of warranties they contain are discussed later in this chapter.)

Plant Life and Vegetation

Plant life, both natural and cultivated, is also considered to be real property. In many instances, the natural vegetation, such as trees, adds greatly to the value of the realty.

---

1. *Butler v. Frontier Telephone Co.*, 186 N.Y. 486, 79 N.E. 716 (1906).
2. *Herrin v. Sutherland*, 74 Mont. 587, 241 P. 328 (1925). Shooting over a person's land constitutes trespass.
3. *United States v. Causby*, 328 U.S. 256, 66 S.Ct. 1062, 90 L.Ed. 1206 (1946).

When a parcel of land is sold and the land has growing crops on it, the sale includes the crops, unless otherwise specified in the sales contract. When crops are sold by themselves, however, they are considered to be personal property or goods. Consequently, the sale of crops is a sale of goods, and therefore it is governed by the Uniform Commercial Code rather than by real property law.[4]

Fixtures

Certain personal property can become so closely associated with the real property to which it is attached that the law views it as real property. Such property is known as a **fixture**—a thing *affixed* to realty, meaning it is attached to it by roots; embedded in it; or permanently attached by means of cement, plaster, bolts, nails, or screws. The fixture can be physically attached to real property, be attached to another fixture, or even be without any actual physical attachment to the land (such as a statue). As long as the owner *intends* the property to be a fixture, normally it will be a fixture.

Fixtures are included in the sale of land if the sales contract does not provide otherwise. The sale of a house includes the land and the house and the garage on the land, as well as the cabinets, plumbing, and windows. Because these are permanently affixed to the property, they are considered to be a part of it. Unless otherwise agreed, however, the curtains and throw rugs are not included. Items such as drapes and window-unit air conditioners are difficult to classify. Thus, a contract for the sale of a house or commercial realty should indicate which items of this sort are included in the sale. The following case illustrates the court's interpretation of whether a grain storage silo became a fixture to the realty or remained personal property.

FIXTURE
A thing that was once personal property but that has become attached to real property in such a way that it takes on the characteristics of real property and becomes part of that real property.

---

4.   See UCC 2–107(2).

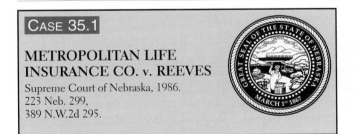

CASE 35.1

METROPOLITAN LIFE INSURANCE CO. v. REEVES
Supreme Court of Nebraska, 1986.
223 Neb. 299,
389 N.W.2d 295.

HISTORICAL AND TECHNOLOGICAL SETTING   *As a foundation, one type of grain storage silo uses a concrete slab that is partially embedded in the ground. The steel structures in which the grain is dried and stored are sometimes transported unassembled to the slab. The structures are then bolted together (with over a thousand bolts in each storage bin), lifted into the air, and hoisted onto the slab, where they are bolted into place. Some silos consist of three compartments: a dryer and two storage bins. To move the grain from the dryer into either of the bins, it may be necessary to pump air electronically through fifty or more feet of underground tubing. To take the silo apart and remove the steel structures can take more than two weeks.*

FACTS   Lawrence Reeves was a landowning farmer whose land was being foreclosed upon by his mortgage holder, Metropolitan Life Insurance Company. Prior to the foreclosure, Reeves had contracted with Production Sale Company to erect a grain storage facility on the farm. Its total cost was $171,185.30, of which Reeves had paid only $16,137.77. When Metropolitan brought the foreclosure proceedings, the question arose as to whether the grain storage facility was a fixture to the realty or personal property. If it was considered to be a fixture, Metropolitan would receive the proceeds from the sale; if it was considered to be personal property, the proceeds would go to Production Sale Company. A Nebraska state trial court held that the facility was a fixture. Production Sale Company appealed to the Supreme Court of Nebraska.

ISSUE   Was the facility a fixture to the real property, or was it personal property?

DECISION   The Supreme Court of Nebraska, reversing the district court's ruling, deemed the storage facility to be personal property.

(Continued)

Case 35.1—Continued

REASON The court cited three factors that determine whether an article, or combination of articles, is a fixture: (1) whether the article was actually annexed to the realty, (2) whether the article had been appropriated to the use or purpose of that part of the realty with which it was connected, and (3) whether it was the intention of the parties making the contract to affix the article permanently to the land. The last factor was the most important in determining this case, and the court gave much weight to the circumstances of the purchase agreement between Reeves and Production Sale. The court concluded that under the provisions of the purchase agreement, the parties had not intended the grain storage facility to become a part of the real property until full payment had been made. Because full payment had not been made, the facility had not become a fixture.

FOR CRITICAL ANALYSIS—Social Consideration *In determining whether an article of property is a fixture, why would the intent factor be more important than whether the article was actually annexed to the realty?*

Ownership of Real Property

"The institution called property guards the troubled boundary between [the] individual . . . and the state."

Charles A. Reich, 1928–
(American legal scholar)

Ownership of property is an abstract concept that cannot exist independently of the legal system. No one can actually possess or *hold* a piece of land, the air above it, the earth below it, and all the water contained on it. The legal system therefore recognizes certain rights and duties that constitute ownership interests in real property.

Recall from Chapter 34 that property ownership is often viewed as a bundle of rights. One who possesses the entire bundle of rights is said to hold the property in *fee simple*, which is the most complete form of ownership. When only some of the rights in the bundle are transferred to another person, the effect is to limit the ownership rights of both the one transferring the rights and the one receiving them.

Ownership in Fee Simple

The most common type of property ownership today is the fee simple. Generally, the term *fee simple* is used to designate a **fee simple absolute,** in which the owner has the greatest possible aggregation of rights, privileges, and power. The fee simple is limited absolutely to a person and his or her heirs and is assigned forever without limitation or condition. The rights that accompany a fee simple include the right to use the land for whatever purpose the owner sees fit, subject to laws that prevent the owner from unreasonably interfering with another person's land and subject to applicable zoning laws. Furthermore, the owner has the rights of *exclusive* possession and use of the property. A fee simple is potentially infinite in duration and can be disposed of by deed or by will (by selling or giving away). When there is no will, the fee simple passes to the owner's legal heirs.

Ownership in fee simple may become limited whenever the property is transferred to another *conditionally*. When this occurs, the fee simple is known as a **fee simple defeasible** (the word *defeasible* means capable of being terminated or annulled). For example, a **conveyance,** or transfer of real property, "to A and his heirs as long as the land is used for charitable purposes" creates a fee simple defeasible, because ownership of the property is conditioned on the land's being used for charitable purposes. The original owner retains a *partial* ownership interest, because if the specified condition does not occur (if the land ceases to be used for charitable purposes), then the land reverts, or returns, to the original owner. If the original owner is not living at the time, the land passes to his or her heirs.

FEE SIMPLE ABSOLUTE
An ownership interest in land in which the owner has the greatest possible aggregation of rights, privileges, and power. Ownership in fee simple absolute is limited absolutely to a person and his or her heirs.

FEE SIMPLE DEFEASIBLE
An ownership interest in real property that can be taken away (by the prior grantor) upon the occurrence or nonoccurrence of a specified event.

CONVEYANCE
The transfer of a title to land from one person to another by deed; a document (such as a deed) by which an interest in land is transferred from one person to another.

Life Estates

A **life estate** is an estate that lasts for the life of some specified individual. A conveyance "to A for his life" creates a life estate.[5] In a life estate, the life tenant has fewer rights of ownership than the holder of a fee simple defeasible, because the rights necessarily cease to exist on the life tenant's death. The life tenant has the right to use the land, provided that he or she commits no waste (injury to the land). In other words, the life tenant cannot injure the land in a manner that would adversely affect its value. The life tenant can use the land to harvest crops or, if mines and oil wells are already on the land, can extract minerals and oil from it, but the life tenant cannot exploit the land by creating new wells or mines. The life tenant has the right to mortgage the life estate and create liens, easements, and leases; but none can extend beyond the life of the tenant. In addition, with few exceptions, the owner of a life estate has an exclusive right to possession during his or her life.

Along with these rights, the life tenant also has some duties—to keep the property in repair and to pay property taxes. In short, the owner of the life estate has the same rights as a fee simple owner except that he or she must maintain the value of the property during his or her tenancy, less the decrease in value resulting from the normal use of the property allowed by the life tenancy.

Future Interests

When an owner in fee simple absolute conveys the estate conditionally to another (such as with a fee simple defeasible) or for a limited period of time (such as with a life estate), the original owner still retains an interest in the land. The owner retains the right to repossess ownership of the land if the conditions of the fee simple defeasible are not met or when the life of the life-estate holder ends. The residuary (or leftover) interest in the property that the owner retains is called a **future interest,** because if it arises, it will only arise in the future.

If the owner retains ownership of the future interest, then the future interest is described as a **reversionary interest,** because the property will *revert* to the original owner if the condition specified in a fee simple defeasible fails or when a life tenant dies. If, however, the owner of the future interest transfers ownership rights in that future interest to another, the future interest is described as a **remainder.** For example, a conveyance "to A for life, then to B" creates a life estate for A and a remainder (future interest) for B. An **executory interest** is a type of future interest very similar to a remainder, the difference being that an executory interest does not take effect immediately on the expiration of another interest, such as a life estate. For example, a conveyance "to A and his (or her) heirs, as long as the premises are used for charitable purposes, and if not so used for charitable purposes, then to B" creates an executory interest in the property for B.

Nonpossessory Interests

In contrast to the types of property interests just described, some interests in land do not include any rights to possess the property. These interests are thus known as *nonpossessory interests.* Two forms of nonpossessory interests are easements and profits. A license to come onto property is also a nonpossessory interest.

An **easement** is the right of a person to make limited use of another person's real property without taking anything from the property. An easement, for example, can be the right to travel over another's property. In contrast, a **profit**[6] is the right to go onto

LIFE ESTATE
An interest in land that exists only for the duration of the life of some person, usually the holder of the estate.

FUTURE INTEREST
An interest in real property that is not at present possessory but will or may become possessory in the future.

REVERSIONARY INTEREST
A future interest in property retained by the original owner.

REMAINDER
A future interest in property held by a person other than the original owner.

EXECUTORY INTEREST
A future interest, held by a person other than the grantor, that begins after the termination of the preceding estate.

EASEMENT
A nonpossessory right to use another's property in a manner established by either express or implied agreement.

PROFIT
In real property law, the right to enter upon and remove things from the property of another (for example, the right to enter onto a person's land and remove sand and gravel therefrom).

---

5. A less common type of life estate is created by the conveyance "to A for the life of B." This is known as an estate *pur autre vie,* or an estate for the duration of the life of another.

6. The term *profit,* as used here, does not refer to the "profits" made by a business firm. Rather, it means a gain or an advantage.

land in possession of another and take away some part of the land itself or some product of the land. For example, Akmed, the owner of Sandy View, gives Carmen the right to go there and remove all the sand and gravel that she needs for her cement business. Carmen has a profit. Easements and profits can be classified as either *appurtenant* or *in gross*. Because easements and profits are similar and the same rules apply to both, they are discussed together.

EASEMENT OR PROFIT APPURTENANT　An easement or profit appurtenant arises when the owner of one piece of land has a right to go onto (or to remove things from) an *adjacent* piece of land owned by another. Suppose that Acosta, the owner of Juniper Hills, has a right to drive his car across Green's land, Greenacres, which is adjacent to Juniper Hills. This right-of-way over Green's property is an easement appurtenant to Juniper Hills and can be used only by the owner of Juniper Hills. Acosta can convey the easement when he conveys Juniper Hills. Now suppose that the highway is on the other side of Bancroft's property, which is on the other side of Green's property. To reach the highway, Acosta has an easement across both Green's and Bancroft's properties. Juniper Hills and Bancroft's property are not adjacent, but Green's and Bancroft's properties are, so Acosta has an easement appurtenant.

CONTRAST An easement appurtenant requires two pieces of land owned by two different persons, but an easement in gross needs only one piece of land owned by someone other than the owner of the easement.

EASEMENT OR PROFIT IN GROSS　An easement or profit in gross exists when one's right to use or take things from another's land does not depend on one's owning an adjacent tract of land. Suppose that Avery owns a parcel of land with a marble quarry. Avery conveys to XYZ Corporation, which owns no land, the right to come onto his land and remove up to five hundred pounds of marble per day. XYZ Corporation owns a profit in gross. When a utility company is granted an easement to run its power lines across another's property, it obtains an easement in gross.

EFFECT OF A SALE OF PROPERTY　When a parcel of land that is *benefited* by an easement or profit appurtenant is sold, the property carries the easement or profit along with it. Thus, if Acosta sells Juniper Hills to Thomas and includes the appurtenant right-of-way across Green's property in the deed to Thomas, Thomas will own both the property and the easement that benefits it.

When a parcel of land that has the *burden* of an easement or profit appurtenant is sold, the new owner must recognize its existence only if he or she knew or should have known of it or if it was recorded in the appropriate office of the county. Thus, if Acosta records his easement across Green's property in the appropriate county office before Green conveys the land, the new owner of Green's property will have to allow Acosta, or any subsequent owner of Juniper Hills, to continue to use the path across Green's property.

CREATION OF AN EASEMENT OR PROFIT　Easements and profits can be created by deed, by will, or by implication, necessity, or prescription. Creation by *deed* or *will* simply involves the delivery of a deed or a disposition in a will by the owner of an easement stating that the grantee (the person receiving the profit or easement) is granted the owner's rights in the easement or profit.

An easement or profit may be created by *implication* when the circumstances surrounding the division of a parcel of property imply its creation. If Barrow divides a parcel of land that has only one well for drinking water and conveys the half without a well to Jarad, a profit by implication arises, because Jarad needs drinking water.

An easement may also be created by *necessity*. An easement by necessity does not require division of property for its existence. A person who rents an apartment, for example, has an easement by necessity in the private road leading up to it.

Easements and profits by *prescription* are created in much the same way as title to property is obtained by *adverse possession* (discussed later in this chapter). An easement arises by prescription when one person exercises an easement, such as a right-of-way, on another person's land without the landowner's consent, and the use is apparent and continues for a period of time equal to the applicable statute of limitations.

TERMINATION OF AN EASEMENT OR PROFIT   An easement or profit can be terminated or extinguished in several ways. The simplest way is to deed it back to the owner of the land that is burdened by it. Another way is to abandon it and create evidence of intent to relinquish the right to use it. Mere nonuse will not extinguish an easement or profit *unless the nonuse is accompanied by an intent to abandon.* Finally, when the owner of an easement or profit becomes the owner of the property burdened by it, then it is merged into the property.

LICENSE   A **license** is the revocable right of a person to come onto another person's land. It is a personal privilege that arises from the consent of the owner of the land and that can be revoked by the owner. A ticket to attend a movie at a theater is an example of a license. Assume that a Broadway theater owner issues to Carla a ticket to see a play. If Carla is refused entry into the theater because she is improperly dressed, she has no right to force her way into the theater. The ticket is only a revocable license, not a conveyance of an interest in property.

LICENSE
A revocable right or privilege of a person to come on another person's land.

▍Transfer of Ownership

Ownership of real property can pass from one person to another in a number of ways. Commonly, ownership interests in land are transferred by sale, in which case the terms of the transfer are specified in a real estate sales contract. When real property is sold or transferred as a gift, title to the property is conveyed by means of a **deed**—the instrument of conveyance of real property. We look here at transfers of real property by deed, as well as some other ways in which ownership rights in real property can be transferred.

DEED
A document by which title to property (usually real property) is passed.

Deeds

A valid deed must contain the following elements:

1.   The names of the buyer (grantee) and seller (grantor).
2.   Words evidencing an intent to convey the property (for example, "I hereby bargain, sell, grant, or give").
3.   A legally sufficient description of the land.
4.   The grantor's (and usually the spouse's) signature.

Additionally, to be valid, a deed must be delivered to the person to whom the property is being conveyed or to his or her agent.

WARRANTY DEEDS   Different types of deeds provide different degrees of protection against defects of title. A **warranty deed** warrants the greatest number of things and thus provides the greatest protection for the buyer, or grantee. In most states, special language is required to make a deed a general warranty deed; normally, the deed must include a written promise to protect the buyer against all claims of ownership of the property. A sample warranty deed is shown in Exhibit 35–1. Warranty deeds commonly include a number of *covenants*, or promises, that the grantor makes to the grantee.

A *covenant of seisin*[7] and a *covenant of the right to convey* warrant that the seller has title to the estate that the deed describes and the power to convey the estate,

WARRANTY DEED
A deed in which the grantor guarantees to the grantee that the grantor has title to the property conveyed in the deed, that there are no encumbrances on the property other than what the grantor has represented, and that the grantee will enjoy quiet possession of the property; a deed that provides the greatest amount of protection for the grantee.

---

7.   Pronounced *see*-zuhn.

◆ Exhibit 35–1
   A Sample Warranty Deed

Date: May 31, 1998

Grantor: GAYLORD A. JENTZ AND WIFE, JOANN H. JENTZ

Grantor's Mailing Address (including county):
        4106 North Loop Drive
        Austin, Travis County, Texas

Grantee: DAVID F. FRIEND AND WIFE, JOAN E. FRIEND AS JOINT TENANTS
        WITH RIGHT OF SURVIVORSHIP
Grantee's Mailing Address (including county):
        5929 Fuller Drive
        Austin, Travis County, Texas

Consideration:
For and in consideration of the sum of Ten and No/100 Dollars ($10.00) and other
valuable consideration to the undersigned paid by the grantees herein named, the
receipt of which is hereby acknowledged, and for which no lien is retained, either
express or implied.

Property (including any improvements):
Lot 23, Block "A", Northwest Hills, Green Acres Addition, Phase 4, Travis County,
Texas, according to the map or plat of record in volume 22, pages 331-336 of the
Plat Records of Travis County, Texas.

Reservations from and Exceptions to Conveyance and Warranty:

This conveyance with its warranty is expressly made subject to the following:

Easements and restrictions of record in Volume 7863, Page 53, Volume 8430,
Page 35, Volume 8133, Page 152 of the Real Property Record of Travis County,
Texas; Volume 22, Pages 335-339, of the Plat Records of Travis County, Texas;
and to any other restrictions and easements affecting said property which are
of record in Travis County, Texas.

Grantor, for the consideration and subject to the reservations from and exceptions to conveyance and warranty, grants,
sells, and conveys to Grantee the property, together with all and singular the rights and appurtenances thereto in any wise
belonging, to have and hold it to Grantee, Grantee s heirs, executors, administrators, successors, or assigns forever.
Grantor binds Grantor and Grantor s heirs, executors, administrators, and successors to warrant and forever defend all and
singular the property to Grantee and Grantee s heirs, executors, administrators, successors, and assigns against every
person whomsoever lawfully claiming or to claim the same or any part thereof, except as to the reservations from and
exceptions to conveyance and warranty.

When the context requires, singular nouns and pronouns include the plural.

                                    BY: *Gaylord A. Jentz*
                                        Gaylord A. Jentz

                                    BY: *John H. Jentz*
                                        JoAnn H. Jentz

                        (Acknowledgment)

STATE OF TEXAS
COUNTY OF TRAVIS

        This instrument was acknowledged before me on the   31st day of May   . 1998

                        Rosemary Potter
                        Notary Public.State of Texas
                        Notary s name (printed): Rosemary Potter

            Notary Seal
                        Notary s commission expires: 1/31/2002

respectively. The covenant of seisin specifically assures the buyer that the grantor has the property in the purported quantity and quality.

A *covenant against encumbrances* is a covenant that the property being sold or conveyed is not subject to any outstanding rights or interests that will diminish the value of the land, except as explicitly stated. Examples of common encumbrances include mortgages, liens, profits, easements, and private deed restrictions on the use of the land.

A *covenant of quiet enjoyment* guarantees that the buyer will not be disturbed in his or her possession of the land by the seller or any third persons. For example, assume that Julio sells a two-acre lot and office building by warranty deed. Subsequently, a third person shows better title than Julio had and proceeds to evict the buyer. Here, the covenant of quiet enjoyment has been breached, and the buyer can recover the purchase price of the land plus any other damages incurred as a result of the eviction.

QUITCLAIM DEEDS   A **quitclaim deed** offers the least amount of protection against defects in the title. Basically, a quitclaim deed conveys to the grantee whatever interest the grantor had; so if the grantor had no interest, then the grantee receives no interest. Quitclaim deeds are often used when the seller, or grantor, is uncertain as to the extent of his or her rights in the property.

RECORDING STATUTES   Every jurisdiction has **recording statutes**, which allow deeds to be recorded. Recording a deed gives notice to the public that a certain person is now the owner of a particular parcel of real estate. Thus, prospective buyers can check the public records to see whether there have been earlier transactions creating interests or rights in specific parcels of real property. Placing everyone on notice as to the identity of the true owner is intended to prevent the previous owners from fraudulently conveying the land to other purchasers. Deeds are recorded in the county in which the property is located. Many state statutes require that the grantor sign the deed in the presence of two witnesses before it can be recorded.

Will or Inheritance

Property that is transferred on an owner's death is passed either by will or by state inheritance laws. If the owner of land dies with a will, the land passes in accordance with the terms of the will. If the owner dies without a will, state inheritance statutes prescribe how and to whom the property will pass. Transfers of property by will or inheritance are examined in detail in Chapter 36.

Adverse Possession

Adverse possession is a means of obtaining title to land without delivery of a deed. Essentially, when one person possesses the property of another for a certain statutory period of time (three to thirty years, with ten years being most common), that person, called the *adverse possessor*, acquires title to the land and cannot be removed from it by the original owner. The adverse possessor is vested with a perfect title just as if there had been a conveyance by deed.

For property to be held adversely, four elements must be satisfied:

1.   Possession must be actual and exclusive; that is, the possessor must take sole physical occupancy of the property.
2.   The possession must be open, visible, and notorious, not secret or clandestine. The possessor must occupy the land for all the world to see.
3.   Possession must be continuous and peaceable for the required period of time. This requirement means that the possessor must not be interrupted in the occupancy by the true owner or by the courts.

QUITCLAIM DEED
A deed intended to pass any title, interest, or claim that the grantor may have in the property but not warranting that such title is valid. A quitclaim deed offers the least amount of protection against defects in the title.

RECORDING STATUTES
Statutes that allow deeds, mortgages, and other real property transactions be recorded so as to provide notice to future purchasers or creditors of an existing claim on the property.

ADVERSE POSSESSION
The acquisition of title to real property by occupying it openly, without the consent of the owner, for a period of time specified by a state statute. The occupation must be actual, open, notorious, exclusive, and in opposition to all others, including the owner.

4. Possession must be hostile and adverse. In other words, the possessor must claim the property as against the whole world. He or she cannot be living on the property with the permission of the owner.

There are a number of public-policy reasons for the adverse possession doctrine. These reasons include society's interest in resolving boundary disputes and determining ownership rights when title to property is in question and in assuring that real property remains in the stream of commerce. More fundamentally, policies behind the doctrine include not rewarding owners who sit on their rights too long and rewarding possessors for putting land to productive use. In the following case, the question before the court was whether a couple had obtained title to a certain portion of land by adverse possession.

CASE 35.2

KLOS v. MOLENDA

Superior Court of Pennsylvania, 1986.
355 Pa.Super. 399,
513 A.2d 490.

HISTORICAL AND CULTURAL SETTING *After World War II ended in 1945, members of the armed forces returned to their families or began families, and the birthrate increased dramatically each year for a time. Many of the former servicepeople went to college, but even those who did not go back to school needed relatively low-cost housing. In 1947, a builder, Abraham Levitt, and his sons developed Levittown—a community on Long Island consisting of inexpensive houses and a playground, shops, and other amenities. Over the next few years, other builders began to imitate Levitt's idea, and by 1950, suburban developments were sprawling across the American landscape.*

FACTS In September 1950, Michael and Albina Klos purchased part of some property in Pennsylvania owned by John and Anne Molenda. The Kloses' lot was 50 feet wide and 135 feet deep. Rather than surveying the property, the seller and buyer paced off the lot and placed stakes in the ground as boundary markers. The Kloses built a house on the lot in 1952 and put in a sidewalk along the full front. They also put in a driveway thirty inches from the stake line. They planted grass in that thirty inches and maintained it until 1984. In 1983, John Molenda died, and his widow hired a surveyor to inventory the landholdings. The survey located the rightful property line between the Molendas' and the Kloses' land as being thirty inches closer to the Kloses' house than the line established earlier. This placed the property line right along the Kloses' driveway, instead of thirty inches to the side of the driveway. Upon learning this, Anne Molenda erected a fence right along the Kloses' driveway to mark the property line. The Kloses brought an action in a Pennsylvania state court challenging Anne Molenda's conduct, claiming that they held title to the land by adverse possession. The trial court held that the Kloses had title to the land. Anne Molenda appealed.

ISSUE Who held title to the thirty-inch strip of land?

DECISION The Kloses held rightful title to the land. The appellate court affirmed the trial court's decision.

REASON The rule of adverse possession holds that if a person has actual, continuous, exclusive, visible, notorious, distinct, and hostile possession of land for a long period of time (in Pennsylvania, twenty-one years), that person gains title to the land. This means that the adverse possessor must use the land in a regular, normal, and obvious manner so that the original title owner would know, on inspection, of the possessor's use. If the original title owner does not evict the possessor or otherwise exercise his or her ownership rights, then the possessor will obtain title once the statutory time period has lapsed. Here, the Kloses were certainly open, hostile, and notorious in their possession of the land in question, and they possessed the land for over thirty years. They therefore obtained title to the land by adverse possession.

FOR CRITICAL ANALYSIS—Ethical Consideration *If the Kloses had known from the outset that the Molendas actually owned the thirty-inch strip of land, would this have affected the outcome in this case?*

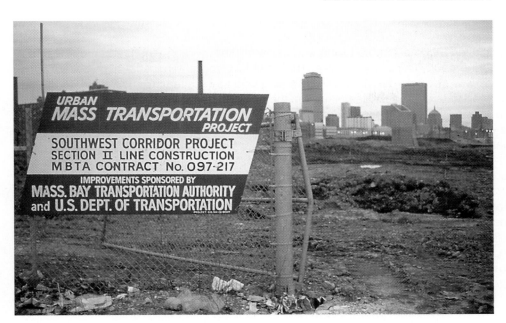

A local government undertakes a mass transit project. Why is the government prohibited from taking private land for public uses without paying the owner?

Eminent Domain

Even ownership in real property in fee simple absolute is limited by a superior ownership. Just as in medieval England the king was the ultimate landowner, so in the United States the government has an ultimate ownership right in all land. This right is known as **eminent domain**, and it is sometimes referred to as the condemnation power of the government to take land for public use. It gives the government a right to acquire possession of real property in the manner directed by the Constitution and the laws of the state whenever the public interest requires it. Property may be taken only for public use.

When the government takes land owned by a private party for public use, it is referred to as a **taking**, and the government must compensate the private party. Under the so-called *takings clause* of the Fifth Amendment, the government may not take private property for public use without "just compensation."

The power of eminent domain is generally invoked through condemnation proceedings. For example, when a new public highway is to be built, the government must decide where to build it and how much land to condemn. After the government determines that a particular parcel of land is necessary for public use, it brings a judicial proceeding to obtain title to the land. Then, in another proceeding, the court determines the *fair value* of the land, which is usually approximately equal to its market value.

In an attempt to preserve the natural beauty and resources of the land, environmental laws have increasingly prohibited private parties from using certain lands (wetlands and coastal lands, for example) in specific ways. Does imposing such limitations on landowners' rights constitute a taking by the government? This question is explored in this chapter's *Business Law in Action* on page 916.

EMINENT DOMAIN
The power of a government to take land for public use from private citizens for just compensation.

TAKING
The taking of private property by the government for public use. Under the Fifth Amendment to the Constitution, the government may not take private property for public use without "just compensation."

Homeowners, particularly in high-crime areas, sometimes face a difficult—and expensive—situation. Police officers in pursuit of a wrongdoer may damage the homes of innocent persons in the process. The ethical question here is who should assume responsibility for these damages, the government or the innocent homeowners? Some homeowners have alleged that the reduction in the value of their property

Ethical Perspective

(Continued)

Ethical Perspective—Continued

constitutes a compensable taking on the part of the government. Is it? According to at least one court, the answer is yes. The case involved a Minnesota homeowner whose house was severely damaged by the police when they attempted to capture a suspect who had entered and hidden himself in the home. To force the suspect out of the house, the police and a SWAT team fired rounds of tear gas into the home and threw grenades as well. The Supreme Court of Minnesota held that the damages constituted a taking and that the homeowner should be compensated for the damages to her home.[a]

In another case, however, the court held differently. The owner of a California convenience store had to spend $275,000 to repair the damages caused by police officers who were trying to capture a robbery suspect. The Supreme Court of California held that the damages were not a compensable taking. It held that the takings clause was not designed to compensate innocent persons for damages resulting from "routine efforts to enforce the criminal laws."[b]

For Critical Analysis: *What might be the effect on society if courts routinely held that damage to property owned by innocent persons was a compensable taking?*

a.　*Wegner v. Milwaukee Mutual Insurance Co.,* 479 N.W.2d 38 (Minn. 1991).
b.　*Customer Co. v. City of Sacramento,* 10 Cal.4th 368, 895 P.2d 900, 41 Cal.Rptr.2d 658 (1995).

▍Leasehold Estates

LEASE
In real property law, a contract by which the owner of real property (the landlord, or lessor) grants to a person (the tenant, or lessee) an exclusive right to use and possess the property, usually for a specified period of time, in return for rent or some other form of payment.

Often, real property is used by those who do not own it. A **lease** is a contract by which the owner of real property (the landlord, or lessor) grants to a person (the tenant, or lessee) an exclusive right to use and possess the property, usually for a specified period of time, in return for rent or some other form of payment. Property in the possession of a tenant is referred to as a **leasehold estate.**

The respective rights and duties of the landlord and tenant that arise under a lease agreement will be discussed shortly. Here we look at the types of leasehold estates, or tenancies, that can be created when real property is leased.

LEASEHOLD ESTATE
An estate in realty held by a tenant under a lease. In every leasehold estate, the tenant has a qualified right to possess and/or use the land.

Tenancy for Years

TENANCY FOR YEARS
A type of tenancy under which property is leased for a specified period of time, such as a month, a year, or a period of years.

A **tenancy for years** is created by an express contract by which property is leased for a specified period of time, such as a month, a year, or a period of years. For example, signing a one-year lease to occupy an apartment creates a tenancy for years. At the end of the period specified in the lease, the lease ends (without notice), and possession of the apartment returns to the lessor. If the tenant dies during the period of the lease, the lease interest passes to the tenant's heirs as personal property. Often, leases include renewal or extension provisions.

Periodic Tenancy

PERIODIC TENANCY
A lease interest in land for an indefinite period involving payment of rent at fixed intervals, such as week to week, month to month, or year to year.

A **periodic tenancy** is created by a lease that does not specify how long it is to last but does specify that rent is to be paid at certain intervals. This type of tenancy is automatically renewed for another rental period unless properly terminated. For example, a periodic tenancy is created by a lease that states, "Rent is due on the tenth day of every month." This provision creates a tenancy from month to month. This type of tenancy can also extend from week to week or from year to year.

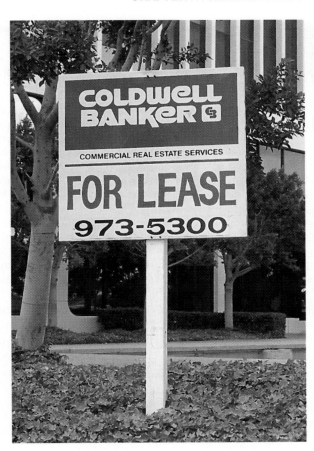

How does a leasehold estate differ from ownership in fee simple, from a life estate, and from such nonpossessory interests as easements and profits?

Under the common law, to terminate a periodic tenancy, the landlord or tenant must give one period's notice to the other party. If the tenancy extends from month to month, for example, one month's notice must be given. State statutes may require a different period for notice of termination in a periodic tenancy, however.

Tenancy at Will

Suppose that a landlord rents an apartment to a tenant "for as long as both agree." In such a situation, the tenant receives a leasehold estate known as a **tenancy at will.** Under the common law, either party can terminate the tenancy without notice (that is, "at will"). This type of estate usually arises when a tenant who has been under a tenancy for years retains possession after the termination date of that tenancy with the landlord's consent. Before the tenancy has been converted into a periodic tenancy (by the periodic payment of rent), it is a tenancy at will, terminable by either party without notice. Once the tenancy is treated as a periodic tenancy, termination notice must conform to the one already discussed for that type of tenancy. The death of either party or the voluntary commission of waste by the tenant will terminate a tenancy at will.

Tenancy at Sufferance

The mere possession of land without right is called a **tenancy at sufferance.** It is not a true tenancy. A tenancy at sufferance is not an estate, because it is created when a tenant *wrongfully* retains possession of property. Whenever a tenancy for years, periodic tenancy, or tenancy at will ends and the tenant continues to retain possession of the premises without the owner's permission, a tenancy at sufferance is created.

TENANCY AT WILL
A type of tenancy under which either party can terminate the tenancy without notice; usually arises when a tenant who has been under a tenancy for years retains possession, with the landlord's consent, after the tenancy for years has terminated.

TENANCY AT SUFFERANCE
A type of tenancy under which one who, after rightfully being in possession of leased premises, continues (wrongfully) to occupy the property after the lease has been terminated. The tenant has no rights to possess the property and occupies it only because the person entitled to evict the tenant has not done so.

Private versus Public Property Rights

Environmental regulations and other legislation to control land use are prevalent throughout the United States. Generally, these laws reflect the public's interest in preserving the beauty and natural resources of the land and in allowing the public to have access to and enjoy limited natural resources, such as coastal areas. Although few would disagree with the rationale underlying these laws, the owners of the private property directly affected by the laws may feel that they should be compensated for the limitation imposed on their right to do as they wish with their land. Several cases have been brought by private-property owners who allege that regulations limiting their control over their own land essentially constitute a taking of private-property rights in the public interest. Therefore, the private-property owners should receive the just compensation guaranteed under the Fifth Amendment.

For example, in one case a New Jersey property developer, Loveladies Harbor, Inc., owned fifty-one acres of land and planned to construct thirty-

five single-family homes on fifty of the acres. A significant portion of the land (twelve-and-a-half acres) consisted of wetlands that would need to be filled. Loveladies sought a permit from the Army Corps of Engineers to fill these wetlands, as required under the Clean Water Act (see Chapter 31). The Corps denied the permit, and ultimately Loveladies brought an action alleging that the refusal to allow it to develop the twelve-and-a-half acres constituted a compensable taking under the Fifth Amendment.

The trial court held that when the Corps denied the permit to fill the wetlands, a taking had occurred. In affirming the trial court's decision, the federal appellate court phrased the essential question in the case as follows: "[W]hen the Government fulfills its obligation to preserve and protect the public interest, may the cost of obtaining that public benefit fall solely upon the affected property owner, or is it to be shared by the community at large[?]" The court, adopting the view of an increasing number of other courts, concluded that the expense should be borne by the public.[a]

For years, courts evaluating similar claims brought by private-property

owners alleging regulatory takings generally sided with the public authorities and held that no compensable takings had occurred. Beginning in the 1980s, however, the tide began to turn, and the courts now give a little more weight to the interests of private property owners.[b] This trend was bolstered by a United States Supreme Court ruling in 1994 in which the Court held that the city of Tigard, Oregon (a Portland suburb), could not require a property owner to dedicate a portion of her property for public use without compensation.[c]

For Critical Analysis: *Why are courts more willing today than in the past to consider the rights of private property owners in regard to alleged regulatory takings?*

a. *Loveladies Harbor, Inc. v. United States*, 28 F.3d 1171 (Fed.Cir. 1994).

b. See, for example, *Bell v. Town of Wells*, 557 A.2d 168 (Me. 1989); *Nollan v. California Coastal Commission*, 483 U.S. 825, 107 S.Ct. 3141, 97 L.Ed.2d 677 (1987); and *Lucas v. South Carolina Coastal Council*, 505 U.S. 1003, 112 S.Ct. 2886, 120 L.Ed.2d 798 (1992).

c. *Dolan v. City of Tigard*, 512 U.S. 374, 114 S.Ct. 2309, 129 L.Ed.2d 304 (1994).

▌Landlord-Tenant Relationships

In the past several decades, landlord-tenant relationships have become much more complex than they were before, as has the law governing them. Generally, the law has come to apply contract doctrines, such as those providing for implied warranties and unconscionability, to the landlord-tenant relationship. Increasingly, landlord-tenant relationships have become subject to specific state and local statutes and ordinances as well. In 1972, in an effort to create more uniformity in the law governing landlord-tenant relationships, the National Conference of Commissioners on Uniform State Laws issued the Uniform Residential Landlord and Tenant Act (URLTA). We look now at how a landlord-tenant relationship is created and at the respective rights and duties of landlords and tenants.

Creating the Landlord-Tenant Relationship

A landlord-tenant relationship is established by a lease contract. As mentioned, a lease contract arises when a property owner (landlord) agrees to give another party (the tenant) the exclusive right to possess the property—usually for a price and for a specified term.

FORM OF THE LEASE   A lease contract may be oral or written. Under the common law, an oral lease is valid. As with most oral contracts, however, a party who seeks to enforce an oral lease may have difficulty proving its existence. In most states, statutes mandate that leases be in writing for some tenancies (such as those exceeding one year). To ensure the validity of a lease agreement, it should therefore be in writing and do the following:

NOTE Sound business practice dictates that a lease for commercial property should be written carefully and should clearly define the parties' rights and obligations.

1.   Express an intent to establish the relationship.
2.   Provide for the transfer of the property's possession to the tenant at the beginning of the term.
3.   Provide for the landlord's reversionary interest, which entitles the property owner to retake possession at the end of the term.
4.   Describe the property—for example, give its street address.
5.   Indicate the length of the term, the amount of the rent, and how and when it is to be paid.

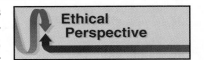

Because lease contracts are commonly drafted by the landlord, prospective tenants who are unfamiliar with certain terms and clauses may not realize the legal consequences of signing a lease. The *unconscionability* concept, founded in contract law, helps protect tenants from contracts in which they have signed away, without realizing it, important rights.

Basically, as applied to leases in some jurisdictions, the unconscionability concept follows the unconscionability provision of the Uniform Commercial Code (UCC). Under UCC 2–302, a court may declare an entire contract or any of its clauses unconscionable and thus illegal, depending on the circumstances surrounding the transaction and the parties' relative bargaining positions. For example, in a residential lease, a clause claiming to absolve a landlord from responsibility for interruptions in such essential services as central heating or air conditioning will not shield the landlord from liability if the systems break down when they are needed most.

For Critical Analysis: *In landlord-tenant disputes, courts tend to be more protective of residential tenants than commercial tenants. Why is this?*

LEGAL REQUIREMENTS   State or local law often dictates permissible lease terms. For example, a statute or ordinance might prohibit the leasing of a structure that is in a certain physical condition or is not in compliance with local building codes. Similarly, a statute may prohibit the leasing of property for a particular purpose. For instance, a state law might prohibit gambling houses. Thus, if a landlord and tenant intend that the leased premises be used only to house an illegal betting operation, their lease is unenforceable.

A property owner cannot legally discriminate against prospective tenants on the basis of race, color, national origin, religion, gender, or disability. Similarly, a tenant cannot legally promise to do something counter to laws prohibiting discrimination. A tenant, for example, cannot legally promise to do business only with members of a particular race. The public policy underlying these prohibitions is to treat all people equally.

Often, rental properties are leased by agents of the landowner. Recall from Chapter 23 that under the theory of *respondeat superior*, a principal (a landlord, with respect to leases) is liable for the wrongful actions of his or her agent if the actions occurred within the scope of employment. At issue in the following case is whether a landlord can be held liable for his agent's discrimination on the basis of sex against a woman who sought to rent a particular apartment.

CASE 35.3

WALKER v. CRIGLER
United States Court of Appeals,
Fourth Circuit, 1992.
976 F.2d 900.

HISTORICAL AND SOCIAL SETTING   *At common law, a landlord was free to rent, or refuse to rent, to anyone for any reason. For example, a landlord was not required to rent an apartment to someone with a considerable number of unpaid bills. Today, that rule still generally applies: a landlord does not need a particularly good reason to refuse to rent his or her property to someone. Over the last forty years, however, the federal government has recognized that persons have a right not to be denied a housing opportunity because of race, color, religion, gender, national origin, mental or physical disability, marital status, or the presence of children. Some states protect against discrimination on the basis of other characteristics as well, such as age.*

FACTS   Darlene Walker, a single parent with one son, was looking for an apartment in Falls Church, Virginia. A real estate agent, John Moore, was assisting her in her search and took Walker to view an apartment owned by Frank Whitesell III and managed by Constance Crigler. Walker liked the apartment because it was near a school for her son and near transportation, and Moore called Crigler and told her that he had an applicant for the apartment. Crigler told Moore, and later Walker, that she would never rent to a woman in any circumstances. Walker asked Crigler if she was speaking for the owner, and Crigler said that she was. Walker sued Crigler and Whitesell in a federal district court for violating federal laws prohibiting discrimination in housing. The trial court found Crigler liable for damages in the amount of $5,000 but held that Whitesell was not liable for Crigler's actions, because he had previously instructed her, in writing, not to discriminate illegally against any potential renters. Walker appealed. (Shortly after the appeal was filed, Crigler filed for Chapter 7 bankruptcy, and a few months later the $5,000 judgment against her was discharged.)

ISSUE   Can Whitesell be held liable for Crigler's discrimination against Walker?

DECISION   Yes. The U.S. Court of Appeals for the Fourth Circuit reversed the trial court's decision on this issue. Whitesell was ordered to pay $5,000 in damages to Walker.

REASON   The trial jury had found that Crigler, because she disobeyed Whitesell's instructions, had acted outside the scope of her employment. The appellate court stated that this was an erroneous reading of the law. For one thing, the appellate court doubted whether the "mere act of instructing Crigler not to discriminate would be sufficient to justify a ruling that she was acting outside the scope of employment." In any event, whether Crigler was acting within the scope of her employment was irrelevant in this case, because the duty not to discriminate was nondelegable. The court noted that just as property owners cannot avoid responsibilities for paying taxes and meeting health and safety requirements by delegating those responsibilities to others, neither can owners avoid the duty not to discriminate through delegation of the duty. In sum, said the court, "Whitesell could not insulate himself from liability for sex discrimination in regard to living premises owned by him and managed for his benefit merely by relinquishing the responsibility for preventing such discrimination to another party."

FOR CRITICAL ANALYSIS—Ethical Consideration
For what policy reasons do courts impose liability on landlords for their agents' actions?

Rights and Duties

The rights and duties of landlords and tenants generally pertain to four broad areas of concern—the possession, use, and maintenance of leased property and, of course, rent.

POSSESSION　Possession involves both the obligation of the landlord to deliver possession to the tenant at the beginning of the lease term and the right of the tenant to obtain possession and retain it until the lease expires.

The covenant of quiet enjoyment mentioned previously also applies to leased premises. Under this covenant, the landlord promises that during the lease term, neither the landlord nor anyone having a superior title to the property will disturb the tenant's use and enjoyment of the property. This covenant forms the essence of the landlord-tenant relationship, and if it is breached, the tenant can terminate the lease and sue for damages.

If the landlord deprives the tenant of the tenant's possession of the leased property or interferes with the tenant's use or enjoyment of it, an **eviction** occurs. An eviction occurs, for example, when the landlord changes the lock and refuses to give the tenant a new key. A **constructive eviction** occurs when the landlord wrongfully performs or fails to perform any of the undertakings the lease requires, thereby making the tenant's further use and enjoyment of the property exceedingly difficult or impossible. Examples of constructive eviction include a landlord's failure to provide heat in the winter, light, or other essential utilities.

USE AND MAINTENANCE OF THE PREMISES　If the parties do not limit by agreement the uses to which the property may be put, the tenant may make any use of it, as long as the use is legal and reasonably relates to the purpose for which the property is adapted or ordinarily used and does not injure the landlord's interest.

The tenant is responsible for any damages to the premises that he or she causes, intentionally or negligently, and the tenant may be held liable for the cost of returning the property to the physical condition it was in at the lease's inception. Unless the parties have agreed otherwise, the tenant is not responsible for ordinary wear and tear and the property's consequent depreciation in value.

Usually, the landlord must comply with state statutes and city ordinances that delineate specific standards for the construction and maintenance of buildings. Typically, these codes contain structural requirements common to the construction, wiring, and plumbing of residential and commercial buildings. In some jurisdictions, landlords of residential property are required by statute to maintain the premises in good repair.

EVICTION
A landlord's act of depriving a tenant of possession of the leased premises.

CONSTRUCTIVE EVICTION
A form of eviction that occurs when a landlord fails to perform adequately any of the undertakings (such as providing heat in the winter) required by the lease, thereby making the tenant's further use and enjoyment of the property exceedingly difficult or impossible.

Unlike the law in the United States governing landlord-tenant relationships, much of which evolved under the common law, English landlord-tenant law has been created, to a great extent, by statute. English law traditionally adhered to the principle of *caveat tenant* ("let the tenant beware"). In other words, tenants had little recourse against landlords who refused to keep the leased premises in good repair. In 1985, however, the English Parliament enacted the Landlord and Tenant Act. The act sets forth details related to the landlord's obligations to maintain and repair leased premises. The act also requires that leased premises be fit for human habitation, a concept similar to the implied warranty of habitability in some U.S. jurisdictions (to be discussed shortly). Although the English Landlord and Tenant Act applies mainly to dwellings rented for very low rates, it has improved, to some extent, the rights of all tenants in that country.

International Perspective

(Continued)

International Perspective—Continued

For Critical Analysis: *Given that tenants in the United States have traditionally had rights under the common law, why has it been necessary to regulate landlord-tenant relationships in the United States so extensively by statutory law?*

IMPLIED WARRANTY OF HABITABILITY
An implied promise by a landlord that rented residential premises are fit for human habitation— that is, in a condition that is safe and suitable for people to live in.

IMPLIED WARRANTY OF HABITABILITY   The **implied warranty of habitability** requires a landlord who leases residential property to deliver the premises to the tenant in a habitable condition—that is, in a condition that is safe and suitable for people to live in—at the beginning of a lease term and to maintain them in that condition for the lease's duration. Some state legislatures have enacted this warranty into law. In other jurisdictions, courts have based the warranty on the existence of a landlord's statutory duty to keep leased premises in good repair, or they have simply applied it as a matter of public policy.

Generally, this warranty applies to major, or *substantial*, physical defects that the landlord knows or should know about and has had a reasonable time to repair—for example, a large hole in the roof. An unattractive or annoying feature, such as a crack in the wall, may be unpleasant, but unless the crack is a structural defect or affects the residence's heating capabilities, it is probably not sufficiently substantial to make the place uninhabitable. At issue in the following case is whether specific conditions in an apartment basement constituted a violation of the implied warranty of habitability.

CASE 35.4

WEINGARDEN v. EAGLE RIDGE CONDOMINIUMS
Toledo Municipal Court,
Lucas County, Ohio, 1995.
71 Ohio Misc.2d 7,
653 N.E.2d 759.

HISTORICAL AND SOCIAL SETTING   *Landlord-tenant law grew out of medieval property law. From the Middle Ages until 1970, a lease was held to convey to a tenant primarily an interest in land—the value of a lease was the land itself. In truth, however, the value of a lease for an apartment is that it gives someone a place to live. The tenant has little interest in the land. He or she wants secure walls, windows, and doors, and adequate heat, light, ventilation, and plumbing. U.S. courts began to recognize this truth in 1970 and subsequently revolutionized landlord-tenant law. Today, anyone who leases an apartment expects it to be habitable.*

FACTS   Don Weingarden notified his landlord, Eagle Ridge Condominiums, that his apartment basement leaked when it rained or when snow melted. The water soaked the carpeting and caused the growth of mildew; this rendered the basement—which was one-third of the apartment—useless and spread odor throughout the

apartment. For these and other reasons, Weingarden vacated the premises before the end of the term. When his security deposit was not returned, Weingarden filed a suit in an Ohio state court against Eagle Ridge.

ISSUE   Did the conditions in the basement violate the implied warranty of habitability?

DECISION   Yes. The court ruled in Weingarden's favor.

REASON   The court pointed out that "the apartment was rented to the plaintiff with a carpeted basement, leading the tenant to believe that the basement was indeed a habitable part of the unit." The court concluded that the continuing leak, "resulting in thoroughly soaked carpeting and resultant mildew and its odors," made the basement uninhabitable. "[T]his breach of the warranty of habitability resulted in a constructive eviction of the tenant."

FOR CRITICAL ANALYSIS—Ethical Consideration
What policy reasons justify imposing an implied warranty of habitability on landlords?

Rent   *Rent* is the tenant's payment to the landlord for the tenant's occupancy or use of the landlord's real property. Generally, the tenant must pay the rent even if he or she refuses to occupy the property or moves out, as long as the refusal or the move is unjustifiable and the lease is in force.

Under the common law, destruction by fire or flood of a building leased by a tenant did not relieve the tenant of the obligation to pay rent and did not permit the termination of the lease. Today, however, state statutes have altered the common law rule. If the building burns down, apartment dwellers in most states are not continuously liable to the landlord for the payment of rent.

In some situations, such as when a landlord breaches the implied warranty of habitability, a tenant is allowed to withhold rent as a remedy. When rent withholding is authorized under a statute (sometimes referred to as a "rent-strike" statute), the tenant must usually put the amount withheld into an *escrow account*. This account is held in the name of the depositor (in this case, the tenant) and an *escrow agent* (in this case, usually the court or a government agency), and the funds are returnable to the depositor if the third person (in this case, the landlord) fails to fulfill the escrow condition. Generally, the tenant may withhold an amount equal to the amount by which the defect rendering the premises unlivable reduces the property's rental value. How much that is may be determined in different ways, and the tenant who withholds more than is legally permissible is liable to the landlord for the excessive amount withheld.

NOTE Options that may be available to a tenant on a landlord's breach of the implied warranty of habitability include repairing the defect and deducting the amount from the rent, canceling the lease, and suing for damages.

Transferring Rights to Leased Property

Either the landlord or the tenant may wish to transfer his or her rights to the leased property during the term of the lease.

Transferring the Landlord's Interest   Just as any other real property owner can sell, give away, or otherwise transfer his or her property, so can a landlord—who is, of course, the leased property's owner. If complete title to the leased property is transferred, the tenant becomes the tenant of the new owner. The new owner may collect subsequent rent but must abide by the terms of the existing lease agreement.

Transferring the Tenant's Interest   The tenant's transfer of his or her entire interest in the leased property to a third person is an *assignment of the lease*. A lease assignment is an agreement to transfer all rights, title, and interest in the lease to the assignee. It is a complete transfer. Many leases require that the assignment have the landlord's written consent, and an assignment that lacks consent can be avoided (nullified) by the landlord. A landlord who knowingly accepts rent from the assignee, however, will be held to have waived the requirement. An assignment does not terminate a tenant's liabilities under a lease agreement, however, because the tenant may assign rights but not duties. Thus, even though the assignee of the lease is required to pay rent, the original tenant is not released from the contractual obligation to pay the rent if the assignee fails to do so.

The tenant's transfer of all or part of the premises for a period shorter than the lease term is a **sublease.** The same restrictions that apply to an assignment of the tenant's interest in leased property apply to a sublease. To illustrate, a student named Derek leases an apartment for a two-year period. Although Derek had planned on attending summer school, he is offered a job in Europe for the summer months and accepts. Because he does not wish to pay three months' rent for an unoccupied apartment, Derek subleases the apartment to Darwin (the sublessee). (Derek may have to obtain his landlord's consent for this sublease if the lease requires it.) Darwin is bound by the same terms of the lease as Derek, but as in a lease assignment, Derek remains liable for the obligations under the lease if Darwin fails to fulfill them.

SUBLEASE
A lease executed by the lessee of real estate to a third person, conveying the same interest that the lessee enjoys but for a shorter term than that held by the lessee.

Application

Law and the Entrepreneur— How to Negotiate a Favorable Lease*

Generally, an entrepreneur first starting a business is well advised to lease rather than buy property, because the future success of the business is uncertain. By leasing instead of purchasing property, persons just starting out in business allow themselves some time to determine whether business profits will warrant the outright purchase of property.

One thing to keep in mind when leasing property is that lease contracts are usually form contracts that favor the landowner. That means that, as a prospective tenant, you need to think about negotiating terms more favorable to you. Before negotiating the terms of the lease, do some comparison shopping to see what the rent for other comparable properties in the area is. Usually, rental prices for business property are stated as so many dollars per square foot (per month or per year). In commercial leases to retail stores, it is common for part or all of the rent to consist of a percentage of the tenant's sales made on the premises during the term of the lease. Bear in mind, too, that the nature of your business should determine, to a great extent, the location of the leased premises. If you are involved in a mail-order business, for example, you need not pay the extra price for a prime location that might be required for a restaurant business.

When negotiating a lease, you must also determine who will pay property taxes and insurance on the property and who will be responsible for repairs of the property and

utility payments. These terms are generally negotiable, and depending on who takes responsibility, the rent payment may be adjusted accordingly. Generally, your success in negotiating favorable lease terms will depend on the market. If the rental market is "good" (that is, if you have numerous other rental options at favorable rates), you may be able to convince the landlord that he or she should be responsible for taxes, insurance, maintenance, and the like, and possibly for improvements to the property necessary for your business. Therefore, it is important to investigate the status of the market before you begin negotiations with a potential landlord.

 Checklist for the Lessee of Business Property

1. When you are entering into business, leasing rather than buying property has advantages, because it reduces your liability in the event that your business is unsuccessful.
2. Realize that although lease contracts normally favor the landlord, you usually can negotiate favorable terms for your lease of the premises.
3. Make sure that the lease contract clearly indicates whether the landlord or tenant is to be responsible for taxes on the property, costs relating to necessary maintenance and repairs, and utility costs. By comparison shopping, you should be able to judge which lease terms are favorable and which are not.
4. To protect yourself in the event your business is unsuccessful, start with a short-term initial lease, perhaps with an option to renew the lease in the future.

*This *Application* is not meant to substitute for the services of an attorney who is licensed to practice law in your state.

▌Key Terms

▌Chapter Summary: Real Property

The Nature of Real Property *(See pages 904–906.)*	Real property (also called real estate or realty) is immovable. It includes land, subsurface and air rights, plant life and vegetation, and fixtures.
Ownership of Real Property *(See pages 906–909.)*	1. *Fee simple absolute*—The most complete form of ownership. 2. *Fee simple defeasible*—Ownership in fee simple that can end if a specified event or condition occurs. 3. *Life estate*—An estate that lasts for the life of a specified individual; ownership rights in a life estate are subject to the rights of the future-interest holder. 4. *Future interest*—A residuary interest not granted by the grantor in conveying an estate to another for life, for a specified period of time, or on the condition that a specific event does or does not occur. The grantor may retain the residuary interest (which is then called a reversionary interest) or transfer ownership rights in the future interest to another (the interest is then referred to as a remainder). 5. *Nonpossessory interest*—An interest that involves the right to use real property but not to possess it. Easements, profits, and licenses are nonpossessory interests.
Transfer of Ownership *(See pages 909–914.)*	1. *By deed*—When real property is sold or transferred as a gift, title to the property is conveyed by means of a deed. A deed must meet specific legal requirements. A *warranty deed* warrants the most extensive protection against defects of title. A *quitclaim deed* conveys to the grantee whatever interest the grantor had; it warrants less than any other deed. A deed may be recorded in the manner prescribed by *recording statutes* in the appropriate jurisdiction to give third parties notice of the owner's interest. 2. *By will or inheritance*—If the owner dies after having made a valid will, the land passes as specified in the will. If the owner dies without having made a will, the heirs inherit according to state inheritance statutes. 3. *By adverse possession*—When a person possesses the property of another for a statutory period of time (three to thirty years, with ten years being the most common), that person acquires title to the property, provided the possession is actual and exclusive, open and visible, continuous and peaceable, and hostile and adverse (without the permission of the owner). 4. *By eminent domain*—The government can take land for public use, with just compensation, when the public interest requires the taking.
Leasehold Estates *(See pages 914–916.)*	A leasehold estate is an interest in real property that is held only for a limited period of time, as specified in the lease agreement. Types of tenancies relating to leased property include the following: 1. *Tenancy for years*—Tenancy for a period of time stated by express contract. 2. *Periodic tenancy*—Tenancy for a period determined by the frequency of rent payments; automatically renewed unless proper notice is given. 3. *Tenancy at will*—Tenancy for as long as both parties agree; no notice of termination is required. 4. *Tenancy at sufferance*—Possession of land without legal right.

Landlord-Tenant Relationships *(See pages 916–921.)*	1. *Lease agreement*—The landlord-tenant relationship is created by a lease agreement. State or local laws may dictate whether the lease must be in writing and what lease terms are permissible.
	
	2. *Rights and duties*—The rights and duties that arise under a lease agreement generally pertain to the following areas:
	  a. Possession—The tenant has an exclusive right to possess the leased premises, which must be available to the tenant at the agreed-on time. Under the covenant of quiet enjoyment, the landlord promises that during the lease term neither the landlord nor anyone having superior title to the property will disturb the tenant's use and enjoyment of the property.
	  b. Use and maintenance of the premises—Unless the parties agree otherwise, the tenant may make any legal use of the property. The tenant is responsible for any damage that he or she causes. The landlord must comply with laws that set specific standards for the maintenance of real property. The implied warranty of habitability requires that a landlord furnish and maintain residential premises in a habitable condition (that is, in a condition safe and suitable for human life).
	
	(Continued)

▌Chapter Summary: Real Property—Continued

Landlord-Tenant Relationships— Continued	c. Rent—The tenant must pay the rent as long as the lease is in force, unless the tenant justifiably refuses to occupy the property or withholds the rent because of the landlord's failure to maintain the premises properly. 3. *Transferring rights to leased property*— 　a. If the landlord transfers complete title to the leased property, the tenant becomes the tenant of the new owner. The new owner may then collect the rent but must abide by the existing lease. 　b. Generally, tenants may assign their rights (but not their duties) under a lease contract to a third person. Tenants may also sublease leased property to a third person, but the original tenant is not relieved of any obligations to the landlord under the lease. In either case, the landlord's consent may be required.

▌For Review

1. What can a person who holds property in fee simple absolute do with the property? Can a person who holds property as a life estate do the same?

2. What are the requirements for acquiring property by adverse possession?

3. What limitations may be imposed on the rights of property owners?

4. What is a leasehold estate? What types of leasehold estates, or tenancies, can be created when real property is leased?

5. What are the respective duties of the landlord and tenant concerning the use and maintenance of leased property? Is the tenant responsible for all damages that he or she causes, intentionally or negligently?

▌Questions and Case Problems

35–1. Tenant's Rights and Responsibilities. You are a student in college and plan to attend classes for nine months. You sign a twelve-month lease for an apartment. Discuss fully each of the following situations.

(a) You have a summer job in another town and wish to assign the balance of your lease (three months) to a fellow student who will be attending summer school. Can you do so?

(b) You are graduating in May. The lease will have three months remaining. Can you terminate the lease without liability by giving a thirty-day notice to the landlord?

35–2. Property Ownership. Antonio is the owner of a lakeside house and lot. He deeds the house and lot "to my wife, Angela, for life, then to my son, Charles." Given these facts, answer the following questions:

(a) Does Antonio have any ownership interest in the lakeside house after making these transfers? Explain.

(b) What is Angela's interest called? Is there any limitation on her rights to use the property as she wishes?

(c) What is Charles's interest called? Why?

35–3. Property Ownership. Lorenz was a wanderer twenty-two years ago. At that time, he decided to settle down on an unoccupied, three-acre parcel of land that he did not own. People in the area indicated to him that they had no idea who owned the property. Lorenz built a house on the land, got married, and raised three children while living there. He fenced in the land, placed a gate with a sign above it that read "Lorenz's Homestead," and had trespassers removed. Lorenz is now con-

fronted by Joe Reese, who has a deed in his name as owner of the property. Reese, claiming ownership of the land, orders Lorenz and his family off the property. Discuss who has the better "title" to the property.

35–4. Deeds. Wiley and Gemma are neighbors. Wiley's lot is extremely large, and his present and future use of it will not involve the entire area. Gemma wants to build a single-car garage and driveway along the present lot boundary. Because of ordinances requiring buildings to be set back fifteen feet from an adjoining property line, and because of the placement of her existing structures, Gemma cannot build the garage. Gemma contracts to purchase ten feet of Wiley's property along their boundary line for $3,000. Wiley is willing to sell but will give Gemma only a quitclaim deed, whereas Gemma wants a warranty deed. Discuss the differences between these deeds as they would affect the rights of the parties if the title to this ten feet of land later proved to be defective.

35–5. Leased Property. The landlord of an apartment building leased a building he owned nearby for use as a cocktail lounge. The residential tenants complained to the landlord about the late evening and early morning music and disturbances coming from the lounge. Although the lease for the lounge provided that entertainment had to be conducted so that it could not be heard outside the building and would not disturb the apartment tenants, the landlord was unsuccessful in remedying the problem. The tenants vacated their apartments. Was the landlord successful in his suit to collect rent from the tenants who vacated the premises? Discuss. [*Blackett v. Olanoff*, 371 Mass. 714, 358 N.E.2d 817 (1977)]

35–6. Easements. In 1882, Moses Webster owned a parcel of land that extended down to the Atlantic Ocean. He conveyed the strip of the property fronting the ocean to another party. The deed included the following statement: "Reserve being had for said Moses Webster the right of way by land or water." The strip of property is now owned by Margaret Williams, and the portion retained by Webster now belongs to Thomas O'Neill. Williams is denying O'Neill access to the ocean. O'Neill has brought an action to establish his title to an easement over Williams's property. What should the court decide? Discuss fully. [*O'Neill v. Williams*, 527 A.2d 322 (Me. 1987)]

35–7. Adverse Possession. As the result of a survey in 1976, the Nolans discovered that their neighbor's garage extended more than a foot onto their property. Nolan requested that his neighbor, Naab, tear down the garage. The Naabs refused to do this, stating that the garage had been built in 1952 and had been on the property when the Naabs purchased it in 1973. In West Virginia, where these properties were located, there is a ten-year statute of limitations covering adverse possession of property. Were the Naabs able to claim title to the land on which the garage was situated by adverse possession? Explain. [*Naab v. Nolan*, 327 S.E.2d 151 (W.Va.1985)]

35–8. Maintenance of Leased Premises. Inwood North Professional Group—Phase I leased medical office space to Joseph Davidow, a physician. The terms of the five-year lease specified that Inwood would provide electricity, hot water, air conditioning, janitorial and maintenance services, light fixtures, and security services. During his tenancy, Davidow encountered a number of problems. The roof leaked, and the air conditioning did not function properly. The premises were not cleaned and maintained by Inwood as promised in the lease agreement, and as a consequence, rodents and pests infested the premises, and trash littered the parking area. There was frequently no hot water, and at one point Davidow was without electricity for several days because Inwood had not paid the bill. About a year prior to the lease's expiration, Davidow moved to another office building and refused to pay the remaining rent due under the lease. Inwood sued for the unpaid rent. Must Davidow pay the remaining rent due under the lease? Discuss. [*Davidow v. Inwood North Professional Group—Phase I*, 747 S.W.2d 373 (Tex. 1988)]

35–9. The Lease Contract. Christine Callis formed a lease agreement with Colonial Properties, Inc., to lease property in a shopping center in Montgomery, Alabama. Callis later alleged that before signing the lease agreement, she had told a representative of Colonial that she wanted to locate in a shopping center that would attract a wealthy clientele, and the representative had assured her that no discount stores would be allowed to lease space in the shopping center. The written lease agreement, which Callis signed, contained a clause stating that "[n]o representation, inducement, understanding or anything of any nature whatsoever made, stated or represented on Landlord's behalf, either orally or in writing (except this Lease), has induced Tenant to enter into this lease." The lease also stipulated that Callis would not conduct any type of business commonly called a discount store, surplus store, or other similar business. Later, Colonial did, in fact, lease space to discount stores, and Callis sued Colonial for breach of the lease contract. Will Callis succeed in her claim? Discuss fully. [*Callis v. Colonial Properties, Inc.*, 597 So.2d 660 (Ala. 1991)]

35–10. Easements. Merton Peterson owned a golf course, a supper club, and the parking lot between them. Both golfers and club patrons always parked in the lot. Peterson sold the club and the lot to the American Legion, which sold them to VBC, Inc. (owned by Richard Beck and others). When VBC demanded rent from Peterson for use of the lot, Peterson filed a suit in a South Dakota state court to determine title. On what basis might the court hold that Peterson has an easement for the use of the lot? Does Peterson have an easement? [*Peterson v. Beck*, 537 N.W.2d 375 (S.Dak. 1995)]

A QUESTION OF ETHICS AND SOCIAL RESPONSIBILITY

35–11. *The Stanards have owned lakeshore property since 1963. In 1969, the Urbans purchased lakeshore property adjoining the Stanards' lot and since that time have used a grassy area of land—part of which belonged to the Stanards—up to a wooded area between the two houses. Between 1969 and 1988, the Urbans mowed the grassy area and kept the weeds down, let their children and grandchildren play in the grassy area, and in the winter stored their boat dock on the grassy area. In 1981, the Urbans constructed a white tin storage shed—mounted on a concrete slab—on the grassy area. Most of the shed was located on the Stanards' property. In 1988, the Stanards sued the Urbans for trespass and sought removal of the white shed. The Urbans claimed that they had acquired ownership of the property by adverse possession, because they had used the property since 1969 (the state's statutory period for adverse possession was fifteen years). The Stanards claimed that the statutory period should begin in 1981, when the storage shed was constructed. Given these circumstances, consider the following questions. [Stanard v. Urban, 453 N.W.2d 733 (Minn.App. 1990)]*

1. Do you think that the Urbans' use of the Stanards' property prior to 1981 (when the shed was built) met the requirements for adverse possession? That is, was the use actual, open, hostile, continuous, and exclusive during those years? Or is this situation similar to many others in which there are no fences between neighboring lots, and the owners and their families occasionally trespass on each other's property?

2. Would the fact that the Urbans, sometime between 1980 and 1982, offered to purchase the parcel of property in question from the Stanards affect your answer to the above question?

3. At what point should trespass on another's property constitute adverse possession? For example, if your neighbors customarily store their boat partially on your property, and you do not object, should this circumstance trigger a statutory period for adverse possession? What if your neighbors' children also customarily play on your side of the boundary line between your property and your neighbors' property?

4. Why do you think that state statutes permit people to acquire title to property by adverse possession? What public policy is reflected in these statutes?

FOR CRITICAL ANALYSIS

35–12. *Real property law dates back hundreds of years. What changes have occurred in society, including business and technological changes, that have affected the development and application of real property law? (Hint: Was airspace an issue three hundred years ago?)*

▌Accessing the Internet: Business Law and Legal Environment

Several law firms offer Web sites that include, among other things, information on real estate law. For information from Heller, et al. on real estate, go to

http://gnn.digital.com/gnn/bus/hewm/index.html

Additional information can be found at a Web site maintained by Reinhart, et al. at the following:

http://www.rbvdnr.com/

The commercial service GEnie provides information on real estate law. Once you are in GEnie, select the following:

Career/Professional Services

Then select

Law RT

Another site on the Web for real estate law is

http://www.panix.com~novick

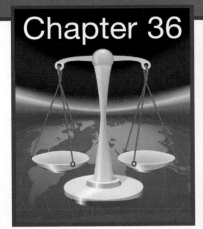

Chapter 36

Insurance, Wills, and Trusts

"Insurance is part charity and part business, but all common sense."

> Calvin Coolidge, 1872–1933
> (*Thirtieth president of the United States, 1923–1929*)

CHAPTER OBJECTIVES

After reading this chapter, you should be able to:

1. Indicate when an insurable interest arises in regard to life and property insurance.
2. Distinguish between an insurance broker and an insurance agent.
3. Summarize some of the clauses that are typically included in insurance contracts.
4. Describe the requirements of a valid will.
5. Explain how property is transferred when a person dies without a valid will.

Most individuals insure both real and personal property (as well as their lives). As Calvin Coolidge asserted in the opening quotation above, insurance is "all common sense"—by insuring our property, we protect ourselves against damage and loss. After discussing insurance, which is a foremost concern of all property owners, we examine how property is transferred on the death of its owner. Certainly, the laws of succession of property are a necessary corollary to the concept of private ownership of property. Our laws require that on death, title to the property of a decedent (one who has recently died) must be delivered in full somewhere. In this chapter we see that this can be done by will, through trusts, or through state laws prescribing distribution of property among heirs or next of kin.

▮ Insurance

Insurance is a contract by which the insurance company (the insurer) promises to pay a sum of money or give something of value to another (either the insured or the

INSURANCE
A contract in which, for a stipulated consideration, one party agrees to compensate the other for loss on a specific subject by a specified peril.

RISK
A prediction concerning potential loss based on known and unknown factors.

RISK MANAGEMENT
Planning that is undertaken to protect one's interest should some event threaten to undermine its security. In the context of insurance, risk management involves transferring certain risks from the insured to the insurance company.

beneficiary) in the event that the insured is injured, dies, or sustains damage to his or her property as a result of particular, stated contingencies. Basically, insurance is an arrangement for *transferring and allocating risk*. In many cases, **risk** can be described as a prediction concerning potential loss based on known and unknown factors. Insurance, however, involves much more than a game of chance.

Many precautions may be taken to protect against the hazards of life. For example, an individual may wear a seat belt to protect against automobile injuries or install smoke detectors to guard against injury from the risk of fire. Of course, no one can predict whether an accident or a fire will ever occur, but individuals and businesses must establish plans to protect their personal and financial interests should some event threaten to undermine their security. This concept is known as **risk management.** The most common method of risk management is the transfer of certain risks from the individual to the insurance company.

Risk is transferred to an insurance company by a contractual agreement. The insurance contract and its provisions will be examined shortly. First, however, we look at the different types of insurance that can be obtained, insurance terminology, and the concept of insurable interest.

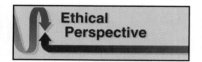
Ethical Perspective

A major ethical concern in the area of insurance involves *moral hazard*. In the insurance industry, moral hazard occurs when insurance coverage reduces the incentive of individuals or companies to act cautiously or to guard against destruction or loss that will be paid for by their insurance companies.

For example, the businessperson who takes out a large insurance policy on a building has less incentive to take care that the building is protected from fire than an individual without any insurance policy. Similarly, the property owner who takes out property insurance may have less incentive to install alarm systems, to pay for private patrol service, and so on. Additionally, the smaller the *deductible* (a specified amount that the policyholder must pay on a claim—for example, the first $250 of a claim) in an insurance policy, the less incentive the policyholder has to prevent losses from fire or theft. Moral hazard exists with medical insurance as well. The smaller the deductible, the greater the incentive for the individual to neglect the practice of preventive medicine.

For Critical Analysis: *Who ultimately pays for the losses resulting from the moral hazard created by insurance?*

POLICY
In insurance law, a contract between the insurer and the insured in which, for a stipulated consideration, the insurer agrees to compensate the insured for loss on a specific subject by a specified peril.

PREMIUM
In insurance law, the price paid by the insured for insurance protection for a specified period of time.

UNDERWRITER
In insurance law, the insurer, or the one assuming a risk in return for the payment of a premium.

Classifications of Insurance

Insurance is classified according to the nature of the risk involved. For example, fire insurance, casualty insurance, life insurance, and title insurance apply to different types of risk. Furthermore, policies of these types differ in the persons and interests that they protect. This is reasonable, because the types of losses that are expected and the types that are foreseeable or unforeseeable vary with the nature of the activity. Exhibit 36–1 presents a list of insurance classifications.

Insurance Terminology

An insurance contract is called a **policy;** the consideration paid to the insurer is called a **premium;** and the insurance company is sometimes called an **underwriter.**

The parties to an insurance policy are the *insurer* (the insurance company) and the *insured* (the person covered by the insurer's provisions or the holder of the policy).

♦ Exhibit 36–1
Insurance Classifications

TYPE OF INSURANCE	COVERAGE
Accident	Covers expenses, losses, and suffering incurred by the insured because of accidents causing physical injury and any consequent disability; sometimes includes a specified payment to heirs of the insured if death results from an accident.
All-risk	Covers all losses that the insured may incur except those resulting from fraud on the part of the insured.
Automobile	May cover damage to automobiles resulting from specified hazards or occurrences (such as fire, vandalism, theft, or collision); normally provides protection against liability for personal injuries and property damage resulting from the operation of the vehicle.
Casualty	Protects against losses that may be incurred by the insured as a result of being held liable for personal injuries or property damage sustained by others.
Credit	Pays to a creditor the balance of a debt on the disability, death, insolvency, or bankruptcy of the debtor; often offered by lending institutions.
Decreasing-term life	Provides life insurance; requires uniform payments over the life (term) of the policy, but with a decreasing face value (amount of coverage).
Employer's liability	Insures employers against liability for injuries or losses sustained by employees during the course of their employment; covers claims not covered under workers' compensation insurance.
Fidelity or guaranty	Provides indemnity against losses in trade or losses caused by the dishonesty of employees, the insolvency of debtors, or breaches of contract.
Fire	Covers losses caused to the insured as a result of fire.
Floater	Covers movable property, as long as the property is within the territorial boundaries specified in the contract.
Group	Provides individual life, medical, or disability insurance coverage but is obtainable through a group of persons, usually employees; the policy premium is paid either entirely by the employer or partially by the employer and partially by the employee.

(Continued)

Insurance contracts are usually obtained through an *agent*, who ordinarily works for the insurance company, or through a *broker*, who is ordinarily an *independent contractor*. When a broker deals with an applicant for insurance, the broker is, in effect, the applicant's agent. In contrast, an insurance agent is an agent of the insurance company, not of the applicant. As a general rule, the insurance company is bound by the acts of its agents when they act within the agency relationship (discussed in Chapter 23). A broker, however, normally has no relationship with the insurance company and is an agent of the insurance applicant. In most situations, state law determines the status of all parties writing or obtaining insurance.

Insurable Interest

A person can insure anything in which he or she has an **insurable interest**. Without this insurable interest, there is no enforceable contract, and a transaction to insure would have to be treated as a wager. In regard to real and personal property, an insurable interest exists when the insured derives a pecuniary benefit (a benefit consisting of or relating to money) from the preservation and continued existence of the property. Put another way, one has an insurable interest in property when one would sustain a pecuniary loss from its destruction. In regard to life insurance, a person must have a

INSURABLE INTEREST
An interest either in a person's life or well-being or in property that is sufficiently substantial that insuring against injury to (or the death of) the person or against damage to the property does not amount to a mere wagering (betting) contract.

♦ Exhibit 36–1
Insurance Classifications—Continued

Health	Covers expenses incurred by the insured resulting from physical injury or illness and other expenses relating to health and life maintenance.
Homeowners'	Protects homeowners against some or all risks of loss to their residences and the residences' contents or liability arising from the use of the property.
Key-person	Protects a business in the event of the death or disability of a key employee.
Liability	Protects against liability imposed on the insured resulting from injuries to the person or property of another.
Life	Covers the death of the policyholder. Upon the death of the insured, an amount specified in the policy is paid by the insurer to the insured's beneficiary.
Major medical	Protects the insured against major hospital, medical, or surgical expenses.
Malpractice	Protects professionals (doctors, lawyers, and others) against malpractice claims brought against them by their patients or clients; a form of liability insurance.
Marine	Covers movable property, including ships, freight, and cargo, against certain perils or navigation risks during a specific voyage or time period.
Mortgage	Covers a mortgage loan; the insurer pays the balance of the mortgage to the creditor on the death or disability of the debtor.
No-fault auto	Covers personal injury and (sometimes) property damage resulting from automobile accidents. The insured submits his or her claims to his or her own insurance company, regardless of who was at fault. A person may sue the party at fault or that party's insurer only in cases involving serious medical injury and consequent high medical costs. Governed by state "no-fault" statutes.
Term life	Provides life insurance for a specified period of time (term) with no cash surrender value; usually renewable.
Title	Protects against any defects in title to real property and any losses incurred as a result of existing claims against or liens on the realty at the time of purchase.

reasonable expectation of benefit from the continued life of another in order to have an insurable interest in that person's life. The benefit may be pecuniary (as with so-called *key-person insurance*, which insures the lives of important employees, usually in small companies), or it may be founded on the relationship between the parties (by blood or affinity).

For property insurance, the insurable interest must exist at the time the loss occurs but need not exist when the policy is purchased. In contrast, for life insurance, the insurable interest must exist at the time the policy is obtained. The existence of an insurable interest is a primary concern in determining liability under an insurance policy.

The Insurance Contract

An insurance contract is governed by the general principles of contract law, although the insurance industry is heavily regulated by each state. Several aspects of the insurance contract will be treated here, including the application for insurance, when the contract takes effect, important contract provisions, cancellation of the policy, and defenses that can be raised by insurance companies against payment on a policy.

NOTE The federal government has the power to regulate the insurance industry under the commerce clause of the U.S. Constitution. Instead of exercising this power itself, Congress allows the states to regulate insurance.

APPLICATION   The filled-in application form for insurance is usually attached to the policy and made a part of the insurance contract. Thus, an insurance applicant is bound by any false statements that appear in the application (subject to certain exceptions). Because the insurance company evaluates the risk factors based on the information included in the insurance application, misstatements or misrepresentations can void a policy, especially if the insurance company can show that it would not have extended insurance if it had known the true facts.

EFFECTIVE DATE   The effective date of an insurance contract is important. In some instances, the insurance applicant is not protected until a formal written policy is issued. In other situations, the applicant is protected between the time the application is received and the time the insurance company either accepts or rejects it. Four facts should be kept in mind:

1.   A broker is merely the agent of an applicant. Therefore, until the broker obtains a policy, the applicant normally is not insured.
2.   A person who seeks insurance from an insurance company's agent will usually be protected from the moment the application is made, provided—in the case of life insurance—that some form of premium has been paid. Between the time the application is received and either rejected or accepted, the applicant is covered (possibly subject to medical examination). Usually, the agent will write a memorandum, or **binder,** indicating that a policy is pending and stating its essential terms.
3.   If the parties agree that the policy will be issued and delivered at a later time, the contract is not effective until the policy is issued and delivered or sent to the applicant, depending on the agreement. Thus, any loss sustained between the time of application and the delivery of the policy is not covered.
4.   Parties may agree that a life insurance policy will be binding at the time the insured pays the first premium, or the policy may be expressly contingent on the applicant's passing a physical examination. In the latter situation, if the applicant pays the premium and passes the examination, then the policy coverage is in effect. If the applicant pays the premium but dies before having the physical examination, then to collect, the applicant's estate must show that the applicant would have passed the examination had he or she not died.

BINDER
A written, temporary insurance policy.

In the following case, the court had to decide whether a policy that required an applicant to be "still insurable" on the effective date of the policy should prevent the beneficiary from recovering.

CASE 36.1

LIFE INSURANCE CO. OF NORTH AMERICA v. CICHOWLAS

District Court of Appeal of Florida, Fourth District, 1995.
659 So.2d 1333.

HISTORICAL AND GLOBAL SETTING   *The United States leads the world in insurance coverage. Over 3,500 U.S. companies sell property insurance, and more than 2,200 offer life insurance. Thirty-three of these companies have been selling insurance for more than one hundred years and control more than half of the insurance market. In the 1980s, some of these companies tripled the amount that they take in annually in premiums. Despite these glowing figures, some insurers claim that they are losing money writing insurance in certain markets.*

FACTS   Waldemar Cichowlas applied to the Life Insurance Company of North America (LINA) for insurance

naming his wife Ewa as beneficiary. The application asked if he had been hospitalized during the past five years and if he had ever been treated for lung disease. A yes answer would have affected his insurability. Waldemar truthfully answered no. The policy required that an applicant be "still insurable" on the effective date of the policy. Three weeks before the policy took effect, Waldemar was hospitalized with a lung disease. He did not tell LINA. When he died of other causes, LINA refused to pay Ewa. She filed a suit in a Florida state court against the insurer. The court ordered LINA to pay. The insurer appealed.

ISSUE   Did the requirement that Waldemar be "still insurable" on the effective date of the policy prevent Ewa from recovering?

DECISION   Yes. The District Court of Appeal of Florida reversed the judgment of the lower court and remanded the case.

REASON   The state intermediate appellate court explained that "[c]lauses requiring that an applicant

(Continued)

Case 36.1—Continued

remain insurable between the filing of the application and the delivery of the policy have traditionally been approved by Florida courts." The court noted that "Mr. Cichowlas was not insurable on the effective date of the policy." Thus, "the 'still insurable' clause precluded recovery for" Ewa.

FOR CRITICAL ANALYSIS—Ethical Consideration
What effect might it have had on the outcome of this case if the court had held that LINA had a continuing duty to ask about the health of its applicants?

PROVISIONS AND CLAUSES   Some of the important provisions and clauses contained in insurance contracts are listed and defined in Exhibit 36–2. The courts are increasingly cognizant of the fact that most people do not have the special training necessary to understand the intricate terminology used in insurance policies. Thus, the words used in an insurance contract have their ordinary meanings. They are interpreted by the courts in light of the nature of the coverage involved.

When there is an ambiguity in the policy, the provision generally is interpreted against the insurance company. When the written policy has not been delivered and it is unclear whether an insurance contract actually exists, the uncertainty normally will be resolved against the insurance company. The court will presume that the policy is in effect unless the company can show otherwise. Similarly, an insurer must take care to make sure that the insured is adequately notified of any change in coverage under an existing policy (see this chapter's *Business Law in Action*).

CANCELLATION   The insured can cancel a policy at any time, and the insurer can cancel under certain circumstances. When an insurance company can cancel its insurance contract, the policy or a state statute usually requires that the insurer give advance written notice of the cancellation to the insured.

♦ **Exhibit 36–2**
Insurance Contract Provisions and Clauses

Incontestability clause	An incontestability clause provides that after a policy has been in force for a specified length of time—usually two or three years—the insurer cannot contest statements made in the application.
Coinsurance clause	A coinsurance clause provides that if the owner insures his or her property up to a specified percentage—usually 80 percent—of its value, he or she will recover any loss up to the face amount of the policy. If the insurance is for less than the fixed percentage, the owner is responsible for a proportionate share of the loss.
Appraisal clause	Insurance policies frequently provide that if the parties cannot agree on the amount of a loss covered under the policy or the value of the property lost, an appraisal, or estimate, by an impartial and qualified third party can be demanded.
Arbitration clause	Many insurance policies include clauses that call for arbitration of disputes that may arise between the insurer and the insured concerning the settlement of claims.
Antilapse clause	An antilapse clause provides that the policy will not automatically lapse if no payment is made on the date due. Ordinarily, under such a provision, the insured has a *grace period* of thirty or thirty-one days within which to pay an overdue premium before the policy is canceled.
Cancellation	Cancellation of an insurance policy can occur for various reasons, depending on the type of insurance. When an insurance company can cancel its insurance contract, the policy or a state statute usually requires that the insurer give advance written notice of the cancellation. An insurer cannot cancel—or refuse to renew—a policy because of the national origin or race of an applicant or because the insured has appeared as a witness in a case against the company.

BUSINESS LAW IN ACTION

"Caveat Insurer"

In disputes involving ambiguous insurance clauses, courts generally decide in favor of the insured. This is because insurance contracts, in a sense, are adhesion contracts—that is, they are offered to the insurer on a "take it or leave it" basis. There is rarely any opportunity for a person seeking insurance coverage to negotiate over the contract's terms. Whenever a dispute arises concerning how a particular clause in an insurance contract should be interpreted, the watchword is therefore *"caveat* insurer"—or "let the insurer beware."

Similarly, if an insurance company sends a notice of a change in coverage under a policy, the notice must clearly indicate what the change is. The case of *Koski v. Allstate Insurance Co.*[a] provides a good example of this requirement. Allstate Insurance Company refused to pay a claim submitted by the insured, Thomas Koski, because the coverage had changed—and Allstate had notified Koski of the change. The

a.   213 Mich.App. 166, 539 N.W.2d 561 (1995).

policy was a homeowners' policy, which Koski had initially purchased in 1976 and renewed each year since then.

In 1982, Allstate made some changes to its coverage under the policy. It sent a packet to Koski that included a cover letter, a brochure describing the changes in coverage, and a copy of the revised insurance policy that would be effective on receipt of Koski's 1982 premium payment. The cover letter invited the reader to "take a few minutes to read your new policy [and] the enclosed booklet," and it set forth several features of the new policy without mentioning any exclusions from coverage. The enclosed brochure contained the following language: "An exclusion has been added stating that we will not provide liability protection when members of the same household are engaged in a liability suit against each other." Koski renewed the policy without reading the brochure.

In 1984, Koski's daughter, Nikki, was seriously injured in an accident involving machinery being operated by Koski. In 1986, Nikki and her mother, Marsha, sued Koski for negligence, and a judgment was entered in their favor. Allstate refused to pay on Koski's claim because of the 1982 change in coverage. Koski sued Allstate for breach of contract, and the question before the court was whether Allstate had adequately notified Koski of the policy change in 1982.

The court acknowledged that an insured "is obligated to read the insurance policy and to raise questions concerning coverage within a reasonable time after issuance of the policy." The court stated, however, that an exception to this rule exists "where a policy is renewed without actual notice to the insured that the policy has been altered. Where a renewal policy is issued without calling the insured's attention to a reduction in coverage, the insurer is bound to the greater coverage in the earlier policy." "In this case," stated the court, "the notice to plaintiff of the new exclusion consisted of a single unemphasized reference in a twelve-page booklet." The court concluded that the notice provided by Allstate "was inadequate as a matter of law."

For Critical Analysis: *What did the judge mean by the phrase "as a matter of law"?*

The insurer may cancel an insurance policy for various reasons, depending on the type of insurance. For example, automobile insurance can be canceled for nonpayment of premiums or suspension of the insured's driver's license. Property insurance can be canceled for nonpayment of premiums or for other reasons, including the insured's fraud or misrepresentation, conviction for a crime that increases the hazard insured against, or gross negligence that increases the hazard insured against. Life and health policies can be canceled because of false statements made by the insured in the application. An insurer cannot cancel—or refuse to renew—a policy for discriminatory reasons or other reasons that violate public policy, or because the insured has appeared as a witness in a case against the company.

State laws normally impose specific requirements relating to insurance policy cancellations. In the following case, the plaintiff claimed that the insurer had not complied with the state's statutory requirements governing policy cancellation.

CASE 36.2

CLYBURN v. ALLSTATE INSURANCE CO.

United States District Court,
District of South Carolina, 1993.
826 F.Supp. 955.

COMPANY PROFILE *The Allstate Corporation sells life and property insurance in the United States, Puerto Rico, Canada, Japan, and South Korea. Allstate sells reinsurance (insurance for insurers) worldwide through the Allstate Reinsurance Company in London. In the United States, Allstate also offers annuities, as well as other business and retirement benefits insurance. Allstate was started by Sears, Roebuck, and Company in the 1930s to sell auto insurance through the mail and is today the second largest auto—and home—insurer in the United States.*

FACTS William Clyburn's house burned to the ground. Because two years had passed since he had paid a premium on his policy with the Allstate Insurance Company, Allstate refused to cover the loss. Clyburn sued Allstate in a federal district court, claiming that the policy had not been canceled. To cancel a policy, a state statute required an insurer to send written notice to both the insured and the insured's agent of record. Allstate argued that it had properly notified Clyburn in writing of

the cancellation and had also notified Clyburn's agent of record, Thomas Young, by sending Young a computer diskette containing the cancellation notice. The jury found in Clyburn's favor, concluding that Allstate had sent written notice to Clyburn but not to Young, the agent of record. Allstate moved for either a new trial or a judgment notwithstanding the verdict (*n.o.v.*).

ISSUE Can notice included on a computer diskette constitute "written notice"?

DECISION Yes. Because the factual issue of whether Allstate had actually sent a diskette to its agent still needed to be resolved, however, the court granted Allstate's motion for a new trial.

REASON The district court held that notice on a diskette could constitute written notice. The court pointed out that "other media forms," including videotapes and tape recordings, "are recognized as 'writings.'" Referring to "today's 'paperless' society of computer generated information," the court reasoned that "[t]he storage of information on tape recordings and videotapes is not that much different from that on floppy diskettes for computers, but rather is more a difference in the devices used to read the information."

FOR CRITICAL ANALYSIS—Technological Consideration *Can you think of other examples of how technological changes have challenged traditional legal terminology?*

DEFENSES AGAINST PAYMENT In attempting to avoid payment on a policy claim, an insurance company can raise any of the defenses that would be valid in any ordinary action on a contract, as well as some defenses that do not apply in ordinary contract actions. If the insurance company can show that the policy was procured by fraud, misrepresentation, or violation of warranties, it may have a valid defense for not paying on a claim. Improper actions, such as those that are against public policy or that are otherwise illegal, can also give the insurance company a defense against the payment of a claim or allow it to rescind the contract.

An insurance company can be prevented from asserting some defenses that are normally available, however. For example, if a company tells an insured that information requested on a form is optional, and the insured provides it anyway, the company cannot use the information to avoid its contractual obligation under the insurance contract. Similarly, incorrect statements as to the age of the insured normally do not allow the insurer to avoid payment on the death of the insured.

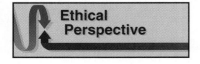
Ethical Perspective

An insurance company that resorts to unfair tactics to avoid payment on a policy may find a less than warm reception in the courtroom. Good faith is required in all contracts, including insurance contracts. Insurers must exercise good faith in the processing and payment of claims. In some states, statutory penalties may be imposed on insurers

Ethical Perspective—Continued

who act in bad faith; additionally, insurers may be required to pay the claimants' attorneys' fees.

For example, in one case the insured had described his male lover and beneficiary as simply his "business partner." The insurance company brought an action against the executor of the insured's estate to rescind the insurance contract on the ground that the insured had misrepresented his relationship with his beneficiary. The court concluded that the insurance company's actions evidenced "a gross disregard for its policy obligation." "Even if there was misrepresentation," stated the court, "it was not material." The court ordered the insurance company not only to pay on the policy but also to pay the executor's attorneys' fees, stating that attorneys' fees can be awarded to the insured "where there has been an unreasonable bad faith denial of coverage."[a]

For Critical Analysis: *How can a court decide whether an insurance company is acting in bad faith when it denies a claim?*

a. *New England Mutual Life Insurance Co. v. Johnson*, 589 N.Y.S.2d 736 (1992).

▌ Wills

Private ownership of property leads logically to both the protection of that property by insurance coverage while the owner is alive and the transfer of that property on the death of the owner to those designated in the owner's will. A **will** is the final declaration of how a person desires to have his or her property disposed of after death.

At common law, people had no way to control the distribution of their property after death. The power of transfer or distribution is derived solely from statutes originating in feudal England that strictly controlled the transfer of property at death. The heir (the one who inherited) was required to pay the feudal lord a sum of money[1] for the privilege of succeeding to his or her ancestor's lands. When a tenant died without heirs, title to the land reverted to the feudal lord of the manor.

Sweeping land reforms in England during the 1920s replaced inheritance payments and reversion of title to the feudal lord with the right of the Crown to receive inheritance taxes and to take the property of an **intestate** (one who dies without a valid will) who died without heirs. Modern legislation has changed the terminology but not the result. Today, in the United States, title to the land of persons who die intestate and without heirs reverts to the state.

A will, because it is a person's "last will and testament," is referred to as a *testamentary disposition* of property. It is a formal instrument that must follow exactly the requirements of state law to be effective. The reasoning behind such a strict requirement is obvious. A will becomes effective only after death. No attempts to modify it after the death of the maker are allowed, because the court cannot ask the maker to confirm the attempted modifications. (Sometimes, however, the wording of the will must be "interpreted" by the courts.) A will can serve other purposes besides the distribution of property. It can appoint a guardian for minor children or incapacitated adults. It can also appoint a *personal representative* to settle the affairs of the deceased. Exhibit 36–3 presents a copy of one of the many wills purportedly written by Howard Hughes, the reclusive American film producer and manufacturer.

"The only authentic evidence which we have of the survival of life after death is the ability of the judges to read the intention of the testator long after he has been buried."

**Frederick E. Crane,
1869–1947
(American jurist)**

WILL
An instrument directing what is to be done with the testator's property upon his or her death, made by the testator and revocable during his or her lifetime. No interests in the testator's property pass until the testator dies.

INTESTATE
As a noun, one who has died without having created a valid will; as an adjective, the state of having died without a will.

---

1.   The sum, called a *relief*, was usually equivalent to one year's rent.

♦ **Exhibit 36–3**
A Sample Will

Jan. 11/72

      This is my Last Will and Testament

(1)   I hereby revoke all Wills and testamentary dispositions of every nature or kind whatsoever made by me before this date.

(2)   I nominate, constitute, and appoint my counsel Chester C. Davis, sole executor and trustee of this my Last Will and Testament . . .

(3)   I give, devise, and bequeath all my monies, holdings, property of every nature and kind, all of my possessions and any profits of the before mentioned to the Howard Hughes Medical Institute for the use of medical research and the betterment of medical and health standards around the world.

(4)   I hereby direct my trustee Chester Davis and my assistants Nadine Henley and Frank Gay to continue in their positions and duties, and to also assume a controlling interest in management in the Medical Institute, to decide, direct, and implement policies and funds for the proper uses of the Medical Institute in the areas of medical research and the betterment of world health and medical standards.

(5)   I hereby request that my trustee make known to any business associates, aides, or confidants who wish to, or have undertaken a written documentation of any or all parts of my life, the terms of the Rosemont Enterprises agreement and possible infringements thereof—because of the conditions of that document.

(6)   I hereby direct my trustee to instruct Rosemont Enterprises to complete all written, visual, and audio documentation in the presentation of the factual representation of my life for public release two years to the day, after my death.

(7)   I authorize my trustee to make funds available limited to one quarter of the total estate to a private agency of my trustee's choice, in the event of my death by unnatural or man-made causes; to apprehend such person or group of persons and to bring them within full prosecution of the law; the funds being made available for legal expenses and costs incurred on behalf of the trustee's appointed agency.

(8)   I wish to make known to my trustee that I did not at any time enter into any contracts, agreements, or promises either oral or written, that transferred gave or bequeathed the bulk or any part of my estate to any person, persons, organizations, or whatever other than the Howard Hughes Medical Institute. I sign this as my Last Will and Testament.

                                          /S/ Howard R. Hughes
                                                Jan. 11,1972

Terminology of Wills

A person who makes out a will is known as a **testator** (from the Latin *testari*, "to make a will"). The court responsible for administering any legal problems surrounding a will is called a *probate court,* as mentioned in Chapter 3. When a person dies, a personal representative administers the estate and settles finally all of the decedent's (deceased person's) affairs. An **executor** is a personal representative named in the will; an **administrator** is a personal representative appointed by the court for a decedent who dies without a will, who fails to name an executor in the will, who names an executor lacking the capacity to serve, or who writes a will that the court refuses to admit to probate.

A gift of real estate by will is generally called a **devise,** and a gift of personal property by will is called a **bequest,** or **legacy.** The recipient of a gift by will is a **devisee** or **legatee,** depending on whether the gift was a devise or a legacy.

Types of Gifts

Gifts by will can be specific, general, or residuary. A *specific* devise or bequest (legacy) describes particular property (such as "Eastwood Estate" or "my gold pocket watch") that can be distinguished from all the rest of the testator's property. A *general* devise or bequest (legacy) uses less restrictive terminology. For example, "I devise all my lands" is a general devise. A general bequest often specifies a sum of money instead of a particular item of property, such as a watch or an automobile. For example, "I give to my nephew, Carleton, $30,000" is a general bequest.

If the assets of an estate are insufficient to pay in full all general bequests provided for in the will, an *abatement*, by which the legatees receive reduced benefits, takes place. If a legatee dies prior to the death of the testator or before the legacy is payable, a *lapsed legacy* results. At common law, the legacy failed. Today, the legacy may not lapse if the legatee is in a certain blood relationship to the testator (such as a child, grandchild, brother, or sister) and has left a child or other surviving descendant.

Sometimes a will provides that any assets remaining after specific gifts have been made and debts are paid—called the *residuum*—are to be distributed through a *residuary* clause. A residuary clause is used when the exact amount to be distributed cannot be determined until all of the other gifts and payouts have been made. A residuary clause can pose problems, however, when the will does not specifically name the beneficiaries to receive the residuum. In such a situation, if the court cannot determine the testator's intent, the residuum passes according to state laws of intestacy.

Probate Procedures

To *probate* a will means to establish its validity and to carry the administration of the estate through a court process. Probate laws vary from state to state. In 1969, however, the American Bar Association and the National Conference of Commissioners on Uniform State Laws approved the Uniform Probate Code (UPC). The UPC codifies general principles and procedures for the resolution of conflicts in settling estates and relaxes some of the requirements for a valid will contained in earlier state laws. About a third of the states have adopted some form of the UPC. Because succession and inheritance laws vary widely among states, one should always check the particular laws of the state involved.[2] Typically, probate procedures vary, depending on the size of the decedent's estate.

INFORMAL PROBATE   For smaller estates, most state statutes provide for the distribution of assets without formal probate proceedings. Faster and less expensive methods

TESTATOR
One who makes and executes a will.

EXECUTOR
A person appointed by a testator to see that his or her will is administered appropriately.

ADMINISTRATOR
One who is appointed by a court to handle the probate (disposition) of a person's estate if that person dies intestate (without a valid will) or if the executor named in the will cannot serve.

DEVISE
To make a gift of real property by will.

BEQUEST
A gift by will of personal property (from the verb—*to bequeath*).

LEGACY
A gift of personal property under a will.

DEVISEE
One designated in a will to receive a gift of real property.

LEGATEE
One designated in a will to receive a gift of personal property.

"If you want to see a man's true character, watch him divide an estate."

Benjamin Franklin, 1706–1790 (American diplomat, author, and scientist)

are then used. For example, property can be transferred by affidavit (a written statement taken before a person who has authority to affirm it), and problems or questions can be handled during an administrative hearing. In addition, some state statutes provide that title to cars, savings and checking accounts, and certain other property can be passed merely by filling out forms.

A majority of states also provide for *family settlement agreements*, which are private agreements among the beneficiaries. Once a will is admitted to probate, the family members can agree to settle among themselves the distribution of the decedent's assets. Although a family settlement agreement speeds the settlement process, a court order is still needed to protect the estate from future creditors and to clear title to the assets involved. The use of these and other types of summary procedures in estate administration can save time and money.

FORMAL PROBATE   For larger estates, normally formal probate proceedings are undertaken, and the probate court supervises every aspect of the settlement of the decedent's estate. Additionally, in some situations—such as when a guardian for minor children or for an incompetent person must be appointed, and a trust has been created to protect the minor or the incompetent person—more formal probate procedures cannot be avoided. Formal probate proceedings may take several months to complete, and as a result, a sizable portion of the decedent's assets (up to perhaps 10 percent) may have to go toward payment of court costs and fees charged by attorneys and personal representatives.

PROPERTY TRANSFERS OUTSIDE THE PROBATE PROCESS   In the ordinary situation, a person can employ various will substitutes to avoid the cost of probate—for example, *inter vivos* trusts (discussed later in this chapter), life insurance policies with named beneficiaries, or joint-tenancy arrangements. Not all methods are suitable for every estate, but there are alternatives to complete probate administration.

Requirements for a Valid Will

A will must comply with statutory formalities designed to ensure that the testator understood his or her actions at the time the will was made. These formalities are intended to help prevent fraud. Unless they are followed, the will is declared void, and the decedent's property is distributed according to the laws of intestacy of that state. The requirements are not uniform among the jurisdictions. Most states, however, uphold certain basic requirements for executing a will. We now look at these requirements.

RECALL In most states, the age of majority for contractual purposes is also eighteen years.

TESTAMENTARY CAPACITY   For a will to be valid, the testator must have testamentary capacity—that is, the testator must be of legal age and sound mind *at the time the will is made*. The legal age for executing a will varies, but in most states and under the UPC the minimum age is eighteen years [UPC 2–501]. Thus, the will of a twenty-one-year-old decedent written when the person was sixteen is invalid if, under state law, the legal age for executing a will is eighteen.

The concept of "being of sound mind" refers to the testator's ability to formulate and to comprehend a personal plan for the disposition of property. Generally, a testator must (1) intend the document to be his or her last will and testament, (2) comprehend the kind and character of the property being distributed, and (3) comprehend and remember the "natural objects of his or her bounty" (usually, family members and persons for whom the testator has affection).

In the following case, the question before the court was whether the testator had the required testamentary capacity. As the court notes, testamentary capacity will be presumed unless sufficient evidence exists to call such capacity into question.

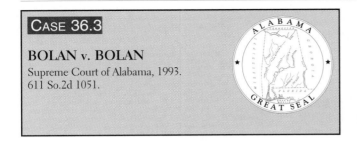

CASE 36.3

BOLAN v. BOLAN
Supreme Court of Alabama, 1993.
611 So.2d 1051.

HISTORICAL AND CULTURAL SETTING *In cases involving contested wills, English courts did not allow trial by jury. In actions of* ejectment *(in which a plaintiff seeks the removal of the defendant from land), English courts did allow trial by jury, even when one of the issues in the case was title to land that had been part of a testamentary disposition. When wills involving title to land came to be probated in the United States, it was believed that if those wills were contested, trial by jury should be allowed. Thus, trial by jury in will-contest cases came to be allowed in many states, including Alabama. Juries answer questions of fact. Incapacity is a question of fact. Because appellate courts do not generally consider questions of fact, an appellate court will normally not overturn the finding of a jury on the issue of incapacity as long as there is evidence to support the finding.*

FACTS On Charley Bolan's death, he was survived by six children. His will left one dollar to each of three of his children and to each child of his deceased son ("the contestants") and the remainder of his estate to the other three children ("the proponents"). The contestants claimed that the will was invalid, alleging, among other things, that Charley lacked testamentary capacity at the time he made the will. The evidence before the court was conflicting. Witnesses present at the time the will was executed testified that Charley was in sound mental condition on that occasion, and other family members testified to the same effect. Other testimony, including statements made by the contestants, indicated that Charley was "in poor health before the date of execution; that he repeatedly held conversations with his dead wife; that he refused to bathe, change his clothes, or otherwise take care of himself; and that he had rigged up a dangerous spring-gun to protect himself from intruders when no real threat existed." The case was transferred from a probate court to an Alabama state trial court, and the trial jury held for the contestants. The proponents appealed.

ISSUE Was there sufficient evidence to support a finding that Charley Bolan lacked testamentary capacity?

DECISION Yes. The Supreme Court of Alabama affirmed the trial court's judgment.

REASON The court stated that every testator is presumed to have the capacity to make a will, and the burden is on the contestant of a will to prove that testamentary capacity is lacking. "The contestant need not show that the testator suffered from permanent insanity," said the court. All that the contestant must do is show that the testator lacked testamentary capacity at the time the will was made. After reviewing the record, the court concluded that "[a]lthough the evidence was conflicting, the contestants presented sufficient evidence of a lack of testamentary capacity to support the submission of the contest to the jury on this ground."

FOR CRITICAL ANALYSIS—Social Consideration
What policy considerations underlie the courts' presumption that testamentary capacity exists?

WRITING REQUIREMENTS Generally, a will must be in writing. The writing itself can be informal as long as it substantially complies with the statutory requirements. In some states, a will can be handwritten in crayon or ink. It can be written on a sheet or scrap of paper, on a paper bag, or on a piece of cloth. A will that is completely in the handwriting of the testator is called a **holographic will** (sometimes referred to as an *olographic will*).

In some cases, oral wills are found valid. A **nuncupative will** is an oral will made before witnesses. It is not permitted in most states. Where authorized by statute, such wills are generally valid only if made during the last illness of the testator and are therefore sometimes referred to as *deathbed wills*. Normally, only personal property can be transferred by a nuncupative will. Statutes frequently permit soldiers and sailors to make nuncupative wills when on active duty.

HOLOGRAPHIC WILL
A will written entirely in the signer's handwriting and usually not witnessed.

NUNCUPATIVE WILL
An oral will (often called a deathbed will) made before witnesses; usually limited to transfers of personal property.

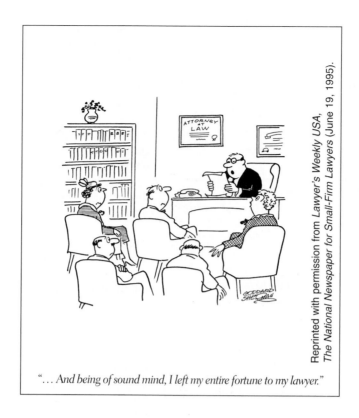

Reprinted with permission from *Lawyer's Weekly USA,*
The National Newspaper for Small-Firm Lawyers (June 19, 1995).

"*...And being of sound mind, I left my entire fortune to my lawyer.*"

SIGNATURE REQUIREMENTS It is a fundamental requirement that the testator's signature appear, generally at the end of the will. Each jurisdiction dictates by statute and court decision what constitutes a signature. Initials, an X or other mark, and words like "Mom" have all been upheld as valid when it was shown that the testators *intended* them to be signatures.

WITNESS REQUIREMENTS A will must be attested (sworn to) by two, and sometimes three, witnesses. The number of witnesses, their qualifications, and the manner in which the witnessing must be done are generally set out in a statute. A witness can be required to be disinterested—that is, not a beneficiary under the will. The UPC, however, provides that a will is valid even if it is attested by an interested witness [UPC 2–505]. There are no age requirements for witnesses, but witnesses must be mentally competent.

The purpose of witnesses is to verify that the testator actually executed (signed) the will and had the requisite intent and capacity at the time. A witness does not have to read the contents of the will. Usually, the testator and all witnesses must sign in the sight or the presence of one another, but the UPC deems it sufficient if the testator acknowledges his or her signature to the witnesses [UPC 2–502]. The UPC does not require all parties to sign in the presence of one another.

PUBLICATION REQUIREMENTS A will is *published* by an oral declaration by the maker to the witnesses that the document they are about to sign is his or her "last will and testament." Publication is becoming an unnecessary formality in most states, and it is not required under the UPC.

Undue Influence

A valid will is one that represents the maker's intention to transfer and distribute his or her property. When it can be shown that the decedent's plan of distribution was the result of improper pressure brought by another person, the will is declared invalid. Undue influence may be inferred by the court if the testator ignored blood relatives and named as beneficiary a nonrelative who was in constant close contact and in a position to influence the making of the will. For example, if a nurse or friend caring for the deceased at the time of death was named as beneficiary to the exclusion of all family members, the validity of the will might well be challenged on the basis of undue influence.

DON'T FORGET Undue influence can also occur in the making of a contract. The essential feature in all situations is that the party of whom advantage is taken does not exercise free will.

Revocation of Wills

An executed will is revocable by the maker at any time during the maker's lifetime. The maker may revoke a will by a physical act, such as tearing up the will, or by a subsequent writing. Wills can also be revoked by operation of law. Revocation can be partial or complete, and it must follow certain strict formalities.

REVOCATION BY A PHYSICAL ACT OF THE MAKER A testator may revoke a will by intentionally burning, tearing, canceling, obliterating, or otherwise destroying it, or by having someone else do so in the presence of the maker and at the maker's direction.[3] In some states, partial revocation by physical act of the maker is recognized. Thus, those portions of a will lined out or torn away are dropped, and the remaining parts of the will are valid. In no circumstances, however, can a provision be crossed out and an additional or substitute provision written in. Such altered portions require reexecution (re-signing) and reattestation (rewitnessing). To revoke a will by physical act, it is necessary to follow the mandates of a state statute exactly. When a state statute prescribes the exact methods for revoking a will by physical act, those are the only methods that will revoke the will.

REVOCATION BY A SUBSEQUENT WRITING A will may also be wholly or partially revoked by a **codicil**, a written instrument separate from the will that amends or revokes provisions in the will. A codicil eliminates the necessity of redrafting an entire will merely to add to it or amend it. It can also be used to revoke an entire will. The codicil must be executed with the same formalities required for a will, and it must refer expressly to the will. In effect, it updates a will, because the will is "incorporated by reference" into the codicil.

CODICIL
A written supplement or modification to a will. A codicil must be executed with the same formalities as a will.

A new will (second will) can be executed that may or may not revoke the first or a prior will, depending on the language used. To revoke a prior will, the second will must use language specifically revoking other wills, such as, "This will hereby revokes all prior wills." If the second will is otherwise valid and properly executed, it will revoke all prior wills. If the express *declaration of revocation* is missing, then both wills are read together. If any of the dispositions made in the second will are inconsistent with the prior will, the second will controls.

REVOCATION BY OPERATION OF LAW Revocation by *operation of law* occurs when marriage, divorce or annulment, or the birth of a child takes place after a will has been executed. In most states, when a testator marries after executing a will that does not include the new spouse, on the testator's death the spouse can still receive the amount he or she would have taken had the testator died intestate (how an intestate's property is distributed under state laws will be discussed shortly). In effect, this revokes the will to the point of providing the spouse with an intestate share. The rest of the estate is passed under the will [UPC 2–301, 2–508]. If, however, the new spouse is otherwise

---

3.   The destruction cannot be inadvertent. The maker's intent to revoke must be shown. Consequently, when a will has been burned or torn accidentally, it is normally recommended that the maker have a new document created so that it will not falsely appear that the maker intended to revoke the will.

provided for in the will (or by transfer of property outside the will), the new spouse will not be given an intestate amount.

At common law and under the UPC, divorce does not necessarily revoke the entire will. A divorce or an annulment occurring after a will has been executed will revoke those dispositions of property made under the will to the former spouse [UPC 2–508].

If a child is born after a will has been executed and if it appears that the deceased parent would have made a provision for the child, then the child is entitled to receive whatever portion of the estate he or she is allowed under state laws providing for the distribution of an intestate's property. Most state laws allow a child to receive some portion of a parent's estate if no provision is made in the parent's will, unless it appears from the terms of the will that the testator intended to disinherit the child. Under the UPC, the rule is the same.

Intestacy Laws

Each state regulates by statute how property will be distributed when a person dies intestate (without a valid will). These statutes are called statutes of descent and distribution, or more simply, **intestacy laws.** Intestacy laws attempt to carry out the likely intent and wishes of the decedent. These laws assume that deceased persons would have intended that their natural heirs (spouses, children, grandchildren, or other family members) inherit their property. Therefore, intestacy statutes set out rules and priorities under which these heirs inherit the property. If no heirs exist, the state will assume ownership of the property. The rules of descent vary widely from state to state.

SURVIVING SPOUSE AND CHILDREN   Usually, state statutes provide that first the debts of the decedent must be satisfied out of his or her estate, and then the remaining assets will pass to the surviving spouse and to the children. A surviving spouse usually receives only a share of the estate—one-half if there is also a surviving child and one-third if there are two or more children. Only if no children or grandchildren survive the decedent will a surviving spouse succeed to the entire estate.

Assume that Allen dies intestate and is survived by his wife, Della, and his children, Duane and Tara. Allen's property passes according to intestacy laws. After Allen's outstanding debts are paid, Della will receive the homestead (either in fee simple or as a life estate) and ordinarily a one-third (to one-half) interest in all other property. The remaining real and personal property will pass to Duane and Tara in equal portions. Under most state intestacy laws and under the UPC, in-laws do not share in an estate. If a child dies before his or her parents, the child's spouse will not receive an inheritance upon the parents' death. For example, if Duane died before his father (Allen), Duane's spouse would not inherit Duane's share of Allen's estate.

When there is no surviving spouse or child, the order of inheritance is grandchildren, then brothers and sisters, and in some states, parents of the decedent. These relatives are usually called *lineal descendants.* If there are no lineal descendants, then *collateral heirs*—nieces, nephews, aunts, and uncles of the decedent—make up the next group to share. If there are no survivors in any of these groups, most statutes provide for the property to be distributed among the next of kin of the collateral heirs.

STEPCHILDREN, ADOPTED CHILDREN, AND ILLEGITIMATE CHILDREN   Under intestacy laws, stepchildren are not considered kin. Legally adopted children, however, are recognized as lawful heirs of their adoptive parents. Statutes vary from state to state in regard to the inheritance laws governing illegitimate children. Generally, an illegitimate child is treated as the child of the mother and can inherit from her and her relatives. The child is usually not regarded as the legal child of the father with the right of inheritance unless paternity is established through some legal proceeding prior to the father's death. The following *Landmark in the Law* discusses a leading case in regard to the rights of illegitimate children.

"Land was never lost for want of an heir."

(English proverb)

INTESTACY LAWS
State statutes that specify how property will be distributed when a person dies intestate (without a valid will); also called statutes of descent and distribution.

Trimble v. Gordon (1977)

At common law, the illegitimate child was regarded as a *filius nullius* (Latin for "child of no one") and had no right to inherit. Over time, this attitude changed. A landmark case in establishing the rights of illegitimate children in the United States was decided by the United States Supreme Court in 1977. In *Trimble v. Gordon,*[a] an illegitimate child sought to inherit property from her deceased natural father on the ground that an Illinois statute prohibiting inheritance by illegitimate children in the absence of a will was unconstitutional.

The child was Deta Mona Trimble, daughter of Jessie Trimble and Sherman Gordon. The paternity of the father had been established before a Cook County, Illinois, circuit court in 1973. Gordon died intestate in 1974. The mother filed a petition on behalf of the child in the probate division of the county circuit court; the petition was denied by the court on the basis of an Illinois law disallowing the child's inheritance because she was illegitimate. Had she been legitimate, she would have been her father's sole heir. The Illinois Supreme Court in 1975 affirmed the petition's dismissal.

When the case came before the United States Supreme Court in 1977, the Court acknowledged that the "judicial task here is the difficult one of vindicating constitutional rights without interfering unduly with the State's primary responsibility in this area . . . [a]nd the need for the States to draw 'arbitrary lines . . . to facilitate potentially difficult problems of proof.'" The Court held that the section of the Illinois Probate Act that forbade Deta Mona Trimble to inherit her father's property was unconstitutional, because it "cannot be squared with the command of the Equal Protection Clause of the Fourteenth Amendment." The Court "expressly considered and rejected the argument that a State may attempt to influence the actions of men and women by imposing sanctions on the children born of their illegitimate relationships."

By declaring the Illinois statute unconstitutional, the Court invalidated similar laws of several other states. That does not mean that all illegitimate children will have inheritance rights identical to those of legitimate children. Those state statutes that discriminate between the two classes for legitimate state purposes have been thus far allowed to stand, in the interests of each state's need to create an appropriate legal framework for the legal disposition of property at death.[b]

For Critical Analysis: *Can there ever be a legitimate state purpose for discriminating between legitimate and illegitimate children? Explain.*

a. 430 U.S. 762, 97 S.Ct. 1459, 52 L.Ed.2d 31 (1977).
b. UPC 2–109; *White v. Randolph,* 59 Ohio St.2d 6, 391 N.E.2d 333 (1979).

DISTRIBUTION TO GRANDCHILDREN   When an intestate is survived by descendants of deceased children, a question arises as to what share these descendants (that is, grandchildren of the intestate) will receive. **Per stirpes** is a method of dividing an intestate share by which, within a class or group of distributees (for example, grandchildren), the children of any one descendant take the share that their deceased parent *would have been* entitled to inherit. For example, assume that Michael, a widower, has two children, Scott and Jonathan. Scott has two children (Becky and Holly), and Jonathan has one child (Paul). Scott and Jonathan die before their father, and then Michael dies. If Michael's estate is distributed *per stirpes*, Becky and Holly will each receive one-fourth of the estate (dividing Scott's one-half share). Paul will receive one-half of the estate (taking Jonathan's one-half share). Exhibit 36–4 illustrates the *per stirpes* method of distribution.

An estate may also be distributed on a **per capita** basis, which means that each person in a class or group takes an equal share of the estate. If Michael's estate is

PER STIRPES
A Latin term meaning "by the roots." In the law governing estate distribution, a method of distributing an intestate's estate in which each heir in a certain class (such as grandchildren) takes the share to which his or her deceased ancestor (such as a mother or father) would have been entitled.

PER CAPITA
A Latin term meaning "per person." In the law governing estate distribution, a method of distributing the property of an intestate's estate in which each heir in a certain class (such as grandchildren) receives an equal share.

♦ **Exhibit 36–4**
Per Stirpes **Distribution**
Under this method of distribution, an heir takes the share that his or her deceased parent would have been entitled to inherit, had the parent lived. This may mean that a class of distributees—the grandchildren in this example—will not inherit in equal portions. Note that Becky and Holly only receive one-fourth of Michael's estate while Paul inherits one-half.

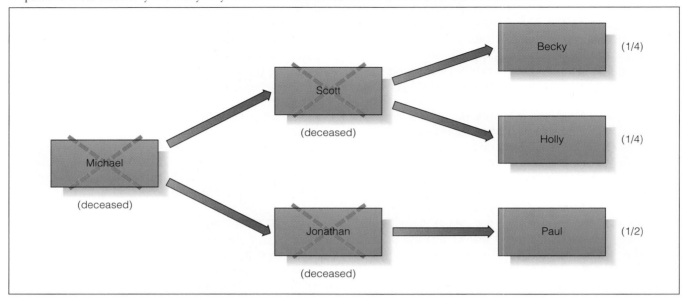

distributed *per capita*, Becky, Holly, and Paul will each receive a one-third share. Exhibit 36–5 illustrates the *per capita* method of distribution.

▌ Trusts

"Put not your trust in money, but put your money in trust."

Oliver Wendell Holmes, Jr., 1841–1935
(*Associate justice of the United States Supreme Court, 1902–1932*)

TRUST
An arrangement in which title to property is held by one person (a trustee) for the benefit of another (a beneficiary).

A **trust** is any arrangement through which property is transferred from one person to a trustee to be administered for the transferor's or another party's benefit. It can also be defined as a right or property, real or personal, held by one party for the benefit of another. A trust can be created for any purpose that is not illegal or against public policy. Its essential elements are as follows:

1. A designated beneficiary.
2. A designated trustee.
3. A fund sufficiently identified to enable title to pass to the trustee.
4. Actual delivery by the settlor or grantor to the trustee with the intention of passing title.

If James conveys his farm to the First Bank of Minnesota to be held for the benefit of his daughters, he has created a trust. James is the settlor, the First Bank of Minnesota is the trustee, and James's daughters are the beneficiaries. This arrangement is illustrated in Exhibit 36–6. Numerous types of trusts can be established. In this section, we look at some of the major types of trusts and their characteristics.

Express Trusts

An *express trust* is one created or declared in explicit terms, usually in writing. Express trusts fall into two categories: *inter vivos* (living) trusts and testamentary trusts (trusts provided for in a last will and testament).

◆ **Exhibit 36–5**
Per Capita **Distribution**
Under this method of distribution, all heirs in a certain class—in this case, the grandchildren—inherit equally. Note that Becky and Holly in this situation each inherit one-third, as does Paul.

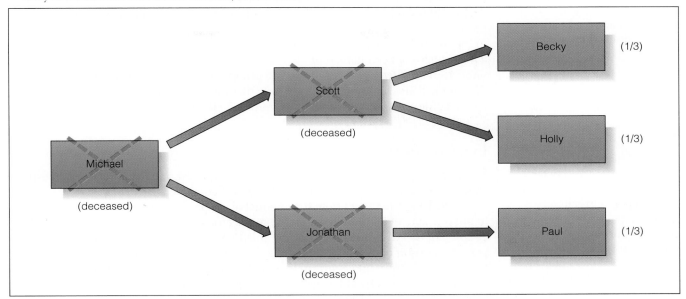

An *inter vivos* **trust** is a trust executed by a grantor during his or her lifetime. The grantor (settlor) executes a *trust deed,* and legal title to the trust property passes to the named trustee. The trustee has a duty to administer the property as directed by the grantor for the benefit and in the interest of the beneficiaries. The trustee must preserve the trust property, make it productive, and if required by the terms of the trust agreement, pay income to the beneficiaries, all in accordance with the terms of the

INTER VIVOS TRUST
A trust created by the grantor (settlor) and effective during the grantor's lifetime; a trust not established by a will.

◆ **Exhibit 36–6**
Trust Arrangement
In a trust, there is a separation of interests in the trust property. The trustee takes *legal* title, which is the complete ownership and possession but which does not include the right to receive any benefits from the property. The beneficiary takes *equitable* title, which is the right to receive benefits from the property.

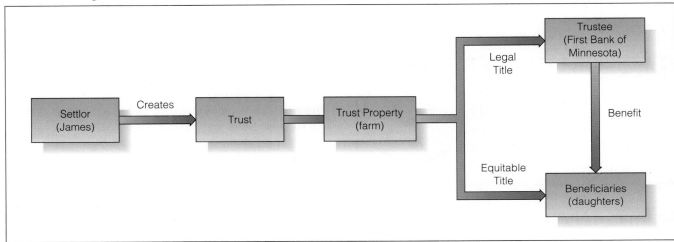

trust. Once the *inter vivos* trust is created, the grantor has, in effect, given over the property for the benefit of the beneficiaries. Often, tax-related benefits exist in setting up this type of trust.

A **testamentary trust** is a trust created by a will to come into existence on the settlor's death. Although a testamentary trust has a trustee who maintains legal title to the trust property, actions of the trustee are subject to judicial approval. This trustee can be named in the will or be appointed by the court. Thus, a testamentary trust does not fail because a trustee has not been named in the will. The legal responsibilities of the trustee are the same as in an *inter vivos* trust. If the will setting up a testamentary trust is invalid, then the trust will also be invalid. The property that was supposed to be in the trust will then pass according to intestacy laws, not according to the terms of the trust.

TESTAMENTARY TRUST
A trust that is created by will and therefore does not take effect until the death of the testator.

Implied Trusts

Sometimes, a trust will be imposed (implied) by law, even in the absence of an express trust. Implied trusts include resulting trusts and constructive trusts.

A **resulting trust** arises from the conduct of the parties. Suppose that Garrison wants to put one acre of land she owns on the market for sale. Because she is going out of the country for two years and would not be able to deed the property to a buyer during that period, Garrison conveys the property to her good friend Oswald. Oswald will attempt to sell the property while Garrison is gone. Because the intent of the transaction to convey the property to Oswald is neither a sale nor a gift, the property will be held in trust (a resulting trust) by Oswald for the benefit of Garrison. Therefore, on Garrison's return, Oswald will be required either to deed back the property to Garrison or, if the property has been sold, to turn over the proceeds (held in trust) to Garrison. Here, the trust arises (*results* from) the *apparent intention* of the parties.

RESULTING TRUST
An implied trust arising from the conduct of the parties. A trust in which a party holds the actual legal title to another's property but only for that person's benefit.

A **constructive trust** is an equitable trust imposed in the interests of fairness and justice. If someone wrongfully holds legal title to property—for example, if the property was obtained through fraud or in breach of a legal duty—a court may require that owner to hold the property in trust for the person or persons who rightfully should own the property. For instance, suppose that Kraft is a partner in a partnership that purchases and develops real estate. Kraft learns in a partners' meeting that the partnership is considering the purchase of a vacant lot that will soon come on the market. Kraft secretly purchases the property in his own name, thus violating his fiduciary duty of loyalty to the partnership. If the partnership discovers what Kraft has done and brings a legal action against Kraft, a court may impose a constructive trust, thus requiring Kraft to hold the property in trust for the partnership.

Constructive trusts may be imposed for a variety of reasons. In the following case, the issue concerns whether a constructive trust should be imposed to counter the effects of an insurance company's failure to change the beneficiary on a life insurance policy after the insured had requested the change.

CONSTRUCTIVE TRUST
An equitable trust that is imposed in the interests of fairness and justice when someone wrongfully holds legal title to property. A court may require the owner to hold the property in trust for the person or persons who rightfully should own the property.

CASE 36.4

ZEIGLER v. CARDONA
United States District Court,
Middle District of Alabama, 1993.
830 F.Supp. 1395.

COMPANY PROFILE *In 1927, in Birmingham, Alabama, Frank Samford founded an insurance company*

called the Heralds of Liberty. Two years later, the Heralds of Liberty became the Liberty National Life Insurance Company. Then and now, Liberty National markets its life, accident, and health-insurance policies in rural regions to lower-income customers. Liberty National concentrates its marketing in seven southern states and does half its business in Alabama. Liberty National life insurance costs three times more than other insurers' life insurance and ten times more than others' group coverage. But Liberty National sells policies without a physical examination and offers personal, monthly premium-collection service. Liberty National is the ninth

Case 36.4—Continued

largest life insurer in the United States; in the early 1990s, its profit margin was twice as high as the average life insurance company. Liberty National is owned by Torchmark, a diversified insurance and financial services company headquartered in Birmingham.

FACTS In March 1990, Antonio Suarez, Sr., bought a $50,000 life insurance policy from Liberty National Life Insurance Company. The beneficiary was Suarez's mother, Guarina Cardona. At the time, Suarez was living with his aunt, Ruby Zeigler. Suarez and Zeigler later met with the insurance agent to change the beneficiary to Zeigler. At the meeting, Suarez made it clear that he wanted the proceeds of the policy to be used for the benefit of his children, Antonio and Ebony, and after Zeigler agreed to implement his wishes, Suarez signed the change-of-beneficiary form. Apparently due to a clerical error, Liberty National never acted on the change-of-beneficiary request. Zeigler paid the premiums. Suarez died in January 1991. Because of Liberty National's error, Cardona was the beneficiary of record. A suit was brought in a federal district court to establish who had rights in the insurance proceeds. The children sought to have the proceeds placed in a constructive trust on their behalf.

ISSUE Who is entitled to the insurance proceeds?

DECISION The court held that Zeigler was the proper beneficiary under the policy and was entitled to $10,000. A constructive trust on the remainder of the proceeds was imposed for the benefit of Antonio and Ebony. Cardona received nothing.

REASON The court explained that "the law of equity regards as having been done that which ought to be done and the courts will give effect to the intention of the insured by holding that a change of beneficiary has been accomplished where he or she has done all that he or she could do in order to comply with the provisions of the policy." The court concluded that in this case, Suarez had done all that he could do, which made Zeigler the beneficiary. In imposing the constructive trust, the court noted that the evidence is undisputed that Suarez intended that the proceeds be used for the children and pointed out that "[a] constructive trust may be imposed on life insurance proceeds even though the designated beneficiary is not guilty of fraud or wrongdoing."

FOR CRITICAL ANALYSIS—Social Consideration *If Suarez had no proof that he had ever signed a change-of-beneficiary form, would the outcome in this case be different?*

Special Types of Trusts

Certain trusts are created for special purposes. Three of these trusts that warrant discussion are charitable, spendthrift, and Totten trusts. A trust designed for the benefit of a segment of the public or of the public in general is a **charitable trust.** Usually, to be deemed a charitable trust, a trust must be created for charitable, educational, religious, or scientific purposes.

A trust created to provide for the maintenance of a beneficiary by preventing his or her improvidence with the bestowed funds is a **spendthrift trust.** Essentially, the beneficiary is permitted to draw only a certain portion of the total amount to which he or she is entitled at any one time. The majority of states allow spendthrift trust provisions that prohibit creditors from attaching such trusts.

A **Totten trust**[4] is created when one person deposits money in his or her own name as a trustee for another. This trust is tentative in that it is revocable at will until the depositor dies or completes the gift in his or her lifetime by some unequivocal act or declaration (for example, delivery of the funds to the intended beneficiary). If the depositor should die before the beneficiary dies and if the depositor has not revoked the trust expressly or impliedly, the beneficiary obtains property rights to the balance on hand.

CHARITABLE TRUST
A trust in which the property held by a trustee must be used for a charitable purpose, such as the advancement of health, education, or religion.

SPENDTHRIFT TRUST
A trust created to protect the beneficiary from spending all the money to which he or she is entitled. Only a certain portion of the total amount is given to the beneficiary at any one time, and most states prohibit creditors from attaching assets of the trust.

TOTTEN TRUST
A trust created by the deposit of a person's own money in his or her own name as a trustee for another. It is a tentative trust, revocable at will until the depositor dies or completes the gift in his or her lifetime by some unequivocal act or declaration.

---

4. This type of trust derives its unusual name from *In the Matter of Totten*, 179 N.Y. 112, 71 N.E. 748 (1904).

Application

Law and the Partner or Shareholder— Key-Person Insurance*

Life insurance on the lives of partners or shareholders may be a valuable tool for those who are partners in a partnership or shareholders in a closely held corporation. Typically, should one partner or co-shareholder die, the others will want to buy that person's interest, particularly if they wish to continue in the business. The partnership or corporation may wish to purchase key-person life insurance on each partner or co-shareholder to help fund the buy-out. Problems arise, however, when the partners or co-shareholders are not all the same age or do not all have the same financial interest in the partnership or corporation. How does one arrange an insurance and buy-out agreement that is fair to everyone?

If you are a partner or a shareholder in a close corporation, you must first determine the current value of the business and then provide a method for determining the value of the business when one of the owners dies. There are numerous ways to accomplish such a valuation. The important point is that all of the partners or shareholders agree on the method to be used. Each participant must be satisfied that if he or she is the first to die, the valuation method will provide a fair and equitable way to buy that interest from the estate.

Next, you must determine how much life insurance to purchase. Insurance can be used to fund the entire amount of the purchase price of the deceased's interest

in the firm or just a part of that purchase price. Because the premiums for some of the owners may cost more (due to more advanced age or poorer health), an agreement may be reached to buy less insurance for them to reduce the current cost of the life insurance policy. The agreement could specify that the remaining part of the buy-out purchase price would be paid to the deceased's heirs in the form of installments, including interest payments at current interest rates.

Owners can negotiate a variety of payment plans to fit the needs of each partner or shareholder in the event a buy-out becomes necessary. For example, for an older partner, the payments may be spread over only a few years, and for younger partners, over a longer period of time. All of these points are negotiable. It should be possible to draft an agreement that provides for insurance and/or a buy-out purchase plan that protects the interest of each person.

✓ Checklist for Partners and Close Corporation Shareholders

1. If anyone in your partnership or closely held corporation can be considered a key person, then you should probably buy key-person life insurance on that individual.
2. Estimate the amount of loss that the partnership or closely held corporation would suffer if a key person died or became incapacitated. Insure that person for only that amount (the partnership or close corporation should not benefit from a partner's or shareholder's death but rather be left in an equal financial position compared with its position prior to the death).
3. Establish a buy-out purchase plan for the partnership or close corporation members in the event of one key person's death.

*This *Application* is not meant to substitute for the services of an attorney who is licensed to practice law in your state.

▮ Key Terms

▍Chapter Summary: Insurance, Wills, and Trusts

INSURANCE	
Classifications *(See pages 928, 929–930.)*	See Exhibit 36–1.
Terminology *(See pages 928–929.)*	1. *Policy*—The insurance contract. 2. *Premium*—The consideration paid to the insurer for a policy. 3. *Underwriter*—The insurance company. 4. *Parties*—Include the insurer (the insurance company), the insured (the person covered by insurance), an agent (a representative of the insurance company) or a broker (ordinarily an independent contractor), and a beneficiary (the person to receive proceeds under the policy).
Insurable Interest *(See pages 929–930.)*	An insurable interest exists whenever an individual or entity benefits from the preservation of the health or life of the insured or the property to be insured. For life insurance, an insurable interest must exist at the time the policy is issued. For property insurance, an insurable interest must exist at the time of the loss.
The Insurance Contract *(See pages 930–935.)*	1. *Laws governing*—The general principles of contract law are applied; the insurance industry is also heavily regulated by the states. 2. *Application*—An insurance applicant is bound by any false statements that appear in the application (subject to certain exceptions), which is part of the insurance contract. Misstatements or misrepresentations may be grounds for voiding the policy. 3. *Effective date*—Coverage on an insurance policy can begin when the binder (a written memorandum indicating that a formal policy is pending and stating its essential terms) is written; when the policy is issued; or depending on the terms of the contract, when certain conditions are met. 4. *Provisions and clauses*—See Exhibit 36–2. Words will be given their ordinary meanings, and any ambiguity in the policy will be interpreted against the insurance company. When the written policy has not been delivered and it is unclear whether an insurance contract actually exists, the uncertainty will be determined against the insurance company. The court will presume that the policy is in effect unless the company can show otherwise. 5. *Defenses against payment to the insured*—Defenses include misrepresentation, fraud, or violation of warranties by the applicant.
WILLS	
Terminology *(See page 937.)*	1. *Intestate*—One who dies without a valid will. 2. *Testator*—A person who makes out a will. 3. *Personal representative*—A person appointed in a will or by a court to settle the affairs of a decedent. A personal representative named in the will is an *executor*; a personal representative appointed by the court for an intestate decedent is an *administrator*. 4. *Devise*—A gift of real estate by will; may be general or specific. The recipient of a devise is a *devisee*. 5. *Bequest, or legacy*—A gift of personal property by will; may be general or specific. The recipient of a bequest (legacy) is a *legatee*.
Probate Procedures *(See pages 937–938.)*	To probate a will means to establish its validity and to carry the administration of the estate through a court process. Probate laws vary from state to state. Probate procedures may be informal or formal, depending on the size of the estate and other factors, such as whether a guardian for minor children must be appointed.
Requirements for a Valid Will *(See pages 938–941.)*	1. The testator must have testamentary capacity (be of legal age and sound mind at the time the will is made). 2. A will must be in writing (except for nuncupative wills). A holographic will is completely in the handwriting of the testator. 3. A will must be signed by the testator; what constitutes a signature varies from jurisdiction to jurisdiction. *(Continued)*

▌Chapter Summary: Insurance, Wills, and Trusts—Continued

Requirements for a Valid Will— Continued	4. A nonholographic will (an attested will) must be witnessed in the manner prescribed by state statute. 5. A will may have to be *published*—that is, the testator may be required to announce to witnesses that this is his or her "last will and testament." Not required under the UPC.

Revocation of Wills *(See pages 941–942.)*	1. By *physical act of the maker*—Tearing up, canceling, obliterating, or deliberately destroying part or all of a will.
	
	2. By *subsequent writing*—
	  a. Codicil—A formal, separate document to amend or revoke an existing will.
	  b. Second will or new will—A new, properly executed will expressly revoking the existing will.
	
	3. By *operation of law*—
	  a. Marriage—Generally revokes part of a will written before the marriage.
	  b. Divorce or annulment—Revokes dispositions of property made under a will to a former spouse.
	  c. Subsequently born child—It is *implied* that the child is entitled to receive the portion of the estate granted under intestacy distribution laws.

Intestacy Laws *(See pages 942–944.)*	1. Vary widely from state to state. Usually, the law provides that the surviving spouse and children inherit the property of the decedent (after the decedent's debts are paid). The spouse usually will inherit the entire estate if there are no children, one-half of the estate if there is one child, and one-third of the estate if there are two or more children. 2. If there is no surviving spouse or child, then, in order, lineal descendants (grandchildren, brothers and sisters, and—in some states—parents of the decedent) inherit. If there are no lineal descendants, then collateral heirs (nieces, nephews, aunts, and uncles of the decedent) inherit.
TRUSTS	
Definition *(See page 944.)*	A trust is any arrangement through which property is transferred from one person to be administered by a trustee for another party's benefit. The essential elements of a trust are (1) a designated beneficiary, (2) a designated trustee, (3) a fund sufficiently identified to enable title to pass to the trustee, and (4) actual delivery to the trustee with the intention of passing title.
Express Trusts *(See page 944–946.)*	Express trusts are created by expressed terms, usually in writing, and fall into two categories: 1. *Inter vivos trust*—A trust executed by a grantor during his or her lifetime. 2. *Testamentary trust*—A trust created by will and coming into existence on the death of the grantor.
Implied Trusts *(See pages 946–947.)*	Implied trusts, which are imposed by law in the interests of fairness and justice, include the following: 1. *Resulting trust*—Arises from the conduct of the parties when an *apparent intention* to create a trust is present. 2. *Constructive trust*—Arises by operation of law whenever a transaction takes place in which the person who takes title to property is in equity not entitled to enjoy the beneficial interest therein.
Special Types of Trusts *(See page 947.)*	1. *Charitable trust*—A trust designed for the benefit of a public group or the public in general. 2. *Spendthrift trust*—A trust created to provide for the maintenance of a beneficiary by allowing only a certain portion of the total amount to be received by the beneficiary at any one time. 3. *Totten trust*—A trust created when one person deposits money in his or her own name as a trustee for another.

For Review

1. What is an insurable interest? To obtain life insurance, when must an insurable interest exist—at the time that the policy is obtained, at the time that the loss occurs, or both? To obtain property insurance, when must an insurable interest exist—at the time that the policy is obtained, at the time that the loss occurs, or both?

2. Is an insurance broker the agent of the insurance applicant or the agent of the insurer? If the broker accepts an applicant's initial premium but fails to obtain coverage, and the applicant is damaged as a result, who may be liable for the damage?

3. Who can make a will? What are the basic requirements for executing a will? How may a will be revoked?

4. What is the difference between a *per stirpes* and a *per capita* distribution of an estate to the grandchildren of the deceased?

5. What are the four essential elements of a trust? What is an express trust? How do implied trusts arise?

Questions and Case Problems

36–1. Timing of Insurance Coverage. On October 10, Joleen Vora applied for a $50,000 life insurance policy with Magnum Life Insurance Co.; she named her husband, Jay, as the beneficiary. Joleen paid the insurance company the first year's policy premium upon making the application. Two days later, before she had a chance to take the physical examination required by the insurance company and before the policy was issued, Joleen was killed in an automobile accident. Jay submitted a claim to the insurance company for the $50,000. Can Jay collect? Explain.

36–2. Validity of Wills. Merlin Winters had three sons. Merlin and his youngest son, Abraham, had a falling out in 1994 and had not spoken to each other since. Merlin made a formal will in 1996, leaving all his property to the two older children and deliberately excluding Abraham. Merlin's health began to deteriorate, and by 1997 he was under the full-time care of a nurse, Julia. In 1998, he made a new will expressly revoking the 1996 will and leaving all his property to Julia. On Merlin's death, the two older children contested the 1998 will, claiming that Julia had exercised undue influence over their father. Abraham claimed that both wills were invalid, because the first one had been revoked by the second will, and the second will was invalid on the ground of undue influence. Is Abraham's contention correct? Explain.

36–3. Wills. Gary Mendel drew up a will in which he left his favorite car, a 1966 red Ferrari, to his daughter, Roberta. A year prior to his death, Mendel sold the 1966 Ferrari and purchased a 1969 Ferrari. Discuss whether Roberta will inherit the 1969 Ferrari under the terms of her father's will.

36–4. Estate Distribution. Benjamin is a widower who has two married children, Edward and Patricia. Patricia has two children, Perry and Paul. Edward has no children. Benjamin dies, and his typewritten will leaves all his property equally to his children, Edward and Patricia, and provides that should a child predecease him, the grandchildren are to take *per stirpes*. The will was witnessed by Patricia and by Benjamin's lawyer and was signed by Benjamin in their presence. Patricia has predeceased Benjamin. Edward claims the will is invalid.

(a) Discuss whether the will is valid.

(b) Discuss the distribution of Benjamin's estate if the will is invalid.

(c) Discuss the distribution of Benjamin's estate if the will is valid.

36–5. Validity of Wills. An elderly, childless widow had nine nieces and nephews. Her will divided her entire estate equally among two nieces and the husband of one of the nieces, who was also the attorney who drafted the will and the executor named in the will. The testator was definitely of sound mind when the will was executed. If you were one of the seven nieces or nephews omitted from the will, could you think of any way to have the will invalidated? [*Estate of Eckert*, 93 Misc.2d 677, 403 N.Y.S.2d 633 (Surrogate's Ct. 1978)]

36–6. Revocation of Wills. Myrtle Courziel executed a valid will that provided for the establishment of a scholarship fund designed to encourage the study of corrosion as it affects metallurgical engineering. The recipients were to be students in the upper halves of their classes at the University of Alabama. Subsequently, Courziel died. John Calhoun, the eventual administrator of her estate, obtained access to her safe-deposit box to search for her will. He found the will intact, except that the last page of the will, which had contained Courziel's signature and the signatures of the witnesses, had been removed from the document and was not in the safe-deposit box or anywhere else to be found. Because Courziel had had sole control over the will, should it be presumed that her removal of the last page (or her having allowed it to be removed) effectively revoked the will? Discuss. [*Board of Trustees of University of Alabama v. Calhoun*, 514 So.2d 895 (Ala. 1987)]

36–7. Insurer's Defenses. Kirk Johnson applied for life insurance with New York Life Insurance Co. on October 7, 1986. In answer to a question about smoking habits, Johnson stated that he had not smoked in the past twelve months and that he had never smoked cigarettes. In fact, Johnson had smoked for thirteen years, and during the month prior to the insurance application, he was smoking approximately ten cigarettes per day. Johnson died on July 17, 1988, for reasons unrelated to smoking. Johnson's father, Lawrence Johnson, who was the beneficiary of the policy, filed a claim for the insurance proceeds. While investigating the claim, New York Life discovered Kirk Johnson's misrepresentation and denied the claim. The company canceled the policy and sent Lawrence Johnson a check for the premiums that had been paid. Lawrence Johnson refused to accept the check, and New York Life brought an action for a declaratory judgment (a court determination of a plaintiff's rights). What should the court decide? Discuss fully. [*New York Life Insurance Co. v. Johnson*, 923 F.2d 279 (3d Cir. 1991)]

36–8. Testamentary Trusts. Edwin Fickes died in 1943. His will provided for the creation of a trust, half of which was to be divided, on the death of Fickes's last surviving child, "in equal portions between [the testator's] grandchildren then living." At the time of the death of Fickes's last surviving child, there were four biological grandchildren and four adopted grandchildren living. Two of the adopted grandchildren, both boys, had been adopted prior to Fickes's death. The other two, both girls, had been adopted after Fickes died. The trustee, Connecticut National Bank and Trust Co., sought a court determination of whether the adopted grandchildren were entitled to share in the trust distribution. The trial court found that the testator, Fickes, had intended to include his adopted grandsons as "grandchildren" within the meaning of his will but could not have intended to include his adopted granddaughters as "grandchildren," so they were not entitled to a share of the trust. What will happen on appeal? Discuss fully. [*Connecticut National Bank and Trust Co. v. Chadwick*, 217 Conn. 260, 585 A.2d 1189 (1991)]

36–9. Spendthrift Trusts. Billy Putman rented and occupied a house trailer owned by Douglas Sanders. Because Putman damaged the trailer while it was in his possession, Sanders sought and acquired a judgment against Putman for $2,429.36 in damages, plus court costs and interest. Sanders garnished Putman's bank account and learned of a certificate of deposit (CD) worth $20,000, which was held by a trustee (Georgia Putman) on behalf of Billy Putman as the beneficiary. The CD was purchased with the proceeds from Billy Putman's deceased father's life insurance policy. Sanders claimed that the insurance proceeds, or the CD, could be garnished. Billy Putman argued that the CD funds were part of a spendthrift trust and therefore could not be reached by creditors, including Sanders. The only evidence in support of a spendthrift trust was the insurance company's check made payable to Billy Putman's trustee. How should the court decide? Explain. [*Sanders v. Putman*, 315 Ark. 251, 866 S.W.2d 827 (1993)]

36–10. Validity of Wills. In the last fourteen years of Evelyn Maheras's life, William Cook, a Baptist pastor, became her spiritual adviser and close personal friend. Cook—and no one else—actively participated in helping Maheras draft her will. He gave Maheras a church-sponsored booklet on will drafting, recommended an attorney (a church member) to do the drafting, and reviewed the terms of the will with Maheras. When Maheras died, she left most of her estate to Cook's church. Cook personally received nothing under the will. Maheras's nephew and only heir, Richard Suagee, filed a suit against Cook in an Oklahoma state court to contest the will, arguing that Cook unduly influenced Maheras. Can a party who receives nothing under a will be regarded as having exercised undue influence over the testator? What should the court in Maheras's case do? [*Estate of Maheras*, 897 P.2d 268 (Okla. 1995)]

A QUESTION OF ETHICS AND SOCIAL RESPONSIBILITY

36–11. *Heber Burke and his wife Evelyn had been married for fifty-three years. Evelyn died, and about five months later, Heber married Lexie Damron, a widow who attended his church. Seven days after the marriage, Heber executed a will, which was drawn up by Lexie's attorney, in which he left all of his property to Lexie. Heber died three weeks later. Heber's children, Donald Burke and Beatrice Bates, contested the will, alleging that Heber lacked testamentary capacity and that Heber's will resulted from Lexie's undue influence over him. Friends and relatives of Heber testified that they had never known Heber to drink and that, although he seemed saddened by his first wife's death, he was not incapacitated by it. According to the children's witnesses, however, after Evelyn's death, Heber drank heavily and constantly, had frequent crying spells, repeatedly visited his wife's grave, tried to dig her up so that he could talk to her, and had hallucinations. The jury found the will to be invalid on the ground of undue influence, and Lexie appealed. [Burke v. Burke, 801 S.W.2d 691 (Ken.App. 1990)]*

1. The appellate court had to weigh two conflicting policies in deciding this issue. What are these two policies, and what criteria should be used in resolving the issue?
2. Given the circumstances described above, would you infer undue influence on the part of Lexie if you were the judge? Would you conclude that Heber lacked testamentary capacity? What would be the fairest solution, in your opinion?
3. Heber's first wife, Evelyn, contributed substantially to the acquisition of the property subject to Heber's will. A natural assumption would be that Evelyn would want their children to inherit the jointly acquired property. If Heber were found to be of sound mind and not the victim of any undue influence, however, the court would allow him to disregard the children totally, if he wished, in his will. Is this fair to Evelyn's presumed intentions? To the children? Is there any solution to the possible unfairness that can result from giving people the right to disregard natural heirs in their wills?

FOR CRITICAL ANALYSIS

36–12. *Statistics show that the extent of risk assumed by insurance companies varies depending on the gender of the insured. Many people contend that laws prohibiting gender-based insurance rates are thus fundamentally unfair. Do you agree with this contention? Why or why not?*

▌ Unit Nine—Cumulative Hypothetical Problem

36–13. *Joel and Marsha Cummings operate a consulting business out of their home. Most of their work consists of creating and maintaining "home pages" on the Internet for various clients. Business is thriving, and to obtain tax benefits, they recently organized their business as an S corporation. They are contemplating leasing office space and hiring some assistants.*

1. Joel and Marsha own their home and both of their cars as joint tenants. They have never gotten around to making a will. Assume that Joel dies and is survived by his wife (Marsha) and their two children. Who will inherit the home and the two automobiles?

2. One day, Marsha's computer malfunctions, and she takes it to a computer shop for repairs. The next day, the computer technician calls Marsha and tells her that her computer is missing. Marsha claims that the shop is liable for the value of the computer. The shop contends that it was not negligent in any way and therefore cannot be held liable. Will Marsha succeed in a suit against the shop? Explain.

3. Marsha and Joel, having decided to move their business out of their home, lease office space in a building owned by Dan Silver. The written lease contract, a brief form contract, provides that the term of the lease is one year; that the monthly rent is $900, to be paid on the first of each month; and that Marsha and Joel will pay all utility bills. After they have moved to the new office space, Marsha and Joel learn that the electrical wiring is deficient, that the roof leaks, and that the furnace does not function properly. Silver refuses to make any repairs. What legal options do Marsha and Joel have in this situation? Can they break the lease without liability? Discuss fully.

4. Marsha and Joel are concerned about the potential liability they will incur if a customer is injured while on their business premises. They also want to protect against the loss of income that they would suffer if one of them were disabled or died. What types of insurance policies would best meet each of these needs? Why?

5. Joel dies intestate, and his property is distributed under intestacy laws. Marsha decides she had better write a will so that she will have more control over how her property will be transferred on her death. She particularly wants to make sure that one of her children, Sam, inherits nothing, because he has been so unaffectionate and unhelpful to his parents over the years. In her will, Marsha designated her daughter, Julie, as her sole heir, and said nothing about Sam. If Sam contests the will, will he succeed in obtaining any of his mother's property?

6. Assume that Marsha, before she died, had a change of heart. She wrote a new will in which she left everything she owned to both of her children in equal shares. In the new will, she said nothing about revoking her prior will. Who will inherit what in these circumstances?

▌ Accessing the Internet: Business Law and Legal Environment

A commercial service called Butterworth Legal Publishers allows you to search for titles over the Internet. Then you can order them by fax. For more information, go to

gopher://igopher.infor.com:4800/1

The gopher address is

Gopher.infor.com

Once you are in the gopher, select the following:

Butterworth Legal Publishers

A law firm by the name of Advice and Counsel, Inc., with offices in San Francisco and San Diego, offers information about frequently asked questions concerning wills, trusts, and estate planning. It can be found on the Web at

http://starbase.ingress.com/adviceco

If you are using the commercial service GEnie, you can access Wills, Trusts, and Estates. Simply select the following:

Career/Professional Services

And then select

Law RT

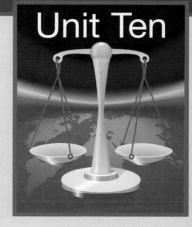

The International Legal Environment

Unit Ten

UNIT OUTLINE

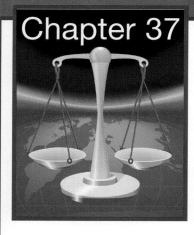

Chapter 37

International Law
in a Global Economy

*"Our interests are those of the open door—a door of
friendship and mutual advantage. This is the only
door we care to enter."*

**Woodrow Wilson, 1856–1924
(Twenty-eighth president of the United
States, 1913–1921)**

CHAPTER OBJECTIVES

After reading this chapter, you should be able to:

1. Identify and discuss some basic principles and doctrines that frame international business transactions.
2. Describe some ways in which U.S. businesspersons do business internationally.
3. Explain how parties to international contracts protect against various risks through contractual clauses and letters of credit.
4. Discuss how specific types of international business activities are regulated by governments.
5. Give examples of the extraterritorial application of certain U.S. laws.

Since ancient times, independent peoples and nations have traded their goods and wares with one another. In other words, international business transactions are not unique to the modern world, because people have always found that they can benefit from exchanging goods with others, as suggested by President Woodrow Wilson's statement in the opening quotation. What is new in our time is that, particularly since World War II, business has become increasingly *multinational*. It is not uncommon, for example, for a U.S. corporation to have investments or manufacturing plants in a foreign country, or for a foreign corporation to have operations within the United States.

Transacting business on an international level is considerably different from transacting business within the boundaries of just one nation. Buyers and sellers face far greater risks in the international marketplace than they do in a domestic context because the laws governing these transactions are more complex and uncertain. For example, the Uniform Commercial Code will govern many disputes that arise between U.S. buyers and sellers of goods unless they have provided otherwise in their contracts. What happens, however, if a U.S. buyer breaches a contract formed with a British seller? What law will govern the dispute—British or American? What if an investor owns substantial assets in a developing nation and the government of that nation decides to nationalize—assert its ownership over—the property? What recourse does the investor have against the actions of a foreign government? Questions such as these, which normally do not arise in a domestic context, can become critical in international business dealings.

Because the exchange of goods, services, and ideas on a global level is now a common phenomenon, it is important for the student of business law to be familiar with the laws pertaining to international business transactions. In this chapter, we first examine the legal context of international business transactions. We then look at some selected areas relating to business activities in a global context, including international sales contracts, civil dispute resolution, letters of credit, and investment protection. We conclude the chapter with a discussion of the application of certain U.S. laws in a transnational setting.

▍International Principles and Doctrines

Recall from our discussion of international law in Chapter 1 that *international law* is a body of written and unwritten laws that are observed by otherwise independent nations and that govern the acts of individuals as well as states. We also discussed in that chapter the major sources of international law, including international customs, treaties between nations, and international organizations and conferences. Here, we look at some other legal principles and doctrines that have evolved over time and that the courts of various nations have employed—to a greater or lesser extent—to resolve or reduce conflicts that involve a foreign element. The three important legal principles and doctrines discussed in the following sections are based primarily on courtesy and respect and are applied in the interests of maintaining harmonious relations among nations.

The Principle of Comity

Under what is known as the principle of **comity,** one nation will defer and give effect to the laws and judicial decrees of another country, as long as those laws and judicial decrees are consistent with the law and public policy of the accommodating nation. This recognition is based primarily on courtesy and respect. For example, assume that a Swedish seller and an American buyer have formed a contract, which the buyer breaches. The seller sues the buyer in a Swedish court, which awards damages. The buyer's assets, however, are in the United States and cannot be reached unless the judgment is enforced by a U.S. court of law. In this situation, if it is determined that the procedures and laws applied in the Swedish court were consistent with U.S. national law and policy, a court in the United States will likely defer to (and enforce) the foreign court's judgment.

COMITY
A deference by which one nation gives effect to the laws and judicial decrees of another nation. This recognition is based primarily upon respect.

The Act of State Doctrine

The **act of state doctrine** is a judicially created doctrine that provides that the judicial branch of one country will not examine the validity of public acts committed by a recognized foreign government within its own territory. This doctrine is premised on the theory that the judicial branch should not "pass upon the validity of foreign acts when to do so would vex the harmony of our international relations with that foreign nation."[1]

ACT OF STATE DOCTRINE
A doctrine that provides that the judicial branch of one country will not examine the validity of public acts committed by a recognized foreign government within its own territory.

---

1. *Libra Bank, Ltd. v. Banco Nacional de Costa Rica, S.A.,* 570 F.Supp. 870 (S.D.N.Y. 1983).

EXPROPRIATION
The seizure by a government of privately owned business or personal property for a proper public purpose and with just compensation.

CONFISCATION
A government's taking of privately owned business or personal property without a proper public purpose or an award of just compensation.

The act of state doctrine can have important consequences for individuals and firms doing business with, and investing in, other countries. For example, this doctrine is frequently employed in cases involving expropriation or confiscation. **Expropriation** occurs when a government seizes a privately owned business or privately owned goods for a proper public purpose and awards just compensation. When a government seizes private property for an illegal purpose or without just compensation, the taking is referred to as a **confiscation**. The line between these two forms of taking is sometimes blurred because of differing interpretations of what is illegal and what constitutes just compensation.

To illustrate: Tim Flaherty, an American businessperson, owns a mine in Brazil. The government of Brazil seizes the mine for public use and claims that the profits that Tim has realized from the mine in *preceding* years constitute just compensation. Tim disagrees, but the act of state doctrine may prevent Tim's recovery in a U.S. court of law.

When applicable, both the act of state doctrine and the doctrine of sovereign immunity (to be discussed shortly) tend to immunize foreign nations from the jurisdiction of U.S. courts. What this means is that firms or individuals who own property overseas often have little legal protection against government actions in the countries in which they operate. The applicability of the act of state doctrine is at issue in the following case.

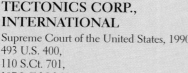

CASE 37.1

W. S. KIRKPATRICK & CO. v. ENVIRONMENTAL TECTONICS CORP., INTERNATIONAL
Supreme Court of the United States, 1990.
493 U.S. 400,
110 S.Ct. 701,
107 L.Ed.2d 816.

HISTORICAL AND POLITICAL SETTING   *Once a colony of Great Britain, Nigeria gained its independence in 1960, which was also the year of the first meeting of the Organization of Petroleum Exporting Countries (OPEC). Nigeria, which possesses the greatest oil resources in Africa, later joined OPEC. In 1963, Nigeria became a federal republic, but between 1966 and 1979, the government changed hands four times in military coups. In 1975, the military announced that it would gradually return the government to civilian democratic rule, which finally occurred in 1979. Nigeria, benefiting from the increase in oil prices during the 1970s, began an intense program of modernization and construction. Among other problems that Nigeria has endured since its independence is internal corruption.*

FACTS   In 1981, W. S. Kirkpatrick & Company learned that the Republic of Nigeria was interested in contracting

for the construction and equipment of a medical center in Nigeria. Kirkpatrick, with the aid of a Nigerian citizen, secured the contract as a result of bribing Nigerian officials. Nigerian law prohibits both the payment and the receipt of bribes in connection with the awarding of government contracts, and the U.S. Foreign Corrupt Practices Act of 1977 expressly prohibits U.S. firms and their agents from bribing foreign officials to secure favorable contracts. Environmental Tectonics Corporation, International (ETC), an unsuccessful bidder for the contract, learned of the bribery and sued Kirkpatrick in a U.S. federal court for damages. The district court granted summary judgment for Kirkpatrick, because resolution of the case in favor of ETC would require imputing to foreign officials an unlawful motivation (the obtaining of bribes) and accordingly might embarrass the Nigerian government or interfere with the conduct of U.S. foreign policy. ETC appealed, and the appellate court reversed the judgment of the district court. Kirkpatrick appealed to the United States Supreme Court.

ISSUE   Is ETC's action barred by the act of state doctrine?

DECISION   No. The United States Supreme Court held that the action was not barred by the act of state doctrine.

REASON   The Court stated that in every case in which it had held the act of state doctrine applicable, "the relief sought * * * would have required a court in the United States to declare invalid the official act of a for-

Case 37.1—Continued

eign [government] performed within its own territory." In the present case, the Court held that the validity of a foreign government's act was not in question. "The short of the matter is this: Courts in the United States have the power, and ordinarily the obligation, to decide cases and controversies properly presented to them. The act of state doctrine does not establish an exception for cases and controversies that may embarrass foreign govern-

ments, but merely requires that, in the process of deciding, the acts of foreign [governments] taken within their own jurisdictions shall be deemed valid. That doctrine has no application to the present case because the validity of no foreign [government] act is at issue."

FOR CRITICAL ANALYSIS—International Consideration
What does the United States have to gain by presuming the validity of the actions of foreign governments?

The Doctrine of Sovereign Immunity

Under certain conditions, the doctrine of **sovereign immunity** immunizes (protects) foreign nations from the jurisdiction of the U.S. courts. In 1976, Congress codified this rule in the Foreign Sovereign Immunities Act (FSIA). The FSIA exclusively governs the circumstances in which an action may be brought in the United States against a foreign nation, including attempts to attach a foreign nation's property.

Section 1605 of the FSIA sets forth the major exceptions to the jurisdictional immunity of a foreign state or country. A foreign state is not immune from the jurisdiction of the courts of the United States when the state has "waived its immunity either explicitly or by implication" or when the action is "based upon a commercial activity carried on in the United States by the foreign state."[2]

Issues frequently arise as to what entities fall within the category of a foreign state. The question of what is a commercial activity has also been the subject of dispute. Under Section 1603 of the FSIA, a *foreign state* is defined to include both a political subdivision of a foreign state and an instrumentality of a foreign state. A *commercial activity* is broadly defined under Section 1603 to mean a commercial activity that is carried out by a foreign state within the United States. The act, however, does not define the particulars of what constitutes a commercial activity. Rather, it is left up to the courts to decide whether a particular activity is governmental or commercial in nature. (See this chapter's *Business Law in Action* on page 961 for a further discussion of this issue.) In the following case, the court had to determine whether the defense of sovereign immunity was available under the FSIA.

SOVEREIGN IMMUNITY
A doctrine that immunizes foreign nations from the jurisdiction of U.S. courts when certain conditions are satisfied.

---

2. 28 U.S.C. Section 1605(a)(1), (2).

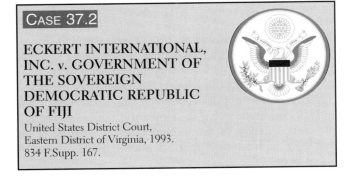

CASE 37.2

ECKERT INTERNATIONAL, INC. v. GOVERNMENT OF THE SOVEREIGN DEMOCRATIC REPUBLIC OF FIJI

United States District Court,
Eastern District of Virginia, 1993.
834 F.Supp. 167.

HISTORICAL AND POLITICAL SETTING   *A British colony for nearly a century, Fiji gained its independence*

in 1970. Ratu Sir Kamisese Mara became prime minister at the time of independence. In 1987, a coalition led by members of the Indian majority gained political power but was overthrown in October in a military coup led by native Fijian Sitivina Rambuka. Rambuka proclaimed Fiji a republic, and the nation withdrew from the British Commonwealth. A new constitution was adopted in 1990. In 1992, Rambuka replaced Mara as the head of government.

FACTS   In 1988, Eckert International, Inc., an American corporation, entered into a three-year contract with the

(Continued)

Case 37.2—Continued

government of Fiji to provide Fiji with public-relations consulting services in Washington, D.C., for annual payments of $250,000. In 1991, the contract was renewed without change for three more years. In 1992, Fiji's new prime minister terminated the contract and refused to pay Eckert for the remaining two years. Eckert sued Fiji in a U.S. district court for breach of contract. Fiji moved to dismiss the suit, asserting, among other things, that it was immunized from the jurisdiction of U.S. courts by the Foreign Sovereign Immunities Act (FSIA).

ISSUE Is Fiji immune from the jurisdiction of U.S. courts under the FSIA?

DECISION No. The district court denied Fiji's motion.

REASON The court concluded that the contract was a "garden-variety consulting contract," essentially commercial in nature, and thus fell under the FSIA's "commercial activities" exception to sovereign immunity. The court stated that "[t]his exception differentiates between a foreign state's public acts performed in its sovereign capacity and a foreign state's private acts performed as a market participant. * * * [T]he focus in drawing the distinction between public and private acts must be on the nature of the act performed rather than on its purpose." The court reasoned that Fiji's entering into the contract was "plainly a private act," which was "inherently commercial in nature" and "governed by the rules of the marketplace." Fiji argued that the contract was governmental in nature, because Eckert represented Fiji in its "political and diplomatic relationship" with the United States. "This reasoning," said the court, "mistakenly focuses on the contract's purpose." The court concluded that "[t]he FSIA neither permits nor contemplates * * * a misuse of sovereign immunity. To the contrary, where as here, a foreign state has entered into an essentially commercial contract for the performance of consulting services, it may not claim sovereign immunity under the FSIA."

FOR CRITICAL ANALYSIS—Political Consideration
Does the "commercial activities" exception to the FSIA conflict with the act of state doctrine?

▌Doing Business Internationally

EXPORT
To sell products to buyers located in other countries.

A U.S. domestic firm can engage in international business transactions in a number of ways. The simplest way to engage in international business transactions is to seek out foreign markets for domestically produced products or services. In other words, U.S. firms can look abroad for **export** markets for their goods and services. Alternatively, a U.S. firm can establish foreign production facilities so as to be closer to the foreign market or markets in which its products are sold. The advantages may include lower labor costs, fewer government regulations, and lower taxes and trade barriers. It is also possible to obtain business from abroad through the licensing of technology that has been developed and is owned by a domestic firm to an existing foreign company. Yet another way to expand abroad is by selling franchises to overseas entities. The presence of McDonald's, Burger King, and KFC franchises throughout the world attests to the popularity of franchising.

Exporting

The initial foray into international business by most U.S. companies is through exporting. Exporting can take two forms: direct exporting and indirect exporting. In *direct exporting*, a U.S. company signs a sales contract with a foreign purchaser that provides for the conditions of shipment and payment for the goods. (How payments are made in international transactions is discussed later in this chapter.) If business develops sufficiently in foreign countries, a U.S. corporation may develop a specialized marketing organization that, for example, sells directly to consumers in that country. Such *indirect exporting* can be undertaken by the appointment of a foreign agent or a foreign distributor.

FOREIGN AGENT When a U.S. firm desires a limited involvement in an international market, it will typically establish an *agency relationship* with a foreign firm. In an

BUSINESS LAW IN ACTION

What Is a "Commercial Activity"?

Unlike the economy of the United States, which is primarily controlled by private interests, the economies of many other countries, particularly developing nations, are often extensively controlled by government. This means that if a U.S. plaintiff sues a business or institution that is controlled by a foreign government, the foreign defendant may assert the defense of sovereign immunity under the Foreign Sovereign Immunities Act (FSIA) of 1976. In this situation, a U.S. court cannot exercise jurisdiction over the dispute unless the plaintiff can prove, among other things, that the defendant's actions constituted a "commercial activity." What, however, is a "commercial activity"?

Although the FSIA does not define this phrase with any precision, the United States Supreme Court has provided some guidance on the issue. For example, in *Saudi Arabia v. Nelson*,[a] the Court addressed the

question of whether the Saudi Arabian government's allegedly wrongful arrest, imprisonment, and torture of an American employee of a Saudi hospital constituted a commercial activity. The court concluded that it did not, holding that a state engages in commercial activity "where it exercises 'only those powers that can also be exercised by private citizens,' as distinct from those 'powers peculiar to sovereigns.'" The Court held that the alleged tortious actions of the Saudi government against the American employee were "sovereign" in character, and thus the Saudi government was immune from liability under the FSIA.

In 1995, the District of Columbia Court of Appeals applied this distinction between activities of a "sovereign character" and a "commercial character" in *Janini v. Kuwait University*.[b] The plaintiffs in the case were an American citizen, George Janini, and other former professors and employees of Kuwait University (KU). The plaintiffs were terminated from their positions when the government of Kuwait, following Iraq's invasion of Kuwait in August 1990, issued a decree stating, among other things, that "contracts

concluded between the Government and those non-Kuwaiti workers who worked for it . . . shall be considered automatically abrogated because of the impossibility of enforcement due to the Iraqi invasion."

The plaintiffs sued KU in a U.S. court, alleging that their termination breached their employment contracts, which required nine months' notice before termination. The plaintiffs sought back pay and other benefits to which they were entitled under their contracts. The question before the court was whether terminating the professors' positions constituted a commercial activity. The court held that it did. The court concluded that "there is nothing 'peculiarly sovereign' about unilaterally terminating an employment contract. Private parties often repudiate contracts in everyday commerce and may be held liable therefor. That the termination here may have been accomplished by a formal decree of abrogation does not affect its commercial nature."

For Critical Analysis: *In addition to finding that a government-controlled foreign defendant has engaged in a commercial activity, what other requirement must be met before a U.S. court can exercise jurisdiction over the defendant?*

a. 507 U.S. 349, 113 S.Ct. 1471, 123 L.Ed.2d 47 (1993).

b. 43 F.3d 1534, 310 U.S.App.D.C. 109 (D.C. Cir. 1995).

agency relationship (discussed in Chapter 23), one person (the agent) agrees to act on behalf of another (the principal). The foreign agent is thereby empowered to enter into contracts in the agent's country on behalf of the U.S. principal.

FOREIGN DISTRIBUTOR   When a substantial market exists in a foreign country, a U.S. firm may wish to appoint a distributor located in that country. The U.S. firm and the distributor enter into a **distribution agreement,** which is a contract between the seller and the distributor setting out the terms and conditions of the distributorship—for example, price, currency of payment, availability of supplies, and method of payment. The terms and conditions primarily involve contract law. Disputes concerning distribution agreements may involve jurisdictional or other issues (discussed in detail later in this chapter). In addition, some **exclusive distributorships**—in which distributors agree to distribute only the sellers' goods—have raised antitrust problems.

Manufacturing Abroad

An alternative to direct or indirect exporting is the establishment of foreign manufacturing facilities. Typically, U.S. firms want to establish manufacturing plants abroad if

DISTRIBUTION AGREEMENT
A contract between a seller and a distributor of the seller's products setting out the terms and conditions of the distributorship.

EXCLUSIVE DISTRIBUTORSHIP
A distributorship in which the seller and distributor of the seller's products agree that the distributor has the exclusive right to distribute the seller's products in a certain geographic area.

A worker sews a garment at a Levi's plant in Poland. Why would a U.S. domestic firm set up a manufacturing facility abroad?

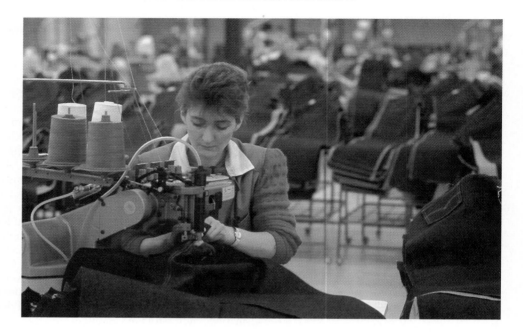

they believe that by doing so they will reduce costs—particularly for labor, shipping, and raw materials—and thereby be able to compete more effectively in foreign markets. Apple Computer, IBM, General Motors, and Ford are some of the many U.S. companies that have established manufacturing facilities abroad. Foreign firms have done the same in the United States. Sony, Nissan, and other Japanese manufacturers have established U.S. plants to avoid import duties that the U.S. Congress may impose on Japanese products entering this country.

There are several ways in which an American firm can manufacture goods in other countries. They include licensing and franchising, as well as investing in a wholly owned subsidiary or a joint venture.

TECHNOLOGY LICENSING
Allowing another to use and profit from intellectual property (patents, copyrights, trademarks, innovative products or processes, and so on) for consideration. In the context of international business transactions, technology licensing is sometimes an attractive alternative to the establishment of foreign production facilities.

LICENSING   It is possible for U.S. firms to license their technologies to foreign manufacturers. **Technology licensing** may involve a process innovation that lowers the cost of production, or it may involve a product innovation that generates a superior product. Technology licensing may be an attractive alternative to establishing foreign production facilities, particularly if the process or product innovation has been patented, because the patent protects—at least to some extent—against the possibility that the innovation might be pirated. Like any licensing agreement, a licensing agreement with a foreign-based firm calls for a payment of royalties on some basis—such as so many cents per unit produced or a certain percentage of profits from units sold in a particular geographical territory.

In certain circumstances, even in the absence of a patent, a firm may be able to license the "know-how" associated with a particular manufacturing process—for example, a plant design or a secret formula. The foreign firm that agrees to sign the licensing agreement further agrees to keep the know-how confidential and to pay royalties. For example, the Coca-Cola Bottling Company licenses firms worldwide to use (and keep confidential) its secret formula for the syrup used in that soft drink, in return for a percentage of the income gained from the sale of Coca-Cola by those firms.

The licensing of technology benefits all parties to the transaction. Those who receive the license can take advantage of an established reputation for quality, and the firm that grants the license receives income from the foreign sales of the firm's products, as well as establishing a worldwide reputation. Additionally, once a firm's trademark is known worldwide, the demand for other products manufactured or sold by that firm may increase—obviously an important consideration.

The licensing of technology allows U.S. owners of intellectual property (such as patents, trademarks, and copyrights) to benefit from sales of their products in other countries. Much intellectual property, however, is "pirated"—that is, unauthorized copies of the property (such as a software program) are made and sold. In 1994, to protect intellectual property rights on a worldwide basis, more than one hundred nations signed the international agreement on Trade-Related Aspects of Intellectual Property Rights (TRIPS), which is administered by the World Trade Organization (WTO). These nations pledged to pass and enforce laws protecting patents, copyrights, and trademarks (see the *Landmark in the Law* in Chapter 6).

The attempted enforcement of intellectual property rights on a worldwide basis, however, raises some ethical concerns. For example, in a developing country, the welfare of small business firms and consumers may be enhanced by the ability to purchase pirated (less expensive) copies of high-tech products. Although the owners of the pirated intellectual property lose out, it may be that the owners would have received nothing anyway—if no authorized copies (at higher prices) could have been sold in the poorer country. Furthermore, laws governing intellectual property rights are necessarily somewhat arbitrary. For example, if the United States grants copyright protection for a longer period of time than Japan, does this mean that U.S. law is "right" and Japanese law is "wrong"?

For Critical Analysis: *The piracy of another's property rights constitutes the crime of theft. Can this crime ever be justified?*

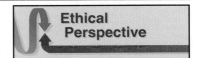

Ethical Perspective

BE AWARE A foreign manufacturer who is licensed to make and sell goods with a U.S. firm's trademark or name in a foreign country may attempt to sell those goods in the United States in direct competition with the U.S. firm. Such goods are known as "gray market" goods.

FRANCHISING   Franchising is a well-known form of licensing. Recall from Chapter 24 that a franchise can be defined as an arrangement in which the owner of a trademark, trade name, or copyright (the franchisor) licenses another (the franchisee) to use the trademark, trade name, or copyright—under certain conditions or limitations—in the selling of goods or services in exchange for a fee, usually based on a percentage of gross or net sales. Examples of international franchises include McDonald's, the Coca-Cola Bottling Company, Holiday Inn, Avis, and Hertz.

INVESTING IN A WHOLLY OWNED SUBSIDIARY OR A JOINT VENTURE   One way to expand into a foreign market is to establish a wholly owned subsidiary firm in a foreign

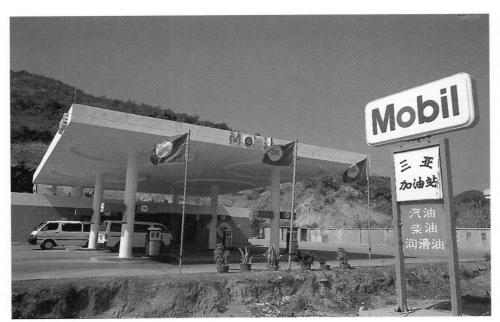

A Mobil station operates on Hainan Island in China. What benefits can a U.S. domestic firm realize from selling a franchise to an overseas entity?

country. The European subsidiary would likely take the form of the *société anonyme* (S.A.), which is similar to a U.S. corporation. In German-speaking nations, it would be called an *Aktiengesellschaft* (A.G.). When a wholly owned subsidiary is established, the parent company, which remains in the United States, retains complete ownership of all the facilities in the foreign country, as well as complete authority and control over all phases of the operation.

The expansion of a U.S. firm into international markets can also take the form of a joint venture. In a joint venture, the U.S. company owns only part of the operation; the rest is owned either by local owners in the foreign country or by another foreign entity. In a joint venture, all of the firms involved share responsibilities, as well as profits and liabilities.

Commercial Contracts in an International Setting

Like all commercial contracts, an international contract should be in writing. The sample form shown in Exhibit 37–1 illustrates the typical terms and conditions that might be contained in an international contract. *(For an example of an actual international sales contract, refer back to the fold-out contract in Chapter 14.)*

> **RECALL** The interpretation of the words in a contract can be the basis for a dispute even when both parties communicate in the same language.

Language and legal differences among nations can create special problems for parties to international contracts when disputes arise. It is possible to avoid these problems by including in a contract special provisions designating the official language of the contract, the legal forum (court or place) in which disputes under the contract will be settled, and the substantive law that will be applied in settling any disputes. Parties to international contracts should also indicate in their contracts what acts or events will excuse the parties from performance under the contract and whether disputes under the contract will be arbitrated or litigated.

Choice of Language

> **CHOICE-OF-LANGUAGE CLAUSE**
> A clause in a contract designating the official language by which the contract will be interpreted in the event of a future disagreement over the contract's terms.

A deal struck between a U.S. company and a company in another country normally involves two languages. The complex contractual terms involved may not be understood by one party in the other party's language. Typically, many phrases in one language are not readily translatable into another. To make sure that no disputes arise out of this language problem, an international sales contract should have a **choice-of-language clause** designating the official language by which the contract will be interpreted in the event of disagreement.

International Perspective

In 1995, France implemented a law making the use of the French language mandatory in certain legal documents. Documents relating to securities offerings, such as prospectuses, for example, must be written in French. So must instruction manuals and warranties for goods and services offered for sale in France. Additionally, all agreements entered into with French state or local authorities, with entities controlled by state or local authorities, and with private entities carrying out a public service (such as providing utilities) must be written in French. The law has posed problems for some businesspersons because certain legal terms or phrases in documents governed by, say, U.S. or English law, have no equivalent terms or phrases in the French legal system.

For Critical Analysis: *How might language differences affect the meaning of certain terms or phrases in an international contract?*

♦ **Exhibit 37–1**
Sample International Purchase Order Form (Front)
Caution: This form contains a typical set ot terms written from the buyer's point of view, but it is not applicable to all factual situations and the laws of all states. Terms and conditions of sale or purchase must be custom drafted to be appropriate for the type of business and type of goods involved.

Sample International Purchase Order Terms & Conditions*
The _____ Company, Inc.
International Terms and Conditions of Purchase

1. *Acceptance.* Acceptance of this order is expressly limited to the terms and conditions contained herein, including all terms and conditions set forth on the face hereof. Acceptance of this order by Seller may be made by signing and returning the attached acknowledgement copy hereof, by other express acceptance, or by shipment of goods hereunder. If Seller uses its own order acknowledgement or other form to accept this order, it is understood that said form shall be used for convenience only and any terms or conditions contained therein inconsistent with or in addition to those contained herein shall be of no force or effect whatsoever between the parties hereto.

2. *Warranty.* Seller warrants the goods covered by this Agreement and their packaging and labelling shall be in merchantable condition and shall be free from defects in workmanship and materials and shall be in conformity with the specifications, drawings, samples and descriptions attached hereto or referred to on the face hereof, if any. Seller warrants that the goods covered by this Agreement shall be fit for such particular purposes and uses, if any, as specified by BUYER or otherwise known to Seller. Seller warrants that the goods shall be free and clear of any lien or other adverse claim against title, and to the extent not manufactured to detailed designs furnished by BUYER shall be free from defects in design. All warranties contained herein shall survive inspection, test and acceptance by BUYER. Seller agrees, at its own costs and expense, to defend and hold BUYER harmless from and against any and all claims made against BUYER based upon, relating to, or arising out of any claimed defects in the goods or services ordered hereunder. Seller's warranties (and any consumer warranties, service policies, or similar undertakings of Seller) shall be enforceable by BUYER'S customers and any subsequent owner or operator of the goods as well as by BUYER.

3. *Shipping Instructions.* No charge shall be made to BUYER for draying and packaging unless authorized by BUYER. Merchandise shipped by freight or express shall be packed, marked and described and the carrier shall be selected, so as to obtain the lowest rate possible under freight or express classifications or regulations except when otherwise specified by BUYER, and penalties or increased charges due to failure so to do will be charged to Seller. The foregoing notwithstanding, Seller shall comply with all instructions of BUYER as to packaging, marking, shipping and insurance. Prior to passage of title to BUYER the goods shall be held by Seller without risk or expense to BUYER.

4. *Invoices, Other Documents and Charges.* Seller shall invoice in duplicate. Originals of all invoices, government and commercial bills of lading and air express receipts shall be air mailed to the Purchasing Department of BUYER when goods are shipped. Packing slips must accompany item number, and a complete description of its contents. Except as otherwise provided on the face hereof, the contract price includes all costs and charges to be paid or reimbursed to Seller by BUYER, including without limitation, all applicable taxes and duties and all charges for packing, loading and transportation. Transportation charges and taxes and duties, when applicable, and when agreed on the face hereof to be borne by BUYER shall be billed as separate items on Seller's invoices.

5. *Inspection—Nonconformity.* BUYER may inspect the goods and, with respect to nonconforming goods, may return them or hold them at the Seller's risk and expense, and may in either event charge the Seller with cost of transportation, shipping, unpacking, examining, repacking, reshipping, and other like expense. Promptly upon BUYER's written request, and without expense to BUYER, Seller agrees to replace or correct defects of any rejected goods or other goods not conforming to the warranty set forth above. In the event of failure of Seller to replace or correct defects in nonconforming goods promptly, BUYER after reasonable notice to Seller, may make such corrections or replace such goods and charge Seller for the costs incurred by BUYER in doing so. Time is of the essence in this transaction. In addition to its remedies of breach of contract, BUYER reserves the right to return any or all goods in unopened original packing to Seller if delivered to BUYER more than five (5) days after the delivery date shown in shipping instructions. If the delivery date shown in shipping instructions is revised by BUYER by notification to Seller, the such five (5) day period shall not commence to run until such revised delivery date. Also, BUYER reserves the right to refuse goods delivered contrary to instructions or not in recognized standard containers. BUYER shall be under no duty to inspect goods prior to BUYER's use or resale, and neither retention, use nor resale of such goods shall be construed to constitute an acceptance of goods not in compliance with the requirements of this order.

6. *Changes.* Unless agreed in writing by BUYER, Seller shall not purchase materials, or make material commitments, or production arrangements, in excess of the amount, or in advance of the time necessary to meet BUYER'S delivery schedule. BUYER shall have the right at any time to make changes in drawings, designs, specifications, materials, packaging, time and place of delivery and method of transportation. If any such changes cause an increase or decrease in the cost, or the time required for the performance, an equitable adjustment shall be made and this agreement shall be modified in writing accordingly. Seller agrees to accept any such changes subject to this paragraph. This right to an adjustment shall be deemed waived unless asserted within thirty (30) days after the change is ordered. BUYER reserves the right to terminate this order or any part hereof for its sole convenience. In the event of such termination, Seller shall immediately stop all work hereunder, and shall immediately cause any of its suppliers or subcontractors to cease such work. Seller shall be paid a reasonable termination charge consisting of a percentage of the order price reflecting the percentage of the work performed prior to the notice of termination. Such charge shall be Seller's only remedy for such termination. Seller shall not be paid for any work done after receipt of the notice of termination nor for any work done by Seller's suppliers or subcontractor which Seller could reasonable have avoided.

7. *Default.* BUYER may also terminate this order or any part hereof for cause in the event of any default by the Seller of if the Seller fails to comply with any of the terms and conditions of this offer. Late deliveries, deliveries of goods which are defective or which do not conform to this order, and failure to provide BUYER, upon request, reasonable assurances of future performance shall all be causes allowing BUYER to terminate this order for cause. In the event of termination for cause, BUYER shall not be liable to Seller for any amount and Seller shall be liable to BUYER for any and all damage sustained by reason of the default which gave rise to the termination.

♦ Exhibit 37–1—Continued
Sample International Purchase Order Form (Back)

8.   *Indemnity*. Seller will defend and indemnify BUYER, upon demand, against all claims, actions, liability, damage, loss and expense (including investigative expense and attorney's fees incurred in litigation or because of threatened litigation) as the result of BUYER'S purchase and/or use of goods and arising or alleged to arise from patent, trademark or copyright infringement; unfair competition; the failure or alleged failure of the goods to comply with specifications or with any express or implied warranties of Seller; the alleged violation by such goods or in its manufacture or sale of any statute, ordinance, or administrative order, rule or regulation; defects, whether latent or patent, in material or workmanship; defective design; defective warnings or instructions; or Seller's negligence.

9.   *Price Reduction*. Seller will give BUYER the benefit of any price reductions occurring before the specified shipping date or to actual time of shipment, whichever is later. Likewise, if Seller accepts this order as a commission merchant, Seller shall obtain for BUYER from the manufacturer of such goods the benefit of price reductions to the specified date or to actual time of shipment, whichever is later. Seller warrants that the price for the articles sold BUYER hereunder are not less favorable than those currently extended to any other customer for the same or similar articles in similar quantities.

10.   *Information*. Seller shall consider all information furnished by BUYER to be confidential and shall not disclose any such information to any other person, or use such information itself for any purpose other than performing this order unless Seller obtains written permission from BUYER to do so. This confidential requirement shall also apply to drawings, specifications, or other documents prepared by Seller for BUYER in connection with this order. Seller shall provide confidential information only to those of its agents, servants and employees who have been informed of the requirements of this paragraph and have agreed to be bound by them. Upon completion or termination of this order, Seller shall make such disposition of all such information and items as may be directed by BUYER. Seller shall not advertise or publish the fact that BUYER has ordered goods from Seller nor shall any information relating to this order be disclosed without BUYER'S written permission. Unless otherwise agreed in writing, no commercial, financial or technical information disclosed in any manner or at any time by Seller to BUYER shall be deemed secret or confidential and Seller shall have no rights against BUYER with respect thereto except such rights as may exist under patent laws.

11.   *Tools, Dies, Etc.* Seller agrees that the information, tools, jigs, dies, etc., drawings, patterns and specifications supplied or paid for by BUYER shall be and remain BUYER'S property, shall be used only on BUYER'S orders, and shall be held by Seller for BUYER unless directed otherwise. Seller will account for such items and keep them in good working condition and fully covered by insurance at all times without expense to BUYER. In the event Seller devises and incorporates any new features design into any goods made under this order, Seller grants to BUYER the right of reproduction of such goods, together with a royalty-free, nonexclusive, irrevocable license to use such new features of design.

12.   *General Provisions.*

(a)   Seller and BUYER shall be independent contractors. This transaction does not create a principal-agent or partnership relationship between them, and neither one may legally commit the other in any matter.

(b)   BUYER may deduct from any payment due to Seller or set-off against any claim by Seller any amount which is due to BUYER by Seller for any reason, including, among other reasons, any excess transportation charges caused by deviations from BUYER'S shipping instructions or the shipping of partial shipments.

(c)   Seller shall comply with all laws, regulations and policies applicable to it by any jurisdiction and shall obtain all permits needed to complete this transaction under the laws of the country from which the shipment is made, including among other things, any required export permits and Central Bank approvals.

(d)   All billings and payments shall be made in U.S. Dollars.

(e)   In the event the importation of the goods results in the assessment of a countervailing duty on BUYER as the importer, Seller shall reimburse such countervailing duty to BUYER, provided such reimbursement is permitted under U.S. laws and regulations.

(f)   Goods ordered hereunder to be made with use of BUYER'S confidential information, BUYER'S designs, BUYER'S trademarks or tradenames or BUYER'S customer's trademarks or tradenames shall be furnished by Seller exclusively to BUYER. Any excess of such inventory shall be destroyed by Seller at its own expense.

(g)   Seller warrants that it has accepted no gratuities of any kind from any employee of BUYER in connection with placement of this order.

(h)   Seller shall cooperate fully with BUYER at Seller's expense in obtaining approvals of the goods requested by BUYER from certifying organizations such as Underwriters Laboratories.

(i)   Any goods that are hazardous will be packaged, marked and shipped by Seller to comply with all U.S. federal, state and local regulations and will further comply with all special BUYER requirements. Seller shall furnish BUYER a Material Hazard Data Sheet covering all such goods.

(j)   BUYER shall not be liable to Seller for any loss incurred by Seller due to strikes, riots, storms, fires, explosions, acts of God, war, embargo, government boycott or other governmental action or any other causes similar thereto beyond the reasonable control of BUYER. Any failure or delay in performance of any of the foregoing shall not be a default hereunder.

(k)   BUYER may waive performance of any condition, but waiver by BUYER of a condition shall not be considered a waiver of that condition for succeeding performance. None of BUYER'S remedies hereunder shall exclude its pursuit of its other legal remedies.

(l)   This document and any other documents mentioned on the face hereof, constitute the entire agreement between the parties on this subject. All prior representations, negotiations or arrangements on this subject matter are superseded by these terms and shall not form a basis for interpretation of these terms. All amendments to these terms must be agreed to in writing by BUYER.

(m)   If any manufacturer's excise tax, value added tax or other tax measured by selling price is included in or added to the price of the goods paid by BUYER, then, in the event all or any part of that tax shall be refunded to Seller, Seller shall promptly remit such refund in full to BUYER.

(n)   This order is nonassignable. Any attempt to assign without BUYER'S written consent is void.

(o)   This transaction and all its terms shall be construed in accordance with and all disputes shall be governed by the laws of the State of _____ , U.S.A., specifically including the provisions of the Uniform Commercial Code, as adopted by that state, and excluding the provisions of the Convention on the International Sale of Goods. Seller submits to the jurisdiction of the courts located in the State of _____ in the event of any proceedings therein in connection herewith.

(p)   Any and all disputes arising between BUYER and Seller in connection with this transaction (other than actions for contribution or indemnity with respect to court actions involving third parties) shall be exclusively and finally decided by arbitration in _____ under the rules of the American Arbitration Association. The arbitration award shall be final and nonappealable. There shall be three arbitrators, one chosen by each party and the third chosen by the first two, or in the event of their failure to agree, by the _____ state court of general jurisdiction. The arbitrators shall reach their decision, and state it in writing with reason for it, within twelve months after the appointment of the third arbitrator.

(q)   This order shall expire in thirty (30) days from the date of issuance by BUYER, unless earlier revoked by BUYER or accepted by Seller. ■

Choice of Forum

When several countries are involved, litigation may be sought in courts in different nations. There are no universally accepted rules regarding the jurisdiction of a particular court over subject matter or parties to a dispute. Consequently, parties to an international transaction should always include in the contract a **forum-selection clause** indicating what court, jurisdiction, or tribunal will decide any disputes arising under the contract. It is especially important to indicate specifically what court will have jurisdiction. The forum does not necessarily have to be within the geographical boundaries of either of the parties' nations.

FORUM-SELECTION CLAUSE
A provision in a contract designating the court, jurisdiction, or tribunal that will decide any disputes arising under the contract.

Choice of Law

A contractual provision designating the applicable law—such as the law of Germany or England or California—is called a **choice-of-law clause.** Every international contract typically includes a choice-of-law clause. At common law (and in European civil law systems), parties are allowed to choose the law that will govern their contractual relationship provided that the law chosen is the law of a jurisdiction that has a substantial relationship to the parties and to the international business transaction.

CHOICE-OF-LAW CLAUSE
A clause in a contract designating the law (such as the law of a particular state or nation) that will govern the contract.

Under Section 1–105 of the Uniform Commercial Code, parties may choose the law that will govern the contract as long as the choice is "reasonable." Article 6 of the United Nations Convention on Contracts for the International Sale of Goods (discussed in Chapter 14), however, imposes no limitation on the parties in their choice of what law will govern the contract. The 1986 Hague Convention on the Law Applicable to Contracts for the International Sale of Goods—often referred to as the Choice-of-Law Convention—allows unlimited autonomy in the choice of law. The Hague Convention indicates that whenever a choice of law is not specified in a contract, the governing law is that of the country in which the *seller's* place of business is located.

Force Majeure Clause

Every contract, particularly those involving international transactions, should have a *force majeure* clause. *Force majeure* is a French term meaning "impossible or irresistible force"—which sometimes is loosely identified as "an act of God." In international business contracts, *force majeure* clauses commonly stipulate that in addition to acts of God, a number of other eventualities (such as governmental orders or regulations, embargoes, or shortages of materials) may excuse a party from liability for nonperformance.

FORCE MAJEURE CLAUSE
A provision in a contract stipulating that certain unforeseen events—such as war, political upheavals, acts of God, or other events—will excuse a party from liability for nonperformance of contractual obligations.

Civil Dispute Resolution

International contracts frequently include arbitration clauses. By means of such clauses, the parties agree in advance to be bound by the decision of a specified third party in the event of a dispute, as discussed in Chapter 3. The third party may be a neutral entity (such as the International Chamber of Commerce), a panel of individuals representing both parties' interests, or some other group or organization. (For an example of an arbitration clause in an international contract, refer to Exhibit 37–1, *as well as to the fold-out exhibit in Chapter 14.*) The United Nations Convention on the Recognition and Enforcement of Foreign Arbitral Awards (often called the New York Convention) assists in the enforcement of arbitration clauses, as do provisions in specific treaties between nations. The New York Convention has been implemented in nearly one hundred countries, including the United States.

If no arbitration clause is contained in the sales contract, litigation may occur. If forum-selection and choice-of-law clauses are included in the contract, the lawsuit will be heard by a court in the forum specified and decided according to that forum's law. If no forum and choice of law have been specified, however, legal proceedings will be more complex and attended by much more uncertainty. For example, litigation may take place in two or more countries, with each country applying its own choice-of-law rules to determine which substantive law will be applied to the particular transactions. Even if a plaintiff wins a favorable judgment in a lawsuit litigated in the plaintiff's country, there is no way to predict whether the court's judgment will be enforced by judicial bodies in the defendant's country. As discussed earlier in this chapter, under the principle of comity, the judgment may be enforced in the defendant's country, particularly if the defendant's country is the United States and the foreign court's decision is consistent with U.S. national law and policy. Other nations, however, may not be as accommodating as the United States in this respect.

International Perspective

One of the reasons many businesspersons find it advantageous to include arbitration clauses in their international contracts is because arbitration awards are usually easier to enforce than court judgments. As mentioned, the New York Convention provides for the enforcement of arbitration awards in those countries that have signed the convention. Enforcement of court judgments, however, normally depends on the principle of comity and bilateral agreements providing for such enforcement. How the principle of comity is applied, however, varies from one nation to another, and many countries have not agreed, in bilateral agreements, to enforce judgments rendered in U.S. courts.

For Critical Analysis: *What might be some other advantages of arbitration in the context of international transactions? Are there any disadvantages?*

Making Payment on International Transactions

Currency differences between nations and the geographical distance between parties to international sales contracts add a degree of complexity to international sales that does not exist within the domestic market. Because international contracts involve greater financial risks, special care should be taken in drafting these contracts to specify both the currency in which payment is to be made and the method of payment.

Monetary Systems

While it is true that our national currency, the U.S. dollar, is one of the primary forms of international money, any U.S. firm undertaking business transactions abroad must be prepared to deal with one or more other currencies. After all, just as a U.S. firm wants to be paid in U.S. dollars for goods and services sold abroad, so, too, does a Japanese firm want to be paid in Japanese yen for goods and services sold outside Japan. Both firms therefore must rely on the convertibility of currencies.

FOREIGN EXCHANGE MARKETS   Currencies are convertible when they can be freely exchanged one for the other at some specified market rate in a **foreign exchange market.** Foreign exchange markets are a worldwide system for the buying and selling of foreign currencies. At any point in time, the foreign exchange rate is set by the forces of supply and demand in unrestricted foreign exchange markets. The foreign exchange rate is simply the price of a unit of one country's currency in terms of

FOREIGN EXCHANGE MARKET
A worldwide system in which foreign currencies are bought and sold.

another country's currency. For example, if today's exchange rate is one hundred Japanese yen for one dollar, that means that anybody with one hundred yen can obtain one dollar, and vice versa.

CORRESPONDENT BANKING   Often, a U.S. company can deal directly with its domestic bank, which will take care of the international money flow problem. Commercial banks sometimes have **correspondent banks** in other countries. Correspondent banking is a major means of transferring funds internationally. Suppose, for example, that a customer of Citibank wishes to pay a bill in French francs to a company in Paris. Citibank can draw a bank check payable in francs on its account in Crédit Lyonnais, a Paris correspondent bank, and then send it to the French company to which its customer owes the money. Alternatively, Citibank's customer can request a wire transfer of the funds to the French company. Citibank instructs Crédit Lyonnais by wire to pay the necessary amount in French francs. The Clearinghouse Interbank Payment System (CHIPS) handles about 90 percent of both national and international interbank transfers of U.S. funds. In addition, the Society for Worldwide International Financial Telecommunications (SWIFT) is a communication system that provides banks with messages concerning transactions.

CORRESPONDENT BANK
A bank in which another bank has an account (and vice versa) for the purpose of facilitating fund transfers.

Letters of Credit

Because buyers and sellers engaged in international business transactions are often separated by thousands of miles, special precautions are often taken to ensure performance under the contract. Sellers want to avoid delivering goods for which they might not be paid. Buyers desire the assurance that sellers will not be paid until there is evidence that the goods have been shipped. Thus, **letters of credit** are frequently used to facilitate international business transactions. In a simple letter-of-credit transaction, the *issuer* (a bank) agrees to issue a letter of credit and to ascertain whether the *beneficiary* (seller) performs certain acts. In return, the *account party* (buyer) promises to reimburse the issuer for the amount paid to the beneficiary. There may also be an *advising bank* that transmits information, and a *paying bank* may be involved to expedite payment under the letter of credit. Exhibit 37–2 summarizes the "life cycle" of a letter of credit.

LETTER OF CREDIT
A written instrument, usually issued by a bank on behalf of a customer or other person, in which the issuer promises to honor drafts or other demands for payment by third persons in accordance with the terms of the instrument.

Under a letter of credit, the issuer is bound to pay the beneficiary (seller) when the beneficiary has complied with the terms and conditions of the letter of credit. The beneficiary looks to the issuer, not to the account party (buyer), when it presents the documents required by the letter of credit. Typically, the letter of credit will require that the beneficiary deliver to the issuing bank a *bill of lading* to prove that shipment has been made. Letters of credit assure beneficiaries (sellers) of payment while at the same time assuring account parties (buyers) that payment will not be made until the beneficiaries have complied with the terms and conditions of the letter of credit.

THE VALUE OF A LETTER OF CREDIT   The basic principle behind letters of credit is that payment is made against the documents presented by the beneficiary and not against the facts that the documents purport to reflect. Thus, in a letter-of-credit transaction, the issuer does not police the underlying contract; a letter of credit is independent of the underlying contract between the buyer and the seller. Eliminating the need for banks (issuers) to inquire into whether or not actual conditions have been satisfied greatly reduces the costs of letters of credit. Moreover, the use of a letter of credit protects both buyers and sellers.

DON'T FORGET A letter of credit is independent of the underlying contract between the buyer and the seller.

COMPLIANCE WITH A LETTER OF CREDIT   In a letter-of-credit transaction, generally at least three separate and distinct contracts are involved: the contract between the account party (buyer) and the beneficiary (seller); the contract between the issuer (bank) and the account party (buyer); and finally, the letter of credit itself, which

♦ Exhibit 37–2
The "Life Cycle" of a Letter of Credit

> Although the letter of credit appears quite complex at first, it is not difficult to understand. This cycle merely involves the exchange of documents (and money) through intermediaries. The following steps depict the letter-of-credit procurement cycle.
>
> Step 1: The buyer and seller agree on the terms of sale. The sales contract dictates that a letter of credit is to be used to finance the transaction.
>
> Step 2: The buyer completes an application for a letter of credit and forwards it to his or her bank, which will issue the letter of credit.
>
> Step 3: The issuing (buyer's) bank then forwards the letter of credit to a correspondent bank in the seller's country.
>
> Step 4: The correspondent bank relays the letter of credit to the seller.
>
> Step 5: Having received assurance of payment, the seller makes the necessary shipping arrangements.
>
> Step 6: The seller prepares the documents required under the letter of credit and delivers them to the correspondent bank.
>
> Step 7: The correspondent bank examines the documents. If it finds them in order, it sends them to the issuing bank and pays the seller in accordance with the terms of the letter of credit.
>
> Step 8: The issuing bank, having received the documents, examines them. If they are in order, the issuing bank will charge the buyer's account and send the documents on to the buyer or his or her customs broker. The issuing bank also will reimburse the correspondent bank.
>
> Step 9: The buyer or broker receives the documents and picks up the merchandise from the shipper (carrier).
>
> *Source*: National Association of Purchasing Management.

involves the issuer (bank) and the beneficiary (seller). These contracts are separate and distinct, and the issuer's obligations under the letter of credit do not concern the underlying contract between the buyer and the seller. Rather, it is the issuer's duty to ascertain whether the documents presented by the beneficiary (seller) comply with the terms of the letter of credit.

If the documents presented by the beneficiary comply with the terms of the letter of credit, the issuer (bank) must honor the letter of credit. Sometimes, however, it is difficult to determine exactly what a letter of credit requires. Moreover, the courts are divided as to whether *strict* or *substantial* compliance with the terms of the letter of credit is required. Traditionally, courts required strict compliance with the terms of a letter of credit, but in recent years, some courts have moved to a standard of *reasonable* compliance.

If the issuing bank refuses to pay the seller (beneficiary) even though the seller has complied with all the requirements of the letter, the seller can bring an action to enforce payment. In the international context, the fact that the issuing bank may be thousands of miles distant from the seller's business location can pose difficulties for the seller—as the following case illustrates.

CASE 37.3

PACIFIC RELIANT INDUSTRIES, INC. v. AMERIKA SAMOA BANK
United States Court of Appeals,
Ninth Circuit, 1990.
901 F.2d 735.

HISTORICAL AND POLITICAL SETTING *Originally inhabited by Polynesians, Samoa is a group of islands 2,610 miles south of Hawaii. In 1899, the islands were divided into Western Samoa and American Samoa by the Treaty of Berlin, which was signed by Great Britain, Germany, and the United States. Thus, the United States acquired American Samoa. In 1960, American Samoa adopted a constitution, which it revised in 1967, but it*

Case 37.3—Continued

remains a non-self-governing, unincorporated territory of the United States. Its currency is the U.S. dollar, its languages are Samoan and English, and it is administered by the U.S. Department of the Interior. The population of American Samoa is less than fifty thousand.

FACTS Pacific Reliant Industries, Inc., an Oregon company, sold building materials to Paradise Development Company, a company located in American Samoa. Pacific was reluctant to make several large deliveries, totaling more than $1 million in value, without some protection against nonpayment. Accordingly, representatives from Pacific, Paradise, and Amerika Samoa Bank (ASB) met in American Samoa on two occasions to discuss the supply contract and a letter of credit. Following these negotiations, ASB issued a letter of credit in favor of Pacific on Paradise's account. Later, alleging that ASB had wrongfully dishonored the letter of credit, Pacific brought suit in the U.S. district court for the district of Oregon against ASB to recover payment. The court dismissed the suit for lack of personal jurisdiction, holding that ASB lacked sufficient "minimum contacts" (see Chapter 3) with the state of Oregon to subject it to a lawsuit in that state.[a] Pacific appealed, contending that this case was not typical of other letter-of-credit cases

a. State law governs some cases that may be brought in a federal court because the parties to the case are citizens of different states or are aliens. In such a case, the federal court normally applies the law of the state in which the court is located.

because ASB had participated in forming the underlying contract, had had personal contact with the beneficiary (Pacific), and had known that Pacific would not extend credit or ship goods from Oregon without the letter of credit.

ISSUE Did ASB have sufficient minimum contacts with the state of Oregon to justify the state's jurisdiction over the dispute?

DECISION No. The U.S. Court of Appeals for the Ninth Circuit affirmed the lower court's ruling. Pacific could not bring suit against ASB in Oregon.

REASON The court stated that ASB lacked sufficient minimum contacts with Oregon to satisfy jurisdictional requirements. ASB did not initiate the transactions between itself, Paradise, and Pacific, nor did ASB take any significant actions in Oregon. The court noted that "both the negotiations for the underlying contract and the letter of credit occurred in American Samoa." The court reasoned that ASB could not have reasonably expected to be hauled into court in Oregon and "that ASB's conduct as an issuing bank of a letter of credit does not subject it to suit in Oregon."

FOR CRITICAL ANALYSIS—Political Consideration
If a court could exercise jurisdiction over a nonresident corporation that did not have minimum contacts with the jurisdiction in which the suit was brought, what might result?

▮ Regulation of Specific Business Activities

Doing business abroad can affect the economies, foreign policy, domestic politics, and other national interests of the countries involved. For this reason, nations impose laws to restrict or facilitate international business. Controls may also be imposed by international agreement. We discuss here how different types of international activities are regulated.

Investing

Investing in foreign nations involves a risk that the foreign government may take possession of the investment property. Expropriation, as already mentioned, occurs when property is taken and the owner is paid just compensation for what is taken. This does not violate generally observed principles of international law. Confiscation occurs when property is taken and no (or inadequate) compensation is paid. International legal principles are violated when property is confiscated. Few remedies are available for confiscation of property by a foreign government. Claims are often resolved by lump-sum settlements after negotiations between the United States and the taking nation.

To counter the deterrent effect that the possibility of confiscation may have on potential investors, many countries guarantee that foreign investors will be compensated if their property is taken. A guaranty can take the form of national constitutional or statutory laws or provisions in international treaties. As further protection for foreign investments, some countries provide insurance for their citizens' investments abroad.

Export Restrictions and Incentives

The U.S. Constitution provides in Article I, Section 9, that "No Tax or Duty shall be laid on Articles exported from any State." Thus, Congress cannot impose any export taxes. Congress can, however, use a variety of other devices to control exports. Congress may set export quotas on various items, such as grain being sold abroad. Under the Export Administration Act of 1979,[3] restrictions can be imposed on the flow of technologically advanced products and technical data.

Devices to stimulate exports and thereby aid domestic businesses include export incentives and subsidies. The Revenue Act of 1971,[4] for example, gave tax benefits to firms marketing their products overseas through certain foreign sales corporations, exempting income produced by the exports. Under the Export Trading Company Act of 1982,[5] U.S. banks are encouraged to invest in export trading companies. An export trading company consists of exporting firms joined to export a line of goods. The Export-Import Bank of the United States provides financial assistance, which consists primarily of credit guaranties given to commercial banks that in turn loan funds to U.S. exporting companies.

NOTE Most countries restrict exports for the same reasons: to protect national security; to project foreign policy, to prevent the spread of nuclear weapons, and to preserve scarce commodities.

Import Restrictions

All nations have restrictions on imports, and the United States is no exception. Restrictions include strict prohibitions, quotas, and tariffs. Under the Trading with the Enemy Act of 1917,[6] for example, no goods may be imported from nations that have been designated enemies of the United States. Other laws prohibit the importation of illegal drugs, books that urge insurrection against the United States, and agricultural products that pose dangers to domestic crops or animals.

"The notion dies hard that in some sort of way exports are patriotic but imports are immoral."

Lord Harlech (David Ormsley Gore), 1918–1985 (English writer)

QUOTAS AND TARIFFS   Quotas are limits on the amounts of goods that can be imported. Tariffs are taxes on imports. A tariff is usually a percentage of the value of the import, but it can be a flat rate per unit (for example, per barrel of oil). Tariffs raise the prices of goods, which causes some consumers to purchase less expensive, domestically manufactured goods.

DUMPING   The United States has specific laws directed at what it sees as unfair international trade practices. **Dumping**, for example, is the sale of imported goods at "less than fair value." "Fair value" is usually determined by the price of those goods in the exporting country. Foreign firms that engage in dumping in the United States hope to undersell U.S. businesses to obtain a larger share of the U.S. market. To prevent this, an extra tariff—known as an antidumping duty—may be assessed on the imports.

DUMPING
The selling of goods in a foreign country at a price below the price charged for the same goods in the domestic market.

MINIMIZING TRADE BARRIERS   Restrictions on imports are also known as trade barriers. The elimination of trade barriers is sometimes seen as essential to the world's economic well-being. To minimize trade barriers among nations, most of the world's leading trade nations abide by the General Agreement on Tariffs and Trade (GATT),

---

3.   50 U.S.C. Sections 2401–2420.
4.   26 U.S.C. Sections 991–994.
5.   15 U.S.C. Sections 4001, 4003.
6.   12 U.S.C. Section 95a.

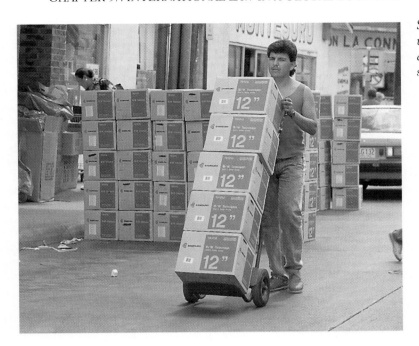

Samsung televisions are unloaded in Laredo, Texas. Why are quotas and tariffs placed on some imported goods?

which became the World Trade Organization (WTO) in 1995. (See Chapter 6 for a discussion of GATT and the WTO in respect to intellectual property rights.) Under Article I of GATT, each member country is required to grant **most-favored-nation status** to other member countries. This article obligates each member to treat other members at least as well as it treats that country that receives its most favorable treatment with regard to imports or exports.

Various regional trade agreements, or associations, also help to minimize trade barriers between nations. The European Union (EU), for example, attempts to minimize or remove barriers to trade among European member countries. The EU is the result of negotiations undertaken by European nations since the 1950s. By 1997, the EU had become a single integrated European trading unit made up of fifteen European nations. Another important regional trade agreement is the North American Free Trade Agreement (NAFTA). NAFTA, which became effective on January 1, 1994, created a regional trading unit consisting of Mexico, the United States, and Canada. The primary goal of NAFTA is to eliminate tariffs among these three countries on substantially all goods over a period of fifteen to twenty years.

MOST-FAVORED-NATION STATUS
A status granted in an international treaty by a provision stating that the citizens of the contracting nations may enjoy the privileges accorded by either party to citizens of the most favored nations. Generally, most-favored-nation clauses are designed to establish equality of international treatment.

Bribing Foreign Officials

Giving cash or in-kind benefits to foreign government officials to obtain business contracts and other favors is often considered normal practice. To reduce such bribery by representatives of U.S. corporations, Congress enacted the Foreign Corrupt Practices Act (FCPA) in 1977.[7] This act and its implications for American businesspersons engaged in international business transactions are discussed in detail in the *Landmark in the Law* in Chapter 4.

▍U.S. Laws in a Global Context

The internationalization of business raises questions of the extraterritorial effect of a nation's laws—that is, the effect of the country's laws outside the country. To what

7. 15 U.S.C. Sections 78m–78ff.

PROFILE

Mizuho Fukushima (1956–   )

"The era of seemingly shy, weak women in Japan is over," says Mizuho Fukushima, a human rights lawyer. "Sleeping Beauty has awakened."[a]

Fukushima is the leading advocate in Japan for victims of sexual harassment in the workplace. Male-dominated Japanese society has long been known for its chauvinism. Recognition of basic women's rights is far behind that of other countries.

a.   Louis Kraar, "Dedicated to Their Work: Meet 20 CEOs, Managers, and Technocrats Who Help Drive the Economies of the Pacific Rim," *Fortune*, September 22, 1990; and Louise do Rosario, "Mizuho Fukushima—Petite Lady Lawyer Fights Sex Harassment," *Far Eastern Economic Review*, August 12, 1993.

Fukushima helped introduce the concept of sexual harassment to the Japanese public by translating American articles on the subject and helped introduce the term *seku hara*—sexual harassment—into the Japanese vocabulary. She joined three other lawyers to set up a shelter and counseling center for battered women in Tokyo, which offers special help to women from Southeast Asia who are brought illegally to Japan to work as prostitutes.

Other causes included her effort to change the law that required women to give up their maiden and professional names after marriage. This law symbolized how Japanese women are deprived of their individuality, she believed. In conservative Japan, where women are expected to be submissive, such positions are shocking. "At least people are starting to talk about these things openly. That's progress," she says.

After attending the University of Tokyo, Fukushima was one of the few women to pass the tough examination for admission to the Legal Training and Research Institute, which is the only path to a legal career in Japan. Following her graduation from the institute, Fukushima approached Tokyo law firms for a job, only to be told that females need not apply.

Fukushima points out that the situation has improved for women in the law over the last few years. She also says that sexism has not impeded her career as an advocate for women. "The kind of work I'm doing is actually easy for a woman to do, because no one has ever done it before."[b]

For Critical Analysis: *How does the recognition of basic rights for women benefit all societies?*

b.   Karl Schoenberger, "For Every Action of the Crowd There Is an Opposite—If Unequal—Reaction: Four Tales from the Front Lines of Individualism in the Land of Conformity," *Los Angeles Times*, May 3, 1992.

extent do U.S. domestic laws affect other nations' businesses? To what extent are U.S. businesses affected by domestic laws when doing business abroad? The following sub-sections discuss these questions in the context of U.S. antitrust law. We also look at the extraterritorial application of U.S. laws prohibiting employment discrimination.

U.S. Antitrust Laws

U.S. antitrust laws (discussed in Chapter 30) have a wide application. They may *subject* persons in foreign nations to their provisions, as well as *protect* foreign consumers and competitors from violations committed by U.S. citizens. Consequently, *foreign persons*, a term that by definition includes foreign governments, may sue under U.S. antitrust laws in U.S. courts.

Section 1 of the Sherman Act provides for the extraterritorial effect of the U.S. antitrust laws. The United States is a major proponent of free competition in the global economy, and thus any conspiracy that has a substantial effect on U.S. commerce is within the reach of the Sherman Act. The violation may even occur outside the United States, and foreign governments as well as persons can be sued for violations of U.S. antitrust laws. Before U.S. courts will exercise jurisdiction and apply antitrust laws, it must be shown that the alleged violation had a *substantial effect* on U.S.

commerce. U.S. jurisdiction is automatically invoked, however, when a *per se* violation occurs.[8] A *per se* violation may consist of resale price fixing and tying, or tie-in, contracts. If a domestic firm, for example, joins a foreign cartel to control the production, price, or distribution of goods, and this cartel has a *substantial restraining effect* on U.S. commerce, a *per se* violation may exist. Hence, both the domestic firm and the foreign cartel may be sued for violation of the U.S. antitrust laws. Likewise, if foreign firms doing business in the United States enter into a price-fixing or other anticompetitive agreement to control a portion of U.S. markets, a *per se* violation may exist.

An alleged conspiracy on the part of Japanese television manufacturers to gain control of the electronic products market in the United States—in possible violation of the Sherman Act and other antitrust and tariff legislation—was considered by the United States Supreme Court in the following case.

---

8.   Certain types of restrictive contracts, such as price-fixing agreements, are deemed inherently anti-competitive and thus in restraint of trade as a matter of law. When such a restrictive contract is entered into, there is said to be a *per se* violation of the antitrust laws. See Chapter 30.

CASE 37.4

MATSUSHITA ELECTRIC INDUSTRIAL CO. v. ZENITH RADIO CORP.

Supreme Court of the United States, 1986.
475 U.S. 574,
106 S.Ct. 1348,
89 L.Ed.2d 538.

HISTORICAL AND ECONOMIC SETTING *Zenith Electronics Corporation began broadcasting with the first all-electronic television station, W9XZV, in 1939. In 1948, Zenith introduced its first television sets. By 1960, there were twenty-seven U.S. companies manufacturing television sets. The technology improved, and sales increased. By 1980, virtually every American home had a television set, and many had two or three. During the 1970s, however, some of the companies that based their products entirely on U.S. technology had begun losing their market shares to foreign competition. During the early 1980s, purchases of television sets manufactured by U.S. companies fell dramatically. While other U.S. manufacturers ceased selling television sets or sold their brands to foreign companies, Zenith fought its foreign competitors in the marketplace, in Congress, and in the United States Supreme Court. (Note that today, Zenith is no longer a U.S. manufacturer.)*

FACTS Zenith Radio Corporation and several other U.S. manufacturers of television sets filed suit in a U.S. federal district court, alleging that Matsushita Electric Industrial Company and other Japanese firms had violated U.S. antitrust laws. Zenith and the other U.S. firms contended that the Japanese firms had "illegally conspired to drive American firms from the consumer electronic products market" by means of a "scheme to raise, fix and maintain artificially high prices for television receivers sold by [Matsushita and others] in Japan and, at the same time, to fix and maintain low prices for television receivers exported to and sold in the United States." The alleged conspiracy began, according to Zenith, in 1953. The American firms claimed that the Japanese were engaged in a "predatory pricing" arrangement whereby the losses sustained by selling at such low prices in the United States were offset by monopoly profits obtained in Japan. Once the Japanese gained control over an overwhelming portion of the American market for electronic products, their monopoly power would enable them to recover their losses by charging artificially high prices in the United States as well. The district court granted summary judgment in favor of the Japanese firms, and the case was appealed. The appellate court reversed the judgment of the district court, and the case was appealed to the United States Supreme Court.

ISSUE Were the Japanese firms engaging in a price-fixing scheme in violation of U.S. antitrust laws?

DECISION No. The United States Supreme Court reversed the decision of the appellate court and remanded the case.

REASON The Supreme Court found little evidence to support the argument that Japanese electronic products manufacturers were engaged in a conspiracy to drive American competitors out of business by charging artificially low prices, because the alleged conspiracy had

(Continued)

Case 37.4—Continued

failed "to achieve its ends in the two decades of its asserted operation." The Court also noted that the American firms that brought the suit had seen their collective market share increase substantially during the same period of time.

FOR CRITICAL ANALYSIS—Economic Consideration
Why should the United States apply its antitrust laws to business firms owned by citizens or the government of another nation?

Discrimination Laws

As explained in Chapter 33, there are laws in the United States prohibiting discrimination on the basis of race, color, national origin, religion, sex, age, and disability. These laws, as they affect employment relationships, generally apply extraterritorially. Since 1984, for example, the Age Discrimination in Employment Act (ADEA) of 1967 has covered U.S. employees working abroad for U.S. employers. The Americans with Disabilities Act of 1990, which requires employers to accommodate the needs of workers with disabilities, also applies to U.S. nationals working abroad for U.S. firms.

For some time, it was uncertain whether the major U.S. law regulating discriminatory practices in the workplace, Title VII of the Civil Rights Act of 1964, applied extraterritorially. The Civil Rights Act of 1991 addressed this issue. The act provides that Title VII applies extraterritorially to all U.S. employees working for U.S. employers abroad. Generally, U.S. employers must abide by U.S. discrimination laws *unless* to do so would violate the laws of the country in which their workplaces are located. This "foreign laws exception" allows employers to avoid being subjected to conflicting laws.

What happens if a Japanese firm doing business in the United States allegedly discriminates against U.S. employees in favor of Japanese citizens, which is permitted under a treaty between the United States and Japan? Is discrimination on the basis of citizenship the same thing as discrimination on the basis of national origin? These questions were addressed in the following case.

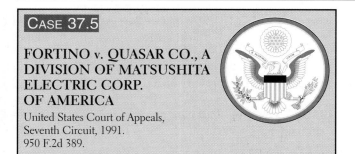

CASE 37.5

FORTINO v. QUASAR CO., A DIVISION OF MATSUSHITA ELECTRIC CORP. OF AMERICA

United States Court of Appeals, Seventh Circuit, 1991.
950 F.2d 389.

HISTORICAL AND ECONOMIC SETTING *Motorola, Inc., manufactured automobile radios, police radios, and walkie-talkies before and during World War II, which ended in 1945. In the early years of television, Motorola marketed the first television sets priced under $200. By the 1970s, however, Motorola had begun losing its share of the television market to Japanese manufacturers, and in 1974, the company sold its Quasar television manufacturing facilities in Franklin Park, Illinois, to Matsushita*

Electric Industrial Company, which is based in Osaka, Japan. Matsushita made more than a million television sets in the Quasar plant in 1988. The next year, Matsushita appointed an American, who had worked for Quasar before its sale by Motorola, to Matsushita's second highest executive position in North America.

FACTS In 1953, the United States and Japan entered into a Treaty of Friendship, Commerce, and Navigation. The treaty provides, among other things, that Japanese companies doing business in the United States and U.S. companies doing business in Japan have the right to choose citizens of their own nations as executives for their firms. Quasar Company, doing business in the United States as a subsidiary of the Japanese company Matsushita Electric Industrial Company, employed U.S. workers and management personnel but was largely controlled by executives of Matsushita. After Matsushita suffered a $20 million loss in 1985, Matsushita executives restructured Quasar and cut its work force dramatically.

Case 37.5—Continued

Of eighty-nine managers working for the company, sixty-six were fired. None of the company's ten Japanese executives was laid off, and some of them received raises. John Fortino and two other American executives who had been fired (the plaintiffs) sued Quasar in a U.S. district court for, among other things, discriminating against them on the basis of national origin in violation of Title VII. Quasar defended by asserting that discrimination on the basis of citizenship, as allowed under the Treaty of Friendship, Commerce, and Navigation, did not violate Title VII. The trial court held for the American executives, and Quasar appealed.

ISSUE   Did Quasar's discrimination on the basis of citizenship constitute discrimination on the basis of national origin in violation of Title VII?

DECISION   No. The U.S. Court of Appeals for the Seventh Circuit reversed the trial court's decision. The plaintiffs had no cause of action under Title VII.

REASON   The court stressed that the discrimination on the basis of citizenship permitted by the treaty is not prohibited by Title VII. Title VII prohibits discrimination on the basis of national origin but not preference based on citizenship. The court conceded that most Japanese citizens are likely to be of Japanese national origin but concluded that discrimination on the basis of citizenship is conceptually distinct from bias based on national origin. Japanese companies were expressly given the right to choose citizens from their own nation as executives of their foreign subsidiaries in the United States. "That right would be empty," said the court, "if the subsidiary could be punished for treating its citizen executives differently from American executives on the ground that, since the former were of Japanese national origin and the latter were not, it was discriminating on the basis of national origin. Title VII would be taking back from the Japanese with one hand what the treaty had given them with the other. This collision is avoided by holding national origin and citizenship separate."

FOR CRITICAL ANALYSIS—Ethical Consideration
What fundamental policies are in conflict in this case?

▌ Key Terms

▌ Chapter Summary: International Law in a Global Economy

International Principles and Doctrines *(See pages 957–960.)*	1. *The principle of comity*—Under this principle, nations give effect to the laws and judicial decrees of other nations for reasons of courtesy and international harmony. 2. *The act of state doctrine*—A doctrine under which American courts avoid passing judgment on the validity of public acts committed by a recognized foreign government within its own territory. 3. *The doctrine of sovereign immunity*—When certain conditions are satisfied, foreign nations are immune from U.S. jurisdiction under the Foreign Sovereign Immunities Act of 1976. Exceptions are made (a) when the foreign state has "waived its immunity either explicitly or by implication" or (b) when the action is "based upon a commercial activity carried on in the United States by the foreign state."
Doing Business Internationally *(See pages 960–964.)*	Ways in which U.S. domestic firms engage in international business transactions include (a) exporting, which may involve foreign agents or distributors, and (b) manufacturing abroad through licensing arrangements, franchising operations, wholly owned subsidiaries, or joint ventures.

(Continued)

▌ Chapter Summary: International Law in a Global Economy—Continued

Commercial Contracts in an International Setting (*See pages 964–968.*)	Choice-of-language, forum-selection, and choice-of-law clauses are often included in international business contracts to reduce the uncertainties associated with interpreting the language of the agreement and dealing with legal differences. *Force majeure* clauses are included in most domestic and international contracts. They commonly stipulate that certain events, such as floods, fire, accidents, labor strikes, and shortages, may excuse a party from liability for nonperformance of the contract. Arbitration clauses are also frequently found in international contracts.
Making Payment on International Transactions (*See pages 968–971.*)	1. *Currency conversion*—Because nations have different monetary systems, payment on international contracts requires currency conversion at a rate specified in a foreign exchange market. 2. *Correspondent banking*—Correspondent banks facilitate the transfer of funds from a buyer in one country to a seller in another. 3. *Letters of credit*—Letters of credit facilitate international transactions by ensuring payment to sellers and ensuring to buyers that payment will not be made until the sellers have complied with the terms of the letters of credit. Typically, compliance occurs when a bill of lading is delivered to the issuing bank.
Regulation of Specific Business Activities (*See pages 971–973.*)	In the interests of their economies, foreign policies, domestic policies, or other national priorities, nations impose laws that restrict or facilitate international business. Such laws regulate foreign investments; exporting and importing activities; and in the United States, the bribery of foreign officials to obtain favorable contracts. The General Agreement on Tariffs and Trade (now the World Trade Organization) attempts to minimize trade barriers among nations, as do regional trade agreements, including the European Union and the North American Free Trade Agreement.
U.S. Laws in a Global Context (*See pages 973–977.*)	1. *Antitrust laws*—U.S. antitrust laws may be applied beyond the borders of the United States. Any conspiracy that has a substantial effect on commerce within the United States may be subject to the Sherman Act, even if the violation occurs outside the United States. 2. *Discrimination laws*—The major U.S. laws prohibiting employment discrimination, including Title VII of the Civil Rights Act of 1964, the Age Discrimination in Employment Act of 1967, and the Americans with Disabilities Act of 1990, cover U.S. employees working abroad for U.S. firms—*unless* to apply the U.S. laws would violate the laws of the host country.

▌ For Review

1. What is the principle of comity, and why do courts deciding disputes involving a foreign law or judicial decree apply this principle?

2. What is the act of state doctrine? In what circumstances is this doctrine applied?

3. A foreign nation is not immune from the jurisdiction of U.S. courts if the nation waives its immunity. Under the Foreign Sovereign Immunities Act

of 1976, on what other basis might a foreign state be considered subject to the jurisdiction of U.S. courts?

4. In what circumstances will U.S. antitrust laws be applied extraterritorially?

5. Do U.S. laws prohibiting employment discrimination apply in all circumstances to U.S. employees working for U.S. employers abroad?

▌ Questions and Case Problems

37–1. Letters of Credit. James Reynolds entered into an agreement to purchase dental supplies from Tooth-Tech, Inc. Reynolds also secured a letter of credit from Central Bank to pay for the supplies. Tooth-Tech placed sixty crates of dental supplies on board a steamship and received in return the invoices required under the letter of credit. The purchaser, Reynolds, subsequently learned that Tooth-Tech, Inc., had filled the sixty crates with rubbish, not dental supplies. Given the fact that an issuer's obligation under a letter of credit is

independent of the underlying contract between the buyer and the seller, would the issuer be required to pay the seller in this situation? Explain.

37–2. Sovereign Immunity. Texas Trading & Milling Corp. and other companies brought an action for breach of contract against the Federal Republic of Nigeria and its central bank. Nigeria, a rapidly developing and oil-rich nation, had over-bought huge quantities of cement from Texas Trading and others. Unable to accept delivery of the cement, Nigeria repudiated the contract, alleging immunity under the Foreign Sovereign Immunities Act of 1976. Because the buyer of the cement was the Nigerian government, did the doctrine of sovereign immunity remove the dispute from the jurisdiction of U.S. courts? [*Texas Trading & Milling Corp. v. Federal Republic of Nigeria*, 647 F.2d 300 (2d Cir. 1981)]

37–3. Letters of Credit. The Swiss Credit Bank issued a letter of credit in favor of Antex Industries to cover the sale of 92,000 electronic integrated circuits manufactured by Electronic Arrays. The letter of credit specified that the chips would be transported to Tokyo by ship. Antex shipped the circuits by air. Payment on the letter of credit was dishonored because the shipment by air did not fulfill the precise terms of the letter of credit. Should a court compel payment? Explain. [*Board of Trade of San Francisco v. Swiss Credit Bank*, 728 F.2d 1241 (9th Cir. 1984)]

37–4. Act of State Doctrine. Sabbatino, an American, contracted with a Cuban corporation that was largely owned by U.S. residents to buy Cuban sugar. When the Cuban government expropriated the corporation's property and rights in retaliation against a U.S. reduction of the Cuban sugar quota, Sabbatino entered into a new contract to make payment for the sugar to Banco Nacional de Cuba, a government-owned Cuban bank. Sabbatino refused to make the promised payment, and Banco subsequently filed an action in a U.S. district court seeking to recover payment for the sugar. The issue was whether the act of state doctrine should apply when a foreign state violates international law. (If the doctrine were applied, the Cuban government's action would be presumed valid, and thus Banco's claim would be legitimate.) Should the act of state doctrine be applied in these circumstances? Discuss. [*Banco Nacional de Cuba v. Sabbatino*, 376 U.S. 398, 84 S.Ct. 923, 11 L.Ed.2d 804 (1964)]

37–5. Antitrust Claims. Billy Lamb and Carmon Willis (the plaintiffs) were tobacco growers in Kentucky. Phillip Morris, Inc., and B.A.T. Industries, PLC, routinely purchased tobacco not only from Kentucky but also from producers in several foreign countries. In 1982, subsidiaries of Phillip Morris and B.A.T. (the defendants) entered into an agreement with La Fundacion Del Niño (the Children's Foundation) of Caracas, Venezuela, headed by the wife of the president of Venezuela. The agreement provided that the two subsidiaries would donate a total of approximately $12.5 million to the Children's Foundation, and in exchange, the subsidiaries would obtain price controls on Venezuelan tobacco, elimination of controls on retail cigarette prices in Venezuela, tax deductions for the donations, and assurances that existing tax rates applicable to tobacco companies would not be increased. The plaintiffs brought an action, alleging that the Venezuelan arrangement was an inducement designed to restrain trade in violation of U.S. antitrust laws. Such an arrangement, the plaintiffs contended, would result in the artificial depression of tobacco prices to the detriment of domestic tobacco growers, while ensuring lucrative retail prices for tobacco products sold abroad. The trial court held that the plaintiffs' claim was barred by the act of state doctrine. What will result on appeal? Discuss. [*Lamb v. Phillip Morris, Inc.*, 915 F.2d 1024 (6th Cir. 1990)]

37–6. Sovereign Immunity. The Bank of Jamaica, which is wholly owned by the government of Jamaica, contracted with Chisholm & Co. in January 1981 for Chisholm to arrange for lines of credit from various U.S. banks and to obtain $50 million in credit insurance from the Export-Import Bank of the United States. This Chisholm successfully did, but subsequently the Bank of Jamaica refused the deals arranged by Chisholm, and the bank refused to pay Chisholm for its services. Chisholm sued the bank in a federal district court for breach of an implied contract. The bank moved to dismiss the case, claiming, among other things, that it was immune from the jurisdiction of U.S. courts under the doctrine of sovereign immunity. What factors will the court consider in deciding whether the bank is immune from the jurisdiction of U.S. courts under the doctrine of sovereign immunity? Will the court agree? Discuss fully. [*Chisholm & Co. v. Bank of Jamaica*, 643 F.Supp. 1393 (S.D.Fla. 1986)]

37–7. Forum-Selection Clauses. Royal Bed and Spring Co., a Puerto Rican distributor of furniture products, entered into an exclusive distributorship agreement with Famossul Industria e Comercio de Moveis Ltda., a Brazilian manufacturer of furniture products. Under the terms of the contract, Royal Bed was to distribute in Puerto Rico the furniture products manufactured by Famossul in Brazil. The contract contained choice-of-forum and choice-of-law clauses, which designated the judicial district of Curitiba, State of Paraná, Brazil, as the judicial forum and the Brazilian Civil Code as the law to be applied in the event of any dispute. Famossul terminated the exclusive distributorship and suspended the shipment of goods without just cause. Under Puerto Rican law, forum-selection clauses providing for foreign venues are not enforced as a matter of public policy. In what jurisdiction should Royal Bed bring suit? Discuss fully. [*Royal Bed and Spring Co. v. Famossul Industria e Comercio de Moveis Ltda.*, 906 F.2d 45 (5th Cir. 1990)]

37–8. Discrimination Claims. Radio Free Europe and Radio Liberty (RFE/RL), a U.S. corporation doing business in Germany, employs more than three hundred U.S. citizens at its principal place of business in Munich, Germany. The concept of mandatory retirement is deeply embedded in German labor policy, and a contract formed in 1982 between RFE/RL and a German labor union contained a clause that required workers to be retired when they reach the age of sixty-five. When William Mahoney and other American employees (the plaintiffs) reached the age of sixty-five, RFE/RL terminated their employment as required under its contract with the labor union. The plaintiffs sued RFE/RL for discriminating against them on the basis of age, in violation of the Age Discrimination in Employment Act of 1967. Will the plaintiffs succeed in their suit? Discuss fully. [*Mahoney v. RFE/RL, Inc.*, 47 F.3d 447 (D.C. Cir. 1995)]

37–9. Sovereign Immunity. Reed International Trading Corp., a New York corporation, agreed to sell down jackets to Alink, a Russian business. Alink referred Reed to the Bank for Foreign and Economic Affairs of the Russian Federation for payment and gave Reed a letter of credit payable in New York. When Reed tried to collect, the bank refused to pay. Reed (and others) filed a suit in a federal district court against the bank (and others). The bank qualified as a "sovereign" under the Foreign Sovereign Immunities Act and thus claimed in part that it was immune from suit in U.S. courts. On what basis might the court hold that the bank was *not* immune? Explain. [*Reed International Trading Corp. v. Donau Bank, A.G.*, 866 F.Supp. 750 (S.D.N.Y. 1994)]

A QUESTION OF ETHICS AND SOCIAL RESPONSIBILITY

37–10. *Ronald Riley, an American citizen, and Council of Lloyd's, a British insurance corporation with its principal place of business in London, entered into an agreement in 1980 that allowed Riley to underwrite insurance through Lloyd's. The agreement provided that if any dispute arose between Lloyd's and Riley, the courts of England would have exclusive jurisdiction, and the laws of England would apply. Over the next decade, some of the parties insured under policies that Riley underwrote experienced large losses, for which they filed claims. Instead of paying his share of the claims, Riley filed a lawsuit in a U.S. district court against Lloyd's and its managers and directors (all British citizens or entities), seeking, among other things, rescission of the 1980 agreement. Riley alleged that the defendants had violated the Securities Act of 1933, the Securities Exchange Act of 1934, and Rule 10b-5. The defendants asked the court to enforce the forum-selection clause in the agreement. Riley argued that if the clause was enforced, he would be deprived of his rights under the U.S. securities laws. The court held that the parties were to resolve their dispute in England.* [Riley v. Kingsley Underwriting Agencies, Ltd., 969 F.2d 953 (10th Cir. 1992)]

1. Did the court's decision fairly balance the rights of the parties? How would you argue in support of the court's decision in this case? How would you argue against it?
2. Should the fact that an international transaction may be subject to laws and remedies different from or less favorable than those of the United States be a valid basis for denying enforcement of forum-selection and choice-of-law clauses?
3. All parties to this litigation other than Riley were British. Should this fact be considered by the court in deciding this case?

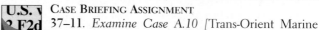

CASE BRIEFING ASSIGNMENT

37–11. *Examine Case A.10* [Trans-Orient Marine Corp. v. Star Trading & Marine, Inc., 731 F.Supp. 619 (S.D.N.Y. 1990)] *in Appendix A. The case has been excerpted there in great detail. Review and then brief the case, making sure that you include answers to the following questions in your brief.*

1. What specific circumstances led to this lawsuit?
2. What was the central international legal issue addressed by the court?
3. How did the court distinguish a "succession of state" from a "succession of government," and what was the effect of the distinction on executory contracts of the state?
4. What "seminal decision" on this issue was referred to by the court? On what other cases did the court rely in its reasoning?

FOR CRITICAL ANALYSIS

37–12. *Business cartels and monopolies that are legal in some countries may engage in practices that violate U.S. antitrust laws. In view of this fact, what are some of the implications of applying U.S. antitrust laws extraterritorially?*

▌Unit Ten—Cumulative Hypothetical Problem

37–13. *JB Mediquip, Inc., is a U.S. manufacturer of hospital equipment. JB does business throughout the world and has manufacturing plants in several other countries.*

1. JB forms a contract with a business firm in Pardum, a foreign country, to purchase components for certain equipment that JB manufactures. The contract includes a choice-of-language clause, a choice-of-law clause, and a forum-selection clause. What do these clauses provide for, and what are their legal effects?
2. JB agrees to sell fifty hospital beds to a health-care facility operated on a military base in Zamboria, a foreign country. The health-care facility is owned and operated by the Zamborian government. JB ships the beds, but the health-care facility refuses to pay for them. To recover the price of the beds, JB sues the health-care facility in a U.S. district court. Zamboria moves to dismiss JB's action, contending that a U.S. court cannot exercise jurisdiction over the matter. On what ground might Zamboria base its assertion? Is Zamboria correct?
3. Many of the employees in JB's plant in Algoton, a foreign country, are American citizens. JB blatantly discriminates against the female employees in regard to salary and promotions. Several female employees sue JB in a U.S. court, alleging gender-based discrimination in violation of Title VII of the Civil Rights Act of 1964. JB contends that such discrimination is not illegal in Algoton, and therefore its actions are not illegal. Is JB correct? Explain.

▌Accessing the Internet: Business Law and Legal Environment

You can access the original 1947 General Agreement on Tariffs and Trade (GATT) by going to

**gopher://gopher.law.cornell.edu:70/00/0/foreign/
flectcher/BH209.txt**

The gopher address is

Gopher.law.cornell.edu

Then you should select

**Foreign and International Law: Primary Documents and
Commentary.**

Next, select

Multilateral treaties by category

Then you should select

Trade and Commercial Relations

Finally, you should select

The General Agreement on Tariffs and Trade

If you use the commercial service CompuServe, you can obtain information on legal aspects of importing and exporting goods by doing the following. Type in

Go itforum

From your Library Menu, you should choose

Browse

Then select

IT Practices

Then you should select

Legal Aspects of U.S. Importing

or

Legal Aspects of U.S. Exporting

You can get information about, and the text of, the North American Free Trade Agreement at the following Web site:

http://the=tech.mit.edu/Bulletins/nafta.html

If you want to know more about international trade law, the best place to go is probably the following Web site:

http://ananse.irv.uit.no/trade_law/nav/trade.html

PERSONAL LAW HANDBOOK

Contents

Note to Student*

Business law and the legal environment do not just consist of theoretical concepts and vague statutes. Rather, you will find that you can use what you have learned from your course in many practical ways throughout your life. In this *Personal Law Handbook* you will discover suggestions for preventing costly legal problems, as well as ideas about how to handle those legal problems that you have not been able to avoid. To a large extent, personal law is preventive—the more you know about the legal consequences of your actions and the actions of those with whom you have dealings, the better you will be able to prevent legal problems.

In no way should you take this *Handbook* to be a substitute for licensed, professional legal assistance. Whenever you think that you have a legal problem, you should consult an attorney.

---

* This handbook was written by Frank B. Cross of the University of Texas at Austin.

Topic 1   Renting a Home

Like millions of Americans, you may decide not to own your own home. Instead, you may choose to rent a house, an apartment, a mobile home, or some other form of housing. As a tenant, your relationship with your landlord is *generally governed by the law of the state in which you live.*

▮ Leases

The **lease** is the agreement between you and your landlord that sets out rights and duties regarding the rental property. A written lease is a legal document enforceable in court—a signature on a lease is generally proof that the person who signed it read it and agreed to it. Thus, if you sign a lease, you are bound to do what it says. For this reason, you should read an entire lease carefully before you sign it.

Most leases are written to favor the landlord's interests. If you are unsure of the meaning or effect of any of the terms, before signing the lease you should seek the advice of a lawyer, a tenants' rights organization, a legal aid office, or others experienced with leases.

Oral Leases

In almost all states, an oral lease for a period of less than a year is valid and enforceable. The basic problem with an oral lease is the same as the basic problem with other oral contracts: it is difficult to prove the terms of the oral agreement. Generally, it is assumed an oral lease that requires rent to be paid monthly creates a **month-to-month tenancy.** This means that, with a month's written notice, a landlord can raise the rent or end the tenancy. Of course, you can also end the tenancy with a month's written notice. The notice must be given a month (or, if a local statute states thirty days, then thirty days) before the rent is due.

Lease Terms

Leases include such terms as the following items:

1. The names of the parties to the agreement.
2. The address of the rental property.
3. The amount and the due date of the rent.
4. Other fees and charges.
5. The period of time for which the property is rented.
6. The rights and duties of the parties, which relate to use of the premises, alterations, maintenance, repairs, and other areas of responsibility.
7. The amount of a security deposit.
8. The conditions under which the rent can be raised.
9. Provisions for subleasing the property and terminating the lease.

ALTERATIONS   Can you make changes to rental property after you move in? In most circumstances, the answer depends on the terms of the lease. Most leases include a provision that prohibits alterations without the landlord's written approval. If you do not get the landlord's approval before making alterations, you will violate the lease and may be liable for any presumed destruction of the property. If there is no lease provision concerning alterations, you can make changes to the property that do not reduce the value of the property to the landlord.

If no lease provision applies and you have made a change—for example, if you have added bookshelves or installed new cabinets—who owns the new addition? If you cannot come to an agreement with your landlord, and you ask a court to decide the question, the court will look at the laws of your state to determine who owns what. In some states, the addition may be the property of the landlord; in other states, it may be yours, and you can sell it to the landlord or remove it. If it is your property and you choose to remove it, you should do so carefully to avoid any damage to the rental property. If the property is damaged, you are responsible.

SUBLEASES   Normally, a lease contains a provision that prohibits a tenant from **subleasing** the rental property without the landlord's written approval. If the lease does not require the landlord's approval, in most cases you can sublease for whatever period of time you could remain on the property under the lease. A sublease cannot be for a longer period than you could stay on the property. For instance, if you signed a one-year lease that contains no provision regarding subleasing and there are six months left before the lease expires, you could sublease the property for six months or less. *As the original tenant, however, you are still liable for the rent and any damage to the property.*

Whether or not your lease prohibits subleasing, can you move out before the lease expires? Generally, the answer is yes. You will be liable for the rent for the rest of the lease, however. There may be a limit on how much you pay: in some states, a landlord must make a reasonable effort to find a new tenant for the same amount of rent and the same period of time. If the property can be rented only for a smaller amount of money or a shorter time, you will be liable for the difference.

To minimize your losses, as soon as you know you will be moving out, send the landlord written notice (via certified or registered mail) of your plan to allow as much time as possible to find a new tenant. Keep a copy of the notice. You might also help find a new tenant by advertising that the property will be available.

RENEWAL   Typically, a lease requires that you move out when it expires. A lease can provide, however, that it renews automatically unless you tell the landlord in advance that you plan to move out. If you do not give the landlord this notice, you will be renewing the lease on the same terms for the same period of time. A different lease might provide that if you stay on the property after the lease expires and the landlord accepts a payment of rent, the lease renews according to the original terms.

If the lease does not mention renewal, in some states the landlord does not need to give you notice that the lease is ending. In these states, the reasoning is that you know when the lease expires because you signed it, and thus you must leave the property when the lease ends without additional notice. In other states, if you remain on the property after the lease ends and the landlord accepts a payment of rent, a new month-to-month tenancy is created or, in some states, the lease renews according to its original terms.

OTHER RIGHTS   You may have other rights and responsibilities as a tenant. Leases often cover such subjects as pets, parking, cleaning, noise, and so on. If you violate any of these rules, the landlord can give you notice to move or take you to court to have you evicted. The other tenants are probably subject to the same rules. If you have any complaints regarding other tenants' behavior under the lease, contact your landlord. If you are unhappy with the landlord's response, or if the complaint concerns a neighbor who is not a tenant, contact your attorney, a legal aid office, or a local tenants' rights organization.

Illegal Terms

A landlord cannot legally discriminate against you on the basis of your race, color, religion, national origin, or gender. Also, a landlord cannot discriminate against you if you have a handicap or, in most cases, if you have children. Similarly, as a tenant, you cannot legally promise to do something counter to the laws prohibiting discrimination. The public policy underlying these prohibitions is to treat all people equally.

One of the reasons to read a lease carefully is to look for, and avoid, illegal terms. Generally, any clause that purports to waive your legal rights is unenforceable. For this reason, clauses that attempt to do any or all of the following may be unenforceable in your state:

1.   Waiving your right to a jury trial in eviction proceedings.
2.   Permitting your landlord to evict you in a court proceeding without your presence.
3.   Providing for a nonrefundable security deposit.
4.   Limiting your landlord's liability for hazardous conditions that injure you or your guests.
5.   Requiring that you pay an unreasonably high fee or penalty for a late rent payment.
6.   Requiring that you assume your landlord's responsibility for maintenance and repair of a private residence.
7.   Requiring that you pay your landlord's attorneys' fees if the landlord sues to enforce the lease.

A lease is enforceable in most cases even if it contains an illegal clause. A court will strike the illegal clause from the lease and enforce the other terms. For example, some states prohibit a clause under which you agree to pay the landlord's attorneys' fees if the landlord sues to enforce the lease. If you fail to pay the rent and the landlord sues, the court could enforce the lease but order the landlord to pay his or her own attorneys' fees.

▌Eviction

Eviction is a legal process by which your landlord can get you off the rental property. In most states, the procedure involves a written notice to you and a hearing in court.

Reasons for Eviction

Your landlord can have you evicted for violating the lease, the law, or other rules that apply to the rental property. Reasons that your landlord might want to evict you include:

1. Failing to pay the rent.
2. Remaining on the property after the lease expires.
3. Damaging the property.
4. Disturbing your neighbors' quiet enjoyment.

The most common reason for eviction is nonpayment of rent. Paying rent late, paying less than is due, and paying it to the wrong person or at the wrong place are related reasons that a landlord might want to evict you. Failing to pay a valid rent increase may justify eviction. If you believe that an increase is not valid, you may defend against an eviction on that ground. Another course of action is to pay the increase under protest and challenge it in court.

Can your landlord refuse to accept rent that is offered on time and evict you for nonpayment of rent? If your landlord refuses to accept your payment, send the landlord a certified, return-receipt-requested letter offering again to pay the rent. Keep a copy of the letter. If your landlord tries to evict you, you can show the copy of the letter and receipt to the court to prove that you offered the rent and it was refused.

Your landlord can evict you for staying on the property after your lease expires. You might avoid an eviction after the last month of the term by offering the landlord the next month's rent. If the landlord accepts the payment, a new month-to-month tenancy begins or, in some states, the lease is renewed.

Eviction Notice

Ordinarily, your landlord has to give you written notice before beginning an eviction, to give you a chance to correct the violation. For example, if you have not paid the rent, you must be given an opportunity to pay it. The notice period is usually short—three days, in most states. Of course, if the lease has expired, in most states the landlord is not required to give notice. Many states have strict requirements about how the notice must be given. Sometimes it must be given to you personally or sent to you by registered or certified mail.

Eviction Proceedings

In most states, eviction requires going to court. An eviction proceeding is generally a brief proceeding in which the court acts quickly to determine who has the right to the rental property. In some states and in some cases, you have the right to a jury trial (ask the clerk of the court). You are not entitled to a court-appointed lawyer in an eviction proceeding, and you are not required to have one, but it is a good idea to be represented because the landlord will probably have an attorney. If you choose to represent yourself, you can do anything an attorney could do, but you will be expected to do it competently. If you do not show up to defend yourself, you normally automatically lose.

In the proceeding, your landlord must prove the truth of what he or she claims and show that what is proved is a cause for eviction. You have a right to prove that the landlord is wrong. For example, if the landlord is attempting to evict you for not paying all of the rent or not paying a rent increase, you might defend yourself on any of the following grounds:

1. You paid the rent.
2. No rent was owed.
3. You rightfully deducted the cost of a repair to the property from the amount of the rent.
4. The landlord's motive for the eviction or the rent increase violated the lease or was otherwise illegal.
5. The eviction notice did not give you necessary information within the required time.

The court decides whom to believe and if what is proved is a sufficient cause for eviction or a sufficient defense against it. The court can issue an order to the landlord to leave you alone, or the court can issue a judgment in favor of the landlord for the amount of the rent. The court can also issue an order to an officer (usually a sheriff) to put you out on the street. The officer may give you notice a few days before acting, depending on local law. In many states, the court can order a **stay of eviction,** which temporarily postpones execution of the judgment, usually on the basis of a hardship such as cold winter weather or the lack of another place to live. The entire process, from the day you receive the notice of eviction to the day the sheriff appears at your door, may take as little as three weeks or as much as three months. Either party may appeal the judgment.

▌ Substandard Housing

Landlords must maintain rental property to meet certain minimum health and safety standards. These standards are generally established in state or local laws known as housing codes. In most states, the **implied warranty of habitability** also guarantees that landlords will provide decent, safe, sanitary, and livable housing, as defined by local housing codes.

Local Housing Codes

Housing codes normally include regulations that cover such details as the following:

1. Room temperature.
2. Water temperature, water pressure, and plumbing.
3. Electrical wiring and fire safety, including smoke alarms.
4. Rodent and insect infestation.
5. The number of garbage cans.
6. Building structure and related features, such as the kind of locks required on apartment doors.

To learn the exact requirements of your local housing code, contact your attorney, a legal aid office, a local tenants' rights organization, or the city or county building inspection department. Your local library may also have a reference copy of the housing code and other state and local laws.

The Implied Warranty of Habitability

The implied warranty of habitability applies whether or not it is mentioned in your lease, and a clause in the lease that attempts to reject the warranty is unenforceable. Generally, this warranty covers only the most serious problems—a lack of heat in the winter, for example, rather than a few ants on the kitchen floor. If your landlord fails to fix a serious problem, you can go to court and charge the landlord with violation of the warranty. Your best evidence to prove the substandard condition of your home is your copy of the building inspection department's report (discussed below).

Steps to Take to Fix the Situation

What can you do if your landlord fails to provide decent, safe, sanitary, and livable housing? You can contact the city or county to enforce your local housing code. There are steps you can take on your own, or with other tenants, to remedy the situation. Possible steps that you can take include moving out; repairing the condition that makes the housing unsafe, unsanitary, or unlivable and deducting the cost of the repair from the rent; reducing the amount of the rent that you pay; getting a court order to have the property repaired; and suing your landlord. Your landlord may challenge what you do, and this challenge may involve court action, but if you choose your remedy carefully and follow the appropriate steps, you should have a good defense.

CONTACT YOUR LOCAL BUILDING INSPECTION DEPARTMENT If you believe that your landlord is in violation of your local housing code, contact your local building inspection department. Explain what you think is wrong and ask for an inspection. When the inspector arrives, point out the conditions that need repair and ask the inspector to check the rest of the building for other violations. When the inspector files a report, get a copy from the building inspection department. If there are mistakes or something is missing, ask for a new inspection.

Your landlord will be given a copy of the report and an order to repair violations within a certain period of time (usually thirty days). The building inspection department and the courts are responsible for seeing that your landlord makes the repairs, but if there will be a hearing, you may want to go to explain what you think is wrong. A landlord who does not make the repairs is subject to a fine. If the violations are very serious, the property may be condemned and the building demolished.

MOVE OUT If the property is essentially uninhabitable, you can move out. Generally, it does not matter what caused the property to become uninhabitable—a fire, a storm, a flood, or your landlord's failure to maintain the property—so long as the cause was not something that you did. Frequently, you can move out without giving the landlord notice and without being liable for future rent. You should be aware, however, that the option to move out was created by the courts as the **doctrine of constructive eviction.** Its availability varies from state to state and from case to case. If you move out and your landlord sues you, the court may decide that the property was habitable, and you can be held liable for unpaid and future rent.

MAKE REPAIRS AND DEDUCT THE COST FROM THE RENT In some states, if the rental property includes a defective condition that will affect your health or safety (that is, if the condition violates the warranty of habitability), you can pay for the repairs and deduct the cost from the rent. To use this remedy, take the following steps:

1. Determine that the problem is the landlord's responsibility. This will depend on your local law or lease terms to the contrary. In some states, the condition must concern a basic service, such as heat or water.
2. Notify the landlord about the problem in writing (certified or registered mail), explaining that you intend to use this remedy if repairs are not made within a rea-

sonable time. Normally, thirty days is sufficient. An emergency might warrant less time.

3. Make repairs (or hire someone to make repairs) if the landlord does not take steps to fix the problem. Some states require that you get written estimates first. Save all receipts and other paperwork.

4. Deduct the cost of the repairs from your next rent payment. Give the receipts to the landlord but keep copies. In some states, the deductible amount is restricted to a month's rent or some other fixed amount. To avoid this restriction in making a major repair, you and other tenants might act together and deduct a portion of the cost from each tenant's rent. Before doing so, however, ask your attorney, or someone else familiar with your local law, about this possibility.

If your landlord tries to evict you for nonpayment of rent, you can explain your side of the story in court. Generally, if you have followed the law and used common sense, you should have few problems. If the court decides that you were wrong, you will have to pay the entire rent, regardless of how much you spent on repairs.

WITHHOLD RENT In some states, if the rental property includes a defective condition that violates the warranty of habitability, you can withhold some of the rent. To use this remedy, take the following steps:

1. Determine that the condition violates the warranty of habitability.
2. Notify the landlord of the problem in writing (certified or registered mail).
3. Allow the landlord a reasonable time to make repairs.
4. Withhold all or part of your next rental payment. In some states, you may be able to withhold amounts for past months when the property was uninhabitable and you paid the rent. In a few states, you must deposit any withheld amounts in a special **escrow account.** The money in the account will be returned to you if the landlord does not make the repairs.

The basic difficulty with using this remedy is determining how much rent to withhold. Often, the decision is made by a court because usually, when rent is withheld, a landlord tries to evict the tenant for nonpayment of rent or asks a court to order the tenant to pay back rent. The court reviews the condition of the property and decides whether the amount withheld was correct. Generally, the court considers how much the defective condition affects the habitability of the property. There is no penalty for withholding too much rent if you act in good faith. If the court determines that you withheld too much, you pay the difference to the landlord.

SUE THE LANDLORD You can sue your landlord anytime you believe that the implied warranty of habitability has been breached. In your suit, you can ask the court for any of the following remedies:

1. A declaration of your rights and remedies in the relationship with your landlord.
2. An order to the landlord to pay you money for any injury to you or any damage to your property.
3. An order to the landlord to fix the condition of the property or to stop doing whatever it is that makes the property uninhabitable.

Before asking a court for relief, you should be aware that a court will usually declare parties' rights and remedies, but courts are reluctant to order landlords to do something or to stop doing something when constant supervision is required to ensure that the orders are followed. Also, although a lawsuit is always a possible course of action, it is not always economical.

If a serious dispute develops between you and your landlord, and the dispute cannot be resolved, you may take the matter to court. In some circumstances, this may be required. In most cases and in most states, the appropriate court is a small claims court. When taking a matter to small claims court, you should keep the following points in mind:

1. In many states, no attorney is necessary. In some states, an attorney cannot appear on behalf of a client in small claims court. Assistance can be obtained from the clerk of the court or some other designated official.
2. The proper party must be notified about the suit. You may know only the resident manager of the property, not the actual owner, or you may know the owner only as the name of a corporation. An owner's name may be available through the local tax assessor's office or the county clerk.
3. All relevant documents should be kept available for the court. These may include a copy of the lease, rent receipts, an inventory of the condition of the premises taken before you moved in, canceled checks, receipts and estimates for repairs, and notes taken during any negotiations between you and your landlord.
4. You might be able to recover attorneys' fees, if an attorney was consulted and paid. In some cases, you may recover double or triple the amount of a security deposit wrongfully retained by your landlord. For more information about small claims courts, see the discussion of consumer law later in this *Handbook*.

Retaliatory Eviction

Retaliatory eviction occurs if your landlord evicts you for complaining to a government agency about the condition of the property. If you can prove that your landlord's primary purpose in evicting or attempting to evict you is retaliation for reporting violations—of a housing or sanitation code, for example—you may be entitled to stop the eviction proceedings or collect damages. This can be difficult to prove, unless your landlord admits his or her purpose in a note, in a statement to another person, or in testimony to a court.

In many states, a landlord is presumed to be acting in retaliation if the eviction proceedings are begun within a certain period of time (six to twelve months, in some states) after a tenant has contacted a government agency. In this case, the landlord must prove that he or she did not have a retaliatory purpose. If your landlord shows that you did not pay the rent or that you violated the lease, you could be evicted. If you win, however, you can stay on the premises.

When your lease comes up for renewal, the landlord may raise the rent to help cover the cost of the repairs. Your landlord cannot raise the rent simply to punish you for reporting the violations, however. In most of the states that protect tenants from retaliatory eviction, courts would consider this retaliatory and subject to the same limitations as a retaliatory eviction.

∎ Rent

The primary obligation of the tenant is to pay the agreed-upon rent at the time specified. You retain this obligation even after you have subleased the apartment. If the sublessee fails to pay, your lease obliges you to make payment. Rent is typically due on a certain date of the month. If payments are late, the landlord may charge interest for being late. Most leases provide that if rent is late by more than a certain amount, you will be charged a penalty fee. The amount and nature of this fee must be specified in the lease. The amount must also be reasonable. One Vermont case held that a dollar-a-day charge for late rent payments was excessive.

Raising the Rent

As a general rule, your landlord cannot raise your rent during the term of your lease. An exception would exist if the lease itself provides some procedure for rent increases during its term. Such a provision is typically called an **escalation clause,** which permits periodic increases that usually are based upon rising costs for fuel or building upkeep.

After a lease expires, you may continue, with the landlord's consent, renting on a month-to-month basis. This means that the terms of the old lease continue in operation but can be terminated at any time either by you or the landlord (usually with one month's or thirty days' notice). Alternatively, you may execute a new lease with your landlord, who may require a higher rental payment. This is a matter to be negotiated.

Rent Control

While landlords may generally charge whatever the market will bear, many large cities have rent control laws that restrain rent increases. These ordinances place limits on how much rent can be raised by landlords, even after a lease expires. Rent can be increased only by a set percentage, which may be tied to the cost of living. Because the existence and substance of these ordinances vary from place to place and can change over time, those renting property should become familiar with their local laws.

∎ Security Deposits

Before renting an apartment, you probably will be required to make a **security deposit** in an amount such as one month's rent. The landlord holds this money during your lease to protect against damage that you may do to the property. Theoretically, you recover this deposit when you move out of the apartment. All security deposits must be potentially refundable. If you caused more damage than covered by your security deposit, the landlord may sue you for the remainder.

Use of the Security Deposit

You may lose your security deposit if the landlord requires the money to repair damages that you have done to the premises. The security deposit is not applied to **ordinary wear and tear.** This term applies to ordinary deterioration of an apartment over time, such as fading paint, carpet wear, etc. The landlord may take your security deposit for larger damages, such as permanent stains or cigarette burns in carpeting, broken appliances or window frames, or holes punched in walls. Even a small hole to hang a picture might permit withholding (though repair costs would be quite small). Some landlords might attempt to use your security deposit to recover fees for late payment of rent, but this is illegal in most states.

Protecting Your Security Deposit

When you attempt to recover your security deposit, a dispute may arise over the nature of damages and the condition of the apartment when you moved in. The following steps will help you protect your deposit:

1. Get a receipt for the amount of the deposit.
2. Before moving in, make a list of existing defects or problems and provide a copy of the list to your landlord.
3. Before moving out, clean the apartment and repair damages insofar as possible.

4.   Before moving out, inspect the apartment yourself along with the landlord or other witness.
5.   After moving out, leave a forwarding address and your keys to the apartment with the landlord.

You might also ask your landlord for interest on your deposit during your lease. This is required only in a few states.

Withholding Your Deposit

The landlord may decide to withhold some of your security deposit for repairs. Most jurisdictions require the landlord to provide you with an itemized list of repairs and their costs. In many states, to avoid a penalty, the landlord must provide this list or refund the deposit within thirty days of the date that you moved out and gave the landlord a forwarding address. If the landlord does not do this, he or she may forfeit the right to withhold any of your security deposit.

You may dispute your landlord's assessment. You may file suit against your landlord for withholding your deposit, probably in small claims court. You can question either the need for the repairs or whether the cost of the repairs was reasonable.

▌Liability for Injuries

What if a guest of yours is injured while in your apartment? The guest might sue the landlord, or you, or both. Either one of you could be liable.

Common Areas

Liability for injuries in apartments depends on who has legal control over the area in question. **Common areas** are under the control of the landlord, who will be liable for injuries in this area. If your guest trips over a defective stair step on the way to your apartment, the landlord is liable and you probably are not. The landlord may also be responsible for slippery surfaces, inadequate lighting, or rotting wood.

Structural Defects

Even if the injury occurs inside your apartment, the landlord may be liable. A defective water heater or outside railing, for example, is within the landlord's control. Similarly, if the landlord undertakes certain repairs in your apartment and performs the repairs negligently, the landlord is responsible for resultant damages.

Tenant Liability

You are potentially liable for certain injuries occurring within your apartment. You have some control over this area and are responsible for maintaining its safe condition. You are responsible for any injuries resulting from your furnishings or from your misuse of apartment fixtures, such as lights or plumbing. You may purchase renters' insurance to cover this liability, as well as to insure against the damage, loss, or destruction of your belongings.

▌Lockouts

If a dispute with your landlord has reached an extreme level, your landlord may lock you out of your apartment and seize your possessions. In the vast majority of states, such lockouts are unlawful. The laws provide that a tenant has a right to notice and a hearing, but some landlords continue to conduct illegal lockouts. If you suffer an illegal lockout, you should call the police and complain of a criminal trespass and conversion of your personal property. If the police are unhelpful, you can get an attorney to obtain an order recovering possession. You may recover all your costs from the landlord and may continue to pursue a tort action.

In lieu of a lockout, the landlord may conduct a **utility shutoff,** in an effort to force you off the premises. This action is also illegal, and states provide both civil and criminal penalties against the offending landlord. As with a lockout, you may need to go to court to enforce your rights and get your utilities turned back on.

Topic 2   **Family Law**

Families ideally work out their relationships internally and settle their own problems without resorting to legal process. In reality, however, courts often become involved in family disputes. Moreover, the law establishes a basic framework through which parties may voluntarily resolve their disputes without going before a judge.

∎ Getting Married

The decision to get married has changed in recent decades. Couples are more frequently living together, or cohabiting, without first marrying. This is generally legal, though some states have normally unenforced laws prohibiting extramarital cohabitation. Most couples still get married and there are some practical advantages to marriage. Married couples may have an easier time obtaining insurance, credit, etc. Married partners, upon divorce, are more likely to receive child custody. Married couples also have more adoption opportunities. Many companies offer health insurance to spouses but not to unmarried partners.

Engagement

There are few legal requirements governing engagement. Traditionally, one left at the altar could sue a fiancé for breach of promise to marry. Today, most states have done away with this cause of action. If an engagement is broken, the law probably would force the party to return certain gifts, such as engagement rings, shower gifts, etc.

Marriage Requirements

States place some limitations upon who may marry. The betrothed must be man and woman, currently unmarried, not closely related by blood, and over a certain age (often eighteen). State laws differ, and some actually prohibit marriages among those closely related even if the relation is only by marriage. Those who are underage may marry with parental consent or if judicially emancipated from their parents. Below a certain age, such as fourteen or sixteen, marriage may be absolutely prohibited by state law except with court approval.

Marriage Ceremony

Certain procedures are generally required for a legally recognized marriage. The parties must first obtain a marriage license from the state government. Some states also require a blood test, in which the government checks for diseases, such as venereal diseases. Some states require a waiting period before getting the license or between the time of acquiring the license and officially getting married. In thirteen states and the District of Columbia, a license is the only requirement for a marriage.

In the other thirty-seven states, some form of marriage ceremony is also required. The parties must present the license to someone authorized to perform marriages (a state official or member of the clergy). The ceremony must involve a public statement of agreement to marriage. The remainder of the ceremony is generally within the couple's discretion. After the ceremony, the marriage license must be recorded.

Common Law Marriage

About fifteen states recognize a **common law marriage,** a procedure by which parties become married without a license or ceremony. There are four general requirements for a common law marriage:

1. The parties must be eligible to marry.
2. The parties must have a present and continuing intention and agreement to be husband and wife.
3. The parties must live together as husband and wife.
4. The parties must hold themselves out to the public as husband and wife.

There are a number of misapprehensions about common law marriage. Cohabitation alone cannot produce a common law marriage; the parties must additionally hold themselves out to others as husband and wife. There is no minimum time period required for a common law marriage. The parties may become married as soon as they both live as husband and wife and hold themselves out to the public as married.

There is no common law divorce. Once a couple is regarded as married—and particularly once a court has recognized them as married by common law—they must obtain a court decree to dissolve the marriage.

Duties of Marriage

The law considers marriage to be a form of contract, and historically the marriage contract came complete with a full set of duties for the husband and wife. Formerly, the husband had the duty to be the provider, and could not purchase luxuries for himself until the family was provided with necessities. The wife had certain duties in the home. Times have changed, and courts today enforce few duties arising from the marriage contract. Spouses are generally allowed to arrange their own affairs however they see fit.

The law still holds that a spouse has a duty of financial support, providing such basics as food, shelter, and medical care, insofar as he or she is able. In many states, this duty lasts throughout the marriage, even if the spouses are living apart. Failure to provide support for a child may be a criminal violation. (In non-community property states, except for these basics, one spouse is not responsible for the debts of the other spouse unless he or she is ordered to pay them as part of a divorce decree.)

Additional duties may be created by a separate agreement between the spouses. Some decisions have held that a spouse may not deny sexual relations without good cause, though courts are becoming more hesitant to enforce such a requirement.

Traditional common law provided for **interspousal immunity.** This means that one spouse could not sue the other for torts, such as assault and battery. Most states now have modified this law and permit one spouse to sue the other for at least intentional torts. Interspousal immunity still means that one partner may not be required to testify against a spouse in court, though a spouse may voluntarily so testify. An increasing number of states recognizes the crime of marital rape.

It is, of course, illegal to batter a spouse. Unlawful abuse has been extended to include extreme cases of harassment and threats of physical beating or confinement. A victim of spousal battering should call the police and may seek other legal protection against the abuser, including an emergency restraining order, which requires the abusing spouse to stay away from the victim. Many shelters are available to assist an abused spouse.

Financial Aspects of Marriage

Prenuptial Agreements

Brides and grooms are increasingly bringing substantial assets into a marriage, which has led to greater use of the **prenuptial,** or premarital, **agreement.** A prenuptial agreement is a contract between the parties entered into before the wedding occurs. Such an agreement generally provides for disposition of property in the event of the divorce or death of one spouse. One typical use of a prenuptial agreement would be to guarantee that children from a previous marriage receive a certain share of their parent's estate. Prenuptial agreements must be in writing to be enforceable.

There are certain advantages to prenuptial agreements. Such contracts enable the parties to settle possible disagreements in advance and provide some long-term financial certainty to the parties. Note, though, that prenuptial agreements are criticized for evincing a lack of mutual trust and for being unromantic. Such agreements may even prove unfair to a spouse in the event of divorce.

As with any contract, prenuptial agreements are presumptively valid but are not always so. While traditional courts refused to recognize prenuptial agreements, most states now uphold such contracts, even if they eliminate financial support in the event of divorce. Courts do look closely at the agreement for evidence of unfairness. There are several circumstances when courts have refused to enforce prenuptial agreements, such as:

● When the agreement would so impoverish the spouse as to make him or her eligible for welfare.
● When there was unfair bargaining at the time of the agreement, such as a failure to disclose all money and property assets.
● When one party was not represented by counsel.
● When the agreement was entered into immediately

before the marriage (such agreements should be made weeks or months in advance).

In general, a party must show that the prenuptial agreement was made voluntarily and without threats or unfair pressure.

Property Ownership

Separate property is property that a spouse owned before the marriage, plus inheritances and gifts acquired during the marriage. This property belongs to the spouse personally and not to the marital unit. Upon dissolution of the marriage, separate property is not divided but retained by the owner.

The separate property right may be lost during marriage, however. If the couple combines separate property with that acquired during the marriage, the two properties may be merged into jointly held property. Suppose that a wife owns a lot on which the couple builds a house after their marriage. The wife has lost her separate property rights in the land. Merely renovating a separately held property (e.g., sprucing up a vacation home) may transform the separate property into joint property. Placing separate property into a jointly held bank account may also transform the money into joint property. The separate property issue is important even if the couple is happy and trusting. For example, a wife's creditors may not attach her husband's separate property but may reach at least a portion of jointly held property.

The converse of separate property occurs when one spouse brings debts into the marriage. In most states, you are not liable for your spouse's premarital debts. In community property states (described below), under certain circumstances, a spouse may become liable for premarital debts.

Ten jurisdictions (Arizona, California, Idaho, Louisiana, Nebraska, New Mexico, Texas, Washington, Wisconsin, and Puerto Rico) have the system known as **community property.** In these jurisdictions, each spouse shares equally in all income earned and most property acquired during the marriage. This is true even if one party supplied all the income and assets. The community property system is significant both for creditors and for the parties upon divorce. In community property states, one spouse may encumber the other with debts. In other states, one party generally may not incur debts for the other.

Separation and Divorce

Divorce is generally preceded by a separation period. Such separation may be due to abandonment or may be through mutual consent. States may require a separation period prior to granting a divorce.

A divorce is a formal court proceeding used to legally dissolve a marriage. Divorce laws vary considerably among the states, with some having much easier procedures. All states provide for some form of **no-fault divorce.** This eliminates the requirement that divorce be justified by some demonstrable reason, such as abuse or abandonment. The most common basis for a no-fault divorce is irreconcilable differences. No-fault divorce laws make it practically impossible for one spouse to prevent a divorce desired by the other. Even in these states, courts may look to fault in deciding financial settlements between the parties.

Lawyers are not strictly required for a divorce proceeding. Most states permit "do-it-yourself divorces," sometimes called *pro se* **divorces.** In this process, the individuals handle everything themselves before the court. Couples can obtain the necessary forms at the local courthouse (or in form books). If a significant amount of money is at stake, however, the divorcing spouses should obtain professional legal and accounting advice.

Most divorces are not actually tried in court. Only about ten percent of divorces go to trial. The parties typically settle their outstanding claims, though often only after lengthy negotiations. Divorcing spouses increasingly use **mediation** to settle disagreements. A mediator is typically trained and meets with the parties in the absence of lawyers. The mediator does not make decisions but tries to prod the parties into a mutually acceptable agreement.

In a divorce settlement, some written agreement is reached on contested issues, such as property settlement, child custody, continued support, etc. This agreement must be presented to the court for its approval. The court may disapprove the agreement as unconscionable (extremely unfair), though this is very rare. If only one side of the divorce had legal representation, courts will scrutinize settlement agreements more closely.

An **annulment** is more than a divorce and means that the marriage was never effective in the first place. Annulment may be available if the marriage is based upon fraud, if the marriage was unconsummated, if there was **bigamy,** and for a limited set of other reasons. Obtaining an annulment is especially significant for those belonging to certain religions (such as Catholicism) in order for a person to remarry.

Property Division and Alimony

Although most divorcing parties settle their financial disputes, this settlement is colored by the requirements of the law. Whether the state has community property laws or not, the court may divide marital property without respect to formal papers of ownership. Judges have almost unlimited discretion in deciding which person receives what property, as long as the division is reasonably equitable.

Courts divide marital property and, in most circumstances, separate property remains with the owner.

When deciding how to divide the common property, however, judges consider the existence of the separate property and its effect on the wealth and needs of the divorcing spouses. Retirement benefits are generally considered to be marital property, divided between the spouses. In community property states, the property is presumptively split equally. Judges may change this division to suit the circumstances, however. Courts use a variety of standards in considering how to divide property, including the following:

- The duration of the marriage.
- The health of the parties.
- The individuals' occupations and vocational skills.
- The individuals' relative wealth and income.
- The standard of living during the marriage.
- The relative contributions to the marriage, both financially and in homemaker contributions.
- Needs and concerns of any children.
- Tax and inheritance considerations.

Marital debts must also be divided according to similar criteria.

A typical property controversy in divorce cases concerns rights to the marital residence. If there are minor children, the house is usually given to the parent with custody of the children. It may be difficult to balance the grant of the house with other property (many families have few substantial assets other than their homes). Once the children are grown, the court may order the house to be sold and the proceeds divided.

Alimony is money paid for support of the former spouse. Historically, the husband was the wage earner and was expected to pay alimony to his former wife, to permit her to maintain her standard of living. There are well-known cases involving wealthy entertainers, such as former NBC late-night T.V. host Johnny Carson, who have been directed to pay their ex-wives (or, in a few cases, ex-husbands) hundreds of thousands of dollars in annual alimony. Alimony ends when the recipient remarries.

The law of alimony is changing. One common form of alimony today is called **rehabilitative support.** Rather than providing indefinite support payments, rehabilitative support is designed to provide the ex-spouse with the education, training, or job experience necessary to support himself or herself. This form of alimony assists spouses who devoted their lives to homemaking or who left lucrative opportunities because of the marriage. Such rehabilitative support may only last for a limited period, particularly if the spouse finds a good job. Such temporary rehabilitative support has been criticized, because many divorcees are of an age that hampers their prospects of developing a new career. Many courts still award permanent support, if the recipient's earning prospects are far less than those of the wealthier spouse or if the recipient is of relatively advanced age. About half the states also consider fault in the divorce as a factor in awarding spousal support such as alimony. Alimony may be modified as the parties' situations change.

A common controversy involves one spouse supporting another through graduate school (such as law or medical school), followed by a divorce. The supporting spouse may claim a share of the income subsequently earned by the supported spouse as a lawyer or a doctor. Courts have been hesitant to grant the supporting spouse some property right in the advanced or professional degree obtained by the other spouse but have awarded payments to compensate for the supporting spouse's contributions to the education. One New York decision did hold that an academic degree earned by the husband was marital property.

Palimony

Palimony is a common but nonlegal name for claims made by a member of an unmarried couple after they have split up. After cohabiting for years, a partner may claim some interest in the other's property. There is no statutory provision for such a claim, and courts have been reluctant to recognize an automatic right to palimony. Unmarried couples may enter a contract that specifies legal rights should they break up. Such contracts may be valid, but courts have tended to scrutinize them closely for legality. These contracts should be in writing, although this is not strictly required at law. The California Supreme Court has held that a contract between a cohabiting couple may even be implied from conduct or unspoken understandings. Other states, such as Illinois, are unwilling to recognize palimony actions. Palimony may be especially important for homosexual couples, who are barred from marrying legally.

Child Custody

The most contentious issue in many divorces is child custody—the right to live with and to care for the children on an everyday basis. Traditionally, the mother almost always received custody. Forty-four states have now adopted the Uniform Marriage and Divorce Act, which governs custody determinations. Mothers still usually receive custody, but courts now explicitly consider a list of factors, including:

- The wishes of the child.
- The nature of the relationship and emotional ties with each parent.
- The ability and interest of the parents in providing for the child's needs and education.
- Any required adjustments to a new house or community.

- The stability of the family relationship.

Family stability is probably the most important factor. Some recent decisions have put increased emphasis on whether one parent was a smoker, because secondary smoke may damage the child's lungs. Courts may appoint a **guardian** *ad litem,* usually an attorney, who directly represents the child's interests in court. Custody decisions are not permanent and may be changed by a court.

The noncustodial parent generally receives visitation rights. The parent may get to spend weekends or other time periods with the child. Visitation is denied in extreme cases, such as child abuse or when there is a reasonable fear of child snatching by the noncustodial parent.

The court may provide a system of **joint custody,** which many states now prefer. Joint legal custody means that both parents together make major decisions about the child. Some procedure, such as mediation, is available in the event of disagreement. In some states, including California, mediation is mandatory in child custody disputes. This may also involve joint physical custody, in which both parents maintain a home for the child and have roughly comparable time with the child.

Regardless of the custody arrangements, a court must make some provision for financial **child support.** Child support obligations arise even if the parents were never married. States have official guidelines to determine child support duties. These guidelines are often percentage formulas based on parental income. Judges must follow the guidelines, unless special facts justify a departure. Children with particularly large needs (for example, the disabled) may require a greater support award.

It is a common misconception that if one ex-spouse fails to meet his or her obligations under a divorce decree or other court order (such as withholding visitation rights), the other party can withhold payment of child support. Child support is a separate court order—it cannot be withheld because an ex-spouse does something that the other ex-spouse does not like. (What a parent can do is ask the court to modify a decree in some way.) A large number of noncustodial parents are failing to make their child support payments, and states are providing for automatic withholding of support payments from the wages of the parent. Child support orders may also be revised and adjusted according to need and ability to pay. The Uniform Reciprocal Enforcement of Support Act assists states in recovering support payments from parents living in other states. The failure to make child support payments is a crime.

▌ Children

The decision whether to have children is a central part of the family relationship. The law of childbearing has become increasingly complex with the advent of new arrangements, such as surrogate parenthood and artificial insemination. The law here is still unsettled. Within a marriage, the decision to have children obviously should be mutually reached. The woman ultimately has the right to use contraceptive devices or to go ahead and bear a child, and she does not need to obtain the husband's permission.

Paternity

If a couple is married, the law presumes that any newborn child is the husband's, and he must support the child unless he can prove that he is not the biological father. Some states do not even allow the husband an opportunity to prove his lack of paternity. An unmarried mother may file a suit to establish the **paternity** of her child. If the unwed mother is on public welfare aid, the government may file a paternity suit to be reimbursed.

The paternity of a child may be proved scientifically. Science has advanced beyond historically used blood tests and now uses DNA testing or comparable procedures that check for genetic factors. Such tests reportedly are 98 to 99 percent accurate in determining parenthood. The biological father of the child has a legal obligation to provide support, regardless of marital status. These obligations are just as great as for married fathers and are determined by the child support guidelines of the state. The obligations usually last until the child is no longer a minor. The mother's subsequent marriage to another man does not necessarily extinguish the child support obligations of the biological father.

While all biological fathers have an obligation to provide child support regardless of marital status, children born out of wedlock still suffer disadvantages. Legally, an illegitimate child has no presumptive right to inherit as an heir of the father. An increasing number of children are born to unmarried parents (about one-third of all first births). In response, the law is evolving to provide added rights and protections to children born out of wedlock. Courts have held that the government cannot discriminate against illegitimate children and that such children have a right to recover damages for the deaths of their parents. In most states, the eventual marriage of the parents "legitimizes" a previous child of theirs.

Adoption

Adoption is a procedure in which persons become the official legal parents of a child that is not their biological child. Adoption may be contrasted with **foster care,** which is a temporary arrangement in which a family is paid by the state to care for a child over a limited time period, often pending adoption. There are three minimum requirements for an adoption to be legal:

1. The legal rights of the biological parents must have been terminated by death or judicial decree.
2. The adopting parents must follow all procedures required by the state of adoption.
3. The adoption must be formally approved by a judge.

There may be additional requirements in specific circumstances. For example, adopting a teenage child generally requires the child's official consent.

Adoption is often done through a public or private agency that has received authority to agree to the adoption of children in its custody. The biological parents may convey the authority to the agency to find legal parents for their child. The agency investigates potential adopters and chooses a set of parents. In other circumstances, potential parents may pursue independent adoption, when a doctor or lawyer or other individual puts adopting parents together with a pregnant woman who must give up her child. These parties make their own private arrangements, which usually involve the adopting parents paying for the legal and medical expenses associated with childbirth and adoption. The intermediary also generally receives a fee. This approach has the potential for abuse and is prohibited by some states. There is a growing number of black market adoptions from developing nations (such as China and Romania).

Even entirely independent adoptions must be approved in court. The primary standard for approving an adoption is the best interests of the child. The court (and applicable private agency) considers the financial resources of the adopting parents, their family stability and home environment, their ages, religious and racial compatibility, and other factors relevant to the child's future health and welfare. Most states permit single persons to adopt, though married couples are generally preferred.

After the adoption, many states place the new parents on probation for a time. This period is usually from six months to one year. The agency or court appoints an individual to ensure that the adoptive parents are caring appropriately for the child's well-being. If not, the child may be removed and returned to an agency for placement in another home.

Once an adoption is formally completed, the adoptive parents have all the responsibilities of biological parents. Should they divorce, each adoptive parent still has all the child support obligations associated with biological parents. Depending on the state, the child may retain some legal connection with the biological parents, such as inheritance rights upon their deaths. The adopted child also has rights of inheritance from the adoptive parents.

Children's Rights

The law has special concern for children. Legally, a child is an unmarried minor (under the age of eighteen), who is not emancipated. **Emancipation** occurs when children leave home to support themselves. Parents have duties toward their children to provide food, shelter, clothing, medical care, and other necessities. Parents must also ensure that their children attend school (normally until the age of sixteen). Parents are prohibited from abusing or neglecting their children. Parental duties to children generally end at age eighteen, but these duties may continue longer if the child is seriously disabled.

Along with these duties, parents have certain rights of control over children. Parents can direct the upbringing of their children and control where they live, what school they attend, and even what religion they practice. Parents also generally control the medical care to be given, though parents' refusal to provide for such care in life-threatening situations (usually for religious reasons) can be a crime. Parents have broad legal authority to control the behavior of their children, though this lessens as the children age and become more mature. Parents may punish children but not excessively.

Historically, children could not sue their parents for negligence, due to a governmental interest in family harmony. Today, most states permit such lawsuits, which are generally covered by insurance. The traditional common law rule was that parents were not liable for the tortious actions of their children. About half the states now provide partial parental liability for their children's intentional torts, up to a limit of about $10,000 (depending upon the state).

Child Abuse and Neglect

All states have laws that prohibit the abuse and neglect of children by their parents or others. Child abuse primarily covers severe physical beatings and sexual molestation of minors by anyone. Child abuse may even extend to emotional abuse, when a person publicly humiliates a child in an extreme way. Child neglect occurs when parents or legal guardians fail to provide for basic needs, such as food, shelter, clothing, and medical treatment. Laws now require doctors and social workers to report suspected cases of child abuse.

In serious cases of child abuse or neglect, the government may remove the child from his or her parents. Ideally, this is temporary and the objective is to reunite the family after the parents' problems have been corrected through counseling or otherwise. If the parents are unrepentant, the state may ask the court to terminate all parental rights and make the children available for adoption.

▌ Wills and Estates

In a marriage, each spouse should have a will. State intestacy laws provide that surviving spouses automatically inherit a share of a decedent's property. These laws apply if a person dies **intestate** (without a will). The adjudication of inheritance rights is known as **probate**, and legal probate battles may be protracted and costly. If there is no will, a court will appoint someone to manage the estate. Couples also should revise the terms of their wills to take advantage of changes in the tax laws and the changing needs of their heirs. A will is even more important for unmarried couples. An unmarried partner has no automatic right to assets on death and will inherit only if provided for in a will.

In the absence of a will, the deceased's property is distributed according to a state's intestate succession law. The surviving spouse has a legal right to a certain share of the estate (usually one-third or one-half, depending upon the state). In the absence of a will, children also have a right to a share of the property.

When there is a will, the law restricts its terms in order to protect the surviving family. A married person cannot will an entire estate to charity, for example. The surviving spouse has a right to what is known as the **elective share.** The elective share is a certain guaranteed minimum of the deceased's estate. It is called elective, because the spouse may choose to take what is provided in the will or may elect the minimum share specified by state law. A spouse may lose this elective share option if he or she signed the deceased's will. A child may be disinherited, even when he or she is a minor, and thereby be denied a share of the deceased parent's estate. Such disinheritance must be clearly intended, however. Mere failure to mention a child in the will does not constitute disinheritance. In limited circumstances, the contents of a will may be challenged by potential heirs.

Some families partially avoid probate and wills by using a **living trust.** The living trust is a device in which a person known as the **trustee** holds legal title to property and manages it in the interest of named beneficiaries of the trust. A wife might establish such a trust with herself and her husband as beneficiaries for life. After her death, her husband may receive the property directly or continue the trust, with himself as beneficiary. The latter option requires appointment of a new trustee. The trust option may allow greater flexibility than a will and also avoid certain taxes.

▌ Homosexual Families

Some of the most controversial family law topics involve gay or lesbian families. Many homosexual couples live in stable, long-term relationships. They may wish to formally recognize their relationships through a wedding ceremony. No state legally recognizes such same-sex marriages, although Hawaii may soon pass legislation allowing such marriages. Gays and lesbians may hold what have become known as "commitment ceremonies," which are similar to marriage ceremonies. Such commitment ceremonies do not invoke the legal protections surrounding marriage, however. There is no legal provision for community property or alimony in such cases. Homosexual couples may provide for similar protections through a contract.

Some homosexual couples wish to adopt children, though this can be difficult. Two states, Florida and New Hampshire, have explicitly prohibited homosexual adoptions, but some local Florida courts have struck down that state's law as being unconstitutional. Even in the absence of such a law, an Ohio judge held in 1988 that gays and lesbians were ineligible to adopt. Despite the roadblocks, over two hundred homosexual couples have successfully adopted children. Gays and lesbians are also at a disadvantage in child custody battles that follow a divorce.

Topic 3   **Consumer Law**

The typical American undertakes hundreds of consumer transactions every year. Most such purchases prove ordinary and uncontroversial, but an occasional purchase goes awry. The product may be worthless or even dangerous. In these instances, the consumer may need the protection of the law. The traditional common law embraced the doctrine of *caveat emptor*, meaning "let the buyer beware." Consumers had little recourse when purchases went sour. Today, there is an increasing number of consumer protection laws.

▌The Consumer Contract

Whenever you purchase groceries or any other product, you enter a contract. Although grocery shopping does not involve a formal written contract, such purchases are contracts and are governed by the principles of contract law. Consumer purchases must meet all of the requirements of a contract in order to be binding on you and the seller. Most purchases easily satisfy the main requirements of contract law and present no loopholes for escaping a deal. An exception exists when a purchaser is a minor. The general rule is that a minor (someone under eighteen years of age) may disavow and escape a contract even after it has been completed.

Fraud

You can escape a contract if you were fraudulently induced into making the contract. Fraud requires proof of the following elements:

1. A misrepresentation of material fact.
2. An intent to deceive.
3. Justifiable reliance.

A seller who lies about the attributes of a product to make a sale may commit fraud. You must distinguish fraudulent lying from **puffing,** which refers to the seller's qualitative statements about the product. A seller who promises that its product is "of great quality" or "fantastic" is merely puffing about the product. To show fraud you would have to demonstrate a more specific statement of fact, such as a false statement about the number of miles on a used car. If you can prove fraud, you may either rescind (escape) the contract or collect the damages that you suffered as a consequence of the fraud.

Unconscionability

The law ordinarily does not look into the fairness of contracts. It is the responsibility of the parties to obtain the best deal for themselves. Courts usually will not strike down contracts simply for unfairness. A limited exception exists for **unconscionability,** which means such extreme unfairness as to "shock the conscience" of a court. Courts can refuse to enforce unconscionable contracts.

Unconscionability may be found when there is a great disparity of bargaining power. Such disparity may arise with **contracts of adhesion.** These exist when a seller presents you with a "take-it-or-leave-it" form contract and refuses to negotiate over the terms on the form. You have little bargaining power in this circumstance. Note that not all contracts of adhesion are unconscionable—you could simply walk away from the deal. If circumstances force you to make a contract and you cannot bargain over the terms, and if those terms seem manifestly unfair to you, the contract may be deemed unconscionable.

▌ Warranties

Most products that you purchase will come with some form of warranty or promise regarding the quality of the product. If the product does not meet the warranted standard, you have a right to a remedy. Generally this remedy is readily provided by the manufacturer or retailer, but in some cases you may need to go to court. Warranties may come in several forms.

Express Warranties

An **express warranty** is any explicit factual assurance about a product. The express warranty may be a written promise of quality and performance or may be an oral assurance from a salesperson. An express warranty may even be visual. If the retailer shows you a model of the product, it is creating an express warranty that the item purchased will conform to that model. Of course, a written warranty is easier to enforce in court. You should also be aware that puffing does not create a warranty but is merely sales talk.

Many warranties contain a specific remedy should something go wrong with the product. A **full warranty** means that the product will be repaired or replaced free of charge within a reasonable time, or else you will receive a refund. Even a full warranty does not provide absolute protection, because the warranty will also set forth terms and conditions. For example, a microwave oven may be under full warranty for 180 days. After that time you are unprotected. A limited warranty provides even less protection. A limited warranty might provide for repair but not a refund. Moreover, to take advantage of such a warranty you may have to deliver or mail the product to a designated site.

Beware of disclaimers. Even after a salesperson makes detailed promises about a product, you may be expected to sign a written contract that disclaims all express warranties. Although this may seem unfair, it is a legal practice and can nullify anything that the salesperson said, as well as eliminate any other warranty protection. Disclaimers are discussed below. Be sure to read any warranty and understand your rights before you make a purchase.

Implied Warranties

Many consumer contracts come with implied warranties that automatically come with the product. These warranties protect you even if the salesperson made no promises about the product. The law implies these warranties in sales of goods. Implied warranties of merchantability are created only by sellers who are merchants. Thus, a garage sale in your neighborhood would not include such a warranty.

The **implied warranty of merchantability** means that your purchase will be of at least average quality for that type of product and will perform its intended function. This means that if you buy a camera, it will successfully take pictures. The **implied warranty of fitness** applies when the salesperson helps you select a product for a particular purpose. If you inform the retailer of your purpose and rely on him or her to choose a suitable product, the company warrants that the product is suited for that purpose. If you ask for an underwater camera, the product a salesperson picks out must function under water. The **implied warranty of title** simply means that the seller warrants that he or she is the owner (or authorized agent) of the item for sale.

Disclaimers

Companies may choose to disclaim warranties or to limit their potential liability. The disclaimer may bluntly declare that there are no warranties on the product or may state that your only remedy is repair or replacement of the product. Merchants may even disclaim the implied warranties discussed above, but they must use specific and conspicuous language to do so. The implied warranties of merchantability and fitness may be disclaimed by declaring that the product is sold "as is." This language is understood to state that the product is being sold with possible flaws and that the buyer assumes the risk of the flaws.

Most disclaimers are legally effective and prevent you from claiming breach of warranty, but many disclaimers must be conspicuous (for example, in capital letters on the front page of the contract) or in clear and understandable language to be effective. In any event, you are expected to read the contract and be aware of any disclaimers.

▌ Product Liability

If you are physically injured by a product, you may bring a product liability action. Under modern law, you may sue even if you did not personally purchase the product that injured you. This is the doctrine of **strict product liability.**

Under strict product liability, you need not prove that the manufacturer was negligent or careless, but you must show that the product contained a defect causing an unreasonable danger. Suppose that you received from your toaster a nasty shock that required medical attention. You might recover these damages in strict product liability. You could not get a new toaster, however. You cannot recover if you or anyone else altered the product after it was purchased.

You may recover product liability damages in negligence, though negligence tends to be difficult to prove. A breach of warranty action may also be available for unsafe products. Warranties often are limited to the actual purchasers of the product or family members, however. Warranty actions are limited by the scope of the warranty and any disclaimers.

▌ Deceptive Sales Practices

Most of the protections discussed above are limited by the sales contract. In recent years, many legislatures have passed statutes that provide further protection to consumers against a variety of deceptive sales practices used by merchants.

Bait and Switch

Bait and switch is a sales tactic that has been outlawed. The typical bait-and-switch scheme begins with a store advertising a popular product at an extremely low price. This is the "bait." Consumers see the advertisement and go to the store to purchase the advertised product. The store informs the consumers that it is sold out of the advertised product or otherwise discourages the sale of this product. Salespersons attempt to convince the consumer to purchase an alternative product that has a higher profit margin (the "switch"). The bait-and-switch scheme lures customers into the store, where they can be persuaded to "buy up" by the salesperson.

The federal government has prohibited bait-and-switch tactics. If you believe that a store is using this method, you should complain to the Federal Trade Commission, which enforces the law. Most states and many local government consumer protection agencies also act against unlawful bait-and-switch tactics.

Note the differences between illegal bait-and-switch scams and legal *loss-leader tactics*. Grocery stores may offer a very low price on milk or some other staple to get you into the store. Their theory is that once you buy the milk, you are also likely to purchase other groceries that have higher markups. You should be aware of this tactic, but as long as the milk is available for your purchase, the tactic is a sound business practice and perfectly legal.

Mail Order Sales

Mail order sales are growing rapidly, as tens of millions of Americans rely on the convenience of ordering at home. Mail order purchases obviously represent some risk to consumers, however, because you don't obtain immediate possession of the product. Some laws have been passed to protect against mail order fraud.

A Federal Trade Commission rule states that the seller must inform you when the purchase will be shipped and must conform to promises about shipping. If no shipping date is given, the merchandise must be sent within thirty days. If the product is not shipped within thirty days, you have a right to cancel the order.

Sometimes, unsolicited products are sent to you by mail. You may treat these as gifts, and you have no obligation to pay for the unrequested merchandise. Sending you a bill for free samples may be mail fraud, which is a federal crime. This rule does not apply if you belong to a club, such as a book-of-the-month club or a record club. When you joined this club, it is likely that you contractually agreed to purchase the month's selection unless you took affirmative action and sent in a card rejecting the selection. If you failed to send in the card, you are legally obligated to pay for the selection shipped.

"Free" Offers

From time to time, you may receive what appear to be remarkable offers for free merchandise. One common form of such offers is a promise that if you visit a condominium complex you will receive one of a selection of valuable-sounding gifts. These offers are seldom as they appear. In one reported case, a person was promised an "all-terrain vehicle," but this proved to be a lawn chair on wheels. You might have a fraud action in response to such an offer, but it is wisest simply to have a healthy skepticism and protect yourself in the first place. Be particularly suspicious if you must pay any money to take advantage of some later offer.

Door-to-Door Sales

Door-to-door sales occur when a salesperson goes from house to house in a neighborhood offering a product. The law offers special protections for consumers in these transactions.

The law establishes a three-day **cooling-off period** for sales made in your home or anywhere that is not a fixed place of business for the seller. Under this rule, you may cancel the contract for any or no reason within three days of entering into the deal. The three-day period does not begin to run until you have been informed of your cooling-off-period rights. There can be no charge for your canceling the deal. If you have already made payment, the salesperson must refund your money in full within ten business days. If you have received the merchandise, you must make it available to be picked up during this time.

In addition to the cooling-off period, federal and state laws dictate that the door-to-door salesperson provide you with certain information on a receipt or otherwise. This information includes:

● A description of the goods or services sold.
● The seller's identity and place of business.

- The amount of money you paid or the value of the goods delivered to you.
- Your cooling-off-period rights.

Consumer Credit

A large proportion of purchases in today's market is made with credit. While use of credit is convenient, the process creates its own legal issues. Several laws have been passed to settle credit issues.

Credit Cards

Most consumers use credit cards for purchases. These cards may be issued by a specific store or may be all-purpose cards, such as Visa or American Express. While such cards make shopping convenient, be sure that you understand how the cards operate.

Many credit cards, such as Visa and Mastercard and most department store credit cards, use a **revolving credit** system. Each month's purchases are added and a bill is sent to you. Many cards grant you a "free ride period," meaning you need not pay interest during the weeks before you receive the bill. You may pay all or a minimum portion of the bill. The remaining unpaid balance represents a loan to you. Be careful about maintaining an unpaid balance on your charge cards. Interest rates charged on credit cards continue to be high, compared with market rates for bank loans. You may end up paying a considerable premium for use of your credit card. Some companies reserve the right to change their interest rates over time.

Some companies, such as American Express, issue cards that do not permit a revolving credit balance and require you to pay off your debts in full every month. If you fail to pay in full on these cards, you will be charged a contractual penalty that may well exceed the high interest rates of charge cards. Many cards also charge an annual fee for possession of the card. You should compare interest rates and other features before choosing a charge card for regular use.

One concern with credit-card ownership is theft. If your card is stolen, the thief could make many purchases and bill them to you. Indeed, a thief does not need your actual card—learning your card number enables such a person to make mail order purchases on your card. Credit-card theft is increasingly common. The law provides some strong protections for the consumer who suffers from credit-card theft.

Under the Truth-in-Lending Act, you have no liability on your credit card unless the granting company has followed required procedures. The credit grantor must prove that you used the card at least once yourself, that the company notified you of your potential liability, and that the company notified you of how to inform the company in the event the card was stolen or lost. Even if the company follows all these requirements, your potential liability is still quite limited.

The law normally restricts your total liability for improper use of your charge cards to $50 per card. Moreover, you have no liability for any charges that occur after you have reported the card as stolen. Consequently, you should report lost or stolen charge cards as soon as you discover them to be missing.

Another potential credit-card problem involves **billing errors.** Billing errors could include being charged for products you did not purchase, mistakes in computations, or failure to give credit for your payments or returned purchases. If you believe that you have discovered a billing error, the Fair Credit Billing Act provides procedures for you to use.

First, notify the credit-card company in writing within sixty days after the bill was mailed to you. Notification must be in writing—telephone calls do not protect your rights under the statute. Be sure to include your account number, the date of the error, and a specification of the nature of the error. The credit-card company must acknowledge your letter or correct the error within thirty days. If the error is not corrected, the company must explain to you within ninety days why it believes the bill to be correct. You may continue to correspond with the company. If you protest the company's explanation within ten days, your credit record will reflect the presence of the dispute. The following table summarizes the time limits of the law.

• Notify company of error—*in writing, sixty days from error*
• Company acknowledgment to you—*thirty days from notification*
• Company correction or final response—*ninety days from notification*
• Your notice of protest—*ten days from final response*

If the company fails to follow the required legal procedures, it cannot collect the first $50 of the disputed amount or finance charges but can bill you for any remainder. If you fail to pay the remainder, the company may institute collection proceedings against you. At this point, your choice may be to pay or to go to court.

If you use a credit card to buy goods that are defective or damaged or services that are poor quality, you may withhold payment for the disputed item. You cannot withhold payment, however, unless you notify the merchant of your complaint at the same time and make a real attempt to resolve the problem with the merchant. If you bought the goods or services with a credit card other than the store's credit card, the right to withhold payment is limited to purchases over $50 that occurred in your state, or outside your state within one hundred miles of your home address.

Credit Reports

After using credit cards or paying off other loans, you will establish a **credit record.** It is important to make payments on time, as this will create a good credit record and make it much easier to obtain a loan in the future. If you have a bad credit record, you may face difficulty getting a loan, even if you are gainfully employed.

Your credit record is summarized on **credit reports** that are maintained by credit bureaus and other companies. Despite your best efforts to pay responsibly, there is a risk that an error in your credit report could make you appear to have an unreliable credit record. To help correct this problem, Congress passed the Fair Credit Reporting Act in 1970.

The Fair Credit Reporting Act requires that those who deny you credit based on credit-bureau information must inform you of the name and address of the credit bureau. If you inquire of the bureau, it must disclose the substance of the information in your file, though you do not have a right to actual copies of the file. If the information in your credit record is inaccurate or incomplete, you can demand that the credit bureau investigate and correct these errors. If the disagreement continues, you can have your position included in your file. If the credit bureau refuses to cooperate at all, you may complain to the Federal Trade Commission, which enforces the act.

Bill Collection Practices

If you have an overdue debt, a company may assign it to a debt collector. This is a person or company that effectively receives a percentage of the debt in exchange for efforts to collect overdue debts. In the past, collection agencies have been quite abusive in their efforts to collect past-due accounts.

In response to past abuses, Congress passed the Fair Debt Collection Practices Act in 1978. This act requires the debt collector to notify you of the following facts within five days of the initial contact:

1. The amount that you owe.
2. To whom you owe the money.
3. That the collector accepts the debt as authentic unless you challenge it within thirty days.
4. What to do if you dispute the debt.

Perhaps you accept that you owe the debt but are simply unable to pay at this time. You may be able to negotiate a payment schedule with the debt collector. The act prohibits a specific series of debt-collection practices, such as:

- Informing employers or others of the debt.
- Using obscene or harassing language.
- Using threats to harm you or your reputation.
- Making harassing telephone calls at inconvenient times.
- Misrepresenting the amount of the debt or the collector's identity.
- Threatening you with imprisonment or garnishment other than that provided at law.

If the debt-collection agency violates these provisions you may sue the collector and recover up to $1,000. You should also inform the Federal Trade Commission, any state or local consumer protection departments, and if appropriate, the telephone company.

You may choose to send a letter to the debt collector telling the agency not to contact you any further. The collector must also stop contacting you if you write within thirty days that you dispute the existence or amount of the debt. The collector may respond by sending you proof of the debt. In any event, the collector still may commence a legal collection action against you for the unpaid debt.

If you are sued for an unpaid debt, you should contact a lawyer or go to a legal aid office if you cannot afford an attorney. You may have defenses to the alleged debt, such as your belief that you purchased a defective product. If the court enters a judgment against you for the debt, it may allow the creditor to seize your nonexempt property in the amount owed and sell it to satisfy the debt. In most states, the court might **garnish** your bank accounts or wages. This permits the creditor automatically to receive a portion of your take-home pay from your employer (up to a maximum of 25 percent).

▌Small Claims Court

Some defective products may cause great harm, such as bodily injury, and these damages should be pursued with a lawyer in a general state court. Many consumer transactions, such as the purchase of a nonfunctioning product, result in only small damages, which make it impractical to hire a lawyer and pursue an ordinary claim. For these smaller harms, every state provides some form of **small claims court** (sometimes called *pro se* courts or magistrate courts).

There are many advantages to the use of small claims court. The cost of bringing an action is much less than in regular court, and you probably will receive a decision much sooner. A typical small claims case is resolved in a couple of months, while ordinary litigation may take years. In small claims court, you will not need to retain a lawyer to represent you; many states prohibit the use of attorneys in small claims court. You will not need complicated forms or special language. You do make some sacrifices, however, such as the absence of a jury trial and pretrial discovery.

Jurisdictional Limits

Not every case can be filed in small claims court. The court's jurisdiction is limited to truly small claims and varies by state. The typical dollar limit for small claims court is about $2,500, which means you may not bring an action seeking more than that amount in damages. Some states have higher limits—for example, Tennessee, which permits small claims court to hear cases for up to $10,000, and Illinois, which places the limit at $15,000. Other states have lower limits, such as Arizona and Ohio, which limit jurisdiction to claims of under $1,000.

You may voluntarily choose to reduce your claim to slip under the jurisdiction of the small claims court. If you believe that you are owed $3,000, you might file a claim for only $2,500 in small claims court. While you lose the opportunity to recover the $500 difference, you gain the reduced costs of proceeding in small claims court. You cannot split a single claim into two separate cases and then try to bring them both in small claims court. In about half the states, small claims cases are limited to damages and the court cannot issue injunctions or other equitable remedies.

Filing a Claim

As in a general court, a small claims court action begins with the filing of a claim at a specific office. Before filing this claim, you should notify the prospective defendant through a **demand letter** that states the amount that you believe you are owed. The claim need follow few formalities but must contain certain essential information, such as:

● Your name and address.
● The correct name and address of the person that you are suing.
● The reason that you are owed money, such as when and where your damages arose or a debt was incurred.
● The amount of damages that you are claiming.

Some states give you a form on which you supply this information. Keep copies of all letters, forms, and other papers for your files.

Statutes of limitations apply to small claims actions. This means that you must bring your case within a reasonably prompt time after you suffered damages or learned of your claim. The statutes of limitations vary by state. In most states, the limitations period for actions under a written contract is four years; under an oral contract it is two years; and for a tort action it is two or three years, depending upon the tort.

There is a fee associated with filing a claim in small claims court. The amount of this fee is typically small (about $25 to $50), and the fee may vary based on the amount of your claim. You must pay this fee at the time that you file the claim. If you win, the fee may be refunded or added to the judgment.

After the claim is filed, the court will notify the person you are suing. That party will receive a summons to appear before the court. You must provide the court with the correct address, however, which is not always easy to obtain for out-of-state corporations. You may obtain this information from your state's secretary of state office, which maintains a roster of companies doing business in the state. In some states, the defendant must respond to your claim (if only by filing a general denial), but in most jurisdictions, the defendant need file no papers in response to your claim.

Pretrial Procedures

In the traditional legal action, trial is preceded by extensive discovery, in which the parties exchange documents, question witnesses, etc. The small claims court dispenses with most of this expensive and time-consuming process. As a litigant, you can **subpoena** documents if necessary. While this procedure is seldom used in small claims court, it could be that the defendant or other party has documents that you need for your case. You can require the party to turn over these documents, but don't abuse this authority. If extensive discovery is necessary, you should go to a more traditional court.

You should also identify and arrange for the appearance of relevant witnesses. Go over their testimony with witnesses in advance of trial so that you are prepared for what they will say. You can have a subpoena issued to uncooperative witnesses. If a question of value is at issue, you may need an expert witness. If you are disputing the efficacy of an automobile repair, you should have your own mechanic render an opinion.

You will probably receive a hearing on your claim within thirty days. In most jurisdictions, this is an informal pretrial hearing without witnesses. The court may try to arrange a settlement between you and the defendant. If the defendant fails to appear, you can win a **default judgment,** which is a victory without a trial. If you fail to appear, your case may be dismissed. In the absence of a settlement, your case will promptly advance to trial.

Some states do not provide for these pretrial procedures. If the defendant does respond, the matter is scheduled for trial.

Trial Procedures

Because you will be presenting the case in small claims court, you should do some preparation. Arrange all your documentary evidence of support (receipts, canceled checks, contracts, etc.) and other physical evidence, such as the damaged product. Outline your case and go over your presentation. You should also consider sitting in on a few cases before your own trial, in order to familiarize yourself with the court's methods. Sitting in can also alert you to potential pitfalls.

When the trial time comes, you will stand up and present your case, along with your documents, witnesses, and other evidence. You and your witnesses can speak freely, without the constraints of the formal rules of evidence. Indeed, your witness need not appear in person but might provide a written statement. You may prepare maps or charts or write on a court blackboard. The defendant will have an opportunity to present its case to the court as well. The judge will ask questions of both sides.

When presenting your case, stand up. Be clear, organized, and concise. Limit yourself to the facts and treat the defendant with courtesy. Provide only that evidence which is relevant to your particular claim. Present your facts in a conversational manner; do not attempt to read or memorize every word of a prepared statement. Don't act like Perry Mason but simply present your facts in a straightforward fashion.

Judgment and Appeal

After deliberating, the small claims judge will render a decision. If you prevail, you will receive a **final judgment,** which is a document that states that you are authorized to recover a certain amount from the party that you sued. This amount will be whatever the court found you were owed, plus court fees and **prejudgment interest.** The court may provide that the judgment is to be paid out in installments over a period of time.

Even if you win and receive the final judgment, you still must collect the claim. The court does not serve as a collection agency. The court will inform you of how to go about collecting your judgment. If the defendant refuses to pay, you must go back to court to obtain a **writ of execution**—a legal document that you can present to the sheriff, who will seize the defendant's nonexempt property for you. When payment is complete, you file a **satisfaction of judgment** form with the court.

In most states, if you lose your case in small claims court, you may appeal. Some states, including Michigan and California, do not permit plaintiffs to appeal a small claims judgment. If appeal is allowed, you must file a notice of appeal within a brief time following the judgment, such as thirty days. There will be an additional fee to file an appeal, and attorneys may be used on appeal.

Topic 4   Owning and Operating Motor Vehicles

Motor vehicles are a significant part of the average American's life. In many areas of the country, a car or motorcycle is a necessity for commuting, shopping, etc. A car is also one of the most significant expenses that you may have. The laws of owning and operating motor vehicles vary by state jurisdiction, but the state requirements have many common features.

∎ Buying a New Car

When shopping for a new motor vehicle, you will inevitably be drawn to dealer advertising in newspapers or on television. Some states regulate automobile ads, requiring that they state the duration of a sale or the number of vehicles that the dealer has available. Automobile ads may nevertheless mislead you. Published prices may omit necessary or factory-installed option packages, dealer preparation costs, taxes, and other fees.

Once you have settled on a new motor vehicle, its purchase is a fairly standard contractual arrangement in which you obtain title to the vehicle in exchange for cash or loan financing. The contract must be in writing and should clearly set forth all important terms (such as total cost, value for trade-in, terms of financing, etc.). The contract also should set forth the vehicle identification number ("VIN") and any other fundamental understandings between the buyer and seller. For example, the contract should state that the car is in fact new and has not been used as a demonstrator or rental car. Also, be sure to get promised warranties in writing in the contract.

Financing

Most individuals cannot pay cash for a new car and must therefore arrange for financing. You may obtain such financing through a bank, savings and loan, or credit union, but many dealers now offer their own financing, often at a discount rate, in order to attract customers. Compare rates and be aware that dealers may increase the purchase price of the car to compensate for discount financing.

Federal law regulates contracts for financing products such as automobiles. The lender must inform you of the following facts:

1. The annual percentage rate charged.
2. How the lender sets the finance charge.
3. The balance on which the finance charge is computed.
4. The finance charge amount.
5. The amount to be financed.
6. The total dollar amount to be paid.
7. The number, amounts, and due dates of payments.

Lenders who violate the law owe you any damages you have suffered, plus a fine and court costs.

Title

Once financing has been arranged, you obtain the vehicle plus a certificate of title to the vehicle. This title serves as proof of ownership and should be safely kept by the buyer. The title alone does not give you the right to drive the vehicle, however. States require that the car be registered with the state and be issued license plates. The driver also must have a driver's license.

If you fail to make required loan payments, the seller may take back the title and repossess the car. After a car is repossessed, you have a chance to redeem it by paying all overdue payments (and possibly the entire balance due), plus repossession costs.

Warranties

Most new cars come with some form of **express warranty.** This is a promise of quality or service that should be stated in the contract. A typical express warranty would provide that the seller will replace any defective parts without charge, for a certain time period or until the car has been driven a certain number of miles.

Automobile purchasers also automatically receive certain **implied warranties.** These warranties are presumed to be included in all contracts and need not be stated explicitly. The **implied warranty of title** declares that the seller is the true owner of the car and has legal right to transfer that ownership to you. The **implied warranty of merchantability** states that the vehicle at least meets ordinary standards of mechanical efficiency. This assures you that the car won't break down as soon as you drive it off the seller's lot.

While these implied warranties generally accompany any sale of a new car, the seller may avoid such warranties by using a **disclaimer.** A provision in the contract of sale, if properly worded, could clearly declare that the seller is making no warranties. The sale of a used car "as is" disclaims implied warranties. If you sign such a contract, you lose the legal protections associated with implied warranties of merchantability.

If a warranty or other contract provision is violated, you may cancel the sale of the car within a reasonable time after you have obtained it. A reasonable time is usually no more than a week or two. Alternatively, you may provide the dealer an opportunity to "cure" the defect. Once you cancel the sale of the car, it is no longer yours and you must stop using it.

If the warranty violation is discovered too late for cancellation, you can seek damages. As a general rule, you must continue to make your car payments while seeking legal recourse. If the violation is significant or costly to correct, you may need a lawyer to help you enforce your contractual rights.

Lemon Laws

Forty-five states have passed **lemon laws** to protect those who purchase defective vehicles. These laws provide you protection over and above any warranties. The precise terms of lemon laws vary from state to state. In general, a "lemon" is a vehicle that has a defect substantially affecting its use, value, or safety, even after reasonable efforts of repair. This may mean as many as four repair attempts on the same problem before repair is deemed futile. Alternatively, some states consider a car a lemon if it is out of commission for more than thirty days during the first year of ownership.

In order to take advantage of a lemon law, you must notify the dealer of the defect and keep a copy of all repair records and receipts. In most states, you will be required to take the dispute to **arbitration** before suing. If you win, you may obtain a satisfactory replacement vehicle or a refund of the purchase price plus associated taxes and fees (minus some allowance for the value of your use of the car). The states also provide other consumer protection laws that offer larger damages than those under lemon laws (such as triple the cost of the car), though these laws may require you to prove that the dealer knowingly or willfully sold you a defective vehicle.

▌Buying or Selling a ▌Used Car

Used vehicles represent a significant percentage of sales, and nonmerchants may be on both sides of a used-car sale. The law provides some basic requirements for such a contract. First, if the price is $500 or more, the contract must be in writing to be enforceable in court. Second, the transaction must include a written **bill of sale.** The bill of sale should state the amount paid, the method of payment, and identifying details about the car, including its VIN. The bill of sale or transfer of title should be signed and dated and generally must be submitted to a specific government agency for registration. Note that applicable sales tax must be paid on used-car sales.

Used-car sales are subject to many of the same buyer-protection laws as are new-car sales. Lemon laws are increasingly being extended to apply to used-car sales. Warranties also apply to many used car sales. If you are selling a car with a material latent defect (one that is not readily discoverable by the buyer), you have a duty to disclose that defect. Otherwise you may be liable for fraud. The implied warranty of merchantability, however, only applies to merchants and does not exist if the sale is by an individual who is not in the business of selling used cars. Although an individual seller makes no implied warranty of quality, the seller may make an express warranty of quality.

Additional regulatory requirements apply to dealers in used cars and provide further buyer protection. A dealer is anyone who sells six or more used cars in a twelve-month period. The Federal Trade Commission requires that dealers post a **Buyer's Guide** on the side window of each used car they sell. This includes a warning that oral promises are difficult to enforce as a practical matter and a recommendation that you get all promises in unambiguous writing. The Guide also lists the terms of any warranties provided and supplies details about any service contracts and significant recurrent problems with the car's mechanical or safety systems.

▌ Renting or Leasing a Car

A short-term automobile rental is another form of contractual arrangement subject to the agreement of the parties. Most automobile rental companies require that you have a driver's license and a major credit card, and some require that you be at least twenty-five years old before they will rent you a vehicle. These companies often waive the age requirement if the rental is business related or if you are a member of an established auto club.

The rental agreement contract will contain a variety of detailed terms and provide you some options. The most significant of these options is the **collision damage waiver.** If you pay for this collision protection, you are not liable for accidental damages to the rental car. The coverage does not extend to personal injuries or damage to others' property, however. Accepting the company's collision damage insurance may be unnecessary. Your existing automobile insurance policy may already provide for this

coverage, as may your employer's policy (if this is a business rental) or your credit card itself.

Automobile leasing is a growing business and typically substitutes for the purchase of a car. Under a typical lease, you make monthly payments to the dealer for two to four years. These payments are in place of and typically much less than the monthly payments you would make on a new-car loan. Unlike such loan payments, however, lease payments do not provide you with an **equity (ownership) interest** in the vehicle. Leasing a car may in some states avoid the need to pay sales tax and avoid a down payment (although one- or two-months' advance lease payments are typically required).

When the lease expires, you return the vehicle to the dealer. You no longer have any obligation or interest in this car. If you want to keep the car, you may buy it from the dealer at the end of the lease. Some leases specify an end-of-lease purchase price. For other leases, you simply must negotiate a price with the dealer.

The terms of a lease are like any other contract. Many leases provide that you must make additional payments if you drive more than 15,000 miles per year or cause some irreparable damage to the vehicle. Other terms may include insurance, maintenance agreements, loaner-car arrangements, etc. These may be negotiated, but some dealers may be unwilling to modify their standard form leases.

In some respects, a lease of a motor vehicle may be as much of a commitment as a purchase. The contract binds you to keep the car for the duration of the lease, unless you can sublease the vehicle. Some lease contracts contain an early termination clause through which you may escape the lease early if you don't like the car. These clauses typically require you to pay a penalty, however. If your leased car is stolen or destroyed, it is considered to be an early termination, and your insurance probably will not cover the early termination penalty. **Gap insurance** is available to cover this possibility.

▌ Insuring a Car

Categories of Insurance

Many states require you to have automobile **liability insurance** and others require you to demonstrate "financial responsibility" (such as obtaining insurance or posting a bond). The laws specify a minimum basic level of coverage that is required. These requirements vary by state. Insurance laws are designed to ensure that you can pay damages if injury occurs to another person as a result of your careless driving. Failure to maintain such insurance is a driving violation that subjects you to a fine and potential loss of your license.

When you acquire liability insurance, your insurance company must pay for the damages that you caused. If you are sued for negligent driving, your insurance company generally will take charge of the suit and supply its own lawyer. You remain personally liable, however, for damages over and above the policy limits (which may be as low as $50,000). The compulsory liability insurance laws also help protect your ability to recover damages if you are injured by others.

When you obtain insurance, your periodic payment rate will be based upon a number of factors. These include type of car, your age, gender, driving record, and primary use of car, plus local accident rates. Although it may seem unfair, all young males pay an extra premium, because so many young males get into accidents. You may pay a higher rate if your type of car is particularly expensive to repair or especially likely to be stolen. As with any business deal, you can shop around to find the best rates.

When acquiring insurance, you may obtain **uninsured motorist coverage.** Indeed, seventeen states require you to have such a policy. This uninsured motorist coverage enables you to collect for your damages if you are injured by a negligent driver who lacks his or her own insurance. Even in states in which liability insurance is required, a significant number of drivers lack coverage. Under uninsured motorist coverage, your own insurance company pays for your damages and then attempts to recover this payment in an action against the uninsured driver. You are thus covered even if the negligent driver lacks the ability to pay.

To collect under uninsured motorist coverage, you generally must show that the other driver was at fault and lacked liability insurance. Many uninsured motorist policies provide protection even when the other party has insurance, but the party's policy limits are insufficient to cover all your damages. You can recover your damages only once, however, and cannot duplicate payments from both your own and the other party's insurers.

In addition to liability and uninsured motorist coverage, you have other insurance options. Many individuals purchase **collision insurance,** through which the insurer pays for any damages to your car from a collision, regardless of who was at fault. **Comprehensive insurance** protects against non-collision damage to your vehicle (including theft, vandalization, and hail damage). These policies generally do *not* cover personal items left in your vehicle. These policies also generally contain a **deductible,** which means that you must pay a certain amount of your loss, such as the first $200 of damages. You may also obtain insurance to cover medical payments for you and your passengers after an accident.

About half of the states have a system of **no-fault insurance.** This system largely eliminates lawsuits for negligence and requires every driver to carry insurance to pay for his or her own damages, regardless of who was at fault in the accident. Under this system, parties need not go to court to recover and need not worry that the other driver lacks insurance. Damage compensation in no-fault systems tends to be lower than in traditional jurisdictions.

Insurance Coverage

If you obtain automobile insurance and inform your insurance company that others may drive your car, they too are protected by the policy. An automobile insurance policy typically extends coverage to the following parties:

● You and your spouse.
● Other residents of your household that you have declared to the insurance company.
● Other undeclared persons who drive the car with your permission (though this may be limited to infrequent borrowings).
● Nondrivers who may be liable due to your negligence, such as your employer.

If you fail to inform the insurance company that another party will be a regular driver of your car, that person may not be covered by the insurance.

If you purchase a new car, your old automobile insurance policy continues in effect for at least thirty days, while a new policy may be written and acquired. You should notify your insurance company of your purchase and obtain a new policy promptly in order to ensure continued protection. Your policy will also cover you when you drive an automobile owned by another person. If you go on vacation and have an accident while driving your sister's car, you will probably be covered by both your policy and her policy. In many cases, your policy will not provide coverage for driving in foreign countries (except Canada).

∎ Repairing a Car

When your car is damaged and requires repair, you will need to choose a mechanic. In some areas, auto mechanics are notorious for questionable or fraudulent practices. To defend yourself against such practices, investigate the reputation and past practices of mechanics and negotiate a repair contract that legally protects your interests.

The repair contract is often called a **repair order.** This order is customarily a form standard in the industry that describes the work to be done on your vehicle. Signing the order creates a contract authorizing the mechanic to make the described repairs. The repair order contains necessary identifying information about you and your car but does not generally state a price for the repairs.

It is a good practice to receive a cost estimate for repairs before authorizing the work, though some repair shops will charge for such estimates. At common law, this estimate is not binding, and if the cost proves greater than the estimate, you are still bound to pay the difference. Some states have legislation that provides that actual costs cannot exceed the estimate by more than a certain percentage.

After repair work, complaints may arise over the quality of the work, the cost, or warranties made by the mechanic. Most states have laws requiring that you be provided with a detailed invoice of parts and labor as well as the right to receive parts that have been replaced. If you believe that you have been cheated, you may be able to sue in contract or under a deceptive trade practices statute. If you inform your state attorney general, he or she may take action on your behalf.

If you refuse to pay for the repairs, the mechanic may keep your car through an **artisan's lien** (or mechanic's lien), which gives the repair shop the right to sell your car to satisfy your debt. This lien is available only if the shop has complied with legal requirements for repair authorization. If you make payments, or the mechanic has agreed to do the repairs on credit, the mechanic must return your car.

▌ Driving Violations

A long list of criminal laws governs driving. These laws vary greatly in seriousness and in penalties. For the most significant violations, penalties may include prison time.

Stop and Search

The police have a broad right to stop you while you are driving. When you see the police flashing lights in your rearview mirror, you should pull over to the side of the road as promptly and safely as possible. The police have a right to see your driver's license and to have you step out of the car.

After a stop, the officer may want to search your car. The officer need not have a warrant. Your car can only be searched, however, if either (a) you consent or (b) the officer has probable cause to believe that your vehicle contains incriminating evidence. If an illegal item (such as drugs or guns) is in plain view in your car, the officer may seize it without the need for a search warrant. The law defining the scope of police searches is ever changing as new cases are brought. At a minimum, the police may search the area within the driver's reach, including the glove compartment. Under some circumstances, the police can impound your car. If so, they may do a thorough search without a warrant or even probable cause.

Speeding

A common driving violation is excessive speed. If you are caught speeding, you may be subject to a substantial fine.

The officer may choose not to cite you for speeding if you have a particularly good reason (such as a health emergency). Most speeding violations are demonstrated by radar readings of your speed. You may have heard of cases in which radar results were thrown out of court for improper maintenance or other reasons. In the vast majority of cases, however, courts accept the results of radar guns as virtually conclusive evidence that you were speeding. In many jurisdictions, you may take a defensive driving course in lieu of a fine for speeding. Completion of the course may also keep the ticket off your driving record and avoid an increase in insurance rates.

Some people use radar detectors to avoid getting caught speeding. Connecticut and Virginia have outlawed the use of such radar detectors. In a recent New Jersey case, a person was arrested for flashing his headlights to warn oncoming traffic of the presence of a radar trap. The court, however, held that his actions were perfectly legal.

Driving While Intoxicated

Perhaps the most serious driving violation is driving while intoxicated with alcohol or other drugs. Some states call this crime "driving under the influence." Intoxication is typically defined by blood-alcohol level, and different states have different standards for defining intoxication. Drunk driving is responsible for about 20,000 deaths annually.

The blood-alcohol level defining intoxication varies somewhat by state, with most using a .10 standard (meaning one-tenth of one percent blood-alcohol concentration). California and some other states have lowered this threshold to .08. Your blood-alcohol level is a function of your weight and alcohol consumption, plus some other factors. Having two regular-sized drinks (one ounce of alcohol each) within one hour may put you in the danger zone of violation.

The police may pull you over if your driving appears erratic, such as weaving from lane to lane. Indeed, the police may establish roadblocks in areas frequented by drinkers and stop cars randomly to check for drunk driving. Once you are stopped they will observe your coordination, your speech, whether you smell of alcohol, and the appearance of your eyes. They may administer a simple test of your ability to walk a straight line or your ability to focus your eyes on a point. If they continue to suspect that you were driving while intoxicated, they will ask you to take a breathalyzer examination.

You are not required to take the breathalyzer test, due to the constitutional protection against self-incrimination. If you refuse, however, states are authorized to suspend your driver's license, usually for several months. Many attorneys advise that you should refuse the breathalyzer if you suspect that you are indeed intoxicated beyond the legal limit. If you fail a breathalyzer test, your attorney may subsequently challenge the results, but the test is often powerful evidence. In many states, you have a right to a second, confirmatory test if you fail the first breathalyzer exam. If you refuse the breathalyzer, the case against you will be built upon the testimony of the police officer and others who observed your condition at the time.

Penalties

The penalty for most driving violations is a fine, ranging from tens to hundreds of dollars. If you have accumulated a number of driving violations, the state may also suspend your license temporarily or revoke your license indefinitely. Revocation is generally limited to serious violations, such as driving while intoxicated, fleeing the police, or using a vehicle to commit a felony crime. You are entitled to notice and a hearing before revocation takes effect.

If you drive without a license (because it has been suspended or revoked), you may be arrested and held in jail until you can post bond. The amount of this bond will depend on your driving record and the nature of any other violation you may have committed to provoke the arrest. In this event, you should find an attorney as promptly as possible.

Serious violations, such as driving while intoxicated, may result in imprisonment. Fourteen states require mandatory imprisonment after the first offense of drunk driving. (The requirement may be only a few days.) Numerous other states require imprisonment after repeat violations and potential penalties include months or years in prison. A drunk-driving conviction also results in a substantial increase in insurance premiums or even insurance cancellation.

▌ Driving Accidents
....

Liability

Under the law, you have a duty to drive with reasonable care. If your negligent driving injures someone, you and/or your insurance company may be liable for the resultant damages. Negligence is a general term covering any sort of carelessness including driving violations. It is also negligence if you fail to keep your vehicle in good repair. If the accident was unavoidable, you are not liable.

You may be liable even if you were not the driver. The doctrine of **negligent entrustment** applies if you permit an underage, intoxicated, or other incapable person to use your car. In about half the states, parents or guardians are automatically liable if they have signed the driver's license application for their children who subsequently cause an accident. An employer is also typically liable for accidents caused by an employee acting within the scope of employment.

In many accidents, both involved parties were negligent in some manner. In this circumstance, the law provides for **comparative negligence.** Under this doctrine, each party must pay damages in proportion to his or her negligence. In most states, you cannot recover any damages if you were more than 50 percent to blame. Even in these states, the damages you owe will be reduced by the proportion of negligence assigned to the other driver. You also may be liable to passengers in your own car who are injured in an accident that was your fault.

Reporting Requirements

The law requires that you report some driving accidents. A written report is required if the accident causes personal injury or if property damage exceeds a minimum threshold (usually about $250). This report generally must be filed with a specific government agency within five or ten days of the accident, depending on the state. To help ensure the report's accuracy, take careful note of weather and road conditions, speed estimates, time, and other relevant factors.

Failure to file the report is a misdemeanor and may be punishable by suspension of your driver's license. When you submit the report, you are automatically verifying that all the reported facts are true and that you are not omitting any material facts about the accident. Knowingly providing false information may be a felony.

What to Do after Your Accident

If you are in a significant accident, you should first park your car out of traffic, if possible. Driving away from the scene of the accident is illegal. Post warning flares by the side of the road or have a person warn oncoming vehicles. Exchange information with the other driver involved in the accident. This information should include the names and addresses of all passengers, vehicle license number, vehicle registration, and proof of insurance. Today's laws require a person to provide such identification. If police officers arrive on the scene, ask for their names and badge numbers. If you have a camera in your car, take pictures of the scene.

Do not make statements about fault to the other driver, bystanders, or the police. If you have injured someone, you may feel bad. There is nothing to be gained, however, by confessing fault immediately after the accident. At this time, you may be unaware of the true cause of the accident, and an admission of fault may be used against you even if you later realize that you were not at fault. After you are familiar with all the relevant facts and you have consulted with your insurance company and an attorney, you may choose to admit fault.

If someone is hurt or killed in the accident, you should alert the police and emergency medical services immediately. Be cautious about attempting to provide medical assistance unless you are qualified—you could aggravate an injury. After emergency concerns have been addressed, you should file required reports, contact your insurance company, and possibly contact an attorney.

Even if you do not seem to be injured, you should see a doctor for possible hidden or delayed conditions. If the insurance claims adjustor for the other party contacts you, refer the adjustor to your attorney. If you don't have an attorney, be careful what you say. Make no settlement until you have sufficiently explored your medical condition and legal opportunities. If you suspect that the accident was caused by a defect in your own vehicle, do not have the car repaired until after consulting with an attorney. In any event, keep careful records of any repairs done following the accident and retain replaced parts.

Rendering Assistance to Others

If you come across an accident while driving, you may consider stopping and rendering assistance. As a general rule, you have no duty to provide assistance if you were uninvolved in the accident. If you were involved in the accident, all states require you to stop and render assistance, even if you do not believe that you were at fault. Rendering assistance may simply involve telephoning the police and emergency medical services.

If you witness an accident, you may render assistance even when it is not legally required. If you stop and provide assistance to an accident victim, theoretically you could subsequently be sued by the victim for negligence in the manner of providing such assistance. The vast majority of states have adopted **Good Samaritan laws,** which shield you from any liability for simple negligence in assisting an accident victim. You could still be sued, though, for extreme or gross negligence in providing assistance.

Topic 5   Criminal Law

It is wise to obey the law and avoid the criminal justice system. Should you be charged with a crime, it is crucial for you to understand the charges and your constitutional rights. Except for the most minor crimes, you must consult an attorney.

▊ The Nature of Crimes

A criminal act is one that is prohibited by the legislature in a statute. An act does not become criminal simply because it is unethical or reprehensible—it must be specifically outlawed to be a crime.

There is considerable overlap between criminal law and civil law. If a person steals your car, that action is the crime of auto theft and also the civil tort of conversion. The responsible party may be prosecuted for the crime and also sued for the tort in separate judicial actions. The criminal action will be brought by the state government and tried by a **prosecutor** employed by the government. If convicted, the defendant will be required to pay a fine and/or do time in jail. The civil action must be brought by you and litigated by your lawyer. If you win, the defendant must pay you damages. The defendant cannot be sentenced to jail in a civil case. Although the two cases deal with the same action, they are pursued independently and employ different procedures, such as different burdens of proof.

Either the state or the federal legislature may make a certain action criminal. Most crimes are state crimes, prosecuted by the state and heard in state court. Other crimes, such as mail fraud or failure to pay federal income tax, are uniquely federal and enforced by federal authorities. A few crimes, such as possession of illegal drugs and bank robbery, are both federal and state crimes.

Types of Crimes

A wide range of activities have been outlawed as criminal acts. The best known are the most serious and violent crimes, such as murder, rape, and kidnapping. These crimes are punishable by death or by an imprisonment sentence for a period such as twenty years to life. The **felony murder rule** makes a person guilty of murder, even if he or she does not personally murder anyone. Suppose an armed robbery of a convenience store involves three persons—two go into the store and one stays in the "getaway car." No violence is planned, but one of the robbers shoots and kills the clerk. All three persons are guilty of murder, even the one who did not go into the store.

The criminal justice system considers lesser but still severe crimes to include those such as armed robbery and manslaughter (for example, murder through negligence). Careless driving that results in a fatal accident may give rise to a negligent manslaughter prosecution. The sentence for these crimes may be three to five years or longer in prison.

Some crimes against property are also punished severely. For example, arson and extortion may be punished by years of imprisonment. Robbery, the taking of money or property by force from a person, is a more serious crime than burglary, the taking of property from a home in that person's absence. A burglary conviction may have greater penalties if it was conducted with a weapon, at night, or when the home was occupied. Receiving or buying property that you know or should know has been stolen is itself a crime sometimes referred to as obtaining stolen goods.

Crimes against public health, safety, and welfare form another category of criminal action. This category includes the possession, manufacture, or sale of certain prohibited drugs, such as cocaine or heroin. Selling alcohol to a minor is another example of this type of crime. Many of the laws against such crimes are aimed at businesses that may violate environmental laws or food safety laws.

Among the most controversial crimes are those "against public decency and morals." Such crimes include bigamy, prostitution, and illegal gambling. A controversial Supreme Court decision held that it was constitutional to prohibit homosexual sodomy, even in private. A number of states still have statutes that outlaw both homosexual and heterosexual sodomy, but these laws are seldom enforced. By contrast, molestation or other lewd and lascivious behavior toward a child is illegal and strictly enforced.

Misdemeanors versus Felonies

Crimes are deemed to be either **misdemeanors** or **felonies.** A felony is a particularly serious crime. Examples of felonies are homicide, rape, and armed robbery. Misdemeanors are somewhat less serious crimes. Shoplifting, public drunkenness, and mildly resisting arrest are examples of misdemeanors.

The general distinction between felonies and misdemeanors is based upon the potential sentence for the crime. Offenses punishable by a prison sentence of more than one year are considered felonies. Misdemeanors are punishable by sentences of a year or less, and incarceration is in a county or municipal jail rather than a state prison. Those convicted of felonies may also lose other significant rights, including the right to vote or to serve on a jury.

The same basic action may be a misdemeanor or a felony, depending on the circumstances. For example, petty theft involves stealing less than a certain dollar amount and is a misdemeanor. Stealing goods worth more than the statutorily specified dollar amount is grand theft and constitutes a felony. For other crimes, the first offense may be considered a misdemeanor, but subsequent offenses become felonies.

❚ Arrest and Prosecution

Stop and Arrest

The criminal process often commences with a procedure known as **stop and frisk**. This occurs when the police have reason to suspect that you are engaged in a criminal activity and that you may be armed. Such suspicion may arise if you were loitering outside a home or business in a manner to suggest that you might be "casing" the place for a break-in. After the police have stopped you, they may ask you questions. They may also conduct a frisk, which is a patting down of the outside of your clothing. If they feel something that might be a weapon, the police are permitted to reach into your pocket and remove it. If they feel something soft that could not be a dangerous weapon, the police generally cannot search for it. In June 1993, the Supreme Court expanded police authority to allow removal and seizure of a package of drugs felt during a frisk.

Except for the stop-and-frisk rule, the police may not search you, unless you are under arrest or the police have a **search warrant.** The police may ask you to consent to a search, but there is no reason for you to agree. Refusal to cooperate with a stop and frisk, however, may represent independent grounds to arrest you.

The stop and frisk may be followed by an **arrest**. An arrest occurs when a suspect is taken into custody. The police may obtain an arrest warrant in advance, then seek out and arrest the suspect. If a person is caught in the act of committing a crime and the police lack time to obtain a warrant, the police may perform a **warrantless arrest.** A warrantless arrest must be based upon **probable cause.** Probable cause is a concept meaning that the police have a reasonable belief that a specific person has committed a crime. Probable cause is based on more than just a hunch or a stereotype, but involves far less than the evidence required to convict at trial. A tip from an informer is one way of establishing probable cause. Those subjected to warrantless arrest have an opportunity for a prompt hearing on the presence of probable cause.

Warrantless arrests are generally limited to public situations. For the police to seek you out and arrest you in a private place, an arrest warrant is generally required. The police may put you under surveillance at your house and then arrest you without a warrant after you leave home.

If you are arrested, you should be very careful of what you say or do. Don't resist the arrest or fingerprinting, and give the police your name and address. Don't say anything about the arrest to the police until after you have consulted with an attorney. If you are held in jail, you will have an opportunity to call a friend or relative. Inform them of the situation and arrange for legal representation. Be scrupulously honest with your lawyer—confessions to your lawyer cannot be used against you, due to the attorney-client privilege. Have your lawyer present at any police questioning or lineups at which you might be identified by the purported crime victim.

The police may seek to question you immediately after the arrest, before you have an opportunity to consult with an attorney. The U.S. Constitution guarantees you a right against self-incrimination, so that you cannot be forced to testify against yourself, and you need not respond to such questioning. Historically, the police have sometimes used physical or psychological pressure to coerce confessions even from the innocent. To avoid this scenario, the Supreme Court has required that persons in custody be given a set of **Miranda warnings** (named for the case that created the requirement). Police initially carried a "Miranda card" to remind them of the language, but these warnings are now quite well known to police and many ordinary citizens.

MIRANDA WARNINGS

● You have the right to remain silent. Anything you say can be used against you.
● You have the right to a lawyer and to have one present during questioning.
● If you cannot afford a lawyer, one will be appointed for you before questioning commences.

If the police fail to provide Miranda warnings, a suspect may still be prosecuted and convicted. The Miranda warnings are required only for use at trial of statements made by the accused.

Search and Seizure

The Fourth Amendment to the United States Constitution protects the privacy of Americans and restricts the government's ability to conduct searches. The government may search your home if it obtains a *search warrant*. Such a warrant generally must be obtained from a judge. The police go before the court and present evidence of its probable cause to believe that evidence of a crime is present. This warrant must particularly describe the place or person to be searched and the evidence to be seized. With such a warrant, the police may thoroughly search you, your home, your car, your business, or other places.

Under certain defined circumstances, the police may conduct a warrantless search. The stop and frisk is a limited form of such a warrantless search. Some examples of lawful warrantless searches are:

1. When the police are in hot pursuit of a felon trying to escape the scene of a crime.
2. When the police have probable cause to believe that a vehicle contains illegal items, the police may search the vehicle without a warrant.
3. When an item is in plain view of an officer, it may be seized without a warrant.
4. When the police make a proper arrest, they may search the area immediately surrounding the arrested person.
5. When a person consents to the search and seizure.
6. Searches in some special locations, such as at the national border or at an airport.

What if a search is illegal, due to the absence of a warrant or grounds for a warrantless search, and the police then find evidence of a crime? Under the **exclusionary rule,** evidence from the illegal search cannot be introduced at the criminal trial.

▌Pretrial Procedures

After the arrest, the accused typically is **booked,** fingerprinted, and photographed at the local police station. Booking is the official police processing of the arrest. The defendant may be strip-searched.

Hearing Right

Soon after the booking, the accused has a right to a first appearance before a court. At this point, the judge explains the charges to be brought and the defendant's rights. The court will appoint a lawyer for the defendant if necessary. In a felony case, this appearance is often called a **presentment** or **preliminary arraignment.** This hearing may serve as an **arraignment,** when the defendant is formally advised of the charges and given an opportunity to respond by pleading guilty or not guilty. When the government's case is weak, the judge may dismiss the case in this first appearance.

Release before Trial

The key aspect of this first-appearance hearing is whether the defendant will be released from custody automatically, or if **bail** will be set. Bail involves the payment of a bond by the defendant in order to secure release from custody. The core function of bail is to ensure that the accused does not go into hiding to avoid trial. In many cases, the defendant may obtain a **release on his or her own recognizance** (without posting a bond). This occurs when the defendant promises to return for trial and convinces the court that he or she is a good risk.

In some cases, even bail may be denied and the defendant held in custody without prospect for release. Bail may be denied for particularly horrendous crimes, if the defendant is considered a threat to the community. Bail may also be denied if the defendant was already on parole or probation and if the defendant presents a particular danger of flight from the jurisdiction before trial.

The next major step in a criminal prosecution is either to present the case to a grand jury for indictment or to hold a preliminary hearing. Both events require a closer investigation of the charges against the defendant. A grand jury is a group of up to twenty-three ordinary citizens who hear testimony and evidence presented only by the prosecution. The grand jury then decides whether to indict the accused and send the defendant to trial, or to "no bill" the defendant, releasing the accused from the charges.

At a preliminary hearing, the prosecutor, in the presence of a judge, must present sufficient evidence and witnesses to establish the probable guilt of the defendant. The accused is represented by counsel, who may present witnesses and evidence and may cross-examine prosecution witnesses. The judge decides whether to bind the defendant over for trial. Grand jury indictments are required in federal prosecution of felonies.

If the prosecution proceeds and the defendant maintains innocence, the parties then undergo discovery of evidence. Lawyers may file pretrial motions to the court. For example, the defense may contend that the prosecution's evidence is inadmissible and ask the judge to dismiss the action. If the prosecution prevails, the next step is the criminal trial.

▌ Trial and Defenses

Defendants have a right to a speedy trial which must quickly follow the indictment or arraignment. Typically, a state might guarantee that the trial begin within sixty days. It is common, however, for defendants to waive their right to be tried so promptly, in order to obtain more time to prepare their defenses.

The Trial

The Constitution has been interpreted to give the defendant the right to a jury trial for significant crimes (punishable by imprisonment of six months or more). The defendant has a right to a jury of peers, but this does not mean individuals in the same financial or social position

as the defendant. A jury of peers simply means that the jury is selected from residents of the accused's community and that no groups have been artificially excluded from serving on the jury. If the crime has received extensive pretrial publicity, the defendant may ask for a **change of venue,** so that the trial can be held in another location where jurors may not be so prejudiced by media coverage of the crime.

Eventually, the criminal case will come to trial. The prosecution will present its evidence. Such evidence may be in the form of eyewitness testimony; namely, individuals who claim to have seen the defendant commit the crime. The prosecution may present documentary evidence of guilt. The prosecution may also present circumstantial evidence, facts that create a strong inference that the defendant must have committed the crime. The defendant has the **presumption of innocence.** This means that the prosecution has the burden of proof to establish guilt beyond a reasonable doubt.

Defenses

Several constitutional protections extend to the trial of the accused. The Fifth Amendment contains a general right to **due process,** which requires procedural fairness, such as an impartial judge. The Sixth Amendment gives the accused a right to confront and cross-examine the witnesses against them. As noted, the defendant has a right to an attorney and the right not to testify. The defendant may seek to exclude some prosecution evidence as inadmissible. The exclusionary rule means that most illegally obtained evidence cannot be introduced against you in trial. This includes evidence from illegal searches and seizures or confessions obtained through coercion or without first giving the accused his or her Miranda warnings.

Criminal defendants may have available other procedural or constitutional defenses. One such defense is known as **entrapment.** Defendants often claim entrapment but seldom succeed. The defense is quite narrow, and the defendant has the burden of proof to demonstrate entrapment. It is not enough to show that government agents suggested the commission of a crime. A police officer offering to sell drugs to a college student is generally not a case of entrapment. Entrapment means that the government somehow induced a person to commit a crime that he or she otherwise would never have considered committing. If the government merely affords a person the opportunity to commit a crime, and the person seizes that opportunity, entrapment is not established.

Entrapment might exist when the government continues at great length in its efforts to catch an individual. Suppose that an undercover agent arrived at your door and offered to sell you a stolen stereo. You declined. The agent then appeared at your door and made the same offer day after day. After you declined to purchase the stereo many times, you finally relented. This degree of government perseverance might constitute entrapment.

The accused may of course maintain that no crime was committed or that he or she is not the guilty party. This defense may involve undermining the testimony of the prosecution witnesses, such as challenging the accuracy of eyewitness testimony. The defendant may also present evidence of his or her innocence. This may consist, for example, of an **alibi,** showing that the defendant was somewhere else at the time of the crime's commission. The defendant may testify but is not required to do so.

Another defense to crime is **self-defense** or the defense of others. It is not unlawful to attack someone in self-defense. To demonstrate self-defense, a defendant must show that he or she had a reasonable fear of an imminent danger of bodily harm from an attacker. This same defense is available if you come to the defense of others endangered by an attack. The force used in self-defense must be reasonable. If the attacker runs away from you, you generally may not pursue him to strike him further. Deadly force (such as a gun or knife) may be used in self-defense only when you are threatened with deadly force. You can also use some force in the defense of your property, but you usually cannot use deadly force in defense of property. Some states have exceptions to this rule. In Texas, you can use deadly force if a person is seeking to enter your property at night.

Another defense is available if the defendant is not responsible for his or her actions. Extreme cases of intoxication may mean that the defendant lacked the state of mind to commit certain crimes. Slight drunkenness is not a defense, though, and some states hold that voluntary intoxication cannot be a defense, no matter how drunk the defendant is. Another such defense is **insanity.** The insanity defense is actually rather narrow, and even a significant psychological problem may not qualify. Standards differ somewhat by state but a common test is that the defendant be so insane as to lack the ability to appreciate the nature of the criminal act or that the conduct was wrongful. Insanity is judged as pertaining to the time of the crime. If the defendant remains insane, a trial cannot proceed, because due process requires that the defendant be able to understand the charges brought. Such a defendant is typically held in an institution until sanity is regained.

Yet another defense is the passage of too much time between the act and the prosecution. The **statute of limitations** is a law that requires that legal proceedings (such as a complaint) commence within a certain period of time. A typical state statute of limitations would be one year for misdemeanors and three years for certain felonies. The statute stops running if the defendant is out of the state during this period or changes his or her identity. For very serious crimes, such as murder, there is no statute of limitations.

∎ Sentencing

After a person is convicted of a crime, the court metes out some form of sentence. Sentencing has a variety of purposes. Some of the objectives of sentencing are rehabilitation of the offender, incapacitation of the offender so that the crime is not repeated, and deterrence of future crimes by the offender and others.

Types of Sentences

The law provides for a broad range of sentencing options, depending upon the nature of the crime. The most severe is capital punishment, in which the defendant is executed. Other serious crimes provide for imprisonment for a specified term, often a number of years. Felony sentences are commonly served in state prison, while misdemeanor sentences are typically served in a local jail. In many other cases, the defendant must pay a fine to the state.

A variety of lesser sentences are also available for less serious crimes or first offenders. **Probation** refers to a sentence by which an offender does not go to jail or prison but is released under the supervision of a probation officer. States prohibit probation for certain serious offenses. The offender also agrees to follow certain conditions, such as not carrying a gun, not using illegal drugs, getting a job, and checking in regularly with the probation officer. Probation is for a set period of time, such as one year. If the offender violates the terms of probation during this period, probation may be revoked and he or she may be sent to prison. Revocation of probation requires a hearing to establish the presence of a violation.

In some cases, the convicted criminal may receive a **suspended sentence.** The offender first receives a particular prison sentence (for example, two years in prison), which is then suspended by the judge. The offender is then released without conditions or supervision by a probation officer. In a suspended sentence, the conviction and sentence is a matter of public record and may hamper the job prospects of the convicted. Another procedure is called **deferred sentencing.** After a conviction, the judge will elect to defer sentencing for a period such as a year. If the offender commits no more violations during that year, the judge imposes no sentence at all.

States are increasingly turning to innovative forms of punishment. Many states have **restitution statutes.** Such laws require defendants to pay the victims to compensate them for the losses suffered from the crimes. While conceptually appealing, restitution statutes have limits for the reason that many convicted criminals lack the resources to make restitution. Judges have also turned to public humiliation as a sanction. A convicted criminal may be forced to wear a sign or take out an advertisement in the newspaper confessing his or her guilt. Convicted drunk drivers have been compelled to apply bumper stickers declaring themselves guilty of that crime.

The Eighth Amendment to the Constitution prohibits **cruel and unusual punishment.** This typically concerns punishments such as torture, but courts are extending the amendment to unreasonable prison conditions if the government exhibits "deliberate indifference" to the conditions. A 1993 Supreme Court decision held that being confined to a cell with a smoker could be cruel and unusual punishment if the prisoner could show that the secondhand tobacco smoke presented a serious risk to his or her health.

▌Juvenile Justice

The United States provides a justice system for juveniles separate from that for adults. This system tends to be more lenient and often refers to "delinquent acts" rather than crimes. Sentences are also lighter. As juveniles are increasingly committing heinous crimes, the relative lenience of juvenile courts has fallen into some disfavor.

The Juvenile

Each state sets its own age limit for determination of whether an accused person should be tried as an adult or as a juvenile. In most states the age of maturity is eighteen, but a number of states have reduced this age to sixteen or seventeen. Underage individuals are presumptively treated as youths and tried in juvenile court. Most states provide that some juveniles may be tried in an adult court and subjected to the full range of penalties. The juvenile may be transferred to adult court, depending on certain factors. The relevant factors include the seriousness of the crime, the criminal record of the defendant, the age of the defendant, and the likelihood that juvenile status will better enable the rehabilitation of the defendant.

Pretrial

The apprehension of a juvenile is not called an arrest but *a taking into custody.* Juveniles may be taken into custody for the very same criminal acts that would result in the arrest of an adult. Juveniles may also be taken into custody for **status offenses.** Status offenses are not criminal acts proscribed by the legislature but are problems such as repeated truancy at school or habitual disobedience

and may apply to those minors who have run away from home. A single episode of misbehavior does not render a youth a status offender. Consistent misbehavior is required. Juveniles charged with status offenses have basically the same legal protections as those charged with crimes.

As juvenile criminal behavior has grown, status offenses have taken a back seat. Such offenses are still significant, however, as they often reflect an emotionally troubled life that may be amenable to rehabilitation. Various programs, such as youth shelters and counseling, have been established to assist runaways and other troubled youths.

After a juvenile is taken into custody for either a crime or a status offense, the police may choose to file a formal charge, refer the case to social workers, or release the youth to the care of parents. If the police detain the juvenile, a process known as **intake** follows. At this stage the authorities question the juvenile, to assess the seriousness of the problem. Many complaints are eliminated at this stage, and the youth may be referred to a social service agency or have the charges dismissed.

Juvenile Court Procedures

Juveniles in custody must first receive an initial hearing on the validity of their detention. The youth has a right to an attorney and may have one appointed by the court if necessary. Instead of a trial, a juvenile is given an **adjudication hearing.** This functions much like an adult trial, and the juvenile has a constitutional right to due process, including the right to present evidence, cross-examine witnesses, and be represented by an attorney. In contrast to the trial of an adult, a juvenile adjudication hearing is not public.

A juvenile may be found delinquent, rather than guilty. In this event juveniles undergo a **dispositional hearing** in which the judge decides what disposition (sentence) the youth should receive. Juvenile dispositions tend to place more emphasis on rehabilitation and less on deterrence or incarceration as compared to adult sentencing. Probation is a common disposition, and the conditions of probation may be particularly strict, such as a curfew. The juvenile may be sentenced to a juvenile institution for an indeterminate amount of time, up to the maximum statutorily allowed for the violation committed. The youth may instead be sent to a halfway house or foster home for rehabilitation.

Disposition is more limited for status offenders, who have committed no adult crime. Parents may actually take their child to a local prosecutor and ask that a status offender complaint be filed against the juvenile. Such a petition might request that the youth be removed from the home and placed in some sort of government institution or foster home. Many states allow such a ruling for a child who continually refuses to obey the directions of parents or fails to attend school. Such a juvenile might be declared a **person in need of supervision.**

Juveniles have many, but not all, of the constitutional protections afforded adults. The Supreme Court has held that juveniles cannot be found in violation of a criminal act without proof beyond a reasonable doubt, though this does not extend to status offenses. Juveniles also have the right to an attorney and to confront their accusers. Juveniles do not have the right to trial by jury, however. An adult can never be tried for status offenses. Most states permit juveniles to appeal their dispositions, but the Supreme Court has never held that this is constitutionally required.

Topic 6   Jury Duty

The jury system is central to the American system of justice. Serving on a jury is both a privilege and a responsibility of citizenship. While such service may be a temporary inconvenience, the willingness of citizens to serve is essential to preserve constitutional rights and is reflective of democracy. Community participation in justice is important to public confidence in the system.

▌ Jury *Venire* and Selection

The process of jury selection can be lengthy and confusing to the ordinary person. While parts of the process may appear arbitrary, they are designed to help select an impartial jury of the defendant's peers.

Jury *Venire*

Jury selection must begin with a pool of possible jurors. This pool of potential jurors is often called a jury *venire*. Choosing the individuals in this pool for any given case requires a list of all possible jurors in the community. There is no such convenient list. In the past, some communities used lists of property taxpayers or telephone book listings. Such lists created a bias toward the wealthier citizens, who are more likely to own property and have more telephone lines. Consequently, exclusive reliance on such lists may violate the constitutional requirement of a **jury of peers.**

A defendant's right to a jury of peers does not mean that the jurors must come from the same walk of life as the defendant. A hot-rodder charged with drunk driving has no right to a jury composed of automobile fanciers. Rather, the term "jury of peers" simply means that no group in the community has been systematically excluded from the jury. The jury pool must represent a "fair cross section" of the community. Suppose that the jury pool was drawn from all those who voted in the last two presidential elections. The hot-rodder might reasonably complain that this unfairly excluded a large number of younger persons in their twenties.

There is no perfect list for a jury *venire*. Many communities still use phone books but supplement them with lists of registered voters, census rolls, and motor vehicle registration lists. Whatever the list used, the jury pool is selected randomly from the list. The *venire* may consist of hundreds of names, depending on the number of trials to be covered and the potential difficulty of finding impartial individuals. A highly publicized trial may require a larger initial *venire* of potential jurors, because many individuals may already have formed a strong opinion of the case.

If you are in the *venire* of jurors for a given case or cases, you will first receive a card in the mail summoning you to the courthouse. Many people ignore this card—over 50 percent of those summoned to jury duty fail to appear on the designated day and time. It is your civic duty to appear, however, and it is normally a crime if you fail to appear in response to the summons. Failure to appear may result in your arrest, though it is more common for the government to issue a contempt-of-court letter that may result in a fine. Many people on the *venire* will not actually be selected for a jury. One New Jersey study found that 63 percent of those summoned for jury duty never served.

Jury Selection

After responding to your summons to jury duty, you probably will sit in a large courtroom and listen to a judge lecture you on the importance of jury service and your duties. At this point, some jurors will be removed from the pool because of exemptions from jury service. An exemption is a statutory provision declaring that certain groups need not serve on juries, often because their jobs are considered so important that the individuals cannot be taken away from their employment.

Historically, states provided a large number of exemptions from jury service. Even in this century, women were exempted for a variety of reasons, including their duties to home and family. The exemption for women was deemed unconstitutional, but many professional groups are still excluded. A representative list of exemptions might include the clergy, doctors, lawyers, teachers, pharmacists, firefighters, and even embalmers. These professional exemptions do not mean that the individuals *cannot* serve on a jury. The exemptions mean that the professionals are not required to serve.

There is currently a trend toward abolishing all these exemptions. The exclusion of professionals obviously makes the jury less than representative of the community. In some states, even judges serve on juries when summoned. These states still provide some exemption for individuals who would be removed from work necessary for the public health or safety of the community or who can establish some other good cause for being exempted.

States also provide for other exemptions in addition to the named professions. Felons, minors, noncitizens, and those who cannot understand English are typically exempted. Most states also exempt severely disabled individuals. Single parents with minor children or others with special cause may also be excluded. Fear of losing one's job is not a basis for exemption from jury duty.

Suppose that you are summoned for jury duty and have no professional exemption. It also happens that the next month is particularly critical to your business and requires your close attention. You probably can receive a deferral of jury service until a later, more convenient date. Such deferrals are routinely granted.

Voir Dire

Once the exemption process is completed, the court commences *voir dire*. This is a process of questioning jurors to elicit any prejudices that could preclude the individual's impartiality. In some states, the attorneys conduct *voir dire* and question the potential jurors directly. In other states, the attorneys for the parties submit questions to the judge, who does the direct questioning of the *venire*.

Voir dire questions might inquire about whether the individual had a strong prejudice against members of a given race or religion. Other questions relate to the facts of the case, such as whether the juror would be willing to consider imposing capital punishment. A common question is whether the potential jurors have read about the case in the papers and formed an opinion about the guilt or innocence of a criminal defendant. Merely reading about a case does not disqualify a juror as biased, but the formation of a strong opinion about guilt will undermine impartiality. The court or lawyers also will ask about education, relevant experiences, family background, and other factors.

If you wish to avoid jury service, you might be tempted to state that you are biased about the case. In addition to being dishonest, this approach might not work. In a Massachusetts case, a doctor openly sought to avoid jury service for financial reasons. He stated that he would be biased in the case. The judge believed that he was lying and ordered the doctor to sit in the courtroom as a spectator for the duration of the trial.

Challenges

After a juror is questioned, the attorneys may accept him or her or they may attempt to challenge the individual. Such a challenge may prevent the person from serving on the jury. Each side of the case may raise an unlimited number of **challenges for cause.** A challenge for cause involves the attorney asking the judge to excuse the juror because of disqualifying bias or lack of competence for jury service. The judge makes the ultimate decision whether the individual should serve or not.

Each side of the case also gets a limited number of **peremptory challenges.** In capital cases, the defendant may have as many as twenty peremptories, while for misdemeanors peremptories may be limited to four. In a peremptory challenge, an attorney may excuse a prospective juror from service without giving any reason at all. Lawyers typically use peremptory challenges when they have a hunch that a juror will favor the other side but cannot establish this bias sufficiently to convince the judge to accept a challenge for cause.

The theory of jury selection is to find an impartial jury. In reality, each side is seeking to identify and seat jurors who favor its case, even if only subconsciously. Some lawyers hire psychologists for jury selection to help choose favorable jurors. The tobacco industry, for example, has discovered that current smokers tend to be unsympathetic to smokers suing cigarette companies for health harms. It is hoped that the efforts of both sides will balance each other out so that the resulting jury will be reasonably impartial.

Lawyers' use of peremptory challenges is limited by the Constitution. Such challenges cannot be used to exclude a given race or gender from the jury. For example, in a case when an African American is on trial for a crime, there might be only a few African Americans in the jury *venire*. A prosecutor who uses all his or her peremptory challenges against these African Americans, ensuring an all-white jury, violates the Constitution and denies the defendant a jury of peers.

Alternate Jurors and Jury Size

The *voir dire* and challenge process continues until a full jury can be seated. In complicated cases, *voir dire* can last for weeks. Most juries consist of twelve persons, though a court usually selects a couple of alternate jurors as well. The alternates sit in the courtroom and observe the case just like the real jurors. Should a juror fall sick during the trial or become disqualified for other reasons, an alternate juror may sit in. This avoids the waste of restarting the trial from the beginning with a new jury.

The twelve-person jury is historically traditional but not constitutionally required. Many states today, however, have approved juries of less than twelve persons. A reduced number makes it easier and quicker to empanel a jury.

▌Trial

Once you are selected for a jury, you sit through the trial in a designated spot in the courtroom. You will likely discover that trials are not as exciting as portrayed on television or in movies. Nevertheless, your close attention is required in order that the parties get a fair verdict.

Trial Procedures

The trial usually will begin with opening arguments from the attorneys for each side in the case. These arguments are not evidence but are persuasive appeals that help you understand the theories of the parties. Each side then will present its evidence in the form of physical exhibits, documents, and witnesses. The witnesses probably will be cross-examined. You must follow this presentation closely and decide which witnesses are believable. It is likely that you will be prohibited from taking notes, so you must struggle to remember key facts. After the evidence, the attorneys will present closing arguments, which are not evidence but which summarize the case and seek to persuade you.

Jury Instructions

At the end of the trial, the judge will give you instructions to help decide the case. These instructions inform you of the law that should be applied to the facts, based upon the testimony. A judge's instructions might tell you that you have to find certain facts before you may decide the case for a given side.

It is the jury's general responsibility to apply the law, even if you disagree with the law. Some juries have been known to ignore the law, a process known as jury nullification. Such a jury might decide that marijuana should be legal and therefore refuse to convict a person for possession of that drug. Jury nullification is often criticized, but jury deliberations are secret and there is no known way to prevent a jury from nullifying the law and acquitting a defendant. If the jury obviously ignores the law in

a civil case, the decision is more likely to be overturned on appeal.

Deliberations

Different juries may adopt very different approaches to deliberations. Whatever procedure is chosen, you should speak openly about your views and listen closely to the opinions of fellow jurors. You must decide the case on the evidence presented at trial, not on prejudices or outside sources of information known to you. If you forget something that occurred during the trial, you may ask the judge for information. If you wish to examine an exhibit, it generally will be provided. In contrast, courts commonly deny jury requests for transcripts of trial testimony.

It is expected that there will be disagreement among the jurors. After discussion and give-and-take, the jury is expected to reach a verdict. In criminal cases, the verdict must be unanimous. In civil cases, states provide for verdicts by a **supermajority** of the jury, such as a three-fourths or two-thirds vote. In a criminal case, if you cannot reach a verdict it is called a hung jury, and the judge must declare a **mistrial.** This means that the trial must be conducted again before a new jury. For obvious reasons, courts try to avoid such deadlocks and will urge you to compromise and reach a verdict.

It is very difficult to challenge a jury verdict after the fact. It is important that verdicts have finality and not be subject to constant reopening. Suppose that a juror evinces extreme racial bias toward the defendant during deliberations. Courts are still unsettled about whether evidence of such bias will even be considered. Some judges have refused even to listen to such evidence of bias. This makes it all the more important that unbiased jurors work to ensure a fair result. Courts are more likely to overturn a verdict if a juror lied in *voir dire* about a significant fact such as that he or she has been convicted of a felony. A $45 million verdict against Lockheed Corporation was overturned because of such a lie.

▌Jurors' Rights

Jury service is a duty that may inconvenience you. In the best case you will lose some time at work. In the worst case, you may be penalized or even fired by your employer for losing this time. The law increasingly provides some protections for jurors.

Employment

In the past under common law, an employer could fire a worker for any reason whatsoever. Today, courts recognize a **wrongful discharge** action that makes it illegal to fire employees for certain public-policy reasons. Courts have consistently found that it is wrongful to fire a person for serving on a jury. The juror will, of course, have to prove that jury service was indeed the cause of the termination. In a 1992 Oklahoma case, the juror successfully proved this point and received $175,000 in actual damages for being fired and another $175,000 in punitive damages.

In addition to private wrongful discharge actions, a number of states make it illegal to fire a worker because of jury duty. In Arizona, for example, companies are prohibited from dismissing workers, demoting workers, or taking away seniority rights for time on jury service. Breaking this law is punishable by both a fine and imprisonment of the responsible individual.

Pay

Jurors are paid a *per diem* (an allowance for daily expenses) for their service. The rate of pay for jury service is set by state law and is far below the minimum wage. A common *per diem* is $5 per day of jury duty. There is momentum to increase the *per diem*, but the most generous states pay only about $30 per day.

Firms are not necessarily required to pay wages for employees' time spent on jury service. Most cases last only two or three days, however, and companies often pay for this time. When a Los Angeles law firm refused to pay a worker for extended jury duty in 1992, the federal district court reprimanded the firm for evading its civic responsibility. The judge declared that he would "make them" pay her.

Secrecy

Traditionally, the law provides for the **sequestration** of jurors in order to maintain their objectivity. If a trial was receiving great publicity, the jurors would be confined to hotel rooms and denied access to newspapers and television, to prevent them from reading public accounts of their trial. This helped ensure that the jury decided the case only on the facts presented in court.

Today, a more extreme form of sequestration may occur for a different reason. In organized crime prosecutions, jurors have been bribed or threatened by criminals in order to gain an acquittal. In response, the identities of jurors in such trials are kept secret, and the jury may even sit behind a screen. A similar approach may be used in extremely controversial cases, such as certain police-brutality prosecutions. If such a case may produce rioting, jurors may have concern for their safety or fear public blame for bringing in an unpopular verdict. These jurors also may have their identities shielded by the court.

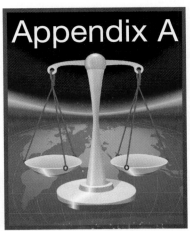

Appendix A

How to Brief a Case and Selected Cases

How to Brief a Case

To fully understand the law with respect to business, you need to be able to read and understand court decisions. To make this task easier, you can use a method of case analysis that is called *briefing*. There is a fairly standard procedure that you can follow when you "brief" any court case. You must first read the case opinion carefully. When you feel you understand the case, you can prepare a brief of it.

Although the format of the brief may vary, typically it will present the essentials of the case under headings such as those listed below.

1. **Citation.** Give the full citation for the case, including the name of the case, the date it was decided, and the court that decided it.
2. **Facts.** Briefly indicate (a) the reasons for the lawsuit; (b) the identity and arguments of the plaintiff(s) and defendant(s), respectively; and (c) the lower court's decision—if appropriate.
3. **Issue.** Concisely phrase, in the form of a question, the essential issue before the court. (If more than one issue is involved, you may have two—or even more—questions here.)
4. **Decision.** Indicate here—with a "yes" or "no," if

possible—the court's answer to the question (or questions) in the *Issue* section above.
5. **Reason.** Summarize as briefly as possible the reasons given by the court for its decision (or decisions) and the case or statutory law relied on by the court in arriving at its decision.

Sample Annotated Case

As a guide to briefing cases, we present here excerpts from the actual words of the court in the "sample court case" provided (in a "briefed" version) in the Appendix to Chapter 1. We have added annotations in the margin to explain the meaning of certain terms or phrases, or certain portions of the opinion.

Court opinions can run from a few pages to hundreds of pages in length. For reasons of space, only the essential parts of the opinions are presented in the annotated case as well as in the selected cases for briefing that follow. A series of three asterisks indicates that a portion of the text—other than citations and footnotes—has been omitted. Four asterisks indicate the omission of an entire paragraph (or more). Additionally, when an opinion cites another case or legal source, the citation to the referenced case or source has been omitted to save space and to improve the flow of the text.

SUGGS v. SERVICEMASTER EDUCATION FOOD MANAGEMENT
United States Court of Appeals, Sixth Circuit, 1996.
72 F.3d 1228.

BATCHELDER, Circuit Judge.
   * * * *
   This action originated when Sharon L. Suggs * * * filed * * * an employment discrimination charge against ServiceMaster Education Food Management

> The first part of the court opinion normally summarizes the facts of the case. The facts include the identities of the plaintiff (the party initiating the lawsuit) and the defendant (the party against whom the suit is brought), the reason for the action, the contentions of the parties, and the judgment of the lower court.

A–1

Title VII of the Civil Rights Act of 1964 is a federal law that prohibits employment discrimination on the basis of race, color, national origin, religion, or gender.

("ServiceMaster"), claiming that her termination was based on sex or race * * *, in violation of Title VII of the Civil Rights Act of 1964. Following a two-day * * * trial, the district court awarded judgment to Suggs and ordered ServiceMaster to reinstate her. The court awarded Suggs $100,460.03 in back pay from the time of her termination * * * to the end of trial. In addition, the court * * * required ServiceMaster to pay Suggs "additional backpay based on an annual salary of $44,409.63 for the period from the conclusion of trial * * * through the effective date of an offer of reinstatement by ServiceMaster to Ms. Suggs." ServiceMaster timely appealed * * * the district court's judgment in favor of Suggs * * *.

* * * *

Suggs has a B.S. degree in food and nutritional sciences from Tuskegee Institute. ServiceMaster, a corporate/institutional food catering service, hired Suggs as an assistant-director in 1984. In 1988, she was promoted to director and was given responsibility for the ServiceMaster account at Tennessee State University ("TSU"). * * * In September 1989, the health department closed the main campus cafeteria at TSU for several hours to correct significant problems with the facility conditions. Terry Van Booven, the ServiceMaster area manager to whom Suggs reported, conceded that the facilities were a "significant part" of the reason for the shut-down and that Suggs was not authorized to order repairs.

One week after the shut-down, Van Booven approved a four percent pay raise for Suggs. Van Booven then ranked the directors under his supervision according to the profitability of their facilities and quality of service provided to their clients. Suggs was ranked fifth among the twelve directors * * *. Van Booven approved another four percent pay increase for Suggs in October 1990. He rated Suggs' performance in the area of client relations as "satisfactory" on her November 1990 evaluation. * * * Suggs was terminated on January 17, 1991, and was given ten days' severance pay. According to her employment contract, Suggs would have been eligible for severance pay only if she had performed her job adequately. * * * ServiceMaster stated that "major issues concerning [her] separation * * * were: (1) client dissatisfaction; (2) continuing unresolved operational problems; [and] (3) failure to meet financial and budget commitments."

Gordon, the man who replaced Suggs as director of the TSU account * * *, testified that Van Booven told him * * * it was time to show that a man could run the operation better. * * * When ServiceMaster lost the TSU account to another company in June 1991, ServiceMaster offered the male production supervisor of the TSU account three different director positions, in New York, Kentucky, and North Carolina. * * *

Bryant, a male director who had been ranked below Suggs, was promoted to area manager in 1992. Herman, who had been ranked last among the twelve directors, was promoted and transferred when he lost the account for which he was responsible.
* * *

* * * *

Under Title VII of the Civil Rights Act of 1964, *protected class* is the legal term used to denote any persons classified because of race, color, national origin, religion, or gender.

To prevail on her * * * claim of discriminatory discharge, the plaintiff must prove the following elements: she belongs to a protected class; she was qualified for her position; she was discharged by the defendant; * * * after she was discharged, she was replaced with a similarly qualified person or her employer sought a similarly qualified replacement, who was not a member of her protected class; and her treatment differed from that accorded to otherwise similarly-situated individuals outside her protected group. After a * * * trial, the district court * * * analyzed the evidence * * *, finding that the female plaintiff in this case was indisputably a member of a protected class, that she had been terminated by the defendant and replaced by a man, and that she had demonstrated that she was qualified for the position from which she had been discharged. * * * [T]he district court concluded * * * that ServiceMaster's proffered reasons for removing Suggs from her position and terminating her employment were a pretext to mask unlawful discrimination.

> The lower court's decision.

* * * *

The evidence does not support a claim that ServiceMaster's client TSU was dissatisfied with Suggs * * *. Although ServiceMaster's contract with TSU provided that the client could request removal of ServiceMaster employees from the TSU account, no TSU official ever made such a request, and Suggs' manager had, only weeks before her termination, given her a satisfactory rating on client satisfaction. Competent evidence in the record concerning "operational problems" points to the TSU facility itself, rather than to Suggs' management * * *. As to Suggs' purported failure to meet financial and budget commitments, * * * the problems * * * had been ongoing for many years prior to Suggs' promotion to director of the account. She had recently been evaluated favorably for profitability. Suggs received merit raises throughout her period of employment with ServiceMaster. Suggs' manager had consistently rated her performance favorably and had recently approved another increase in her salary. When she was terminated, Suggs was given ten days of severance pay to which she would not have been entitled if she had been discharged for failing to perform her duties adequately.

> The appellate court's conclusion on the first part of the issue.

> The court's conclusion on the second part of the issue.

The evidence supports Suggs' claim that ServiceMaster's stated reasons for terminating her employment were pretextual and that Suggs was actually terminated because she was a female. Suggs was qualified for the position she held. She was replaced by a man and was not offered another position with the company when she was removed from the TSU account and later terminated, although ServiceMaster had identified positions available at other locations. In contrast to ServiceMaster's treatment of Suggs, other directors in Suggs' area, who had been ranked below Suggs for profitability and client satisfaction, were offered transfers and relocations when their accounts were lost. Those directors were men. * * *

* * * *

The district court's judgment that Suggs was terminated in violation of Title VII is AFFIRMED * * *.

> The judgment of the lower court is affirmed.

▌ Selected Cases for Briefing

• •

The cases presented in the following pages have all been referenced in *Case Briefing Assignments* within the text.

Case A.1   Reference: *Problem 2–12.*

AUSTIN v. BERRYMAN

United States Court of Appeals, Fourth Circuit, 1989.
878 F.2d 786.

MURNAGHAN, Circuit Judge:

We have before us for *en banc* reconsideration [consideration by the whole court] an appeal taken from an action successfully brought by Barbara Austin in the United States

District Court for the Western District of Virginia against the Virginia Employment Commission, challenging a denial of unemployment compensation benefits. * * * In brief, Austin charged, *inter alia* [among other things], that the denial of her claim for unemployment benefits, based on a Virginia statute specifically precluding such benefits for any individual who voluntarily quits work to join his or her spouse in a new location, was an unconstitutional infringement upon the incidents of marriage protected by the fourteenth amendment and an unconstitutional burden on her first amendment right to the free exercise of her religion. Her religion happened to command that she follow her spouse wherever he might go and the sincerity of her religious belief was not questioned. The district court found in Austin's favor and awarded injunctive relief and retroactive benefits.

On appeal, Judge Sprouse, writing for a panel majority, found that the denial of benefits did not implicate Austin's fourteenth amendment rights, but that it did unconstitutionally burden Austin's right to the free exercise of her religion. The panel also found, however, that any award of retroactive benefits was barred by the eleventh amendment. One panel member concurred with the panel majority as to the fourteenth and eleventh amendment issues, but dissented as to the existence of a free exercise violation. The panel opinion now, of course, has been vacated by a grant of rehearing *en banc*.

After careful consideration of the additional arguments proffered by both sides, the Court, *en banc*, is convinced that the panel majority correctly concluded that denying Austin unemployment benefits did not infringe upon fundamental marital rights protected by the fourteenth amendment. To this extent, we adopt the majority panel opinion. We also find, however, that the denial of benefits did not unconstitutionally burden Austin's first amendment right to the free exercise of her religion. We are persuaded that the views expressed on the first amendment, free exercise of religion claim in the opinion dissenting in part from the panel majority are correct, and we hereby adopt that opinion as that of the *en banc* court. As we find that Austin is not entitled to any relief, we need not address whether the eleventh amendment bars an award of retroactive benefits.

The decisive consideration, as we see it, is that the proximate cause of Austin's unemployment is geographic distance, not her religious beliefs. There is no conflict between the circumstances of work and Austin's religious precepts. Austin's religious beliefs do not "require" her "to refrain from the work in question." Austin is unable to work simply because she is now too far removed from her employer to make it practical. In striking contrast, if one, for genuine religious beliefs, moves to a new residence in order to continue to live with a spouse, and that residence is not geographically so removed as to preclude regular attendance at the worksite, no unemployment, and hence no unemployment benefits, will arise. That amounts to proof that extent of geographical [distance], not religious belief, led to Austin's disqualification for unemployment benefits.

Austin voluntarily decided to quit her job and join her spouse in a new geographic location 150 miles away. Virginia has stated that every individual who follows such a course, no matter what the reason, religious or non-religious, is disqualified for unemployment benefits. To craft judicially a statutory exception only for those individuals who profess Austin's religious convictions, particularly in the absence of a direct conflict between a given employment practice and a religious belief, would, in our view, result in a subsidy to members of a particular religious belief, impermissible under the Establishment Clause.

Accordingly, the judgment of the district court is REVERSED.

Case A.2   *Reference: Problem 5–13.*

BURLINGHAM v. MINTZ
Supreme Court of Montana, 1995.
891 P.2d 527.

HUNT, Justice.

* * * *

On March 21, 1990, Candance Burlingham visited Dr. Mintz for a check-up and teeth cleaning. Dr. Mintz determined that she needed further treatment. Dr. Mintz also determined that Candance suffered from temporomandibular joint (TMJ) pain. On April 20, 1990, Candance returned to Dr. Mintz for treatment of her upper left rear molar. After applying a local anesthetic, Dr. Mintz noted that Candance had difficulty keeping her mouth open. To help keep her mouth open, Dr. Mintz placed a bite block between Candance's jaws. A bite block is a rubber coated tapered device with a serrated surface to keep it in place. The bite block was left in for approximately 45 minutes to one hour while Dr. Mintz completed the work. Later that day Candance began to suffer severe TMJ pain which did not abate. Dr. Mintz filled several more of Candance's teeth over the next few months, although he was hindered by her TMJ pain. In October 1990, Dr. Mintz referred Candance to a * * * specialist [in Kalispell, Montana,] who attempted, without success, to relieve Candance's pain. Eventually, Candance underwent restorative arthroscopic surgery in Spokane, Washington, to alleviate her TMJ pain.

On September 18, 1992, appellants filed suit alleging that Dr. Mintz's negligence caused Candance's TMJ injury. Appellants' first standard of care expert, Dr. James McGivney, was deposed on June 11, 1993. On August 12, 1993, appellants filed a motion asking the District Court to qualify Dr. McGivney as an **expert** [a person whose professional training or experience qualifies him or her to testify on a particular subject]. * * *

On February 8, 1994, the District Court denied appellants' motion[,] finding that Dr. McGivney, a suburban St. Louis dentist, was not familiar with the standards of practice or medical facilities available in Eureka, Montana, in a similar locality in Montana, or a similar locality anywhere in the country. The District Court granted appellants until the end of February to find another expert.

* * * *

On June 7, 1994, respondent filed a motion for summary judgment, arguing that appellants were not able to present expert testimony to meet their burden of proof to establish * * * a violation by respondent of his standard of care. The District Court granted respondent's motion. Appellants appeal from the order granting summary judgment.

* * * *

The District Court concluded that appellants' proposed experts had no idea of the standards of practice in Eureka, Montana, in a similar locality in Montana, or in a similar place anywhere else in the country. A review of the testimony of respondent's and appellants' standard of care experts reveals little, if any, contradictory testimony as to the applicable standard of care for a dentist treating a patient suffering from TMJ pain

in Eureka, Montana, or any other community in the country. Respondent's first standard of care expert testified that, with the exception of limited specialties, the same standard of care that applies to dentists in San Francisco and Kalispell, applies to dentists in Eureka. He agreed that the standard of care required in the diagnosis of and the treatment decisions regarding TMJ pain would be the same in San Francisco, Kalispell, and Eureka. Respondent's second standard of care expert testified that in non-emergency situations the standard of care for dentists in Eureka is the same as the non-emergency standard of care anywhere else in the United States.

* * * *

We conclude that appellants' standard of care experts were familiar with the applicable non-emergency standard of care for dentists in Eureka if, by either direct or indirect knowledge, they were familiar with the applicable non-emergency standard of care for dentists in their communities, regardless of size or location. As a result, we hold that the District Court erred by excluding appellants' standard of care experts.

* * * *

* * * We reverse the summary judgment and remand this case to the District Court for further proceedings.

Case A.3   Reference: Problem 13–12.

POTTER v. OSTER
Supreme Court of Iowa, 1988.
426 N.W.2d 148.

NEUMAN, Justice.

This is a suit in equity brought by the plaintiffs to rescind an installment land contract based on the seller's inability to convey title. The question on appeal is whether, in an era of declining land values, returning the parties to the status quo works an inequitable result. We think not. Accordingly, we affirm the district court judgment for rescission and restitution.

The facts are largely undisputed. Because the case was tried in equity, our review is *de novo* [as if the case had not been heard and no decision rendered before]. We give weight to the findings of the trial court, particularly where the credibility of witnesses is concerned, but we are not bound thereby.

The parties, though sharing a common interest in agribusiness, present a study in contrasts. We think the disparity in their background and experience is notable insofar as it bears on the equities of the transaction in issue. Plaintiff Charles Potter is a farm laborer and his wife, Sue, is a homemaker and substitute teacher. They have lived all their lives within a few miles of the real estate in question. Defendant Merrill Oster is an agricultural journalist and recognized specialist in land investment strategies. He owns Oster Communications, a multimillion dollar publishing concern devoted to furnishing farmers the latest in commodity market analysis and advice on an array of farm issues.

In May 1978, Oster contracted with Florence Stark to purchase her 160-acre farm in Howard County, Iowa, for $260,000 on a ten-year contract at seven percent interest. Oster then sold the homestead and nine acres to Charles and Sue Potter for $70,000. Potters paid $18,850 down and executed a ten-year installment contract for the balance at 8.5% interest. Oster then executed a contract with Robert Bishop for the sale of the remaining 151 acres as part of a package deal that included the sale of seventeen farms for a sum exceeding $5.9 million.

These back-to-back contracts collapsed like dominoes in March 1985 when Bishop failed to pay Oster and Oster failed to pay Stark the installments due on their respective contracts. Stark commenced **forfeiture proceedings** [proceedings to retake the property, in this case because Oster failed to perform a legal obligation—payment under the contract—and thus forfeited his right to the land]. Potters had paid every installment when due under their contract with Oster and had included Stark as a **joint payee** [one of two or more payees—persons to whom checks or notes are payable] with Oster on their March 1, 1985, payment * * * [The Potters'] interest in the real estate was forfeited along with Oster's and Bishop's and they were forced to move from their home in August 1985.

Potters then sued Oster to rescind their contract with him, claiming restitution damages for all consideration paid * * *

Trial testimony * * * revealed that the market value of the property had decreased markedly since its purchase. Expert appraisers valued the homestead and nine acres between $27,500 and $35,000. Oster himself placed a $28,000 value on the property; Potter $39,000. Evidence was also received placing the reasonable rental value of the property at $150 per month, or a total of $10,800 for the six-year Potter occupancy.

The district court concluded the Potters were entitled to rescission of the contract and return of the consideration paid including principal and interest, cost of improvements, closing expenses, and taxes for a total of $65,169.37. From this the court deducted $10,800 for six years' rental, bringing the final judgment to $54,369.37.

On appeal, Oster challenges the judgment. * * * [H]e claims Potters had an adequate remedy at law for damages which should have been measured by the actual economic loss sustained * * *.

* * * *

Rescission is a restitutionary remedy which attempts to restore the parties to their positions at the time the contract was executed. The remedy calls for a return of the land to the seller, with the buyer given judgment for payments made under the contract plus the value of improvements, less reasonable rental value for the period during which the buyer was in possession. The remedy has long been available in Iowa to buyers under land contracts when the seller has no title to convey.

Rescission is considered an extraordinary remedy, however, and is ordinarily not available to a litigant as a matter of right but only when, in the discretion of the court, it is necessary to obtain equity. Our cases have established three requirements that must be met before rescission will be granted. First, the injured party must not be in default. Second, the breach must be substantial and go to the heart of the contract. Third, remedies at law must be inadequate.

The first two tests are easily met in the present case. Potters are entirely without fault in this transaction. They tendered their 1985 installment payment to Oster before the forfeiture, and no additional payments were due until 1986. On the question of materiality, Oster's loss of **equitable title** [ownership rights protected in equity] to the homestead by forfeiture caused not only substantial, but total breach of his obligation to insure **peaceful possession** [an implied promise made by a landowner, when selling or renting land, that the buyer or tenant will not be evicted or disturbed by the landowner or a person having a lien or superior title] and convey marketable title under the Oster-Potter contract.

Only the third test—the inadequacy of damages at law—is contested by Oster on appeal. * * *

Restoring the status quo is the goal of the restitutionary remedy of rescission. Here, the district court accomplished the goal

by awarding Potters a sum representing all they had paid under the contract rendered worthless by Oster's default. Oster contends that in an era of declining land values, such a remedy goes beyond achieving the status quo and results in a windfall to the Potters. Unwilling to disgorge the benefits he has received under the unfulfilled contract, Oster would have the court shift the **"entrepreneural risk"** [the risk assumed by one who initiates, and provides or controls the management of, a business enterprise] of market loss to the Potters by limiting their recovery to the difference between the property's market value at breach ($35,000) and the contract balance ($27,900). In other words, Oster claims the court should have awarded * * * damages. * * *

* * * *

* * * [L]egal remedies are considered inadequate when the damages cannot be measured with sufficient certainty. Contrary to Oster's assertion that Potters' compensation should be limited to the difference between the property's fair market value and contract balance at time of breach, * * * damages are correctly calculated as the difference between contract price and market value at the time for performance. Since the time of performance in this case would have been March 1990, the market value of the homestead and acreage cannot be predicted with any certainty, thus rendering such a formulation inadequate.

Most importantly, the fair market value of the homestead at the time of forfeiture is an incorrect measure of the benefit Potters lost. It fails to account for the special value Potters placed on the property's location and residential features that uniquely suited their family. For precisely this reason, remedies at law are presumed inadequate for breach of a real estate contract. Oster has failed to overcome that presumption here. His characterization of the transaction as a mere market loss for Potters, compensable by a sum which would enable them to make a nominal down payment on an equivalent homestead, has no legal or factual support in this record. * * *

* * * *

In summary, we find no error in the trial court's conclusion that Potters were entitled to rescission of the contract and return of all benefits allowed thereunder, less the value of reasonable rental for the period of occupancy * * *.

AFFIRMED.

Case A.4   *Reference: Problem 14–13.*

GOLDKIST, INC. v. BROWNLEE

Court of Appeals of Georgia, 1987.
182 Ga.App. 287,
355 S.E.2d 733.

BEASLEY, Judge.

The question is whether the two defendant farmers, who as a partnership both grew and sold their crops, were established

by the undisputed facts as not being "merchants" as a matter of law, according to the definition in OCGA [Section] 11-2-104(1) [Official Code of Georgia Annotated; Section 11-2-104(1) corresponds to UCC 2-104(1)]. We are not called upon here to consider the other side of the coin, whether farmers or these farmers in particular are "merchants" as a matter of law.

In November 1983, Goldkist sued under OCGA [Section] 11-2-712 for losses arising out of the necessity to cover [a remedy of the buyer in a breached sales contract; if the seller fails to deliver the goods contracted for, the buyer can purchase them elsewhere and recover any additional price paid, plus damages, from the breaching seller (see Chapter 16)] a contract for soybeans. It produced a written confirmation dated July 22 for 5,000 bushels of soybeans to be delivered to it by defendants between August 22 and September 22 at $6.88 per bushel. A defense was that there was no writing signed by either of the Brownlees, as required by OCGA [Section] 11-2-201(1).

* * * [T]he court agreed with the Brownlees that the circumstances did not fit any of the exceptions provided for in Section 201 and granted summary judgment. On appeal, Goldkist asserts that defendants came within subsection (2), relating to dealings "between merchants."

Appellees admit that their crops are "goods" as defined in OCGA [Section] 11-2-105. The record establishes the following facts. The partnership had been operating the row crop farming business for 14 years, producing peanuts, soybeans, corn, milo, and wheat on 1,350 acres, and selling the crops.

It is also established without dispute that Barney Brownlee, whose deposition was taken, was familiar with the marketing procedure of "booking" crops, which sometimes occurred over the phone between the farmer and the buyer, rather than in person, and a written contract would be signed later. He periodically called plaintiff's agent to check the price, which fluctuated. If the price met his approval, he sold soybeans. At this time the partnership still had some of its 1982 crop in storage, and the price was rising slowly. Mr. Brownlee received a written confirmation in the mail concerning a sale of soybeans and did not contact plaintiff to contest it but simply did nothing. In addition to the agricultural business, Brownlee operated a gasoline service station.

In dispute are the facts with respect to whether or not an oral contract was made between Barney Brownlee for the partnership and agent Harrell for the buyer in a July 22 telephone conversation. The plaintiff's evidence was that it occurred and that it was discussed soon thereafter with Brownlee at the service station on two different occasions, when he acknowledged it, albeit reluctantly, because the market price of soybeans had risen. Mr. Brownlee denies booking the soybeans and denies the nature of the conversations at his service station with Harrell and the buyer's manager.

In this posture, of course, the question of whether an oral contract was made would not yield to summary adjudication, as apparently recognized by the trial court, which based its decision on the preliminary question of whether the Brownlee partnership was a "merchant."

Whether or not the farmers in this case are "merchants" as a matter of law, which is not before us, the evidence does not demand a conclusion that they are outside of that category which is excepted from the requirement of a signed writing to bind a buyer and seller of goods. * * *

* * * *

Defendants' narrow construction of "merchant" would, given the booking procedure used for the sale of farm products, thus guarantee to the farmers the best of both possible worlds (fulfill booking if price goes down after booking and reject it if price improves) and to the buyers the worst of both possible worlds. On the other hand, construing "merchants" in OCGA [Section] 11-2-104(1) as not excluding as a matter of law farmers such as the ones in this case, protects them equally as well as the buyer. If the market price declines after the booking, they are assured of the higher booking price; the buyer cannot renege, as OCGA [Section] 11-2-201(2) would apply.

* * * *

We believe this is the proper construction to give the two statutes, OCGA [Sections] 11-2-104(1) and 11-2-201(2), as taken together they are thus further branches stemming from the centuries-old simple legal idea *pacta servanda sunt*—agreements are to be kept. So construed, they evince the legislative intent to enforce the accepted practices of the marketplace among those who frequent it.

Judgment reversed.

Case A.5   *Reference: Problem 18–13.*

FEDERAL DEPOSIT INSURANCE CORP. v. TRANS PACIFIC INDUSTRIES, INC.

United States Court of Appeals, Fifth Circuit, 1994.
14 F.3d 10.

POLITZ, Chief Judge:

The FDIC [Federal Deposit Insurance Corporation,] as receiver for Harris County Bank—Houston, N.A.[,] filed suit to enforce two promissory notes payable to the Bank, one for $67,500 and the other for $100,000. The suit sought recovery from Trans Pacific Industries, Inc. [TPI,] and [W. K.] Robbins, TPI's board chairman. On cross-motions for summary judg-ment the district court held both defendants liable. Robbins appealed.

* * * *

The top left corner of each note contains a block for designation of "Borrower(s) Name(s) & Address(es)." The only borrower identified in that block is TPI. Underneath, the text begins with the sentence "The undersigned Borrower(s) (if more than one, jointly and severally and hereinafter, whether one or more, called Borrower) promises to pay to the order of the above-named Lender * * * ." The signature block in the bottom right corner has three lines with the designation "Borrower" at the end of each. On each note "TRANS PACIFIC INDUSTRIES" is typewritten on the first line and the name "W. K. Robbins, Jr." is typed and signed below. On the reverse side there is a guaranty which is unsigned.

Robbins contends that he signed only in his capacity as agent for TPI. The government contends that he is bound in his individual capacity as well.

The import of a signature by an authorized representative is governed by section 3-403 of the Uniform Commercial Code. That section provides in pertinent part: ["](2) An authorized representative who signs his own name to an instrument . . . .(b) except as otherwise established between the immediate parties, is personally obligated if the instrument names the person represented but does not show that the representative signed in a representative capacity * * * .["] The FDIC contends that Robbins is personally liable under subsection (2)(b) because the note did not show that Robbins signed in a representative capacity. We are not persuaded.

In order to avoid personal responsibility, the general rule is that an individual signing in a representative capacity must name his principal and must place "by:" before his signature or must follow it with a display of agency status, preferably his title in the represented institution. Thus, "TPI, W. K. Robbins, Jr.," without more, would bind Robbins. Section 3-403(2)(b), however, requires that we consider the face of the entire instrument. When we do so in the context of business expectations, we find it abundantly clear that Robbins signed in a representative capacity only.

The face of the note unambiguously shows that TPI was the sole borrower; it is the only entity listed in the upper left-hand identification block. The FDIC attempts to nullify the import of the identification block by arguing that the first sentence of the text—"The undersigned Borrower(s) * * * promises to pay"—renders each signatory a borrower. It is a basic tenet of contract interpretation, however, that one part of a writing cannot be read to nullify another. Interpreted in harmony with the identification block, the first sentence of the text must mean: TPI, which signs below, promises to pay . . . . The instrument therefore indicates on its face that TPI is the sole borrower and maker of the note.

A corporation can act only through agents. Assuming **per arguendo** [for the sake of argument] that the typewritten name of the organization conceivably might pass muster as a signature under U.C.C. section 3-401(2), there are few if any lenders who would accept it as binding. That is both understandable and prudent. The usual business practice is to bind the corporation with the signature of an officer authorized by the corporation to sign on its behalf. On the notes before us, TPI was bound by the signature of Robbins. That Robbins signed on TPI's behalf would be apparent to any holder of the note. It must have been apparent to the FDIC that Robbins signed for TPI for it sued TPI on the note. The district court agreed for it rendered summary judgment against TPI. "Having secured a judgment on that basis against the corporate defendant, we are at a loss to see how [the FDIC] may now contend that [Robbins'] signature was on his individual behalf and not in a representative capacity. * * *

* * * *

The judgment of the district court is REVERSED, judgment is RENDERED in favor of W. K. Robbins, Jr., and the case is REMANDED for further proceedings consistent herewith.

Case A.6   Reference: Problem 22–11.

HAWLEY v. CEMENT INDUSTRIES, INC.
United States Court of Appeals, Eleventh Circuit, 1995.
51 F.3d 246.

PER CURIAM:

* * * *

In September 1990, Appellant Phillip E. Hawley ("Appellant") filed a Chapter 7 bankruptcy petition, claiming less than $20,000 in assets. In a signed statement dated June 15, 1989, Appellant listed his total assets at $13,822,477, total liabilities at $1,876,814, and total net worth at $11,945,663. Later in 1990, one of Appellant's creditors, Cement Industries, Inc. ("Appellee"), filed an adversary proceeding pursuant to 11 U.S.C. s 727(a)(5), urging the court to deny Appellant's discharge based on his failure to satisfactorily explain the loss of his assets between the filings of his financial statement and his bankruptcy petition.

Section 727(a)(5) of the Bankruptcy Code provides as follows: * * * ["](a) the court shall grant the debtor a discharge, unless— * * * the debtor has failed to explain satisfactorily, before determination of denial of discharge under this paragraph, any loss of assets or deficiency of assets to meet the debtor's liabilities.["]

* * * *

The bankruptcy court denied Appellant's discharge, observing that the Appellant, a "sophisticated and experienced businessman," had been unable to present documentation to explain the discrepancy between the value of his assets as listed in 1989 and the value he had listed in his bankruptcy petition in 1990. The court found a "complete lack of documentation to support the Debtor's loss of assets" and determined that "when examining the totality of the circumstances, this Court finds a pattern which leads this Court to conclude that the Debtor has not satisfactorily explained the loss or diminution of his assets."

The Appellant appealed to the district court. The district court affirmed and adopted the opinion of the bankruptcy court "as fully as if copied verbatim." The district court dismissed the appeal and Appellant then appealed to this Court * * * .

* * * *

* * * Appellant argues that Appellee failed to carry its burden in showing that Appellant's explanations for the loss of his assets were unsatisfactory. In its [Section] 727(a)(5) action, Appellee had the initial burden of proving its objection to Appellant's discharge. Appellee sustained this burden by showing the vast discrepancies between Appellant's 1989 financial statement and his 1990 Chapter 7 schedules. Once the party objecting to the discharge establishes the basis for its objection, the burden then shifts to the debtor "to explain satisfactorily the loss." "To be satisfactory, 'an explanation' must convince the judge." "Vague and indefinite explanations of losses that are based on estimates uncorroborated by documentation are unsatisfactory." Obviously, Appellant's explanations did not "convince the judge." The bankruptcy judge clearly found Appellant's testimony and complete lack of documentation unconvincing. Upon review of the record, we find that the bankruptcy judge did not clearly err in finding that Appellant's explanation of his loss of more than $13 million in assets over the course of fifteen months was too vague and indefinite to be "satisfactory." Therefore, the judgment of the district court is AFFIRMED.

Case A.7   Reference: Problem 27–13.

MASCHMEIER v. SOUTHSIDE PRESS, LTD.

Court of Appeals of Iowa, 1989.
435 N.W.2d 377.

HABHAB, Judge.

Defendant Kenneth E. Maschmeier and Charlotte A. Maschmeier created a corporation, Southside Press, Ltd., that did business at 1220 Second Avenue North in Council Bluffs. This building is owned by Kenneth and Charlotte and was leased by them to the corporation. Kenneth and Charlotte are the majority shareholders, with each having 1300 shares. They are the only officers and directors of the corporation.

They gifted to their two sons [Marty and Larry] each 1200 shares of stock. All the parties were employed by Southside Press until the summer of 1985 when, because of family disagreements, Marty and Larry were terminated as employees. * * *

The parents on August 2, 1985, created a new corporation, Southside Press of the Midlands, Ltd. They are its only officers and directors. As individuals they terminated the lease of their building * * * with Southside and leased the same premises to Midlands. In addition, Kenneth, as president of Southside, entered into a lease with himself as president of Midlands whereby the printing equipment and two of the vehicles were leased to Midlands for $22,372 per year for five years, with an option to buy such assets at the end of the lease term at their fair market value but not to exceed $20,000. In addition, the inventory and two other vehicles owned by Southside were sold by it to Midlands. Notwithstanding the fact that a substantial part of the assets of Southside had been disposed of, the parents still received an annual salary from it of more than $20,000.

After Marty and Larry's employment with Southside had terminated, each obtained employment with other printing companies in the same metropolitan area. The family disagreement continued. All stockholders were employed by companies that were competitive to Southside. Ultimately, the parents, as majority shareholders, offered to buy the sons' shares of stock for $20 per share. Their sons felt that this amount was inadequate. Thus, this lawsuit.

In 1985, Southside Press had gross sales of more than $600,000. The trial court found that in 1985 the corporate assets had a fair market value of $160,745. Shareholders' equity was found to be $236,502.92, and divided by the number of shares equals $47.30 per share. The court found that the majority shareholders had been abusive and oppressive to the minority shareholders by wasting the corporate assets and leaving Southside Press only a shell of a corporation. The court ordered the majority shareholders to pay $47.30 per share to the sons, or $56,760 to each son, plus interest at the maximum legal rate from the date of the filing of the petition.

* * * *

* * * [D]efendants state that the shares were valued at $20 pursuant to the corporate bylaws and should be enforced as an agreement of the shareholders. * * *

* * * *

Whenever a situation exists which is contrary to the principles of equity and which can be redressed within the scope of judicial action, a court of equity will devise a remedy to meet the situation though no similar relief has been granted before. The district court has the power to liquidate a corporation under [Iowa Code] section 496A.94(1). This statute also allows the district court to fashion other equitable relief.

It is contended that, in order for the trial court to have properly invoked the powers under section 496A.94(1), it had to find either the majority shareholders were oppressive in their conduct towards the minority shareholders, or that the majority shareholders misapplied or wasted corporate assets.

* * * The alleged oppressive conduct by those in control of a close corporation must be analyzed in terms of "fiduciary duties" owed by majority shareholders to the minority shareholders and "reasonable expectations" held by minority shareholders in committing capital and labor to the particular enterprise, in light of the predicament in which minority shareholders in a close corporation can be placed by a "freeze-out" situation.

* * * The trial court found * * * here [that] the majority shareholders attempted to "freeze out" or "squeeze out" the minority shareholders by terminating their employment and not permitting them to participate in the business.

* * * *

We concur with the trial court's findings that the majority shareholders acted oppressively toward the minority shareholders and wasted corporate assets. In this respect, we further determine that the trial court properly invoked Iowa Code section 496A.94 when it fashioned the remedy requiring the majority shareholders to purchase the shares of the minority.

But that does not resolve the problem, for as stated above, the plaintiff does not on appeal challenge that part of the court's ruling that ordered the majority shareholders to purchase the minority's stock. The appellant challenges the method fashioned by the trial court in fixing the value of the stock and payment thereof by asserting it should be governed by the bylaws.

The articles of incorporation of Southside vested in the directors of the corporation the "authority to make provisions in the Bylaws of the corporation restricting the transfer of shares of this corporation." This the board of directors did when they adopted the following bylaw that relates to restrictions on the transferability of stock. * * *

* * * *

Section 3 [of the corporate bylaws] is a restriction on stock transfer. If a shareholder intends to sell his stock, he must first offer it to the corporation at a price "agreed upon by the shareholders at each annual meeting." The shareholders must agree on the value of the stock and if they are unable to do so, each has a right to select an appraiser and the appraisers shall appoint another and in this instance the five appraisers are to act as a Board of Appraisers to value the stock.

* * * Since none of the shareholders requested appraisers, we deem this, as the trial court did, to be a waiver. We concur with this statement from the trial court's ruling: "All parties have left the Court with the burden of evaluating the corporate stock."

* * * *

We agree with the defendants that a contractual formula price is enforceable even if the formula price is less than its fair market value. But here the parties were unable to agree to a price, i.e., at the last meeting of the stockholders. Thus the trial court was called upon to do so.

Courts have generally held that no one factor governs the valuation of shares; but that all factors, such as market value, asset value, future earning prospects, should be considered. In this case, the parties relied rather heavily on what is referred to in the record as book value (shareholders' equity) in arriving at stock value. The trial court likewise used shareholder equity but adjusted that amount by the present day fair market value of corporate assets.

* * * *

We determine that under the circumstances here the valuation per share as fixed by the trial court and the method it employed in arriving at value is fair and reasonable. However, we further conclude that the amount Larry and Marty are to receive must be reduced by the total amount of loans made to them as they appear on the corporate books.

* * * *

We affirm and modify.

Case A.8   Reference: Problem 31–13.
ROBERTS v. WALMART STORES, INC.
United States District Court, E.D. Missouri, 1990.
736 F.Supp. 1527

LIMBAUGH, District Judge.

Plaintiffs are black citizens of the United States. Defendant is a retail department store. On December 5, 1989 plaintiffs were customers at a store operated by defendant in St. Charles, Missouri. During this visit plaintiffs purchased several items and presented defendant with a check in payment for the merchandise. Defendant recorded the race of plaintiffs on the check. Plaintiffs, upon becoming aware that their race was being recorded on the check, returned the merchandise and retrieved the check. Plaintiffs then filed a two-count amended complaint against defendant alleging that defendant's practice of recording the race of black citizens who pay for merchandise by check violates the Thirteenth Amendment. * * *

The Thirteenth Amendment is implicated when it is alleged that a private individual or entity deliberately acted in a way to segregate, humiliate or belittle a person of the black race in a way that prevented such a person from freely exercising a right guaranteed to all citizens. * * * Plaintiffs may not maintain a cause of action against defendant, a private corporation, directly under the Thirteenth Amendment. Instead, plaintiffs must base their claims on one of the implementing statutes of the Thirteenth Amendment. * * *

* * * *

Defendant asserts that its recording the race of the plaintiffs on the check is post-formation conduct which is no longer actionable. * * * [The] resolution of this civil rights claim turns on an interpretation of the Missouri Commercial Code to determine whether the contract was formed at the time the alleged violation occurred. The court does not possess enough information about the retail transaction to ascertain whether a contract was already formed at the time defendant recorded the race of plaintiffs on the check. Therefore, defendant's motion to dismiss plaintiffs" claim * * * is denied.

* * * *

First, defendant asserts that plaintiffs have failed to plead that blacks were treated any differently than whites. Although plaintiffs did not plead that whites purchasing merchandise by check do not have their race recorded on their check, plaintiffs' complaint should not be dismissed unless it appears that plaintiffs could "prove no set of facts in support of the claim which would entitle them to relief." * * *

Second, defendant asserts that plaintiffs failed to plead a cause of action * * * because plaintiffs were able to purchase the merchandise with a check. Therefore, although defendant recorded plaintiffs' race on the check, no civil rights violation occurred because defendant did not refuse to sell plaintiffs the merchandise due to their race. * * * Although defendant was willing to consummate the retail transaction with plaintiffs, defendant is not absolved from liability * * * if defendant's motives in recording the race of plaintiffs was infected with racial discrimination. * * *

* * * *

There is no authority for plaintiffs' argument that payment by check, absent an agreement by the seller to hold the check for a period of time before presentment to the drawee, constitutes an extension of credit rather than a cash transaction. * * *

* * * *

Defendant seeks for the Court to require plaintiffs to file a second amended complaint because "plaintiffs' amended complaint is so vague and ambiguous that defendant cannot reasonably be required to frame a responsive pleading." * * * The Court has reviewed plaintiffs' amended complaint and concludes that plaintiffs' allegations are clear and plain and are undoubtedly sufficient to satisfy the requirements of notice pleading * * *.

[The district court granted defendant's motion to dismiss in part and denied defendant's motion to dismiss in part.]

Case A.9   Reference: Problem 34–12.

STRANG v. HOLLOWELL

Court of Appeals of North Carolina, 1990.
387 S.E.2d 664.

WELLS, Judge.

On 2 January 1987 plaintiff met with defendants Hollowell and Jones in Cary, North Carolina to negotiate a consignment agreement for the sale of plaintiff's 1974 Pantera automobile which had an estimated value of $23,000 to $25,000. A written consignment contract was executed between plaintiff and Hollowell Auto Sales. Defendant Jones, then employed by Hollowell Auto Sales, signed the contract on behalf of Hollowell Auto Sales. Plaintiff gave defendants the keys to his automobile and they transported it by flatbed trailer to the Hollowell Auto Sales lot in Morehead City. Defendants Jones and Hollowell were unable to sell the Pantera and it was returned to plaintiff in August 1987. At that time plaintiff discovered that the automobile had been damaged to an extent which reduced its value to between $10,000 and $12,000.

On 23 December 1987 plaintiff sued defendants Jones and Hollowell for negligence in their bailment of his automobile. Plaintiff was unaware that Hollowell Auto Sales was a trade name for Solar Center, Inc., whose principal place of business is in Carteret County. Plaintiff was under the impression that Hollowell Auto Sales was a sole proprietorship operated by defendant Hollowell. On motion of defendant Hollowell in open court, defendant Solar Center, Inc. was added as an additional party prior to trial.

Defendant Jones did not file an answer to plaintiff's complaint and default judgment was subsequently entered against him. At a non-jury trial, judgment in the amount of $11,000 was entered against defendants Jones and Hollowell, jointly and severally. Defendant Gene Hollowell appeals.

* * * *

The only issue presented in this appeal is whether defendant Hollowell can be held individually liable for plaintiff's damages. Defendant contends that he was acting as an agent of Hollowell Auto Sales and therefore cannot be held personally liable. Defendant further asserts that, regardless of the fact that plaintiff was unaware that Hollowell Auto Sales was a trade name for Solar Center, Inc., defendant is nevertheless shielded from individual liability because Solar Center, Inc. fulfilled its legal obligation to disclose its relationship with Hollowell Auto Sales by filing an assumed name certificate in [the appropriate county office]. For the following reasons, we disagree.

When plaintiff gave possession of his automobile to defendant under the consignment contract a bailment for the mutual benefit of bailor and bailee was created. This bailment continued until the automobile was returned to plaintiff in August 1987. Defendant was therefore a bailee of plaintiff's automobile while it was in his custody in Morehead City. A bailee is obligated to exercise due care to protect the subject of the bailment from negligent loss, damage, or destruction. His liability depends on the presence or absence of ordinary negligence. While this obligation arises from the relationship created by the contract of bailment, breach of this contractual duty results in a tort. It is well settled that one is personally liable for all torts committed by him, including negligence, notwithstanding that he may have acted as agent for another or as an officer for a corporation. Furthermore, the potential for corporate liability, in addition to individual liability, does not shield the individual tortfeasor from liability. Rather, it provides the injured party a choice as to which party to hold liable for the tort.

Here there is no dispute that plaintiff's automobile was returned to him in a damaged condition. Defendant does not except to the trial court's findings and conclusions that a bailment was created between plaintiff and defendant and that "defendants were negligent in their care and control of the vehicle while it was in their possession." We therefore hold that the trial court correctly ruled that by failing to exercise due care and allowing the automobile to be damaged while in his custody, defendant committed a tort for which he can be held individually liable.

Because the resolution of this case is in tort for negligence, rather than in contract for breach, we need not reach the issue of whether defendant had sufficiently disclosed his agency with Hollowell Auto Sales or with Solar Center, Inc. However, we note that our Supreme Court has said that use of a trade name is not sufficient as a matter of law to disclose the identity of the principal and the fact of agency.

Likewise, the existence of means by which the fact of agency might be discovered is also insufficient to disclose agency.

* * * *

Affirmed.

Case A.10   *Reference: Problem 37–11.*

TRANS-ORIENT MARINE CORP. v. STAR TRADING & MARINE, INC.

United States District Court, Southern District of New York, 1990. 731 F.Supp. 619.

WILLIAM C. CONNER, District Judge:

Defendant Republic of the Sudan moves this Court to dismiss the complaint for failure to state a claim or for summary judgment. It claims that the new Republic of the Sudan, as successor state, is not liable for the alleged breach of a five-year exclusive agency contract entered into by the prior sovereign state of Sudan. Defendant further asserts that a fundamental change in circumstances relieves it of any prior contractual obligations.

FACTS

Plaintiff's cause of action for breach of contract arises from an alleged five-year exclusive agency agreement to represent the Sudan in the United States P.L. 480 program [an agricultural trade development and assistance program]. The alleged October 14, 1983 agreement was effective from October 1, 1984 through September 30, 1989. In April 1985, a military coup deposed the then head of state, declaring a state of emergency and suspending the constitution. A twelve-month transitional military regime followed, which was then replaced by a civilian coalition government. The name of the state was changed from the Sudan to the Republic of Sudan. In June 1989, there was another military coup in which the present military regime overthrew the former civilian administration and suspended the constitution. Both parties agree that the Republic of the Sudan is a foreign sovereign state.

On January 3 and 4, 1985, the then Sudanese government sent letters advising plaintiff that a new agent, CIDCO, had been appointed to handle the contracts under P.L. 480 and that CIDCO would select the shipping agent. This alleged termination of the then-executory contract did not provide the one-year termination notice required under the original contract. Since January 1985, the Sudan has awarded CIDCO a continuing series of contracts to handle the wheat and wheat flour transportation under P.L. 480, in alleged violation of plaintiff's exclusive agency contract. No additional facts are relevant to the present motion.

DISCUSSION

The present Sudanese government asserts that it is not liable for the contractual obligations of the prior sovereign, pointing to the two military coups of 1985 and 1989 to sustain its position that both the 1985 military regime and the present administration are successor states and that there has been a fundamental change in circumstances. Plaintiff contends that neither the 1985 regime nor the present regime is a successor state but that they represent mere changes in government which do not relieve the present regime from the prior government's contractual obligations. Plaintiff further argues that even if either regime is a successor state, they have ratified the prior government's contract. For the following reasons, summary judgment is denied.

Whether a new administration may terminate the executory portions of its predecessor's contracts is based on the succession of state theory. International law sharply distinguishes the succession of state, which may create a discontinuity of statehood, from a succession of government, which leaves statehood unaffected. It is generally accepted that a change in government, regime or ideology has no effect on that state's international rights and obligations because the state continues to exist despite the change. * * *

However, where one sovereign succeeds another, and a new state is created, the rights and obligations of the successor state are affected. The rule with regard to contracts with private foreign individuals involves a balancing of competing interests. While the successor state is permitted to terminate existing contracts originally executed by the former sovereign and the private party, the successor state is liable to that party only for any amount due him as of the date of the change of sovereignty. But if the contract is totally executory, the successor state is released from the contract.

The Restatement of Foreign Relations Law describes a successor state to include: a state that wholly absorbs another state, that takes over part of the territory of another state, that becomes independent of another state of which it had formed a part, or that arises because of the dismemberment of the state of which it had been a part.

Careful study of defendant's submission reveals that the state of Sudan has not (1) wholly absorbed or been wholly absorbed by another state; (2) partly taken over or been partly taken over by another state; (3) become independent from another state of which it had formed a part; or (4) arisen out of dismemberment of a state of which it had been a part since the date of plaintiff's contract. Under the Restatement's definition, the state of Sudan has remained the same entity since its independence in 1956. Defendant's own exhibit in support of its motion substantiates that only a change in government was effected by the two military coups * * *.

Accordingly, the only changes in the Sudan since its independence in 1956 have been in the government, with seven distinct successive administrations. But there has been only one state.

Defendant unpersuasively emphasizes various aspects of the relevant transitions to reflect the creation of a new state: that the transitions resulted by way of military coups as opposed to routine, constitutional processes, the re-naming of the nation, the suspension of the constitution, the closing of the borders and the declaration of a state of emergency. Treatises, as well as applicable case law, demonstrate that such features do not effect a succession of state. * * *

Furthermore, the Restatement's comparative chart in a Recognition of States section illustrates that a change in government by armed force or fraud, as well as institution of another regime following a civil war, leaves "no question of the existence of the state." It offers as contemporary examples of mere changes in government: Pinochet's 1973 ouster of Allende in Chile, Franco's 1936–39 takeover of Spain, and the Communist revolution in China.

The seminal decision on the distinction between a succession of state versus a change in government is the U. S. Supreme Court decision in *The Sapphire*. In *The Sapphire*, the Supreme Court considered whether a lawsuit begun by the French Emperor, Napoleon III, was abated by the overthrow of the Emperor during the course of litigation. In holding that the action was not extinguished, the Supreme Court stated that, "on the [Emperor's] deposition the sovereignty does not change, but merely the person or persons in whom it resides. . . .

A change in such representative works no change in the national sovereignty or its rights."

* * * *

* * * In *United States v. National City Bank of New York*, the district court held the post-revolutionary State of Russia liable on the treasury notes of the pre-revolutionary state. Similarly, in *Jackson v. People's Republic of China*, the district court determined that the People's Republic, as successor government to the Imperial Chinese Government, was successor to its obligations, specifically, payment of principal due on the prior government-issued bonds. The law is clear that the obligations of a state are unaffected by a mere change in government. It is of no consequence that the Sudan allegedly breached an executory contract. The distinction between executed and executory contracts only applies where there has been a succession of state. The military coups of 1985 and 1989 did not effect a succession of state of the Sudan but merely changed the state's governing body, leaving the state's obligations undisturbed.

Defendant's alternative claim that a fundamental change of circumstances has occurred since October, 1983 relieving it of any prior contractual obligations is unsubstantiated. Defendant presents no explanation as to what "circumstances constituted an essential basis of the consent of the parties to be bound by the agreement" or what changes have "radically transform[ed] the extent of obligations still to be performed under the agreement." Having failed to demonstrate a fundamental change in circumstances, the present government is therefore contractually obligated to plaintiff under the October 14, 1983 five-year extension of agency contract if its predecessor indeed breached that agreement.

CONCLUSION

For the reasons discussed above, summary judgment is denied.

SO ORDERED.

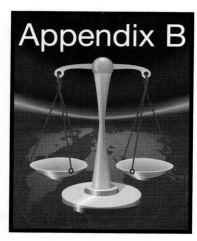

Appendix B

The Constitution of the United States

We the People of the United States, in Order to form a more perfect Union, establish Justice, insure domestic Tranquility, provide for the common defence, promote the general Welfare, and secure the Blessings of Liberty to ourselves and our Posterity, do ordain and establish this Constitution for the United States of America.

ARTICLE I

Section 1. All legislative Powers herein granted shall be vested in a Congress of the United States, which shall consist of a Senate and House of Representatives.

Section 2. The House of Representatives shall be composed of Members chosen every second Year by the People of the several States, and the Electors in each State shall have the Qualifications requisite for Electors of the most numerous Branch of the State Legislature.

No Person shall be a Representative who shall not have attained to the Age of twenty five Years, and been seven Years a Citizen of the United States, and who shall not, when elected, be an Inhabitant of that State in which he shall be chosen.

Representatives and direct Taxes shall be apportioned among the several States which may be included within this Union, according to their respective Numbers, which shall be determined by adding to the whole Number of free Persons, including those bound to Service for a Term of Years, and excluding Indians not taxed, three fifths of all other Persons. The actual Enumeration shall be made within three Years after the first Meeting of the Congress of the United States, and within every subsequent Term of ten Years, in such Manner as they shall by Law direct. The Number of Representatives shall not exceed one for every thirty Thousand, but each State shall have at Least one Representative; and until such enumeration shall be made, the State of New Hampshire shall be entitled to chuse three, Massachusetts eight, Rhode Island and Providence Plantations one, Connecticut five, New York six, New Jersey four, Pennsylvania eight, Delaware one, Maryland six, Virginia ten, North Carolina five, South Carolina five, and Georgia three.

When vacancies happen in the Representation from any State, the Executive Authority thereof shall issue Writs of Election to fill such Vacancies.

The House of Representatives shall chuse their Speaker and other Officers; and shall have the sole Power of Impeachment.

Section 3. The Senate of the United States shall be composed of two Senators from each State, chosen by the Legislature thereof, for six Years; and each Senator shall have one Vote.

Immediately after they shall be assembled in Consequence of the first Election, they shall be divided as equally as may be into three Classes. The Seats of the Senators of the first Class shall be vacated at the Expiration of the second Year, of the second Class at the Expiration of the fourth Year, and of the third Class at the Expiration of the sixth Year, so that one third may be chosen every second Year; and if Vacancies happen by Resignation, or otherwise, during the Recess of the Legislature of any State, the Executive thereof may make temporary Appointments until the next Meeting of the Legislature, which shall then fill such Vacancies.

No Person shall be a Senator who shall not have attained to the Age of thirty Years, and been nine Years a Citizen of the United States, and who shall not, when elected, be an Inhabitant of that State for which he shall be chosen.

The Vice President of the United States shall be President of the Senate, but shall have no Vote, unless they be equally divided.

The Senate shall chuse their other Officers, and also a President pro tempore, in the Absence of the Vice President, or when he shall exercise the Office of President of the United States.

The Senate shall have the sole Power to try all Impeachments. When sitting for that Purpose, they shall be on Oath or Affirmation. When the President of the United States is tried, the Chief Justice shall preside: And no Person shall be convicted without the Concurrence of two thirds of the Members present.

Judgment in Cases of Impeachment shall not extend further than to removal from Office, and disqualification to hold and enjoy any Office of honor, Trust, or Profit under the United States: but the Party convicted shall nevertheless be liable and subject to Indictment, Trial, Judgment, and Punishment, according to Law.

Section 4. The Times, Places and Manner of holding Elections for Senators and Representatives, shall be prescribed in each State by the Legislature thereof; but the Congress may at any time by Law make or alter such Regulations, except as to the Places of chusing Senators.

The Congress shall assemble at least once in every Year, and such Meeting shall be on the first Monday in December, unless they shall by Law appoint a different Day.

Section 5.   Each House shall be the Judge of the Elections, Returns, and Qualifications of its own Members, and a Majority of each shall constitute a Quorum to do Business; but a smaller Number may adjourn from day to day, and may be authorized to compel the Attendance of absent Members, in such Manner, and under such Penalties as each House may provide.

Each House may determine the Rules of its Proceedings, punish its Members for disorderly Behavior, and, with the Concurrence of two thirds, expel a Member.

Each House shall keep a Journal of its Proceedings, and from time to time publish the same, excepting such Parts as may in their Judgment require Secrecy; and the Yeas and Nays of the Members of either House on any question shall, at the Desire of one fifth of those Present, be entered on the Journal.

Neither House, during the Session of Congress, shall, without the Consent of the other, adjourn for more than three days, nor to any other Place than that in which the two Houses shall be sitting.

Section 6.   The Senators and Representatives shall receive a Compensation for their Services, to be ascertained by Law, and paid out of the Treasury of the United States. They shall in all Cases, except Treason, Felony and Breach of the Peace, be privileged from Arrest during their Attendance at the Session of their respective Houses, and in going to and returning from the same; and for any Speech or Debate in either House, they shall not be questioned in any other Place.

No Senator or Representative shall, during the Time for which he was elected, be appointed to any civil Office under the Authority of the United States, which shall have been created, or the Emoluments whereof shall have been increased during such time; and no Person holding any Office under the United States, shall be a Member of either House during his Continuance in Office.

Section 7.   All Bills for raising Revenue shall originate in the House of Representatives; but the Senate may propose or concur with Amendments as on other Bills.

Every Bill which shall have passed the House of Representatives and the Senate, shall, before it become a Law, be presented to the President of the United States; If he approve he shall sign it, but if not he shall return it, with his Objections to the House in which it shall have originated, who shall enter the Objections at large on their Journal, and proceed to reconsider it. If after such Reconsideration two thirds of that House shall agree to pass the Bill, it shall be sent together with the Objections, to the other House, by which it shall likewise be reconsidered, and if approved by two thirds of that House, it shall become a Law. But in all such Cases the Votes of both Houses shall be determined by Yeas and Nays, and the Names of the Persons voting for and against the Bill shall be entered on the Journal of each House respectively. If any Bill shall not be returned by the President within ten Days (Sundays excepted) after it shall have been presented to him, the Same shall be a Law, in like Manner as if he had signed it, unless the Congress by their Adjournment prevent its Return in which Case it shall not be a Law.

Every Order, Resolution, or Vote, to which the Concurrence of the Senate and House of Representatives may be necessary (except on a question of Adjournment) shall be presented to the President of the United States; and before the Same shall take Effect, shall be approved by him, or being disapproved by him, shall be repassed by two thirds of the Senate and House of Representatives, according to the Rules and Limitations prescribed in the Case of a Bill.

Section 8.   The Congress shall have Power To lay and collect Taxes, Duties, Imposts and Excises, to pay the Debts and provide for the common Defence and general Welfare of the United States; but all Duties, Imposts and Excises shall be uniform throughout the United States;

To borrow Money on the credit of the United States;

To regulate Commerce with foreign Nations, and among the several States, and with the Indian Tribes;

To establish an uniform Rule of Naturalization, and uniform Laws on the subject of Bankruptcies throughout the United States;

To coin Money, regulate the Value thereof, and of foreign Coin, and fix the Standard of Weights and Measures;

To provide for the Punishment of counterfeiting the Securities and current Coin of the United States;

To establish Post Offices and post Roads;

To promote the Progress of Science and useful Arts, by securing for limited Times to Authors and Inventors the exclusive Right to their respective Writings and Discoveries;

To constitute Tribunals inferior to the supreme Court;

To define and punish Piracies and Felonies committed on the high Seas, and Offenses against the Law of Nations;

To declare War, grant Letters of Marque and Reprisal, and make Rules concerning Captures on Land and Water;

To raise and support Armies, but no Appropriation of Money to that Use shall be for a longer Term than two Years;

To provide and maintain a Navy;

To make Rules for the Government and Regulation of the land and naval Forces;

To provide for calling forth the Militia to execute the Laws of the Union, suppress Insurrections and repel Invasions;

To provide for organizing, arming, and disciplining, the Militia, and for governing such Part of them as may be employed in the Service of the United States, reserving to the States respectively, the Appointment of the Officers, and the Authority of training the Militia according to the discipline prescribed by Congress;

To exercise exclusive Legislation in all Cases whatsoever, over such District (not exceeding ten Miles square) as may, by Cession of particular States, and the Acceptance of Congress, become the Seat of the Government of the United States, and to exercise like Authority over all Places purchased by the Consent of the Legislature of the State in which the Same shall be, for the Erection of Forts, Magazines, Arsenals, dock-Yards, and other needful Buildings;—And

To make all Laws which shall be necessary and proper for carrying into Execution the foregoing Powers, and all other Powers vested by this Constitution in the Government of the United States, or in any Department or Officer thereof.

Section 9.   The Migration or Importation of such Persons as any of the States now existing shall think proper to admit, shall not be prohibited by the Congress prior to the Year one thousand eight hundred and eight, but a Tax or duty may be imposed on such Importation, not exceeding ten dollars for each Person.

The privilege of the Writ of Habeas Corpus shall not be suspended, unless when in Cases of Rebellion or Invasion the public Safety may require it.

No Bill of Attainder or ex post facto Law shall be passed.

No Capitation, or other direct, Tax shall be laid, unless in Proportion to the Census or Enumeration herein before directed to be taken.

No Tax or Duty shall be laid on Articles exported from any State.

No Preference shall be given by any Regulation of Commerce or Revenue to the Ports of one State over those of another: nor shall Vessels bound to, or from, one State be obliged to enter, clear, or pay Duties in another.

No Money shall be drawn from the Treasury, but in Consequence of Appropriations made by Law; and a regular Statement and Account of the Receipts and Expenditures of all public Money shall be published from time to time.

No Title of Nobility shall be granted by the United States: And no Person holding any Office of Profit or Trust under them, shall, without the Consent of the Congress, accept of any present, Emolument, Office, or Title, of any kind whatever, from any King, Prince, or foreign State.

Section 10.   No State shall enter into any Treaty, Alliance, or Confederation; grant Letters of Marque and Reprisal; coin Money; emit Bills of Credit; make any Thing but gold and silver Coin a Tender in Payment of Debts; pass any Bill of Attainder, ex post facto Law, or Law impairing the Obligation of Contracts, or grant any Title of Nobility.

No State shall, without the Consent of the Congress, lay any Imposts or Duties on Imports or Exports, except what may be absolutely necessary for executing its inspection Laws: and the net Produce of all Duties and Imposts, laid by any State on Imports or Exports, shall be for the Use of the Treasury of the United States; and all such Laws shall be subject to the Revision and Controul of the Congress.

No State shall, without the Consent of Congress, lay any Duty of Tonnage, keep Troops, or Ships of War in time of Peace, enter into any Agreement or Compact with another State, or with a foreign Power, or engage in War, unless actually invaded, or in such imminent Danger as will not admit of delay.

Article II

Section 1.   The executive Power shall be vested in a President of the United States of America. He shall hold his Office during the Term of four Years, and, together with the Vice President, chosen for the same Term, be elected, as follows:

Each State shall appoint, in such Manner as the Legislature thereof may direct, a Number of Electors, equal to the whole Number of Senators and Representatives to which the State may be entitled in the Congress; but no Senator or Representative, or Person holding an Office of Trust or Profit under the United States, shall be appointed an Elector.

The Electors shall meet in their respective States, and vote by Ballot for two Persons, of whom one at least shall not be an Inhabitant of the same State with themselves. And they shall make a List of all the Persons voted for, and of the Number of Votes for each; which List they shall sign and certify, and transmit sealed to the Seat of the Government of the United States, directed to the

President of the Senate. The President of the Senate shall, in the Presence of the Senate and House of Representatives, open all the Certificates, and the Votes shall then be counted. The Person having the greatest Number of Votes shall be the President, if such Number be a Majority of the whole Number of Electors appointed; and if there be more than one who have such Majority, and have an equal Number of Votes, then the House of Representatives shall immediately chuse by Ballot one of them for President; and if no Person have a Majority, then from the five highest on the List the said House shall in like Manner chuse the President. But in chusing the President, the Votes shall be taken by States, the Representation from each State having one Vote; A quorum for this Purpose shall consist of a Member or Members from two thirds of the States, and a Majority of all the States shall be necessary to a Choice. In every Case, after the Choice of the President, the Person having the greater Number of Votes of the Electors shall be the Vice President. But if there should remain two or more who have equal Votes, the Senate shall chuse from them by Ballot the Vice President.

The Congress may determine the Time of chusing the Electors, and the Day on which they shall give their Votes; which Day shall be the same throughout the United States.

No person except a natural born Citizen, or a Citizen of the United States, at the time of the Adoption of this Constitution, shall be eligible to the Office of President; neither shall any Person be eligible to that Office who shall not have attained to the Age of thirty five Years, and been fourteen Years a Resident within the United States.

In Case of the Removal of the President from Office, or of his Death, Resignation or Inability to discharge the Powers and Duties of the said Office, the same shall devolve on the Vice President, and the Congress may by Law provide for the Case of Removal, Death, Resignation or Inability, both of the President and Vice President, declaring what Officer shall then act as President, and such Officer shall act accordingly, until the Disability be removed, or a President shall be elected.

The President shall, at stated Times, receive for his Services, a Compensation, which shall neither be increased nor diminished during the Period for which he shall have been elected, and he shall not receive within that Period any other Emolument from the United States, or any of them.

Before he enter on the Execution of his Office, he shall take the following Oath or Affirmation: "I do solemnly swear (or affirm) that I will faithfully execute the Office of President of the United States, and will to the best of my Ability, preserve, protect and defend the Constitution of the United States."

Section 2.   The President shall be Commander in Chief of the Army and Navy of the United States, and of the Militia of the several States, when called into the actual Service of the United States; he may require the Opinion, in writing, of the principal Officer in each of the executive Departments, upon any Subject relating to the Duties of their respective Offices, and he shall have Power to grant Reprieves and Pardons for Offenses against the United States, except in Cases of Impeachment.

He shall have Power, by and with the Advice and Consent of the Senate to make Treaties, provided two thirds of the Senators present concur; and he shall nominate, and by and with the Advice and Consent of the Senate, shall appoint Ambassadors, other public Ministers and Consuls, Judges of the supreme Court, and all other Officers of the United States, whose Appointments are not herein otherwise provided for, and which shall be established by Law; but the Congress may by Law vest the Appointment of such inferior Officers, as they think proper, in the President alone, in the Courts of Law, or in the Heads of Departments.

The President shall have Power to fill up all Vacancies that may happen during the Recess of the Senate, by granting Commissions which shall expire at the End of their next Session.

Section 3. He shall from time to time give to the Congress Information of the State of the Union, and recommend to their Consideration such Measures as he shall judge necessary and expedient; he may, on extraordinary Occasions, convene both Houses, or either of them, and in Case of Disagreement between them, with Respect to the Time of Adjournment, he may adjourn them to such Time as he shall think proper; he shall receive Ambassadors and other public Ministers; he shall take Care that the Laws be faithfully executed, and shall Commission all the Officers of the United States.

Section 4. The President, Vice President and all civil Officers of the United States, shall be removed from Office on Impeachment for, and Conviction of, Treason, Bribery, or other high Crimes and Misdemeanors.

ARTICLE III

Section 1. The judicial Power of the United States, shall be vested in one supreme Court, and in such inferior Courts as the Congress may from time to time ordain and establish. The Judges, both of the supreme and inferior Courts, shall hold their Offices during good Behaviour, and shall, at stated Times, receive for their Services a Compensation, which shall not be diminished during their Continuance in Office.

Section 2. The judicial Power shall extend to all Cases, in Law and Equity, arising under this Constitution, the Laws of the United States, and Treaties made, or which shall be made, under their Authority;—to all Cases affecting Ambassadors, other public Ministers and Consuls;—to all Cases of admiralty and maritime Jurisdiction;—to Controversies to which the United States shall be a Party;—to Controversies between two or more States;—between a State and Citizens of another State;—between Citizens of different States;—between Citizens of the same State claiming Lands under Grants of different States, and between a State, or the Citizens thereof, and foreign States, Citizens or Subjects.

In all Cases affecting Ambassadors, other public Ministers and Consuls, and those in which a State shall be a Party, the supreme Court shall have original Jurisdiction. In all the other Cases before mentioned, the supreme Court shall have appellate Jurisdiction, both as to Law and Fact, with such Exceptions, and under such Regulations as the Congress shall make.

The Trial of all Crimes, except in Cases of Impeachment, shall be by Jury; and such Trial shall be held in the State where the said Crimes shall have been committed; but when not committed within any State, the Trial shall be at such Place or Places as the Congress may by Law have directed.

Section 3. Treason against the United States, shall consist only in levying War against them, or, in adhering to their Enemies, giving them Aid and Comfort. No Person shall be convicted of Treason unless on the Testimony of two Witnesses to the same overt Act, or on Confession in open Court.

The Congress shall have Power to declare the Punishment of Treason, but no Attainder of Treason shall work Corruption of Blood, or Forfeiture except during the Life of the Person attainted.

ARTICLE IV

Section 1. Full Faith and Credit shall be given in each State to the public Acts, Records, and judicial Proceedings of every other State. And the Congress may by general Laws prescribe the Manner in which such Acts, Records and Proceedings shall be proved, and the Effect thereof.

Section 2. The Citizens of each State shall be entitled to all Privileges and Immunities of Citizens in the several States.

A Person charged in any State with Treason, Felony, or other Crime, who shall flee from Justice, and be found in another State, shall on Demand of the executive Authority of the State from which he fled, be delivered up, to be removed to the State having Jurisdiction of the Crime.

No Person held to Service or Labour in one State, under the Laws thereof, escaping into another, shall, in Consequence of any Law or Regulation therein, be discharged from such Service or Labour, but shall be delivered up on Claim of the Party to whom such Service or Labour may be due.

Section 3. New States may be admitted by the Congress into this Union; but no new State shall be formed or erected within the Jurisdiction of any other State; nor any State be formed by the Junction of two or more States, or Parts of States, without the Consent of the Legislatures of the States concerned as well as of the Congress.

The Congress shall have Power to dispose of and make all needful Rules and Regulations respecting the Territory or other Property belonging to the United States; and nothing in this Constitution shall be so construed as to Prejudice any Claims of the United States, or of any particular State.

Section 4. The United States shall guarantee to every State in this Union a Republican Form of Government, and shall protect each of them against Invasion; and on Application of the Legislature, or of the Executive (when the Legislature cannot be convened) against domestic Violence.

ARTICLE V

The Congress, whenever two thirds of both Houses shall deem it necessary, shall propose Amendments to this Constitution, or, on the Application of the Legislatures of two thirds of the several States, shall call a Convention for proposing Amendments, which, in either Case, shall be valid to all Intents and Purposes, as part of this Constitution, when ratified by the Legislatures of three fourths of the several States, or by Conventions in three fourths thereof, as the one or the other Mode of Ratification may be proposed by the Congress; Provided that no Amendment which may be made prior to the Year One thousand eight hundred and eight shall in any Manner affect the first and fourth Clauses in the Ninth Section of the first Article; and that no State, without its Consent, shall be deprived of its equal Suffrage in the Senate.

ARTICLE VI

All Debts contracted and Engagements entered into, before the Adoption of this Constitution shall be as valid against the United States under this Constitution, as under the Confederation.

This Constitution, and the Laws of the United States which shall be made in Pursuance thereof; and all Treaties made, or which shall be made, under the Authority of the United States, shall be the supreme Law of the Land; and the Judges in every State shall be bound thereby, any Thing in the Constitution or Laws of any State to the Contrary notwithstanding.

The Senators and Representatives before mentioned, and the Members of the several State Legislatures, and all executive and judicial Officers, both of the United States and of the several States, shall be bound by Oath or Affirmation, to support this Constitution; but no religious Test shall ever be required as a Qualification to any Office or public Trust under the United States.

ARTICLE VII

The Ratification of the Conventions of nine States shall be sufficient for the Establishment of this Constitution between the States so ratifying the Same.

AMENDMENT I [1791]

Congress shall make no law respecting an establishment of religion, or prohibiting the free exercise thereof; or abridging the freedom of speech, or of the press; or the right of the people peaceably to assembly, and to petition the Government for a redress of grievances.

AMENDMENT II [1791]

A well regulated Militia, being necessary to the security of a free State, the right of the people to keep and bear Arms, shall not be infringed.

AMENDMENT III [1791]

No Soldier shall, in time of peace be quartered in any house, without the consent of the Owner, nor in time of war, but in a manner to be prescribed by law.

AMENDMENT IV [1791]

The right of the people to be secure in their persons, houses, papers, and effects, against unreasonable searches and seizures, shall not be violated, and no Warrants shall issue, but upon probable cause, supported by Oath or affirmation, and particularly describing the place to be searched, and the persons or things to be seized.

AMENDMENT V [1791]

No person shall be held to answer for a capital, or otherwise infamous crime, unless on a presentment or indictment of a Grand Jury, except in cases arising in the land or naval forces, or in the Militia, when in actual service in time of War or public danger; nor shall any person be subject for the same offence to be twice put in jeopardy of life or limb; nor shall be compelled in any criminal case to be a witness against himself, nor be deprived of life, liberty, or property, without due process of law; nor shall private property be taken for public use, without just compensation.

AMENDMENT VI [1791]

In all criminal prosecutions, the accused shall enjoy the right to a speedy and public trial, by an impartial jury of the State and district wherein the crime shall have been committed, which district shall have been previously ascertained by law, and to be informed of the nature and cause of the accusation; to be confronted with the witnesses against him; to have compulsory process for obtaining witnesses in his favor, and to have the Assistance of Counsel for his defence.

AMENDMENT VII [1791]

In Suits at common law, where the value in controversy shall exceed twenty dollars, the right of trial by jury shall be preserved, and no fact tried by jury, shall be otherwise re-examined in any Court of the United States, than according to the rules of the common law.

AMENDMENT VIII [1791]

Excessive bail shall not be required, nor excessive fines imposed, nor cruel and unusual punishments inflicted.

AMENDMENT IX [1791]

The enumeration in the Constitution, of certain rights, shall not be construed to deny or disparage others retained by the people.

AMENDMENT X [1791]

The powers not delegated to the United States by the Constitution, nor prohibited by it to the States, are reserved to the States respectively, or to the people.

AMENDMENT XI [1798]

The Judicial power of the United States shall not be construed to extend to any suit in law or equity, commenced or prosecuted against one of the United States by Citizens of another State, or by Citizens or Subjects of any Foreign State.

AMENDMENT XII [1804]

The Electors shall meet in their respective states, and vote by ballot for President and Vice-President, one of whom, at least, shall not be an inhabitant of the same state with themselves; they shall name in their ballots the person voted for as President, and in distinct ballots the person voted for as Vice-President, and they shall make distinct lists of all persons voted for as President, and of all persons voted for as Vice-President, and of the number of votes for each, which lists they shall sign and certify, and transmit sealed to the seat of the government of the United States, directed to the President of the Senate;—The President of the Senate shall, in the presence of the Senate and House of Representatives, open all the certificates and the votes shall then be counted;—The person having the greatest number of votes for President, shall be the President, if such number be a majority of the whole number of Electors appointed; and if no person have such majority, then from the persons having the highest numbers not exceeding three on the list of those voted for as President, the House of Representatives shall choose immediately, by ballot, the President. But in choosing the President, the votes shall be taken by states, the representation from each state having one vote; a quorum for this purpose shall consist of a member or members from two-thirds of the states, and a majority of all states shall be necessary to a choice. And if the House of Representatives shall not choose a President whenever the right of choice shall devolve upon them, before the fourth day of March next following, then the Vice-President shall act as President, as in the case of the death or other constitutional disability of the President.—The person having the greatest number of votes as Vice-President, shall be the Vice-President, if such number be a majority of the whole number of Electors appointed, and if no person have a majority, then from the two highest numbers on the list, the Senate shall choose the

Vice-President; a quorum for the purpose shall consist of two-thirds of the whole number of Senators, and a majority of the whole number shall be necessary to a choice. But no person constitutionally ineligible to the office of President shall be eligible to that of Vice-President of the United States.

AMENDMENT XIII [1865]

Section 1. Neither slavery nor involuntary servitude, except as a punishment for crime whereof the party shall have been duly convicted, shall exist within the United States, or any place subject to their jurisdiction.

Section 2. Congress shall have power to enforce this article by appropriate legislation.

AMENDMENT XIV [1868]

Section 1. All persons born or naturalized in the United States, and subject to the jurisdiction thereof, are citizens of the United States and of the State wherein they reside. No State shall make or enforce any law which shall abridge the privileges or immunities of citizens of the United States; nor shall any State deprive any person of life, liberty, or property, without due process of law; nor deny to any person within its jurisdiction the equal protection of the laws.

Section 2. Representatives shall be apportioned among the several States according to their respective numbers, counting the whole number of persons in each State, excluding Indians not taxed. But when the right to vote at any election for the choice of electors for President and Vice President of the United States, Representatives in Congress, the Executive and Judicial officers of a State, or the members of the Legislature thereof, is denied to any of the male inhabitants of such State, being twenty-one years of age, and citizens of the United States, or in any way abridged, except for participation in rebellion, or other crime, the basis of representation therein shall be reduced in the proportion which the number of such male citizens shall bear to the whole number of male citizens twenty-one years of age in such State.

Section 3. No person shall be a Senator or Representative in Congress, or elector of President and Vice President, or hold any office, civil or military, under the United States, or under any State, who having previously taken an oath, as a member of Congress, or as an officer of the United States, or as a member of any State legislature, or as an executive or judicial officer of any State, to support the Constitution of the United States, shall have engaged in insurrection or rebellion against the same, or given aid or comfort to the enemies thereof. But Congress may by a vote of two-thirds of each House, remove such disability.

Section 4. The validity of the public debt of the United States, authorized by law, including debts incurred for payment of pensions and bounties for services in suppressing insurrection or rebellion, shall not be questioned. But neither the United States nor any State shall assume or pay any debt or obligation incurred in aid of insurrection or rebellion against the United States, or any claim for the loss or emancipation of any slave; but all such debts, obligations and claims shall be held illegal and void.

Section 5. The Congress shall have power to enforce, by appropriate legislation, the provisions of this article.

AMENDMENT XV [1870]

Section 1. The right of citizens of the United States to vote shall not be denied or abridged by the United States or by any State on account of race, color, or previous condition of servitude.

Section 2. The Congress shall have power to enforce this article by appropriate legislation.

AMENDMENT XVI [1913]

The Congress shall have power to lay and collect taxes on incomes, from whatever source derived, without apportionment among the several States, and without regard to any census or enumeration.

AMENDMENT XVII [1913]

Section 1. The Senate of the United States shall be composed of two Senators from each State, elected by the people thereof, for six years; and each Senator shall have one vote. The electors in each State shall have the qualifications requisite for electors of the most numerous branch of the State legislatures.

Section 2. When vacancies happen in the representation of any State in the Senate, the executive authority of such State shall issue writs of election to fill such vacancies: *Provided,* That the legislature of any State may empower the executive thereof to make temporary appointments until the people fill the vacancies by election as the legislature may direct.

Section 3. This amendment shall not be so construed as to affect the election or term of any Senator chosen before it becomes valid as part of the Constitution.

AMENDMENT XVIII [1919]

Section 1. After one year from the ratification of this article the manufacture, sale, or transportation of intoxicating liquors within, the importation thereof into, or the exportation thereof from the United States and all territory subject to the jurisdiction thereof for beverage purposes is hereby prohibited.

Section 2. The Congress and the several States shall have concurrent power to enforce this article by appropriate legislation.

Section 3. This article shall be inoperative unless it shall have been ratified as an amendment to the Constitution by the legislatures of the several States, as provided in the Constitution, within seven years from the date of the submission hereof to the States by the Congress.

AMENDMENT XIX [1920]

Section 1. The right of citizens of the United States to vote shall not be denied or abridged by the United States or by any State on account of sex.

Section 2. Congress shall have power to enforce this article by appropriate legislation.

AMENDMENT XX [1933]

Section 1. The terms of the President and Vice President shall end at noon on the 20th day of January, and the terms of Senators and Representatives at noon on the 3d day of January, of the years in which such terms would have ended if this article had not been ratified; and the terms of their successors shall then begin.

Section 2. The Congress shall assemble at least once in every year, and such meeting shall begin at noon on the 3d day of January, unless they shall by law appoint a different day.

Section 3. If, at the time fixed for the beginning of the term of the President, the President elect shall have died, the Vice President elect shall become President. If the President shall not have been chosen before the time fixed for the beginning of his term, or if the President elect shall have failed to qualify, then the Vice President elect shall act as President until a President shall have qualified; and the Congress may by law provide for the case wherein neither a President elect nor a Vice President elect shall have qualified, declaring who shall then act as President, or the manner in which one who is to act shall be selected, and such person shall act accordingly until a President or Vice President shall have qualified.

Section 4.   The Congress may by law provide for the case of the death of any of the persons from whom the House of Representatives may choose a President whenever the right of choice shall have devolved upon them, and for the case of the death of any of the persons from whom the Senate may choose a Vice President whenever the right of choice shall have devolved upon them.

Section 5.   Sections 1 and 2 shall take effect on the 15th day of October following the ratification of this article.

Section 6.   This article shall be inoperative unless it shall have been ratified as an amendment to the Constitution by the legislatures of three-fourths of the several States within seven years from the date of its submission.

AMENDMENT XXI [1933]

Section 1.   The eighteenth article of amendment to the Constitution of the United States is hereby repealed.

Section 2.   The transportation or importation into any State, Territory, or possession of the United States for delivery or use therein of intoxicating liquors, in violation of the laws thereof, is hereby prohibited.

Section 3.   This article shall be inoperative unless it shall have been ratified as an amendment to the Constitution by conventions in the several States, as provided in the Constitution, within seven years from the date of the submission hereof to the States by the Congress.

AMENDMENT XXII [1951]

Section 1.   No person shall be elected to the office of the President more than twice, and no person who has held the office of President, or acted as President, for more than two years of a term to which some other person was elected President shall be elected to the office of President more than once. But this Article shall not apply to any person holding the office of President when this Article was proposed by the Congress, and shall not prevent any person who may be holding the office of President, or acting as President, during the term within which this Article becomes operative from holding the office of President or acting as President during the remainder of such term.

Section 2.   This article shall be inoperative unless it shall have been ratified as an amendment to the Constitution by the legislatures of three-fourths of the several States within seven years from the date of its submission to the States by the Congress.

AMENDMENT XXIII [1961]

Section 1.   The District constituting the seat of Government of the United States shall appoint in such manner as the Congress may direct:

A number of electors of President and Vice President equal to the whole number of Senators and Representatives in Congress to which the District would be entitled if it were a State, but in no event more than the least populous state; they shall be in addition to those appointed by the states, but they shall be considered, for the purposes of the election of President and Vice President, to be electors appointed by a state; and they shall meet in the District and perform such duties as provided by the twelfth article of amendment.

Section 2.   The Congress shall have power to enforce this article by appropriate legislation.

AMENDMENT XXIV [1964]

Section 1.   The right of citizens of the United States to vote in any primary or other election for President or Vice President, for electors for President or Vice President, or for Senator or Representative in Congress, shall not be denied or abridged by the United States, or any State by reason of failure to pay any poll tax or other tax.

Section 2.   The Congress shall have power to enforce this article by appropriate legislation.

AMENDMENT XXV [1967]

Section 1.   In case of the removal of the President from office or of his death or resignation, the Vice President shall become President.

Section 2.   Whenever there is a vacancy in the office of the Vice President, the President shall nominate a Vice President who shall take office upon confirmation by a majority vote of both Houses of Congress.

Section 3.   Whenever the President transmits to the President pro tempore of the Senate and the Speaker of the House of Representatives his written declaration that he is unable to discharge the powers and duties of his office, and until he transmits to them a written declaration to the contrary, such powers and duties shall be discharged by the Vice President as Acting President.

Section 4.   Whenever the Vice President and a majority of either the principal officers of the executive departments or of such other body as Congress may by law provide, transmit to the President pro tempore of the Senate and the Speaker of the House of Representatives their written declaration that the President is unable to discharge the powers and duties of his office, the Vice President shall immediately assume the powers and duties of the office as Acting President.

Thereafter, when the President transmits to the President pro tempore of the Senate and the Speaker of the House of Representatives his written declaration that no inability exists, he shall resume the powers and duties of his office unless the Vice President and a majority of either the principal officers of the executive department or of such other body as Congress may by law provide, transmit within four days to the President pro tempore of the Senate and the Speaker of the House of Representatives their written declaration and the President is unable to discharge the powers and duties of his office. Thereupon Congress shall decide the issue, assembling within forty-eight hours for that purpose if not in session. If the Congress, within twenty-one days after receipt of the latter written declaration, or, if Congress is not in session, within twenty-one days after Congress is required to assemble, determines by two-thirds vote of both Houses that the President is unable to discharge the powers and duties of his office, the Vice

President shall continue to discharge the same as Acting President; otherwise, the President shall resume the powers and duties of his office.

AMENDMENT XXVI [1971]

Section 1. The right of citizens of the United States, who are eighteen years of age or older, to vote shall not be denied or abridged by the United States or by any State on account of age.

Section 2. The Congress shall have power to enforce this article by appropriate legislation.

AMENDMENT XXVII [1992]

No law, varying the compensation for the services of the Senators and Representatives, shall take effect, until an election of Representatives shall have intervened.

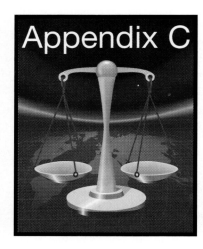

Appendix C

The Uniform Commercial Code

(Adopted in fifty-two jurisdictions; all fifty States, although Louisiana has adopted only Articles 1, 3, 4, 7, 8, and 9; the District of Columbia; and the Virgin Islands.)

The Code consists of the following articles:

Art.

1. General Provisions
2. Sales
2A. Leases
3. Commercial Paper
4. Bank Deposits and Collections
4A. Funds Transfers
5. Letters of Credit
6. Bulk Transfers (including Alternative B)
7. Warehouse Receipts, Bills of Lading and Other Documents of Title
8. Investment Securities
9. Secured Transactions: Sales of Accounts and Chattel Paper
10. Effective Date and Repealer
11. Effective Date and Transition Provisions

Article 1
GENERAL PROVISIONS

Part 1 Short Title, Construction, Application and Subject Matter of the Act

§ 1—101. **Short Title.**

This Act shall be known and may be cited as Uniform Commercial Code.

§ 1—102. **Purposes; Rules of Construction; Variation by Agreement.**

(1) This Act shall be liberally construed and applied to promote its underlying purposes and policies.

(2) Underlying purposes and policies of this Act are

(a) to simplify, clarify and modernize the law governing commercial transactions;

(b) to permit the continued expansion of commercial practices through custom, usage and agreement of the parties;

(c) to make uniform the law among the various jurisdictions.

(3) The effect of provisions of this Act may be varied by agreement, except as otherwise provided in this Act and except that the obligations of good faith, diligence, reasonableness and care prescribed by this Act may not be disclaimed by agreement but the parties may by agreement determine the standards by which the performance of such obligations is to be measured if such standards are not manifestly unreasonable.

(4) The presence in certain provisions of this Act of the words "unless otherwise agreed" or words of similar import does not imply that the effect of other provisions may not be varied by agreement under subsection (3).

(5) In this Act unless the context otherwise requires

(a) words in the singular number include the plural, and in the plural include the singular;

(b) words of the masculine gender include the feminine and the neuter, and when the sense so indicates words of the neuter gender may refer to any gender.

§ 1—103. **Supplementary General Principles of Law Applicable.**

Unless displaced by the particular provisions of this Act, the principles of law and equity, including the law merchant and the law relative to capacity to contract, principal and agent, estoppel, fraud, misrepresentation, duress, coercion, mistake, bankruptcy, or other validating or invalidating cause shall supplement its provisions.

§ 1—104. **Construction Against Implicit Repeal.**

This Act being a general act intended as a unified coverage of its subject matter, no part of it shall be deemed to be impliedly repealed by subsequent legislation if such construction can reasonably be avoided.

§ 1—105. **Territorial Application of the Act; Parties' Power to Choose Applicable Law.**

(1) Except as provided hereafter in this section, when a transaction bears a reasonable relation to this state and also to another state or nation the parties may agree that the law either of this state or of such other state or nation shall govern their rights and duties. Failing such agreement this Act applies to transactions bearing an appropriate relation to this state.

(2) Where one of the following provisions of this Act specifies the applicable law, that provision governs and a contrary agreement is effective only to the extent permitted by the law (including the conflict of laws rules) so specified:

Rights of creditors against sold goods. Section 2—402.

Applicability of the Article on Leases. Sections 2A—105 and 2A—106.

Applicability of the Article on Bank Deposits and Collections. Section 4—102.

Governing law in the Article on Funds Transfers. Section 4A—507.

Letters of Credit, Section 5—116.

Bulk sales subject to the Article on Bulk Sales. Section 6—103.

Applicability of the Article on Investment Securities. Section 8—106.

Perfection provisions of the Article on Secured Transactions. Section 9—103.

§ 1—106. **Remedies to Be Liberally Administered.**

(1) The remedies provided by this Act shall be liberally administered to the end that the aggrieved party may be put in as good a position as if the other party had fully performed but neither consequential or special nor penal damages may be had except as specifically provided in this Act or by other rule of law.

(2) Any right or obligation declared by this Act is enforceable by action unless the provision declaring it specifies a different and limited effect.

§ 1—107. **Waiver or Renunciation of Claim or Right After Breach.**

Any claim or right arising out of an alleged breach can be discharged in whole or in part without consideration by a written waiver or renunciation signed and delivered by the aggrieved party.

§ 1—108. **Severability.**

If any provision or clause of this Act or application thereof to any person or circumstances is held invalid, such invalidity shall not affect other provisions or applications of the Act which can be given effect without the invalid provision or application, and to this end the provisions of this Act are declared to be severable.

§ 1—109. **Section Captions.**

Section captions are parts of this Act.

Part 2   General Definitions and Principles of Interpretation

§ 1—201. **General Definitions.**

Subject to additional definitions contained in the subsequent Articles of this Act which are applicable to specific Articles or Parts thereof, and unless the context otherwise requires, in this Act:

(1) "Action" in the sense of a judicial proceeding includes recoupment, counterclaim, set-off, suit in equity and any other proceedings in which rights are determined.

(2) "Aggrieved party" means a party entitled to resort to a remedy.

(3) "Agreement" means the bargain of the parties in fact as found in their language or by implication from other circumstances including course of dealing or usage of trade or course of performance as provided in this Act (Sections 1—205 and 2—208). Whether an agreement has legal consequences is determined by the provisions of this Act, if applicable; otherwise by the law of contracts (Section 1—103). (Compare "Contract".)

(4) "Bank" means any person engaged in the business of banking.

(5) "Bearer" means the person in possession of an instrument, document of title, or certificated security payable to bearer or indorsed in blank.

(6) "Bill of lading" means a document evidencing the receipt of goods for shipment issued by a person engaged in the business of transporting or forwarding goods, and includes an airbill. "Airbill" means a document serving for air transportation as a bill of lading does for marine or rail transportation, and includes an air consignment note or air waybill.

(7) "Branch" includes a separately incorporated foreign branch of a bank.

(8) "Burden of establishing" a fact means the burden of persuading the triers of fact that the existence of the fact is more probable than its non-existence.

(9) "Buyer in ordinary course of business" means a person who in good faith and without knowledge that the sale to him is in violation of the ownership rights or security interest of a third party in the goods buys in ordinary course from a person in the business of selling goods of that kind but does not include a pawnbroker. All persons who sell minerals or the like (including oil and gas) at wellhead or minehead shall be deemed to be persons in the business of selling goods of that kind. "Buying" may be for cash or by exchange of other property or on secured or unsecured credit and includes receiving goods or documents of title under a pre-existing contract for sale but does not include a transfer in bulk or as security for or in total or partial satisfaction of a money debt.

(10) "Conspicuous": A term or clause is conspicuous when it is so written that a reasonable person against whom it is to operate ought to have noticed it. A printed heading in capitals (as: NON-NEGOTIABLE BILL OF LADING) is conspicuous. Language in the body of a form is "conspicuous" if it is in larger or other contrasting type or color. But in a telegram any stated term is "conspicuous". Whether a term or clause is "conspicuous" or not is for decision by the court.

(11) "Contract" means the total legal obligation which results from the parties' agreement as affected by this Act and any other applicable rules of law. (Compare "Agreement".)

(12) "Creditor" includes a general creditor, a secured creditor, a lien creditor and any representative of creditors, including an assignee for the benefit of creditors, a trustee in bankruptcy, a receiver in equity and an executor or administrator of an insolvent debtor's or assignor's estate.

(13) "Defendant" includes a person in the position of defendant

in a cross-action or counterclaim.

(14) "Delivery" with respect to instruments, documents of title, chattel paper, or certificated securities means voluntary transfer of possession.

(15) "Document of title" includes bill of lading, dock warrant, dock receipt, warehouse receipt or order for the delivery of goods, and also any other document which in the regular course of business or financing is treated as adequately evidencing that the person in possession of it is entitled to receive, hold and dispose of the document and the goods it covers. To be a document of title a document must purport to be issued by or addressed to a bailee and purport to cover goods in the bailee's possession which are either identified or are fungible portions of an identified mass.

(16) "Fault" means wrongful act, omission or breach.

(17) "Fungible" with respect to goods or securities means goods or securities of which any unit is, by nature or usage of trade, the equivalent of any other like unit. Goods which are not fungible shall be deemed fungible for the purposes of this Act to the extent that under a particular agreement or document unlike units are treated as equivalents.

(18) "Genuine" means free of forgery or counterfeiting.

(19) "Good faith" means honesty in fact in the conduct or transaction concerned.

(20) "Holder" with respect to a negotiable instrument, means the person in possession if the instrument is payable to bearer or, in the cases of an instrument payable to an identified person, if the identified person is in possession. "Holder" with respect to a document of title means the person in possession if the goods are deliverable to bearer or to the order of the person in possession.

(21) To "honor" is to pay or to accept and pay, or where a credit so engages to purchase or discount a draft complying with the terms of the credit.

(22) "Insolvency proceedings" includes any assignment for the benefit of creditors or other proceedings intended to liquidate or rehabilitate the estate of the person involved.

(23) A person is "insolvent" who either has ceased to pay his debts in the ordinary course of business or cannot pay his debts as they become due or is insolvent within the meaning of the federal bankruptcy law.

(24) "Money" means a medium of exchange authorized or adopted by a domestic or foreign government and includes a monetary unit of account established by an intergovernmental organization or by agreement between two or more nations.

(25) A person has "notice" of a fact when

(a) he has actual knowledge of it; or

(b) he has received a notice or notification of it; or

(c) from all the facts and circumstances known to him at the time in question he has reason to know that it exists.

A person "knows" or has "knowledge" of a fact when he has actual knowledge of it. "Discover" or "learn" or a word or phrase of similar import refers to knowledge rather than to reason to know. The time and circumstances under which a notice or notification may cease to be effective are not determined by this Act.

(26) A person "notifies" or "gives" a notice or notification to another by taking such steps as may be reasonably required to inform the other in ordinary course whether or not such other actually comes to know of it. A person "receives" a notice or noti-

fication when

(a) it comes to his attention; or

(b) it is duly delivered at the place of business through which the contract was made or at any other place held out by him as the place for receipt of such communications.

(27) Notice, knowledge or a notice or notification received by an organization is effective for a particular transaction from the time when it is brought to the attention of the individual conducting that transaction, and in any event from the time when it would have been brought to his attention if the organization had exercised due diligence. An organization exercises due diligence if it maintains reasonable routines for communicating significant information to the person conducting the transaction and there is reasonable compliance with the routines. Due diligence does not require an individual acting for the organization to communicate information unless such communication is part of his regular duties or unless he has reason to know of the transaction and that the transaction would be materially affected by the information.

(28) "Organization" includes a corporation, government or governmental subdivision or agency, business trust, estate, trust, partnership or association, two or more persons having a joint or common interest, or any other legal or commercial entity.

(29) "Party", as distinct from "third party", means a person who has engaged in a transaction or made an agreement within this Act.

(30) "Person" includes an individual or an organization (See Section 1—102).

(31) "Presumption" or "presumed" means that the trier of fact must find the existence of the fact presumed unless and until evidence is introduced which would support a finding of its nonexistence.

(32) "Purchase" includes taking by sale, discount, negotiation, mortgage, pledge, lien, issue or re-issue, gift or any other voluntary transaction creating an interest in property.

(33) "Purchaser" means a person who takes by purchase.

(34) "Remedy" means any remedial right to which an aggrieved party is entitled with or without resort to a tribunal.

(35) "Representative" includes an agent, an officer of a corporation or association, and a trustee, executor or administrator of an estate, or any other person empowered to act for another.

(36) "Rights" includes remedies.

(37) "Security interest" means an interest in personal property or fixtures which secures payment or performance of an obligation. The retention or reservation of title by a seller of goods notwithstanding shipment or delivery to the buyer (Section 2—401) is limited in effect to a reservation of a "security interest". The term also includes any interest of a buyer of accounts or chattel paper which is subject to Article 9. The special property interest of a buyer of goods on identification of those goods to a contract for sale under Section 2—401 is not a "security interest", but a buyer may also acquire a "security interest" by complying with Article 9. Unless a consignment is intended as security, reservation of title thereunder is not a "security interest," but a consignment is in any event subject to the provisions on consignment sales (Section 2—326).

Whether a transaction creates a lease or security interest is determined by the facts of each case; however, a transaction creates a security interest if the consideration the lessee is to pay the lessor for the right to possession and use of the goods is an obligation for the term of the lease not subject to termination by the lessee, and

(a) the original term of the lease is equal to or greater than the remaining economic life of the goods,

(b) the lessee is bound to renew the lease for the remaining economic life of the goods or is bound to become the owner of the goods,

(c) the lessee has an option to renew the lease for the remaining economic life of the goods for no additional consideration or nominal additional consideration upon compliance with the lease agreement, or

(d) the lessee has an option to become the owner of the goods for no additional consideration or nominal additional consideration upon compliance with the lease agreement.

A transaction does not create a security interest merely because it provides that

(a) the present value of the consideration the lessee is obligated to pay the lessor for the right to possession and use of the goods is substantially equal to or is greater than the fair market value of the goods at the time the lease is entered into,

(b) the lessee assumes risk of loss of the goods, or agrees to pay taxes, insurance, filing, recording, or registration fees, or service or maintenance costs with respect to the goods,

(c) the lessee has an option to renew the lease or to become the owner of the goods,

(d) the lessee has an option to renew the lease for a fixed rent that is equal to or greater than the reasonably predictable fair market rent for the use of the goods for the term of the renewal at the time the option is to be performed, or

(e) the lessee has an option to become the owner of the goods for a fixed price that is equal to or greater than the reasonably predictable fair market value of the goods at the time the option is to be performed.

For purposes of this subsection (37):

(x) Additional consideration is not nominal if (i) when the option to renew the lease is granted to the lessee the rent is stated to be the fair market rent for the use of the goods for the term of the renewal determined at the time the option is to be performed, or (ii) when the option to become the owner of the goods is granted to the lessee the price is stated to be the fair market value of the goods determined at the time the option is to be performed. Additional consideration is nominal if it is less than the lessee's reasonably predictable cost of performing under the lease agreement if the option is not exercised;

(y) "Reasonably predictable" and "remaining economic life of the goods" are to be determined with reference to the facts and circumstances at the time the transaction is entered into; and

(z) "Present value" means the amount as of a date certain of one or more sums payable in the future, discounted to the date certain. The discount is determined by the interest rate specified by the parties if the rate is not manifestly unreasonable at the time the transaction is entered into; otherwise, the discount is determined by a commercially reasonable rate that takes into account the facts and circumstances of each case at the time the transaction was entered into.

(38) "Send" in connection with any writing or notice means to deposit in the mail or deliver for transmission by any other usual means of communication with postage or cost of transmission provided for and properly addressed and in the case of an instrument to an address specified thereon or otherwise agreed, or if there be none to any address reasonable under the circumstances. The receipt of any writing or notice within the time at which it would have arrived if properly sent has the effect of a proper sending.

(39) "Signed" includes any symbol executed or adopted by a party with present intention to authenticate a writing.

(40) "Surety" includes guarantor.

(41) "Telegram" includes a message transmitted by radio, teletype, cable, any mechanical method of transmission, or the like.

(42) "Term" means that portion of an agreement which relates to a particular matter.

(43) "Unauthorized" signature means one made without actual, implied or apparent authority and includes a forgery.

(44) "Value". Except as otherwise provided with respect to negotiable instruments and bank collections (Sections 3—303, 4—210 and 4—211) a person gives "value" for rights if he acquires them

(a) in return for a binding commitment to extend credit or for the extension of immediately available credit whether or not drawn upon and whether or not a chargeback is provided for in the event of difficulties in collection; or

(b) as security for or in total or partial satisfaction of a preexisting claim; or

(c) by accepting delivery pursuant to a preexisting contract for purchase; or

(d) generally, in return for any consideration sufficient to support a simple contract.

(45) "Warehouse receipt" means a receipt issued by a person engaged in the business of storing goods for hire.

(46) "Written" or "writing" includes printing, typewriting or any other intentional reduction to tangible form.

§1—202. **Prima Facie Evidence by Third Party Documents.**

A document in due form purporting to be a bill of lading, policy or certificate of insurance, official weigher's or inspector's certificate, consular invoice, or any other document authorized or required by the contract to be issued by a third party shall be prima facie evidence of its own authenticity and genuineness and of the facts stated in the document by the third party.

§ 1—203. **Obligation of Good Faith.**

Every contract or duty within this Act imposes an obligation of good faith in its performance or enforcement.

§ 1—204. **Time; Reasonable Time; "Seasonably".**

(1) Whenever this Act requires any action to be taken within a reasonable time, any time which is not manifestly unreasonable may be fixed by agreement.

(2) What is a reasonable time for taking any action depends on the nature, purpose and circumstances of such action.

(3) An action is taken "seasonably" when it is taken at or within the time agreed or if no time is agreed at or within a reasonable time.

§ 1—205. **Course of Dealing and Usage of Trade.**

(1) A course of dealing is a sequence of previous conduct between

the parties to a particular transaction which is fairly to be regarded as establishing a common basis of understanding for interpreting their expressions and other conduct.

(2) A usage of trade is any practice or method of dealing having such regularity of observance in a place, vocation or trade as to justify an expectation that it will be observed with respect to the transaction in question. The existence and scope of such a usage are to be proved as facts. If it is established that such a usage is embodied in a written trade code or similar writing the interpretation of the writing is for the court.

(3) A course of dealing between parties and any usage of trade in the vocation or trade in which they are engaged or of which they are or should be aware give particular meaning to and supplement or qualify terms of an agreement.

(4) The express terms of an agreement and an applicable course of dealing or usage of trade shall be construed wherever reasonable as consistent with each other; but when such construction is unreasonable express terms control both course of dealing and usage of trade and course of dealing controls usage trade.

(5) An applicable usage of trade in the place where any part of performance is to occur shall be used in interpreting the agreement as to that part of the performance.

(6) Evidence of a relevant usage of trade offered by one party is not admissible unless and until he has given the other party such notice as the court finds sufficient to prevent unfair surprise to the latter.

§ 1—206. Statute of Frauds for Kinds of Personal Property Not Otherwise Covered.

(1) Except in the cases described in subsection (2) of this section a contract for the sale of personal property is not enforceable by way of action or defense beyond five thousand dollars in amount or value of remedy unless there is some writing which indicates that a contract for sale has been made between the parties at a defined or stated price, reasonably identifies the subject matter, and is signed by the party against whom enforcement is sought or by his authorized agent.

(2) Subsection (1) of this section does not apply to contracts for the sale of goods (Section 2—201) nor of securities (Section 8—113) nor to security agreements (Section 9—203).

§ 1—207. Performance or Acceptance Under Reservation of Rights.

(1) A party who with explicit reservation of rights performs or promises performance or assents to performance in a manner demanded or offered by the other party does not thereby prejudice the rights reserved. Such words as "without prejudice", "under protest" or the like are sufficient.

(2) Subsection (1) does not apply to an accord and satisfaction.

§ 1—208. Option to Accelerate at Will.

A term providing that one party or his successor in interest may accelerate payment or performance or require collateral or additional collateral "at will" or "when he deems himself insecure" or in words of similar import shall be construed to mean that he shall have power to do so only if he in good faith believes that the prospect of payment or performance is impaired. The burden of establishing lack of good faith is on the party against whom the

power has been exercised.

§ 1—209. Subordinated Obligations.

An obligation may be issued as subordinated to payment of another obligation of the person obligated, or a creditor may subordinate his right to payment of an obligation by agreement with either the person obligated or another creditor of the person obligated. Such a subordination does not create a security interest as against either the common debtor or a subordinated creditor. This section shall be construed as declaring the law as it existed prior to the enactment of this section and not as modifying it. Added 1966.

Note: *This new section is proposed as an optional provision to make it clear that a subordination agreement does not create a security interest unless so intended.*

Article 2
SALES

Part 1   Short Title, General Construction and Subject Matter

§ 2—101.   Short Title.

This Article shall be known and may be cited as Uniform Commercial Code—Sales.

§ 2—102.   Scope; Certain Security and Other Transactions Excluded From This Article.

Unless the context otherwise requires, this Article applies to transactions in goods; it does not apply to any transaction which although in the form of an unconditional contract to sell or present sale is intended to operate only as a security transaction nor does this Article impair or repeal any statute regulating sales to consumers, farmers or other specified classes of buyers.

§ 2—103.   Definitions and Index of Definitions.

(1) In this Article unless the context otherwise requires

   (a) "Buyer" means a person who buys or contracts to buy goods.

   (b) "Good faith" in the case of a merchant means honesty in fact and the observance of reasonable commercial standards of fair dealing in the trade.

   (c) "Receipt" of goods means taking physical possession of them.

   (d) "Seller" means a person who sells or contracts to sell goods.

(2) Other definitions applying to this Article or to specified Parts thereof, and the sections in which they appear are:

"Acceptance". Section 2—606.
"Banker's credit". Section 2—325.
"Between merchants". Section 2—104.
"Cancellation". Section 2—106(4).
"Commercial unit". Section 2—105.
"Confirmed credit". Section 2—325.
"Conforming to contract". Section 2—106.
"Contract for sale". Section 2—106.
"Cover". Section 2—712.
"Entrusting". Section 2—403.

"Financing agency". Section 2—104.
"Future goods". Section 2—105.
"Goods". Section 2—105.
"Identification". Section 2—501.
"Installment contract". Section 2—612.
"Letter of Credit". Section 2—325.
"Lot". Section 2—105.
"Merchant". Section 2—104.
"Overseas". Section 2—323.
"Person in position of seller". Section 2—707.
"Present sale". Section 2—106.
"Sale". Section 2—106.
"Sale on approval". Section 2—326.
"Sale or return". Section 2—326.
"Termination". Section 2—106.

(3) The following definitions in other Articles apply to this Article:

"Check". Section 3—104.
"Consignee". Section 7—102.
"Consignor". Section 7—102.
"Consumer goods". Section 9—109.
"Dishonor". Section 3—507.
"Draft". Section 3—104.

(4) In addition Article 1 contains general definitions and principles of construction and interpretation applicable throughout this Article.

§ 2—104. **Definitions: "Merchant"; "Between Merchants"; "Financing Agency".**

(1) "Merchant" means a person who deals in goods of the kind or otherwise by his occupation holds himself out as having knowledge or skill peculiar to the practices or goods involved in the transaction or to whom such knowledge or skill may be attributed by his employment of an agent or broker or other intermediary who by his occupation holds himself out as having such knowledge or skill.

(2) "Financing agency" means a bank, finance company or other person who in the ordinary course of business makes advances against goods or documents of title or who by arrangement with either the seller or the buyer intervenes in ordinary course to make or collect payment due or claimed under the contract for sale, as by purchasing or paying the seller's draft or making advances against it or by merely taking it for collection whether or not documents of title accompany the draft. "Financing agency" includes also a bank or other person who similarly intervenes between persons who are in the position of seller and buyer in respect to the goods (Section 2—707).

(3) "Between merchants" means in any transaction with respect to which both parties are chargeable with the knowledge or skill of merchants.

§ 2—105. **Definitions: Transferability; "Goods"; "Future" Goods; "Lot"; "Commercial Unit".**

(1) "Goods" means all things (including specially manufactured goods) which are movable at the time of identification to the contract for sale other than the money in which the price is to be paid, investment securities (Article 8) and things in action. "Goods" also includes the unborn young of animals and growing crops and other identified things attached to realty as described in the sec-

tion on goods to be severed from realty (Section 2—107).

(2) Goods must be both existing and identified before any interest in them can pass. Goods which are not both existing and identified are "future" goods. A purported present sale of future goods or of any interest therein operates as a contract to sell.

(3) There may be a sale of a part interest in existing identified goods.

(4) An undivided share in an identified bulk of fungible goods is sufficiently identified to be sold although the quantity of the bulk is not determined. Any agreed proportion of such a bulk or any quantity thereof agreed upon by number, weight or other measure may to the extent of the seller's interest in the bulk be sold to the buyer who then becomes an owner in common.

(5) "Lot" means a parcel or a single article which is the subject matter of a separate sale or delivery, whether or not it is sufficient to perform the contract.

(6) "Commercial unit" means such a unit of goods as by commercial usage is a single whole for purposes of sale and division of which materially impairs its character or value on the market or in use. A commercial unit may be a single article (as a machine) or a set of articles (as a suite of furniture or an assortment of sizes) or a quantity (as a bale, gross, or carload) or any other unit treated in use or in the relevant market as a single whole.

§ 2—106. **Definitions: "Contract"; "Agreement"; "Contract for Sale"; "Sale"; "Present Sale"; "Conforming" to Contract; "Termination"; "Cancellation".**

(1) In this Article unless the context otherwise requires "contract" and "agreement" are limited to those relating to the present or future sale of goods. "Contract for sale" includes both a present sale of goods and a contract to sell goods at a future time. A "sale" consists in the passing of title from the seller to the buyer for a price (Section 2—401). A "present sale" means a sale which is accomplished by the making of the contract.

(2) Goods or conduct including any part of a performance are "conforming" or conform to the contract when they are in accordance with the obligations under the contract.

(3) "Termination" occurs when either party pursuant to a power created by agreement or law puts an end to the contract otherwise than for its breach. On "termination" all obligations which are still executory on both sides are discharged but any right based on prior breach or performance survives.

(4) "Cancellation" occurs when either party puts an end to the contract for breach by the other and its effect is the same as that of "termination" except that the cancelling party also retains any remedy for breach of the whole contract or any unperformed balance.

§ 2—107. **Goods to Be Severed From Realty: Recording.**

(1) A contract for the sale of minerals or the like (including oil and gas) or a structure or its materials to be removed from realty is a contract for the sale of goods within this Article if they are to be severed by the seller but until severance a purported present sale thereof which is not effective as a transfer of an interest in land is effective only as a contract to sell.

(2) A contract for the sale apart from the land of growing crops or other things attached to realty and capable of severance without material harm thereto but not described in subsection (1) or of timber to be cut is a contract for the sale of goods within this Article whether the subject matter is to be severed by the buyer or by

the seller even though it forms part of the realty at the time of con-tracting, and the parties can by identification effect a present sale before severance.

(3) The provisions of this section are subject to any third party rights provided by the law relating to realty records, and the con-tract for sale may be executed and recorded as a document trans-ferring an interest in land and shall then constitute notice to third parties of the buyer's rights under the contract for sale.

Part 2 Form, Formation and Readjustment of Contract

§ 2—201. Formal Requirements; Statute of Frauds.

(1) Except as otherwise provided in this section a contract for the sale of goods for the price of $500 or more is not enforceable by way of action or defense unless there is some writing sufficient to indicate that a contract for sale has been made between the parties and signed by the party against whom enforcement is sought or by his authorized agent or broker. A writing is not insufficient because it omits or incorrectly states a term agreed upon but the contract is not enforceable under this paragraph beyond the quan-tity of goods shown in such writing.

(2) Between merchants if within a reasonable time a writing in confirmation of the contract and sufficient against the sender is received and the party receiving it has reason to know its contents, its satisfies the requirements of subsection (1) against such party unless written notice of objection to its contents is given within ten days after it is received.

(3) A contract which does not satisfy the requirements of subsec-tion (1) but which is valid in other respects is enforceable

(a) if the goods are to be specially manufactured for the buyer and are not suitable for sale to others in the ordinary course of the seller's business and the seller, before notice of repudia-tion is received and under circumstances which reasonably indicate that the goods are for the buyer, has made either a substantial beginning of their manufacture or commitments for their procurement; or

(b) if the party against whom enforcement is sought admits in his pleading, testimony or otherwise in court that a contract for sale was made, but the contract is not enforceable under this provision beyond the quantity of goods admitted; or

(c) with respect to goods for which payment has been made and accepted or which have been received and accepted (Sec. 2—606).

§ 2—202. Final Written Expression: Parol or Extrinsic Evidence.

Terms with respect to which the confirmatory memoranda of the parties agree or which are otherwise set forth in a writing intended by the parties as a final expression of their agreement with respect to such terms as are included therein may not be contradicted by evidence of any prior agreement or of a contemporaneous oral agreement but may be explained or supplemented

(a) by course of dealing or usage of trade (Section 1—205) or by course of performance (Section 2—208); and

(b) by evidence of consistent additional terms unless the court finds the writing to have been intended also as a com-plete and exclusive statement of the terms of the agreement.

§ 2—203. Seals Inoperative.

The affixing of a seal to a writing evidencing a contract for sale or an offer to buy or sell goods does not constitute the writing a sealed instrument and the law with respect to sealed instruments does not apply to such a contract or offer.

§ 2—204. Formation in General.

(1) A contract for sale of goods may be made in any manner suf-ficient to show agreement, including conduct by both parties which recognizes the existence of such a contract.

(2) An agreement sufficient to constitute a contract for sale may be found even though the moment of its making is undetermined.

(3) Even though one or more terms are left open a contract for sale does not fail for indefiniteness if the parties have intended to make a contract and there is a reasonably certain basis for giving an appropriate remedy.

§ 2—205. Firm Offers.

An offer by a merchant to buy or sell goods in a signed writing which by its terms gives assurance that it will be held open is not revocable, for lack of consideration, during the time stated or if no time is stated for a reasonable time, but in no event may such period of irrevocability exceed three months; but any such term of assurance on a form supplied by the offeree must be separately signed by the offeror.

§ 2—206. Offer and Acceptance in Formation of Contract.

(1) Unless other unambiguously indicated by the language or cir-cumstances

(a) an offer to make a contract shall be construed as inviting acceptance in any manner and by any medium reasonable in the circumstances;

(b) an order or other offer to buy goods for prompt or current shipment shall be construed as inviting acceptance either by a prompt promise to ship or by the prompt or current shipment of conforming or nonconforming goods, but such a shipment of non-conforming goods does not constitute an acceptance if the seller seasonably notifies the buyer that the shipment is offered only as an accommodation to the buyer.

(2) Where the beginning of a requested performance is a reason-able mode of acceptance an offeror who is not notified of accep-tance within a reasonable time may treat the offer as having lapsed before acceptance.

§ 2—207. Additional Terms in Acceptance or Confirmation.

(1) A definite and seasonable expression of acceptance or a writ-ten confirmation which is sent within a reasonable time operates as an acceptance even though it states terms additional to or dif-ferent from those offered or agreed upon, unless acceptance is expressly made conditional on assent to the additional or different terms.

(2) The additional terms are to be construed as proposals for addi-tion to the contract. Between merchants such terms become part of the contract unless:

(a) the offer expressly limits acceptance to the terms of the offer;

(b) they materially alter it; or

(c) notification of objection to them has already been given or is given within a reasonable time after notice of them is received.

(3) Conduct by both parties which recognizes the existence of a contract is sufficient to establish a contract for sale although the writings of the parties do not otherwise establish a contract. In such case the terms of the particular contract consist of those terms on which the writings of the parties agree, together with any supplementary terms incorporated under any other provisions of this Act.

§ 2—208. **Course of Performance or Practical Construction.**

(1) Where the contract for sale involves repeated occasions for performance by either party with knowledge of the nature of the performance and opportunity for objection to it by the other, any course of performance accepted or acquiesced in without objection shall be relevant to determine the meaning of the agreement.

(2) The express terms of the agreement and any such course of performance, as well as any course of dealing and usage of trade, shall be construed whenever reasonable as consistent with each other; but when such construction is unreasonable, express terms shall control course of performance and course of performance shall control both course of dealing and usage of trade (Section 1—205).

(3) Subject to the provisions of the next section on modification and waiver, such course of performance shall be relevant to show a waiver or modification of any term inconsistent with such course of performance.

§ 2—209. **Modification, Rescission and Waiver.**

(1) An agreement modifying a contract within this Article needs no consideration to be binding.

(2) A signed agreement which excludes modification or rescission except by a signed writing cannot be otherwise modified or rescinded, but except as between merchants such a requirement on a form supplied by the merchant must be separately signed by the other party.

(3) The requirements of the statute of frauds section of this Article (Section 2—201) must be satisfied if the contract as modified is within its provisions.

(4) Although an attempt at modification or rescission does not satisfy the requirements of subsection (2) or (3) it can operate as a waiver.

(5) A party who has made a waiver affecting an executory portion of the contract may retract the waiver by reasonable notification received by the other party that strict performance will be required of any term waived, unless the retraction would be unjust in view of a material change of position in reliance on the waiver.

§ 2—210. **Delegation of Performance; Assignment of Rights.**

(1) A party may perform his duty through a delegate unless otherwise agreed or unless the other party has a substantial interest in having his original promisor perform or control the acts required by the contract. No delegation of performance relieves the party delegating of any duty to perform or any liability for breach.

(2) Unless otherwise agreed all rights of either seller or buyer can be assigned except where the assignment would materially change the duty of the other party, or increase materially the burden or risk imposed on him by his contract, or impair materially his chance of obtaining return performance. A right to damages for breach of the whole contract or a right arising out of the assignor's

due performance of his entire obligation can be assigned despite agreement otherwise.

(3) Unless the circumstances indicate the contrary a prohibition of assignment of "the contract" is to be construed as barring only the delegation to the assignee of the assignor's performance.

(4) An assignment of "the contract" or of "all my rights under the contract" or an assignment in similar general terms is an assignment of rights and unless the language or the circumstances (as in an assignment for security) indicate the contrary, it is a delegation of performance of the duties of the assignor and its acceptance by the assignee constitutes a promise by him to perform those duties. This promise is enforceable by either the assignor or the other party to the original contract.

(5) The other party may treat any assignment which delegates performance as creating reasonable grounds for insecurity and may without prejudice to his rights against the assignor demand assurances from the assignee (Section 2—609).

Part 3 General Obligation and Construction of Contract

§ 2—301. **General Obligations of Parties.**

The obligation of the seller is to transfer and deliver and that of the buyer is to accept and pay in accordance with the contract.

§ 2—302. **Unconscionable Contract or Clause.**

(1) If the court as a matter of law finds the contract or any clause of the contract to have been unconscionable at the time it was made the court may refuse to enforce the contract, or it may enforce the remainder of the contract without the unconscionable clause, or it may so limit the application of any unconscionable clause as to avoid any unconscionable result.

(2) When it is claimed or appears to the court that the contract or any clause thereof may be unconscionable the parties shall be afforded a reasonable opportunity to present evidence as to its commercial setting, purpose and effect to aid the court in making the determination.

§ 2—303. **Allocations or Division of Risks.**

Where this Article allocates a risk or a burden as between the parties "unless otherwise agreed", the agreement may not only shift the allocation but may also divide the risk or burden.

§ 2—304. **Price Payable in Money, Goods, Realty, or Otherwise.**

(1) The price can be made payable in money or otherwise. If it is payable in whole or in part in goods each party is a seller of the goods which he is to transfer.

(2) Even though all or part of the price is payable in an interest in realty the transfer of the goods and the seller's obligations with reference to them are subject to this Article, but not the transfer of the interest in realty or the transferor's obligations in connection therewith.

§ 2—305. **Open Price Term.**

(1) The parties if they so intend can conclude a contract for sale even though the price is not settled. In such a case the price is a reasonable price at the time for delivery if

    (a) nothing is said as to price; or

(b) the price is left to be agreed by the parties and they fail to agree; or

(c) the price is to be fixed in terms of some agreed market or other standard as set or recorded by a third person or agency and it is not so set or recorded.

(2) A price to be fixed by the seller or by the buyer means a price for him to fix in good faith.

(3) When a price left to be fixed otherwise than by agreement of the parties fails to be fixed through fault of one party the other may at his option treat the contract as cancelled or himself fix a reasonable price.

(4) Where, however, the parties intend not to be bound unless the price be fixed or agreed and it is not fixed or agreed there is no contract. In such a case the buyer must return any goods already received or if unable so to do must pay their reasonable value at the time of delivery and the seller must return any portion of the price paid on account.

§ 2—306. **Output, Requirements and Exclusive Dealings.**

(1) A term which measures the quantity by the output of the seller or the requirements of the buyer means such actual output or requirements as may occur in good faith, except that no quantity unreasonably disproportionate to any stated estimate or in the absence of a stated estimate to any normal or otherwise comparable prior output or requirements may be tendered or demanded.

(2) A lawful agreement by either the seller or the buyer for exclusive dealing in the kind of goods concerned imposes unless otherwise agreed an obligation by the seller to use best efforts to supply the goods and by the buyer to use best efforts to promote their sale.

§ 2—307. **Delivery in Single Lot or Several Lots.**

Unless otherwise agreed all goods called for by a contract for sale must be tendered in a single delivery and payment is due only on such tender but where the circumstances give either party the right to make or demand delivery in lots the price if it can be apportioned may be demanded for each lot.

§ 2—308. **Absence of Specified Place for Delivery.**

Unless otherwise agreed

(a) the place for delivery of goods is the seller's place of business or if he has none his residence; but

(b) in a contract for sale of identified goods which to the knowledge of the parties at the time of contracting are in some other place, that place is the place for their delivery; and

(c) documents of title may be delivered through customary banking channels.

§ 2—309. **Absence of Specific Time Provisions; Notice of Termination.**

(1) The time for shipment or delivery or any other action under a contract if not provided in this Article or agreed upon shall be a reasonable time.

(2) Where the contract provides for successive performances but is indefinite in duration it is valid for a reasonable time but unless otherwise agreed may be terminated at any time by either party.

(3) Termination of a contract by one party except on the happening of an agreed event requires that reasonable notification be received by the other party and an agreement dispensing with notification is invalid if its operation would be unconscionable.

§ 2—310. **Open Time for Payment or Running of Credit; Authority to Ship Under Reservation.**

Unless otherwise agreed

(a) payment is due at the time and place at which the buyer is to receive the goods even though the place of shipment is the place of delivery; and

(b) if the seller is authorized to send the goods he may ship them under reservation, and may tender the documents of title, but the buyer may inspect the goods after their arrival before payment is due unless such inspection is inconsistent with the terms of the contract (Section 2—513); and

(c) if delivery is authorized and made by way of documents of title otherwise than by subsection (b) then payment is due at the time and place at which the buyer is to receive the documents regardless of where the goods are to be received; and

(d) where the seller is required or authorized to ship the goods on credit the credit period runs from the time of shipment but post-dating the invoice or delaying its dispatch will correspondingly delay the starting of the credit period.

§ 2—311. **Options and Cooperation Respecting Performance.**

(1) An agreement for sale which is otherwise sufficiently definite (subsection (3) of Section 2—204) to be a contract is not made invalid by the fact that it leaves particulars of performance to be specified by one of the parties. Any such specification must be made in good faith and within limits set by commercial reasonableness.

(2) Unless otherwise agreed specifications relating to assortment of the goods are at the buyer's option and except as otherwise provided in subsections (1)(c) and (3) of Section 2—319 specifications or arrangements relating to shipment are at the seller's option.

(3) Where such specification would materially affect the other party's performance but is not seasonably made or where one party's cooperation is necessary to the agreed performance of the other but is not seasonably forthcoming, the other party in addition to all other remedies

(a) is excused for any resulting delay in his own performance; and

(b) may also either proceed to perform in any reasonable manner or after the time for a material part of his own performance treat the failure to specify or to cooperate as a breach by failure to deliver or accept the goods.

§ 2—312. **Warranty of Title and Against Infringement; Buyer's Obligation Against Infringement.**

(1) Subject to subsection (2) there is in a contract for sale a warranty by the seller that

(a) the title conveyed shall be good, and its transfer rightful; and

(b) the goods shall be delivered free from any security interest or other lien or encumbrance of which the buyer at the time of contracting has no knowledge.

(2) A warranty under subsection (1) will be excluded or modified only by specific language or by circumstances which give the

buyer reason to know that the person selling does not claim title in himself or that he is purporting to sell only such right or title as he or a third person may have.

(3) Unless otherwise agreed a seller who is a merchant regularly dealing in goods of the kind warrants that the goods shall be delivered free of the rightful claim of any third person by way of infringement or the like but a buyer who furnishes specifications to the seller must hold the seller harmless against any such claim which arises out of compliance with the specifications.

§ 2—313. **Express Warranties by Affirmation, Promise, Description, Sample.**

(1) Express warranties by the seller are created as follows:

(a) Any affirmation of fact or promise made by the seller to the buyer which relates to the goods and becomes part of the basis of the bargain creates an express warranty that the goods shall conform to the affirmation or promise.

(b) Any description of the goods which is made part of the basis of the bargain creates an express warranty that the goods shall conform to the description.

(c) Any sample or model which is made part of the basis of the bargain creates an express warranty that the whole of the goods shall conform to the sample or model.

(2) It is not necessary to the creation of an express warranty that the seller use formal words such as "warrant" or "guarantee" or that he have a specific intention to make a warranty, but an affirmation merely of the value of the goods or a statement purporting to be merely the seller's opinion or commendation of the goods does not create a warranty.

§ 2—314. **Implied Warranty: Merchantability; Usage of Trade.**

(1) Unless excluded or modified (Section 2—316), a warranty that the goods shall be merchantable is implied in a contract for their sale if the seller is a merchant with respect to goods of that kind. Under this section the serving for value of food or drink to be consumed either on the premises or elsewhere is a sale.

(2) Goods to be merchantable must be at least such as

(a) pass without objection in the trade under the contract description; and

(b) in the case of fungible goods, are of fair average quality within the description; and

(c) are fit for the ordinary purposes for which such goods are used; and

(d) run, within the variations permitted by the agreement, of even kind, quality and quantity within each unit and among all units involved; and

(e) are adequately contained, packaged, and labeled as the agreement may require; and

(f) conform to the promises or affirmations of fact made on the container or label if any.

(3) Unless excluded or modified (Section 2—316) other implied warranties may arise from course of dealing or usage of trade.

§ 2—315. **Implied Warranty: Fitness for Particular Purpose.**

Where the seller at the time of contracting has reason to know any particular purpose for which the goods are required and that the buyer is relying on the seller's skill or judgment to select or furnish suitable goods, there is unless excluded or modified under the next section an implied warranty that the goods shall be fit for such purpose.

§ 2—316. **Exclusion or Modification of Warranties.**

(1) Words or conduct relevant to the creation of an express warranty and words or conduct tending to negate or limit warranty shall be construed wherever reasonable as consistent with each other; but subject to the provisions of this Article on parol or extrinsic evidence (Section 2—202) negation or limitation is inoperative to the extent that such construction is unreasonable.

(2) Subject to subsection (3), to exclude or modify the implied warranty of merchantability or any part of it the language must mention merchantability and in case of a writing must be conspicuous, and to exclude or modify any implied warranty of fitness the exclusion must be by a writing and conspicuous. Language to exclude all implied warranties of fitness is sufficient if it states, for example, that "There are no warranties which extend beyond the description on the face hereof."

(3) Notwithstanding subsection (2)

(a) unless the circumstances indicate otherwise, all implied warranties are excluded by expressions like "as is", "with all faults" or other language which in common understanding calls the buyer's attention to the exclusion of warranties and makes plain that there is no implied warranty; and

(b) when the buyer before entering into the contract has examined the goods or the sample or model as fully as he desired or has refused to examine the goods there is no implied warranty with regard to defects which an examination ought in the circumstances to have revealed to him; and

(c) an implied warranty can also be excluded or modified by course of dealing or course of performance or usage of trade.

(4) Remedies for breach of warranty can be limited in accordance with the provisions of this Article on liquidation or limitation of damages and on contractual modification of remedy (Sections 2—718 and 2—719).

§ 2—317. **Cumulation and Conflict of Warranties Express or Implied.**

Warranties whether express or implied shall be construed as consistent with each other and as cumulative, but if such construction is unreasonable the intention of the parties shall determine which warranty is dominant. In ascertaining that intention the following rules apply:

(a) Exact or technical specifications displace an inconsistent sample or model or general language of description.

(b) A sample from an existing bulk displaces inconsistent general language of description.

(c) Express warranties displace inconsistent implied warranties other than an implied warranty of fitness for a particular purpose.

§ 2—318. **Third Party Beneficiaries of Warranties Express or Implied.**

Note: If this Act is introduced in the Congress of the United States this section should be omitted. (States to select one alternative.)

Alternative A

A seller's warranty whether express or implied extends to any natural person who is in the family or household of his buyer or who is a guest in his home if it is reasonable to expect that such person may use, consume or be affected by the goods and who is injured in person by breach of the warranty. A seller may not exclude or limit the operation of this section.

Alternative B

A seller's warranty whether express or implied extends to any natural person who may reasonably be expected to use, consume or be affected by the goods and who is injured in person by breach of the warranty. A seller may not exclude or limit the operation of this section.

Alternative C

A seller's warranty whether express or implied extends to any person who may reasonably be expected to use, consume or be affected by the goods and who is injured by breach of the warranty. A seller may not exclude or limit the operation of this section with respect to injury to the person of an individual to whom the warranty extends. As amended 1966.

§ 2—319. F.O.B. and F.A.S. Terms.

(1) Unless otherwise agreed the term F.O.B. (which means "free on board") at a named place, even though used only in connection with the stated price, is a delivery term under which

(a) when the term is F.O.B. the place of shipment, the seller must at that place ship the goods in the manner provided in this Article (Section 2—504) and bear the expense and risk of putting them into the possession of the carrier; or

(b) when the term is F.O.B. the place of destination, the seller must at his own expense and risk transport the goods to that place and there tender delivery of them in the manner provided in this Article (Section 2—503);

(c) when under either (a) or (b) the term is also F.O.B. vessel, car or other vehicle, the seller must in addition at his own expense and risk load the goods on board. If the term is F.O.B. vessel the buyer must name the vessel and in an appropriate case the seller must comply with the provisions of this Article on the form of bill of lading (Section 2—323).

(2) Unless otherwise agreed the term F.A.S. vessel (which means "free alongside") at a named port, even though used only in connection with the stated price, is a delivery term under which the seller must

(a) at his own expense and risk deliver the goods alongside the vessel in the manner usual in that port or on a dock designated and provided by the buyer; and

(b) obtain and tender a receipt for the goods in exchange for which the carrier is under a duty to issue a bill of lading.

(3) Unless otherwise agreed in any case falling within subsection (1)(a) or (c) or subsection (2) the buyer must seasonably give any needed instructions for making delivery, including when the term is F.A.S. or F.O.B. the loading berth of the vessel and in an appropriate case its name and sailing date. The seller may treat the failure of needed instructions as a failure of cooperation under this Article (Section 2—311). He may also at his option move the goods in any reasonable manner preparatory to delivery or shipment.

(4) Under the term F.O.B. vessel or F.A.S. unless otherwise

agreed the buyer must make payment against tender of the required documents and the seller may not tender nor the buyer demand delivery of the goods in substitution for the documents.

§ 2—320. C.I.F. and C. & F. Terms.

(1) The term C.I.F. means that the price includes in a lump sum the cost of the goods and the insurance and freight to the named destination. The term C. & F. or C.F. means that the price so includes cost and freight to the named destination.

(2) Unless otherwise agreed and even though used only in connection with the stated price and destination, the term C.I.F. destination or its equivalent requires the seller at his own expense and risk to

(a) put the goods into the possession of a carrier at the port for shipment and obtain a negotiable bill or bills of lading covering the entire transportation to the named destination; and

(b) load the goods and obtain a receipt from the carrier (which may be contained in the bill of lading) showing that the freight has been paid or provided for; and

(c) obtain a policy or certificate of insurance, including any war risk insurance, of a kind and on terms then current at the port of shipment in the usual amount, in the currency of the contract, shown to cover the same goods covered by the bill of lading and providing for payment of loss to the order of the buyer or for the account of whom it may concern; but the seller may add to the price the amount of the premium for any such war risk insurance; and

(d) prepare an invoice of the goods and procure any other documents required to effect shipment or to comply with the contract; and

(e) forward and tender with commercial promptness all the documents in due form and with any indorsement necessary to perfect the buyer's rights.

(3) Unless otherwise agreed the term C. & F. or its equivalent has the same effect and imposes upon the seller the same obligations and risks as a C.I.F. term except the obligation as to insurance.

(4) Under the term C.I.F. or C. & F. unless otherwise agreed the buyer must make payment against tender of the required documents and the seller may not tender nor the buyer demand delivery of the goods in substitution for the documents.

§ 2—321. C.I.F. or C. & F.: "Net Landed Weights"; "Payment on Arrival"; Warranty of Condition on Arrival.

Under a contract containing a term C.I.F. or C. & F.

(1) Where the price is based on or is to be adjusted according to "net landed weights", "delivered weights", "out turn" quantity or quality or the like, unless otherwise agreed the seller must reasonably estimate the price. The payment due on tender of the documents called for by the contract is the amount so estimated, but after final adjustment of the price a settlement must be made with commercial promptness.

(2) An agreement described in subsection (1) or any warranty of quality or condition of the goods on arrival places upon the seller the risk of ordinary deterioration, shrinkage and the like in transportation but has no effect on the place or time of identification to the contract for sale or delivery or on the passing of the risk of loss.

(3) Unless otherwise agreed where the contract provides for pay-

ment on or after arrival of the goods the seller must before payment allow such preliminary inspection as is feasible; but if the goods are lost delivery of the documents and payment are due when the goods should have arrived.

§ 2—322. **Delivery "Ex-Ship".**

(1) Unless otherwise agreed a term for delivery of goods "ex-ship" (which means from the carrying vessel) or in equivalent language is not restricted to a particular ship and requires delivery from a ship which has reached a place at the named port of destination where goods of the kind are usually discharged.

(2) Under such a term unless otherwise agreed

(a) the seller must discharge all liens arising out of the carriage and furnish the buyer with a direction which puts the carrier under a duty to deliver the goods; and

(b) the risk of loss does not pass to the buyer until the goods leave the ship's tackle or are otherwise properly unloaded.

§ 2—323. **Form of Bill of Lading Required in Overseas Shipment; "Overseas".**

(1) Where the contract contemplates overseas shipment and contains a term C.I.F. or C. & F. or F.O.B. vessel, the seller unless otherwise agreed must obtain a negotiable bill of lading stating that the goods have been loaded on board or, in the case of a term C.I.F. or C. & F., received for shipment.

(2) Where in a case within subsection (1) a bill of lading has been issued in a set of parts, unless otherwise agreed if the documents are not to be sent from abroad the buyer may demand tender of the full set; otherwise only one part of the bill of lading need be tendered. Even if the agreement expressly requires a full set

(a) due tender of a single part is acceptable within the provisions of this Article on cure of improper delivery (subsection (1) of Section 2—508); and

(b) even though the full set is demanded, if the documents are sent from abroad the person tendering an incomplete set may nevertheless require payment upon furnishing an indemnity which the buyer in good faith deems adequate.

(3) A shipment by water or by air or a contract contemplating such shipment is "overseas" insofar as by usage of trade or agreement it is subject to the commercial, financing or shipping practices characteristic of international deep water commerce.

§ 2—324. **"No Arrival, No Sale" Term.**

Under a term "no arrival, no sale" or terms of like meaning, unless otherwise agreed,

(a) the seller must properly ship conforming goods and if they arrive by any means he must tender them on arrival but he assumes no obligation that the goods will arrive unless he has caused the non-arrival; and

(b) where without fault of the seller the goods are in part lost or have so deteriorated as no longer to conform to the contract or arrive after the contract time, the buyer may proceed as if there had been casualty to identified goods (Section 2—613).

§ 2—325. **"Letter of Credit" Term; "Confirmed Credit".**

(1) Failure of the buyer seasonably to furnish an agreed letter of credit is a breach of the contract for sale.

(2) The delivery to seller of a proper letter of credit suspends the buyer's obligation to pay. If the letter of credit is dishonored, the seller may on seasonable notification to the buyer require payment directly from him.

(3) Unless otherwise agreed the term "letter of credit" or "banker's credit" in a contract for sale means an irrevocable credit issued by a financing agency of good repute and, where the shipment is overseas, of good international repute. The term "confirmed credit" means that the credit must also carry the direct obligation of such an agency which does business in the seller's financial market.

§ 2—326. **Sale on Approval and Sale or Return; Consignment Sales and Rights of Creditors.**

(1) Unless otherwise agreed, if delivered goods may be returned by the buyer even though they conform to the contract, the transaction is

(a) a "sale on approval" if the goods are delivered primarily for use, and

(b) a "sale or return" if the goods are delivered primarily for resale.

(2) Except as provided in subsection (3), goods held on approval are not subject to the claims of the buyer's creditors until acceptance; goods held on sale or return are subject to such claims while in the buyer's possession.

(3) Where goods are delivered to a person for sale and such person maintains a place of business at which he deals in goods of the kind involved, under a name other than the name of the person making delivery, then with respect to claims of creditors of the person conducting the business the goods are deemed to be on sale or return. The provisions of this subsection are applicable even though an agreement purports to reserve title to the person making delivery until payment or resale or uses such words as "on consignment" or "on memorandum". However, this subsection is not applicable if the person making delivery

(a) complies with an applicable law providing for a consignor's interest or the like to be evidenced by a sign, or

(b) establishes that the person conducting the business is generally known by his creditors to be substantially engaged in selling the goods of others, or

(c) complies with the filing provisions of the Article on Secured Transactions (Article 9).

(4) Any "or return" term of a contract for sale is to be treated as a separate contract for sale within the statute of frauds section of this Article (Section 2—201) and as contradicting the sale aspect of the contract within the provisions of this Article on parol or extrinsic evidence (Section 2—202).

§ 2—327. **Special Incidents of Sale on Approval and Sale or Return.**

(1) Under a sale on approval unless otherwise agreed

(a) although the goods are identified to the contract the risk of loss and the title do not pass to the buyer until acceptance; and

(b) use of the goods consistent with the purpose of trial is not acceptance but failure seasonably to notify the seller of election to return the goods is acceptance, and if the goods conform to the contract acceptance of any part is acceptance of the whole; and

(c) after due notification of election to return, the return is at the seller's risk and expense but a merchant buyer must follow any reasonable instructions.

(2) Under a sale or return unless otherwise agreed

(a) the option to return extends to the whole or any commercial unit of the goods while in substantially their original condition, but must be exercised seasonably; and

(b) the return is at the buyer's risk and expense.

§ 2—328. **Sale by Auction.**

(1) In a sale by auction if goods are put up in lots each lot is the subject of a separate sale.

(2) A sale by auction is complete when the auctioneer so announces by the fall of the hammer or in other customary manner. Where a bid is made while the hammer is falling in acceptance of a prior bid the auctioneer may in his discretion reopen the bidding or declare the goods sold under the bid on which the hammer was falling.

(3) Such a sale is with reserve unless the goods are in explicit terms put up without reserve. In an auction with reserve the auctioneer may withdraw the goods at any time until he announces completion of the sale. In an auction without reserve, after the auctioneer calls for bids on an article or lot, that article or lot cannot be withdrawn unless no bid is made within a reasonable time. In either case a bidder may retract his bid until the auctioneer's announcement of completion of the sale, but a bidder's retraction does not revive any previous bid.

(4) If the auctioneer knowingly receives a bid on the seller's behalf or the seller makes or procures such as bid, and notice has not been given that liberty for such bidding is reserved, the buyer may at his option avoid the sale or take the goods at the price of the last good faith bid prior to the completion of the sale. This subsection shall not apply to any bid at a forced sale.

Part 4 Title, Creditors and Good Faith Purchasers

§ 2—401. **Passing of Title; Reservation for Security; Limited Application of This Section.**

Each provision of this Article with regard to the rights, obligations and remedies of the seller, the buyer, purchasers or other third parties applies irrespective of title to the goods except where the provision refers to such title. Insofar as situations are not covered by the other provisions of this Article and matters concerning title became material the following rules apply:

(1) Title to goods cannot pass under a contract for sale prior to their identification to the contract (Section 2—501), and unless otherwise explicitly agreed the buyer acquires by their identification a special property as limited by this Act. Any retention or reservation by the seller of the title (property) in goods shipped or delivered to the buyer is limited in effect to a reservation of a security interest. Subject to these provisions and to the provisions of the Article on Secured Transactions (Article 9), title to goods passes from the seller to the buyer in any manner and on any conditions explicitly agreed on by the parties.

(2) Unless otherwise explicitly agreed title passes to the buyer at the time and place at which the seller completes his performance with reference to the physical delivery of the goods, despite any reservation of a security interest and even though a document of title is to be delivered at a different time or place; and in particular and despite any reservation of a security interest by the bill of lading

(a) if the contract requires or authorizes the seller to send the goods to the buyer but does not require him to deliver them at destination, title passes to the buyer at the time and place of shipment; but

(b) if the contract requires delivery at destination, title passes on tender there.

(3) Unless otherwise explicitly agreed where delivery is to be made without moving the goods,

(a) if the seller is to deliver a document of title, title passes at the time when and the place where he delivers such documents; or

(b) if the goods are at the time of contracting already identified and no documents are to be delivered, title passes at the time and place of contracting.

(4) A rejection or other refusal by the buyer to receive or retain the goods, whether or not justified, or a justified revocation of acceptance revests title to the goods in the seller. Such revesting occurs by operation of law and is not a "sale".

§ 2—402. **Rights of Seller's Creditors Against Sold Goods.**

(1) Except as provided in subsections (2) and (3), rights of unsecured creditors of the seller with respect to goods which have been identified to a contract for sale are subject to the buyer's rights to recover the goods under this Article (Sections 2—502 and 2—716).

(2) A creditor of the seller may treat a sale or an identification of goods to a contract for sale as void if as against him a retention of possession by the seller is fraudulent under any rule of law of the state where the goods are situated, except that retention of possession in good faith and current course of trade by a merchant-seller for a commercially reasonable time after a sale or identification is not fraudulent.

(3) Nothing in this Article shall be deemed to impair the rights of creditors of the seller

(a) under the provisions of the Article on Secured Transactions (Article 9); or

(b) where identification to the contract or delivery is made not in current course of trade but in satisfaction of or as security for a pre-existing claim for money, security or the like and is made under circumstances which under any rule of law of the state where the goods are situated would apart from this Article constitute the transaction a fraudulent transfer or voidable preference.

§ 2—403. **Power to Transfer; Good Faith Purchase of Goods; "Entrusting".**

(1) A purchaser of goods acquires all title which his transferor had or had power to transfer except that a purchaser of a limited interest acquires rights only to the extent of the interest purchased. A person with voidable title has power to transfer a good title to a good faith purchaser for value. When goods have been delivered under a transaction of purchase the purchaser has such power even though

(a) the transferor was deceived as to the identity of the purchaser, or

(b) the delivery was in exchange for a check which is later dishonored, or

(c) it was agreed that the transaction was to be a "cash sale", or

(d) the delivery was procured through fraud punishable as larcenous under the criminal law.

(2) Any entrusting of possession of goods to a merchant who deals in goods of that kind gives him power to transfer all rights of the entruster to a buyer in ordinary course of business.

(3) "Entrusting" includes any delivery and any acquiescence in retention of possession regardless of any condition expressed between the parties to the delivery or acquiescence and regardless of whether the procurement of the entrusting or the possessor's disposition of the goods have been such as to be larcenous under the criminal law.

(4) The rights of other purchasers of goods and of lien creditors are governed by the Articles on Secured Transactions (Article 9), Bulk Transfers (Article 6) and Documents of Title (Article 7).

Part 5 Performance

§ 2—501. Insurable Interest in Goods; Manner of Identification of Goods.

(1) The buyer obtains a special property and an insurable interest in goods by identification of existing goods as goods to which the contract refers even though the goods so identified are non-conforming and he has an option to return or reject them. Such identification can be made at any time and in any manner explicitly agreed to by the parties. In the absence of explicit agreement identification occurs

(a) when the contract is made if it is for the sale of goods already existing and identified;

(b) if the contract is for the sale of future goods other than those described in paragraph (c), when goods are shipped, marked or otherwise designated by the seller as goods to which the contract refers;

(c) when the crops are planted or otherwise become growing crops or the young are conceived if the contract is for the sale of unborn young to be born within twelve months after contracting or for the sale of crops to be harvested within twelve months or the next normal harvest season after contracting whichever is longer.

(2) The seller retains an insurable interest in goods so long as title to or any security interest in the goods remains in him and where the identification is by the seller alone he may until default or insolvency or notification to the buyer that the identification is final substitute other goods for those identified.

(3) Nothing in this section impairs any insurable interest recognized under any other statute or rule of law.

§ 2—502. Buyer's Right to Goods on Seller's Insolvency.

(1) Subject to subsection (2) and even though the goods have not been shipped a buyer who has paid a part or all of the price of goods in which he has a special property under the provisions of the immediately preceding section may on making and keeping good a tender of any unpaid portion of their price recover them from the seller if the seller becomes insolvent within ten days after receipt of the first installment on their price.

(2) If the identification creating his special property has been made by the buyer he acquires the right to recover the goods only if they conform to the contract for sale.

§ 2—503. Manner of Seller's Tender of Delivery.

(1) Tender of delivery requires that the seller put and hold conforming goods at the buyer's disposition and give the buyer any notification reasonably necessary to enable him to take delivery. The manner, time and place for tender are determined by the agreement and this Article, and in particular

(a) tender must be at a reasonable hour, and if it is of goods they must be kept available for the period reasonably necessary to enable the buyer to take possession; but

(b) unless otherwise agreed the buyer must furnish facilities reasonably suited to the receipt of the goods.

(2) Where the case is within the next section respecting shipment tender requires that the seller comply with its provisions.

(3) Where the seller is required to deliver at a particular destination tender requires that he comply with subsection (1) and also in any appropriate case tender documents as described in subsections (4) and (5) of this section.

(4) Where goods are in the possession of a bailee and are to be delivered without being moved

(a) tender requires that the seller either tender a negotiable document of title covering such goods or procure acknowledgment by the bailee of the buyer's right to possession of the goods; but

(b) tender to the buyer of a non-negotiable document of title or of a written direction to the bailee to deliver is sufficient tender unless the buyer seasonably objects, and receipt by the bailee of notification of the buyer's rights fixes those rights as against the bailee and all third persons; but risk of loss of the goods and of any failure by the bailee to honor the non-negotiable document of title or to obey the direction remains on the seller until the buyer has had a reasonable time to present the document or direction, and a refusal by the bailee to honor the document or to obey the direction defeats the tender.

(5) Where the contract requires the seller to deliver documents

(a) he must tender all such documents in correct form, except as provided in this Article with respect to bills of lading in a set (subsection (2) of Section 2—323); and

(b) tender through customary banking channels is sufficient and dishonor of a draft accompanying the documents constitutes non-acceptance or rejection.

§ 2—504. Shipment by Seller.

Where the seller is required or authorized to send the goods to the buyer and the contract does not require him to deliver them at a particular destination, then unless otherwise agreed he must

(a) put the goods in the possession of such a carrier and make such a contract for their transportation as may be reasonable having regard to the nature of the goods and other circumstances of the case; and

(b) obtain and promptly deliver or tender in due form any document necessary to enable the buyer to obtain possession of the goods or otherwise required by the agreement or by usage of trade; and

(c) promptly notify the buyer of the shipment.

Failure to notify the buyer under paragraph (c) or to make a proper contract under paragraph (a) is a ground for rejection only if material delay or loss ensues.

§ 2—505. **Seller's Shipment under Reservation.**

(1) Where the seller has identified goods to the contract by or before shipment:

(a) his procurement of a negotiable bill of lading to his own order or otherwise reserves in him a security interest in the goods. His procurement of the bill to the order of a financing agency or of the buyer indicates in addition only the seller's expectation of transferring that interest to the person named.

(b) a non-negotiable bill of lading to himself or his nominee reserves possession of the goods as security but except in a case of conditional delivery (subsection (2) of Section 2—507) a non-negotiable bill of lading naming the buyer as consignee reserves no security interest even though the seller retains possession of the bill of lading.

(2) When shipment by the seller with reservation of a security interest is in violation of the contract for sale it constitutes an improper contract for transportation within the preceding section but impairs neither the rights given to the buyer by shipment and identification of the goods to the contract nor the seller's powers as a holder of a negotiable document.

§ 2—506. **Rights of Financing Agency.**

(1) A financing agency by paying or purchasing for value a draft which relates to a shipment of goods acquires to the extent of the payment or purchase and in addition to its own rights under the draft and any document of title securing it any rights of the shipper in the goods including the right to stop delivery and the shipper's right to have the draft honored by the buyer.

(2) The right to reimbursement of a financing agency which has in good faith honored or purchased the draft under commitment to or authority from the buyer is not impaired by subsequent discovery of defects with reference to any relevant document which was apparently regular on its face.

§ 2—507. **Effect of Seller's Tender; Delivery on Condition.**

(1) Tender of delivery is a condition to the buyer's duty to accept the goods and, unless otherwise agreed, to his duty to pay for them. Tender entitles the seller to acceptance of the goods and to payment according to the contract.

(2) Where payment is due and demanded on the delivery to the buyer of goods or documents of title, his right as against the seller to retain or dispose of them is conditional upon his making the payment due.

§ 2—508. **Cure by Seller of Improper Tender or Delivery; Replacement.**

(1) Where any tender or delivery by the seller is rejected because non-conforming and the time for performance has not yet expired, the seller may seasonably notify the buyer of his intention to cure and may then within the contract time make a conforming delivery.

(2) Where the buyer rejects a non-conforming tender which the seller had reasonable grounds to believe would be acceptable with or without money allowance the seller may if he seasonably noti-

fies the buyer have a further reasonable time to substitute a conforming tender.

§ 2—509. **Risk of Loss in the Absence of Breach.**

(1) Where the contract requires or authorizes the seller to ship the goods by carrier

(a) if it does not require him to deliver them at a particular destination, the risk of loss passes to the buyer when the goods are duly delivered to the carrier even though the shipment is under reservation (Section 2—505); but

(b) if it does require him to deliver them at a particular destination and the goods are there duly tendered while in the possession of the carrier, the risk of loss passes to the buyer when the goods are there duly so tendered as to enable the buyer to take delivery.

(2) Where the goods are held by a bailee to be delivered without being moved, the risk of loss passes to the buyer

(a) on his receipt of a negotiable document of title covering the goods; or

(b) on acknowledgment by the bailee of the buyer's right to possession of the goods; or

(c) after his receipt of a non-negotiable document of title or other written direction to deliver, as provided in subsection (4)(b) of Section 2—503.

(3) In any case not within subsection (1) or (2), the risk of loss passes to the buyer on his receipt of the goods if the seller is a merchant; otherwise the risk passes to the buyer on tender of delivery.

(4) The provisions of this section are subject to contrary agreement of the parties and to the provisions of this Article on sale on approval (Section 2—327) and on effect of breach on risk of loss (Section 2—510).

§ 2—510. **Effect of Breach on Risk of Loss.**

(1) Where a tender or delivery of goods so fails to conform to the contract as to give a right of rejection the risk of their loss remains on the seller until cure or acceptance.

(2) Where the buyer rightfully revokes acceptance he may to the extent of any deficiency in his effective insurance coverage treat the risk of loss as having rested on the seller from the beginning.

(3) Where the buyer as to conforming goods already identified to the contract for sale repudiates or is otherwise in breach before risk of their loss has passed to him, the seller may to the extent of any deficiency in his effective insurance coverage treat the risk of loss as resting on the buyer for a commercially reasonable time.

§ 2—511. **Tender of Payment by Buyer; Payment by Check.**

(1) Unless otherwise agreed tender of payment is a condition to the seller's duty to tender and complete any delivery.

(2) Tender of payment is sufficient when made by any means or in any manner current in the ordinary course of business unless the seller demands payment in legal tender and gives any extension of time reasonably necessary to procure it.

(3) Subject to the provisions of this Act on the effect of an instrument on an obligation (Section 3—310), payment by check is conditional and is defeated as between the parties by dishonor of the check on due presentment.

§ 2—512. **Payment by Buyer Before Inspection.**

(1) Where the contract requires payment before inspection non-conformity of the goods does not excuse the buyer from so making payment unless

    (a) the non-conformity appears without inspection; or

    (b) despite tender of the required documents the circumstances would justify injunction against honor under the provisions of this Act (Section 5—114).

(2) Payment pursuant to subsection (1) does not constitute an acceptance of goods or impair the buyer's right to inspect or any of his remedies.

§ 2—513. Buyer's Right to Inspection of Goods.

(1) Unless otherwise agreed and subject to subsection (3), where goods are tendered or delivered or identified to the contract for sale, the buyer has a right before payment or acceptance to inspect them at any reasonable place and time and in any reasonable manner. When the seller is required or authorized to send the goods to the buyer, the inspection may be after their arrival.

(2) Expenses of inspection must be borne by the buyer but may be recovered from the seller if the goods do not conform and are rejected.

(3) Unless otherwise agreed and subject to the provisions of this Article on C.I.F. contracts (subsection (3) of Section 2—321), the buyer is not entitled to inspect the goods before payment of the price when the contract provides

    (a) for delivery "C.O.D." or on other like terms; or

    (b) for payment against documents of title, except where such payment is due only after the goods are to become available for inspection.

(4) A place or method of inspection fixed by the parties is presumed to be exclusive but unless otherwise expressly agreed it does not postpone identification or shift the place for delivery or for passing the risk of loss. If compliance becomes impossible, inspection shall be as provided in this section unless the place or method fixed was clearly intended as an indispensable condition failure of which avoids the contract.

§ 2—514. When Documents Deliverable on Acceptance; When on Payment.

Unless otherwise agreed documents against which a draft is drawn are to be delivered to the drawee on acceptance of the draft if it is payable more than three days after presentment; otherwise, only on payment.

§ 2—515. Preserving Evidence of Goods in Dispute.

In furtherance of the adjustment of any claim or dispute

    (a) either party on reasonable notification to the other and for the purpose of ascertaining the facts and preserving evidence has the right to inspect, test and sample the goods including such of them as may be in the possession or control of the other; and

    (b) the parties may agree to a third party inspection or survey to determine the conformity or condition of the goods and may agree that the findings shall be binding upon them in any subsequent litigation or adjustment.

Part 6 Breach, Repudiation and Excuse

§ 2—601. Buyer's Rights on Improper Delivery.

Subject to the provisions of this Article on breach in installment contracts (Section 2—612) and unless otherwise agreed under the sections on contractual limitations of remedy (Sections 2—718 and 2—719), if the goods or the tender of delivery fail in any respect to conform to the contract, the buyer may

    (a) reject the whole; or

    (b) accept the whole; or

    (c) accept any commercial unit or units and reject the rest.

§ 2—602. Manner and Effect of Rightful Rejection.

(1) Rejection of goods must be within a reasonable time after their delivery or tender. It is ineffective unless the buyer seasonably notifies the seller.

(2) Subject to the provisions of the two following sections on rejected goods (Sections 2—603 and 2—604),

    (a) after rejection any exercise of ownership by the buyer with respect to any commercial unit is wrongful as against the seller; and

    (b) if the buyer has before rejection taken physical possession of goods in which he does not have a security interest under the provisions of this Article (subsection (3) of Section 2—711), he is under a duty after rejection to hold them with reasonable care at the seller's disposition for a time sufficient to permit the seller to remove them; but

    (c) the buyer has no further obligations with regard to goods rightfully rejected.

(3) The seller's rights with respect to goods wrongfully rejected are governed by the provisions of this Article on Seller's remedies in general (Section 2—703).

§ 2—603. Merchant Buyer's Duties as to Rightfully Rejected Goods.

(1) Subject to any security interest in the buyer (subsection (3) of Section 2—711), when the seller has no agent or place of business at the market of rejection a merchant buyer is under a duty after rejection of goods in his possession or control to follow any reasonable instructions received from the seller with respect to the goods and in the absence of such instructions to make reasonable efforts to sell them for the seller's account if they are perishable or threaten to decline in value speedily. Instructions are not reasonable if on demand indemnity for expenses is not forthcoming.

(2) When the buyer sells goods under subsection (1), he is entitled to reimbursement from the seller or out of the proceeds for reasonable expenses of caring for and selling them, and if the expenses include no selling commission then to such commission as is usual in the trade or if there is none to a reasonable sum not exceeding ten per cent on the gross proceeds.

(3) In complying with this section the buyer is held only to good faith and good faith conduct hereunder is neither acceptance nor conversion nor the basis of an action for damages.

§ 2—604. Buyer's Options as to Salvage of Rightfully Rejected Goods.

Subject to the provisions of the immediately preceding section on perishables if the seller gives no instructions within a reasonable time after notification of rejection the buyer may store the rejected goods for the seller's account or reship them to him or resell them for the seller's account with reimbursement as provided in the preceding section. Such action is not acceptance or conversion.

§ 2—605. Waiver of Buyer's Objections by Failure to Particularize.

(1) The buyer's failure to state in connection with rejection a particular defect which is ascertainable by reasonable inspection precludes him from relying on the unstated defect to justify rejection or to establish breach

(a) where the seller could have cured it if stated seasonably; or

(b) between merchants when the seller has after rejection made a request in writing for a full and final written statement of all defects on which the buyer proposes to rely.

(2) Payment against documents made without reservation of rights precludes recovery of the payment for defects apparent on the face of the documents.

§ 2—606. What Constitutes Acceptance of Goods.

(1) Acceptance of goods occurs when the buyer

(a) after a reasonable opportunity to inspect the goods signifies to the seller that the goods are conforming or that he will take or retain them in spite of their nonconformity; or

(b) fails to make an effective rejection (subsection (1) of Section 2—602), but such acceptance does not occur until the buyer has had a reasonable opportunity to inspect them; or

(c) does any act inconsistent with the seller's ownership; but if such act is wrongful as against the seller it is an acceptance only if ratified by him.

(2) Acceptance of a part of any commercial unit is acceptance of that entire unit.

§ 2—607. Effect of Acceptance; Notice of Breach; Burden of Establishing Breach After Acceptance; Notice of Claim or Litigation to Person Answerable Over.

(1) The buyer must pay at the contract rate for any goods accepted.

(2) Acceptance of goods by the buyer precludes rejection of the goods accepted and if made with knowledge of a non-conformity cannot be revoked because of it unless the acceptance was on the reasonable assumption that the non-conformity would be seasonably cured but acceptance does not of itself impair any other remedy provided by this Article for non-conformity.

(3) Where a tender has been accepted

(a) the buyer must within a reasonable time after he discovers or should have discovered any breach notify the seller of breach or be barred from any remedy; and

(b) if the claim is one for infringement or the like (subsection (3) of Section 2—312) and the buyer is sued as a result of such a breach he must so notify the seller within a reasonable time after he receives notice of the litigation or be barred from any remedy over for liability established by the litigation.

(4) The burden is on the buyer to establish any breach with respect to the goods accepted.

(5) Where the buyer is sued for breach of a warranty or other obligation for which his seller is answerable over

(a) he may give his seller written notice of the litigation. If the notice states that the seller may come in and defend and that if the seller does not do so he will be bound in any action against him by his buyer by any determination of fact common to the two litigations, then unless the seller after seasonable receipt of the notice does come in and defend he is so bound.

(b) if the claim is one for infringement or the like (subsection (3) of Section 2—312) the original seller may demand in writing that his buyer turn over to him control of the litigation including settlement or else be barred from any remedy over and if he also agrees to bear all expense and to satisfy any adverse judgment, then unless the buyer after seasonable receipt of the demand does turn over control the buyer is so barred.

(6) The provisions of subsections (3), (4) and (5) apply to any obligation of a buyer to hold the seller harmless against infringement or the like (subsection (3) of Section 2—312).

§ 2—608. Revocation of Acceptance in Whole or in Part.

(1) The buyer may revoke his acceptance of a lot or commercial unit whose non-conformity substantially impairs its value to him if he has accepted it

(a) on the reasonable assumption that its nonconformity would be cured and it has not been seasonably cured; or

(b) without discovery of such non-conformity if his acceptance was reasonably induced either by the difficulty of discovery before acceptance or by the seller's assurances.

(2) Revocation of acceptance must occur within a reasonable time after the buyer discovers or should have discovered the ground for it and before any substantial change in condition of the goods which is not caused by their own defects. It is not effective until the buyer notifies the seller of it.

(3) A buyer who so revokes has the same rights and duties with regard to the goods involved as if he had rejected them.

§ 2—609. Right to Adequate Assurance of Performance.

(1) A contract for sale imposes an obligation on each party that the other's expectation of receiving due performance will not be impaired. When reasonable grounds for insecurity arise with respect to the performance of either party the other may in writing demand adequate assurance of due performance and until he receives such assurance may if commercially reasonable suspend any performance for which he has not already received the agreed return.

(2) Between merchants the reasonableness of grounds for insecurity and the adequacy of any assurance offered shall be determined according to commercial standards.

(3) Acceptance of any improper delivery or payment does not prejudice the party's right to demand adequate assurance of future performance.

(4) After receipt of a justified demand failure to provide within a reasonable time not exceeding thirty days such assurance of due performance as is adequate under the circumstances of the particular case is a repudiation of the contract.

§ 2—610. Anticipatory Repudiation.

When either party repudiates the contract with respect to a performance not yet due the loss of which will substantially impair the value of the contract to the other, the aggrieved party may

(a) for a commercially reasonable time await performance by the repudiating party; or

(b) resort to any remedy for breach (Section 2—703 or Section 2—711), even though he has notified the repudiating party that he would await the latter's performance and has urged retraction; and

(c) in either case suspend his own performance or proceed in accordance with the provisions of this Article on the seller's right to identify goods to the contract notwithstanding breach or to salvage unfinished goods (Section 2—704).

§ 2—611. Retraction of Anticipatory Repudiation.

(1) Until the repudiating party's next performance is due he can retract his repudiation unless the aggrieved party has since the repudiation cancelled or materially changed his position or otherwise indicated that he considers the repudiation final.

(2) Retraction may be by any method which clearly indicates to the aggrieved party that the repudiating party intends to perform, but must include any assurance justifiably demanded under the provisions of this Article (Section 2—609).

(3) Retraction reinstates the repudiating party's rights under the contract with due excuse and allowance to the aggrieved party for any delay occasioned by the repudiation.

§ 2—612. "Installment Contract"; Breach.

(1) An "installment contract" is one which requires or authorizes the delivery of goods in separate lots to be separately accepted, even though the contract contains a clause "each delivery is a separate contract" or its equivalent.

(2) The buyer may reject any installment which is non-conforming if the non-conformity substantially impairs the value of that installment and cannot be cured or if the non-conformity is a defect in the required documents; but if the non-conformity does not fall within subsection (3) and the seller gives adequate assurance of its cure the buyer must accept that installment.

(3) Whenever non-conformity or default with respect to one or more installments substantially impairs the value of the whole contract there is a breach of the whole. But the aggrieved party reinstates the contract if he accepts a non-conforming installment without seasonably notifying of cancellation or if he brings an action with respect only to past installments or demands performance as to future installments.

§ 2—613. Casualty to Identified Goods.

Where the contract requires for its performance goods identified when the contract is made, and the goods suffer casualty without fault of either party before the risk of loss passes to the buyer, or in a proper case under a "no arrival, no sale" term (Section 2—324) then

(a) if the loss is total the contract is avoided; and

(b) if the loss is partial or the goods have so deteriorated as no longer to conform to the contract the buyer may nevertheless demand inspection and at his option either treat the contract as voided or accept the goods with due allowance from the contract price for the deterioration or the deficiency in quantity but without further right against the seller.

§ 2—614. Substituted Performance.

(1) Where without fault of either party the agreed berthing, loading, or unloading facilities fail or an agreed type of carrier becomes unavailable or the agreed manner of delivery otherwise becomes commercially impracticable but a commercially reasonable substitute is available, such substitute performance must be tendered and accepted.

(2) If the agreed means or manner of payment fails because of domestic or foreign governmental regulation, the seller may withhold or stop delivery unless the buyer provides a means or manner of payment which is commercially a substantial equivalent. If delivery has already been taken, payment by the means or in the manner provided by the regulation discharges the buyer's obligation unless the regulation is discriminatory, oppressive or predatory.

§ 2—615. Excuse by Failure of Presupposed Conditions.

Except so far as a seller may have assumed a greater obligation and subject to the preceding section on substituted performance:

(a) Delay in delivery or non-delivery in whole or in part by a seller who complies with paragraphs (b) and (c) is not a breach of his duty under a contract for sale if performance as agreed has been made impracticable by the occurrence of a contingency the nonoccurrence of which was a basic assumption on which the contract was made or by compliance in good faith with any applicable foreign or domestic governmental regulation or order whether or not it later proves to be invalid.

(b) Where the causes mentioned in paragraph (a) affect only a part of the seller's capacity to perform, he must allocate production and deliveries among his customers but may at his option include regular customers not then under contract as well as his own requirements for further manufacture. He may so allocate in any manner which is fair and reasonable.

(c) The seller must notify the buyer seasonably that there will be delay or non-delivery and, when allocation is required under paragraph (b), of the estimated quota thus made available for the buyer.

§ 2—616. Procedure on Notice Claiming Excuse.

(1) Where the buyer receives notification of a material or indefinite delay or an allocation justified under the preceding section he may by written notification to the seller as to any delivery concerned, and where the prospective deficiency substantially impairs the value of the whole contract under the provisions of this Article relating to breach of installment contracts (Section 2—612), then also as to the whole,

(a) terminate and thereby discharge any unexecuted portion of the contract; or

(b) modify the contract by agreeing to take his available quota in substitution.

(2) If after receipt of such notification from the seller the buyer fails so to modify the contract within a reasonable time not exceeding thirty days the contract lapses with respect to any deliveries affected.

(3) The provisions of this section may not be negated by agreement except in so far as the seller has assumed a greater obligation under the preceding section.

Part 7 Remedies

§ 2—701. Remedies for Breach of Collateral Contracts Not Impaired.

Remedies for breach of any obligation or promise collateral or ancillary to a contract for sale are not impaired by the provisions of this Article.

§ 2—702. Seller's Remedies on Discovery of Buyer's Insolvency.

(1) Where the seller discovers the buyer to be insolvent he may refuse delivery except for cash including payment for all goods theretofore delivered under the contract, and stop delivery under this Article (Section 2—705).

(2) Where the seller discovers that the buyer has received goods on credit while insolvent he may reclaim the goods upon demand made within ten days after the receipt, but if misrepresentation of solvency has been made to the particular seller in writing within three months before delivery the ten day limitation does not apply. Except as provided in this subsection the seller may not base a right to reclaim goods on the buyer's fraudulent or innocent misrepresentation of solvency or of intent to pay.

(3) The seller's right to reclaim under subsection (2) is subject to the rights of a buyer in ordinary course or other good faith purchaser under this Article (Section 2—403). Successful reclamation of goods excludes all other remedies with respect to them.

§ 2—703. Seller's Remedies in General.

Where the buyer wrongfully rejects or revokes acceptance of goods or fails to make a payment due on or before delivery or repudiates with respect to a part or the whole, then with respect to any goods directly affected and, if the breach is of the whole contract (Section 2—612), then also with respect to the whole undelivered balance, the aggrieved seller may

(a) withhold delivery of such goods;

(b) stop delivery by any bailee as hereafter provided (Section 2—705);

(c) proceed under the next section respecting goods still unidentified to the contract;

(d) resell and recover damages as hereafter provided (Section 2—706);

(e) recover damages for non-acceptance (Section 2—708) or in a proper case the price (Section 2—709);

(f) cancel.

§ 2—704. Seller's Right to Identify Goods to the Contract Notwithstanding Breach or to Salvage Unfinished Goods.

(1) An aggrieved seller under the preceding section may

(a) identify to the contract conforming goods not already identified if at the time he learned of the breach they are in his possession or control;

(b) treat as the subject of resale goods which have demonstrably been intended for the particular contract even though those goods are unfinished.

(2) Where the goods are unfinished an aggrieved seller may in the exercise of reasonable commercial judgment for the purposes of avoiding loss and of effective realization either complete the manufacture and wholly identify the goods to the contract or cease manufacture and resell for scrap or salvage value or proceed in any other reasonable manner.

§ 2—705. Seller's Stoppage of Delivery in Transit or Otherwise.

(1) The seller may stop delivery of goods in the possession of a car-

rier or other bailee when he discovers the buyer to be insolvent (Section 2—702) and may stop delivery of carload, truckload, planeload or larger shipments of express or freight when the buyer repudiates or fails to make a payment due before delivery or if for any other reason the seller has a right to withhold or reclaim the goods.

(2) As against such buyer the seller may stop delivery until

(a) receipt of the goods by the buyer; or

(b) acknowledgment to the buyer by any bailee of the goods except a carrier that the bailee holds the goods for the buyer; or

(c) such acknowledgment to the buyer by a carrier by reshipment or as warehouseman; or

(d) negotiation to the buyer of any negotiable document of title covering the goods.

(3) (a) To stop delivery the seller must so notify as to enable the bailee by reasonable diligence to prevent delivery of the goods.

(b) After such notification the bailee must hold and deliver the goods according to the directions of the seller but the seller is liable to the bailee for any ensuing charges or damages.

(c) If a negotiable document of title has been issued for goods the bailee is not obliged to obey a notification to stop until surrender of the document.

(d) A carrier who has issued a non-negotiable bill of lading is not obliged to obey a notification to stop received from a person other than the consignor.

§ 2—706. Seller's Resale Including Contract for Resale.

(1) Under the conditions stated in Section 2—703 on seller's remedies, the seller may resell the goods concerned or the undelivered balance thereof. Where the resale is made in good faith and in a commercially reasonable manner the seller may recover the difference between the resale price and the contract price together with any incidental damages allowed under the provisions of this Article (Section 2—710), but less expenses saved in consequence of the buyer's breach.

(2) Except as otherwise provided in subsection (3) or unless otherwise agreed resale may be at public or private sale including sale by way of one or more contracts to sell or of identification to an existing contract of the seller. Sale may be as a unit or in parcels and at any time and place and on any terms but every aspect of the sale including the method, manner, time, place and terms must be commercially reasonable. The resale must be reasonably identified as referring to the broken contract, but it is not necessary that the goods be in existence or that any or all of them have been identified to the contract before the breach.

(3) Where the resale is at private sale the seller must give the buyer reasonable notification of his intention to resell.

(4) Where the resale is at public sale

(a) only identified goods can be sold except where there is a recognized market for a public sale of futures in goods of the kind; and

(b) it must be made at a usual place or market for public sale if one is reasonably available and except in the case of goods which are perishable or threaten to decline in value speedily the seller must give the buyer reasonable notice of the time and place of the resale; and

(c) if the goods are not to be within the view of those attending the sale the notification of sale must state the place where the goods are located and provide for their reasonable inspection by prospective bidders; and

(d) the seller may buy.

(5) A purchaser who buys in good faith at a resale takes the goods free of any rights of the original buyer even though the seller fails to comply with one or more of the requirements of this section.

(6) The seller is not accountable to the buyer for any profit made on any resale. A person in the position of a seller (Section 2—707) or a buyer who has rightfully rejected or justifiably revoked acceptance must account for any excess over the amount of his security interest, as hereinafter defined (subsection (3) of Section 2—711).

§ 2—707. "Person in the Position of a Seller".

(1) A "person in the position of a seller" includes as against a principal an agent who has paid or become responsible for the price of goods on behalf of his principal or anyone who otherwise holds a security interest or other right in goods similar to that of a seller.

(2) A person in the position of a seller may as provided in this Article withhold or stop delivery (Section 2—705) and resell (Section 2—706) and recover incidental damages (Section 2—710).

§ 2—708. Seller's Damages for Non-Acceptance or Repudiation.

(1) Subject to subsection (2) and to the provisions of this Article with respect to proof of market price (Section 2—723), the measure of damages for non-acceptance or repudiation by the buyer is the difference between the market price at the time and place for tender and the unpaid contract price together with any incidental damages provided in this Article (Section 2—710), but less expenses saved in consequence of the buyer's breach.

(2) If the measure of damages provided in subsection (1) is inadequate to put the seller in as good a position as performance would have done then the measure of damages is the profit (including reasonable overhead) which the seller would have made from full performance by the buyer, together with any incidental damages provided in this Article (Section 2—710), due allowance for costs reasonably incurred and due credit for payments or proceeds of resale.

§ 2—709. Action for the Price.

(1) When the buyer fails to pay the price as it becomes due the seller may recover, together with any incidental damages under the next section, the price

(a) of goods accepted or of conforming goods lost or damaged within a commercially reasonable time after risk of their loss has passed to the buyer; and

(b) of goods identified to the contract if the seller is unable after reasonable effort to resell them at a reasonable price or the circumstances reasonably indicate that such effort will be unavailing.

(2) Where the seller sues for the price he must hold for the buyer any goods which have been identified to the contract and are still in his control except that if resale becomes possible he may resell them at any time prior to the collection of the judgment. The net proceeds of any such resale must be credited to the buyer and payment of the judgment entitles him to any goods not resold.

(3) After the buyer has wrongfully rejected or revoked acceptance of the goods or has failed to make a payment due or has repudiated (Section 2—610), a seller who is held not entitled to the price under this section shall nevertheless be awarded damages for non-acceptance under the preceding section.

§ 2—710. Seller's Incidental Damages.

Incidental damages to an aggrieved seller include any commercially reasonable charges, expenses or commissions incurred in stopping delivery, in the transportation, care and custody of goods after the buyer's breach, in connection with return or resale of the goods or otherwise resulting from the breach.

§ 2—711. Buyer's Remedies in General; Buyer's Security Interest in Rejected Goods.

(1) Where the seller fails to make delivery or repudiates or the buyer rightfully rejects or justifiably revokes acceptance then with respect to any goods involved, and with respect to the whole if the breach goes to the whole contract (Section 2—612), the buyer may cancel and whether or not he has done so may in addition to recovering so much of the price as has been paid

(a) "cover" and have damages under the next section as to all the goods affected whether or not they have been identified to the contract; or

(b) recover damages for non-delivery as provided in this Article (Section 2—713).

(2) Where the seller fails to deliver or repudiates the buyer may also

(a) if the goods have been identified recover them as provided in this Article (Section 2—502); or

(b) in a proper case obtain specific performance or replevy the goods as provided in this Article (Section 2—716).

(3) On rightful rejection or justifiable revocation of acceptance a buyer has a security interest in goods in his possession or control for any payments made on their price and any expenses reasonably incurred in their inspection, receipt, transportation, care and custody and may hold such goods and resell them in like manner as an aggrieved seller (Section 2—706).

§ 2—712. "Cover"; Buyer's Procurement of Substitute Goods.

(1) After a breach within the preceding section the buyer may "cover" by making in good faith and without unreasonable delay any reasonable purchase of or contract to purchase goods in substitution for those due from the seller.

(2) The buyer may recover from the seller as damages the difference between the cost of cover and the contract price together with any incidental or consequential damages as hereinafter defined (Section 2—715), but less expenses saved in consequence of the seller's breach.

(3) Failure of the buyer to effect cover within this section does not bar him from any other remedy.

§ 2—713. Buyer's Damages for Non-Delivery or Repudiation.

(1) Subject to the provisions of this Article with respect to proof of market price (Section 2—723), the measure of damages for non-

delivery or repudiation by the seller is the difference between the market price at the time when the buyer learned of the breach and the contract price together with any incidental and consequential damages provided in this Article (Section 2—715), but less expenses saved in consequence of the seller's breach.

(2) Market price is to be determined as of the place for tender or, in cases of rejection after arrival or revocation of acceptance, as of the place of arrival.

§ 2—714. Buyer's Damages for Breach in Regard to Accepted Goods.

(1) Where the buyer has accepted goods and given notification (subsection (3) of Section 2—607) he may recover as damages for any non-conformity of tender the loss resulting in the ordinary course of events from the seller's breach as determined in any manner which is reasonable.

(2) The measure of damages for breach of warranty is the difference at the time and place of acceptance between the value of the goods accepted and the value they would have had if they had been as warranted, unless special circumstances show proximate damages of a different amount.

(3) In a proper case any incidental and consequential damages under the next section may also be recovered.

§ 2—715. Buyer's Incidental and Consequential Damages.

(1) Incidental damages resulting from the seller's breach include expenses reasonably incurred in inspection, receipt, transportation and care and custody of goods rightfully rejected, any commercially reasonable charges, expenses or commissions in connection with effecting cover and any other reasonable expense incident to the delay or other breach.

(2) Consequential damages resulting from the seller's breach include

    (a) any loss resulting from general or particular requirements and needs of which the seller at the time of contracting had reason to know and which could not reasonably be prevented by cover or otherwise; and

    (b) injury to person or property proximately resulting from any breach of warranty.

§ 2—716. Buyer's Right to Specific Performance or Replevin.

(1) Specific performance may be decreed where the goods are unique or in other proper circumstances.

(2) The decree for specific performance may include such terms and conditions as to payment of the price, damages, or other relief as the court may deem just.

(3) The buyer has a right of replevin for goods identified to the contract if after reasonable effort he is unable to effect cover for such goods or the circumstances reasonably indicate that such effort will be unavailing or if the goods have been shipped under reservation and satisfaction of the security interest in them has been made or tendered.

§ 2—717. Deduction of Damages From the Price.

The buyer on notifying the seller of his intention to do so may deduct all or any part of the damages resulting from any breach of the contract from any part of the price still due under the same contract.

§ 2—718. Liquidation or Limitation of Damages; Deposits.

(1) Damages for breach by either party may be liquidated in the agreement but only at an amount which is reasonable in the light of the anticipated or actual harm caused by the breach, the difficulties of proof of loss, and the inconvenience or nonfeasibility of otherwise obtaining an adequate remedy. A term fixing unreasonably large liquidated damages is void as a penalty.

(2) Where the seller justifiably withholds delivery of goods because of the buyer's breach, the buyer is entitled to restitution of any amount by which the sum of his payments exceeds

    (a) the amount to which the seller is entitled by virtue of terms liquidating the seller's damages in accordance with subsection (1), or

    (b) in the absence of such terms, twenty per cent of the value of the total performance for which the buyer is obligated under the contract or $500, whichever is smaller.

(3) The buyer's right to restitution under subsection (2) is subject to offset to the extent that the seller establishes

    (a) a right to recover damages under the provisions of this Article other than subsection (1), and

    (b) the amount or value of any benefits received by the buyer directly or indirectly by reason of the contract.

(4) Where a seller has received payment in goods their reasonable value or the proceeds of their resale shall be treated as payments for the purposes of subsection (2); but if the seller has notice of the buyer's breach before reselling goods received in part performance, his resale is subject to the conditions laid down in this Article on resale by an aggrieved seller (Section 2—706).

§ 2—719. Contractual Modification or Limitation of Remedy.

(1) Subject to the provisions of subsections (2) and (3) of this section and of the preceding section on liquidation and limitation of damages,

    (a) the agreement may provide for remedies in addition to or in substitution for those provided in this Article and may limit or alter the measure of damages recoverable under this Article, as by limiting the buyer's remedies to return of the goods and repayment of the price or to repair and replacement of non-conforming goods or parts; and

    (b) resort to a remedy as provided is optional unless the remedy is expressly agreed to be exclusive, in which case it is the sole remedy.

(2) Where circumstances cause an exclusive or limited remedy to fail of its essential purpose, remedy may be had as provided in this Act.

(3) Consequential damages may be limited or excluded unless the limitation or exclusion is unconscionable. Limitation of consequential damages for injury to the person in the case of consumer goods is prima facie unconscionable but limitation of damages where the loss is commercial is not.

§ 2—720. Effect of "Cancellation" or "Rescission" on Claims for Antecedent Breach.

Unless the contrary intention clearly appears, expressions of "cancellation" or "rescission" of the contract or the like shall not be construed as a renunciation or discharge of any claim in damages for an antecedent breach.

§ 2—721. **Remedies for Fraud.**

Remedies for material misrepresentation or fraud include all remedies available under this Article for non-fraudulent breach. Neither rescission or a claim for rescission of the contract for sale nor rejection or return of the goods shall bar or be deemed inconsistent with a claim for damages or other remedy.

§ 2—722. **Who Can Sue Third Parties for Injury to Goods.**

Where a third party so deals with goods which have been identified to a contract for sale as to cause actionable injury to a party to that contract

(a) a right of action against the third party is in either party to the contract for sale who has title to or a security interest or a special property or an insurable interest in the goods; and if the goods have been destroyed or converted a right of action is also in the party who either bore the risk of loss under the contract for sale or has since the injury assumed that risk as against the other;

(b) if at the time of the injury the party plaintiff did not bear the risk of loss as against the other party to the contract for sale and there is no arrangement between them for disposition of the recovery, his suit or settlement is, subject to his own interest, as a fiduciary for the other party to the contract;

(c) either party may with the consent of the other sue for the benefit of whom it may concern.

§ 2—723. **Proof of Market Price: Time and Place.**

(1) If an action based on anticipatory repudiation comes to trial before the time for performance with respect to some or all of the goods, any damages based on market price (Section 2—708 or Section 2—713) shall be determined according to the price of such goods prevailing at the time when the aggrieved party learned of the repudiation.

(2) If evidence of a price prevailing at the times or places described in this Article is not readily available the price prevailing within any reasonable time before or after the time described or at any other place which in commercial judgment or under usage of trade would serve as a reasonable substitute for the one described may be used, making any proper allowance for the cost of transporting the goods to or from such other place.

(3) Evidence of a relevant price prevailing at a time or place other than the one described in this Article offered by one party is not admissible unless and until he has given the other party such notice as the court finds sufficient to prevent unfair surprise.

§ 2—724. **Admissibility of Market Quotations.**

Whenever the prevailing price or value of any goods regularly bought and sold in any established commodity market is in issue, reports in official publications or trade journals or in newspapers or periodicals of general circulation published as the reports of such market shall be admissible in evidence. The circumstances of the preparation of such a report may be shown to affect its weight but not its admissibility.

§ 2—725. **Statute of Limitations in Contracts for Sale.**

(1) An action for breach of any contract for sale must be commenced within four years after the cause of action has accrued. By the original agreement the parties may reduce the period of limi-

tation to not less than one year but may not extend it.

(2) A cause of action accrues when the breach occurs, regardless of the aggrieved party's lack of knowledge of the breach. A breach of warranty occurs when tender of delivery is made, except that where a warranty explicitly extends to future performance of the goods and discovery of the breach must await the time of such performance the cause of action accrues when the breach is or should have been discovered.

(3) Where an action commenced within the time limited by subsection (1) is so terminated as to leave available a remedy by another action for the same breach such other action may be commenced after the expiration of the time limited and within six months after the termination of the first action unless the termination resulted from voluntary discontinuance or from dismissal for failure or neglect to prosecute.

(4) This section does not alter the law on tolling of the statute of limitations nor does it apply to causes of action which have accrued before this Act becomes effective.

Article 2A
LEASES

Part 1   General Provisions

§ 2A—101. **Short Title.**

This Article shall be known and may be cited as the Uniform Commercial Code—Leases.

§ 2A—102. **Scope.**

This Article applies to any transaction, regardless of form, that creates a lease.

§ 2A—103. **Definitions and Index of Definitions.**

(1) In this Article unless the context otherwise requires:

(a) "Buyer in ordinary course of business" means a person who in good faith and without knowledge that the sale to him [or her] is in violation of the ownership rights or security interest or leasehold interest of a third party in the goods buys in ordinary course from a person in the business of selling goods of that kind but does not include a pawnbroker. "Buying" may be for cash or by exchange of other property or on secured or unsecured credit and includes receiving goods or documents of title under a pre-existing contract for sale but does not include a transfer in bulk or as security for or in total or partial satisfaction of a money debt.

(b) "Cancellation" occurs when either party puts an end to the lease contract for default by the other party.

(c) "Commercial unit" means such a unit of goods as by commercial usage is a single whole for purposes of lease and division of which materially impairs its character or value on the market or in use. A commercial unit may be a single article, as a machine, or a set of articles, as a suite of furniture or a line of machinery, or a quantity, as a gross or carload, or any other unit treated in use or in the relevant market as a single whole.

(d) "Conforming" goods or performance under a lease contract means goods or performance that are in accordance with the obligations under the lease contract.

(e) "Consumer lease" means a lease that a lessor regularly engaged in the business of leasing or selling makes to a lessee who is an individual and who takes under the lease primarily for a personal, family, or household "purpose [, if" the total payments to be made under the lease contract, excluding payments for options to renew or buy, do not exceed. . . .

(f) "Fault" means wrongful act, omission, breach, or default.

(g) "Finance lease" means a lease with respect to which:

(i) the lessor does not select, manufacture or supply the goods;

(ii) the lessor acquires the goods or the right to possession and use of the goods in connection with the lease; and

(iii) one of the following occurs:

(A) the lessee receives a copy of the contract by which the lessor acquired the goods or the right to possession and use of the goods before signing the lease contract;

(B) the lessee's approval of the contract by which the lessor acquired the goods or the right to possession and use of the goods is a condition to effectiveness of the lease contract;

(C) the lessee, before signing the lease contract, receives an accurate and complete statement designating the promises and warranties, and any disclaimers of warranties, limitations or modifications of remedies, or liquidated damages, including those of a third party, such as the manufacturer of the goods, provided to the lessor by the person supplying the goods in connection with or as part of the contract by which the lessor acquired the goods or the right to possession and use of the goods; or

(D) if the lease is not a consumer lease, the lessor, before the lessee signs the lease contract, informs the lessee in writing (a) of the identity of the person supplying the goods to the lessor, unless the lessee has selected that person and directed the lessor to acquire the goods or the right to possession and use of the goods from that person, (b) that the lessee is entitled under this Article to any promises and warranties, including those of any third party, provided to the lessor by the person supplying the goods in connection with or as part of the contract by which the lessor acquired the goods or the right to possession and use of the goods, and (c) that the lessee may communicate with the person supplying the goods to the lessor and receive an accurate and complete statement of those promises and warranties, including any disclaimers and limitations of them or of remedies.

(h) "Goods" means all things that are movable at the time of identification to the lease contract, or are fixtures (Section 2A—309), but the term does not include money, documents, instruments, accounts, chattel paper, general intangibles, or minerals or the like, including oil and gas, before extraction. The term also includes the unborn young of animals.

(i) "Installment lease contract" means a lease contract that authorizes or requires the delivery of goods in separate lots to be separately accepted, even though the lease contract contains a clause "each delivery is a separate lease" or its equivalent.

(j) "Lease" means a transfer of the right to possession and use of goods for a term in return for consideration, but a sale, including a sale on approval or a sale or return, or retention or creation of a security interest is not a lease. Unless the context clearly indicates otherwise, the term includes a sublease.

(k) "Lease agreement" means the bargain, with respect to the lease, of the lessor and the lessee in fact as found in their language or by implication from other circumstances including course of dealing or usage of trade or course of performance as provided in this Article. Unless the context clearly indicates otherwise, the term includes a sublease agreement.

(l) "Lease contract" means the total legal obligation that results from the lease agreement as affected by this Article and any other applicable rules of law. Unless the context clearly indicates otherwise, the term includes a sublease contract.

(m) "Leasehold interest" means the interest of the lessor or the lessee under a lease contract.

(n) "Lessee" means a person who acquires the right to possession and use of goods under a lease. Unless the context clearly indicates otherwise, the term includes a sublessee.

(o) "Lessee in ordinary course of business" means a person who in good faith and without knowledge that the lease to him [or her] is in violation of the ownership rights or security interest or leasehold interest of a third party in the goods, leases in ordinary course from a person in the business of selling or leasing goods of that kind but does not include a pawnbroker. "Leasing" may be for cash or by exchange of other property or on secured or unsecured credit and includes receiving goods or documents of title under a pre-existing lease contract but does not include a transfer in bulk or as security for or in total or partial satisfaction of a money debt.

(p) "Lessor" means a person who transfers the right to possession and use of goods under a lease. Unless the context clearly indicates otherwise, the term includes a sublessor.

(q) "Lessor's residual interest" means the lessor's interest in the goods after expiration, termination, or cancellation of the lease contract.

(r) "Lien" means a charge against or interest in goods to secure payment of a debt or performance of an obligation, but the term does not include a security interest.

(s) "Lot" means a parcel or a single article that is the subject matter of a separate lease or delivery, whether or not it is sufficient to perform the lease contract.

(t) "Merchant lessee" means a lessee that is a merchant with respect to goods of the kind subject to the lease.

(u) "Present value" means the amount as of a date certain of one or more sums payable in the future, discounted to the date certain. The discount is determined by the interest rate specified by the parties if the rate was not manifestly unreasonable at the time the transaction was entered into; otherwise, the discount is determined by a commercially reasonable rate that takes into account the facts and circumstances of each case at the time the transaction was entered into.

(v) "Purchase" includes taking by sale, lease, mortgage, security interest, pledge, gift, or any other voluntary transaction creating an interest in goods.

(w) "Sublease" means a lease of goods the right to possession and use of which was acquired by the lessor as a lessee under an existing lease.

(x) "Supplier" means a person from whom a lessor buys or leases goods to be leased under a finance lease.

(y) "Supply contract" means a contract under which a lessor buys or leases goods to be leased.

(z) "Termination" occurs when either party pursuant to a power created by agreement or law puts an end to the lease contract otherwise than for default.

(2) Other definitions applying to this Article and the sections in which they appear are:

"Accessions". Section 2A–310(1).
"Construction mortgage". Section 2A–309(1)(d).
"Encumbrance". Section 2A–309(1)(e).
"Fixtures". Section 2A–309(1)(a).
"Fixture filing". Section 2A–309(1)(b).
"Purchase money lease". Section 2A–309(1)(c).

(3) The following definitions in other Articles apply to this Article:

"Accounts". Section 9–106.
"Between merchants". Section 2–104(3).
"Buyer". Section 2–103(1)(a).
"Chattel paper". Section 9–105(1)(b).
"Consumer goods". Section 9–109(1).
"Document". Section 9–105(1)(f).
"Entrusting". Section 2–403(3).
"General intangibles". Section 9–106.
"Good faith". Section 2–103(1)(b).
"Instrument". Section 9–105(1)(i).
"Merchant". Section 2–104(1).
"Mortgage". Section 9–105(1)(j).
"Pursuant to commitment". Section 9–105(1)(k).
"Receipt". Section 2–103(1)(c).
"Sale". Section 2–106(1).
"Sale on approval". Section 2–326.
"Sale or return". Section 2–326.
"Seller". Section 2–103(1)(d).

(4) In addition Article 1 contains general definitions and principles of construction and interpretation applicable throughout this Article.

As amended in 1990.

§ 2A–104. Leases Subject to Other Law.

(1) A lease, although subject to this Article, is also subject to any applicable:

(a) certificate of title statute of this State: (list any certificate of title statutes covering automobiles, trailers, mobile homes, boats, farm tractors, and the like);

(b) certificate of title statute of another jurisdiction (Section 2A–105); or

(c) consumer protection statute of this State, or final consumer protection decision of a court of this State existing on the effective date of this Article.

(2) In case of conflict between this Article, other than Sections 2A–105, 2A–304(3), and 2A–305(3), and a statute or decision referred to in subsection (1), the statute or decision controls.

(3) Failure to comply with an applicable law has only the effect specified therein.

As amended in 1990.

§ 2A–105. Territorial Application of Article to Goods Covered by Certificate of Title.

Subject to the provisions of Sections 2A–304(3) and 2A–305(3), with respect to goods covered by a certificate of title issued under a statute of this State or of another jurisdiction, compliance and the effect of compliance or noncompliance with a certificate of title statute are governed by the law (including the conflict of laws rules) of the jurisdiction issuing the certificate until the earlier of (a) surrender of the certificate, or (b) four months after the goods are removed from that jurisdiction and thereafter until a new certificate of title is issued by another jurisdiction.

§ 2A–106. Limitation on Power of Parties to Consumer Lease to Choose Applicable Law and Judicial Forum.

(1) If the law chosen by the parties to a consumer lease is that of a jurisdiction other than a jurisdiction in which the lessee resides at the time the lease agreement becomes enforceable or within 30 days thereafter or in which the goods are to be used, the choice is not enforceable.

(2) If the judicial forum chosen by the parties to a consumer lease is a forum that would not otherwise have jurisdiction over the lessee, the choice is not enforceable.

§ 2A–107. Waiver or Renunciation of Claim or Right After Default.

Any claim or right arising out of an alleged default or breach of warranty may be discharged in whole or in part without consideration by a written waiver or renunciation signed and delivered by the aggrieved party.

§ 2A–108. Unconscionability.

(1) If the court as a matter of law finds a lease contract or any clause of a lease contract to have been unconscionable at the time it was made the court may refuse to enforce the lease contract, or it may enforce the remainder of the lease contract without the unconscionable clause, or it may so limit the application of any unconscionable clause as to avoid any unconscionable result.

(2) With respect to a consumer lease, if the court as a matter of law finds that a lease contract or any clause of a lease contract has been induced by unconscionable conduct or that unconscionable conduct has occurred in the collection of a claim arising from a lease contract, the court may grant appropriate relief.

(3) Before making a finding of unconscionability under subsection (1) or (2), the court, on its own motion or that of a party, shall afford the parties a reasonable opportunity to present evidence as to the setting, purpose, and effect of the lease contract or clause thereof, or of the conduct.

(4) In an action in which the lessee claims unconscionability with respect to a consumer lease:

(a) If the court finds unconscionability under subsection (1) or (2), the court shall award reasonable attorney's fees to the lessee.

(b) If the court does not find unconscionability and the lessee claiming unconscionability has brought or maintained an action he [or she] knew to be groundless, the court shall award reasonable attorney's fees to the party against whom the claim is made.

(c) In determining attorney's fees, the amount of the recovery on behalf of the claimant under subsections (1) and (2) is not controlling.

§ 2A—109. Option to Accelerate at Will.

(1) A term providing that one party or his [or her] successor in interest may accelerate payment or performance or require collateral or additional collateral "at will" or "when he [or she] deems himself [or herself] insecure" or in words of similar import must be construed to mean that he [or she] has power to do so only if he [or she] in good faith believes that the prospect of payment or performance is impaired.

(2) With respect to a consumer lease, the burden of establishing good faith under subsection (1) is on the party who exercised the power; otherwise the burden of establishing lack of good faith is on the party against whom the power has been exercised.

Part 2 Formation and Construction of Lease Contract

§ 2A—201. Statute of Frauds.

(1) A lease contract is not enforceable by way of action or defense unless:

(a) the total payments to be made under the lease contract, excluding payments for options to renew or buy, are less than $1,000; or

(b) there is a writing, signed by the party against whom enforcement is sought or by that party's authorized agent, sufficient to indicate that a lease contract has been made between the parties and to describe the goods leased and the lease term.

(2) Any description of leased goods or of the lease term is sufficient and satisfies subsection (1)(b), whether or not it is specific, if it reasonably identifies what is described.

(3) A writing is not insufficient because it omits or incorrectly states a term agreed upon, but the lease contract is not enforceable under subsection (1)(b) beyond the lease term and the quantity of goods shown in the writing.

(4) A lease contract that does not satisfy the requirements of subsection (1), but which is valid in other respects, is enforceable:

(a) if the goods are to be specially manufactured or obtained for the lessee and are not suitable for lease or sale to others in the ordinary course of the lessor's business, and the lessor, before notice of repudiation is received and under circumstances that reasonably indicate that the goods are for the lessee, has made either a substantial beginning of their manufacture or commitments for their procurement;

(b) if the party against whom enforcement is sought admits in that party's pleading, testimony or otherwise in court that a lease contract was made, but the lease contract is not enforceable under this provision beyond the quantity of goods admitted; or

(c) with respect to goods that have been received and accepted by the lessee.

(5) The lease term under a lease contract referred to in subsection (4) is:

(a) if there is a writing signed by the party against whom enforcement is sought or by that party's authorized agent spec-

ifying the lease term, the term so specified;

(b) if the party against whom enforcement is sought admits in that party's pleading, testimony, or otherwise in court a lease term, the term so admitted; or

(c) a reasonable lease term.

§ 2A—202. Final Written Expression: Parol or Extrinsic Evidence.

Terms with respect to which the confirmatory memoranda of the parties agree or which are otherwise set forth in a writing intended by the parties as a final expression of their agreement with respect to such terms as are included therein may not be contradicted by evidence of any prior agreement or of a contemporaneous oral agreement but may be explained or supplemented:

(a) by course of dealing or usage of trade or by course of performance; and

(b) by evidence of consistent additional terms unless the court finds the writing to have been intended also as a complete and exclusive statement of the terms of the agreement.

§ 2A—203. Seals Inoperative.

The affixing of a seal to a writing evidencing a lease contract or an offer to enter into a lease contract does not render the writing a sealed instrument and the law with respect to sealed instruments does not apply to the lease contract or offer.

§ 2A—204. Formation in General.

(1) A lease contract may be made in any manner sufficient to show agreement, including conduct by both parties which recognizes the existence of a lease contract.

(2) An agreement sufficient to constitute a lease contract may be found although the moment of its making is undetermined.

(3) Although one or more terms are left open, a lease contract does not fail for indefiniteness if the parties have intended to make a lease contract and there is a reasonably certain basis for giving an appropriate remedy.

§ 2A—205. Firm Offers.

An offer by a merchant to lease goods to or from another person in a signed writing that by its terms gives assurance it will be held open is not revocable, for lack of consideration, during the time stated or, if no time is stated, for a reasonable time, but in no event may the period of irrevocability exceed 3 months. Any such term of assurance on a form supplied by the offeree must be separately signed by the offeror.

§ 2A—206. Offer and Acceptance in Formation of Lease Contract.

(1) Unless otherwise unambiguously indicated by the language or circumstances, an offer to make a lease contract must be construed as inviting acceptance in any manner and by any medium reasonable in the circumstances.

(2) If the beginning of a requested performance is a reasonable mode of acceptance, an offeror who is not notified of acceptance within a reasonable time may treat the offer as having lapsed before acceptance.

§ 2A—207. Course of Performance or Practical Construction.

(1) If a lease contract involves repeated occasions for performance

by either party with knowledge of the nature of the performance and opportunity for objection to it by the other, any course of performance accepted or acquiesced in without objection is relevant to determine the meaning of the lease agreement.

(2) The express terms of a lease agreement and any course of performance, as well as any course of dealing and usage of trade, must be construed whenever reasonable as consistent with each other; but if that construction is unreasonable, express terms control course of performance, course of performance controls both course of dealing and usage of trade, and course of dealing controls usage of trade.

(3) Subject to the provisions of Section 2A—208 on modification and waiver, course of performance is relevant to show a waiver or modification of any term inconsistent with the course of performance.

§ 2A—208. **Modification, Rescission and Waiver.**

(1) An agreement modifying a lease contract needs no consideration to be binding.

(2) A signed lease agreement that excludes modification or rescission except by a signed writing may not be otherwise modified or rescinded, but, except as between merchants, such a requirement on a form supplied by a merchant must be separately signed by the other party.

(3) Although an attempt at modification or rescission does not satisfy the requirements of subsection (2), it may operate as a waiver.

(4) A party who has made a waiver affecting an executory portion of a lease contract may retract the waiver by reasonable notification received by the other party that strict performance will be required of any term waived, unless the retraction would be unjust in view of a material change of position in reliance on the waiver.

§ 2A—209. **Lessee under Finance Lease as Beneficiary of Supply Contract.**

(1) The benefit of the supplier's promises to the lessor under the supply contract and of all warranties, whether express or implied, including those of any third party provided in connection with or as part of the supply contract, extends to the lessee to the extent of the lessee's leasehold interest under a finance lease related to the supply contract, but is subject to the terms warranty and of the supply contract and all defenses or claims arising therefrom.

(2) The extension of the benefit of supplier's promises and of warranties to the lessee (Section 2A–209(1)) does not: (i) modify the rights and obligations of the parties to the supply contract, whether arising therefrom or otherwise, or (ii) impose any duty or liability under the supply contract on the lessee.

(3) Any modification or rescission of the supply contract by the supplier and the lessor is effective between the supplier and the lessee unless, before the modification or rescission, the supplier has received notice that the lessee has entered into a finance lease related to the supply contract. If the modification or rescission is effective between the supplier and the lessee, the lessor is deemed to have assumed, in addition to the obligations of the lessor to the lessee under the lease contract, promises of the supplier to the lessor and warranties that were so modified or rescinded as they existed and were available to the lessee before modification or rescission.

(4) In addition to the extension of the benefit of the supplier's promises and of warranties to the lessee under subsection (1), the lessee retains all rights that the lessee may have against the supplier which arise from an agreement between the lessee and the supplier or under other law.

As amended in 1990.

§ 2A—210. **Express Warranties.**

(1) Express warranties by the lessor are created as follows:

(a) Any affirmation of fact or promise made by the lessor to the lessee which relates to the goods and becomes part of the basis of the bargain creates an express warranty that the goods will conform to the affirmation or promise.

(b) Any description of the goods which is made part of the basis of the bargain creates an express warranty that the goods will conform to the description.

(c) Any sample or model that is made part of the basis of the bargain creates an express warranty that the whole of the goods will conform to the sample or model.

(2) It is not necessary to the creation of an express warranty that the lessor use formal words, such as "warrant" or "guarantee," or that the lessor have a specific intention to make a warranty, but an affirmation merely of the value of the goods or a statement purporting to be merely the lessor's opinion or commendation of the goods does not create a warranty.

§ 2A—211. **Warranties Against Interference and Against Infringement; Lessee's Obligation Against Infringement.**

(1) There is in a lease contract a warranty that for the lease term no person holds a claim to or interest in the goods that arose from an act or omission of the lessor, other than a claim by way of infringement or the like, which will interfere with the lessee's enjoyment of its leasehold interest.

(2) Except in a finance lease there is in a lease contract by a lessor who is a merchant regularly dealing in goods of the kind a warranty that the goods are delivered free of the rightful claim of any person by way of infringement or the like.

(3) A lessee who furnishes specifications to a lessor or a supplier shall hold the lessor and the supplier harmless against any claim by way of infringement or the like that arises out of compliance with the specifications.

§ 2A—212. **Implied Warranty of Merchantability.**

(1) Except in a finance lease, a warranty that the goods will be merchantable is implied in a lease contract if the lessor is a merchant with respect to goods of that kind.

(2) Goods to be merchantable must be at least such as

(a) pass without objection in the trade under the description in the lease agreement;

(b) in the case of fungible goods, are of fair average quality within the description;

(c) are fit for the ordinary purposes for which goods of that type are used;

(d) run, within the variation permitted by the lease agreement, of even kind, quality, and quantity within each unit and among all units involved;

(e) are adequately contained, packaged, and labeled as the lease agreement may require; and

(f) conform to any promises or affirmations of fact made on the container or label.

(3) Other implied warranties may arise from course of dealing or usage of trade.

§ 2A—213. Implied Warranty of Fitness for Particular Purpose.

Except in a finance of lease, if the lessor at the time the lease contract is made has reason to know of any particular purpose for which the goods are required and that the lessee is relying on the lessor's skill or judgment to select or furnish suitable goods, there is in the lease contract an implied warranty that the goods will be fit for that purpose.

§ 2A—214. Exclusion or Modification of Warranties.

(1) Words or conduct relevant to the creation of an express warranty and words or conduct tending to negate or limit a warranty must be construed wherever reasonable as consistent with each other; but, subject to the provisions of Section 2A—202 on parol or extrinsic evidence, negation or limitation is inoperative to the extent that the construction is unreasonable.

(2) Subject to subsection (3), to exclude or modify the implied warranty of merchantability or any part of it the language must mention "merchantability", be by a writing, and be conspicuous. Subject to subsection (3), to exclude or modify any implied warranty of fitness the exclusion must be by a writing and be conspicuous. Language to exclude all implied warranties of fitness is sufficient if it is in writing, is conspicuous and states, for example, "There is no warranty that the goods will be fit for a particular purpose".

(3) Notwithstanding subsection (2), but subject to subsection (4),

(a) unless the circumstances indicate otherwise, all implied warranties are excluded by expressions like "as is" or "with all faults" or by other language that in common understanding calls the lessee's attention to the exclusion of warranties and makes plain that there is no implied warranty, if in writing and conspicuous;

(b) if the lessee before entering into the lease contract has examined the goods or the sample or model as fully as desired or has refused to examine the goods, there is no implied warranty with regard to defects that an examination ought in the circumstances to have revealed; and

(c) an implied warranty may also be excluded or modified by course of dealing, course of performance, or usage of trade.

(4) To exclude or modify a warranty against interference or against infringement (Section 2A—211) or any part of it, the language must be specific, be by a writing, and be conspicuous, unless the circumstances, including course of performance, course of dealing, or usage of trade, give the lessee reason to know that the goods are being leased subject to a claim or interest of any person.

§ 2A—215. Cumulation and Conflict of Warranties Express or Implied.

Warranties, whether express or implied, must be construed as consistent with each other and as cumulative, but if that construction is unreasonable, the intention of the parties determines which warranty is dominant. In ascertaining that intention the following rules apply:

(a) Exact or technical specifications displace an inconsistent sample or model or general language of description.

(b) A sample from an existing bulk displaces inconsistent general language of description.

(c) Express warranties displace inconsistent implied warranties other than an implied warranty of fitness for a particular purpose.

§ 2A—216. Third-Party Beneficiaries of Express and Implied Warranties.

Alternative A

A warranty to or for the benefit of a lessee under this Article, whether express or implied, extends to any natural person who is in the family or household of the lessee or who is a guest in the lessee's home if it is reasonable to expect that such person may use, consume, or be affected by the goods and who is injured in person by breach of the warranty. This section does not displace principles of law and equity that extend a warranty to or for the benefit of a lessee to other persons. The operation of this section may not be excluded, modified, or limited, but an exclusion, modification, or limitation of the warranty, including any with respect to rights and remedies, effective against the lessee is also effective against any beneficiary designated under this section.

Alternative B

A warranty to or for the benefit of a lessee under this Article, whether express or implied, extends to any natural person who may reasonably be expected to use, consume, or be affected by the goods and who is injured in person by breach of the warranty. This section does not displace principles of law and equity that extend a warranty to or for the benefit of a lessee to other persons. The operation of this section may not be excluded, modified, or limited, but an exclusion, modification, or limitation of the warranty, including any with respect to rights and remedies, effective against the lessee is also effective against the beneficiary designated under this section.

Alternative C

A warranty to or for the benefit of a lessee under this Article, whether express or implied, extends to any person who may reasonably be expected to use, consume, or be affected by the goods and who is injured by breach of the warranty. The operation of this section may not be excluded, modified, or limited with respect to injury to the person of an individual to whom the warranty extends, but an exclusion, modification, or limitation of the warranty, including any with respect to rights and remedies, effective against the lessee is also effective against the beneficiary designated under this section.

§ 2A—217. Identification.

Identification of goods as goods to which a lease contract refers may be made at any time and in any manner explicitly agreed to by the parties. In the absence of explicit agreement, identification occurs:

(a) when the lease contract is made if the lease contract is for a lease of goods that are existing and identified;

(b) when the goods are shipped, marked, or otherwise designated by the lessor as goods to which the lease contract refers, if the lease contract is for a lease of goods that are not existing and identified; or

(c) when the young are conceived, if the lease contract is for a lease of unborn young of animals.

§ 2A—218. Insurance and Proceeds.

(1) A lessee obtains an insurable interest when existing goods are identified to the lease contract even though the goods identified are nonconforming and the lessee has an option to reject them.

(2) If a lessee has an insurable interest only by reason of the lessor's identification of the goods, the lessor, until default or insolvency or notification to the lessee that identification is final, may substitute other goods for those identified.

(3) Notwithstanding a lessee's insurable interest under subsections (1) and (2), the lessor retains an insurable interest until an option to buy has been exercised by the lessee and risk of loss has passed to the lessee.

(4) Nothing in this section impairs any insurable interest recognized under any other statute or rule of law.

(5) The parties by agreement may determine that one or more parties have an obligation to obtain and pay for insurance covering the goods and by agreement may determine the beneficiary of the proceeds of the insurance.

§ 2A—219. Risk of Loss.

(1) Except in the case of a finance lease, risk of loss is retained by the lessor and does not pass to the lessee. In the case of a finance lease, risk of loss passes to the lessee.

(2) Subject to the provisions of this Article on the effect of default on risk of loss (Section 2A—220), if risk of loss is to pass to the lessee and the time of passage is not stated, the following rules apply:

(a) If the lease contract requires or authorizes the goods to be shipped by carrier

(i) and it does not require delivery at a particular destination, the risk of loss passes to the lessee when the goods are duly delivered to the carrier; but

(ii) if it does require delivery at a particular destination and the goods are there duly tendered while in the possession of the carrier, the risk of loss passes to the lessee when the goods are there duly so tendered as to enable the lessee to take delivery.

(b) If the goods are held by a bailee to be delivered without being moved, the risk of loss passes to the lessee on acknowledgment by the bailee of the lessee's right to possession of the goods.

(c) In any case not within subsection (a) or (b), the risk of loss passes to the lessee on the lessee's receipt of the goods if the lessor, or, in the case of a finance lease, the supplier, is a merchant; otherwise the risk passes to the lessee on tender of delivery.

§ 2A—220. Effect of Default on Risk of Loss.

(1) Where risk of loss is to pass to the lessee and the time of passage is not stated:

(a) If a tender or delivery of goods so fails to conform to the lease contract as to give a right of rejection, the risk of their loss remains with the lessor, or, in the case of a finance lease, the supplier, until cure or acceptance.

(b) If the lessee rightfully revokes acceptance, he [or she], to the extent of any deficiency in his [or her] effective insurance coverage, may treat the risk of loss as having remained with the lessor from the beginning.

(2) Whether or not risk of loss is to pass to the lessee, if the lessee as to conforming goods already identified to a lease contract repudiates or is otherwise in default under the lease contract, the lessor, or, in the case of a finance lease, the supplier, to the extent of any deficiency in his [or her] effective insurance coverage may treat the risk of loss as resting on the lessee for a commercially reasonable time.

§ 2A—221. Casualty to Identified Goods.

If a lease contract requires goods identified when the lease contract is made, and the goods suffer casualty without fault of the lessee, the lessor or the supplier before delivery, or the goods suffer casualty before risk of loss passes to the lessee pursuant to the lease agreement or Section 2A—219, then:

(a) if the loss is total, the lease contract is avoided; and

(b) if the loss is partial or the goods have so deteriorated as to no longer conform to the lease contract, the lessee may nevertheless demand inspection and at his [or her] option either treat the lease contract as avoided or, except in a finance lease that is not a consumer lease, accept the goods with due allowance from the rent payable for the balance of the lease term for the deterioration or the deficiency in quantity but without further right against the lessor.

Part 3 Effect Of Lease Contract

§ 2A—301. Enforceability of Lease Contract.

Except as otherwise provided in this Article, a lease contract is effective and enforceable according to its terms between the parties, against purchasers of the goods and against creditors of the parties.

§ 2A—302. Title to and Possession of Goods.

Except as otherwise provided in this Article, each provision of this Article applies whether the lessor or a third party has title to the goods, and whether the lessor, the lessee, or a third party has possession of the goods, notwithstanding any statute or rule of law that possession or the absence of possession is fraudulent.

§ 2A—303. Alienability of Party's Interest Under Lease Contract or of Lessor's Residual Interest in Goods; Delegation of Performance; Transfer of Rights.

(1) As used in this section, "creation of a security interest" includes the sale of a lease contract that is subject to Article 9, Secured Transactions, by reason of Section 9—102(1)(b).

(2) Except as provided in subsections (3) and (4), a provision in a lease agreement which (i) prohibits the voluntary or involuntary transfer, including a transfer by sale, sublease, creation or enforcement of a security interest, or attachment, levy, or other judicial process, of an interest of a party under the lease contract or of the lessor's residual interest in the goods, or (ii) makes such a transfer an event of default, gives rise to the rights and remedies provided in subsection (5), but a transfer that is prohibited or is an event of default under the lease agreement is otherwise effective.

(3) A provision in a lease agreement which (i) prohibits the creation or enforcement of a security interest in an interest of a party under the lease contract or in the lessor's residual interest in the goods, or (ii) makes such a transfer an event of default, is not

enforceable unless, and then only to the extent that, there is an actual transfer by the lessee of the lessee's right of possession or use of the goods in violation of the provision or an actual delegation of a material performance of either party to the lease contract in violation of the provision. Neither the granting nor the enforcement of a security interest in (i) the lessor's interest under the lease contract or (ii) the lessor's residual interest in the goods is a transfer that materially impairs the prospect of obtaining return performance by, materially changes the duty of, or materially increases the burden or risk imposed on, the lessee within the purview of subsection (5) unless, and then only to the extent that, there is an actual delegation of a material performance of the lessor.

(4) A provision in a lease agreement which (i) prohibits a transfer of a right to damages for default with respect to the whole lease contract or of a right to payment arising out of the transferor's due performance of the transferor's entire obligation, or (ii) makes such a transfer an event of default, is not enforceable, and such a transfer is not a transfer that materially impairs the prospect of obtaining return performance by, materially changes the duty of, or materially increases the burden or risk imposed on, the other party to the lease contract within the purview of subsection (5).

(5) Subject to subsections (3) and (4):

(a) if a transfer is made which is made an event of default under a lease agreement, the party to the lease contract not making the transfer, unless that party waives the default or otherwise agrees, has the rights and remedies described in Section 2A—501(2);

(b) if paragraph (a) is not applicable and if a transfer is made that (i) is prohibited under a lease agreement or (ii) materially impairs the prospect of obtaining return performance by, materially changes the duty of, or materially increases the burden or risk imposed on, the other party to the lease contract, unless the party not making the transfer agrees at any time to the transfer in the lease contract or otherwise, then, except as limited by contract, (i) the transferor is liable to the party not making the transfer for damages caused by the transfer to the extent that the damages could not reasonably be prevented by the party not making the transfer and (ii) a court having jurisdiction may grant other appropriate relief, including cancellation of the lease contract or an injunction against the transfer.

(6) A transfer of "the lease" or of "all my rights under the lease," or a transfer in similar general terms, is a transfer of rights and, unless the language or the circumstances, as in a transfer for security, indicate the contrary, the transfer is a delegation of duties by the transferor to the transferee. Acceptance by the transferee constitutes a promise by the transferee to perform those duties. The promise is enforceable by either the transferor or the other party to the lease contract.

(7) Unless otherwise agreed by the lessor and the lessee, a delegation of performance does not relieve the transferor as against the other party of any duty to perform or of any liability for default.

(8) In a consumer lease, to prohibit the transfer of an interest of a party under the lease contract or to make a transfer an event of default, the language must be specific, by a writing, and conspicuous.

As amended in 1990.

§ 2A—304. **Subsequent Lease of Goods by Lessor.**

(1) Subject to Section 2A—303, a subsequent lessee from a lessor of goods under an existing lease contract obtains, to the extent of the leasehold interest transferred, the leasehold interest in the goods that the lessor had or had power to transfer, and except as provided in subsection (2) and Section 2A—527(4), takes subject to the existing lease contract. A lessor with voidable title has power to transfer a good leasehold interest to a good faith subsequent lessee for value, but only to the extent set forth in the preceding sentence. If goods have been delivered under a transaction of purchase the lessor has that power even though:

(a) the lessor's transferor was deceived as to the identity of the lessor;

(b) the delivery was in exchange for a check which is later dishonored;

(c) it was agreed that the transaction was to be a "cash sale"; or

(d) the delivery was procured through fraud punishable as larcenous under the criminal law.

(2) A subsequent lessee in the ordinary course of business from a lessor who is a merchant dealing in goods of that kind to whom the goods were entrusted by the existing lessee of that lessor before the interest of the subsequent lessee became enforceable against that lessor obtains, to the extent of the leasehold interest transferred, all of that lessor's and the existing lessee's rights to the goods, and takes free of the existing lease contract.

(3) A subsequent lessee from the lessor of goods that are subject to an existing lease contract and are covered by a certificate of title issued under a statute of this State or of another jurisdiction takes no greater rights than those provided both by this section and by the certificate of title statute.

As amended in 1990.

§ 2A—305. **Sale or Sublease of Goods by Lessee.**

(1) Subject to the provisions of Section 2A—303, a buyer or sublessee from the lessee of goods under an existing lease contract obtains, to the extent of the interest transferred, the leasehold interest in the goods that the lessee had or had power to transfer, and except as provided in subsection (2) and Section 2A—511(4), takes subject to the existing lease contract. A lessee with a voidable leasehold interest has power to transfer a good leasehold interest to a good faith buyer for value or a good faith sublessee for value, but only to the extent set forth in the preceding sentence. When goods have been delivered under a transaction of lease the lessee has that power even though:

(a) the lessor was deceived as to the identity of the lessee;

(b) the delivery was in exchange for a check which is later dishonored; or

(c) the delivery was procured through fraud punishable as larcenous under the criminal law.

(2) A buyer in the ordinary course of business or a sublessee in the ordinary course of business from a lessee who is a merchant dealing in goods of that kind to whom the goods were entrusted by the lessor obtains, to the extent of the interest transferred, all of the lessor's and lessee's rights to the goods, and takes free of the existing lease contract.

(3) A buyer or sublessee from the lessee of goods that are subject to an existing lease contract and are covered by a certificate of title issued under a statute of this State or of another jurisdiction takes

no greater rights than those provided both by this section and by the certificate of title statute.

§ 2A—306. **Priority of Certain Liens Arising by Operation of Law.**

If a person in the ordinary course of his [or her] business furnishes services or materials with respect to goods subject to a lease contract, a lien upon those goods in the possession of that person given by statute or rule of law for those materials or services takes priority over any interest of the lessor or lessee under the lease contract or this Article unless the lien is created by statute and the statute provides otherwise or unless the lien is created by rule of law and the rule of law provides otherwise.

§ 2A—307. **Priority of Liens Arising by Attachment or Levy on, Security Interests in, and Other Claims to Goods.**

(1) Except as otherwise provided in Section 2A—306, a creditor of a lessee takes subject to the lease contract.

(2) Except as otherwise provided in subsections (3) and (4) and in Sections 2A—306 and 2A—308, a creditor of a lessor takes subject to the lease contract unless:

(a) the creditor holds a lien that attached to the goods before the lease contract became enforceable,

(b) the creditor holds a security interest in the goods and the lessee did not give value and receive delivery of the goods without knowledge of the security interest; or

(c) the creditor holds a security interest in the goods which was perfected (Section 9—303) before the lease contract became enforceable.

(3) A lessee in the ordinary course of business takes the leasehold interest free of a security interest in the goods created by the lessor even though the security interest is perfected (Section 9—303) and the lessee knows of its existence.

(4) A lessee other than a lessee in the ordinary course of business takes the leasehold interest free of a security interest to the extent that it secures future advances made after the secured party acquires knowledge of the lease or more than 45 days after the lease contract becomes enforceable, whichever first occurs, unless the future advances are made pursuant to a commitment entered into without knowledge of the lease and before the expiration of the 45-day period.

§ 2A—308. **Special Rights of Creditors.**

(1) A creditor of a lessor in possession of goods subject to a lease contract may treat the lease contract as void if as against the creditor retention of possession by the lessor is fraudulent under any statute or rule of law, but retention of possession in good faith and current course of trade by the lessor for a commercially reasonable time after the lease contract becomes enforceable is not fraudulent.

(2) Nothing in this Article impairs the rights of creditors of a lessor if the lease contract (a) becomes enforceable, not in current course of trade but in satisfaction of or as security for a pre-existing claim for money, security, or the like, and (b) is made under circumstances which under any statute or rule of law apart from this Article would constitute the transaction a fraudulent transfer or voidable preference.

(3) A creditor of a seller may treat a sale or an identification of goods to a contract for sale as void if as against the creditor reten-tion of possession by the seller is fraudulent under any statute or rule of law, but retention of possession of the goods pursuant to a lease contract entered into by the seller as lessee and the buyer as lessor in connection with the sale or identification of the goods is not fraudulent if the buyer bought for value and in good faith.

§ 2A—309. **Lessor's and Lessee's Rights When Goods Become Fixtures.**

(1) In this section:

(a) goods are "fixtures" when they become so related to particular real estate that an interest in them arises under real estate law;

(b) a "fixture filing" is the filing, in the office where a mortgage on the real estate would be filed or recorded, of a financing statement covering goods that are or are to become fixtures and conforming to the requirements of Section 9—402(5);

(c) a lease is a "purchase money lease" unless the lessee has possession or use of the goods or the right to possession or use of the goods before the lease agreement is enforceable;

(d) a mortgage is a "construction mortgage" to the extent it secures an obligation incurred for the construction of an improvement on land including the acquisition cost of the land, if the recorded writing so indicates; and

(e) "encumbrance" includes real estate mortgages and other liens on real estate and all other rights in real estate that are not ownership interests.

(2) Under this Article a lease may be of goods that are fixtures or may continue in goods that become fixtures, but no lease exists under this Article of ordinary building materials incorporated into an improvement on land.

(3) This Article does not prevent creation of a lease of fixtures pursuant to real estate law.

(4) The perfected interest of a lessor of fixtures has priority over a conflicting interest of an encumbrancer or owner of the real estate if:

(a) the lease is a purchase money lease, the conflicting interest of the encumbrancer or owner arises before the goods become fixtures, the interest of the lessor is perfected by a fixture filing before the goods become fixtures or within ten days thereafter, and the lessee has an interest of record in the real estate or is in possession of the real estate; or

(b) the interest of the lessor is perfected by a fixture filing before the interest of the encumbrancer or owner is of record, the lessor's interest has priority over any conflicting interest of a predecessor in title of the encumbrancer or owner, and the lessee has an interest of record in the real estate or is in possession of the real estate.

(5) The interest of a lessor of fixtures, whether or not perfected, has priority over the conflicting interest of an encumbrancer or owner of the real estate if:

(a) the fixtures are readily removable factory or office machines, readily removable equipment that is not primarily used or leased for use in the operation of the real estate, or readily removable replacements of domestic appliances that are goods subject to a consumer lease, and before the goods become fixtures the lease contract is enforceable; or

(b) the conflicting interest is a lien on the real estate obtained by legal or equitable proceedings after the lease contract is enforceable; or

(c) the encumbrancer or owner has consented in writing to the lease or has disclaimed an interest in the goods as fixtures; or

(d) the lessee has a right to remove the goods as against the encumbrancer or owner. If the lessee's right to remove terminates, the priority of the interest of the lessor continues for a reasonable time.

(6) Notwithstanding paragraph (4)(a) but otherwise subject to subsections (4) and (5), the interest of a lessor of fixtures, including the lessor's residual interest, is subordinate to the conflicting interest of an encumbrancer of the real estate under a construction mortgage recorded before the goods become fixtures if the goods become fixtures before the completion of the construction. To the extent given to refinance a construction mortgage, the conflicting interest of an encumbrancer of the real estate under a mortgage has this priority to the same extent as the encumbrancer of the real estate under the construction mortgage.

(7) In cases not within the preceding subsections, priority between the interest of a lessor of fixtures, including the lessor's residual interest, and the conflicting interest of an encumbrancer or owner of the real estate who is not the lessee is determined by the priority rules governing conflicting interests in real estate.

(8) If the interest of a lessor of fixtures, including the lessor's residual interest, has priority over all conflicting interests of all owners and encumbrancers of the real estate, the lessor or the lessee may (i) on default, expiration, termination, or cancellation of the lease agreement but subject to the agreement and this Article, or (ii) if necessary to enforce other rights and remedies of the lessor or lessee under this Article, remove the goods from the real estate, free and clear of all conflicting interests of all owners and encumbrancers of the real estate, but the lessor or lessee must reimburse any encumbrancer or owner of the real estate who is not the lessee and who has not otherwise agreed for the cost of repair of any physical injury, but not for any diminution in value of the real estate caused by the absence of the goods removed or by any necessity of replacing them. A person entitled to reimbursement may refuse permission to remove until the party seeking removal gives adequate security for the performance of this obligation.

(9) Even though the lease agreement does not create a security interest, the interest of a lessor of fixtures, including the lessor's residual interest, is perfected by filing a financing statement as a fixture filing for leased goods that are or are to become fixtures in accordance with the relevant provisions of the Article on Secured Transactions (Article 9).

As amended in 1990.

§ 2A—310. **Lessor's and Lessee's Rights When Goods Become Accessions.**

(1) Goods are "accessions" when they are installed in or affixed to other goods.

(2) The interest of a lessor or a lessee under a lease contract entered into before the goods became accessions is superior to all interests in the whole except as stated in subsection (4).

(3) The interest of a lessor or a lessee under a lease contract entered into at the time or after the goods became accessions is superior to all subsequently acquired interests in the whole except

as stated in subsection (4) but is subordinate to interests in the whole existing at the time the lease contract was made unless the holders of such interests in the whole have in writing consented to the lease or disclaimed an interest in the goods as part of the whole.

(4) The interest of a lessor or a lessee under a lease contract described in subsection (2) or (3) is subordinate to the interest of

(a) a buyer in the ordinary course of business or a lessee in the ordinary course of business of any interest in the whole acquired after the goods became accessions; or

(b) a creditor with a security interest in the whole perfected before the lease contract was made to the extent that the creditor makes subsequent advances without knowledge of the lease contract.

(5) When under subsections (2) or (3) and (4) a lessor or a lessee of accessions holds an interest that is superior to all interests in the whole, the lessor or the lessee may (a) on default, expiration, termination, or cancellation of the lease contract by the other party but subject to the provisions of the lease contract and this Article, or (b) if necessary to enforce his [or her] other rights and remedies under this Article, remove the goods from the whole, free and clear of all interests in the whole, but he [or she] must reimburse any holder of an interest in the whole who is not the lessee and who has not otherwise agreed for the cost of repair of any physical injury but not for any diminution in value of the whole caused by the absence of the goods removed or by any necessity for replacing them. A person entitled to reimbursement may refuse permission to remove until the party seeking removal gives adequate security for the performance of this obligation.

§ 2A—311. **Priority Subject to Subordination.**

Nothing in this Article prevents subordination by agreement by any person entitled to priority.

As added in 1990.

Part 4 Performance Of Lease Contract: Repudiated, Substituted And Excused

§ 2A—401. **Insecurity: Adequate Assurance of Performance.**

(1) A lease contract imposes an obligation on each party that the other's expectation of receiving due performance will not be impaired.

(2) If reasonable grounds for insecurity arise with respect to the performance of either party, the insecure party may demand in writing adequate assurance of due performance. Until the insecure party receives that assurance, if commercially reasonable the insecure party may suspend any performance for which he [or she] has not already received the agreed return.

(3) A repudiation of the lease contract occurs if assurance of due performance adequate under the circumstances of the particular case is not provided to the insecure party within a reasonable time, not to exceed 30 days after receipt of a demand by the other party.

(4) Between merchants, the reasonableness of grounds for insecurity and the adequacy of any assurance offered must be determined according to commercial standards.

(5) Acceptance of any nonconforming delivery or payment does not prejudice the aggrieved party's right to demand adequate assurance of future performance.

§ 2A—402. Anticipatory Repudiation.

If either party repudiates a lease contract with respect to a performance not yet due under the lease contract, the loss of which performance will substantially impair the value of the lease contract to the other, the aggrieved party may:

(a) for a commercially reasonable time, await retraction of repudiation and performance by the repudiating party;

(b) make demand pursuant to Section 2A—401 and await assurance of future performance adequate under the circumstances of the particular case; or

(c) resort to any right or remedy upon default under the lease contract or this Article, even though the aggrieved party has notified the repudiating party that the aggrieved party would await the repudiating party's performance and assurance and has urged retraction. In addition, whether or not the aggrieved party is pursuing one of the foregoing remedies, the aggrieved party may suspend performance or, if the aggrieved party is the lessor, proceed in accordance with the provisions of this Article on the lessor's right to identify goods to the lease contract notwithstanding default or to salvage unfinished goods (Section 2A—524).

§ 2A—403. Retraction of Anticipatory Repudiation.

(1) Until the repudiating party's next performance is due, the repudiating party can retract the repudiation unless, since the repudiation, the aggrieved party has cancelled the lease contract or materially changed the aggrieved party's position or otherwise indicated that the aggrieved party considers the repudiation final.

(2) Retraction may be by any method that clearly indicates to the aggrieved party that the repudiating party intends to perform under the lease contract and includes any assurance demanded under Section 2A—401.

(3) Retraction reinstates a repudiating party's rights under a lease contract with due excuse and allowance to the aggrieved party for any delay occasioned by the repudiation.

§ 2A—404. Substituted Performance.

(1) If without fault of the lessee, the lessor and the supplier, the agreed berthing, loading, or unloading facilities fail or the agreed type of carrier becomes unavailable or the agreed manner of delivery otherwise becomes commercially impracticable, but a commercially reasonable substitute is available, the substitute performance must be tendered and accepted.

(2) If the agreed means or manner of payment fails because of domestic or foreign governmental regulation:

(a) the lessor may withhold or stop delivery or cause the supplier to withhold or stop delivery unless the lessee provides a means or manner of payment that is commercially a substantial equivalent; and

(b) if delivery has already been taken, payment by the means or in the manner provided by the regulation discharges the lessee's obligation unless the regulation is discriminatory, oppressive, or predatory.

§ 2A—405. Excused Performance.

Subject to Section 2A—404 on substituted performance, the following rules apply:

(a) Delay in delivery or nondelivery in whole or in part by a lessor or a supplier who complies with paragraphs (b) and (c) is not a default under the lease contract if performance as agreed has been made impracticable by the occurrence of a contingency the nonoccurrence of which was a basic assumption on which the lease contract was made or by compliance in good faith with any applicable foreign or domestic governmental regulation or order, whether or not the regulation or order later proves to be invalid.

(b) If the causes mentioned in paragraph (a) affect only part of the lessor's or the supplier's capacity to perform, he [or she] shall allocate production and deliveries among his [or her] customers but at his [or her] option may include regular customers not then under contract for sale or lease as well as his [or her] own requirements for further manufacture. He [or she] may so allocate in any manner that is fair and reasonable.

(c) The lessor seasonably shall notify the lessee and in the case of a finance lease the supplier seasonably shall notify the lessor and the lessee, if known, that there will be delay or nondelivery and, if allocation is required under paragraph (b), of the estimated quota thus made available for the lessee.

§ 2A—406. Procedure on Excused Performance.

(1) If the lessee receives notification of a material or indefinite delay or an allocation justified under Section 2A—405, the lessee may by written notification to the lessor as to any goods involved, and with respect to all of the goods if under an installment lease contract the value of the whole lease contract is substantially impaired (Section 2A—510):

(a) terminate the lease contract (Section 2A—505(2)); or

(b) except in a finance lease that is not a consumer lease, modify the lease contract by accepting the available quota in substitution, with due allowance from the rent payable for the balance of the lease term for the deficiency but without further right against the lessor.

(2) If, after receipt of a notification from the lessor under Section 2A—405, the lessee fails so to modify the lease agreement within a reasonable time not exceeding 30 days, the lease contract lapses with respect to any deliveries affected.

§ 2A—407. Irrevocable Promises: Finance Leases.

(1) In the case of a finance lease that is not a consumer lease the lessee's promises under the lease contract become irrevocable and independent upon the lessee's acceptance of the goods.

(2) A promise that has become irrevocable and independent under subsection (1):

(a) is effective and enforceable between the parties, and by or against third parties including assignees of the parties, and

(b) is not subject to cancellation, termination, modification, repudiation, excuse, or substitution without the consent of the party to whom the promise runs.

(3) This section does not affect the validity under any other law of a covenant in any lease contract making the lessee's promises irrevocable and independent upon the lessee's acceptance of the goods.

As amended in 1990.

Part 5 Default
A. In General
§ 2A—501. Default: Procedure.

(1) Whether the lessor or the lessee is in default under a lease contract is determined by the lease agreement and this Article.

(2) If the lessor or the lessee is in default under the lease contract, the party seeking enforcement has rights and remedies as provided in this Article and, except as limited by this Article, as provided in the lease agreement.

(3) If the lessor or the lessee is in default under the lease contract, the party seeking enforcement may reduce the party's claim to judgment, or otherwise enforce the lease contract by self-help or any available judicial procedure or nonjudicial procedure, including administrative proceeding, arbitration, or the like, in accordance with this Article.

(4) Except as otherwise provided in Section 1–106(1) or this Article or the lease agreement, the rights and remedies referred to in subsections (2) and (3) are cumulative.

(5) If the lease agreement covers both real property and goods, the party seeking enforcement may proceed under this Part as to the goods, or under other applicable law as to both the real property and the goods in accordance with that party's rights and remedies in respect of the real property, in which case this Part does not apply.

As amended in 1990.

§ 2A—502. Notice After Default.

Except as otherwise provided in this Article or the lease agreement, the lessor or lessee in default under the lease contract is not entitled to notice of default or notice of enforcement from the other party to the lease agreement.

§ 2A—503. Modification or Impairment of Rights and Remedies.

(1) Except as otherwise provided in this Article, the lease agreement may include rights and remedies for default in addition to or in substitution for those provided in this Article and may limit or alter the measure of damages recoverable under this Article.

(2) Resort to a remedy provided under this Article or in the lease agreement is optional unless the remedy is expressly agreed to be exclusive. If circumstances cause an exclusive or limited remedy to fail of its essential purpose, or provision for an exclusive remedy is unconscionable, remedy may be had as provided in this Article.

(3) Consequential damages may be liquidated under Section 2A—504, or may otherwise be limited, altered, or excluded unless the limitation, alteration, or exclusion is unconscionable. Limitation, alteration, or exclusion of consequential damages for injury to the person in the case of consumer goods is prima facie unconscionable but limitation, alteration, or exclusion of damages where the loss is commercial is not prima facie unconscionable.

(4) Rights and remedies on default by the lessor or the lessee with respect to any obligation or promise collateral or ancillary to the lease contract are not impaired by this Article.

As amended in 1990.

§ 2A—504. Liquidation of Damages.

(1) Damages payable by either party for default, or any other act or omission, including indemnity for loss or diminution of anticipated tax benefits or loss or damage to lessor's residual interest, may be liquidated in the lease agreement but only at an amount or by a formula that is reasonable in light of the then anticipated

harm caused by the default or other act or omission.

(2) If the lease agreement provides for liquidation of damages, and such provision does not comply with subsection (1), or such provision is an exclusive or limited remedy that circumstances cause to fail of its essential purpose, remedy may be had as provided in this Article.

(3) If the lessor justifiably withholds or stops delivery of goods because of the lessee's default or insolvency (Section 2A—525 or 2A—526), the lessee is entitled to restitution of any amount by which the sum of his [or her] payments exceeds:

(a) the amount to which the lessor is entitled by virtue of terms liquidating the lessor's damages in accordance with subsection (1); or

(b) in the absence of those terms, 20 percent of the then present value of the total rent the lessee was obligated to pay for the balance of the lease term, or, in the case of a consumer lease, the lesser of such amount or $500.

(4) A lessee's right to restitution under subsection (3) is subject to offset to the extent the lessor establishes:

(a) a right to recover damages under the provisions of this Article other than subsection (1); and

(b) the amount or value of any benefits received by the lessee directly or indirectly by reason of the lease contract.

§ 2A—505. Cancellation and Termination and Effect of Cancellation, Termination, Rescission, or Fraud on Rights and Remedies.

(1) On cancellation of the lease contract, all obligations that are still executory on both sides are discharged, but any right based on prior default or performance survives, and the cancelling party also retains any remedy for default of the whole lease contract or any unperformed balance.

(2) On termination of the lease contract, all obligations that are still executory on both sides are discharged but any right based on prior default or performance survives.

(3) Unless the contrary intention clearly appears, expressions of "cancellation," "rescission," or the like of the lease contract may not be construed as a renunciation or discharge of any claim in damages for an antecedent default.

(4) Rights and remedies for material misrepresentation or fraud include all rights and remedies available under this Article for default.

(5) Neither rescission nor a claim for rescission of the lease contract nor rejection or return of the goods may bar or be deemed inconsistent with a claim for damages or other right or remedy.

§ 2A—506. Statute of Limitations.

(1) An action for default under a lease contract, including breach of warranty or indemnity, must be commenced within 4 years after the cause of action accrued. By the original lease contract the parties may reduce the period of limitation to not less than one year.

(2) A cause of action for default accrues when the act or omission on which the default or breach of warranty is based is or should have been discovered by the aggrieved party, or when the default occurs, whichever is later. A cause of action for indemnity accrues when the act or omission on which the claim for indemnity is based is or should have been discovered by the indemnified party,

whichever is later.

(3) If an action commenced within the time limited by subsection (1) is so terminated as to leave available a remedy by another action for the same default or breach of warranty or indemnity, the other action may be commenced after the expiration of the time limited and within 6 months after the termination of the first action unless the termination resulted from voluntary discontinuance or from dismissal for failure or neglect to prosecute.

(4) This section does not alter the law on tolling of the statute of limitations nor does it apply to causes of action that have accrued before this Article becomes effective.

§ 2A—507. Proof of Market Rent: Time and Place.

(1) Damages based on market rent (Section 2A—519 or 2A—528) are determined according to the rent for the use of the goods concerned for a lease term identical to the remaining lease term of the original lease agreement and prevailing at the times specified in Sections 2A–519 and 2A–528.

(2) If evidence of rent for the use of the goods concerned for a lease term identical to the remaining lease term of the original lease agreement and prevailing at the times or places described in this Article is not readily available, the rent prevailing within any reasonable time before or after the time described or at any other place or for a different lease term which in commercial judgment or under usage of trade would serve as a reasonable substitute for the one described may be used, making any proper allowance for the difference, including the cost of transporting the goods to or from the other place.

(3) Evidence of a relevant rent prevailing at a time or place or for a lease term other than the one described in this Article offered by one party is not admissible unless and until he [or she] has given the other party notice the court finds sufficient to prevent unfair surprise.

(4) If the prevailing rent or value of any goods regularly leased in any established market is in issue, reports in official publications or trade journals or in newspapers or periodicals of general circulation published as the reports of that market are admissible in evidence. The circumstances of the preparation of the report may be shown to affect its weight but not its admissibility.

As amended in 1990.

B. Default by Lessor

§ 2A—508. Lessee's Remedies.

(1) If a lessor fails to deliver the goods in conformity to the lease contract (Section 2A—509) or repudiates the lease contract (Section 2A—402), or a lessee rightfully rejects the goods (Section 2A—509) or justifiably revokes acceptance of the goods (Section 2A—517), then with respect to any goods involved, and with respect to all of the goods if under an installment lease contract the value of the whole lease contract is substantially impaired (Section 2A—510), the lessor is in default under the lease contract and the lessee may:

(a) cancel the lease contract (Section 2A—505(1));

(b) recover so much of the rent and security as has been paid and is just under the circumstances;

(c) cover and recover damages as to all goods affected whether or not they have been identified to the lease contract

(Sections 2A—518 and 2A—520), or recover damages for nondelivery (Sections 2A—519 and 2A—520);

(d) exercise any other rights or pursue any other remedies provided in the lease contract..

(2) If a lessor fails to deliver the goods in conformity to the lease contract or repudiates the lease contract, the lessee may also:

(a) if the goods have been identified, recover them (Section 2A—522); or

(b) in a proper case, obtain specific performance or replevy the goods (Section 2A—521).

(3) If a lessor is otherwise in default under a lease contract, the lessee may exercise the rights and pursue the remedies provided in the lease contract, which may include a right to cancel the lease, and in Section 2A–519(3).

(4) If a lessor has breached a warranty, whether express or implied, the lessee may recover damages (Section 2A—519(4)).

(5) On rightful rejection or justifiable revocation of acceptance, a lessee has a security interest in goods in the lessee's possession or control for any rent and security that has been paid and any expenses reasonably incurred in their inspection, receipt, transportation, and care and custody and may hold those goods and dispose of them in good faith and in a commercially reasonable manner, subject to Section 2A—527(5).

(6) Subject to the provisions of Section 2A—407, a lessee, on notifying the lessor of the lessee's intention to do so, may deduct all or any part of the damages resulting from any default under the lease contract from any part of the rent still due under the same lease contract.

As amended in 1990.

§ 2A—509. Lessee's Rights on Improper Delivery; Rightful Rejection.

(1) Subject to the provisions of Section 2A—510 on default in installment lease contracts, if the goods or the tender or delivery fail in any respect to conform to the lease contract, the lessee may reject or accept the goods or accept any commercial unit or units and reject the rest of the goods.

(2) Rejection of goods is ineffective unless it is within a reasonable time after tender or delivery of the goods and the lessee seasonably notifies the lessor.

§ 2A—510. Installment Lease Contracts: Rejection and Default.

(1) Under an installment lease contract a lessee may reject any delivery that is nonconforming if the nonconformity substantially impairs the value of that delivery and cannot be cured or the nonconformity is a defect in the required documents; but if the nonconformity does not fall within subsection (2) and the lessor or the supplier gives adequate assurance of its cure, the lessee must accept that delivery.

(2) Whenever nonconformity or default with respect to one or more deliveries substantially impairs the value of the installment lease contract as a whole there is a default with respect to the whole. But, the aggrieved party reinstates the installment lease contract as a whole if the aggrieved party accepts a nonconforming delivery without seasonably notifying of cancellation or brings an action with respect only to past deliveries or demands performance as to future deliveries.

§ 2A—511. Merchant Lessee's Duties as to Rightfully Rejected Goods.

(1) Subject to any security interest of a lessee (Section 2A—508(5)), if a lessor or a supplier has no agent or place of business at the market of rejection, a merchant lessee, after rejection of goods in his [or her] possession or control, shall follow any reasonable instructions received from the lessor or the supplier with respect to the goods. In the absence of those instructions, a merchant lessee shall make reasonable efforts to sell, lease, or otherwise dispose of the goods for the lessor's account if they threaten to decline in value speedily. Instructions are not reasonable if on demand indemnity for expenses is not forthcoming.

(2) If a merchant lessee (subsection (1)) or any other lessee (Section 2A—512) disposes of goods, he [or she] is entitled to reimbursement either from the lessor or the supplier or out of the proceeds for reasonable expenses of caring for and disposing of the goods and, if the expenses include no disposition commission, to such commission as is usual in the trade, or if there is none, to a reasonable sum not exceeding 10 percent of the gross proceeds.

(3) In complying with this section or Section 2A—512, the lessee is held only to good faith. Good faith conduct hereunder is neither acceptance or conversion nor the basis of an action for damages.

(4) A purchaser who purchases in good faith from a lessee pursuant to this section or Section 2A—512 takes the goods free of any rights of the lessor and the supplier even though the lessee fails to comply with one or more of the requirements of this Article.

§ 2A—512. Lessee's Duties as to Rightfully Rejected Goods.

(1) Except as otherwise provided with respect to goods that threaten to decline in value speedily (Section 2A—511) and subject to any security interest of a lessee (Section 2A—508(5)):

(a) the lessee, after rejection of goods in the lessee's possession, shall hold them with reasonable care at the lessor's or the supplier's disposition for a reasonable time after the lessee's seasonable notification of rejection;

(b) if the lessor or the supplier gives no instructions within a reasonable time after notification of rejection, the lessee may store the rejected goods for the lessor's or the supplier's account or ship them to the lessor or the supplier or dispose of them for the lessor's or the supplier's account with reimbursement in the manner provided in Section 2A—511; but

(c) the lessee has no further obligations with regard to goods rightfully rejected.

(2) Action by the lessee pursuant to subsection (1) is not acceptance or conversion.

§ 2A—513. Cure by Lessor of Improper Tender or Delivery; Replacement.

(1) If any tender or delivery by the lessor or the supplier is rejected because nonconforming and the time for performance has not yet expired, the lessor or the supplier may seasonably notify the lessee of the lessor's or the supplier's intention to cure and may then make a conforming delivery within the time provided in the lease contract.

(2) If the lessee rejects a nonconforming tender that the lessor or the supplier had reasonable grounds to believe would be acceptable with or without money allowance, the lessor or the supplier may have a further reasonable time to substitute a conforming tender if he [or she] seasonably notifies the lessee.

§ 2A—514. Waiver of Lessee's Objections.

(1) In rejecting goods, a lessee's failure to state a particular defect that is ascertainable by reasonable inspection precludes the lessee from relying on the defect to justify rejection or to establish default:

(a) if, stated seasonably, the lessor or the supplier could have cured it (Section 2A—513); or

(b) between merchants if the lessor or the supplier after rejection has made a request in writing for a full and final written statement of all defects on which the lessee proposes to rely.

(2) A lessee's failure to reserve rights when paying rent or other consideration against documents precludes recovery of the payment for defects apparent on the face of the documents.

§ 2A—515. Acceptance of Goods.

(1) Acceptance of goods occurs after the lessee has had a reasonable opportunity to inspect the goods and

(a) the lessee signifies or acts with respect to the goods in a manner that signifies to the lessor or the supplier that the goods are conforming or that the lessee will take or retain them in spite of their nonconformity; or

(b) the lessee fails to make an effective rejection of the goods (Section 2A—509(2)).

(2) Acceptance of a part of any commercial unit is acceptance of that entire unit.

§ 2A—516. Effect of Acceptance of Goods; Notice of Default; Burden of Establishing Default after Acceptance; Notice of Claim or Litigation to Person Answerable Over.

(1) A lessee must pay rent for any goods accepted in accordance with the lease contract, with due allowance for goods rightfully rejected or not delivered.

(2) A lessee's acceptance of goods precludes rejection of the goods accepted. In the case of a finance lease, if made with knowledge of a nonconformity, acceptance cannot be revoked because of it. In any other case, if made with knowledge of a nonconformity, acceptance cannot be revoked because of it unless the acceptance was on the reasonable assumption that the nonconformity would be seasonably cured. Acceptance does not of itself impair any other remedy provided by this Article or the lease agreement for nonconformity.

(3) If a tender has been accepted:

(a) within a reasonable time after the lessee discovers or should have discovered any default, the lessee shall notify the lessor and the supplier, if any, or be barred from any remedy against the party notified;

(b) except in the case of a consumer lease, within a reasonable time after the lessee receives notice of litigation for infringement or the like (Section 2A—211) the lessee shall notify the lessor or be barred from any remedy over for liability established by the litigation; and

(c) the burden is on the lessee to establish any default.

(4) If a lessee is sued for breach of a warranty or other obligation for which a lessor or a supplier is answerable over the following apply:

(a) The lessee may give the lessor or the supplier, or both, written notice of the litigation. If the notice states that the person notified may come in and defend and that if the person notified does not do so that person will be bound in any action against that person by the lessee by any determination of fact common to the two litigations, then unless the person notified after seasonable receipt of the notice does come in and defend that person is so bound.

(b) The lessor or the supplier may demand in writing that the lessee turn over control of the litigation including settlement if the claim is one for infringement or the like (Section 2A—211) or else be barred from any remedy over. If the demand states that the lessor or the supplier agrees to bear all expense and to satisfy any adverse judgment, then unless the lessee after seasonable receipt of the demand does turn over control the lessee is so barred.

(5) Subsections (3) and (4) apply to any obligation of a lessee to hold the lessor or the supplier harmless against infringement or the like (Section 2A—211).

As amended in 1990.

§ 2A—517. Revocation of Acceptance of Goods.

(1) A lessee may revoke acceptance of a lot or commercial unit whose nonconformity substantially impairs its value to the lessee if the lessee has accepted it:

(a) except in the case of a finance lease, on the reasonable assumption that its nonconformity would be cured and it has not been seasonably cured; or

(b) without discovery of the nonconformity if the lessee's acceptance was reasonably induced either by the lessor's assurances or, except in the case of a finance lease, by the difficulty of discovery before acceptance.

(2) Except in the case of a finance lease that is not a consumer lease, a lessee may revoke acceptance of a lot or commercial unit if the lessor defaults under the lease contract and the default substantially impairs the value of that lot or commercial unit to the lessee.

(3) If the lease agreement so provides, the lessee may revoke acceptance of a lot or commercial unit because of other defaults by the lessor.

(4) Revocation of acceptance must occur within a reasonable time after the lessee discovers or should have discovered the ground for it and before any substantial change in condition of the goods which is not caused by the nonconformity. Revocation is not effective until the lessee notifies the lessor.

(5) A lessee who so revokes has the same rights and duties with regard to the goods involved as if the lessee had rejected them.

As amended in 1990.

§ 2A—518. Cover; Substitute Goods.

(1) After a default by a lessor under the lease contract of the type described in Section 2A—508(1), or, if agreed, after other default by the lessor, the lessee may cover by making any purchase or lease of or contract to purchase or lease goods in substitution for those due from the lessor.

(2) Except as otherwise provided with respect to damages liquidated in the lease agreement (Section 2A—504) or otherwise

determined pursuant to agreement of the parties (Sections 1—102(3) and 2A—503), if a lessee's cover is by lease agreement substantially similar to the original lease agreement and the new lease agreement is made in good faith and in a commercially reasonable manner, the lessee may recover from the lessor as damages (i) the present value, as of the date of the commencement of the term of the new lease agreement, of the rent under the new lease agreement applicable to that period of the new lease term which is comparable to the then remaining term of the original lease agreement minus the present value as of the same date of the total rent for the then remaining lease term of the original lease agreement, and (ii) any incidental or consequential damages, less expenses saved in consequence of the lessor's default.

(3) If a lessee's cover is by lease agreement that for any reason does not qualify for treatment under subsection (2), or is by purchase or otherwise, the lessee may recover from the lessor as if the lessee had elected not to cover and Section 2A—519 governs.

As amended in 1990.

§ 2A—519. Lessee's Damages for Non-Delivery, Repudiation, Default, and Breach of Warranty in Regard to Accepted Goods.

(1) Except as otherwise provided with respect to damages liquidated in the lease agreement (Section 2A—504) or otherwise determined pursuant to agreement of the parties (Sections 1—102(3) and 2A—503), if a lessee elects not to cover or a lessee elects to cover and the cover is by lease agreement that for any reason does not qualify for treatment under Section 2A—518(2), or is by purchase or otherwise, the measure of damages for non-delivery or repudiation by the lessor or for rejection or revocation of acceptance by the lessee is the present value, as of the date of the default, of the then market rent minus the present value as of the same date of the original rent, computed for the remaining lease term of the original lease agreement, together with incidental and consequential damages, less expenses saved in consequence of the lessor's default.

(2) Market rent is to be determined as of the place for tender or, in cases of rejection after arrival or revocation of acceptance, as of the place of arrival.

(3) Except as otherwise agreed, if the lessee has accepted goods and given notification (Section 2A—516(3)), the measure of damages for non-conforming tender or delivery or other default by a lessor is the loss resulting in the ordinary course of events from the lessor's default as determined in any manner that is reasonable together with incidental and consequential damages, less expenses saved in consequence of the lessor's default.

(4) Except as otherwise agreed, the measure of damages for breach of warranty is the present value at the time and place of acceptance of the difference between the value of the use of the goods accepted and the value if they had been as warranted for the lease term, unless special circumstances show proximate damages of a different amount, together with incidental and consequential damages, less expenses saved in consequence of the lessor's default or breach of warranty.

As amended in 1990.

§ 2A—520. Lessee's Incidental and Consequential Damages.

(1) Incidental damages resulting from a lessor's default include expenses reasonably incurred in inspection, receipt, transporta-

tion, and care and custody of goods rightfully rejected or goods the acceptance of which is justifiably revoked, any commercially reasonable charges, expenses or commissions in connection with effecting cover, and any other reasonable expense incident to the default.

(2) Consequential damages resulting from a lessor's default include:

(a) any loss resulting from general or particular requirements and needs of which the lessor at the time of contracting had reason to know and which could not reasonably be prevented by cover or otherwise; and

(b) injury to person or property proximately resulting from any breach of warranty.

§ 2A—521. Lessee's Right to Specific Performance or Replevin.

(1) Specific performance may be decreed if the goods are unique or in other proper circumstances.

(2) A decree for specific performance may include any terms and conditions as to payment of the rent, damages, or other relief that the court deems just.

(3) A lessee has a right of replevin, detinue, sequestration, claim and delivery, or the like for goods identified to the lease contract if after reasonable effort the lessee is unable to effect cover for those goods or the circumstances reasonably indicate that the effort will be unavailing.

§ 2A—522. Lessee's Right to Goods on Lessor's Insolvency.

(1) Subject to subsection (2) and even though the goods have not been shipped, a lessee who has paid a part or all of the rent and security for goods identified to a lease contract (Section 2A—217) on making and keeping good a tender of any unpaid portion of the rent and security due under the lease contract may recover the goods identified from the lessor if the lessor becomes insolvent within 10 days after receipt of the first installment of rent and security.

(2) A lessee acquires the right to recover goods identified to a lease contract only if they conform to the lease contract.

C. Default by Lessee

§ 2A—523. Lessor's Remedies.

(1) If a lessee wrongfully rejects or revokes acceptance of goods or fails to make a payment when due or repudiates with respect to a part or the whole, then, with respect to any goods involved, and with respect to all of the goods if under an installment lease contract the value of the whole lease contract is substantially impaired (Section 2A—510), the lessee is in default under the lease contract and the lessor may:

(a) cancel the lease contract (Section 2A—505(1));

(b) proceed respecting goods not identified to the lease contract (Section 2A—524);

(c) withhold delivery of the goods and take possession of goods previously delivered (Section 2A—525);

(d) stop delivery of the goods by any bailee (Section 2A—526);

(e) dispose of the goods and recover damages (Section 2A—527), or retain the goods and recover damages (Section

2A—528), or in a proper case recover rent (Section 2A—529)

(f) exercise any other rights or pursue any other remedies provided in the lease contract.

(2) If a lessor does not fully exercise a right or obtain a remedy to which the lessor is entitled under subsection (1), the lessor may recover the loss resulting in the ordinary course of events from the lessee's default as determined in any reasonable manner, together with incidental damages, less expenses saved in consequence of the lessee's default.

(3) If a lessee is otherwise in default under a lease contract, the lessor may exercise the rights and pursue the remedies provided in the lease contract, which may include a right to cancel the lease. In addition, unless otherwise provided in the lease contract:

(a) if the default substantially impairs the value of the lease contract to the lessor, the lessor may exercise the rights and pursue the remedies provided in subsections (1) or (2); or

(b) if the default does not substantially impair the value of the lease contract to the lessor, the lessor may recover as provided in subsection (2).

As amended in 1990.

§ 2A—524. Lessor's Right to Identify Goods to Lease Contract.

(1) After default by the lessee under the lease contract of the type described in Section 2A—523(1) or 2A—523(3)(a) or, if agreed, after other default by the lessee, the lessor may:

(a) identify to the lease contract conforming goods not already identified if at the time the lessor learned of the default they were in the lessor's or the supplier's possession or control; and

(b) dispose of goods (Section 2A—527(1)) that demonstrably have been intended for the particular lease contract even though those goods are unfinished.

(2) If the goods are unfinished, in the exercise of reasonable commercial judgment for the purposes of avoiding loss and of effective realization, an aggrieved lessor or the supplier may either complete manufacture and wholly identify the goods to the lease contract or cease manufacture and lease, sell, or otherwise dispose of the goods for scrap or salvage value or proceed in any other reasonable manner.

As amended in 1990.

§ 2A—525. Lessor's Right to Possession of Goods.

(1) If a lessor discovers the lessee to be insolvent, the lessor may refuse to deliver the goods.

(2) After a default by the lessee under the lease contract of the type described in Section 2A—523(1) or 2A—523(3)(a) or, if agreed, after other default by the lessee, the lessor has the right to take possession of the goods. If the lease contract so provides, the lessor may require the lessee to assemble the goods and make them available to the lessor at a place to be designated by the lessor which is reasonably convenient to both parties. Without removal, the lessor may render unusable any goods employed in trade or business, and may dispose of goods on the lessee's premises (Section 2A—527).

(3) The lessor may proceed under subsection (2) without judicial process if that can be done without breach of the peace or the lessor may proceed by action.

As amended in 1990.

§ 2A—526. Lessor's Stoppage of Delivery in Transit or Otherwise.

(1) A lessor may stop delivery of goods in the possession of a carrier or other bailee if the lessor discovers the lessee to be insolvent and may stop delivery of carload, truckload, planeload, or larger shipments of express or freight if the lessee repudiates or fails to make a payment due before delivery, whether for rent, security or otherwise under the lease contract, or for any other reason the lessor has a right to withhold or take possession of the goods.

(2) In pursuing its remedies under subsection (1), the lessor may stop delivery until

    (a) receipt of the goods by the lessee;

    (b) acknowledgment to the lessee by any bailee of the goods, except a carrier, that the bailee holds the goods for the lessee; or

    (c) such an acknowledgment to the lessee by a carrier via reshipment or as warehouseman.

(3) (a) To stop delivery, a lessor shall so notify as to enable the bailee by reasonable diligence to prevent delivery of the goods.

    (b) After notification, the bailee shall hold and deliver the goods according to the directions of the lessor, but the lessor is liable to the bailee for any ensuing charges or damages.

    (c) A carrier who has issued a nonnegotiable bill of lading is not obliged to obey a notification to stop received from a person other than the consignor.

§ 2A—527. Lessor's Rights to Dispose of Goods.

(1) After a default by a lessee under the lease contract of the type described in Section 2A—523(1) or 2A–523(3)(a) or after the lessor refuses to deliver or takes possession of goods (Section 2A—525 or 2A—526), or, if agreed, after other default by a lessee, the lessor may dispose of the goods concerned or the undelivered balance thereof by lease, sale, or otherwise.

(2) Except as otherwise provided with respect to damages liquidated in the lease agreement (Section 2A—504) or otherwise determined pursuant to agreement of the parties (Sections 1—102(3) and 2A—503), if the disposition is by lease agreement substantially similar to the original lease agreement and the new lease agreement is made in good faith and in a commercially reasonable manner, the lessor may recover from the lessee as damages (i) accrued and unpaid rent as of the date of the commencement of the term of the new lease agreement, (ii) the present value, as of the same date, of the total rent for the then remaining lease term of the original lease agreement minus the present value, as of the same date, of the rent under the new lease agreement applicable to that period of the new lease term which is comparable to the then remaining term of the original lease agreement, and (iii) any incidental damages allowed under Section 2A—530, less expenses saved in consequence of the lessee's default.

(3) If the lessor's disposition is by lease agreement that for any reason does not qualify for treatment under subsection (2), or is by sale or otherwise, the lessor may recover from the lessee as if the lessor had elected not to dispose of the goods and Section 2A—528 governs.

(4) A subsequent buyer or lessee who buys or leases from the lessor in good faith for value as a result of a disposition under this section takes the goods free of the original lease contract and any

rights of the original lessee even though the lessor fails to comply with one or more of the requirements of this Article.

(5) The lessor is not accountable to the lessee for any profit made on any disposition. A lessee who has rightfully rejected or justifiably revoked acceptance shall account to the lessor for any excess over the amount of the lessee's security interest (Section 2A—508(5)).

As amended in 1990.

§ 2A—528. Lessor's Damages for Non-acceptance, Failure to Pay, Repudiation, or Other Default.

(1) Except as otherwise provided with respect to damages liquidated in the lease agreement (Section 2A—504) or otherwise determined pursuant to agreement of the parties (Section 1—102(3) and 2A—503), if a lessor elects to retain the goods or a lessor elects to dispose of the goods and the disposition is by lease agreement that for any reason does not qualify for treatment under Section 2A—527(2), or is by sale or otherwise, the lessor may recover from the lessee as damages for a default of the type described in Section 2A—523(1) or 2A—523(3)(a), or if agreed, for other default of the lessee, (i) accrued and unpaid rent as of the date of the default if the lessee has never taken possession of the goods, or, if the lessee has taken possession of the goods, as of the date the lessor repossesses the goods or an earlier date on which the lessee makes a tender of the goods to the lessor, (ii) the present value as of the date determined under clause (i) of the total rent for the then remaining lease term of the original lease agreement minus the present value as of the same date of the market rent as the place where the goods are located computed for the same lease term, and (iii) any incidental damages allowed under Section 2A—530, less expenses saved in consequence of the lessee's default.

(2) If the measure of damages provided in subsection (1) is inadequate to put a lessor in as good a position as performance would have, the measure of damages is the present value of the profit, including reasonable overhead, the lessor would have made from full performance by the lessee, together with any incidental damages allowed under Section 2A—530, due allowance for costs reasonably incurred and due credit for payments or proceeds of disposition.

As amended in 1990.

§ 2A—529. Lessor's Action for the Rent.

(1) After default by the lessee under the lease contract of the type described in Section 2A—523(1) or 2A—523(3)(a) or, if agreed, after other default by the lessee, if the lessor complies with subsection (2), the lessor may recover from the lessee as damages:

    (a) for goods accepted by the lessee and not repossessed by or tendered to the lessor, and for conforming goods lost or damaged within a commercially reasonable time after risk of loss passes to the lessee (Section 2A—219), (i) accrued and unpaid rent as of the date of entry of judgment in favor of the lessor (ii) the present value as of the same date of the rent for the then remaining lease term of the lease agreement, and (iii) any incidental damages allowed under Section 2A—530, less expenses saved in consequence of the lessee's default; and

    (b) for goods identified to the lease contract if the lessor is unable after reasonable effort to dispose of them at a reasonable price or the circumstances reasonably indicate that effort will be unavailing, (i) accrued and unpaid rent as of the date of entry of judgment in favor of the lessor, (ii) the present value as of the same date of the rent for the then remaining lease term of the lease agreement, and (iii) any incidental damages allowed under Section 2A—530, less expenses saved in consequence of the lessee's default.

(2) Except as provided in subsection (3), the lessor shall hold for the lessee for the remaining lease term of the lease agreement any goods that have been identified to the lease contract and are in the lessor's control.

(3) The lessor may dispose of the goods at any time before collection of the judgment for damages obtained pursuant to subsection (1). If the disposition is before the end of the remaining lease term of the lease agreement, the lessor's recovery against the lessee for damages is governed by Section 2A—527 or Section 2A—528, and the lessor will cause an appropriate credit to be provided against a judgment for damages to the extent that the amount of the judgment exceeds the recovery available pursuant to Section 2A—527 or 2A—528.

(4) Payment of the judgment for damages obtained pursuant to subsection (1) entitles the lessee to the use and possession of the goods not then disposed of for the remaining lease term of and in accordance with the lease agreement.

(5) After default by the lessee under the lease contract of the type described in Section 2A—523(1) or Section 2A—523(3)(a) or, if agreed, after other default by the lessee, a lessor who is held not entitled to rent under this section must nevertheless be awarded damages for non-acceptance under Sections 2A—527 and 2A—528.

As amended in 1990.

§ 2A—530. Lessor's Incidental Damages.

Incidental damages to an aggrieved lessor include any commercially reasonable charges, expenses, or commissions incurred in stopping delivery, in the transportation, care and custody of goods after the lessee's default, in connection with return or disposition of the goods, or otherwise resulting from the default.

§ 2A—531. Standing to Sue Third Parties for Injury to Goods.

(1) If a third party so deals with goods that have been identified to a lease contract as to cause actionable injury to a party to the lease contract (a) the lessor has a right of action against the third party, and (b) the lessee also has a right of action against the third party if the lessee:

> (i) has a security interest in the goods;

> (ii) has an insurable interest in the goods; or

> (iii) bears the risk of loss under the lease contract or has since the injury assumed that risk as against the lessor and the goods have been converted or destroyed.

(2) If at the time of the injury the party plaintiff did not bear the risk of loss as against the other party to the lease contract and there is no arrangement between them for disposition of the recovery, his [or her] suit or settlement, subject to his [or her] own interest, is as a fiduciary for the other party to the lease contract.

(3) Either party with the consent of the other may sue for the benefit of whom it may concern.

§ 2A—532. Lessor's Rights to Residual Interest.

In addition to any other recovery permitted by this Article or other law, the lessor may recover from the lessee an amount that will fully compensate the lessor for any loss of or damage to the lessor's residual interest in the goods caused by the default of the lessee.

As added in 1990.

Revised Article 3
NEGOTIABLE INSTRUMENTS

Part 1 General Provisions and Definitions

§ 3—101. Short Title.

This Article may be cited as Uniform Commercial Code—Negotiable Instruments.

§ 3—102. Subject Matter.

(a) This Article applies to negotiable instruments. It does not apply to money, to payment orders governed by Article 4A, or to securities governed by Article 8.

(b) If there is conflict between this Article and Article 4 or 9, Articles 4 and 9 govern.

(c) Regulations of the Board of Governors of the Federal Reserve System and operating circulars of the Federal Reserve Banks supersede any inconsistent provision of this Article to the extent of the inconsistency.

§ 3—103. Definitions.

(a) In this Article:

> (1) "Acceptor" means a drawee who has accepted a draft.

> (2) "Drawee" means a person ordered in a draft to make payment.

> (3) "Drawer" means a person who signs or is identified in a draft as a person ordering payment.

> (4) "Good faith" means honesty in fact and the observance of reasonable commercial standards of fair dealing.

> (5) "Maker" means a person who signs or is identified in a note as a person undertaking to pay.

> (6) "Order" means a written instruction to pay money signed by the person giving the instruction. The instruction may be addressed to any person, including the person giving the instruction, or to one or more persons jointly or in the alternative but not in succession. An authorization to pay is not an order unless the person authorized to pay is also instructed to pay.

> (7) "Ordinary care" in the case of a person engaged in business means observance of reasonable commercial standards, prevailing in the area in which the person is located, with respect to the business in which the person is engaged. In the case of a bank that takes an instrument for processing for collection or payment by automated means, reasonable commercial standards do not require the bank to examine the instrument if the failure to examine does not violate the bank's prescribed procedures and the bank's procedures do not vary unreasonably from general banking usage not disapproved by this Article or Article 4.

(8) "Party" means a party to an instrument.

(9) "Promise" means a written undertaking to pay money signed by the person undertaking to pay. An acknowledgment of an obligation by the obligor is not a promise unless the obligor also undertakes to pay the obligation.

(10) "Prove" with respect to a fact means to meet the burden of establishing the fact (Section 1—201(8)).

(11) "Remitter" means a person who purchases an instrument from its issuer if the instrument is payable to an identified person other than the purchaser.

(b);(c) [Other definitions' section references deleted.]

(d) In addition, Article 1 contains general definitions and principles of construction and interpretation applicable throughout this Article.

§ 3—104. Negotiable Instrument.

(a) Except as provided in subsections (c) and (d), "negotiable instrument" means an unconditional promise or order to pay a fixed amount of money, with or without interest or other charges described in the promise or order, if it:

(1) is payable to bearer or to order at the time it is issued or first comes into possession of a holder;

(2) is payable on demand or at a definite time; and

(3) does not state any other undertaking or instruction by the person promising or ordering payment to do any act in addition to the payment of money, but the promise or order may contain (i) an undertaking or power to give, maintain, or protect collateral to secure payment, (ii) an authorization or power to the holder to confess judgment or realize on or dispose of collateral, or (iii) a waiver of the benefit of any law intended for the advantage or protection of an obligor.

(b) "Instrument" means a negotiable instrument.

(c) An order that meets all of the requirements of subsection (a), except paragraph (1), and otherwise falls within the definition of "check" in subsection (f) is a negotiable instrument and a check.

(d) A promise or order other than a check is not an instrument if, at the time it is issued or first comes into possession of a holder, it contains a conspicuous statement, however expressed, to the effect that the promise or order is not negotiable or is not an instrument governed by this Article.

(e) An instrument is a "note" if it is a promise and is a "draft" if it is an order. If an instrument falls within the definition of both "note" and "draft," a person entitled to enforce the instrument may treat it as either.

(f) "Check" means (i) a draft, other than a documentary draft, payable on demand and drawn on a bank or (ii) a cashier's check or teller's check. An instrument may be a check even though it is described on its face by another term, such as "money order."

(g) "Cashier's check" means a draft with respect to which the drawer and drawee are the same bank or branches of the same bank.

(h) "Teller's check" means a draft drawn by a bank (i) on another bank, or (ii) payable at or through a bank.

(i) "Traveler's check" means an instrument that (i) is payable on demand, (ii) is drawn on or payable at or through a bank, (iii) is designated by the term "traveler's check" or by a substantially similar term, and (iv) requires, as a condition to payment, a countersignature by a person whose specimen signature appears on the instrument.

(j) "Certificate of deposit" means an instrument containing an acknowledgment by a bank that a sum of money has been received by the bank and a promise by the bank to repay the sum of money. A certificate of deposit is a note of the bank.

§ 3—105. Issue of Instrument.

(a) "Issue" means the first delivery of an instrument by the maker or drawer, whether to a holder or nonholder, for the purpose of giving rights on the instrument to any person.

(b) An unissued instrument, or an unissued incomplete instrument that is completed, is binding on the maker or drawer, but nonissuance is a defense. An instrument that is conditionally issued or is issued for a special purpose is binding on the maker or drawer, but failure of the condition or special purpose to be fulfilled is a defense.

(c) "Issuer" applies to issued and unissued instruments and means a maker or drawer of an instrument.

§ 3—106. Unconditional Promise or Order.

(a) Except as provided in this section, for the purposes of Section 3—104(a), a promise or order is unconditional unless it states (i) an express condition to payment, (ii) that the promise or order is subject to or governed by another writing, or (iii) that rights or obligations with respect to the promise or order are stated in another writing. A reference to another writing does not of itself make the promise or order conditional.

(b) A promise or order is not made conditional (i) by a reference to another writing for a statement of rights with respect to collateral, prepayment, or acceleration, or (ii) because payment is limited to resort to a particular fund or source.

(c) If a promise or order requires, as a condition to payment, a countersignature by a person whose specimen signature appears on the promise or order, the condition does not make the promise or order conditional for the purposes of Section 3—104(a). If the person whose specimen signature appears on an instrument fails to countersign the instrument, the failure to countersign is a defense to the obligation of the issuer, but the failure does not prevent a transferee of the instrument from becoming a holder of the instrument.

(d) If a promise or order at the time it is issued or first comes into possession of a holder contains a statement, required by applicable statutory or administrative law, to the effect that the rights of a holder or transferee are subject to claims or defenses that the issuer could assert against the original payee, the promise or order is not thereby made conditional for the purposes of Section 3—104(a); but if the promise or order is an instrument, there cannot be a holder in due course of the instrument.

§ 3—107. Instrument Payable in Foreign Money.

Unless the instrument otherwise provides, an instrument that states the amount payable in foreign money may be paid in the foreign money or in an equivalent amount in dollars calculated by using the current bank-offered spot rate at the place of payment for the purchase of dollars on the day on which the instrument is paid.

§ 3—108. Payable on Demand or at Definite Time.

(a) A promise or order is "payable on demand" if it (i) states that it is payable on demand or at sight, or otherwise indicates that it is payable at the will of the holder, or (ii) does not state any time of payment.

(b) A promise or order is "payable at a definite time" if it is payable on elapse of a definite period of time after sight or acceptance or at a fixed date or dates or at a time or times readily ascertainable at the time the promise or order is issued, subject to rights of (i) prepayment, (ii) acceleration, (iii) extension at the option of the holder, or (iv) extension to a further definite time at the option of the maker or acceptor or automatically upon or after a specified act or event.

(c) If an instrument, payable at a fixed date, is also payable upon demand made before the fixed date, the instrument is payable on demand until the fixed date and, if demand for payment is not made before that date, becomes payable at a definite time on the fixed date.

§ 3—109. Payable to Bearer or to Order.

(a) A promise or order is payable to bearer if it:

(1) states that it is payable to bearer or to the order of bearer or otherwise indicates that the person in possession of the promise or order is entitled to payment;

(2) does not state a payee; or

(3) states that it is payable to or to the order of cash or otherwise indicates that it is not payable to an identified person.

(b) A promise or order that is not payable to bearer is payable to order if it is payable (i) to the order of an identified person or (ii) to an identified person or order. A promise or order that is payable to order is payable to the identified person.

(c) An instrument payable to bearer may become payable to an identified person if it is specially indorsed pursuant to Section 3—205(a). An instrument payable to an identified person may become payable to bearer if it is indorsed in blank pursuant to Section 3—205(b).

§ 3—110. Identification of Person to Whom Instrument Is Payable.

(a) The person to whom an instrument is initially payable is determined by the intent of the person, whether or not authorized, signing as, or in the name or behalf of, the issuer of the instrument. The instrument is payable to the person intended by the signer even if that person is identified in the instrument by a name or other identification that is not that of the intended person. If more than one person signs in the name or behalf of the issuer of an instrument and all the signers do not intend the same person as payee, the instrument is payable to any person intended by one or more of the signers.

(b) If the signature of the issuer of an instrument is made by automated means, such as a check-writing machine, the payee of the instrument is determined by the intent of the person who supplied the name or identification of the payee, whether or not authorized to do so.

(c) A person to whom an instrument is payable may be identified in any way, including by name, identifying number, office, or account number. For the purpose of determining the holder of an instrument, the following rules apply:

(1) If an instrument is payable to an account and the account is identified only by number, the instrument is payable to the person to whom the account is payable. If an instrument is payable to an account identified by number and by the name of a person, the instrument is payable to the named person, whether or not that person is the owner of the account identified by number.

(2) If an instrument is payable to:

(i) a trust, an estate, or a person described as trustee or representative of a trust or estate, the instrument is payable to the trustee, the representative, or a successor of either, whether or not the beneficiary or estate is also named;

(ii) a person described as agent or similar representative of a named or identified person, the instrument is payable to the represented person, the representative, or a successor of the representative;

(iii) a fund or organization that is not a legal entity, the instrument is payable to a representative of the members of the fund or organization; or

(iv) an office or to a person described as holding an office, the instrument is payable to the named person, the incumbent of the office, or a successor to the incumbent.

(d) If an instrument is payable to two or more persons alternatively, it is payable to any of them and may be negotiated, discharged, or enforced by any or all of them in possession of the instrument. If an instrument is payable to two or more persons not alternatively, it is payable to all of them and may be negotiated, discharged, or enforced only by all of them. If an instrument payable to two or more persons is ambiguous as to whether it is payable to the persons alternatively, the instrument is payable to the persons alternatively.

§ 3—111. Place of Payment.

Except as otherwise provided for items in Article 4, an instrument is payable at the place of payment stated in the instrument. If no place of payment is stated, an instrument is payable at the address of the drawee or maker stated in the instrument. If no address is stated, the place of payment is the place of business of the drawee or maker. If a drawee or maker has more than one place of business, the place of payment is any place of business of the drawee or maker chosen by the person entitled to enforce the instrument. If the drawee or maker has no place of business, the place of payment is the residence of the drawee or maker.

§ 3—112. Interest.

(a) Unless otherwise provided in the instrument, (i) an instrument is not payable with interest, and (ii) interest on an interest-bearing instrument is payable from the date of the instrument.

(b) Interest may be stated in an instrument as a fixed or variable amount of money or it may be expressed as a fixed or variable rate or rates. The amount or rate of interest may be stated or described in the instrument in any manner and may require reference to information not contained in the instrument. If an instrument provides for interest, but the amount of interest payable cannot be ascertained from the description, interest is payable at the judgment rate in effect at the place of payment of the instrument and at the time interest first accrues.

§ 3—113. Date of Instrument.

(a) An instrument may be antedated or postdated. The date stated determines the time of payment if the instrument is payable at a fixed period after date. Except as provided in Section 4—401(c), an instrument payable on demand is not payable before the date of the instrument.

(b) If an instrument is undated, its date is the date of its issue or, in the case of an unissued instrument, the date it first comes into possession of a holder.

§ 3—114. Contradictory Terms of Instrument.

If an instrument contains contradictory terms, typewritten terms prevail over printed terms, handwritten terms prevail over both, and words prevail over numbers.

§ 3—115. Incomplete Instrument.

(a) "Incomplete instrument" means a signed writing, whether or not issued by the signer, the contents of which show at the time of signing that it is incomplete but that the signer intended it to be completed by the addition of words or numbers.

(b) Subject to subsection (c), if an incomplete instrument is an instrument under Section 3—104, it may be enforced according to its terms if it is not completed, or according to its terms as augmented by completion. If an incomplete instrument is not an instrument under Section 3—104, but, after completion, the requirements of Section 3—104 are met, the instrument may be enforced according to its terms as augmented by completion.

(c) If words or numbers are added to an incomplete instrument without authority of the signer, there is an alteration of the incomplete instrument under Section 3—407.

(d) The burden of establishing that words or numbers were added to an incomplete instrument without authority of the signer is on the person asserting the lack of authority.

§ 3—116. Joint and Several Liability; Contribution.

(a) Except as otherwise provided in the instrument, two or more persons who have the same liability on an instrument as makers, drawers, acceptors, indorsers who indorse as joint payees, or anomalous indorsers are jointly and severally liable in the capacity in which they sign.

(b) Except as provided in Section 3—419(e) or by agreement of the affected parties, a party having joint and several liability who pays the instrument is entitled to receive from any party having the same joint and several liability contribution in accordance with applicable law.

(c) Discharge of one party having joint and several liability by a person entitled to enforce the instrument does not affect the right under subsection (b) of a party having the same joint and several liability to receive contribution from the party discharged.

§ 3—117. Other Agreements Affecting Instrument.

Subject to applicable law regarding exclusion of proof of contemporaneous or previous agreements, the obligation of a party to an instrument to pay the instrument may be modified, supplemented, or nullified by a separate agreement of the obligor and a person entitled to enforce the instrument, if the instrument is issued or the obligation is incurred in reliance on the agreement or as part of the same transaction giving rise to the agreement. To the extent an obligation is modified, supplemented, or nullified by an agreement under this section, the agreement is a defense to the obligation.

§ 3—118. Statute of Limitations.

(a) Except as provided in subsection (e), an action to enforce the obligation of a party to pay a note payable at a definite time must be commenced within six years after the due date or dates stated in the note or, if a due date is accelerated, within six years after the accelerated due date.

(b) Except as provided in subsection (d) or (e), if demand for payment is made to the maker of a note payable on demand, an action to enforce the obligation of a party to pay the note must be commenced within six years after the demand. If no demand for payment is made to the maker, an action to enforce the note is barred if neither principal nor interest on the note has been paid for a continuous period of 10 years.

(c) Except as provided in subsection (d), an action to enforce the obligation of a party to an unaccepted draft to pay the draft must be commenced within three years after dishonor of the draft or 10 years after the date of the draft, whichever period expires first.

(d) An action to enforce the obligation of the acceptor of a certified check or the issuer of a teller's check, cashier's check, or traveler's check must be commenced within three years after demand for payment is made to the acceptor or issuer, as the case may be.

(e) An action to enforce the obligation of a party to a certificate of deposit to pay the instrument must be commenced within six years after demand for payment is made to the maker, but if the instrument states a due date and the maker is not required to pay before that date, the six-year period begins when a demand for payment is in effect and the due date has passed.

(f) An action to enforce the obligation of a party to pay an accepted draft, other than a certified check, must be commenced (i) within six years after the due date or dates stated in the draft or acceptance if the obligation of the acceptor is payable at a definite time, or (ii) within six years after the date of the acceptance if the obligation of the acceptor is payable on demand.

(g) Unless governed by other law regarding claims for indemnity or contribution, an action (i) for conversion of an instrument, for money had and received, or like action based on conversion, (ii) for breach of warranty, or (iii) to enforce an obligation, duty, or right arising under this Article and not governed by this section must be commenced within three years after the [cause of action] accrues.

§ 3—119. Notice of Right to Defend Action.

In an action for breach of an obligation for which a third person is answerable over pursuant to this Article or Article 4, the defendant may give the third person written notice of the litigation, and the person notified may then give similar notice to any other person who is answerable over. If the notice states (i) that the person notified may come in and defend and (ii) that failure to do so will bind the person notified in an action later brought by the person giving the notice as to any determination of fact common to the two litigations, the person notified is so bound unless after seasonable receipt of the notice the person notified does come in and defend.

Part 2 Negotiation, Transfer, and Indorsement

§ 3—201. Negotiation.

(a) "Negotiation" means a transfer of possession, whether voluntary or involuntary, of an instrument by a person other than the issuer to a person who thereby becomes its holder.

(b) Except for negotiation by a remitter, if an instrument is payable to an identified person, negotiation requires transfer of possession of the instrument and its indorsement by the holder. If an instrument is payable to bearer, it may be negotiated by transfer of possession alone.

§ 3—202. **Negotiation Subject to Rescission.**

(a) Negotiation is effective even if obtained (i) from an infant, a corporation exceeding its powers, or a person without capacity, (ii) by fraud, duress, or mistake, or (iii) in breach of duty or as part of an illegal transaction.

(b) To the extent permitted by other law, negotiation may be rescinded or may be subject to other remedies, but those remedies may not be asserted against a subsequent holder in due course or a person paying the instrument in good faith and without knowledge of facts that are a basis for rescission or other remedy.

§ 3—203. **Transfer of Instrument; Rights Acquired by Transfer.**

(a) An instrument is transferred when it is delivered by a person other than its issuer for the purpose of giving to the person receiving delivery the right to enforce the instrument.

(b) Transfer of an instrument, whether or not the transfer is a negotiation, vests in the transferee any right of the transferor to enforce the instrument, including any right as a holder in due course, but the transferee cannot acquire rights of a holder in due course by a transfer, directly or indirectly, from a holder in due course if the transferee engaged in fraud or illegality affecting the instrument.

(c) Unless otherwise agreed, if an instrument is transferred for value and the transferee does not become a holder because of lack of indorsement by the transferor, the transferee has a specifically enforceable right to the unqualified indorsement of the transferor, but negotiation of the instrument does not occur until the indorsement is made.

(d) If a transferor purports to transfer less than the entire instrument, negotiation of the instrument does not occur. The transferee obtains no rights under this Article and has only the rights of a partial assignee.

§ 3—204. **Indorsement.**

(a) "Indorsement" means a signature, other than that of a signer as maker, drawer, or acceptor, that alone or accompanied by other words is made on an instrument for the purpose of (i) negotiating the instrument, (ii) restricting payment of the instrument, or (iii) incurring indorser's liability on the instrument, but regardless of the intent of the signer, a signature and its accompanying words is an indorsement unless the accompanying words, terms of the instrument, place of the signature, or other circumstances unambiguously indicate that the signature was made for a purpose other than indorsement. For the purpose of determining whether a signature is made on an instrument, a paper affixed to the instrument is a part of the instrument.

(b) "Indorser" means a person who makes an indorsement.

(c) For the purpose of determining whether the transferee of an instrument is a holder, an indorsement that transfers a security interest in the instrument is effective as an unqualified indorsement of the instrument.

(d) If an instrument is payable to a holder under a name that is not the name of the holder, indorsement may be made by the holder in the name stated in the instrument or in the holder's name or both, but signature in both names may be required by a person paying or taking the instrument for value or collection.

§ 3—205. **Special Indorsement; Blank Indorsement; Anomalous Indorsement.**

(a) If an indorsement is made by the holder of an instrument, whether payable to an identified person or payable to bearer, and the indorsement identifies a person to whom it makes the instrument payable, it is a "special indorsement." When specially indorsed, an instrument becomes payable to the identified person and may be negotiated only by the indorsement of that person. The principles stated in Section 3—110 apply to special indorsements.

(b) If an indorsement is made by the holder of an instrument and it is not a special indorsement, it is a "blank indorsement." When indorsed in blank, an instrument becomes payable to bearer and may be negotiated by transfer of possession alone until specially indorsed.

(c) The holder may convert a blank indorsement that consists only of a signature into a special indorsement by writing, above the signature of the indorser, words identifying the person to whom the instrument is made payable.

(d) "Anomalous indorsement" means an indorsement made by a person who is not the holder of the instrument. An anomalous indorsement does not affect the manner in which the instrument may be negotiated.

§ 3—206. **Restrictive Indorsement.**

(a) An indorsement limiting payment to a particular person or otherwise prohibiting further transfer or negotiation of the instrument is not effective to prevent further transfer or negotiation of the instrument.

(b) An indorsement stating a condition to the right of the indorsee to receive payment does not affect the right of the indorsee to enforce the instrument. A person paying the instrument or taking it for value or collection may disregard the condition, and the rights and liabilities of that person are not affected by whether the condition has been fulfilled.

(c) If an instrument bears an indorsement (i) described in Section 4—201(b), or (ii) in blank or to a particular bank using the words "for deposit," "for collection," or other words indicating a purpose of having the instrument collected by a bank for the indorser or for a particular account, the following rules apply:

(1) A person, other than a bank, who purchases the instrument when so indorsed converts the instrument unless the amount paid for the instrument is received by the indorser or applied consistently with the indorsement.

(2) A depositary bank that purchases the instrument or takes it for collection when so indorsed converts the instrument unless the amount paid by the bank with respect to the instrument is received by the indorser or applied consistently with the indorsement.

(3) A payor bank that is also the depositary bank or that takes the instrument for immediate payment over the counter from a person other than a collecting bank converts the instrument unless the proceeds of the instrument are received by the

indorser or applied consistently with the indorsement.

(4) Except as otherwise provided in paragraph (3), a payor bank or intermediary bank may disregard the indorsement and is not liable if the proceeds of the instrument are not received by the indorser or applied consistently with the indorsement.

(d) Except for an indorsement covered by subsection (c), if an instrument bears an indorsement using words to the effect that payment is to be made to the indorsee as agent, trustee, or other fiduciary for the benefit of the indorser or another person, the following rules apply:

(1) Unless there is notice of breach of fiduciary duty as provided in Section 3—307, a person who purchases the instrument from the indorsee or takes the instrument from the indorsee for collection or payment may pay the proceeds of payment or the value given for the instrument to the indorsee without regard to whether the indorsee violates a fiduciary duty to the indorser.

(2) A subsequent transferee of the instrument or person who pays the instrument is neither given notice nor otherwise affected by the restriction in the indorsement unless the transferee or payor knows that the fiduciary dealt with the instrument or its proceeds in breach of fiduciary duty.

(e) The presence on an instrument of an indorsement to which this section applies does not prevent a purchaser of the instrument from becoming a holder in due course of the instrument unless the purchaser is a converter under subsection (c) or has notice or knowledge of breach of fiduciary duty as stated in subsection (d).

(f) In an action to enforce the obligation of a party to pay the instrument, the obligor has a defense if payment would violate an indorsement to which this section applies and the payment is not permitted by this section.

§ 3—207. **Reacquisition.**

Reacquisition of an instrument occurs if it is transferred to a former holder, by negotiation or otherwise. A former holder who reacquires the instrument may cancel indorsements made after the reacquirer first became a holder of the instrument. If the cancellation causes the instrument to be payable to the reacquirer or to bearer, the reacquirer may negotiate the instrument. An indorser whose indorsement is canceled is discharged, and the discharge is effective against any subsequent holder.

Part 3 Enforcement of Instruments

§ 3—301. **Person Entitled to Enforce Instrument.**

"Person entitled to enforce" an instrument means (i) the holder of the instrument, (ii) a nonholder in possession of the instrument who has the rights of a holder, or (iii) a person not in possession of the instrument who is entitled to enforce the instrument pursuant to Section 3—309 or 3—418(d). A person may be a person entitled to enforce the instrument even though the person is not the owner of the instrument or is in wrongful possession of the instrument.

§ 3—302. **Holder in Due Course.**

(a) Subject to subsection (c) and Section 3—106(d), "holder in due course" means the holder of an instrument if:

(1) the instrument when issued or negotiated to the holder does not bear such apparent evidence of forgery or alteration or is not otherwise so irregular or incomplete as to call into question its authenticity; and

(2) the holder took the instrument (i) for value, (ii) in good faith, (iii) without notice that the instrument is overdue or has been dishonored or that there is an uncured default with respect to payment of another instrument issued as part of the same series, (iv) without notice that the instrument contains an unauthorized signature or has been altered, (v) without notice of any claim to the instrument described in Section 3—306, and (vi) without notice that any party has a defense or claim in recoupment described in Section 3—305(a).

(b) Notice of discharge of a party, other than discharge in an insolvency proceeding, is not notice of a defense under subsection (a), but discharge is effective against a person who became a holder in due course with notice of the discharge. Public filing or recording of a document does not of itself constitute notice of a defense, claim in recoupment, or claim to the instrument.

(c) Except to the extent a transferor or predecessor in interest has rights as a holder in due course, a person does not acquire rights of a holder in due course of an instrument taken (i) by legal process or by purchase in an execution, bankruptcy, or creditor's sale or similar proceeding, (ii) by purchase as part of a bulk transaction not in ordinary course of business of the transferor, or (iii) as the successor in interest to an estate or other organization.

(d) If, under Section 3—303(a)(1), the promise of performance that is the consideration for an instrument has been partially performed, the holder may assert rights as a holder in due course of the instrument only to the fraction of the amount payable under the instrument equal to the value of the partial performance divided by the value of the promised performance.

(e) If (i) the person entitled to enforce an instrument has only a security interest in the instrument and (ii) the person obliged to pay the instrument has a defense, claim in recoupment, or claim to the instrument that may be asserted against the person who granted the security interest, the person entitled to enforce the instrument may assert rights as a holder in due course only to an amount payable under the instrument which, at the time of enforcement of the instrument, does not exceed the amount of the unpaid obligation secured.

(f) To be effective, notice must be received at a time and in a manner that gives a reasonable opportunity to act on it.

(g) This section is subject to any law limiting status as a holder in due course in particular classes of transactions.

§ 3—303. **Value and Consideration.**

(a) An instrument is issued or transferred for value if:

(1) the instrument is issued or transferred for a promise of performance, to the extent the promise has been performed;

(2) the transferee acquires a security interest or other lien in the instrument other than a lien obtained by judicial proceeding;

(3) the instrument is issued or transferred as payment of, or as security for, an antecedent claim against any person, whether or not the claim is due;

(4) the instrument is issued or transferred in exchange for a negotiable instrument; or

(5) the instrument is issued or transferred in exchange for the incurring of an irrevocable obligation to a third party by the person taking the instrument.

(b) "Consideration" means any consideration sufficient to support a simple contract. The drawer or maker of an instrument has a defense if the instrument is issued without consideration. If an instrument is issued for a promise of performance, the issuer has a defense to the extent performance of the promise is due and the promise has not been performed. If an instrument is issued for value as stated in subsection (a), the instrument is also issued for consideration.

§ 3—304. Overdue Instrument.

(a) An instrument payable on demand becomes overdue at the earliest of the following times:

> (1) on the day after the day demand for payment is duly made;

> (2) if the instrument is a check, 90 days after its date; or

> (3) if the instrument is not a check, when the instrument has been outstanding for a period of time after its date which is unreasonably long under the circumstances of the particular case in light of the nature of the instrument and usage of the trade.

(b) With respect to an instrument payable at a definite time the following rules apply:

> (1) If the principal is payable in installments and a due date has not been accelerated, the instrument becomes overdue upon default under the instrument for nonpayment of an installment, and the instrument remains overdue until the default is cured.

> (2) If the principal is not payable in installments and the due date has not been accelerated, the instrument becomes overdue on the day after the due date.

> (3) If a due date with respect to principal has been accelerated, the instrument becomes overdue on the day after the accelerated due date.

(c) Unless the due date of principal has been accelerated, an instrument does not become overdue if there is default in payment of interest but no default in payment of principal.

§ 3—305. Defenses and Claims in Recoupment.

(a) Except as stated in subsection (b), the right to enforce the obligation of a party to pay an instrument is subject to the following:

> (1) a defense of the obligor based on (i) infancy of the obligor to the extent it is a defense to a simple contract, (ii) duress, lack of legal capacity, or illegality of the transaction which, under other law, nullifies the obligation of the obligor, (iii) fraud that induced the obligor to sign the instrument with neither knowledge nor reasonable opportunity to learn of its character or its essential terms, or (iv) discharge of the obligor in insolvency proceedings;

> (2) a defense of the obligor stated in another section of this Article or a defense of the obligor that would be available if the person entitled to enforce the instrument were enforcing a right to payment under a simple contract; and

> (3) a claim in recoupment of the obligor against the original payee of the instrument if the claim arose from the transaction that gave rise to the instrument; but the claim of the obligor may be asserted against a transferee of the instrument only to reduce the amount owing on the instrument at the time the action is brought.

(b) The right of a holder in due course to enforce the obligation of a party to pay the instrument is subject to defenses of the obligor stated in subsection (a)(1), but is not subject to defenses of the obligor stated in subsection (a)(2) or claims in recoupment stated in subsection (a)(3) against a person other than the holder.

(c) Except as stated in subsection (d), in an action to enforce the obligation of a party to pay the instrument, the obligor may not assert against the person entitled to enforce the instrument a defense, claim in recoupment, or claim to the instrument (Section 3—306) of another person, but the other person's claim to the instrument may be asserted by the obligor if the other person is joined in the action and personally asserts the claim against the person entitled to enforce the instrument. An obligor is not obliged to pay the instrument if the person seeking enforcement of the instrument does not have rights of a holder in due course and the obligor proves that the instrument is a lost or stolen instrument.

(d) In an action to enforce the obligation of an accommodation party to pay an instrument, the accommodation party may assert against the person entitled to enforce the instrument any defense or claim in recoupment under subsection (a) that the accommodated party could assert against the person entitled to enforce the instrument, except the defenses of discharge in insolvency proceedings, infancy, and lack of legal capacity.

§ 3—306. Claims to an Instrument.

A person taking an instrument, other than a person having rights of a holder in due course, is subject to a claim of a property or possessory right in the instrument or its proceeds, including a claim to rescind a negotiation and to recover the instrument or its proceeds. A person having rights of a holder in due course takes free of the claim to the instrument.

§ 3—307. Notice of Breach of Fiduciary Duty.

(a) In this section:

> (1) "Fiduciary" means an agent, trustee, partner, corporate officer or director, or other representative owing a fiduciary duty with respect to an instrument.

> (2) "Represented person" means the principal, beneficiary, partnership, corporation, or other person to whom the duty stated in paragraph (1) is owed.

(b) If (i) an instrument is taken from a fiduciary for payment or collection or for value, (ii) the taker has knowledge of the fiduciary status of the fiduciary, and (iii) the represented person makes a claim to the instrument or its proceeds on the basis that the transaction of the fiduciary is a breach of fiduciary duty, the following rules apply:

> (1) Notice of breach of fiduciary duty by the fiduciary is notice of the claim of the represented person.

> (2) In the case of an instrument payable to the represented person or the fiduciary as such, the taker has notice of the breach of fiduciary duty if the instrument is (i) taken in payment of or as security for a debt known by the taker to be the personal debt of the fiduciary, (ii) taken in a transaction

known by the taker to be for the personal benefit of the fiduciary, or (iii) deposited to an account other than an account of the fiduciary, as such, or an account of the represented person.

(3) If an instrument is issued by the represented person or the fiduciary as such, and made payable to the fiduciary personally, the taker does not have notice of the breach of fiduciary duty unless the taker knows of the breach of fiduciary duty.

(4) If an instrument is issued by the represented person or the fiduciary as such, to the taker as payee, the taker has notice of the breach of fiduciary duty if the instrument is (i) taken in payment of or as security for a debt known by the taker to be the personal debt of the fiduciary, (ii) taken in a transaction known by the taker to be for the personal benefit of the fiduciary, or (iii) deposited to an account other than an account of the fiduciary, as such, or an account of the represented person.

§ 3—308. Proof of Signatures and Status as Holder in Due Course.

(a) In an action with respect to an instrument, the authenticity of, and authority to make, each signature on the instrument is admitted unless specifically denied in the pleadings. If the validity of a signature is denied in the pleadings, the burden of establishing validity is on the person claiming validity, but the signature is presumed to be authentic and authorized unless the action is to enforce the liability of the purported signer and the signer is dead or incompetent at the time of trial of the issue of validity of the signature. If an action to enforce the instrument is brought against a person as the undisclosed principal of a person who signed the instrument as a party to the instrument, the plaintiff has the burden of establishing that the defendant is liable on the instrument as a represented person under Section 3—402(a).

(b) If the validity of signatures is admitted or proved and there is compliance with subsection (a), a plaintiff producing the instrument is entitled to payment if the plaintiff proves entitlement to enforce the instrument under Section 3—301, unless the defendant proves a defense or claim in recoupment. If a defense or claim in recoupment is proved, the right to payment of the plaintiff is subject to the defense or claim, except to the extent the plaintiff proves that the plaintiff has rights of a holder in due course which are not subject to the defense or claim.

§ 3—309. Enforcement of Lost, Destroyed, or Stolen Instrument.

(a) A person not in possession of an instrument is entitled to enforce the instrument if (i) the person was in possession of the instrument and entitled to enforce it when loss of possession occurred, (ii) the loss of possession was not the result of a transfer by the person or a lawful seizure, and (iii) the person cannot reasonably obtain possession of the instrument because the instrument was destroyed, its whereabouts cannot be determined, or it is in the wrongful possession of an unknown person or a person that cannot be found or is not amenable to service of process.

(b) A person seeking enforcement of an instrument under subsection (a) must prove the terms of the instrument and the person's right to enforce the instrument. If that proof is made, Section 3—308 applies to the case as if the person seeking enforcement had produced the instrument. The court may not enter judgment in favor of the person seeking enforcement unless it finds that the person required to pay the instrument is adequately protected against loss that might occur by reason of a claim by another person to enforce the instrument. Adequate protection may be provided by any reasonable means.

§ 3—310. Effect of Instrument on Obligation for Which Taken.

(a) Unless otherwise agreed, if a certified check, cashier's check, or teller's check is taken for an obligation, the obligation is discharged to the same extent discharge would result if an amount of money equal to the amount of the instrument were taken in payment of the obligation. Discharge of the obligation does not affect any liability that the obligor may have as an indorser of the instrument.

(b) Unless otherwise agreed and except as provided in subsection (a), if a note or an uncertified check is taken for an obligation, the obligation is suspended to the same extent the obligation would be discharged if an amount of money equal to the amount of the instrument were taken, and the following rules apply:

(1) In the case of an uncertified check, suspension of the obligation continues until dishonor of the check or until it is paid or certified. Payment or certification of the check results in discharge of the obligation to the extent of the amount of the check.

(2) In the case of a note, suspension of the obligation continues until dishonor of the note or until it is paid. Payment of the note results in discharge of the obligation to the extent of the payment.

(3) Except as provided in paragraph (4), if the check or note is dishonored and the obligee of the obligation for which the instrument was taken is the person entitled to enforce the instrument, the obligee may enforce either the instrument or the obligation. In the case of an instrument of a third person which is negotiated to the obligee by the obligor, discharge of the obligor on the instrument also discharges the obligation.

(4) If the person entitled to enforce the instrument taken for an obligation is a person other than the obligee, the obligee may not enforce the obligation to the extent the obligation is suspended. If the obligee is the person entitled to enforce the instrument but no longer has possession of it because it was lost, stolen, or destroyed, the obligation may not be enforced to the extent of the amount payable on the instrument, and to that extent the obligee's rights against the obligor are limited to enforcement of the instrument.

(c) If an instrument other than one described in subsection (a) or (b) is taken for an obligation, the effect is (i) that stated in subsection (a) if the instrument is one on which a bank is liable as maker or acceptor, or (ii) that stated in subsection (b) in any other case.

§ 3—311. Accord and Satisfaction by Use of Instrument.

(a) If a person against whom a claim is asserted proves that (i) that person in good faith tendered an instrument to the claimant as full satisfaction of the claim, (ii) the amount of the claim was unliquidated or subject to a bona fide dispute, and (iii) the claimant obtained payment of the instrument, the following subsections apply.

(b) Unless subsection (c) applies, the claim is discharged if the person against whom the claim is asserted proves that the instrument or an accompanying written communication contained a conspicuous statement to the effect that the instrument was tendered as full satisfaction of the claim.

(c) Subject to subsection (d), a claim is not discharged under subsection (b) if either of the following applies:

(1) The claimant, if an organization, proves that (i) within a reasonable time before the tender, the claimant sent a conspicuous statement to the person against whom the claim is asserted that communications concerning disputed debts, including an instrument tendered as full satisfaction of a debt, are to be sent to a designated person, office, or place, and (ii) the instrument or accompanying communication was not received by that designated person, office, or place.

(2) The claimant, whether or not an organization, proves that within 90 days after payment of the instrument, the claimant tendered repayment of the amount of the instrument to the person against whom the claim is asserted. This paragraph does not apply if the claimant is an organization that sent a statement complying with paragraph (1)(i).

(d) A claim is discharged if the person against whom the claim is asserted proves that within a reasonable time before collection of the instrument was initiated, the claimant, or an agent of the claimant having direct responsibility with respect to the disputed obligation, knew that the instrument was tendered in full satisfaction of the claim.

§ 3—312. Lost, Destroyed, or Stolen Cashier's Check, Teller's Check, or Certified Check.

(a) In this section:

(1) "Check" means a cashier's check, teller's check, or certified check.

(2) "Claimant" means a person who claims the right to receive the amount of a cashier's check, teller's check, or certified check that was lost, destroyed, or stolen.

(3) "Declaration of loss" means a written statement, made under penalty of perjury, to the effect that (i) the declarer lost possession of a check, (ii) the declarer is the drawer or payee of the check, in the case of a certified check, or the remitter or payee of the check, in the case of a cashier's check or teller's check, (iii) the loss of possession was not the result of a transfer by the declarer or a lawful seizure, and (iv) the declarer cannot reasonably obtain possession of the check because the check was destroyed, its whereabouts cannot be determined, or it is in the wrongful possession of an unknown person or a person that cannot be found or is not amenable to service of process.

(4) "Obligated bank" means the issuer of a cashier's check or teller's check or the acceptor of a certified check.

(b) A claimant may assert a claim to the amount of a check by a communication to the obligated bank describing the check with reasonable certainty and requesting payment of the amount of the check, if (i) the claimant is the drawer or payee of a certified check or the remitter or payee of a cashier's check or teller's check, (ii) the communication contains or is accompanied by a declaration of loss of the claimant with respect to the check, (iii) the communication is received at a time and in a manner affording the bank a reasonable time to act on it before the check is paid, and (iv) the claimant provides reasonable identification if requested by the obligated bank. Delivery of a declaration of loss is a warranty of the truth of the statements made in the declaration. If a claim

is asserted in compliance with this subsection, the following rules apply:

(1) The claim becomes enforceable at the later of (i) the time the claim is asserted, or (ii) the 90th day following the date of the check, in the case of a cashier's check or teller's check, or the 90th day following the date of the acceptance, in the case of a certified check.

(2) Until the claim becomes enforceable, it has no legal effect and the obligated bank may pay the check or, in the case of a teller's check, may permit the drawee to pay the check. Payment to a person entitled to enforce the check discharges all liability of the obligated bank with respect to the check.

(3) If the claim becomes enforceable before the check is presented for payment, the obligated bank is not obliged to pay the check.

(4) When the claim becomes enforceable, the obligated bank becomes obliged to pay the amount of the check to the claimant if payment of the check has not been made to a person entitled to enforce the check. Subject to Section 4—302(a)(1), payment to the claimant discharges all liability of the obligated bank with respect to the check.

(c) If the obligated bank pays the amount of a check to a claimant under subsection (b)(4) and the check is presented for payment by a person having rights of a holder in due course, the claimant is obliged to (i) refund the payment to the obligated bank if the check is paid, or (ii) pay the amount of the check to the person having rights of a holder in due course if the check is dishonored.

(d) If a claimant has the right to assert a claim under subsection (b) and is also a person entitled to enforce a cashier's check, teller's check, or certified check which is lost, destroyed, or stolen, the claimant may assert rights with respect to the check either under this section or Section 3—309.

Part 4 Liability of Parties

§ 3—401. Signature.

(a) A person is not liable on an instrument unless (i) the person signed the instrument, or (ii) the person is represented by an agent or representative who signed the instrument and the signature is binding on the represented person under Section 3—402.

(b) A signature may be made (i) manually or by means of a device or machine, and (ii) by the use of any name, including a trade or assumed name, or by a word, mark, or symbol executed or adopted by a person with present intention to authenticate a writing.

§ 3—402. Signature by Representative.

(a) If a person acting, or purporting to act, as a representative signs an instrument by signing either the name of the represented person or the name of the signer, the represented person is bound by the signature to the same extent the represented person would be bound if the signature were on a simple contract. If the represented person is bound, the signature of the representative is the "authorized signature of the represented person" and the represented person is liable on the instrument, whether or not identified in the instrument.

(b) If a representative signs the name of the representative to an instrument and the signature is an authorized signature of the represented person, the following rules apply:

(1) If the form of the signature shows unambiguously that the

signature is made on behalf of the represented person who is identified in the instrument, the representative is not liable on the instrument.

(2) Subject to subsection (c), if (i) the form of the signature does not show unambiguously that the signature is made in a representative capacity or (ii) the represented person is not identified in the instrument, the representative is liable on the instrument to a holder in due course that took the instrument without notice that the representative was not intended to be liable on the instrument. With respect to any other person, the representative is liable on the instrument unless the representative proves that the original parties did not intend the representative to be liable on the instrument.

(c) If a representative signs the name of the representative as drawer of a check without indication of the representative status and the check is payable from an account of the represented person who is identified on the check, the signer is not liable on the check if the signature is an authorized signature of the represented person.

§ 3–403. Unauthorized Signature.

(a) Unless otherwise provided in this Article or Article 4, an unauthorized signature is ineffective except as the signature of the unauthorized signer in favor of a person who in good faith pays the instrument or takes it for value. An unauthorized signature may be ratified for all purposes of this Article.

(b) If the signature of more than one person is required to constitute the authorized signature of an organization, the signature of the organization is unauthorized if one of the required signatures is lacking.

(c) The civil or criminal liability of a person who makes an unauthorized signature is not affected by any provision of this Article which makes the unauthorized signature effective for the purposes of this Article.

§ 3–404. Impostors; Fictitious Payees.

(a) If an impostor, by use of the mails or otherwise, induces the issuer of an instrument to issue the instrument to the impostor, or to a person acting in concert with the impostor, by impersonating the payee of the instrument or a person authorized to act for the payee, an indorsement of the instrument by any person in the name of the payee is effective as the indorsement of the payee in favor of a person who, in good faith, pays the instrument or takes it for value or for collection.

(b) If (i) a person whose intent determines to whom an instrument is payable (Section 3–110(a) or (b)) does not intend the person identified as payee to have any interest in the instrument, or (ii) the person identified as payee of an instrument is a fictitious person, the following rules apply until the instrument is negotiated by special indorsement:

(1) Any person in possession of the instrument is its holder.

(2) An indorsement by any person in the name of the payee stated in the instrument is effective as the indorsement of the payee in favor of a person who, in good faith, pays the instrument or takes it for value or for collection.

(c) Under subsection (a) or (b), an indorsement is made in the name of a payee if (i) it is made in a name substantially similar to that of the payee or (ii) the instrument, whether or not indorsed, is deposited in a depositary bank to an account in a name substantially similar to that of the payee.

(d) With respect to an instrument to which subsection (a) or (b) applies, if a person paying the instrument or taking it for value or for collection fails to exercise ordinary care in paying or taking the instrument and that failure substantially contributes to loss resulting from payment of the instrument, the person bearing the loss may recover from the person failing to exercise ordinary care to the extent the failure to exercise ordinary care contributed to the loss.

§ 3–405. Employer's Responsibility for Fraudulent Indorsement by Employee.

(a) In this section:

(1) "Employee" includes an independent contractor and employee of an independent contractor retained by the employer.

(2) "Fraudulent indorsement" means (i) in the case of an instrument payable to the employer, a forged indorsement purporting to be that of the employer, or (ii) in the case of an instrument with respect to which the employer is the issuer, a forged indorsement purporting to be that of the person identified as payee.

(3) "Responsibility" with respect to instruments means authority (i) to sign or indorse instruments on behalf of the employer, (ii) to process instruments received by the employer for bookkeeping purposes, for deposit to an account, or for other disposition, (iii) to prepare or process instruments for issue in the name of the employer, (iv) to supply information determining the names or addresses of payees of instruments to be issued in the name of the employer, (v) to control the disposition of instruments to be issued in the name of the employer, or (vi) to act otherwise with respect to instruments in a responsible capacity. "Responsibility" does not include authority that merely allows an employee to have access to instruments or blank or incomplete instrument forms that are being stored or transported or are part of incoming or outgoing mail, or similar access.

(b) For the purpose of determining the rights and liabilities of a person who, in good faith, pays an instrument or takes it for value or for collection, if an employer entrusted an employee with responsibility with respect to the instrument and the employee or a person acting in concert with the employee makes a fraudulent indorsement of the instrument, the indorsement is effective as the indorsement of the person to whom the instrument is payable if it is made in the name of that person. If the person paying the instrument or taking it for value or for collection fails to exercise ordinary care in paying or taking the instrument and that failure substantially contributes to loss resulting from the fraud, the person bearing the loss may recover from the person failing to exercise ordinary care to the extent the failure to exercise ordinary care contributed to the loss.

(c) Under subsection (b), an indorsement is made in the name of the person to whom an instrument is payable if (i) it is made in a name substantially similar to the name of that person or (ii) the instrument, whether or not indorsed, is deposited in a depositary bank to an account in a name substantially similar to the name of that person.

§ 3–406. Negligence Contributing to Forged Signature or Alteration of Instrument.

(a) A person whose failure to exercise ordinary care substantially contributes to an alteration of an instrument or to the making of a forged signature on an instrument is precluded from asserting the alteration or the forgery against a person who, in good faith, pays the instrument or takes it for value or for collection.

(b) Under subsection (a), if the person asserting the preclusion fails to exercise ordinary care in paying or taking the instrument and that failure substantially contributes to loss, the loss is allocated between the person precluded and the person asserting the preclusion according to the extent to which the failure of each to exercise ordinary care contributed to the loss.

(c) Under subsection (a), the burden of proving failure to exercise ordinary care is on the person asserting the preclusion. Under subsection (b), the burden of proving failure to exercise ordinary care is on the person precluded.

§ 3—407. Alteration.

(a) "Alteration" means (i) an unauthorized change in an instrument that purports to modify in any respect the obligation of a party, or (ii) an unauthorized addition of words or numbers or other change to an incomplete instrument relating to the obligation of a party.

(b) Except as provided in subsection (c), an alteration fraudulently made discharges a party whose obligation is affected by the alteration unless that party assents or is precluded from asserting the alteration. No other alteration discharges a party, and the instrument may be enforced according to its original terms.

(c) A payor bank or drawee paying a fraudulently altered instrument or a person taking it for value, in good faith and without notice of the alteration, may enforce rights with respect to the instrument (i) according to its original terms, or (ii) in the case of an incomplete instrument altered by unauthorized completion, according to its terms as completed.

§ 3—408. Drawee Not Liable on Unaccepted Draft.

A check or other draft does not of itself operate as an assignment of funds in the hands of the drawee available for its payment, and the drawee is not liable on the instrument until the drawee accepts it.

§ 3—409. Acceptance of Draft; Certified Check.

(a) "Acceptance" means the drawee's signed agreement to pay a draft as presented. It must be written on the draft and may consist of the drawee's signature alone. Acceptance may be made at any time and becomes effective when notification pursuant to instructions is given or the accepted draft is delivered for the purpose of giving rights on the acceptance to any person.

(b) A draft may be accepted although it has not been signed by the drawer, is otherwise incomplete, is overdue, or has been dishonored.

(c) If a draft is payable at a fixed period after sight and the acceptor fails to date the acceptance, the holder may complete the acceptance by supplying a date in good faith.

(d) "Certified check" means a check accepted by the bank on which it is drawn. Acceptance may be made as stated in subsection (a) or by a writing on the check which indicates that the check is certified. The drawee of a check has no obligation to certify the check, and refusal to certify is not dishonor of the check.

§ 3—410. Acceptance Varying Draft.

(a) If the terms of a drawee's acceptance vary from the terms of the draft as presented, the holder may refuse the acceptance and treat the draft as dishonored. In that case, the drawee may cancel the acceptance.

(b) The terms of a draft are not varied by an acceptance to pay at a particular bank or place in the United States, unless the acceptance states that the draft is to be paid only at that bank or place.

(c) If the holder assents to an acceptance varying the terms of a draft, the obligation of each drawer and indorser that does not expressly assent to the acceptance is discharged.

§ 3—411. Refusal to Pay Cashier's Checks, Teller's Checks, and Certified Checks.

(a) In this section, "obligated bank" means the acceptor of a certified check or the issuer of a cashier's check or teller's check bought from the issuer.

(b) If the obligated bank wrongfully (i) refuses to pay a cashier's check or certified check, (ii) stops payment of a teller's check, or (iii) refuses to pay a dishonored teller's check, the person asserting the right to enforce the check is entitled to compensation for expenses and loss of interest resulting from the nonpayment and may recover consequential damages if the obligated bank refuses to pay after receiving notice of particular circumstances giving rise to the damages.

(c) Expenses or consequential damages under subsection (b) are not recoverable if the refusal of the obligated bank to pay occurs because (i) the bank suspends payments, (ii) the obligated bank asserts a claim or defense of the bank that it has reasonable grounds to believe is available against the person entitled to enforce the instrument, (iii) the obligated bank has a reasonable doubt whether the person demanding payment is the person entitled to enforce the instrument, or (iv) payment is prohibited by law.

§ 3—412. Obligation of Issuer of Note or Cashier's Check.

The issuer of a note or cashier's check or other draft drawn on the drawer is obliged to pay the instrument (i) according to its terms at the time it was issued or, if not issued, at the time it first came into possession of a holder, or (ii) if the issuer signed an incomplete instrument, according to its terms when completed, to the extent stated in Sections 3—115 and 3—407. The obligation is owed to a person entitled to enforce the instrument or to an indorser who paid the instrument under Section 3—415.

§ 3—413. Obligation of Acceptor.

(a) The acceptor of a draft is obliged to pay the draft (i) according to its terms at the time it was accepted, even though the acceptance states that the draft is payable "as originally drawn" or equivalent terms, (ii) if the acceptance varies the terms of the draft, according to the terms of the draft as varied, or (iii) if the acceptance is of a draft that is an incomplete instrument, according to its terms when completed, to the extent stated in Sections 3—115 and 3—407. The obligation is owed to a person entitled to enforce the draft or to the drawer or an indorser who paid the draft under Section 3—414 or 3—415.

(b) If the certification of a check or other acceptance of a draft states the amount certified or accepted, the obligation of the acceptor is that amount. If (i) the certification or acceptance does not state an amount, (ii) the amount of the instrument is subsequently raised, and (iii) the instrument is then negotiated to a holder in due course, the obligation of the acceptor is the amount of the instrument at the time it was taken by the holder in due course.

§ 3—414. Obligation of Drawer.

(a) This section does not apply to cashier's checks or other drafts drawn on the drawer.

(b) If an unaccepted draft is dishonored, the drawer is obliged to pay the draft (i) according to its terms at the time it was issued or, if not issued, at the time it first came into possession of a holder, or (ii) if the drawer signed an incomplete instrument, according to its terms when completed, to the extent stated in Sections 3—115 and 3—407. The obligation is owed to a person entitled to enforce the draft or to an indorser who paid the draft under Section 3—415.

(c) If a draft is accepted by a bank, the drawer is discharged, regardless of when or by whom acceptance was obtained.

(d) If a draft is accepted and the acceptor is not a bank, the obligation of the drawer to pay the draft if the draft is dishonored by the acceptor is the same as the obligation of an indorser under Section 3—415(a) and (c).

(e) If a draft states that it is drawn "without recourse" or otherwise disclaims liability of the drawer to pay the draft, the drawer is not liable under subsection (b) to pay the draft if the draft is not a check. A disclaimer of the liability stated in subsection (b) is not effective if the draft is a check.

(f) If (i) a check is not presented for payment or given to a depositary bank for collection within 30 days after its date, (ii) the drawee suspends payments after expiration of the 30-day period without paying the check, and (iii) because of the suspension of payments, the drawer is deprived of funds maintained with the drawee to cover payment of the check, the drawer to the extent deprived of funds may discharge its obligation to pay the check by assigning to the person entitled to enforce the check the rights of the drawer against the drawee with respect to the funds.

§ 3—415. Obligation of Indorser.

(a) Subject to subsections (b), (c), and (d) and to Section 3—419(d), if an instrument is dishonored, an indorser is obliged to pay the amount due on the instrument (i) according to the terms of the instrument at the time it was indorsed, or (ii) if the indorser indorsed an incomplete instrument, according to its terms when completed, to the extent stated in Sections 3—115 and 3—407. The obligation of the indorser is owed to a person entitled to enforce the instrument or to a subsequent indorser who paid the instrument under this section.

(b) If an indorsement states that it is made "without recourse" or otherwise disclaims liability of the indorser, the indorser is not liable under subsection (a) to pay the instrument.

(c) If notice of dishonor of an instrument is required by Section 3—503 and notice of dishonor complying with that section is not given to an indorser, the liability of the indorser under subsection (a) is discharged.

(d) If a draft is accepted by a bank after an indorsement is made, the liability of the indorser under subsection (a) is discharged.

(e) If an indorser of a check is liable under subsection (a) and the check is not presented for payment, or given to a depositary bank for collection, within 30 days after the day the indorsement was made, the liability of the indorser under subsection (a) is discharged.

§ 3—416. Transfer Warranties.

(a) A person who transfers an instrument for consideration warrants to the transferee and, if the transfer is by indorsement, to any subsequent transferee that:

(1) the warrantor is a person entitled to enforce the instrument;

(2) all signatures on the instrument are authentic and authorized;

(3) the instrument has not been altered;

(4) the instrument is not subject to a defense or claim in recoupment of any party which can be asserted against the warrantor; and

(5) the warrantor has no knowledge of any insolvency proceeding commenced with respect to the maker or acceptor or, in the case of an unaccepted draft, the drawer.

(b) A person to whom the warranties under subsection (a) are made and who took the instrument in good faith may recover from the warrantor as damages for breach of warranty an amount equal to the loss suffered as a result of the breach, but not more than the amount of the instrument plus expenses and loss of interest incurred as a result of the breach.

(c) The warranties stated in subsection (a) cannot be disclaimed with respect to checks. Unless notice of a claim for breach of warranty is given to the warrantor within 30 days after the claimant has reason to know of the breach and the identity of the warrantor, the liability of the warrantor under subsection (b) is discharged to the extent of any loss caused by the delay in giving notice of the claim.

(d) A [cause of action] for breach of warranty under this section accrues when the claimant has reason to know of the breach.

§ 3—417. Presentment Warranties.

(a) If an unaccepted draft is presented to the drawee for payment or acceptance and the drawee pays or accepts the draft, (i) the person obtaining payment or acceptance, at the time of presentment, and (ii) a previous transferor of the draft, at the time of transfer, warrant to the drawee making payment or accepting the draft in good faith that:

(1) the warrantor is, or was, at the time the warrantor transferred the draft, a person entitled to enforce the draft or authorized to obtain payment or acceptance of the draft on behalf of a person entitled to enforce the draft;

(2) the draft has not been altered; and

(3) the warrantor has no knowledge that the signature of the drawer of the draft is unauthorized.

(b) A drawee making payment may recover from any warrantor damages for breach of warranty equal to the amount paid by the drawee less the amount the drawee received or is entitled to receive from the drawer because of the payment. In addition, the drawee is entitled to compensation for expenses and loss of interest resulting from the breach. The right of the drawee to recover damages under this subsection is not affected by any failure of the drawee to exercise ordinary care in making payment. If the drawee accepts the draft, breach of warranty is a defense to the obligation of the acceptor. If the acceptor makes payment with respect to the draft, the acceptor is entitled to recover from any warrantor for breach of warranty the amounts stated in this subsection.

(c) If a drawee asserts a claim for breach of warranty under subsection (a) based on an unauthorized indorsement of the draft or an alteration of the draft, the warrantor may defend by proving that the indorsement is effective under Section 3—404 or 3—405 or the drawer is precluded under Section 3—406 or 4—406 from asserting against the drawee the unauthorized indorsement or alteration.

(d) If (i) a dishonored draft is presented for payment to the drawer or an indorser or (ii) any other instrument is presented for payment to a party obliged to pay the instrument, and (iii) payment is received, the following rules apply:

> (1) The person obtaining payment and a prior transferor of the instrument warrant to the person making payment in good faith that the warrantor is, or was, at the time the warrantor transferred the instrument, a person entitled to enforce the instrument or authorized to obtain payment on behalf of a person entitled to enforce the instrument.

> (2) The person making payment may recover from any warrantor for breach of warranty an amount equal to the amount paid plus expenses and loss of interest resulting from the breach.

(e) The warranties stated in subsections (a) and (d) cannot be disclaimed with respect to checks. Unless notice of a claim for breach of warranty is given to the warrantor within 30 days after the claimant has reason to know of the breach and the identity of the warrantor, the liability of the warrantor under subsection (b) or (d) is discharged to the extent of any loss caused by the delay in giving notice of the claim.

(f) A [cause of action] for breach of warranty under this section accrues when the claimant has reason to know of the breach.

§ 3—418. Payment or Acceptance by Mistake.

(a) Except as provided in subsection (c), if the drawee of a draft pays or accepts the draft and the drawee acted on the mistaken belief that (i) payment of the draft had not been stopped pursuant to Section 4—403 or (ii) the signature of the drawer of the draft was authorized, the drawee may recover the amount of the draft from the person to whom or for whose benefit payment was made or, in the case of acceptance, may revoke the acceptance. Rights of the drawee under this subsection are not affected by failure of the drawee to exercise ordinary care in paying or accepting the draft.

(b) Except as provided in subsection (c), if an instrument has been paid or accepted by mistake and the case is not covered by subsection (a), the person paying or accepting may, to the extent permitted by the law governing mistake and restitution, (i) recover the payment from the person to whom or for whose benefit payment was made or (ii) in the case of acceptance, may revoke the acceptance.

(c) The remedies provided by subsection (a) or (b) may not be asserted against a person who took the instrument in good faith and for value or who in good faith changed position in reliance on the payment or acceptance. This subsection does not limit remedies provided by Section 3—417 or 4—407.

(d) Notwithstanding Section 4—215, if an instrument is paid or accepted by mistake and the payor or acceptor recovers payment or revokes acceptance under subsection (a) or (b), the instrument is deemed not to have been paid or accepted and is treated as dishonored, and the person from whom payment is recovered has rights as a person entitled to enforce the dishonored instrument.

§ 3—419. Instruments Signed for Accommodation.

(a) If an instrument is issued for value given for the benefit of a party to the instrument ("accommodated party") and another party to the instrument ("accommodation party") signs the instrument for the purpose of incurring liability on the instrument without being a direct beneficiary of the value given for the instrument, the instrument is signed by the accommodation party "for accommodation."

(b) An accommodation party may sign the instrument as maker, drawer, acceptor, or indorser and, subject to subsection (d), is obliged to pay the instrument in the capacity in which the accommodation party signs. The obligation of an accommodation party may be enforced notwithstanding any statute of frauds and whether or not the accommodation party receives consideration for the accommodation.

(c) A person signing an instrument is presumed to be an accommodation party and there is notice that the instrument is signed for accommodation if the signature is an anomalous indorsement or is accompanied by words indicating that the signer is acting as surety or guarantor with respect to the obligation of another party to the instrument. Except as provided in Section 3—605, the obligation of an accommodation party to pay the instrument is not affected by the fact that the person enforcing the obligation had notice when the instrument was taken by that person that the accommodation party signed the instrument for accommodation.

(d) If the signature of a party to an instrument is accompanied by words indicating unambiguously that the party is guaranteeing collection rather than payment of the obligation of another party to the instrument, the signer is obliged to pay the amount due on the instrument to a person entitled to enforce the instrument only if (i) execution of judgment against the other party has been returned unsatisfied, (ii) the other party is insolvent or in an insolvency proceeding, (iii) the other party cannot be served with process, or (iv) it is otherwise apparent that payment cannot be obtained from the other party.

(e) An accommodation party who pays the instrument is entitled to reimbursement from the accommodated party and is entitled to enforce the instrument against the accommodated party. An accommodated party who pays the instrument has no right of recourse against, and is not entitled to contribution from, an accommodation party.

§ 3—420. Conversion of Instrument.

(a) The law applicable to conversion of personal property applies to instruments. An instrument is also converted if it is taken by transfer, other than a negotiation, from a person not entitled to enforce the instrument or a bank makes or obtains payment with respect to the instrument for a person not entitled to enforce the instrument or receive payment. An action for conversion of an instrument may not be brought by (i) the issuer or acceptor of the instrument or (ii) a payee or indorsee who did not receive delivery of the instrument either directly or through delivery to an agent or a co-payee.

(b) In an action under subsection (a), the measure of liability is presumed to be the amount payable on the instrument, but recovery may not exceed the amount of the plaintiff's interest in the instrument.

(c) A representative, other than a depository bank, who has in good faith dealt with an instrument or its proceeds on behalf of one who was not the person entitled to enforce the instrument is not liable in conversion to that person beyond the amount of any proceeds that it has not paid out.

Part 5 Dishonor

§ 3–501. **Presentment.**

(a) "Presentment" means a demand made by or on behalf of a person entitled to enforce an instrument (i) to pay the instrument made to the drawee or a party obliged to pay the instrument or, in the case of a note or accepted draft payable at a bank, to the bank, or (ii) to accept a draft made to the drawee.

(b) The following rules are subject to Article 4, agreement of the parties, and clearing-house rules and the like:

(1) Presentment may be made at the place of payment of the instrument and must be made at the place of payment if the instrument is payable at a bank in the United States; may be made by any commercially reasonable means, including an oral, written, or electronic communication; is effective when the demand for payment or acceptance is received by the person to whom presentment is made; and is effective if made to any one of two or more makers, acceptors, drawees, or other payors.

(2) Upon demand of the person to whom presentment is made, the person making presentment must (i) exhibit the instrument, (ii) give reasonable identification and, if presentment is made on behalf of another person, reasonable evidence of authority to do so, and (. . .) sign a receipt on the instrument for any payment made or surrender the instrument if full payment is made.

(3) Without dishonoring the instrument, the party to whom presentment is made may (i) return the instrument for lack of a necessary indorsement, or (ii) refuse payment or acceptance for failure of the presentment to comply with the terms of the instrument, an agreement of the parties, or other applicable law or rule.

(4) The party to whom presentment is made may treat presentment as occurring on the next business day after the day of presentment if the party to whom presentment is made has established a cut-off hour not earlier than 2 P.M. for the receipt and processing of instruments presented for payment or acceptance and presentment is made after the cut-off hour.

§ 3–502. **Dishonor.**

(a) Dishonor of a note is governed by the following rules:

(1) If the note is payable on demand, the note is dishonored if presentment is duly made to the maker and the note is not paid on the day of presentment.

(2) If the note is not payable on demand and is payable at or through a bank or the terms of the note require presentment, the note is dishonored if presentment is duly made and the note is not paid on the day it becomes payable or the day of presentment, whichever is later.

(3) If the note is not payable on demand and paragraph (2) does not apply, the note is dishonored if it is not paid on the day it becomes payable.

(b) Dishonor of an unaccepted draft other than a documentary draft is governed by the following rules:

(1) If a check is duly presented for payment to the payor bank otherwise than for immediate payment over the counter, the check is dishonored if the payor bank makes timely return of the check or sends timely notice of dishonor or nonpayment under Section 4–301 or 4–302, or becomes accountable for the amount of the check under Section 4–302.

(2) If a draft is payable on demand and paragraph (1) does not apply, the draft is dishonored if presentment for payment is duly made to the drawee and the draft is not paid on the day of presentment.

(3) If a draft is payable on a date stated in the draft, the draft is dishonored if (i) presentment for payment is duly made to the drawee and payment is not made on the day the draft becomes payable or the day of presentment, whichever is later, or (ii) presentment for acceptance is duly made before the day the draft becomes payable and the draft is not accepted on the day of presentment.

(4) If a draft is payable on elapse of a period of time after sight or acceptance, the draft is dishonored if presentment for acceptance is duly made and the draft is not accepted on the day of presentment.

(c) Dishonor of an unaccepted documentary draft occurs according to the rules stated in subsection (b)(2), (3), and (4), except that payment or acceptance may be delayed without dishonor until no later than the close of the third business day of the drawee following the day on which payment or acceptance is required by those paragraphs.

(d) Dishonor of an accepted draft is governed by the following rules:

(1) If the draft is payable on demand, the draft is dishonored if presentment for payment is duly made to the acceptor and the draft is not paid on the day of presentment.

(2) If the draft is not payable on demand, the draft is dishonored if presentment for payment is duly made to the acceptor and payment is not made on the day it becomes payable or the day of presentment, whichever is later.

(e) In any case in which presentment is otherwise required for dishonor under this section and presentment is excused under Section 3–504, dishonor occurs without presentment if the instrument is not duly accepted or paid.

(f) If a draft is dishonored because timely acceptance of the draft was not made and the person entitled to demand acceptance consents to a late acceptance, from the time of acceptance the draft is treated as never having been dishonored.

§ 3–503. **Notice of Dishonor.**

(a) The obligation of an indorser stated in Section 3–415(a) and the obligation of a drawer stated in Section 3–414(d) may not be enforced unless (i) the indorser or drawer is given notice of dishonor of the instrument complying with this section or (ii) notice of dishonor is excused under Section 3–504(b).

(b) Notice of dishonor may be given by any person; may be given by any commercially reasonable means, including an oral, written, or electronic communication; and is sufficient if it reasonably identifies the instrument and indicates that the instrument has been dishonored or has not been paid or accepted. Return of an instrument given to a bank for collection is sufficient notice of dishonor.

(c) Subject to Section 3—504(c), with respect to an instrument taken for collection by a collecting bank, notice of dishonor must be given (i) by the bank before midnight of the next banking day following the banking day on which the bank receives notice of dishonor of the instrument, or (ii) by any other person within 30 days following the day on which the person receives notice of dishonor. With respect to any other instrument, notice of dishonor must be given within 30 days following the day on which dishonor occurs.

§ 3—504. Excused Presentment and Notice of Dishonor.

(a) Presentment for payment or acceptance of an instrument is excused if (i) the person entitled to present the instrument cannot with reasonable diligence make presentment, (ii) the maker or acceptor has repudiated an obligation to pay the instrument or is dead or in insolvency proceedings, (iii) by the terms of the instrument presentment is not necessary to enforce the obligation of indorsers or the drawer, (iv) the drawer or indorser whose obligation is being enforced has waived presentment or otherwise has no reason to expect or right to require that the instrument be paid or accepted, or (v) the drawer instructed the drawee not to pay or accept the draft or the drawee was not obligated to the drawer to pay the draft.

(b) Notice of dishonor is excused if (i) by the terms of the instrument notice of dishonor is not necessary to enforce the obligation of a party to pay the instrument, or (ii) the party whose obligation is being enforced waived notice of dishonor. A waiver of presentment is also a waiver of notice of dishonor.

(c) Delay in giving notice of dishonor is excused if the delay was caused by circumstances beyond the control of the person giving the notice and the person giving the notice exercised reasonable diligence after the cause of the delay ceased to operate.

§ 3—505. Evidence of Dishonor.

(a) The following are admissible as evidence and create a presumption of dishonor and of any notice of dishonor stated:

   (1) a document regular in form as provided in subsection (b) which purports to be a protest;

   (2) a purported stamp or writing of the drawee, payor bank, or presenting bank on or accompanying the instrument stating that acceptance or payment has been refused unless reasons for the refusal are stated and the reasons are not consistent with dishonor;

   (3) a book or record of the drawee, payor bank, or collecting bank, kept in the usual course of business which shows dishonor, even if there is no evidence of who made the entry.

(b) A protest is a certificate of dishonor made by a United States consul or vice consul, or a notary public or other person authorized to administer oaths by the law of the place where dishonor occurs. It may be made upon information satisfactory to that person. The protest must identify the instrument and certify either that presentment has been made or, if not made, the reason why it was not made, and that the instrument has been dishonored by nonacceptance or nonpayment. The protest may also certify that notice of dishonor has been given to some or all parties.

Part 6 Discharge and Payment

§ 3—601. Discharge and Effect of Discharge.

(a) The obligation of a party to pay the instrument is discharged as stated in this Article or by an act or agreement with the party which would discharge an obligation to pay money under a simple contract.

(b) Discharge of the obligation of a party is not effective against a person acquiring rights of a holder in due course of the instrument without notice of the discharge.

§ 3—602. Payment.

(a) Subject to subsection (b), an instrument is paid to the extent payment is made (i) by or on behalf of a party obliged to pay the instrument, and (ii) to a person entitled to enforce the instrument. To the extent of the payment, the obligation of the party obliged to pay the instrument is discharged even though payment is made with knowledge of a claim to the instrument under Section 3—306 by another person.

(b) The obligation of a party to pay the instrument is not discharged under subsection (a) if:

   (1) a claim to the instrument under Section 3—306 is enforceable against the party receiving payment and (i) payment is made with knowledge by the payor that payment is prohibited by injunction or similar process of a court of competent jurisdiction, or (ii) in the case of an instrument other than a cashier's check, teller's check, or certified check, the party making payment accepted, from the person having a claim to the instrument, indemnity against loss resulting from refusal to pay the person entitled to enforce the instrument; or

   (2) the person making payment knows that the instrument is a stolen instrument and pays a person it knows is in wrongful possession of the instrument.

§ 3—603. Tender of Payment.

(a) If tender of payment of an obligation to pay an instrument is made to a person entitled to enforce the instrument, the effect of tender is governed by principles of law applicable to tender of payment under a simple contract.

(b) If tender of payment of an obligation to pay an instrument is made to a person entitled to enforce the instrument and the tender is refused, there is discharge, to the extent of the amount of the tender, of the obligation of an indorser or accommodation party having a right of recourse with respect to the obligation to which the tender relates.

(c) If tender of payment of an amount due on an instrument is made to a person entitled to enforce the instrument, the obligation of the obligor to pay interest after the due date on the amount tendered is discharged. If presentment is required with respect to an instrument and the obligor is able and ready to pay on the due date at every place of payment stated in the instrument, the obligor is deemed to have made tender of payment on the due date to the person entitled to enforce the instrument.

§ 3—604. Discharge by Cancellation or Renunciation.

(a) A person entitled to enforce an instrument, with or without consideration, may discharge the obligation of a party to pay the instrument (i) by an intentional voluntary act, such as surrender of the instrument to the party, destruction, mutilation, or cancellation of the instrument, cancellation or striking out of the party's signature, or the addition of words to the instrument indicating discharge, or (ii) by agreeing not to sue or otherwise renouncing rights against the party by a signed writing.

(b) Cancellation or striking out of an indorsement pursuant to subsection (a) does not affect the status and rights of a party derived from the indorsement.

§ 3—605. Discharge of Indorsers and Accommodation Parties.

(a) In this section, the term "indorser" includes a drawer having the obligation described in Section 3—414(d).

(b) Discharge, under Section 3—604, of the obligation of a party to pay an instrument does not discharge the obligation of an indorser or accommodation party having a right of recourse against the discharged party.

(c) If a person entitled to enforce an instrument agrees, with or without consideration, to an extension of the due date of the obligation of a party to pay the instrument, the extension discharges an indorser or accommodation party having a right of recourse against the party whose obligation is extended to the extent the indorser or accommodation party proves that the extension caused loss to the indorser or accommodation party with respect to the right of recourse.

(d) If a person entitled to enforce an instrument agrees, with or without consideration, to a material modification of the obligation of a party other than an extension of the due date, the modification discharges the obligation of an indorser or accommodation party having a right of recourse against the person whose obligation is modified to the extent the modification causes loss to the indorser or accommodation party with respect to the right of recourse. The loss suffered by the indorser or accommodation party as a result of the modification is equal to the amount of the right of recourse unless the person enforcing the instrument proves that no loss was caused by the modification or that the loss caused by the modification was an amount less than the amount of the right of recourse.

(e) If the obligation of a party to pay an instrument is secured by an interest in collateral and a person entitled to enforce the instrument impairs the value of the interest in collateral, the obligation of an indorser or accommodation party having a right of recourse against the obligor is discharged to the extent of the impairment. The value of an interest in collateral is impaired to the extent (i) the value of the interest is reduced to an amount less than the amount of the right of recourse of the party asserting discharge, or (ii) the reduction in value of the interest causes an increase in the amount by which the amount of the right of recourse exceeds the value of the interest. The burden of proving impairment is on the party asserting discharge.

(f) If the obligation of a party is secured by an interest in collateral not provided by an accommodation party and a person entitled to enforce the instrument impairs the value of the interest in collateral, the obligation of any party who is jointly and severally liable with respect to the secured obligation is discharged to the extent the impairment causes the party asserting discharge to pay more than that party would have been obliged to pay, taking into account rights of contribution, if impairment had not occurred. If the party asserting discharge is an accommodation party not entitled to discharge under subsection (e), the party is deemed to have a right to contribution based on joint and several liability rather than a right to reimbursement. The burden of proving impairment is on the party asserting discharge.

(g) Under subsection (e) or (f), impairing value of an interest in collateral includes (i) failure to obtain or maintain perfection or recordation of the interest in collateral, (ii) release of collateral without substitution of collateral of equal value, (iii) failure to perform a duty to preserve the value of collateral owed, under Article 9 or other law, to a debtor or surety or other person secondarily liable, or (iv) failure to comply with applicable law in disposing of collateral.

(h) An accommodation party is not discharged under subsection (c), (d), or (e) unless the person entitled to enforce the instrument knows of the accommodation or has notice under Section 3—419(c) that the instrument was signed for accommodation.

(i) A party is not discharged under this section if (i) the party asserting discharge consents to the event or conduct that is the basis of the discharge, or (ii) the instrument or a separate agreement of the party provides for waiver of discharge under this section either specifically or by general language indicating that parties waive defenses based on suretyship or impairment of collateral.

ADDENDUM TO REVISED ARTICLE 3

Notes to Legislative Counsel

1. If revised Article 3 is adopted in your state, the reference in Section 2—511 to Section 3—802 should be changed to Section 3—310.

2. If revised Article 3 is adopted in your state and the Uniform Fiduciaries Act is also in effect in your state, you may want to consider amending Uniform Fiduciaries Act § 9 to conform to Section 3—307(b)(2)(iii) and (4)(iii). See Official Comment 3 to Section 3—307.

Revised Article 4
BANK DEPOSITS AND COLLECTIONS

Part 1 General Provisions and Definitions

§ 4—101. Short Title.

This Article may be cited as Uniform Commercial Code—Bank Deposits and Collections.

§ 4—102. Applicability.

(a) To the extent that items within this Article are also within Articles 3 and 8, they are subject to those Articles. If there is conflict, this Article governs Article 3, but Article 8 governs this Article.

(b) The liability of a bank for action or non-action with respect to an item handled by it for purposes of presentment, payment, or collection is governed by the law of the place where the bank is located. In the case of action or non-action by or at a branch or separate office of a bank, its liability is governed by the law of the place where the branch or separate office is located.

§ 4—103. Variation by Agreement; Measure of Damages; Action Constituting Ordinary Care.

(a) The effect of the provisions of this Article may be varied by agreement, but the parties to the agreement cannot disclaim a bank's responsibility for its lack of good faith or failure to exercise ordinary care or limit the measure of damages for the lack or failure. However, the parties may determine by agreement the standards by which the bank's responsibility is to be measured if those standards are not manifestly unreasonable.

(b) Federal Reserve regulations and operating circulars, clearing-house rules, and the like have the effect of agreements under subsection (a), whether or not specifically assented to by all parties interested in items handled.

(c) Action or non-action approved by this Article or pursuant to Federal Reserve regulations or operating circulars is the exercise of ordinary care and, in the absence of special instructions, action or non-action consistent with clearing-house rules and the like or with a general banking usage not disapproved by this Article, is prima facie the exercise of ordinary care.

(d) The specification or approval of certain procedures by this Article is not disapproval of other procedures that may be reasonable under the circumstances.

(e) The measure of damages for failure to exercise ordinary care in handling an item is the amount of the item reduced by an amount that could not have been realized by the exercise of ordinary care. If there is also bad faith it includes any other damages the party suffered as a proximate consequence.

§ 4—104. Definitions and Index of Definitions.

(a) In this Article, unless the context otherwise requires:

(1) "Account" means any deposit or credit account with a bank, including a demand, time, savings, passbook, share draft, or like account, other than an account evidenced by a certificate of deposit;

(2) "Afternoon" means the period of a day between noon and midnight;

(3) "Banking day" means the part of a day on which a bank is open to the public for carrying on substantially all of its banking functions;

(4) "Clearing house" means an association of banks or other payors regularly clearing items;

(5) "Customer" means a person having an account with a bank or for whom a bank has agreed to collect items, including a bank that maintains an account at another bank;

(6) "Documentary draft" means a draft to be presented for acceptance or payment if specified documents, certificated securities (Section 8—102) or instructions for uncertificated securities (Section 8—102), or other certificates, statements, or the like are to be received by the drawee or other payor before acceptance or payment of the draft;

(7) "Draft" means a draft as defined in Section 3—104 or an item, other than an instrument, that is an order;

(8) "Drawee" means a person ordered in a draft to make payment;

(9) "Item" means an instrument or a promise or order to pay money handled by a bank for collection or payment. The term does not include a payment order governed by Article 4A or a credit or debit card slip;

(10) "Midnight deadline" with respect to a bank is midnight on its next banking day following the banking day on which it receives the relevant item or notice or from which the time for taking action commences to run, whichever is later;

(11) "Settle" means to pay in cash, by clearing-house settlement, in a charge or credit or by remittance, or otherwise as agreed. A settlement may be either provisional or final;

(12) "Suspends payments" with respect to a bank means that it has been closed by order of the supervisory authorities, that a public officer has been appointed to take it over, or that it ceases or refuses to make payments in the ordinary course of business.

(b);(c) [Other definitions' section references deleted.]

(d) In addition, Article 1 contains general definitions and principles of construction and interpretation applicable throughout this Article.

§ 4—105. "Bank"; "Depositary Bank"; "Payor Bank"; "Intermediary Bank"; "Collecting Bank"; "Presenting Bank".

In this Article:

(1) "Bank" means a person engaged in the business of banking, including a savings bank, savings and loan association, credit union, or trust company;

(2) "Depositary bank" means the first bank to take an item even though it is also the payor bank, unless the item is presented for immediate payment over the counter;

(3) "Payor bank" means a bank that is the drawee of a draft;

(4) "Intermediary bank" means a bank to which an item is transferred in course of collection except the depositary or payor bank;

(5) "Collecting bank" means a bank handling an item for collection except the payor bank;

(6) "Presenting bank" means a bank presenting an item except a payor bank.

§ 4—106. Payable Through or Payable at Bank: Collecting Bank.

(a) If an item states that it is "payable through" a bank identified in the item, (i) the item designates the bank as a collecting bank and does not by itself authorize the bank to pay the item, and (ii) the item may be presented for payment only by or through the bank.

Alternative A

(b) If an item states that it is "payable at" a bank identified in the item, the item is equivalent to a draft drawn on the bank.

Alternative B

(b) If an item states that it is "payable at" a bank identified in the item, (i) the item designates the bank as a collecting bank and does not by itself authorize the bank to pay the item, and (ii) the item may be presented for payment only by or through the bank.

(c) If a draft names a nonbank drawee and it is unclear whether a bank named in the draft is a co-drawee or a collecting bank, the bank is a collecting bank.

§ 4—107. Separate Office of Bank.

A branch or separate office of a bank is a separate bank for the purpose of computing the time within which and determining the place at or to which action may be taken or notices or orders shall be given under this Article and under Article 3.

§ 4—108. **Time of Receipt of Items.**

(a) For the purpose of allowing time to process items, prove balances, and make the necessary entries on its books to determine its position for the day, a bank may fix an afternoon hour of 2 P.M. or later as a cutoff hour for the handling of money and items and the making of entries on its books.

(b) An item or deposit of money received on any day after a cutoff hour so fixed or after the close of the banking day may be treated as being received at the opening of the next banking day.

§ 4—109. **Delays.**

(a) Unless otherwise instructed, a collecting bank in a good faith effort to secure payment of a specific item drawn on a payor other than a bank, and with or without the approval of any person involved, may waive, modify, or extend time limits imposed or permitted by this [act] for a period not exceeding two additional banking days without discharge of drawers or indorsers or liability to its transferor or a prior party.

(b) Delay by a collecting bank or payor bank beyond time limits prescribed or permitted by this [act] or by instructions is excused if (i) the delay is caused by interruption of communication or computer facilities, suspension of payments by another bank, war, emergency conditions, failure of equipment, or other circumstances beyond the control of the bank, and (ii) the bank exercises such diligence as the circumstances require.

§ 4—110. **Electronic Presentment.**

(a) "Agreement for electronic presentment" means an agreement, clearing-house rule, or Federal Reserve regulation or operating circular, providing that presentment of an item may be made by transmission of an image of an item or information describing the item ("presentment notice") rather than delivery of the item itself. The agreement may provide for procedures governing retention, presentment, payment, dishonor, and other matters concerning items subject to the agreement.

(b) Presentment of an item pursuant to an agreement for presentment is made when the presentment notice is received.

(c) If presentment is made by presentment notice, a reference to "item" or "check" in this Article means the presentment notice unless the context otherwise indicates.

§ 4—111. **Statute of Limitations.**

An action to enforce an obligation, duty, or right arising under this Article must be commenced within three years after the [cause of action] accrues.

Part 2 **Collection of Items: Depositary and Collecting Banks**

§ 4—201. **Status of Collecting Bank As Agent and Provisional Status of Credits; Applicability of Article; Item Indorsed "Pay Any Bank".**

(a) Unless a contrary intent clearly appears and before the time that a settlement given by a collecting bank for an item is or becomes final, the bank, with respect to an item, is an agent or sub-agent of the owner of the item and any settlement given for the item is provisional. This provision applies regardless of the form of indorsement or lack of indorsement and even though credit given for the item is subject to immediate withdrawal as of right or is in fact withdrawn; but the continuance of ownership of an item by its owner and any rights of the owner to proceeds of the item are subject to rights of a collecting bank, such as those resulting from outstanding advances on the item and rights of recoupment or setoff. If an item is handled by banks for purposes of presentment, payment, collection, or return, the relevant provisions of this Article apply even though action of the parties clearly establishes that a particular bank has purchased the item and is the owner of it.

(b) After an item has been indorsed with the words "pay any bank" or the like, only a bank may acquire the rights of a holder until the item has been:

(1) returned to the customer initiating collection; or

(2) specially indorsed by a bank to a person who is not a bank.

§ 4—202. **Responsibility for Collection or Return; When Action Timely.**

(a) A collecting bank must exercise ordinary care in:

(1) presenting an item or sending it for presentment;

(2) sending notice of dishonor or nonpayment or returning an item other than a documentary draft to the bank's transferor after learning that the item has not been paid or accepted, as the case may be;

(3) settling for an item when the bank receives final settlement; and

(4) notifying its transferor of any loss or delay in transit within a reasonable time after discovery thereof.

(b) A collecting bank exercises ordinary care under subsection (a) by taking proper action before its midnight deadline following receipt of an item, notice, or settlement. Taking proper action within a reasonably longer time may constitute the exercise of ordinary care, but the bank has the burden of establishing timeliness.

(c) Subject to subsection (a)(1), a bank is not liable for the insolvency, neglect, misconduct, mistake, or default of another bank or person or for loss or destruction of an item in the possession of others or in transit.

§ 4—203. **Effect of Instructions.**

Subject to Article 3 concerning conversion of instruments (Section 3—420) and restrictive indorsements (Section 3—206), only a collecting bank's transferor can give instructions that affect the bank or constitute notice to it, and a collecting bank is not liable to prior parties for any action taken pursuant to the instructions or in accordance with any agreement with its transferor.

§ 4—204. **Methods of Sending and Presenting; Sending Directly to Payor Bank.**

(a) A collecting bank shall send items by a reasonably prompt method, taking into consideration relevant instructions, the nature of the item, the number of those items on hand, the cost of collection involved, and the method generally used by it or others to present those items.

(b) A collecting bank may send:

(1) an item directly to the payor bank;

(2) an item to a nonbank payor if authorized by its transferor; and

(3) an item other than documentary drafts to a nonbank payor, if authorized by Federal Reserve regulation or operating circular, clearing-house rule, or the like.

(c) Presentment may be made by a presenting bank at a place where the payor bank or other payor has requested that presentment be made.

§ 4—205. Depositary Bank Holder of Unindorsed Item.

If a customer delivers an item to a depositary bank for collection:

(1) the depositary bank becomes a holder of the item at the time it receives the item for collection if the customer at the time of delivery was a holder of the item, whether or not the customer indorses the item, and, if the bank satisfies the other requirements of Section 3—302, it is a holder in due course; and

(2) the depositary bank warrants to collecting banks, the payor bank or other payor, and the drawer that the amount of the item was paid to the customer or deposited to the customer's account.

§ 4—206. Transfer Between Banks.

Any agreed method that identifies the transferor bank is sufficient for the item's further transfer to another bank.

§ 4—207. Transfer Warranties.

(a) A customer or collecting bank that transfers an item and receives a settlement or other consideration warrants to the transferee and to any subsequent collecting bank that:

(1) the warrantor is a person entitled to enforce the item;

(2) all signatures on the item are authentic and authorized;

(3) the item has not been altered;

(4) the item is not subject to a defense or claim in recoupment (Section 3—305(a)) of any party that can be asserted against the warrantor; and

(5) the warrantor has no knowledge of any insolvency proceeding commenced with respect to the maker or acceptor or, in the case of an unaccepted draft, the drawer.

(b) If an item is dishonored, a customer or collecting bank transferring the item and receiving settlement or other consideration is obliged to pay the amount due on the item (i) according to the terms of the item at the time it was transferred, or (ii) if the transfer was of an incomplete item, according to its terms when completed as stated in Sections 3—115 and 3—407. The obligation of a transferor is owed to the transferee and to any subsequent collecting bank that takes the item in good faith. A transferor cannot disclaim its obligation under this subsection by an indorsement stating that it is made "without recourse" or otherwise disclaiming liability.

(c) A person to whom the warranties under subsection (a) are made and who took the item in good faith may recover from the warrantor as damages for breach of warranty an amount equal to the loss suffered as a result of the breach, but not more than the amount of the item plus expenses and loss of interest incurred as a result of the breach.

(d) The warranties stated in subsection (a) cannot be disclaimed with respect to checks. Unless notice of a claim for breach of warranty is given to the warrantor within 30 days after the claimant has reason to know of the breach and the identity of the warrantor, the warrantor is discharged to the extent of any loss caused by the delay in giving notice of the claim.

(e) A cause of action for breach of warranty under this section accrues when the claimant has reason to know of the breach.

§ 4—208. Presentment Warranties.

(a) If an unaccepted draft is presented to the drawee for payment or acceptance and the drawee pays or accepts the draft, (i) the person obtaining payment or acceptance, at the time of presentment, and (ii) a previous transferor of the draft, at the time of transfer, warrant to the drawee that pays or accepts the draft in good faith that:

(1) the warrantor is, or was, at the time the warrantor transferred the draft, a person entitled to enforce the draft or authorized to obtain payment or acceptance of the draft on behalf of a person entitled to enforce the draft;

(2) the draft has not been altered; and

(3) the warrantor has no knowledge that the signature of the purported drawer of the draft is unauthorized.

(b) A drawee making payment may recover from a warrantor damages for breach of warranty equal to the amount paid by the drawee less the amount the drawee received or is entitled to receive from the drawer because of the payment. In addition, the drawee is entitled to compensation for expenses and loss of interest resulting from the breach. The right of the drawee to recover damages under this subsection is not affected by any failure of the drawee to exercise ordinary care in making payment. If the drawee accepts the draft (i) breach of warranty is a defense to the obligation of the acceptor, and (ii) if the acceptor makes payment with respect to the draft, the acceptor is entitled to recover from a warrantor for breach of warranty the amounts stated in this subsection.

(c) If a drawee asserts a claim for breach of warranty under subsection (a) based on an unauthorized indorsement of the draft or an alteration of the draft, the warrantor may defend by proving that the indorsement is effective under Section 3—404 or 3—405 or the drawer is precluded under Section 3—406 or 4—406 from asserting against the drawee the unauthorized indorsement or alteration.

(d) If (i) a dishonored draft is presented for payment to the drawer or an indorser or (ii) any other item is presented for payment to a party obliged to pay the item, and the item is paid, the person obtaining payment and a prior transferor of the item warrant to the person making payment in good faith that the warrantor is, or was, at the time the warrantor transferred the item, a person entitled to enforce the item or authorized to obtain payment on behalf of a person entitled to enforce the item. The person making payment may recover from any warrantor for breach of warranty an amount equal to the amount paid plus expenses and loss of interest resulting from the breach.

(e) The warranties stated in subsections (a) and (d) cannot be disclaimed with respect to checks. Unless notice of a claim for breach of warranty is given to the warrantor within 30 days after the claimant has reason to know of the breach and the identity of the warrantor, the warrantor is discharged to the extent of any loss caused by the delay in giving notice of the claim.

(f) A cause of action for breach of warranty under this section accrues when the claimant has reason to know of the breach.

§ 4—209. Encoding and Retention Warranties.

(a) A person who encodes information on or with respect to an item after issue warrants to any subsequent collecting bank and to the payor bank or other payor that the information is correctly encoded. If the customer of a depository bank encodes, that bank also makes the warranty.

(b) A person who undertakes to retain an item pursuant to an agreement for electronic presentment warrants to any subsequent collecting bank and to the payor bank or other payor that retention and presentment of the item comply with the agreement. If a customer of a depository bank undertakes to retain an item, that bank also makes this warranty.

(c) A person to whom warranties are made under this section and who took the item in good faith may recover from the warrantor as damages for breach of warranty an amount equal to the loss suffered as a result of the breach, plus expenses and loss of interest incurred as a result of the breach.

§ 4—210. Security Interest of Collecting Bank in Items, Accompanying Documents and Proceeds.

(a) A collecting bank has a security interest in an item and any accompanying documents or the proceeds of either:

(1) in case of an item deposited in an account, to the extent to which credit given for the item has been withdrawn or applied;

(2) in case of an item for which it has given credit available for withdrawal as of right, to the extent of the credit given, whether or not the credit is drawn upon or there is a right of charge-back; or

(3) if it makes an advance on or against the item.

(b) If credit given for several items received at one time or pursuant to a single agreement is withdrawn or applied in part, the security interest remains upon all the items, any accompanying documents or the proceeds of either. For the purpose of this section, credits first given are first withdrawn.

(c) Receipt by a collecting bank of a final settlement for an item is a realization on its security interest in the item, accompanying documents, and proceeds. So long as the bank does not receive final settlement for the item or give up possession of the item or accompanying documents for purposes other than collection, the security interest continues to that extent and is subject to Article 9, but:

(1) no security agreement is necessary to make the security interest enforceable (Section 9—203(1)(a));

(2) no filing is required to perfect the security interest; and

(3) the security interest has priority over conflicting perfected security interests in the item, accompanying documents, or proceeds.

§ 4—211. When Bank Gives Value for Purposes of Holder in Due Course.

For purposes of determining its status as a holder in due course, a bank has given value to the extent it has a security interest in an item, if the bank otherwise complies with the requirements of Section 3—302 on what constitutes a holder in due course.

§ 4—212. Presentment by Notice of Item Not Payable by, Through, or at Bank; Liability of Drawer or Indorser.

(a) Unless otherwise instructed, a collecting bank may present an item not payable by, through, or at a bank by sending to the party to accept or pay a written notice that the bank holds the item for acceptance or payment. The notice must be sent in time to be received on or before the day when presentment is due and the bank must meet any requirement of the party to accept or pay under Section 3—501 by the close of the bank's next banking day after it knows of the requirement.

(b) If presentment is made by notice and payment, acceptance, or request for compliance with a requirement under Section 3—501 is not received by the close of business on the day after maturity or, in the case of demand items, by the close of business on the third banking day after notice was sent, the presenting bank may treat the item as dishonored and charge any drawer or indorser by sending it notice of the facts.

§ 4—213. Medium and Time of Settlement by Bank.

(a) With respect to settlement by a bank, the medium and time of settlement may be prescribed by Federal Reserve regulations or circulars, clearing-house rules, and the like, or agreement. In the absence of such prescription:

(1) the medium of settlement is cash or credit to an account in a Federal Reserve bank of or specified by the person to receive settlement; and

(2) the time of settlement is:

(i) with respect to tender of settlement by cash, a cashier's check, or teller's check, when the cash or check is sent or delivered;

(ii) with respect to tender of settlement by credit in an account in a Federal Reserve Bank, when the credit is made;

(iii) with respect to tender of settlement by a credit or debit to an account in a bank, when the credit or debit is made or, in the case of tender of settlement by authority to charge an account, when the authority is sent or delivered; or

(iv) with respect to tender of settlement by a funds transfer, when payment is made pursuant to Section 4A—406(a) to the person receiving settlement.

(b) If the tender of settlement is not by a medium authorized by subsection (a) or the time of settlement is not fixed by subsection (a), no settlement occurs until the tender of settlement is accepted by the person receiving settlement.

(c) If settlement for an item is made by cashier's check or teller's check and the person receiving settlement, before its midnight deadline:

(1) presents or forwards the check for collection, settlement is final when the check is finally paid; or

(2) fails to present or forward the check for collection, settlement is final at the midnight deadline of the person receiving settlement.

(d) If settlement for an item is made by giving authority to charge the account of the bank giving settlement in the bank receiving settlement, settlement is final when the charge is made by the bank receiving settlement if there are funds available in the account for the amount of the item.

§ 4—214. Right of Charge-Back or Refund; Liability of Collecting Bank: Return of Item.

(a) If a collecting bank has made provisional settlement with its customer for an item and fails by reason of dishonor, suspension of payments by a bank, or otherwise to receive settlement for the item which is or becomes final, the bank may revoke the settlement given by it, charge back the amount of any credit given for the item to its customer's account, or obtain refund from its customer, whether or not it is able to return the item, if by its midnight deadline or within a longer reasonable time after it learns the facts it returns the item or sends notification of the facts. If the return or notice is delayed beyond the bank's midnight deadline or a longer reasonable time after it learns the facts, the bank may revoke the settlement, charge back the credit, or obtain refund from its customer, but it is liable for any loss resulting from the delay. These rights to revoke, charge back, and obtain refund terminate if and when a settlement for the item received by the bank is or becomes final.

(b) A collecting bank returns an item when it is sent or delivered to the bank's customer or transferor or pursuant to its instructions.

(c) A depositary bank that is also the payor may charge back the amount of an item to its customer's account or obtain refund in accordance with the section governing return of an item received by a payor bank for credit on its books (Section 4–301).

(d) The right to charge back is not affected by:

(1) previous use of a credit given for the item; or

(2) failure by any bank to exercise ordinary care with respect to the item, but a bank so failing remains liable.

(e) A failure to charge back or claim refund does not affect other rights of the bank against the customer or any other party.

(f) If credit is given in dollars as the equivalent of the value of an item payable in foreign money, the dollar amount of any charge-back or refund must be calculated on the basis of the bank-offered spot rate for the foreign money prevailing on the day when the person entitled to the charge-back or refund learns that it will not receive payment in ordinary course.

§ 4–215. **Final Payment of Item by Payor Bank; When Provisional Debits and Credits Become Final; When Certain Credits Become Available for Withdrawal.**

(a) An item is finally paid by a payor bank when the bank has first done any of the following:

(1) paid the item in cash;

(2) settled for the item without having a right to revoke the settlement under statute, clearing-house rule, or agreement; or

(3) made a provisional settlement for the item and failed to revoke the settlement in the time and manner permitted by statute, clearing-house rule, or agreement.

(b) If provisional settlement for an item does not become final, the item is not finally paid.

(c) If provisional settlement for an item between the presenting and payor banks is made through a clearing house or by debits or credits in an account between them, then to the extent that provisional debits or credits for the item are entered in accounts between the presenting and payor banks or between the presenting and successive prior collecting banks seriatim, they become final upon final payment of the item by the payor bank.

(d) If a collecting bank receives a settlement for an item which is or becomes final, the bank is accountable to its customer for the amount of the item and any provisional credit given for the item

in an account with its customer becomes final.

(e) Subject to (i) applicable law stating a time for availability of funds and (ii) any right of the bank to apply the credit to an obligation of the customer, credit given by a bank for an item in a customer's account becomes available for withdrawal as of right:

(1) if the bank has received a provisional settlement for the item, when the settlement becomes final and the bank has had a reasonable time to receive return of the item and the item has not been received within that time;

(2) if the bank is both the depositary bank and the payor bank, and the item is finally paid, at the opening of the bank's second banking day following receipt of the item.

(f) Subject to applicable law stating a time for availability of funds and any right of a bank to apply a deposit to an obligation of the depositor, a deposit of money becomes available for withdrawal as of right at the opening of the bank's next banking day after receipt of the deposit.

§ 4–216. **Insolvency and Preference.**

(a) If an item is in or comes into the possession of a payor or collecting bank that suspends payment and the item has not been finally paid, the item must be returned by the receiver, trustee, or agent in charge of the closed bank to the presenting bank or the closed bank's customer.

(b) If a payor bank finally pays an item and suspends payments without making a settlement for the item with its customer or the presenting bank which settlement is or becomes final, the owner of the item has a preferred claim against the payor bank.

(c) If a payor bank gives or a collecting bank gives or receives a provisional settlement for an item and thereafter suspends payments, the suspension does not prevent or interfere with the settlement's becoming final if the finality occurs automatically upon the lapse of certain time or the happening of certain events.

(d) If a collecting bank receives from subsequent parties settlement for an item, which settlement is or becomes final and the bank suspends payments without making a settlement for the item with its customer which settlement is or becomes final, the owner of the item has a preferred claim against the collecting bank.

Part 3 Collection of Items: Payor Banks

§ 4–301. **Deferred Posting; Recovery of Payment by Return of Items; Time of Dishonor; Return of Items by Payor Bank.**

(a) If a payor bank settles for a demand item other than a documentary draft presented otherwise than for immediate payment over the counter before midnight of the banking day of receipt, the payor bank may revoke the settlement and recover the settlement if, before it has made final payment and before its midnight deadline, it

(1) returns the item; or

(2) sends written notice of dishonor or nonpayment if the item is unavailable for return.

(b) If a demand item is received by a payor bank for credit on its books, it may return the item or send notice of dishonor and may revoke any credit given or recover the amount thereof withdrawn by its customer, if it acts within the time limit and in the manner specified in subsection (a).

(c) Unless previous notice of dishonor has been sent, an item is dishonored at the time when for purposes of dishonor it is returned or notice sent in accordance with this section.

(d) An item is returned:

(1) as to an item presented through a clearing house, when it is delivered to the presenting or last collecting bank or to the clearing house or is sent or delivered in accordance with clearing-house rules; or

(2) in all other cases, when it is sent or delivered to the bank's customer or transferor or pursuant to instructions.

§ 4—302. Payor Bank's Responsibility for Late Return of Item.

(a) If an item is presented to and received by a payor bank, the bank is accountable for the amount of:

(1) a demand item, other than a documentary draft, whether properly payable or not, if the bank, in any case in which it is not also the depositary bank, retains the item beyond midnight of the banking day of receipt without settling for it or, whether or not it is also the depositary bank, does not pay or return the item or send notice of dishonor until after its midnight deadline; or

(2) any other properly payable item unless, within the time allowed for acceptance or payment of that item, the bank either accepts or pays the item or returns it and accompanying documents.

(b) The liability of a payor bank to pay an item pursuant to subsection (a) is subject to defenses based on breach of a presentment warranty (Section 4—208) or proof that the person seeking enforcement of the liability presented or transferred the item for the purpose of defrauding the payor bank.

§ 4—303. When Items Subject to Notice, Stop-Payment Order, Legal Process, or Setoff; Order in Which Items May Be Charged or Certified.

(a) Any knowledge, notice, or stop-payment order received by, legal process served upon, or setoff exercised by a payor bank comes too late to terminate, suspend, or modify the bank's right or duty to pay an item or to charge its customer's account for the item if the knowledge, notice, stop-payment order, or legal process is received or served and a reasonable time for the bank to act thereon expires or the setoff is exercised after the earliest of the following:

(1) the bank accepts or certifies the item;

(2) the bank pays the item in cash;

(3) the bank settles for the item without having a right to revoke the settlement under statute, clearing-house rule, or agreement;

(4) the bank becomes accountable for the amount of the item under Section 4—302 dealing with the payor bank's responsibility for late return of items; or

(5) with respect to checks, a cutoff hour no earlier than one hour after the opening of the next banking day after the banking day on which the bank received the check and no later than the close of that next banking day or, if no cutoff hour is fixed, the close of the next banking day after the banking day on which the bank received the check.

(b) Subject to subsection (a), items may be accepted, paid, certified, or charged to the indicated account of its customer in any order.

Part 4 Relationship Between Payor Bank and its Customer

§ 4—401. When Bank May Charge Customer's Account.

(a) A bank may charge against the account of a customer an item that is properly payable from the account even though the charge creates an overdraft. An item is properly payable if it is authorized by the customer and is in accordance with any agreement between the customer and bank.

(b) A customer is not liable for the amount of an overdraft if the customer neither signed the item nor benefited from the proceeds of the item.

(c) A bank may charge against the account of a customer a check that is otherwise properly payable from the account, even though payment was made before the date of the check, unless the customer has given notice to the bank of the postdating describing the check with reasonable certainty. The notice is effective for the period stated in Section 4—403(b) for stop-payment orders, and must be received at such time and in such manner as to afford the bank a reasonable opportunity to act on it before the bank takes any action with respect to the check described in Section 4—303. If a bank charges against the account of a customer a check before the date stated in the notice of postdating, the bank is liable for damages for the loss resulting from its act. The loss may include damages for dishonor of subsequent items under Section 4—402.

(d) A bank that in good faith makes payment to a holder may charge the indicated account of its customer according to:

(1) the original terms of the altered item; or

(2) the terms of the completed item, even though the bank knows the item has been completed unless the bank has notice that the completion was improper.

§ 4—402. Bank's Liability to Customer for Wrongful Dishonor; Time of Determining Insufficiency of Account.

(a) Except as otherwise provided in this Article, a payor bank wrongfully dishonors an item if it dishonors an item that is properly payable, but a bank may dishonor an item that would create an overdraft unless it has agreed to pay the overdraft.

(b) A payor bank is liable to its customer for damages proximately caused by the wrongful dishonor of an item. Liability is limited to actual damages proved and may include damages for an arrest or prosecution of the customer or other consequential damages. Whether any consequential damages are proximately caused by the wrongful dishonor is a question of fact to be determined in each case.

(c) A payor bank's determination of the customer's account balance on which a decision to dishonor for insufficiency of available funds is based may be made at any time between the time the item is received by the payor bank and the time that the payor bank returns the item or gives notice in lieu of return, and no more than one determination need be made. If, at the election of the payor bank, a subsequent balance determination is made for the purpose of reevaluating the bank's decision to dishonor the item, the account balance at that time is determinative of whether a dishonor for insufficiency of available funds is wrongful.

§ 4—403. Customer's Right to Stop Payment; Burden of Proof of Loss.

(a) A customer or any person authorized to draw on the account if there is more than one person may stop payment of any item drawn on the customer's account or close the account by an order to the bank describing the item or account with reasonable certainty received at a time and in a manner that affords the bank a reasonable opportunity to act on it before any action by the bank with respect to the item described in Section 4–303. If the signature of more than one person is required to draw on an account, any of these persons may stop payment or close the account.

(b) A stop-payment order is effective for six months, but it lapses after 14 calendar days if the original order was oral and was not confirmed in writing within that period. A stop-payment order may be renewed for additional six-month periods by a writing given to the bank within a period during which the stop-payment order is effective.

(c) The burden of establishing the fact and amount of loss resulting from the payment of an item contrary to a stop-payment order or order to close an account is on the customer. The loss from payment of an item contrary to a stop-payment order may include damages for dishonor of subsequent items under Section 4–402.

§ 4–404. Bank Not Obliged to Pay Check More Than Six Months Old.

A bank is under no obligation to a customer having a checking account to pay a check, other than a certified check, which is presented more than six months after its date, but it may charge its customer's account for a payment made thereafter in good faith.

§ 4–405. Death or Incompetence of Customer.

(a) A payor or collecting bank's authority to accept, pay, or collect an item or to account for proceeds of its collection, if otherwise effective, is not rendered ineffective by incompetence of a customer of either bank existing at the time the item is issued or its collection is undertaken if the bank does not know of an adjudication of incompetence. Neither death nor incompetence of a customer revokes the authority to accept, pay, collect, or account until the bank knows of the fact of death or of an adjudication of incompetence and has reasonable opportunity to act on it.

(b) Even with knowledge, a bank may for 10 days after the date of death pay or certify checks drawn on or before the date unless ordered to stop payment by a person claiming an interest in the account.

§ 4–406. Customer's Duty to Discover and Report Unauthorized Signature or Alteration.

(a) A bank that sends or makes available to a customer a statement of account showing payment of items for the account shall either return or make available to the customer the items paid or provide information in the statement of account sufficient to allow the customer reasonably to identify the items paid. The statement of account provides sufficient information if the item is described by item number, amount, and date of payment.

(b) If the items are not returned to the customer, the person retaining the items shall either retain the items or, if the items are destroyed, maintain the capacity to furnish legible copies of the items until the expiration of seven years after receipt of the items. A customer may request an item from the bank that paid the item, and that bank must provide in a reasonable time either the item or, if the item has been destroyed or is not otherwise obtainable, a legible copy of the item.

(c) If a bank sends or makes available a statement of account or items pursuant to subsection (a), the customer must exercise reasonable promptness in examining the statement or the items to determine whether any payment was not authorized because of an alteration of an item or because a purported signature by or on behalf of the customer was not authorized. If, based on the statement or items provided, the customer should reasonably have discovered the unauthorized payment, the customer must promptly notify the bank of the relevant facts.

(d) If the bank proves that the customer failed, with respect to an item, to comply with the duties imposed on the customer by subsection (c), the customer is precluded from asserting against the bank:

(1) the customer's unauthorized signature or any alteration on the item, if the bank also proves that it suffered a loss by reason of the failure; and

(2) the customer's unauthorized signature or alteration by the same wrongdoer on any other item paid in good faith by the bank if the payment was made before the bank received notice from the customer of the unauthorized signature or alteration and after the customer had been afforded a reasonable period of time, not exceeding 30 days, in which to examine the item or statement of account and notify the bank.

(e) If subsection (d) applies and the customer proves that the bank failed to exercise ordinary care in paying the item and that the failure substantially contributed to loss, the loss is allocated between the customer precluded and the bank asserting the preclusion according to the extent to which the failure of the customer to comply with subsection (c) and the failure of the bank to exercise ordinary care contributed to the loss. If the customer proves that the bank did not pay the item in good faith, the preclusion under subsection (d) does not apply.

(f) Without regard to care or lack of care of either the customer or the bank, a customer who does not within one year after the statement or items are made available to the customer (subsection (a)) discover and report the customer's unauthorized signature on or any alteration on the item is precluded from asserting against the bank the unauthorized signature or alteration. If there is a preclusion under this subsection, the payor bank may not recover for breach or warranty under Section 4–208 with respect to the unauthorized signature or alteration to which the preclusion applies.

§ 4–407. Payor Bank's Right to Subrogation on Improper Payment.

If a payor has paid an item over the order of the drawer or maker to stop payment, or after an account has been closed, or otherwise under circumstances giving a basis for objection by the drawer or maker, to prevent unjust enrichment and only to the extent necessary to prevent loss to the bank by reason of its payment of the item, the payor bank is subrogated to the rights

(1) of any holder in due course on the item against the drawer or maker;

(2) of the payee or any other holder of the item against the drawer or maker either on the item or under the transaction out of which the item arose; and

(3) of the drawer or maker against the payee or any other holder of the item with respect to the transaction out of which the item arose.

Part 5 Collection of Documentary Drafts

§ 4—501. Handling of Documentary Drafts; Duty to Send for Presentment and to Notify Customer of Dishonor.

A bank that takes a documentary draft for collection shall present or send the draft and accompanying documents for presentment and, upon learning that the draft has not been paid or accepted in due course, shall seasonably notify its customer of the fact even though it may have discounted or bought the draft or extended credit available for withdrawal as of right.

§ 4—502. Presentment of "On Arrival" Drafts.

If a draft or the relevant instructions require presentment "on arrival", "when goods arrive" or the like, the collecting bank need not present until in its judgment a reasonable time for arrival of the goods has expired. Refusal to pay or accept because the goods have not arrived is not dishonor; the bank must notify its transferor of the refusal but need not present the draft again until it is instructed to do so or learns of the arrival of the goods.

§ 4—503. Responsibility of Presenting Bank for Documents and Goods; Report of Reasons for Dishonor; Referee in Case of Need.

Unless otherwise instructed and except as provided in Article 5, a bank presenting a documentary draft:

(1) must deliver the documents to the drawee on acceptance of the draft if it is payable more than three days after presentment, otherwise, only on payment; and

(2) upon dishonor, either in the case of presentment for acceptance or presentment for payment, may seek and follow instructions from any referee in case of need designated in the draft or, if the presenting bank does not choose to utilize the referee's services, it must use diligence and good faith to ascertain the reason for dishonor, must notify its transferor of the dishonor and of the results of its effort to ascertain the reasons therefor, and must request instructions.

However, the presenting bank is under no obligation with respect to goods represented by the documents except to follow any reasonable instructions seasonably received; it has a right to reimbursement for any expense incurred in following instructions and to prepayment of or indemnity for those expenses.

§ 4—504. Privilege of Presenting Bank to Deal With Goods; Security Interest for Expenses.

(a) A presenting bank that, following the dishonor of a documentary draft, has seasonably requested instructions but does not receive them within a reasonable time may store, sell, or otherwise deal with the goods in any reasonable manner.

(b) For its reasonable expenses incurred by action under subsection (a) the presenting bank has a lien upon the goods or their proceeds, which may be foreclosed in the same manner as an unpaid seller's lien.

Article 4A
FUNDS TRANSFERS

Part 1 Subject Matter and Definitions

§ 4A—101. Short Title.

This Article may be cited as Uniform Commercial Code—Funds Transfers.

§ 4A—102. Subject Matter.

Except as otherwise provided in Section 4A—108, this Article applies to funds transfers defined in Section 4A—104.

§ 4A—103. Payment Order—Definitions.

(a) In this Article:

(1) "Payment order" means an instruction of a sender to a receiving bank, transmitted orally, electronically, or in writing, to pay, or to cause another bank to pay, a fixed or determinable amount of money to a beneficiary if:

(i) the instruction does not state a condition to payment to the beneficiary other than time of payment,

(ii) the receiving bank is to be reimbursed by debiting an account of, or otherwise receiving payment from, the sender, and

(iii) the instruction is transmitted by the sender directly to the receiving bank or to an agent, funds-transfer system, or communication system for transmittal to the receiving bank.

(2) "Beneficiary" means the person to be paid by the beneficiary's bank.

(3) "Beneficiary's bank" means the bank identified in a payment order in which an account of the beneficiary is to be credited pursuant to the order or which otherwise is to make payment to the beneficiary if the order does not provide for payment to an account.

(4) "Receiving bank" means the bank to which the sender's instruction is addressed.

(5) "Sender" means the person giving the instruction to the receiving bank.

(b) If an instruction complying with subsection (a)(1) is to make more than one payment to a beneficiary, the instruction is a separate payment order with respect to each payment.

(c) A payment order is issued when it is sent to the receiving bank.

§ 4A—104. Funds Transfer—Definitions.

In this Article:

(a) "Funds transfer" means the series of transactions, beginning with the originator's payment order, made for the purpose of making payment to the beneficiary of the order. The term includes any payment order issued by the originator's bank or an intermediary bank intended to carry out the originator's payment order. A funds transfer is completed by acceptance by the beneficiary's bank of a payment order for the benefit of the beneficiary of the originator's payment order.

(b) "Intermediary bank" means a receiving bank other than the originator's bank or the beneficiary's bank.

(c) "Originator" means the sender of the first payment order in a funds transfer.

(d) "Originator's bank" means (i) the receiving bank to which the payment order of the originator is issued if the originator is not a bank, or (ii) the originator if the originator is a bank.

§ 4A—105. Other Definitions.

(a) In this Article:

(1) "Authorized account" means a deposit account of a customer in a bank designated by the customer as a source of payment of payment orders issued by the customer to the bank. If a customer does not so designate an account, any account of the customer is an authorized account if payment of a payment order from that account is not inconsistent with a restriction on the use of that account.

(2) "Bank" means a person engaged in the business of banking and includes a savings bank, savings and loan association, credit union, and trust company. A branch or separate office of a bank is a separate bank for purposes of this Article.

(3) "Customer" means a person, including a bank, having an account with a bank or from whom a bank has agreed to receive payment orders.

(4) "Funds-transfer business day" of a receiving bank means the part of a day during which the receiving bank is open for the receipt, processing, and transmittal of payment orders and cancellations and amendments of payment orders.

(5) "Funds-transfer system" means a wire transfer network, automated clearing house, or other communication system of a clearing house or other association of banks through which a payment order by a bank may be transmitted to the bank to which the order is addressed.

(6) "Good faith" means honesty in fact and the observance of reasonable commercial standards of fair dealing.

(7) "Prove" with respect to a fact means to meet the burden of establishing the fact (Section 1—201(8)).

(b) Other definitions applying to this Article and the sections in which they appear are:

"Acceptance"	Section 4A—209
"Beneficiary"	Section 4A—103
"Beneficiary's bank"	Section 4A—103
"Executed"	Section 4A—301
"Execution date"	Section 4A—301
"Funds transfer"	Section 4A—104
"Funds-transfer system rule"	Section 4A—501
"Intermediary bank"	Section 4A—104
"Originator"	Section 4A—104
"Originator's bank"	Section 4A—104
"Payment by beneficiary's bank to beneficiary"	Section 4A—405
"Payment by originator to beneficiary"	Section 4A—406
"Payment by sender to receiving bank"	Section 4A—403
"Payment date"	Section 4A—401
"Payment order"	Section 4A—103
"Receiving bank"	Section 4A—103
"Security procedure"	Section 4A—201
"Sender"	Section 4A—103

(c) The following definitions in Article 4 apply to this Article:

"Clearing house"	Section 4—104
"Item"	Section 4—104
"Suspends payments"	Section 4—104

(d) In addition, Article 1 contains general definitions and principles of construction and interpretation applicable throughout this Article.

§ 4A—106. **Time Payment Order Is Received.**

(a) The time of receipt of a payment order or communication cancelling or amending a payment order is determined by the rules applicable to receipt of a notice stated in Section 1—201(27). A receiving bank may fix a cut-off time or times on a funds-transfer business day for the receipt and processing of payment orders and communications cancelling or amending payment orders. Different cut-off times may apply to payment orders, cancellations, or amendments, or to different categories of payment orders, cancellations, or amendments. A cut-off time may apply to senders generally or different cut-off times may apply to different senders or categories of payment orders. If a payment order or communication cancelling or amending a payment order is received after the close of a funds-transfer business day or after the appropriate cut-off time on a funds-transfer business day, the receiving bank may treat the payment order or communication as received at the opening of the next funds-transfer business day.

(b) If this Article refers to an execution date or payment date or states a day on which a receiving bank is required to take action, and the date or day does not fall on a funds-transfer business day, the next day that is a funds-transfer business day is treated as the date or day stated, unless the contrary is stated in this Article.

§ 4A—107. **Federal Reserve Regulations and Operating Circulars.**

Regulations of the Board of Governors of the Federal Reserve System and operating circulars of the Federal Reserve Banks supersede any inconsistent provision of this Article to the extent of the inconsistency.

§ 4A—108. **Exclusion of Consumer Transactions Governed by Federal Law.**

This Article does not apply to a funds transfer any part of which is governed by the Electronic Fund Transfer Act of 1978 (Title XX, Public Law 95—630, 92 Stat. 3728, 15 U.S.C. § 1693 et seq.) as amended from time to time.

Part 2 Issue and Acceptance of Payment Order

§ 4A—201. **Security Procedure.**

"Security procedure" means a procedure established by agreement of a customer and a receiving bank for the purpose of (i) verifying that a payment order or communication amending or cancelling a payment order is that of the customer, or (ii) detecting error in the transmission or the content of the payment order or communication. A security procedure may require the use of algorithms or other codes, identifying words or numbers, encryption, callback procedures, or similar security devices. Comparison of a signature on a payment order or communication with an authorized specimen signature of the customer is not by itself a security procedure.

§ 4A—202. **Authorized and Verified Payment Orders.**

(a) A payment order received by the receiving bank is the authorized order of the person identified as sender if that person authorized the order or is otherwise bound by it under the law of agency.

(b) If a bank and its customer have agreed that the authenticity of payment orders issued to the bank in the name of the customer as sender will be verified pursuant to a security procedure, a payment order received by the receiving bank is effective as the order of the customer, whether or not authorized, if (i) the security procedure is a commercially reasonable method of providing security against unauthorized payment orders, and (ii) the bank proves that it accepted the payment order in good faith and in compliance with the security procedure and any written agreement or instruction of the customer restricting acceptance of payment orders issued in the name of the customer. The bank is not required to follow an instruction that violates a written agreement with the customer or notice of which is not received at a time and in a manner affording the bank a reasonable opportunity to act on it before the payment order is accepted.

(c) Commercial reasonableness of a security procedure is a question of law to be determined by considering the wishes of the customer expressed to the bank, the circumstances of the customer known to the bank, including the size, type, and frequency of payment orders normally issued by the customer to the bank, alternative security procedures offered to the customer, and security procedures in general use by customers and receiving banks similarly situated. A security procedure is deemed to be commercially reasonable if (i) the security procedure was chosen by the customer after the bank offered, and the customer refused, a security procedure that was commercially reasonable for that customer, and (ii) the customer expressly agreed in writing to be bound by any payment order, whether or not authorized, issued in its name and accepted by the bank in compliance with the security procedure chosen by the customer.

(d) The term "sender" in this Article includes the customer in whose name a payment order is issued if the order is the authorized order of the customer under subsection (a), or it is effective as the order of the customer under subsection (b).

(e) This section applies to amendments and cancellations of payment orders to the same extent it applies to payment orders.

(f) Except as provided in this section and in Section 4A—203(a)(1), rights and obligations arising under this section or Section 4A—203 may not be varied by agreement.

§ 4A—203. Unenforceability of Certain Verified Payment Orders.

(a) If an accepted payment order is not, under Section 4A—202(a), an authorized order of a customer identified as sender, but is effective as an order of the customer pursuant to Section 4A—202(b), the following rules apply:

(1) By express written agreement, the receiving bank may limit the extent to which it is entitled to enforce or retain payment of the payment order.

(2) The receiving bank is not entitled to enforce or retain payment of the payment order if the customer proves that the order was not caused, directly or indirectly, by a person (i) entrusted at any time with duties to act for the customer with respect to payment orders or the security procedure, or (ii) who obtained access to transmitting facilities of the customer or who obtained, from a source controlled by the customer and without authority of the receiving bank, information facilitating breach of the security procedure, regardless of how the information was obtained or whether the customer was at fault. Information includes any access device,

computer software, or the like.

(b) This section applies to amendments of payment orders to the same extent it applies to payment orders.

§ 4A—204. Refund of Payment and Duty of Customer to Report with Respect to Unauthorized Payment Order.

(a) If a receiving bank accepts a payment order issued in the name of its customer as sender which is (i) not authorized and not effective as the order of the customer under Section 4A—202, or (ii) not enforceable, in whole or in part, against the customer under Section 4A—203, the bank shall refund any payment of the payment order received from the customer to the extent the bank is not entitled to enforce payment and shall pay interest on the refundable amount calculated from the date the bank received payment to the date of the refund. However, the customer is not entitled to interest from the bank on the amount to be refunded if the customer fails to exercise ordinary care to determine that the order was not authorized by the customer and to notify the bank of the relevant facts within a reasonable time not exceeding 90 days after the date the customer received notification from the bank that the order was accepted or that the customer's account was debited with respect to the order. The bank is not entitled to any recovery from the customer on account of a failure by the customer to give notification as stated in this section.

(b) Reasonable time under subsection (a) may be fixed by agreement as stated in Section 1—204(1), but the obligation of a receiving bank to refund payment as stated in subsection (a) may not otherwise be varied by agreement.

§ 4A—205. Erroneous Payment Orders.

(a) If an accepted payment order was transmitted pursuant to a security procedure for the detection of error and the payment order (i) erroneously instructed payment to a beneficiary not intended by the sender, (ii) erroneously instructed payment in an amount greater than the amount intended by the sender, or (iii) was an erroneously transmitted duplicate of a payment order previously sent by the sender, the following rules apply:

(1) If the sender proves that the sender or a person acting on behalf of the sender pursuant to Section 4A—206 complied with the security procedure and that the error would have been detected if the receiving bank had also complied, the sender is not obliged to pay the order to the extent stated in paragraphs (2) and (3).

(2) If the funds transfer is completed on the basis of an erroneous payment order described in clause (i) or (iii) of subsection (a), the sender is not obliged to pay the order and the receiving bank is entitled to recover from the beneficiary any amount paid to the beneficiary to the extent allowed by the law governing mistake and restitution.

(3) If the funds transfer is completed on the basis of a payment order described in clause (ii) of subsection (a), the sender is not obliged to pay the order to the extent the amount received by the beneficiary is greater than the amount intended by the sender. In that case, the receiving bank is entitled to recover from the beneficiary the excess amount received to the extent allowed by the law governing mistake and restitution.

(b) If (i) the sender of an erroneous payment order described in subsection (a) is not obliged to pay all or part of the order, and

(ii) the sender receives notification from the receiving bank that the order was accepted by the bank or that the sender's account was debited with respect to the order, the sender has a duty to exercise ordinary care, on the basis of information available to the sender, to discover the error with respect to the order and to advise the bank of the relevant facts within a reasonable time, not exceeding 90 days, after the bank's notification was received by the sender. If the bank proves that the sender failed to perform that duty, the sender is liable to the bank for the loss the bank proves it incurred as a result of the failure, but the liability of the sender may not exceed the amount of the sender's order.

(c) This section applies to amendments to payment orders to the same extent it applies to payment orders.

§ 4A—206. Transmission of Payment Order through Funds-Transfer or Other Communication System.

(a) If a payment order addressed to a receiving bank is transmitted to a funds-transfer system or other third party communication system for transmittal to the bank, the system is deemed to be an agent of the sender for the purpose of transmitting the payment order to the bank. If there is a discrepancy between the terms of the payment order transmitted to the system and the terms of the payment order transmitted by the system to the bank, the terms of the payment order of the sender are those transmitted by the system. This section does not apply to a funds-transfer system of the Federal Reserve Banks.

(b) This section applies to cancellations and amendments to payment orders to the same extent it applies to payment orders.

§ 4A—207. Misdescription of Beneficiary.

(a) Subject to subsection (b), if, in a payment order received by the beneficiary's bank, the name, bank account number, or other identification of the beneficiary refers to a nonexistent or unidentifiable person or account, no person has rights as a beneficiary of the order and acceptance of the order cannot occur.

(b) If a payment order received by the beneficiary's bank identifies the beneficiary both by name and by an identifying or bank account number and the name and number identify different persons, the following rules apply:

(1) Except as otherwise provided in subsection (c), if the beneficiary's bank does not know that the name and number refer to different persons, it may rely on the number as the proper identification of the beneficiary of the order. The beneficiary's bank need not determine whether the name and number refer to the same person.

(2) If the beneficiary's bank pays the person identified by name or knows that the name and number identify different persons, no person has rights as beneficiary except the person paid by the beneficiary's bank if that person was entitled to receive payment from the originator of the funds transfer. If no person has rights as beneficiary, acceptance of the order cannot occur.

(c) If (i) a payment order described in subsection (b) is accepted, (ii) the originator's payment order described the beneficiary inconsistently by name and number, and (iii) the beneficiary's bank pays the person identified by number as permitted by subsection (b)(1), the following rules apply:

(1) If the originator is a bank, the originator is obliged to pay its order.

(2) If the originator is not a bank and proves that the person identified by number was not entitled to receive payment from the originator, the originator is not obliged to pay its order unless the originator's bank proves that the originator, before acceptance of the originator's order, had notice that payment of a payment order issued by the originator might be made by the beneficiary's bank on the basis of an identifying or bank account number even if it identifies a person different from the named beneficiary. Proof of notice may be made by any admissible evidence. The originator's bank satisfies the burden of proof if it proves that the originator, before the payment order was accepted, signed a writing stating the information to which the notice relates.

(d) In a case governed by subsection (b)(1), if the beneficiary's bank rightfully pays the person identified by number and that person was not entitled to receive payment from the originator, the amount paid may be recovered from that person to the extent allowed by the law governing mistake and restitution as follows:

(1) If the originator is obliged to pay its payment order as stated in subsection (c), the originator has the right to recover.

(2) If the originator is not a bank and is not obliged to pay its payment order, the originator's bank has the right to recover.

§ 4A—208. Misdescription of Intermediary Bank or Beneficiary's Bank.

(a) This subsection applies to a payment order identifying an intermediary bank or the beneficiary's bank only by an identifying number.

(1) The receiving bank may rely on the number as the proper identification of the intermediary or beneficiary's bank and need not determine whether the number identifies a bank.

(2) The sender is obliged to compensate the receiving bank for any loss and expenses incurred by the receiving bank as a result of its reliance on the number in executing or attempting to execute the order.

(b) This subsection applies to a payment order identifying an intermediary bank or the beneficiary's bank both by name and an identifying number if the name and number identify different persons.

(1) If the sender is a bank, the receiving bank may rely on the number as the proper identification of the intermediary or beneficiary's bank if the receiving bank, when it executes the sender's order, does not know that the name and number identify different persons. The receiving bank need not determine whether the name and number refer to the same person or whether the number refers to a bank. The sender is obliged to compensate the receiving bank for any loss and expenses incurred by the receiving bank as a result of its reliance on the number in executing or attempting to execute the order.

(2) If the sender is not a bank and the receiving bank proves that the sender, before the payment order was accepted, had notice that the receiving bank might rely on the number as the proper identification of the intermediary or beneficiary's bank even if it identifies a person different from the bank identified by name, the rights and obligations of the sender and the receiving bank are governed by subsection (b)(1), as though the sender were a bank. Proof of notice may be made by any admissible evidence. The receiving bank satisfies the burden of proof if it proves that the sender, before the payment order

was accepted, signed a writing stating the information to which the notice relates.

(3) Regardless of whether the sender is a bank, the receiving bank may rely on the name as the proper identification of the intermediary or beneficiary's bank if the receiving bank, at the time it executes the sender's order, does not know that the name and number identify different persons. The receiving bank need not determine whether the name and number refer to the same person.

(4) If the receiving bank knows that the name and number identify different persons, reliance on either the name or the number in executing the sender's payment order is a breach of the obligation stated in Section 4A—302(a)(1).

§ 4A—209. Acceptance of Payment Order.

(a) Subject to subsection (d), a receiving bank other than the beneficiary's bank accepts a payment order when it executes the order.

(b) Subject to subsections (c) and (d), a beneficiary's bank accepts a payment order at the earliest of the following times:

(1) When the bank (i) pays the beneficiary as stated in Section 4A—405(a) or 4A—405(b), or (ii) notifies the beneficiary of receipt of the order or that the account of the beneficiary has been credited with respect to the order unless the notice indicates that the bank is rejecting the order or that funds with respect to the order may not be withdrawn or used until receipt of payment from the sender of the order;

(2) When the bank receives payment of the entire amount of the sender's order pursuant to Section 4A—403(a)(1) or 4A—403(a)(2); or

(3) The opening of the next funds-transfer business day of the bank following the payment date of the order if, at that time, the amount of the sender's order is fully covered by a withdrawable credit balance in an authorized account of the sender or the bank has otherwise received full payment from the sender, unless the order was rejected before that time or is rejected within (i) one hour after that time, or (ii) one hour after the opening of the next business day of the sender following the payment date if that time is later. If notice of rejection is received by the sender after the payment date and the authorized account of the sender does not bear interest, the bank is obliged to pay interest to the sender on the amount of the order for the number of days elapsing after the payment date to the day the sender receives notice or learns that the order was not accepted, counting that day as an elapsed day. If the withdrawable credit balance during that period falls below the amount of the order, the amount of interest payable is reduced accordingly.

(c) Acceptance of a payment order cannot occur before the order is received by the receiving bank. Acceptance does not occur under subsection (b)(2) or (b)(3) if the beneficiary of the payment order does not have an account with the receiving bank, the account has been closed, or the receiving bank is not permitted by law to receive credits for the beneficiary's account.

(d) A payment order issued to the originator's bank cannot be accepted until the payment date if the bank is the beneficiary's bank, or the execution date if the bank is not the beneficiary's bank. If the originator's bank executes the originator's payment order before the execution date or pays the beneficiary of the originator's payment order before the payment date and the payment

order is subsequently cancelled pursuant to Section 4A—211(b), the bank may recover from the beneficiary any payment received to the extent allowed by the law governing mistake and restitution.

§ 4A—210. Rejection of Payment Order.

(a) A payment order is rejected by the receiving bank by a notice of rejection transmitted to the sender orally, electronically, or in writing. A notice of rejection need not use any particular words and is sufficient if it indicates that the receiving bank is rejecting the order or will not execute or pay the order. Rejection is effective when the notice is given if transmission is by a means that is reasonable in the circumstances. If notice of rejection is given by a means that is not reasonable, rejection is effective when the notice is received. If an agreement of the sender and receiving bank establishes the means to be used to reject a payment order, (i) any means complying with the agreement is reasonable and (ii) any means not complying is not reasonable unless no significant delay in receipt of the notice resulted from the use of the noncomplying means.

(b) This subsection applies if a receiving bank other than the beneficiary's bank fails to execute a payment order despite the existence on the execution date of a withdrawable credit balance in an authorized account of the sender sufficient to cover the order. If the sender does not receive notice of rejection of the order on the execution date and the authorized account of the sender does not bear interest, the bank is obliged to pay interest to the sender on the amount of the order for the number of days elapsing after the execution date to the earlier of the day the order is cancelled pursuant to Section 4A—211(d) or the day the sender receives notice or learns that the order was not executed, counting the final day of the period as an elapsed day. If the withdrawable credit balance during that period falls below the amount of the order, the amount of interest is reduced accordingly.

(c) If a receiving bank suspends payments, all unaccepted payment orders issued to it are are deemed rejected at the time the bank suspends payments.

(d) Acceptance of a payment order precludes a later rejection of the order. Rejection of a payment order precludes a later acceptance of the order.

§ 4A—211. Cancellation and Amendment of Payment Order.

(a) A communication of the sender of a payment order cancelling or amending the order may be transmitted to the receiving bank orally, electronically, or in writing. If a security procedure is in effect between the sender and the receiving bank, the communication is not effective to cancel or amend the order unless the communication is verified pursuant to the security procedure or the bank agrees to the cancellation or amendment.

(b) Subject to subsection (a), a communication by the sender cancelling or amending a payment order is effective to cancel or amend the order if notice of the communication is received at a time and in a manner affording the receiving bank a reasonable opportunity to act on the communication before the bank accepts the payment order.

(c) After a payment order has been accepted, cancellation or amendment of the order is not effective unless the receiving bank agrees or a funds-transfer system rule allows cancellation or amendment without agreement of the bank.

(1) With respect to a payment order accepted by a receiving

bank other than the beneficiary's bank, cancellation or amendment is not effective unless a conforming cancellation or amendment of the payment order issued by the receiving bank is also made.

(2) With respect to a payment order accepted by the beneficiary's bank, cancellation or amendment is not effective unless the order was issued in execution of an unauthorized payment order, or because of a mistake by a sender in the funds transfer which resulted in the issuance of a payment order (i) that is a duplicate of a payment order previously issued by the sender, (ii) that orders payment to a beneficiary not entitled to receive payment from the originator, or (iii) that orders payment in an amount greater than the amount the beneficiary was entitled to receive from the originator. If the payment order is cancelled or amended, the beneficiary's bank is entitled to recover from the beneficiary any amount paid to the beneficiary to the extent allowed by the law governing mistake and restitution.

(d) An unaccepted payment order is cancelled by operation of law at the close of the fifth funds-transfer business day of the receiving bank after the execution date or payment date of the order.

(e) A cancelled payment order cannot be accepted. If an accepted payment order is cancelled, the acceptance is nullified and no person has any right or obligation based on the acceptance. Amendment of a payment order is deemed to be cancellation of the original order at the time of amendment and issue of a new payment order in the amended form at the same time.

(f) Unless otherwise provided in an agreement of the parties or in a funds-transfer system rule, if the receiving bank, after accepting a payment order, agrees to cancellation or amendment of the order by the sender or is bound by a funds-transfer system rule allowing cancellation or amendment without the bank's agreement, the sender, whether or not cancellation or amendment is effective, is liable to the bank for any loss and expenses, including reasonable attorney's fees, incurred by the bank as a result of the cancellation or amendment or attempted cancellation or amendment.

(g) A payment order is not revoked by the death or legal incapacity of the sender unless the receiving bank knows of the death or of an adjudication of incapacity by a court of competent jurisdiction and has reasonable opportunity to act before acceptance of the order.

(h) A funds-transfer system rule is not effective to the extent it conflicts with subsection (c)(2).

§ 4A—212. Liability and Duty of Receiving Bank Regarding Unaccepted Payment Order.

If a receiving bank fails to accept a payment order that it is obliged by express agreement to accept, the bank is liable for breach of the agreement to the extent provided in the agreement or in this Article, but does not otherwise have any duty to accept a payment order or, before acceptance, to take any action, or refrain from taking action, with respect to the order except as provided in this Article or by express agreement. Liability based on acceptance arises only when acceptance occurs as stated in Section 4A—209, and liability is limited to that provided in this Article. A receiving bank is not the agent of the sender or beneficiary of the payment order it accepts, or of any other party to the funds transfer, and the bank owes no duty to any party to the funds transfer except as provided in this Article or by express agreement.

Part 3 Execution of Sender's Payment Order by Receiving Bank

§ 4A—301. Execution and Execution Date.

(a) A payment order is "executed" by the receiving bank when it issues a payment order intended to carry out the payment order received by the bank. A payment order received by the beneficiary's bank can be accepted but cannot be executed.

(b) "Execution date" of a payment order means the day on which the receiving bank may properly issue a payment order in execution of the sender's order. The execution date may be determined by instruction of the sender but cannot be earlier than the day the order is received and, unless otherwise determined, is the day the order is received. If the sender's instruction states a payment date, the execution date is the payment date or an earlier date on which execution is reasonably necessary to allow payment to the beneficiary on the payment date.

§ 4A—302. Obligations of Receiving Bank in Execution of Payment Order.

(a) Except as provided in subsections (b) through (d), if the receiving bank accepts a payment order pursuant to Section 4A—209(a), the bank has the following obligations in executing the order:

(1) The receiving bank is obliged to issue, on the execution date, a payment order complying with the sender's order and to follow the sender's instructions concerning (i) any intermediary bank or funds-transfer system to be used in carrying out the funds transfer, or (ii) the means by which payment orders are to be transmitted in the funds transfer. If the originator's bank issues a payment order to an intermediary bank, the originator's bank is obliged to instruct the intermediary bank according to the instruction of the originator. An intermediary bank in the funds transfer is similarly bound by an instruction given to it by the sender of the payment order it accepts.

(2) If the sender's instruction states that the funds transfer is to be carried out telephonically or by wire transfer or otherwise indicates that the funds transfer is to be carried out by the most expeditious means, the receiving bank is obliged to transmit its payment order by the most expeditious available means, and to instruct any intermediary bank accordingly. If a sender's instruction states a payment date, the receiving bank is obliged to transmit its payment order at a time and by means reasonably necessary to allow payment to the beneficiary on the payment date or as soon thereafter as is feasible.

(b) Unless otherwise instructed, a receiving bank executing a payment order may (i) use any funds-transfer system if use of that system is reasonable in the circumstances, and (ii) issue a payment order to the beneficiary's bank or to an intermediary bank through which a payment order conforming to the sender's order can expeditiously be issued to the beneficiary's bank if the receiving bank exercises ordinary care in the selection of the intermediary bank. A receiving bank is not required to follow an instruction of the sender designating a funds-transfer system to be used in carrying out the funds transfer if the receiving bank, in good faith, determines that it is not feasible to follow the instruction or that following the instruction would unduly delay completion of the funds transfer.

(c) Unless subsection (a)(2) applies or the receiving bank is otherwise instructed, the bank may execute a payment order by transmitting its payment order by first class mail or by any means reasonable in the circumstances. If the receiving bank is instructed to execute the sender's order by transmitting its payment order by a particular means, the receiving bank may issue its payment order by the means stated or by any means as expeditious as the means stated.

(d) Unless instructed by the sender, (i) the receiving bank may not obtain payment of its charges for services and expenses in connection with the execution of the sender's order by issuing a payment order in an amount equal to the amount of the sender's order less the amount of the charges, and (ii) may not instruct a subsequent receiving bank to obtain payment of its charges in the same manner.

§ 4A—303. Erroneous Execution of Payment Order.

(a) A receiving bank that (i) executes the payment order of the sender by issuing a payment order in an amount greater than the amount of the sender's order, or (ii) issues a payment order in execution of the sender's order and then issues a duplicate order, is entitled to payment of the amount of the sender's order under Section 4A—402(c) if that subsection is otherwise satisfied. The bank is entitled to recover from the beneficiary of the erroneous order the excess payment received to the extent allowed by the law governing mistake and restitution.

(b) A receiving bank that executes the payment order of the sender by issuing a payment order in an amount less than the amount of the sender's order is entitled to payment of the amount of the sender's order under Section 4A—402(c) if (i) that subsection is otherwise satisfied and (ii) the bank corrects its mistake by issuing an additional payment order for the benefit of the beneficiary of the sender's order. If the error is not corrected, the issuer of the erroneous order is entitled to receive or retain payment from the sender of the order it accepted only to the extent of the amount of the erroneous order. This subsection does not apply if the receiving bank executes the sender's payment order by issuing a payment order in an amount less than the amount of the sender's order for the purpose of obtaining payment of its charges for services and expenses pursuant to instruction of the sender.

(c) If a receiving bank executes the payment order of the sender by issuing a payment order to a beneficiary different from the beneficiary of the sender's order and the funds transfer is completed on the basis of that error, the sender of the payment order that was erroneously executed and all previous senders in the funds transfer are not obliged to pay the payment orders they issued. The issuer of the erroneous order is entitled to recover from the beneficiary of the order the payment received to the extent allowed by the law governing mistake and restitution.

§ 4A—304. Duty of Sender to Report Erroneously Executed Payment Order.

If the sender of a payment order that is erroneously executed as stated in Section 4A—303 receives notification from the receiving bank that the order was executed or that the sender's account was debited with respect to the order, the sender has a duty to exercise ordinary care to determine, on the basis of information available to the sender, that the order was erroneously executed and to notify the bank of the relevant facts within a reasonable time not exceeding 90 days after the notification from the bank was received by the sender. If the sender fails to perform that duty, the bank is not obliged to pay interest on any amount refundable to the sender

under Section 4A—402(d) for the period before the bank learns of the execution error. The bank is not entitled to any recovery from the sender on account of a failure by the sender to perform the duty stated in this section.

§ 4A—305. Liability for Late or Improper Execution or Failure to Execute Payment Order.

(a) If a funds transfer is completed but execution of a payment order by the receiving bank in breach of Section 4A—302 results in delay in payment to the beneficiary, the bank is obliged to pay interest to either the originator or the beneficiary of the funds transfer for the period of delay caused by the improper execution. Except as provided in subsection (c), additional damages are not recoverable.

(b) If execution of a payment order by a receiving bank in breach of Section 4A—302 results in (i) noncompletion of the funds transfer, (ii) failure to use an intermediary bank designated by the originator, or (iii) issuance of a payment order that does not comply with the terms of the payment order of the originator, the bank is liable to the originator for its expenses in the funds transfer and for incidental expenses and interest losses, to the extent not covered by subsection (a), resulting from the improper execution. Except as provided in subsection (c), additional damages are not recoverable.

(c) In addition to the amounts payable under subsections (a) and (b), damages, including consequential damages, are recoverable to the extent provided in an express written agreement of the receiving bank.

(d) If a receiving bank fails to execute a payment order it was obliged by express agreement to execute, the receiving bank is liable to the sender for its expenses in the transaction and for incidental expenses and interest losses resulting from the failure to execute. Additional damages, including consequential damages, are recoverable to the extent provided in an express written agreement of the receiving bank, but are not otherwise recoverable.

(e) Reasonable attorney's fees are recoverable if demand for compensation under subsection (a) or (b) is made and refused before an action is brought on the claim. If a claim is made for breach of an agreement under subsection (d) and the agreement does not provide for damages, reasonable attorney's fees are recoverable if demand for compensation under subsection (d) is made and refused before an action is brought on the claim.

(f) Except as stated in this section, the liability of a receiving bank under subsections (a) and (b) may not be varied by agreement.

Part 4 Payment

§ 4A—401. Payment Date.

"Payment date" of a payment order means the day on which the amount of the order is payable to the beneficiary by the beneficiary's bank. The payment date may be determined by instruction of the sender but cannot be earlier than the day the order is received by the beneficiary's bank and, unless otherwise determined, is the day the order is received by the beneficiary's bank.

§ 4A—402. Obligation of Sender to Pay Receiving Bank.

(a) This section is subject to Sections 4A—205 and 4A—207.

(b) With respect to a payment order issued to the beneficiary's bank, acceptance of the order by the bank obliges the sender to pay the bank the amount of the order, but payment is not due until the payment date of the order.

(c) This subsection is subject to subsection (e) and to Section 4A—303. With respect to a payment order issued to a receiving bank other than the beneficiary's bank, acceptance of the order by the receiving bank obliges the sender to pay the bank the amount of the sender's order. Payment by the sender is not due until the execution date of the sender's order. The obligation of that sender to pay its payment order is excused if the funds transfer is not completed by acceptance by the beneficiary's bank of a payment order instructing payment to the beneficiary of that sender's payment order.

(d) If the sender of a payment order pays the order and was not obliged to pay all or part of the amount paid, the bank receiving payment is obliged to refund payment to the extent the sender was not obliged to pay. Except as provided in Sections 4A—204 and 4A—304, interest is payable on the refundable amount from the date of payment.

(e) If a funds transfer is not completed as stated in subsection (c) and an intermediary bank is obliged to refund payment as stated in subsection (d) but is unable to do so because not permitted by applicable law or because the bank suspends payments, a sender in the funds transfer that executed a payment order in compliance with an instruction, as stated in Section 4A—302(a)(1), to route the funds transfer through that intermediary bank is entitled to receive or retain payment from the sender of the payment order that it accepted. The first sender in the funds transfer that issued an instruction requiring routing through that intermediary bank is subrogated to the right of the bank that paid the intermediary bank to refund as stated in subsection (d).

(f) The right of the sender of a payment order to be excused from the obligation to pay the order as stated in subsection (c) or to receive refund under subsection (d) may not be varied by agreement.

§ 4A—403. Payment by Sender to Receiving Bank.

(a) Payment of the sender's obligation under Section 4A—402 to pay the receiving bank occurs as follows:

(1) If the sender is a bank, payment occurs when the receiving bank receives final settlement of the obligation through a Federal Reserve Bank or through a funds-transfer system.

(2) If the sender is a bank and the sender (i) credited an account of the receiving bank with the sender, or (ii) caused an account of the receiving bank in another bank to be credited, payment occurs when the credit is withdrawn or, if not withdrawn, at midnight of the day on which the credit is withdrawable and the receiving bank learns of that fact.

(3) If the receiving bank debits an account of the sender with the receiving bank, payment occurs when the debit is made to the extent the debit is covered by a withdrawable credit balance in the account.

(b) If the sender and receiving bank are members of a funds-transfer system that nets obligations multilaterally among participants, the receiving bank receives final settlement when settlement is complete in accordance with the rules of the system. The obligation of the sender to pay the amount of a payment order transmitted through the funds-transfer system may be satisfied, to the extent permitted by the rules of the system, by setting off and applying against the sender's obligation the right of the sender to receive payment from the receiving bank of the amount of any other payment order transmitted to the sender by the receiving bank through the funds-transfer system. The aggregate balance of obligations owed by each sender to each receiving bank in the funds-transfer system may be satisfied, to the extent permitted by the rules of the system, by setting off and applying against that balance the aggregate balance of obligations owed to the sender by other members of the system. The aggregate balance is determined after the right of setoff stated in the second sentence of this subsection has been exercised.

(c) If two banks transmit payment orders to each other under an agreement that settlement of the obligations of each bank to the other under Section 4A—402 will be made at the end of the day or other period, the total amount owed with respect to all orders transmitted by one bank shall be set off against the total amount owed with respect to all orders transmitted by the other bank. To the extent of the setoff, each bank has made payment to the other.

(d) In a case not covered by subsection (a), the time when payment of the sender's obligation under Section 4A—402(b) or 4A—402(c) occurs is governed by applicable principles of law that determine when an obligation is satisfied.

§ 4A—404. Obligation of Beneficiary's Bank to Pay and Give Notice to Beneficiary.

(a) Subject to Sections 4A—211(e), 4A—405(d), and 4A—405(e), if a beneficiary's bank accepts a payment order, the bank is obliged to pay the amount of the order to the beneficiary of the order. Payment is due on the payment date of the order, but if acceptance occurs on the payment date after the close of the funds-transfer business day of the bank, payment is due on the next funds-transfer business day. If the bank refuses to pay after demand by the beneficiary and receipt of notice of particular circumstances that will give rise to consequential damages as a result of nonpayment, the beneficiary may recover damages resulting from the refusal to pay to the extent the bank had notice of the damages, unless the bank proves that it did not pay because of a reasonable doubt concerning the right of the beneficiary to payment.

(b) If a payment order accepted by the beneficiary's bank instructs payment to an account of the beneficiary, the bank is obliged to notify the beneficiary of receipt of the order before midnight of the next funds-transfer business day following the payment date. If the payment order does not instruct payment to an account of the beneficiary, the bank is required to notify the beneficiary only if notice is required by the order. Notice may be given by first class mail or any other means reasonable in the circumstances. If the bank fails to give the required notice, the bank is obliged to pay interest to the beneficiary on the amount of the payment order from the day notice should have been given until the day the beneficiary learned of receipt of the payment order by the bank. No other damages are recoverable. Reasonable attorney's fees are also recoverable if demand for interest is made and refused before an action is brought on the claim.

(c) The right of a beneficiary to receive payment and damages as stated in subsection (a) may not be varied by agreement or a funds-transfer system rule. The right of a beneficiary to be notified as stated in subsection (b) may be varied by agreement of the beneficiary or by a funds-transfer system rule if the beneficiary is notified of the rule before initiation of the funds transfer.

§ 4A—405. Payment by Beneficiary's Bank to Beneficiary.

(a) If the beneficiary's bank credits an account of the beneficiary of a payment order, payment of the bank's obligation under Section 4A—404(a) occurs when and to the extent (i) the beneficiary is notified of the right to withdraw the credit, (ii) the bank lawfully applies the credit to a debt of the beneficiary, or (iii) funds with respect to the order are otherwise made available to the beneficiary by the bank.

(b) If the beneficiary's bank does not credit an account of the beneficiary of a payment order, the time when payment of the bank's obligation under Section 4A—404(a) occurs is governed by principles of law that determine when an obligation is satisfied.

(c) Except as stated in subsections (d) and (e), if the beneficiary's bank pays the beneficiary of a payment order under a condition to payment or agreement of the beneficiary giving the bank the right to recover payment from the beneficiary if the bank does not receive payment of the order, the condition to payment or agreement is not enforceable.

(d) A funds-transfer system rule may provide that payments made to beneficiaries of funds transfers made through the system are provisional until receipt of payment by the beneficiary's bank of the payment order it accepted. A beneficiary's bank that makes a payment that is provisional under the rule is entitled to refund from the beneficiary if (i) the rule requires that both the beneficiary and the originator be given notice of the provisional nature of the payment before the funds transfer is initiated, (ii) the beneficiary, the beneficiary's bank, and the originator's bank agreed to be bound by the rule, and (iii) the beneficiary's bank did not receive payment of the payment order that it accepted. If the beneficiary is obliged to refund payment to the beneficiary's bank, acceptance of the payment order by the beneficiary's bank is nullified and no payment by the originator of the funds transfer to the beneficiary occurs under Section 4A—406.

(e) This subsection applies to a funds transfer that includes a payment order transmitted over a funds-transfer system that (i) nets obligations multilaterally among participants, and (ii) has in effect a loss-sharing agreement among participants for the purpose of providing funds necessary to complete settlement of the obligations of one or more participants that do not meet their settlement obligations. If the beneficiary's bank in the funds transfer accepts a payment order and the system fails to complete settlement pursuant to its rules with respect to any payment order in the funds transfer, (i) the acceptance by the beneficiary's bank is nullified and no person has any right or obligation based on the acceptance, (ii) the beneficiary's bank is entitled to recover payment from the beneficiary, (iii) no payment by the originator to the beneficiary occurs under Section 4A—406, and (iv) subject to Section 4A—402(e), each sender in the funds transfer is excused from its obligation to pay its payment order under Section 4A—402(c) because the funds transfer has not been completed.

§ 4A—406. Payment by Originator to Beneficiary; Discharge of Underlying Obligation.

(a) Subject to Sections 4A—211(e), 4A—405(d), and 4A—405(e), the originator of a funds transfer pays the beneficiary of the originator's payment order (i) at the time a payment order for the benefit of the beneficiary is accepted by the beneficiary's bank in the funds transfer and (ii) in an amount equal to the amount of the order accepted by the beneficiary's bank, but not more than the amount of the originator's order.

(b) If payment under subsection (a) is made to satisfy an obligation, the obligation is discharged to the same extent discharge would result from payment to the beneficiary of the same amount in money, unless (i) the payment under subsection (a) was made by a means prohibited by the contract of the beneficiary with respect to the obligation, (ii) the beneficiary, within a reasonable time after receiving notice of receipt of the order by the beneficiary's bank, notified the originator of the beneficiary's refusal of the payment, (iii) funds with respect to the order were not withdrawn by the beneficiary or applied to a debt of the beneficiary, and (iv) the beneficiary would suffer a loss that could reasonably have been avoided if payment had been made by a means complying with the contract. If payment by the originator does not result in discharge under this section, the originator is subrogated to the rights of the beneficiary to receive payment from the beneficiary's bank under Section 4A—404(a).

(c) For the purpose of determining whether discharge of an obligation occurs under subsection (b), if the beneficiary's bank accepts a payment order in an amount equal to the amount of the originator's payment order less charges of one or more receiving banks in the funds transfer, payment to the beneficiary is deemed to be in the amount of the originator's order unless upon demand by the beneficiary the originator does not pay the beneficiary the amount of the deducted charges.

(d) Rights of the originator or of the beneficiary of a funds transfer under this section may be varied only by agreement of the originator and the beneficiary.

Part 5 Miscellaneous Provisions

§ 4A—501. Variation by Agreement and Effect of Funds-Transfer System Rule.

(a) Except as otherwise provided in this Article, the rights and obligations of a party to a funds transfer may be varied by agreement of the affected party.

(b) "Funds-transfer system rule" means a rule of an association of banks (i) governing transmission of payment orders by means of a funds-transfer system of the association or rights and obligations with respect to those orders, or (ii) to the extent the rule governs rights and obligations between banks that are parties to a funds transfer in which a Federal Reserve Bank, acting as an intermediary bank, sends a payment order to the beneficiary's bank. Except as otherwise provided in this Article, a funds-transfer system rule governing rights and obligations between participating banks using the system may be effective even if the rule conflicts with this Article and indirectly affects another party to the funds transfer who does not consent to the rule. A funds-transfer system rule may also govern rights and obligations of parties other than participating banks using the system to the extent stated in Sections 4A—404(c), 4A—405(d), and 4A—507(c).

§ 4A—502. Creditor Process Served on Receiving Bank; Setoff by Beneficiary's Bank.

(a) As used in this section, "creditor process" means levy, attachment, garnishment, notice of lien, sequestration, or similar process issued by or on behalf of a creditor or other claimant with respect to an account.

(b) This subsection applies to creditor process with respect to an authorized account of the sender of a payment order if the creditor process is served on the receiving bank. For the purpose of determining rights with respect to the creditor process, if the receiving bank accepts the payment order the balance in the authorized account is deemed to be reduced by the amount of the payment order to the extent the bank did not otherwise receive payment of the order, unless the creditor process is served at a time and in a manner affording the bank a reasonable opportunity to act on it before the bank accepts the payment order.

(c) If a beneficiary's bank has received a payment order for payment to the beneficiary's account in the bank, the following rules apply:

(1) The bank may credit the beneficiary's account. The amount credited may be set off against an obligation owed by the beneficiary to the bank or may be applied to satisfy creditor process served on the bank with respect to the account.

(2) The bank may credit the beneficiary's account and allow withdrawal of the amount credited unless creditor process with respect to the account is served at a time and in a manner affording the bank a reasonable opportunity to act to prevent withdrawal.

(3) If creditor process with respect to the beneficiary's account has been served and the bank has had a reasonable opportunity to act on it, the bank may not reject the payment order except for a reason unrelated to the service of process.

(d) Creditor process with respect to a payment by the originator to the beneficiary pursuant to a funds transfer may be served only on the beneficiary's bank with respect to the debt owed by that bank to the beneficiary. Any other bank served with the creditor process is not obliged to act with respect to the process.

§ 4A—503. Injunction or Restraining Order with Respect to Funds Transfer.

For proper cause and in compliance with applicable law, a court may restrain (i) a person from issuing a payment order to initiate a funds transfer, (ii) an originator's bank from executing the payment order of the originator, or (iii) the beneficiary's bank from releasing funds to the beneficiary or the beneficiary from withdrawing the funds. A court may not otherwise restrain a person from issuing a payment order, paying or receiving payment of a payment order, or otherwise acting with respect to a funds transfer.

§ 4A—504. Order in Which Items and Payment Orders May Be Charged to Account; Order of Withdrawals from Account.

(a) If a receiving bank has received more than one payment order of the sender or one or more payment orders and other items that are payable from the sender's account, the bank may charge the sender's account with respect to the various orders and items in any sequence.

(b) In determining whether a credit to an account has been withdrawn by the holder of the account or applied to a debt of the holder of the account, credits first made to the account are first withdrawn or applied.

§ 4A—505. Preclusion of Objection to Debit of Customer's Account.

If a receiving bank has received payment from its customer with respect to a payment order issued in the name of the customer as sender and accepted by the bank, and the customer received notification reasonably identifying the order, the customer is precluded from asserting that the bank is not entitled to retain the payment unless the customer notifies the bank of the customer's objection to the payment within one year after the notification was received by the customer.

§ 4A—506. Rate of Interest.

(a) If, under this Article, a receiving bank is obliged to pay interest with respect to a payment order issued to the bank, the amount payable may be determined (i) by agreement of the sender and receiving bank, or (ii) by a funds-transfer system rule if the payment order is transmitted through a funds-transfer system.

(b) If the amount of interest is not determined by an agreement or rule as stated in subsection (a), the amount is calculated by multiplying the applicable Federal Funds rate by the amount on which interest is payable, and then multiplying the product by the number of days for which interest is payable. The applicable Federal Funds rate is the average of the Federal Funds rates published by the Federal Reserve Bank of New York for each of the days for which interest is payable divided by 360. The Federal Funds rate for any day on which a published rate is not available is the same as the published rate for the next preceding day for which there is a published rate. If a receiving bank that accepted a payment order is required to refund payment to the sender of the order because the funds transfer was not completed, but the failure to complete was not due to any fault by the bank, the interest payable is reduced by a percentage equal to the reserve requirement on deposits of the receiving bank.

§ 4A—507. Choice of Law.

(a) The following rules apply unless the affected parties otherwise agree or subsection (c) applies:

(1) The rights and obligations between the sender of a payment order and the receiving bank are governed by the law of the jurisdiction in which the receiving bank is located.

(2) The rights and obligations between the beneficiary's bank and the beneficiary are governed by the law of the jurisdiction in which the beneficiary's bank is located.

(3) The issue of when payment is made pursuant to a funds transfer by the originator to the beneficiary is governed by the law of the jurisdiction in which the beneficiary's bank is located.

(b) If the parties described in each paragraph of subsection (a) have made an agreement selecting the law of a particular jurisdiction to govern rights and obligations between each other, the law of that jurisdiction governs those rights and obligations, whether or not the payment order or the funds transfer bears a reasonable relation to that jurisdiction.

(c) A funds-transfer system rule may select the law of a particular jurisdiction to govern (i) rights and obligations between participating banks with respect to payment orders transmitted or processed through the system, or (ii) the rights and obligations of some or all parties to a funds transfer any part of which is carried out by means of the system. A choice of law made pursuant to clause (i) is binding on participating banks. A choice of law made pursuant to clause (ii) is binding on the originator, other sender, or a receiving bank having notice that the funds-transfer system might be used in the funds transfer and of the choice of law by the system when the originator, other sender, or receiving bank issued or accepted a payment order. The beneficiary of a funds transfer is bound by the choice of law if, when the funds transfer is initiated, the beneficiary has notice that the funds-transfer system might be used in the funds transfer and of the choice of law by the system. The law of a jurisdiction selected pursuant to this subsection may govern, whether or not that law bears a reasonable relation to the matter in issue.

(d) In the event of inconsistency between an agreement under subsection (b) and a choice-of-law rule under subsection (c), the agreement under subsection (b) prevails.

(e) If a funds transfer is made by use of more than one funds-transfer system and there is inconsistency between choice-of-law rules of the systems, the matter in issue is governed by the law of the selected jurisdiction that has the most significant relationship to the matter in issue.

[Articles 5, 6, 7, and 8 are not includeed here.]

Article 9
SECURED TRANSACTIONS; SALES OF ACCOUNTS AND CHATTEL PAPER

Note: *The adoption of this Article should be accompanied by the repeal of existing statutes dealing with conditional sales, trust receipts, factor's liens where the factor is given a nonpossessory lien, chattel mortgages, crop mortgages, mortgages on railroad equipment, assignment of accounts and generally statutes regulating security interests in personal property.*

Where the state has a retail installment selling act or small loan act, that legislation should be carefully examined to determine what changes in those acts are needed to conform them to this Article. This Article primarily sets out rules defining rights of a secured party against persons dealing with the debtor; it does not prescribe regulations and controls which may be necessary to curb abuses arising in the small loan business or in the financing of consumer purchases on credit. Accordingly there is no intention to repeal existing regulatory acts in those fields by enactment or re-enactment of Article 9. See Section 9—203(4) and the Note thereto.

Part 1 Short Title, Applicability and Definitions

§ 9—101. Short Title.

This Article shall be known and may be cited as Uniform Commercial Code—Secured Transactions.

§ 9—102. Policy and Subject Matter of Article.

(1) Except as otherwise provided in Section 9—104 on excluded transactions, this Article applies

(a) to any transaction (regardless of its form) which is intended to create a security interest in personal property or fixtures including goods, documents, instruments, general intangibles, chattel paper or accounts; and also

(b) to any sale of accounts or chattel paper.

(2) This Article applies to security interests created by contract including pledge, assignment, chattel mortgage, chattel trust, trust deed, factor's lien, equipment trust, conditional sale, trust receipt, other lien or title retention contract and lease or consignment intended as security. This Article does not apply to statutory liens except as provided in Section 9—310.

(3) The application of this Article to a security interest in a secured obligation is not affected by the fact that the obligation is itself secured by a transaction or interest to which this Article does not apply.

§ 9—103. Perfection of Security Interest in Multiple State Transactions.

(1) Documents, instruments and ordinary goods.

(a) This subsection applies to documents, instruments, rights to proceeds of written letters of credit, and goods other than those covered by a certificate of title described in subsection (2), mobile goods described in subsection (3), and minerals described in subsection (5).

(b) Except as otherwise provided in this subsection, perfection and the effect of perfection or non-perfection of a security interest in collateral are governed by the law of the jurisdiction where the collateral is when the last event occurs on which is based the assertion that the security interest is perfected or unperfected.

(c) If the parties to a transaction creating a purchase money security interest in goods in one jurisdiction understand at the time that the security interest attaches that the goods will be kept in another jurisdiction, then the law of the other jurisdiction governs the perfection and the effect of perfection or non-perfection of the security interest from the time it attaches until thirty days after the debtor receives possession of the goods and thereafter if the goods are taken to the other jurisdiction before the end of the thirty-day period.

(d) When collateral is brought into and kept in this state while subject to a security interest perfected under the law of the jurisdiction from which the collateral was removed, the security interest remains perfected, but if action is required by Part 3 of this Article to perfect the security interest,

(i) if the action is not taken before the expiration of the period of perfection in the other jurisdiction or the end of four months after the collateral is brought into this state, whichever period first expires, the security interest becomes unperfected at the end of that period and is thereafter deemed to have been unperfected as against a person who became a purchaser after removal;

(ii) if the action is taken before the expiration of the period specified in subparagraph (i), the security interest continues perfected thereafter;

(iii) for the purpose of priority over a buyer of consumer goods (subsection (2) of Section 9—307), the period of the effectiveness of a filing in the jurisdiction from which the collateral is removed is governed by the rules with respect to perfection in subparagraphs (i) and (ii).

(2) Certificate of title.

(a) This subsection applies to goods covered by a certificate of title issued under a statute of this state or of another jurisdiction under the law of which indication of a security interest on the certificate is required as a condition of perfection.

(b) Except as otherwise provided in this subsection, perfection and the effect of perfection or non-perfection of the security interest are governed by the law (including the conflict of laws rules) of the jurisdiction issuing the certificate until four months after the goods are removed from that jurisdiction and thereafter until the goods are registered in another jurisdiction, but in any event not beyond surrender of the certificate. After the expiration of that period, the goods are not covered by the certificate of title within the meaning of this section.

(c) Except with respect to the rights of a buyer described in the next paragraph, a security interest, perfected in another jurisdiction otherwise than by notation on a certificate of title, in goods brought into this state and thereafter covered by a certificate of title issued by this state is subject to the rules stated in paragraph (d) of subsection (1).

(d) If goods are brought into this state while a security interest therein is perfected in any manner under the law of the jurisdiction from which the goods are removed and a certificate of title is issued by this state and the certificate does not show that the goods are subject to the security interest or that they may be subject to security interests not shown on the certificate, the security interest is subordinate to the rights of a buyer of the goods who is not in the business of selling goods of that kind to the extent that he gives value and receives delivery of the goods after issuance of the certificate and without knowledge of the security interest.

(3) Accounts, general intangibles and mobile goods.

(a) This subsection applies to accounts (other than an account described in subsection (5) on minerals) and general intangibles (other than uncertificated securities) and to goods which are mobile and which are of a type normally used in more than one jurisdiction, such as motor vehicles, trailers, rolling stock, airplanes, shipping containers, road building and construction machinery and commercial harvesting machinery and the like, if the goods are equipment or are inventory leased or held for lease by the debtor to others, and are not covered by a certificate of title described in subsection (2).

(b) The law (including the conflict of laws rules) of the jurisdiction in which the debtor is located governs the perfection and the effect of perfection or non-perfection of the security interest.

(c) If, however, the debtor is located in a jurisdiction which is not a part of the United States, and which does not provide for perfection of the security interest by filing or recording in that jurisdiction, the law of the jurisdiction in the United States in which the debtor has its major executive office in the United States governs the perfection and the effect of perfection or non-perfection of the security interest through filing. In the alternative, if the debtor is located in a jurisdiction which is not a part of the United States or Canada and the collateral is accounts or general intangibles for money due or to become due, the security interest may be perfected by notification to the account debtor. As used in this paragraph, "United States" includes its territories and possessions and the Commonwealth of Puerto Rico.

(d) A debtor shall be deemed located at his place of business if he has one, at his chief executive office if he has more than one place of business, otherwise at his residence. If, however, the debtor is a foreign air carrier under the Federal Aviation Act of 1958, as amended, it shall be deemed located at the designated office of the agent upon whom service of process may be made on behalf of the foreign air carrier.

(e) A security interest perfected under the law of the jurisdiction of the location of the debtor is perfected until the expiration of four months after a change of the debtor's location to another jurisdiction, or until perfection would have ceased by the law of the first jurisdiction, whichever period first expires. Unless perfected in the new jurisdiction before the end of that period, it becomes unperfected thereafter and is deemed to have been unperfected as against a person who became a purchaser after the change.

(4) Chattel paper.

The rules stated for goods in subsection (1) apply to a possessory security interest in chattel paper. The rules stated for accounts in subsection (3) apply to a nonpossessory security interest in chattel paper, but the security interest may not be perfected by notification to the account debtor.

(5) Minerals.

Perfection and the effect of perfection or non-perfection of a security interest which is created by a debtor who has an interest in minerals or the like (including oil and gas) before extraction and which attaches thereto as extracted, or which attaches to an account resulting from the sale thereof at the wellhead or minehead are governed by the law (including the conflict of laws rules) of the jurisdiction wherein the wellhead or minehead is located.

(6) Investment property.

(a) This subsection applies to investment property.

(b) Except as otherwise provided in paragraph (f), during the time that a security certificate is located in a jurisdiction, perfection of a security interest, the effect of perfection or non-perfection, and the priority of a security interest in the certificated security represented thereby are governed by the local law of that jurisdiction.

(c) Except as otherwise provided in paragraph (f), perfection of a security interest, the effect of perfection or non-perfection, and the priority of a security interest in an uncertificated security are governed by the local law of the issuer's jurisdiction as specified in Section 8—110(d).

(d) Except as otherwise provided in paragraph (f), perfection of a security interest, the effect of perfection or non-perfection, and the priority of a security interest in a security entitlement or securities account are governed by the local law of the securities intermediary's jurisdiction as specified in Section 8—110(e).

(e) Except as otherwise provided in paragraph (f), perfection of a security interest, the effect of perfection or non-perfection, and the priority of a security interest in a commodity contract or commodity account are governed by the local law of the commodity intermediary's jurisdiction. The following rules determine a "commodity intermediary's jurisdiction" for purposes of this paragraph:

(i) If an agreement between the commodity intermediary and commodity customer specifies that it is governed by the law of a particular jurisdiction, that jurisdiction is the commodity intermediary's jurisdiction.

(ii) If an agreement between the commodity intermediary and commodity customer does not specify the governing law as provided in subparagraph (i), but expressly specifies that the commodity account is maintained at an office in a particular jurisdiction, that jurisdiction is the commodity intermediary's jurisdiction.

(iii) If an agreement between the commodity intermediary and commodity customer does not specify a jurisdiction as provided in subparagraphs (i) or (ii), the commodity intermediary's jurisdiction is the jurisdiction in which is located the office identified in an account statement as the office serving the commodity customer's account.

(iv) If an agreement between the commodity intermediary and commodity customer does not specify a jurisdiction as provided in subparagraphs (i) or (ii) and an account statement does not identify an office serving the commodity customer's account as provided in subparagraph (iii), the commodity intermediary's jurisdiction is the jurisdiction in which is located the chief executive office of the commodity intermediary.

(f) Perfection of a security interest by filing, automatic perfection of a security interest in investment property granted by a broker or securities intermediary, and automatic perfection of a security interest in a commodity contract or commodity account granted by a commodity intermediary are governed by the local law of the jurisdiction in which the debtor is located.

§ 9—104. **Transactions Excluded From Article.**

This Article does not apply

(a) to a security interest subject to any statute of the United States, to the extent that such statute governs the rights of parties to and third parties affected by transactions in particular types of property; or

(b) to a landlord's lien; or

(c) to a lien given by statute or other rule of law for services or materials except as provided in Section 9—310 on priority of such liens; or

(d) to a transfer of a claim for wages, salary or other compensation of an employee; or

(e) to a transfer by a government or governmental subdivision or agency; or

(f) to a sale of accounts or chattel paper as part of a sale of the business out of which they arose, or an assignment of accounts or chattel paper which is for the purpose of collection only, or a transfer of a right to payment under a contract to an assignee who is also to do the performance under the contract or a transfer of a single account to an assignee in whole or partial satisfaction of a preexisting indebtedness; or

(g) to a transfer of an interest in or claim in or under any policy of insurance, except as provided with respect to proceeds (Section 9—306) and priorities in proceeds (Section 9—312); or

(h) to a right represented by a judgment (other than a judgment taken on a right to payment which was collateral); or

(i) to any right of set-off; or

(j) except to the extent that provision is made for fixtures in Section 9—313, to the creation or transfer of an interest in or lien on real estate, including a lease or rents thereunder; or

(k) to a transfer in whole or in part of any claim arising out of tort; or

(l) to a transfer of an interest in any deposit account (subsection (1) of Section 9—105), except as provided with respect to proceeds (Section 9—306) and priorities in proceeds (Section 9—312).

(m) to a transfer of an interest in a letter of credit other than the rights to proceeds of a written letter of credit.

§ 9—105. **Definitions and Index of Definitions.**

(1) In this Article unless the context otherwise requires:

(a) "Account debtor" means the person who is obligated on an account, chattel paper or general intangible;

(b) "Chattel paper" means a writing or writings which evidence both a monetary obligation and a security interest in or a lease of specific goods, but a charter or other contract involving the use or hire of a vessel is not chattel paper. When a transaction is evidenced both by such a security agreement or a lease and by an instrument or a series of instruments, the group of writings taken together constitutes chattel paper;

(c) "Collateral" means the property subject to a security interest, and includes accounts and chattel paper which have been sold;

(d) "Debtor" means the person who owes payment or other performance of the obligation secured, whether or not he owns or has rights in the collateral, and includes the seller of accounts or chattel paper. Where the debtor and the owner of the collateral are not the same person, the term "debtor" means the owner of the collateral in any provision of the Article dealing with the collateral, the obligor in any provision dealing with the obligation, and may include both where the context so requires;

(e) "Deposit account" means a demand, time, savings, passbook or like account maintained with a bank, savings and loan association, credit union or like organization, other than an account evidenced by a certificate of deposit;

(f) "Document" means document of title as defined in the general definitions of Article 1 (Section 1—201), and a receipt of the kind described in subsection (2) of Section 7—201;

(g) "Encumbrance" includes real estate mortgages and other liens on real estate and all other rights in real estate that are not ownership interests;

(h) "Goods" includes all things which are movable at the time the security interest attaches or which are fixtures (Section 9—313), but does not include money, documents, instruments, investment property, commodity contracts accounts, chattel paper, general intangibles, or minerals or the like (including oil and gas) before extraction. "Goods" also includes standing timber which is to be cut and removed under a conveyance or contract for sale, the unborn young of animals, and growing crops;

(i) "Instrument" means a negotiable instrument (defined in Section 3—104), or any other writing which evidences a right to the payment of money and is not itself a security agreement or lease and is of a type which is in ordinary course of business transferred by delivery with any necessary indorsement or assignment. The term does not include investment property.

(j) "Mortgage" means a consensual interest created by a real estate mortgage, a trust deed on real estate, or the like;

(k) An advance is made "pursuant to commitment" if the secured party has bound himself to make it, whether or not a subsequent event of default or other event not within his control has relieved or may relieve him from his obligation;

(l) "Security agreement" means an agreement which creates or provides for a security interest;

(m) "Secured party" means a lender, seller or other person in whose favor there is a security interest, including a person to whom accounts or chattel paper have been sold. When the holders of obligations issued under an indenture of trust, equipment trust agreement or the like are represented by a trustee or other person, the representative is the secured party;

(n) "Transmitting utility" means any person primarily engaged in the railroad, street railway or trolley bus business, the electric or electronics communications transmission business, the transmission of goods by pipeline, or the transmission or the production and transmission of electricity, steam, gas or water, or the provision of sewer service.

(2) Other definitions applying to this Article and the sections in which they appear are:

"Account". Section 9—106.

"Attach". Section 9—203.

"Commodity contract". Section 9—115.

"Commodity customer". Section 9—115.

"Commodity intermediary". Section 9—115.

"Construction mortgage". Section 9—313(1).

"Consumer goods". Section 9—109(1).

"Control". Section 9—115.

"Equipment". Section 9—109(2).

"Farm products". Section 9—109(3).

"Fixture". Section 9—313(1).

"Fixture filing". Section 9—313(1).

"General intangibles". Section 9—106.

"Inventory". Section 9—109(4).

"Investment property". Section 9—115.

"Lien creditor". Section 9—301(3).

"Proceeds". Section 9—306(1).

"Purchase money security interest". Section 9—107.

"United States". Section 9—103.

(3) The following definitions in other Articles apply to this Article:

"Broker". Section. 8—102.

"Certified security". Section 8—102.

"Check". Section 3—104.

"Clearing corporation". Section 8—102.

"Contract for sale". Section 2—106.

"Control". Section 8—106.

"Delivery". Section 8—301.

"Entitlement holder". Section 8—102.

"Financial asset". Section 8—102.

"Holder in due course". Section 3—302.

"Letter of credit". Section 5—102.

"Note". Section 3—104.

"Proceeds of a letter of credit". Section 5—114(a).

"Sale". Section 2—106.

"Securities intermediary". Section 8—102.

"Security". Section 8—102.

"Security certificate". Section 8—102.

"Security entitlement". Section 8—102.

"Uncertificated security". Section 8—102.

(4) In addition Article 1 contains general definitions and principles of construction and interpretation applicable throughout this Article.

§ 9—106. **Definitions: "Account"; "General Intangibles".**

"Account" means any right to payment for goods sold or leased or for services rendered which is not evidenced by an instrument or chattel paper, whether or not it has been earned by performance. "General intangibles" means any personal property (including things in action) other than goods, accounts, chattel paper, documents, instruments, investment property, rights to proceeds of written letters of credit, and money. All rights to payment earned or unearned under a charter or other contract involving the use or hire of a vessel and all rights incident to the charter or contract are accounts.

§ 9—107. **Definitions: "Purchase Money Security Interest".**

A security interest is a "purchase money security interest" to the extent that it is

(a) taken or retained by the seller of the collateral to secure all or part of its price; or

(b) taken by a person who by making advances or incurring an obligation gives value to enable the debtor to acquire rights in or the use of collateral if such value is in fact so used.

§ 9—108. **When After-Acquired Collateral Not Security for Antecedent Debt.**

Where a secured party makes an advance, incurs an obligation, releases a perfected security interest, or otherwise gives new value which is to be secured in whole or in part by after-acquired property his security interest in the after-acquired collateral shall be deemed to be taken for new value and not as security for an antecedent debt if the debtor acquires his rights in such collateral either in the ordinary course of his business or under a contract of purchase made pursuant to the security agreement within a reasonable time after new value is given.

§ 9—109. **Classification of Goods; "Consumer Goods"; "Equipment"; "Farm Products"; "Inventory".**

Goods are

(1) "consumer goods" if they are used or bought for use primarily for personal, family or household purposes;

(2) "equipment" if they are used or bought for use primarily in business (including farming or a profession) or by a debtor who is a non-profit organization or a governmental subdivision or agency or if the goods are not included in the definitions of inventory, farm products or consumer goods;

(3) "farm products" if they are crops or livestock or supplies used or produced in farming operations or if they are products of crops or livestock in their unmanufactured states (such as ginned cotton, wool-clip, maple syrup, milk and eggs), and if they are in the possession of a debtor engaged in raising, fattening, grazing or other farming operations. If goods are farm products they are neither equipment nor inventory;

(4) "inventory" if they are held by a person who holds them for sale or lease or to be furnished under contracts of service or if he has so furnished them, or if they are raw materials, work in process or materials used or consumed in a business. Inventory of a person is not to be classified as his equipment.

§ 9—110. **Sufficiency of Description.**

For purposes of this Article any description of personal property or real estate is sufficient whether or not it is specific if it reasonably identifies what is described.

§ 9—111. Applicability of Bulk Transfer Laws.

The creation of a security interest is not a bulk transfer under Article 6 (see Section 6—103).

§ 9—112. Where Collateral Is Not Owned by Debtor.

Unless otherwise agreed, when a secured party knows that collateral is owned by a person who is not the debtor, the owner of the collateral is entitled to receive from the secured party any surplus under Section 9—502(2) or under Section 9—504(1), and is not liable for the debt or for any deficiency after resale, and he has the same right as the debtor

(a) to receive statements under Section 9—208;

(b) to receive notice of and to object to a secured party's proposal to retain the collateral in satisfaction of the indebtedness under Section 9—505;

(c) to redeem the collateral under Section 9—506;

(d) to obtain injunctive or other relief under Section 9—507(1); and

(e) to recover losses caused to him under Section 9—208(2).

§ 9—113. Security Interests Arising Under Article on Sales or Under Article on Leases.

A security interest arising solely under the Article on Sales (Article 2) or the Article on Leases is subject to the provisions of this Article except that to the extent that and so long as the debtor does not have or does not lawfully obtain possession of the goods

(a) no security agreement is necessary to make the security interest enforceable; and

(b) no filing is required to perfect the security interest; and

(c) the rights of the secured party on default by the debtor are governed (i) by the Article on Sales (Article 2) in the case of a security interest arising solely under such Article or (ii) by the Article on Leases (Article 2A) in the case of a security interest arising solely under such Article.

§ 9—114. Consignment.

(1) A person who delivers goods under a consignment which is not a security interest and who would be required to file under this Article by paragraph (3)(c) of Section 2—326 has priority over a secured party who is or becomes a creditor of the consignee and who would have a perfected security interest in the goods if they were the property of the consignee, and also has priority with respect to identifiable cash proceeds received on or before delivery of the goods to a buyer, if

    (a) the consignor complies with the filing provision of the Article on Sales with respect to consignments (paragraph (3)(c) of Section 2—326) before the consignee receives possession of the goods; and

    (b) the consignor gives notification in writing to the holder of the security interest if the holder has filed a financing statement covering the same types of goods before the date of the filing made by the consignor; and

    (c) the holder of the security interest receives the notification within five years before the consignee receives possession of the goods; and

    (d) the notification states that the consignor expects to deliver goods on consignment to the consignee, describing the goods by item or type.

(2) In the case of a consignment which is not a security interest and in which the requirements of the preceding subsection have not been met, a person who delivers goods to another is subordinate to a person who would have a perfected security interest in the goods if they were the property of the debtor.

§ 9—115. Investment Property.

(1) In this Article:

    (a) "Commodity account" means an account maintained by a commodity intermediary in which a commodity contract is carried for a commodity customer.

    (b) "Commodity contract" means a commodity futures contract, an option on a commodity futures contract, a commodity option, or other contract that, in each case, is:

        (i) traded on or subject to the rules of a board of trade that has been designated as a contract market for such a contract pursuant to the federal commodities laws; or

        (ii) traded on a foreign commodity board of trade, exchange, or market, and is carried on the books of a commodity intermediary for a commodity customer.

    (c) "Commodity customer" means a person for whom a commodity intermediary carries a commodity contract on its books.

    (d) "Commodity intermediary" means:

        (i) a person who is registered as a futures commission merchant under the federal commodities laws; or

        (ii) a person who in the ordinary course of its business provides clearance or settlement services for a board of trade that has been designated as a contract market pursuant to the federal commodities laws.

    (e) "Control" with respect to a certificated security, uncertificated security, or security entitlement has the meaning specified in Section 8—106. A secured party has control over a commodity contract if by agreement among the commodity customer, the commodity intermediary, and the secured party, the commodity intermediary has agreed that it will apply any value distributed on account of the commodity contract as directed by the secured party without further consent by the commodity customer. If a commodity customer grants a security interest in a commodity contract to its own commodity intermediary, the commodity intermediary as secured party has control. A secured party has control over a securities account or commodity account if the secured party has control over all security entitlements or commodity contracts carried in the securities account or commodity account.

    (f) "Investment property" means:

        (i) a security, whether certificated or uncertificated;

        (ii) a security entitlement;

        (iii) a securities account;

        (iv) a commodity contract; or

        (v) a commodity account.

(2) Attachment or perfection of a security interest in a securities account is also attachment or perfection of a security interest in all

security entitlements carried in the securities account. Attachment or perfection of a security interest in a commodity account is also attachment or perfection of a security interest in all commodity contracts carried in the commodity account.

(3) A description of collateral in a security agreement or financing statement is sufficient to create or perfect a security interest in a certificated security, uncertificated security, security entitlement, securities account, commodity contract, or commodity account whether it describes the collateral by those terms, or as investment property, or by description of the underlying security, financial asset, or commodity contract. A description of investment property collateral in a security agreement or financing statement is sufficient if it identifies the collateral by specific listing, by category, by quantity, by a computational or allocational formula or procedure, or by any other method, if the identity of the collateral is objectively determinable.

(4) Perfection of a security interest in investment property is governed by the following rules:

(a) A security interest in investment property may be perfected by control.

(b) Except as otherwise provided in paragraphs (c) and (d), a security interest in investment property may be perfected by filing.

(c) If the debtor is a broker or securities intermediary a security interest in investment property is perfected when it attaches. The filing of a financing statement with respect to a security interest in investment property granted by a broker or securities intermediary has no effect for purposes of perfection or priority with respect to that security interest.

(d) If a debtor is a commodity, intermediary, a security interest in a commodity contract or a commodity account is perfected when it attaches. The filing of a financing statement with respect to a security interest in a commodity contract or a commodity account granted by a commodity intermediary has no effect for purposes of perfection or priority with respect to that security interest.

(5) Priority between conflicting security interests in the same investment property is governed by the following rules:

(a) A security interest of a secured party who has control over investment property has priority over a security interest of a secured party who does not have control over the investment property.

(b) Except as otherwise provided in paragraphs (c) and (d), conflicting security interests of secured parties each of whom has control rank equally.

(c) Except as otherwise agreed by the securities intermediary, a security interest in a security entitlement or a securities account granted to the debtor's own securities intermediary has priority over any security interest granted by the debtor to another secured party.

(d) Except as otherwise agreed by the commodity intermediary, a security interest in a commodity contract or a commodity account granted to the debtor's own commodity intermediary has priority over any security interest granted by the debtor to another secured party.

(e) Conflicting security interests granted by a broker, a securities intermediary, or a commodity intermediary which are perfected without control rank equally.

(f) In all other cases, priority between conflicting security interests in investment property is governed by Section 9—312(5), (6), and (7). Section 9—312(4) does not apply to investment property.

(6) If a security certificate in registered form is delivered to a secured party pursuant to agreement, a written security agreement is not required for attachment or enforceability of the security interest, delivery suffices for perfection of the security interest, and the security interest has priority over a conflicting security interest perfected by means other than control, even if a necessary indorsement is lacking.

§ 9—116. **Security Interest Arising in Purchase or Delivery of Financial Asset.**

(1) If a person buys a financial asset through a securities intermediary in a transaction in which the buyer is obligated to pay the purchase price to the securities intermediary at the time of the purchase, and the securities intermediary credits the financial asset to the buyer's securities account before the buyer pays the securities intermediary, the securities intermediary has a security interest in the buyer's security entitlement securing the buyer's obligation to pay. A security agreement is not required for attachment or enforceability of the security interest, and the security interest is automatically perfected.

(2) If a certificated security, or other financial asset represented by a writing which in the ordinary course of business is transferred by delivery with any necessary indorsement or assignment is delivered pursuant to an agreement between persons in the business of dealing with such securities or financial assets and the agreement calls for delivery versus payment, the person delivering the certificate or other financial asset has a security interest in the certificated security or other financial asset securing the seller's right to receive payment. A security agreement is not required for attachment or enforceability of the security interest, and the security interest is automatically perfected.

Part 2 Validity of Security Agreement and Rights of Parties Thereto

§ 9—201. **General Validity of Security Agreement.**

Except as otherwise provided by this Act a security agreement is effective according to its terms between the parties, against purchasers of the collateral and against creditors. Nothing in this Article validates any charge or practice illegal under any statute or regulation thereunder governing usury, small loans, retail installment sales, or the like, or extends the application of any such statute or regulation to any transaction not otherwise subject thereto.

§ 9—202. **Title to Collateral Immaterial.**

Each provision of this Article with regard to rights, obligations and remedies applies whether title to collateral is in the secured party or in the debtor.

§ 9—203. **Attachment and Enforceability of Security Interest; Proceeds; Formal Requisites.**

(1) Subject to the provisions of Section 4—210 on the security interest of a collecting bank, Sections 9—115 and 9—116 on security interests in investment property, and Section 9—113 on a security interest arising under the Articles on Sales and Leases, a security interest is not enforceable against the debtor or third par-

ties with respect to the collateral and does not attach unless:

(a) the collateral is in the possession of the secured party pursuant to agreement, the collateral is investment property and the secured party has control pursuant to agreement, or the debtor has signed a security agreement which contains a description of the collateral and in addition, when the security interest covers crops growing or to be grown or timber to be cut, a description of the land concerned;

(b) value has been given; and

(c) the debtor has rights in the collateral.

(2) A security interest attaches when it becomes enforceable against the debtor with respect to the collateral. Attachment occurs as soon as all of the events specified in subsection (1) have taken place unless explicit agreement postpones the time of attaching.

(3) Unless otherwise agreed a security agreement gives the secured party the rights to proceeds provided by Section 9—306.

(4) A transaction, although subject to this Article, is also subject to . . . .*, and in the case of conflict between the provisions of this Article and any such statute, the provisions of such statute control. Failure to comply with any applicable statute has only the effect which is specified therein.

Note: At * in subsection (4) insert reference to any local statute regulating small loans, retail installment sales and the like.

The foregoing subsection (4) is designed to make it clear that certain transactions, although subject to this Article, must also comply with other applicable legislation.

This Article is designed to regulate all the "security" aspects of transactions within its scope. There is, however, much regulatory legislation, particularly in the consumer field, which supplements this Article and should not be repealed by its enactment. Examples are small loan acts, retail installment selling acts and the like. Such acts may provide for licensing and rate regulation and may prescribe particular forms of contract. Such provisions should remain in force despite the enactment of this Article. On the other hand if a retail installment selling act contains provisions on filing, rights on default, etc., such provisions should be repealed as inconsistent with this Article except that inconsistent provisions as to deficiencies, penalties, etc., in the Uniform Consumer Credit Code and other recent related legislation should remain because those statutes were drafted after the substantial enactment of the Article and with the intention of modifying certain provisions of this Article as to consumer credit.

§ 9—204. After-Acquired Property; Future Advances.

(1) Except as provided in subsection (2), a security agreement may provide that any or all obligations covered by the security agreement are to be secured by after-acquired collateral.

(2) No security interest attaches under an after-acquired property clause to consumer goods other than accessions (Section 9—314) when given as additional security unless the debtor acquires rights in them within ten days after the secured party gives value.

(3) Obligations covered by a security agreement may include future advances or other value whether or not the advances or value are given pursuant to commitment (subsection (1) of Section 9—105).

§ 9—205. Use or Disposition of Collateral Without Accounting Permissible.

A security interest is not invalid or fraudulent against creditors by reason of liberty in the debtor to use, commingle or dispose of all or part of the collateral (including returned or repossessed goods) or to collect or compromise accounts or chattel paper, or to accept the return of goods or make repossessions, or to use, commingle or dispose of proceeds, or by reason of the failure of the secured party to require the debtor to account for proceeds or replace collateral. This section does not relax the requirements of possession where perfection of a security interest depends upon possession of the collateral by the secured party or by a bailee.

§ 9—206. Agreement Not to Assert Defenses Against Assignee; Modification of Sales Warranties Where Security Agreement Exists.

(1) Subject to any statute or decision which establishes a different rule for buyers or lessees of consumer goods, an agreement by a buyer or lessee that he will not assert against an assignee any claim or defense which he may have against the seller or lessor is enforceable by an assignee who takes his assignment for value, in good faith and without notice of a claim or defense, except as to defenses of a type which may be asserted against a holder in due course of a negotiable instrument under the Article on Negotiable Instruments (Article 3). A buyer who as part of one transaction signs both a negotiable instrument and a security agreement makes such an agreement.

(2) When a seller retains a purchase money security interest in goods the Article on Sales (Article 2) governs the sale and any disclaimer, limitation or modification of the seller's warranties.

§ 9—207. Rights and Duties When Collateral is in Secured Party's Possession

(1) A secured party must use reasonable care in the custody and preservation of collateral in his possession. In the case of an instrument or chattel paper reasonable care includes taking necessary steps to preserve rights against prior parties unless otherwise agreed.

(2) Unless otherwise agreed, when collateral is in the secured party's possession

(a) reasonable expenses (including the cost of any insurance and payment of taxes or other charges) incurred in the custody, preservation, use or operation of the collateral are chargeable to the debtor and are secured by the collateral;

(b) the risk of accidental loss or damage is on the debtor to the extent of any deficiency in any effective insurance coverage;

(c) the secured party may hold as additional security any increase or profits (except money) received from the collateral, but money so received, unless remitted to the debtor, shall be applied in reduction of the secured obligation;

(d) the secured party must keep the collateral identifiable but fungible collateral may be commingled;

(e) the secured party may repledge the collateral upon terms which do not impair the debtor's right to redeem it.

(3) A secured party is liable for any loss caused by his failure to meet any obligation imposed by the preceding subsections but does not lose his security interest.

(4) A secured party may use or operate the collateral for the purpose of preserving the collateral or its value or pursuant to the order of a court of appropriate jurisdiction or, except in the case of consumer goods, in the manner and to the extent provided in the security agreement.

§ 9—208. Request for Statement of Account or List of Collateral.

(1) A debtor may sign a statement indicating what he believes to be the aggregate amount of unpaid indebtedness as of a specified date and may send it to the secured party with a request that the statement be approved or corrected and returned to the debtor. When the security agreement or any other record kept by the secured party identifies the collateral a debtor may similarly request the secured party to approve or correct a list of the collateral.

(2) The secured party must comply with such a request within two weeks after receipt by sending a written correction or approval. If the secured party claims a security interest in all of a particular type of collateral owned by the debtor he may indicate that fact in his reply and need not approve or correct an itemized list of such collateral. If the secured party without reasonable excuse fails to comply he is liable for any loss caused to the debtor thereby; and if the debtor has properly included in his request a good faith statement of the obligation or a list of the collateral or both the secured party may claim a security interest only as shown in the statement against persons misled by his failure to comply. If he no longer has an interest in the obligation or collateral at the time the request is received he must disclose the name and address of any successor in interest known to him and he is liable for any loss caused to the debtor as a result of failure to disclose. A successor in interest is not subject to this section until a request is received by him.

(3) A debtor is entitled to such a statement once every six months without charge. The secured party may require payment of a charge not exceeding $10 for each additional statement furnished.

Part 3 Rights of Third Parties; Perfected and Unperfected Security Interests; Rules of Priority

§ 9—301. Persons Who Take Priority Over Unperfected Security Interests; Rights of "Lien Creditor".

(1) Except as otherwise provided in subsection (2), an unperfected security interest is subordinate to the rights of

(a) persons entitled to priority under Section 9—312;

(b) a person who becomes a lien creditor before the security interest is perfected;

(c) in the case of goods, instruments, documents, and chattel paper, a person who is not a secured party and who is a transferee in bulk or other buyer not in ordinary course of business or is a buyer of farm products in ordinary course of business, to the extent that he gives value and receives delivery of the collateral without knowledge of the security interest and before it is perfected;

(d) in the case of accounts, general intangibles, and investment property a person who is not a secured party and who is a transferee to the extent that he gives value without knowledge of the security interest and before it is perfected.

(2) If the secured party files with respect to a purchase money security interest before or within ten days after the debtor receives possession of the collateral, he takes priority over the rights of a transferee in bulk or of a lien creditor which arise between the time the security interest attaches and the time of filing.

(3) A "lien creditor" means a creditor who has acquired a lien on the property involved by attachment, levy or the like and includes an assignee for benefit of creditors from the time of assignment, and a trustee in bankruptcy from the date of the filing of the petition or a receiver in equity from the time of appointment.

(4) A person who becomes a lien creditor while a security interest is perfected takes subject to the security interest only to the extent that it secures advances made before he becomes a lien creditor or within 45 days thereafter or made without knowledge of the lien or pursuant to a commitment entered into without knowledge of the lien.

§ 9—302. When Filing Is Required to Perfect Security Interest; Security Interests to Which Filing Provisions of This Article Do Not Apply.

(1) A financing statement must be filed to perfect all security interests except the following:

(a) a security interest in collateral in possession of the secured party under Section 9—305;

(b) a security interest temporarily perfected in instruments, certificated securities, or documents without delivery under Section 9—304 or in proceeds for a 10 day period under Section 9—306;

(c) a security interest created by an assignment of a beneficial interest in a trust or a decedent's estate;

(d) a purchase money security interest in consumer goods; but filing is required for a motor vehicle required to be registered; and fixture filing is required for priority over conflicting interests in fixtures to the extent provided in Section 9—313;

(e) an assignment of accounts which does not alone or in conjunction with other assignments to the same assignee transfer a significant part of the outstanding accounts of the assignor;

(f) a security interest of a collecting bank (Section 4—210) or arising under the Articles on Sales and Leases (see Section 9—113) or covered in subsection (3) of this section;

(g) an assignment for the benefit of all the creditors of the transferor, and subsequent transfers by the assignee thereunder.

(h) a security interest in investment property which is perfected without filing under Section 9—115 or Section 9—116.

(2) If a secured party assigns a perfected security interest, no filing under this Article is required in order to continue the perfected status of the security interest against creditors of and transferees from the original debtor.

(3) The filing of a financing statement otherwise required by this Article is not necessary or effective to perfect a security interest in property subject to

(a) a statute or treaty of the United States which provides for a national or international registration or a national or international certificate of title or which specifies a place of filing different from that specified in this Article for filing of the security interest; or

(b) the following statutes of this state; [list any certificate of title statute covering automobiles, trailers, mobile homes, boats, farm tractors, or the like, and any central filing statute.]; but during any period in which collateral is inventory held for sale by a person who is in the business of selling goods of that kind, the filing provisions of this Article (Part 4) apply to a security interest in that collateral created by him as debtor; or

(c) a certificate of title statute of another jurisdiction under the law of which indication of a security interest on the certificate is required as a condition of perfection (subsection (2) of Section 9—103).

(4) Compliance with a statute or treaty described in subsection (3) is equivalent to the filing of a financing statement under this Article, and a security interest in property subject to the statute or treaty can be perfected only by compliance therewith except as provided in Section 9—103 on multiple state transactions. Duration and renewal of perfection of a security interest perfected by compliance with the statute or treaty are governed by the provisions of the statute or treaty; in other respects the security interest is subject to this Article.

§ 9—303. **When Security Interest Is Perfected; Continuity of Perfection.**

(1) A security interest is perfected when it has attached and when all of the applicable steps required for perfection have been taken. Such steps are specified in Sections 9—115, 9—302, 9—304, 9—305 and 9—306. If such steps are taken before the security interest attaches, it is perfected at the time when it attaches.

(2) If a security interest is originally perfected in any way permitted under this Article and is subsequently perfected in some other way under this Article, without an intermediate period when it was unperfected, the security interest shall be deemed to be perfected continuously for the purposes of this Article.

§ 9—304. **Perfection of Security Interest in Instruments, Documents, Proceeds of a Written Letter of Credit, and Goods Covered by Documents; Perfection by Permissive Filing; Temporary Perfection Without Filing or Transfer of Possession.**

(1) A security interest in chattel paper or negotiable documents may be perfected by filing. A security interest in the rights to proceeds of a written letter of credit can be perfected only by the secured party's taking possession of the letter of credit. A security interest in money or instruments (other than instruments which constitute part of chattel paper) can be perfected only by the secured party's taking possession, except as provided in subsections (4) and (5) of this section and subsections (2) and (3) of Section 9—306 on proceeds.

(2) During the period that goods are in the possession of the issuer of a negotiable document therefor, a security interest in the goods is perfected by perfecting a security interest in the document, and any security interest in the goods otherwise perfected during such period is subject thereto.

(3) A security interest in goods in the possession of a bailee other than one who has issued a negotiable document therefor is perfected by issuance of a document in the name of the secured party or by the bailee's receipt of notification of the secured party's interest or by filing as to the goods.

(4) A security interest in instruments, certificated securities, or negotiable documents is perfected without filing or the taking of possession for a period of 21 days from the time it attaches to the extent that it arises for new value given under a written security agreement.

(5) A security interest remains perfected for a period of 21 days without filing where a secured party having a perfected security interest in an instrument, a certificated security, a negotiable doc-

ument or goods in possession of a bailee other than one who has issued a negotiable document therefor

(a) makes available to the debtor the goods or documents representing the goods for the purpose of ultimate sale or exchange or for the purpose of loading, unloading, storing, shipping, transshipping, manufacturing, processing or otherwise dealing with them in a manner preliminary to their sale or exchange, but priority between conflicting security interests in the goods is subject to subsection (3) of Section 9—312; or

(b) delivers the instrument or certificated security to the debtor for the purpose of ultimate sale or exchange or of presentation, collection, renewal or registration of transfer.

(6) After the 21 day period in subsections (4) and (5) perfection depends upon compliance with applicable provisions of this Article.

§ 9—305. **When Possession by Secured Party Perfects Security Interest Without Filing.**

A security interest in goods, instruments, money, negotiable documents, or chattel paper may be perfected by the secured party's taking possession of the collateral. A security interest in the right to proceeds of a written letter of credit may be perfected by the secured party's taking possession of the letter of credit. If such collateral other than goods covered by a negotiable document is held by a bailee, the secured party is deemed to have possession from the time the bailee receives notification of the secured party's interest. A security interest is perfected by possession from the time possession is taken without a relation back and continues only so long as possession is retained, unless otherwise specified in this Article. The security interest may be otherwise perfected as provided in this Article before or after the period of possession by the secured party.

§ 9—306. **"Proceeds"; Secured Party's Rights on Disposition of Collateral.**

(1) "Proceeds" includes whatever is received upon the sale, exchange, collection or other disposition of collateral or proceeds. Insurance payable by reason of loss or damage to the collateral is proceeds, except to the extent that it is payable to a person other than a party to the security agreement. Any payments or distributions made with respect to investment property collateral are proceeds. Money, checks, deposit accounts, and the like are "cash proceeds". All other proceeds are "noncash proceeds".

(2) Except where this Article otherwise provides, a security interest continues in collateral notwithstanding sale, exchange or other disposition thereof unless the disposition was authorized by the secured party in the security agreement or otherwise, and also continues in any identifiable proceeds including collections received by the debtor.

(3) The security interest in proceeds is a continuously perfected security interest if the interest in the original collateral was perfected but it ceases to be a perfected security interest and becomes unperfected ten days after receipt of the proceeds by the debtor unless

(a) a filed financing statement covers the original collateral and the proceeds are collateral in which a security interest may be perfected by filing in the office or offices where the financing statement has been filed and, if the proceeds are acquired with cash proceeds, the description of collateral in the financing statement indicates the types of property constituting the proceeds; or

(b) a filed financing statement covers the original collateral and the proceeds are identifiable cash proceeds; or

(c) the original collateral was investment property and the proceeds are identifiable cash proceeds; or

(d) the security interest in the proceeds is perfected before the expiration of the ten day period.

Except as provided in this section, a security interest in proceeds can be perfected only by the methods or under the circumstances permitted in this Article for original collateral of the same type.

(4) In the event of insolvency proceedings instituted by or against a debtor, a secured party with a perfected security interest in proceeds has a perfected security interest only in the following proceeds:

(a) in identifiable noncash proceeds and in separate deposit accounts containing only proceeds;

(b) in identifiable cash proceeds in the form of money which is neither commingled with other money nor deposited in a deposit account prior to the insolvency proceedings;

(c) in identifiable cash proceeds in the form of checks and the like which are not deposited in a deposit account prior to the insolvency proceedings; and

(d) in all cash and deposit accounts of the debtor in which proceeds have been commingled with other funds, but the perfected security interest under this paragraph (d) is

(i) subject to any right to set-off; and

(ii) limited to an amount not greater than the amount of any cash proceeds received by the debtor within ten days before the institution of the insolvency proceedings less the sum of (I) the payments to the secured party on account of cash proceeds received by the debtor during such period and (II) the cash proceeds received by the debtor during such period to which the secured party is entitled under paragraphs (a) through (c) of this subsection (4).

(5) If a sale of goods results in an account or chattel paper which is transferred by the seller to a secured party, and if the goods are returned to or are repossessed by the seller or the secured party, the following rules determine priorities:

(a) If the goods were collateral at the time of sale, for an indebtedness of the seller which is still unpaid, the original security interest attaches again to the goods and continues as a perfected security interest if it was perfected at the time when the goods were sold. If the security interest was originally perfected by a filing which is still effective, nothing further is required to continue the perfected status; in any other case, the secured party must take possession of the returned or repossessed goods or must file.

(b) An unpaid transferee of the chattel paper has a security interest in the goods against the transferor. Such security interest is prior to a security interest asserted under paragraph (a) to the extent that the transferee of the chattel paper was entitled to priority under Section 9—308.

(c) An unpaid transferee of the account has a security interest in the goods against the transferor. Such security interest is

subordinate to a security interest asserted under paragraph (a).

(d) A security interest of an unpaid transferee asserted under paragraph (b) or (c) must be perfected for protection against creditors of the transferor and purchasers of the returned or repossessed goods.

§ 9—307. **Protection of Buyers of Goods.**

(1) A buyer in ordinary course of business (subsection (9) of Section 1—201) other than a person buying farm products from a person engaged in farming operations takes free of a security interest created by his seller even though the security interest is perfected and even though the buyer knows of its existence [subject to the Food Security Act of 1985 (7 U.S.C. Section 1631)].

(2) In the case of consumer goods, a buyer takes free of a security interest even though perfected if he buys without knowledge of the security interest, for value and for his own personal, family or household purposes unless prior to the purchase the secured party has filed a financing statement covering such goods.

(3) A buyer other than a buyer in ordinary course of business (subsection (1) of this section) takes free of a security interest to the extent that it secures future advances made after the secured party acquires knowledge of the purchase, or more than 45 days after the purchase, whichever first occurs, unless made pursuant to a commitment entered into without knowledge of the purchase and before the expiration of the 45 day period.

§ 9—308. **Purchase of Chattel Paper and Instruments.**

A purchaser of chattel paper or an instrument who gives new value and takes possession of it in the ordinary course of his business has priority over a security interest in the chattel paper or instrument

(a) which is perfected under Section 9—304 (permissive filing and temporary perfection) or under Section 9—306 (perfection as to proceeds) if he acts without knowledge that the specific paper or instrument is subject to a security interest; or

(b) which is claimed merely as proceeds of inventory subject to a security interest (Section 9—306) even though he knows that the specific paper or instrument is subject to the security interest.

§ 9—309. **Protection of Purchasers of Instruments, Documents and Securities.**

Nothing in this Article limits the rights of a holder in due course of a negotiable instrument (Section 3—302) or a holder to whom a negotiable document of title has been duly negotiated (Section 7—501) or a bona fide purchaser of a security (Section 8—302) and the holders or purchasers take priority over an earlier security interest even though perfected. Filing under this Article does not constitute notice of the security interest to such holders or purchasers.

§ 9—310. **Priority of Certain Liens Arising by Operation of Law.**

When a person in the ordinary course of his business furnishes services or materials with respect to goods subject to a security interest, a lien upon goods in the possession of such person given by statute or rule of law for such materials or services takes priority over a perfected security interest unless the lien is statutory and the statute expressly provides otherwise.

§ 9—311. **Alienability of Debtor's Rights: Judicial Process.**

The debtor's rights in collateral may be voluntarily or involuntarily transferred (by way of sale, creation of a security interest, attachment, levy, garnishment or other judicial process) notwithstanding a provision in the security agreement prohibiting any transfer or making the transfer constitute a default.

§ 9—312. Priorities Among Conflicting Security Interests in the Same Collateral.

(1) The rules of priority stated in other sections of this Part and in the following sections shall govern when applicable: Section 4—208 with respect to the security interests of collecting banks in items being collected, accompanying documents and proceeds; Section 9—103 on security interests related to other jurisdictions; Section 9—114 on consignments.

(2) A perfected security interest in crops for new value given to enable the debtor to produce the crops during the production season and given not more than three months before the crops become growing crops by planting or otherwise takes priority over an earlier perfected security interest to the extent that such earlier interest secures obligations due more than six months before the crops become growing crops by planting or otherwise, even though the person giving new value had knowledge of the earlier security interest.

(3) A perfected purchase money security interest in inventory has priority over a conflicting security interest in the same inventory and also has priority in identifiable cash proceeds received on or before the delivery of the inventory to a buyer if

(a) the purchase money security interest is perfected at the time the debtor receives possession of the inventory; and

(b) the purchase money secured party gives notification in writing to the holder of the conflicting security interest if the holder had filed a financing statement covering the same types of inventory (i) before the date of the filing made by the purchase money secured party, or (ii) before the beginning of the 21 day period where the purchase money security interest is temporarily perfected without filing or possession (subsection (5) of Section 9—304); and

(c) the holder of the conflicting security interest receives the notification within five years before the debtor receives possession of the inventory; and

(d) the notification states that the person giving the notice has or expects to acquire a purchase money security interest in inventory of the debtor, describing such inventory by item or type.

(4) A purchase money security interest in collateral other than inventory has priority over a conflicting security interest in the same collateral or its proceeds if the purchase money security interest is perfected at the time the debtor receives possession of the collateral or within ten days thereafter.

(5) In all cases not governed by other rules stated in this section (including cases of purchase money security interests which do not qualify for the special priorities set forth in subsections (3) and (4) of this section), priority between conflicting security interests in the same collateral shall be determined according to the following rules:

(a) Conflicting security interests rank according to priority in time of filing or perfection. Priority dates from the time a filing is first made covering the collateral or the time the security interest is first perfected, whichever is earlier, provided

that there is no period thereafter when there is neither filing nor perfection.

(b) So long as conflicting security interests are unperfected, the first to attach has priority.

(6) For the purposes of subsection (5) a date of filing or perfection as to collateral is also a date of filing or perfection as to proceeds.

(7) If future advances are made while a security interest is perfected by filing, the taking of possession, or under Section 8—321 on securities, the security interest has the same priority for the purposes of subsection (5) with respect to the future advances as it does with respect to the first advance. If a commitment is made before or while the security interest is so perfected, the security interest has the same priority with respect to advances made pursuant thereto. In other cases a perfected security interest has priority from the date the advance is made.

§ 9—313. Priority of Security Interests in Fixtures.

(1) In this section and in the provisions of Part 4 of this Article referring to fixture filing, unless the context otherwise requires

(a) goods are "fixtures" when they become so related to particular real estate that an interest in them arises under real estate law

(b) a "fixture filing" is the filing in the office where a mortgage on the real estate would be filed or recorded of a financing statement covering goods which are or are to become fixtures and conforming to the requirements of subsection (5) of Section 9—402

(c) a mortgage is a "construction mortgage" to the extent that it secures an obligation incurred for the construction of an improvement on land including the acquisition cost of the land, if the recorded writing so indicates.

(2) A security interest under this Article may be created in goods which are fixtures or may continue in goods which become fixtures, but no security interest exists under this Article in ordinary building materials incorporated into an improvement on land.

(3) This Article does not prevent creation of an encumbrance upon fixtures pursuant to real estate law.

(4) A perfected security interest in fixtures has priority over the conflicting interest of an encumbrancer or owner of the real estate where

(a) the security interest is a purchase money security interest, the interest of the encumbrancer or owner arises before the goods become fixtures, the security interest is perfected by a fixture filing before the goods become fixtures or within ten days thereafter, and the debtor has an interest of record in the real estate or is in possession of the real estate; or

(b) the security interest is perfected by a fixture filing before the interest of the encumbrancer or owner is of record, the security interest has priority over any conflicting interest of a predecessor in title of the encumbrancer or owner, and the debtor has an interest of record in the real estate or is in possession of the real estate; or

(c) the fixtures are readily removable factory or office machines or readily removable replacements of domestic appliances which are consumer goods, and before the goods become fixtures the security interest is perfected by any method permitted by this Article; or

(d) the conflicting interest is a lien on the real estate obtained by legal or equitable proceedings after the security interest was perfected by any method permitted by this Article.

(5) A security interest in fixtures, whether or not perfected, has priority over the conflicting interest of an encumbrancer or owner of the real estate where

(a) the encumbrancer or owner has consented in writing to the security interest or has disclaimed an interest in the goods as fixtures; or

(b) the debtor has a right to remove the goods as against the encumbrancer or owner. If the debtor's right terminates, the priority of the security interest continues for a reasonable time.

(6) Notwithstanding paragraph (a) of subsection (4) but otherwise subject to subsections (4) and (5), a security interest in fixtures is subordinate to a construction mortgage recorded before the goods become fixtures if the goods become fixtures before the completion of the construction. To the extent that it is given to refinance a construction mortgage, a mortgage has this priority to the same extent as the construction mortgage.

(7) In cases not within the preceding subsections, a security interest in fixtures is subordinate to the conflicting interest of an encumbrancer or owner of the related real estate who is not the debtor.

(8) When the secured party has priority over all owners and encumbrancers of the real estate, he may, on default, subject to the provisions of Part 5, remove his collateral from the real estate but he must reimburse any encumbrancer or owner of the real estate who is not the debtor and who has not otherwise agreed for the cost of repair of any physical injury, but not for any diminution in value of the real estate caused by the absence of the goods removed or by any necessity of replacing them. A person entitled to reimbursement may refuse permission to remove until the secured party gives adequate security for the performance of this obligation.

§ 9–314. Accessions.

(1) A security interest in goods which attaches before they are installed in or affixed to other goods takes priority as to the goods installed or affixed (called in this section "accessions") over the claims of all persons to the whole except as stated in subsection (3) and subject to Section 9–315(1).

(2) A security interest which attaches to goods after they become part of a whole is valid against all persons subsequently acquiring interests in the whole except as stated in subsection (3) but is invalid against any person with an interest in the whole at the time the security interest attaches to the goods who has not in writing consented to the security interest or disclaimed an interest in the goods as part of the whole.

(3) The security interests described in subsections (1) and (2) do not take priority over

(a) a subsequent purchaser for value of any interest in the whole; or

(b) a creditor with a lien on the whole subsequently obtained by judicial proceedings; or

(c) a creditor with a prior perfected security interest in the whole to the extent that he makes subsequent advances

if the subsequent purchase is made, the lien by judicial proceedings obtained or the subsequent advance under the prior perfected security interest is made or contracted for without knowledge of the security interest and before it is perfected. A purchaser of the whole at a foreclosure sale other than the holder of a perfected security interest purchasing at his own foreclosure sale is a subsequent purchaser within this section.

(4) When under subsections (1) or (2) and (3) a secured party has an interest in accessions which has priority over the claims of all persons who have interests in the whole, he may on default subject to the provisions of Part 5 remove his collateral from the whole but he must reimburse any encumbrancer or owner of the whole who is not the debtor and who has not otherwise agreed for the cost of repair of any physical injury but not for any diminution in value of the whole caused by the absence of the goods removed or by any necessity for replacing them. A person entitled to reimbursement may refuse permission to remove until the secured party gives adequate security for the performance of this obligation.

§ 9–315. Priority When Goods Are Commingled or Processed.

(1) If a security interest in goods was perfected and subsequently the goods or a part thereof have become part of a product or mass, the security interest continues in the product or mass if

(a) the goods are so manufactured, processed, assembled or commingled that their identity is lost in the product or mass; or

(b) a financing statement covering the original goods also covers the product into which the goods have been manufactured, processed or assembled.

In a case to which paragraph (b) applies, no separate security interest in that part of the original goods which has been manufactured, processed or assembled into the product may be claimed under Section 9–314.

(2) When under subsection (1) more than one security interest attaches to the product or mass, they rank equally according to the ratio that the cost of the goods to which each interest originally attached bears to the cost of the total product or mass.

§ 9–316. Priority Subject to Subordination.

Nothing in this Article prevents subordination by agreement by any person entitled to priority.

§ 9–317. Secured Party Not Obligated on Contract of Debtor.

The mere existence of a security interest or authority given to the debtor to dispose of or use collateral does not impose contract or tort liability upon the secured party for the debtor's acts or omissions.

§ 9–318. Defenses Against Assignee; Modification of Contract After Notification of Assignment; Term Prohibiting Assignment Ineffective; Identification and Proof of Assignment.

(1) Unless an account debtor has made an enforceable agreement not to assert defenses or claims arising out of a sale as provided in Section 9–206 the rights of an assignee are subject to

(a) all the terms of the contract between the account debtor and assignor and any defense or claim arising therefrom; and

(b) any other defense or claim of the account debtor against the assignor which accrues before the account debtor receives notification of the assignment.

(2) So far as the right to payment or a part thereof under an assigned contract has not been fully earned by performance, and notwithstanding notification of the assignment, any modification of or substitution for the contract made in good faith and in accordance with reasonable commercial standards is effective against an assignee unless the account debtor has otherwise agreed but the assignee acquires corresponding rights under the modified or substituted contract. The assignment may provide that such modification or substitution is a breach by the assignor.

(3) The account debtor is authorized to pay the assignor until the account debtor receives notification that the amount due or to become due has been assigned and that payment is to be made to the assignee. A notification which does not reasonably identify the rights assigned is ineffective. If requested by the account debtor, the assignee must seasonably furnish reasonable proof that the assignment has been made and unless he does so the account debtor may pay the assignor.

(4) A term in any contract between an account debtor and an assignor is ineffective if it prohibits assignment of an account or prohibits creation of a security interest in a general intangible for money due or to become due or requires the account debtor's consent to such assignment or security interest.

Part 4 Filing

§ 9—401. Place of Filing; Erroneous Filing; Removal of Collateral.

First Alternative Subsection (1)

(1) The proper place to file in order to perfect a security interest is as follows:

(a) when the collateral is timber to be cut or is minerals or the like (including oil and gas) or accounts subject to subsection (5) of Section 9—103, or when the financing statement is filed as a fixture filing (Section 9—313) and the collateral is goods which are or are to become fixtures, then in the office where a mortgage on the real estate would be filed or recorded;

(b) in all other cases, in the office of the [Secretary of State].

Second Alternative Subsection (1)

(1) The proper place to file in order to perfect a security interest is as follows:

(a) when the collateral is equipment used in farming operations, or farm products, or accounts or general intangibles arising from or relating to the sale of farm products by a farmer, or consumer goods, then in the office of the . . . . in the county of the debtor's residence or if the debtor is not a resident of this state then in the office of the . . . . in the county where the goods are kept, and in addition when the collateral is crops growing or to be grown in the office of the . . . . in the county where the land is located;

(b) when the collateral is timber to be cut or is minerals or the like (including oil and gas) or accounts subject to subsection (5) of Section 9—103, or when the financing statement is filed as a fixture filing (Section 9—313) and the collateral is goods which are or are to become fixtures, then in the office where a mortgage on the real estate would be filed or recorded;

(c) in all other cases, in the office of the [Secretary of State].

Third Alternative Subsection (1)

(1) The proper place to file in order to perfect a security interest is as follows:

(a) when the collateral is equipment used in farming operations, or farm products, or accounts or general intangibles arising from or relating to the sale of farm products by a farmer, or consumer goods, then in the office of the . . . . in the county of the debtor's residence or if the debtor is not a resident of this state then in the office of the . . . . in the county where the goods are kept, and in addition when the collateral is crops growing or to be grown in the office of the . . . . in the county where the land is located;

(b) when the collateral is timber to be cut or is minerals or the like (including oil and gas) or accounts subject to subsection (5) of Section 9—103, or when the financing statement is filed as a fixture filing (Section 9—313) and the collateral is goods which are or are to become fixtures, then in the office where a mortgage on the real estate would be filed or recorded;

(c) in all other cases, in the office of the [Secretary of State] and in addition, if the debtor has a place of business in only one county of this state, also in the office of . . . . of such county, or, if the debtor has no place of business in this state, but resides in the state, also in the office of . . . . of the county in which he resides.

Note: *One of the three alternatives should be selected as subsection (1).*

(2) A filing which is made in good faith in an improper place or not in all of the places required by this section is nevertheless effective with regard to any collateral as to which the filing complied with the requirements of this Article and is also effective with regard to collateral covered by the financing statement against any person who has knowledge of the contents of such financing statement.

(3) A filing which is made in the proper place in this state continues effective even though the debtor's residence or place of business or the location of the collateral or its use, whichever controlled the original filing, is thereafter changed.

Alternative Subsection (3)

[(3) A filing which is made in the proper county continues effective for four months after a change to another county of the debtor's residence or place of business or the location of the collateral, whichever controlled the original filing. It becomes ineffective thereafter unless a copy of the financing statement signed by the secured party is filed in the new county within said period. The security interest may also be perfected in the new county after the expiration of the four-month period; in such case perfection dates from the time of perfection in the new county. A change in the use of the collateral does not impair the effectiveness of the original filing.]

(4) The rules stated in Section 9—103 determine whether filing is necessary in this state.

(5) Notwithstanding the preceding subsections, and subject to subsection (3) of Section 9—302, the proper place to file in order to perfect a security interest in collateral, including fixtures, of a transmitting utility is the office of the [Secretary of State]. This filing constitutes a fixture filing (Section 9—313) as to the collateral described therein which is or is to become fixtures.

(6) For the purposes of this section, the residence of an organiza-

tion is its place of business if it has one or its chief executive office if it has more than one place of business.

Note: *Subsection (6) should be used only if the state chooses the Second or Third Alternative Subsection (1).*

§ 9—402. Formal Requisites of Financing Statement; Amendments; Mortgage as Financing Statement.

(1) A financing statement is sufficient if it gives the names of the debtor and the secured party, is signed by the debtor, gives an address of the secured party from which information concerning the security interest may be obtained, gives a mailing address of the debtor and contains a statement indicating the types, or describing the items, of collateral. A financing statement may be filed before a security agreement is made or a security interest otherwise attaches. When the financing statement covers crops growing or to be grown, the statement must also contain a description of the real estate concerned. When the financing statement covers timber to be cut or covers minerals or the like (including oil and gas) or accounts subject to subsection (5) of Section 9—103, or when the financing statement is filed as a fixture filing (Section 9—313) and the collateral is goods which are or are to become fixtures, the statement must also comply with subsection (5). A copy of the security agreement is sufficient as a financing statement if it contains the above information and is signed by the debtor. A carbon, photographic or other reproduction of a security agreement or a financing statement is sufficient as a financing statement if the security agreement so provides or if the original has been filed in this state.

(2) A financing statement which otherwise complies with subsection (1) is sufficient when it is signed by the secured party instead of the debtor if it is filed to perfect a security interest in

(a) collateral already subject to a security interest in another jurisdiction when it is brought into this state, or when the debtor's location is changed to this state. Such a financing statement must state that the collateral was brought into this state or that the debtor's location was changed to this state under such circumstances; or

(b) proceeds under Section 9—306 if the security interest in the original collateral was perfected. Such a financing statement must describe the original collateral; or

(c) collateral as to which the filing has lapsed; or

(d) collateral acquired after a change of name, identity or corporate structure of the debtor (subsection (7)).

(3) A form substantially as follows is sufficient to comply with subsection (1):

Name of debtor (or assignor) . . . .
Address . . . .
Name of secured party (or assignee) . . . .
Address . . . .
1. This financing statement covers the following types (or items) of property:
      (Describe) . . . .
2. (If collateral is crops) The above described crops are growing or are to be grown on:
      (Describe Real Estate) . . . .
3. (If applicable) The above goods are to become fixtures on *
*Where appropriate substitute either "The above timber is standing on . . . ." or "The above minerals or the like (including oil and gas) or accounts will be financed at the wellhead or minehead of the well or mine located on . . . ."

(Describe Real Estate) . . . .
and this financing statement is to be filed [for record] in the real estate records. (If the debtor does not have an interest of record) The name of a record owner is . . . .
4. (If products of collateral are claimed) Products of the collateral are also covered.

(use
whichever   . . . .
                        Signature of Debtor (or Assignor)

is   . . . .
applicable)   Signature of Secured Party
                              (or Assignee)

(4) A financing statement may be amended by filing a writing signed by both the debtor and the secured party. An amendment does not extend the period of effectiveness of a financing statement. If any amendment adds collateral, it is effective as to the added collateral only from the filing date of the amendment. In this Article, unless the context otherwise requires, the term "financing statement" means the original financing statement and any amendments.

(5) A financing statement covering timber to be cut or covering minerals or the like (including oil and gas) or accounts subject to subsection (5) of Section 9—103, or a financing statement filed as a fixture filing (Section 9—313) where the debtor is not a transmitting utility, must show that it covers this type of collateral, must recite that it is to be filed [for record] in the real estate records, and the financing statement must contain a description of the real estate [sufficient if it were contained in a mortgage of the real estate to give constructive notice of the mortgage under the law of this state]. If the debtor does not have an interest of record in the real estate, the financing statement must show the name of a record owner.

(6) A mortgage is effective as a financing statement filed as a fixture filing from the date of its recording if

(a) the goods are described in the mortgage by item or type; and

(b) the goods are or are to become fixtures related to the real estate described in the mortgage; and

(c) the mortgage complies with the requirements for a financing statement in this section other than a recital that it is to be filed in the real estate records; and

(d) the mortgage is duly recorded.

No fee with reference to the financing statement is required other than the regular recording and satisfaction fees with respect to the mortgage.

(7) A financing statement sufficiently shows the name of the debtor if it gives the individual, partnership or corporate name of the debtor, whether or not it adds other trade names or names of partners. Where the debtor so changes his name or in the case of an organization its name, identity or corporate structure that a filed financing statement becomes seriously misleading, the filing is not effective to perfect a security interest in collateral acquired by the debtor more than four months after the change, unless a new appropriate financing statement is filed before the expiration of that time. A filed financing statement remains effective with respect to collateral transferred by the debtor even though the secured party knows of or consents to the transfer.

(8) A financing statement substantially complying with the requirements of this section is effective even though it contains minor errors which are not seriously misleading.

Note: *Language in brackets is optional.*

Note: *Where the state has any special recording system for real estate other than the usual grantor-grantee index (as, for instance, a tract system or a title registration or Torrens system) local adaptations of subsection (5) and Section 9—403(7) may be necessary. See Mass.Gen.Laws Chapter 106, Section 9—409.*

§ 9—403. What Constitutes Filing; Duration of Filing; Effect of Lapsed Filing; Duties of Filing Officer.

(1) Presentation for filing of a financing statement and tender of the filing fee or acceptance of the statement by the filing officer constitutes filing under this Article.

(2) Except as provided in subsection (6) a filed financing statement is effective for a period of five years from the date of filing. The effectiveness of a filed financing statement lapses on the expiration of the five year period unless a continuation statement is filed prior to the lapse. If a security interest perfected by filing exists at the time insolvency proceedings are commenced by or against the debtor, the security interest remains perfected until termination of the insolvency proceedings and thereafter for a period of sixty days or until expiration of the five year period, whichever occurs later. Upon lapse the security interest becomes unperfected, unless it is perfected without filing. If the security interest becomes unperfected upon lapse, it is deemed to have been unperfected as against a person who became a purchaser or lien creditor before lapse.

(3) A continuation statement may be filed by the secured party within six months prior to the expiration of the five year period specified in subsection (2). Any such continuation statement must be signed by the secured party, identify the original statement by file number and state that the original statement is still effective. A continuation statement signed by a person other than the secured party of record must be accompanied by a separate written statement of assignment signed by the secured party of record and complying with subsection (2) of Section 9—405, including payment of the required fee. Upon timely filing of the continuation statement, the effectiveness of the original statement is continued for five years after the last date to which the filing was effective whereupon it lapses in the same manner as provided in subsection (2) unless another continuation statement is filed prior to such lapse. Succeeding continuation statements may be filed in the same manner to continue the effectiveness of the original statement. Unless a statute on disposition of public records provides otherwise, the filing officer may remove a lapsed statement from the files and destroy it immediately if he has retained a microfilm or other photographic record, or in other cases after one year after the lapse. The filing officer shall so arrange matters by physical annexation of financing statements to continuation statements or other related filings, or by other means, that if he physically destroys the financing statements of a period more than five years past, those which have been continued by a continuation statement or which are still effective under subsection (6) shall be retained.

(4) Except as provided in subsection (7) a filing officer shall mark each statement with a file number and with the date and hour of filing and shall hold the statement or a microfilm or other photographic copy thereof for public inspection. In addition the filing officer shall index the statement according to the name of the debtor and shall note in the index the file number and the address of the debtor given in the statement.

(5) The uniform fee for filing and indexing and for stamping a copy furnished by the secured party to show the date and place of filing for an original financing statement or for a continuation statement shall be $. . . . . . . if the statement is in the standard form prescribed by the [Secretary of State] and otherwise shall be $. . . . . . ., plus in each case, if the financing statement is subject to subsection (5) of Section 9—402, $. . . . . . . The uniform fee for each name more than one required to be indexed shall be $. . . . . . . The secured party may at his option show a trade name for any person and an extra uniform indexing fee of $. . . . . . . shall be paid with respect thereto.

(6) If the debtor is a transmitting utility (subsection (5) of Section 9—401) and a filed financing statement so states, it is effective until a termination statement is filed. A real estate mortgage which is effective as a fixture filing under subsection (6) of Section 9—402 remains effective as a fixture filing until the mortgage is released or satisfied of record or its effectiveness otherwise terminates as to the real estate.

(7) When a financing statement covers timber to be cut or covers minerals or the like (including oil and gas) or accounts subject to subsection (5) of Section 9—103, or is filed as a fixture filing, [it shall be filed for record and] the filing officer shall index it under the names of the debtor and any owner of record shown on the financing statement in the same fashion as if they were the mortgagors in a mortgage of the real estate described, and, to the extent that the law of this state provides for indexing of mortgages under the name of the mortgagee, under the name of the secured party as if he were the mortgagee thereunder, or where indexing is by description in the same fashion as if the financing statement were a mortgage of the real estate described.

Note: *In states in which writings will not appear in the real estate records and indices unless actually recorded the bracketed language in subsection (7) should be used.*

§ 9—404. Termination Statement.

(1) If a financing statement covering consumer goods is filed on or after . . . ., then within one month or within ten days following written demand by the debtor after there is no outstanding secured obligation and no commitment to make advances, incur obligations or otherwise give value, the secured party must file with each filing officer with whom the financing statement was filed, a termination statement to the effect that he no longer claims a security interest under the financing statement, which shall be identified by file number. In other cases whenever there is no outstanding secured obligation and no commitment to make advances, incur obligations or otherwise give value, the secured party must on written demand by the debtor send the debtor, for each filing officer with whom the financing statement was filed, a termination statement to the effect that he no longer claims a security interest under the financing statement, which shall be identified by file number. A termination statement signed by a person other than the secured party of record must be accompanied by a separate written statement of assignment signed by the secured party of record complying with subsection (2) of Section 9—405, including payment of the required fee. If the affected secured party fails to file such a termination statement as required by this subsection, or to send such a termination statement within

ten days after proper demand therefor, he shall be liable to the debtor for one hundred dollars, and in addition for any loss caused to the debtor by such failure.

(2) On presentation to the filing officer of such a termination statement he must note it in the index. If he has received the termination statement in duplicate, he shall return one copy of the termination statement to the secured party stamped to show the time of receipt thereof. If the filing officer has a microfilm or other photographic record of the financing statement, and of any related continuation statement, statement of assignment and statement of release, he may remove the originals from the files at any time after receipt of the termination statement, or if he has no such record, he may remove them from the files at any time after one year after receipt of the termination statement.

(3) If the termination statement is in the standard form prescribed by the [Secretary of State], the uniform fee for filing and indexing the termination statement shall be $. . . . ., and otherwise shall be $. . . . ., plus in each case an additional fee of $. . . . . . . for each name more than one against which the termination statement is required to be indexed.

Note: *The date to be inserted should be the effective date of the revised Article 9.*

§ 9—405. Assignment of Security Interest; Duties of Filing Officer; Fees.

(1) A financing statement may disclose an assignment of a security interest in the collateral described in the financing statement by indication in the financing statement of the name and address of the assignee or by an assignment itself or a copy thereof on the face or back of the statement. On presentation to the filing officer of such a financing statement the filing officer shall mark the same as provided in Section 9—403(4). The uniform fee for filing, indexing and furnishing filing data for a financing statement so indicating an assignment shall be $. . . . . . . if the statement is in the standard form prescribed by the [Secretary of State] and otherwise shall be $. . . . ., plus in each case an additional fee of $. . . . . . . for each name more than one against which the financing statement is required to be indexed.

(2) A secured party may assign of record all or part of his rights under a financing statement by the filing in the place where the original financing statement was filed of a separate written statement of assignment signed by the secured party of record and setting forth the name of the secured party of record and the debtor, the file number and the date of filing of the financing statement and the name and address of the assignee and containing a description of the collateral assigned. A copy of the assignment is sufficient as a separate statement if it complies with the preceding sentence. On presentation to the filing officer of such a separate statement, the filing officer shall mark such separate statement with the date and hour of the filing. He shall note the assignment on the index of the financing statement, or in the case of a fixture filing, or a filing covering timber to be cut, or covering minerals or the like (including oil and gas) or accounts subject to subsection (5) of Section 9—103, he shall index the assignment under the name of the assignor as grantor and, to the extent that the law of this state provides for indexing the assignment of a mortgage under the name of the assignee, he shall index the assignment of the financing statement under the name of the assignee. The uniform fee for filing, indexing and furnishing filing data about such a separate statement of assignment shall be $. . . . . if the state-

ment is in the standard form prescribed by the [Secretary of State] and otherwise shall be $. . . . ., plus in each case an additional fee of $. . . . . for each name more than one against which the statement of assignment is required to be indexed. Notwithstanding the provisions of this subsection, an assignment of record of a security interest in a fixture contained in a mortgage effective as a fixture filing (subsection (6) of Section 9—402) may be made only by an assignment of the mortgage in the manner provided by the law of this state other than this Act.

(3) After the disclosure or filing of an assignment under this section, the assignee is the secured party of record.

§ 9—406. Release of Collateral; Duties of Filing Officer; Fees.

A secured party of record may by his signed statement release all or a part of any collateral described in a filed financing statement. The statement of release is sufficient if it contains a description of the collateral being released, the name and address of the debtor, the name and address of the secured party, and the file number of the financing statement. A statement of release signed by a person other than the secured party of record must be accompanied by a separate written statement of assignment signed by the secured party of record and complying with subsection (2) of Section 9—405, including payment of the required fee. Upon presentation of such a statement of release to the filing officer he shall mark the statement with the hour and date of filing and shall note the same upon the margin of the index of the filing of the financing statement. The uniform fee for filing and noting such a statement of release shall be $. . . . . . if the statement is in the standard form prescribed by the [Secretary of State] and otherwise shall be $. . . . ., plus in each case an additional fee of $. . . . . for each name more than one against which the statement of release is required to be indexed.

§ 9—407. Information From Filing Officer.

[(1) If the person filing any financing statement, termination statement, statement of assignment, or statement of release, furnishes the filing officer a copy thereof, the filing officer shall upon request note upon the copy the file number and date and hour of the filing of the original and deliver or send the copy to such person.]

[(2) Upon request of any person, the filing officer shall issue his certificate showing whether there is on file on the date and hour stated therein, any presently effective financing statement naming a particular debtor and any statement of assignment thereof and if there is, giving the date and hour of filing of each such statement and the names and addresses of each secured party therein. The uniform fee for such a certificate shall be $. . . . . . if the request for the certificate is in the standard form prescribed by the [Secretary of State] and otherwise shall be $. . . . . . Upon request the filing officer shall furnish a copy of any filed financing statement or statement of assignment for a uniform fee of $. . . . . per page.]

Note: *This section is proposed as an optional provision to require filing officers to furnish certificates. Local law and practices should be consulted with regard to the advisability of adoption.*

§ 9—408. Financing Statements Covering Consigned or Leased Goods.

A consignor or lessor of goods may file a financing statement using the terms "consignor," "consignee," "lessor," "lessee" or the like instead of the terms specified in Section 9—402. The provisions of this Part shall apply as appropriate to such a financing statement but its filing shall not of itself be a factor in determining whether or not the consignment or lease is intended as security (Section 1—201(37)). However, if it is determined for other reasons that the consignment or lease is so intended, a security interest of the consignor or lessor which attaches to the consigned or leased goods is perfected by such filing.

Part 5 Default

§ 9—501. Default; Procedure When Security Agreement Covers Both Real and Personal Property.

(1) When a debtor is in default under a security agreement, a secured party has the rights and remedies provided in this Part and except as limited by subsection (3) those provided in the security agreement. He may reduce his claim to judgment, foreclose or otherwise enforce the security interest by any available judicial procedure. If the collateral is documents the secured party may proceed either as to the documents or as to the goods covered thereby. A secured party in possession has the rights, remedies and duties provided in Section 9—207. The rights and remedies referred to in this subsection are cumulative.

(2) After default, the debtor has the rights and remedies provided in this Part, those provided in the security agreement and those provided in Section 9—207.

(3) To the extent that they give rights to the debtor and impose duties on the secured party, the rules stated in the subsections referred to below may not be waived or varied except as provided with respect to compulsory disposition of collateral (subsection (3) of Section 9—504 and Section 9—505) and with respect to redemption of collateral (Section 9—506) but the parties may by agreement determine the standards by which the fulfillment of these rights and duties is to be measured if such standards are not manifestly unreasonable:

(a) subsection (2) of Section 9—502 and subsection (2) of Section 9—504 insofar as they require accounting for surplus proceeds of collateral;

(b) subsection (3) of Section 9—504 and subsection (1) of Section 9—505 which deal with disposition of collateral;

(c) subsection (2) of Section 9—505 which deals with acceptance of collateral as discharge of obligation;

(d) Section 9—506 which deals with redemption of collateral; and

(e) subsection (1) of Section 9—507 which deals with the secured party's liability for failure to comply with this Part.

(4) If the security agreement covers both real and personal property, the secured party may proceed under this Part as to the personal property or he may proceed as to both the real and the personal property in accordance with his rights and remedies in respect of the real property in which case the provisions of this Part do not apply.

(5) When a secured party has reduced his claim to judgment the lien of any levy which may be made upon his collateral by virtue of any execution based upon the judgment shall relate back to the date of the perfection of the security interest in such collateral. A judicial sale, pursuant to such execution, is a foreclosure of the security interest by judicial procedure within the meaning of this section, and the secured party may purchase at the sale and thereafter hold the collateral free of any other requirements of this Article.

§ 9—502. Collection Rights of Secured Party.

(1) When so agreed and in any event on default the secured party is entitled to notify an account debtor or the obligor on an instrument to make payment to him whether or not the assignor was theretofore making collections on the collateral, and also to take control of any proceeds to which he is entitled under Section 9—306.

(2) A secured party who by agreement is entitled to charge back uncollected collateral or otherwise to full or limited recourse against the debtor and who undertakes to collect from the account debtors or obligors must proceed in a commercially reasonable manner and may deduct his reasonable expenses of realization from the collections. If the security agreement secures an indebtedness, the secured party must account to the debtor for any surplus, and unless otherwise agreed, the debtor is liable for any deficiency. But, if the underlying transaction was a sale of accounts or chattel paper, the debtor is entitled to any surplus or is liable for any deficiency only if the security agreement so provides.

§ 9—503. Secured Party's Right to Take Possession After Default.

Unless otherwise agreed a secured party has on default the right to take possession of the collateral. In taking possession a secured party may proceed without judicial process if this can be done without breach of the peace or may proceed by action. If the security agreement so provides the secured party may require the debtor to assemble the collateral and make it available to the secured party at a place to be designated by the secured party which is reasonably convenient to both parties. Without removal a secured party may render equipment unusable, and may dispose of collateral on the debtor's premises under Section 9—504.

§ 9—504. Secured Party's Right to Dispose of Collateral After Default; Effect of Disposition.

(1) A secured party after default may sell, lease or otherwise dispose of any or all of the collateral in its then condition or following any commercially reasonable preparation or processing. Any sale of goods is subject to the Article on Sales (Article 2). The proceeds of disposition shall be applied in the order following to

(a) the reasonable expenses of retaking, holding, preparing for sale or lease, selling, leasing and the like and, to the extent provided for in the agreement and not prohibited by law, the reasonable attorneys' fees and legal expenses incurred by the secured party;

(b) the satisfaction of indebtedness secured by the security interest under which the disposition is made;

(c) the satisfaction of indebtedness secured by any subordinate security interest in the collateral if written notification of demand therefor is received before distribution of the proceeds is completed. If requested by the secured party, the holder of a subordinate security interest must seasonably furnish reasonable proof of his interest, and unless he does so, the secured party need not comply with his demand.

(2) If the security interest secures an indebtedness, the secured party must account to the debtor for any surplus, and, unless otherwise agreed, the debtor is liable for any deficiency. But if the

underlying transaction was a sale of accounts or chattel paper, the debtor is entitled to any surplus or is liable for any deficiency only if the security agreement so provides.

(3) Disposition of the collateral may be by public or private proceedings and may be made by way of one or more contracts. Sale or other disposition may be as a unit or in parcels and at any time and place and on any terms but every aspect of the disposition including the method, manner, time, place and terms must be commercially reasonable. Unless collateral is perishable or threatens to decline speedily in value or is of a type customarily sold on a recognized market, reasonable notification of the time and place of any public sale or reasonable notification of the time after which any private sale or other intended disposition is to be made shall be sent by the secured party to the debtor, if he has not signed after default a statement renouncing or modifying his right to notification of sale. In the case of consumer goods no other notification need be sent. In other cases notification shall be sent to any other secured party from whom the secured party has received (before sending his notification to the debtor or before the debtor's renunciation of his rights) written notice of a claim of an interest in the collateral. The secured party may buy at any public sale and if the collateral is of a type customarily sold in a recognized market or is of a type which is the subject of widely distributed standard price quotations he may buy at private sale.

(4) When collateral is disposed of by a secured party after default, the disposition transfers to a purchaser for value all of the debtor's rights therein, discharges the security interest under which it is made and any security interest or lien subordinate thereto. The purchaser takes free of all such rights and interests even though the secured party fails to comply with the requirements of this Part or of any judicial proceedings

    (a) in the case of a public sale, if the purchaser has no knowledge of any defects in the sale and if he does not buy in collusion with the secured party, other bidders or the person conducting the sale; or

    (b) in any other case, if the purchaser acts in good faith.

(5) A person who is liable to a secured party under a guaranty, indorsement, repurchase agreement or the like and who receives a transfer of collateral from the secured party or is subrogated to his rights has thereafter the rights and duties of the secured party. Such a transfer of collateral is not a sale or disposition of the collateral under this Article.

§ 9—505. Compulsory Disposition of Collateral; Acceptance of the Collateral as Discharge of Obligation.

(1) If the debtor has paid sixty per cent of the cash price in the case of a purchase money security interest in consumer goods or sixty per cent of the loan in the case of another security interest in consumer goods, and has not signed after default a statement renouncing or modifying his rights under this Part a secured party who has taken possession of collateral must dispose of it under Section 9—504 and if he fails to do so within ninety days after he takes possession the debtor at his option may recover in conversion or under Section 9—507(1) on secured party's liability.

(2) In any other case involving consumer goods or any other collateral a secured party in possession may, after default, propose to retain the collateral in satisfaction of the obligation. Written notice of such proposal shall be sent to the debtor if he has not signed after default a statement renouncing or modifying his rights under this subsection. In the case of consumer goods no other notice need be given. In other cases notice shall be sent to any other secured party from whom the secured party has received (before sending his notice to the debtor or before the debtor's renunciation of his rights) written notice of a claim of an interest in the collateral. If the secured party receives objection in writing from a person entitled to receive notification within twenty-one days after the notice was sent, the secured party must dispose of the collateral under Section 9—504. In the absence of such written objection the secured party may retain the collateral in satisfaction of the debtor's obligation. Amended in 1972.

§ 9—506. Debtor's Right to Redeem Collateral.

At any time before the secured party has disposed of collateral or entered into a contract for its disposition under Section 9—504 or before the obligation has been discharged under Section 9—505(2) the debtor or any other secured party may unless otherwise agreed in writing after default redeem the collateral by tendering fulfillment of all obligations secured by the collateral as well as the expenses reasonably incurred by the secured party in retaking, holding and preparing the collateral for disposition, in arranging for the sale, and to the extent provided in the agreement and not prohibited by law, his reasonable attorneys' fees and legal expenses.

§ 9—507. Secured Party's Liability for Failure to Comply With This Part.

(1) If it is established that the secured party is not proceeding in accordance with the provisions of this Part disposition may be ordered or restrained on appropriate terms and conditions. If the disposition has occurred the debtor or any person entitled to notification or whose security interest has been made known to the secured party prior to the disposition has a right to recover from the secured party any loss caused by a failure to comply with the provisions of this Part. If the collateral is consumer goods, the debtor has a right to recover in any event an amount not less than the credit service charge plus ten per cent of the principal amount of the debt or the time price differential plus 10 per cent of the cash price.

(2) The fact that a better price could have been obtained by a sale at a different time or in a different method from that selected by the secured party is not of itself sufficient to establish that the sale was not made in a commercially reasonable manner. If the secured party either sells the collateral in the usual manner in any recognized market therefor or if he sells at the price current in such market at the time of his sale or if he has otherwise sold in conformity with reasonable commercial practices among dealers in the type of property sold he has sold in a commercially reasonable manner. The principles stated in the two preceding sentences with respect to sales also apply as may be appropriate to other types of disposition. A disposition which has been approved in any judicial proceeding or by any bona fide creditors' committee or representative of creditors shall conclusively be deemed to be commercially reasonable, but this sentence does not indicate that any such approval must be obtained in any case nor does it indicate that any disposition not so approved is not commercially reasonable.

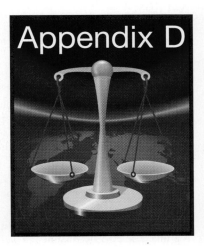

Appendix D

The Uniform Partnership Act

(Adopted in forty-nine states [all of the states except Louisiana], the District of Columbia, the Virgin Islands, and Guam. The adoptions by Alabama and Nebraska do not follow the official text in every respect, but are substantially similar, with local variations.)

The Act consists of 7 Parts as follows:

I. Preliminary Provisions

II. Nature of Partnership

III. Relations of Partners to Persons Dealing with the Partnership

IV. Relations of Partners to One Another

V. Property Rights of a Partner

VI. Dissolution and Winding Up

VII. Miscellaneous Provisions

An Act to make uniform the Law of Partnerships

Be it enacted, etc.:

Part I Preliminary Provisions

Sec. 1. Name of Act

This act may be cited as Uniform Partnership Act.

Sec. 2. Definition of Terms

In this act, "Court" includes every court and judge having jurisdiction in the case.

"Business" includes every trade, occupation, or profession.

"Person" includes individuals, partnerships, corporations, and other associations.

"Bankrupt" includes bankrupt under the Federal Bankruptcy Act or insolvent under any state insolvent act.

"Conveyance" includes every assignment, lease, mortgage, or encumbrance.

"Real property" includes land and any interest or estate in land.

Sec. 3. Interpretation of Knowledge and Notice

(1) A person has "knowledge" of a fact within the meaning of this act not only when he has actual knowledge thereof, but also when he has knowledge of such other facts as in the circumstances shows bad faith.

(2) A person has "notice" of a fact within the meaning of this act when the person who claims the benefit of the notice:

(a) States the fact to such person, or

(b) Delivers through the mail, or by other means of communication, a written statement of the fact to such person or to a proper person at his place of business or residence.

Sec. 4. Rules of Construction

(1) The rule that statutes in derogation of the common law are to be strictly construed shall have no application to this act.

(2) The law of estoppel shall apply under this act.

(3) The law of agency shall apply under this act.

(4) This act shall be so interpreted and construed as to effect its general purpose to make uniform the law of those states which enact it.

(5) This act shall not be construed so as to impair the obligations of any contract existing when the act goes into effect, nor to affect any action or proceedings begun or right accrued before this act takes effect.

Sec. 5. Rules for Cases Not Provided for in This Act.

In any case not provided for in this act the rules of law and equity, including the law merchant, shall govern.

Part II Nature of Partnership

Sec. 6. Partnership Defined

(1) A partnership is an association of two or more persons to carry on as co-owners a business for profit.

(2) But any association formed under any other statute of this state, or any statute adopted by authority, other than the authority of this state, is not a partnership under this act, unless such association would have been a partnership in this state prior to the adoption of this act; but this act shall apply to limited partnerships except in so far as the statutes relating to such partnerships are inconsistent herewith.

Sec. 7. Rules for Determining the Existence of a Partnership

In determining whether a partnership exists, these rules shall apply:

(1) Except as provided by Section 16 persons who are not partners as to each other are not partners as to third persons.

(2) Joint tenancy, tenancy in common, tenancy by the entireties, joint property, common property, or part ownership does not of itself establish a partnership, whether such co-owners do or do not share any profits made by the use of the property.

(3) The sharing of gross returns does not of itself establish a partnership, whether or not the persons sharing them have a joint or common right or interest in any property from which the returns are derived.

(4) The receipt by a person of a share of the profits of a business is prima facie evidence that he is a partner in the business, but no such inference shall be drawn if such profits were received in payment:

(a) As a debt by installments or otherwise,

(b) As wages of an employee or rent to a landlord,

(c) As an annuity to a widow or representative of a deceased partner,

(d) As interest on a loan, though the amount of payment vary with the profits of the business,

(e) As the consideration for the sale of a good-will of a business or other property by installments or otherwise.

Sec. 8. **Partnership Property**

(1) All property originally brought into the partnership stock or subsequently acquired by purchase or otherwise, on account of the partnership, is partnership property.

(2) Unless the contrary intention appears, property acquired with partnership funds is partnership property.

(3) Any estate in real property may be acquired in the partnership name. Title so acquired can be conveyed only in the partnership name.

(4) A conveyance to a partnership in the partnership name, though without words of inheritance, passes the entire estate of the grantor unless a contrary intent appears.

Part III   Relations of Partners to Persons Dealing with the Partnership

Sec. 9. **Partner Agent of Partnership as to Partnership Business**

(1) Every partner is an agent of the partnership for the purpose of its business, and the act of every partner, including the execution in the partnership name of any instrument, for apparently carrying on in the usual way the business of the partnership of which he is a member binds the partnership, unless the partner so acting has in fact no authority to act for the partnership in the particular matter, and the person with whom he is dealing has knowledge of the fact that he has no such authority.

(2) An act of a partner which is not apparently for the carrying on of the business of the partnership in the usual way does not bind the partnership unless authorized by the other partners.

(3) Unless authorized by the other partners or unless they have abandoned the business, one or more but less than all the partners have no authority to:

(a) Assign the partnership property in trust for creditors or on

the assignee's promise to pay the debts of the partnership,

(b) Dispose of the good-will of the business,

(c) Do any other act which would make it impossible to carry on the ordinary business of a partnership,

(d) Confess a judgment,

(e) Submit a partnership claim or liability to arbitration or reference.

(4) No act of a partner in contravention of a restriction on authority shall bind the partnership to persons having knowledge of the restriction.

Sec. 10. **Conveyance of Real Property of the Partnership**

(1) Where title to real property is in the partnership name, any partner may convey title to such property by a conveyance executed in the partnership name; but the partnership may recover such property unless the partner's act binds the partnership under the provisions of paragraph (1) of section 9, or unless such property has been conveyed by the grantee or a person claiming through such grantee to a holder for value without knowledge that the partner, in making the conveyance, has exceeded his authority.

(2) Where title to real property is in the name of the partnership, a conveyance executed by a partner, in his own name, passes the equitable interest of the partnership, provided the act is one within the authority of the partner under the provisions of paragraph (1) of section 9.

(3) Where title to real property is in the name of one or more but not all the partners, and the record does not disclose the right of the partnership, the partners in whose name the title stands may convey title to such property, but the partnership may recover such property if the partners' act does not bind the partnership under the provisions of paragraph (1) of section 9, unless the purchaser or his assignee, is a holder for value, without knowledge.

(4) Where the title to real property is in the name of one or more or all the partners, or in a third person in trust for the partnership, a conveyance executed by a partner in the partnership name, or in his own name, passes the equitable interest of the partnership, provided the act is one within the authority of the partner under the provisions of paragraph (1) of section 9.

(5) Where the title to real property is in the names of all the partners a conveyance executed by all the partners passes all their rights in such property.

Sec. 11. **Partnership Bound by Admission of Partner**

An admission or representation made by any partner concerning partnership affairs within the scope of his authority as conferred by this act is evidence against the partnership.

Sec. 12. **Partnership Charged with Knowledge of or Notice to Partner**

Notice to any partner of any matter relating to partnership affairs, and the knowledge of the partner acting in the particular matter, acquired while a partner or then present to his mind, and the knowledge of any other partner who reasonably could and should have communicated it to the acting partner, operate as notice to or knowledge of the partnership, except in the case of a fraud on the partnership committed by or with the consent of that partner.

Sec. 13. **Partnership Bound by Partner's Wrongful Act**

Where, by any wrongful act or omission of any partner acting in the ordinary course of the business of the partnership or with the authority of his co-partners, loss or injury is caused to any person, not being a partner in the partnership, or any penalty is incurred, the partnership is liable therefor to the same extent as the partner so acting or omitting to act.

Sec. 14. **Partnership Bound by Partner's Breach of Trust**

The partnership is bound to make good the loss:

(a) Where one partner acting within the scope of his apparent authority receives money or property of a third person and misapplies it; and

(b) Where the partnership in the course of its business receives money or property of a third person and the money or property so received is misapplied by any partner while it is in the custody of the partnership.

Sec. 15. **Nature of Partner's Liability**

All partners are liable

(a) Jointly and severally for everything chargeable to the partnership under sections 13 and 14.

(b) Jointly for all other debts and obligations of the partnership; but any partner may enter into a separate obligation to perform a partnership contract.

Sec. 16. **Partner by Estoppel**

(1) When a person, by words spoken or written or by conduct, represents himself, or consents to another representing him to any one, as a partner in an existing partnership or with one or more persons not actual partners, he is liable to any such person to whom such representation has been made, who has, on the faith of such representation, given credit to the actual or apparent partnership, and if he has made such representation or consented to its being made in a public manner he is liable to such person, whether the representation has or has not been made or communicated to such person so giving credit by or with the knowledge of the apparent partner making the representation or consenting to its being made.

> (a) When a partnership liability results, he is liable as though he were an actual member of the partnership.

> (b) When no partnership liability results, he is liable jointly with the other persons, if any, so consenting to the contract or representation as to incur liability, otherwise separately.

(2) When a person has been thus represented to be a partner in an existing partnership, or with one or more persons not actual partners, he is an agent of the persons consenting to such representation to bind them to the same extent and in the same manner as though he were a partner in fact, with respect to persons who rely upon the representation. Where all the members of the existing partnership consent to the representation, a partnership act or obligation results; but in all other cases it is the joint act or obligation of the person acting and the persons consenting to the representation.

Sec. 17. **Liability of Incoming Partner**

A person admitted as a partner into an existing partnership is liable for all the obligations of the partnership arising before his admission as though he had been a partner when such obligations were incurred, except that this liability shall be satisfied only out of partnership property.

Part IV Relations of Partners to One Another

Sec. 18. **Rules Determining Rights and Duties of Partners**

The rights and duties of the partners in relation to the partnership shall be determined, subject to any agreement between them, by the following rules:

(a) Each partner shall be repaid his contributions, whether by way of capital or advances to the partnership property and share equally in the profits and surplus remaining after all liabilities, including those to partners, are satisfied; and must contribute towards the losses, whether of capital or otherwise, sustained by the partnership according to his share in the profits.

(b) The partnership must indemnify every partner in respect of payments made and personal liabilities reasonably incurred by him in the ordinary and proper conduct of its business, or for the preservation of its business or property.

(c) A partner, who in aid of the partnership makes any payment or advance beyond the amount of capital which he agreed to contribute, shall be paid interest from the date of the payment or advance.

(d) A partner shall receive interest on the capital contributed by him only from the date when repayment should be made.

(e) All partners have equal rights in the management and conduct of the partnership business.

(f) No partner is entitled to remuneration for acting in the partnership business, except that a surviving partner is entitled to reasonable compensation for his services in winding up the partnership affairs.

(g) No person can become a member of a partnership without the consent of all the partners.

(h) Any difference arising as to ordinary matters connected with the partnership business may be decided by a majority of the partners; but no act in contravention of any agreement between the partners may be done rightfully without the consent of all the partners.

Sec. 19. **Partnership Books**

The partnership books shall be kept, subject to any agreement between the partners, at the principal place of business of the partnership, and every partner shall at all times have access to and may inspect and copy any of them.

Sec. 20. **Duty of Partners to Render Information**

Partners shall render on demand true and full information of all things affecting the partnership to any partner or the legal representative of any deceased partner or partner under legal disability.

Sec. 21. **Partner Accountable as a Fiduciary**

(1) Every partner must account to the partnership for any benefit, and hold as trustee for it any profits derived by him without the consent of the other partners from any transaction connected with the formation, conduct, or liquidation of the partnership or from any use by him of its property.

(2) This section applies also to the representatives of a deceased partner engaged in the liquidation of the affairs of the partnership as the personal representatives of the last surviving partner.

Sec. 22. Right to an Account

Any partner shall have the right to a formal account as to partnership affairs:

(a) If he is wrongfully excluded from the partnership business or possession of its property by his co-partners,

(b) If the right exists under the terms of any agreement,

(c) As provided by section 21,

(d) Whenever other circumstances render it just and reasonable.

Sec. 23. Continuation of Partnership beyond Fixed Term

(1) When a partnership for a fixed term or particular undertaking is continued after the termination of such term or particular undertaking without any express agreement, the rights and duties of the partners remain the same as they were at such termination, so far as is consistent with a partnership at will.

(2) A continuation of the business by the partners or such of them as habitually acted therein during the term, without any settlement or liquidation of the partnership affairs, is prima facie evidence of a continuation of the partnership.

Part V Property Rights of a Partner

Sec. 24. Extent of Property Rights of a Partner

The property rights of a partner are (1) his rights in specific partnership property, (2) his interest in the partnership, and (3) his right to participate in the management.

Sec. 25. Nature of a Partner's Right in Specific Partnership Property

(1) A partner is co-owner with his partners of specific partnership property holding as a tenant in partnership.

(2) The incidents of this tenancy are such that:

(a) A partner, subject to the provisions of this act and to any agreement between the partners, has an equal right with his partners to possess specific partnership property for partnership purposes; but he has no right to possess such property for any other purpose without the consent of his partners.

(b) A partner's right in specific partnership property is not assignable except in connection with the assignment of rights of all the partners in the same property.

(c) A partner's right in specific partnership property is not subject to attachment or execution, except on a claim against the partnership. When partnership property is attached for a partnership debt the partners, or any of them, or the representatives of a deceased partner, cannot claim any right under the homestead or exemption laws.

(d) On the death of a partner his right in specific partnership property vests in the surviving partner or partners, except where the deceased was the last surviving partner, when his right in such property vests in his legal representative. Such surviving partner or partners, or the legal representative of the last surviving partner, has no right to possess the partnership property for any but a partnership purpose.

e) A partner's right in specific partnership property is not subject to dower, curtesy, or allowances to widows, heirs, or next of kin.

Sec. 26. Nature of Partner's Interest in the Partnership

A partner's interest in the partnership is his share of the profits and surplus, and the same is personal property.

Sec. 27. Assignment of Partner's Interest

(1) A conveyance by a partner of his interest in the partnership does not of itself dissolve the partnership, nor, as against the other partners in the absence of agreement, entitle the assignee, during the continuance of the partnership, to interfere in the management or administration of the partnership business or affairs, or to require any information or account of partnership transactions, or to inspect the partnership books; but it merely entitles the assignee to receive in accordance with his contract the profits to which the assigning partner would otherwise be entitled.

(2) In case of a dissolution of the partnership, the assignee is entitled to receive his assignor's interest and may require an account from the date only of the last account agreed to by all the partners.

Sec. 28. Partner's Interest Subject to Charging Order

(1) On due application to a competent court by any judgment creditor of a partner, the court which entered the judgment, order, or decree, or any other court, may charge the interest of the debtor partner with payment of the unsatisfied amount of such judgment debt with interest thereon; and may then or later appoint a receiver of his share of the profits, and of any other money due or to fall due to him in respect of the partnership, and make all other orders, directions, accounts and inquiries which the debtor partner might have made, or which the circumstances of the case may require.

(2) The interest charged may be redeemed at any time before foreclosure, or in case of a sale being directed by the court may be purchased without thereby causing a dissolution:

(a) With separate property, by any one or more of the partners, or

(b) With partnership property, by any one or more of the partners with the consent of all the partners whose interests are not so charged or sold.

(3) Nothing in this act shall be held to deprive a partner of his right, if any, under the exemption laws, as regards his interest in the partnership.

Part VI Dissolution and Winding up

Sec. 29. Dissolution Defined

The dissolution of a partnership is the change in the relation of the partners caused by any partner ceasing to be associated in the carrying on as distinguished from the winding up of the business.

Sec. 30. Partnership not Terminated by Dissolution

On dissolution the partnership is not terminated, but continues until the winding up of partnership affairs is completed.

Sec. 31. Causes of Dissolution

Dissolution is caused:

(1) Without violation of the agreement between the partners,

(a) By the termination of the definite term or particular undertaking specified in the agreement,

(b) By the express will of any partner when no definite term or particular undertaking is specified,

(c) By the express will of all the partners who have not assigned their interests or suffered them to be charged for their separate debts, either before or after the termination of any specified term or particular undertaking,

(d) By the expulsion of any partner from the business bona fide in accordance with such a power conferred by the agreement between the partners;

(2) In contravention of the agreement between the partners, where the circumstances do not permit a dissolution under any other provision of this section, by the express will of any partner at any time;

(3) By any event which makes it unlawful for the business of the partnership to be carried on or for the members to carry it on in partnership;

(4) By the death of any partner;

(5) By the bankruptcy of any partner or the partnership;

(6) By decree of court under section 32.

Sec. 32. **Dissolution by Decree of Court**

(1) On application by or for a partner the court shall decree a dissolution whenever:

(a) A partner has been declared a lunatic in any judicial proceeding or is shown to be of unsound mind,

(b) A partner becomes in any other way incapable of performing his part of the partnership contract,

(c) A partner has been guilty of such conduct as tends to affect prejudicially the carrying on of the business,

(d) A partner wilfully or persistently commits a breach of the partnership agreement, or otherwise so conducts himself in matters relating to the partnership business that it is not reasonably practicable to carry on the business in partnership with him,

(e) The business of the partnership can only be carried on at a loss,

(f) Other circumstances render a dissolution equitable.

(2) On the application of the purchaser of a partner's interest under sections 28 or 29 [should read 27 or 28];

(a) After the termination of the specified term or particular undertaking,

(b) At any time if the partnership was a partnership at will when the interest was assigned or when the charging order was issued.

Sec. 33. **General Effect of Dissolution on Authority of Partner**

Except so far as may be necessary to wind up partnership affairs or to complete transactions begun but not then finished, dissolution terminates all authority of any partner to act for the partnership,

(1) With respect to the partners,

(a) When the dissolution is not by the act, bankruptcy or death of a partner; or

(b) When the dissolution is by such act, bankruptcy or death of a partner, in cases where section 34 so requires.

(2) With respect to persons not partners, as declared in section 35.

Sec. 34. **Rights of Partner to Contribution from Copartners after Dissolution**

Where the dissolution is caused by the act, death or bankruptcy of a partner, each partner is liable to his copartners for his share of any liability created by any partner acting for the partnership as if the partnership had not been dissolved unless

(a) The dissolution being by act of any partner, the partner acting for the partnership had knowledge of the dissolution, or

(b) The dissolution being by the death or bankruptcy of a partner, the partner acting for the partnership had knowledge or notice of the death or bankruptcy.

Sec. 35. **Power of Partner to Bind Partnership to Third Persons after Dissolution**

(1) After dissolution a partner can bind the partnership except as provided in Paragraph (3).

(a) By any act appropriate for winding up partnership affairs or completing transactions unfinished at dissolution;

(b) By any transaction which would bind the partnership if dissolution had not taken place, provided the other party to the transaction

(I) Had extended credit to the partnership prior to dissolution and had no knowledge or notice of the dissolution; or

(II) Though he had not so extended credit, had nevertheless known of the partnership prior to dissolution, and, having no knowledge or notice of dissolution, the fact of dissolution had not been advertised in a newspaper of general circulation in the place (or in each place if more than one) at which the partnership business was regularly carried on.

(2) The liability of a partner under paragraph (1b) shall be satisfied out of partnership assets alone when such partner had been prior to dissolution

(a) Unknown as a partner to the person with whom the contract is made; and

(b) So far unknown and inactive in partnership affairs that the business reputation of the partnership could not be said to have been in any degree due to his connection with it.

(3) The partnership is in no case bound by any act of a partner after dissolution

(a) Where the partnership is dissolved because it is unlawful to carry on the business, unless the act is appropriate for winding up partnership affairs; or

(b) Where the partner has become bankrupt; or

(c) Where the partner has no authority to wind up partnership affairs; except by a transaction with one who

(I) Had extended credit to the partnership prior to dissolution and had no knowledge or notice of his want of authority; or

(II) Had not extended credit to the partnership prior to dissolution, and, having no knowledge or notice of his want of authority, the fact of his want of authority has not been advertised in the manner provided for advertising the fact of dissolution in paragraph (1bII).

(4) Nothing in this section shall affect the liability under Section 16 of any person who after dissolution represents himself or consents to another representing him as a partner in a partnership engaged in carrying on business.

Sec. 36. **Effect of Dissolution on Partner's Existing Liability**

(1) The dissolution of the partnership does not of itself discharge the existing liability of any partner.

(2) A partner is discharged from any existing liability upon dissolution of the partnership by an agreement to that effect between himself, the partnership creditor and the person or partnership continuing the business; and such agreement may be inferred from the course of dealing between the creditor having knowledge of the dissolution and the person or partnership continuing the business.

(3) Where a person agrees to assume the existing obligations of a dissolved partnership, the partners whose obligations have been assumed shall be discharged from any liability to any creditor of the partnership who, knowing of the agreement, consents to a material alteration in the nature or time of payment of such obligations.

(4) The individual property of a deceased partner shall be liable for all obligations of the partnership incurred while he was a partner but subject to the prior payment of his separate debts.

Sec. 37. **Right to Wind Up**

Unless otherwise agreed the partners who have not wrongfully dissolved the partnership or the legal representative of the last surviving partner, not bankrupt, has the right to wind up the partnership affairs; provided, however, that any partner, his legal representative or his assignee, upon cause shown, may obtain winding up by the court.

Sec. 38. **Rights of Partners to Application of Partnership Property**

(1) When dissolution is caused in any way, except in contravention of the partnership agreement, each partner, as against his co-partners and all persons claiming through them in respect of their interests in the partnership, unless otherwise agreed, may have the partnership property applied to discharge its liabilities, and the surplus applied to pay in cash the net amount owing to the respective partners. But if dissolution is caused by expulsion of a partner, bona fide under the partnership agreement and if the expelled partner is discharged from all partnership liabilities, either by payment or agreement under section 36(2), he shall receive in cash only the net amount due him from the partnership.

(2) When dissolution is caused in contravention of the partnership agreement the rights of the partners shall be as follows:

(a) Each partner who has not caused dissolution wrongfully shall have,

(I) All the rights specified in paragraph (1) of this section, and

(II) The right, as against each partner who has caused the dissolution wrongfully, to damages for breach of the agreement.

(b) The partners who have not caused the dissolution wrongfully, if they all desire to continue the business in the same name, either by themselves or jointly with others, may do so, during the agreed term for the partnership and for that purpose may possess the partnership property, provided they secure the payment by bond approved by the court, or pay to any partner who has caused the dissolution wrongfully, the value of his interest in the partnership at the dissolution, less

any damages recoverable under clause (2a II) of the section, and in like manner indemnify him against all present or future partnership liabilities.

(c) A partner who has caused the dissolution wrongfully shall have:

(I) If the business is not continued under the provisions of paragraph (2b) all the rights of a partner under paragraph (1), subject to clause (2a II), of this section,

(II) If the business is continued under paragraph (2b) of this section the right as against his co-partners and all claiming through them in respect of their interests in the partnership, to have the value of his interest in the partnership, less any damages caused to his co-partners by the dissolution, ascertained and paid to him in cash, or the payment secured by bond approved by the court, and to be released from all existing liabilities of the partnership; but in ascertaining the value of the partner's interest the value of the good-will of the business shall not be considered.

Sec. 39. **Rights Where Partnership Is Dissolved for Fraud or Misrepresentation**

Where a partnership contract is rescinded on the ground of the fraud or misrepresentation of one of the parties thereto, the party entitled to rescind is, without prejudice to any other right, entitled,

(a) To a lien on, or right of retention of, the surplus of the partnership property after satisfying the partnership liabilities to third persons for any sum of money paid by him for the purchase of an interest in the partnership and for any capital or advances contributed by him; and

(b) To stand, after all liabilities to third persons have been satisfied, in the place of the creditors of the partnership for any payments made by him in respect of the partnership liabilities; and

(c) To be indemnified by the person guilty of the fraud or making the representation against all debts and liabilities of the partnership.

Sec. 40. **Rules for Distribution**

In settling accounts between the partners after dissolution, the following rules shall be observed, subject to any agreement to the contrary:

(a) The assets of the partnership are:

(I) The partnership property,

(II) The contributions of the partners necessary for the payment of all the liabilities specified in clause (b) of this paragraph.

(b) The liabilities of the partnership shall rank in order of payment, as follows:

(I) Those owing to creditors other than partners,

(II) Those owing to partners other than for capital and profits,

(III) Those owing to partners in respect of capital,

(IV) Those owing to partners in respect of profits.

(c) The assets shall be applied in the order of their declaration in clause (a) of this paragraph to the satisfaction of the liabilities.

(d) The partners shall contribute, as provided by section 18(a) the amount necessary to satisfy the liabilities; but if any, but not all, of the partners are insolvent, or, not being subject to process, refuse to contribute, the other partners shall contribute their share of the liabilities, and, in the relative proportions in which they share the profits, the additional amount necessary to pay the liabilities.

(e) An assignee for the benefit of creditors or any person appointed by the court shall have the right to enforce the contributions specified in clause (d) of this paragraph.

(f) Any partner or his legal representative shall have the right to enforce the contributions specified in clause (d) of this paragraph, to the extent of the amount which he has paid in excess of his share of the liability.

(g) The individual property of a deceased partner shall be liable for the contributions specified in clause (d) of this paragraph.

(h) When partnership property and the individual properties of the partners are in possession of a court for distribution, partnership creditors shall have priority on partnership property and separate creditors on individual property, saving the rights of lien or secured creditors as heretofore.

(i) Where a partner has become bankrupt or his estate is insolvent the claims against his separate property shall rank in the following order:

  (I) Those owing to separate creditors,

  (II) Those owing to partnership creditors,

  (III) Those owing to partners by way of contribution.

Sec. 41. Liability of Persons Continuing the Business in Certain Cases

(1) When any new partner is admitted into an existing partnership, or when any partner retires and assigns (or the representative of the deceased partner assigns) his rights in partnership property to two or more of the partners, or to one or more of the partners and one or more third persons, if the business is continued without liquidation of the partnership affairs, creditors of the first or dissolved partnership are also creditors of the partnership so continuing the business.

(2) When all but one partner retire and assign (or the representative of a deceased partner assigns) their rights in partnership property to the remaining partner, who continues the business without liquidation of partnership affairs, either alone or with others, creditors of the dissolved partnership are also creditors of the person or partnership so continuing the business.

(3) When any partner retires or dies and the business of the dissolved partnership is continued as set forth in paragraphs (1) and (2) of this section, with the consent of the retired partners or the representative of the deceased partner, but without any assignment of his right in partnership property, rights of creditors of the dissolved partnership and of the creditors of the person or partnership continuing the business shall be as if such assignment had been made.

(4) When all the partners or their representatives assign their rights in partnership property to one or more third persons who promise to pay the debts and who continue the business of the dissolved partnership, creditors of the dissolved partnership are also creditors of the person or partnership continuing the business.

(5) When any partner wrongfully causes a dissolution and the remaining partners continue the business under the provisions of section 38(2b), either alone or with others, and without liquidation of the partnership affairs, creditors of the dissolved partnership are also creditors of the person or partnership continuing the business.

(6) When a partner is expelled and the remaining partners continue the business either alone or with others, without liquidation of the partnership affairs, creditors of the dissolved partnership are also creditors of the person or partnership continuing the business.

(7) The liability of a third person becoming a partner in the partnership continuing the business, under this section, to the creditors of the dissolved partnership shall be satisfied out of partnership property only.

(8) When the business of a partnership after dissolution is continued under any conditions set forth in this section the creditors of the dissolved partnership, as against the separate creditors of the retiring or deceased partner or the representative of the deceased partner, have a prior right to any claim of the retired partner or the representative of the deceased partner against the person or partnership continuing the business, on account of the retired or deceased partner's interest in the dissolved partnership or on account of any consideration promised for such interest or for his right in partnership property.

(9) Nothing in this section shall be held to modify any right of creditors to set aside any assignment on the ground of fraud.

(10) The use by the person or partnership continuing the business of the partnership name, or the name of a deceased partner as part thereof, shall not of itself make the individual property of the deceased partner liable for any debts contracted by such person or partnership.

Sec. 42. Rights of Retiring or Estate of Deceased Partner When the Business Is Continued

When any partner retires or dies, and the business is continued under any of the conditions set forth in section 41 (1, 2, 3, 5, 6), or section 38(2b) without any settlement of accounts as between him or his estate and the person or partnership continuing the business, unless otherwise agreed, he or his legal representative as against such persons or partnership may have the value of his interest at the date of dissolution ascertained, and shall receive as an ordinary creditor an amount equal to the value of his interest in the dissolved partnership with interest, or, at his option or at the option of his legal representative, in lieu of interest, the profits attributable to the use of his right in the property of the dissolved partnership; provided that the creditors of the dissolved partnership as against the separate creditors, or the representative of the retired or deceased partner, shall have priority on any claim arising under this section, as provided by section 41(8) of this act.

Sec. 43. Accrual of Actions

The right to an account of his interest shall accrue to any partner, or his legal representative, as against the winding up partners or the surviving partners or the person or partnership continuing the business, at the date of dissolution, in the absence of any agreement to the contrary.

Part VII Miscellaneous Provisions

Sec. 44. When Act Takes Effect

This act shall take effect on the ___ day of ___ one thousand nine hundred and ___.

Sec. 45. Legislation Repealed

All acts or parts of acts inconsistent with this act are hereby repealed.

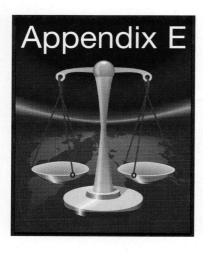

Appendix E

The Revised Model Business Corporation Act

Chapter 1.
GENERAL PROVISIONS

Subchapter A. Short Title and Reservation of Power

§ 1.01 Short Title

This Act shall be known and may be cited as the "[name of state] Business Corporation Act."

§ 1.02 Reservation of Power to Amend or Repeal

The [name of state legislature] has power to amend or repeal all or part of this Act at any time and all domestic and foreign corporations subject to this Act are governed by the amendment or repeal.

Subchapter B. Filing Documents

§ 1.20 Filing Requirements

(a) A document must satisfy the requirements of this section, and of any other section that adds to or varies these requirements, to be entitled to filing by the secretary of state.

(b) This Act must require or permit filing the document in the office of the secretary of state.

(c) The document must contain the information required by this Act. It may contain other information as well.

(d) The document must be typewritten or printed.

(e) The document must be in the English language. A corporate name need not be in English if written in English letters or Arabic or Roman numerals, and the certificate of existence required of foreign corporations need not be in English if accompanied by a reasonably authenticated English translation.

(f) The document must be executed:

(1) by the chairman of the board of directors of a domestic or foreign corporation, by its president, or by another of its officers;

(2) if directors have not been selected or the corporation has not been formed, by an incorporator; or

(3) if the corporation is in the hands of a receiver, trustee, or other court-appointed fiduciary, by that fiduciary.

(g) The person executing the document shall sign it and state beneath or opposite his signature his name and the capacity in which he signs. The document may but need not contain: (1) the corporate seal, (2) an attestation by the secretary or an assistant secretary, (3) an acknowledgement, verification, or proof.

(h) If the secretary of state has prescribed a mandatory form for the document under section 1.21, the document must be in or on the prescribed form.

(i) The document must be delivered to the office of the secretary of state for filing and must be accompanied by one exact or conformed copy (except as provided in sections 5.03 and 15.09), the correct filing fee, and any franchise tax, license fee, or penalty required by this Act or other law.

§ 1.21 Forms

(a) The secretary of state may prescribe and furnish on request forms for: (1) an application for a certificate of existence, (2) a foreign corporation's application for a certificate of authority to transact business in this state, (3) a foreign corporation's application for a certificate of withdrawal, and (4) the annual report. If the secretary of state so requires, use of these forms is mandatory.

(b) The secretary of state may prescribe and furnish on request forms for other documents required or permitted to be filed by this Act but their use is not mandatory.

§ 1.22 Filing, Service, and Copying Fees

(a) The secretary of state shall collect the following fees when the documents described in this subsection are delivered to him for filing:

Document	Fee
(1) Articles of incorporation	$_____.
(2) Application for use of indistinguishable name	$_____.
(3) Application for reserved name	$_____.
(4) Notice of transfer of reserved name	$_____.
(5) Application for registered name	$_____.
(6) Application for renewal of registered name	$_____.
(7) Corporation's statement of change of registered agent or registered	

THE REVISED MODEL BUSINESS CORPORATION ACT

office or both $_____.

(8) Agent's statement of change of registered office for each affected corpor-
ation not to exceed a total of $_____.

(9) Agent's statement of resignation   No fee.

(10) Amendment of articles of incorporation $_____.

(11) Restatement of articles of incorporation
with amendment of articles $_____.

(12) Articles of merger or share exchange $_____.

(13) Articles of dissolution $_____.

(14) Articles of revocation of dissolution $_____.

(15) Certificate of administrative dissolution No fee.

(16) Application for reinstatement following
administrative dissolution $_____.

(17) Certificate of reinstatement   No fee.

(18) Certificate of judicial dissolution   No fee.

(19) Application for certificate of authority   No fee.

(20) Application for amended certificate
of authority $_____.

(21) Application for certificate of withdrawal $_____.

(22) Certificate of revocation of authority
to transact business   No fee.

(23) Annual report $_____

(24) Articles of correction $_____.

(25) Application for certificate of existence
or authorization $_____.

(26) Any other document required or
permitted to be filed by this Act. $_____.

(b) The secretary of state shall collect a fee of $_____ each time process is served on him under this Act. The party to a proceeding causing service of process is entitled to recover this fee as costs if he prevails in the proceeding.

(c) The secretary of state shall collect the following fees for copying and certifying the copy of any filed document relating to a domestic or foreign corporation:

(1) $_____ a page for copying; and

(2) $_____ for the certificate.

§ 1.23 **Effective Time and Date of Document**

(a) Except as provided in subsection (b) and section 1.24(c), a document accepted for filing is effective:

(1) at the time of filing on the date it is filed, as evidenced by the secretary of state's date and time endorsement on the original document; or

(2) at the time specified in the document as its effective time on the date it is filed.

(b) A document may specify a delayed effective time and date, and if it does so the document becomes effective at the time and date specified. If a delayed effective date but no time is specified, the document is effective at the close of business on that date. A delayed effective date for a document may not be later than the 90th day after the date it is filed.

§ 1.24 **Correcting Filed Document**

(a) A domestic or foreign corporation may correct a document filed by the secretary of state if the document (1) contains an incorrect statement or (2) was defectively executed, attested, sealed, verified, or acknowledged.

(b) A document is corrected:

(1) by preparing articles of correction that (i) describe the document (including its filing date) or attach a copy of it to the articles, (ii) specify the incorrect statement and the reason it is incorrect or the manner in which the execution was defective, and (iii) correct the incorrect statement or defective execution; and

(2) by delivering the articles to the secretary of state for filing.

(c) Articles of correction are effective on the effective date of the document they correct except as to persons relying on the uncorrected document and adversely affected by the correction. As to those persons, articles of correction are effective when filed.

§ 1.25 **Filing Duty of Secretary of State**

(a) If a document delivered to the office of the secretary of state for filing satisfies the requirements of section 1.20, the secretary of state shall file it.

(b) The secretary of state files a document by stamping or otherwise endorsing "Filed," together with his name and official title and the date and time of receipt, on both the original and the document copy and on the receipt for the filing fee. After filing a document, except as provided in sections 5.03 and 15.10, the secretary of state shall deliver the document copy, with the filing fee receipt (or acknowledgement of receipt if no fee is required) attached, to the domestic or foreign corporation or its representative.

(c) If the secretary of state refuses to file a document, he shall return it to the domestic or foreign corporation or its representative within five days after the document was delivered, together with a brief, written explanation of the reason for his refusal.

(d) The secretary of state's duty to file documents under this section is ministerial. His filing or refusing to file a document does not:

(1) affect the validity or invalidity of the document in whole or part;

(2) relate to the correctness or incorrectness of information contained in the document;

(3) create a presumption that the document is valid or invalid or that information contained in the document is correct or incorrect.

§ 1.26 **Appeal From Secretary of State's Refusal to File Document**

(a) If the secretary of state refuses to file a document delivered to his office for filing, the domestic or foreign corporation may appeal the refusal to the [name or describe] court [of the county where the corporation's principal office (or, if none in this state, its registered office) is or will be located] [of _____ county]. The appeal is commenced by petitioning the court to compel filing the document and by attaching to the petition the document and the secretary of state's explanation of his refusal to file.

(b) The court may summarily order the secretary of state to file the document or take other action the court considers appropriate.

(c) The court's final decision may be appealed as in other civil proceedings.

§ 1.27 Evidentiary Effect of Copy of Filed Document

A certificate attached to a copy of the document filed by the secretary of state, bearing his signature (which may be in facsimile) and the seal of this state, is conclusive evidence that the original document is on file with the secretary of state.

§ 1.28 Certificate of Existence

(a) Anyone may apply to the secretary of state to furnish a certificate of existence for a domestic corporation or a certificate of authorization for a foreign corporation.

(b) A certificate of existence or authorization sets forth:

(1) the domestic corporation's corporate name or the foreign corporation's corporate name used in this state;

(2) that (i) the domestic corporation is duly incorporated under the law of this state, the date of its incorporation, and the period of its duration if less than perpetual; or (ii) that the foreign corporation is authorized to transact business in this state;

(3) that all fees, taxes, and penalties owed to this state have been paid, if (i) payment is reflected in the records of the secretary of state and (ii) nonpayment affects the existence or authorization of the domestic or foreign corporation;

(4) that its most recent annual report required by section 16.22 has been delivered to the secretary of state;

(5) that articles of dissolution have not been filed; and

(6) other facts of record in the office of the secretary of state that may be requested by the applicant.

(c) Subject to any qualification stated in the certificate, a certificate of existence or authorization issued by the secretary of state may be relied upon as conclusive evidence that the domestic or foreign corporation is in existence or is authorized to transact business in this state.

§ 1.29 Penalty for Signing False Document

(a) A person commits an offense if he signs a document he knows is false in any material respect with intent that the document be delivered to the secretary of state for filing.

(b) An offense under this section is a [_____] misdemeanor [punishable by a fine of not to exceed _____].

Subchapter C. Secretary of State

§ 1.30 Powers

The secretary of state has the power reasonably necessary to perform the duties required of him by this Act.

Subchapter D. Definitions

§1.40 Act Definitions

In this Act:

(1) "Articles of incorporation" include amended and restated articles of incorporation and articles of merger.

(2) "Authorized shares" means the shares of all classes a domestic or foreign corporation is authorized to issue.

(3) "Conspicuous" means so written that a reasonable person

against whom the writing is to operate should have noticed it. For example, printing in italics or boldface or contrasting color, or typing in capitals or underlined, is conspicuous.

(4) "Corporation" or "domestic corporation" means a corporation for profit, which is not a foreign corporation, incorporated under or subject to the provisions of this Act.

(5) "Deliver" includes mail.

(6) "Distribution" means a direct or indirect transfer of money or other property (except its own shares) or incurrence of indebtedness by a corporation to or for the benefit of its shareholders in respect of any of its shares. A distribution may be in the form of a declaration or payment of a dividend; a purchase, redemption, or other acquisition of shares; a distribution of indebtedness; or otherwise.

(7) "Effective date of notice" is defined in section 1.41.

(8) "Employee" includes an officer but not a director. A director may accept duties that make him also an employee.

(9) "Entity" includes corporation and foreign corporation; not-for-profit corporation; profit and not-for-profit unincorporated association; business trust, estate, partnership, trust, and two or more persons having a joint or common economic interest; and state, United States, and foreign government.

(10) "Foreign corporation" means a corporation for profit incorporated under a law other than the law of this state.

(11) "Governmental subdivision" includes authority, county, district, and municipality.

(12) "Includes" denotes a partial definition.

(13) "Individual" includes the estate of an incompetent or deceased individual.

(14) "Means" denotes an exhaustive definition.

(15) "Notice" is defined in section 1.41.

(16) "Person" includes individual and entity.

(17) "Principal office" means the office (in or out of this state) so designated in the annual report where the principal executive offices of a domestic or foreign corporation are located.

(18) "Proceeding" includes civil suit and criminal, administrative, and investigatory action.

(19) "Record date" means the date established under chapter 6 or 7 on which a corporation determines the identity of its shareholders and their shareholdings for purposes of this Act. The determinations shall be made as of the close of business on the record date unless another time for doing so is specified when the record date is fixed.

(20) "Secretary" means the corporate officer to whom the board of directors has delegated responsibility under section 8.40(c) for custody of the minutes of the meetings of the board of directors and of the shareholders and for authenticating records of the corporation.

(21) "Share" means the unit into which the proprietary interests in a corporation are divided.

(22) "Shareholder" means the person in whose name shares are registered in the records of a corporation or the beneficial owner of shares to the extent of the rights granted by a nominee certificate on file with a corporation.

(23) "State," when referring to a part of the United States, includes a state and commonwealth (and their agencies and

governmental subdivisions) and a territory, and insular possession (and their agencies and governmental subdivisions) of the United States.

(24) "Subscriber" means a person who subscribes for shares in a corporation, whether before or after incorporation.

(25) "United States" includes district, authority, bureau, commission, department, and any other agency of the United States.

(26) "Voting group" means all shares of one or more classes or series that under the articles of incorporation or this Act are entitled to vote and be counted together collectively on a matter at a meeting of shareholders. All shares entitled by the articles of incorporation or this Act to vote generally on the matter are for that purpose a single voting group.

§ 1.41 Notice

(a) Notice under this Act shall be in writing unless oral notice is reasonable under the circumstances.

(b) Notice may be communicated in person; by telephone, telegraph, teletype, or other form of wire or wireless communication; or by mail or private carrier. If these forms of personal notice are impracticable, notice may be communicated by a newspaper of general circulation in the area where published; or by radio, television, or other form of public broadcast communication.

(c) Written notice by a domestic or foreign corporation to its shareholder, if in a comprehensible form, is effective when mailed, if mailed postpaid and correctly addressed to the shareholder's address shown in the corporation's current record of shareholders.

(d) Written notice to a domestic or foreign corporation (authorized to transact business in this state) may be addressed to its registered agent at its registered office or to the corporation or its secretary at its principal office shown in its most recent annual report or, in the case of a foreign corporation that has not yet delivered an annual report, in its application for a certificate of authority.

(e) Except as provided in subsections (c) and (d), written notice, if in a comprehensible form, is effective at the earliest of the following:

(1) when received;

(2) five days after its deposit in the United States Mail, as evidenced by the postmark, if mailed postpaid and correctly addressed;

(3) on the date shown on the return receipt, if sent by registered or certified mail, return receipt requested, and the receipt is signed by or on behalf of the addressee.

(f) Oral notice is effective when communicated if communicated in a comprehensible manner.

(g) If this Act prescribes notice requirements for particular circumstances, those requirements govern. If articles of incorporation or bylaws prescribe notice requirements, not inconsistent with this section or other provisions of this Act, those requirements govern.

§ 1.42 Number of Shareholders

(a) For purposes of this Act, the following identified as a shareholder in a corporation's current record of shareholders constitutes one shareholder:

(1) three or fewer co-owners;

(2) a corporation, partnership, trust, estate, or other entity;

(3) the trustees, guardians, custodians, or other fiduciaries of a single trust, estate, or account.

(b) For purposes of this Act, shareholdings registered in substantially similar names constitute one shareholder if it is reasonable to believe that the names represent the same person.

Chapter 2.
INCORPORATION

§ 2.01 Incorporators

One or more persons may act as the incorporator or incorporators of a corporation by delivering articles of incorporation to the secretary of state for filing.

§ 2.02 Articles of Incorporation

(a) The articles of incorporation must set forth:

(1) a corporate name for the corporation that satisfies the requirements of section 4.01;

(2) the number of shares the corporation is authorized to issue;

(3) the street address of the corporation's initial registered office and the name of its initial registered agent at that office; and

(4) the name and address of each incorporator.

(b) The articles of incorporation may set forth:

(1) the names and addresses of the individuals who are to serve as the initial directors;

(2) provisions not inconsistent with law regarding:

(i) the purpose or purposes for which the corporation is organized;

(ii) managing the business and regulating the affairs of the corporation;

(iii) defining, limiting, and regulating the powers of the corporation, its board of directors, and shareholders;

(iv) a par value for authorized shares or classes of shares;

(v) the imposition of personal liability on shareholders for the debts of the corporation to a specified extent and upon specified conditions;

(3) any provision that under this Act is required or permitted to be set forth in the bylaws; and

(4) a provision eliminating or limiting the liability of a director to the corporation or its shareholders for money damages for any action taken, or any failure to take any action, as a director, except liability for (A) the amount of a financial benefit received by a director to which he is not entitled; (B) an intentional infliction of harm on the corporation or the shareholders; (C) a violation of section 8.33; or (D) an intentional violation of criminal law.

(c) The articles of incorporation need not set forth any of the corporate powers enumerated in this Act.

§ 2.03 Incorporation

(a) Unless a delayed effective date is specified, the corporate existence begins when the articles of incorporation are filed.

(b) The secretary of state's filing of the articles of incorporation is conclusive proof that the incorporators satisfied all conditions precedent to incorporation except in a proceeding by the state to cancel or revoke the incorporation or involuntarily dissolve the corporation.

§ 2.04 Liability for Preincorporation Transactions

All persons purporting to act as or on behalf of a corporation, knowing there was no incorporation under this Act, are jointly and severally liable for all liabilities created while so acting.

§ 2.05 Organization of Corporation

(a) After incorporation:

(1) if initial directors are named in the articles of incorporation, the initial directors shall hold an organizational meeting, at the call of a majority of the directors, to complete the organization of the corporation by appointing officers, adopting bylaws, and carrying on any other business brought before the meeting;

(2) if initial directors are not named in the articles, the incorporator or incorporators shall hold an organizational meeting at the call of a majority of the incorporators:

(i) to elect directors and complete the organization of the corporation; or

(ii) to elect a board of directors who shall complete the organization of the corporation.

(b) Action required or permitted by this Act to be taken by incorporators at an organizational meeting may be taken without a meeting if the action taken is evidenced by one or more written consents describing the action taken and signed by each incorporator.

(c) An organizational meeting may be held in or out of this state.

§ 2.06 Bylaws

(a) The incorporators or board of directors of a corporation shall adopt initial bylaws for the corporation.

(b) The bylaws of a corporation may contain any provision for managing the business and regulating the affairs of the corporation that is not inconsistent with law or the articles of incorporation.

§ 2.07 Emergency Bylaws

(a) Unless the articles of incorporation provide otherwise, the board of directors of a corporation may adopt bylaws to be effective only in an emergency defined in subsection (d). The emergency bylaws, which are subject to amendment or repeal by the shareholders, may make all provisions necessary for managing the corporation during the emergency, including:

(1) procedures for calling a meeting of the board of directors;

(2) quorum requirements for the meeting; and

(3) designation of additional or substitute directors.

(b) All provisions of the regular bylaws consistent with the emergency bylaws remain effective during the emergency. The emergency bylaws are not effective after the emergency ends.

(c) Corporate action taken in good faith in accordance with the emergency bylaws:

(1) binds the corporation; and

(2) may not be used to impose liability on a corporate director, officer, employee, or agent.

(d) An emergency exists for purposes of this section if a quorum of the corporation's directors cannot readily be assembled because of some catastrophic event.

Chapter 3.
PURPOSES AND POWERS

§ 3.01 Purposes

(a) Every corporation incorporated under this Act has the purpose of engaging in any lawful business unless a more limited purpose is set forth in the articles of incorporation.

(b) A corporation engaging in a business that is subject to regulation under another statute of this state may incorporate under this Act only if permitted by, and subject to all limitations of, the other statute.

§ 3.02 General Powers

Unless its articles of incorporation provide otherwise, every corporation has perpetual duration and succession in its corporate name and has the same powers as an individual to do all things necessary or convenient to carry out its business and affairs, including without limitation power:

(1) to sue and be sued, complain and defend in its corporate name;

(2) to have a corporate seal, which may be altered at will, and to use it, or a facsimile of it, by impressing or affixing it or in any other manner reproducing it;

(3) to make and amend bylaws, not inconsistent with its articles of incorporation or with the laws of this state, for managing the business and regulating the affairs of the corporation;

(4) to purchase, receive, lease, or otherwise acquire, and own, hold, improve, use, and otherwise deal with, real or personal property, or any legal or equitable interest in property, wherever located;

(5) to sell, convey, mortgage, pledge, lease, exchange, and otherwise dispose of all or any part of its property;

(6) to purchase, receive, subscribe for, or otherwise acquire; own, hold, vote, use, sell, mortgage, lend, pledge, or otherwise dispose of; and deal in and with shares or other interests in, or obligations of, any other entity;

(7) to make contracts and guarantees, incur liabilities, borrow money, issue its notes, bonds, and other obligations (which may be convertible into or include the option to purchase other securities of the corporation), and secure any of its obligations by mortgage or pledge of any of its property, franchises, or income;

(8) to lend money, invest and reinvest its funds, and receive and hold real and personal property as security for repayment;

(9) to be a promoter, partner, member, associate, or manager of any partnership, joint venture, trust, or other entity;

(10) to conduct its business, locate offices, and exercise the powers granted by this Act within or without this state;

(11) to elect directors and appoint officers, employees, and agents of the corporation, define their duties, fix their com-

pensation, and lend them money and credit;

(12) to pay pensions and establish pension plans, pension trusts, profit sharing plans, share bonus plans, share option plans, and benefit or incentive plans for any or all of its current or former directors, officers, employees, and agents;

(13) to make donations for the public welfare or for charitable, scientific, or educational purposes;

(14) to transact any lawful business that will aid governmental policy;

(15) to make payments or donations, or do any other act, not inconsistent with law, that furthers the business and affairs of the corporation.

§ 3.03 Emergency Powers

(a) In anticipation of or during an emergency defined in subsection (d), the board of directors of a corporation may:

(1) modify lines of succession to accommodate the incapacity of any director, officer, employee, or agent; and

(2) relocate the principal office, designate alternative principal offices or regional offices, or authorize the officers to do so.

(b) During an emergency defined in subsection (d), unless emergency bylaws provide otherwise:

(1) notice of a meeting of the board of directors need be given only to those directors whom it is practicable to reach and may be given in any practicable manner, including by publication and radio; and

(2) one or more officers of the corporation present at a meeting of the board of directors may be deemed to be directors for the meeting, in order of rank and within the same rank in order of seniority, as necessary to achieve a quorum.

(c) Corporate action taken in good faith during an emergency under this section to further the ordinary business affairs of the corporation:

(1) binds the corporation; and

(2) may not be used to impose liability on a corporate director, officer, employee, or agent.

(d) An emergency exists for purposes of this section if a quorum of the corporation's directors cannot readily be assembled because of some catastrophic event.

§ 3.04 Ultra Vires

(a) Except as provided in subsection (b), the validity of corporate action may not be challenged on the ground that the corporation lacks or lacked power to act.

(b) A corporation's power to act may be challenged:

(1) in a proceeding by a shareholder against the corporation to enjoin the act;

(2) in a proceeding by the corporation, directly, derivatively, or through a receiver, trustee, or other legal representative, against an incumbent or former director, officer, employee, or agent of the corporation; or

(3) in a proceeding by the Attorney General under section 14.30.

(c) In a shareholder's proceeding under subsection (b)(1) to enjoin an unauthorized corporate act, the court may enjoin or set aside the act, if equitable and if all affected persons are parties to the proceeding, and may award damages for loss (other than anticipated profits) suffered by the corporation or another party because of enjoining the unauthorized act.

Chapter 4.
NAME

§ 4.01 Corporate Name

(a) A corporate name:

(1) must contain the word "corporation," "incorporated," "company," or "limited," or the abbreviation "corp.," "inc.," "co.," or "ltd.," or words or abbreviations of like import in another language; and

(2) may not contain language stating or implying that the corporation is organized for a purpose other than that permitted by section 3.01 and its articles of incorporation.

(b) Except as authorized by subsections (c) and (d), a corporate name must be distinguishable upon the records of the secretary of state from:

(1) the corporate name of a corporation incorporated or authorized to transact business in this state;

(2) a corporate name reserved or registered under section 4.02 or 4.03;

(3) the fictitious name adopted by a foreign corporation authorized to transact business in this state because its real name is unavailable; and

(4) the corporate name of a not-for-profit corporation incorporated or authorized to transact business in this state.

(c) A corporation may apply to the secretary of state for authorization to use a name that is not distinguishable upon his records from one or more of the names described in subsection (b). The secretary of state shall authorize use of the name applied for if:

(1) the other corporation consents to the use in writing and submits an undertaking in form satisfactory to the secretary of state to change its name to a name that is distinguishable upon the records of the secretary of state from the name of the applying corporation; or

(2) the applicant delivers to the secretary of state a certified copy of the final judgment of a court of competent jurisdiction establishing the applicant's right to use the name applied for in this state.

(d) A corporation may use the name (including the fictitious name) of another domestic or foreign corporation that is used in this state if the other corporation is incorporated or authorized to transact business in this state and the proposed user corporation:

(1) has merged with the other corporation;

(2) has been formed by reorganization of the other corporation; or

(3) has acquired all or substantially all of the assets, including the corporate name, of the other corporation.

(e) This Act does not control the use of fictitious names.

§ 4.02 Reserved Name

(a) A person may reserve the exclusive use of a corporate name, including a fictitious name for a foreign corporation whose corporate name is not available, by delivering an application to the secretary of state for filing. The application must set forth the name and address of the applicant and the name proposed to be reserved. If the secretary of state finds that the corporate name applied for is available, he shall reserve the name for the applicant's exclusive use for a nonrenewable 120-day period.

(b) The owner of a reserved corporate name may transfer the reservation to another person by delivering to the secretary of state a signed notice of the transfer that states the name and address of the transferee.

§ 4.03 Registered Name

(a) A foreign corporation may register its corporate name, or its corporate name with any addition required by section 15.06, if the name is distinguishable upon the records of the secretary of state from the corporate names that are not available under section 4.01(b)(3).

(b) A foreign corporation registers its corporate name, or its corporate name with any addition required by section 15.06, by delivering to the secretary of state for filing an application:

(1) setting forth its corporate name, or its corporate name with any addition required by section 15.06, the state or country and date of its incorporation, and a brief description of the nature of the business in which it is engaged; and

(2) accompanied by a certificate of existence (or a document of similar import) from the state or country of incorporation.

(c) The name is registered for the applicant's exclusive use upon the effective date of the application.

(d) A foreign corporation whose registration is effective may renew it for successive years by delivering to the secretary of state for filing a renewal application, which complies with the requirements of subsection (b), between October 1 and December 31 of the preceding year. The renewal application renews the registration for the following calendar year.

(e) A foreign corporation whose registration is effective may thereafter qualify as a foreign corporation under that name or consent in writing to the use of that name by a corporation thereafter incorporated under this Act or by another foreign corporation thereafter authorized to transact business in this state. The registration terminates when the domestic corporation is incorporated or the foreign corporation qualifies or consents to the qualification of another foreign corporation under the registered name.

Chapter 5.
OFFICE AND AGENT

§ 5.01 Registered Office and Registered Agent

Each corporation must continuously maintain in this state:

(1) a registered office that may be the same as any of its places of business; and

(2) a registered agent, who may be:

(i) an individual who resides in this state and whose business office is identical with the registered office;

(ii) a domestic corporation or not-for-profit domestic corporation whose business office is identical with the registered office; or

(iii) a foreign corporation or not-for-profit foreign corporation authorized to transact business in this state whose business office is identical with the registered office.

§ 5.02 Change of Registered Office or Registered Agent

(a) A corporation may change its registered office or registered agent by delivering to the secretary of state for filing a statement of change that sets forth:

(1) the name of the corporation;

(2) the street address of its current registered office;

(3) if the current registered office is to be changed, the street address of the new registered office;

(4) the name of its current registered agent;

(5) if the current registered agent is to be changed, the name of the new registered agent and the new agent's written consent (either on the statement or attached to it) to the appointment; and

(6) that after the change or changes are made, the street addresses of its registered office and the business office of its registered agent will be identical.

(b) If a registered agent changes the street address of his business office, he may change the street address of the registered office of any corporation for which he is the registered agent by notifying the corporation in writing of the change and signing (either manually or in facsimile) and delivering to the secretary of state for filing a statement that complies with the requirements of subsection (a) and recites that the corporation has been notified of the change.

§ 5.03 Resignation of Registered Agent

(a) A registered agent may resign his agency appointment by signing and delivering to the secretary of state for filing the signed original and two exact or conformed copies of a statement of resignation. The statement may include a statement that the registered office is also discontinued.

(b) After filing the statement the secretary of state shall mail one copy to the registered office (if not discontinued) and the other copy to the corporation at its principal office.

(c) The agency appointment is terminated, and the registered office discontinued if so provided, on the 31st day after the date on which the statement was filed.

§ 5.04 Service on Corporation

(a) A corporation's registered agent is the corporation's agent for service of process, notice, or demand required or permitted by law to be served on the corporation.

(b) If a corporation has no registered agent, or the agent cannot with reasonable diligence be served, the corporation may be served by registered or certified mail, return receipt requested, addressed to the secretary of the corporation at its principal office. Service is perfected under this subsection at the earliest of:

(1) the date the corporation receives the mail;

(2) the date shown on the return receipt, if signed on behalf of the corporation; or

(3) five days after its deposit in the United States Mail, if mailed postpaid and correctly addressed.

(c) This section does not prescribe the only means, or necessarily the required means, of serving a corporation.

Chapter 6.
SHARES AND DISTRIBUTIONS

Subchapter A. Shares

§ 6.01 Authorized Shares

(a) The articles of incorporation must prescribe the classes of shares and the number of shares of each class that the corporation is authorized to issue. If more than one class of shares is authorized, the articles of incorporation must prescribe a distinguishing designation for each class, and prior to the issuance of shares of a class the preferences, limitations, and relative rights of that class must be described in the articles of incorporation. All shares of a class must have preferences, limitations, and relative rights identical with those of other shares of the same class except to the extent otherwise permitted by section 6.02.

(b) The articles of incorporation must authorize (1) one or more classes of shares that together have unlimited voting rights, and (2) one or more classes of shares (which may be the same class or classes as those with voting rights) that together are entitled to receive the net assets of the corporation upon dissolution.

(c) The articles of incorporation may authorize one or more classes of shares that:

(1) have special, conditional, or limited voting rights, or no right to vote, except to the extent prohibited by this Act;

(2) are redeemable or convertible as specified in the articles of incorporation (i) at the option of the corporation, the shareholder, or another person or upon the occurrence of a designated event; (ii) for cash, indebtedness, securities, or other property; (iii) in a designated amount or in an amount determined in accordance with a designated formula or by reference to extrinsic data or events;

(3) entitle the holders to distributions calculated in any manner, including dividends that may be cumulative, noncumulative, or partially cumulative;

(4) have preference over any other class of shares with respect to distributions, including dividends and distributions upon the dissolution of the corporation.

(d) The description of the designations, preferences, limitations, and relative rights of share classes in subsection (c) is not exhaustive.

§ 6.02 Terms of Class or Series Determined by Board of Directors

(a) If the articles of incorporation so provide, the board of directors may determine, in whole or part, the preferences, limitations, and relative rights (within the limits set forth in section 6.01) of (1) any class of shares before the issuance of any shares of that class or (2) one or more series within a class before the issuance of any shares of that series.

(b) Each series of a class must be given a distinguishing designation.

(c) All shares of a series must have preferences, limitations, and relative rights identical with those of other shares of the same series and, except to the extent otherwise provided in the description of the series, of those of other series of the same class.

(d) Before issuing any shares of a class or series created under this section, the corporation must deliver to the secretary of state for filing articles of amendment, which are effective without shareholder action, that set forth:

(1) the name of the corporation;

(2) the text of the amendment determining the terms of the class or series of shares;

(3) the date it was adopted; and

(4) a statement that the amendment was duly adopted by the board of directors.

§ 6.03 Issued and Outstanding Shares

(a) A corporation may issue the number of shares of each class or series authorized by the articles of incorporation. Shares that are issued are outstanding shares until they are reacquired, redeemed, converted, or cancelled.

(b) The reacquisition, redemption, or conversion of outstanding shares is subject to the limitations of subsection (c) of this section and to section 6.40.

(c) At all times that shares of the corporation are outstanding, one or more shares that together have unlimited voting rights and one or more shares that together are entitled to receive the net assets of the corporation upon dissolution must be outstanding.

§ 6.04 Fractional Shares

(a) A corporation may:

(1) issue fractions of a share or pay in money the value of fractions of a share;

(2) arrange for disposition of fractional shares by the shareholders;

(3) issue scrip in registered or bearer form entitling the holder to receive a full share upon surrendering enough scrip to equal a full share.

(b) Each certificate representing scrip must be conspicuously labeled "scrip" and must contain the information required by section 6.25(b).

(c) The holder of a fractional share is entitled to exercise the rights of a shareholder, including the right to vote, to receive dividends, and to participate in the assets of the corporation upon liquidation. The holder of scrip is not entitled to any of these rights unless the scrip provides for them.

(d) The board of directors may authorize the issuance of scrip subject to any condition considered desirable, including:

(1) that the scrip will become void if not exchanged for full shares before a specified date; and

(2) that the shares for which the scrip is exchangeable may be sold and the proceeds paid to the scripholders.

Subchapter B. Issuance of Shares

§ 6.20 Subscription for Shares before Incorporation

(a) A subscription for shares entered into before incorporation is irrevocable for six months unless the subscription agreement provides a longer or shorter period or all the subscribers agree to revocation.

(b) The board of directors may determine the payment terms of subscriptions for shares that were entered into before incorporation, unless the subscription agreement specifies them. A call for payment by the board of directors must be uniform so far as practicable as to all shares of the same class or series, unless the subscription agreement specifies otherwise.

(c) Shares issued pursuant to subscriptions entered into before incorporation are fully paid and nonassessable when the corporation receives the consideration specified in the subscription agreement.

(d) If a subscriber defaults in payment of money or property under a subscription agreement entered into before incorporation, the corporation may collect the amount owed as any other debt. Alternatively, unless the subscription agreement provides otherwise, the corporation may rescind the agreement and may sell the shares if the debt remains unpaid more than 20 days after the corporation sends written demand for payment to the subscriber.

(e) A subscription agreement entered into after incorporation is a contract between the subscriber and the corporation subject to section 6.21.

§ 6.21 Issuance of Shares

(a) The powers granted in this section to the board of directors may be reserved to the shareholders by the articles of incorporation.

(b) The board of directors may authorize shares to be issued for consideration consisting of any tangible or intangible property or benefit to the corporation, including cash, promissory notes, services performed, contracts for services to be performed, or other securities of the corporation.

(c) Before the corporation issues shares, the board of directors must determine that the consideration received or to be received for shares to be issued is adequate. That determination by the board of directors is conclusive insofar as the adequacy of consideration for the issuance of shares relates to whether the shares are validly issued, fully paid, and nonassessable.

(d) When the corporation receives the consideration for which the board of directors authorized the issuance of shares, the shares issued therefor are fully paid and nonassessable.

(e) The corporation may place in escrow shares issued for a contract for future services or benefits or a promissory note, or make other arrangements to restrict the transfer of the shares, and may credit distributions in respect of the shares against their purchase price, until the services are performed, the note is paid, or the benefits received. If the services are not performed, the note is not paid, or the benefits are not received, the shares escrowed or restricted and the distributions credited may be cancelled in whole or part.

§ 6.22 Liability of Shareholders

(a) A purchaser from a corporation of its own shares is not liable to the corporation or its creditors with respect to the shares except to pay the consideration for which the shares were authorized to be issued (section 6.21) or specified in the subscription agreement (section 6.20).

(b) Unless otherwise provided in the articles of incorporation, a shareholder of a corporation is not personally liable for the acts or debts of the corporation except that he may become personally liable by reason of his own acts or conduct.

§ 6.23 Share Dividends

(a) Unless the articles of incorporation provide otherwise, shares may be issued pro rata and without consideration to the corporation's shareholders or to the shareholders of one or more classes or series. An issuance of shares under this subsection is a share dividend.

(b) Shares of one class or series may not be issued as a share dividend in respect of shares of another class or series unless (1) the articles of incorporation so authorize, (2) a majority of the votes entitled to be cast by the class or series to be issued approve the issue, or (3) there are no outstanding shares of the class or series to be issued.

(c) If the board of directors does not fix the record date for determining shareholders entitled to a share dividend, it is the date the board of directors authorizes the share dividend.

§ 6.24 Share Options

A corporation may issue rights, options, or warrants for the purchase of shares of the corporation. The board of directors shall determine the terms upon which the rights, options, or warrants are issued, their form and content, and the consideration for which the shares are to be issued.

§ 6.25 Form and Content of Certificates

(a) Shares may but need not be represented by certificates. Unless this Act or another statute expressly provides otherwise, the rights and obligations of shareholders are identical whether or not their shares are represented by certificates.

(b) At a minimum each share certificate must state on its face:

(1) the name of the issuing corporation and that it is organized under the law of this state;

(2) the name of the person to whom issued; and

(3) the number and class of shares and the designation of the series, if any, the certificate represents.

(c) If the issuing corporation is authorized to issue different classes of shares or different series within a class, the designations, relative rights, preferences, and limitations applicable to each class and the variations in rights, preferences, and limitations determined for each series (and the authority of the board of directors to determine variations for future series) must be summarized on the front or back of each certificate. Alternatively, each certificate may state conspicuously on its front or back that the corporation will furnish the shareholder this information on request in writing and without charge.

(d) Each share certificate (1) must be signed (either manually or in facsimile) by two officers designated in the bylaws or by the board of directors and (2) may bear the corporate seal or its facsimile.

(e) If the person who signed (either manually or in facsimile) a share certificate no longer holds office when the certificate is issued, the certificate is nevertheless valid.

§ 6.26 Shares without Certificates

(a) Unless the articles of incorporation or bylaws provide otherwise, the board of directors of a corporation may authorize the issue of some or all of the shares of any or all of its classes or series without certificates. The authorization does not affect shares already represented by certificates until they are surrendered to the corporation.

(b) Within a reasonable time after the issue or transfer of shares without certificates, the corporation shall send the shareholder a written statement of the information required on certificates by section 6.25(b) and (c), and, if applicable, section 6.27.

§ 6.27 Restriction on Transfer or Registration of Shares and Other Securities

(a) The articles of incorporation, bylaws, an agreement among shareholders, or an agreement between shareholders and the corporation may impose restrictions on the transfer or registration of transfer of shares of the corporation. A restriction does not affect shares issued before the restriction was adopted unless the holders of the shares are parties to the restriction agreement or voted in favor of the restriction.

(b) A restriction on the transfer or registration of transfer of shares is valid and enforceable against the holder or a transferee of the holder if the restriction is authorized by this section and its existence is noted conspicuously on the front or back of the certificate or is contained in the information statement required by section 6.26(b). Unless so noted, a restriction is not enforceable against a person without knowledge of the restriction.

(c) A restriction on the transfer or registration of transfer of shares is authorized:

    (1) to maintain the corporation's status when it is dependent on the number or identity of its shareholders;

    (2) to preserve exemptions under federal or state securities law;

    (3) for any other reasonable purpose.

(d) A restriction on the transfer or registration of transfer of shares may:

    (1) obligate the shareholder first to offer the corporation or other persons (separately, consecutively, or simultaneously) an opportunity to acquire the restricted shares;

    (2) obligate the corporate or other persons (separately, consecutively, or simultaneously) to acquire the restricted shares;

    (3) require the corporation, the holders of any class of its shares, or another person to approve the transfer of the restricted shares, if the requirement is not manifestly unreasonable;

    (4) prohibit the transfer of the restricted shares to designated persons or classes of persons, if the prohibition is not manifestly unreasonable.

(e) For purposes of this section, "shares" includes a security convertible into or carrying a right to subscribe for or acquire shares.

§ 6.28 Expense of Issue

A corporation may pay the expenses of selling or underwriting its shares, and of organizing or reorganizing the corporation, from the consideration received for shares.

Subchapter C. Subsequent Acquisition of Shares by Shareholders and Corporation

§ 6.30 Shareholders' Preemptive Rights

(a) The shareholders of a corporation do not have a preemptive right to acquire the corporation's unissued shares except to the extent the articles of incorporation so provide.

(b) A statement included in the articles of incorporation that "the corporation elects to have preemptive rights" (or words of similar import) means that the following principles apply except to the extent the articles of incorporation expressly provide otherwise:

    (1) The shareholders of the corporation have a preemptive right, granted on uniform terms and conditions prescribed by the board of directors to provide a fair and reasonable opportunity to exercise the right, to acquire proportional amounts of the corporation's unissued shares upon the decision of the board of directors to issue them.

    (2) A shareholder may waive his preemptive right. A waiver evidenced by a writing is irrevocable even though it is not supported by consideration.

    (3) There is no preemptive right with respect to:

        (i) shares issued as compensation to directors, officers, agents, or employees of the corporation, its subsidiaries or affiliates;

        (ii) shares issued to satisfy conversion or option rights created to provide compensation to directors, officers, agents, or employees of the corporation, its subsidiaries or affiliates;

        (iii) shares authorized in articles of incorporation that are issued within six months from the effective date of incorporation;

        (iv) shares sold otherwise than for money.

    (4) Holders of shares of any class without general voting rights but with preferential rights to distributions or assets have no preemptive rights with respect to shares of any class.

    (5) Holders of shares of any class with general voting rights but without preferential rights to distributions or assets have no preemptive rights with respect to shares of any class with preferential rights to distributions or assets unless the shares with preferential rights are convertible into or carry a right to subscribe for or acquire shares without preferential rights.

    (6) Shares subject to preemptive rights that are not acquired by shareholders may be issued to any person for a period of one year after being offered to shareholders at a consideration set by the board of directors that is not lower than the consideration set for the exercise of preemptive rights. An offer at a lower consideration or after the expiration of one year is subject to the shareholders' preemptive rights.

(c) For purposes of this section, "shares" includes a security convertible into or carrying a right to subscribe for or acquire shares.

§ 6.31 Corporation's Acquisition of Its Own Shares

(a) A corporation may acquire its own shares and shares so acquired constitute authorized but unissued shares.

(b) If the articles of incorporation prohibit the reissue of acquired shares, the number of authorized shares is reduced by the number of shares acquired, effective upon amendment of the articles of incorporation.

(c) Articles of amendment may be adopted by the board of directors without shareholder action, shall be delivered to the secretary of state for filing, and shall set forth:

    (1) the name of the corporation;

(2) the reduction in the number of authorized shares, itemized by class and series; and

(3) the total number of authorized shares, itemized by class and series, remaining after reduction of the shares.

Subchapter D. Distributions

§ 6.40 Distributions to Shareholders

(a) A board of directors may authorize and the corporation may make distributions to its shareholders subject to restriction by the articles of incorporation and the limitation in subsection (c).

(b) If the board of directors does not fix the record date for determining shareholders entitled to a distribution (other than one involving a purchase, redemption, or other acquisition of the corporation's shares), it is the date the board of directors authorizes the distribution.

(c) No distribution may be made if, after giving it effect:

(1) the corporation would not be able to pay its debts as they become due in the usual course of business; or

(2) the corporation's total assets would be less than the sum of its total liabilities plus (unless the articles of incorporation permit otherwise) the amount that would be needed, if the corporation were to be dissolved at the time of the distribution, to satisfy the preferential rights upon dissolution of shareholders whose preferential rights are superior to those receiving the distribution.

(d) The board of directors may base a determination that a distribution is not prohibited under subsection (c) either on financial statements prepared on the basis of accounting practices and principles that are reasonable in the circumstances or on a fair valuation or other method that is reasonable in the circumstances.

(e) Except as provided in subsection (g), the effect of a distribution under subsection (c) is measured:

(1) in the case of distribution by purchase, redemption, or other acquisition of the corporation's shares, as of the earlier of (i) the date money or other property is transferred or debt incurred by the corporation or (ii) the date the shareholder ceases to be a shareholder with respect to the acquired shares;

(2) in the case of any other distribution of indebtedness, as of the date the indebtedness is distributed;

(3) in all other cases, as of (i) the date the distribution is authorized if the payment occurs within 120 days after the date of authorization or (ii) the date the payment is made if it occurs more than 120 days after the date of authorization.

(f) A corporation's indebtedness to a shareholder incurred by reason of a distribution made in accordance with this section is at parity with the corporation's indebtedness to its general, unsecured creditors except to the extent subordinated by agreement.

(g) Indebtedness of a corporation, including indebtedness issued as a distribution, is not considered a liability for purposes of determinations under subsection (c) if its terms provide that payment of principal and interest are made only if and to the extent that payment of a distribution to shareholders could then be made under this section. If the indebtedness is issued as a distribution, each payment of principal or interest is treated as a distribution, the effect of which is measured on the date the payment is actually made.

Chapter 7.
SHAREHOLDERS

Subchapter A. Meetings

§ 7.01 Annual Meeting

(a) A corporation shall hold annually at a time stated in or fixed in accordance with the bylaws a meeting of shareholders.

(b) Annual shareholders' meetings may be held in or out of this state at the place stated in or fixed in accordance with the bylaws. If no place is stated in or fixed in accordance with the bylaws, annual meetings shall be held at the corporation's principal office.

(c) The failure to hold an annual meeting at the time stated in or fixed in accordance with a corporation's bylaws does not affect the validity of any corporate action.

§ 7.02 Special Meeting

(a) A corporation shall hold a special meeting of shareholders:

(1) on call of its board of directors or the person or persons authorized to do so by the articles of incorporation or bylaws; or

(2) if the holders of at least 10 percent of all the votes entitled to be cast on any issue proposed to be considered at the proposed special meeting sign, date, and deliver to the corporation's secretary one or more written demands for the meeting describing the purpose or purposes for which it is to be held.

(b) If not otherwise fixed under sections 7.03 or 7.07, the record date for determining shareholders entitled to demand a special meeting is the date the first shareholder signs the demand.

(c) Special shareholders' meetings may be held in or out of this state at the place stated in or fixed in accordance with the bylaws. If no place is stated or fixed in accordance with the bylaws, special meetings shall be held at the corporation's principal office.

(d) Only business within the purpose or purposes described in the meeting notice required by section 7.05(c) may be conducted at a special shareholders' meeting.

§ 7.03 Court-Ordered Meeting

(a) The [name or describe] court of the county where a corporation's principal office (or, if none in this state, its registered office) is located may summarily order a meeting to be held:

(1) on application of any shareholder of the corporation entitled to participate in an annual meeting if an annual meeting was not held within the earlier of 6 months after the end of the corporation's fiscal year or 15 months after its last annual meeting; or

(2) on application of a shareholder who signed a demand for a special meeting valid under section 7.02 if:

(i) notice of the special meeting was not given within 30 days after the date the demand was delivered to the corporation's secretary; or

(ii) the special meeting was not held in accordance with the notice.

(b) The court may fix the time and place of the meeting, determine the shares entitled to participate in the meeting, specify a record date for determining shareholders entitled to notice of and to vote at the meeting, prescribe the form and content of the meeting notice, fix the quorum required for specific matters to be considered at the meeting (or direct that the votes represented at the meeting constitute a quorum for action on those matters), and enter other orders necessary to accomplish the purpose or purposes of the meeting.

§ 7.04 **Action without Meeting**

(a) Action required or permitted by this Act to be taken at a shareholders' meeting may be taken without a meeting if the action is taken by all the shareholders entitled to vote on the action. The action must be evidenced by one or more written consents describing the action taken, signed by all the shareholders entitled to vote on the action, and delivered to the corporation for inclusion in the minutes or filing with the corporate records.

(b) If not otherwise determined under sections 7.03 or 7.07, the record date for determining shareholders entitled to take action without a meeting is the date the first shareholder signs the consent under subsection (a).

(c) A consent signed under this section has the effect of a meeting vote and may be described as such in any document.

(d) If this Act requires that notice of proposed action be given to nonvoting shareholders and the action is to be taken by unanimous consent of the voting shareholders, the corporation must give its nonvoting shareholders written notice of the proposed action at least 10 days before the action is taken. The notice must contain or be accompanied by the same material that, under this Act, would have been required to be sent to nonvoting shareholders in a notice of meeting at which the proposed action would have been submitted to the shareholders for action.

§ 7.05 **Notice of Meeting**

(a) A corporation shall notify shareholders of the date, time, and place of each annual and special shareholders' meeting no fewer than 10 nor more than 60 days before the meeting date. Unless this Act or the articles of incorporation require otherwise, the corporation is required to give notice only to shareholders entitled to vote at the meeting.

(b) Unless this Act or the articles of incorporation require otherwise, notice of an annual meeting need not include a description of the purpose or purposes for which the meeting is called.

(c) Notice of a special meeting must include a description of the purpose or purposes for which the meeting is called.

(d) If not otherwise fixed under sections 7.03 or 7.07, the record date for determining shareholders entitled to notice of and to vote at an annual or special shareholders' meeting is the day before the first notice is delivered to shareholders.

(e) Unless the bylaws require otherwise, if an annual or special shareholders' meeting is adjourned to a different date, time, or place, notice need not be given of the new date, time, or place if the new date, time, or place is announced at the meeting before adjournment. If a new record date for the adjourned meeting is or must be fixed under section 7.07, however, notice of the adjourned meeting must be given under this section to persons who are shareholders as of the new record date.

§ 7.06 **Waiver of Notice**

(a) A shareholder may waive any notice required by this Act, the articles of incorporation, or bylaws before or after the date and time stated in the notice. The waiver must be in writing, be signed by the shareholder entitled to the notice, and be delivered to the

corporation for inclusion in the minutes or filing with the corporate records.

(b) A shareholder's attendance at a meeting:

(1) waives objection to lack of notice or defective notice of the meeting, unless the shareholder at the beginning of the meeting objects to holding the meeting or transacting business at the meeting;

(2) waives objection to consideration of a particular matter at the meeting that is not within the purpose or purposes described in the meeting notice, unless the shareholder objects to considering the matter when it is presented.

§ 7.07 **Record Date**

(a) The bylaws may fix or provide the manner of fixing the record date for one or more voting groups in order to determine the shareholders entitled to notice of a shareholders' meeting, to demand a special meeting, to vote, or to take any other action. If the bylaws do not fix or provide for fixing a record date, the board of directors of the corporation may fix a future date as the record date.

(b) A record date fixed under this section may not be more than 70 days before the meeting or action requiring a determination of shareholders.

(c) A determination of shareholders entitled to notice of or to vote at a shareholders' meeting is effective for any adjournment of the meeting unless the board of directors fixes a new record date, which it must do if the meeting is adjourned to a date more than 120 days after the date fixed for the original meeting.

(d) If a court orders a meeting adjourned to a date more than 120 days after the date fixed for the original meeting, it may provide that the original record date continues in effect or it may fix a new record date.

Subchapter B. Voting

§ 7.20 **Shareholders' List for Meeting**

(a) After fixing a record date for a meeting, a corporation shall prepare an alphabetical list of the names of all its shareholders who are entitled to notice of a shareholders' meeting. The list must be arranged by voting group (and within each voting group by class or series of shares) and show the address of and number of shares held by each shareholder.

(b) The shareholders' list must be available for inspection by any shareholder, beginning two business days after notice of the meeting is given for which the list was prepared and continuing through the meeting, at the corporation's principal office or at a place identified in the meeting notice in the city where the meeting will be held. A shareholder, his agent, or attorney is entitled on written demand to inspect and, subject to the requirements of section 16.02(c), to copy the list, during regular business hours and at his expense, during the period it is available for inspection.

(c) The corporation shall make the shareholders' list available at the meeting, and any shareholder, his agent, or attorney is entitled to inspect the list at any time during the meeting or any adjournment.

(d) If the corporation refuses to allow a shareholder, his agent, or attorney to inspect the shareholders' list before or at the meeting (or copy the list as permitted by subsection (b)), the [name or describe] court of the county where a corporation's principal office (or, if none in this state, its registered office) is located, on application of the shareholder, may summarily order the inspection or copying at the corporation's expense and may postpone the meeting for which the list was prepared until the inspection or copying is complete.

(e) Refusal or failure to prepare or make available the shareholders' list does not affect the validity of action taken at the meeting.

§ 7.21 Voting Entitlement of Shares

(a) Except as provided in subsections (b) and (c) or unless the articles of incorporation provide otherwise, each outstanding share, regardless of class, is entitled to one vote on each matter voted on at a shareholders' meeting. Only shares are entitled to vote.

(b) Absent special circumstances, the shares of a corporation are not entitled to vote if they are owned, directly or indirectly, by a second corporation, domestic or foreign, and the first corporation owns, directly or indirectly, a majority of the shares entitled to vote for directors of the second corporation.

(c) Subsection (b) does not limit the power of a corporation to vote any shares, including its own shares, held by it in a fiduciary capacity.

(d) Redeemable shares are not entitled to vote after notice of redemption is mailed to the holders and a sum sufficient to redeem the shares has been deposited with a bank, trust company, or other financial institution under an irrevocable obligation to pay the holders the redemption price on surrender of the shares.

§ 7.22 Proxies

(a) A shareholder may vote his shares in person or by proxy.

(b) A shareholder may appoint a proxy to vote or otherwise act for him by signing an appointment form, either personally or by his attorney-in-fact.

(c) An appointment of a proxy is effective when received by the secretary or other officer or agent authorized to tabulate votes. An appointment is valid for 11 months unless a longer period is expressly provided in the appointment form.

(d) An appointment of a proxy is revocable by the shareholder unless the appointment form conspicuously states that it is irrevocable and the appointment is coupled with an interest. Appointments coupled with an interest include the appointment of:

(1) a pledgee;

(2) a person who purchased or agreed to purchase the shares;

(3) a creditor of the corporation who extended it credit under terms requiring the appointment;

(4) an employee of the corporation whose employment contract requires the appointment; or

(5) a party to a voting agreement created under section 7.31.

(e) The death or incapacity of the shareholder appointing a proxy does not affect the right of the corporation to accept the proxy's authority unless notice of the death or incapacity is received by the secretary or other officer or agent authorized to tabulate votes before the proxy exercises his authority under the appointment.

(f) An appointment made irrevocable under subsection (d) is revoked when the interest with which it is coupled is extinguished.

(g) A transferee for value of shares subject to an irrevocable appointment may revoke the appointment if he did not know of its existence when he acquired the shares and the existence of the irrevocable appointment was not noted conspicuously on the certificate representing the shares or on the information statement for shares without certificates.

(h) Subject to section 7.24 and to any express limitation on the proxy's authority appearing on the face of the appointment form, a corporation is entitled to accept the proxy's vote or other action as that of the shareholder making the appointment.

§ 7.23 Shares Held by Nominees

(a) A corporation may establish a procedure by which the beneficial owner of shares that are registered in the name of a nominee is recognized by the corporation as the shareholder. The extent of this recognition may be determined in the procedure.

(b) The procedure may set forth:

(1) the types of nominees to which it applies;

(2) the rights or privileges that the corporation recognizes in a beneficial owner;

(3) the manner in which the procedure is selected by the nominee;

(4) the information that must be provided when the procedure is selected;

(5) the period for which selection of the procedure is effective; and

(6) other aspects of the rights and duties created.

§ 7.24 Corporation's Acceptance of Votes

(a) If the name signed on a vote, consent, waiver, or proxy appointment corresponds to the name of a shareholder, the corporation if acting in good faith is entitled to accept the vote, consent, waiver, or proxy appointment and give it effect as the act of the shareholder.

(b) If the name signed on a vote, consent, waiver, or proxy appointment does not correspond to the name of its shareholder, the corporation if acting in good faith is nevertheless entitled to accept the vote, consent, waiver, or proxy appointment and give it effect as the act of the shareholder if:

(1) the shareholder is an entity and the name signed purports to be that of an officer or agent of the entity;

(2) the name signed purports to be that of an administrator, executor, guardian, or conservator representing the shareholder and, if the corporation requests, evidence of fiduciary status acceptable to the corporation has been presented with respect to the vote, consent, waiver, or proxy appointment;

(3) the name signed purports to be that of a receiver or trustee in bankruptcy of the shareholder and, if the corporation requests, evidence of this status acceptable to the corporation has been presented with respect to the vote, consent, waiver, or proxy appointment;

(4) the name signed purports to be that of a pledgee, beneficial owner, or attorney-in-fact of the shareholder and, if the corporation requests, evidence acceptable to the corporation of the signatory's authority to sign for the shareholder has been presented with respect to the vote, consent, waiver, or proxy appointment;

(5) two or more persons are the shareholder as co-tenants or fiduciaries and the name signed purports to be the name of at least one of the coowners and the person signing appears to be acting on behalf of all the coowners.

(c) The corporation is entitled to reject a vote, consent, waiver, or proxy appointment if the secretary or other officer or agent authorized to tabulate votes, acting in good faith, has reasonable basis for doubt about the validity of the signature on it or about the signatory's authority to sign for the shareholder.

(d) The corporation and its officer or agent who accepts or rejects a vote, consent, waiver, or proxy appointment in good faith and in accordance with the standards of this section are not liable in damages to the shareholder for the consequences of the acceptance or rejection.

(e) Corporate action based on the acceptance or rejection of a vote, consent, waiver, or proxy appointment under this section is valid unless a court of competent jurisdiction determines otherwise.

§ 7.25 Quorum and Voting Requirements for Voting Groups

(a) Shares entitled to vote as a separate voting group may take action on a matter at a meeting only if a quorum of those shares exists with respect to that matter. Unless the articles of incorporation or this Act provide otherwise, a majority of the votes entitled to be cast on the matter by the voting group constitutes a quorum of that voting group for action on that matter.

(b) Once a share is represented for any purpose at a meeting, it is deemed present for quorum purposes for the remainder of the meeting and for any adjournment of that meeting unless a new record date is or must be set for that adjourned meeting.

(c) If a quorum exists, action on a matter (other than the election of directors) by a voting group is approved if the votes cast within the voting group favoring the action exceed the votes cast opposing the action, unless the articles of incorporation or this Act require a greater number of affirmative votes.

(d) An amendment of articles of incorporation adding, changing, or deleting a quorum or voting requirement for a voting group greater than specified in subsection (b) or (c) is governed by section 7.27.

(e) The election of directors is governed by section 7.28.

§ 7.26 Action by Single and Multiple Voting Groups

(a) If the articles of incorporation or this Act provide for voting by a single voting group on a matter, action on that matter is taken when voted upon by that voting group as provided in section 7.25.

(b) If the articles of incorporation or this Act provide for voting by two or more voting groups on a matter, action on that matter is taken only when voted upon by each of those voting groups counted separately as provided in section 7.25. Action may be taken by one voting group on a matter even though no action is taken by another voting group entitled to vote on the matter.

§ 7.27 Greater Quorum or Voting Requirements

(a) The articles of incorporation may provide for a greater quorum or voting requirement for shareholders (or voting groups of shareholders) than is provided for by this Act.

(b) An amendment to the articles of incorporation that adds, changes, or deletes a greater quorum or voting requirement must meet the same quorum requirement and be adopted by the same vote and voting groups required to take action under the quorum and voting requirements then in effect or proposed to be adopted, whichever is greater.

§ 7.28 Voting for Directors; Cumulative Voting

(a) Unless otherwise provided in the articles of incorporation, directors are elected by a plurality of the votes cast by the shares entitled to vote in the election at a meeting at which a quorum is present.

(b) Shareholders do not have a right to cumulate their votes for directors unless the articles of incorporation so provide.

(c) A statement included in the articles of incorporation that "[all] [a designated voting group of] shareholders are entitled to cumulate their votes for directors" (or words of similar import) means that the shareholders designated are entitled to multiply the number of votes they are entitled to cast by the number of directors for whom they are entitled to vote and cast the product for a single candidate or distribute the product among two or more candidates.

(d) Shares otherwise entitled to vote cumulatively may not be voted cumulatively at a particular meeting unless:

> (1) the meeting notice or proxy statement accompanying the notice states conspicuously that cumulative voting is authorized; or

> (2) a shareholder who has the right to cumulate his votes gives notice to the corporation not less than 48 hours before the time set for the meeting of his intent to cumulate his votes during the meeting, and if one shareholder gives this notice all other shareholders in the same voting group participating in the election are entitled to cumulate their votes without giving further notice.

Subchapter C. Voting Trusts and Agreements

§ 7.30 Voting Trusts

(a) One or more shareholders may create a voting trust, conferring on a trustee the right to vote or otherwise act for them, by signing an agreement setting out the provisions of the trust (which may include anything consistent with its purpose) and transferring their shares to the trustee. When a voting trust agreement is signed, the trustee shall prepare a list of the names and addresses of all owners of beneficial interests in the trust, together with the number and class of shares each transferred to the trust, and deliver copies of the list and agreement to the corporation's principal office.

(b) A voting trust becomes effective on the date the first shares subject to the trust are registered in the trustee's name. A voting trust is valid for not more than 10 years after its effective date unless extended under subsection (c).

(c) All or some of the parties to a voting trust may extend it for additional terms of not more than 10 years each by signing an extension agreement and obtaining the voting trustee's written consent to the extension. An extension is valid for 10 years from the date the first shareholder signs the extension agreement. The voting trustee must deliver copies of the extension agreement and list of beneficial owners to the corporation's principal office. An extension agreement binds only those parties signing it.

§ 7.31 Voting Agreements

(a) Two or more shareholders may provide for the manner in which they will vote their shares by signing an agreement for that purpose. A voting agreement created under this section is not subject to the provisions of section 7.30.

(b) A voting agreement created under this section is specifically enforceable.

§ 7.32 Shareholder Agreements

(a) An agreement among the shareholders of a corporation that complies with this section is effective among the shareholders and the corporation even though it is inconsistent with one or more other provisions of this Act in that it:

(1) eliminates the board of directors or restricts the discretion or powers of the board of directors;

(2) governs the authorization or making of distributions whether or not in proportion to ownership of shares, subject to the limitations in section 6.40;

(3) establishes who shall be directors or officers of the corporation, or their terms of office or manner of selection or removal;

(4) governs, in general or in regard to specific matters, the exercise or division of voting power by or between the shareholders and directors or by or among any of them, including use of weighted voting rights or director proxies;

(5) establishes the terms and conditions of any agreement for the transfer or use of property or the provision of services between the corporation and any shareholder, director, officer or employee of the corporation or among any of them;

(6) transfers to one or more shareholders or other persons all or part of the authority to exercise the corporate powers or to manage the business and affairs of the corporation, including the resolution of any issue about which there exists a deadlock among directors or shareholders;

(7) requires dissolution of the corporation at the request of one or more of the shareholders or upon the occurrence of a specified event or contingency; or

(8) otherwise governs the exercise of the corporate powers or the management of the business and affairs of the corporation or the relationship among the shareholders, the directors and the corporation, or among any of them, and is not contrary to public policy.

(b) An agreement authorized by this section shall be:

(1) set forth (A) in the articles of incorporation or bylaws and approved by all persons who are shareholders at the time of the agreement or (B) in a written agreement that is signed by all persons who are shareholders at the time of the agreement and is made known to the corporation;

(2) subject to amendment only by all persons who are shareholders at the time of the amendment, unless the agreement provides otherwise; and

(3) valid for 10 years, unless the agreement provides otherwise.

(c) The existence of an agreement authorized by this section shall be noted conspicuously on the front or back of each certificate for outstanding shares or on the information statement required by section 6.26(b). If at the time of the agreement the corporation has shares outstanding represented by certificates, the corporation shall recall the outstanding certificates and issue substitute certificates that comply with this subsection. The failure to note the existence of the agreement on the certificate or information statement shall not affect the validity of the agreement or any action taken pursuant to it. Any purchaser of shares who, at the time of purchase, did not have knowledge of the existence of the agreement shall be entitled to rescission of the purchase. A purchaser shall be deemed to have knowledge of the existence of the agreement if its existence is noted on the certificate or information statement for the shares in compliance with this subsection and, if the shares are not represented by a certificate, the information statement is delivered to the purchaser at or prior to the time of purchase of the shares. An action to enforce the right of rescission authorized by this subsection must be commenced within the earlier of 90 days after discovery of the existence of the agreement or two years after the time of purchase of the shares.

(d) An agreement authorized by this section shall cease to be effective when shares of the corporation are listed on a national securities exchange or regularly traded in a market maintained by one or more members of a national or affiliated securities association. If the agreement ceases to be effective for any reason, the board of directors may, if the agreement is contained or referred to in the corporation's articles of incorporation or bylaws, adopt an amendment to the articles of incorporation or bylaws, without shareholder action, to delete the agreement and any references to it.

(e) An agreement authorized by this section that limits the discretion or powers of the board of directors shall relieve the directors of, and impose upon the person or persons in whom such discretion or powers are vested, liability for acts or omissions imposed by law on directors to the extent that the discretion or powers of the directors are limited by the agreement.

(f) The existence or performance of an agreement authorized by this section shall not be a ground for imposing personal liability on any shareholder for the acts or debts of the corporation even if the agreement or its performance treats the corporation as if it were a partnership or results in failure to observe the corporate formalities otherwise applicable to the matters governed by the agreement.

(g) Incorporators or subscribers for shares may act as shareholders with respect to an agreement authorized by this section if no shares have been issued when the agreement is made.

Subchapter D. Derivative Proceedings

§ 7.40 Subchapter Definitions

In this subchapter:

(1) "Derivative proceeding" means a civil suit in the right of a domestic corporation or, to the extent provided in section 7.47, in the right of a foreign corporation.

(2) "Shareholder" includes a beneficial owner whose shares are held in a voting trust or held by a nominee on the beneficial owner's behalf.

§ 7.41 Standing

A shareholder may not commence or maintain a derivative proceeding unless the shareholder:

(1) was a shareholder of the corporation at the time of the act or omission complained of or became a shareholder through transfer by operation of law from one who was a shareholder at that time; and

(2) fairly and adequately represents the interests of the corporation in enforcing the right of the corporation.

§ 7.42 Demand

No shareholder may commence a derivative proceeding until:

(1) a written demand has been made upon the corporation to take suitable action; and

(2) 90 days have expired from the date the demand was made unless the shareholder has earlier been notified that the demand has been rejected by the corporation or unless irreparable injury to the corporation would result by waiting for the expiration of the 90 day period.

§ 7.43 Stay of Proceedings

If the corporation commences an inquiry into the allegations made in the demand or complaint, the court may stay any derivative proceeding for such period as the court deems appropriate.

§ 7.44 Dismissal

(a) A derivative proceeding shall be dismissed by the court on motion by the corporation if one of the groups specified in subsections (b) or (f) has determined in good faith after conducting a reasonable inquiry upon which its conclusions are based that the maintenance of the derivative proceeding is not in the best interests of the corporation.

(b) Unless a panel is appointed pursuant to subsection (f), the determination in subsection (a) shall be made by:

(1) a majority vote of independent directors present at a meeting of the board of directors if the independent directors constitute a quorum; or

(2) a majority vote of a committee consisting of two or more independent directors appointed by majority vote of independent directors present at a meeting of the board of directors, whether or not such independent directors constituted a quorum.

(c) None of the following shall by itself cause a director to be considered not independent for purposes of this section:

(1) the nomination or election of the director by persons who are defendants in the derivative proceeding or against whom action is demanded;

(2) the naming of the director as a defendant in the derivative proceeding or as a person against whom action is demanded; or

(3) the approval by the director of the act being challenged in the derivative proceeding or demand if the act resulted in no personal benefit to the director.

(d) If a derivative proceeding is commenced after a determination has been made rejecting a demand by a shareholder, the complaint shall allege with particularity facts establishing either (1) that a majority of the board of directors did not consist of independent directors at the time the determination was made or (2) that the requirements of subsection (a) have not been met.

(e) If a majority of the board of directors does not consist of independent directors at the time the determination is made, the corporation shall have the burden of proving that the requirements of subsection (a) have been met. If a majority of the board of directors consists of independent directors at the time the determination is made, the plaintiff shall have the burden of proving that the requirements of subsection (a) have not been met.

(f) The court may appoint a panel of one or more independent persons upon motion by the corporation to make a determination whether the maintenance of the derivative proceeding is in the best interests of the corporation. In such case, the plaintiff shall have the burden of proving that the requirements of subsection (a) have not been met.

§ 7.45 Discontinuance or Settlement

A derivative proceeding may not be discontinued or settled without the court's approval. If the court determines that a proposed discontinuance or settlement will substantially affect the interests of the corporation's shareholders or a class of shareholders, the court shall direct that notice be given to the shareholders affected.

§ 7.46 Payment of Expenses

On termination of the derivative proceeding the court may:

(1) order the corporation to pay the plaintiff's reasonable expenses (including counsel fees) incurred in the proceeding if it finds that the proceeding has resulted in a substantial benefit to the corporation;

(2) order the plaintiff to pay any defendant's reasonable expenses (including counsel fees) incurred in defending the proceeding if it finds that the proceeding was commenced or maintained without reasonable cause or for an improper purpose; or

(3) order a party to pay an opposing party's reasonable expenses (including counsel fees) incurred because of the filing of a pleading, motion or other paper, if it finds that the pleading, motion or other paper was not well grounded in fact, after reasonable inquiry, or warranted by existing law or a good faith argument for the extension, modification or reversal of existing law and was interposed for an improper purpose, such as to harass or to cause unnecessary delay or needless increase in the cost of litigation.

§ 7.47 Applicability to Foreign Corporations

In any derivative proceeding in the right of a foreign corporation, the matters covered by this subchapter shall be governed by the laws of the jurisdiction of incorporation of the foreign corporation except for sections 7.43, 7.45 and 7.46.

Chapter 8.
DIRECTORS AND OFFICERS

Subchapter A. Board of Directors

§ 8.01 Requirement for and Duties of Board of Directors

(a) Except as provided in subsection (c), each corporation must have a board of directors.

(b) All corporate powers shall be exercised by or under the authority of, and the business and affairs of the corporation managed under the direction of, its board of directors, subject to any limitation set forth in the articles of incorporation.

(c) A corporation having 50 or fewer shareholders may dispense with or limit the authority of a board of directors by describing in its articles of incorporation who will perform some or all of the duties of a board of directors.

§ 8.02 Qualifications of Directors

The articles of incorporation or bylaws may prescribe qualifications for directors. A director need not be a resident of this state or a shareholder of the corporation unless the articles of incorporation or bylaws so prescribe.

§ 8.03 Number and Election of Directors

(a) A board of directors must consist of one or more individuals, with the number specified in or fixed in accordance with the articles of incorporation or bylaws.

(b) If a board of directors has power to fix or change the number of directors, the board may increase or decrease by 30 percent or less the number of directors last approved by the shareholders, but only the shareholders may increase or decrease by more than 30 percent the number of directors last approved by the shareholders.

(c) The articles of incorporation or bylaws may establish a variable range for the size of the board of directors by fixing a minimum and maximum number of directors. If a variable range is established, the number of directors may be fixed or changed from time to time, within the minimum and maximum, by the shareholders or the board of directors. After shares are issued, only the shareholders may change the range for the size of the board or change from a fixed to a variable-range size board or vice versa.

(d) Directors are elected at the first annual shareholders' meeting and at each annual meeting thereafter unless their terms are staggered under section 8.06.

§ 8.04 Election of Directors by Certain Classes of Shareholders

If the articles of incorporation authorize dividing the shares into classes, the articles may also authorize the election of all or a specified number of directors by the holders of one or more authorized classes of shares. Each class (or classes) of shares entitled to elect one or more directors is a separate voting group for purposes of the election of directors.

§ 8.05 Terms of Directors Generally

(a) The terms of the initial directors of a corporation expire at the first shareholders' meeting at which directors are elected.

(b) The terms of all other directors expire at the next annual shareholders' meeting following their election unless their terms are staggered under section 8.06.

(c) A decrease in the number of directors does not shorten an incumbent director's term.

(d) The term of a director elected to fill a vacancy expires at the next shareholders' meeting at which directors are elected.

(e) Despite the expiration of a director's term, he continues to serve until his successor is elected and qualifies or until there is a decrease in the number of directors.

§ 8.06 Staggered Terms for Directors

If there are nine or more directors, the articles of incorporation may provide for staggering their terms by dividing the total number of directors into two or three groups, with each group containing one-half or one-third of the total, as near as may be. In that event, the terms of directors in the first group expire at the first annual shareholders' meeting after their election, the terms of the second group expire at the second annual shareholders' meeting after their election, and the terms of the third group, if any, expire at the third annual shareholders' meeting after their election. At each annual shareholders' meeting held thereafter, directors shall be chosen for a term of two years or three years, as the case may be, to succeed those whose terms expire.

§ 8.07 Resignation of Directors

(a) A director may resign at any time by delivering written notice to the board of directors, its chairman, or to the corporation.

(b) A resignation is effective when the notice is delivered unless the notice specifies a later effective date.

§ 8.08 Removal of Directors by Shareholders

(a) The shareholders may remove one or more directors with or without cause unless the articles of incorporation provide that directors may be removed only for cause.

(b) If a director is elected by a voting group of shareholders, only the shareholders of that voting group may participate in the vote to remove him.

(c) If cumulative voting is authorized, a director may not be removed if the number of votes sufficient to elect him under cumulative voting is voted against his removal. If cumulative voting is not authorized, a director may be removed only if the number of votes cast to remove him exceeds the number of votes cast not to remove him.

(d) A director may be removed by the shareholders only at a meeting called for the purpose of removing him and the meeting notice must state that the purpose, or one of the purposes, of the meeting is removal of the director.

§ 8.09 Removal of Directors by Judicial Proceeding

(a) The [name or describe] court of the county where a corporation's principal office (or, if none in this state, its registered office) is located may remove a director of the corporation from office in a proceeding commenced either by the corporation or by its shareholders holding at least 10 percent of the outstanding shares of any class if the court finds that (1) the director engaged in fraudulent or dishonest conduct, or gross abuse of authority or discretion, with respect to the corporation and (2) removal is in the best interest of the corporation.

(b) The court that removes a director may bar the director from reelection for a period prescribed by the court.

(c) If shareholders commence a proceeding under subsection (a), they shall make the corporation a party defendant.

§ 8.10 Vacancy on Board

(a) Unless the articles of incorporation provide otherwise, if a vacancy occurs on a board of directors, including a vacancy resulting from an increase in the number of directors:

   (1) the shareholders may fill the vacancy;

   (2) the board of directors may fill the vacancy; or

   (3) if the directors remaining in office constitute fewer than a quorum of the board, they may fill the vacancy by the affirmative vote of a majority of all the directors remaining in office.

(b) If the vacant office was held by a director elected by a voting group of shareholders, only the holders of shares of that voting group are entitled to vote to fill the vacancy if it is filled by the shareholders.

(c) A vacancy that will occur at a specific later date (by reason of a resignation effective at a later date under section 8.07(b) or otherwise) may be filled before the vacancy occurs but the new director may not take office until the vacancy occurs.

§ 8.11 Compensation of Directors

Unless the articles of incorporation or bylaws provide otherwise, the board of directors may fix the compensation of directors.

Subchapter B. Meetings and Action of the Board

§ 8.20 Meetings

(a) The board of directors may hold regular or special meetings in or out of this state.

(b) Unless the articles of incorporation or bylaws provide otherwise, the board of directors may permit any or all directors to participate in a regular or special meeting by, or conduct the meeting through the use of, any means of communication by which all directors participating may simultaneously hear each other during the meeting. A director participating in a meeting by this means is deemed to be present in person at the meeting.

§ 8.21 Action without Meeting

(a) Unless the articles of incorporation or bylaws provide otherwise, action required or permitted by this Act to be taken at a board of directors' meeting may be taken without a meeting if the action is taken by all members of the board. The action must be evidenced by one or more written consents describing the action taken, signed by each director, and included in the minutes or filed with the corporate records reflecting the action taken.

(b) Action taken under this section is effective when the last director signs the consent, unless the consent specifies a different effective date.

(c) A consent signed under this section has the effect of a meeting vote and may be described as such in any document.

§ 8.22 Notice of Meeting

(a) Unless the articles of incorporation or bylaws provide otherwise, regular meetings of the board of directors may be held without notice of the date, time, place, or purpose of the meeting.

(b) Unless the articles of incorporation or bylaws provide for a longer or shorter period, special meetings of the board of directors must be preceded by at least two days' notice of the date, time, and place of the meeting. The notice need not describe the purpose of the special meeting unless required by the articles of incorporation or bylaws.

§ 8.23 Waiver of Notice

(a) A director may waive any notice required by this Act, the articles of incorporation, or bylaws before or after the date and time stated in the notice. Except as provided by subsection (b), the waiver must be in writing, signed by the director entitled to the notice, and filed with the minutes or corporate records.

(b) A director's attendance at or participation in a meeting waives any required notice to him of the meeting unless the director at the beginning of the meeting (or promptly upon his arrival) objects to holding the meeting or transacting business at the meeting and does not thereafter vote for or assent to action taken at the meeting.

§ 8.24 Quorum and Voting

(a) Unless the articles of incorporation or bylaws require a greater number, a quorum of a board of directors consists of:

   (1) a majority of the fixed number of directors if the corporation has a fixed board size; or

   (2) a majority of the number of directors prescribed, or if no number is prescribed the number in office immediately before the meeting begins, if the corporation has a variable-range size board.

(b) The articles of incorporation or bylaws may authorize a quorum of a board of directors to consist of no fewer than one-third of the fixed or prescribed number of directors determined under subsection (a).

(c) If a quorum is present when a vote is taken, the affirmative vote of a majority of directors present is the act of the board of directors unless the articles of incorporation or bylaws require the vote of a greater number of directors.

(d) A director who is present at a meeting of the board of directors or a committee of the board of directors when corporate action is taken is deemed to have assented to the action taken unless: (1) he objects at the beginning of the meeting (or promptly upon his arrival) to holding it or transacting business at the meeting; (2) his dissent or abstention from the action taken is entered in the minutes of the meeting; or (3) he delivers written notice of his dissent or abstention to the presiding officer of the meeting before its adjournment or to the corporation immediately after adjournment of the meeting. The right of dissent or abstention is not available to a director who votes in favor of the action taken.

§ 8.25 Committees

(a) Unless the articles of incorporation or bylaws provide otherwise, a board of directors may create one or more committees and appoint members of the board of directors to serve on them. Each committee may have two or more members, who serve at the pleasure of the board of directors.

(b) The creation of a committee and appointment of members to it must be approved by the greater of (1) a majority of all the directors in office when the action is taken or (2) the number of directors required by the articles of incorporation or bylaws to take action under section 8.24.

(c) Sections 8.20 through 8.24, which govern meetings, action without meetings, notice and waiver of notice, and quorum and voting requirements of the board of directors, apply to committees and their members as well.

(d) To the extent specified by the board of directors or in the articles of incorporation or bylaws, each committee may exercise the authority of the board of directors under section 8.01.

(e) A committee may not, however:

   (1) authorize distributions;

   (2) approve or propose to shareholders action that this Act requires to be approved by shareholders;

   (3) fill vacancies on the board of directors or on any of its committees;

   (4) amend articles of incorporation pursuant to section 10.02;

   (5) adopt, amend, or repeal bylaws;

   (6) approve a plan of merger not requiring shareholder approval;

(7) authorize or approve reacquisition of shares, except according to a formula or method prescribed by the board of directors; or

(8) authorize or approve the issuance or sale or contract for sale of shares, or determine the designation and relative rights, preferences, and limitations of a class or series of shares, except that the board of directors may authorize a committee (or a senior executive officer of the corporation) to do so within limits specifically prescribed by the board of directors.

(f) The creation of, delegation of authority to, or action by a committee does not alone constitute compliance by a director with the standards of conduct described in section 8.30.

Subchapter C. Standards of Conduct

§ 8.30 General Standards for Directors

(a) A director shall discharge his duties as a director, including his duties as a member of a committee:

(1) in good faith;

(2) with the care an ordinarily prudent person in a like position would exercise under similar circumstances; and

(3) in a manner he reasonably believes to be in the best interests of the corporation.

(b) In discharging his duties a director is entitled to rely on information, opinions, reports, or statements, including financial statements and other financial data, if prepared or presented by:

(1) one or more officers or employees of the corporation whom the director reasonably believes to be reliable and competent in the matters presented;

(2) legal counsel, public accountants, or other persons as to matters the director reasonably believes are within the person's professional or expert competence; or

(3) a committee of the board of directors of which he is not a member if the director reasonably believes the committee merits confidence.

(c) A director is not acting in good faith if he has knowledge concerning the matter in question that makes reliance otherwise permitted by subsection (b) unwarranted.

(d) A director is not liable for any action taken as a director, or any failure to take any action, if he performed the duties of his office in compliance with this section.

§ 8.33 Liability for Unlawful Distributions

(a) A director who votes for or assents to a distribution made in violation of section 6.40 or the articles of incorporation is personally liable to the corporation for the amount of the distribution that exceeds what could have been distributed without violating section 6.40 or the articles of incorporation if it is established that he did not perform his duties in compliance with section 8.30. In any proceeding commenced under this section, a director has all of the defenses ordinarily available to a director.

(b) A director held liable under subsection (a) for an unlawful distribution is entitled to contribution:

(1) from every other director who could be held liable under subsection (a) for the unlawful distribution; and

(2) from each shareholder for the amount the shareholder accepted knowing the distribution was made in violation of section 6.40 or the articles of incorporation.

(c) A proceeding under this section is barred unless it is commenced within two years after the date on which the effect of the distribution was measured under section 6.40(e) or (g).

Subchapter D. Officers

§ 8.40 Required Officers

(a) A corporation has the officers described in its bylaws or appointed by the board of directors in accordance with the bylaws.

(b) A duly appointed officer may appoint one or more officers or assistant officers if authorized by the bylaws or the board of directors.

(c) The bylaws or the board of directors shall delegate to one of the officers responsibility for preparing minutes of the directors' and shareholders' meetings and for authenticating records of the corporation.

(d) The same individual may simultaneously hold more than one office in a corporation.

§ 8.41 Duties of Officers

Each officer has the authority and shall perform the duties set forth in the bylaws or, to the extent consistent with the bylaws, the duties prescribed by the board of directors or by direction of an officer authorized by the board of directors to prescribe the duties of other officers.

§ 8.42 Standards of Conduct for Officers

(a) An officer with discretionary authority shall discharge his duties under that authority:

(1) in good faith;

(2) with the care an ordinarily prudent person in a like position would exercise under similar circumstances; and

(3) in a manner he reasonably believes to be in the best interests of the corporation.

(b) In discharging his duties an officer is entitled to rely on information, opinions, reports, or statements, including financial statements and other financial data, if prepared or presented by:

(1) one or more officers or employees of the corporation whom the officer reasonably believes to be reliable and competent in the matters presented; or

(2) legal counsel, public accountants, or other persons as to matters the officer reasonably believes are within the person's professional or expert competence.

(c) An officer is not acting in good faith if he has knowledge concerning the matter in question that makes reliance otherwise permitted by subsection (b) unwarranted.

(d) An officer is not liable for any action taken as an officer, or any failure to take any action, if he performed the duties of his office in compliance with this section.

§ 8.43 Resignation and Removal of Officers

(a) An officer may resign at any time by delivering notice to the corporation. A resignation is effective when the notice is delivered unless the notice specifies a later effective date. If a resignation is made effective at a later date and the corporation accepts the future effective date, its board of directors may fill the pending vacancy before the effective date if the board of directors provides that the successor does not take office until the effective date.

(b) A board of directors may remove any officer at any time with or without cause.

§ 8.44 Contract Rights of Officers

(a) The appointment of an officer does not itself create contract rights.

(b) An officer's removal does not affect the officer's contract rights, if any, with the corporation. An officer's resignation does not affect the corporation's contract rights, if any, with the officer.

Subchapter E. Indemnification

§ 8.50 Subchapter Definitions

In this subchapter:

(1) "Corporation" includes any domestic or foreign predecessor entity of a corporation in a merger or other transaction in which the predecessor's existence ceased upon consummation of the transaction.

(2) "Director" means an individual who is or was a director of a corporation or an individual who, while a director of a corporation, is or was serving at the corporation's request as a director, officer, partner, trustee, employee, or agent of another foreign or domestic corporation, partnership, joint venture, trust, employee benefit plan, or other enterprise. A director is considered to be serving an employee benefit plan at the corporation's request if his duties to the corporation also impose duties on, or otherwise involve services by, him to the plan or to participants in or beneficiaries of the plan. "Director" includes, unless the context requires otherwise, the estate or personal representative of a director.

(3) "Expenses" include counsel fees.

(4) "Liability" means the obligation to pay a judgment, settlement, penalty, fine (including an excise tax assessed with respect to an employee benefit plan), or reasonable expenses incurred with respect to a proceeding.

(5) "Official capacity" means: (i) when used with respect to a director, the office of director in a corporation; and (ii) when used with respect to an individual other than a director, as contemplated in section 8.56, the office in a corporation held by the officer or the employment or agency relationship undertaken by the employee or agent on behalf of the corporation. "Official capacity" does not include service for any other foreign or domestic corporation or any partnership, joint venture, trust, employee benefit plan, or other enterprise.

(6) "Party" includes an individual who was, is, or is threatened to be made a named defendant or respondent in a proceeding.

(7) "Proceeding" means any threatened, pending, or completed action, suit, or proceeding, whether civil, criminal, administrative, or investigative and whether formal or informal.

§ 8.51 Authority to Indemnify

(a) Except as provided in subsection (d), a corporation may indemnify an individual made a party to a proceeding because he is or was a director against liability incurred in the proceeding if:

(1) he conducted himself in good faith; and

(2) he reasonably believed:

(i) in the case of conduct in his official capacity with the corporation, that his conduct was in its best interests; and

(ii) in all other cases, that his conduct was at least not opposed to its best interests; and

(3) in the case of any criminal proceeding, he had no reasonable cause to believe his conduct was unlawful.

(b) A director's conduct with respect to an employee benefit plan for a purpose he reasonably believed to be in the interests of the participants in and beneficiaries of the plan is conduct that satisfies the requirement of subsection (a)(2)(ii).

(c) The termination of a proceeding by judgment, order, settlement, conviction, or upon a plea of nolo contendere or its equivalent is not, of itself, determinative that the director did not meet the standard of conduct described in this section.

(d) A corporation may not indemnify a director under this section:

(1) in connection with a proceeding by or in the right of the corporation in which the director was adjudged liable to the corporation; or

(2) in connection with any other proceeding charging improper personal benefit to him, whether or not involving action in his official capacity, in which he was adjudged liable on the basis that personal benefit was improperly received by him.

(e) Indemnification permitted under this section in connection with a proceeding by or in the right of the corporation is limited to reasonable expenses incurred in connection with the proceeding.

§ 8.52 Mandatory Indemnification

Unless limited by its articles of incorporation, a corporation shall indemnify a director who was wholly successful, on the merits or otherwise, in the defense of any proceeding to which he was a party because he is or was a director of the corporation against reasonable expenses incurred by him in connection with the proceeding.

§ 8.53 Advance for Expenses

(a) A corporation may pay for or reimburse the reasonable expenses incurred by a director who is a party to a proceeding in advance of final disposition of the proceeding if:

(1) the director furnishes the corporation a written affirmation of his good faith belief that he has met the standard of conduct described in section 8.51;

(2) the director furnishes the corporation a written undertaking, executed personally or on his behalf, to repay the advance if it is ultimately determined that he did not meet the standard of conduct; and

(3) a determination is made that the facts then known to those making the determination would not preclude indemnification under this subchapter.

(b) The undertaking required by subsection (a)(2) must be an unlimited general obligation of the director but need not be secured and may be accepted without reference to financial ability to make repayment.

(c) Determinations and authorizations of payments under this section shall be made in the manner specified in section 8.55.

§ 8.54 Court-Ordered Indemnification

Unless a corporation's articles of incorporation provide otherwise, a director of the corporation who is a party to a proceeding may apply for indemnification to the court conducting the proceeding or to another court of competent jurisdiction. On receipt of an application, the court after giving any notice the court considers necessary may order indemnification if it determines:

(1) the director is entitled to mandatory indemnification under section 8.52, in which case the court shall also order the corporation to pay the director's reasonable expenses incurred to obtain court-ordered indemnification; or

(2) the director is fairly and reasonably entitled to indemnification in view of all the relevant circumstances, whether or not he met the standard of conduct set forth in section 8.51 or was adjudged liable as described in section 8.51(d), but if he was adjudged so liable his indemnification is limited to reasonable expenses incurred.

§ 8.55 Determination and Authorization of Indemnification

(a) A corporation may not indemnify a director under section 8.51 unless authorized in the specific case after a determination has been made that indemnification of the director is permissible in the circumstances because he has met the standard of conduct set forth in section 8.51.

(b) The determination shall be made:

(1) by the board of directors by majority vote of a quorum consisting of directors not at the time parties to the proceeding;

(2) if a quorum cannot be obtained under subdivision (1), by majority vote of a committee duly designated by the board of directors (in which designation directors who are parties may participate), consisting solely of two or more directors not at the time parties to the proceeding;

(3) by special legal counsel:

(i) selected by the board of directors or its committee in the manner prescribed in subdivision (1) or (2); or

(ii) if a quorum of the board of directors cannot be obtained under subdivision (1) and a committee cannot be designated under subdivision (2), selected by majority vote of the full board of directors (in which selection directors who are parties may participate); or

(4) by the shareholders, but shares owned by or voted under the control of directors who are at the time parties to the proceeding may not be voted on the determination.

(c) Authorization of indemnification and evaluation as to reasonableness of expenses shall be made in the same manner as the determination that indemnification is permissible, except that if the determination is made by special legal counsel, authorization of indemnification and evaluation as to reasonableness of expenses shall be made by those entitled under subsection (b)(3) to select counsel.

§ 8.56 Indemnification of Officers, Employees, and Agents

Unless a corporation's articles of incorporation provide otherwise:

(1) an officer of the corporation who is not a director is entitled to mandatory indemnification under section 8.52, and is entitled to apply for court-ordered indemnification under section 8.54, in each case to the same extent as a director;

(2) the corporation may indemnify and advance expenses under this subchapter to an officer, employee, or agent of the corporation who is not a director to the same extent as to a director; and

(3) a corporation may also indemnify and advance expenses to an officer, employee, or agent who is not a director to the extent, consistent with public policy, that may be provided by its articles of incorporation, bylaws, general or specific action of its board of directors, or contract.

§ 8.57 Insurance

A corporation may purchase and maintain insurance on behalf of an individual who is or was a director, officer, employee, or agent of the corporation, or who, while a director, officer, employee, or agent of the corporation, is or was serving at the request of the corporation as a director, officer, partner, trustee, employee, or agent of another foreign or domestic corporation, partnership, joint venture, trust, employee benefit plan, or other enterprise, against liability asserted against or incurred by him in that capacity or arising from his status as a director, officer, employee, or agent, whether or not the corporation would have power to indemnify him against the same liability under section 8.51 or 8.52.

§ 8.58 Application of Subchapter

(a) A provision treating a corporation's indemnification of or advance for expenses to directors that is contained in its articles of incorporation, bylaws, a resolution of its shareholders or board of directors, or in a contract or otherwise, is valid only if and to the extent the provision is consistent with this subchapter. If articles of incorporation limit indemnification or advance for expenses, indemnification and advance for expenses are valid only to the extent consistent with the articles.

(b) This subchapter does not limit a corporation's power to pay or reimburse expenses incurred by a director in connection with his appearance as a witness in a proceeding at a time when he has not been made a named defendant or respondent to the proceeding.

Subchapter F. Directors' Conflicting Interest Transactions

§ 8.60 Subchapter Definitions

In this subchapter:

(1) "Conflicting interest" with respect to a corporation means the interest a director of the corporation has respecting a transaction effected or proposed to be effected by the corporation (or by a subsidiary of the corporation or any other entity in which the corporation has a controlling interest) if

(i) whether or not the transaction is brought before the board of directors of the corporation for action, the director knows at the time of commitment that he or a related person is a party to the transaction or has a beneficial financial interest in or so closely linked to the transaction and of such financial significance to the director or a related person that the interest would reasonably be expected to exert an influence on the director's judgment if he were called upon to vote on the transaction; or

(ii) the transaction is brought (or is of such character and significance to the corporation that it would in the normal course be brought) before the board of directors of the corporation for action, and the director knows at the time of commitment that any of the following persons is either a party to the transaction or has a beneficial financial interest in or so closely linked to the transaction and of such financial significance to the person that the interest would reasonably be expected to exert an influence on the director's judgment if he were called upon to vote on the transaction: (A) an entity (other than the corporation) of which the director is a director, general partner, agent, or employee; (B) a person that controls one or more of the entities specified in subclause (A) or an entity that is controlled by, or is under common control with, one or more of the entities specified in subclause (A); or (C) an individual who is a general partner, principal, or employer of the director.

(2) "Director's conflicting interest transaction" with respect to a corporation means a transaction effected or proposed to be effected by the corporation (or by a subsidiary of the corporation or any other entity in which the corporation has a controlling interest) respecting which a director of the corporation has a conflicting interest.

(3) "Related person" of a director means (i) the spouse (or a parent or sibling thereof) of the director, or a child, grandchild, sibling, parent (or spouse of any thereof) of the director, or an individual having the same home as the director, or a trust or estate of which an individual specified in this clause (i) is a substantial beneficiary; or (ii) a trust, estate, incompetent, conservatee, or minor of which the director is a fiduciary.

(4) "Required disclosure" means disclosure by the director who has a conflicting interest of (i) the existence and nature of his conflicting interest, and (ii) all facts known to him respecting the subject matter of the transaction that an ordinarily prudent person would reasonably believe to be material to a judgment about whether or not to proceed with the transaction.

(5) "Time of commitment" respecting a transaction means the time when the transaction is consummated or, if made pursuant to contract, the time when the corporation (or its subsidiary or the entity in which it has a controlling interest) becomes contractually obligated so that its unilateral withdrawal from the transaction would entail significant loss, liability, or other damage.

§ 8.61 **Judicial Action**

(a) A transaction effected or proposed to be effected by a corporation (or by a subsidiary of the corporation or any other entity in which the corporation has a controlling interest) that is not a director's conflicting interest transaction may not be enjoined, set aside, or give rise to an award of damages or other sanctions, in a proceeding by a shareholder or by or in the right of the corporation, because a director of the corporation, or any person with whom or which he has a personal, economic, or other association, has an interest in the transaction.

(b) A director's conflicting interest transaction may not be enjoined, set aside, or give rise to an award of damages or other sanctions, in a proceeding by a shareholder or by or in the right of the corporation, because the director, or any person with whom or which he has a personal, economic, or other association, has an interest in the transaction, if:

(1) directors' action respecting the transaction was at any time taken in compliance with section 8.62;

(2) shareholders' action respecting the transaction was at any time taken in compliance with section 8.63; or

(3) the transaction, judged according to the circumstances at the time of commitment, is established to have been fair to the corporation.

§ 8.62 **Directors' Action**

(a) Directors' action respecting a transaction is effective for purposes of section 8.61(b)(1) if the transaction received the affirmative vote of a majority (but no fewer than two) of those qualified directors on the board of directors or on a duly empowered committee of the board who voted on the transaction after either required disclosure to them (to the extent the information was not known by them) or compliance with subsection (b); provided that action by a committee is so effective only if:

(1) all its members are qualified directors; and

(2) its members are either all the qualified directors on the board or are appointed by the affirmative vote of a majority of the qualified directors on the board.

(b) If a director has a conflicting interest respecting a transaction, but neither he nor a related person of the director specified in section 8.60(3)(i) is a party to the transaction, and if the director has a duty under law or professional canon, or a duty of confidentiality to another person, respecting information relating to the transaction such that the director may not make the disclosure described in section 8.60(4)(ii), then disclosure is sufficient for purposes of subsection (a) if the director (1) discloses to the directors voting on the transaction the existence and nature of his conflicting interest and informs them of the character and limitations imposed by that duty before their vote on the transaction, and (2) plays no part, directly or indirectly, in their deliberations or vote.

(c) A majority (but no fewer than two) of all the qualified directors on the board of directors, or on the committee, constitutes a quorum for purposes of action that complies with this section. Directors' action that otherwise complies with this section is not affected by the presence or vote of a director who is not a qualified director.

(d) For purposes of this section, "qualified director" means, with respect to a director's conflicting interest transaction, any director who does not have either (1) a conflicting interest respecting the transaction, or (2) a familial, financial, professional, or employment relationship with a second director who does have a conflicting interest respecting the transaction, which relationship would, in the circumstances, reasonably be expected to exert an influence on the first director's judgment when voting on the transaction.

§ 8.63 **Shareholders' Action**

(a) Shareholders' action respecting a transaction is effective for purposes of section 8.61(b)(2) if a majority of the votes entitled to be cast by the holders of all qualified shares were cast in favor of the transaction after (1) notice to shareholders describing the director's conflicting interest transaction, (2) provision of the information referred to in subsection (d), and (3) required disclosure to the shareholders who voted on the transaction (to the extent the information was not known by them).

(b) For purposes of this section, "qualified shares" means any shares entitled to vote with respect to the director's conflicting interest transaction except shares that, to the knowledge, before the vote, of the secretary (or other officer or agent of the corporation authorized to tabulate votes), are beneficially owned (or the

the vote, of the secretary (or other officer or agent of the corporation authorized to tabulate votes), are beneficially owned (or the voting of which is controlled) by a director who has a conflicting interest respecting the transaction or by a related person of the director, or both.

(c) A majority of the votes entitled to be cast by the holders of all qualified shares constitutes a quorum for purposes of action that complies with this section. Subject to the provisions of subsections (d) and (e), shareholders' action that otherwise complies with this section is not affected by the presence of holders, or the voting, of shares that are not qualified shares.

(d) For purposes of compliance with subsection (a), a director who has a conflicting interest respecting the transaction shall, before the shareholders' vote, inform the secretary (or other office or agent of the corporation authorized to tabulate votes) of the number, and the identity of persons holding or controlling the vote, of all shares that the director knows are beneficially owned (or the voting of which is controlled) by the director or by a related person of the director, or both.

(e) If a shareholders' vote does not comply with subsection (a) solely because of a failure of a director to comply with subsection (d), and if the director establishes that his failure did not determine and was not intended by him to influence the outcome of the vote, the court may, with or without further proceedings respecting section 8.61(b)(3), take such action respecting the transaction and the director, and give such effect, if any, to the shareholders' vote, as it considers appropriate in the circumstances.

Chapter 9.
[RESERVED]

Chapter 10.
AMENDMENT OF ARTICLES OF INCORPORATION AND BYLAWS

Subchapter A. Amendment of Articles of Incorporation

§ 10.01 Authority to Amend

(a) A corporation may amend its articles of incorporation at any time to add or change a provision that is required or permitted in the articles of incorporation or to delete a provision not required in the articles of incorporation. Whether a provision is required or permitted in the articles of incorporation is determined as of the effective date of the amendment.

(b) A shareholder of the corporation does not have a vested property right resulting from any provision in the articles of incorporation, including provisions relating to management, control, capital structure, dividend entitlement, or purpose or duration of the corporation.

§ 10.02 Amendment by Board of Directors

Unless the articles of incorporation provide otherwise, a corporation's board of directors may adopt one or more amendments to the corporation's articles of incorporation without shareholder action:

(1) to extend the duration of the corporation if it was incorporated at a time when limited duration was required by law;

(2) to delete the names and addresses of the initial directors;

(3) to delete the name and address of the initial registered agent or registered office, if a statement of change is on file with the secretary of state;

(4) to change each issued and unissued authorized share of an outstanding class into a greater number of whole shares if the corporation has only shares of that class outstanding;

(5) to change the corporate name by substituting the word "corporation," "incorporated," "company," "limited," or the abbreviation "corp.," "inc.," "co.," or "ltd.," for a similar word or abbreviation in the name, or by adding, deleting, or changing a geographical attribution for the name; or

(6) to make any other change expressly permitted by this Act to be made without shareholder action.

§ 10.03 Amendment by Board of Directors and Shareholders

(a) A corporation's board of directors may propose one or more amendments to the articles of incorporation for submission to the shareholders.

(b) For the amendment to be adopted:

(1) the board of directors must recommend the amendment to the shareholders unless the board of directors determines that because of conflict of interest or other special circumstances it should make no recommendation and communicates the basis for its determination to the shareholders with the amendment; and

(2) the shareholders entitled to vote on the amendment must approve the amendment as provided in subsection (e).

(c) The board of directors may condition its submission of the proposed amendment on any basis.

(d) The corporation shall notify each shareholder, whether or not entitled to vote, of the proposed shareholders' meeting in accordance with section 7.05. The notice of meeting must also state that the purpose, or one of the purposes, of the meeting is to consider the proposed amendment and contain or be accompanied by a copy or summary of the amendment.

(e) Unless this Act, the articles of incorporation, or the board of directors (acting pursuant to subsection (c)) require a greater vote or a vote by voting groups, the amendment to be adopted must be approved by:

(1) a majority of the votes entitled to be cast on the amendment by any voting group with respect to which the amendment would create dissenters' rights; and

(2) the votes required by sections 7.25 and 7.26 by every other voting group entitled to vote on the amendment.

§ 10.04 Voting on Amendments by Voting Groups

(a) The holders of the outstanding shares of a class are entitled to vote as a separate voting group (if shareholder voting is otherwise required by this Act) on a proposed amendment if the amendment would:

(1) increase or decrease the aggregate number of authorized shares of the class;

(2) effect an exchange or reclassification of all or part of the shares of the class into shares of another class;

(3) effect an exchange or reclassification, or create the right of exchange, of all or part of the shares of another class into shares of the class;

(4) change the designation, rights, preferences, or limitations of all or part of the shares of the class;

(5) change the shares of all or part of the class into a different number of shares of the same class;

(6) create a new class of shares having rights or preferences with respect to distributions or to dissolution that are prior, superior, or substantially equal to the shares of the class;

(7) increase the rights, preferences, or number of authorized shares of any class that, after giving effect to the amendment, have rights or preferences with respect to distributions or to dissolution that are prior, superior, or substantially equal to the shares of the class;

(8) limit or deny an existing preemptive right of all or part of the shares of the class; or

(9) cancel or otherwise affect rights to distributions or dividends that have accumulated but not yet been declared on all or part of the shares of the class.

(b) If a proposed amendment would affect a series of a class of shares in one or more of the ways described in subsection (a), the shares of that series are entitled to vote as a separate voting group on the proposed amendment.

(c) If a proposed amendment that entitles two or more series of shares to vote as separate voting groups under this section would affect those two or more series in the same or a substantially similar way, the shares of all the series so affected must vote together as a single voting group on the proposed amendment.

(d) A class or series of shares is entitled to the voting rights granted by this section although the articles of incorporation provide that the shares are nonvoting shares.

§ 10.05 Amendment before Issuance of Shares

If a corporation has not yet issued shares, its incorporators or board of directors may adopt one or more amendments to the corporation's articles of incorporation.

§ 10.06 Articles of Amendment

A corporation amending its articles of incorporation shall deliver to the secretary of state for filing articles of amendment setting forth:

(1) the name of the corporation;

(2) the text of each amendment adopted;

(3) if an amendment provides for an exchange, reclassification, or cancellation of issued shares, provisions for implementing the amendment if not contained in the amendment itself;

(4) the date of each amendment's adoption;

(5) if an amendment was adopted by the incorporators or board of directors without shareholder action, a statement to that effect and that shareholder action was not required;

(6) if an amendment was approved by the shareholders:

(i) the designation, number of outstanding shares, number of votes entitled to be cast by each voting group entitled to vote separately on the amendment, and number of votes of each voting group indisputably represented at the

meeting;

(ii) either the total number of votes cast for and against the amendment by each voting group entitled to vote separately on the amendment or the total number of undisputed votes cast for the amendment by each voting group and a statement that the number cast for the amendment by each voting group was sufficient for approval by that voting group.

§ 10.07 Restated Articles of Incorporation

(a) A corporation's board of directors may restate its articles of incorporation at any time with or without shareholder action.

(b) The restatement may include one or more amendments to the articles. If the restatement includes an amendment requiring shareholder approval, it must be adopted as provided in section 10.03.

(c) If the board of directors submits a restatement for shareholder action, the corporation shall notify each shareholder, whether or not entitled to vote, of the proposed shareholders' meeting in accordance with section 7.05. The notice must also state that the purpose, or one of the purposes, of the meeting is to consider the proposed restatement and contain or be accompanied by a copy of the restatement that identifies any amendment or other change it would make in the articles.

(d) A corporation restating its articles of incorporation shall deliver to the secretary of state for filing articles of restatement setting forth the name of the corporation and the text of the restated articles of incorporation together with a certificate setting forth:

(1) whether the restatement contains an amendment to the articles requiring shareholder approval and, if it does not, that the board of directors adopted the restatement; or

(2) if the restatement contains an amendment to the articles requiring shareholder approval, the information required by section 10.06.

(e) Duly adopted restated articles of incorporation supersede the original articles of incorporation and all amendments to them.

(f) The secretary of state may certify restated articles of incorporation, as the articles of incorporation currently in effect, without including the certificate information required by subsection (d).

§ 10.08 Amendment Pursuant to Reorganization

(a) A corporation's articles of incorporation may be amended without action by the board of directors or shareholders to carry out a plan of reorganization ordered or decreed by a court of competent jurisdiction under federal statute if the articles of incorporation after amendment contain only provisions required or permitted by section 2.02.

(b) The individual or individuals designated by the court shall deliver to the secretary of state for filing articles of amendment setting forth:

(1) the name of the corporation;

(2) the text of each amendment approved by the court;

(3) the date of the court's order or decree approving the articles of amendment;

(4) the title of the reorganization proceeding in which the order or decree was entered; and

(5) a statement that the court had jurisdiction of the proceed-

ing under federal statute.

(c) Shareholders of a corporation undergoing reorganization do not have dissenters' rights except as and to the extent provided in the reorganization plan.

(d) This section does not apply after entry of a final decree in the reorganization proceeding even though the court retains jurisdiction of the proceeding for limited purposes unrelated to consummation of the reorganization plan.

§ 10.09 Effect of Amendment

An amendment to articles of incorporation does not affect a cause of action existing against or in favor of the corporation, a proceeding to which the corporation is a party, or the existing rights of persons other than shareholders of the corporation. An amendment changing a corporation's name does not abate a proceeding brought by or against the corporation in its former name.

Subchapter B. Amendment of Bylaws

§ 10.20 Amendment by Board of Directors or Shareholders

(a) A corporation's board of directors may amend or repeal the corporation's bylaws unless:

(1) the articles of incorporation or this Act reserve this power exclusively to the shareholders in whole or part; or

(2) the shareholders in amending or repealing a particular bylaw provide expressly that the board of directors may not amend or repeal that bylaw.

(b) A corporation's shareholders may amend or repeal the corporation's bylaws even though the bylaws may also be amended or repealed by its board of directors.

§ 10.21 Bylaw Increasing Quorum or Voting Requirement for Shareholders

(a) If expressly authorized by the articles of incorporation, the shareholders may adopt or amend a bylaw that fixes a greater quorum or voting requirement for shareholders (or voting groups of shareholders) than is required by this Act. The adoption or amendment of a bylaw that adds, changes, or deletes a greater quorum or voting requirement for shareholders must meet the same quorum requirement and be adopted by the same vote and voting groups required to take action under the quorum and voting requirement then in effect or proposed to be adopted, whichever is greater.

(b) A bylaw that fixes a greater quorum or voting requirement for shareholders under subsection (a) may not be adopted, amended, or repealed by the board of directors.

§ 10.22 Bylaw Increasing Quorum or Voting Requirement for Directors

(a) A bylaw that fixes a greater quorum or voting requirement for the board of directors may be amended or repealed:

(1) if originally adopted by the shareholders, only by the shareholders;

(2) if originally adopted by the board of directors, either by the shareholders or by the board of directors.

(b) A bylaw adopted or amended by the shareholders that fixes a greater quorum or voting requirement for the board of directors may provide that it may be amended or repealed only by a specified vote of either the shareholders or the board of directors.

(c) Action by the board of directors under subsection (a)(2) to

adopt or amend a bylaw that changes the quorum or voting requirement for the board of directors must meet the same quorum requirement and be adopted by the same vote required to take action under the quorum and voting requirement then in effect or proposed to be adopted, whichever is greater.

Chapter 11.
MERGER AND SHARE EXCHANGE

§ 11.01 Merger

(a) One or more corporations may merge into another corporation if the board of directors of each corporation adopts and its shareholders (if required by section 11.03) approve a plan of merger.

(b) The plan of merger must set forth:

(1) the name of each corporation planning to merge and the name of the surviving corporation into which each other corporation plans to merge;

(2) the terms and conditions of the merger; and

(3) the manner and basis of converting the shares of each corporation into shares, obligations, or other securities of the surviving or any other corporation or into cash or other property in whole or part.

(c) The plan of merger may set forth:

(1) amendments to the articles of incorporation of the surviving corporation; and

(2) other provisions relating to the merger.

§ 11.02 Share Exchange

(a) A corporation may acquire all of the outstanding shares of one or more classes or series of another corporation if the board of directors of each corporation adopts and its shareholders (if required by section 11.03) approve the exchange.

(b) The plan of exchange must set forth:

(1) the name of the corporation whose shares will be acquired and the name of the acquiring corporation;

(2) the terms and conditions of the exchange;

(3) the manner and basis of exchanging the shares to be acquired for shares, obligations, or other securities of the acquiring or any other corporation or for cash or other property in whole or part.

(c) The plan of exchange may set forth other provisions relating to the exchange.

(d) This section does not limit the power of a corporation to acquire all or part of the shares of one or more classes or series of another corporation through a voluntary exchange or otherwise.

§ 11.03 Action on Plan

(a) After adopting a plan of merger or share exchange, the board of directors of each corporation party to the merger, and the board of directors of the corporation whose shares will be acquired in the share exchange, shall submit the plan of merger (except as provided in subsection (g)) or share exchange for approval by its shareholders.

(b) For a plan of merger or share exchange to be approved:

(1) the board of directors must recommend the plan of merger or share exchange to the shareholders, unless the board of directors determines that because of conflict of interest or other special circumstances it should make no recommendation and communicates the basis for its determination to the shareholders with the plan; and

(2) the shareholders entitled to vote must approve the plan.

(c) The board of directors may condition its submission of the proposed merger or share exchange on any basis.

(d) The corporation shall notify each shareholder, whether or not entitled to vote, of the proposed shareholders' meeting in accordance with section 7.05. The notice must also state that the purpose, or one of the purposes, of the meeting is to consider the plan of merger or share exchange and contain or be accompanied by a copy or summary of the plan.

(e) Unless this Act, the articles of incorporation, or the board of directors (acting pursuant to subsection (c)) require a greater vote or a vote by voting groups, the plan of merger or share exchange to be authorized must be approved by each voting group entitled to vote separately on the plan by a majority of all the votes entitled to be cast on the plan by that voting group.

(f) Separate voting by voting groups is required:

(1) on a plan of merger if the plan contains a provision that, if contained in a proposed amendment to articles of incorporation, would require action by one or more separate voting groups on the proposed amendment under section 10.04;

(2) on a plan of share exchange by each class or series of shares included in the exchange, with each class or series constituting a separate voting group.

(g) Action by the shareholders of the surviving corporation on a plan of merger is not required if:

(1) the articles of incorporation of the surviving corporation will not differ (except for amendments enumerated in section 10.02) from its articles before the merger;

(2) each shareholder of the surviving corporation whose shares were outstanding immediately before the effective date of the merger will hold the same number of shares, with identical designations, preferences, limitations, and relative rights, immediately after;

(3) the number of voting shares outstanding immediately after the merger, plus the number of voting shares issuable as a result of the merger (either by the conversion of securities issued pursuant to the merger or the exercise of rights and warrants issued pursuant to the merger), will not exceed by more than 20 percent the total number of voting shares of the surviving corporation outstanding immediately before the merger; and

(4) the number of participating shares outstanding immediately after the merger, plus the number of participating shares issuable as a result of the merger (either by the conversion of securities issued pursuant to the merger or the exercise of rights and warrants issued pursuant to the merger), will not exceed by more than 20 percent the total number of participating shares outstanding immediately before the merger.

(h) As used in subsection (g):

(1) "Participating shares" means shares that entitle their holders to participate without limitation in distributions.

(2) "Voting shares" means shares that entitle their holders to vote unconditionally in elections of directors.

(i) After a merger or share exchange is authorized, and at any time before articles of merger or share exchange are filed, the planned merger or share exchange may be abandoned (subject to any contractual rights), without further shareholder action, in accordance with the procedure set forth in the plan of merger or share exchange or, if none is set forth, in the manner determined by the board of directors.

§ 11.04 **Merger of Subsidiary**

(a) A parent corporation owning at least 90 percent of the outstanding shares of each class of a subsidiary corporation may merge the subsidiary into itself without approval of the shareholders of the parent or subsidiary.

(b) The board of directors of the parent shall adopt a plan of merger that sets forth:

(1) the names of the parent and subsidiary; and

(2) the manner and basis of converting the shares of the subsidiary into shares, obligations, or other securities of the parent or any other corporation or into cash or other property in whole or part.

(c) The parent shall mail a copy or summary of the plan of merger to each shareholder of the subsidiary who does not waive the mailing requirement in writing.

(d) The parent may not deliver articles of merger to the secretary of state for filing until at least 30 days after the date it mailed a copy of the plan of merger to each shareholder of the subsidiary who did not waive the mailing requirement.

(e) Articles of merger under this section may not contain amendments to the articles of incorporation of the parent corporation (except for amendments enumerated in section 10.02).

§ 11.05 **Articles of Merger or Share Exchange**

(a) After a plan of merger or share exchange is approved by the shareholders, or adopted by the board of directors if shareholder approval is not required, the surviving or acquiring corporation shall deliver to the secretary of state for filing articles of merger or share exchange setting forth:

(1) the plan of merger or share exchange;

(2) if shareholder approval was not required, a statement to that effect;

(3) if approval of the shareholders of one or more corporations party to the merger or share exchange was required:

(i) the designation, number of outstanding shares, and number of votes entitled to be cast by each voting group entitled to vote separately on the plan as to each corporation; and

(ii) either the total number of votes cast for and against the plan by each voting group entitled to vote separately on the plan or the total number of undisputed votes cast for the plan separately by each voting group and a statement that the number cast for the plan by each voting group was sufficient for approval by that voting group.

(b) Unless a delayed effective date is specified, a merger or share exchange takes effect when the articles of merger or share exchange are filed.

§ 11.06 Effect of Merger or Share Exchange

(a) When a merger takes effect:

(1) every other corporation party to the merger merges into the surviving corporation and the separate existence of every corporation except the surviving corporation ceases;

(2) the title to all real estate and other property owned by each corporation party to the merger is vested in the surviving corporation without reversion or impairment;

(3) the surviving corporation has all liabilities of each corporation party to the merger;

(4) a proceeding pending against any corporation party to the merger may be continued as if the merger did not occur or the surviving corporation may be substituted in the proceeding for the corporation whose existence ceased;

(5) the articles of incorporation of the surviving corporation are amended to the extent provided in the plan of merger; and

(6) the shares of each corporation party to the merger that are to be converted into shares, obligations, or other securities of the surviving or any other corporation or into cash or other property are converted and the former holders of the shares are entitled only to the rights provided in the articles of merger or to their rights under chapter 13.

(b) When a share exchange takes effect, the shares of each acquired corporation are exchanged as provided in the plan, and the former holders of the shares are entitled only to the exchange rights provided in the articles of share exchange or to their rights under chapter 13.

§ 11.07 Merger of Share Exchange with Foreign Corporation

(a) One or more foreign corporations may merge or enter into a share exchange with one or more domestic corporations if:

(1) in a merger, the merger is permitted by the law of the state or country under whose law each foreign corporation is incorporated and each foreign corporation complies with that law in effecting the merger;

(2) in a share exchange, the corporation whose shares will be acquired is a domestic corporation, whether or not a share exchange is permitted by the law of the state or country under whose law the acquiring corporation is incorporated;

(3) the foreign corporation complies with section 11.05 if it is the surviving corporation of the merger or acquiring corporation of the share exchange; and

(4) each domestic corporation complies with the applicable provisions of sections 11.01 through 11.04 and, if it is the surviving corporation of the merger or acquiring corporation of the share exchange, with section 11.05.

(b) Upon the merger or share exchange taking effect, the surviving foreign corporation of a merger and the acquiring foreign corporation of a share exchange is deemed:

(1) to appoint the secretary of state as its agent for service of process in a proceeding to enforce any obligation or the rights of dissenting shareholders of each domestic corporation party to the merger or share exchange; and

(2) to agree that it will promptly pay to the dissenting shareholders of each domestic corporation party to the merger or share exchange the amount, if any, to which they are entitled under chapter 13.

(c) This section does not limit the power of a foreign corporation to acquire all or part of the shares of one or more classes or series of a domestic corporation through a voluntary exchange or otherwise.

Chapter 12.
SALE OF ASSETS

§ 12.01 Sale of Assets in Regular Course of Business and Mortgage of Assets

(a) A corporation may, on the terms and conditions and for the consideration determined by the board of directors:

(1) sell, lease, exchange, or otherwise dispose of all, or substantially all, of its property in the usual and regular course of business;

(2) mortgage, pledge, dedicate to the repayment of indebtedness (whether with or without recourse), or otherwise encumber any or all of its property whether or not in the usual and regular course of business; or

(3) transfer any or all of its property to a corporation all the shares of which are owned by the corporation.

(b) Unless the articles of incorporation require it, approval by the shareholders of a transaction described in subsection (a) is not required.

§ 12.02 Sale of Assets Other Than in Regular Course of Business

(a) A corporation may sell, lease, exchange, or otherwise dispose of all, or substantially all, of its property (with or without the good will), otherwise than in the usual and regular course of business, on the terms and conditions and for the consideration determined by the corporation's board of directors, if the board of directors proposes and its shareholders approve the proposed transaction.

(b) For a transaction to be authorized:

(1) the board of directors must recommend the proposed transaction to the shareholders unless the board of directors determines that because of conflict of interest or other special circumstances it should make no recommendation and communicates the basis for its determination to the shareholders with the submission of the proposed transaction; and

(2) the shareholders entitled to vote must approve the transaction.

(c) The board of directors may condition its submission of the proposed transaction on any basis.

(d) The corporation shall notify each shareholder, whether or not entitled to vote, of the proposed shareholders' meeting in accordance with section 7.05. The notice must also state that the purpose, or one of the purposes, of the meeting is to consider the sale, lease, exchange, or other disposition of all, or substantially all, the property of the corporation and contain or be accompanied by a description of the transaction.

(e) Unless the articles of incorporation or the board of directors (acting pursuant to subsection (c)) require a greater vote or a vote by voting groups, the transaction to be authorized must be approved by a majority of all the votes entitled to be cast on the transaction.

(f) After a sale, lease, exchange, or other disposition of property is authorized, the transaction may be abandoned (subject to any contractual rights) without further shareholder action.

(g) A transaction that constitutes a distribution is governed by section 6.40 and not by this section.

Chapter 13.
DISSENTERS' RIGHTS

Subchapter A. Right to Dissent and Obtain Payment for Shares

§ 13.01 Definitions

In this chapter:

(1) "Corporation" means the issuer of the shares held by a dissenter before the corporate action, or the surviving or acquiring corporation by merger or share exchange of that issuer.

(2) "Dissenter" means a shareholder who is entitled to dissent from corporate action under section 13.02 and who exercises that right when and in the manner required by sections 13.20 through 13.28.

(3) "Fair value," with respect to a dissenter's shares, means the value of the shares immediately before the effectuation of the corporate action to which the dissenter objects, excluding any appreciation or depreciation in anticipation of the corporate action unless exclusion would be inequitable.

(4) "Interest" means interest from the effective date of the corporate action until the date of payment, at the average rate currently paid by the corporation on its principal bank loans or, if none, at a rate that is fair and equitable under all the circumstances.

(5) "Record shareholder" means the person in whose name shares are registered in the records of a corporation or the beneficial owner of shares to the extent of the rights granted by a nominee certificate on file with a corporation.

(6) "Beneficial shareholder" means the person who is a beneficial owner of shares held in a voting trust or by a nominee as the record shareholder.

(7) "Shareholder" means the record shareholder or the beneficial shareholder.

§ 13.02 Right to Dissent

(a) A shareholder is entitled to dissent from, and obtain payment of the fair value of his shares in the event of, any of the following corporate actions:

(1) consummation of a plan of merger to which the corporation is a party (i) if shareholder approval is required for the merger by section 11.03 or the articles of incorporation and the shareholder is entitled to vote on the merger or (ii) if the corporation is a subsidiary that is merged with its parent under section 11.04;

(2) consummation of a plan of share exchange to which the corporation is a party as the corporation whose shares will be acquired, if the shareholder is entitled to vote on the plan;

(3) consummation of a sale or exchange of all, or substantially all, of the property of the corporation other than in the usual and regular course of business, if the shareholder is enti-

tled to vote on the sale or exchange, including a sale in dissolution, but not including a sale pursuant to court order or a sale for cash pursuant to a plan by which all or substantially all of the net proceeds of the sale will be distributed to the shareholders within one year after the date of sale;

(4) an amendment of the articles of incorporation that materially and adversely affects rights in respect of a dissenter's shares because it:

(i) alters or abolishes a preferential right of the shares;

(ii) creates, alters, or abolishes a right in respect of redemption, including a provision respecting a sinking fund for the redemption or repurchase, of the shares;

(iii) alters or abolishes a preemptive right of the holder of the shares to acquire shares or other securities;

(iv) excludes or limits the right of the shares to vote on any matter, or to cumulate votes, other than a limitation by dilution through issuance of shares or other securities with similar voting rights; or

(v) reduces the number of shares owned by the shareholder to a fraction of a share if the fractional share so created is to be acquired for cash under section 6.04; or

(5) any corporate action taken pursuant to a shareholder vote to the extent the articles of incorporation, bylaws, or a resolution of the board of directors provides that voting or nonvoting shareholders are entitled to dissent and obtain payment for their shares.

(b) A shareholder entitled to dissent and obtain payment for his shares under this chapter may not challenge the corporate action creating his entitlement unless the action is unlawful or fraudulent with respect to the shareholder or the corporation.

§ 13.03 Dissent by Nominees and Beneficial Owners

(a) A record shareholder may assert dissenters' rights as to fewer than all the shares registered in his name only if he dissents with respect to all shares beneficially owned by any one person and notifies the corporation in writing of the name and address of each person on whose behalf he asserts dissenters' rights. The rights of a partial dissenter under this subsection are determined as if the shares as to which he dissents and his other shares were registered in the names of different shareholders.

(b) A beneficial shareholder may assert dissenters' rights as to shares held on his behalf only if:

(1) he submits to the corporation the record shareholder's written consent to the dissent not later than the time the beneficial shareholder asserts dissenters' rights; and

(2) he does so with respect to all shares of which he is the beneficial shareholder or over which he has power to direct the vote.

Subchapter B. Procedure for Exercise of Dissenters' Rights

§ 13.20 Notice of Dissenters' Rights

(a) If proposed corporate action creating dissenters' rights under section 13.02 is submitted to a vote at a shareholders' meeting, the meeting notice must state that shareholders are or may be entitled to assert dissenters' rights under this chapter and be accompanied by a copy of this chapter.

(b) If corporate action creating dissenters' rights under section 13.02 is taken without a vote of shareholders, the corporation shall notify in writing all shareholders entitled to assert dissenters' rights that the action was taken and send them the dissenters' notice described in section 13.22.

§ 13.21 Notice of Intent to Demand Payment

(a) If proposed corporate action creating dissenters' rights under section 13.02 is submitted to a vote at a shareholders' meeting, a shareholder who wishes to assert dissenters' rights (1) must deliver to the corporation before the vote is taken written notice of his intent to demand payment for his shares if the proposed action is effectuated and (2) must not vote his shares in favor of the proposed action.

(b) A shareholder who does not satisfy the requirements of subsection (a) is not entitled to payment for his shares under this chapter.

§ 13.22 Dissenters' Notice

(a) If proposed corporate action creating dissenters' right under section 13.02 is authorized at a shareholders' meeting, the corporation shall deliver a written dissenters' notice to all shareholders who satisfied the requirements of section 13.21.

(b) The dissenters' notice must be sent no later than 10 days after the corporate action was taken, and must:

(1) state where the payment demand must be sent and where and when certificates for certificated shares must be deposited;

(2) inform holders of uncertificated shares to what extent transfer of the shares will be restricted after the payment demand is received;

(3) supply a form for demanding payment that includes the date of the first announcement to news media or to shareholders of the terms of the proposed corporate action and requires that the person asserting dissenters' rights certify whether or not he acquired beneficial ownership of the shares before that date;

(4) set a date by which the corporation must receive the payment demand, which date may not be fewer than 30 nor more than 60 days after the date the subsection (a) notice is delivered; and

(5) be accompanied by a copy of this chapter.

§ 13.23 Duty to Demand Payment

(a) A shareholder sent a dissenters' notice described in section 13.22 must demand payment, certify whether he acquired beneficial ownership of the shares before the date required to be set forth in the dissenter's notice pursuant to section 13.22(b)(3), and deposit his certificates in accordance with the terms of the notice.

(b) The shareholder who demands payment and deposits his shares under section (a) retains all other rights of a shareholder until these rights are cancelled or modified by the taking of the proposed corporate action.

(c) A shareholder who does not demand payment or deposit his share certificates where required, each by the date set in the dissenters' notice, is not entitled to payment for his shares under this chapter.

§ 13.24 Share Restrictions

(a) The corporation may restrict the transfer of uncertificated shares from the date the demand for their payment is received until the proposed corporate action is taken or the restrictions released under section 13.26.

(b) The person for whom dissenters' rights are asserted as to uncertificated shares retains all other rights of a shareholder until these rights are cancelled or modified by the taking of the proposed corporate action.

§ 13.25 Payment

(a) Except as provided in section 13.27, as soon as the proposed corporate action is taken, or upon receipt of a payment demand, the corporation shall pay each dissenter who complied with section 13.23 the amount the corporation estimates to be the fair value of his shares, plus accrued interest.

(b) The payment must be accompanied by:

(1) the corporation's balance sheet as of the end of a fiscal year ending not more than 16 months before the date of payment, an income statement for that year, a statement of changes in shareholders' equity for that year, and the latest available interim financial statements, if any;

(2) a statement of the corporation's estimate of the fair value of the shares;

(3) an explanation of how the interest was calculated;

(4) a statement of the dissenter's right to demand payment under section 13.28; and

(5) a copy of this chapter.

§ 13.26 Failure to Take Action

(a) If the corporation does not take the proposed action within 60 days after the date set for demanding payment and depositing share certificates, the corporation shall return the deposited certificates and release the transfer restrictions imposed on uncertificated shares.

(b) If after returning deposited certificates and releasing transfer restrictions, the corporation takes the proposed action, it must send a new dissenters' notice under section 13.22 and repeat the payment demand procedure.

§ 13.27 After-Acquired Shares

(a) A corporation may elect to withhold payment required by section 13.25 from a dissenter unless he was the beneficial owner of the shares before the date set forth in the dissenters' notice as the date of the first announcement to news media or to shareholders of the terms of the proposed corporate action.

(b) To the extent the corporation elects to withhold payment under subsection (a), after taking the proposed corporate action, it shall estimate the fair value of the shares, plus accrued interest, and shall pay this amount to each dissenter who agrees to accept it in full satisfaction of his demand. The corporation shall send with its offer a statement of its estimate of the fair value of the shares, an explanation of how the interest was calculated, and a statement of the dissenter's right to demand payment under section 13.28.

§ 13.28 Procedure If Shareholder Dissatisfied with Payment or Offer

(a) A dissenter may notify the corporation in writing of his own estimate of the fair value of his shares and amount of interest due, and demand payment of his estimate (less any payment under section 13.25), or reject the corporation's offer under section 13.27 and demand payment of the fair value of his shares and interest due, if:

> (1) the dissenter believes that the amount paid under section 13.25 or offered under section 13.27 is less than the fair value of his shares or that the interest due is incorrectly calculated;

> (2) the corporation fails to make payment under section 13.25 within 60 days after the date set for demanding payment; or

> (3) the corporation, having failed to take the proposed action, does not return the deposited certificates or release the transfer restrictions imposed on uncertificated shares within 60 days after the date set for demanding payment.

(b) A dissenter waives his right to demand payment under this section unless he notifies the corporation of his demand in writing under subsection (a) within 30 days after the corporation made or offered payment for his shares.

Subchapter C. Judicial Appraisal of Shares

§ 13.30 Court Action

(a) If a demand for payment under section 13.28 remains unsettled, the corporation shall commence a proceeding within 60 days after receiving the payment demand and petition the court to determine the fair value of the shares and accrued interest. If the corporation does not commence the proceeding within the 60-day period, it shall pay each dissenter whose demand remains unsettled the amount demanded.

(b) The corporation shall commence the proceeding in the [name or describe] court of the county where a corporation's principal office (or, if none in this state, its registered office) is located. If the corporation is a foreign corporation without a registered office in this state, it shall commence the proceeding in the county in this state where the registered office of the domestic corporation merged with or whose shares were acquired by the foreign corporation was located.

(c) The corporation shall make all dissenters (whether or not residents of this state) whose demands remain unsettled parties to the proceeding as in an action against their shares and all parties must be served with a copy of the petition. Nonresidents may be served by registered or certified mail or by publication as provided by law.

(d) The jurisdiction of the court in which the proceeding is commenced under subsection (b) is plenary and exclusive. The court may appoint one or more persons as appraisers to receive evidence and recommend decision on the question of fair value. The appraisers have the powers described in the order appointing them, or in any amendment to it. The dissenters are entitled to the same discovery rights as parties in other civil proceedings.

(e) Each dissenter made a party to the proceeding is entitled to judgment (1) for the amount, if any, by which the court finds the fair value of his shares, plus interest, exceeds the amount paid by the corporation or (2) for the fair value, plus accrued interest, of his after-acquired shares for which the corporation elected to withhold payment under section 13.27.

§ 13.31 Court Costs and Counsel Fees

(a) The court in an appraisal proceeding commenced under section 13.30 shall determine all costs of the proceeding, including the reasonable compensation and expenses of appraisers appointed by the court. The court shall assess the costs against the corporation, except that the court may assess costs against all or some of the dissenters, in amounts the court finds equitable, to the extent the court finds dissenters acted arbitrarily, vexatiously, or not in good faith in demanding payment under section 13.28.

(b) The court may also assess the fees and expenses of counsel and experts for the respective parties, in amounts the court finds equitable:

> (1) against the corporation and in favor of any or all dissenters if the court finds the corporation did not substantially comply with the requirements of sections 13.20 through 13.28; or

> (2) against either the corporation or a dissenter, in favor of any other party, if the court finds that the party against whom the fees and expenses are assessed acted arbitrarily, vexatiously, or not in good faith with respect to the rights provided by this chapter.

(c) If the court finds that the services of counsel for any dissenter were of substantial benefit to other dissenters similarly situated, and that the fees for those services should not be assessed against the corporation, the court may award to these counsel reasonable fees to be paid out of the amounts awarded the dissenters who were benefited.

Chapter 14.
DISSOLUTION

Subchapter A. Voluntary Dissolution

§ 14.01 Dissolution by Incorporators or Initial Directors

A majority of the incorporators or initial directors of a corporation that has not issued shares or has not commenced business may dissolve the corporation by delivering to the secretary of state for filing articles of dissolution that set forth:

> (1) the name of the corporation;

> (2) the date of its incorporation;

> (3) either (i) that none of the corporation's shares has been issued or (ii) that the corporation has not commenced business;

> (4) that no debt of the corporation remains unpaid;

> (5) that the net assets of the corporation remaining after winding up have been distributed to the shareholders, if shares were issued; and

> (6) that a majority of the incorporators or initial directors authorized the dissolution.

§ 14.02 Dissolution by Board of Directors and Shareholders

(a) A corporation's board of directors may propose dissolution for submission to the shareholders.

(b) For a proposal to dissolve to be adopted:

> (1) the board of directors must recommend dissolution to the shareholders unless the board of directors determines that because of conflict of interest or other special circumstances it should make no recommendation and communicates the basis for its determination to the shareholders; and

> (2) the shareholders entitled to vote must approve the proposal to dissolve as provided in subsection (e).

(c) The board of directors may condition its submission of the proposal for dissolution on any basis.

(d) The corporation shall notify each shareholder, whether or not entitled to vote, of the proposed shareholders' meeting in accordance with section 7.05. The notice must also state that the purpose, or one of the purposes, of the meeting is to consider dissolving the corporation.

(e) Unless the articles of incorporation or the board of directors (acting pursuant to subsection (c)) require a greater vote or a vote by voting groups, the proposal to dissolve to be adopted must be approved by a majority of all the votes entitled to be cast on that proposal.

§ 14.03 Articles of Dissolution

(a) At any time after dissolution is authorized, the corporation may dissolve by delivering to the secretary of state for filing articles of dissolution setting forth:

(1) the name of the corporation;

(2) the date dissolution was authorized;

(3) if dissolution was approved by the shareholders;

(i) the number of votes entitled to be cast on the proposal to dissolve; and

(ii) either the total number of votes cast for and against dissolution or the total number of undisputed votes cast for dissolution and a statement that the number cast for dissolution was sufficient for approval.

(4) If voting by voting groups is required, the information required by subparagraph (3) shall be separately provided for each voting group entitled to vote separately on the plan to dissolve.

(b) A corporation is dissolved upon the effective date of its articles of dissolution.

§ 14.04 Revocation of Dissolution

(a) A corporation may revoke its dissolution within 120 days of its effective date.

(b) Revocation of dissolution must be authorized in the same manner as the dissolution was authorized unless that authorization permitted revocation by action by the board of directors alone, in which event the board of directors may revoke the dissolution without shareholder action.

(c) After the revocation of dissolution is authorized, the corporation may revoke the dissolution by delivering to the secretary of state for filing articles of revocation of dissolution, together with a copy of its articles of dissolution, that set forth:

(1) the name of the corporation;

(2) the effective date of the dissolution that was revoked;

(3) the date that the revocation of dissolution was authorized;

(4) if the corporation's board of directors (or incorporators) revoked the dissolution, a statement to that effect;

(5) if the corporation's board of directors revoked a dissolution authorized by the shareholders, a statement that revocation was permitted by action by the board of directors alone pursuant to that authorization; and

(6) if shareholder action was required to revoke the dissolution, the information required by section 14.03(3) or (4).

(d) Unless a delayed effective date is specified, revocation of dissolution is effective when articles of revocation of dissolution are filed.

(e) When the revocation of dissolution is effective, it relates back to and takes effect as of the effective date of the dissolution and the corporation resumes carrying on its business as if dissolution had never occurred.

§ 14.05 Effect of Dissolution

(a) A dissolved corporation continues its corporate existence but may not carry on any business except that appropriate to wind up and liquidate its business and affairs, including:

(1) collecting its assets;

(2) disposing of its properties that will not be distributed in kind to its shareholders;

(3) discharging or making provision for discharging its liabilities;

(4) distributing its remaining property among its shareholders according to their interests; and

(5) doing every other act necessary to wind up and liquidate its business and affairs.

(b) Dissolution of a corporation does not:

(1) transfer title to the corporation's property;

(2) prevent transfer of its shares or securities, although the authorization to dissolve may provide for closing the corporation's share transfer records;

(3) subject its directors or officers to standards of conduct different from those prescribed in chapter 8;

(4) change quorum or voting requirements for its board of directors or shareholders; change provisions for selection, resignation, or removal of its directors or officers or both; or change provisions for amending its bylaws;

(5) prevent commencement of a proceeding by or against the corporation in its corporate name;

(6) abate or suspend a proceeding pending by or against the corporation on the effective date of dissolution; or

(7) terminate the authority of the registered agent of the corporation.

§ 14.06 Known Claims against Dissolved Corporation

(a) A dissolved corporation may dispose of the known claims against it by following the procedure described in this section.

(b) The dissolved corporation shall notify its known claimants in writing of the dissolution at any time after its effective date. The written notice must:

(1) describe information that must be included in a claim;

(2) provide a mailing address where a claim may be sent;

(3) state the deadline, which may not be fewer than 120 days from the effective date of the written notice, by which the dissolved corporation must receive the claim; and

(4) state that the claim will be barred if not received by the deadline.

(c) A claim against the dissolved corporation is barred:

(1) if a claimant who was given written notice under subsection (b) does not deliver the claim to the dissolved corporation

by the deadline;

(2) if a claimant whose claim was rejected by the dissolved corporation does not commence a proceeding to enforce the claim within 90 days from the effective date of the rejection notice.

(d) For purposes of this section, "claim" does not include a contingent liability or a claim based on an event occurring after the effective date of dissolution.

§ 14.07 **Unknown Claims against Dissolved Corporation**

(a) A dissolved corporation may also publish notice of its dissolution and request that persons with claims against the corporation present them in accordance with the notice.

(b) The notice must:

(1) be published one time in a newspaper of general circulation in the county where the dissolved corporation's principal office (or, if none in this state, its registered office) is or was last located;

(2) describe the information that must be included in a claim and provide a mailing address where the claim may be sent; and

(3) state that a claim against the corporation will be barred unless a proceeding to enforce the claim is commenced within five years after the publication of the notice.

(c) If the dissolved corporation publishes a newspaper notice in accordance with subsection (b), the claim of each of the following claimants is barred unless the claimant commences a proceeding to enforce the claim against the dissolved corporation within five years after the publication date of the newspaper notice:

(1) a claimant who did not receive written notice under section 14.06;

(2) a claimant whose claim was timely sent to the dissolved corporation but not acted on;

(3) a claimant whose claim is contingent or based on an event occurring after the effective date of dissolution.

(d) A claim may be enforced under this section:

(1) against the dissolved corporation, to the extent of its undistributed assets; or

(2) if the assets have been distributed in liquidation, against a shareholder of the dissolved corporation to the extent of his pro rata share of the claim or the corporate assets distributed to him in liquidation, whichever is less, but a shareholder's total liability for all claims under this section may not exceed the total amount of assets distributed to him.

Subchapter B. Administrative Dissolution

§ 14.20 **Grounds for Administrative Dissolution**

The secretary of state may commence a proceeding under section 14.21 to administratively dissolve a corporation if:

(1) the corporation does not pay within 60 days after they are due any franchise taxes or penalties imposed by this Act or other law;

(2) the corporation does not deliver its annual report to the secretary of state within 60 days after it is due;

(3) the corporation is without a registered agent or registered office in this state for 60 days or more;

(4) the corporation does not notify the secretary of state within 60 days that its registered agent or registered office has been changed, that its registered agent has resigned, or that its registered office has been discontinued; or

(5) the corporation's period of duration stated in its articles of incorporation expires.

§ 14.21 **Procedure for and Effect of Administrative Dissolution**

(a) If the secretary of state determines that one or more grounds exist under section 14.20 for dissolving a corporation, he shall serve the corporation with written notice of his determination under section 5.04.

(b) If the corporation does not correct each ground for dissolution or demonstrate to the reasonable satisfaction of the secretary of state that each ground determined by the secretary of state does not exist within 60 days after service of the notice is perfected under section 5.04, the secretary of state shall administratively dissolve the corporation by signing a certificate of dissolution that recites the ground or grounds for dissolution and its effective date. The secretary of state shall file the original of the certificate and serve a copy on the corporation under section 5.04.

(c) A corporation administratively dissolved continues its corporate existence but may not carry on any business except that necessary to wind up and liquidate its business and affairs under section 14.05 and notify claimants under sections 14.06 and 14.07.

(d) The administrative dissolution of a corporation does not terminate the authority of its registered agent.

§ 14.22 **Reinstatement Following Administrative Dissolution**

(a) A corporation administratively dissolved under section 14.21 may apply to the secretary of state for reinstatement within two years after the effective date of dissolution. The application must:

(1) recite the name of the corporation and the effective date of its administrative dissolution;

(2) state that the ground or grounds for dissolution either did not exist or have been eliminated;

(3) state that the corporation's name satisfies the requirements of section 4.01; and

(4) contain a certificate from the [taxing authority] reciting that all taxes owed by the corporation have been paid.

(b) If the secretary of state determines that the application contains the information required by subsection (a) and that the information is correct, he shall cancel the certificate of dissolution and prepare a certificate of reinstatement that recites his determination and the effective date of reinstatement, file the original of the certificate, and serve a copy on the corporation under section 5.04.

(c) When the reinstatement is effective, it relates back to and takes effect as of the effective date of the administrative dissolution and the corporation resumes carrying on its business as if the administrative dissolution had never occurred.

§ 14.23 **Appeal from Denial of Reinstatement**

(a) If the secretary of state denies a corporation's application for reinstatement following administrative dissolution, he shall serve the corporation under section 5.04 with a written notice that explains the reason or reasons for denial.

(b) The corporation may appeal the denial of reinstatement to the [name or describe] court within 30 days after service of the notice of denial is perfected. The corporation appeals by petitioning the court to set aside the dissolution and attaching to the petition copies of the secretary of state's certificate of dissolution, the corporation's application for reinstatement, and the secretary of state's notice of denial.

(c) The court may summarily order the secretary of state to reinstate the dissolved corporation or may take other action the court considers appropriate.

(d) The court's final decision may be appealed as in other civil proceedings.

Subchapter C. Judicial Dissolution

§ 14.30 Grounds for Judicial Dissolution

The [name or describe court or courts] may dissolve a corporation:

(1) in a proceeding by the attorney general if it is established that:

(i) the corporation obtained its articles of incorporation through fraud; or

(ii) the corporation has continued to exceed or abuse the authority conferred upon it by law;

(2) in a proceeding by a shareholder if it is established that:

(i) the directors are deadlocked in the management of the corporate affairs, the shareholders are unable to break the deadlock, and irreparable injury to the corporation is threatened or being suffered, or the business and affairs of the corporation can no longer be conducted to the advantage of the shareholders generally, because of the deadlock;

(ii) the directors or those in control of the corporation have acted, are acting, or will act in a manner that is illegal, oppressive, or fraudulent;

(iii) the shareholders are deadlocked in voting power and have failed, for a period that includes at least two consecutive annual meeting dates, to elect successors to directors whose terms have expired; or

(iv) the corporate assets are being misapplied or wasted;

(3) in a proceeding by a creditor if it is established that:

(i) the creditor's claim has been reduced to judgment, the execution on the judgment returned unsatisfied, and the corporation is insolvent; or

(ii) the corporation has admitted in writing that the creditor's claim is due and owing and the corporation is insolvent; or

(4) in a proceeding by the corporation to have its voluntary dissolution continued under court supervision.

§ 14.31 Procedure for Judicial Dissolution

(a) Venue for a proceeding by the attorney general to dissolve a corporation lies in [name the county or counties]. Venue for a proceeding brought by any other party named in section 14.30 lies in the county where a corporation's principal office (or, if none in this state, its registered office) is or was last located.

(b) It is not necessary to make shareholders parties to a proceeding to dissolve a corporation unless relief is sought against them

individually.

(c) A court in a proceeding brought to dissolve a corporation may issue injunctions, appoint a receiver or custodian pendente lite with all powers and duties the court directs, take other action required to preserve the corporate assets wherever located, and carry on the business of the corporation until a full hearing can be held.

§ 14.32 Receivership or Custodianship

(a) A court in a judicial proceeding brought to dissolve a corporation may appoint one or more receivers to wind up and liquidate, or one or more custodians to manage, the business and affairs of the corporation. The court shall hold a hearing, after notifying all parties to the proceeding and any interested persons designated by the court, before appointing a receiver or custodian. The court appointing a receiver or custodian has exclusive jurisdiction over the corporation and all its property wherever located.

(b) The court may appoint an individual or a domestic or foreign corporation (authorized to transact business in this state) as a receiver or custodian. The court may require the receiver or custodian to post bond, with or without sureties, in an amount the court directs.

(c) The court shall describe the powers and duties of the receiver or custodian in its appointing order, which may be amended from time to time. Among other powers:

(1) the receiver (i) may dispose of all or any part of the assets of the corporation wherever located, at a public or private sale, if authorized by the court; and (ii) may sue and defend in his own name as receiver of the corporation in all courts of this state;

(2) the custodian may exercise all of the powers of the corporation, through or in place of its board of directors or officers, to the extent necessary to manage the affairs of the corporation in the best interests of its shareholders and creditors.

(d) The court during a receivership may redesignate the receiver a custodian, and during a custodianship may redesignate the custodian a receiver, if doing so is in the best interests of the corporation, its shareholders, and creditors.

(e) The court from time to time during the receivership or custodianship may order compensation paid and expense disbursements or reimbursements made to the receiver or custodian and his counsel from the assets of the corporation or proceeds from the sale of the assets.

§ 14.33 Decree of Dissolution

(a) If after a hearing the court determines that one or more grounds for judicial dissolution described in section 14.30 exist, it may enter a decree dissolving the corporation and specifying the effective date of the dissolution, and the clerk of the court shall deliver a certified copy of the decree to the secretary of state, who shall file it.

(b) After entering the decree of dissolution, the court shall direct the winding up and liquidation of the corporation's business and affairs in accordance with section 14.05 and the notification of claimants in accordance with sections 14.06 and 14.07.

Subchapter D. Miscellaneous

§ 14.40 Deposit with State Treasurer

Assets of a dissolved corporation that should be transferred to a creditor, claimant, or shareholder of the corporation who cannot be found or who is not competent to receive them shall be reduced to cash and deposited with the state treasurer or other appropriate state official for safekeeping. When the creditor, claimant, or shareholder furnishes satisfactory proof of entitlement to the amount deposited, the state treasurer or other appropriate state official shall pay him or his representative that amount.

[Chapter 15.
FOREIGN CORPORATIONS. OMITTED.]

Chapter 16.
RECORDS AND REPORTS

Subchapter A. Records

§ 16.01 Corporate Records

(a) A corporation shall keep as permanent records minutes of all meetings of its shareholders and board of directors, a record of all actions taken by the shareholders or board of directors without a meeting, and a record of all actions taken by a committee of the board of directors in place of the board of directors on behalf of the corporation.

(b) A corporation shall maintain appropriate accounting records.

(c) A corporation or its agent shall maintain a record of its shareholders, in a form that permits preparation of a list of the names and addresses of all shareholders, in alphabetical order by class of shares showing the number and class of shares held by each.

(d) A corporation shall maintain its records in written form or in another form capable of conversion into written form within a reasonable time.

(e) A corporation shall keep a copy of the following records at its principal office:

(1) its articles or restated articles of incorporation and all amendments to them currently in effect;

(2) its bylaws or restated bylaws and all amendments to them currently in effect;

(3) resolutions adopted by its board of directors creating one or more classes or series of shares, and fixing their relative rights, preferences, and limitations, if shares issued pursuant to those resolutions are outstanding;

(4) the minutes of all shareholders' meetings, and records of all action taken by shareholders without a meeting, for the past three years;

(5) all written communications to shareholders generally within the past three years, including the financial statements furnished for the past three years under section 16.20;

(6) a list of the names and business addresses of its current directors and officers; and

(7) its most recent annual report delivered to the secretary of state under section 16.22.

§ 16.02 Inspection of Records by Shareholders

(a) Subject to section 16.03(c), a shareholder of a corporation is entitled to inspect and copy, during regular business hours at the corporation's principal office, any of the records of the corporation described in section 16.01(e) if he gives the corporation written notice of his demand at least five business days before the date on which he wishes to inspect and copy.

(b) A shareholder of a corporation is entitled to inspect and copy, during regular business hours at a reasonable location specified by the corporation, any of the following records of the corporation if the shareholder meets the requirements of subsection (c) and gives the corporation written notice of his demand at least five business days before the date on which he wishes to inspect and copy:

(1) excerpts from minutes of any meeting of the board of directors, records of any action of a committee of the board of directors while acting in place of the board of directors on behalf of the corporation, minutes of any meeting of the shareholders, and records of action taken by the shareholders or board of directors without a meeting, to the extent not subject to inspection under section 16.02(a);

(2) accounting records of the corporation; and

(3) the record of shareholders.

(c) A shareholder may inspect and copy the records identified in subsection (b) only if:

(1) his demand is made in good faith and for a proper purpose;

(2) he describes with reasonable particularity his purpose and the records he desires to inspect; and

(3) the records are directly connected with his purpose.

(d) The right of inspection granted by this section may not be abolished or limited by a corporation's articles of incorporation or bylaws.

(e) This section does not affect:

(1) the right of a shareholder to inspect records under section 7.20 or, if the shareholder is in litigation with the corporation, to the same extent as any other litigant;

(2) the power of a court, independently of this Act, to compel the production of corporate records for examination.

(f) For purposes of this section, "shareholder" includes a beneficial owner whose shares are held in a voting trust or by a nominee on his behalf.

§ 16.03 Scope of Inspection Right

(a) A shareholder's agent or attorney has the same inspection and copying rights as the shareholder he represents.

(b) The right to copy records under section 16.02 includes, if reasonable, the right to receive copies made by photographic, xerographic, or other means.

(c) The corporation may impose a reasonable charge, covering the costs of labor and material, for copies of any documents provided to the shareholder. The charge may not exceed the estimated cost of production or reproduction of the records.

(d) The corporation may comply with a shareholder's demand to inspect the record of shareholders under section 16.02(b)(3) by providing him with a list of its shareholders that was compiled no earlier than the date of the shareholder's demand.

§ 16.04 Court-Ordered Inspection

(a) If a corporation does not allow a shareholder who complies with section 16.02(a) to inspect and copy any records required by that subsection to be available for inspection, the [name or describe court] of the county where the corporation's principal office (or, if none in this state, its registered office) is located may summarily order inspection and copying of the records demanded at the corporation's expense upon application of the shareholder.

(b) If a corporation does not within a reasonable time allow a shareholder to inspect and copy any other record, the shareholder who complies with section 16.02(b) and (c) may apply to the [name or describe court] in the county where the corporation's principal office (or, if none in this state, its registered office) is located for an order to permit inspection and copying of the records demanded. The court shall dispose of an application under this subsection on an expedited basis.

(c) If the court orders inspection and copying of the records demanded, it shall also order the corporation to pay the shareholder's costs (including reasonable counsel fees) incurred to obtain the order unless the corporation proves that it refused inspection in good faith because it had a reasonable basis for doubt about the right of the shareholder to inspect the records demanded.

(d) If the court orders inspection and copying of the records demanded, it may impose reasonable restrictions on the use or distribution of the records by the demanding shareholder.

Subchapter B. Reports

§ 16.20 Financial Statements for Shareholders

(a) A corporation shall furnish its shareholders annual financial statements, which may be consolidated or combined statements of the corporation and one or more of its subsidiaries, as appropriate, that include a balance sheet as of the end of the fiscal year, an income statement for that year, and a statement of changes in shareholders' equity for the year unless that information appears elsewhere in the financial statements. If financial statements are prepared for the corporation on the basis of generally accepted accounting principles, the annual financial statements must also be prepared on that basis.

(b) If the annual financial statements are reported upon by a public accountant, his report must accompany them. If not, the statements must be accompanied by a statement of the president or the person responsible for the corporation's accounting records:

(1) stating his reasonable belief whether the statements were prepared on the basis of generally accepted accounting principles and, if not, describing the basis of preparation; and

(2) describing any respects in which the statements were not prepared on a basis of accounting consistent with the statements prepared for the preceding year.

(c) A corporation shall mail the annual financial statements to each shareholder within 120 days after the close of each fiscal year. Thereafter, on written request from a shareholder who was not mailed the statements, the corporation shall mail him the latest financial statements.

§ 16.21 Other Reports to Shareholders

(a) If a corporation indemnifies or advances expenses to a director under section 8.51, 8.52, 8.53, or 8.54 in connection with a proceeding by or in the right of the corporation, the corporation shall report the indemnification or advance in writing to the shareholders with or before the notice of the next shareholders' meeting.

(b) If a corporation issues or authorizes the issuance of shares for promissory notes or for promises to render services in the future, the corporation shall report in writing to the shareholders the number of shares authorized or issued, and the consideration received by the corporation, with or before the notice of the next shareholders' meeting.

§ 16.22 Annual Report for Secretary of State

(a) Each domestic corporation, and each foreign corporation authorized to transact business in this state, shall deliver to the secretary of state for filing an annual report that sets forth:

(1) the name of the corporation and the state or country under whose law it is incorporated;

(2) the address of its registered office and the name of its registered agent at that office in this state;

(3) the address of its principal office;

(4) the names and business addresses of its directors and principal officers;

(5) a brief description of the nature of its business;

(6) the total number of authorized shares, itemized by class and series, if any, within each class; and

(7) the total number of issued and outstanding shares, itemized by class and series, if any, within each class.

(b) Information in the annual report must be current as of the date the annual report is executed on behalf of the corporation.

(c) The first annual report must be delivered to the secretary of state between January 1 and April 1 of the year following the calendar year in which a domestic corporation was incorporated or a foreign corporation was authorized to transact business. Subsequent annual reports must be delivered to the secretary of state between January 1 and April 1 of the following calendar years.

(d) If an annual report does not contain the information required by this section, the secretary of state shall promptly notify the reporting domestic or foreign corporation in writing and return the report to it for correction. If the report is corrected to contain the information required by this section and delivered to the secretary of state within 30 days after the effective date of notice, it is deemed to be timely filed.

Chapter 17.
TRANSITION PROVISIONS

§ 17.01 Application to Existing Domestic Corporations

This Act applies to all domestic corporations in existence on its effective date that were incorporated under any general statute of this state providing for incorporation of corporations for profit if power to amend or repeal the statute under which the corporation was incorporated was reserved.

§ 17.02 Application to Qualified Foreign Corporations

A foreign corporation authorized to transact business in this state on the effective date of this Act is subject to this Act but is not required to obtain a new certificate of authority to transact business under this Act.

§ 17.03 Saving Provision

(a) Except as provided in subsection (b), the repeal of a statute by this Act does not affect:

(1) the operation of the statute or any action taken under it before its repeal;

(2) any ratification, right, remedy, privilege, obligation, or liability acquired, accrued, or incurred under the statute before its repeal;

(3) any violation of the statute, or any penalty, forfeiture, or punishment incurred because of the violation, before its repeal;

(4) any proceeding, reorganization, or dissolution commenced under the statute before its repeal, and the proceeding, reorganization, or dissolution may be completed in accordance with the statute as if it had not been repealed.

(b) If a penalty or punishment imposed for violation of a statute repealed by this Act is reduced by this Act, the penalty or punishment if not already imposed shall be imposed in accordance with this Act.

§ 17.04 Severability

If any provision of this Act or its application to any person or circumstance is held invalid by a court of competent jurisdiction, the invalidity does not affect other provisions or applications of the Act that can be given effect without the invalid provision or application, and to this end the provisions of the Act are severable.

§ 17.05 Repeal

The following laws and parts of laws are repealed: [to be inserted].

§ 17.06 Effective Date

This Act takes effect _____.

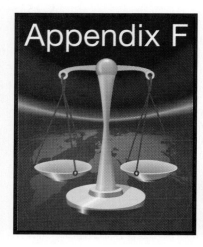

Appendix F

Restatement (Second) of Torts (Excerpts)

Section 402 A. Special liability of seller of product for physical harm to user or consumer.

(1) One who sells any product in a defective condition unreasonably dangerous to the consumer or to his property is subject to liability for physical harm thereby caused to the ultimate user or consumer, or to his property, if

(a) the seller is engaged in the business of selling such a product, and

(b) it is expected to and does reach the user or consumer without substantial change in the condition in which it is sold.

(2) The rule stated in Subsection (1) applies although

(a) the seller has exercised all possible care in the preparation and sale of his product, and

(b) the user or consumer has not bought the product from or entered into any contractual relation with the seller.

Section 402 B. Misrepresentation by seller of chattels to consumer.

One engaged in the business of selling chattels who, by advertising, labels, or otherwise, makes to the public a misrepresentation of a material fact concerning the character or quality of a chattel sold by him is subject to liability for physical harm to a consumer of the chattel caused by justifiable reliance upon the misrepresentation, even though

(a) it is not made fraudulently or negligently, and

(b) the consumer has not bought the chattel from or entered into any contractual relations with the seller.

Sherman Antitrust Act of 1890 (Excerpts)

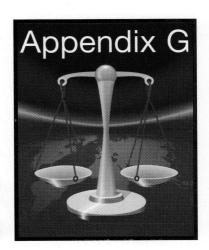

Section. 1 Every contract, combination in the form of trust or otherwise, or conspiracy, in restraint of trade or commerce among the several States, or with foreign nations, is hereby declared to be illegal. Every person who shall make any such contract or engage in any such combination or conspiracy shall be deemed guilty of a felony, and, on conviction thereof, shall be punished by fine not exceeding one million dollars if a corporation, or, if any other person, one hundred thousand dollars or by imprisonment not exceeding three years, or by both said punishments in the discretion of the court.

Section 2. Every person who shall monopolize, or attempt to monopolize, or conspire with any other person or persons, to monopolize any part of the trade or commerce among the several States, or with foreign nations, shall be deemed guilty of a felony, and, on conviction thereof, shall be punished by fine not exceeding one million dollars if a corporation, or, if any other person, one hundred thousand dollars or by imprisonment not exceeding three years, or by both said punishments, in the discretion of the court.

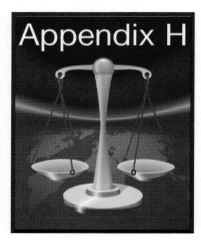

Appendix H

Securities Act of 1933 (Excerpts)

Definitions

Section 2. When used in this title, unless the context requires—

(1) The term "security" means any note, stock, treasury stock, bond, debenture, evidence of indebtedness, certificate of interest or participation in any profit-sharing agreement, collateral-trust certificate, preorganization certificate or subscription, transferable share, investment contract, voting-trust certificate, certificate of deposit for a security, fractional undivided interest in oil, gas, or other mineral rights, any put, call, straddle, option, or privilege on any security, certificate of deposit, or group or index of securities (including any interest therein or based on the value thereof), or any put, call, straddle, option, or privilege entered into on a national securities exchange relating to foreign currency, or, in general, any interest or participation in, temporary or interim certificate for, receipt for, guarantee of, or warrant or right to subscribe to or purchase, any of the foregoing.

Exempted Securities

Section 3. (a) Except as hereinafter expressly provided the provisions of this title shall not apply to any of the following classes of securities:

* * * *

(2) Any security issued or guaranteed by the United States or any territory thereof, or by the District of Columbia, or by any State of the United States, or by any political subdivision of a State or Territory, or by any public instrumentality of one or more States or Territories, or by any person controlled or supervised by and acting as an instrumentality of the Government of the United States pursuant to authority granted by the Congress of the United States; or any certificate of deposit for any of the foregoing; or any security issued or guaranteed by any bank; or any security issued by or representing an interest in or a direct obligation of a Federal Reserve Bank. * * *

(3) Any note, draft, bill of exchange, or banker's acceptance which arises out of a current transaction or the proceeds of which have been or are to be used for current transactions, and which has a maturity at the time of issuance of not exceeding nine months, exclusive of days of grace, or any renewal thereof the maturity of which is likewise limited;

(4) Any security issued by a person organized and operated exclusively for religious, educational, benevolent, fraternal, charitable, or reformatory purposes and not for pecuniary profit, and no part of the net earnings of which inures to the benefit of any person, private stockholder, or individual;

* * * *

(11) Any security which is a part of an issue offered and sold only to persons resident within a single State or Territory, where the issuer of such security is a person resident and doing business within, or, if a corporation, incorporated by and doing business within, such State or Territory.

(b) The Commission may from time to time by its rules and regulations and subject to such terms and conditions as may be described therein, add any class of securities to the securities exempted as provided in this section, if it finds that the enforcement of this title with respect to such securities is not necessary in the public interest and for the protection of investors by reason of the small amount involved or the limited character of the public offering; but no issue of securities shall be exempted under this subsection where the aggregate amount at which such issue is offered to the public exceeds $5,000,000.

Exempted Transactions

Section 4. The provisions of section 5 shall not apply to—

(1) transactions by any person other than an issuer, underwriter, or dealer.

(2) transactions by an issuer not involving any public offering.

(3) transactions by a dealer (including an underwriter no longer acting as an underwriter in respect of the security involved in such transactions), except—

(A) transactions taking place prior to the expiration of forty days after the first date upon which the security was bona fide offered to the public by the issuer or by or through an underwriter.

(B) transactions in a security as to which a registration statement has been filed taking place prior to the expiration of forty days after the effective date of such registration statement or prior to the expiration of forty days after the first date upon which the security was bona fide offered to the public by the issuer or by or through an underwriter after such effective date, whichever is later (excluding in the computation of such forty days any time during which a stop order issued under section 8 is in effect as to the security), or such shorter period as the Commission may specify by rules and regulations or order, and

(C)   transactions as to the securities constituting the whole or a part of an unsold allotment to or subscription by such dealer as a participant in the distribution of such securities by the issuer or by or through an underwriter.

With respect to transactions referred to in clause (B), if securities of the issuer have not previously been sold pursuant to an earlier effective registration statement the applicable period, instead of forty days, shall be ninety days, or such shorter period as the Commission may specify by rules and regulations or order.

(4) brokers' transactions, executed upon customers' orders on any exchange or in the over-the-counter market but not the solicitation of such orders.

*   *   *   *

(6) transactions involving offers or sales by an issuer solely to one or more accredited investors, if the aggregate offering price of an issue of securities offered in reliance on this paragraph does not exceed the amount allowed under Section 3(b) of this title, if there is no advertising or public solicitation in connection with the transaction by the issuer or anyone acting on the issuer's behalf, and if the issuer files such notice with the Commission as the Commission shall prescribe.

Prohibitions Relating to Interstate Commerce and the Mails

Section 5. (a) Unless a registration statement is in effect as to a security, it shall be unlawful for any person, directly or indirectly—

(1) to make use of any means or instruments of transportation or communication in interstate commerce or of the mails to sell such security through the use or medium of any prospectus or otherwise; or

(2) to carry or cause to be carried through the mails or in interstate commerce, by any means or instruments of transportation, any such security for the purpose of sale or for delivery after sale.

(b) It shall be unlawful for any person, directly or indirectly—

(1) to make use of any means or instruments of transportation or communication in interstate commerce or of the mails to carry or transmit any prospectus relating to any security with respect to which a registration statement has been filed under this title, unless such prospectus meets the requirements of section 10, or

(2) to carry or to cause to be carried through the mails or in interstate commerce any such security for the purpose of sale or for delivery after sale, unless accompanied or preceded by a prospectus that meets the requirements of subsection (a) of section 10.

(c) It shall be unlawful for any person, directly, or indirectly, to make use of any means or instruments of transportation or communication in interstate commerce or of the mails to offer to sell or offer to buy through the use or medium of any prospectus or otherwise any security, unless a registration statement has been filed as to such security, or while the registration statement is the subject of a refusal order or stop order or (prior to the effective date of the registration statement) any public proceeding of examination under section 8.

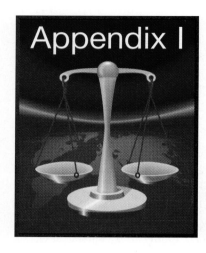

Securities Exchange Act of 1934 (Excerpts)

Definitions and Application of Title

Section 3. (a) When used in this title, unless the context otherwise requires—

* * * *

(4) The term "broker" means any person engaged in the business of effecting transactions in securities for the account of others, but does not include a bank.

(5) The term "dealer" means any person engaged in the business of buying and selling securities for his own account, through a broker or otherwise, but does not include a bank, or any person insofar as he buys or sells securities for his own account, either individually or in some fiduciary capacity, but not as part of a regular business.

* * * *

(7) The term "director" means any director of a corporation or any person performing similar functions with respect to any organization, whether incorporated or unincorporated.

(8) The term "issuer" means any person who issues or proposes to issue any security; except that with respect to certificates of deposit for securities, voting-trust certificates, or collateral-trust certificates, or with respect to certificates of interest or shares in an unincorporated investment trust not having a board of directors or the fixed, restricted management, or unit type, the term "issuer" means the person or persons performing the acts and assuming the duties of depositor or manager pursuant to the provisions of the trust or other agreement or instrument under which such securities are issued; and except that with respect to equipment-trust certificates or like securities, the term "issuer" means the person by whom the equipment or property is, or is to be, used.

(9) The term "person" means a natural person, company, government, or political subdivision, agency, or instrumentality of a government.

Regulation of the Use of Manipulative and Deceptive Devices

Section 10. It shall be unlawful for any person, directly or indirectly, by the use of any means or instrumentality of interstate commerce or of the mails, or of any facility of any national securities exchange—

(a) To effect a short sale, or to use or employ any stop-loss order in connection with the purchase or sale, of any security registered on a national securities exchange, in contravention of such rules and regulations as the Commission may prescribe as necessary or appropriate in the public interest or for the protection of investors.

(b) To use or employ, in connection with the purchase or sale of any security registered on a national securities exchange or any security not so registered, any manipulative or deceptive device or contrivance in contravention of such rules and regulations as the Commission may prescribe as necessary or appropriate in the public interest or for the protection of investors.

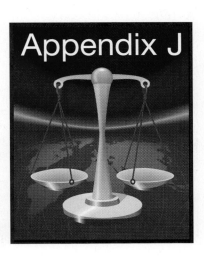

Appendix J

Title VII of the Civil Rights Act of 1964 (Excerpts)

Section 703. Unlawful Employment Practices. (a) It shall be an unlawful employment practice for an employer—

(1) to fail or refuse to hire or to discharge any individual, or otherwise to discriminate against any individual with respect to his compensation, terms, conditions, or privileges of employment, because of such individual's race, color, religion, sex, or national origin; or

(2) to limit, segregate, or classify his employees or applicants for employment in any way which would deprive or tend to deprive any individual of employment opportunities or otherwise adversely affect his status as an employee, because of such individual's race, color, religion, sex, or national origin.

(b) It shall be an unlawful employment practice for an employment agency to fail or refuse to refer for employment, or otherwise to discriminate against, any individual because of his race, color, religion, sex, or national origin, or to classify or refer for employment any individual on the basis or his race, color, religion, sex, or national origin.

(c) It shall be an unlawful employment practice for a labor organization—

(1) to exclude or to expel from its membership, or otherwise to discriminate against, any individual because of his race, color, religion, sex, or national origin;

(2) to limit, segregate, or classify its membership or applicants for membership, or to classify or fail or refuse to refer for employment any individual, in any way which would deprive or tend to deprive any individual of employment opportunities, or would limit such employment opportunities or otherwise adversely affect his status as an employee or as an applicant for employment, because of such individual's race, color, religion, sex, or national origin; or

(3) to cause or attempt to cause an employer to discriminate against an individual in violation of this section.

(d) It shall be an unlawful employment practice for any employer, labor organization, or joint labor-management committee controlling apprenticeship or other training or retraining, including on-the-job training programs to discriminate against any individual because of his race, color, religion, sex, or national origin in admission to, or employment in, any program established to provide apprenticeship or other training.

(e) Notwithstanding any other provision of this subchapter—

(1) it shall not be an unlawful employment practice for an employer to hire and employ employees, for an employment agency to classify, or refer for employment any individual, for a labor organization to classify its membership or to classify or refer for employment any individual, or for an employer, labor organization, or joint labor-management committee controlling apprenticeship or other training or retraining programs to admit or employ any individual in any such program, on the basis of his religion, sex, or national origin in those certain instances where religion, sex, or national origin is a bona fide occupational qualification reasonably necessary to the normal operation of that particular business or enterprise, and

(2) it shall not be an unlawful employment practice for a school, college, university, or other educational institution or institution of learning to hire and employ employees of a particular religion if such school, college, university, or other educational institution or institution of learning is, in whole or in substantial part, owned, supported, controlled, or managed by a particular religion or by a particular religious corporation, association, or society, or if the curriculum of such school, college, university, or other educational institution or institution of learning is directed toward the propagation of a particular religion.

(f) As used in this subchapter, the phrase "unlawful employment practice" shall not be deemed to include any action or measure taken by an employer, labor organization, joint labor-management committee, or employment agency with respect to an individual who is a member of the Communist Party of the United States or of any other organization required to register as a Communist-action or Communist-front organization. * * *

(g) Notwithstanding any other provision of this subchapter, it shall not be an unlawful employment practice for an employer to fail or refuse to hire and employ any individual for any position, for an employer to discharge any individual from any position, or for an employment agency to fail or refuse to refer any individual for employment in any position, or for a labor organization to fail or refuse to refer any individual for employment in any position, if—

(1) the occupancy of such position, or access to the premises in or upon which any part of the duties of such position is performed or is to be performed, is subject to any requirement imposed in the

interest of the national security of the United States * * * and

(2) such individual has not fulfilled or has ceased to fulfill that requirement.

(h) Notwithstanding any other provision of this subchapter, it shall not be an unlawful employment practice for an employer to apply different standards of compensation, or different terms, conditions, or privileges of employment pursuant to a bona fide seniority or merit system, or a system which measures earnings by quantity or quality of production or to employees who work in different locations, provided that such differences are not the result of an intention to discriminate because of race, color, religion, sex, or national origin, nor shall it be an unlawful employment practice for an employer to give and act upon the results of any professionally developed ability test provided that such test, its administration or action upon the results is not designed, intended or used to discriminate because of race, color, religion, sex, or national origin. * * *

(j) Nothing contained in this subchapter shall be interpreted to require any employer, employment agency, labor organization, or joint labor-management committee subject to this subchapter to grant preferential treatment to any individual or to any group because of the race, color, religion, sex, or national origin of such individual or group on account of an imbalance which may exist with respect to the total number or percentage of persons of any race, color, religion, sex, or national origin employed by any employer, referred or classified for employment by any employment agency or labor organization, or admitted to, or employed in, any apprenticeship or other training program, in comparison with the total number or percentage of persons of such race, color, religion, sex, or national origin in any community, State, section, or other area, or in the available work force in any community, State, section, or other area.

* * * *

Section 704. Other Unlawful Employment Practices. (a) It shall be an unlawful employment practice for an employer to discriminate against any of his employees or applicants for employment, for an employment agency, or joint labor-management committee controlling apprenticeship or other training or retraining, including on-the-job training programs, to discriminate against any individual, or for a labor organization to discriminate against any member thereof or applicant for membership, because he has opposed any practice made an unlawful employment practice by this subchapter, or because he has made a charge, testified, assisted, or participated in any manner in an investigation, proceeding, or hearing under this subchapter.

(b) It shall be an unlawful employment practice for an employer, labor organization, employment agency, or joint labor-management committee controlling apprenticeship or other training or retraining, including on-the-job training programs, to print or publish or cause to be printed or published any notice or advertisement relating to employment by such an employer or membership or any classification or referral for employment by such a labor organization, or relating to any classification or referral for employment by such an employment agency, or relating to admission to, or employment in, any program established to provide apprenticeship or other training by such a joint labor-management committee, indicating any preference, limitation, specification, or discrimination, based on race, color, religion, sex, or national origin, except that such a notice or advertisement may indicate a preference, limitation, specification, or discrimination based on religion, sex or national origin when religion, sex, or national origin is a bona fide occupational qualification for employment.

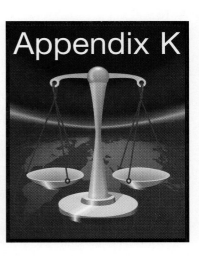

Appendix K

Americans with Disabilities Act of 1990 (Excerpts)

TITLE I—EMPLOYMENT

Sec. 101. Definitions.

As used in this title: * * *

(8) **Qualified individual with a disability.**—The term "qualified individual with a disability" means an individual with a disability who, with or without reasonable accommodation, can perform the essential functions of the employment position that such individual holds or desires. For the purposes of this title, consideration shall be given to the employer's judgment as to what functions of a job are essential, and if an employer has prepared a written description before advertising or interviewing applicants for the job, this description shall be considered evidence of the essential functions of the job.

(9) **Reasonable accommodation.**—The term "reasonable accommodation" may include—

(A) making existing facilities used by employees readily accessible to and usable by individuals with disabilities; and

(B) job restructuring, part-time or modified work schedules, reassignment to a vacant position, acquisition or modification of equipment or devices, appropriate adjustment or modifications of examinations, training materials or policies, the provision of qualified readers or interpreters, and other similar accommodations for individuals with disabilities.

(10) **Undue Hardship.**—

(A) **In general.**—The term "undue hardship" means an action requiring significant difficulty or expense, when considered in light of the factors set forth in subparagraph (B).

(B) **Factors to be considered.**—In determining whether an accommodation would impose an undue hardship on a covered entity, factors to be considered include—

(i) the nature and cost of accommodation needed under this Act;

(ii) the overall financial resources of the facility or facilities involved in the provision of the reasonable accommodation; the number of persons employed at such facility; the effect on expenses and resources, or the impact otherwise of such accommodation upon the operation of the facility;

(iii) the overall financial resources of the covered entity; the overall size of the business of a covered entity with respect to the number of its employees; the number, type, and location of its facilities; and

(iv) the type of operation or operations of the covered entity, including the composition, structure, and functions of the workforce of such entity; the geographic separateness, administrative, or fiscal relationship of the facility or facilities in question to the covered entity.

Sec. 102. Discrimination.

(a) **General Rule.**—No covered entity shall discriminate against a qualified individual with a disability because of the disability of such individual in regard to job application procedures, the hiring, advancement, or discharge of employees, employee compensation, job training, and other terms, conditions, and privileges of employment.

(b) **Construction.**—As used in subsection (a), the term "discriminate" includes—

(1) limiting, segregating, or classifying a job applicant or employee in a way that adversely affects the opportunities or status of such applicant or employee because of the disability of such applicant or employee;

(2) participating in a contractual or other arrangement or relationship that has the effect of subjecting a covered entity's qualified applicant or employee with a disability to the discrimination prohibited by this title (such relationship includes a relationship with an employment or referral agency, labor union, an organization providing fringe benefits to an employee of the covered entity, or an organization providing training and apprenticeship programs);

(3) utilizing standards, criteria, or methods of administration—

(A) that have the effect of discrimination on the basis of disability; or

(B) that perpetuate the discrimination of others who are subject to common administrative control;

(4) excluding or otherwise denying equal jobs or benefits to a qualified individual because of the known disability of an individual with whom the qualified individual is known to have a relationship or association;

(5)

(A) not making reasonable accommodations to the known physical or mental limitations of an otherwise qualified individual with a disability who is an applicant or employee, unless such covered entity can demonstrate that the accommodation would impose an undue hardship on the operation of the business of such covered entity; or

(B) denying employment opportunities to a job applicant or employee who is an otherwise qualified individual with a disability, if such denial is based on the need of such covered entity to make reasonable accommodation to the physical or mental impairments of the employee or applicant;

(6) using qualification standards, employment tests or other selection criteria that screen out or tend to screen out an individual with a disability or a class of individuals with disabilities unless the standard, test or other selection criteria, as used by the covered entity, is shown to be job-related for the position in question and is consistent with business necessity; and

(7) failing to select and administer tests concerning employment in the most effective manner to ensure that, when such test is administered to a job applicant or employee who has a disability that impairs sensory, manual, or speaking skills, such test results accurately reflect the skills, aptitude, or whatever other factor of such applicant or employee that such test purports to measure, rather than reflecting the impaired sensory, manual, or speaking skills of such employee or applicant (except where such skills are the factors that the test purports to measure). * * *

Sec. 104. Illegal Use of Drugs and Alcohol. * * *

(b) **Rules of Construction.**—Nothing in subsection (a) shall be construed to exclude as a qualified individual with a disability an individual who—

(1) has successfully completed a supervised drug rehabilitation program and is no longer engaging in the illegal use of drugs, or has otherwise been rehabilitated successfully and is no longer engaging in such use;

(2) is participating in a supervised rehabilitation program and is no longer engaging in such use; or

(3) is erroneously regarded as engaging in such use, but is not engaging in such use; except that it shall not be a violation of this Act for a covered entity to adopt or administer reasonable policies or procedures, including but not limited to drug testing, designed to ensure that an individual described in paragraph (1) or (2) is no longer engaging in the illegal use of drugs. * * *

Sec. 107. Enforcement.

(a) **Powers, Remedies, and Procedures.**—The powers, remedies, and procedures set forth in sections 705, 706, 707, 709, and 710 of the Civil Rights Act of 1964 (42 U.S.C. 2000e-4, 2000e-5, 2000e-6, 2000e-8, and 2000e-9) shall be the powers, remedies, and procedures this title provides to the Commission, to the Attorney General, or to any person alleging discrimination on the basis of disability in violation of any provision of this Act, or regulations promulgated under section 106, concerning employment.

(b) **Coordination.**—The agencies with enforcement authority for actions which allege employment discrimination under this title and under the Rehabilitation Act of 1973 shall develop procedures to ensure that administrative complaints filed under this title and under the Rehabilitation Act of 1973 are dealt with in a manner that avoids duplication of effort and prevents imposition of inconsistent or conflicting standards for the same requirements under this title and the Rehabilitation Act of 1973. The Commission, the Attorney General, and the Office of Federal Contract Compliance Programs shall establish such coordinating mechanisms (similar to provisions contained in the joint regulations promulgated by the Commission and the Attorney General at part 42 of title 28 and part 1691 of title 29, Code of Federal Regulations, and the Memorandum of Understanding between the Commission and the Office of Federal Contract Compliance Programs dated January 16, 1981 (46 Fed. Reg. 7435, January 23, 1981)) in regulations implementing this title and Rehabilitation Act of 1973 not later than 18 months after the date of enactment of this Act.

Sec. 108. Effective Date.

This title shall become effective 24 months after the date of enactment.

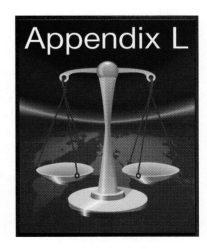

Civil Rights Act of 1991 (Excerpts)

Section 3. Purposes.

The purposes of this Act are—

(1) to provide appropriate remedies for intentional discrimination and unlawful harassment in the workplace;

(2) to codify the concepts of "business necessity" and "job related" enunciated by the Supreme Court in *Griggs v. Duke Power Co.*, 401 U.S. 424 (1971), and in the other Supreme Court decisions prior to *Wards Cove Packing Co. v. Atonio*, 490 U.S. 642 (1989);

(3) to confirm statutory authority and provide statutory guidelines for the adjudication of disparate impact suits under title VII of the Civil Rights Act of 1964 (42 U.S.C. 2000e *et seq.*); and

(4) to respond to recent decisions of the Supreme Court by expanding the scope of relevant civil rights statutes in order to provide adequate protection to victims of discrimination.

Section 101. Prohibition against All Racial Discrimination in the Making and Enforcement of Contracts.

Section 1977 of the Revised Statutes (42 U.S.C. 1981) is amended * * * by adding at the end the following new subsections:

(b) For purposes of this section, the term "make and enforce contracts" includes the making, performance, modification, and termination of contracts, and the enjoyment of all benefits, privileges, terms, and conditions of the contractual relationship.

(c) The rights protected by this section are protected against impairment by nongovernmental discrimination and impairment under color of State law.

Section 102. Damages in Cases of Intentional Discrimination.

The Revised Statutes are amended by inserting after section 1977 (42 U.S.C.1981) the following new section:

Section 1977A. Damages in Cases of Intentional Discrimination in Employment.

(a) Right of Recovery.—

(1) Civil Rights.—In an action brought by a complaining party under section 706 or 717 of the Civil Rights Act of 1964 (42 U.S.C. 2000e-5) against a respondent who engaged in unlawful intentional discrimination (not an employment practice that is unlawful because of its disparate impact) prohibited under section 703, 704, or 717 of the Act (42 U.S.C. 2000e-2

or 2000e-3), and provided that the complaining party cannot recover under section 1977 of the Revised Statutes (42 U.S.C.1981), the complaining party may recover compensatory and punitive damages as allowed in subsection (b), in addition to any relief authorized by section 706(g) of the Civil Rights Act of 1964, from the respondent.

* * * *

(b) Compensatory and Punitive Damages.—

(1) Determination of Punitive Damages.—A complaining party may recover punitive damages under this section against a respondent (other than a government, government agency or political subdivision) if the complaining party demonstrates that the respondent engaged in a discriminatory practice or discriminatory practices with malice or with reckless indifference to the federally protected rights of an aggrieved individual.

(2) Exclusions from Compensatory Damages.—Compensatory damages awarded under this section shall not include backpay, interest on backpay, or any other type of relief authorized under section 706(g) of the Civil Rights Act of 1964.

(3) Limitations.—The sum of the amount of compensatory damages awarded under this section for future pecuniary losses, emotional pain, suffering, inconvenience, mental anguish, loss of enjoyment of life, and other nonpecuniary losses, and the amount of punitive damages awarded under this section, shall not exceed, for each complaining party—

(A) in the case of a respondent who has more than 14 and fewer than 101 employees in each of 20 or more calendar weeks in the current or preceding calendar year, $50,000;

(B) in the case of a respondent who has more than 100 and fewer than 201 employees in each of 20 or more calendar weeks in the current or preceding calendar year, $100,000; and

(C) in the case of a respondent who has more than 200 and fewer than 501 employees in each of 20 or more calendar weeks in the current or preceding calendar year, $200,000; and

(D) in the case of a respondent who has more than 500 employees in each of 20 or more calendar weeks in the current or preceding calendar year, $300,000.

*   *   *   *

Section 105. Burden of Proof in Disparate Impact Cases.

(a) Section 703 of the Civil Rights Act of 1964 (42 U.S.C. 2000e-2) is amended by adding at the end the following new [subsections to 703(k)(1)]—

(A) An unlawful employment practice based on disparate impact is established under this title only if—

(i) a complaining party demonstrates that a respondent uses a particular employment practice that causes a disparate impact on the basis of race, color, religion, sex, or national origin and the respondent fails to demonstrate that the challenged practice is job related for the position in question and consistent with business necessity; or

(ii) the complaining party makes the demonstration described in subparagraph (C) with respect to an alternative employment practice and the respondent refuses to adopt such alternative employment practice.

*   *   *   *

(C) The demonstration referred to by subparagraph (A)(ii) shall be in accordance with the law as it existed on June 4, 1989, with respect to the concept of "alternative employment practice."

*   *   *   *

Section 107. Clarifying Prohibition against Impermissible Consideration of Race, Color, Religion, Sex, or National Origin in Employment Practices.

(a) In General.—Section 703 of the Civil Rights Act of 1964 (42 U.S.C. 2000e-2) (as amended by sections 105 and 106) is further amended by adding at the end the following new subsection:

(m) Except as otherwise provided in this title, an unlawful employment practice is established when the complaining party demonstrates that race, color, religion, sex, or national origin was a motivating factor for any employment practice, even though other factors also motivated the practice.

*   *   *   *

Section 109. Protection of Extraterritorial Employment.

(a) Definition of Employee.—Section 701(f) of the Civil Rights Act of 1964 (42 U.S.C. 2000e(f)) and section 101(4) of the Americans with Disabilities Act of 1990 (42 U.S.C. 12111(4)) are each amended by adding at the end the following: "With respect to employment in a foreign country, such term includes an individual who is a citizen of the United States."

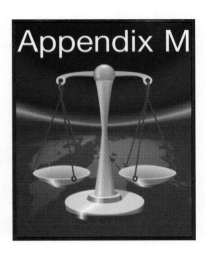

United Nations Convention on Contracts For the International Sale of Goods (Excerpts)

Part I. SPHERE OF APPLICATION AND GENERAL PROVISIONS

* * * *

Chapter II—General Provisions

* * * *

Article 8

(1) For the purposes of this Convention statements made by and other conduct of a party are to be interpreted according to his intent where the other party knew or could not have been unaware what that intent was.

(2) If the preceding paragraph is not applicable, statements made by and other conduct of a party are to be interpreted according to the understanding that a reasonable person of the same kind as the other party would have had in the same circumstances.

(3) In determining the intent of a party or the understanding a reasonable person would have had, due consideration is to be given to all relevant circumstances of the case including the negotiations, any practices which the parties have established between themselves, usages and any subsequent conduct of the parties.

Article 9

(1) The parties are bound by any usage to which they have agreed and by any practices which they have established between themselves.

(2) The parties are considered, unless otherwise agreed, to have impliedly made applicable to their contract or its formation a usage of which the parties knew or ought to have known and which in international trade is widely known to, and regularly observed by, parties to contracts of the type involved in the particular trade concerned.

* * * *

Article 11

A contract of sale need not be concluded in or evidenced by writing and is not subject to any other requirement as to form. It may be proved by any means, including witnesses.

* * * *

Part II. FORMATION OF THE CONTRACT

Article 14

(1) A proposal for concluding a contract addressed to one or more specific persons constitutes an offer if it is sufficiently definite and indicates the intention of the offeror to be bound in case of acceptance. A proposal is sufficiently definite if it indicates the goods and expressly or implicitly fixes or makes provision for determining the quantity and the price.

(2) A proposal other than one addressed to one or more specific persons is to be considered merely as an invitation to make offers, unless the contrary is clearly indicated by the person making the proposal.

Article 15

(1) An offer becomes effective when it reaches the offeree.

(2) An offer, even if it is irrevocable, may be withdrawn if the withdrawal reaches the offeree before or at the same time as the offer.

Article 16

(1) Until a contract is concluded an offer may be revoked if the revocation reaches the offeree before he has dispatched an acceptance.

(2) However, an offer cannot be revoked:

  (a) If it indicates, whether by stating a fixed time for acceptance or otherwise, that it is irrevocable; or

  (b) If it was reasonable for the offeree to rely on the offer as being irrevocable and the offeree has acted in reliance on the offer.

Article 17

An offer, even if it is irrevocable, is terminated when a rejection reaches the offeror.

Article 18

(1) A statement made by or other conduct of the offeree indicating assent to an offer is an acceptance. Silence or inactivity does not in itself amount to acceptance.

(2) An acceptance of an offer becomes effective at the moment the indication of assent reaches the offeror. An acceptance is not effec-

tive if the indication of assent does not reach the offeror within the time he has fixed or, if no time is fixed, within a reasonable time, due account being taken of the circumstances of the transaction, including the rapidity of the means of communication employed by the offeror. An oral offer must be accepted immediately unless the circumstances indicate otherwise.

(3) However, if, by virtue of the offer or as a result of practices which the parties have established between themselves or of usage, the offeree may indicate assent by performing an act, such as one relating to the dispatch of the goods or payment of the price, without notice to the offeror, the acceptance is effective at the moment the act is performed, provided that the act is performed within the period of time laid down in the preceding paragraph.

Article 19

(1) A reply to an offer which purports to be an acceptance but contains additions, limitations or other modifications is a rejection of the offer and constitutes a counter-offer.

(2) However, a reply to an offer which purports to be an acceptance but contains additional or different terms which do not materially alter the terms of the offer constitutes an acceptance, unless the offeror, without undue delay, objects orally to the discrepancy or dispatches a notice to that effect. If he does not so object, the terms of the contract are the terms of the offer with the modifications contained in the acceptance.

(3) Additional or different terms relating, among other things, to the price, payment, quality and quantity of the goods, place and time of delivery, extent of one party's liability to the other or the settlement of disputes are considered to alter the terms of the offer materially.

* * * *

Article 22

An acceptance may be withdrawn if the withdrawal reaches the offeror before or at the same time as the acceptance would have become effective.

* * * *

Part III. SALE OF GOODS

Chapter I—General Provisions

Article 25

A breach of contract committed by one of the parties is fundamental if it results in such detriment to the other party as substantially to deprive him of what he is entitled to expect under the contract, unless the party in breach did not foresee and a reasonable person of the same kind in the same circumstances would not have foreseen such a result.

* * * *

Article 28

If, in accordance with the provisions of this Convention, one party is entitled to require performance of any obligation by the other party, a court is not bound to enter a judgment for specific performance unless the court would do so under its own law in respect of similar contracts of sale not governed by this Convention.

Article 29

(1) A contract may be modified or terminated by the mere agreement of the parties.

(2) A contract in writing which contains a provision requiring any modification or termination by agreement to be in writing may not be otherwise modified or terminated by agreement. However, a party may be precluded by his conduct from asserting such a provision to the extent that the other party has relied on that conduct.

Chapter II—Obligations of the Seller

* * * *

Section II. Conformity of the Goods and Third Party Claims

Article 35

(1) The seller must deliver goods which are of the quantity, quality and description required by the contract and which are contained or packaged in the manner required by the contract.

(2) Except where the parties have agreed otherwise, the goods do not conform with the contract unless they:

(a) Are fit for the purposes for which goods of the same description would ordinarily be used;

(b) Are fit for any particular purpose expressly or impliedly made known to the seller at the time of the conclusion of the contract, except where the circumstances show that the buyer did not rely, or that it was unreasonable for him to rely, on the seller's skill and judgment;

(c) Possess the qualities of goods which the seller has held out to the buyer as a sample or model;

(d) Are contained or packaged in the manner usual for such goods or, where there is no such manner, in a manner adequate to preserve and protect the goods.

(3) The seller is not liable under subparagraphs (a) to (d) of the preceding paragraph for any lack of conformity of the goods if at the time of the conclusion of the contract the buyer knew or could not have been unaware of such lack of conformity.

* * * *

Article 64

(1) The seller may declare the contract avoided:

(a) If the failure by the buyer to perform any of his obligations under the contract or this Convention amounts to a fundamental breach of contract; or

(b) If the buyer does not, within the additional period of time fixed by the seller in accordance with paragraph (1) of article 63, perform his obligation to pay the price or take delivery of the goods, or if he declares that he will not do so within the period so fixed.

(2) However, in cases where the buyer has paid the price, the seller loses the right to declare the contract avoided unless he does so:

(a) In respect of late performance by the buyer, before the seller has become aware that performance has been rendered; or

(b) In respect of any breach other than late performance by the buyer, within a reasonable time:

(i) After the seller knew or ought to have known of the breach; or

(ii) After the expiration of any additional period of time fixed by the seller in accordance with paragraph (1) of article 63, or after the buyer has declared that he will not perform his obligations within such an additional period.

* * * *

Chapter IV—Passing of Risk

* * * *

Article 67

(1) If the contract of sale involves carriage of the goods and the seller is not bound to hand them over at a particular place, the risk passes to the buyer when the goods are handed over to the first carrier for transmission to the buyer in accordance with the contract of sale. If the seller is bound to hand the goods over to a carrier at a particular place, the risk does not pass to the buyer until the goods are handed over to the carrier at that place. The fact that the seller is authorized to retain documents controlling the disposition of the goods does not affect the passage of the risk.

(2) Nevertheless, the risk does not pass to the buyer until the goods are clearly identified to the contract, whether by markings on the goods, by shipping documents, by notice given to the buyer or otherwise.

* * * *

Chapter V—Provisions Common to the Obligations of the Seller and of the Buyer

Section I. **Anticipatory Breach and Instalment Contracts**

Article 71

(1) A party may suspend the performance of his obligations if, after the conclusion of the contract, it becomes apparent that the other party will not perform a substantial part of his obligations as a result of:

(a) A serious deficiency in his ability to perform or in his creditworthiness; or

(b) His conduct in preparing to perform or in performing the contract.

(2) If the seller has already dispatched the goods before the grounds described in the preceding paragraph become evident, he may prevent the handing over of the goods to the buyer even though the buyer holds a document which entitles him to obtain them. The present paragraph relates only to the rights in the goods as between the buyer and the seller.

(3) A party suspending performance, whether before or after dispatch of the goods, must immediately give notice of the suspension to the other party and must continue with performance if the other party provides adequate assurance of his performance.

Article 72

(1) If prior to the date for performance of the contract it is clear that one of the parties will commit a fundamental breach of contract, the other party may declare the contract avoided.

(2) If time allows, the party intending to declare the contract avoided must give reasonable notice to the other party in order to permit him to provide adequate assurance of his performance.

(3) The requirements of the preceding paragraph do not apply if the other party has declared that he will not perform his obligations.

Article 73

(1) In the case of a contract for delivery of goods by instalments, if the failure of one party to perform any of his obligations in respect of any instalment constitutes a fundamental breach of contract with respect to that instalment, the other party may declare the contract avoided with respect to that instalment.

(2) If one party's failure to perform any of his obligations in respect of any instalment gives the other party good grounds to conclude that a fundamental breach of contract will occur with respect to future instalments, he may declare the contract avoided for the future, provided that he does so within a reasonable time.

(3) A buyer who declares the contract avoided in respect of any delivery may, at the same time, declare it avoided in respect of deliveries already made or of future deliveries if, by reason of their interdependence, those deliveries could not be used for the purpose contemplated by the parties at the time of the conclusion of the contract.

Section II. **Damages**

Article 74

Damages for breach of contract by one party consist of a sum equal to the loss, including loss of profit, suffered by the other party as a consequence of the breach. Such damages may not exceed the loss which the party in breach foresaw or ought to have foreseen at the time of the conclusion of the contract, in the light of the facts and matters of which he then knew or ought to have known, as a possible consequence of the breach of contract.

Article 75

If the contract is avoided and if, in a reasonable manner and within a reasonable time after avoidance, the buyer has bought goods in replacement or the seller has resold the goods, the party claiming damages may recover the difference between the contract price and the price in the substitute transaction as well as any further damages recoverable under article 74.

Article 76

(1) If the contract is avoided and there is a current price for the goods, the party claiming damages may, if he has not made a purchase or resale under article 75, recover the difference between the price fixed by the contract and the current price at the time of avoidance as well as any further damages recoverable under article 74. If, however, the party claiming damages has avoided the contract after taking over the goods, the current price at the time of such taking over shall be applied instead of the current price at the time of avoidance.

(2) For the purposes of the preceding paragraph, the current price is the price prevailing at the place where delivery of the goods should have been made or, if there is no current price at that place, the price at such other place as serves as a reasonable substitute, making due allowance for differences in the cost of transporting the goods.

Article 77

A party who relies on a breach of contract must take such measures as are reasonable in the circumstances to mitigate the loss, including loss of profit, resulting from the breach. If he fails to take such measures, the party in breach may claim a reduction in the damages in the amount by which the loss should have been mitigated.

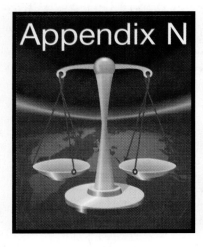

Appendix N

Spanish Equivalents for Important Legal Terms in English

Abandoned property: bienes abandonados
Acceptance: aceptación; consentimiento; acuerdo
Acceptor: aceptante
Accession: toma de posesión; aumento; accesión
Accommodation indorser: avalista de favor
Accommodation party: firmante de favor
Accord: acuerdo; convenio; arregio
Accord and satisfaction: transacción ejecutada
Act of state doctrine: doctrina de acto de gobierno
Administrative law: derecho administrativo
Administrative process: procedimiento o metódo administrativo
Administrator: administrador (-a)
Adverse possession: posesión de hecho susceptible de proscripción adquisitiva
Affirmative action: acción afirmativa
Affirmative defense: defensa afirmativa
After-acquired property: bienes adquiridos con posterioridad a un hecho dado
Agency: mandato; agencia
Agent: mandatorio; agente; representante
Agreement: convenio; acuerdo; contrato
Alien corporation: empresa extranjera
Allonge: hojas adicionales de endosos
Answer: contestación de la demande; alegato
Anticipatory repudiation: anuncio previo de las partes de su imposibilidad de cumplir con el contrato
Appeal: apelación; recurso de apelación
Appellate jurisdiction: jurisdicción de apelaciones

Appraisal right: derecho de valuación
Arbitration: arbitraje
Arson: incendio intencional
Articles of partnership: contrato social
Artisan's lien: derecho de retención que ejerce al artesano
Assault: asalto; ataque; agresión
Assignment of rights: transmisión; transferencia; cesión
Assumption of risk: no resarcimiento por exposición voluntaria al peligro
Attachment: auto judicial que autoriza el embargo; embargo

Bailee: depositario
Bailment: depósito; constitución en depósito
Bailor: depositante
Bankruptcy trustee: síndico de la quiebra
Battery: agresión; física
Bearer: portador; tenedor
Bearer instrument: documento al portador
Bequest or legacy: legado (de bienes muebles)
Bilateral contract: contrato bilateral
Bill of lading: conocimiento de embarque; carta de porte
Bill of Rights: declaración de derechos
Binder: póliza de seguro provisoria; recibo de pago a cuenta del precio
Blank indorsement: endoso en blanco
Blue sky laws: leyes reguladoras del comercio bursátil
Bond: título de crédito; garantía; caución
Bond indenture: contrato de emisión de bonos; contrato del amprésтito
Breach of contract: incumplimiento de contrato
Brief: escrito; resumen; informe

Burglary: violación de domicilio
Business judgment rule: regla de juicio comercial
Business tort: agravio comercial

Case law: ley de casos; derecho casuístico
Cashier's check: cheque de caja
Causation in fact: causalidad en realidad
Cease-and-desist order: orden para cesar y desistir
Certificate of deposit: certificado de depósito
Certified check: cheque certificado
Charitable trust: fideicomiso para fines benéficos
Chattel: bien mueble
Check: cheque
Chose in action: derecho inmaterial; derecho de acción
Civil law: derecho civil
Close corporation: sociedad de un solo accionista o de un grupo restringido de accionistas
Closed shop: taller agremiado (emplea solamente a miembros de un gremio)
Closing argument: argumento al final
Codicil: codicilo
Collateral: garantía; bien objeto de la garantía real
Comity: cortesía; cortesía entre naciones
Commercial paper: instrumentos negociables; documentos a valores commerciales
Common law: derecho consuetudinario; derecho común; ley común
Common stock: acción ordinaria
Comparative negligence: negligencia comparada
Compensatory damages: daños y perjuicios reales o compensatorios

Concurrent conditions: condiciones concurrentes
Concurrent jurisdiction: competencia concurrente de varios tribunales para entender en una misma causa
Concurring opinion: opinión concurrente
Condition: condición
Condition precedent: condición suspensiva
Condition subsequent: condición resolutoria
Confiscation: confiscación
Confusion: confusión; fusión
Conglomerate merger: fusión de firmas que operan en distintos mercados
Consent decree: acuerdo entre las partes aprobado por un tribunal
Consequential damages: daños y perjuicios indirectos
Consideration: consideración; motivo; contraprestación
Consolidation: consolidación
Constructive delivery: entrega simbólica
Constructive trust: fideicomiso creado por aplicación de la ley
Consumer protection law: ley para proteger el consumidor
Contract: contrato
Contract under seal: contrato formal o sellado
Contributory negligence: negligencia de la parte actora
Conversion: usurpación; conversión de valores
Copyright: derecho de autor
Corporation: sociedad anónima; corporación; persona juridica
Co-sureties: cogarantes
Counterclaim: reconvención; contrademanda
Counteroffer: contraoferta
Course of dealing: curso de transacciones
Course of performance: curso de cumplimiento
Covenant: pacto; garantía; contrato
Covenant not to sue: pacto or contrato a no demandar
Covenant of quiet enjoyment: garantía del uso y goce pacífico del inmueble
Creditors' composition agreement: concordato preventivo
Crime: crimen; delito; contravención
Criminal law: derecho penal
Cross-examination: contrainterrogatorio
Cure: cura; cuidado; derecho de remediar un vicio contractual
Customs receipts: recibos de derechos aduaneros

Damages: daños; indemnización por daños y perjuicios
Debit card: tarjeta de dé bito
Debtor: deudor
Debt securities: seguridades de deuda
Deceptive advertising: publicidad engañosa
Deed: escritura; título; acta translativa de domino
Defamation: difamación
Delegation of duties: delegación de obligaciones
Demand deposit: depósito a la vista
Depositions: declaración de un testigo fuera del tribunal
Devise: legado; deposición testamentaria (bienes inmuebles)
Directed verdict: veredicto según orden del juez y sin participación activa del jurado
Direct examination: interrogatorio directo; primer interrogatorio
Disaffirmance: repudiación; renuncia; anulación
Discharge: descargo; liberación; cumplimiento
Disclosed principal: mandante revelado
Discovery: descubrimiento; producción de la prueba
Dissenting opinion: opinión disidente
Dissolution: disolución; terminación
Diversity of citizenship: competencia de los tribunales federales para entender en causas cuyas partes intervinientes son cuidadanos de distintos estados
Divestiture: extinción premature de derechos reales
Dividend: dividendo
Docket: orden del día; lista de causas pendientes
Domestic corporation: sociedad local
Draft: orden de pago; letrade cambio
Drawee: girado; beneficiario
Drawer: librador
Duress: coacción; violencia

Easement: servidumbre
Embezzlement: desfalco; malversación
Eminent domain: poder de expropiación
Employment discrimination: discriminación en el empleo
Entrepreneur: empresario
Environmental law: ley ambiental
Equal dignity rule: regla de dignidad egual
Equity security: tipo de participación en una sociedad
Estate: propiedad; patrimonio; derecho
Estop: impedir; prevenir
Ethical issue: cuestión ética

Exclusive jurisdiction: competencia exclusiva
Exculpatory clause: cláusula eximente
Executed contract: contrato ejecutado
Execution: ejecución; cumplimiento
Executor: albacea
Executory contract: contrato aún no completamente consumado
Executory interest: derecho futuro
Express contract: contrato expreso
Expropriation: expropriación

Federal question: caso federal
Fee simple: pleno dominio; dominio absoluto
Fee simple absolute: dominio absoluto
Fee simple defeasible: dominio sujeta a una condición resolutoria
Felony: crimen; delito grave
Fictitious payee: beneficiario ficticio
Fiduciary: fiduciaro
Firm offer: oferta en firme
Fixture: inmueble por destino, incorporación a anexación
Floating lien: gravamen continuado
Foreign corporation: sociedad extranjera; U.S. sociedad constituída en otro estado
Forgery: falso; falsificación
Formal contract: contrato formal
Franchise: privilegio; franquicia; concesión
Franchisee: persona que recibe una concesión
Franchisor: persona que vende una concesión
Fraud: fraude; dolo; engaño
Future interest: bien futuro

Garnishment: embargo de derechos
General partner: socio comanditario
General warranty deed: escritura translativa de domino con garantía de título
Gift: donación
Gift *causa mortis*: donación por causa de muerte
Gift *inter vivos*: donación entre vivos
Good faith: buena fe
Good faith purchaser: comprador de buena fe

Holder: tenedor por contraprestación
Holder in due course: tenedor legítimo
Holographic will: testamento ológrafico
Homestead exemption laws: leyes que exceptúan las casas de familia de ejecución por duedas generales
Horizontal merger: fusión horizontal

Identification: identificación
Implied-in-fact contract: contrato implícito en realidad
Implied warranty: guarantía implícita
Implied warranty of merchantability: garantía implícita de vendibilidad
Impossibility of performance: imposibilidad de cumplir un contrato
Imposter: imposter
Incidental beneficiary: beneficiario incidental; beneficiario secundario
Incidental damages: daños incidentales
Indictment: auto de acusación; acusación
Indorsee: endorsatario
Indorsement: endoso
Indorser: endosante
Informal contract: contrato no formal; contrato verbal
Information: acusación hecha por el ministerio público
Injunction: mandamiento; orden de no innovar
Innkeeper's lien: derecho de retención que ejerce el posadero
Installment contract: contrato de pago en cuotas
Insurable interest: interés asegurable
Intended beneficiary: beneficiario destinado
Intentional tort: agravio; cuasi-delito intenciónal
International law: derecho internaciónal
Interrogatories: preguntas escritas sometidas por una parte a la otra o a un testigo
Inter vivos **trust:** fideicomiso entre vivos
Intestacy laws: leyes de la condición de morir intestado
Intestate: intestado
Investment company: compañia de inversiones
Issue: emisión

Joint tenancy: derechos conjuntos en un bien inmueble en favor del beneficiario sobreviviente
Judgment *n.o.v.*: juicio no obstante veredicto
Judgment rate of interest: interés de juicio
Judicial process: acto de procedimiento; proceso jurídico
Judicial review: revisión judicial
Jurisdiction: jurisdicción

Larceny: robo; hurto
Law: derecho; ley; jurisprudencia
Lease: contrato de locación; contrato de alquiler
Leasehold estate: bienes forales
Legal rate of interest: interés legal

Legatee: legatario
Letter of credit: carta de crédito
Levy: embargo; comiso
Libel: libelo; difamación escrita
Life estate: usufructo
Limited partner: comanditario
Limited partnership: sociedad en comandita
Liquidation: liquidación; realización
Lost property: objetos perdidos

Majority opinion: opinión de la mayoría
Maker: persona que realiza u ordena; librador
Mechanic's lien: gravamen de constructor
Mediation: mediación; intervención
Merger: fusión
Mirror image rule: fallo de reflejo
Misdemeanor: infracción; contravención
Mislaid property: bienes extraviados
Mitigation of damages: reducción de daños
Mortgage: hypoteca
Motion to dismiss: excepción parentoria
Mutual fund: fondo mutual

Negotiable instrument: instrumento negociable
Negotiation: negociación
Nominal damages: daños y perjuicios nominales
Novation: novación
Nuncupative will: testamento nuncupativo

Objective theory of contracts: teoria objetiva de contratos
Offer: oferta
Offeree: persona que recibe una oferta
Offeror: oferente
Order instrument: instrumento o documento a la orden
Original jurisdiction: jurisdicción de primera instancia
Output contract: contrato de producción

Parol evidence rule: regla relativa a la prueba oral
Partially disclosed principal: mandante revelado en parte
Partnership: sociedad colectiva; asociación; asociación de participación
Past consideration: causa o contraprestación anterior
Patent: patente; privilegio
Pattern or practice: muestra o práctica
Payee: beneficiario de un pago
Penalty: pena; penalidad
Per capita: por cabeza

Perfection: perfeción
Performance: cumplimiento; ejecución
Personal defenses: excepciones personales
Personal property: bienes muebles
Per stirpes: por estirpe
Plea bargaining: regateo por un alegato
Pleadings: alegatos
Pledge: prenda
Police powers: poders de policia y de prevención del crimen
Policy: póliza
Positive law: derecho positivo; ley positiva
Possibility of reverter: posibilidad de reversión
Precedent: precedente
Preemptive right: derecho de prelación
Preferred stock: acciones preferidas
Premium: recompensa; prima
Presentment warranty: garantía de presentación
Price discrimination: discriminación en los precios
Principal: mandante; principal
Privity: nexo jurídico
Privity of contract: relación contractual
Probable cause: causa probable
Probate: verificación; verificación del testamento
Probate court: tribunal de sucesiones y tutelas
Proceeds: resultados; ingresos
Profit: beneficio; utilidad; lucro
Promise: promesa
Promisee: beneficiario de una promesa
Promisor: promtente
Promissory estoppel: impedimento promisorio
Promissory note: pagaré; nota de pago
Promoter: promotor; fundador
Proximate cause: causa inmediata o próxima
Proxy: apoderado; poder
Punitive, or exemplary, damages: daños y perjuicios punitivos o ejemplares

Qualified indorsement: endoso con reservas
Quasi contract: contrato tácito o implícito
Quitclaim deed: acto de transferencia de una propiedad por finiquito, pero sin ninguna garantía sobre la validez del título transferido

Ratification: ratificación
Real property: bienes inmuebles
Reasonable doubt: duda razonable
Rebuttal: refutación
Recognizance: promesa; compromiso; reconocimiento

Recording statutes: leyes estatales sobre registros oficiales
Redress: reporacíon
Reformation: rectificación; reforma; corrección
Rejoinder: dúplica; contrarréplica
Release: liberación; renuncia a un derecho
Remainder: substitución; reversión
Remedy: recurso; remedio; reparación
Replevin: acción reivindicatoria; reivindicación
Reply: réplica
Requirements contract: contrato de suministro
Rescission: rescisión
Res judicata: cosa juzgada; res judicata
Respondeat superior: responsabilidad del mandante o del maestro
Restitution: restitución
Restrictive indorsement: endoso restrictivo
Resulting trust: fideicomiso implícito
Reversion: reversión; sustitución
Revocation: revocación; derogación
Right of contribution: derecho de contribución
Right of reimbursement: derecho de reembolso
Right of subrogation: derecho de subrogación
Right-to-work law: ley de libertad de trabajo
Robbery: robo
Rule 10b-5: Regla 10b-5

Sale: venta; contrato de compreventa
Sale on approval: venta a ensayo; venta sujeta a la aprobación del comprador
Sale or return: venta con derecho de devolución
Sales contract: contrato de compraventa; boleto de compraventa
Satisfaction: satisfacción; pago
Scienter: a sabiendas
S corporation: S corporación
Secured party: acreedor garantizado
Secured transaction: transacción garantizada
Securities: volares; titulos; seguridades
Security agreement: convenio de seguridad
Security interest: interés en un bien dado en garantía que permite a quien lo detenta venderlo en caso de incumplimiento
Service mark: marca de identificación de servicios

Shareholder's derivative suit: acción judicial entablada por un accionista en nombre de la sociedad
Signature: firma; rúbrica
Slander: difamación oral; calumnia
Sovereign immunity: immunidad soberana
Special indorsement: endoso especial; endoso a la orden de una person en particular
Specific performance: ejecución precisa, según los términos del contrato
Spendthrift trust: fideicomiso para pródigos
Stale check: cheque vencido
Stare decisis: acatar las decisiones, observar los precedentes
Statutory law: derecho estatutario; derecho legislado; derecho escrito
Stock: acciones
Stock warrant: certificado para la compra de acciones
Stop-payment order: orden de suspensión del pago de un cheque dada por el librador del mismo
Strict liability: responsabilidad unconditional
Summary judgment: fallo sumario

Tangible property: bienes corpóreos
Tenancy at will: inguilino por tiempo indeterminado (según la voluntad del propietario)
Tenancy by sufferance: posesión por tolerancia
Tenancy by the entirety: locación conyugal conjunta
Tenancy for years: inguilino por un término fijo
Tenancy in common: specie de copropiedad indivisa
Tender: oferta de pago; oferta de ejecución
Testamentary trust: fideicomiso testamentario
Testator: testador (-a)
Third party beneficiary contract: contrato para el beneficio del tercero-beneficiario
Tort: agravio; cuasi-delito
Totten trust: fideicomiso creado por un depósito bancario
Trade acceptance: letra de cambio aceptada
Trademark: marca registrada
Trade name: nombre comercial; razón social

Traveler's check: cheque del viajero
Trespass to land: ingreso no authorizado a las tierras de otro
Trespass to personal property: violación de los derechos posesorios de un tercero con respecto a bienes muebles
Trust: fideicomiso; trust

Ultra vires: ultra vires; fuera de la facultad (de una sociedad anónima)
Unanimous opinion: opinión unámine
Unconscionable contract or clause: contrato leonino; cláusula leonino
Underwriter: subscriptor; asegurador
Unenforceable contract: contrato que no se puede hacer cumplir
Unilateral contract: contrato unilateral
Union shop: taller agremiado; empresa en la que todos los empleados son miembros del gremio o sindicato
Universal defenses: defensas legitimas o legales
Usage of trade: uso comercial
Usury: usura

Valid contract: contrato válido
Venue: lugar; sede del proceso
Vertical merger: fusión vertical de empresas
Voidable contract: contrato anulable
Void contract: contrato nulo; contrato inválido, sin fuerza legal
Voir dire: examen preliminar de un testigo a jurado por el tribunal para determinar su competencia
Voting trust: fideicomiso para ejercer el derecho de voto

Waiver: renuncia; abandono
Warranty of habitability: garantía de habitabilidad
Watered stock: acciones diluídos; capital inflado
White-collar crime: crimen administrativo
Writ of attachment: mandamiento de ejecución; mandamiento de embargo
Writ of *certiorari*: auto de avocación; auto de certiorari
Writ of execution: auto ejecutivo; mandamiento de ejecutión
Writ of mandamus: auto de mandamus; mandamiento; orden judicial

Glossary

A

Abandoned property Property with which the owner has voluntarily parted, with no intention of recovering it.

Acceleration clause A clause that allows a payee or other holder of a time instrument to demand payment of the entire amount due, with interest, if a certain event occurs, such as a default in the payment of an installment when due.

Acceptance A voluntary act by the offeree that shows assent, or agreement, to the terms of an offer; may consist of words or conduct.

Acceptor A drawee that promises to pay an instrument when the instrument is presented later for payment.

Accession Occurs when an individual adds value to personal property by either labor or materials. In some situations, a person may acquire ownership rights in another's property through accession.

Accommodation party A person who signs an instrument for the purpose of lending his or her name as credit to another party on the instrument.

Accord and satisfaction An agreement for payment (or other performance) between two parties, one of whom has a right of action against the other. After the payment has been accepted or other performance has been made, the "accord and satisfaction" is complete and the obligation is discharged.

Accredited investors In the context of securities offerings, "sophisticated" investors, such as banks, insurance companies, investment companies, the issuer's executive officers and directors, and persons whose income or net worth exceeds certain limits.

Act of state doctrine A doctrine that provides that the judicial branch of one country will not examine the validity of public acts committed by a recognized foreign government within its own territory.

Actionable Capable of serving as the basis of a lawsuit.

Actual malice Real and demonstrable evil intent. In a defamation suit, a statement made about a public figure normally must be made with actual malice (with either knowledge of its falsity or a reckless disregard of the truth) for liability to be incurred.

Adhesion contract A "standard form" contract, such as that between a large retailer and a consumer, in which the stronger party dictates the terms.

Adjudicate To render a judicial decision. In the administrative process, the proceeding in which an administrative law judge hears and decides on issues that arise when an administrative agency charges a person or a firm with violating a law or regulation enforced by the agency.

Administrative agency A federal or state government agency established to perform a specific function. Administrative agencies are authorized by legislative acts to make and enforce rules to administer and enforce the acts.

Administrative law The body of law created by administrative agencies (in the form of rules, regulations, orders, and decisions) in order to carry out their duties and responsibilities.

Administrative law judge (ALJ) One who presides over an administrative agency hearing and who has the power to administer oaths, take testimony, rule on questions of evidence, and make determinations of fact.

Administrative process The procedure used by administrative agencies in the administration of law.

Administrator One who is appointed by a court to handle the probate (disposition) of a person's estate if that person dies intestate (without a valid will) or if the executor named in the will cannot serve.

Adverse possession The acquisition of title to real property by occupying it openly, without the consent of the owner, for a period of time specified by a state statute. The occupation must be actual, open, notorious, exclusive, and in opposition to all others, including the owner.

Affirmative action Job-hiring policies that give special consideration to members of protected classes in an effort to overcome present effects of past discrimination.

After-acquired property Property of the debtor that is acquired after the execution of a security agreement.

Agency A relationship between two parties in which one party (the agent) agrees to represent or act for the other (the principal).

Agent A person who agrees to represent or act for another, called the principal.

Agreement A meeting of two or more minds in regard to the terms of a contract; usually broken down into two events—an offer by one party to form a contract, and an acceptance of the offer by the person to whom the offer is made.

Alien corporation   A designation in the United States for a corporation formed in another country but doing business in the United States.

Alienation   In real property law, a term used to define the process of transferring land out of one's possession (thus "alienating" the land from oneself).

Allonge (pronounced uh-*lohnj*)   A piece of paper firmly attached to a negotiable instrument, upon which transferees can make indorsements if there is no room left on the instrument itself.

Alternative dispute resolution (ADR)   The resolution of disputes in ways other than those involved in the traditional judicial process. Negotiation, mediation, and arbitration are forms of ADR.

Answer   Procedurally, a defendant's response to the plaintiff's complaint.

Anticipatory repudiation   An assertion or action by a party indicating that he or she will not perform an obligation that the party is contractually obligated to perform at a future time.

Antitrust laws   Laws protecting commerce from unlawful restraints.

Appraisal right   The right of a dissenting shareholder, if he or she objects to an extraordinary transaction of the corporation (such as a merger or consolidation), to have his or her shares appraised and to be paid the fair value of his or her shares by the corporation.

Appropriation   In tort law, the use by one person of another person's name, likeness, or other identifying characteristic without permission and for the benefit of the user.

Arbitration   The settling of a dispute by submitting it to a disinterested third party (other than a court), who renders a decision that is (usually) legally binding.

Arbitration clause   A clause in a contract that provides that, in case of a dispute, the parties will submit the dispute to arbitration rather than litigate the dispute in court.

Arson   The malicious burning of another's dwelling. Some statutes have expanded this to include any real property regardless of ownership and the destruction of property by other means—for example, by explosion.

Articles of incorporation   The document filed with the appropriate governmental agency, usually the secretary of state, when a business is incorporated; state statutes usually prescribe what kind of information must be contained in the articles of incorporation.

Articles of partnership   A written agreement that sets forth each partner's rights and obligations with respect to the partnership.

Artisan's lien   A possessory lien given to a person who has made improvements and added value to another person's personal property as security for payment for services performed.

Assault   Any word or action intended to make another person fearful of immediate physical harm; a reasonably believable threat.

Assignment   The act of transferring to another all or part of one's rights arising under a contract.

Assumption of risk   A defense against negligence that can be used when the plaintiff is aware of a danger and voluntarily assumes the risk of injury from that danger.

Attachment   In the context of secured transactions, the process by which a security interest in the property of another becomes enforceable. In the context of judicial liens, a court-ordered seizure and taking into custody of property prior to the securing of a judgment for a past-due debt.

Attempted monopolization   Any actions by a firm to eliminate competition and gain monopoly power.

Automatic stay   In bankruptcy proceedings, the suspension of virtually all litigation and other action by creditors against the debtor or the debtor's property; the stay is effective the moment the debtor files a petition in bankruptcy.

Award   In the context of litigation, the amount of money awarded to a plaintiff in a civil lawsuit as damages. In the context of arbitration, the arbitrator's decision.

B

Bailee   One to whom goods are entrusted by a bailor. Under the UCC, a party who, by a bill of lading, warehouse receipt, or other document of title, acknowledges possession of goods and contracts.

Bailment   A situation in which the personal property of one person (a bailor) is entrusted to another (a bailee), who is obligated to return the bailed property to the bailor or dispose of it as directed.

Bailor   One who entrusts goods to a bailee.

Bait-and-switch advertising   Advertising a product at a very attractive price (the "bait") and then informing the consumer, once he or she is in the store, that the advertised product is either not available or is of poor quality; the customer is then urged to purchase ("switched" to) a more expensive item.

Bankruptcy court   A federal court of limited jurisdiction that handles only bankruptcy proceedings. Bankruptcy proceedings are governed by federal bankruptcy law.

Battery   The unprivileged, intentional touching of another.

Bearer   A person in the possession of an instrument payable to bearer or indorsed in blank.

Bearer instrument   Any instrument that is not payable to a specific person, including instruments payable to the bearer or to "cash."

Bequest   A gift by will of personal property (from the verb—to bequeath).

Beyond a reasonable doubt   The standard of proof used in criminal cases. If there is any reasonable doubt that a criminal defendant did not commit the crime with which he or she has been charged, then the verdict must be "not guilty."

Bilateral contract   A type of contract that arises when a promise is given in exchange for a return promise.

Bill of Rights   The first ten amendments to the U.S. Constitution.

Binder   A written, temporary insurance policy.

Binding authority   Any source of law that a court must follow when deciding a case. Binding authorities include constitutions, statutes, and regulations that govern the issue being decided, as well as court decisions that are controlling precedents within the jurisdiction.

Blank indorsement An indorsement that specifies no particular indorsee and that can consist of a mere signature. An order instrument that is indorsed in blank becomes a bearer instrument.

Blue laws State or local laws that prohibit the performance of certain types of commercial activities on Sunday.

Blue sky laws State laws that regulate the offer and sale of securities.

Bona fide occupational qualification (BFOQ) Identifiable characteristics reasonably necessary to the normal operation of a particular business. These characteristics can include gender, national origin, and religion, but not race.

Bond A certificate that evidences a corporate (or government) debt. It is a security that involves no ownership interest in the issuing entity.

Bond indenture A contract between the issuer of a bond and the bondholder.

Bounty payment A reward (payment) given to a person or persons who perform a certain service—such as informing legal authorities of illegal actions.

Breach of contract The failure, without legal excuse, of a promisor to perform the obligations of a contract.

Brief A formal legal document submitted by the attorney for the appellant or the appellee (in answer to the appellant's brief) to an appellate court when a case is appealed. The appellant's brief outlines the facts and issues of the case, the judge's rulings or jury's findings that should be reversed or modified, the applicable law, and the arguments on the client's behalf.

Burglary The unlawful entry into a building with the intent to commit a felony. (Some state statutes expand this to include the intent to commit any crime.)

Business ethics Ethics in a business context; a consensus of what constitutes right or wrong behavior in the world of business and the application of moral principles to situations that arise in a business setting.

Business invitees Those people, such as customers or clients, who are invited onto business premises by the owner of those premises for business purposes.

Business judgment rule A rule that immunizes corporate management from liability for actions that result in corporate losses or damages if the actions are undertaken in good faith and are within both the power of the corporation and the authority of management to make.

Business necessity A defense to allegations of employment discrimination in which the employer demonstrates that an employment practice that discriminates against members of a protected class is related to job performance.

Business tort The wrongful interference with another's business rights.

Bylaws A set of governing rules adopted by a corporation or other association.

C

Case law The rules of law announced in court decisions. Case law includes the aggregate of reported cases that interpret judicial precedents, statutes, regulations, and constitu-

tional provisions.

Cashier's check A check drawn by a bank on itself.

Categorical imperative A concept developed by the philosopher Immanuel Kant as an ethical guideline for behavior. In deciding whether an action is right or wrong, or desirable or undesirable, a person should evaluate the action in terms of what would happen if everybody else in the same situation, or category, acted the same way.

Causation in fact An act or omission without which an event would not have occurred.

Cease-and-desist order An administrative or judicial order prohibiting a person or business firm from conducting activities that an agency or court has deemed illegal.

Certificate of deposit (CD) A note of a bank in which a bank acknowledges a receipt of money from a party and promises to repay the money, with interest, to the party on a certain date.

Certificate of incorporation The primary document that evidences corporate existence (referred to as articles of incorporation in some states).

Certificate of limited partnership The basic document filed with a designated state official by which a limited partnership is formed.

Certified check A check that has been accepted by the bank on which it is drawn. Essentially, the bank, by certifying (accepting) the check, promises to pay the check at the time the check is presented.

Charitable trust A trust in which the property held by a trustee must be used for a charitable purpose, such as the advancement of health, education, or religion.

Chattel All forms of personal property.

Check A draft drawn by a drawer ordering the drawee bank or financial institution to pay a certain amount of money to the holder on demand.

Checks and balances The national government is composed of three separate branches: the executive, the legislative, and the judicial branches. Each branch of the government exercises a check upon the actions of the others.

Choice-of-language clause A clause in a contract designating the official language by which the contract will be interpreted in the event of a future disagreement over the contract's terms.

Choice-of-law clause A clause in a contract designating the law (such as the law of a particular state or nation) that will govern the contract.

Chose in action A right that can be enforced in court to recover a debt or to obtain damages.

Citation A reference to a publication in which a legal authority—such as a statute or a court decision—or other source can be found.

Civil law The branch of law dealing with the definition and enforcement of all private or public rights, as opposed to criminal matters.

Civil law system A system of law derived from that of the Roman Empire and based on a code rather than case law; the predominant system of law in the nations of continental Europe and the nations that were once their colonies. In the United States, Louisiana is the only state that has a civil law system.

Clearinghouse   A system or place where banks exchange checks and drafts drawn on each other and settle daily balances.

Close corporation   A corporation whose shareholders are limited to a small group of persons, often including only family members. The rights of shareholders of a close corporation usually are restricted regarding the transfer of shares to others.

Closed shop   A firm that requires union membership by its workers as a condition of employment. The closed shop was made illegal by the Labor-Management Relations Act of 1947.

Codicil   A written supplement or modification to a will. A codicil must be executed with the same formalities as a will.

Collateral   Under Article 9 of the UCC, the property subject to a security interest, including accounts and chattel paper that have been sold.

Collateral promise   A secondary promise that is ancillary (subsidiary) to a principal transaction or primary contractual relationship, such as a promise made by one person to pay the debts of another if the latter fails to perform. A collateral promise normally must be in writing to be enforceable.

Collecting bank   Any bank handling an item for collection, except the payor bank.

Collective bargaining   The process by which labor and management negotiate the terms and conditions of employment, including working hours and workplace conditions.

Comity   A deference by which one nation gives effect to the laws and judicial decrees of another nation. This recognition is based primarily upon respect.

Commerce clause   The provision in Article I, Section 8, of the U.S. Constitution that gives Congress the power to regulate interstate commerce.

Commingle   To mix together. In corporate law, if personal and corporate interests are commingled to the extent that the corporation has no separate identity, a court may "pierce the corporate veil" and expose the shareholders to personal liability.

Common carrier   An owner of a truck, railroad, airline, ship, or other vehicle who is licensed to offer transportation services to the public, generally in return for compensation or a payment.

Common law   That body of law developed from custom or judicial decisions in English and U.S. courts, not attributable to a legislature.

Common stock   Shares of ownership in a corporation that give the owner of the stock a proportionate interest in the corporation with regard to control, earnings, and net assets; shares of common stock are lowest in priority with respect to payment of dividends and distribution of the corporation's assets upon dissolution.

Community property   A form of concurrent ownership of property in which each spouse technically owns an undivided one-half interest in property acquired during the marriage. This form of joint ownership occurs in only nine states and Puerto Rico.

Comparative negligence   A theory in tort law under which the liability for injuries resulting from negligent acts is shared by all parties who were negligent (including the injured party), on the basis of each person's proportionate negligence.

Compensatory damages   A money award equivalent to the actual value of injuries or damages sustained by the aggrieved party.

Complaint   The pleading made by a plaintiff alleging wrongdoing on the part of the defendant; the document that, when filed with a court, initiates a lawsuit.

Computer crime   Any act that is directed against computers and computer parts, that uses computers as instruments of crime, or that involves computers and constitutes abuse.

Concurrent conditions   Conditions in a contract that must occur or be performed at the same time; they are mutually dependent. No obligations arise until these conditions are simultaneously performed.

Concurrent jurisdiction   Jurisdiction that exists when two different courts have the power to hear a case. For example, some cases can be heard in a federal or a state court.

Condition   A qualification, provision, or clause in a contractual agreement, the occurrence of which creates, suspends, or terminates the obligations of the contracting parties.

Condition precedent   A condition in a contract that must be met before a party's promise becomes absolute.

Condition subsequent   A condition in a contract that operates to terminate a party's absolute promise to perform.

Confession of judgment   The act of a debtor in permitting a judgment to be entered against him or her by a creditor, for an agreed sum, without the institution of legal proceedings.

Confiscation   A government's taking of privately owned business or personal property without a proper public purpose or an award of just compensation.

Confusion   The mixing together of goods belonging to two or more owners so that the separately owned goods cannot be identified.

Conglomerate merger   A merger between firms that do not compete with each other because they are in different markets (as opposed to horizontal and vertical mergers).

Consent   Voluntary agreement to a proposition or an act of another. A concurrence of wills.

Consequential damages   Special damages that compensate for a loss that is not direct or immediate (for example, lost profits). The special damages must have been reasonably foreseeable at the time the breach or injury occurred in order for the plaintiff to collect them.

Consideration   Generally, the value given in return for a promise. The consideration, which must be present to make the contract legally binding, must be something of legally sufficient value and bargained for and must result in a detriment to the promisee or a benefit to the promisor.

Consignment   A transaction in which an owner of goods (the consignor) delivers the goods to another (the consignee) for the consignee to sell. The consignee pays the consignor for the goods when they are sold by the consignee.

Consolidation   A contractual and statutory process in which two or more corporations join to become a completely new corporation. The original corporations cease to exist, and the new corporation acquires all their assets and liabilities.

Constitutional law   Law based on the U.S. Constitution and the constitutions of the various states.

Constructive delivery   An act equivalent to the actual, physical delivery of property that cannot be physically delivered because of difficulty or impossibility; for example, the transfer of a key to a safe constructively delivers the contents of the safe.

Constructive eviction   A form of eviction that occurs when a landlord fails to perform adequately any of the undertakings (such as providing heat in the winter) required by the lease, thereby making the tenant's further use and enjoyment of the property exceedingly difficult or impossible.

Constructive trust   An equitable trust that is imposed in the interests of fairness and justice when someone wrongfully holds legal title to property. A court may require the owner to hold the property in trust for the person or persons who rightfully should own the property.

Consumer-debtor   An individual whose debts are primarily consumer debts (debts for purchases made primarily for personal or household use).

Continuation statement   A statement that, if filed within six months prior to the expiration date of the original financing statement, continues the perfection of the original security interest for another five years. The perfection of a security interest can be continued in the same manner indefinitely.

Contract   An agreement that can be enforced in court; formed by two or more parties who agree to perform or to refrain from performing some act now or in the future.

Contractual capacity   The threshold mental capacity required by the law for a party who enters into a contract to be bound by that contract.

Contributory negligence   A theory in tort law under which a complaining party's own negligence contributed to or caused his or her injuries. Contributory negligence is an absolute bar to recovery in a minority of jurisdictions.

Conversion   The wrongful taking, using, or retaining possession of personal property that belongs to another.

Conveyance   The transfer of a title to land from one person to another by deed; a document (such as a deed) by which an interest in land is transferred from one person to another.

"Cooling off" laws   Laws that allow buyers a period of time, such as two to three days, in which to cancel door-to-door sales contracts.

Copyright   The exclusive right of "authors" to publish, print, or sell an intellectual production for a statutory period of time. A copyright has the same monopolistic nature as a patent or trademark, but it differs in that it applies exclusively to works of art, literature, and other works of authorship (including computer programs).

Corporate social responsibility   The concept that corporations can and should act ethically and be accountable to society for their actions.

Corporate charter   The document issued by a state agency or authority (usually the secretary of state) that grants a cor-

poration legal existence and the right to function.

Corporation   A legal entity formed in compliance with statutory requirements. The entity is distinct from its shareholders-owners.

Correspondent bank   A bank in which another bank has an account (and vice versa) for the purpose of facilitating fund transfers.

Cost-benefit analysis   A decision-making technique that involves weighing the costs of a given action against the benefits of the action.

Co-surety   A joint surety; a person who assumes liability jointly with another surety for the payment of an obligation.

Counteradvertising   New advertising that is undertaken pursuant to a Federal Trade Commission order for the purpose of correcting earlier false claims that were made about a product.

Counterclaim   A claim made by a defendant in a civil lawsuit that in effect sues the plaintiff.

Counteroffer   An offeree's response to an offer in which the offeree rejects the original offer and at the same time makes a new offer.

Course of dealing   Prior conduct between parties to a contract that establishes a common basis for their understanding.

Course of performance   The conduct that occurs under the terms of a particular agreement; such conduct indicates what the parties to an agreement intended it to mean.

Covenant not to sue   An agreement to substitute a contractual obligation for some other type of legal action based on a valid claim.

Cover   Under the UCC, a remedy of the buyer that allows the buyer or lessee, on the seller's or lessor's breach, to purchase the goods from another seller or lessor and substitute them for the goods due under the contract. If the cost of cover exceeds the cost of the contract goods, the breaching seller or lessor will be liable to the buyer or lessee for the difference. In obtaining cover, the buyer or lessee must act in good faith and without unreasonable delay.

Cram-down provision   A provision of the Bankruptcy Code that allows a court to confirm a debtor's Chapter 11 reorganization plan even though only one class of creditors has accepted it. To exercise the court's right under this provision, the court must demonstrate that the plan does not discriminate unfairly against any creditors and is fair and equitable.

Creditors' composition agreement   An agreement formed between a debtor and his or her creditors in which the creditors agree to accept a lesser sum than that owed by the debtor in full satisfaction of the debt.

Crime   A wrong against society proclaimed in a statute and, if committed, punishable by society through fines and/or imprisonment—and, in some cases, death.

Criminal law   Law that defines and governs actions that constitute crimes. Generally, criminal law has to do with wrongful actions committed against society for which society demands redress.

Cure   The right of a party who tenders nonconforming performance to correct his or her performance within the contract period [UCC 3–508].

D

Damages Money sought as a remedy for a breach of contract or for a tortious act.

Debtor Under Article 9 of the UCC, a debtor is any party who owes payment or performance of a secured obligation, whether or not the party actually owns or has rights in the collateral.

Debtor in possession (DIP) In Chapter 11 bankruptcy proceedings, a debtor who is allowed to continue in possession of the estate in property (the business) and to continue business operations.

Deceptive advertising Advertising that misleads consumers, either by unjustified claims concerning a product's performance or by the omission of a material fact concerning the product's composition or performance.

Deed A document by which title to property (usually real property) is passed.

Defamation Anything published or publicly spoken that causes injury to another's good name, reputation, or character.

Default The failure to observe a promise or discharge an obligation. The term is commonly used to mean the failure to pay a debt when it is due.

Default judgment A judgment entered by a court against a defendant who has failed to appear in court to answer or defend against the plaintiff's claim.

Defendant One against whom a lawsuit is brought; the accused person in a criminal proceeding.

Defense That which a defendant offers and alleges in an action or suit as a reason why the plaintiff should not recover or establish what he or she seeks.

Deficiency judgment A judgment against a debtor for the amount of a debt remaining unpaid after collateral has been repossessed and sold.

Delegation of duties The act of transferring to another all or part of one's duties arising under a contract.

Depositary bank The first bank to receive a check for payment.

Deposition The testimony of a party to a lawsuit or a witness taken under oath before a trial.

Destination contract A contract for the sale of goods in which the seller is required or authorized to ship the goods by carrier and deliver them at a particular destination. The seller assumes liability for any losses or damage to the goods until they are tendered at the destination specified in the contract.

Devise To make a gift of real property by will.

Devisee One designated in a will to receive a gift of real property.

Disaffirmance The legal avoidance, or setting aside, of a contractual obligation.

Discharge The termination of an obligation. In contract law, discharge occurs when the parties have fully performed their contractual obligations or when events, conduct of the parties, or operation of the law releases the parties from performance. In bankruptcy proceedings, the extinction of the debtor's dischargeable debts.

Disclosed principal A principal whose identity is known to a third party at the time the agent makes a contract with the third party.

Discovery A phase in the litigation process during which the opposing parties may obtain information from each other and from third parties prior to trial.

Disparagement of property An economically injurious falsehood made about another's product or property. A general term for torts that are more specifically referred to as slander of quality or slander of title.

Disparate-impact discrimination A form of employment discrimination that results from certain employer practices or procedures that, although not discriminatory on their face, have a discriminatory effect.

Disparate-treatment discrimination A form of employment discrimination that results when an employer intentionally discriminates against employees who are members of protected classes.

Dissolution The formal disbanding of a partnership or a corporation. It can take place by (1) acts of the partners or, in a corporation, of the shareholders and board of directors; (2) the death of a partner; (3) the expiration of a time period stated in a partnership agreement or a certificate of incorporation; or (4) judicial decree.

Distribution agreement A contract between a seller and a distributor of the seller's products setting out the terms and conditions of the distributorship.

Diversity of citizenship Under Article III, Section 2, of the Constitution, a basis for federal court jurisdiction over a lawsuit between (1) citizens of different states, (2) a foreign country and citizens of a state or of different states, or (3) citizens of a state and citizens or subjects of a foreign country. The amount in controversy must be more than $50,000 before a federal court can take jurisdiction in such cases.

Divestiture The act of selling one or more of a company's parts, such as a subsidiary or plant; often mandated by the courts in merger or monopolization cases.

Dividend A distribution to corporate shareholders of corporate profits or income, disbursed in proportion to the number of shares held.

Docket The list of cases entered on a court's calendar and thus scheduled to be heard by the court.

Document of title Paper exchanged in the regular course of business that evidences the right to possession of goods (for example, a bill of lading or a warehouse receipt).

Domestic corporation In a given state, a corporation that does business in, and is organized under the law of, that state.

Dominion Ownership rights in property, including the right to possess and control the property.

Double jeopardy A situation occurring when a person is tried twice for the same criminal offense; prohibited by the Fifth Amendment to the Constitution.

Draft Any instrument drawn on a drawee (such as a bank) that orders the drawee to pay a certain sum of money, usually to a third party (the payee), on demand or at a definite future time.

Dram shop act A state statute that imposes liability on the owners of bars and taverns, as well as those who serve alcoholic drinks to the public, for injuries resulting from accidents caused by intoxicated persons when the sellers or servers of alcoholic drinks contributed to the intoxication.

Drawee   The party that is ordered to pay a draft or check. With a check, a financial institution is always the drawee.

Drawer   The party that initiates a draft (such as a check), thereby ordering the drawee to pay.

Due process clause   The provisions of the Fifth and Fourteenth Amendments to the Constitution that guarantee that no person shall be deprived of life, liberty, or property without due process of law. Similar clauses are found in most state constitutions.

Dumping   The selling of goods in a foreign country at a price below the price charged for the same goods in the domestic market.

Duress   Unlawful pressure brought to bear on a person, causing the person to perform an act that he or she would not otherwise perform.

Duty of care   The duty of all persons, as established by tort law, to exercise a reasonable amount of care in their dealings with others. Failure to exercise due care, which is normally determined by the "reasonable person standard," constitutes the tort of negligence.

E

Early neutral case evaluation   A form of alternative dispute resolution in which a neutral third party evaluates the strengths and weakness of the disputing parties' positions; the evaluator's opinion forms the basis for negotiating a settlement.

Easement   A nonpossessory right to use another's property in a manner established by either express or implied agreement.

Electronic fund transfer (EFT)   A transfer of funds with the use of an electronic terminal, a telephone, a computer, or magnetic tape.

Emancipation   In regard to minors, the act of being freed from parental control; occurs when a child's parent or legal guardian relinquishes the legal right to exercise control over the child. Normally, a minor who leaves home to support himself or herself is considered emancipated.

Embezzlement   The fraudulent appropriation of money or other property by a person to whom the money or property has been entrusted.

Eminent domain   The power of a government to take land for public use from private citizens for just compensation.

Employment at will   A common law doctrine under which either party may terminate an employment relationship at any time for any reason, unless a contract specifies otherwise.

Employment discrimination   Treating employees or job applicants unequally on the basis of race, color, national origin, religion, gender, age, or disability; prohibited by federal statutes.

Enabling legislation   A statute enacted by Congress that authorizes the creation of an administrative agency and specifies the name, composition, purpose, and powers of the agency being created.

Entrapment   In criminal law, a defense in which the defendant claims that he or she was induced by a public official— usually an undercover agent or police officer—to commit a crime that he or she would otherwise not have committed.

Environmental impact statement (EIS)   A statement required by the National Environmental Policy Act for any major federal action that will significantly affect the quality of the environment. The statement must analyze the action's impact on the environment and explore alternative actions that might be taken.

Equal dignity rule   In most states, a rule stating that express authority given to an agent must be in writing if the contract to be made on behalf of the principal is required to be in writing.

Equal protection clause   The provision in the Fourteenth Amendment to the Constitution that guarantees that no state will "deny to any person within its jurisdiction the equal protection of the laws." This clause mandates that the state governments treat similarly situated individuals in a similar manner.

Equitable principles and maxims   General propositions or principles of law that have to do with fairness (equity).

Establishment clause   The provision in the First Amendment to the Constitution that prohibits Congress from creating any law "respecting an establishment of religion."

Estate in property   In bankruptcy proceedings, all of the debtor's legal and equitable interests in property presently held, wherever located, together with certain jointly owned property, property transferred in transactions voidable by the trustee, proceeds and profits from the property of the estate, and certain property interests to which the debtor becomes entitled within 180 days after filing for bankruptcy.

Estopped   Barred, impeded, or precluded.

Estray statute   A statute defining finders' rights in property when the true owners are unknown.

Ethics   Moral principles and values applied to social behavior.

Eviction   A landlord's act of depriving a tenant of possession of the leased premises.

Exclusionary rule   In criminal procedure, a rule under which any evidence that is obtained in violation of the accused's constitutional rights guaranteed by the Fourth, Fifth, and Sixth Amendments, as well as any evidence derived from illegally obtained evidence, will not be admissible in court.

Exclusive distributorship   A distributorship in which the seller and the distributor of the seller's products agree that the distributor has the exclusive right to distribute the seller's products in a certain geographic area.

Exclusive jurisdiction   Jurisdiction that exists when a case can be heard only in a particular court or type of court.

Exclusive-dealing contract   An agreement under which a seller forbids a buyer to purchase products from the seller's competitors.

Exculpatory clause   A clause that releases a contractual party from liability in the event of monetary or physical injury, no matter who is at fault.

Executed contract   A contract that has been completely performed by both parties.

Execution   An action to carry into effect the directions in a court decree or judgment.

Executive agency An administrative agency within the executive branch of government. At the federal level, executive agencies are those within the cabinet departments.

Executor A person appointed by a testator to see that his or her will is administered appropriately.

Executory contract A contract that has not as yet been fully performed.

Executory interest A future interest, held by a person other than the grantor, that or begins some time after the termination of the preceding estate.

Export To sell products to buyers located in other countries.

Express contract A contract in which the terms of the agreement are fully and explicitly stated in words, oral or written.

Express warranty A seller's or lessor's oral or written promise, ancillary to an underlying sales or lease agreement, as to the quality, description, or performance of the goods being sold or leased.

Expropriation The seizure by a government of privately owned business or personal property for a proper public purpose and with just compensation.

Extension clause A clause in a time instrument that allows the instrument's date of maturity to be extended into the future.

F

Federal form of government A system of government in which the states form a union and the sovereign power is divided between a central government and the member states.

Federal question A question that pertains to the U.S. Constitution, acts of Congress, or treaties. A federal question provides a basis for federal jurisdiction.

Federal Reserve System A network of twelve central banks, located around the country and headed by the Federal Reserve Board of Governors. Most banks in the United States have Federal Reserve accounts.

Fee simple An absolute form of property ownership entitling the property owner to use, possess, or dispose of the property as he or she chooses during his or her lifetime. Upon death, the interest in the property descends to the owner's heirs; a fee simple absolute.

Fee simple absolute An ownership interest in land in which the owner has the greatest possible aggregation of rights, privileges, and power. Ownership in fee simple absolute is limited absolutely to a person and his or her heirs; a fee simple absolute.

Fee simple defeasible An ownership interest in real property that can be taken away (by the prior grantor) upon the occurrence or nonoccurrence of a specified event.

Felony A crime—such as arson, murder, rape, or robbery—that carries the most severe sanctions, usually ranging from one year in a state or federal prison to the forfeiture of one's life.

Fictitious payee A payee on a negotiable instrument whom the maker or drawer does not intend to have an interest in the instrument. Indorsements by fictitious payees are not treated as unauthorized under Article 3 of the UCC.

Fiduciary As a noun, a person having a duty created by his or her undertaking to act primarily for another's benefit in matters connected with the undertaking. As an adjective, a relationship founded upon trust and confidence.

Financing statement A document prepared by a secured creditor and filed with the appropriate state or local official to give notice to the public that the creditor claims an interest in collateral belonging to the debtor named in the statement. The financing statement must be signed by the debtor, contain the addresses of both the debtor and the creditor, and describe the collateral by type or item.

Firm offer An offer (by a merchant) that is irrevocable without consideration for a period of time (not longer than three months). A firm offer by a merchant must be in writing and must be signed by the offeror.

Fixture A thing that was once personal property but that has become attached to real property in such a way that it takes on the characteristics of real property and becomes part of that real property.

Floating lien A security interest in proceeds, after-acquired property, or property purchased under a line of credit (or all three); a security interest in collateral that is retained even when the collateral changes in character, classification, or location.

Force majeure (pronounced mah-*zhure*) **clause** A provision in a contract stipulating that certain unforeseen events—such as war, political upheavals, acts of God, or other events—will excuse a party from liability for nonperformance of contractual obligations.

Foreign corporation In a given state, a corporation that does business in the state without being incorporated therein.

Foreign exchange market A worldwide system in which foreign currencies are bought and sold.

Forgery The fraudulent making or altering of any writing in a way that changes the legal rights and liabilities of another.

Formal contract A contract that by law requires for its validity a specific form, such as executed under seal.

Forum-selection clause A provision in a contract designating the court, jurisdiction, or tribunal that will decide any disputes arising under the contract..

Franchise Any arrangement in which the owner of a trademark, trade name, or copyright licenses another to use that trademark, trade name, or copyright, under specified conditions or limitations, in the selling of goods and services.

Franchisee One receiving a license to use another's (the franchisor's) trademark, trade name, or copyright in the sale of goods and services.

Franchisor One licensing another (the franchisee) to use his or her trademark, trade name, or copyright in the sale of goods or services.

Fraudulent misrepresentation (fraud) Any misrepresentation, either by misstatement or omission of a material fact, knowingly made with the intention of deceiving another and on which a reasonable person would and does rely to his or her detriment.

Free exercise clause The provision in the First Amendment to the Constitution that prohibits Congress from making any law "prohibiting the free exercise" of religion.

Fungible goods Goods that are alike by physical nature, by agreement, or by trade usage. Examples of fungible goods are wheat, oil, and wine that are identical in type and quality.

Future interest An interest in real property that is not at present possessory but will or may become possessory in the future.

G

Garnishment A legal process used by a creditor to collect a debt by seizing property of the debtor (such as wages) that is being held by a third party (such as the debtor's employer).

General partner In a limited partnership, a partner who assumes responsibility for the management of the partnership and liability for all partnership debts.

Gift Any voluntary transfer of property made without consideration, past or present.

Gift *causa mortis* A gift made in contemplation of death. If the donor does not die of that ailment, the gift is revoked.

Gift *inter vivos* A gift made during one's lifetime and not in contemplation of imminent death, in contrast to a gift *causa mortis*.

Good faith purchaser A purchaser who buys without notice of any circumstance that would put a person of ordinary prudence on inquiry as to whether the seller has valid title to the goods being sold.

Good Samaritan statute A state statute that provides that persons who rescue or provide emergency services to others in peril—unless they do so recklessly, thus causing further harm—cannot be sued for negligence.

Grand jury A group of citizens called to decide, after hearing the state's evidence, whether a reasonable basis (probable cause) exists for believing that a crime has been committed and whether a trial ought to be held.

Group boycott The refusal to deal with a particular person or firm by a group of competitors; prohibited by the Sherman Act.

Guarantor A person who agrees to satisfy the debt of another (the debtor) only after the principal debtor defaults; a guarantor's liability is thus secondary.

H

Herfindahl-Hirschman Index (HHI) An index of market power used to calculate whether a merger of two corporations will result in sufficient monopoly power to violate antitrust laws.

Holder Any person in the possession of an instrument drawn, issued, or indorsed to him or her, to his or her order, to bearer, or in blank.

Holder in due course (HDC) A holder who acquires a negotiable instrument for value; in good faith; and without notice that the instrument is overdue, that it has been dishonored, that any person has a defense against it or a claim to it, or that the instrument contains unauthorized signa-

tures, alterations, or is so irregular or incomplete as to call into question its authenticity.

Holographic will A will written entirely in the signer's handwriting and usually not witnessed.

Homestead exemption A law permitting a debtor to retain the family home, either in its entirety or up to a specified dollar amount, free from the claims of unsecured creditors or trustees in bankruptcy.

Horizontal merger A merger between two firms that are competing in the same marketplace.

Horizontal restraint Any agreement that in some way restrains competition between rival firms competing in the same market.

Hot-cargo agreement An agreement in which employers voluntarily agree with unions not to handle, use, or deal in nonunion-produced goods of other employers; a type of secondary boycott explicitly prohibited by the Labor-Management Reporting and Disclosure Act of 1959.

I

Identification In a sale of goods, the express designation of the goods provided for in the contract.

Implied warranty A warranty that the law derives by implication or inference from the nature of the transaction or the relative situation or circumstances of the parties.

Implied warranty of fitness for a particular purpose A warranty that goods sold or leased are fit for a particular purpose. The warranty arises when any seller or lessor knows the particular purpose for which a buyer or lessee will use the goods and knows that the buyer or lessee is relying on the skill and judgment of the seller or lessor to select suitable goods.

Implied warranty of habitability An implied promise by a landlord that rented residential premises are fit for human habitation—that is, in a condition that is safe and suitable for people to live in.

Implied warranty of merchantability A warranty that goods being sold or leased are reasonably fit for the general pupose for which they are sold or leased, are properly packaged and labeled, and are of proper quality. The warranty automatically arises in every sale or lease of goods made by a merchant who deals in goods of the kind sold or leased.

Implied-in-fact contract A contract formed in whole or in part from the conduct of the parties (as opposed to an express contract).

Impossibility of performance A doctrine under which a party to a contract is relieved of his or her duty to perform when performance becomes impossible or totally impracticable (through no fault of either party).

Imposter One who, by use of the mails, telephone, or personal appearance, induces a maker or drawer to issue an instrument in the name of an impersonated payee. Indorsements by imposters are not treated as unauthorized under Article 3 of the UCC.

Incidental beneficiary A third party who incidentally benefits from a contract but whose benefit was not the reason the contract was formed; an incidental beneficiary has no rights in a contract and cannot sue to have the contract enforced.

Incidental damages   Damages resulting from a breach of contract, including all reasonable expenses incurred because of the breach.

Independent contractor   One who works for, and receives payment from, an employer but whose working conditions and methods are not controlled by the employer. An independent contractor is not an employee but may be an agent.

Independent regulatory agency   An administrative agency that is not considered part of the government's executive branch and is not subject to the authority of the president. Independent agency officials cannot be removed without cause.

Indictment (pronounced in-*dyte*-ment)   A charge by a grand jury that a named person has committed a crime.

Indorsee   The person to whom a negotiable instrument is transferred by indorsement.

Indorsement   A signature placed on an instrument for the purpose of transferring one's ownership rights in the instrument.

Indorser   A person who transfers an instrument by signing (indorsing) it and delivering it to another person.

Informal contract   A contract that does not require a specified form or formality in order to be valid.

Information   A formal accusation or complaint (without an indictment) issued in certain types of actions (usually criminal actions involving lesser crimes) by a law officer, such as a magistrate.

Innkeeper's lien   A possessory lien placed on the luggage of hotel guests for hotel charges that remain unpaid.

Insider trading   The purchase or sale of securities on the basis of "inside information" (information that has not been made available to the public) in violation of a duty owed to the company whose stock is being traded.

Insolvent   Under the UCC, a term describing a person who ceases to pay "his debts in the ordinary course of business or cannot pay his debts as they become due or is insolvent within the meaning of federal bankruptcy law" [UCC 1–201(23)].

Installment contract   Under the UCC, a contract that requires or authorizes delivery in two or more separate lots to be accepted and paid for separately.

Insurable interest   An interest either in a person's life or well-being or in property that is sufficiently substantial that insuring against injury to (or the death of) the person or against damage to the property does not amount to a mere wagering (betting) contract.

Insurance   A contract in which, for a stipulated consideration, one party agrees to compensate the other for loss on a specific subject by a specified peril.

Integrated contract   A written contract that constitutes the final expression of the parties' agreement. If a contract is integrated, evidence extraneous to the contract that contradicts or alters the meaning of the contract in any way is inadmissible.

Intellectual property   Property resulting from intellectual, creative processes. Patents, trademarks, and copyrights are examples of intellectual property.

Intended beneficiary   A third party for whose benefit a contract is formed; an intended beneficiary can sue the promisor if such a contract is breached.

Intentional tort   A wrongful act knowingly committed.

Inter vivos trust   A trust created by the grantor (settlor) and effective during the grantor's lifetime; a trust not established by a will.

Intermediary bank   Any bank to which an item is transferred in the course of collection, except the depositary or payor bank.

International law   The law that governs relations among nations. National laws, customs, treaties, and international conferences and organizations are generally considered to be the most important sources of international law.

Interrogatories   A series of written questions for which written answers are prepared and then signed under oath by a party to a lawsuit, usually with the assistance of the party's attorney.

Intestacy laws   State statutes that specify how property will be distributed when a person dies intestate (without a valid will); also called statutes of descent and distribution.

Intestate   As a noun, one who has died without having created a valid will; as an adjective, the state of having died without a will.

Investment company   A company that acts on behalf of many smaller shareholders-owners by buying a large portfolio of securities and professionally managing that portfolio.

J

Joint tenancy   The joint ownership of property by two or more co-owners of property in which each co-owner owns an undivided portion of the property. Upon the death of one of the joint tenants, his or her interest automatically passes to the surviving joint tenants.

Joint and several liability   In partnership law, a doctrine under which a plaintiff may sue, and collect a judgment from, one or more of the partners separately (severally, or individually) or all of the partners together (jointly). This is true even if one of the partners sued did not participate in, ratify, or know about whatever it was that gave rise to the cause of action.

Joint liability   Shared liability. In partnership law, partners incur joint liability for partnership obligations and debts. For example, if a third party sues a partner on a partnership debt, the partner has the right to insist that the other partners be sued with him or her.

Judicial review   The process by which a court decides on the constitutionality of legislative enactments and actions of the executive branch.

Jurisdiction   The authority of a court to hear and decide a specific action.

Jurisprudence   The science or philosophy of law.

Justiciable (pronounced jus-*tish*-a-bul) controversy   A controversy that is not hypothetical or academic but real and substantial; a requirement that must be satisfied before a court will hear a case.

L

Larceny   The wrongful taking and carrying away of another person's personal property with the intent to permanently deprive the owner of the property. Some states classify larceny as either grand or petit, depending on the property's value.

Law   A body of enforceable rules governing relationships among individuals and between individuals and their society.

Lease   In real property law, a contract by which the owner of real property (the landlord, or lessor) grants to a person (the tenant, or lessee) an exclusive right to use and possess the property, usually for a specified period of time, in return for rent or some other form of payment.

Lease agreement   In regard to the lease of goods, an agreement in which one person (the lessor) agrees to transfer the right to the possession and use of property to another person (the lessee) in exchange for rental payments.

Leasehold estate   An estate in realty held by a tenant under a lease. In every leasehold estate, the tenant has a qualified right to possess and/or use the land.

Legacy   A gift of personal property under a will.

Legal positivism   A school of legal thought centered on the assumption that there is no law higher than the laws created by the government. Laws must be obeyed, even if they are unjust, to prevent anarchy.

Legal realism   A school of legal thought of the 1920s and 1930s that generally advocated a less abstract and more realistic approach to the law, an approach that takes into account customary practices and the circumstances in which transactions take place. The school left a lasting imprint on American jurisprudence.

Legatee   One designated in a will to receive a gift of personal property.

Lessee   A person who acquires the right to the possession and use of another's property in exchange for rental payments.

Lessor   A person who sells the right to the possession and use of property to another in exchange for rental payments.

Letter of credit   A written instrument, usually issued by a bank on behalf of a customer or other person, in which the issuer promises to honor drafts or other demands for payment by third persons in accordance with the terms of the instrument.

Levy   The obtaining of money by legal process through the seizure and sale of property, usually done after a writ of execution has been issued.

Libel   Defamation in written form.

License   A revocable right or privilege of a person to come on another person's land.

Lien (pronounced *leen*)   An encumbrance upon a property to satisfy a debt or protect a claim for payment of a debt.

Life estate   An interest in land that exists only for the duration of the life of some person, usually the holder of the estate.

Limited liability company (LLC)   A hybrid form of business enterprise that offers the limited liability of the coporation but the tax advantages of a partnership.

Limited liability partnership   A form of partnership that allows professionals to enjoy the tax benefits of a partnership while avoiding personal liability for the malpractice of other partners.

Limited partner   In a limited partnership, a partner who contributes capital to the partnership but has no right to participate in the management and operation of the business. The limited partner assumes no liability for partnership debts beyond the capital contributed.

Limited partnership   A partnership consisting of one or more general partners (who manage the business and are liable to the full extent of their personal assets for debts of the partnership) and one or more limited partners (who contribute only assets and are liable only to the extent of their contributions).

Liquidated damages   An amount, stipulated in the contract, that the parties to a contract believe to be a reasonable estimation of the damages that will occur in the event of a breach.

Liquidation   In regard to corporations, the process by which corporate assets are converted into cash and distributed among creditors and shareholders according to specific rules of preference. In regard to bankruptcy, the sale of all of the nonexempt assets of a debtor and the distribution of the proceeds to the debtor's creditors. Chapter 7 of the Bankruptcy Code provides for liquidation bankruptcy proceedings.

Litigation   The process of resolving a dispute through the court system.

Long arm statute   A state statute that permits a state to obtain personal jurisdiction over nonresident defendants. A defendant must have certain "minimum contacts" with that state for the statute to apply.

Lost property   Property with which the owner has involuntarily parted and then cannot find or recover.

M

Mailbox rule   A rule providing that an acceptance of an offer becomes effective upon dispatch (upon being placed in a mailbox), if mail is, expressly or impliedly, an authorized means of communication of acceptance to the offeror.

Maker   One who promises to pay a certain sum to the holder of a promissory note or certificate of deposit (CD).

Malpractice   Professional misconduct or the lack of the requisite degree of skill as a professional. Negligence—the failure to exercise due care—on the part of a professional, such as a physician or an attorney, is commonly referred to as malpractice.

Market power   The power of a firm to control the market price of its product. A monopoly has the greatest degree of market power.

Market-share test   The primary measure of monopoly power. A firm's market share is the percentage of a market that the firm controls.

Mechanic's lien   A statutory lien upon the real property of another, created to ensure payment for work performed and materials furnished in the repair or improvement of real property, such as a building.

Mediation   A method of settling disputes outside of court by using the services of a neutral third party, who acts as a communicating agent between the parties and assists the parties in negotiating a settlement.

Merchant   A person who is engaged in the purchase and sale of goods. Under the UCC, a person who deals in goods of the kind involved in the sales contract; for further definitions, see UCC 2–104.

Merger   A contractual and statutory process in which one corporation (the surviving corporation) acquires all of the assets and liabilities of another corporation (the merged corporation). The shareholders of the merged corporation receive either payment for their shares or shares in the surviving corporation.

Mini-trial   A private proceeding in which each party to a dispute argues its position before the other side and vice versa. A neutral third party may be present and act as an adviser if the parties fail to reach an agreement.

Minimum wage   The lowest wage, either by government regulation or union contract, that an employer may pay an hourly worker.

Mirror image rule   A common law rule that requires, for a valid contractual agreement, that the terms of the offeree's acceptance adhere exactly to the terms of the offeror's offer.

Misdemeanor   A lesser crime than a felony, punishable by a fine or imprisonment for up to one year in other than a state or federal penitentiary.

Mislaid property   Property with which the owner has voluntarily parted and then cannot find or recover.

Mitigation of damages   A rule requiring a plaintiff to have done whatever was reasonable to minimize the damages caused by the defendant.

Money laundering   Falsely reporting income that has been obtained through criminal activity as income obtained through a legitimate business enterprise—in effect, "laundering" the "dirty money."

Monopolization   The possession of monopoly power in the relevant market and the willful acquisition or maintenance of the power, as distinguished from growth or development as a consequence of a superior product, business acumen, or historic accident.

Monopoly   A term generally used to describe a market in which there is a single seller or a limited number of sellers.

Monopoly power   The ability of a monopoly to dictate what takes place in a given market.

Mortgagee   Under a mortgage agreement, the creditor who takes a security interest in the debtor's property.

Mortgagor   Under a mortgage agreement, the debtor who gives the creditor a security interest in the debtor's property in return for a mortgage loan.

Most-favored-nation status   A status granted in an international treaty by a provision stating that the citizens of the contracting nations may enjoy the privileges accorded by either party to citizens of the most favored nations. Generally, most-favored-nation clauses are designed to establish equality of international treatment.

Motion for a directed verdict   In a jury trial, a motion for the judge to take the decision out of the hands of the jury and direct a verdict for the moving party on the ground that the other party has not produced sufficient evidence to support his or her claim.

Motion for a new trial   A motion asserting that the trial was so fundamentally flawed (because of error, newly discovered evidence, prejudice, or other reason) that a new trial is necessary to prevent a miscarriage of justice.

Motion for judgment N.O.V.   A motion requesting the court to grant judgment in favor of the party making the motion on the ground that the jury verdict against him or her was unreasonable and erroneous.

Motion for judgment on the pleadings   A motion by either party to a lawsuit at the close of the pleadings requesting the court to decide the issue solely on the pleadings without proceeding to trial. The motion will be granted only if no facts are in dispute.

Motion for summary judgment   A motion requesting the court to enter a judgment without proceeding to trial. The motion can be based on evidence outside the pleadings and will be granted only if no facts are in dispute.

Motion to dismiss   A pleading in which a defendant asserts that the plaintiff's claim fails to state a cause of action (that is, has no basis in law) or that there are other grounds on which a suit should be dismissed.

Mutual fund   A specific type of investment company that continually buys or sells to investors shares of ownership in a portfolio.

N

National law   Law that pertains to a particular nation (as opposed to international law).

Natural law   The belief that government and the legal system should reflect universal moral and ethical principles that are inherent in human nature. The natural law school is the oldest and one of the most significant schools of legal thought.

Necessaries   Necessities required for life, such as food, shelter, clothing, and medical attention; may include whatever is believed to be necessary to maintain a person's standard of living or financial and social status.

Negligence   The failure to exercise the standard of care that a reasonable person would exercise in similar circumstances.

Negligence *per se*   An act (or failure to act) in violation of a statutory requirement.

Negotiable instrument   A signed writing that contains an unconditional promise or order to pay an exact sum of money, on demand or at an exact future time, to a specific person or order, or to bearer.

Negotiation   In regard to dispute settlement, a process in which parties attempt to settle their dispute informally, with or without attorneys to represent them. In regard to instruments, the transfer of an instrument in such a way that the transferee (the person to whom the instrument is transferred) becomes a holder.

No-par shares   Corporate shares that have no face value—that is, no specific dollar amount is printed on their face.

Nominal damages   A small monetary award (often one dollar) granted to a plaintiff when no actual damage was suffered.

Notary public   A public official authorized to attest to the authenticity of signatures.

Novation The substitution, by agreement, of a new contract for an old one, with the rights under the old one being terminated. Typically, there is a substitution of a new person who is responsible for the contract and the removal of an original party's rights and duties under the contract.

Nuisance A common law doctrine under which persons may be held liable for using their property in a manner that unreasonably interferes with others' rights to use or enjoy their own property.

Nuncupative will An oral will (often called a deathbed will) made before witnesses; usually limited to transfers of personal property.

O

Objective theory of contracts A theory under which the intent to form a contract will be judged by outward, objective facts (what the party said when entering into the contract, how the party acted or appeared, and the circumstances surrounding the transaction) as interpreted by a reasonable person, rather than by the party's own secret, subjective intentions.

Offer A promise or commitment to perform or refrain from performing some specified act in the future.

Offeree A person to whom an offer is made.

Offeror A person who makes an offer.

Option contract A contract under which the offeror cannot revoke his or her offer for a stipulated time period, and the offeree can accept or reject the offer during this period without fear that the offer will be made to another person. The offeree must give consideration for the option (the irrevocable offer) to be enforceable.

Order for relief A court's grant of assistance to a complainant. In bankruptcy proceedings, the order relieves the debtor of the immediate obligation to pay the debts listed in the bankruptcy petition.

Order instrument A negotiable instrument that is payable "to the order of an identified person" or "to an identified person or order."

Output contract An agreement in which a seller agrees to sell and a buyer agrees to buy all or up to a stated amount of what the seller produces.

Overdraft A check written on a checking account in which there are insufficient funds to cover the amount of the check.

P

Par-value shares Corporate shares that have a specific face value, or formal cash-in value, written on them, such as one dollar.

Parol evidence rule A substantive rule of contracts under which a court will not receive into evidence the parties' prior negotiations, prior agreements, or contemporaneous oral agreements if that evidence contradicts or varies the terms of the parties' written contract.

Partially disclosed principal A principal whose identity is unknown by a third person, but the third person knows that the agent is or may be acting for a principal at the time the agent and the third person form a contract.

Partnership An agreement by two or more persons to carry on, as co-owners, a business for profit.

Past consideration An act done before the contract is made, which ordinarily, by itself, cannot be consideration for a later promise to pay for the act.

Patent A government grant that gives an inventor the exclusive right or privilege to make, use, or sell his or her invention for a limited time period. The word patent usually refers to some invention and designates either the instrument by which patent rights are evidenced or the patent itself.

Payee A person to whom an instrument is made payable.

Payor bank The bank on which a check is drawn (the drawee bank).

Penalty A sum inserted into a contract, not as a measure of compensation for its breach but rather as punishment for a default. The agreement as to the amount will not be enforced, and recovery will be limited to actual damages.

Per capita A Latin term meaning "per person." In the law governing estate distribution, a method of distributing the property of an intestate's estate in which each heir in a certain class (such as grandchildren) receives an equal share.

Per stirpes A Latin term meaning "by the roots." In the law governing estate distribution, a method of distributing an intestate's estate in which each heir in a certain class (such as grandchildren) takes the share to which his or her deceased ancestor (such as a mother or father) would have been entitled.

Per se violation A type of anticompetitive agreement—such as a horizontal price-fixing agreement—that is considered to be so injurious to the public that there is no need to determine whether it actually injures market competition; rather, it is in itself (*per se*) a violation of the Sherman Act.

Perfection The legal process by which secured parties protect themselves against the claims of third parties who may wish to have their debts satisfied out of the same collateral; usually accomplished by the filing of a financing statement with the appropriate government official.

Performance In contract law, the fulfillment of one's duties arising under a contract with another; the normal way of discharging one's contractual obligations.

Periodic tenancy A lease interest in land for an indefinite period involving payment of rent at fixed intervals, such as week to week, month to month, or year to year.

Personal defenses Defenses that can be used to avoid payment to an ordinary holder of a negotiable instrument but not a holder in due course (HDC) or a holder with the rights of an HDC.

Personal property Property that is movable; any property that is not real property.

Persuasive authority Any legal authority or source of law that a court may look to for guidance but on which it need not rely in making its decision. Persuasive authorities include cases from other jurisdictions and secondary sources of law.

Petition in bankruptcy The document that is filed with a bankruptcy court to initiate bankruptcy proceedings. The official forms required for a petition in bankruptcy must be completed accurately, sworn to under oath, and signed by the debtor.

Petty offense   In criminal law, the least serious kind of criminal offense, such as a traffic or building-code violation.

Plaintiff   One who initiates a lawsuit.

Plea bargaining   The process by which a criminal defendant and the prosecutor in a criminal case work out a mutually satisfactory disposition of the case, subject to court approval; usually involves the defendant's pleading guilty to a lesser offense in return for a lighter sentence.

Pleadings   Statements made by the plaintiff and the defendant in a lawsuit that detail the facts, charges, and defenses involved in the litigation; the complaint and answer are part of the pleadings.

Pledge   A common law security device (retained in Article 9 of the UCC) in which personal property is turned over to the creditor as security for the payment of a debt and retained by the creditor until the debt is paid.

Police powers   Powers possessed by states as part of their inherent sovereignty. These powers may be exercised to protect or promote the public order, health, safety, morals, and general welfare.

Policy   In insurance law, a contract between the insurer and the insured in which, for a stipulated consideration, the insurer agrees to compensate the insured for loss on a specific subject by a specified peril.

Positive law   The body of conventional, or written, law of a particular society at a particular point in time.

Potentially responsible party (PRP)   A liable party under the Comprehensive Environmental Response, Compensation, and Liability Act (CERCLA). Any person who generated the hazardous waste, transported the hazardous waste, owned or operated a waste site at the time of disposal, or currently owns or operates a site may be responsible for some or all of the clean-up costs involved in removing the hazardous chemicals.

Power of attorney   A written document, which is usually notarized, authorizing another to act as one's agent; can be special (permitting the agent to do specified acts only) or general (permitting the agent to transact all business for the principal).

Precedent   A court decision that furnishes an example or authority for deciding subsequent cases involving identical or similar facts.

Predatory behavior   Business behavior, such as the entry into business, that is undertaken with the intention of unlawfully driving competitors out of the market.

Predatory pricing   The pricing of a product below cost with the intent to drive competitors out of the market.

Preemption   A doctrine under which certain federal laws preempt, or take precedence over, conflicting state or local laws.

Preemptive rights   Rights held by shareholders that entitle them to purchase newly issued shares of a corporation's stock, equal in percentage to shares presently held, before the stock is offered to any outside buyers. Preemptive rights enable shareholders to maintain their proportionate ownership and voice in the corporation.

Preference   In bankruptcy proceedings, property transfers or payments made by the debtor that favor (give preference to) one creditor over others. The bankruptcy trustee is allowed to recover payments made both voluntarily and involuntarily to one creditor in preference over another.

Preferred stock   Classes of stock that have priority over common stock both as to payment of dividends and distribution of assets upon the corporation's dissolution.

Premium   In insurance law, the price paid by the insured for insurance protection for a specified period of time.

Prenuptial agreement   An agreement made before marriage that defines each partner's ownership rights in the other partner's property. Prenuptial agreements must be in writing to be enforceable.

Presentment   The act of presenting an instrument to the party liable on the instrument to collect payment; presentment also occurs when a person presents an instrument to a drawee for acceptance.

Presentment warranties   Implied warranties, made by any person who presents an instrument for payment or acceptance, that (1) the person obtaining payment or acceptance is entitled to enforce the instrument or is authorized to obtain payment or acceptance on behalf of a person who is entitled to enforce the instrument, (2) the instrument has not been altered, and (3) the person obtaining payment or acceptance has no knowledge that the signature of the drawer of the instrument is unauthorized.

Price discrimination   Setting prices in such a way that two competing buyers pay two different prices for an identical product or service.

Price-fixing agreement   An agreement between competitors in which the competitors agree to fix the prices of products or services at a certain level; prohibited by the Sherman Act.

Prima facie **case**   A case in which the plaintiff has produced sufficient evidence of his or her conclusion that the case can go to to a jury; a case in which the evidence compels the plaintiff's conclusion if the defendant produces no evidence to disprove it.

Primary source of law   A document that establishes the law on a particular issue, such as a constitution, a statute, an administrative rule, or a court decision.

Principal   In agency law, a person who agrees to have another, called the agent, act on his or her behalf.

Privilege   In tort law, the ability to act contrary to another person's right without that person's having legal redress for such acts. Privilege may be raised as a defense to defamation.

Privity of contract   The relationship that exists between the promisor and the promisee of a contract.

Probable cause   Reasonable grounds to believe the existence of facts warranting certain actions, such as the search or arrest of a person.

Probate court   A state court of limited jurisdiction that conducts proceedings relating to the settlement of a deceased person's estate.

Procedural law   Law that establishes the methods of enforcing the rights established by substantive law.

Proceeds   Under Article 9 of the UCC, whatever is received when the collateral is sold or otherwise disposed of, such as by exchange.

Product liability   The legal liability of manufacturers, sellers, and lessors of goods to consumers, users, and bystanders for injuries or damages that are caused by the goods.

Profit   In real property law, the right to enter upon and remove things from the property of another (for example, the right to enter onto a person's land and remove sand and gravel therefrom).

Promise   A declaration that something either will or will not happen in the future.

Promisee   A person to whom a promise is made.

Promisor   A person who makes a promise.

Promissory estoppel   A doctrine that applies when a promisor makes a clear and definite promise on which the promisee justifiably relies; such a promise is binding if justice will be better served by the enforcement of the promise.

Promissory note   A written promise made by one person (the maker) to pay a fixed sum of money to another person (the payee or a subsequent holder) on demand or on a specified date.

Promoter   A person who takes the preliminary steps in organizing a corporation, including (usually) issuing a prospectus, procuring stock subscriptions, making contract purchases, securing a corporate charter, and the like.

Property   Legally protected rights and interests in anything with an ascertainable value that is subject to ownership.

Prospectus   A document required by federal or state securities laws that describes the financial operations of the corporation, thus allowing investors to make informed decisions.

Proximate cause   Legal cause; exists when the connection between an act and an injury is strong enough to justify imposing liability.

Proxy   In corporation law, a written agreement between a stockholder and another under which the stockholder authorizes the other to vote the stockholder's shares in a certain manner.

Puffery   A salesperson's often exaggerated claims concerning the quality of property offered for sale. Such claims involve opinions rather than facts and are not considered to be legally binding promises or warranties.

Punitive damages   Money damages that may be awarded to a plaintiff to punish the defendant and deter future similar conduct.

Purchase-money security interest (PMSI)   A security interest that arises when a seller or lender extends credit for part or all of the purchase price of goods purchased by a buyer.

Q

Qualified indorsement   An indorsement on a negotiable instrument in which the indorser disclaims any contract liability on the instrument; the notation "without recourse" is commonly used to create a qualified indorsement.

Quasi contract   A fictional contract imposed on parties by a court in the interests of fairness and justice; usually, quasi contracts are imposed to avoid the unjust enrichment of one party at the expense of another.

Quitclaim deed   A deed intended to pass any title, interest, or claim that the grantor may have in the property but not warranting that such title is valid. A quitclaim deed offers the least amount of protection against defects in the title.

Quorum   The number of members of a decision-making body that must be present before business may be transacted.

R

Ratification   The act of accepting and giving legal force to an obligation that previously was not enforceable.

Real property   Land and everything attached to it, such as foliage and buildings.

Reasonable person standard   The standard of behavior expected of a hypothetical "reasonable person." The standard against which negligence is measured and that must be observed to avoid liability for negligence.

Receiver   In a corporate dissolution, a court-appointed person who winds up corporate affairs and liquidates corporate assets.

Recording statutes   Statutes that allow deeds, mortgages, and other real property transactions be recorded so as to provide notice to future purchasers or creditors of an existing claim on the property.

Red herring   A preliminary prospectus that can be distributed to potential investors after the registration statement (for a securities offering) has been filed with the Securities and Exchange Commission. The name derives from the red legend printed across the prospectus stating that the registration has been filed but has not become effective.

Reformation   A court-ordered correction of a written contract so that it reflects the true intentions of the parties.

Regulation Z   A set of rules promulgated by the Federal Reserve Board to implement the provisions of the Truth-in-Lending Act.

Release   A contract in which one party forfeits the right to pursue a legal claim against the other party.

Remainder   A future interest in property held by a person other than the original owner.

Remedy   The relief given to an innocent party to enforce a right or compensate for the violation of a right.

Replevin (pronounced ruh-*pleh*-vin)   An action to recover specific goods in the hands of a party who is wrongfully withholding them from the other party.

Reply   Procedurally, a plaintiff's response to a defendant's answer.

Requirements contract   An agreement in which a buyer agrees to purchase and the seller agrees to sell all or up to a stated amount of what the buyer needs or requires.

Res ipsa loquitur   A doctrine under which negligence may be inferred simply because an event occurred, if it is the type of event that would not occur in the absence of negligence. Literally, the term means "the facts speak for themselves."

Resale price maintenance agreement   An agreement between a manufacturer and a retailer in which the manufacturer specifies the minimum retail price of its products. Resale price maintenance agreements are illegal *per se* under the Sherman Act.

Rescission (pronounced reh-*sih*-zhen)   A remedy whereby a contract is canceled and the parties are returned to the positions they occupied before the contract was made; may be effected through the mutual consent of the parties, by their conduct, or by court decree.

Respondeat superior (pronounced ree-*spahn*-dee-uht soo-*peer*-ee-your)   In Latin, "Let the master respond." A doctrine under which a principal or an employer is held liable for the wrongful acts committed by agents or employees while acting within the scope of their agency or employment.

Restitution   An equitable remedy under which a person is restored to his or her original position prior to loss or injury, or placed in the position he or she would have been in had the breach not occurred.

Restrictive indorsement   Any indorsement on a negotiable instrument that requires the indorsee to comply with certain instructions regarding the funds involved. A restrictive indorsement does not prohibit the further negotiation of the instrument.

Resulting trust   An implied trust arising from the conduct of the parties. A trust in which a party holds the actual legal title to another's property but only for that person's benefit.

Retained earnings   The portion of a corporation's profits that has not been paid out as dividends to shareholders.

Reversionary interest   A future interest in property retained by the original owner.

Revocation   In contract law, the withdrawal of an offer by an offeror; unless the offer is irrevocable, it can be revoked at any time prior to acceptance without liability.

Right of first refusal   The right to purchase personal or real property—such as corporate shares or real estate—before the property is offered for sale to others.

Right of contribution   The right of a co-surety who pays more than his or her proportionate share upon a debtor's default to recover the excess paid from other co-sureties.

Right of reimbursement   The legal right of a person to be restored, repaid, or indemnified for costs, expenses, or losses incurred or expended on behalf of another.

Right of subrogation   The right of a person to stand in the place of (be substituted for) another, giving the substituted party the same legal rights that the original party had.

Right-to-work law   A state law providing that employees are not to be required to join a union as a condition of obtaining or retaining employment.

Risk   A prediction concerning potential loss based on known and unknown factors.

Risk management   Planning that is undertaken to protect one's interest should some event threaten to undermine its security. In the context of insurance, risk management involves transferring certain risks from the insured to the insurance company.

Robbery   The act of forcefully and unlawfully taking personal property of any value from another; force or intimidation is usually necessary for an act of theft to be considered a robbery.

Rule of four   A rule of the United States Supreme Court under which the Court will not issue a writ of *certiorari* unless at least four justices approve of the decision to issue the writ.

Rule of reason   A test by which a court balances the positive effects (such as economic efficiency) of an agreement against its potentially anticompetitive effects. In antitrust litigation, many practices are analyzed under the rule of reason.

Rulemaking   The process undertaken by an administrative agency when formally adopting a new regulation or amending an old one. Rulemaking involves notifying the public of a proposed rule or change and receiving and considering the public's comments.

S

S corporation   A close business corporation that has met certain requirements as set out by the Internal Revenue Code and thus qualifies for special income-tax treatment. Essentially, an S corporation is taxed the same as a partnership, but its owners enjoy the privilege of limited liability.

Sale   The passing of title from the seller to the buyer for a price.

Sale on approval   A type of conditional sale in which the buyer may take the goods on a trial basis. The sale becomes absolute only when the buyer approves of (or is satisfied with) the goods being sold.

Sale or return   A type of conditional sale in which title and possession pass from the seller to the buyer; however, the buyer retains the option to return the goods during a specified period even though the goods conform to the contract.

Sales contract   A contract for the sale of goods under which the ownership of goods is transferred from a seller to a buyer for a price.

Scienter (pronounced sy-en-ter)   Knowledge by the misrepresenting party that material facts have been falsely represented or omitted with an intent to deceive.

Search warrant   An order granted by a public authority, such as a judge, that authorizes law-enforcement personnel to search particular premises or property.

Seasonably   Within a specified time period, or, if no period is specified, within a reasonable time.

SEC Rule 10b-5   A rule of the Securities and Exchange Commission that makes it unlawful, in connection with the purchase or sale of any security, to make any untrue statement of a material fact or to omit a material fact if such omission causes the statement to be misleading.

Secondary boycott   A union's refusal to work for, purchase from, or handle the products of a secondary employer, with whom the union has no dispute, for the purpose of forcing that employer to stop doing business with the primary employer, with whom the union has a labor dispute.

Secondary source of law   A publication that summarizes or interprets the law, such as a legal encyclopedia, a legal treatise, or an article in a law review.

Secured party   A lender, seller, or any other person in whose favor there is a security interest, including a person to whom accounts or chattel paper has been sold.

Secured transaction   Any transaction in which the payment of a debt is guaranteed, or secured, by personal property owned by the debtor or in which the debtor has a legal interest.

Security Generally, a stock certificate, bond, note, debenture, warrant, or other document given as evidence of an ownership interest in a corporation or as a promise of repayment by a corporation.

Security agreement An agreement that creates or provides for a security interest between the debtor and a secured party.

Security interest Any interest "in personal property or fixtures which secures payment or performance of an obligation" [UCC 1–201(37)].

Self-defense The legally recognized privilege to protect one's self or property against injury by another. The privilege of self-defense protects only acts that are reasonably necessary to protect one's self or property.

Seniority system In regard to employment relationships, a system in which those who have worked longest for the company are first in line for promotions, salary increases, and other benefits; they are also the last to be laid off if the work force must be reduced.

Service mark A mark used in the sale or the advertising of services, such as to distinguish the services of one person from the services of others. Titles, character names, and other distinctive features of radio and television programs may be registered as service marks.

Sexual harassment In the employment context, the granting of job promotions or other benefits in return for sexual favors or language or conduct that is so sexually offensive that it creates a hostile working environment.

Shareholder's derivative suit A suit brought by a shareholder to enforce a corporate cause of action against a third person.

Shelter principle The principle that the holder of a negotiable instrument who cannot qualify as a holder in due course (HDC), but who derives his or her title through an HDC, acquires the rights of an HDC.

Shipment contract A contract for the sale of goods in which the seller is required or authorized to ship the goods by carrier. The buyer assumes liability for any losses or damage to the goods after they are delivered to the carrier.

Short-form merger A merger between a subsidiary corporation and a parent corporation that owns at least 90 percent of the outstanding shares of each class of stock issued by the subsidiary corporation. Short-form mergers can be accomplished without the approval of the shareholders of either corporation.

Signature Under the UCC, "any symbol executed or adopted by a party with a present intention to authenticate a writing."

Slander Defamation in oral form.

Slander of quality (trade libel) The publication of false information about another's product, alleging that it is not what its seller claims.

Slander of title The publication of a statement that denies or casts doubt upon another's legal ownership of any property, causing financial loss to that property's owner.

Small claims courts Special courts in which parties may litigate small claims (usually, claims involving $2,500 or less). Attorneys are not required in small claims courts, and in many states attorneys are not allowed to represent the parties.

Sole proprietorship The simplest form of business, in which the owner is the business; the owner reports business income on his or her personal income tax return and is legally responsible for all debts and obligations incurred by the business.

Sovereign immunity A doctrine that immunizes foreign nations from the jurisdiction of U.S. courts when certain conditions are satisfied.

Special indorsement An indorsement on an instrument that indicates the specific person to whom the indorser intends to make the instrument payable; that is, it names the indorsee.

Specific performance An equitable remedy requiring exactly the performance that was specified in a contract; usually granted only when money damages would be an inadequate remedy and the subject matter of the contract is unique (for example, real property).

Spendthrift trust A trust created to protect the beneficiary from spending all the money to which he or she is entitled. Only a certain portion of the total amount is given to the beneficiary at any one time, and most states prohibit creditors from attaching assets of the trust.

Stale check A check, other than a certified check, that is presented for payment more than six months after its date.

Standing to sue The requirement that an individual must have a sufficient stake in a controversy before he or she can bring a lawsuit. The plaintiff must demonstrate that he or she either has been injured or threatened with injury.

Stare decisis (pronounced *ster*-ay dih-*si*-ses) A common law doctrine under which judges are obligated to follow the precedents established in prior decisions.

Statute of Frauds A state statute under which certain types of contracts must be in writing to be enforceable.

Statute of limitations A federal or state statute setting the maximum time period during which a certain action can be brought or certain rights enforced.

Statutory law The body of law enacted by legislative bodies (as opposed to constitutional law, administrative law, or case law).

Stock An equity (ownership) interest in a corporation, measured in units of shares.

Stock certificate A certificate issued by a corporation evidencing the ownership of a specified number of shares in the corporation.

Stock warrant A certificate that grants the owner the option to buy a given number of shares of stock, usually within a set time period.

Stop-payment order An order by a bank customer to his or her bank not to pay or certify a certain check.

Strict liability Liability regardless of fault. In tort law, strict liability may be imposed on defendants in cases involving abnormally dangerous activities, dangerous animals, or defective products.

Strike An extreme action undertaken by unionized workers when collective bargaining fails; the workers leave their jobs, refuse to work, and (typically) picket the employer's workplace.

Sublease A lease executed by the lessee of real estate to a third person, conveying the same interest that the lessee enjoys but for a shorter term than that held by the lessee.

Substantive law   Law that defines, describes, regulates, and creates legal rights and obligations.

Summary jury trial (SJT)   A method of settling disputes in which a trial is held, but the jury's verdict is not binding. The verdict acts only as a guide to both sides in reaching an agreement during the mandatory negotiations that immediately follow the summary jury trial.

Summons   A document informing a defendant that a legal action has been commenced against him or her and that the defendant must appear in court on a certain date to answer the plaintiff's complaint. The document is delivered by a sheriff or any other person so authorized.

Supremacy clause   The provision in Article VI of the Constitution that provides that the Constitution, laws, and treaties of the United States are "the supreme Law of the Land." Under this clause, state and local laws that directly conflict with federal law will be rendered invalid.

Surety   A person, such as a cosigner on a note, who agrees to be primarily responsible for the debt of another.

Suretyship   An express contract in which a third party to a debtor-creditor relationship (the surety) promises to be primarily responsible for the debtor's obligation.

T

Taking   The taking of private property by the government for public use. Under the Fifth Amendment to the Constitution, the government may not take private property for public use without "just compensation."

Tangible property   Property that has physical existence and can be distinguished by the senses of touch, sight, and so on. A car is tangible property; a patent right is intangible property.

Target corporation   The corporation to be acquired in a corporate takeover; a corporation to whose shareholders a tender offer is submitted.

Technology licensing   Allowing another to use and profit from intellectual property (patents, copyrights, trademarks, innovative products or processes, and so on) for consideration. In the context of international business transactions, technology licensing is sometimes an attractive alternative to the establishment of foreign production facilities.

Tenancy at sufferance   A type of tenancy under which one who, after rightfully being in possession of leased premises, continues (wrongfully) to occupy the property after the lease has been terminated. The tenant has no rights to possess the property and occupies it only because the person entitled to evict the tenant has not done so.

Tenancy at will   A type of tenancy under which either party can terminate the tenancy without notice; usually arises when a tenant who has been under a tenancy for years retains possession, with the landlord's consent, after the tenancy for years has terminated.

Tenancy by the entirety   The joint ownership of property by a husband and wife. Neither party can transfer his or her interest in the property without the consent of the other.

Tenancy for years   A type of tenancy under which property is leased for a specified period of time, such as a month, a year, or a period of years.

Tenancy in common   Co-ownership of property in which each party owns an undivided interest that passes to his or her heirs at death.

Tender   An unconditional offer to perform an obligation by a person who is ready, willing, and able to do so.

Tender offer   An offer to purchase made by one company directly to the shareholders of another (target) company; often referred to as a "takeover bid."

Testamentary trust   A trust that is created by will and therefore does not take effect until the death of the testator.

Testator   One who makes and executes a will.

Third party beneficiary   One for whose benefit a promise is made in a contract but who is not a party to the contract.

Tippee   A person who receives inside information.

Tombstone ad   An advertisement, historically in a format resembling a tombstone, of a securities offering. The ad informs potential investors of where and how they may obtain a prospectus.

Tort   A civil wrong not arising from a breach of contract. A breach of a legal duty that proximately causes harm or injury to another.

Tortfeasor   One who commits a tort.

Totten trust   A trust created by the deposit of a person's own money in his or her own name as a trustee for another. It is a tentative trust, revocable at will until the depositor dies or completes the gift in his or her lifetime by some unequivocal act or declaration.

Trade acceptance   A draft that is drawn by a seller of goods ordering the buyer to pay a specified sum of money to the seller, usually at a stated time in the future. The buyer accepts the draft by signing the face of the draft, thus creating an enforceable obligation to pay the draft when it comes due. On a trade acceptance, the seller is both the drawer and the payee.

Trade name   A term that is used to indicate part or all of a business's name and that is directly related to the business's reputation and goodwill. Trade names are protected under the common law (and under trademark law, if the name is the same as the firm's trademarked property).

Trade secrets   Information or processes that give a business an advantage over competitors who do not know the information or processes.

Trademark   A distinctive mark, motto, device, or implement that a manufacturer stamps, prints, or otherwise affixes to the goods it produces so that they may be identified on the market and their origins made known. Once a trademark is established (under the common law or through registration), the owner is entitled to its exclusive use.

Transfer warranties   Implied warranties, made by any person who transfers an instrument for consideration to subsequent transferees and holders who take the instrument in good faith, that (1) the transferor is entitled to enforce the instrument, (2) all signatures are authentic and authorized, (3) the instrument has not been altered, (4) the instrument is not subject to a defense or claim of any party that can be asserted against the transferor, and (5) the transferor has no knowledge of any insolvency proceedings against the maker, the acceptor, or the drawer of the instrument.

Traveler's check A check that is payable on demand, drawn on or payable through a bank, and designated as a traveler's check.

Treaty An agreement formed between two or more independent nations.

Trespass to land The entry onto, above, or below the surface of land owned by another without the owner's permission or legal authorization.

Trespass to personal property The unlawful taking or harming of another's personal property; interference with another's right to the exclusive possession of his or her personal property.

Trust An arrangement in which title to property is held by one person (a trustee) for the benefit of another (a beneficiary).

Trust indorsement An indorsement for the benefit of the indorser or a third person; also known as an agency indorsement. The indorsement results in legal title vesting in the original indorsee.

Tying arrangement An agreement between a buyer and a seller in which the buyer of a specific product or service becomes obligated to purchase additional products or services from the seller.

U

U.S. trustee A government official who performs certain administrative tasks that a bankruptcy judge would otherwise have to perform.

Ultra vires (pronounced uhl-trah vye-reez) A Latin term meaning "beyond the powers"; in corporate law, acts of a corporation that are beyond its express and implied powers to undertake.

Unconscionable (pronounced un-kon-shun-uh-bul) contract (or unconscionable clause) A contract or clause that is void on the basis of public policy because one party, as a result of his or her disproportionate bargaining power, is forced to accept terms that are unfairly burdensome and that unfairly benefit the dominating party.

Underwriter In insurance law, the insurer, or the one assuming a risk in return for the payment of a premium.

Undisclosed principal A principal whose identity is unknown by a third person, and the third person has no knowledge that the agent is acting for a principal at the time the agent and the third person form a contract.

Unenforceable contract A valid contract rendered unenforceable by some statute or law.

Unilateral contract A contract that results when an offer can only be accepted by the offeree's performance.

Union shop A place of employment in which all workers, once employed, must become union members within a specified period of time as a condition of their continued employment.

Universal defenses Defenses that are valid against all holders of a negotiable instrument, including holders in due

course (HDCs) and holders with the rights of HDCs.

Unreasonably dangerous product In product liability, a product that is defective to the point of threatening a consumer's health and safety. A product will be considered unreasonably dangerous if it is dangerous beyond the expectation of the ordinary consumer or if a less dangerous alternative was economically feasible for the manufacturer, but the manufacturer failed to produce it.

Usage of trade Any practice or method of dealing having such regularity of observance in a place, vocation, or trade as to justify an expectation that it will be observed with respect to the transaction in question.

Usury Charging an illegal rate of interest.

Utilitarianism An approach to ethical reasoning in which ethically correct behavior is not related to any absolute ethical or moral values but to an evaluation of the consequences of a given action on those who will be affected by it. In utilitarian reasoning, a "good" decision is one that results in the greatest good for the greatest number of people affected by the decision.

V

Valid contract A contract that results when elements necessary for contract formation (agreement, consideration, legal purpose, and contractual capacity) are present.

Venue (pronounced ven-yoo) The geographical district in which an action is tried and from which the jury is selected.

Vertical merger The acquisition by a company at one stage of production of a company at a higher or lower stage of production (such as a company merging with one of its suppliers or retailers).

Vertical restraint Any restraint on trade created by agreements between firms at different levels in the manufacturing and distribution process.

Vertically integrated firm A firm that carries out two or more functional phases (manufacture, distribution, retailing, and so on) of a product.

Vesting The creation of an absolute or unconditional right or power.

Void contract A contract having no legal force or binding effect.

Voidable contract A contract that may be legally avoided (canceled, or annulled) at the option of one of the parties.

Voir dire (pronounced vwahr-deehr) A French phrase meaning "to speak the truth." In jury trials, the phrase refers to the process in which the attorneys question prospective jurors to determine whether they are biased or have any connection with a party of the action or with a prospective witness.

Voting trust An agreement (trust contract) under which legal title to shares of corporate stock is transferred to a trustee who is authorized by the shareholders to vote the shares on their behalf.

W

Warranty deed A deed in which the grantor guarantees to the grantee that the grantor has title to the property conveyed in the deed, that there are no encumbrances on the property other than what the grantor has represented, and that the grantee will enjoy quiet possession of the property; a deed that provides the greatest amount of protection for the grantee.

Watered stock   Shares of stock issued by a corporation for which the corporation receives, as payment, less than the stated value of the shares.

Wetlands   Areas of land designated by government agencies (such as the Army Corps of Engineers or the Environmental Protection Agency) as protected areas that support wildlife and that therefore cannot be filled in or dredged by private contractors or parties.

Whistleblowing   An employee's disclosure to government, the press, or upper-management authorities that the employer is engaged in unsafe or illegal activities.

White-collar crime   Nonviolent crime committed by individuals or corporations to obtain a personal or business advantage.

Will   An instrument directing what is to be done with the testator's property upon his or her death, made by the testator and revocable during his or her lifetime. No interests in the testator's property pass until the testator dies.

Winding up   The second of two stages involved in the termination of a partnership or corporation. Once the firm is dissolved, it continues to exist legally until the process of winding up all business affairs (collecting and distributing the firm's assets) is complete.

Workers' compensation laws   State statutes establishing an administrative procedure for compensating workers' injuries that arise out of—or in the course of—their employment, regardless of fault.

Workout   An out-of-court agreement between a debtor and his or her creditors in which the parties work out a payment plan or schedule under which the debtor's debts can be discharged.

Writ of attachment   A court's order, prior to a trial to collect a debt, directing the sheriff or other officer to seize nonexempt property of the debtor; if the creditor prevails at trial, the seized property can be sold to satisfy the judgment.

Writ of *certiorari* (pronounced sur-shee-uh-*rah*-ree)   A writ from a higher court asking the lower court for the record of a case.

Writ of execution   A court's order, after a judgment has been entered against the debtor, directing the sheriff to seize (levy) and sell any of the debtor's nonexempt real or personal property. The proceeds of the sale are used to pay off the judgment, accrued interest, and costs of the sale; any surplus is paid to the debtor.

Wrongful discharge   An employer's termination of an employee's employment in violation of an employment contract or laws that protect employees.

Table of Cases

The principal cases (those presented within the chapters) are in bold type. Cases cited or discussed within the text or in case problems are in roman type.

Index